CONTEMPORARY
WORLD WRITERS

Contemporary Writers of the English Language

Contemporary Poets
Contemporary Novelists
   (including short-story writers)
Contemporary Dramatists
Contemporary Literary Critics
Contemporary World Writers

CONTEMPORARY
WORLD WRITERS

SECOND EDITION

PREFACE
SUSAN BASSNETT

EDITOR
TRACY CHEVALIER

St J

St James Press

Detroit   London   Washington DC

04363

While every effort has been made to ensure the reliability of the information presented in this publication, St James Press does not guarantee the accuracy of the data contained herein. St James Press accepts no payment for listing; and inclusion in the publication of any organization, agency, institution, publication, service, or individual does not imply endorsement of the editors or publisher. Errors brought to the attention of the publisher and verified to the satisfaction of the publisher will be corrected in future editions.

Gale Research International Ltd.
PO Box 699
Cheriton House
North Way
Andover
Hants SP10 5YE
United Kingdom

or

Gale Research Inc.
835 Penobscot Bldg.
Detroit, MI 48226–4094
U.S.A.

ST. JAMES PRESS is an imprint of Gale Research International Ltd.
An Affiliated Company of Gale Research Inc.

A CIP catalogue record for this book is available from the British Library.

ISBN 1–55862–200–4

Library of Congress Cataloging-in-Publication Data

Contemporary world writers / editor. Tracy Chevalier.
    p.   cm.
   Contains biographical and bibliographical information on 345 authors.
   Includes bibliographical references and index.
   ISBN 1–55862–200–4
   1. Authors—Biography—Dictionaries.   2. Literature, Modern—20th century—Bio-bibliography—Dictionaries.   I. Chevalier, Tracy.
PN51.C6235 1993
809′.04—dc20
[B]
                                                  93–5352
                                                    CIP

First edition published as *Contemporary Foreign-Language Writers*, 1984

Typeset by Spartan Press, Lymington, Hants, U.K.
Printed in the United States

Published simultaneously in the United Kingdom and the United States of America

The paper used in this publication meets the minimum requirements of American National Standard for Information Sciences — Permanence Paper for printed Library Materials, ANSI Z39.48–1984.

CONTENTS

PREFACE

The compilation of a volume on world literature is a very delicate task, fraught with all kinds of problems, the principal of which is the fundamental question of whom to include and whom to leave out. For although there are a few well-known names, some of whom are on the international bestseller lists and some of whom have been awarded major international literary prizes, there is no canon of world literature, nor could there be. The multitude of languages, of types of text, of varieties of writing, of readers' expectations in the world today are constant reminders of the infinite variety of literary production that comes under the general heading of "world literature." So much is always going on that it is impossible for any one reader to keep pace with new developments, and most of us feel doomed to exist in a state of not-knowing, aware that there are surely wonderful writers throughout the world that we have never heard of, or, frustratingly, who are inaccessible to us because of the constraints of our knowledge of other languages.

The present volume is an attempt to alleviate such feelings of readerly inadequacy. *Contemporary World Writers* is an encyclopaedic collection of short essays and basic information on some 340 living writers from over 60 countries whose work has, at least in part, been translated into English. This list includes Nobel prize winners such as Gabriel García Márquez and Nagīb Mafūz, writers who are leading political figures in their own countries such as Václav Havel and Blaga Dimitrova, writers whose poetry reflects their powerful commitment to human rights such as Mahmūd Darwīsh, Irina Ratushinskaia, and Claribel Alegría, writers like Tove Jansson whose work has delighted children throughout the world, writers like Umberto Eco and Patrick Süskind whose novels have been read by millions, writers who have raised our awareness of gender politics such as Nicole Brossard, Hélène Cixous, and Zhang Ailing, or of the politics of negritude and the legacy of post-colonialism such as Aimé Césaire and Léopold Senghor.

The enormous changes caused by the spread of electronic media throughout the world are constantly remarked upon by politicians and scholars alike; access to satellite television, computer networking systems, and teleconferencing have all contributed to a revolution in mass communications which ensures that people in remote villages are put in touch with events taking place at the other ends of the earth almost instantaneously. Children in developed nations today are computer literate from an early age and television has increased their knowledge of places, peoples, and events in other countries beyond anything an earlier generation could have ever imagined. And an important aspect of that increased knowledge is an increased desire for cultural exchange, a growing need to share experiences as represented by creative artists in different lands.

Changes in communications systems have had an obvious impact upon publishing policies. Indeed, it is probably fair to say that the revolution in communications that we have lived through in the 20th century is comparable to the revolution in the 15th century caused by the invention in the Western world of printing. We can no longer sit quietly in our homes and ignore the world outside, or wait until it comes to us in the form of colourful stamps on foreign envelopes or picture books or travellers' tales, as our grandparents did. National pride is still a powerful force for good, of course, but the excesses of narrow nationalist thinking that excludes other cultures are all too painfully obvious to us all. Religious sectarianism, bigotry, chauvinism, racism, and belief in ethnic superiority are still killing and maiming millions of people, as they have always done, but the difference today is that we can see it happening on our television screens. We bear witness to atrocities committed by other human beings in ways that no previous generation has ever been able to do, because today the evidence of violence is brought to us through direct images, into our own homes.

Yet even at this moment when mass communication is inexorably changing how we perceive the world and our place in it, the written word is as vitally important as ever. For despite the advances in information technology, the power of writers to influence people remains unchanged. Few images are more terrifying than the sight of books being thrown onto a bonfire by a fanatical crowd, for that has become a symbol of repression, while another sign of the power of literature is the number of writers who are thrown into gaol, tortured, driven into exile, and sometimes even murdered simply because they chose to take up the pen and write.

Writing, as has often been observed, is about entertainment and about instruction, and also about bearing witness. As we become more immediately aware of what is happening out in the world, unable to close our eyes to shut out the sight of people starving to death because of man-made or natural disasters, so we are seeking to discover more about other cultures through their writers. More and more works are becoming available in a wide range of languages, and so finally we are being granted access to the work of writers from the Indian subcontinent, Central Asia, China, Eastern Europe, the Middle East, and Latin America. In that process, we as readers are able to share in experiences beyond our own, and become through the very act of reading part of other cultures.

The dominance of English as a world language in the 19th and 20th centuries served ironically to isolate English speakers from other literatures. The teaching of other languages declined and the number of texts translated decreased. Whereas in the 16th and 17th centuries translation was viewed as a high art — and indeed Shakespeare could not have written his plays without translations — by the 18th century as the United Kingdom began to become an imperial power and the United States came into being, more works came to be translated out of English than into English. The export of literature all but eclipsed the import, a phenomenon not shared by other languages which continued to translate abundantly, even where political differences accentuated physical frontiers.

That situation is now, happily, changing. The English-speaking world has belatedly begun to recognize the need for greater involvement with other cultures. The boom in Latin American literature of the 1960s, for example, has resulted in the translation of the work of large numbers of writers previously relatively unknown to English readers. Sometimes political events affect translation policies; so, for example, the great changes in China over the last 30 years or the more recent changes in Eastern and Central Europe have led to a surge of interest expressed in increased translations of well-known writers. Czesław Miłosz once remarked that Poland was the white space on the map of Europe because nobody except a Pole ever quite knew for certain where it was. That has now changed completely, and with the redrawing of the map of the world comes a desire to become more acquainted with the literature and culture of those places previously ignored. Writers do indeed put their cultures on the map.

Fundamental to any increased awareness of world literature is the role of the translator. Here again, the English-speaking world has been behind other cultures, and translation has all too often been seen as a secondary activity, a craft rather than an art, a process that diminishes the original text. There has been much talk of what is lost in translation, as though interlingual transfer necessarily entails the loss of literary qualities that mark the original as unique. But the emphasis on loss devalues the importance of translation, which is crucial for the development of any culture. It is notable that whenever a culture is developing, either during a period of intense nationalist resurgence or during a period of relatively low literary production, at such times translation becomes a vital source of regeneration. Great periods of transition such as the Renaissance or the Enlightenment are also great periods of translation. The capacity of one writer to influence another frequently happens through translation. So, for example, the impact of the 19th-century Russian novel on prose writers throughout the world occurred because Leo Tolstoi and Fedor Dostoevskii were translated into other languages, and not because millions of readers learned a Slavonic language. We may talk about reading Sanskrit poetry or Japanese fiction or the latest novel by Milan Kundera or Christa Wolf, but what we are actually saying is that we have read and enjoyed those works in translation.

The spread of English as a language has led to a certain complacency about the value of translated texts. Now at last we are coming to see that without translation, and the vital regenerative processes that translation brings, no literary system can survive in today's world. The terminology surrounding translation has also begun to change in significant ways; instead of describing translating as copying or imitating or serving an original, we now recognize the value of Walter Benjamin's image of the translation as afterlife, as the survival of the text. Just as nations need other nations in order to ensure the survival of their economies and their cultures, so writers need to be in touch with what other writers are doing, and they need translators to keep them in touch. It does not matter where the term "magic realism" first came from; what does matter is that Latin American magic realist novelists are read throughout the world, and there are Indian, African, Chinese, Russian, Danish, and Hungarian writers who can also be described as magic realists.

Influence rarely happens in a straight line; it is a complex process of interweaving, as writers encounter the work of other writers in all sorts of strange and unexpected ways. The history of literatures is full of patterns of connection and as translation gives us greater access to writing in other languages, so those patterns are diversified. Unable to read the poetry of Tomas Tranströmer or Nina Cassian or Adūnīs in their original Swedish, Romanian, or Arabic, we can nevertheless make contact with these inspiring writers through the work of their translators. Nor do we pause to reflect on what may or may not have been lost; what remains is more than enough, and any doubts about the creative power of translation are dispelled when we reflect on García Márquez's comment that the English version of his *One Hundred Years of Solitude* was better than the Spanish original, or on Haraldo de Campos's image of the translation as a transfusion of blood, granting new healthy life to a text in a new context.

In the past, idealists have suggested that literature is a civilizing force, that writing knows no frontiers, even that greater understanding between nations will be encouraged by exchanges of books. Today, we look at such propositions rather more cynically. The export of Shakespeare as a literary master in the 19th century took place at the expense of the great works of other cultures, and the extolling of European masters as exemplary writers has been challenged in the age of post-colonialism by writers from other continents who question the basis of Eurocentric evaluation. Greater literacy across the globe has not resulted in a lessening of violence and struggle; books are still flung onto bonfires and writers are still shot by snipers in passing cars. But greater access to other literatures does make a difference, for the moment we read a text by an Iranian writer, for example, or a Russian or a Paraguayan, we are making contact with another culture that takes us far beyond the representation of that culture in the mass media and serves in a very fundamental way to transcend prejudices and stereotypes.

Writers may not be able to change the world, but the world is changed by writing. It is changed because as readers meet writers, whether in the same language or in translation, they share experiences, emotions, images, dreams, and desires, and that sharing is nothing less than the birth of a new relationship. This present book is an important element in that regenerative process.

SUSAN BASSNETT

EDITOR'S NOTE

The selection of writers included in this book is based on the recommendations of the advisers listed on page xiii several of whom helped on the first edition. I have also taken advice from contributors when appropriate.

The entry for each writer consists of a biography, a complete list when possible of separately published books, a list of published bibliographies and critical studies (in English) when available, and a signed essay. In addition, entrants were invited to comment on their work. Some replied in English; other statements have been translated into English from the original language.

For certain language groups entrants have been listed by their transliterated name, with alternative forms of the name also listed. Cross-references are provided as appropriate. All diacritical marks (whether for pronunciation or stress) have been ignored when alphabetising names.

Chinese, Japanese, and Korean entrants are listed last name then first name with no separating comma, as is standard academic practice. Icelandic writers are referred to by their last names rather than by first name (as is the practice in Iceland). Again, cross-references are provided when needed to avoid confusion.

The original edition of each book in the original language has been listed, as well as original British and United States editions of all English translations.

Some book lists (particularly for Japanese and Russian entrants, and some of the samizdat underground publishing in Central and Eastern Europe) contain works that were first published in journals, as is the custom in many countries.

All book titles mentioned in essays include a literal English translation or the published English translation title listed after the first mention of the book. In addition, book lists for entrants in languages other than French, German, Spanish, and Italian contain when possible literal English translations of titles in square brackets after each title.

Some bibliographies used in research referred to dates of publication using non-Roman calendar dates. When it was not possible to find out the Roman year of publication both possibilities are listed.

The book contains two indexes: the nationality index lists entrants by all their nationalities (current and past); the title index lists titles of all works in the fiction, verse, and plays sections of each entry, as well as selected important works of non-fiction.

I would like to thank the following people for their help with languages and/or research on the book: Cristina Ashby, Harry Bucknall, Krystyna Carter, Christine Garabedian, Janet Garton, Sarah M. Hall, Bernard Johnson, Ulla Munck Jorgensen, Ahmed Al-Khashem, Gill Kitley, Parvin Loloi, Susan Mackervoy, Sean McCullough, David McDuff, Rory McTurk, Patricia Anne Odber de Baubeta, Francesca Orsini, Robert Shannan Peckham, Robert Rabinowitz, Ian Raeside, Péter Siklós, Annika Small, Fiona Worthington, and Jackie Wrout.

I would also like to thank the entrants and contributors for their patience and cooperation in helping to compile this book.

ADVISERS

A. James Arnold
Thomas G. Bergin
Gordon Brotherston
Pierre Cachia
Mary Ann Caws
Ruby Cohn
Delia Davin
Wallace Fowlie
Michael Freeman
Janet Garton
Igor Hájek
Peter Hutchinson
Harry Levin
Felicia Hardison Londré

Stuart McGregor
Doris Meyer
Earl Miner
Janet Pérez
Christopher R. Pike
Dušan Puvačić
Olga Ragusa
Judy Rawson
Anthony Rudolf
Josef Škvorecký
James Russell Stamm
Daniel Weissbort
David Young

CONTRIBUTORS

Kamal Abu-Deeb
Robin Allan
Gunilla M. Anderman
Hans Christian Andersen
Merle Lyn Bachman
Chris Banfield
Stanisław Barańczak
Enikő Molnár Basa
Lucille Frackman Becker
David J. Bond
Richard C. Borden
Sandra Maria Boschetto-Sandoval
Issa J. Boullata
Denis Brass
Peter Broome
Suzanne Burgoyne
Glenn S. Burne
Yvonne Burns
Anthony Bushell
Christopher Cairns
Nick Caistor
Sue-Ellen Case
Mary Ann Caws
David Coward
Joyce Crick
Delia Davin
Barbara Day
Thomas J. Donahue
Leonard E. Doucette
Kevin Elstob

Bente Elsworth
John Fletcher
Albert H. Friedlander
Deborah Fronko
Samba Gadjigo
Janet Garton
David Gillespie
Barbara Godard
Marketa Goetz-Stankiewicz
George Gömöri
Helena Goscilo
Marlene Gottlieb
Peter Graves
Peter J. Graves
Brita Green
Güneli Gün
David T. Haberly
Sabry Hafez
Igor Hájek
Talat S. Halman
Celia Hawkesworth
Peter Hertz-Ohmes
David K. Herzberger
James Higgins
Richard G. Hodgson
Marian Peter Holt
Aamer Hussein
William M. Hutchins
Peter Hutchinson
Neil Jackson

Regina Janes
David Jiang
Bernard Johnson
D. Barton Johnson
Margaret E. W. Jones
W. Glyn Jones
A. S. Kalsi
Amy Kaminsky
Maia Kipp
Robert Kirsner
George L. Kline
Patricia N. Klingenberg
Charles Klopp
Manfred K. Kremer
Celita Lamar
André Lefevere
Harry Levin
Bart L. Lewis
Tim Lewis
Li Ruru
Parvin Loloi
Felicia Hardison Londré
Jennifer Lorch
Sharon Magnarelli
Heitor Martins
Igor Maver
Mercedes Mazquiarán de Rodríguez
Bonnie S. McDougall
David McDuff
Stuart McGregor
Keith McMahon
George R. McMurray
Rory McTurk
Patrick Miles
Valerie Minogue
Michael Mitchell
Oscar Montero
Anne W. Mullen
Susan J. Napier
Kirsten F. Nigro
David A. Norris
Patricia Anne Odber de Baubeta
John O'Leary
Lois Oppenheim
Carys Owen
Augustus Pallotta
Shirley J. Paolini
Robert Shannan Peckham
Janet Pérez
Kerstin Petersson
Donald Pirie
Valentina Polukhina

Giovanni Pontiero
Robert Porter
Sabrina Prielaida
Glyn Pursglove
Michael Pursglove
Robert B. Pynsent
Michael L. Quinn
Ian Raeside
James Raeside
Girdhar Rathi
Judy Rawson
Michael Robinson
David Rock
Francesca Ross
Patricia Rubio
Christine A. Rydel
Barry P. Scherr
Grace Schulman
Claude Schumacher
Kessel Schwartz
Irene Scobbie
Juris Silenieks
G. Singh
Hans H. Skei
Christopher Smith
Raymond D. Souza
Satyendra Śrīvāstava
James Russell Stamm
Mary E. Stewart
Arrigo V. Subiotto
Philip Swanson
Takahashi Yasunari
Anna-Marie Taylor
Birgitta Thompson
Laurie Thompson
Bjarne T. Thomsen
Michael Tilby
Egil Törnqvist
Heather Valencia
Hugo J. Verani
Maïr Verthuy
Paul Vincent
Jennifer Waelti-Walters
Anthony Waine
I. Robin Warner
Daniel Weissbort
George E. Wellwarth
Theresa Werner
Mark Williams
Jason Wilson
George Woodyard
Leon I. Yudkin
Phyllis Zatlin

CONTEMPORARY WORLD WRITERS

Adūnīs
Ilse Aichinger
Chingiz Aitmatov
Bella Akhmadulina
Vasilii Aksenov
Rafael Alberti
Claribel Alegría
Isabel Allende
Jorge Amado
Yehuda Amichai
Katerina Anghelaki-Rooke
Aharon Appelfeld
Manlio Argueta
Homero Aridjis
Fernando Arrabal
Juan José Arreola
Upendranāth "Aśk"
Werner Aspenström
Francisco Ayala

Ba Jin
Salwā Bakr
Stanisław Barańczak
Giorgio Bassani
'Abd al-Wahhāb al-Bayāti
Jurek Becker
Bei Dao
Gioconda Belli
Tahar Ben Jelloun
H. C. ten Berge
Ingmar Bergman
Dharmvīr Bhārtī
Wolf Biermann
Adolfo Bioy Casares
Marie-Claire Blais
Ana Blandiana
Anders Bodelsen
Yves Bonnefoy
Gerd Brantenberg
Volker Braun
Breyten Breytenbach
Iosif Brodskii
Suzanne Brøgger
Nicole Brossard
Antonio Buero Vallejo
Gesualdo Bufalino
Michel Butor

G. Cabrera Infante
Elias Canetti
Cao Yu
Emilio Carballido
Ernesto Cardenal
Marie Cardinal
José Cardoso Pires
T. Carmi
Bo Carpelan
Nina Cassian
Camilo José Cela
Gianni Celati
Aimé Césaire
Rosa Chacel
Chen Ruoxi
Jacques Chessex
Driss Chraïbi
Antonio Cisneros
Hélène Cixous

Hugo Claus
Carmen Conde
Maryse Condé
Dobrica Ćosić
Sándor Csoóri

Bernard Dadié
Fazıl Hüsnü Dağlarca
Sīmīn Dāneshvar
Mahmūd Darwīsh
Mahmūd Dawlatābādi
Michel Deguy
Miguel Delibes
René Depestre
Jorge Díaz
Blaga Dimitrova
José Donoso
Ariel Dorfman
Jacques Dupin
Marguerite Duras

Umberto Eco
Odysseus Elytis
Endō Shūsaku
Per Olov Enquist
Hans Magnus Enzensberger
Luciano Erba
Péter Esterházy
Evgenii Evtushenko

Knut Faldbakken
Aminata Sow Fall
Feng Jicai
Rosario Ferré
Kjartan Fløgstad
Dario Fo
André Frénaud
Carlos Fuentes

Antonio Gala
Griselda Gambaro
Gabriel García Márquez
Jacques Garelli
Elena Garro
Armand Gatti
Édouard Glissant
Árpád Göncz
Natalia Gorbanevskaia
Juan Goytisolo
Luis Goytisolo
Julien Gracq
Günter Grass
Julien Green
I. Grekova
David Grossman
Eugène Guillevic
Haim Guri
Lars Gustafsson
Gyānrañjan

Paavo Haavikko
Imīl Ḥabībi
Peter Hacks
Qurratulain Haidar
Peter Handke
Hao Ran
Győző Határ

Olav H. Hauge
Václav Havel
Buland al-Ḥaydari
Anne Hébert
Christoph Hein
Piet Hein
Jens Pauli Heinesen
Zbigniew Herbert
Willem Frederik Hermans
Luisa Josefina Hernández
Judith Herzberg
Stefan Heym
Rolf Hochhuth
Miroslav Holub
Bohumil Hrabal
Abdullāh Hussein
Jeanne Hyvrard

Ibuse Masuji
Eugène Ionesco

Jabrā Ibrāhīm Jabrā
Philippe Jaccottet
Rolf Jacobsen
Svava Jakobsdóttir
Tove Jansson
P. C. Jersild
Matthías Johannessen
Ferenc Juhász

Amalia Kahana-Carmon
Kamleśvar
Yaşar Kemal
Sarah Kirsch
Ivan Klíma
Blaže Koneski
György Konrád
Tadeusz Konwicki
Franz Xaver Kroetz
Karl Krolow
Ku Sang
Milan Kundera
Günter Kunert
Reiner Kunze
Aleksandr Kushner

Carmen Laforet
Ivan V. Lalić
André Langevin
Halldór Laxness
J. -M. G. Le Clézio
Stanisław Lem
Siegfried Lenz
Sara Lidman
Astrid Lindgren
Ewa Lipska
Liu Binyan
Liu Xinwu
Cecilie Løveid
Lucebert
Arnošt Lustig
Mario Luzi

Muhammad al-Māghūt
Naġīb Mahfūz
Antonine Maillet
Françoise Mallet-Joris

Eduardo Manet
Dacia Maraini
Carmen Martín Gaite
Ana María Matute
Claude Mauriac
João Cabral de Melo Neto
Albert Memmi
Slavko Mihalić
Czesław Miłosz
Ladislav Mňačko
Patrick Modiano
Sławomir Mrożek
Harry Mulisch
Heiner Müller
'Abd al-Rahmān Munīf
Murakami Haruki
Jan Myrdal

Nāgārjun
Francisco Nieva
Henrik Nordbrandt
Lars Norén

Silvina Ocampo
Ōe Kenzaburō
Juan Carlos Onetti
Sembène Ousmane
Guillaume Oyônô-Mbia
Amos Oz

José Emilio Pacheco
Heberto Padilla
Orhan Pamuk
Nicanor Parra
Fernando del Paso
Milorad Pavić
Miodrag Pavlović
Octavio Paz
Śripad Nārāyaṇ Peṇḍse
Cristina Peri Rossi
György Petri
Liudmila Petrushevskaia
Robert Pinget
Nélida Piñón
Elena Poniatowska
Michele Prisco
Amritā Pritam

Nizār Qabbāni
Qian Zhongshu
Rachel de Queiroz
Elena Quiroga

Edvard Radzinskii
Sergio Ramírez
Valentin Rasputin
Irina Ratushinskaia
Dahlia Ravikovitch
Gerard Reve
João Ubaldo Ribeiro
Klaus Rifbjerg
Augusto Roa Bastos
Alain Robbe-Grillet
Christiane Rochefort
Tadeusz Różewicz
José Ruibal

Ernesto Sabato
Nawal al-Saʿdāwi
Juan José Saer
Françoise Sagan
Tomaž Šalamun
al-Tayyib Sālih
José Saramago
Severo Sarduy
Nathalie Sarraute
Alfonso Sastre
Solveig von Schoultz
Léopold Senghor
Ahmad Shāmlū
Ḥanān al-Shaykh
Shen Rong
Claude Simon
Andrei Siniavskii
Badal Sircar
Antonio Skármeta
Josef Škvorecký
Yehoshua Sobol
Sasha Sokolov
Mario Soldati
Philippe Sollers
Carlos Solórzano
Vladimir Soloukhin
Aleksandr Solzhenitsyn
Piotr Sommer
Villy Sørensen
Marin Sorescu
Satyendra Śrīvāstava
Henrik Stangerup
Botho Strauss
Patrick Süskind
András Sütő
Abraham Sutzkever
Wisława Szymborska

Antonio Tabucchi
Pia Tafdrup
Jean Tardieu
Lygia Fagundes Telles
Agnar Þórðarson
Kirsten Thorup
Aleksandar Tišma
Tatiana Tolstaia
Miguel Torga
Michel Tournier

Tomas Tranströmer
Michel Tremblay
Dea Trier Mørch
Tsushima Yūko
Esther Tusquets

Dubravka Ugrešić

Ludvík Vaculík
Luisa Valenzuela
Nils Aslak Valkeapää
Blanca Varela
Mario Vargas Llosa
Nirmal Varmā
Ana Lydia Vega
Halldis Moren Vesaas
Bjørg Vik
Thor Vilhjálmsson
Michel Vinaver
Vladimir Voinovich
Paolo Volponi
Andrei Voznesenskii

Martin Walser
Wang Meng
Per Wästberg
Elie Wiesel
Paul Willems
Monique Wittig
Gabriele Wohmann
Christa Wolf
Jan Wolkers

Rājendra Yādav
Yang Lian
Yang Mo
Yasuoka Shōtarō
Ye Junjian
A. B. Yehoshua
Yoshioka Minoru

Nathan Zach
Andrea Zanzotto
Zhang Ailing
Zhang Jie
Zhang Kangkang
Zhang Xianliang
Zhang Xinxin

A

ADONIS. *See* ADŪNĪS.

ADŪNĪS. Also Adonis. Pseudonym for Ali Ahmad Sa'id. Lebanese. Born in Qassabin, Syria, in 1930. Educated at a school in Latakia, Syria; French Lycée, Tartus, 1944–50, graduated 1950; University of Damascus, 1950–54, licence-ès-lettres 1954; the Sorbonne, Paris, 1960–61; St. Joseph University, Beirut, Ph.D. 1973. Married Khālida Ṣāliḥ in 1956; two daughters. Imprisoned, then exiled to Beirut, 1956; became Lebanese citizen; founder, with Yūsuf al-Khāl, *Shi'r* [Poetry] journal, 1957; founder, *Mawāqif* [Positions] journal, 1968; Professor of Arabic literature, Lebanese University, Beirut, from 1971; also taught at Collège de France, University of Damascus, Georgetown University, Washington, D.C., and the Sorbonne, Paris. Since 1985 has lived in Paris; part-time teacher, University of Geneva. Recipient: International Poetry Forum Syria-Lebanon award, 1971; Jean Malrieu prize for poetry (France), 1991. Address: c/o al-Saqi Books, 26 Westbourne Grove, London W2 5RH, England.

PUBLICATIONS

Verse

Dalīla [Delilah]. 1950.
Qālat al-ard [The Earth Has Said]. 1952.
Qasā'id ūla [First Poems]. 1957.
Iza qultu ya Sūriyya [When I Say, Syria]. 1958.
Al-ba'th wa al-ramād [Resurrection and Ashes]. 1958.
Awrāq fil-rīḥ [Leaves in the Wind]. 1958.
Aghānī Mihyār al-Dimashqī [Songs of Mihyar the Damascene]. Beirut, Dār Majallat Shi'r, 1961.
Kitāb al-taḥawwulāt wal-hijra fi aqālīm an-nahar wal-lail [The Book of Metamorphosis and Migration in the Regions of Day and Night]. 1965.
Al-masraḥ wa'l marāya [The Stage and the Mirrors]. 1968.
Waqt bain al-ramād wa'l ward [A Time Between Ashes and Roses]. 1970.
Qabr min ajl New York [A Tomb for New York]. 1971.
Al-āthār al-kāmilah: al-shi'r [The Complete Works: Poetry]. Beirut, 3 vols., 1971.
The Blood of Adonis, translated by Samuel Hazo. Pittsburgh, Pittsburgh University Press, 1971.
Mirrors, translated by Abdullah al-Udhari. London, TR Press, 1976.
Iḥtifa'an bil-ashyā' al-wādiḥa wal-ghāmida [In Celebration of Things Clear and Obscure]. Beirut, Dār al-Ādāb, 1980.
Transformations of the Lover, translated by Samuel Hazo. Athens, Swallow Press-Ohio University Press, 1982.

Victims of a Map (bilingual edition), with Mahmūd Darwīsh and Samīh al-Qāsim. London, Al-Saqi, 1984.
Kitāb al-ḥisār [The Book of the Siege]. Beirut, Dār al-Ādāb, 1985.
Shahwa tataqadam fi kharā'iṭ al-mādda. Al-dār al-Bayda, Dār Tuqbāl, 1987.

Other

Muqadima lil-shi'r al-Arabi [Introduction to Arabic Poetry]. 1971.
Zamān al shi'r [The Time for Poetry]. Beirut, Dār al-'Awdah, 1972.
Al-thabit wal-mutawārath [The Static and the Dynamic] (vol. 1: *Al-usūl*; vol. 2: *Ta'sīl al-usūl*; vol. 3: *Sadmat al-hadathah* [The Shock of Modernity]). Beirut, Dār al-'Awdah, 3 vols., 1974–78.
Fātiha li-nihāyāt al-qarn. Beirut, Dār al-'Awdah, 1980.
Ahmad Shawqi. Beirut, Dār al-' Ilm lil-Malayīn, 1982.
Siyāsat ash-Shi'r: dirāsa fil-shi'riyāt al-Arabiyya al-mu'aṣira [The Policy of Poetry: A Study in Contemporary Arabic Poetry]. 1985.
An Introduction to Arab Poetics. London, Al-Saqi, 1990.
Al-Islam wal-hadātha [A Symposium on Islam and Modernism]. London, Al-Saqi, 1990.
Al-Ṣufiyya wal-siryaliyya [Sophism and Surrealism]. London, Al-Saqi, 1992.

Editor, *Dīwan al-shi'r al-'Arabi* [Diwan of Arabic Poetry]. 1964.
Editor, with Khālida Sa'īd, *Al-Kawākibi, Abdul-Raḥmān bin Ahmad. Dīwan al-Nahda: al-Kwakibi*. Beirut, n. p., 1982.

*

Critical Studies: "Adonis and the New Poetry" by M. M. Badawi, in his *Modern Arabic Poetry*, Cambridge, Cambridge University Press, 1975; "The Perplexity of the All-Knowing: A Study of Adonis" by Kamal Abu-Deeb, in *Mundus Artium* (Athens, Ohio), 10(1), 1977; "Textual Intentions: A Reading of Adonis' Poem 'Unintended Worship Ritual'" by Issa J. Boullata, in *International Journal of Middle East Studies* (Salt Lake City, Utah), 21(4), 1989.

* * *

Adūnīs (Adonis) is the assumed name of Ali Ahmad Sa'id, possibly the most important poet in the Arab world in the second half of the 20th century. Born in 1930 in Qassabin, a small village in the district of Latakia, Syria, and educated at Damascus University, Adūnīs moved to Beirut in 1956 at a time of crucial importance for the modernist current of thought. He was to play a major role in articulating the concepts and principles underlying modernist writing and modes of thinking, through both his literary output and his involvement in cultural journalism. On the latter level, his most important contribution has perhaps been the role he

1

played in the publication of the avant-garde journal *Sh'ir* (Poetry) which was edited by his close friend the poet Yusuf al-Khal. Launched in 1957, *Shi'r* was soon to gather around it a remarkable group of poets, critics, artists, and some philosophers most of whom have since become prominent figures in Arab cultural life. In 1968, after the *Shi'r* group had broken up, and in the wake of the Six-Day War with Israel, Adūnīs launched *Mawāqif* (Positions), a more culturally oriented journal which has become the finest avant-garde publication in the Arab world. Having for 10 years resisted the idea of leaving Lebanon during the civil war (1975–90), in 1985 Adūnīs moved to Paris. His disillusionment with the Arab world has become total, and he seems to have despaired of the struggle for change, freedom, modernity, and the emergence of the "brave new world" of his dreams. The years he has spent in France, however, have greatly enhanced his reputation as a poet of international standing.

Adūnīs's education and intellectual make-up represent a synthesis of Arabic and European cultures. He is equally at home with Arab Sufi writings and European Symbolist and Surrealist literature. His literary output, in its variety and artistic qualities, embodies his rather unusual fusion of cultural elements. In fact, his entire intellectual position rests on the belief in the necessity of evolving a positive dialogue between cultures. In his prose writings he has explored the common sources for what he believes to be the most creative currents in Western and Arabic poetry, arguing that the visionary dimension, the spirituality, and the transcendental and metaphysical yearning which underlie the most creative currents in Western poetry and philosophy derived originally from the East.

Although first and foremost a poet, Adūnīs has written extensively on literature, culture, politics, and intellectual history; he has also produced one of the finest anthologies of Arabic poetry throughout the ages and translated some major Western poets as well as a number of Arab poets writing in French. His influence as a theorist is superseded only by the influence his poetry has exerted on younger poets throughout the Arab world. And in everything he has done, he has been driven by an overwhelming desire to achieve a radical and total transformation of Arab society, Arabic literature, particularly poetry, and the Arabic language itself. In an age of great revolutionary fervour, he has often argued that a social and political revolution is impossible in the absence of a revolution within language and creative writing. He believes the structure of language embodies a structure of thought which moulds our view of the world and which, unless revolutionized, makes revolutionary change an unattainable goal. The role he assigns to poetry, and writing in general, may be considered by many too ambitious and even unrealistic. Yet it is to the fulfillment of this very role that he has devoted his energy and creative powers in a rather missionary, prophetic fashion. And he, more than any other figure over the past four decades, has made the transformation to which he has aspired possible.

While rooted in the traditions of ancient Arabic poetry, Adūnīs's work has become synonymous with modernity, rejection (both as an overall intellectual position and as a concrete stand vis-à-vis authority, preconceived models, and rules), and the search for change and the quest for the beyond. Although he often appears to advocate a view of poetry as an autonomous space, requiring a high degree of formal craftsmanship, a refined language, distilled rhythmic formulations, and imagery unbounded by any inherited criteria, he has always been a politically and socially involved poet. In his youth he engaged in political activity, and because of his links with the Syrian Nationalist Socialist Party he suffered arbitrary imprisonment in the notorious Mazza prison in Damascus in 1956. He remained politically active after his escape to

Lebanon. From the late 1960s, his views began to take a pan-Arab, and at times a Marxist, bent. But he remained throughout an anti-ideologue and a champion of the cause of freedom, unrestricted creativity, and human dignity. He has always sought to generate in his cultural environment a spirit of restlessness, skepticism, questioning, and yearning for the unknown. As part of his radical project he has reinterpreted the Arabic tradition, in its literary, intellectual, and religious components, aspiring to revive the creative spirit of rejection and opposition to the dominant culture, which he believes to be underlined by a static, conservative, and more specifically Islamic, religious view of the world.

Adūnīs's early poetry was imbued with a spirit of anxiety and longing in some ways akin to the current of writing generated by Jubran Khalil Jubran (Kahlil Gibran) and the early romantic and symbolist poets; but his verse distinguished itself from the outset by its lack of sentimentality, its aesthetic purity, and its worldliness. A growing tendency to use ancient Syrian mythology at this early stage was to be intensified later on with the discovery of the universal significance of the Middle Eastern myths of sacrificial death and rebirth in the work of major Western poets like T. S. Eliot. This point of fusion climaxed in a text of crucial importance in the development of Adūnīs's poetry, *Al-ba'th wa al-ramād* (Resurrection and Ashes), published in 1958.

But the vital transformation of his poetry crystallized at the beginning of the 1960s and was truly remarkable, representing a major break with both the traditions of classical Arabic poetry and the dominant idiom of the poetry of his immediate historical period. His poetry became steeped in the language of Sufism and symbolism but revealed a higher degree of artistic refinement, subtlety, economy of phrase, and a visionary type of imagery which seemed to appear from nowhere. The spirit of quest, yearning, search for the incomplete and the unknown was given its perfect embodiment in a little-used metre, *al-mutadarak*, which Adūnīs made his own and through which a new Adonisian tone began to permeate poetic writing throughout the Arab world. All this was incarnated in the character of Mihyar the Damascene: a mystical, prophetic, restless explorer and sacrificial redeemer, reminiscent of Jubran's prophet but with a modernist outlook and poetic idiom and a revolutionary temperament. Mihyar derived his name from a real historical and marginal figure, Mihyar al-Daylami, but bore very little similarity to him on any other level except, perhaps, for his consciousness of being an outsider. The influence of Adūnīs's *Aghānī Mihyār al-Dimashqī* (Songs of Mihyar the Damascene) was to prove crucial for the development of Arabic poetry over the following three decades.

Adūnīs's fusion of poetic prose with regular *taf'ilat* (feet) opened a new direction for free verse (which had burst out in the late 1940s after decades of indecisive attempts to free Arabic verse from symmetry, mono-rhyme, and almost absolute regularity of metrical composition). Over the following 15 years, Adūnīs went on to produce extremely complex poetic structures, seeking in every new text to transcend the structures he developed in his previous texts, in what appeared to be an act of permanent revolution. His poems of this period have remained without parallel in Arabic poetry both in their sheer length and in their complexity and exploration of new rhythmic and syntactic structures, fresh imagery, and language. But above all, these texts have remained unrivalled on the level of their vision of man, nature, culture, the metaphysical world, the relationship of a culture to its own past, and the agonies and ecstasies generated by its increasingly intense confrontation with other, more aggressive, cultures.

His more recent poetry reveals a growing tendency towards the poetics of place and a little less preoccupation with time and history; in *Kitāb al-ḥiṣār* (The Book of the Siege) he explores the more intimate and personal aspects of living in a specific place (Beirut) through the tragedy of civil war, the destruction caused by Israeli occupation, and the heroic resistance to this occupation by the Lebanese and Palestinians. At the same time, however, Adūnīs goes on exploring the more mysterious regions of man's presence in the world with the same power and energy but with a greater degree of torment and doubt and with a sense of a fissured soul which has little of the earlier faith in its ability to destroy the ossified world and re-create it in its own image.

At the heart of Adūnīs's poetry lies a paradoxical vision of the universe, of man and his world. His verse is dominated by two opposing forces: a lyrical, contemplative, peaceful tone with a falling rhythm, progressing in a highly controlled fashion and unfolding as a fusing and unifying force; and an explosive, dramatic, rising and falling, sweeping rhythm releasing an immense energy powered by a violent desire to confuse, destroy, and obliterate: a structuring movement confronted by a deconstructive movement. These two occasionally mingle in a complex fashion to celebrate what Adūnīs calls "*al-kharab al-jamil*" (beautiful destruction) with its promise of a new, enchanting beginning; but more often they occupy separate spaces and alternate in gaining prominence at different historical points in his development.

In a recent volume of prose poems, *Iḥtifa'an bil-ashyā' al-wādiḥa wal-ghāmida* (In Celebration of Things Clear and Obscure), the lyrical, unifying tone completely takes over; his texts become highly economical and elliptical, condensing an entire sphere of being into a concisely constructed statement approaching the brevity and syntactic simplicity of aphorisms. Here, Adūnīs seems to transcend experience and history altogether and concentrate on distilling his visions into striking, proverb-like formulations which possess the power to survive as timeless testimonies about the world, man, nature, and their interwoven presence within the same confined space of existence. Recently Adūnīs embarked on a massive project exploring the complex personality of the poet al-Mutanabbi and attempting a reinterpretation of Arab history while probing the agonies and ecstasies of the estranged, prophetic personality of the outsider in history. The master, at 62, and despite all the disillusionment and despair, is far from exhausted; in fact, according to him, he has not yet written the poem he dreams of writing. He has just embarked, for the thousand-and-first time, on trying to achieve that ever-illusive goal.

—Kamal Abu-Deeb

———

AGNAR ÞÓRÐARSON. *See* ÞÓRÐARSON, Agnar.

———

AICHINGER, Ilse. Austrian. Born in Vienna, 1 November 1921. Educated at a gymnasium in Vienna, graduated 1939;

University of Vienna, 1945/6–48. Married Günter Eich in 1953 (died 1972); two children. Publisher's reader, S. Fischer publishers, Frankfurt, East Germany, and Vienna, 1949–50; assistant to founder Inge Scholl, Hochschule für Gestaltung, Ulm. Member, Grupe 47, from 1951. Recipient: Gruppe 47 prize, 1952; Austrian State prize, 1952; City of Bremen prize, 1955; Immermann prize, 1955; Bavarian Academy of Fine Arts prize, 1961, 1991; Wildgans prize, 1969; Nelly Sachs prize, 1971; City of Vienna prize, 1974; City of Dortmund prize, 1975; Trackle prize, 1979; Petrarca prize, 1982; Belgian Europe Festival prize, 1987; Weilheim prize, 1987; Town of Solothurn prize, 1991; Roswitha Medal. Address: c/o Fischer Verlag, Postfach 700480, 6000 Frankfurt, Germany.

PUBLICATIONS

Fiction

Die größere Hoffnung. Amsterdam, Bermann-Fischer, 1948; as *Herod's Children*, New York, Atheneum, 1963.
Rede unter dem Galgen. Vienna, Jungbrunnen, 1952; as *Der Gefesselte*, Frankfurt, Fischer, 1953; as *The Bound Man, and Other Stories*, London, Secker and Warburg, 1955; New York, Farrar Straus, 1956.
Eliza, Eliza. Frankfurt, Fischer, 1965.
Selected Short Stories and Dialogue (in German), edited by James C. Alldridge. Oxford, Pergamon, 1966.
Nachricht vom Tag: Erzählungen. Frankfurt, Fischer, 1970.
Schlechte Wörter (includes radio plays). Frankfurt, Fischer, 1976.
Meine Sprache und ich: Erzählungen. Frankfurt, Fischer, 1978.
Spiegelgeschichte: Erzählungen und Dialoge. Leipzig, Kiepenheuer, 1979.

Plays

Zu keiner Stunde (dialogues). Frankfurt, Fischer, 1957; enlarged edition, 1980.
Besuch im Pfarrhaus: Ein Hörspiel, Drei Dialoge. Frankfurt, Fischer, 1961.
Auckland: 4 Hörspiele (radio plays). Frankfurt, Fischer, 1969.
Knöpfe (radio play). Published in *Hörspiele*, Frankfurt, Fischer, 1978.
Weisse Chrysanthemum. Published in *Kurzhörspiele*, St. Pölten, Niederösterreichisches Pressehaus, 1979.

Radio Plays: *Knöpfe*, 1953; *Auckland*, 1969; *Gare maritime*, 1973; *Belvedere*; *Weisse Chrysanthemum.*

Verse

Verschenkter Rat. Frankfurt, Fischer, 1978.

Other

Wo ich wohne: Erzählungen, Gedichte, Dialoge (includes stories, poems, dialogues). Frankfurt, Fischer, 1963.
Dialoge, Erzählungen, Gedichte (includes dialogues, stories, poems). Stuttgart, Reclam, 1971.
Gedichte und Prosa. Weilheim, Deutschlehrer am Gymnasium Weilheim, 1980.
Selected Poetry and Prose of Ilse Aichinger, translated by Allen H. Chappel. Durango, Colorado, Logbridge Rhodes, 1983.

Grimmige Märchen, with Martin Walser, edited by Wolfgang
  Mieder.   Frankfurt, Fischer, 1986.
Kleist, Moos, Fasane.   Frankfurt, Fischer, 1987.
Gesammalte Werke, edited by Richard Reichensperger.
  Frankfurt, Fischer, 8 vols., 1991.

Editor, *Gedichte*, by Günter Eich.   Frankfurt, Suhrkamp,
  1973.

                                    *

Critical Studies: *Ilse Aichinger* by James C. Alldridge,
London, Wolff, and Chester Springs, Pennsylvania, Dufour,
1969; "A Structural Approach to Aichinger's *Spiegelgesch-
ichte*" by Michael W. Resler, in *Unterrichtspraxis* (Fay-
etteville, Arkansas), 12(1), 1979; "Freedom vs. Meaning:
Aichinger's 'Bound Man' and the Old Order Amish" by Marc
A. Olshan, in *Internal and External Perspectives on Amish and
Mennonite Life, II*, edited by Werner Enninger, Joachim
Raith, and Karl-Heinz Wandt, Essen, Unipress, 1986; "The
Reception of the Works of Ilse Aichinger in the United States"
by U. Henry Gerlach, in *Modern Austrian Literature* (River-
side, California), 20(3–4), 1987; "*Spiegelgeschichte*: A Lin-
guistic Analysis" by Maurice Aldridge, in *International Review
of Applied Linguistics in Language Teaching* (Stuttgart),
May 1988; "Recent Works by Ilse Aichinger" by Brian
Keith-Smith, in *German Life and Letters* (London), July 1988.

                              *   *   *

Austrian writer Ilse Aichinger's work is difficult to subject to
critical exegesis and literary classification. There are traces of
the literary styles of writers such as Franz Kafka, Adalbert
Stifter, and Georg Trakl in her work, and some critics have
detected ideas that draw on Freud's and Jung's psychoanalytic
theories and on Wittgenstein's repudiation of the logic of
language. With contemporary Austrian writers such as
Thomas Bernhard and Peter Handke (*q.v.*), she shares a
sceptical attitude towards the shared possibilities of linguistic
expression. However, attempts to explain her work perhaps
reveal more about the critic than the writer, since Aichinger's
work is well and truly her own, providing a self-contained and
often impenetrable literary universe with its own private
codes.

Aichinger's first and longest work, *Die größere Hoffnung*
(*Herod's Children*), is her only novel so far, and was one of the
first literary evaluations of Jewish suffering under Nazi rule in
Austria. A young half-Jewish girl, whose mother has emigrated to the United States and who is living with her
grandmother, seeks comradeship with a group of abandoned
Jewish children. She is not fully accepted by them, and
eventually is killed during enemy action. This brief description
may suggest that *Herod's Children*, like other examples of
German-language *Trümmerliteratur* (rubble literature), is a
piece of extended social realism. However, Aichinger's novel
is far from socially realistic in style, as it frequently inter-
changes reality and fantasy, in an attempt to invade a child's
view of the world, and does not present us with psychologically
motivated characters and naturalistic dialogue. The novel is
structured rather like the Expressionist "station dramas" of the
playwrights Friedrich Kaiser and August Strindberg, showing
in a number of tableaux Ellen's dreamlike and marginal
participation in various aspects of the "real world" she
inhabits. What is most striking about the novel is the way
Aichinger transfigures reality, using Ellen's *anomie* as neither
fully Jewish nor pure Aryan, not only to describe actual

historical circumstances, but also to represent a much wider
sense of existential uncertainty and doubt.

Despite the choice of the novel form for this confident early
work, Aichinger has expressed herself through much more
compressed forms in her subsequent career, preferring the
poem, short story, radio play, and very much her own
contribution to modern literary forms, a reworking of the
Platonic dialogue. However, *Herod's Children* shares many
features with Aichinger's later work, not least the de-familiar-
isation of the contemporary, material world by untoward
events and unexpected linguistic usages. The majority of
Aichinger's narratives take place in unnamed and sparely
described, but clearly terrestrial, surroundings, which are
imbued with dreamlike and fantastical qualities. As in dreams,
and in Franz Kafka's work, the arenas of bourgeois life —
streets, hallways, cellars, stairways, offices, flats, and attics —
take on hidden and often macabre meanings. Similarly, the
platitudes and banalities of social dialogue reveal uncertainties, word associations, and guilty truths, their cheery confidences unable to disguise the instability and inadequacy of the
language that is being used. More acutely even than Kafka,
Aichinger creates a grotesque, enclosed, and highly individual
universe, characterised by recurring motifs and preoccupations that include particular colours, children and dwarfs, the
sea, the moon, students, and animals.

One of the most uinsettling aspects of Aichinger's short
stories is the position of the narrator. The stories are often
recounted in the first-person, yet there is surprisingly little
authorial intervention or attempt to create a realistic narrator.
Although the language is unadorned and laconic, and employs
the immediacy of the present tense or the imperative, the
subject-matter related is often very bizarre. The collections of
short stories, dialogues, and poems, *Wo ich wohne* (Where I
Live) and *Eliza, Eliza* show Aichinger at her recondite best. In
"The Mouse" the narrative "I" turns out to be a rodent with
more developed human characteristics and fears than many an
Aichinger *Homo sapiens*, while the child's toy in "Die Puppe"
(The Doll) seems to have taken on human emotion from its
owner. One of Aichinger's best-known pieces, the haunting
"Mirror Story," is told by a woman on the point of death after
an abortion, who re-enacts her life in reverse. In her own
inimitable way, Aichinger actualizes the improbable in stories
such as "The Green Donkey," "Lake Spirits," and "Mein
Vater aus Stroh" (My Father of Straw), presenting tentative
sightings of a donkey, lake inhabitants locked into previous
lives, and a far from comfortable father-figure in entirely
matter-of-fact tones. In these collections Aichinger also
employs less opaque parable forms; good examples of which
are "The Bound Man" and "Where I Live," which are initiated
by the invasion of the everyday through the occurrence and
subsequent acceptance of grotesque events.

Aichinger's most creative period has been from the late
1940s to the late 1960s, and it was during this time that she
produced a number of dramatic dialogues and radio plays as
well as poems and short stories. These dramatic pieces are also
characterised by uncertain viewpoints, the sense of the familiar
turned strange, and a desire to test the boundaries of what can
be expressed. The radio play *Knöpfe* (Buttons) is a good
illustration of Aichinger's imaginative method. Here female
workers in a button factory disappear, and are later discovered
to have been changed into buttons. The mass-produced
buttons contain the personality of the erstwhile worker. In
Aichinger's play, the workers accept these circumstances; the
button firm increasingly becomes the one and only world for
the women who have not yet been transformed. Most of her
dramatic work consists of dialogues, found in collections such
as *Zu keiner Stunde* (Not at Any Hour) and *Auckland*, where

the questioning, exchanges, and word associations reveal the instability of any shared "truth" and linguistic consensus. Her poetry from 1955 to 1977, characterised by its terseness, and tantalising combination of direct address and enigmatic content, is collected in *Verschenkter Rat* (Advice Given Away).

In the last 20 years or so, Aichinger's work has shown an even more pronounced scepticism about the possibilities of expression, and, rather like Samuel Beckett in his later years, she has written less and less. Some critics see her collection of writings, *Schlechte Wörter* (Bad Words) as the most radical of her statements about the difficulties of communicating experience and imagination through words. Therefore, her most recent collection of work, *Kleist, Moos, Fasane* (Kleist, Moss, Pheasant) — street names in her grandmother's district — comes as a surprise. The book is arranged in three parts, the first of which contains early memories and reveals Aichinger at her most accessible, with a warmly evoked description of her grandmother's house in the title story, a poignant remembering of what Christmas was like for a half-Jewish child during the *Anschluss* in *Vor der langen Zeit* (A Long Time Ago), and a recollection of the comfortable and ordinary Viennese world in "der 1. September 1939" (The First of September 1939). The second part of the volume is given over to aphoristic writings that span the years 1950–1985, while the final section contains more extended pieces, including highly personal essays on Joseph Conrad, Franz Kafka, Adalbert Stifter, Georg Trakl, and Nelly Sachs (many of whose prizes she has also won). Included also is the essay "Schnee" (Snow) that like "Schlechte Wörter" shows Aichinger paring down language and discarding words that do not evoke pleasure or yield immediate meaning, perhaps attempting, as she admits at the end of "Mirror Story" is one of the most difficult tasks, to get to the prelinguistic stage of human development.

Aichinger has maintained that "Reading and writing are like searching and finding in their relationship to one another." Because of the hermetic nature of her writing, and the great responsibility placed on the reader to construct meaning, "searching" in Aichinger's intriguing work can both exhilarate and frustrate.

—Anna-Marie Taylor

––––––

AITMATOV, Chingiz (Torekulovich). Also Chinghiz Aitmatov. Kirghizstani. Born in Sheker, Kirghizstan, 12 December 1928. Educated at Kirghiz Agricultural Institute, degree in animal husbandry 1953; Gorky Literary Institute, Moscow, 1956–58. Married 1) Keres Aitmatova, two sons; 2) Maria Urmatova in 1974, one son and one daughter. Assistant to secretary of Sheker Village Soviet, from 1943; editor, *Literaturnyi Kyrghyzstan* magazine, late 1950s; correspondent, *Pravda*, for five years; member of the Communist Party of the Soviet Union, 1959–91; deputy to Supreme Soviet, 1966–89; People's Writer of Kirghiz Soviet Socialist Republic, 1968; candidate member, 1969–71, and member, 1971–90, Central Committee, Kirghiz S.S.R.; vice chair, Committee of Solidarity with Peoples of Asian and African Countries, 1974–89; member, Congress of People's Deputies of the U.S.S.R., 1989–91; member of Mikhail Gorbachev's Presidential Council, 1990–91. Since 1990 Ambassador to Luxembourg. Member of the editorial board, *Novyi mir* and *Literaturnaia gazeta* literary journals; editor, *Druzhba*

narodov; editor-in-chief, *Inostrannaia literatura*, 1988–90. First secretary, 1964–69, and chair, 1969–86, Cinema Union of Kirghiz S.S.R.; since 1986 chair, Union of Writers of Kirghizstan, and Issyk-Kul Forum. Recipient: Lenin prize, 1963; Order of the Red Banner of Labor (twice); State prize, 1968, 1977, 1983; Hero of Socialist Labour, 1978. Member of Kirghiz Academy of Science, 1974, European Academy of Arts, Science, and Humanities, 1983, and World Academy of Art and Science, 1987. Address: Russian Embassy, 1719 Luxembourg.

PUBLICATIONS

Fiction

Litsom k litsu [Face to Face]. Published in *Oktiabr'* (Moscow), 3, 1958.
Rasskazy [Stories]. Moscow, Sovetskii pisatel', 1958.
Dzhamilia. Moscow, Pravda, 1959; as *Jamilia*, Moscow, Foreign Languages Publishing House, 1960.
Melodiia [Melody]. Frunze, Kirgizdosizdat, 1959.
Verbliuzhii glaz [The Camel's Eye]. Moscow, Sovetskii pisatel', 1962.
Povesti gor i stepei. Moscow, Goslitizdat, 1962; as *Tales of the Mountains and Steppes*, Moscow, Progress, 1969.
Materinskoe pole. Moscow, Pravda, 1963; as *Mother-Earth*, in *Novels*, 1965; in *Mother Earth and Other Stories*, 1989.
Samanchy zholu. Basmasy, n.p., 1963.
Mlechnyi put' [Milky Way]. Frunze, Kirgizgosizdat, 1963.
Pervyi uchitel' [The First Master]. Frunze, Kirgizuchpedgiz, 1963.
Ballada o pervom uchitele [Ballad About the First Teacher]. Moscow, Progress, 1964.
Korotkie novelly [Short Novels]. Moscow, Progress, 1964.
Topolek moi v krasnoi kosynke [My Little Poplar in a Red Headscarf]. Moscow, Znanie, 1964.
Tri povesti [Three Short Stories]. Erevan, Aistan, 1965; as *Short Novels: To Have and to Lose; Duishen; Mother-Earth*, Moscow, Progress, 1965.
Povesti [Novellas]. Kazan', Tatknigoizdat, 1965.
Proschai, Gul'sary! Published in *Novyi mir* (Moscow), 3, 1966; Moscow, Molodaia gvardiia, 1967; as *Farewell, Gul'sary!*, London, Hodder and Stoughton, 1970.
Otvetstvennost' pered budushchim [Responsibility for the Future]. Published in *Voprosy literatury* (Moscow), 9, 1967.
Povesti i rasskazy [Novellas and Stories]. Moscow, Molodaia gvardiia, 1970.
Syn soldata [The Son of a Soldier]. Frunze, Mektep, 1970.
Belyi parokhod. Published in *Novyi mir* (Moscow), 1, 1970; as *The White Ship*, New York, Crown, 1972; as *The White Steamship*, London, Hodder and Stoughton, 1972.
Posle skazki [After the Fairytale]. Riga, Liesma, 1971.
Izbrannoe [Collection]. Moscow, Progress, 1973.
The Lament of a Migrating Bird, Felixstowe, Premier Press, 1973, as *Rannie zhuravli*, Moscow, Molodaia gvardiia, 1976; as *The Cranes Fly Early*, Moscow, Raduga, 1983.
Posle skazki (Belyi parokhod); Materinskoe pole; Proshchai, Gul'sary!; Pervyi uchitel'; Litsom k litsu; Dzhamilia; Topolek moi v krasnoi kosynke; Verbliuzhii glaz; Svidanie s synom; Soldatenok. Frunze, Kyrgyzstan, 1974.
Soldatenok [The Soldier]. Frunze, Mektep, 1974.
Nochnoi poliv [Night Dew]. Frunze, Kyrgyzstan, 1975.
Povesti [Short Stories]. Moscow, Detskaia literatura, 1976.
Lebedi nad Issyk-Kulem [Swans Above Issyk-Kulem]. Moscow, Progress, 1976.

Pegii pes, begushchii kraem moria. Moscow, Sovetskii pisatel', 1977; as *Piebald Dog Running Along the Shore and Other Stories*, Moscow, Raduga, 1989.

Izbrannye proizvedeniia [Collected works]. Tashkent, Izdatal'stvo Literatury i Iskusstvo, 2 vols., 1978.

Legenda o rogatoi materi-olenizhe [The Legend of the Horned Mother Deer]. Alma-Ata, Zhalyn, 1979.

I dol'she veka dlitsia den'. Frunze, Kyrgyzstan, 1981; as *The Day Lasts More than a Hundred Years*, Bloomington, Indiana University Press, and London, Macdonald, 1983.

Burannyi polustanok (I dol'she veka dlitsia den') [The Snowstorm Halt]. Frunze, Kyrgyzstan, 1981.

Izbrannoe. Minsk, Iunatstva, 1981.

Povesti [Short Stories]. Moscow, Molodaia gvardiia, 1982.

Sobranie sochinenii v 3-kh tomakh [Collected Works in 3 Volumes]. Moscow, Molodaia gvardiia, 3 vols., 1982–84.

Mat'-olenikha: legenda (iz povesti "Belyi parokhod") [Mother Deer: Legend (from the novel *White Steamship*)]. Frunze, Mektep, 1983.

Povesti [Short Stories]. Frunze, Mektep, 1983.

Rasskazy [Stories]. Frunze, Mektep, 1983.

Rasskazy, ocherki, publitsistika [Stories, Essays, Publications]. Moscow, Molodaia gvardiia, 1984.

Povesti, rasskazy [Novellas, Stories]. Frunze, Kyrgyzstan, 1985.

Ekho mira: povesti, rasskazy, publitsistika [Echo of the World: Novellas, Stories, Publications]. Moscow, Pravda, 1985.

Krasnoe iabloko [The Red Apple]. Frunze, Mektep, 1985.

Mal'chik s pal'chik. Frunze, Mektep, 1985.

Plakha. Riga, "Liesma," 1986; as *The Place of the Skull*, London, Faber, and New York, Grove Press, 1989.

Povesti [Short Stories]. Moscow, Sovetskii pisatel', 1987.

Bogoroditsa v snegakh [Madonna in the Snows]. 1987.

Legenda o ptitse Donenbai: iz romana "I dol'she veka dlitsia den'" [The Legend of the Donenbay Bird: From the Novel *The Day Lasts More than a Hundred Years*]. Frunze, Mektep, 1987.

Svidania s synom [An Appointment with the Son]. Frunze, Mektep, 1987.

Sineglazaia volchitsa: Otr. iz romana "Plakha" [Blue-Eyed She-Wolf: From the Novel *The Block*]. Frunze, Mektep, 1987.

Shestevo i sed'moi: Otr. iz romana "Plakha" [Sixth and Seventh: From the Novel *The Block*]. Frunze, Mektep, 1987.

Chas slova. Moscow, Progress, 1988; as *The Time to Speak Out*, Moscow, Progress, 1988; as *Time to Speak*, New York, International Publishers, 1989.

Mother Earth and Other Stories. London, Faber, 1989.

Beloe oblako Chingiskhana [The White Cloud of Chingiskhan]. Published in *Znamia* (Moscow), 8, 1990.

Play

Voskhozhdenie na Fudzhiiamu, with Kaltai Mukhamedzhanov (produced Moscow, 1973). As *The Ascent of Mount Fuji* (produced Washington, D.C., 1975), New York, Farrar Straus, 1975.

Other

Atadan kalgan tuiak. Frunze, Mektep, 1970.

V soavtorstve s zemleiu i vodoiu [In Co-Authorship with the Earth and Water] (essays and lectures). Frunze, Kyrgyzstan, 1978.

Do the Russians Want War? Moscow, Progress, 1985.

My izmeniaem mir, mir izmeniaet nas [We Change the World, the World Changes Us] (essays, articles, interviews). Frunze, Kyrgyzstan, 1985.

On Craftsmanship, with *Chinghiz Aitmatov* by V. Novikov. Moscow, Raduga, 1987.

Biz duinonu zhangyrtabyz, duino bizdi zhangyrtat. Frunze, Kyrgyzstan, 1988.

Stat'i, vystupleniia, dialogi, interv'iu [Articles, Statements, Dialogues, Interviews]. Moscow, Agenstva pechati Novosti, 1988.

*

Critical Studies: "Am I Not in My Own Home?" by Boris Pankin, in *Soviet Studies in Literature* (Armonk, New York), 18(3), 1981; "The Child Narrator in the Novels of Chingiz Aitmatov" by Nina Kolesnikoff, and "A Poetic Vision in Conflict: Chingiz Aitmatov's Fiction" by Constantin V. Ponomareff, both in *Russian Literature and Criticism*, edited by Evelyn Bristol, Berkeley, California, Berkeley Slavic Specialties, 1982; "Chingiz Aitmatov: A Feeling for the Times" by Nikolai Khokhlov, in *Soviet Literature* (Brooklyn, New York), 4[421], 1983; "Both Are Primary: An 'Author's Translation' Is a Creative Re-Creation" by Munavvarkhon Dadazhanova, in *Soviet Studies in Literature* (Armonk, New York), 20(4), 1984; "Time to Speak Out" (interview) by Vladimir Korkin, in *Soviet Literature* (Brooklyn, New York), 5[434], 1984; "Chingiz Aitmatov's First Novel: A New Departure?" by Stewart Paton, in *Slavonic and East European Review* (London), October 1984; "Prose Has Two Wings" by Keneshbek Asanliyev, in *Soviet Literature* (Brooklyn, New York), 2[443], 1985; "Chingiz Aitmatov's *Proshchay, Gul'sary*" by Shellagh Duffin Graham, in *Journal of Russian Studies* (Rugby, Warwickshire), 49, 1985; "India Has Become Near" by Miriam Salganik, in *Soviet Literature* (Brooklyn, New York), 12[453], 1985; *Chinghiz Aitmatov* by V. Novkov, Moscow, Raduga, 1987; "Chingiz Aitmatov's *The Execution Block*: Religion, Opium and the People" by Robert Porter, in *Scottish Slavonic Review* (Glasgow), 8, 1987; "On Chinghiz Aitmatov and His Characters: For the Author's 60th Birthday" by Evgenii Sidorov, in *Soviet Literature* (Brooklyn, New York), 11[488], 1988.

*   *   *

From the mid-1960s to the 1980s Chingiz Aitmatov was one of the most popular prose writers in the Soviet Union. In some measure his special appeal can be attributed to the fact that he is a Kirghiz and thus represents one of the smallest and most remote Soviet peoples. He became one of the best examples of how Soviet cultural policy benefited ethnic minorities. To all intents and purposes Kirghizia did not acquire its own written language until after the Russian Revolution. However, there had been a strong oral literary tradition, and Aitmatov's achievement can be seen in part as blending folk legend and myth with the modern novel. His work has sometimes been classified as magic realism. The epic qualities of some of his stories have also led to his being likened to Homer and Tolstoi. Early works such as *Materinskoe pole* (*Mother-Earth*) and *Topolek moi v krasnoi kosynke* (My Little Poplar in a Red Headscarf) were written in Kirghiz and then translated into Russian, while his more mature works are written in Russian. The author has often discussed the phenomenon of bilingualism and also the problems arising when a "young" literature comes into contact with an established one. It is his view that the Russian and Kirghiz languages live in co-existence and that through Russian his writing and indeed the culture of his native land have reached a worldwide audience. Aitmatov was a prominent, though liberal, Communist, yet his homeland is predominantly Muslim, and such conflicts are occasionally glimpsed in his writing, which overall explores the broad interface of the ancient and modern worlds. Never in any sense a "dissident," Aitmatov occasionally attracted censure from conservative quarters.

Dzhamilia tells of the sympathetic eponymous heroine abandoning her thoroughly unworthy husband and making a new life with another man. Louis Aragon called this piece, all the more daring given its Islamic setting, "the most splendid love story in the world." It was *Proschai, Gul'sary!* (*Farewell, Gul'sary!*), however, that established Aitmatov's world reputation. Ostensibly the story of a horse (Gul'sary) and his master, this short novel examines one of the most painful episodes in Soviet history — collectivisation. Tanabai is an overzealous yet honest Communist whose horse is taken from him, gelded, and used merely as a status symbol by the collective farm chairman. Though there is an implication that the Communist system in the post-Stalin era is now capable of reforming itself, the overriding impression the story leaves is of mankind's talent for injustice, mistakes, and waste. Gul'sary is returned to his rightful owner, but dies. The thoroughly realistic narrative is interspersed with Tanabai's wife songs, which tell of Grey She-Goat luring a wantonly destructive hunter to his death and of a camel that has lost her young. Here we have a key notion in Aitmatov — the moral superiority of the animal kingdom.

Allegory and legend are used to perfection in Aitmatov's other major short novel, *Belyi parokhod* (*The White Steamship*, also known as *After the Fairy Tale*). The hero, a seven-year-old boy, is cared for by his grandfather Momun, who nourishes him on folk legends, particularly one concerning the Horned-Deer Mother and the origins of the Kirghiz people. The boy invents his own fairy story, in which he will turn into a fish and swim out on Lake Issyk-Kul to meet his (long-departed) father, who was once a sailor. The boy's innocence is brutally violated by the adult world. His uncle, a drunkard and wife-beater with a nostalgia for the well-ordered era of Stalin, slaughters a maral deer and initiates a drunken orgy in which Momun is induced to eat the deer meat. Horrified by this desecration of the "Horned-Mother Deer," the protector of the Kirghiz nation, the boy enacts his own fairytale and drowns. The strong educative value of the story along with its emphasis on cultural heritage and moral concerns offer a powerful challenge to the narrowly utilitarian and materialistic establishment values.

Aitmatov's later, lengthier novels are not as successful in artistic terms, but they aroused a good deal of discussion when they first appeared. *I dol'she veka dlitsia den'* (*The Day Lasts More than a Hundred Years*) combines a conventional narrative (the lives of a few characters from the 1950s to the 1970s), a science-fiction story, and an ancient legend concerning the Mankurts, who when captured by a foreign tribe are tortured either to death or until they lose all memory and become slaves and zombies. These three strands are pulled neatly together at the end of the book when the hero, Yedigei, returns to his ancestral grounds to bury his friend, only to discover that a space station has been built there. The novel depicts cooperation between East and West in the face of contact with extraterrestrials, and taken as a whole can be seen as an attempt to portray a Soviet Union that is now prepared to come to terms with its past and to implement Brezhnev's policy of détente.

Plakha (*The Place of the Skull*) is similarly loose in structure, attempting to address topical issues while still presenting the author's traditional preoccupations: cultural heritage, the importance of myth, moral awareness, and the animal world.

Published in 1986, it is a good example of glasnost early fiction, confronting the problems of drug abuse, general criminality, and environmental destruction. Religion is another fundamental concern of the book. The hero Avdii (Obadiah) is a religious idealist who is expelled from his seminary before he has time to leave of his own accord. He tries to "do good" by infiltrating a group of drug dealers, but is beaten up by them. Later he joins a work team that slaughters antelope herds to fulfil the meat quota. He is "crucified" on a tree by his workmates when he objects to the wholesale destruction. These two stories are bound together somewhat by a third storyline involving a pair of wolves, personified, trying to raise a litter despite the obstacles placed in their path by mankind. The work contains graphic and engaging passages, but also some shallow and contrived philosophising ("People seek out fate, but fate seeks out people").

Aitmatov's fiction is set primarily in his native land, though *The Day Lasts More than a Hundred Years* takes place largely in Kazakhstan, and a short powerful work, *Pegii pes, begushchii kraem moria* (*Piebald Dog Running Along the Shore*) is about a family of Gilyaks, the tiny nation living on the mouth of the Amur river and on part of Sakhalin Island, very near Japan. Thus nationalism and patriotism are celebrated in his work, but only to the extent that they contribute to a greater understanding of human beings everywhere. *Piebald Dog*, an account of an ill-fated seal-culling expedition, attains an almost timeless, universal quality, and critics have understandably likened it to Ernest Hemingway's *The Old Man and the Sea*.

—Robert Porter

AKHMADULINA, Bella (Isabella Akhatovna Akhmadulina). Also Bella Axmadulina. Russian. Born in Moscow, 10 April 1937. Educated at the Gorky Literary Institute, Moscow, until 1960. Married 1) Evgenii Evtushenko (*q.v.*) in 1954 (divorced); 2) Iurii Nagibin (divorced); 3) Gennadii Mamlin; 4) Boris Messerer in 1974. Delegate, All-Russian Congress of Writers, 1965; secretary, Union of Soviet Writers, since 1986. Recipient: State prize, 1989. Honorary member, American Academy of Arts and Letters, 1977. Address: Cherniachovskogo str. 4, apt. 37, 125319 Moscow, Russia.

PUBLICATIONS

Verse

El' — Zhaleika [Fir Tree — Zhaleika].   Published in *Grani* (Frankfurt), 38, 1958.
Struna [String].   Moscow, Sovetskii pisatel', 1962.
Stikhi [Poems].   Tbilisi, Nakaduli, 1962.
Skazka o dozhde [Tale of the Rain].   1963.
Moia rodoslovnaia [My Genealogy].   1963.
Prikliuchenie v antikvarnom magazine [Adventure in an Antique Store].   1967.
Oznob (includes prose, and *Skazka o dozhde, Moia rodoslovnaia*, and *Prikliuchenie v antikvarnom magazine*). Frankfurt, Posev, 1968; as *Fever and Other New Poems*, translated by Geoffrey Dutton, Melbourne, Sun, 1968; New York, Morrow, 1969; London, Owen, 1970.

Stikhi [Poems].   Erevan, Aiastan, 1968.
Snegopad [Snowstorm].   Published in *Novyi mir* (Moscow), 5, 1968.
Uroki muzyki [Music Lessons].   Moscow, Sovetskii pisatel', 1969.
Stikhi [Poems].   Moscow, Khudozhestvennaia literatura, 1975.
Tri stikhtvoreniia [Three Poems].   Published in *Grani* (Frankfurt), 74, 1977.
Metel' [Snowstorm].   Moscow, Sovetskii pisatel', 1977.
Svecha [Candle].   Moscow, Sovetskaia Rossiia, 1977.
Sny o Gruzii [Dreams of Georgia].   Tbilisi, Merani, 1977.
Three Russian Poets, with Margarite Aliger and Iunna Morits, translated by Elaine Feinstein.   Manchester, Carcanet, 1979.
Three Russian Women Poets, with Anna Akhmatova and Marina Tsvetaeva, translated by Mary Maddock.-Trumansburg, New York, Crossing Press, 1983.
Taina: novye stikhi [Secret: New Poems].   Moscow, Sovetskii pisatel', 1983.
Sad: novye stikhi [The Garden: New Poems].   Moscow, Sovetskii pisatel', 1987.
Stikhotvoreniia [Poems].   Moscow, Khudozhestvennaia literatura, 1988.
Izbrannoe: stikhi [Selections].   Moscow, Sovetskii pisatel', 1988.
The Garden: New and Selected Poetry and Prose, edited and translated by F. D. Reeve.   New York, Holt, 1990; London, Boyars, 1991.
Poberezh'e [Seashore].   Moscow, n.p., 1991.

Fiction

Mnogo sobak i sobaka.   Published in *Metropol'* (Moscow), 1979; as *The Many Dogs and the Dog*, in *Metropol'*, 1982.

Play

Screenplay: *Clear Ponds*, 1965.

*

Bibliographies: by Christine A. Rydel, in *Russian Literature Triquarterly* (Ann Arbor, Michigan), 1, 1971; in *Ten Bibliographies of Twentieth Century Russian Literature*, Ann Arbor, Michigan, Ardis, 1977.

Critical Studies: "The Metapoetical World of Bella Akhmadulina" by Christine Rydel, in *Russian Literature Triquarterly* (Ann Arbor, Michigan), 1, 1971; "Poetic Creation in Bella Axmadulina," in *Slavic and East European Journal* (Minneapolis), 28(1), 1984, and "The Wonder of Nature and Art: Bella Axmadulina's *Secret*," in *New Studies in Russian Language and Literature*, edited by Anna Lisa Crone and Catherine V. Chvany, Columbus, Ohio, Slavica, 1986, both by Sonia Ketchian; "Axmadulina's *Poèmy*: Poems of Transformation and Origins" by Nancy Condee, in *Slavic and East European Journal* (Minneapolis), 29(2), 1985; "Have the Poets Yielded Their Former Position?" (interview) by Anatoli Ivanushkin, in *Soviet Literature* (Brooklyn, New York), 6[483], 1988.

*   *   *

Bella Akhmadulina's writing has a highly personal tone. Often identified with the poet herself, Akhmadulina's lyrical narrator steps into the longer narrative poems, and recounts her fantastic adventures. In "Adventure in an Antique Store" she meets the ancient owner who takes her back to the age of Aleksandr Pushkin's Ethiopian ancestor, Gannibal, while in "A Summer Home Romance" she enters into a romantic triangle with Pushkin himself and Anna Kern, a woman to whom he dedicated some important lyrics. Bella observes the actions of her Italian and Tatar precursors in *Moia rodoslovnaia* (My Genealogy); she suffers from a malady so severe that her violent shaking alienates the neighbors by causing their furniture to rattle so loudly that it prevents their children from sleeping in "Chill." But one of her best and most popular poems, *Skazka o dozhde* (Tale of the Rain) combines all of her early favorite symbols in a highly structured work that describes the joy and pain of poetic inspiration.

The poem describes the process of creation that Rain (inspiration) activates within her. Akhmadulina describes how the Rain's all-encompassing presence alienates her from those around her. Because she somehow feels it is improper to be "soaked to the skin" while everyone else suffers from the drought, she sends the Rain away. Only after she enters a house full of philistines who interrogate her about her "gift" does she realize how much she loves and needs the Rain. Heeding her summons the Rain enters the house only to have the other guests destroy it, mop it up with rags, and pour it down the commode. Left without the Rain, the narrator runs into the street and demonstrates her love for her former companion by kissing a puddle of water on the dry asphalt. This puddle alone remains as a reminder of the Rain; and "plunged into fear, the weather bureau never again predicted precipitation."

Unfortunately Akhmadulina also suffered a period of drought in which she produced almost no poetry. Her works after *Skazka o dozhde* explore the themes of sickness, insomnia, and suffering over her inability to write in an atmosphere of muteness, shadows, and darkness. In the mid-1970s, however, her poems again began to appear regularly in the press and in a number of collections. In these poems some of her old themes and images reappear, but new ones also gradually emerge.

In her recent works Akhmadulina returns to the themes of writing; her love of foreign lands — especially Georgia; evocations of the past through visions of the specific Russian poets who influenced her; the joys and rewards of friendship. Always displaying a profound sense of integrity and morality, her poems now are acquiring an even deeper spiritual cast. Almost Romantic in tone, Akhmadulina's poems find God and virtue in nature. Throughout her career she has been able to transform the mundane into the whimsical, the sublime, and the wonderful. She continues her miracles of transformation; now, however, she performs them in a more mature, reflective manner.

Since Akhmadulina began writing in the mid-1950s, her poems have become more dense, complex, and difficult. Always prone to wordplay, especially puns, she now mixes her own remarkable neologisms with archaisms and intertwines colloquial speech and slang with highblown poetic diction — often in the same poem. Her tendency to use elliptical phrases along with ambiguous and/or convoluted syntax contributes to the linguistic virtuosity of her poems. The classically elegant form of her early poetic exercises, with their short iambic lines rich in soundplay and innovative rhymes, has given way to more daring, elaborate structures. Akhmadulina has recently been experimenting with ternary meters and longer iambic lines. While her rhymes have always been intricate, they have become more varied with their approximations, consonant reversals, compound, deep and internal assonances and alliterations.

Akhmadulina's symbolic system has developed in a similar vein. The puppies which featured in her early works have grown into a variety of dogs which sometimes stand for poetic conscience and other times for inspiration itself. Rain still appears, but in many guises: snow, dew, the damp earth, and Russia's rivers, especially the Oka and Neva. Her playful children have grown up with her and have turned into orphans. The flying she did around the tops of buildings in Moscow and St. Petersburg now takes her further out into the night sky. All of her recurring images change to reflect Akhmadulina's own growth and maturation as a poet; however, her treatment of flowers best reflects three main stages in her poetic life.

For Akhmadulina, flowers have always represented poems. In the early lyrics they grow in greenhouses, protected from the elements. As she becomes more daring as a poet, she finds herself more often in gardens where the flowers grow in the open air. The motifs of flowers and gardens all but disappear in her collections *Snegopad* (Snowstorms) and *Svecha* (Candle). But in the first poem of her dazzling collection *Taina* (Secret), "I have a secret that arises from a miraculous flowering," the lyrical narrator bypasses gardens and runs out into the fields to greet the first spring blooms from which she learns a valuable secret. Only in the collection *Sad* (The Garden) does each poem provide a clue to the revelation of the secret: flowers act simultaneously as the source of inspiration as well as its result — the poems themselves. The entire volume is called "The Garden" because each poem is a flower lying within its pages.

Akhmadulina has also gained renown as a translator — especially from Georgian. In addition she has written excellent prose, both journalistic and belletristic in nature. The remarkable story *Mnogo sobak i sobaka* (*The Many Dogs and the Dog*) appeared in the unofficial 1979 almanac *Metropol'*, whose chief editor was her long-time friend Vasilii Aksenov (*q.v.*). This Proustian, synesthetic, multi-leveled tale relates the plight of the main character, Shelaputov, who has lost all of his senses as well as his memory. His search for identity reveals the main theme of the work: the pain of creation, of "how the song is sung." And whereas inspiration earlier appeared as an affectionate puppy, it has now aged into a scarred, careworn, old, but magnificent dog. In *Skazka o dozhde* the philistines try to eliminate inspiration, but a puddle remains; in the later story an enemy shoots and kills Shelaputov's dog. Though Akhmadulina never overtly refers to political systems, the various subtexts of the work make her implications clear. In this story, as well as in the complete body of her work, Akhmadulina consistently ponders questions of good and evil and champions artistic freedom.

Throughout her poetic career Akhmadulina has been able to retain her integrity as a poet, even when the political climate has been hostile to the arts. Through her metapoetry she not only ponders the act of creation, but also defines herself as a poet. She has identified with some of her predecessors, especially Anna Akhmatova and Marina Tsvetaeva. She marvels at the poetic talents of Pushkin, Mikhail Lermontov, and Osip Mandel'shtam. Conscious of her destiny as an heir to her masters, she seeks her place in the rich tradition of Russian literature. Bella Akhmadulina certainly belongs in the ranks of Russia's most gifted poets.

—Christine A. Rydel

AKSENOV, Vasilii (Pavlovich). Also Vasily Aksyonov. Russian; son of the writer Evgenia Ginzburg. Born in Kazan, 20 August 1932. Educated at Pavlov Medical Institute, Leningrad, medical degree 1956. Married 1) Kira Mendeleva in 1957 (divorced 1979), one son; 2) Maia Karmen in 1979. Physician in the far north, 1956–60, then in Leningrad, in a tuberculosis clinic, Moscow, six months, and in Moscow; travelled to Poland, Japan, and India, 1962; editor, *Iunost'* [Youth] magazine, from 1962; Regent Lecturer and Visiting Professor, University of California, Los Angeles, 1975; work banned as a result of contributing to (also editor of) *Metropol'* journal (samizdat), 1979; exiled to United States, July 1980; writer-in-residence, University of Michigan, Ann Arbor, University of Southern California, Los Angeles, and Woodrow Wilson Center, George Washington University, Washington, D.C., all 1981, and Goucher College, Baltimore, Maryland, 1984; Soviet citizenship restored, 1990; returned to Russia, early 1990s. Member, Writers' Union (resigned in protest, 1979). Recipient: International Competition of Satirical Authors golden prize (Bulgaria), 1967; Woodrow Wilson International Center fellow, 1982. Address: Krasnoiarmeskaia st. 21, apt. 20, 125319 Moscow, Russia.

PUBLICATIONS

Fiction

Kollegi. Moscow, Sovetskii pisatel', 1961; as *Colleagues*, Moscow, Foreign Languages Publishing House, 1961; New York and London, Putnam, 1962.
Zvezdnyi bilet. Published in *Iunost'* (Moscow), 1961; as *A Starry Ticket*, New York and London, Putnam, 1962; as *A Ticket to the Stars*, New York, New American Library, 1963.
Na polputi k lune. Published in *Novyi mir* (Moscow), 7, 1962; as "Halfway to the Moon," in *The New Writing in Russia*, edited by Thomas Whitney, Ann Arbor, University of Michigan Press, 1964.
Apel'siny iz Marokko [Oranges from Morocco]. Published in *Iunost'* (Moscow), 1963.
Katapul'ta [Catapult]. Moscow, Sovetskii pisatel', 1964.
Tovarishch Krasivii Furazhkin [Comrade Krasivii Furazhkin]. Published in *Iunost'* (Moscow), 12, 1964.
Pora, moi drug, pora. Moscow, Molodaia gvardiia, 1965; as *It's Time, My Friend, It's Time*, London, Macmillan, 1969; as *It's Time, My Love, It's Time*, Nashville, Tennessee, Aurora, 1969.
Malen'kii kit — lakirovshchik deistvitel'nosti [The Little Whale — The Varnisher of Reality]. Tallin, Periodika, 1965.
Mestnyi "khuligan" Abramashvili [The Local "Hooligan" of Abramashvil]. Tbilisi, Nakaduli, 1966.
Zatovarennaia bochkotara. Published in *Iunost'* (Moscow), 3, 1968; with *Randevu*, New York, Serebrianyi vek, 1980; as *Surplussed Barrelware*, Ann Arbor, Michigan, Ardis, 1985.
Zhal', chto vas ne bylo s nami [A Pity That You Were Not with Us]. Moscow, Sovetskii pisatel', 1969.
Liubov' k elektrichestvu [Love to the Electricity]. Published in *Iunost'* (Moscow), 1971.
Dzhin Grin — neprikasaemii [Gene Green — The Untouchable] (as Grivadii Gorpozhaks), with O. Gorchakov and G. Pozhenian. Moscow, n.p., 1972.
Samson and Samsoness. In *The Young Russians*, New York, Macmillan, 1972.
Kruglye sutki non-stop [Around the Clock Non-Stop]. Published in *Novyi mir* (Moscow), 8, 1976.
Poiski zhanra [In Search of a Genre]. Published in *Novyi mir* (Moscow), 1, 1977.

Stal'naia ptitsa. Published in *Glagol* (Michigan), 1, 1977; as *The Steel Bird, and Other Stories*, Ann Arbor, Michigan, Ardis, 1979.

Zolotaia nasha Zhelezka. Ann Arbor, Michigan, Ardis, 1980; as *Our Golden Ironburg*, Ann Arbor, Michigan, Ardis, 1988.

Ozhog. Ann Arbor, Michigan, Ardis, 1980; as *The Burn*, Boston, Houghton Mifflin, and London, Hutchinson, 1984.

Ostrov Krym. Ann Arbor, Michigan, Ardis, 1981; as *The Island of Crimea*, New York, Random House, 1983; London, Hutchinson, 1985.

Pravo na ostrov: rasskazy. Ann Arbor, Hermitage, 1983; as *Quest for an Island*, New York, Performing Arts Journal Publishing, 1987.

Bumazhnyi peizazh [The Paperscape]. Ann Arbor, Michigan, Ardis, 1983.

Skazhi izium: roman v moskovskikh traditsiiakh. Ann Arbor, Michigan, Ardis, 1985; as *Say Cheese!*, New York, Random House, 1989; London, Bodley Head, 1990.

Sobranie sochinenii [Collected Works]. Ann Arbor, Michigan, Ardis, 1987–.

Den' pervogo snegopada [The Day of the First Snowfall]. Leningrad, Sovetskii pisatel', 1990.

Kapital'noe peremeshchenie [Capitalist Displacement]. Published in *Voprosy literatury* (Moscow), August 1990.

Rai devu. Moscow, Tekst, 1991.

Zheltok iaitsa [The Yolk of an Egg]. Published in *Znamia* (Moscow), 8, 1991.

Moskovskaia saga [Moscow Saga]. Published in *Iunost'* (Moscow), 5–11, 1991.

Ran-devu [Rendezvous]. Moscow, Tekst, 1991.

Plays

Kollegi, from his own novel (produced Paris, 1962).

Vsegda v prodazhe [Always on Sale] (produced Moscow, 1965).

Vash ubiytsa [Your Murderer]. Published in *Performing Arts Journal* (New York), Spring 1977.

Chetyre temperamenta [The Four Temperaments]. Published in *Metropol'* (Moscow), 1979.

Aristofaniana s liagushkami [Aristophaniana and the Frogs]. Ann Arbor, Michigan, Hermitage, 1981.

Tsaplia [The Heron] (produced Paris, 1984). Published in *Sovremennaia dramaturgiia* (Moscow), 3, 1990.

Bliuz s russkim aksentom [The Blues with a Russian Accent] (film script). Published in *Grani* (Frankfurt), 139, 1986.

Other

Moi dedushka pamiatnik [My Grandfather Is a Monument] (for children). Moscow, Detskaia literatura, 1969.

Geografia liubovi: dialog v 2 chasti [Geography of Love: Dialogue in 2 Parts]. Moscow, VAAP, 1975.

Sunduchok v kotorom chto-to stuchit [The Box in Which Something Thumps] (for children). Moscow, Detskaia literatura, 1976.

The Paperscape: A View from the Flag Tower of the Smithsonian Institution Building: An Attempt at Introspection, or, How Some Stack of Paper Turns into a Russian Novel. Washington, D.C., Woodrow Wilson Center/Kennan Institute, 1982.

Progulka v Kalashnyi riad [A Walk in Kalashnii Row]. Published in *Grani* (Frankfurt), 133, 1984.

Afisha glasila: k 125-letiiu Chekhova [The Poster Read: To 125 Years of Chekhov]. Published in *Grani* (Frankfurt), 135, 1985.

V poiskakh grustnogo bebi: knigi ob Amerike. New York, Liberty, 1987; as *In Search of Melancholy Baby*, New York, Random House, 1987.

Editor, with Viktor Erofeev, Fazil Iskander, Andrei Bitov, and Evgenii Popov, *Metropol': literaturnyi al'manakh.* Ann Arbor, Michigan, Ardis, 1979; as *Metropol: A Literary Almanac*, New York, Norton, 1982.

Translator, *Buran*, by T. Akhtanov. Alma-Ata, n.p., 1971.
Translator, *Indiiskaia povest'*, by T. Akhtanov. Alma-Ata, Zhazushy, 1972.

*

Critical Studies: *The Function of the Grotesque in Vasilij Aksenov* by Peter Dalgård, Aarhus, Arkona, 1982; "Aksenov and Stalinism: Political, Moral and Literary Power" by Priscilla Meyer, in *Slavic and East European Journal* (Minneapolis), 30, 1986; *Vasiliy Pavlovich Aksenov: A Writer in Quest of Himself*, edited by Edward Możejko, Boris Brikev, and Peter Dalgård, Columbus, Ohio, Slavica, 1986; "Vasilij Aksionov's Aviary: *The Heron* and *The Steel Bird*" by D. Barton Johnson, in *Scando-Slavica* (Copenhagen), 33, 1987; "Aksenov Beyond 'Youth Prose' Subversion Through Popular Culture" by Greta N. Slobin, in *Slavic and East European Journal* (Minneapolis), 31(1), 1987; "Vasilii Aksenov and the Literature of Convergence: *Ostrov Krym* as Self-Criticism" by Olga Matich, in *Slavic Review* (Austin, Texas), 47(4), 1988; *The Artist and the Tyrant: Vassily Aksenov's Works in the Brezhnev Era* by Konstantin Kustanovich, Columbus, Ohio, Slavica, 1992.

*   *   *

Vassilii Aksenov has long been regarded as one of the most talented prose writers to emerge during what might be called the "post-Stalinist" era in Russian literature. His first novels, which appeared at the very beginning of the 1960s, brought him almost immediate fame, while his continuing reputation has been based on his short stories as well, especially a handful of widely anthologized works from that decade. Less well known but also significant are this prolific writer's plays and essays, the former dating primarily from the 1960s, the latter more typical of the late 1970s and 1980s, when the boundary in his writing between fictional and non-fictional genres at times becomes fluid. He has also tried his hand at English-Russian translation, including a Russian rendition of E. L. Doctorow's *Ragtime*.

Indeed, *Ragtime*, with its stylistic virtuosity as well as its unpredictable and often irreverent mixture of history and fiction, is a work particularly congenial to Aksenov's sensibility. *Ostrov Krym* (*The Island of Crimea*), written during the years that led up to his forced emigration from the Soviet Union in 1980, remains highly typical of his mature style. The novel changes one small aspect of post-revolutionary Soviet history, asking what would have happened had the Crimea remained controlled by the anti-revolutionary Whites and developed as a Western enclave — where people enjoy both personal freedoms and all the excesses of materialism — on the very edge of the Soviet Union. Aksenov takes advantage of the opportunities afforded by fiction to create sharply exaggerated pictures of both Communist and Western society; by nature he is a satirist, with a satirist's love of grotesque distortion as a method of highlighting flaws in both the social and political order. The contrasts in tone are also a general feature of Aksenov's writing: the lively style and the comic quality of individual scenes mask dark underpinnings and eventually give way to a somber message.

The Island of Crimea must be ranked among the more accessible of Aksenov's mature novels. His subsequent *Skazhi izium* (*Say Cheese!*) is equally humorous, equally swift-moving, and perhaps shows off Aksenov's wonderful sense of language to still greater advantage—few can equal his ability to catch the nuances of political slogans or the rhythms of contemporary speech. The key historical event here is very close to Aksenov: the attempt by himself and other writers at the end of the 1970s to put out *Metropol'*, a miscellany of writings that had not been submitted to Soviet censorship for approval. Here photography replaces fiction as the art form, but many of the figures are clearly based on real figures or are composites of people whom Aksenov knew. While the action and the verbal brilliance are themselves entertaining, anyone not intimately familiar with Moscow literary life of the period feels constantly aware that much of the humor is based on satirical thrusts at unrecognizable targets. Thus even after settling in the United States Aksenov continued to write fiction that could be fully appreciated only by the audience that he had left behind. Under glasnost and even more so after the collapse of the Communist regime, the barriers to publishing his work in Russia have fallen away; thus, even if his popularity abroad is never likely to match the renown he once achieved in the Soviet Union, he is likely to remain a major figure in contemporary Russian literature.

At the same time it needs to be stressed that much of Aksenov's writing from the mid-1960s on is difficult and unlikely to appeal to the mass reader. He established his reputation at the beginning of that decade with generally realistic novels and stories that captured the spirit of teenagers and young adults in the decade following Stalin's death. Thematically, the works were considered daring for questioning the supposed ideals of Communist society. Thus in his first novel, *Kollegi* (*Colleagues*), he writes of three young doctors who find that the actual life they encounter outside school contains the corruption, poverty, and violence that the older generation pretends do not exist. The gap between age groups is even wider in *Zvezdnyi bilet* (*A Ticket to the Stars* or *A Starry Ticket*), where the teenage protagonists simply "drop out" for the summer. Here Aksenov first revealed the full degree of his knack for depicting both the actual speech and the interests of ordinary people in modern Russia. The novel is full of slang and references to primarily low Western culture; the topic is alienated young people (reminiscent of those in Western works from the 1950s) living in a society where alienation is not supposed to exist. The older, far less sheltered hero of what is perhaps Aksenov's best known story, *Na polputi k lune* ("Halfway to the Moon"), is no less adrift; having fallen in love with a stewardess he encounters briefly, he spends his entire vacation flying back and forth the several thousand miles between Khabarovsk and Moscow in an attempt to catch another glimpse of her.

After this early period Aksenov's writing turns more self-consciously literary; fantasy and the grotesque become integral to his method. Typical in this regard are stories such as *Stal'naia ptitsa* ("The Steel Bird") (a 1965 work that could not be published in pre-glasnost Russia), in which a semi-human bird of steel tyrannizes the inhabitants of an apartment house, using methods not unlike those of the "man of steel," Stalin. While the overall message is sufficiently clear, the plot—with its frequent digressions and illogical turns—makes for difficult reading. Individual moments of the story are inconsistent with others; at times the hero resembles an ordinary person, at others the fantastic elements come to the fore. The style and the narrative as well as the descriptions employ elements of the grotesque. This manner reaches an apogee in *Ozhog* (*The Burn*),

Aksenov's longest novel. Like many of his longer works, it is in part autobiographical—here describing his late 1940s stay with his mother, imprisoned and exiled in the Kolyma region of the Far East—but it frequently veers between dream and reality, particularly in the pages dealing with the Moscow intelligentsia. The five major figures in the Moscow portion all have the same patronymic, which would indicate that they share a common father, and all have the same memories of the stay in Magadan. Are they different characters or versions of the same person? In this and many other ways, the novel resists easy interpretation.

Both Aksenov's avant-garde plays and his memoir dealing with life in America, *V poiskakh grustnogo bebi* (*In Search of Melancholy Baby*), maintain the manner found in his other writing. Satirical, filled with references to social and political themes, purposefully disjointed in terms of structure and plot, and as challenging to stage as his most difficult stories are to read, the plays owe their strength to Aksenov's linguistic gifts. *In Search of Melancholy Baby* includes "Sketches for a Future Novel" that separate the chapters; this mixture of fiction and non-fiction is indicative of his constant efforts to explore new narrative possibilities.

It is possible to divide his career roughly by period: the realistic if fresh early works give way to the extremely dense, often fantastic writings of the next 10 years, followed by pieces that are equally inventive but usually clearer in their story line. However, whatever the period or genre, Aksenov's distinguishing traits remain his ear for language, a satirical bent, sharp humor blended with an ultimately bleak outlook, the efforts to elucidate the legacy of Communism for Russian society, and a willingness to place demands on his audience.

—Barry P. Scherr

———

AKSYONOV, Vasily. *See* **AKSENOV, Vasilii.**

———

AL-BAYĀTI, 'Abdal-Wahhāb. *See* **BAYĀTI, 'Abdal-Wahhāb al-.**

———

AL-ḤAYDARI, Buland. *See* **ḤAYDARI, Buland al-.**

———

AL-MĀGHŪT, Muhammad. *See* **MĀGHŪT, Muhammad al-.**

———

AL-SA'DĀWI, Nawal. *See* **SA'DĀWI, Nawal al-.**

————

AL-SHAYKH, Ḥanān. *See* **SHAYKH, Ḥanān al-.**

————

ALBERTI (Merello), Rafael. Spanish. Born in Puerto de Santa María, 16 December 1902. Educated at the Colegio de San Luís Gonzaga, Puerto de Santa María, to age 15; studied painting in Madrid, 1917, and worked as an impressionist and cubist painter until 1923; joined Residencia de Estudiantes, Madrid. Married María Teresa León c. 1930; one daughter. Ill with tuberculosis, 1923–24; founded, with his wife, *Octubre* magazine, 1934, and involved in revolutionary politics; director, Museo Romántico, Madrid, from 1936; lived in Paris, 1939–40, Buenos Aires, 1940–63, and Rome, 1963–77; returned to Spain, 1977; elected Deputy for province of Cádiz, 1977. Also a painter. Recipient: National literature prize, 1925; Lenin prize, 1965; Etna-Taormina prize, 1975; Struga prize, 1976; Kristo Botev de Bulgaria prize, 1980; National theatre prize, 1981; Pedro Salinas prize, 1981; Cervantes prize, 1983. Honorary doctorate: University of Toulouse, 1982; University of Cádiz, 1985. Commandeur de l'Ordre des Arts et des Lettres (France), 1982. Agent: Agencia Literaria Carmen Balcells, Diagonal 580, 08021 Barcelona, Spain.

PUBLICATIONS

Verse

Marinero en tierra.   Madrid, Biblioteca Nueva, 1925.
La amante: canciones.   Malaga, n.p., 1926.
El alba del alhelí.   Santander, Ediciones para Amigos de J. M. de Cossío, 1927.
Sobre los ángeles.   Madrid, CIAP, 1929; as *Concerning the Angels*, translated by Geoffrey Connell, London, Rapp and Carroll, 1967.
Cal y canto.   Madrid, Revista de Occidente, 1929.
Consignas.   Madrid, Octubre, 1933.
Un fantasma recorre Europa. Madrid, La Tentativa Poética, 1933; as *A Spectre Is Haunting Europe: Poems of Revolutionary Spain*, edited by Angel Flores, New York, Critics Group, 1936.
Poesía 1924–1930.   Madrid, Cruz y Raya, 1934.
Verte y no verte.   Madrid, Aguirre, 1935.
13 bandas y 48 estrellas.   Madrid, n.p., 1936.
Poesía 1924–1937.   Madrid, Signo, 1938.
Poesía 1924–1938. Buenos Aires, Losada, 1940.
Entre el clavel y la espada 1939–1940.   Buenos Aires, Losada, 1941.
Pleamar 1942–1944.   Buenos Aires, Losada, 1944.
Selected Poems, translated by Lloyd Mallan.   New York, New Directions, 1944.

A la pintura: cantata de la línea y del color.   Buenos Aires, Lopez, 1945; revised edition, Buenos Aires, Losada, 1948, 1953; Madrid, Aguilar, 1968; in English, translated by Ben Belitt, West Islip, New York, Universal Art Editions, 1972.
Antología poética 1924–1944.   Buenos Aires, Losada, 1945; revised edition, 1959.
Poesía 1924–1944.   Buenos Aires, Losada, 1946.
El ceñidor de Venus desceñido.   Buenos Aires, Botella al Mar, 1947.
Coplas de Juan Panadero (Libro I).   Montevideo, Pueblos Unidos, 1949.
Buenos Aires en tinta china, edited by Attilio Rossi.   Buenos Aires, Losada, 1951.
Retornos de lo vivo lejano 1948–1952.   Buenos Aires, Losada, 1952; revised edition, Barcelona, Libres de Sinera, 1972.
Ora marítima.   Buenos Aires, Losada, 1953.
Baladas y canciones del Paraná.   Buenos Aires, Losada, 1954.
Diez liricografías.   Buenos Aires, Bonino, 1954.
María Carmen Portela.   Buenos Aires, Losada, 1956.
Sonríe China, with María Teresa León, illustrated by Alberti. Buenos Aires, Muchnok, 1958.
Cal y canto, Sobre los ángeles, Sermones y moradas.   Buenos Aires, Losada, 1959.
El otoño otra vez.   Lima, n.p., 1960.
Los viejos olivos.   Caracas, Dirección de Cultura y Bella Artes, 1960.
Poesías completas.   Buenos Aires, Losada, 1961; and later editions.
Poemas escénicos.   Buenos Aires, Losada, 1962.
Diez sonetos romanos.   Buenos Aires, Bonino, 1964.
Abierto a todas horas 1960–1963.   Madrid, Aguado, 1964.
El poeta en la calle: poesía civil 1931–1965.   Paris, Globe, 1966.
Selected Poems, edited and translated by Ben Belitt. Berkeley, University of California Press, 1966.
Poemas de amor.   Madrid, Alfaguara, 1967.
Roma, peligro para caminantes 1964–1967.   Mexico City, Mortiz, 1968.
Libro del mar, edited by Aitana Alberti.   Barcelona, Lumen, 1968.
Poesía anteriores a Marinero en tierra 1920–1923.   N.p., V.A., 1969.
Los 8 nombres de Picasso, y No digo más que lo que no digo 1966–1970.   Barcelona, Kairós, 1970.
Canciones del alto valle del Aniene, y otros versos y prosas 1967–1972.   Buenos Aires, Losada, 1972.
Poesía 1924–1967.   Madrid, Aguilar, 1972.
The Owl's Insomnia, edited and translated by Mark Strand. New York, Atheneum, 1973.
Poemas del destierro y de la espera, edited by J. Corredor-Matheos.   Madrid, Espasa-Calpe, 1976.
Poesía.   Havana, Arte y Literatura, 1976.
Coplas de Juan Panadero 1949–1977; Vida bilingüe de un refugiado español en Francia 1939–1940.   Madrid, Mayoría, 1977; *Coplas de Juan Panadero* published as *Poética de Juan Panadero*, El Ferrol, Sociedad de Cultura Valle-Inclán, 1987.
Poesía 1924–1977.   Madrid, Aguilar, 1977.
Los cinco destacagados.   Seville, Calle del Aire, 1978.
Signos del día; La primavera de los muebles.   Barcelona, Seix Barral, 1978.
Poemas anteriores a Marinero en tierra.   Barcelona, Seix Barral, 1978.
El matador: poemas escénicos 1961–1965.   Barcelona, Seix Barral, 1979.

Fustigada luz (1972–78).   Barcelona, Seix Barral, 1980.
Canto de siempre.   Madrid, Espasa-Calpe, 1980.
101 sonetos (1924–75). Barcelona, Seix Barral, 1980.
The Other Shore: 100 Poems, edited by Kosrof Chantikian, translated by José A. Elgorriaga and Paul Martin.   San Francisco, Kosmos, 1981.
Versos sueltos de cada día (1979–82).   Barcelona, Seix Barral, 1982.
XaX: una correspondencia en verso (inedita) Roma-Madrid, with José Bergamín.   Torremolinos, Litoral, 1982.
Robert Motherwell, el Negro, illustrated by Robert Motherwell.   Bedford Village, New York, Tyler Graphics, 1983.
Antología poética, edited by Natalia Calamaí.   Madrid, Alianza, 1983.
Todo el mar.   Barcelona, Círculo de Lectores, 1986.
Los hijos del drago y otros poemas.   Granada, Diputación Provincial de Granada, 1986.
Golfo de sombras.   Madrid, Villamonte, 1986.
Retornos de un isla dichosa y otros poemas.   Eivissa, Caixa de Balears "Sa Nostra," 1987.
Cuatro canciones.   Málaga, Librería Anticuaria, 1987.
Accidente: poemas del hospital.   Málaga, Librería Anticuaria, 1987.
Canciones par Altair.   Madrid, Hiperión, 1989.
Antología comentada, edited by María Asunción Mateo.   Madrid, Torre, 1990.

Plays

El hombre deshabitado (produced Madrid, 1931).   Madrid, Gama, 1930.
Fermín Galán (produced Madrid, 1931).   Madrid, Chulilla y Angel, 1931.
La pájara pinta (produced Madrid, 1931?).   Included in *Lope de Vega y la poesía contemporánea*, 1964.
Bazar de la providencia (includes *Farsa de los Reyes Magos*).   Madrid, Octubre, 1934.
De un momento a otro: poesía y historia.   Madrid, Europa-America, 1937.
Numancia, from the play by Miguel de Cervantes (produced Madrid, 1937).   Madrid, Signo, 1937.
El ladrón de niños, from a play by Jules Supervielle (produced Montevideo, 1943).
El adefesio.   Buenos Aires, Losada, 1944.
Teatro (includes *El hombre deshabitado*; *El trébol florido*; *La gallarda*).   Buenos Aires, Losada, 1950; enlarged edition (includes *El adefesio*), 1959.
Noche de guerra en el Museo del Prado.   Buenos Aires, Losada, 1956.
Las picardías de Scapin, from the play by Molière (produced Buenos Aires, 1958).
Teatro 2 (includes *Lozana andaluza*; *De un momento a otro*; *Noche de guerra en el Museo del Prado*).   Buenos Aires, Losada, 1964.
Farsa del licenciado Pathelin, from a French work (produced Buenos Aires, 1970).   Buenos Aires, Centro Editor de América Latina, 1970.

Screenplay: *La dama duende*, with María Teresa León, 1944.

Fiction

Imagen primera de . . .   Buenos Aires, Losada, 1945.
Relatos y prosa.   Barcelona, Bruguera, 1980.
Prosas.   Madrid, Alianza, 1980.

Other

La poesía popular en la lírica española contemporánea.   N.p., Gronan, 1933.
Nuestra diaria palabra.   Madrid, Héroe, 1936.
El poeta en la España de 1931.   Buenos Aires, Patronato Hispano-Argentino de Cultura, 1942.
La arboleda perdida y otras prosas.   Mexico City, Seneca, 1942; revised edition, Buenos Aires, Fabril, 1959; Barcelona, Seix Barral, 2 vols., 1987–89; as *The Lost Grove: Autobiography of a Spanish Poet in Exile*, Berkeley, University of California Press, 1976.
Vida bilingüe de un refugiado español en Francia.   Buenos Aires, Bajel, 1942.
Eh, los toros!, illustrated by Luis Seoane.   Buenos Aires, Emecé, 1942.
Suma taurina: verso, prosa, teatro, illustrated by the author, edited by Rafael Montesinos.   Barcelona, RM, 1963.
Lope de Vega y la poesía contemporánea (includes the play *La pájara pinta*).   Paris, Centre de Recherches de l'Institut d'Études Hispaniques, 1964.
Prosas encontradas 1924–1942, edited by Robert Marrast.   Madrid, Ayuso, 1970.
A Year of Picasso's Paintings.   New York, Abrams, 1971.
Obras completas.   Madrid, Aguilar, 7 vols., 1972–88.
Picasso, el rayo que no cesa. Parets del Vallés, Polígrafa, 1975.
Maravillas con variaciones acrósticas en el jardín de Miró.   Parets del Vallés, Polígrafa, 1975.
Cuaderno de Rute (1925): un libro inédito.   Málaga, Litoral, 1977.
Lo que conté y dije de Picasso.   Barcelona, Bruguera, 1981.
Aire, que me lleva el aire (for children).   Barcelona, Labor, 1981.
Federico García Lorca, poeta y amigo.   Granada, Andaluzas Unidas and Seville, EAUSA, 1984.
Otra Andalucía, with Julio Anguita.   Madrid, Ayuso, 1986.
La palabra y el signo.   Madrid, A–Z, 1989.

Editor, *Églogas y fábulas castellanas*.   Buenos Aires, Mirto, 2 vols., 1944.
Editor, *Romancero general de la guerra española*.   Buenos Aires, Patronato Hispano-Argentino de Cultura, 1944.
Editor, with Guillermo de Torre, *Antología poética 1918–1936*, by Federico García Lorca.   Buenos Aires, Losada, 1957.
Editor and Translator, *Doinas y baladas populares rumanas*.   Buenos Aires, Losada, 1964.
Editor, *Poesías*, by Lope de Vega.   Buenos Aires, Losada, 1965.
Editor, *Antología poética: Antonio Machado, Juan Ramón Jiménez, Federico García Lorca*. Barcelona, Nauta, 1970.
Editor, *Antología poética*, by Pablo Neruda.   Madrid, Espasa-Calpe, 1982.

Translator, *Visages*, by Gloria Alcorta.   Buenos Aires, Botella al Mar, 1951.
Translator, *Homenaje a la pintura*, by Robert Motherwell.   Barcelona, Círculo de Lectores, 1991.

*

Critical Studies: *Rafael Alberti's "Sobre los ángeles": Four Major Themes* by C. B. Morris, Hull, University of Hull, 1966; *The Theatre of Rafael Alberti* by Louise B. Popkin, London, Tamesis, 1975; *The Poetry of Rafael Alberti: A Visual Approach* by Robert C. Manteiga, London, Tamesis, 1978; Alberti issue of *Malahat Review*, July 1978; *Revolution and*

Tradition: The Poetry of Rafael Alberti by Pieter Wesseling, Valencia, Albatros Hispanófila, 1981; *Multiple Spaces: The Poetry of Rafael Alberti* by Salvador Jiménez Fajardo, London, Tamesis, 1985; *Rafael Alberti's Poetry of the Thirties: The Poet's Public Voice* by Judith Nantell, Athens, University of Georgia Press, 1986.

* * *

Rafael Alberti, a member of the Generation of 1927, has written thousands of poems from the early 1920s to the present. A master of poetic technique and with an almost unlimited range, he fuses the cultured with the popular in graceful poems of great verbal beauty and striking visual imagery, especially involving descriptions of the sea. Often an intellectual poet, Alberti has nonetheless treated the quotidian, the comic, the pageantry of bullfighting, the form and technique of painting and the arts, experiences in China, and, less successfully, social protest.

In *Marinero en tierra* (Sailor on Land), his first prize-winning volume of poetry, he combines joy and nostalgia and the popular ballad tradition with an elaborate metaphorical technique, evoking with longing and musical, colorful lines the sea of his dreams, of youthful innocence and freedom. In another early colorful collection, *El alba del alhelí* (Gillyflower Dawn), Alberti mixes merriment and mystery in poems about the Andalusian countryside. *Cal y canto* (Quicklime and Song) contains many dehumanized, baroque poems, but beyond the hermetic form and formal beauty we discover an anguished poet unable to find love, to comprehend both the tangible *cal* and the poetic *canto*, or to create order out of chaos. Alberti's dislocated and destructive symbology in this volume prepared the way for *Sobre los ángeles* (Concerning the Angels), his acknowledged masterpiece.

Concerning the Angels treats of a personal and universal spiritual crisis. The poet, having lost Paradise, love, and religious faith, confronts potential death. Angry and frustrated at his loss of innocence and facing the emptiness of life, he sinks into an anguished and despairing spiritual abyss. The angels, representing human drives and affects and both the positive and negative of human potential, sometimes obfuscate and impede, but one leads him from darkness and despair. The poet, recovering from chaotic time and space, achieves a kind of reintegration of faith and redemption in a dehumanized world of disintegrating values. Surrealistic and almost mystical, this collection contains at times incoherent and almost irrational imagery to convey an apocalyptic vision of existential mortality.

Exiled in 1939, Alberti sought peace in South America, but he was unable to forget his native land. *Entre el clavel y la espada* (Between the Carnation and the Sword) reveals that the Spanish Civil War for him is still an unbearable memory, and his obsession with Spain as a lost Paradise prevents his enjoyment of a new land. In several other collections of American poetry, not as profound as his early works, Alberti continues to remember the sea of Cádiz and the civil war. The best of these collections, *Retornos de lo vivo lejano* (Recurrences of Painful Recall), stresses memories of childhood, friends, and fellow poets. As the soul of other landscapes passes before his eyes, Alberti exudes sadness, resignation, and melancholy, for the past continues to exist in an eternal present of poetic fantasy, a memory which sustains him in his present life.

In the 1960s, Alberti wrote, among many collections, *Abierto a todas horas* (Open All Hours), a continuation of his themes of an exile's yearning for Spain, reminiscences, and the sea, but the poet also quests for life as he considers the passing years and the implications of age and approaching death. Another important volume, *Roma, peligro para caminantes* (Rome, a Threat to Travellers), offers us an ambivalent view of Rome in its positive and negative aspects, but as Alberti demystifies that ancient city and presents us with its sights and sounds, he nonetheless identifies with it and its artists.

In the 1970s Alberti continued to write thematic anthologies and original poetry which increasingly took on the form of a poetic diary. Typical of such poetry, *Canciones del alto valle del Aniene* (Songs from the High Valley of the Aniene), written in Italy between 1967 and 1971, contains memories of friends and visits to Picasso, but in addition to the autobiography, explores nature in all of its manifestations. The poet describes dreams and death and contemplates the anguish and solitude of the world.

Representative of Alberti's poetry in the 1980s are *Fustigada luz* (Wounded Light) and *Versos sueltos de cada día* (Loose Verses for Every Day). In the first volume he deals with fellow poets, painters, the changing seasons, passing time, life and death, and his search for light in a world of darkness. In the second volume the poet focuses on his daily life, solitude, the passing seasons, the reality of New York and the exterior world, and death.

Less well known as a dramatist, Alberti nevertheless succeeded in *El hombre deshabitado* (The Uninhabited Man) in creating an expressionistic allegory of man in a meaningless world. In several historical plays, he stresses ideological passion and the intolerance engendered by the Spanish Civil War.

—Kessel Schwartz

———

ALEGRÍA, Claribel. Salvadoran and Nicaraguan. Born in Estelí, Nicaragua, 12 May 1924. Grew up in El Salvador; moved to the United States, 1943. Educated at George Washington University, Washington, D.C., B.A. 1948. Married Darwin J. Flakoll in 1947; three daughters and one son. Has lived in the U.S., Paris, Mexico, Chile, Uruguay, and Mallorca; now lives in Nicaragua. Recipient: Casa de las Américas award, 1978. Agent: Alexander Taylor, Curbstone Press, 321 Jackson Street, Willimantic, Connecticut 06226, U.S.A. Address: Apartado Postal A-36, Managua, Nicaragua.

PUBLICATIONS

Verse

Anillo de silencio.   Mexico City, Botas, 1948.
Suite.   San Rafael, Mendoza, Brigadas Líricas, 1951.
Vigilias.   Mexico City, Poesía de América, 1953.
Acuario.   Santiago, Editorial Universitaria, 1955.
Huésped de mi tiempo.   Buenos Aires, Américalee, 1961.
Vía unica.   Montevideo, Alfa, 1965.
Aprendizaje.   San Salvador, Editorial Universitaria, 1970.
Pagaré a cobrar.   Barcelona, Sinera, 1973.
Sobrevivo.   Havana, Casa de la Américas, 1978.
Suma y sigue.   Madrid, Visor, 1981.
Flores del volcán/Flowers from the Volcano (bilingual edition), translated by Carolyn Forché.   Pittsburgh, University of Pittsburgh Press, 1982.

Poesía viva (bilingual edition).　London, El Salvador Solidarity Campaign, 1984(?).
Despierta mi bien despierta.　San Salvador, UCA, 1986.
Y este poema río.　Managua, Nueva Nicaragua, 1988.
Woman of the River (bilingual edition), translated by Darwin J. Flakoll. Pittsburgh, University of Pittsburgh Press, 1989.

Fiction

Cenizas de Izalco, with Darwin J. Flakoll.　Barcelona, Seix Barral, 1966; as *Ashes of Izalco*, Willimantic, Connecticut, Curbstone Press, 1989.
El detén.　Barcelona, Lumen, 1977.
Album familiar.　San José, Costa Rica, EDUCA, 1982; as *Family Album*, 1990.
Pueblo de Dios y de Mandinga.　Mexico City, Era, 1985; as *Village of God and the Devil*, in *Family Album*, 1990.
Luisa en el país de la realidad.　Mexico City, Boldó i Climent, 1987; as *Luisa in Realityland*, Willimantic, Connecticut, Curbstone Press, 1987.
Family Album (collection). London, Women's Press, 1990; Willimantic, Connecticut, Curbstone Press, 1991.

Other

Tres cuentos (for children).　San Salvador, Ministry of Culture, 1958.
La encrucijada salvadoreña, with Darwin J. Flakoll. Barcelona, Seix Barral, 1980.
Nicaragua, la revolución sandinista: una crónica política, 1855–1979, with Darwin J. Flakoll.　Mexico City, Era, 1982.
No me agarran viva: la mujer salvadoreña en lucha, with Darwin J. Flakoll.　Mexico City, Era, 1983; as *They Won't Take Me Alive: Salvadoran Women in Struggle for National Liberation*, London, Women's Press, 1987.
Para romper el silencio.　Mexico City, Era, 1984.

Editor and Translator, with Darwin J. Flakoll, *New Voices of Hispanic America*.　Boston, Beacon Press, 1962; as *Nuevas noces de norteamérica*, Barcelona, Plaza & Janés, 1981.
Editor and Translator, with Darwin J. Flakoll, *On the Front Line*.　Willimantic, Connecticut, Curbstone Press, 1990.

Translator, with Darwin J. Flakoll, *The Cyclone*, by Miguel A. Asturias.　London, Owen, 1967.

*

Critical Studies: "Two Poets of the Sandinista Struggle" by Electra Arenal, in *Feminist Studies* (College Park, Maryland), 7(1), 1981; "Interview with Claribel Alegría" by Carolyn Forché, in *Index on Censorship* (London), 13(2), 1984; *Claribel Alegría and Central American Literature: Critical Essays*, edited by Sandra M. Boschetto and Marcia P. McGowan, Athens, Ohio University Press, 1993.

*　*　*

Claribel Alegría, born in 1924 in Nicaragua but raised from early childhood in El Salvador, is one of the richest and most versatile literary voices of Central America. She is a poet, essayist, journalist, novelist, and writer of *testimonio* (testimonies). While living in the United States in the early 1960s, she published (in collaboration with her husband Darwin J. Flakoll) *New Voices of Hispanic America*, an anthology that included the early work of writers who have

since become major figures in contemporary Latin American literature. Her book of poetry *Sobrevivo* (I Survive) won the prestigious Casa de las Américas prize in 1978. American readers are perhaps best acquainted with Alegría through the publication of the bilingual edition of her book of poetry *Flores del volcán/Flowers from the Volcano*, translated by the poet Carolyn Forché, who quotes Alegría in the preface as saying: "I have no *fusil* (rifle) in my hand, but only my testimony."

Alegría began her literary career as a poet, under the mentorship of the Spanish lyricist Juan Ramón Jimenez. Alegría attributes to her "maestro" the lyrical discipline of her first books of poetry: *Anillo de silencio* (Ring of Silence), *Suite*, *Vigilias* (Vigils), and *Acuario* (Aquarium). Regarding the last of these, Alegría notes that it differs greatly from previous volumes. "There is more humor in it, for one thing, and I began to pay more attention to what was happening around me, rather than gazing at my own navel and my interior, subjective states." The real jolt to her literary career came in 1959 with the Cuban Revolution and the literary renewal which was its aftermath. While living in Paris (1962–1966) with her husband, she also came in contact with many Latin American writers living in exile at the time, among them Julio Cortázar, Carlos Fuentes (*q.v.*), Saul Yukievich, and Mario Benedetti. It was also in Paris that Alegría, instigated by Fuentes, determined to exorcise a childhood obsession: the peasant massacre in El Salvador in 1932 by the then military dictator Maximiliano Hernández Martínez. The result of her efforts (in collaboration with Flakoll) was the novel *Cenizas de Izalco* (*Ashes of Izalco*). Critics have noted that the publication of *Ashes of Izalco*, which interweaves a love story with sociopolitical critique, signalled the end of social realism for Central American fiction — subsequent to the publication of the book, it was no longer enough to write about "political themes." The literary work had to be aesthetically pleasing and innovative as well, conscious of the aesthetic quality of language, and opposed to a utilitarian "linear style" where language pretends to be nonexistent, transparent, or unseductive. The narrative transition and innovation inaugurated by *Ashes of Izalco* involved the substitution of an authoritarian voice by an internally persuasive one.

The assassination of Archbishop Oscar Arnulfo Romero by a member of the Salvadoran death squads in March of 1980 marked another crossroads in Alegría's personal life and literary career. Alegría herself marks this moment as the beginning of her "political career." Subsequent to the assassination, Alegría's publications have, in fact, been primarily concerned with testimonial voicings of the voiceless and the denunciation of government-sponsored terrorism in both her region and elsewhere. In addition to writing *Nicaragua, la revolución sandinista: una crónica política, 1855–1979* (Nicaragua, the Sandinista Revolution: A Political Chronicle), she and Darwin Flakoll have collaborated on a number of historical/testimonial books: *La encrucijada salvadoreña* (Salvadoran Crossroads), *No me agarran viva* (*They Won't Take Me Alive*), and *Para romper el silencio* (To Break the Silence: The History of Salvador's Political Prisoners). In 1990 she and Flakoll translated and published *On the Front Line*, an anthology of Salvadoran guerrilla poetry. Her more recently published and translated works also include the prose/verse novel *Luisa en el país de la realidad* (*Luisa in Realityland*), and the fantastic novellas *Album familiar* (*Family Album*) and *Pueblo de Dios y de Mandinga* (*Village of God and the Devil*).

To situate Alegría's opus within its Latin American sociohistoric and political context is to retrieve and reconstruct not only a particular history of oppression and colonial restructurization; it is also to ground reality in a specific historic moment when subjects come to see themselves as integral parts of a collective process of intervention in history. The "struggle for a better world" is what characterizes both the project of popular historiography and the poetic itinerary of Claribel Alegría. As poet, essayist, journalist, novelist of fantastic fiction, and writer of *testimonio*, Alegría functions in a manner very similar to that of a cartographer. Tracing the heights, depths, and contours of her memory, Alegría charts the most recondite and trauma-laden regions of her psyche. The effect is not unlike that of a series of symmetrical mirrors, simultaneously reflecting inward and outward. The maps she draws, while subversive, are necessarily anchored, however, in her own discontinuous locations, both personal and political.

There are several ways to consider Alegría's work as a whole. One of these consists in looking for an explanation of its variety, for the reasons why a writer cannot express certain themes and concerns in a particular genre, but can do it in another, as is the case with Alegría. Another question is that of how this choice of a particular genre marks different territories: the personal and the collective, the public and the private. A second way of examining her writing involves looking at the unity of her work. If her work is diverse, perhaps it is because it reflects the diversity and multiplicity of the very world that it describes, and because such a world, in turn, demands diverse forms of expression to reveal its true nature. *Village of God and the Devil*, for example, fulfills a function very different from that of the testimonial, and in it is realized a notably unique style. At the same time, it accomplishes a literary feat worth mentioning: it destroys the myth that defines "magical realism" as a phenomenon and style specifically Latin American, illustrating that in ancient Europe, precisely in Mediterranean Mallorca where the story takes place, "strange things" also happen and that the fantasy of the location nourishes and fertilizes a restless and creative imagination such as Alegría's. Public and private are different dimensions of life which she manages excellently in very different texts. This difference is not oppositional but complementary. The reader cannot sense a contradiction between the two dimensions.

To read the literary collage of a writer deeply committed to both incantation and elegy, such as Claribel Alegría, is to learn to look twice at the world, to unveil its transparency, the vague clarity of things, the unmasking possibilities of the mask. To read Alegría's work is also to share in the politics of survivorship. Survivorship, positively defined, is the project of everyday life, a "life among the ruins," but one that is intensely meaningful because it presents us with critical understandings other than victimization, understandings that raise issues not only of resistance but of healing, both for oneself and for other members of society.

—Sandra Maria Boschetto-Sandoval

—————

ALEPOUDELIS, Odysseus. *See* **ELYTIS, Odysseus.**

—————

ALLENDE, Isabel. Chilean; niece of former Chilean President Salvador Allende (assassinated 1973). Born in Lima, Peru, 2 August 1942. Educated at a private high school, Santiago, graduated 1959. Married 1) Miguel Frias in 1962 (divorced 1987), one daughter (deceased) and one son; 2) William Gordon in 1988. Secretary, United Nations Food and Agricultural Organization, Santiago, 1959–65; journalist, editor, and advice columnist, *Paula* magazine, Santiago, 1967–74; television interviewer, Canal 13/Canal 7 television station, 1970–75; worked on movie newsreels, 1973–75; administrator, Colegio Marroco, Caracas, 1979–82; guest teacher, Montclair State College, New Jersey, Spring 1985, and University of Virginia, Charlottesville, Fall 1988; Gildersleeve Lecturer, Barnard College, New York, Spring 1988; creative writing teacher, University of California, Berkeley, Spring 1989. Recipient: Panorama Literario novel of the year (Chile), 1983; Author of the Year, 1984, 1986, and Book of the Year, 1984 (Germany); Grand Prix d'Évasion (France), 1984; Colima for best novel (Mexico), 1985; Point de Mire (Belgium), 1985; Mulheres Best Novel (Portugal), 1987. Agent: Carmen Balcells, Diagonal 580, 08021 Barcelona, Spain. Address: 15 Nightingale Lane, San Rafael, California 94901, U.S.A.

PUBLICATIONS

Fiction

La casa de los espíritus.   Barcelona, Plaza & Janés, 1982; as *The House of the Spirits*, New York, Knopf, and London, Cape, 1985.
De amor y de sombra.   Barcelona, Plaza & Janés, 1984; as *Of Love and Shadows*, New York, Knopf, and London, Cape, 1987.
Eva Luna.   Barcelona, Plaza & Janés, 1987; in English, New York, Knopf, 1988; London, Hamish Hamilton, 1989.
Los cuentos de Eva Luna.   Barcelona, Plaza & Janés, 1990; as *The Stories of Eva Luna*, New York, Atheneum, and London, Hamish Hamilton, 1991.
El plan infinito.   Barcelona, Plaza & Janés, 1991; as *The Infinite Plan*, New York and London, Harper Collins, 1993.

Other

Civilice a su troglodita: los impertinentes de Isabel Allende. Santiago, Lord Cochran, 1974.
La gorda de porcelana (for children).   Madrid, Alfaguara, 1984.

*

Critical Studies: "Isabel Allende and the Testimonial Novel" by Michael Moody, in *Confluencia* (Greeley, Colorado), 2(1), 1986; "Literature as Survival: Allende's *The House of the Spirits*" by Peter Earle, in *Contemporary Literature* (Madison, Wisconsin), 28(4), 1987; "Isabel Allende on Love and Shadow" by Ambrose Gordon, in *Contemporary Literature* (Madison, Wisconsin), 28(4), 1987; "Parody or Piracy: The Relation of the House of the Spirits to One Hundred Years of Solitude" by Robert Antoni, in *Latin American Literary Review* (Pittsburgh), 16(32), 1988; "Isabel Allende Unveiled" by Douglas Foster, in *Mother Jones* (San Francisco), 13(10), 1988; "Exile and the Female Condition in Isabel Allende's *De amor y de sombra*" by Doris Meyer, in *International Fiction Review* (Fredericton, New Brunswick), 15(2), 1988; "Isabel Allende's *La casa de los espíritus* and the Literature of

Matrilineage" by Mary Gómez Parham, in *Discurso Literario* (Stillwater, Oklahoma), 6(1), 1988; in *Interviews with Latin American Writers* by Marie-Lise Gazarian Gautier, Elmwood Park, Illinois, Dalkey Archive Press, 1989; "The House of the Truebas" by Sascha Talmor, in *Durham University Journal* (Durham, England), 81(2), 1989; "A Passage to Androgyny: Isabel Allende's *La casa de los espíritus*" by Linda Gould Levine, in *In the Feminine Mode: Essays on Hispanic Women Writers*, Lewisburg, Pennsylvania, Bucknell University Press, 1990; "Ink, Blood, and Kisses: *La casa de los Espíritus* and the Myth of Disunity" by E. Thomson Shields, Jr., in *Hispanófila* (Chapel Hill, North Carolina), 33(3[99]), 1990; "Isabel Allende's 'The Judge's Wife': Heroine or Female Stereotype?" by Tony Spanos, in *Encyclia* (Provo, Utah), 67, 1990; "'The responsibility to tell you': An Interview with Isabel Allende" by John Rodden, in *Kenyon Review* (Gambier, Ohio), 13(1), 1991; "Two Modes of Writing the Female Self: Isabel Allende's *The House of the Spirits* and Clarice Lispector's *The Stream of Life*" by Flora H. Schiminovich, in *Redefining Autobiography in 20th-Century Women's Fiction*, New York, Garland, 1991.

* * *

Isabel Allende broke into the ranks of the bestsellers with her first novel, *La casa de los espíritus* (*The House of the Spirits*), a book that confirmed the link between Latin American writing and the label "magic realism" imposed on it by critics. The novel is written in the hyperbolic style inaugurated by *Cien años de soledad* (*One Hundred Years of Solitude*) (1967) by Gabriel García Márquez (*q.v.*), and deals with the rise and fall of a family dynasty over several generations. Some of the female characters practice magic, predict events, talk to the dead, and have green hair. Allende's fluid, readable prose shares certain stylistic tics with García Márquez, such as sudden leaps into the future, long lists, and pithy dialogue. Allende, however, pegs the family history to a specific country, Chile, and a specific event in history: elected Marxist president (and Isabel Allende's uncle) Salvador Allende's overthrow and murder in 1973. There is an epigraph from Chile's great poet Pablo Neruda, who also died in 1973 and appears as the Poet in the novel.

Despite these influences, Allende does not plagiarize. Her first novel contains such a wide range of characters and destinies, described in such rich detail, that it is clearly something unique. The central male character — and sometimes narrator — Esteban Trueba, whose long life spans the entire novel, struggles to become rich after the death of his first love. He marries Clara who keeps a diary that becomes the source of the novel as narrated by her politically-minded granddaughter. Clara is the female antithesis to macho Trueba, with his violations of country girls, inability to love, and indifference to peasants. By the end Trueba is horrified by what Pinochet is doing to his country, but he cannot undo the damage he has caused in his own relationship, and prevent Clara's total withdrawal from him.

If Trueba's experience lies at the centre of the novel, it is the lives of the women that dominate; they constitute a secret power within this patriarchal family. Clara's daughter Blanca takes as her secret lover a peasant, the left-wing folk-singer Pedro García III (possibly based on Victor Jara), and their illegitimate daughter Alba falls for left-wing student organizer Miguel. The pregnant Blanca is forced to marry a homosexual to conceal her guilt. The novel is packed with incidents: a duel between peasant Pedro García and landowner Trueba, first menstruations, an abortion, secret political meetings, life on a *fundo* or farm ("Las Tres Marías"), eccentric uncles, book

burnings . . . interwoven with the always surprising unfolding of the family's history. The novel ends with Alba surviving torture thanks to women's solidarity but pregnant either from a rape or from her lover, and beginning to write the novel as the reader finishes it. The closer the novel gets to Allende's 1970 election and three years in power, the less "magical" the style, as if the magical qualities are related to the past, while the present demands a more realistic treatment.

Allende's second novel, *De amor y de sombra* (*Of Love and Shadows*), is a protest novel, written from exile in Venezuela and based on a real event, the discovery of 15 assassinated corpses in a cave in Lonquén, Chile. This second novel maintains an uneasy balance between historical record (the evils of Pinochet) and sentimental popular fiction, with its happy ending. The protagonist Irene is a journalist from a rich background, engaged to an army officer, who slowly realizes through a friendship, then love for Francisco, a photographer, that her class version of events does not correspond to what actually happened. By the end she has to flee incognito over the Andes with her lover Francisco, after narrowly escaping death. The novel attempts to chart Irene's change in consciousness. She is not entirely convincing, however, for instead of being a believable character she seems to serve a polemical need on Allende's part to re-interpret and re-present political events.

Of Love and Shadows continues to explore Allende's fascination with Chile's human variety where one of the "disappeared" is a peasant girl called Evangelina, from the vividly depicted Ranquileo family, whose fits attract local people hoping for miraculous cures and the fulfilment of wishes. Francisco Leal's Spanish anarchist family is also drawn acutely. Allende's Latin America is conditioned by an outrageous geography, a postponed modernity, and a mixture of cultures and races, with Indians, Negros, Chinese, Turks, and other immigrants living under atrocious oppression in a continent "blessed by so many passions."

Allende's third novel, *Eva Luna*, is set in a tropical land (Venezuela) that combines Stone Age tribes with futuristic cities in an unpredictable way: "All ages of history co-exist in this immoderate geography." The novel follows two parallel lives, those of the rebellious orphan Eva and the German-born filmmaking immigrant Rolf, who eventually find happiness as lovers. The plot unfolds in a picaresque way as Eva climbs the social ladder from servant to soap-opera writer with the help of her intelligence and courage. In this novel, storytelling — a woman's skill — protects against often unpleasant realities. A message that emerges from *Eva Luna* is that romantic pulp novels, with their wish fulfilment, are part of facing up to real life. Again Allende packs her novel with larger-than-life characters: street-urchins, mean upper-class spinsters, a harelipped Turkish trader, and a beautiful transvestite. The novel retains journalistic immediacy, however, for the guerrilla action that closes the novel comments on contemporary history. Allende does not avoid the harsh realities of life (there are suicides, for example) but she does assert that escapist soap operas are in fact close to reality: "He strode forward, and kissed me exactly as it happened in romantic novels . . ."

Her fourth book of fiction illustrates the kind of stories that Eva Luna wrote and is called simply *Los cuentos de Eva Luna* (*The Stories of Eva Luna*). A series of linked stories all set in a backwater village called Agua Santa, near oil-fields, recreate the eventful lives of the colourful local characters. These vivid stories are sad, erotic, and sometimes violent, but always immensely readable, like adult fairy stories.

Allende's fifth novel, *El plan infinito* (*The Infinite Plan*), set in the United States, follows the life of Gregory Reeves, son of a travelling preacher offering an "infinite" plan of salvation. Abandoned in a Mexican ghetto in Los Angeles after his father's death, he adopts Mexican macho qualities in order to survive, and becomes such a part of the Morales family that the daughter Carmen becomes his most intimate friend through life, even for a brief period his lover. The novel is also about her quest for love, and, through adopting a child, maternity. After the (well-evoked) horrors of the Vietnam war, Gregory Reeves stumbles through two marriages, problem children, worldly success as a lawyer, then bankruptcy and a breakdown before he meets the nameless narrator and tells her the story we are reading. This novel about destiny and life, about fighting one's problems alone, about finding deep intimacy and companionship, which is love, opens in 1945 and ends in the 1980s. It is dense with facts and people's stories, with a more relentless narrative than Allende's earlier fiction, defending *latinos* against the fashionable liberation of the *gringos*. Allende's fiction follows her around the world (she now lives in California), and breaks new ground by exploring the situation of Latins in the U.S.A., with sympathy and humour. Carmen, she writes, has "five hundred years of Indian and Spanish tradition and a solid Anglo-Saxon common sense." Gregory at the end has learned to cry, release his emotions, break down the macho image, and become a real person through his crisis.

Behind all Allende's writing lies a sheer joy in storytelling, like a latter-day Scheherazade, a fascination with women, politics, the poor, and destiny, and interest in all kinds of lives related to the best gossip, and an exuberant sensuousness that is in part her style, and in part her outlook on life. She believes in happy endings despite the atrocious history of Latin America, and deserves her immense popularity (with almost nine million copies of her books sold around the world).

—Jason Wilson

AMADO, Jorge (Fazenda Auricídia). Brazilian. Born in Ilhéus, Bahia, 10 August 1912. Educated at the Federal University, Rio de Janeiro, J.D. 1935. Married 1) Matilde Garcia Rosa in 1933 (separated 1944), one daughter; 2) Zélia Gattai in 1945, one son and one daughter. Reporter, *Diário da Bahia*, 1927; imprisoned for political reasons, 1935; exiled 1937, 1941–43, 1948–52. Communist deputy of Brazilian parliament, 1945–48; editor, *Para Todos*, Rio de Janeiro, 1956–58. Recipient: Graça Aranha prize; Stalin peace prize, 1951; National literary prize, 1958; Gulbenkian prize (Portugal), 1971; Italian-Latin American Institute prize, 1976; Nonnino literary prize (Italy), 1983; Neruda prize, 1989; Volterra prize (Italy), 1989; Sino del Duca prize (Paris), 1990; Mediterranean prize, 1990. Member, Brazilian Academy of Letters, since 1961; Commander, Légion d'Honneur (France), 1984. Address: Rua Alagoinhas 33, Rio Vermelho, Salvador, Bahia, Brazil.

PUBLICATIONS

Fiction

Lenita, with Dias da Costa and Edison Carneiro.   Rio de Janeiro, Coelho Branco Filho, 1930.
O país do carnaval.   Rio de Janeiro, Schmidt, 1931.

Cacáu.   Rio de Janeiro, Olympio, 1933.
Suor.   Rio de Janeiro, Ariel, 1934.
Jubiabá.   Rio de Janeiro, Olympio, 1935; in English, New York, Avon, 1984.
Mar morto.   Rio de Janeiro, Olympio, 1936; as *Sea of Death*, New York, Avon, 1984.
Capitães de Areia.   Rio de Janeiro, Olympio, 1937; as *Captains of the Sands*, New York, Avon, 1988.
Terras do sem fim.   São Paulo, Martins, 1943; as *The Violent Land*, New York, Knopf, 1945; revised edition, 1965; London, Collins Harvill, 1989.
São Jorge dos Ilhéus.   São Paulo, Martins, 1944.
Seara vermelha.   São Paulo, Martins, 1946.
Gabriela, cravo e canela.   São Paulo, Martins, 1958; as *Gabriela, Clove and Cinnamon*, New York, Knopf, 1962; London, Chatto and Windus, 1963.
Os velhos marinheiros.   São Paulo, Martins, 1961; as *Home Is the Sailor*, New York, Knopf, and London, Chatto and Windus, 1964.
A morte e a morte de Quincas Berro d'Água.   Rio de Janeiro, Sociedade dos Cem Bibliófilos do Brasil, 1962; as *The Two Deaths of Quincas Wateryell*, New York, Knopf, 1965.
Os pastores da noite.   São Paulo, Martins, 1964; as *Shepherds of the Night*, New York, Knopf, 1966; London, Collins Harvill, 1989.
Dona Flor e seus dois maridos: história moral e de amor.   São Paulo, Martins, 1966; as *Dona Flor and Her Two Husbands: A Moral and Amorous Tale*, New York, Knopf, 1969; London, Weidenfeld and Nicolson, 1970.
Tenda dos milagres.   São Paulo, Martins, 1969; as *Tent of Miracles*, New York, Knopf, 1971; London, Collins Harvill, 1989.
Tereza Batista, cansada de guerra.   São Paulo, Martins, 1972; as *Tereza Batista, Home from the Wars*, New York, Knopf, 1975; London, Souvenir Press, 1982.
O gato malhado e a andorinha sinha.   Rio de Janeiro, Record, 1976; as *The Swallow and the Tom Cat: A Grown-Up Love Story*, New York, Delacorte Press, 1982.
Tiêta do Agreste.   Rio de Janeiro, Record, 1977; as *Tieta the Goat Girl*, New York, Knopf, 1979; London, Souvenir Press, 1981.
Farda, fardão, camisola de dormir: fábula para acender uma esperança.   Rio de Janeiro, Record, 1979; as *Pen, Sword, Camisole: A Fable to Kindle a Hope*, New York, Godine, 1985.
The Miracle of the Birds.   New York, Targ, 1983.
Tocaia grande: a face obscura.   Rio de Janeiro, Record, 1984; as *Showdown*, Toronto, New York, and London, Bantam, 1988.
O sumiço da santa: uma história de feitiçaria: romance baiano.   Rio de Janeiro, Record, 1988; as *The Golden Harvest*, New York, Avon, 1992.

Verse

A estrada do mar.   Sergipe, Tipografia Popular, 1938.

Play

O amor de Castro Alves.   Rio de Janeiro, Povo, 1947; as *O amor do soldado*, São Paulo, Martins, 1958.

Other

ABC de Castro Alves.   São Paulo, Martins, 1941.

Vida de Luis Carlos Prestes, o cavaleiro da esperança. São Paulo, Martins, 1942.

Obras. São Paulo, Martins, 17 vols., 1944–67.

O Cavaleiro da Esperança. São Paulo, Martins, 1945.

Bahia de todos os santos: guia das ruas e dos mistérios da cidade do Salvador. São Paulo, Martins, 1945.

Homens e coisas do Partido Comunista. Rio de Janeiro, Horizonte, 1946.

O mundo da paz: União Soviética e democracias populares. Rio de Janeiro, Vitoria, 1951.

Os subterrâneos da liberdade: Os ásperos tempos, Agonia da noite, A luz no túnel. São Paulo, Martins, 3 vols., 1954.

Trinta anos de literatura (selection). São Paulo, Martins, 1961.

O poeta ze trinidade. Rio de Janeiro, Ozon, 1965.

Bahia boa terra Bahia. Rio de Janeiro, Image, 1967.

O compadre de Ogun. Rio de Janeiro, Sociedade dos Cem Bibliófilos do Brasil, 1969.

Bahia (bilingual edition). São Paulo, Brunner, 1971.

Quarenta anos de literature (selection). São Paulo, Martins, 1972.

Porto Seguro recriado por Sergio Telles, with Luis Viana Filho and Jeanine Warnod. Rio de Janeiro, Bolsa de Arte, 1976.

Iconografia dos deuses africanos no Candomblé da Bahia, with Pierre Verger and Waldeloir Rego. São Paulo, Raízes, 1980.

O Menino Grapiúna. Rio de Janeiro, Record, 1982.

A cidade de Bahia, with Carybé, photographs by Mário Cravo Neto. Salvador, Aries, 1984.

Terra mágica da Bahia, with Alain Draeger. São Paulo, Banco Francês e Brasileiro, 1984.

A bola e o goleiro (for children). Rio de Janeiro, Record, 1984.

Navegação de cabotagem: apontamentos para um livro de memórias que jamais escreverei. Rio de Janeiro, Record, 1992.

*

Bibliography: in *Jorge Amado: vida e obra* by Miécio Táti, Belo Horizonte, Itatiaia, 1960.

Critical Studies: *Brazil's New Novel: Four Northeastern Masters* by Fred P. Ellison, Berkeley, University of California Press, 1954; "Poetry and Progress in Jorge Amado's *Gabriela, cravo e canela*" by Richard A. Mazzara, in *Hispania* (Los Angeles), 46, 1963; "Narrative Focus in Jorge Amado's Story of Vasco Moscoso Aragão" by Judith Bernard, in *Romance Notes* (Chapel Hill, North Carolina), 8, 1966; "Afro-Brazilian Cults in the Novels of Jorge Amado" by Russell G. Hamilton, in *Hispania* (Los Angeles), 50, 1967; "The 'New' Jorge Amado" by Elizabeth Schlomann Lowe, in *Luso-Brazilian Review*, 6, 1969; "Allegory in Two Works of Jorge Amado," and "Moral Dilemma in Jorge Amado's *Dona Flor e seus dois maridos*," both in *Romance Notes* (Lexington, Kentucky), 13, 1971, and "Duality in Jorge Amado's *The Two Deaths of Quincas Wateryell*," in *Studies in Short Fiction*, 15, 1978, all by Malcolm Noel Silverman; "The Preservation of African Culture in Brazilian Literature: The Novels of Jorge Amado" by Maria Luísa Nunes, in *Luso-Brazilian Review*, 10, 1973; "The Problem of the Unreliable Narrator in Jorge Amado's *Tenda dos milagres*," in *Romance Quarterly* (Lexington, Kentucky), 30, 1983, and "Structural Ambiguity in Jorge Amado's *A morte e a morte de Quincas Berro d'Água*," in *Hispania* (Los Angeles), 67, 1984, both by Earl E. Fitz; "The Guys and Dolls of Jorge Amado" by L. Clark Keating, in *Hispania* (Los Angeles), 66, 1983; "Jorge Amado: Morals and Marvels" by Daphne Patai, in *Myth and Ideology in Contemporary Brazilian Fiction*, Rutherford, New Jersey, Fairleigh Dickinson University Press, 1983; "Jorge Amado: Populism and Prejudice" by David Brookshaw, in *Race and Color in Brazilian Literature*, Metuchen, New Jersey, Scarecrow Press, 1986.

*   *   *

Jorge Amado is rightly described as Brazil's best-known novelist. An exceedingly prolific writer whose work has spanned seven decades, Amado has been writing since 1931 when he published his first novel, *O país do carnaval* (Carnival Country); in 1992, the year of his 80th birthday, he published a volume of memoirs, *Navegação de cabotagem* (Coastwise Shipping), and a novella, "A descoberta da América pelos turcos ou de como o árabe Jamil Bichara, desbravador de florestas, de visita à cidade de Itabuna para dar abasto ao corpo, ali lhe ofereceram fartura e casamento ou ainda os esponsais de Adma" (America's Discovery by the Turks, or How the Arab Jamil Bichara, Clearer of Forests, on a Visit to the City of Itabuna to Fortify His Body, Was offered Abundance and Marriage, or Even The Marriage Vows of Adma), destined to mark the quincentenary of Christopher Columbus's discovery of America. His works have been translated into some 40 languages, adapted for film, and serialised for television. There is some disagreement among critics about the "literariness" of his work, but this has affected neither his popularity nor, indeed, his immense readability. Several controversies surround his literary output, and critical opinion is divided as to whether or not his early novels are little more than crude exposés of sociopolitical conditions driven by left-wing ideology, whether he is sexist in his attitude to women, and whether his works, regardless of how well-intentioned, enshrine and perpetrate racist attitudes.

Amado made his literary debut as an exponent of the Northeastern Novel, and the greater part of his work has retained this regional bias. Few of his novels do not have as their geographical setting Salvador, capital of Bahia, or the cacao-producing region of Northeastern Brazil.

It is usual to separate Amado's work into two main phases. The first, stemming from a strong ideological commitment to depict the Northeastern reality as faithfully as possible, begins with *O país do carnaval* and ends with *Capitães da Areia* (*Captains of the Sands*) of 1937. In these novels he chooses as his subject-matter some of the typical motifs of the Northeast: the drought and its effects on the inhabitants of the region; the plight of the hired plantation workers, and the urban poor; the situation of the black man in Brazil. His later works, from *Terras do sem fim* (*The Violent Land*) of 1943 onwards, are characterised by a greater preoccupation with style and technique, incorporating elements of lyricism, humour, irony, and what some critics have tagged "magical socialism."

Any attempt to evaluate Amado's writing must inevitably lead to the conclusion that his major achievement is the group of novels that constitute his "cacao cycle." In *Cacáu* (Cacao), the situation in the Northeast is interpreted very much in terms of the class struggle. Although this work is not an aesthetic success, it introduces the themes that find a fuller, more artistic expression 10 years later in *The Violent Land*, a "tropical western" considered by many to be Amado's best work. It deals with the conquest of the land, when ruthless men cleared the jungle to plant cacao, then fought for political control over their empires. *The Violent Land* focuses on the bloodthirsty struggle between two such planters, Colonel Horácio Silveira and Juca Badaró. The emphasis is on epic deeds rather than denunciation of social evils, and the main protagonist of the novel is the land itself.

São Jorge dos Ilhéus (St. George of the Islanders) continues the story told in *The Violent Land*, with more political content than its predecessor. It chronicles the transition from the pioneering days to the emergence of a new ruling class, the exporters, who employ different means to conquer the land. Whereas Amado views the pioneers with mingled affection and respect, it is clear that he feels a profound antipathy for the new order.

Gabriela, cravo e canela (*Gabriela, Clove and Cinnamon*) takes as its subject the city of Ilhéus during the period 1925 to 1926. This is very much a work of Amado's maturity, and romanticism and humour take precedence over social and political comment. The background of the novel is one of social change, with an ongoing conflict between defenders of the status quo and those who desire progress. Against the backdrop is narrated the love story of Nacib, the son of immigrants, and Gabriela, the picaresque *mulata* who comes out of the backlands to fuel male fantasies.

In 1984 Amado returned to the early days of the cacao region in *Tocaia grande: a face obscura* (*Showdown*), whose tone is predominantly nostalgic.

In his later works, Amado becomes increasingly interested in the art of storytelling, introducing elements of fantasy and popular culture into his novels. He is particularly interested in presenting strong female protagonists who symbolize for him the struggle against exploitation — the most notable being Tereza Batista in *Tereza Batista, cansada de guerra* (*Tereza Batista, Home from the Wars*) and Tiêta in *Tiêta do Agreste* (*Tieta the Goat Girl*) — and showing how they overcome adversity by using their sexuality as a weapon. However, as feminist critics have pointed out, the author is not advocating a radical change in the situation of women; rather he tends to emphasize the traditional stereotype of women as dependent on men for emotional and financial security.

The importance of Afro-Brazilian elements in Amado's work should not be overlooked — for instance in *Jubiabá*, *Gabriela, Clove and Cinnamon*, and *Tenda dos milagres* (*Tent of Miracles*). In the numerous interviews he has given over the years, Amado has always insisted that Brazilian society, just as Brazilian Portuguese, must be understood as the product of the intermingling of various cultures, religions, and traditions. Thus he makes much of the religious syncretism to be found in the Northeast. It has, however, been suggested that his novels also reinforce white myths about the Afro-Brazilian containing what might be perceived as elements of prejudice.

Amado selects very specific aspects of the Brazilian social reality, focusing on the poor and disadvantaged, on blacks and women, as well as the rich and powerful. He might almost be described as the Master of the Brazilian picaresque, concentrating on the marginal elements of society and recounting their adventures with evident gusto, for instance, the escapades of Vadinho in *Dona Flor e seus dois maridos* (*Dona Flor and Her Two Husbands*), or the eponymous Quincas Berro d'Água (*The Two Deaths of Quincas Wateryell*).

Amado's writing derives much of its vigour from oral narrative tradition and his subject-matter is unashamedly popular and picturesque. His overall achievement has been to write with exuberance and affection about the region and society he knows best. He will be remembered above all for his rich and creative use of the Brazilian idiom and for the essentially Brazilian characters he has created.

—Patricia Anne Odber de Baubeta

————

AMICHAI, Yehuda. Israeli. Born in Würzburg, Germany, in 1924; emigrated to Palestine in 1935: naturalized Israeli citizen. Educated at Bet Sefer Maaleh, Jerusalem; Hebrew University, Jerusalem. Served with the Jewish Brigade in the British Army during World War II, and as an infantryman in the Israeli War of Independence: Sergeant-Major in reserve. Married 1) Tamar Horn, one son; 2) Chang Sokolov, one son and one daughter. Former teacher of Hebrew literature and the Bible in secondary schools, Jerusalem; visiting poet, University of California, Berkeley, 1971, 1976; Dorot Visiting Fellowship, 1983–84, and visiting poet, 1987, New York University. Recipient: Shlonsky prize; Acum prize (twice); Bialik prize; Israel prize; Brenner prize, 1985; Agnon prize, 1986. Honorary doctorate: Hebrew University, 1990. Distinguished Associate Fellow, American Academy for the Arts and Sciences, 1987. Address: 26 Malki Street, Yemin Moshe, Jerusalem, Israel.

PUBLICATIONS

Verse

Achshav ubayamin na'acherim [Now and in Other Days]. Tel Aviv, n.p., 1955.
Bemerchak shetey tikvot [Two Hopes Away]. Tel Aviv, n.p., 1958.
Beginah hatsiburit [In the Park]. Jerusalem, n.p., 1959.
Shirim 1948–1962 [Poetry 1948–1962]. Jerusalem, n.p., 1962/63.
Selected Poems, translated by Assia Gutmann. London, Cape Goliard Press, 1968; as *Poems*, New York, Harper, 1969.
Achshav bara'nsh [Now in the Turmoil]. 1968.
Selected Poems, translated by Ted Hughes, Assia Gutmann, and Harold Schimmel. London, Penguin, 1971.
Velo al menat lizkor [And Not in Order to Remember]. 1971.
Songs of Jerusalem and Myself, translated by Harold Schimmel. New York, Harper, 1973.
Me'achorey kol zeh mistater osher gadol [Behind All This Hides Great Happiness]. 1974.
Mas'ot Binyamin ha'acharon mitudelah. As *Travels of a Latter-Day Benjamin of Tudela*, Toronto, House of Exile, 1976; Webster Groves, Missouri, Webster Review, 1977; as *Travels* (bilingual edition), translated by Ruth Nevo, New York, Sheep Meadow Press, 1986.
Amen, translated by the author and Ted Hughes. New York, Harper, and London, Oxford University Press, 1978.
On New Year's Day, Next to a House Being Built. Bedford, Sceptre Press, 1979.
Time, translated by the author and Ted Hughes. New York, Harper, and London, Oxford University Press, 1979.
Love Poems (bilingual edition). Tel Aviv, Schocken, and New York, Harper, 1981.
She'at hachesed [Hour of Charity]. Tel Aviv, Schocken, 1982.
Great Tranquillity: Questions and Answers, translated by Glenda Abramson and Tudor Parfitt. New York, Harper, 1983.

Me'Adam atah ve'el Adam tashuv [From Man You Come, and to Man You Will Return].   Tel Aviv, Schocken, 1985.
The Selected Poetry of Yehuda Amichai, edited and translated by Stephen Mitchell and Chana Bloch. New York, Harper, 1986; London, Viking, 1987; as *Selected Poems*, London, Penguin, 1988.
Shirey Yerushalayim/Poems of Jerusalem (bilingual edition), translated by Alizah Orbakh.   Tel Aviv, Schocken, 1987; New York, Perennial Library, 1988.
Gam ha'egrof hayah pa'am yad petuchah.   Tel Aviv, Schocken, 1989; as *Even a Fist Was Once an Open Palm with Fingers*, translated by Barbara and Benjamin Harshav, New York, Harper Perennial, and London, Harper Collins, 1991.

Plays

Mas'a leNinveh [Journey to Nineveh] (produced Tel Aviv, 1964).   Jerusalem, n.p., 1962.
Pa'amonim verakavot (radio play).   As *Bells and Trains*, in *Midstream*, October 1966.

Fiction

Beruach hanora'ah chazot. Tel Aviv, Merhavya, 1961; as *The World Is a Room (and Other Stories)*, Philadelphia, Jewish Publication Society, 1984.
Lo me'achshav, lo mikan. Tel Aviv, n.p., 1963; as *Not of This Time, Not of This Place*, New York, Harper, 1968; London, Vallentine Mitchell, 1973.
Mi yitneni malon [Hotel in the Wilderness].   1971.

Other

Mah she-karah le-roni bi-Nyu-York.   1968.
Sefer halaylah hagadol [The Big Night-Time Book] (for children).   Tel Aviv, Schocken, 1988.

Editor, with Allen Mandelbaum, *The Syrian-African Rift and Other Poems*, by Avoth Yeshurun.   Philadelphia, Jewish Publication Society, 1980.
Editor, with Allen Mandelbaum, *Points of Departure*, by Dan Pagis.   Philadelphia, Jewish Publication Society, 1982.

Has translated works by Rolf Hochhuth and Else Lasker-Schüler.

*

Critical Studies: "Yehuda Amichai" by Sholom J. Kahn, in *Literature East and West* (Austin, Texas), 14(1), 1970; "An Interview with Yehuda Amichai" by Harry James Cargas, in *Webster Review*, 2(1), 1975; "Elements of Poetic Self-Awareness in Modern Poetry" by Shimon Levy, in *Modern Hebrew Literature* (Ramat-Gan, Israel), 3, 1976; "Saul and David in the Early Poetry of Yehuda Amichai" by Noam Flinker, in *The David Myth in Western Literature*, edited by Raymond-Jean Frontain and Jan Wojcik, West Lafayette, Indiana, Purdue University Press, 1980; "Poet at the Window" by Edward Hirsch, in *American Poetry Review* (Philadelphia), 10(3), 1981; "In the Great Wilderness" by Nikki Stiller, in *Parnassus* (New York), 11(2), 1983–84; "Images in Transformation in the Recent Poetry of Yehuda Amichai" by Nili Scharf Gold, in *Prooftexts* (College Park, Maryland), 4(2), 1984; "On Amichai's 'El male rahamin'" by Naomi B. Sokoloff, in *Prooftexts* (College Park, Maryland), 4(2), 1984; "The Poet as Prose Writer" by H. Halkin, in *Ariel* (Calgary, Alberta), 61,

1985; "Farewell to Arms and Sentimentality: Reflections of Israel's Wars in Yehuda Amichai's Poetry" by Yari Mazar, in *World Literature Today* (Norman, Oklahoma), 60(1), 1986; *The Writing of Yehuda Amichai* by Glenda Abramson, Binghamton, State University of New York Press, 1989; "Yehuda Amichai: Neither Prophet nor Guru" by Chaim Chertok, in his *We Are All Close: Conversations with Israeli Writers*, New York, Fordham University Press, 1989; in *Voices of Israel* by Joseph Cohen, Albany, State University of New York Press, 1990.

*   *   *

Yehuda Amichai, who has published 11 volumes of poetry as well as novels, short stories, and plays, is the most popular and important, and certainly the most widely translated, contemporary Israeli poet.

His career epitomises the creation and battle for existence of the State of Israel and the shaping of Israeli literary culture. A pre-World War II émigré from Germany, but from an orthodox Jewish family and with a fluent knowledge of Hebrew, Amichai served in the British Army during the war and afterwards fought the British as a member of the Hagganah's commando organization, the Palmah. Subsequently, this most pacific of men served in two other Israeli wars (1956 and 1973). Even such bare biographical facts are of particular significance in this case, since, as Ted Hughes — Amichai's most influential fan abroad and an occasional translator of his work — has recently remarked: "There's a depth, breadth and weighty momentum in these subtle and intricate poems of his . . . that sounds more and more like the undersong of a people." In a 1992 interview, Amichai himself acknowledged: "I am, in a way, like the State of Israel — I have a poem which says, 'when I was young, the country was young' . . . My personal history has coincided with a larger history. For me it's always been one and the same."

From his debut with *Achshav ubayamin na'acherim* (Now and in Other Days), Amichai has displayed a prolific ability to create imagery, drawing on biblical and historical Jewish sources. His diction and prosody have also blended biblical elements with the formalism of the Spanish Golden Age and the evolving vernacular of contemporary Israel. The personal opens up into the historical and the mythical, but there is nothing portentous about Amichai's work, no self-conscious seeking out of significant themes. Even his irony more often than not has a tender ring to it. His strength seems to come from an undefensive recognition of weakness and vulnerability. The flow of his imagination is guided and controlled by an unaffected judiciousness, an ingenuous self-awareness.

Amichai is thus a man *in* the world, rather than *of* the world. At the same time, his wryness about himself does not suggest self-hatred or self-castigation. He is the enemy of exaggeration, the exponent of level-headedness, though he is also well known for his elaborate use of metaphor and has been accused of shock tactics . . . a kind of superabundance, sometimes overabundance in his works . . . a feeling that the richness of the metaphorical display sometimes exceeds the emotional matter with which it is designed to deal" (Arieh Sachs). But as Michael Hamburger has commented in his astute and prescient introduction to Amichai's *Selected Poems*, his first major collection in English: "[this quality] strikes me as a resort analogous to the simultaneity rendered by the narrative structure of his novels: seemingly incompatible images are juxtaposed or telescoped in order to enact Amichai's essential awareness of simultaneity . . . the metaphors do their job of relating and contrasting the everyday with the mythical, heroic and exemplary, the poet's own experience with that of Biblical or mediaeval paradigms, King Saul to Ibn Gabirol." Amichai himself is fond of quoting the Talmud in this connection, as in the following: "'There's nothing early or late in the Bible', which means that everything, all events, are ever present, that the past and future converge on the present, especially in language."

Perhaps the closest Amichai comes to a kind of formalism is in his metaphors. He has remarked: "A metaphor is like a little poem. To me, the core of the poem is really the image . . . The invention of the metaphor is the greatest human invention, because it establishes some kind of dual existence, opening up an endless richness." Drawing on material that ranges from the intimately personal to the historical or mythological, Amichai's poems are particularly rich — entertaining, in the highest sense of the word. What unifies them is a tone of voice, a compound of human considerateness and sheer good sense.

So, celebrating his likeness with other men, though in an unassertive manner (to be assertive would be to lift himself above them), Amichai does not try to make more of historical or personal circumstances than need be; that is, he does not dramatize, because the drama is within and all about him and need not be added. But sometimes his memory, his predicament as a kind of focal point or meeting place for memories, becomes a burden, albeit one which he shoulders lovingly. He is not so much overwhelmed or overawed by the multi-dimensionality, the historical density of things, as he is simply tired, weary almost unto death — yet even then, not quite, because this tiredness too is part of the human condition, just as the burden itself is inescapable.

Amichai's sense of his own history, that of his family, and that of his people, is almost physical. In an early poem, "My Parents' Migration," he writes:

> And my parents' migration has not yet calmed in me.
> My blood goes on shaking at its walls,
> As the bowl after it is set down.

In "National Thoughts," another early poem, he encapsulates the linguistic dilemma of Israeli literature, as well as giving expression to his own dilemma as a poet:

> To speak, now, in this tired language,
> Torn from its sleep in the Bible —
> Blinded, it lurches from mouth to mouth —
> The language which described God and the Miracles,
> Says:
> Motor car, bomb, God.

And his recent book, *Gam ha'egrof hayah pa'am yad petuchah* (*Even a Fist Was Once an Open Palm with Fingers*), contains a poem, "Summer Evening in the Jerusalem Mountains," in which he again identifies with his times but, as usual, with a wryness that undercuts any suggestion of self-importance:

> I open my mouth and sing into the world,
> I have a mouth, the world has no mouth.
> It must use mine if it wants
> to sing into me. I and the world are equivalent.
>
> I am more.

Amichai concludes his poem "I Am a Poor Prophet." from the same volume:

> I started my life so low.
> When I climb high with my intoxicated soul,
> when I reach the peak of my vision,
> I find myself with everyday people
> who have children and work, family cares,
> household chores. These are my vision.
> I am a poor prophet.

Yes, but it is that climb, that journey — Amichai frequently refers to himself as a "traveller" — that accounts for the universality of his vision. This poet's work, in its expansiveness and humanity, enriches all its readers and has been crucial in enabling the new literature of Israel to engage in a creative dialogue with the entire problematical and paradoxical history of the Jewish people.

—Daniel Weissbort

––––––––

ANGHELAKI-ROOKE, Katerina. Greek. Born in Athens, 22 February 1939. Educated at the University of Nice, 1957–58, diploma in French as a second language; University of Athens, 1958–59; University of Geneva, 1959–62, diploma in translation and interpretation. Married Rodney J. Rooke in 1963. Since 1962 freelance translator, Athens. Participated in International Writing Program, University of Iowa, Iowa City, 1974–75; Fulbright Visiting Lecturer, Harvard University, Cambridge, Massachusetts, University of Utah, Salt Lake City, and San Francisco State University, 1980–81; Visiting Fellow, Princeton University, New Jersey, 1987. Recipient: City of Geneva prize, 1962; Ford Foundation grant, 1972–73, 1975–76; Fulbright fellowship, 1980–81; Greek National poetry prize, 1985. Address: Synesiou Kyrenes 4, 114 71 Athens, Greece.

PUBLICATIONS

Verse

Liki ke Sinnefa [Wolves and Clouds]. Athens, Zarvanos, 1963.
Piimata 63–69 [Poems 1963–1969]. Athens, Ermias, 1971.
Magdalini, to Megalo Thilastiko (Magdalene, the Vast Mammal]. Athens, Ermeias, 1974.
The Body Is the Victory and the Defeat of Dreams (bilingual edition), translated by Philip Ramp. San Francisco, Wire Press, 1975.
Ta Skorpia Hartia tis Pinelopis [The Scattered Papers of Penelope]. Thessaloniki, Tram, 1977.
O Thriamvos tis Statheris Apolias [The Triumph of Constant Loss]. Athens, Kedros, 1978.
Enantios Erotas [Counter Love]. Athens, Kedros, 1982.
Oi Mnistires [The Suitors]. Athens, Kedros, 1984.
Beings and Things on Their Own, translated by the author and Jackie Willcox. Brockport, New York, BOA, 1986.
Otan to Soma [When the Body]. Athens, Ypsilon, 1988.
Epilogos Aeras [Wind Epilogue]. Athens, Kedros, 1990.
A Spring Offering for Yiannoussa (trilingual edition in Greek, Hebrew, and English). Tel Aviv, Lushy, 1991.

Plays

Mia Isorropia Tromou, translation of *A Delicate Balance* by
Edward Albee (produced Athens, 1979).
To Imeroma tis Stringlas, translation of *The Taming of the
Shrew* by William Shakespeare (produced 1988).

Other

Editor, *Sighroni Amerikani piites* [20 Contemporary
American Poets]. Athens, Ypsilon, 1983.

Translator, *O Drakos* [*Dragon*], by Eugene Schwarz. Athens,
Kalvos, 1968.
Translator, *O Proust* (into Greek), by Samuel Beckett.
Athens, Ermias, 1971.
Translator, *Kato apo to Galatodasos* [*Under Milk Wood*], by
Dylan Thomas. Athens, Ermias, 1972.
Translator, *Epilegmena Piimata* [Selected Poems], by Andrei
Voznesenskii. Athens, Boukoumanis, 1974.
Translator, with Philip Ramp, *The Suffering God*, by Nikos
Kazantzakis. New Rochelle, Caratzas, 1979.
Translator, *Nikos Kazantzakis* (into Greek), by Peter
Bien. Athens, Kedros, 1983.
Translator, *Féline* (into Greek), by Jean-Marie Drot. Athens,
Kedros, 1984.
Translator, *Where Burning Sappho Loved* (into Greek), by
Irving Layton. Athens, Libro, 1985.
Translator, *To Fidi tou Theou* [*God's Snake*], by Irene
Spanidou. Athens, Kedros, 1987.
Translator, *Pos Ftiahnonte i Stihi* [*How Are Verses Made?*], by
Vladimir Maiakovskii. Athens, Ypsilon, 1988.
Translator, *Les Amants d'Avignon* (into Greek), by Elsa
Triolet. Athens, Ermias, 1992.

*

Critical Studies: "Modernity: The Third Stage, the New Poets"
by Andonis Decavalles, in *The Charioteer* (New York), 20,
1978; "Greek Women Poets and the Language of Silence" by
Helen Kolias, in *Translation Perspectives IV*, Binghamton,
New York, State University of New York Press, 1988;
"Knives, Forks, and Photographs: The Appropriation and
Loss of Traditional Laments in the Writings of Palamas,
Ritsos, Anghelaki-Rooke, and Dimoula" by Gail Holst-
Warhaft, in *Journal of Modern Greek Studies* (Baltimore,
Maryland), 9(2), 1991.

Katerina Anghelaki-Rooke comments:
One of our best poets, Nikos Karouzos (who died in 1990),
said, "Poems are the shreds of the absolute." I would add that,
since I conceive the absolute as pure truth, poems are the little
titbits that we get from it. One principle: never lie in poetry.
Meaning, never exaggerate sentiment or hope. Meaning,
never exaggerate *language*. Inspiration is a more or less total
opening to the true dimension of things, that is *nature*. A poet's
guide, nature.

* * *

The autobiographical drama enacted in Katerina
Anghelaki-Rooke's poems suggests a subjective, confessional
genre of writing. Indeed, in the introduction to her collection
of translations *Sighroni Amerikani piites* (20 Contemporary
American Poets), she explicitly identifies the shift towards a
more self-referential discourse as a distinguishing feature of
poetry composed in the 1960s and 1970s. Anghelaki-Rooke,

however, is acutely conscious of the contradictions behind the
term autobiography. In the same preface, for example, she
emphasizes the rhetorical aspects of any poetic "voice."
Similarly, her recent volume *Epilogos Aeras* (Wind Epilogue)
contains a cycle of 13 poems entitled "I Diigisi Tou Ego" (The
Narration of an I) and subtitled "autobiographical attempts."
If such an assertion intimates the limitations of autobiographical writing, this sequence is followed by a series of
poems that centres on the imaginary persona of "Yiannousa"
and in which overtly fictional and mythological characters
interact with real situations.

Preoccupations with an autobiographical past recur
throughout Anghelaki-Rooke's poetry, as demonstrated by
the pervasive motif of her parents' premature death. "Simiosis
Yia To Vivlio Tou Patera" (Notes for Father's Book), for
example, is a lament to her dying father. The image of the
poet's deceased mother is particularly conspicuous in early
poems like "I Mana Mou Ke O Satanas" (My Mother and
Satan). In this poem, Anghelaki-Rooke subverts the conventions of religious and folk laments. Indeed, her engagement
with the Orthodox tradition contrasts with that of a poet like
Yannis Ritsos, whose poem "Epitaphios" focuses on a
mother's dirge for her dead son. Conversely, in Anghelaki-
Rooke's poem, the orphan mourns her dead mother, while the
focus is almost exclusively on the lamenting subject.

For Anghelaki-Rooke, the past represents a source of
creativity. As the protagonist remarks in the poem "O
Skiouros Apantai Sti Yineka" (The Squirrel Answers the
Woman), memory and dream are inseparable. This very
admission, however, engenders a poignant realization. Precisely because creativity is inextricably bound up with memory, it can never align itself completely with the present.
Paradoxically, the poet becomes "nostalgic for the future as if
it was the past" — a sentiment that echoes the poem "Nostalgia
for the Present" by Andrei Voznesenskii (a selection of whose
verse Anghelaki-Rooke has translated).

Like the future, the past is portrayed as an expansive storage
room. In another prose poem entitled "I Akrotites Tou
Mellontos" (The Extremities of the Future) the protagonist
sits back to back with the future, like a passenger facing
backwards in a train:

> We will never sit side by side with life, or
> with it. Its back will only warm our back
> for a while, until we arrive.

Anghelaki-Rooke's dilemma is thus an ontological one, as
she strives to evade the solipsistic confines of her autobiographical experiences. From this perspective Anghelaki-
Rooke's poetry can be interpreted as an investigation of the
temporal and spatial boundaries inscribed by the term autobiography. "What's the world like" the protagonist inquires in
one poem, "when we are absent?" The wheel comes full circle
here, for birth and death are both envisaged as discontinuities,
blank spaces that demand to be filled imaginatively.

The poet's ambiguous relationship to the past is dramatized
as a series of binary oppositions that pervade her poetry, from
her earliest collection *Liki ke Sinnefa* (Wolves and Clouds) to
Epilogos Aeras. Existence is construed by Anghelaki-Rooke
in terms of a perpetual Heraclitean struggle between birth and
death, light and dark; opposites which wrestle "like two wild
animals." At the same time, such neat polarities are undermined by an intuition that, however contradictory, these
antithetical forces are nevertheless inseparable. As
Anghelaki-Rooke expresses it, the cries of jackals and nightin-
gales intermingle, just as her mother is both a reminder of
mortality and an affirmation of motherhood as a generative

source. In one poem Anghelaki-Rooke describes a cat giving birth, her newborn kittens drenched in blood. Here overtly sexual details merge with images of death and violation and recall the poet's description of her own caesarean birth.

Anghelaki-Rooke's poetry is full of such violent but striking inversions, whereby the traditional symbolic resonance of specific images is turned inside out: the moon resembles the yellow cover of a transparent chamberpot, or luminous butter that melts over the protagonists' bodies. Mundane physical details are juxtaposed to abstract images, just as the protagonist's juvenile world is divided between the kitchen with its familiar household sounds and smells and an ideal world peopled with imaginary figures: "The kitchen and my paper fantasy,/are the poles inscribed so early then?"

Many of Anghelaki-Rooke's most successful poems are love poems pervaded with sensual, often brazenly erotic imagery:

the small blossoms of the acacias
lying on the ground
remind me
of your juices
dried upon me —

In these texts, the body becomes the poet's presiding image, encapsulating the paradoxical nature of experience. As a metaphor the body delineates the twin poles of death and desire which Anghelaki-Rooke posits as her central concerns. If it elicits pleasure, the body is also the object of longing and an inspiration for poetry. It simultaneously attracts and repels. In fact this repellent aspect of the body is conveyed in poems which confront the poet's own physical deformities. Thus, while the body gives satisfaction, it is also perceived as a "cage," or an obstacle to absolute communion: "only by losing the body/will I receive you completely."

This perceptive ambiguity can be traced throughout Anghelaki-Rooke's poetry and extends to the individual's double-life. Just as the mother is both a symbol of chastity and promiscuity, so gender definitions are equally permeable. It is fitting, therefore, that Anghelaki-Rooke concludes her volume *Piimata 63–69* (Poems 1963–1969) with a poem entitled "Diyenis": the name of the eponymous Byzantine hero, which in Greek means twice-born. Similarly, the protagonist in Anghelaki-Rooke's poetry reveals the split nature of her personality, which is both angelic and demonic, sensual and intellectual. In turn, this antithesis extends to a pastoral dichotomy between the city (Athens) and the country (Aegina) and between the summer and the winter.

—Robert Shannan Peckham

APPELFELD, Aharon. Israeli. Born in Czernowitz, Bukovina, in 1932. Held in Transnistria concentration camp, Romania, for three years during World War II; escaped, wandered for several years, hiding in the Ukrainian countryside and then joining the Russian army; arrived in Palestine, 1947; served in Israeli army. Educated at Hebrew University, Jerusalem; Visiting Fellowship for Israeli Writers, St. Cross College, Oxford University, 1967–68. Visiting Lecturer, School of Oriental and African Studies, University of London, Oxford University, and Cambridge University, 1984. Currently Lecturer in Hebrew literature, Be'er Shev'a University.

Recipient: Youth Aliyah prize; Prime Minister's prize for creative writing, 1969; Anne Frank literary prize (twice); Brenner prize, 1975; Milo prize; Israel prize, 1983; Jerusalem prize; H. H. Wingate literary award, 1987, 1989. Address: c/o Keter Publishing House, P.O. Box 7145, Jerusalem 91071, Israel.

PUBLICATIONS

Fiction

Ashan [Smoke].   1962; in English, in *In the Wilderness*, 1965.
Bagay haporeh [In the Fertile Valley].   1964; in English, in *In the Wilderness*, 1965.
In the Wilderness.   Tel Aviv, Achshav Publishing House, 1965.
Kafor al ha'aretz [Frost on the Land].   Ramat-Gan, Masadah, 1965.
Bekumat hakark'a [At Ground Level].   Tel Aviv, Dagah, 1968.
Chamishah sipurim [Five Stories].   Jerusalem, Histadrut, 1969–70.
Ha'or vehakutonet [The Skin and the Gown].   Tel Aviv, Am Oved, 1971.
Adoni hanahar [My Master the River].   Tel Aviv, Hakibuts haMe'uchad, 1971.
Ke'ishon ha'ayin [Like the Pupil of an Eye].   Tel Aviv, Hakibuts haMe'uchad, 1972.
Shanim vesha'ot [Years and Hours].   Tel Aviv, Hakibuts haMe'uchad, 1974–75.
Keme'ah edim: mivchar [Like a Hundred Witnesses: A Selection].   Tel Aviv, Hakibuts haMe'uchad, 1975.
Tor hapela'ot.   Tel Aviv, Hakibuts haMe'uchad, 1978; as *The Age of Wonders*, Boston, Godine, 1981; London, Weidenfeld and Nicolson, 1987.
Badenheim, ir nofesh.   Tel Aviv, Hakibuts haMe'uchad, 1979; as *Badenheim 1939*, Boston, Godine, 1980; London, Dent, 1981.
Michvat ha'or [A Burn on the Skin].   Tel Aviv, Hakibuts haMe'uchad, 1980.
Tzili, the Story of a Life.   New York, Dutton, 1983.
Hakutonet vehapasim [The Shirt and the Stripes].   Tel Aviv, Hakibuts haMe'uchad, 1983.
The Retreat.   New York, Dutton, 1984; London, Quartet, 1985.
Ba'et uve'onah achat [At One and the Same Time].   Jerusalem, Keter, 1985; as *The Healer*, London, Weidenfeld and Nicolson, 1990.
To the Land of the Cattails.   New York, Weidenfeld and Nicolson, 1986; as *To the Land of the Reeds*, London, Weidenfeld and Nicolson, 1987.
Bartfus ben ha'almavet.   As *The Immortal Bartfuss*, New York and London, Weidenfeld and Nicolson, 1988.
Ritspat esh [Tongue of Fire].   Jerusalem, Keter, 1988.
Al kol hapesha'im.   As *For Every Sin*, New York and London, Weidenfeld and Nicolson, 1989.
Katerinah.   Jerusalem, Keter, 1989; as *Katerina*, New York, Random House, 1992.
Mesilat barzel [The Railway].   Jerusalem, Keter, 1991.

Other

Mas'ot beguf rish'on [Essays in First-Person].   Jerusalem, Hasifriyah Hatsiyonit, 1979.
Writing and the Holocaust.   New York, Holmes and Meier, 1988.

Editor, *From the World of Rabbi Nahman of Bratslav*. Jerusalem, World Zionist Organization, 1973.

*

Critical Studies: "The Shirt and the Stripes" by Rochelle Furstenberg, in *Modern Hebrew Literature* (Ramat-Gan, Israel), 9(1–2), 1983; "Aharon Appelfeld, Survivor" by Ruth R. Wisse, in *Commentary* (New York), 75(8), 1983; "Aharon Appelfeld: The Search for a Language" by Sidra DeKoven Ezrahi, in *Studies in Contemporary Jewry*, 1, 1984; "Applefeld [*sic*] and Affirmation," in *Ariel* (Calgary, Alberta), 61, 1985, and "Aharon Appelfeld: Not to the Left, Not to the Right," in his *We Are All Close: Conversations with Israeli Writers*, New York, Fordham University Press, 1989, both by Chaim Chertok; "Aharon Appelfeld and the Uses of Language and Silence" by Lawrence Langer, in *Remembering the Future*, Oxford, Pergamon Press, 1989; "Literary Device Used for Effects of Subtlety and Restraint in an Emotion-Loaded Narrative Text: 'The Burn of Light' by A. Appelfeld" by Rina Dudai, in *Hebrew Linguistics* (Ramat-Gan, Israel), January 1990; "Impossible Mourning: Two Attempts to Remember Annihilation" by James Hatley, in *Centennial Review* (East Lansing, Michigan), 35(3), 1990.

*   *   *

Aharon Appelfeld was born in Romania and is considered a Hebrew writer. His early work, *Ashan* (Smoke), *Bagay haporeh* (In the Fertile Valley), and other works collected in the English translation *In the Wilderness*, show a writer of allegories dealing with a Holocaust which resides outside of time, a permanent darkness of the human soul. Behind the allegory, one finds the reality of the murdered family, the child fleeing from the camp into the forest for two years of silence, away from humans except for chance encounters: "I know I loved the trees and the animals," Appelfeld said in an interview. "At least one could know that they were not the enemy!" Appelfeld became estranged from the world then, with Yiddish as a secret language and memories of his neighbour Paul Celan (at home and in the transit camp) making his later texts about Israel somehow distant from the Israeli situation. His Jewish characters remain vessels bearing the contents of the past.

Appelfeld's language is often poetic and sometimes obscure. The events described are not placed in a specific time and location; often they are dream sequences. They move between generations and journey across strange landscapes. Appelfeld remains a stranger; he pushes against the world he creates in a desperate effort to escape that world. The novel *Badenheim, ir nofesh* (*Badenheim 1939*) may give us a clear sequence of familiar events because it brings to mind the places where they did take place. But what happened? The quiet horror of the text is that almost nothing happens, but we know what will happen after the last page of the book. The goldfish bowl with its trapped fish is a central symbol of Jewish life in *Badenheim 1939*, and the reader experiences what the protagonists do not yet know. As Sidra DeKoven Ezrahi explains: "Appelfeld exhibits in his fiction both linguistic estrangement and profound geographic disorientation. A struggle recurs in his stories between public language and collective memory on the one hand and the mother language and private memory on the other."

Badenheim 1939 is a paradigmatic text for the reader as much as for the writer. If the protagonists of the novel are trapped within an invalid language, the reader also experiences the helplessness that comes from our special knowledge and insights which we cannot share with the individuals trapped on a stage outside of time and beyond our reach. The reader is trapped in many of Appelfeld's novels, since they somehow reach into areas of our own family life and involve us in the events beyond our control. Writing in Israel, Appelfeld portrays a Europe in this ironic narrative where the Jew is shown in his full helplessness: once defined as Jews, the protagonists of *Badenheim 1939* can no longer claim to be judged as Austrians. They rationalize the projected journey towards Poland as a place which is somehow "healthier," where they can be themselves, even as they acknowledge that the outer environment has become a threat to which they cannot respond.

That theme of the outer darkness recurs throughout Appelfeld's writings. We are alone in a world of inexorable patterns that do not acknowledge us. There is also the survivor, the protagonist of *Bartfus ben ha'almavet* (*The Immortal Bartfuss*) who is isolated and alone in the world after the Holocaust. As Lawrence Langer notes: "Bartfuss, at least, has experienced the somber tones of Celan's 'Death Fugue'; we have his creator's word to confirm it. 'The survivor, Bartfuss,' said Appelfeld in a recent interview with Philip Roth, 'has swallowed the Holocaust whole, and he walks about with it in all his limbs. He drinks the "black milk" of the poet Paul Celan, morning, noon, and night. He has an advantage over anyone else, but he still hasn't lost his human face. That isn't a great deal, but it's something.' This is a minimal tribute, perhaps; but one must turn to the text to determine how having 'swallowed the Holocaust whole' affects one's spiritual digestion." For Appelfeld, Bartfuss represents the survivor who actually internalizes the events of his life. Even when he talks, he remains a silent witness, touched by Appelfeld's irony of being "immortal," legendary, paradigmatic: "He withdrew, and words he had once used withered within him." Once again, we are within inner and outer landscapes.

Appelfeld lives in exile, occupying a no-man's land between those landscapes, with a passport not recognized by readers who view his world as "imaginary," the "fairie land" of Keats where an unattainable truth and beauty are one. Alienation is part of the writer's stance here, particularly in Israel where Appelfeld writes in Hebrew for a reading public that wants affirmation of the new, vital culture rather than an evocation of Old World revenants. Yet Appelfeld is determined to carry them through the guilt and anxiety of the past into the future.

Appelfeld's *To the Land of the Cattails* is such a text. Again, inner and outer landscapes merge; the past becomes present; the unspeakable is almost said — and that last tremor of silence brings us into awareness. This story parallels *Badenheim 1939* and has a similar landscape. In the summer of 1938, a woman insists upon going back to the land of her childhood, "the land of the cattails" not far from the Bukovina: Ruthenia. Her son goes with her on that doomed journey into the Europe under Hitler's shadow; fights against the trip, escapes into drunkenness, and loses the mother who has been caught and shipped off by that mysterious train to the unknown destination. The landscape is fear; and the son Tony wavers between his Jewish and Gentile heritage. His suffering makes him affirm his Jewishness where Israel again becomes an aching cry addressed to humanity. In his review of the book, Bernard Levin wrote: ". . . a chill comes off the pages, akin to Tony's inexplicable fear. Suppose someone who had never heard of the Holocaust were to read this book; I believe it would provoke a very deep unease, a realization that some terrible thing was waiting in the wings at the end . . . it is the measure of Mr. Appelfeld's power that no reader could fail to understand that there was a reality to guess at."

Appelfeld's testimony is not only alive within scholarship

testing the nuances, but also open to a general public trying to come to terms with the despair and debris left in today's world by the Holocaust. Ultimately, one reads Appelfeld because he is one of the great storytellers of our time. The narrative swallows us up, much like the old train at the end of *To the Land of the Cattails*, which "goes from station to station, scrupulously gathering up the remainder."

Inevitability is part of the atmosphere of an Appelfeld text. History is cyclical, and the seasons become important because they show pre-determination as well as a return to the beginning. The European Holocaust thus lies underneath the land and new life of Israel and makes its re-appearance in the next generation. Some scholars view this aspect of his work as obsession; but it is no more than the realization that the discrete experience draws the totality of Jewish history into its dimension, particularly when viewed through the poetry, the allegory, the movement from the short story which Appelfeld has mastered into the novel where stories intermingle in a seamless pattern. And, at some point in all of these works, one encounters a page of silence where we meet the child crying silently in its forest hiding place.

—Albert H. Friedlander

ARGUETA, Manlio. El Salvadoran. Born in San Miguel, 24 November 1935. Educated at the Universidad Nacional, San Salvador. Founding member, Universidad Nacional Literary Circle. Has lived in exile in Costa Rica since 1973. Recipient: Certamen Cultural Centroamericano award, 1968; Casa de las Américas prize, 1977; University of Central America/EDITORES prize, 1980. Address: c/o Chatto and Windus, 20 Vauxhall Bridge Road, London SW1N 2SA, England.

PUBLICATIONS

Fiction

El valle de las hamacas. Buenos Aires, Sudamericana, 1970.
Caperucita en la zona rosa. Havana, Casa de las Américas, 1977.
Un día en la vida. San Salvador, University of Central America, 1980; as *One Day of Life*, New York, Vintage, 1983; London, Chatto and Windus, 1984.
Cuzcatlán: donde bate la Mar del Sur. Tegucigalpa, Honduras, Guaymuras, 1986; as *Cuzcatlán: Where the Southern Sea Beats*, New York, Vintage, and London, Chatto and Windus, 1987.

Verse

Poemas. N.p., n.p., 1967.
En el costado de la luz. San Salvador, Editorial Universitaria de El Salvador, 1968.
La bellas armas reales. N.p., n.p., 1979.
El Salvador, photographs by Adam Kufeld. New York, Norton, 1990.

Other

Editor, *Poesía de El Salvador.* San José, Costa Rica, Editorial Universitaria Centroamericana, 1983.

*   *   *

The troubled political reality of Central America has provided a literary opportunity for the Salvadoran writer Manlio Argueta. Like most Central Americans with literary aspirations, he first began writing as a poet, and has edited an anthology of poetry from El Salvador. He started his literary career with other young writers like Roque Dalton at the University of San Salvador in the late 1950s, sharing a wish to write verse which sometimes humorously, sometimes angrily expressed their rejection of the social and political inequalities suffered by many of their fellow countrymen. In these early poems, Argueta used everyday language and situations to share his hope that reality could be transformed for the better by revolution. As with many of his generation, Argueta saw literature as a weapon which acted directly within society; the literary skills he cultivated were those of direct, forceful expression, put at the service of a political aim that was always more open-minded and generous than strictly doctrinaire.

In the 1970s Argueta also wrote two novels in a similar vein: *El valle de las hamacas* (The Valley of the Hammocks) and *Caperucita en la zona roja* (Little Red Riding Hood in the Red Light District), which won the important Casa de las Américas prize in 1977. As the political situation in El Salvador worsened at the end of the decade, Argueta left to live in exile in nearby Costa Rica, and it was there that the idea of the writer as a social historian who records the testimonies of his own people came to the fore. As he has said in interview: "the writer should give a voice to a people who are only now beginning to realise they have a history. They are only just starting to emerge from oppression, and part of this is the discovery that they have their own history. I want to help write that forgotten history."

Argueta has achieved this with great success in several novels, most notably *Un día en la vida* (*One Day of Life*) and *Cuzcatlán: donde bate la Mar del Sur* (*Cuzcatlán: Where the Southern Sea Beats*). As its title suggests, *One Day of Life* focuses on a peasant family in rural El Salvador and depicts the hardship and violence of their lives as reflected in the passage of 24 hours. *Cuzcatlán* takes one of the characters from that book, and by tracing back four generations of his family, examines how the Salvadoran people have generated not only the rebel fighters struggling to bring about a more just society, but also the very people who are active in repressing them. Argueta's expert knowledge of the Salvadoran peasants' lively patterns of speech, their everyday activities, as well as their customs and legends, enables him to portray convincingly the life of a whole nation. The degree of empathy Argueta achieves with his central characters enables him to create unforgettable portraits (Guadalupe, the heroine of *One Day of Life*, has been called the "Mother Courage of Central America") and helps to carry forward the action of the novels and rescue them from any overly schematic political intention. In the final chapters of a book such as *Cuzcatlán*, however, the sense that the writer is anxious to convey a definite political moral does detract from the literary qualities of the book, as events and dialogue are forced in directions imposed by preconceived ideas.

It seems also to be true that Argueta has suffered from being cut off for so many years from the reality he wishes to write about. Like other Latin American literary exiles, he keenly feels the lack of voices and experiences with which he can immediately identify and turn into his own hard-hitting literature. Thus in recent years Argueta has turned to writing screenplays for an international audience interested in the political turmoil in El Salvador, and has also returned to his first love, poetry. Perhaps with the new possibilities for peace to El Salvador he will be able to live there once again, and to find fresh inspiration in the stories generated by the changing social situation of the 1990s.

—Nick Caistor

————

ARIDJIS, Homero. Mexican. Born in Mexico, 6 April 1940. Educated at the National Autonomous University of Mexico, Mexico City, degree 1961. Married Betty Ferber in 1965; two daughters. Editor-in-chief, *Correspondencias*, Mexico, 1957–61; assistant editor, *Diálogos*, 1966; Visiting Lecturer, University of Indiana, Bloomington, 1969, and New York University, 1967–71; director, Festival Internacional de Poesía, 1981, 1982, 1987. Recipient: Xavier Villaurrutia prize, 1964; Guggenheim fellowship, 1966, 1979; Novela Novedades prize, 1988. Commander of Royal Order of the Polar Star (Sweden), 1986. Address: Sierra Jiutepec 155B, Lomas Barrilaco, Mexico City 11010, Mexico.

PUBLICATIONS

Verse

Los ojos desdoblados. Mexico City, La Palabra, 1960.
Antes del reino. Mexico City, Era, 1963.
La difícil ceremonia. N.p., Pájaro Cascabel, 1963.
Los espacios azules. Mexico City, Mortiz, 1968; as *Blue Spaces: Selected Poems of Homero Aridjis*, edited by Kenneth Rexroth, New York, Seabury Press, 1974.
Ajedrez; Navegaciones (includes short sketches). Mexico City, Siglo Veintiuno, 1969.
Quemar las naves. Mexico City, Mortiz, 1975.
Antología, edited by Cristina Peri Rossi. Barcelona, Lumen, 1976.
Vivir para ver. Mexico City, Mortiz, 1977; as *Exaltation of Light*, translated by Eliot Weinberger, New York, BOA, 1981.
Construir la muerte. Mexico City, Mortiz, 1982.
República de poetas. Mexico City, Casillas, 1985.
Obra poética, 1960–1986. Mexico City, Mortiz, 1987.
Imágenes para el fin del milenio; Nueva expulsión del paraíso. Mexico City, Mortiz, 1990.

Fiction

Ta, i.e. La tumba de Filidor. Mexico City, La Palabra, 1961.
Mirándola dormir; Pavana por la amada presente. Mexico City, Mortiz, 1964.
Perséfone. Mexico City, Mortiz, 1967; as *Persephone*, New York, Vintage, 1986.
El encantador solitario. Mexico City, Fondo de Cultura Económica, 1972.
Playa nudista; El último Adán. Barcelona, Argos Vergara, 1982.

1492. Vida y tiempos de Juan Cabezón de Castilla. Madrid, Siglo Veintiuno, 1985; as *1492*, New York, Summit, 1991.
El último Adán; Noche de independencia; Playa nudista. Mexico City, Mortiz, 1986.
Memorias del Nuevo Mundo. Mexico City, Diana, 1988.

Play

Espectáculo del año dos mil. Mexico City, Mortiz, 1981.

Other

El poeta niño: narración. Mexico City, Fondo de Cultura Económica, 1971.
Sobre una ausencia. Barcelona, Seix Barral, 1976.
Gran teatro del fin del mundo. Mexico City, Mortiz, 1990.

Editor, *Seis poetas latinoamericanos de hoy.* New York, Harcourt Brace, 1972.
Editor, *Antología del Primer Festival International de Poesía, Morelia, 1981.* Mexico City, Mortiz, 1982.

*

Bibliography: in *Mexican Literature: A Bibliography of Secondary Sources* by David William Foster, Metuchen, New Jersey, Scarecrow Press, 1992.

Critical Studies: "A Hovering Imagination" by John Fandel, in *Review* (New York), 15, 1975; "Four Contemporary Mexican Poets: Marco Antonio Montes de Oca, Gabriel Zaid, José Emilio Pacheco, Homero Aridjis" by Merlin H. Forster, in *Tradition and Renewal: Essays on 20th-Century Latin American Literature and Culture*, Urbana, University of Illinois Press, 1975; "Homero Aridjis: Blue Spaces of Illumination" by Kenneth Rexroth, in *Review* (New York), 14, 1975.

*   *   *

Homero Aridjis published his first collection of poems when he was 20 years old, and since then has continued ceaselessly to publish both poetry and fiction. He was one of three collaborators with Octavio Paz (*q.v.*) on the anthology *Poesía en movimiento* (1966) (*New Poetry of Mexico*), where Paz characterized Aridjis's early love poetry as the most original of his generation but hinted that he ought to concentrate his gifts rather than let them run loose. There is a torrential quality to Aridjis's early poetry that suggests a litany, almost a lyrical narrative. "Mirándola dormir" (Seeing Her Sleep) exemplifies this broad scope. The poem is the poet's meditation on a sleeping woman, borrowing magical insights from Paz's view of woman in *Piedra de sol* (1957) (*Sun Stone*), and the surrealist leader André Breton's elegy to his wife, "Ma Femme" (1932). The long poem incorporates dialogues, monologues, and mind-flow sequences in long lines with repeated words and leitmotifs. Woman becomes all women, Eve and Bérenice, man's opposite without whom there is neither revelation nor poetry.

This lyrical expansion reaches its climax in *Perséfone* (*Persephone*). In this erotic, lyrical novel without a plot or well-defined characters Aridjis recreates the Goddess of the Dead and the Underworld, an insatiable amorous woman turned into a whore in a brothel. Aridjis privileges the gaze, and names erotic parts in a hypnotic litany. Several passages embody his theory of regenerative love pulling people back to their "confused beginning" and origins. At times he borders on the outrageous, and links himself with a long French tradition of this kind of writing (Marquis de Sade, Georges Bataille, the surrealists). *Persephone* charts a descent into a more meaningful self. The men who arrive at the brothel "had left their brains, hearts and teeth in a closet, had put on their sense at random and in haste, putting memory on their knees and souls in their genitals." All the time Persephone, slightly absent and mysterious, controls this erotic ritual of self-knowledge.

Aridjis has also mastered the short lyric. In *Los espacios azules* (*Blue Spaces: Selected Poems*), and especially in *Quemar las naves* (Burning the Boats) and *Vivir para ver* (*Exaltation of Light*), we see how vision predominates in a poetry of celebration of light, the world, and the here and now: "Birds in the rain are/brief dark flashes/that flock at day's end/ to the tree of life/and willow fog or pine/each tree the light reveals/in the damp of the shadows/is the tree of life." In "Burn the Boats" Aridjis moves from Cortés's daring act of burning his boats to impersonate several Mexican figures from Aztec deities to the revolutionary Emilio Zapata. The poem "Letter from Mexico" captures Aridjis at his best:

> Invisible ancestors
> walk with us
> through these back streets
> car-noises
> the stares of children
> young girls' bodies
> cross through them
> Weightless vague
> we travel through them
> at doorways that no longer are
> on bridges that are empty
> while with the sun on our faces
> we too
> move toward transparency.

Though still dependent on Paz for his poetics, Aridjis is more genuinely lyrical, not letting his intellect interfere with the poem's music. However, he tends to be inconcise, and to expand endlessly and rely on a piling-up of images and repetitions to create sense.

A clear narrative temptation in Aridjis's verse inevitably led him to write a novel. *1492. Vida y tiempos de Juan Cabezón de Castilla* (*1492. The Life and Times of Juan Cabezón of Castile*) is an extraordinary recreation of detailed Spanish history in the picaresque mode. Aridjis has worked diligently at getting his documentary-realist base right as he covers a century from a pogrom in Seville in 1391 to Columbus's departure from Palos de Moguer in 1492. The novel relates the history of a persecuted couple of Jewish converts — Juan Cabezón, on the run from the inquisition, who seeks Isabel de la Vega and their child all over Spain. The success of Aridjis's enterprise lies in the utter and hypnotic density he gives to the Spain of that hectic period with its multi-cultured fissions. He skilfully invents several kinds of documents so that we almost participate in the period through this trick of immediacy. This novel is undoubtedly the most convincing portrait of what 1492 actually felt like. By fusing the reconquest of Spain from the Moors and the imminent discovery of the "New World" with the expulsion of the Jews, he achieves contemporary echoes and relevances. The novel ends with an appendix that purports to be an original document, thus overturning the old Cervantine opposition between the lies of fiction and truth. Not least of Aridjis's felicities is his recreation of a wonderfully free Spanish language that avoids pastiche and collage.

Juan Cabezón's peregrinations continue in *Memorias del Nuevo Mundo* (Memories of the New World) as Aridjis's protagonist Juan Cabezón sets sail with Columbus in 1492 for the Caribbean, and then accompanies Cortés to Mexico and the sacking of the canal city of Tenochtitlan. Aridjis grounds this follow-up on the same rich documentation given in a five-page appendix at the end. Read together, the two novels recreate this extraordinary period more vividly than any other genre could, and justify the combination of well-researched material with picaresque inventions. At the heart of all Aridjis's work lies a verbal dexterity never just playfully baroque, but always subservient to vital concerns like love, light, self-knowledge, and understanding history.

—Jason Wilson

———

ARRABAL (Terán), Fernando. Born in Melilla, Spanish Morocco, 11 August 1932. Educated at a school in Getafe; a military academy; Escuela Teórico-Práctica de la Industria del Papel, Valencia; studied law at the University of Madrid. Married Luce Moreau in 1958; one daughter and one son. Writer, and theatre and film director; moved to France in 1955; co-founder, Panic Movement, 1963; jailed for several months in 1967 during a trip to Spain; taught at the University of California, Santa Cruz, 1971. Editor, *Le Théâtre*, 1968. Recipient: Superdotado prize, 1942; Ford grant, for travel to the USA, 1959; Lugné-Poë theatre prize, 1966; Society of Authors prize, 1966; Grand Prix du Théâtre, 1967; Grand Prix de Humour Noir, 1968; Obie award, 1976; Nadal prize, 1983; World's Theatre prize, 1984; Fine Arts Gold Medal (Spain), 1989. Chevalier de l'Ordre des Arts et des Lettres. Address: 22 rue Jouffroy, 75017 Paris, France.

PUBLICATIONS

Plays

Théâtre I (includes *Oraison*; *Les Deux Bourreaux*; *Fando et Lis*; *Le Cimetière des voitures*).   Paris, Julliard, 1958.
Oraison.   Included in *Théâtre I*, 1958; as *Orison* (produced London, 1961; Lock Haven, Pennsylvania, 1967; New York, 1968), in *Four Plays*, 1962.
Les Deux Bourreaux.   Included in *Théâtre I*, 1958; as *The Two Executioners* (produced New York, 1960; London, 1966), with *The Automobile Graveyard*, 1960; in *Four Plays*, 1962.
Fando et Lis (produced Paris, 1961).   Included in *Théâtre I*, 1958; as *Fando and Lis* (produced London, 1961; New York, 1967), in *Four Plays*, 1962.
Le Cimetière des voitures (produced Dijon, 1966; Paris, 1967).   Included in *Théâtre I*, 1958; as *The Automobile Graveyard* (produced New York, 1961), with *The Two Executioners*, 1960; as *The Car Cemetery* (produced London, 1969), in *Four Plays*, 1962.
Le Tricycle (produced Madrid, 1958). Included in *Théâtre II*, 1961; as *The Tricycle* (produced New York, 1970), in *Plays*, 1967; in *Guernica and Other Plays*, 1969.
Pique-nique en campagne (produced 1959).   Included in *Théâtre II*, 1961; as *Picnic on the Battlefield* (produced London, 1964; New York, 1967), in *Plays*, 1967; in *Guernica and Other Plays*, 1969.

The Automobile Graveyard, and The Two Executioners. New York, Grove Press, 1960.

Orchestration théâtrale (produced Paris, 1960). Published as *Dieu tenté par les mathématiques*, in *Théâtre VIII*, 1970.

Guernica (produced Celle, 1960). Included in *Théâtre II*, 1961; in English (produced New York, 1969), in *Plays*, 1967; in *Guernica and Other Plays*, 1969.

Théâtre II (includes *Guernica*; *Le Labyrinthe*; *Le Tricycle*; *Pique-nique en campagne*; *La Bicyclette du condamné*). Paris, Julliard, 1961.

Le Labyrinthe (produced Vincennes, 1967). Included in *Théâtre II*, 1961; as *The Labyrinth* (produced London and Waltham, Massachusetts, 1968), in *Plays*, 1967; in *Guernica and Other Plays*, 1969.

La Bicyclette du condamné (produced Paris, 1966). Included in *Théâtre II*, 1961; as *The Condemned Man's Bicycle* (produced London, 1968), in *Plays*, 1967.

Four Plays (includes *Orison*; *The Two Executioners*; *Fando and Lis*; *The Car Cemetery*). London, Calder, 1962.

La Communion solennelle (produced Paris, 1964). Included in *Théâtre V*, 1967; as *The Solemn Communion* (produced Lock Haven, Pennsylvania, 1967; London, 1970), in *The Architect and the Emperor of Assyria*, 1970.

Strip-tease de la jalousie (produced Paris, 1964). Included in *Théâtre V*, 1967; as *Striptease of Jealousy*, in *Drama Review*, Fall 1968.

Le Couronnement (produced Paris, 1965). Included in *Théâtre III*, 1965; revised version, as *Le Lai de Barabbas*, in *Théâtre IV*, 1969.

Théâtre III: Théâtre panique (includes *Le Couronnement*; *Le Grand Cérémonial*; *Concert dans un œuf*; *Cérémonie pour un noir assassiné*). Paris, Julliard, 1965.

Cérémonie pour un noir assassiné (produced Nancy, 1966). Included in *Théâtre III*, 1965; as *Ceremony for a Murdered Black* (produced New York, 1972; London, 1973).

Les Amours impossibles (produced Paris, 1965). Included in *Théâtre V*, 1967; as *Impossible Loves* (produced London, 1971), in *Drama Review*, Fall 1968.

Le Grand Cérémonial (produced Paris, 1966). Included in *Théâtre III*, 1965.

Concert dans un oeuf (produced Bordeaux, 1966). Included in *Théâtre III*, 1965.

Une Chèvre sur un nuage (produced Paris, 1966). Included in *Théâtre V*, 1967.

La Princesse (produced Paris, 1966).

La Jeunesse illustrée (produced Vincennes, 1967). Included in *Théâtre V*, 1967.

Plays (includes *Guernica*; *The Labyrinth*; *The Tricyle*; *Picnic on the Battlefield*; *The Condemned Man's Bicycle*). London, Calder and Boyars, 1967.

L'Architecte et l'empereur d'Assyrie (produced Paris, 1967). Included in *Théâtre V*, 1967; as *The Architect and the Emperor of Assyria* (produced London, 1967; San Francisco, 1968), New York, Grove Press, 1969; London, Calder and Boyars, 1970.

Théâtre V (includes *Théâtre panique — La Communion solennelle*; *Les Amours impossibles*; *Une Chèvre sur un nuage*; *La Jeunesse illustrée*; *Dieu est-il devenu fou?*; *Strip-tease de la jalousie*; *Les Quatres Cubes* — and *L'Architecte et l'empereur d'Assyrie*). Paris, Bourgois, 1967.

Théâtre IV (includes *La Lai de Barabbas*; *Concert dans un oeuf*). Paris, Bourgois, 1969.

Revolution-Imagination (produced Brussels, 1969).

Le Jardin des délices (produced Paris, 1969). Included in *Théâtre VI*, 1969; as *Garden of Delights*, New York, Grove Press, 1974.

Bestialité érotique (produced Paris, 1969). Included in *Théâtre VI*, 1969.

Une Tortue nommée Dostoievsky (produced Paris, 1969). Included in *Théâtre VI*, 1969.

Théâtre VI (includes *Le Jardin des délices*; *Bestialité érotique*; *Une Tortue nommée Dostoievsky*). Paris, Bourgois, 1969.

Et Ils passèrent des menottes aux fleurs (produced Paris, 1969). Included in *Théâtre VII*, 1969; as *And They Put Handcuffs on the Flowers* (produced New York, 1971; London, 1973), New York, Grove Press, 1973.

L'Aurore rouge et noire (produced Brussels, 1969). Included in *Théâtre VII*, 1969; as *Dawn: Red and Black* (produced New York, 1971); section entitled *Groupuscule of My Heart* published in *Drama Review*, Summer 1969.

Théâtre VII: Théâtre de guerilla (includes *Et Ils passèrent des menottes aux fleurs*; *L'Aurore rouge et noire*). Paris, Bourgois, 1969.

Théâtre 1969 (includes *La Contestation*; *Le Grand Guignol*). Paris, Bourgois, 2 vols., 1969.

Guernica and Other Plays (includes *The Labyrinth*; *The Tricycle*; *Picnic on the Battlefield*). New York, Grove Press, 1969.

Théâtre VIII: Deux opéras paniques (includes *Ars Amandi*; *Dieu tenté par les mathématiques*). Paris, Bourgois, 1970.

Ars Amandi. Included in *Théâtre VIII*, 1970; in English, London, Calder, 1983.

Théâtre 1970: Théâtre en marge. Paris, Bourgois, 1970.

The Architect and the Emperor of Assyria, The Grand Ceremonial, The Solemn Communion. London, Calder and Boyars, 1970.

Viva la muerte (screenplay), with *Baal Babylone*. Paris, Bourgois, 1971.

Théâtre 1971: Les Monstres. Paris, Bourgois, 1971.

Théâtre IX (includes *Le Ciel et la merde*; *La Grande Revue du XXe siécle*). Paris, Bourgois, 1972.

Bella Ciao: la guerre de mille ans (produced Paris, 1972). Paris, Bourgois, 1972.

La Marche royale (produced Paris, 1973). Included in *Théâtre XI*, 1976.

Sur le Fil; ou, La Ballade du train fantôme (produced Paris, 1974). Paris, Bourgois, 1974.

Théâtre X (includes *La Guerre du mille ans*; *Sur le Fil, ou, La Ballade du train fantôme*; *Jeunes Barbares d'aujourd'hui*). Paris, Bourgois, 1975.

Jeunes Barbares d'aujourd'hui (produced Paris, 1975). Included in *Théâtre X*, 1975.

La Tour de Babel (produced São Paulo, 1977; Paris, 1979). Included in *Théâtre XI*, 1976.

La Gloire en images, music by Graziano Mandozzi (produced Paris, 1976). Included in *Théâtre XI*, 1976.

Théâtre XI: La Tour de Babel (includes *La Marche royale*; *Une Orange sur le Mont de Vénus*; *La Gloire en images*). Paris, Bourgois, 1976.

Le Ciel et la merde II (produced Paris, 1976). Included in *Théâtre XIII*, 1981.

Vole-Moi un petit milliard (produced Paris, 1977). Included in *Théâtre XII*, 1978.

Théâtre XII: Théâtre bouffe (includes *Vole-Moi un petit milliard*; *La Pastaga des loufs, ou, Ouverture orang-outan*; *Punk et punk et Colégram*). Paris, Bourgois, 1978.

Le Roi de Sodome (produced Paris, 1979). Included in *Théâtre XIII*, 1981.

Baal Babylone, from his own novel (produced Paris, 1980).

Inquisición (produced Barcelona, 1980). Granada, Don Quichote, 1982, as *Inquisition* (produced New York, 1983).

Théâtre XIII (includes *Mon doux royaume saccagé*; *Le Roi de Sodome*; *Le Ciel et la merde II*). Paris, Bourgois, 1981.

L'Extravagante Réussite de Jésus-Christ, Karl Marx, et William Shakespeare. Included in *Théâtre XIV*, 1982; as *The Extravagant Triumph of Jesus Christ, Karl Marx, and William Shakespeare* (produced New York, 1981).
Théâtre XIV (includes *L'Extravagante Réussite de Jésus-Christ, Karl Marx, et William Shakespeare*; *Lève-Toi et rêve*). Paris, Bourgois, 1982.
Théâtre XV (includes *Les Délices de la chair*; *La Ville dont le prince était une princesse*). Paris, Bourgois, 1984.
Théâtre XVI (includes *Bréviaire d'amour d'un haltérophile*; *Apokalyptica*; *La Charge de centaures*). Paris, Bourgois, 1986.
Théâtre XVII (includes *Les "Cucarachas" de Yale*; *Une Pucelle pour un gorille*; *The Red Madonna* [sic]; *La Traversée de l'empire*). Paris, Bourgois, 1987.
La Nuit est aussi un soleil; Roues d'infortune. Arles, Actes Sud-Papiers, 1990.

Screenplays: *Viva la muerte*, 1971; *The Tricycle*; *J'irai comme un cheval fou*, 1973; *L'Arbre de Guernica*, 1975; *Odyssey of the Pacific*, 1982; *La Cimetière des voitures.*

Fiction

Baal Babylone. Paris, Julliard, 1959; in English, New York, Grove Press, 1961.
L'Enterrement de la sardine. Paris, Julliard, 1961; as *The Burial of the Sardine*, London, Calder and Boyars, 1965; New York, Riverrun Press, 1980.
Arrabal celebrando la ceremonia de la confusión. Madrid, Alfaguara, 1966; as *Fêtes et rites de la confusion*, Paris, Le Terrain Vague, 1967.
La torre herida por el rayo. Barcelona, Destino, 1983; as *La Tour prends garde*, Paris, Grasset, 1983; as *The Tower Struck by Lightning*, New York, Viking, 1988.
La Reverdie. Paris, Bourgois, 1985.
La piedra iluminada. Barcelona, Destino, 1985; as *The Compass Stone*, New York, Grove Press, 1987.
La Vierge rouge. Paris, Acropole, 1986.
La Fille de King Kong. Paris, Acropole, 1988; as *La hija de King Kong*, Barcelona, Seix Barral, 1988.
L'Extravagante Croisade d'un castrat amoureux, ou, comme un lys entre les épines. Ramsay, Cortanze, 1989.

Verse

La Pierre de la folie. Paris, Julliard, 1963.
Le New York d'Arrabal. Paris, Balland, 1973.
Humbles Paradis: première anthologie poétique. Paris, Bourgois, 1985; as *Mis humildes paraísos*, Barcelona, Destino, 1985.

Other

Lettre au General Franco. Paris, Union Générale d'Éditions, 1972.
Sur Fischer: initiation aux échecs. Monaco, Éditions du Rocher, 1973.
Carta a los militantes comunistas españoles. Barcelona, Actuales, 1978.
Les Échecs féeriques et libertaires: chronique de l'express. Monaco, Éditions du Rocher, 1980.
Teatro, o seu demônio e beato, with Mariângela Alves de Lima. São Paulo, Brasiliense, 1983.
Lettre à Fidel Castro. Paris, Bourgois, 1984.
Echecs et mythe. Paris, Payot, 1984.

Devoirs de vacances, été 85, with Jean Miotte. Paris, Galilée, 1986.
La travesia del imperio, o, la guerra de las estrellas con Puerto Rico en las trincheras. Madrid, Burdeos, 1988.
El Greco. Paris, Flohic, 1991.

Editor, *Le "Panique".* Paris, Union Générale d'Éditions, 1973.

*

Bibliography: *Bibliographie d'Arrabal* by Joan P. Berenguer, Grenoble, Presses Universitaires de Grenoble, 1978.

Critical Studies: *Fernando Arrabal* by Peter L. Podol, Boston, Twayne, 1978; *The Theatre of Fernando Arrabal: A Garden of Earthly Delights* by Thomas John Donahue, New York, New York University Press, 1980; *The Festive Play of Fernando Arrabal* by Luis Oscar Arata, Lexington, University Press of Kentucky, 1982.

*   *   *

Only a few years ago, Fernando Arrabal was at the cutting edge of the avant-garde theater. Today, although his bimonthly column on chess in the French news magazine *Express* keeps him in the public eye, he is no longer so much in the limelight. As the self-appointed "prince of panic," Arrabal's presence, nevertheless, shows that his quirky brand of humanity and his surreal musings continue to satisfy a demand among the reading and theater-going public as well as among the aficionados of chess. Besides the theater, Arrabal has expanded his artistic output into film, novels, and poetry, but with less stunning success. Despite his years of exile — first imposed by the Franco regime, now apparently voluntary — Arrabal has not lost qualities that were part of his vision in the late 1950s and early 1960s. The insertion in his works of autobiographical material, almost exclusively drawn from recollections of his youth, still creates a tone of playfulness mixed with harshness. His characters maintain the aura of street urchins searching for some lost paradise. His language is at once lyrical, scatological and raucous. He seeks large metaphors on which he can hang a series of themes.

In one of his earliest plays, *Le Cimetière des voitures* (*The Automobile Graveyard*), Arrabal uses the theatrical metaphor of a city of decrepit autos, peopled by adults who talk and play like children, to comment on the progressive choking of artistic freedom by anyone so foolish as to oppose the prevailing authority. A naive representation of Christ's Passion and death, the action of the play places Emmanou (Emanuel) in a constant race with the police who want him both for murder and for playing his trumpet for the poor wretches who live in the automobile graveyard. In the end he is betrayed by a friend with a kiss and strung up on a bicycle frame. The basic themes of Arrabal's canon are already in place: a master-slave relationship, sadomasochism, moral ambiguity, and erotic love, all encased in a framework of theatricality and surreal poetry. Victor García's Paris production of the play, with the audience seated in swivel chairs so that they could watch the high-pitched action taking place on platforms erected on the perimeter of the auditorium, marked Arrabal's theater as Artaudian in concept.

Much of the Panic Theater of Arrabal has been placed by critics under the aegis of Antonin Artaud — despite some protestations by Arrabal to the contrary. Its surreal origins can be readily found in Arrabal's musings on the theater: "I dream of a theater in which the human and poetry, panic and love are united . . . like the humanoid dreams that haunt the night of an IBM machine." From the Panic Theater comes one of his most critically acclaimed plays, *L'Architecte et l'empereur d'Assyrie* (*The Architect and Emperor of Assyria*). In this work Arrabal uses a familiar trope: a survivor of an airplane crash stranded on an island encounters a savage islander. Prospero meets Caliban; civilization meets the natural world. The savage islander, the Architect, as it turns out, is several thousand years old and has a firm command of nature — he can actually whistle the birds out of the trees and make the sun rise and set. The pitiful Emperor can only work out the guilt from the murder of his mother. In this theatrical *pas de deux*, Arrabal takes aim at many of the ills that western civilization has brought upon itself. As the two characters play multiple roles in the trial and conviction of the Emperor, a whirligig of activities leads eventually to the Emperor's confession of guilt and its expiation. After executing the Emperor with a hammer blow to his skull, the Architect-judge consumes the body of his civilized friend and takes on his memory, his past, and his sorrowful qualities. The work ends with another horrendous crash and the action begins again. Arrabal's theatrical games here open an entire trunkful of themes, but his surreal celebration of humankind's imaginative genius stands out as one of the foremost aspects of the play.

The events of May 1968 in Paris may have galvanized some of Arrabal's political thinking, but his arrest and imprisonment in Spain by Franco's police for having dedicated a book with the inscription "I shit on God, the Fatherland, and everything else" pushed Arrabal's creative energies into the area of guerilla theater. This mixture of "panic" and politics is best displayed in *Et Ils passèrent des menottes aux fleurs* (*And They Put Handcuffs on the Flowers*), a play which describes the horrors of life in a Spanish prison, older men's nightmares, and younger men's shattered lives. The centers of power: the State, the Church, and the Banks, are vilified for their tyrannical roles in society. The central figure, Tosan, a political prisoner, is condemned to die and, despite his wife's fervent efforts to stay the execution, he is garotted. The play ends with the ritual washing of the prisoners in Tosan's blood and urine. Tosan, like many of Arrabal's heros, becomes a Christ-figure, not merely a victim of ideology.

Panic mixed with politics and a generous dose of playfulness marks most of Arrabal's works in more recent years. In his *Théâtre bouffe*, Arrabal treats — and frequently parodies — such themes as the women's liberation movement, DNA research, and chess, while using traditional techniques of fast-moving plots and mistaken identity. In *Vole-Moi un petit milliard* (Steal Me a Million) researchers from the National Institute of Scientific Research mix with toreadors and liberated Carmelite nuns. In a light, mocking tone, Arrabal takes on the "business" of scientific research and pollution. *La Pastaga des loufs, ou Ouverture ourang-outan* (Orangutang Opening) contrasts the criminal underworld and the cerebral world of chess. The game of chess turns wild when large chess figures are found to be filled with cocaine and a woman becomes world chess champion.

In *La Vierge rouge* (Red Madonna), Arrabal returns to the theme of disillusionment with modern Spain, a theme he treated with theatrical poetry in *Sur le Fil; ou, La Ballade du train fantôme* (On the Highwire, or, the Ballad of the Phantom Train). In this intriguing metaphor, a mother slays her daughter, a prodigy of sorts who has taken an interest in alchemy. The mother here represents Spain and the daughter the playwright. In a strange twist the daughter pleads to be slain because she has been corrupted by the world and lost her purity. Arrabal revisits the world of games, androgyny, and love in *Bréviaire d'amour d'un haltérophile* (The Body

Builder's Book of Love). Once again he returns to the *pas de deux* of two male characters with a controlling force exercised by an unseen woman. Job, the body builder, wants nothing more than to pass into a mystic world beyond desire and pain. His partner, Tao, an androgynous masseur, plays the tormentor. Phylis (from a large family of Lis and Lys found in Arrabal's canon) is the unseen woman. For Job she is the means by which he will find his paradise, while for Tao she is the source of all erotic love. Although billed as a comedy, the play shows moments of sadistic cruelty as Tao goads the innocent Job into greater and greater challenges of physical strength, ending with a bloody scene in which Job tries to free the enchained Tao with his teeth.

Note should be made of Arrabal's more recent novels, especially *La torre herida por el rayo* (*The Tower Struck by Lightning*). Author of several novels of an experimental nature written in French, Arrabal had hoped to "re-enter" the Spanish literary community with this tale of two chess champions, Elias Tarsis and Marc Amary, who face off in a chess tournament. The real story, though, deals with the sordid life of Tarsis and the self-possessed and intellectual Amary. Using themes he had explored thoroughly in many of his plays, Arrabal concocts a novel that is at times ingenious as the reader follows the chessboard moves of the champions, but in the end is disappointing.

Clearly, Arrabal's works defy easy classification. His years of exile place him outside the Spanish literary world and his Spanishness situates him on the margins of the French literary scene. Eccentric, polemical, and playful, he continues to provoke his audiences with a brand of theater whose black humor supports a harsh attitude toward modern society. Mixing the oniric and the political, Arrabal creates a strange brew. Neither of the political left or the right, he has marked out a territory that is unique in both its thematic and formal dimensions, a territory that borders on the land of the surreal and the absurd, the ludic and the political.

—Thomas J. Donahue

***

ARREOLA, Juan José. Mexican. Born in Ciudad Guzmán, Jalisco, 12 September 1918. Studied theatre in Paris, 1945. Teacher in Ciudad Guzmán, from 1941; worked on a newspaper in Guadalajara, 1943–45; editor, with Juan Rulfo, *Pan* magazine, and *Eos* magazine, 1940s; proofreader, Fondo de Cultura Económica publishing house, Mexico City, 1946; director of creative writing workshop, National Autonomous University of Mexico, Mexico City; founding member and actor, Poesía en Voz Alta group. Recipient: Institute of Fine Arts Drama Festival prize, and El Colegio de México fellowship, late 1940s; Xavier Villaurrutia prize, 1963. Address: c/o Editorial Joaquín Mortiz, Ave Insurgentes Sur 1162-3, Col del Valle, 03100 Mexico City, Mexico.

PUBLICATIONS

Fiction

Gunther Stapenhorst: viñetas de Isidoro Ocampo. Mexico City, n.p., 1946.

Varia invención. Mexico City, Tezontle, 1949; enlarged edition, Mexico City, Mortiz, 1971.

Cinco cuentos. Mexico City, Los Presentes, 1951.

Confabulario. Mexico City, Fondo de Cultura Económica, 1952; revised edition, published with *Varia invención*, as *Confabulario y Varia invención: 1951–1955*, Fondo de Cultura Económica, 1955; published with *Bestiario* and *Punta de plata*, as *Confabulario total, 1941–1961*, Fondo de Cultura Económica, 1962; as *Confabulario and Other Inventions*, Austin, University of Texas Press, 1964; revised edition, as *Confabulario definitivo*, Madrid, Cátedra, 1986.

Bestiario. Mexico City, Universidad Nacional Autónoma de México, 1958; published with *Confabulario* and *Punta de plata*, as *Confabulario total, 1941–1961*, Mexico City, Fondo de Cultura Económica, 1962; revised edition, Mexico City, Mortiz, 1981.

Punta de plata. Mexico City, n.p., 1958; published with *Confabulario* and *Bestiario*, as *Confabulario total, 1941–1961*, Mexico City, Fondo de Cultura Económica, 1962.

La feria. Mexico City, Mortiz, 1963; as *The Fair*, Austin, University of Texas Press, 1977.

Cuentos. Havana, Casa de las Américas, 1969.

Antología de Juan José Arreola, edited by Jorge Arturo Ojeda. Mexico City, Oasis, 1969.

Palindroma (includes play). Mexico City, Mortiz, 1971.

Mujeres, animales, y fantasías mecánicas. Barcelona, Tusquets, 1972.

Confabulario antológico. Madrid, Círculo de Lectores, 1973.

Mi confabulario. Mexico City, Promexa, 1979.

Confabulario personal. Barcelona, Bruguera, 1980.

Imagen y obra escogida. Mexico City, Universidad Nacional Autónoma de México, 1984.

Estas páginas mías. Mexico City, Fondo de Cultura Económica, 1985.

Play

La hora de todos: juguete cómico en un acto. Mexico City, Los Presentes, 1954.

Other

La palabra educación. Mexico City, Secretaria de Educación Pública, 1973.

Y ahora, la mujer. Mexico City, Utopía, 1975.

Inventario. Mexico City, Grijalbo, 1976.

Ramón López Velarde: una lectura parcial. Mexico City, Cultural Bancen, 1988.

El arte de Nicolás Moreno, with Carlos Pellicer and Elisa García Barragán. Mexico City, Banco Nacional de Obras y Servicios Públicos, 1990.

Editor, *Cuadernos del unicornio.* Mexico City, n.p., 5 vols., 1958–60.

Editor, *Lectura en voz alta.* Mexico City, Porrúa, 1968.

Editor, *La ciudad de Querétaro*, by Fernando Pereznieto Castro. Mexico City, Mortiz, 1975.

*

Bibliography: in *Mexican Literature: A Bibliography of Secondary Sources* by David William Foster, Metuchen, New Jersey, Scarecrow Press, 1992.

Critical Studies: "The Estranged Man: Kafka's Influence on Arreola" by Thomas J. Tomanek, in *Revue des Langues Vivantes*, 37, 1971; "An Ancient Mold for Contemporary Casting: The Beast Book of Juan José Arreola," in *Hispania* (Los Angeles), 56, 1973, and *Juan José Arreola*, Boston, Twayne, 1983, both by Yulan M. Washburn; "An Independent Author" by Andrée Conrad, in *Review* (New York), 14, 1975; "Continuity in Evolution: Juan José Arreola as Dramatist," in *Latin American Theatre Review* (Lawrence, Kansas), 8(2), 1975, "René Avilés Fabila in the Light of Juan José Arreola: A Study in Spiritual Affinity," in *Journal of Spanish Studies: 20th Century*, 7, 1979, and "Artistic Iconoclasm in Mexico: Countertexts of Arreola, Agustín, Avilés and Hiriart," in *Chasqui* (Provo, Utah), 18(1), 1989, all by Theda Mary Herz; "Albert Camus' Concept of the Absurd and Juan José Arreola's 'The Switchman'" by George R. McMurray, in *Latin American Literary Review* (Pittsburgh), 11, 1977; "The Little Girl and the Cat: 'Kafkaesque' Elements in Arreola's 'The Switchman'" by Leonard A. Cheever, in *American Hispanist* (Clear Creek, Indiana), 34–35, 1979; "Absurdist Techniques in the Short Stories of Juan José Arreola" by Read G. Gilgen, in *Journal of Spanish Studies: 20th Century*, 8, 1980; "*Los de abajo* [Mariano Azuela], *La feria*, and the Notion of Space-Time Categories in the Narrative Text" by Floyd Merrell, in *Hispanófila* (Chapel Hill, North Carolina), 79, 1983; "Juan José Arreola: Allegorist in an Age of Uncertainty" by Paula R. Heusinkveld, in *Chasqui* (Provo, Utah), 13(2–3), 1984; "Arreola's 'The Switchman' — The Train and the Desert Experience" by Bettina Knapp, in *Confluencia* (Greeley, Colorado), 3(1), 1987; "This Is No Way to Run a Railroad: Arreola's Allegorical Railroad and a Possible Source" by John R. Burt, in *Hispania* (Los Angeles), 71, 1988; "Arreola's *La feria*: The Author and the Reader in the Text" by Carol Clark D'Lugo, in *Hispanófila* (Chapel Hill, North Carolina), 97, 1989.

*   *   *

Juan José Arreola's reputation as one of Mexico's foremost contemporary writers rests on a few volumes of short stories produced at sporadic intervals over a lengthy career. Impressive as these are, Arreola has undoubtedly managed to create a legend around his own work that has often seemed to exempt it from criticism, particularly within Mexico itself.

When Arreola published his first collection of short stories *Varia Invención* (Various Inventions) in 1949, Mexican literature was still dominated by realist works centred around the events and themes of the social turmoil which characterized the revolutionary years of the early decades of this century. The determinedly non-realist experimentalism and the mixture of styles and tones in the 18 stories of Arreola's book immediately set him apart from most of his predecessors, although critical attention at the time was scant.

It was Arreola's next book, *Confabulario*, that firmly established Arreola's reputation in Mexico. Once again, the range and variety of the stories demonstrates the author's originality. There are stories centred on animals, imaginary biographies from various historical periods, stories of metaphysical suspense which show Arreola to have been an assiduous reader of Franz Kafka, tales of horror and fantasy, as well as others that read more like essays on modern Mexican life and customs.

The fantastic vein Arreola explored in *Confabulario* was especially novel in Mexican literature at the time, and he pursued it successfully in the books that followed. Also unusual was his fidelity to the short-story form, usually seen by Mexican writers simply as a stage of apprenticeship before they launch on more "serious" novel writing. In this esteem for the short-story form as allowing both greater liberty and being more demanding, Arreola was joining such important Latin American contemporaries as Jorge Luis Borges and Julio Cortázar.

In 1955 Arreola initiated what has become a common practice for him: he brought out a revised version of his first two books, adding new material he had written since their first publication, and revising all the texts. The collection now included some of his best-known stories, such as "Parable of the Exchange" and "A Tamed Woman."

On a different tack, 1958 saw the publication of *Punta de plata* (Silverpoint), a series of observations on animals in the Mexico City zoo. In this bestiary, Arreola uses the animals as metaphors for human conduct, which he regards with generally sardonic amusement. This collection has also been brought out in various editions.

Arreola has so far made only one attempt at novel writing, *La feria* (*The Fair*). The novel is a poetic invocation and satire on life in his home town Zapotlán, but its lack of structure and unified plot have left most critics rather bewildered. As the academic John S. Brushwood has written: "the only thing I am certain about is that the book raises many questions that probably only time will answer. It is not a collection of short stories. If it is a novel, we must change our understanding of what a novel is. Still, it is unquestionably a form of fiction" (*Mexico in Its Novel*, 1966).

In more recent years, Arreola has continued to write mostly short fables and fantastic pieces. His influence on younger generations has been considerable, to the point where it might be said that the wheel has come full circle, and young Mexican writers need to explore fresh ways to create a more realist kind of fiction.

—Nick Caistor

"AŚK," Upendranāth. Indian. Born in Jalandhar, Panjab, 14 December 1910. Educated at Saindass Anglo-Sanskrit High School, Jalandhar, graduated 1927; Dayanand Anglovedic Vedic College, Jalandhar, graduated 1931; University of the Panjab, Lahore, LL.B. 1936. Married 1) Śilā Devī in 1932 (died 1936); 2) Śyāmā in 1941 (separated 1941), one daughter and one son; 3) Kauśalyā Devī in 1941, one son. Member of the editorial board, *Bhiṣam* newspaper, Lahore; began writing in Urdu, 1927, in Hindi, 1935; staff member, *Bandemataram*, Lahore, two years; editor, *Prīt Lahrī*, Pritnagar (now Amritsar), 1939–41; playwright for All India Radio, Lahore, 1941–44; editor, *Sainik Samacār* journal, Delhi, 1944–45; screenwriter, Filmistan, Bombay, 1945–47; founder Nīlābh Prakasan publishing house, Allahabad, 1949. Recipient: GOI award; Panjab Government award, 1959; Uttar Prades Government award; Saṅgīt Nāṭak prize, 1965; Soviet Land Nehru award, 1972; Uttar Prades Urdū Akādemi award, 1979; Uttar Prades Sāhitya Varidhi; Hindī Sāhitya Sammelan; Bhāṣā Vibhāg award; Bihar Urdū award, 1981; Bengal Urdū Akādemī award, 1983; Lakhnau Urdū Academi award; Uttar Prades Hindī Sansthān award; Hindī Sāhitya Sammelan Sāhitya Varhaspati, 1987; Mahā Urdū award, 1988. Fellow, Uttar Prades Saṅgīt Nāṭak Akādemī, 1981. Address: 15A Mahatma Gandhi Marg, Allahabad 211001, India.

PUBLICATIONS

Fiction

Sitārō ke khel [The Games of the Stars].   Delhi, n.p., 1938.
Ḍācī [The She-Camel].   1939.
Kōpal [Sprouts] (in Urdu).   Lahore, n.p., 1940; as *Aṅkur* (in Hindi), Benares, Sarasvatī Press, n.p., 1945.
Piñjrā [The Cage].   Lahore, n.p., 1945.
Niśāniyā [Aims].   Bombay, National Information, n.p., 1947.
Cetan cycle.
   Girtī dīvārē [Falling Walls].   Allahabad, n.p., 1947.
   Śahar mē ghūmtā ainā [A Mirror in the City].   Allahabad, Nīlābh, 1961.
   Ek nanhī kiṇḍīl [A Tiny Lamp].   Allahabad, Nīlābh, 1969.
   Bandho na nāv is ṭhā̃v [Don't Moor the Boat Here].   Allahabad, Nīlābh, 2 vols., 1974.
Ṛnjatā.   Allahabad, Bhārtī Bhaṇḍār, 1949.
Cı̄te [Ants].   Allahabad, Bhārtī Bhaṇḍār, 1949.
Do dhārā [Two Streams], with Kauśalyā Aśk.   Allahabad, Nīlābh, 1949.
Kāle sāhab [Native Sahab].   Allahabad, Nīlābh, 1950.
Judāī kī śām kā gīt [A Farewell's Night Song].   Allahabad, Nīlābh, 1951.
Garm rākh [Hot Ashes].   Allahabad, Nīlābh, 1952.
Baṛī baṛī ā̃khē [Two Big Eyes].   Allahabad, Nīlābh, 1952.
Baigan kā paudhā [Eggplant].   Allahabad, Nīlābh, 1952.
Kahānī-lekhikā aur Jhelam ke sāt pul [A Woman Writer and Jhelam's Seven Bridges].   Allahabad, Nīlābh, 1957.
Patthar-alpatthar.   Allahabad, Nīlābh, 1957; as *Sorrow of the Snows*, Calcutta, Writers' Workshop, 1971.
Sattar śreṣṭh kahāniyā [70 of the Best Stories].   Allahabad, Nīlābh, 1958.
Aśk kī sarvaśreṣṭh kahāniyā [The Best Stories from Aśk].   Allahabad, Nīlābh, 1960.
Saṅgharṣ kā satya [The Truth of Struggle].   Allahabad, Nīlābh, 1960.
Palaṅg [The Bed].   Allahabad, Nīlābh, 1961.
Tūfānī lahrō mē hāstā mājhī [A Boatman Laughing Among Shattering Waves] (based on the life of Mark Twain).   Allahabad, Nīlābh, 1966.
Udās phūl kī muskān [The Smile of a Sad Flower] (based on the life of O. Henry).   Allahabad, Nīlābh, 1966.
Robdāb [Arrogance].   Allahabad, Nīlābh, 1966.
Ākāścārī [Dwelling in the Clouds].   Allahabad, Nīlābh, 1966.
Ugte sūraj kā darśak [Watching the Rising Sun] (based on the life of Ernest Hemingway).   Allahabad, Nīlābh, 1967.
Ek rāt kā narak [One Night's Hell].   Allahabad, Nīlābh, 1968.
Ubāl aur anya kahāniyā [Seething and Other Stories]. Allahabad, Nīlābh, 1968.
Merī priy kahāniyā [My Favourite Short Stories].   New Delhi, Rājpāl & Sons, 1970.
Nanhī-sī lau [A Tender Light].   Allahabad, Nīlābh, 1979.
Nimiṣā [A Moment].   Allahabad, Nīlābh, 1980.
Ye rāje ye ṛṣi [These Kings, These Seers].   Allahabad, Nīlābh, 1981.
Cācā Rāmditā [Uncle Ramdita].   Allahabad, Nīlābh, 1981.
Durdarśī log tathā anya kahāniyā [Farsighted People and Other Stories].   Allahabad, Nīlābh, 1982.
Ustād kī jagah khālī hai [The Master's Seat Is Empty].   Allahabad, Nīlābh, 1985.
Terrace par baiṭhī śām [An Evening on the Terrace].   Allahabad, Nayā Ādārah, 1987.

Plays

Jay-parājay [Victory-Defeat]. Lahore, Motīlāl Banarsīdās, 1937.
Lakṣmī ka svāgat [Welcoming Lakṣmī]. 1938.
Adhikār kī rakṣak [The Custodian of Right]. 1938.
Svarg ki jhalak [A Glimpse of Paradise]. Lahore, Motīlāl Banarsīdās, 1939.
Joṅk [Leech]. 1939.
Āpas kā samjhautā [Mutual Compromise]. 1939.
Pahelī [Riddle]. 1939.
Vivāh ke din [Married Days]. 1940.
Devtāō kī chāyā mē [In the Shadow of the Gods]. 1940.
Chatā beṭā [The Sixth Son]. 1940.
Tauliye [Towels]. 1943.
Bhāvar [Whirlpool]. 1943.
Tūfān se pahle [Before the Hurricane]. 1946.
Carvāhe [Shepherds]. Allahabad, Bhārtī Bhaṇḍār, 1948.
Andhī galī ke āṭh ekāṅkī [Eight One-Act Plays for a Blind Alley]. Allahabad, Nīlābh, 1949.
Pratinidhi ekāṅkī [Representative One-Act Plays]. Allahabad, Nīlābh, 1950.
Pardā uthāo, pardā girāo [Raise the Curtain, Lower the Curtain]. Allahabad, Nīlābh, 1950.
Pakkā gānā [Mature Song]. Allahabad, Nīlābh, 1950.
Qaid aur Uṛān [Prison, and Flight]. Allahabad, Nīlābh, 1950.
Ādi mārg [The First Path]. Allahabad, Nīlābh, 1950.
Kasbe ke cricket-club kā udghāṭan [The Cricket Club Is Inaugurated in the Small Town]. Allahabad, Nīlābh, 1950.
Maskebajō ka svarg [The Flatterers' Paradise]. Allahabad, Nīlābh, 1951.
Paintre [Tricks]. Allahabad, Nīlābh, 1952.
Alag-alag rāste [Separate Paths]. Allahabad, Nīlābh, 1953.
Ādarś aur yathārtha [Ideal and Reality]. Allahabad, Nīlābh, 1953.
Añjo dīdī [Añjo the Elder Sister]. Allahabad, Nīlābh, 1954.
Raṅg-ekāṅkī [One-Act Plays]. Allahabad, Nīlābh, 1956.
Sāhab ko zukām hai (includes *Kiskī bāt*; *Fadarza*; *Kusum kā sapnā*; *Ghaplē*; *Sāhab ko zukām hai*) [includes Whose Matter; Fadarza; A Flower's Dream; Mess; Sahab Has a Cold]. Allahabad, Nīlābh, 1959.
Ye naye raṅg-ekāṅkī [New One-Act Plays]. Allahabad, Nīlābh, 1961.
Bebāt kī bāt [Nonsense] (collection of one-act plays). New Delhi, Hind Pocket Books, 1963.
Baṛe khilāṛī [Great Players]. Allahabad, Nīlābh, 1967.
Paccīs śreṣṭh ekāṅkī [25 Choice One-Act Plays]. Allahabad, Nīlābh, 1969.
Lauṭṭā huā din [The Same Day Once Again]. Allahabad, Nīlābh, 1972.
Mere śreṣṭh ekāṅkī [My Best One-Act Plays]. New Delhi, National Publishing House, 1978.
Taulie [Towels]. Allahabad, Nayā Ādārah, 1979.
Mukhṛā badal gayā (includes *Paṛosin kā koṭā*; *Fāltū mohrā*; *Mukhṛā badal gayā*; *Travika kalā*; *Lakṣmaṇ rekhā*) [includes The Neighbour's Share; Useless Pawn; The Face Has Changed; Travika kala; The Crossing Line]. Allahabad, Anāmikā, 1980.
Girdab. Allahabad, Nayā Ādārah, 1981.

Verse

Urmiyā̃ [Waves]. Allahabad, Leader Press, 1941.
Bargad kī beṭī [Daughter of the Bargad Tree]. Allahabad, Nīlābh, 1949.
Dīp jalegā [The Lamp Will Glow]. Allahabad, Nīlābh, 1950.
Cādnī rāt aur ajgar [A Full-Moon Night and a Python]. Allahabad, Nīlābh, 1952.
Sarakō pe ḍhāle sāyē [Dusk Hanging on the Streets]. Allahabad, Nīlābh, 1960.
Khoyā huā prabhā-maṇḍal [The Lost Aura]. Allahabad, Nīlābh, 1965.
Adṛśya nadī [The Invisible River]. Allahabad, Nīlābh, 1977.
Pīlī coñcavālī ciṛiyā ke nām [The Yellow-Beak Bird's Name]. Allahabad, Nīlābh, 1990.
Svarga ek talghar hai [Heaven Is a Basement]. Allahabad, Nīlābh, 1991.

Other

Rekhāē aur citr [Lines and Images]. Allahabad, Nīlābh, 1955.
Maṇṭo merā duśman [My Enemy Maṇṭoo]. Allahabad, Nīlābh, 1956.
Rekhaē aur raṅgsamāj [Lines and Society]. Allahabad, Nīlābh, 1958.
Zyādā apnī, kam parāyī [More About Me, Less About Others]. Allahabad, Nīlābh, 1959.
Hindī kahāniyā̃ aur fashion [Hindi Short Stories and Fashion]. Allahabad, Nīlābh, 1964.
Partō ke ār-pār [Across the Layers]. Allahabad, Nīlābh, 1965.
Śikāyatē aur śikāyatē [Queries and Queries], with Kauśalyā Aśk. Allahabad, Nīlābh, 1966.
Hindī kahānī: ek antaraṅg paricay [The Hindi Short Story: An Intimate Introduction] (articles, letters, comments). Allahabad, Nīlābh, 1967.
Kuch dusrō ke lie [Something for the Others]. Allahabad, Nīlābh, 1968.
Choṭī-sī pahcān [A Little Recognition] (articles, reminiscences). Allahabad, Nīlābh, 1971.
Kahānī ke ird-gird [About the Short Story] (interviews). Allahabad, Nīlābh, 1971.
Āsmān aur bhī hai [There Are Other Skies, Too] (reminiscences). Allahabad, Nīlābh, 1973.
Aṅveṣan kī sah-yātrā [A Common Journey] (literary essays). Allahabad, Nīlābh, 1973.
Filmī duniyā kī jhalkiyā̃ [Glimpse from the Cinema World]. Allahabad, Nīlābh, 1976.
Cehre: anek [Many Faces]. Allahabad, Nīlābh, 1977.
Upendranāth Aśk (selected works). Allahabad, Hindī Sāhitya Sammelan, 1978.
Āmne sāmne [Face to Face] (interviews), with Sudhīndra Rastogī and others. Allahabad, Nīlābh, 1981.
Khone aur pāne ke bīc [Between Losing and Finding]. Allahabad, Nīlābh, 1982.
Ham kahe, āp kaho [Let Us Speak, Let You Speak]. Allahabad, Subodh, 1985.
Bedī, merā hamdam merā dost [Bedi, My Companion, My Friend]. Allahabad, Nīlābh, 1986.
Vivādō ke ghere mē [Inside Polemics] (interviews), with Ravīndra Kāliyā. Allahabad, Nīlābh, 1986.
Aśk 75 (selected works). New Delhi, Rādhākṛṣṇa, 1986–.

Editor, *Urdū kāvya kī ek naī dhārā* [A New Current in Urdu Poetry] (collection of Urdu poems). Allahabad, Hindustānī Akādemī, 1941.
Editor, *Merī duniyā* [My World] (anthology of short stories). Allahabad, Upāsanā Prakāśan, 1957.
Editor, with Mahmūd Ahmad Hunar, *Saṅket* [Sign]. Allahabad, Nīlābh, 1962.

Editor, *Urdū kā behtarin hasya-vyaṅgyu* [The Best of Urdu
    Humour].   Allahabad, Nīlābh, 1962.
Editor, *Urdū ke behtarin ekāṅkī* [The Best of Urdu One-Act
    Plays].   Allahabad, Nīlābh, 1962.
Editor, *Urdū kī behtarin ghazalē* [The Best Urdu Ghazals].
    Allahabad, Nīlābh, 1962.
Editor, *Urdū ke behtarin saṃsmaraṇ* [The Best of Reminis-
    cences in Urdu].   Allahabad, Nīlābh, 1962.
Editor, *Urdu kī behtarin nazmē* [The Best Urdu
    Poems].   Allahabad, Nīlābh, 1962.

Translator, *Hitcintak* [The Matchmaker], by Thornton
    Wilder.   Allahabad, Nīlābh, 1955.
Translator, *Raṅgsāz* (short stories), by Anton Chekhov.
    Allahabad, Nīlābh, 1958.
Translator, *Ye ādmī: ye cūhe* [Of Mice and Men], by John
    Steinbeck.   Allahabad, Nīlābh, 1960.
Translator, *Lambe din kī yātrā* [Long Day's Journey into
    Night], by Eugene O'Neill.   Allahabad, Nīlābh, 1963.
Translator, *Kṣitij ke pār* [Beyond the Horizon], by Eugene
    O'Neill.   Allahabad, Nīlābh, 1964.
Translator, with Bhairavprasad Gupta, *His Excellency*, by
    Fedor Dostoevskii.   Allahabad, Nīlābh, 1978(?).

*   *   *

Upendranāth "Aśk" holds an important place in modern
Hindi literature, especially in fiction. A prolific writer, he
compels attention by the originality and single-mindedness of
his approach in many of his novels, and by his success among
the Hindi reading public. He has been successful also as a
dramatist, and in 1965 was the first Hindi writer to be awarded
the Saṅgīt Nāṭak prize for drama. He has in addition produced
a great number of short stories, several volumes of critical and
other essays, and some collections of poems.

Aśk began his literary career as a writer of Urdu short
stories, but switched to Hindi in the 1930s, as Premcand had
done some 20 years earlier. His work has been influenced by
Premcand's: both the early short stories, such as *Ḍācī* (The
She-Camel) with which he first made his name as a Hindi
writer, and his later novels. These, the main part of Aśk's
work, show appreciable gifts of realistic observation and
description and an introspective insight into character. The
suffering and exploitation of the individual are prominent
themes in Aśk's early writing, as is a vein of sardonic comment
on social abuses and human failings that distinguishes him
among Hindi writers.

Aśk's favourite themes are found in the lower class milieu of
the Panjab towns in which he grew up. He was one of the first
Hindi writers to take up this subject-matter. His major
endeavour has been the production from 1947 onwards of a
series of novels, semi-autobiographical in character, dealing
with life in the towns of the Panjab during the years of his own
early adulthood. Some consider the extensive *Girtī dīvārē*
(Falling Walls) to be his best work, but this judgment fails to do
justice to some of Aśk's later writing and reflects, rather, the
novel's immediate impact on the Hindi reading public of the
1950s. The theme of *Girtī dīvārē* is a young man's personal
struggle with frustrations of family and social life as experienced among less well-educated urban communities. The
members of this section of society struggle with both their own
personal problems and those of the society itself, uneasily
aspiring to rise towards social norms received from above. The
tensions they feel are often sublimated in crude or coarse
behaviour or in inward romantic escapism. Disappointments
and frustrations punctuate their lives, which are led largely out
of touch with the wider world of concerns of the better-

educated: public life and service, education, literature, and
politics. Aśk is overwhelmingly conscious here of adverse
influences and aspects of life. One peculiarity of *Girtī dīvārē*
that throws light on the author's long-term objective in this
series is that Aśk leaves his young hero Cetan largely a victim
of events that have shaped his life hitherto, with the innate
qualities of his character still to be asserted. The following
volume of the Cetan cycle, *Śahar mē ghūmtā ainā* (A Mirror in
the City) largely fulfils expectations awakened but left un-
satisfied in its predecessor. Presentation of Cetan is more
dispassionate and balanced, and his experiences in wandering
for a day through the city of Jalandhar encourage a dimension
of social analysis which had been neglected earlier out of
single-minded concern with the hero. The picture presented of
the life of Jalandhar is kaleidoscopic in variety and detail. Aśk
turns here towards portrayal both of a more mature Cetan, and
of a more balanced and hopeful view of society.

The later novels of the Cetan cycle, *Ek nanhī kiṇḍīl* (A Tiny
Lamp) and *Bandho na nāv is ṭhāv* (Don't Moor the Boat
Here), show a development in the author's approach. Aśk's
attention now moves towards deeper human experiences, and
moral issues posed by life; yet he continues to work in the same
local urban context and with the same fixation on small periods
of time taken from the years of his early life.

Among Aśk's other novels, *Garm rākh* (Hot Ashes) and the
satirical, prize-winning *Baṛī baṛī ākhē* (Two Big Eyes) are
again based on early personal experiences of the author in
Lahore or Amritsar. More significant is the short *Patthar-
alpatthar* (*Sorrow of the Snows*), not connected with the Cetan
cycle but resembling the Cetan novels in its concern with social
pressures and conflicts and in focusing upon a single character.
The plot of this work contrasts the different worlds of an
uneducated Kashmiri groom (horse-keeper) and of two of his
tourist clients and their families from Delhi, representatives
respectively of more traditional and more westernised ways.
Aśk challenges the validity of various assumptions in this
untypical and unpretentious novel, and gives a memorable
portrayal of the thought processes, and the humanity, of an
uneducated man.

Aśk takes full advantage in his plays of his ability to define
social issues and human dilemmas. *Añjo dīdī* (Añjo the Elder
Sister), one of the most effective of a dozen one-act plays,
explores the recreation of attitudes and personality types in
successive generations of a strongly controlling family.

Aśk's work represents a continuation of the realistic approach which was strong in Premcand's work, and an application of that approach to new subject-matter. Not moved by the
same idealistic zeal as Premcand, he has sought in the events
and settings of his own early life a theme capable of universal-
isation. His gifts of introspective analysis and observation have
won him significant success, and his popularity shows that the
problems of Cetan and his world have remained real ones in
north India, despite all that has changed since the 1930s in
society and literature. With a broader sweep of sympathies and
perhaps of subject-matter Aśk would have won even greater
success.

—Stuart McGregor

ASPENSTRÖM, (Karl) Werner. Swedish. Born in Norrbärke,
13 November 1918. Educated at Sigtuna Folk High School,

1936–38; University of Stockholm, B.A. 1945. Married Signe Lund in 1946. Editor, *40-tal* [Forties] literary journal, 1944–47. Honorary doctorate: University of Stockholm, 1976. Member, Swedish Academy, 1981. Address: c/o Bonniers Förlag, Box 3159, 103 63 Stockholm, Sweden.

PUBLICATIONS

Verse

Förberedelse [Preparation].   Stockholm, Bonnier, 1943.
Skriket och tystnaden [The Scream and the Silence].   Stockholm, Bonnier, 1946.
Snölegend [Snow Legend].   Stockholm, Bonnier, 1949.
Litania [Litany].   Stockholm, Bonnier, 1952.
Hundarna [The Dogs].   Stockholm, Bonnier, 1954.
Dikter, 1946–1954 [Poems, 1946–1954].   Stockholm, Bonnier, 1955.
Dikter under träden [Poems Under the Trees].   Stockholm, Bonnier, 1956.
Om dagen om natten [By Day by Night].   Stockholm, Bonnier, 1961.
66 dikter [66 Poems].   Stockholm, Bonnier, 1964.
Trappan [The Stairs].   Stockholm, Bonnier, 1964.
Dikter [Poems].   Stockholm, Bonnier, 1966.
Inre [Within].   Stockholm, Bonnier, 1969.
Skäl [Reasons] (includes essays).   Stockholm, Bonnier, 1970.
Under tiden [Meanwhile].   Stockholm, Bonnier, 1972.
Jordvagga — himmelstak [Earth Cradle — Sky Ceiling].   Stockholm, FIB:s Lyrikklubb, 1973.
Ordbok [Dictionary].   Stockholm, Bonnier, 1976.
Selected Poems, translated by Robin Fulton.   London, Oasis, 1976.
Dikter [Poems].   Stockholm, Bonnier, 1978.
Tidigt en morgon sent på jorden: dikter, 1976–1980 [Early One Morning Late on Earth: Poems 1976–1980].   Stockholm, Bonnier, 1980.
You and I and the World, translated by Siv Cedering.   Merrick, New York, Cross Cultural Communications, 1980.
Sorl [Murmur].   Stockholm, Bonnier, 1983.
Poems 1946–1983 (bilingual edition), translated by David L. Emblen.   Santa Rosa, California, Clamshell Press, 1987.
Varelser [Beings].   Stockholm, Bonnier, 1988.

Plays

Platsen är inhöljd i rök [The Place Is Enveloped in Smoke] (radio play).   Stockholm, Bonnier, 1948.
En clown måste ha gått vilse [A Clown Must Have Lost His Way].   Stockholm, Bonnier, 1949.
Tre kortpjäser (includes *Snaran*; *Arken*; *Poeten och kejsaren*).   Stockholm, Bonnier, 1955.
Poeten och kejsaren (radio play).   Stockholm, Sveriges Radio, 1956; as *The Poet and the Emperor*, Sveriges Radio, 1957.
Snaran [The Snare] (television play).   Stockholm, Eklund, 1959.
Arken [The Ark] (television play).   Stockholm, Eklund, 1959.
Teater I (includes *De lyckliga bröderna*; *Auktionen*; *Stjärnan*; *Det eviga*; *Trädet*; *Skuggorna*; *Trollet*) [Theatre I: The Happy Brother; The Auction; Stjärnan; Det eviga; The Tree; The Shadows; The Troll].   Stockholm, Bonnier, 1959.

Teater II (includes *Hemma över julen*; *Ett ovanligt fall*; *Trappan*; *Vågspel*; *Källan*; *Flugsmällan*; *Snaskpartyt*) [Theatre II: At Home During Christmas; An Unusual Case; The Staircase; Venture; The Cellar; The Fly-Swat; The Candy Party].   Stockholm, Bonnier, 1963.
Mattan [The Carpet] (produced 1964).   Stockholm, Bonnier, 1963.
Skådespelarens död [The Death of the Actor] (radio play).   Stockholm, Bonnier, 1964.
Spindlarna samt en kortpjäs [The Spiders and a Short Play] (produced 1966).   Included in *Teater III*, 1966.
Teater III (includes *Huset*; *Spindlarna samt en kortpjäs*; *Dårarnas natt*) [Theatre III: The House; The Spiders and a Short Play; The Fools' Night].   Stockholm, Bonnier, 1966.
Med egna ögon [With One's Own Eyes] (television play).   Stockholm, Bonnier, 1967.
Jag måste till Berlin [I Must Go to Berlin] (produced 1968).   Stockholm, Bonnier, 1967.
Stackars Job [Poor Job] (produced 1969).   Stockholm, Bonnier, 1971.
Näsan [The Nose] (television play).   Stockholm, Bonnier, 1971.
Stå upp och gå till Nya Nineve [Stand Up and Go to New Nineveh] (radio play).   Stockholm, Bonnier, 1972.
Inte så ung längre [Not So Young Anymore] (television play).   Stockholm, Bonnier, 1972.
Väntarna [Those Who Wait] (produced Stockholm, 1976)   Included in *Teater IV*, 1978.
Teater IV (includes *Väntarna*; *Faster och forskaren*) [Theatre IV: Those Who Wait; Aunt and the Researcher].   Stockholm, Bonnier, 1978.
Teater V (includes *Höga berg och låga kullar*; *Snömannen*; *Moder åt oss alla*; *Hos frisören*) [Theatre V: High Mountains and Low Hills; The Snowman; Mother to Us All; At the Hairdressers].   Stockholm, Bonnier, 1985.

Radio Plays: *Den stora resan* [The Great Journey], 1945; *Branden* [The Fire], 1947; *Platsen är inhöljd i rök* [The Place is Enveloped in Smoke], 1948; *Hyresgästen* [The Lodger], 1951; *Poeten och kejsaren* (*The Poet and the Emperor*), 1956; *Han som inte for till månen* [The One Who Didn't Go to the Moon], 1962; *Skådespelarens död* [The Death of the Actor], 1964; *Stå upp och gå till Nya Nineve* [Stand Up and Go to New Nineveh], 1972; *Vågspel* [Venture], 1982.

Television Plays: *Snaran* [The Snare], 1955; *Arken* [The Ark], 1957; *Med egna ögon* [With One's Own Eyes], 1967; *Näsan* [The Nose], 1971; *Inte så ung längre* [Not So Young Anymore], 1972.

Fiction

Oändligt är vårt äventyr [Endless Is Our Adventure].   Stockholm, Bonnier, 1945.
Förebud [Omen].   Stockholm, Bonnier, 1953.
Blåvalen: halvsagor och andra prosastycken.   Stockholm, Bonnier, 1975; as *The Blue Whale and Other Prose Pieces*, London, Oasis, 1981.

Other

Bäcken [The Brook].   Stockholm, Bonnier, 1958.
Motsägelser [Contradictions].   Stockholm, Bonnier, 1961; revised edition, Stockholm, Bokförlaget Aldus/Bonnier, 1968.
Gula tassen [The Yellow Paw] (for children).   Stockholm, Rabén & Sjögren, 1965.

Sommar: om naturen, människan och tidens gång [Summer: Of Nature, People, and the Passage of Time]. Stockholm, Bonnier, 1968.

Vissa sidor och ovissa: artiklar och essäer [Certain Pages and Uncertain Ones: Articles and Essays]. Stockholm, Bonnier, 1979.

Ögonvittnen [Eye-Witnesses]. Stockholm, Bonnier, 1980.

Sten Lindroth: inträdestal i Svenska Akademien [Sten Lindroth: Introductory Speech at the Swedish Academy]. Stockholm, Norstedt, 1981.

Det röda molnet: drömmar och drömlikt ur "De svarta böckerna" [The Red Cloud]. Stockholm, Bonnier, 1986.

Bertil Malmberg. Stockholm, Norstedt, 1987.

Fragmentarium [Fragmentation]. Stockholm, Bonnier, 1987.

Sidoljus: ett prosaurval [Sidelights: A Selection of Prose]. Stockholm, Bonnier, 1989.

Editor, with K. G. Vennberg, *Kritiskt 40-tal*. Stockholm, Bonnier, 1948.

Editor, *Verner von Heidenstams dikter* [The Selected Poems of Verner von Heidenstam]. Stockholm, Bonnier, 1959.

Translator, with G. Lundström, *Ett moln i byxor* [A Cloud in Trousers], by Vladimir Maiakovskii. Stockholm, FIB:s Lyrikklubb, 1958.

Translator, *Sex ungerska poeter: modern ungersk lyrik i urval av Géza Thinsz* [Six Hungarian Poets]. Stockholm, Bonnier, 1968.

Translator, *Oas i öknen* [Oasis in the Desert], by Joseph Brodskii. Stockholm, FIB:s Lyrikklubb/Tiden, 1977.

*

Critical Studies: "Poet in the Space Age: A Theme in Aspenström's Plays" by Egil Törnqvist, in *Scandinavian Studies* (Madison, Wisconsin), 39(1), 1967; "Werner Aspenström: A Writer for All Seasons" by Leif Sjöberg, in *American-Scandinavian Review*, 57, 1969; "Werner Aspenström: Making a Pillow from the Darkness" by Brita Green, in *Swedish Book Review* (Lampeter, Wales), 2, 1983.

* * *

Werner Aspenström is one of the leading poets in Sweden today. He has also published short stories and essays and a book for children, and is an effective dramatist with some 40 plays to his name, most of which have been written for and performed on radio or television.

Aspenström first made his name during World War II. He was one of the editors of the influential journal *40-tal* (Forties), in which the younger poets made their voices heard. They dissociated themselves from conventional beliefs and viewpoints, and depicted the chaotic and splintered world around them through a sometimes impenetrable symbolic language and surrealistic imagery, as in the lines "Blown to pieces in the fibres of the tree/I live" from his second book of poems, *Skriket och tystnaden* (The Scream and the Silence).

Alongside a cryptic symbolic form, Aspenström developed a more direct style:

> Old rib-backed sofas and cathedrals,
> bagpipes and zeppelins,
> windmills without vanes,
> men with bearskin caps,
> women with peacock hats,
> children thinner than wire.

How could the skipper possibly remember
all the legends about sunken islands?
Europe?
What year did it happen?
Was it summer or winter?

This is a style he employs to great effect in his nature vignettes. Although Aspenström himself has claimed that the following often-anthologised poem is a straightforward nature study about "an altogether unsymbolic" inch-worm — in Swedish named "measurer" — it has often been interpreted as a self-portrait:

> I stretch out from my cherry leaf
> and peer towards eternity:
> eternity is much too vast today,
> much too blue and thousand-leagued.
> I think I'll stay here on my cherry-leaf
> and measure my green cherry-leaf.

Miniature with a universal perspective is a description that could also be applied to Aspenström's plays, which are often short and superficially simple, with a burlesque satirical or folkloristic tone. In *Höga berg och låga kullar* (High Mountains and Low Hills), a married couple is seen climbing in the Himalayas, the man driven by idealistic ambition and the wife, more reluctantly, by loyalty to her husband. Halfway up, they have an argument about toothpaste tubes. "He snatches the tube from her and demonstrates how it should *properly* be squeezed, from the end. And this happens, not only in full view of the sherpa, but in full view of eternity, represented by the high mountains."

Aspenström holds up a mirror to our times, our weaknesses and prejudices.

> THE REDEEMER LIVETH
> In the vacant space after the Father
> there's a parked Mercedes.
> The space after the Mother in the kitchen
> is filled by a refrigerator.
> Swivelling armchairs replace
> Brothers and Sisters.
> The fitted carpet:
> Grass.
> The reading lamp gives truer light than the Sun.
> The radio out-voices the Voices.
> The TV shows pictures from the World.
>
> Free at last.
> Your navel is a wound that's been healed.

He gently satirises our faith in the sciences and our arrogant rationalism and materialism, and reminds us that there is another aspect to life.

> IS THAT BURNING I CAN SMELL?
> No doubt the flesh-eater's bright lad
> grilling midges at a candle-flame
> and dreaming grander dreams.
>
> Like the Pyramids!
> The Chinese Wall!
> The Pentagon!
>
> And not a green leaf on earth.

In *Snölegend* (Snow Legend), Aspenström proclaims "I speak on nobody's behalf/I belong to no vanguard/I belong to no rearguard/I simply make it known/that something has been lost." This does not mean that he is apolitical, however; rather, he distrusts big words and ostensive gesturing. He has taken an active part in the political debate. In 1951 he and others published *Tredje ståndpunkten* (The Third Viewpoint), claiming the right not to take sides in the international power struggle between East and West.

Seeing both sides of an argument extends beyond politics for Aspenström; in fact it is a fundamental feature of all his writing.

> AS FAR AS I'VE GOT
> There he is again,
> bird of the border country,
> half in light,
> half in shadow,
> and I hear a double note
> of a riven bird:
> black wing,
> white wing,
> flying for a moment
> side by side.
> And whoever searches for a meaning
> finds two.
> Which is as far as I've got,
> though the spring has gone
> and summer passed.

Doubts and scepticism recur in his writing. *Motsägelser* (Contradictions) is the title of one of his books of essays, and contradictions occur in several of the titles of his collections of poetry. It is the feature Nina Burton emphasises in her thesis *Mellan eld och skugga, studier i den lyriska motsägelsen hos Werner Aspenström* (Between Fire and Shadow, Studies in Lyrical Contradiction in Werner Aspenström, 1984) in which she contrasts idealism with despair, mysticism with rationalism, the universal with the familiar, and catastrophe with idyll.

Aspenström's scepticism also embraces religion. He has compared himself to trolls in fairytales, standing on a rock at the edge of the forest, fascinated by the sound of the churchbells, curious but uncomprehending. However, he is no stranger to the irrational and mystical dimensions of our existence. He has described religion and poetry as two different ways of gaining insight into the world. And he assures us that he knows more than the astronauts:

> . . . on the other side, the turned-away side,
> the giant blue toad still sat
> with a crown on his head
> and *dreamed* us and *thought* the world

Folklore and fantasy, or whimsical reality, also figure in Aspenström's prose, both in his autobiographical childhood sketches (e.g., *Bäcken* [The Brook]) and the books of essays and prose passages, which cover such areas as philosophy, religion, language, visual arts, and dreams, and often take the form of diarylike musing.

Aspenström is an accessible, humorous, and serious writer. His achievement can be summed up in Ingemar Algulin's words (*A History of Swedish Literature*, 1989): "In a thought-provoking and often amusing way, Aspenström succeeds in playing out the chaotic absurdity of modern existence against experiences of timelessness and mysticism. His world is that of chance and paradox, and it is filled with genuine poetic revelations and ever fresh impressions of nature."

—Brita Green

AYALA, Francisco. Spanish. Born in Granada, 16 March 1906. Educated at the University of Madrid, law degree 1929, doctorate 1931. Married Etelvina Silva in 1931; one daughter. Professor of law, University of Madrid, 1932–35; diplomat for Spanish Republic, 1937; exiled in Argentina, 1939–50, Puerto Rico, 1950–58, New York, 1958–66, and Chicago, 1966–73; Professor at Rutgers University, New Brunswick, New Jersey, Bryn Mawr College, Pennsylvania, University of Chicago, and New York University. U.S. representative to Unesco. Recipient: National Critics' prize, 1972; National Literature prize, 1983; National Prize of Spanish Letters, 1988; Cervantes prize, 1991. Elected to the Spanish Royal Academy, 1983. Address: c/o Alianza Editorial, Apdo 9107, 28043 Madrid, Spain.

PUBLICATIONS

Fiction

Tragicomedia de un hombre sin espíritu. Madrid, Industrial Grafica, 1925.
Historia de un amanecer. Madrid, Castilla, 1926.
El boxeador y un ángel. Madrid, Cuadernos Literarios de la Lectura, 1929.
Cazador en el alba. Madrid, Ulises, 1930.
El hechizado. Buenos Aires, Emecé, 1944.
La cabeza del cordero. Buenos Aires, Losada, 1949; as *The Lamb's Head*, Austin, University of Texas, 1971.
Los usurpadores. Buenos Aires, Sudamericana, 1949; as *Usurpers*, New York, Schocken, 1987.
Historia de macacos. Madrid, Revista de Occidente, 1955.
Muertes de perro. Buenos Aires, Sudamericana, 1958; as *Death as a Way of Life*, New York, Macmillan, 1964; London, Michael Joseph, 1965.
El fondo del vaso. Buenos Aires, Sudamericana, 1962.
El As de Bastos. Buenos Aires, Sur, 1963.
El rapto. Madrid, La Novela Popular, 1965.
Mis paginas mejores. Madrid, Gredos, 1965.
De raptos, violaciones y otras inconveniencias. Madrid, Alfaguara, 1966.
Cuentos. Salamanca, Anaya, 1966; as *El inquisidor y otras narraciones españolas*, Anaya, 1970.
Obras narrativas completas, edited by Andrés Amorós. Mexico City, Aguilar, 1969.
El jardín de las delicias. Barcelona, Seix Barral, 1971.
El rapto; Fragancia de jazmines; Diálogo entre el amor y un viejo, edited by Estelle Irizarry. Barcelona, Labor, 1974.
El jardín de las delicias; El tiempo y yo. Madrid, Espasa-Calpe, 1978.
El jardín de las malicias. Madrid, Montena, 1988.

Other

Indagación del cinema. Madrid, Mundo Latino, 1929.
El derecho social en la constitución de la República española. Madrid, Minuesa de los Riós, 1932.

El pensamiento vivo de Saavedra Fajardo. Buenos Aires, Losada, 1941.

El problema del liberalismo. Mexico City, Fondo de Cultura Económica, 1941.

Historia de la libertad. Buenos Aires, Atlántida, 1942.

Oppenheimer. Mexico City, Fondo de Cultura Económica, 1942.

Razón del mundo (La preocupación de España). Buenos Aires, Losada, 1944.

Histrionismo y representación. Buenos Aires, Sudamericana, 1944.

Los políticos. Buenos Aires, Depalma, 1944.

Una doble experiencia política: España e Italia. Mexico City, El Colegio de Mexico, 1944.

Jovellanos. Buenos Aires, Centro Asturiano, 1945.

Ensayo sobre la libertad. Mexico City, Fondo de Cultura Económica, 1945.

Tratado de sociología. Buenos Aires, Losada, 1947.

La invención del "Quijote". Río Piedras, Puerto Rico, Editorial Universitaria, 1950.

Ensayos de sociología política. Mexico City, Universidad Nacional, 1952.

Introducción a las ciencias sociales. Madrid, Aguilar, 1952.

Derechos de la persona individual para una sociedad de masas. Buenos Aires, Perrot, 1953.

El escritor en la sociedad de masas; Breve teoría de la traducción. Mexico City, Obregón, 1956; as *Problemas de la traducción*, Madrid, Taurus, 1965.

La integración social en América. Buenos Aires, Perrot, 1958.

La crisis actual de la enseñanza. Buenos Aires, Nova, 1958.

Tecnología y libertad. Madrid, Taurus, 1959.

Experiencia e invención. Madrid, Taurus, 1960.

Realidad y ensueño. Madrid, Gredos, 1963.

La evasión de los intelectuales, with H. A. Murena. Mexico City, Centro de Estudios y Documentación Sociales, 1963.

De este mundo y el otro. Barcelona, Edhasa, 1963.

España, a la fecha. Buenos Aires, Sur, 1965; enlarged edition, Madrid, Tecnos, 1977.

El cine: arte y espectáculo. Xalapa, Mexico, Universidad Veracruzana, 1966.

España y la cultura germánica; España a la fecha. Mexico City, Finisterre, 1968.

Reflexiones sobre la estructura narrativa. Madrid, Taurus, 1970.

El "Lazarillo": Nuevo examen de algunos aspectos. Madrid, Taurus, 1971.

Confrontaciones. Barcelona, Seix Barral, 1972.

Hoy ya es ayer (includes *Libertad y liberalismo*; *Razón del mundo*; *La crisis de la enseñanza*). Madrid, Moneday Crédito, 1972.

Los ensayos: teoría y crítica literaria. Madrid, Aguilar, 1972.

La novela: Galdós y Unamuno. Barcelona, Seix Barral, 1974.

Cervantes y Quevesdo. Barcelona, Seix Barral, 1974.

El escritor y su imagen: Ortega y Gasset, Azorín, Valle-Inclán, Machado. Madrid, Guadarrama, 1975.

El escritor y el cine. Madrid, Centro, 1975.

Galdós en su tiempo. Santander, Universidad Internacional Menéndez Pelayo, 1978.

España 1975–1980: conflictos y logros de la democracia. Madrid, Libertarias, 1982.

De triunfos y penas. Barcelona, Seix Barral, 1982.

Conversaciones con Francisco Ayala. Madrid, Espasa-Calpe, 1982.

Recuerdos y olvidos: I: Del paraíso al destierro; II: El exilio (memoirs). Madrid, Alianza, 2 vols., 1982.

Palabras y letras. Barcelona, Edhasa, 1983.

La estructura narrativa, y otras experiencias literarias.- Barcelona, Crítica, 1984.

La retórica del periodismo y otras retóricas. Madrid, Espasa-Calpe, 1985.

La imagen de España: continuidad y cambio en la sociedad española. Madrid, Alianza, 1986.

Mi cuarto a espadas. Madrid, El País/Aguilar, 1988.

Las plumas del fénix: estudios de literatura española. Madrid, Alianza, 1989.

El escritor en su siglo. Madrid, Alianza, 1990.

Editor, *Diccionario Atlántico.* Buenos Aires, Sudamericana, 1977.

*

Bibliographies: *Bibliografía de Francisco Ayala* by Andrés Amorós, New York, Syracuse University, 1973; *Bibliografía de Francisco Ayala* by José Alvarez Calleja, Madrid, Serie Bibliografias, 1983.

Critical Studies: *Francisco Ayala*, Boston, Twayne, 1977, and "The Ubiquitous Trickster Archetype in the Narrative of Francisco Ayala," in *Hispania* (Los Angeles), 70(2), 1987, both by Estelle Irizarry; *Narrative Perspective in the Post-Civil War Novels of Francisco Ayala: "Muertes de perro" and "El fondo del vaso"* by Maryellen Bieder, Chapel Hill, University of North Carolina, 1979; "Historicity and Historiography in F. Ayala's *Los usurpadores*" by Nelson Orringer, in *Letras Peninsulares*, 3(1), 1990.

*   *   *

A professor of law, diplomat, political scientist, and sociologist before being forced into exile by the Spanish Civil War, Francisco Ayala achieved early literary success with his first novel, written when he was only 18. Subsequently he established a reputation as an essayist, professional Hispanist, and literary critic, as well as renewing his career as novelist and diplomat with even greater distinction. For Ayala, the category "novel" includes long and short fiction alike; he rejects arbitrary distinctions of genre, including categorization of his briefer works as novelettes, tales, or short stories. His wide-ranging essays observe no clear demarcation between socio-political phenomena and literary theory; nearly all provide important insights into his creative process. A wide and voracious reader, Ayala is equally familiar with Spanish literary classics and contemporary European philosophy, with current politics and culture in Latin America and the United States; both well-read and a cosmopolitan with vast international experience, he is an intellectual citizen of the world.

Important philosophical ingredients in Ayala's writing include the perspectivism of José Ortega y Gasset and the major tenets of existentialism. Major literary models (as often parodied as imitated) are Miguel de Cervantes, Francisco Quevedo, Benito Pérez Galdós, and Miguel de Unamuno. Ayala's pre-Civil War fiction was written largely under the aegis of European Modernism and reflects then prevailing experimentalism, vanguardist innovations, and abstractions; fiction produced in exile following a 14-year hiatus is radically different: deceptively mimetic, deeply ironic, skeptical, and humorous. Ayala's first novel *Tragicomedia de un hombre sin espíritu* (Tragicomedy of a Man Without Spirit) inaugurated the framework of literary allusions and metaliterary devices which reappear in much of Ayala's mature fiction, and characteristic social and political considerations are enunciated early in *Historia de un amanecer* (The Story of a Dawn), although they do not completely prevail until the postwar works. The five pieces of vanguard fiction published in *El boxeador y un ángel* (The Boxer and an Angel) (virtuoso exercises of diverse metaphorical brilliance) reflect contemporary technological progress and social mechanization, with dehumanization of man and humanization of objects accompanied by traces of surrealism, coincidences with futurism's emphasis on machinery, velocity, and the radically new underscored by cinematic changes of scene, headlong pace, and the juxtaposition of disconcertingly disparate objects. These early works evince Ayala's exceptional stylistic skill, foreshadowing his postwar recognition as one of the Spanish language's foremost living prose writers. Nevertheless, his reputation today rests not on the prewar experimentation (frequently fantastic or allegorical and abstract, sometimes hermetic) and portrayals of imaginary worlds, but on comparably unpretentious, straightforward, seemingly matter-of-fact "historical" narratives with tremendous subversive charge, written largely in exile.

In Ayala's mature work, stylistic considerations are no longer paramount but subject to thematic and philosophical ends. Ayala masters the difficult art of simplicity and clarity counseled by his master, Ortega, offering both enormous narrative economy and seeming transparency, yet these works are far from simple or transparent. The 17th-century world recreated in the masterful, demythologizing novelette, *El hechizado* (The Bewitched), and the frequent medieval and Renaissance settings employed in the 10 "exemplary tales" of *Los usurpadores* (Usurpers) contain no identifiable distortions of accepted historical accounts; they appear almost bereft of literary artifice, yet they are enormously subversive in their implications (via astute psychological perceptions), undermining the Franco regime's idealization of Spain's past days of glory and of empire. Abrupt transitions, brilliant imagery, and experimentalism are replaced by rare moral and philosophical intensity. The unifying theme of usurpation of power underlies these seemingly innocuous recreations of familiar figures from Spain's past, illustrating how power corrupts those who hold it, while the apocryphal prologue (a Cervantine device often utilized by Ayala) indicates that all control exercised by one man over another involves such usurpation. The four novelettes of *La cabeza del cordero* (*The Lamb's Head*), united by the common background of the Spanish Civil War, illustrate various means whereby human shortcomings (cowardice, selfishness, errors in judgment, egotism, and weakness) may play a more important role in historical events than acknowledged by historiographers. *Historia de macacos* (Story of Victims) contains six stories whose common theme is the all-too-human tendency to abuse, ridicule, humiliate, and debase others, while ethical concerns with outrages both moral and physical (deception, robbery, kidnapping, rape) perpetrated against one's neighbors unify the sardonic tales of *El As de Bastos* (Bastos's Ace).

Ayala's two interconnected novels, *Muertes de perro* (*Death as a Way of Life*) and *El fondo del vaso* (The Bottom of the Glass) portray tyranny, demagoguery, and existential alienation in an imaginary Latin American dictatorship (replaced in the sequel by the worst kind of "popular democracy"). Ayala's erstwhile experience as a journalist in exile and his socio-philosophical concerns with the mission and influence of the mass media are highly visible; the writer's enduring preoccupation with the abuse of power reappears not only at the level of government but in abuses of the power of the press and in outrages by juvenile gangs. Aesthetic, critical, and pedagogical concerns embodied in such essays as *El escritor en la sociedad de masas* (The Writer in the Society of the Masses), *La crisis actual de la enseñanza* (The Current Crisis in Teaching), and *Tecnología y libertad* (Technology and Freedom) underlie the two novels and evoke specific current events inspiring incidents in these Ayala masterpieces. Satiric and even sarcastic, yet deceptively simple with their occasional recreation of journalistic style and mentality, Ayala's novels explore difficult questions of the rights of the individual in a society of masses, examine complex issues of politics and sociology, and illuminate the many ways whereby contemporary man falls short of existential authenticity.

—Janet Pérez

B

BA JIN. Pseudonym for Li Feikan and Li Yaotang. Chinese. Born in Chengdu, Sichuan, 25 November 1904 (some sources say 1905). Educated at Foreign Language School, Chengdu; Southeastern University, Nanjing, graduated 1925; graduate study in France, 1927–28. Married Chen Yunchen (some sources say Xiao Shan) in 1944 (died 1972); one daughter and one son. Editor, *Ban Yue*, 1928; editor-in-chief, Wenhua shenghuo [Cultural Life Publishing House], Shanghai, 1935–38, 1946; member of editorial board, *Feng-huo* [Beacon], 1937–38, *Na han* [Outcry], from 1937, *Jing chun* [Warning the People], and *Pingmin zhisheng* [Voice of the Proletariat]; chief editor, People's Literature Publishing House, Beijing, 1957–58, and Shanghai Literature, 1961; in disgrace, 1967–77; vice chair, 5th Municipal Congress, 1977–83, member of Presidium, 6th National Congress, 1983–88, and vice chair, 7th National Congress, since 1988, all Chinese Communist Party. Founder, Chinese Writers Anti-Aggression Association, 1938; committee member, China Association of Literary Workers, 1949, and Cultural and Educational Commission, 1949–54; vice chair, All-China Federation of Literary and Art Circles, 1953; vice chair, from 1953, and chair, 1958–68, China People's Union of Chinese Writers, Shanghai; deputy chief, Afro-Asian Writers' Congress, 1958; vice president, Sino-Soviet Friendship Association, 1959–68; member of executive council, China Welfare Institute, since 1978; vice chair, China Federation of Literary and Art Circles, since 1978; president, China PEN, 1980–91, and National Literary Foundation, 1986–89. Recipient: Medal of International Friendship (U.S.S.R.), 1990. Honorary member, American Academy of Arts and Sciences, 1985. Address: c/o China PEN, Shatan Beije 2, Beijing, China.

PUBLICATIONS

Fiction

Mie wang [Destruction]. 1929.
Sichu de taiyang [The Setting Sun]. 1930.
Aiqing de san bu chu [Love: A Trilogy]. N.p., Kaiming, 1939.
    Wu [Fog]. 1931.
    Yu [Rain]. 1932.
    Dian [Thunder]. 1933.
Fuzhou [First Love]. 1931.
Guangming [Glory]. 1931.
Jiliu [Turbulent Stream] trilogy.
    Jia. 1931; as *The Family*, Beijing, Foreign Languages Press, 1958, as *Family*, Garden City, New York, Anchor, 1972.
    Chun [Spring]. 1938.
    Qiu [Autumn]. 1940.
Hai de meng [Dream on the Sea]. N.p., Kaiming, 1932.
Chuntian li de qiutian [Autumn Day Comes in the Spring]. 1932.
Sha ding [Sand Hogs]. 1932.
Dian yi [Electric Chair]. 1932.

Mobu [A Duster]. 1932.
Yue ye [A Moonlight Night]. 1933.
Xin sheng [New Life]. 1933.
Jiangjun [The General]. 1933.
Mengya [Germs]. N.p., Xiandai, 1933; as *Xue* [Snow], Shanghai, Cultural Life Publishing House, 1946.
Chenmo [Deep Silence]. 2 vols., 1934.
Lina [Lena]. 1934.
Shen, gui, ren [Gods, Spirits, Men]. Shanghai, Cultural Life Publishing House, 1935.
Chen luo [Sinking Down]. 1935.
Fa de gushi [Story of Hair]. 1936.
Lun luo [Fall from Grace]. 1936.
Chuang xia [Underneath the Window]. 1936.
Chang sheng ta [Pagoda of Long Life]. 1937.
Hei tu [Black Earth]. 1939.
Ba Jin duanpian xiaoshuo xuanji [Collection of Ba Jin's Short Stories]. N.p., Kaiming, 1940.
Short Stories by Ba Jin, edited by Wen Yi. Shanghai, Chongying Publishing House, 1941.
Long, hu, gou [Dragon, Tiger, Dog]. 1941.
Huo [Fire]. N.p., Kaiming, 3 vols., 1941–45.
Feiyuan wai [Behind a Desolate Garden]. N.p., Nanfang, 1942.
Qi yuan [Garden of Rest]. 1944.
Huanhun cao [The Grass of Resurrection]. Shanghai, Cultural Life Publishing House, 1945.
Yaliannuo. 1945.
Di-si bingshi [Ward Number Four]. 1946.
Xiao ren xiao shi [Little Men, Little Things]. Shanghai, Cultural Life Publishing House, 1947.
Han ye. 1947; as *Cold Nights*, Hong Kong, Chinese University Press, and Seattle, University of Washington Press, 1978.
Bai niao zhi ge [The Song of the White Bird]. 1947.
Qingye de bei ju [Tragedy in a Quiet Night]. Shanghai, Cultural Life Publishing House, 1948.
Ba Jin xuanji [Collection of Ba Jin's Works]. N.p., Kaiming, 1951.
Piao bo [Drifting]. 195-(?).
Women huishen liao Peng Dehuai si ling yuan [Our Meeting with Commander Peng Denhuai]. N.p., Literature Publishing House, 1953.
Fu yu zi [Turgenev]. 1953.
Ba Jin duanpian xiaoshuo xuan [Selected Short Stories by Ba Jin]. 1955.
Baowei heping de renmen [People Guarding Peace]. Zhongqing, Zhongqing Publishing House, 1955.
Mingzhu he Yuji [Mingzhu and Yuji]. N.p., China People's Publishing House, 1957.
Luoche shang [On the Mule Cart]. N.p., Xinyue, 1959.
Li Dahai. Beijing, Writers' Publishing House, 1961.
Short Stories (bilingual edition). Hong Kong, Hui Tong Bookstore, 1978(?).
Autumn in Spring and Other Stories. Beijing, Chinese Literature/Panda, 1981.
Sanwen suibi xuan [Selected Prose and Essays]. Chengdu, Sichuan People's Publishing House, 1982.

Duanpian xiaoshuo xuan [Selected Short Stories].   Chengdu, Sichuan People's Publishing House, 1982.
Bing zhong ji [In Sickness].   Beijing, People's Literature Publishing House, 1984.

Other

Zhiqiaogeko de canju [The Chicago Tragedy] (as Li Feikan).   N.p., Pingshe, 1926.
Wuzhengfuzhuyi yu shiji wenti [Anarchism and Reality: A Problem] (as Li Feikan), with Wu and Hui-lin.   N.p., Minzhong, 1927.
Duantoutai shang [On the Scaffold] (as Li Feikan).   N.p., Ziyou, 1929.
Cong zibenzhuyi dao annaqizhuyi [From Capitalism to Anarchism] (as Li Feikan).   N.p., Pingshe, 1930.
Hai xing zaji [Sea Voyage Notebook].   1932.
Lutu suibi [Random Notes of a Voyage].   1934.
Ba Jin zizhuan [Ba Jin's Autobiography].   1934; enlarged edition, as *I* [Memoirs], Shanghai, Cultural Life Publishing House, 1936.
Diandi [Fragments].   1935.
Menjianir [The Threshold] (collected translations).   Shanghai, Cultural Life Publishing House, 1935.
Ba Jin xuanji [Ba Jin's Selected Works].   N.p., Central Bookstore, 1936.
Sheng zhi chanhui [Confessions of a Life].   Shanghai, Commercial Press, 1936.
Eguo xuwuzhuyi yundong shihua [History of the Russian Nihilist Movement].   Shanghai, Cultural Life Publishing House, 1936.
Ziyou xue: wuyi xundaozhe de wu shu zhounian [Blood of Freedom: On the 50th Anniversary of the Martyrdom of Five Comrades] (as Li Feikan).   N.p., Ziyou, 1937.
Zhanzheng yu jingji.   1937.
Duan jian [Short Conversations].   2 vols., 1937.
Meng yu zui [Dreams and Inebriation].   N.p., Kaiming, 1938.
Xibanya de shuguang [Dawn in Spain].   N.p., Pingming Publishing House, 1939.
Lutu tongxun [Letters from the Road].   Shanghai, Cultural Life Publishing House, 2 vols., 1940.
Wu ti [Unnamed].   1941.
Kong su [Denunciation].   Shanghai, Cultural Life Publishing House, 1941.
Lutu zaji [Travel Notebook].   N.p., Wen ye ban, 1946.
Huainian [Reminiscences].   N.p., Kaiming, 1947.
Huashacheng de jieji [Warsaw Diary].   Beijing, People's Literature Publishing House, 1951.
Ba Jin xuanji [Ba Jin's Selected Works].   N.p., Kaiming, 1951.
Ba Jin daibiao zuoxuan [Selection of Representative Works of Ba Jin].   N.p., Chuan chui, 1951.
Shenghuo de hui L (autobiography).   1953.
Yingxiong de gushi.   N.p., Pingming Publishing House, 1953; as *Living Amongst Heroes*, Beijing, Foreign Languages Press, 1954.
Tan Jiehefu [Chekhov].   N.p., Pingming Publishing House, 1955.
Ba Jin sanwen xuan [Ba Jin's Selected Essays].   Beijing, Xinhua, 1955.
Da huanle de rizi [Days of Great Joy].   Beijing, Writers' Publishing House, 1957.
Ba Jin wenji [Ba Jin's Collected Works].   Beijing, People's Literature Publishing House, 14 vols., 1958–62; revised edition of vol. 14, Nanguo, Nanguo Publishing House, 1970.
Xin sheng ji [New Voices Collection].   Beijing, People's Literature Publishing House, 1959.

Youyi ji [Friendship Collection].   Beijing, Writers' Publishing House, 1959.
Zan ge ji [Songs of Praise].   Cambridge, Massachusetts, Harvard University Chinese-Japanese Library, 1960.
Qingtu bu jin de ganqing [Inexhaustible Friendship].   Tianjin, Baihua Literature and Arts Publishing House, 1963.
Xianliang qiao pan [At the Xianliang Bridge].   Beijing, Writers' Publishing House, 1964.
Sui xiang lu.   Hong Kong, Shenghuo, dushu xinzhi san lian shudian, 1979; as *Random Thoughts*, Hong Kong, Joint Publishing, 1984.
Tan zi ji [Talking About Myself].   Chengdu, Sichuan People's Publishing House, 1982.
Ba Jin lun chuangzuo [Ba Jin Discusses His Work].   Shanghai, Shanghai Literature and Arts Publishing House, 1983.
Xiezuo shenghuo de huigu [Looking Back at My Writing Career].   Shanghai, Hunan People's Publishing House, 1984.
Tong nian de huiyi [Memories of My Childhood] (for children).   Chengdu, Sichuan People's Publishing House, 1984.
Bing zhong ji: 1982.7–84.2 [In Sickness].   Hong Kong, Shenghuo, dushu, xinzhi san lian Publishing House, 1984.
Bei chuang ji shi.   Taibei, Lianhe baoshe, 1985.
Ba Jin quan ji (collected works).   Beijing, People's Literature Publishing House, 8 vols., 1986–90.
Dangdai zawen xuancui [Collection of Short Stories].   Shanghai, Hunan Literature and Arts Publishing House, 1986.
Ren sheng de taiyang: zuojia yishujia zhi qingshao nian [Sun of Life: A Message from Writers and Artists to the Young Generation], with Ping Xin.   Beijing, People's Literature Publishing House, 1988.
Selected Works of Ba Jin.   Beijing, Foreign Languages Press, 2 vols., 1988.
Chang he bu jin liu: huainian Shen Congwen xiansheng [The Long River Always Flows: Remembering Shen Congwen], with Huang Yongyu.   Shanghai, Hunan Literature and Arts Publishing House, 1989.
Kangzhan jishi [Account of the War of Resistance], with Ping Xin.   Beijing, China Friendship Publishing House, 1989.

Editor, *Tao huang*, by Ai Wu.   1942.

*

Critical Studies: *Ba Jin and His Writings: Chinese Youth Between the Two Revolutions* by O. Lang, Cambridge, Massachusetts, Harvard University East Asian Research Center, 1967; *Ba Jin* by Nathan K. Mao, Boston, Twayne, 1978; "Europeanized Grammar in Ba Jin's Novel *Jia*" by Cornelius C. Kubler, in *Journal of the Chinese Language Teachers' Association* (Columbus, Ohio), 20(1), 1985; "Ba Jin and Turgenev" by Naixiou Shun, in *Foreign Literatures* (Beijing), 11, 1986.

*   *   *

Ba Jin, originally named Li Yaotang and Li Feikan, is one of contemporary China's most famous and influential writers. His name is familiar throughout China, and his work has been included in school and university textbooks for more than five decades.

Ba Jin began to publish poems, prose writings, and short stories in newspapers in 1922. In 1927 he wrote his first novella, *Mie wang* (Destruction), which concerns the conflicts between young intellectuals and the old power structures and feudal system, and their sufferings, struggles, and failures. Ba Jin was influenced by political events in China and abroad; he had been profoundly upset by the execution of the anarchists Nicola Sacco and Bartolomeo Vanzetti by the U.S. government. In the novella, Ba Jin gives vent to his loneliness, indignation, suffering, and the dilemmas he feels; indeed, it is a kind of *cri de coeur*. Though *Mie wang* is based on social reality, it has something of the quality of a legend, with characters who play stock roles of hero and villain, and has a romantic and symbolistic flavour. Because it treats subjects which concerned many young people at that time and is imbued with passionate feeling, it attracted widespread attention and praise. In this novella Ba Jin was already using literature as a weapon to fight against what he saw as irrational systems which hinder the progress and development of society and human nature. Later he published novellas such as *Aiqing de san bu chu* (Love: A Trilogy), consisting of *Wu* (Fog), *Yu* (Rain), and *Dian* (Thunder), and *Xin sheng* (New Life), as well as several short stories, prose works, and essays. In these, too, he rails against traditional attitudes and ideas in a way which struck a chord in many people of his radical, reforming generation.

Ba Jin wrote his best-known work, *Jia* (*Family*), in 1931. It chronicles the decline and division of a large family in an inaccessible inland city at a time when the tide of social reform is finally reaching the interior of China. He shows how the old system is routed and the young generation is influenced by the new outlook of the time. This novel draws on Ba Jin's own family background and personal experience, and bears the stamp of authenticity. It focuses on family life and presents ordinary people living their everyday lives rather than the heroic characters of his earlier work. Three kinds of young people are represented in *Family*: the radical who boldly seeks progress; the compromiser who submits to the still-powerful forces of family and propriety for the sake of peace and in doing so destroys himself, as well as other people; and the sentimental women whose youthful dreams are cruelly shattered by reality.

Family was enormously influential in the 1930s. It depicted young people's struggles against the authoritarian family in general and arranged marriages in particular — subjects of great concern to the predominantly young reading public of the period. The novel mixes passion and protest with despair and sadness. Ba Jin's writing is natural, fluent, and simple, without extravagant embellishment, yet it deals at a profound level with the complex issue of the forces of good and evil.

After 1949 Ba Jin tried to adapt his writing to the requirements of "being in the service of the proletarian politics." His work in this period presents a blandly positive picture of the new socialist system, the new life, and the "heroes of the new era"; he has lost his depth of thought and feeling. Ba Jin endured harsh persecution during the Cultural Revolution (1966–76), yet in 1978, already well into his 70s, he began to write and publish again. *Sui xiang lu* (*Random Thoughts*), a collection of prose writings, contains Ba Jin's reflections on China's historical experience and his sober self-analysis. It is authentic, pithy, and vivid, and shows a great maturity both in the depth of its thought and in its language. He recognizes that for 30 years he has told many lies against his conscience and vows that from now on he will tell only the truth.

—David Jiang

BAKR, Salwā. Egyptian. Born in Matareya, Cairo, June 1949. Educated at Ayn Shams University, Cairo, B.A. in management 1972, B.A. in drama criticism 1976. Married to Munīr al-Shaʿrānī; one daughter and one son. Government rationing inspector, 1974–80; freelance film and theatre critic in Cyprus, 1980–86; returned to Egypt, 1986; founder, *Hagar* journal, 1993. Address: c/o Atelier of Writers and Artists, Karim al-Dawla Street, Off Talat Harb Square, Cairo, Egypt.

PUBLICATIONS

Fiction

Zinātfī jināzat al-raʾīs [Zinat at the President's Funeral]. Cairo, privately printed, 1986.
Maqām ʿAṭiyyah [ʿAṭiyyah's Shrine]. Cairo, Dār al-Fikr li-l-Dirāsāt wa-l-Nashr, 1986.
ʿAn al-rūḥ allatī suriqat tadrījiyyā [About the Soul That Was Spirited Away]. Cairo, Masriyyah li-l-Nashr wa-l-Tawzīʾ, 1989.
Al-ʿarabah al-dhahabiyyah lā taṣʿad ilā al-samāʾ. Cairo, Sīnā li-l-Nashr, 1991; as *The Golden Chariot Does Not Ascend to Heaven*, Reading, Berkshire, Garnet, 1994.
The Wiles of Men and Other Stories. London, Quartet, 1992.
ʿAjīn al-fallāḥah [Monkey Business]. Cairo, Sīnā li-l-Nashr, 1992.
Waṣf al-bulbul [Depicting the Nightingale]. Cairo, Sīnā li-l-Nashr, 1993.

*

Critical Studies: "A Walk on the Downside" by Mohamed Ragheb, in *Cairo Today*, August 1990; "Women Enslaved by Law and Tradition" by Hoda El-Sada, in *Al-Ahram* (London), 2 May 1991; "Madness as a Strategy in Female Discourse" by Dinah Manisty, in *Alif: Journal of Comparative Poetics*, Cairo, University of Cairo Press, 1994.

*   *   *

Salwā Bakr is probably the most gifted woman writer of her generation in Egypt. She started writing short stories in the 1970s, encountered severe opposition from the state, and was imprisoned several times. This delayed the appearance of her first collection, *Zīnātfī jināzat al-raʾīs* (Zinat at the President's Funeral), which she published at her own expense despite her limited means. The insistence on publishing her first work independently in the face of tremendous odds paid off when *Zīnāt* received wide critical acclaim both in Egypt and in other parts of the Arab world. This led to the publication of Bakr's first novel, *Maqām ʿAṭiyyah* (ʿAṭiyyah's Shrine), in the same year, to even wider critical acclaim. In these first two books it became evident that Bakr's energy and talent was aimed at taking women's literature beyond the simple "feminist" discourse of Nawal al-Saʿdāwi (*q.v.*) and her generation.

Unlike the feminist writing of her predecessors, Bakr produces a sophisticated female narrative, a discourse of difference which expresses itself in a rich variety of techniques. She sees feminists as women who crave power and social legitimation to grant them respect and a place in the prevalent but faulty patriarchal system. Instead, she develops in her three collections of short stories — *Zīnāt*, *ʿAn al-rūḥ allatī suriqat tadrī jiyyā* (About the Soul That Was Spirited Away), and *ʿAjīn al-fallāḥah* (Monkey Business) — a fascinating narrative of self-discovery concerned with granting the voiceless female a mature voice that is truly her own. Her subtle, shrewd, and artistically mature techniques for subverting the prevalent order result in some of the most interesting female writing in Arabic, for it offers its discourse in the context of changing national realities and is careful not to alienate the other gender. The main feature of this reality is the disintegration of the old nationalist, rational, and liberal project and the emergence of new forms of traditionalism. The rational approach is rapidly making way to a new sectarian thinking whose rising forms of belligerence use the sacred to consolidate the shaky old order and manipulate a religious discourse to serve the patriarchal system.

Bakr is aware that narrative discourse, by its very nature, is both secular and liberal. In her varied and highly sophisticated narrative, the textual strategies capable of undermining the rising traditionalism and furthering the secular are numerous. One of these strategies is the glorification of the female, a literary device that aspires to break the male's monopoly on the divine and provide the sacred with a feminine aspect. This also humanizes the sacred and reflects a fundamental change in the perception of the female in the culture. This is evident in Bakr's novel *Maqām 'Aṭiyyah*, in which the narrative structure itself is based on multiplicity of testimonies. It is enhanced by the selection of an androgynous name, 'Aṭiyyah, which is used in Arabic for both men and women — a feature the text is keen should not escape the reader's attention — and often extends this androgynous nature to the heroine.

The narrative structure uses the polyphony of narrative voices neither to establish the various facets of truth nor to demonstrate its relativity, but to defer any application of patriarchal binary thought. Ths novel resorts to a significant technique which acknowledges the absence of the woman and turns it with the dexterity of narrative treatment into a sign of its overwhelming presence. The main character of the novel, 'Aṭiyyah, is deliberately absent, as if to conform to the prevalent social norm, in an attempt to investigate this norm by taking its tenets as its point of departure. The primary concern of the novel is to exorcise this absence and turn it into a stark form of presence, superior in quality and significance to that of the omnipresent male. By taking absence as its point of departure the novel equates the writing of the story of the deceased 'Aṭiyyah with that of realizing the potential of the narrator of the story, 'Azzah, in an attempt to suggest the vital connection between rewriting the story of their foremothers and reshaping that of the present generation. The multiple identification of 'Azzah and 'Aṭiyyah with the ancient Egyptian Goddess Isis involves the reader in the relational network of the text and its intertextual implications. The identification with Isis is in constant interaction with its presentation as the female version of Osiris, for the inversion of roles in "female" writing is achieved without alienating the woman from her female self. This is enhanced on the text's ideological plane by positing the popular belief with its feminine synthesizing nature, in which the ancient Egyptian creeds are blended with the tenets of Christianity and Islam and integrated in their practice, against the dogmatic male version of Islam with its inherent fundamentalism.

The novel succeeds in creating a textual equivalent of the social conditions in which sexual politics arc structured around the suppression of the female voice, yet is able to write this voice into the very texture of the narrative. The presentation of narrative discourse constructs the textual space in a manner reproducing the structural order of patriarchy, while at the same time subverting its very authority. It gives the male voices the function of starting and ending the story, and squeezes the females, who are outnumbered by the males, into the middle. By cutting up the continuity of the male voice, and giving the female the interruptive role, it is possible to achieve the real inversion of the prevalent order by turning its structure against

itself. In addition, grouping the female voices in the centre of the narrative sequence assures the continuity of their voices and the centrality of their position within the hierarchy of the textual order.

This technique of subtle inversion, ostensible fragmentation, and profound intertextuality has continued in her two other novels, *Al-'arabah al-dhahabiyyah lā taṣ'ad ilā al-samā'* (*The Golden Chariot Does Not Ascend to Heaven*) and *Waṣf al-bulbul* (Depicting the Nightingale). In the former, Bakr ventures into the taboo area of female sexuality and aggression, which has never been treated in Arabic with such clarity and candour. She selects the oppressive atmosphere of a women's prison, of which she has had first-hand experience, as the location of her narrative, and tells the stories of its women who trespassed the boundaries of the patriarchal order. Through the accumulation of stories of constant violation of the female body and soul, Bakr is able to transform the ostensible madness of her narrator into a counter-logic capable of revealing the inherent contradiction of the penal patriarchal system.

Like *The Arabian Nights*, the novel has a unique structure of autonomous tales linked together by their constant dialogue with the frame story of Aziza and her imaginary chariot. Her fantasy of escaping from the gloomy reality of prison in a golden chariot and ascending to a heavenly utopia links the diverse narrative of 15 different prisoners. Yet her fantasy of escape and utopian existence, which verges on the brink of madness, serves other narrative functions. It shows how madness is an inherent part of the condition of women in society and manifests their yearning for a different world, free from the oppression of both the actual prison and the harsher one of the external reality that forced them into prison. It also staves off the harsh impact of the gallery of horrors which each story exhibits and involves the reader in the inner web of social madness imposed on them. But its main role is to suspend the closed social horizon, from which women have no escape, and to intensify the effect of the novel's depressing ending. The constant interaction between fantasy and reality reveals the hidden aspects of reality and enables the text to subvert them at the same time.

Bakr's most recent novel, *Waṣf al-bulbul*, is a fascinating tale of self-discovery and rebellion against the prescribed norms of feminine behaviour. It ventures into another taboo area, the re-examination of the Qur'anic discourse on women, and conducts a profound intertextual dialogue between the story of its heroine, Hājir, and the Qur'anic version of the story of Joseph and the wife of the Pharaoh which led to his imprisonment in Egypt. The constant dialogue between the narrative and its Qur'anic counterpart enables the author to violate the sacred and rewrite its story of the female while developing her own narrative of self-realisation and fulfilment. The heroine's journey to another unidentified Arab country (probably Morocco) takes her to a new space, a fresh experience, and an intriguing trip of self-discovery. The novel is the account of the six days of her visit to the unidentified Arab country, during which she falls in love with a waiter of a hotel. But beneath this simple story, one reads of the search for the suppressed female self submerged under social conventions and family obligations. The six days of the narrative recall the six days of creation, and the author rests on the seventh day, leaving the rest of the work to her reader. The new story of the creation of woman and her world emerges, and with it a new and highly imaginative form of "female" writing.

—Sabry Hafez

BARAŃCZAK, Stanisław. Polish. Born in Poznań, 13 November 1946. Educated at Adam Mickiewicz University, Poznań, 1964–69, M.A. in Polish literature 1969, Ph.D. 1973. Married Anna Barańczak in 1968; one son and one daughter. Assistant Professor, Adam Mickiewicz University, 1970–77, 1980–81; Associate Professor, 1981–84, and since 1984 Professor, Harvard University, Cambridge, Massachusetts. Recipient: Kościelski Foundation prize, 1973; Jurzykowski prize, 1981; Terrence des Pres award, 1989; Polish PEN Club award, 1990. Address: Department of Slavic Languages, 301 Boylston Hall, Harvard University, Cambridge, Massachusetts 02138, U.S.A.

PUBLICATIONS

Verse

Korekta twarzy [Proofreading of a Face]. Poznań, Wydawnictwo Poznańskie, 1968.
Jednym tchem [In One Breath]. Warsaw, Universitas, 1970.
Dziennik poranny: wiersze 1967–1971 [A Morning Diary: Poems 1967–1971]. Poznań, Wydawnictwo Poznańskie, 1972.
Ja wiem, że to niesłuszne: wiersze z lat 1975–1976 [I Know It Is Not Right: Poems from 1975–1976]. Paris, Instytut Literacki, 1977.
Sztuczne oddychanie [Artificial Breathing]. London, Aneks, 1978.
Tryptyk z betonu, zmęczenia i śniegu [A Tryptych of Cement, Exhaustion and Snow]. Cracow, Kos, 1980.
Wiersze prawie zebrane [Poems Almost Collected]. Warsaw, Niezależna Oficyna Wydanicza, 1981.
Atlantyda i inne wiersze z lat 1981–1985 [Atlantis and Others Verses from 1981–1985]. London, Puls, 1986.
Widokówka z tego świata i inne rymy z lat 1986–1988 [A Postcard from This World and Other Rhymes from 1986–1988]. Paris, Zeszyty Literackie, 1988.
The Weight of the Body: Selected Poems. Evanston, Illinois, TriQuarterly, 1989.
159 wierszy: 1968–1988 [159 Poems: 1968–1988]. Cracow, Znak, 1990.

Other

Nieufni i zadufani: romantyzm i klascycyzm w młodej poezji lat sześćdziesiątych [Mistrustful Ones and Presumptuous Ones: Romanticism and Classicism of Young Polish Poetry of the 1960s]. Wrocław, Zakład Narodowy Imienia Ossolińskich-Wydawnictwo Polskiej Akademii Nauk, 1971.
Ironia i harmonia: szkice o najnowszej literaturze polskiej [Irony and Harmony: Essays on Modern Polish Literature]. Warsaw, Czytelnik, 1973.
Język poetycki Mirona Białoszewskiego [Miron Białoszewski's Poetic Language]. Wrocław, Zakład Narodowy Imienia Ossolińskich-Wydawnictwo Polskiej Akademii Nauk, 1974.
Etyka i poetyka: szkice 1970–1979 [Ethics and Poetics, Essays 1970–1978]. Paris, Instytut Literacki, 1979.
Książki najgorsze [The Worst Books]. Cracow, Kos, 1981.
Czytelnik ubezwłasnowolniony: perswazja w masowej kulturze literackiej PRL [Incapacitated Reader: Persuasion in the Polish People's Republic's Mass Literary Culture]. Paris, Libella, 1983.
Uciekinier z utopii: o poezji Zbigniewa Herberta. London, Polonia, 1984; as *A Fugitive from Utopia: The Poetry of Zbigniew Herbert*, Cambridge, Massachusetts, Harvard University Press, 1987.

Przed i po: szkice o poezji krajowej przeło mu lat siedemdziesiątych i osiemdziesiątych [Before and After: Essays on Polish Poetry of the Turn of the 1970s/80s]. London, Aneks, 1988.
Breathing Under Water and Other East European Essays. Cambridge, Massachusetts, Harvard University Press, 1990.
Tablica z Macondo: osiem naście prób wytłumaczenia, po co i dlaczego się pisze [The Slab from Macondo: 18 Ways of Trying to Explain the Reasons for Writing]. London, Aneks, 1990.
Ocalone w tłumaczeniu. Poznań, Wydawnictwo a5, 1992.

Editor and Translator, *Wiersze wybrane* [Selected Poems], by Dylan Thomas. Cracow, Wydawnictwo Literackie, 1974.
Editor and Translator, *Późne wiersze* [The Late Poems], by Osip Mandelshtam. London, Oficyna Poetów i Malarzy, 1977.
Editor and Translator, *Wiersze i poematy* [Poems, Short and Long], by Iosif Brodskii. Warsaw, Niezależna Oficyna Wydawnicza, 1979.
Editor and Translator, *Wybór poezji* [Selected Poems], by Gerard Manley Hopkins. Cracow, Znak, 1981.
Editor and Translator, *Antologia angielskiej poezji metafizycznej XVII stulecia* [An Anthology of 17th-Century English Metaphysical Poetry]. Warsaw, Państwowy Instytut Wydawniczy, 1982; enlarged edition, 1991.
Editor and Translator, *150 wierszy*, by e. e. cummings. Cracow, Wydawnictwo Literackie, 1983.
Editor and Translator, *Nieposłuszna mama i inne wierszyki dla dzieci* [When We Were Very Young], by A. A. Milne. Warsaw, Nasza Księgarnia, 1983.
Editor and Translator, *Wiersze wybrane* [Selected Poems], by John Donne. Cracow, Wydawnictwo Literackie, 1984.
Editor, *Poeta pamięta: antologia poezji świadectwa i sprzeciwu 1944–1984* [A Poet Remembers: An Anthology of Poetry of Testimony and Protest 1944–1984]. London, Puls, 1984.
Editor and Translator, with Clare Cavanagh, *Citizen R. K. Does Not Live: Poems*, by Ryszard Krynicki. Forest Grove, Oregon, Mr. Cogito Press, 1985.
Editor and Translator, *82 wiersze i poematy* [82 Poems], by Iosif Brodskii. Paris, Zeszyty Literackie, 1988.
Editor and Translator, *Rozmowa w zimie: wybór wierszy* [The Winter Talk: Selected Poems], by Tomas Venclova. Paris, Zeszyty Literackie, 1989.
Editor and Translator, *Wiersze wybrane* [Selected Poems], by George Herbert. Cracow, Znak, 1990.
Editor and Translator, *100 wierszy* [100 Poems], by Emily Dickinson. Cracow, Wydawnictwo Arka, 1990.
Editor and Translator, *Wybór poezji* [Selected Poems], by James Merrill. Paris, Zeszyty Literackie, 1990.
Editor and Translator, *"Zwierzę słucha zwierzeń": małe bestiarium z angielskiego* ["The Animal Confessors": A Little English and American Bestiary]. Warsaw, Itaka-PEN, 1991.
Editor and Translator, *44 wiersze* [44 Poems], by Philip Larkin. Cracow, Wydawnictwo Arka, 1991.
Editor and Translator, *"Z Tobą więc ze Wszystkim": 222 arcydzieła angielskiej i amerykańskiej liryki religijnej* ["With Thee, Therefore with All": 222 Masterpieces of English and American Religious Verse]. Cracow, Znak, 1992.
Editor and Translator, with Clare Cavanagh, *Spoiling Cannibals' Fun: Polish Poetry of the Last Two Decades of Communist Rule.* Evanston, Illinois, Northwestern University Press, 1992.
Editor and Translator, *77 wierszy* [77 Poems], by Robert Herrick. Cracow, Wydawnictwo Arka, 1992.

Editor and Translator, *55 wierszy* [55 Poems], by Robert Frost.   Cracow, Wydawnictwo Arka, 1992.

Editor and Translator, *Madonny z dorysowaną szpicbródką oraz inne wiersze, prozy poetyckie i eseje* [Madonnas Touched Up with a Goatee, and Other Poems, Prose Poems, and Essays], by Charles Simic.   Poznań, Wydawnictwo a5, 1992.

Translator, *Hamlet*, by William Shakespeare.   Poznań, Wydawnictwo Drodze, 1990.

Translator, *Romeo i Julia* [Romeo and Juliet], by William Shakespeare.   Poznań, Wydawnictwo Drodze, 1990.

Translator, *Król Lear* [King Lear], by William Shakespeare.   Poznań, Wydawnictwo Drodze, 1991.

Translator, *Burza*; *Zimowa opowieść* [The Tempest; The Winter's Tale], by William Shakespeare.   Poznań, Wydawnictwo Drodze, 1991.

Translator, *Sen nocy letniej*; *Kupiec wenecki* [A Midsummer Night's Dream; The Merchant of Venice], by William Shakespeare.   Poznań, Wydawnictwo Drodze, 1992.

Translator, *Makbet* [Macbeth], by William Shakespeare.   Poznań, Wydawnictwo Drodze, 1992.

*

Stanisław Barańczak comments:

Poetry is nothing less than a way of challenging the injustice inherent in the order of the universe — the order that, depending on your philosophy, may be "natural" or "scientific" or "God-given" but is always contrary to or at least divergent from what we expect from life. These expectations may be narrow and naive but they are our own — they are human. They may mean nothing against the vastness of the universe and its intricate designs but they offer the only scale of measuring things that is accessible to us — a scale graduated with various degrees of pain. Political utopias, laws of nature, or providential decrees are too vast and all-encompassing to bother with my individual self — only when I painfully bump into their corners or fall into their traps, do I have tangible proof of their validity. And only this pain is irrefutably real, a hard evidence of both their and my own existence.

From this point of view, there is probably no real difference between my poems written in Poland and those composed on American soil, even though, superficially speaking, the former were understandably more focused on specific "political" themes. A standard explanation pointing out that in the countries of the Eastern Bloc every area of life, from housing and shopping to love or religious faith, is in any event indelibly tainted by "politics," by the omnipresence of oppressive social institutions, reveals only a part of the truth. The other, more essential part is perhaps that regardless of its theme and specific address, poetry is always some kind of a protest. It does not really matter whether the pain it protests against has been inflicted by a policeman's truncheon or by a realization of the inevitability of death. Whatever the world treats him with, the poet reacts the same way: he tries, against all odds and all logic, to defend his human birthright to what he considers normal, to his human norm imposed insolently upon the universe. (from the preface to *The Weight of the Body*, 1989)

*   *   *

Stanisław Barańczak is one of the best poets and essayists of the Polish "1968 Generation." His first book of poetry, *Korekta twarzy* (Proofreading of a Face), was published in that year, but it was really the next collection, *Jednym tchem* (In One Breath), that focused attention on the work of this young linguist from Poznań. His poems expressed the deep mistrust felt by a generation which was too young to be seriously influenced by World War II and the post-war Stalinist regime, but attached high hopes to the "rebirth of genuine Socialism" promised by Władysław Gomułka in 1956. Barańczak finds the gap between slogans and reality too wide to leave him unconcerned: indeed, he discredits altogether the language of officialdom as used in the press and other media. In his poems he confronts the language of the human body and of individual existence with officialese, completely undermining the latter's veracity. An excellent example of Barańczak's ingenious use of the language in this period is the poem "Wypełnić czytelnym pismem" (Fill It in in Legible Writing) which mimics an official questionnaire with ironic twists and turns.

Between the years 1972 and 1980 Barańczak could publish only in samizdat (underground, unofficial publishing) — a fact which did not impair his poetic development. On the contrary: in *Sztuczne oddychanie* (Artificial Breathing) and *Tryptyk z betonu, zmęczenia i śniegu* (A Tryptych of Cement, Exhaustion and Snow) he managed to tell much about the world and himself. The first of these cycles is written about a fictitious person, a certain N.N. whose anonimity allows Barańczak to describe both the everyday life and concerns of the so-called "grey citizen" of Poland, as well as the surrounding reality, or rather unreality, of a Communist regime surviving on foreign loans and trying to stem the growing dissatisfaction of the population. In the "Tryptych," on the other hand, Barańczak returns to the first-person singular and in short but formally diverse poems manages to show the "Polish hell of everyday life." Some of these poems actually have the subtitle "How to Get to the Counter," indicating that in these years a large amount of a Pole's time was spent in queues, just waiting for something to buy.

In 1981 Barańczak emigrated to the United States, where a Chair in Polish Literature was waiting for him at Harvard University. His poetry since then has illustrated that while his work is very much rooted in reality, he is not a poet of constant political commitment. He still writes poems about Poland and primarily Polish problems, but much of his new work is preoccupied with the self-definition of an expatriate who "can see the matter from two points of view." So Barańczak's "American" poems, while they introduce new themes and new landscapes, also deepen his commitment to private life and to concerns which, for the first time, can exist for him outside a collective — socialist or national — framework.

Barańczak is also an accomplished critic and essayist. His first critical work, *Nieufni i zadufani* (Mistrustful Ones and Presumptuous Ones), rejected the compromise which most Polish poets struck with the authorities after 1956: "if you allow us to experiment we shall not query fundamental issues." Here Barańczak showed the greatest appreciation for those poets whose praxis involved a critique of the language in any form. While the collection *Etyka i poetyka* (Ethics and Poetics) was devoted to problems of contemporary Polish literature and European culture, Barańczak also wrote persuasively about the poetic language of Miron Białoszewski, and about the poetry of Zbigniew Herbert (*q.v.*) in *Uciekinier z utopii* (*A Fugitive from Utopia*). A collection of Barańczak's essays was published in English under the title *Breathing Under Water*; it reveals the author not only as a sharp-eyed critic tackling a broad range of problems, but also as an excellent mediator of values between different cultures.

This picture would not be complete without mentioning the third area in which Barańczak has done valuable work — translation. He has translated into Polish both from Russian and English, making available the poetry of Osip Mandelshtam and Iosif Brodskii (*q.v.*), John Donne, Gerard

Manley Hopkins, e. e. cummings, and Dylan Thomas, not to mention a number of Metaphysical poets from whose work he produced a much praised anthology. His skill as a translator and his achievements in other genres define Barańczak as a central figure in contemporary Polish literature.

—George Gömöri

BASSANI, Giorgio. Italian. Born in Bologna, 4 April 1916. Educated at the University of Bologna, degree in literature. Imprisoned, 1943; after release took part in the Resistance. Used pseudonym Giacomo Marchi for several years to avoid Nazi–Fascist persecution. Married Valeria Sinigallia in 1943; one son and one daughter. Lived in Ferrara until 1943, then in Rome; after World War II worked as scriptwriter and film dubbing editor; editor, Feltrinelli publishers, Milan, 1958–64; Instructor in history of the theatre, Academy of Dramatic Art, Rome, 1957–68; vice president, Radio Televisione Italiana, Rome, 1964–65. Editor, *Botteghe Oscure*, Rome, 1948–60; co-editor, *Paragone*, Milan, 1953–55. President, from 1966, and currently honorary president, Italia Nostra. Recipient: Veillon prize, 1956; Strega prize, 1956; Viareggio prize, 1962; Campiello prize, 1969; Sachs prize, 1969; Bagutta prize, 1983. Address: Via G. B. De Rossi 33, Rome, Italy.

PUBLICATIONS

Fiction

Una città di pianura (as Giacomo Marchi).   Milan, Lucini, 1940.
La passeggiata prima di cena.   Florence, Sansoni, 1953.
Gli ultimi anni di Clelia Trotti.   Pisa, Nistri Lischi, 1955.
Cinque storie ferraresi.   Turin, Einaudi, 1956; as *A Prospect of Ferrara*, London, Faber, 1962; as *Five Stories of Ferrara*, New York, Harcourt Brace, 1971.
Gli occhiali d'oro.   Turin, Einaudi, 1958; as *The Gold-Rimmed Spectacles*, New York, Atheneum, and London, Faber, 1960.
Una notte del '43.   Turin, Einaudi, 1960.
Il giardino dei Finzi-Contini.   Turin, Einaudi, 1962; as *The Garden of the Finzi-Continis*, New York, Atheneum, and London, Faber, 1965.
Dietro la porta.   Turin, Einaudi, 1964; as *Behind the Door*, New York, Harcourt Brace, 1972; London, Weidenfeld and Nicolson, 1973.
Due novelle.   Venice, Stamperia di Venezia, 1965.
L'airone.   Milan, Mondadori, 1968; as *The Heron*, New York, Harcourt Brace, and London, Weidenfeld and Nicolson, 1970.
L'odore del fieno.   Milan, Mondadori, 1972; as *The Smell of Hay* (with *The Gold-Rimmed Spectacles*), New York, Harcourt Brace, and London, Weidenfeld and Nicolson, 1975.
Il romanzo di Ferrara (collection).   Milan, Mondadori, 1974; revised edition, 1980.
Di là dal cuore.   Milan, Mondadori, 1984.

Play

Screenplay: *The Stranger's Hands*, with Guy Elmes and Graham Greene, 1954.

Verse

Storie dei poveri amanti e altri versi.   Rome, Astrolabio, 1946.
Te lucis ante.   Rome, Ubaldini, 1947.
Un'altra libertà.   Milan, Mondadori, 1951.
L'alba ai vetri: poesie 1942–1950.   Turin, Einaudi, 1963.
Epitaffio.   Milan, Mondadori, 1974.
In gran segreto.   Milan, Mondadori, 1978.
In rima e senza.   Milan, Mondadori, 1982.
Rolls Royce and Other Poems (bilingual edition).   Toronto, Aya Press, 1982.

Other

Le parole preparate e altri scritti di letteratura.   Turin, Einaudi, 1966.

*

Critical Studies: "The *Storie ferraresi* of Giorgio Bassani," in *Italica* (Madison, Wisconsin), 49, 1972, and "Bassani's Ironic Mode," in *Canadian Journal of Italian Studies* (Hamilton, Ontario), 1, 1978, both by Marianne Shapiro; "*The Garden of the Finzi-Continis*" by Stanley G. Eskin, in *Literature/Film Quarterly* (Salisbury, Maryland), 1, 1973; "Mythical Dimensions of Micòl Finzi-Contini," in *Italica* (Madison, Wisconsin), 51, 1974, "A Conversion to Death: Giorgio Bassani's *L'airone*," in *Canadian Journal of Italian Studies* (Hamilton, Ontario), 1, 1978, and *Vengeance of the Victim: History and Symbol in Giorgio Bassani's Fiction*, Minneapolis, University of Minnesota Press, 1986, all by Marilyn Schneider; "Transformation in Bassani's Garden," in *Modern Fiction Studies* (West Lafayette, Indiana), 21, 1975, "The Closed World of Giorgio Bassani," in *Italian Culture* (Kent, Ohio), 3, 1981, "Exile in the Narrative Writings of Giorgio Bassani," in *Italian Culture* (Kent, Ohio), 5, 1984, "Bassani: The Motivation of Language," in *Italica* (Madison, Wisconsin), 62(2), 1985, *The Exile into Eternity: A Study of the Narrative Writings of Giorgio Bassani*, Rutherford, New Jersey, Fairleigh Dickinson University Press, 1987, and "Bassani: The Guilt Beyond the Door," in *Gradiva* (Stony Brook, New York), 4(2[6]), 1988, all by Douglas Radcliff-Umstead; "Art and Death in Bassani's Poetry" by Stelio Cro, in *Canadian Journal of Italian Studies* (Hamilton, Ontario), 1, 1978; "Giorgio Bassani: The Record of a Confession" by Diego L. Bastianutti, in *Queen's Quarterly* (Kingston, Ontario), 88(4), 1981; "Insiders and Outsiders: Discourses of Oppression in Giorgio Bassani's *Gli occhiali d'oro*" by Mirna Cicioni, in *Italian Studies* (Leeds), 41, 1986; "Visual Memory and the Nature of the Epitaph: Bassani's *Epitaffio*" by Linda Nemerow-Ulman, in *Italian Quarterly* (New Brunswick, New Jersey), 27(106), 1986; "Narrated and Narrating I in *Il giardino dei Finzi-Contini*" by Harry Davis, in *Italian Studies* (Leeds), 43, 1988.

*   *   *

Although he has also written poetry and essays and held important editorial posts, Giorgio Bassani is best known both in Italy and abroad (where he has been widely translated) for his narrative fiction. The stories collected in 1956 as *Cinque storie ferraresi* (*Five Stories of Ferrara*) are his earliest writing of this sort. Most of them were composed in the decade immediately following World War II, but all of them have been thoroughly, even obsessively, reworked for republication since. The focus in each of these stories is on the relationship of a central character with some larger social entity — the family, the Ferrarese Jewish community (whose unofficial modern chronicler Bassani has in many ways become), or Ferrara itself, especially during the Fascist era. This partly imaginary, partly historical city in the Po valley during the 1920s and 1930s is the setting for virtually all of Bassani's fiction. It is also, in some ways, the most important character in the on-going "novel" or "romance" of Ferrara Bassani has been slowly and meticulously creating throughout his career. Several collections of these short stories bear the subtitle "inside the walls," a reference not only to their physical setting, but also to the social and psychological barriers which separate Bassani's characters from one another as well as protect them from a world usually, but not always, beyond their ken. Although most of the action in these stories occurs before World War II, the narrator who recounts them does so from a perspective after the war, Italian Civil War, and Holocaust. This retrospective view makes possible their characteristically elegiac tone which is designed to awaken pity rather than condemnation of the often petty cruelties and banal disappointments of a time "before" which has now disappeared forever.

This same spatial-historical setting and temporal perspective are present also in *Gli occhiali d'oro* (*The Gold-Rimmed Spectacles*), a longer "Ferrarese story" in which Bassani introduces for the first time the unnamed but clearly autobiographical narrator whose fall from innocence into a world of infectious but enigmatic Evil will be traced in two other novels of the early 1960s — *Il giardino dei Finzi-Contini* (*The Garden of the Finzi-Continis*) and *Dietro la porta* (*Behind the Door*). In all three of these novels the adolescent protagonist is struggling to establish his identity in a world outside the protective circle of his family. Here he encounters increasingly complex social configurations of inclusion and exclusion which have the power not only to wound emotionally, but also to destroy physically, as in the case of both the homosexual Doctor Fadigati and the 183 Ferrarese Jews deported to Buchenwald from Ferrara. In *The Garden of the Finzi-Continis*, set at the time of the anti-Semitic proclamations, the narrator makes the not uncommon but nonetheless extremely painful error of mistaking expressions of fraternal solidarity for signs of the unqualified love he is desperately seeking — a personal tragedy which is given special poignancy by the ominous political storm clouds gathering on the horizon. The *cupio dissolvi* which hangs over these pages becomes even more explicit in *L'airone* (The Heron), which is set entirely in the post-war period, and a chronicle of the last day in the life of a survivor of the war and Holocaust who is nonetheless unable to cope with the anguish of his existential condition and so commits suicide.

Bleak as these themes of loneliness, exclusion, and death may seem, the elegance and moral seriousness of Bassani's writings give the actions they recount considerable dignity in a memorialization meant to redeem these characters and their tragic vicissitudes from the indifference of time and history.

—Charles Klopp

BASTOS, Augusto Roa. *See* **ROA BASTOS, Augusto.**

BAYĀTI, 'Abdal-Wahhāb al-. Iraqi. Born in Baghdad, in 1926. Educated at Baghdad Teachers Training College. Married; two sons and one daughter. Teacher of Arabic, 1950–53; sentenced to prison and concentration camp for revolutionary activities; escaped, lived in Beirut and Cairo; member of editorial staff, *Al Jumhūria* newspaper, Cairo, 1956; returned to Iraq, 1958; translations and publishing director, Ministry of Education, Baghdad; cultural attaché, Moscow; lecturer, Asian People's Institute, Moscow, 1961; lived in exile in Moscow, then Cairo; returned to Iraq, 1972; cultural adviser, Ministry of Culture and Fine Arts, Baghdad. Address: c/o Georgetown University Press, Intercultural Center, Room 111, Washington, D.C. 20057, U.S.A.

PUBLICATIONS

Verse

Malā'ika wa shayāṭīn [Angels and Devils].   1950.
Abārīq muhashshamah [Broken Pitchers].   1954.
Al-majd lil-atfāl wa z-zaytūn [Glory Be to Children and the Olive Branch].   1956.
Ash'ār fi al-manfā [Poems in Exile].   1957.
Khamsata 'ashara qasīda min Viyana [15 Poems from Vienna].   1958.
'Ishrūn qasīda min Berlin [20 Poems from Berlin].   1959.
Kalimāt la tamūt [Words That Never Die].   1960.
Al-nār wa-al-kalimāt [Fire and Words].   1964.
Sifr al-faqr wa-al-thawrah [The Book of Poverty and Revolution].   1965.
Allazi ya' ti wa-lā ya' ti [That Which Comes and Does Not Come].   1966.
Al-mawt fil-ḥayāh [Death in Life].   1968.
'Uyūn al-kilāb al-mayyita [Dead Dogs' Eyes].   1969.
Al-kitābah 'ala al-ṭīn [The Writing on Clay].   1970.
Qasa' id 'ala bawwabat al-'ālam al-sab' [Love Poems on the Seven Gates of the World].   1971.
Dīwan 'Abdul-Wahhāb al-Bayāti [Collected Poems].   Beirut, n. p., 2 vols., 1971.
Lilies and Death, translated by Mohammed Bakir Alwān. Baghdad, Al-Adīb Print Press, 1972.
Qamar shīraz [The Moon of Shiraz].   1975.
The Singer and the Moon, translated by Abdullah al-Uzari.   London, TR Press, 1976.
Poet of Iraq, Abdul Wahab al-Bayāti: An Introductory Essay with Translations, translated by Desmond Stewart. London, Gazelle, 1976.
Eye of the Sun.   Copenhagen, privately printed, 1978.
Abdul Wahab al-Bayāti.   London, UR Magazine, 1979.
Mamlakat al-sunbulah [Kingdom of the Spike].   Beirut, Dār al-'Awdah, 1979.
Al-ḥubb taḥta al-matar [Love in the Rain].   Madrid, Oriental, 1985.
Bustān 'Ā'isha ['Ā'isha's Orchard].   Cairo, Dar al-Shurūq, 1989.
Love, Death and Exile.   Washington, D.C., Georgetown University Press, 1990.

Play

Muḥākama fī Nīsabūr [Trial in Nishapur].   1963.

Other

Al-Jaza' ir arḍ al-lahab wa-al-dam [Algeria, the Land of Flame and Blood], with Muhammad 'Udah.   1957.
Tajribati ash-shī' riya [My Poetic Experiment].   1968.

Al-dawlah al-qānuniyah wa-al-niḍham al-siyāsi al-Islāmi [The Law State and the Islamic Political System]. Baghdad, Al-Dār al-'Arabiyah lil-Ṭiba'ah, 1979.

*

Critical Studies: "Bayyati and the Committed Poets" by M. M. Badawi, in his *Modern Arabic Poetry*, Cambridge, Cambridge University Press, 1975; in *Poet of Iraq, Abdul Wahab al-Bayati: An Introductory Essay with Translations*, essay by Desmond Stewart, London, Gazelle, 1976.

*   *   *

One of the best-known leaders of the Socialist Realist movement in modern Arabic poetry, 'Abd al-Wahhāb al-Bayāti has been writing for over four decades, never swerving from his basic message of sympathy with the struggle of the workers and the poor against exploitation, and of calling for the liberation of Arabs and other Third World peoples from injustices visited upon them by domestic and foreign forces. His tone and his technique may have changed over the years, but not his commitment to radical transformation in Arab society and other societies like it in the modern world.

Al-Bayāti began his literary career in Iraq as a Romantic poet, following the popular general trend in the late 1940s led by Ilyās Abū Shabaka in Lebanon and 'Alī Maḥmūd Ṭāhā in Egypt. His first collection, *Malā'ika wa shayāṭīn* (Angels and Devils), abounds with the Romantic themes of the unheeding sweetheart and the forlorn lover; on dreams of an ideal world, memories of childhood, and reminiscences of the lost past; on the suffering poet, sorrows of the night, the death of a nightingale, and so on. Mostly in free verse, these poems generally followed the traditional prosody, often maintaining one rhyme throughout the poem. Al-Bayāti soon shook off this Romanticism and adopted free verse as a medium, in which he wrote most of the poems of his second collection, *Abārīq muhashshamah* (Broken Pitchers), and all later collections.

As he was beginning to find his own poetic voice, he developed a style known for its economy of words and for its sequence of images joined by conjunctions and forming a montage often complemented with snatches of dialogue, popular proverbs, facile comments, or common wise sayings. In *Abārīq muhashshamah*, this is how he begins his poem "The Village Market":

> The sun, the lean donkeys, the flies
> A soldier's old shoes passing
> From hand to hand, a peasant staring blankly:
> "In the new year
> My hand will certainly be full of money
> And I shall buy those shoes."
> The cry of a cock escaping from a cage . . .

His realism in this early period dwells on the ugly things in life that are so common they have come to dull the senses and are no longer perceived, so that the poet must draw attention to them. The dreams they contain are no longer romantic ones or those of the poet himself, but those of the poor and the wretched hoping for better times, like the peasant of "The Village Market" or the Palestinian refugees in "The Twentieth Shelter", another poem in the same collection.

In his next five or six collections, mostly written when, for political reasons, he was outside Iraq in Moscow and Eastern Europe and later in Egypt, al-Bayāti's voice occasionally becomes strident as he celebrates the rise of Nassir and Arab nationalism, the struggle of workers everywhere, and the national aspirations of the Iraqis and other Arabs. Even his personal poems addressed from exile to his wife and children, who lived away from him in Iraq, are set in the context of the struggle of the oppressed and the hopes of better days for them. And so are other poems addressed to Mao Zedong, Maxim Gorkii, Vladimir Maiakovskii, Nādhzim Ḥikmat, T. S. Eliot, Ernest Hemingway, and others. But imagery becomes a more effective element of his poetry and is enhanced by a more flexible usage of simple language and a better control of it.

With the publication in 1965 of his collection *Sifr al-faqr wa-al-thawrah* (The Book of Poverty and Revolution), al-Bayāti achieves new heights in his development, both in poetic techniques and themes. Not only does his voice soften, but his manner becomes oblique. The title poem of the collection begins thus:

> From the depths I call out to you,
> With my tongue dried up, and
> My butterflies scorched over your mouth.
> Is this snow from the coldness of your nights?
> Is this poverty from the generosity of your hands,
> With its shadow racing mine at the gate of night,
> Crouching hungry and naked in the field,
> Pursuing me to the river?

Although most of al-Bayāti's poems in previous collections have been short, this title poem is long and consists of six parts. In the same collection, there are other long poems, each in several parts, such as "'Aẓāb al-Ḥallāj" (The Suffering of al-Ḥallāj) in six parts, and "Miḥnat Abī al-'Alā'" (The Ordeal of Abū al-'Alā') in 10 parts. In both poems, al-Bayāti adopts a figure from the past to be his mask; without necessarily being historically exact regarding the figure's identity, he uses it as a persona to express his own thoughts and feelings in relation to modern problems.

This becomes a regular feature of his poetry in his later collections. His *Allaẓī ya'ti wa-lā ya'ti* (That Which Comes and Does Not Come) is subtitled "An internal autobiography of Omar Khayyam who lived in all ages waiting for that which comes and does not come." The following collection, *Al-mawt fil-ḥayāh* (Death in Life), is subtitled "The other aspect of Khayyam's contemplations on existence and nonexistence." Other figures appear in later collections such as al-Mutanabbī, Waḍḍāḥ al-Yaman, Ibn 'Arabī, and his beloved 'Ayn al-Shams, as well as Hamlet, Pablo Picasso, Federico García Lorca, and others. Through them al-Bayāti speaks more freely about contemporary matters, criticizes the depravity of the modern world, denounces the evils of Arab society and politics, comments on the human condition in the 20th century, and identifies with the aspirations of the weak and the poor everywhere for a better life. The use of the mask allows him to appear objective in what he writes without sounding ideological or didactic. But his passion for justice, freedom, human dignity, and peace is no less genuine.

In his more recent poetry, the figure of 'Ā'isha, Khayyam's beloved, appears often. She seems to symbolize al-Bayāti's love for all that is good, beautiful, and ideal. 'Ā'isha is not only the poet's beloved but also the eternal female man seeks throughout history. She is the symbol of divine love mystically experienced by human beings as well as the earthy love they feel for country and homeland. She is the embodiment of harmony and perfection that the poet seeks as he continues his life journey. In his collection *Bustān 'Ā'isha* ('Ā'isha's Orchard), al-Bayāti says in his poem "Ṣūra Jānibiyya li-'Ā'isha" ('Ā'isha's Profile):

She appeared in my dreams, I said: A butterfly
Fluttering in the summer of my childhood
Premature
She incarnated all faces
And travelled/sleeping in my blood
A saint fleeing in the middle of the darkness
To embrace the shattered idol

A prolific poet with over 20 collections to his name, al-Bayāti remains one of the most important, avant-garde poetic voices in the Arab world.

—Issa J. Boullata

BECKER, Jurek. German. Born in Lodz, 30 September 1937. Held in Ravensbrück and Sachsenhausen concentration camps during World War II. Educated at a school in East Berlin, diploma 1955; Humboldt University, Berlin, 1957–60; Filmhochschule, Potsdam-Babelsberg. Married Christine Harsch-Niemeyer in 1986 (second marriage); three sons (two by previous marriage). Joined Socialist Unity party, 1957: expelled, 1976; resigned from the Writers' Union, 1976; left East Germany, 1977; writer-in-residence, Oberlin College, Ohio, 1978, Cornell University, Ithaca, New York, 1984, and University of Texas, Austin, 1987; Visiting Professor, University of Essen, one semester, 1978, and University of Augsburg, 1982–83; resident writer, Bergen-Enkheim, 1987. Recipient: Heinrich Mann prize, 1971; Veillon prize (Switzerland), 1971; West Berlin Film Festival Silver Bear award, 1974; City of Bremen prize, 1974; National Prize for Literature, 1975; Grimme prize, 1988; Fallada prize, 1990; Bayerischer prize, 1990; Bundesfilmpreis, 1991. Member, German Academy for Languages and Literature, since 1983, and Academy of Arts, Berlin, 1990. Address: c/o Suhrkamp Verlag, Postfach 101945, 6000 Frankfurt, Germany.

PUBLICATIONS

Fiction

Jakob der Lügner.   Berlin, Aufbau, 1969; as *Jacob the Liar*, New York, Harcourt Brace, 1975.
Irreführung der Behörden.   Rostock, Hinstorff, and Frankfurt, Suhrkamp, 1973.
Der Boxer.   Rostock, Hinstorff, and Frankfurt, Suhrkamp, 1976.
Schlaflose Tage.   Frankfurt, Suhrkamp, 1978; as *Sleepless Days*, New York, Harcourt Brace, and London, Secker and Warburg, 1979.
Nach der ersten Zukunft.   Frankfurt, Suhrkamp, 1980.
Aller Welt Freund. Frankfurt, Suhrkamp, 1982.
Bronsteins Kinder. Frankfurt, Suhrkamp, 1986; as *Bronstein's Children*, San Diego, Harcourt Brace, 1988.
Erzählungen.   Rostock, Hinstorff, 1986.
Die beliebteste Familiengeschichte.   Frankfurt, Insel, 1991.

Plays

Screenplays: *Jakob der Lügner*, 1974; *Neuner*, 1991.

Television Plays: many, including *Liebling Kreuzberg*, 1986.

Other

Warnung vor dem Schriftsteller.   Frankfurt, Frankfurter Vorlesungen, 1990.

*

Critical Studies: "Interview with Jurek Becker" and "Jurek Becker — Writer with a Cause," both by R. A. Zipser, in *Dimension* (Columbia, South Carolina), 11(3), 1978; Becker issue of *Seminar* (Kingston, Ontario), 19(4), 1983; "Where Did the Wife Go? Reading Jurek Becker's 'Parkverbot'" by Sabine Gölz, in *Germanic Review* (New York), Winter 1987; "Radios and Trees: A Note to Jurek Becker's Ghetto Fiction," in *Germanic Notes* (Bemidji, Minnesota), 19(1–2), 1988, and "Jurek Becker's Holocaust Fiction: A Father and Son Survive," in *Critique* (Washington, D.C.), Spring 1989, both by Russell E. Brown; *The Works of Jurek Becker: A Thematic Analysis* by Susan M. Johnson, New York, Lang, 1988.

*   *   *

With the publication of his first novel, *Jakob der Lügner* (*Jacob the Liar*), Jurek Becker's reputation grew rapidly from that of a relatively unknown scriptwriter of East German films to that of a prize-winning novelist of international standing. His works are rooted in his own unusual personal history: his childhood experiences in the Lodz Ghetto and in concentration camps, and his life in the former German Democratic Republic, where he changed from a loyal Socialist Unity Party member to an outspoken critic of hardline trends.

It is true that Becker, in his essay "My Way of Being a Jew," denies any religious or emotional attachment to Judaism (Becker himself is an atheist) and resists the label of "Jewish" writer. However, many of his fictional works testify to a quest for his Jewish identity.

Becker claims to have almost no memory of his childhood in Lodz, admitting that his works set in this period are largely the product of a combination of his own imagination, his father's anecdotes, and historical research. Yet in *Jacob the Liar*, he reconstructs remarkably the lost world of his childhood in a story about an unheroic hero in a Polish ghetto during World War II. The shopkeeper Jakob Heym is able to fill the desperate people around him with hope ("suddenly there is a tomorrow") by inventing the existence of a radio and supplying them with mostly fictitious news about the advance of the Russians. Becker recreates something of the Yiddish oral tradition of storytelling in the narrative technique of the novel and in its style; individual Yiddish words and Old Testament imagery are woven into a language in which he "tried to transfer some of the rules of colloquial Yiddish to High German." As his first-person narrator, Becker employs a 46-year-old survivor of the Holocaust who, in his portrayal of everyday life in the Ghetto, avoids sensational brutality and tells his story in a disarmingly casual, conversational tone. His frequent touches of delicate irony and humour create distance and avoid sentimentality, but also bring home the horror of the historical situation. The form of the novel underlines its central theme of hope as resistance to barbarity by employing techniques associated with Jewish culture in order to affirm its survival of its attempted destruction by the Nazis.

Memory is examined as a means of unlocking the past in the story "The Wall," in which an adult narrator pretends to become a child again and to re-experience events in a ghetto through the eyes of himself as a five-year-old. Although the vividness of his memories makes the past appear to come alive, he admits that they may create a fiction which never existed in reality. The act of narration itself becomes a theme both in this story and in Becker's first novel, where the narrator parallels his hero Jacob by paradoxically employing fiction in order to authenticate reality.

The notion of the past living on in the present is central to the novels *Der Boxer* (The Boxer) and *Bronsteins Kinder* (*Bronstein's Children*), and Becker is probably unique among German authors in relating the problem of coming to terms with Nazism from the perspective of victims rather than perpetrators. *Der Boxer* demonstrates the inability of a survivor of the concentration camps to overcome his psychological scars from the past, despite his attempts to obliterate his Jewish identity. The novel's formal diffuseness, for which it was initially criticised, is quite deliberate: it is written in the form of a loosely constructed protocol of a series of interviews. With its thematic emphasis on the subjective nature of individual experience which resists easy categorisation, both the form and the content of the novel give the lie to the principles of Socialist Realism and its naïve assumption that all outsiders could be integrated into the socialist society of the GDR.

Bronstein's Children is a provocative portrayal of a Jewish victim of Nazism as an oppressor who takes revenge on his former persecutor. Becker originally intended to give the novel the ironic title *How I Became a German* — it is told from the perspective of the victim's son, a citizen of the GDR who was born after the Holocaust. He tries to ignore his Jewish identity but discovers that he is unable to disconnect himself from his father's fate and that he too is an outsider. With its technical control and laconic style, *Bronstein's Children* is Becker's finest achievement after *Jacob the Liar*.

Dishonesty, which was justified in the world of the ghetto as life-sustaining, receives no such defence in Becker's first novel about the GDR. *Irreführung der Behörden* (Misleading the Authorities) exposes the development of a writer's self-deception when he succumbs to the pressure to conform and produce the kind of literature the Party wants. Becker makes this opportunist the first-person narrator of his own story, and, through the use of irony, subjects the narrative voice itself to critical scrutiny by mimicking the popular style of his successful writer-protagonist. Criticism of conditions in the GDR is more radical in *Schlaflose Tage* (Sleepless Days), in which the existentialist hero suddenly experiences a "desire for the future," a desire to overcome his habitual ways of thinking and mechanical behaviour, to break out of his rigidly conformist shell and enter into a dynamic state of constant change through self-reflection. The protagonist's increasing alienation from the society around him is impressively reflected in the narrative technique: although written in the third person, the perspective is limited exclusively to that of the protagonist.

The influence of Ernst Bloch's philosophy of hope is discernible in *Jacob the Liar*, *Sleepless Days*, and also in the title of Becker's collection of short stories, *Nach der ersten Zukunft* (After the Initial Future), with its echo of Bloch's dialectic concept of a "memory of the future." Written at the time of his move to the West, many of the stories spring from Becker's experience of disillusionment with the GDR. His first-person narrators are often submissive subjects of the state who become its victims, threatened with loss of identity. The wide range of formal, stylistic, and thematic approaches that Becker adopts in the stories demonstrates his talent as a storyteller. Frequently, as in his novel *Aller Welt Freund* (Everybody's Friend), Becker leaves the social and political context in which events occur intentionally vague in order to direct his readers' attention to universal issues. Becker is

recognised as one of the outstanding writers to emerge from the GDR, but his works invariably make political statements which transcend narrow GDR concerns.

—David Rock

BEI DAO. Pseudonym for Zhao Zhenkai. Chinese. Born in Beijing, 2 August 1949. Educated at the Fourth Middle School, Beijing. Married to Shao Fei; one daughter. Founder, with Mang Ke, *Today* journal (banned), 1978–79. Since 1989 no longer resident in China. Agent: Jacqueline Korn, David Higham Associates, 5–8 Lower John Street, Golden Square, London W1R 4HA, England.

PUBLICATIONS

Verse

Notes from the City of the Sun, translated by Bonnie S. McDougall. Ithaca, New York, Cornell University East Asia Papers, 1983.
Bei Dao shi xuan [Collected Poems]. Canton, Xiushiji Chubanshe, 1986; as *The August Sleepwalker*, translated by Bonnie S. McDougall, London, Anvil Press Poetry, 1988; revised edition, New York, New Directions, 1990.
Bei Dao shi ji [Poems by Bei Dao]. Taibei, Xindi Chubanshe, 1988.
Old Snow. New York, New Directions, 1991; London, Anvil Press Poetry, 1992.

Fiction

Bodong. Hong Kong, Chinese University Press, 1985; as *Waves*, London, Heinemann, 1987.

Other

Translator, *Bei-ou Xiandai shi xuan* [Contemporary Scandinavian Poetry]. Hunan, Renmin Chubanshe, 1987.

*

Critical Studies: "Zhao Zhenkai's Fiction: A Study in Cultural Alienation," in *Modern Chinese Literature* (San Francisco), 1(1), 1984, and "Bei Dao's Poetry: Revelation and Communication," in *Modern Chinese Literature* (San Francisco), 1(2), 1985, both by Bonnie S. McDougall.

*   *   *

Zhao Zhenkai is best known under his pen name Bei Dao (North Island), one of several pseudonyms he assumed in the 1970s as an underground writer. As a child he received what passed for a good education at the Fourth Middle School in Beijing, but his formal education was interrupted during his last year at school by the outbreak of the Cultural Revolution in 1966. Briefly a Red Guard, and for a short time after that a construction worker, he began writing as an alternative to political action and also to the official literature of his time. By the time the Cultural Revolution ended shortly after Mao

Zedong's death in 1976, Bei Dao was already well known among literary youth as one of the originators of a new kind of poetry and prose.

Dubbed "shadows poetry" (*menglongshi*: literally, dim or obscure poetry) by its critics, the new poetry spoke of dreams and illusions rather than direct praise or criticism of the social reality of its time. But not to address political issues in China during the 1950s, 1960s, and 1970s was itself a political statement, and Bei Dao and his colleagues were closely associated with the democratic movements in China of the late 1970s. To his readers at this time, Bei Dao was the voice of his generation, expressing a fierce but despairing desire for freedom, love, and autonomy of the self. His most famous poem of the 1970s, "The Answer," declared, "I don't believe the sky is blue," and a sense of nihilism runs throughout his work.

Bei Dao's younger readers had no trouble in working out the underlying meaning of lines like the one above, but when "shadows poetry" made the transition from "underground" to "unofficial" to "official" publications in the late 1970s and early 1980s, hostile critics representing the establishment complained that it was impossible to understand. Bei Dao and his fellow poets rejected the public voice of orthodox Chinese poetry of the 1950–70s, drawing on a sometimes private imagery usually expressed in brief, tightly constructed lines depicting natural phenomena and the urban furniture of their daily lives. In these early poems, Bei Dao rarely resorts to literary allusions, though the structure and use of imagery in his poetry clearly have precedents in classical Chinese and modernist Western verse. One favourite device, for instance, is to refer to what is not present, or what does not happen, by pointing out what is present or what does happen, as in the famous lines, "Life: The sun rises too," where the sun refers to Mao Zedong (known during the Cultural Revolution as "the red sun in our hearts"); Bei Dao's lines imply that there is more to life than the sun alone.

Employing devices from classical Chinese poetic grammar and Western free verse patterns, Bei Dao also experimented with creating a new prosody in an attempt to resolve the age-old problem of Chinese poetry: the constantly renewed gulf between spoken and written Chinese due to the nature of the Chinese written script and its peculiar grammar. To some older readers, Bei Dao's poetic syntax and vocabulary were irritatingly Westernised; to a younger generation of poets, his style came to sound too stiff and formal. Nevertheless, Bei Dao's verse remains an outstanding achievement in the history of modern Chinese poetry.

Bei Dao's fiction is less celebrated, although the novella *Bodong* (*Waves*), written and circulated underground during the Cultural Revolution, is no less innovatory than his poetry. Using the devices of multiple narrators and interior monologue, it successfully breaks away from the traditionally univocal and closed didacticism of both serious and entertainment fiction in China. *Waves* was followed by five shorter pieces written between 1980 and 1985, on contemporary themes such as the distortion to family and marriage relationships caused by official campaigns and policies, the rigidly hierarchical nature of class distinctions in a so-called socialist China, corruption of various kinds in the official literary scene, and the sinister brutality of the Chinese police state.

During the 1980s, Bei Dao was able to publish his poetry openly, but despite the notable relaxation of political controls during most of this period (with the equally notable exception of the campaigns against spiritual pollution in 1983–84 and against bourgeois liberalism in 1986–87), his poetry became more, not less, pessimistic. At the same time, his language became harsher, and his imagery featured illness, old age,

madness, and the more obtrusive streetscapes of urban China. This culminated in the nightmarish "Daydream" (1986), a long sequence of poems with a repeated motif of unfulfilled expectations.

To outward appearances, Bei Dao's life may have seemed quite fulfilled during the second part of the 1980s. He married, fathered a child, was accepted into the official Chinese Writers' Association, and frequently travelled abroad. Nevertheless he remained stubbornly and unfashionably conscious of the underlying political tensions in China, and towards the end of 1988 expressed his forebodings: "I watch the process of apples spoiling." His support for imprisoned democratic activist Wei Jingshen in early 1989 was one of the events that sparked the student protests of the spring, and his lines from the 1970s, "I will not kneel on the ground,/Allowing the executioners to look tall,/The better to obstruct the wind of freedom" appeared on banners in Tiananmen Square.

Bei Dao was in Berlin at the time of the Tiananmen massacre in June 1989. Since then he has travelled constantly, stopping for brief periods in Oslo, Stockholm, Århus, and most recently Leiden, in the shelter of Chinese studies departments in Western universities. His poems express grief, outrage, and personal anguish at his separation from family and home. Although written in his customary abstract and abbreviated style, they have proved remarkably effective in poetry readings both in the original and in translation. Bei Dao's genius as a poet lies primarily in his striking and universally comprehensible imagery, so that despite the usual caveat about the loss of effect in translation, translations of his poems into over a dozen languages have been warmly received. Bei Dao is thus one of the very few Chinese writers of this century to gain a truly international audience.

—Bonnie S. McDougall

BELLI, Gioconda. Nicaraguan. Born in 1948. Educated in Europe and the United States. Married at age 18 (divorced); three children. Member, Sandinista Front for National Liberation (FSLN); exiled to Costa Rica in 1975; worked for Foreign Affairs Commission, FSLN, Costa Rica; helped build European support for Sandinistas, 1975–79; returned to Nicaragua, 1979; has worked for *Barricada* newspaper, Ministry of Planning, Association of Nicaraguan Women, and national broadcasting companies. Recipient: Casa de las Américas prize, 1978. Address: c/o Curbstone Press, 321 Jackson Street, Willimantic, Connecticut 06226, U.S.A.

PUBLICATIONS

Verse

Sobre la grama.   Managua, n.p., 1974.
Línea de fuego.   Havana, Casa de las Américas, 1978.
Truenos y arco iris.   Managua, Nueva Nicaragua, 1982.
Amor insurrecto.   Managua, Nueva Nicaragua, 1984.
De la costilla de Eva.   Managua, Nueva Nicaragua, 1987; as *From Eve's Rib*, translated by Steven F. White, Willimantic, Connecticut, Curbstone Press, 1989.
Poesía reunida.   Mexico, Diana, 1989.
Nicaragua Under Fire.   Warwick, Greville, 1989.

Fiction

La mujer habitada.   Managua, Vanguardia, 1988.

Other

Nicaragua in Reconstruction and at War.   Minneapolis, MEP, 1985.

*

Critical Studies: "Two Poets of the Sandinista Struggle" by Electra Arenal, in *Feminist Studies* (College, Park, Maryland), 7(1), 1982; "Gioconda Belli: The Erotic Politics of the Great Mother" by Kathleen March, in *Monographic Review/Revista Monográfica* (Odessa, Texas), 6, 1990; "A Place for Eve in the Revolution: Giaconda Belli [sic] and Rosario Murillo" by Patricia Murray, in *Knives and Angels: Women Writers in Latin America,* edited by Susan Bassnett, London, Zed, 1990; "Giaconda Belli [sic], *La mujer habitada*" by W. Nick Hill, in *World Literature Today* (Norman, Oklahoma), 65(1), 1991.

*   *   *

With a single novel and several books of poetry to her credit, Gioconda Belli has emerged as a major figure in contemporary Central American literature. Her work engages two key issues of our time — revolutionary politics and women's subjectivity — and as a result has caught the attention of both popular audiences and literary critics.

It is easy to identify the source of Belli's popular appeal. Her writing is accessible, direct, and often erotic. It speaks to a common experience and a common cause: the Sandinista struggle told in terms of human relationships. Belli writes as a woman claiming her own place in the revolution and struggling with the realigning of gender arrangements. Her poetry has been embraced by readers who delight in a woman's claim to her own sexuality, but it has been criticized on that same account by critics who note that the terms of her claim seem bound by conventional heterosexual expectations. In many of Belli's poems the speaker's experience of revolutionary struggle is mediated by her lover.

Belli's early poetry is characterized by its energy and vitality. *Sobre la grama* (On the Grama Grass) contains poems that celebrate the pure pleasure the speaker takes in her body, her sexuality, and her physical presence in the world. The youthful exuberance of these poems reconfigures the traditional hoary identification of women with nature, infusing both the speaker and the landscape with an energy that challenges the conventional passivity of "woman" and "nature." Later poems in the collection, dealing with sex, menstruation, pregnancy, childbirth, and lactation, are early attempts to make poetry out of that which has been erased and silenced. Rather than rewritings of old myths, they represent a first attempt to write what until now has been left unspoken.

Línea de fuego (Line of Fire) was written during the height of the Sandinista revolution, in which Belli participated as a forced exile. She writes of Nicaragua as beloved and the beloved as revolutionary in language that is unusually passionate and direct, though it turns to metaphor and euphemism to describe sex organs and sexual intercourse. Belli's representation of heterosexual desire tends to be conventional, but not entirely so. Even when the speaker seems to subordinate herself to the lover, as in "Yo, la que te quiere" (I, the One Who Loves You), the speaker asserts her own power and subjectivity with her insistence on the emphatic "yo," a subject pronoun that in Spanish need not be enunciated but here is,

over and over. That forceful "I" is, furthermore, figured as the most powerful of nature's forces — electrical storm, fire, volcano — in control of her own desire and her lover's.

Truenos y arco iris (Thunder and Rainbow) contains poems of the consolidation of a revolution whose sacrifices are personally and deeply felt. The collection is infused with a sense of loss, and of those poems not written in the past, many are written in a present that is also immersed in reconstruction and recall. Where the poems of *Sobre la grama* luxuriated in the subject's *being* as a natural fact, poems such as "Nueva construcción del presente" (New Construction of the Present) struggle with her *becoming* within the terms of a deliberately and painstakingly elaborated social pact. The explosive erotic pleasure of the earlier collections is first domesticated ("Como gata boca arriba" [Like a Cat on Its Back]) and later settles into a sense of loss, anger, and disillusionment ("Eva advierte sobre manzanas" [Eve Warns About Apples]).

De la costilla de Eva (*From Eve's Rib*) continues the double themes of sexuality and revolution in poems denser and richer than those of the earlier collections. Here Belli begins to imagine an egalitarian partnership with the lover, one that goes beyond her speaker's assertion of sexual desire and pleasure. One brave poem exhorts the new man, forged in the crucible of revolution, to respect women's independence and individuality and to share responsibility for tasks traditionally assigned to women. But in others the speaker still awaits, or mourns, her warrior lover.

In her novel *La mujer habitada* (The Inhabited Woman), Belli invests the relationship between gender, sex, and revolution with greater complexity than in any of her poems. The novel's protagonist Lavinia is caught up in conflicting forces, some of which she can name and others of which she is unaware, that enable her to act toward a reshaping of self and nation. Although she perceives the need for profound social, economic, political, and interpersonal change and can even find a way to help make those changes, Lavinia is not given access to the history that shapes her own participation in the struggle. Inhabited by the spirit of an indigenous woman who fought against the invading Spanish conquistadors but who has been forgotten by the official histories of the country (even in its oppositional form history appears to contain only male actors), Lavinia is largely impelled to act by a force she experiences only as the trace of subconscious activity — dreams, automatic drawing, irrational impulse. Lavinia is likewise captive to existing constructions of sex. She desires her lover not simply because he is intelligent, creative, and committed to the revolution, but because like any hero of romance he is powerful, dominant, and a little dangerous. Although she cannot determine through will who the object of her sexual desire is to be, she can and does actively direct the nature of their relationship, first to claim her own sexual pleasure and later to resist her lover's desire to relegate her to conventional femininity.

One of Belli's achievements in *La mujer habitada* is to chart the complexity of the interplay among power relations between men and women, the rich and the poor, the government and the people, in a country where these dichotomies seem beyond reconciliation. Belli's work, taken whole, is a compelling testament to the transitional period in Nicaraguan history and in women's consciousness. It is a period that wants to call itself post-revolutionary and post-feminist, but Belli's writing shows that it is neither, yet.

—Amy Kaminsky

BEN JELLOUN, Tahar. Moroccan. Born in Fès, 21 December 1944. Educated at the Collège Ibn Al Khatib et Lycée Regnault, Tangier; University of Mohammed V, Rabat, licencié et certificat d'aptitude in teaching of philosophy; doctorate in social psychiatry. Professor of philosophy, Tétouan and Casablanca, 1968–71; Professor of sociology, University of Paris X, Nanterre, 1971–72; Professor of social psychiatry, l'École Pratique des Hautes Études, Paris, 1972–75. Contributor to *Le Monde* newspaper, Paris, since 1973; member of l'Académie Mallarmé, 1976, and the Conseil Supérieur de la Langue Française, since 1989. Recipient: Franco-Arab prize, 1976; Association of French Booksellers prize, 1978; Goncourt prize, 1987; Community of Mediterranean Universities prize. Chevalier de la Légion d'Honneur, and de l'Ordre des Arts et des Lettres. Lives in Paris. Address: c/o Éditions Seuil, 27 rue Jacob, 75261 Paris Cedex 06, France.

PUBLICATIONS

Fiction

Harrouda.   Paris, Denoël, 1973.
La Réclusion solitaire.   Paris, Denoël, 1976; as *Solitaire*, London, Quartet, 1988.
Moha le fou, Moha le sage.   Paris, Seuil, 1978.
La Prière de l'absent.   Paris, Seuil, 1981.
L'Enfant du sable.   Paris, Seuil, 1983; as *The Sandchild*, San Diego, Harcourt Brace, 1987; London, Quartet, 1988.
La Nuit sacrée.   Paris, Seuil, 1987; as *The Sacred Night*, San Diego, Harcourt Brace, and London, Quartet, 1989.
Jour de silence à Tanger.   Paris, Seuil, 1990; as *Silent Day in Tangier*, San Diego, Harcourt Brace, and London, Quartet, 1991.
Les Yeux baissés.   Paris, Seuil, 1991.

Plays

Chronique d'une solitude (produced Avignon, 1976).
La Fiancée de l'eau; Entretien avec Monsieur Saïd Hammadi, ouvrier algérien.   Arles, Actes Sud/Théâtre Populaire de Lorraine, 1984.

Verse

Hommes sous linceul de silence.   Casablanca, Atlantes, 1971.
Cicatrices du soleil.   Paris, Maspero, 1972.
Le Discours du chameau.   Paris, Maspero, 1974.
Les Amandiers sont morts de leurs blessures. Paris, Maspero, 1976.
A l'Insu du souvenir.   Paris, Maspero, 1980.

Other

La Plus Haute des solitudes: misère sexuelle d'émigrés nord-africains.   Paris, Seuil, 1977.
Haut Atlas: l'exil de pierres, photographs by Philippe Lafond. Paris, Chêne/Hachette, 1982.
L'Écrivain public: récit.   Paris, Seuil, 1983.
Hospitalité française: racisme et immigration maghrébine. Paris, Seuil, 1984.
Marseille: comme un matin d'insomnie, photographs by Thierry Ibert.   St. Maximin, Le Temps Parallèle, 1986.

Editor, *La Mémoire future: Anthologie de la nouvelle poésie du Maroc.*   Paris, Maspero, 1976.

Editor and translator, *Le Pain nu: récit autobiographique*, by Mohamed Choukri.   Paris, Maspero, 1980.

*

Critical Study: "Tahar Ben Jelloun and the Poetry of Refusal" by Janis L. Pallister, in *Revue Celfan/Celfan Review* (Philadelphia), May 1983.

* * *

An expatriate Moroccan who has spent much of his adult life in Paris, Tahar Ben Jelloun writes in French, but the landscape of his imagination is North African, and the lyrical cadences of his prose are reminiscent of Arabic poetry. A psychiatrist by training, he has also researched mental disorders among North African migrants in France, and his mature work reflects his multiple insights; he frequently deals with displacement and exile, conflict between genders and cultures, the oppressive nature of family or clan, the on-going problem of racial discrimination. However, he deftly avoids documentary realism in his fiction: his writings are equally preoccupied with language and its allusions and metaphors, the passing of time, and the nature of memory. The early novella *La Réclusion solitaire* (*Solitaire*) is a good, if not always successful, attempt to reconcile his poetic and political concerns. Focussing upon a single figure, an isolated migrant worker in France, the novella employs fragmented narrative and a subjective, erotic lyricism to convey the protagonist's shifting states of mind, his homesickness, and his violent sexual loneliness. The novel's dense, allusive style is often in marked contrast to the stark realism of its theme.

Ben Jelloun's two interlocking narratives of the fantastic, *L'Enfant du sable* (*The Sandchild*) and the prize-winning *La Nuit sacrée* (*The Sacred Night*), move deeply into the enchanted hinterlands of Arab folklore and Latin American-inspired magic realism. Written at the peak of the trend for the fantastic narratives ably produced by such renowned practitioners as Salman Rushdie and Nuruddin Farah, *The Sandchild* is nevertheless an entirely new departure in style and technique in Francophone Arab literature, employing the voices of no fewer than six storytellers, telling and retelling the story of the legendary Zahra, who was born a woman and brought up as a man by her phallocentric father. Thus, the structure and symbols of the novel reflect the oral culture of its context and also borrow from traditional story cycles such as *The Arabian Nights*. Though it is concerned with the construction of gender, the nature of patriarchy, and the heritage of a culture that exalts the sensual but secludes its women, *The Sandchild* is above all an entrancing tale interwoven with the modish conceits of metafiction. *The Sacred Night* is formally and thematically a more sober performance; Zahra herself tells her story in her own voice, correcting the varying versions of her life and fate recounted in the earlier volume. The questions of sexuality and gender raised in *The Sandchild* are here foregrounded, as is the metaphysical dimension of the story, which draws equally upon the philosophical games of Jorge Luis Borges (a recurring presence in both novels) and the Sufi Muslim spiritual tradition.

In the 1990s, Ben Jelloun has made a salutary shift from the fabulous to a highly personal form of realism. In *Jour de silence à Tanger* (*Silent Day in Tangier*), the carnivalesque and timeless backdrop of earlier fictions is replaced by the chaotic setting of modern Moroccan city life, and the central figure is an old seller of jellabas, bitter and bound to the past. Closer in style and substance to the work of Samuel Beckett or Peter Handke (*q.v.*) than to the exuberance of Gabriel García

Márquez (*q.v.*) or Rushdie , the novel is highly compressed in structure, its lyricism all the more effective for its restraint; Ben Jelloun never allows his rich imagery to overwhelm the text, as he has occasionally been guilty of doing in earlier works. Narrated in the third person, the novel moves between a modified third-person stream of consciousness, extended first-person interior monologue, snatches of dialogue real or imagined, and the occasional omniscient authorial comment. The city is falling apart, social and religious values are declining, his old friends are dying, his house decaying, and history has failed to fulfill its promises: such is the old man's world. Only the idealised past makes sense.

Ben Jelloun's realism remains that of the impressionist rather than of the news photographer, and is well contained within the subjectivity of a mind given to wandering and digressions. His following work, however, is even more deeply anchored in the real: *Les Yeaux baissés* (Eyes Lowered) adopts the voice and person of a young Moroccan woman from a Berber village, telling the story of her painful childhood, her separation from her father who has migrated to France, and her dream of discovering a treasure hidden in a neighbouring mountain. Taken to France by her father, she faces culture shock but also the freedom to read, encounters racism but also love and the freedom to choose her own sexual partners. The novel evokes the dilemma of the immigrant unable to belong entirely to the society of adoption and aware of the impossibility of returning to severed roots: the solution lies in a third place, a metaphor for the expatriate's imagination. Three worlds constantly co-exist in Ben Jelloun's fictional universe: the past and the present, the abandoned homeland and the inhospitable port of arrival, the stony pavement beneath torn shoes and the distant fire-streaked skies of the imagination.

—Aamer Hussein

BERGE, H(ans) C(ornelis) ten. Dutch. Born Alkmaar, 24 December 1938. Teacher, Academy of Dramatic Art, Amsterdam, 1968–70, and Art Academy, Arnhem, 1970–90; visiting scholar, National Museum of Man, Ottawa, Ontario, 1974–75; Visiting Professor, University of Texas, Austin, 1981. Founder and editor, *Raster* [Grid] literary journal. Recipient: Society of Dutch Literature prize, 1968; City of Amsterdam prize, 1971; Jan Campert Foundation prize, 1972; Multatuli prize, 1987. Agent: Meulenhoff Nederland, P.O. Box 100, 1000 AC Amsterdam, The Netherlands.

PUBLICATIONS

Verse

Zwartkruis. Amsterdam, Polak & Van Gennep, 1966.
Personages [Characters]. Amsterdam, Polak & Van Gennep, 1966.
Gedichten 1964–1967 [Poems 1964–1967]. Amsterdam, Athenaeum, 1969.
De witte sjamaan [The White Shaman]. Amsterdam, Bezige Bij, 1973.
Va-banque. Amsterdam, Bezige Bij, 1977.
Nieuwe Gedichten [New Poems]. Amsterdam, Bezige Bij, 1981.

Tramontane: vijf triptieken en een liefdesverklaring [Tramontana: Five Triptychs and a Declaration of Love]. Baarn, Atalanta, 1983.
Texaanse elegieën [Texan Elegies]. Amsterdam, Bezige Bij, 1983.
Acht liederen van angst en vertwijfeling [Eight Songs of Anguish and Despair]. Baarn, Atalanta, 1987; as *Liederen van angst en vertwijfeling*, Amsterdam, Meulenhoff, 1988.
We dromen weg in blauw en grijs: een drieluik voor M.B. [We Dream Away in Blue and Grey]. Oosterhesselen, De Klencke, 1991.
The White Shaman: Selected Poems. London, Forest, 1991.
Overgangsriten [Rites of Passage]. Amsterdam, Meulenhoff, 1992.

Fiction

Canaletto, en andere verhalen [Canaletto, and Other Stories]. Amsterdam, Athenaeum, 1969.
Een geval van verbeelding [A Question of Imagination]. Amsterdam, Bezige Bij, 1970.
Het meisje met de korte vlechten [The Girl with the Short Braids]. Amsterdam, Bezige Bij, 1977.
Der beren van Churchill [Churchill's Bears]. Amsterdam, Bezige Bij, 1978.
Matglas [Frosted Glass]. Amsterdam, Athenaeum, 1981.
Zelfportret met witte muts [Self-Portrait with White Cap]. Amsterdam, Meulenhoff, 1985.
Het geheim van en opgewekt humeur [The Secret of a Cheerful Mood]. Amsterdam, Meulenhoff, 1986.
Een Italiaan in Zutphen [An Italian in Zutphen]. Amsterdam, Meulenhoff, 1991.

Other

Een schrijver als grenskozak: F. C. Terborgh over zichself en zijn werk [A Writer as Border Cossack: F. C. Terborgh on Himself and His Work] (interview). Amsterdam, Bezige Bij, 1977.
Levenstekens en doodssinjalen [Signs of Life and Signals of Death]. Amsterdam, Bezige Bij, 1980.
De Mannenschrik: over het motief van de verslindende vrouw in literatuur en mythe [On Devouring Women in Literature and Mythology]. Zutphen, ten Bosch, 1984.
De verdediging van de poëzie, en andere essays [The Defence of Poetry and Other Essays]. Leiden , Nijhoff, 1988.
Zutphen, illustrated by Elizabeth de Vaal. Arnhem, Stichting Beeldende Kunst Gelderland, 1988.

Editor and Translator, *15 Cantos*, by Ezra Pound. Amsterdam, Bezige Bij, 1970.
Editor and Translator, *Poëzie van de Azteken* [Poetry of the Aztecs]. Amsterdam, Bezige Bij, 1972.
Editor, *Mythen en fabels van noordelijke volken* [Myths and Fables of Northern Peoples]. Amsterdam, Bezige Bij, 3 vols., 1974–79; revised and enlarged edition, Amsterdam, Meulenhoff, 3 vols., 1987.

Translator, *De dood is de jager: Indiaanse mythen van Noordwestr-Amerika* [Death Is the Hunter: Indian Myths from Northwest America]. Amsterdam, Bezige Bij, 1974.
Translator, *Laat op aarde* [Late on Earth], by Gunnar Ekelöf. Amsterdam, n.p., 1975.
Translator, *In het geheime huis en andere gedichten* [In the Secret House and Other Poems], by Christopher Middleton. Amsterdam, Marsyas, 1983.

Translator, *De danseres van Izu* [The Dancer from Izu], by Kawabata Yasunari.   Zutphen, ten Bosch, 1983.

Translator, *Een lakse bries*, by Mark Strand.   Amsterdam, Marsyas, 1983.

Translator, with Marguérite Törnqvist, *De Byzantijnse trilogie* [The Byzantine Trilogy], by Gunnar Ekelöf.   Amsterdam, Meulenhoff, 1985.

Translator, *Canto XLIX*, by Ezra Pound.   Wijhe, Elferink, 1985.

Translator, *Kerkhof in de sneeuw* [Graveyard in the Snow], by Xavier Villaurrutia y González.   Wijhe, Elferink, 1986.

Translator, *Mijn naam is Schurft, voorafgegaan door Het verhaal van Asdiwál* [My Name Is Scurvy, Two Mythical Tales].   Amsterdam, Meulenhoff, 1990.

*

Bibliography: published by The Hague, Dutch Literary Museum and Documentation Centre.

Critical Study: "Anonymous Restless Forms: The Dutch Writer H. C. ten Berge" by Wam de Moor, in *Books Abroad* (Norman, Oklahoma), 57, 1973.

H. C. ten Berge comments:

Where do I stand? Between tradition and experiment. It is my aim to accept novelties and to further integrate them, in more trusted forms and patterns, into what already exists. Radical, but not reckless. Resolute, but with respect for old, even archaic forms.

Forms that have been exhausted and burnt out become truly distant and hidden in the silent corners of the mind, where if they so wish they can later sprout in the ground that calls for them.

*   *   *

H. C. ten Berge is an important figure on the contemporary Dutch literary scene. His poetry is precise, well-crafted, and masterful in its deployment of the unexpected, gripping image. His narrative prose shows the same characteristics. His criticism is of high intellectual and scholarly quality, and his work as founder and editor of the Dutch literary journal *Raster* has contributed to changing the climate for the reception of his kind of poetry in the Dutch language area forever.

Ten Berge has much in common with the American poet Ezra Pound. Pound combined the actual writing of poetry with theoretical pronouncements on the art of writing it, as does ten Berge. Pound was interested in different cultures, often relatively unknown to the Western reader of his time, as is ten Berge. Ten Berge's favorite non-Western culture is that of the Eskimos; he has written a book about his experience of living with them, and he constantly refers to their literature and culture in his own poetry and prose. The Eskimos have, over the years, become the main source of material for the multicultural, multidimensional montages that constitute most of ten Berge's poems.

Ten Berge makes use of montage for a number of reasons. Combining one's own text with fragments taken from other texts allows the author to keep his distance from his creation. The montage creates an "alienation effect" of sorts. In ten Berge's own words, "a quotation is also a mask." He needs distance because he does not believe emotion should play a large part in the creation of poetry, at least not in the form of sentiment. Rather, emotion should be crystallized into form

through the process of writing. The "soft" emotion that may act as stimulus, triggering the process of artistic creation, needs to be turned into "hard" emotion.

Ten Berge's favorite Pound quotation is: "There is no intelligence without emotion." This kind of intelligence, though, is very much akin to the "concrete intelligence" ten Berge claims to find in Eskimo literature, which is an oral literature. The written literatures of Europe have lost this kind of intelligence, but some strands of North American poetry have preserved it to a greater extent. Ten Berge believes that Western civilization is very much in need of this kind of intelligence, which he considers the only antidote to the growing cynicism and arrogance with which the West treats not only other cultures, but also those who participate in its own culture. Arrogance and cynicism thrive in a civilization in which poetry is no longer an integral and necessary component of culture as a whole.

To achieve this integration is ten Berge's mission as a poet, and he sees that mission as all the more urgent and important in the medium of the Dutch language precisely because that language is not spoken by many people, and its very existence may be threatened in the future.

If ten Berge — or any other poet, for that matter — is to take that mission seriously, he or she will also have to live it, to a great extent. Poetry is not an activity one can slip into and out of, almost at will. Rather poetry has to become a way of life, in which the artistic or spiritual meets the material, the physical. The poet as maker, language as his tool, and reality as his material must form the unity that is also found in the art — not least the Eskimo art — that the West has called primitive for so long.

From this perspective reality, the poet's material, is filtered through the poet's own creativity. Ten Berge does not describe; he juxtaposes. He does not participate; he withdraws. This stance also explains the predominance of masks and rituals in his poetry. The ritual is an activity which allows the observer to don a mask and to withdraw behind it, while registering what he sees and projecting it onto other times and other places. In this way ten Berge's multicultural collages achieve a mythical dimension. They no longer belong only to one time and one place; rather, the juxtaposition of historical periods and geographical locations allows them to belong to all times and all places. This mythical dimension, not infrequently expressed through the use of animals as symbols, potentially heightens the didactic value of ten Berge's work.

Ten Berge himself would deny that he is actively trying to "teach." In the Poundian vein, he "affirms." In fact, he holds that all creation has to be of necessity anarchic, if it is not to become ossified soon after it has been created. Poetry both crystallizes emotion into form, and then proceeds to "free what is caught in form"; it consists of a continuous dialectic of creation and re-creation.

Yet what has often been perceived as the didactic tendency in his work has also, not infrequently, militated against a wide and positive reception of that work in his homeland. Dutch critics often find his poetry "scholarly," an epithet that denotes respect rather than enthusiasm, the more so since this kind of "scholarly" poetry, written in the Eliot-Pound vein of Anglo-American high modernism, has been rather conspicuously absent from Dutch poetry before ten Berge.

—André Lefevere

BERGMAN, (Ernst) Ingmar. Swedish. Born in Uppsala, 14 July 1918. Educated at Palmgrens School, Östermalm, 1934–37; University of Stockholm, 1938–40. Served in the Swedish military, 1938. Married 1) Else Fisher in 1943 (divorced 1945), one daughter; 2) Ellen Lundström in 1945 (divorced 1950), two sons and three daughters; 3) Gun Hagberg (i.e. Gun Grut) in 1951, one son; 4) Käbi Laretei in 1959 (separated 1965), one son; 5) Ingrid von Rosen in 1971; also one daughter by the actress Liv Ullmann. Production assistant, Stockholm Opera, from 1939; scriptwriter, 1943, and artistic adviser, 1961, Svensk Filmindustri; director, Helsingborg City Theatre, 1944–46, Gothenburg City Theatre, 1946–49, and Malmö City Theatre, 1952–58; director, 1959–63, and head, 1963–66, Royal Dramatic Theatre, Stockholm; settled on island of Faro, 1966; founder, Cinematograph production company, 1968, and Personafilm production company, 1977; moved to Munich because of charges of tax evasion in Sweden, 1976–82; director, Munich Residenzteater, 1977–82. Recipient: Cannes Festival Special Jury prize, 1956, 1957; Berlin Festival Golden Bear, 1958; Swedish Film Academy Gold Medal, 1958, 1977; Academy award, 1961, 1962, 1984; Erasmus prize (Netherlands), 1965; Irving Thalberg memorial award, 1971; Goethe prize, 1976; Meadows award, 1981. Honorary Ph.D., 1975, and Honorary Professor, 1985, Stockholm University. Address: c/o Norstedts Förlag, Box 2052, 103 12 Stockholm, Sweden.

PUBLICATIONS

Plays

Scapin, Pimpel, and Kasper (also director; produced Helsingborg, 1945).
Jack hos skådespelarna [Jack at the Actors']. Stockholm, Bonnier, 1946.
Dagen slutar tidigt [The Day Ends Early] (also director; produced Gothenburg, 1947). Included in *Moraliteter*, 1948.
Mig till skräck [To My Terror] (also director; produced Gothenburg, 1947). Included in *Moraliteter*, 1948.
Dra en nit [Draw Blank] (also director; produced Helsingborg, 1948).
Moraliteter: tre pjäser (includes *Rakel och biografvakt-mästaren*; *Dagen slutar tidigt*; *Mig till skräck*) [Moralities: Three Plays: Rakel and the Cinema Caretaker; The Day Ends Early; To My Terror]. Stockholm, Bonnier, 1948.
Mordet i Barjärna [The Murder in Barjärna] (also director; produced Malmö, 1952).
Trämålning [Painting on Wood] (also director; produced Malmö, 1955). Stockholm, Bonnier, 1954.
Sommarnattens leende (screenplay). As *Smiles of a Summer Night*, in *Four Screen Plays of Ingmar Bergman*, 1960.
Det sjunde inseglet (screenplay). As *The Seventh Seal*, in *Four Screen Plays of Ingmar Bergman*, 1960.
Smultronstället (screenplay). As *Wild Strawberries*, in *Four Screen Plays of Ingmar Bergman*, 1960.
Ansiktet (screenplay). As *The Magician*, in *Four Screen Plays of Ingmar Bergman*, 1960.
Four Screen Plays of Ingmar Bergman (includes *Smiles of a Summer Night*; *The Seventh Seal*; *Wild Strawberries*; *The Magician*). New York, Simon and Schuster, and London, Secker and Warburg, 1960.
En filmtrilogi (includes *Såsom i en spegel*; *Nattvardsgästerna*; *Tystnaden*). Stockholm, Norstedt, 1963; as *A Film Trilogy* (includes *Through a Glass Darkly*; *Winter Light*; *The Silence*), New York, Orion Press, and London, Calder and

Boyars, 1967; as *Three Films*, New York, Grove Press, 1970.
Persona (screenplay). Stockholm, Norstedt, 1966; in English, with *Shame*, New York, Grossman, and London, Calder and Boyars, 1972.
Skammen (screenplay). As *Shame*, with *Persona*, New York, Grossman, and London, Calder and Boyars, 1972.
Riten; Reservatet; Beröringen; Viskningar och rop [The Ritual; The Reservation; The Touch; Cries and Whispers] (screenplays). Stockholm, PAN/Norstedt, 1973.
Scener ur ett äktenskap (screenplay; stage version produced Munich, 1981). Stockholm, Norstedt, 1973; as *Scenes from a Marriage* (produced London, 1990), New York, Pantheon, and London, Calder and Boyars, 1974.
Ansikte mot ansikte (screenplay). Stockholm, PAN/Norstedt, 1973; as *Face to Face*, New York, Pantheon, and London, Calder and Boyars, 1976.
A Dream Play, adaptation of the play by August Strindberg. London, Secker and Warburg, 1973.
Filmberättelser [Film Stories]. Stockholm, PAN/Norstedt, 3 vols., 1973.
Vargtimmen (screenplay). As *Hour of the Wolf*, in *Four Stories of Ingmar Bergman*, 1976.
En pasion (screenplay). As *The Passion of Anna*, in *Four Stories of Ingmar Bergman*, 1976.
Beröringen (screenplay). As *The Touch*, in *Four Stories of Ingmar Bergman*, 1976.
Viskningar och rop (screenplay). As *Cries and Whispers*, in *Four Stories of Ingmar Bergman*, 1976.
Four Stories of Ingmar Bergman (screenplays; includes *Hour of the Wolf*; *The Passion of Anna*; *The Touch*; *Cries and Whispers*). New York, Anchor Press, 1976; London, Calder and Boyars, 1977.
Ormens ägg (screenplay). Stockholm, PAN/Norstedt, 1977; as *The Serpent's Egg*, New York, Pantheon, 1977; London, Calder and Boyars, 1978.
Höstsonaten (screenplay). Stockholm, PAN/Norstedt, 1978; as *Autumn Sonata*, New York, Pantheon, 1978.
Ur marionetternas liv (screenplay). Stockholm, PAN/Norstedt, 1980; as *From the Life of the Marionettes*, New York, Pantheon, 1980.
Fanny och Alexander (screenplay). Stockholm, Norstedt, 1982; as *Fanny and Alexander*, New York, Pantheon, 1982; London, Penguin, 1989.
The Marriage Scenarios (screenplays; includes *Scenes from a Marriage*; *Face to Face*; *Autumn Sonata*). New York, Pantheon, 1983; London, Aurum Press, 1989.
A Project for the Theatre (includes *Nora*, adaptation of *A Doll's House* by Henrik Ibsen; *Julie*, adaptation of *Miss Julie* by August Strindberg; *Scenes from a Marriage*), edited by Frederick J. Marker and Lise-Lone Marker. New York, Ungar, 1983.

Screenplays (also director): *Kris* (*Crisis*), 1946; *Det regnar på vår kärlek* (*It Rains on Our Love* or *The Man with an Umbrella*), 1946; *Skepp till Indialand* (*A Ship Bound for India* or *The Land of Desire*), 1947; *Fängelse* (*Prison* or *The Devil's Wanton*), 1949; *Till glädje* (*To Joy*), 1950; *Sommarlek* (*Summer Interlude* or *Illicit Interlude*), 1951; *Kvinnors väntan* (*Secrets of Women* or *Waiting Women*), 1952; *Sommaren med Monika* (*Monika* or *Summer with Monika*), 1953; *Gycklarnas afton* (*The Naked Night* or *Sawdust and Tinsel*), 1953; *En lektion i kärlek* (*A Lesson in Love*), 1954; *Kvinnodröm* (*Dreams* or *Journey into Autumn*), 1955; *Sommarnattens leende* (*Smiles of a Summer Night*), 1955; *Det sjunde inseglet* (*The Seventh Seal*), 1957; *Smultronstället* (*Wild Strawberries*), 1957; *Nära livet* (*Brink of Life* or *So Close to Life*), 1958;

Ansiktet (*The Magician* or *The Face*), 1958; *Djävulens öga* (*The Devil's Eye*), 1960; *Jungfrukäkken* (*The Virgin Spring*), 1960; *Såsom i en spegel* (*Through a Glass Darkly*), 1961; *Nattvardsgästerna* (*Winter Light*), 1963; *Tystnaden* (*The Silence*), 1963; *För att inte tala om alla dessa kvinnor* (*All These Women* or *Now About These Women*), as Buntel Eriksson, with Erland Josephson, 1964; *Persona*, 1966; *Vargtimmen* (*Hour of the Wolf*), 1968; *Skammen* (*Shame*), 1968; *Riten* (*The Ritual* or *The Rite*), 1969; *En passion* (*The Passion of Anna* or *The Passion*), 1969; *Fårö-dokument* (*The Fårö Document*), 1969; *Beröringen* (*The Touch*), 1971; *Viskningar och rop* (*Cries and Whispers*), 1973; *Scener ur ett äktenskap* (*Scenes from a Marriage*), from his television series, 1973; *Das Schlangenei* (*The Serpent's Egg* or *Ormens ägg*), 1977; *Herbstsonate* (*Autumn Sonata*, or *Höstsonaten*), 1978; *Fårö-dokument 1979* (*Fårö 1979*), 1979; *Aus dem Leben der Marionetten* (*From the Life of the Marionettes*), 1980; *Fanny och Alexander* (*Fanny and Alexander*), 1982.

Screenplays (writer only): *Hets* (*Torment* or *Frenzy*), 1944; *Kvinna utan ansikte* (*Woman Without a Face*), 1947; *Eva*, 1948; *Medan staden sover* (*While the City Sleeps*), 1950; *Frånskild* (*Divorced*), 1951; *Sista paret ut* (*Last Couple Out*), 1956; *Lustgården* (*The Pleasure Garden*), as Buntel Eriksson, 1961; *Den goda viljan* (*Best Intentions*), 1992; *Söndagsbarn* (*Sunday's Children*), 1992.

Radio Plays: *Dra en nit* [Draw Blank], 1949; *Staden* [The City], 1951.

Television Plays: *Lögnen* [The Lie], 1970; *Scener ur ett äktenskap*, 1973, as *Scenes from a Marriage*, 1974; *Trollflöjten* [The Magic Flute], 1974; *Ansikte mot ansikte* [Face to Face], 1976.

Fiction

The Best Intentions (novelization of his screenplay). New York, Arcade, 1993.

Other

Bergman om Bergman, with Stig Björkman, Torsten Manns, and Jonas Sima. Stockholm, Norstedt, 1970; as *Bergman on Bergman*, New York, Simon and Schuster, and London, Secker and Warburg, 1973.
Ingmar Bergman, My Story, with Alan Burgess. New York, Delacorte Press, 1980.
Talking with Ingmar Bergman, edited by G. William Jones. Dallas, Texas, Southern Methodist University Press, 1983.
Laterna magica. Stockholm, Norstedt, 1987; as *The Magic Lantern: An Autobiography*, New York, Viking, and London, Hamish Hamilton, 1988.
Bilder. Stockholm, Norstedt, 1990.

*

Critical Studies: *The Personal Vision of Ingmar Bergman* by Jörn Donner, Bloomington, Indiana University Press, 1962; *Antonioni, Bergman, Resnais*, London, Tantivy Press, and New York, Barnes, 1964, and *Ingmar Bergman*, London, Secker and Warburg, 1982, and New York, Scribner, 1983, both by Peter Cowie; *Ingmar Bergman*, Boston, Twayne, 1968, and *Ingmar Bergman: A Guide to References and Resources*, Boston, Hall, 1987, both by Birgitta Steene; *The Silence of God: Creative Response to the Films of Ingmar Bergman* by Arthur Gibson, New York, Harper, 1969; *Ingmar*

Bergman by Robin Wood, New York, Praeger, 1969; *Cinema Borealis: Ingmar Bergman and the Swedish Ethos* by Vernon Young, New York, David Lewis, 1971; *The Lutheran Milieu of the Films of Ingmar Bergman* by Richard Aloysius Blake, New York, Arno, 1972; *Ingmar Bergman Directs* by John Simon, New York, Harcourt Brace, 1972, London, Davis-Poynter, 1973; *Ingmar Bergman: Essays in Criticism*, edited by Stuart Kaminsky, London, Oxford University Press, 1975; *Ingmar Bergman and Society* by Maria Bergom-Larsson, London, Tantivy Press, and South Brunswick, New Jersey, Barnes, 1978; *Mindscreen: Bergman, Godard and First-Person Film* by Bruce Kawin, Princeton, New Jersey, Princeton University Press, 1978; *Ingmar Bergman: An Appreciation* by Roger Manvell, New York, Ayer, 1980; *Ingmar Bergman: The Cinema as Mistress* by Philip Mosley, London, Boyars, 1981; *Film and Dreams: An Approach to Ingmar Bergman*, edited by Vlada Petrić, South Salem, New York, Redgrave, 1981; *Ingmar Bergman and the Rituals of Art* by Paisley Livingston, Ithaca, New York, Cornell University Press, 1982; *Ingmar Bergman: Four Decades in the Theater* by Lise-Lone Marker, Cambridge, Cambridge University Press, 1982; *Persona: The Transcendent Image* by Marilyn Johns Blackwell, Urbana, University of Illinois Press, 1986; *The Passion of Ingmar Bergman* by Frank Gado, Durham, North Carolina, Duke University Press, 1986; *The Influence of Existentialism on Ingmar Bergman: An Analysis of the Theological Ideas Shaping a Filmmaker's Art* by Charles B. Ketcham, Lewiston, New York, Mellen, 1986; *God, Death, Art & Love: The Philosophical Vision of Ingmar Bergman* by Robert E. Lauder, Mahwah, New Jersey, Paulist Press, 1989.

Theatrical Activities:
Director: **Films** — as listed above, and *Musik i mörker* (*Music in Darkness* or *Night Is My Future*), 1948; *Törst* (*Thirst* or *Three Strange Loves*), 1949; *Sånt händer inte här* (*High Tension* or *This Doesn't Happen Here*), 1950; **Plays** — many, since 1938, most recently *Long Day's Journey into Night* by Eugene O'Neill, 1988.

*   *   *

Ingmar Bergman might have become a considerable author, but found the best outlet for his talents in the theatre and cinema. Unlike most outstanding film directors, he writes nearly all his own scripts (although the published versions of his screenplays often bear little resemblance to the films themselves and give few indications of the effects Bergman achieved on film). He has also had a very successful career as a stage director, with some of his best productions, notably of plays by August Strindberg and Henrik Ibsen, touring the world.

Many of Bergman's films tend to be grim and harrowing, and detractors accuse him of Scandinavian "gloom and doom." Nevertheless, many of them have comic interludes, and he has made a handful of comedies. There is a lyrical quality about several of his films — the nostalgic memories of the old professor in *Smultronstället* (*Wild Strawberries*), the halcyon summer days in the Stockholm archipelago in *Sommaren med Monika* (*Summer with Monika*), for example — and he occasionally uses the stark landscape of his favourite island Fårö to haunting effect.

He inspires great loyalty among his associates, and assembled a sort of repertory group of players, with the same actors taking leading roles in film after film. One of them, Max von Sydow, has commented (in *Chaplin*, 1989) that "you have to get more involved in a Bergman film than you do in others, because it deals with much deeper and more philosophic questions than the average movie. He also establishes a much closer relationship with his actors and technicians than would ever be possible on a larger production."

Bergman achieved his greatest international fame as a filmmaker in the 1950s and 1960s, with a number of stark, emotionally intense, hauntingly symbolic films shot in black and white. *Det sjunde inseglet* (*The Seventh Seal*) is widely thought to be one of his finest works, and it contains many typical themes: the credibility of religious faith, the constant threat of tragedy and death, the role of love, the precarious and ambiguous situation of the artist. Cowie characterises the film admirably in his biography of Bergman: ". . . the ideas that dominate the film arise from a tension of opposites: faith versus atheism, death versus life, innocence versus corruption, light versus darkness, comedy versus tragedy, hope versus despair, love versus infidelity, vengeance versus magnanimity, sadism versus suffering." Several scenes haunt the mind's eye long after the film has been seen, especially the final Dance of Death on a distant hilltop, and the chess game between Death and the Knight: there can only be one winner, but the Knight plays for time and extracts his small triumphs.

The existence of God is also questioned in the impressive trilogy *Såsom i en spegel* (*Through a Glass Darkly*), *Nattvardsgästerna* (*Winter Light*), and *Tystnaden* (*The Silence*). By the end, the characters seem to have lost all hope of contact with the outside world, which is mysteriously threatening — uniformed soldiers and tanks move ominously in the background, and people speak an incomprehensible tongue; the only contact between the main characters and the world around them is the animal passion of Anna and someone she has picked up. Ester dies, the extent of her isolation depicted in a masturbation scene thought shocking at the time, and little Johan is completely bewildered as the film ends as he and Anna board the train to leave this ghostly hell on earth. God is silent, unable to help.

In the mid 1960s, Bergman stopped making black-and-white films — reluctantly, one suspects — and went over to colour. *Persona* takes up once more the theme of silence, and as the title suggests, it is full of references to the theories of Carl Jung about masks and split personalities. It highlights the failure of language as a link between people, and also embodies another favourite theme, the inadequate artist. As Birgitta Steene has stressed, Bergman's attitude towards artists is ambiguous and reflects his ambivalent approach to filmmaking: the artist can control the emotions of his audience, and yet is at their mercy.

Persona included a great deal of extemporisation, and Bergman said his script was more like the melody line of a piece of music, which had to be elaborated as the actors went along. Apart from the cinema, Bergman's great passion is classical music, and the musical accompaniment of his films is always an important part of the overall effect. Bergman was able to combine his three great loves — the film, theatre, and music — in a highly successful version of Mozart's *The Magic Flute*, made for television at the Drottningholm Theatre just outside Stockholm.

In the richly colourful and often funny *Fanny och Alexander* (*Fanny and Alexander*), his last film as director, Bergman recreates the constricting and oppressive atmosphere of his childhood: his father was a Lutheran minister with an authoritarian bent (the Bishop in the film), and his mother more emotional but also dominant in a different way. As Peter Cowie suggests (*Swedish Book Review*, 2, 1987) "From his father stemmed, one feels, the compulsive attraction to religious issues, from his mother, the sensitivity and emotional fervour of his work." Echoes from his childhood frequently recur in his films, which tend to deal with inner conflict and psychological probing. A part of Ingmar Bergman is to be found in virtually all of his characters, and when two or more seem to be at war with each other, the real battle is often within the author himself.

Recently Bergman has written the screenplays for two more overtly autobiographical films, *Den goda viljan* (*Best Intentions*, directed by Bille August), about his parents' stormy courtship and marriage, and *Söndagsbarn* (*Sunday's Children*, the directorial debut by Bergman's son Daniel), which draws from Bergman's memoirs, *Laterna magica* (*The Magic Lantern*). *The Magic Lantern* is well written, especially when Bergman avoids direct speech which often seems stilted on the page. He recreates scenes, atmospheres, and people most effectively, but confuses his readers by concentrating in great detail on certain aspects of his life while barely mentioning the films for which he is best known, and various people who played an important part in his life are conspicuous by their absence.

Ingmar Bergman is an enigma, but is also one of the great creative artists of the 20th century.

—Laurie Thompson

BERNSTEIN, Ingrid. *See* **KIRSCH, Sarah.**

BHĀRTĪ, Dharmvīr. Indian. Born in 1926. Educated at the University of Allahabad, M.A. 1947, Ph.D. in Hindi medieval mystical literature. Taught at university level for several years. Founder member, *Parimal* literary club, 1944–69; founder and editor, *Dharmayug*, 30 years; assistant editor, with Ilācandra Jośī, *Saṅgam* weekly; editor, with Lakṣmīkānt Varmā, *Nikaṣ* literary magazine, 1955; editor, *Ālocnā* quarterly. Address: c/o *Dharmayug*, Bennett, Coleman & Co., Times Building, Dr. D. N. Road, Bombay 400001, India.

PUBLICATIONS

Verse

Ṭhaṇḍā lohā [Cold Iron].   Allahabad, Sāhitya Bhavan, 1952.
Kanupriyā [The Beloved of Krishna].   Benares, Bhārtīy Jñānpīṭh, 1959.
Sāt gīt varṣā [Seven Years of Lyrics].   Benares, Bhārtīy Jñānpīṭh, 1959.

Fiction

Murdō kā gāv [The Village of the Dead].   Allahabad, Kitāb Mahal, 1946.
Gunāhō kā devtā [The God of Sins].   Allahabad, Sāhitya Bhavan, 1949.
Sūraj kā sātvā ghoṛā [The Seventh Horse of the Sun God].   Allahabad, Sāhitya Sadan, 1952.
Amar putra [Immortal Son].   Jalandhar, n.p., 1952.

Cād aur ṭūṭe hue log [The Moon and Broken People]. Allahabad, Kitāb Mahal, 1965.
Svarg aur pṛthvī [Heaven and Earth].   Benares, Nandkiśor & Sons, n.d.

Plays

Nadī pyāsī thī [The River Was Thirsty].   Allahabad, Kitāb Mahal, 1954.
Andhāyug [The Blind Age] (play in verse).   Allahabad, Kitāb Mahal, 1954.

Other

Ṭhele par Himālay [Himalayas on a Cart] (travelogue). Benares, Bhārtīy Jñānpīth, n.d.
Paśyanti (essays).   New Delhi, Bhārtīy Jñānpīth, n.d.
Siddha sāhitya [Siddha Literature] (Ph.D. dissertation on the mystical literature of India].   Allahabad, Kitāb Mahal, 1955.
Manav mūlya aur sāhitya [Literature and Human Values]. New Delhi, Bhārtīy Jñānpīth, 1960.

*   *   *

Dharmvīr Bhārtī is a leading Hindi poet, novelist, playwright, and essayist. The recipient of many prestigious awards, he has been a major influence on many new Hindi writers of post-independence India.

Born in 1926, Bhārtī began his literary career as a poet. His poetry is a happy blending of romanticism and realism, sentimentality and rationality. He is one of the trend setters of a new kind of Hindi poetry which emerged in the 1950s, called *Naī Kavitā*, or New Poetry, which in all its composite nature is essentially individualistic. The varied aspects of humanist temper reflected in Bhārtī's poetry shows that he recognizes no restriction in the choice of subjects for poetry. Bhārtī's poems have a lyrical and sometimes sensual charm, although in some of his early poems the use of clichés on the pattern of Urdu poetry has reduced the seriousness of his subject-matter. In his early verse the main attraction lay in the excellence of diction and form, whereas in his later poems ideas take precedence over style.

Bhārtī has published four poetical works: *Andhāyug* (The Blind Age), *Ṭhaṇḍā lohā* (Cold Iron), *Kanupriyā* (The Beloved of Krishna), and *Sāt gīt varṣā* (Seven Years of Lyrics). In these poems Bhārtī sings of beauty and revolution. He is deeply frustrated by the state of Indian society and depicts the ugly and unhealthy aspects of human life, but is always ready to face the challenge of life. In his poem "Ṭūṭā Pahiyā" (The Broken Wheel), he writes:

I am
the broken wheel of a chariot.
But do not throw me away.
Who knows,
one day some valorous Abhimanyu might get trapped
while challenging the impregnable circular array of troops . . .
then I
the broken chariot wheel
in his hand will face bravely
the aggression of infallible weapons.

Bhārtī has provided original interpretations of the Sanskrit epic the *Mahābhārata* in the form of a verse play, *Andhāyug*, and a long poem, *Kanupriyā*. In the latter he narrates the love of Rādhā with exquisite tenderness of emotion and sensitivity,

while commenting on the social issues that still frustrate mankind.

In the verse play *Andhāyug*, Bhārtī's best work, his social awareness is shown more markedly through the effect of war on the individual as well as on society. The plot is taken from various episodes of the *Mahābhārata* and contains many layers of mythological references from the great Sanskrit epic. The aim of this work is not to retell the well-known story, but to adapt it in such a way that it depicts man's struggle in asserting himself, against all the odds, in face of the problems of contemporary life: rejection of values, the reality of being in a continuous state of doubt, the loneliness arising from the divisions of society, the growing materialism of modern life. In this work most of the characters represent behaviour patterns that arise from their struggle. At one point the character Ashvatthama, who symbolises the moral destruction of the warring peoples, admits after murdering sleeping warriors and their children:

Mine was the sin
I committed murders
But my hands were not mine
My heart was not mine either
The blind age had taken abode in me
Becoming an avenger's blind force.

In his prose writing Bhārtī sprang into the limelight with his novel *Gunāhō kā devtā* (The God of Sins), in which he traces the development of a man who makes his way against great odds. Here idealism is shown as a counterpart of realism. The novel was much discussed at the time of its publication because of its bold plot: a student falls in love with his professor's daughter and she returns his love, but he persuades her to marry another man out of respect for his teacher. The marriage of the girl to a man she does not love, and her subsequent death during pregnancy, brings home to the student the shortcomings of his own character in that he was never able to unite feeling with the courage to act and so caused destruction and pain to others and himself.

Bhārtī's second novel *Sūraj kā satvā ghoṛā* (The Seventh Horse of the Sun God) is more remarkable from the point of view of technique and style. Its novelty lies in the resurrection of an old style of story telling. Bhārtī depicts a gathering of friends where on six successive days a narrator tells three love stories. The old method of narrating parables or moral fables has been re-orientated by using stories of contemporary life in the old framework. After every story, friends comment on it from a liberal point of view. To depict the reality of common life and to project his own beliefs and ideas, Bhārtī uses the legendary symbols of the seven horses of the sun and the scriptural methods of story telling. The contemporary aspect of the work is re-emphasized by the story teller explaining, "Listen, these stories are really not love stories. But they depict the life of our lower middle class, where economic struggle and moral disintegration are more prominent than love-making."

Bhārtī has written some notable short stories which lay bare the social inequalities and anomalies that make day-to-day living a Herculean task, especially for those with modest means. "Gulkī Banno" is a love story about a condemned, forsaken, ugly wife. The story's power lies in the fact that in the midst of her poverty, the ridicule and contempt of the local boys, and absolute neglect and indifference from her husband, Gulkī remains firm in her love for him. Bhārtī carries the same spirit of individual struggle against social complexities in his much discussed one-act play *Āvāz kā nīlām*.

—Satyendra Śrīvāstava

BIERMANN, Wolf. German. Born in Hamburg, 15 November 1936. Moved to East Germany in 1953. Educated at Humboldt University, Berlin, 1959–63. Married to Christine Bark; two sons and one daughter. Singer, composer, and guitar virtuoso. Assistant director, Brecht's Berliner Ensemble, 1957–59; member, Socialist Unity party: expelled, 1963; forbidden to perform or be published in East Germany, 1965–76; performed in concert, Cologne, and as a result had citizenship taken away, November 1976: decision reversed, 1989. Recipient: Fontane prize, 1969; Offenbach prize, 1974; German Record award, 1975, 1977; Deutscher Keinkunstpreis, 1979; Hölderlin award, 1989; Mörike prize, 1991; Büchner prize, 1991. Address: c/o Verlag Kiepenheuer und Witsch, Rondorfer Straße 5, 5000 Cologne-Marienburg, Germany.

PUBLICATIONS

Verse

Die Drahtharfe: Balladen, Gedichte, Lieder. Berlin, Wagenbach, 1965; as *The Wire Harp*, translated by Eric Bentley, New York, Harcourt Brace, 1968.
Mit Marx- und Engelszungen: Gedichte, Balladen, Lieder. Berlin, Wagenbuch, 1968.
Für meine Genossen: Hetzlieder, Balladen, Gedichte. Berlin, Wagenbuch, 1972.
Deutschland: Ein Wintermärchen. Berlin, Wagenbuch, 1972.
Nachlaß I (songs). Cologne, Kiepenheuer und Witsch, 1977.
Wolf Biermann: Poems and Ballads, translated by Steve Gooch. London, Pluto Press, 1977.
Loblieder und Haßgesänge, edited by Andreas M. Reinhard. N.p., Bange, 1977.
Preußischer Ikarus: Lieder, Balladen, Gedichte, Prosa. Cologne, Kiepenheuer und Witsch, 1978.
Verdrehte Welt — das seh' ich gerne. Cologne, Kiepenheuer und Witsch, 1982.
Und als ich von Deutschland nach Deutschland: Lieder mit Noten, Gedichte, Balladen aus dem Osten, aus dem Westen. Gütersloh, Bertelsmann-Club, 1984.
Three Contemporary German Poets: Wolf Biermann, Sarah Kirsch, Reiner Kunze, edited by Peter J. Graves. Leicester, Leicester University Press, 1985.
Affenfels und Barrikade: Gedichte, Lieder, Balladen. Cologne, Kiepenheuer und Witsch, 1986.
Alle Lieder. Cologne, Kiepenheuer und Witsch, 1991.
Vier neue Lieder. Berlin, Wagenbuch, n.d.

Fiction

Das Märchen vom kleinen Herrn Moritz. Munich, Parabel, 1972.

Play

Der Dra-Dra: Die grosse Drachentöterschau in 8 Akten mit Musik (produced Munich, 1971). Berlin, Wagenbuch, 1970.

Other

Das Märchen von dem Mädchen mit dem Holzbein: ein Bilderbuch. Cologne, Kiepenheuer und Witsch, 1979.
Klartexte im Getümmel: 13 Jahre im Westen. Cologne, Kiepenheuer und Witsch, 1990.
Über das Geld und andere Herzensdinge: 5 prosaische Versuche über Deutschland. Cologne, Kiepenheuer und Witsch, 1991.
Ich hatte viel Bekümmernis: Meditation zur Kantate Nr.21 von J. S. Bach. N.p., TVZ, 1991.

Translator, *Berichte aus dem sozialistischen Lager*, by Daniel Julij. Hamburg, Hoffmann und Campe, 1972.

*

Critical Studies: "The Songs of Wolf Biermann: The Poet as Composer" by Michael Moreley, in *Journal of the Australasian Universities Language and Literature Association*, 48, 1977; "'I'd rather be dead than think the way Kunert does': Interview with Wolf Biermann and Günter Kunert" by Fritz J. Raddatz, in *New German Critique* (Ithaca, New York), Spring-Summer 1981; "Wolf Biermann and 'Die zweite deutsche Exilliteratur': An Appraisal After Nine Years" by Dennis R. McCormick, in *Selected Papers from the Eleventh New Hampshire Symposium on the German Democratic Republic*, edited by Margy Gerber and others, Lanham, Maryland, University Press of America, 1986.

* * *

The former East German poet and songwriter Wolf Biermann shot to international prominence in 1976 when the withdrawal of his citizenship of the German Democratic Republic provoked an outcry among the intelligentsia of that state and led to a growing outflow of artistic talent to the West. During a West German tour he was unexpectedly allowed to make in November of that year, Biermann gave a song-and-guitar performance before an enthusiastic audience of several thousand in Cologne. The East German authorities deemed it provocative, refused Biermann re-entry into the GDR, and effectively exiled him. Such an extreme measure led to a storm of international protest against the suppression of dissident views and, gradually, to a loosening of the bureaucratic stranglehold on opinion. This *cause célèbre* brought about the most serious crisis of legitimacy for the GDR since the building of the Berlin Wall in 1961.

The "Biermann affair" was preceded by a decade of harassment of the singer by the cultural authorities as well as the Stasi security police. Biermann, whose father died in Auschwitz, came from a staunchly communist background and went from Hamburg to East Germany in 1953, only to find that his brand of non-conformist communist thinking was uncongenial to the official line. He began writing in the early 1960s and was soon expelled from the Socialist Unity Party in 1963. In 1965 a blanket ban was imposed, forbidding all performances and publication by Biermann in East Germany. He was accused of anarchistic individualism, and his intimate friendship with the outspoken East German academic Robert Havemann only exacerbated his position.

Up to 1976 Biermann's reputation grew in a curious vacuum; his books and records found a wide and receptive audience in West Germany (especially in the turbulent late 1960s of student revolt and social upheaval), but he lacked the resonance and response of contact with an immediate audience. The need for this was particularly acute as Biermann sang his ballads in public to his own guitar accompaniment in an unmistakably idiosyncratic manner, singing "against" the music, alternating rasping harshness with gentle tones, prose with poetry. West German propaganda interests also created an artificial distortion by highlighting his criticisms of East Germany while at the same time suppressing his passionate condemnation of the realities of capitalism.

During the 10 years he was silenced in his own country Biermann published several collections in the West — gathered in one volume in 1977, ironically titled *Nachlaß I* (Posthumous Works I) — which testified to his insouciant, exuberant support for a light-hearted, pleasurable communism. These often sensual verses drew the opprobrium of the plodding, heavyhanded men in power in the GDR; the cultural minister Abusch described them as "besmirching the party of the working-class" and Höpcke called his work "pornographic and anti-communist." The poems and songs in *Die Drahtharfe* (*The Wire Harp*), *Mit Marx- und Engelszungen* (With Tongues of Marx and Engels), and *Für meine Genossen* (For My Comrades) span a wide variety of public and private topics, and range from indulgent, hopeful criticisms of faults in the communist system of his country to harshly virulent and aggressive rejection of its intolerable darker aspects. Certain themes emerged as dominant concerns of the poet and he was not afraid to expose them mercilessly: the Stalinist bureaucrats, the deformation of socialism engendered by obsession with rigid ideology, and above all the suppression of the citizen's right to speak out were constant targets in Biermann's witty, caustic ballads. But he also directed his attention to events in the wider world: topical happenings like the assassination attempt on Rudi Dutschke, the Vietnam conflict, the Chile coup, and the charisma of Che Guevara all found a formulation in Biermann's verses.

In common with many fellow-writers, Biermann's attitude was one of "critical solidarity" with the state that had banned his work. His scepticism never became total resignation, though he was possessed of a powerful strain of pessimism in the mid-1960s. His sorrowful regret at the division of Germany persisted into exile, and he continued his prolific output with *Preußischer Ikarus* (Prussian Icarus), *Verdrehte Welt* (Crazy World), and *Affenfels und Barrikade* (Monkey Rock and Barricade). These volumes bear testimony to Biermann's ability to mesh personal experience with the wider situation in society; history is for him the interface between private sphere and public concern. In exile Biermann has demonstrated a sensitive, vulnerable, even lonely personality in his work; his hopes are now "crow-black" and he is by no means an acquiescent participant in the flawed freedom of the West. He has taken into his repertoire themes that dog the affluent torpor of the Federal Republic: strikes and unemployment, terrorism and its backlash, uneasy guilt about recent history, the "daily tiny fascism" and the "lesser evil," armaments and aggression — all are fodder to his rasping voice. "German Miserere" lambasts both East and West evenhandedly: "Here they roll over on their backs/There they crawl on their bellies/And I have come/oh! I have come/from the frying-pan into the fire."

The genre Biermann cultivates is that of the *chansonnier*, a tradition strong in the political cabaret in Germany and France, and reaching back through the street ballad to figures like Heinrich Heine and François Villon; *Deutschland: Ein Wintermärchen* (Germany: A Winter's Tale) is directly inspired by Heine, and Biermann often portrays himself as a Villon-like figure. The political song has the characteristics of courage, melancholy, and cheekiness, and relies on colloquial idiom, plebeian language, and topical allusion. These Biermann shares with Bertolt Brecht, whose Marxist beliefs and dialectic structures of thought and formulation are ever-present models. An integral part of the songs is the performance, again indebted to Brecht and the composer Hanns Eisler, who used music not as a mere vehicle for the text, but as a contrapuntal contradiction to its meaning, actively encouraging alertness, detachment, and scepticism. Text, music, and performance, working against each other, create life and resonance.

The reunification of Germany brought no solace to Biermann, who looked beyond the euphoria and foresaw continuing division and inequality ("The West powers on and booms and whoops/The East limps whimpering on"). Nostalgia for the barricades, a glimmer of hope in a socialist future, the comradely solidarity of the commune continue to inform Biermann's writing and give verve to his music; and his resiliently combative idealism counterbalances the frustrations of the shackled imagination in the real political world: "I have never stopped singing the resurrection of the oppressed and my indestructible belief in a more just society — in spite of everything!"

—Arrigo V. Subiotto

BIOY CASARES, Adolfo. Also writes as Javier Miranda; Martin Sacastru; H. Bustos Domecq; B. Lynch Davis; B. Suárez Lynch (joint pseudonym with Jorge Luis Borges). Argentinian. Born in Buenos Aires, 15 September 1914. Educated at the University of Buenos Aires, 1933–34. Married Silvina Ocampo (*q.v.*) in 1940; one daughter. Founder, with Jorge Luis Borges, *Destiempo* literary magazine, 1936, and "The Seventh Circle" detective series, Emecé Editores, Buenos Aires, 1943–56. Recipient: City of Buenos Aires municipal prize, 1941; National literature prize, 1969; Argentine Society of Writers grand prize of honour, 1975; Mondello prize, 1984; IILA prize (Italy), 1986; Cervantes prize, 1990, 1991; Echeverría prize; Konex prize. Elected to Légion d'Honneur (France), 1981. Address: Posadas 1650, 1112 Buenos Aires, Argentina.

PUBLICATIONS

Fiction

17 disparos contra lo porvenir (as Martin Sacastru).   Buenos Aires, Tor, 1933.
Caos.   Buenos Aires, Viau y Zona, 1934.
La nueva tormenta, o La vida múltiple de Juan Ruteno. Buenos Aires, Colombo, 1935.
Luis Greve, muerto.   Buenos Aires, Destiempo, 1937.
La invención de Morel.   Buenos Aires, Losada, 1940; with stories from *La trama celeste*, as *The Invention of Morel, and Other Stories from "La trama celeste"*, Austin, University of Texas Press, 1964.

Seis problemas para don Isidro Parodi, with Jorge Luis Borges (jointly as H. Bustos Domecq).   Buenos Aires, Sur, 1942; as *Six Problems for Don Isidro*, New York, Dutton, and London, Allen Lane, 1981.

El perjurio de la nieve.   Buenos Aires, La Quimera, 1945; as *The Perjury of the Snow*, New York, Vanishing Rotating Triangle, 1964.

Plan de evasión.   Buenos Aires, Emecé, 1945; as *A Plan for Escape*, New York, Dutton, 1975.

Dos fantasías memorables, with Jorge Luis Borges (jointly as H. Bustos Domecq).   Buenos Aires, Oportet y Haereses, 1946.

Un modelo para la muerte, with Jorge Luis Borges (jointly as B. Suárez Lynch).   Buenos Aires, Oportet y Haereses, 1946.

Los que aman, odian, with Silvina Ocampo.   Buenos Aires, Emecé, 1946.

La trama celeste.   Buenos Aires, Sur, 1948; part, with *La invención de Morel*, as *The Invention of Morel, and Other Stories from "La trama celeste"*, Austin, University of Texas Press, 1964.

Las visperas de Fausto.   Buenos Aires, La Perdiz, 1949.

El sueño de héroes.   Buenos Aires, Losada, 1954; as *The Dream of Heroes*, London, Quartet, 1987; New York, Dutton, 1988.

Historia prodigiosa.   Mexico City, Obregón, 1956; enlarged edition, Buenos Aires, Emecé, 1961.

Guirnalda con amores: cuentos.   Buenos Aires, Emecé, 1959.

El lado de la sombra.   Buenos Aires, Emecé, 1962.

Adolfo Bioy Casares (omnibus), edited by Ofelia Kovacci.   Buenos Aires, Ministry of Education and Justice, 1963.

El gran serafín.   Buenos Aires, Emecé, 1967.

Crónicas de Bustos Domecq, with Jorge Luis Borges. Buenos Aires, Losada, 1967; as *Chronicles of Bustos Domecq*, New York, Dutton, 1976; London, Allen Lane, 1982.

Diario de la guerra del cerdo.   Buenos Aires, Emecé, 1969; as *Diary of the War of the Pig*, New York, McGraw Hill, 1972; London, Allison and Busby, 1989.

Adversos milagros: relatos.   Caracas, Monte Avila, 1969.

Historias de amor.   Buenos Aires, Emecé, 1972.

Historias fantásticas.   Buenos Aires, Emecé, 1972.

Dormir al sol.   Buenos Aires, Emecé, 1973; as *Asleep in the Sun*, New York, Persea, 1978.

Nuevos contos de Bustos Domecq, with Jorge Luis Borges. Buenos Aires, La Ciudad, 1977.

El heroe de las mujeres.   Buenos Aires, Emecé, 1978.

Los afanes.   Buenos Aires, Arte Gaglianone, 1983.

La aventura de un fotógrafo en La Plata.   Buenos Aires, Emecé, 1985; as *The Adventures of a Photographer in La Plata*, New York, Dutton, 1989; London, Bloomsbury, 1991.

Páginas (selections).   Buenos Aires, Celtia, 1985.

Historias desaforadas.   Buenos Aires, Emecé, 1986.

La invención y la trama.   Mexico City, Fondo de Cultura Económica, 1988.

Una muñeca rusa.   Buenos Aires, Tusquets, 1991.

Plays

Los orilleros; El paraíso de los creyentes (screenplays), with Jorge Luis Borges.   Buenos Aires, Losada, 1955.

Les Autres (screenplay), with Jorge Luis Borges and Hugo Santiago.   Paris, Bourgois, 1974.

Screenplays: *Les Autres*, with Jorge Luis Borges and Hugo Santiago, 1974; *Los orilleros*, with Jorge Luis Borges, 1975.

Other

Prologo.   Buenos Aires, Biblos, 1929.

La estatua casera.   Buenos Aires, Jacaranda, 1936.

Antes del novecientos (recuerdos).   Buenos Aires, n.p., 1958.

Años de mocedad: recuerdos.   Buenos Aires, Nuevo Cabildo, 1963.

La otra aventura.   Buenos Aires, Galerna, 1968.

Memoria sobre la pampa y los gauchos.   Buenos Aires, Sur, 1970.

Breve diccionario del argentino exquisito (as Javier Miranda).   Buenos Aires, Barros Merino, 1971; enlarged edition (as Bioy Casares), Buenos Aires, Emecé, 1978, 1990.

Aventuras de la imaginación (interviews), with Noemí Ulla.   Buenos Aires, Corregidor, 1990.

Editor, with Jorge Luis Borges and Silvina Ocampo, *Antología de la literatura fantástica*.   Buenos Aires, Sudamericana, 1940; as *The Book of Fantasy*, New York, Viking, and London, Xanadu, 1988.

Editor, with Jorge Luis Borges and Silvina Ocampo, *Antología poética argentina*.   Buenos Aires, Sudamericana, 1941; as *Antología de la poesia argentina*, Sudamericana, 1948.

Editor and translator, with Jorge Luis Borges, *Los mejores cuentos policiales*.   Buenos Aires, Emecé, 2 vols., 1943–51.

Editor, with Jorge Luis Borges, *Prosa y verso*, by Francisco Quevedo.   Buenos Aires, Emecé, 1948.

Editor and translator, with Jorge Luis Borges, *Poesía gauchesca*.   Mexico City, Fondo de Cultura Económica, 2 vols., 1955.

Editor, with Jorge Luis Borges, *Cuentos breves y extraordinarios*.   Buenos Aires, Raigal, 1955; as *Extraordinary Tales*, New York, Herder, 1971; London, Souvenir Press, 1973.

Editor, with Jorge Luis Borges, *El libro del cielo y del infierno*.   Buenos Aires, Sur, 1960.

Editor, with Jorge Luis Borges, *Hilario Ascasubi, Aniceto el gallo y Santos Vega*.   N.p., Eudeba Siglo y Medio, 1960.

*

Bibliographies: "Bibliografía de y sobre Adolfo Bioy Casares" by Raquel Puig Zaldívar, in *Revista Iberoamericana* (Pittsburgh), 40, 1974; "Bibliografía sobre Adolfo Bioy Casares (Algunas nuevas fichas)" by Rodolfo A. Borello, in *Revista Iberoamericana* (Pittsburgh), 91, 1975.

Critical Studies: "The Mirror and the Lie: Two Stories by Jorge Luis Borges and Adolfo Bioy Casares" by Alfred J. MacAdam, in *Modern Fiction Studies* (West Lafayette, Indiana), 19, 1973; "The Novels and Short Stories of Adolfo Bioy Casares" by David P. Gallagher, in *Bulletin of Hispanic Studies* (Liverpool), 52, 1975; in *Jorge Luis Borges: A Literary Biography* by Emir R. Monegal, New York, Dutton, 1978; "The Narrator as Creator and Critic in *The Invention of Morel*" by Margaret L. Snook, in *Latin American Literary Review* (Pittsburgh), 7, 1979; "Parody Island: Two Novels by Adolfo Bioy Casares" by Suzanne Jill Levine, in *Hispanic Journal* (Indiana, Pennsylvania), 4, 1983; *From the Ashen Land of the Virgin* by Raul Galvez, Oakville, Ontario, Mosaic Press, 1989.

*   *   *

Adolfo Bioy Casares is one of the chief exponents of the "fantastic literature" which has been a striking characteristic of writing from the Rio de la Plata region (Argentina and

Uruguay) for much of the 20th century. To many Argentine writers, from Bioy Casares's close friend and collaborator Jorge Luis Borges, to Julio Cortázar or Manuel Puig, fantasy in literature is not simply an escape from everyday concerns, but an attempt to define another reality which is hidden within our everyday world, often providing it with a deeper meaning. As Bioy Casares has written: "the world is inexhaustible; it is made up of an infinite number of worlds in the manner of Russian dolls" ("Guirnalda").

The task of the writer then becomes one of uncovering the laws of this infinite world, as Bioy Casares says in his prologue to the *Antología de la literatura fantástica* (*The Book of Fantasy*) (compiled in conjunction with his wife Silvina Ocampo [*q.v.*] and Borges): "these laws exist, to write is to be constantly discovering them or to fail . . . the writer therefore should look on his work as a problem to be solved partly in accordance with these general, pre-established laws, and partly through new ones which he himself discovers and fulfils."

This attitude led Bioy Casares to an exploration of the detective genre as a paradigm for the kind of investigation involved in the process of writing itself. In several works, such as *Seis problemas para don Isidro Parodi* (*Six Problems for Don Isidro*), he collaborated with Borges under the pseudonym of H. Bustos Domecq. In an essay on Borges's work, Bioy Casares explained why he thought this kind of literature was such a good discipline for a writer: "it may be that the detective novel has never produced a masterpiece. But it has produced an ideal: an ideal of invention, of rigour, of elegance (in the sense of the term as it is used in mathematics) in the plots. To emphasize the importance of construction: that is perhaps the main contribution the genre has made to literary history." This insistence on the clarity and solid construction of Bioy Casares's writing, be it novels or short stories, underpins its fantastic elements to great effect, lending it credibility and heightening the contrasts convincingly in a way that is reminiscent of Robert Louis Stevenson or H. G. Wells.

Among the fantastic elements that most interested Bioy Casares are those of the interpenetrability of different time scales, and the haunting idea of an eternal present. This idea formed the theme of one of his early novels, *La invención de Morel* (*The Invention of Morel*), and has resurfaced frequently in his short stories. As the critic Ofelia Kovacci has written, this fascination is double-edged: "these images bring up to date the myth of eternal renewal, of the possibility of life into the infinite, with the future always before one. However, from the usual perspective of man conscious of his finite being, at the mercy of his idea of consecutive time, this idea of being able to achieve immortality arouses a secret terror."

This anxiety is often linked to an even more deep-seated existential concern: that of personal identity. Bioy Casares returns again and again to the idea of an individual who in fact turns out to be a "sosie," the stand-in or replica of a lost original, presenting the reader with a world almost entirely populated by these imaginary beings, with whom the possibilities of contact or meaningful exchange are nil. This underlying pessimism adds a desperate note to much of Bioy Casares's work, although it is often offset by a sense of humour and surprising attention to the everyday details of Argentine life and society.

It is this irony which sustains his best novels, in which the fantastic elements are often of secondary importance. *Diario de la guerra del cerdo* (*Diary of the War of the Pig*), for example, can be read as a mordant satire of the Peronist regime in Argentina which imposed a straitjacket of intellectual conformity on the country in the early 1950s. A novel of the 1980s, *La aventura de un fotógrafo en La Plata* (*The Adventures of a Photographer in La Plata*), while on one level once more exploring the author's fascination with the nature of the reality of photographic images, is also a perfect description of the unreal atmosphere prevalent in Argentina during the military governments of the late 1970s when many thousands of people simply "disappeared" after being kidnapped by security forces.

In many ways it seems Bioy Casares has come to see that everyday reality can be even more extraordinary than any fantastic devices he could invent to convey his existential uncertainties. His ability to welcome reality, and to continue to distil and invent fictions that display all the rigour and elegance of which he spoke at the start of his career, has won him the Cervantes prize for literature (the Spanish-speaking world's most important literary award) and recognition by many Latin American writers as a writer equal in stature to his much better-known friend Jorge Luis Borges.

—Nick Caistor

———

BLAIS, Marie-Claire. Canadian. Born in Quebec, 5 October 1939. Educated at Pensionnat St. Roch and Laval University, both Quebec. Clerical worker, 1956–59; lived in the United States 1963–74; now lives in Quebec. Recipient: Canada council fellowship, 1960; French language prize, 1961; Guggenheim grant, 1963, 1965; France-Quebec prize, 1966; Medicis prize (France), 1966; Governor-General's award, 1969, 1979; Belgium-Canada prize, 1976; Athanase David prize, 1982; Académie Française prize, 1983; Nessim Habif prize (Belgium), 1991. Honorary doctorate: York University, Toronto, 1975; Victoria University, 1990; honorary professor: University of Calgary, 1978. Companion, Order of Canada, 1975; member, Royal Society of Canada, 1990. Agent: John C. Goodwin and Associates, 839 Sherbrooke Est, Suite 2, Montreal, Quebec H2L 1K6, Canada.

PUBLICATIONS

Fiction

La Belle Bête. Quebec, Institut Littéraire, 1959; as *Mad Shadows*, Toronto, McClelland and Stewart, and London, Cape, 1960; Boston, Little Brown, 1961.
Tête blanche. Quebec, Institut Littéraire, 1960; in English, Toronto, McClelland and Stewart, and Boston, Little Brown, 1961; London, Cape, 1962.
Le Jour est noir. Montreal, Jour, 1962; in *The Day Is Dark, and Three Travelers*, 1967.
Une Saison dans la vie d'Emmanuel. Montreal, Jour, 1965; as *A Season in the Life of Emmanuel*, New York, Farrar Straus, 1966; London, Cape, 1967.
Les Voyageurs sacrés. Montreal, HMH, 1966; in *The Day Is Dark, and Three Travelers*, 1967.
L'Insoumise. Montreal, Jour, 1966; as *The Fugitive*, Ottawa, Oberon Press, 1978.
The Day Is Dark, and Three Travelers. New York, Farrar Straus, 1967; Markham, Ontario, and London, Penguin, 1985.
David Sterne. Montreal, Jour, 1967; in English, Toronto, McClelland and Stewart, 1973.

Manuscrits de Pauline Archange:
1. *Manuscrits de Pauline Archange*. Montreal, Jour, 1968.
2. *Vivre! Vivre!* Montreal, Jour, 1969.
3. *The Manuscripts of Pauline Archange* (includes translations of *Manuscrits de Pauline Archange* and *Vivre! Vivre!*). New York, Farrar Straus, 1970.
4. *Les Apparences*. Montreal, Jour, 1970; as *Durer's Angel*, Vancouver, Talonbooks, 1976.

Le Loup. Montreal, Jour, 1972; as *The Wolf*, Toronto, McClelland and Stewart, 1974.

Un Joualonais, sa joualonie. Montreal, Jour, 1973; as *À cœur joual*, Paris, Laffont, 1974; as *St. Lawrence Blues*, New York, Farrar Straus, 1974; London, Harrap, 1975.

Une Liaison parisienne. Montreal, Stanké, 1975; as *A Literary Affair*, Toronto, McClelland and Stewart, 1979.

Les Nuits de l'Underground. Montreal, Stanké, 1978; as *Nights in the Underground*, Don Mills, Ontario, Musson, 1979.

Le Sourd dans la ville. Montreal, Stanké, 1979; as *Deaf to the City*, Toronto, Lester Orpen Dennys, 1981; Woodstock, New York, Overlook, 1987.

Visions d'Anna, ou, Le Vertige. Montreal, Stanké, 1982; as *Anna's World*, Toronto, Lester Orpen Dennys, 1985.

Pierre, la guerre du printemps 81. Montreal, Primeur, 1984; as *Pierre*, Paris, Acropole, 1986; Montreal, Boréal, 1991.

L'Ange de la solitude. Montreal, VLB, 1989.

Plays

Le Roulotte aux poupées (produced Montreal, 1962); as *The Puppet Caravan* (televised 1967).

Eleonor (produced Quebec, 1962).

L'Éxécution (produced Montreal, 1967). Montreal, Jour, 1968; as *The Execution*, Vancouver, Talon, 1976.

Fièvre et autres textes dramatiques: théâtre radiophonique (includes *L'Envahisseur*; *Le Disparu*; *Deux Destins*; *Un Couple*). Montreal, Jour, 1974.

La Nef des sorcières (Marcelle), with others (produced Montreal, 1976). Montreal, Quinze, 1976; as *A Clash of Symbols*, Toronto, Coach House Press, 1979.

L'Océan; Murmures (broadcast, 1976). Montreal, Quinze, 1977; *L'Océan* translated as *The Ocean*, Toronto, Exile, 1977; *Murmures* translated, in *Canadian Drama* (Guelph, Ontario), Fall 1979.

Sommeil d'hiver. Montreal, Pleine Lune, 1984.

L'Île (produced Montreal, 1991). Montreal, VLB, 1988; as *The Island*, Ottawa, Oberon Press, 1991.

Un Jardin dans la tempête (broadcast 1990).

Radio Plays: *Le Disparu*, 1971; *L'Envahisseur*, 1972; *Deux Destins*, 1973; *Fièvre*, 1973; *Une Autre Vie*, 1974; *Un Couple*, 1975; *Une Femme et les autres*, 1976; *L'Océan, suivi de Murmures*, 1976; *L'Enfant*, 1980.

Television Plays: *L'Océan*, 1976; *Journal en images froides*, 1978; *L'Exil, l'escale*, 1979.

Verse

Pays voilés. Quebec, Garneau, 1963; with *Existences*, as *Veiled Countries; Lives*, translated by Michael Harris, Montreal, Signal, 1984.

Existences. Quebec, Garneau, 1964; with *Pays voilés*, as *Veiled Countries; Lives*, translated by Michael Harris, Montreal, Signal, 1984.

Other

Voies de pères, voix de filles. Saint-Laurent, Quebec, Lacomb, 1988.

*

Bibliography: "Bibliographie de Marie-Claire Blais" by Aurélien Boivin, Lucie Robert, and Ruth Major-Lapierre, in *Voix et Images*, Winter 1983.

Manuscript Collection: National Library of Canada, Ottawa.

Critical Studies: *Marie-Claire Blais* by Philip Stratford, Toronto, Forum House, 1971; "Fiction as Autobiography in Québec: Notes on Pierre Vallières and Marie-Claire Blais" by James Kraft, in *Novel* (Providence, Rhode Island), 6, 1972; "*Mad Shadows* as Psychological Fiction" by Joan Caldwell, and "The Shattered Glass: Mirror and Illusion in *Mad Shadows*" by Douglas H. Parker, both in *Journal of Canadian Fiction* (Montreal), 2(4), 1973; "Marie-Claire Blais, French Canadian Naturalist" by L. Clark Keating, in *Romance Notes* (Chapel Hill, North Carolina), 15, 1973; "The Church in Marie-Claire Blais's *A Season in the Life of Emmanuel*" by Margaret Anderson, in *Sphinx* (Regina, Saskatchewan), 7, 1977; "Marie-Claire Blais' *Une Liaison parisienne*: An Ambiguous Discovery" by Camille R. La Bossière, in *Selecta* (Corvallis, Oregon), 2, 1981; "The Censored Word and the Body Politic: Reconsidering the Fiction of Marie-Claire Blais" by Karen Gould, in *Journal of Popular Culture* (Bowling Green, Ohio), Winter 1981; "From Shattered Reflections to Female Bonding: Mirroring in Marie-Claire Blais's *Visions d'Anna*" by Paula Gilbert Lewis, in *Québec Studies*, 2, 1984; "Redefining the Maternal: Women's Relationships in the Fiction of Marie-Claire Blais" by Mary Jean Green, in *Traditionalism, Nationalism and Feminism: Women Writers of Quebec*, edited by Paula Gilbert Lewis, Westport, Connecticut, Greenwood, 1985; "Atomized Lives in Limbo: An Analysis of *Mad Shadows* by Marie-Claire Blais" by Coomie S. Vevaina, in *Literary Criterion* (Mysore, India), 22(1), 1987.

*   *   *

Marie-Claire Blais has attracted national and international attention since the appearance of her first novel, *La Belle Bête* (*Mad Shadows*), published when she was barely 20 years old. Since then she has continued to publish, mainly novels but also television and stage plays, at almost yearly intervals at first, and at a slower rhythm in recent years.

From the beginning she has revealed her preoccupation with the lives of those who live on the fringes of, or in opposition to, an oppressive, stifling society, variously symbolised by the Church, parents, school, marriage, and other social institutions. In almost all cases, the young are victims of their elders, although in some writings the horrors of solitary old age are also depicted.

Some of her characters are outcasts, rejected by society for nonconformity to a prevailing norm. For Isabelle in *Mad Shadows*, it is her ugliness that sets her apart. Elsewhere it is sexual preference or the mere fact of youth. Others choose to reject what they see as mediocrity and freely assume marginal lives. In both *David Sterne* and her play *L'Exécution* (*The Execution*), for instance, the central characters, in a gesture reminiscent of Leopold and Loeb, perform gratuitous murders. Similarly, in *Pierre, la guerre du printemps 81* (Pierre in the War of Spring 81) a young man who can find no other way to assert his manhood rallies a group of macho skinhead bikers in a round of mindless violence that parodies the violent events taking place in the world around them.

Blais's writing before 1977 conjures up a picture of a bleak, despairing universe in which individual suffering is the mirror of larger horrors stalking the world, like racism or war. Hope is limited. Perhaps the ordered perfection of mathematics can offer temporary release (*David Sterne*) or, for the privileged few, the act of writing itself, which offers escape into the future — for instance in the first volume of her Pauline Archange triptych, *Manuscrits de Pauline Archange* (*The Manuscripts of Pauline Archange*).

The publication of *Les Nuits de l'Underground* (*Nights in the Underground*) in 1978 reveals a shift in her writing that becomes even more apparent in *Visions d'Anna* (*Anna's World*) of 1982. If the world has not improved, Blais's new feminism allows her for a short period both to posit a variety of warm, loving relationships between women and to offer positive, nurturing values in opposition to the legalised violence of army and state that, in her view, are inherent in a society organised on a patriarchal basis.

Gradually, however, Blais's earlier pessimism has returned, has deepened even. Neither in her recent plays nor in her recent novels does she show any sign of optimism. *L'Ange de la solitude* (The Angel of Solitude) ends with a group of young women scattering on the river the ashes of one of their group, dead in mysterious circumstances, then lighting the candles on the 20th birthday cake the dead girl would never see. *Pierre . . .* shows that even revolt is futile, as Pierre at the end of Spring joins the ranks of those he despises. One may note here Blais's apparent fear that women are about to become victims of a significant backlash.

Blais has chosen to give her writing a universal dimension. Only rarely does she evoke a specific neighbourhood or city, and the few country or cityscapes she offers are symbolic rather than real, frequently shrouded in mist or snow. Even her occasional preoccupation with *joual* (a popular form of French spoken in the Montreal area) stems less from a wish to localize her text than from the desire both to explore the social dimension of language and to revitalise written French.

One of the most important characteristics of her work is her constant experimentation with form, which frequently involves the visual dimension of the printed page as much as other more properly linguistic or stylistic effects. Her concern is, of course, aesthetic; it is also part and parcel of her general questioning of accepted norms.

Blais is one of the first women to have ventured successfully into what was traditionally a masculine field. Not only do her formalist innovations belong to the tradition of writers such as Louis-Ferdinand Céline or Guillaume Apollinaire, but the themes she favours are frequently reminiscent of Friedrich Nietzsche or J. D. Salinger. Female and male characters in her writings live on the dangerous edges of society. This particular aspect of her originality has not always received the notice it deserves.

—Maïr Verthuy

————

BLANDIANA, Ana. Pseudonym for Otilia Valeria Rusan. Romanian. Born in Timişoara, Transylvania, 25 March 1942. Educated at Oradea high school, graduated 1959; University of Cluj, 1962–67, degree in philology 1967. Married to Romulus Rusan. Editor, *Viaţa studenţească*, 1968, and *Amfiteatru*, 1968–74; librarian, Institute of Fine Arts, Bucharest, from 1975. Columnist, *Contemporanul*, 1968–73, and Writers' Union *România literară* magazine, 1974–88. Recipient: Writers' Union poetry prize, 1969, 1980, and journalism prize, 1984; Romanian Academy prize, 1970; Mihai Eminescu Academy prize; Herder prize (Austria), 1982. Address: c/o Cartea Românească, Str Nuferilor 41, 79721 Bucharest, Romania.

PUBLICATIONS

Verse

Persoana întîia plural [First-Person Plural].   Bucharest, Editura de Stat pentru Literatură şi Artă, 1964.
Călcîiul vulnerabil [The Vulnerable Heel].   Bucharest, Editura pentru Literatură, 1966.
A treia taină [The Third Sacrament].   Bucharest, Editura Tineretului, 1969.
Cincizeci de poeme [50 Poems].   Bucharest, Eminescu, 1970.
Octombrie, noiembrie, decembrie [October, November, December].   Bucharest, Cartea Românească, 1972.
Poezii [Poems].   Bucharest, Cartea Românească, 1974.
Somnul din somn [The Sleep Within the Sleep].   Bucharest, Cartea Românească, 1977.
Poeme [Poems].   Bucharest, Albatros, 1978.
Întîmplări din grădina mea [Goings-On in My Garden].   Bucharest, n.p., 1980.
Ochiul de greier [The Cricket's Eye].   Bucharest, Albatros, 1981.
Poems (bilingual edition), translated by Dan Duţescu.   Bucharest, Eminescu, 1982.
Ora de nisip [The Hour of Sand].   Bucharest, Eminescu, 1983.
Stea de pradă [Star of Prey].   Bucharest, Carta Românească, 1985.
Poezii [Poems].   Bucharest, Minerva, 1989.
The Hour of Sand: Selected Poems 1969–1989, translated by Peter Jay and Anca Cristofivici.   London, Anvil Press Poetry, 1990.

Fiction

Cele patru anotimpuri [The Four Seasons].   Bucharest, Albatros, 1977.
Proiecte de trecut: proză [Projects for the Past].   Bucharest, Carta Românească, 1982.

Other

Calitatea de martor [To Be a Witness].   Bucharest, Carta Românească, 1970.
Convorbiri subiective, with Romulus Rusan.   Bucharest, Albatros, 1972.
Eu scriu, tu scrii, el ea scrie [I Write, You Write, He, She Writes].   Bucharest, n.p., 1975.
Cea mai frumoasă dintre lumile posibile [The Most Beautiful of All Possible Worlds].   Bucharest, Carta Românească, 1978.
Coridoare de oglinzi [Corridors of Mirrors], with Romulus Rusan.   Bucharest, Carta Românească, 1984.
Autoportret cu palimpsest.   Bucharest, Eminescu, 1986.

*

Critical Study: "Flights from Reality: Three Romanian Women Poets of the New Generation" by Michael H. Impey, in *Books Abroad* (Norman, Oklahoma), 50, 1976.

* * *

Ana Blandiana is one of the most prominent, lyrical poets writing in Romania today. Hers is a steady, searching voice that echoes some of the thematic and stylistic traditions of her forebears and speaks from a neo-Romantic sensibility. Her poetry is set primarily in the natural world, and explores the relationship between the terrestrial and the spiritual. More recently, however, the political situation in her country has led Blandiana to speak out, however indirectly, and her writings were banned three times in the years leading to the 1989 revolution. As her translators Peter Jay and Anca Cristofovici write in their postscript to *The Hour of Sand*, an English edition of selected poems published in 1990, "Blandiana is at heart an apolitical writer whom the times forced into a political role."

Blandiana published her first book of poems, *Persoana întîia plural* (First-Person Plural), at a lenient, post-Stalin period of Romanian history. Well-received, the poems are youthful and confessional. In subsequent collections such as *A treia taină* (The Third Sacrament), *Octombrie, noiembrie, decembrie* (October, November, December), *Somnul din somn* (The Sleep Within the Sleep), and *Ochiul, de greier* (The Cricket's Eye), Blandiana establishes a vocabulary of imagery and metaphor with which she relentlessly probes the cycle of life. Nature and the seasons play a large part in her imagery of change: fruit which ripens and rots, trees, grass, hay (dead grass) appear again and again. "Una, două, trei" ("One, Two, Three") directly addresses this cycle and how it differs from the human cycle of life and death. Plums fall from the tree and "wait dutifully/To become alcohol," shedding their stones which plant themselves in a regenerative act. The poet concludes wistfully:

> For a plum
> Dying is such an easy and safe thing!
> Her life to come begins every next spring.

Angels recur throughout Blandiana's poetry, but while her concerns are spiritual, they are not necessarily religious. Two early poems depict Jesus speaking to his mother, but the emphasis is on his relationship with her rather than any philosophy he embodies. Nor is Blandiana's spirituality pantheistic; instead she uses nature metaphorically to seek a spiritual reconciliation with the very tangible cycle of life and death as exhibited in nature. From nature she learns of her own death, as in "Eu nu cînt frunza" ("I Do Not Sing the Leaf"):

> I
> Do not sing the leaf,
> I only sing the frail death
> That it hides
> As if it were a country of intoxicating breath,
> And whoever travels to it
> Forgets to return and dies there
> So that he may go
> Even farther
> And be happier . . .

In the 1980s her poems become darker and more pessimistic. While not blatantly political Blandiana begins to be more critical, as in "Inside" from the 1985 collection *Stea de pradă* (Star of Prey):

> And everything known for millennia,
> The beautiful millennia of yesteryear
> When were running in the woods . . .
> Now, only into our own entrails.

Then, more directly, "The Cold Melt" from early 1989 starts:

> Entire decades waiting for
> The turning of the key in the lock;
> More and more rusted,
> Lying in wait for entire decades
> Without words,
> Without a destiny.

and ends: "History in slow motion."

Since the 1989 revolution Romania has been locked in the difficult process of breaking from the past with no guarantees for a brighter future. Time will tell if Blandiana's poetry will be inextricably linked with that of the mood of her country. Nonetheless, her continuing lyricism in the face of uncertainty can be only an aid to Romania's future.

—Theresa Werner

BODELSEN, Anders. Danish. Born in Copenhagen, 11 February 1937. Educated at Ordrup Gymnasium, graduated 1956; University of Copenhagen, 1956–60. Married Eva Sindahl-Pedersen in 1975. Freelance journalist for *Aktuelt*, *Ekstra Bladet*, and *Berlingske Aftenavis*, 1959–64; editor, *Perspektiv*, 1963–65; staff member, *Information*, 1964–67, and *Politiken*, from 1967. Member of Litteraturkritikernes Lav, 1966–69, and Filmrådet, 1969. Recipient: Prix Italia (for radio play), 1967; Danish Critics prize, 1968; Danish Booksellers' Association Golden Laurels, 1969; Grand Prix de la Littérature Policière, 1971; Gyldendal prize, 1981; Danish State Art Foundation lifelong grant, from 1986; Golden Handcuffs, 1986; Oehlenschläger award, 1988; Danish Society for the Blind prize (for radio play), 1989; Swedish Crime Writers Academy prize, 1990; Simon Spies Foundation award, 1990. Address: Christiansholms Parkvej 12, 2930 Klampenborg, Denmark.

PUBLICATIONS

Fiction

De lyse nætters tid [The Time of the Light Nights]. Copenhagen, Thaning & Appel, 1959.
Villa Sunset. Copenhagen, Gyldendal, 1964.
Drivhuset [The Greenhouse]. Copenhagen, Thaning & Appel, 1965.
Rama Sama. Copenhagen, Thaning & Appel, 1967.
Tænk på et tal. Copenhagen, Gyldendal, 1968; as *Think of a Number*, New York, Harper, and London, Joseph, 1969; as *The Silent Partner*, London, Penguin, 1978.
Hændeligt uheld. Copenhagen, Gyldendal, 1968; as *One Down*, New York, Harper, 1970; as *Hit and Run, Run, Run*, London, Joseph, 1970.

Frysepunktet. Copenhagen, Gyldendal, 1969; as *Freezing Down*, New York, Harper, 1971; as *Freezing Point*, London, Joseph, 1971.

Ferie [Holiday]. Copenhagen, Gyldendal, 1970.

Straus. Copenhagen, Gyldendal, 1971; in English, New York, Harper, 1974.

Hjælp: syv noveller [Help: Seven Stories]. Copenhagen, Gyldendal, 1971.

Pigerne på broen [The Girls on the Bridge]. Copenhagen, Gyldendal, 1972.

Uden for nummer [Outside Number]. Copenhagen, Forening for Boghaandværk, 1972.

Bevisets stilling. Copenhagen, Gyldendal, 1973; as *Consider the Verdict*, New York, Harper, 1976.

Lov og orden [Law and Order]. Copenhagen, Gyldendal, 1973.

Alt hvad du ønsker dig [Everything You Wish]. Copenhagen, Gyldendal, 1974.

Blæsten i alleen [The Wind in the Alley]. Copenhagen, Gyldendal, 1975.

Operation Cobra. Copenhagen, Gyldendal, 1975; in English, London, Pelham, 1976; New York, Elsevier, 1979.

Pengene og livet [Money and the Life]. Copenhagen, Gyldendal, 1976.

De gode tider [The Good Times]. Copenhagen, Gyldendal, 1977.

År for år [Year by Year]. Copenhagen, Gyldendal, 1978.

Borte borte [Gone Gone]. Copenhagen, Gyldendal, 1980.

Over regnbuen [Over the Rainbow]. Copenhagen, Gyldendal, 1982.

Domino. Copenhagen, Gyldendal, 1984.

Beskyttelsesrummet [The Shelter]. Vejle, Schweitzers Bogtrykkeri, 1984.

Revision. Copenhagen, Gyldendal, 1985.

Guldregn [Gold Rain/Laburnum] (novelization of television series). Copenhagen, Gyldendal, 1986.

Jeg kommer til at løbe [I Must Run]. Copenhagen, Gyldendal, 1987.

Den blå time [The Blue Hour]. Vejle, Schweitzers Bogtrykkeri, 1987.

Mørk lægning [Blackout]. Copenhagen, Gyldendal, 1988.

Byen uden ildebrande [The Town Without Fires]. Copenhagen, Gyldendal, 1989.

Rød september [Red September]. Copenhagen, Gyldendal, 1991.

Plays

Lørdag aften [Saturday Night]. Copenhagen, Dansk Amatør Teater Samvirke, 1969.

Professor Mancinis hemmelighed og to andre hørespil [Professor Mancini's Secret and Two Other Radio Plays]. Copenhagen, Gyldendal, 1987.

Radio Plays: *En hård dags nat* [A Hard Day's Night], 1966; *Professor Mancinis hemmelighed* [Professor Mancini's Secret], 1971; *Overhøring* [Examination], 1979; *Passageren* [The Passenger], 1979; *Radio*, 1983; *Mørklægning* [Blackout], from his own novel, 1988.

Television Plays: *Skygger* [Shadows], 1972; *Fjernsynet flimrer* [The Television Flickers], 1974; episodes of *En by i provinsen* [A Provincial Town] series, 1977–79; *Guldregn* [Gold Rain/ Laburnum] series, with Søren Kragh-Jacobsen, 1986; *Domino* series, from his own novel, 1991.

Other

Editor, with Ivan Malinovski and Peter Seeberg, *Gruppe 66: introduktion: en antologi* [Group 66: Introduction: An Anthology]. Fredensborg, Arena/Forfatternes, 1966.

Editor, *Filmen nu* [New Films]. Copenhagen, Danmarks Radios Grundbøger, 1966.

*

Critical Study: "Three Danish Authors Examine the Welfare State: Finn Søeborg, Leif Panduro, and Anders Bodelsen" by Frank Hugus, in *Scandinavian Studies* (Madison, Wisconsin), 62(2), 1990.

*   *   *

The Danish novelist Anders Bodelsen has been at the forefront of Scandinavian literary realism for more than three decades. He has put the suspense novel firmly on the literary agenda as a forum for social, psychological, and moral investigation. A prolific author, he has developed a journalistic, mainstream style of writing in opposition to the technique found in the modernistic novel. Bodelsen's skilfulness in reflecting almost seismographically the changes in the socio-psychological climate of post-war Denmark has secured him large audiences, and the idea of art reaching beyond the elite has indeed been emphasized by Bodelsen more than once.

The typical Bodelsen protagonist is a well-adapted, if somewhat lonely male belonging to the new middle classes that mushroomed in the wake of the Danish welfare boom of the 1960s. Although the boom was led by the public sector (in 1960 Denmark had approximately 300,000 public employees, in 1990 about 800,000), the Bodelsen protagonist is employed privately more often than publicly; sometimes he even runs his own business. He is a bank clerk, engineer, factory owner, shopkeeper, journalist, student, civil servant in one of the ministries, or even a competitive fiction writer. As Bodelsen sees it, these middle classes have legitimate expectations to be represented realistically in literature. Bodelsen — who was himself born into an academic family of liberal orientation — has become their portrayer.

A typical Bodelsen novel is located in the new suburbia of greater Copenhagen with high-rise buildings, detached brick houses, modern terraces, shopping and service centres, motorways and metropolitan trains to the city centre. This orderly and recognizable suburbia is, however, juxtaposed by a nearby, almost futuristic cityscape with overtones of physical danger and existential pain: airfields, labyrinthine road complexes, dumping grounds, town moors and parks with viaducts and bridges, lines of railway track cutting through the city, asphalt deserts with closed-down filling stations and pubs out of place, poor neighbourhoods, etc. On excursions into these locations the protagonist, and the reader in his footsteps, encounter the system's outcasts or subversives, who are ambiguously portrayed and frequently linked to illegal money in one form or another.

The typical plot of a Bodelsen novel revolves around the fall of the decent, cautious, and seemingly satisfied protagonist from affluent normality into criminality and crisis, either his own or others — or both. Bodelsen employs the suspense technique to expose the criminal potential in all of us, such as in the novels *Tænk på et tal* (*Think of a Number* or *The Silent Partner*) and *Hændeligt uheld* (*Hit and Run, Run, Run*). As the title suggests, *Hit and Run, Run, Run* addresses the dilemma of the hit-and-run driver, his consequent guilt, and the blackmailing of him. A similar theme can be found in *The*

Silent Partner, which gave Bodelsen his popular breakthrough and has been filmed and translated into many languages. The novel elegantly narrates the story of the bank clerk who cheats the bank robber simply by telling the authorities that more money was stolen than was actually the case — and keeping the difference. He subsequently even steals the robber's girlfriend and has the robber imprisoned! A psychological power struggle then develops between the two men and in the end the past, represented by the released robber and a detective on the trail, seems to catch up with the protagonist, who is forced to commit murder. Thus the novel raises the question of who is the victim and who is the culprit — an existential concern that is more far-reaching than some would expect to find in the suspense genre. Bodelsen's crime novels are, however, characterized precisely by their psychological and moral pursuit: they frequently focus on the paradoxical attachment and similarity between the hunter and the hunted, the blackmailer and the blackmailed. This attachment is, for example, the main theme in *Pengene og livet* (Money and the Life), a direct continuation of *The Silent Partner*, written eight years later.

Bodelsen could be classed as a state-of-the-nation novelist; his best fiction takes the varying pulse of Danishness. (*Revision*) presents its thoroughly researched version of a notorious, unsolved Copenhagen double murder committed in the restless and directionless late 1940s. The novel *Ferie* (Holiday) and the short stories in *Blæsten i Alleen* depict the modest, but also discreetly oppressive 1950s. In the connected novels *De gode tider* (The Good Times) and *År for år* (Year by Year) Bodelsen attempts his most comprehensive treatment of the Danish welfare development, from 1959 to 1971, seen from the point of view of two young and enterprising, though not very successful industrialists. *Borte borte* (Gone Gone) tells the story of the shopkeeper whose trade declines during the oil-crisis of the 1970s and who is persuaded to collect the shop's insurance through arson. *Rød september* (Red September) presents its picture of the uninspired, visionless 1990s, seen through the double pair of eyes of two very different brothers, whose paths cross once again. One is a moderately reformist civil servant in the Danish Ministry of Taxation, while the other is a former revolutionary of the New Left, now an Islamic convert, who returns to his native country on a secret mission. The novel is a tale about the duality of modern society and of modern man as he enters the last decade of the 20th century.

Bodelsen employs the crime genre to expose the shallowness and dark side of prosperity. In the course of a Bodelsen plot, the main characters' quest for happiness is juxtaposed to their actual experience of the alienation, emptiness, loneliness, greediness, and brutality of the new society. Thus Bodelsen stays a long way away from equating happiness and welfare, although an honest fascination with the good life, new technology, and the details of modern living is doubtless also a factor that contributes to popularity of his fiction.

—Bjarne T. Thomsen

———

BONNEFOY, Yves. French. Born in Tours, 24 June 1923. Educated at the Lycée Descartes, Tours; University of Poitiers; University of Paris, degree in philosophy. Married Lucille Vine in 1968; one daughter. Has taught literature at many universities, including Brandeis University, Waltham, Massachusetts, 1962–64, Centre Universitaire, Vincennes, 1969–70, Johns Hopkins University, Baltimore, Princeton University, New Jersey, Yale University, New Haven, Connecticut, University of Geneva, University of Nice, 1973–76, University of Provence, Aix, 1979–81, Collège de France, Paris, since 1981, and Graduate School, City University of New York, since 1986. Co-founder, *L'Éphémère*, Paris, 1967. Recipient: *L'Express* prize, for essays, 1959; Cecil Hemley prize, 1967; Critics prize (France), 1971; Fémina-Vacaresco prize, 1977; Montaigne-prize (Hamburg), 1978; Académie Française grand poetry prize, 1981; Société des Gens de Lettres grand prize, 1987. Address: c/o Collège de France, 11 place Marcelin-Berthelot, 75005 Paris, France.

PUBLICATIONS

Verse

Du mouvement et de l'immobilité de Douve.   Paris, Mercure, 1953; as *On the Motion and Immobility of Douve*, translated by Galway Kinnell, Athens, Ohio University Press, 1968.
Hier régnant désert.   Paris, Mercure, 1958.
Anti-Platon.   Paris, Maeght, 1962.
Pierre écrite.   Paris, Mercure, 1965; as *Pierre écrite/Words in Stone*, translated by Susanna Lang, Amherst, University of Massachusetts Press, 1976.
Selected Poems, translated by Anthony Rudolf.   London, Cape, 1968; New York, Grossman, 1969.
Dans le Leurre du seuil.   Paris, Mercure, 1975; with *Pierre écrite*, as *Poems 1959–1975*, translated by Richard Pevear, New York, Random House, 1985.
Poèmes.   Paris, Mercure, 1978.
Things Dying Things Newborn, translated by Anthony Rudolf.   London, Menard Press, 1985.
Ce qui fut sans lumière.   Paris, Mercure, 1987; as *In the Shadow's Light*, translated by John T. Naughton, Chicago, University of Chicago Press, and Newcastle-upon-Tyne, Bloodaxe, 1991.
Là où retombe la flèche.   Paris, Mercure, 1988.
Early Poems 1947–1959, translated by Galway Kinnell and Richard Pevear.   Athens, Ohio University Press, 1991.
Début et fin de la neige; Là où retombe la flèche.   Paris, Mercure, 1991.

Other

Traité du pianiste.   Paris, Révolution la Nuit, 1946.
Peintures murales de la France gothique.   Paris, Hartmann, 1954.
L'Improbable.   Paris, Mercure, 1959.
La Seconde Simplicité.   Paris, Mercure, 1961.
Rimbaud par lui-même.   Paris, Seuil, 1961; as *Rimbaud*, New York, Harper, 1973.
Miró.   Paris, Bibliothèque des Arts, 1964; in English, New York, Viking Press, 1967.
Un Rêve fait à Mantoue.   Paris, Mercure, 1967.
La Poésie française et le principe d'identité.   Paris, Maeght, 1967.
Rome 1630: L'Horizon du premier baroque.   Paris, Flammarion, 1970.
L'Arrière-pays.   Geneva, Skira, 1972.
Garache, with Jacques Thuillier.   Paris, Maeght, 1975.
L'Ordalie, illustrated by Claude Garache.   Paris, Maeght, 1975.

Terre seconde. Ratilly, Association des Amis de Ratilly, 1976.

Rue traversière. Paris, Mercure, 1977.

Le Nuage rouge: essais sur la poétique. Paris, Mercure, 1977.

Entretiens sur la poésie. Neuchâtel, À la Baconnière, 1981.

La Présence et l'image. Paris, Mercure, 1983.

La Poésie et l'université. Fribourg, Éditions Universitaires Fribourg Suisse, 1984.

Récits en rêve. Paris, Mercure, 1987.

Une Autre Époque de l'écriture. Paris, Mercure, 1988.

La Vérité de parole. Paris, Mercure, 1988.

Sur un Sculpteur et des peintres. Paris, Plon, 1989.

The Act and the Place of Poetry: Selected Essays, edited by John T. Naughton. Chicago and London, University of Chicago Press, 1989.

Eduardo Chillida (exhibition catalogue). Paris, Galerie Lelong, 1990.

Giacometti. Paris, Flammarion, 1991; in English, London, Thames and Hudson, 1991.

Editor, *Dictionnaire des mythologies et des religions des sociétés traditionelles et du monde antique.* Paris, Flammarion, 2 vols., 1981; as *Mythologies*, edited by Wendy Doniger, Chicago, University of Chicago Press, 1991.

Editor, *Poésies*, by Marceline Desbordes-Valmore. Paris, Gallimard, 1983.

Editor and Translator, *Quarante-cinq Poèmes de W. B. Yeats.* Paris, Hermann, 1989.

Translator, *Une Chemise de nuit de flanelle.* Paris, Les Pas Perdus, 1951.

Translator, *1 Henri IV*, *Jules César*, *Hamlet*, *Le Conte d'hiver*, *Vénus et Adonis*, and *Le Viol de Lucrèce*, by Shakespeare. Paris, Club Français du Livre, 6 vols., 1957–60.

Translator, *Jules César*, *Hamlet*, *Le Roi Lear*, *Roméo et Juliette*, and *Macbeth*, by Shakespeare. Paris, Mercure, 5 vols., 1960–83.

*

Critical Studies: *The Inner Theatre of Recent French Poetry*, Princeton, New Jersey, Princeton University Press, 1972, and *Yves Bonnefoy*, Boston, Twayne, 1984, both by Mary Ann Caws; *The Poetics of Yves Bonnefoy* by John T. Naughton, Chicago, University of Chicago Press, 1984.

*   *   *

France's best-loved and most widely translated contemporary poet, Yves Bonnefoy writes both poetry and critical prose in a style at once deceptively simple and powerful in its metaphysical reverberation, in its few figures, and against the few elements of its backdrop.

His first well-known volume of poems, *Du Mouvement et de l'immobilité de Douve* (*On the Motion and Immobility of Douve*), creates for us a figure at once a woman loved, the moat of defense for a castle, a deepening of the earth, and of poetry itself. In his next volumes, the desert dryness that reigned only yesterday leaves its needed ardor, and promises, for tomorrow, a future less arid (*Hier régnant désert*). Then, against a landscape of always greater metaphysical depth, a stone is inscribed, written like the pages (*Pierre écrite*/*Words in Stone*). In his next volume of poems, the scene is cast in a dry landscape but is moving with the sight of the river, where a child is found and poetry is reborn (*Dans le Leurre du seuil*). It seems that always, in his poems, the dark (*Ce qui fut sans lumière* [*In the Shadow's Light*] finds its complementary

illumination. These volumes are made up of successive and simple poems seeming to join together all the voices essential to Bonnefoy's universe, voices of a phoenix and a maenad, of myth and of a real landscape. The ideas on which Bonnefoy's poetics are based hold in an extremely complex and yet apparently simple equilibrium. Our "excarnation" outside ourselves, when we are extended in the world by our collective passions, is balanced by our "incarnation" as we are one with our senses and our intellect; the passion of our art and writing is set against the "unwriting" characteristic of our present critical moment; our literary and artistic past, as it infuses its traditional values into the present by means of intertextual visual and verbal references, may clash with but be included in the future projection of our path. This delicate balance must influence any critical study of Bonnefoy, as that study itself must respond to the various contrary and yet interrelated impulses.

In a writer whose own critical production is known for its perception and deeply human values, the apparent modes of difference — poems and literary essays, tales and critical commentary on art — have their own coherence and even their forms of repetition, so that the reassembling view of what might have seemed dispersed efforts retells and recalls an integrity we already sensed, underlying all the parts.

A strong emphasis should be laid on the idea of place: the place of the essay, of the poem, of the critical vision, and the place of the reader in response to these texts, each related to a time and a space, a now and a here. Each image in the world Bonnefoy's texts inhabit has the power to indicate the whole, so that one stone, a cloud, or a salamander is able to speak of far more than itself. So too any commentary on Bonnefoy's work should, in fact must, reach out past its individual parts to the function and the place of poetry as a whole.

In some remarkable way, Bonnefoy's criticism, both literary and artistic, reflects the simple engagement of the poems and the massive power of a thought fully involved in a morally luminous consideration of what it is to create and to be, here and now on this earth. As we respond to our actual condition, we transcend it, but never for some heaven, only for what humans are able to make with human thought and love and perception. So Bonnefoy suggests we consider the Tombs of Ravenna for their statement about death as a part of life and about the lies of the concept, or the abstract idea, that bloodless refusal of what most counts: being here, using the language we love, seeing the red cloud Mondrian, for example, taught us to see, or hearing the ant scurrying across the leaves, as a haiku might have had us listen to the smallest detail. Just so, the radical sparseness of Giacometti's figures inspires Bonnefoy's most moving meditations.

As he celebrates the small and the available, as well as what is unseen but sensed, that back country (*L'Arrière-pays*) beyond the one in which we live, but which — as we feel it present — gives our time and our space its meaning and its loveliness, Bonnefoy makes of himself one of the great teachers as he is already one of the great poets of our time.

—Mary Ann Caws

BRANTENBERG, Gerd. Norwegian. Born in Oslo, 27 October 1941. Educated at the University of Oslo, arts degree 1971. High school teacher, Copenhagen, 1971–74, and

Oslo, 1974–82. Since 1982 full-time writer. Co-founder of refugee center for women, the Women's High School, Denmark, and Literary Women's Forum, Norway. Recipient: Mads Wiel Nygård prize, 1983; Norwegian Writers' Union scholarship, 1983–88; Thit prize (Denmark), 1986; Sarpsborg prize, 1989. Agent: Aschehougs Forlag, Sehestedsgt. 3, Oslo, Norway. Address: Nils Bays vei 66, 0855 Oslo 8, Norway.

PUBLICATIONS

Fiction

Opp alle jordens homofile. Oslo, Gyldendal, 1973; as *What Comes Naturally*, London, Women's Press, 1986.
Egalias døtre. Oslo, Pax, 1977; as *The Daughters of Egalia*, London, Journeyman, 1985; as *Egalia's Daughters*, Seattle, Seal Press, 1985.
Ja vi slutter [Stop Smoking]. Oslo, Pax, 1978.
Sangen om St. Croix [The Song of St. Croix]. Oslo, Aschehoug, 1979.
Favntak [Embraces]. Oslo, Aschehoug, 1983.
Ved fergestedet [At the Ferry Crossing]. Oslo, Aschehoug, 1985.
For alle vinder [Scattered by the Winds]. Oslo, Aschehoug, 1989.

Play

Egalia, from her own novel (produced Oslo, 1982).

*

Critical Study: "A Norwegian Women's Fantasy: Gerd Brantenberg's *Egalias døtre* as 'kvinneskelig' Utopia" by Verne Moberg, in *Scandinavian Studies* (Madison, Wisconsin), 57(3), 1985.

Gerd Brantenberg comments:

My novels clearly fall in two periods — the first three being satirical feminist works (*What Comes Naturally*, *The Daughters of Egalia*, and *Ja vi slutter*) — 1973–78. After this I've written epic fiction, starting the trilogy with *Sangen om St. Croix* (1979). The trilogy covers the years 1948–65, and is an attempt at portraying those years and the post-war generation.

*   *   *

Central to everything Gerd Brantenberg writes is an active engagement in sexual politics; she is the most well-known contemporary Norwegian writer who has openly declared herself to be lesbian. In fiction and in her articles and speeches she has made an important contribution towards a greater tolerance of alternative sexuality in Norwegian society.

Her first novel, *Opp alle jordens homofile* (*What Comes Naturally*), is the story of a girl discovering what it is like to be a lesbian in Oslo in the 1960s, the so-called decade of sexual liberation which, in fact, only liberated heterosexuals. It is not, however, a serious tract, but a very funny story, in which the narrator continually finds herself in absurd situations, and has as much difficulty in explaining her actions to her own well-brought-up self as she does to her reader.

Brantenberg's breakthrough came with her next novel, *Egalias døtre* (*The Daughters of Egalia*), which became an international bestseller. It takes place in an imaginary world, Egalia, a matriarchy in which women literally wear the trousers. Yet this is no utopia; it is a parody, which turns our

familiar society on its head to expose its absurdity. In a world in which God is female and society was founded by the Moulding Mothers, it is the men who wear tight skirts and uncomfortable shoes, curl their beards, and remove their chest hair. Selective breeding favours men who are short, fat, and gentle, and women who are tall and strong. The novel describes a revolt against this inequality which leads to the founding of the masculist movement, and the burning of penis holders.

It is not only social structures with which the author takes issue here. Language, as feminist theorists know, is one of the subtlest forms of oppression, which structures the way people conceive of themselves; it is impossible to change the way people think without changing the language in which they think. In order to give authentic expression to a woman-centred world view, Brantenberg found that she had to abandon "phallocentric" language and invent her own. In Egalia, the dominant form is the female; thus instead of deriving "woman" from "man" and "female" from "male," she derives "manwom" from "wom" and "mafele" from "fele." (In Norwegian, the problems are different; but the author worked with the English translator to produce ingenious alternatives.) The hero Petronius's suggestion that he wants to become a mafele seawom is ridiculed by his aggressive sister Ba, while Director Bram demands peace to read the paper and her housebound Christopher tries to placate everyone. Petronius's thoughts are soon directed in a more seemly fashion towards the maidmen's ball, in which the young lordies hope to be carried off by the wom of their dreams, to escape the dire fate of ending up an elderly spinnerman. The masculist rebellion is a shock to society's rulers, who cannot understand what the menwim are complining about, as they are so well looked after. The novel is the best example in Norwegian literature of the effectiveness of humour as a weapon in the fight for sexual equality.

After this, Brantenberg returned to realism with her trilogy *Sangen on St. Croix* (The Song of St. Croix), *Ved fergestedet* (At the Ferry Crossing), and *For alle vinder* (Scattered by the Winds), a semi-autobiographical account of growing up in Brantenberg's home town of Fredrikstad. The novels trace the story of Inger, her family and friends, from the day she begins school through to her experiences as a student at the University of Oslo. Inger's unwillingness to accept her growing awareness that she is different, that she does not fall in love with boys like the other girls but with girls instead, forms the core of the story; she carries the awareness with her like a catastrophe, feeling that she must be the only one singled out for such misery. It is not until the age of 22 that she manages to begin to talk about it, and to discover that she is not alone in the world. For here too, the problem is one of language; there are no words for this love which literally has no name, and while others can indulge in all the effusions of romance, Inger is reduced to silence. In a sense, this is what makes her a writer, as she begins to write what she cannot say.

The trilogy puts Inger's experiences into a broader social perspective of life in a provincial town in the 1950s and in Oslo in the 1960s. It follows a class of children through their school careers, demonstrating unobtrusively how — with the best of motives — school and home subtly pressurize both boys and girls into traditional life and work patterns. The independence of girls is stifled not by decree but by the images they are presented with: "It wasn't school that curbed the rebellion. It was make-up" (*Sangen om St. Croix*). The mothers' generation is also described — those who had even less hope than their daughters of breaking the mould. Inger's mother Evelyn gave up her acting career to marry and have children too young, and has been reduced by her husband's tyrannical behaviour to a nervous wreck, who eventually loses the will to live: "Papa got the woman he loved. Mamma. And then he destroyed her."

By the end of the trilogy, Inger is building up an identity which does not falsify her real inclinations; but it has been a long and painful process. Brantenberg's fiction demonstrates how far there is still to go before society extends its tolerance to its ugly ducklings: "When would the ice finally break up so that they could see themselves, mirror themselves in the water and see that they were fine? When would a flock of youngsters stand on the shore and call to them: 'There's a new one!'" (*For alle vinder*).

—Janet Garton

BRAUN, Volker. German. Born in Dresden, 7 May 1939. Educated at German high school, graduated 1957; University of Leipzig, 1960–64. Has one daughter. Worked as a machine operator and construction worker; travelled to Siberia, 1964, France, 1971, Cuba, Peru, and Italy, 1976, and England, 1980; reader or assistant director, Berliner Ensemble, 1965–66 and from 1977, Leipzig Municipal Theatre, 1971–72, and Deutsches Theater, Berlin, 1972–77. Recipient: Heine prize, 1971; Heinrich Mann prize, 1980; Berliner prize, 1989; Lessing prize; City of Bremen prize; GDR National prize. Member, Academy of Arts, Berlin, and Mainz Academy of Sciences and Literature. Address: Wolfshagener Straße 68, 1100 Berlin, Germany.

PUBLICATIONS

Plays

Kipper Paul Bauch. Published in *Deutsches Theater der Gegenwart*, Frankfurt, Suhrkamp, 1967; as *Die Kipper* (produced Zurich, 1972), Berlin, Aufbau, 1972.
Hans Furst (produced Weimar, 1968).
Hinze und Kunze (produced Weimar, 1968). Berlin, Henschel, 1972.
Freunde (produced 1972). Published in *Neue Stücke der deutschen Demokratischen Republik*, Berlin, Henschel, 1971.
Stücke 1 (includes *Die Kipper*; *Hinze und Kurze*; *Tinka*). Frankfurt, Suhrkamp, 1975.
Tinka (produced Karl-Marx-Stadt, 1976). In *Stücke 1*, 1975.
Guevara, oder, Der Sonnenstaat (produced Mannheim, 1977). Frankfurt, Suhrkamp, 1977.
Grosser Frieden (produced Berlin, 1979). Berlin, Henschel, 1979; as *The Great Peace* (produced Colchester, 1983).
Simplex Deutsch (produced Berlin, 1980). Berlin, Henschel, 1982(?).
Schmitten (produced Leipzig, 1982). In *Stücke 2*, 1981.
Stücke 2 (includes *Schmitten*; *Guevara, oder, Der Sonnenstaat*; *Grosser Frieden*; *Simplex Deutsch*). Frankfurt, Suhrkamp, 1981.
Dmitri, adaptation of an unfinished play by Günter Schiller (produced Karlsruhe, 1982). Frankfurt, Suhrkamp, 1982.
Stücke (vol. 1 includes *Die Kipper*; *Hinze und Kunze*; *Schmitten*; *Tinka*; *Guevara, oder, Der Sonnenstaat*; *Grosser Frieden*; *Simplex Deutsch*; *Dmitri*; vol. 2 includes *Der Eisenwagen*; *Lenins Tod*; *Totleben*; *Die Übergangs-*

gesellschaft; *Siegfried*; *Frauenprotokolle*; *Deutscher Furor*; *Transit Europa*). Berlin, Henschel, 2 vols., 1983–89.
Siegfried; Frauenprotokolle; Deutscher Furor (produced Weimar, 1986). Berlin, Henschel, 1987.
Übergangsgesellschaft (produced Bremen, 1987). Berlin, Henschel, 1987.
Stücke 3. Frankfurt, Suhrkamp, 1987.
Transit Europa, adaptation of the novel *Transit* by Anne Seghers (produced Berlin, 1988). Berlin, Henschel, 1987.
Lenins Tod (produced Berlin, 1988). Berlin, Henschel, 1988.
Das Denkmal. Published in *Texte*, 6, 1991.

Verse

Provokation für mich. Halle, Mitteldeutscher, 1965; enlarged edition, as *Vorläufiges*, Frankfurt, Suhrkamp, 1966.
Kriegserklärung. Halle, Mitteldeutscher, 1967.
Wir und nicht sie. Halle, Mitteldeutscher, 1970; enlarged edition, 1979.
Gedichte, edited by Christel and Walfried Hartinger. Leipzig, Reclam, 1972; enlarged edition, 1976.
Gegen die symmetrische Welt. Halle, Mitteldeutscher, 1974.
Zeit-Gedichte. Munich, Damnitz, 1977.
Der Stoff zum Leben. Pffaffenweiler, Pfaffenweiler Presse, 1977.
Gedichte. Frankfurt, Suhrkamp, 1979.
Training des aufrechten Gangs. Halle, Mitteldeutscher, 1979.
Rimbaud: ein psalm der aktualität. Stuttgart, Steiner, 1985.
Langsamer knirschender Morgen. Halle, Mitteldeutscher, and Frankfurt, Suhrkamp, 1987.
Annatomie. Bremen, Neuer Bremer Presse, 1989.

Fiction

Das ungezwungne Leben Kasts: Drei Berichte. Berlin, Aufbau, 1972; enlarged edition, 1979.
Unvollendete Geschichte. Frankfurt, Suhrkamp, 1977.
Berichte von Hinze und Kunze. Halle, Mitteldeutscher, 1983.
Hinze-Kunze-Roman. Frankfurt, Suhrkamp, 1985.
Bodenloser Satz. Frankfurt, Suhrkamp, 1990.

Other

Es genügt nicht die einfache Wahrheit: Notate. Leipzig, Reclam, 1975.
Im Querschnitt: Gedichte, Prosa, Stücke, Aufsätze, edited by Holger J. Schubert. Halle, Mitteldeutscher, 1978.
Verheerende Folgen mangelnden Anscheins innerbetrieblicher Demokratie: Schriften. Leipzig, Reclam, and Frankfurt, Suhrkamp, 1988.
Texte: in zeitlicher Folge. Halle, Mitteldeutscher, 7 vols., 1989–91.

*

Bibliography: "Bibliographie Volker Braun" by Winifred Hönes, in *Text und Kritik* (Munich), 55, 1977.

Critical Studies: "Volker Braun's *Tinka*: Two Views" by Margaret E. Ward, in *University of Dayton Review* (Dayton, Ohio), 13(2), 1978; "Theater of Provocation: The Plays of Volker Braun" by Christine Cosentino, in *West Virginia University Philological Papers* (Morgantown), 25, 1979;

"Volker Braun's Lyric Poetry: Problems of Reception" by Ian Wallace, in *Studies in GDR Culture and Society, III: Selected Papers from the Eighth International Symposium on the German Democratic Republic*, edited by Margy Gerber and others, Lanham, Maryland, University Press of America, 1983; "Back to the Future: Volker Braun and the German Theatrical Tradition" by Julian Hilton, in *A Radical Stage: Theatre in Germany in the 1970s and 1980s*, edited by W. G. Sebald, Oxford, Berg, 1988.

* * *

Volker Braun has been one of the most innovative and controversial of the many authors in the former German Democratic Republic who in the past 30 years outpaced the sometimes moribund writing of the Federal Republic. Born in 1939, he belonged to a generation young enough to be free of the taint of fascism and to have grown up within the structures of a nascent socialist state. This also meant that, though a convinced Marxist himself, he did not need to defend at all costs the often rigid, narrow thinking of the old guard of communists who had established the GDR and held the reins of power. Indeed, it was his mordant denunciation of them and their successors that earned him a great deal of official dislike and suspicion.

The difficulty of integrating Braun harmoniously into officially endorsed modes of thinking can be attributed to his fierce predilection for dialectic. This is of course the keystone of Marxist-Leninist theory and is inherent in the concepts of contradiction, revolution, progress; in practice there is a tendency for achieved positions to settle into lethargy and complacency. For Braun, the very structure of society in all its aspects is a constant dialectical process in which nothing is at rest or complete, where the "consolidation of achievements" means calling those achievements into question. Over three decades Braun has turned his hand to all the major genres, publishing several plays and collections of poetry as well as a handful of prose works. They all consistently embody his overriding impulse to dialectic, but it is the lyric form that, by his own confession, offers him the most effective mode of expressing it.

Braun's acute sense of realism tempered his faith in progress and enabled him to perceive clearly the dialectic deep in the new society. The collision between ideals and utopian projections on the one hand and the irksome, irritating subjection to mediocre leadership and dour economic facts on the other was an inevitable theme in the political context of the GDR, and Braun articulated the impatience of his generation in uncompromising terms. The conflicts associated with the process of evolving a socialist consciousness, the hurt of change, were focused on the workplace. Here the contradictions intrinsic to the division of labour, the role of women, demands for codetermination by the workforce, and above all the exercise of authority were tackled by Braun with blunt and forthright honesty. His enthusiastic advocacy of the *process* of revolution made it impossible for him to assimilate to any establishment and ranked him with a younger generation that could not accept the achievements of its elders as the final goal. For this reason he was the *enfant terrible* of GDR literature, asserting his affinity with earlier rebels in German culture, Friedrich Klopstock, Friedrich Hölderlin and Georg Büchner, and finding in Arthur Rimbaud, that scourge of the Second Empire in France, a paradigm — even a symbol — for his own situation in the GDR.

Braun's evocation of the dilemmas of Hölderlin and Büchner had already posed some awkward leading questions in the 1970s. The prose work *Unvollendete Geschichte* (Un-

finished Story) deals with two young people pressurized to conform to imposed patterns of behaviour; social alienation, hostility, attempted suicide, and isolation are the result. In drama too he was moving away from "production pieces" (which investigated the frictions accompanying the transition to collective industry) to broader historical and parabolic themes. In the 1970s Braun felt that the GDR, still in the slow process of socialist formation, had ossified into rigid structures in which the ordinary person was deprived of a decision-making role. This aroused in him a mood of melancholy resignation, but also prompted a harder satirical tone. The smothering of lively participation by an overwhelming state apparatus was expressed in the recurring images of "Schlamm," "Brei," "ewiger Schnee," "Eis der Strukturen" (mud, mush, unending snow, frozen structures), and he sought new strategies of writing to demolish illusions and give vent to a widespread sense of frustration and impotence. The volume of poems *Training des aufrechten Gangs* (Training of an Upright Stance), with its ambiguous title, is a concentration of Braun's almost palpable invective against bureaucracy and at the same time of his unquenchable hope. The dominant tone of these poems is that of a sad and angry rebelliousness against a static system, but also a belief in the organic evolution of a real socialism from the confined larva to the wondrous flight of the butterfly.

The last years of the GDR gave Braun no cause to modify his attacks on the sluggish self-complacency of its society, and his work consequently often had to fight its way to publication. His *Hinze-Kunze-Roman* (Dick-and-Harry Novel) reiterates in the relationship of Hinze and Kunze the theme of power and subordination. This pair had appeared in different genres from Braun's earliest writing; now Kunze is made a high-ranking, overbearing, and sexually pleasure-seeking official whose slightest order his chauffeur Hinze has to obey (echoes of Brecht's Puntila and Matti). Again the vitality, resourcefulness, and down-to-earth common sense of the ordinary man is presented as superior to and capable of surmounting the abuse of power endemic to those in privileged and protected positions.

Unlike Rimbaud, Braun did not opt out; his "innermost Africa" is a vision of liberation in images of the open sea and the frontier, a breaking out from the shell of constraints. For him, utopia is not a predetermined goal in the distance we must strive to reach, but an ever-present potential, in our very bones. If there is a spiritual dimension to Braun's writing it resides in the humanistic certainty that each individual, equal to every other, has the right to a continuing voice in his or her own destiny as a single entity and as part of a community. The complacent trumpeting of achievements must give way to the sense of process, the perpetual living movement of change.

On the disintegration of the GDR Braun quickly spoke out on the elated but unstable freedoms newly found, advocating a system of citizens' forums and people's committees, and seeking to dissuade his fellow countrymen from embracing too eagerly a meretricious Western ethos. The circumstances of German reunification seem to indicate that Braun will remain a lone poetic voice in an ideological wilderness.

—Arrigo V. Subiotto

BREYTENBACH, Breyten. South African and French. Born in Bonnievale, 16 September 1939. Educated at the University of Cape Town, until 1959. Married Yolande Ngo Thi Hoang

Lien in 1964. Lived in Paris, 1961–75; founder, Okhela anti-apartheid organization; on incognito visit to South Africa, arrested and imprisoned for anti-apartheid activities, 1975–82. Recipient: A.P.B. literary prize, 1964; Afrikaans Press Corps prize, 1964; South African Central News Agency prize, 1967, 1970; Van der Hoogt prize (Netherlands), 1972; Perskor newspaper group prize, 1976; Pris des Sept, 1977; Hertzog prize, 1984; *Rapport* prize, 1986. Lives in Paris. Address: c/o Faber and Faber Ltd., 3 Queen Square, London WC1N 3AU, England.

PUBLICATIONS

Verse

Die ysterkoei moet sweet [The Iron Cow Must Sweat]. Johannesburg, Afrikaanse Pers, 1964.
Die huis van die dowe [House of the Deaf]. Cape Town, Human & Rousseau, 1967.
Kouevuur [Gangrene]. Cape Town, Buren-Uitgewers, 1969.
Oorblyfsels. Cape Town, Buren-Uitgewers, 1970.
Lotus (as Jan Blom). Cape Town, Buren-Uitgewers, 1970.
Skryt: om 'n sinkende skip blou te verf [Sky/Write: To Paint a Sinking Ship Blue]. Amsterdam, Meulenhoff, 1972.
Met ander woorde: vrugte van die droom van stilte [In Other Words: Fruits from the Dream of Silence] (includes some prose). Cape Town, Buren, 1973.
Voetskrif [Footscript]. Johannesburg, Perskor, 1976.
Blomskryf: uit die gedigte van Breyten Breytenbach en Jan Blom [Flower Writing] (as Breytenbach and Jan Blom). Emmarentia, Taurus, 1977.
Sinking Ship Blues. Toronto, Oasis, 1977.
And Death White as Words: An Anthology of the Poetry of Breyten Breytenbach (bilingual edition), edited by A. J. Coetzee. London, Collings, 1978.
In Africa Even the Flies Are Happy: Selected Poems, 1964–1977, translated by Denis Hirson. London, Calder, 1978.
Vingermaan: tekeningen uit Pretoria [Fingermoon: Drawings from Pretoria]. Amsterdam, Meulenhoff, 1980.
Eklips: die derde bundel van die ongedanste dans. Emmarentia, Taurus, 1983.
Lewendood: kantlynkarteling by 'n digbundel. Emmarentia, Taurus, 1985.

Fiction

Katastrofes [Catastrophes]. Johannesburg, Afrikaanse Pers, 1964; parts published as *Die miernes swel op; Ja die fox-terrier kry 'n weekend*, Emmarentia, Taurus, 1980.
Om te vlieg: 'n opstel in vyf ledemate en 'n ode. Cape Town, Buren-Uitgewers, 1971.
Memory of Snow and of Dust. New York, Farrar Straus, and London, Faber, 1989.

Other

'N Seisoen in die paradys (includes some prose). Johannesburg, Perskor, 1976; as *A Season in Paradise*, London, Cape, and New York, Persea, 1980.
Mouroir: bespieëlende nota's van 'n roman. Emmarentia, Taurus, 1983; as *Mouroir: Mirrornotes of a Novel*, New York, Farrar Straus, and London, Faber, 1984.
Buffalo Bill: panem et circenses. Emmarentia, Taurus, 1984.

The True Confessions of an Albino Terrorist (includes verse). Emmarentia, Taurus, and London, Faber, 1984; New York, Farrar Straus, 1985.
End Papers: Essays, Letters, Articles of Faith, Workbook Notes. London, Faber, and New York, Farrar Straus, 1986.
Boek: dryfpunt (essays). Emmarentia, Taurus, 1987.
Judas Eye; Self Portrait, Deathwatch (verse and essays). New York, Penguin, and London, Faber, 1988.
All One Horse. Emmarentia, Taurus, and London, Faber, 1990.

Translator, *Titus Andronicus*, by William Shakespeare. Cape Town, Buren-Uitgewers, 1970.

*

Critical Studies: "Breyten Breytenbach and the Poet Revolutionary" by P. P. van der Merwe, in *Theoria* (Natal), May 1981; "The Martian Descends: The Poetry of Breyten Breytenbach" by Gerald Moore, in *Ariel* (Calgary, Alberta), April 1985; "Breyten Breytenbach and the South African Prison Book" by J. U. Jacobs, in *Theoria* (Natal), December 1986; "Breyten Breytenbach's Prison Literature" by Sheila Roberts, in *Centennial Review* (East Lansing, Michigan), Spring 1986; "Breytenbach's *Mouroir*: The Novel as Autobiography" by Susanna Egan, in *Journal of Narrative Technique* (Ypsilanti, Michigan), Spring 1988.

* * *

Breyten Breytenbach is, if not South Africa's undisputed leading poet, at least one of the most conspicuous and widely read poets. This is all the more surprising because he writes in Afrikaans, a language confined to about 13 million people inside South Africa. His work has, however, been widely translated into English and other major languages because of his early and uncompromising opposition against apartheid. This oppositional stance to the ruling Afrikaner establishment in South Africa, which felt utterly betrayed by the fact that one of its main poets, one of the guardians of the Afrikaans language, turned against both it and them. Small wonder that Breytenbach spent seven years in jail in South Africa, and lived in exile in Paris for many years.

Yet Breytenbach is a political poet only by necessity. The common theme of most of his poetry more often than not is love. Though this "love" encompasses love between the sexes, it is by no means limited to this one expression of what appears as a cosmic principle in Breytenbach's work. Rather, in much of his work, which from an early stage has exhibited the distinct influence of both Zen Buddhism and Indian Tantrism, the physical union of man and woman is sublimated in the union of the male earth-bound god and the female creative principle, of Shiva and Shakti respectively. Breytenbach has undoubtedly written some of the most moving, because inventive, tender, creative, childlike, and playful love poetry of the 20th century. In these poems sexual love becomes an extended meditation or, as Breytenbach himself puts it, "copulation is meditation." This also explains why so many of his best love poems are "daybreak poems," in which the mind wanders freely between sleep and wakefulness and expresses itself in unusual juxtapositions of words, neologisms, allusions, and quotations.

Poetry is, as Breytenbach puts it, the very "breath of his being," which appears in "the shape of his voice." On a less exalted level of discourse he has referred to his writing of poetry as a "normal bodily function." It is perhaps the combination of his view of himself as the "inescapable" poet, and of his strong conviction of the existence of love as the cosmic principle that joins subject and object in a bond they cannot destroy without destroying each other, that has made Breytenbach the natural spokesman of those who do not have a voice, who, until very recently, were not allowed to speak for themselves inside South Africa.

Breytenbach's anger, disappointment, grief at what has been happening in South Africa, and the sometimes vitriolic invective in which those emotions have expressed themselves, may well stem from the realization that the country he was born in and grew up in did not practice the form of love preached in the Calvinist Bible read and revered by its Afrikaner establishment. Breytenbach's political poetry is always biting, direct, and dripping with either irony or sarcasm, depending on the strength of the emotion that prompted the writing of a particular poem.

And yet there is another dimension also to his political poetry. In accordance with his Zen views, Breytenbach sees decay and dissolution as the potential source of new life, hence perhaps his vituperative anger at the "verkrampte" politicians of his homeland, who tried for so long to prevent a process of necessary decay, which could lead to a new beginning.

Apart from the love he celebrates in so many of his poems, Breytenbach also shows another side of his persona in his work, the side that is forever connected with the very South Africa that is the villain of his political poetry, the South Africa of parents, family, and friends, all or most of whom could be tarred with the same brush as "oppressors." The poems connected with this side of Breytenbach's persona deal with exile, the lack of love and understanding, and a sometimes poignantly expressed nostalgia for the land of his birth. For Breytenbach exile is a matter of artistic life and death. Especially in some of the poems written shortly before F. W. de Klerk came to power in South Africa, the poet sounds a note of despair, since exile may ultimately imply the loss of connection with the living Afrikaans that is spoken by whites, "coloureds," and blacks in South Africa, and not by many people in Paris, where Breytenbach has spent most of his years in exile. The very loss of this connection might mean nothing less than artistic death for the poet, and the fear of this kind of death is a powerful motif in some of Breytenbach's "poems of exile." With the recent changes in South Africa, however, the threat of artistic death has become more and more remote for Breytenbach, who has become a frequent visitor to his native country.

—André Lefevere

———

BRODSKII, Iosif (Alexandrovich). Also Joseph Brodsky. Russian and American. Born in Leningrad, 24 May 1940; emigrated to the United States in 1972, naturalized 1977. Educated at schools in Leningrad to age 15. Married; one son and one daughter. Convicted as a "social parasite" in 1964 and served 20 months of a five-year sentence of hard labour in the far north; later exiled by the Soviet government; poet-in-residence and Special Lecturer, University of Michigan, Ann Arbor, 1972–73, 1974–80; has taught at Queen's College, City University of New York, Columbia University, New York, New York University, Smith College, Northampton, Massachusetts, Amherst College, Massachusetts, and Hampshire College. Currently Professor of literature, Mount Holyoke College, South Hadley, Massachusetts. Recipient: Guggenheim fellowship; MacArthur fellowship; Mondello prize (Italy), 1979; National Book Critics' Circle award, 1987; Nobel prize for literature, 1987. D.Litt.: Yale University, New Haven, Connecticut, 1978. Member, American Academy of Arts and Letters: resigned in 1987 to protest Evgenii Evtushenko (q.v.) being made an honorary member; corresponding member, Bavarian Academy of Sciences; U.S. Poet Laureate, 1991–92. Address: Department of English, Mount Holyoke College, South Hadley, Massachusetts 01075–1496, U.S.A.

PUBLICATIONS

Verse

Stikhotvoreniia i poemy [Longer and Shorter Poems]. Washington, D.C., Inter-Language, 1965.
Elegy to John Donne and Other Poems, translated by Nicholas Bethell. London, Longman, 1967.
Ostanovka v pustyne [A Halt in the Wilderness]. New York, Chekhov, 1970; corrected edition, Ann Arbor, Michigan, Ardis, 1988.
Selected Poems, translated by George L. Kline, foreword by W. H. Auden. New York, Harper, and London, Penguin, 1973.
Debut, translated by Carl R. Proffer. Ann Arbor, Michigan, Ardis, 1973.
Three Slavic Poets, with Tymoteusz Karpowicz and Djordje Nikolic. Chicago, Elpenor, 1975.
Konets prekrasnoi epokhi: stikhotvoreniia 1964–1971 [The End of the Belle Epoque: Poems 1964–1971]. Ann Arbor, Michigan, Ardis, 1977.
Chast' rechi: stikhotvoreniia 1972–1976. Ann Arbor, Michigan, Ardis, 1977.
A Part of Speech. London, Oxford University Press, and New York, Farrar Straus, 1980.
V Anglii [In England]. Ann Arbor, Michigan, Ardis, 1977.
Verses on the Winter Campaign 1980. London, Anvil Press Poetry, 1981.
Rimskie elegii [Roman Elegies]. New York, Russica, 1982.
Novye stansy k Avguste: stikhi k M.B. 1962–1982 [New Stanzas to Augusta: Poems to M.B. 1962–1982]. Ann Arbor, Michigan, Ardis, 1983.
Uraniia [Urania]. Ann Arbor, Michigan, Ardis, 1987.
To Urania (selected poems). Toronto, Collins, New York, Farrar Straus, and London, Viking, 1988.
Primechaniia paporotnika [A Fern's Commentary]. Bromma, Sweden, Hylaea, 1990.
Osennii krik iastreba [The Hawk's Cry in Autumn]. Leningrad, n.p., 1990.
Stikhotvoreniia [Poems]. Leningrad, Alga-Fond, 1990.
Chast' rechi: izbrannye stikhi 1962–1989 [A Part of Speech: Selected Poems 1962–1989]. Moscow, Khudozhestvennaia literatura, 1990.
Bog sokhraniaet vse [God Preserves All Things]. Moscow, Mif, 1991.
Forma vremeni [The Form of Time] (vol. 2 includes essays and plays). Minsk, Eridan, 2 vols., 1992.
Sochineniia [Works]. St. Petersburg, Pushkinskii fond & Tret'ia volna, 1992.

Plays

Mramor. Ann Arbor, Michigan, Ardis, 1984; as *Marbles: A*

Play in Three Acts, New York, Farrar Straus, and London, Penguin, 1989.

Demokratiia/Démocratie (bilingual edition in Russian and French).   Paris, Éditions à Die, 1990; as *Democracy* (produced London, 1990), published in *Granta* (London), 30, 1990.

Other

Less than One: Selected Essays.   New York, Farrar Straus, and London, Viking, 1986.

The Nobel Lecture.   New York, Farrar Straus, 1988.

Razmerom podlinnike [In the Meter of the Original] (essays; includes essays by others about his work).   Tallin, Estonia, n.p., 1990.

Tragicheskii elegik (o poezii Evgeniia Reina) [A Tragic Elegist (on the Poetry of Evgenii Rein)].   Published in *Znamia* (Moscow), 7, 1991.

Watermark.   New York, Farrar Straus, and London, Hamish Hamilton, 1992; in Russian, Moscow, Slovo, 1992.

Vspominaia Akhmatova [Remembering Akhmatova].   Moscow, Nezavisimaia gazeta, 1992.

Editor, with Carl Proffer, *Modern Russian Poets on Poetry: Blok, Mandelstam, Pasternak, Mayakovsky, Gumilev, Tsvetaeva*.   Ann Arbor, Michigan, Ardis, 1982.

Editor, *An Age Ago: A Selection of Nineteenth-Century Russian Poetry*.   New York, Farrar Straus, 1988.

*

Bibliographies: by George L. Kline, in *Ten Bibliographies of Twentieth Century Russian Literature*, Ann Arbor, Michigan, Ardis, 1977; in *Joseph Brodsky: A Poet for Our Time* by Valentina Polukhina, Cambridge, Cambridge University Press, 1989.

Critical Studies: "A Struggle Against Suffocation" by Czesław Miłosz, in *New York Review*, 14 August 1980; *Joseph Brodsky: A Poet for Our Time*, Cambridge, Cambridge University Press, 1989, and *Brodsky Through the Eyes of His Contemporaries*, London, Macmillan, 1992, both by Valentina Polukhina; *Joseph Brodsky's Poetics and Aesthetics*, edited by Lev Loseff and Valentina Polukhina, London, Macmillan, 1990; *Joseph Brodsky and the Creation of Exile* by David M. Bethea, Princeton, New Jersey, Princeton University Press, 1994.

*   *   *

Iosif Brodskii has been powerfully influenced by such major Russian poets as the 18th-century Gavriil Derzhavin, the 19th-century Evgenii Baratynskii, and the three 20th-century giants: Boris Pasternak, Osip Mandel'shtam, and Marina Tsvetaeva. But the influence of a number of Western poets has been equally strong, from John Donne and Andrew Marvell, through Robert Frost, Dylan Thomas, and T. S. Eliot, to the emigré Polish poet Czesław Miłosz. Brodskii was personally close to Anna Akhmatova from 1960 until the time of her death (in 1966) and to W. H. Auden from June 1972 until the latter's death (in September 1973). For the younger poet the

two older poets served not as direct literary models but rather as vivid exemplars of what it means to be a great poet, and a great human being, living with courage and dignity in desperate times.

As an exiled poet, Brodskii stands consciously in the tradition of Joseph Conrad rather than in that of Ovid. He has not — like Ovid in Scythia yearning for Rome — spent himself in nostalgia for his unrecoverable homeland. Instead he has immersed himself, with notable energy and imagination, in the literature and culture of the West. The latest evidence of this is the brilliant and sensitive meditation on the culture and architecture of Venice contained in his slim volume *Watermark*. Although for Brodskii exile is in a sense the poet's "natural condition," one notes a sharp difference between the poems written during his internal exile (1964–65), those written (in early 1972) in anticipation of his permanent foreign exile, and those written, beginning late in 1972, after he found himself in the West. The first group of poems conveys a sense of shock and loss, a sense of "being overboard" and in "no-man's land," of going deaf, blind, even mad, of losing his memory. But in these poems there is no hint of becoming *mute*, of lapsing into silence — a theme powerfully expressed in the third group of poems of exile.

The second group of poems poignantly expresses Brodskii's anticipation of painful personal losses — loss of the woman he loves, who is the mother of his young son, and of that son. Other poems in this group advance a Brodskiian theme which was to be more fully developed in later poems: that of the "Empire" — a huge, amoral, menacing force standing in opposition to the free, or freedom-seeking, individual.

The third group of poems expresses a set of themes new to the then 32-year-old poet: a sense of growing old and decrepit, of lapsing into "non-speaking" (*molchanie*). Physical attrition is linked to cultural and literary loss in Brodskii's catalogue of the things he is losing — "volosy, zuby, glagoly, suffiksy" ("my teeth and hair, my verbs and endings"). The last symbolize the absolute control of his native language that a poet, to be a poet, must retain. At the same time, Brodskii has made it clear from the beginning that the poet is an instrument of language (as of culture generally), rather than the other way around, as is frequently assumed.

In certain poems dating from 1974–76 the poet is tacitly identified, or at least closely associated, with three historical figures — Dante, Mary Queen of Scots, and Marshal Zhukov — who, despite their obvious differences, have in common the fact that they were abused (exiled, imprisoned, or executed) by the city or country which they loved and served, and which came belatedly to reverse its harsh judgment and pay them the high honors that were their due. In Brodskii's case recognition and honor in his homeland began in 1988 and accelerated in 1990, with conferences devoted to his work and the publication of numerous books, poems, and articles by and about him in Moscow, St. Petersburg, Tallin, Minsk, and other cities of the former Soviet Union.

Poetry, for Brodskii, is a revelation of "what time does to the existing individual" — as manifested in loss, separation, deformity, disease, madness, old age, and death. Some of his most powerful poems evoke, in controlled "classical" form, a series of disturbing "existentialist" and even "absurdist" visions of the "horrors and atrocities" of human existence and the "infernal nothingness" of death. Yet it is poetry which offers a way, in the end perhaps the *only* way, of enduring these horrors and atrocities.

As a verse translator, Brodskii has produced splendid Russian versions of Donne, Marvell, Miłosz, and the Lithuanian-born poet Tomas Venclova. He has written (in Russian before the mid-1970s, in English since that time) penetrating critical essays on Mandel'shtam, Tsvetaeva, Akhmatova, Cavafy, Montale, Miłosz, Auden, and Derek Walcott. Although he continues to write poetry predominantly in Russian, he has in recent years taken an increasingly active part in the translation of his Russian poetry into English. He has also written moving elegies — to Auden and to Robert Lowell — directly in English.

—George L. Kline

————

BRODSKY, Joseph. *See* BRODSKII, Iosif.

————

BRØGGER, Suzanne. Danish. Born in Copenhagen, 18 November 1944. Educated at Bernadotteskolen, Hellerup; schools in southeast Asia; Th. Langs Kostskole, Silkeborg; University of Copenhagen. Married Keld Zeruneith in 1991. Freelance journalist in the Soviet Union and the Middle East. Has also worked as an actress. Recipient: Poul Henningsen prize, 1975; Selskabet til de Skjønne og Nyttige Videnskaber prize, 1981; Danish Booksellers' Association Golden Laurels, 1982; Rhodos prize, 1984; Jespersen award, 1984; Tagea Brandt travel award, 1985; Danish State Art Foundation lifelong grant, 1985; Gabor prize, 1987. Address: Knudstrup Gl. Skole, 4270 Høng, Denmark.

PUBLICATIONS

Fiction

Fri os fra kærligheden. Copenhagen, Rhodos, 1973; as *Deliver Us from Love*, New York, Delacorte, 1976; London, Quartet, 1977.
Ja [Yes]. Copenhagen, Rhodos, 1984.
Den pebrede susen: flydende fragmenter og fixeringer [The Pepper Whistle: Floating Fragments and Fixations]. Copenhagen, Rhodos, 1986.
Min verden i en nøddeskal [My World in a Nutshell]. Copenhagen, Rhodos, 1991.

Play

Efter orgiet [After the Orgy] (produced Stockholm, 1991). Copenhagen, Rhodos, 1991.

Verse

Tone: epos. Copenhagen, Rhodos, 1981.
Edvard og Elvira: en ballade [Edward and Elvira: A Ballad]. Copenhagen, Rhodos, 1988.

Other

Kærlighedens veje og vildveje [The Right and Wrong Ways of Love]. Copenhagen, Rhodos, 1975.
Crême fraiche. Copenhagen, Rhodos, 1978.

En gris som har været oppe at slås kan man ikke stege [A Pig That's Been Fighting Can't Be Roasted]. Copenhagen, Rhodos, 1979.
Brøg: 1965–1980 [Brew]. Copenhagen, Rhodos, 1980.
Et Grønlands — essay og tre digte [A Greenland — Essay and Three Other Poems], poems by Sven Holm. Copenhagen, Rhodos, 1982.
Kvælstof: 1980–1990 [Nitrogen]. Copenhagen, Rhodos, 1990.

Translator, *Katte især* [Particularly Cats], by Doris Lessing. Copenhagen, Brøndum, 1977.
Translator, *Syv vise mestre og kælighed* [Seven Wise Masters and Love], by Lars Gyllensten. Copenhagen, Rhodos, 1987.

*

Critical Study: "Suzanne Brøgger: You Shouldn't Be Allowed to Put Up with It!" by Jens Kistrup, in *Out of Denmark: Isak Dinesen/Karen Blixen 1885–1985 and Danish Women Writers Today*, edited by Bodil Wamberg, Copenhagen, Danish Cultural Institute, 1985.

Theatrical Activities:
Actress: **Play** — Helena in *Troilus and Cressida*, 1968; film and television roles.

*   *   *

Theories emerging from the women's movement had a strong impact on Danish literature in the 1970s. Danish critics say that women's literature had two functions at this time. One was to register oppression and suffering in the form of confessional literature; the other was to evoke a potential for change. Women writers also changed the feminist catchphrase "the personal is political" to "politicize the personal."

According to Danish critic May Schack, Suzanne Brøgger dissolves the distinction between the personal and the political by presenting her life as an alternative to the traditional woman's life. Her first book, *Fri os fra kærligheden* (*Deliver Us from Love*), contains essays, interviews, autobiographical material, and fiction on the theme of sexual liberation, which in Brøgger's opinion should mean liberation from a fixation with sexuality. The strongest pieces in this book, according to Schack, are the essays analyzing typical phenomena in Western culture such as marriage and family. Brøgger believes it is fatal to associate marriage with love. Her definition of love is a meeting between two people in the widest and deepest sense. Eros implies going beyond the self, by allowing oneself to be seduced and transformed; however, this erotic power is lost as soon as it is systematized into a permanent arrangement like family, marriage, or monogamy.

Kærlighedens veje og vildveje (The Right and Wrong Ways of Love) is in form and content a continuation of *Deliver Us from Love*. The opening essay describes the painful process of saying no to a man the author loves, because he requires her to conform to a traditional woman's role, which conflicts with the realities of contemporary life. In this book, Brøgger examines sexuality's variations, using examples that are not particularly excessive, but which nonetheless led the Danish press to portray her as the high priestess of sexuality, thereby rendering her social criticism ineffective.

Brøgger has also written two autobiographical works — *Crême fraiche* and *En gris som har været oppe at slås kan man ikke stege* (A Pig That's Been Fighting Can't Be Roasted) — which initially appear vastly different, yet actually share the same theme. *Crême fraiche* describes Brøgger's travels in her youth, the people she meets, and her changing view of life and eroticism. May Schack explains that while many women writers at the time were describing the wretched state of the world, Brøgger presents the world as a large candy store, in which eroticism is candy for adults. *En gris* . . . portrays an uneventful life in a rural Danish town, where Brøgger lived for 20 years. The two books complement each other: on the one hand, travel, change, and the hustle and bustle of major cities, and on the other, peace, meditative quiet, and unchanging country life. The theme shared by both books has been summed up by Brøgger as "how one sets about living in the *least* unhappy way, and in the *most* interesting way, before one dies." In *En gris* . . . Brøgger finds the intensity of life in deep introspection, while in *Crême fraiche* she finds it in sexual pleasure and erotic play.

Brøg (Brew) is a collection of articles which ends with an essay influenced by the French philosopher Michel Foucault. It criticizes free sexuality, which Foucault claims has become as banal as part of a general health routine. Eros has lost his wings, has become impotent, and eroticism has been reduced to mechanical orgasms. Brøgger pessimistically declares, "Everything we liberate disappears."

Tone is an epic poem which gained attention from the academic world with its structure and innovation. *Tone* makes public the private life of a Danish woman, her love of life, and struggle against death. Her friends, a wig maker, and others in her home town describe her in segments and anecdotes, creating a mosaic-like portrait. Tone is a woman who fights against the traditional life she has been forced to live, and paves her own path to liberation. On the surface she appears to be an extravagant, eccentric, and egocentric woman, bourgeois and at the same time bohemian. Once the motives behind her actions are revealed, however, the reader understands that such characteristics are a result of her conscientiousness, consideration, hospitality, and self-sacrifice—in other words, traditional traits expected in a woman.

In the title essay to *Kærlighedens veje og vildveje* Brøgger maintains that people like Tone who realize their potential are above selfishness and unselfishness. Danish critic Bjarne Sandstrøm says that Tone's egocentricity and generosity represent for Brøgger the personification of a theoretical-ideological ideal, the harmonization of opposites. Sandstrøm compares this balance to the voltage that develops between two poles of a battery, and feels that this is the source of energy in *Tone*.

Sandstrøm characterizes the style of the poem as rhythmic, musical prose, graphically presented as free verse. The poem is set in a contemporary environment, but the language is full of mythological allusions and archaisms, together with the colloquialisms and jargons of the Copenhagen dialect. As a result the language gives an antique character to a contemporary subject and environment.

Tone presents an individual answer to the conditions of life. In this sense the poem is, as Brøgger says, a *kvindekvad*, a song of a woman, depicting change brought about within the scope of a woman's personality.

Brøgger's latest books include the novels *Ja* (Yes) and *Den pebrede susen* (The Pepper Whistle), the short story collection *Min verden i en nøddeskal* (My World in a Nutshell), and *Edvard och Elvira* (Edvard and Elvira), subtitled "a ballad." The essay collection *Kvælstof* (Nitrogen) contains portraits of personalities she has known, such as Henry Miller, who influenced her literary style. Her first drama *Efter orgiet* (After the Orgy) is written in the form of a tragedy, with all the humor and catharsis found in the ancient Greek tragedies. It has been described as an obscene, baroque play with an apocalyptic atmosphere.

Brøgger unites her occupation as a writer with her life in general, and presents her own life in literary form as an experiment in living. Her goal in her writing is not to convey aesthetic pleasure and knowledge, but rather to present woman as subject-matter, and to describe experiences that are particular to women.

—Deborah Fronko

———

BROSSARD, Nicole. Canadian. Born in Montreal, 27 November 1943. Educated at the Collège Marguerite-Bourgeoys, Montreal, from 1956; University of Montreal, from 1962, B.A. 1965, Licence ès lettres 1968, M.A. 1972; University of Quebec, Montreal, 1969–71, baccalauréat in pedagogy 1971. Married Roger Soublière in 1966 (divorced); one daughter. Co-founder, with Marcel Saint-Pierre, Roger Soublière, and Jan Stafford, *La Barre du Jour* journal, 1965–75; director, with Luce Guilbeault, *Some American Feminists: New York 1976* (film), 1975; founding member, *Les Têtes de Pioche* feminist editorial collective, 1976–79; co-editor, with Michel Gay and Jean-Yves Collette, *La Nouvelle Barre du Jour*, 1977–79; director, 1977–79, and vice president, 1983–85, Union des Écrivains Québécois; founder, L'Intégrale publishing house, 1982; Visiting Professor of French, Queen's University, Kingston, Ontario, 1982–84; short-term fellow, Princeton University, New Jersey, 1991. Recipient: Governor General's award, for poetry, 1974, 1984; Fondation des Forges grand prize, 1989; Athanase-David prize, 1991; Harbourfront Festival prize, 1991. Address: 34 avenue Robert, Outremont, Quebec H3S 2P2, Canada.

PUBLICATIONS

Verse

Aube à la saison. Published in *Trois*, Montreal, A.G.E.U.M., 1965.
Mordre en sa chair. Montreal, Esterel, 1966.
L'Écho bouge beau. Montreal, Esterel, 1968.
Suite logique. Montreal, Hexagone, 1970.
Le Centre blanc. Montreal, Orphée, 1970.
Mécanique jongleuse. Paris, Génération, 1973.
Mécanique jongleuse; Masculin grammaticale. Montreal, Hexagone, 1974; as *Daydream Mechanics*, Toronto, Coach House Press, 1980.
La Partie pour le tout. Montreal, L'Aurore, 1975.
D'Arcs de cycle la dérive, illustrated by Francine Simonin. St.-Jacques-le-Mineur, Maison, 1979.
Amantes. Montreal, Les Quinze, 1980; as *Lovhers*, Montreal, Guernica, 1986.
Double Impression: poèmes et textes 1967–1984. Montreal, Hexagone, 1984.
L'aviva. Montreal, nbj, 1985.
Mauve, with Daphne Marlatt. Montreal, njb/writing, 1985.
Jeu de lettres/Character, with Daphne Marlatt. Montreal, njb/writing, 1986.
Sous la Langue/Under Tongue. Montreal, Essentielle, 1987.
À Tout Regard, with Daphne Marlatt. Montreal, BQ, 1989.

Installations (avec et sans pronoms). Trois-Rivières, Quebec, Forges, 1989.
Typhon dru.   Paris, Génération, 1990(?).
Langues obscures.   Montreal, Hexagone, 1992.

Fiction

Un Livre.   Montreal, Jour, 1970; as *A Book*, Toronto, Coach House Press, 1976.
Sold-Out.   Montreal, Jour, 1973; as *Turn of a Pang*, Toronto, Coach House Press, 1976.
French Kiss.   Montreal, Jour, 1974; as *French Kiss, or, A Pang's Progress*, Toronto, Coach House Press, 1986.
L'Amèr, ou, Le Chapitre effrité.   Montreal, Quinze, 1977; revised edition, Montreal, Hexagone, 1988; as *These Our Mothers, or, The Disintegrating Chapter*, Toronto, Coach House Press, 1983.
Le Sens apparent.   Paris, Flammarion, 1980; as *Surfaces of Sense*, Toronto, Coach House Press, 1989.
Picture Theory.   Montreal, Nouvelle Optique, 1982; revised and enlarged edition, Montreal, Hexagone, 1989; in English, New York, Roof, and Montreal, Guernica, 1991.
La Lettre aérienne.   Montreal, Remue-Ménage, 1985; as *The Aerial Letter*, Toronto, Women's Press, 1988.
Le Désert mauve.   Montreal, Hexagone, 1987; as *Mauve Desert*, Toronto, Coach House Press, 1990.

Plays

L'Écrivain.   Published in *La Nef des sorcières*, Montreal, Quinze, 1976; as *The Writer* (produced Toronto, 1979), in *A Clash of Symbols*, Toronto, Coach House Press, 1979.

Radio Plays: *Narrateur et personnages*, 1971; *Une Impression de fiction dans le rétroviseur*, 1978; *Journal intime*, 1983.

Other

Journal intime, ou, Voilà donc un manuscrit.   Montreal, Herbes Rouges, 1984.
Domaine d'écriture.   Montreal, nbj, 1985.
Le Forum des femmes.   Montreal, njb, 1986.
La Nuit verte du parc labyrinthe.   Laval, Quebec, Trois, 1992.
La Nuit Verte du parc labyrinthe (trilingual edition in French, English, Spanish).   Laval, Quebec, Trois, 1992.

Editor, *The Story So Far/Les Stratégies du réel*.   Toronto, Coach House Press, and Montreal, La Nouvelle Barre du Jour, 1979.
Editor, with Lisette Girouard, *Anthologie de la poésie des femmes au Québec*.   Montreal, Remue-Ménage, 1991.

*

Critical Studies: "Subversion Is the Order of the Day" by Caroline Bayard, in *Essays on Canadian Writing* (Montreal), 7–8, 1977, and "Nicole Brossard" by Bayard and Jack David, in *Avant-Postes/Out-Posts*, Erin, Ontario, Porcupine Press, 1978; "The Novels of Nicole Brossard: An Active Voice," in *Room of One's Own* (Vancouver), 4(12), 1978, "Beyond the Myths and Fictions of Traditionalism and Nationalism: The Political in the Work of Nicole Brossard," in *Traditionalism, Nationalism, and Feminism: Women Writers of Quebec*, edited by Paula Gilbert Lewis, Westport, Connecticut, Greenwood, 1985, and "Deconstructing Formal Space/Accelerating Motion in the Work of Nicole Brossard," in *A Mazing Space:*

Writing Canadian Women Writing, edited by Shirley Neuman, Edmonton, Alberta, Longspoon, 1986, all by Louise Forsyth; "The Avant-Garde in Canada: *Open Letter* and *La Barre du Jour*," in *Ellipse* (Sherbrooke, Quebec), 23, 1979, "The Translator as Ventriloquist," in *Prism International* (Vancouver), 20(3), 1982, "Women Loving Women Writing: Nicole Brossard," in *Resources for Feminist Research*, Spring 1983, and "L'Amèr or the Exploding Chapter: Nicole Brossard at the Site of Feminist Deconstruction," in *Atlantis* (Halifax, Nova Scotia), Spring 1984, all by Barbara Godard; "From Picture to Hologram: Nicole Brossard's Grammar of Utopia" by Lorraine Weir, in *A Mazing Space: Writing Canadian Women Writing*, edited by Shirley Neuman, Edmonton, Alberta, Longspoon, 1986.

*   *   *

The awarding of the 1991 Athanase-David prize of Quebec for the totality of her work acknowledged Nicole Brossard's leadership among a generation of poets who transformed Quebec poetics from 1965–70, through her editorship of the influential periodical, *La Barre du Jour* (and *La Nouvelle Barre du Jour*), and her poetic innovations exploring the production of meaning and work of gender in language and textuality. Translated into many languages, including English, German, Italian, and Spanish, Brossard has developed an international reputation as a feminist theorist.

Despite such official recognition, Brossard's writing has situated itself as an interrogation of received practices and of the text as commodity. Working from Marxist theories of the material production of cultural work and post-structuralist theories about the way language constructs our worlds and inscribes power relations, Brossard has engaged, first through Quebec nationalism and later through feminism, in writing as resistance and transformation of literary and social institutions. By self-reflexively drawing attention to established conventions of reading and writing, Brossard disrupts habitual knowledge relations. Through play on the textual surface — neologisms and typographical variations — Brossard exposes the constructedness of texts, and undermines the referential power of language and the mimetic aspect of literature in a textual practice that demands an active reader. Reading, like writing, is research, an engagement with the process, not the product of meaning-making. Indeed, Brossard explores the work of notation systems of mathematics as well as of phonetic alphabets in her work, considering fiction as hypothesis-generating that orders relationships among entities, such fictions being taken for reality that establish truth-claims and organize social relations. In its interrogation of narrative and its preoccupation with surfaces, with simulacra, Brossard's poetics are postmodernist.

The more than 30 works by Brossard may be divided into roughly three periods. During the 1960s, influenced by surrealism, she wrote poetry characterized by an associative flux of images in surprising juxtapositions and by sexuality as a mode of consciousness. The female body experiencing desire and pain in *Mordre en sa chair* (To Bite into the Flesh) challenges the dominant Quebec poetry of the period which celebrated a Quebec national homeland in a land-as-woman metaphor that poses problems for a woman poet as speaking subject. While sharing the prevalent view of avant-garde art forms as revolutionary political activity, Brossard attempted to undermine the symbolic Woman to examine women's desires. With her peers, Brossard was aware of language in the production of a national culture and the need to renew poetic language turning, though, not to the popular dialect *joual*, as did many Quebec writers, but to disruption of formal elements in language — the subject-verb-complement rule (the predicative logic of the copula, the grammar of narrative) — and subsequently to gender rules in French (where the masculine takes precedence over the feminine), to challenge all forms of textual decorum, all notions of the "proper," especially those of identity. Transgression, she advances (following Michel Foucault), is the assertion of a subject whose desire realigns power relations.

In the 1970s, Brossard's work entered a formalist phase stimulated by French post-structuralism, especially the work of Roland Barthes which, following Ferdinand de Saussure, stressed the non-referentiality of signs (words) articulated as a system of differences. Brossard realized that words could never capture the private life of her body: they could, however, combine in an infinite number of ways to create multiple networks. Brossard explored these possibilities of language in several works around the paradox of absence/presence, the white space and the black marks, through puns on *personne* as both "person" and "nobody," through verbal fragments adrift from syntactical connections, especially in *Le Centre blanc* (The White Centre) and *Suite logique* (Logical Sequence). The latter is anything but a logical sequence: disjunctive, it forces the reader to examine meaning making processes. The former engages the vanishing point which is nonetheless a vortex for energy, the energy of the mind contemplating its own processes in the consciousness of self-consciousness. In the same year Brossard published her first fiction, *Un Livre* (*A Book*), a meditation on the conventions of the novel. Characters here with names like *Or* (Now) or sharing the same name "Dominique" are verbal fabrications, word beings, that function as points of connection for other words. Anecdotes are incomplete as the text insists on its lack of "depth": the only reality is words and they "take place. On a surface," accessible through the physical activities of writing and reading. These words may be conscripted by various ideologies, as Brossard explores in her next fiction, *Sold-Out* (*Turn of a Pang*). Juxtaposing an associative stream on the word *roux* (reddish)/*roue* (wheel) to fragments of an historical narrative of the 1943 conscription crisis, it considers the ways in which *inscrire* is simultaneously to inscribe and to conscript: words have power as political slogans and sexual putdowns. *French Kiss*, a fiction of the automobile and the city as an allegory of women's desire circulating in the public space, continues this articulation of language as power and the disruptive force of transgressive sexualities to constitute "a sapphic semantic chain" where the erotic centre of the body is no longer the vagina, vehicle for reproduction, but tongues, whose encounter is the French kiss. Brossard moves beyond the critique of masculinist language in *Masculin grammaticale* (*Daydream Mechanics*) to posit a different order of signs within relations of female desire.

The third phase of Brossard's writing takes up this call to "make the difference" and develops a poetics and politics of sexual difference. Influenced by French feminist philosophers such as Luce Irigaray and Hélène Cixous (*q.v.*), Brossard developed a mode of writing she calls "fiction/theory," fiction as hypothesis forming potential worlds. *L'Amèr, ou, Le Chapitre effrité* (*These Our Mothers, or, The Disintegrating Chapter*), the first volume in Brossard's "lesbian triptych," is an exercise in self-defence in a patriarchal society where women are limited to the role of symbolic mother. In a fragmented text ranging from lyric utterance to prose poem to analytic essay, Brossard disintegrates the patriarchal Mother in order to posit the possibilities for relationships among women figured in the embrace of three generations of women and in the lesbian embrace. The text works to inscribe women in the trajectory of the species, to write them into history.

Exploring difference as alterity and deferral, demonstrating an absence of closure and an economy of multiple meanings, Brossard's text has been an influential work of feminist theory as well as of experimental fiction. While it centres on the thought of emotion, *Le Sens apparent* (*Surfaces of Sense*) articulates the sensation of emotion and thought. A narrative that constantly digresses, a manifesto that is not quite a manifesto in its refusal of clarity, the text circles around the writing of a number of feminist writers, in the "spiral pattern in books written by women," in the activity of reading women writing. The text develops the image of skin, emphasizing surfaces of body and text on which desire is inscribed, open to the world. Model for the "superposition" of texts, it also shapes *Amantes* (*Lovhers*) which, as poetry, celebrates the emotion of thought.

These motifs are deployed again in *Picture Theory*, Brossard's major work to date, a complex theoretical fiction based on Wittgenstein's statement that "a proposition is a picture of reality," exploring the superposition of Monique Wittig's (*q.v.*) Amazonian island on anecdotes of the family of "Dérive Stein" (Stein Derivative, Stein Adrift). A book of light, it rewrites the great modernist books of the night, especially the works of James Joyce. The temptation towards the anecdote is once again displaced by the networks of metonymies around skin/screen/scream and their French versions *peau/écran/cri/écrit* in what is another method of notation. The text is composed through the repetition of verbal fragments recombined in different permutations, the text as combinatory. In this, Brossard explicitly draws on the mathematical theory of quantum physics to construct a text as hologram that will produce from these fragments a virtual woman. This offers a model for the text as a process of transformation, central to Brossard's aesthetic.

Brossard has published a number of theoretical essays on the problem of representation for women. Women's writing must inevitably be fiction, feigning, visionary, self-conscious artifice, to avoid the trap of naturalization, of pretending to be reality, that has made literature traditionally an extension of the symbolic and party to the subjugation of women and reality. Fiction is the way to fight such containing fictions, Brossard suggests in *La Lettre aérienne* (*The Aerial Letter*), by exposing their fictionality to open a space for alternate fictions, Brossard's fictionalizing and theorizing aim to produce a space for fictions that will create a reality which allows women the free expression of their desire, which empowers women as subjects. The possibilities for a feminist, specifically a lesbian, aesthetics are further developed in essays in *Double Impression* and *La Nuit verte du parc labyrinthe* (*The Green Night of the Labyrinth Park*). Questions of representation and of narrative are also pursued in *Journal intime* (Intimate Journal), a diary which is not a diary, disrupting the sequential temporal imperative and confessional convention of life-writing genres, underlining the way in which the book as text is shaped by language, not "life." These concerns with the way subjectivity is produced in/by language are addressed in Brossard's most recent poetry, *Installations* and especially *Langues obscures* (Obscure Tongues) which explores the adventures of "I," "pure marvel," the subjective pronoun, shifter through which is effected the work of relating a speaker with others, with a world.

Brossard's work on language and codes took another route during the 1980s to explore translation both as textual practice and as metaphor for transcoding, for transformation, through the proliferation of chains of signification across languages. Many of her texts introduce words in English, Spanish, and Italian, as Brossard considers what reality might be like if lived in another tongue. Experiment with homolinguistic translation or the play with the recombinant possibilities of syllables in *L'aviva* was followed by translation of texts by poet Daphne Marlatt in *Mauve* and *Jeu de lettres/Character* and by a fiction, *Le Désert mauve* (*Mauve Desert*), about a translator's work upon a text from Spanish to French, a text about a violent murder in the Arizona desert that links atomic explosions to an attack on a lesbian. Drawing on her common motif of reading as desiring from the French pun on "délire" as "delirium" and "un-reading," Brossard's fiction develops in three parts involving a translator's discovery of another woman's text, a meditation on the processes of transformative reading in her transfer of the text into a different network of signification, and the product of this work, which is a semantic reworking of the first section, the sort of recombinant work effected by the shift from *Laure* Angestelle to Maude *Laure*. Drawing together in the metaphor of translation, especially pertinent to the Quebec literary scene, midway between Paris and New York — an axis crucial to feminist theorizing too — *Mauve Desert* has been the most popular of Brossard's novels and perhaps the most accessible, for the narrative of the translation process is less fragmented than those of the scene of writing in other texts. In her dramatic monologue, *L'Écrivain* (*The Writer*), however, the actor's body on stage bridged the gaps with gestures. Brossard's only dramatic text, it focuses, like all her work, self-reflexively on the work of writing, of ordering words and worlds, as this is gendered activity.

—Barbara Godard

BUERO VALLEJO, Antonio. Spanish. Born in Guadalajara, 29 September 1916. Educated at the Instituto de Segunda Enseñanza, Guadalajara; studied painting at San Fernando School of Fine Arts, Madrid, 1934–36. Served as medical corpsman in Loyalist forces during Spanish Civil War, 1937–39; imprisoned for 5 years at end of war, released 1946. Married Victoria Rodríguez in 1959; two sons. Writer. Recipient: Lope de Vega prize, 1949; Amigos de los Quintero prize, 1949; Rolland prize, 1956, 1958, 1960; National Theatre prize, 1957, 1958, 1959, 1980; March Foundation prize, 1959; Barcelona Critics' prize, 1960; Larra prize, 1962; *El Espectador y la Crítica* prize, 1967, 1970, 1974, 1976, 1977, 1981, 1984, 1986; Leopoldo Cano prize, 1968, 1972, 1974, 1975, 1977; Mayte prize, 1974; Foro Teatral prize, 1974; "Gaceta Ilustrada" Gold Medal, 1976; Ercilla prize, 1985; Valle-Inclán Medal, 1985; Iglesias prize, 1986; Cervantes prize, 1986; Gold Medal and Favourite Son of Guadalajara, 1987; Gold Medal of Castilla-La Mancha, 1988. Member, Royal Spanish Academy, 1971, and Hispanic Society of America, 1971; Honorary Fellow, Modern Language Association (USA), 1978; Officier, Palmes Académiques (France), 1980. Agent: Sociedad General de Autores de España, Fernando VI 4, Madrid 28080, Spain. Address: Calle General Díaz Porlier 36, Madrid 28001, Spain.

PUBLICATIONS

Plays

Historia de una escalera (produced Madrid, 1949). Barcelona, Janés, 1950.

Las palabras en la arena (produced Madrid, 1949). With *Historia de una escalera*, Madrid, Alfil, 1952.

En la ardiente oscuridad (produced Madrid, 1950). Madrid, Alfil, 1951; as *In the Burning Darkness*, in *Three Plays*, 1985.

La tejedora de sueños (produced Madrid, 1952). Madrid, Alfil, 1952; as *The Dream Weaver*, in *Masterpieces of the Modern Spanish Theatre*, edited by Robert W. Corrigan, New York, Macmillan, 1967.

La señal que se espera (produced Madrid, 1952). Madrid, Alfil, 1953.

Casi un cuento de hadas: una glosa de Perrault (produced Madrid, 1953). Madrid, Alfil, 1953.

Madrugada (produced Madrid, 1953). Madrid, Alfil, 1954.

El terror inmóvil. Madrid, Alfil, 1954; complete version, Murcia, Universidad, 1979.

Irene; o, El tesoro (produced Madrid, 1954). Madrid, Alfil, 1955.

Aventura en lo gris. Madrid, Puerta del Sol, 1955; revised version (produced Madrid, 1963), Madrid, Alfil, 1964.

Hoy es fiesta (produced Madrid, 1956). Madrid, Alfil, 1957; as *Today's a Holiday*, Lanham, Maryland, University Press of America, 1987.

Las cartas boca abajo (produced Madrid, 1957). Madrid, Alfil, 1958.

Un soñador para un pueblo (produced Madrid, 1958). Madrid, Alfil, 1959.

Teatro (vol. 1 includes *En la ardiente oscuridad*; *Madrugada*; *Hoy es fiesta*; *Las cartas boca abajo*; vol. 2 includes *Historia de una escalera*; *La tejedora de sueños*; *Irene; o, El tesoro*; *Un soñador para un pueblo*). Buenos Aires, Losada, 2 vols., 1959–62.

Las Meninas (produced Madrid, 1960). Madrid, Alfil, 1961; in English, San Antonio, Texas, Trinity University Press, 1987.

Hamlet, from the play by Shakespeare (produced Madrid, 1961). Madrid, Alfil, 1962.

El concierto de San Ovidio (produced Madrid, 1962). Madrid, Alfil, 1963; as *The Concert at Saint Ovide* (produced London, 1973), in *The Modern Spanish Stage*, edited by Marion Holt, New York, Hill and Wang, 1970.

Madre Coraje y sus hijos, from the play *Mother Courage* by Brecht (produced Madrid, 1966). Madrid, Alfil, 1967.

Teatro selecto (includes *Historia de una escalera*; *Las cartas boca abajo*; *Un soñador para un pueblo*; *Las Meninas*; *El concierto de San Ovidio*), edited by Luce Moreau-Arrabal. Madrid, Escelicer, 1966.

La doble historia del Doctor Valmy (produced Madrid, 1976). Philadelphia, Center for Curriculum Development, 1970; as *The Double Case History of Doctor Valmy* (produced Chester, 1968), in *Artes Hispánicas I*, 2, 1967.

El tragaluz (produced Madrid, 1967). Madrid, Alfil, 1968; as *The Basement Window*, in *Plays of Protest from the Franco Era*, edited by Patricia W. O'Connor, Madrid, S.G.E.L., 1981.

Mito, libro para una ópera. Madrid, Alfil, 1968.

El sueño de la razón (produced Madrid, 1970). Madrid, Escelicer, 1970; as *The Sleep of Reason*, in *Three Plays*, 1985.

Llegada de los dioses (produced Madrid, 1972). Published in *Teatro español, 1971–72*, Madrid, Aguilar, 1973.

La fundación (produced Madrid, 1974). With *El concierto de San Ovidio*, Madrid, Espasa-Calpe, 1974; as *The Foundation*, in *Three Plays*, 1985.

La detonación (produced Madrid, 1977). Madrid, Espasa-Calpe, 1979; as *The Shot*, Warminster, Wiltshire, Aris and Phillips, 1989.

Jueces en la noche (produced Madrid, 1979). Madrid, Vox, 1979.

Caimán (produced Madrid, 1981). Madrid, Espasa-Calpe, 1981.

El pato silvestre, from the play *The Wild Duck* by Ibsen (produced Madrid, 1982). Málaga, Rev. Canente, 1990.

Diálogo secreto (produced San Sebastián, 1984). Madrid, Espasa-Calpe, 1985.

Marginalia (includes *La señal que se espera*; *Diana*; poems). N.p., Club Internacional de Libro, 1984.

Three Plays (includes *The Sleep of Reason*; *The Foundation*; *In the Burning Darkness*). San Antonio, Texas, Trinity University Press, 1985.

Lazaro en el laberinto (produced Madrid, 1986). Madrid, Espasa-Calpe, 1987.

Música cercana (produced Bilbao, 1989). Madrid, Espasa-Calpe, 1990.

Other

García Lorca ante el esperpento (address). Madrid, Real Academia Español, 1972.

Tres maestros ante el público (Valle-Inclán, Velázquez, Lorca). Madrid, Alianza, 1973.

*

Bibliographies: "Antonio Buero Vallejo: A Bibliography (1949–70)" by John W. Kronik, in *Hispania* (Los Angeles), December 1971; *Antonio Buero Vallejo and Alfonso Sastre: An Annotated Bibliography* by Marsha Forys, Metuchen, New Jersey, Scarecrow Press, 1988.

Critical Studies: "The Ironic Structure of *Historia de una escalera*" by Farris Anderson, in *Romance Quarterly* (Lexington, Kentucky), 18, 1971; "Antonio Buero Vallejo's Theory of Tragedy in *El tragaluz*" by Gerard R. Weiss, in *Revista de Estudios Hispánicos* (Poughkeepsie, New York), 5, 1971; "Symbols of Hope in Three Plays of Antonio Buero Vallejo" by David Ling, in *Romance Notes* (Chapel Hill, North Carolina), 13, 1972; *The Tragic Stages of Antonio Buero Vallejo*, Chapel Hill, University of North Carolina Press, 1972, "Antonio Buero-Vallejo: Stages, Illusions and Hallucinations," in *The Contemporary Spanish Theater*, edited by Martha T. Halsey and Phyllis Zatlin, Lanham, Maryland, University Press of America, 1988, and "History as Image and Sound: Three Plays of Antonio Buero Vallejo," in *Estreno* (University Park, Pennsylvania), 14(1), 1988, all by Robert L. Nicholas; *Antonio Buero Vallejo: The First Fifteen Years* by Joelyn Roeple, New York, Eliseo Torres, 1972; *Antonio Buero Vallejo*, New York, Twayne, 1973, "Two Sonnets of Antonio Buero Vallejo," in *Romance Notes* (Chapel Hill, North Carolina), 21, 1980, "Buero, Olmo and the Dialectics of Hope," in *South Atlantic Bulletin*, 45(2), 1980, "Landscapes of the Imagination: Images of Hope in the Theater of Antonio Buero Vallejo," in *Hispania* (Los Angeles), 68(2), 1985, and "Dictatorship to Democracy in the Recent Theater of Antonio Buero Vallejo (*La fundación* to *Diálogo secreto*)," in *Estreno* (University Park, Pennsylvania), 13(9), 1987, all by Martha T. Halsey; "Antonio Buero Vallejo's *El tragaluz* and Man's Existence in History" by John W. Kronik, in *Hispanic Review* (Philadelphia), 41, 1973; "The Significance of Insanity in Four Plays by Antonio Buero Vallejo" by Kenneth Brown, in *Revista de Estudios Hispánicos* (Poughkeepsie, New York), 8, 1974; "The Dialectical Structure of Antonio Buero Vallejo's Multi-Faceted Definition of Tragedy," in *Romance Quarterly* (Lexington, Kentucky), 22, 1975, and "Vita activa and vita contemplativa: Antonio Buero Vallejo's *El tragaluz* and Herman Hesse's *Magister Lundi*," in *Hispanófila* (Chapel Hill, North Carolina), 53, 1975, both by Ida Molina; "Tragic Conflict and Progressive Synthesis in Antonio Buero Vallejo's *En la ardiente oscuridad*" by Reed Anderson, in *Symposium* (Washington, D.C.), 29, 1975; Buero Vallejo issues of *Estreno* (University Park, Pennsylvania), 5(1), 1979, and 12(2), 1986; "Antonio Buero Vallejo: Good Mistresses and Bad Wives" by John A. Moore, in *Romance Notes* (Chapel Hill, North Carolina), 21, 1980; "Antonio Buero Vallejo's Use of Biblical Archetypes," in *Notes on Contemporary Literature* (Carrollton, Georgia), 10(4), 1980, "The Role of Music in *El concierto de San Ovidio*," in *Romance Notes* (Chapel Hill, North Carolina), 26(1), 1985, and "Art and Music in Antonio Buero Vallejo's *Diálogo secreto*," in *Hispanic Journal* (Indiana, Pennsylvania), 9(1), 1987, all by Eric Pennington; "The Humanization of Archetypes in Buero Vallejo's *La tejedora de sueños*," in *Revista de Estudios Hispánicos* (Poughkeepsie, New York), 15(3), 1981, and "Role Constraints versus Self-Identity in *La tejedora de sueños* and *Anillos para una dama*," in *Modern Drama* (Toronto), 26(3), 1983, both by Elizabeth S. Rogers; "Shades of Plays to Come: Antonio Buero Vallejo's *El terror inmóvil*" by Patricia W. O'Connor, in *Crítica Hispánica* (Pittsburgh), 5(1), 1983; "Blindness and Insight: A Re-Reading of Antonio Buero Vallejo's *En la ardiente oscuridad*," in *Modern Languages* (Leeds), 64(3), 1983, and "Patriarchy, Sexuality and Oedipal Conflict in Antonio Buero Vallejo's *El concierto de San Ovidio*," in *Modern Drama* (Toronto), 28(3), 1985, both by Barry Jordan; "Dramatic Point of View and Antonio Buero Vallejo's *La fundación*" by Barry E. Weingarten, in *Hispanic Journal* (Indiana, Pennsylvania), 5(2), 1984; "The Painterly Vision of Antonio Buero Vallejo's *El sueño de la razón*" by David K. Herzberger, in *Symposium* (Washington, D.C.), 39(2), 1985; "Psychological and Visual Planes in Antonio Buero Vallejo's *Diálogo secreto*" by Margaret E. W. Jones, in *Estreno* (University Park, Pennsylvania), 12(1), 1986; "Death and Dying in *El la ardiente oscuridad*" by John Philip Gabriele, in *Language Quarterly* (Tampa, Florida), 26(1–2), 1987; "Provocations to Audience Response: Narrators in the Plays of Antonio Buero Vallejo" by Susan G. Polansky, in *Letras Peninsulares* (East Lansing, Michigan), 1(2), 1988.

Antonio Buero Vallejo comments:

The war and the post-war period in Spain led me gradually to change my first vocation as artist to that of writer, and especially as writer for the theatre. Despite a lack of comprehension from both within and without, an attitude still alive and which was born of the simple prejudice that it was impossible to create anything worthwhile under Franco's censorship, many independent writers among us decided not to stay silent, either artistically or socially. So there was an increasing and extended collective struggle for cultural rebirth, a struggle more positive, we believe, than some are still willing to recognize. As for me, I dared to present myself for the Lope de Vega award in 1949; I won and have since presented 25 works. In my theatre the central theme is usually tragic, but on a deeper level it does not exclude the possibility of hope or resolution, just as the Greeks, if we can understand them, teach us in their conciliatory tragedies. Although the theme of Spain is elemental in nearly all my works, through it I am always interested in exploring more general human conflicts and enigmas as well as certain theatrical forms. Successes I have had from time to time have allowed me to keep my place in Spanish theatre and even to open the door for some of my works to be performed in different parts of the world. To give pleasure is the fundamental role of the theatre, as are, in my opinion, to criticise or disturb. All three have, in sum, been the driving forces behind my writing.

* * *

Antonio Buero Vallejo is Spain's leading post-Lorcan dramatist and scenic innovator. The production of *Historia de una escalera* (Story of a Stairway) in 1949 brought him immediate recognition and created expectations that he would be the leader of a new Spanish theatre, one which would be socially committed and provide a voice of political protest in spite of the strict censorship that prevailed. Although Buero Vallejo wrote his earliest works within a dramatic mode that he himself has called "symbolic realism," several contain striking dramatic moments that depart from conventional realism and anticipate the imaginative scenic concepts that are associated with his mature plays.

Buero Vallejo quickly ran into problems with the censors, and when they prevented him from producing his politically slanted *Aventura en lo gris* (Adventure in Greyness) he began a period of experimentation with plays on mythic, metaphysical, and psychological themes that sometimes proved puzzling to both audiences and critics. One of the best but least understood is *Irene; o, El tesoro* (Irene, or The Treasure), in which a desperate young widow quixotically fictionalizes her existence, influenced by childhood stories. This play is also the first of a group of works labelled "fábulas" (fables), all dealing with mental aberrations, obsessions, or flights of illusionistic fantasy that are conveyed through visual or aural scenic devices.

Buero Vallejo's increasing international recognition accompanied his turn to historical drama in 1958 to present conflicts from which parallels could be drawn with the political and social concerns of the Spain of Franco. In *Las Meninas*, one of a series of plays that Buero Vallejo calls "fantasías," the predicament of the creative artist (or writer) frustrated by censorship is illuminated through his treatment of Velázquez, under attack for painting nudes and for aspiring to create the painting that gives the play its title. *El concierto de San Ovidio* (*The Concert at Saint Ovide*) explores the tragic relationships of a group of blind musicians exploited by a French impresario on the eve of the French Revolution. This play contains two of Buero Vallejo's most memorable scenes: the mocking reception of the blind musicians' performance by a dehumanized on-stage audience, and the murder of the drunken impresario by the blind protagonist in total darkness. The epilogue delivered by Valentin Haüy, teacher of the blind and an historical witness to the concert, has been criticized as being superfluous, but it reveals Buero Vallejo's willingness to thwart audiences' conventional expectations and his true dramatic purpose in demanding not only catharsis but social action from the spectator.

Early critical attention to Buero Vallejo's theatre focused on his precepts for writing modern tragedies, such as *Hoy es fiesta* (*Today's a Holiday*), in which a modicum of hope prevails in the face of death or irreversible loss, and on his recourse to dramatic situations in which individuals struggle against physical disabilities — most often blindness. But his individuality is most apparent in his scenic concepts for a highly personal type of total theatre in which the visual and the aural (music and non-verbal sounds) reinforce the dialogic elements of his plays. Central to the Buerian mode are recurring dramatic devices that the Spanish critic Ricardo Doménech has labelled "efectos de inmersión" (immersion effects). The earliest example occurs in *En la ardiente oscuridad* (*In the Burning Darkness*), when every light in the theatre fades briefly to total darkness, placing the audience in the physical condition of the two blind characters on stage. Until his masterful multimedia play on Goya, *El sueño de la razón* (*The Sleep of Reason*) of 1970, these affects tended to be discrete, momentarily erasing the proscenium barrier and helping the audience to identify more closely with a character's physical or psychological state. In *The Sleep of Reason*, Buero Vallejo provides a pervasive identification with the deaf painter through multiple projections of his "Black Paintings." When Goya is on stage, the lines of the other characters are mouthed, and the audience hears only Goya's responses. Also audible are the sounds the painter imagines — voices and animal cries — as well as his heartbeats, speeded up and amplified at times to suggest his increasing fear. In his next play, *Llegada de los dioses* (The Arrival of the Gods), the action the audience sees when the protagonist is on stage is his distorted vision of the other characters, who wear animal masks and interact in ways that contradict their dialogue. Buero Vallejo is decidedly Artaudian in his assaults on the audience's sensibilities in these plays, and he has acknowledged to the American critic Robert Nicholas that both Artaud and the Living Theatre may have exerted some influence on his writing at this point — though in the same statement he emphatically rejects the type of actor-audience contact practiced on occasion by the Living Theatre.

Buero Vallejo was an active participant in the Spanish Civil War, but only one of his plays, *El tragaluz* (*The Basement Window*), relates significantly to events occurring during that conflict. Even in this work the war years are recalled rather than recreated, and the entire action is framed by scenes in which "researchers" from some distant future recapture and attempt to learn from events of the past. However, in a number of Buero's plays, elements remind the audience of his long imprisonment at the end of the war. *La fundación* (*The Foundation*) deals specifically with the interactions of political prisoners within a bare cell that the youngest of the group denies metatheatrically by imagining comfortable surroundings and a Turner-like landscape. In other plays, such as *In the Burning Darkness* and *The Sleep of Reason*, the environment is claustrophobic and closed, and recurring in his dramas is the presence of a closed or partially open door, hinting at inaccessible and sometimes mysterious alternative existences.

The existentialist struggle of Buero Vallejo's alienated and often guilt-ridden protagonists has its roots in Miguel de Unamuno's "tragic sense of life," but his acknowledged master is Henrik Ibsen — even though his structural approach to drama has evolved far beyond Ibsen's dramaturgy. His Goya echoes both Brand and Rubek, and repeatedly he counterbalances characters bent on defining truth with others who survive through their "life-lie." Such confrontations occur in plays ranging from the early *In the Burning Darkness* to *Diálogo secreto* (Secret Dialogue) and *Lazaro en el laberinto* (Lazarus in the Labyrinth), both written in the 1980s. These plays also illustrate Buero's artistic trajectory over more than three decades from essentially realistic works in a three-act format to the two-act plays in which musical motifs, contrapuntal dialogue, and multiple levels of "reality" are the norm.

—Marion Peter Holt

———

BUFALINO, Gesualdo. Italian. Born in Comiso, Sicily, 15 November 1920. Educated at the universities of Catania and Palermo, 1939–46. Fought with the partisans in northern Italy,

1942–43: captured by Germans, but escaped. Married Giovanna Leggio in 1982. Professor of Italian and history, Istituto Magistrale di Vittoria, 1949–75. Recipient: Campiello prize, 1981; Scanno prize, 1986; Castiglione di Sicilia, 1987; Strega prize, 1988. Agent: Agenzia Letteraria Internazionale, Via Fratelli Gabba 3, 20121 Milan, Italy. Address: Via Architetto Mancini 26, 97013 Comiso, Italy.

PUBLICATIONS

Fiction

Diceria dell'untore. Palermo, Sellerio, 1981; as *The Plague Sower*, Hygiene, Colorado, Eridanos Press, 1988.
Museo d'ombre. Palermo, Sellerio, 1982.
Argo il cieco, ovvero I sogni della memoria. Palermo, Sellerio, 1984; as *Blind Argus, or, The Fables of the Memory*, London, Collins Harvill, 1989.
L'uomo invaso e altre invenzioni. Milan, Bompiani, 1986.
Le menzogne della notte. Milan, Bompiani, 1988; as *Night's Lies*, London, Collins Harvill, 1990; as *Lies of the Night*, New York, Atheneum, 1991.
Qui pro quo. Milan, Bompiani, 1991.
Calende greche. Milan, Bompiani, 1992.

Plays

Trittico. Catania, Sanfilippo, 1989.

Screenplay: *Diceria dell'untore*, from his own novel.

Verse

L'amaro miele. Turin, Einaudi, 1982.
Rondò della felicità. N.p., La Corda Pazza, 1991.

Other

Cere perse. Palermo, Sellerio, 1985.
La luce e il lutto. Palermo, Sellerio, 1988.
L'isola nuda, with Giuseppe Leone. Milan, Bompiani, 1989.
Saldi d'autunno. Milan, Bompiani, 1990.

Editor, *Due preghiere*, by Ernest Renan and Jean Giraudoux. Palermo, Sellerio, 1981.
Editor, *Dizionario dei personaggi di romanzo*. Milan, Mondadori, 1982.
Editor, *Il malpensante: lunario dell'anno che fu*. Milan, Bompiani, 1987.

Translator, with Paola Masino, *L'amor geloso: tre racconti*, by Marie Madeleine Pioche de la Vergne, Comtesse de La Fayette. Palermo, Sellerio, 1980.
Translator, *Susanna e il Pacifico* [Suzanne et le Pacifique], by Jean Giraudoux. Palermo, Sellerio, 1980.
Translator, *Le controrime* [Les Contrerimes], by Paul-Jean Toulet. Palermo, Sellerio, 1981.
Translator, *Fiori del male* [Les Fleurs du mal], by Charles Baudelaire. Milan, Mondadori, 1983.
Translator, *Per Poe* [On Edgar Allan Poe], by Charles Baudelaire. Palermo, Sellerio, 1988.

*

Bibliography: *Bibliografia de Gesualdo Bufalino* by Antonella Moncada, Catania, University of Catania Press, 1987.

Manuscript Collection: University of Pavia.

*   *   *

My work is a journey within my soul, within my heart, within me, a fragile human creature who is not the voice of all others, who does not even know how to depict them. My ambition is to be recognised as a European writer, an Italian writer and a Sicilian writer, in that order. Of course, every writer wants to appeal to all men and since my traditional cultural background is Western European, then I cling to that, to Europe and especially to France and Italy. My own past and memories are naturally Sicilian and so I speak out as a Sicilian.

Gesualdo Bufalino belongs to that group of contemporary Sicilian writers who are now emerging as literary successes in later life. Born in 1920 in the town of Comiso (Cruisetown) in the Sicilian province of Ragusa, Bufalino won the Campiello prize in 1981 with his first novel, *Diceria dell'untore* (*The Plague Sower*). In the words of the Sicilian writer Leonardo Sciascia, who discovered him, Bufalino writes "perfectly."

Bufalino's writing to date comprises five novels: *The Plague Sower*, *Argo il cieco* (*Blind Argus*), *Le menzogne della notte* (*Night's Lies* or *Lies of the Night*), *Qui pro quo*, and *Calende greche* (Greek Calends). *Museo d'ombre* (Museum of Shadows) is a very personal collection of short prose pieces recalling his Sicilian youth. Other prose writing includes *Cere perse* (Lost Candles) and *La luce e il lutto* (Light and Sorrow), and he has also written a book of short stories, *L'uomo invaso* (Man Invaded), and some poetry, *L'amaro miele* (Bitter Honey).

His first two novels (*The Plague Sower* and *Blind Argus*) are his most autobiographical, and are set respectively in immediate post-war Sicily and 1951. His third novel, *Night's Lies*, is set at the time of the Risorgimento (1860) but is by no means another lesson on the political cynicism of that period; instead it is a challenging and complex congeries of all Bufalino's principal notions on writing.

Bufalino's main themes are recognisably Sicilian and by extension universal. However, unlike Leonardo Sciascia, who maintained a moral stance against injustice and in particular against the criminality of the Mafia and political powers in collusion with it, Bufalino is not in any way ideologically or politically committed. (In this way he is a fine example of 20th-century postmodernism.) He could not be called provincial and indeed does not depict his Sicily in Lampedusian tones of "voluptuous immobility." Nor does he uphold the typical tragic vision of Sicilian history — that is, of Sicily constantly oppressed by outside forces and having to combat endemic forms of corruption and injustice. The influence of his Sicilian background is more manifest in literary terms, in particular, Luigi Pirandello and Vitaliano Brancati. Bufalino explains, "I am more than aware of their very active presence. Pirandello for me is essentially and unequivocally the only true interpreter of the Sicilian spirit as a kind of painful, sophist way of understanding, in part from the ancient Gorgias, as well as Empedocles. Brancati on the other hand is filled with the spirit of irony, a bitter kind of carnality. Life is assailed and voluptuously savoured with all the senses, yet a kind of bleak pessimism prevails. Brancati displays an ironic, amusing vitality, portraying the gaiety of life, tinged with bitterness. I consider myself to be between them both."

Easily identifiable in Bufalino's work are those themes such as the multiplicity of character, the "mask," the search for identity and for the meaning of one's existence, coupled with powerful erotic and sensual evocations of his native Sicily. Most dramatic of all is the all-pervading theme of death:

"Death for a Sicilian is a contradiction of his natural thirst for life. It is something which is unjust; it is a scandal and it is unnatural. Our fate under a difficult sky is an unjust one."

Bufalino considers himself a "lyricist, a poet disguised as a narrator," and his "perfect language" is Sicilian baroque: exuberant, excessive, and opulent. Form and language are the key elements of his literariness. He rarely uses familiar forms of narrative: instead he manipulates and parodies a variety of literary forms, from high, classical literature to more popular forms such as the detective novel. His melancholic and elegiac recollections of Sicily contrast with the deliberate theatricality and vanity of his later novels.

"I am a pessimist, even worse, a nihilist," he says. "I see the void and burnt-out ashes at the heart of everything yet there is one phrase which pounds away inside my head — *il faut tenter de vivre* — and because of this, inasmuch as I see life as a living lie, a form of madness, made up of anguish, suffering and despair, I have it within me to smile wryly at life. It is an illness and writing is a type of medicine, a toy even, to forget the sickness."

—Anne W. Mullen

BUSTOS DOMECQ, H. *See* **BIOY CASARES, Adolfo.**

BUTOR, Michel (Marie François). French. Born in Mons-en-Baroeul, 14 September 1926. Educated at the Collège Saint-François-de-Sales, Evreux; Lycée Louis-le-Grand, Paris, until 1945; the Sorbonne, Paris, 1945–49, licence 1946 and diploma 1947 in philosophy. Married Marie-Josèphe Mas in 1958; four daughters. Philosophy teacher, Sens, 1950; French teacher, Al Minya, Egypt, 1950–51, University of Manchester, England, 1951–53, in Salonika, 1954–55, École Normale Supérieure, Paris, 1955, and Geneva, 1956–57; Associate Professor, Centre Universitaire, Vincennes, 1969; Adjunct Professor, 1970–73, and Assistant Professor, 1973–75, University of Nice. Since 1975 Professor, University of Geneva. Visiting Professor of French, Bryn Mawr College, Pennsylvania, and Middlebury College, Vermont, 1960, State University of New York, Buffalo, 1962, Northwestern University, Evanston, Illinois, 1965, University of New Mexico, Albuquerque, 1969–70 and 1973–74. Since 1958 advisory editor, Gallimard publishers, Paris. Recipient: Fénéon prize, 1957; Renaudot prize, 1957; Grand prize for Literary Criticism, 1960, Ford Foundation grant, 1964. Chevalier, National Order of Merit. Address: À l'écart, 74380 Lucinges, France.

PUBLICATIONS

Fiction

Passage de Milan.   Paris, Minuit, 1954.
L'Emploi du temps.   Paris, Minuit, 1956; as *Passing Time*, London, Faber, and New York, Simon and Schuster, 1960.
La Modification.   Paris, Minuit, 1957; as *Second Thoughts*, London, Faber, 1958; as *A Change of Heart*, New York, Simon and Schuster, 1959.
Degrés.   Paris, Gallimard, 1960; as *Degrees*, New York, Simon and Schuster, 1961; London, Methuen, 1962.
Portrait de l'artiste en jeune singe: capriccio.   Paris, Gallimard, 1967.
Intervalle.   Paris, Gallimard, 1973.
Matière de rêves:
   1. *Matière de rêves.*   Paris, Gallimard, 1975.
   2. *Second Sous-sol.*   Paris, Gallimard, 1976.
   3. *Troisième Dessous.*   Paris, Gallimard, 1977.
   4. *Quadruple fond.*   Paris, Gallimard, 1981.
   5. *Mille et un plis.*   Paris, Gallimard, 1985.
La Rêve d'Irénée.   Paris, Cercles, 1979.
Vanité: conversation dans les Alpes-Maritimes.   Paris, Balland, 1980.
Explorations (includes verse).   Lausanne, l'Aire, 1981.
L'Embarquement de la Reine de Saba: d'après le tableau de Claude Lorrain.   Paris, la Différence, 1989.

Plays

Réseau aérien (broadcast 1962).   Paris, Gallimard, 1962.
Votre Faust . . . (opera), music by Henri Pousseur.   Paris, Gallimard, 1962.
6 810 000 Litres d'eau par seconde: étude stéréophonique.   Paris, Gallimard, 1965; as *Niagara*, Chicago, Regnery, 1969.
Elseneur: Suite dramatique.   La Chaux-de-Cossonay, Volumen, 1979.

Radio Play: *Réseau aérien*, 1962.

Verse

Cycle sur neuf gouaches d'Alexandre Calder.   Paris, la Hune, 1962.
Illustrations 1–4.   Paris, Gallimard, 4 vols., 1964–76.
Litanie d'eau.   Paris, la Hune, 1964.
Dans les flammes: chanson du moine à Madame Nhu.   Stuttgart, Belser, 1965.
Comme Shirley.   Paris, la Hune, 1966.
La Banlieue de l'aube à l'aurore; Mouvement brownien.   Montpellier, Fata Morgana, 1968.
Tourmente.   Montpellier, Fata Morgana, 1968.
Travaux d'approche.   Paris, Gallimard, 1972.
Envois.   Paris, Gallimard, 1980.
Brassée d'avril.   Paris, la Différence, 1982.
Luminaires et préliminaires: 21 ballades et 7 chansons.   Gourdon, Bedou, 1983.
Exprès.   Paris, Gallimard, 1983.
Herbier lunaire.   Paris, la Différence, 1984.
Victor Hugo écartelé, illustrated by Baltazar.   Nice, Matarasso, 1984.
Hors d'œuvre.   Rouen, l'Instant Perpétuel, 1985.
Les Jouets du vent.   Ginasservis, la Garonne, 1985.
Roberte et Gulliver.   Fontfroide-le-Haut, Fata Morgana, 1987.
Ailes, illustrated by Guido Llinás.   Paris, Brocéliande, 1987.
Zone franche.   Fontfroide-le-Haut, Fata Morgana, 1989.
La Forme courte.   Marseille, Temps Parallèle, 1990.

Other

Zanartu.   Geneva, Galerie Éditions, 1958.

Le Génie du lieu:

> *Le Génie du lieu.* Paris, Grasset, 1958; as *The Spirit of Mediterranean Places*, Marlboro, Vermont, Marlboro Press, 1986.
>
> *Mobile: étude pour un représentation des États Unis.* Paris, Gallimard, 1962; as *Mobile: Study for a Representation of the United States*, New York, Simon and Schuster, 1963.
>
> *Description de San Marco.* Paris, Gallimard, 1963; as *Description of San Marco*, New York, French and European Publications, 1983; Fredericton, New Brunswick, York Press, 1983.
>
> *Où.* Paris, Gallimard, 1971.
>
> *Boomerang.* Paris, Gallimard, 1978; translated in part as *Letters from the Antipodes*, St. Lucia, University of Queensland Press, and Athens, Ohio University Press, 1981.

Répertoire 1–5. Paris, Minuit, 4 vols., 1960–82.

Une Histoire extraordinaire: Essai sur un rêve de Baudelaire. Paris, Gallimard, 1961; as *Histoire extraordinaire: Essay on a Dream of Baudelaire's*, London, Cape, 1969.

Hérold. Paris, Fall, 1964.

Les Œuvres d'art imaginaires chez Proust (lecture). London, Athlone Press, 1964.

Essais sur les modernes. Paris, Gallimard, 1964.

Le Masque, with Harold Rosenberg. Paris, Maeght, 1966.

Entretiens avec Michel Butor, with Georges Charbonnier. Paris, Gallimard, 1967.

Dialogues des règnes. Paris, Brunidor, 1967.

Paysage de répons; Dialogues de règnes. Albeuve, Castella, 1968.

Essais sur Les Essais (on Montaigne). Paris, Gallimard, 1968.

Inventory: Essays, edited by Richard Howard. New York, Simon and Schuster, 1968; London, Cape, 1970.

Essais sur le roman. Paris, Gallimard, 1969.

Les Mots dans la peinture. Geneva, Skira, 1969.

La Rose des vents: 32 rhumbs pour Charles Fourier. Paris, Gallimard, 1970.

Dialogue avec 33 variations de Ludwig van Beethoven sur une valse de Diabelli. Paris, Gallimard, 1971.

Les Sept Femmes de Gilbert le Mauvais. Montpellier, Fata Morgana, 1972.

Rabelais: ou, C'était pour rire. Paris, Larousse, 1972.

Les Compagnons de Pantagruel (lecture). Oxford, Clarendon Press, 1976.

Dotrement et ses écritures: entretiens sur les logogrammes, with Michel Sicard. Paris, Place, 1978.

Matières et talismans (interview), with Michel Sicard. Paris, Place, 1978.

Michel Butor, voyageur à la roue (interviews), with J. M. Le Sidaner, Paris, Encre, 1979.

Filaments sensibles. Paris, Luc Moreau, 1981.

Treize à la douzaine. Montreal, Esterel, 1981.

Sept à la demi-douzaine. Draguignan, Lettres de Casse, 1982.

Naufragés de l'arche. Paris, la Différence, 1982.

Fenêtres sur le passage intérieur. Bois-de-Champ, Æncrages, 1982.

Vieira da Silva: peintures. Paris, l'Autre Musée, 1983.

Voyage avec Michel Butor (interviews), with Madeleine Santschi. Lausanne, l'Age d'Homme, 1983.

Problèmes de l'art contemporain à partir des trauvaux d'Henri Maccheroni, with Michel Sicard. Paris, Bourgois, 1983.

Résistances: conversations aux antipodes, with Michel Launay. Paris, Presses Universitaires de France, 1983.

La Vision de Namur: à l'intention de la Rose des voix, with Henri Pousseur. Yverdon-les-Bains, La Thièle, 1983.

Loisirs et brouillons (1964–1984). Boît-les-Orgues, Bastin-Gouet, 1984.

Improvisations sur Flaubert, with *Michel Butor à Mayence*, by René Andrianne and others. Paris, la Différence, 1984.

Le Chien roi, illustrated by Pierre Alechinsky. Paris, Galerie Lelong, 1984.

Alechinsky dans le texte, with Michel Sicard. Paris, Galilée, 1984.

Dimanche matin. Rouen, L'Instant Perpétuel, 1984.

L'Office des mouettes, illustrated by Cesare Peverelli. Geneva, Blanco, 1984.

La Quinte major: le temps qui passe. Montpellier, CMS, 1984.

Improvisations sur Henri Michaux. Fontfroide-le-Haut, Fata Morgana, 1985.

Frontières: [entretiens avec Christian Jacomino]. St. Maximin, Temps Parallèle, 1985.

Chantier. Gourdon, Bedou, 1985.

La Famille Grabouillage, with Stéphane Bastin. Gourdon, Bedou, 1985.

Trajet du héraut, with *Maltraité du peinture*, by Jacques Hérold. Fontfroide-le-Haut, Fata Morgana, 1985.

Avant-goût, I-II-III-IV. Rennes, Ubacs, 4 vols., 1985–90.

L'Œil de Prague: dialogue avec Charles Baudelaire autour des travaux de Jiří Kolář; suivi de, Réponses; et de, La Prague de Kafka par Jiří Kolář. Paris, la Différence, 1986.

Le Congrès des cuillers. Geneva, Musée Barbier-Mueller, 1986.

Menace intime, illustrated by Jean Lecoultre. N.p., Au Verseau Un sur Un, 1986.

ABC de correspondance, with Michel Sicard, illustrated by Pierre Alechinsky. Paris, Galerie Lelong, 1986.

Cartes et lettres: correspondance 1966–1979, with Christian Dotrement. Paris, Galilée, 1986.

Klasen: rétrospective de l'œuvre peint de 1960 à 1987 (exhibition catalogue), with Gilbert Cascault and Carole Naggar. Aix-en-Provence, Présence Contemporaine, 1987.

Triple Suite en jaune à la gloire de van Gogh 1981-1985-1986, with Michel Sicard. Paris, Traversière, 1987.

Une Visite chez Pierre Klossowski le samedi 25 avril 1987, photographs by Maxime Godard. Paris, la Différence, 1987.

D'un Jour à l'autre. Rosporden, Hôtel Continental, 1987.

Angkor silencieux, with Nouth Narang, photographs by Philippe Gras. Paris, Sous le Vent, 1988.

Le Retour de Boomerang. Paris, Presses Universitaires de France, 1988.

Improvisations sur Rimbaud. Paris, la Différence, 1989.

Au Jour le jour: carnets 1985. Paris, Plon, 1989.

Alechinsky: frontières et bordures, with Michel Sicard. Paris, Galilée, 1989.

De la Distance: (déambulation), with Frédéric-Yves Jeannet. Rennes, Ubacs, 1990.

Andre-Pierre Arnal: progrès du jeu assez lent, with Jean-Paul Carnier and Bernard Teulon-Nouailles. Montpellier, Galerie Wimmer, and Paris, la Différence, 1990.

Editor, *Essais*, by Montaigne. Paris, Union Générale de Éditions, 1964.

Translator, with Lucien Goldmann, *Brève Histoire de la littérature allemande*, by Georg Lukács. Paris, Nagel, 1949.

Translator, *La Théorie du champ de la conscience*, by Aaron Gurwitsch. Brussels, Desclée de Brouwer, 1957.

Translator, *Tout est bien qui finit bien*, by William Shake-
speare.   Paris, Formes et Reflets, 1958.
Translator, *De l'Origine des dieux*, by Bernardino de Sahagún.
Montpellier, Fata Morgana, 1981.

*

Bibliography: *Michel Butor: A Checklist* by Barbara Mason,
London, Grant and Cutler, 1979.

Critical Studies: *Michel Butor* by Leon S. Roudiez, New York,
Columbia University Press, 1965; *The French New Novel:
Claude Simon, Michel Butor, Alain Robbe-Grillet* by John
Sturrock, London, Oxford University Press, 1969; *Michel
Butor: L'Emploi du temps* by Marion A. Grant, London,
Arnold, 1973; *Michel Butor* by Michael Spencer, Boston,
Twayne, 1974; *Michel Butor* by Jennifer Waelti-Walters,
Victoria, British Columbia, Sono Nis Press, 1977; *The Narra-
tive of Michel Butor: The Writer as Janus* by Dean McWilliams,
Athens, Ohio University Press, 1978; *Address: Rimbaud,
Mallarmé, Butor* by Liliane Welch, Victoria, British Col-
umbia, Sono Nis, 1979; *Perpetuum Mobile: A Study of the
Novels and Aesthetics of Michel Butor* by Mary Lydon,
Edmonton, University of Alberta Press, 1980; *Intentionality
and Intersubjectivity: A Phenomenological Study of Michel
Butor's La Modification* by Lois Oppenheim, Lexington,
Kentucky, French Forum, 1980; Butor issue of *World
Literature Today* (Norman, Oklahoma), Spring 1982, and
Kentucky Romance Quarterly, 38(1), 1985.

*   *   *

Michel Butor became known in the late 1950s among the
writers of the *nouveau roman*, the group who were famous for
their refusal of traditional concepts of plot, characterization,
and use of chronology. Thus began Butor's systematic exploration and description of the networks of relationships that make
up our perception of the world: an exploration that has
continued until this time, involving him in collaboration with
other artists, experiments in structure and typography and a
total rejection of any concept of *genre*.

By tradition Butor has been spoken of as novelist, poet,
critic, dramatist, and experimental writer, but this is not
satisfactory, for in his hands each of these categories spills over
into the next. The distinctions they draw are not those which
matter in his growing body of work. It would perhaps be better
to think of Butor as "Notre Faust," defining Faust as an
explorer of the universe and a famous teacher, for his work is
voluntarily didactic and operates on all the planes of a good
education; it requires the reader to attend to what he is being
told, make an active attempt to follow instructions in the
manipulation of the material at hand, understand symbolic
communication of all kinds, utilize the resources of the outside
world in his study, and finally take what he has achieved out
into his daily life.

The novels *Passage de Milan*, *L'Emploi du temps* (*Passing
Time*), *La Modification* (*A Change of Heart*), and *Degrés*
(*Degrees*) demonstrate how architecture, myth, literature,
geography form the context in which we live and create
networks of interconnecting experience where each person is a
single junction or knot. Having adjusted his readers' perception of the world in this way and presented to them the
complexities of understanding, Butor proceeds to examine
human creativity from as many aspects as he can in series of
inter-connected texts. The *Répertoire* series of critical essays
and the volumes on Montaigne, Baudelaire, Rabelais, and
others provide an analysis of the development of individual
creative expression; the *Illustrations* series are personal texts
(frequently poems) in response to works by other artists
(creativity growing from creative expression); the *Génie du
lieu* (Spirit of Place) series, *Description de San Marco* (*Description of San Marco*), and *Intervalle* show the importance
of landscape, myth, culture on collective expression of experience — the growth of cities, sacred places, and so on — while
the *Matière de rêves* (Material of Dreams) series ventures into
the psychology of creativity by the way the ironic pseudo-
dreams are described.

The immensity of Butor's undertaking and the systematic
way in which he works are expressed clearly in the organization
pf the special Butor issue of the journal *L'Arc* which Butor was
invited to edit himself. He divided the volume into five
chapters: "Arts and Crafts," "Sites," "Museums," "Spectacles," "Books," and his interests — craftsmanship and
technique, collective expression in the past, individual
creativity from the past, living collective expression, contemporary works of art — can be studied under those headings,
although it very soon becomes evident that the categories are
indivisible and that the resonances between them are all
important.

In the breadth of his vision Butor defies classification. Sartre
was quite right when, in 1960, he said that Butor was the only
contemporary writer capable of formulating the problem of
totality.

—Jennifer Waelti-Walters

C

CABRAL DE MELO NETO, João. *See* **MELO NETO, João Cabral de.**

————

CABRERA INFANTE, G(uillermo). British. Born in Gibara, Cuba, 22 April 1929; emigrated to England in 1966: British citizen. Educated at the University of Havana, 1949, 1950–54. Married 1) Marta Calvo in 1953 (divorced 1961), two daughters; 2) Miriam Gomez in 1961. Professor of English literature, School of Journalism, Havana, 1960–61; cultural attaché, 1962–64, and chargé d'affaires, 1964–65, Cuban Embassy, Brussels; scriptwriter, 20th Century-Fox and Cupid Productions, 1967–72; Visiting Professor, University of Virginia, Charlottesville, Spring 1982. Film reviewer (as G. Cain), 1954–60, and fiction editor, 1957–60, *Carteles* magazine, Cuba; editor, *Lunes* (weekly literary supplement of *Revolución*), 1959–61. Recipient: Biblioteca Breve prize, 1964; Guggenheim fellowship, 1970; Foreign book prize (France), 1971. Agent: Carmen Balcells, Diagonal 580, 08021 Barcelona, Spain. Address: 53 Gloucester Road, London SW7 4QN, England.

PUBLICATIONS

Fiction

Así en la paz como en la guerra: cuentos. Havana, Revolución, 1960.
Tres tristes tigres. Barcelona, Seix Barral, 1965; as *Three Trapped Tigers*, New York, Harper, 1971; London, Pan, 1980.
Vista del amanecer en el trópico. Barcelona, Seix Barral, 1974; as *A View of Dawn in the Tropics*, New York, Harper, 1978; London, Faber, 1988.
La Habana para un infante difunto. Barcelona, Seix Barral, 1979; as *Infante's Inferno*, New York, Harper, and London, Faber, 1984.

Plays

Screenplays (as G. Cain): *Wonderwall*, 1968; *Vanishing Point*, 1970.

Other

Un oficio del siglo veinte (as G. Cain). Havana, Revolución, 1960; revised edition, Barcelona, Seix Barral, 1973; as *A Twentieth-Century Job* (as Cabrera Infante), London, Faber, 1991.
O. Barcelona, Seix Barral, 1975.
Exorcismos de estil(l)o. Barcelona, Seix Barral, 1976.

Arcadia todas las noches. Barcelona, Seix Barral, 1978.
Vidas de un héroe. N.p., n.p., 1984(?).
Holy Smoke (on the cigar). London, Faber, and New York, Harper, 1985.

Editor, *Mensajes de libertad: ¡La España rebelde! ensayos selectos.* Lima, Movimiento Universitario Revolucionario, 1961.

Translator, *Dublineses* [Dubliners], by James Joyce. Barcelona, Lumen, 1972.

*

Bibliography: in *Cuban Literature: A Research Guide* by David William Foster, New York, Garland, 1985.

Critical Studies: "Heilsgeschichte and the Structure of *Tres tristes tigres*," in *Romance Quarterly* (Lexington, Kentucky), 22, 1975, "Women as Cosmic Phenomena in *Tres tristes tigres*," in *Journal of Spanish Studies: 20th Century*, 3, 1975, and "Guillermo Cabrera Infante: *Tres tristes tigres*," in his *The Worlds Reborn: The Hero in the Modern Spanish American Novel*, Morgantown, West Virginia University Press, 1984, all by William L. Siemens; "Cabrera Infante: Creation in Progress" by Raymond D. Souza, in his *Major Cuban Novelists: Innovation and Tradition*, Columbia, University of Missouri Press, 1976; "Intratextual Distance in *Tres tristes tigres*" by Jonathan Tittler, in *Modern Language Notes* (Baltimore, Maryland), 93, 1978; "*Tres tristes tigres*, or the Treacherous Play on Carnival" by M.-Pierrette Malcuzynski, in *Ideologies and Literature*, 3(15), 1980; "A Secret Idiom: The Grammar and Role of Language in *Tres tristes tigres*," in *Latin American Literary Review* (Pittsburgh), 8, 1980, and *Logos and the Word: The Novel of Language and Linguistic Motivation in Grande Sertão: Veredas* [by J. Guimarães] *and Tres tristes tigres*, Berne, Lang, 1983, both by Stephanie Merrim; "The Literary Exorcisms of Guillermo Cabrera Infante" by Edna Acosta-Belén, in *Crítica Hispánica* (Pittsburgh), 3(2), 1981; *G. Cabrera Infante in the Menippean Tradition* by Ardis L. Nelson, Newark, Delaware, Juan de la Cuesta, 1983; "La Habana para un infante difunto: Cabrera Infante's Self-Conscious Narrative," in *Hispania* (Los Angeles), 68, 1985, and "The Pícaro's Journey in *La Habana para un infante difunto*," in *Hispanófila* (Chapel Hill, North Carolina), 30, 1987, both by Isabel Alvarez-Borland; *Novel Lives: The Fictional Autobiographies of G. Cabrera Infante and Mario Vargas Llosa* by Rosemary Geisdorfer Feal, Chapel Hill, University of North Carolina, 1986; Cabrera Infante issue of *World Literature Today* (Norman, Oklahoma), 61, 1987; "Squared Circles, Encircling Bowls: Reading Figures in *Tres tristes tigres*" by Jacques Lezra, in *Latin American Literary Review* (Pittsburgh), 16, 1988; *Guillermo Cabrera Infante and the Cinema* by Kenneth E. Hall, Newark, Delaware, Juan de la Cuesta, 1989.

*   *   *

G. Cabrera Infante is a versatile writer whose audacious works have continually surprised his readers. Under his influence even a deceptively innocent book like *Un oficio del siglo veinte* (*A Twentieth-Century Job*), a collection of film reviews originally published in Cuba between 1954 and 1960, is transformed into something more than criticism as the author, the critic (Cain), and films continually merge and separate in a cultural dialogue of change and identity. *Tres tristes tigres* (*Three Trapped Tigers*), which the publisher labels a novel and Cabrera Infante prefers to call a book, is widely recognized for its explosive humor and experimental form. And *Vista del amanecer en el trópico* (*A View of Dawn in the Tropics*) presents a pessimistic panorama of Cuban history by adeptly using vignettes as the basic structural unit.

His most recent novel, *La Habana para un infante difunto* (*Infante's Inferno*), blurs the distinctions between autobiography and fiction. Set in Havana during the 1940s and 1950s, it makes numerous direct references to people, places, and events which form important aspects of the author's personal past. His parents and their activities in the Cuban Communist Party, their residence at Zulueta 408 in Havana, and his association with the mazagine *Carteles* are examples of an extraordinary number of autobiographical references. Just where the autobiography ends and the fiction begins is difficult to ascertain, and it is doubtful that the author always knows. When the writer of this article broached the subject, Cabrera Infante professed to be confused about the matter — perhaps with good reason, since much of the novel concerns a young man's obsession with sexual escapades. *Infante's Inferno* demythologizes the Don Juan legend in Hispanic culture, or at least the aspiration of many to be a Don Juan. As far as autobiographical elements are concerned, it is best to say that Cabrera Infante maintains a dialogue in this work with his own past. That is, rather than simply attempting to recreate the past, he maintains a dialogue with it and the emphasis is on the dynamic quality of the relationship. At times a desire to recapture an element from the past seems to predominate; at others, a device from the past is merely used as a springboard for creative fiction. Memory and the transformation of the past is also a theme in *Three Trapped Tigers* and *A View of Dawn in the Tropics*, and at times these concerns are combined with a preoccupation with history.

Three Trapped Tigers, Cabrera Infante's most widely acclaimed and recognized work, contains a section which is entitled "The Death of Trotsky as Described by Various Cuban Writers, Several Years after the Event and Before." This section, which is supposedly a tape recording made by some of the main characters, uses the literary style of several Cuban writers to narrate the assassination of Trotsky in Mexico City in August 1940. "The Death of Trotsky" parodies the literary styles and personalities of several important Cuban literary figures, but it also brings into question the relativity of historical truth. In "The Death of Trotsky" we see the presentation of an historical event according to the stylistic norms of different writers, and each is based on its own conceptualization or stylization of reality. This section maintains a dialogue with both the historical and literary past and is indicative of the innovative and experimental nature of Cabrera Infante's works, as well as his remarkable ability to manipulate language.

—Raymond D. Souza

CANETTI, Elias. Born in Ruse (Ruschuk), Bulgaria, 25 July 1905. Educated at schools in England, Austria, Switzerland, and Germany; University of Vienna, Ph.D. 1929. Married 1) Venetia Taubner-Calderón in 1934 (died 1963); 2) Hera Buschor in 1971; one daughter. Full-time writer; resident in England since 1939. Recipient: Foreign Book prize (France), 1949; Vienna prize, 1966; Critics prize (Germany), 1967; Great Austrian State prize, 1967; Bavarian Academy of Fine Arts prize, 1969; Büchner prize, 1972; Nelly Sachs prize, 1975; Franz Nabl prize (Graz), 1975; Keller prize, 1977; Order of Merit (Bonn), 1979; Europa Prato prize (Italy), 1980; Order of Merit, Germany, 1980(?); Hebbel prize, 1980; Nobel prize for literature, 1981; Kafka prize, 1981; Great Service Cross (Germany), 1983. D.Litt.: University of Manchester; honorary Ph.D.: University of Munich. Agent: John Wolfers, 3 Regent Square, London WC1H 8HZ, England. Address: 8 Thurlow Road, London N.W.3, England.

PUBLICATIONS

Fiction

Die Blendung. Vienna, Reichner, 1936; translated as *Auto-da-Fé*, London, Cape, 1946; Briarcliff Manor, New York, Stein and Day, 1964; as *The Tower of Babel*, New York, Knopf, 1947.

Plays

Hochzeit (produced Brunswick, 1965). Berlin, Fischer, 1932; as *The Wedding*, New York, Performing Arts, 1986.
Komödie der Eitelkeit (produced Brunswick, 1965). Munich, Weismann, 1950; as *Comedy of Vanities*, with *Life-Terms*, New York, Performing Arts, 1983.
Die Befristeten (produced Vienna, 1967). Included in *Dramen*, 1964; as *The Numbered* (produced Oxford, 1956), London and New York, Boyars, 1984; as *Life-Terms*, with *Comedy of Vanities*, New York, Performing Arts, 1982.
Dramen (includes *Hochzeit*; *Komödie der Eitelkeit*; *Die Befristeten*). Munich, Hanser, 1964.

Other

Fritz Wotruba. Vienna, Rosenbaum, 1955.
Masse und Macht. Hamburg, Claassen, 1960; as *Crowds and Power*, New York, Viking Press, and London, Gollancz, 1962.
Welt im Kopf (selection), edited by Erich Fried. Graz, Stiasny, 1962.
Aufzeichnungen 1942–1948. Munich, Hanser, 1965.
Die Stimmen von Marrakesch: Aufzeichnungen nach einer Reise. Munich, Hanser, 1967; as *The Voices of Marrakesh*, London, Calder and Boyars, and New York, Seabury, 1978.
Der andere Prozess: Kafkas Briefe an Felice. Munich, Hanser, 1969; as *Kafka's Other Trial. The Letters to Felice*, New York, Schocken, and London, Calder and Boyars, 1974.
Alle vergeudete Verehrung: Aufzeichnungen 1949–1960. Munich, Hanser, 1970.
Die gespaltene Zukunft: Aufsätze und Gespräche. Munich, Hanser, 1972.
Macht und Überleben: drei Essays. Berlin, Literarisches Colloquium, 1972.
Die Provinz des Menschen: Aufzeichnungen 1942–1972. Munich, Hanser, 1973; as *The Human Province*, New York, Seabury, 1978; London, Deutsch, 1986.

Der Ohrenzeuge: 50 Charaktere.   Munich, Hanser, 1974; as *Earwitness: Fifty Characters*, New York, Seabury, and London, Deutsch, 1979.

Das Gewissen der Worte: Essays.   Munich, Hanser, 1975; as *The Conscience of Words*, New York, Seabury, 1979; London, Deutsch, 1986.

Der Überlebende.   Frankfurt, Suhrkamp, 1975.

Der Beruf des Dichters.   Munich, Hanser, 1976.

Die gerettete Zunge: Geschichte einer Jugend.   Munich, Hanser, 1977; as *The Tongue Set Free: Remembrance of a European Childhood*, New York, Seabury Press, 1979; London, Deutsch, 1988.

Die Fackel im Ohr: Lebensgeschichte 1921–1931.   Munich, Hanser, 1980; as *The Torch in My Ear*, New York, Farrar Straus, 1982; London, Deutsch, 1989.

Das Augenspiel: Lebensgeschichte 1931–1937.   Munich, Hanser, 1985; as *The Play of the Eyes*, New York, Farrar Straus, 1986; London, Deutsch, 1990.

Das Geheimherz der Uhr: Aufzeichnungen 1973–1985. Munich, Hanser, 1987; as *The Secret Heart of the Clock: Notes, Aphorisms, Fragments 1973–1985*, New York, Farrar Straus, 1989; London, Deutsch, 1991.

Translator, *Leidweg der Liebe*, by Upton Sinclair. Berlin, Malik, 1930.

Translator, *Das Geld schreibt: eine Studie über die amerikanische Literatur*, by Upton Sinclair.   Berlin, Malik, 1930.

Translator, *Alkohol*, by Upton Sinclair.   Berlin, Malik, 1932.

*

Critical Studies: "Elias Canetti's Novel *Die Blendung*" by Idris Parry, in *Essays on German Literature*, edited by F. Norman, London, University of London Institute of German Studies, 1965; "Grotesque Comedy in Canetti's *Auto-da-Fé*" by Mark Sacharoff, in *Critique* (Washington, D.C.), 14(1), 1972; "Elias Canetti's *Die Blendung* and the Changing Image of Madness" by Edward Thompson, in *German Life and Letters* (London), 26, 1973; "Doubting Death: On Elias Canetti's Drama *The Deadlined*" by Dagmar Barnouw, in *Mosaic* (Winnipeg, Manitoba), 7(2), 1974; "The Vision of Man in Elias Canetti's *Die Blendung*" by Peter Russell, in *German Life and Letters* (London), 28, 1974–75; "Remembering Times Past: Canetti, Sperber, and 'A World That Is No More'" by Peter Stenberg, in *Seminar* (Kingston, Ontario), November 1981; Canetti issue of *Modern Austrian Literature* (Riverside, California), 16(3–4), 1983; "Acoustic Masks: Strategies and Language in the Theater of Canetti, Bernhard and Handke" by Gitta Honegger, in *Modern Austrian Literature* (Riverside, California), 18(2), 1985; "Becoming Elias Canetti" by Roger Kimball, in *New Criterion* (New York), September 1986; "Notes on *Die Blendung* by Elias Canetti" by Kathleen Thorpe, in *Theoria* (Natal), October 1986; *Essays in Honor of Elias Canetti*, translated by Michael Hulse, New York, Farrar Straus, and London, Deutsch, 1987; "Aspects of Confucianism in Elias Canetti's Notes and Essays" by Reinhard Düssel, in *Tamkang Review* (Taipei), Autumn 1987–Summer 1988; "Elias Canetti: Exile and the German Language" by Yaier Cohen, in *German Life and Letters* (London), October 1988.

*   *   *

Although Elias Canetti has been publishing since the 1930s, his writings have only received sustained critical attention in the last 20 years or so. Canetti's belated fame may have been to do with his position as a German-language writer who lived in England for most of his literary career. The late interest in his work, though, is probably more to do with the way it resists easy categorisation, either in its literary forms or in an adherence to particular intellectual trends. He is the author of only one novel, *Die Blendung* (*Auto-da-Fé*); it is, however, now regarded alongside key works of Modernism such as James Joyce's *Ulysses* (1922) and Robert Musil's *The Man Without Qualities* (1930). As well as being a translator, essayist, dramatist, and writer of memoirs, Canetti has written one of this century's major studies of human behaviour, *Masse und Macht* (*Crowds and Power*). This work of immense scholarship has proved difficult to classify, in that it synthesizes findings from social anthropology and comparative religion, behavioural psychology and historical study, as well as from sociobiology and philosophical speculation.

Despite the discontinuity of Canetti's work (a discontinuity that was not only a result of Canetti's life on the move across Europe, but was also caused by his relentlessly shifting search for knowledge and method), it is possible to locate a recurrent concern with the position of the individual in modern mass societies in much of his writing. Like other German-language thinkers such as Erich Fromm and Wilhelm Reich, Canetti concerns himself with the sociopathology of contemporary life, locating individual behaviour within its historical context. His work has also been seen by critics as being preoccupied with the affirmation of life in the face of death's omnipotence, as well as displaying a recognizably Middle-European concern with language's ability (and failure) to communicate meaning. Such a preoccupation, as David Turner points out in *Modern Austrian Writing* (1980), may stem from Canetti's own complex position of identification and distance as a German-language writer who, like fellow Viennese exile poet Erich Fried, was resident in London for most of his later life. However, Canetti was further removed from the process of writing and communication, in that he did not have German as his birth tongue but the sephardic Jewish language Ladino.

In *Auto-da-Fé* Canetti uses the central irony of a scholar who has devoted himself to the study of ancient and oriental languages, but is unable to decipher the distinctly mundane occidental voices that surround him. The central figure Peter Kien exists apart from the populace of his city (probably Vienna but equally Berlin for its sense of claustrophobia and chaos), alive only in his windowless private library. Remote from everyday existence, the intellectual Kien fears social and physical contact, both at conversational and sexual level. Abruptly, however, this solitary bibliophile's life (and with it Kien's reason) are invaded by the outside world, as a consequence of his misguided decision to marry his housekeeper, the grotesque representative of the petit bourgeosie, Therese Krummholz. Kien's library is taken over and appropriated by his harridan of a wife, aided by the brutal, proto-fascist caretaker of the apartment block, Benedikt Pfaff. In order to reclaim his books, Kien descends to the city's underworld where he enlists the help of a hunchbacked dwarf, Fischerle. Kien's world and wits disintegate, and in the final part of this trilogy of novels, his brother Georges, a successful psychiatrist in Paris, arrives to effect a cure. Georges's arrival, though, is to no avail, and the by now completely deluded brother (whose name "resinous pine" Canetti chose to suggest ignitability) eventually sets fire to the priceless library and to himself.

Originally conceived as an eight-part *comedie humaine*, the three novels of *Auto-da-Fé* are by no means works of Balzac-inspired realism. Critics (among others Klaus Völker in *Text und Kritik* [1973]) have pointed out how the characterisation in Canetti's work of the 1930s has its visual equivalent in the harsh caricatures of George Grosz. Social roles, thoughts, and pretensions are exaggerated and distorted, and in the small cast of characters, Canetti presents us with a mad spectacle of particularly intense forms of monomaniac behaviour. The isolated individuals here all have their own *idées fixes*, ranging from Fischerle's desire to become world chess champion through to Therese's obsession with acquiring property and affecting propriety. When it exists at all, communication between characters is partial, leading to absurd misunderstandings and, as the German title *Die Blendung* (the Blinding/Delusion) indicates, a nightmarish tumble into private and mass fantasies. Canetti has a very acute ear for colloquialisms and the banalities of everyday speech, creating what he terms an "acoustic mask" for each figure, a core vocabulary of a few hundred words that marks out a character's habits of thought and behaviour. Canetti's penetration of his various social representative's linguistic habits is quite remarkably sustained, creating a world of complete self-absorption, vanity, and personal and public insanity.

Because of its unrelenting depiction of a world gone mad, critics have been divided as to the meaning — if any unified meaning can be imposed on such an elaborate text — of Canetti's idiosyncratic and grimly comic work. Some have seen it as a work of Swiftian satire deprecating all aspects of Austro-German society, others an allegory about the position of the intellectual and the devaluation of knowledge in a wholly mercantile world. Whatever its overall significance, *Auto-da-Fé* is one of the most remarkable studies of the possibly inflammatory madness of Middle Europe in the 1930s, with its tragi-comic depiction of the isolation of individuals in a fragmented culture with no common language, and, as such, deserves to be even more widely read.

The relationship of the individual to the mass was duly pursued by Canetti in his best-known work *Crowds and Power*. By bringing together extensive material from many disciplines, Canetti attempts in this exhilarating survey to draw up a typology of the crowd and to anatomise different sorts of power. His starting point is that crowd instinct is as natural as sexual instinct, and the human need to seek sustenance and support in crowds stems from a wish to conquer a (Kien-like?) fear of being touched by strangers. Through self-annihilation in belonging to a group, be it an army, religious sect, or audience being entertained, such a fear is abolished. From this premise, Canetti describes and analyses all manner of human crowd behaviours, and in particular the possibilities for violence in such human groupings, incorporating source material from many cultures. From a general classification of types of crowds, Canetti moves to historically- and culturally-specific assemblages, speculating on the mass under National Socialism in chapters such as "Germany and Versailles" and "Inflation and the Crowd." In this section of the work, Canetti also dissects the nature of modern parliamentarism, seeing it as a substitute for earlier warlike behaviours. The latter part of the study deals with manifestations of power and control, both in terms of overt authority and covert government; interestingly, in view of *Auto-da-Fé*'s depiction of group madness, it includes case studies of tyrannical and paranoic rule.

The tortured fear of renouncing individual isolation and belonging to the group is seen by Canetti as the motivating factor behind Franz Kafka's unhappiness in his insightful examination of Kafka's letters to his fiancée Felice Bauer in *Der andere Prozess* (*Kafka's Other Trial*). Canetti explores Kafka's dual response to comfortable middle-class life, as evident in the difficult real-life and letter relationship he had with Felice. Feeling frightened by loss of self within the life that surrounded him (and all that a marriage to Felice offered), yet unable to renounce his class's background, Kafka used this

complicated response to belonging as a creative impulse for his work. As Kien experiences in *Auto-da-Fé*, Kafka too felt invaded by the bourgeoisie's smug self-assurance in the shape of its solid furnishings. Furthermore, rather in the way that the ascetic Kien is cowed by the massive and physically powerful Therese, Kafka saw himself as weak and puny compared to the strength of the Bauer family.

The distinctly uncharming life of the bourgeoisie is paraded in the play *Hochzeit* (*The Wedding*), Canetti's disturbing variation on the Viennese comedy of manners. The first performance in Brunswick met with considerable hostility for the way that it exposed the pettinesses, self-conceits, and animalistic natures of a group of *Spiesser* (philistines) from an apartment block who attend a wedding party. Eventually Canetti subjects the whole grasping group to an earthquake. Equally critical of vanity, self-seeking, and greed, Canetti's other two plays also speculate on what living would be like in particular dystopian societies. *Komödie der Eitelkeit* (*Comedy of Vanities*) deals with a world of inadequate self-reflection in a society devoid of mirrors and photographs, while *Die Befristeten* (*The Numbered* or *Life-Terms*) speculates upon what it would be like to be spared the uncertainty of death, in a group where people know the exact date of their deaths.

Canetti's writings can be measured against his novel *Auto-da-Fé*, not so much in literary and philosophical achievement, but rather in the way they attempt to forge order out of chaos. The distillation of a society's pandemonium into a few representative figures in his novel and early plays (and in the surreal city types of the later *Der Ohrenzeuge* [*Earwitness*]) makes way in later works for calmer and more expansive methods of analysis, above all in *Crowds and Power* and in his compelling three-part autobiography. The mass of evidence for the first work, and the turbulent events of his own displaced life that he details in his memoirs are shaped, refined, and ordered, and are used to illustrate considerable conclusions about individual and social behaviour. Hence, Bushmen's transformations into animals, the voyage into madness of a Dresden judge, the behaviour of boarders at table in a Frankfurt guesthouse, the relationship of a Czech writer to his girlfriends, and the sighting of a comet as a child in Bulgaria, all these different occurrences enlighten Canetti, and help him to comprehend people's forbearance, folly, and faith.

—Anna-Marie Taylor

CAO YU. Pseudonym for Wan Jiabao. Chinese. Born in Qianjian, Hubei Province, 24 September 1910. Educated at Nankai School, Tianjin, 1922–28; Nankai University, 1928–30; Qinghua University, Beijing, 1930–33. Married 1) Zheng Xiu in 1939 (divorced 1951), two daughters; 2) Deng Yisheng in 1951 (died 1980), two daughters, 3) Li Yuru. English teacher, Women's Normal College, Hebei Province, 1934; teacher, then Dean, National Drama Training School, Nanjing, 1936–38, Chongqing, 1938–39, Jiangnan, 1939–42, and Fudan University, during World War II; travelled to the United States and Canada, 1946; screenwriter, and drama teacher, Shanghai; after 1949 worked at Academy of Dramatic Art, and Chinese Dramatists Association; director, People's Art Theatre, Beijing; joined Communist Party, 1956; sent to country reform school during Cultural Revolution, 1966–76; restored to literary and theatrical prominence after 1976;

travelled to Britain, 1980. Currently chair, Chinese Dramatists Association; vice president, China PEN, since 1982; president, Beijing People's Art Theatre; permanent member, 7th CPPCC, since 1988. Address: c/o China PEN, Shatan Beije 2, Beijing, China.

PUBLICATIONS

Plays

Leiyu (produced Beijing, 1935). Shanghai, Cultural Life Publishing House, 1934; as *Thunderstorm*, Beijing, Foreign Languages Press, 1958.
Richu (produced 1936). Shanghai, Cultural Life Publishing House, 1936; as *The Sunrise*, Shanghai, Commercial Press, 1940; as *Sunrise*, Beijing, Foreign Languages Press, 1960.
Yuanye (produced 1937). Shanghai, Cultural Life Publishing House, 1937; as *The Wilderness*, Hong Kong, Hong Kong University Press, and Bloomington, Indiana University Press, 1980.
Quanmin zongdongyuan [Mobilisation of the Whole People], with Song Zhidi. 1938.
Zhengzai xiang [Just Thinking]. 1940; Shanghai, Cultural Life Publishing House, 1946.
Beijingren. Shanghai, Cultural Life Publishing House, 1940; as *Peking Man*, New York, n.p., 194-?; Honolulu, University of Hawaii, 1959; New York, Columbia University Press, 1986.
Tuibian [Decay]. Shanghai, Cultural Life Publishing House, 1940.
Jia [Family], adaptation of the novel by Ba Jin. Shanghai, Cultural Life Publishing House, 1942.
Dujin [Goldplated]. 1943.
Qiao [Bridge]. Shanghai, Cultural Life Publishing House, 1947.
Heizi ershiba [Black Character 28] with Song Zhidi. 1947.
Cao Yu xuanji [Collected Works by Cao Yu]. 1951–52.
Cao Yu juben xuan [Selected Plays by Cao Yu]. 1954.
Minglang de tian. Beijing, People's Literature Publishing House, 1956; as *Bright Skies*, Beijing, Foreign Languages Press, 1960.
Jiandan pian [The Gall and the Sword]. Beijing, People's Literature Publishing House, 1962.
Wang Zhaojun. 1978; as *The Consort of Peace*, Hong Kong, Kelly & Walsh, 1980.
Cao Yu wenji [Collected Works of Cao Yu]. Beijing, China Theatre Publishing House, 2 vols., 1989.

Screenplay: *Yanyangtian* [Bright Sunny Days], 1948.

Other

Yingchun ji [Welcoming Spring]. 1958.
Meihao de ganqing [Beautiful Feelings], with Yu Ling and Liu Housheng. Beijing, China Literature and Arts United Press, 1983.

Editor, *Huangxiuqiu*, by I-so chu. Zhengzhou, Zhengzhou Classics Publishing House, 1987.

Translator, *Luomiou yu Jiuliye* [Romeo and Juliet], by William Shakespeare. Shanghai, Cultural Life Publishing House, 1949.

*

Critical Studies: "The Trilogy of Cao Yu and Western Drama" by David Y. Chen, in *Asia and the Humanities*, edited by Horst Frenz, Bloomington, Indiana University, 1959; "Interview: The Playwright Cao Yu" by Yang Yu, in *Chinese Literature* (San Francisco), November 1963; *Cao Yu: The Reluctant Disciple of Chekhov and O'Neill: A Study in Literary Influence* by Joseph Shiu-ming Lau, Hong Kong, University of Hong Kong, 1970; *Cao Yu* by John Y. Hu, Boston, Twayne, 1972; "On the Sources and Motives Behind Ts'ao Yü's *Thunderstorm*: A Qualitative Analysis" by Lewis S. Robinson, in *Tamkang Review* (Taibei), 16, 1985.

*   *   *

Cao Yu (the pen name of Wan Jiabao) is one of the most influential playwrights in Chinese theatre today. Modern Chinese theatre only began to emerge in 1907 when China's cultural continuity was first disrupted by the influence of new forms and ideas from the West. The new form of theatre was called *huaju*, or spoken drama, to distinguish it from the operatic forms of the traditional Chinese theatre. The pioneers of this new form produced interesting work, but it was Cao Yu who brought it to full maturity. His plays were very popular with urban Chinese audiences and have been translated into many languages and staged in Japan, the former Soviet Union, Romania, the United States, and other countries.

Cao Yu's first full-length play, *Leiyu* (*Thunderstorm*), was written in 1933 when he was an undergraduate at Qinghua University, studying western literature. Appearing at a time when modern drama was at a low point, it immediately received tremendous acclaim. Its success elevated the new theatrical form to unprecedented heights of prestige and influence. *Thunderstorm* is a densely constructed tragedy depicting the disintegration of a wealthy family following the adultery of some of its members. Their spiritual destruction is dramatically highlighted by concentrating the complicated action of the play, which covers 20 years, into 18 hours set against the physical menace of a gathering storm. The success of *Thunderstorm* encouraged Cao Yu into further writing for the theatre, and his next play was *Richu* (*Sunrise*), a realistic piece, portraying a group of characters in a big city. The heroine is a girl who, although eager for the brightness of the sun and freedom of life, wastes her youth among the evils and temptations of the city. She commits suicide at the end of the play when she realizes that the future holds nothing for her. *Yuanye* (*The Wilderness*), Cao Yu's third play, symbolizes man's struggle against fate through a young peasant's unruly passions and his tragedy in which he seeks revenge.

The above three plays comprise the first phase of Cao Yu's career. *Beijingren* (*Peking Man*) and *Jia* (Family) are the best plays in his second period (1937–47), and these were again well received by both readers and audiences. The former, deceptively relaxed on the surface, is actually built on a number of tense incidents leading towards a tragic outcome in this satirical story of the decline of a traditional scholar-official family. The play reflects the maturity of its author's dramatic skills, is written with great assurance and adroitness with regard to plot structure, and displays great confidence in the use of dialogue. *Jia*, an adaptation of Ba Jin's (*q.v.*) novel of the same title, describes unfulfilled love and condemns conventional Chinese family ethics. Cao Yu has only written three plays since 1947, in addition to many essays required for various occasions. Like all the writers of his generation in mainland China, his creativity as a writer has been impaired to an extent by restrictive Communist literary policies; hence his reputation as a dramatist rests on the plays he wrote in his early years.

The author wrote in the preface to *Thunderstorm* (1936 edition), "I was seized by a sudden passion so overwhelming that I could not but give vent to my rage that had been suppressed for so long a time. I am launching an attack on the Chinese family and society." This rage runs like a thread through all his early plays. By emphasising human tragedy and degradation and the hatefulness of feudal tradition, Cao Yu exposes the anguish and darkness of life and cries out for freedom and genuine love, yet his writing also holds out the promise of redemption.

Cao Yu's great achievements in modern Chinese drama owe much to his skill in adapting the methods of Western drama to Chinese themes, his stage experience acquired as an active member of students' drama clubs, and his profound knowledge of indigenous Chinese literature and drama. The declaration, a combination of modesty and artistic pride, which appears in the preface to the 1936 edition of *Thunderstorm*, illustrates his thoughts about the influences he has received: "Possibly, I have subconsciously stolen thread after thread of golden yarn from the master's house, used them to mend my ugly and coarse garments and then denied that these discoloured threads (for they have now become mine) originally belonged to the master."

Cao Yu shows courage as a writer in using different constructions and styles in his plays. Boldly ignoring his previous successes, he is always ready to try new devices and techniques; while *Thunderstorm* is carefully constructed, *Sunrise* is the author's conscious effort to reject the mechanical techniques of a well-made play. As he declared in his postscript to the 1936 edition of *Sunrise*, "I want to write something more straightforward." *The Wilderness* draws on Cao Yu's idea that "the heart of a person who has a black face is not black," and is regarded as the earliest experimental work of expressionism in China. *Peking Man* is one of the few plays in modern Chinese theatre that has achieved the delicate balance between tragedy and comedy.

Cao Yu's characterization is memorable. He was the first playwright in China to dredge up the inner conflicts of human beings. Most of his characters suffer as a result of their own passions and desires; "they are made into fools by their own conduct (emotional and rational) and by some sort of unknown power (casual or circumstantial), and living in a cramped cage with ostentatious conceit . . ." (preface to *Thunderstorm*, 1936).

Cao Yu is also a translator and a poet. He not only writes poems but also uses the medium of drama to create his own poetry. He employs a wide variety of symbols in his plays (weather, buildings, flowers, trees, birds, kites), and most of the titles of his works are the images of a particular theme. His prose dialogues convey the rhythm and beauty of classic Chinese poetry, but are written in a simple yet poignant vernacular. Cao Yu has also translated and adapted a number of western plays; his *Romeo and Juliet* is regarded as one of the most successful attempts to translate Shakespeare into Chinese.

Cao Yu's plays are constantly revived in China. His influence on modern Chinese theatre, whether direct or indirect, can hardly be overestimated.

—Li Ruru

CARBALLIDO (Fentanes), Emilio. Mexican. Born in Córdoba, Veracruzana, 22 May 1925. Educated at the National Autonomous University of Mexico, Mexico City, 1945–49, M.A. in dramatic art. Has one son. Assistant director, School of Theatre, 1954, member of Editorial Council, from 1959, Professor, Faculty of philosophy and letters, 1960–61, and director of the Faculty of Arts, 1974–76, University of Veracruzana, Xalapa; Professor at theatre school, National Institute of Fine Arts, Mexico City, from 1955; literary adviser, from 1957, and public relations representative on European and Asian tours, 1957–58, Mexican National Ballet; staff member, Departamento de Difusión Cultural, 1960–74, and director, Taller de Composición Dramática, 1969–74, Instituto Politécnico Nacional, Mexico City; Professor of dramatic theory and composition and head of Seminario de Teatro Mexicano, National Autonomous University of Mexico, Mexico City, 1965–68; Visiting Professor, Rutgers University, New Brunswick, New Jersey, 1965–66, and University of Pittsburgh, Pennsylvania, 1970–71. Director, *Tramoya* magazine, University of Veracruzana, since 1974. Recipient: Rockefeller fellowship, 1950; Centro Mexicano de Escritores fellowship, 1951–52, 1955–56; Universidad Nacional Autónoma de México contest prize, 1954; *El Nacional* prize, 1954, 1958; National Institute of Fine Arts Regional Festival prize, 1955; Ruíz de Alarcón Critics' prize, 1957, 1966, 1968, 1978, 1984, 1986, 1991; Non-Associated Critics' prize, 1960; Menorah de Oro prize, 1961; Instituto Internacional de Teatro prize, 1962; Casa de las Américas prize, 1962; *El Heraldo* prize, 1967, 1975; Asociación de Críticos y Cronistas prize, 1976. Address: c/o CREA, Fondo de Cultura Económica, Ave Universidad 975, Apdo 44975, 03100 Mexico City 12, Mexico.

PUBLICATIONS

Plays

La triple porfía (produced Mexico City, 1948). With *La zona intermedia: auto sacramental* and *Escribir, por ejemplo*, 1951.
El triángulo sutil (produced Mexico City, 1948).
La zona intermedia: auto sacramental (produced Mexico City, 1950). With *Escribir, por ejemplo* and *La triple porfía*, 1951; as *The Intermediate Zone*, in *The Golden Thread and Other Plays*, 1970.
Escribir, por ejemplo (produced Mexico City, 1950). With *La zona intermedia: auto sacramental* and *La triple porfía*, 1951.
El suplicante (produced Mexico City, 1950). Published in *Universidad de México*, 13, 1958.
Rosalba y los Llaveros (produced Mexico City, 1950). Included in *Teatro*, 1960.
La triple porfía; *La zona intermedia: auto sacramental*; *Escribir, por ejemplo*. Mexico City, Colección Teatro Mexicano, 1951.
El invisible (ballet scenario; produced Mexico City, 1952).
Ermesinda (ballet scenario; produced Mexico City, 1952).
El pozo (opera libretto; produced Mexico City, 1953).
La sinfonía doméstica (produced Mexico City, 1953).
El viaje de Nocresida, with Sergio Magaña (produced Mexico City, 1953).
Felicidad (produced Mexico City, 1955). Published in *Concurso Mexicano de teatro: obras premiadas*, Mexico City, National Institute of Fine Arts, 1956.

La danza que sueña la tortuga (produced as *Palabras cruzadas*, Mexico City, 1955). Mexico City, Fondo de Cultura Económica, 1957.

La hebra de oro (produced Mexico City, 1956). Included in *La hebra de oro*, 1957; as *The Golden Thread*, in *The Golden Thread and Other Plays*, 1970.

Selaginela (produced Mexico City, 1959). Included in *D.F.*, 1957.

El censo (produced Mexico City, 1959; New York, 1977). Included in *D.F.*, 1957.

Parásitas (produced in German as *Die Parasiten*, Kiel, West Germany, 1963). Included in *D.F.*, 1957.

El lugar y la hora (trilogy including *La bodega*; *El amor muerto*; *El glacier*). With *La hebra de oro*, 1957; as *Tangentes*, in *D.F.*, 1957; as *The Time and the Place: Dead Love, The Glacier, The Wine Cellar*, in *The Golden Thread and Other Plays*, 1970.

La hebra de oro (includes *La hebra de oro*; *El lugar y la hora*). Mexico City, Imprenta Universitara, Universidad Nacional Autónoma de México, 1957.

D.F. (includes *Misa primera*; *Selaginela*; *El censo*; *Escribir, por ejemplo*; *El espejo*; *Hipolito*; *Tangentes*; *Parásitas*; *La medalla*). Mexico City, Colección Teatro Mexicano, 1957; enlarged edition (also includes *La perfecta casada*; *Paso de madrugada*; *El solitario en octubre*; *Un cuento de Navidad*; *Pastores de la cuidad*), Xalapa, Universidad Veracruzana, 1962; revised and enlarged edition (also includes *El final de un idilio*; *Delicioso domingo*; *Dificultades*; *Un mujer de malas*; *Sõnar*; *Las noticias del día*; *La miseria*; *La pesadilla*; *Antes cruzaban ríos*; *Una rosa con otro nombre*; *¡Únete, Pueblo!*; *Por si alguna vez soñamos*), Mexico City, Grijalbo, 1978.

Cinco pasos al cielo, with Luisa Bauer and Fernando Wagner (produced Mexico City, 1959). As *Las lámparas del cielo y de la tierra*, in *El arca de Noé*, Mexico City, Secretaría de Educación Pública, 1974.

Las estatuas de marfil (produced Mexico City, 1960). Xalapa, Universidad Veracruzana, 1960.

El relojero de Córdoba (produced Mexico City, 1960). Included in *Teatro*, 1960; as *The Clockmaker from Córdoba*, in *The Golden Thread and Other Plays*, 1970.

La lente maravillosa (produced Mexico City, 1960).

El jardinero y los pájaros (produced Mexico City, 1960).

Guillermo y el nahual (produced Mexico City, 1960).

Homenaje a Hidalgo, music by Rafael Elizondo (produced Mexico City, 1960; revised version produced Mexico City, 1965). Included in *A la epopeya, un gajo: 5 obras dramáticas*, 1983.

Medusa (produced Ithaca, New York, 1966). Included in *Teatro*, 1960; in English, in *An English Translation of Three Plays by Emilio Carballido*, 1974.

El día que se soltaron los leones (produced Havana, 1963). Included in *Teatro*, 1960; as *The Day They Let the Lions Loose*, in *New Voices in Latin American Theatre*, Austin, University of Texas Press, 1971.

Teatro (includes *El relojero de Córdoba*; *Medusa*; *Rosalba y los Llaveros*; *El día que se soltaron los leones*). Mexico City, Fondo de Cultura Económica, 1960; New York, French and European Publications, 1969.

Teseo (produced Mexico City, 1962). Published in *La palabra y el hombre* (Mexico City), 24, 1962; as *Theseus*, in *The Golden Thread and Other Plays*, 1970.

Un pequeño día de ira (broadcast on Cuban television, 1969; produced Mexico City, 1976). Havana, Casa de las Américas, 1962; as *A Short Day's Anger* (produced Pittsburgh, Pennsylvania, 1970).

La perfecta casada (produced Xalapa, 1963). Included in *D.F.*, 1962.

Misa de seis, musica by Carlos Jiménez Mabarak (opera libretto; produced Mexico City, 1962).

Pastores de la ciudad, with Luisa Josefina Hernández (produced Mexico City, 1972). Included in *D.F.*, 1962.

"¡Silencio, pollos pelones, ya les van a echar su maíz!" (produced Ciudad Juárez, Mexico, 1963). Mexico City, Aguilar, 1963; as *Shut Up, You Plucked Chickens, You're Going to Be Fed!* (produced Claremont, California, 1969), in *An English Translation of Three Plays by Emilio Carballido*, 1974.

Los hijos del capitán Grant, adaptation of a novel by Jules Verne (produced Mexico City, 1964). Published in *5 obras para teatro escolar-II*, Mexico City, National Institute of Fine Arts, 1972.

Yo también hablo de la rosa (produced Mexico City, 1966). Mexico City, National Institute of Fine Arts, 1966; as *I Also Speak About the Rose* (produced Northridge, California, 1972); as *I, Too, Speak of the Rose*, in *Drama and Theatre*, 8(1), 1969; in *The Modern Stage in Latin America: Six Plays*, edited by George Woodyard, New York, Dutton, 1971.

Te juro, Juana, que tengo ganas (produced Mexico City, 1967; New York, 1977). Mexico City, Novaro, 1970; in English, in *An English Translation of Three Plays by Emilio Carballido*, 1974.

Almanaque de Juárez (produced Mexico City, 1968). Monterrey, Sierra Madre, 1972.

¡Tianguis! (produced Mexico City, 1968).

Macario (screenplay). Mexico City, Azteca, 1968.

Las noticias del día. Mexico City, Colección Teatro de Bolsillo, 1968.

Acapulco, los lunes (produced Mexico City, 1970). Monterrey, Sierra Madre, 1969.

Un vals sin fin por el planeta (produced Mexico City, 1970). Included in *Tres comedias*, 1981.

La fonda de las siete cabrillas, adaptation of *Don Bonifacio* by Manuel Eduardo de Gorostiza (produced Mexico City, 1970).

The Golden Thread and Other Plays (includes *The Mirror*; *The Time and the Place: Dead Love, The Glacier, The Wine Cellar*; *The Golden Thread*; *The Intermediate Zone*; *The Clockmaker from Córdoba*; *Theseus*). Austin, University of Texas Press, 1970.

Conversación entre las ruinas (produced as *Conversation Among the Ruins*, Kalamazoo, Michigan, 1971; New York, 1989).

An English Translation of Three Plays by Emilio Carballido: Te juro, Juana, que tengo ganas; *Medusa*; *¡Silencio, pollos pelones, ya les van a echar su maíz!"*. Denver, University of Denver, 1974.

Las cartas de Mozart (produced Mexico City, 1975). With *Orinoco!* and *Felicidad*, 1985.

Numancia, adaptation of the play by Miguel de Cervantes (produced Guanajuato, Mexico, 1975).

Nahui Ollin (produced Caracas, 1977). Included in *A la epopeya, un gajo: 5 obras dramáticas*, 1983.

Tres comedias (includes *Un vals sin fin por el planeta*; *La danza que sueña la tortuga*; *Felicidad*). Mexico City, Extemporáneos, 1981.

Orinoco! (produced Mexico City, 1982). With *Las cartas de Mozart* and *Felicidad*, 1985.

A la epopeya, un gajo: 5 obras dramáticas (includes *Homenaje a Hidalgo*; *Hoy canta el fénix en nuestro gallinero*; *Teseo*; *Almanaque de Juárez*; *Nahui Ollin*). Mexico City, Universidad Autónoma del Estado de México, 1983.

Fotografía en la playa (produced Mexico City, 1984).

Orinoco!; Las cartas de Mozart; Felicidad. Mexico City, Mexicanos Unidos, 1985.

Ceremonia en el tiempo del tigre; Rosa de dos aromas; Un pequeño día de ira. Mexico City, Mexicanos Unidos, 1986.

Rosa de dos aromas. With *Ceremonia en el tiempo del tigre* and *Un pequeño día de ira*, 1986; as *Rose of Two Aromas* (produced New York, 1987).

Teatro 2 (includes *Un vals sin fin por el planeta*; *La danza que sueña la tortuga*; *Las estatuas de marfil*). Mexico City, Fondo de Cultura Económica, 1988.

Screenplays: *Macario*, 1968; *Felicidad*, from his own play; *Los novios*, 1970; *Las visitaciones del diablo*, from his own novel; *Rosa Blanca*; *El águila descalza*; *La torre de marfil*.

Television Plays: *El relojero de Córdoba* and *Un pequeño día de ira* (Cuban television), 1967; *La danza que sueña la tortuga*, 1975.

Fiction

La veleta oxidada. Mexico City, Los Presentes, 1956.

El norte. Xalapa, Universidad Veracruzana, 1958; as *The Norther*, Austin, University of Texas Press, 1968.

La caja vacía. Mexico City, Fondo de Cultura Económica, 1962.

La visitaciones del diablo: folletín románico en XV partes. Mexico City, Mortiz, 1965.

El sol. Mexico City, Mortiz, 1970.

Los zapatos de fierro. Mexico City, Mortiz, 1977.

El tren que corría. Mexico City, Fondo de Cultura Económica, 1984.

Other

Tiempo de ladrones: la historia de Chucho el Roto. Mexico City, Grijalbo, 1983.

El pizarrón encantado (for children). Mexico City, CID CLI, 1984.

Editor, *Teatro joven de México.* Mexico City, Novaro, 1973.

Editor, *El arca de Noé.* Mexico City, Secretaría de Educación Pública, 1974.

Editor, *Más teatro joven de México.* Mexico City, Mexicanos Unidos, 1982.

Editor, *Nueve obras jóvenes.* Mexico City, Mexicanos Unidos, 1985.

Editor, *Avanzada: más teatro joven.* Mexico City, Mexicanos Unidos, 1985.

Editor, *Teatro para obreros.* Mexico City, Mexicanos Unidos, 1985.

*

Bibliography: "Emilio Carballido, Curriculum Operum" by Margaret Sayers Peden, in *Texto Crítico* (Xalapa, Mexico), 3, 1976.

Critical Studies: "Theory and Practice in Artaud and Carballido," in *Modern Drama* (Toronto), 11, 1968, "Greek Myth in Contemporary Mexican Theater," in *Modern Drama* (Toronto), 12, 1969, and *Emilio Carballido*, Boston, Twayne, 1980, all by Margaret Sayers Peden; "A Mexican Medusa" by Tamara Holzapfel, in *Modern Drama* (Toronto), 12, 1969; "The Theatre of Emilio Carballido: Spinning a Web" by Eugene R. Skinner, in *Dramatists in Revolt: The New Latin American Theater*, edited by Leon F. Lyday and George W. Woodyard, Austin, University of Texas Press, 1976; "Existential Irony in Three Carballido Plays" by Karen Peterson, in *Latin American Theatre Review* (Lawrence, Kansas), 10(2), 1977; "Freedom and Fantasy: A Structural Approach to the Fantastic in Carballido's *Las cartas de Mozart*," in *Latin American Theatre Review* (Lawrence, Kansas), Fall 1980, "A Theatre of Contradictions: The Recent Works of Emilio Carballido," in *Latin American Theatre Review* (Lawrence, Kansas), 18, 1985, and "Carballido's *Acapulco, los lunes* and the Darker Side of Comedy," in *Chasqui* (Provo, Utah), 19(2), 1990, all by Jacqueline Eyring Bixler.

*   *   *

Emilio Carballido is generally acknowledged to be the leading contemporary Mexican dramatist, one whose plays have significantly influenced modern Mexican theatre. His numerous awards and prizes include *El Nacional* for the best play in 1954 and 1958. Founder and editor of Mexico's leading theatre periodical *Tramoya*, he has also written novels, short stories, screenplays, and critical essays, and has edited collections of plays for children and plays for workers.

When Carballido began writing plays in 1946, realism was the dominant mode in commercial theatre while small companies were open to experimentation. Many of Carballido's early plays were written in a vein of fantasy that was considered experimental. However, he also won acclaim for his plays of psychological realism or comedies of customs like *Rosalba y los Llaveros* (Rosalba and the Llavero Family). For him, *La hebra de oro* (*The Golden Thread*) represented a major breakthrough in that he succeeded there in combining the realistic with the fantastic. In her book-length study of Carballido (1980), Margaret Sayers Peden claims that "his real contribution has been the introduction of a vein of fantasy and humor into the realistic tradition, a very personal blend that creates plays that transcend the specifically realistic and restrictively Mexican to achieve a theater that can be called modern, contemporary, and universal, while never losing the specificity of its Mexican origin."

The Golden Thread begins as a realistic drama. Adela and Leonor are both grandmothers of Silvestre, who has been missing for several years. During the women's visit to his decaying estate, spirits appear, perhaps as projections of the high-strung Leonor's mental state, or perhaps as a product of the radio's energy field in the storm-threatening atmosphere. Scenes conjured from their pasts serve to reveal the women's true natures and to put across Carballido's theme: all people are bound together by invisible threads of memories, dreams, desires. The thread breaks only when someone — like Silvestre — is unable to fulfill his or her potential. Similarly, *El día que se soltaron los leones* (*The Day They Let the Lions Loose*) rests upon the psychologically truthful portrayals of 65-year-old Ana and a middle-aged Woman. It is their encounter with the fantastic — picnicking with lions that have escaped from their cages in the zoo — that enables both women to gain some objectivity about their own lives. There is a delightfully whimsical quality about this "didactic farce," with its cartoon-like musical interlude, and yet the political subtext is unmistakable.

Carballido's finest blending of fantasy and realism is a brilliant tour-de-force in one act, *Yo también hablo de la rosa* (*I, Too, Speak of the Rose*). A Medium dressed in peasant costume unifies the various episodes that present different perspectives on the derailment of a freight train by two youngsters. At play in a junkyard while skipping school, Polo and Tonya impetuously roll a tub full of cement onto the train tracks. The incident is replayed with a Marxist interpretation, and then presented again in Freudian terms. Finally, the metaphor of the rose suggests that there is no absolute reality, "only a fusion of miraculous fictions" that bind together all people, things, and actions.

Among the strictly realistic plays, *Rosalba y los Llaveros* remains especially popular. Visiting her provincial relatives, the urbane young Rosalba creates havoc by challenging their fear of scandal. In her efforts to restore equilibrium and to win back the love of her cousin Lázaro, she learns something about herself. Also in the realistic mode are most of the one-act plays collected in several different editions of *D.F.* The title refers to Mexico City as the Federal District (*Distrito Federal*) of Mexico. *Una rosa con otro nombre* (A Rose, by Any Other Name), for example, is a drama of two women, both committed to the same man who demonstrates little regard for either of them. Through their joint effort to earn the money that will buy his release from prison, they also earn a sense of self-worth that allows them to break free of him. A more recent, full-length play, *Orinoco!*, traces a similar emotional trajectory between two showgirls, Mina and Fifi, drifting down the Orinoco River on an abandoned boat.

Carballido's first published play, *La zona intermedia* (*The Intermediate Zone*), is an engaging example of his plays of pure fantasy. Set in a cosmic way-station between death and final judgment, this one-act brings together a Virgin, a Critic, an Ineffectual Man, and a Fallen Woman, all relegated to the intermediate zone for failing to realize their potential. In the course of the action, the Ineffectual Man is carried away by devils, the Virgin begins her slow process of vaporizing into nothingness, and the Critic is eaten by a Nahual, a protean creature from Aztec mythology. Only the Fallen Woman is able to overcome her obsessive love and move on to judgment. *El lugar y la hora* (*The Place and the Time*) is the umbrella title for three short pieces — *El amor muerto* (*Dead Love*), *El glacier* (*The Glacier*), and *La bodega* (*The Wine Cellar*) — in which an element of horror enters the fantasy.

The diversity of Carballido's dramatic canon extends to historical drama. *Teseo* (*Theseus*) and *Medusa* are based upon Greek myth. *El relojero de Córdoba* (*The Clockmaker from Córdoba*) is based upon a Chinese story, but the action is transposed to 17th-century Mexico. In this gripping tale, the clockmaker narrowly escapes execution for a crime he only imagined, but which turns out to have actually occurred. The experience tempers his excessive dreaminess with an appreciation for the small realities of life.

Carballido's best-known novel, *El norte* (*The Norther*), reiterates a number of themes from the plays. Aristeo, a young man willingly caught up in an affair with an older woman, breaks off the relationship and experiences a new oneness with nature. The narrative echoes one of the ideas in *I, Too, Speak of the Rose*: "Between one choice and the next there are many roads. We always find ourselves some place else and not where we meant to be . . . nor do we know how we got there. Can we tell what fruits our acts will bear?"

Carballido's thematic concerns might be summed up as the reconciliation of opposites in a vast interconnecting web of human endeavor. Thus, both angel and demon, the rational and the irrational, have their place in each individual and in nature on a grand scale. When a sensitive character comes to an awareness that his or her potential has been limited by narrowness of outlook or experience, rebellion and change bring self-realization as well as a vast network of linkages. Such characters include Ana in *The Day They Let the Lions Loose*, Lázaro in *Rosalba y los Llaveros*, the Fallen Woman in *The Intermediate Zone*, and Aristeo in *The Norther*.

—Felicia Hardison Londré

CARDENAL, Ernesto. Nicaraguan. Born in Granada, 20 January 1925. Educated at the National Autonomous University of Mexico, Mexico City, 1944–48; Columbia University, New York, 1948–49. Trappist novice, Gethsemani, Kentucky, 1957–59; member of Benedictine monastery of Santa María de la Resurrección, Cuernavaca, Mexico, and a seminary in Colombia, 1961; ordained Roman Catholic priest, 1965; founder of religious community, Solentiname Archipelago; Former Minister of culture for Nicaragua. Recipient: Christopher Book award, 1972; Premio de la Paz grant, 1980. Address: Apartado Postal A-252, Managua, Nicaragua.

PUBLICATIONS

Verse

La ciudad deshabitada.   1946.
Proclama del conquistador.   1947.
Ansias lengua de la poesía nueva nicaragüense.   Managua, n.p., 1948.
Gethsemani, Ky.   Mexico City, Ediciones Ecuador, 1960.
La hora O.   Mexico City, Revista Mexicana de Literatura, 1960.
Epigramas: poemas.   Mexico City, Universidad Nacional Autónoma de México, 1961.
Oración por Marilyn Monroe, y otros poemas.   Medellín, Colombia, La Tertulia, 1965.
El estrecho dudoso.   Madrid, Ediciones Cultura Hispánica, 1966.
Antología.   Santiago, Chile, Editora Santiago, 1967.
Poemas.   Havana, Casa de las Américas, 1967.
Salmos.   Avila, Institución Gran Duque de Alba, 1967; as *Psalms of Struggle and Liberation*, translated by Emile G. McAnany, New York, Herder, 1971; as *Psalms*, translated by Thomas Blackburn, London, Sheed and Ward, and New York, Crossroad, 1981.
Mayapán.   Managua, Alemana, 1968.
Poemas reunidos 1949–1969.   Valencia, Venezuela, Universidad de Carabobo, 1969.
Homenaje a los índios americanos.   León, Universidad Nacional Autónoma de Nicaragua, 1969; as *Homage to the American Indians*, translated by Carlos and Monique Altschul, Baltimore, Johns Hopkins University Press, 1973.
La hora cero y otros poemas.   Barcelona, Saturno, 1971; as *Zero Hour and Other Documentary Poems*, New York, New Directions, 1980.
Antología, edited by Pablo Antonio Cuadro.   Buenos Aires, Lohlé, 1971.
Poemas.   Barcelona, Ocnos, 1971.
Antología.   San José, Costa Rica, EDUCA, 1972.
Canto nacional.   Buenos Aires, Lohlé, 1973.
Oráculo sobre Managua.   Buenos Aires, Lohlé, 1973.
Poesía escogida.   Barcelona, Seix Barral, 1975.

Marilyn Monroe and Other Poems, edited and translated by Robert Pring-Mill.   London, Search Press, 1975.
Apocalypse and Other Poems, edited and translated by Robert Pring-Mill and Donald D. Walsh.   New York, New Directions, 1977.
Antología.   Barcelona, Laia, 1978.
Canto a un país que nace.   Puebla, Universidad Autónoma de Puebla, 1978.
Poesía de uso: antología, 1949–1978.   Buenos Aires, El Cid, 1979.
Poesía.   Havana, Casa de las Américas, 1979.
Nueva antología poética.   Mexico City, Siglo Veintiuno, 1979.
Tocar el cielo.   Salamanca, Loguez, 1981.
Waslala, translated by Fidel López-Criado and R. A. Kerr.   Winter Park, Florida, Chase Avenue Press, 1983.
Antología: Ernesto Cardenal.   Managua, Nueva Nicaragua-Monimbó, 1983.
Poesía de la nueva Nicaragua.   Mexico City, Siglo Veintiuno, 1983.
Vuelos de Victoria.   Madrid, Visor, 1984; as *Flights of Victory: Songs of Celebration of the Nicaraguan Revolution*, translated by Marc Zimmerman, Mary Knoll, New York, Orbis, 1985.
Quetzalcóatl.   Managua, Nueva Nicaragua-Monimbó, 1985.
With Walker in Nicaragua and Other Early Poems, 1949–1954, translated by Jonathan Cohen.   Middletown, Connecticut, Wesleyan University Press, 1985.
From Nicaragua with Love: Poems, 1976–1986, translated by Jonathan Cohen.   San Francisco, City Lights, 1987.
Cántico cósmico.   Managua, Nueva Nicaragua, 1989.
Los ornis de oro.   Managua, Nicarao, 1991.
Golden UFOs: The Indian Poems, translated by Carlos and Monique Altschul, edited by Russell O. Salmon.   Bloomington, Indiana University Press, 1992.

Other

Vida en el amor.   Buenos Aires, Lohlé, 1970; as *To Live Is to Love*, New York, Herder, 1972; as *Love = Vida en el amor*, London, Search Press, 1974.
En Cuba.   Buenos Aires, Lohlé, 1972; as *In Cuba*, New York, New Directions, 1974.
Cristianismo y revolución, with Fidel Castro.   Buenos Aires, Quetzal, 1974.
Cardenal en Valencia (interviews).   Valencia, Venezuela, Universidad de Carabobo, 1974.
El evangelio en Solentiname.   Salamanca, Sígueme, 1975; as *The Gospel in Solentiname*, Mary Knoll, New York, Orbis, 1976; as *Love in Practice: The Gospel in Solentiname*, London, Search Press, 1977; selections as *Evangelio, pueblo, y arte*, Salamanca, Lóguez, 1983; selections as *The Gospel in Art by the Peasants of Solentiname*, edited by Philip and Sally Sharper, Orbis, 1984.
La santidad de la revolución.   Salamanca, Sígueme, 1976.
La paz mundial y la revolución de Nicaragua.   Managua, Ministry of Culture, 1981.
Nostalgia del futuro: pintura y buena noticia en Solentiname.   Managua, Nueva Nicaragua, 1982.
La democratización de la cultura.   Managua, Ministry of Culture, 1982.
Nicaragua: la guerra de liberación — der Befreiungskrieg, with Richard Cross.   Managua, Ministry of Culture, 1982(?).
Nuevo cielo y tierra nueva.   Managua, Nueva Nicaragua-Monimbó, 1985.

Editor, with José Coronel Urtecho, *Antología de la poesía norteamericana*.   Madrid, Aguilar, 1963.
Editor, with Jorge Montoya Toro, *Literatura indígena americana: antología*.   Medellín, Colombia, Universidad de Antioquía, 1964.
Editor, *Poesía nicaragüense*.   Havana, Casa de las Américas, 1973.
Editor, *Poesía nueva de Nicaragua*.   Buenos Aires, Lohlé, 1974.
Editor, *Poesía cubana de la revolución*.   Mexico City, Extemporáneos, 1976.
Editor, *Antología de poesía primitiva*.   Madrid, Alianza, 1979.
Editor, *Poemas de un joven*, by Joaquín Pasos.   Managua, Nueva Nicaragua, 1983.
Editor, *Antología: Azarias H. Pallais*.   Managua, Nueva Nicaragua, 1986.

Translator, *Catulo-Marcial en versión de Ernesto Cardenal*.   Barcelona, Laia, 1978.
Translator, *Tu paz es mi paz*, by Ursula Schulz.   Managua, Nueva Nicaragua-Monimbó, 1982.

*

Bibliography: *An Annotated Bibliography of and About Ernesto Cardenal* by Janet Lynne Smith, Tempe, Arizona State University, 1979.

Critical Studies: "Pound and Cardenal" by Isabel Fraire, in *Review* (New York), 18, 1976; "Typology and Narrative Techniques in Cardenal's *El estrecho dudoso*" by James J. Alstrum, in *Journal of Spanish Studies: 20th Century*, 8, 1980; "Daniel Boone, Moses and the Indians: Ernesto Cardenal's Evolution from Alienation to Social Commitment," in *Chasqui* (Provo, Utah), 11(1), 1981, and "The Image of the United States in the Poetry of René Depestre and Ernesto Cardenal," in *Revista/Review Interamericana* (San German, Puerto Rico), 11(2), 1981, both by Henry Cohen; "The Evolution of Ernesto Cardenal's Prophetic Poetry," in *Latin American Literary Review* (Pittsburgh), 12(23), 1983, "Cardenal's Poetic Style: Cinematic Parallels," in *Revista Canadiense de Estudios Hispánicos* (Toronto), 11(1), 1986, and "Cardenal's Exteriorismo: The Ideology Underlying the Esthetic," in *Mid Hudson Languages Studies* (Westchester, Pennsylvania), 10, 1987, all by Jorge H. Valdés; "Prophecy of Liberation: The Poetry of Ernesto Cardenal" by Edward Elias, in *Poetic Prophecy in Western Literature*, edited by Jan Wojcik and R.-J. Frontain, Rutherford, New Jersey, Fairleigh Dickinson University Press, 1984; "Poetry in the Central American Revolution: Ernesto Cardenal and Roque Dalton" by John Beverley, in *Literature and Contemporary Revolutionary Culture* (Minneapolis), 1, 1984–85; "Peace, Poetry and Popular Culture: Ernesto Cardenal and the Nicaraguan Revolution" by Claudia Scharfer-Rodríguez, in *Latin American Literary Review* (Pittsburgh), 13(26), 1985, "Political Poetry and the Example of Ernesto Cardenal" by Reginald Gibbons, in *Critical Inquiry* (Chicago), 13(3), 1987.

*   *   *

Ernesto Cardenal's work falls into a number of distinct phases — before and after his religious conversion, after the death of Thomas Merton, after his visit to Cuba, before and after the Nicaraguan Revolution. Yet one can recognise an overarching continuity to the work, a continuity which is itself a kind of validation of his integrity as a poet. His essential themes — such as the possibility of human and social renewal through love, the evil of human greed and violence, the American Indians — remain largely constant. In poetic manner, too, there is a recognisable singleness of purpose. After the early work which he has now rejected, Cardenal has been consistent in the pursuit of a kind of poetic objectivity — one version of which he and José Coronel Urtecho christened *exteriorismo* — for which the model of Ezra Pound offered an alternative to the subjectivity represented by Rubén Darío.

In most of the phases of his work Cardenal has written fine short poems (most obviously in the early volume of *Epigramas* [Epigrams]), but he is perhaps seen at his best in the rhetorical idiom of his longer poems. In such poems his instincts for politico-religious prophecy, exhortation or celebration find most fitting incarnation. *La hora O* (*Zero Hour*), for example, is powerful and direct in its political and social statements, more sophisticated than might at first appear in its Pound-like juxtaposition of material from a variety of different sources and of linguistic idioms from many different registers. It is characteristic that the poem's political "facts" should be located alongside an apt quotation from *Isaiah* (or, to give it its relevant full title, *The Book of the Prophet Isaiah Concerning the Fall of Judah*):

> San Salvador, at night: distrust and spying,
> muttering in the homes and small hotels,
> and screams in police stations.
> The crowd stoned the palace of Carías,
> breaking just one window of his office,
> but the police opened fire on the crowd.
> And Managua: covered by deployed machine-guns
> from its palace, which is like a chocolate cake:
> steel helmets out patrolling in the streets.
> *Watchman, what of the night?*
> *Watchman, what of the night?*

Cardenal's work — and life — offers a clear statement of the positive values by which he judges contemporary capitalism. If we call Cardenal a "protest" poet it must be on the understanding that his is never a merely negative voice. The very activity of poetry — even when devoted to subjects not explicitly political — has an inescapable political significance, since it is a commitment to the truthfulness of language. The point is effectively made in an early epigram, and is central to the whole of Cardenal's work:

> Haven't you read, my love, in the *News*:
> SENTINEL OF PEACE, GENIUS OF WORK
> PALADIN OF DEMOCRACY IN AMERICA
> DEFENDER OF CATHOLICISM IN AMERICA
> THE PROTECTOR OF THE PEOPLE
>   THE BENEFACTOR . . . ?
> They plunder the people's language.
> And they falsify the people's words.
> (Just like the people's money.)
> That's why we poets do so much polishing on a poem.
> And that's why my love poems are important.

It is, in the last resort, Love which Cardenal elevates as the means to human and social redemption. The prose of *Vida en el amor* (*To Live Is to Love*) has a Franciscan warmth and simplicity; it is a vision which the life of the community Cardenal founded at Solentiname sought to put into practice. It is also the vision which underlies most of Cardenal's later poetry. It is Love which he opposes to human greed and self-destructiveness. In the moving "Prayer for Marilyn Monroe" the filmstar is seen as the victim of a loveless and spiritually desolate society — "She was hungry for love and we offered her tranquillizers." In the "Coplas on the Death of Merton" — a dense and allusive piece, richly argued and musical — Death and Love are treated as mutually necessary fulfilments:

> Love, love above all, an anticipation
> of death
>   There was a taste of death in the kisses
>   being
>   is being
>   in another being
>   we exist only in love
> But in this life we love only briefly
> and feebly
>   We love or exist only when we stop being
> when we die
>   nakedness of the whole being in order to make love
>   *make love not war*
>   that go empty into the love
>   that is life

All areas of human thought and activity seem to be inextricably linked for Cardenal. In his work as a poet he is never afraid of the big subject, nor of the grand and "simple" statement. For Cardenal "the God who exists is of the proletariat" ("Psalm 57"); he celebrates "matter's holiness" and in the over 500 pages of his *Cántico cósmico* (Cosmic Canticle) he attempts a kind of integrated philosophy on a grand scale. It is a vision of "the delighted dance of things," of a world of rhythm and change, not of static and discrete entities:

> Animals and plants, we all
> have the same microscopic ancestor.
>   We are notes in the same music.
> A universe harmonious as a harp —
>   wings, neck and tail
>   all keeping time —
> heart and aorta have rhythm
> like a musical instrument.

Cardenal is a remarkable figure, rich in paradoxes and creative contradictions. By turns he seems ultra-sophisticated and naive. He has been head of a rural religious community and active revolutionary; he has been Trappist novice and government minister. Through it all he has remained a poet; and his poetry has continued to grow so as to embrace and articulate the range of his experience and the growth of his ideas. It is in the poetry that one can see the organic continuity of his development.

—Glyn Pursglove

CARDINAL, Marie. French and Algerian. Born in Algiers, 9 March 1929. Educated at the Cours Fénelon, Algiers; Institut Maintenon, Paris; University of Algiers, licence and diplôme d'études supérieures in philosophy; the Sorbonne, Paris. Married Jean-Pierre Ronfard in 1953; two sons and one daughter. Taught French language and literature in Thessaloniki, Greece, 1957–58, Lisbon, 1958–61, Vienna, 1961–62, and Montreal; freelance writer in Paris during 1960s; moved to Canada; teacher, Continuing Education Division, University of Montreal, Autumn semesters. Recipient: International prize for first novel, 1962; Prix Littré, 1976. Address: 831 Viger Est, Montreal, Quebec H2L 2P5, Canada.

PUBLICATIONS

Fiction

Écoutez la mer.   Paris, Julliard, 1962.
La Mûle de Corbillard.   Paris, Julliard, 1963.
La Souricière.   Paris, Julliard, 1965.
La Clé sur la porte.   Paris, Grasset, 1972.
Les Mots pour le dire.   Paris, Grasset, 1975; as *The Words to Say It*, Cambridge, Massachusetts, VanVactor and Goodheart, 1983; London, Picador, 1984.
Une Vie pour deux.   Paris, Grasset, 1978.
Le Passé empiété.   Paris, Grasset, 1983.
Les Grands Désordres.   Paris, Grasset, 1987; as *Devotion and Disorder*, London, Women's Press, 1991.
Comme si de rien n'était.   Paris, Grasset, 1990.

Play

Screenplay: *Les Mots pour le dire*, from her own novel, 1983.

Other

Guide junior de Paris, with Christiane Cardinal.   Paris, Julliard, 1964.
Cet Été-là, with *Deux ou Trois Choses que je sais d'elle*, by Jean-Luc Godard.   Paris, Julliard, 1967.
Mao, with Lucien Bodard.   Paris, Gallimard, 1970.
Autrement Dit.   Paris, Grasset, 1977.
Au Pays de mes racines, with *Au Pays de Moussia*, by Bénédicte Ronfard.   Paris, Grasset, 1980.
Les Pieds-Noirs: Algérie 1920–1954.   Paris, Belfond, 1988.

Editor, *La Cause des Femmes*, by Gisèle Halimi.   Paris, Grasset, 1973.

Translator, *La Médée d'Euripide*.   Montreal, Éditions Victor-Lévy Beaulieu, 1986; Paris, Grasset, 1987.
Translator, *Peer Gynt*, by Henrik Ibsen.   Arles, Actes Sud, 1991.

*

Critical Studies: "Mothers, Madness, and the Middle Class in *The Bell Jar* and *Les Mots pour le dire*" by Elaine A. Martin, in *French-American Review*, Spring 1981; "Feminism and Formalism: Dialectical Structures in Marie Cardinal's *Une Vie pour deux*," in *Tulsa Studies in Women's Literature* (Oklahoma), Spring 1985, and "Patterns of Influence: Simone de Beauvoir and Marie Cardinal," in *French Review* (Santa Barbara, California), February 1987, both by Carolyn A. Durham; "In the Eye of Abjection: Marie Cardinal's *The Words to Say It*" by Patricia Elliot, in *Mosaic* (Winnipeg, Manitoba), Fall 1987.

*   *   *

Marie Cardinal came to fame in 1975 with her novel *Les Mots pour le dire* (*The Words to Say It*). The title refers to the course of psychoanalysis that the heroine successfully under-

goes, and may be interpreted as an echo of the expression "the talking cure." That name was commonly given to such treatment when it first came into vogue at the beginning of the century. In retrospect it appears, in fact, that the psychoanalytic element comes a little too pat and is used rather too obviously as a structuring device, yet there is no questioning the power of the narrative. In *The Words to Say It*, just as in *La Souricière* (The Mouse-Trap), which was not greatly appreciated when it first appeared in 1965, Cardinal tells a story with which many a Frenchwoman at the time could easily identify. The heroine is an intelligent young woman who grew up close to nature, married quite early, and is now on the point of collapse as a result of all the pressures that bear in upon her, especially the strains of pregnancies. Her mental anguish is reflected in acute physical decline, and at the start of the novel she is faced with the imminent threat of a hysterectomy. This she is able to avoid only because she finds a psychiatrist who hastens to assure her that her condition is psychosomatic and then sets out to discover the deep-seated causes of her malaise.

Now begins a fascinating exploration. While the heroine stays in Paris making a regular succession of visits to the psychiatrist, who remains a shadowy figure and refuses to allow anything more than a strictly professional attitude to develop between himself and his patient, we are taken further and further back into her past.

The basic problem lies, as it so often turns out to be where psychoanalysis is concerned, in childhood traumas in a distinctly odd family. For French readers in the 1960s, there was, however, an important additional factor. The perennial problems of this woman who struggles to reconcile her own claims for independence with the demands of her children and her husband's career are complicated by the difficulties she is experiencing in coming to terms with a profoundly disorientating experience. Her family had long been settled in Algeria, but had been obliged to leave as the colonial period came to its painful end, and for Cardinal expulsion from what she has regarded as her home land was nothing less than exile. Cardinal has, then, an interesting story to tell, and she skilfully contrasts her heroine's gradual restoration to health and confidence with the sometimes alarming revelations of her past. She evokes scenes and situations with great vividness and puts real dynamism into a quest for the truth about the past which places her novel directly in the grand French tradition of psychological investigation.

The Words to Say It is a first-person novel. Many elements in it are plainly related to its author's personal experiences, and though Cardinal insists that her work is not directly autobiographical, her readers responded to what they recognized as the voice of authenticity. *The Words to Say It* was also in accord with the prevailing current of feminism in France at the time. Gynaecological matters are treated with unusual frankness, to give the novel a very striking beginning, and in her acceptance of heterosexuality as a norm Cardinal was able to appeal to the vast majority of her compatriots at the time.

After the success of *The Words to Say It*, which was followed up by interviews that were printed in *Autrement Dit* (In Other Words), Cardinal became a noted figure in feminist circles. This is reflected in her being invited to write the preface to Suzanne Horer's *La Sexualité des femmes*, a study based on a nationwide attitudes survey, and she also worked with Gisèle Halimi on the text of *La Cause des femmes* (The Right to Choose), one of the key texts of the pro-abortion movement in France. There was also a resurgence of interest in Cardinal's earlier books, above all in *La Clé sur la porte* (The Key in the Door), which is an investigation of a 40-year-old mother's efforts to retain the affection of her teenaged children. Set in the Paris that had been shaken by the abortive student uprising of 1968, the novel takes as its theme the burning issue of permissiveness.

After *Une Vie pour deux* (One Life for Two), which is set in Ireland and explores marital relationships under stress, Cardinal wrote a sympathetic account of her return to post-colonial Algeria in *Au Pays de mes racines* (In the Country of My Roots), the very title of which explains a good deal about her attitudes. No less significant was her decision to call her next novel *Le Passé empiété* (The Past Encroached On), which takes as the starting point for its explorations the pressures that build up on a middle-aged woman after she has bought her children a motorcycle on which they have a serious accident. *Les Grands Désordres* (*Devotion and Disorder*) takes on another set of issues with which every mother can readily identify as it tells how a child psychologist who had been widowed when her husband was killed in Algeria must now cope with the problems arising from the discovery that her grown-up daughter is a heroin addict.

Cardinal tackles issues that many of her readers have to face up to in real life, and she has the knack of combining insight into the way human beings feel and behave with great skill in the description of scenes and actions. Some feminists might wish that she could see beyond the conventions of the family, which are particularly deeply rooted in France, and other critics might feel that she is somewhat too ready to use concepts derived from Freud. All the same, there can be no doubt that Marie Cardinal has deserved her popularity.

—Christopher Smith

CARDOSO PIRES, José (Augusto Neves). Portuguese. Born in Peso, Castelo Branco, 2 October 1925. Educated at the Faculty of Sciences, University of Lisbon, studies in mathematics. Served in the Merchant Marines. Literary director of publishing houses in Lisbon; director, *Almanaque* magazine; editor, *Gazeta Musical e de Todas as Artes* magazine; lecturer, King's College, London, 1969; adjunct director, *Diário de Lisboa*, 1974–75. Elected member of the board, Society of Portuguese Writers, 1961; vice president of the Portuguese delegation, European Community of Writers, 1962. Recipient: Camilo Castelo Branco prize, 1964; Grande Prémio do Romance e da Novela, 1983. Address: Rua São João de Brito, 7-1.°, 1700 Lisbon, Portugal.

PUBLICATIONS

Fiction

Os caminheiros e outros contos.   Lisbon, Bibliográfico, 1949.
Histórias de amor.   Lisbon, Gleba, 1952 (banned).
Estrada 43.   Lisbon, Organizações, 1955.
A anjo ancorado.   Lisbon, Ulisseia, 1958.
Jogos de azar.   Lisbon, Arcádia, 1963.
O hóspede de Job.   Lisbon, Arcádia, 1963.
O delfim.   Lisbon, Moraes, 1968.
Dinossauro excelentíssimo.   Lisbon, Arcádia, 1972.
O burro-em-pé.   Lisbon, Moraes, 1978.
Balada da Praia dos Cães: [dissertação sobre um crime].   Lisbon, O Jornal, 1982; as *Ballad of Dogs' Beach:*

dossier of a Crime, London, Dent, 1986; New York, Beaufort, 1987.
Alexandra Alpha.   Lisbon, Dom Quixote, 1987.
A República dos Corvos.   Lisbon, Dom Quixote, 1988.

Plays

O render dos heróis.   Lisbon, Europa-América, 1960.
Corpo-delito na sala de espelhos.   Lisbon, Moraes, 1980.

Other

Cartilha do Marialva, ou das negações libertinas.   Lisbon, Ulisseia, 1960.
Gente, photographs by Eduardo Gageiro.   Lisbon, O Século, 1971.
E agora, José?   Lisbon, Moraes, 1977.

Translator, with Vitor Palla, *Morte dum caixeiro viajante*, by Arthur Miller.   Lisbon, Europa-América, 1963.

*

Critical Studies: "The Portuguese Revolution Seen Through the Eyes of Three Contemporary Writers" by Alice Clemente, in *Proceedings of the Fourth National Portuguese Conference*, Providence, Rhode Island, Multilingual Multicultural Resource and Training Center, 1979; "Time and Voice in the Work of José Cardoso Pires" by Óscar Lopes, in *Portuguese Studies* (London), 2, 1986.

*   *   *

For over 40 years José Cardoso Pires has been one of the most consistently impressive Portuguese writers. Although regularly appearing in new editions, his novels are few in number, each reflecting a long period of gestation and attention to details of composition, and his similarly limited output of short stories includes some outstanding examples of a genre richly cultivated in contemporary Portuguese prose fiction.

Even in the original versions (they were thoroughly revised and combined in *Jogos de azar* (Games of Chance) over a decade after their first appearance), the contents of *Os caminheiros e outros contos* (The Tramps and Other Stories) and *Histórias de amor* (Love Stories) constitute an innovative and personal approach to socially committed writing, based on an imaginative re-evaluation of neo-realist techniques and topics. While Cardoso Pires's narrative has evolved considerably in terms of narrative sophistication, his broad conception of the writer's craft — a term which carries ethical as well as technical connotations — has remained substantially the same. Perhaps the most salient feature is a reliance on effabulation (in the double sense of powers of observation allied to storytelling skills, and an ability to invest narrative material with a dimension of fable or allegory) to convey the thrust of moral and sociopolitical commentary. The "ideal reader" with whom, as Cardoso Pires affirms in one of the essays of *E agora, José?* (What Now, José?), "the novelist carries on a dialogue as he writes," is sometimes drawn into strategies of complicity with the author, but there is no straightforward attempt to manipulate his sympathies; nor is he offered easy interpretations. Where characterization is concerned, psychological motivation is presented as inseparable from social and historical, that is, ideological influences, but the link is a subtle and sometimes enigmatic one. Symbolic connotations arise unobtrusively from the narrated situation and function to point up ironic contradictions rather than to emphasize single meanings. The overall effect is of a scrupulously stylized narrative integrity, however involving or occasionally shocking the subject-matter.

In the works from the period when the Portuguese dictator António de Oliviera Salazar was in power (1936–68), there is a tendency to bring into sharp focus the contrast between the bleak living conditions of an underclass whose very existence was concealed by the official media, and the convoluted forms of legitimization and self-justification practised by members of a privileged middle class who, whether complacently, cynically, or with a sense of frustrated impotence, connive at the continuation of a regime which treated the majority of its citizens only marginally better than the indigenous population of its colonies. Such a schema is particularly evident in Cardoso Pires's first two novels *A anjo ancorado* (The Anchored Angel) and *O hóspede de Job* (Job's Guest), both set in backward and impoverished areas, in which more advantaged characters appear as selfish and uncomprehending intruders. On the other hand, the novels of the democratic era — the chilling "exposition of a crime" *Balada da Praia dos Cães* (*Ballad of Dogs' Beach*), and *Alexandra Alpha*—tend to analyze patterns of interaction among a cast of urban characters. While still concerned with sinister features of the authoritarian past (and, especially in *Alexandra Alpha*, with some of its unsavoury hangovers), the later novels are also powerful reminders that such a legacy cannot be simply forgotten, but must be accepted and understood before it can be truly left behind. While Cardoso Pires's broad political sympathies are clear, their expression, in his essays as well as his fiction, is by no means simplistic. The underlying values of socialist humanism provide a method for investigating reality (the narrator of *O delfim* [The Dolphin] considers himself a "writer-ferret") rather than a prescription for categorizing it. The main critique is centred not so much on flagrant examples of inequality, or the dehumanizing pressure of economic deprivation, as on the workings of meaning in the service of power. There is a consistent attention to the ideological nature of a wide range of symbolic practices, from the very human propensity to "make sense" of direct experience of the world, and the effects of socially determined assumptions on interpersonal communication and understanding, to the semiotics of institutionalized deception, persuasion, and coercion. By bringing into view the constructed nature of social reality, including the status of subjective accounts, reported utterances, and narrative devices, Cardoso Pires invites his readers to reflect on their own norms of interpretation. As Maria Lúcia Lepecki has remarked, "with their high degree of complexity, points of view, in Cardoso Pires, are meanings."

However strong his belief in writing as a form of social action, Cardoso Pires's views are rigorously balanced against a demanding concept of authorial responsibility. The narrator of *O delfim*, perhaps the most multi-layered of his novels, provides a revealing definition:

No writer likes creating complications, of whatever sort, and he likes simplifying things even less. Whether his blow strikes home depends on such precision "And so do his tribulations," I add under my breath.

Such comments reveal a writer for whom keeping faith with his art is inseparable from keeping faith with his convictions.

—I. Robin Warner

CARMI, T. Israeli. Born Carmi Charny in New York City, 31 December 1925; settled in Israel in 1947. Educated at Yeshiva University, New York, B.A. 1946; Columbia University, New York, 1946; the Sorbonne, Paris, 1946–47; Hebrew University, Jerusalem, 1949–51. Served in the Israeli Defense Forces, 1947–49: Captain. Married 1) Shoshana Heiman, one child; 2) Tamara Rikman, one child; 3) Lilach Peled, one child. Worked in children's homes in France, 1946; co-editor, *Massa*, Tel Aviv, 1952–54; editor, *Orot*, Jerusalem, 1955, and *Ariel*, 1971–74; editor, Sifriyat Po'alim Publishers, Tel Aviv, 1957–62, and Am Oved Publishers, Tel Aviv, 1963–70; Ziskind Visiting Professor, Brandeis University, Waltham, Massachusetts, 1970; Associate Professor, Institute for Arts and Communications, Tel Aviv University, 1973; Visiting Fellow, Oxford Centre for Post-Graduate Hebrew Studies, 1974–76; poet-in-residence, Hebrew University, Spring 1977; since 1978 Visiting Professor of Hebrew literature, Hebrew Union College, Jewish Institute of Religion, Jerusalem; Visiting Professor, Stanford University, California, 1979, New York University, Winter 1986, Reconstructionist Rabbinical College, Wyncote, Pennsylvania, Winter 1986, and Yale University, New Haven, Connecticut, Spring 1986; Senior Lecturer, University of Texas, Austin, Spring 1987. Recipient: Shlonsky prize, 1958; National Translation Center commission, 1966, and fellowship, 1968; Littauer Foundation grant, 1971, 1989; Matz Foundation grant, 1971; Brenner prize, 1972; Prime Minister's award, 1973; Jewish Book Council Kovner award, 1978; Irving and Bertha Neuman award, 1982; *Present Tense* Kenneth Smilen award, for translation; Guggenheim fellowship, 1987–88; Tel Aviv Foundation for Literature and Art grant, 1988; Bialik prize, 1990. Address: Hebrew Union College, Jewish Institute of Religion, 13 King David Street, Jerusalem 94101, Israel.

PUBLICATIONS

Verse

Mum vechalom [Blemish and Dream]. Tel Aviv, Mahbarot Lesifrut, 1951.
Eyn perachim shechorim [There Are No Black Flowers]. Tel Aviv, Mahbarot Lesifrut, 1953.
Sheleg bi-Yrushalayim [Snow in Jerusalem]. Tel Aviv, Sifriyat Po'alim, 1956.
Hayam ha'acharon [The Last Sea]. Tel Aviv, Mahbarot Lesifrut, 1958.
Nechash hanechoshet. Jerusalem, Tarshish Books, 1961; as *The Brass Serpent*, translated by Dom Moraes, London, Deutsch, and Athens, Ohio University Press, 1964.
Ha'unicorn mistakel bamar'ah [The Unicorn Looks in the Mirror]. Jerusalem, Tarshish Books, 1967.
Tevi'ah [The Claim]. Jerusalem, Tarshish Books, 1967.
Davar acher [Another Version: Selected Poems and Translations 1951–1969]. Tel Aviv, Am Oved, 1970.
Somebody Like You, translated by Stephen Mitchell. London, Deutsch, 1971.
Hitnatslut hamechaber [Author's Apology]. Tel Aviv, Dvir, 1974.
Selected Poems (with Dan Pagis), translated by Stephen Mitchell. London, Penguin, 1976.
El erets acheret [Into Another Land]. Tel Aviv, Dvir, 1977.
Leyad even hato'im [At the Stone of Losses]. Tel Aviv, Dvir, 1981.
At the Stone of Losses (selected edition), translated by Grace Schulman. Berkeley, University of California Press, and Manchester, Carcanet, 1983.

Achat hi li [One to Me].   Tel Aviv, Sifriyat Po'alim, 1985.
Shirim min ha-'azuvah [Monologues and Other Poems].   Tel Aviv, Dvir, 1988.

Plays

The Firstborn, from the play by Christopher Fry.   Tel Aviv, Israel Anniversary Committee, 1958.
Herr Puntila und sein Knecht Matti (Hebrew version), from the play by Bertolt Brecht.   Jerusalem, Tarshish Books, 1962.
Pantagleize (Hebrew version), from the play by Michel de Ghelderode.   Tel Aviv, Amikam Books, 1963.
A Midsummer Night's Dream (Hebrew version), from the play by William Shakespeare.   Tel Aviv, Sifriyat Po'alim, 1964.
Antigone (Hebrew version), from the Robert Fitzgerald and Dudley Fitts version of the play by Sophocles.   Tel Aviv, Dvir, 1969.
Measure for Measure (Hebrew version), from the play by William Shakespeare.   Tel Aviv, Sifriyat Po'alim, 1979.
La Folle de Chaillot (Hebrew version), from the play by Jean Giraudoux.   Tel Aviv, Dvir, 1979.
Hamlet (Hebrew version), from the play by William Shakespeare.   Tel Aviv, Dvir, 1981.
Much Ado About Nothing (Hebrew version), from the play by William Shakespeare.   Tel Aviv, Dvir, 1983.
Cyrano de Bergerac (Hebrew version), from the play by Edmond Rostand.   Tel Aviv, Zmora-Beitan, 1986.
Othello (Hebrew version), from the play by William Shakespeare.   Tel Aviv, Dvir, 1991.

Also made Hebrew versions of the following works for stage production: *Spoon River Anthology* by Edgar Lee Masters, *Noé* by André Obey, *Rosencrantz and Guildenstern Are Dead* by Tom Stoppard, *The Beaux' Stratagem* by George Farquhar, *The Zoo Story* by Edward Albee, *Look Back in Anger* by John Osborne, *The Hostage* by Brendan Behan, and *The Little Foxes* by Lillian Hellman.

Other

Editor, with Stanley Burnshaw and Ezra Spicehandler, *The Modern Hebrew Poem Itself, from the Beginnings to the Present*.   New York, Holt Rinehart, 1965; revised edition, Cambridge, Massachusetts, Harvard University Press, 1989.
Editor and Translator, *The Penguin Book of Hebrew Verse*. London, Penguin, and New York, Viking, 1981.

Translator, *Selected Poetry* (Hebrew version), by Nazim Hikmet.   Tel Aviv, Sifriyat Po'alim, 1958.

*

Critical Studies: "Elements of Poetic Self-Awareness in Modern Poetry" by Shimon Levy, in *Modern Hebrew Literature* (Ramat-Gan, Israel), 3, 1976; "'The Voice Inside': Translating the Poetry of T. Carmi" by Grace Schulman, in *Translating Poetry: The Double Labyrinth*, edited by Daniel Weissbort, Iowa City, University of Iowa Press, 1989.

*   *   *

T. Carmi is a poet whose vision is simultaneously historical and miraculous. He has, like others of his time and place, an acute awareness of human suffering, and he recognizes the absurdity of individual lives in the context of social and political events. At the same time, his focus is intensely personal, and in many ways close to the surrealist mode of pursuing the marvelous in everyday life by discovering and using strange images close to subconscious thought.

Carmi has an international background, and has absorbed French and English literary traditions. Born in New York, having lived in Paris, the poet settled in Israel in 1947, where he expressed formal ideas in language he heard in parks and cafés, from bartenders and taxicab drivers. He was familiar not only with biblical and midrashic tradition, but with the full range of Hebrew poetry. As editor and translator of *The Penguin Book of Hebrew Verse*, Carmi read those texts for years to represent, in the anthology, an uninterrupted tradition in Hebrew poetry from biblical times to the present.

Throughout Carmi's poetry, there is a startling fusion of tradition and modern speech. For example, the poem "At the Stone of Losses" begins:

> I search
> for what I have not lost.
>
> For you, of course.
> I would stop
> if I knew how.
> I would stand
> at the Stone of Losses
> and proclaim,
> shouting:
>
> Forgive me.
> I've troubled you for nothing.

The poem refers to a real stone of losses (*even hato'im*) in Jerusalem, a kind of "lost-and-found" connected with the return of lost property during the Second Temple period, as mentioned in the Talmud. The language is reminiscent of Pascal's *Pensées* ("Console toi; tu ne me chercherais pas, si tu ne m'avais pas trouvé"), and, incidentally, of a talmudic passage about an old man searching for his youth. At the same time, the language is characterized by a bareness of utterance that is in keeping with the central situation: that of a lost modern man searching for wholeness in the other.

One of the striking characteristics of his poetry is the unexpected transposition of sacred images and religious ideas into erotic experience. In his poetic sequence, "I say 'Love,'" for example, the opening lines are:

> You untie the vows
> within me.
>
> You erase my handwriting
> from the old drafts.

They are, of course, a portrayal of a modern love scene, and are spoken by a man to his woman. At the same time, they are a transmutation of the Kol Nidre prayer for the Eve of the Day of Atonement ("Let our personal vows, pledges, and oaths, be considered neither vows nor pledges nor oaths . . .").

Carmi's knowledge of the sacred, and of Hebrew literature and legend, affords images that are used as agents of transmutation, enabling him to focus on a divided world and see the wonder in daily life. Even in his poems of historical awareness, he is concerned with people not as nameless victims, not as ennobled human beings, but as ordinary men and women turning slightly away from the tragedy of public events.

In all of his poems, Carmi envisions two worlds. These may be, for example, the world of the immediate present and the luminous world beyond it, as in an early poem, "Story," whose two worlds are metaphor and experience. It is one of his most compelling techniques, early and late, to present one world as metaphor for the other, with the mysteries of an unfragmented life suggested by the terms of the metaphor.

Seeing a world that is divided by time and by the notions of being and becoming. Carmi focuses his gaze on ordinary things in the struggle to redeem a broken universe. His hallucinatory clarity calls back the surrealists, as do many of his images of flaming visionary change, despite their origin in midrashic sources. "I Say 'Love'" and "Song of Thanks," with their images of sun and fire, exemplify this method. However, while the surrealists unified a divided world, often using fiery images of transformation to illuminate contradictions and make them whole, Carmi's opposites are never reconciled. His poetry is a quest for a day that is alive, that does not end in death.

—Grace Schulman

CARMON, Amalia Kahana. *See* **KAHANA-CARMON, Amalia.**

CARPELAN, Bo (Gustaf Bertellsson). Finnish (Swedish language). Born in Helsinki, 25 October 1926. Educated at the University of Helsinki, B.A. 1948, M.A. 1956, Ph.D. 1960; studied in England, 1950, France, 1952, and the United States, 1961. Married Barbro Eriksson in 1954; one son and one daughter. Head of department, 1960–64, assistant chief librarian, 1964–80, and since 1980 Professor of arts, City Library, Helsinki. Literary critic, Hufvudstadsbladet, 1950–64. Recipient: Finnish State prize, 1969; Holgersson prize, 1969; Nordic Council prize, 1977; Ovralid prize, 1978; Ferlin prize, 1980; Pro Finlandia Medal, 1980. Address: Nyckelpigvaagen 2B, 02770 Espoo, Finland.

PUBLICATIONS

Verse

Som en dunkel värme [Like a Dim Warmth]. Helsinki, Schildt, and Stockholm, Bonnier, 1946.
Du mörka överlevande [O Dark Survivor]. Stockholm, Bonnier, 1947.
Variationer [Variations]. Helsinki, Schildt, and Stockholm, Bonnier, 1950.
Minus sju [Minus Seven]. Stockholm, Bonnier, 1952.
Objekt för ord [Objects for Words]. Stockholm, Bonnier, 1954.
Landskapets förvandlingar [Transformations of the Landscape]. Helsinki, Schildt, and Stockholm, Bonnier, 1957.
Den svala dagen [The Chilly Day]. Helsinki, Schildt, and Stockholm, Bonnier, 1961.
73 dikter [73 Poems]. Helsinki, Schildt, and Stockholm, Bonnier, 1966.

Gården. Helsinki, Schildt, and Stockholm, Bonnier, 1969; as *Gården = The Courtyard* (bilingual edition), translated by Samuel Charters, Gothenburg, Swedish Books, 1982.
Källan [The Spring]. Helsinki, Schildt, and Stockholm, Bonnier, 1973.
I de mörka rummen, i de ljusa [In the Dark Rooms, in the Light Ones]. Helsinki, Schildt, and Stockholm, Bonnier, 1976.
Dikter från trettio år [Poems from 30 Years]. Helsinki, Schildt, 1980.
Trösklar = Kynnyksiä [Thresholds] (bilingual edition in Swedish and Finnish). Helsinki, Tröskehn, 1982.
Poesi — Poeså: dikter för stora och små [Verses Spoken, Verses Sung: Poetry for Old and Young] (for children). Stockholm, Bonnier, 1982.
Dagen vänder [The Turning of the Day]. Helsinki, Schildt, and Stockholm, Bonnier, 1983.
Valda dikter 1946–1983 [Selected Poems 1946–1983], edited by Rolando Pieraccini. Helsinki, Eurographica, 1987.
Room Without Walls: Selected Poems, translated by Anne Born. London, Forest, 1987.
Måla himlen, vers för stora och små [Paint the Sky: Verses for Big and Small] (for children). Stockholm, Bonnier, 1988.
År som löv [Years Like Leaves]. Helsinki, Schildt, and Stockholm, Bonnier, 1989.

Fiction

Rösterna i den sena timmen. Helsinki, Schildt, and Stockholm, Bonnier, 1971; as Voices at the Late Hour, Athens, University of Georgia Press, 1988.
Din gestalt bakom dörren [Your Figure Behind the Door]. Helsinki, Schildt, and Stockholm, Bonnier, 1975.
Vandrande skugga: en småstadsberättelse [Wandering Shadows: A Small-Town Story]. Helsinki, Schildt, and Stockholm, Bonnier, 1977.
Axel. Helsinki, Schildt, and Stockholm, Bonnier, 1986; in English, Manchester, Carcanet, 1989.
Armbandsuret [The Wrist Watch]. Bromma, Fripress, Helsinki, Schildt, and Stockholm, Bonnier, 1986.

Plays

Paluu nuoruuteen [Back to Youth] (produced Helsinki, 1971).

Radio Play: *Rösterna i den sena timmen* [Voices at the Late Hour], from his own novel.

Other

Anders på ön [Andrew on the Island] (for children). Stockholm, Bonnier, 1959.
Studier i Gunnar Björlings diktning 1922–1933 [Studies of Gunnar Björling's Poems 1922–1933]. Helsinki, Söderström, 1960.
Anders i stan [Andrew in the City] (for children). Stockholm, Bonnier, 1962.
Bågen: berättelsen om en sommar som var annorlunda (for children). Helsinki, Schildt, and Stockholm, Bonnier, 1968; as Bow Island: The Story of a Summer That Was Different, New York, Delacorte Press, 1971; as The Wide Wings of Summer, London, Heinemann, 1972.
Paradiset: berättelsen om Marvins och Johns vänskap (for children). Helsinki, Schildt, and Stockholm, Bonnier, 1973; as Dolphins in the City, New York, Delacorte Press, 1976.
Jag minns att jag drömde [I Remember I Dreamt] (includes verse). Helsinki, Schildt, and Stockholm, Bonnier, 1979.

Helsingfors [Helsinki], with Matti A. Pitkänen.   Helsinki, Helsingfors Stad, 1979.

Julius Blom, ett huvud för sig [Julius Blom Has a Will of His Own] (for children).   Stockholm, Bonnier, 1982.

Marginalia till grekisk och romersk diktning [Notes on Greek and Latin Poetry].   Helsinki, Schildt, and Stockholm, Bonnier, 1984.

Marvins bok [Marvin's Book] (for children).   Stockholm, Bonnier, 1990.

Editor, *Finlandssvenska lyrikboken* [The Finnish-Swedish Book of Lyrics].   Stockholm, Forum, and Helsinki, Söderström, 1967.

Editor, *Den stora enklas dag: dikter och prosa* [The Great Day of the Ordinary Man: Poetry and Prose], by Gunnar Björling.   Stockholm, Rabén & Sjögren, 1975.

Editor, *Dikter* [Poems], by Paavo Haavikko.   Stockholm, Forum, 1977.

Editor and Translator, *Modern finsk lyrik* [Modern Finnish Poetry].   Helsinki, Schildt, and Stockholm, Bonnier, 1984.

Editor and Translator, *Dikter* [Poems], by Paavo Haavikko.   Stockholm, Atlantis, and Helsinki, Schildt, 1985.

Editor, with Claes Andersson, *Modern finlandssvensk lyrik: en antologi* [Modern Finland-Swedish Poetry: An Anthology].   Helsinki, Söderström, 1986.

Editor and Translator, *Dikter* [Poems], by Tuomas Anhava.   Helsinki, Schildt, and Stockholm, Bonnier, 1988.

Editor and Translator, with Johan Bargum, *Den svarta måsen: 30 moderna finska berättare* [The Black Seagull: 30 Modern Finnish Stories].   Stockholm, Alba, and Helsinki, Schildt, 1989.

Translator, *Ny finsk lyrik* [New Finnish Poetry], edited by Eino S. Repo and N. B. Stormbom.   Stockholm, FIB:s Lyrikklub, 1960.

Translator, *Beskrivning av en tågresa och fem andra noveller* [Description of a Train Journey and Five Other Novellas], by Antti Hyry.   Stockholm, Bonnier, 1964.

Translator, *Sök dig själv hos tystnaden* [Search for Yourself in the Silence], by Helena Anhava.   Helsinki, Schildt, and Stockholm, Bonnier, 1980.

Translator, *Framför lampor och nävar* [In Front of Lamps and Fists], by Sándor Csoóri.   Bromma, Fripress, 1982.

Translator, *Dubbelbild* [Double Picture], by Lassi Nummi.   Helsinki, Schildt, 1985.

Translator, *Livet är ett i vinden vacklande hus* [Life Is Like a House Rattling in the Wind], by Sirkka Turkka.   Stockholm, Wahlström & Widstrand, and Helsinki, Schildt, 1987.

Translator, *Prospero: försök till självporträtt* [Prospero: An Attempt at Self-Portrait], by Paavo Haavikko.   Stockholm, Atlantis, 1989.

*

Critical Studies: "Two Poets of Finland: Paavo Haavikko and Bo Carpelan" by Jaakko A. Ahokas, in *Books Abroad* (Norman, Oklahoma), 46(1), 1972; "Poems from *Jag minns att jag drömde*" by Kai Laitinen, in *Books from Finland* (Helsinki), 3, 1977.

*   *   *

Bo Carpelan is one of the most distinguished poets writing in Finland today; he is also an acclaimed novelist and writer of short fiction. He writes in Swedish, Finland's second language, which is spoken by a minority of the population, and in which a large and significant part of Finland's literature is written.

Carpelan began his literary career in the tense, umpromising atmosphere of Finland in the years immediately after the end of World War II. The political future was so uncertain that most writers tended to avoid direct statement or engagement of any kind, and it was perhaps inevitable that the influence of the Swedish poetic modernist movement known as *fyrtiotal-isme*, or "1940s-ism" — a subjective and hermetic tendency whose leading representatives were Gunnar Ekelöf, Erik Lindegren, Karl Vennberg, and Artur Lundkvist — made itself felt. The poems of Carpelan's earliest collections, *Som en dunkel värme* (Like a Dim Warmth), *Du mörka överlevande* (O Dark Survivor), and *Variationer* (Variations), show strong traces of his reading of these poets, and for the most part they focus upon the creation of a rhetorical and aesthetic universe in which symbols and key words play a prominent role. Even this early, somewhat derivative work shows a skilled and practised hand, however, and in it are established the characteristics that are typical of the later Carpelan, and which the Finland-Swedish critic Thomas Warburton has designated in his *Åttio år finlandssvensk litteratur* (80 Years of Finland-Swedish Literature, 1984) as "the apostrophizing of rest, evening, coolness, events that take place slowly, the dying impression."

In the collection *Minus sju* (Minus Seven) of 1952, Carpelan broke with Swedish modernism and struck out along a more individual road. The short prose poems making up the collection exercise his innate sense of humour and his eye for the bizarre and the absurd, and move away from subjectivism towards a much more down-to-earth appraisal of both self and reality. In the subsequent collections *Objekt för ord* (Objects for Words) and *Landskapets förvandlingar* (Transformations of the Landscape) this objectivizing tendency is further reinforced and is joined to a lyrical impulse towards directness and simplicity of expression. Taking his lead from the Finland-Swedish Dadaist poet of the 1920s, Gunnar Björling, Carpelan sought to shear his poetic language of every form of "beautiful-ness," in preparation for an authentic, personal voice that would be his own. He himself considers that he first achieved this in the collection *Den svala dagen* (The Chilly Day), which opens with a poem, "Höst promenad" (Autumn Walk), where objectivity and personal statement are fused into one with the utmost economy of means:

> A man walks through the wood
> one day of shifting light.
> Encounters few people,
> stops, considers the autumn sky.
> He is making for the graveyard
> and no one is following him.

In his 1966 collection, *73 dikter* (73 Poems), Carpelan goes even further in this direction, and one of its poems invokes a tree in only two one-word lines: "branched/light." There was obviously a limit to such minimalism, and the poet's next collection, *Gården* (*The Courtyard*), looks towards a kind of documentary realism, where emotional objectivity is main-tained by the emulation of some of the devices proper to photography, an art that has always had a peculiar fascination for Carpelan. The poems of *The Courtyard* form, in War-burton's words, "a kind of social document, both in and between their lines," and describe the poet's childhood in pre-World War II Helsingfors (Helsinki), spent for the most part in an old apartment house on Sjötullsgatan (Meritullinkatu), in the harbour area of the city. Each poem is a kind of verbal photograph, and the collection consists of sets of interiors with figures, broken by shots of the courtyard itself and by fragments of overheard dialogue. Carpelan himself considers *The Courtyard* to be his most important collection of poetry, and he has characterized it as an evocation of "the rooms we have been living in during our lives, where contact with things is as important as contact with people."

Carpelan's collections of the 1970s and 1980s are marked by an ever-increasing musicality of expression and a quiet mastery of form and language. His most recent collection, *År som löv* (Years Like Leaves), displays a darker colouring than many of its predecessors. In it one sees and hears the poet confronting his own existence and the fact of his mortality. But there is also a sense of a task accomplished, and of a return to a familiar soil. This verse has a classical, almost Homeric ring:

> This they taught me, the words that came:
> farewells are parts of everything that lives
> and, when I have dreamt most strongly,
> a homecoming.

Although he considers poetry to be his "true homeland," Carpelan has also developed a career as a writer of imaginative prose. The fantastical colorations of *Jag minns att jag drömde* (I Remember I Dreamt), a collection of subjective dreamlike essays, show him as a writer of "pure" prose. But he is also the author of two detective novels and of the lyrical and psychologically exploratory *Rösterna i den sena timmen* (*Voices at the Late Hour*), which concerns the threat of nuclear catastrophe. But Carpelan's principal oeuvre in this genre to date is undoubtedly the historical novel *Axel*, concerning the story of the dedication of the composer Jean Sibelius's Second Symphony to Axel Carpelan, the poet's great-uncle. Through a fictive diary, which reveals to us the workings of Axel's mind and emotions as he develops from childhood into adulthood, we become acquainted not only with the musical life of Helsinki and St. Petersburg, but also with the personality of Sibelius, who befriends Axel, and with the details of Finland's struggle for independence from Russia. The novel blends Carpelan's gift for nostalgic lyricism with an acute sense of human reality, and also displays the visual, "photographic" characteristics first evidenced in *The Courtyard*.

—David McDuff

CASARES, Adolfo Bioy. *See* **BIOY CASARES, Adolfo.**

CASSIAN, Nina. Romanian. Born in Galați, 27 September 1924. Educated at the Pompilian Institute; University of Bucharest and the Conservatory of Music. Married 1) Vladimir Colin in 1943 (divorced 1948); 2) Alexandru Ştefănescu in 1948(?) (died 1984). Journalist, film critic, and translator; also composer and musician. Visiting Professor, New York University, 1985–86; exiled in United States in 1985 as result of the murder of friend by government who discovered satirical verse by Cassian in his diary; participant in International Writing Program, University of Iowa, Iowa City, 1987. Lives in New York City. Recipient: Romanian state prize, 1952; Writers' Union award, 1969, 1983; Writers'

Association award, 1982; Fulbright grant, 1986; Yaddo fellowship, 1986. Address: c/o Norton & Company, 500 Fifth Avenue, New York, New York 10110, U.S.A.

PUBLICATIONS

Verse

La scara 1/1 [On the Scale of 1/1]. Bucharest, Forum, 1948.
Sufletul nostru [Our Soul]. Bucharest, Editura pentru Literatură, 1949.
An viu, nouă sute şi şaptesprezece [Vital Year, 1917]. Bucharest, Editura pentru Literatură, 1949.
Cîntece pentru Republică [Songs for the Republic]. Bucharest, Editura pentru Literatură, 1949.
Horea nu mai este singur [Horea Not Alone Anymore]. Bucharest, Editura de Stat pentru Literatură şi Artă, 1952.
Tinereţe [Youth]. Bucharest, Editura Tineretului, 1953.
Versuri alese [Selected Poems]. Bucharest, Editura de Stat pentru Literatură şi Artă, 1955.
Vîrstele anului [The Measures of the Year]. Bucharest, Editura de Stat pentru Literatură şi Artă, 1957.
Dialogul vîntului cu marea: motive bulgare [The Dialogue of Wind and Sea: Bulgarian Motives]. Bucharest, Editura de Stat pentru Literatură şi Artă, 1957.
Spectacol în aer liber [Outdoor Performance — A Monograph of Love]. Bucharest, Editura pentru Literatură, 1961.
Sărbătorile zilnice [Everyday Holidays]. Bucharest, Editura Tineretului, 1961.
Să ne facem daruri [Gift Giving]. Bucharest, Editura pentru Literatură, 1963.
Cele mai frumoase poezii [The Most Beautiful Poems]. Bucharest, Editura Tineretului, 1963.
Disciplina harfei [The Discipline of the Harp]. Bucharest, Editura pentru Literatură, 1965.
Sîngele [Blood]. Bucharest, Editura Tineretului, 1966.
Destinele paralele [Parallel Destinies]. With *La scara 1/1*, Bucharest, Editura pentru Literatură, 1967.
Ambitus [Ambit]. Bucharest, Editura pentru Literatură, 1969.
Cronofagie, 1944–1969 [Chronophagy, 1944–1969]. Bucharest, Eminescu, 1970.
Marea conjugare [The Big Conjugation]. Cluj, Dacia, 1971.
Recviem [Requiem]. Bucharest, Eminescu, 1971.
Loto-poeme [Lottery Poems]. Bucharest, Albatros, 1972.
Spectacol în aer liber — o altă monografie a dragostei [Outdoor Performance — Another Monograph of Love]. Bucharest, Albatros, 1974.
O sută de poeme [100 Poems]. Bucharest, Eminescu, 1974.
Suave. Bucharest, Carta Românească, 1977.
Viraje [Orbits]. Bucharest, n.p., 1978.
De îndurare [Mercy]. Bucharest, Eminescu, 1981.
Lady of Miracles, translated by Laura Schiff. Berkeley, California, Cloud Marauder Press, 1982.
Numărătoarea inversă [Countdown]. Bucharest, Eminescu, 1983.
Call Yourself Alive?, translated by Andrea Deletant and Brenda Walker. London, Forest, 1988.
Life Sentence: Selected Poems, edited by William Jay Smith. New York, Norton, and London, Anvil Press Poetry, 1990.
Cheer Leader for a Funeral. London, Forest, 1992.

Verse (for children)

Ce-a văzut Oana: versuri şi cîntece [What Oana Saw: Poems and Songs]. Bucharest, n.p., 1952.

Florile patriei [Flowers of Homeland].   Bucharest, Editura Tineretului, 1954.
Nică fără frică [Fearless Niki]. Bucharest, Editura Tineretului, 1956.
Prinţul Miorlau [Prince Miaow].   Bucharest, n.p., 1957.
Bot Gros, căţel fricos [Big Muzzle, the Fearful Puppy].   Bucharest, Editura Tineretului, 1957.
Chipuri hazlii pentru copii [Funny Faces for Kids]. Bucharest, Editura Muzicală, 1958.
Aventurile lui Trompişor [The Adventures of Trunky the Elephant].   Bucharest Editura Tineretului, 1959.
Încurcă-lume [The Mischief Maker].   Bucharest, n.p., 1961.
Curcubeu [Rainbow].   Bucharest, n.p., 1962.
Poveştea a doi pui de tigru numiţi Ninigra şi Aligru. Bucharest, n.p., 1969; as *Tigrino and Tigrene*, in *The Lion and the Unicorn* (Brooklyn, New York), 1987.
Pisica la televizor [T.V. Cat].   Bucharest, n.p., 1971.
Intre noi copiii [Between Us Kids].   Bucharest, n.p., 1974.

Plays

Puppet Plays: *Elefănţelul curios* [The Curious Little Elephant], adaptation of a Kipling story, 1964; *Pisica de una singură* [The Cat Alone], adaptation of a Kipling story, 1967; *Ninigra si Aligru* [Tigrino and Tigrene], 1972; *Nacă fără frică* [Fearless Niki], 1984.

Fiction

Atît de grozavă şi adio: confidenţe fictive [You're Wonderful — Adieu: Fictitious Confidences]. Bucharest, Carta Românească, 1971; enlarged edition, as *Confidenţe fictive* [Fictitious Confidences], Carta Românească, 1976.
Jocuri de vacanţă [Parlour Games] (includes verse). Bucharest, Carta Românească, 1983.

Other

Has translated Paul Celan, William Shakespeare, Molière, Guillaume Apollinaire, Iannis Ritsos, Max Jacob, Vladimir Maiakovskii, Bertolt Brecht, and others.

*

Critical Study: "Writing Children's Literature in Romania: Interview with Nina Cassian" by Geraldine DeLuca and Roni Natov, in *The Lion and the Unicorn* (Brooklyn, New York), 10, 1986.

*   *   *

Nina Cassian is an artist of extraordinary creative energy — she is not only a poet and a translator of works by Paul Celan, William Shakespeare (*Hamlet*, and *The Tempest*), Molière, Guillaume Apollinaire, and others, but also a writer of fiction and children's books (and puppet plays!), a composer, and an illustrator of her own writings. Her critical writings (on music, film, and books) and her fiction (e.g., *Confidenţe fictive* [Fictitious Confidences]) is of considerable merit; it is as a lyrical poet, however, that her achievement is most remarkable.

As one might expect from a skilled musician, her work is rhythmically sophisticated and powerful. She presents us with images of a dynamic and intense world, registered in intense sensations. It is a world where one can "feel light gliding across the cornea/like the train of a dress" and be "deafened by dust falling on the furniture" and in which one is "riveted by the immense nails of the sun" (quoted from translations by Andrea Deletant and Brenda Walker). All her work registers an acute sense of human physicality. Speech itself is a physical, even sexual, activity:

> Please God take pity
> on the roof of my mouth,
> on my tongue,
> on my glottis,
> on the clitoris in my throat
> vibrating, sensitive, pulsating,
> exploding in the orgasm of Romania.
>   ("Licentiousness")

Everywhere in her work is a passionate appetite for life and sensation:

> I'm greedy, I gulp things down, I fly,
> and I'm proud that on my small lapel
> occasionally a decoration glitters —
> call it rapture, that golden rosette.

Cassian is perhaps at her most impressive as a love poet. The rapture of shared love and the pain of betrayal and loss are articulated alike in poems characterised by an extraordinary intensity and violence of image. She is a supreme poet of passion:

> You're him — the rainmaker.
> Your arms pour down my body,
> your eyes rinse my throat,
> your mouth blossoms on my hip
> like a moist blue flower.
> You tore off the golden ring
> that wedded me to drought,
> that ring of arid gold
> engraved with ashen thorns.
> The restlessness of harvest swells my breasts,
> Water-tassels hang from the ends of my fingers.
> Faint thunder travels in and through us.
>   ("The Rainmaker")

The kisses of lovers are "battles . . ./heavy, slow, hurtful,/ where blood, voice and memory all take part" ("Kisses"); lovers "could chase flames on the curve of their hips,/thrusting kisses where bones met" ("The First and Last Night of Love"). Pleasure and pain are effectively indistinguishable: "everything hurts,/mouth — from longing,/eyes — from light" ("Longing"). Tenderness and savagery are aspects of one and the same experience — "I scraped off your smile with nails./ Licked away your eyes" ("Capital Punishment").

Cassian's work fuses a sophisticated modern intelligence with a powerful strain of imagery and symbolism which is deeply rooted in the traditions of folklore and myth. It is in such traditions that one finds anticipations of the elemental intensity of imagery characteristic of Cassian. Through both her intuition and her intelligence Cassian has, as it were, tapped into a realm of archetypes which validates the individuality of her own poetic personality. Poems such as "The Dialogue of the Wind and the Sea" or the wry "Ballad of Jack of Diamonds" well exemplify this fusion of modern and post-Freudian with native and traditional. Cassian's essential subjects — "love and loss, life and death" as William Jay Smith puts it (*Life Sentence*) — are hardly new. The poet herself recognises the fact: "This ballad seems at least twice-told./ Well, all Romanian plots are old" ("Ballad of the Jack of Diamonds"). Writing in first-person lyrics or third-person ballads Cassian creates poems in which the oldest of human stories takes on a new freshness and vividness of colour:

> She was beautiful and wicked.
> He was wicked and beautiful.
> From head to toe
> they were smeared with viper honey.
> ("She was Beautiful and Wicked")

Whether in celebration:

> With you, my man,
> through your person, your presence,
> I share all legends, all myths
> of this universe and beyond
> ("With You")

or in curse:

> Forgive me for making you weep,
> I should have murdered you,
> I should have dragged out your soul
> and battered you with it
> ("Romance")

Cassian writes with peculiar intensity of the central experiences of human love and sexuality; she does so in language of a genuinely singing lyricism. In her, some of the most fundamental and ancient concerns of poetry find successful modern expression; she draws on modern techniques but avoids the dangers of excessive subjectivity.

—Glyn Pursglove

———

CELA (y Trulock), Camilo José. Spanish. Born in Iria Flavia, La Coruña, 11 May 1916. Educated at the University of Madrid, 1933–36, 1939–43. Served in Franco's forces, 1936–39: Corporal. Married 1) María del Rosario Conde Picavea in 1944 (marriage ended 1989), one son; 2) Marina Castaño in 1991. Freelance writer in Madrid until 1954, then in Mallorca; founder, *Papeles de Son Armadans*, 1956–79. Recipient: National Critics' prize, 1956; National literature prize, 1984; Prince of Asturias prize for literature, 1987; Nobel prize for literature, 1989. Honorary doctorate: Syracuse University, 1964; University of Birmingham, 1976; John F. Kennedy University, Buenos Aires, 1978; Interamericana University, Puerto Rico, 1980; University of Palma, Mallorca, 1980; Hebrew University, Jerusalem, 1986; University of Miami, University of Tel Aviv, University of San Marcos, Lima, Dowling College, Long Island, New York, and Millersville University, Pennsylvania, all 1990; Universidad Complutense, Madrid, and La Trobe University, Australia, 1991. Honorary Professor, University of Santo Domingo, 1990. Member, Spanish Royal Academy, since 1957. Address: Finca el Espinar, Carretera de Fontanar, Guadalajara, Spain.

PUBLICATIONS

Fiction

La familia de Pascual Duarte. Madrid, Aldecoa, 1942; as *Pascual Duarte's Family*, London, Eyre and Spottiswoode, 1946; as *The Family of Pascual Duarte*, Boston, Little Brown, 1964.

Pabellón de reposo. Madrid, Afrodisio Aguado, 1943; as *Rest Home*, New York, Las Américas, 1961.

Nuevas andanzas y desventuras de Lazarillo de Tormes. Madrid, La Nave, 1944.

Esas nubes que pasan. Madrid, Afrodisio Aguado, 1945.

El bonito crimen del carabinero, y otras invenciones. Barcelona, Janés, 1947.

El gallego y su cuadrilla, y otros apuntes carpetovetónicos. Madrid, Aguilera, 1949.

La colmena. Buenos Aires, Emecé, 1951; as *The Hive*, New York, Farrar Straus, and London, Gollancz, 1953.

Santa Balbina 37, gas en cada piso. Melilla, Mirto y Laurel, 1952.

Timoteo el incomprendido. Madrid, Rollán, 1952.

Café de artistas. Madrid, Tecnos, 1953.

Mrs. Caldwell habla con su hijo. Barcelona, Destino, 1953; as *Mrs. Caldwell Speaks to Her Son*, Ithaca, New York, Cornell University Press, 1968.

Baraja de invenciones. Valencia, Castalia, 1953.

La catira. Barcelona, Noguer, 1955.

El molino de viento, y otras novelas cortas. Barcelona, Noguer, 1956.

Nuevo retablo de don Cristobita: invenciones, figuraciones, y alucinaciones. Barcelona, Destino, 1957.

Cajón de sastre. Madrid, Cid, 1957.

Historias de España: Los ciegos, Los tontos. Madrid, Arión, 1958; as *A la pata de palo: Historias de España, La familia del héroe, El ciudadano Iscariote Reclús, Viaje a U.S.A.*, Madrid, Alfaguara, 4 vols., 1965–67; as *El tacatá oxidado: florilegio de carpetovetonismos y otras lindezas*, Barcelona, Noguer, 1973.

Los viejos amigos. Barcelona, Noguer, 2 vols., 1960–61.

Gavilla de fábulas sin amor. Palma de Mallorca, Papeles de Son Armadans, 1962.

Tobogán de hambrientos. Barcelona, Noguer, 1962.

Once cuentos de fútbol. Madrid, Nacional, 1963.

Las compañías convenientes, y otros fingimientos y cegueras. Barcelona, Destino, 1963.

El solitario, Los sueños de Quesada. Palma de Mallorca, Papeles de Son Armadans, 1963.

Garito de hospicianos; o, Guirigay de imposturas y bambollas. Barcelona, Noguer, 1963.

Toreo de salón. Barcelona, Lumen, 1963.

Izas, rabizas, y colipoterras. Barcelona, Lumen, 1964.

Cuentos 1941–1953, Nuevo retablo de don Cristobita. Barcelona, Destino, 1964.

Apuntes carpetovetónicos: novelas cortas 1949–1956. Barcelona, Destino, 1965.

Nuevas escenas matritenses. Madrid, Alfaguara, 7 vols., 1965–66; as *Fotografías al minuto*, Madrid, Sala, 1972.

San Camilo, 1936: vísperas, festividad, y octava de San Camilo del año 1936 en Madrid. Madrid, Alfaguara, 1969; as *San Camilo, 1936: The Eve, Feast and Octave of St. Camillus of the Year 1936 in Madrid*, Durham, North Carolina, Duke University Press, 1992.

Café des artistas y otros cuentos. Pamplona, Salvat/Alianza, 1969.

Timoteo el incomprendido y otros papeles ibéricos. Madrid, Magisterio Español, 1970.

Obras selectas.   Madrid, Alfaguara, 1971.
Oficio de tinieblas 5; o, Novela de tesis escrita para ser cantada por un coro de enfermos.   Barcelona, Noguer, 1973.
Cuentos para leer despues del baño.   Barcelona, La Gaya Ciencia, 1974.
Prosa, edited Jacinto-Luis Guerña.   Madrid, Narcea, 1974.
Café de artistas y otros papeles volanderos.   Madrid, Alce, 1978.
El espejo y otros cuentos.   Madrid, Espasa-Calpe, 1981.
Mazurca para dos muertos.   Barcelona, Seix Barral, 1983.
Cristo versus Arizona.   Barcelona, Seix Barral, 1988.
Desde el palomar de Hita.   Barcelona, Plaza & Janés, 1991.
Cachondeos, escareos y otros meneos.   Madrid, Temas de Hoy, 1991.
O Camaleón solteiro.   Santiago de Compostela, El Correo Gallego, 1991.

Play

Homenaje al Bosco I: El carro de heno, o, El inventor de la guillotina.   Palma de Mallorca, Papeles de Son Armadans, 1969.

Verse

Poemas de una adolescencia cruel.   Barcelona, Zodiaco, 1945; as *Pisando la dudosa luz del día*, 1945.
Maria Sabina.   Palma de Mallorca, Papeles de Son Armadans, 1967.
Cancionero de la Alcarria.   Barcelona, Círculo de Lectores, 1987.

Other

Mesa revuelta.   Madrid, Sagitario, 1945; enlarged edition, Madrid, Taurus, 1957.
San Juan de la Cruz (as Matilde Verdú).   Madrid, n.p., 1948.
Viaje a la Alcarria.   Madrid, Revista de Occidente, 1948; as *Journey to the Alcarria*, Madison, University of Wisconsin Press, 1964.
Ávila.   Barcelona, Noguer, 1952; revised edition, 1968.
Del Miño al Bidasoa: notas de un vagabundaje.   Barcelona, Noguer, 1952.
Ensueños y figuraciones.   Barcelona, G.P., 1954.
Vagabundo por Castilla.   Barcelona, Seix Barral, 1955.
Mis páginas preferidas.   Madrid, Gredos, 1956.
Judíos, moros, y cristianos: notas de un vagabundaje por Ávila, Segovia, y sus tierras.   Barcelona, Destino, 1956.
La rueda de los ocios.   Barcelona, Mateu, 1957.
La obra literaria del pintor Solana.   Palma de Mallorca, Papeles de Son Armadans, 1957.
Recuerdo de don Pío Baroja.   Mexico City, De Andrea, 1958.
La cucaña: memorias.   Barcelona, Destino, 1959.
Primer viaje andaluz: notas de un vagabundaje por Jaen, Córdoba, Sevilla, Huelva, y sus tierras.   Barcelona, Noguer, 1959.
Cuaderno del Guadarrama.   Madrid, Arión, 1959.
Cuatro figuras del '98: Unamuno, Valle-Inclán, Baroja, Azorín, y otros retratos y ensayos españoles.   Barcelona, Aedos, 1961.
Obra completa.   Barcelona, Destino, 14 vols., 1962–83.
Páginas de geografía errabunda.   Madrid, Alfaguara, 1965.
Viaje al Pirineo de Lérida: notas de un paseo a pie por el Pallars Sobira, el Valle de Aran, y el Condado de Ribagorza.   Madrid, Alfaguara, 1965.
Viajes por España.   Barcelona, Destino, 3 vols., 1965–68.
Madrid.   Madrid, Alfaguara, 1966.

Calidoscopio callejero, marítimo y campestre de Camilo José Cela para el reino y ultramar.   Madrid, Alfaguara, 1966.
Xam, with Cesáreo Rodríguez Aguilera.   Palma de Mallorca, Daedalus, 1966.
Diccionario secreto.   Madrid, Alfaguara, 2 vols., 1968–72.
Al servicio de algo.   Madrid, Alfaguara, 1969.
La bandada de palomas (for children).   Barcelona, Labor, 1969.
Barcelona, illustrated by Federico Lloveras.   Madrid, Alfaguara, 1970.
La Mancha en el corazón y en los ojos.   Barcelona, Edivsen, 1971.
La bola del mundo: escenas cotidianas.   Madrid, Sala, 1972.
A vueltas con España.   Madrid, Seminarios y Ediciones, 1973.
Cristina Mallo (monograph).   Madrid, Theo, 1973.
Balada del vagabundo sin suerte y otros papeles volanderos.   Madrid, Espasa-Calpe, 1973.
Diccionari manual castellá-catalá, catalá-castellá.   Barcelona, Bibliograf, 1974.
Danza de las gigantas amorosas.   Barcelona, Luchán, 1975.
Rol de cornudos.   Barcelona, Noguer, 1976.
Crónica del cipote de Archidona.   Madrid, Gisa, 1977.
La rosa.   Barcelona, Destino, 1979.
Los sueños vanos, los ángeles curiosos.   Barcelona, Argos Vergara, 1980.
Vuelta de hoja.   Barcelona, Destino, 1981.
Los vasos comunicantes.   Barcelona, Bruguera, 1981.
Album de taller (art commentary).   Barcelona, Ambit, 1981.
Enciclopedia de erotismo.   Barcelona, Destino, 3 vols., 1982–86; revised edition, as *Diccionario del erotismo*, Barcelona, Grijalbo, 2 vols., 1988.
El juego de los tres madroños.   Barcelona, Destino, 1983.
Madrid, color y siluta.   Sabadell, AUSA, 1985.
Nuevo viaje a la Alcarria.   Barcelona, Plaza & Janés, 1986.
El asno de Buridán (articles).   Madrid, El País, 1986.
Of Genes, Gods, and Tyrants: The Biological Causation of Reality.   Norwell, Massachusetts, Kleiwer Academic, 1987.
Conversaciones españoles.   Barcelona, Plaza & Janés, 1987.
Los caprichos de Francisco de Goya y Lucientes.   Madrid, Sílex, 1989.
Las orejas del niño Raúl.   Madrid, Debate, 1989.
Vocación de repartidor.   Madrid, Debate, 1989.
Obras completas.   Barcelona, Planeta-Agostini, 25 vols., 1989–90.
Galicia.   Madrid, Vigo, 1990.
Blanquito, peón de Brega.   Madrid, Calambur, 1991.
Páginas escogidas (anthology).   Madrid, Espasa-Calpe, 1991.
Torerías; El gallego y su cuadrilla; Madrid toreo de salón.   Madrid, Espasa-Calpe, 1991.

Editor, *Homenaje y recuerdo a Gregorio Marañón (1887–1960)*.   Palma de Mallorca, Papeles de Son Armadans, 1961.

Translator, *La Celestina*, by Fernando de Rojas.   Barcelona, Destino, 1979.
Translator, *La resistible ascensión de Arturo Ui*, by Bertolt Brecht.   Madrid, Júcar, 1986.

*

Critical Studies: *The Novels and Travels of Camilo José Cela*, Chapel Hill, University of North Carolina Press, 1963, and "Camilo José Cela's Quest for a Tragic Sense of Life," in

Romance Quarterly (Lexington, Kentucky), 17, 1970, both by Robert Kirsner; "Social Criticism, Existentialism and Tremendismo in Camilo José Cela's *La familia de Pascual Duarte*," in *Romance Quarterly* (Lexington, Kentucky), 13 (Supplement), 1967, and *Forms of the Novel in the Work of Camilo José Cela*, Columbia, University of Missouri Press, 1967, both by David W. Foster; "Mode of Existence and the Concept of Morality in *La familia de Pascual Duarte*," in *OPLLL* (Athens, Ohio), A9, 1968, "Camilo José Cela's *La colmena*: The Creative Process as Message," in *Hispania* (Los Angeles), 55, 1972, and "Systematic Doubt: The Moral Art of *La familia de Pascual Duarte*," in *Hispanic Review* (Philadelphia), 40, 1972, all by Robert C. Spires; *Camilo José Cela* by D. W. McPheeters, New York, Twayne, 1969; "The Figure of the Civil Guard in the Novels of Camilo José Cela," in *OPLLL* (Athens, Ohio), A14, 1971, and "Camilo José Cela's *La familia del héroe*, the *nouveau roman* and the Creative Act," in *Modern Language Notes* (Baltimore, Maryland), 88, 1973, both by Thomas R. Franz; "Camilo José Cela's Portrayal of Martin Marco in *La colmena*," in *Neophilologus* (Amsterdam), 55, 1971, "*La colmena*: An Oversight on the Part of Camilo José Cela," in *Romance Notes* (Chapel Hill, North Carolina), 13, 1972, and "Theme and Structure in *La colmena*," in *Forum for Modern Language Studies* (St. Andrews, Scotland), 8, 1972, all by David Henn; "Two Recurring Structures in Camilo José Cela's *Prólogos*" by Brian D. Steel, in *Revista de Estudios Hispánicos* (Poughkeepsie, New York), 6, 1972; "Tremendismo and Symbolic Imagery in Camilo José Cela's 'Marcelo Brito': An Analysis" by Fred Abrams, in *Romance Notes* (Chapel Hill, North Carolina), 14, 1973; "Confession and Inaction in *San Camilo*" by J. S. Bernstein, in *Hispanófila* (Chapel Hill, North Carolina), 51, 1974; "*La familia de Pascual Duarte* and the Prominence of Fate" by Cedric Busette, in *Revista de Estudios Hispánicos* (Poughkeepsie, New York), 8, 1974; "The Antisocial Humanism of Camilo José Cela and Hemingway" by Lynette Hubbard Seator, in *Revista de Estudios Hispánicos* (Poughkeepsie, New York), 9, 1975; "Form and Structure in *La colmena*: From Alienation to Community" by Dru Dougherty, and "The Politics of Obscenity in *San Camilo, 1936*" by Paul Ilie, both in *Anales de la Novela de Posguerra*, 1, 1976; "Narrative Tension and Structural Unity in Camilo José Cela's *La familia de Pascual Duarte*" by Michael D. Thomas, in *Symposium* (Washington, D.C.), 31, 1977; "*La familia de Pascual Duarte* and *L'Étranger*: A Contrast" by Michael Fody, III, in *West Virginia University Philological Papers* (Morgantown, West Virginia), 24, 1977; "The Onomastic Devices of Camilo José Cela" by Luis A. Oyarzun, in *Literary Onomastics Studies* (Brockport, New York), 9, 1982; "Bleak House Revisited: Camilo José Cela's *La colmena*" by Norma G. Kobzina, in *Hispanófila* (Chapel Hill, North Carolina), 28(1[82]), 1984; "Camilo José Cela and the Case of Sergiusz Piasecki" by Florian L. Smieja, in *Essays in Honour of Robert Brian Tate*, Nottingham, University of Nottingham Department of Hispanic Studies, 1984; "Implications of the Autobiographical Form in *La familia de Pascual Duarte*" by Rosa Marie Marcone, in *Language Quarterly* (Tampa, Florida), 24(1–2), 1985; "The Function of the Simile in Camilo José Cela's *La familia de Pascual Duarte*" by Catherine R. Perricone, in *Language Quarterly* (Tampa, Florida), 24(3–4), 1986; "Narrators and Fragmentation in Camilo José Cela's *Mrs. Caldwell habla con su hijo*" by Susan G. Polansky, in *Revista de Estudios Hispánicos* (Poughkeepsie, New York), 21(3), 1987; "Primitivism in *La familia de Pascual Duarte*" by William M. Sherzer, in *Discurso Literario* (Stillwater, Oklahoma), 5(2), 1988; "*Mazurca para dos muertos*: Demythologization of the Civil War, History and Narrative Reliability" by Janet Pérez, in *Anales de la Literatura Española Contemporánea* (Boulder, Colorado), 13(1–2), 1988; "Camilo José Cela's *San Camilo, 1936* as Anti-History" by J. H. R. Polt, in *Anales de Literature Española* (Alicante), 6, 1988; "Camilo José Cela's 'Anti-Novelette' *Café de artistas*" by Kenneth G. Eller, in *Hispanófila* (Chapel Hill, North Carolina), 33(1[97]), 1989; "La Politique des auteurs: Narrative Point of View in *Pascual Duarte*, Novel and Film" by Kathleen M. Vernon, in *Hispania* (Los Angeles), 72(1), 1989.

* * *

Camilo José Cela has been the dominant novelist of Spain for 50 years. Since 1942, when his first novel, *La familia de Pascual Duarte* (*The Family of Pascual Duarte*), made its appearance, Cela has prevailed as the foremost figure among prose writers in Spain. Actually, his writing extends beyond fiction; for instance, he has also dedicated himself to valuable but explosive scholarship, such as *Diccionario secreto* (Secret Dictionary), a veritable thesaurus of forbidden words and expressions. In erudition as in fiction, Cela is forever the iconoclast who seeks to shock his audiences by awakening them to the horrors of our existence. Small wonder that he is regarded as the father of *Tremendismo*, a literary movement identified with unseemly and unforeseen outbursts of brutality. Nonetheless, it would be inaccurate to perceive the art of Cela in simplistic terms as a revelling in ruthlessness, for his writing also touches innermost sympathetic chords. Incongruous as it might seem, love and tenderness permeate the most obvious acts of cruelty.

To be sure, *The Family of Pascual Duarte* stunned readers with its seemingly senseless savagery. Pío Baroja, who was at the time the best-known Spanish novelist, was too frightened to write a prologue for the novel, which was destined to incur the wrath of the Spanish government after the second edition became available. (Apparently, the Franco censors had not read carefully or had not understood the work when it was first printed.) The blood baths celebrated in the narrative of family relationships vividly bore on the bloody carnage that characterized the Spanish Civil War. The fact that Cela had been a soldier on the Franco side might have kept him out of prison, but it did not prevent his impressive novel from earning under a despotic regime the honorable appellation of being "non-grata."

Though equally critical of the social circumstances created by the triumphant tyrannical forces, Cela's most accomplished novel, *La colmena* (*The Hive*), recreated daily existence in Madrid in the aftermath of the civil war with gentleness and feeling for every aspect of life, however insignificant or incongruous. Whatever the occasion, be it in sadness as in joy, the experience of the event stands out as a homage to life. Lest it be misunderstood, *Tremendismo*, a sort of Hispanic Existentialism, constitutes a toast to the living, even when the libation is composed of bitter leaves. The consciousness of one's existence, for all its disparity, is the ultimate reality.

Cela's zest for life reveals itself in person as in his art and erudition. His imposing personality, distinguished by his propensity for candidness, has not always endeared him to colleagues and critics. Unquestionably, Cela is considered to be a forceful, combative person. Although he is a Nobel Laureate, for some time it appeared that he was destined to suffer the same unhappy fate as Benito Pérez Galdós who, nearly a century earlier, was prevented by some of his countrymen from receiving the coveted award. Still, Cela's literary genius has not been truly recognized in Spain.

In his literature as in person, Cela has championed unpopular causes. As a member of the prestigious Spanish Royal Academy since 1957 — where he has maintained the rights of *all* literary words, be they nice or not so nice, to be included in the official dictionary of the academy — or as a former Senator by direct appointment of the King, Cela has been in the midst of bio-political activities. As though he were the protagonist of his literary accomplishments, his sensitivity to suffering and social disservice has made him appear as the feared Conscience of his peers.

Cela's output is vast and varied: poetry, novels, books of travels (not to be confused with travel books), operas, and articles in popular publications as well as in scholarly journals. At present he is actively engaged in writing his memoirs. Yet, notwithstanding the great merits of his writings in forms of novels, essays, and operas, as well as his scholarly achievements, it can be said that the four works which have commanded the greatest attention are *The Family of Pascual Duarte*, *Viaje a la Alcarria* (*Journey to the Alcarria*), *The Hive*, and *San Camilo, 1936*. Any one of these would suffice to give the author a lasting place in the annals of Spanish literary history; however, together they embody an outstanding collection which affords its author a unique place in 20th-century literature in Spain, and in the world. With his art, Cela has objectively perpetuated an historical epoch which by its reflection of inhumanity could well serve as a conscience for us all.

—Robert Kirsner

CELATI, Gianni. Italian. Born in Sondrio, Ferrara, in 1937. Lecturer in Anglo-American literature, University of Bologna. Recipient: Bagutta prize, 1974; Mondello prize, 1990. Address: c/o Feltrinelli, Via Andegari 6, 20121 Milan, Italy.

PUBLICATIONS

Fiction

Comiche. Turin, Einaudi, 1971.
Le avventure di Guizzardi. Turin, Einaudi, 1971.
Il chiodo in testa, with Carlo Gajani. Polenza, La Nuova Foglio, 1975(?).
La banda dei sospiri. Turin, Einaudi, 1976.
Lunario del paradiso. Turin, Einaudi, 1978.
Narratori delle pianure. Milan, Feltrinelli, 1985; as *Voices from the Plains*, London, Serpent's Tail, 1989.
Quattro novelle sulle apparenze. Milan, Feltrinelli, 1987; as *Appearances*, London, Serpent's Tail, 1991.
Verso la foce. Milan, Feltrinelli, 1989.

Other

Finzioni occidentali: fabulazioni, comicità e scrittura. Turin, Einaudi, 1975.
La bottega dei mimi, with Lino Gabellone and Nicole Fiéloux. Pollenza, La Nuova Foglio, 1977.
Parlamenti buffi. Milan, Feltrinelli, 1989.
Profili delle nuvole: immagini di un paesaggio, with Luigi Ghirri. Milan, Feltrinelli, 1989.

Editor, *Alice disambientata*. Milan, L'Erba Voglio, 1978.
Editor, *Narratori della riserva*. Milan, Feltrinelli, 1992.

Translator, *Futilità*, by William Alexander Gerhardi. Turin, Einaudi, 1969.
Translator, *Il linguaggio silenzioso* [The Silent Language], by Edward T. Hall. Milan, Bompiani, 1969.
Translator, with Lino Gabellone, *Colloqui con il professor Y* [Entretiens avec le Professor Y], by Louis-Ferdinand Céline. Turin, Einaudi, 1971.
Translator, with Lino Gabellone, *Il ponte di Londra* [Le Pont de Londres], by Louis-Ferdinand Céline. Turin, Einaudi, 1971.
Translator, *Barthes di Roland Barthes*. Turin, Einaudi, 1980.
Translator, *Guignol's band*, by Louis-Ferdinand Céline. Turin, Einaudi, 1982.

*

Critical Study: "Gianni Celati's Silence, Space, Motion and Relief" by Pina Piccolo, in *Gradiva* (Stony Brook, New York), 4(2[6]), 1988.

*   *   *

Everything that is written is already dust at the very moment it is written and it is right that it should be lost with all the other dusts and ashes of this world. Writing is a way of passing time, paying the homage that is due to it: it gives and takes and what it gives is only what it takes — so the sum is always zero, the insubstantial.

We wish only to be able to celebrate this insubstantial thing and the void, the shadow, the dry grass, the stones of crumbling walls and the dust we breathe. (From *Quattro novelle sulle apparenze* [*Appearances*])

Gianni Celati's recent works of fiction, *Narratori delle pianure* (*Voices from the Plains*) and *Quattro novelle sulle apparenze* (*Appearances*), display certain traits of contemporary Italian fiction — in particular the work of a younger generation, who do not adhere to any particular movement and who manipulate various genres. While there has certainly been a return to the narrative form, any political or ideological allegiances seem to be subordinate to more aesthetic, philosophical concerns. In Celati's case, his earlier fiction was experimental, but as a contemporary writer of the 1980s and 1990s, he has been communicating his dissatisfaction with literature as a commercial project and with the loss, among other things, of individual self-worth and the most basic human values, which include man's place in the universe.

Celati's career began in the early 1970s, and his production of fantastic, comic fictions bore the stamp of his involvement with the Italian Neo-Avantgarde movement of the 1960s. He was also influenced by the slapstick comedy of the silent films. His linguistic experiments in these novels demanded not so much intense intellectual endeavour, but more physical participation in order to understand their verbal slapstick and body language.

Celati then turned to more theoretical and critical considerations of literature, questioning the validity of contemporary writing and its place within Western literature. His period of silence for seven years between *Lunario del paradiso* (Almanac of Paradise) and *Voices from the Plains* was indicative of his disillusionment with "industrial literature," literature produced for the purpose of selling books. He felt such work lacked subtlety and was not sensitive to language as a "continual parody of voices . . . rhythms, voices and tonalities." Language for Celati is fragile and should not be subjected to strict organization under grammatical rules. What is internal has to interact with what is external, and that is forever changing: "Phrases come and go and make the thoughts come which then go. Talk and talk, think and think and then there's nothing left. The head is nothing — it all happens in the open."

In 1985 Celati produced *Voices from the Plains*, and two years later *Appearances*. These collections contain stories told in a simple manner using basic present and perfect tenses, each self-contained, dealing with ordinary people in ordinary settings. The encouragement and influence of Italo Calvino is apparent in these two collections.

Voices from the Plains has its roots in Celati's travels along the Po valley. His characters are part of this landscape and are able to feel themselves in harmony with their environment because they discover and use their ability to communicate. Similar themes are conveyed in the four stories which make up *Appearances*. It is not enough to accept society at face value: is everything not just "an immense piece of make-believe? A whole comedy of appearances that makes us believe all sorts of things and instead none of it is true?" The stories are ultimately about communication, the ability not only to listen to and understand what is happening but to be able then to situate oneself within the wide spectrum of life, to assert one's own individuality and worth.

As Michael Caesar has said (referring to *Voices from the Plains*), "The tales are told with an extraordinary lightness . . . Celati has created a mode of story-telling which shakes off the weight of narrative in what is a conscious and consistent effort to pare away the superstructure of ideology and 'that homogeneous and totalizing continuity that is called history.'"

—Anne W. Mullen

———

CÉSAIRE, Aimé (Fernand). Martiniquais. Born in Basse-Pointe, Martinique, West Indies, 25 June 1913. Educated at Lycée Schoelcher, Fort-de-France, Martinique, 1924–31; Lycée Louis-le-Grand, Paris, 1931–35; École Normale Supérieure, Paris, 1935–39, licence ès lettres 1936. Married Suzanne Roussy in 1937 (died 1966); four sons and two daughters. Teacher, Lycée Schoelcher, Fort-de-France, 1939–45; member of the two French constituent assemblies, 1945–46, and since 1946 Deputy for Martinique in the French National Assembly; member of the Communist bloc, 1946–56, and since 1978 founding member, later president, Parti Progressiste Martiniquais; Mayor of Fort-de-France (councillor for 4th Canton, 1956–70), 1945–83: re-elected, but result invalidated by Tribunal, 1983; re-elected, 1984; President, Conseil Régional Martinique, 1983–86. Founder, with Léopold Senghor and Léon Damas, *L'Étudiant Noir*, Paris, 1934; editor, *Tropiques*, Fort-de-France, 1941–45; president, Society of African Culture, Paris. Recipient: Laporte prize, 1960; Viareggio-Versilia prize, 1968; National grand prize for poetry, 1982. Address: Assemblée Nationale, 75007 Paris, France; or, La Mairie, 97200 Fort-de-France, Martinique, West Indies.

PUBLICATIONS

Verse

Les Armes miraculeuses. Paris, Gallimard, 1946; revised edition, 1970.
Cahier d'un retour au pays natal. Paris, Bordas, 1947; revised edition, Paris, Présence Africaine, 1956; as *Memorandum on My Martinique*, translated by Ivan Goll and Lionel Abel, New York, Brentano's, 1947; as *Return to My Native Land*, translated by Emil Snyder, Présence Africaine, 1968; translated by John Berger and Anna Bostock, London, Penguin, 1969; as *Notebook of a Return to the Native Land*, translated by Clayton Eshleman and Annette Smith, New York, Montemora, 1979.
Soleil cou-coupé. Paris, K, 1948; revised version, in *Cadastre*, 1961.
Corps perdu, illustrated by Picasso. Paris, Fragrance, 1950; revised version, in *Cadastre*, 1961; as *Lost Body*, translated by Clayton Eshleman and Annette Smith, New York, Braziller, 1986.
Ferrements. Paris, Seuil, 1960.
Cadastre. Paris, Seuil, 1961; in English, translated by Emile Snyder and Sanford Upson, New York, Third Press, 1973.
State of the Union, translated by Clayton Eshleman and Denis Kelly. Bloomington, Indiana, Caterpillar, 1966.
Aimé Césaire: Écrivain martiniquais (selected poems). Paris, Nathan, 1977.
Moi, Laminaire. Paris, Seuil, 1982.
Aimé Césaire: The Collected Poetry, translated by Clayton Eshleman and Annette Smith. Berkeley, University of California Press 1983.
Non-Vicious Circle: Twenty Poems, translated by Gregson Davis. Stanford, California, Stanford University Press, 1984.
Lyric and Dramatic Poetry 1946–82, translated by Clayton Eshleman and Annette Smith. Charlottesville, University Press of Virginia, 1990.

Plays

Et les Chiens se taisaient. Paris, Présence Africaine, 1956.
La Tragédie du roi Christophe (produced Salzburg, 1964; Paris, 1965). Paris, Présence Africaine, 1963; revised edition, 1970; as *The Tragedy of King Christophe*, New York, Grove Press, 1970.
Une Saison au Congo (produced Brussels, 1966; Paris, 1967). Paris, Seuil, 1966; as *A Season in the Congo* (produced New York, 1970), New York, Grove Press, 1968.
Une Tempête: adaptation pour un théâtre nègre, adaptation of *The Tempest* by William Shakespeare (produced Hammamet, Tunisia, 1969). Paris, Seuil, 1969; as *A Tempest*, New York, Borchardt, 1985.

Other

Discours sur le colonialisme. Paris, Réclame, 1950; 5th edition, Paris, Présence Africaine, 1970; as *Discourse on Colonialism*, New York, Monthly Review Press, 1972.
Lettre ouverte à Maurice Thorez. Paris, Présence Africaine, 1956; as *Letter to Maurice Thorez*, 1957.
Toussaint Louverture: la révolution française et le problème colonial. Paris, Club Français du Livre, 1960; revised edition, Paris, Présence Africaine, 1962.
Oeuvres complètes. Fort-de-France, Désormeaux, 3 vols., 1976.

Culture and Colonization. Yaoundé, Université de Yaoundé, 1978.

*

Bibliographies: *Aimé Césaire: Bibliographie* by Frederick I. Case, Toronto, Manna, 1973; "Les Écrits d'Aimé Césaire" by Thomas A. Hale, in *Études Littéraires 14*, October 1978.

Critical Studies: *Aimé Césaire: Black Between Worlds* by Susan Frutkin, Coral Gables, Florida, University of Miami Center for Advanced International Studies, 1973; *Modernism and Negritude: The Poetry and Poetics of Aimé Césaire* by A. James Arnold, Cambridge, Massachusetts, Harvard University Press, 1981; *The Poet's Africa: Africanness in the Poetry of Nicolás Guillén and Aimé Césaire* by Josaphat B. Kubayanda, New York, Greenwood, 1990; *Critical Perspectives on Aimé Césaire*, edited by Thomas Hale, Washington, D.C., Three Continents Press, 1992.

*   *   *

Aimé Césaire's work registers a remarkable fusion of European and non-European presences. The native traditions of his birthplace on the island of Martinique, and behind them the traditions of Black Africa, formed a kind of core of sensibility and knowledge around which were later to be added Césaire's studies in Paris — he spent several years at the Sorbonne in the 1930s as a student of Latin, Greek, and French literature — and his creative encounter with French surrealism. Poetic (and human) growth have for Césaire not been a matter of leaving anything behind; rather his growth has been like that of a tree, layer added to layer.

Césaire's first major work (and perhaps still that with which the newcomer to Césaire should begin) was *Cahier d'un retour au pays natal* (*Notebook of a Return to the Native Land*). This is a symphonic poem, of some 1055 lines, in three movements. The first is an evocative account of the psychic, physical, and moral damage inflicted on Martinique by colonialism; the second presents the poet's determination to rid himself of his westernised preoccupation with the merely rational, to rediscover his *négritude*, to find a fuller black consciousness, both personal and racial, and thus to grow to full awareness of distinctively Negro-African cultural values. A transitional point comes when the poet finds himself treating with scorn a degraded Negro; the third movement is a headlong, rhythmically exciting affirmation of renewal, of the "primitive" and the magical, of blackness. André Breton described the *Notebook* as "the greatest lyrical monument of our time," and such an endorsement, from such a source, has perhaps encouraged too ready a description of it as a surrealist work. Certainly much of the writing reveals Césaire's familiarity with the French traditions of Comte de Lautréamont and Arthur Rimbaud and of surrealism itself; there is though a clear underlying structure of thought, even if that structure has more affinities with music than with prose argument. Much of Césaire's work is not best served by being described as surrealist; it is, though, poetry that would probably have been impossible without the example of Surrealism.

Césaire is most strikingly a poet of metamorphosis and transformation. "The Thoroughbreds," for example, is a striking mythological narrative in which the protagonist achieves a kind of loss of ego, and eventual fusion with the vegetal spirit of growth, by means of a series of metamorphoses through animal and fish, culminating in an experience of the "sacred/whirling primordial streaming/at the second beginning of everything," celebrated in language of great power:

> I grow like a plant
> remorseless and unwarped
> toward the ungnarled hours of day
> pure and confident as a plant
> uncrucifiable
> toward the ungnarled hours of evening
>
> The end!
> My feet follow the wormy meandering
> plant
> my woody limbs circulate strange saps
> plant plant
>
> and I speak
> and my word is peace
> and I speak and my word is earth
> and I speak
> and
> Joy
> bursts in the new sun
> and I speak

Césaire is generally at his most impressive in the long poem; the sweep and momentum of such works articulates the almost "prophetic" dimension of much of his thought, and allows him to effect abrupt transitions between extremes — one minute savage, the next delicate — while achieving an overall balance and design. Césaire's essays on poetry have defined it as the means to the "replenishing" of knowledge; he opposes it to scientific knowledge, a matter of mere numbers which "classifies and kills"; poetry's concern is with "everything that ever existed, that is ever possible . . . [with] all pasts, all possible futures in all fluxes, all radiations." It seeks to affirm "the cosmic totality." Césaire's "antirationalism" is part of his attempt to use his work as the means to such an enquiry, to encounter and understand the processes of change, energy, and growth — cosmic, human, and political. At a time when so much purely "western" poetry has settled for the anecdotal and the trivial, the scope of Césaire's thought and the related linguistic excitement of his work constitute an exhilarating challenge. The esoteric quality of much of his vocabulary (Clayton Eshleman and Annette Smith describe his translators "bent over various encyclopaedias, dictionaries of several languages [including African and Creole], botanical indexes, atlases and history texts") is not merely a matter of "aureate" diction; like his disruptions of "normal" French syntax it is an enactment of what the poetry exists to express, a sense of the world's plenitude and of the impotence of the merely rational to encompass that abundance, of the existence of forms of knowledge to which the western mind has effectively closed itself.

The political themes which are largely implicit in Césaire's verse find more explicit statement in his prose works — such as *Discours sur le colonialisme* (*Discourse on Colonialism*) — and in his plays. The series of plays which includes such works as *Et les Chiens se taisaient* (And the Dogs Were Quiet), *La Tragédie du roi Christophe* (*The Tragedy of King Christophe*) and *Une Saison au Congo* (*A Season in the Congo*) all explore the problems of power confronting peoples and individuals as black nations emerge from colonial subjection. They are, like his poetry, both analyses of a situation and a vision of possibilities.

An active politician, as well as a prolific writer, Césaire's career has been an extraordinary one. His life and thought have, in effect, been the building of a bridge between the European and the African; or perhaps we should say that they have worked towards the recognition of those most profoundly universal levels of humanity at which there exists a unity which transcends not merely the racial categories of human beings but the distinct species of life itself, the division between animate and inanimate. Sartre's phrase "Orphée Noir" (Black Orpheus) applies to no figure more fully than to Césaire.

—Glyn Pursglove

CHACEL (Arimón), Rosa. Spanish. Born in Valladolid, 3 June 1898. Educated at the Escuela de Artes y Oficios, and Escuela Superior de Bellas Artes de San Fernando, Madrid, 1908–18. Married Timoteo Pérez Rubio in 1921 (died 1977); one son. Lived in Italy, 1921–27; lived in France during Spanish Civil War, 1936–39, and after, then in Greece; lived in Rio de Janeiro and Buenos Aires, 1940–77, then returned to Spain. Recipient: Guggenheim fellowship, 1959–60; March Foundation fellowship, 1974–76; National Critics' prize, 1977; National literature prize, 1987. Honorary doctorate: University of Valladolid, 1989. Address: c/o Editorial Seix Barral, Córcega 270, 4°, 08008 Barcelona, Spain.

PUBLICATIONS

Fiction

Estación, ida y vuelta.   Madrid, Ulises, 1930.
Teresa.   Buenos Aires, Nueva Romance, 1941.
Memorias de Leticia Valle.   Buenos Aires, Emecé, 1945.
Sobre el piélago.   Buenos Aires, Imán, 1952; enlarged edition, as *Ofrenda a una virgen loca*, Xalapa, Universidad Veracruzana, 1961; enlarged edition, as *Icada, Nevda, Diada*, Barcelona, Seix Barral, 1971.
La sinrazón.   Buenos Aires, Losada, 1960.
Barrio de maravillas.   Barcelona, Seix Barral, 1976.
Novelas antes de tiempo (includes non-fiction).   Barcelona, Bruguera, 1981.
Acrópolis.   Barcelona, Seix Barral, 1984.
Ciencias naturales.   Barcelona, Seix Barral, 1988.
Balaam y otros cuentos.   Madrid, Montena, 1989.

Verse

A la orilla de un pozo.   Madrid, Héroe, 1936.
Versos prohibidos.   Madrid, Caballo Griego, 1978.
Poesías 1931–1991.   Barcelona, Tusquets, 1992.

Other

La confesión.   Barcelona, Edhasa, 1970.
Saturnal.   Barcelona, Seix Barral, 1972.
Desde el amanecer.   Madrid, Revista de Occidente, 1972.
Timoteo Pérez Rubio y sus retratos de jardín.   Madrid, Cátedra, 1980.

Ramón en cuatro entregas (Obra completa).   Madrid, Museo Municipal de Madrid, 4 vols., 1980.
Los títulos, edited by Clara Janés.   Barcelona, Edhasa, 1981.
Alcancía: I: Ida; *II: Vuelta.*   Barcelona, Seix Barral, 2 vols., 1982.
Rebañaduras: colección de artículos de Rosa Chacel, edited by Moisés Mori. Salamanca, Junta de Castilla y León, Consejería de Educación y Cultura, 1986.
La lectura es secreto.   Madrid, Júcar, 1989.
Obra completa.   Valladolid, Diputación Provincial, 1989.

Translator, *La Peste*, by Albert Camus.   Barcelona, Edhasa, 1977.
Translator, *Seis tragedias*, by Jean Racine.   Madrid, Alfaguara, 1983.

*

Critical Studies: "Narcissism and the Quest for Identity in Rosa Chacel's *La sinrazón*," in *Perspectives on Contemporary Literature*, 8, 1982, "*Estación, ida y vuelta*: Rosa Chacel's Apprenticeship Novel," in *Hispanic Journal* (Indiana, Pennsylvania), Spring 1983, and "*Teresa*: Rosa Chacel's Novel of Exile and Alienation," in *Monographic Review/Revista Mongráfica* (Odessa, Texas), 2, 1986, all by Eunice D. Myers; "Women and Spanish Modernism: The Case of Rosa Chacel" by Shirley Mangini, in *Anales de la Literatura Española Contemporánea* (Boulder, Colorado), 12(1–2), 1987; "Rosa Chacel's *Barrio de maravillas*: The Role of the Arts and the Problem of Spain" by Wilma Newberry, in *Hispanic Journal* (Indiana, Pennsylvania), 9(2), 1988.

*   *   *

One of the last survivors and most significant woman of the "Generation of 1927" (including Federico García Lorca, Vicente Aleixandre, Rafael Alberti (*q.v.*), and other famous poets), Rosa Chacel frequented their circles and her work, like theirs, is vanguardist and experimental. Surrealism reached Spain in 1928, affecting several members of the Generation of 1927, including Chacel, whose style has changed but little.

Chacel's writing features intellectualism and concern for formal perfection, befitting a disciple of philosopher-essayist José Ortega y Gasset. Her contact during the 1920s with European Modernism, especially the works of James Joyce and Marcel Proust, was decisive. Cosmopolitanism and aestheticism come naturally to Chacel, who lived decades as an expatriate in intimate contact with the world of art. Her youthful studies of painting and sculpture have produced pictorial conception and painterly execution of her fiction.

Chacel's first novel, *Estación, ida y vuelta* (Station, Round Trip), was directly influenced by Joyce's *Portrait of the Artist as a Young Man*. Secondary influences include Proust's slowed rhythm, internalized focus, and minimal action, and Miguel de Unamuno's treatment of *aboulia*, proto-existential elements and experiments with character autonomy. The title alludes not only to a round trip by the young male protagonist but also to the round of seasons and to the novel's cyclic nature. Also influenced by Chacel's readings of Freud, this *Künstlerroman* depicts the formation of a disoriented and somewhat petulant, aspiring intellectual. Chacel related this first novel to *La sinrazón*, a more successful mature work some three times longer: *Estación* contains the seed developed later. Both exhibit influence by psychoanalysis as her narrative advances and retreats, exploring the hidden depths of personality. The confluence of Joyce, surrealism, and Freud in Chacel's prose imparts a special density.

Chacel lived in Spain from 1927 to 1936, associating with Republican intellectuals; during the Spanish Civil War she volunteered as a Red Cross nurse and later traveled in Europe while her husband helped Republican cultural agencies rescue Spain's artistic treasures. Chacel contributed to leading Republican literary magazines such as *Revista de Occidente, Ultra*, Neruda's *Caballo verde para la poesía, El mono azul*, and the wartime *Hora de España*. Her book of sonnets, *A la orilla de un pozo* (Shore of the Well), reflected the Baroque style of Don Luis de Góngora, whose obscurity and Latinate syntax briefly influenced the Generation of 1927. Chacel's 30 sonnets echo the original's obscure classical allusions and exceptionally learned lexicon; many are dedicated to intellectual contemporaries.

Before the civil war, Chacel began a literary biography of Teresa Mancha (tragic lover of the Romantic poet, José de Espronceda). *Teresa* finally appeared in Buenos Aires in 1941, possibly modified by Chacel's own exile, which becomes a major theme. Teresa left her husband and children to become Espronceda's companion but found herself helpless and alienated when the poet abandoned her to die alone. Chacel inserts implicit feminist concerns and existential notes, developing characterization so extensively that the result is often deemed a novel.

From 1939 to 1960 Chacel contributed essays, poetry, and fiction to the Argentine literary review *Sur*, collaborated in *La Nación* and *Realidad*, and began publishing novels. *Memorias de Leticia Valle* (Memoirs of Leticia Valle) is in a diary format and recounts the memoirs of a precocious adolescent. 11-year-old Leticia resembles Chacel in being the gifted, brilliant, only child of a bourgeois Valladolid family. The apocryphal autobiography recalls the girl's psychological seduction and incipient sexual relationship with a married professor, based on an incident Chacel heard of in her youth. Themes include coming-of-age, artistic apprenticeship, and adolescent moral ambiguity, as well as possible child molestation — a daring topic for the day.

Chacel's short-story collections, *Sobre el piélago* (On the High Seas) and *Ofrenda a una virgen loca* (Offering to a Mad Virgin) were subsequently incorporated in *Icada, Nevda, Diada*, together with other narratives. The title (three variations of a word meaning nothing) evokes the abstract concept of nothingness, and abstraction appears in characterization and setting; plot is minimal, but themes include impressions, the mind's ability to create its own reality, double suicide, the strength of will, and views of the world from particular perspectives such as the artist, the child, and alienated mentalities. A similar work (brief fiction, not originally intended as brief) is *Novelas antes de tiempo* (Novels Before Their Time), containing four unfinished novels and two schematic outlines. Chacel's preface discussing the creative process indicates that she feared she might not have time to finish them (she was then 82).

La sinrazón (Without Reason), first published in Buenos Aires and perhaps Chacel's best novel, received the Spanish Critics' prize when republished in Spain in 1977. A diary format purveys the male protagonist's confession, retracing his passage from adolescence to adulthood and loss of innocence. The introspective, internalized action spans the years 1918–1941, focusing on the psychological turmoil of his search for self-understanding which eventually becomes an existential search for meaning, and for God. The title echoes an Unamuno essay affirming the ontological quest, with or without reason, or even against it.

Barrio de maravillas (Parish of Miracles), the first of a three-part history of Chacel's generation, follows the experiences of two adolescent girls in the Madrid neighborhood where Chacel's family lived in her maternal grandmother's house up to 1914, depicting the era's music, painting, sculpture, cinema, and new literature of the day. Spanish critics saw Chacel's portrayal of female adolescence as sufficiently significant to distinguish the work with the 1976 Critics' prize (followed in 1977 by a second such distinction for *La sinrazón*). *Acrópolis*, the second part of the trilogy, follows the same girls from 1914 to 1931, as they encounter modernist art, take excursions with mentors, begin their own artistic careers, and mature personally and academically. Chacel entitled her trilogy "The Platonic School," an inspiration visible in the abundant Platonic dialogues, philosophical concerns, and aesthetic discussions. The third part, *Ciencias naturales* (Natural Sciences), demands much of the reader, given its intellectual density, interior monologue, and the challenges of Chacel's lexicon.

After her husband's death in 1977, Chacel returned permanently to Spain and devoted herself to a book-length study of her husband's art, *Timoteo Pérez Rubio y sus retratos de jardín* (Pérez Rubio's Garden Portraits). Her essay collections include *La confesión*, on the confessional genre, *Saturnal* (Saturnalia), on love, eroticism, and gender equity, and *Rebañaduras* (Slices), aesthetic and ideological reflections. Shorter critical essays by Chacel were edited by younger poet-novelist Clara Janés and published as *Los títulos* (Titles); the most recent essay collection is *La lectura es secreto* (Reading Is Secret). An autobiography of Chacel's first 10 years, *Desde el amanecer* (Since Dawn) is supplemented by a two-volume diary, *Alcancía* (Piggy Bank), subtitled *Ida* (Departure) and *Vuelta* (Return). Chacel's prose, both fiction and non-fiction, exhibits her love of language per se, an almost sensual pleasure in seeking out the most exact, beautiful, and appropriate words, giving her style an intensely personal character. Had it not been for her exile and expatriation, Chacel would have been recognized decades ago as one of Spain's leading writers; she is nonetheless, unquestionably, the dean of Spanish women novelists.

—Janet Pérez

CHANG, Eileen. *See* **ZHANG AILING.**

CHANG HSIN-HSIN. *See* **ZHANG XINXIN.**

CHARNY, Carmi. *See* **CARMI, T.**

CHEN JO-HSI. *See* **CHEN RUOXI.**

CHEN RUOXI. Taiwanese. Born in Taiwan, 15 November 1938. Educated at Taiwan National University, B.A. 1961; Johns Hopkins University, Baltimore, Maryland, M.A. 1965. Married S.Y. Tuann in 1964; two sons. Moved to China, 1966; Lecturer, Huatong Hydro College, China, 1969–73; teacher, New Method College, Hong Kong, 1972–73; Lecturer, University of California, Berkeley, 1983. Chief editor, *Far-East Times*, 1981–82. Recipient: Zhong Shan literary prize, 1977; *United Daily* literature prize, 1978; Wu's literature prize, 1978; Wu Zhuoliu prize, 1981. Address: 428 Boynton Avenue, Berkeley, California 94707, U.S.A.

PUBLICATIONS

Fiction

Yin xianzhang [Mayor Yin].   Taibei, Yuan Jing, 1976.
Chen Ruoxi zixuan chi [Selected Works by Chen Ruoxi].   Taibei, Lian Jing, 1976.
Lao ren [The Old Man].   Taibei, Lian Jing, 1978.
Gui [Repatriation].   Taibei, Lian Jing, 1978.
The Execution of Mayor Yin, and Other Stories from The Great Proletarian Cultural Revolution.   Bloomington, Indiana University Press, 1978; London, Allen and Unwin, 1979.
Chengli chengwai [Inside and Outside the Wall].   Taibei, Time Publisher, 1981.
Tu wei.   Hong Kong, Joint Publishing, 1983; as *Breaking Out*, Taibei, Yuan Jing, 1983.
Chen Ruoxi duanpian xiaoshuo xuan [Selected Short Stories by Chen Ruoxi].   Beijing, Guanbo, 1983.
Yuan jian.   Taibei, Yuan Jing, 1984; as *Foresight*, Taibei, Joint Publishing, 1984.
Er Hu.   N.p., Gaoxiong shi, 1985; as *The Two Hus*, Taibei, Dunli, 1985.
Zhi hun [Paper Marriage].   Taibei, Zili Wanbao, 1986.
The Old Man and Other Stories.   Hong Kong, Chinese University Press, 1986.

Other

Wenge zaji [Reminiscences of the Cultural Revolution].   Taibei, Hongfan, 1979.
Two Writers and the Cultural Revolution, with Lao She (also includes critical essays on Chen Ruoxi and Lao She). Hong Kong, Chinese University Press, 1980.
Shenghuo suibi [Random Notes].   Taibei, Time Publisher, 1981.
Ethics and Rhetoric of the Chinese Cultural Revolution, with Lowell Dittmer.   Berkeley, University of California Institute of East Asian Studies, 1981.
Democracy Wall and the Unofficial Journals.   Berkeley, University of California Center for Chinese Studies, 1982.
Wuliao cai dushu [Read to Kill Time].   Hong Kong, Diandi, 1983.
Tianran shengchu de huaduo [Flower Grown Naturally].   Tianjin, Baihua Literature and Arts Publishing House, 1987.

Xicang xing [Trip to Tibet].   Hong Kong, Xianggang Publishing House, 1988.
Neimeng zhi xing [Trip to Inner Mongolia].   Taibei, Time Publisher, 1988.
Qing Cang gaoyuan de yuhuo [Temptation of the Tibetan Plateau].   Taibei, Lian Jing, 1989.

Editor, with Liang Shijiu, *Xing xing zhao yu wo*.   Jiulong, Wen Guang, 1983.
Editor, *Hong chen ren huo*.   Gaoxiong, Dunli, 1985.

*

Manuscript Collections: Literary Museum, Beijing; National Central Library, Taibei.

Critical Study: *Two Writers and the Cultural Revolution*, with Lao She (includes critical essays on Chen Ruoxi and Lao She), Hong Kong, Chinese University Press, 1980.

Chen Ruoxi comments:
My fiction exposes the sufferings of the Chinese people under the Communist regime. My prose and weekly columns deal with current Chinese affairs. The writer represents the people's voice.

*   *   *

Chen Ruoxi occupies a unique place in modern Chinese fiction because she is able to write with authority and sensitivity about the three very different worlds in which she has lived: the People's Republic of China, Taiwan, and the Chinese expatriate society in North America.

Chen Ruoxi's first stories were published when she was still a student in Taiwan in the early 1960s and part of a group which brought out its own literary journal. She gained the attention of a wider audience many years later with the publication of "The Execution of Mayor Yin" and other stories which deal with the experiences of ordinary Chinese during the Cultural Revolution.

As Chen Ruoxi now lives in the United States, her testimony is uninhibited by political factors. Her tone is low-key; her plots usually deal with everyday life, and tend to understate their drama. She conveys both the warmth and the cruelty of Chinese society. Her characters, especially the intellectuals, are understandably fearful and suffer the sense of being constantly under observation. Even those who are critical of the lack of sincerity around them often feel the pressure to act hypocritically in the interests of self-preservation.

Chen Ruoxi's most successful writing draws on her own experience of living in China as a returnee in the period when distrust of returnees from overseas was at its height. In stories such as "Gen Er in Beijing," "Chairman Mao Is a Rotten Egg," and "Night Duty" and in her novel *Gui* (Repatriation), the narrator or the protagonist is a Chinese who has returned to the motherland to contribute to its development. The disillusion of these idealists, and the suspicion, criticism, and even persecution they undergo, is a major theme in Chen Ruoxi's writing, and one which gives it a particular resonance for Chinese outside China. In addition, the perspective of the returned overseas Chinese allows her to employ an authorial voice both familiar with the current realities of life in China, and acutely aware, in a way more typical of the outsider, of its outrageous aspects.

In "Geng Er in Beijing," Geng, a scientist who returned to China after 20 years in the United States, has been unable to marry because his status as an intellectual with overseas connections makes him an undesirable partner. His worker girlfriend dropped him, claiming that "people were talking about them." When colleagues try to arrange a match for him with a widow, the institute for which he works vetoes the marriage because her class background turns out to be even more suspect than his own. An overseas Chinese colleague visiting from America, sympathetic, but mystified by Geng's single state, represents the total outsider, offering advice on a situation which he cannot understand. Geng, who understands all too well, cannot explain any of the constraints under which he lives to the visitor: "In the final analysis I am Chinese, he told himself: how I feel is my own business, but defending the national image is a moral obligation."

In *Gui* (Repatriation), Chen Ruoxi again depicts the difficulty for returned Chinese of maintaining a genuine relationship with people from their past. When Wei Ming, a Taiwanese on a trip to China from America, asks to see Xinmei, an old schoolfriend who has returned to live in Nanjing, Xinmei is visited by a "foreign affairs comrade." This man checks on her family life, her apartment and its sanitary arrangements, and insists that she must borrow an extra chair for Wei Ming to sit on before reluctantly agreeing to arrange the visit. He admonishes Xinmei and her husband, "Now be sure you don't forget our policy of distinguishing between insiders and outsiders, and whatever you do remember you must preserve confidentiality. There's no reason for us to tell these foreign guests everything . . ." When the visit takes place, a gap yawns between these former friends, caused not only by official interference, but also by Wei Ming's determined blindness to China's faults. He is very critical of their mutual friends, the Fangs, returnees who now wish to leave China. He says their return to the United States will be bad for China's image, and besides, life in the U.S. is not so easy — only in China is a person's livelihood guaranteed. Yet, when asked if he himself will stay permanently in China, Wei Ming explains that his wife would not be able to bear the hardship and that anyway he is more useful as a propagandist in the U.S.

The total politicisation of life in China and its impact on family relationships is another of Chen Ruoxi's themes. For the female narrator in "Chairman Mao Is A Rotten Egg," birthdays have become a thing of the past since her return from the U.S. The only one she still celebrates is Chairman Mao's for which a special issue of noodles is made available. Yet she is taken aback when she realises that her little boy, soon to be four, doesn't know what a birthday is. She explains and promises him an outing, only to start worrying when her excited son chatters to a neighbour about his treat.

I was beginning to regret having mentioned the outing to Jingjing. If he were to go around telling everyone about celebrating his birthday, people would think that his parents were still full of decadent capitalist ideas. So I quickly pulled him inside the house and told him not to mention his birthday again or one day he would become an old counter-revolutionary. He couldn't understand why he mustn't talk about his birthday, but he knew exactly what an "old counter-revolutionary" was. His face tightened immediately and he nodded gravely.

The way children are affected by Chinese politics is portrayed chillingly in "Ren Xiulan," the story of a former college Party secretary who has escaped from detention during the Cultural Revolution. Most of the staff of the college have been sent to the countryside and only their children are left to conduct a search. There is "an element of precocious seriousness" in their excitement at being given such responsibility. When the poor woman is discovered dead in a cesspit a

meeting is held to denounce her suicide. Later, others in her political group are politically rehabilitated, but she is already forgotten. The narrator feels weighed down by this meaningless death; she has moved from being a half-acquiescent participant in the hunt at the start of the story to sad alienation by the end.

Chen Ruoxi also exposes the faults of Chinese expatriates in the United States. In "Another Fortress Besieged" a Stanford University faculty wife who is a native of Taiwan is asked to entertain an academic delegation from China to dinner. She is pleased by the honour, which she thinks will help her husband's career. Then she is besieged for invitations by local Chinese, all anxious to gain some advantage by meeting the delegation. After the delicious dinner has been eaten, the guests from China reveal they have their own agenda. When their political minder is out of the room the two academics ask for help to get young relatives to the United States. Finally, as they leave, the minder himself slips a note into his hostess's hand: he too has a son who wants to study abroad.

In common with most modern Chinese writers of fiction, Chen Ruoxi is concerned to reflect society as she sees it. Implicitly she also offers her criticism of it. She makes effective use of flashback, but her narrative is otherwise straightforward, spare, and plain, in striking contrast to the flowery style of much modern Chinese fiction. Her best writing has come out of her most traumatic experiences. In all her work she is preoccupied with what it means to be Chinese in the modern world, whether as an expatriate, in the People's Republic, or in Taiwan. Paradoxically, it is perhaps this theme which gives her work its international appeal. Although Chen Ruoxi deals with a particular version of it, the problem of identity is universal in modern societies.

—Delia Davin

———

CHESSEX, Jacques. Swiss. Born in Payerne, 1 March 1934. Educated at the Collège Classique Cantonal, Lausanne, certificate 1950; Collège Saint-Michel, Fribourg, baccalaureate 1952; University of Lausanne, licence ès lettres 1961. Married Elisabeth Reichenbach in 1975. Teacher, Béthusy secondary school, Lausanne, for several years; Professor of French literature, Gymnase Cantonal de la Cité, from 1969. Founder, with Bertil Galland. *Écriture* review, Lausanne, 1964. Recipient: Schiller prize, 1963; Alpes-Jura prize, 1971; Goncourt prize, 1973. Address: c/o Éditions Grasset, 61 rue des Sts .-Pères, 75006 Paris, France.

PUBLICATIONS

Fiction

La Tête ouverte.   Paris, Gallimard, 1962.
La Confession du pasteur Burg.   Paris, Bourgois, 1967.
L'Ogre.   Paris, Grasset, 1973; as *A Father's Love*, New York, Bobbs Merrill, 1975.
L'Ardent Royaume.   Paris, Grasset, 1975.
Le Séjour des morts.   Paris, Grasset, 1977.
Les Yeux jaunes.   Paris, Grasset, 1979.
Où vont mourir les oiseaux.   Paris, Grasset, 1980.

Judas le transparent.   Paris, Grasset, 1982.
Jonas.   Paris, Grasset, 1987.
Morgane Madrigal.   Paris, Grasset, 1990.

Verse

Le Jour proche.   N.p., Aux Miroirs Partagés, 1954.
Chant de printemps.   Geneva, n.p., 1955.
Une Voix la nuit.   Lausanne, Mermod, 1957.
Batailles dans l'air.   Lausanne, Mermod, 1959.
Le Jeûne de huit nuits.   Lausanne, Payot, 1966.
L'Ouvert obscur.   Lausanne, L'Age d'Homme, 1967.
Élégie, soleil du regret.   Lausanne, Galland, 1976.
Le Calviniste.   Paris, Grasset, 1983.
Feux d'orée.   Lausanne, L'Aire, 1984.
Comme l'Os.   Paris, Grasset, 1988.

Other

Écriture: cahier de littérature et de poésie, with Bertil Galland.
    Lausanne, Cahiers de la Renaissance Vaudoise, 1964.
Reste avec nous, précédé de Carnet de terre.   Lausanne,
    Cahiers de la Renaissance Vaudoise, 1967.
Charles-Albert Cingria.   Paris, Seghers, 1967.
Portrait des Vaudois.   Lausanne, Cahiers de la Renaissance
    Vaudoise, 1969.
Carabas.   Paris, Grasset, 1971.
Les Saintes Écritures. Lausanne, Galland, 1972.
Le Renard qui disait non à la lune (for children).   Paris,
    Grasset, 1974.
Les Dessins d'Étienne Delessert.   Lausanne, Galland, 1974.
Bréviaire (includes verse).   Vevey, Galland, 1976.
Adieu à Gustave Roud, with Maurice Chappaz and Philippe
    Jaccottet.   Vevey, Galland, 1977.
Marie et le chat sauvage (for children).   Paris, Grasset, 1979;
    as *Mary and the Wild Cat*, London, Gollancz, 1980.
Entretiens avec Jacques Chessex, with Jérôme Garcin.   Paris,
    La Différence, 1979.
Maupassant et les autres.   Paris, Ramsay, 1981.
Mort d'un cimetière, with Luc Chessex.   Lausanne, 24
    Heures, 1989.
Neuf, l'œuf (for children).   Paris, Grasset, 1990.
Flaubert, ou, le désert en abîme.   Paris, Grasset, 1991.

Editor, *Hommage à Gustave Roud.*   Lausanne, n.p., 1957.
Editor, with Marcel Raymond, *Claude Aubert.*   Lausanne,
    Galland, 1974.

*

Critical Study: "The Dualistic Vision of Jacques Chessex's
Fiction" by David J. Bond, in *Swiss-French Studies* (Wolfville,
Ontario), November 1981.

*   *   *

Jacques Chessex traces the inspiration of his poetry and
fiction to his origins in that part of Switzerland called the Vaud.
"I need this land as Baudelaire needed Paris," he has said in his
autobiography *Carabas*. The setting of most of his fiction is the
Vaud, and descriptions of its natural beauty fill many of his
pages. Yet his love of the Vaud is mixed with hatred of the
Calvinism that he associates with it and that he believes is the
heritage of all Vaudois of his generation. By Calvinism he does
not mean a personal belief, but a cultural influence. He says in
an interview in David Bevan's *Écrivains d'aujourd'hui* (1986):
"In the cantons with a Protestant tradition, there exists a
Calvinist heritage that is absolutely not the result of church
attendance or even the practice of a faith, but of a cultural
tradition." Alexandre Dumur in *Les Yeux jaunes* (Yellow
Eyes) could be speaking for Chessex, and for most of
Chessex's other characters, when he says: "What other
categories can we think in? I was linked to this sad belief by my
birth and the blood of my race."

This Calvinism is an excessively severe religion that is
obsessed with sin, and especially sins of the flesh. "Mortal
malediction is attached to the flesh, that's the Calvinist
heritage," writes Chessex in *Les Saintes Écritures* (Holy Writ),
and Alexandre Dumur in *Les Yeux jaunes* never escapes the
belief that the body is "a cesspool that God despises and
punishes." Woman is directly linked to sin because she is a
temptress, and Pastor Burg in *La Confession du pasteur Burg*
(The Confession of Pastor Burg) avoids women precisely for
this reason. The devil is seen as the inspiration for men's acts,
and the main character in *Jonas* (Jonah) says that belief in
Satan is "blood of my race, mother's milk." He is to be found
particularly in the natural world, and, in *Les Yeux jaunes* he is
symbolised by an outbreak of rabies, a disease that infects and
drives living things to madness and death.

The God of Calvinism is seen as a jealous and vengeful deity
from whom there is no escape. Jean Calmet in *L'Ogre* (A
Father's Love) projects on to his father the characteristics of
this God. He is an all-seeing, dominating figure in whose
presence Jean has always felt guilty. When he was a child, he
was aware that his father's "implacable gaze rested on
everyone in his family," and that this man "knew all about him
because he was the master." The perfect representation of
Jean's father and of the Calvinist God is the statue that Jean
sees in Bern: an enormous ogre devouring a child. One may
interpret Jean's feelings as a classic Oedipus complex, especially as, when the novel opens, Jean feels suddenly free because
his father has just died. However, Jean's sense of guilt is typical
of the Calvinist conscience, which is dominated by what
Chessex describes in *Bréviaire* (Breviary) as "the feeling of sin,
remorse, solitude and being steeped in sin." It is also dominated by death, which is the punishment for sin, particularly for
sins of the flesh. Death is frequently associated with sex, and
Chessex has said in *Carabas*, "I have never held a body in my
embrace without imagining the bones that it will become in the
grave."

Yet Chessex's texts also demonstrate a determined effort to
escape the influence of Calvinism. They affirm life and love in
the face of death, and one poem in *Une Voix la nuit* (A Voice at
Night) says: "Before death we may believe in the world/Love
this sand you speak of, these plants, these clouds." Jonas
Carex in *Jonas* leaves his Calvinist birthplace for Catholic
Fribourg, which he associates with a period in his life when he
knew love and freedom. Jean Calmet in *A Father's Love* seeks
life and freedom in his love for Thérèse, as does Mange in
L'Ardent Royaume (The Ardent Kingdom) when he falls in
love with Monna. Women thus become representatives of love
and liberty as well as of sin. When Mange sits in an old church,
surrounded by reminders of death and "that smell of sin spread
over everything," he turns to Monna, and his fear disappears.
Nature too, while being the devil's dwelling place, is also a
source of beauty and delight. It is associated with life, and with
what Jean Calmet in *A Father's Love* calls "the great telluric
forces that rise and gush forth."

Combined with this rejection of Calvinism is an attack on
those whom Chessex calls "Les Justes." These are the leaders
of Calvinist society, who preach a strict morality but whose
main concern is to turn a quick profit. They are the par-
ishioners who dislike Burg's attacks on their materialism and
the authorities who have Mange drummed out of the legal

profession for immorality. They are the profiteers who destroy the Swiss countryside to build ski resorts and hotels. In *Portrait des Vaudois* (Portrait of the Vaudois) Chessex looks at the land he loves, and laments: "The land is dying," and he points to "bulldozers, bunkers, motels, sheds, factories . . . and clouds of supershell."

Chessex's love of his native region, and the cultural influence of that region, are important for an understanding of his texts. But he also believes himself to be in a French tradition. "I feel myself very clearly attached to France through my writing, my language and my heritage," he says in *Écrivains d'aujourd'hui*. He particularly appreciates the Naturalists, and he says in an interview with Jean-Louis Ézine (*Les Nouvelles Littéraires*, 24 December 1973): "I belong to the Naturalist tradition." His early work is influenced by the French writers Francis Ponge and Jean Paulhan, and, like their work, his style is noticeably concise and spare, and avoids excessive emotion. Beginning with *Carabas* in 1971, however, Chessex's style becomes much more exuberant and flamboyant.

Whatever the changes in style, however, and whatever the national influences, the struggle against a certain kind of Calvinism remains a constant throughout Chessex's work.

—David J. Bond

CH'IEN CHUNG-SHU. *See* **QIAN ZHONGSHU.**

CHRAÏBI, Driss. Moroccan and French.   Born in El Jadida, Morocco, 15 July 1926. Educated at a Koranic school; Lycée Lyautey, Casablanca; a grande école, Paris, degree in chemical engineering 1950. Married Sheena McCallion in 1978 (second marriage); five children from first marriage. Worked as a photographer, journalist, teacher, labourer, and insurance salesman. Since 1954 writer; Professor, University of Laval, Quebec, 1969–70. Recipient: Rivages prize, 1958; Association des Écrivains de la Langue Française prize; Franco-Arab prize; Mediterranean Africa prize, 1973; Société des Auteurs prize, 1990. Address: 15 rue Paul Pons, 26400 Crest, France.

PUBLICATIONS

Fiction

Le Passé simple.   Paris, Denoël, 1954; as *The Simple Past*, Washington, D.C., Three Continents Press, 1990.
Les Boucs.   Paris, Denoël, 1955; as *The Butts*, Washington, D.C., Three Continents Press, 1983.
L'Âne.   Paris, Denoël, 1956.
De Tous les Horizons.   Paris, Denoël, 1958.
La Foule.   Paris, Denoël, 1961.
Succession ouverte.   Paris, Denoël, 1962; as *Heirs to the Past*, London, Heinemann, 1971.
Un Ami viendra vous voir.   Paris, Denoël, 1966.

La Civilisation, ma mère! . . .   Paris, Denoël, 1972; as *Mother Comes of Age*, Washington, D.C., Three Continents Press, 1984.
Mort au Canada.   Paris, Denoël, 1974.
Une Enquête au pays.   Paris, Seuil, 1981; as *Flutes of Death*, Washington, D.C., Three Continents Press, 1985.
La Mère du printemps.   Paris, Seuil, 1982; as *Mother Spring*, Washington, D.C., Three Continents Press, 1989.
Naissance à l'aube.   Paris, Seuil, 1986; as *Birth at Dawn*, Washington, D.C., Three Continents Press, 1990.
L'Homme du livre.   Paris, Seuil, 1992.

Plays

Radio Plays: many scripts for Radio France, including adaptations of works by M. Chokolov, Ernest Hemingway, Norman Mailer, Jack London, and others.

Other

Contes pour enfants.   Paris, Seuil, 1992.

*

Critical Studies: Chraïbi issue of *Revue Celfan/Celfan Review* (Philadelphia), February 1986; "Women in a Man's Exploration of His Country, His World: Chraïbi's *Succession ouverte*" by Rafika Merini, in *Ngambika: Studies of Women in African Literature*, edited by Carole Boyce Davies, Trenton, New Jersey, Africa World, 1986; "Master of the Maghreb" by Hedi Abdel-Jaouad, in *Book World*, October 1991.

*   *   *

Driss Chraïbi was one of the first Francophone writers from North Africa to have an impact on the world of letters. His early novels derived their themes from his personal experience of life in Morocco and then in France. Later, presumably because he decided to pursue a career in France, he abandoned the North African inspiration of his writing and set a series of novels in a purely Western context. His more recent novels have, however, returned to the North African vein, although the choice of subject and the general tone of the writing are very different from those of the early novels.

For many of the North African writers who began their careers in the 1950s, the act of writing signified a revolt against the France whose colonial system had long dominated their countries. While the revolt would also, in Algeria at least, take a military form, there is no doubt that these writers saw their work as possessing a consciousness-raising function, challenging Western culture and reasserting indigenous values. While some of them may now seem to have indulged excessively in local colour, concentrating on the traditions and beliefs of their peoples, others — including Chraïbi — sought to address the very real problems of North African society at a turning point in its history.

Chraïbi's first novel, *Le Passé simple* (*The Simple Past*), has as its narrator a character-type much portrayed by this group of writers, an "acculturé," a North African granted the rare favour of a French-style education but then finding himself stranded between cultures and languages. Not only is Chraïbi's narrator alienated from his origins, but he makes the painful discovery that the foreign culture which has been thrust upon him denies him full integration. But what sets Chraïbi's novel apart from others with the same theme is the ruthlessness with which it targets both the foreign oppressor and Moroccan society itself, particularly the feudalism of its family structures, the hypocrisy of the followers of Islam, and the exploitation practised at every level of social interaction. That Chraïbi could produce such an attack at a time when his country was striving to re-establish belief in itself was considered treason by his fellow Moroccans, and Chraïbi found it advisable to move to France to continue his writing career there.

His second novel, *Les Boucs* (*The Butts*) was, however, equally polemical, denouncing the treatment of North African immigrants in France. The novel nevertheless pursues the criticism of North Africans themselves, alleging their complicity in their victimization. *The Butts* also highlights the relationship of literature and the writer to political oppression. Its narrator, himself an Algerian writer, longs to give hope to his vilified fellow-countrymen but their illiteracy denies him that contact. Chraïbi also portrays a prestigious French writer (apparently based on François Mauriac) who, despite his offers of support to his young North African *protégé*, never seriously questions the cultural (or political) hegemony of Europe.

While Chraïbi's later novels were less iconoclastic than his first two, the criticism of society continued. The accusation in *The Butts* that Western society destroys individuality reappears in a number of books, notably *La Foule* (The Crowd) and *Un Ami viendra vous voir* (A Friend Will Come See you), in which Chraïbi exposes various processes, from media techniques to psychiatric medicine, whereby Western civilization has progressively created a faceless, mindless mass.

While these novels show Chraïbi to be an acute observer of the post-1950 phenomenon of a consumer society that consumed the consumer, there is less scope for his own particular skills in the handling of character and anecdote, and it may be considered fortunate that he has gradually turned again to North Africa for his inspiration. *La Civilisation, ma mère!* . . . (*Mother Comes of Age*) is an entertaining (if optimistic) account of the emancipation of a Moroccan housewife, while *Une Enquête au pays* (*Flutes of Death*) relates, often hilariously, a police investigation into the whereabouts of a political subversive. More recently, Chraïbi has attempted, like various other North African novelists, to recreate the historical past of North Africa in order to dispel the notion of a void long promoted by Western powers as a justification for colonization. *La Mère du printemps* (*Mother Spring*) and *Naissance à l'aube* (*Birth at Dawn*) both start with a character borrowed from the detective story and then take the reader back to the early centuries of Islam. Both the historical and the modern tales demonstrate Chraïbi's gift for the depiction of character and action. The novelist continues to suggest that the "backward" have a savour lost to those adulterated by "civilization."

The North African Francophone novel became a force in its own right just as the *nouveau roman* was being born in France. The technical innovation of the Maghrebian novelists perhaps owed less, however, to the influence of the *nouveau roman* than to the fact that they were borrowing a form unknown in oriental literature and did not feel constrained to respect all the conventions of that form. Chraïbi was one of the first to show that he contested both Western ideas and the mould in which those ideas were cast. *The Simple Past* already reveals some disorientating processes, while the brutal disruption of chronology and style in *The Butts* plays a significant role in destroying the reader's complacency. The technical experimentation in *L'Âne* (The Ass), however, tried its readers' patience, and thereafter Chraïbi limited his excesses, although continuing a gentle subversiveness that warns the reader against passive acceptance of the text. It does not appear that writing in French ever induced in Chraïbi the sense of a linguistic oppression that drove other North African authors either to contemplate abandoning writing or to opt eventually

for Arabic, but it is noticeable that his recent historical tales incorporate words written in Arabic script and without translations being supplied for the benefit of non-Arabic-speaking readers.

—Carys Owen

CISNEROS, Antonio. Peruvian. Born in Lima, 27 December 1942. Educated at the Catholic University, Lima; National University of San Marcos, Lima, Ph.D. 1974. Married twice; one daughter. Teacher of literature, University of Huamanga, Avacucho, 1965, University of Southampton, 1967–70, University of Nice, 1970–72, and University of San Marcos, since 1972; Exchange Professor, University of Budapest, 1974–75. Recipient: National Poetry prize (Peru), 1965; Casa de las Américas prize, 1968. Address: Literature Department, Universidad Nacional Mayor de San Marcos de Lima, Avda República de Chile 295, Of. 506, Casilla 454, Lima, Peru.

PUBLICATIONS

Verse

Destierro.   Lima, Cuadernos del Hontanar, 1961.
David.   Lima, El Timonel, 1962.
Comentarios reales.   Lima, La Rama Florida/Universitaria, 1964.
Canto ceremonial contra un oso hormiguero.   Havana, Casa de las Américas, 1968.
The Spider Hangs Too Far from the Ground, translated by Maureen Ahern, William Rowe, and David Tipton. London, Cape Goliard, 1970.
Agua que no has de beber.   Barcelona, Milla Batres, 1971.
Como higuera en un campo de golf.   Lima, Instituto Nacional de Cultura, 1972.
El libro de Dios y los húngaros.   Lima, Libre-1, 1978.
Cuatro poetas: Victor García Robles, Antonio Cisneros, Pedro Shimose, Armando Tejada Gómez.   Havana, Casa de las Américas, 1979.
Helicopters in the Kingdom of Peru, translated by Maureen Ahern, William Rowe, and David Tipton.   Bradford, Rivelin/Equatorial, 1981.
La crónica del Niño Jesús de Chilca.   Mexico City, Premià, 1981.
At Night the Cats, edited and translated by Maureen Ahern, William Rowe, and David Tipton.   New York, Red Dust, 1985.
Land of Angels, translated by Maureen Ahern, William Rowe, and David Tipton.   Portree, Aquila, 1985.
Monólogo de la casta Susana y otros poemas.   Lima, National Institute of Culture, 1986.
Propios como ajenos: poesia 1962–1988.   Lima, PEISA, 1989.
El arte de envolver pescado.   Lima, Caballo Rojo, 1990.
Poesía, una historia de locos: 1962–1986.   Madrid, Hiperión, 1990.

*

Critical Study: in *The Poet in Peru* by James Higgins, Liverpool, Liverpool Monographs in Hispanic Studies, 1982.

*   *   *

Antonio Cisneros is the leading figure among the new generation of Peruvian poets who emerged in the 1960s. Reflecting the changing climate of that decade, his work breaks with the prevailing Hispanic tradition and opens up Peruvian verse to outside, notably Anglo-Saxon, influences. A more open and cosmopolitan spirit expresses itself through a free-flowing discourse and intertextual dialogue, while a relaxed and irreverent conversational manner is deployed to voice nonconformity with the established social order and its antiquated lifestyle.

One of Cisneros's main concerns is to affirm a modern Peruvian identity by defining where he stands in relation to the forces that have shaped the country's history. His first major book, *Comentarios reales* (Royal Commentaries), starts from the premise that to free itself from dependency and underdevelopment Peru must rid itself of the mythologies propagated by the ruling establishment. Written in a manner reminiscent of Bertolt Brecht, the book ironically debunks the official version of national history, its main targets being Spanish colonialism and the Creole oligarchy who carried on its legacy. "Question of Time," for example, strips the Conquest of its legendary glory to depict the conquistadores as rapacious but inept adventurers who initiated a tradition of exploitation and underdevelopment, while "Prayers of a Repentant Gentleman" satirises the hypocrisy that manipulated religion as a justification for social and racial oppression. Similarly, "Tupac Amaru Relegated" and "Description of a Plaza, a Monument and Allegories in Bronze" demythologise Peruvian Independence, revealing it to be a sham which perpetuated an unjust social order behind a façade of noble ideals.

Canto ceremonial contra un oso hormiguero (Ceremonial Song Against an Ant-Eater), his most important book, is informed by the central experience of the 60s generation, the dashing of the expectation of radical change which had been generated by a liberalisation of the international climate, the example of the Cuban Revolution, and the election of the reformist Fernando Belaúnde Terry to the Peruvian presidency in 1963. "In Memoriam" is a sardonic lament on the demise of the revolutionary dream, killed by the Belaúnde government's suppression of the left-wing guerrilla movement and epitomised by the death of Cisneros's fellow poet, Javier Heraud, at the hands of counter-insurgency forces in 1963. Disenchantment with half-hearted liberal reformism is likewise expressed in the title poem, where the corruption and exploitation of the traditional ruling oligarchy are satirised in the predatory activities of an ageing homosexual, depicted as an antediluvian monster who has somehow outlived the historical changes which should logically have made it extinct.

From *Canto ceremonial* onwards Cisneros's poetry becomes more confessional in manner. In "Poem on Jonah and the Disalienated," for example, the story of Jonah is invoked as a metaphor of his existence in the stiflingly conservative and provincial world of Lima's middle classes, while the poem that follows it constitutes a postscript in which, with characteristic self-deprecation, he acknowledges that his moments of rebelliousness have always ended in a whimper and that like everyone else he has accommodated himself to the system.

Residence in Europe was to bring to the fore another of Cisneros's preoccupations, the relationship between the Third World and the developed West. As is indicated by the title of *Como higuera en un campo de golf* (Like a Fig-Tree on a Golf Course), contact with Europe made him acutely aware of his Third World status, and in one poem he complains of continually coming across "Triumphal arches celebrating my condition of slave, of son of the rice-eaters." In "Weighing and Measuring the Differences on This Side of the Channel," from *Canto ceremonial*, he addresses the issue of the underdeveloped countries' cultural dependency on the imperialist West and posits the need for Latin Americans to forge a cultural identity of their own. He himself eschews any complex of cultural inferiority and in other poems simultaneously puts himself on equal footing with Western writers and asserts his independence by drawing on the Western literary tradition while at the same time treating it with healthy irreverence, as, for example, when he highlights the pain of homesickness by contrasting it with the vapid laments of Garcilaso de la Vega's lovelorn shepherds.

In *La crónica del Niño Jesús de Chilca* (Chronicle of the Infant Jesus of Chilca) Cisneros returns to the project of writing an alternative history of Peru. Here he presents what he regards as the real history of the country, the unspectacular history of ordinary men and women recounted from their own perspective. Chilca was a once-flourishing coastal community which fell on hard times as a result of the flooding of its salt-pans and was subsequently pushed into extinction by capitalist development of the area. Evoking its golden age of Chilca as recalled by its few remaining survivors, Cisneros puts forward a model of popular democracy as an alternative to the official mythology which he had subverted in his earlier books. However, the flooding of the salt-pans takes on the proportions of a Fall, provoking the distintegration of the community, and the book becomes a lament for the depopulation of the Peruvian countryside and for a tradition of popular democracy destroyed by uncontrolled capitalist development. Cisneros is not entirely successful in conveying the popular consciousness, but, nonetheless, the book represents an important attempt to create a new national mythology.

—James Higgins

———

CIXOUS, Hélène. French. Born in Oran, Algeria, 5 June 1937. Educated: received agrégation in English 1959; Doctorat d'état in English literature 1968. Married in 1955 (divorced); one daughter and one son. Assistante, University of Bordeaux, 1962–65; maître assistante, the Sorbonne, Paris, 1965–67; maître de conférence, University of Paris X, Nanterre, 1967–68. Founder of experimental branch, 1968, since 1968 Professor of English literature, and since 1974 founder and director of Centre de Recherche en Études Féminines, University of Paris VIII, St. Denis. Founder, with Tzvetan Todorov and Gérard Genette, *Poétique*, 1969. Recipient: Medicis prize, 1969. Doctor honoris causa: Queen's University, Kingston, Ontario, 1991. Address: 14–16 Villa Leblanc, 92120 Montrouge, France.

PUBLICATIONS

Fiction

Le Prénom de Dieu. Paris, Grasset, 1967.

Dedans. Paris, Grasset, 1969; as *Inside*, New York, Schocken, 1986.
Le Troisième Corps. Paris, Grasset, 1970.
Les Commencements. Paris, Grasset, 1970.
Un Vrai Jardin. Paris, L'Herne, 1971.
Neutre. Paris, Grasset, 1972.
Tombe. Paris, Seuil, 1973.
Portrait du soleil. Paris, Denoël, 1974.
Révolutions pour plus d'un Faust. Paris, Seuil, 1975.
Un K. incompréhensible: Pierre Goldman. Paris, Bourgois, 1975.
Souffles. Paris, Des Femmes, 1975.
La. Paris, Gallimard, 1976.
Partie. Paris, Des Femmes, 1976.
Angst. Paris, Des Femmes, 1977; in English, London, Calder, and New York, Riverrun, 1985.
Préparatifs de noces au delà de l'abîme. Paris, Des Femmes, 1978.
Vivre l'orange = To Live the Orange (bilingual edition). Paris, Des Femmes, 1979.
Anankè. Paris, Des Femmes, 1979.
Illa. Paris, Des Femmes, 1980.
With; ou, L'Art de l'innocence. Paris, Des Femmes, 1981.
Limonade tout était si infini. Paris, Des Femmes, 1982.
Le Livre de Promethea. Paris, Gallimard, 1983; as *The Book of Promethea*, Lincoln, University of Nebraska Press, 1991.
La Bataille d'Arcachon. Laval, Quebec, Trois, 1986.
Manne aux Mandelstams aux Mandelas. Paris, Des Femmes, 1988.
Jours de l'an. Paris, Des Femmes, 1990.
L'Ange au secret. Paris, Des Femmes, 1991.

Plays

La Pupille. Paris, Gallimard, 1972.
Portrait de Dora (produced Paris, 1976). Paris, Des Femmes, 1976; as *Portrait of Dora*, in *Benmussa Directs*, London, Calder, and Dallas, Riverrun, 1979.
Le Non d'Oedipe: Chant du corps interdit (libretto), music by André Boucourechliev (produced Avignon, 1978). Paris, Des Femmes, 1978; as *The Name of Oedipus*, in *Women's Theater in French*, Ann Arbor, University of Michigan Press, 1991.
La Prise de l'école de Madhubaï (produced Paris, 1983). Paris, Avant-Scène, 1984.
Celui que ne parle pas (produced Grenoble, 1984).
L'Histoire terrible mais inachevée de Norodom Sihanouk, roi du Cambodge (produced Paris, 1985). Paris, Théâtre du Soleil, 1985.
Thèâtre (includes *Portrait de Dora*; *La Prise de l'école de Madhubaï*). Paris, Des Femmes, 1986.
L'Indiade; ou, L'Inde de leurs rêves (produced Paris, 1987). Paris, Théâtre du Soleil, 1987.
Karine Saporta, with Daniel Dobbels and Bérénice Reynaud. Paris, Armand Colin, 1990.
On ne part pas, on ne revient pas. Paris, Des Femmes, 1991.

Television Play: *La Nuit miraculeuse*, with Ariane Mnouchkine, 1989.

Radio Play: *Amour d'une délicatesse*, 1982.

Other

L'Exil de James Joyce; ou, L'Art du remplacement. Paris, Grasset, 1968; as *The Exile of James Joyce*, New York, Lewis, 1972; London, Calder, 1976.

Les États-Unis d'aujourd'hui, with Pierre Dommergues and Mariane Debouzy. Paris, Colin, 1969.
Prénoms de personne. Paris, Seuil, 1974.
La Jeune Née, with Catherine Clément. Paris, Union Générale d'Editions, 1977; as *The Newly Born Woman*, Minneapolis, University of Minnesota Press, and Manchester, Manchester University Press, 1986.
La Venue à l'Écriture, with Madeleine Gagnon and Annie Leclerc. Paris, Union Générale d'Editions, 1977.
Rykiel, with Madeleine Chapsal and Sonia Rykiel, edited by Daniele Flis. Paris, Herscher, 1985.
Entre l'Écriture. Paris, Des Femmes, 1986.
L'Heure de Clarice Lispector. Paris, Des Femmes, 1989; as *Reading with Clarice Lispector*, London, Harvester Wheatsheaf, and Minneapolis, University of Minnesota Press, 1990.
"Coming to Write" and Other Essays, edited by Deborah Jenson. Cambridge, Massachusetts, Harvard University Press, 1991.
Readings: The Poetics of Blanchot, Joyce, Kafka, Kleist, Lispector, and Tsvetayeva. Minneapolis, University of Minnesota Press, 1991.
The Ladder of Writing. New York, Columbia University Press, 1992.

*

Critical Studies: interview by Christiane Makward, in *Sub-Stance* (Santa Barbara, California), Autumn 1976; "Cixous and Gertrude Stein" by Anna Gibbs, in *Meanjin* (Parkville, Victoria), September 1979; "Cixous' Exorbitant Texts" by Brian Duren, in *Sub-Stance* (Santa Barbara, California), 10, 1981; "Writing and Body: Toward an Understanding of *L'écriture féminine*" by Ann Rosalind Jones, in *French Studies* (Oxford), Summer 1981; "Introduction to Hélène Cixous's 'Castration or Decapitation?'" by Annette Kuhn, in *Signs* (Durham, North Carolina), Autumn 1981; "Portrait of Dora: Freud's Case History as Reviewed by Hélène Cixous" by Martha Noel Evans, in *Sub-Stance* (Santa Barbara, California), 11, 1982; "Amazons and Mothers? Monique Wittig, Hélène Cixous and Theories of Women's Writing" by Diane Griffin Crowder, in *Contemporary Literature* (Madison, Wisconsin), Summer 1983; Cixous issue of *Boundary 2*, Winter 1984; *Hélène Cixous: Writing the Feminine* by Verena Andermatt Conley, Lincoln, University of Nebraska Press, 1984; "I Want Vulva! Cixous and the Poetics of the Body" by Vivian Kogan, in *Esprit Créateur* (Baton Rouge, Louisiana), Summer 1985; "Jean Cocteau and Hélène Cixous" by Judith G. Miller, in *Drama, Sex and Politics*, edited by James Redmond, Cambridge, Cambridge University Press, 1985; "Cixous: An Imaginary Utopia" by Toril Moi, in *Sexual/Textual Politics*, London, Methuen, 1985; "Hélène Cixous's *Portrait de Dora*: The Unseen and the Un-Scene," in *Theater Journal* (Madison, Wisconsin), October 1985, and "Mistranslation: *Vivre l'Orange*," in *Sub-Stance* (Santa Barbara, California), 16, 1987, both by Sharon Willis; "Hélène Cixous and North African Origin: Writing *L'Orange*" by Deborah W. Carpenter, in *Revue Celfan/Celfan Review* (Philadelphia), November 1986; *Writing Differences*, edited by Susan Sellers, New York, St. Martin's Press, and Milton Keynes, Open University Press, 1988; "The Mystic Aspect of *l'écriture féminine*: Hélène Cixous' *Vivre l'Orange*" by Anu Aneja, in *Qui Parle* (Berkeley, California), Spring 1989; "The Reverse Side of a Portrait: The Dora of Freud and Cixous" by Rosette C. Lamont, and "In Search of a Feminist Theater: *Portrait of Dora*" by Jeannette Laillou Savona, both in *Feminine Focus: The New Women Playwrights*, Oxford, Oxford University

Press, 1989; "History and Hysteria: Writing the Body in *Portrait of Dora* and *Signs of Life*" by Ann Wilson, in *Modern Drama* (Downsview, Ontario), March 1989; *The Body and the Text: Hélène Cixous, Reading and Teaching*, London, Harvester Wheatsheaf, 1990.

*   *   *

Hélène Cixous is one of the primary champions of *l'écriture féminine*, within the French feminist literary movement. She shares the effort to promote "feminine writing" with other major theorists, such as Luce Irigaray, Monique Wittig (*q.v.*), and Julia Kristeva.

Cixous resents being labelled a "feminist" because of the term's negative connotation in France, and she rejects the role imposed upon her to support feminist analytical discourse, having claimed, "I do not have to produce theory." Cixous places herself on the side of poetic freedom — not a poetry in opposition to prose, but in subversion of a language which would reduce and flatten experience. To Cixous, poetry is necessary to social transformation, as it confers the power to deconstruct the coded, systematic tyranny of ordinary language. Despite her reluctance to wear the feminist label, Cixous's writing is strongly political. Her continual commitment to discussing women's issues in France, through both teaching and publishing, as well as the very nature of her criticism of patriarchal literary hegemony, demonstrates her position within the feminist movement.

Anglophone readers were first introduced to Cixous in 1972 with the publication of her doctoral thesis, *The Exile of James Joyce*. It was during the 1970s that Cixous's explorations first focused on and publicly challenged the definition of femininity, feminism, and the written text, on both political and cultural fronts in France. She is known to anglophone readers mainly through journal articles and because of her "theoretical" writing, such as "The Laugh of the Medusa" and *The Newly Born Woman*. Although Cixous writes primarily fiction, most of it has not yet been translated into English.

L'écriture féminine has evolved mainly from the tenet that Western thought has been based on a systematic suppression of women's experience. This suppression is evidenced in literary works by the phallocentric nature of masculinist discourse. *L'écriture féminine* proposes to overthrow patriarchal ideologies by evolving new female discourses, rooted in the belief that women's psyche is completely different from men's and that difference is based in psychosexual specificity. Much of *l'écriture féminine* borrows from the theoretical frameworks set out by Jacques Lacan, Roland Barthes, and Jacques Derrida, who were the main teachers of the new generation of French female theorists. Such academic borrowing is not without criticism of its sources; *l'écriture féminine* refashions many of the ideas to its own ends. Thus, one of the main ideas promoted by feminists to overthrow masculinist privilege is the notion of *jouissance*, slightly expanded from Barthes's original, "The Pleasure of the Text," to include a feminine specificity. This anti-phallic writing posits the capability of finding pleasure in many places, not only within the text, but within the source of that text, in this case being the woman's own body.

Cixous promotes a body-centered form of literary revolt: that women must discover and express the libidinal impulses inherent in their own unconscious in order to understand the nature of what has been repressed in them. This discovery begins in the body, with the genital and libidinal differences women have from men. Women's writing does not compete with men's writing, for it is motivated by a completely different experience of bodily expressiveness: ". . . it's with her body

that she vitally supports the 'logic' of her speech. Her flesh speaks true. She lays herself bare. In fact, she physically materializes what she's thinking; she signifies it with her body. In a certain way she *inscribes* what she's saying." ("Medusa")

Cixous makes an effort in all her writing to expose the tyranny of what she calls "patriarchal binary thought." This is a system of oppositions in which a hierarchy emerges, painting the "feminine" side as the negative, the powerless: Activity/Passivity; Sun/Moon; Culture/Nature; Day/Night; Father/Mother. According to Cixous, this system invariably collapses in death, for in order for one term to acquire meaning, the other must be destroyed. Thus, the Female is perpetually placed in the role of Other or of Non-existent. Against this binary, Cixous proposes a scheme of multiple, heterogeneous *différence*, by which identity is measured along a continuum. She uses this as part of her effort to move, not exclusively to a feminine writing, but to what she suggests might someday be called "bisexual writing."

Cixous considers writing to be both a personal and a political liberating gesture by which women can finally reawaken to themselves, wrest language away from men, and transform it to their own uses. She is concerned with language as the locus for the basic dynamic of oppression. While masculine logic promotes a discourse of clarity and unity, a monolith, Cixous insists that "there will not be one feminine discourse."

In collaboration with such major directors as Ariane Mnouchkine and Simone Benmussa, Cixous has also explored the possibilities of drama. This genre has allowed her not only the freedom to explore the body-presence but, as with *Portrait de Dora* (*Portrait of Dora*), the opportunity to constitute woman as speaking subject. Cixous robs Freud of the monolithic certainty of his narrative, "Fragment of an Analysis of a Case of Hysteria," not only by allowing Dora to speak for herself, but also by inviting all voices within the story to battle over the reconstruction of the event. Not only is Dora the emotional locus of that struggle, but her body is presented as the bartered object by which men, especially Freud, gain legitimacy for their actions.

Cixous anticipates a theater which will challenge gender roles rather than reinscribe women as silent objects of exchange. In her dramatic manifesto, "Aller à la Mer," originally published in *Le Monde* (April 1977), Cixous rejects a theater "which is built according to the dictates of male fantasy . . . (in which) it is always necessary for a woman to die in order for the play to begin." Cixous equates this kind of theater-going with going to her own funeral. She longs for a theater in which "Woman is Whole, where instead of being acted out, life is lived." She explains:

If I go to the theatre now, it must be a political gesture, with a view to changing, with the help of other women, its means of production and expression. It is high time that women gave back to the theatre its fortunate position, its *raison d'être* and what makes it different — the fact that there it is possible to get across the living, breathing, speaking body.

Cixous's writing promotes *l'écriture féminine* through its own example. The flow of words, the *jouissance* of expression exemplify her own fascination with language, as well as the way in which it affects her personally and physically. However, it is not merely textual pleasure which fuels her to write but the conviction that through writing she can assert the feminine voice and subvert the forces which so easily relegate women to silence.

—Sabrina Prielaida

———

CLAUS, Hugo (Maurice Julien). Belgian. Born in Bruges, 5 April 1929. Educated at schools in Eke, Aalbeke, Kortrijk, Deinze, and Ghent. Married Elly Overzier in 1955; one son. Worked as a housepainter, agricultural worker, actor, etc., then full-time writer: editor, *Tijd en Mens*, 1949-55, and *Nieuw Vlaams Tijdshrift*. Recipient: Krijn prize, 1951; Lugné-Poë prize (France), 1955; Triennial Belgian State prize, for drama, 1955, 1967, 1973, for verse, 1971; Roland Holst prize, 1965; Huygens prize, 1979; Prize for Dutch Letters, 1986. Address: Kasteelstraat 166, 9000 Ghent, Belgium.

PUBLICATIONS

Plays

De getuigen [The Witnesses] (produced Brussels, 1955).
Een bruid in de morgen (produced Rotterdam, 1955). Antwerp, Ontwikkeling, and Amsterdam, Bezige Bij, 1955; as *A Bride in the Morning* (produced New York, 1960).
Het lied van de moordenaar [The Song of the Murderer] (produced Rotterdam, 1957). Antwerp, Ontwikkeling, and Amsterdam, Bezige Bij, 1957.
Dantons dood, adaptation of a play by Georg Büchner. Amsterdam, Bezige Bij, 1958.
Suiker [Sugar]. Antwerp, Ontwikkeling, and Amsterdam, Bezige Bij, 1958.
Mama, kijk, zonder handen! [Look, Ma, No Hands] (produced Brussels, 1960). Amsterdam, Bezige Bij, 1959.
Het mes [The Knife] (scenario). Amsterdam, Bezige Bij, 1961.
De dans van de reiger [The Heron's Dance]. Amsterdam, Bezige Bij, 1962; adapted as screenplay, 1966.
Uilenspiegel, adaptation of a work by Charles de Coster (produced Leiden, 1965). Amsterdam, Bezige Bij, 1965.
Thyestes, adaptation of the play by Seneca (produced 1966). Amsterdam, Bezige Bij, and Antwerp, Contact, 1966.
Het Goudland [The Gold Country], adaptation of a novel by Henrik Conscience (produced Antwerp, 1966). Amsterdam, Bezige Bij, 1966.
Acht toneelstukken [Eight Stageplays]. Amsterdam, Bezige Bij, 1966.
De vijanden [The Enemies] (screenplay). Amsterdam, Bezige Bij, 1967.
Masscheroen (produced Knokke, 1967). Amsterdam, Bezige Bij, 1968.
Wrrraak!, adaptation of the play *The Revenger's Tragedy* by Cyril Tourneur (produced Eindhoven, 1968). Amsterdam, Bezige Bij, 1968.
Morituri (as *Hyperion en het geweld*, produced Brussels, 1968). Amsterdam, Bezige Bij, 1968.
Motet (produced Ghent, 1969).
Reconstructie [Reconstruction] (libretto), with others (produced Amsterdam, 1969). Amsterdam, Bezige Bij, 1969.

Vrijdag (produced Amsterdam, 1969). Amsterdam, Bezige Bij, 1969; as *Friday*, London, Davis Poynter, 1972; in *Four Plays for the Theatre by Hugo Claus*, 1990.
Tand om tand [A Tooth for a Tooth]. Amsterdam, Bezige Bij, 1970.
Het leven en de werken van Leopold II: 29 taferelen uit de Belgische oudheid. Amsterdam, Bezige Bij, 1970; as *The Life and Works of Leopold II: 29 Scenes from Belgian Antiquity*, in *An Anthology of Contemporary Belgian Plays 1970–1982*, edited by David Willinger, New York, Whitston, 1984.
De Spaanse hoer [The Spanish Whore], adaptation of *La Celestina* by Fernando de Rojas (produced Eindhoven, 1970). Amsterdam, Bezige Bij, 1970.
Interieur [Interior], from his novel *Omtrent Deedee* [About Deedee] (produced Amsterdam, 1971). Amsterdam, Bezige Bij, 1971.
Oedipus, adaptation of the play by Seneca. Amsterdam, Bezige Bij, 1971.
De vossejacht [The Foxhunt], adaptation of the play *Volpone* by Ben Jonson. Amsterdam, Bezige Bij, 1972.
Blauw blauw [Blue Blue], adaptation of the play *Private Lives* by Noël Coward. Amsterdam, Bezige Bij, 1973.
Pas de deux. Amsterdam, Bezige Bij, 1973.
Thuis [Home]. Amsterdam, Bezige Bij, 1975; as *Back Home*, in *An Anthology of Contemporary Belgian Plays, 1970–1982*, edited by David Willinger, New York, Whitston, 1984.
Orestes, adaptation of the play by Euripides. Amsterdam, Bezige Bij, 1976.
Jessica! Amsterdam, Ziggurat, 1977.
Het huis van Labdakos [The House of Labdakos], adaptation of a scenario by Frans Marijnen. Amsterdam, Bezige Bij, 1977.
Phaedra, adaptation of the play by Seneca. Amsterdam, Bezige Bij, 1980.
Ontmoetingen met Corneille en Karel Appel [Meetings with Corneille and Karel Appel]. Antwerp, Manteau, 1980.
Het haar van de hond. Amsterdam, Bezige Bij, 1982; as *The Hair of the Dog*, in *Four Works for the Theatre by Hugo Claus*, 1990.
Serenade. Amsterdam, Bezige Bij, 1984; in English, in *Four Works for the Theatre by Hugo Claus*, 1990.
Blindeman [Blind Man]. Amsterdam, Bezige Bij, 1985.
Georg Faust (libretto), music by Konrad Boehmer. Amsterdam, Bezige Bij, 1985.
Gilles!, adapted from his novel *Gilles en de nacht* (produced Brussels, 1988). Antwerp, Nioba, 1988.
Toneel (vol. 1 includes *Acht toneelstukken*; vol. 2 includes *Morituri*; *Vrijdag*; *Tand om tand*; *Het leven en de werken van Leopold II*; *Interieur*; *Pas de deux*; vol. 3 includes *Blauw blauw*; *Thuis*; *Jessica!*; *Het haar van de hond*; *Serenade*; *Blindeman*). Amsterdam, Bezige Bij, 3 vols., 1988–91.
Het schommelpaard. Amsterdam, Bezige Bij, 1988.
Four Works for the Theatre by Hugo Claus (includes *The Temptation*; *Friday*; *Serenade*; *The Hair of the Dog*), edited by David Willinger. New York, CASTA, 1990.
The Temptation, adapted from his novel *De verzoeking*. Included in *Four Works for the Theatre by Hugo Claus*, 1990.

Fiction

De metsiers. Brussels, Manteau, 1950; as *The Duck Hunt*, New York, Random House, 1965; as *Sister of Earth*, London, Panther, 1966.
De hondsdagen [The Dog Days]. Amsterdam, Bezige Bij, 1952.

Natuurgetrouw: Schetsen, verhalen, fabels . . . [True to Life: Sketches, Stories, Fables . . .].   Amsterdam, Bezige Bij, 1954.
De koele minnaar [The Cool Lover].   Amsterdam, Bezige Bij, 1956.
De zwarte keizer [The Black King].   Amsterdam, Bezige Bij, 1958.
Omtrent Deedee [About Deedee].   Amsterdam, Bezige Bij, 1963.
De verwondering [Wonderment].   Amsterdam, Bezige Bij, 1963.
Het jaar van de kreeft [The Year of the Cancer].   Amsterdam, Bezige Bij, 1972.
Schaamte [Shame].   Amsterdam, Bezige Bij, 1972.
Gebed om geweld: verhalen [Calling to Violence: Stories]. Amsterdam, Bezige Bij, 1972.
In het wijde westen [In the Wide West].   Amsterdam, Rap, 1973.
Aan de evenaar [At the Equator].   Amsterdam, Rap/Bezige Bij, 1973.
De groene ridder en de paladijnen [The Green Knight and the Paladins].   Amsterdam, Rap, 1973.
Jessica! Amsterdam, Bezige Bij, 1977.
De vluchtende Atalanta [Atalanta in Flight].   Antwerp, Pink Editions, 1977.
Het verlangen [Longing].   Amsterdam, Bezige Bij, 1978.
De verzoeking [The Temptation].   Antwerp, Pink Editions, 1980.
Het verdriet van België.   Amsterdam, Bezige Bij, 1983; as *The Sorrow of Belgium*, London, Viking, and New York, Pantheon, 1990.
Een overtreding [An Offence].   Amstelveen, AMO, 1985.
De mensen hiernaast: verhalen [The People Next Door: Stories].   Amsterdam, Bezige Bij, 1985.
Een zachte vernieling [A Gentle Destruction].   Amsterdam, Bezige Bij, 1988.
Gilles en de nacht [Gilles and the Night].   Amsterdam, Bezige Bij, 1989.

Verse

Kleine reeks [Small Series].   Moeskroen, Aurora, 1947.
Registreren [Registration].   Ostend, Carillon, 1948.
Zonder vorm van proces [Without Trial].   Brussels, Draak, 1950.
De blijde en onvoorziene week [The Happy, Unexpected Week], illustrated by Karel Appel.   Paris, Cobra, 1950.
Tancredo infrasonic.   The Hague, Stols, 1952.
Een huis dat tussen nacht en morgen staat [A House Between Night and Morning].   Antwerp, De Sikkel, 1953.
Paal en perk [Limits].   The Hague, De Sikkel, 1955.
De Oostakkerse gedichten [Poems from Oostakker]. Amsterdam, Bezige Bij, 1955.
Een geverfde ruiter [A Painted Horseman].   Amsterdam, Bezige Bij, 1961.
Love Song, illustrated by Karel Appel.   New York, Abrams, 1963.
Oog om oog [An Eye for an Eye], photographs by Sanne Sannes.   Amsterdam, Bezige Bij, 1964.
Gedichten [Poems].   Amsterdam, Bezige Bij, 1965.
Relikwie [Relic].   Antwerp, Monas, 1967.
Heer Everzwijn [Lord Boar].   Amsterdam, Bezige Bij, 1970.
Van horen zeggen [On Hearsay].   Amsterdam, Bezige Bij, 1970.
Dag, jij [Hello, Love].   Amsterdam, Bezige Bij, 1971.
Figuratief [Figurative].   Amsterdam, Bezige Bij, 1973.
Het Jansenisme [Jansenism].   Antwerp, Pink Editions, 1977.

De wangebeden [No-Good Prayers].   Amsterdam, Bezige Bij, 1977.
Van de koude grond [Outdoor Grown].   Antwerp, Ziggurat, 1978.
Het teken van de hamster.   Antwerp, Lotus, 1979; as *The Sign of the Hamster*, Leuven, Leuvense Schrijversaktie, 1986.
Gedichten 1969–1978 [Poems].   Amsterdam, Bezige Bij, 1979.
Claustrum: 222 knittelverzen [Claustrum: 222 Doggerel Verses].   Antwerp, Pink Editions, 1980.
Dertien manieren om een fragment van Alechinsky te zien [Thirteen Ways of Looking at a Fragment of Alechinsky's].   Antwerp, Ziggurat, 1980.
Jan de Lichte [Jan the Light One].   Antwerp, Ziggurat, 1981.
Almanak: 366 knittelverzen [Almanach: 366 Doggerel Verses].   Amsterdam, Bezige Bij, 1982.
Alibi.   Amsterdam, Bezige Bij, 1985.
Een weerzinwekkend bezoek [A Disgusting Visit].   Aalst, De Gele Limonade, 1985.
Wyckaert, with Freddy de Vree.   Tielt, Lannoo, 1986.
Bewegen [Moving], photographs by Willy Legendre. Bruges, van de Wiele, 1986.
Selected Poems 1953–1973; edited by Theo Hermans, translated by Hermans, Paul Brown, and Peter Nifmeijer. Portree, Scotland, Aquila, 1986.
Gedichten van Hugo Claus [Poems by Hugo Claus] (series).   Amstelveen, AMO, 22 Pamphlets, 1986–90.
Evergreens.   Amstelveen, AMO, 1986.
Het verschijnsel [The Apparition].   Amstelveen, AMO, 1986.
Sporen [Traces].   Wommelgen, Den Gulden Engel, 1987.
Mijn honderd gedichten [My Hundred Poems].   Amsterdam, Bezige Bij, 1987.
Sonnetten [Sonnets].   Amsterdam, Bezige Bij, 1987.
Voor Pierre [For Pierre].   Amstelveen, AMO, 1987.
Hymen.   Amsterdam and Amstelveen, SUD/De 23 Gratiën/AMO, 1987.

Other

Over het werk van Corneille [On the Work of Corneille].   Amsterdam, Martinet en Michels, 1951.
Karel Appel, schilder.   Amsterdam, Strengholt, 1964; as *Karel Appel, Painter*, Strengholt, 1962; London, Thames and Hudson, 1963.
De man van Tollund: schilderijen 1962–1963 [The Tollund Man: Paintings].   Rotterdam, Galerie Delta, 1963.
Louis Paul Boon.   Brussels, Manteau, 1964.
De schilderijen van Roger Raveel [The Paintings of Roger Raveel].   Amsterdam, Galerie Espace, 1965.
Het landschap [The Landscape] (on Maurice Wyckaert).   Amsterdam, Galerie M.A.S., 1965.
De avonturen van Belgman I [The Adventures of Belgman I] (strip cartoon), drawings by Hoguké.   Antwerp, Standaard, 1967.
Schola Nostra (as Dorothea van Male).   Amsterdam, Bezige Bij, 1971.
Mexico vandaag: land van Posada [Mexico Today, Land of Posada], with Freddy de Vree.   Brussels, BRT, 1982.
Beelden [Images].   Haarlem, Becht, 1988.
De zwaardvis [The Swordfish].   N.p., Stichting Collective Propaganda van het Nederlandse Boek, 1989.
Kort dagboek [Short Diary].   Amstelveen, AMO, 1989.
Perte totale [Total Loss].   Amstelveen, AMO, 1989.

Translator, *Onder het melkwoud* [Under Milkwood], by Dylan Thomas.   Amsterdam, Bezige Bij, 1958.

Translator, *Als een jonge hond* [Portrait of the Artist as a Young Dog], by Dylan Thomas. Rotterdam, Donker, 1958.

Translator, *Het hooglied* [The Song of Solomon]. Antwerp, Pink Editions, 1982.

Translator, *Lysistrata*, by Aristophanes. Antwerp, Pink Editions, 1982.

Translator, *Hamlet*, by Shakespeare. Berchem, Dedalus, 1986.

Translator, *In Kolonos* [Oedipus in Kolonos], by Sophocles. Amsterdam, Bezige Bij, 1986.

Translator, with Freddy de Vree, *De anderehand* [The Other Hand], by Pierre Alechinsky. Amsterdam, Meulenhoff, 1987.

*

Critical Studies: *Claus-Reading* by Paul Claes, Antwerp, Manteau, 1984; "Hugo Claus' *The Temptation* and Flemish Mysticism," in *Sacred Theatre*, edited by Daniel Gerould, Bettina Knapp, and Jane House, New York, n.p., 1989, and "Introducing Hugo Claus," in *Western European Stages*, Spring 1990, both by David Willinger.

* * *

As poet, novelist, playwright, translator, scriptwriter, theatre director, filmmaker, and painter, Hugo Claus is one of the most versatile and prolific figures on the contemporary Dutch cultural scene, bringing to each of his manifold activities the same restless energy, inventiveness, and cosmopolitan erudition, together with a shrewd feel for publicity and commercial appeal.

His experimentalist *De Oostakkerse gedichten* (Poems from Oostakker), with their abundance of primitive, often grotesque nature images, have, like the work of many contemporaries, links with the painting of the Cobra group, but a powerfully individual voice is already unmistakable. No less striking than the linguistic and rhythmical virtuosity of these poems is their urgent physicality: few poets in Dutch can match Claus's evocation, at his best, of an animal eroticism which alternates with bleakness and futility. In subsequent collections the discovery of T. S. Eliot and above all Ezra Pound leads Claus to seek a more sophisticated, mythically rooted synthesis of instinct and reason, as in the long, canto-like *Het teken van de hamster* (The Sign of the Hamster). Much of his later poetry is more outward-looking and explicit in its social criticism and political allegiances, the latter always more instinctively anti-authoritarian and individualist than systematic. A collection of accomplished sonnets showed his mastery of a stricter verse form than he has been wont to use.

A dense, sometimes cryptic allusiveness also characterises much of Claus's varied output of fiction, and works like the nightmarish collage *De verwondering* (Wonderment) in which a Flemish school teacher journeys back through a private inferno to a National Socialist past, have been criticised as well as admired for their baroqueness and (over)arch allegorising. Nevertheless, works as diverse as his Faulkner-inspired debut, *De metsiers* (The Duck Hunt or Sister of Earth), with its alternating narrative, *Schaamte* (Shame), an obliquely understated commentary on the moral bankruptcy of modern Western man set in the Caribbean during the filming of Christ's passion, and the more conventional bestseller *Het jaar van de kreeft* (The Year of the Cancer), based on a love affair between the author and a well-known actress, have established Claus as a considerable novelist. Of his more recent work, the novellas *De verzoeking* (The Temptation) and *Gilles en de nacht* (Gilles

and the Night), monologues by a decrepit nun and the historical figure of Gilles de Rais respectively, have both been successfully adapted for the stage. These "chamber" works are as impressive in their way as Claus's magnum opus, *Het verdriet van België* (*The Sorrow of Belgium*), an episodic but gripping account of occupation and collaboration in World War II Flanders seen through the eyes of a young boy at a Catholic boarding school similar to the one the author himself attended.

It is as a playwright that Claus's reputation is, at least at present, most secure: his stagecraft and gift for dialogue have produced a dramatic oeuvre unmatched in this century in an area which cannot boast of an abundance of indigenous modern theatre. Highlights of his wide-ranging production, in which the early influences of Antonin Artaud and Samuel Beckett are apparent without being obtrusive, are the poignant melodrama *Suiker* (Sugar), set among migrant agricultural workers in France, the tragi-comic family dramas *Een bruid in de morgen* (*A Bride in the Morning*), *De dans van de reiger* (The Heron's Dance), and *Vrijdag* (*Friday*) (the last successfully performed in London in an adaptation by Christopher Logue), an epic debunking of King Leopold II's colonial exploits in the Congo, and classical adaptations, *Thyestes*, *Oedipus*, *Phaedra*, *Blindeman*, and *In Kolonos*.

Hailed as a prodigy on his first emergence in the 1950s, Claus has been accused of profligacy of talent and on occasion wilful mystification. Yet despite, or perhaps partly by virtue of, the intense Flemishness of his language, imagery, and themes (central among them his love-hate relationship with Belgium, whose provincialism and religious bigotry in particular he mercilessly evokes and castigates), he has received wide public as well as critical acclaim throughout the Low Countries.

Rather than "dig one plot" like some of his (especially Northern) contemporaries, Claus prefers unashamedly to "flit," attaching as much value to the creative process as to the finished artefact. Such adventurousness, with the challenges and risks it implies, may account for Claus's ability repeatedly to surprise, disturb, and, at his best, enthral.

—Paul Vincent

———

CONDE (Abellán), Carmen. Has also written as Florentina del Mar. Spanish. Born in Cartagena, Murcia, 15 August 1907. Educated at the Escuela Normal, Albacete, degree in pedagogy. Married Antonio Oliver Belmas (died 1968) in 1931. Co-founder, *El Gallo Crisis* magazine. Recipient: Elisendo de Montcada prize, 1953; Simon Bolivar international poetry prize, 1954; Primo de Rivera, 1967; Seville Athenaeum prize, 1980; National prize, for children's and teenage literature, 1987. Elected to the Spanish Royal Academy, 1978. Address: c/o Plaza & Janés, Virgen de Guadalupe 21–33, 08950 Esplugas de Llobregat, Barcelona, Spain.

PUBLICATIONS

Verse

Brocal. Madrid, Cuadernos Literarios, 1929.
Júbilos. Murcia, Sudeste, 1934.

Pasión del verbo. Madrid, Marsiega, 1944.
Honda memoria de mí. Madrid, Romo, 1944.
Ansia de la gracia. Madrid, Adonais, 1945.
Mujer sin Edén. Madrid, Jura, 1947; as *Woman Without Eden,* translated by Alexis Levitin and José R. de Armas, Miami, Universal, 1986.
Sea la luz. Madrid, Mensaje, 1947.
Mi fin en el viento. Madrid, Adonais, 1947.
Iluminada tierra. Private printed, 1951.
Vivientes de los siglos. Privately printed, 1954.
Mi fin en el viento. Madrid, Adonais, 1957.
Los monólogos de la hija. Privately printed, 1959.
En un mundo de fugitivos. Buenos Aires, Losada, 1960.
Derribado Arcángel. Madrid, Revista de Occidente, 1960.
En la tierra de nadie. Murcia, Laurel del Sureste, 1960.
Los poemas del Mar Menor. Murcia, Catedra Saavedra Fajardo/Universidad de Murcia, 1962.
Su voz le doy a la noche. Privately printed, 1962.
Viejo venís y florido . . . (as Florentina del Mar). Alicante, Caja de Ahorros del Sureste, 1963.
Obra poética de Carmen Conde, 1929–1966. Madrid, Biblioteca Nueva, 1967.
A este lado de la eternidad. Madrid, Biblioteca Nueva, 1970.
Corrosión. Madrid, Biblioteca Nueva, 1975.
Cita con la vida. Madrid, Biblioteca Nueva, 1976.
Días por la tierra: antología incompleta. Madrid, Nacional, 1977.
El tiempo es un río lentísimo de fuego. Barcelona, Ediciones 29, 1978.
La noche oscura del cuerpo. Madrid, Biblioteca Nueva, 1980.
Desde nunca. Barcelona, Rio Nuevo, 1982.
Derramen su sangre las sombras. Madrid, Torremozas, 1983.
Del obligado dolor. Madrid, Almarabu, 1984.
Brocal, y Poemas a María, edited by Rosario Hiriart. Madrid, Biblioteca Nueva, 1984.
La calle de los balcones azules. Barcelona, Plaza & Janés, 1985.
Cráter. Madrid, Biblioteca Nueva, 1985.
Hermosos días en China. Madrid, Torremozas, 1985.
Antología poética, edited by Rosario Hiriart. Madrid, Espasa-Calpe, 1985.
Canciones de nana y desvelo. Valladolid, Miñon, 1985.
Memoria puesta en olvido: antología personal. Madrid, Torremozas, 1987.
Una palabra tuya. Madrid, Torremozas, 1988.

Fiction

Vidas contra su espejo (as Florentina del Mar). Madrid, Alhambra, 1944.
Soplo que va y no vuelve (as Florentina del Mar). Madrid, Alhambra, 1944.
En manos del silencio. Barcelona, Plaza & Janés, 1950.
Mientras los hombres mueren. Milan, Cisalpino, 1953.
Cobre. Madrid, Grifón, 1954.
Las oscuras raíces. Barcelona, Garbo, 1954.
La rambla. Madrid, Magisterio Español/Novelas y Cuentos, 1977.
Creció espesa la yerba. Barcelona, Planeta, 1979.
Soy la madre. Barcelona, Planeta, 1980.

Plays

Aladino (as Florentina del Mar). Madrid, Hesperia, 1945.
Belén. Madrid, ENAG, 1953.

A la estrella por la cometa, with Antonio Oliver. Madrid, Doncel, 1961.

Other

Por la escuela renovada. Valencia, Embajador Vich, 1931.
Doña Centenioto, gato salvaje (for children). Madrid, Alhambra, 1943.
Los enredos de Chismecita (for children; as Florentina del Mar). Madrid, Alhambra, 1943.
Don Juan de Austria (as Florentina del Mar). Madrid, Hesperia, 1943.
La amistad en la literatura española (as Florentina del Mar). Madrid, Alhambra, 1944.
Dios en la poesía española. Madrid, Alhambra, 1944.
La poesía ante la eternidad. Madrid, Alhambra, 1944.
El Cristo de Medinaceli (as Magdalena Noguera). Madrid, Alhambra, 1944.
Don Alvaro de Luna. Madrid, Hesperia, 1945.
El santuario del Pilar (as Magdalena Noguera). Madrid, Alhambra, 1945.
Cartas a Katherine Mansfield. Zaragoza, Doncel, 1948.
El escorial: una meditación más. Madrid, Raíz, 1948.
Mi libro de El Escorial. Valladolid, Colegio Mayor Universitario de Santa Cruz, 1949.
Obras escogidas. Madrid, Plenitud, 1949.
Juan Ramón Jiménez (as Florentina del Mar). Bilbao, Conferencias y Ensayos, 1952.
Empezando la vida: memorias de una infancia en Marruecos, 1914–1920. Tetuán, Morocco, Al-Motamid, 1955.
Jaguar puro inmarchito. Privately printed, 1963.
Acompañando a Francisca Sánchez: resumen de una vida junto a Rubén Darío. Managua, Unión, 1964.
Un pueblo que lucha y canta. Madrid, Nacional, 1967.
Menéndez Pidal. Madrid, Unión, 1969.
Gabriela Mistral. Madrid, Unión, 1970.
Cancionero de la enamorada. Avila, Torro de Granito, 1971.
El caballito y la luna (for children). Madrid, CVS, 1974.
Al encuentro de Santa Teresa. Murcia, Belmar, 1978.
Poesía ante el tiempo y la inmortalidad. Madrid, Real Academia, 1979.
Una niña oye su voz. Madrid, Escuela Española, 1979.
Un conejo soñador rompe con la tradición. Madrid, Escucla Española, 1979.
El mundo empieza fuera del mundo. Madrid, Escuela Española, 1979.
El Conde Sol. Madrid, Escuela Española, 1979.
Zoquetín y Martina (for children). Barcelona, Ediciones 29, 1979.
El monje y el pajarillo. Madrid, Escuela Española, 1980.
Cuentos para niños de buena fe. Madrid, Escuela Española, 1982.
Por el camino, viendo sus orillas (memoirs). Barcelona, Plaza & Janés, 3 vols., 1986.
Centenito. Madrid, Escuela Española, 1987.
Cuentos del romancero. Madrid, Escuela Española, 1987.
Cantando al amanecer. Madrid, Escuela Española, 1988.

Editor, *Poesía femenina española viviente.* Madrid, Anroflo, 1955.
Editor, *Once grandes poetisas americohispanas.* Madrid, Cultura Hispanica, 1967.
Editor, *Poesía femenina española, 1939–1950.* Barcelona, Bruguera, 1967.
Editor, *Antología de poesia amorosa contemporánea.* Barcelona, Bruguera, 1969.

Editor, *Poesía femenina española, 1950–1960.* Barcelona, Bruguera, 1971.

Editor, *Memoria puesta en el olvido.* Madrid, Torremozas, 1987.

*

Critical Studies: *Carmen Conde and the Sea* by Josefina Inclán, Miami, Universal, 1980; "Carmen Conde's *En la tierra de nadie*: A Journey Through Death and Solitude" by Bonnie M. Brown, in *Revista Review Interamericana* (San German, Puerto Rico), 12, 1982; "Twentieth-Century Hispanic Women Poets: An Introduction" by Maria Nowakowska Stycos, in *Revista Review Interamericana* (San German, Puerto Rico), 12, 1982; "The World Without End: Mythic and Linguistic Revision in Carmen Conde Abellán's *Mujer sin Edén*" by Judith C. Richards, in *Monographic Review/Revista Monografica* (Odessa, Texas), 6, 1990.

*   *   *

Although obliged to write secretly because of her mother's opposition, the Spanish writer Carmen Conde began to publish her first poems in the local newspaper while still in her teens. *Brocal* (Well-Stone), her first book, combines passion for the sea and for her future husband in prose poems much influenced by her admiration for Juan Ramón Jiménez and Gabriel Miró. This early work, along with poems and stories published in the periodical press before her marriage in 1931, is viewed by Conde as her "first period." Conde first visited Madrid and made contact with the literary world there in 1929, meeting poet Ernestina de Champourcín, her contemporary, and her idol, Jiménez (a friendship which continued until 1936, when Jiménez and his wife went into exile).

Conde identifies a second period in her poetry following her marriage to fellow poet Antonio Oliver in 1931, a time when she was totally absorbed by poetry and by vanguard experimentation. *Júbilos* (Jubilation) is the primary example of this period; traces of ultraism and surrealist touches are noticeable. Conde also worked with her husband to create the Public University of Cartagena (an enterprise ended by the civil war; it was finally reopened in 1981, with Conde as honorary president). Conde and her husband collaborated with vanguard poet Miguel Hernández and Ramon Sijé in founding the important review, *El Gallo Crisis.* Her first novel for adults, *Vidas contra su espejo*, was written in 1935 but remained unpublished for nearly a decade. Resembling the "pure" fiction of the Generation of 1927, it is lyric, abstract, passive, comprised primarily of meditations. The ambient of Levante and impressionistic prose style evoke writings of Gabriel Miró; major characters are aesthetes influenced by decadentism, and issues are primarily intellectual (the question of instinctual passion as opposed to an intellectual love).

In 1936, Conde received a grant from the Republic to continue her studies of pedagogy in France and Belgium (a project truncated by the outbreak of the civil war). The war changed her life in other ways: her husband fought in the Loyalist army, and both wrote for the Republican daily, *El Sol*, for which they were subsequently tried by Franco's military tribunals. *Mientras los hombres mueren* (While Men Die) was written during a time of intense suffering for what the war was destroying, under the conviction that such suffering is futile. Conde and her husband were obliged to use pseudonyms for a number of years in order to continue publishing. Conde's literary production changed as a result of the war, suffusing her work with pain and sorrow and a preoccupation with Truth,

especially as she saw old truths replaced by new as military and political fortunes changed.

Ansia de la gracia (Desire for Grace), one of her most important collections, marks the resumption of her poetic career; its major themes are love (love of life and fellow creatures) and destiny, cosmic identification and mystical longing, dialogue with nature and the Creator.

Mujer sin Edén (*Woman Without Eden*) is one of Conde's most significant and controversial works, a feminist rewriting of the biblical myth of the Fall from Grace in which Eve's side of the story is privileged and the image of oppressed women throughout history reappears in each of the five cantos. Conde incarnates herself in the symbolic Woman representing all the women of the world, who constantly laments woman's suffering but also creates an image of an eternal, transcendent body; she ends by demanding that the flaming sword of the angel that cast her out of Eden be turned against her womb so that she may cease bearing children who grow into men of violence, war, and hate.

Sea la luz (Let There Be Light) and *Mi fin en el viento* (My Purpose in the Wind) both treat the need for a mystical dying to oneself, as well as the topic of physical death, the great paradox of destiny, death and resurrection, darkness into light. Nature reappears: the poet's process of soulful identification with nature whereby body and spirit are detached is expressed through a favorite Conde image, the archangels. Love of nature also inspires *Iluminada tierra* (Lighted Land) expressed through a dialogue with God. *Derribado Arcángel* (Fallen Archangel) is especially concerned with the conflict between good and evil, while *En un mundo de fugitivos* (In a World of Fugitives) brings together poems written during the years of the civil war as well as the period 1939–57, and expresses the poet's sense of identification with the losers.

Some of Conde's poetry of the 1960s belongs to the "social" literature of the 1950s and 1960s in Spain, in which covert opposition to the regime is conveyed via a concentration on injustice, economic exploitation, and inequities, but personal and religious concerns prevent complete *engagement*. Growing recognition of Conde's importance as a poet led to publication of her *Obra poética* in 1967, which was awarded the National prize for literature. The death of her husband in 1968 was not alleviated by her literary success; *A este lado de la eternidad* (This Side of Eternity) expresses her profound grieving. *Corrosión* continues the poet's exploration of the cosmic struggle between death and life.

Conde's novels are less significant than her poetry, although she is skilled at maintaining narrative interest. The dramatic novel *En manos del silencio* (In the Hands of Silence) was considered especially audacious in its day with its treatment of themes usually censored by the Franco regime: guilty passion, incest, adultery. A "friend of the family" seduces the wife and daughter of his associate and leaves both women pregnant. No one is held blameless, including the husband/father of the two women: all end tragically in death and madness. *Las oscuras raíces* (Dark Roots) treats the themes of destiny and all-consuming love, recreating the histories of four couples who have lived in the same accursed house by the sea, seemingly responsible for destroying the happiness of those who live inside, through ill-fated love triangles. *Creció espesa la yerba* (Thick Grows the Grass) presents a woman who returns years after a family trauma to confront a past incestuous relationship and recover her identity through the painful process of remembering a suppressed tragedy. The power of the past to change and even destroy the present appears in *La rambla* (The Avenue), in which a woman's discovery that her husband had killed a man two decades before destroys the foundations of their marriage. *Soy la madre* (I'm the Mother) further explores the power of past events, together with the themes of maternal love, rape, and *caciquismo* (bossism). Most of Conde's mature novels are in the realist vein, and show her at her best when drawing psychological portraits of women.

In 1978 Conde became the first woman ever elected to the Spanish Royal Academy. Now, with some 80 books to her credit, she remains active and creative. Although she has attempted various other genres, her major contribution and fame is as a poet. But poetry as a genre is relatively neglected, and women poets almost entirely so; thus despite being unquestionably the dean of living Spanish woman poets and rivaled only by Rafael Alberti among the masculine poets, Conde is largely unknown and surprisingly little studied.

—Janet Pérez

CONDÉ, Maryse (née Boucolon). Guadeloupian. Born in Pointe-à-Pitre, 11 February 1934. Educated at the Sorbonne, Paris, M.A., Ph.D. in comparative literature 1976. Married 1) Mamadou Conde in 1958 (divorced 1981), four children; 2) Richard Philcox in 1982. Instructor, École Normale Supérieure, Conakry, Guinea, 1960–64, Ghana Institute of Languages, Accra, 1966–68, and Lycée Charles de Gaulle, Saint Louis, Senegal, 1966–68; program producer, French Services of the BBC, London, 1968–70; assistant at Jussieu, 1970–72, lecturer at Nanterre, 1972–80, and chargé de cours at the Sorbonne, 1980–85, all University of Paris; editor, Présence Africaine publishers, Paris, 1972; program producer, Radio France Internationale, from 1980. Since 1990 Professor, University of California, Berkeley. Recipient: Fulbright scholar, 1985–86; Prix Littéraire de la Femme, 1986; Boucheron prize, 1986; Rockefeller Foundation fellowship, 1987; Guggenheim fellowship, 1987–88; Académie Française prize, 1988. Address: Montebello, 97170 Petit Bourg, Guadeloupe, French West Indies.

PUBLICATIONS

Fiction

Hérémakhonon. Paris, Union Générale d'Éditions, 1976; in English, Washington, D.C., Three Continents Press, 1982.
Une Saison à Rihata. Paris, Laffont, 1981; as *A Season in Rihata,* London, Heinemann, 1988.
Ségou: les murailles de terre. Paris, Laffont, 1984; as *Segu,* New York, Viking, 1987.
Ségou II: la terre en miettes. Paris, Laffont, 1985; as *The Children of Segu,* New York, Viking, 1989.
Pays mêlé; Nanna-ya. Paris, Hatier, 1985.
Moi, Tituba, sorcière noire de Salem. Paris, Mercure, 1986; as *I, Tituba, Black Witch of Salem,* Charlottesville, University Press of Virginia, 1992.
La Vie scélérate. Paris, Seghers, 1987; as *Tree of Life,* New York, Ballantine, 1992.
Traversée de la mangrove. Paris, Mercure, 1989.
No Woman No Cry. Paris, Le Serpent à Plumes, 1991.
Les Derniers Rois Mages. Paris, Mercure, 1992.

Plays

Dieu nous l'a donné (produced Fort de France, Martinique, 1973). Paris, Oswald, 1972.

Mort d'Oluwémi d'Ajumako (produced Haiti, 1975). Paris, Oswald, 1973.
Pension les Alizés (produced Pointe-à-Pitre, 1989). Paris, Mercure, 1988.
An Tan Revolisyon (produced Pointe-à-Pitre, 1989). Pointe-à-Pitre, Conseil Régional, 1989.
The Hills of Massabielle (produced New York, 1991).

Other

La Civilisation du bossale. Paris, L'Harmattan, 1978.
Le Profil d'une œuvre: cahier d'un retour au pays natal. Paris, Hatier, 1978.
La Parole des femmes: essai sur des romancières des Antilles de langue française. Paris, L'Harmattan, 1979.
Haïti chérie (for children). Paris, Bayard, 1987.
Guadeloupe, photographs by Jean Du Boisberranger. Paris, Richer/Hoa Qui, 1988.
Victor et les barricades (for children). Paris, Bayard, 1989.

Editor, *La Poésie antillaise.* Paris, Nathan, 1977.
Editor, *Le Roman antillais.* Paris, Nathan, 1977.
Editor, with Alain Rutil, *Bouquet de voix pour Guy Tirolien.* Pointe-à-Pitre, Jasor, 1990.
Editor, *L'Héritage de Caliban.* Pointe-à-Pitre, Jasor, 1992.

Translator, *De Christophe Colombe à Fidel Castro: l'histoire des Caraïbes, 1492–1969,* by Eric Williams. Paris, Présence Africaine, 1975.

*

Critical Studies: "Maryse Condé: Creative Writer in a Political World" by David K. Bruner, in *L'Esprit Créateur* (Baton Rouge, Louisiana), Summer 1977; "Buchi Emecheta and Maryse Condé: Contemporary Writing from Africa and the Caribbean" by Charlotte and David K. Bruner, in *World Literature Today* (Norman, Oklahoma), 59(1), 1985; "Maryse Condé and Africa: The Making of a Recalcitrant Daughter?" by Jonathan Ngaté, in *Current Bibliography on African Affairs* (Washington, D.C.), 19(1), 1986–87; "Reading Below the Belt: Sex and Sexuality in Françoise Éga and Maryse Condé" by Arthur Flannigan, in *French Review* (Santa Barbara, California), December 1988; "Maryse Condé's *Hérémakhonon*: A Triangular Structure of Alienation" by Arlette M. Smith, in *College Language Association Journal* (Atlanta, Georgia), September 1988; "'Je me suis réconcilié avec mon île'/'I have made peace with my island': An Interview with Maryse Condé" by VeVe A. Clark and Cecile Daheny, in *Callaloo* (Baltimore, Maryland), Winter 1989; "History, Identity and the Constitution of the Female Subject: Maryse Condé's *Tituba*" by Jeanne Snitgen, in *Matatu* (Frankfurt), 3(6), 1989.

*   *   *

The author of what Charles Larson in the *New York Times Book Review* (31 May 1987) called "the most significant historical novel about black Africa published in many a year," *Ségou* (*Segu*) is not by a native African as one might expect, but rather by the Guadeloupian writer Maryse Condé. She grew up on the island of Guadeloupe in the West Indies, was educated at the Sorbonne, lived for many years in West Africa (home of her ancestors), and in Paris, before returning to live on Guadeloupe in 1986. In 1990 she accepted a professorship at Berkeley, but maintains a home on her native island. The settings of her fiction range as widely as she has herself, but there is a clear movement in the course of her fiction from an exploration of her African roots to an acceptance and renewed interest in her homeland and her more immediate family.

This movement from what Arlette M. Smith has described as a "yearning for Africa as the depository of black culture" to an acceptance of the need to make peace with one's home and family is begun in Condé's first novel, *Hérémakhonon*. It is the story of Veronica, a young Guadeloupian woman, educated in Paris, who journeys to an unnamed country in West Africa to search for her history and a sense of belonging that will replace the alienation she has felt in both Guadeloupe and France. As a teenager she had had to leave Guadeloupe after having what was seen by bourgeois blacks on the island as a scandalous affair with a mulatto. In Paris she had a white lover, and felt very much apart from French culture. In Africa she becomes the mistress of Ibrahima Sory, the Minister of Defence, who is from an ancient, established family. Veronica has a romantic notion of Africa, and sees Sory as a symbol of the noble past who will introduce her to a culture that will make her feel complete. However, as often happens to those who search for answers in their roots, the past they seek is no longer so important to the present culture. Sory is more interested in the politics of an African country struggling to join the 20th century, open to Western ideas and exploitation. Only belatedly does Veronica allow herself to admit that Sory is a corrupt oppressor and murderer of his people. In the end she returns to France, having failed to find solace, but with a new understanding that she cannot look for spiritual answers in the past. This ending, so often seen negatively, can be read positively if we abandon the notion of it as a quest novel, and see it instead as an apprenticeship novel, where mistakes are useful to the character. As Arlette Smith explains, "Awareness of one's errors is in itself a gain."

Given that Veronica's spiritual growth in the novel follows Condé's own throughout her writing career, it is interesting that Condé has vigorously protested against the suggestion that Veronica is an autobiographical character. Still, Condé says she and Veronica share only their childhoods; otherwise Veronica is a "negative character, the opposite of myself: a person lacking in will power, energy, and dynamism . . ."

Condé's second novel, *Une Saison à Rihata* (*A Season in Rihata*), is also set in West Africa, and follows the misfortunes of a family in a country rife with corruption.

It is *Segu*, however, that has established Condé's reputation as a formidable writer. Written in two volumes, and set in the African kingdom of Segou (now in Mali) between 1797 and 1860, it is a massive and masterly undertaking. The story follows four sons of a royal family torn apart by various outside forces that assault the country, including Islam, Christianity, slave trade, and European colonization. Conversion, slavery, corruption, incest, murder, suicide, rape — many personal stories are set against the panorama of a larger history. Condé's research has been thorough and well-absorbed into the story; bits of historical documents are skillfully interwoven into the narrative. The exploitation and subjugation of women is particularly well drawn, and Condé's insistence on reserving authorial judgement and instead telling the stories objectively and dispassionately makes our own responses all the more powerful for being unforced.

Although criticised by some as simply a soap opera saga with little analysis of the underlying forces that drive the machine, *Segu* is nonetheless a powerful story, and a rich re-enactment of a little-known history.

Segu appears to have exorcised Condé's obsession with her African roots. Since then her fiction has been set in Guadeloupe (she returned to Guadeloupe to live in 1986), or in the United States and Barbados in *Moi, Tituba, sorcière noire de Salem* (*I, Tituba, Black Witch of Salem*). Condé heard about Tituba while teaching in the United States and was inspired to write about her story. Several authors have written about the Salem witch trials (most famously Arthur Miller in his play *The Crucible*), but few have shown particular interest in Tituba, a slave from Barbados who was arrested for witchcraft along with the white girls but was later released from jail rather than hanged. There are no certain records of what happened to her afterwards, the part of the story Condé found most interesting. She has created a moving tale about a woman caught in a culture clash: in Barbados Tituba was seen to have healing powers, which in Puritan New England were interpreted as witchcraft. In Condé's version of the story, after her release from jail Tituba manages to return to Barbados, only to be arrested and hung by English colonists putting down a rebellion on the island.

La Vie scélérate (*Tree of Life*) announces Condé's homecoming; the novel is set on Guadeloupe and is based on Condé's own family, as well as on West Indian historical events such as the use of West Indians to work on the Panama Canal in the early 20th century. It is to be hoped that this new yet familiar setting and new peace with her immediate past will continue to be inspiring territory for both Condé and her readers.

—Theresa Werner

———

CORREIA DA ROCHA, Adolfo. *See* **TORGA, Miguel.**

———

ĆOSIĆ, Dobrica. Serbian. Born in Velika Drenova, 29 December 1921. Political commissar for partisans during World War II; after the war held various Communist Party and cultural positions, and was a representative to the Yugoslav Parliament; member of the Central Committee, League of Communists of Serbia (expelled 1968). Since 1992 President, Federal Republic of Yugoslavia. Member of the editorial board, *Delo* literary periodical, 1955–63, and *Danas* literary monthly, 1961–63. Member, Serbian Academy of Sciences and Arts, 1977. Address: Federal Assembly, Belgrade, Serbia.

PUBLICATIONS

Fiction

Daleko je sunce. Belgrade, Prosveta, 1951; as *Far Away Is the Sun*, Belgrade, Jugoslavija, and New York, Praeger, 1963.
Koreni [Roots]. Belgrade, Prosveta, 1954.
Deobe [Divisions]. Belgrade, Prosveta, 1961.
Bajka [Fairytale]. Belgrade, Prosveta, 1966.
Vreme smrti. Belgrade, Prosveta, 4 vols., 1972–79; as *A Time of Death, Reach to Eternity*, and *South to Destiny*, New York, Harcourt Brace, 3 vols., 1978–81; as *This Land, This Time*, Harcourt Brace, 4 vols., 1983.
Grešnik [Sinner]. Belgrade, Beogradski Izdovačko-Grafički Zavod, 1985.

Otpadnik [Renegade]. Belgrade, Beogradski Izdovačko-Grafički Zavod, 1986.
Vernik [Believer]. Belgrade, Beogradski Izdovačko-Grafički Zavod, 1990.

Other

Sedam dona u Budimpešti [Seven Days in Budapest]. Belgrade, Nolit, 1957.
Akcija [Action]. Belgrade, Prosveta, 1965.
Sabrana dela [Collected Works]. Belgrade, Prosveta, 8 vols., 1966.
Moć i strepnje [Power and Foreboding]. N.p., n.p., 1972.
Stvarno i moguće [The Real and the Possible]. Rijeka, Keršovani, 1982.
The Historical Turning Point for the Serbian People: Interview to "Politika" Given by Mr. Dobrica Ćosić, Academician, Great Serbian Writer. Belgrade, n.p., 1991.

*

Critical Study: "Aspects of Nationalism in Dobrica Ćosić's Novel *A Time of Death*" by Vasa D. Mihailovich, in *World Literature Today* (Norman, Oklahoma), 60(3), 1986.

*   *   *

The central concern of Dobrica Ćosić as a writer has been the political life of his native Serbia. He was a prominent member of the League of Communists of Yugoslavia until 1968, when he was expelled from the Central Committee, accused of "nationalism." Until 1990, Ćosić was a controversial figure, outspoken and independent-minded, representing an unofficial, intellectual opposition, although his open championing of the Serbs became increasingly acceptable, and eventually adopted as the central platform of the blatantly nationalist President of Serbia, Slobodan Milošević. With the elections, in 1990, the first since World War II, it was possible for Ćosić to play a more openly political role, and in 1992 he was appointed the first President of the new Federal Republic of Yugoslavia, consisting of the two former Socialist Federal Yugoslav republics of Serbia and Montenegro.

Ćosić's fundamentally political orientation is reflected in his fiction. His work represents an examination of the fate of his country and its people, its history, and the forces shaping its destiny. Ćosić sees the upheavals of the 20th century as having driven people to a new concern with history as an all-powerful force governing their lives in the place of a lost God. By offering a poetic transposition of history, Ćosić believes that literature can "revitalize the spiritual life of the people." Most of Ćosić's fiction has been concerned with the recent past of Serbia, as are his essays and the allegory *Bajka* (Fairytale). His first novel, *Daleko je sunce* (*Far Away Is the Sun*), examines the process of decision-making among the Partisans and their relations with the peasant population during World War II. An insubstantial work, the novel nevertheless demonstrates Ćosić's readiness to explore sensitive areas. This is still more clearly the case with his second novel about World War II, the three-volume study *Deobe* (Divisions), in which he considers the various reasons which drove the Chetniks (guerrillas loyal to the king) to turn their arms against their fellow Serbs, the Partisans. *Koreni* (Roots) focuses on the years of Serbia's emergence from a patriarchal agricultural province of the Ottoman Empire and the beginnings of its development as an independent state.

Ćosić's next work was his lengthy study of World War I in Serbia, published in four volumes as *Vreme smrti* (*This Land, This Time*). The novel takes up the set of characters introduced in *Koreni*, and draws on official documents, diaries, and letters, merging historical and fictitious characters. It covers the whole spectrum of Serbian society, following the decision-making processes of the government and army commanders, portraying the generals, King Peter, Prime Minister Pašić and their closest associates. At the same time, it describes the life of the village and the fate of its population. The novel offers a detailed and moving account of the little kingdom's struggle against the Habsburg forces, its unexpected successes in the first year of the war, the appalling scale of its losses in battle and through disease, the devastation of the army and civilian population in the great retreat through the mountains of Montenegro and Albania in the winter of 1915, and the regrouping of the remains of the army to fight again with the allies. The epic scale of the work can be seen as reflecting the cultural heritage of the South Slavs. The style is discursive and at times overstated but it is a powerful story, movingly told, of wide general interest and appeal.

Ćosić's recent novels continue the pattern set in his earlier works: a history of the political ideas of 20th-century Serbia as they affect the lives of the Katić family. The trilogy, *Grešnik* (Sinner), *Otpadnik* (Renegade), and *Vernik* (Believer), deals with the dilemmas faced by communists in the light of Stalin's purges, the expulsion of Yugoslavia from the Cominform, and the Yugoslav "Gulag," *Goli otok* (Barren Island). As in his earlier novels, Ćosić personifies and debates all the issues confronting left-wing intellectuals in mid-20th-century Yugoslavia through individual characters. His fiction provides a remarkably comprehensive account of the political life of his people.

—Celia Hawkesworth

———

CSOÓRI, Sándor. Hungarian. Born in Zámoly, Transbanubia, 3 February 1930. Educated at the Calvinist grammar school, Pápa, from 1943; Lenin Institute, from 1951. Staff member, *Pápai Néplap* [Pápa Popular News], from 1949, *Veszprém Megyei Népújság* [Veszprém County Popular Newspaper], from 1949, *Szabad Ifjúság* [Free Youth], from 1952, and *Irodalmi Újság* [Literary News], 1953–54; head of poetry section, *Új Hang* [New Voice], 1955–56; dramaturge, Hungarian Film Studio, from 1971. Recipient: Attila József prize, 1954; Cannes Film Festival prize, 1964, 1968; Herder prize (Austria), 1981. Address: c/o Magvető Könyvkiadó, Vörösmarty tér 1, 1806 Budapest V, Hungary.

PUBLICATIONS

Verse

Felröppen a madár [The Bird Takes Wing]. Budapest, Szépirodalmi, 1954.
Ördögpille [Devil's Moth]. Budapest, Magvető, 1957.
Menekülés a magányból [Flight from Solitude]. Budapest, Magvető, 1962.
Szigorú korban élünk [We Live in Harsh Times], with Frigyes Hidas. Budapest, NPI, 1967.

Második születésem [My Second Birth].   Budapest, Magvető, 1967.
Lekvárcirkusz bohócai [Clowns of a Jam Circus].   Budapest, Móra, 1969.
Párbeszéd, sötétben [Dialogue, in the Dark].   Budapest, Magvető, 1973.
A látogató emlékei [The Memories of a Visitor].   Budapest, Magvető, 1977.
Jóslás a te idődről [Predictions About Your Time].   Budapest, Magvető, 1979.
A tizedik este [The 10th Evening].   Budapest, Magvető, 1980.
Wings of Knives and Nails, edited and translated by I. L. Halász de Béky. Toronto, Vox Humana, 1981.
Elmaradt lázálom [Nightmare Postponed].   Budapest, Magvető, 1982.
Várakozás a tavaszban [Waiting in the Spring].   Budapest, Magvető, 1983.
Memory of Snow, translated by Nicholas Kolumban.   Great Barrington, Massachusetts, Penmaen Press, 1983.
Kezemben zöld ág [In My Hand a Green Branch].   Budapest, Magvető, 1985.
Lábon járó verőfény [Bright Sunshine on Foot].   Budapest, Móra, 1987.
Csoóri Sándor breviárium [Breviary] (includes prose).   Budapest, Eötvös, 1988.
A világ emlékművei [Monuments of the World].   Budapest, Magvető, 1989.
Selected Poems of Sándor Csoóri, translated by Len Roberts. Port Townsend, Washington, Copper Canyon Press, 1992.

Plays

Ítélet [Sentence] (screenplay), with Ferenc Kósa.   Budapest, Mafilm, 1967.
Nincs idő [There Is No Time] (screenplay), with Ferenc Kósa.   Budapest, Hunnia Filmstúdió, 1972.
Forradás [Scars] (screenplay), with *Ítélet* and *Nincs idő*, with Ferenc Kósa.   Budapest, Magvető, 1972.
80 huszár [80 Hussars] (screenplay), with Sándor Sára.   Budapest, Magvető, 1980.
Tüske a köröm alatt [Thorn Under the Fingernail] (screenplay), with Sándor Sára.   Budapest, Budapest Stúdió, 1987.

Screenplays: *Tízezer nap* [10,000 Days], 1968; *80 huszár* [80 Hussars], with Sándor Sára; *Ítélet*, with Ferenc Kósa; *Nincs idő*, with Ferenc Kósa; *Forradás*, with Ferenc Kósa; *Tüske a köröm alatt*, with Sándor Sára.

Fiction

Faltól falig [From Wall to Wall].   Budapest, Magvető, 1969.
Utazás, félálomban [Journey While Half-Asleep].   Budapest, Magvető, 1974.
Iszapeső [Mud-Rain].   Budapest, Magvető, 1981.

Other

Tudósítás a toronyból [Report from the Tower].   Budapest, Magvető, 1963.
Kubai napló [Cuban Diary].   Budapest, Magvető, 1965.
A költő és a majompofa [The Poet and the Monkey Face].   Budapest, Magvető, 1966.
Biztató [Reassurance].   Lyndhurst, New Jersey, Kaláka, 1973.
Nomád napló [The Wanderer's Diary].   Budapest, Magvető, 1979.

Tenger és diólevél [The Sea and the Walnut Leaf].   New York, Püski, 1982.
Készülődés a számadásra [Preparation for the Day of Reckoning].   Budapest, Magvető, 1987.

Editor, *Szárny és piramis* [Wing and Pyramid], by László Nagy.   Budapest, Helikon, 1980.
Editor, *Mert szemben ülsz velem* [Because You Sit Opposite Me], by Gyula Illyés.   Budapest, Helikon, 1982.

*   *   *

"The good writer is the one who, like history, makes us wiser but doesn't explain . . ." So says Sándor Csoóri, one of Hungary's most respected contemporary poets. History is of the greatest importance to Csoóri; by comparing the present to the past he reveals the alienation of man faced with a relentlessly evolving world. Csoóri says that his writing has always contained "a general sense of unease. About how to maintain the existence of the human personality in the world amid the great campaigns of depersonalization" (*ARION* [Budapest], 12, 1980). But his poetry is not necessarily pessimistic; he also commemorates the strength of the human will to adapt and survive. As Len Roberts explains in his foreword to *Barbarian Prayer*, "Csoóri's poetry, in its best moments, is redeeming, for it represents man's spirit coming to terms with the hardships of his existence."

Csoóri grew up in a small village in Transbanubia. He won a scholarship to study at a Calvinist school in Pápa — a step up for a boy from peasant stock. Indeed, on returning to his village years later because of illness, he was shocked by the poverty and hardship of the life he had left. His first book, *Felröppen a madár* (The Bird Takes Wing), was published in 1954, during the artistic thaw across Central and Eastern Europe following Stalin's death. Since the mid-1960s Csoóri has published collections regularly. He has also written several screenplays with Ferenc Kósa, and worked for a time in the early 1970s for the Hungarian Film Studio.

Csoóri's first poems concerned national, political issues and events. With time, however, he turned inward to link the socioeconomic world with more personal dilemmas and responses, often using nature as a setting that is able to contain images from both personal and political worlds. The poem "Várakozás" ("The Wait") is a good example:

I'm waiting, I don't know what for.
A train clatters by in front of your house,
soldiers wave out of windows,
their hair whips in the wind then settles
like the flame of a match.
Things go on
when moments ago time stood still:
a cow is chewing its cud
trees stand around dumbfounded in the summer
like newspaper readers
free from illusion under a wide sky.
They invoke the end of the world.
. . .
something has happened,
something that hasn't reached me
but it ought to soar before my eyes
as the words, the starlings,
the moaning waves of the Atlantic swished once
or war's fires,
burning out the eyes of insects.

But now only a whitewashed pigeon flies by,
at an angle,
in front of my face.

The cow, the trees, the pigeon and starlings, the insects are both witnesses and somehow implicated by their very existence. They wait with the poet, but they also act — the waves swish, the pigeon flies. They embody both the private and public responses to the suggested apocalypse.

Death underlies much of Csoóri's poetry, and again nature provides an evocative setting, pointing up the contrast between "natural" and "unnatural" dying. He is determined, however, that his own death will be a personal issue, his to control. In "Last Will and Testament — May" he brings nature on his side to explain:

I've always loved clouds gathering in May,
why shouldn't I have a little rain
when I die, too? . . .
. . . The torrent would beat down
on your eyes like windows thrown open waiting.

. . .
As you dried on the long way home
the road with its chestnuts — my displaced

and denounced life — would rise to evaporate
from you, into the heights of May.

Such control over the way the poet wants his death to be portrayed goes a long way towards redressing the forces that have made his life "displaced and denounced."

Nature then often plays a redemptive role in Csoóri's poems. He also finds solace in personal relationships, and in particular writes lovingly about women, for example in "Eleven emlékem marad" ("It Will Remain a Lively Memory"): "It will be good to gaze upon/the inviting duel of your lovely breasts:/it will remain a living memory/my pattern of all perishable things." Granted, Csoóri is fixing an image of the woman in his mind so that he will be able to remember her when she is dead; nevertheless the poem manages to rise above the moroseness the subject demands, for the poet is concerned that it be a "living" and "lively" memory. In the end, for all his talk of death, Csoóri's poems actually celebrate life.

—Theresa Werner

D

DADIÉ, Bernard (Binlin). Ivorian. Born in Assinie, in 1916. Educated at l'École Normale William-Ponty, Gorée, Senegal. Married Rosa Assamala Koutoua in 1950; nine children. Librarian and archivist, Institut Français d'Afrique Noire (IFAN), University of Dakar, 1936–47; co-founder, Théâtre Indigène de la Côte d'Ivoire, 1938, and Cercle Culturel et Folklorique de la Côte d'Ivoire, 1953; press secretary to the Committee Director, PDCI-RDA, Ivory Coast, 1947–53; head of Cabinet, 1957–59, and director of Cultural Affairs, from 1961, Ministry of National Education, Ivory Coast; director of Information Services, Government of the Ivory Coast, 1959–61. Member and vice president of Executive Council, Unesco, 1964–72; director, Commission Nationale de la Fondation Félix Houphouet-Boigny; member, Conseil Économique et Social, 1976–77; president, Conférence Générale de l'Agence de Coopération Culturelle et Technique, 1977–79; president, Association Internationale pour le Développement de la Documentation des Bibliothèques et des Archives en Afrique, Association Générale des Arts et Lettres de la Côte d'Ivoire, Association Internationale pour le Développement de la Documentation des Bibliothèques, des Archives, et des Musées de la Côte d'Ivoire, and Société Africaine de Culture (Ivory Coast chapter). Recipient: Lauréat du Grand Prix Littéraire de l'Afrique Noire, 1965; Academy of Trevise Gold Medal; Ville de Paris Silver Medal; Ville de Bordeaux Silver Medal; Marciano Moreno prize (Argentina); Unesco Gold Medal; Académie Populaire de Guyenne et Gascogne Gold Medal; Haute Académie Internationale de Lutèce Gold Medal; Edgar Allan Poe poetry prize, 1975; Académie des Sciences d'Outre-Mer Cross; Cross of Honor for Science and Art (Austria); Alfonso X El Sabio Medal. Commandeur de l'Ordre National de la Côte d'Ivoire; Commandeur de l'Ordre du Mérite de l'Éducation Nationale; Chevalier de l'Ordre des Arts et des Lettres; Troubadour d'Honneur du Collège des Troubadours; Officier de l'Ordre des Arts et des Lettres (France); Commandeur de l'Ordre du Mérite Français d'Outre-Mer, 1964; Commandeur de Pléiade de l'Ordre de la Francophonie et du Dialogue des Cultures; Commandeur de l'Ordre National de la Légion d'Honneur (France); Grand Officier de l'Ordre de Léopold (Belgium); Grand Officier de l'Ordre National du Mérite (France); Grand Officier de l'Ordre du Mérite de la République Féderale d'Allemagne. Address: Direction des Affaires Culturelles, BP V39 Abidjan, Ivory Coast.

Publications

Plays

Les Villes (produced Ivory Coast, 1934).
Assémien Déhylé, roi du Sanwi (produced Paris, 1937). N.p., Album Officiel de la Mission Pontificale, 1936.
Min Adja-O (c'est mon héritage!) (produced 1960). Published in *Le Théâtre populaire en République de Côte d'Ivoire*, Abidjan, Cercle Culturel et Folklorique de Côte d'Ivoire, 1965.

Papassidi maître-escroc (produced 1960). Paris, Nouvelles Éditions Africaines, 1975.
Serment d'amour (produced Abidjan, 1965). Published in *Le Théâtre populaire en République de Côte d'Ivoire*, Abidjan, Cercle Culturel et Folklorique de Côte d'Ivoire, 1965.
Situation difficile (produced in Abidjan, 1965). Published in *Le Théâtre populaire en République de Côte d'Ivoire*, Abidjan, Cercle Culturel et Folklorique de Côte d'Ivoire, 1965.
Monsieur Thôgô-Gnini (produced Algiers, 1969). Paris, Présence Africaine, 1970; in English, New York, Ubu Repertory, 1986.
Les Voix dans le vent (produced 1969). Abidjan, Clé, 1970.
Béatrice du Congo (produced 1969; Avignon, 1971). Paris, Présence Africaine, 1970.
Îles de tempête. Paris, Présence Africaine, 1973.
Mhoi-Ceul. Paris, Présence Africaine, 1979.

Fiction

Légendes africaines. Paris, Seghers, 1954.
Le Pagne noir. Paris, Présence Africaine, 1955; as *Les Belles Histoires de Kacou Ananze l'araignée* (with stories by André Terrisse), Paris, Nathan, 1963; as *The Black Cloth*, Amherst, University of Massachusetts Press, 1987.
Climbié. Paris, Seghers, 1956; in English, New York, Africana, and London, Heinemann, 1971.
Un Nègre à Paris. Paris, Présence Africaine, 1956.
Patron de New York. Paris, Présence Africaine, 1964.
La Ville où nul ne meurt. Paris, Présence Africaine, 1968; as *The City Where No One Dies*, Washington, D.C., Three Continents Press, 1986.
Commandant Taureault et ses nègres. Abidjan, CEDA, 1980.
Les Jambes du fils de Dieu. Abidjan, CEDA, 1980.
Les Contes de Koutou-as-Samala. Paris, Présence Africaine, 1982.

Verse

Afrique debout. Paris, Seghers, 1950.
La Ronde des jours. Paris, Seghers, 1956.
Hommes de tous les continents. Paris, Présence Africaine, 1957.

Other

Légendes et poèmes (includes fiction and verse). Paris, Seghers, 1966.
Opinions d'un nègre: aphorismes 1934–1946. Dakar, Club Afrique Loisirs, 1980.
Carnet de prison. Abidjan, CEDA, 1981.

*

Critical Studies: "Bernard Dadié and the Aesthetics of the Chronique: An Affirmation of Cultural Identity" by Janis

A. Mayes, in *Présence Africane/Cultural Review of the Negro World* (Paris), 101–102, 1977, and *Critical Perspectives on Bernard Dadié*, edited by Mayes, Washington, D.C., Three Continents Press, 1991; *Mythology and Cosmology in the Narratives of Bernard Dadié and Birago Diop: A Structural Approach* by Marie S. Tollerson, Washington, D.C., Three Continents Press, 1992.

* * *

Ivory Coast writer Bernard Dadié published his first literary work in 1936 — the historical play *Assémien Dehylé, roi du Sanwi* (Assémien Dehylé, King of the Sanwi), written while he was still a pupil at the École Normale William-Ponty in Gorée, Senegal, where he was studying to become an administrator. In 1937 it was produced in Paris, at the Théâtre des Champs Élysées. Since then, in a writing career lasting more than four decades, Dadié has repeatedly returned to the theatre and is, by some accounts, Africa's most prolific playwright. He has also produced work in a range of other genres, including the novel, autobiography, poetry, and fable. Of his novels, the best is without doubt *Climbié*, a semi-autobiographical account of the rise to adulthood of an educated young man from the Ivory Coast in the 1930s and 1940s. The book is also a critique of the alienating nature of colonialism. It is memorable in particular for a number of set pieces in which Dadié evokes such episodes as the visit of a European conjuror to Grand-Bassam, the death of the Commissioner of Police, or even a typical Saturday evening dance. These are literary *tours de force*, but the work also expresses memorable ideas, most notably in a series of conversations between the young Climbié and his uncle, a former soldier turned farmer who has asserted his independence from the colonizing power at the price of a harsh and impoverished existence. He acquaints the young boy with the first stirrings of black consciousness on the other side of the Atlantic. *Climbié* offers a personal and at times vivid account of a particular historical epoch. By comparison, Dadié's later novels — *Un Nègre à Paris* (A Negro in Paris), *Patron de New York* (Boss of New York), and *La Ville où nul ne meurt* (*The City Where No One Dies*), seem rather sterile, even somewhat circumstantial, literary exercises.

Dadié has also published two collections of folk tales or fables, *Légendes africaines* (African Legends) and *Le Pagne noir* (*The Black Cloth*). These are interesting works, half fairytale, half creation myth. One cannot help but feel, however, that the transformation of what were presumably vernacular narratives into literary texts has resulted in a certain loss of power. Structurally, they retain an episodic, even diffuse character, which stamps them as quintessentially oral.

A similar tendency to conventional rhetoric also mars some of Dadié's poetry. The chief theme of *Hommes de tous les continents* (Men of All Continents) — as suggested by its title — is a call to fraternity among peoples. The sentiments it expresses are admirable, but the collection is spoiled by its reliance on a number of rather hackneyed devices. At their worst, they are reminiscent of Victor Hugo at his least inspired. Dadié the scholar is no friend to Dadié the artist.

Climbié apart, it is for the stage that Dadié has written his most telling work. Dramatic construction is not his forté; his plots tend to be perfunctory. But Dadié's plays do offer evidence of a sense of humour not apparent in his other works and which ranges from the droll to the sharp. Those of his plays which deal with post-colonial reality are marked by an apparent indirectness of aim, a perhaps prudent blurring of the satirical focus. Yet their targets are readily identifiable and their message remains clear. Among Dadié's strategies is the classic one of using a historical situation in order to expose present evils. He adopts precisely this approach in his best-known play, *Monsieur Thôgô-Gnini*, which is set in West Africa in the 1840s. The protagonist of the play (his name means "the opportunist") starts as the intermediary between an African ruler and the white colonial interests who are anxious to do business with him. Increasingly, however, it is Thôgô-Gnini himself who acts as the exploiter and oppressor of his people, by exercising monopoly control over palm oil, peanuts, and cocoa. The rather sketchy plot of the play is provided by the hostility between Thôgô-Gnini and Paul Nzekou, a young man whose palm oil he has refused to pay for. This results in a courtroom confrontation, which provides the play with its last scene. Here, a Molièresque *deus ex machina* puts an end to the depredations of M. Thôgô-Gnini. The setting of the play may be the 19th century, but its resonance is clearly contemporary. The crops monopolized by Thôgô-Gnini are the present-day staples of the Ivory Coast, which has little natural mineral wealth and an economy based on agriculture.

In similar vein is *Papassidi, maître-escroc* (Papassidi, Master Crook), a fairly coarse-grained farce. Here, however, the obliquity of Dadié's attack stems from geographical and ethnic factors, rather than from historical displacement. Ostensibly about a fraudulent fortune teller from the North, it is actually a critique of government arbitrariness and bureaucratic corruption and indolence. Its protagonist is not Papassidi (who appears in only three of its seven *tableaux*), but the congenial everyman figure of Aka, a public scribe, who is forced to struggle with the dire consequences of a government ban on his profession. As a dramatist, Dadié's talent is nothing if not diverse. *Béatrice du Congo* (Beatrice of the Congo) is an altogether more sombre play, in which he again uses a historical situation (the Portuguese colonization of Africa) to mount a pointed critique of neocolonialism. The play contains a number of highly theatrical scenes. Its third act in particular, which recounts the brutal suppression of an early rebellion, is marked by an impressively solemn pageantry. However, unshielded this time by comic invention, Dadié's limitations as a constructor are more severely exposed.

One of Dadié's hallmarks as a writer is his earnestness. Paradoxically, it may be for some of his least solemn works that he will be longest remembered.

—Tim Lewis

———

DAĞLARCA, Fazıl Hüsnü. Turkish. Born in Istanbul, in 1914. Educated at the Military College. Career officer, to Captain, in the Turkish Army, 1935–50; inspector for Ministry of Labour, 1952–60; owner and manager of bookstore, Istanbul, 1959–70. Recipient: Yeditepe poetry award, 1956; Turkish Language Society award, 1958; International Poetry Forum award (U.S.A.), 1967; Struga Poetry Festival Golden Wreath, 1974; Rotterdam Poetry International Poet of the Year, 1977; Simavi literature prize, 1987. Address: P.K. 33, Kadiköy, Istanbul, Turkey.

PUBLICATIONS

Verse

Havaya çizilen dünya [A World Sketched on Air].   1935.
Çocuk ve Allah [Child and God].   1940.

Daha [More]. Istanbul, Lâtif Dinçbaş Matbaasï, 1943.
Çakırın destanı [The Epic of Çakir]. Istanbul, Marmara Kitabevi, 1945.
Taş devri [The Stone Age]. Istanbul, Marmara Kitabevi, 1945.
Üç şehitler destanı [The Epic of the Three Martyrs]. Istanbul, Varlïk, 1949.
Toprak ana [Mother Earth]. Istanbul, Varlïk, 1950.
Bağımsızlık savaşı: Samsun'dan Ankara'ya. 1951.
Bağımsızlık savaşı: Inönüler. 1951.
Aç yazı [Hungry Writing]. Istanbul, Varlïk, 1951.
İstiklâl savaşı [The War of Independence]. 1951.
Sıvaslı karınca [Ant from Sivas]. 1951.
İstanbul: fetih destanı [The Epic of the Conquest of Istanbul]. Istanbul, Varlïk, 1953.
Anıtkabir [Mausoleum]. Istanbul, Yenilik, 1953.
Âsû. Istanbul, Yenilik, 1955.
Delice böcek [The Insane Insect]. Istanbul, Varlïk, 1957.
Batı acısı [The Agony of the West]. Istanbul, Varlïk, 1958.
Mevlâna'da olmak — Gezi [Voyage — Alive in Mevlana]. Konya, Çagrı, 1958.
Hoo'lar [Ho-os]. Istanbul, Kitap, 1960.
Özgürlük alanı [Freedom Square]. Istanbul, Yenilik, 1960.
Cezayir türküsü = Chanson d'Algérie = Song of Algeria (trilingual edition in Turkish, French, and English). Istanbul, Kitap, 1961.
Aylam [Moon Life]. Istanbul, Kitap, 1962.
Karşı-duvar dergisi: Türk olmak [Being a Turk]. Istanbul, Kitap, 1963.
Yedi memetler [Seven Heroes]. Istanbul, Kitap, 1964.
Yeryağ [Soil Oil]. Istanbul, Kitap, 1965.
Dışardan gazel [A Jarring Song]. Istanbul, Kitap, 1965.
Kazmalama [Give It the Axe]. Istanbul, Kitap, 1965.
Çanakkale destanı [The Epic of the Dardanelles]. Istanbul, Kitap, 1965.
Vietnam savaşımız. Istanbul, Yenilik, 1966; as *Our Vietnam War,* Istanbul, Izlem, 1966.
Açıl susam açıl [Open, Sesame, Open]. 1967.
Kubilay destanı [The Epic of Kubilay]. Istanbul, Kitap, 1968.
Haydi [Come On]. Istanbul, Kitap, 1968.
19 mayıs destanı [The Epic of May 19]. 1969.
Seçme şiirler = Selected Poems (bilingual edition), translated by Talat Sait Halman. Pittsburgh, University of Pittsburgh Press, 1969.
Vietnam, körü [Blind in Vietnam]. Istanbul, Kitap, 1970.
Hiroşima: atom bombasının 25. yılı [Hiroshima: 25th Anniversary of the Atomic Bomb] (trilingual edition in Turkish, French, and English]. Istanbul, Kitap, 1970.
Dört kanatlı kuş [Four-Winged Bird] (selected poems). Istanbul, Varlïk, 1970.
Malazgirt ululaması [Manzikert Exaltation]. Ankara, University of Ankara Press, 1971.
Kuş ayak. Istanbul, Milliyet, 1971.
Kınalı kuzu ağıdı [Elegy for the Hennaed Lamb]. Istanbul, Cem, 1972.
Haliç. 1972.
Gazi Mustafa Kemal Atatürk [Atatürk]. Ankara, Tüık Dil Kurumu, 1973.
Bağımsızlık savaşı: Sakarya kıyıları. Istanbul, Cem, 1973.
Bağımsızlık savaşı: 30 ağustos. 1973.
Bağımsızlık savaşı: İzmir yollarinda. 1973.
Yeryüzü çocukları. Istanbul, Cem, 1974.
Arkaüstü. Istanbul, Cem, 1974.
Dağlarca: Critical Approaches, Interviews, Selected Poems (bilingual edition). Istanbul, Cem, 1974.
Horoz [Rooster]. Istanbul, Cem, 1977.

Yanık çocuklar koçaklaması. 1977.
Ağrı dağı bildirisi. 1977.
Alamanyalarda çöpçülerimiz. 1977.
İkili anlaşma anıtı. 1977.
Pir Sultan Abdal günleri. 1977.
Karşı duvar dergisi. 1977.
Balina ile mandalina. 1977.
Hollandalı dörtlüker = Quatrains of Holland (bilingual edition). 1977.
Yazıları seven ayı. 1978.
Göz masalı. 1979.
Yaramaz sözcükler. Ankara, Kültür Bakanlığı, 1979.
Çukurova kocaklamasi [Heroic Song of Chukurova]. Istanbul, Cem, 1979.
The Bird and I, translated by Talat Sait Halman. Merrick, New York, Cross-Cultural Communications, 1980.
Nötron bombasi; Çiplak; Yunus Emre'de olmak; Uzun kindi [Neutron Bomb; Naked; Alive in Yunus Emre]. Istanbul, Cem, 1981.
Akşamci [Boozer]. 1985.
İlk yapıtla 50 yıl sonrakiler [First Work and Those 50 Years Later]. Istanbul, Üzgür, 1985.
Şeyh Galib'e çiçekler [Flowers for Sheikh Ghalib]. 1986.
Takma yaşamalar çagı [The Age of Fake Lives]. 1986.
Yurdana [Motherland]. 1988.
Uzaklarla giyinmek [Clad in Distances]. 1990.
Dikdeki bilgisayar [The Computer in the Language]. 1992.

*

Critical Studies: in *Literature East and West* (Austin, Texas), 17, 1973; *Dağlarca: Critical Approaches, Interviews, Selected Poems* (bilingual edition), Istanbul, Cem, 1974.

* * *

One of the eminent figures of modern Turkish poetry, Fazıl Hüsnü Dağlarca has devoted his entire literary life to poetry in a career which has spanned more than six decades. He has been extraordinarily prolific (many thousands of poems, with many more thousands awaiting publication) and versatile (an unusually broad spectrum of types and techniques). His poetic gift has, from the outset, been so unique that he cannot be said to show any influences of his predecessors or contemporaries in Turkey or abroad.

Dağlarca has received all of his country's major poetry awards. In 1967, a jury composed of five prominent Turkish men of letters named him "the foremost living poet of Turkey," for the 1968 "Turkish award" of the International Poetry Forum in Pittsburgh. In the 1990s he continues to enjoy that designation. His international prestige has also grown with numerous honors and awards abroad and with his selected poems published in book form in many languages.

The diversity of Dağlarca's themes and aesthetic strategies has been astounding. He has explored the mysteries of the ancient world and dealt with the immediacy of contemporary political issues. He is equally at home with philosophical speculation and children's ditties. He has produced exquisite lyrics of romantic love as well as the most biting satire. Some of his poems are dominated by a patriotic spirit; yet he is a compelling universalist as well. From the epigrammatic to the epic, his output embraces a range that few Turkish poets have ever achieved.

In his first decade as a young poet he exhibited an engrossing metaphysical curiosity which expressed itself in a heightened lyrical formulation. His cosmic consciousness amassed into a private world is clearly dominant in these earliest poems.

Çocuk ve Allah (Child and God), his second collection, which stands as one of the most significant and enduring books of modern Turkish poetry, depicts a fearful, sensitive child confronted with God's mysteriousness and life's enigmas. *Daha* (More), three years later, expanded Dağlarca's thematic horizons, and became memorable for a number of splendid poems evoking the dramas of Ottoman history. Two collections, *Çakırın destanı* (The Epic of Çakir) and *Taş devri* (The Stone Age), both published in 1945, explore the world of the ancient man and the vicissitudes faced by Everyman. In these gripping poems Dağlarca ranges from pagan passions to pantheistic urges.

Until 1955, Dağlarca's second decade was spent discovering the epic themes of Turkish history and the realities of his country and other cultures in contemporary times. He produced two epics of the Turkish struggle for independence, and a stirring epic of the 1453 Ottoman conquest of Istanbul (Constantinople). He also wrote a cycle of poems, *Anıtkabir* (Mausoleum), eulogizing Mustafa Kemal (Atatürk), the founder and first President of the Turkish Republic. *Toprak ana* (Mother Earth) of 1950, virtually a magnum opus, secured a permanent place for Dağlarca. It exposes the tragic conditions of rural Anatolia and its human dramas. The following year also saw the publication of *Aç yazı* (Hungry Writing), a collection of exquisite poems out of the Turkish experience, and *Sıvaslı karınca* (Ant from Sivas), an eloquent expression of Dağlarca's internationalist spirit and interest in other cultures. *Âsû*, a large collection, contains some of Dağlarca's most impressive poems. His lyric formulations of thoughts on love and death are remarkable for their powerful images, symbols, rhythms, and evocations.

From the late 1950s onwards, Dağlarca's art turned like a prism in all directions. In *Batı acısı* (The Agony of the West), he gives glimpses of European culture and a neo-romantic appreciation of the Mediterranean milieu following a voyage which took him to Italy and France. Also in 1958 he published his neo-mystical poems which avowedly drew inspiration from the humanitarian mysticism of the Anatolian poet-philosopher Mevlana Jalal ud Din Rumi (1207–1273). His political consciousness relating to developments at home and abroad became more acute during this period; he wrote powerful verses about the upheaval which led to a revolution in Turkey in 1960, and also a short epic about the Algerian revolution. The starting conquest of outer space, with its promise of man's landing on the moon, inspired in Dağlarca a long cycle of poems which he collected in a fascinating volume entitled *Aylam* (Moon Life) in 1962.

Dağlarca's later output continued to maintain his astonishing diversity of themes, concerns, and expressive techniques. In the 1960s and 1970s he became one of Turkey's most influential voices of social protest. Starting out with poem-posters he pasted periodically on the window of his bookstore in Istanbul's Aksaray section, he caught the public imagination with numerous small volumes of stirring criticism and satire directed against the powers that be, the government and the West, capitalism and colonialism. He also published two volumes denouncing the United States for the Vietnam War and for Hiroshima. He struck hard at Turkey's religious reactionaries in a cycle of poems entitled "The Epic of Kubilay," about the assassination and lynching of a young progressive teacher, Kubilay, by Islamic zealots.

In many volumes he celebrated patriotic episodes in Turkish history, including the Turkish victory at the Dardanelles and other achievements by Mustafa Kemal (Atatürk). Between 1967 and 1992, he published several dozen children's books (all in verse), becoming Turkey's leading children's poet. In other volumes, Dağlarca attempted to strengthen his links with some of the great figures of Turkish poetry, such as Yunus Emre (d. 1321), an Anatolian mystic who composed spiritual and humanistic poems of love and ecumenism, and Şeyh Galib (d. 1799), a late classical Ottoman poet renowned for rhapsodical mysticism.

Dağlarca's most impressive work late in his career is a very large number of epigrammatic poems. His *Haydi* (Come On), a collection of 1243 quatrains, is an unusual display of distilled intellect. His probing mind is also at work in *Uzaklarla giyinmek* (Clad in Distances), which contains many effectively crafted lyrics of philosophical inquiry.

Like most leading poets, Dağlarca exhibits his poetic prowess best in tastefully made selections from his vast corpus. As such, *Dört kanatlı kuş* (Four-Winged Bird) is highly impressive. Many of his important poems have been published in English translation in *Selected Poems* and *The Bird and I*.

Yaşar Nabi Nayir (d. 1981), one of Turkey's foremost literary critics, wrote in his introduction to the *Selected Poems* that Dağlarca "contributed to Turkish literature a unique aesthetic sensibility, new concepts of substance and form, and an inimitable style" and that "his versatility and originality have been matched by few Turkish literary figures, past or present."

—Talat S. Halman

DĀNESHVAR, Sīmīn. Iranian.   Born in Shiraz, 23 April 1921. Educated at the University of Tehran, Ph.D. in Persian literature 1949; Fulbright Fellow, Stanford University, California 1952. Married Jala Al-e Ahmad in 1950 (died 1969). Teacher at Tehran Conservatory; Professor, Department of Archeology, University of Tehran, until 1979. Co-founder, Writers' Association of Iran, 1968. Address: c/o Mage Books, 1032 29th Street, N.W., Washington, D.C. 20007, U.S.A.

PUBLICATIONS

Fiction

Atash-e khamoush [The Extinguished Fire].   1948.
Shahrī chon behesht [A City Like Paradise].   1961.
Savushun. Tehran, Kharazmi, 1969; in English, Washington, D.C., Mage, 1990; as *A Persian Requiem*, London, Peter Halban, 1991.
Be kī salam konam? [Whom Should I Salute?].   Tehran, Kharazmi, 1980.
Ghorub-e-Jalal [Jalal's Sunset].   1981.
Daneshvar's Playhouse: A Collection of Stories. Washington, D.C., Mage, 1989.

Other

Has translated into Persian *Arms and the Man* by George Bernard Shaw, *The Cherry Orchard* and *The Enemies* by Anton Chekhov, *The Scarlet Letter* by Nathaniel Hawthorne, *The Human Comedy* by William Saroyan, *Cry, the Beloved Country* by Alan Paton, and *Beatrice* by Arthur Schnitzler.

*

Critical Study: "Power, Prudence and Print: Censorship and Simin Daneshvar" by Farzaneh Milani, in *Iranian Studies* (New York), 18(2–4), 1985.

*   *   *

A pioneer in modern Persian fiction, Sīmīn Dāneshvar's first book of short stories, *Atash-e khamoush* (The Extinguished Fire), was actually the first to be published by a Persian woman. It contains 16 stories, seven of which are directly influenced by O. Henry. The volume is very much the work of a beginner; her characters possess no individual identity, and are no more than types. However, *Shahrī chon behesht* (A City Like Paradise), published 13 years later, shows a marked improvement in both style and content.

Dāneshvar's fame as the first woman novelist in Iran was established with the publication of her novel *Savushun* (*A Persian Requiem*) in 1969. The book is set during the World War II Allied occupation of Iran, in Shiraz, the cradle of Persian civilization. Within a historical context the novel portrays the reaction of the community as a whole to the arrogance of the foreign powers, and how some locals are willing to sell themselves, as it were, to the British. It also explores the struggle between the landlords and peasants, as well as the different environments of city, village, and tribal life. Above all, *A Persian Requiem* is the story of an educated land-owning family, whose head, Yusof, is unwilling to succumb to the pressure of the foreign forces and their Iranian allies. Yusof refuses their demands to hand over his crops to feed the occupying army, knowing that if he did his own peasants would starve to death. He is eventually assassinated on a visit to his village. His funeral instigates a demonstration which is swiftly quashed by the government forces, and the body has to be taken back to the house by Yusof's brother and his pregnant wife Zari, to be buried unceremoniously at night. The novel marks a departure point in Persian fiction, in that for the first time the social, political, and traditional Iranian customs are all seen through the eyes of a woman — Zari, the narrator and the real protagonist of the book. She, while supporting her idealistic and obstinate husband, tries very hard to keep her family intact. It is Zari's struggle for self-identification and independence in a male-dominated society that is portrayed in the novel. She only succeeds in achieving this after the death of her husband. The grief-stricken Zari, who thinks she is going mad, is consoled by their elderly family doctor:

> . . . my dear. In this world, everything is in one's own hands. Madness, fear, even love. A human being can if he so desires, move mountains, dry up the waters, create havoc everywhere. A human life is a chronicle . . . a sweet one, a bitter one, an ugly one . . . or a heroic one. The human body is fragile, but no force in this world can equal man's spiritual power. As long as he has a strong will and some awareness."

On leaving, Dr. Abdullah Khan informs Zari that her young midwife, who had gone to the brink of suicide through madness, has been discharged from the asylum, and will have recovered by the time Zari gives birth. It is at this moment that revelation comes to her: "Zari felt as if she'd been freed from a cage . . . Not one but a thousand stars were lit in her mind. She knew now that she feared no-one and nothing in the world." Dāneshvar employs the themes of madness and suicide in her fiction to portray the fate of educated women who rebel against their suppression in a traditional society which rejects them as outcasts.

The portrayal of the deprived classes of society through black characters is an important feature of Dāneshvar's fiction. "The Playhouse" particularly displays her typical wit and perception, presenting the life of a lower class actor, whose job is to blacken his face every night and play the role of either a servant or a guard, but whose true sensibility is demonstrated in his improvised jokes, which are somewhat reminiscent of the wisdom of Shakespeare's fools.

Dāneshvar's fiction presents a general image of the social and historical events of modern Iran; her particular concern, however, is with the women of the country, with their social dilemmas and their spiritual development. Her female characters come from varying backgrounds — from the well-educated upper classes to the servants and black slaves who work for them. The Islamic Revolution was naturally a matter of concern for all Iranian writers; in "The Traitor's Intrigue" we are shown some of the forces which brought about this revolution. Despite the adversities she writes about, Dāneshvar is an optimist, and an idealist. This is perhaps most evident in the final words of *A Persian Requiem* written, ironically, by the Irish war correspondent MacMahon, a drunkard and a poet, in the form of his condolences to Zari: "Do not weep, my sister. A tree will take root in your home and many trees in your town and even more in your land. And the wind will bring the messages of each tree to the other, and the trees will ask the wind, 'did you see the dawn as you were coming on your way?'"

Dāneshvar's prose is generally simple and colloquially idiomatic, and her occasional use of traditional literary vocabulary gives it a vitality and eloquence all of its own. Her characters are, with the one or two exceptions, uncomplicated, but each has his or her own distinct personality, and displays an individual set of weaknesses and strengths.

As well as being the foremost female writer in Persian, Dāneshvar is also a very able translator — among others, she has translated works by G. B. Shaw, Nathaniel Hawthorne, and Anton Chekhov. In her translations she displays the lucidity and elegance which characterise her own fiction.

—Parvin Loloi

———

DARWĪSH, Mahmūd. Palestinian. Born in al-Birwa, Palestine, in 1942. Refugee in Lebanon, 1948–49. Married Rana Qabbani (marriage ended). Journalist in Haifa, until 1971: editor, *Al-Ittihad* [Unity] newspaper; arrested and jailed, 1961, 1965, 1966, 1967; lived in Egypt, 1971, and Beirut, 1972–82; editor, *Shu'un Filastiniyya*, Beirut, and *Al Jadid* magazine; now lives in Paris; editor, *Al-Karmal* magazine, Paris. Recipient: Lotus prize, 1969; Mediterranean prize, 1980; Lenin Peace prize, 1983. Address: c/o Riad el-Rayyes Books, 56 Knightsbridge, London SW1X 7NJ, England.

PUBLICATIONS

Verse

'Aṣāfīr bilā ajniḥah [Sparrows Without Wings].   1960.
Awrāq al-zaytūn [Olive Branches].   1965.
'Āshiq min Filastīn [A Lover from Palestine].   1966.
Ākhir al-layl [The End of Night].   1967.
Al-'aṣāfīr tamūt fi al-Jalīl [Sparrows Die in Galilee].   1970.

A Letter from Exile. New Delhi, League of Arab States Mission, 1970(?).
Ḥabībati tanhaḍ min nawmihā [My Beloved Wakes Up]. 1971.
Uḥibuk aw lā uḥibuk [Love You, Love You Not]. 1972.
The Palestinian Chalk Circle. Beirut, Arab Women's Information Committee, 1972(?).
Selected Poems, translated by Ian Wedde and Fawwaz Tuqan. Manchester, Carcanet, 1973.
Muḥāwalah raqm sabʿah [The Seventh Attempt]. 1973.
Splinters of Bone, edited and translated by B. M. Bennani. New York, Greenfield Review Press, 1974; as *Ahmad al-Zaʾtar* (bilingual edition), translated by Rana Kabbani, Beirut, al-Ittihad al-'Āmm lil-Kuttāb al-Suhufiyīn al-Filastīniyīn, 1977(?).
Tilk ṣūratōhā wa-hadhā intiḥār al-ʿāshiq [That Is Her Picture and This Is Her Lover's Suicide]. 1975.
Aʿrās [Weddings]. 1977.
Dīwan Mahmūd Darwīsh [Collected Poems]. Beirut, Dār al-'Awdah, 1977.
The Music of Human Flesh, edited and translated by Denys Johnson-Davis. London, Heinemann, and Washington, D.C., Three Continents Press, 1980.
Madīh al-ḍhill al-'āli. Beirut, Dār al-'Awdah, 1983.
Victims of a Map (bilingual edition), with Adūnīs and Samīh al-Qāsim, translated by Abdullah al-Udhari. London, Al-Saqi, 1984.
Ḥiṣār li-madā' ih al-bahr [Ban on Panegyrics to the Sea]. 'Akka, al-Aswār/'Arabask, 1984.
Wadā' an ayyatuha al-ḥarb, wadā'an ayyuha al-salām [Farewell War, Farewell Peace]. 'Akka, Manshurat al-Aswār, 1985.
Ward aqal [Lesser Roses]. 1986.
Sand and Other Poems, edited and translated by Rana Kabbani. London, KPI, 1986.
Hiyā ughniyah, hiyā ughniyah [It Is a Song, It Is a Song]. Beirut, Dār al-Kalimah lil-Nashr, 1986.
Ma'sāt al-Nirjis wa-malhat al-fiddah [The Tragedy of Narcissus and the Comedy of Silver]. London, Riad el-Rayyes, 1989.
Arā mā urīd [I See What I Want]. 1990.
Ihdā 'ashar kawkabā 11 Planets]. 1992.

Other

Shay' 'an al-waṭan [Something About Home]. 1971.
Yawmiyyāt al-ḥuzn al-'ādi [Diaries of Ordinary Grief]. 1973.
Ẓākirah lil-nisyān [A Memory fo Oblivion]. Beirut, Al Mu'assasah al-'Arabiyyah lil-Dirāsāt wa-al-Nashr, 1987.

*   *   *

Mahmūd Darwīsh is arguably the most important Arab poet writing today. He has succeeded in achieving wide popularity throughout the Arab world while showing constant concern for innovation and poetic experimentation in language and form. From the early years of his poetic career, Darwīsh was destined to devote his poetic talent to the cause of Palestine. He is one of the few poets whose life is inseparable from their poetry and their cause. His very emergence as a major Arab poet who spent his formative years under Israeli control is a testimony to the resilience and perseverance of the Palestinian character. Indeed, Darwīsh's childhood in an Israeli controlled area of Palestine enhanced his sense of being an Arab and a Palestinian despite his Hebrew-language education. He was six when the state of Israel was created and his village was completely destroyed. His father, who was a wealthy farmer and land owner, was dispossessed and forced to work as a labourer in a quarry to sustain his family of eight children.

Darwīsh's first poem, which he read at his school's annual party when he was only 14, put him in direct confrontation with Israeli military rule. It was a heartfelt cry from an Arab child to his Jewish peer at school about the simple things denied to an Arab boy and allowed to his Jewish counterpart. The following day, he was summoned to the office of the military ruler of the area and threatened that if he persisted in writing poetry, they would prevent his father from working at the local quarry. From this early age, Darwīsh realised that poetry is action and relished the impact of his simple, innocent words on the mighty establishment. At the age of 19 he published his first collection of poetry, *'Aṣāfir bilā ajniḥah* (Sparrows Without Wings); the following year he was arrested and given his first taste of Israeli prison. The conflict between the poet and his jailer continued: between 1965–67 he published three more books of poetry and was arrested and imprisoned three more times. His life became a series of poems and cells, and when he was out of prison his freedom of movement and expression were curtailed and he was subjected to long periods of house arrest.

In his diary, *Yawmiyyāt al-ḥuzn al-'ādi* (Diaries of Ordinary Grief), he talks about life under house arrest as a pattern in which he has his days and "they" have control over his nights, for he was not allowed to leave his house between sunset and sunrise. This established the poet as the prince of light and his jailer as the figure of darkness. The more his words were feared by the Israeli authorities, the more he became aware of the power of poetry and of the importance of Arabic language as an expression of his identity. In 1970, the pattern of poems and prison was broken when he published his collection, *Al-'aṣāfir tamūt fi al-Jalīl* (Sparrows Die in Galilee) and left immediately for Moscow to complete his education which was denied him in Israel. Having completed his one-year course in Moscow, he dreaded going back to the old pattern of poetry and prison, and decided to join his people in the diaspora. In 1971 he moved to Egypt and a year later to Beirut where he stayed until the Israeli invasion of Lebanon in 1982. In his words, he "joined Ulysses in his search for Ithaca," and developed as the voice of the Palestinian consciousness.

In his diaries he states "he who turned me into a refugee changed me into a bomb," and he has continued to explode in strong poetry ever since. Since 1971 he has published 10 more collections of poetry and two books of prose. His rich output of poetry can be divided into three different stages: the Israeli phase (1960–71), the Beirut phase (1972–82), and the post-Beirut phase (1982–92). In the first phase, which comprises his first five collections and *Ḥabībati tanhaḍ min nawmihā* (My Beloved Wakes Up), his poetry was marked by its lyrical iconography of simple Palestininian objects redolent with significance and symbolism. It took pride in its Arabic language and celebrated the simple fact of being Palestinian in an atmosphere hostile to everything Palestinian. In this phase, the intellectual structure of his poetry owes much to Karl Marx and Antonio Gramsci, and he drew his poetic inspiration from Pablo Neruda and Federico García Lorca in particualr. Like them, he was not converted to Marxism but found in it an answer to his own dark emotions; it was an ordering and granting of purpose to his life. His poetry during this time is overtly political, with luxuriant sensual language, a "daylight" poetry of visual, tactile things. It has a characteristically didactic, diagnostic tone, and its technique combines the sophisticated exploitation of traditional lyrical resonance with vivid images or vignettes. Yet it is charged with the power to evoke tremendous resistance, which enabled it to capture and even inflame the imagination of its readers throughout the Arab world.

Darwīsh's lyrical poetry in the 1960s was inseparable from the structure of a politics in which political and individual codes interpenetrated to a remarkable degree. His resistance poetry had a politicised lyrical structure inscribed within a complex national mode of existence of the exceptionally free and rebellious Palestinian in an Arab world ruled by dictators. The 1970s witnessed the cynical maturity of the poet and the dissipation of the simple optimism of revolutionary innocence, for this was the phase of inter-Arab conflicts with more Palestinians being killed by Arabs than by Israelis. Like T. S. Eliot's "Unreal city" of *The Waste Land*, Darwīsh's Beirut amalgamates the spirit of the Arab city and the ethos of Hell, and is entangled in mythological and intertextual allusions. In the poetry of this second phase, the poetic structure became refined and tense, as the task of the poet became more difficult with reality growing more prosaic by the hour. The poet became increasingly conscious of his poetic endeavour and attempted to develop a new poetic form capable of conveying the prevalent sense of disconnectedness and apathy. The loss of the collective dream of an optimistic future removed from the poetic horizon not only a sense of meaning but also a whole category of imagery, vocabulary, and poetic structures. The lyrical diction and the positive imagery of the 1960s rang false in the desolate reality of the 1970s. Towards the end of this phase, the poet became increasingly aware of the apathy of his reader, (in Baudelaire's words) "*hypocrite lecteur! — mon semblable — mon frère!*"

This hypocrisy became the hallmark of the post-Beirut phase from 1982 onward. The poetry of collections published during this time oscillates between long dramatic poems and tense short ones in which he invokes the biblical lyric of lament and turns it against itself, so that it ceases to sound euphonious and lyrical. The psalm-like poems sing of an abandoned people in Babylonian exile and captivity, and pierce like shrapnel. His long poems, with their epic quality, crystallize the sense of physical dislocation, political chaos, and failure of Arab politics, especially in the aftermath of the Israeli invasion of Lebanon in 1982, and thus define some fundamental aspects of literary modernism's pervasive negativity and pessimism. In this later poetry he became, as T. S. Eliot advocates, "more and more comprehensive, more allusive, more indirect, in order to force, to dislocate if necessary, language into his meaning." In the disjunctive perturbed poems of the post-Beirut phase, he became clearly preoccupied with a sense of the disjunction of the Arab/Palestinian self.

In his poetry Darwīsh advocated greater precision in the use of words and eschewed all types of decorative language. He also realized that the transposition from the auditory to the visual is a textual phenomenon, one that is entirely encoded in the poetic text — hence his resort to fresh strategies of poetic representation and new rules of reference to extrinsic elements, be they historical, realistic, or even textual. Musical mimesis replaced old forms of poetic representation and led the poet to explore various aspects of the poeticality of words and to create new rhythms as the expression of new modes of experience. In his recent poetry, even the nature of poetic obscurity underwent radical change. Rational obscurity presupposes a framework of intelligibility in which problems can be attributed to the absence of knowledge, and once the necessary arcane knowledge is supplied, the poem becomes rationally coherent. This was replaced by a different type of obscurity which was more philosophical, for the modern poems of this period

involve a discourse that belongs irreducibly to a system of new referentiality and requires fresh conventions. As a result Darwīsh's poetry has become more pensive and sophisticated, for he thinks of himself as a maker of symbols rather than a receiver of symbols made by external reality.

In his recent work, Darwīsh opens new venues for poetic experimentation and continues to play a leading role in the development of the modern and postmodern sensibility. But unlike many Arab poets, his innovative endeavours do not isolate him from the wide reading public who continue to turn his poetry readings into magnificent events.

—Sabry Hafez

———

DAVIS, B. Lynch. *See* **BIOY CASARES, Adolfo.**

———

DAWLATĀBĀDI, Mahmūd. Also Mahmud Dowlatabadi. Iranian. Born in Dawlatābād, in 1940. Worked as a farm labourer; worked in odd jobs for cinemas and theatres in Tehran; completed course (with honours) with Anahita Troup theatre study group; actor for a time; arrested and imprisoned for a few years because of writings. Address: c/o Bazurgmihr Publishers, Tehran, Iran.

PUBLICATIONS

Fiction

Aqīl, Aqīl [The Chief, the Chief].   Tehran, Chāp-e Payk-e Irān, 1974.
Az kham-e chambar [From the Bend of Chambar]. Tehran, Payvand, 1977.
Lāyah 'hā-ye biyābānī [The Layers of the Desert].   Tehran, Payvand, 1978 or 1979.
Gāvārehbān [The Herdsman].   Tehran, Aftāb, 1978.
Tangnā [The Narrow Pass].   Tehran, Payvand, 1978 or 1979.
Kelīdar.   10 vols., 1978–84.
Jā-ye khālī sūlūch [The Empty Place of Sūlūch].   Tehran, Nashr-e Naw, 1982 or 1983.
Kārnāmeh-'e sipanj: majmū'eh-'e dāstān [The 15-Year Record: Collected Stories]   Tehran, Bazurgmihr, 1990.

Play

Qaqnūs [The Phoenix].   Tehran, Nashr-e Naw, 1982 or 1983.

*   *   *

Fiction based on rural life and its harsh realities has become an established form in contemporary Persian literature. Mahmūd Dawlatābādi (Mahmud Dowlatabadi) is at the forefront of a number of writers in this mode. His short stories and novels are largely set in the northeastern regions of Iran, concerned with the people who live on the edge of the great desert and their struggle for survival. In an innovative way, and with a fresh outlook on the life of nomads and villagers, Dawlatābādī presents a vivid picture of their life at a specific moment in time.

His early short stories share a common starting point; in most of them a social crisis of some sort is introduced at the very beginning, and all the other events branch out from this central theme. The characters also develop in relation to the first event of the book; thus we are given a precise picture of the characters and their social milieu, and the way these deprived and simple people try to survive. The social upheavals of the late 1960s and the 1970s, which culminated in the late Shah's so-called White Revolution, play an important part in his fiction. The disintegration of the peasant community and their families formed in a feudal society, as a direct result of the forceful economic changes, form the background of these stories. "Ausaneh Baba Subhan" (The Legend of Baba Subhan) is a typically well-formed and eloquent long story. It opens with tragic news, brought home by Saleh, Baba Subhan's son, that the rich widow Adeleh — the owner of "their" land — is going to take it from them and give it to a young city man, Ghulam, who is completely ignorant of the land and its working. Adeleh, however, is only interested in receiving a greater income from her land so that she can spend it on her life in the city. In what follows, Saleh is killed by Ghulam, and Baba Subhan returns to their village with his corpse, and with his fatally wounded second son. The old man, who has tried very hard to preserve his family and their livelihood, is now left with nothing. The only winner in this struggle is the landowner, who has usurped Saleh's piece of land. Baba Subhan, on the other hand, is now left with only his sorrow and despair: "He did not kindle the light anymore at night, because there was nobody to look at. He did not even put on the oven, because there was nobody to sit opposite him at dinner time."

In this story, the tragedy is the culmination of the events narrated. In another story, "Gavarehban" (The Herdsman), the tragic crisis is, contrastingly, the starting point for a new life. Here as in the previous story the tragedy focuses on the disintegration of the family, but the one who loses his life (at the hands of ruthless army sergeants) is the father and not the son; the son himself has been taken by force to serve his period of conscription, but escapes from the camp, only to arrive in his village just as his father is being buried. He is moved through this tragedy to rebel against the social injustices of his small world. In this short story Dawlatābādī has departed from his usual pessimistic realism and tried to explore the possibilities of the creation of order out of chaos. As is also the case in "Mard" (Man), he portrays small and humble men who can rise above their tragic lives, and display the full potential of human nature, in their capacity to endure and to live in hopes of a better life.

Dawlatābādī completed his masterpiece in 1984; its first volume had been published in 1978. *Kelīdar* (the name of a mountain in the region of Khorasan) is written in 10 volumes (bound in five), and is 3000 pages long. It is a turning point in Persian fiction, insofar as it combines two major literary genres, the novel and the epic. It portrays the desert, and the nomadic lives of a hundred people, who share their griefs, pains, and joys during the 1940s when the influence of the Communists had infiltrated different layers of society. Central to the story is the Kalmīshī household with its extended family. Their lives and destinies are inevitably interwoven with the lives of others in the community, from their fellow nomads and villagers to the local gendarmes. The climatic extremes of the desert are both cause of, and backcloth to, their sufferings and their labour.

Gol Muhammad, the second son of the family, and the main protagonist and hero of the novel, is imprisoned for killing two representatives of the government, who have come to collect taxes on the cattle which the drought has destroyed. With the help of an enigmatic cobbler, Sattar (implicitly identified as a communist), he escapes, and is forced to take up arms against the government. He and his bandit supporters are eventually gunned down. His tragic life is encompassed in a series of heroic acts against the injustices of nature, society, and the government. His name inspires awe among the villagers, who love him dearly because they see him as a symbol of justice. (His character is actually based on the life of a real bandit hero of the same name.) Sattar, disappointed by the ineffectiveness of the Communist party, joins his friend, whom he has come to idealize.

Kelīdar is also a remarkable linguistic achievement. Its language, in the tradition of the great epic poet Firdowsi, is predominantly pure Persian (purged as far as possible of Arabic diction) into which is fused the dialect of Khorāsān. Dawlatābādī's artistry lies in the way he unites the colloquial language of modern fiction with the idiom of the literary epic, so as to create a rhythmic and musical language akin to poetry. Similarly, both his familiarity with the northeastern regions of Iran and his interest in the theatre contribute to the realistic and vivid pictures of the windswept landscape, and its inhabitants which characterise his novels.

—Parvin Loloi

———

DE QUEIROZ, Rachel. *See* **QUEIROZ, Rachel de.**

———

DEDALUS. *See* **ECO, Umberto.**

———

DEGUY, Michel. French. Born in Paris, 23 May 1930. Educated at the University of Paris, docteur ès lettres. Married to Monique Brossollet; two daughters and one son. Professor, University of Paris VIII; President, Collège International de Philosophie, Paris. Co-founder, *La Revue de la Poésie*, Paris; member of the editorial board, *Po&sie*; formerly reader for Gallimard publishers. Recipient: Fénéon prize, 1961; Max Jacob prize, 1962; Ministry of Culture poetry prize, 1989; Académie Mallarmé prize. Address: 48 rue de Vaugirard, 75006 Paris, France.

PUBLICATIONS

Verse

Les Meurtrières.   Paris, Oswald, 1959.
Fragments du cadastre.   Paris, Gallimard, 1960.
Poèmes de la presqu'île.   Paris, Gallimard, 1961.
Biefs.   Paris, Gallimard, 1964.
Ouï-dire.   Paris, Gallimard, 1966.
Figurations.   Paris, Gallimard, 1969.
Poèmes 1960–1970.   Paris, Gallimard, 1973.
Jumelages; Made in USA.   Paris, Seuil, 1978.
Given Giving: Selected Poems, translated by Clayton Eshleman.   Berkeley, University of California Press, 1984.
Gisants.   Paris, Gallimard, 1985.
Poèmes II: 1970–1980.   Paris, Gallimard, 1986.
Arrêts fréquents.   Paris, Métailié, 1990.

Other

Le Monde de Thomas Mann.   Paris, Plon, 1962.
Actes.   Paris, Gallimard, 1966.
Tombeau de Du Bellay.   Paris, Gallimard, 1973.
Reliefs.   Paris, Atelier, 1975.
Donnant donnant: cartes, aires, brevets.   Paris, Gallimard, 1981.
La Machine matrimoniale, ou, Marivaux.   Paris, Gallimard, 1982.
Brevets.   Seyssel, Champ Vallon, 1986.
Choses de la poésie et affaire culturelle.   Paris, Hachette, 1986.
Le Comité de lecture: confessions d'un lecteur de Grande Maison.   Seyssel, Champ Vallon, 1988.
La Poésie n'est pas seule.   Paris, Seuil, 1988.
Aux Heures d'affluence, with Bernard Dorny.   Paris, Chez Dutrou, 1991.
Axiomatique rosace, with Michel Canteloup.   Paris, Carte Blanche, 1991.
Un Poléoscope.   Paris, Collectif Génération, 1991.

Editor, with Jean-Pierre Dupuy, *René Girard et le problème du mal*.   Paris, Grasset, 1982.

Translator, with Jacques Roubald, *Vingt Poètes américains*.   Paris, Gallimard, 1980.
Translator, *La Langue greffée*, by John Montague.   Paris, Belin, 1988.

*

Critical Studies: "Musing: Michel Deguy's Language as Mask and Matrix" by Mary Ann Caws, in *The Language of Poetry*, edited by Michael Bishop, Amsterdam, Rodopi, n.d.; "The Coherence of (R)evolution: The Poetics of Michel Deguy" by Michael Bishop, in *Forum for Modern Language Studies* (St. Andrews, Fife), January 1983; "Poetics into Practice with Michel Deguy" by Steven Winspur, in *Poesis*, 5(4), 1984; "Michel Deguy and the Ethics of Figuration" by Wilson Baldridge, in *Symposium* (Syracuse, New York), Summer 1987; "The Sublime in Michel Deguy's Aural Calligrams," in *Language and Style* (Flushing, New York), Spring 1987, and "The Poetry of Michel Deguy," in *World Literature Today* (Norman, Oklahoma), Winter 1988, both by Gabriella Bedetti.

*   *   *

Poet, philosopher, critic Michel Deguy is the author of numerous works of great diversity. He figures among the most important of our postmodernist poets, among the most significant practitioners of philosophy in the continental (Heideggerian) tradition, and among the most active editors of and collaborators in the influential literary and cultural journals of France.

Deguy's practice of poetry is inseparable from his contemplation of it, and his work both reflects his philosophic concerns and reveals a soundly constructed poetics. It focuses on what has been termed the pre-reflexive or pre-cognitive mode of being common to all, and on the articulation of the relation of individual to world. Auto-reflexive, his poetry reveals a consistent effort to demarcate the site of poetisation which, for him, lies in metaphor: since language is fundamentally irreducible to and unidentifiable with that of which it speaks, poetry can express only through comparison. For Deguy, it is the *comme* (the "like" or "as") of the comparison that constitutes the primary operation of the poetic utterance, and the act of making poems consists therefore in transferring the inherently poetic dimension of the world into language. A phenomenological exploration of creative expression combines in his poetry with a highly energetic and often ludic or playful synthesizing of contemporary culture. It is this combination of density and intensity, on the one hand, and playfulness and comprehensiveness, on the other, that, along with the often labyrinthic structuring of his poems, has led to Deguy's reputation as a "difficult" poet.

Fragments du cadastre (Fragments of the Cadastre) and *Poèmes de la presqu'île* (Peninsular Poems) are among Deguy's first volumes of poetry. In both, the poet tries to come to terms with the "spectacle" of the world and with what Michael Bishop, in *Michel Deguy* (Amsterdam, Rodopi, 1988) calls, "une dialectique ontologique et scripturale qui reste — toujours, à chaque instant — à résoudre" (an ontological and scriptural dialectic which remains — always, at every instant — to resolve.) The poet's global vision of the world, his contemplation of it as distinct from and yet forever linked to its articulation in poetic writing, leads him to seek "a truth" at once unifying and differentiating. The problem of alterity, of the other, whether the otherness of the world or that of another human or material presence within it, haunts these volumes and leads the poet to consider not only the essential relation of word to world, but of self to all that is not the self, and of individual to universal. From this vast enterprise, Deguy erects an at times anxious, but always lucid cosmography devoid of nostalgia in its persistent neutrality.

Deguy's poetics achieve a new depth in his third major collection of poems, *Biefs*, where the allegorical depiction of expressivity reveals a reality forever in dissolution and the poet as the only possible giver of meaning. As in his other volumes, Deguy's spatial preoccupation and geometrization of the world is most evident—the juxtaposition, proximity, and overlapping of "things" creating a *lieu* (place), a "zone" whose contemplation gives rise to a circularity (what Bishop calls "une réciprocité vertigineuse mais richement lucide" [a vertiginous but richly lucid reciprocity]) of word and world, part and whole, symbol and meaning. Here, as in the soon to follow volumes *Ouï-dire* (By Word of Mouth), *Actes* (Acts), and *Figurations*, the word, speech, like any other "thing" of the world, is material and spatial, while simultaneously not being so. As Deguy claims in an essay whose title — "Ce qui a lieu d'être ne va pas sans dire" (That meant to be does not go without saying) — unveils much that is both characteristic of his play with language and his thinking on poetry, poetic language is not spatial insofar as it opens space, says space, and originates that place expressible, only by expressions comparable but irreducible to it.

In *Jumelages; Made in USA* (Twinnings/Made in USA) and *Given Giving*, the complexities of Deguy's poetics — above all, the paradoxal notion of poetry as a (rhetorical) figuration of the world that cannot figure (i.e., ex-press) what it is not — are rendered all the more apparent by an insistence on the infinite possibilities of language, on the freedom of verbal and typographical choice. As in the more recent *Gisants*, the poet seeks a connection between the "sublimation" necessarily operative within the poetic utterance and the non-verbal recognition of the figure as such: the "'comme *comme* comme'" (the like *like* like). In *Gisants*, death becomes the site of the (re)enactment of the poetic act, the place — beyond the insufficiency, impotency, and failure of language to re-present — of the originating function of poetry and thus of the configuring of the world and the transfiguring of being in language. *Brevets* (Patents) and Deguy's other recent volumes are further illustrations of the vastness, the richness of this uniquely panoramic vision.

Throughout most of his writings, Deguy's effort consists in uncovering the ways and means of the fundamental metaphorical functioning of poetic language, a functioning defined as the seizing hold of the order of the disposition of things of the world. The language of the poet operates, therefore, in that space, that undefinable interval, that defines the proximity of things, that reveals them as similar, yet different; as Deguy has written, ". . . the poem is in the figure, and not the figure in the poem."

—Lois Oppenheim

———

DEL PASO, Fernando. *See* **PASO, Fernando del.**

———

DELIBES (Setien), Miguel. Spanish. Born in Valladolid, 17 October 1920. Educated at Hermanos Doctrina Christiana School, Bachillerato; University of Valladolid, doctor of law 1944; Escuela Altos Estudios Mercantiles; Escuela Periodismo. Served in the Spanish Navy, 1938–39. Married Angeles de Castro Ruiz in 1946 (died 1974); five sons and two daughters. Taught mercantile law at Valladolid; visiting professor, University of Maryland, College Park, 1964. Director, El Norte de Castilla, Valladolid. Recipient: Nadal prize, 1948; Ministry of Information Cervantes prize, 1955; Fastenrath prize, 1959; National Critics' prize, 1963; Prince of Asturias prize for literature, 1983; Castilla y León de las letras prize, 1984; City of Barcelona prize, 1987. Honorary doctorate: universities of Valladolid, Madrid, and Saarbrücken. Member, Royal Academy of Language. Agent: Ediciones Destino, Consejo de Ciento 425, 08009 Barcelona, Spain. Address: Dos de Mayo 10, Valladolid, Spain.

PUBLICATIONS

Fiction

La sombra del ciprés es alargada.   Barcelona, Destino, 1948.

Aún es de día.   Barcelona, Destino, 1949.
El camino.   Barcelona, Destino, 1950; as *The Path*, New York, Day, and London, Hamish Hamilton, 1961.
Mi idolatrado hijo Sisí.   Barcelona, Destino, 1953.
El loco.   Madrid, Prensa Española, 1953.
La partida.   Barcelona, Caralt, 1954.
Los raíles.   Madrid, Prensa Española, 1954.
Diario de un cazador.   Barcelona, Destino, 1955.
Siestas con viento sur.   Barcelona, Destino, 1957.
Diario de un emigrante.   Barcelona, Destino, 1958.
La hoja roja.   Barcelona, Destino, 1959.
Las ratas.   Barcelona, Destino, 1962; as *Smoke on the Ground*, New York, Doubleday, 1972.
Cinco horas con Mario.   Barcelona, Destino, 1966; as *Five Hours with Mario*, New York, Columbia University Press, 1988.
La mortaja.   Madrid, Alianza, 1969; enlarged edition, Madrid, Cátedra, 1984.
Parábola del náufrago.   Barcelona, Destino, 1969; as *The Hedge*, New York, Columbia University Press, 1983.
El principe destronado.   Barcelona, Destino, 1973; as *The Prince Dethroned*, Madrid, Iberia, 1986.
Las guerras de nuestros antepasados.   Barcelona, Destino, 1975.
El disputado voto del señor Cayo.   Barcelona, Destino, 1978.
Los santos inocentes.   Barcelona, Planeta, 1981.
El otro fútbol.   Barcelona, Destino, 1982.
Tres pájaros de cuenta.   Valladolid, Miñon, 1982.
Cartas de amor de un sexagenario voluptuoso.   Barcelona, Destino, 1983.
El tesoro.   Barcelona, Destino, 1985.
377A, madera de héroe.   Barcelona, Destino, 1987; as *The Stuff of Heroes*, New York, Pantheon, 1990.
Señora de rojo sobre fondo gris.   Barcelona, Destino, 1991.

Plays

Cinco horas con Mario, from his own novel (produced Madrid, 1980).
La hoja roja, from his own novel.   Barcelona, Destino, 1987.

Television Plays: *Tierras de Valladolid*, 1966; *La Mortaja*; *Castilla, esta es mi tierra*, 1983.

Other

Un novelista descubre América: Chile en el ojo ajeno.   Madrid, Nacional, 1956.
La barbería.   Barcelona, G.P., 1957.
Castilla, photographs by Ramon Masats.   Barcelona, Lumen, 1960; as *Viejas historias de Castilla la Vieja*, 1964.
La caza de la perdiz roja, photographs by Oriol Maspons.   Barcelona, Lumen, 1963.
Europa: parada y fonda.   Madrid, Cid, 1963.
El libro de la caza menor.   Barcelona, Destino, 1964.
Obras completas.   Barcelona, Destino, 5 vols., 1964–75.
USA y yo.   Barcelona, Destino, 1966.
Vivir al día.   Barcelona, Destino, 1968.
La primavera de Praga.   Madrid, Alianza, 1968.
Con la escopeta al hombro.   Barcelona, Destino, 1970.
Un año de mi vida.   Barcelona, Destino, 1972.
La caza en España.   Madrid, Alianza, 1972.
Castilla en mi obra.   Madrid, Editorial Magisterio Español, 1972.
S.O.S.: el sentido del progreso desde mi obra.   Barcelona, Destino, 1975.

Aventuras, venturas, y desventuras de un cazador a rabo. Barcelona, Destino, 1977.

Mis amigas las truchas. Barcelona, Destino, 1977.

Castilla, lo castellano, y los castellanos. Barcelona, Planeta, 1979.

Un mundo que agoniza. Barcelona, Plaza & Janés, 1979; as *El mundo en la agonía*, Barcelona, Círculo de Lectores, 1988.

Las perdices del domingo. Barcelona, Destino, 1981.

Dos viajes en automóvil: Suecia y países bajos. Barcelona, Plaza & Janés, 1982.

La censura de prensa en los años 40, y otros ensayos. Valladolid, Ambito, 1985.

Cinco horas con Miguel Delibes (interviews), with Javier Goñi. Madrid, Anjana, 1985.

Castilla habla. Barcelona, Destino, 1986.

Mi vida al aire libre: memorias deportivas de un hombre sedentario. Barcelona, Destino, 1989.

Pegar la hebra. Barcelona, Destino, 1990.

El conejo. Madrid, Compañía Europa de Comunicación e Información, 1991.

*

Critical Studies: "The Religious Significance of Miguel Delibes's *Las ratas*" by Dorothy Ewing, in *Romance Notes* (Chapel Hill, North Carolina), 11, 1970; *Miguel Delibes*, New York, Twayne, 1971, "Miguel Delibes' Vision of Castilla," in *South Atlantic Bulletin*, 36(3), 1971, and "Thematic Reiteration and Linguistic Preoccupation in Miguel Delibes' Latest Novel," in *Crítica Hispánica* (Pittsburgh), 1, 1979, all by Janet W. Díaz, and "Structural and Thematic Reiteration in Miguel Delibes' Recent Fiction" by Díaz and Ricardo Landeira, in *Hispania* (Los Angeles), 63, 1980; "Environmental Concerns in Miguel Delibes" by Michael H. Handelsman, in *South Atlantic Bulletin*, 40(4), 1975; "Miguel Delibes' *Parábola del náufrago*: Utopia Redreamed," in *Studies in 20th-Century Literature* (Manhattan, Kansas), 1, 1976, and "Cinco horas con Mario and the Dynamics of Irony," in *Anales de la Novela de Posguerra*, 2, 1977, both by H. L. Boudreau; "Language Manipulation and Social Order in Miguel Delibes' *Parábola del náufrago*" by Roberta A. Quance, in *Essays in Literature* (Macomb, Illinois), 3, 1976; "Language and Communication in Miguel Delibes' *Parábola del náufrago*" by John W. Kronik, in *The American Hispanist* (Clear Creek, Indiana), 1(1), 1977; "Miguel Delibes' Two Views of the Spanish Mother" by Phyllis Zatlin-Boring, in *Hispanófila* (Chapel Hill, North Carolina), 63, 1978; "Automatization and Defamiliarization in Miguel Delibes' *Parábola del náufrago*" by David K. Herzberger, in *Modern Language Notes* (Baltimore, Maryland), 95, 1980; "An Archetypal Interpretation of *La hoja roja*," in *University of Dayton Review* (Dayton, Ohio), 15(1), 1981, and "Eliade's Concept of the Sacred in Miguel Delibes' *Las ratas*," in *La Chispa '81*, edited by Gilbert Paolini, New Orleans, Tulane University, 1981, both by Elizabeth Rogers, "Foregrounding as a Performative Device in *Las ratas*" by Leo Hickey, in *Hispanófila* (Chapel Hill, North Carolina), 31(2[92]), 1988; "The Emergence of Women in the Novels of Miguel Delibes" by Donald W. Tucker, in *Hispania* (Los Angeles), 71(1), 1988; "Narrative and Technology in Miguel Delibes' *The Hedge*: Can Humankind Have Any Hope?" by Barbara Currier Bell, in *Ometeca*, 1(1), 1989.

*   *   *

Miguel Delibes, one of Spain's best novelists, has also written essays, travel books, and non-fiction. Some of his

characters, whose psychological penetration is central to his novels, are innocent and idealistic; others are solitary and alienated; but simple or complicated, they personify the fight for human dignity and freedom.

La sombra del ciprés es alargada (The Cypress's Shadow Is Lengthened), his first and partly autobiographical novel, follows the tenets of traditional Spanish fiction. Delibes's characters seek in vain for the affirmation of love and faith in a world of solitude and death. *El camino* (The Path), based on the recollections of an 11-year-old boy just before his trip from country to city, idealizes small village life in contrast with so-called progress. Through picturesque and at times poetic anecdotal incidents, told with greath warmth and humor, Delibes stresses the importance of nature in the process of growing up. *Diario de un cazador* (Diary of a Hunter), another early work, concerns the passion for the hunt of a non-intellectual but proud beadle. Delibes, masterfully transcribing oral and colloquial language, shows that man, overwhelmed by civilization, must from time to time seek out his primitive roots.

Many consider *Cinco horas con Mario* (*Five Hours with Mario*) to be his masterpiece and a sample of Delibes's new sophistication as a novelist. The long interior monologue (a kind of free association conveyed through a chaotic temporal technique) by Carmen before the corpse of her husband becomes a dialogue between the living and the dead. Carmen, who presumably typifies the Spanish middle class and its hypocritical and vulgar viewpoints, is shallow, bigoted, and unforgiving. Delibes contrasts, through appropriate biblical passages at the beginning of each chapter, Christian charity with her own false values. An attack on Franco Spain, the novel, in spite of its irony, may be read as a defense of individual liberties.

Parábola del náufrago (The Hedge), a fantasy of modern man trapped in a dehumanizing Orwellian State, depicts the author's nightmare vision of technology and authoritarianism which turns men into helpless beasts. In this, his most experimental novel, Delibes employs free association, allegory, and oneiric imagery, together with distorted grammar and punctuation.

Among Delibes's later works, *Las guerras de nuestros antepasados* (The Wars of Our Ancestors), told through seven taped conversations between the protagonist, a marginal victim of society, and a psychiatrist, shows how modern Spaniards were prepared by tradition to indulge in violence, an integral part of humanity, which each man carries in his soul. Continuing his commentary on Spanish hatred and violence, Delibes, in *El disputado voto del señor Cayo* (The Disputed Vote of Mr. Cayo), contrasts rural wisdom with urban sophistry, and in *El tesoro* (The Treasure), a short novel, he again reflects the violence and greed at an archeological site and the continuing friction between city and country. One of Delibes's best novels, *377A, madera de héroe* (The Stuff of Heroes), attempts to decipher personal guilt and betrayal and determine true heroism before and during the Spanish Civil War, through a portrayal of the life of Gervasio García de Lastra, assigned the number 377A in the navy.

In Delibes's novels rural Old Castile and nature suffer from the destruction caused by an ever more technological world. Humanity, says Delibes, must learn to accommodate its thirst for liberty with the needs of society, but, in spite of his pessimism, he has not given up hope that man may yet find happiness, even in a grotesque and dehumanized world.

—Kessel Schwartz

DEPESTRE, René. Haitian and French. Born in Jacmel, Haiti, 29 August 1926. Became French citizen in 1991. Educated at the Lycée Pinchinat, Jacmel, and the Lycée Pétion, Port-au-Prince, 1939–44; the Sorbonne and the Institut d'Études Politiques, University of Paris, 1946–51. Married 1) Edith Sorel in 1950 (divorced 1961); 2) Nelly Campano in 1962, two sons. Journalist in Haiti, various Latin American countries, and Cuba; founder, with Jacques Stephen Alexis, Haitian Communist Party; participated in Haitian revolution, 1946: imprisoned, then expelled, 1946; expelled twice from France, once from Cuba, then lived in Chile, Argentina, and Brazil, 1951–55; returned to Haiti, 1958; moved to Cuba, 1959; teacher and editor, Cuba, 1959–78; also worked for Ministry of External Relations, National Cultural Council, and Radio Havana; expelled from Cuba, 1978; member of the Secretariat, 1979–86, attaché to the Office of the Director General, 1979–82, and to the Office of Culture, 1982–86, Unesco, Paris. Recipient: Goncourt prize, 1982; Renaudot prize, 1988; Société des Gens de Lettres prize, 1988; City of Montpellier Antigone prize, 1988; Académie Royale prize (Belgium), 1988. Address: 31 bis, Route de Roubia, 11200 Lézignan-Corbières, France.

PUBLICATIONS

Verse

Étincelles. Port-au-Prince, Imprimerie de l'État, 1945.
Gerbe de sang. Port-au-Prince, Imprimerie de l'État, 1946.
Végétations de clarté. Paris, Seghers, 1951; as *Vegetations of Splendor*, New York, Vanguard, 1981.
Minerai noir. Paris, Présence Africaine, 1956.
Journal d'un animal marin. Paris, Seghers, 1964.
Un Arc-en-ciel pour l'Occident chrétien. Paris, Présence Africaine, 1967; as *A Rainbow for the Christian West*, translated by Jack Hirschman, Fairfax, California, Red Hill Press, 1972.
Cantate d'octobre à la vie et à la mort du commandant Ernesto Che Guevara. Havana, Institut du Livre, 1968; revised edition, Algiers, SNED, 1969.
Poète à Cuba. Paris, Oswald, 1976.
En État de poésie. Paris, Les Éditeurs Français Réunis, 1980.
Journal d'un animal marin: choisi de poèmes, 1956–1990. Paris, Gallimard, 1990.
Au Matin de la négritude. Luxembourg, Euroeditor, 1990.
Anthologie personnelle. Arles, Actes Sud, 1992.

Fiction

Le Mât de cocagne. Paris, Gallimard, 1979; as *The Festival of the Greasy Pole*, Charlottesville, University Press of Virginia, 1990.
Alléluia pour une femme-jardin. Paris, Gallimard, 1982.
Hadriana dans tous mes rêves. Paris, Gallimard, 1988.
Éros dans un train chinois: neuf histoires d'amour et un conte de sorcier. Paris, Gallimard, 1990.

Other

Por la revolución, por la poesía. Montevideo, Marcha, 1970; as *Pour la Révolution, pour la poésie*, Montreal, Leméac, 1974.
Influencia del Africa en las literaturas antillanas, with Henry Bangou and George Lamming. Montevideo, ILAC, 1972.

Problemas de la indentidad del hombre negro en las literaturas antillanas. Mexico City, Universidad Nacional Autónoma de México, 1978.
Bonjour et adieu à la négritude: travaux d'identité. Paris, Laffont, 1980.

Editor and Translator, *Poésie cubaine, 1959–1966.* Havana, Institut du Livre, 1967.

Translator, *Le Grand Zoo*, by Nicolas Guillén. Paris, Seghers, 1967.
Translator, *Avec les Mêmes Mains*, by Roberto F. Retamar. Paris, Oswald, 1969.
Translator, *Un Catalogue de vieilles automobiles*, by César Fernandez Moreno. Paris, Unesco/Cherche-Midi, 1992.

*

Bibliography: in *René Depestre*, by Claude Couffon, Paris, Seghers, 1986.

Critical Studies: *Cultural Identity, Négritude, and Decolonization: The Haitian Situation in the Light of the Socialist Humanism of Jacques Roumain and René Depestre* by Guy Viêt Levilain, New York, American Institute for Marxist Studies, 1978; "The New Political Statement in Haitian Fiction" by Joseph Ferdinand, in *Voices from Under: Black Narrative in Latin America and the Caribbean*, edited by William Luis, Westport, Connecticut, Greenwood, 1984; "'Hallelujah for a Garden-Woman': The Caribbean Adam and His Pretext" by Joan Dayan, in *French Review* (Santa Barbara, California), March 1986; "The Umbrella, the Night World, and the Lonely Moon" by Milan Kundera, in *The New York Review*, 19 December 1991.

*   *   *

Haitian writer René Depestre seems to have been expelled from more countries than he has lived in! Born in Haiti in 1926, he and fellow writer Jacques Stephen Alexis enthusiastically founded the Haitian Communist Party in 1946 when Depestre was barely 20, and were expelled from Haiti that same year after the country's revolution. Depestre then lived in and was thrown out of several countries, finally spending almost 20 years in Cuba, his "second homeland," as he called it. However, his collection of poetry *Poète à Cuba* (Poet in Cuba), published in France in 1976, was openly critical of certain aspects of Cuban Communism; it was banned from publication in Cuba, and Depestre was eventually obliged to leave the country in 1978. He then moved to France, where he still lives.

Depestre began writing fiery, militant poetry as a teenager, publishing *Étincelles* (Sparks) when he was 19. From the start he wrote about issues that have remained central to his work: the social, economic, and political exploitation of the underprivileged in general and black people in particular.

> Here I stand
> a proletarian
> I feel within me the rumble
> of the breathing of the masses
> I feel vibrating in me
> the rage of the exploited
> the blood of the whole black humanity
> is bursting my blue veins
> I have melted all races
> in my burning heart.

This passionate rage is not simply a product of youthful energy, however; it has remained a constant, energising power throughout Depestre's work.

Depestre quickly gained a reputation as Haiti's most militant poet, writing with spirit about revolution, justice, and *négritude*, the term coined by the Martiniquais poet Aimé Césaire (*q.v.*) to describe a movement towards fuller awareness of a distinctive black consciousness rooted in Africanness. In *Un Arc-en-ciel pour l'Occident chrétien* (*A Rainbow for the Christian West*), a long poetic work condemning the nuclear proliferation of the 1950s and 1960s, Depestre defines his role as the "Negro-Tempest" who, as Guy Viêt Levilain describes it, proclaims his "noble wrath":

> Yes, I am the Negro-Tempest
> a Negro-root of rainbow
> my heart clenches like a fist
> to smash the faces of the false gods
> at the end of my sadness
> there are growing claws.

Rainbow takes on a Whitman-like intensity and momentum as it begins likening the power of the Negro-Tempest to figures from Haitian mythology as well as revolutionaries from the past, both black and white. In the end, however, Depestre acknowledges that the answer to evil in the world is not violence, but wisdom:

> come back prodigal daughter of knowledge
> to rule over our most familiar beacons
> come back to give our wisdom
> the shape and perfume of roses
> come back to raise with our most gentle tides
> a new age of human heart!

With time Depestre's poetry becomes calmer, tempered by the maturity that comes with experience of a painful world. What his style loses in manic energy, however, it gains in elegance and grace, as in the elegiac "Ode to the 20th Century," from the banned collection *Poète à Cuba*. He mourns the loss of innocence, love, and light in the world:

> My century, my love and my cross
> Here I am lying in its darkness
> I am an animal who grazes on its grass.
> The pain I suffer is the lack of tenderness
> That chokes this age, I am
> sick from a world where one is never loved.

Depestre no longer plays the role of the inspired and inspiring revolutionary: the Negro-Tempest has given way to the martyr, the poet-sacrifice. He says

> O my 20th century, my assassin,
> You can quench your thirst for fresh blood in my veins,
> You can assuage your hatred upon my body
> But to men keep your promises of happiness,
> Sow new seeds in the furrows of the rights of man,
> Attach the sun to the mill of their dreams
> Attach my life to the wheel of darkness . . .

His tone is not completely resigned, however; he still holds on to the belief that it is still possible for the world to change for the better, even if he will have to sacrifice taking part in it.

More recent poems combine his early passion with a mature lyricism. At times his poetry is celebratory, as in poems to his wife, and to other poets like Léon Damas and Aimé Césaire ("I sing Aimé Césaire: I laugh, I dance for joy/for the man with a head full of roots and justice").

Depestre's move to France in 1978 marked two new directions for him. He began working at Unesco, where he could direct his desire for justice and human rights to concrete ends. And he began writing fiction for the first time, publishing in 1979 *Le Mât de cocagne* (*The Festival of the Greasy Pole*), a political novel set in Haiti. In 1982 his collection of short stories *Alléluia pour une femme-jardin* (Hallelujah for a Garden-Woman) won the Goncourt prize, and those who didn't know him already as a poet discovered writing suffused with bold imagery and a frank eroticism that had been apparent but never central in his poetry. Milan Kundera (*q.v.*) has called Depestre "a true master of the marvellous," and describes *Alléluia pour une femme-jardin* as "a world where vice and innocence are one and the same thing."

With his second novel, *Hadriana dans tous mes rêves* (Hadriana in All My Dreams), winning rave reviews and many prizes, Depestre is now established as a master of passionate writing in two genres.

—Theresa Werner

DÍAZ (Gutierrez), Jorge. Chilean and Spanish. Born in Rosario, Argentina, 20 February 1930; moved to Chile in 1934. Educated at the Catholic University, Santiago, degree in architecture 1956. Painter, briefly; actor and set designer, from 1959, and president, 1963–64, ICTUS theatre group, Santiago; emigrated to Spain, 1965; director, Teatro del Nuevo Mundo theatre group, 1969–71, and Teatro Trabalenguas, 1972–81. Since 1980 scriptwriter for radio and television. Recipient: Critics' prize (Chile), 1961; Municipality of Santiago prize, 1963; Calaf prize, 1964; Golden Laurels (Chile), 1965; 18 prizes for theatre in Spain; two prizes for stories. Address: c/. Cava Baja, 1 — Apartamento 410, 28005 Madrid, Spain.

PUBLICATIONS

Plays

Un hombre llamado Isla (produced Santiago, 1961).
El cepillo de dientes (one-act version produced Santiago, 1961; two-act version produced Madrid, 1966).   Included in *La víspera de degüello*, 1967; Philadelphia, Center for Curriculum Development, 1971.
Réquiem para un girasol (produced Santiago, 1961). Santiago, n.p., 1963.
El velero en la botella (produced Santiago, 1962). With *El cepillo de dientes; o, Náufragos en el parque de atracciones*, Santiago, Universitaria, 1973.
Chumingo y el pirata de lata (for children), with Mónica Echeverría (produced Santiago, 1963). Revised version, as *El pirata de hojalata* (produced Huelva, Spain, 1972).
El lugar donde mueren los mamíferos (produced Santiago, 1963).   Published in *Conjunto* (Havana), 1, 1964.
Variaciones para muertos de persecución (produced Santiago, 1964).
Serapio y Yerbabuena (for children) (produced Santiago, 1964).

La mala nochebuena de don Etcétera (for children) (produced Santiago, 1964).

El nudo ciego (produced Santiago, 1965).

Canción de cuna para un decapitado (produced 1966).

Topografía de un desnudo: esquema para una indagación inútil (produced Santiago, 1967). Santiago, Editora Santiago, 1967.

La víspera del degüello (produced Madrid, 1970). Madrid, Taurus, 1967; as *The Eve of the Execution; or, Genesis Was Tomorrow*, in *Modern One-Act Plays from Latin America*, Los Angeles, University of California, 1974.

La víspera de degüello (includes *El cepillo de dientes*; *Réquiem por un girasol*; *La víspera de degüello*). Madrid, Taurus, 1967.

Introducción al elefante y otras zoologías (produced Chile, 1968).

La orgástula (produced 1970).

Liturgia para cornudos (produced Santiago, 1970). Revised version, as *Ceremonia ortopédica* (produced Pamplona, 1976), included in *Teatro, ceremonias de la soledad*, 1978.

Los ángeles ladrones (for children) (produced Santiago, 1970).

Pirueta y Voltereta (for children) (produced Léon, 1970).

La pancarta (produced Madrid, 1971). Included in *Teatro difícil*, Madrid, Escelicer, 1971.

Americaliente (produced Puerto Rico, 1971).

Algo para contar en Navidad (produced Barcelona, 1972). Barcelona, Don Bosco, 1974.

Antropofagia de salón; o, Electroshock para gente de orden (produced Madrid, 1973).

Amaos los unos sobre los otros. Published as *Love Yourself Above All Others*, in *One-Act Plays*, Pittsburgh, University of Pittsburgh Press, 1973.

Los alacranes; Las hormigas (produced Madrid, 1973).

Os anxos cómense crús, music by Vittorio Cintolesi. Vigo, Galaxia, 1973.

Rascatripa (for children) (produced Madrid, 1973).

La barraca de Jipi Japa (for children) (produced Madrid, 1974).

Educastración de Supermán (produced 1975).

El supercoco (for children) (produced Córdoba, 1975).

Cuentos para armar entre todos (for children) (produced Madrid, 1975).

Mata a tu prójimo como a ti mismo (produced Valencia, 1976). Madrid, Cultura Hispánica, 1977; as *Esplendor carnal de la ceniza* (produced Santiago, 1984).

Contrapunto para dos voces cansadas; o, El locutorio (produced as *El locutorio*, Valladolid, 1979). As *El locutorio*, with *El cerco de la peste*, by José González Torices, Valladolid, Caja de Ahorros Provincial, 1976.

Mear contra el viento, with Francisco Javier Uriz (produced Lisbon, 1976).

Rinconete y Cortadillo, adaptation of a work by Miguel de Cervantes (for children) (produced Vigo, 1976).

La puñeta (produced Pamplona, 1977).

La ciudad que tiene la cara sucia (for children) (produced Madrid, 1977).

Un día es un día; o, Los sobre vivientes (produced Madrid, 1978).

Teatro, ceremonias de la soledad (includes *El locutorio*; *Mata a tu prójimo como a ti mismo*; *Ceremonia ortopédica*). Santiago, Nascimento, 1978.

La manifestación (produced Valladolid, 1979).

El espantajo (produced Nîmes, 1979).

Equación (produced Zaragoza, 1979).

El mariscalito; o, El generalito (for children) (produced Madrid, 1979).

Séneca, ratón de biblioteca (for children) (produced Córdoba, 1979).

La dragonera (for children) (produced Barcelona, 1980).

El imperio del humo (for children) (produced Caracas, 1980).

Toda esta larga noche (produced Munich, 1981).

Estuias o trabajas?, with Rafael Herrero (produced Madrid, 1981).

Los juguetes olvidados (for children) (produced Barcelona, 1981).

"Piel contra piel" (produced Santiago, 1982).

Un ombligo para dos (produced Madrid, 1982).

Oscuro vuelo compartido (produced Spain, 1982).

Ligeros de equipaje (produced Sitges, 1982). Published in *Primer Acto*, 1985.

Viaje alrededor de un pañuelo (for children) (produced Madrid, 1983).

La ciudad al revés (for children) (produced 1983).

El guirigay; o, Zambacanuta (for children) (produced Santiago, 1983).

Entre pícaros (for children) (produced 1983).

Desde la sangre y el silencio; o, Fulgor y muerte de Pablo Neruda (produced Rostock, 1984).

Las cicatrices de la memoria (finale, allegro ma non troppo) (produced Spain, 1985). Madrid, Cultura Hispánica, Instituto de Cooperación Iberoamericana, 1986.

Ulises en el titirimundo (for children) (produced Madrid, 1985).

Dicen que la distancia es el olvido (produced Madrid, 1986).

Los tiempos oscuros (produced Montreal, 1986).

La otra orilla. Spain, Junta de Comunidades de Castilla-La Mancha, 1988(?).

Muero, luego existo (produced Spain, 1990).

Un corazón lleno de lluvia (produced Spain, 1991).

A imagen y semejanza (produced Spain, 1991).

Pablo Neruda viene volando (produced Chile, 1991).

Screenplay: *La rosa de los vientos*, 1984.

Radio Plays: *Contrapunto para dos voces cansadas*, 1987; *El abrazo del Winnipeg*, 1989; *Lugares*, 1989; *Los habitantes de la memoria*, 1990.

Television Plays: *El próximo verano*, 1984; *Cosas de dos*, 1986.

Other

El cambio en una empresa del APS, with Manuel Barrera and Gustavo Aranda. Santiago, Instituto de Economía y Planificación, 1973(?).

*

Bibliographies: in *A Bibliographical Guide to the Spanish American Theater* by Frank F. Hebblethwaite, Washington, D.C., Pan American Union, 1969; in *Bibliografía hispanoamericano* by Fernando de Toro and Peter Roster, Frankfurt, Vervuert, 2 vols., 1985.

Critical Studies: "Jorge Díaz and the Liturgy of Violence," in *Dramatists in Revolt: The New Latin American Theatre*, edited by George W. Woodyard and Leon F. Lyday, Austin, University of Texas Press, 1976, and "Ritual as Reality in Díaz's *Mata a tu prójimo como a ti mismo*," in *Estreno: Cuadernos del Teatro Español Contemporáneo*, Autumn 1983, both by George W. Woodyard; "*El cepillo de dientes*: Empty Words, Empty Games?" by Ronald D. Burgess, in *Estreno: Cuadernos del Teatro Español Contemporáneo*, Autumn 1983;

"Stage and Audience: Jorge Díaz's *El lugar donde mueren los mamíferos* and *Topografía de un desnudo*" by Kirsten F. Nigro, in *Estreno: Cuadernos del Teatro Español Contemporáneo*, Autumn 1983; "Inversion in the Absurdist Plays of Jorge Díaz" by Leon F. Lyday, in *Romance Notes* (Chapel Hill, North Carolina), Autumn 1986; "Crest or Pepsodent: Jorge Díaz's *El cepillo de dientes*" by Becky Boling, in *Latin American Theatre Review* (Lawrence, Kansas), 24(1), 1990.

Jorge Díaz comments:

Until very recently, I was governed by two feelings alone: anger and a sense of ridicule. But now the anger has changed to a feeling of tenderness and the sense of ridicule to a smile.

I am growing older and my characters are growing older with me to become, like me, more vulnerable.

Language attracts me as a means of *defining* characters. I never define them by their ideas, nor by their acts, and even less by their psychology (a hateful little word), but in the way in which they speak.

Vague feelings of guilt have led me to write moralizing, epic works, but this is only a disguise; I prefer the incomprehensible, the sudden flash of a phrase or the fleeting quality of a feeling hidden behind a sarcastic comment.

They say that I write about death and sex . . . but is there anything else to write about?

I enjoy collecting scrap materials. My works are always "pastiches," a "collage" of things I have read, of articles. I love "sticking together" (as in a scrapbook) other people's articles that have caught my attention. Just as in a box of odds and ends, you can find in all my works consumer literature, comic strips, my favourite writers.

Perhaps they are only "collages to be read," as I hate performances of the theatre. A theatre performance always makes me run, covered in embarrassment from head to toe.

Sitting at my typewriter I'm perfectly happy, but faced with an open curtain I get embarrassed. Literature is a "con-trick," but to laugh in the company of others is almost as good as making love.

*   *   *

Latin American theatre in the mid-20th century could well find its representative history recorded in the career of a single dramatist, the Argentine-born Chilean playwright Jorge Díaz, who has spent a large part of his adult life living and writing in Spain. Díaz's absurdist works, alive with political sensitivity, creating new forms of dramatic presentation, and challenging the very medium of theatrical expression, language itself, synthesize the experimentations of all Latin American dramatists who have sought since World War II to bring quality and social awareness to artistic theatre in Latin America.

Díaz's early career as designer, actor, author, and director with the Santiago theatrical company ICTUS also parallels the active involvement of contemporary Latin American playwrights with the creation of a non-commercial theatre for audiences receptive to timely political themes. And in a further alignment of Díaz and his colleagues, he ardently calls for the establishment of a continental identity among Latin American dramatists, one that would transcend strictly national concerns. Performed internationally more than any other Chilean playwright, Díaz forcefully articulates Latin American theatre's desire to stir and provoke: "We must give back to the theatre its ritual confrontation with us, its critical ceremonial. And it must be passionate and entertaining" ("Reflections on the Chilean Theatre," *Drama Review*, 14(2), 1970).

The features that characterize the whole of Díaz's production — experimentation with form and the assertive expression of social themes — are evident from the beginning of his career. *El cepillo de dientes* (The Toothbrush), one of his first produced plays and perhaps his most famous, lacks a discernible plot, and relies on the confusions of meaningless language and obliterated personalities to impart its message of the vacuity of a modern capitalist, consumeristic society. As is the case with other of his plays, Díaz rewrote *El cepillo de dientes*, adding a second act and a subtitle, *Náufragos en el parque de atracciones* (Shipwrecked in an Amusement Park), and premiered it in Madrid in 1966. The style of this absurdist play, a classic of the genre, indicates the close attention that Latin American dramatists have paid to their European counterparts, whose theatrical mixtures of violence, humor, and groaning despair achieve additional resonance, social and political, in Latin America. Indeed, Díaz's most overtly political works, such as *Introducción al elefante y otras zoologías* (Introduction to the Elephant and Other Zoologies) and *Americaliente* (Hotamerica), censure repressive U.S. policies in Latin America, and, in the case of the former, invite an open discussion among cast and audience members of the issues dramatized.

But the universality evident in Díaz's works, resulting from his desire both to replace theatre's strictly commercial appeal with artistic substance and to honor his commitment to a Latin American aesthetic, finds its finest expression in his treatment of the themes of communication and alienation. Language, the literary art's only matter and humanity's only source of understanding, is put forth as communication's paramount obstacle. Díaz exposes language for what it is — an arbitrary, conventional construct subject to collapse at any time — and sets about examining its other, neglected qualities: density, sudden poetry, erosion through use, senselessness. Gulping and stammering, falling silent and babbling, human beings strive mightily to make themselves understood. Formalized language such as slogans and jingles remove us further from something approaching a pure transmission of meaning. In *El nudo ciego* (The Blind Knot) characters' inner thoughts are heard through headsets used by the spectators.

La orgástula (The Orgastula), with its male and female characters bound together in white gauze forming one body, transforms this linguistic theme into a philosophical one, that of alienation in confinement: small numbers of characters create great torment for each other. *El lugar donde mueren los mamíferos* (The Place Where the Mammals Die) presents a long sought-after poor man, who is made a model of Latin American penury by the director of a charitable organization; in death, his cadaver will continue to represent the presence of poverty. With glib rhetorical cant and boardroom chatter, the director speaks all of his prefabricated words to a man whose soul is never acknowledged. And Díaz's definitive play on the subject of language and alienation, *El cepillo de dientes*, pits its two characters named only He and She, in endless verbal battles where violence and death are routine solutions to the far more pressing problem of who said what.

In sum, Díaz's plays are varied and extensive, successfully produced and widely performed. His continual experimentations with staging techniques, the absurdist tone and style of his works, and his preponderant themes of language, communication, and the lived despair of the modern world all link him closely to the other Latin American playwrights of his time. A man defined by his political commitment, belief in a continental community of artists, complete immersion into theatrical production, and surrender to the art of drama at all costs, Jorge Díaz represents the best that Latin America can produce as it struggles to mature theatrically.

—Bart L. Lewis

DIMITROVA, Blaga. Bulgarian. Born in Byala Slatina, 2 January 1922. Educated at the Classical Secondary School, Sofia, graduated 1941; University of Sofia, degree in philology 1945; Gorky Literary Institute, Moscow, degree 1951. Married to Iordan Vasilev; one adopted daughter. Editor of poetry department, *Septemvri* [September] literary magazine, two years; construction worker in Rhodope Mountains, two years; editor, Bŭlgarski pisatel [The Bulgarian Writer] publishing house, from 1962, and Narodna Kultura [National Culture] publishing house, from 1963. Writings were banned several times. Since 1992 Vice President of Bulgaria. Member of leadership of Poets' Section, Bulgarian Writers' Union, 1954–56. Recipient: Bulgarian Writers' Union prize, 1959; *Vecherni Novini* [Evening News] Silver Ring, 1962; Order of Red Banner of Labour, 1972; Honoured Cultural Worker, 1974; Polish PEN Club award, 1978. Member, Order of People's Republic of Bulgaria, 1981. Address: c/o Bŭlgarski pisatel, ul 6 Septemvri 35, 1000 Sofia, Bulgaria.

PUBLICATIONS

Verse

Stikhove za vozhda [Verses About the Leader].   Sofia, n.p., 1950.
S Nazum Khikmet v Bulgariya: ocherk [With Nazim Hikmet in Bulgaria].   Sofia, n.p., 1952.
Pesni za rodopite [In the Open].   Sofia, n.p., 1954.
Na otkrito.   Sofia, n.p., 1956.
Do utre [Until Tomorrow].   Sofia, n.p., 1959.
Lilyana [Liliana].   Sofia, n.p., 1959.
Svetut v shepa [World in My Palm].   Sofia, n.p., 1962.
Ekspeditsiya kum idniya den [Expedition into Tomorrow].   Sofia, n.p., 1964.
Obratno vreme [Reverse Time].   Sofia, Bŭlgarski pisatel, 1966.
Osadeni na lyubov [Condemned to Love: Poems About Vietnam].   Sofia, Narodna mladezh, 1967.
Migove [Moments].   Sofia, Bŭlgarski pisatel, 1968.
Stikhotvoreniya [Poems].   Sofia, n.p., 1968.
Impulsi [Impulses].   Sofia, Bŭlgarski pisatel, 1972.
Kak [How].   Sofia, n.p., 1973.
Gong.   Sofia, Narodna mladezh, 1976.
Zabraneno more [Forbidden Sea].   Varna, Bakalov, 1976.
Prostranstva [Spaces].   Sofia, Bŭlgarski pisatel, 1980.
Pamet: poeziia [Memory: Poems].   Sofia, Bŭlgarski pisatel, 1982.
Izbrani tvorbi.   Sofia, Bŭlgarski pisatel, 2 vols., 1982.
Glas [Voice].   Plovdiv, Danov, 1985.
Nove stikhove [New Verses].   Sofia, 1985.
Izbrani stikhotvoreniia [Selected Poems].   Varna, Bakalov, 1986.
Labirint [Labyrinth].   Sofia, Bŭlgarski pisatel, 1987.
Otvŭd liubovta.   Sofia, Narodna mladezh, 1987.

Because the Sea Is Black, edited and translated by Niko Boris and Heather McHugh. Middletown, Connecticut, Wesleyan University Press, 1989.
Tranzit.   Sofia, Kadiiski, 1990.
Mezhdu.   Sofia, Bŭlgarski pisatel, 1990.
The Last Rock Eagle, translated by Brenda Walker and Vladimir Levchev.   London, Forest, 1992.

Fiction

Pŭtuvane kŭm sebe si.   Sofia, Bŭlgarski pisatel, 1965; as *Journey to Oneself*, London, Cassell, 1969.
Otklonenie [Detour].   Sofia, Bŭlgarski pisatel, 1967.
Strashniyat sud [Judgement Day].   Sofia, Narodna Kultura, 1968.
Lavina [Avalanche].   Sofia, n.p., 1971.
Dni cherni i beli [Black and White Days], with Iordan Vasilev.   Sofia, Nauka i izkustvo, 1975.
Mladostta na Bagriana i neinite sputnitsi [Bagriana's Youth], with Iordan Vasilev.   Plovdiv, Danov, 1975.
Litse [Face].   Sofia, Bŭlgarski pisatel, 1981.
Otklonenie; Lavina [Digression: Avalanche].   Sofia, Bŭlgarski pisatel, 1982.

Plays

Doktor Faustina [Dr. Faustina].   Sofia, n.p., 1971.
Nechakana srehta [Unpremeditated Meeting].   Sofia, n.p., 1975.

Screenplays: *Otklonenie* [Detour]; *Lavina* [Avalanche], 1973.

Other

Podzemno nebe [Underground Sky].   Sofia, Partezdat, 1972.
Vietnamski dnevnik [Vietnamese Diary].   Sofia, n.p., 1972.

Has translated works by Homer and various Soviet, Swedish, and German poets.

*   *   *

Blaga Dimitrova has been an important figure in Bulgarian literature for some 40 years. Her work as a novelist, a dramatist, and a critic has been widely influential and much translated. She has herself been a prolific and able translator into Bulgarian — including works by Mickiewicz, Homer, and contemporary poetry from Swedish and German. She has written film scripts. She has been well-known as a campaigner for democracy and human rights. It is her work as a poet, however, that has perhaps constituted her greatest claim for international attention and recognition.

Stylistically dense — her language full of puns, coinages, and complex sound patterns — Dimitrova's verse is sophisticated and rigorously intelligent. Yet she is also capable of great human warmth, and her writing is characterised by the depth and range of her compassion. Her fellow Bulgarian Julia Kristeva has observed that "seldom has a woman's writing been at once more cerebral and more sensual." There is a strong moral core to her work, a passionate concern for human suffering. This finds expression on a variety of levels, both political and personal. In the late 1960s she was much involved in campaigns against the war in Vietnam, and two novels and many poems grew from her visits there. The best of the poems of this period avoid the obvious dangers of mere propaganda and in their attention to the particularities of human situations produce compelling images of pain, endurance, and hope. In "A Woman Pregnant," for example:

> She walks, slow and solemn,
> gravid with the sorrows of the world.
> Amidst that roaring she alone can hear
> what's inside of her,
> that echo beating there.
>
> . . .
>
> She passes through ruins
> and through the felled forests of the killed.
>
> . . .
>
> She walks, wise and anxious,
> containing in herself as in a chalice
> that frail laughter of the future,
> And carries the globe of the world ahead.

It was perhaps only with the work of Elissaveta Bagriana in the 1920s that women first achieved any degree of prominence in Bulgarian poetry. Dimitrova views the history of women in her land as one of "cruel silences," of "the girl grown mute/in wedlock," of "the bride/sworn in her home to be/dumb as a doornail all her life." Now, in poetry, they can find their voice:

> there are so many poets
> among women in my land.
> The mute whose speech
> is suddenly restored
> will rend the air
> with a moan or a shout —
> centuries of silence
> crying to come out.
> ("The Women Who Are Poets in My Land")

Dimitrova's work constitutes an eloquent exploration of the roles of relationships of woman's life — woman as daughter, lover, wife, and mother. Especially poignant are sequences of poems on the old age and death of the poet's mother and father. Now, in her mother's old age their previous relationship has been reversed; in "Lullaby for My Mother" there is a touching simplicity and directness of a kind Dimitrova does not always achieve:

> At night I make her bed
> in the folds of old age.
> Her skinny hand
> pulls mine into the dark.
>
> Before her dreams begin,
> from a brain erased of speech,
> a small cracked voice calls *mama*
> and I become my mother's mother.

The sequence "Requiem," on the death of her father, similarly contains poetry of exact and unsentimental, but tender, emotion.

At the very heart of Dimitrova's work is a fundamental concern for the values both of individuality and of a balanced interaction among individuals. So she celebrates the music of Bach as one which gives "equal rights to every kind of voice" and which can therefore continue for centuries:

> sounding
> that pure, supreme harmony, welding together
> free, independent varied voices
> into a prayer-like, sovereign unity of spirit.
> ("Bach's Harmony")

In language resides any proper understanding of human values, and Dimitrova has no doubts as to the role of the poet in the preservation of language and thus of social and moral values:

> Nothing can be
> unless in a word reborn.
>
> The present isn't,
> unless represented,
>
> there's no past unless
> recalled into a word.
>
> . . .
>
> Meanwhile, word murderers have their designs
> on human being.
> ("Creation of the Word")

It is out of the full realisation of the weight and responsibility of what this perception involves that Dimitrova's poetry is written. Her poetry is the product of necessity — not only personal psychological necessity, but the necessity of the role she sees as demanded of the poet. These are needs which her work very potently succeeds in meeting.

—Glyn Pursglove

———

DOMECQ, H. Bustos. *See* **BIOY CASARES, Adolfo.**

———

DONNADIEU, Marguerite. *See* **DURAS, Marguerite.**

———

DONOSO (Yañez), José. Chilean. Born in Santiago, 5 October 1924. Educated at the Grange School, Santiago; University of Chile Instituto Pedagógio, 1947; Princeton University, New Jersey (Doherty scholar), A.B. 1951. Married María del Pilar Serrano in 1961; one daughter. Worked as a shepherd in Patagonia; taught English, Catholic University of Chile, 1954, and journalism at University of Chile; staff member, *Revista Ercilla*, Santiago, 1959–64; and at Colorado State University, Fort Collins, 1969; literary critic, *Siempre* magazine, 1964–66; participant in Writers' Workshop, University of Iowa, Iowa City, 1965–67. Recipient: City of Santiago prize, 1955; Chile-Italy prize, for journalism, 1960; William Faulkner Foundation prize, 1962; Guggenheim fellowship, 1968, 1973; Critics' prize (Spain), 1979; Encomienda con Placa de la Orden de Alfonso X el Sabio, 1987; National Literature prize (Chile), 1990; Woodrow Wilson Foundation fellow, 1992. Chevalier de l'Ordre des Arts et des Lettres (France), 1986. Agent: Agencia

Carmen Balcells, Diagonal 580, 08021 Barcelona, Spain. Address: Galvarino Gallardo 1747, Santiago, Chile.

PUBLICATIONS

Fiction

Veraneo y otros cuentos.   Santiago, n.p., 1955.
Coronación.   Santiago, Nascimiento, 1957; as *Coronation*, New York, Knopf, and London, Bodley Head, 1965.
El charleston.   Santiago, Nascimiento, 1960; as *Charleston and Other Stories*, Boston, Godine, 1977.
Los mejores cuentos.   Santiago, Zig-Zag, 1966.
El lugar sin límites.   Mexico, Moritz, 1966; as *Hell Hath No Limits*, in *Triple Cross*, New York, Dutton, 1972.
Este domingo.   Santiago, Zig-Zag, 1966; as *This Sunday*, New York, Knopf, 1967; London, Bodley Head, 1968.
El obsceno pájaro de la noche.   Barcelona, Seix Barral, 1970; as *The Obscene Bird of Night*, New York, Knopf, 1973; London, Cape, 1974.
Cuentos.   Barcelona, Seix Barral, 1971.
Tres novelitas burguesas.   Barcelona, Seix Barral, 1973; as *Sacred Families*, New York, Knopf, 1977; London, Gollancz, 1978.
Casa de campo.   Barcelona, Seix Barral, 1978; as *A House in the Country*, New York, Knopf, and London, Allen Lane, 1984.
La misteriosa desaparición de la marquesita de Loria.   Barcelona, Seix Barral, 1980.
El jardín de al lado.   Barcelona, Seix Barral, 1981; as *The Garden Next Door*, New York, Grove, 1992.
Cuatro para Delfina.   Barcelona, Seix Barral, 1982.
Cuentos.   Barcelona, Seix Barral, 1985.
La desesperanza.   Barcelona, Seix Barral, 1986; as *Curfew*, New York, Weidenfeld and Nicolson, 1988; London, Picador, 1990.
Taratuta; Naturaleza muerta con cachimba.   Madrid, Mondadori, 1990; as *Taratuta; Still Life with Pipe*, New York, Norton, 1993.

Plays

Sueños de mala muerte (produced Santiago, 1982).   Santiago, Universitaria, 1985.
Este domingo, with Carlos Cerda from his own novel (produced Santiago, 1990).   Santiago, Bello, 1990.

Screenplay: *The Moon in the Mirror*.

Verse

Poemas de un novelista.   Barcelona, Seix Barral, 1981.

Other

Historia personal del "boom".   Barcelona, Anagrama, 1972; as *The Boom in Spanish American Literature: A Personal History*, New York, Columbia University Press, 1977.

Editor, with others, *The Tri-Quarterly Anthology of Contemporary Latin American Literature*.   New York, Dutton, 1969.

Has translated works by John Dickson Carr, Isak Dinesen, Nathaniel Hawthorne, and Françoise Mallet-Joris.

*

Bibliography: in *José Donoso: originales y metáforas* by Carlos Cerda, Santiago, Planeta, 1988.

Manuscript Collection: Princeton University, New Jersey.

Critical Studies: "The Novel as Happening: An Interview with José Donoso" by Rodríguez Monegal, in *Review* (New York), 73, 1973; *José Donoso* by George R. McMurray, Boston, Twayne, 1979; "*El obsceno pájaro de la noche*: A Willed Process of Evasion" by Pamela Bacarisse, in *Contemporary Latin American Fiction*, edited by Salvador Bacarisse, Edinburgh, Scottish Academic Press, 1980; "Structure and Meaning in *La misteriosa desaparición de la marquesita de Loria*," in *Bulletin of Hispanic Studies* (Liverpool), 3, 1986, and "Donoso and the Post-Boom: Simplicity and Subversion," in *Contemporary Literature* (Madison, Wisconsin), 4, 1987, both by Philip Swanson; "Countries of the Mind: Literary Space in Joseph Conrad and José Donoso" by Alfred J. MacAdam, in his *Textual Confrontations*, Chicago, University of Chicago Press, 1987; *Studies on the Works of José Donoso: An Anthology of Critical Essays*, Lewiston, New York, Mellen, 1990; "Aesthetics, Ethics, and Politics in Donoso's *El jardín de al lado*" by Ricardo Gutiérrez Mouat, in *PMLA* (New York), 106, 1991; *Understanding José Donoso* by Sharon Magnarelli, Columbia, University of South Carolina Press, 1992.

*   *   *

Though George McMurray's 1979 study describes José Donoso as an "eclectic," the variety of content and narrative technique in his work really points to a pattern of development which is emblematic of the evolution of the modern Latin American novel as a whole. As his important essay of 1974, *Historia personal del "boom"* (*The Boom in Spanish American Literature*), implies, Donoso's literary career has to be understood in the context of the growth of the Latin American "new novels," emerging against a traditional background of regionalist social realism, culminating in the so-called "Boom" of technically innovative writing in the 1960s and continuing from the 1970s onwards in the form of what is now commonly termed the "Post-Boom."

While there are regionalist undertones in some of the early short stories, Donoso's first novel *Coronación* (*Coronation*) has an urban context. At first sight it may seem a realist novel written in a Dickensian or Galdosian mode, but a strong line of existential subtext and the grotesque climax of the absurd coronation scene reveal an awareness of new approaches. Indeed, Donoso has remarked that the novel was completed under the influence of Alejo Carpentier's more experimental work *Los pasos perdidos* (*The Lost Steps*). Not surprisingly, then, one of Donoso's next works, *Este domingo* (*This Sunday*), applies a much more formally complex narrative framework to a setting and subject-matter which is essentially similar to the first novel. The big break, however, occurred with *El lugar sin límites* (*Hell Hath No Limits*), published in the same year, 1966. The social backdrop is now rural, still clearly defined, yet structure zigzags, narrative viewpoint is problematized, and characters and situations are heavily symbolic. This is an inverted, uncertain world where a decrepit brothel replaces the patriarchal family home of the traditional novel as the central reference point. The whorehouse is run by an ageing male transvestite and his frigid virgin daughter; the powerful God-like local landowner is revealed to be ailing and without influence; and the village tough guy turns out to be a coward and latent homosexual.

The climax of this pattern of overturning conventional values — at a thematic and formal level — came in 1970 with the publication of Donoso's most important work, *El obsceno pájaro de la noche* (*The Obscene Bird of Night*). Inversion and fragmentation are now taken to the point where the novel seems chaotic and bewildering. In part this can be explained by the madness of the schizophrenic narrator, Humberto Peñaloza or Mudito. More importantly, it reflects a view of reality that is opposed to that presupposed by conventional realism: far from being ordered and coherent, it is now perceived as fluid, ambiguous, and subjectively generated. This has obvious political implications, since it challenges a fixed notion of a given social and moral order, mirrored in the thematic portrayal of the breakdown of an almost feudal social system. A deeper social or sociopsychological significance, meanwhile, is the novel's exposure of the process of disintegration which follows man's confrontation with a subconscious which is normally suppressed so as to secure the smooth running of a precariously stable society. Taking it a stage further, the undermining of rational thought has a clear existential or metaphysical dimension: men and women are seen to be desperately struggling to cling to a rational interpretation of the cosmos, while the evidence around them points to chaos and futility. At whatever level the novel is read, though, the basic pattern remains one of a constant rupturing of binary logic and a consequent erosion of any sense of order — be it social, psychological, or existential.

This tendency to problematize reality and literature's relationship to it is, in many ways, the hallmark of the "Boom": the intense degree of tortuousness and complexity in *The Obscene Bird of Night* marks it out as the culmination of this tradition. Indeed, the word "tradition" is appropriate because — as Donoso himself would later argue — the formal experimentalism of the Latin American "new novel" had itself settled, to some extent, into a new set of conventions. The unity of the Boom was, in any case, disintegrating due to ideological or personal rifts and practical problems caused by the arrest in Cuba of the poet Heberto Padilla (*q.v.*) for alleged counter-revolutionary activities and the break at the influential Seix Barral publishing house in Spain. Changes in direction were soon underway and before long critics were talking of a "Post-Boom." Though there was no clear and unequivocal switch or transition, there was an undeniable evolution of emphasis away from formal complexity.

Donoso's work since 1970 is certainly more accessible, though the characteristic subversion of conventional notions of reality remains. The key Post-Boom work by Donoso is *Casa de campo* (*A House in the Country*) from 1978. In keeping with the Post-Boom's often more direct engagement with social and political themes, the novel is on one level an allegory of Latin American history, in particular modern Chilean history up to the period immediately after the Pinochet coup. At the same time, though, the role of the narrator — who repeatedly intervenes directly to reveal his own narratorial machinations and remind us of the artificiality of his text — is a clear commentary on the new novel's exhausted attempts to create an autonomous narrative and at the same time a reminder of the failure and limitations of traditional realism. Other works from this period subvert realism in a similar way, while equally eschewing extreme formal complexity. For example, the jovial sex romp *La misteriosa desaparición de la marquesita de Loria* (The Mysterious Disappearance of the Young Marchioness of Loria) alarmingly gives way to obscure, unfathomable symbolism as the protagonist abandons her sexual adventures for a strange (and non-sexual) relationship with a dog, while *El jardín de al lado* (*The Garden Next Door*) — an apparently straightforward psychological realist novel — ends up revealing that the first-person narrator is a character totally different from the one the reader has been led to believe it is. The problem is that many of these works rely on principles of "story" or "realism," only then to undermine them. In particular, one might argue that *A House in the Country* claims that literature cannot reflect reality while it simultaneously offers a concrete social, political, and historical analysis of a specific reality. This is a fundamental dilemma underlying much modern Latin American fiction and is, perhaps, a further explanation for the apparent eclecticism of Donoso's work. It may not be surprising therefore that, after returning to his native land, Donoso reverted largely to realism with his 1986 novel on Pinochet's Chile, *La desesperanza* (*Curfew*). Though disappointing on a literary level, the novel is a reminder that formal experimentation is not a prerequisite of politically alternative fiction. Indeed, the Post-Boom as a whole suggests that the opposite is true. One conclusion to be drawn is that what made the "new novel" (and Donoso's best-known works) different was not any unusual political vision but their literary, formal qualities. Perhaps in the long run Donoso and his contemporaries will be remembered not so much for what they said but for how they said it.

—Philip Swanson

* * *

DORFMAN, Ariel. Chilean. Born in Buenos Aires, 6 May 1942. Lived as a child for 10 years in the United States; moved to Chile, 1954; became Chilean citizen, 1967. Educated at the University of Chile, Santiago, licenciado in philosophy (summa cum laude) 1967. Married María Angélica Malinarich in 1966; two sons. Research scholar, University of California, Berkeley, 1968–69; Professor of Spanish-American studies, University of Chile, 1970–73; exiled from Chile by Pinochet regime, 1973; research fellow, Friedrich Ebert Stiftung, 1974–76; maître des conférences (replacement) of Spanish-American literature, the Sorbonne, Paris, 1975–76; head of scientific research, Spaans Seminarium, University of Amsterdam, 1976–80; fellow, Woodrow Wilson Center for International Scholars, Washington, D.C., 1980–81; visiting fellow, Institute for Policy Studies, Washington, D.C., 1981–84; Visiting Professor, University of Maryland, College Park, 1983; Visiting Professor, 1984, and since 1985 (spring semesters) Professor of literature and Latin American studies, Duke University, Durham, North Carolina. Recipient: Chile Films award, for screenplay, 1972; *La Opinión* Ampliado Sudamericana prize, 1973; Israeli Alternative Theatre Festival prize, 1987; Kennedy Center-American Express New American Plays award, 1988; *Time Out* award, for play, 1991; Olivier award, for play, 1992. Honorary doctorate: Illinois Wesleyan University, Bloomington, 1989. Agent: Andrew Wylie, 250 West 57th Street, Suite 2106, New York, New York 10109, U.S.A. Address: Department of International Studies, Duke University, Durham, North Carolina 27706, U.S.A.

PUBLICATIONS

Fiction

Moros en la costa. Buenos Aires, Sudamericana, 1973; as *Hard Rain*, London and Columbia, Louisiana, Readers International, 1990.

Cría ojos. Mexico City, Nueva Imagen, 1979; as *My House Is on Fire*, New York, Viking, 1990.

Viudas. Mexico City, Siglo XXI, 1981; as *Widows*, New York, Pantheon, and London, Pluto, 1983.

La última canción de Manuel Sendero. Mexico City, Siglo XXI, 1982; as *The Last Song of Manuel Sendero*, New York, Viking, 1987.

Dorando la píldora. Santiago, Ediciones del Ornitorrinco, 1985.

Travesía. Montevideo, Banda Oriental, 1986.

Cuentos paramilitares: La batalla de los colores y otros cuentos. Santiago, Emisión, 1986.

Máscaras. Buenos Aires, Sudamericana, 1988; as *Mascara*, New York, Viking, 1988.

Plays

Widows, from his own novel (produced Williamstown, Massachusetts, 1988; revised version produced Los Angeles, 1991).

Death and the Maiden, (produced London, 1991; New York, 1992). London, Hern, 1991; New York, Viking Penguin, 1992.

Reader, from his own story (produced Williamstown, Massachusetts, 1992).

Verse

Aus den Augen Verlieren/Desaparecer. Bonn, Lamuv, 1979; as *Missing*, translated by Edie Grossman, London, Amnesty International British Section, 1982.

Pruebas al canto. Mexico City, Nueva Imagen, 1980.

Pastel de choclo. Santiago, Sinfronteras, 1986.

Last Waltz in Santiago and Other Poems of Exile and Disappearance, translated by the author and Edie Grossman. New York, Viking, 1988.

Other

El absurdo entre cuatro paredes: el teatro de Harold Pinter. Santiago, Universitaria, 1968.

Imaginación y violencia en América. Santiago, Universitaria, 1970; as *Some Write to the Future*, Durham, North Carolina, Duke University Press, 1991.

Para leer al Pato Donald, with Armand Mattelart. Valparaíso, Ediciones Universitaria de Valparaíso, 1971; as *How to Read Donald Duck: Imperialist Ideology in the Disney Comic*, New York, International General, 1975; revised edition, 1984.

Ensayos quemados en Chile: inocencia y neocolonialismo. Buenos Aires, Flor, 1974.

Superman y sus amigos del alma, with Manuel Jofré. Buenos Aires, Galerna, 1974.

La última aventura del llanero solitario. San José, Costa Rica, Ciudad Universitaria Rodrigo Facio, 1979.

Reader's Nuestro que estás en la tierra: ensayos sobre el imperialismo cultural. Mexico City, Nueva Imagen, 1980; enlarged edition, as *The Empire's Old Clothes: What the Lone Ranger, Babar, and Other Innocent Heroes Do to Our Minds*, New York, Pantheon, and London, Pluto, 1983; revised edition, as *Patos, elefantes y heroes: La infancia como subdesarrollo*, Buenos Aires, Flor, 1985.

Hacia la liberación del lector latinoamericano. Hanover, New Hampshire, Ediciones del Norte, 1984.

Sin ir más lejos. Santiago, Pehuén, 1986.

La rebelión de los conejos mágicos (for children). Buenos Aires, Flor, 1987.

*

Critical Studies: "Ariel Dorfman: A Conversation" by S. L. Wisenberg, in *Another Chicago Magazine*, 18, 1988; "Ideology, Exile, Language: An Interview with Ariel Dorfman" by Peggy Boyers and Juan Carlos Lértora, in *Salmagundi* (Saratoga Springs, New York), Spring-Summer 1989; "Liberating the Reader: A Conversation with Ariel Dorfman" by John Incledon, in *Chasqui* (Provo, Utah), 20(1), 1990.

*   *   *

With the recent London staging of *Death and the Maiden*, and with subsequent productions of the play in New York and around the world, Ariel Dorfman has joined the handful of Latin American writers who are widely known outside their native continent. While the success of *Death and the Maiden* is gratifying, there is a danger that it will obscure Dorfman's work in other fields. This would be a pity, for his novels, poems, stories, and essays are as urgent and compelling as any in modern writing.

Dorfman first came to public notice with *Para leer al Pato Donald* (*How to Read Donald Duck*), a polemical attack on the cultural imperialism of Walt Disney's famous cartoon character. Witty and exuberant, the essay lays out many of the concerns — the importance of children's literature in shaping adult attitudes, the insidious nature of economic colonialism — that Dorfman has since explored more widely in essays such as *The Empire's Old Clothes*. At the same time he began writing *Moros en la costa* (*Hard Rain*), an experimental novel whose fragmented structure was meant to mirror the turbulence and dislocation of the Allende years. *Hard Rain* is not an easy book — its difficulty derives in part from the fact that Dorfman was obliged to complete it while sheltering in a foreign embassy — but it is important because it foreshadows later, more accomplished works such as *La última canción de Manuel Sendero* (*The Last Song of Manuel Sendero*) in its use of multiple narrators, fantasy, and non-fictional elements. Dedicated to those who struggled and died in Pinochet's coup it is, perhaps, best seen as a monument to crushed hopes and lost dreams.

With exile Dorfman's writing underwent a change of direction and alteration of tone. No longer the brilliant expression of an optimistic radical, it became a sombre, often anguished chronicle of Chile's descent into brutality and totalitarianism. The stark, simple poems of *Desaparecer* (*Missing*) and *Pruebas al canto* (*Last Waltz in Santiago*) belong to this period; also the short stories of *Cría ojos* (*My House Is on Fire*) and the novel *Viudas* (*Widows*). This last is, perhaps, the best of Dorfman's books: while lacking the exuberance and imaginative invention of, say, *The Last Song of Manuel Sendero*, it has a clarity and force unequalled until *Death and the Maiden*. Set in Greece, or a country very like Greece, it tells of the struggle of a group of village women to recover the bodies of their men from the clutches of the local military, who would like these inconvenient corpses to disappear as quickly and anonymously as possible. Against the soldiers' weapons the women have only their patient obstinacy, yet they do succeed; at the end, as the foremost matriarch claims her man, there is a sense of triumph and new life springing, magically, from the midst of defeat and death. At one level a tribute to the women of Chile, who have searched so patiently and obstinately for their "disappeared ones" it is, more generally, a homage to all those women in totalitarian states who keep their own and others' humanity alive.

With the return of Chile to democracy, and the end of his exile, Dorfman's writing has shifted its focus once again. The problem now is not how to survive and resist and bear witness abroad, but how to live and be happy at home when the perpetrators of so many terrible crimes are allowed to go unpunished. This is the problem of *Death and the Maiden*, a play (Dorfman's first) of classical unity and force. Paulina, a torture victim, is married to Gerardo, a lawyer charged with investigating human rights abuses committed by his country's previous military regime. One evening he brings home a new friend, Roberto, whom Paulina believes to be the doctor who tortured her years before. Horrified, yet determined to bring Roberto to justice, Paulina organizes an on-the-spot trial. What follows is a tense drama of accusation, denial, and confession — a drama of an explicitly cathartic nature designed, in Dorfman's words, to purge and cleanse. It is, altogether, a superb play; one hopes its success will stimulate Dorfman to write others.

—John O'Leary

————

DOWLATABADI, Mahmud. *See* **DAWLATĀBĀDI, Mahmūd.**

————

DUPIN, Jacques. French. Born in Privas, Ardèche, 4 March 1927. Educated at the Collège de Privas; University of Paris, from 1945. Married Christine Rousset in 1951; two daughters. Formerly editorial secretary, *Émpédocle* review and *Cahiers d'Art* review, both Paris; publications editor, Galérie Maeght, Paris, from 1954; editor, *L'Ephémère* review, Paris. Address: c/o POL Éditeur, 8 villa d'Alesia, 75014 Paris, France.

PUBLICATIONS

Verse

Cendrier du voyage.   Paris, GLM, 1950.
Le Nuage en échec.   Paris, Pierre à Feu, 1956.
Les Brisants.   Paris, GLM, 1958.
L'Épervier.   Paris, GLM, 1960.
Saccades.   Paris, Maeght, 1962.
Gravir.   Paris, Gallimard, 1963; part as "To Climb: Poems from *Gravir*," in *Cronopios* (Madison, Wisconsin), 7, 1970.
La Nuit grandissante.   Saint-Gall, Switzerland, Erker-Presse, 1968.
L'Embrasure.   Paris, Gallimard, 1969.
L'Embrasure; Gravir; La Ligne de rupture; L'Onglée.   Paris, Gallimard, 1971.
Fits and Starts: Selected Poems, translated by Paul Auster.   Berkeley, California, Book People, 1973; Salisbury, Wiltshire, Compton Press, 1974.

Jacques Dupin (selections).   Paris, Seghers, 1974.
Dehors.   Paris, Gallimard, 1975.
Ballast.   Paris, Le Collet de Buffle, 1976.
Du Nul Lieu et du Japon.   Montpellier, Fata Morgana, 1981.
Une Apparence de soupirail.   Paris, Gallimard, 1982.
L'Espace autrement dit.   Paris, Galilée, 1982.
De Singes et de mouches.   St. Clément-la-Rivière, Fata Morgana, 1983.
Les Mères.   St. Clément-la-Rivière, Fata Morgana, 1986.
Contumace.   Paris, POL, 1986.
Chansons troglodytes.   Fontfroide-le-Haut, Fata Morgana, 1989.
Enchancré.   Paris, POL, 1991.
Rien encore, toujours déjà.   Fontfroide-le-Haut, Fata Morgana, 1991.

Play

L'Éboulement.   Paris, Galilée, 1977.

Other

Art poétique.   Paris, Benoit, 1956.
Miró.   Paris, Flammarion, 1961; in English, New York, Abrams, and London, Thames and Hudson, 1962.
Alberto Giacometti.   Paris, Maeght, 1962.
Les Peintures sur carton de Miró.   Paris, Maeght, 1965.
Adami.   Paris, Maeght, 1970.
Steinberg.   Paris, Maeght, 1971.
Miró: peintures sur papier, with Pierre Alechinsky.   Paris, Maeght, 1971.
Alberto Giacometti (exhibition catalogue).   Chur, Bündner Kunstmuseum, 1978.
Chagall, lithographies originales: sur 14 lithographies de Chagall.   Paris, Maeght, 1981.
Juan Miró, with Michel Leiris.   Paris, Galerie Lelong, 1983.
Juan Miró.   Zurich, Kunsthaus, 1986.
Henri Michaux.   Paris, Galerie Lelong, 1990.

Editor, with Bernard Pingaud, *René Char*.   Aix-en-Provence, n.p., 1963.
Editor, *Miró graveur*: vol. 1: *1928–1960*; vol. 2: *1961–1976*.   Paris, Galerie Lelong, 2 vols., 1984–89; as *Miró Engraver*, New York, Rizzoli, 2 vols., 1989.
Editor, with Michel Leiris, *Écrits*, by Alberto Giacometti.   Paris, Hermann, 1990.

*

Critical Studies: "Jacques Dupin: The Word Engraved," in *Dalhousie French Studies* (Halifax, Nova Scotia), 1, 1979, and "Jacques Dupin: Access, or Speaking It Through," in *Poesis*, 5(3), 1984, both by Mary Ann Caws; "*Proximité du murmure*: Dupin and [Raoul] Ubac Collaborate," in *Visible Language* (Medin, Pennsylvania), Autumn 1906, "*Les Brisants*, Framing the Poem and the Print," in *Dalhousie French Studies* (Halifax, Nova Scotia), Spring-Summer 1987, "Jacques Dupin and the Rhetoric of Landscape Poetry," in *Symposium* (Syracuse, New York), Winter 1987–88, and "Jacques Dupin and a New Kind of Lyricism," in *French Forum* (Lexington, Kentucky), May 1989, all by Maryann De Julio; "'La Terreur d'écrire': The Primeval Experience of Language in the Poetry of Jacques Dupin" by Michael Brophy, in *Forum for Modern Language Studies* (St. Andrews, Fife), April 1989.

*   *   *

The landscape evoked in Jacques Dupin's poetry is an unfamiliar, primordial setting of rocks, mountains, and sea. Like his contemporaries Yves Bonnefoy (q.v.) and André du Bouchet, the scope of imagery in Dupin's work is consciously minimalist. At the same time, the lapidary quality of Dupin's writing reflects the poet's interest in the plastic arts. Indeed, Dupin has written studies and exhibition catalogues on Juan Miró, Alberto Giacometti, and other artists.

Many of Dupin's poems are concerned with the act of writing and represent a genre of reflexive meditation on the process of poetic composition. Bearing little resemblance to his native Ardèche, Dupin's poetic geography is depicted figuratively in terms of a linguistic landscape. Although the poems are characterized by a hermeticism and remain syntactically taut, there is a pervasive sense of aggression and anguish. His landscape is punctuated with traces of past confrontations. Indeed, the motif of disruption, or *brisure*, is conspicuous in Dupin's verse where images of tearing, uprooting, explosion, rupture, and dislocation abound. If such antagonistic gestures denote the combative nature of his poetry, this violence is reflected textually in the poet's assertive and belligerent use of syntax. Titles of collections and poems such as *Saccades* (Fits and Starts) and "La Ligne de Rupture" (The Line of Rupture) exemplify this predilection.

The persistent aggression enacted in these texts is not inflicted by some hostile force against the poet-protagonist. On the contrary, violence and creativity are construed as concomitant activities. In his volume *De Singes et de mouches* (Of Monkeys and Flies) Dupin speaks of "the terror of writing" and likens words to knives. As the protagonist observes in a poem entitled "La Trêve" (The Truce): "The dogs that sleep in my voice/Are always mad dogs." Language in Dupin's poetry brims with potentially destructive energy. Similarly, language is associated with fire, a pernicious element that is nevertheless charged with rejuvenating potential.

Dupin's poems are conceived as types of *embrasures* or gun-ports: strategic vantage-points from where an assault is launched against the notion of a referential language. In fact the architectural tension suggested in the image of the window, between the interior and the exterior, can be traced throughout Dupin's poetry, and is particularly prominent in the long sequence "Moraines" and through his collection *Dehors* (Outside):

You won't escape me, says the book. You open me and close me, and you think you're outside, but you are incapable of leaving because there is no inside.

Published in the volume *L'Embrasure* this prose-poem clearly reflects many of the philosophical preoccupations which were being articulated by the so-called *Tel-Quel* group in the 1960s. In this passage the poet focuses on the conventions within which he operates, persistently interrogating the poetic text itself and undermining what Dupin calls "the fossilized horizon of a book." The poet's emphasis on disruption, or as he puts it on "the act of writing as rupture," is also pertinent in this context: "To demolish the writing of this oppressive space/and lose oneself writing it" ("La Ligne de Rupture").

Poetry is thus construed by Dupin as a war zone for contending impulses within language. On the one hand rhetorical resources are manipulated to evoke the immanence of external phenomena. Yet Dupin's verse registers an anxiety that the landscape depicted may in the final analysis amount to nothing more than the contrivances of a theatrical performance ("la machinerie du thèâtre mental"). As Dupin observes, "the word doesn't separate itself from the thing."

The protagonist of Dupin's poetry therefore struggles with a rhetoricity that threatens to engulf him. He is conscious of the rhetorical layers that have accumulated and stratified in a genre of linguistic geology. Indeed, Dupin's protagonist seeks to rupture this artificial "pact" between signs and meaning, and expose "the imperceptible fracture" which he describes elsewhere as "a clearing free from all diseased shadow." Paradoxically, he does so by harnessing the disruptive energies within language.

The danger of Dupin's ambitious venture is clear, as the poet evokes nightmare scenarios where communication is ruptured. Words are free-standing and "migrate" across a landscape itself characterized by sliding (*glissement*) and drift (*dérive*). This is the chaos of "a night country where the path is lost." It resembles an underworld and is associated with the malignant presence of "the black widow" or "the blind mother."

In fact, this female figure that recurs in Dupin's poetry, perhaps most notably in *Les Mères* (The Mothers), is also a creative source. In the same way, the potentially inhibiting hermeticism of Dupin's verse is countered by a dynamic configuration of light and dark, visibility and obscurity. In the final analysis it is precisely the opacity of the poet's landscape that sets his utterances in relief:

To walk in the night, to speak through the uproar,
so that the ray of the rising sun fuses and
answers my step, designates the branch, breaks off
the fruit.

In another sequence entitled "La Nuit grandissante" (The Lengthening Night) the poet remarks: "As long as my speech is obscure, it breathes."

The poetic dilemma enacted in Dupin's poetry is resolved in one of his most arresting images of an "open house, inaccessible,/which the fire builds and maintains." Contradictions are poised in this metaphor that balances immobility and mobility, closure and openness, destruction and construction. The rigour of Dupin's poetic inquiry, however, compels him to acknowledge that even this hard-fought-for resolution is a trope. In this way resolution necessitates its own destruction, or as Dupin expresses it more succinctly: "To break up and recapture, and thus to tie up again."

—Robert Shannan Peckham

DURAS, Marguerite. French. Born Marguerite Donnadieu in Gia Dinh, near Saigon, Indo-China (now Vietnam), 4 April 1914. Educated at Lycée de Saigon, baccalaureate 1931; the Sorbonne, Paris, 1933–34, degree in law and political science 1935. Married Robert Antelme in 1939 (divorced 1946); one son (by Dionys Mascolo). Moved to France, 1932. Secretary, Ministry of Colonies, Paris, 1935–41; then freelance writer; journalist, *Observateur*; also film writer and director. Member, French Communist Party, expelled 1950. Recipient: Cocteau prize, 1954/55; Ibsen prize, 1970; Cannes Film Festival special prize, for *India Song*, 1975; French Academy grand prize for theatre, 1983; Goncourt prize, 1984; Ritz Paris Hemingway prize, 1986. Address: c/o Éditions Gallimard, 5 rue Sébastien-Bottin, 75007 Paris, France.

PUBLICATIONS

Fiction

Les Impudents. Paris, Plon, 1943.

La Vie tranquille. Paris, Gallimard, 1944.

Un Barrage contre le Pacifique. Paris, Gallimard, 1950; as *The Sea Wall*, New York, Pellegrini and Cudahy, 1952; London, Faber, 1986; as *A Sea of Troubles*, London, Methuen, 1953.

Le Marin de Gibraltar. Paris, Gallimard, 1952; as *The Sailor from Gibraltar*, London, Calder and Boyars, 1966; New York, Grove Press, 1967.

Les Petits Chevaux de Tarquinia. Paris, Gallimard, 1953; as *The Little Horses of Tarquinia*, London, Calder, 1960; New York, Riverrun, 1985.

Des Journées entières dans les arbres. Paris, Gallimard, 1954; as *Whole Days in the Trees*, New York, Riverrun, 1983; London, Calder, 1984.

Le Square. Paris, Gallimard, 1955; as *The Square*, New York, Grove Press, and London, Calder, 1959.

Moderato cantabile. Paris, Minuit, 1958; in English, New York, Grove Press, 1960; London, Calder, 1966.

Dix Heures et demi du soir en été. Paris, Gallimard, 1960; as *Ten-Thirty on a Summer Night*, London, Calder, 1962; New York, Grove Press, 1963.

L'Après-midi de Monsieur Andesmas. Paris, Gallimard, 1962; as *The Afternoon of Monsieur Andesmas*, with *The Rivers and Forests*, London, Calder, 1964; in *Four Novels*, 1965.

Le Ravissement de Lol V. Stein. Paris, Gallimard, 1964; as *The Ravishing of Lol V. Stein*, New York, Grove Press, 1967; as *The Rapture of Lol V. Stein*, London, Hamish Hamilton, 1967.

Four Novels (includes *The Square*; *Moderato Cantabile*; *Ten-Thirty on a Summer Night*; *The Afternoon of Mr. Andesmas*). New York, Grove Press, 1965.

Le Vice-Consul. Paris, Gallimard, 1966; as *The Vice-Consul*, London, Hamish Hamilton, 1968; New York, Pantheon, 1987.

L'Amante anglaise. Paris, Gallimard, 1967; in English, New York, Grove Press, 1968.

Détruire, dit-elle. Paris, Minuit, 1969; as *Destroy, She Said*, New York, Grove Press, and London, Hamish Hamilton, 1970.

Abahn Sabana David. Paris, Gallimard, 1970.

L'Amour. Paris, Gallimard, 1971.

Ah! Ernesto, with Bernard Bonhomme. Paris, Ruy-Vidal, 1971.

La Maladie de la mort. Paris, Minuit, 1983; as *The Malady of Death*, New York, Grove Press, 1986.

L'Amant. Paris, Minuit, 1984; as *The Lover*, New York, Pantheon, and London, Collins, 1985.

Les Yeux bleus cheveux noirs. Paris, Minuit, 1986; as *Blue Eyes, Black Hair*, New York, Pantheon, 1987; London, Collins, 1900.

Emily L. Paris, Minuit, 1987; in English, New York, Pantheon, and London, Collins, 1989.

La Pluie d'été. Paris, POL, 1990; as *Summer Rain*, New York, Scribner, and London, Harper Collins, 1992.

L'Amant de la Chine du Nord. Paris, Gallimard, 1991.

Plays and Texts for Voices

Le Square, with Claude Martin, from her own novel (produced Paris, 1957; revised version produced Paris, 1965). Included in *Théâtre I*, 1965; as *The Square* (produced Bromley, Kent, 1961; London, 1963), in *Three Plays*, 1967.

Hiroshima mon amour (screenplay). Paris, Gallimard, 1960; in English, New York, Grove Press, 1961; with *Une Aussi Longue Absence*, London, Calder and Boyars, 1966.

Les Viaducs de la Seine-et-Oise (produced Paris, 1960). Paris, Gallimard, 1960; as *The Viaducts of Seine-et-Oise* (as *The Viaduct*, produced Guildford, Surrey, 1967), in *Three Plays*, 1967.

Une Aussi Longue Absence (screenplay), with Gérard Jarlot. Paris, Gallimard, 1961; in English, with *Hiroshima Mon Amour*, London, Calder and Boyars, 1966.

Les Papiers d'Aspern, with Robert Antelme, adaptation of the play *The Aspern Papers* by Michael Redgrave based on the story by Henry James (produced Paris, 1961). Paris, Paris-Théâtre, 1970.

Miracle en Alabama, with Gérard Jarlot, adaptation of the play *The Miracle Worker* by William Gibson (produced Paris, 1961). Published with *L'Homme qui se taisait*, by Pierre Gaillot, Paris, L'Avant-Scène, 1962.

La Bête dans la jungle, with James Lord, adaptation of the story *The Beast in the Jungle* by Henry James (produced Paris, 1962).

Théâtre I (includes *Les Eaux et fôrets*; *Le Square*; *La Musica*). Paris, Gallimard, 1965.

Les Eaux et fôrets (produced Paris, 1965). Included in *Théâtre I*, 1965; as *The Rivers and Forests* (produced London, 1976), with *The Afternoon of Monsieur Andesmas*, London, Calder, 1964.

La Musica (produced Paris, 1965). Included in *Théâtre I*, 1965; as *The Music* (produced Edinburgh and London, 1966; New York, 1967); in *Suzanna Andler, La Musica, and L'Amante Anglaise*, 1975.

Des Journées entières dans les arbres (produced Paris, 1965). Included in *Théâtre 2*, 1968; as *Days in the Trees* (produced London, 1966), in *Three Plays*, 1967; as *Whole Days in the Trees*, London, Calder, and New York, Riverrun, 1984.

Three Plays. London, Calder and Boyars, 1967.

Théâtre 2 (includes *Susanna Andler*; *Yes, peut-être*; *Le Shaga*; *Des Journées entières dans les arbres*; *Un Homme est venu me voir*). Paris, Gallimard, 1968.

Le Shaga (also director: produced Paris, 1968). Included in *Théâtre 2*, 1968.

Susanna Andler (produced Paris, 1969). Included in *Théâtre 2*, 1968; as *Suzanna Andler* (produced Cambridge and London, 1973; New York, 1984), in *Suzanna Andler, La Musica, and L'Amante Anglaise*, 1975.

L'Amante Anglaise, from her own novel (produced Paris, 1969). Paris, Théâtre National Populaire, 1968; as *A Place Without Doors* (produced New Haven, Connecticut, and New York, 1970); as *The Lovers of Viorne*, produced London, 1971); included in *Suzanna Andler, La Musica, and L'Amante Anglaise*, 1975.

Yes, peut-être (produced Paris, 1968; Edinburgh, 1986). Included in *Théâtre 2*, 1968.

La Danse de mort, d'après August Strindberg (produced Paris, 1970). Included in *Théâtre III*, 1984.

Nathalie Granger; *La Femme du Gange* (screenplays). Paris, Gallimard, 1973.

India Song (in French). Paris, Gallimard, 1973; in English, New York, Grove Press, 1976; with *Eden Cinema* (bilingual edition), Arles, Actes Sud, 1988.

Home (in French), from the play by David Storey. Paris, Gallimard, 1973.

Suzanna Andler, La Musica, and L'Amante Anglaise. London, Calder, 1975.

L'Eden Cinéma (produced Paris, 1977). Paris, Mercure,

1977; with *India Song* (bilingual edition), Arles, Actes Sud, 1988.

Le Camion (screenplay).   Paris, Minuit, 1977.

Le Navire Night, Césarée, Les Mains négatives, Aurélia Steiner, Aurélia Steiner, Aurélia Steiner.   Paris, Mercure, 1979.

Véra Baxter; ou, Les Plages de l'Atlantique (screenplay). Paris, Albatros, 1980; as *Véra Baxter* (produced London, 1989).

L'Homme assis dans le couloir.   Paris, Minuit, 1980.

Agatha.   Paris, Minuit, 1981.

L'Homme Atlantique.   Paris, Minuit, 1982.

Savannah Bay.   Paris, Minuit, 1982; revised edition, 1983 (produced London, 1984).

Théâtre III (includes *La Bête dans la jungle, d'après Henry James*, with James Lord; *Les Papiers d'Aspern, d'après Henry James*, with Robert Antelme; *La Danse de mort, d'après August Strindberg*).   Paris, Gallimard, 1984.

La Musica deuxième (produced Paris, 1985; London, 1989). Paris, Gallimard, 1985.

Screenplays: *Hiroshima mon amour*, 1959; *Moderato cantabile*, with Gérard Jarlot and Peter Brook, 1960; *Une Aussi Longue Absence* (*The Long Absence*), with Gérard Jarlot, 1961; *10:30 P.M. Summer*, with Jules Dassin, 1966; *La Musica*, 1966; *Les Rideaux blancs*, 1966; *Détruire, dit-elle* (*Destroy, She Said*), 1969; *Jaune le soleil*, 1971; *Nathalie Granger*, 1972; *La ragazza di Passaggio/La Femme du Gange*, 1973; *Ce que savait Morgan*, with others, 1974; *India Song*, 1975; *Des Journées entières dans les arbres*, 1976; *Son Nom de Venises dans Calcutta désert*, 1976; *Baxter — Véra Baxter*, 1977; *Le Camion*, 1977; *La Navire Night*, 1978; *Césarée*; *Les Mains négatives*; *Aurélia Steiner*; *L'Homme assis dans le couloir*, 1980; *Agatha et les lectures illimitées*, 1981; *L'Homme Atlantique*, 1981; *Dialogue de Rome*, 1982.

Television Play: *Sans Merveille*, with Gérard Jarlot, 1964.

Other

Les Parleuses (interviews), with Xaviere Gauthier.   Paris, Minuit, 1974; as *Woman to Woman*, Lincoln, University of Nebraska Press, 1987.

Étude sur l'oeuvre littéraire, théâtrale, et cinématographique de Marguerite Duras, with Jacques Lacan and Maurice Blanchot.   Paris, Albatros, 1975.

Territoires du féminin, with Marcelle Marini.   Paris, Minuit, 1977.

Les Lieux de Marguerite Duras (interview), with Michelle Porte.   Paris, Minuit, 1978.

L'Été 80.   Paris, Minuit, 1980.

Les Yeux ouverts (special Duras issue).   Paris, Les Cahiers du Cinéma 312–313, June 1980.

Outside: papiers d'un jour.   Paris, Michel, 1981; revised edition, Paris, POL, 1984; as *Outside: Selected Writings*, Boston, Beacon Press, 1986; London, Fontana, 1987.

Marguerite Duras à Montréal (interviews and lectures), edited by Suzanne Lamy and André Roy.   Montreal, Spirale, 1981.

La Douleur.   Paris, POL, 1985; as *The War*, New York, Pantheon, and London, Collins, 1986.

La Pute de la côte normande.   Paris, Minuit, 1986.

La Vie matérielle: Marguerite Duras parle à Jérôme Beaujour.   Paris, POL, 1987; as *Practicalities: Marguerite Duras Speaks to Jérôme Beaujour*, New York, Grove Weidenfeld, and London, Collins, 1990.

Les Yeux verts.   Paris, Cahiers du Cinéma, 1987; as *Green Eyes*, New York, Columbia University Press, 1990.

Marguerite Duras (interview).   San Francisco, City Lights, 1987.

Translator, *La Mouette*, by Anton Chekhov.   Paris, Gallimard, 1985.

*

Critical Studies: *Marguerite Duras* by Alfred Cismaru, New York, Twayne, 1971; *Marguerite Duras: Moderato Cantabile* by David Coward, London, Grant and Cutler, 1981; *Alienation and Absence in the Novels of Marguerite Duras* by Carol J. Murphy, Lexington, Kentucky, French Forum, 1982; *Marguerite Duras: Writing on the Body* by Sharon Willis, Urbana, University of Illinois Press, 1987; *The Other Woman: Femininity in the Work of Marguerite Duras* by Trista Selous, New Haven, Connecticut, Yale University Press, 1988; *Remains to Be Seen: Essays on Marguerite Duras*, edited by Sanford Scribner Ames, New York, Lang, 1988.

Theatrical Activities:
Director: **Film** — *Les Enfants*, 1985.

*   *   *

Marguerite Duras has always responded positively to current intellectual trends. Her first war-time novels trailed wisps of existentialism and in the 1950s her writing reflected trends associated with the rejection by the *nouveau roman* of the props of realistic fiction: linear plots and conventional psychology. A member of the Communist Party until she was expelled for revisionism in 1950, she has remained on the left, though in many ways she is best described as a radical, since her mistrust of totalitarianism has proved as great as her opposition to bourgeois imperialism. Understandably, therefore, she took an anti-colonial line on Algeria and in May 1968 supported the students. During the 1970s, she became sympathetic to feminism, which she then abandoned in the early 1980s. In 1971, she renounced the novel for the cinema, though, since 1980, she has returned triumphantly to written texts, first finding her voice in brief, elusive fictions before embarking on more accessible forms which advance her preoccupations with individualism and personal freedom.

Like Samuel Beckett, Duras has never written a literary manifesto, though she has discussed her work in magazine articles and interviews. Her first novels were relatively traditional, owing much to writers as diverse as Fran- çois Mauriac, Ernest Hemingway, and Virginia Woolf, but were remarkable for the use of elliptic dialogue and their insistence on inner states and struggles. By the early 1960s, the dialogue had become almost cinematographic and her plots minimal. Her characters are defined against the con- certed symbolism of nature and the occurrence of ex- traneous events which trigger highly personal responses. Between 1952 and 1962, the pattern of her novels and plays shows a middle-class wife in her thirties, often with a child, who exists in a state of spiritual *ennui*. Alcohol, violence, or the pressures of a routine life bring her to the point of revolt. She commits an action (adultery, willed or real, is a popular choice) through which she glimpses the intense self-fulfilment she has been seeking. But the "death" of the self brings only temporary relief. Since it is impossible to exist permanently in a state of total freedom, she sinks into a contemplative trance (called "madness").

It was this "entrancement" which Duras next explored in two novels, *Le Ravissement de Lol V. Stein* (*The Ravishing of*

Lol V. Stein) and *Le Vice-Consul* (*The Vice-Consul*), which marked the beginnings of a new intensity in her work. From them emerge a preoccupation with her adolescence in Indo-China which, first expressed in *Un Barrage contre le Pacifique* (*The Sea Wall*; also published as *A Sea of Troubles*), has dominated so much of her later work. Her mother and her brothers, the role model of the liberated Anne-Marie Stretter and the haunting presence of the Vietnamese beggar woman, have been, directly or indirectly, the secret source of her deepest obsessions. In immediate terms, the first "Indian" novels inaugurated a cycle of interrelated novels, plays, and films — notably *India Song*, which links colonial oppression with the impoverishment of personal lives, a theme already expressed in the film *Hiroshima mon amour* which made Duras an international figure. The horror of Hiroshima and the tragedy of the French girl are two faces of the same universal disaster, just as the poverty of the East and the poverty of the lives of Duras's characters are two expressions of the same despair. For what is true of love — that it is "impossible" — will henceforth also be true of politics.

Détruire, dit-elle (*Destroy, She Said*), Duras's most overtly political work, states the necessity for the "impossible revolution," but though political commitment is explored subsequently in feminist, revolutionary, and colonial contexts in her novels, plays, and especially films of the 1970s, it is to the theme of "impossible love" that Duras has always most insistently returned. The short fictions, dense and sensuous, with which she began the 1980s, gave way to plainer and more direct expressions of her compulsions which gained for her a new generation of admirers. *L'Amant* (*The Lover*), a further return to her Vietnamese adolescence, won the Goncourt prize of 1984 and sold 1.5 million copies. Since then, her powers of invention within the self-imposed limits of her closed world have enabled her to return to her earlier, "impossible" manner — for instance in *Emily L.* — to explore the theme of the marginal social outsider of *La Pluie d'été* (*Summer Rain*), and to provide yet another version of her Vietnamese experience, *L'Amant de la Chine du Nord* (The Lover from Northern China).

No less inventive have been her experiments with form. Duras acts on her belief that distinctions between different modes of expression are artificial. An early novel, *Le Square* (*The Square*), transferred almost verbatim to the stage and subsequently Duras followed the logic of such flexibility. Much of her work since the mid-1970s defies categorisation. What is offered to the private reader may equally serve as a performance text. Her plays, bereft of action, work best as orchestrations of the voice. Voices are central also to her avant-garde films, which are technically as bold as any produced since the time of the silent pioneers. Equally remarkable has been her ability to return to the same material — turning earlier works of different genres into new plays, novels, and films — and re-present it in startlingly different ways. With each new telling, the story acquires new depth and significance. In particular, the dozen or so meditations on her Vietnamese rites of passage, real or imagined, may be read as a fascinating, multi-dimensional sequence of reflected images which, taken together, constitute a single work of singular, poetic power.

Always a controversial figure, stronger on understated passion than on feeling, continually experimenting with new forms of expression, Duras commands attention by the intensity of her commitment and the evocative power of her unhurried, incantatory prose style.

—David Coward

E

ECO, Umberto. Also writes as Dedalus. Italian. Born in Alessandria, 5 January 1932. Educated at the University of Turin, Ph.D. 1954. Served in the Italian Army, 1958–59. Married Renate Ramge in 1962; one son and one daughter. Editor of cultural programs, RAI Italian Radio-Television, Milan, 1954–59; assistant lecturer, 1956–63, and lecturer in aesthetics, 1963–64, University of Turin; lecturer in architecture, University of Milan, 1964–65; Professor of visual communications, University of Florence, 1965–69; Professor of semiotics, Milan Polytechnic, 1969–71; Associate Professor, 1971–75, since 1975 Professor of semiotics, and currently director, Istituto di Discipline della Comunicazioni e dello Spettacolo, University of Bologna. Visiting Professor, New York University, 1969, 1976, Northwestern University, Evanston, Illinois, 1972, University of California, San Diego, 1975, New York University, 1976, Yale University, New Haven, Connecticut, 1977, 1980, 1981, and Columbia University, New York, 1978, 1984. Non-fiction senior editor, Bompiani publishing house, Milan, 1959–75; co-founder, *Marcatré* review, 1961, and *Quindici* review, 1967; editor, *Versus*, from 1971; member of editorial board, *Semiotica, Poetics Today, Degrès, Structuralist Review, Text, Communication, Problemi dell'informazione,* and *Alfabeta*. Secretary-general, 1972–79, and since 1979 vice president, International Association for Semiotic Studies. Recipient: Strega prize, 1981; Viareggio prize, 1981; Anghiari prize, 1981; Medicis prize, 1982; McLuhan Teleglobe prize, 1985. Honorary doctorate: University of Odense, 1986; Loyola University, Chicago, 1987; University of Glasgow, 1990; University of Kent, Canterbury, 1992. Named honorary citizen of Monte Cerignone, 1982. Address: Istituto della Comunicazioni e dello Spettacolo, Universita di Bologna, Via Guerrazzi 20, 40125 Bologna, Italy.

PUBLICATIONS

Fiction

Il nome della rosa. Milan, Bompiani, 1980; as *The Name of the Rose*, San Diego, Harcourt Brace, and London, Secker and Warburg, 1983.
Il pendolo di Foucault. Milan, Bompiani, 1988; as *Foucault's Pendulum*, San Diego, Harcourt Brace, and London, Secker and Warburg, 1989.

Verse

Filisofi in libertà (as Dedalus). Turin, Taylor, 1958.

Other

Il problema estetico in San Tommaso. Turin, Edizioni di Filosofia, 1956; as *Il problema estetico in Tommaso d'Aquino*, Milan, Bompiani, 1970; as *The Aesthetics of Thomas Aquinas*, London, Radius, 1988.
Opera aperta: forma e indeterminazione nelle poetiche contemporanee. Milan, Bompiani, 1962; revised edition, 1967, 1972; as *The Open Work*, Cambridge, Massachusetts, Harvard University Press, and London, Hutchinson Radius, 1989.
Storiografia medievale ed estetica teorica: appunti metodologici su Jacques Maritain. Turin, Edizioni di Filosofia, 1962(?).
Diario minimo. Milan, Mondadori, 1963; revised edition, 1976.
Apocalittici e integrati: comunicazioni di massa e teoria della cultura di massa. Milan, Bompiani, 1964; revised edition, 1977.
Le poetiche di Joyce. Milan, Bompiani, 1965; as *Le poetiche di Joyce dalla "Summa" al "Finnegans Wake"*, 1966; as *The Middle Ages of James Joyce: The Aesthetics of Chaosmos*, Tulsa, University of Tulsa, 1982; London, Hutchinson Radius, 1989.
Appunti per una semiologia delle comunicazioni visive. Milan, Bompiani, 1967.
La struttura assente. Milan, Bompiani, 1968; revised edition, 1983.
La definizione dell'arte. Milan, Mursia, 1968.
De consolatione picturae: A Conversation Between Umberto Eco and Gianfranco Baruchello. Milan, Galleria Schwarz, 1970.
Le forme del contenuto. Milan, Bompiani, 1971.
Il segno. Milan, Istituto Editoriale Internazionale, 1971.
Il costume di casa: evidenze e misteri dell'ideologia italiano. Milan, Bompiani, 1973.
Beato di Liébana: miniature del Beato de Fernando I y Sancha. Milan, Ricci, 1973.
Eugenio Carmi: una pittura di paesaggio? Milan, Prearo, 1973.
Ammazza l'uccellino: letture scolastiche per i bambini della maggioranza silenziosa (as Dedalus). Milan, Bompiani, 1973.
Looking for a Logic of Culture. Lisse, Ridder, 1975.
Trattato di semiotica generale. Milan, Bompiani, 1975; as *A Theory of Semiotics*, Bloomington, Indiana University Press, 1976; London, Macmillan, 1977.
Il superuomo di massa: studi sul romanzo popolare. Milan, Cooperativa Scrittori, 1976; revised edition, as *Il superuomo di massa: retorica e ideologia nel romanzo popolare*, Milan, Bompiani, 1978.
Dalla periferia dell'Impero. Milan, Bompiani, 1976.
Stelle & [i.e.] Stellette: la via lattea mormorò. Conegliano, Quadragono, 1976.
Cristianesimo e politica: esame della presente situazione culturale (as Dedalus). Naples, Vico, 1976.
Come si fa una tesi di laurea. Milan, Bompiani, 1977.
Perché continuiamo a fare e a insegnare arte?, with others. Bologna, Cappelli, 1979.
The Role of the Reader: Explorations in the Semiotics of Texts. Bloomington, Indiana University Press, 1979; London, Hutchinson, 1981; revised edition, as *Lector in fabula: la cooperazione interpretativa nei testi narrativi*, Milan, Bompiani, 1979.

Informazione: consenso e dissenso, with Marino Livolsi and Giovanni Panozzo.   Milan, Il Saggiatore, 1979.

Strutture ed eventi dell'economica alessandrina.   Milan, La Pietra, 1981.

De bibliotheca.   Milan, Biblioteca Comunale di Milano, 1981.

Testa a testa.   Padua, Mastrogiacomo, 1981.

Environmental Information: A Methodological Proposal, with Paolo Fabbri and Mauro Wolf.   Paris, Unesco, 1981.

Miei teatri, with Sylvano Bussotti and Luciano Morini.   Palermo, Novecento, 1982.

Cremonini: peintures, 1978–1982 (exhibition catalogue). Paris, Galerie Claude Bernard, 1983.

Sette anni di desiderio.   Milan, Bompiani, 1983.

Carnival!, with V. V. Ivanov and Monica Rector, edited by Thomas A. Sebeok.   Berlin, Mouton, 1984.

La riscoperta dell'America, with G. P. Ceserani and B. Placido.   Bari, Laterza, 1984.

Postille a "Il nome della rosa".   Milan, Bompiani, 1984; as *Postscript to "The Name of the Rose"*, San Diego, Harcourt Brace, 1984; as *Reflections on "The Name of the Rose"*, London, Secker and Warburg, 1985.

Cremonini: opere dal 1960–1984, with Italo Calvino and Bruno Mantura.   Bologna, Grafis, 1984.

Semiotica e filosofia del linguaggio.   Turin, Einaudi, 1984; as *Semiotics and the Philosophy of Language*, Bloomington, Indiana University Press, and London, Macmillan, 1984.

Sugli specchi e altri saggi.   Milan, Bompiani, 1985.

Art and Beauty in the Middle Ages.   New Haven, Connecticut, Yale University Press, 1986; as *Arte e bellezza nell'estetica medievale*, Milan, Bompiani, 1987.

Faith in Fakes: Essays.   London, Secker and Warburg, 1986.

Travels in Hyper Reality.   San Diego, Harcourt Brace, 1986.

Le ragioni della retorica, with Paolo Rossi and Renato Barilli.   Modena, Mucchi, 1987.

Tre cosmonauti; La bomba e il generale (for children), illustrated by Eugenio Carmi.   Milan, Bompiani, n.d.; as *The Bomb and the General; The Three Astronauts*, San Diego, Harcourt Brace, and London, Secker and Warburg, 2 vols., 1989.

Lo strano caso della Hanau 1609.   Milan, Bompiani, 1989.

I limiti dell'interpretazione.   Milan, Bompiani, 1990; as *The Limits of Interpretation*, Bloomington, Indiana University Press, 1990.

Out of Chaos.   Arlington, Texas, Liberal Arts Press, 1991.

Vocali — soluzioni felici, with P. D. Malvinni.   Naples, Guida, 1991.

Diario minimo secondo.   Milan, Bompiani, 1992.

Interpretation and Overinterpretation, with Richard Rorty, Jonathan Cullter, and Christine Brooke-Rose, edited by Stefan Collini.   Cambridge, Cambridge University Press, 1992.

Editor, with G. B. Zorzoli, *Storia figurata delle invenzioni dalla selce scheggiata al volo spaziali*.   Milan, Bompiani, 1961; as *A Pictorial History of Inventions from Plough to Polaris*, London, Weidenfeld and Nicolson, 1962; as *The Picture History of Inventions from Plough to Polaris*, New York, Macmillan, 1963.

Editor, with Oreste del Buono, *Il caso Bond*.   Milan, Bompiani, 1965; as *The Bond Affair*, London, Macdonald, 1966.

Editor, *Noi vivi*, by Mimmo Castellano.   Bari, Dedalo, 1967.

Editor, *L'arte come mestiere*.   Milan, Bompiani, 1969.

Editor, with Remo Faccani, *I sistemi di segni e lo strutturalismo sovietico*.   Milan, Bompiani, 1969; as *Semiotica della letteratura in URSS*, 1974.

Editor, *Socialismo y consolación: reflexiones en torno a "Los misterios de Paris" de Eugene Sue*.   Barcelona, Tusquets, 1970.

Editor, with Cesare Sughi, *Cent'anni dopo: il ritorno dell'intreccio*.   Milan, Bompiani, 1971.

Editor, with Jean Chesneaux and Gino Nebiolo, *I fumetti di Mao*.   Bari, Laterza, 1971; as *The People's Comic Book: Red Women's Detachment, Hot on the Trail, and Other Chinese Comics*, Garden City, New York, Anchor Press, 1973.

Editor, *Estetica e teoria dell'informazione*.   Milan, Bompiani, 1972.

Editor, *Il falcone sardese: Big Sleeping in una nuova avventura di Panebarco*.   Milan, Longanesi, 1977.

Editor, *Apocalisse*, by Enrico Baj.   Milan, Mazzotta, 1979.

Editor, with Seymour Chatman and Jean-Marie Klinkenberg, *A Semiotic Landscape*.   The Hague, Mouton, 1979.

Editor, with Thomas A. Sebeok, *Sign of the Three: Dupin, Holmes, Pierce*.   Bloomington, Indiana University Press, 1983.

Editor, *Trent'anni di costume*.   Rome, L'Espresso, 1985.

Editor, with Marco Santambrogio and Patrizia Violi, *Meaning and Mental Representations*.   Bloomington, Indiana University Press, 1988.

Editor, with Constantino Marmo, *On the Medieval Theory of Signs*.   Amsterdam, Benjamin, 1989.

Translator, with C. Berberian, *Il complesso facile; Passionella; Giorgio nella luna* [Sick Sick Sick; Passionella and Other Stories; The Explainers], by Jules Feiffer.   Milan, Bompiani, 1974.

*

Critical Studies: "Faith, Reason and Desire" by Franco Schiavoni, in *Meanjin* (Parkville, Victoria), December 1984; Eco issue of *SubStance* (Madison, Wisconsin), 47, 1985; "Eco's Echoes: Semiotic Theory and Detective Practice in *The Name of the Rose*" by David H. Richter, in *Studies in 20th-Century Literature* (Manhattan, Kansas), Spring 1986; *The Key to "The Name of the Rose"* by Adele J. Haft, Jane G. White, and Robert J. White, Huntington Park, New Jersey, Ampersand, 1987; *Naming the Rose: Eco, Medieval Signs, and Modern Theory* by Theresa Coletti, Ithaca, New York, Cornell University Press, 1988; *Naming the Rose: Essays on Umberto Eco's "The Name of the Rose"*, edited by M. Thomas Inge, Jackson, University Press of Mississippi, 1988.

*   *   *

An Italian novelist, critic, and academic, who studied philosophy at the University of Turin, Umberto Eco's thesis subject on an aspect of medieval philosophy eventually provided the basis for his first book, *Il problema estetico in San Tommaso* (*The Aesthetics of Thomas Aquinas*). In the late 1950s and in the 1960s he worked on cultural programmes for Radio Televisione Italiana, and as an editor for the publishing house Bompiani, before taking up a university teaching post at the University of Bologna, where he is now Professor of semiotics. His output, on a wide range of academic, intellectual, and cultural subjects, has been prodigious, and although some of his best work (both philosophical and creative) has been concerned with medieval subjects, always prominent too has been a keen engagement with modern society and ideas.

In 1971 Eco became editor of *Versus*, a journal committed to the newly emerging intellectual discipline of semiotics. By that time he had published a number of books which indicate the range of his interests and the liveliness and originality of his critical strategies, including *Diario minimo* (Minimal Diary), a collection of short satirical articles and parodies, *La struttura assente* (The Missing Structure), an analysis of the current state of semiological research, and *La definizione dell'arte* (The Definition of Art) which seeks to advance an aesthetics attuned to contemporary art and experience. Most notably, Eco produced the vigorous and engaging *Opera aperta* (*The Open Work*), an essay in critical theory which attempts to engage with the governing characteristics and ideological implications of 20th-century avant-garde and neo-avant-garde art, embracing work as apparently diverse as symbolist poetry, the novels of James Joyce, modern experimental literature, serial music, and mid-century movements in the fine arts, to develop an aesthetic based upon an interaction of contemporary critical, philosophical, and scientific ideas. A seminal work, it made a substantial contribution to the debates which have characterised much discussion of late 20th-century postmodernism.

Eco's output in the 1970s and 1980s continued to maintain a remarkably catholic range, and although apparently writing at different times for quite separate audiences — general readers on the one hand, and academic specialists on the other — he has sustained an all-embracing consistency in his work, the formal philosophical investigations informing his more readily accessible journalistic writings, and the former enlivened and illuminated by his engagement with the immediacies of contemporary fads, preoccupations, arts, and mass media. In his later critical and philosophical work Eco has consistently interrogated, with admirable intellectual rigour and engagement, his own earlier conclusions, providing a veritable model of ongoing intellectual enquiry: it is interesting, for example, to note the continuities and refinements in his thinking between, say, his conception of the dialectical relationship between text and interpreter in *The Open Work*, and that in the more recent *I limiti dell'interpretazione* (*The Limits of Interpretation*), and in his Tanner lectures in Stefan Collini's collection *Interpretation and Overinterpretation*, where he sees in some modern theory a tendency to accord the interpreter an overly dominant role.

For one whose engagement had for more than 20 years been with philosophical, critical, and social issues, then, Eco's shift into the field of novel writing was as unexpected as it was successful. *Il nome della rosa* (*The Name of the Rose*), a kind of "who-done-it" with a medieval monastic setting and pronounced but palatable metaphysical and ideological overtones, won worldwide acclaim. The plot is ingenious and most skilfully worked out, a complex and intellectually demanding tale carried through with a verbal and narrative *brio* that makes it highly readable. The time is 1327, the setting a Benedictine abbey in northern Italy, at a time of intellectual turbulence: a break-away sect, the Fraticelli, with the support of secular powers threaten, by their espousal of an austere poverty, the wealth and political influence of the Church. When an English Franciscan arrives to investigate suspected Fraticellian influence, he is persuaded to investigate the death of one of the monks, his enquiries leading him to the very centre of the abbey, its library, and a possible explanation for a series of murders.

Critical opinion of the novel has been various, some considering it an overly brilliant display of intellectual pyrotechnics parading (if in a highly imaginative and engaging way) the great erudition, intellectual brilliance, and rich command of language and image which characterise Eco's non-fiction work, while others have seen it as a seminal breakthrough in the novel form, an application of the techniques of popular fiction to the exploration of arcane academic and philosophical subject-matter in order to make the novel of serious concerns accessible to a wide readership. But there is general agreement that in the course of telling a rich and fascinating tale Eco also explores the diversity, contradictions, and complexity of the medieval world, and in the course of doing so raises questions about our own: not least, from the library, repository of past learning and current speculation, about what constitutes culture, what is transmitted, by whom, and for what purposes.

Eight years later Eco confounded those who suspected *The Name of the Rose* of being a one-off *jeu d'esprit* by producing a second novel, *Il pendolo di Foucault* (*Foucault's Pendulum*). Ranging between the present — driven by information technology and an insatiable curiosity about meanings and predictions in history — and the past with its cults, myths, and mysteries, more particularly the machinations of puzzle-obsessed transmitters down the ages of the medieval Templar's secret for world domination, this second novel, if less warmly received by a wide public, has all the wit, verbal buoyancy, and narrative ingenuity of Eco's first. The delight in learned play with words and ideas, with associations and interconnections, literary allusions and exemplary tables, makes the novel, in the invitation it extends to various decodings, seem like an illustration of the concept of the literary work as a project open to multiple readings. Much of the pleasure of the tale lies in the game of making. Eco clearly has a creative gift from which much more can be expected.

—Francesca Ross

EL-SAADAWI, Nawal. *See* SA'DĀWI, Nawal al-.

ELYTIS, Odysseus. Pseudonym for Odysseus Alepoudelis. Greek. Born in Heraklion, Crete, 2 November 1911. Educated at the University of Athens, 1930–33; the Sorbonne, Paris, 1948–52. Served in the First Army Corps, in Albania, 1940–41: Lieutenant. Program director, National Broadcasting Institution, 1945–47, 1953–54; art and literary critic, *Kathimerini* newspaper, 1946–48; adviser to Art Theatre, 1955–56, and Greek National Theatre, 1965–68. President of the Governing Board, Greek Ballet, 1956–58, and Greek Broadcasting and Television, 1974; member of the Administrative Board, Greek National Theatre, 1974–76. Recipient: National prize in poetry, 1960; Nobel prize for literature, 1979; Royal Society of Literature Benson Medal (UK), 1981. D.Litt.: University of Thessaloniki, 1976; the Sorbonne, 1980; University of London, 1981. Member, Order of the Phoenix, 1965; Grand Commander, Order of Honour, 1979; Commandeur de l'Ordre des Arts et des Lettres (France), 1984; Commandeur de la Légion d'Honneur (France), 1989. Address: Skoufa Street 23, Athens, Greece.

PUBLICATIONS

Verse

Prosanatolismi [Orientations].   Athens, Pirsos, 1939.
O Ilios o Protos, mazi me tis Parallayes pano se mian Ahtida [Sun the First Together with Variations on a Sunbeam].   Athens, Glaros, 1943.
Asma Iroiko ke Penthimo yia ton Hameno Anthipolohago tis Alvanias [Heroic and Elegiac Song for the Lost Second Lieutenant of the Albanian Campaign].   Published in *Notebook* (Athens), 2, August-September 1945.
I Kalosini stis Likopories [Kindness in the Wolfpasses].   Published in *Notebook* (Athens), December 1946.
To Axion Esti.   Athens, Ikaros, 1959; as *The Axion Esti*, translated by Edmund Keeley and G. P. Savidis, Pittsburgh, University of Pittsburgh Press, 1974; London, Anvil Press Poetry, 1980.
Exi ke Mia Tipsis yia ton Ourano [Six and One Regrets for the Sky].   Athens, Ikaros, 1960.
To Fotodendro ke i Dekati Tetarti Omorfia [The Light Tree and the Fourteenth Beauty].   Athens, Ikaros, 1971.
O Ilios o Iliatoras [The Sovereign Sun].   Athens, Ikaros, 1971.
Thanatos ke Anastasis tou Konstantinou Paleologou [Death and Resurrection of Constantine Palaiologos].   Thessaloniki, Tram, 1971, and Geneva, Duo d'Art S.A., 1971.
To Monogramma [The Monogram].   Athens, Ikaros, 1972.
Ta Ro tou Erota [The Ro of Eros].   Athens, Asterias, 1972.
Clear Days: Poems by Palamas and Elytis, in Versions by Nikos Tselepides, edited by Kenneth O. Hanson.   Portland, Oregon, Press-22, 1972.
Villa Natacha.   Thessaloniki, Tram, 1973.
O Fillomantis [The Leaf Diviner].   Athens, Asterias, 1973.
Ta Eterothali [The Stepchildren].   Athens, Ikaros, 1974.
The Sovereign Sun: Selected Poems, edited by Kimon Friar.   Philadelphia, Temple University Press, 1974.
Maria Nefeli.   Athens, Ikaros, 1978; in English, translated by Athan Anagnostopoulos, Boston, Houghton Mifflin, 1981.
Selected Poems, edited by Edmund Keeley and Philip Sherrard.   London, Anvil Press Poetry, and New York, Viking, 1981.
Tria Piimata me Simea Evkerias [Three Poems Under a Flag of Convenience].   Athens, Ikaros, 1982.
Imeroloyio enos Atheatou Apriliou [Diary of an Invisible April].   Athens, Ypsilon, 1984.
O Mikros Naftilos.   Athens, Ikaros, 1985; as *The Little Mariner*, Port Townsend, Washington, Copper Canyon Press, 1988.
What I Love: Selected Poems of Odysseus Elytis, translated by Olga Broumas.   Port Townsend, Washington, Copper Canyon Press, 1986.
Krinagoras.   Athens, Ypsilon, 1987.
Ta Elegia tis Oxopetras [The Elegies of Oxopetras].   Athens, Ikaros, 1991.

Other

O Zografos Theofilos [The Painter Theophilos].   Athens, Asterias, 1973.
Anihta Hartia [The Open Book].   Athens, Asterias, 1974.
I Mayia tou Papadiamanti [The Magic of Papadiamantis].   Athens, Ermias, 1976.
Anafora ston Andrea Embiriko [Report to Andreas Embiriko]. Athens, Ypsilon, 1980.

To Domatio me tis Ikones [The Room of Images].   Athens, Ikaros, 1986.
Ta Dimosia ke ta Idiotika [Public and Private Matters].   Athens, Ikaros, 1990.
I Idiotiki Odos [Private Way].   Athens, Ypsilon, 1990.
En Lefko [In White].   Athens, Ikaros, 1992.

Translator, *Defteri Graphi* [The Second Writing], by Arthur Rimbaud and others.   Athens, Ikaros, 1976.
Translator, *Sappho — Anasinthesi ke Apodosi* (from ancient to modern Greek).   Athens, Ikaros, 1985.
Translator, *Ioannis, I Apokalipsi* (from ancient to modern Greek).   Athens, Ypsilon, 1985.

*

Critical Studies: Elytis issue of *Books Abroad* (Norman, Oklahoma), Autumn 1975; *Odysseus Elytis: Anthologies of Light*, edited by Ivar Ivask, Norman, University of Oklahoma Press, 1981; "Maria Nefeli and the Changeful Sameness of Elytis' Variations on a Theme" by Andonis Decavalles, and "Elytis and the Greek Tradition" by Edmund Keeley, both in *Charioteer* (New York), 1982–83; "Odysseus Elytis and the Discovery of Greece" by Philip Sherrard, in *Journal of Modern Greek Studies* (Baltimore, Maryland), 1(2), 1983; "Eliot and Elytis: Poet of Time, Poet of Space" by Karl Malkoff, in *Comparative Literature* (Eugene, Oregon), 36(3), 1984; "Odysseus Elytis in the 1980s" by Andonis Decavalles, in *World Literature Today* (Norman, Oklahoma), 62(1), 1988.

*   *   *

The recipient of the Nobel prize for literature in 1979, Odysseus Elytis is undoubtedly Greece's most important living poet, with a major international reputation.

Elytis's poetry is often read in the context of Surrealism. Indeed, he is the translator of numerous surrealist texts into Greek and has written extensively on the subject, many of these essays collected in the volume *Anihta Hartia* (The Open Book). Significantly, in 1991 an exhibition of Greek poetry and painting, including work by Elytis, was staged at the Georges Pompidou Centre, Paris, and entitled "Surréalistes Grecs."

Elytis's first poems appeared in 1935, a year which also saw the publication by Andreas Embirikos of the prose poems *Ipsikaminos* (Blast-Furnace), a collection of automatic writing reminiscent of André Breton. At the same time, the impact of surrealism is conspicuous throughout Elytis's verse, especially in his early volumes *Prosanatolismi* (Orientations) and *O Ilios o Protos* (Sun the First). These collections include the well-known lyrics "Of the Aegean," "Body of Summer," and "The Mad Pomegranate Tree," in which the poet formulates for the first time his "solar metaphysics."

Nevertheless, although Elytis engages with contemporary Surrealism in these poems, it would be misleading to exaggerate the extent of the poet's commitment to any movement. Even in the early verse, Surrealism is adapted (to borrow Elytis's own term) as the poet confronts "Greek reality," drawing upon the resources of a native poetic tradition. In fact Elytis has been outspoken in stressing his intimate poetic relationship to Greek literary figures as diverse as Andreas Kalvos (1946) and Alexandros Papadiamantis (1976). Moreover, echoes from Greek folk poetry, Byzantine hymns, and liturgical texts reverberate through his poetry. As Elytis remarked in his Nobel acceptance speech in 1979, the poet must simultaneously ". . . recast the elements of the Greek tradition and on the other hand give expression to the social and psychological requirements of [his] age. This assertion intimates the ambitious scope of Elytis's poetry where rigorous attentiveness to detail is set against an expansive context of literary allusions. Elytis's latest collection, *Ta Elegia tis Oxopetras* (The Elegies of Oxopetras) can be read as a protracted meditation on Romanticism. Echoes from the German poets Friedrich Hölderlin and Novalis interact with allusions to the national Greek poet Dionysios Solomos.

In 1940–41 Elytis served as a lieutenant in the Albanian campaign against the invading Italian forces, an experience which had a decisive impact upon his poetry. The serenity of his earlier lyrical verse is complicated by an awareness of death and the necessity for struggle. These tendencies are noticeable in his collection *Asma Iroiko ke Penthimo yia ton Hameno Anthipolohago tis Alvanias* (Heroic And Elegiac Song for the Lost Second Lieutenant of the Albanian Campaign) where the poet develops a dialectic of struggle and conciliation, death and resurrection. In this poem the young protagonist is slaughtered in battle and emerges at the end, transfigured through his suffering, as a Christ-like figure. These thematic configurations of suffering and resurrection can be traced throughout Elytis's major works and most obviously in *To Axion Esti* (The Axion Esti) and *Thanatos ke Anastasis tou Konstantinou Paleologou* (Death and Resurrection of Constantine Palaiologos).

In 1960 Elytis's long poem *The Axion Esti* was awarded the National prize for poetry, and despite his more recent output such as *O Mikros Naftilos* (*The Little Mariner*) and *Ta Elegia tis Oxopetras*, it remains in many respects his most complex and, paradoxically, his most popular work. Part of its popularity is due to its having been set to music by the Greek composer Mikis Theodorakis.

Comprising three sections, "The Genesis," "The Passion," and "The Gloria," Elytis's long poem combines a multiplicity of poetic forms, meters, and styles ranging from epic to lyric to prose. The text's ingenious, mathematical organization anticipates the title poem of his later volume *To Monogramma* (The Monogram). "The Passion" section, for example, alternates between hymns, psalms, odes, and prose passages referred to as "anagnosmata" (readings). Thematically, too, *The Axion Esti* is densely structured, focusing both on the world's mythical creation and on the poet's personal history: his birth, confrontation with death, and survival through struggle. The importance of poetry in this contest is crucial, for the poetic act is dramatized as a constant endeavour to elicit shape and coherence in an otherwise chaotic material world. The first-person drama, however, assumes broader dimensions as a national and indeed emblematic confrontation of man with history. This latter preoccupation is further developed in the long poem *Maria Nefeli* which evokes a contemporary milieu where a young girl's monologue is juxtaposed against the voice of a "counter-speaker."

Perhaps the most fruitful way of approaching a poem of such complexity as *The Axion Esti*, however, is to view it in the context of Elytis's longstanding preoccupation with art. An art critic and prolific painter, Elytis has also collaborated with many of Greece's outstanding artists. Picasso himself provided an original sketch for his volume *Villa Natacha*. Many of Elytis's own collages are collected in the book *To Domatio me tis Ikones* (The Room of Images), while a recent collection of prose writings *I Idiotiki Odos* (Private Way) contains 35 colour illustrations by Elytis and can be read as a series of interconnected reflections on art's relationship to poetry.

In *The Axion Esti*, the correspondence between artistic representation and poetic expression is made explicit from the beginning, with the choice of title. Axion Esti, meaning literally "it is worth," derives from the Orthodox ecclesiastical tradition, being the title of a Byzantine hymn. Secondly,

however, it is the name of a celebrated icon of the Virgin on Mount Athos. If references to icons pervade the text, in *The Axion Esti* Elytis articulates an aesthetics based upon an appreciation of language as a form of iconography. This is evident, perhaps most strikingly, in *The Little Mariner* where words appear as a concordance. Similarly, the associations clustering around specific letters are drawn out in a manner reminiscent of Rimbaud's poem "Voyelles." Elsewhere, place names are listed and accompanied by elliptic entries, as in a genre of hermetic guidebook. In fact the relationship between language and place is one of Elytis's pervasive preoccupations and the central concern of the short prose collection *Ta Dimosia ke ta Idiotika* (Public and Private Matters).

For Elytis, therefore, iconographic poetry becomes a way of reconciling personal and public experience, or as he puts it elsewhere, of bringing the "sur" and the "realism" that constitute Surrealism into a satisfactory relationship.

—Robert Shannan Peckham

ENDŌ Shūsaku. Japanese. Born in Tokyo, 27 March 1923. Educated at Keio University, Tokyo, B.A. in French literature 1949; University of Lyon, 1950–53. Married Junto Okado in 1955; one son. Contracted tuberculosis in 1959. Former editor, *Mita bungaku* literary journal; chair, Bungeika Kyōkai (Literary Artists' Association); manager, Kiza amateur theatrical troupe; President, Japan PEN. Recipient: Akutagawa prize, 1955; Tanizaki prize, 1967; Gru de Oficial da Ordem do Infante dom Henrique (Portugal), 1968; Sanct Silvestri (award by Pope Paul VI), 1970; Noma prize, 1980. Member, Japanese Arts Academy, 1981. Honorary doctorate: Georgetown University, Washington, D.C.; University of California, Santa Clara. Address: c/o Japanese PEN Club, Room 265 Syuwa Residential Hotel, 9-1-7 Akasaka, Minato-ku, Tokyo, Japan.

PUBLICATIONS

Fiction

Aden made [Till Aden].   Published in *Mita bungaku* (Tokyo), November 1954.
Shiroi hito [White Man].   Tokyo, Kōdansha, 1955.
Kiiroi hito [Yellow Man].   1955.
Aoi chiisana budō [Green Little Grapes].   Published in *Bungakukai* (Tokyo), January-June 1956.
Umi to dokuyaku.   Tokyo, Bungei Shunjū Shinsha, 1958; as *The Sea and Poison*, London, Peter Owen, 1972; Tokyo, Tuttle, 1973; New York, Taplinger, 1980.
Kazan.   1959; as *Volcano*, London, Peter Owen, 1978; New York, Taplinger, 1980.
Obakasan.   Published in *Asahi shinbun* (Tokyo), April-August 1959; as *Wonderful Fool*, London, Peter Owen, 1974; New York, Harper, 1983.
Otoko to kyūkanchō [Three Men and a Starling].   Published in *Bungakukai* (Tokyo), January 1963.
Watashi ga suteta onna [The Girl I Left Behind].   1963; as "Mine," in *Japan Christian Quarterly* (Tokyo), 40(4), 1974.
Aika [Elegies].   1965.
Ryūgaku.   Published in *Gunzō* (Tokyo), March 1965; as *Foreign Studies*, London, Peter Owen, 1989.

Chimmoku. Tokyo, Shinchōsha, 1966; as *Silence*, Tokyo, Sophia University Press, and London, Prentice Hall, 1969; New York, Taplinger, 1979.
Taihen daa [Good Grief!]. 1969.
Shikai no hotori [By the Dead Sea]. 1973.
Iesu no shōgai. 1973; as *A Life of Jesus*, New York, Paulist Press, 1978.
Yumoa shōsetsu shū. Tokyo, Kōdansha, 1973.
Waga seishun ni kui ari. Tokyo, Kadokawa, 1974.
Kuchibue o fuku toki. Tokyo, Kōdansha, 1974; as *When I Whistle*, London, Peter Owen, and New York, Taplinger, 1979.
Sekai kikō. Tokyo, Kōdansha, 1975.
Hechimakun. Tokyo, Kōdansha, 1975.
Endō Shūsaku bungaku zenshū [Collected Works]. Tokyo, Shinchōsha, 11 vols., 1975.
Kitsunegata tanukigata. Tokyo, Kōdansha, 1976.
Gūtara mandanshū. Tokyo, Kadokawa Shōten, 1978.
Jūichi no iro garasu [11 Stained Glass Elegies]. Tokyo, Shinchōsha, 1979.
Marie Antoinette. Tokyo, Asahi Shinbunsha, 1979.
Samurai. Tokyo, Shinchōsha, 1980; as *The Samurai*, London, Peter Owen, and New York, Harper, 1982.
Onna no issho. Tokyo, Asahi Shinbunsha, 1982.
Akuryō no gogo. Tokyo, Kōdansha, 1983.
Stained Glass Elegies. London, Peter Owen, 1984; New York, Dodd, 1985.
Sukyandaru. Tokyo, Shinchōsha, 1986; as *Scandal*, London, Peter Owen, and New York, Dodd, 1988.
Hangyaku. Tokyo, Kōdansha, 2 vols., 1989.

Plays

Ōgon no kuni (produced Tokyo, 1966). Tokyo, Shinchōsha, 1969; as *The Golden Country*, Rutland, Vermont and Tokyo, Tuttle, 1970; London, Peter Owen, 1989.
Bara no yakata [A House Surrounded by Roses]. Tokyo, Shinchōsha, 1969.

Other

Furansu no daigakusei [Students in France, 1951–52]. Tokyo, Hayakawa Shobō, 1953.
Seisho no naka no joseitachi. Tokyo, Shinchōsha, 1968.
Korian vs. Mambō, with Kita Morio. Tokyo, Kōdansha, 1974.
Ukiaru kotoba. Tokyo, Shinchōsha, 1976.
Ai no akebono, with Miura Shumon. 1976.
Nihonjin wa kirisuto kyō o shinjirareru ka. Tokyo, Shōgakukan, 1977.
Kirisuto no tanjō. Tokyo, Shinchōsha, 1978.
Ningen no naka no X. Tokyo, Chūō Kōronsha, 1978.
Rakuten taishō. Tokyo, Kōdansha, 1978.
Kare no ikikata. Tokyo, Shinchōsha, 1978.
Jū to jūjika (biography of Pedro Cassini). Tokyo, Chūō Kōronsha, 1979.
Shinran, with Masutani Fumio. 1979.
Sakka no nikki. Tokyo, Tōju-sha, 1980.
Chichioya. Tokyo, Shinchōsha, 1980.
Kekkonron. Tokyo, Shufunotomosha, 1980.
Endō Shūsaku ni yoru Endō Shūsaku. Tokyo, Seidōsha, 1980.
Meiga Iesu junrei. Tokyo, Bungei Shunjū, 1981.
Ai to jinsei o meguru dansō. 1981.
Okuku e no michi. 1981.
Fuyu no yasashisa. Tokyo, Bunka Shuppakyoku, 1982.
Watakushi ni totte kami to wa. Tokyo, Kōdansha, 1983.

Kokoro. Tokyo, Sakuhinsha, 1984.
Ikuru gakkō. Tokyo, Bungei Shunjū, 1984.
Watakushi no aishita shōsetsu. Tokyo, Shinchōsha, 1985.
Rakudai bōzu no rirekisho. Tokyo, Nihon Keizai Shinbunsha, 1989.
Kawaru mono to kawaranu mono: hanadokei. Tokyo, Bungei Shunjū, 1990.

*

Critical Studies: "Shusaku Endo: The Second Period" by Francis Mathy, in *Japan Christian Quarterly*, 40, 1974; "Tradition and Contemporary Consciousness: Ibuse, Endo, Kaiko, Abe" by J. Thomas Rimer, in his *Modern Japanese Fiction and Its Traditions*, Princeton, New Jersey, Princeton University Press, 1978; "Mr. Shusaku Endo Talks About His Life and Works as a Catholic Writer" (interview), in *Chesterton Review* (Saskatoon, Saskatchewan), 12(4), 1986; "The Roots of Guilt and Responsibility in Shusaku Endo's *The Sea and Poison*" by Hans-Peter Breuer, in *Literature and Medicine* (Galveston, Texas), 7, 1988; "Rediscovering Japan's Christian Tradition: Text-Immanent Hermeneutics in Two Short Stories by Shusaku Endo" by Rolf J. Goebel, in *Studies in Language and Culture*, 14(63), 1988; "Graham Greene: *The Power and the Glory*: A Comparative Essay with *Silence* by Shusaku Endo" by Kazuie Hamada, in *Collected Essays by the Members of the Faculty (Kyoritsu Women's Junior College)*, 31, February 1988; "Christianity in the Intellectual Climate of Modern Japan" by Shunichi Takayanagi, in *Chesterton Review* (Saskatoon, Saskatchewan), 14(3), 1988; "Salvation of the Weak: Endo Shusaku," in *The Sting of Life: Four Contemporary Japanese Novelists*, New York, Columbia University Press, 1989, and "The Voice of the Doppelgänger," in *Japan Quarterly* (Tokyo), 38(2), 1991, both by Van C. Gessel.

*   *   *

Ever since his emergence on the literary scene. Endō Shūsaku has consistently sought resolution of the conflict he has perceived between, on the one hand, his "adopted" religion, Christianity, and, on the other, his chosen profession as author. Derived in part from his study of several French Catholic novelists, the desire for a reconciliation between his perceived duty, as Christian, to seek within man the potential for salvation and the necessity, accruing to him as author, to remain totally honest to his observations of human nature informs his entire oeuvre. In the case of Endō, a Japanese national, moreover, the tension was further exacerbated by the need to operate within a cultural and spiritual framework that provides little encouragement for the development of literary themes dealing with the spiritual drama of the relationship between God and man, leading him to conclude: "As a Christian, Japanese and an author, I am constantly concerned with the relationship and conflict created by these three tensions . . . Unfortunately, these three tensions continue to appear as contradictory in my mind."

The result in the case of Endō is an author whose self-professed desire "to find God on the streets of Shinjuku and Shibuya, districts which seem so far removed from Him" has been constantly tempered by a realisation that he was "not writing in order to proselytise" — and that, if he were, his "works would certainly suffer as literature." Thereafter, the more he has found himself drawn to privilege his obligations as literary artist, the more he has come to recognise the need to create "living human beings," a task that required, not merely external observation, but also scrutiny of the internal psychology of his creations, a faithful depiction of their inner being, however unattractive. The result is a body of work that increasingly mirrors Endō's conviction that "to describe man's inner self, we must probe to the third dimension [within the unconscious] . . . to the territory of demons. One cannot describe man's inner being completely unless one closes in on this demonic part."

The paradox is readily apparent: in focusing on a realm in which "our desire for Good conflicts with our penchant for Evil, where our appreciation of Beauty conflicts with our attachment to the Ugly," Endō was drawn increasingly to focus on the weakness of human nature, in the belief that only thus could he portray, behind the sin depicted, "the glimmer of light . . . the light of God's grace" — the potential for salvation which he saw as underlying the entire human drama. The consequent vision of the unconscious as both the fount of all sin and the "place where God works and has His being" is reflected in the Endō text by an increasing focus on the "monstrous duality of man," this assuming the literary guise of a gradual fusion of two qualities, initially established as in opposition. In several texts, like *Chimmoku* (*Silence*) and *Samurai* (*The Samurai*), the central dichotomy thus established is that between East and West, with the distance between the two, initially depicted as unfathomable (as evidenced by the Western missionaries appearing unable to penetrate the "mudswamp" of Japan), steadily eroded during the course of the novels as a result of the author's increasing focus, not on external distinctions, but on internal similarities that allow for meaningful communication across various national, religious, and cultural divides. Thus, at the outset of *Silence*, Rodrigues, the Portuguese missionary, is portrayed as entirely confident of his own inner resources. Confronted by the choice, imposed upon him by the Japanese shogunate authorities, between on the one hand adherence to his faith and the consequent death of the Japanese converts being tortured before his eyes, and, on the other, renunciation of all that his life to date had stood for, Rodrigues ultimately succumbs and tramples on the crucifix that had been placed before him in an outward act of apostasy. Internally, however, there is evidence, supported in the text by the erosion of the apparently irreconcilable distinction between the "strong" martyr and the "weak" apostate, of the protagonist's augmented love of God at the end of the novel, the narrator acknowledging of Rodrigues's decision, following shortly after his act of public apostasy, to hear the confession of the Japanese man who had betrayed him to the authorities: "He may have been betraying [his fellow priests], but he was not betraying 'that man [Christ]'. He loved Him now in a totally different way. 'Everything in my life to date was necessary in order to know that love. I am still the last priest in this land'."

A similar process can be seen at work in *The Samurai*, a novel in which the distance between the "Western" missionary, Velasco, and the lower-ranking samurai, symbol of "Eastern" values, is initially portrayed as unfathomable. As the novel progresses, however, so Endō's narrator succeeds in breaking down the various obstacles to reconciliation, this being acknowledged at the personal level by Velasco in his eventual recognition: "It was as if a firm bond of solidarity had formed between the envoys and myself."

In these, and other examples of oppositions subjected to similar fusion in Endō's novels, the emphasis is on a steady growth in self-awareness and as the Endō protagonist becomes more and more aware of some previously unconscious aspect of his being, so he appears increasingly well equipped to participate in this process of reconciliation. Seen in this light, the focus of Endō's 1986 novel *Sukyandaru* (*Scandal*), a text heralded by several critics as an abrupt abandonment of earlier Endō motifs, comes to appear rather as a progression, a work that addresses more directly than ever before the inherent human duality. During the course of the novel, the protagonist Suguro grows steadily in his conviction that the "imposter" he initially dismisses as a chance lookalike is none other than his own double — that "he could no longer conceal that part of himself, no longer deny its existence" — the pervading impression being of an author confident in the assessment of human nature he offered at the time: "Man is a splendid and beautiful being, and, at the same time, man is a terrible being as we recognised in Auschwitz — God knows well this monstrous dual quality of man."

—Mark Williams

ENQUIST, Per Olov. Swedish. Born in Bureå, Västerbotten, 23 September 1934. Educated at the University of Uppsala, 1955–64, Ph.D. Married to Lone Bastholm (second marriage). Literary and theatre critic, Uppsala *Nya Tidning*, 1960–63, *Svenska Dagbladet*, 1966–67, *Expressen*, from 1967, and other newspapers and journals. Member, Swedish Radio Board, and National Arts Council, 1969–73; Visiting Professor, University of California, Los Angeles, 1973. Recipient: Bonniers Literary Magazine prize, 1964; Nordic Council prize, 1969. Address: c/o Norstedts Förlag, Box 2052, 103 12 Stockholm 2, Sweden.

PUBLICATIONS

Fiction

Kristallögat [The Crystal Eye].   Stockholm, Norstedt, 1961.
Färdvägen [The Route].   Stockholm, Norstedt, 1963.
Bröderna Casey [The Casey Brothers], with Torsten Ekbom and Leif Nylén (as Peter Husberg).   Stockholm, Bonnier, 1964.
Magnetisörens femte vinter.   Stockholm, Norstedt, 1964; as *The Magnetist's Fifth Winter*, London, Quartet, 1989.
Hess.   Stockholm, Norstedt, 1966.
Legionärerna.   Stockholm,   Norstedt,   1968;   as   *The Legionnaires*, New York, Delacorte, 1973; London, Cape, 1974.
Sekonden [The Seconder].   Stockholm, Norstedt, 1971.
Berättelser från de inställda upprorens tid [Tales from the Age of Cancelled Rebellions].   Stockholm, Norstedt, 1974.
Musikanternas uttåg.   Stockholm, Norstedt, 1978; as *The March of the Musicians*, London, Collins, 1985.
Doktor Mabuses Nya Testamente [Dr. Mabuse's New Will], with Anders Ehnmark.   Stockholm, Norstedt, 1982.
Nedstörtad ängel: en kärleksroman.   Stockholm, Norstedt, 1985; as *Downfall: A Love Story*, London, Quartet, 1986.
Protagoras sats: på spaning efter det politiska förnuftet [Protagora's Theory: On the Hunt for Political Sense], with Anders Ehnmark.   Stockholm, Norstedt, 1987.
Kapten Nemos bibliotek.   Stockholm, Norstedt, 1991; as *Captain Nemo's Library*, London, Quartet, 1992.

Plays

Tribadernas natt (produced Sweden, 1975).   Stockholm PAN/Norstedt, 1975; as *The Night of the Tribades* (pro duced New York, 1977), New York, Hill and Wang, 1977; as *The Tribades* (produced London, 1978).

Chez nous: bilder från svenskt församlingsliv [Chez Nous: Pictures from Swedish Community Life], with Anders Ehnmark. Stockholm, Norstedt, 1976.

Mannen på trottoaren [Man on the Pavement], with Anders Ehnmark. Stockholm, Norstedt, 1979.

Till Fedra [To Phaedra]. Stockholm, Norstedt, 1980.

Från regnormarnas liv (produced Copenhagen and Stockholm, 1981); as *The Rain Snakes* (produced New York, 1984; London [rehearsed reading], 1992).

En triptyk (includes *Tribadernas natt*; *Från regnormarnas liv*; *Till Fedra*). Stockholm, Norstedt, 1981.

I lodjurets timma (produced Stockholm, 1988). Stockholm, Norstedt, 1988; as *The Hour of the Lynx* (produced Edinburgh, 1990), London, Forest, 1990.

Television Play: *Strindberg — ett liv* [Strindberg — A Life], 1984.

Other

Katedralen i München och andra berättelser [The Cathedral in Munich and Other Stories]. Stockholm, Norstedt, 1972.

Strindberg — ett liv [Strindberg — A Life]. Stockholm, Norstedt, 1984.

Mannen i båten [The Man in the Boat]. Stockholm, Carlsen/if, 1985.

Två reportage om idrott [Two Report on Sport]. Stockholm, Norstedt, 1986.

Editor, *Sextiotals kritik: en antologi* [Criticism of the Sixties: An Anthology]. Stockholm, Norstedt, 1966.

*

Critical Studies: "The Swedish Short Story: Per Olov Enquist," in *Scandinavian Studies* (Madison, Wisconsin), 49(2), 1977, "Putting Together the Puzzle in Per Olov Enquist's *Sekonden*," in *Scandinavian Studies* (Madison, Wisconsin), 49(3), 1977, "Strindberg: The Man and the Myth as Seen in the Mirror of Per Olov Enquist," in *Structures of Influence: A Comparative Approach to August Strindberg*, edited by Marilyn Johns Blackwell, Chapel Hill, North Carolina, University of North Carolina Press, 1981, "Per Olov Enquist's *Hess*," in *Scandinavica* (Norwich), 22(1), 1983, and *Per Olov Enquist: A Critical Study*, Westport, Connecticut, Greenwood, 1984, all by Ross Shideler; "Literature as a Vehicle for Commitment: Per Olov Enquist and Göran Sonnevi" by Janet Mawby, in her *Writers and Politics in Modern Scandinavia*, London, Hodder and Stoughton, 1978.

*   *   *

When in the 1960s Per Olov Enquist's novels first began to be published, his writing clearly reflected the relativism and loss of ideology of the decade. Political, religious, and psychological theories, useful for a neat, compartmentalised organisation of the universe were now demolished, leaving only fragments and shattered pieces. Influenced by the new French novel and Gruppe 47 in Germany, Enquist wrote intellectual, experimental novels, often collage-like in form. At a time when young writers were looking for new forms of literary expression, Enquist settled for an investigative style, an attempt to reconstruct events reported to have happened but where the truth is often too inaccessible, the facts too complex to yield anything but ambiguous answers. It was a

style that was to remain Enquist's literary trademark, characterising both his novels and his plays.

In his first novel, *Kristallögat* (The Crystal Eye), Enquist tells the story of a young woman to whom life and other people seem unreal but who comes to terms with this feeling by investigating her own past. She is, as the last line of the book reads, "coming out of unreality — on her way towards something different." But no investigation of the past is foolproof, and we simply do not know whether we have been given the truth or a past recreated through analysis.

In *Hess*, Enquist takes his discussion of identity a step further. While there is little evidence of the eponymous protagonist, "H" of the novel moves freely in space and time, and just as Hitler's deputy has often been described as a psychological riddle, so is the Hess figure of Enquist's novel.

In *Magnetisörens femte vinter* (*The Magnetist's Fifth Winter*) we encounter another, familiar Enquist theme. Into the spotlessly clean, rational, and sensible town of Seefond in Germany of the 1790s comes Meisner, charismatic faith healer and con man to some but a saviour from increasing alienation to others. We have already encountered this same emotional death in both *Kristallögat* and *Hess*.

With *Legionärerna* (*The Legionnaires*), which won him the prestigious Nordic Council literary prize, Enquist's writing also acquires a clear political profile characteristic of all his work throughout the 1970s. But the conflict between the two opposing forces still remains — scepticism versus mysticism, alienation versus integration, freedom versus security — and in choosing reconstruction through investigation as his literary form, the two forces are successfully kept in balance. In *The Legionnaires*, which concerns the repatriation of the Baltic refugees, Enquist even refers to himself as "the investigator" who, not surprisingly given Enquist's approach, poses more questions than he himself can answer. The investigative method is also employed in *Sekonden* (The Seconder), a novel about a disqualified and discredited hammer-thrower which shares many features with both *Hess* and *The Legionnaires* in its attempt to create a coherent whole out of disparate fragments of reality. There is just one difference: this time Enquist ends his investigation on a hopeful note. Another novel belonging to Enquist's politically committed period in the 1970s is *Musikanternas uttåg* (*The March of the Musicians*), which argues against the thesis that Social Democracy has "failed" the people by abandoning Socialism in favour of watered-down Revisionism.

Enquist also attracted considerable attention in the 1970s as a playwright, applying the same form of investigative reconstruction to his plays as he had previously to his novels. In *Tribadernas natt* (*The Night of the Tribades*), which catapulted Enquist into fame as a dramatist, he dissects August Strindberg's play *Den starkare* (*The Stronger*). Here Enquist's interpretation of events is distinctly at odds with Strindberg's expressed intentions. What Strindberg has tried to do, according to Enquist, is to attempt to change reality by rewriting it in literary form. Again Enquist is concerned with secrets that lurk underneath the surface, recapturing the truth through reconstruction, but a truth that will always fail to be anything but subjective. In *Från regnormarnas liv* (*The Rain Snakes*) Enquist continues his quest for the truth, this time about Hans Christian Andersen, while in *I lodjurets timma* (*The Hour of the Lynx*) he applies the scalpel to an authentic incident from his native Västerbotten.

His latest novel, *Kapten Nemos bibliotek* (*Captain Nemo's Library*), which Enquist informs us is also his last (although there appear to be more plays to come), is a concluding literary interpretation of the shattering events of his childhood which run like a thread through all of his work. Here Enquist achieves the writer's ambition of being at once the observer and the observed, observing his life while participating in his own past. As it turns out, the library of the title is nothing but Enquist's own literary output since his debut as a writer in 1961.

—Gunilla M. Anderman

———

ENZENSBERGER, Hans Magnus. German. Born in Kaufbeuren, 11 November 1929. Educated at schools in Nuremberg; universities of Freiburg, Hamburg, and Erlangen, Ph.D. 1955; the Sorbonne, Paris, 1952–54. Served in the Volkssturm, 1944–45. Married 1) Dagrun Christensen; 2) Maria Makarova (divorced); 3) Katharine Bonitz in 1986; two daughters. Program editor, South German Radio, Stuttgart, 1955–57; guest lecturer, Academy of Design, Ulm, 1956–57; editor, 1960–75, and publisher, 1970–75, Suhrkamp publishers, Frankfurt; professor of poetry, University of Frankfurt, 1965; founder, 1965, and publisher, 1970–90, *Kursbuch* periodical; founding editor, *TransAtlantik*, 1980–82. Since 1985 publisher, Die Andere Bibliothek book series. Fellow, Center for Advanced Studies, Wesleyan University, Middletown, Connecticut (resigned 1968). Lived in Norway, 1961–65, then in Berlin, and since 1979, Munich. Recipient: Villa Massimo grant; Jacobi prize, 1956; Critics prize (Germany), 1962, 1979; Büchner prize, 1963; Etna-Taormina prize, 1967; Nuremberg cultural prize, 1967; Pasolini prize, 1982; Heinrich Böll prize, 1985; Bavarian Academy of Fine Arts award, 1987. Address: c/o Suhrkamp Verlag, Postfach 101945, 6000 Frankfurt am Main, Germany.

PUBLICATIONS

Verse

Verteidigung der Wölfe. Frankfurt, Suhrkamp, 1957.
Landessprache. Frankfurt, Suhrkamp, 1960.
Gedichte. Frankfurt, Suhrkamp, 1962.
Blindenschrift. Frankfurt, Suhrkamp, 1964.
Poems, translated by Michael Hamburger. Newcastle upon Tyne, Northern House, 1966.
Poems for People Who Don't Read Poems, translated by the author, Michael Hamburger, and Jerome Rothenberg. London, Secker and Warburg, and New York, Atheneum, 1968; as *Selected Poems*, London, Penguin, 1968.
Gedichte 1955–1970. Frankfurt, Suhrkamp, 1971.
Mausoleum: 37 Balladen aus der Geschichte des Fortschritts. Frankfurt, Suhrkamp, 1975; in English, translated by Joachim Neugroschel, New York, Urizen Press, 1976.
Der Untergang der Titanic. Frankfurt, Suhrkamp, 1978; as *The Sinking of the Titanic*, translated by the author, Boston, Houghton Mifflin, 1980; Manchester, Carcanet Press, 1981.
Beschreibung eines Dickichts. Berlin, Volk und Welt, 1979.
Die Furie des Verschwindens: Gedichte. Frankfurt, Suhrkamp, 1980.
Dreiunddreißig Gedichte. Stuttgart, Reclam, 1981.
Die Gedichte. Frankfurt, Suhrkamp, 1983.
Hans Magnus Enzensberger, edited by A. V. Subiotto. Leicester, Leicester University Press, 1985.
Gedichte, 1950–1985. Frankfurt, Suhrkamp, 1986.

Diderot und das dunkle Ei: eine Mystifikation. Berlin, Friedenauer Presse, 1990.
Zukunftsmusik. Frankfurt, Suhrkamp, 1991.

Plays

Das Verhör von Habana (produced Essen). Frankfurt, Suhrkamp, 1970; as *The Havana Inquiry*, New York, Holt Rinehart, 1973.
El Cimarron, music by Hans Werner Henze, from a work by Miguel Barnet (produced Aldeburgh, Suffolk, 1970). Mainz, n.p., 1971.
La Cubana, music by Hans Werner Henze (produced Munich, 1975).
Der Menschenfeind, from the play *Le Misanthrope* by Molière (produced Berlin, 1979). Frankfurt, Insel, 1979.
Der Menschenfreund (produced Berlin, 1984). Frankfurt, Suhrkamp, 1984.
Die Tochter der Luft (produced Essen, 1992). Frankfurt, Suhrkamp, 1992.

Radio Play: *Der tote Mann und der Philosoph*, 1978.

Other

Zupp: Eine Geschichte in der sehr viel vorkommt. Olten, Walter, 1959.
Brentanos Poetik. Munich, Hanser, 1961.
Einzelheiten. Frankfurt, Suhrkamp, 1962.
Einzelheiten II: Poesie und Politik. Frankfurt, Suhrkamp, 1964.
Politik und Verbrechen. Frankfurt, Suhrkamp, 1964; as *Politics and Crime*, edited by Michael Roloff, New York, Seabury, 1974.
Politische Kolportagen. Frankfurt, Fischer, 1966.
Deutschland, Deutschland unter anderm: Äusserungen zur Politik. Frankfurt, Suhrkamp, 1967.
Staatsgefährdende Umtriebe. Berlin, Voltaire, 1968.
Der kurze Sommer der Anarchie. Frankfurt, Suhrkamp, 1972.
The Consciousness Industry, edited by Michael Roloff. New York, Seabury, 1973.
Palaver: Politische Überlegungen (1967–1973). Frankfurt, Suhrkamp, 1974.
Raids and Reconstructions: Essays on Politics, Crime, and Culture. London, Pluto Press, 1976.
Baukasten zu einer Theorie der Medien. Bremen(?), Schwarz-Weiss, 1981.
Politische Brosamen. Frankfurt, Suhrkamp, 1982; as *Political Crumbs*, London, Verso, 1990.
Critical Essays, edited by Reinhold Grimm. New York, Continuum, 1982.
Im kleinen Leben liegt der grosse Schmerz: Liederbuch, with Ingrid Craven and Peer Raben. Berlin, Albino, 1983.
Die Deutschen, photographs by René Burri. Munich, Schirmer/Mosel, 1986.
Ach Europa! Frankfurt, Suhrkamp, 1987; as *Europe, Europe: Forays into a Continent*, New York, Pantheon, and London, Radius, 1989.
Dreamers of the Absolute: Essays on Politics, Crime and Culture. London, Radius, 1988.
Mittelmaß und Wahn: gesammelte Zerstrenuungen. Frankfurt, Suhrkamp, 1988; as *Mediocrity and Delusion*, London, Verso, 1992.
Erinnerung an die Zukunft: Poesie und Poetik. Leipzig, Reclam, 1988.

Requiem für eine romantische Frau. Berlin, Friedenauer Presse, 1988.
Der fliegende Robert: Gedichte, Szenen, Essays. Frankfurt, Suhrkamp, 1989.

Editor, *Gedichte, Erzählungen, Briefe*, by Clemens Brentano. Franfurt, Fischer, 1958.
Editor, *Museum der modernen Poesie.* Frankfurt, Suhrkamp, 1960.
Editor, *Allerleirauh: Viele schöne Kinderreime.* Frankfurt, Suhrkamp, 1961.
Editor, *Vorzeichen: Fünf neue deutsche Autoren.* Frankfurt, Suhrkamp, 1962.
Editor, *Gedichte*, by Andreas Gryphius. Frankfurt, Insel, 1962.
Editor, *Poesie*, by Gunnar Ekelöf, translated by Nelly Sachs. Frankfurt, Suhrkamp, 1962.
Editor, *Der Hessische Landbote*, by Georg Büchner. Frankfurt, Insel, 1965.
Editor, *Kurzgefasster Bericht*, by Bartolome de Las Casas. Frankfurt, Insel, 1966; as *The Devastation of the Indies*, New York, Seabury, 1974.
Editor, *Politische Essays*, by Heinrich Mann. Frankfurt, Suhrkamp, 1968.
Editor, *Freisprüche: Revolutionäre vor Gericht.* Frankfurt, Suhrkamp, 1970.
Editor, *Klassenbuch: Ein Lesebuch zu den Klassenkämpfen in Deutschland 1756–1971.* Neuwied, Luchterhand, 1972.
Editor, *Gespräche mit Marx und Engels.* Frankfurt, Insel, 1973.
Editor, *Der Weg ins Freie.* Frankfurt, Suhrkamp, 1975.
Editor, *Ludwig Börne und Heinrich Heine: ein deutsches Zerwürfnis.* Nördlingen, Greno, 1986.
Editor and Translator, *Die Raserei und die Qual: Gedichte*, by Pablo Neruda. Frankfurt, Suhrkamp, 1986.
Editor, *Europa in Trümmern: Augenzeugenberichte aus den Jahren 1944–1948*, by Stig Dagerman. Frankfurt, Eichborn, 1990.

Translator, *Die Bettleroper*, by John Gay, in *Dreigroschenbuch*. Frankfurt, Suhrkamp, 1960.
Translator, *Quoat-Quoat* by Audiberti, in *Theaterstücke 1.* Neuwied, Luchterhand, 1961.
Translator, *Gedichte*, by William Carlos Williams. Frankfurt, Suhrkamp, 1962.
Translator, *Gedichte*, by César Vallejo. Frankfurt, Suhrkamp, 1963.
Translator, *Poesie*, by Franco Fortini. Frankfurt, Suhrkamp, 1963.
Translator, *Die Maschinen: Gedichte*, by Lars Gustafsson. Munich, 1967.
Translator, *Poesie impure: Gedichte*, by Pablo Neruda. Hamburg, Hoffmann und Campe, 1968.
Translator, *Komplette Nonsens*, by Edward Lear. Frankfurt, Insel, 1977.
Translator, *Der Vampir von St. Petersburg*, by Alexander Suchovo-Kobylin. Frankfurt, Autoren, 1978.
Translator, *William Carlos Williams, endlos und unzerstörbar.* Walbrunn, Heiderhoff, 1983.
Translator, *Über die Verfinsterung der Geschichte*, by Alexander Herzen. Berlin, Friedenauer Presse, 1984.
Translator, *Klauenspur: Gedichte und Briefe*, by Edith Södergran. Leipzig, Reclam, 1990.

*

Critical Studies: "The Commitment and Contradiction of Hans Magnus Enzensberger," in *Books Abroad* (Norman, Oklahoma), 47, 1973, and "Hans Magnus Enzensberger," in *Northwest Review* (Eugene, Oregon), 21(1), 1983, both by Reinhold Grimm; "Drowning as One of the Fine Arts" by Paul West, in *Parnassus* (New York), Spring-Summer 1981; "The Crisis" by Joseph B. and Kjersti D. Board, in *Scandinavian Review* (New York), June 1983; "Enzensberger and the Iceberg" by Philip Martin, in *Meanjin* (Parkville, Victoria), June 1983; "Enzensberger: A Self-Taught Lesson" by Charlotte Melin, in *Germanic Notes* (Bemidji, Minnesota), 14(2), 1983; "A Conversation with Hans Magnus Enzensberger," in *Northwest Review* (Eugene, Oregon), 21(1), 1983, and "Writing as Disappearing: Enzensberger's Negative Utopian Move," in *Monatshefte* (Madison, Wisconsin), Summer 1986, both by Lydia K. Schultz; "Watermarks on the Titanic: Hans Magnus Enzensberger's Defence of Poesy" by Philip Brady, in *Publications of the English Goethe Society* (London), 58, 1989.

*   *   *

Hans Magnus Enzensberger's writing career is almost contemporaneous with the existence of the Federal Republic of Germany itself. Just as the latter has undergone several painful yet fascinating mutations (and with the integration of the former East Germany is currently in the midst of yet another phase of change), so too has Enzensberger altered, chameleon-like, often to the consternation and confusion of his critics and admirers alike. His progress, to use one of his own favourite yet loaded terms, is charted with wryness, jejune candidness, and a soupçon of scepticism in his multifaceted literary productions. Furthermore, his intellectual and psychological growth has been fostered by incessant travels, an avid study especially of European writers, thinkers, and scientists, and by an active involvement in the "consciousness industry," to deploy his own provocative coinage from the early 1960s, when his early talent for penetrating essay writing first began to emerge.

Enzensberger is a legitimate heir to the generation of European and American modernist poets writing between 1910 and 1945. In particular he is indebted to Bertolt Brecht and Gottfried Benn. In his poetry, which he began producing in the mid-1950s, he too eschews rhyme, inclines towards irregular rhythms, employs counterpointing and montage techniques, and appeals to the intellect through his elliptical, laconic style. Added to these features is his particular penchant for grotesque verbal distortions which render familiar realities in a new and alarming light.

Not surprisingly, in view of Enzensberger's restless, itinerant lifestyle and involuntary, premature encounters with foreigners — aged 16 he worked as an interpreter and barman for the Royal Air Force in post-war Germany — his work has a distinctly cosmopolitan feel, which is even evident in the titles of several poems such as "Corps diplomatique socialiste," "La Forza del destino," "Doomsday," "Countdown," and "Middle Class Blues." This last poem is typical in a number of respects. It criticizes the materialism and consumerism of contemporary society, while evoking a sense of spiritual emptiness underneath the façade of satiety. Like many of his poems it is a melancholic lament rather than an aggressive indictment, and invalidates the early labelling of Enzensberger as an "angry young man." If "anger" exists in his work, then it is expressed rather as the result of his own frustration as one who seeks self-liberation but finds himself enchained firmly to the middle class.

This frustration boiled over in the mid-1960s when he announced that he was giving up writing poetry in order to make his country "politically literate." Enzensberger was not of course the only West German intellectual who, feeling provoked by the kind of society West Germany was becoming, entered that public arena of conflict in which the representatives of *Geist* (i.e., the intellectuals) confront and expose the entrenched interests of *Macht* (i.e., the political rulers). Martin Walser (*q.v.*), Günter Grass (*q.v.*), Heinrich Böll, Siegfried Lenz (*q.v.*), and indeed the majority of the members of that quintessentially post-war German literary coterie, Gruppe 47 (who met twice a year and from the mid-1950s onwards sought to use their semi-mythical reputation to voice their concern on matters political, social, and cultural) behaved in the same nonconformist mode. But, with the possible exception of Walser, Enzensberger's nonfictional diagnosis of society was not only the most incisive but also the most comprehensive of the group. In particular, he was one of the first writers to gauge the vast power of the media (at the core of the "consciousness industry") to influence not only the material conditions of modern citizens but their immaterial existences too, by impregnating minds with "opinions, judgements and prejudices."

When ultimately he did return to his artistic role of poet-mentor to the German nation, the poems dating from his period of political *engagement* published in the sections "Davor" (Before) and "Danach" (After) in *Die Gedichte* (Collected Poems) of 1983 are the least convincing of his output due to their over intellectualised, narrow focus on radical, leftwing politicking. Here his gift for verbal play and innovation, which truly demasks the way our minds have been infested with the jargon of modern technology, industry, commerce, and, of course, the media, is wasted on facile parody.

Enzensberger's involvement in the Berlin student movement and his well-publicised pilgrimage to Cuba in 1968–69 are put, however, into (self)critical perspective in his remarkable epic poem *Der Untergang der Titanic* (*The Sinking of the Titanic*, characteristically translated into English by the author himself!). Berlin and Cuba, these former idylls of progress, are as quietly shattered by the poet as the ostensibly unsinkable passenger ship was by an iceberg. Manmade symbols of progress, be they a new ship or a new society, are revealed as ephemeral artefacts threatened by failure almost as soon as they are created. But individuals prefer to remain blind to impending disasters because their basic instinct is to live for the present and believe in survival, irrespective of all the lessons of history and the writings on the wall (see for instance his earlier poem "Braille"). The poet's responsibility is therefore to make us face reality and recognize the technological and political icebergs which can sink our entire planet with the same chilling suddenness as the real one which destroyed the *Titanic*.

While the 1980s saw no new poems published, Enzensberger's output of essays was prolific and, tentatively, marked yet a further change in direction for their ever-fertile, yet indefinable author. The humour has increased, the didactic and missionary zeal toned down, and the social and cultural optimism has become more pronounced. For example, he asserts that old conflicts, such as the aforementioned "natural" hostility between writer and politician, have been largely overcome, while the middle classes, far from suffering the blues, have now established themselves as a progressive, heterogeneous, and highly adaptable class — at least in his native country. It is their culture which reigns supreme; as he says in *Mittelmaß und Wahn* (*Mediocrity and Delusion*), "The republic is, sociologically and culturally, characterised by the undisputed hegemony of the middle class." Of course one is never quite certain as to Enzensberger's complete identification with what he says. His ubiquitous irony keeps the reader on her/his toes, as when he enthuses that the infamous *Bild* newspaper is "the artistic work of the avantgarde . . . the break with every traditional form of language . . . is collage, montage, assemblage . . . *objet trouvé* and *écriture automatique* . . . poetry without poetry . . ." Perhaps this last characterisation is indeed the key to his present tongue-in-cheek view of the media and possibly even to an understanding of his own forsaking of poetry for other media such as the essay and indeed journalism in general. Elsewhere in *Mediocrity and Delusion* he writes: "Everywhere poetry is spreading its wings, in the headlines, in pop music, in advertisements . . . unfamiliar feelings, new ways of perception are being invented in the cinema, in all kinds of therapy, in sects and sub-cultures, in the crazy spectacle offered in the streets of our metropolises. In this sense literature has fallen victim to public ownership. The socialisation of literature has brought with it the literarisation of society." No doubt Enzensberger will continue to write and publish poetry but he now acknowledges, seemingly quite happily, that he is no longer an exclusive member of a divinely ordained minority of artists known as "poets."

—Anthony Waine

ERBA, Luciano. Italian. Born in Milan, 18 September 1922. Educated at Liceo Manzoni, Milan, graduated 1940; Catholic University, Milan, Ph.D. 1947. Member of anti-fascist group in Milan, 1943, then refugee in Switzerland, 1944–45. Married Maria Giuseppina Sain in 1961; three daughters. Lecturer in Italian, Lycée Saint-Louis, Paris, 1948–50; Assistant in French, 1953–54, Lecturer, 1954–57, and Associate Professor, 1957–63, Catholic University, Milan; Visiting Professor, 1963–64, and Associate Professor of comparative literature, 1964–65, Rutgers University, New Brunswick, New Jersey; Associate Professor of comparative literature, University of Washington, Seattle, 1965–66, University of Bari, 1967–70, University of Trieste, 1970–71, and University of Bologna, 1971–72; Professor of French literature, University of Trieste, 1972–73, University of Padua, 1973–82, and University of Verona, from 1982. Editor, *Itinerari* magazine, Genoa, 1953–54. Recipient: Carducci prize, 1977; Viareggio prize, 1980; Bagutta prize, 1987. Address: Via Giason del Maino 16, 20146 Milan, Italy.

PUBLICATIONS

Verse

Linea K.   Modena, Guanda, 1951.
Il bel paese.   Milan, Meridiana, 1956.
Il prete di Ratanà.   Milan, Scheiwiller, 1959.
Il male minore.   Milan, Mondadori, 1960.
Il prato più verde.   Milan, Guanda, 1977.
Il nastro di Moebius.   Milan, Mondadori, 1980.
(Selection) in English, in *The New Italian Poetry*, edited and translated by Lawrence R. Smith.   Berkeley, University of California Press, 1981.
Il cerchio aperto.   Milan, All'Insegna del Pesce d'Oro, 1983.
L'ippopotamo.   Turin, Einaudi, 1989.

Plays

Radio Play: *Robinson Crusoe*, 1977.

Television Play: *La valle del Po al tempo dei Galli e dei Romani*, 1983–84.

Fiction

Françoise.   Brescia, Farfengo, 1982.

Other

Magia e Invenzione: note e ricerche su Cyrano de Bergerac e altri autori del primo Seicento francese.   Milan, Scheiwiller, 1967.
Huysmans e la liturgia, e alcune note di letteratura francese contemporanea.   Bari, Adriatica, 1971.
Storia e antologia della letteratura francese: il Novecento.   Milan, Fabbri, 2 vols., 1972.

Editor, *Lettres*, by Cyrano de Bergerac.   Milan, Scheiwiller, 1965.
Editor, *Gli stati e imperi della luna*, by Cyrano de Bergerac.   Rome, Theoria, 1982.
Editor, *Viaggio al centro della terra*, by Jules Verne.   Rome, Theoria, 1983.

Translator, *L'altro mondo*, by Cyrano de Bergerac.   Florence, Sansoni, 1956.
Translator, *Poesie*, by Blaise Cendrars.   Milan, Nuova Accademia, 1961.
Translator, *Vita del testo*, by Francis Ponge.   Milan, Mondadori, 1971.
Translator, *Giles Ragazzo-Capra*, by John Barth.   Milan, Rizzoli, 1972.
Translator, *Tatto*, by Thom Gunn.   Milan, Guanda, 1979.

* * *

In the immediate post-war period, a large circle of younger poets committed to cultural and artistic renewal reacted against hermeticism, the prevailing current in Italian poetry represented by such established figures as Eugenio Montale and Salvatore Quasimodo. Luciano Erba and other poets of the so-called fourth generation — Cattafi, Orelli, Spaziani, and Andrea Zanzotto (*q.v.*) among others — chose a different course. To the quest for social engagement they opposed a disenchanted view of contemporary life; to the perceived need for new modes of experimentation they responded with a continued attachment to the formal means of expression identified with hermetic verse: semantic concentration, understatement, attention to the allusive qualities of the poetic word.

In Erba the adherence to the basic tenets of hermeticism generates a poetry of simple emotions and the epiphany of seemingly insignificant actions and events associated with the past. *Il male minore* (The Lesser Evil), which includes three books of verse issued between 1951 and 1959, is distinguished by a low-key existential disposition and a deep disillusionment with the present often compensated by a mnemonic return to adolescence and early youth. The indulgence in retrospection stands out consistently as an antidote to alienation. Yet the search for an idyllic past, though contemplated, is not seriously nurtured in Erba's work as it is, for instance, in Cesare Pavese's narrative. Memory, while assuring evasive comfort,

serves the functional need of counteracting "the senseless passage of time." In other words, memory is denied a cognitive function inasmuch as Erba's existential consciousness is veined with corrosive irony and a sense of ambivalence, if not mistrust, toward rationality and ideology. When poetic diction takes the form of epigram — as in "Nothing is certain" and "Of Life we knew only its tedium" — it crystallizes a vision of our time so lucidly cognizant of the impotence to arrest the tide of materialism that even art is deemed irrelevant. As Erba puts it, "Poetry changes nothing."

Il prato più verde (The Greenest Grass) reaffirms the poet's conscious estrangement from the mainstream of life and his position in society as a marginal and disaffected observer. But fresh elements are also in evidence. The texture of the verse alternates between spontaneous expression of remarkable simplicity and complex, syntactic constructs in which the signified becomes intelligible only through a patient decoding process. More importantly, the elegiac tone and resigned pessimism of the earlier period give way to a more assertive existential outlook grounded in metaphysical reflection which, even in its recurring moments of negativism, entertains a glimmer of hope for the fate of mankind.

—Augustus Pallotta

ESTERHÁZY, Péter. Hungarian. Born in Hungary, 15 April 1950. Educated at the University of Budapest; Eötvös Loránd University, degree in mathematics 1974. Married to Gitta Reén; two sons and two daughters. Former staff member, Ministry of Foundries and Machine Tools. Since 1978 full-time writer. Recipient: Attila József prize. Address: c/o Hungarian Writers Federation, Bajza-utca 18, 1062 Budapest, Hungary.

PUBLICATIONS

Fiction

Francsiskó és Pinta [Francisco and Pinta].   Budapest, Magvető, 1976.
Pápai vizeken ne kalózkodj! [Don't Be a Pirate in the Waters of Pápa!].   Budapest, Magvető, 1977.
Termelési-regény (kissregény) [Production-Novel (Little Novel)].   Budapest, Magvető, 1979.
Függő [Appendix].   Budapest, Magvető, 1981.
Ki szavatol a lady biztonságáért [Who Can Guarantee the Lady's Safety].   Budapest, Magvető, 1982.
Fuvarosok [Hauliers].   Budapest, Magvető, 1983.
Kis Magyar pornográfia [Little Hungarian Pornography].   Budapest, Magvető, 1984.
A szív segédigéi: bevezetés a szépirodalomba.   Budapest, Magvető, 1985; as *Helping Verbs of the Heart*, New York, Grove Weidenfeld, 1991.
Tizenhét hattyuk [17 Swans] (as Lili Csokonai).   Budapest, Magvető, 1987.
Biztos Island, with Balázs Czeisel.   Budapest, Novotrade, 1989.
Hrabal könyve [Hrabal's Book].   Budapest, Magvető, 1990.

Hahn-Hahn grófnő pillantása [The Glance of Countess Hahn-Hahn]. Budapest, Magvető, 1991.

Play

Daisy: opera semiseria egy felvonásban. Budapest, Magvető, 1984.

Other

A kitömött hattyú: írások [The Stuffed Swan]. Budapest, Magvető, 1988.
A halacska csodálatos élete [The Wonderful Life of the Little Fish]. Budapest, Magvető, 1991.
Az elefánt-csonttoronyból [From the Ivory Tower]. Budapest, Magvető, 1991.

*

Critical Study: "Delicate Balance: Coherence and Mutual Knowledge in a Short Story" by István Siklaki, in *Poetics* (Amsterdam), 17, 1988.

*   *   *

Péter Esterházy is a master of Hungarian prose who has helped to create the modern Hungarian novel, from his first work, *Francsiskó és Pinta* (Francisco and Pinta), a collection of narratives, in 1976, to recent writings. Esterházy is concerned with vocabulary and style much more than with story or explicit message, and in this he brings a new approach to Hungarian literature, which has been perhaps too concerned with the "message," however well-expressed; except for a few notable exceptions "art for art's sake" has had few supporters. But it would be unfair to dismiss Esterházy as merely a clever stylist and innovator, for there is real substance in his work. It demands intense attention, yet is not devoid of humor and irony. Associations, metaphors, allusions and evocative language, quotations and the suggestion of other writers and other works give his writing a rich texture while going to the heart of the ideas he seeks to convey.

As Miklós Béládi has argued in *Válaszutak*, Esterházy knows that he wants to present a curtailed world. He does not consider literary reality to be the same as actual reality, and he does not strive for so-called objective depiction, sociological studies, ideological or ethical evaluation: curtailed literature does not have such lofty goals. Only narrowed reality is felt to be true, convincing, and without illusions. Thus, his emphasis is on the *means* available to depict the world, and Esterházy chooses one possible mirror on reality among many. Through manipulation of text he consistently conveys to the reader that "literature is experience that can be formed into an epic, but at the same time it is opinions, judgement, and intervention."

While he destroys the conventions of the traditional novel, Esterházy seeks to substitute a new order which is valid for this age; in this way he can be said to be postmodern or postavantgarde. To cite Béládi again, "he offers a reevaluation of existence to the reader, stressing the non-recurrence of life, the impossibility of its repetition, that it has to be taken infinitely seriously but can be made bearable if we do not espouse the soap-bubble theory but are attached to past times, do not allow the past to be lost, and preserve ourselves, our independence, the freedom of our conscience, the taking of risks and confrontation."

Esterházy's concern is with language, for which he has a writer's feeling but which he uses with a mathematician's precision, even when indulging in playful twists on the sounds and meanings of words. Words have no meaning, only usage, he notes in *Függő* (Appendix) and *Ágnes*. Thus he is interested in grammar, the mechanics of communication, and to emphasize this point he quotes and echoes other writers and even himself. These interpolations assume a cultural value, but Esterházy often suggests an examination or rethinking of their values. By going beyond the cult of the absurd and deconstruction, he forces the reader to come to grips with the philosophical theses he poses.

Sometimes Esterházy explores, in a reflexive rather than expository way, the contra-logical situation of Eastern and Central Europe in the past 40 years. Yet he is not a political writer: he points out the absurdity of life under the communist system without mounting a campaign against it.

Objectivity and a sense of humor are also characteristic of his work. Both may be a result of his mathematical background and the irony of having worked for several years at the Ministry of Foundries and Machine Tools. In any case, he is able to stand back from his work and poke fun at himself, and at those who lionize him or find him impossible. A similar distancing is seen in Esterházy's use of character and narrator. He emphasizes personal involvement in presenting his text, but as Peter Balassa noted in an article in *Mozgó világ*: "the open revelation of the method and circumstances of composition, its discussion within the text, the insertions, interruptions, interpolations, citations and self-citations, digressions, changes of setting for the dialogue, and the justification of the same *as story*" emphasize the complexity of the experience. "The monologue-like dialogue, the argument, the dispute exist as we happen: events do not happen so much as we experience them" — it is this that Esterházy tries to convey through the many-faceted texture of his narrative.

With Esterházy the infraction of the rules, the presence of apparent errors, and the overblown and frenetic use of language alert us that we ourselves use language in this way. He is known for his unique use of language, for his so-called deformation of everyday phrases, and confusion of similes. But, on close examination of his works, it becomes clear that the language is enriched by this irregular use, and that the reader is challenged to become more aware of the possibilities of language. Esterházy himself said at the Lisbon Conference on Literature, later printed in *Cross Currents* (New Haven, Connecticut):

"As I see it, literature must always stand at its own frontiers, it must question itself from within; but there is also the doubt from without, because it is demanded that literature be not literature at all, but an advocate for our yearning for freedom, for a parliament, for something to provide a solution to our lives!"

—Enikő Molnár Basa

EVTUSHENKO, Evgenii (Alexandrovich). Also Yevgeny Yevtushenko. Russian. Born in Stanzia Zima, Irkutsk region, Siberia, 18 July 1933. Went on geological expeditions with father to Kazakhstan, 1948, and the Altai, 1950. Educated at the Gorky Literary Institute, Moscow, early 1950s. Married 1) Bella Akhmadulina (*q.v.*) in 1954 (divorced); 2) Galina Semionova; 3) Jan Butler in 1978; 4) Maria Novika in 1986; five sons. Member, Congress of People's Deputies of USSR, since 1989; vice president, Russian PEN, since 1990.

Recipient: U.S.S.R. Committee for Defence of Peace award, 1965; Order of Red Banner of Labour (twice); State prize, 1984. Honorary member, American Academy of Arts and Sciences, 1987. Address: Kutuzovskii Prospekt 2/1, Apt. 101, 121248 Moscow, Russia.

PUBLICATIONS

Verse

Razvedchiki griadushchevo [The Prospectors of the Future]. Moscow, Sovetskii pisatel', 1952.
Tretii sneg [Third Snow].   Moscow, Sovetskii pisatel', 1955.
Shosse entuziastov [Highway of the Enthusiasts].   Moscow, Moskovskii rabochii, 1956.
Stantsiia Zima.   Published in *Oktiabr'* (Moscow), 10, 1956; as *Winter Station*, translated by Oliver J. Frederiksen, Munich, Gerber, 1964.
Obeshchanie [Promise].   Moscow, Sovetskii pisatel', 1957.
Dve liubimykh [Two Loves].   Published in *Grani* (Frankfurt), 38, 1958.
Luk i lira [The Bow and the Lyre].   Tbilisi, Zara Vostoka, 1959.
Stikhi raznykh let [Poems of Several Years].   Moscow, Molodaia gvardiia, 1959.
Iabloko [The Apple].   Moscow, Sovetskii pisatel', 1960.
Red Cats.   San Francisco, City Lights, 1961.
Vzmakh ruki [A Wave of the Hand].   Moscow, Molodaia gvardiia, 1962.
(*Selection*), translated by Peter Levi and Robin Milner-Gulland.   London, Penguin, 1962; as *Selected Poems*, New York, Dutton, 1962.
Nezhnost': novye stikhi [Tenderness: New Poems].   Moscow, Sovetskii pisatel', 1962.
Posle Stalina [After Stalin].   Chicago, Russian Language Specialties, 1962.
The Heirs of Stalin.   Published in *Current Digest of the Soviet Press*, 14(40), 1962; as *Nasledniki Stalina*, London, Flegon Press, 1963.
Selected Poems.   London, Penguin, 1962.
Selected Poetry.   Oxford, Pergamon Press, 1963.
Khochu ia stat' nemnozhko staromodym [I Want to Become a Bit Old-Fashioned].   Published in *Novyi mir* (Moscow), 7, 1964.
The Poetry of Yevgeny Yevtushenko, edited and translated by George Reavey.   New York, October House, 1964; London, Calder and Boyars, 1966; revised edition, London, Boyars, 1981; as *Early Poems*, Boyars, 1989.
Bratskaia GES.   Chicago, Russian Language Specialties, 1965; as *Bratsk Station*, New York, Praeger, 1966.
Khotiat li russkie voiny? [Do They Want Russian Wars?].   Moscow, Novosti, 1965.
So mnoiu vot chto proiskhodit: izbrannaia lirika [Here's What Happens to Me].   Moscow, Pravda, 1966.
Kater sviazi [Torpedo Boat Signalling].   Moscow, Molodaia gvardiia, 1966.
Kachka [Swing-Boat].   London, Flegon, 1966.
Yevtushenko Poems (bilingual edition), translated by Herbert Marshall.   Oxford, Pergamon Press, 1966.
New Works: The Bratsk Station, translated by Tina Tupikina-Glaessner and Geoffrey Dutton.   Melbourne, Sun, 1966; as *Bratsk Station and Other New Poems*, New York, Praeger, and London, Hart Davis, 1967.
Poems, translated by Herbert Marshall.   New York, Dutton, 1966; Oxford, Pergamon Press, 1967.

Poems Chosen by the Author, translated by Peter Levi and Robin Milner-Gulland.   London, Collins, 1966; New York, Hill and Wang, 1967.
The City of Yes and the City of No and Other Poems.   Melbourne, Sun, 1966.
Stikhi [Poems].   Moscow, Khudozhestvennaia literatura, 1967.
New Poems.   Melbourne, Sun, 1968.
Tramvai poezii [Tram of Poetry].   1968.
Tiaga val'dshnepov [Roding Woodcock].   Riga, Liesma, 1968.
Idut belye snegi [The White Snows Are Falling].   Moscow, Khudozhestvennaia literatura, 1969.
Flowers and Bullets, and Freedom to Kill.   San Francisco, City Lights, 1970.
Ia sibirskoi porody [I'm of Siberian Stock].   Irkutsk, Vostochno-Sibirskoe knizhnoe izdatel'stvo, 1971.
Stolen Apples, translated by James Dickey.   New York, Doubleday, 1971; London, W. H. Allen, 1972.
Kazanskii universitet.   Tatar, Tarsk Knizhnoe, 1971; as *Kazan University and Other New Poems*, Melbourne, Sun, 1973.
Doroga nomer odin [Highway Number One].   Moscow, Sovremennik, 1972.
Poiushchaia damba [The Singing Dam].   Moscow, Sovetskii pisatel', 1972.
Poet v Rossii — bol'she, chem poet [A Poet in Russia Is More than a Poet].   Moscow, Sovetskaia Rossiia, 1973.
Intimnaia lirika [Intimate Lyrics].   Moscow, Molodaia gvardiia, 1973.
Ottsovskii slukh [Father's Hearing].   Moscow, Sovetskii pisatel', 1975.
Izbrannye proizvedeniia [Selected Works].   Moscow, Khudozhestvennaia literatura, 2 vols., 1975.
Proseka [The Track].   Tbilisi, Nakaduli, 1976.
Spasibo [Thank You].   Moscow, Pravda, 1976.
From Desire to Desire.   New York, Doubleday, 1976; as *Love Poems*, London, Gollancz, 1977.
V polny rost: novaia kniga stikhov i poem [At Full Growth: New Book of Verse and Poetry].   Moscow, Sovremennik, 1977.
Zaklinanie [A Spell].   Tallin, Eesti raamat, 1977.
Utrennyi narod: novaia kniga stikhov [The Morning Crowds: New Book of Poetry].   Moscow, Molodaia gvardiia, 1978.
Prisiaga prostoru: stikhi [An Oath to Space].   Irkutsk, Vostochno-Sibirskoe knizhnoe izdatel'stvo, 1978.
A Choice of Poems by Evgeny Evtushenko.   Culham, privately printed, 1978.
Kompromiss Kompromissovich [Compromise Kompromissovich].   Moscow, Pravda, 1978.
The Face Behind the Face, translated by Arthur Boyars and Simon Franklin.   London, Boyars, and New York, Marek, 1979.
Ivan the Terrible and Ivan the Fool, translated by Daniel Weissbort.   London, Gollancz, 1979.
Tiazhelee zemli [Heavier than Earth].   Tbilisi, Merani, 1979.
Kogda muzhchine sorok let [When a Man Is 40].   Tbilisi, Nakaduli, 1979.
Doroga, ukhodiushchula vdal' [The Road, Leading Far].   Alma-Ata, Zhalyn, 1979.
Svarka vzryvom: stikhotvoreniia i poemy [Explosion Welding].   Moscow, Moskovskii rabochii, 1980.
Tret'ia pamiat' [Third Memory].   Riga, Liesma, 1980.
Poslushaite menia [Listen to Me].   Baku, Iazychy, 1980.
Tochka opory [Fulcrum] (includes *Pirl-kharbor* [Pearl Harbour]).   Moscow, Molodaia gvardiia, 1981.
Ia sibiriak [I'm a Siberian].   Erevan, Sovetakan grokh, 1981.
Dve pary lyzh [A Pair of Skis].   Moscow, Sovremennik, 1982.
Belye snegi [White Snows].   Tashkent, Literatura i iskusstvo, 1982.

A Dove in Santiago (novella in verse), translated by D. M. Thomas. London, Secker and Warburg, 1982; New York, Viking, 1983.

Mama i neitronaiia bomba i drugie poemy [Mother and Neutron Bomb and Other Poems]. Moscow, Sovetskii pisatel', 1983.

Otkuda rodom ia [Where I Come From]. Leningrad, Detskaia literatura, 1983.

Sobranie sochinenii [Selected Poems]. Moscow, Khudozhestvennaia literatura, 3 vols., 1983–84.

Dva goroda [Two Towns]. Tbilisi, Merani, 1985.

More [Sea]. Sukhumi, Alashara, 1985.

Pochti naposledok: novaia kniga. Moscow, Molodaia gvardiia, 1985; as *Almost at the End*, translated by Antonina W. Bouis and Albert C. Todd, London, Boyars, and New York, Holt, 1987.

Poltravinochki [Half a Blade of Grass]. Moscow, Pravda, 1986.

Stikhi [Poems]. Kishinev, Literaturnoe artistike, 1986.

Zavtrashnii veter [Tomorrow's Wind]. Moscow, Pravda, 1987.

Stikhotvoreniia. Moscow, Sovremennik, 1987.

Sud [The Trial]. Published in *Novyi mir* (Moscow), 11, 1987.

Stikhotvoreniia i poemy 1951–1986. Moscow, Sovetskaia Rossiia, 3 vols., 1987.

Posledniaia popytka: stikhotvoreniia iz starykh i novykh tetradei [Last Attempt: Poetry from Old and New Books]. Petrozavodsk, Kareliia, 1988.

Pochti v poslednii mig [Almost at the Last Moment]. Uzhgorod, Karpaty, 1988.

Nezhnost' [Tenderness]. Kiev, Rad. psy'mennyk, 1988.

Poemy o mire [Poems About Peace]. Alma-Ata, Zhalyn, 1989.

Stikhi [Poems]. Dushanbe, Adib., 1989.

Grazhdane, poslushaite menia . . . [Citizens, Listen to Me . . .]. Moscow, Khudozhestvennaia literatura, 1989.

Liubimaia, spi . . . [Loved One, Sleep . . .]. Moscow, SP "Vsia Moskva," 1989.

Pomozhem svobode! [We Will Help Freedom!]. Published in *Znamia* (Moscow), 4, 1990.

The Collected Poems 1952–1990, edited by Albert C. Todd. Edinburgh, Mainstream, 1991.

Ne umirai prezhde smerti [Don't Die Before Death]. Published in *Ogonek* (Moscow), 10, 1992.

Fiction

Chetvertaia meshchanskaia [Four Vulgar Women]. Published in *Iunost'* (Moscow), 2, 1959.

Iagodnye mesta. Moscow, Sovetskii pisatel', 1982; as *Wild Berries*, New York, Morrow, and London, Macmillan, 1984.

Ardabiola. London, Granada, and New York, St. Martin's Press, 1984.

Plays

Bratskaia GES (produced Moscow, 1968). Moscow, Sovetskii pisatel', 1967.

Under the Skin of the Statue of Liberty (produced Moscow, 1972).

Screenplays: *Kindergarten*, 1984; *Detskii sad Moscow*, 1989.

Other

Avtobiografiia. London, Flegon Press, 1963; as *A Precocious Autobiography*, New York, Dutton, 1963.

Yevtushenko's Reader: The Spirit of Elbe, A Precocious Autobiography, Poems. New York, Dutton, 1966.

Talent est' chudo nesluchainoe [Talent Is a Miracle Coming Not by Chance]. Moscow, Sovetskii pisatel', 1980.

Invisible Threads. London, Secker and Warburg, and New York, Macmillan, 1981.

Voina — eto antikultura [War Is Anti-Culture]. Moscow, Sovetskaia Rossiia, 1983.

Divided Twins = Razdel ennye blizne t sy: Alaska and Siberia, photographs by the author and Boyd Norton. London, Viking Studio, 1988; New York, Viking, 1989.

Politika privilegiia vsekh [Everybody's Privilege]. Moscow, Izdatel'stvo APN, 1990.

Propast' — v dva pryzhka? [The Precipice — in Two Leaps?]. Kharkov, Prapor, 1990.

Fatal Half Measures: The Culture of Democracy in the Soviet Union, with Antonina W. Bouis. Boston, Little Brown, 1991.

Translator, *Mlechnyi put'*, by D. Ulzytuev. Moscow, Sovetskii pisatel', 1961.

Translator, *Seti zvezd*, by T. Chiladze. Tbilisi, Zaria Vostoka, 1961.

Translator, *Na koleni ne padat!*, by G. Dzhagarov. Moscow, Molodaia gvardiia, 1961.

Translator, *Tiazhelee zemli: stikhi o Gruzii, poety Gruzii.* Tbilisi, Merani, 1979.

*

Critical Studies: "Herbert and Yevtushenko: On Whose Side Is History?" by George Gömöri, in *Mosaic* (Winnipeg, Manitoba), 3(1), 1969; "The Politics of Poetry: The Sad Case of Yevgeny Yevtushenko" by Robert Conquest, in *New York Times Magazine*, 30 September 1973; "An Interview with Evgeniy Evtushenko" by Gordon McVay, in *Journal of Russian Studies* (Rugby, Warwickshire), 33, 1977; "Women in Evtushenko's Poetry" by Vickie A. Rebenko, in *Russian Review* (Columbus, Ohio), 36, 1977; "Yevtushenko as a Critic" by Vladimir Ognev, in *Soviet Studies in Literature* (Armonk, New York), 18(3), 1981; "Yevgeni Yevtushenko's Solo: On His 50th Birthday" by Yevgeni Sidorov, in *Soviet Literature* (Brooklyn, New York), 7[424], 1983; "Two Opinions About Evgenii Evtushenko's Narrative Poem: 'Man and the Neutron Bomb': And What If This Is Prose? And What If It Is Not?" by Adol'f Urban and Gennadii Krasnikov, in *Soviet Studies in Literature* (Armonk, New York), 20(1), 1983–84; "The Poetry of Yevgeny Yevtushenko in the 1970's" by Irma Mercedes Kaszuba, in *USF Language Quarterly* (San Francisco), 25(1–2), 1986; "Evtušenko's *Jagodnye mesta*: The Poet as Prose Writer" by Richard N. Porter, in *Russian Language Journal* (East Lansing, Michigan), 40(135), 1986; "'Queuing for Hope': About Yevgeni Yevtushenko's Poem 'Fuku!'" by Pavel Ulyashov, in *Soviet Literature* (Brooklyn, New York), 9[462], 1986; "Yevtušenko's *Stantsiya Zima*: A Reassessment" by Michael Pursglove, in *New Zealand Slavonic Journal* (Wellington), 2, 1988.

Theatrical Activities:
Director: **Films** — *Kindergarten*, 1984; *Stalin's Funeral*, 1990.
Actor: **Films** — *Tsiolkovskii*, 1978; *Take Off*, 1979.

*   *   *

Evgenii Evtushenko is one of Russia's most celebrated living poets. He became famous after the publication of his autobiographical long poem "Zima Junction" (1956). This "noisy

Siberian François Villon," as he describes himself, was at the centre of the polemics about truth, ethics, and the duty of a poet during Khrushchev's "thaw." Like Vladimir Maiakovskii, he belongs to the tradition of "civic" poetry. For him "poetry is not a tranquil chapel, poetry is civil war. The poet is a warrior." He writes with a strong rhetorical note about the burning topics of the day. In "Babi Iar" (1961) he evoked the horrors of the massacre in Kiev. The poem lent itself to interpretation as an attack on antisemitism in the Soviet Union. In his *Nasledniki Stalina* (*The Heirs of Stalin*) he demanded that the guards around Stalin's grave be doubled and tripled lest the dictator rise from the dead and bring back the past with him. More recently, however, Evtushenko has tended to criticise his country only indirectly, often by means of historical parallel, as in the poem "The Calicos from Ivanovo" (1976). He peers into the heart of Russia's tumultuous history with clear political resonances: "For Russians to live in Russia is past bearing, but it is more so to live without her." Whether in or out of official favour, he maintains, as he has put it, "a proud and difficult faith in the revolution." His lyrical hero is a committed participant in all that happens both in his own country and in the world at large.

But, as Andrei Siniavskii (*q.v.*) said, ". . . we are often astonished at his skill in touching the acute and painful questions of our time without stating them profoundly, we are also astonished by his ability to meditate on everything in the world but not to speak to the essence of anything." His greed for new experience often leads to superficiality. He is well aware of this. "We are all suffering from the same disease of soul: superficiality which is worse than dumbness." Having admitted this however he goes on producing superficial work. "Seventy per cent of what I wrote I don't like," he says. His public-oriented poems often lapse into the commonplace and sentimental: "O my Russian people! You are really international in heart! But the unclean have often loudly taken in vain your most pure name." His lyrical poems are more emotionally credible. He has fully realized what Pasternak called "the idea of a poet's biography as spectacle." With stunning frankness and directness he has introduced into his poetry the details of his private life. His poetics seem to waver between the folk style of Sergei Esenin and rather unsuccessful attempts to utilize that of Maiakovskii. There is no lack of vigour and skill in his verse but there is almost an excess of clarity. He repeatedly declares that his essential aim is to communicate with his fellow men, and he tends to simplify his language and imagery. As a result, there is nothing hidden or enigmatic about his poetry. He is still amazingly productive: he writes critical prose for the *Literary Gazette*; satirical verse for *Krokodil*; he has taken part in dramatisations of his verse in the Taganka Theatre; played the leading role in the film *Tsiolkovskii* (1978). In his book *Invisible Threads* he attempts to combine poetry and photography. And he has published a novel *Iagodnye mesta* (*Wild Berries*).

Evtushenko continues to elicit a wide range of value judgments, some of which are too severe — "cynical opportunist," "an ambassador for the Kremlin." A more serious criticism is that in every aspect of his writing — his technique, his cultural accoutrements, and aesthetic outlook — there are the signs of a manifest regression.

—Valentina Polukhina

F

FAGUNDES TELLES, Lygia. *See* **TELLES, Lygia Fagundes.**

———

FALDBAKKEN, Knut (Robert). Norwegian. Born in Oslo, 31 August 1941. Studied psychology, 1960–62; journalist, 1963–65; lived abroad, 1965–75; literary reviewer, *Dagbladet*, since 1972; editor, *Vinduet* literary periodical, 1975–80. Recipient: Riksmål prize, 1978. Address: c/o Gyldendal Norsk Forlag, Postboks 6860, St. Olavs Plass, 0130 Oslo 1, Norway.

PUBLICATIONS

Fiction

Den grå regnbuen [The Grey Rainbow].   Oslo, Gyldendal, 1967.

Sin mors hus [His Mother's House].   Oslo, Gyldendal, 1969.

Eventyr [Fairytales].   Oslo, Gyldendal, 1970.

Maude danser.   Oslo, Gyldendal, 1971; as *The Sleeping Prince*, London, Owen, 1988.

Insektsommer.   Oslo, Gyldendal, 1972; as *Insect Summer*, London, Owen, 1991; Chester Springs, Pennsylvania, Dufour, 1992.

Uår: 1. Aftenlandet; 2: Sweetwater [Famine: 1. The Evening Country; 2. Sweetwater].   Oslo, Gyldendal, 2 vols., 1974–76.

Adams dagbok.   Oslo, Gyldendal, 1978; as *Adam's Diary*, Lincoln, University of Nebraska Press, 1988; London, Owen, 1989.

E 18.   Oslo, Gyldendal, 1980.

Bryllupsreisen.   Oslo, Gyldendal, 1982; as *The Honeymoon*, New York, St. Martin's Press, 1987.

Glahn.   Oslo, Gyldendal, 1985.

Bad Boy.   Oslo, Gyldendal, 1988.

Evig din [Forever Yours].   Oslo, Gyldendal, 1990.

Til verdens ende [To the End of the World].   Oslo, Gyldendal, 1991.

Plays

Tyren og jomfruen (Den gamle historien) [The Bull and the Virgin (The Old Story)] (produced Bergen, 1976).   Oslo, Gyldendal, 1976.

To skuespill: Kort opphold i Verona; Den siste landhandleren [Two Plays: Short Stopover in Verona; The Last Country Storekeeper].   Oslo, Gyldendal, 1981.

Livet med Marilyn [Life with Marilyn].   Oslo, Gyldendal, 1987.

*

Critical Studies: "The Crippled Children: A Study of the Underlying Myths in Knut Faldbakken's Fiction" by Mary Kay Norseng, in *Scandinavica* (Norwich), 22(2), 1983; "Knut Faldbakken: A Norwegian Contemporary" by Ronald E. Peterson, in *Scandinavian Review* (New York), 73(3), 1985.

*   *   *

Knut Faldbakken has one of the widest audiences abroad of any Norwegian writer of his generation: his books have been translated into many languages, and have been well received in both the United States and Britain. Faldbakken writes in a conventional narrative style about life and love, conflict, marital problems, and the particular difficulties men suffer in an age when women's rights are becoming increasingly important. His early books are psychological novels in which Freudian issues are central, while his later books have freed themselves from this influence, and reflect issues and interests not only of the writer himself, but of leading groups in the literary and cultural life of his time.

Faldbakken's first novel, *Den grå regnbuen* (The Grey Rainbow), went largely unnoticed, whereas his second novel, *Sin mors hus* (His Mother's House), provoked interest and debate, not least because it described an incestuous relationship. With his next two novels, *Maude danser* (*The Sleeping Prince*) and *Insektsommer* (*Insect Summer*), Faldbakken continued his examination of sexual fantasies and strong emotional drives which frequently prove destructive.

With his two novels about a young couple who move to a waste land outside a big city (probably in England) — *Uår: Aftenlandet* (Famine: The Evening Country) and *Uår: Sweetwater* (Famine: Sweetwater) — Faldbakken turns to social and environmental problems. He describes a dystopia set in the near future, a world slowly breaking down, until its inhabitants have to make a fresh start, and try to create a new and different society. Artistic creativity seems to be a necessary element in this vision of a better world. These books established his international reputation, which has grown ever since. The *Uår* books could still be said to be Faldbakken's best, although his novels from different periods vary so greatly that it is difficult to compare them directly.

A number of Faldbakken's later novels deal with problems in the lives of men and women: marriage, children, sex, new ways of handling increasingly complex pressures and expectations. *Adams dagbok* (*Adam's Diary*) is a penetrating analysis of the many roles into which a man may escape when confronted with the new-won freedom and strength of women. Some of Faldbakken's characters discover that they are living false lives, with surprising consequences; *Bryllupsreisen* (*The Honeymoon*) tells the story of a married couple who make such an unsettling discovery. Critics have disagreed violently as to the merits of this book, and *Glahn*, a parody of Knut Hamsun's *Pan*, also created problems for many critics and readers because it both uses Hamsun's text and questions some of the basic myths on which the original book rests.

Faldbakken's latest novels — *Bad Boy*, *Evig din* (Forever Yours), and *Til verdens ende* (To the End of the World) — have all been considerable successes, and have reached a wide audience through book club distribution. Their fairly conventional narratives and their subject-matter — strong emotions which lead to crises and new solutions — seem to appeal to many readers. Faldbakken's characters are sometimes outsiders who refuse to live by normal standards, and very often sexuality is a strong force in their lives. *Bad Boy* begins by narrating the downfall of a 40-year-old man, and then turns into an action-filled novel about seduction and deceit. The well-behaved and considerate mother's boy becomes the "bad boy," and both the metamorphosis and the complexities of the plot are skilfully handled. *Til verdens ende* is about the explorer Christopher Columbus; from the perspective of one of the sailors we are allowed to follow the hero to the New World.

Faldbakken has also written short stories and a number of plays. He has worked as a book reviewer, and has been editor of the Norwegian literary journal *Vinduet*. Two of his novels, *Insect Summer* and *Uår: Sweetwater*, have been made into films.

—Hans H. Skei

———

FALL, Aminata Sow. Senegalese. Born in Saint-Louis, Senegal, 27 April 1941. Educated at the Lycée Faidherbe, Saint-Louis, and Lycée Van Vollenhoven, baccalauréat 1962; the Sorbonne, Paris, degree in French literature 1967. Married Samba Sow in 1963; two daughters and two sons. Worked for the Senegalese National Commission; French teacher in schools and grandes écoles in Senegal; director of Letters and Intellectual Ownership, Ministry of Culture. Recipient: Grand Prix de l'Afrique Noire, 1980; Alioune Diop grand prize. Address: Sicap Amitié III, no. 4438, Dakar, Senegal.

PUBLICATIONS

Fiction

Le Revenant.   Paris, Nouvelles Éditions Africaines, 1976.
La Grève des bàttu.   Paris, Nouvelles Éditions Africaines, 1979; as *The Beggars' Strike*, London, Longman, 1981.
L'Appel des arènes.   Paris, Nouvelles Éditions Africaines, 1982.
L'Ex-père de la nation.   Paris, L'Harmattan, 1987.
Le Jujubier du patriarche.   Dakar, Khoudia, 1993.

*

Critical Study: "Social Vision in Aminata Sow Fall's Literary Work" by Samba Gadjigo, in *World Literature Today* (Norman, Oklahoma), 63(3), 1989.

*   *   *

It was in 1976, at the height of a successful career as a cultural worker, that Aminata Sow Fall turned to fiction writing and opened a new chapter in African literary history.

Her novel *Le Revenant* (The Ghost) was the first work of fiction ever published by a Francophone African woman.

However, Fall did not come to world attention until her second novel *La Grève des bàttu* (*The Beggars' Strike*) was translated into English, Chinese, and Russian. Nominated twice for the Goncourt prize and awarded the Grand Prix de l'Afrique Noire and the Grand Prix International Alioune Diop, Fall is considered today to be one of the most prestigious Senegalese women writers. In addition to the two pioneering works already mentioned, Fall has published three more novels: *L'Appel des arènes* (The Call of the Arena), *L'Ex-père de la nation* (The Former Head of the Nation), and *Le Jujubier du patriarche* (The Patriarch's Jujube Tree).

For Fall, writing in a "third" world, post-colonial context means, first of all, subverting the image of Africa mirrored in metropolitan literary imagination. In her own words, "writing should not be an act of justification but an activity by which the individual reveals the self, one's conditions of living, one's people." This realist narrative tradition derives from Fall's conviction that ethnicity is the *sine qua non* for universality and humanism.

Fundamentally grounded in a Senegalese, Muslim, and Wolof ethos, Fall's prose fiction is at the surface level a poignant tale of disintegration, a vitriolic portrayal of a corrupt social and moral fabric. Set in the urban space of Dakar, *Le Revenant* is the opening of a five-act play in which Fall depicts a shifting society whose founding values are giving way to new and corrupt ones. Born and raised to believe in the regulatory values of dignity, nobility, and pride, Bakar the narrator suddenly finds himself in an unrecognizable society in which a market economy has commodified human and family relationships. In that wasteland, money becomes the only measure of human worth. Financially exploited and pushed to embezzle money to satisfy his family's greed, Bakar ends up in jail and is rejected by his "loved ones." In the final pages of the book, he too resorts to counterfeit in order to get at the heart of things. At a deeper, more symbolic level, Fall's first work sounds the anguished outcry of a writer faced with the tormenting consciousness of human alienation in a changing world.

Yet, perhaps because of her Islamic upbringing, Fall's recording of a sense of loss does not generate despair or a sense of absurd *à la* Camus. Indeed, starting with *The Beggars' Strike* she engages in a quest, a programmatic search to restore her society's lost wholeness. Depicting a strike organized by beggars in response to the insensitivity of local leaders, Fall asserts her profound conviction that the enduring value of the past is necessary for the preservation of cultural identity. Against the authorities' zeal to get rid of the beggars in order to promote tourism and economic development, a female character interjects: "You know . . . You are wasting your time with the beggars. They have been here since the time of our great-great-grand fathers. They were there when you came into this world and they will be there when you leave it. You can't do anything about them."

Indeed, in her effort to reach a comprehensive macro-sociological explanation of Senegalese society, Fall rejects the possibility of changing the social order. Rather, her basic sociological paradigm appears as one which "sees society as a system operating much like an organism with interdependent components." Thus, Fall hints that the cultural survival of post-colonial societies like Senegal should rely on "functional" integration of the old and the new, based on value-consensus. Her work does not then project "historic systemic change" as a solution to the African predicament caused, in her thinking, by "modernization."

The historical thrust of her novels is in effect a conservative effort to preserve the old Wolof social structures and the values they embody. In *L'Appel des arènes*, for instance, the contrast Fall offers between the past and the present, the city and the village, serves to demonstrate the failure of society to maintain vital links with the marvellous world of the past "où la sérénité procure une vie toute heureuse" (where serenity provides an entirely happy life). However, unable to look forward and to place such a promised land in the future, Fall deliberately turns to the past, in an idealized quest for a lost paradise.

However, if from *Le Revenant* to *L'Ex-père de la nation* Fall's work has focussed on the recherche du temps perdu, *Le Jujubier du patriarche* seems to announce a new dawn, a temps retrouvé through art. Like Baudelaire's *Les fleurs du mal*, *Le Jujubier* is indeed a beautiful bouquet brought back from Fall's long dive into the abysses of a decaying society. Unable to recapture the past, she chooses to pursue immortality through a renewed poetics that infuses the legacy of the African epic tradition into the art of fiction writing. In this new novel Fall's prose appears as a live and colorful jujube tree whose roots are nourished by the rich humus of the Natange river, symbol of past African glory.

—Samba Gadjigo

———

FENG JICAI. Chinese. Born in Tianjin, 9 February 1942. Educated at Number One High School, Tanggu, Tianjin, diploma 1961. Married Gu Tongzhao in 1967; one son. Member of Tianjin Men's Basketball Team, 1961–62; painter, Tianjin Society of Calligraphy and Painting, 1962–74; teacher, Tianjin Workers' College of Arts and Crafts, 1974–78. Since 1978 writer, Tianjin Federation of Literature and Art Circles. Recipient: National prize for best short story, 1980, for novelette, 1981; First Round prize for romance, 1987. Agent: Tianjin Federation of Literature and Art Circles, 237 Xinhua Road, Tianjin, China. Address: 801 Yun-Feng-Lou A, Nanjing Road, Tianjin, China.

PUBLICATIONS

Fiction

Yihequan [The Boxers], with Li Dingxing.   1977.
Puhuade qilu [Flowering Branch Road].   Beijing, People's Publishing House, 1979.
Ah! [A Letter].   Tianjin, Baihua Literature and Art Publishing House, 1980.
Shendeng [The Magic Lantern].   Beijing, People's Literature Publishing House, 1981.
Diaohua yandou [The Carved Pipe].   Guangdong, Guangdong People's Publishing House, 1981.
Wuzhong ren [Man in the Fog].   Tianjin, Baihua Literature and Art Publishing House, 1983.
Zuojin baofengyu [Into the Storm].   Beijing, Youth Publishing House, 1983.
Shen bian [The Miraculous Pigtail].   Tianjin, Baihua Literature and Art Publishing House, 1984.
Gao nuren he ta de ai zhangfu [The Tall Woman and Her Short Husband].   Shanghai, Shanghai Literature and Arts Publishing House, 1984.
Chrysanthemums.   San Diego, Harcourt Brace, 1985.
Ganxie shenghuo [Thanks to Life].   1985.

San cun jinlian [Three-Inch Golden Lotus].   Chengdu, Sichuan Literature and Art Publishing House, 1986.
Yinyang Bagua [The Eight Diagrams of Yin and Yang].   Tianjin, Baihua Literature and Art Publishing House, 1988.

Plays

Shendeng [The Magic Lantern], from his own novel (produced Tianjin, 1982).

Screenplays: *Zuojin baofengyu* [Into the Storm]; *Shen bian* [The Miraculous Pigtail]; *Beyond Love* (in Chinese).

Radio Play: *Beyond Love* (in Chinese).

Television Play: *An Italian Violin* (in Chinese).

Other

Voices from the Whirlwind.   New York, Random House, 1991.

*

Manuscript Collection: Tianjin Federation of Literature and Art Circles.

Feng Jicai comments:
Those who are unfortunate in life can be very fortunate in literature. Those who again and again are flooded by the dirty water of life have the potential to become shining stars. Only when life has wantonly plundered you will you be presented with the gift of writing. Literature is the bitter fruit of life, yet it has the sweetest taste.

*   *   *

Feng Jicai published his first novel in 1977, although he began writing much earlier. Like many intellectuals of his time, having lived for a decade in the stifling atmosphere of the Cultural Revolution (1966–76), he had a strong desire to give vent to his feelings and found that writing was the best way to do so. His first publication was a historical novel, *Yihequan* (The Boxers), co-written with Li Dingxing. This, and his later novels *Shendeng* (The Magic Lantern) and *Shen bian* (The Miraculous Pigtail), were reworkings of historical stories set in Tianjin, Feng Jicai's home town, during the Qing dynasty. He focused on legends because they were less politically sensitive. These lively novels were well-received, perhaps because they employ the storytelling techniques of traditional popular narrative. *Shen bian*, the most successful of the novels, is set during the Boxer Rebellion which the Eight Power Allied Army invaded China to crush. Feng Jicai uses a historical allegory to express ideas about contemporary China and the psychology of its people. The hero's long pigtail is a family heirloom which has magical powers. It has defeated numerous enemies in the past, and has come to be regarded as a "miraculous whip." When it is used against the guns and cannons of the foreign invaders, some people retain a firm faith in it, while others hesitate, or doubt its efficacy. This novel mixes somewhat absurd episodes with convincingly described scenes. Parallels with current events and debates are clearly suggested, as China faces the problems of modernization and reform.

Much of Feng's important writing focuses on the Cultural Revolution and expresses his ideas about human life and the human soul. *Puhuade qilu* (Flowering Branch Road) tells of a young girl who gets involved with so-called "rebels" in the early days of the Cultural Revolution and cruelly beats a female teacher. At this point she is filled with a fanatical belief in Mao Zedong's call to the Red Guards, but later she comes to doubt and reject her thoughts and actions. This novella was praised for its perceptive treatment of the girl's inner emotional world, although its plot is somewhat melodramatic: after the girl assaults her teacher, she falls in love with a young man whom she eventually discovers to be the teacher's son. On this revelation the couple split up, but in the end he forgives her. Another of Feng Jicai's novellas, *Ah!* (A Letter), demonstrates more mature skills in its structure and character portrayal. It is the story of an intellectual faced with the horror of class struggle. At the beginning of the story the protagonist has lost a letter from his disgraced brother which will get him into trouble if anyone else finds and reads it. In his terror, the intellectual makes many stupid mistakes with tragic and ridiculous consequences before he discovers finally that he hasn't lost the letter after all. The story accurately describes the psychological state of fear and tension of that time.

Feng Jicai's long connections with the world of fine art (he had been a painter before he became a writer) are reflected in his style. He builds up his descriptions of scenery and characters with fine brushwork, and his writing has an aesthetic quality suggestive of painting. Props play important symbolic roles in Feng Jicai's stories, for example the pipe in *Diaohua yandou* (The Carved Pipe), the pigtail in *Shen bian*, the letter in *Ah!*, and the porcelain in *Ganxie shenghuo* (Thanks to Life). In this last story Feng Jicai reaches new heights in his literary technique. The tragic fate of his hero, an artist, is no longer the only focus of the story; instead the most important issue is how the artist derives inspiration and discovers a new world for his art from his contact with the "lower people" during his difficult times. As Feng Jicai has himself said, literature should not only touch on life, it should also reach to the human soul. *Ganxie shenghuo* shows that Feng Jicai has matured as a writer.

—David Jiang and Li Ruru

———

FERRÉ, Rosario. Puerto Rican. Born in Ponce, 28 July 1942 (some sources say 1938 or 1940). Educated at Manhattanville College, Bronx, New York, B.A.; University of Puerto Rico, San Juan, M.A.; University of Maryland, College Park, Ph.D. 1986. Married Benigno Trigo in 1960 (divorced); one daughter and two sons. Founder and editor, *Zona de carga y descarga* journal, 1970s. Agent: Tomás Colchie, 5 rue de la Villette, 75019 Paris, France.

PUBLICATIONS

Fiction

Papeles de Pandora. Mexico City, Mortiz, 1976; as *The Youngest Doll*, Lincoln, University of Nebraska Press, 1991.
Los cuentos de Juan Bobo. Río Piedras, Huracán, 1981.
La mona que le pisaron la cola. Río Piedras, Huracán, 1981.
La caja de cristal. Mexico City, La Máquina de Escribir, 1982.

Maldito amor. Mexico City, Mortiz, 1986; revised edition, as *Sweet Diamond Dust*, New York, Ballantine, 1988.

Verse

Fábulas de la garza desangrada. Mexico City, Mortiz, 1982.
Sonatinas. Río Piedras, Huracán, 1989.

Other

El medio pollito: siete cuentos infántiles (for children). Río Piedras, Huracán, 1976.
Sitio a Eros: trece ensayos literarios. Mexico City, Mortiz, 1980.
El acomodador: una lectura fantástica de Felisberto Hernández. Mexico City, Fondo de Cultura Económica, 1986.
El árbol y sus sombras. Mexico City, Fondo de Cultura Económica, 1989.
El coloquio de las perras. San Juan, Cultural, 1990.

*

Critical Studies: "From a Woman's Perspective: The Short Stories of Rosario Ferré and Ana Lydia Vega," in *Contemporary Women Authors of Latin America*, Brooklyn, Brooklyn College Press, 1983, and "Constructing Heroines: Rosario Ferré's cuentos infántiles and Feminine Instruments of Change," in *The Lion and the Unicorn* (Brooklyn, New York), 10, 1986, both by Margarite Fernández Olmos; "Interpreting Puerto Rico's Cultural Myths: Rosario Ferré and Manuel Rámos Otero" by Edward Mullen, in *The Americas Review* (Houston), 17(3–4), 1989; "Madness and Colonization: Ferré's Ballet" by Jill Netchinsky, in *Revista de Estudios Hispánicos* (Poughkeepsie, New York), 25(3), 1991.

*   *   *

Born into a prominent, upper-class Puerto Rican family, Rosario Ferré rejected her traditional upbringing and the oppressive role assigned to women in a patriarchal society. Thus many of her female characters are depicted as adornments trapped in confining marriages from which they escape either through open rebellion or retreat into fantasy. Other important themes in her works include the racial discrimination she has observed in her native land and the pernicious presence of American culture. Although Ferré is known for her essays and poetry, she considers herself primarily a writer of stories and novelettes. Major influences on her works include Simone de Beauvoir, Virginia Woolf, Julio Cortázar, and Mario Varga Llosa (q.v.).

Ferré's two best novelettes are "Sleeping Beauty," first published in *Papeles de Pandora* (*The Youngest Doll*), and *Maldito amor* (*Sweet Diamond Dust*). The protagonist of the former, María de los Angeles, is the only child of a wealthy Puerto Rican couple, who expect their daughter to marry and provide them with a male heir to the family fortune. María de los Angeles, however, aspires to become a ballet dancer, an ambition that shocks both her parents and the Reverenda Madre Martínez, the director of the Catholic academy María de los Angeles attends. The girl's marriage ends in tragedy when her egotistical husband Felisberto impregnates her by force to prove his machismo, and María de los Angeles is killed — along with Felisberto — while imitating the free lifestyle of her ideal, a circus acrobat named Carmen Merengue.

The principal theme, María de los Angeles's rebellion against antiquated bourgeois values, is underscored by Ferré's adept use of intertextuality and modern literary techniques. Thus the Sleeping Beauty legend is ironically integrated into the text when the protagonist is awakened from a coma by Felisberto's kiss. As seen above, however, the two lovers do not live happily ever after. Equally important are the fractured structure, satirical humor, and collage of multiple narrative perspectives provided by society columns, letters, and interior monologues, all of which make this work poetically satisfying and challenging.

Sweet Diamond Dust is also a technically complex work of art with elements of intertextuality; the original Spanish title *Maldito amor* (Cursed Love) derives from a popular Puerto Rican dance. Depicted in this novelette are several generations of the De la Valle family, members of which first represent the sugarcane oligarchy and then the industrialists and bankers allied with present-day American interests. Major characters, include Julio Font, founder of the dynasty, his son and grandchildren and, ultimately, his grandson's wife Gloria who, having been widowed, inherits the family estate. Like "Sleeping Beauty," *Sweet Diamond Dust* is esthetically enhanced by multiple narrative voices and a disjointed structure which present the action from different angles. Moreover, one of the narrators, the family lawyer, Don Hermenegildo, is an amateur novelist who contributes to the fictive quality of the text. This work's apocalyptic ending (Gloria rejects her inheritance and burns down the coveted estate) conveys the meaning of the Spanish title, that is, the love-hate relationship not only between lovers and family members, but also between Puerto Ricans and their American invaders.

"The Youngest Doll" is one of Ferré's most anthologized tales. The protagonist is an aging aunt who never married because of an infection that made her leg swell grotesquely when she was bitten by prawns. She has thus spent her life making beautiful dolls for her nieces, the youngest of whom marries a greedy, unscrupulous doctor. The story ends on a fantastic note of revenge when the doctor mutilates "the youngest doll" by excising its diamond eyes and, instead of sugar and spice, "out of the empty sockets . . . came the frenzied antennae of all those prawns."

Perhaps Ferré's best story, "The Gift," like "Sleeping Beauty," satirizes Puerto Rico's frivolous upper class and its alliance with the Catholic Church, but it also exposes racial prejudice. The main characters are two young girls, Merceditas Cáceres, the daughter of a rich, traditional family, and Carlota Rodríguez, a mulatta whose father is one of the nouveaux riches. Carlota, moreover, is the first mulatta to attend the Sacred Heart Academy where the two girls become fast friends. The eponymous gift is a mango Carlota gives to Merceditas, who breaks the rules when she leaves it in her desk where it is discovered by the school's director, Madre Artigas. Soon thereafter Carlota's unorthodox behavior leads to her expulsion from the academy and the story's final episode. Accompanied by Merceditas, Carlota is about to take leave of her schoolmates when she finds herself confronted by Madre Artigas who, in a fury, cuts off her long tresses, rips her clothing, and insults her in the vilest language. Then Merceditas, her arm around her friend, reverently extends to Madre Artigas a gift symbolic of the Sacred Heart Academy: the rotten mango.

Sitio a Eros (Eros Besieged) is a collection of essays on women writers who achieved success despite many obstacles, including Mary Shelley, George Sand, Sylvia Plath, Lillian Hellman, and Virginia Woolf. In perhaps her most famous essay, "The Writer's Kitchen," Ferré discusses a variety of subjects: the evolution of Puerto Rican society over the past century; feminist criticism; the importance of imagination in the creative process; and how she came to write her first story, "The Youngest Doll."

In her book of poems, *Fábulas de la garza desangrada* (Fables of the Bled Heron), Ferré reinterprets literary classics, often changing the endings so that the female characters are not victimized. Unlike the original myth of Ariadne and Theseus, for example, Ferré's version presents Ariadne as a heroine who abandons Theseus in the labyrinth and follows the thread to the exit.

A feminist who considers feminism the most important revolution of the 20th century, Ferré is one of the major talents to achieve prominence in Latin American fiction since the so-called "Boom" of the 1960s. The future augurs well for this writer.

—George R. McMurray

———

FLIEG, Helmut. *See* **HEYM, Stefan.**

———

FLØGSTAD, Kjartan. Has also written as Kjartan Villum. Norwegian. Born in Sauda, 7 June 1944. Educated at the University of Oslo, M.A. in philology 1971. Served in the Royal Norwegian Guards, 1964. Married Anne Kathrine Nore in 1977; two children. Has worked as a sailor and in industry. Recipient: Aschehoug prize, 1974; Nordic Council prize, 1977; Norwegian Critics' prize, 1980; Melsom prize, 1980; Pegasus prize, 1988. Agent: Gyldendal Norsk Forlag, Postboks 6860, St. Olavs Plass, 0130 Oslo 1, Norway.

PUBLICATIONS

Fiction

Fangliner [Mooring Lines]. Oslo, Det Norske Samlaget, 1972.
Rasmus. Oslo, Det Norske Samlaget, 1974.
Døden ikke heller [Not Even Death] (as Kjartan Villum). Oslo, Gyldendal, 1975.
Ein for alle [One for All] (as Kjartan Villum). Oslo, Det Norske Samlaget, 1976.
Dalen Portland. Oslo, Det Norske Samlaget, 1977; as *Dollar Road*, Baton Rouge, Louisiana State University Press, 1989.
Fyr og flamme [Fire and Flame]. Oslo, Det Norske Samlaget, 1980.
U3. Oslo, Det Norske Samlaget, 1983.
Det 7. klima: Salim Mahmood i Media Thule [The Seventh Climate: Salim Mahmood in Media Thule]. Oslo, Det Norske Samlaget, 1986.
Kniven på strupen [The Knife at the Throat]. Oslo, Gyldendal, 1991.

Verse

Valfart [Pilgrimage].   Oslo, Det Norske Samlaget, 1968.
Seremoniar [Ceremonies].   Oslo, Det Norske Samlaget, 1969.

Other

Den hemmelege jubel [The Secret Cheering].   Oslo, Det Norske Samlaget, 1970.
Loven vest for Pecos, og andre essays om populær kunst og kulturindustri [The Law West of Pecos, and Other Essays on Popular Art and the Culture Industry].   Oslo, Gyldendal, 1981.
Ordlyden [Wording].   Oslo, Det Norske Samlaget, 1983.
Tyrannosaurus Text.   Oslo, Det Norske Samlaget, 1988.
Portrett av eit magisk liv: poeten Claes Gill [Portrait of a Magic Life: The Poet Claes Gill].   Oslo, Aschehoug, 1988.
Arbeidets lys [The Light of Work].   Oslo, Det Norske Samlaget, 1990.

Translator, *De tre røvarane* [The Three Robbers], by Jean Thomas Ungerer.   Oslo, Bokklubbens Barn, 1973.
Translator, *Litteratur i revolusjonen: dikt frå Cuba* [Literature and Revolution: Poetry from Cuba].   Oslo, Pax, 1973.
Translator, *Dikt i utval* [Selected Poetry], by Pablo Neruda.   Oslo, Mariendal, 1973.

*   *   *

Kjartan Fløgstad is widely recognized as one of the foremost novelists of the generation which dominated the revolutionary 1970s, and has remained in the forefront of literary life in Norway in the 1980s and early 1990s. Fløgstad did not go as far as some novelists in his description of a class society which only revolution could save. His parodic and playful use of language, together with his use of the conventions of popular fiction, was first displayed in collections of short stories and novels, including crime novels. His early prose fiction draws on his knowledge of Sauda, a small industrial city on the western coast of Norway, his experience as a sailor, and his wide-ranging education. His familiarity with Latin-American fiction (he has translated poetry by Pablo Neruda) also left its mark on his early fiction, and in later books his knowledge of linguistics and philosophy as well as his use of Mikhail Bakhtin's Rabelais studies have been as influential as the tradition of social realism. The central theme of Fløgstad's best novels is the rapid and almost complete change from an agricultural to an industrial society in some areas of Norway early this century.

Fløgstad began as a poet, however, in a symbolist tradition. The collections *Valfart* (Pilgrimage) and *Seremoniar* (Ceremonies) are clearly related to his experience of the "modern" in exotic environments and big cities, and in his next work, this time in prose, *Den hemmelege jubel* (The Secret Cheering), he explains and defends modernism and symbolism and the complexities of art against programmatic and fashionable writing. Much later in his career, in 1988, he put his understanding of modernism to good use in biography of the early Norwegian modernist poet Claes Gill, *Portrett av eit magisk liv* (Portrait of a Magic Life).

In 1972 Fløgstad published a collection of short stories, *Fangliner* (Mooring Lines), a mixture of down-to-earth accounts of the lives of factory workers and sailors, and more fantastic stories using elements from popular fiction and mass media. Two years later his first novel, *Rasmus*, appeared, and since then all his major works have been in this genre. *Rasmus* depicts the everyday lives of working-class people in the 1960s and 1970s. The style is realistic, and the descriptions tough and naturalistic. The workers do not discuss solidarity or work for high ideals: they work to get their pay, discuss football, watch TV, and brag about women. The transition from life on the small farms to working in big factories in growing industrial towns is at the centre of this first novel, as it is in a number of later novels.

Vacillation between the realistic and the fantastic is typical of Fløgstad's work, yet the novels are very much rooted in a Norwegian experience. *Dalen Portland* (*Dollar Road*), which won the annual prize of the Nordic Council, is a convincing and entertaining story of working-class life. Fløgstad combines magic realism, wild exaggeration, popular wisdom, and humour with a tough realism. In *Fyr og flamme* (Fire and Flame) carnivalistic exaggeration colours a story about workers. Compared to the mimetic realism of conventional story-telling, Fløgstad's novels may also be seen as a response to the social realism of many Norwegian novelists in the 1970s.

Fløgstad is a good stylist, and he handles the most complex of narrative structures with ease. His word games, his propensity for strange, descriptive names, and his parodic use of myths and tales make heavy demands on his readers. He has always had a large audience, but some readers may have found his 1986 novel, *Det 7. klima: Salim Mahmood i Media Thule* (The Seventh Climate: Salim Mahmood in Media Thule), too sophisticated. In this novel the author's wide reading in linguistics and literary theory is combined with the usual parodic playfulness. The novel pretends to be the biography of Salim, and even includes an index. Fløgstad's next book was a *real* biography, of Claes Gill, although even here Fløgstad stretches the limits of the genre.

In the mid 1970s Fløgstad published two crime novels under the pseudonym Kjartan Villum, *Døden ikke heller* (Not Even Death) and *Ein for alle* (One for All). He has also published several collections of essays, including *Loven vest for Pecos* (The Law West of Pecos) and *Tyrannosaurus Text*. In 1990 he published *Arbeidets lys* (The Light of Work), a book about the factory in Sauda, the industrial city where he grew up. Besides documenting the history of the factory, the book also strongly criticises multinational capitalism.

Returning to the structure of the crime story or detective novel, Fløgstad's latest book, *Kniven på strupen* (The Knife at the Throat), is an elegant exposé of post-industrial, postmodern life in Norway near the end of this century. Whether this novel secures Fløgstad's position as one of the leading Norwegian novelists has been debated, but there are few novelists with his talent, capacity, and ambition in Norwegian literature.

—Hans H. Skei

———

FO, Dario. Italian. Born in San Giano, Lombardy, 24 March 1926. Educated at the Academy of Fine Arts, Milan; Brera Art Academy. Married the actress and playwright Franca Rame in 1954; one son. Wrote for cabarets and theatres, including Piccolo Teatro, Milan; wrote and performed *Poer nano* radio program, RAI Italian Radio, 1951; co-founder, I Dritti revue company, 1953; screenwriter, Rome, 1956–58; artistic director, *Chi l'ha visto?* weekly television musical revue, 1959; founder, with Rame, Compagnia Dario Fo-Franca Rame, 1959, and Nuova Scena theatre cooperative (associated with

Italian Communist Party); performed comic sketches with Rame on *Canzonissima* television program, 1962; left Italian Communist Party; founder, La Comune theatre collective, Milan, 1970–73. Recipient: Sonning award (Denmark), 1981; Obie award, 1987. Agent: Michael Imison Playwrights Ltd., 28 Almeida Street, London N1 1TD, England. Address: c/o C.T.F.R., Viale Piave 11, 20129, Milan, Italy.

PUBLICATIONS

Plays

Poer nano ed altre storie (radio series; stage version produced Milan, 1952). As *Poer nano*, Milan, Ottaviano, 1976.
Il dito nell'occhio (produced Milan, 1953). Published in *Teatro d'oggi* (Milan), 2(3), 1954.
I sani da legare (produced Milan, 1954). Published in *Sipario* (Milan), 1955.
Ladri, manichini e donne nude (4 short plays; produced Milan, 1957). Included in *Teatro comico*, 1962; part as *Not All Burglars Have Bad Intentions* (produced New York, 1969); as *The Virtuous Burglars*, in *Plays One*, 1992; part as *One Was Nude and One Wore Tails*, and *Women Undressed, Bodies Ready to Be Dispatched* (produced Edinburgh and London, 1986); *One Was Nude and One Wore Tails* published separately, London, Theatretexts, 1985.
Comico finale (4 short plays; produced Turin, 1958). Included in *Teatro comico*, 1962; part as *Marcolfa* (produced New York, 1969); part as *Corpse for Sale* (produced Derby, 1986).
Gli arcangeli non giocano a flipper (produced Milan, 1959; Zagreb, 1960). Included in *Le commedie I* (Struzzi series 54), 1966; as *Archangels Don't Play Pinball* (produced Bristol, 1986; Cambridge, Massachusetts, 1987; London, 1988), London, Methuen, 1987.
Aveva due pistole con gli occhi bianchi e neri (produced Milan, 1960). Included in *Le commedie I* (Struzzi series 54), 1966; as *Two Pistols* (produced Cardiff, 1985).
Chi ruba un piede è fortunato in amore (produced Milan, 1961). Included in *Le commedie I* (Struzzi series 54), 1966; as *He Who Steals a Foot Is Lucky in Love* (produced Glasgow, 1983).
Teatro comico (includes *La Marcolfa*; *Gli imbianchini non hanno ricordi*; *I tre bravi*; *Non tutti i ladri vengono per nuocere*; *Un morto da vendere*; *I cadaveri si spediscono e le donne si spogliano*; *L'uomo nudo e l'uomo in frak*). Milan, Garzanti, 1962; as *Le commedie VI* (Struzzi series 289), 1984.
Isabella, tre caravelle e un cacciaballe (produced Milan, 1963). Included in *Le commedie II* (Struzzi series 55), 1966.
Settimo, ruba un po' meno (produced Milan, 1964). Included in *Le commedie II* (Struzzi series 55), 1966; as *Seventh Commandment: Thou Shalt Steal a Bit Less* (produced St. Lucia, Queensland, 1973).
La colpa è sempre del diavolo (produced Milan, 1965). Included in *Le commedie II* (Struzzi series 55), 1966.
Le commedie:
    I (Struzzi series 54): *Gli arcangeli non giocano a flipper*; *Aveva due pistole con gli occhi bianchi e neri*; *Chi ruba un piede è fortunato in amore*. Turin, Einaudi, 1966.
    II (Struzzi series 55): *Isabella, tre caravelle e un cacciaballe*; *Settimo, ruba un po' meno*; *La colpa è sempre del diavolo*. Turin, Einaudi, 1966.

    III (Struzzi series 78): *Grande pantomima con bandiere e pupazzi piccoli e medi*; *L'operaio conosce 300 parole il padrone 1000 per questo lui è il padrone*; *Legami pure che tanto io spacco tutto lo stesso*. Turin, Einaudi, 1975.
    IV (Struzzi series 125): *Vorrei morire anche stasera se dovessi pensare che non è servito a niente*; *Tutti uniti! Tutti insieme! Ma scusa, quello non è il padrone?*; *Fedayn*. Turin, Einaudi, 1977.
    V (Struzzi series 131): *Mistero buffo*; *Ci ragiono e canto*. Turin, Einaudi, 1977.
    VI (Struzzi series 289): *La Marcolfa*; *Gli imbianchini non hanno ricordi*; *I tre bravi*; *Non tutti i ladri vengono per nuocere*; *Un morto da vendere*; *I cadaveri si spediscono e le donne si spogliano*; *L'uomo nudo e l'uomo in frak*; *Canzoni e ballate*. Turin, Einaudi, 1984.
    VII (Struzzi series 330): *Morte accidentale di un anarchico*; *La signora è da buttare*. Turin, Einaudi, 1988.
    VIII (Struzzi series 356): *25 monologhi per una donna*: *Tutta casa, letto e chiesa*; *Altre storie*; *Fabulazioni della resistenza*; *Discorsi sul terrorismo e la repressione*; *Giullarate religiose*, all with Franca Rame. Turin, Einaudi, 1989; as *"A Woman Alone" and Other Plays* (includes all but *Giullarate religiose*), London, Methuen, 1991.
    IX (Struzzi series 398): *Coppia aperta, quasi spalancata*; several other short plays, all with Franca Rame. Turin, Einaudi, 1991.
Ci ragiono e canto (produced Turin, 1966). Verona, Bertani, 1972; revised versions (produced Milan, 1969; Genoa, 1973).
La Signora è da buttare (produced Milan, 1967). Turin, Einaudi, 1976.
Grande pantomima con bandiere e pupazzi piccoli e medi (produced Milan, 1968). Included in *Le commedie III* (Struzzi series 78), 1975; revised version, as *Morte e resurrezione di un pupazzo* (produced Milan, 1971), Milan, Sapere, 1971.
Legami pure che tanto io spacco tutto lo stesso (produced Genoa, 1969). Included in *Le commedie III* (Struzzi series 78), 1975; as *Il funerale del padrone*, in *Campagni senza censura*, 1970; as *The Boss's Funeral* (produced Kensington, New South Wales, 1984; Colchester, Essex, 1987).
Mistero Buffo (produced Milan, 1969). Included in *Campagni senza censura 1*, 1970; in English (produced Glasgow, 1983; London, 1984; New York, 1986), London, Methuen, 1988.
L'operaio conosce 300 parole il padrone 1000 per questo lui è il padrone (produced Genoa, 1969). Included in *Campagni senza censura 1*, 1970; as *The Worker Knows 300 Words, the Boss 1000, That's Why He's the Boss* (produced Coventry, 1983; London, 1984).
Morte accidentale di un anarchico (produced Milan, 1970). Verona, Bertani, 1970; as *Accidental Death of an Anarchist* (produced London, 1979; Los Angeles, 1983; Washington, D.C., and New York, 1984), London, Pluto Press, 1980; New York, French, 1987.
Vorrei morire anche stasera se dovessi pensare che non è servito a niente (produced Milan, 1970). Verona, Bertani, 1970.
Compagni senza censura:
    1. *Mistero Buffo*; *L'operaio conosce 300 parole il padrone 1000 per questo lui è il padrone*; *Il Telaio*; *Il funerale del padrone*. Milan, Marzotta, 1970.

2. *Morte accidentale di un anarchico*; *Vorrei morire anche stasera se dovessi pensare che non è servito a niente*; *Morte e resurrezione di un pupazzo*; *Tutti uniti! Tutti insieme! Ma scusa, quello non è il padrone?*; *Fedayn*. Milan, Marzotta, 1972.

Tutti uniti! Tutti insieme! Ma scusa, quello non è il padrone? (produced Varese, 1971). Verona, Bertani, 1971.

Fedayn (produced Milan, 1972). Milan, Sapere, 1972.

Pum pum! Chi e? La polizia! (produced Rome, 1972). Verona, Bertani, 1972; revised edition, 1974.

Ordine! Per Dio.000.000.000 (produced Milan, 1972). Verona, Bertani, 1972.

Basta con i fascisti (toured Northern Italy, 1973).

Guerra di popolo in Cile (produced Bolzano, 1973). Verona, Bertani, 1973.

The Bawd (produced Sassari, Sardinia, 1973). Included in *"A Woman Alone" and Other Plays*, 1991.

Porta e belle (produced Italy, 1974).

Non si paga, non si paga (produced Milan, 1974). Verona, Bertani, 1974; as *We Can't Pay We Won't Pay!* (produced London, 1978; Los Angeles, 1981; Chicago, 1985), London, Pluto Press, 1978; as *Can't Pay? Won't Pay!* (produced London, 1981), London, Pluto Press, 1982; as *We Won't Pay! We Won't Pay!* (produced New York, 1980), New York, French, 1984; as *Don't Pay! Don't Pay!* (produced Canberra, 1985).

Canzoni e ballate (produced Italy, 1974). Included in *Le commedie VI* (Struzzi series 289), 1984.

Il caso Marini. Verona, Bertani, 1974.

Il fanfari rapito (produced Milan, 1975). Verona, Bertani, 1975.

La guillarata (produced Milan, 1975). Verona, Bertani, 1975.

La marijuana della mamma è la più bella (produced Milan, 1976). Verona, Bertani, 1976.

Tutta casa, letto e chiesa, with Franca Rame (produced Milan, 1977). Verona, Bertani, 1978; as *Female Parts: One Woman Plays* (includes *Waking Up*; *A Woman Alone*; *The Same Old Story*) (produced London, 1981; Novoton, USA, 1982), London, Pluto Press, 1981; as *The Fourth Wall* (produced London, 1983); *A Woman Alone* (produced London, 1984); *The Same Old Story, and Medea* (produced London, 1984); *Waking Up* (produced London, 1987); part as *Adult Orgasm Escapes from the Zoo* (produced New York, 1983), New York, Broadway Play Publishing, 1985; part published in *All Home Bed and Church* section, *"A Woman Alone" and Other Plays*, 1991.

Il teatro politico di Dario Fo (includes *Mistero Buffo*; *Isabella, tre caravelle e un cacciaballe*). Milan, Mazzotta, 1977.

La storia di un soldato, adaptation of the chamber opera by Igor Stravinsky (produced Cremona, 1978). Milan, Electa, 1979.

Storia della tigre et altre storie (produced Milan, 1978). Milan, La Comune, 1980; as *The Tale of a Tiger* (produced Colchester, Essex, 1987), London, Theatretexts, 1984.

Betty (produced Edinburgh, 1980).

Clacson, trombette e pernacchi (produced Milan, 1981). As *About Face* (produced New Haven, Connecticut, 1983; San Francisco, 1986; New York, 1987), New York, French, 1989; as *Trumpets and Raspberries* (produced London, 1984), London, Pluto Press, 1984.

L'opera dello sghignazzo, with Franca Rame, adaptation of *The Beggar's Opera* by John Gay (produced Prato, 1981; revised version produced Milan, 1982). Milan, La Comune, 1982.

Storia vera di Piero d'Angera: che alla crociata non c'era (produced Genoa, 1984). Milan, La Comune, 1981.

Una madre (produced Italy, 1982); as *The Mother*, with *Coming Home*, with Franca Rame (produced London, 1984); *The Mother* published London, Theatretexts, 1984; as *A Mother*, in *"A Woman Alone" and Other Plays*, 1991.

Fabulazzo osceno, with Franca Rame (produced Milan, 1982). Milan, La Comune, 1982; as *Obscene Fables* (produced Edinburgh, 1986; London, 1987).

Coppia aperta, quasi spalancata, with Franca Rame (produced Milan, 1983). Included in *Le commedie IX* (Struzzi series 398), 1991; as *The Open Couple* (produced London, 1985; San Francisco, 1987), London, Theatretexts, 1984.

Quasi per caso una donna: Elisabetta (produced Riccione, 1984). As *Elizabeth: Almost by Chance a Woman* (produced London, 1986; New Haven, Connecticut, 1987), London, Methuen, 1987; New York, French, 1989.

The History of Masks (produced London, 1984).

Diario di Eva (produced Northern Italy, 1984); as *Eve's Diary* (produced Massachusetts, 1985).

Hellequin, Harlekin, Arlechino (produced Venice, 1985). Published in *Alcatraz News* (Perugia), 1985.

25 monologhi per una donna, with Franca Rame (produced Italy, from 1989). Included in *Le commedie VIII* (Struzzi series 356), 1989; part as *The Whore in the Madhouse* (produced London, 1985), in *"A Woman Alone" and Other Plays*, 1991; part as *I'm Ulrike, Screaming* (produced London, 1985), in *"A Woman Alone" and Other Plays*, 1991.

Una giornata qualunque (produced Milan, 1986); as *An Ordinary Day* (produced San Francisco, 1988), with *The Open Couple*, London, Methuen, 1990.

Il ratto della Francesca (produced Trieste, 1986). Milan, La Comune, 1986.

La parte del Leone (produced Bologna, 1987).

Lettera dalla Cina (produced Italy, 1989).

Il papa e la strega (produced Italy, 1989); as *The Pope and the Witch* (produced London, 1991), London, Methuen, 1992.

Zitti! stiamo precipitando! (produced Italy, 1990).

Johan Padan a la descoverta de le Americhe (produced Italy, 1991). Florence, Giunti, 1991.

Parliamo di donne: L'eroina — grassa è bello, with Franca Rame (produced Italy, 1991).

"A Woman Alone" and Other Plays. London, Methuen, 1991.

Plays One (includes *Mistero Buffo*; *Accidental Death of an Anarchist*; *Trumpets and Raspberries*; *The Virtuous Burglars*; *One Was Nude and One Wore Tails*). London, Methuen, 1992.

Screenplay: *Lo svitato*, 1956.

Radio Plays: *Poer nano ed altre storie* (series), from 1951.

Television Plays: *Monetine da 5 lire*, 1956; *Chi l'ha visto?*, 1959; *Il teatro di Dario Fo*, with Franca Rame, 1977; *Parliamo di donne*, 1977; *Buona sera*, with Franca Rame, 1979–80; *La professione della Signora Warren*, 1981; *The Tricks of the Trade*, 1985; *Trasmissione forzata* (variety), 1988; *Una lepre con la faccia da bambina*, with Franca Rame, 1989; *Parti femminili*, 1989; *Promessi sposi*, 1989; *Coppia aperta*, with Franca Rame, 1990; *Settimo ruba un po' meno*, 1991; *Mistero Buffo*, 1991.

Other

Manuale minimo dell'attore. Turin, Einaudi, 1987; as *The Tricks of the Trade*, London, Methuen, 1991.

Dialogo provocatorio sul comico, il tragico, la follia e la ragione (interviews), with Luigi Allegri.   Rome, Laterza, 1990; as *Provocative Dialogue on the Comic, the Tragic, Folly and Reason*, London, Methuen, 1993.

*

Bibliography: "Dario Fo: Bibliography, Biography, Playography" by Suzanne Cowan, in *Theatre Checklist*, 17, 1978.

Critical Studies: *Dario Fo and Franca Rame: Theatre Workshops at Riverside Studios, London*, London, Red Notes, 1983; *Dario Fo: People's Court Jester* by Tony Mitchell, London, Methuen, 1984, revised edition, 1986; *File on Fo*, edited by Simon Trussler, London, Methuen, 1989; *Dario Fo and Franca Rame* by David L. Hirst, London, Macmillan, 1989.

Theatrical Activities:
Director: **Plays** — *Gli amici della battoneria*, 1962; *Chi ruba un piede è fortunato in amore*, 1963; *La passeggiata della domenica*, 1967; *Enzo Jannacci: 22 canzoni*, 1968; *La storia di un soldato*, 1978; *L'opera dello sghignazzo*, 1981; *Tutta casa, letto e chiesa*, 1986; *Il barbiere di siviglia*, 1987, 1988, 1989, 1990, 1992; *Gli arcangeli non giocano a flipper*, 1987; *Il medico per forza/Il medico volante*, 1990, 1991; *Isabella, tre caravelle e un cacciaballe*, 1992.

*   *   *

Coming from the world of revue and radio, and already renowned for the radio character *Poer nano* (Poor Dwarf) and the revue *Il dito nell'occhio* (The Finger in the Eye), Dario Fo's activity as a satirical actor and playwright crossed the Italian frontier to achieve international recognition in 1960 with *Gli arcangeli non giocano a flipper* (*Archangels Don't Play Pinball*), which was performed in Zagreb in Yugoslavia. Since then his reputation has grown steadily until today it is widely believed that he is the most performed playwright alive today in any language. Fo came to the theatre after studying architecture (he still designs his own sets, and is an accomplished artist), evolving his own individual brand of farce and combining the grotesque, music, mime, and satire to develop a distinctly subversive and satirical image, placed at the service (since the momentous political events of the late 1960s) of the militant left. Now, with his wife Franca Rame, herself an accomplished actress from a theatrical family, he includes the rights of women in Europe and the preoccupations of "feminist" thinking among his targets in the political struggle.

Archangels Don't Play Pinball mocks the oppressive hierarchy and obstructionist bureaucracy of post-war Italy through the hilarious adventures of a petty criminal who dreams he has suffered from a loss of identity (and thus has no papers) and is buffeted this way and that by the inexorable machinery of the state. But this was good-natured satire, on a Pirandellian theme, hardly militant protest. *Isabella, tre caravelle e un cacciaballe* (Isabella, Three Sailing Ships and a Con Man), however, first performed in Milan in 1963, used historical research to present a fictional Christopher Columbus in his dealings with the power base to show, through commentary and songs, the plight of the individual at the mercy of the ruling class. In 1958, Fo and Rame had formed the Compagnia Dario Fo-Franca Rame and were performing to bourgeois audiences, but by 1962, in the now famous story of the television programme, *Canzonissima*, in which their satire of Italian institutions and named individuals proved too hot for the Italian censor, the way forward was indicated when they refused to accept such "editing" and walked out after a few episodes.

Continuing to cement his reputation — now firmly established throughout Europe — Fo continued to create satirical shows throughout the 1960s until *La Signora è da buttare* (Throw the Lady Out), an anti-American satire, brought them firmly to the forefront of the 1967–68 political movements in Italy. A characteristic mixture of satire, topical comment (Vietnam, Lee Harvey Oswald, the Kennedy assassination), and circus acts, the play had such an effect that Fo was accused of disrespect towards a foreign head of state (President Lyndon B. Johnson) and was for a long time denied a visa for entry to the United States. Dissatisfied with what they saw as their role as entertainers of the bourgeoisie, Fo and Rame disbanded their company and formed the Nuova Scena theatre cooperative in order to put their efforts at the service of the proletariat, performing in workers' clubs, occupied factories, and football stadia, always with a political ambition, often with a specific purpose to highlight the issue of workers' rights. At this time, Fo's *Grande pantomima con bandiere e pupazzi piccoli e medi* (Grand Pantomime with Flags and Small and Middle-Sized Puppets) was their most overtly political play, and projected the struggle between the proletariat (as puppets manipulated by strings in full view of the audience) and a monster puppet representing fascism which "gave birth" to other forms of repression, such as a king and queen, the middle class, a bishop, a general, a bishop, and the Italian equivalent of the Confederation of British Industry.

But the most enduring results of Fo's experience of the events of 1968 were certainly *Morte accidentale di un anarchico* (*Accidental Death of an Anarchist*), his best-known play, now performed in about 40 countries, including (remarkably for a piece which savagely satirizes the forces of law and order) Argentina, Chile, South Africa, and Ceausescu's Romania, and his one-man *Mistero Buffo* (The Comic Mysteries), the most long-running of Fo's shows and considered by many his masterpiece. *Accidental Death of an Anarchist* got as close as Fo ever has to contemporary reality, dramatising a police cover-up of the fall from a police station window of an anarchist accused of complicity in the Milan terrorist bombing in 1969. The immediacy of the events was unique in modern theatre: the play was performed during the actual trial following the assertion of the left-wing *Lotta Continua* that an inspector had pushed the anarchist, and the newspaper was being sued by the inspector. The play uses the device of a certified lunatic who, by impersonating various establishment figures, strips away the fabric of pretence, lies, and fabricated evidence in a travesty of cross-examination which turns the legal system on its head. *Mistero Buffo*, on the other hand, is a tour-de-force of Fo's own acting style, using mime and a comically effective dialect form of language to represent the medieval *giullare* (jester) function, and combining the introductory lecturette with performance sketches culled from medieval sources as well as from the Bible, to show the exploitation of the worker down the long course of Western European history. This one-man show, constantly updated, has been performed many times (including on most of the television services in Europe) and in many languages.

Since 1970, Fo has followed these, his greatest successes, with other plays on similarly committed themes. *Non si paga, non si paga* (*Can't Pay? Won't Pay!*) was an international success, as was *Clacson, trombette e pernacchi* (*Trumpets and Raspberries*), the former highlighting the plight of workers oppressed by economic forces (they steal from supermarkets), and the latter using the classic personality-doubling device to pillory an industrial baron (Agnelli). Fo has suffered continual harassment as a result of his committed political stand, being imprisoned briefly in Sardinia, while Franca Rame was abducted and beaten up on one occasion. In Italy, the one-man show format was continued with Fo's *Storia della tigre* (*The Tale of a Tiger*), *Fabulazzo osceno* (*Obscene Fables*), and most recently the further elaboration of the Columbus myth —timed to coincide with the 1992 celebrations—*Johan Padan a la descoverta de le Americhe* (Johan Padan and the Discovery of America). In 1985, he and Rame accepted the suggestion that he was today's equivalent of Harlequin and mounted a *Commedia dell'Arte* show. Since then, he has highlighted more international social and political issues in his plays, and has returned in a sense (since the collapse of the Berlin Wall) to the regular theatre circuit, to point to the international scandal of the drug scene in a hilarious satire of the Pope and Vatican attitudes (*Il papa e la strega* [*The Pope and the Witch*]), as well as the preoccupation of contemporary society with the spread of Aids (and a farcical send-up of the classic pretensions of the Italian macho male), in *Zitti! stiamo precipitando!* (Hush, We're Falling).

—Christopher Cairns

———

FRÉNAUD, André. French. Born in Montceau-les-Mines, Saône-et-Loire, 26 July 1907. Educated at the University of Dijon; the Sorbonne, Paris, degree in law. Served in the French Army during World War II: prisoner-of-war, 1940–42. Married Monique Mathieu in 1971 (second marriage). Lecturer, University of Lvov, 1930; civil administrator, Ministry of Transport, Paris, 1937–64. Member of the executive committee, Communauté Européenne des Écrivains, 1963–68. Recipient: Etna-Taormina prize, 1973; Académie Française grand poetry prize, 1973; Ministry of Culture and Communication poetry prize, 1988; Société des Gens de Lettres grand prize, 1989. Address: 52 rue de Bourgogne, 75007 Paris, France.

PUBLICATIONS

Verse

Les Rois Mages.   Paris, Seghers, 1943; revised edition, Paris, Gallimard, 1966, 1977.
Les Mystères de Paris.   Paris, Seuil, 1944.
Soleil irréductible.   Neuchâtel and Paris, Ides et Calendes, 1946.
La Femme de ma vie.   N.p., Blaizot, 1947.
Poèmes de Brandebourg.   Paris, Gallimard, 1947.
Poèmes de dessous le plancher; La Noce noire.   Paris, Gallimard, 1949.
L'Énorme Figure de la Déesse Raison, illustrated by Raoul Ubac. Privately printed, 1950.
Les Paysans.   N.p., Jean Aubier, 1951.
Source entière.   Paris, Seghers, 1953.
André Frénaud (selections), edited by G. E. Clancier.   Paris, Seghers, 1953.
Dans l'Arbre ténébreux.   Alès, Benoit, 1956.
La Nuit des prestiges.   Alès, Benoit, 1956.
Chemins du vain espoir.   N.p., De Romilly, 1956.
Passage de la visitation.   Paris, GLM, 1956.
Cœur mal fléché.   Alès, Benoit, 1957.

Pays retrouvé.   Alès, Benoit, 1957.
Excrétion, misère et facéties.   Caltanissetta and Rome, Sciascia, 1958.
Noël au chemin de fer.   Alès, Benoit, 1959.
L'Agonie du Général Krivitski, illustrated by André Masson. Paris, Oswald, 1960.
L'Amitié d'Italie.   Milan, Strenna per Gli Amici, 1961.
Pour l'Office des morts.   Alès, Benoit, 1961.
Il n'y a pas de paradis.   Paris, Gallimard, 1962.
L'Étape dans la clairière; Pour une Plus Haute Flamme par le défi.   Paris, Gallimard, 1966.
Vieux pays; Campagne.   Paris, Maeght, 1967.
La Sainte Face.   Paris, Gallimard, 1968; revised edition, 1985.
Depuis Toujours déjà: poèmes, 1953–1968.   Paris, Gallimard, 1970.
Le Miroir de l'homme par les bêtes.   Paris, Maeght, 1972.
Qui possède quoi? (bilingual edition in French and English), translated by Serge Gavronsky.   San Francisco, Greenwood Press, 1972.
La Sorcière de Rome.   Paris, Gallimard, 1973.
Mines de rien, petits délires.   Veilhes, Puel, 1974.
A Round O, translated by Keith Bosley.   Egham, Surrey, Interim Press, 1977.
November, translated by John Montague and Evelyn Robson. Cork, Golden Stone Press, 1977.
La Vie comme elle tourne et par exemple.   Paris, Maeght, 1979.
Alentour de la montagne.   Paris, Galanis, 1980.
Le Tombeau de mon père.   Paris, Galanis, n.d.
Haeres.   Paris, Gallimard, 1982.
Nul ne s'égare; La Vie comme elle tourne et par exemple; Comme un Serpent remonte les rivières.   Paris, Gallimard, 1986.
André Frénaud ontologique: 11 poèmes.   Gourdon, Bedou, 1986.

Other

Bazaine, Estève, Lapicque, with Jean Lescure and Jean Tardieu.   Paris, Carré, 1945.
C'est à valoir, with Maurice Estève.   Alès, Benoit, 1955.
A. Beaudin, peinture 1927–1957 (exhibition catalogue).   Paris, Galerie Leiris, 1957.
Le Château et la quête du poète.   Alès, Benoit, 1957.
Chant de Marc Chagall.   Paris, Maeght, 1969.
Notre Inhabileté fatale (interview), with Bernard Pingaud. Paris, Gallimard, 1979.
Miró, comme un enchanteur.   Paris, Maeght, 1983.
Ubac et les fondements de son art.   Paris, Maeght, 1985.

*

Bibliography: in *André Frénaud* by G. E. Clancier and J. Y. Debreuille, Paris, Seghers, 1989.

Manuscript Collection: Harvard University, Cambridge, Massachusetts.

Critical Studies: "Maximum and Minimum: The Poetics of André Frénaud" by Michael Bishop, in *French Forum* (Lexington, Kentucky), 5, 1980; *André Frénaud* by Peter Broome, Amsterdam, Rodopi, 1987; "André Frénaud's Plural Voice" by Roger Little, in *Studies in 20th-Century Literature* (Manhattan, Kansas), Winter 1989.

André Frénaud comments:

A poem surpasses the person who forms it but in the end it
expresses that person! In constructing this object-microcosm
the author constructs himself and discovers himself different
— and united with the world by different links — but he still
knows himself as he is, with his resources which are also his
limits, his light depth.

These unexpected little verbal monuments, the consciousness that bore them is that of a unique man with his experiences
and his desires, his monsters, his preoccupations, everything
that has marked him profoundly in life and which remains
irreducible, with his tastes, his intelligence, his tradition, his
prejudices and his words, with his courage and his personal
misery — from these things stems the fact that each creator has
his themes and his style. And of course a poem is made in the
changing duration of a lifetime. If it always brings about a
transfiguration (to the point even of mockery) the work takes
on a different tonality according to the degree of sensitivity
which is created in the surpassing of the creator. So it is that the
greatest joy and simple pleasure, wonderment, nostalgia,
bitterness or despair, revolt and rage, kindness, all the
emotions that can be felt can predominate in turn. (from
Passage de la visitation, Paris, GLM, 1956)

* * *

André Frénaud came to poetry comparatively late in his
career, on the verge of World War II, with a piece entitled
"Epitaph": a poetic beginning, a birth, paradoxically drawing
its energy from the anticipation and acceptance of his own end,
and already establishing the tragic dimension and illusionless
stoicism of his work, with its lucid face-to-face with the
inevitability of nothingness. It is a poetry poised "between the
question and the void," reverberating into the dark enigma: a
dialectic poetry, a strenuous debate, caught in the jaws of
contradiction and finding its rhythms and structures in the play
of opposite polarities to which it can give no false resolution.
Hence the integrity of Frénaud's writing, which refuses hope
(in any Christian or philosophical sense) but refuses equally to
silence or abandon the futile questioning voice. It refuses also
the evasions, self-deceptions and impostures which serve to
defuse or alleviate the human predicament. At the same time it
resists the impostures of poetry itself (its verbal pretentions,
suave notes, consoling idealizations, aesthetically pleasing
forms), partly by leaving it to fall prey to its inner contradictions and discrepancies, and partly by making room for the
ironic humour, grating tones, parodic jingles and mocking
voices of a character such as the "little old man" in "Les
Poèmes du petit vieux" (The Poems of the Little Old Man,
from *La Sainte Face* [The Holy Face]) which come periodically
to subvert the more high-flown or ambitious expressions of
poetic aspiration.

Frénaud's main theme is that of the never-ending quest,
epically illustrated in *Les Rois Mages* (The Magi) a quest
which, unlike the biblical version, loses its way, destroys itself
as it advances, feeds on its own privation, stutters amidst
impediments, confusions, and intermittences, only to be
reborn again and again, hopelessly. It is illustrated, too, in his
magnificent "city-poems," of which *La Sorcière de Rome* (The
Sorceress of Rome) is the most grandiose and resonant
example: a journey through the labyrinth of time and space,
through the signs and ruins of history, through the fissures of
consciousness and a multiplicity of obscure voices, in search of
a potent, disturbing presence constantly glimpsed and lost.
Such texts are an indication of the mythical dimension of
Frénaud's work: myth not simply as a reworking of inherited
material now deeply embedded as a model in the cultural or
spiritual psyche, nor as a delving into the secret life of the
fragmentary myths of Rome, strewn between ancient and
modern, but as the ability to see (in the everyday streets of
Paris, Prague, Genoa, or Venice) deep patterns of significance, compulsive images which loom and tempt one, however
inconclusively, beyond mere appearances.

The titles of Frénaud's major collections, *Les Rois Mages*, *Il
n'y a pas de paradis* (There Is No Paradise), or *La Sainte Face*
(The Holy Face) suggest a religious preoccupation. In one
sense, this is true: one poem "Chuchotements aux Oliviers"
(Whispers on the Mount of Olives) is an orchestration of voices
between God the Father, Christ, and the Holy Spirit. But,
while fired by a burning question mark, this is an impetus
which negates itself, sees no afterlife, end, or redemption. It
would be more appropriate to speak of an obscure sense of the
sacré: the deep instinct for celebration, for raising structures in
honour of the unknown, for rising above oneself momentarily
in an inflagration which consumes itself, crumbles as ash, and
leaves one abandoned. Hence the number of poems, seen
particularly in the latest collections *Haeres* (Inherited) and *Nul
ne s'égare* (No One Is Lost), which interrogate the plaintive
sign language of fragments of religious sculpture, architecture,
and iconography: like broken beads of the human spirit on a
network of paths leading nowhere.

Frénaud is also a militant poet: not only by the martial,
aggressive, rebellious mood which infuses much of his work
and refuses to be quenched, nor by the productive spirit of
self-rejection which leads him to say "I am unacceptable to
myself," but also in a more politically committed sense. His
Poèmes de Brandebourg (Brandenburg Poems) are a private
resistance movement sprung from imprisonment in a German
labour camp between 1940 and 1942; his "civic" poems (from
La Sainte Face) give voice to the tragedy of the Spanish Civil
War, the rape of Prague, and the widowhood of Poland;
L'Agonie du Général Krivitski (The Agony of General
Krivitski) evokes the anguish and dilemmas of a Russian secret
agent now on the run from the long arms of the Moscow purges
and reprisals; while *L'Énorme Figure de la Déesse Raison*
(The Huge Figure of the Goddess Reason) sets on stage the
awesome, irrepressible force of Revolution forever inciting
change and the overthrow of status quos. But through all these
one senses a further dimension, transcending the pains and
tensions of the particular times and places of history: an
enquiry into the energies of rebirth and death, faith and
nihilism, order and chaos, humanity and inhumanity.

Frénaud's love poetry is among the most distinctive of recent
years, intense and perturbing. It may have recourse to ancient
myth as in "La Mort d'Actéon" (The Death of Actæon), from
Depuis Toujours déjà [Since Always Already] or "Jeune
Amazone et son ombre" (Young Amazon and Her Shadow), it
may take the voice of a woman aching with the absence of the
eternally missing partner, or it may become the epic personal
search of *Pour une Plus Haute Flamme par le défi* (For a Higher
Flame, through Defiance). Rarely does it transcend solitude or
exorcize the haunting and tormented images of a restless
subconscious, but rarely have deprivation and distance generated a more powerful yearning for the impossible unity.

A native Burgundian, Frénaud has never broken his bonds
with the provincial earth, and sequences such as "Novembre"
(November), and "Où Dieu répose" (Where God Rests), from
Depuis Toujours déjà are delicate, intuitive captures of the
luminous, mobile seasonal expressions of Nature, which we
can never join and from which we shall be finally erased as the
cycles revolve towards nothingness: so many shafts of light, so
many small clearings in the wood as one moves on.

One should mention, finally, Frénaud as tireless critic of
himself: commentating on his own work, rediscovering its

possible structures and significances, restoring it to the cycles of rebirth. His recorded interviews with Bernard Pingaud, published as *Notre Inhabileté fatale* (Our Fateful Inability), are a fertile dialogue with himself, and his unfinished glosses on several of the movements of *La Sorcière de Rome* illustrate the extent to which poetry will continue to uncover depth upon depth of its own possibility, revaluing and enriching its own definition: the supreme example of the quest.

—Peter Broome

FUENTES, Carlos. Mexican. Born in Panama City, 11 November 1928. As a child lived in the United States, Chile, and Argentina; returned to Mexico at age 16. Educated at Colegio Frances Morelos; National Autonomous University of Mexico, Mexico City, LL.B. 1948; Institut des Hautes Études Internationales, Geneva. Married 1) Rita Macedo in 1959 (divorced 1966), one daughter; 2) Sylvia Lemus in 1973, one son and one daughter. Member, then Secretary, Mexican delegation, International Labor Organization, Geneva, 1950–52; assistant chief of press section, Ministry of Foreign Affairs, Mexico City, 1954; press secretary, United Nations Information Center, Mexico City, 1954; secretary, then assistant director of Cultural Department, National Autonomous University of Mexico, 1955–56; Head of Department of Cultural Relations, Ministry of Foreign Affairs, 1957–59; Mexican Ambassador to France, 1974–77; Fellow, Woodrow Wilson International Center for Scholars, 1974; Virginia Gildersleeve Visiting Professor, Barnard College, New York, 1977; Norman Maccoll Lecturer, 1977, and Simón Bolívar Professor of Latin American studies, 1986–87, Cambridge University; Henry L. Tinker Lecturer, Columbia University, New York, 1978; Professor of English, University of Pennsylvania, Philadelphia, 1978–83; Fellow of the Humanities, Princeton University, New Jersey; Professor of comparative literature, 1984–86, and Robert F. Kennedy Professor of Latin American studies, since 1987, Harvard University, Cambridge, Massachusetts. Editor, *Revista Mexicana de Literatura*, 1954–58, *El Espectador*, 1959–61, *Siempre*, from 1960, and *Política*, from 1960. President, Modern Humanities Research Association, since 1989. Recipient: Mexican Writers Center fellowship, 1956; Biblioteca Breve prize, 1967; Xavier Villaurrutia prize, 1975; Rómulo Gallegos prize (Venezuela), 1977; Alfonso Reyes prize, 1979; Mexican National award for literature, 1984; Cervantes prize, 1987; Rubén Darío prize, 1988; Italo-Latino Americano Instituto prize, 1988; New York City National Arts Club Medal of Honor, 1988; Order of Cultural Independence (Nicaragua), 1988; IUA prize, 1989. D.Litt.: Wesleyan University, Middletown, Connecticut, 1982; Cambridge University, 1987; D.Univ.: University of Essex, Wivenhoe, 1987; LL.D.: Harvard University; other honorary doctorates: Columbia College; Chicago State University; Washington University, St. Louis. Member, El Colegio Nacional, since 1974; American Academy and Institute of Arts and Letters, 1986. Agent: Carl Brandt, Brandt & Brandt, 1501 Broadway, New York, New York 10036, U.S.A. Address: 401 Boylston Hall, Harvard University, Cambridge, Massachusetts 02138, U.S.A.

PUBLICATIONS

Fiction

Los días emmascarados. Mexico City, Los Presentes, 1954.
La región más transparente. Mexico City, Fondo de Cultura Económica, 1958; as *Where the Air Is Clear*, New York, Obolensky, 1960; London, Deutsch, 1986.
Las buenas conciencias. Mexico City, Fondo de Cultura Económica, 1959; as *The Good Conscience*, New York, Obolensky, 1961; London, Deutsch, 1986.
La muerte de Artemio Cruz. Mexico City, Fondo de Cultura Económica, 1962; as *The Death of Artemio Cruz*, New York, Farrar Straus, and London, Collins, 1964.
Aura. Mexico City, Era, 1962; in English, New York, Farrar Straus, 1965; London, Deutsch, 1990.
Cantar de ciegos. Mexico City, Mortiz, 1964.
Zona sagrada. Mexico City, Siglo Veintiuno, 1967; as *Holy Places*, in *Triple Cross*, New York, Dutton, 1972.
Cambio de piel. Mexico City, Mortiz, 1967; as *A Change of Skin*, New York, Farrar Straus, and London, Cape, 1968.
Cumpleaños. Mexico City, Mortiz, 1969.
Chac Mool y otros cuentos. Estella, Salvat, 1973.
Terra nostra. Barcelona, Seix Barral, 1975; in English, New York, Farrar Straus, 1976; London, Secker and Warburg, 1977.
La cabeza de la hidra. Mexico City, Mortiz, 1978; as *The Hydra Head*, New York, Farrar Straus, 1978; London, Secker and Warburg, 1979.
Una familia lejana. Mexico City, Era, 1980; as *Distant Relations*, New York, Farrar Straus, and London, Secker and Warburg, 1982.
Agua quemada. Mexico City, Fondo de Cultura Económica, 1981; as *Burnt Water*, New York, Farrar Straus, and London, Secker and Warburg, 1981.
El gringo viejo. Mexico City, Fondo de Cultura Económica, 1985; as *The Old Gringo*, New York, Farrar Straus, 1985; London, Deutsch, 1986.
Cristóbal nonato. Mexico City, Fondo de Cultura Económica, 1987; as *Christopher Unborn*, New York, Farrar Straus, and London, Deutsch, 1989.
Constancia, y otras novelas para vírgenes. Madrid, Mondadori, 1989; as *Constancia and Other Stories for Virgins*, New York, Farrar Straus, and London, Deutsch, 1990.
La campaña. Madrid, Mondadori, 1990; as *The Campaign*, New York, Farrar Straus, and London, Deutsch, 1991.

Plays

Todos los gatos son pardos. Mexico City, Siglo Veintiuno, 1970.
El tuerto es rey. Mexico City, Mortiz, 1970.
Los reinos originarios (includes *Todos los gatos son pardos* and *El tuerto es rey*). Barcelona, Seix Barral, 1971.
Orquídeas a la luz de la luna. Barcelona, Seix Barral, 1982; as *Orchids in the Moonlight* (produced Cambridge, Massachusetts, 1982; London, 1989).

Screenplays: *Pedro Paramo*, 1966; *Tiempo de morir*, 1966; *Los caifanes*, 1967.

Television Series: *The Buried Mirror* (on Christopher Columbus), 1991.

Verse

Poemas de amor: cuentos del alma. Madrid, Cruces, 1971.

Other

The Argument of Latin America: Words for North Americans. N.p., Radical Education Project, 1963.
Paris: la revolución de Mayo. Mexico City, Era, 1968.
La nueva novela hispanoamericana. Mexico City, Mortiz, 1969.
El mundo de Jose Luis Cuevas. Mexico City, Tudor, 1969.
Casa con dos puertas. Mexico City, Mortiz, 1970.
Tiempo mexicano. Mexico City, Mortiz, 1971.
Cuerpos y ofrendas. Madrid, Alianza, 1972.
Cervantes; o, La crítica de la lectura. Mexico City, Mortiz, 1976; as *Don Quixote; or, The Critique of Reading,* Austin, University of Texas Institute of Latin American Studies, 1976.
High Noon in Latin America. Los Angeles, Manas, 1983.
Juan Soriano y su obra, with Teresa del Conde. Mexico City, Institute of Fine Arts, 1984.
On Human Rights: A Speech. Dallas, Somesuch Press, 1984.
Latin America: At War with the Past. Montreal, CBC Enterprises, 1985.
Palacio Nacional, with Guillermo Tovar y de Teresa. Mexico City, Presidencia de la República, Dirección General de Comunición Social, 1986.
Gabriel García Marquez and the Invention of America (lecture). Liverpool, Liverpool University Press, 1987.
Myself with Others: Selected Essays. New York, Farrar Straus, and London, Deutsch, 1988.
The Buried Mirror: Reflections on Spain and the New World. Boston, Houghton Mifflin, 1992.

Editor, *Los signos en rotación y otra ensayos,* by Octavio Paz. Madrid, Alianza, 1971.

*

Bibliographies: "Carlos Fuentes: A Bibliography" by Sandra L. Dunn, in *Review of Contemporary Fiction* (Elmwood Park, Illinois), 8, 1988; in *Mexican Literature: A Bibliography of Secondary Sources* by David William Foster, Metuchen, New Jersey, Scarecrow Press, 1992.

Critical Studies: *Carlos Fuentes* by Daniel de Guzman, New York, Twayne, 1972; *The Archetypes of Carlos Fuentes: From Witch to Androgyne* by Gloria Durán, Hamden, Connecticut, Archon (Shoestring), 1980; *Carlos Fuentes: A Critical View* edited by Robert Brody and Charles Rossman, Austin, University of Texas Press, 1982; *Carlos Fuentes* by Wendy D. Faris, New York, Ungar, 1983; *Carlos Fuentes: Life, Work, and Criticism* by Alfonso González, Fredericton, New Brunswick, York, 1987.

* * *

Carlos Fuentes for some years now has been one of the most imposing figures in Latin America. His fame extends beyond literary achievements, and certainly beyond his mother country Mexico (actually he was born in Panama where his father, who was in the diplomatic service, was stationed at the time). He belongs to the Latin American generation of great writers who are known as the authors of "the Boom." Along with Fuentes, other such luminaries as Gabriel García Márquez and Octavio Paz (*qq.v.*) (both Nobel Prize winners) have made the world aware of the great accomplishments of Latin American literature. In 1987 Fuentes was awarded Spain's most prestig-

ious literary prize, "el premio Cervantes." He has received numerous other prestigious prizes from many countries, including the Venezuelan Rómulo Gallegos national prize, equivalent to the Cervantes prize in Spain.

Fuentes's professional life defies description. He is equally at home when speaking French, English, or Spanish, and equally at home in literature, history, politics, or journalism. He has been visiting Professor in the United States at some of the most distinguished universities, and has received honorary degrees from many more. In matters of diplomatic positions, he has attained the highest cultural post available to any artist in a Latin American country, as his nation's Ambassador to France. In England and France he has been involved with the intellectual pursuits of the intelligentsia. Moreover, he has been quite active in meetings and conferences in underdeveloped countries. His passion, of course, has been his dedication to understanding, and expressing in literary form the essence of Mexican civilization, and by extension the substance of Latin American life and thought. His quest is inexorably linked to capturing the spiritual structure of those countries, Spain and the United States in particular, whose values are interwoven by patrimony as in the case of Spain, or by propinquity and political dominance as in the case of the U.S., with the destiny of Latin America.

Although Fuentes had already distinguished himself as a writer of note with his earlier work, in 1962 when his novel *La muerte de Artemio Cruz* (*The Death of Artemio Cruz*) appeared, he became a truly international figure as a man of letters. *The Death of Artemio Cruz,* which depicts the dying days of a former general of the Mexican Revolution, recreates the history of Mexico since 1910, when the Revolution broke out. As the old moribund patriot of the struggle for freedom chronicles the idealistic quest for liberty and for an equitable distribution of land, he wonders, as did Don Quixote towards the end of his life, what, if anything, was accomplished. At the same time that Artemio Cruz reflects on the uselessness of the past, he comments on his surviving heirs to whom the impending death of an old man is essentially nothing but an annoying event that interferes with their immediate pursuit of personal happiness. Unbeknownst to the young, the dying patriot is able to listen in on the conversations around him. Yet there is no bitterness; *The Death of Artemio Cruz* smiles ironically on humanity. Disillusionment is conceived as but an inexorable experience of living. Idealism is as necessary as disenchantment is inevitable.

The 1985 novel *El gringo viejo* (*The Old Gringo*), which was subsequently made into a movie starring Jane Fonda and Gregory Peck, projected the continuity of personal tyranny in Mexico. Revolutions and more revolutions fail to quench the thirst for power among the brave Mexican *machos.* Idealism, fuelled by adulation, makes despots or political bosses ("caciques") of them all. Here we have the microcosm of the apparent never-ending growth of caciques throughout Latin America. Principles and ideals give way to personal hegemony, and all members of society in one way or another participate in creating a form of government that befits the abiding faith that one man can inspire. In the person of the character who is "the old gringo" we have the naïve, innocent observer who cannot fully grasp the prevailing form of life in a Latin American country. Even when the gringo means well, he is basically lost in another culture.

Fuentes's writings are indeed varied and numerous. However, his recent book *The Buried Mirror: Reflections on Spain and the New World* stands out as a most ambitious project. It is a kind of celebration of what has become the polemical quincentenary observance of Christopher Columbus's arrival in the New World. *The Buried Mirror* is akin to a self-examining quest for truth and reality. In the highest humanistic tradition, with a sense of compassion for human imperfection, Fuentes feelingly recreates history for all participants, victors and vanquished alike. Perhaps they are all mere victims of their own passions. In the long run, the distinction between them is blurred. New World countries as well as Spain have experienced — and survived — all sorts of leaders and seemingly untenable situations. While not "history" in the traditional scientific tradition, Fuentes's account affords us a living experience of the essence of the Hispanic and Hispanic American way of life.

—Robert Kirsner

G

GAITE, Carmen Martín. *See* **MARTÍN GAITE, Carmen.**

GALA (Vetasco), Antonio. Spanish. Born in Córdoba, in 1936. Educated at the University of Seville, law degree; University of Madrid, degrees in history and political science. Taught religion, philosophy, and art history at secondary schools, Madrid; columnist, *Sábado Gráfico* magazine, from 1973, and *El País*. Recipient: Calderón de la Barca prize, 1963; City of Barcelona prize, 1965; Planeta prize, 1990. Address: c/o Editorial Planeta, Córcega 273–277, 08008 Barcelona, Spain.

Publications

Plays

Los verdes campos del Edén (produced Madrid, 1963). Madrid, Escelicer, 1964; as *The Green Fields of Eden*, in *The Contemporary Spanish Theater: The Social Comedies of the Sixties*, edited by Patricia W. O'Connor, Madrid, SGEL, 1983.

El sol en el hormiguero (produced Madrid, 1966). With *El caracol en el espejo* and *Noviembre y un poco de yerba*, Madrid, Taurus, 1970.

Noviembre y un poco de yerba (produced Madrid, 1967). With *El caracol en el espejo* and *El sol en el hormiguero*, Madrid, Taurus, 1970.

Píldora nupcial; Corazones y diamantes; El "weekend" de Andrómaca; Vieja se muere la alegría (television plays). Madrid, Escelicer, 1968.

Esa mujer (screenplay). Madrid, Proesa, 1968.

Un delicado equilibrio, adaptation of a play by Edward Albee (produced Madrid, 1969).

Spain's Strip-Tease (produced Madrid, 1970). Included in *Obras escogidas*, 1981.

Los buenos días perdidos (produced Madrid, 1972). Madrid, Escelicer, 1973; as *The Bells of Orleans*, in *Estreno* (University Park, Pennsylvania), 1992.

Anillos para una dama (produced Madrid, 1973). Madrid, Júcar, 1974.

Canta, gallo acorralado, adaptation of a play by Sean O'Casey (produced Madrid, 1973).

Cantar de Santiago para todos (television play). Madrid, MK, 1974.

Las cítaras colgadas de los árboles (produced Madrid, 1974). With *¿Por qué corres, Ulises?*, Madrid, Espasa-Calpe, 1977.

¿Por qué corres, Ulises? (produced Madrid, 1975). With *Las cítaras colgadas de los árboles*, Madrid, Espasa-Calpe, 1977.

4 conmemoraciones: Eterno Tuy; Auto del Santo Reino; Oratorio de Fuenterrabía; Retablo de Santa Teresa (television plays). Madrid, Adra, 1976.

Trilogía de la libertad. Madrid, Espasa-Calpe, 1983.
  Petra Regalada (produced Madrid, 1980). Madrid, MK, 1980.
  La vieja señorita del Paraíso (produced Madrid, 1981). Madrid, MK, 1981.
  El cementerio de los pájaros (produced Madrid, 1982). Madrid, MK, 1982.

Obras escogidas (includes *Los verdes campos del Edén*; *El caracol en el espejo*; *El sol en el hormiguero*; *Noviembre y un poco de yerba*; *Spain's Strip-Tease*; *Los buenos días perdidos*; *Anillos para una dama*; *Las cítaras colgadas de los árboles*; *¡Suerte, campeón!*; *¿Por qué corres, Ulises?*; *Petra Regalada*; *La vieja señorita del Paraíso*). Madrid, Aguilar, 1981.

Paisaje andaluz con figuras (television play). Andalucía, Andaluzas Unidas, 2 vols., 1984.

Samarkanda (produced Madrid, 1985). With *El hotelito*, Madrid, Espasa-Calpe, 1985.

El hotelito (produced Madrid, 1985). With *Samarkanda*, Madrid, Espasa-Calpe, 1985.

Paisaje con figuras (television series). Madrid, Espasa-Calpe, 2 vols., 1985.

El sombrero de tres picos, with Enrique Jiménez. Madrid, Léon, 1986.

Séneca, o el beneficio de la duda (produced Madrid, 1987). Madrid, Espasa-Calpe, 1987.

Carmen, Carmen (produced Madrid, 1988). Madrid, Espasa-Calpe, 1988.

Cristóbal Colón (opera libretto), music by Leonardo Balada (produced Madrid, 1989). Madrid, Espasa-Calpe, 1989.

La truhana (produced Madrid, 1992).

Screenplays: *Digan lo que digan*, with Miguel Rubio and Mario Camús, 1968; *Esa mujer*, 1968; *Pepa Doncel*, with Luis Lucia, 1969; *Los buenos días perdidos*, from his own play, with Miguel Rubio, 1975.

Fiction

El manuscrito carmesí. Barcelona, Planeta, 1990.

Verse

Enemigo íntimo. Madrid, Rialp, 1960.

Other

Córdoba para vivir. N.p., Publicaciones Españolas, 1965.

El teatro de Lorca. Salamanca, Publicaciones de los cursos de verano de la Universidad, 1972.

Vicente vela. Madrid, Rayuela, 1975.

Barrera-Wolff: [exposición] enero 1976. Madrid, Galeria Kreisler, 1975.

Texto y Pretexto. Madrid, Sedmay, 1977.

Teatro de hoy, teatro de mañana. Almería, Ateneo de
   Almería/Univers, 1978.
Charlas con Troylo. Madrid, Espasa-Calpe, 1981.
En propia mano. Madrid, Espasa-Calpe, 1983.
Cuaderno de la Dama de Otoño. Madrid, El País, 1985.
Dedicado a Tobías. Barcelona, Planeta, 1988.
La soledad sonora. Barcelona, Planeta, 1991.
La Granada de los nazaríes. Barcelona, Planeta, 1992.

Translator, *El zapato de raso*, by Paul Claudel. Madrid,
   Escelicer, 1965.

*

Manuscript Collection: Theatre collection, Biblioteca Nacional, Madrid.

Critical Studies: "From Protest to Resignation" by Farris
Anderson, in *Estreno* (University Park, Pennsylvania), 2(2),
1976; "The Theater and Politics of Antonio Gala," in *Hispanic
Literature and Politics*, Indiana, Indiana University of
Pennsylvania, 1976, and "The Function of Children in Three
Representative Plays by Antonio Gala," in *El niño en las
literaturas hispánicas*, edited by J. Cruz Mendizábal, Indiana,
Indiana University of Pennsylvania, 1978, both by David
M. Kirsner; "The Theater of Antonio Gala: In Search of
Paradise" by Phyllis Zatlin-Boring, in *Romance Quarterly*
(Lexington, Kentucky), 24, 1977; "Petra Regalada: Madonna
or Whore?," and "Myth of Penélope and Ulysses in *La
tejedora de sueños*, *¿Por qué corres, Ulises?*, and *Ulises no
vuelve*," in *Estreno* (University Park, Pennsylvania), 11, 1985,
both by Iride Lamartina-Lens; "Antonio Gala's *El cementerio
de los párajos* and the Problem of Freedom" by Wilma
Newberry, in *Hispania* (Los Angeles), 70(3), 1987; "Antonio
Gala and the New Catholicism," in *The Contemporary Spanish
Theater: A Collection of Critical Essays*, edited by Martha
T. Halsey and Phyllis Zatlin, Lanham, Maryland and London,
University Press of America, 1988, and "Antonio Gala's
Cristóbal Colón: A Preliminary Note," in *Estreno* (University
Park, Pennsylvania), 18(2), 1992, both by Robert Louis
Sheehan.

*   *   *

Virtually all critical studies of Antonio Gala focus on his
theatre. Nevertheless, Gala affirms that he is not a playwright,
but rather an author who sometimes writes for the stage. His
prolific writing supports his statement. His works include
poetry, short stories, a novel, essays, and journalistic commentary. His theatrical texts include translations, television
series, movie scripts, and librettos for musical comedies, and
an opera, as well as original stage plays. In Spain he has
enjoyed celebrity status since the early 1970s, based primarily
on his television appearances and his weekly essays in the
popular press. At Madrid's annual book fair, crowds line up to
have him sign collections of his articles from the Sunday
supplement of *El País*. His personal charisma, combined with
his witty and elegant style, invariably makes him one of the
fair's best-selling authors.

At the University of Seville, Gala completed the law degree
chosen by his father, but also took specializations in political
science and history. These latter interests underscore much of
his work, both popular and creative. In addition to his weekly
essays — begun in 1973 with the series *Texto y Pretexto* for the
magazine *Sábado Gráfico* and continued since then, under
various titles, in Spain's most important newspaper, *El País* —
he prepares a brief statement for another Madrid daily in

which he reacts to current events. In his journalistic writings he
often takes controversial stands on political issues.

Contemporary Spain's sociopolitical reality also informs
much of his theatre. *El hotelito* (The Little Family Manor)
verged on agitprop: a riotously funny satire of democratic
Spain's autonomous regions and the decision (misguided, in
Gala's view) to enter the European Community. However, in
general Gala's theatre, which typically blends sparkling
surface humor with an underlying tragic reality, presents a
more subtle political allegory. In *Los verdes campos del Edén*
(*The Green Fields of Eden*), he caricatures the Franco regime
while giving a poetic portrayal of a liberal reformer doomed to
failure. *Noviembre y un poco de yerba* (November and a Bit of
Grass), a response to amnesty for soldiers on the losing side in
the Spanish Civil War (1936–1939), revolves around a man
who has lived in hiding for 30 years. *Los buenos días perdidos*
(*The Bells of Orleans*) confronts hypocrisy and materialism
with an idealistic desire for love and freedom. *Petra Regalada*
is a not-so-subtle criticism both of the Franco regime and of the
self-serving "reformer" who would replace one tyranny with
another; atypically, the play ends on an optimistic note as the
much exploited Petra and her allies kill the would-be tyrant
and take charge. Two other works following *Petra Regalada* in
the "trilogy of freedom" — *La vieja señorita del Paraíso* (The
Elderly Miss of "The Paradise") and *El cementerio de los
pájaros* (The Bird Cemetery) — return to the pattern of his
earlier plays. The attempt to escape repression and confinement, to establish an earthly paradise where each individual
will have the liberty to find self-realization and love, is
inevitably defeated by the materialistic interests of those in
power.

In parallel with such commentaries on contemporary Spanish political reality are Gala's historical works. These
encompass his popular television series — *Si las piedras
hablaran* (If Stones Could Talk) and *Paisajes con figuras*
(Landscapes with Human Figures) — as well as stage plays, an
opera about Christopher Columbus, and his first novel. *Anillos
para una dama* (Rings for a Lady) is a debunking of the Cid
myth, told from the perspective of Jimena, the epic hero's
widow. *Las cítaras colgadas de los árboles* (Zithers Hung in the
Trees) demythifies the "glorious" period of Spain's conquest of
the Americas; it focuses on the degeneracy of those left
behind, especially on the persecution of "new Christians" —
the Jews forced to convert to or be expelled from their homeland.
In the opera libretto *Cristóbal Colón* Gala supports the thesis
that the explorer was of Jewish descent; he also highlights the
often overlooked contribution of the Andalusian Pinzón to
Columbus's voyage of discovery. Gala's extensive knowledge
of Andalusian history, as well as his sympathy for the Jews and
Arabs displaced by the Catholic Monarchs' Reconquest of
Spain in 1492, culminates in his monumental novel *El
manuscrito carmesí* (The Crimson Manuscript), the fictional
memoirs of Boabdil, the last sultan of Granada. While the
first-person account does not ignore factionalism among the
Moorish leaders or Arab acts of violence and deceit, the
perspective of the Andalusian king tends both to demythify the
image of the Catholic victors and to create a greater appreciation for Moorish culture in general and the ill-fated, sensitive
Boabdil in particular. The non-fictional *La Granada de los
nazaríes* (Granada Under the Nasrid Kings) was conceived as a
companion volume to the novel.

Throughout his career, Gala has shown a strong concern for
individual freedom, particularly the right to love the person of
one's choice. Many of his stage and television plays have
featured female protagonists who have voiced their desires and
rebellion with exceptional wit and eloquence. Jimena in
Anillos para una dama notably expresses a feminist

deconstruction of official History, as imposed by the patriarchy. The musical *Carmen, Carmen*, written in 1975 but not
staged until 1988, contains four stories; in each of them
Carmen, symbol of happiness, is rejected by male values:
honor, power, religion, fame. In democratic Spain, Gala has
expanded his plea for tolerance to include the rights of
homosexuals. The title character of *La vieja señorita del
Paraíso* attempts to protect various pairs of lovers, including
mixed-race and gay couples. The play *Samarkanda* goes so far
as to present an incestuous relationship between two brothers.
In *El manuscrito carmesí*, Gala contrasts the sensual bisexu-
ality of Boabdil with the absolute intolerance of the Christians,
who burn homosexuals at the stake. Courageously, Gala
continues to ask his readers to re-evaluate Spanish history and
their own prejudices.

—Phyllis Zatlin

GAMBARO, Griselda. Argentinian. Born in Buenos Aires,
28 July 1928. Married to Juan Carlos Distéfano; one daughter
and one son. Office worker for publishing company, 1943, and
sports club, 1947–56; drama teacher, Universidad Nacional del
Litoral, Santa Fé, 1969; lived in Italy, 1969–70; lecturer on
contemporary drama, 1973, and juror in national competi-
tions, 1973–75, National Endowment for the Arts; lived in
exile in Europe and the United States because of ban on
Ganarse la muerte, 1977–80. Recipient: National Endowment
for the Arts prize, 1963; Emecé Publishers prize, 1964;
Argentores prize, 1968, 1976; Municipality of Buenos Aires
prize, 1968; *Talía* magazine prize; Municipal Radio of Buenos
Aires prize; Guggenheim fellowship, 1982. Address: c/o
Argentores, Virrey Pacheco De Melo, 1126 Buenos Aires,
Argentina.

PUBLICATIONS

Plays

Matrimonio (produced Buenos Aires, 1965).
El desatino, from her short story (produced Buenos Aires,
    1966). Buenos Aires, Centro de Experimentación
    Audiovisual del Instituto Torcuato Di Tella, 1965.
Las paredes, from her short story (produced Buenos Aires,
    1966). Included in *Teatro*, 1979; as *The Walls*, in *Informa-
    tion for Foreigners: Three Plays*, 1992.
Los siameses (produced Buenos Aires, 1967). Buenos Aires,
    Insurrexit, 1967.
El campo (produced Buenos Aires, 1968). Buenos Aires,
    Insurrexit, 1967; as *The Camp*, in *Voices of Change in the
    Spanish American Theater*, Austin, University of Texas
    Press, 1971.
Nada que ver, from her novel *Nada que ver con otra historia*
    (produced Buenos Aires, 1972). Included in *Teatro*, 1983.
Sólo un aspecto (produced Buenos Aires, 1974). Included in
    Teatro, 1989.
El viaje a Bahía Blanca (produced Buenos Aires, 1975).
El nombre (produced Buenos Aires, 1976).
Sucede lo que pasa (produced Buenos Aires, 1976). Included
    in *Teatro*, 1983; as *Putting Two and Two Together* (pro-
    duced London, 1991).

Teatro: Las paredes; El desatino; Los siameses. Barcelona,
    Argonauta, 1979.
Decir sí (produced Buenos Aires, 1981). Included in *Teatro*,
    1989.
El despojamiento. Published in *Tramoya*, November-
    December 1981.
La malasangre (produced Buenos Aires, 1982). Included in
    Teatro, 1984; as *Bad Blood* (produced London, 1992).
Real envido (produced Buenos Aires, 1983). Included in
    Teatro, 1984.
Teatro (includes *Nada que ver*; *Sucede lo que pasa*). Ottawa,
    Girol, 1983.
Del sol naciente (produced Buenos Aires, 1984). Included in
    Teatro, 1984.
Teatro. Buenos Aires, Flor, 4 vols., 1984–90.
    vol. 1: *Real envido*; *La malasangre*; *Del sol naciente*.
    vol. 2: *Dar la vuelta*; *Información para extranjeros*; *Puesta en
        claro*; *Sucede lo que pasa*.
    vol. 3: *Viaje de invierno*; *Sólo un aspecto*; *La gracia*; *El
        miedo*; *Decir sí*; *Antígona furiosa*; and several other short
        plays.
    vol. 4: *Las paredes*; *El desatino*; *Los siameses*; *El campo*;
        Nada que ver.
Información para extranjeros. Included in *Teatro*, 1986; as
    Information for Foreigners, in *Information for Foreigners:
    Three Plays*, 1992.
The Impenetrable Madam X. Detroit, Wayne State Uni-
    versity Press, 1991.
Information for Foreigners: Three Plays (includes *Information
    for Foreigners*; *The Walls*; *Antígona furiosa*), edited and
    translated by Marguerite Feitlowitz. Evanston, Illinois,
    Northwestern University Press, 1992.

Fiction

Cuentos. Buenos Aires, Américalee, 1953.
Madrigal en ciudad. Buenos Aires, Goyanarte, 1963.
El desatino. Buenos Aires, Emecé, 1965.
Un felicidad con menos pena. Buenos Aires, Sudamericana,
    1968.
Nada que ver con otra historia. Buenos Aires, Noé, 1972.
Ganarse la muerte. Buenos Aires, Flor, 1976.
Dios no nos quiere contentos. Barcelona, Lumen, 1979.
Lo impenetrable. Buenos Aires, Torres Agüero, 1984.

Other

La cola mágica (stories for children). Buenos Aires, Flor,
    1975.
*Conversaciones con chicos: sobre la sociedad, los padres, los
    afectos, la cultura*. Buenos Aires, Timerman, 1977.

*

Critical Studies: "Griselda Gambaro's Theatre of the Absurd"
by Tamara Holzapfel, in *Latin American Theatre Review*
(Lawrence, Kansas), Fall 1970; "Three Female Playwrights
Explore Contemporary Latin American Reality: Myrna
Casas, Griselda Gambaro, Luisa Josefina Hernández" by
Gloria Feiman Waldman, in *Latin American Women Writers:
Yesterday and Today*, Pittsburgh, Latin American Literary
Review Press, 1972; "Physical Imagery in the Works of
Griselda Gambaro," in *Modern Drama* (Toronto), 17, 1975,
and "The Plays of Griselda Gambaro," in *Dramatists in Revolt*,
edited by Leon F. Lyday and George Woodyard, Austin,
University of Texas Press, 1976, both by Sandra M. Cypess; in
Women's Voices from Latin America: Interviews with Six

Contemporary Authors by Evelyn Picon Garfield, Detroit, Wayne State University Press, 1985; in *Interviews with Contemporary Women Playwrights*, edited by Kathleen Betsko and Rachel Koenig, New York, Beech Tree, 1987; "From Pin-Ups to Striptease in Gambaro's *El despojamiento*" by Becky Boling, in *Latin American Theatre Review* (Lawrence, Kansas), Spring 1987; in *Theatre of Crisis: Drama and Politics in Latin America* by Diana Taylor, Lexington, University Press of Kentucky, 1991.

*   *   *

Griselda Gambaro has seen her work both banned and awarded the highest literary prizes in Argentina. During the 1970s, even when she was living abroad after her novel *Ganarse la muerte* (To Earn Death) was banned by the president of Argentina, she withheld worldwide production rights to her play *Información para extranjeros* (*Information for Foreigners*) in order not to endanger her family in Argentina. While she does not focus on specific political issues or events, her novels, short stories, and plays are permeated with an atmosphere of repression and violence reflecting her experience of life under military dictatorships, including the "Dirty War" of 1976–83 when an estimated 30 thousand people disappeared, undoubtedly victims of torture and murder. All Argentine theatre is "more or less political," she told Kathleen Betsko and Rachel Koenig in *Interviews with Contemporary Women Playwrights* (1987). "One feeds oneself with the information provided by one's surrounding reality. One transmits, transfers, this information into one's work."

Gambaro's earliest published writing was a collection of short stories that she dismisses as the work of an "immature" 24-year-old. 10 years later, her career was launched in earnest with *Madrigal en ciudad* (Madrigal in the City), a collection of three short novels that won the El Fondo Nacional de las Artes prize in 1963. A 1964 collection of stories and short novels, *El desatino* (The Blunder), also won a prize and provided the impetus for her first plays, *Las paredes* (*The Walls*) and *El desatino*, both based upon short novels of the same titles. "I turned to theatre because I felt the necessity; I didn't ask myself why," she recalls. "I saw that the themes in those narratives were not exhausted." Subsequently, she began writing *Los siameses* (The Siamese Twins) as a novel, but could not complete it and so turned it into a play. Although she continues to write novels (and devoted herself exclusively to narrative fiction during her 1977–80 exile from Argentina), it is as a playwright that Gambaro has earned international renown.

Among the constant features of Gambaro's work are a preoccupation with violence, an ethical concern that arises from situations of confrontation, and a rational or realistic foundation against which the outrageous behavior and action can only be seen as "grotesque." Gambaro acknowledges the influence of the Argentine literary tradition of *el grotesco*, while she categorically rejects attempts to link her plays to the theatre of the absurd. Franz Kafka is perhaps the European writer with whom she is most frequently compared. A persistent theme from her earliest work to the present is humankind's failure to assume responsibility for oneself or one's social environment. It seems safer to go along with existing conditions, as Gambaro shows, because evil is often depicted with a smiling face. Avoiding any reference to Argentina or to any other specific place or time, Gambaro achieves a mythic or allegorical quality even as her plays abound with precise indications for the setting, lighting, sound, and costuming.

Gambaro's drama has evolved in three phases, according to Diana Taylor in her *Theatre of Crisis: Drama and Politics in Latin America* (1991). The plays of the 1960s include the four that have excited the most critical commentary: *The Walls*, *El desatino*, *Los siameses* and, most importantly, *El campo* (*The Camp*). Each of these plays follows a pattern of action in which an ordinary man suddenly finds himself victimized, both psychologically and physically, by a person or group professing to have his best interests at heart. In some sequences, two authority figures play the roles of "good cop" and "bad cop" toward the victim. As the torment intensifies, the victim deludes himself about what is happening and adopts a propitiary manner toward his victimizer, passively accepting his own destruction. In *The Walls*, a Young Man is detained in an attractively furnished but windowless room. As he loses all sense of time, the room becomes progressively smaller and more spartan. Finally, he awaits the death that his victimizers have described as "the walls falling in on someone." In *El desatino*, a young man inexplicably finds himself immobilized in his home by a large iron trap on one foot; in his progressive degeneration he becomes the passive victim of his comic mother, his loutish friend, and certainly of himself. *Los siameses* juxtaposes a good brother, Ignacio, and a bad brother, Lorenzo. Ignacio continues to respect Lorenzo, even when the latter sets him up to be beaten, arrested, and finally killed. The horror is virtually unmitigated in *The Camp*, a powerful drama with overlapping evocations of rural summer camps for children and Nazi concentration camps. Martin, hired as an accountant at the camp, offers no resistance to the increasingly bizarre circumstances into which he is drawn by his Nazi-uniformed employer, tellingly named Franco. In a powerfully grotesque scene, he sits in an audience of Gestapo officers and concentration camp inmates for a silent "piano concert" given by an emaciated woman in prison garb, wearing a wig over her shaved head. Despite her wounded hand and evident suffering, the woman speaks like a character in a drawing-room comedy. Such disparity between words and action is a frequent device that Gambaro uses to powerful effect.

Taylor characterizes Gambaro's plays of the early 1970s as "a drama of disappearance, obsessed with the 'missing'," which includes not only people, but "everything that has previously made sense — from life-sustaining values to reason itself." Prominent among the plays of this period is *Information for Foreigners*, "a chronicle in twenty scenes." The scenes are performed in various rooms of a house and are seen in different order by various small groups of audience members who are conducted by actors playing Guides. In this "guided tour of the places of repression and indignity," the Guides prove to be, according to Feitlowitz, "untrustworthy characters on whom we nevertheless must depend." Actual case histories of kidnappings and torture are cited for some scenes, while other scenes blatantly signal their artifice as if reifying what Taylor has called "the theatricality of terrorism." In another play of this period, *Nada que ver* (Nothing to Do), loosely based upon Gambaro's novel, *Nada que ver con otra historia*), Gambaro takes an uncharacteristic comic approach, only to end up with the agonizing absence of one of the three central characters. Among the many short dramatic pieces of the 1970s are one-woman plays like *El nombre* (The Name) and *El viaje a Bahía Blanca* (Trip to Bahía Blanca).

Women are more prominently featured in the later works, and Gambaro herself admits to an increasing "tenderness," as if she had acquired "greater understanding of certain things, more sensitivity to what it is to be a human organism." She also notes a tendency to more introspection and reflectivity in her more recent writing. Structurally, her plays are far less linear, more complex, without clear beginnings and endings. Taylor shows that while the victim-victimizer relationship persists in the plays of the 1980s, the victims no longer delude themselves; their physical powerlessness is no longer synonymous with passive acceptance.

—Felicia Hardison Londré

GARCÍA MÁRQUEZ, Gabriel. Colombian. Born in Aracataca, 6 March 1928. Educated at Colegio San José, Barranquilla, 1940–42; Colegio Nacional, Zipaquirá, to 1946; studied law and journalism at the National University of Colombia, Bogotá, 1947–48; University of Cartagena, 1948–49. Married Mercedes Barcha in 1958; two sons. Journalist, 1947–50, 1954, and foreign correspondent in Paris, 1955, *El Espectador*; journalist, *El Heraldo*, Barranquilla, 1950–54; founder, Prensa Latina (Cuban press) agency, Bogotá: worked in Prensa Latina office, Havana, 1959, and New York, 1961. Lived in Venezuela, Cuba, the United States, Spain, and Mexico; returned to Colombia in 1982. Founder, 1979, and since 1979 president, Fundación Habeas. Recipient: Colombian Association of Writers and Artists award, 1954; Concurso Nacional de Cuento short story prize, 1955; Esso literary prize, 1961; Chianciano prize (Italy), 1968; Foreign Book prize (France), 1970; Rómulo Gallegos prize (Venezuela), 1972; Neustadt international prize, 1972; Nobel prize for literature, 1982; Los Angeles *Times* prize, 1988. LL.D.: Columbia University, New York, 1971. Member, American Academy. Agent: Agencia Carmen Balcells, Diagonal 580, 08021 Barcelona, Spain.

PUBLICATIONS

Fiction

La hojarasca. Bogotá, Sipa, 1955.
El coronel no tiene quien le escriba. Mexico City, Era, 1957; as *No One Writes to the Colonel*, in *No One Writes to the Colonel and Other Stories*, 1968; with *Big Mama's Funeral*, 1971.
La mala hora. Madrid, Pérez, 1962; as *In Evil Hour*, New York, Harper, 1979; London, Cape, 1980.
Los funerales de la Mamá Grande. Xalapa, Universidad Veracruzana, 1962; as *Big Mama's Funeral*, with *No One Writes to the Colonel*, 1971.
Isabel viendo llover en Macondo. Buenos Aires, Editorial Estuario, 1967.
Cien años de soledad. Buenos Aires, Sudamericana, 1967; as *One Hundred Years of Solitude*, New York, Harper, and London, Cape, 1970.
No One Writes to the Colonel and Other Stories. New York, Harper, 1968.
No One Writes to the Colonel; Big Mama's Funeral. London, Cape, 1971.
Leaf Storm and Other Stories. New York, Harper, and London, Cape, 1972.
La increíble y triste historia de la cándida Eréndira y de su abuela desalmada: siete cuentos. Barcelona, Seix Barral, 1972; as *Innocent Erendira and Other Stories*, New York, Harper, 1978; London, Cape, 1979.

El negro qui hizo esperar a los ángeles. Montevideo, Alfil, 1972.
Ojos de perro azul: nueve cuentos desconocidos. Buenos Aires, Equis, 1972.
Cuatro cuentos. Mexico City, Comunidad Lationoamericana de Escritores, 1974.
Todo los cuentos 1947–1972. Barcelona, Plaza & Janés, 1975.
El otoño del patriarca. Barcelona, Plaza & Janés, 1975; as *The Autumn of the Patriarch*, New York, Harper, 1976; London, Cape, 1977.
El último viaje del buque fantasma. Parets del Vallés, Polígrafa, 1976.
Crónica de una muerte anunciada. Bogotá, Oveja Negra, 1981; as *Chronicle of a Death Foretold*, London, Cape, 1982; New York, Knopf, 1983.
El rastro de tu sangre en la nieve: el verano feliz de la señora Forbes. Bogotá, W. Dampier Editores, 1982.
Collected Stories. New York, Harper, 1984; revised edition, London, Cape, 1991.
El amor en los tiempos del cólera. Bogotá, Oveja Negra, 1985; as *Love in the Time of Cholera*, New York, Knopf, and London, Cape, 1988.
El general en su laberinto. Bogotá, Oveja Negra, 1989; as *The General in His Labyrinth*, New York, Knopf, 1990; London, Cape, 1991.
Collected Novellas. New York, Harper Collins, 1990.

Plays

Viva Sandino. Managua, Nueva Nicaragua, 1982; as *El asalto: el operativo con que el FSLN se lanzo al mundo*, Nueva Nicaragua, 1983.
El secuestro (screenplay). Salamanca, Lóquez, 1982.
Erendira (screenplay, from his own novella). N.p., Les Films du Triangle, 1983.
Diatribe of Love Against a Seated Man (produced Buenos Aires, 1988).

Screenplays: *El secuestro*, 1982; *María de mi corazón* (*Mary My Dearest*), with J. H. Hermosillo, 1983; *Erendira*, from his own novella, 1983.

Other

La novela en América Latina: diálogo, with Mario Vargas Llosa. Lima, Carlos Milla Batres, 1968.
Relato de un náufrago. Barcelona, Tusquets, 1970; as *The Story of a Shipwrecked Sailor*, New York, Knopf, and London, Cape, 1986.
Cuando era feliz e indocumentado. Caracas, El Ojo del Camello, 1973.
De viaje por los países socialistas: 90 días en la "Cortina de Hierro." Cali, Macondo, 1978.
Crónicas y reportajes. Bogotá, Oveja Negra, 1978.
Periodismo militante. Bogotá, Son de Máquina Editores, 1978.
La batalla de Nicaragua, with Gregorio Selser and Daniel Waksman Schinca. Mexico City, Bruguera Mexicana, 1979.
García Márquez habla de García Márquez. Bogotá, Rentería, 1979.
Obra periodística (includes vol. 1: *Textos constenos*; vols. 2–3: *Entre cachacos*; vol. 4: *De Europa y América (1955–1960)*), edited by Jacques Gilard. Buenos Aires, Bruguera, 4 vols., 1981–83.
El olor de la guayaba, with Plinio Apuleyo Mendoza.

Bogotá, Oveja Negra, 1982; as *The Fragrance of Guava*, London, Verso-New Left, 1983.

La soledad de América Latina; Brindis por la poesía. Cali, Corporación Editorial Universitaria de Colombia, 1983.

Persecución y muerte de minorías, with Guillermo Nolasco-Juárez. Buenos Aires, Juárez, 1984.

La aventura de Miguel Littín, clandestino en Chile: un reportaje. Bogotá, Oveja Negra, 1986; as *Clandestine in Chile: The Adventures of Miguel Littín*, New York, Holt, 1987; London, Granta, 1989.

El cataclismo de Damocles = The Doom of Damocles. San José, Costa Rica, Universitaria Centroamericana, 1986.

Textos costeños. Buenos Aires, Sudamericana, 1987.

Dialogo sobre la novela latinoamericana, with Mario Vargas Llosa. Lima, Perú Andino, 1988.

*

Bibliographies: *Gabriel García Márquez: An Annotated Bibliography 1947–1979* by Margaret Eustella Fau, Westport, Connecticut, Greenwood Press, 1980; *A Bibliographical Guide to Gabriel García Márquez 1979–1985* by Margaret Eustella Fau and Nelly Sfeir de González, Westport, Connecticut, Greenwood Press, 1986.

Critical Studies: *Gabriel García Márquez* by George R. McMurray, New York, Ungar, 1977; *Gabriel García Márquez: Revolutions in Wonderland* by Regina Janes, Columbia, University of Missouri Press, 1981; *The Evolution of Myth in García Márquez from La hojarasca to Cien años de soledad* by Robert Lewis Sims, Miami, Universal, 1981; *Gabriel García Márquez* by Raymond L. Williams, Boston, Hall, 1984; *Critical Essays on Gabriel García Márquez*, Boston, Hall, 1987; *Gabriel García Márquez and Latin America* edited by Alok Bhalla, New Delhi, Sterling, 1987; *Gabriel García Márquez and the Invention of America* by Carlos Fuentes, Liverpool, Liverpool University Press, 1987; *Gabriel García Márquez: New Readings* edited by Bernard McGuirk and Richard Cardwell, New York and Cambridge, Cambridge University Press, 1987; *Gabriel García Márquez, Writer of Colombia* by Stephen Minta, London, Cape, 1987; *Gabriel García Márquez and the Powers of Fiction* edited by Julio Ortega, Austin, University of Texas Press, 1988; *Understanding Gabriel García Márquez* by Kathleen McNerney, Columbia, University of South Carolina Press, 1989; *Gabriel García Márquez: The Man and His Work* by Gene H. Bell-Villada, Chapel Hill, University of North Carolina Press, 1990; *Gabriel García Márquez: One Hundred Years of Solitude* by Michael Wood, Cambridge, Cambridge University Press, 1990; *Gabriel García Márquez: A Study of the Short Fiction* by Harley D. Oberhelman, Boston, Twayne, 1991.

*   *   *

Novelist, polemical journalist, recipient of the Nobel prize for literature, Gabriel García Márquez has been among the most influential of 20th-century Latin American writers. The author of a varied and substantial body of work, his influence originates in his fourth novel, *Cien años de soledad* (*One Hundred Years of Solitude*). That syncretic and innovative work made "magic realism" a common critical term and generated imitators from Chile to London, Bombay to Massachusetts. Simultaneously an account of a nation, a town, a family, a house, and a book, the novel integrated the literary, temporal, and political interests of its period in a narrative of dazzling inventiveness, intricacy, and lucidity. Violating the Aristotelian precept that a probable impossibility is preferable to an improbable possibility, the novel set out to restore a sense of wonder relative both to the objects of representation and to the surface of the text. In the process, it established an alternative to the conventions of social or psychological realism and modernist fragmentation. Especially invigorating to writers whose societies are not entirely modern by western industrial standards, that alternative also spoke to writers oppressed and bored by the entire modernity of their western industrial societies. Transforming a continuing concern in Latin American writing, *One Hundred Years of Solitude* provided a way to represent people of the cultural margin without condescending to them as primitive, mythologizing them as nobly mysterious, or pitying them as deprived.

García Márquez's realistic story of development and decline included episodes conventionally excluded by those rationalist criteria that, developing in the 17th and 18th centuries along with the novel, separated the novel from the romance. Creating a town, Macondo, where it seemed almost anything could happen, García Márquez's new epic narrator reintegrated events long ruled out as too bizarre because they do not happen at all; because they are no longer believed to happen; because although they do happen, they fail to fit into dominant rationalist categories. He also made appear wonderful events or objects that modernity takes for granted and that no longer seem strange (the original sense of "magic realism" in art criticism). When characters now levitate or fly away, move surrounded by butterflies, bleed strange colors, marry their aunts, watch dead birds rain from the skies, or suffer from the winds of disillusion. García Márquez's spirit has touched the page, directly or indirectly.

From his earliest short stories, García Márquez manifested his impatience with meat-and-potatoes realism. The earliest fictions evoke dreams, doubles, and ghosts, altered states of consciousness, "real" hallucinations in stories that omit or barely allude to their most crucial concern. Under the helpfully foreign influence of William Faulkner and Ernest Hemingway, he turned to more realistic representations and subjects: the history of a family and town in the Faulknerian monologues of *La hojarasca* (*Leafstorm*), of a town and *la violencia* in the intercut episodic structure of *La mala hora* (*In Evil Hour*) and the spare short stories of *Los funerales de la Mamá Grande* (*Big Mama's Funeral*). In some of the stories of that volume and the short novel *El coronel no tiene quien le escriba* (*No One Writes to the Colonel*), García Márquez discovered the power of humor and ironic juxtaposition to give some relief to the oppressive political atmosphere he also intended to communicate. Through *One Hundred Years of Solitude*, *El otoño del patriarca* (*The Autumn of the Patriarch*), *La increíble y triste historia de la cándida Eréndira* (*Innocent Erendira*), and some short stories, García Márquez deployed the fantastic or impossible element often taken to characterize his fiction and then abandoned it.

The abandonment is characteristic. In addition to the inventiveness and originality of his fictional fabling, García Márquez is a master craftsman, intent on locating unique shapes or structures for each fiction. While certain stylistic features remain constant (and have become perhaps too habitual for the writer himself), he works very hard not to give his readers what many of them wanted: a dozen *One Hundred Years of Solitude*. Each work operates on a distinct structural principle, not generated by character or a character's history, but by the desire to make an artificial form an integral aspect of character and theme. *One Hundred Years of Solitude* depends on the making of a book through the destruction of the town, family, and house that are the subject of the book; *The Autumn of the Patriarch* on the swirl of voices and constant resurrections that constitute the power of dictators; *Crónica de una muerte anunciada* (*Chronicle of a Death Foretold*) on the predictive shape of classical Greek tragedy; *El amor en los tiempos del cólera* (*Love in the Time of Cholera*) on an impossible openness established by the refusal to close off the fiction; *El general en su laberinto* (*The General in His Labyrinth*) on a journey to an ending that attempts to start again and cannot. As Phil West has observed, myths always provide a second chance; history never does.

Often humorous, at times bitterly ironic or grotesque, occasionally tinged with pathos, García Márquez's work is marked by fullness, achieved through exaggeration, precise enumeration, rhetorical symmetry in characters, phrases, events, and repetition, always with variation. His episodic structures are packed with incident and striking images illuminated by an unexpected detail, where incongruity now replaces impossibility. (In *The General in His Labyrinth*, the "impossibilities" have become the historical errors pointed out for exclusion by helpful historian-readers and included as the climax to the thankful afterword.) Profiting from pioneers in the realist tradition like Venezuela's Rómulo Gallegos and even more from the ingenious anti-realism of Argentina's Jorge Luis Borges, García Márquez at his best achieves continuous surprise in the elaboration of a rococo, tesselated prose surface.

Structural artifice, episodic variety, and vibrant prose compensate for García Márquez's lack of interest in communicating the psychological and social density characteristic of the realistic novel and some other modernisms. Structure and surface virtuosity replace the illusion of penetrated depths, and the reader is stimulated instead by the constant necessity of shifting interpretive codes.

García Márquez's work is in the regionalist tradition, rooted in the Caribbean litoral, the hot, dusty, isolated towns periodically mired in endless seasonal rains, set against icy precipices, the blue gleam of distant islands, the languid pressure of suffocating vines. As Emir Rodríguez Monegal pointed out, García Márquez's fictions have moved further and further into the past since *One Hundred Years of Solitude* and *The Autumn of the Patriarch*. In *Love in the Time of Cholera* he retreated to the early years of the 20th century to celebrate a love that had a second chance; in *The General in His Labyrinth*, an historical novel on Bolívar's last trip down the Magdalena River, he moved into the 19th century to explore the last days of a man of power, a patriarch who failed. Love, death, power, and entrapment remain his crucial themes, whether they are explored in novels or in polemical journalism or, recently, in screenplays and plays, usually derived from stories or fragments of stories.

—Regina Janes

GARELLI, Jacques. French. Professor of philosophy, University of Picardie, Amiens; also taught literature at New York University and Yale University, New Haven, Connecticut, for 11 years. Address: Department of Philosophy, University of Picardie, rue Solomon Mahlangu, 80025 Amiens Cedex, France.

PUBLICATIONS

Verse

Brèche.   Paris, Mercure, 1966.
Les Dépossessions; Prender appui.   Paris, Mercure, 1968.

Lieux précaires; La Pluie belliqueuse de souviendras.   Paris, Mercure, 1972.
L'Ubiquité d'être; Difficile Séjour: poème composé sur l'œuvre sculpturale de Gonzalo Fonseca.   Paris, Corti, 1986.
Les Archives du silence; Récurrences du songe.   Paris, Corti, 1989.

Other

La Gravitation poétique.   Paris, Mercure, 1966.
Le Recel et la dispersion: essai sur le champ de lecture poétique.   Paris, Gallimard, 1978.
Artaud et la question du lieu: essay sur le théâtre et la poésie d'Artaud.   Paris, Corti, 1982.
Le Temps des signes.   Paris, Klincksieck, 1983.
A Nos Dirigéants.   Paris, Albatros, 1986.
Rythmes et mondes: au revers de l'identité et de l'altérité.   Grenoble, Millon, 1991.

*

Critical Study: "The Field of Poetic Constitution" by Lois Oppenheim, in *The Existential Coordinates of the Human Condition*, edited by Anna-Teresa Tymieniecka, Dordrecht, Reidel, 1984.

*   *   *

A philosopher and poet of Corsican heritage, Jacques Garelli combines thought and the recording of it in what might be called an autoconstitutional act of creation. In his critical works — for example, *La Gravitation poétique* (Poetic Gravitation), *Le Recel et la dispersion* (Withdrawing, Scattering), and *Le Temps des signes* (Time of the Signs) — he manages to combine an existential and humanistic bent with a Bergsonian vocabulary based on three elements, roughly speaking: intentionality, temporality, and ontology. The poem, as he sees it, is a "temporalizing structuration whose motif is ontological," tinged by what he calls "mondanéité," or the situation of being in the world. This "worldifying" of his thought and writing translates in practice into an uncompromising, indeed absolute commitment to the moment and what it contains. The whole creation, constituting itself as it goes along, confident of its direction, is reminiscent of the rugged land of Corsica with its unforgiving harsh beauty.

Garelli quotes Rilke in one of his characteristic sayings which is as apparently simple as it is all-demanding: "And we have basically only to be there, but simply, but in the moment, as the earth is there." This is not poetry that wills itself the mirror of the world, but rather poetry that is sure the world will find itself through poetic agency.

Already in an early volume of poetry, *Brèche* (Breach), Garelli was calling on words to break apart under the violence of foundational meaning. Gaps in structure, meaning, and rhythm are sought, left, pointed out: through this very unevenness, the *fault* shows through, read as a positive element because it is the foundation of Garelli's poetics, determining his most effective texts. "Convoi" (Convoy) begins in strength like a one-line manifesto: "No matter who, in any sentence, here or there, over these coals, for a lack." That lacking sense — a missing element, a default, a mistake, akin, etymologically and semantically, to the pitiless geological fault — is treasured as the starting point of lyricism as well as philosophy.

Even lying has its place: in the next volume, *Les Dépossessions* (Dispossessions), the lie is also the link: ("Linked, liar, linked, to the oblique string of words.") The fissure moving towards the work requires a new sort of truth; in the moving volume of *Lieux précaires* (Precarious Places), the emptiness of the fissure, the gap, the fault is sensed as devouring the words of the poem itself and the philosophic text. The poet sees himself as waiting both for what he terms an immense tidal wave and for the gentle smile of the painter Duccio. The latter sense is as important as the first one; for Garelli increasingly turns towards the eye, seemingly the most precious part of this "body which has become through a long stammering an error of itself." Looking is what opens, what contains, what makes a meaningful effort.

In *L'Ubiquité d'être; Difficile Séjour* (The Ubiquity of Being; Difficult Stay), we are called upon to accept that it is our seeing and listening which constitute us as they constitute the poem making itself. Garelli turns to the monumental stone constructions of the Uruguayan artist Gonzalo Fonseca to ground the poem in their place, in these enormous blocks of Order—Night—Time. It feels like a return to the primordial place of origin.

The strength of Garelli's writing is apparent as it now issues forth in parallel with the artist he has chosen. The same is true of the prison constructions of Piranesi in Garelli's *Les Archives du silence; Récurrences du songe* (Archives of Silence; Recurrences of Dream), where the complexities of his own thought work in and out of his poetic approach to the work. Garelli states the lyricism and the randomness of his own meetings with art in a passage which gives the flavor of his own intense marvelling—it too is simple, like Rilke's requirement about our being, like and on the earth. He marvels at conjunctions, at "the agreement between the vaporous color of a certain Japanese cherry tree and the word 'Blossom' suddenly said, musically charged with perfumes, mists, and flowering colors. Or then, the memory of one city with its perfumes and sounds taking over the peeling walls of another. The conjunction of the first measures of some Quartet and the memory of a walk in the fog." His demand is that the poem will, in its condensation, get these things right. Garelli's poems seem to do just that.

—Mary Ann Caws

GARRO, Elena. Mexican. Born in Puebla, Mexico, in 1920. Married Octavio Paz (*q.v.*) in 1937 (divorced); one daughter. Playwright for Poesía en Voz Alta theatre group; choreographer for Teatro de la Universidad; journalist. Recipient: Xavier Villaurrutia prize, 1963. Left Mexico in 1971; lives in France. Address: c/o Editorial Grijalbo, Apdo 17-568, Mexico City 17, Mexico.

PUBLICATIONS

Fiction

Los recuerdos del porvenir. Mexico City, Mortiz, 1963; as *Recollections of Things to Come*, Austin, University of Texas Press, 1969.
La semana de colores. Xalapa, Universidad Veracruzana, 1964.
Andamos huyendo Lola. Mexico City, Mortiz, 1980.
Testimonios sobre Mariana. Mexico City, Grijalbo, 1981.
Reencuentro de personajes. Mexico City, Grijalbo, 1982.
La casa junto al río. Mexico City, Grijalbo, 1983.

Plays

Felipe Angeles (produced 1954). Mexico City, Difusión Cultural/Universidad Nacional Autónoma de México, 1979.
Un hogar sólido, y otras piezas en un acto (includes *Un hogar sólido*; *Los pilares de doña Blanca*; *El rey mago*; *Andarse por las ramas*; *Ventura Allende*; *El encanto, tendajón mixto*; *Los perros*; *El árbol*; *La dama boba*; *El rastro*; *Benito Fernández*; *La mudanza*). Xalapa, Universidad Veracruzana, 1958; as *Un hogar sólido, y otras piezas*, Universidad Veracruzana, 1983.
La señora en su balcón. Madrid, Aguilar, 1970; as *The Lady on Her Balcony*, in *Shantih* (New York), Fall-Winter 1976.
Y Matarazo no llamó —. Mexico City, Grijalbo, 1991.

*

Critical Studies: "The Theatre of the Absurd in Spanish America [Garro inter alios]" by George Woodyard, in *Comparative Drama* (Kalamazoo, Michigan), 3(3), 1969; "Form and Content in Elena Garro's *Los recuerdos del porvenir*" by Harry L. Rosser, in *Revista Canadiense de Estudios Hispánicos* (Toronto), 2, 1975; "A Thematic Exploration of the Works of Elena Garro" by Gabriela Mora, in *Latin American Women Writers Yesterday and Today*, edited by Y. Miller and C. Tatum, Pittsburgh, Latin American Review Press, 1977; "Elena Garro's Attitudes Towards Mexican Society" by Harvey L. Johnson, in *South Central Bulletin*, 40(4), 1980; "Analytical Psychology and Garro's *Los pilares de doña Blanca*" by Richard J. Callan, in *Latin American Theatre Review* (Lawrence, Kansas), 16(2), 1983; "Myth and Archetype in *Recollections of Things to Come*" by Robert K. Anderson, in *Studies in 20th-Century Literature* (Manhattan, Kansas), 9(2), 1985; "Visual and Verbal Distances in the Mexican Theatre: The Plays of Elena Garro" by Sandra Messinger Cypess, in *Woman as Myth and Metaphor in Latin American Literature*, edited by C. Virgilio and N. Lindstrom, Columbia, University of Missouri Press, 1985; "Alienation and Escape in Elena Garro's *La semana de colores*" by Doris Meyer, in *Hispanic Review* (Philadelphia), 55, 1987; "In *illo tempore*: Elena Garro's *La semana de colores*" by Carmen Salazar, in *Retrospect: Essays on Latin American Literature*, York, South Carolina, Spanish Literature Publications, 1987; "The New Historical Novel: History and Fantasy in *Los recuerdos del porvenir*" by Daniel Balderston, in *Bulletin of Hispanic Studies* (Liverpool), 66(1), 1989; "Recollections of Plays to Come: Time in the Theater of Elena Garro" by Catherine Larson, in *Latin American Theatre Review* (Lawrence, Kansas), 22(2), 1989; *A Different Reality: Essays on the Works of Elena Garro* edited by Anita Stoll, Lewisburg, Bucknell University Press, 1990; "Lope de Vega and Elena Garro: The Doubling of *La dama boba*" by Catherine Larson, in *Hispania* (Los Angeles), 74(1), 1991.

*   *   *

Elena Garro's works belong to the so-called literature of magic realism. Rooted in the pre-Columbian Mexican tradition, her earlier writings — *Los recuerdos del porvenir* (*Recollections of Things to Come*), the short stories of *La semana de colores* (Week of Colors), and the one-act plays of *Un hogar sólido* (A Solid Home) — weave magic and myth with the objective dimensions of reality. In her later novels, *Testimonios sobre Mariana* (Testimonies About Mariana) and *La casa junto al río* (The House by the River), magic yields to the fantastic, which also co-exists with the rational and the ordinary, thus proposing eccentric worlds, where multivalence replaces unity. The ambiguity of her fictive worlds is emphasized by the manner in which suprarealist events belonging to the realms of magic, fantasy, or dream are depicted as if they were ordinary or common experience.

Garro's treatment of time is one of the main elements contributing to such diffuseness. In *Recollections of Things to Come*, for example, which takes place in Ixtepec, a rural town occupied by the forces of the Calles regime during the Cristero War, the characters experience multiple chronologies. The infinite time of an irredeemable Indian past — forever lost after the conquest — causes Ixtepec to exist "in a dimension of time which remains still." The time escaping the clock's computation, as experienced by the Moncadas, one of the mestizo families, is "a new and melancholic time where gestures and voices begin to move in the past." There is no future in this dimension, as demonstrated by the destiny of the Moncadas. Both Juan and Nicolás are killed by the military, and Isabel turns into stone — thus placing herself outside of time — after becoming the lover of General Rosas, her brothers' assassin. There is also the timelessness of mythical time, as experienced by Hurtado — the outsider who brings imagination and poetry to Ixtepec — and Julia — Rosas's lover who mystifies the town. As they escape the town also transcends time for a place "where the roses are paralyzed under the air of a fixed sky."

The characters in the short stories of *La semana de colores* may live simultaneously in two different historical periods, such as in "La culpa es de los tlaxcaltecas" (It's the Tlaxcaltecs' Fault) where the protagonist escapes the present of an unfulfilling and oppressive marriage by joining her lover in the Aztec past. Children are particularly prone to entering and exiting various dimensions of time. The girls of "El día que fuimos perros" (The Day We Were Dogs) live in "one day which has two days inside." As the two sisters of "Antes de la guerra de Troya" (Before the Trojan War) grow older, they lose their mutual identification in a common perception of time.

Garro's treatment of time, then, has both positive and negative implications. On the one hand it contributes to the expansion of reality; on the other it also adds to individual isolation, as demonstrated by her characters who often exist in divergent chronological spheres. This also adds to the sense of hopelessness pervading so many of her stories: "They would never find each other because they would all fall at different times" ("El duende" [The Goblin]).

Her later works, *Testimonios sobre Mariana*, *Reencuentro de personajes* (Gathering of Characters), *La casa junto al río*, and the short stories of *Andamos huyendo Lola* (Lola, We Are on the Run), deal more exclusively with the plight of women who often find themselves on the margins of society. Irreconcilable differences separate women and men, differences that threaten the legitimacy of the patriarchal order and feed men's resentment and aggressiveness towards women. Both Mariana, the protagonist of *Testimonios*, and Verónica, of *Reencuentro*, are destroyed by their male counterparts. Mariana, a Russian dancer, is married to a Mexican anthropologist with a promising career. His principal objective is to destroy his wife as punishment for her silent but firm resistance to his effort to make her submissive. Mariana is verbally, psychologically, and physically abused; she is subject to public humiliation and constant harassment. Verónica, on the other hand, enters a sadomasochistic relationship with a bisexual man who, by means of verbal and physical abuse and constant persecution, terrorizes her into submission. It is unclear whether Mariana commits suicide or is killed by Augusto, her husband. Verónica, however, has lost even the will to end her life.

The women of *Andamos huyendo Lola* are the victims of politics and of governmental policies. As depicted in most of her works, the patriarchy derives much of its strength from the implementation of exclusionary policies. The characters in these short stories — five of them share the same protagonists — are women in exile escaping persecution in their countries of origin, only to find poverty, isolation, and uprootedness in hostile, foreign nations.

Persecution and defeat are also the topics of *La casa junto al río*. Consuelo, the sole survivor of her family, returns from Mexico to her hometown in Asturias in search for her roots, her identity, and a possible new meaning to her life. She encounters, however, the hostility of the locals, understanding only too late that they will kill her in order to lay legitimate claim to her inheritance. As with most of her other protagonists, Consuelo is alone in battling insurmountable forces which ultimately defeat her.

A consideration of the structural and stylistic complexities of Garro's work lies beyond the scope of this brief thematic survey. However, her works cannot be fully appreciated or thoroughly understood without a careful consideration of their technical sophistication and stylistic richness. One should remember that her first novel, *Recollections of Things to Come*, predates *Cien años de soledad* (*One Hundred Years of Solitude*) (1967), the cornerstone of contemporary Spanish American fiction, and that Gabriel García Márquez (*q.v.*) himself acknowledges its influence on his own work.

—Patricia Rubio

GATTI, Armand. Moroccan and French. Born Daute Gatti in Morocco, 26 January 1924; naturalized French citizen, 1956. Educated at a seminary of Saint Paul, Super-Cannes, 1939. Member of the Resistance during World War II: arrested by the Gestapo and imprisoned in various labour camps, including Neuengamme camp, near Hamburg — escaped; joined French SAS, until 1945. Journalist 1945–59: international correspondent in Korea, 1950, and Siberia, 1957; also travelled to South America and China; lived in Belgium, 1969–73, and Germany, 1974–75. Recipient: Albert Londres prize, for journalism, 1954; Fénéon prize, 1959. Address: c/o L'Éther Vague, c/o Patrice-Thierry, 37 rue Jean-Sizabuire, 31400 Toulouse, France.

PUBLICATIONS

Plays

Le Poisson noir (revised version produced Toulouse, 1964). Paris, Seuil, 1958.
Le Crapaud buffle (produced Paris, 1959). Paris, L'Arche, 1959.
Le Quetzal. Published in *Europe*, June 1960.
Théâtre:
    vol. 1: includes *L'Enfant-rat*; *Le Voyage du Grand Tchou*. Paris, Seuil, 1960.
    vol. 2: includes *La Vie imaginaire de l'éboueur Auguste G.*; *Chroniques d'une planète provisoire*; *La Deuxième Existence du Camp de Tatenberg*. Paris, Seuil, 1962.

vol. 3: includes *Chant public devant deux chaises électriques*. Paris, Seuil, 1964.
L'Enfant-rat (produced Vienna, 1961). Included in *Théâtre*, vol. 1, 1960.
La Vie imaginaire de l'éboueur Auguste G. (produced Villeurbanne, 1961). Included in *Théâtre*, vol. 2, 1962.
L'Enclos (screenplay). Paris, Fayard, 1962.
Le Voyage du Grand Tchou (produced Marseilles, 1962). Included in *Théâtre*, vol. 1, 1960.
La Deuxième Existence du Camp de Tatenberg (produced Lyon, 1962). Included in *Théâtre*, vol. 2, 1962.
Chroniques d'une planète provisoire (produced Toulouse, 1963). Included in *Théâtre*, vol. 2, 1962.
Chant public devant deux chaises électriques (revised version produced Paris, 1966). Included in *Théâtre*, vol. 3, 1964; as *Public Performance Before Two Electric Chairs*, n.p., n.p., 197–?.
Un Homme seul (produced Paris, 1966). Paris, Seuil, 1969.
V comme Vietnam (produced Toulouse, 1967). Paris, Seuil, 1967.
La Passion du Général Franco (original version banned in France; produced Kassel, 1967). Paris, Seuil, 1968; revised version as *La Passion du Général Franc par les émigrés eux-mêmes* (produced Paris, 1976). Paris, Seuil, 1975.
Les 13 Soleils de la rue Sainte-Blaise (produced Paris, 1968). Paris, Seuil, 1968.
La Cigogne (produced Strasbourg, 1968). Paris, Seuil, 1971.
La Naissance (produced Villejuif, 1968). Paris, Seuil, 1969.
Pourquoi les animaux domestiques? ou, La Journée d'une infirmière (performed in various hospitals in France by Groupe V theatre group, 1968; Avignon, 1970). Published in *Partisans*, November–December 1970.
La Machine excavatrice pour entrer dans le plan de défrichement de la colonne d'invasion Che Guevara (produced Turn, 1970).
Ne pas perdre du temps sur un titre (produced Bremen, 1970).
Rosa collective (produced Kassel, 1971). Paris, Seuil, 1973.
La Colonne Durruti (produced Louvain, 1972). Published in *Cahiers-Théâtre de Louvain*, 14–17, 1973.
Quatre Schizophrénies à la recherche d'un pays dont l'existence est contestée (produced in German, West Berlin, 1974).
Le Joint (produced Ris-Orangis, 1975).
Armand Gatti dans le Brabant Wallon: L'Arche d'Adelin. Published in *Cahiers-Théâtre de Louvain*, 26–29, 1977.
Le Cheval qui se suicide par le feu (produced Avignon, 1977).
Le Labyrinthe (produced Genoa, 1982); revised version, as *Le Labyrinthe tel qu'il a été écrit par les habitants de l'Histoire de Derry; Notes de travail en Ulster*. Toulouse, Terres Hérétiques, 1983.
Opéra avec titre long (produced Montreal, 1986). Toulouse, L'Éther Vague, 1986.
Les Arches de Noé (produced Toulouse, 1986).
Le Train (produced Vienna, 1987).
Le Passage des oiseaux dans le ciel (produced Montreal, 1987).
Les 7 Possibilités du train 713 en partance d'Auschwitz. Seyssel, COMP'ACT, 1989; as *Train 713* (produced Rochester, New York, 1988).
Œuvres théâtrales, edited by Michel Séonnet. Lagrasse, Verdier, 3 vols., 1991.

Screenplays: *Morambong*, 1958; *L'Enclos* (also director), 1960; *El otro Cristobal*, 1962; *Le Lion, sa cage et ses ailes* (6 video films; also director), 1975–77; *Nous étions tous des noms d'arbres*, 1981; *Ton Nom était Joi*, 1987.

Television Plays: *Übergang über den Ebro*, 1970; *La Première Lettre* (7 films; also director), 1978–84.

Other

La Vie de Churchill, with Pierre Joffroy. Paris, Seuil, 1954.
Envoyé spécial dans la cage aux fauves. Paris, Seuil, 1955.
Chine. Paris, Seuil, 1957.
Sibérie – zéro + l'infini. Paris, Seuil, 1958.
Max Schoendorff, with Jean-Jacques Lerrant and Robert Droguet. N. p., Losfeld, 1969.
L'Aventure de la parole errante, with Marc Kravetz. Toulouse, L'Éther Vague, 1987.
Les Analogues du réel. Toulouse, L'Éther Vague, 1988.

*

Critical Studies: "Armand Gatti: Multiplicity of vision in Action Theatre" by Bettina L. Knapp, in *Modern Drama* (Downsview, Ontario), 12, 1969; "Portrait of a Pugnacious Playwright" by François Pasqualini, in *Trace*, 70, 1969; "Armand Gatti: Brecht and the Cultural Revolution" by Victoria W. Hill, in her *Bertolt Brecht and Postwar French Drama*, Stuttgart, Heinz, 1978; "Armand Gatti: Theatre Without Walls" by Joseph Long, in *Threshold* (Belfast), 30, 1979; *Armand Gatti in the Theatre: Wild Duck Against the Wind* by Dorothy Knowles, London, Athlone Press, 1989.

*   *   *

"There is a corridor in a French prison somewhere that in spite of all my efforts I have never quite got out of." Poet, playwright, and, most importantly, political thinker, Armand Gatti has been fuelled by his own struggles with personal identity, from the physical and spiritual battering of surviving a Nazi work camp to the confusion of being a "working-class intellectual." His work is centered on the exploration of History as a construction which depends entirely upon the individual to revolutionize. Gatti sees revolution not as a result of violence but as the fruit of individual creation — the birth of a new conscience in every actor/spectator of the world event.

Gatti began writing professionally as a journalist, which allowed him to travel to the non-Western countries that subsequently became the loci of his dramatic investigation. However, his relationship with the written word started much earlier, as part of his war experience. Gatti used literature to build up a defensive linguistic wall between himself and his torturers. They laughed at his ramblings, and he learned that literature could be more vital than a mere escape from reality; he found it to be a potent protection against the madness of human cruelty.

Gatti began writing plays in 1954 with *Le Quetzal*, a play exploring guerrilla struggle in Guatemala, based upon Gatti's own observations as a journalist in Central America. Throughout the 1960s, Gatti continued to explore and expose the positive gesture of political revolt, to give voice to the struggles of the invisible warriors of many countries enveloped in postwar upheaval. His plays did not necessarily reflect contemporary events, but rather turned attention to historical moments that foregrounded parallel struggles with each country's own identity. In *Le Poisson noir* (The Black Fish), he consciously reconstructs revolt in feudal China during the building of the Great Wall. *Chant public devant deux chaises électriques* (*Public Performance Before Two Electric Chairs*) juxtaposes the Sacco and Vanzetti story with American union battles. *La Passion du Général Franco* (The Passion of General Franco), *V comme Vietnam* (V as in Vietnam), and *La Cigogne* (The Stork) (about the bombing of Nagasaki) are all equally politicized.

May 1968 was for Gatti, as for most of France, a turning point in political and cultural awareness and shaped the course of his own artistic endeavors. His dissatisfaction with professional theater and drama as a bourgeois commodity led to his formulation of a "spectacle without spectators." He has dedicated his efforts to the project of realizing that "spectacle" since 1973. His method encourages collective creation, by which he means to demystify theatrical and cinematic creation by teaching people — entire communities — how to create themselves. Gatti moves into a community — such as Wallon in Brabant, or Londonderry in Northern Ireland — and learns about the inhabitants of the region, eliciting their own stories and histories. With the contribution of all, he then stages something like a medieval pageant in which no one watches, but everyone participates.

Gatti conceives theater as a dying *affaire du cul*, where a comfortable posterior is essential to appreciation. This passivity is equivalent to prison on Gatti's thematic scale. While captivity was explored in his early works, Gatti has dramatized the theme of being imprisoned by everyday habits in subsequent texts. The prison metaphor extends to encompass all forms of the restrictions, patterns, and defenses that permit the perpetuation of indifference — the hegemony of the closed mind and the cult of passive spectatorship. The passive voyeurism of a spectator who consumes the theatrical vision, only to expulse it upon exiting the theatre is anathema to his ideas and goals as a theater artist. For this reason, many have aligned Gatti's agenda with that of Brecht.

Like Brecht's, Gatti's theater is devoted to exploring and framing the dialectical play between Individual and History. Gatti's images thrive on contradiction; even solitude, for example, is resolved only in the dialectical contradiction: we are always alone/we are never alone. Such contradictions are constantly renegotiated as Gatti explores his attitudes towards Fact/Fiction. Whereas Gatti strives to expose the way reality is constructed on an ideological level, he also celebrates the individual's power to create an alternate history, hence subverting the ideology which tries to dictate experience. Creation itself is valued as the triumph of the individual, and Gatti believes that History is not what is written but what is lived. These two operations are played out in the two major movements of Gatti's work: the early plays reflect the playwright's attempts to promote awareness of global ideological forces at play, whereas the movement towards "spectacle without spectators" has purported to empower people with their own construction of reality.

Gatti defies a commodified theater that feeds its spectators a neat package of unified plot and unified subject. His idea of theater and the theatrical subject was shaped by his own experience in a concentration camp where the individual had no sense of past or future, only an "undernourished present." Gatti's *théâtre éclaté* fragments its subject in a world where all the possible pasts and futures shape the present, continuously reposturing and denying the spectator the satisfaction of unity or wholeness. Gatti calls upon the spectator to wander actively through the possibilities raised by his texts. His manipulation and multiplication of time, space, and character demand the active, alert participation of the audience member.

Language is important to Gatti because it unites the human subject with action. He seeks for a new critical, dialectical language, which will liberate the subject from "the ideologies that condition his/her thought and expression." One of the major reasons that Gatti relocated his theatrical "tribe" to countries such as Northern Ireland and Germany (and set about discovering the local people) was to explore the specificity of their language. Through this distancing effect, Gatti hoped to find out how people learn and repeat the ideological codes built into the linguistic apparatus. Conversely, he also hoped to discover how and where opposition to the dominant discourse found expression, and by doing so, hoped to encourage dissent and challenge passivity.

Gatti emphasizes that the theater is a medium; it is both the place and the event which gets the process of critical evaluation started. The role of theater is not to provide answers or dictate what one should do upon leaving its confines. It must place issues before the spectator and encourage questioning, as opposed to perpetuating the passive expectation of an answer/product. The Question is Gatti's first step to opening the prison door, to altering the mechanisms of ideology which entrap the human being. It is that moment of questioning which marks the birth of a new consciousness, because "when a person starts asking questions s/he is beginning to change, and s/he could one day want to change the world."

—Sabrina Prielaida

GATTI, Daute. *See* **GATTI, Armand.**

GLISSANT, Édouard. Martiniquais. Born in Sainte-Marie, 21 September 1928. Educated at the Lycée Schoelcher, Fort-de-France; the Sorbonne, Musée de l'Homme, Paris, licence ès philosophie and certificat in ethnological studies. Married Maryse Glissant in 1944(?) (second marriage); two sons and one daughter, and one son from a previous marriage. Founder and director, Institut Martiniquais d'Études, from 1967; editor *Acoma* journal; formerly principal of a private school, Fort-de-France. Recipient: Renaudot prize, 1958; Veillon prize, 1965. Address: c/o Éditions Seuil, 27 rue Jacob, 75261 Paris Cedex 06, France.

PUBLICATIONS

Fiction

La Lézarde.   Paris, Seuil, 1958; as *The Ripening*, New York, Braziller, 1959; London, Heinemann, 1985.
Le Quatrième Siècle.   Paris, Seuil, 1964.
Malemort.   Paris, Seuil, 1975.
La Case du commandeur.   Paris, Seuil, 1981.
Mahagony.   Paris, Seuil, 1987.

Play

Monsieur Toussaint.   Paris, Seuil, 1961; Washington, D.C., Three Continents Press, 1981; as screenplay (in French), Seuil, 1986.

Verse

Un Champ d'îles.   Paris, Dragon, 1953.
La Terre inquiète.   Paris, Dragon, 1954.

Les Indes. Paris, Scuil, 1956.
Le Sel noir. Paris, Seuil, 1960.
Le Sang rivé. Paris, Présence Africaine, 1961.
Édouard Glissant (selected poems). Paris, Seghers, 1982.
Pays rêvé, pays réel. Paris, Seuil, 1985.

Other

Soleil de la conscience. Paris, Seuil, 1955.
L'Intention poétique. Paris, Seuil, 1969.
Le Discours antillais. Paris, Seuil, 1981; as *Caribbean Discourse*, Charlottesville, University Press of Virginia, 1989.
Poétique de la relation. Paris, Gallimard, 1990.

Editor, *Mémoires de M. d'Artagnan*, by Gatien de Courtilz.
   Paris, Bonnot, 1966.

*

Critical Studies: "The Image of Africa in the Writings of Édouard Glissant" by Wilbert J. Roget, in *College Language Association Journal* (Atlanta, Georgia), 21, 1978; Glissant issue of *World Literature Today* (Norman, Oklahoma), Autumn 1989.

*   *   *

Édouard Glissant's oeuvre is almost totally informed by his native land, the Caribbean island of Martinique, its landscapes and the destinies of its people. His early poetry and essays reveal his preoccupations with the ambiguities of his personal situation as an Antillean intellectual immersed in French culture, a thematic strand that weaves through his work. But Glissant is more than an introspective regional writer. In 1956 he published a long epic poem, *Les Indes* (*The Indies*), which retraces Columbus's voyage to America and poses questions on the destinies of the New World and its relations to the world.

The notion of relation has become increasingly central in Glissant's work. Thus the tiny island of Martinique, to which Glissant refers as an "immensité de cet espace minuscule" (immensity of this minuscule space), becomes emblematic of the relationships that characterize societies and cultures. The land and the people of Martinique have an ontological reciprocity, essential and yet so precarious. The history of the people of Martinique, most of whom were forcefully transplanted from Africa, reveals a series of discontinuities. So much of their past has been lost, or misrepresented through Eurocentric historiography. Thus, as Glissant states in one of his early essays: "It is essential for us to recover our authentic past." The poet must look for traces of this past in the collective unconscious of the people and its folklore, as well as in the landscape, which is like a cadastre where the deeds of the people are inscribed.

Glissant's first novel, *La Lézarde* (*The Ripening*), which, not without controversy, won the author the much-coveted Renaudot prize, is an exploration of Martiniquals space. The journey starts from the heights in the mountains where the maroons—the fugitive slaves—took refuge. It follows the river Lézarde on its downward journey to the sea, along sugar plantations where the slaves from Africa and later indentured workers from India were forced to work, down to the city and finally to the sea which still harbors traces of the Caribs, the first inhabitants of the region who were quickly exterminated by the early European colonists. Contrasting features, like the rain forests in the north, with rich fauna and flora, and the arid desert in the south mark the Martiniquais landscape, rife with

significance. The main characters of this first novel and its partial sequel *Le Quatrième Siècle* (The Fourth Century) come from two lineages: the Beluses represent the plantation slaves, who "accepted," as Glissant puts it, their condition, and the Longoués, who "refused" and upon arrival in Martinique escaped to the mountains to become the much-dreaded and admired maroons. The destinies of the two families are intertwined through murders and marriages, and their descendants reappear in virtually all Glissant's novels, like the intellectual Mathieu, his companion Marie Celat, a woman of great moral fortitude, Raphaël, the solitary shepherd in the mountains, imbued with the old legends, and the *quimboiseur*, the ancient medicine man, Papa Longoué, who embodies uncompromising refusal and lives on the margin of society. The first two novels explore basically the relationship of Martiniquais with their land. In the following novels, new preoccupations emerge with the presence of other races, principally the French settlers, popularly called the békés and the East Indians, as well as the Syrians and other peoples of the region. The relatively buoyant mood of Glissant's first two novels changes to somber reflections in his subsequent work.

In *Malemort* (Foul Death), in a series of disrupted sequences not unlike the history of the Martiniquais people itself, in wry moods and a poignant sense of helplessness, sarcastic and tragic, Glissant describes the cultural assimilation and socio-economic exploitation that the Martiniquais suffer willy-nilly and the loss of their cultural identity with the onslaught of urbanization, industrialization, and the tourist industry, much promoted by metropolitan interests. Alarmed by these trends, Glissant increasingly probes folkloric materials, stories, legends, being particularly interested in rehabilitating the much maligned maroon, the only authentic Antillean hero.

In *Mahogany*, Glissant's latest novel, the mahogany tree, which used to provide shelter and comfort for the maroon, becomes a polyvalent symbol for steadfastness and courage in the face of oppression and unfairness. The novel ends with a vision of mahogany trees growing in steppes, tundras, sierras, pampas, anywhere where people care for man's freedom and dignity.

In a way, *Poétique de la relation* (Poetics of Relation), one of Glissant's latest collections of essays, offers the true circumference of his work's significance. Glissant's analysis of the Antillean situation, at the crossroads of many cultures and linguistic codes, reinforces the notion of the world's diversity. The notion of relation resists all attempts at homogenization and standardization and rejects the Eurocentric ideals of uniformity, monopoly, and hierarchy. It affirms the inevitability of intercontamination, the creolization of cultures and values.

Glissant emerges as a profound thinker of our contemporary civilization. With the passing of *Négritude*, established by black writers of an earlier generation such as Léopold Senghor and Aimé Césaire (*qq v*), as a viable cultural notion, Glissant's ideas have given rise to a new generation of writers and intellectuals in the region who call themselves *Créolistes* and acknowledge their spiritual indebtedness to Glissant. The recognition of Glissant as the most visible intellectual figure in the Francophone Caribbean and even beyond is incontestable.

—Juris Silenieks

GOKÇELI, Yaşar Kemal. *See* **KEMAL, Yaşar.**

GÖNCZ, Árpád. Hungarian. Born in Budapest, 10 February 1922. Educated at the University of Budapest, 1938–44, law degree 1944; Gödöllo University, 1951–56, studies in soil reclamation. Served in the army during World War II; became member of Hungarian underground resistance. Married Susan Maria Göntér, in 1946; four children. Clerk, Land Credit Institute, after World War II; factory steel worker, Budapest; took part in Hungarian uprising following Russian invasion, 1956: imprisoned, 1956–63; translator, from 1965: has translated over 150 books from English into Hungarian; member and president of Hungarian Parliament, 1989; Acting President of Hungary, 1989, and since 1990 President of Hungary. President, Hungarian Writers Federation, 1989–90. Recipient: Wheatland prize, for translation; Attila József prize. Address: Office of the President, Kossuth Lajos tér 1, 1055 Budapest, Hungary.

PUBLICATIONS

Plays

Magyar Médeia (produced Budapest, 1975). With *Sarusok* and *Rácsok*, Budapest, Magvető, 1979; as *Hungarian Medea*, in *Voices of Dissent*, 1989.
Magyar Médeia; *Sarusok*; *Rácsok* [Hungarian Medea; Sandalled Ones (from his own novel); Iron Bars]. Budapest, Magvető, 1979.
Voices of Dissent (includes *Hungarian Medea*; *Iron Bars*). Lewisburg, Pennsylvania, Bucknell University Press, 1989.
Mérleg [Scales]. Budapest, Magvető, 1990.
Plays and Other Writings (includes *Man of God*; *Persephone*; also fiction). New York, Garland, 1990; fiction published as *The Homecoming and Other Stories*, Budapest, Corvina, 1991.

Fiction

Sarusok [The Sandalled Ones]. Budapest, Magvető, 1974.
Találkozások [Encounter]. Budapest, Magvető, 1980.

Other

Translator, *A szépek még nem születtek meg* [The Beautiful Ones Are Not Yet Born], by Ayi Kwei Armah. Budapest, Európa, 1975.
Translator, *A tó* [Mizuumi], by Kawabata Yasunari. Budapest, Európa, 1978.
Translator, *Egy hibbant vénember naplója* [Futen rojin nikki], by Dzsunicsiró Tanidzaki. Budapest, Európa, 1980.
Translator, *Nirmalá: elbeszélések*, by Premchand. Budapest, Európa, 1980.
Translator, with István Hürkecz and Erzsébet Teleki, *A vadlúd: elbeszélések*, by Ógai Mori. Budapest, Európa, 1983.

Has also translated over 150 books from English into Hungarian, including works by William Golding, Ernest Hemingway, John Updike, E. M. Forster, J. R. R. Tolkien, Agatha Christie, J. B. Priestley, Robert Louis Stevenson, William Faulkner, Peter Shaffer, E. L. Doctorow, John Cheever, John Synge, Willa Cather, D. H. Lawrence, Thomas Wolfe, William Styron, Alan Sillitoe, Susan Sontag, Arthur C. Clarke, Malcolm Lowry, W. Somerset Maugham, and others.

*   *   *

Árpád Göncz is one of those writers whose biography is inseparable from his literary achievement. He became a writer relatively late in life — first he studied law and then agronomy, and he was well over 40 when his first writings were published. Between 1956 and 1963 he was jailed by the Communist authorities for "anti-state activities," but while in jail he learned English and after his release emerged as an excellent translator of English and American literature. He was elected President of the Hungarian Writers' Federation in 1989, and a year later he became President of the independent Hungarian Republic — apart from Václav Havel (*q.v.*) the only writer in East Central Europe to hold such high political office.

Göncz is a playwright and a prose writer of short stories and one novel, *Sarusok* (The Sandalled Ones), which Göncz later turned into a play (translated as *Man of God* in English). The novel is an imaginative recreation of a case of heresy by 15th-century Waldensians in and around the West Hungarian town of Sopron. The central character. Master Nicholas, a goldsmith, is a self-styled "Man of God" who "really believes in nothing else but his own conscience which he regards as God." The most dramatic part of the plot is Master Nicholas's confrontation with the Monk who investigates his case. The Monk tries to understand and in his own way help the accused, but fails in his attempt; this is a case in which several "truths" clash and must be evaluated. As Göncz says in *Sarusok*, "When two truths are equal, the persecuted truth is always the truer truth."

Just as in *Man of God*, in the monodrama *Magyar Médeia* (*Hungarian Medea*) the heroine is punished for infringement of the norms of the community. The daughter of a pre-war general, she is deported to the country by the Communist authorities during the 1950s. There she falls in love with an ambitious peasant lad, András Jászó (note the similarity with "Jason"), and "betrays" her class by marrying him. 25 years later, on the day her divorce comes through, she evokes the past and remonstrates with her present in a series of bitter monologues. Her tragedy is sealed by the death of her only son, a teenager deeply upset by the row between his parents, who drives his parents' car recklessly and is killed, committing a kind of suicide.

Of Göncz's other plays, *Rácsok* (Iron Bars) is the most directly political, yet its message is somewhat camouflaged by the choice of an unnamed South American country as its stage. The plot revolves around the diverse and often ridiculous attempts of the authorities to break the spirit of an imprisoned poet whose former friend is now president of the régime that keeps him in jail. According to critic Clara Györgyey, Göncz "portrays prison life and methods of interrogation with haunting accuracy" (*World Literature Today* [Norman, Oklahoma], 64(2)), a skill gained, no doubt, during the long prison term he served after the events of 1956. The play *Persephone* presents the dilemma of a man torn between two goddesses, between uneventful domestic bliss and exciting but potentially fateful adventure. In all his plays Göncz uses the technique of "cutting" to great advantage, contrasting modern colloquial and classical choral passages, and thereby stressing the eternal nature of passions that vex the human soul.

In his short stories and prose sketches Göncz usually focuses on a dramatic situation which he then handles with controlled passion and a commendable economy of words. Most of his stories deal with human problems such as loneliness, the meeting of former lovers who now live in different countries, and the humiliating disabilities of old age. In the compassionate story "Front," a middle-aged peasant woman in war-time Hungary "tames" a young Russian soldier attempting to rape her. Another story gives Göncz the chance to use his historical imagination once again: *Találkozások* (Encounter) sets up a new confrontation between Joan of Arc and her French judge just before her canonization in the 20th century. Göncz's prose style demonstrates his affinity with the theatre — his laconic dialogues build up often unresolved tension, and the internal monologues of his characters reveal the weight of the enormous burden that loyalty often places on human relationships.

—George Gömöri

GORBANEVSKAIA, Natalia (Evgen'evna). Also Natalya Gorbanevskaya, Natalja Gorbanevskaja. Russian. Born in Moscow, in 1936. Educated at the University of Moscow, expelled twice; University of Leningrad, external degree 1964. Has two sons. Librarian, All-Union Book Center, 1958–64; acute fear of heights led to a short stay in Kashchenko psychiatric hospital, 1959; translator and editor, State Institute of Experimental Pattern Design and Technical Research, 1964–68; co-founder and editor, *Khronika Tekushchikh Sobytii* samizdat journal, 1968–75; arrested for civil rights activities, 1969; in prison hospital, 1970–72; has lived in France since 1975; editor, *Kontinent, Pamiat* magazine, and *La Pensée Russe*, all Paris. Address: c/o Ardis Publishers, 2901 Heatherway, Ann Arbor, Michigan 48104, U.S.A.

PUBLICATIONS

Verse

Piat' stikhotvorenii [Five Poems]. Published in *Grani* (Frankfurt), 69, 1968.
V sumasshedshem dome [In the Mad House]. Published in *Grani* (Frankfurt), 67, 1968.
Stikhi [Poems]. Frankfurt, Posev, 1969.
Sharmanka, poi, sharmanka voi [Street-Organ Sing, Street-Organ Howl]. Published in *Grani* (Frankfurt), 70, 1969.
Stikhi, ne sobrannye v knigi [Poems, Not Collected in Books]. Published in *Grani* (Frankfurt), 76, 1971.
Selected Poems, translated by Daniel Weissbort. Oxford, Carcanet, 1972.
Poberezh'e [The Littoral]. Ann Arbor, Michigan, Ardis, 1973.
Ne spi na zakate [Don't Sleep in the Sunset]. Published in *Grani* (Frankfurt), August–December 1974.
Tri tetradi stikhotvoreniia [Three Books of Poetry]. Bremen, K Presse, 1975.
Chetyre stikhtvoreniia [Four Poems]. Published in *Grani* (Frankfurt), 100, 1976.
Pereletia snezhnuiu granitsu: stikhi 1974–1978. Paris, YMCA Press, 1979.

Angel dereviannyi [Wooden Angel]. Ann Arbor, Michigan, Ardis, 1982.
Poeticheskii traktat [Poetical Treatise]. Ann Arbor, Michigan, Ardis, 1982.
Chuzhie kamni: stikhi 1979–1982 [Alien Stoves: Poems 1979–1982]. New York, Russica, 1983.
Peremennaia oblachnost': stikhi osen' 1982–vesna 1983 [Occasional Cloudiness]. Paris, Kontakt, 1985.
Gde i kogda: stikhi iiun 1983–mart 1985 [Where and When]. Paris, Kontakt, 1985.
I vremia zhit', i vremia povtoriat' [And a Time to Live, and a Time to Repeat]. Published in *Oktiabr'* (Moscow), 7, 1990.
Iz raznykh sbornikov [From Various Collections]. Published in *Znamia* (Moscow), 8, 1990.
Iz stikhov poslednikh let [From Poetry of the Last Years]. Published in *Novyi mir* (Moscow), 11, 1992.
Stikhi poslednikh let [Poems of the Last Years]. Published in *Oktiabr'* (Moscow), 11, 1992.

Other

Polden': Delo o demonstratsii 25 avgusta 1968 goda na krasnoi ploshchadi. Samizdat, 1969; Frankfurt, Posev, 1970; as *Red Square at Noon*, London, Deutsch, and New York, Holt, 1972.

*

Critical Study: "The Early Poems of Natalja Gorbanevskaja" by Christine A. Rydel, in *Russian Language Journal* (East Lansing, Michigan), 123–124, 1982.

*   *   *

The Russian emigré poet Natalia Gorbanevskaia underwent a cruel literary apprenticeship in the Soviet Union where only a handful of her poems ever officially appeared in print. She published most of her poems in Western journals, an offense which alone would have earned her government censure if her political activities had not already made her a target of official persecution. Active in the "dissident" movement, she protested against the closed trials of other dissidents, signed letters of protest against incidents of injustice in the Soviet Union, and even demonstrated in Red Square against the Soviet invasion of Czechoslovakia in 1968. She described the events of this demonstration in her book *Polden'* (*Red Square at Noon*). Arrested and sent to psychiatric hospitals for observation, she was there diagnosed as a schizophrenic. Gorbanevskaia recounts her sufferings in these hospitals in a series of letters ironically called "Free Health Service." Except in a poem against Soviet treatment of Poles and Czechs and a few works called "prison poems," Gorbanevskaia's poetry is not political; instead it explores the themes of love, poetry, and self-definition in a world full of suffering. Since her emigration to France, she has continued to write in the same vein. A sense of loss permeates the poems in which she feels the melancholy of her "transient" state in misty, rainy Paris.

Understandably Gorbanevskaia's poems evoke a sense of despair, disillusionment, confinement, frustration, melancholy and loneliness. In her poetic world love is rare and rejection — even by God — is normal. She can find relief and consolation in poetry, but she repeatedly tells of the pain and torture she must undergo to write. Gorbanevskaia counterbalances the bleakness of her vision of life with ornate, luxurious, musical language and a complex symbolic system which generates new images, almost like a chain reaction.

Gorbanevskaia's symbolic system is based on a contrast between images of heat and cold. Within this framework exist subsystems of image clusters which depend on the primary recurring symbols: burning, flames, and intense heat. However, other motifs cluster around symbolic candles, ashes, and soot, and dryness which in turn generates another group of images relating to tears and grass. But grass also takes on its own special meaning which sometimes relates to the basic images of heat and cold. Her symbolic subsystems often form independent sets.

Images of coldness form the same type of generative system. Gorbanevskaia's primary symbols of chills and snowbanks contain a network of motifs relating to metallically cold settings, wind, and the icy waters of oblivion. Water imagery dominates poems about oblivion and nothingness. Gorbanevskaia usually bemoans a sad and loveless state in settings that are cold and frigid; sometimes, though, she finds passion, love, and affection in settings that are warm or hot. Even though these images may seem conventional, Gorbanevskaia does not use them in a trite manner. Occasionally she even seems to confuse the images, but is always consistent within the context of each poem. For example, in one work she gives her lover a handful of snow but she feels warmth since this shared snow is a sign of affection. Sometimes she combines images oxymoronically to produce an ambiguous effect; in one poem she sheds dry tears.

Even though Gorbanevskaia expresses her feelings in tactile images, soundplay brings real richness to her poetry. Alliteration and assonance appear in each poem, often forming symmetric patterns. She also uses repeated sounds as transitions among stanzas to produce a true welding of sound and sense. Often she repeats entire words or composes paronomastic repetitions. Not surprisingly, her favorite trope is anaphora. Gorbanevskaia also pays special attention to rhymes which are highly assonantal and rarely banal. She likes to use various parts of speech in rhymes that are both rich and deep.

Gorbanevskaia also combines soundplay with similes and metaphors to strengthen her comparisons. In her poetry similes are a rare but varied phenomenon. They are usually not part of her main symbolic system but consistent with it. Sometimes her complex, epic similes generate even more comparisons. Occasionally she uses a simile to introduce a poem, the first stanza of which becomes the tenor of a metaphor realized in the second stanza.

Meter is another important structural device in Gorbanevskaia's poetry. In contrast to most Russian poets, she frequently writes free verse, but many of these free forms are really meters she invents as symmetric patterns of combinations of trochees and iambs. She has written one poem entirely in trochees except for the rhymed words which are all iambs. Almost all meters appear in her poetry from the standard iambic tetrameters and pentameters to trochaic trimeters and even anapaestic hexameters.

Gorbanevskaia is an experimental poet whose formal innovations turn her poems into music. But this is appropriate since she herself tells us in one of her most famous and characteristic works that music is the only consolation in her bleak world:

> There is music, but nothing else —
> neither happiness, nor peace, nor will,
> in all of this dulled, glassy sea of pain
> only music is salvation, so mind it.
>
> Yes, for an hour or an hour and a half,
> when there is neither a tomorrow, nor a yesterday,
> in the midst of winter, mind the flute
> that sings of golden summer like a woodland oriole.

> But an end comes to this brief oblivion,
> the human nestling grows silent,
> and again we walk into the wilderness, the blizzard, the
>   shadows,
> completely barefoot on the broken glass.
>
> A star from the skies or a delightful sonnet,
> nothing will fool you anymore,
> and you utter "Peaceful night,"
> but silently you shout out "there is no Peace."

—Christine A. Rydel

GORBANEVSKAYA, Natalya. *See* **GORBANEVSKAIA, Natalia.**

GOURI, Haim. *See* **GURI, Haim.**

GOYTISOLO, Juan. Spanish. Born in Barcelona, 5 January 1931; brother of the writer Luis Goytisolo (*q.v.*). Educated at the universities of Madrid and Barcelona, 1948–52. Member of Turia literary group, with Ana María Matute (*q.v.*) and others, Barcelona, 1951; emigrated to France, 1957; staff member, Gallimard publishers, Paris, 1958–68; travelled to Cuba, Europe, the Middle East, and Africa; Visiting Professor at universities in the United States. Recipient: Young literature prize, 1953; Indice prize, 1955; Europalia international prize, 1985. Address: c/o Editorial Seix Barral, Córcega 270, 4°, 08008 Barcelona, Spain.

PUBLICATIONS

Fiction

Juegos de manos. Barcelona, Destino, 1954; as *The Young Assassins*, New York, Knopf, 1959; London, MacGibbon and Kee, 1960.
Duelo en el paraíso. Barcelona, Planeta, 1955; as *Children of Chaos*, London, MacGibbon and Kee, 1958.
El circo. Barcelona, Destino, 1957.
La resaca. Paris, Club de Libro Español, 1958.
Fiestas. Buenos Aires, Emecé, 1958; in English, New York, Knopf, 1960; London, MacGibbon and Kee, 1961.
Para vivir aquí. Buenos Aires, Sur, 1960.
La isla. Barcelona, Seix Barral, 1961; as *Island of Women*, New York, Knopf, 1962; as *Sands of Torremolinos*, London, Cape, 1962.

Fin de fiesta: tentativas de interpretación de una historia amorosa. Barcelona, Seix Barral, 1962; as *The Party's Over: Four Attempts to Define a Love Story*, New York, Grove Press, and London, Weidenfeld and Nicolson, 1966.

Señas de identidad. Mexico City, Mortiz, 1966; as *Marks of Identity*, New York, Grove Press, 1969; London, Serpent's Tail, 1988.

Reivindicación del Conde don Julián. Mexico City, Mortiz, 1970; as *Count Julian*, New York, Viking Press, 1974; London, Serpent's Tail, 1989.

Juan sin tierra. Barcelona, Seix Barral, 1975; as *Juan the Landless*, New York, Viking Press, 1977; London, Serpent's Tail, 1990.

Obras completas (fiction). Madrid, Aguilar, 1977.

Makbara. Barcelona, Seix Barral, 1980; in English, New York, Seaver, 1981.

Paisajes después de la batalla. Mexico City, Montesinos, 1982; as *Landscapes After the Battle*, London, Serpent's Tail, and New York, Seaver, 1987.

Las virtudes del pájaro solitario. Barcelona, Seix Barral, 1988; as *The Virtues of the Solitary Bird*, London, Serpent's Tail, 1991.

La cuarentena. Madrid, Mondadori, 1991.

Other

Problemas de la novela. Barcelona, Seix Barral, 1959.

Campos de Níjar. Barcelona, Seix Barral, 1960; as *The Countryside of Nijar*, with *La chanca*, Plainfield, Indiana, Alembic Press, 1987.

La chanca. Paris, Librería Española, 1962; in English, with *The Countryside of Nijar*, Plainfield, Indiana, Alembic Press, 1987.

Las mismas palabras. Barcelona, Seix Barral, 1963.

Pueblo en marcha: instantáneas de un viaje a Cuba. Paris, Librería Española, 1963.

El furgón de cola. Paris, Ruedo Ibérico, 1967.

Disidencias. Barcelona, Seix Barral, 1977.

Libertad, libertad, libertad. Barcelona, Anagrama, 1978.

España y los españoles. Barcelona, Lumen, 1979.

El problema del Sahara. Barcelona, Anagrama, 1979.

Crónicas sarracinas. Madrid, Ruedo Ibérico, 1982.

Coto vedado (autobiography). Barcelona, Seix Barral, 1985; as *Forbidden Territory: The Memoirs of Juan Goytisolo 1931–1956*, San Francisco, North Point Press, and London, Quartet, 1989.

Contracorrientes. Barcelona, Montesinos, 1985.

En los reinos de Taifa (autobiography). Barcelona, Seix Barral, 1986; as *Realms of Strife: The Memoirs of Juan Goytisolo, 1957–1982*, London, Quartet, and San Francisco, North Point Press, 1990.

Space in Motion. New York, Lumen, 1987.

Estambul otomano. Barcelona, Planeta, 1989.

Aproximaciones a Gaudí en Capadocia. Madrid, Mondadori, 1990.

Editor, *Obra inglesa de José María Blanco White.* Buenos Aires, Formentor, 1972.

*

Critical Studies: *Juan Goytisolo* by Kessel Schwartz, New York, Twayne, 1970; *Formalist Elements in the Novels of Juan Goytisolo* by Genaro J. Pérez, Madrid, José Porrúa Turanzas, 1979; *Trilogy of Treason: An Intertextual Study of Juan Goytisolo* by Michael Ugarte, Columbia, University of Missouri Press, 1982; *Juan Goytisolo: The Case for Chaos* by

Abigail Lee Six, New Haven, Connecticut, Yale University Press, 1990.

*   *   *

Juan Goytisolo, who has written short stories, travel books, and several volumes of non-fiction prose, in his early novels concentrates on social realism and a Spain haunted by the civil war, contrasting the world of reality with one of make-believe and lyric force. Through the eyes of children and adolescents he gives us a pessimistic view of the misery in his native land. *Juegos de manos* (*The Young Assassins*) brilliantly analyzes a group of disillusioned, frustrated, and guilt-ridden middle-class adolescents who rebel against a stultifying adult world. Their plan to kill a politician fails, and they immolate the sensitive member who was unable to pull the trigger. *Duelo en el paraíso* (*Children of Chaos*), set during the Spanish Civil War, treats the theme of innocence destroyed in an evil war.

About 1963, disavowing aspects of social realism, Goytisolo adopted many of the formalist and structuralist doctrines, but both his early and later novels involve also criticism of the Catholic Church, capitalism, tourism, and Spanish culture. Throughout he insists on descriptions of bodily secretions and excretions and explicit sexual situations. Most of Goytisolo's protagonists search in vain for a mother figure, and their sense of guilt and frustration gives rise to various oedipal and incestuous fantasies.

In *Señas de identidad* (*Marks of Identity*) Alvaro Mendiola, through recall, dream, and reverie, searches his family past for identity. An outspoken attack on the Franco regime, the novel combines myth with various kinds of stylistic devices to assail a petrified culture and language. In the second volume of the Mendiola trilogy, *Reivindicación del Conde don Julián* (*Count Julian*), Goytisolo, combining free association with temporal dislocations, presents as an alter-ego the modern reincarnation of Spain's betrayer to the Arabs in the 8th century. With hallucinatory intensity, he attacks Spanish orthodoxy in an effort to demolish his country's hypocritical ideas about spiritual and physical purity together with Spain's sacrosanct literary heroes. In the novel, a corruscating collage of incoherent dissolving dream states, Julian, both victim and executioner, cannot fully destroy the language. *Juan sin tierra* (*Juan the Landless*), the third volume, intensifies the literary discourse and intertextuality of the first two novels as the narrator discusses the art of writing the very novel being created. The novel parodies a Spain no longer his, and the protagonist, finally managing to disintegrate language itself, achieves the possibility of freedom. A fantastic, hallucinatory, spatial-temporal travelogue, the novel glorifies sodomy, anal aggression, and the defecatory process. In all of these novels Goytisolo engages in linguistic experimentation, employing non-sentences, associative chains, foreign languages, and first-, second-, and third-person discourse.

Makbara, a defense of the pariahs of the world, explores the relations between a fallen angel and a phallic Moor, *Paisajes después de la batalla* (*Landscapes After the Battle*), a post-structuralist experiment, plays with the concept of literary text and authorship, here involving Lewis Carroll, Juan Goytisolo, and the reader. Closing the decade of the 1980s, *Las virtudes del pájaro solitario* (*The Virtues of the Solitary Bird*) covers a cornucopia of complexities. It deals with the duality of the corporeal and spiritual. Christianity, mysticism, sensuality, St. John of the Cross, and Sufi poetry.

Aside from his works on literary theory and criticism, travel literature, and social and political commentary, Goytisolo, in his two-volume autobiography, *Coto vedado* (*Forbidden Territory*) and *En los reinos de Taifa* (*Realms of Strife*), acknowledges his homosexuality and elucidates his creative process.

Best known for his 12 novels, Goytisolo ultimately writes about personal conflicts, but in the process, as one of the masters of contemporary fiction, he has created magnificent and unusual works of great imagination.

—Kessel Schwartz

GOYTISOLO (Gay), Luis. Spanish. Born in Barcelona, 17 March 1935; brother of the writer Juan Goytisolo (*q.v.*). Studied law at university. Recipient: Sésamo prize, 1956; Biblioteca Breve prize, 1958; City of Barcelona prize, 1977; National Critics' prize, 1981. Address: c/o Editorial Seix Barral, Córcega 270, 4°, 08008 Barcelona, Spain.

PUBLICATIONS

Fiction

Las afueras.   Barcelona, Seix Barral, 1958.
Las mismas palabras.   Barcelona, Seix Barral, 1963.
Antagonía.   Barcelona, Seix Barral, 1981.
   Recuento.   Barcelona, Seix Barral, 1973.
   Los verdes de mayo hasta el mar.   Barcelona, Seix Barral, 1976.
   La cólera de Aquiles.   Barcelona, Seix Barral, 1979.
   Teoría del conocimiento.   Barcelona, Seix Barral, 1981.
Devoraciones.   Barcelona, Anagrama, 1976.
Fábulas.   Barcelona, Bruguera, 1981.
Estela del fuego que se aleja.   Barcelona, Anagrama, 1984.
Investigaciones y conjeturas de Claudio Mendoza.   Barcelona, Anagrama, 1985.
La paradoja del ave migratoria.   Madrid, Alfaguera, 1987.

*

Critical Studies: "Luis Goytisolo's *Recuento*: Towards a Reconciliation of the Word/World Dialectic" by David K. Herzberger, in *Anales de la Novela de Posguerra*, 3, 1978, and "Luis Goytisolo's *Antagonía*: A Portrait of the Artist as a Young Man," by Herzberger and M. Carmen Rodríguez-Margenot, in *Revista Canadiense de Estudios Hispánicos* (Toronto), 13(1), 1988; "The Masks of Eros: Luis Goytisolo's *Antagonía*" by Kathleen M. Vernon, in *Revista de Estudios Hispánicos* (Poughkeepsie, New York), 21(1), 1987; "Luis Goytisolo's *Antagonía* and Radical Change" by Randolph D. Pope, in *Anales de la Literatura Española Contemporánea* (Boulder, Colorado), 13(1–2), 1988.

*   *   *

Luis Goytisolo is widely considered one of the most innovative novelists of post-Civil War Spain. From the late 1950s, when he published his first novel of social realism, to his experimental works of the 1970s and 1980s, Goytisolo has been both a theoretical force in the invention of the contemporary Spanish novel and one of its most imaginative practitioners.

Goytisolo's early writing reflects the predominant view of the spanish novel during the 1950s and 1960s that literature is a form of social and political commitment whose specific intention was to reveal the tragedy of Spain under the Franco dictatorship. Like many other novelists of this time, Goytisolo conceived the novel as a verbal reproduction of external social phenomena. Drawing upon 20th-century metaphor, however, he envisioned the novel less as a mirror held up along the road than as a series of images recorded and projected by the impersonal eye of a camera. Hence the limits of the novel generally coincided with the limits of reality, and the most important fiction during this period portrayed the everyday reality of Spain expressed in conventional novelistic forms. Both of Goytisolo's social realistic novels, *Las mismas palabras* (The Same Words) and *Las afueras* (The Outskirts), are set in present-day Barcelona, and both reveal the decadence of the bourgeoisie and the poverty of lower-class workers. Goytisolo's aim in these works is social revelation: by depicting the hypocrisy and repressive values of the middle class or the degrading poverty of farmers, Goytisolo seeks to project the novel into the very heart of social dissidence during the Franco years.

By the 1970s in Spain the novel of social realism (and its overt social pleading) gives way to a more experimental view of fiction. During this time of novelistic change Goytisolo begins to conceive his masterpiece, the tetralogy *Antagonía*. Following his arrest in 1960 for participating in "anti-government" activities (he was imprisoned for four months but released after intense international pressure), Goytisolo wrote the outline of *Antagonía* and parts of its first novel (*Recuento* [The Retelling]) while in prison. *Antagonía* is a key work in post-war fiction, not only because it articulates a theory of the novel within the frame of metafiction, but also because the individual novels that constitute it represent some of the most complex and demanding fiction written in Spain during the past 50 years.

Goytisolo asserts repeatedly in his tetralogy that both in theory and practice the novel transcends its own esthetics. In contrast to pure metafictionists on the one hand, and to social novelists on the other, he assumes that the writer has something to say, both about the world and about his literary creation. Goytisolo's earlier view of literature as a form of social action now yields to a far more complex system of norms that takes into account the existential functioning of the writer-as-creator as well as the role of language and intrinsic structural patterns in forming a literary world with its self-referring energies. This metafictional focus is clear throughout *Antagonía* and is represented primarily through Raul Ferrer-Gaminde, writer/protagonist of the work and principal agent for expressing Goytisolo's theory. For Raul, *Antagonía* in fact becomes a portrait of the artist as a young man.

In *Recuento* Raul confronts literary tradition (realism) in order to reject it, and he begins to write a novel based upon structuralist and formalist poetics. *Recuento* is a crucial work for Goytisolo because in it he transcends the referential pull of language that shaped his social realistic fiction and begins to explore literary discourse as a complex, self-generating paradigm. In the next two works of the tetralogy he examines fiction from two opposing (but complementary) postures: in *Los verdes de mayo hasta el mar* (The Greens of May unto the Sea) Raul writes a highly self-referential text that commingles his "real" life with the fictional life of his characters. The different levels of reality and fiction play against one another throughout the novel as Raul explores the intimacies between narration and self. In *La cólera de Aquiles* (The Wrath of Achilles) Goytisolo explores the nature of reading through one of the most intriguing characters of postwar fiction, Matilde

Moret (Raul's cousin). Goytisolo sees reading here as a function closely linked to the act of writing: multiple meanings of a text move to the fore through reading, as well as the existential and creative aspect of reader reception that in many ways parallels the process of writing.

The final work of the tetralogy, *Teoría del conocimiento* (Theory of Knowledge), is offered by Goytisolo as Raul's first completed novel. In large part, the work recapitulates many of the ideas asserted in the first three works, but focuses more specifically on the relationship between author, text, and reader in the creation of literary meaning. Goytisolo clearly asserts here both the metafictional and existential base of his work, and in the end offers an intelligent reconciliation between the word as a self-referring sign in literary discourse and the world as necessary referent for both the text and its readers. As one of the three different narrators of Raul's novel notes: "In a work of fiction the final meaning should not be sought in the text, nor in the author, nor in the reader, but in the relationship that ties one to the other, a relationship through which the work gains life, is vivified, at the same that it illuminates both the figure of the author and the reader."

Since the completion of *Antagonía* Goytisolo has continued to explore in his novels the reciprocity between literature and life. The convergence of the two outside of a purely linguistic or a purely existential paradigm creates in his works both a fictionalization of theory and a theory of fictionalization that scrutinizes the literary process at close range. This dual focus gives to Goytisolo's writing a rich configuration of literary ideas and a creative thickness matched by few other novelists of postwar Spain.

—David K. Herzberger

———

GRACQ, Julien. Pseudonym for Louis Poirier. French. Born in Saint-Florent-le-Vieil, 27 July 1910. Educated at the Lycée Clemenceau, Nantes; Lycée Henri IV, Paris; École des Sciences Politiques, diploma 1933; École Normale Supérieure, Paris, agrégation 1934. Served in the French Army, 1939–40: lieutenant; taken prisoner at Dunkerque, repatriated to France 1941. History and geography teacher at Lycées in Nantes, 1937–38, Quimper, 1937–39, and Amiens, 1941–48, and Lycée Claude-Bernard, Paris, 1947–70; Guest Professor of literature, University of Wisconsin, Madison, 1970. Recipient: Goncourt prize, 1951 (refused). Address: 3 rue du Grenier à Sel, 49410 Saint-Florent-le-Vieil, France.

PUBLICATIONS

Fiction

Au Château d'Argol. Paris, Corti, 1938; as *The Castle of Argol*, New York, New Directions, and London, Owen, 1951.
Un Beau ténébreux. Paris, Corti, 1945; as *A Dark Stranger*, New York, New Directions, and London, Owen, 1951.
Le Rivage des Syrtes. Paris, Corti, 1951; as *The Opposing Shore*, New York, Columbia University Press, 1986.
Un Balcon en forêt. Paris, Corti, 1958; as *Balcony in the Forest*, New York, Braziller, 1959; London, Hutchinson, 1960.

La Presqu'île (stories). Paris, Corti, 1970.

Plays

Le Roi pêcheur (produced Paris, 1949). Paris, Corti, 1948.
Penthésilée, translation of the play by Heinrich von Kleist (produced Paris, 1955). Paris, Corti, 1954.

Other

Liberté grande. Paris, Corti, 1946.
André Breton. Paris, Corti, 1948.
La Littérature à l'estomac. Paris, Corti, 1950.
La Terre habitable, with Jacques Hérold. Paris, Corti, 1951.
Prose pour l'étrangère. Paris, Corti, 1952.
Farouche à quatre feuilles, with others. Paris, Grasset, 1954.
Préférences. Paris, Corti, 1961; enlarged edition, 1969.
Lettrines. Paris, Corti, 2 vols., 1967–74.
Les Eaux étroites. Paris, Corti, 1976.
En lisant, en écrivant. Paris, Corti, 1981.
La Forme d'une ville. Paris, Corti, 1985.
Proust considéré comme terminus. Brussels, Complexe, 1986.
Aubrac, photographs by Jacques Dubois. Paris, Nathan, 1987.
Autour des Sept Collines. Paris, Corti, 1988.
Oeuvres complètes. Paris, Gallimard, 1989.

*

Bibliography: *Gracq: Essai de bibliographie 1938–1972* by Peter C. Hoy, London, Grant and Cutler, 1973.

Critical Studies: "Reality and Dream in Julien Gracq: A Stylistic Study" by Annie-Claude Dobbs, in *20th-Century French Fiction*, edited by George Stambolian, New Brunswick, New Jersey, Rutgers University Press, 1975; "A Surrealist Synthesis of History: *Au Château d'Argol*" by Eugenia V. Osgood, in *L'Esprit Créateur* (Lawrence, Kansas), 15, 1975; "The Quest for Happiness and the Grail Myth in Julien Gracq's *Le Rivage des Syrtes* and *Un Balcon en forêt*" by Robert L. Sims, in *Perspective on Contemporary Literature*, 8, 1982; "Metamorphosis in Julien Gracq's *Un Beau ténébreux*," in *Symposium* (Syracuse, New York), Spring 1983, and "The Doubles in Julien Gracq's *Au Château d'Argol*," in *Studies in 20th-Century Literature* (Manhattan, Kansas), Spring 1984, both by Andrée Douchin-Shahin; "Louis Poirier/Julien Gracq: The Surreality of History in *Un Balcon en forêt*," in *French Forum* (Lexington, Kentucky), September 1985, and "Gracq's Fictional Historian: Textuality as History in *Le Rivage des Syrtes*," in *Romanic Review* (New York), March 1989, both by Carol J. Murphy; "Spatial Images of Time in Julien Gracq's *La Presqu'île*" by Anthony Zielonka, in *Romance Quarterly* (Lexington, Kentucky), February 1989.

*   *   *

By temperament an individualist who chose to go his own way, Julien Gracq pursued his personal vision in a relatively small number of works produced at a slow rate over the years from just before World War II. Though he has been chary of identifying himself with any party, group, or movement, critics are unanimous in recognising in him traits which link him with the second generation of the Surrealists. He was a friend of André Breton, on whom he published an important study in 1948. There is further evidence of Gracq's literary affiliations in some of his minor writings. He contributed a preface to an edition of the Comte de Lautréamont's *Les Chants de Maldoror*, and accepted Jean-Louis Barrault's challenging invitation to translate *Penthesilea*, the powerful and erotic tragedy by the German Romantic dramatist Heinrich von Kleist. In *Le Roi pêcheur* of 1948, a play whose Arthurianism has distinct Wagnerian overtones, he reworked the Grail theme in characteristically free and individual fashion. Another significant influence on Gracq was the "magic realism" of Ernst Jünger's fiction, especially *Auf den Marmorklippen* (On the Cliffs of Marble).

Gracq has one play to his credit and wrote prose poems and attractive and trenchant criticism of literature and literary life. But his reputation rests on four novels. Though different in many ways, they share certain distinct similarities. They show small groups of people set apart from the rest of humanity in situations which are mysterious and tense. Placed within an environment that seems to mirror his psychological state, the hero sets out, whether intentionally or not, in search of the meaning of life in ominous circumstances. The theme of the quest is predominant, and the prevailing mood is one of tense anticipation rather than of fulfilment. Forests and restless water are the backcloth to the human emotions as Gracq seeks to convey a poetic intuition of the one-ness of man and the cosmos which transcends rationality. Though sometimes, especially in early works, verging on the Gothic in its symbol-laden descriptions of natural forces, its brooding atmosphere and strange implausibilities, Gracq's fiction recreates myth for the modern reader.

Au Château d'Argol (*The Castle of Argol*), Gracq's first novel, presents the disturbing story of a young man who comes to Brittany and purchases a mysterious château in the depths of the forests where he is visited by his friend Herminien and a beautiful woman. Tensions mount, and there is bloodshed, yet behind the fantastic tale lies the major theme of the search for the ideal. *Un Beau ténébreux* (*A Dark Stranger*) is also set in Brittany, and the hero of the novel, whose Romantic associations are clear even from its title, is a fated man who can find no satisfactions in life and concludes a suicide pact. In *Le Rivage des Syrtes* (*The Opposing Shore*), which won Gracq the Goncourt prize, though he refused to accept it, personal discovery is given an imaginary historical setting. For *Un Balcon en forêt* (*Balcony in the Forest*) Gracq was able to draw on his personal experiences of serving in the French army in 1940. Yet though there is much reflection of actuality, the hero becomes increasingly detached from mundane detail as the novel explores the development of his inner life as rationality is displaced by reverie that seems to open up more valid perspectives.

After *Balcony in the Forest* Gracq turned from the novel proper, and though his later books continue to reflect his customary brilliant handling of language and his particular personality, he has not really added a great deal to an already considerable reputation. *La Presqu'île* (The Peninsula) is a collection of short stories. A fragment from an unfinished novel, "La Route" (The Road) takes up the theme of the quest. "Le Roi Cophuéta" (King Cophuéta), set in the France of 1917, is a moving account of two people whose encounter, we come to realise, reflects aspects of the classic dilemma evoked by the title of the tale. The title story "La Presqu'île" is yet another poignant evocation of human relationships, set, this time, against the background of the coast and countryside of Brittany. *Les Eaux étroites* (Narrow Waters) and *La Forme d'une ville* (The Shape of a City) are quasi-autobiographical works, the first comprising a series of lyric descriptions of the countryside on the banks of the River Eure and the other recalling its author's wanderings in his home town of Nantes

during his adolescence. *Autour des Sept Collines* (Around the Seven Hills) is an account of travels in Italy.

—Christopher Smith

GRASS, Günter (Wilhelm). German. Born in Danzig (now Gdańsk, Poland), 16 October 1927. Educated at Volksschule and Gymnasium, Danzig; trained as stone mason and sculptor; attended Academy of Art, Dusseldorf, 1948–52, and State Academy of Fine Arts, Berlin, 1953–55. Served in World War II: prisoner of war, Marienbad, Czechoslovakia 1945–46. Married 1) Anna Margareta Schwarz in 1954, three sons and one daughter; 2) Ute Grunert in 1979. Worked as farm labourer, miner, apprentice stonecutter, jazz musician; speechwriter for Willy Brandt when Mayor of West Berlin; writer-in-residence, Columbia University, New York, 1966; also artist and illustrator; co-editor, *L*, since 1976, and Verlages L'80 publishing house, since 1980. Member, Gruppe 47. Recipient: Süddeutscher Rundfunk Lyrikpreis, 1955; Gruppe 47 prize, 1958; City of Bremen prize, 1959 (withdrawn); Critics prize (Germany), 1960; Foreign Book prize (France), 1962; Büchner prize, 1965; Fontane prize, 1968; Heuss prize, 1969; Mondello prize (Palermo), 1977; Carl von Ossiersky Medal, 1977; International Literature award, 1978; Viareggio-Versilia prize, 1978; Majkowski Medal, 1978; Vienna literature prize, 1980; Feltrinelli prize, 1982; Leonhard Frank Ring, 1988. Honorary doctorate: Kenyon College, Gambier, Ohio, 1965; Harvard University, Cambridge, Massachusetts, 1976; Adam Mieckiewicz University, Poznań. Member, 1963, and President, 1983–86 (resigned), Academy of Art, Berlin; Member, American Academy of Arts and Sciences. Address: Niedstraße 13, 1000 Berlin 41, Germany.

PUBLICATIONS

Fiction

Danziger Trilogie. Neuwied, Luchterhand, 1980; as *The Danzig Trilogy*, London, Secker and Warburg, and San Diego, Harcourt Brace, 1987.
    Die Blechtrommel. Neuwied, Luchterhand, 1959; as *The Tin Drum*, London, Secker and Warburg, and New York, Random House, 1962.
    Katz und Maus. Neuwied, Luchterhand, 1961; as *Cat and Mouse*, London, Secker and Warburg, and New York, Harcourt Brace, 1963.
    Hundejahre. Neuwied, Luchterhand, 1963; as *Dog Years*, London, Secker and Warburg, and New York, Harcourt Brace, 1965.
Geschichten (as Artur Knoff). Berlin, Literarisches Colloquium Berlin, 1968.
Örtlich betäubt. Neuwied, Luchterhand, 1969; as *Local Anaesthetic*, London, Secker and Warburg, 1969; New York, Harcourt Brace, 1970.
Aus dem Tagebuch einer Schnecke. Neuwied, Luchterhand, 1972; as *From the Diary of a Snail*, New York, Harcourt Brace, 1973; London, Secker and Warburg, 1974.
Der Butt. Neuwied, Luchterhand, 1977; as *The Flounder*, London, Secker and Warburg, and New York, Harcourt Brace, 1978.

Das Treffen in Telgte. Neuwied, Luchterhand, 1979; as *The Meeting at Telgte*, London, Secker and Warburg, and New York, Harcourt Brace, 1981.

Kopfgeburten; oder die Deutschen sterben aus. Neuwied, Luchterhand, 1980; as *Headbirths; or, The Germans Are Dying Out*, London, Secker and Warburg, and New York, Harcourt Brace, 1982.

Die Rättin. Neuwied, Luchterhand, 1986; as *The Rat*, London, Secker and Warburg, and San Diego, Harcourt Brace, 1987.

Tierschutz. Ravensburg, Maier, 1990.

Unkenrufe. Göttingen, Steidl, 1992; as *The Call of the Toad*, London, Secker and Warburg, 1992.

Plays

Hochwasser (produced Frankfurt, 1957). Frankfurt, Suhrkamp, 1963; as *Flood* (produced New York, 1986), in *Four Plays*, 1967.

Onkel, Onkel (produced Cologne, 1958). Berlin, Wagenbach, 1965; in English, in *Four Plays*, 1967.

Noch zehn Minuten bis Buffalo (produced Bochum, 1959). Included in *Theaterspiele*, 1970; as *Only Ten Minutes to Buffalo* (produced Edinburgh, 1969), in *Four Plays*, 1967.

Beritten und zurück (produced Frankfurt, 1959).

Die bösen Köche (produced Berlin, 1961). Included in *Theaterspiele*, 1970; as *The Wicked Cooks* (produced New York, 1967; Birmingham, 1979), in *Four Plays*, 1967.

Goldmäuchen (produced Munich, 1964).

Die Plebejer proben den Aufstand (produced Berlin, 1966). Neuwied, Luchterhand, 1966; as *The Plebeians Rehearse the Uprising* (produced Cambridge, Massachusetts, 1967; Kingston, Rhode Island, and Oxford, 1968; London, 1970), New York, Harcourt Brace, and London, Secker and Warburg, 1966.

Four Plays (includes *Flood*; *Onkel, Onkel*; *Only Ten Minutes to Buffalo*; *The Wicked Cooks*). New York, Harcourt Brace, 1967; London, Secker and Warburg, 1968.

Davor (produced Berlin, 1969). Included in *Theaterspiele*, 1970; as *Max* (as *Uptight*, produced Austin, Texas, 1970), New York, Harcourt Brace, 1972.

Theaterspiele. Neuwied, Luchterhand, 1970.

Die Blechtrommel als Film, with Volker Schlöndorff. Frankfurt, Zweitausendeins, 1979.

Screenplays: *Katz und Maus*, 1967; *Die Blechtrommel*, with Volker Schlöndorff, 1979.

Ballet Scenarios: *Fünf Köche*, 1957; *Stoffreste*, 1959; *Die Vogelscheuchen*, 1970.

Radio Plays: *Zweiunddreißig Zähne*, 1959; *Noch zehn Minuten nach Buffalo*, 1962, *Eine öffentliche Diskussion*, 1963; *Die Plebejer proben den Aufstand*, 1966; *Hochwasser*, 1977.

Verse

Die Vorzüge der Windhühner. Neuwied, Luchterhand, 1956.

Gleisdreieck. Neuwied, Luchterhand, 1960.

Selected Poems, translated by Michael Hamburger and Christopher Middleton. London, Secker and Warburg, and New York, Harcourt Brace, 1966; as *Poems of Günter Grass*, London, Penguin, 1969; as *Selected Poems*, 1980.

März. Neuwied, Luchterhand, 1966.

Ausgefragt. Neuwied, Luchterhand, 1967; as *New Poems*, translated by Michael Hamburger, New York, Harcourt Brace, 1968.

Danach. Neuwied, Luchterhand, 1968.

Die Schweinekopfsülze. Hamburg, Merlin, 1969.

Gesammelte Gedichte. Neuwied, Luchterhand, 1971.

Mariazuehren/Hommageàmarie Inmarypraise. Munich, Bruckmann, 1973; as *Inmarypraise*, translated by Christopher Middleton, New York, Harcourt Brace, 1974.

Liebe geprüft. Bremen, Schünemann, 1974.

Mit Sophie in die Pilze gegangen: Lithographien und Gedichte. Mailand, Upiglio, 1976; revised edition, Göttingen, Steidl, 1987.

In the Egg and Other Poems, translated by Michael Hamburger and Christopher Middleton. New York, Harcourt Brace, 1977; London, Secker and Warburg, 1978.

Kinderlied: Verse and Etchings. Northridge, California, Lord John Press, 1982.

Nachruf auf einen Handschuh: Sieben Radierungen und ein Gedicht. Berlin, Galerie Andre, 1982.

Ach, Butt, dein Märchen geht böse aus. Neuwied, Luchterhand, 1983.

Mädchen, pfeif auf den Prinzen!, with Sarah Kirsch. Cologne, Diederichs, 1984.

Aua, zum Fürchten, mannomann, illustrated by Arik Brauer. Homburg/Saar, Beck, 1985.

Gedichte. Stuttgart, Reclam, 1985.

Die Rättin: 3 Radierungen und 1 Gedicht. Homburg/Saar, Beck, 1985.

Die Gedichte 1955–1986. Neuwied, Luchterhand, 1988.

Tierschutz. Ravensburg, Maier, 1990.

Other

O Susanna: Ein Jazzbilderbuch: Blues, Balladen, Spirituals, Jazz, with H. Geldmacher and H. Wilson. Cologne, Kiepenheuer und Witsch, 1959.

Die Ballerina. Berlin, Friedenauer Presse, 1963.

Rede über das Selbstverständliche. Neuwied, Luchterhand, 1965.

Dich singe ich. Demokratie (pamphlets). Neuwied, Luchterhand, 5 vols., 1965.

Der Fall Axel C. Springer am Beispiel Arnold Zweig. Berlin, Voltaire, 1967.

Briefe über die Grenze: Versuch eines Ost-West-Dialogs, with Pavel Kohout. Hamburg, Wegner, 1968.

Über meinen Lehrer Döblin und andere Vorträge. Berlin, Literarisches Colloquium, 1968.

Über das Selbstverständliche: Reden, Aufsätze, Offene Briefe, Kommentare. Neuwied, Luchterhand, 1968; revised and enlarged edition, as *Über das Selbstverständliche: Politische Schriften*, Munich, Deutscher Taschenbuch, 1969; translated in part as *Speak Out! Speeches, Open Letters, Commentaries*, London, Secker and Warburg, and New York, Harcourt Brace, 1969.

Dokumente zur politischen Wirkung, edited by Heinz Ludwig Arnold and Franz Josef Görtz. Munich, Text und Kritik, 1971.

Der Schriftsteller als Bürger — eine Siebenjahresbilanz. Vienna, Dr.-Karl-Renner-Institut, 1973.

Der Bürger und seine Stimme. Neuwied, Luchterhand, 1974.

Denkzettel: Politische Reden und Aufsätze 1965–76. Neuwied, Luchterhand, 1978.

Aufsätze zur Literatur. Neuwied, Luchterhand, 1980.

Werkverzeichnis der Radierungen (catalogue). Berlin, Galerie Andre, 1980.

Bin ich nun Schreiber oder Zeichner? (exhibition catalogue). Regensburg, Galerie Schürer, 1982.

Vatertag (lithographs). Homburg/Saar, Beck, 1982.

Zeichnen und Schreiben: das bildnerische Werk des Schriftstellers Günter Grass:

  Vol. 1: *Zeichnungen und Texte 1954–1977*. Neuwied, Luchterhand, 1982; as *Drawings and Words 1954–1977*, San Diego, Harcourt Brace, 1983.

  Vol. 2: *Radierungen und Texte, 1972–1982*. Neuwied, Luchterhand, 1984; as *Etchings and Words, 1972–1982*, San Diego, Harcourt Brace, 1985.

Günter Grass: Lithographien: 19. Juni bis 24. Juli 1983 (exhibition catalogue). Ulm, der Kunstverein, 1983.

Die Vernichtung der Menschheit hat begonnen. Hauzenberg, Pongratz, 1983.

Widerstand lernen: Politische Gegenreden, 1980–1983. Neuwied, Luchterhand, 1984.

Geschenkte Freiheit: Rede zum 8. Mai 1945. Berlin, Akademie der Künste, 1985.

On Writing and Politics 1967–1983. London, Secker and Warburg, and San Diego, Harcourt Brace, 1985.

Erfolgreiche Musterreden für den Bürgermeister. Kissing, WEKA, 1986.

In Kupfer, auf Stein. Göttingen, Steidl, 1986.

Werkausgabe in zehn Bänden, edited by Volker Neuhaus. Neuwied, Luchterhand, 10 vols., 1987.

Günter Grass: Radierungen, Lithographien, Zeichnungen, Plastiken, Gedichte (exhibition catalogue). Berlin, Kunstamt Berlin-Tempelhof, 1987.

Es war einmal ein Land: Lyrik und Prosa, Schlagzeug und Perkussion, with Günter "Baby" Sommer. Göttingen, Steidl, 1987.

Zunge Zeigen (travel). Neuwied, Luchterhand, 1988; as *Show Your Tongue*, London, Secker and Warburg, and San Diego, Harcourt Brace, 1989.

Skizzenbuch. Göttingen, Steidl, 1989.

Meine grüne Wiese: Kurzprosa. Zurich, Manesse, 1989.

Wenn wir von Europa sprechen: ein Dialog, with Françoise Giroud. Neuwied, Luchterhand, 1989.

Alptraum und Hoffnung: zwei Reden vor dem Club of Rome, with T. Aitmatow. Göttingen, Steidl, 1989.

Deutscher Lastenausgleich: wider das dumpfe Einheitsgebot: Reden und Gespräche. Neuwied, Luchterhand, 1990; as *Two States — One Nation? The Case Against German Reunification*, London, Secker and Warburg, and San Diego, Harcourt Brace, 1990.

Totes Holz: ein Nachruf. Göttingen, Steidl, 1990.

Ausstellung Günter Grass, Kahlschlag in Unseren Köpfen (1990–1991 Berlin) (exhibition catalogue). Berlin, Kunstamt Reinickendorf, 1990.

Deutschland, einig Vaterland? Ein Streitgespräch, with Rudolph Augstein. Göttingen, Steidl, 1990.

Erfolgreiche Mustergrußworte und Musterbriefe für Bürgermeister und Kommunalpolitiker. Kissing, WEKA, 1990.

Droht der deutsche Einheitstaat? Berlin, Zimmermann, 1990.

Ein Schnäppchen namens DDR: Letzte Reden vorm Glockengeläut. Neuwied, Luchterhand, 1990.

Schreiben nach Auschwitz: Frankfurter Poetik-Vorlesung. Neuwied, Luchterhand, 1990.

Gegen die verstreichende Zeit: Reden, Aufsätze und Gespräche 1989–1991. Neuwied, Luchterhand, 1991.

Vier Jahrzehte: Ein Werkstattbericht. Göttingen, Steidl, 1991.

Editor, with Elisabeth Borchers and Klaus Roehler,

Luchterhands Loseblatt Lyrik: eine Auswahl. Neuwied, Luchterhand, 2 vols., 1983.

*

Bibliography: *Grass: A Bibliography 1955–1975* by P. O'Neill, Toronto, University of Toronto Press, 1976; *Grass in America: The Early Years* edited by Ray Lewis White, Hildesheim, Olms, 1981; in *Erstausgaben deutscher Dichtung*, Stuttgart, Kröner, 1992.

Manuscript Collection: Deutsches Literaturarchiv, Marbach am Neckar.

Critical Studies: "Günter Grass" by Arrigo V. Subiotto, in *German Men of Letters 4*, edited by Brian Keith-Smith, London, Wolff, 1966; *Günter Grass: A Critical Essay* by Norris W. Yates, Grand Rapids, Michigan, Eerdmans, 1967; *Günter Grass* by W. Gordon Cunliffe, New York, Twayne, 1969; *Günter Grass* by Kurt Lothar Tank, New York, Ungar, 1969; *A Günter Grass Symposium* edited by A. Leslie Willson, Austin, University of Texas Press, 1971; *Günter Grass* by Irène Leonard, Edinburgh, Oliver and Boyd, 1974; *A Mythic Journey: Günter Grass's Tin Drum* by Edward Diller, Lexington, University Press of Kentucky, 1974; *Günter Grass* by Keith Miles, London, Vision, 1975; *The "Danzig Trilogy" of Günter Grass* by John Reddick, London, Secker and Warburg, 1975; *The Writer and Society: Studies in the Fiction of Günter Grass and Heinrich Böll* by Charlotte W. Ghurye, Bern, Lang, 1976; *Günter Grass: The Writer in a Pluralist Society* by Michael Hollington, London, Boyars, 1980; *Adventures of a Flounder: Critical Essays on Günter Grass' "Der Butt"*, edited by Gertrude Bauer Pickar, Munich, Fink, 1982; *The Narrative Works of Günter Grass: A Critical Interpretation* by Noel Thomas, Amsterdam, Benjamins, 1982; *The Fisherman and His Wife: Günter Grass's "The Flounder" in Critical Perspective*, edited by Siegfried Mews, New York, AMS Press, 1983; *Günter Grass* by Ronald Hayman, London, Methuen, 1985; *Günter Grass* by Richard H. Lawson, New York, Ungar, 1985; *Grass and Grimmelshausen: Günter Grass's "Das Treffen in Telgte" and Rezeptionstheorie* by Susan C. Anderson, Columbia, South Carolina, Camden House, 1986; *Critical Essays on Günter Grass*, edited by Patrick O'Neill, Boston, Hall, 1987; *Understanding Günter Grass* by Alan Frank Keele, Columbia, University of South Carolina Press, 1988; *Günter Grass's "Der Butt": Sexual Politics and the Male Myth of History*, edited by Philip Brady, Timothy McFarland, and John J. White, Oxford, Clarendon Press, 1990.

*   *   *

Ever since his first literary success with *Die Blechtrommel* (*The Tin Drum*) Günter Grass has been one of the most significant and at times most controversial figures in the field of German literature. Although a truly multi-talented artist, being a gifted poet, graphic designer, etcher, sculptor, and playwright, it is in the field of prose fiction that Grass has made his major impact.

While his first three narrative works — *The Tin Drum* was quickly joined by *Katz und Maus* (*Cat and Mouse*) and *Hundejahre* (*Dog Years*) to form a kind of trilogy — were all thematically concerned with the Nazi and post-war era, and located in his native Danzig (Gdansk) and western Germany after 1945, he later shifted his interests towards "socio-political" topics. Most of his concerns were reflected in his literary work: protests against the East Berlin uprising of 1953 in the play *Die Plebejer proben den Aufstand* (*The Plebeians Rehearse the Uprising*), for instance, and against the Vietnam War in the short story *Örtlich betäubt* (*Local Anaesthetic*). Grass's interpretation of the history of the relationship between men and women from the Stone Age to the age of feminism is captured in *Der Butt* (*The Flounder*). Finally he sums up the fears of a nuclear holocaust and concerns about impending environmental disasters in the doomsday prophecy of *Die Rättin* (*The Rat*).

What caught the interest of the critics, besides his sharp political satire and his fierce anti-Fascism with its merciless accounting of the abominations of the Third Reich, was his unusual narrative style. Grass exemplifies the viability of traditional prose fiction — which had been questioned ever since the turn of the century — by consciously rejecting all formal experiments. At the beginning of *The Tin Drum* when talking about the crisis of the novel in the 20th century and especially about the role of the hero, the narrator says, ". . . you can declare at the very start that it's impossible to write a novel nowadays, but then, behind your own back so to speak, give birth to a whopper . . . that a novel can't have a hero any more because there are no more individualists . . . all men lumped together make up a 'lonely mass' without names and without heroes . . . But as far as I and Bruno my keeper are concerned we are both heroes . . ." However, Grass makes up for this structural "conformity" by expanding an apparent realism through an abundance of fantastic, magic, and surrealistic elements, thus creating his own brand of "magic realism." Virtually all his fiction is rooted in satire and the stylistic elements of his prose comprise the standard repertoire of this mode: exaggeration, parody, irony, sarcasm, the grotesque and, above all, a scurrilous, iconoclastic humour. Perhaps the most remarkable trait of Grass's prose is a digressive style which he generates by employing the associative powers of the language, setting forth the products of the seemingly inexhaustible imagination that has become his trademark. This characteristic makes him part of a rich literary tradition which includes such giants of prose fiction as Lawrence Sterne and Jean Paul.

When Grass made his major public debut with *The Tin Drum* he immediately became controversial; because of the greater sensitivities of the 1950s the public found parts of his novel pornographic and blasphemous. In some instances these allegations were (unsuccessfully) tried in court. While public criticism of this nature quickly subsided with the more liberal thinking of the 1960s and 1970s, it was his political engagement that later raised eyebrows. Like many other Germans of his generation, Grass experienced the totalitarian Nazi state and suffered from it but, unlike many German intellectuals, especially those of the 1920s, he decided that it is not only the right but the duty of the artist to become involved in politics. Thus he is the prototype of the "engaged" writer. Grass is a rationalistic humanist who is aware of the dangers that are constantly threatening a free and decent human existence. While the expressions of these sentiments occupy a central place in his poetry and are everpresent in his fiction, they became most clearly pronounced in his *Aus dem Tagebuch einer Schnecke* (*From the Diary of a Snail*), which is a fictional account of his involvement with Willy Brandt's federal election campaign of 1969, and, more generally, expresses Grass's belief in a slow but steady political progress towards a more humane world. Later his outlook appears to have become much more sceptical, as can be seen in his later novel *The Rat*, where he envisages the ultimate demise of the human race.

Although his active involvement in the federal election campaigns on behalf of the Social Democrats made his sympathy for democratic socialism abundantly clear and found

a certain acceptance, it came as a shock for many that his opposition to the unification of the two German states in 1990 seemed to reveal a latent sympathy for the GDR, a state that few found worth preserving. This attitude isolated him politically from many of his friends of the democratic left, including former chancellor Willy Brandt, who had voiced his unequivocal approval of the unification. Public pronouncements in the years that followed the event have made Grass's attitude a little more understandable. Not only had he apparently hoped, as had many others, that the East German state would eventually evolve into a socialist society "with a human face," but he also feared and still fears that a united Germany, an economic giant of 80 million people, might fall back into her former vices by seeking hegemony in Europe and by threatening her neighbours, especially Poland, for which Grass has a personal affinity. In his view, such a development might give rise to a new German nationalism or fascism.

While his early novels were an unmitigated critical success and have sold hundreds of thousands of copies worldwide, reaction to *The Flounder* was mixed and *The Rat* was to a large degree dismissed as repetitive and boring preaching. His latest novel *Unkenrufe* (*The Call of the Toad*), a love story about an elderly German widower and an elderly Polish widow, set again in Gdansk, was badly received by German critics, but still sold well in Germany.

—Manfred K. Kremer

GREEN, Julien (Hartridge). American. Born Julian Green in Paris, of American parents, 6 September 1900. Educated at the Lycée Janson-de-Sailly, Paris; University of Virginia, Charlottesville, 1919–22; studied drawing at La Grande Chaumière, Paris, 1922–23. Served in the American Field Service, 1917, and the Norton-Harjes Service (later the Red Cross), 1917–18; in the French Army, 1918–19; joined the United States Army, 1942; later with the Office of War Information. Has one son. Freelance writer from 1924. Lectured at Princeton University, New Jersey, Goucher College, Baltimore, Mills College, Oakland, California, and Jesuit College, Baltimore, 1940–42. Recipient: French Academy Paul Flat prize, 1927, and grand prize, 1970; Heinemann prize, 1928; Harper prize, 1929, 1942; Monaco grand prize, 1951; National grand prize for Letters (France), 1966; Ibico Reggino prize, 1968; German Universities prize, 1973; Proust prize, 1974; Polish grand prize, 1988; Italie Cavour grand prize, 1991; Member, Bavarian Academy, 1950, Mainz Academy, 1950, Royal Academy of Belgium, 1951, Académie Française (first foreign member), 1971, American Academy, 1972. Honorary Member, Phi Beta Kappa, 1948. Address: c/o Éditions de la Pléiade, 5 rue Sébastien-Bottin, 75007 Paris, France.

PUBLICATIONS

Fiction

Mont-Cinère. Paris, Plon, 1926; revised edition, 1928, 1984; as *Avarice House*, New York, Harper, 1927; London, Benn, 1928.
Le Voyageur sur la terre (short story). Paris, Gallimard,

1927; as *The Pilgrim on the Earth*, New York, Harper, 1929.

Adrienne Mesurat. Paris, Plon, 1927; as *The Closed Garden*, New York, Harper, and London, Heinemann, 1928; as *Adrienne*, New York, Holmes and Meier, 1990.

La Traversée inutile. Paris, Plon, 1927.

Christine. Abbeville, F. Paillart, 1927; in *Christine and Other Stories*, 1930.

Les Clefs de la mort. Paris, Schiffrin, 1927; as "*The Keys of Death*," in *Christine and Other Stories*, 1930.

Léviathan. Paris, Plon, 1929; as *The Dark Journey*, New York, Harper, and London, Heinemann, 1929.

Le Voyageur sur la terre (collection). Paris, Plon, 1930; as *Christine and Other Stories*, New York, Harper, 1930; London, Heinemann, 1931.

L'Autre Sommeil. Paris, Gallimard, 1931.

Épaves. Paris, Plon, 1932; revised edition, 1978; as *The Strange River*, New York, Harper, 1932; London, Heinemann, 1933.

Le Visionnaire. Paris, Plon, 1934; as *The Dreamer*, New York, Harper, and London, Heinemann, 1934.

Minuit. Paris, Plon, 1936; as *Midnight*, New York, Harper, and London, Heinemann, 1936.

Varouna. Paris, Plon, 1940; revised edition, 1979; as *Then Shall the Dust Return*, New York, Harper, 1941.

Si J'étais vous. Paris, Plon, 1947; revised edition, 1970; as *If I Were You*, New York, Harper, 1949; London, Eyre and Spottiswoode, 1950.

Moïra. Paris, Plon, 1950; in English, New York, Macmillan, and London, Heinemann, 1951.

Le Malfaiteur. Paris, Plon, 1956; revised edition, 1974; as *The Transgressor*, New York, Pantheon, 1957; London, Heinemann, 1958.

Chaque Homme dans sa nuit. Paris, Plon, 1960; as *Each in His Darkness*, New York, Pantheon, and London, Heinemann, 1961; as *Each Man in His Darkness*, London, Quartet, 1990.

L'Autre. Paris, Plon, 1971; as *The Other One*, New York, Harcourt Brace, and London, Collins, 1973.

L'Apprenti psychiâtre (translation by Eric Jourdan of *The Apprentice Psychiatrist*, originally published in *Quarterly Review*, University of Virginia, 1920). Paris, Livre de Poche, 1976.

Le Mauvais Lieu. Paris, Plon, 1977.

Histoires de vertige. Paris, Seuil, 1984.

Les Pays lointains. Paris, Seuil, 1987; as *The Distant Lands*, London, Secker and Warburg, 1990; New York, Boyars, 1991.

Les Étoiles du sud. Paris, Seuil, 1989.

Ralph et la quatrième dimension. Paris, Flammarion, 1991.

Plays

Sud (produced Paris, 1953; opera version, music by Kenton Coe, produced Paris, 1973). Paris, Plon, 1953; as *South* (produced London, 1955), in *Plays of the Year 12*, London, Elek, 1955; London, Boyars, 1991.

L'Ennemi (produced Paris, 1954). Paris, Plon, 1954.

Je est un autre (broadcast 1954). Included in *Oeuvres complètes*, 1973–77.

L'Ombre (produced Paris, 1956). Paris, Plon, 1956.

Léviathan (screenplay). Included in *Les Cahiers du cinéma*, 1962.

Inigo, La Dame de Pique, La Mort d'Ivan Ilytch (screenplays). Included in *Oeuvres complètes*, 1973–77.

Demain n'existe pas; L'Automate. Paris, Seuil, 1985.

Screenplays: *Inigo*, 1947; *Léviathan*, 1962; *La Dame de Pique*, 1965; *La Mort d'Ivan Ilytch*, 1965.

Radio Play: *Je est un autre*, 1954.

Other

Pamphlet contre les Catholiques de France (as Théophile Delaporte). Paris, Revue des Pamphletaires, 1924.

Suite anglaise. Paris, Cahiers de Paris, 1927; revised edition, Paris, Plon, 1972.

Un Puritain Homme de lettres: Nathaniel Hawthorne. Toulouse, Cahiers Libres, 1928.

Journal:

1. *Les Années faciles 1928–1934*. Paris, Plon, 1938; revised edition, as *Les Années faciles 1926–1934*, 1970.
2. *Derniers Beaux Jours 1935–1939*. Paris, Plon, 1939; vols. 1 and 2 as *Personal Record 1928–1939*, New York, Harper, 1939; London, Hamish Hamilton, 1940.
3. *Devant la Porte sombre 1940–1943*. Paris, Plon, 1946.
4. *L'Oeil de l'ouragan 1943–45*. Paris, Plon, 1949.
5. *Le Revenant 1946–1950*. Paris, Plon, 1951.
6. *Le Miroir intérieur 1950–1954*. Paris, Plon, 1955.
7. *Le Bel Aujourd'hui 1955–58*. Paris, Plon, 1958; vols. 1–7 as *Journal: 1928–1958*, 1961; abridged translation as *Diary 1928–1957*, edited by Kurt Wolff, New York, Harcourt Brace, and London, Collins, 1964.
8. *Vers l'Invisible 1958–1967*. Paris, Plon, 1967; vols. 1–8 as *Journal 1928–1966*, 2 vols., 1969.
9. *Ce qui reste de jour 1966–1972*. Paris, Plon, 1972.
10. *La Bouteille à la mer 1972–1976*. Paris, Plon, 1976.
11. *La Terre est si belle 1976–1978*. Paris, Seuil, 1982.
12. *La Lumière du monde 1978–1981*. Paris, Seuil, 1983.
13. *L'Arc-en-ciel 1981–1984*. Paris, Seuil, 1988.
14. *L'Expatrié 1984–1990*. Paris, Seuil, 1990.

Memories of Happy Days. New York, Harper, 1942; London, Dent, 1944.

Quand Nous habitons tous ensemble. New York, Éditions de la Maison Française, 1943.

Gide vivant, with Jean Cocteau. Paris, Amiot Dumont, 1952.

Oeuvres complètes. Paris, Plon, 10 vols., 1954–65.

Jeunes Années (autobiography). Paris, Seuil, 1985.

Partir avant le jour. Paris, Grasset, 1963: revised edition, Paris, Seuil, 1984; as *To Leave Before Dawn*, New York, Harcourt Brace, 1967; London, Owen, 1969.

Mille Chemins ouverts. Paris, Grasset, 1964; revised edition, Paris, Seuil, 1984.

Terre lointaine. Paris, Grasset, 1966; revised edition, Paris, Seuil, 1984.

Jeunesse. Paris, Grasset, 1974; revised edition, Paris, Seuil, 1984.

Qui sommes-nous? Paris, Plon, 1972.

Oeuvres complètes (Pléiade edition), edited by Jacques Petit and Giovanni Lucera. Paris, Gallimard, 6 vols., 1972–90.

Liberté chérie. Paris, Julliard, 1974.

La Nuit des fantômes (for children). Paris, Plon, 1976.

Memories of Evil Days, edited by Jean-Pierre Piriou. Charlottesville, University Press of Virginia, 1976.

Ce qu'il faut d'amour à l'homme. Paris, Plon, 1978.

Dans la gueule du temps (journal 1925–1976). Paris, Plon, 1979.

Une Grande Amitié: correspondance 1926–1972, with Jacques Maritain, edited by Henry Bars and Eric Jourdan. Paris, Plon, 1980; as *The Story of Two Souls: The Correspondence of Jacques Maritain and Julien Green*, Bronx, New York, Fordham University Press, 1988.

Julien Green en liberté (interviews), with Marcel Jullian. Paris, Atelier Marcel Jullian, 1980.

Frère François. Paris, Seuil, 1983; as *God's Fool: The Life and Times of Francis of Assisi*, New York, Harper, 1985; London, Hodder and Stoughton, 1986.

Paris. Paris, Champ Vallon-Seuil, 1983; in English, London, Boyars, and New York, Rizzoli, 1991.

Villes: journal de voyage 1920–1984. Paris, la Différence/Birr, 1985.

Le Langage et son double/The Language and Its Shadow (bilingual edition). Paris, la Différence, 1985.

Diary, 1927–1957. New York, Carroll and Graf, 1985.

Florence. Paris, Autremont, 1987.

Journal du voyageur (selections). Paris, Seuil, 1990.

L'Homme et son ombre. Paris, Seuil, 1991.

Translator, with Anne Green, *Basic Verities: Prose and Poetry*, by Charles Péguy. New York, Pantheon, and London, Kegan Paul, 1943.

Translator, with Anne Green, *Men and Saints*, by Charles Péguy. New York, Pantheon, 1944; London, Kegan Paul, 1947.

Translator, *God Speaks: Religious Poetry*, by Charles Péguy. New York, Pantheon, 1945.

Translator, *The Mystery of the Charity of Joan of Arc*, by Charles Péguy. New York, Pantheon, 1949; London, Hollis and Carter, 1950.

Translator, *Merveilles et démons*, by Edward John Dunsany. Paris, Seuil, 1991.

*

Bibliography: *Julien Green: essai de bibliographie des études en langue française consacrées à Julien Green 1923–1967* by Peter C. Hoy, Paris, Minard, 1970.

Critical Studies: *With Much Love* by Anne Green, New York, Harper, 1948; *Julien Green and the Thorn of Puritanism* by Samuel Stokes, New York, Columbia University Press, 1955; *Hallucination and Death as Motifs of Escape in the Novels by Julien Green* by M. G. Cooke, Washington, D.C., Catholic University of America Press, 1960; *Julien Green* by Glenn S. Burne, New York, Twayne, 1972; *The Exorcism of Sex and Death in Julien Green's Novels* by Nicholas Kostis, The Hague, Mouton, 1973; *The Metamorphoses of the Self: The Mystic, The Sensualist, and the Artist in the Works of Julien Green* by John M. Dunaway, Lexington, University Press of Kentucky, 1978; *Julien Green: Religion and Sensuality* by Anthony H. Newbury, Amsterdam, Rodopi, 1986.

*   *   *

Although Julien Green was born of American parents and has retained his American citizenship, his preferred language has always been French. His published works, with the exception of an early story and two volumes of "memories," have been written in French, and most have been translated into English. The central and unifying theme which runs through Green's writings is his sense of "duality," of a tension between strongly opposing spiritual and sensual impulses. For Green is devoutly religious, having been converted, at age 16, from a puritanical Protestantism to an equally puritanical Catholicism. Obsessed with the idea of purity he was horrified when he experienced strong sexual impulses directed exclusively toward his male schoolmates. For him, the flesh and the senses became the mortal enemy, the Devil incarnate, and he felt that his body was the battleground for a war between Satan — the Impure, the threat of damnation literally believed in — and God, Purity, and Salvation. His novels and plays are partially disguised autobiographies in which he strives to understand and reconcile these painful inner conflicts.

In his early works Green tended to disguise his "emotional bias." The novels *Mont-Cinère* (*Avarice House*), *Adrienne Mesurat* (*The Closed Garden*), and *Léviathan* (*The Dark Journey*) have many female characters whose lives bear little resemblance to Green's, except that they were all victims of powerful emotions, obsessions, tending towards violence, insanity, and suicide. Writing, for Green, was itself an obsession and a necessity, the only means for him to maintain his psychological equilibrium, and he saw it as a means of exorcising the demons of his divided self. And so his plots moved ever closer to autobiography, as in *Épaves* (*The Strange River*), which portrays characters incapable of violent actions — a novel dealing with a man who, in trying to discover his true identity, discovers his own baseness. During the 1930s and 1940s, Green suffered a temporary loss of religious faith, and he sought escape by writing novels of fantasy such as *Le Visionnaire* (*The Dreamer*), *Minuit* (*Midnight*), *Varouna* (*Then Shall the Dust Return*), and *Si J'étais vous* (*If I Were You*). He then returned to the exploration of his emotional bias in the novel *Moïra* and the play *Sud* (*South*), both tragic stories played out against the violence of the American South, and in *Le Malfaiteur* (*The Transgressor*), *Chaque Homme dans sa nuit* (*Each in His Darkness*), and *L'Autre* (*The Other One*).

While some critics have called him a "man of the Middle Ages," an anachronistic solitary obsessed by the temptations of the devil, Green has turned his spiritual-carnal conflicts into powerful and candid psychological studies, sharply focused within the sensibilities of its central figures, rich in vivid imagery with symbolic overtones, and expressed with an intensity which, at times, makes for painful reading. Some scholars believe, however, that Green's journals and autobiographies, which offer fascinating studies of the relations between life and art, will remain the most valuable of his works.

—Glenn S. Burne

———

GREKOVA, I. (Name is a play on words: the Russian *igrek* = mathematical term for unknown "y" from the Latin alphabet.) Pseudonym for Elena Sergeevna Ventsel'. Russian. Born in Reval (Talinn), 21 March 1907. Educated at Moscow University, degree in mathematics 1929; Ph.D. in mathematics 1954. Professor of cybernetics, Moscow Air Force Academy, 1955–67; Professor, Zhukovskii Military Academy, until 1970 (forced to resign). Member, Union of Soviet Writers, since 1967. Address: Leningradskii Prosp. 44, Apt. 29, 125167 Moscow, Russia.

PUBLICATIONS

Fiction

Za prokhodnoi. Published in *Novyi mir* (Moscow), 7, 1962; as *Beyond the Gates*, in *The Young Russians*, New York, Macmillan, 1972.

Damskii master. Published in *Novyi mir* (Moscow), 11, 1963; as *Ladies' Hairdresser*, in *Russian Literature Triquarterly* (Ann Arbor, Michigan), 5, 1973.

Letom v gorode [In Summer in Town].   Published in *Novyi mir* (Moscow), 4, 1965.

Pod fonarem [Under the Streetlight].   Moscow, Sovetskii pisatel', 1966.

Na ispytaniiakh [At the Testing Ground].   Published in *Novyi mir* (Moscow), 7, 1967.

Malen'kii Garusov [Little Garusov].   Published in *Zvezda* (Leningrad), 9, 1970.

Khoziaika gostinitsy.   Published in *Zvezda* (Leningrad), 9, 1976; as *The Hotel Manager*, in *Russian Women: Two Stories*, 1983.

Serezhka u okna [Serezhka by the Window].   Moscow, Detskaia literatura, 1976.

Kafedra [The Department].   Published in *Novyi mir* (Moscow), 9, 1978.

Ania i Mania.   Moscow, Detskaia literatura, 1978.

Vdovii parokhod.   Published in *Novyi mir* (Moscow), 5, 1981; Paris, Institut d'Études Slaves, 1983; as *The Ship of Widows*, London, Virago, 1985.

Russian Women: Two Stories.   New York, Harcourt Brace, 1983.

Porogi [The Rapids].   Published in *Oktiabr'* (Moscow), 10–11, 1984.

Other (as Elena Sergeevna Ventsel')

Teoriia veroiatnostei.   Moscow, Gosudarstvennoe izdatel'-stvo Fiziko-Matematicheskoi literatury, 1958.

Elementy teorii igr.   As *Lectures on Game Theory*, New Delhi, Hindustan, 1961; as *An Introduction to the Theory of Games*, Boston, Heath, 1963; as *Elements of Game Theory*, Moscow, Mir, 1980.

Issledovanie operatsii.   As *Operations Research*, Moscow, Mir, 1983.

Prikladnye zadechi teorii veroiatnostei.   Moscow, Radio i Sviaz, 1983; as *Applied Problems in Probability Theory*, Moscow, Mir, 1986.

Granulometricheskii sostav zagriaznenii kak odin iz Faktorov, opredeliaiushchikh protivoiznosnye svoistva masel [The Granulometric Structure of Pollution as One of the Factors, Showing the Anti-Erosive Features of Oils].   Published in *Trenie i iznos*, 13(4), 1992.

*

Critical Studies: "About I. Grekova's Work" (interview) by Nikolai Nazarov, in *Soviet Literature* (Brooklyn, New York), 4[458], 1986; "Women Without Men in the Writings of Contemporary Soviet Women Writers," in *Russian Literature and Psychoanalysis*, edited by Daniel Rancour-Laferriere, Amsterdam, John Benjamins, 1989, and "Irina [sic] Grekova's *Na Ispytaniiakh*: The History of One Story," in *Slavic Review* (Austin, Texas), 43(3), 1989, both by Adele Barker.

*   *   *

I. Grekova's works frequently reflect the intimate familiarity with both the world of science and that of the university which she possesses thanks to her career as a professor in the field of applied mathematics. Her protagonists are often middle-aged professional women struggling to balance the pressures of their careers with their personal lives. Perhaps more successfully than any writer of her time, she has managed to capture the plight of women old enough to remember the purges and World War II and whose careers span the period from the end of the war through the Brezhnev years. Like many of that generation, her women are usually alone, either through divorce or because of the death of their husbands, and they have been raising children on their own, with few hopes for remarriage. They cope both with the everyday difficulties of life in Russia, where the mere task of buying groceries can take up an inordinate amount of time, and with the special problem of keeping up with their male colleagues, who show little understanding of or sympathy for them.

Damskii master (*Ladies' Hairdresser*), a long story that has often been cited as among her best works, also could be called one of her most typical. The narrator, director of a computer institute, battles with her two sons, just out of their teens, who are as incompetent to assist her at home as her secretary and deputy are to help her at work. While trying to show some concern with her appearance she meets a male hairdresser, the age of her sons, who turns out to be something of a fanatic: his eventual interest in the narrator's secretary is inspired less by love than by the possibilities that her hair offers for testing new coiffures. I. Grekova mines the comic possibilities of the situation with Chekhovian balance — the narrator's foibles are as fair game for her deflating observations as are those of the supporting cast. The story offers a clear display of her gift for creating dialogue and of her unerring ear for the nuances of contemporary Russian speech: each of the figures — the educated but biting narrator, her jocular sons, the other customers at the salon, her obsequious deputy — has a distinct voice. In both technique and theme the story is reminiscent of Iurii Trifonov (1925–81), the modern writer for whom she has expressed the greatest admiration. The first-person narrative subtly conveys the essence of the narrator's lone but successful life at the same time that it provides rich insights into even the most minor characters. Details of everyday life — a lone wilted radish on a refrigerator shelf, a Tchaikovskii violin concerto on the radio — are woven carefully into the fabric of the story and underscore key themes. Also like Trifonov, I. Grekova is ultimately concerned with conveying the malaise of a country where ideology has pervaded and corrupted nearly every corner of people's existence. The narrator's institute is ordered to buy Russian instead of foreign equipment, even though Russian equipment of the type it needs does not exist; the uneducated hairdresser, determined to improve himself, has decided to study dialectical materialism and is reading his way through the collected works of a 19th-century critic.

I. Grekova labels her works as either short stories or novellas, though some of the latter are of sufficient length to qualify as novels. *The Faculty*, one of the longest, resembles *Ladies' Hairdresser* in that the world of computer science again provides the background, but this time the focus shifts to an academic setting. The central figure is once more a woman, Nina Astashova, but here the narrative is more intricate, containing both third- and first-person passages. The issues, too, are more complex: in attempting to uphold the ideals of the former head of the department, whom she deeply admires, Nina Astashova acts with determination and confidence. The work's point, though, is that life does not always offer simple answers, and by the end her assumptions (and the reader's) have been called into question.

It would be wrong to conclude that I. Grekova only writes about the world of science; in *Vdovii parokhod* (*The Ship of Widows*) she tells of five women who share a communal apartment during the years following World War II. One of them has a son, whose personal failings mirror the deep moral decay that has taken hold of Soviet society. Here and in such later works as "Perelom" (Fracture) — where a broken leg leads to a break (or turning point; the Russian title contains both meanings) in the heroine's life — a continuing concern is the elusiveness and the tenuousness of individual happiness.

While the attack on Soviet society in many of her works, as in Trifonov's, is sufficiently subtle that she managed to slip many of her works past the pervasive censorship, such was not always the case. Two stories that could be published only in the late 1980s were originally written much earlier and reveal her willingness to challenge the authorities. In "Masters of Their Lives" (composed in 1960) she describes the tragic fate of those exiled from Leningrad in 1935, just prior to the full onset of the Stalinist purges. "No Smiles" (from 1970) is a more accomplished story, which shows I. Grekova at the height of her powers. It describes an organized, vicious campaign against the female narrator for running foul of the administrators at her institute. The almost jaunty tone of the narrative — characters are referred to not by name, but by characteristics, such as Gnome and Inferno — comes up against the despair of the heroine, who finds comfort in the (actual) writings of a persecuted 19th-century poet. *Na ispytaniakh* (At the Testing Ground), which depicts a Red Army detachment trying out new equipment at a remote site near the end of Stalin's reign, *was* published shortly after it was written, but its daring remarks about Stalinism and the effects that it had on the army led to attacks in the press on I. Grekova, who was forced to resign from her professorship at the Zhukovskii Military Academy. The work was not republished until nearly 20 years later, and then in a moderately censored version; the full text was reprinted only in 1990. Women do play a role in the story, but here the chief characters are two male generals, each of whom embodies an intricate combination of positive and negative qualities. Here and elsewhere, I. Grekova's ability to create deep and compelling portraits of her characters, whether male or female, her eye and ear for the revealing details of everyday life, and her multi-sided portrayal of the personal and professional dilemmas faced by those coping with the legacy of Soviet ideology have established her reputation as a significant figure in the Russian literature of her day.

—Barry P. Scherr

———

GRINBERG, Michel. *See* **VINAVER, Michel.**

———

GROSSMAN, David. Israeli. Born in Jerusalem, in 1954. Recipient: Israel Publishers Association prize, 1985. Address: c/o Hakibuts haMe'uchad Publishing House, P.O. Box 16040, 34 Hayetzirah Street, Tel Aviv 61160, Israel.

PUBLICATIONS

Fiction

Rats [Jogging]. Tel Aviv, Hakibuts haMe'uchad, 1983.
Chiyuch hagediy. Tel Aviv, Hakibuts haMe'uchad, 1983; as *The Smile of the Lamb*, New York, Farrar Straus, 1990; London, Cape, 1991.
Ayen erech: Ahavah. Tel Aviv, Hakibuts haMe'uchad, 1986; as *See Under: Love*, New York, Farrar Straus, 1989; London, Cape, 1990.
Sefer hadikduk hapenimiy [Book of Internal Grammar]. Tel Aviv, Hakibuts haMe'uchad, 1991.

Play

Gan Riki: machazeh bishtey ma'arachot [Riki's Kindergarten]. Tel Aviv, Hakibuts haMe'uchad, 1988.

Other

Itamar metayel al kirot [Itamar Walks on Walls] (for children). Tel Aviv, Am Oved, 1986.
Hazeman hatsahov. Tel Aviv, Hakibuts haMe'uchad, 1987; as *The Yellow Wind*, New York, Farrar Straus, and London, Cape, 1988.
Itamar michtav [Itamar of the Letter] (for children). Tel Aviv, Am Oved, 1988.
Itamar pogesh arnav [Itamar Meets a Rabbit] (for children). Tel Aviv, Am Oved, 1988.
War Diaries. Published in *Cape 1 Magazine* (London), 1991.
Nochechim venifkadim [Present and Absent]. Tel Aviv, Hakibuts haMe'uchad, 1992.

*

Critical Study: in *The Arab in Israeli Literature* by Gila Ramras-Rauch, Bloomington, Indiana University Press, and London, Tauris, 1989.

*   *   *

David Grossman was quickly accepted as one of the most exciting innovators in the Israeli fiction of the 1980s. His first book was a collection of stories, *Rats* (Jogging), written in a plastic prose, adopting the rhythms of thought waves and vernacular in stream-of-consciousness writing. Even at this early stage of his output, the author enters an extreme situation of stress, for example in the title story, where the runner attempts to transcend the limitations of the body in order to continue running. The pace, vocabulary, and syntax match the situation. This use of language has become the hallmark of Grossman's writing. Verbal control, and, in its wake, freedom, is indulged to trace the contours of the imagined mind.

Grossman's writing welds the political with the personal. There are two strands to the work, political (often reportage) and fictional (entering the mind of the character, usually the narrator, often a child). In both the fictional and the journalistic work, the personal situation meets the national, political point of crisis. His first novel, *Chiyuch hagediy* (The Smile of the Lamb), is a fictional representation of life in the West Bank under Israeli occupation. This story is told by the protagonists, Jews and Arabs, governors and governed, where the private lives and conflicts of the characters intersect with the political nexus, creating a tapestry of mixed motives and surprising resolutions. *Hazeman hatsahov* (The Yellow Wind) is the sort of reportage made familiar by Amos Oz (*q.v.*) in *Po vesham beerets Yisrael* (In the Land of Israel), a piece of "straight" reporting, based on interviews and impressions of the material and situation prevailing at that time and place. But whereas Oz deliberately contrived a multi-faceted composite of different views, so as to offer the reader a notion of the complexity of Israeli opinion across the political spectrum, Grossman presents a specific point of view, arguing the case against Israeli military presence and control and in favour of Arab self-determination. Although an earlier work, *The Smile of the*

Lamb can be seen as a fictional equivalent of this reportage, deconstructing the coherent, assured writing set up in the journalistic account, mixing up the motives, casting doubt on certainties and presumptions. The good guy turns out to be ineffective, the bad guy resilient, and all positive thrust questionable. Although it might make for confusion, it does provide one of the touchstones for the difference between fiction and reportage, with the former complex and diverse — in short, representative of the human. Political writing, on the contrary, has to simplify, cohere, and construct a consistent case.

Grossman's later work reinforces this heterodiegetic direction, where stories are told in a multiplicity of modes and voices. The novel *Ayen erech: Ahavah* (*See Under: Love*) is presented not only in four parts by four different voices, but also in four different modes, only tangentially related to each other. The first section, "Momik," establishes the subject, the Holocaust, as reconstructed by the nine-year-old child, through his surviving relative, through the family complex, and through his own imagination. The next three sections are not chronologically sequential but rather parallel and alternative attempts at understanding through fantasy — Bruno Schulz's death now seen as illusory, through the "song of the sea," through the grotesque vision of the relative Anshel Wasserman in Auschwitz, who was unable to die, and, finally, through the encyclopaedic series of definitions of concepts suggested by the novel as a whole. Indubitably experimental, this work enthusiastically challenges traditional narrative standpoint and chronology, so as to offer a full-blooded linguistically exuberant, and imaginatively penetrative account of how reality might be grasped afresh and then conveyed.

One way to see the world anew in Grossman's terms is to enter the child's world. The play *Gan Riki* (Riki's Kindergarten) is set entirely in that kindergarten, where the sole participants are young children, and where there is no mediating adult presence. Thus the world of the child becomes self-authenticating, not seen as subsidiary or as a stage on the way to adulthood.

A further step in this direction is taken by the "novel" *Sefer hadikduk hapenimiy* (Book of Internal Grammar). This fictionalised memoir probes the world of the child through the first-person narrator. The technique of encapsulating and assuming the child view is even more direct than the Momik section of *See Under: Love*. The specific childhood view, with its own tendencies and obsessions, is constantly modified and conditioned by observation and analysis of the adult environment, which inevitably assumes the status of model. In particular this world consists of the meek, not very successful, immigrant father and the dominating, possessive mother. Grossman's love of words affects this world and conjures up a plethora of impressions and reactions, expressing respectful astonishment and eagerness to imbibe and learn.

Nochechim venifkadim (Present and Absent) again moves to the sphere of reportage. While there are clear divisions between the genres, with Grossman's work each genre does impart something of its particular nature to the other. But fiction remains fiction, with its attendant freedom and complexity. Grossman's work, while attaching itself to objective political and national reality, moves freely into the consciousness of the characters in the narrative. It particularly enters the mind of the child, tracing the shape of a child's thought from within, and providing a fresh view of the observed world.

—Leon I. Yudkin

GUÐJÓNSSON, Halldór. *See* **LAXNESS, Halldór.**

GUILLEVIC, Eugène. French. Born in Carnac, Brittany, 5 August 1907. Educated at the Collège d'Altkirch, baccalaureate 1925. Served in the French Army, 1927. Married 1) Alice Munch in 1930, two daughters (one deceased); 2) Lucie Albertini in 1981. Civil servant in Huningen, Bas-Rhin, 1926, and Rocroi and Charleville, 1932–35; worker in ministry of finance, 1935–42, chief of bureau of ministry of national economy, 1942–47, member of cabinet of ministry of reconstruction, 1945–47, and inspector of the national economy for ministry of finance, 1947–63. Member of directing committees of Comité National des Écrivains, and Comité de l'Union des Écrivains; member of French commission for Unesco, 1976–79; member of administration council of Centre National des Lettres, 1978; vice president, Conseil Permanent des Écrivains, 1979; president, l'Académie Mallarmé; member of the council, l'Ordre des Arts et des Lettres, since 1986. Recipient: Nice Book Fair Golden Eagle, 1973; Brittany prize, 1976; l'Academic Française grand prize for poetry, 1976; Couronne d'Or des Soirées Poétiques de Struga (Macedonia), 1976; Medal of Hungarian Republic; Ministry of Culture poetry prize, 1984. Commandeur de la Légion d'Honneur, 1950; Chevalier du Mérite Agricole, c.1960, de l'Économie Nationale, c.1960, and de l'Ordre Hongrois du Drapeau. Address: 47 rue Claude Bernard, 75005 Paris, France.

PUBLICATIONS

Verse

Requiem.   N.p., Tschann, 1938.
Terraqué.   Paris, Gallimard, 1942.
Ensemble.   Paris, Debresse, 1942.
Amulettes.   Paris, Seghers, 1946.
Élégies.   N.p., Pont de Jour, 1946; in English, translated by Maurice O'Meara, Carbondale, Southern Illinois University Press, and London, Feffer and Simons, 1976.
Fractures.   Paris, Minuit, 1947.
Éxécutoire.   Paris, Gallimard, 1947.
Coordonnées.   Geneva, Trois Collines, 1948.
L'Homme qui se ferme.   N.p., Réclame, 1949.
Gagner.   Paris, Gallimard, 1949; revised edition, 1981.
Les Chansons d'Antonin Blond.   Paris, Seghers, 1949.
Les Murs.   N.p., Éditions du Livre, 1950.
Envie de vivre.   Paris, Seghers, 1951.
Le Goût de la paix.   N.p., Au Colporteur, 1951.
Terre à bonheur.   Paris, Seghers, 1951.
31 Sonnets.   Paris, Gallimard, 1954.
L'Âge mûr.   N.p., Cercle d'Art, 1955.
Carnac.   Paris, Gallimard, 1961.
Sphère.   Paris, Gallimard, 1963.
Avec.   Paris, Gallimard, 1966.
Euclidiennes.   Paris, Gallimard, 1967; part as *Six Euclidians*, translated by Teo Savory, Santa Barbara, California, Unicorn Press, 1968; complete as *Euclidians*, translated by Savory, 1975.
Guillevic: A Selection, edited and translated by Teo Savory. Santa Barbara, California, Unicorn Press, 1968.

Selected Poems, translated by Denise Levertov.   New York, New Directions, 1969.
Ville.   Paris, Gallimard, 1969.
Temple du merle.   Paris, Galanis, 1969.
De la prairie.   Paris, Petithory, 1970.
Paroi.   Paris, Gallimard, 1970.
Choses.   Veilhes, Le Bouquet, 1970.
Encoches.   Paris, Français Réunis, 1970.
De l'hiver.   Paris, Galanis, 1971.
Dialogues.   Luxembourg, Origine, 1972.
L'Homme qui se ferme = The Man Closing Up (bilingual edition), translated by Donald Justice.   Iowa City, Stone Wall Press, 1973.
Inclus.   Paris, Gallimard, 1973.
Racines.   Paris, Blanchet, 1973.
Hippo et Hippa.   Paris, Hachette, 1973.
Cymbalum.   Paris, Le Vent d'Arles, 1973.
Supposer.   Asnières, Commune Mesure, 1974.
L'Hubier de la Bretagne.   Paris, Tchou-Laffont, 1974.
Selected Poems, edited and translated by Teo Savory.   London, Penguin, 1974.
Médor. Tudor.   Paris, Farandole, 1975.
La Danse des korrigans.   Paris, Farandole, 1976.
Du Domaine.   Paris, Gallimard, 1977.
Magnificat.   N.p., Carmen Martinez, 1977(?).
Conjugaison.   Asnières, Commune Mesure, 1978.
L'Étier: poèmes, 1965–1975.   Paris, Gallimard, 1979.
Suppose.   N.p., Marc Pessin, 1979.
L'Abeille.   Montreal, Estérel, 1979.
Fifre.   Paris, Maeght, 1980.
Babiolettes.   Paris, Saint-Germain-des-Prés, 1980.
Autres: poèmes, 1969–1979.   Paris, Gallimard, 1980.
Vivre en poésie.   Paris, Stock, 1980.
Harpes.   Paris, Galanis, 1980.
Mammifères.   Paris, Arfuyen, 1981.
Trouées: poèmes 1973–1980.   Paris, Gallimard, 1981.
Blason de chambre.   Paris, Presses d'Aujourd'hui, 1982.
Autrefois.   Rouen, L'Instant Perpétuel, 1983.
Requis: poèmes 1977–1982.   Paris, Gallimard, 1983.
Nuit.   Paris, Le Soufflet Vert, 1983.
Existe un tirage de tête sur chiffon.   Rouen, L'Instant Perpétuel, 1984.
Terre à bonheur.   Paris, Seghers, 1985.
Lexiquer.   Paris, La Tuilerie Tropicale, 1986.
La Plaine.   Draguignan, Lettres de Casse, 1986.
Timbres.   Trois Rivières, Quebec, Écrits des Forges, 1986.
Motifs: poèmes 1981–1984.   Paris, Gallimard, 1987.
Pétrée.   Paris, Créaphis, 1987.
Qui.   Rouen, L'Instant Perpétuel, 1987.
Creusement: poèmes 1977–1986.   Paris, Gallimard, 1987.
Agrestes.   Trois-Rivières, Quebec, Écrits des Forges, 1988.
L'Hôpital.   Paris, Arfuyen, 1988.
Limaille.   N.p., ILM, 1989.
Art poétique.   Paris, Gallimard, 1989.
Le Chant.   Paris, Gallimard, 1990.
Impacts.   Paris, Deyrolle, 1990.

Other

L'Enfant, la poésie (for children).   Paris, Saint-Germain-des-Prés, 1980.
Guillevic: vivre en poésie (interview), with Lucie Albertini and Alain Vircondelet.   Paris, Stock, 1980.
Fabliettes (for children).   Paris, Gallimard, 1981.
Choses parlées: entretiens (interviews; includes some verse), with Raymond Jean.   Seyssel, Champ Vallon, 1982.
Itou et Vicomte (for children).   Paris, Bordas, 1988.

Le Souris sans logis (for children).   Paris, Bordas, 1988.

Editor and Translator, *Tarass Chevtchenko*, by Maxime Rilsky and Alexandre Deitch.   Paris, Seghers, 1964.
Editor and Translator, *Mihai Beniuc*.   Paris, Seghers, 1966.
Editor, *Mes Poètes hongrois*.   Budapest, Corvina, 1967.
Editor, with László Gara, *Endre Ady*.   Paris, Seghers, 1967.
Editor and Translator, *Virages*, by Nina Cassian.   Bucharest, Eminescu, 1978.

Translator, *Contrefables*, by György Somlyó.   Paris, Gallimard, 1973.
Translator, *15 Poèmes*, by Georg Trakl.   Paris, Obsidiane, 1981.

*

Critical Study: "An Introduction to Guillevic" by Teo Savory, in *Books Abroad* (Norman, Oklahoma), 45, 1971.

*   *   *

Eugène Guillevic is a Breton poet of small, sinewy gestures and an arresting, concise manner. Rare in his generation, he was untouched by the surrealist revolution and preferred Charles Baudelaire and the symbolists whom he read avidly as a young man. He also admired Paul Claudel and especially the spare simplicities and directness of Paul Éluard, his immediate inspiration. Soon after arriving in Paris in 1935, he met Jean Follain, who introduced him into literary circles. His first poems appeared in a slim volume, *Requiem*, and the July 1941 issue of the *Nouvelle Revue Française*. In 1939, he met Marcel Arland, a reader for Gallimard publishers, who facilitated the publication of his first collection, *Terraqué*, in 1942. It was admired by readers as different as Drieu de la Rochelle and members of the "École de Rochefort," who printed a number of his poems. He also contributed to the magazine *Poètes* and, under the pseudonym "Serpières", was included in Eluard's clandestine anthology, *Honneur aux poètes*.

From the start, he was temperamentally resistant to the grandiloquence and extravagances of the surrealists whom he regarded as having "scholasticised" Rimbaud. To automatic writing, fantasy, and the obsession with dreams, he preferred to look inside himself with the tools of "intelligence, reason, critical sense and culture." From the start, his poetic vision was rooted in the concrete world of objects which loom menacingly and threaten his precarious place in the natural and social order. Things are solid, impenetrable and dumb in their hostile indifference. A chair, a room "as cold as a carp," or an open cupboard, are self-sufficient and stand in fearsome contrast to the uncertainties of the human condition. There is no commonality between things and man for whom death figures constantly on a none-too-distant horizon. Objects are opaque, unyielding, a source of fear, and Guillevic set himself the task not of demythologising them but of piercing their physical mystery and of finding a route to the elusive relationship between order and disorder, continuity and discontinuity, entropy and negentropy. All language is "foreign" but only through language can the world be made palpable: "Les mots,/C'est pour savoir" (Words are for knowing) (*Exécutoire* [Writ of Execution]).

Guillevic's acute sense of the gap between human impermanence and vulnerability on the one hand, and the density of the material world on the other, an idea clearly articulated in *Terraqué* (with its title suggestive of solid "land" and treacherous "water"), struck an immediate response in occupied France. His manner, stark, resistant to the common sonorities and bereft of adjectives (which dilute) and images (which mislead), marked Guillevic as an exciting new voice. After the war, his resilience was expressed in a warmer compassion for the collective dreams of mankind: "Nous avons à dire,/Nous avons à gagner" (We have things to say,/We have things to gain) (*Gagner* [Gaining]).

By the early 1950s, Guillevic saw the way ahead in communism — he had joined the Party during the war — and his new faith turned him, paradoxically, towards the "truly rhythmic, truly rhymed" forms which, as an exponent of free verse, he had consciously rejected. He broke his always tenuous links with the École de Rochefort in 1954 and his *31 Sonnets* were prefaced by Louis Aragon who described his new manner, approvingly, as "the liquidation of formal individualism in poetry." Guillevic later described his didactic work of the 1950s as "regressive," and it was not until 1961 with the admirably controlled *Carnac* and *Sphère* in 1963 that he resumed his clear-eyed, anguished but undaunted questioning of the material world.

For Guillevic, poetry is not escape but a foray, an exploration, a voyage of discovery, and the road to his goal lies in the lapidary, exact notation of reality and its subjection by language. From the start he mistrusted metaphor which encourages false transpositions of the concrete to the human: one object may be like another but can never be another. In his pared-down verse, Things are placed in proximity to the human, and from them a relationship slowly emerges, a vivifying link which repositions man within a "domain" of much-needed reassurance. If one image may be used to express his overall goal and mood, it is the contrast, implicit in *Terraqué*, central to *Carnac*, and powerful still in *L'Étier* (The Salt Channel) of 1979, between the Breton sea, dangerous and unpredictable, and its graduation to semi-liquid salt marshes and ultimately to firm ground dominated by the menhirs and dolmens which have outlasted the ravages of time and proclaim — at last — a certainty. Guillevic's material world is made of essences — water, plants, geometric figures, birds, metals, stones, towns, cities — and to its silences he gives a voice. In a sense, his materialism was never more than a route to apprehensions of the inner life of things, a means of allowing objects and men to say what they know of man and to reunite him with the "sacred," eternal forces of existence. To achieve this is what he means by "vivre en poésie" ("living through poetry"), a consistent effort to put human nature in touch with its deep self by reference to the impermeability of the external world. He has regretted the tight rein he has kept on emotion, though readers of his most successful collections, *Sphère*, *Avec* (With), *Ville* (Town), or *Trouées* (Breaches), admire his lucid lyricism and the tenacity with which he works constantly towards the "kernel" of things (a rare metaphor). At his best he is a poet of spare forms, almost haiku-like (though he prefers the word "quantas") in their tumescent concision. Guillevic, "Un souffle/Qui essaie de durer" (A human breath/Which strives to endure, from *Art poétique*), reassures the doubting individual that he too has a place in the scheme of things.

—David Coward

———

GURI, Haim. Also Haim Gouri. Israeli. Born in Tel Aviv, 9 October 1923 (some sources say 1921). Served in the Palmach and the Israeli Army, 1941–49; organised Jewish youth movements, recruited immigrants, and trained commando and paratroopers in Hungary, Austria, and Czechoslovakia, 1947. Educated at Hebrew University, Jerusalem, B.A. in Hebrew and French literature and philosophy 1952; the Sorbonne, Paris. Married Aliza Becker in 1952; three children. Columnist, *LeMerchav* newspaper, 1954–70, and *Davar*, from 1970; headed an army brigade in Jerusalem, 1967; army education officer, Sinai, 1973. Former member, Israeli Film Censorship Board. Recipient: Ussishkin prize, 1961; Sokolov prize, 1962; Bialik prize, 1975; Akum prize, 1979; Walenrode prize; Israel prize, 1987. Address: c/o Hakibuts haMe'uchad Publishing House, P.O. Box 16040, 34 Hayetzirah Street, Tel Aviv 61160, Israel.

PUBLICATIONS

Verse

Pirchey esh [Flowers of Fire].   Tel Aviv, Sifriyat Po'alim, 1949.
Ad alot hashachar [Till Dawn Rises] (includes prose).   Tel Aviv, Hakibuts haMe'uchad, 1950.
Shirei chotam [Seal Poems].   Tel Aviv, Hakibuts haMe'uchad, 1954.
Shoshanat haruchot [Rose of the Winds].   Tel Aviv, Hakibuts haMe'uchad, 1960.
Tenu'ah lemag'a [Movement to Contact].   Tel Aviv, Hakibuts haMe'uchad, 1968.
Mar'ot Geychazi [Visions of Gehazi].   Tel Aviv, Hakibuts haMe'uchad, 1974.
Dapim mimachazor nesher [Pages from the Cycle of the Eagle].   Tel Aviv, Hakibuts haMe'uchad, 1974.
Ad kav nesher, 1949–1975 [To the Eagle Line].   Tel Aviv, Hakibuts haMe'uchad, 1975.
Mivchar shirim [Selected Poems].   Tel Aviv, Hakibuts haMe'uchad, 1975.
Ayumah [Terrible].   Tel Aviv, Hakibuts haMe'uchad, 1979.
Ve'od rotzeh otah [And Still He Wants Her].   Tel Aviv, Hakibuts haMe'uchad, 1987.
Machbarot elul [Notebooks of Elul].   Tel Aviv, Hakibuts haMe'uchad, 1988.
Cheshbon over: mivchar shirim 1945–1987.   Tel Aviv, Hakibuts haMe'uchad, 1988.

Fiction

Iskat hashokolad.   Tel Aviv, Hakibuts haMe'uchad, 1965; as *The Chocolate Deal*, New York, Holt, 1968.
Hasefer hameshug'a [The Crazy Book].   Tel Aviv, Am Oved, 1971.
Mi makir et Yosef G.? [Who Knows Joseph G.?].   Tel Aviv, Hakibuts haMe'uchad, 1980.
Hachakirah: sipur Re'uel [The Interrogation: Reuel's Story].   Tel Aviv, Am Oved, 1981.

Other

Mul ta hazechuchit [Facing the Glass Cell].   Tel Aviv, Hakibuts haMe'uchad, 1963.
Dapim Yerushalmiyim [Jerusalem Years].   Tel Aviv, Hakibuts haMe'uchad, 1968.
Mishpachat haPalmach: yalkut alilot vezemer [The Family of the Palmach: A Collection of Songs and Deeds], with Chayim Chefer.   Jerusalem, Keter, 1976.

Has translated French plays, songs, and stories into modern Hebrew.

*

Critical Studies: in *The Modern Hebrew Poem Itself*, edited by Stanley Burnshaw, T. Carmi, and Ezra Spicehandler, New York, Holt Rinehart, 1965, revised edition, Cambridge, Massachusetts, Harvard University Press, 1989; "Property of a Non-Believer: The Poetic Visions of Hayim Guri" by Dov Vardi, in *Modern Hebrew Literature* (Ramat-Gan, Israel), 2, 1975.

*   *   *

Haim Guri was born in what was to become the State of Israel, and accompanied the emergence of the State as an active fighter and member of the Palmach élite corps. He also, more than any other poet, exemplified the new Israeli poetry, committed to the new reality and reflecting the parochial concern of the fighter and comrade, as well as the brute force and savagery of war.

His first volume of poems, *Pirchey esh* (Flowers of Fire), sets the tone for his work. The subjects are romantic and tragic; the ingredients are the romantic tryst, the couple, the night, the landscape, the music. All is enveloped in mist, yet the moon is clearly visible. Time passes in the course of the poem, and the couple awaits the dawn. The poem ends with the statement/request: "Let us stop a while. Approach on your toes and let us kiss suddenly." Although the lines vary in length, a regular rhyme scheme is deployed (this is not always the case in Guri's poetry) — abaacadefee — and sound patterns recur. The assonance invoked by the scene reinforces the slow and heavy beat.

Guri's poetry is always conscious of the potential of the disjunction. Wherever there is joy, another factor makes its presence felt. Wherever there is light, there passes the shadow: "Between me and the light crosses the mist." This again is the voice of the man addressing the woman, and yearning for fulfillment in love.

But Guri's subjects are not exhausted in the immediate and the personal. The time and setting of the poet's early work are the War of Israeli Independence, and some of these early poems are dirges on the fate of fallen comrades. For these the pace of the line slows even further: "Bring blessing to the lads, as time has come./See them silent and ready, with eyes aflame." Perhaps more than any other aspect of his work Guri is remembered for his role as the memorialist of that dreadful war. In one of his most famous poems, he speaks from the point of view of the dead, thus associating intimately with them. In a poem built of anapests, he, the dead, addresses the witness: "See, look, our corpses lined up in one long file, so long./We will not love, nor pluck chords of sounds low and sweet." The themes of love and music here return, after which he invokes a possible resurrection: "We shall then flower, when shriek of the last shot is silenced." Although Guri writes like the traditional romantic poet in this war situation, he is also concerned to quash any possible notion of glory. There can be no such thing when stray bullets hit beloved comrades in arms. This dead soldier acts as witness to those events for other times and places. That time has, paradoxically, become eternal.

The theme of the war is indeed carried far beyond the war itself. Guri also uses prose to convey his message further. The slim volume *Ad alot hashachar* (Till Dawn Rises) is a multi-generic exercise in prose and verse. The theme of the dead in life and the live in death, adapted from an older contemporary,

Natan Alterman, is strengthened and continued. In one of the poems, the dead soldier addresses his beloved Anat, and asserts that at night no borders separate them. The imagery is traditionally religious: "I am crossing with the winds, as is my wont, unseen,/To every forgotten mound of dust, to the abandoned and lonely/Amongst the paths leading to the mount of God./My spirit is held in their chains, and my frame aspires thence,/As to a private sanctuary, my own, abandoned by God and man . . ."

Guri's later work constantly refers back to these foundation experiences, with their own concatenation of associated images. For some his work is nostalgic, stuck in a groove cut during the War of Independence. Certainly Guri's poetry is very different from the stark, paradoxical imagism of Yehuda Amichai (*q.v.*) as well from the modernist and minimalist anti-heroism of Nathan Zach (*q.v.*). In a later volume, *Shoshanat haruchot* (Rose of the Winds), the poet has acquired some modernist trappings (e.g., the use of colours to concretize moods), but he still says in his very personal way: "I think that I am guarding the walls of a city/Which has died long ago./Lights illuminating me now/Are bequests of light extinguished years gone by." The poet sees himself as bearing the message of another time and another place, out of the current context.

Guri is a tragic poet, bearing the implacable message of an unavoidable fate. Like so many other Israeli authors, he also relates to the *aqedah* theme of the binding of Isaac. In *Shoshanat haruchot* he speculates on the people's lot in relating once more the famous story of Abraham and Isaac. Isaac, indeed, was saved, but the conclusion is not quite so simple: "But that moment he passed on to his descendants ./They are born/With knife in heart." A sad lesson is implied, that the Jews have not selected a path, but rather inherited a mission full of pain (the knife, in Hebrew *maakhelet*, the word used in the biblical story for the sacrificial knife taken by Abraham).

In both his poetry and in his idiosyncratic prose, Guri remains the messenger from another place and time. In his later writing, he indeed deploys the image of Odysseus, that great hero who went out to the wars, but who was hardly recognised on his return. Again and again in his work, Guri attempts to invoke and recreate the images of that proto-Israeli past, a time when the young were sacrificed so that the Jewish State might emerge.

—Leon I. Yudkin

———

GUSTAFSSON, Lars (Erik Einar). Swedish. Born in Västerås, 17 May 1936. Educated at the University of Uppsala, filosophie licentiat 1961, Ph.D. 1978. Married 1) Madeleine Lagerberg in 1962; 2) Dena Alexandra Chasnoff in 1982; two sons and two daughters. Co-editor, 1961–65, and editor-in-chief, 1966–72, *Bonniers Litterära Magasin* [Bonniers Literary Magazine], Stockholm; editor, *Expressen* [Expression], 1961–80; freelance writer, from 1972; Thord Gray Professor, 1974, visiting writer, 1979, and since 1983 Adjunct Professor, University of Texas, Austin; research fellow, Bielefeld Institute of Advanced Studies, 1980–81. Vice president, Chasnoff Contacts Systems Inc., Texas, 1985–87; chair, Brindfors Intressenter, since 1988. Recipient: Veillon prize; Heinrich Steffen prize; Övralids prize; Bellman prize. Officier de l'Ordre des Arts et des Lettres (France), 1986; Commander, Bundesverdientszeichens, 1988; member, Academy of the Arts, Berlin. Address: 2312 Tower Drive, Austin, Texas 78203, U.S.A.; or Akademie der Künste, Hanseatenweg 10, 1000 Berlin 21, Germany.

PUBLICATIONS

Fiction

Poeten Brumbergs sista dagar och död: en romantisk berättelse [The Last Days and Death of the Poet Brumberg: A Romantic Story]. Stockholm, Norstedt, 1959.
Bröderna: en allegorisk berättelse [The Brothers: An Allegorical Story]. Stockholm, Norstedt, 1960.
Följeslagarna: en äventyrsberättelse [The Travel Company: An Adventure Story]. Stockholm, Norstedt, 1962.
Den egentliga berättelsen om Herr Arenander [The Essential Story of Mr. Arenander]. Stockholm, Norstedt, 1966.
Förberedelser till flykt och andra berättelser [Preparations for Flight and Other Tales]. Stockholm, Bonnier, 1967.
Sprickorna i muren [Cracks in the Wall].
  1. *Herr Gustafsson själv* [Mr. Gustafsson Himself]. Stockholm, Bonnier, 1971.
  2. *Yllet* [Wool]. Stockholm, Bonnier, 1973.
  3. *Familjefesten* [Family Reunion]. Stockholm, Bonnier, 1975.
  4. *Sigismund: ur en polsk barockfurstes minnen.* Stockholm, Norstedt, 1976; as *Sigismund*, New York, New Directions, 1985.
  5. *En biodlares död.* Stockholm, Norstedt, 1978; as *The Death of a Beekeeper*, New York, New Directions, 1981; London, Collins Harvill, 1990.
Sommar berättelser: sex svenska noveller [Summer Stories: Six Swedish Novellas]. Stockholm, Sveriges Radio, 1973.
Tennisspelarna. Stockholm, Norstedt, 1977; as *The Tennis Players*, New York, New Directions, 1983.
Den lilla världen: om märkvärdigheter uti manniskorna [The Small World]. Stockholm, Alba, 1977.
Berättelser om lyckliga människor. Stockholm, Norstedt, 1981; as *Stories of Happy People*, New York, New Directions, 1986.
Sorgemusik för frimurare. Stockholm, Norstedt, 1983; as *Funeral Music for Freemasons*, translated by Yvonne L. Sandström, New York, New Directions, 1987.
Bernard Foys tredje rockad. Stockholm, Norstedt, 1986; as *Bernard Foy's Third Castling*, New York, New Directions, 1988.
Samlade berättelser [Collected Stories]. Stockholm, Norstedt, 1987.
Det sällsamma djuret från norr och andra science fiction-berättelser [The Strange Animal from the North and Other Science-Fiction Stories]. Stockholm, Norstedt, 1989.

Verse

Ballongfararna [The Balloonists]. Stockholm, Norstedt, 1962.
En förmiddag i Sverige [A Morning in Sweden]. Stockholm, Norstedt, 1963.
En resa till jordens medelpunkt och andra dikter [A Journey to the Centre of the Earth and other Poems]. Stockholm, Norstedt, 1966.
En privatmans dikter [The Poems of a Private Man]. Stockholm, PAN/Norstedt, 1967.

Bröderna Wright uppsöker Kitty Hawk och andra dikter [The Wright Brothers in Search of Kitty Hawk and Other Poems]. Stockholm, Norstedt, 1968.
Dikter [Poems]. Stockholm, Gidlund & Svartengren Trykeri, 1968.
Kärleksförklaring till en sefardisk dam [Declaration of Love to a Sephardic Lady]. Stockholm, Bonnier, 1970.
Selected Poems, translated by Robin Fulton. New York, New Rivers Press, 1972.
Varma rum och kalla. Stockholm, Bonnier, 1972; as *Warm Rooms and Cold*, translated by Yvonne Sandström, Providence, Rhode Island, Copper Beech Press, 1975.
Fosterlandet under jorden [The Native Country Under the Earth]. Stockholm, Bonnier, 1973.
Sonetter [Sonnets]. Stockholm, Norstedt, 1977.
Artesiska brunnar cartesianska drömmar: tjugotvå lärodikter [Artesian Wells Cartesian Dreams]. Stockholm, Norstedt, 1980.
Ur bild i bild: samlade dikter 1950–1980 [Out of the Picture, in the Picture: Collected Poems 1950–1980]. Stockholm, Norstedt, 1982.
Världens tystnad före Bach [The Stillness of the World Before Bach]. Stockholm, Norstedt, 1982.
Fåglarna, och andra dikter [Birds, and Other Poems]. Stockholm, Norstedt, 1984.
The Stillness of the World Before Bach: New Selected Poems, edited by Christopher Middleton. New York, New Directions, 1988.
Den skapande impulsen [The Creative Impulse]. Stockholm, Brindfors, 1989.
Förberedelser för vintersäsongen: elegier och andra dikter [Preparations for the Winter Season: Elegies and Other Poems]. Stockholm, Natur och Kultur, 1990.

Plays

Två maktspel: Tebjudningen som inte ville ta slut; Den nattliga hyllningen [Two Plays on Power: The Tea Party That Did Not Want to End; Celebration at Night] (second play first produced Zurich, 1970). Stockholm, Bonnier, 1970.

Radio Play: *Huset i Oneida* [The House in Oneida], 1973.

Television Play: *Den nattliga hyllningen* [The Evening Tribute], 1971.

Other

Virtus politica: politisk etik och nationellt svärmeri i den tidigare stormaktstidens litteratur [Political Ethics and National Obsessions in the Literature of Previous Periods of Great Power]. Uppsala and Stockholm, Almqvist & Wiksell, 1956.
Järfällaboken [The Järfälla Book]. Järfälla, Järfälla kommunalfullmäktige, 1957.
Vägvila: ett mysteriespel på prosa [A Stop on the Way: A Mysterious Play on Prose]. Uppsala, Siesta, 1957.
Nio brev om romanen [Nine Letters on the Art of the Novel], with Lars Bäckström. Stockholm, Norstedt, 1961.
Predominant Topics of Modern Swedish Debate. Stockholm, Swedish Institute, 1961.
The Public Dialogue in Sweden: Current Issues of Social, Aesthetic, and Moral Debate. Stockholm, Norstedt, 1964.
Konsten att segla med drakar, och andra scener ur privatlivet [The Art of Sailing with Kites, and Other Scenes from Private Life]. Stockholm, Norstedt, 1969.

Utopier, och andra essäer om dikt och liv [Utopias and Other Lectures on Literature and Life]. Stockholm, PAN/Norstedt, 1969.

Kommentarer [Comments]. Stockholm, Gidlund, 1972.

Den onödiga samtiden [The Unnecessary Contemporary World], with Jan Myrdal. Stockholm, PAN/Norstedt, 1974.

Solidaritet med Tjeckoslovakiens folk [Solidarity with the Czechoslovakian People], with Jan Myrdal. Stockholm, Oktober, 1975.

Världsdelar: Reseskildringar [Continents: Travels]. Stockholm, Norstedt, 1975.

Strandhugg in svensk poesi: femton diktanalyser. Stockholm, FIB:s Lyrikklubb/Tiden, 1976; as *Forays into Swedish Poetry*, Austin, University of Texas Press, 1978.

Språk och lögn: en essä om språkfilosofisk extremism in nittonde århundradet [Language and Lies: An Essay on Extremism in the Philosophy of Language in the 19th Century]. Stockholm, Norstedt, 1978.

Kinesisk höst [Chinese Autumn]. Stockholm, Norstedt, 1978.

Filosofier: essäer [Philosophies: Essays]. Stockholm, Norstedt, 1979.

Konfrontationer: stycken om konst, litteratur och politik [Confrontations: Pieces on Art, Literature, and Politics]. Stockholm, PAN/Norstedt, 1979.

I mikroskopet: banaliteter och brottstycken [Under the Microscope: Banalities and Fragments]. Stockholm, Norstedt, 1979.

Afrikanskt försök: en essä om villkoren [African Attempt]. Stockholm, Norstedt, 1980.

För liberalismen: en stridsskrift [For Liberalism: A Controversial Essay]. Stockholm, Norstedt, 1981.

Litteraturhistorikern Schück: vetenskapssyn och historieuppfattning i Henrik Schücks tidigare produktion [The Literary Historian Schück]. Stockholm, Almqvist & Wiksell, 1983.

Sprickorna i muren [Cracks in the Wall]. Stockholm, Norstedt, 1984.

Stunder vid ett trädgårdsbord: stycken om konst och litteratur [Moments at a Garden Table: Pieces on Art and Literature]. Stockholm, Alba, 1984.

Bilderna på Solstadens murar: essäer om ont och gott [Pictures on Solstaden's Walls: Essays of Good and Evil]. Stockholm, Norstedt, 1985.

Frihet och frukten: 22 brev [Freedom and Fear: 22 Letters], with Per Ahlmark. Stockholm, Bonnier, 1985.

Estetik i förvandling: estetik och litteraturhistoria i Uppsala från P.D.A. Atterbom till B.E. Malmström [Aesthetics in Transformation]. Stockholm, Almsqvist & Wiksell, 1986.

Spegelskärvor [Fragments of a Mirror]. Stockholm, Norstedt, 1987.

Editor, with Hans Ylander, *Segla: tretton berättelser om segling i dikt och verklighet* [13 Stories About Sailing in Fiction and Reality]. Stockholm, Norstedt, 1963.

Editor, *Ur mitt inre: eller, Mellan mark och sky* [From My Inner Life: Or, Between Ground and Sky], by Ingemar Willgert. Stockholm, Bonnier, 1964.

Editor, with Daniel Hjorth, *Ny svensk berättarkonst* [New Swedish Prose]. Stockholm, Bonnier, 1966.

Editor, *Svensk dikt: från trollformler till Björn Håkanson: en antologi* [Swedish Poetry: From Magic Formulae to Björn Håkanson: An Anthology]. Stockholm, Wahlström & Widstrand, 1968; revised edition, 1980.

Editor, with Torkel Rasmusson, *Dikterna från 60-talet* [The Poems of the Sixties]. Stockholm, Bonnier, 1970.

Editor, *Forskningsfält och metoder inom litteraturvetenskapen* [The Field of Research and Methods Within Literature]. Stockholm, Wahlström & Widstrand, 1970.

Editor, with Eva Waller, *Delat ansvar: en antologi om människan och miljön* [Shared Responsibility: An Anthology on People and the Environment]. Stockholm, Rabén & Sjögren, 1971.

Editor, *Fransk poesi 1910–1970* [French Poetry 1910–1970]. Stockholm, FIB:s Lyrikklubb, 1974.

Editor, with Wolf Lepenies, *Nemesis divina*, by Carl von Linné. Munich, Hanser, 1981.

Editor, *Frihet och fruktan* [Freedom and Fear], by Per Ahlmark. Stockholm, Bonnier, 1985.

Editor, *Fyra poeter: Gustaf Adolf Fredenlund, Bernard Foy, Ehrmine Wikström, Jan Bohman* [Four Poets]. Stockholm, Norstedt, 1988.

Translator, *Sonetterna till Orfeus* [Sonnets to Orpheus], by Rainer Maria Rilke. Stockholm, Norstedt, 1987.

*

Critical Studies: "Lars Gustafsson: *The Public Dialogue in Sweden: Current Issues of Social, Aesthetic, and Moral Debate*" by Evert Sprinchorn, in *Scandinavica* (Norwich), 4(1), 1965; "The Machine Theme in Some Poems by Lars Gustafsson" by Yvonne Sandström, in *Scandinavian Studies* (Madison, Wisconsin), 44(2), 1972; "The Public Lie, the Truth of Fiction, and *Herr Gustafsson Himself*" by Peter Hertz-Ohmes, in *Pacific Coast Philology* (Portland, Oregon), 17, 1982.

* * *

In an early article, "Richthofen's Problem (1969)," Lars Gustafsson poses a metapoetic dilemma: how can one tell from internal evidence alone whether a protracted confessional narration is a novel or an autobiography? Like Kurt Gödel's metamathematical theorem regarding the consistency and completeness of arithmetic, a decision can only be made by transcending the system. In his doctoral dissertation, *Språk och lögn* (Language and Lies), Gustafsson addresses a similar dilemma, the distinction between what August Strindberg called "the public lie," a state-generated grammar of power, and the elusive truth of fiction, the construction of sometimes fantastic, sometimes reality-simulating alternative possibilities.

On this theoretical basis Gustafsson develops his numerous novels, stories, essays, and poems. His point of departure is a selected social institution (especially aspects of Sweden's hegemonic social engineering) which constitutes a personal hell. An ambitious series of five novels with a strong autobiographical element begins with *Herr Gustafsson själv* (Mr. Gustafsson Himself) and ends with *En biodlares död* (*The Death of a Beekeeper*). Each work is built around a narrator named Lars, all of whom have the same birthday: 17 May 1936. Whether author, school teacher, state environmental inspector, traveling journalist, or beekeeper, each Lars confronts his own perception of personal failure. As the beekeeper remarks, the personality of the hive revolves around expendable and replaceable insects. How then is the insect to assert his own worth over that of the hive?

Using Dante as his model, Gustafsson's protagonists seek a Virgil or a Beatrice to lead them to what he again and again calls "cracks in the wall," a phrase that also designates the novel cycle as a whole. The cracks offer their only hope to pass outside the given system long enough to reconceptualize it, even if, from within, these same cracks signify loss of stature, sanity, or life itself for the individual pilgrim. "We'll try once more, we won't give up" becomes each one's rallying cry in an oppressively ordinary environment where unheroic yet deliberate self-sacrifice becomes the reflexive response to being victimized by a self-perpetuating utopian bureaucracy.

In *Herr Gustafsson själv* the author's somber alter ego maintains a 1960s mentality regarding the pre-established harmony that supposedly links concrete experiences with statements about them. Since language cannot be private if it is communicative, it must follow that an experience also loses its immediacy when translated into speech. This Wittgensteinian hang-up would seem to force all investigation of one's past and present, one's memories and one's daydreams, into the clutches of a monolithic political machinery, exemplified by the way we are herded through airports and school systems, careers and responsibilities. But a chance meeting with a female philosophy instructor brings about the realization that pre-established harmony is more convention than necessity and that many other individuals in his world — student demonstrators in Paris, Cornell, or Berkeley; activists in Palestine or Prague — are also (and more successfully than he) seeking new options for the exercise of personal freedom.

These philosophical ruminations larded with anecdotal reminiscence continue in *Yllet* (Wool), which features an unsuccessful suicide by Lars Herdin, a self-styled outsider, and turn into deeds when Lars Troäng in *Familjefesten* (Family Reunion) makes public a government cover-up on the premise that his attitude will cost him his official position no matter what he does. Troäng's Virgil is a teenage girl he meets at recurrent reunions, with whom he has an out-of-the-ordinary affair. *Sigismund* reminds us that our personal recollections and reconstructions are Quixotic fictions (and sometimes science fiction!) which nevertheless can have a positive effect on others, while *The Death of a Beekeeper* contrasts the closed eternity of the political welfare state with the salutary human need for each person to face death on his own terms as a hope for new beginnings.

Such a new beginning is evident in *Tennisspelarna* (*The Tennis Players*), in which Gustafsson's now self-consciously chummy professorial persona brings Swedish literature to exotic Texas. There he strains the brain of a U.S. government early-warning system computer programmed to compare Strindberg's paranoic *inferno* with a Polish conspiracy diary one of his students claims to have found in the chemistry library. The Gödel-numbered, tennis-textured experiment with alternative accounts and their relative fictionality (i.e., truth) signals, in the foreign environment of Austin, a more playful mien in Gustafsson himself.

This attitude carries over to *Bernard Foys tredje rockad* (*Bernard Foy's Third Castling*), "detective story and reconstruction of *Les Fleurs du mal* by Charles Baudelaire." The novel bears comparison with Umberto Eco's (*q.v.*) *Foucault's Pendulum* (1988) as a tour-de-force of gamesmanship, seriocomic invention, and subversive Popular Culture. The multileveled story itself, distributed among three narrators all named Foy, hasn't the least idea who is telling it; its "satanic" undertone of nonconformism allows the blooming of disparate episodes that in their metamorphoses undermine the reader's assumption of an overriding authorial or genre-based logic. In this novel, as well as in a recent collection of poems, *Världens tystnad före Bach*, (*The Stillness of the World Before Bach*), Gustafsson has moved his emphasis away from the solution of life's problems to the enjoyment of each lived experience as a unique "nodal point." As illustrated in the poem "The Old Tree," the nodal point, out of its singular reality, produces all of its surrounding effects, however illusory. In this regard, the

singularity is not unlike a flame, a momentary illumination in an otherwise uniform darkness.

—Peter Hertz-Ohmes

GYĀNRAÑJAN. Indian; son of litterateur and freedom-fighter Ramnath Suman. Born in Akola, Maharashtra, in 1936. Educated at the University of Allahabad. Lecturer; editor, *Pahal* literary magazine. Address: c/o Parimal Prakashan, Parimal Building, Khadkeshwar, Aurangabad 431001, India.

PUBLICATIONS

Fiction

Fence ke idhar aur udhar [On Either Side of the Fence].   New Delhi, Aksar, 1961.
Yātrā [The Journey].   Allahabad, Racnā, 1966.
Kṣaṇjīvī [Transient Being].   Hapur, Sambhāvnā, 1977.
Sapnā nahī̃ [It's Not a Dream].   Allahabad, Racnā, 1977.
Merī priy kahāniyā̃.   New Delhi, Rājpāl & Sons, 1979.
Pratinidhi kahāniyā̃.   New Delhi, Rājkamal, 1984.

Other

Editor, with Varmā and Svayamprakāśa, *Hindī pragatiśīl kahāniyā̃* [Hindi Progressive Stories]. New Delhi, Rādhākṛṣṇa, 1986.
Editor, with Kamlāprasād, *Nāmvar Singh, vyakti aur ālocak* [Namvar Singh, the Person and the Critic]. Allahabad, Parimal, 1988.

*

Critical Study: "Uncivil Lines: Themes of Discord in the Hindi Short Stories of Gyānrañjan" by Rupert Snell, in *International Journal of Indian Studies*, 1, 1992.

*   *   *

Gyānrañjan came into prominence, primarily as a short story writer, in the middle of the 1960s. This period saw the decline of the *naī kahānī* (the new story) movement. The intellectual vacuum left by its demise was filled by existentialist views of life and notions of alienation. Gyānrañjan's writing shows traces of such influences, but he was able to rise above their superficial manifestations. Among the 1960s generation of writers, Gyānrañjan was foremost in breathing new life into the Hindi short story. His first collection of short stories *Fence ke idhar aur udhar* (On Either Side of the Fence) was followed by *Yātrā* (The Journey) and *Kṣaṇjīvī* (Transient Being). The stories of these three collections have been compiled in a single volume *Sapnā nahī̃* (It's Not a Dream), and also under other titles. The recent history of the Hindi short story has rarely seen a writer earn himself so much literary recognition and accolade by writing so little (25 short stories altogether). Gyānrañjan secures himself such a distinguished place, among other reasons, for the force and quality of analysis of his subject-matter, which he draws from the north Indian Hindu middle classes experiencing a transition in values under the pressure of industrialisation and urbanisation from the 1960s onwards. This analysis is not straight-faced, but laced with barbed humour, a distinguishing feature of his writing.

More than any other writers of his generation, Gyānrañjan is known for his stories of human relationships: the relationship between one individual and another or between family members, the latter being the territory on which he established his reputation. The story "Pitā" (Father) is about the torment of grown-up sons who are exasperated with their father's conservatism. The father, out of a false sense of prestige, shuns and belittles their modernising outlook and styles of life, their economic prosperity and the modern conveniences (such as a shower and wash basin) they have installed in the house. Made to feel insignificant and pitiable, they can neither ignore nor feel at ease with his existence. The differences in the outlook of two generations and the predilection of the second generation for a modern view of life also form the theme of "Amrūd kā per" (The Guava Tree); anger at the superstitious and emotional world of the old is seen as desirable because "it refines life." But where modernism is unassimilated and strikes a note of disharmony, as in "Dilcaspī" (Fascination), it is derided. The changed outlook of the central character in "Sambandh" (Relationships) fills him with terror at the thought of facing his mother: "You see what havoc time plays on human relationships. The woman who has been my mother for a long time now seldom feels like a mother, or an illusion of the mother." Time has also played havoc on the joint family in "Śeṣ hote hue" (Coming to an End), in which the relations between various family members have atrophied. "Several households have sprung up in the same house. On a small scale, the tendency to organise one's affairs oneself is secretly at work." Attenuation of human relationships at a neighbourly level, and the contrast between traditional and urban values, is the subject of "Fens ke idhar aur udhar." The traditional family is baffled and appalled by the self-contained and uninhibited world of their neighbours. When the girl next door, on being married in an unconventional manner, leaves her parental home without crying her eyes out, the father of the narrator observes: "The old times are passing and human heart has become a machine, a machine." The mechanisation of the human heart has also produced a profit-and-loss view of love as illustrated in "Khalnayikā aur bārūd ke phūl" (The Villainess and Fireworks). In this way, Gyānrañjan's short stories not only question the prevailing values but also the new values which are forming, as in "Ghaṇṭā" (Penis), "Bahirgaman" (Exodus), and "Anubhav" (Experience), which, instead of being stories about relationships, are commentaries on the new emerging national culture.

The bulk of Gyānrañjan's short stories are written as first-person narrations. The narrator, from whom the author manages to keep his distance, has his own characteristics: he is self-conscious and self-critical; he is ruminative by nature and has a wry sense of humour; he keeps his cool in highly emotionally charged situations and never ceases to be an objective reporter (e.g., in "Sambandh"); he evaluates and comments on what he observes (e.g., in "Yātrā": "I sometimes imagine vileness in my actions, but to see baseness in actions aimed at preserving human existence does not appear to me to be appropriate"). These characteristics of the narrator give a distinctive flavour to Gyānrañjan's short stories. Above all, he uses powerful language, characterised by a complex accuracy of descriptions. In this example, a can of macaroni is a valuable acquisition in the eyes of the narrator of "Ek namūnā sārthak din" (An Exemplary Successful Day):

On the way, he bought in the high street a can of macaroni, which was probably the only one the shopkeeper had. He felt a slight rage why this thing was available there. If the shopkeeper had said "sorry," he would have felt victorious. In between the can being taken down and his throwing the ten rupee note on the counter with nonchalance, he kept glancing around the shop with a casual disdain, which in fact carried a great deal of hidden interest. He also kept searching whether on being asked for a can of macaroni the shop keeper was startled by him or not.

—A. S. Kalsi

H

HAAVIKKO, Paavo (Juhani). Has also written as Anders Lieksman. Finnish. Born in Helsinki, 25 January 1931. Educated at the University of Helsinki, 1951. Served in the Finnish Army, 1951–52: sergeant. Married 1) Marja-Liisa Vartio Sairanen in 1955 (died 1966), one daughter and one son; 2) Ritva Rainio Hanhineva in 1971. Worked in real estate, 1951–67; literary director, 1967–83, and member of the board of directors, 1968–84, Otava publishing company, Helsinki. Since 1983 director Arthouse publishing group, Helsinki. Member of board, Finnish Writers' Association, 1962–66; member, State Committee for Literature, 1966–67, board of Great Finnish Book Club, 1969, Yhtyneet Kuvalehdet magazine company, 1969–82, and Kalevala Society, from 1976. Recipient: State Literary prize, from 1959 (eight times); Aleksis Kivi Foundation prize, 1966; Pro Finlandia Medal, 1967; State Drama prize, 1969; Knight First Class of the White Rose of Finland, 1978; Neustadt prize, 1984. Honorary doctorate: University of Helsinki, 1969. Address: c/o Arthouse Group, Bulevardi 19C, 00120 Helsinki, Finland.

PUBLICATIONS

Verse

Tiet etäisyyksiin [Roads to Far Away]. Helsinki, Soderström, 1951.
Tuuliöinä [On Windy Nights]. Helsinki, Otava, 1953.
Synnyinmaa [Land of Birth]. Helsinki, Otava, 1955.
Lehdet lehtiä [Leaves, Leaves]. Helsinki, Otava, 1958.
Talvipalatsi. Helsinki, Otava, 1959; as *Winter Palace*, translated by Anselm Hollo, published in *Chelsea* (New York), 1961.
Runot, 1951–1961 [Poems, 1951–1961]. Helsinki, Otava, 1962.
Puut, kaikki heidän vihreytensä [The Trees, All Their Green]. Helsinki, Otava, 1966.
Selected Poems, edited and translated by Anselm Hollo. London, Cape Goliard Press, and New York, Grossman, 1968; revised edition, Manchester, Carcanet, 1991.
Neljätoista hallitsijaa [14 Rulers]. Helsinki, Otava, 1970.
Runoja matkalta salmen ylitse [Poems from a Voyage Across the Sound]. Helsinki, Otava, 1973.
Selected Poems of Paavo Haavikko and Tomas Tranströmer, translated by Anselm Hollo. London, Penguin, 1974.
Kaksikymmentä ja yksi [21]. Helsinki, Otava, 1974.
Runot 1949–1974 [Poems 1949–1974]. Helsinki, Otava, 1975.
Runoelmat [Longer Poems]. Helsinki, Otava, 1975.
Toukokuu, ikuinen [May, Eternal]. Helsinki, Arthouse, 1975.
Kullervon tarina = Kullervo's Story (bilingual edition). Helsinki, Arthouse, 1975.
Viiniä, kirjoitusta [Wine, Writing]. Helsinki, Otava, 1976.
Sillat: valitut runot [Bridges: Selected Poems]. Helsinki, Otava, 1984.

Viisi sarjaa nopeasti virtaavasta elämästä [Five Sequences from Fast-Flowing Life]. Helsinki, Arthouse, 1987.
Rakkaudesta ja kuolemasta [Of Love and Death]. Helsinki, Arthouse, 1989.
Talvirunot [Winter Poems]. Helsinki, Arthouse, 1990.
Runot! runoja [Poems! Poems]. Helsinki, Söderström, 1992.

Fiction

Yksityisiä asioita [Private Affairs]. Helsinki, Otava, 1960.
Toinen taivas ja maa [Another Heaven and Earth]. Helsinki, Otava, 1961.
Vuodet [Years]. Helsinki, Otava, 1962.
Lasi Claudius Civiliksen salaliittolaisten pöydällä [A Glass on the Table of The Conspirators of Claudius Civilis]. Helsinki, Otava, 1964.
Barr-niminen mies [A Man Named Barr] (as Anders Lieksman). Helsinki, Otava, 1976.
Romaanit ja novellit [Novels and Short Stories]. Helsinki, Otava, 1981.
Fleurin konlusyksy [Fleur's Autumn Term]. Helsinki, Arthouse, 1993.

Plays

Münchhausen (produced Helsinki, 1958). With *Nuket*, Hel-sinki, Otava, 1960.
Nuket [The Dolls] (produced Helsinki, 1960). With *Münchhausen*, Helsinki, Otava, 1960.
Agricola ja kettu [Agricola and the Fox] (produced Helsinki, 1968). Included in *Ylilääkäri*, 1968.
Ylilääkäri (television play). Helsinki, Otava, 1968; as *The Superintendent*, in *Modern Nordic Plays*, Oslo, Universitetsforlaget, 1973.
Audun ja jaakarhu [Audun and the Polar Bear] (radio play). Published in *Kahden vuoden aanet*, Helsinki, Otava, 1969.
Brotteruksen perhe [The Brotterus Family] (produced Helsinki, 1969).
Kilpikonna [The Turtle] (radio play). Published in *Aanet myohassa*, Helsinki, Otava, 1970.
Sulka [The Feather] (produced Helsinki, 1973). Privately printed, 1973.
Ratsumies/The Horseman (libretto; bilingual edition), music by Aulis Sallinen (produced Savonlinna, 1975). Privately printed, 1974.
Kuningas lähtee Ranskaan (radio play). Helsinki, Otava, 1974; as *The King Goes Forth to France*, Sevenoaks, Kent, Novello, 1984; opera version, music by Aulis Sallinen (produced Savonlinna, 1984).
Harald Pitkäikäinen [Harald the Long-Lived] (radio play) Helsinki, Otava, 1974.
Ne vahvimmat miehet ei ehjiksi jaa [The Strongest Men Don't Remain Unscathed] (produced Helsinki, 1976). Included in *Näytelmät*, 1978.
Kaisa ja Otto [Kaisa and Otto] (produced Helsinki 1977). Included in *Näytelmät*, 1978.

Kuningas Harald, jaahyvaiset [King Harald's Farewell] (radio play).   Included in *Näytelmät*, 1978.
Soitannollinen ilta Viipurissa 1918 [Soirée in Viipuri 1918] (radio play).   Helsinki, Otava, 1978.
Näytelmät [Plays] (includes *Münchhausen*; *Ylilääkäri*; *Agricola ja kettu*; *Audun ja jaakarhu*; *Kilpikonna*; *Sulka*; *Ratsumies*; *Kuningas lähtee Ranskaan*; *Ne vahvimmat miehet ei ehjiksi jaa*; *Kaisa ja Otto*; *Harald Pitkäikäinen*; *Kuningas Harald, jaahyvaiset*).   Helsinki, Otava, 1978.
Viisi pientä draamallista tekstiä (includes *Kuninkaat, veljekset*; *Naismetsa*; *Herra Ostanskog*; *Viinin karsimykset Venajalla*; *Tilintarkarkastus viini-yhtiossa*) [Five Small Dramatic Pieces: Kings, Brothers; Woman's Forest; Mr. Ostanskog; The Afflictions of Wine in Russia; Audit in the Wine Company].   Helsinki, Otava, 1981.
Rauta-aika [Iron Age] (television play).   Helsinki, Otava, 1982.

Radio Plays: *Lyhytaikaiset lainat* [Short-Term Loans], 1966; *Audun ja jaakarhu* [Audun and the Polar Bear], 1966; *Freijan pelto* [Freya's Field], 1967; *Kilpikonna* [The Turtle], 1968; *Harald Pitkäikäinen* [Harald the Long-Lived], 1974, in English (UK), 1977; *Gottlundin yksi matka länteen ja toinen itään* [Gottlund's Long Voyage West and Another East], 1975; *Kuningas lähtee Ranskaan* [The King Goes Forth to France], 1975; *Kuningas Haraldin pitkä reissu* [King Harald's Long Trip], 1975; *Kertomus siitä miten kuningas Harald käsitteli eräitä hankalia kysymyksiä* [The Story of How King Harald Dealt with Some Tough Problems], 1976; *Kuningas Harald, jaahyvaiset* [King Harald's Farewell], 1976; *Soitannollinen ilta Viipurissa 1918* [Soiree in Viipuri 1918], 1978; *Kuninkaat, veljekset* [Kings, Brothers], 1979; *Herra Ostanskog* [Mr. Ostanskog], 1981; *Viinin karsimykset Venajalla* [The Afflictions of Wine in Russia], 1981; *Tosi kertomus siitä mitä tapahtui kun kuningas Harald näki unta* [The True Story of What Happened When King Harald Dreamed], 1983.

Television Plays: *Ylilääkäri* [The Superintendent], 1966; *Rauta-aika* [Iron Age], 1982.

Other

Puhua, vastata, opettaa [Speak, Answer, Teach].   Helsinki, Otava, 1972; enlarged edition, 1973.
Kansakunnan linja: kommentteja erään tuntemattoman kansan tuntemattomaan historiaan 1904–1975 [The National Line].   Helsinki, Otava, 1977.
Ihmisen aani [The Human Voice].   Helsinki, Söderström, 1977.
Ikuisen rauhan aika [Eternal Peacetime].   Helsinki, Otava, 1981.
Kullervon tarina: moniääninen monologi.   Helsinki, Otava, 1982.
Vuosisadan merikirja: EFFOAn sata ensimmäistä vuotta 1883–1983 [Sea Book of the Century]   Helsinki, EFFOA, 1983.
Wärtsilä 1843–1984 [The Wärtsilä Corporation 1834–1984].   Helsinki, Söderström, 1984.
Pimeys [Darkness] (aphorisms).   Helsinki, Söderström, 1984.
Näkyväistä maailmaa: aforistiset sarjat 1972–1984 [The Visible World: Aphoristic Sequences 1972–1984], edited by Tuomas Anhava.   Helsinki, Söderström, 1985.
Vaella Helsingissä.   Helsinki, Julkaisija Helsingin Kaupunki, 1986; as *In Search of Helsinki*, Helsinki, Söderström, 1986; as *Wanderer in Helsinki*, Helsinki, Söderström, 1986.

Yritys omaksikuvaksi [Attempt at a Self-Portrait].   Helsinki, Arthouse, 1987.
Kansakunnan synty [Birth of a Nation].   Helsinki, Arthouse, 1988.
Erään opportunistin iltapäivä [An Opportunist's After-noon].   Helsinki, Arthouse, 1988.

Editor, with Pentti Huovinen, *Poikien seikkailukirjaston parhaita* [The Best Boys' Adventure Stories].   Helsinki, Otava, 1977.
Editor, *Suomen kansan uusia runoja* [New Finnish Poems].   Savonlinna, Osuuskunta Informaatiokirjakauppa, 1984.

*

Critical Studies: "How Things Are: Paavo Haavikko and His Poetry" by Kai Laitinen, in *Books Abroad* (Norman, Oklahoma), 43(1), 1969; "Two Poets of Finland: Paavo Haavikko and Bo Carpelan" by Jaakko Ahokas, in *Books Abroad* (Norman, Oklahoma), 46(1), 1972; "Dreams Each Within Each: The Finnish Poet Paavo Haavikko," in *Books Abroad* (Norman, Oklahoma), 50(2), 1976, and "A Poet's Playground: The Collected Plays of Paavo Haavikko," in *World Literature Today* (Norman, Oklahoma), 53, 1979, both by Philip Binham; "The Writer and His Works: An Interview with Paavo Haavikko" by Aarne Kinnunen, in *Books from Finland* (Helsinki), 3, 1977; "The View from the Aspen Grove: Paavo Haavikko in National and International Context" by Richard Dauenhauer, in *Snow in May: An Anthology of Finnish Writing*, Rutherford, New Jersey, Fairleigh Dickinson University Press, 1978; Haavikko issue of *World Literature Today* (Norman, Oklahoma), 58(4), 1984; "Haavikko and Saarikoski: Lyrical Strategies" by Herbert Lomas, in *2 Plus 2*, Lausanne, Mylabris Press, 1985.

*   *   *

Paavo Haavikko began his poetic career under the influence of the work of T. S. Eliot, in particular the *Four Quartets*, which he read at the age of 18, and which impressed him with the possibilities of a poetic language that could cover all areas of human experience, from the most subjective and private to the most public and universal. In the cold-war Finland of the early 1950s the opportunities for the public expression of social criticism were severely limited, and Haavikko, like Veijo Meri and, somewhat later, Pentti Saarikoski, saw in the medium of modernist poetry a way of making statements about society and its relation to the individual moral consciousness in terms that were indecipherable to the political leaders of the country, yet able to be understood by a growing number of the country's young, disaffected intellectuals.

For the starting point of his poetic inquiry, which embraced both subjective experience and the life of contemporary Finnish — and European — society, Haavikko chose a period of the historical past that was quite remote: the poems of *Tiet etäisyyksiin* (Roads to Far Away) contain allusions to the history of ancient Rome, yet the fact that it is Finland that is being described and evoked is not concealed:

and days come like time in the great house
where there is little and only sporadic talk,
hours last and last,
the long corridors are saturated with silence.

In subsequent collections Haavikko began to approach present-day reality step by step: the poems of *Synnyinmaa* (Land of Birth) are largely set in 18th- and 19th-century baroque palaces where princes and other aristocrats took refuge before the bourgeois revolution, while those of *Lehdet lehtiä* (Leaves, Leaves) concern a time that is not far from the one in which the poet is writing, and are permeated by a satirical irony that is for the most part directed against the middle class of the young Finnish republic and its holders of governmental power.

It is indeed power that Haavikko sees as man's enemy — the power invested in the state sanctions and authorises deeds and actions that, if performed by individuals in their own name, would be considered crimes. For Haavikko there is a fundamental block, a discrepancy between the individual and the collective which man can, perhaps, never overcome, and which serves as the perpetuating agent of his tragic situation. In the collection *Talvipalatsi* (*Winter Palace*) Haavikko debates the nature of language, and in particular the division he perceives between the "straight word order" imposed by the state and the discourse, both inner and outer, of the private citizen. The eighth poem of the "Winter Palace" sequence contains a despairing outcry against the effort of writing lyrical poetry in a hostile world: "and why should I try to write poems when I am not Musset?"

The poet seems to be willing to renounce the luxurious privacy of lyrical verse in favour of joining the ranks of the "Prince," Satan, and doing battle against the agents of the soul's destruction on their own terms, with their own weapons:

> I know that money doesn't tempt you, and that you
>   want the children to play happily,
> oh let my voice go away from here, I deserve that
> and I don't like it here,
>   in this non-commercial world
> that has been pieced together

Throughout the 1960s Haavikko continued to write poetry of a lyrical, modernistic kind; but increasingly he explored in his poems the tension between personal language and the social idiom of the age, and in the collection *Puut, kaikki heidän vihreytensä* (The Trees, All Their Green) images from politics and economics frequently alternate with those of private, personal experience, or even stand in place of that experience, extending and modifying it. During the 1970s, Haavikko began to move away from the West European stance that had characterized his earlier work, and chose another metaphor with which to interpret the world and the place of the individual in it: that of Ancient Byzantium. The poem sequence *Kaksikymmentä ja yksi* (21) contains an interpretation of Sampo in the *Kalevala* as an East Roman coin-mint that is raided by his Old Finnish heroes. The theme of history becomes an important one, and the poet likens it to a pictorial tapestry in which past and present are woven together — this in defiance of conventional history-writing, which tends to see events as linked by a strictly chronological line of development. Just as he posits the existence of an individual, human language or languages that run counter to the prescriptive language of the state, so Haavikko sees true history as something that lies quite outside the textbooks and official historical accounts, in a personal, human area which perhaps only the poet can describe.

In his flight from the "non-commercial world" of "pure poetry" Haavikko follows his master T. S. Eliot (like Eliot, Haavikko worked for a number of years in a commercial institution), in perceiving that human reality is made up of a blend of biological, socio-economic, and moral-spiritual elements, and that if his voice is to be heard, the poet must be able to move freely between all of them. For Haavikko, as for Eliot, the world is an immutable entity, with laws that are eternal:

only human beings change, and the dynamics of their changing, held firmly within the parameters of "birth, copulation and death," and of commercial relation, are the proper subject for poetry. A recent poem of the late 1980s sums up Haavikko's view of human existence:

> Life being short, poverty and wealth
>   are final verdicts, in that
> poverty and life are of equal duration
>   and wealth and cold indifference
> are perennial and hereditary, like diseases.

In addition to his many collections of poems, Haavikko has produced a large body of other work, including aphorisms, prose narratives, and stage and radio plays. For the most part these deal with the same themes and problems that are encountered in the poems, except that in them one sees more clearly the public nature of Haavikko's endeavour — the plays in particular are characterised by what the critic Aarne Kinnunen has called "institutionalised communication," where an important role is allotted to ritual, ceremony, diplomacy, and business, perhaps again in homage to Eliot's theatrical writing. In Haavikko, Finland possesses a great national poet and international writer, whose voice deserves to be more widely heard and understood throughout the world.

—David McDuff

HABĪBI, Imīl. Also Emile Habiby. Palestinian. Born in 1919 (some sources say 1921 or 1922). Founding member, Israeli Communist Party. Elected three times to Israeli Knesset. Formerly editor-in-chief, *Al-Ittiḥad* [Unity] biweekly periodical. Recipient: Israel literary prize, 1992. Address: c/o Riad el-Rayyes Books, 56 Knightsbridge, London SW1X 7NJ, England.

PUBLICATIONS

Fiction

Sudāsiyat al-ayyām al-sittah [Sextet of the Six Days].   1969.
Al-Waqa' i al-gharībah fi ikhtifā Sa'īd abi al-naḥs al-mutashā'il. Haifa, n.p., 1974; Beirut, Munaḍḍamat al-Tahrir al-Filastīniyah, 1980; as *The Secret Life of Saeed, the Pessoptimist*, New York, Vintage, 1982; London, Zed, 1985.
Akhtiyah. Nicosia, Cyprus, Bisan Baris, 1985.
Sarāya bint al-Ghūl [Saraya the Ogre's Daughter].   London, Riad el-Rayyes, 1992.

Play

Luka' ibn Luka': thalāth jalasāt amāma sundūq al-'ajā'ib: hikāyah masrahiyah [Luka Son of Luka].   Beirut, Dār al-Farabi, 1980.

*

Critical Study: "Symbol and Reality in the Writings of Emile Habibi" by Issa J. Boullata, in *Islamic Culture* (Hyderabad), 62(2–3), 1988.

* * *

Unlike most Palestinian writers, Imīl Ḥabībi started writing late in life, and almost as a challenge to a statement made, after the Arab defeat in the Six Day War of 1967, by a leading Israeli politician who told him that Palestinians do not exist any longer, for if they did they would have produced their own literature. Literature was seen in this exchange as a proof of existence and a document of national identity. Ḥabībi was then in his mid-40s and had devoted most of his active life to the political struggle of his people who stayed behind after the creation of the state of Israel on their land. He was an active member of the Communist Party, the editor of its Arabic language daily, and a Member of Parliament. The denial of the existence of Palestinians, common at the time in Zionist circles, prompted him to produce a document of their survival despite Israeli attempts to erase their identity.

The devastating shock of the 1967 war turned Ḥabībi's left-wing optimism into bitter sarcasm and biting humour which he channelled into his first literary work, *Sudāsiyat al-ayyām al-sittah* (Sextet of the Six Days). In this work, Ḥabībi rejects the outcome of the war and posits narrative account against that of the factual and official version, using narrative as a means of warding off the nightmarish reality. The Sextet is a unique work of narrative using the form of the short-story cycle to present a panoramic view of the contradictions of the Six Day War and its ironic impact on the Palestinians. Each piece is structurally autonomous and can be read as an independent short story, but the subtle link between the pieces offers the work its unity and dynamism. Unlike most short-story cycles which are linked through a character, place, or event, the link generating the structural unity of the Sextet is that of impact, shock, and irony. A fine connection of resonant echoes reverberates throughout the text to enhance the dialectical dialogue between each piece and the other five. This creates a narrative structure similar in its form and effect to that of a hall of mirrors, in which each detail or event has endless reflections throughout the work. The dexterity of the Sextet's structure and the lucidity of its style are as important as the richness of its themes. The dreadful events of the war which turned the Palestinians' hopes and dreams into horrific nightmares are tinged with a fine sense of humour. The constant inversion of every aspect of each tale reflects on the thematic plane the structural effect of the technique of mirroring and demonstrates the illogical and unjust nature of the situation. The Palestinian dream of "return" is accomplished but only ironically when the rest of the Palestinian land falls under Israeli occupation.

The structural irony is also at the core of his second and most famous novel, *Al-Waqa' i al-gharībah fi ikhtifā Sa'īd abi al-nahs al-mutashā'il* (*The Secret Life of Saeed, the Pessoptimist*). In this novel the theme of the immediate shock of the 1967 war recedes into the background, and the survival of the Palestinians in the face of active Zionist attempts to eradicate their identity, erase their culture, and purge their land from any trace of their history comes to the fore. The technique of constant inversion is retained and is provided here with a multi-layered structure aimed at inscribing the cyclical history of the Palestinian tragedy into the very structure of the novel. It consists of three parts, each devoted to a major phase in the recent history of Palestine. Each part is entitled with the name of a woman who is both the beloved of the hero at the time and a symbol of Palestine: the first, "Yu'ād," represents the early period before the loss of Palestine in 1948; the second, "Bāqiyah," embodies the spirit of the Palestinian resistance to the eradication of their national identity after the creation of the state of Israel; and the third, "Yu'ād al-Thāniyah," signifies the new stage of Palestinian consciousness which emerged after 1967 and the armed Palestinian resistance.

The inevitability of resistance is the main theme of the novel. It is confirmed through both the novel's structural development, and its insistence on the impossibility of collaboration. As Ḥabībi presents it, no matter how subservient and accepting Palestinians become, the only fate for them in Israel is oppression and annihilation. Yet the resistance is seen in the novel in its widest sense; it is not confined to overt acts of defiance, for every measure that ensures the continuity of the Palestinian presence and preserves Palestinian identity and culture is an act of resistance, even if it appears as a form of submission and capitulation. In this respect the novel foreshadowed the Palestinian *intifada* (uprising) long before it began in the late 1980s. Unlike most novels, *Saeed, the Pessoptimist* is full of footnotes creating a secondary text which serves as the cultural context of the novel and roots every aspect of the narrative in the historical and geographical reality of Palestine. The detailed information provided in these notes generates an elaborate internal memory which serves as a counter argument against any denial of the existence of Palestine and its identity.

The consolidation of this identity and the preservation of its cultural and oral history seems to be at the heart of Ḥabībi's literary project. It permeates his play, *Luka' ibn Luka'* (Luka Son of Luka), and every aspect of the first two parts of his recent trilogy, *Akhtiyah* and *Sarāya bint al-Ghūl* (Saraya the Ogre's Daughter). In these two novels the textual space becomes an arena for the inscription of what one may call the infrastructure of the Palestinian identity: its history, geography, oral tradition, folk culture, popular lore concerning agriculture and weather, anecdotes, proverbs, and even fragments of its written literature. The collective culture is inscribed as much in the realistic account of daily events as in the flight into fantasy and imagination. The narrative space is present-day Israel with its discriminatory policies towards the Palestinians who have remained there since 1948 or have fallen under its occupation since 1967. But beneath the deformed space of the present, the author invokes through a powerful nostalgia the sacrosanct Palestine around every corner and behind every street name.

In these two novels, Ḥabībi's narrative form has become very dynamic, changing not only from one novel to the next but several times within each novel. The disruptiveness implicit in this random montage of narrative techniques is a structural representation of the dislocation of reality. The constant transformation of form has become one of the characteristics of the narrative of the problematic Palestinian identity. The excessive use of embedded sentences, and its narrative equivalent of embedded episodic tales in a multiplicity of forms, reflect a besieged existence, a sense of entrapment. The fragmentary structure of the novels reveals the author's perception of writing as the renunciation of the individual self and the recreation of the collective one. The "I" in his writing is the "I" of the present involved in the elaborate process of recognizing itself as it sinks into the neutrality of a faceless historic "he" that gives the narrative both its relevance and its obscurity. The absence of being sustains an illusion of being or a redemption of its present condition through a dialectical process of linguistic interaction with historic, literary, and popular discourse. The declared discourse is a discourse of the servile chorus of conformity, of falsehood and misinformation, but Ḥabībi uses the very language of this discourse to show it up and pre-empt its attempt to obliterate the ethos of the Palestinian identity.

Ḥabībi's literary project is still progressing and the third part of his fascinating trilogy has yet to appear. But what he has published so far continues to generate interest and controversy both in the Arab world and among Palestinians and Israelis alike. In 1992, when he was awarded the Israel literary prize, a heated debate commenced as soon as he announced his acceptance. The strong Israeli opposition to his selection for the prize was matched by even stronger objection from Palestinians both in Israeli-controlled areas and in the diaspora for his acceptance. The strength of the controversy and the heated discussion it generated was a testimony of Ḥabībi's importance as a prominent literary figure and a symbol of Palestinian identity. What transpired in all these debates is that he has succeeded in putting the Palestinian question firmly on the literary map.

—Sabry Hafez

————

HABIBY, Emile. *See* **HABĪBI, Imīl.**

————

HACKS, Peter. German. Born in Breslau, 21 March 1928. Educated at the University of Munich, Ph.D. 1951. Married Anna Elisabeth Wiede in 1955. Emigrated to East Germany, 1955. Freelance writer. Recipient: Lessing prize, 1956; Weiskopf prize, 1965; Critics prize (Germany), 1972; GDR National prize, 1974, 1977; Heinrich Mann prize, 1981. Address: c/o Dreimaskenverlag, 2 Heiliggeiststraße, 8000 Munich 2, Germany.

PUBLICATIONS

Plays

Eröffnung des indischen Zeitalters (produced Munich, 1954). Included in *Theaterstücke*, 1957; revised version, as *Columbus* (produced Zaragoza, 1975), in *Ausgewählte Dramen 1*, 1972.
Die Schlacht bei Lobositz (produced Berlin, 1956). Included in *Theaterstücke*, 1957.
Der Held der westlichen Welt, with Anna Wiede, from the play *The Playboy of the Western World* by J. M. Synge (produced Berlin, 1956). Included in *Stücke*, by Synge, Leipzig, Reclam, 1972.
Das Volksbuch vom Herzog Ernst (produced Mannheim, 1967). Included in *Theaterstücke*, 1957.
Theaterstücke. Berlin, Aufbau, 1957.
Der Müller von Sanssouci (produced Berlin, 1958). Included in *Fünf Stücke*, 1965.
Die Kindermörderin, from a play by H. L. Wagner (produced Wuppertal, 1959). Included in *Zwei Bearbeitungen*, 1963.

Die Sorgen und die Macht (produced Senftenberg, 1960; revised version, produced Berlin, 1962). Included in *Fünf Stücke*, 1965.
Der Frieden, from a play by Aristophanes (produced Berlin, 1962). Included in *Zwei Bearbeitungen*, 1963.
Zwei Bearbeitungen (includes *Die Kindermörderin*; *Die Sorgen und die Macht*). Frankfurt, Suhrkamp, 1963.
Die schöne Helena, from the operetta libretto by Meilhac and Halévy (produced Berlin, 1964). Included in *Stücke nach Stücken*, 1965.
Fünf Stücke. Frankfurt, Suhrkamp, 1965.
Stücke nach Stücken (includes *Der Frieden*; *Die Schöne Helena*; *Die Kindermörderin*; *Polly, oder, Die Bataille am Bluewater Creek*). Berlin, Aufbau, 1965.
Poly, oder, die Bataille am Bluewater Creek, from the play by John Gay (produced Halle, 1966). Included in *Stücke nach Stücken*, 1965.
Moritz Tassow (produced Berlin, 1965). Included in *Vier Komödien*, 1971.
Amphitryon (produced Göttingen, 1968; New York, 1970). Berlin, Eulenspiegel, 1969.
Margarete in Aix (produced Basel, 1969). Included in *Vier Komödien*, 1971.
Omphale (produced Frankfurt, 1970). Included in *Vier Komödien*, 1971; revised version, music by S. Matthus (produced Berlin, 1975).
Vier Komödien. Frankfurt, Suhrkamp, 1972.
Ausgewählte Dramen 1–3. Berlin, Aufbau, 3 vols., 1972–81.
Noch einen Löffel Gift, Liebling?, music by S. Matthus (produced Berlin, 1972). Included in *Oper*, 1975.
Adam und Eva (produced Dresden, 1973). Düsseldorf, Claassen, 1976.
Die Vögel, from the play by Aristophanes (produced Dresden, 1981). Included in *Oper*, 1975.
Oper (includes *Geschichten meiner Oper*; *Noch einen Löffel Gift, Liebling?*; *Die Vögel*; *Versuch über das Libretto*). Berlin, Aufbau, 1975.
Prexaspes (produced Dresden, 1975). Included in *Ausgewählte Dramen 2*, 1976.
Das Jahrmarktfest zu Plundersweilern, from the play by Goethe (produced Berlin 1975). With *Rosie träumt*, Berlin, Aufbau, 1976; as *Market Day in Plundersweilern*, in *Gambit* (London), 39–40, 1982.
Rosie träumt, from the plays by Hrosvith von Gandersheim (produced Berlin, 1975). With *Das Jahrmarktsfest zu Plundersweilern*, Berlin, Aufbau, 1976.
Ein Gespräch im Hause Stein über den abwesenden Herrn von Goethe (produced Dresden, 1976). Included in *Ausgewählte Dramen 2*, 1976; as *Conversations About an Absent Lover* (produced Dublin, 1977; as *Charlotte*, produced New York, 1980).
Die Fische (produced Göttingen, 1978). Included in *Sechs Dramen*, 1978.
Sechs Dramen (includes *Numa*; *Prexaspes*; *Adam und Eva*; *Ein Gespräch im Hause Stein über den abwesenden Herrn von Goethe*; *Die Fische*; *Senecas Tod*). Düsseldorf, Claassen, 1978.
Senecas Tod (produced Berlin, 1980). Included in *Sechs Dramen*, 1978.
Armer Ritter (for children; produced Göttingen, 1978). Included in *Märchendramen*, Berlin, Henschel, 1980.
Pandora, from a play by Goethe (produced Göttingen, 1982). Berlin, Aufbau, 1981.
Musen (produced Magdeburg, 1983). Included in *Ausgewählte Dramen 3, 1981*.
Barby, from a play by R. Strahl (produced Halle, 1983). Berlin, Henschel, 1983.

Die Kinder (for children; produced Greifswald, 1984). Berlin, Henschel, 1983.
Die Binsen (produced Berlin, 1985). With *Fredegunde*, Berlin, Aufbau, 1985.
Stücke nach Stücken 2.   Berlin, Aufbau, 1985.
Fredegunde (produced Braunschweig, 1989). With *Die Binsen*, Berlin, Aufbau, 1985.
Maries Baby (for children; produced Nordhausen, 1987). Berlin, Henschel, 1985.
Jona.   Berlin, Aufbau, 1989.

Radio Plays: *Der gestohlene Ton*, 1953; *Das Fell der Zeit*, 1954; *Geschichte eines alten Wittibers in Jahre 1637*, 1957.

Television Plays: *Die unadlige Gräfin*, 1957–58; *Falsche Bärte und Nasen*, 1961.

Fiction

Der Schuhu und die fliegende Prinzessin.   Berlin, Eulenspiegel, 1966.
Die Dinge in Buta.   Berlin, Berliner Handpresse, 1974.
Magister Knauerhase.   Leipzig, Reclam, 1985.

Verse

Lieder zu Stücken.   Berlin, Eulenspiegel, 1967; revised edition, 1978; as *Ich trug eine Rose im Haar*, Munich, Langen-Müller, 1981.
Poesiealbum.   Berlin, Neues Leben, 1972.
Lieder, Briefe, Gedichte.   Wuppertal, Hammer, 1974.
Historien und Romanzen.   Berlin, Aufbau, 1985.
Der blaue Hund, with Anne Heseler.   Frankfurt, Insel, 1987.
Die Gedichte.   Berlin, Aufbau, 1988.

Other (for children)

Das Windloch.   Gütersloh, Bertelsmann, 1956.
Das Turmverlies.   Berlin, Kinderbuch, 1962.
Der Flohmarkt.   Berlin, Kinderbuch, 1965.
Der Affe Oswald.   Munich, Parabel, 1971.
Der Bär auf dem Försterball.   Cologne, Middelhauve, 1972; as *The Bear at the Huntsmen's Ball*, London, Abelard Schuman, 1975.
Die Katze wäscht den Omnibus.   Berlin, Kinderbuch, 1972.
Kathrinchen ging spazieren.   Cologne, Middelhauve, 1973.
Die Sonne.   Berlin, Kinderbuch, 1975.
Meta Morfoss.   Cologne, Middelhauve, 1975.
Das musikalische Nashorn.   Düsseldorf, Claassen, 1977.
Armer Ritter.   Berlin, Kinderbuch, 1979.
Geschichten von Henriette und Onkel Titus.   Berlin, Kinderbuch, 1979.
Leberecht am schiefen Fenster.   Berlin, Kinderbuch, 1979.
Der Mann mit dem schwärzlichen Hintern.   Berlin, Kinderbuch, 1980.
Jules Ratte.   Berlin, Kinderbuch, 1981.
Onkel Mo.   Berlin, Kinderbuch, 1986.
Kinderkurzweil.   Berlin, Kinderbuch, 1986.
Liebkind im Vogelnest.   Berlin and Würzberg, Arena, 1987.

Other

Das Poetische: Ansätze zu einer postrevolutionären Dramaturgie.   Frankfurt, Suhrkamp, 1972.
Die Maßgaben der Kunst: Gesammelte Aufsätze.   Berlin, Henschel, 1977.
Essais.   Leipzig, Reclam, 1983.

Schöne Wirtschaft: Ästhetisch-ökonomische Fragmente.   Berlin, Aufbau, 1988.

*

Critical Studies: *"Enfant Terrible" of Contemporary East German Drama: Peter Hacks in His Role as Adaptor and Innovator* by Judith R. Scheid, Bonn, Bouvier, 1977; "Utopia in Mecklenburg: Peter Hacks' Play *Moritz Tassow*" by Peter Graves, in *Modern Language Review* (London), 75, 1980; "Moritz Tassow and the 'Sturm und Drang' Aspects of Peter Hacks' Socialist Classicism" by Margy Gerber, in *Erkennen und Deuten: Essays zur Literatur und Literaturtheorie*, edited by Martha Woodmansee and Walter F. W. Lohnes, Berlin, Schmidt, 1983; "Aristophanes in East Germany: Peter Hacks's Adaptation of *Peace*" by Ulrich K. Goldsmith, in *Hypatia: Essays in Classics, Comparative Literature and Philosophy*, edited by Goldsmith, William Calder, and Phyllis B. Kerevan, Boulder, Colorado Associated University Press, 1985; *The Children's Literature of Peter Hacks* by Thomas Di Napoli, New York, Lang, 1987.

*   *   *

Peter Hacks was one of the most important playwrights of the recently defunct German Democratic Republic and was also widely performed in West Germany, particularly in the later 1960s and the 1970s. His popularity came from a renewal of poetic drama with larger-than-life characters as images of the future state of mankind, which he saw as developing from the basic liberation he believed had taken place through the common ownership of the means of production under socialism. That it has proved a false dawn does not invalidate his best plays, which are a glorious celebration of creative humanity.

His first four plays, written both before and after he emigrated from West to East Germany in 1955, follow, although not slavishly, the Brechtian method of epic theatre, using historical figures to present models of historical processes seen from a Marxist perspective, while at the same time unmasking the workings of class society. In them his commitment to Marxist theory is demonstrated both with an intellectual wit that has become his hallmark, and with an awareness of the possibilities, especially comic, of the stage.

In his next two major plays, he dealt with the contemporary subjects called for by the cultural functionaries. The theme of the *Die Sorgen und die Macht* (Troubles and Power), for example, is the conflict between the demands for quality and quantity in production during the GDR's reconstruction period. With its positive moral it looks like the kind of play the authorities were trying to encourage, but it was criticized, in particular for the excessively subjective motivation of the hero, whose exemplary development is fuelled by the energy of his own temperament rather than by class consciousness. Hacks's insistence that emancipation includes sexual emancipation always irritated the rather strait-laced socialist establishment; the other main criticism concerned his treatment of the contrast between ideal (future communist society) and reality (the drab present of the GDR).

This contrast, in a more generalised and thus more acceptable form, is the central theme of his later "classical" plays. In the early 1960s Hacks rejected epic theatre for a "socialist classicism," which he saw as the aesthetic correlation of the official view of the GDR as a "mature socialist society"; accepting the Party's premise that the majority had been converted, he deduced that there was no longer any need to preach to them and, therefore, no need for epic theatre. This attitude was criticised by some in the West as conformism and as a retreat from the dangers inherent in treating contemporary subjects. In fact, although it did seem to follow Walter Ulbricht's proclamation of the coming of age of the GDR, it did not bring Hacks immediate acceptance in the East; instead in the late 1960s and early 1970s a number of his plays received their first performances in the West. Although he accepts the authority of the state as necessary in politics, he has always insisted on his own competence in aesthetic matters.

His "classical" plays can be divided into two groups — strict ones observing the unities of time, place, and action and written throughout in verse (*Amphitryon, Adam und Eva* [Adam and Eve], *Senecas Tod* [Seneca's Death], *Fredegunde, Jona*) and others with complex plots, a multiplicity of characters, and a mixture of prose and verse (*Margarete in Aix, Prexaspes, Numa, Die Binsen* [The Rushes]). The former concentrate on great characters as demonstrations of human potential while the latter deal with questions of society, history, and politics. Almost all of Hacks's plays are comedies, which, with his socialist classicism and the poetic theatre he has revived, he sees as an expression of the "self-confidence of the [working] class."

As well as writing his own plays on classical subjects, Hacks has been active as an adaptor. His version of Aristophanes's *Der Frieden* (Peace) was, in the production by Bruno Besson in 1962, one of the great events in East German theatre history, and his "operetta for actors," *Die schöne Helena* (The Beautiful Helen), has been by far the most popular of his works in the East. His main focus during the 1970s was on Goethe, who is the subject of several of his major essays; he clearly sees Goethe's rejection of the Romantics as a model for his own attitude to left-wing Marxists. He has adapted plays by Goethe, and *Adam und Eva* and *Rosie träumt* have echoes of *Faust*. The most enduring expression of his interest in, almost obsession with, Goethe is the one-woman play, *Ein Gespräch im Hause Stein über den abwesenden Herrn von Goethe* (*Conversations About an Absent Lover*), his most widely performed play in the West. It is not dramatised literary history; through a portrait of Goethe and his patroness of the Weimar years, Frau von Stein, Hacks illuminates the position both of women and of the artist in society.

Apart from this *tour de force*, Hacks seemed to lose his way in the 1970s with plays such as *Das Jahrmarktfest zu Plundersweilern* (*Market Day in Plundersweilern*) and *Rosie träumt* which seemed to have more theatricality than substance. However, *Die Binsen* and *Fredegunde* show a renewed vigour in their portrayal of two women who know what they want and make things happen, rather than passively responding to society. In *Die Binsen* Hacks has done, finally but too late, what he has often been criticised for failing to do, and placed one of his active characters within the context of an —admittedly very generalized — GDR society.

Although the cocksure confidence in the inevitable victory of socialism of his early years has eroded, Hacks has never recanted his commitment to Marxism and, not surprisingly, has almost completely disappeared from the repertoire since the unification of the two Germanies. It is likely to be some time before the German theatre is ready to rediscover his poetic theatre.

—Michael Mitchell

HAIDAR, Qurratulain. Also Qurratulain Hyder. Indian. Born in Aligarh, in 1927. Educated in Benares and at Lucknow University, M.A. in English literature 1947; Lucknow Art School; Heatherlay's Art School, London. BBC broadcaster, London; reporter, *The Daily Telegraph*, London, 1953; managing editor, 1964–67, and editor, 1967–68, *Imprint Magazine*, Bombay; member of editorial staff, *Illustrated Weekly of India*, 1968–75; working member, Sāhitya Akādemī, 1968–76; adviser to Chair of Central Board of Film Censor, Government of India, Bombay, 1975–76; member of Advisory Board for Urdu, Central Organisation, All India Radio, New Delhi; Visiting Professor, Jamia Millia Islamia, New Delhi, 1979, and Aligarh Muslim University. Recipient: Sāhitya Akādemī award, 1967; Soviet Land Nehru award, 1969; Uttar Pradeś Urdū Akādemī award, 1981; Padmaśrī, 1984; Ghālib award, 1985; Iqbāl award, 1985; Jñānpīth award, 1989. Address: c/o Sterling Publishers, L-10 Green Park Extension, New Delhi 110016, India.

PUBLICATIONS

Fiction

Sitārō se āge [Before the Stars].   1947.
Mere bhī sanamkhāne [My Temples Too].   Lahore, n.p., 1949.
Śafinā-e-gam-e-dil [Śafinā's Woeful Heart].   1952.
Śīśe ke ghar [Houses of Glass].   1952.
The Exiles: A Novelette.   Pakistan, PEN, 1955.
Āg kā daryā [River of Fire].   Lahore, Maktabah Jadid, 1959.
Patjhar kī āvāz [Autumn's Voice].   1967.
Fasal gul āye ya ajal āye.   Lahore, Khayam, 1968.
Dilrubā [An Instrument].   Lahore, Rabia, 1976.
Kar-i jahān darāz hai [The Task of Life Is Long].   Bombay, Fankar, 2 vols., 1977–79.
Ākhir-e śab ke hamsafar [Last Night's Travellers].   Bombay, Alavi Book Depot, 1979.
Cār novelettes [Four Novelettes].   Aligarh, Educational, 1981.
Rośnī kī raftār [The Light's Speed].   1982.
Gardiś-i raṅg-i caman [Circling the Colours of the Garden].   Karachi, Maktabah-i Daniyal, 1987.
Cāndi Begum.   New Delhi, Educational, 1990.
Jugnuō kī duniyā [The Fireflies' World].   New Delhi, Añjuman Taraqi Urdu, 1990.

Other

Ghalib and His Poetry, with Ali Sardar Jafri.   Bombay, Popular, 1970.
Picture Gallery.   Lahore, Qausain, 1983.

Editor, with Khushwant Singh, *Stories from India*.   New Delhi, Sterling, 1974.

Translator, *The Nautch Girl*, by Hassan Shah.   New Delhi, Sterling, 1992.

*   *   *

Qurratulain Haidar is generally considered to be the Urdu language's greatest living novelist. Her achievements, formidable by any standards, are reflected in her high status among writers in both India and Pakistan; but her work and influence escape categorisation. She emphatically rejects the label of women's writer, perhaps because of her familiarity with it history in Urdu, which began with didactic and corrective fictions depicting servile women circumscribed by the limits of family, marriage, and formal religion. Notable exceptions, such as the tongue-in-cheek fabulist Hijab Ismail and the radical Ismat Chughtai, emerged in the 1930s and 1940s, but Haidar remains as distant from the lavish ahistoricism of the former as she does from the militant critical realism of the latter. It can be said, however, that her influence on contemporaries and successors has removed the tainted aura surrounding women writers, encouraging them to cross the threshold of the inner courtyard of domesticity to navigate territories of identity, culture, and history, hitherto regarded as male preserves. She is equally removed from the trend prevalent at the time of her entry into the literary arena — the largely male-dominated, Marxist-influenced progressive writers' movement. Her novels are polyphonic and polycentric; her concerns, even when her central protagonists are women, are philosophical, political, and above all, historical.

The generally complex structure of Haidar's novels provides spaces for the examination of a multitude of themes — the primacy of (Indian) cultural identity over religious affiliations, the decline of the ruling class and its effect on its erstwhile dependants, the philosophies of successive generations of Indian Society, the relationship between women, men, and their history. Combining her impressive talent for story- telling with her passion for historical research and documentation, she has created a rich and hybrid genre which becomes the locus for the contrapuntal exploration of evolving consciousness and its imperial, colonial, post-colonial, and national contexts.

Concentrating on Muslim characters with a unique understanding of their culture at its most highly evolved, these novels — which are occasionally seen as abstruse and elitist for their often aristocratic settings and their formidable erudition, equally steeped in Western and Eastern discourses and languages — are marked by a distinctive juxtaposition of the narrative and the discursive. Stories and legends collide with digressive passages on peripheral issues; moral matters may be called into question or facets of fading Lucknow life, language, and rituals put on record.

Haidar's early stories and novels established her as an innovator in languages and form; she was credited with the introduction of modernist techniques and sensibility into Urdu fiction. However, early comparisons with Virginia Woolf proved entirely inadequate when her epic Āg kā daryā (River of Fire) challenged every received notion of the novel with its defiance of chronological and formal logistics. Spanning a time from the Buddhist era to the early years of Pakistan, the novel grapples with the entire concept of Indian history; it occupies a place in the South Asian canon analagous to that of Gabriel García Márquez's (q.v.) One Hundred Years of Solitude (1967) in the Western canon. However, the novel preceded García Márquez's masterwork by a decade, and Haidar disclaims all knowledge of magic realism. She questions the boundaries between long and short fiction, stressing that her stories often cover the timespan of novels. Her novels, it may be added, often contain inset stories in the time-hallowed Eastern tradition. In fact, her creative work produced in the decade following the unprecedented success of her novel consists of shorter fictions, and the structural economy and political engagement of the novellas "Housing Society," "Jilavatan," and "Chae ke Bagh" seem to indicate her choice, deliberate or otherwise, of imaginative and formal future directions.

However, critics prepared to dismiss her as a one-novel wonder and essentially a brilliant miniaturist were entirely disproved with Haidar's oeuvre of the 1970s and 1980s. The brilliant Ākhir-e śab ke hamsafar (Last Night's Travellers), set

in Bengal and seen through the eyes of a multitude of characters including several generations of the British Barlow family, chronicles the tortured relationship between India and Britain, the division of Bengal and Partition, and ultimately, the creation of Bangladesh. Haidar's multivocal and multicentred architectonics in this and the novels that follow illustrate her theory of the the blurred boundaries between long and short fictions. One of Ākhir-e śab ke hamsafar's most effective sections is composed of the diary entries of the Bengali dancer Yasmin Belmont, whose feminist odyssey takes her to Europe as the wife of a homosexual Englishman and leads her through a life of dispossession and abandonment of her artistic aspirations for a series of demeaning occupations to eventual suicide. The comments of Yasmin's world-weary half-European daughter follow. (An interesting comparison of Haidar's use of the feminist first person can be made with the title story of the prize-winning collection Patjhar kī āvāz [Autumn's Voice] in which the narrator's social and sexual odyssey parallels her migration to Pakistan and reflects the shattered hopes of the Indian Muslims who left their homeland in search of an ideal; this masterpiece of laconic narration stages the eventual compromise of the transgressive woman rather than the tragic despair of Yasmin's confessions.)

Haidar's rapidly expanding oeuvre is now firmly settled in the grand narrative mode, without, however, foregoing its concern for the marginal, the transgressive, the victimised woman. In Kar-i jahān darāz hai (The Task of Life Is Long) she tells of the ancestors of her father, the writer Yaldaram, recreating, often in their own voices, forgotten personages and remote journeys from Central Asian terrain. Gardiś-i raṅg-i caman (Circling the Colours of the Garden), characteristically ambitious in structure and scope, follows the fortunes of two courtesans of noble origin and the effect of their fortunes on the generations of women that follow. Fact, fantasy, and trenchant satirical humour, diligent research and romantic imagination, baroque pastiche and clipped postmodernism combine in a voluptuous articulation of Haidar's ultimately tragic vision of the collapse of Indo-Muslim culture and its distinguishing values. The moral and metaphysical underpinnings of this collapse are enlarged in Cāndi Begum, in which the eponymous heroine, who makes a paradoxically brief appearance, seemingly symbolises the squandered and brutalised potential of a class and its ultimate inability to survive in conflict with the crass materialism and vulgar opportunism of today's uncomprehending India.

—Aamer Hussein

HANDKE, Peter. Austrian. Born in Griffen, Carinthia, 6 December 1942. Educated at a school in Griffen, 1948–54; Marianum Catholic Boys School, Tanzenberg bei Klagenfurt, 1954–59; Klagenfurt Gymnasium, 1959–61; University of Graz, 1961–65. Married Libgart Schwarz in 1966 (separated 1972); one daughter. Full-time writer since 1966; co-founder, Verlag der Autoren, 1969. Recipient: Hauptmann prize, 1967; Schiller prize, 1972; Steiermark prize, 1972; Büchner prize, 1973; Sadoul prize, 1978; Kafka prize (refused), 1979; Salzburg literary prize, 1986. Address: Mönschberg 17, 5020 Salzburg, Austria.

PUBLICATIONS

Plays

Publikumsbeschimpfung (produced Frankfurt, 1966). Included in *Publikumsbeschimpfung und andere Sprechstück* 1966; as *Offending the Audience* (produced London, 1970; New York, 1974), in *Kaspar and Other Plays*, 1969.
Selbstbezichtigung (produced Oberhausen, 1966). Included in *Publikumsbeschimpfung und andere Sprechstücke*, 1966; as *Self-Accusation* (produced New York, 1970; London, 1973), in *Kaspar and Other Plays*, 1969.
Weissagung (produced Oberhausen, 1966). Included in *Publikumsbeschimpfung und andere Sprechstücke*, 1966; as *Prophecy* (produced London, 1972), in *The Ride Across Lake Constance and Other Plays*, 1976.
Publikumsbeschimpfung und andere Sprechstück. Frankfurt, Suhrkamp, 1966.
Hilferufe (produced Stockholm, 1967). Included in *Stücke 1*, 1972; as *Calling for Help* (produced London, 1972), in *The Ride Across Lake Constance and Other Plays*, 1976.
Kaspar (produced Frankfurt, 1968). Frankfurt, Suhrkamp, 1968; in English (produced New York and London, 1973), in *Kaspar and Other Plays*, 1969; published separately, London, Methuen, 1972.
Hörspiel. Cologne, Kiepenheuer und Witsch, 2 vols., 1968–69.
Das Mündel will Vormund sein (produced Frankfurt, 1969). Included in *Prosa, Gedichte, Theaterstücke, Ho ̈rspiel, Aufsätze*, 1969; as *My Foot My Tutor* (produced London, 1971), in *The Ride Across Lake Constance and Other Plays*, 1976; in *Shakespeare the Sadist and Others*, London, Methuen, 1977.
Kaspar and Other Plays (includes *Offending the Audience*; *Self-Accusation*). New York, Farrar Straus, 1969; as *Offending the Audience and Self-Accusation*, London, Methuen, 1971.
Quodlibet (produced Basel, 1970). Frankfurt, Autoren, 1970; in English, in *The Ride Across Lake Constance and Other Plays*, 1976.
Hörspiel No. 2, 3, und 4. Frankfurt, Autoren, 1970.
Wind und Meer: 4 Hörspiele. Frankfurt, Suhrkamp, 1970.
Der Ritt über den Bodensee (produced Berlin, 1971). Frankfurt, Autoren, 1970; as *The Ride Across Lake Constance* (produced New York, 1972; London, 1973), London, Methuen, 1973; in *The Ride Across Lake Constance and Other Plays*, 1976.
Stücke 1–2. Frankfurt, Suhrkamp, 2 vols., 1972–73.
Die Unvernünftigen sterben aus (produced Zurich, 1974). Frankfurt, Suhrkamp, 1973; as *They Are Dying Out* (produced London, 1976), London, Methuen, 1975; in *The Ride Across Lake Constance and Other Plays*, 1976.
Falsche Bewegung (screenplay). Frankfurt, Suhrkamp, 1975.
The Ride Across Lake Constance and Other Plays (includes *Prophecy*; *Calling for Help*; *My Foot My Tutor*; *Quodlibet*; *They Are Dying Out*). New York, Farrar Straus, 1976.
Über die Dörfer: Dramatisches Gedichte (produced Salzburg, 1982). Frankfurt, Suhrkamp, 1981.
Der Himmel über Berlin (screenplay), with Wim Wenders. Frankfurt, Suhrkamp, 1987.
The Long Way Round, adapted from his own story (produced London 1989). London, Methuen, 1989.
Das Spiel vom Fragen, oder, Die Reise zum sonoren Land. Frankfurt, Suhrkamp, 1989.

Screenplays: *Falsche Bewegung*; *Die linkshändige Frau*, 1977; *Die Angst des Tormanns beim Elfmeter*; *Der kurze Brief zum langen Abschied*; *Der Himmel über Berlin/Wings of Desire*, with Wim Wenders, 1988.

Fiction

Die Hornissen. Frankfurt, Suhrkamp, 1966.
Der Hausierer. Frankfurt, Suhrkamp, 1967.
Begrüßung des Aufsichtsrats: Prosatexte. Salzburg, Residenz, 1967.
Die Angst des Tormanns beim Elfmeter. Frankfurt, Suhrkamp, 1970; as *The Goalie's Anxiety at the Penalty Kick*, New York, Farrar Straus, 1972; London, Methuen, 1977.
Der kurze Brief zum langen Abschied. Frankfurt, Suhrkamp, 1972; as *Short Letter, Long Farewell*, New York, Farrar Straus, 1974; London, Methuen, 1977.
Wunschloses Unglück. Salzburg, Residenz, 1972; as *A Sorrow Beyond Dreams*, New York, Farrar Straus, 1975; London, Souvenir Press, 1976.
Die Stunde der wahren Empfindung. Frankfurt, Suhrkamp, 1975; as *A Moment of True Feeling*, New York, Farrar Straus, 1977.
Die linkshändige Frau. Frankfurt, Suhrkamp, 1976; as *The Left-Handed Woman*, New York, Farrar Straus, 1978; London, Methuen, 1980.
Langsame Heimkehr. Frankfurt, Suhrkamp, 1979; as *The Long Way Around*, in *Slow Homecoming*, 1985.
Die Lehre der Sainte-Victoire. Frankfurt, Suhrkamp, 1980; as *The Lesson of Mont Sainte Victoire*, in *Slow Homecoming*, 1985.
Kindergeschichte. Frankfurt, Suhrkamp, 1981; as *Child's Story*, in *Slow Homecoming*, 1985.
Phantasien der Wiederholung. Frankfurt, Suhrkamp, 1983.
Der Chinese des Schmerzes. Frankfurt, Suhrkamp, 1983; as *Across*, New York, Farrar Straus, and London, Methuen, 1986.
Slow Homecoming (includes *The Long Way Around*; *Child's Story*; *The Lesson of Mont Sainte Victoire*). New York, Farrar Straus, and London, Methuen, 1985.
Die Wiederholung. Frankfurt, Suhrkamp, 1986; as *Repetition*, New York, Farrar and Straus, and London, Methuen, 1988.
Die Abwesenheit. Frankfurt, Suhrkamp, 1987; as *Absence*, New York, Farrar Straus, 1990; London, Methuen, 1991.
Nachmittag eines Schriftstellers. Salzburg, Residenz, 1987; as *The Afternoon of a Writer*, New York, Farrar Straus, and London, Methuen, 1989.
3 x Handke (includes *The Goalie's Anxiety at the Penalty Kick*; *Short Letter, Long Farewell*; *A Sorrow Beyond Dreams*). New York, Macmillan, 1988.

Verse

Die Innenwelt der Aussenwelt der Innenwelt. Frankfurt, Suhrkamp, 1969; as *The Innerworld of the Outerworld of the Innerworld*, New York, Seabury Press, 1974.
Deutsche Gedichte. Frankfurt, Euphorion, 1969.
Das Ende des Flanierens. Vienna, Davidpress, 1976.
Gedichte, 1962–1963. Frankfurt, Suhrkamp, 1983.
Gedicht an die Dauer. Frankfurt, Suhrkamp, 1986.

Other

Prosa, Gedichte, Theaterstücke, Hörspiel, Aufsätze. Frankfurt, Suhrkamp, 1969.
Chronik der laufenden Ereignisse. Frankfurt, Autoren, 1971.

Ich bin ein Bewohner des Elfenbeinturms. Frankfurt, Suhrkamp, 1972.

Wiener Läden, photographs by Didi Petrikat. Munich, Hanser, 1974.

Als das Wünschen noch geholfen hat. Frankfurt, Suhrkamp, 1974; as *Nonsense and Happiness*, New York, Urizen, 1976.

Der Rand der Wörter: Erzählungen, Gedichte, Stücke, edited by Heinz F. Schafroth, Stuttgart, Reclam, 1975.

Das Gewicht der Welt: Ein Journal (November 1975–März 1977). Salzburg, Residenz, 1977; as *The Weight of the World*, New York, Farrar Straus, and London, Secker and Warburg, 1984.

Die Geschichte des Bleistifts. Salzburg, Residenz, 1982.

Aber ich lebe nur von den Zwischenräumen. Zurich, Ammann, 1987.

Versuch über die Müdigkeit. Frankfurt, Suhrkamp, 1989.

Versuch über die Jukebox. Frankfurt, Suhrkamp, 1990.

Noch einmal für Thukydides. Salzburg, Residenz, 1990.

Versuch über den geglückten Tag. Frankfurt, Suhrkamp, 1991.

Editor, *Der gewöhnliche Schrecken: Neue Horrorgeschichten*. Salzburg, Residenz, 1969.

Editor, *Charakter; Der Schwur des Martin Krist, Dokument: Frühe Erzählung*, by Franz Nabl. Salzburg, Residenz, 1975.

Translator, *Der Spiegeltag*, by Georges-Arthur Goldschmidt. Frankfurt, Suhrkamp, 1982.

Translator, *Gedichte 1962–1983*, by Gustav Januš. Frankfurt, Suhrkamp, 1983.

Translator, *Bécon-les-Bruyères eine Vorstadt*, by Emmanuel Bove. Frankfurt, Suhrkamp, 1984.

Translator, *Prometheus, gefesselt*, by Aeschylus. Frankfurt, Suhrkamp, 1986.

Translator, *Das Wintermärchen*, by William Shakespeare. Frankfurt, Suhrkamp, 1991.

*

Bibliography: *Peter Handke: An Annotated Bibliography* by June Schlueter and Ellis Finger, New York, Garland, 1982.

Critical Studies: *Peter Handke: Theatre as Anti-Theatre* by Nicolas Hern, New York, Ungar, 1971; "The 'Grazer Gruppe': Peter Handke and Wolfgang Bauer" by Hugh Rorrison, in *Modern Austrian Writing* edited by Alan Best and Hans Wolfschütz, London, Wolff, 1980; *The Plays and Novels of Peter Handke* by June Schlueter, Pittsburgh, University of Pittsburgh Press, 1981; *Peter Handke and the Postmodern Transformation: The Goalie's Journey Home* by Jerome Klinkowitz, Columbia, University of Missouri Press, 1983; *New German Dramatists* by Denis Calandra, London, Macmillan, and New York, Grove Press, 1983.

*   *   *

A German novelist, poet, playwright, and theatre theorist, Peter Handke's work from the beginning was radically innovative in formal terms, although at the same time firmly rooted in his Austrian cultural background especially 19th- and early 20th-century folk writing and satire of middle-class life. His early novels were much influenced by the minimalist techniques of the French *nouveau roman* of the 1960s, more particularly in the ways in which, while eschewing the more obvious features of narrative, like character and striking incident, they project complex states through emphasis on the apparently insignificant details of everyday life, underscoring the intricate ways in which the individual personality and understanding are shaped. French literary influence is felt, too, in the manner in which works such as *Die Hornissen* (The Hornets) are marked by an existentialist metaphysical tone prominent in much literature of the 1950s and 1960s.

Handke came to international attention in 1966, the year his first novel was published, when he passionately intervened at a meeting of Gruppe 47, an assembly of German writers gathered at Princeton University to discuss new developments in literature. Although he claimed his outburst was spontaneous the vigour of his attack on the domination in contemporary writing of descriptive prose attracted considerable publicity, which in the next couple of years he was able to build upon by turning, at the suggestion of his publisher, to the theatre as a more effective means of maintaining himself economically as a writer. In the mid to late 1960s he produced a number of what he called *Sprechstücke*, "speak plays," the first staged of which, *Publikumsbeschimpfung* (*Offending the Audience*), given at Frankfurt that year, and first performed in London in 1970 made a frontal attack on the accepted conventions and rituals of the theatre. In it, four actors tell the audience that what it sees is not a play, but just a stage with four people on it. Nor, they insist, are they there to fulfill bourgeois expectations of what a theatre is supposed to be, for they present no dramatic plot or characters; rather, they talk about the audience in order to make it aware of itself as an audience, and to underscore how it, as well as the performers, makes the show; at the end, applause comes over loud speakers as a tribute to the audience's contribution.

Other early dramatic pieces include *Weissagung* (*Prophecy*), *Selbstbezichtigung* (*Self-Accusation*) and *Hilferufe* (*Calling for Help*). Evident even in these early plays is not only Handke's hostility to the Brechtian use of theatre for political purposes, but the extent to which his work has been influenced, even if only in part and indirectly, by Ludwig Wittgenstein's thinking about the nature of language, and how words and linguistic forms determine our understanding of the world. But no less important, perhaps, was a more traditional Austrian literary concern with language and, in the theatre, with the uses of space and scenic elements as essentially illustrative means by which to expose the power of conventions. Strongly felt in his theatre work was the influence of earlier Austrian writers and practitioners like Hugo von Hoffmannstahl, Johann Nestroy, Ferdinand Raimund, Karl Krauss, and Ödon von Horváth; indeed Handke was largely responsible for bringing the plays of the last to the attention of a younger generation of playwrights and directors.

Handke's first important full-length play, *Kaspar*, performed in Frankfurt in 1968, draws on that Austrian tradition. It was based on the curious real life story of one Kaspar Hauser, who appeared in 1828 at Nuremberg virtually from nowhere. Apparently isolated for the first 16 years of his life from nearly all human contact, he was therefore a kind of language innocent, not knowing his own name, and able to speak only one sentence, "I want to be a good rider, as my father was": Hauser's end was as curious as his beginning, for he died about five years later, stabbed by an unidentified assailant. His intriguing case history has attracted the attention of many writers, but Handke's play is no representational dramatisation of the case; the world of the play is distinctly non-naturalistic, and his Kaspar is a clown who falls through the theatre curtain as if new-born, repeating throughout much of the action the same sentence, "I want to be someone like someone else once was," an adaptation of the real Hauser's words to Handke's artistic purposes. Speakers called Prompters, harass him verbally over the tannoy, and try to break his hold on the sentence; they try to initiate him into society by giving him their rules and regulations, imposing on him society's ideas of form and order. At first he seems amenable, but is increasingly disturbed by this programming until, after becoming a construct, a kind of automaton, he breaks under the pressure, splits into several Kaspars, mocks attempts to conform to society, and ends shouting Othello's distracted cry at the coming of chaos, "goats and monkeys." Handke resorts to a range of theatrical means to drive home the "making" power of words suggesting in his stage directions that bits of speeches by politicians, religious pundits, and distinguished writers be recited over the tannoy in the intervals. Although hostile to the political project of Brechtian theatre, Handke does not reject theatre's instructional role, seeing in Kaspar's inability to resist the pressure of the Prompters a way of forcing the audience to an awareness of its own need to resist social programming.

Handke's second important full-length play, *Der Ritt über den Bodensee* (*The Ride Across Lake Constance*) is based on a legend of a horse rider who, while searching in snow-bound country for a lake, unwittingly rides across the lake while it is frozen and covered with snow. When he is told that the lake for which he has been searching is behind him, and he has crossed it oblivious of all danger, he dies of shock. Such is the power of words, which prove more powerful than the action the words describe: as a thin covering of ice has supported the rider across an abyss, so a thin linguistic reality and an artificial order sustain social life. It is a difficult play, again eschewing traditional character depiction, with well-known actors of the past appearing as themselves, and consists of a series of apparently unconnected, or only loosely connected dialogues and mimes, of changing moods and erratic pace, reminiscent at times of the expressionistic, dreamlike techniques of August Strindberg. This formal originality proved a handicap in the theatre, and the play divided audiences and critical response alike, many finding it overly obscure and thus in breach of the theatre's obligation to communicate. Similar mixed responses characterised the reception of the seemingly more political play, *Die Unvernünftigen sterben aus* (*They Are Dying Out*), when it was performed in England in 1976 at the National Theatre. More readily accessible, if somewhat untheatrical in its recourse to lengthy monologues was the most recent Handke play at the National in 1989, *The Long Way Round*, a bleak and rather pessimistic exploration in four scenes of lost community and rootless urban living.

For more than 20 years Handke has been a remarkably prolific writer, but from the mid-1970s his preference seems to have been less for drama than for the novel and self-exploratory analytical prose. If the Viennese theatrical tradition is strongly felt in his earlier drama, in Handke's novels the influences are more culturally diverse: those of writers as different as Albert Camus and Raymond Chandler have often been remarked, as too has a strong element of the Kafka-esque. But the mode of enquiry pursued in much of his writing into the relationship between "inner" and "outer" worlds is distinctively his own. Perhaps his most successful novel of the 1970s was *Die Angst des Tormanns beim Elfmeter* (*The Goalie's Anxiety at the Penalty Kick*), made into a film by Wim Wenders. Others included *Der kurze Brief zum langen Abschied* (*Short Letter, Long Farewell*), *Wunschloses Unglück* (*A Sorrow Beyond Dreams*), a sombre account of his mother's life and eventual suicide and *Die linkshändige Frau* (*The Left-Handed Woman*), a compelling portrait of the life of a woman abandoned by her husband and bringing up her son in a world bereft of all save consumerist values. Handke made a film from this under the same title in 1977. Increasingly, he has tended to move between the novel and the journal forms, to the reflective, investigative manner of which last he turned in *Das Gewicht der Welt* (*The Weight of the World*), an account of his life in Paris during the mid-1970s, but with the emphasis on recording mental states rather than everyday activities.

In the 1980s he continued to produce remarkable fiction, like *Der Chinese des Schmerzes* (*Across*), exploring the portal to subjective states, and *Die Abwesenheit* (*Absence*), a novella concerned with a small group of travellers — an old man, a gambler, a soldier, and a woman — journeying through a seemingly alien landscape somewhere in modern Europe. As the plays of the late 1960s and 1970s often explored language as an instrument of conditioning and domination, so too many of Handke's novels and autobiographical writings focus on the problems of communication, and the importance of language conventions to understanding. *Die Wiederholung* (*Repetition*), for example, recounts the journey of one Filip Kobal across the Austrian-Yugoslav border into Slovenia to look for his brother Gregor, taking with him his brother's German-Slovene dictionary in which certain words have been marked, and his brother's notebook written in the Slovene language and kept by him while he was a student for three years at the agricultural college in Maribor. Filip's journey is a search, conducted with the help of language tools, not only for his brother, but for understanding of himself and the world, and of himself in the world — as indeed is much of the work that has made Handke one of the most original and rewarding, if undeniably taxing, of contemporary writers.

—Francesca Ross

HAO JAN. *See* **HAO RAN.**

HAO RAN. Pseudonym for Liang Jinguang. Chinese. Born in Zhaogezhuang, Hebei Province, 25 March 1932. Married Yang Puqiao in 1947; three sons and one daughter. Cadre for eight years; head of Children's Corps, 1946; member of the Communist Party, from 1948; helped set up cooperatives in Jixian County, Hebei Province, early 1950s; staff reporter *Hebei Daily*, from 1954; correspondent and editor for various publishers, 1954–64; editor, *Hongqi* [Red Flag] journal, until 1964. Member of the board of directors, China Writers Association; deputy editor-in-chief, *Oriental Juvenile*; vice president, Folk Literature Society, since 1987. Address: 1–8 Building 6, YueTanBeiJie Street, Beijing, China.

PUBLICATIONS

Fiction

Xique dengzhi [A Magpie on a Branch].   Beijing, Beijing Literature and Arts United Press, 1956.
Xiqiao guozhi [Magpie].   Beijing, Zhongguo qingnian chubanshe, 1958.

Pingguo yao shu le [Apples Are Ripening].   Beijing, Zuojia chubanshe, 1959.
Xin chun qu [New Spring Song].   Beijing, Zhongguo qingnian chubanshe, 1960.
Cai xia ji.   Beijing, Zhongguo qingnian chubanshe, 1963; as *Bright Clouds*, Beijing, Foreign Languages Press, 1974.
Ye yang tian [Bright Sunny Skies].   Beijing, Zuojia Publishing House, vol. 1, 1964; Beijing, People's Literature Publishing House, vols. 2 and 3, 1966.
Jinguang da dao.   Beijing, People's Literature Publishing House, 2 vols., 1972–74; as *The Golden Road*, Beijing, Foreign Languages Press, 1981.
The Call of the Fledgling, and Other Children's Stories.   Beijing, Foreign Languages Press, 1974.
Xisha ernu [Sons and Daughters of the Xisha Islands].   Beijing, People's Literature Publishing House, 1974.
"Little Pebble Is Missing."   Published in *A Student's Companion to "Little Pebble Is Missing"*, Princeton, New Jersey, Princeton University, 1977.
Shan shui qing [Affection for Landscape].   Tianjin, Baihua Literature and Arts Publishing House, 1980.
Fu yun [Floating Clouds].   Changchun, Jilin People's Publishing House, 1983.
Qi sui xiang nenye yiyang [Being Seven Is like Being a Bud].   Tianjin, Xin lei, 1984.
Hao Ran xuanji [Selected Works by Hao Ran].   Tianjin, Baihua Literature and Arts Publishing House, 1984.
Jia bu chuqu de sha yatou [The Silly Girl Who Couldn't Get Married].   Beijing, People's Literature Publishing House, 1985.
Xiang su san bu chu [Trilogy of Rural Customs].   Shenyang, Chunfeng Literature and Arts Publishing House, 1986.
Ta he ta zai chen wu li [He and She in the Morning Mist].   Beijing, Nongcun duwu, 1986.

*   *   *

Hao Ran was the best-known Chinese writer of the Cultural Revolution decade, 1966–76. During this period most professional writers of fiction who had escaped disgrace or detention maintained a nervous silence. Amateur worker and peasant writers produced the few new stories which appeared in these years. China's traditional literature had been condemned as feudal and most modern and foreign literature was also suspect. The range of reading matter available in the bookshops was therefore extremely narrow. These circumstances no doubt contributed to Hao Ran's success, but it would be unfair to imply that his books were bought only because people had no choice. Many read his lively stories of peasant life with great pleasure at a time when life in China was culturally barren and politically frightening.

Himself the son of poor peasants in north China, Hao Ran's great gift is his ability to evoke the sights, sounds, and smells of north China's countryside and to portray the life and character of its people. Hao Ran became a communist cadre during the civil war when he was only 14. He was later assigned to propaganda work and became a reporter in the 1950s. He was a prolific writer who produced over a hundred stories before the publication of his first novel, *Ye yang tian* (Bright Sunny Skies). As a loyal and probably a sincere Party member, Hao Ran wrote on approved topics following the Party line, yet the humour and life in his writing usually save it from hack status.

Some of his heroes are undeniably overdrawn. *Ye yang tian* is set in 1957 during collectivisation movement. The village of Dongshanwu has suffered a natural disaster and its leader, instead of organising the villagers to overcome the difficulty, makes for the city with a few of the other able-bodied men to

find temporary jobs which will allow them to send money to their families. Xiao Changchun, a young Party secretary, is shocked, and throws himself into helping the villagers to recover through dedicated collective effort. During the harvest, when his small son goes missing, Changchun calls off the hunt for the boy, reasoning that harvesting is more important. But the novel also has a wealth of convincing positive characters with their own foibles and faults. Even the negative characters are sketched with a certain subtlety and understanding which makes them far more convincing than the usual crude, two-dimensional villains of this genre.

Hao Ran's second novel, *Jinguang da dao* (The Golden Road), was originally planned to appear in four volumes but only two (each of half a million words) appeared. It again concerned collectivisation, showing loyal poor peasants defending collective property against the machinations of former rich peasants and landlords. Faults already manifest in *Ye yang tian* are more pronounced in *The Golden Road*, which was strongly influenced by norms of the Cultural Revolution. The leading figures are unconvincingly flawless, there is much unnecessary rhetoric, and various quotations from Chairman Mao printed in bold face are scattered through the text. Nonetheless, Hao Ran preserves his storyteller's ability to keep the reader wanting to know what happens next, his vivid colloquial language, and his gift for characterisation.

In *Xisha ernu* (Sons and Daughters of the Xisha Islands), Hao Ran lost this remarkable knack of producing literature of some merit while writing to satisfy political demands. The novella is set in the Xisha Islands, claimed by both Vietnam and China, which China had taken from South Vietnamese forces in 1974. It has none of the authenticity of his stories of the North China Plain because he has strayed beyond the life he knows. Moreover, as this piece was said to have been commissioned by Jiang Qing (Mao Zedong's wife), it associated Hao Ran with the Gang of Four sufficiently closely for him to lose his position when they fell from power in 1976.

Hao Ran, whose books once sold millions of copies, is little read in China today. Neither his political themes nor his focus on rural life hold much interest for the reader in post-reform China, and the heroism of his good characters now seems ridiculous. A longer perspective may produce a rediscovery of his virtues. He remains an outstanding writer for his convincing portrayal of the ordinary peasants who make up the vast majority of the Chinese population.

—Delia Davin

———

HATÁR, Gyözö. Hungarian and British. Born in Gyoma, Hungary, 13 November 1914. Educated at the University of Budapest, degree in architecture. Married to Piroska Prágai. Imprisoned for "anti-state activities," 1943–44, and for illegal border crossing, three years, from 1950; emigrated to the United Kingdom, 1956; broadcaster, BBC, London, 1957–76; resident tutor in Hungarian, Foreign Office, London, 1960–80. Recipient: Hungarian Order of the Star decorated with Golden Wreath, 1989; Kossuth prize, 1991. Agent: Artisjus, Vörösmarty tér 1, 1051 Budapest, Hungary. Address: "Hongriuscule," 12 Edge Hill, Wimbledon, London SW19 4LP, England.

PUBLICATIONS

Fiction

Heliáne. Budapest, Magyar Téka, 1947.
Pepito et Pepita. Paris, Julliard, 1963; as *Pepito és Pepita* [Pepito and Pepita], London, Aurora, 1983.
Bábel tornya [The Tower of Babel]. Stockholm, Hungarian Institute, 1966.
Anibel. Paris, Denoël, 1970; in Hungarian, London, Aurora, 1984.
Az őrző könyve: Egregor [The Book of the Guardian]. Munich, Aurora, 1974.
Archie Dumbarton. Paris, Denoël, 1977; as *Éjszaka minden megnő* [In the Night Everything Looms Larger], London, Aurora, 1984.
Köpönyeg sors [He Who Cannot Shake Off His Destiny]. London, Aurora, 1985.
Angelika kertje [The Garden of Angelica]. London, Aurora, 1987.
A szép Palásthyné a más álmában közösül [Lovely Mrs. Palásthy Goes to Bed with Someone in Somebody Else's Dream]. London, Aurora, 1987.
A fontos ember [A Man of Consequence]. Szeged, Jate, 1989.
Eumolposz [Eumolpus]. London, Aurora, 1990.

Plays

Sírónevető (includes *A kötélvilág*; *A Patkánykirály*; *Hernyóprém*; *Bunkócska*; *Hamu a mamumondó*; *A majomház*; *Az aranypalást*; *Némberköztársaság*; *A libegő*; *Elefántcsorda*; *Gargilianus*; *A ravatal*) [Laughing-Crying Masks: The World of Ropes; The Rat King; Vermine Cloak; Little Cudgel; The Knacker's Yard; Monkey House; The Golden Cloak; The Republic of Shrews; Chairlift; Elephant Herd; Gargilianus; The Bier]. Munich, Aurora, 2 vols., 1972.
A Patkánykirály [The Rat King] (produced Nyíregyháza, 1987). Included in *Sírónevető*, 1972.
Elefántcsorda [Elephant Herd] (produced Budapest, 1992). Included in *Sírónevető*, 1972.
Golghelóghi (cycle of nine full-length plays). Munich, Aurora, 1976.
Görgőszínpad [Rolling Stage], translation of eight early medieval English Mystery plays (produced Békéscsaba, 1989). Budapest, Szent István Társulat, 1988.

Verse

Liturgikon [A Book of Liturgies]. Budapest, Antiqua, 1948.
Hajszálhíd [Gossamer Bridge]. Munich, Aurora, 1970.
Lélekharangjáték [Death Knell Chimes]. London, Aurora, 1986.
Medvedorombolás [Purring of a Bear]. London, Aurora, 1988.
A léleknek rengése (válogatott versek, 1933–1988 [Soul Quake: Selected Poems 1933–1988]. Budapest, Orpheusz, 1990.
Halálfej [Skull]. London, Aurora, 1991.
Üvegkoporsó [Glass Coffin]. London, Aurora, 1992.

Other

Pantarbesz. Munich, Aurora, 1966.
Intra muros [Within the Walls]. London, Aurora, 1978.

Özön közöny [Cosmic Indifference]. London, Aurora, 1980.
A rákóra ideje [Time Crabwise]. London, Aurora, 1982.
Szélhárfa I–II–III [Aeolian Harp]. London, Aurora, 3 vols., 1982–83.
Antisumma. London, Aurora, 1983.
Félreugrók, megtántorodók [Dodgers and Backsliders]. London, Aurora, 1983.
Az ég csarnokai [Hallways of the Sky]. London, Aurora, 1987.
Csodák országa hátsó-Eurázia [On the Outback of Eurasia, Land of Miracles]. London, Aurora, 2 vols., 1988.
Rólunk szól I–II–III [It's About Us]. London, Aurora, 3 vols., 1990.
Filozófiai zárlatok [Philosophical Cadences]. London, Aurora, 1992.

Translator, *Négy szovjet egyfelvonásos* [Four Soviet One-Act Plays]. Budapest, Irodalmi Intézet, 1948.
Translator, with Elek Sárváry and Klára Szőllősy, *Maruszja: három kisregény* [Marusia: Three Novelettes]. Budapest, Révai, 1949.
Translator, *Panfjorov: harc a békéért* [Panfjorov: Fight for Peace], by F. I. Panferov. Budapest, Révai, 1949.
Translator, *Solochov: Akik a hazáért harcoltak* [Sholohov: Those Who Fought for Country], by Mihail Alekszandrovics Solohov. Budapest, Honvédelmi Minisztérium, 1949.
Translator, *Szegény szerelmesek krónikája* [Cronache di poveri amanti], by Vasco Pratolini. Budapest, Móra, 1955.
Translator, with Zoltán Bartos, *Válogatott elbeszélések* [Selected Short Stories], by Jack London. Budapest, Új Magyar Kiadó, 1955.
Translator, *Tristam Shandy* (into Hungarian), by Laurence Sterne. Budapest, Új Magyar Könyvkiadó, 1956.
Translator, *Rókák a szőlőben* [Foxes in the Vineyard], by Lion Feuchtwanger. Budapest, Új Magyar Kiadó, 1956.
Translator, *Érzelmes utazás Francia- és Olaszországban* [A Sentimental Journey Through France and Italy], by Laurence Sterne. Budapest, Európa, 1957.
Translator, with János Benyhe and Endre Szokoly, *Imposztorok tüköre: spanyol kópéregények* [Mirror of Imposters: Spanish Picaresque Novels], edited by Rezső Honti. Budapest, Európa, 1957.
Translator, with István Bart, *Elbeszélések* [Short Stories], by Jack London. Budapest, Athenaeum, 1968.
Translator, *Hajrá!* [Forward!], by Valentin Kataev. Budapest, Európa, 1972.
Translator, with István Bart, *Messze földön* [Tales of the Far North], by Jack London. Budapest, Európa, 1975.

*

Manuscript Collection: Petőfi Museum of Literature Budapest.

Győző Határ comments:
    In both my fiction and poetry I was described as an "avant garde" — provided this term has a validity of three millennia My stage plays are "well-made" plays with a timeless avant garde flavour. In philosophy I belong to the school of Phyrron and Sextus Empiricus; and, while on the one hand my effort went towards demythologizing inherited misconceptions an ingrained, built-in idiotisms of the language, on the other I wa against the aridity of all cul-de-sac philosophies, includin semantics. Founded on a possibly thorough knowledge o

neurology and the working of human sensorium, the highest ranking discipline of philosophy would be ontology — always bearing in mind that philosophy is the privilege of deferred and/or suspended judgement.

With passing several years in both Fascist and Communist prisons and spending four decades in emigration, I have had a chequered life. Yet studies, travels, and experiences never make a polymath unless one has that bent of contemplation which turns one into a philosopher — in the original, Pythagorean sense of the word.

* * *

Győző Határ is undoubtedly the most eminent and prolific Hungarian writer living outside Hungary. An architect by training, Határ wrote his first novel in 1938 but its lithographed copies were impounded by the authorities. His political opposition to the pre-1945 régime landed Határ in jail, which was why his debut took place belatedly after World War II with the publication of the surrealistic novel *Heliáne* and the slim volume of verse and prose poems *Liturgikon* (A Book of Liturgies). They were all that Határ was able to publish before emigrating to England in 1956, but these two books were enough to establish him as one of the most challenging modern Hungarian writers. His literary career, once again interrupted by political developments (a jail sentence for an attempt to escape from Communist Hungary) in the 1950s, took off again in the mid-1960s as he published an increasing number of books in London and Munich. In 1988 Határ began to be published in Hungary again, and in 1991 he was awarded the Hungarian Kossuth prize for his overall achievement.

Határ is a master of nearly all literary genres. If, however, a hierarchy were required, one could say that his most "central" genre around which all others are concentrated is drama. Határ is the author of a large number of plays collected in the two volumes of *Síróneveto* (Laughing-Crying Masks) which, as the title indicates, has room for comedies, tragedies, and most often, tragicomedies. Most of the plays tackle eternal human questions set against different backgrounds: *A kötélvilág* (The World of Ropes) takes place in the cosmic void where human archetypes "dream" about a world which is not yet realized; *A Patkánykirály* (The Rat King) is about the love-hate relationship of a deserter from World War II with the woman who had saved him and keeps him hidden from the world; *Hernyóprém* (Vermine Cloak) is a brilliant parody of political change, the illusory progress of mankind shown from "aristocratic" systems of government through "democracies" back to the monarchy — only the rhetoric changes, while the mechanism of power remains the same. But Határ the playwright attaches most importance to the cycle of mystery plays *Golghelóghi* — the medieval saga of a simple village lad who owns a Book, turns into a Rebel, then attains ever-higher worldly dignities, only to end up in the metaphysical world as a servant of Lord Satan (who is none else but the Creator). Not only is the scale of Golgheloghi impressive — so too are its incredibly rich and variegated language and the multitude of characters who populate this medieval dreamworld. Unfortunately *Golghelóghi* is likely to remain a cycle of plays only to be read, for the task of staging it is probably too taxing for even the most sophisticated European theatre.

The scope of Határ's poetry is baroque; he writes not only poetry in the traditional sense of the word, but also dialogues-in-verse, minidramas, and prose poems. Many of his poems are oneiric in their origin: Határ claims to have composed them in a dream, or at least dreamt of the first few lines. This points to an affinity with surrealism, except that in Határ's case the conscious mind has control over the linguistic

material thrown up by the subconscious. Another characteristic of this poetry is its predilection for impersonation: Határ can assume the voice of the medieval monk with the same ease as that of the 20th-century underworld hero or mythical Eastern emperor. His most representative collections of poetry to date are *Hajszálhíd* (Gossamer Bridge) and *A léleknek rengése* (Soul Quake).

Most readers, and especially French readers of Határ, would know of him as a prose writer above all. (Three of his novels were published first in French between 1963 and 1977.) In fact, the sheer scope and diversity of Határ's prose is astounding. It includes light picaresque novels like the early *Pepito és Pepita* (Pepito and Pepita), fantastic novels about the fate of our civilisation like *Az orzo könyve* (The Book of the Guardian), and ambiguous historical novels such as *Köpönyeg sors* (He Who Cannot Shake Off His Destiny), about the youth of Julian the Apostate. Határ's short prose is also remarkable in its diversity: it includes satirical pieces about western mass culture, metaphysical dreams carried through to their conclusion, and philosophical cameos. The highly amusing long story "Az éjszaka muszaka" (The Night Shift) tackles the problem of dislocation in the context of a foreign journalist working for the World Service of the BBC.

Finally, Határ has published a number of books of philosophical writings and essays critical of contemporary culture and civilization. His empiricist and anti-metaphysical philosophical ideas produced relatively little response among readers, but the critique of culture provided in *Intra muros* (Within the Walls) and *Özön közöny* (Cosmic Indifference) shows him to be an acute observer of the western world which he sees as steeped in cheap consumerism and frighteningly shortsighted in its ignorance of the challenges of the future.

—George Gömöri

———

HAUGE, Olav H(åkonsson). Norwegian. Born in Ulvik, 18 August 1908. Married Bodil Cappelen in 1975. Farmer. Recipient: Norwegian Critics' prize, 1961; Swedish Academy Dobloug prize, 1969; Aschehoug prize, 1978. Address: 5730 Ulvik, Hardanger, Norway.

PUBLICATIONS

Verse

Glør i oska [Ambers in the Ashes]. Oslo, Noregs Boklag, 1946.
Under bergfallet [Under the Mountain]. Oslo, Noregs Boklag, 1951.
Seint rødnar skog i djuvet [Slowly the Woods Redden in the Gorge]. Oslo, Noregs Boklag, 1956.
På ørnetuva [On the Eagle's Hill]. Oslo, Noregs Boklag, 1961.
Dikt i utval; Dogg og dagar [Selected Poems; Dew and Days). Oslo, Noregs Boklag, 1964.
Dropar i austavind [Drops in the East Wind]. Oslo, Noregs Boklag, 1966.
Utanlandske dikt [Poems from Abroad]. Oslo, Noregs Boklag, 1967.
Spør vinden [Ask the Wind]. Oslo, Noregs Boklag, 1971.

Dikt i samling [Collected Poems]. Oslo, Noregs Boklag, 1972.

Syn oss akeren din [Show Us Your Farmland]. Oslo, Den Norske Bokklubben, 1975.

Janglestrå [Straws]. Oslo, Noregs Boklag, 1980.

Dikt i umsetjing [Poems in Translation]. Oslo, Noregs Boklag, 1982.

Regnbogane [The Rainbows], with Wenche Øyen. Oslo, Norske Samlaget, 1983.

Don't Give Me the Whole Truth, translated by Robin Fulton, James Greene, and Siv Hennum. London, Anvil Press Poetry, 1985.

ABC, with Bodil Cappelen. Oslo, DN Samlaget, 1986.

Trusting Your Life to Water and Eternity (bilingual edition), edited and translated by Robert Bly. Minneapolis, Milkweed, 1987.

Other

Noen trekk ved Stavangers kulturhistorie [Aspects of the Cultural History of Stavanger]. Stavanger, n.p., 1976.

Tankar om dikting [Thoughts About Writing], edited by Knut Johansen. Oslo, Per Sivle Forlaget, 1978.

Editor and Translator, *Til ettertidi: 21 dikt*, by Bertolt Brecht. Oslo, Oktober, 1978.

Translator, *Svarte ryttarar*, by Stephen Crane. Oslo, Noregs Boklag, 1974.

*

Critical Study: "Nature Imagery in Olav V. Hauge's Poetry" by Katherine Hanson, in *Proceedings: Pacific Northwest Council on Foreign Languages*, 29, 1978.

*   *   *

Olav H. Hauge is one of the most important Norwegian poets of his generation, and is seen as something of a sage by critics and readers alike. He has always lived far from the mainstream of literary life, making his living as a small farmer and gardener. His reading has been extensive, however, as illustrated by his many — and superb — translations of English, German, and French poetry.

Few readers or critics were aware of Hauge until a new generation of poets and readers discovered his poetry in the 1960s and 1970s. Since then he has achieved an almost mythical status, not least because he has lived on his small farm, growing apples and writing poems without paying much heed to shifting trends. Hauge's special position in Norwegian poetry is related to his being rooted in an old tradition and writing from an experience of the countryside. Much wisdom is often hidden in the simplest of expressions in his concrete poems, including those about objects from his everyday life at the farm.

Hauge's first collection, *Glør i oska* (Ambers in the Ashes), went largely unnoticed. Although a few poems anticipate the economical use of words, sharp observation, and precise expression of his later poetry, most of his work deals with the plight of the poet and with the loneliness and despair of searching for elusive words. The poet calls for inspiration in good romantic tradition, and is most interested in the eternal questions of life, time, and being.

In his next collection of poems, *Under bergfallet* (Under the Mountain), published five years later, the poet's dreams and fears are of a kind not easily shared by his readers. Poem after poem finds new images for a constant problem: the distance

between the dreams and longings and beauty of poetry and the hardships and greyness of everyday life. The poet accepts that some burdens, even failure, are his to carry. One might think that the solidarity of the society Hauge lived in and knew well might help him to overcome such problems, but only later does he solve the conflict between life and art in any meaningful sense.

Seint rødnar skog i djuvet (Slowly the Woods Redden in the Gorge), is characterized by a number of poems in which the relations between people are positive and meaningful. A number of poems describe objects or phenomena in a language purged of symbols or metaphors; the objects remain objects — an axe, a fishing hook, a saw — but they invite the readers to read figuratively, so that the concrete and simple may point to deeper meaning. The wild and rugged landscape of the western parts of Norway is described in poem after poem, and Hauge clearly prefers the spectacular to the calm and quiet. But the landscape is not devoid of its peculiar beauty, which lends a softness to poems in which darkness, cold, and loneliness dominate. Some of these poems are reminiscent of Robert Frost's poetry, and Hauge's strength clearly lies in his ability to combine simplicity of form and expression with a much more profound meaning. *På ørnetuva* (On the Eagle's Hill) is again located in a typical Hauge landscape of mountains, fjords, and rivers, full of dramatic contrasts, and nature is a central theme. The sky above the poet is cold and tense, the moon is threatening, and with so little comfort to find in human relationships, he posits that dreams may be our only solace. Our limitless need for companionship and kindness, for love and compassion, seems to be realized only in the dream world of art.

Later, in *Dropar i austavind* (Drops in the East Wind), Hauge's observations and their poetic expression become more mature, generous, and hopeful. He also makes numerous ironic attempts at modernist poetry, with considerable success. To read and write poetry is now accepted as an activity on a par with everyday duties, and there is much more hope and belief in individual strength in these poems.

In Hauge's later collections, *Spør vinden* (Ask the Wind) and *Janglestrå* (Straws), conflicts from earlier collections have been resolved, although the subject-matter, landscape, and themes are variations of well-known interests in his writing. Typical of these late collections are numerous poems on other poets — William Blake, Gérard de Nerval, Georg Trakl — and poems on poetry itself, now characterized by humour and irony.

Hauge's *Dikt i samling* (Collected Poems) has definitively established the old poet as a Nestor among Norwegian poets.

—Hans H. Ske

———

HAVEL, Václav. Czech. Born in Prague, 5 October 1936. Educated at a technical college, 1955–57; Academy of Arts, Prague, 1962–66. Served in the Czechoslovak Army, 1957–59. Married Olga Šplíchalová in 1964. Chemical laboratory technician, 1951–55; stagehand, ABC Theatre, Prague, 1959–60; stagehand, 1960–61, assistant to the artistic director, 1961–63, literary manager, 1963–68, and resident playwright, 1968, Divadlo na zábradlí [Theatre on the Balustrade], Prague; member of editorial board, *Tvář*, 1965; writings judged subversive: passport confiscated, 1969; worker at Trutno

Brewery, North Bohemia, 1974; co-founder, 1977, and spokesman, 1978, 1989, Charter 77 human rights group; imprisoned for brief terms, 1977, 1978–79; co-founder, Committee for the Defense of the Unjustly Prosecuted (VONS), 1978; sentenced to four and a half years imprisonment for subversion of the republic, 1979: released because of illness, 1983; member of editorial board, and regular contributor, *Lidové noviny* [The People's Paper] samizdat newspaper, 1987–89; arrested and sentenced to nine months imprisonment for incitement and resisting arrest, January 1989: released May 1989; co-founder and leader, Občanské fórum [Civil Forum] political party, 1989; President of the Czech and Slovak Federal Republic, 1989–92, and of the Czech Republic, since 1993. Recipient: Obie award, 1968, 1970; Austrian state prize, 1969; Prix Plaisir du Théâtre (France), 1981; Palach prize, 1981; Erasmus prize, 1986; Olof Palme prize, 1989; Frankfurt Book Fair Peace prize, 1989; Unesco Bolívar prize, 1990; Roosevelt Four Freedom award, 1990; Friedrich-Elbert Foundation Political Book of the Year award, 1990; Malaparte prize, 1990; Man of Peace, 1990; Beyond the War award, 1990; Legion of Honour Grand Cross, 1990; Unesco prize for the teaching of human rights, 1991; Charlemagne prize, 1991; Sonning prize, 1991; Averell Harriman Democracy award (USA), 1991; B'Nai Brith prize (USA), 1991; Freedom award (USA), 1991; Raoul Wallenberg Human Rights award (USA), 1991; International Book award, 1991; Leonhard-Frank-Ring (Germany), 1992. Honorary doctorate: York University, Toronto, 1982; Le Mirail University, Toulouse, 1982; Columbia University, New York, Hebrew University, Jerusalem, Bayreuth University, University of F. Palacký, Olomouc, Charles University, Prague, and University of J. A. Komenský, Bratislava, all 1990; Free University of Brussels, St. Gallen University, LeHigh University, Bethlehem, Pennsylvania, and New York University, all 1991. Agent: Rowohlt Taschenbuch Verlag, Hamburger Straße 17, Postfach 1349, 2057 Reinbek, Germany. Address: Rašínovo nábřeží 78, 120 00 Prague 2, Czech Republic.

PUBLICATIONS

Plays

Autostop [The Hitchhiking], with Ivan Vyskočil (produced Prague, 1961). Prague, Dilia, 1961.
Nejlepší rocky paní Hermannové [The Best "Rock" of Mrs. Hermann], with Miloš Macourek (produced Prague, 1962).
Zahradní slavnost (produced Prague, 1963). Prague, Orbis, 1964; as *The Garden Party*, London, Cape, 1969.
Vyrozumění (produced Prague, 1965). Published in *Protokoly*, Prague, Mladá fronta, 1966; as *The Memorandum* (produced New York, 1968; London, 1970), London, Cape, 1967; New York, Grove Press, 1980.
Ztížená možnost soustředění (produced Prague, 1968). Prague, Orbis, 1969; as *The Increased Difficulty of Concentration* (produced New York, 1970; Richmond, Surrey, 1978; London, 1989), London, Cape, 1972; New York, French, 1976.
Spiklenci [The Conspirators] (produced in German, Baden-Baden, 1974). Shortened version in *Hry*, 1977; full version, Prague, (samizdat) Edice Expedice, 86, 1979.
Audience (produced in German, Vienna, 1976). Prague, (samizdat) Edice Petlice 47, 1975; in *Hry*, 1977; in English (produced London, 1977), in *Sorry*, 1978; as *Conversation* (produced London, 1990).

Vernisáž (produced in German, Vienna, 1976). Prague, (samizdat) Edice Petlice 51, 1975; in *Hry*, 1977; as *A Private View* (produced London, 1977; New York, 1983), in *Sorry*, 1978; as *Unveiling*, in *Three Vaněk Plays*, 1990.
Žebrácká opera (produced in Italian, Trieste, 1976). Prague, (samizdat) Edice Petlice 46 and 10; in *Hry*, 1977; as *The Beggar's Opera* (produced Vancouver, British Columbia, 1992).
Hry 1970–1976 [Plays 1970–1976] (includes *Spiklenci*; *Žebrácká opera*; *Horský hotel*; *Audience*; *Vernisáž*). Toronto, 68 Publishers, 1977.
Horský hotel [The Mountain Resort] (produced in German, Vienna, 1981). Prague, (samizdat) Edice Petlice 62 and 10; in *Hry*, 1977.
Sorry (two one-act plays: includes *Audience*; *Private View*) (produced London, 1986). London, Eyre Methuen, 1978.
Protest (produced in German, Vienna, 1979). Prague, (samizdat) Edice Expedice 89, 1978; in English (produced New York, 1983; London, 1989), in *DRAMA-CONTEMPORARY/Czechoslovakia*, New York, Performing Arts Publications, 1985; in *Three Vaněk Plays*, 1990.
Chyba (produced in Swedish, Stockholm, 1983). Prague, (samizdat) *Obsah*, May 1983; as *The Mistake* (produced London, 1984), in *Selected Plays 1963–1983*, 1991.
Largo desolato (produced in German, Vienna, 1985). Prague, (samizdat) Edice Petlice 281 and 195, 1984; Munich, Obrys/Kontur, 1985; in English (produced New York and Bristol, 1986), New York, Grove Press, and London, Faber, 1987.
Pokoušení (produced in German, Vienna, 1986). Prague, (samizdat) Edice Petlice 306 and 223; Munich, Obrys/Kontur, 1986; as *Temptation* (produced Stratford-upon-Avon, 1987; New York, 1989), London, Faber, 1988; New York, Grove Weidenfeld, 1989.
Ztížené možnosti: (tři hry z šedesátých let) [Worsened Possibilities (Three Plays from the 1960s)]. London, Rozmluvy, 1986.
Asanace (produced in German, Zurich, 1989). Prague, (samizdat) Edice Petlice 361, 1987; Munich, Obrys/Kontur, 1988; as *Redevelopment* (produced Richmond, Surrey, 1990); as *Redevelopment, or, Slum Clearance*, London, Faber, 1990.
The Vaněk Plays, Four Authors, One Character (three one-act plays: includes *Audience*; *Protest*; *Unveiling*). Vancouver, University of British Columbia Press, 1987; as *The Vaněk Plays* (produced London, 1989); as *Three Vaněk Plays*, London, Faber, 1990.
Selected Plays 1963–1983 (includes *The Garden Party*; *The Memorandum*; *The Increased Difficulty of Concentration*; *Audience/Conversation*; *Private View*; *Protest*; *The Mistake*). London, Faber, 1991.

Radio Plays: *Anděl strážý* [The Guardian Angel], 1968; *Audience* and *Private View* (United Kingdom).

Television Plays: *Motýl na anténě* [Butterfly on the Antenna], 1975 (Germany); *Audience* and *Private View*, as *Sorry: Two Plays*, 1978–79 (United Kingdom).

Other

Josef Čapek, with Věra Ptáčková. Prague, Divadclní Ústav, 1963.
Protokoly [Minutes] (miscellany). Prague, Mladá fronta, 1966.

Moc bezmocných. Prague, (samizdat) Edice Petlice 149, 1978; London, Londýnské listy, 1979; as *The Power of the Powerless: Citizens Against the State in Central Eastern Europe*, London, Hutchinson, 1985.

Šestnáct dopisů [16 Letters (abridged)]. Prague, (samizdat) Edice Expedice 157, 1982.

Dopisy Olze (letters to wife from prison). Prague, (samizdat) Edice Petlice 261 and 166, 1983; as *Letters to Olga June 1979 to September 1982*, edited by Paul Wilson, London, Faber, and New York, Knopf, 1988.

Thriller. Prague, (samizdat) *Obsah*, November 1984; in English, in *The Idler*, June–July 1985.

O lidskou identitu: úvahy, fejetony, protesty, polemiky, prohlášení a rozhovory z let 1969–1979 [Towards Human Identity: Essays, Columns, Protests, Polemical Articles, Declarations, and Conversations from the Years 1969–1979]. London, Rozmluvy, 1984.

Politika a svědomí. Published in *Přirozený svět jako politický problém*, Prague, (samizdat) Edice Expedice 188, 1984; as *Politics and Conscience*, Stockholm, Charter 77 Foundation, 1986.

Výzva k transcendenci [Appeal to the Transcendental], with *Consolatio philosophiae hodierna* (as Sidonious). London, Rozmluvy, 1984.

The Anatomy of a Reticence: Eastern European Dissidents and the Peace Movement in the West. Stockholm, Charter 77 Foundation, 1985.

Václav Havel; or, Living in Truth, edited by Jan Vladislav. Amsterdam, Meulenhoff, 1986; London, Faber, 1987.

Děkovná řeč při udělení Erasmovy ceny. Prague, (samizdat) *Obsah*, November 1986; as *Acceptance Speech Written on the Occasion of the Award of the Erasmus Prize 1986*, Amsterdam, Foundation Praemium Erasmianum, 1986.

Dálkový výslech: rozhovor s Karlem Hvížď alou (interviews). Prague, (samizdat) Edice Expedice 233, and London, Rozmluvy, 1986; as *Disturbing the Peace: A Conversation with Karel Hvížď ala*, London, Faber, and New York, Knopf, 1990.

Do různých stran: eseje a články z let 1983–1989 [With Different Destinations: Essays and Articles from 1983–1989]. Scheinfeld-Schwarzenberg, Československé Středisko Nezávislé Literatury, 1989.

Projevy: leden–červen 1990 [Speeches: January–June 1990]. Prague, Vyšehrad, 1990.

Open Letters: Selected Writings 1965–1990, edited by Paul Wilson. New York, Knopf, 1991; as *Open Letters: Selected Prose 1965–1990*, London, Faber, 1991.

Letní přemítaní. Prague, Odeon, 1991; as *Summer Meditations*, New York, Knopf, 1992.

Editor, *Podoby 2.* Prague, Československy spisovatel, 1969.

Editor, *Pohledy I.* Prague, (samizdat) Edice Petlice 74, 1976.

Editor, *Přirozený svět jako politický problém* [The Natural World as a Political Problem], by Václav Bělohradský and others. Prague, (samizdat) Edice Expedice 188, 1984.

Editor, *Hostina: filozofický sborník* [The Banquet: Philosophical Miscellany]. Prague, (samizdat) Edice Expedice 209, 1985; Toronto, 68 Publishers, 1989.

*

Bibliographies: in *Slovník českých spisovatelů*, Toronto, 68 Publishers, 1982; in *Do různých stran: eseje a články z let 1983–1989*, Scheinfeld-Schwarzenberg, Československé Středisko Nezávislé Literatury, 1989; by Jana Kalich, University of Toronto, forthcoming.

Critical Studies: *Czech Drama Since World War II*, White Plains, New York, Sharpe, 1978, and "Havel's *The Garden Party* Revisited," in *Czech Literature Since 1956: A Symposium*, edited by William E. Harkins and Paul I. Trensky, New York, Bohemica, 1980, both by Paul I. Trensky; "Dramaturgy of Models" by Andrzej Wirth, in *Theatre Byways*, edited by C. J. Stevens and Joseph Aurbach, New Orleans, Polyanthos, 1978; *The Silenced Theatre: Czech Playwrights Without a Stage*, Toronto, University of Toronto Press, 1979, "Václav Havel, A Writer for Today's Season," in *World Literature Today* (Norman, Oklahoma), 55(3), 1981, "Ethics at the Cross Roads: The Czech 'Dissident Writer' as Dramatic Character," in *Modern Drama* (Toronto), 27(1), 1984, "Variations of Temptation: Václav Havel's Politics of Language," in *Modern Drama* (Toronto), 33(1), 1990, and "Shall We Dance? Reflections on Václav Havel's Plays," in *Cross Currents* (Ann Arbor, Michigan), 10, 1991, all by Marketa Goetz-Stankiewicz; "I Take the Side of Truth" (interview) by Antoine Spire, in *Index on Censorship* (London), 12(6), 1983; "Havel's *Private View*" by Vera Blackwell, in *Cross Currents* (Ann Arbor, Michigan), 3, 1984; "Václav Havel's Second Wind" by Muriel C. Bradbrook, in *Modern Drama* (Toronto), 27(1), 1984; "'Good Guy, Bad Guy' Effects in Political Theatre" by Ed Tan and Henry Schoenmakers, in *Semiotics of Drama and Theatre: New Perspectives in the Theory of Drama and Theatre*, edited by Herta Schmid and Aloysius van Kesteren, Amsterdam, Benjamins, 1984; "Václav Havel in England" by Barbara Day, in *Cross Currents* (Ann Arbor, Michigan), 7, 1988; "Cops or Robbers: Václav Havel's Beggar's Opera" by Peter Steiner, in *American Contributions to the Tenth International Congress of Slavists, Sofia, September 1988: Literature*, edited by Jane Gary Harris, Columbus, Ohio, Slavica, 1988; *Václav Havel: The Authorized Biography* by Eda Kriseova, Boston, Atlantic Monthly Press, 1991; "'Leave Me Alone!': Chekhovian Echoes in Havel" by Karen E. Lordi, in *Theatre (Yale)* (New Haven, Connecticut), 22(3), 1991; *The Reluctant President: A Political Life of Václav Havel* by Michael Simmons, London, Methuen, 1991.

*   *   *

Ironically, Václav Havel's stature as a major contemporary dramatist has been partly obscured by the attention given to two diametrically opposed aspects of his personal and political experience. Before the downfall of communism in 1989 it was his year-long leading participation in human rights movements in his country, his harassment and imprisonment by the State authorities; after 1989 it was his precipitous rise to the presidency of his country that dominated his image in the public eye. However, though momentarily overshadowed by the oddly sensational extremes of his life, Havel, the playwright, has given unique dramatic shape to some of the burning issues facing us today. Broadly speaking, there is a multi-levelled analysis of three interrelated themes at the core of Havel's plays: first, the complex relationship of the human being and the system he not only lives under but of which he is also part and perpetrator; secondly, the progressive mechanization of the human being; and thirdly, language as a medium that both rules human consciousness and can be used as an instrument of power. On first glance, this hardly seems the stuff that good theatre is made of. But in Havel's plays it is. His texts carry their remarkable moral and intellectual burden very lightly. In fact, one has, as it were, to search for it among the lively action and entertaining histrionics of his plays.

Up to the present Havel's plays can be roughly divided into four overlapping sections. In *Zahradní slavnost* (*The Garden Party*), *Vyrozumění* (*The Memorandum*), and *Horský hotel* (The Mountain Resort) the playwright's interest in language is most obvious. *The Garden Party* shows a protagonist who, by acquiring an "official" language, swiftly rises to bureaucratic fame. In *The Memorandum* Havel puts language itself on display by actually inventing a synthetic language, and then demonstrating how it perpetuates a senseless system. By the time Havel writes *Horský hotel* language has become autonomous, the speakers interchangeable.

The second group of plays reveals Havel's basic concern with mechanizing structures. *Ztížená možnost soustředění* (*The Increased Difficulty of Concentration*) deals with a citizen who has been selected as a sample of computerized behaviour patterns. As his own life becomes increasingly mechanized and predictable, the computer recording his experiences develops "human" qualities. *Spiklenci* (The Conspirators), a play with which Havel is dissatisfied, deals with the suspect motivations of "revolutionaries"; *Žebrácká opera* (*The Beggar's Opera*, recasting Gay and Brecht) shows how clashes between guardians of the law and figures of the underworld turn out to be strategic collaboration.

The third group — three one-act plays frequently staged abroad during their author's lengthy prison sentence — is built around the "dissident" writer Vaněk (a character that has been "borrowed" by other Czech writers), who gets into situations that are both absurd and — in the context of communist Czechoslovakia — realistic. In each play Vaněk's ethical standards are put to the test. In *Audience* a cushier job is offered in return for information for the State police files. The promise of a less harassed existence in return for certain "adjustments" is the subject of *Unveiling*. In *Protest* a successful, "integrated" writer confronts Vaněk with a brilliant self-defence, perhaps the best example of perverted rationality displayed in contemporary theatre.

Of Havel's three latest plays *Largo desolato* is a complex afterthought to the Vaněk plays. The protagonist, another writer, no longer appears clearly as a "dissident" but rather as a prisoner of his own fears and nightmares, who prefers the certainty of prison to the uncertainty of "freedom." In *Pokoušení* (*Temptation*), a version of the Faust myth, the tempter and the tempted hold three razor-sharp dialogues dissecting patterns of strategic reasoning and rationalization processes against a highly theatrical background reflecting the usual Havel themes: the mechanisms of bureaucracy, role-playing tactics within love relationships, seduction by language. Havel's latest play *Asanace* (*Slum Clearance* or *Redevelopment*) is again concerned with bureaucratic constellations. The basic theme here is the levelling and subsequently more sanitary reconstruction of a picturesque but run-down historic village, and in broader terms, the perennial dialectics of destruction and renewal in human life.

Havel's prose writings, of course, show a drastic turn at the end of 1989. Before that there were the searching texts he wrote as "dissident" — their titles speak for themselves: His "Letter to Dr. Gustav Husák, General Secretary of the Czechoslovak Communist Party," the much-quoted essay "The Power of the Powerless," "Responsibility as Destiny," "Politics and Conscience," "Anatomy of a Reticence," "Stories and Totalitarianism," and "A Word About Words" are only a few samples of his writings that have gained the attention of the international readership. Since 1990 there have also been his widely publicized presidential speeches, which are regarded as essays of sorts and are admired for their candour, lack of political clichés, and challenge to the intellect.

Four volumes of prose that appeared in English in Paul Wilson's translation should be mentioned: *Dopisy Olze* (*Letters to Olga*), Havel's letters from prison to his wife tracing, as it were, a victory of mind over matter; *Dálkový výslech* (*Disturbing the Peace*), a book-length interview giving perhaps the deepest insight into Havel's personality; *Open Letters*, a collection of his essays from 1965 to 1990; and *Letní přemítaní* (*Summer Meditations*), Havel's first book as President, consisting of reflections on the nature of politics.

Havel has warned us repeatedly of the "mysterious, ambiguous, ambivalent, and perfidious phenomenon" of words. When using them as playwright, he revealed and illuminated these dubious qualities of language, making them the trademark of his theatre. For the time being the "playwright" has had to fall silent and the "statesman" has been left to speak, having to use much the same potentially treacherous words and making them ring true. This is indeed a unique situation in contemporary literature.

—Marketa Goetz-Stankiewicz

————

ḤAYDARI, Buland al-. Iraqi. Born of a Kurdish family in 1926. Educated in Baghdad. Lived in exile in Beirut, 1963–76, then returned to Baghdad. Now lives in London. Address: c/o Riad el-Rayyes Books, 56 Knightsbridge, London SW1X 7NJ, London.

PUBLICATIONS

Verse

Khuṭwāt fil ghurba [Steps in Exile].   1965.
Khafqāt al-ṭīn [The Throbbing of Clay].   n.d.
Aghāni al-ḥaris al-mut'ab.   Beirut, n.p., 1971; as *Songs of the Tired Guard*, Washington, D.C., Three Continents Press, and London, TR Press, 1977.
Ilā Bayrūt ma'a taḥiyyāti [Greetings to Beirut].   London, Al-Saqi, 1989.
Abwāb ila al-bayt al-dayyiq [Doors to the Narrow House]. London, Riad el-Rayyes, 1990.

Other

Madākhil ila al-sh'ir al-'Irāqi al-ḥadīth [Introduction to Modern Iraqi Poetry].   Cairo, al-Ḥayāh al-Misriyah al-'Āmmah lil-Kitāb, 1987.

*   *   *

One of the pioneers in the free verse movement, Buland al-Ḥaydari's aspirations towards modernising Arabic poetry have involved the freeing of poetry from its traditional restrictions and its élitist position. He has attempted, along with many other Arab poets, to bring poetry to the average man, through the use of vivid imagery and eloquent but simple language, in rhythms close to those of everyday speech.

Al-Ḥaydari's sympathy towards Communism, his political activities, and his subsequent exile first from Iraq to Lebanon, and then to the West are all reflected in his poetry. In exile, especially, his life is viewed as a kind of simple existential being. Thus solitude is a recurring theme in his poetry. Man's solitariness and the inevitability of death dictate al-Ḥaydari's anxious tone in his poem "Twenty Thousand Killed . . . Old News":

> Tomorrow I will die with the flock
> Alone
> My head here
> My leg there
> My hand pressing my hand
> A terrible pain
> I feel the eagerness of Spring
> Dying in me
> Oh death

The theme of the city is a frequent one; it is seen as a centre of political repression and intrigue, as well as a place where the poor are trapped as though in a prison cell and can do no more than seek to survive in a miserable and degraded state. Although a city man himself, al-Ḥaydari describes his unnamed city with such phrases as "the belly of a whale," "a wilderness," and "a human mill." This dehumanized metropolis is above all a place where one feels acutely alone among the crowd. These two themes are deftly interwoven in poems such as "The Lost Footstep," where a small village has been turned into a big city with its glaring lights and its impersonality:

> Nothing knows me or is known to me here
> Nothing remembers me or is remembered by me here
> I will drag my little footsteps in its great streets
> I will be crushed by its blind alleys
> But . . . I will never return
> To whom shall I return, for my village has become a city.

Being consciously aware of the validity of traditional religious values, al-Ḥaydari strongly criticises the old and stagnant beliefs as major obstructions in the way of progress, especially when despotic political and religious leaders use them to gain their own ends, without considering the misery and injustice faced by the ordinary people. In "The Journey of the Yellow Letters," al-Ḥaydari condemns three religions:

> For a thousand years
> we have been the yellowed letters in the New Testament
> and the Torah
> and the Qur'an,
> the letters of mould
> daily manifested
> . . .
> in the oppressor's whip
> in God, in Satan
> but not once in a human being.
>
> For a thousand years, children of my poor village
> we have slept the long sleep of history
> and worshipped our frightful shadows in your eyes

The use of historical, religious, and mythological symbols to express the mental and physical states of the poet is a hallmark of modern Arabic poetry. So, for example, al-Ḥaydari employs the figure of Christ and the crucifixion in "The Disappointment of Ancient Man" to express his own sacrifices for his country and people. At the end of his long path of suffering and exile, the poet achieves the state of a prophet-god:

> Life nailed the cross to each forehead
> and each hour crucified Christ,
> each moment crucified his corpse.
> My pain was a life-long intoxication
> with Him; His skies fell upon my dried eyes.
> A story of a wanderer strangled by his steps —
> and, Sister, I bore my wandering within.
> I prayed,
> fasted
> and in my wandering became a god.

The Greek legend of Sisyphus is also adopted by al-Ḥaydari; the protagonist is no longer a traditional hero so much as an individual who has fallen prey to his own integrity, and is thus doomed to continuous suffering, since "the earth has nothing new/For a fugitive like" him. "And China's Wall still tells its story,/And the earth still has its Sisyphus/Yet the stone doesn't know what it wants" ("The Postman").

al-Ḥaydari's use of reiteration and repetition to emphasise and signify the idea expressed and to unify the rhythm of a poem is in accordance with similar techniques used by other contemporary Arab poets, often under the influence of T. S. Eliot. His two poems, "Guilty Even If I Were Innocent" and "The Dead Witness," are fine examples of this technique. In them the poet employs these devices, not only to create a more musical poem, but also to heighten his poetic experiences in vivid and dramatic images. These poems also display the poet's particular skill in the use of the interior monologue.

Al-Ḥaydari's poetry reveals his acute sensitivity towards the political and social dilemmas which plague the Arab world. His sense of alienation and oppression, above all his deeply felt experiences as an exile, are expressed in an invariably sombre tone. Al-Ḥaydari's vivid imagery and his ability to portray psychological conflict in simple but elegant language have made him an important contributor in the development of contemporary Arabic free verse.

—Parvin Loloi

HÉBERT, Anne. Canadian. Born in Sainte-Catherine-de-Fossambault, Quebec, 1 August 1916. Educated at Collège Saint-Coeur de Marie, Merici, Quebec, and Collège Notre Dame, Bellevue, Quebec. Worked for Radio Canada, 1950–53, and the National Film Board of Canada, 1953–54, 1959–60. Recipient: Canadian Government grant, 1954; France-Canada prize, 1958; Devernay prize, 1958; Canada Council grant, 1960, 1961; Guggenheim grant, 1963; Province of Quebec grant, 1965; Molson prize, 1967; French Booksellers prize, 1971; Governor-General's award, 1975; Académie Française award, 1975; Monaco grand prize, 1976; David prize (Quebec), 1978; Fémina prize, 1982 (France). D.Litt.: University of Toronto, 1967, University of Quebec 1979; McGill University, 1980; University of Laval; University of Laurentienne. Member Royal Society of Canada, 1960. Address: 24 rue de Pontoise, 75005 Paris, France.

PUBLICATIONS

Fiction

Le Torrent.   Montreal, Beauchemin, 1950; as *Le Torrent suiv de deux nouvelles inédites*, Montreal, HMH, 1963; as *Th*

Torrent: Novellas and Short Stories, Montreal, Harvest House, 1973.

Les Chambres de bois. Paris, Seuil, 1958; as *The Silent Rooms*, Don Mills, Ontario, Musson, 1974.

Kamouraska. Paris, Seuil, 1970; in English, Don Mills, Ontario, Musson, and New York, Crown, 1973.

Les Enfants du sabbat. Paris, Seuil, 1975; as *Children of the Black Sabbath*, Don Mills, Ontario, Musson, and New York, Crown, 1977.

Héloïse. Paris, Seuil, 1980; in English, Toronto, Stoddart, 1982.

Les Fous de Bassan. Paris, Seuil, 1982; as *In the Shadow of the Wind*, Toronto, Stoddart, 1983; London, Dent, 1984.

Le Premier Jardin. Paris, Seuil, 1988; as *The First Garden*, Toronto, Anansi, 1990.

L'Enfant chargé de songes. Paris, Seuil, 1992.

Plays

Le Temps sauvage (produced Quebec, 1966). With *La Mercière assassinée* and *Les Invités au procès*, 1967.

Le Temps sauvage; La Mercière assassinée; Les Invités au procès: théâtre. Montreal, HMH, 1967.

La Cage; L'Île de la demoiselle. Montreal, Boréal, 1990.

Screenplays and Commentaries: *Les Indes parmi nous*, 1954; *Drôle de mic-mac*, 1954; *Le Médecin du nord*, 1954; *La Canne à pêche*, 1959; *Saint-Denys-Garneau*, 1960; *Le Déficient mental*, 1960.

Radio Play: *Les Invités au procès*.

Television Plays: *Le Temps sauvage*; *La Mercière assassinée*.

Verse

Les Songes en équilibre. Montreal, L'Arbre, 1942.

Le Tombeau des rois. Quebec, Institut Littéraire, 1953; as *The Tomb of the Kings*, Toronto, Contact Press, 1967.

Poèmes (includes *Le Tombeau des rois* and *Mystère de la parole*). Paris, Seuil, 1960; as *Poems*, Don Mills, Ontario, Musson, 1975.

Saint-Denys-Garneau and Anne Hébert (selected poetry), translated by F. R. Scott. Vancouver, Klanak Press, 1962; revised edition, 1978.

Eve: Poems, translated by A. Poulin, Jr. Princeton, New Jersey, Quarterly Review of Literature, 1980.

Selected Poems, translated by A. Poulin, Jr. Brockport, New York, BOA, 1987; Toronto, Stoddart, 1988.

Other

Dialogue sur la traduction, with F. R. Scott, edited by Jeanne Lapointe. Montreal, HMH, 1970.

*

Bibliography: "Bibliographie d'Anne Hébert" by Janet Paterson, in *Voix et Images*, Spring 1982.

Critical Studies: "The Past: Themes and Symbols of Confrontation in *The Double Hook* and *Le Torrent*" by John W. Lennox, in *Journal of Canadian Fiction* (Montreal), 2(1), 1972; "Anne Hébert: Story and Poem" by F. M. Macri, in *Canadian Literature* (Vancouver), 58, 1973; "Dark Journeys: *Kamouraska* and *Deliverance*" by John Lennox, in *Essays on Canadian Writing* (Montreal), 12, 1978; "Canadian Gothic and

Anne Hébert's *Kamouraska*" by Arnold E. Davidson, in *Modern Fiction Studies* (West Lafayette, Indiana), Summer 1981; "La Lampe dans la fenêtre: The Visualization of Quebec Fiction," in *Canadian Literature* (Vancouver), Spring 1981, and "Repetition and Fragmentation: A Note on Anne Hébert's *Kamouraska*," in *Literary Half-Yearly* (Mysore, India), July 1983, both by Eva-Marie Kröller; "Survival Disguised as Metaphysics: Anne Hébert's Heloïse" by Alexandre L. Amprimoz, in *Waves*, Spring 1982; "Rapunzel in *The Silent Rooms*: Inverted Fairy Tales in Anne Hébert's First Novel" by Arnold E. Davidson, in *Colby Library Quarterly* (Waterville, Maine), March 1983; "My (m)Other, My Self: Strategies for Subversion in Atwood and Hébert" by Barbara Godard, in *Essays on Canadian Writing* (Montreal), Summer 1983; "Anne Hébert and the Discourse of the Unreal" by Janet M. Paterson, in *Yale French Studies* (New Haven, Connecticut), 65, 1983; *Anne Hébert* by Delbert W. Russell, Boston, Twayne, 1983; "Griffin Creek: The English World of Anne Hébert" by Ronald Ewing, in *Canadian Literature* (Vancouver), Summer 1985; "When an Author Chooses French: Hébert and [Andrée] Chédid" by Marilyn Gaddis Rose, in *Québec Studies*, 3, 1985; "Counter-Traditions: The Marginal Poetics of Anne Hébert" by Susan L. Rosenstreich, and "Love on the Rocks: Anne Hébert's *Kamouraska*" by Murray Sachs, both in *Traditionalism, Nationalism and Feminism: Women Writers of Quebec*, edited by Paula Gilbert Lewis, Westport, Connecticut, Greenwood, 1985; "Absence and Meaning in Anne Hébert's *Les Fous de Bassan*" by Karen Gould, in *French Review* (Santa Barbara, California), May 1986; "The Climate of *Viol*/Violence and Madness in Anne Hébert's *Les Fous de Bassan*" by Annabelle M. Rea, in *Québec Studies*, 4, 1986; "Submersion and Resurgence of the Female Other in Anne Hébert's *Les Fous de Bassan*," in *Québec Studies*, 4, 1986, and "Repression, Obsession, and Re-Emergence in Hébert's *Les Fous de Bassan*," in *American Review of Canadian Studies*, Fall 1987, both by Kathryn Slott; "Orphic Elements in Anne Hébert's *Héloïse*" by Janis Pallister, in *Québec Studies*, 5, 1987; "Undoing the Novel of Authority with Anne Hébert" by Steven Winspur, in *Teaching Language Through Literature*, April 1987; "Intentionality and Representation in Anne Hébert's *Kamouraska*" by Elaine Hopkins Garrett, in *Québec Studies*, 6, 1988; "From the First 'Eve' to the New 'Eve': Anne Hébert's Rehabilitation of the Malevolent Female Archetype" by Kathleen Kells, in *Studies in Canadian Literature* (Fredericton, New Brunswick), 14(1), 1989; "The Letter of the Law in Anne Hébert's *Kamouraska*" by Karen McPherson, in *Québec Studies*, 8, 1989.

*   *   *

As a young woman in Quebec, Anne Hébert was involved with the group responsible for *La Relève*, a journal founded by her cousin, Hector de Saint-Denys-Garneau, and dedicated to renewing the spiritual, artistic, and intellectual life of a province isolated from the external world by an all-powerful jansenist Church. Thanks to this coterie and her father Maurice, a well-known literary critic, Hébert enjoyed a broad literary culture not then available to the majority of her compatriots. This is reflected in her first volume of verse, *Les Songes en équilibre* (Dreams in Equilibrium). While the poems now appear to the author herself childish and derivative, a far cry from the post-surrealist poetry of France, the directness of her language and the strength of her imagery reveal a voice strikingly different from that of her predecessors and even her contemporaries in Quebec.

The 10 years following this publication, marked by a series of personal losses, exercised a profound influence on her work. Her most famous short story "Le Torrent" (The Torrent), first published in 1947 as "Au bord du torrent" (Beside the Torrent) and revised for inclusion as the title piece in a volume of collected short stories, The Torrent is now taken as a paradigm of Quebec itself at that earlier period. It conveys the sense of dispossession characteristic of most if not all her later writing, although in her second volume of poetry Le Tombeau des rois (The Tomb of the Kings), devoted to her confrontation with death, the final allusion to dawn (and to a possible rebirth) shows that some hope still exists. This is usually translated, however, as in many of the short stories in The Torrent (e.g., "L'Ange de Dominique" [The Angel of Dominique]), by the idea that "real life is elsewhere."

Indeed, the main character in a recent novel Le Premier Jardin (The First Garden) on returning to her native city (never named, but obviously Quebec), states clearly that life is not to be found where she is and twice expresses in English in the French text her desire to be "Anywhere out of this world." Conversely, in her latest book L'Enfant chargé de songes (The Child Filled with Dreams) the male protagonist, in Paris for the first time, is constantly under the impression that: "the real city is elsewhere." Although such sentiments should not necessarily be read literally, this theme of permanent exile from life, from reality, is consistent with Hébert's own apparent inability to live in her native land, an inability that does not necessarily include the corresponding ability to feel totally at home elsewhere.

In general, the universe she creates, one of physical or temporal isolation, is redolent of violence and despair, both heightened by the sparse, even stark style of the author. Betrayal, murder, incest, madness are among the themes she uses to explore the limits of our existence. In The Tomb of the Kings, she writes, "In an ordered world, the dead below, the quick above, the dead weary me, the quick kill me." Some of these lines reappear in ironic repetition throughout her work, but her world knows no such order. For her characters, there is no absolute distinction between life and death, here and there, present and past, natural and supernatural. The past returns to kill us (La Mercière assassinée [The Assassinated Haberdasher]); vampires, symbolic and "real," stalk their innocent victims in Paris (Les Chambres de bois [The Silent Rooms], Héloïse); the dead haunt us (Kamouraska, Les Fous de Bassan [In the Shadow of the Wind]). The heroine of The First Garden must attempt, not necessarily successfully, to come to terms both with her own expulsion from an earthly paradise and with Quebec's symbolic loss of a Garden of Eden that presumably existed before the Conquest.

Hébert leads her readers on a mythical journey, for some into their individual being, for others into the collective self of Quebec, for all into the death encaged in the heart of human experience. The mythic quality is reinforced by two elements in particular: one, the meticulous reconstruction of those actual events in Quebec history she often uses as a springboard; two, the presence, the demystification even, of many elements from fairytales and folktales, for instance, the Cinderella and Sleeping Beauty stories, the ogres that people a hostile land, the Underworld. As always, exile is the order of the day.

—Maïr Verthuy

HEIN, Christoph. German. Born in Heinzendorf/Schlesien, 8 April 1944. Educated at the University of Leipzig, from 1967; Humboldt University, Berlin, diploma 1971. Married Christiane Hein in 1966; two sons. Literary adviser and playwright, Deutsches Theater, East Berlin, 1971–79. Has also worked as a book dealer, factory worker, and director's assistant. Recipient: Heinrich Mann prize, 1982; West German Critics' prize, 1983; City of Hamburg prize, 1986; Lessing prize, 1989; Andres prize, 1989; Fried prize, 1990. Address: c/o Aufbau-Verlag, Postfach 1217, 1086 Berlin, Germany.

PUBLICATIONS

Fiction

Einladung zum Lever bourgeois. Berlin, Aufbau, 1980; as Nachtfahrt und früher Morgen, Hamburg, Hoffmann und Campe, 1982.
Der fremde Freund. Berlin, Aufbau, 1982; as Drachenblut, Neuwied, Luchterhand, 1983; as The Distant Lover, New York, Random House, 1989; London, Picador, 1991.
Horns Ende. Berlin, Aufbau, and Neuwied, Luchterhand, 1985.
Der Tangospieler. Berlin, Aufbau, and Neuwied, Luchterhand, 1989.

Plays

Schlötel, oder Was solls (produced Berlin, 1974). Neuwied, Luchterhand, 1986.
Vom hungrigen Hennecke. Berlin, Henschel, 1974.
Cromwell (produced Theater der Stadt Cottbus, 1980). Berlin, Henschel, 1977.
Lassalle fragt Herrn Herbert nach Sonja: Eine Szene ein Salon (produced Düsseldorf, 1980). Berlin, Henschel, 1981.
Der neue Menoza oder Geschichte des kumbanischen Prinzen Tandi, adaptation of the play by Jakob Michael Reinhold Lenz (produced Mecklenburg, 1981). Berlin, Henschel, 1981.
Cromwell, und andere Stücke (includes Lassalle fragt Herrn Herbert nach Sonja; Schlötel, oder Was solls; Der neue Menoza oder Geschichte des kumbanischen Prinzen Tandi). Berlin, Aufbau, 1981.
Die wahre Geschichte des Ah Q, based on a novel by Lu Hsun (produced East Berlin, 1983). Berlin, Henschel, 1982; as The True Story of Ah Q (produced London, 1990).
Passage (produced Essen and Dresden, 1987). Berlin, Henschel, 1987.
Die Ritter der Tafelrunde (produced Dresden, 1989). Berlin, Henschel, and Neuwied, Luchterhand, 1989.

Other

Das Wildpferd unterm Kachelofen (for children). Berlin, Altberliner, 1984; as Jamie and His Friends, London, Anderson, 1988.
Öffentlich arbeiten: Essais und Gespräche. Berlin, Aufbau, 1987.
Als Kind habe ich Stalin gesehen. Berlin, Aufbau, 1990.
Die fünfte Grundrechenart: Aufsätze und Reden 1986–1989. Neuwied, Luchterhand, 1990.
Der "Bund proletarisch-revolutionärer Schriftsteller Deutschland": Biographie eines Kulturpolitischen Experiments in der Weimarer Republik. Münster, Lit. Münster, 1991.

Translator, *Britannicus*, by Jean Racine.　Berlin, Henschel, 1980.

*

Critical Studies: "*Einladung zum Lever bourgeois*: Christoph Hein's First Prose Collection" by Bernd Fischer, in *Studies in GDR Culture and Society, III: Selected Papers from the Eighth International Symposium on the German Democratic Republic*, edited by Margy Gerber and others, Lanham, Maryland, University Press of America, 1983; "Alltag, Apathy, Anarchy: GDR Everyday Life as a Provocation in Christoph Hein's Novella *Der fremde Freund*" by Phillip S. McKnight, in *Studies in GDR Culture and Society*, edited by Margy Gerber, Lanham, Maryland, University Press of America, 1988.

*　　*　　*

At the height of East Germany's turmoil in the autumn of 1989, Christoph Hein addressed a huge rally in East Berlin to urge replacement of the country's political structures with ones that more truly reflected socialist values. "If we fail," he was later to say, "we shall be swallowed by McDonalds." Neither his public pronouncements nor his essays had left any doubt about Hein's attachment to a humane socialism, and it was therefore no surprise to see him on this occasion sharing a platform with, among others, the East German novelists Stefan Heym and Christa Wolf (*qq.v.*). But a comparison of their creative writings shows a marked difference in tone. Despite the failures of communism in the German Democratic Republic both Heym and Wolf, Hein's seniors by 31 and 15 years respectively, were able to retain at least traces of the idealist vision and the Utopian hope that had first inspired the older generation of GDR writers. Hein, by contrast, has never been at ease in a prophetic posture and has declined to use literature as a vehicle for moral pronouncements or social didacticism. "Unlike Brecht," he said in 1984, "I cannot instruct my public."

That the role of chronicler, however, can be just as provocative as that of seer or agitator was shown by Hein's novella *Der fremde Freund* (*The Distant Lover*). In this bleak little tale an East German doctor, Claudia, divorced and childless, reflects on her casual affair with Henry, the distant lover of the title, who has been killed in a pub brawl. Their physical intimacy had been accompanied on both sides by a carefully maintained emotional detachment, and Claudia is not unduly perturbed by Henry's death. Indeed, her whole approach to life is marked by the conscious refusal to open herself up to anything that might cause her distress, and although in her eyes the world appears a loveless place devoid of meaning, she has made herself impervious to its intrusions. Secure within her defences she concludes with an affirmation of her self-sufficiency and contentment. There is, of course, much more to her laconic account than meets the eye, but any corrective has to be deduced from behind the narrative, for Claudia's point of view is the only one we are offered, and by and large she has herself firmly under control. It was this aspect which disturbed some East German critics, worried at the story's lack of ideological balance, but it is precisely the closed perspective, Claudia's singleminded defence of her attenuated lifestyle, which gives the tale its perverse fascination. Indeed, the reader's negative response to her attitudes may actually be intensified if it is not pre-empted by ethical position-taking within the text itself.

Individuals with emotional problems are not unique to one kind of society, and there is therefore a universal quality to Hein's story, but it also addresses areas which were particularly sensitive within the East German context. As Claudia recalls her troubled childhood in the 1950s, it becomes apparent that her condition is due, at least in part, to the political repression she encountered then, and the unstated implication is that, like Claudia, East Germany too has a past that must be confronted if it is to be healthy in the present. This interest in history as a key to contemporary attitudes is also evident in Hein's two novels, *Horns Ende* (Horn's End) and *Der Tangospieler* (The Tango-Player). The starting point of the former is the suicide in 1957 of Horn, museum director in a small town in Saxony, but the threads extend backwards to the Nazi period and forwards to the narrative present, the 1980s. The narration is carried by five voices, participants in the events described, but, as in *The Distant Lover*, what seems on the surface a sober chronicle cannot disguise a pervasive misuse of political power, the ambiguous motives of human action, and a desolate absence of community. *Der Tangospieler* is set in 1968 and tells of the attempts of an East German university teacher to seek redress for himself after a period of unjust imprisonment. Against the background of the Warsaw Pact invasion of Czechoslovakia, virtually a taboo subject in GDR literature, it plays in witty and ironic fashion with the shifts in political orthodoxy which could trap even the most wary. Despite the story's setting the principal target of its barbs was the East German regime of the late 1980s, locked in its Stalinist time warp. Some seven months after the book appeared, that regime had been swept away.

In 1989, the same year as *Der Tangospieler*, Hein also published the play *Die Ritter der Tafelrunde* (Knights of the Round Table). Whether portraying 17th-century England (*Cromwell*), 19th-century Germany (*Lassalle*), or a Chinese fable (*Die wahre Geschichte des Ah Q* [*The True Story of Ah Q*]), Hein's plays were unambiguously directed towards topical issues, in particular the aftermath of revolution, with the stagnation and perversion of once noble ideals. His reworking of the Arthurian legend shows the knights as a geriatric clique, corrupt and inert, their belief in the Grail an illusion and their kingdom decaying around them. His allegory could scarcely have been more prescient. Nevertheless, after the collapse of the GDR Hein did not react with the bitterness of some of his older colleagues, instead expressing relief that writers would no longer be expected to act as substitutes for a free press. In one of his favourite phrases, "Literature is when Proust describes how he drinks tea." Despite that modest aspiration, even in a united Germany there is unlikely to be any shortage of material for this cool, sharp-eyed, and mordant observer.

—Peter J. Graves

———

HEIN, Piet. Also writes as Kumbel. Danish. Born in Copenhagen, 16 December 1905. Educated at Metropolitanskolen, graduated 1924; private arts schools; Royal Academy of Arts, Stockholm, 1924–27; Niels Bohr Institute, University of Copenhagen, from 1927; Polytekniske Læreanstalt. Scientist and designer: has worked as design consultant for Fritz Hansen Møbler, Georg Jensens Sølvsmedie, Jay Bojesen, Den kgl. Porcelainsfabrik, Kastrup og Holmegaards Glasværker, 3 M (Germany), and Parker Brothers (United States); holder of patents for technical inventions; designer of "super-ellipse," a rectangular oval used in industrial design. Exhibition of designs: I Ord og Rum [In Words and Space], Kunstindustrimuseet, Copenhagen, 1974. Chair, Frisindet Kulturkamp, 1940, Een Verden [One World], and the Danish department of World Movement for World Federal Government, 1948–49; co-founder and member, Dansk Forening til Fremme af Opfindelser [Danish Association for the Advancement of Inventions], 1968. Has lived and travelled in Asia, North and South America, and Europe; lived in England, 1969–76. Alexander Graham Bell lecturer, Boston University, 1968. Recipient: Aarestrup Medal; Alexander Graham Bell Silver Bell, 1968; ID prize, 1971; De gute Industriform, 1971; Copenhagen Town Hall honorary artisan, 1975; Danish Design Committee prize, 1975; Petersen prize, 1978; Aphia prize (Paris), 1980; Tietgen Medal, 1990. D.H.L.: Yale University, 1972; honorary doctorate: Odense University, 1991. Address: Damsbo, 5683 Hårby, Denmark.

PUBLICATIONS

Verse (grooks published in Danish editions as Kumbel)

Gruk [Grooks]. Copenhagen, Borgen, vols. 1–10, 1940–49; Copenhagen, Gyldendal, vols. 11–20, 1954–63.
Den tiende Muse [The Quiet Muse]. Copenhagen, Naver, 1941.
Vers i verdensrummet [Verse in Space]. Copenhagen, Gyldendal, 1941.
4 digte under sydkorset [Four Poems Under the Southern Cross]. Copenhagen, Naver, 1945.
Helicopteren [The Helicopter]. Copenhagen, Gyldendal, 1947.
Vers af denne verden [Verse of This World]. Copenhagen, Gyldendal, 1948.
Kumbels fødselsdagskalender [Kumbel's Birthday Calendar]. N.p., Ikke i Bogh, 1949.
Kumbels lyre [Kumbel's Lyre]. Copenhagen, Politiken, 1950.
Gruk fra alle årene [Grooks from All the Years]. Copenhagen, Gyldendal, vols. 1–3, 1960–71.
Du skal plante et træ [You Must Plant a Tree]. Copenhagen, Gyldendal, 1960.
Husk at elske [Remember to Love]. Copenhagen, Gyldendal, 1962.
Husk at leve [Remember to Live]. Copenhagen, Borgen, 1965.
Grooks (in English).
    vol. 1: Cambridge, Massachusetts, MIT Press, 1966; London, Hodder and Stoughton, 1969.
    vol. 2: More Grooks, Cambridge, Massachusetts, MIT Press, 1968; London, Hodder and Stoughton, 1969.
    vol. 3: New York, Doubleday, 1970; as Still More Grooks, London, Hodder and Stoughton, 1970.
    vol. 4: New York, Doubleday, 1973; as Motes and Beams, Oxford, Blackwell, 1973.
    vol. 5: New York, Doubleday, 1973; as Mist and Moonshine, Oxford, Blackwell, 1973.
Lad os blive mennesker [Let Us Become Human Beings]. Copenhagen, Borgen, 1967.
Runaway Runes, Short Grooks. Copenhagen, Borgen, 1968.
Korte gruk: I folkemunde; Det kraftens ord [Short Grooks]. Copenhagen, Borgen, 2 vols., 1968–69.
Digte fra alle årene [Poems from All the Years]. Copenhagen, Borgen, vols. 1–2, 1972–78.
Menneskesag [Human Case]. Copenhagen, Bonde, 1975.
Viking Vistas, Short Grooks II. Copenhagen, Borgen, 1983.

Hjertets lyre — Kærlighedsdigte og -gruk [The Lyre of the Heart — Love Poems and Grooks]. Copenhagen, Borgen, 1985.
Lars Løvetand — Gruk [Lars Løvetand — Grook]. Copenhagen, Borgen, 1987.

Fiction

Johannes Buchholtz's urolige hjerte [Johannes Buchholtz's Troubled Heart]. Struer, Johannes Buchholtz Selskabet, 1977.

Other

Kumbel's Almanak 1942. Copenhagen, Grafisk, 1941.
Man skal gaa paa Jorden [One Must Walk on the Ground] (aphorisms). Copenhagen, Gyldendal, 1944.
Selv om den er gloende [Although It Glows]. Copenhagen, Gyldendal, 1950.
Vis electrica. Copenhagen, Elektricitets Selskabet Isefjordværket Interessantskab, 1962.
Kilden og krukken: fabler og essays [The Steam and the Jar: Fables and Essays]. Copenhagen, Gyldendal, 1963.
Man's Communication to Man. Boston, n.p., 1968.

*   *   *

Danish scientist Piet Hein has hobnobbed with Albert Einstein, invented games, and introduced to town planning the "super-ellipse" — a geometric shape that combines aspects of both the rectangle and the circle, and which has been used in Stockholm's rebuilt city centre. Despite his important contributions to science, however, he will probably always be best known for something altogether different — the grook (gruk in Danish — Hein invented the word too).

Grooks are rhyming epigrams that make a witty, meaningful statement about some aspect of life. British writer Sir A. P. Herbert (1890–1971), who penned many a quoted epigram in his time, explained that the rhymed epigram "must have wit, or wisdom — preferably both — compressed into a tiny space, yet perfectly intelligible . . . Then it must have rhyme and it must scan." Hein's grooks fit the definition well. In fact, thanks to the simple rhymes and regular rhythms, they are so easy to remember that Hein has been dubbed "the most quoted Scandinavian."

Hein began writing grooks during the Nazi occupation from 1940 of Denmark, publishing them under the pseudonym "Kumbel," which in Old Norse means a stone with an inscription. (Indeed, grooks would not be out of place on gravestones.) Grooks caught on the world over and have been translated into many languages. The Doubleday editions of Grooks, Grooks II, and Grooks III were bestsellers in their day in the United States. Luckily they have not lost their punch in English translation — Hein translated Grooks into English himself, and in fact wrote some of them in English.

Grooks were actually first published in English by Massachusetts Institute of Technology (M.I.T.) Press — an unusual but appropriate publisher given Hein's desire to combine science and art. As a critic in Life International explains, "He stands astride the two cultures of modern life, contending they are twain only because we make them so, insisting on being an artist and technologist at once and arguing convincingly that the rest of the world should too."

Grooks takes for subject-matter almost anything: missing trains, the nature of love (resembling a pineapple!), common sense, intelligence, progress, the place of poetry, or even low necklines, as in "Foretaste with Aftertaste":

> Corinna's scanty evening dress
> reveals her charms to an excess
> which makes a fellow lust for less.

The taste of the above is a bit questionable — Hein does not always hit the mark. It also reveals the nostalgic, old-fashioned feel of grooks, aided by the accompanying pen-and-ink sketches by Hein that are reminiscent of drawings by James Thurber.

At his best, however, Hein makes a universal, timeless, and unarguable point, as in "That Is the Question (Hamlet Anno Domine)":

> Co-existence
> or no existence.

Or in "The State":

> Nature, our father and mother,
> gave us all we have got.
> The state, our elder brother,
> swipes the lot.

One of Hein's most endearing qualities is his self-deprecating nature. He refuses to take on the mantle of sage, or make out that his grooks should be taken too seriously. Instead he says:

> Shun advice
> at any price
> that's what I call
> good advice.

His grook "Meeting the Eye" perhaps inadvertently sums up the way Hein feels grooks work:

> You'll probably find
>   that it suits your book
> to be a bit cleverer
>   than you look.
> Observe that the easiest
>   method by far
> Is to look a bit stupider
>   than you are.

Their wisdom creeps up on the reader.

—Theresa Werner

HEINESEN, Jens Pauli. Faroese. Born in Tórshavn, 12 November 1932. Educated at the University of Copenhagen, 1953–54; Emdrupborg Statsseminarium, graduated 1955. Married Maud Brimheim in 1956; two daughters. Teacher in Denmark, 1957, and Tórshavn, 1957–70. Chair, Færøernes Forfatterforening, 1968–75. Recipient: Faroese literature prize, 1959, 1969, 1973; Nordic Council prize, 1987. Address: Stoffalág 18, 100 Tórshavn, The Faroe Islands, Via Denmark.

PUBLICATIONS (all self-published)

Fiction

Degningsælið [The Dawn Shower].   1953.
Yrkjarin úr Selvík [The Poet from Selvík].   1958.
Hin vakra kvirran [The Beautiful Calm].   1959.
Tú upphavsins heimur [You, World of Origin].   3 vols., 1962–64.
Gestur [Guest].   1967.
Aldurnar spæla á sandi [The Waves Play on the Shore].   1969.
I aldingarðinum [In the Garden of Eden].   1971.
Frænir eitur ormurin [The Serpent's Name Is Frænir].   1973.
Gamansleikur [Fun and Games].   1974.
Rekamaðurin [The Beachcomber].   1977.
Dropar í lívsins havi [Drops in the Ocean of Life].   1978.
Tey telgja sær gudar [They Carve Their Idols].   1979.
Nú ert tú mansbarn á foldum [Now You Are a Child of Man on Earth].   1980.
Lýsir nú fyri tær heimurin [The World Now Shines Before You].   1981.
Leikur tín er sum hin ljósi dagur [Your Playing Is Like the Bright Day].   1982.
Markleys breiðist nú fyri tær fold [The World Now Stretches Boundless Before You].   1983.
Eitt dýpi av dýrari tíð [A Depth of Precious Time].   1984.
Tann gátuføri kærleikin [The Mysteries of Love].   1986.
Í andgletti [Exposed to the Wind].   1988.
Bláfelli [Blue Mountain].   1992.

Two stories, "Gestur" and "Little Frants Vilhelm," translated into English, in *Faroese Short Stories*, edited by Hedin Brønner, New York, Irvington, 1972.

Plays

Fýra sjónleikir [Four Plays].   1985.
Sníkurin [The Parasite].   1991.

Other

Íkast til 1984 [Contribution to 1984].   1984.
Brúsajøkul (for children) [Sparkling Glacier].   1987.

Editor, *Føroyar í dag: Færøerne i dag* [The Faroes Today].   Tórshavn, Norrøna Felagið, 1966.

*

Critical Studies: "The Novels of Jens Pauli Heinesen," in *Proceedings of the Conference of Scandinavian Studies in Great Britain and Northern Ireland*, Guildford, University of Surrey, 1983, and "Fiction and Fact in the Faroese Novel," in *Bradford Occasional Papers* (University of Bradford), 6, 1984, both by Robin Allan.

*   *   *

Of the current generation of Faroese writers, Jens Pauli Heinesen is not only the most important, but also the most prolific. Since his debut in 1953, he has so far published 14 novels, eight collections of short stories, five plays, and some poetry. His prose works are his most significant literary achievement. Like many other Faroese authors, much of his writing has its roots in Faroese society, and especially in the enormous economic and social changes which have taken place in the islands in the last 80 years or so. His works can be seen as falling into two broad strands: firstly, those which treat universal issues, and yet are placed in a Faroese background (often with some measure of criticism towards his countrymen); and secondly, those which deal with intimate individual human concerns, though again in a specifically Faroese setting.

On the surface, Heinesen's first major novel, *Yrkjarin úr Selvík* (The Poet from Selvík), might be viewed as a deeply personal work, for in it he attempts to come to terms with a problem which he, perhaps especially as an author in a society as small and close-knit as the Faroes, has faced. Like the main character (and poet of the title), Bjarni, Heinesen found that his work was simply not appreciated at all by his compatriots. Bjarni has extreme difficulty in comprehending the prevailing lack of respect for artists and the general Faroese antipathy towards cultural life; he becomes increasingly isolated and alienated from the people around him, and eventually dies an untimely death from tuberculosis. Although one can draw many similarities between Heinesen's artistic situation and that of his fictional poet, Heinesen does not attempt to write solely about himself but rather uses the story and situation of Bjarni to explore the general significance of art for society. In spite of Bjarni's many failings as a human being, Heinesen places most of the blame for what happens to him on his seemingly indifferent audience, and their lack of cultural appreciation is attributed to the rapid economic changes which took place in the Faroes. As the critic Jógvan Isaksen points out (in *Skúlabladið*, 9, 1982), the message of the novel appears to be that advances in the material world should be matched by comparable advances in the cultural and intellectual life of society, for if not, others may begin to control people's thoughts and true culture will perish.

This idea is reinforced in the trilogy *Tú upphavsins heimur* (You, World of Origin). It is set in a small island community which has remained untouched by modern times; the villagers want change, but the authorities refuse to listen. Their cause is championed by Baltasar, who is determined to transform his home village; eventually he succeeds and the community begins to prosper. This is only achieved at some considerable cost, however, for it is not just prosperity which Baltasar brings with him, but also a new philosophy of life; under his influence individual human and cultural values recede, to be replaced by dictatorial principles and doctrines. As well as focusing on and highlighting the cultural impoverishment which the rapid changes in Faroese society have brought in their wake, the trilogy also investigates the mechanics of a totalitarian regime and explores the fundamental interdependence between exploiter and exploited, a recurring theme in much of Heinesen's work, for example in the seminal short story *Gestur* (Guest). The trilogy begins with a graphic, and at times sickening (though deliberately so) description of a traditional Faroese whale hunt, the supreme Faroese metaphor for this interdependence: exploiters need victims, and potential victims invite exploitation.

Frænir eitur ormurin (The Serpent's Name Is Frænir) is both a continuation and culmination of Heinesen's examination of these particular themes, and is perhaps his most ambitious single literary work. Like *Tú upphavsins heimur*, it begins with a thematic metaphor, this time a Spanish bullfight. The plot charts the apparently irresistible rise of a right-wing capitalist business concern (the "Frænir" of the title), which eventually succeeds in taking control of the whole of the Faroes: freedom of speech, civil liberties, newspapers, and even the writing of any form of literature are banned. It is a work which represents the ultimate synthesis of this part of Heinesen's authorship, for here we find his definitive exploration of the concept "freedom," be it artistic, political, or personal. On all counts, it appears that mankind can easily lose out — human under-

standing, compassion, and culture are all fragile commodities, and easy prey for those forces which might wish to destroy them.

Thus Heinesen uses Faroese society as a microcosm to convey his observations on the general condition of man. But, in addition, he wishes to make his fellow countrymen aware of the potential dangers which have arisen from the rapid changes in Faroese society, and in this he is not alone among his fellow Faroese authors. Nonetheless, he imbues his work with a humanism and communality which transcend national boundaries, and as a result the very Faroese essence of his writing can, and does, assume a significance for us all.

After *Frænir eitur ormurin*, Heinesen appears to leave these weighty political, social, and artistic concerns behind him, and moves briefly into a more light-hearted and humorous vein. His next novel, *Rekamadurin* (The Beachcomber), set during World War II, can only be described as typically Faroese and very much in the tradition of the doyen of modern Faroese prose, Heðin Brú, in that it is an affectionate and uncritical portrayal of a traditional facet of Faroese life; yet even here we perceive an intrinsic representation of the author and his own personal struggle, always searching for something outside himself.

In his most recent novels — all of which have the subtitle "Á ferð inn í einn óendaliga søgu" (A Journey into a Story Without End) — Heinesen introduces a new dimension to his work; instead of channelling universal problems into a Faroese context, he now focuses on the life and development of a Faroese boy and explores the way in which he encounters, experiences, and conquers the world surrounding him. Heinesen is now no longer the teacher with a didactic message, but rather the gentle observer who allows the reader to assimilate his material and draw his own conclusions. The novels trace the progress through life of a young Faroeman, Hugin (which in Faroese means "mind" or "thought"), who in many ways is synonymous with Heinesen himself. Some of the personal material they contain has already appeared in his earlier short stories, and yet here it is presented in a more meaningful and personal context; in terms of language and style, these recent works can also be seen as representing a break with the past, for in them we now see a Faroese master craftsman at his very best, displaying all his particular talents as a writer to the full.

—Robin Allan

———

HERBERT, Zbigniew. Polish. Born in Lvov, 29 October 1924. Educated at the University of Cracow, M.A. in economics 1947; Nicholas Copernicus University of Toruń, M.A. in law 1948; University of Warsaw, M.A. in philosophy 1950. Served in the Polish Resistance Home Army during World War II. Married Katarzyna Dzieduszycka in 1968. Worked as a bank clerk, manual labourer, and journalist; staff member, *Twórczość* literary review, Warsaw, 1955–65; co-editor, *Poezja*, Warsaw, 1965–68; Professor of Modern European literature, California State College, Los Angeles, 1970; Visiting Professor, University of Gdańsk, 1972. Member of General Board Foreign Committee, Polish Writers Association, 1955–83. Recipient: Polish Radio Competition prize, 1958; Polish Institute of Arts and Sciences (USA) Millennium prize, 1964; Austrian State prize for European literature

1965; Herder prize, 1973; Knight's Cross, Order of Polonia Resituta, 1974; Petrarch prize, 1979; Jerusalem literary prize, 1991; Jurzykowski Foundation award. Corresponding member, Bavarian Academy. Address: ul. Promenady 21 m. 4, 00 778 Warsaw, Poland.

PUBLICATIONS

Verse

Struna światła [A Chord of Light]. Warsaw, Czytelnik, 1956.
Hermes, pies i gwiazda [Hermes, a Dog and a Star]. Warsaw, Czytelnik, 1957.
Studium przedmiotu [The Study of an Object]. Warsaw, Czytelnik, 1961.
Selected Poems, translated by Czesław Miłosz and Peter Dale Scott. London, Penguin, 1968; New York, Ecco Press, 1986.
Napis [The Inscription]. Warsaw, Czytelnik, 1969.
Wiersze zebrane [Collected Verse]. Warsaw, Czytelnik, 1971; revised edition, 1982.
Pan Cogito [Mr. Cogito]. Warsaw, Czytelnik, 1974.
Selected Poems, edited and translated by John and Bogdana Carpenter. London and New York, Oxford University Press, 1977.
Raport z oblężonego miasta. Paris, Instytut Literacki, 1983; as *Report from the Besieged City and Other Poems*, translated by John and Bogdana Carpenter, New York, Ecco Press, 1985; Oxford, Oxford University Press, 1987.
Wybór Wierszy [Selected Poems]. Warsaw, Państwowy Instytut Wydawniczy, 1983.
18 wierszy [18 Poems]. Cracow, Oficyna Literacka (samizdat), 1983.
Arkusz [A Sheet]. Warsaw, Krąg, 1984.
Report from a Town Under Siege (single poem), translated by Bogusław Rostworowski. Portland, Oregon, Trace, 1984.
Selected Poems. Manchester, Carcanet, 1985.
Elegia na odejście. Paris, Instytut Literacki, 1990.
Hańba domowa [Domestic Shame]. 1991.

Plays

Jaskinia filozofów. Included in *Dramaty*, 1970; as *The Philosophers' Den*, in *The Broken Mirror: A Collection of Writings from Contemporary Poland*, New York, Random House, 1958.
Dramaty (includes *Jaskinia filozofów*; *Rekonstrukcja poety* [The Poet's Reconstruction]; *Drugi pokój* [The Other Room]; *Lalek*). Warsaw, Państwowy Instytut Wydawniczy, 1970.

Other

Barbarzyńca w ogrodzie (essays). Warsaw, Czytelnik, 1962; as *Barbarian in the Garden*, Manchester, Carcanet, 1985; San Diego, Harcourt Brace, 1986.
Wybór poezji; Dramaty [Selected Poems, Plays]. Warsaw, Czytelnik, 1973.

Translator, *Nie ma raju* [Il n'y a pas de paradis], by André Frénaud. Warsaw, Państwowy Instytut, Wydawniczy, 1968.

*

Critical Studies: "Herbert and Yevtushenko: On Whose Side Is History?" by Geroge Gömöri, in *Mosaic* (Winnipeg, Manitoba), 3(1), 1969; "Herbert's 'Study of the Object': A Reading" by Debra Nicholson Czestochowski, in *Polish Review* (New York), 20(4), 1975; "Zbigniew Herbert: The Poet as Conscience," in *Slavic and East European Journal* (Minneapolis), 24, 1980, and "Zbigniew Herbert and the Imperfect Poem," in *Malahat Review* (Victoria, British Columbia), 54, 1980, both by Bogdana and John Carpenter; "A Poet of Exact Meaning" (interview) by Marek Orasmus, in *PN Review* (Manchester), 8(6[26]), 1982; "The Barbarian and the Garden: Zbigniew Herbert's Reevaluations," in *World Literature Today* (Norman, Oklahoma), Summer 1983, "The Prose Poetry of Zbigniew Herbert: Forging a New Genre," in *Slavic and East European Journal* (Minneapolis), Spring 1984, "Zbigniew Herbert's Attack Against Myth," in *Cross Currents* (New Haven, Connecticut), 3, 1984, and "Zbigniew Herbert, the Poet as Witness," in *Polish Review* (New York), 32(1), 1987, all by Bogdana Carpenter; "War as Parable and War as Fact: Herbert and Forché," in *American Poetry Review* (Philadelphia), January-February 1983, and "Strange Days: Zbigniew Herbert in Los Angeles," in *Antioch Review* (Yellow Springs, Ohio), Winter 1987, both by Larry Levis; "Reasons for Poetry and the Reason for Criticism" by William Meredith, in *The Motive for Metaphor: Essays on Modern Poetry*, edited by Francis C. Blessington and Guy L. Rotella, Boston, Northeastern University Press, 1983; "Zbigniew Herbert and the Critics," in *Polish Review* (New York), 30(2), 1985, and *A Fugitive from Utopia: The Poetry of Zbigniew Herbert*, Cambridge, Massachusetts, Harvard University Press, 1987, both by Stanisław Barańczak; "An Atlas of Civilization" by Seamus Heaney, in *Parnassus* (New York), 14(1), 1987; "'Idiots Live More Safely': Seeing Through Zbigniew Herbert's 'The Divine Claudius'" by Andrew Kahn, in *Polish Review* (New York), 32(1), 1987; "Zbigniew Herbert's Poetry and Its Explication Through Antimonies" by C. Prokopczyk, in *Polish Review* (New York), 32(1), 1987; "An Interview with Zbigniew Herbert" by Jacek Trznadel, in *Polish Review* (New York), Fall 1987.

*   *   *

Zbigniew Herbert is among the best poets who emerged in the "new wave" of Polish literature in 1955–56. Although born in 1924 and not much younger than Tadeusz Różewicz, *q.v.* (with whom he shares wartime memories and experiences), Herbert is not an embittered "survivor" but an ironical moralist. It is mainly his critical attachment to history and his firm adherence to classical and Christian values that make Herbert's poetry different from most poets of his generation. While in his first two books of poetry, *Struna światła* and *Hermes, pies i gwiazda* (Hermes, a Dog and a Star), there are still a number of poems about the responsibility of the living towards the dead, and some caustic tales written in poetic prose which hold up to ridicule the absurd logic and Byzantine methods of Stalinism (e.g., "Cesarz," "Mur," "Bajka ruska" — The Emperor, The Wall, Russian Tale), in his later work Herbert often resorts to historical parable to express personal problems (e.g., in "Powrot prokonsula" — The Return of the Proconsul). In the late 1960s and early 1970s — which Herbert mostly spent traveling abroad — his concerns broadened to include meditations on the past and present of Western civilization, while he did not abandon his search for answers to specific Polish problems. The poetic harvest of these years was collected in *Pan Cogito* (Mr. Cogito) and *Raport z oblężonego miasta* (Report from the Besieged City). The latter collection also includes some "Cogito" poems; this fictitious character seems to be Herbert's wiser and more dispassionate alter-ego. Herbert writes on the whole in a rhymeless but vigorous free verse informed by a controlled, often sarcastic rhetoric. "Repeat great words repeat them stubbornly/like those crossing the desert who perished in the sand," he addresses himself in the poem "Przeslanie Pana Cogito," translated by John and Bogdana Carpenter as "The Envoy of Mr. Cogito."

Recently, in the context of an interview given to J. Trznadel and published in the collection *Hańba domowa* (Domestic Shame), more critical attention was paid to Herbert's political stance, expressions of which varied from the implicit antitotalitarianism of "Potwór Pana Cogito" (Mr. Cogito's Monster) to the denunciation of Soviet imperialism for its crimes against the Polish people ("Guziki" — Buttons). Herbert is a tortured classicist who has absorbed and overcome the temptation of the avant-garde with the help of a critically observed tradition.

Herbert's essays were collected in the volume *Barbarzyńca w ogrodzie* (*Barbarian in the Garden*). They are mostly on medieval themes related to Italian and French art, architecture, and history, and are characterized by great lucidity of style and an effortless display of erudition. One of the best essays in this collection investigates the genocide of the Cathar heretics of France ("O Albigensach, inkwizytorach, i trubadurach" — Albigenses, Inquisitors, and Troubadours) — a subject which has a strangely familiar ring for students of modern history. Herbert's plays collected in *Dramaty* deal with contemporary psychological and moral problems; these were written for radio and are probably less effective on stage.

—George Gömöri

HERMANS, Willem Frederik. Dutch. Born in Amsterdam, 1 September 1921. Educated at Barlaeus Gymnasium, Amsterdam; University of Amsterdam, graduated 1950. Ph.D. 1955. Married Emelie Henriette Meurs in 1950. Staff member, *Criterium*, 1946–48, and *Podium*, 1949–50, and after 1963; reader in geography, University of Groningen, 1958–73; then full-time writer. Regular contributor, *NRC/Handelsblad* and *Het Parool* newspapers. Has lived in Paris since 1973. Recipient: Hooft prize, 1971; Ministry of Culture prize, 1977. Address: c/o De Bezige Bij, Postbus 5184, 1071 DW, Amsterdam, The Netherlands.

PUBLICATIONS

Fiction

Conserve [Preserves]. Amsterdam, Salm, 1947; revised edition in *Drie melodrama's*, 1957.
Moedwil en misverstand [Malice and Misunderstanding]. Amsterdam, Meulenhoff, 1948.
De Tranen der acacia's [The Tears of the Acacias]. Amsterdam, Van Oorschot, 1950.
Ik heb altijd gelijk [I Am Always Right]. Amsterdam, Van Oorschot, 1951.
Het behouden huis. Amsterdam, Bezige Bij, 1952; as "The House of Refuge," in *The World of Modern Fiction*; edited by Steven Marcus, New York, Simon and Schuster, 1966.
Paranoia. Amsterdam, Van Oorschot, 1953.

De god Denkbaar, Denkbaar de god [The God Conceivable, Conceivable the God]. Amsterdam, Van Oorschot, 1956.
Een landingspoging op Newfoundland en andere verhalen [An Attempted Landing on Newfoundland and Other Stories]. Amsterdam, Van Oorschot, 1957.
Drie melodrama's: Conserve, De leproos van Molokai, Hermans in hier geweest [Three Melodramas: Preserves, The Leper of Molokai, Hermans Was Here]. Amsterdam, Van Oorschot, 1957.
De donkere kamer van Damokles. Amsterdam, Van Oorschot, 1959; as *The Dark Room of Damocles*, London, Heinemann, 1962.
Nooit meer slapen [Never Sleep Again]. Amsterdam, Bezige Bij, 1966.
Een wonderkind of een total loss [A Child Prodigy or a Total Loss]. Amsterdam, Bezige Bij, 1967.
Herinneringen van een engelbewaarden [Memoirs of a Guardian Angel]. Amsterdam, Bezige Bij, 1971.
Het evangelie van O. Dapper Dapper [The Gospel According to O. Dapper Dapper]. Amsterdam, Bezige Bij, 1973.
Onder professoren [Among Professors]. Amsterdam, Bezige Bij, 1975.
Vijf verhalen [Five Stories]. Utrecht, Knippenberg, 1980.
Dood en weggeraakt [Dead and Gone]. Antwerp, Ziggurat, 1980.
Filip's sonatine [Philip's Sonatina]. Amsterdam, Bezige Bij, 1980.
Homme's hoest [Homme's Cough]. Amsterdam, Bezige Bij, 1980.
Uit talloos veel miljoenen [From Countless Millions]. Amsterdam, Bezige Bij, 1981.
Geyerstein's dynamiek. Amsterdam, Bezige Bij, 1982.
En toch . . . was de machine goed [And Yet The Machine Was Good]. N.p., Piratenpers, 1982.
Waarom schrijven? [Why Write?]. Amsterdam, De Harmonie, 1984.
De zegelring [The Signet Ring]. Amsterdam, Bezige Bij, 1984.
Een heilige van de horlogerie [A Saint from the Cloakroom]. Amsterdam, Bezige Bij, 1987.
Au Pair. Amsterdam, Bezige Bij, 1989.
Naar Magnitogorsk [To Magnitogorsk]. Amsterdam, De Harmonie, 1990.
De laatste roker [The Last Smoker]. Amsterdam, Bezige Bij, 1991.

Plays

Het omgekeerde pension [The Inverted Boarding House]. Published in *Briefgeheim: Vier eenacters* [Confidential: Four One-Act Plays]. Amsterdam, Corvey, 1953.
De woeste wandeling [The Wild Walk] (screenplay). Amsterdam, Bezige Bij, 1962.
Drie drama's [Three Plays]. Amsterdam, Bezige Bij, 1962.
King Kong. Amsterdam, Bezige Bij, 1972.
Periander. Amsterdam, Bezige Bij, 1974.

Verse

Kussen door een rag van woorden [Kissing Through a Web of Words]. Amsterdam, privately printed, 1944.
Horror coeli en andere gedichten [Horror Coeli and Other Poems]. Amsterdam, Meulenhoff, 1946.
Hypnodrome. The Hague, Stols, 1947.
Overgebleven gedichten [Poetic Remnants]. Amsterdam, Rap, 1968; revised edition, 1974, revised edition, Amsterdam, Bezige Bij, 1982.

Other

Fenomenologie van de pin-up girl [Phenomenology of the Pin-Up]. Amsterdam, Van Oorschot, 1950.

Description et genèse des dépôts meubles de surface et du relief de l'Oesling. Luxembourg, Service Géologique, 1955.

Het zonale beginsel in de geografie [The Zonal Principle in Geography]. Groningen, Wolters, 1958.

Misdaad aan de Noordpool [Murder at the North Pole] (as Fjodor Klondyke). N.p., n.d.

De demon van ivoor [The Ivory Demon] (as Fjodor Klondyke). N.p., n.d.

Erosie [Erosion]. Zaandijk, Heijnis, 1960.

Mandarijnen op zwavelzuur [Mandarins in Sulphuric Acid]. Groningen, Mandarijnenpers, 1963; supplement published, 1983.

Het sadistische universum; Van Wittgenstein tot Weinreb [The Sadistic Universe: From Wittgenstein to Weinreb]. Amsterdam, Bezige Bij, 2 vols., 1964–76.

Wittgenstein in de mode en Kazemier niet [Wittgenstein in Fashion, But Not Kazemier]. Amsterdam, Bezige Bij, 1967.

Annum Veritatis (as Pater Anastase Prudhomme, S.J.). Amsterdam, Rap, 1968.

Fotobiografie. Amsterdam, Rap, 1969.

De laatste resten tropisch Nederland [The Last Remnants of Tropical Holland]. Amsterdam, Bezige Bij, 1969.

Hollywood. Amsterdam, Rap, 1970.

Machines in Bikini. Zandvoort, Eliance Pers, 1974.

De raadselachtige Multatuli [The Enigmatic Multatuli]. Amsterdam, Boelen, 1976.

Dinky Toys. Paris, Mandarijnenpers, 1976; Amsterdam, De Harmonie, 1988.

Boze brieven van Bijkaart [Bijkaart's Angry Letters]. Amsterdam, Bezige Bij, 1977.

Bijzondere tekens [Special Signs]. Antwerp, Ziggurat, 1977.

Houten leeuwen en leeuwen van goud [Wooden Lions and Lions of Gold]. Amsterdam, Bezige Bij, 1979.

Ik draag geen helm met vederbos [I Wear No Helmet with a Plume]. Amsterdam, Bezige Bij, 1979.

Scheppend nihilisme: interviews met Willem Frederik Hermans [Scooping Nihilism: Interviews with Willem Frederik Hermans], with Frans A. Jannsen. Amsterdam, Loeb & van der Velden, 1979.

Beertje Bombazijn (as Sita van de Wissel). Amsterdam, De Literaire Loodgieters, 1981.

Het kompas [The Compass]. Amsterdam, Sub Signo Libelli, 1981.

Uitgever oorwurm [Earwig Publisher]. 's-Gravenhage, Presse Illicite, 1982.

Klaas kwam niet [Klaas Didn't Come]. Amsterdam, Bezige Bij, 1983.

Suidafrikaantjies! [South Africans!]. Potchefstroom, Ossewa, 1984.

Relikwieën en documenten: een toespraak [Relics and Documents]. Amsterdam, Bezige Bij, 1985.

De liefde tussen mens en kat [The Love Between Man and Cat]. Amsterdam, Bijenkorf, 1985.

Een steek, een degen en (vooral) een jaargald [A Sting, a Blade and (Especially) an Annuity]. Dunkirk, Uitgaven, 1985.

Het boek der boeken, bij uitstek. Amsterdam, Bezige Bij, 1986.

Koningin eenoog [One-Eyed Queen]. Amsterdam, Bezige Bij, 1986.

Mondelinge mededelingen [Oral Participation]. Amsterdam, Bezige Bij, 1987.

Door gevaarlijke gekken omringd [Surrounded by Dangerous Madmen]. Amsterdam, Bezige Bij, 1988.

De schrijfmachine mijmert gekkepraat [The Typewriter Mimics the Speech of a Madman]. Amsterdam, Rap, 1989.

Vincent literator. Amsterdam, Bezige Bij, 1990.

Wittgenstein (essays). Amsterdam, Bezige Bij, 1990.

Gitaarvissen en Banjoklokken [Guitar-Fish and Banjos] (diaries). Amsterdam, Rap, 1991.

Het hodenparadijs [The Dog-Heaven] (picture book; illustrated by Hermans). Zutphen, De Walburg Press, 1991.

Editor, *Focquenbroch: bloemlezing uit zijn lyriek* [Focquenbroch: An Anthology of His Lyric Poetry]. Amsterdam, Van Oorschot, 1946.

Translator, *Zonlicht op zaterdag* [Daylight on Saturday], by J. B. Priestley. Amsterdam, Arbeiderspers, 1947.

Translator, *Kraters in lichterlaaie* [Craters Ablaze], by H. Tazieff. The Hague, Leopold, 1954.

Translator, *Tractatus logicus-philosophicus*, by Ludwig Wittgenstein. Amsterdam, Athenaeum-Polak & Van Gennep, 1975.

Translator, *De martelgang van de dikzak* [The Fat Man's Ordeal], by Henri Béraud. Amsterdam, Bezige Bij, 1981.

Translator, *Zeven gedichten* [Seven Poems], by Oscar Venceslav de Lubics Miłosz. Amsterdam, Cornamona, 1981.

Translator, *De heilige Maria Juana* [Holy Maria Juana], by Luis Cimatarra. Lelystad, De Watersnip, 1989.

*

Bibliography: *Bibliografie van de verspreide publicaties van Hermans* by Frans A. Janssen and Rob Delvigne, Amsterdam, Rap, 1972.

Critical Study: "Coming to Terms with the Past and Searching for an Identity: The Treatment of the Occupied Netherlands in the Fiction of Hermans, Mulisch and Vestdijk" by John Michielsen, in *Canadian Journal of Netherlandic Studies* (Windsor, Ontario), 7(1–2), 1986.

*   *   *

Although he published some poetry during and just after World War II, Willem Frederik Hermans's favoured medium is fiction. His 12 novels, six novellas, and seven volumes of stories give him a pre-eminent place among living Dutch practitioners. In addition, he is a brilliant and feared polemical essayist, and has written a number of filmscripts and plays.

His fiction explores a universe essentially chaotic and unknowable, loveless, full of violence, hatred, and, above all, confusion. Hermans sees the novelist as engaged in a "science without proofs," and his own undertaking is bedevilled by a distrust of language he shares with the philosopher Wittgenstein, whom he has both translated and written of admiringly. "My greatest regret is that I cannot write with light like a camera," he sighed in his "Preamble" to the collection *Paranoia*, though this very frustration leads him to maximum precision of language, stark clarity of description, and a persistent, even obsessive concern with the visual (not surprisingly, one novel and one story have been filmed). From his bizarre debut, *Conserve* (Preserves), set in a Mormon community in Utah, to his recent novel *Uit talloos veel miljoenen* (From Countless Millions), in which he satirises his own former university, Groningen, Hermans presents us with a memorable array of anti-heroes, outsiders who struggle with a hostile world before succumbing to it. Sometimes their defeat is physically fatal, in other cases the battering is a spiritual and moral one.

In one of Hermans's most succinct and powerful evocations of chaos and futility, the novella *Het behouden huis* ("The House of Refuge"), a partisan fighting in Eastern Europe at the end of World War II seeks to escape the horrors of the front line in a house left intact, whose owners he kills. However, the war catches up with him, and the "refuge" the house seemed to offer proves illusory.

De donkere Kamer van Damokles (*The Dark Room of Damocles*), arguably Hermans's masterpiece to date, has been praised by John le Carré as one of the best spy stories of the period. The main protagonist, an insignificant tobacconist, becomes caught up in underground work during the German occupation, but is subsequently unable to prove the existence of a "double" who he claims recruited and instructed him, but who has since disappeared. Period, place, and atmosphere are vividly captured and the book can be read as an adventure yarn, but what is most impressive and disturbing is the way that the picture of reality shared by protagonist and reader for two-thirds of the novel cannot be substantiated when called into question in the final section.

Disorientation of character and reader is achieved by more radical means in the cryptic fantasy *De god Denkbaar, Denkbaar de god* (The God Conceivable, Conceivable the God) and its satirical sequel *Het evangelie van O. Dapper Dapper* (The Gospel According to O. Dapper Dapper). In *Nooit meer slapen* (Never Sleep Again) Hermans uses a more familiar narrative mode to give a gripping first-person account of a young geologist's abortive expedition to northern Norway in search of meteor craters, which leads him to question the purpose of scientific enquiry.

Hermans's Swift-like onslaughts on the literary and intellectual establishment, in the essay collections *Mandarijnen op zwavelzuur* (Mandarins in Sulphuric Acid) and *Het sadistische universum: Van Wittgenstein tot Weinreb* (The Sadistic Universe: From Wittgenstein to Weinreb) and in a long succession of magazine and newspaper articles, have won him as many enemies as admirers and emulators, while allegedly slighting remarks against Roman Catholics placed in the mouth of a character in the novel *Ik heb altijd gelijk* (I Am Always Right) resulted in (unsuccessful) prosecution. His polemical belligerence sometimes recalls Multatuli, author of the greatest Dutch prose classic, the colonial novel *Max Havelaar* (1860), to whom Hermans devoted a discerning and provocative study.

Some recent work, notably the novella *Filip's sonatine* (Philip's Sonatina) has been a disappointingly uneven reprise of earlier themes, in which the cynicism is occasionally facile, but such strictures are minor ones. The novels *Een heilige van de horlogerie* (A Saint from the Cloakroom) and *Au Pair*, both set in and around Paris, combine narrative elegance and ironic philosophical undertones, while the story collection *De laatste roker* (The Last Smoker) shows the underlying consistency of the author's earlier and later writing.

Hermans has repeatedly shown, in the course of a distinguished career, the capacity to find new and powerful ways of rendering his familiar vision, and one looks forward eagerly to the next version of the "same book" he insists he has been writing all along.

—Paul Vincent

HERNÁNDEZ, Luisa Josefina. Mexican. Born in Mexico City, in 1928. Educated at the National Autonomous University of Mexico, Mexico City, M.A. in English literature and theatre 1955; Columbia University, New York; also studied in Europe. Has one daughter. Professor of drama, National Autonomous University of Mexico, and Institute of Fine Arts, Mexico City. Recipient: *El Nacional* prize, 1954; Institute of Fine Arts Drama Festival prize, 1957. Address: c/o Fondo de Cultura Económica, Ave Universidad 975, Apdo 44975, 03100 Mexico City 12, Mexico.

PUBLICATIONS

Plays

El ambiente jurídico.   1950.
Agonía.   1951.
Aguardiente de caña (produced Mexico City, 1951).
Afuera; Llueve.   1952.
Los sordomudos (produced Mexico City, 1953).
Botica Modelo (produced Mexico City, 1954).   Published in serial form, in *El Nacional* (Mexico City), 1953.
Los frutos caídos (produced 1957).   Published in *Teatro mexicano del siglo XX*, Mexico City, Fondo de Cultura Económica, vol. 27, 1956.
Los duendes (produced 1957; Mexico City, 1963).   Published in *Teatro mexicano 1963*, Mexico City, Aguilar, 1965.
Los huéspedes reales (produced 1968).   Xalapa, Universidad Veracruzana, 1958.
La paz ficticia (produced 1960).   With *Popol Vuh*, Mexico City, Novaro, 1974.
La historia de un anillo.   1961.
Pastores de la ciudad, with Emilio Carballido (produced Mexico City, 1972).   Published in *D.F.*, Xalapa, Universidad Veracruzana, 1962.
La plaza de Puerto Santo, adapted from her own novel (produced 1962).
La calle de la gran ocasión.   Xalapa, Universidad Veracruzana, 1962; second series, 1985.
Clemencia, adaptation of a novel by Ignacio M. Altamirano.   Published in *Cuadernos de Bellas Artes* (Mexico City), 3–4, 1963.
Arpas blancas, conejos dorados.   1963.
La hija del rey.   Published in *Cuarta antologia de obras en un acto*, Mexico City, n.p., 1965.
Quetzalcóatl.   Mexico City, Asuntos Culturales, 1968.
La danza del urogallo múltiple (produced 1971).
Popol Vuh; La paz ficticia.   Mexico City, Novaro, 1974.
Apostasía (produced 1974).   Mexico City, Universidad Nacional Autonóma de México, 1978.
Hécuba (produced 1976).
La fiesta del mulato.   1979.
Ciertas cosas.   1980.
El orden de los factores (produced 1983).
Oriflama.   1988.
Una noche como ésta.   1988.

Fiction

El lugar donde crece la hierba.   Xalapa, Universidad Veracruzana, 1959.
La plaza de Puerto Santo.   Mexico City, Fondo de Cultura Económica, 1961.
Los palacios desiertos.   Mexico City, Mortiz, 1963.
La cólera secreta.   Xalapa, Universidad Veracruzana, 1964.

La primera batalla.   Mexico City, Era, 1965.
El valle que elegimos.   Mexico City, Mortiz, 1965.
La noche exquisita.   Xalapa, Universidad Veracruzana, 1965.
La memoria de Amadís.   Mexico City, Mortiz, 1967.
Nostalgia de Troya.   Mexico City, Siglo Veintiuno, 1970.
Los trovadores.   Mexico City, Mortiz, 1973.
Las fuentes ocultas.   Mexico City, Extemporáneos, 1980.
Apocalipsis cum figuris.   Xalapa, Universidad Veracruzana, 1982.
Cartas de navegaciones submarinas.   Mexico City, Fondo de Cultura Económica, 1987.
La cabalgata.   Mexico City, Océano, 1988.

Other

Caprichos y Disparates de Francisco de Goya.   Mexico City, Universidad Nacional Autonóma de México, 1979.

Translator, *El doctor y los demonios* [The Doctor and the Devils], by Dylan Thomas. Xalapa, Universidad Veracruzana, 1960.
Translator, *Madre Juana de los Angeles*, by Jerzy Kawalerowicz. Xalapa, Universidad Veracruzana, 1964.
Translator, *El rey Lear* [King Lear], by William Shakespeare. Xalapa, Universidad Veracruzana, 1966.

*

Bibliography: in *Mexican Literature: A Bibliography of Secondary Sources* by David William Foster, Metuchen, New Jersey, Scarecrow Press, 1992.

Critical Studies: "Three Female Playwrights Explore Contemporary Latin American Reality: Myrna Casas, Griselda Gambaro, Luisa Josefina Hernández" by Gloria Feiman Waldman, in *Latin American Women Writers: Yesterday and Today*, Pittsburgh, Latin American Literary Review Press, 1972; "Luisa Josefina Hernández: The Labyrinth of Form" by John K. Knowles, in *Dramatists in Revolt*, edited by Leon F. Lyday and George Woodyard, Austin, University of Texas Press, 1976; "Luisa Josefina Hernández: *La cólera secreta*" by Lucía Fox-Lockert, in her *Women Novelists in Spain and Spanish America*, Metuchen, New Jersey, Scarecrow Press, 1979; "Interview with Luisa Josefina Hernández" by Grace M. Bearse, in *Hispania* (Los Angeles), 64, 1981.

*   *   *

The beginning of Luisa Josefina Hernández's career as a playwright coincides with the heyday of stage realism in Mexico. As a student in the 1950s of Rodolfo Usigli, Mexico's foremost playwright and most vocal champion of realism, Hernández's first plays are notable for their almost perfect (although sometimes contrived) three-act structure, their insistence on psychological verisimilitude and believable social types. *Los frutos caídos* (The Fallen Fruit) was her first major stage success, under the very talented Japanese director Seki Sano, who had introduced Mexican theatre artists to Stanislavskii as well as to method acting. The play deals with the conservative values of a Mexico that in the 1950s could not tolerate a woman like Celia, the protagonist, who is twice married and on the verge of taking on a young lover. She returns from Mexico City to the provincial town where she still owns a house that is rented to other family members. This homecoming provides the catalyst for the highly charged confrontations and dramatic revelations so typical of realism,

and which clearly echo the example of Eugene O'Neill's *Long Day's Journey into Night*. Also reminiscent of O'Neill is *Los huéspedes reales* (The Royal Guests), which explores a daughter's rancor towards her mother and subliminal sexual attraction for her father.

Although *Los frutos caídos* remains one of Hernández's better known plays in the United States, inside Mexico she is noted for many of the more experimental plays she wrote in the 1960s and 1970s. During this period also she began to write on a commission basis only, very often for educational institutions or agencies. No longer so interested in individual psychology, Hernández's plays begin to focus on collective social issues, which she often explores through the reconstruction of Mexico's past, and through a variety of theatrical techniques. Works like *Popol Vuh* and *Quetzalcóatl* deal with pre-Columbian Mexico; *La paz ficticia* (The Fictitious Peace) re-creates an incident in which Yaqui indians were duped and robbed of their land; *La historia de un anillo* (The History of a Ring) tells the true story of a rural school teacher who was fired for having taught her students about their constitutional rights. *La fiesta del mulato* (The Mulatto's Orgy) is the finest of these plays and revealing of the strong, positive influence of Brechtian theatre on Mexican and Latin American playwrights at that time. Based on the journal of a friar who in 1799 witnessed the trial of a mulatto accused of embezzling funds from the rich silver mines of Guanajuato, *La fiesta del mulato* denounces a colonial, or any class system based on purity of race and the exploitation of the poor. Far from her early realistic technique, Hernández makes the action here fast-moving and episodic; the stage is nearly bare, with only a few key props. The characters are highly stylized and are dressed in period costumes. *La fiesta del mulato*, however, is not a traditional historical play; instead, like Brecht, Hernández uses alienation techniques to frame the past in relationship to the present.

Through the 1960s and 1970s Hernández's playwriting continued to evolve and absorb a variety of influences or models; for example, *La danza del urogallo múltiple* (The Dance of the Multiple Woodcock) is an experiment in the kind of actor-centred theatre associated with Jerzy Grotowski. Yet in recent years Hernández seems to have come back to her earlier realism, in plays like *El orden de los factores* (The Order of Factors), which deals again with middle-class mores, but with a significant difference: from the 1950s to the 1980s Mexican society had radically changed, having gone through the tumultuous 1960s, the economic boom of the 1970s, and the devastating bust of the 1980s. Divorce may still be frowned upon, but drugs, violence, economic instability, and political corruption — all themes Hernández touches on in her latest plays — are much more of a threat to the Mexican middle class today. According to Hernández, her return to realism is logical, if not inevitable, given the failure of the artistic and political programmes of the two previous decades.

Hernández holds a special position in Mexico, for she is recognized not only as a playwright but also as an award-winning novelist, with over a dozen prose works to her credit. She has also been a major influence in the training of playwrights and actors, in her capacity as a professor of drama at the National Autonomous University and the National Institute of Fine Arts in Mexico City. Her collection of short sketches, *La calle de la gran ocasión* (The Street of the Great Occasion), has been a standard in acting classes and workshops in Mexico; some of these brief pieces have also been used in classes in the United States. And although she does not consider herself a feminist, Luisa Josefina Hernández's early and continued concern with the position of women in Mexico, and her own success cannot help but serve as an example to other aspiring women playwrights and writers.

—Kirsten F. Nigro

———————

HERZBERG, Judith (Frieda Lina). Dutch. Born in Amsterdam, 4 November 1934. Educated at Montessori Lyceum, graduated 1952. Teacher at film schools in Amsterdam and Jerusalem, and at the University of Leiden. Recipient: Jan Campert Foundation prize, for play, 1980, for poetry, 1981; Bayerische film prize, 1980; Dutch Theatre Criticism prize, 1982; Joost van den Vondel prize, 1984; Charlotte Kohler prize, 1988; Cestoda prize, 1988; Netherlands-Vlaamse drama prize, 1989. Address: c/o De Harmonie, Postbus 3547, 1001 AH Amsterdam, The Netherlands.

PUBLICATIONS

Verse

Zeepost [Slow Boat].   Amsterdam, Van Oorschot, 1964.
Beemdgras [Meadow Grass].   Amsterdam, Van Oorschot, 1968.
Vliegen [Flies].   Amsterdam, Rap, 1970.
Strijklicht [Grazing Light].   Amsterdam, Van Oorschot, 1971.
27 liefdesliedjes [27 Love Songs], adaptation of the *Song of Songs*.   Amsterdam, De Harmonie, 1973.
Ethooi.   Amsterdam, Meijer, 1978.
Botshol [Hit and Run].   Amsterdam, Van Oorschot, 1980.
Dagrest [Remains of the Day].   Amsterdam, Van Oorschot, 1984.
Twintig gedichten [Twenty Poems].   Baarn, Atalanta, 1984.
But What: Selected Poems, translated by Shirley Kaufman and the author.   Oberlin, Ohio, Oberlin College Press, 1988.

Plays

Naar Archangel (produced Amsterdam, 1971).
De deur stond open (produced Amsterdam, 1972).   With *Dat het 's ochtends ochtend wordt*, Amsterdam, De Harmonie, 1974.
Het is geen hond [It Is Not a Dog] (produced Amsterdam, 1973).
Dat het 's ochtends ochtend wordt, with *De deur stond open*.   Amsterdam, De Harmonie, 1974; first play published as *That Day May Dawn*, Budapest, Centre Hongrois de l'IIT, 1977.
Leedvermaak [Gloating] (produced Amsterdam, 1982).   Amsterdam, Baal, 1982.
De val van Icarus [The Fall of Icarus].   Amsterdam, Sub Signo Libelli, 1983.
En/of [And/Or] (produced Amsterdam, 1984).   Amsterdam, Baal-De Harmonie, 1985.
Merg [Marrow] (chamber opera) (produced Amsterdam, 1986).   Amsterdam, De Salon, 1986.
De kleine zeemeermin [The Little Mermaid] (produced Amsterdam, 1986).   Amsterdam, De Harmonie, 1986.

De caracal (produced Amsterdam, 1988).   Amsterdam, International Theatre and Film Bookshop, 1988.
Kras [Scratch] (produced Amsterdam, 1989).   Amsterdam, International Theatre and Film Bookshop, 1989.
De tijd en het vertrek [Time and Departure], adaptation of a play by Botho Strauss (produced Amsterdam, 1989).   Amsterdam, Nationale Toneel, 1989.
Lulu: de doos van Pandora [Lulu: Pandora's Box], adaptation of the play by Frank Wedekind (produced Amsterdam, 1989).   Amsterdam, International Theatre and Film Bookshop, 1989.
Het zuiden [The South], adaptation of a work by Julien Green (produced Zuidelijk, 1990).   Eindhoven, Het Zuidelijk Toneel, 1990.
De zomer van Aviya [Aviya's Summer] (produced Holland Festival, 1991).
Een goed hoofd [A Good Head] (produced Haarlem, 1991).   Amsterdam, Orkater, 1991.
Teksten voor toneel en film: 1972–1988 [Texts for the Stage and Film 1972–1988].   Amsterdam, De Harmonie, 1991.

Screenplays: *Rooie sien*; *Mevrouw Katrien*; *Eenvrouw als Eva*; *Charlotte*, 1980; *Leedvermaak*; *Twee vrouwen* [Two Women].

Television Plays: *Het hooglied*, 1971; *Dat het 's ochtend ochtend wordt*, 1974; *Lieve Arthur*, 1976; *En/of*, 1985; *De caracal*, 1989.

Other

Het maken van gedichten en het praten daarover [The Making of Poems and the Talking About Them].   's-Gravenhage, BZZTôH, 1977.
Charlotte: dagboek bij een film [Charlotte: Diary with a Film].   Amsterdam, De Harmonie, 1981.
Dat Engels geen au heeft.   Terhorst, Ser J. L. Prop, 1985.
Hoe de oorlog is verdwenen [How the War Disappeared].   Amsterdam, Van Gennep, 1986.
Tussen Amsterdam en Tel Aviv: artikelen en brieven [Between Amsterdam and Tel Aviv: Articles and Letters].   Amsterdam, Van Gennep, 1988.

Translator, *Wie schoot Roodbaardje Pik* [Who Did Kill Cock Robin], by Peter Vos.   Amsterdam, De Harmonie, 1976.
Translator, *Charlotte Salomon, leven of theater? een autobiografisch zangspel in 769 gouaches* [Charlotte Salomon, Life or Theatre? An Autobiographical Musical in 769 Gouaches].   Maarsen, Schwartz, 1981.
Translator, *Uit den vreemde* [From Afar], by Ernst Jandl.   Amsterdam, Baal, 1982.
Translator, with Heleen ten Holt, *Of sterven we?* (Or Shall We Die?], by Ian MacEwan.   Amsterdam, De Harmonie, 1983.
Translator, *De vrouwen van Troje* [The Trojan Women], by Euripides.   Leiden, Nijhoff, 1984.
Translator, *Moedertje brei* [Little Mother Knit], by Uri Orlev.   Amsterdam, Querido, 1986.
Translator, *Spoken* [Ghosts], by Henrik Ibsen.   Amsterdam, International Theatre and Film Bookshop, and The Hague, Haagse Comedie, 1987.

*   *   *

Judith Herzberg's debut, the collection *Zeepost* (Slow Boat) of 1964, established her as a muted but arrestingly individual voice on the Dutch poetic scene. Her characteristic "mixture of concrete observation and tentative reflection which has always been extremely rare in our poetry" was praised by her fellow writer Adriaan Morriën. The intense focus on the minutiae of existence, the diffident formulations, the (deceptive) formal nonchalance and understatement, contrasted with the sometimes grandiloquent experimentalism of much of the poetry of the 1950s such as that of Lucebert (*q.v.*), and prompted comparisons with the *Barbarber* group's use of "ready made" fragments of reality and with the accessible, quasi-conversational tone of poets like Rutger Kopland and Jan Emmens associated with the magazine *Tirade*. However, the originality with which she blended her influences was not in question. In the poem "Moed" (Courage), for example, disorientation, vulnerability, human solidarity, and resilience meet in a typical synthesis:

> The night has disconcerted me again
> slowly the morning fills
> with words that I'm certain
> meant something — but what? —
> meant something yesterday.
>
> Walking is a tightrope act,
> in the street I see the warm creatures
> who also had the incomprehensible
> courage to get up
> instead of not.
>
> No one is ever sure of anything,
> Of being loved, of being left
> anything's on and anything goes
> everything's in flux.
>
> Now I recall what I wanted to say:
> As long as it doesn't make you too unhappy
> it's a nice feeling. But in fact
> we're soft as Turkish Delight
> in a tin full of nails.

Vliegen (Flies) achieved a studied minimalism in words (and accompanying drawings):

> High above Labrador
> one landed on the edge
> of my plate and sat motionless.
> A fly unaware it was flying.

Beemdgras (Meadow Grass) combines precise evocations of nature (both animals and plants), reminiscent of the work of Christoph van Geel, with experiences of bereavement, ageing, helpless nostalgia triggered by prompts as trivial as the label on a jam jar or a box of crayons (for this mixture of melancholy and rage Herzberg coined the word "weewoed," or "melancholer"). There is regret at the loss of her Yiddish heritage ("Sad, intimate language/I regret that you shrivelled/in this head of mine./It doesn't need you any more/but it still misses you.").

"Big" political statements (for instance on overpopulation, post-Holocaust survival and, later, criticism of Israel's post-1967 borders) are rare but telling. In writing about her own work Herzberg seems to eschew symbolism: "I never try to express anything with images of something else, but simply talk about what I'm talking about without any double bottoms." However, she is capable of striking imagery, while the future accomplished dramatist announces herself in a poem like "Storm" from the collection *Strijklicht* (Grazing Light): "You said, on the phone from Amsterdam:/there's a big storm on the way — /and sure enough, a few words later/

my trees were also tugging at their trunks." Here the literal surface has an intensely erotic subtext. In *Strijklicht* too the liberation of the Netherlands is distilled into a touching emblematic scene:

> 1945
>
> We had heroes to tea
> they sat together on the settee
> they had absolutely no
> conversation, I looked and looked
> till they got embarrassed
> they could not cope
> with such a peace.

While *Strijklicht* was criticised in some quarters as overly sentimental, its successor, *Botshol* (Hit and Run), was acclaimed. Some poems have a raw, almost medieval terseness:

> JULY
>
> I have lost my little ones
> I'd give the world to hear rustling
> My nest's too big for me.

In *27 liefdesliedjes* (27 Love Songs) the poet creates limpidly sensual modern variations on the Song of Songs.

The recent collection *Dagrest* (Remains of the Day) contains the following "mini-drama" with Freudian allusions:

> TIMETABLE
>
> Fear wakes up first. Then wakes
> Reason and plans for the day,
> they tuck it in for a while. Why
> can't calm get up first for a change, or
> joy, why is fear so uncontrolled
> so keen?
>   Miss, Miss, I was first.
> All right, teacher heard you. Just go back to
> your place and don't talk out of turn.
> This afternoon in history, you can
> tell us everything you know about what
> happened.
> In the past.

Herzberg sees her poems and plays as having a common content, "unlived life . . ., which comes to life on paper in poetry, and comes off the page again and stands on its own feet in drama." Her plays, from *Dat het 's ochtends ochtend wordt* (*That Day May Dawn*) of 1974 to *En/of* (And/Or), *Leedvermaak* (Gloating), and the chamber opera *Merg* (Marrow), have the same charged sparseness as many of her poems. Simplicity, however, does not imply overexplicitness. Herzberg has even said that the words "love" and "parting" should be banned from literature as unhelpful. In her plays the characters are searching for a modus vivendi. Michiel, the main character of *That Day May Dawn*, sees the solution in inertia and spends all his time in bed until galvanised into action by his girlfriend's pregnancy. *En/of* is the clipped, schematised view of a love triangle involving one man and two (unnamed) women with its jealousies, sacrifices, compromises, and selfishness, between and beneath the lines. In *Leedvermaak* 14 characters at a party try to come to terms with a post-Auschwitz world. This piece marked a new departure with its effective use of music, which was continued in *Merg*, where a man confronts his impending death from cancer.

In addition to writing poems and plays, Herzberg has established a solid reputation as a scriptwriter for television and films, notably *Twee vrouwen* (Two Women), an adaptation of a Harry Mulisch (*q.v.*) novel, and *Charlotte*, directed by Frans Weisz and based on the brief life and career of the German artist Charlotte Salomon, who died in Auschwitz.

Herzberg's unmonumental but still impressive body of work has remained true to its stated aim of being "a homage to the world, to reality . . . a way of establishing a personal relationship with that reality." Much of her work is informed by what she has called "the gratitude of the survivor." Her literary method has been rightly described as heuristic — a journey of discovery in which the reader is invited to participate. She sums up her aesthetic as follows: "Almost everything intended to be beautiful I find ugly. I like sobriety and extravagance, but not what is in between." These preferences are apparent in the affinity she feels with the English poets Stevie Smith and Philip Larkin, both of whom she has translated.

—Paul Vincent

HEYM, Stefan. German. Born Helmut Flieg in Chemnitz (now Karl-Marx-Stadt), 10 April 1913; name legally changed to Stefan Heym, 1943. Educated at the University of Berlin; University of Chicago, M.A. 1935. Served in the United States Army, 1943–48: Bronze Star. Married 1) Gertrude Peltyn in 1944 (died 1969); 2) Inge Hohn in 1971. Fled to Prague, 1933; clerk, Carson Pirie Scott department store, Chicago, 1936; editor, *Deutsches Volksecho*, New York, 1937–39; salesman, New Union Press printing company, after 1939; became American citizen, 1943; since 1952 has lived in (former) East Berlin; expelled from GDR writers' union, 1977; fined for publishing outside the GDR without government permission, 1979. Wrote all his books to and including *The King David Report* in English; later books written in German. Recipient: Heinrich Mann prize, 1953; GDR National prize; Jerusalem prize, 1993. H.D.D.: University of Berne, 1990; D.Litt.: University of Cambridge, 1991. Address: Rabindranath-Tagore-Strasse 9, 1180 Berlin-Grünau, Germany.

PUBLICATIONS

Fiction

Hostages. New York, Putnam, 1942; London, Putnam, 1943; as *The Glasenapp Case*, Berlin, Seven Seas, 1962; as *Der Fall Glasenapp*, Leipzig, List, 1958.
Of Smiling Peace. Boston, Little Brown, 1944; London, Skeffington, 1946.
The Crusaders. Boston, Little Brown, 1948; London, Cassell, 1950; as *Kreuzfahrer von heute*, Leipzig, List, 1950; as *Der bittere Lorbeer*, Munich, List, 1950.
The Eyes of Reason. Boston, Little Brown, 1951; London, Cassell, 1952; as *Die Augen der Vernunft*, Leipzig, List, 1955.
Goldsborough. In English, Leipzig, List, 1953; in German, 1954; in English, New York, Blue Heron Press, 1954; London, Cassell, 1961.

Die Kannibalen und andere Erzählungen. Leipzig, List, 1953; as *The Cannibals and Other Stories*, Berlin, Seven Seas, 1958.
Schatten und Licht: Geschichten aus einem geteilten Lande. Leipzig, List, 1960; as *Shadows and Lights: Eight Short Stories*, London, Cassell, 1963.
Die Papiere des Andreas Lenz. Leipzig, List, 1963; as *Lenz; oder, Die Freiheit*, Munich, List, 1965; as *The Lenz Papers*, London, Cassell, 1964.
Lassalle. Munich, Bechtle, 1969; as *Uncertain Friend*, London, Cassell, 1969.
Die Schmähschrift; oder, Die Königin gegen Defoe. Zurich, Diogenes, 1970; as *The Queen Against Defoe and Other Stories*, New York, Hill, 1974; London, Hodder and Stoughton, 1975.
Der König-David-Bericht. Munich, Kindler, 1972; as *The King David Report*, New York, Putnam, and London, Hodder and Stoughton, 1973.
Fünf Tage im Juni. Munich, Bertelsmann, 1974; as *Five Days in June*, London, Hodder and Stoughton, 1977; Buffalo, New York, Prometheus, 1978.
Erzählungen. Berlin, Der Morgen, 1976.
Die richtige Einstellung und andere Erzählungen. Munich, Bertelsmann, 1976.
Collin. Munich, Bertelsmann, 1979; in English, New York, Stuart, and London, Hodder and Stoughton, 1980.
Ahasver. Munich, Bertelsmann, 1981; as *The Wandering Jew*, New York, Holt Rinehart, 1984.
Schwarzenberg. Munich, Bertelsmann, 1984.
Gesammelte Erzählungen. Munich, Goldmann, 1984.
Auf Sand gebaut: sieben Geschichten aus der unmittelbaren Vergangenheit. Munich, Bertelsmann, 1990.

Play

Tom Sawyers grosses Abenteuer, with Hanus Burger. Berlin, Henschel, 1952.

Other

Nazis in U.S.A.: An Exposé of Hitler's Aims and Agents in the U.S.A. New York, American Committee for Anti-Nazi Literature, 1938.
Forschungsreise ins Herz der deutschen Arbeiterklasse. Berlin, Tribune, 1953.
Offene Worte: So Liegen die Dinge. Berlin, Tribune, 1953.
Reise ins Land der unbegrenzten Möglichkeiten. Berlin, Tribune, 1954; as *Keine Angst vor Russlands Bären*, Düsseldorf, Brücken, 1955.
Im Kopf sauber: Schriften zum Tage. Leipzig, List, 1954.
Offen Gesagt: Neue Schriften zum Tage. Berlin, Volk und Welt, 1957.
Das kosmische Zeitalter. Berlin, Tribune, 1959; as *A Visit to Soviet Science*, Marzani und Munsell, 1959; as *The Cosmic Age: A Report*, New Delhi, People's Publishing House, 1959.
Casimir und Cymbelinchen: Zwei Märchen (for children). Berlin, Kinderbuch, 1966.
Cymbelinchen; oder, Der Ernst des Lebens: Vier Märchen für kluge Kinder. Munich, Bertelsmann, 1975.
Das Wachsmuth-Syndrom. Berlin, Berliner Handpresse, 1975.
Erich Hückniesel, und das fortgesetzte Rotkäppchen. Berlin, Berliner Handpresse, 1977.
Wege und Umwege: Streitbare Schriften aus fünf Jahrzehnten, edited by Peter Mallwitz. Munich, Bertelsmann, 1980.

Atta Troll: Versuch einer Analyse. Munich, Bertelsmann, 1983.

Münchner Podium in den Kammerspielen '83: Reden über das eigene Land Deutschland. Munich, Bertelsmann, 1983.

Märchen für kluge Kinder (for children). Munich, Goldmann, 1984.

Reden an den Feind. Munich, Bertelsmann, 1986.

Nachruf (autobiography). Munich, Bertelsmann, 1988.

Meine Cousine, die Hexe und weitere Märchen für kluge Kinder (for children). Munich, Bertelsmann, 1989.

Stalin verläßt den Raum: politische Publizistik. Leipzig, Reclam, 1990.

Einmischung: Gespräche, Reden, Essays. Munich, Bertelsmann, 1990.

Editor, *Auskunft 1–2: Neue Prosa aus der DDR.* Munich, Verlag der Autoren, 2 vols., 1974–78; enlarged edition, Munich, Goldmann, 1985.

Editor, with Werner Heiduczek, *Die sanfte Revolution.* Leipzig, Kiepenheuer, 1990.

Translator, *King Leopold's Soliloquy*, by Mark Twain. Berlin, Tribune, 1961.

*

Critical Studies: "Stefan Heym and the Concept of Misunderstanding" by Pavel Petr, in *Journal of the Australasian Universities Language and Literature Association*, 48, 1977; "The State vs. the Writer: Recent Developments in Stefan Heym's Struggle Against the GDR's Kulturpolitik" by M. Dorman, in *Modern Languages* (London), September 1981; "Stefan Heym's Revolutionary Wandering Jew: A Warning and a Hope for the Future" by Nancy A. Lauckner, in *Studies in GDR Culture and Society, IV: Selected Papers from the Ninth New Hampshire Symposium on the German Democratic Republic*, edited by Margy Gerber, Lanham, Maryland, University Press of America, 1984; "Stefan Heym's *Ahasver*: Structure and Principles" by Rodney W. Fisher, in *Seminar* (Kingston, Ontario), September 1986; "Problems of Socialist Historiography: The Example of Stefan Heym's *The King David Report*" by Peter Hutchinson, in *Modern Language Review* (London), January 1986; "Authority, the State and the Individual: Stefan Heym's Novel *Collin*" by Peter J. Graves, in *Forum for Modern Language Studies* (St. Andrews, Scotland), October 1987.

*   *   *

Stefan Heym's fiction owes much to his wide-ranging experience as a highly successful journalist. He is an unashamed realist, he has a fine eye for detail and for the gripping plot, and he can develop his themes through telling use of confrontation and dialogue. Throughout his literary career he has revealed considerable courage in his preparedness to stand against what he felt to be unacceptable in a succession of different societies (National Socialism, US imperialism, Stalinism, dogmatism), and he has repeatedly used the figure of the struggling intellectual as a focus for broad questions on the nature of truth, the influence (and corruption) of power, the reaction of individuals in crisis or revolution, and questions on death and dying.

Although his first language was German, exile in the United States led him to complete his first novel in English; thereafter he tended to use English as first language of literary composition until the 1970s. He has, however, proved to be one of the best self-translators of our age, and all his novels have appeared in two versions. Like many of his heroes, Heym has proved an outsider, a tireless campaigner, and a champion of the individual. Unlike his heroes, however, he has also proved a vigorous survivor, and he was one of the few prominent dissident writers in the German Democratic Republic who had not been forced into exile before the collapse of the Berlin Wall in 1989.

Heym has achieved considerable success with short stories and investigative-reflective journalism, but his major achievement has been his novels. In all of these — from the detective story of the resistance movement in Prague (1942) to the historical, theological, and cultural interpretation-cum-satire of reformation Germany (1981) — Heym has always reached a mass audience through his ability to combine drama and tension with serious questioning of issues relevant to our own age. His works have also carried force through his ability to incorporate much historical detail, which sometimes takes the form of documents. In this respect his novels are thoroughly researched "investigations," and his scholarship has covered such different events as the pillorying of Daniel Defoe, the Baden revolution of 1849, the disturbances in East Germany in 1953, and even the biblical story of King David. The perspective is always socialist. Personal experience has regularly informed a number of his works, and dramatic moments of his career are as striking in his early panoramic treatment of the American advance in Europe (in one of the major novels of World War II, *The Crusaders*), as they are in his late study of Stalinist elements in the GDR (*Collin*). All of these are naturally treated in his enormously successful autobiography, *Nachruf* (Obituary).

Heym's most acclaimed work is *Der König-David-Bericht* (*The King David Report*), which subtly exposes the contradictions of the Books of *Samuel* and *Kings*. The attempt by King Solomon to legitimise his own succession becomes a source of grim comedy in its own right, but Heym reconsiders the biblical evidence in a strikingly unorthodox manner and suggests the relevance of his interpretation for several societies beyond that of ancient Israel. Parody of the style of the Authorised Version enriches the humour of this troubling, and often moving, investigation of primitive totalitarianism.

—Peter Hutchinson

HOCHHUTH, Rolf. German. Born in Eschwege, 1 April 1931. Educated at Realgymnasium, Eschwege, until 1948; studied bookselling at a technical school; universities of Heidelberg and Munich, 1952–55. Married to Dana Pavic; three sons. Worked for mayor of Eschwege, after World War II; staff member, C. Bertelsmann publishers, Gütersloh, from 1955; resident dramatist, Basel Municipal Theater, 1963; founder, with Martin Walser (*q.v.*), Meersburg summer theatre festival. Since 1989 chief cultural correspondent, *Die Welt* newspaper. Recipient: Hauptmann prize, 1962; Young Generation prize, 1963; Berlin prize, 1963; Melcher prize, 1965; Basel Art prize, 1976; Stadt München und der Verbandes bayerischer Verlager prize, 1980; Geschwister-Scholl prize, 1980; Lessing prize, 1981. Address: P.O. Box 661, 4002 Basel, Switzerland.

PUBLICATIONS

Plays

Der Stellvertreter (produced Berlin, 1963). Reinbek,
Rowohlt, 1963; as *The Representative* (produced London,
1963), London, Methuen, 1963; as *The Deputy* (produced
New York, 1964), New York, Grove Press, 1964.
Soldaten: Nekrolog auf Genf (produced Berlin, 1967).
Reinbek, Rowohlt, 1967; as *Soldiers: An Obituary for
Geneva* (produced New York, 1968), New York, Grove
Press, 1968.
Guerillas (produced Stuttgart, 1970). Reinbek, Rowohlt,
1970.
Die Hebamme (produced Zurich, 1972). Reinbek, Rowohlt,
1971.
Lysistrate und die NATO (produced Vienna, 1974).
Reinbek, Rowohlt, 1973.
Tod eines Jägers. Reinbek, Rowohlt, 1976.
Juristen (produced Hamburg, 1980). Reinbek, Rowohlt,
1979.
Ärztinnen (produced Mannheim, 1980). Reinbek, Rowohlt,
1980.
Judith (produced [in English] Glasgow, 1984; [in German]
Kiel, 1985). Reinbek, Rowohlt, 1984.
Unbefleckte Empfängnis: ein Kreidekreis. Reinbek, Rowohlt,
1988.
Sommer 14 ein Totentanz. Reinbek, Rowohlt, 1989.

Fiction

Zwischenspiel in Baden-Baden. Reinbek, Rowohlt, 1959.
Die Berliner Antigone. Reinbek, Rowohlt, 1964.
Eine Liebe in Deutschland. Reinbek, Rowohlt, 1978; as *A
German Love Story*, London, Weidenfeld and Nicolson,
and Boston, Little Brown, 1980.
Atlantik-Novelle: Erzählung. Reinbek, Rowohlt, 1985.
Alan Turing: Erzählung. Reinbek, Rowohlt, 1987.
Jede Zeit baut Pyramiden: Erzählungen und Gedichte.
Berlin, Volk und Welt, 1988.

Other

Krieg und Klassenkrieg: Studien. Reinbek, Rowohlt, 1971.
Die Berliner Antigone: Prose und Verse. Reinbek, Rowohlt,
1975.
Tell '38. Reinbek, Rowohlt, 1979; in English, Boston, Little
Brown, 1984.
Dokumente zur politischen Wirkung, edited by Reinhart
Hoffmeister. Munich, Kindler, 1980.
*Räuber-Rede: drei deutsche Vorwürfe: Schiller, Lessing,
Geschwister Scholl.* Reinbek, Rowohlt, 1982.
Spitze des Eisbergs: ein Reader. Reinbek, Rowohlt, 1982.
Schwarze Segel: Essays und Gedichte. Reinbek, Rowohlt,
1986.
War hier Europa? Reden, Gedichte, Essays. Munich,
Deutscher Taschenbuch, 1987.
*Täter und Denker: Profile und Probleme von Cäsar bis
Jünger.* Stuttgart, Deutsche Verlags-Anstalt, 1987.

Editor, *Sämtliche Werke*, by Wilhelm Busch. Gütersloh,
Mohn, 1959.
Editor, *Lustige Streiche in Versen und Farben*, by Wilhelm
Busch. Hamburg, Ruetten und Loening, 1961.
Editor, *Liebe in unserer Zeit: 16 Erzählungen.* Hamburg,
Ruetten und Loening, 1961.

Editor, *Die Deutschen*, by Otto Flake. Frankfurt, Fischer,
1962.
Editor, *Am grauen Meer: Gesammelte Werke*, by Theodor
Storm. Hamburg, Mosaik, 1963.
Editor, *Dichter und Herrscher*, by Thomas Mann. Munich,
Bertelsmann, 1964.
Editor, *Die grossen Meister.* Cologne, Kiepenheuer und
Witsch, 1966.
Editor, with Peter Härting, *Werke*, by Otto Flake.
Frankfurt, Fischer, 1973.
Editor, with Hans Heinrich Koch, *Kaisers Zeiten: Bilder einer
Epoche aus dem Archiv der Hofphotographen Oscar und
Gustav Tellgmann.* Munich, Herbig, 1973.
Editor, *Die Gegenwarf: 79 deutschsprachige Erzähler der
Jahrgänge 1900–1963.* Cologne, Kiepenheuer und Witsch,
2 vols., 1981.
Editor, *Die Zweite Klassik: deutschsprachige Erzähler der
Jahrgänge 1850–1900.* Cologne, Kiepenheuer und Witsch,
1983.

*

Bibliography: "Auswahlbibliographie zu Rolf Hochhuth" by
Günter Peters, in *Text und Kritik* (Munich), 58, 1978.

Critical Studies: *The Storm over The Deputy*, edited by Eric
Bentley, New York, Grove Press, 1964; *Rolf Hochhuth* by
Rainer Taëni, London, Wolff, 1977; *Rolf Hochhuth* by
M. E. Ward, Boston, Twayne, 1977; "Realists, Idealists and
Political Heroism" by Barry Jay Seltser, in *Soundings*
(Knoxville, Tennessee), Spring 1985; "Hochhuth's
Hemingway: *Tod eines Jägers*" by Wayne Kvam, in *Chiba
Review* (Chiba, Japan), 8, 1986; *Hochhuth's "The Representa-
tive" at the Glasgow Citizen's, 1986*, edited by Claude
Schumacher and Derek Fogg, Glasgow, Theatre Studies
Publications/Goethe-Institut, 1988; "American Mythologies:
Rolf Hochhuth's Plays *Guerillas, Tod eines Jägers*, and *Judith*"
by Manfred Durzak, in *Amerika! New Images in German
Literature*, edited by Heinz D. Osterle, New York, Lang,
1989.

*   *   *

The German dramatist Rolf Hochhuth shot to fame in 1963
in a welter of controversy aroused by his first play, *Der
Stellvertreter* (*The Deputy* or *The Representative*), which
accused Pope Pius XII of condoning the extermination of the
Jews in the Third Reich. Within a year a collection of essays for
and against Hochhuth's "explosive drama" was edited by Eric
Bentley under the title *The Storm over The Deputy*. Produced
by Erwin Piscator in Berlin, this play ushered in the wave of
documentary drama that was to make the theatre a forum for
critical debate in Germany and elsewhere. Despite the topicality of theme and lengthy essayistic reflections in the manner
of Shaw — with whom Hochhuth shares a polemical indignation — there is little that is documentary in the play itself.
Hochhuth writes in the tradition of the Schillerian tragedy
where the individual is shown in the dilemma of a historical
situation having to take the responsibility for decisive moral
actions. The protagonist tends to heroic stature in both Schiller
and Hochhuth, and the structure of *The Deputy* reflects the
pattern of conflict and catastrophe inherent in classical
tragedy. This pattern is only masked by interspersed quotations from such sources as diaries, memoirs, and biographies.
   Hochhuth maintained his controversial impact in his second
play, *Soldaten* (*Soldiers*), in which he pleaded for the exclusion
of civilian targets from modern aerial warfare. The focus of his

attack was another "hero" of history, Winston Churchill, who was alleged by Hochhuth to have personally ordered the massive and militarily unnecessary bombing of Dresden as well as the sabotaging of the plane in which the Polish freedom leader, General Sikorski, was killed. These allegations even led to court cases and the banning of the play from the National Theatre. Hochhuth does not resolve the uneasy marriage of these two themes with the depiction of Churchill as an instrument of destiny, so the central issues of fate and free will, historical necessity and individual moral responsibility, remain confused and unfocused.

As with *The Deputy*, which appeared as the war crimes trials in Germany gathered momentum and helped lift the taboos concealing the national past, Hochhuth showed a perfect sense of timing for topicality of theme by launching *Soldiers* at the height of the American bombings in Vietnam. Subsequent dramas also took as their themes up-to-the-minute topics: the possible scenario of a leftwing putsch in the U.S.A. (*Guerillas*); homeless underdogs struggling against a faceless bureaucracy (*Die Hebamme* [The Midwife]); opposition to the building of a NATO base (*Lysistrate und die NATO* [Lysistrata and NATO]); indictment of the legal profession for active cooperation with the Nazis (*Juristen* [Lawyers]).

In the manner of investigative journalism *Arztinnen* (Lady Doctors) exposed the covert financial links between multinational pharmaceutical giants and unscrupulous doctors who carry out questionable clinical tests. Hochhuth blunted his central thrust by inserting into the play minor attacks on other ills in Germany: the numerus clausus, restricting access to individual subjects in universities, anti-extremist legislation; and the five per cent election clause, which denies representation to any party with less than five per cent of votes cast. The Reagan era featured in *Judith*, where an American President is assassinated by a (Vietnam) war widow who is convinced that the armaments mania in the U.S. threatens mankind. Typically, no major German theatre would risk producing this play — its world premiere was at the Citizens Theatre, Glasgow, in 1984. Yet another phenomenon of the 1980s surfaced in *Unbefleckte Empfängnis* (Immaculate Conception), in which Hochhuth sought to penetrate the prejudices and emotions surrounding the theme of surrogate motherhood; baldly, he propounded the thesis that childlessness is a disease that can be overcome with the aid of modern technologies.

Hochhuth's early training as a historian leads him time and again to underpin his work with what may loosely be termed a philosophy of history. Influenced by Arthur Schopenhauer and Oswald Spengler, he sees history as a chronicle of catastrophes, the result of aimless will, and as a frenetic consumption of human energies, the direction of which is determined by blind drives and chance. This pessimistic view is counterbalanced by the idealistic premises of his plays. The "great" men of history arouse both admiration and censure in Hochhuth; in *Täter und Denker* (Doers and Thinkers) he offers a series of partially laudatory essays on figures from Caesar to Churchill, but most recently, in the play *Sommer 14* (Summer 14), he demonstrates how individual governments and statesmen were responsible for plunging Europe into World War I. This sharp "dance of death" is akin to the biting English satire *Oh, What a Lovely War!* (1964) in ascribing human carnage to the decisions of individuals, not to fate.

Hochhuth's output over the past 30 years is significant as a touchstone of controversial issues that engender acute argument. Turning the stage into a political tribunal, he probes the guilty conscience of a nation that has not yet been salved, and accurately reflects the provocative accusations levelled by a younger generation at those Germans who had carried the power and the responsibility from 1933 to 1945. Hochhuth is most convincing when he is championing the outsiders, those discriminated against, the anonymous participants in history. But his has been called "paper theatre," more concerned with prolix polemic than in creating imaginative scenes and characters. Sometimes a superficial naturalism (his brand of "faction") skirts cheap sensationalism and journalistic transitoriness, and quotation from historical sources substitutes for incisive argument. His plays are often only loosely structured and diffuse, and the characters mouthpieces of abstract political programmes and slogans; it is less their cliché-ridden rhetorical speech and philosophical banalities than their fierce sense of outrage that carries an audience.

—Arrigo V. Subiotto

HOLUB, Miroslav. Czech. Born in Plzeň, 13 September 1923. Educated at Charles University School of Medicine, Prague, 1947–53, M.D. 1953; Czechoslovak Academy of Sciences, Institute of Microbiology, Prague, 1954–57, Ph.D. in immunology 1958. Married 1) Věra Koktová in 1948; 2) Marta Svikruhová in 1963; 3) Jitka Langrová in 1969; two sons and one daughter. Railway worker, 1942–45; clinical pathologist, Bulovka Hospital, Prague, 1953–54; junior scientific worker, 1954–65, and senior scientific worker, 1968–71, Institute of Microbiology; visiting investigator, Public Health Research Institute, New York, 1965–67; worked at Max Planck Institute, Freiburg, 1968–69. Senior scientific worker, from 1972, and since 1990 head of Immunology Department, Institute for Clinical and Experimental Medicine, Prague. Visiting Professor of creative writing, Oberlin College, Ohio, 1979 and 1982. Editor, *Vesmír* [The Universe] (popular science magazine), Prague, 1951–65; president, European Foundation for the Promotion of Poetry, 1990–91, and Pangea-Comenius Foundation, Prague, 1991; vice president, Czechoslovak PEN, 1990, and British Poetry Society, 1991. Recipient: Československý Spisovatel and Mladá Fronta publishers awards, 1963, 1964, 1965, 1969; Czechoslovak Writers' Union prize, 1988; Czechoslovak Academy of Sciences Purkynje Medal, 1988; George Theiner award, 1991. D.Litt.: Oberlin College, 1985; Dr.Sc.: Czechoslovak Academy of Sciences, 1991. Member, Bavarian Academy of Arts, 1969. Address: Svépomocná 107, Hrnčíře, 149 00 Prague 4, Czech Republic.

PUBLICATIONS

Verse

Denní služba [Day Duty]. Prague, Československý spisovatel, 1958

Achilles a želva [Achilles and the Tortoise]. Prague, Mladá fronta, 1960.

Slabikář [Primer]. Prague, Československý spisovatel, 1961.

Jdi a otevři dveře [Go and Open the Door]. Prague, Mladá fronta, 1962.

Kam teče krev [Where the Blood Flows]. Prague, Československý spisovatel, 1963.

Zcela nesoustavná zoologie [A Completely Unsystematic Zoology]. Prague, Mladá fronta, 1963.

Tak zvané srdce [The So-Called Heart]. Prague, Mladá fronta, 1963.

Anamneza: výbor z poezie 1958–1963 [Anamnesis].   Prague,
Mladá fronta, 1964.
Selected Poems, translated by Ian Milner and George Theiner.
London, Penguin, 1967.
Ačkoli.   Prague, Československý spisovatel, 1969; as *Al-
though*, London, Cape, 1971.
Beton: verše z New Yorku a z Prahy [Concrete].   Prague,
Mladá fronta, 1970.
Události [Events].   Prague, VSUP, 1971.
Notes of a Clay Pigeon.   London, Secker and Warburg, 1977.
Sagittal Section, translated by Stuart Friebert and Dana
Hábová. Oberlin, Ohio, Oberlin College Press, 1980.
Naopak.   Prague, Mladá fronta, 1982; as *On the Contrary*,
Newcastle-upon-Tyne, Bloodaxe, 1984.
Interferon; or, On the Theatre, translated by Dana Hábová and
David Young.   Oberlin, Ohio, Oberlin College Press,
1982; as *Interferon čili o divadle*, Prague, Mladá fronta,
1986.
The Fly.   Newcastle-upon-Tyne, Bloodaxe, 1987.
Syndrom mizející plíce.   Prague, Mladá fronta, 1990; as
Vanishing Lung Syndrome, translated by Dana Hábová and
David Young, London, Faber, 1990.
Poems Before and After: Collected English Translations.
Newcastle-upon-Tyne, Bloodaxe, 1990.

Other

Anděl na kolečkách: poloreportáž z USA [Angel on Wheels:
Sketches from the USA].   Prague, Československý
spisovatel, 1963.
Tři kroky po zemi [Three Steps on the Earth].   Prague, Naše
Vojsko, 1965.
Žít v New Yorku [To Live in New York].   Prague,
Melantrich, 1969.
K principu rolničky.   Prague, Melantrich, 1987; as *The Jingle
Bell Principle*, Newcastle-upon-Tyne, Bloodaxe, 1991.
Maxwellův démon, čili o tvořivosti [Maxwell's Demon, or, On
Creativity].   Prague, Československý spisovatel, 1988.
Immunology of Nude Mice.   Boca Raton, Florida, CRC
Press, 1989.
nePatrnene [unSuitably] (aphorisms).   Prague, Českoslo-
venský spisovatel, 1989.
The Dimension of the Present Moment and Other Essays,
edited by David Young.   London, Faber, and Oberlin,
Ohio, Oberlin College Press, 1990.
Skrytá zášť věku [Hidden Hate of the Epoch] (essays). Prague,
Avicenum, 1990.

Translator, *Poe čili údolí neklidu* [Poe; or, The Valley of
Unrest].   Prague, Československý spisovatel, 1971.
Translator, *Živé hodiny* [The Living Clock], by L. M. Ward.
Prague, Mladá fronta, 1979.
Translator, *Buňka, medúza, a ja* [The Cell, The Jellyfish, and
I], by L. Thomas.   Prague, Mladá fronta, 1982.
Translator, *Myšlenky pozdě v noci* [Late Night Thoughts], by
L. Thomas.   Prague, Mladá fronta, 1988.

Author of more than 120 scientific papers and monographs.

*

Critical Studies: "Sytagmatic Structure in the Free Verse of
Miroslav Holub," in *Rackham Literary Studies* (Ann Arbor,
Michigan), 3, 1972, and "Miroslav Holub and William Carlos
Williams," in *Germano-Slavica* (Waterloo, Ontario), 6, 1975,
both by Herbert Eagle; "The Uni(que) Verse of Miroslav
Holub" by Amy Ling, in *Books Abroad* (Norman,
Oklahoma), 48, 1974; "The Fully Exposed Poem" by Seamus
Heaney, in *Parnassus* (Forest Park, Georgia), 11(1), 1983;
"'Collision'" (interview) by Alberta Turner, in *Field* (Oberlin,
Ohio), 30, 1984; "Miroslav Holub" by Dennis O'Driscoll, in
Poetry Review (London), 75(3), 1985.

Miroslav Holub comments:

Both my poetry and my essays were translated into a great
number of languages, but still I feel the closest relation to the
British, American, and Irish literary context. I could not say
exactly why. Maybe the translations are good and I am
intimately involved in the translation process. At some periods
the English translations appeared years before the Czech
originals. I travel a lot into the English-speaking countries. Or,
there is some close relation in terms of images, verbal
economy, black humor, and irony; and all that makes me feel
almost at home in English. Last but not least, English is *the*
scientific language of the world

*   *   *

In the context of Czech poetry, Miroslav Holub is almost an
anomaly. Czech, a language in which the primary role is played
by the verb, capable of expressing through a system of aspects
fine nuances of action, a tongue that can by the use of
diminutives convey both affection and dislike, naturally
tempts those inclined to pour out their heart in verse to
surrender to a lyricism in which the sheer linguistic beauty of
the message may obscure a paucity of ideas. There has never
been a dearth of lyrical poets in Czech literature, and from the
multitude impressive talents occasionally have emerged.

To Holub, however, a sensual enchantment with a flow of
incandescent associations or with pure sound and melody
would be completely alien. His is an unromantic lyricism of the
intellect that does not allow itself to be carried away by
spontaneity. The word is under strict control, and traditional
literary devices are avoided. Poetry is a spectacular way to
demonstrate the human being's most important characteristic
— the capacity to think.

When Holub's work first began to appear in the mid-1950s,
there was a widespread belief that with more effort, knowledge
would prevail upon ignorance and the world could ultimately
be made into a reasonably inhabitable place. Even in Eastern
Europe after Stalin's death rigid dogma was being timidly
replaced with more civilized attitudes. In art, cardboard
heroes set in ideologically devised situations were making way
for more credible characters experiencing the realities of
everyday life. The fake grandeur of the "struggle for socialism"
was abandoned for an unhurried, intimate look at the little
miracles, ironies, and puzzles that the world offers at every
step.

Such detailed examination well suited Holub, a scientist by
profession. The incisive mind summed up its vision in poems
that, although they sometimes employed the language of
laboratory reports, reached the core of the subject by the short
cut of a powerful verbal image. Very much in the spirit of the
times, Holub's analytical observations were conceived as a
scalpel that would cut out any diseased tissue, thus helping the
organism — both individual and social — to heal and to
proceed toward a science-based rational future.

His writing, refined, intricate, sober, and sophisticated, was
permeated with a confidence in the limitless potential of
human endeavour. Poetry itself was regarded as a means of
expanding the realm of intelligence on its rise from the
primeval bog of superstition and ignorance: "A Marathon
runner is more free than a vagabond, and a cosmonaut than a
sage in the state of levitation."

While most of his compatriots regarded him with admiration rather than affection, Holub's cerebral poetics fitted well with the work of similarly oriented American poets of the 1960s, such as Lawrence Ferlinghetti. Perhaps it was the implied optimism, the trust in human progress, the identification of freedom with self-regulation that were at the root of certain reservations at home. Optimism had been officially decreed and therefore became discredited, and progress was an empty word in a country which was stagnating under its banner, while voluntary discipline, some must have felt, could easily be turned into imposed regimentation, despite assurances to the contrary.

Suspicions that reason alone did not provide enough protection to human frailty were sustained when in 1973 a humiliating statement of loyalty to the neo-Stalinist authorities, attributed to Holub, was published in the press. It saved his chance to continue with scientific research, but it still took another nine years before his poetry could again be published at home. Abroad, his reputation steadily grew, although it could not escape notice that his new verse, as concise and pointed as ever, sounded less confident about the previously unquestioned values of rational progress. Complex questions were posed with painstaking exactitude, then left mockingly hanging in the air, and most subjects were now treated with a grain of wry doubt.

The arrival of freedom in 1989 did not essentially affect Holub's stature in Czechoslovakia, where his poetry was still regarded as finely accomplished applied art rather than the revelatory expression of innermost human feelings and thoughts that was expected of poets. The younger generation, racing to catch up with the chimera of postmodernism, were not quite aware of the popularity and respect that Holub's work had gained in the English-speaking world, where it has been perceived as an exceptionally perspicuous comment on life in the second half of the 20th century, achieved by a consummate blending of subtle artistry with intellectual shrewdness.

—Igor Hájek

HRABAL, Bohumil. Czech. Born near Brno, 28 March 1914. Educated at grammar school, and at Charles University, Prague, law degree 1946. Has worked as lawyer's clerk, railwayman, salesman, steel worker in Kladno foundries, laborer, stage hand and extra. Recipient: Gottwald state prize, 1968; Artist of Merit, 1989. Address: Na Hrázi 24, Prague 8-Liben, Czech Republic.

PUBLICATIONS

Fiction

Hovory lidí [People's Conversations].   Prague, Spolek Českých Bibliofilu, 1956.
Perlička na dně [A Pearl at the Bottom].   Prague, Československý spisovatel, 1963.
Pábitelé [Palaverers].   Prague, Mladá fronta, 1964.
Tunečnl hodiny pro starši a pokročilé [Dancing Lessons for the Advanced and the Elderly].   Prague, Československý spisovatel, 1964.

Ostře sledované vlaky.   Prague, Československý spisovatel, 1965; as *A Close Watch on the Trains*, London, Cape, 1968; as *Closely Watched Trains*, New York, Grove Press, 1968.
Inzerát na dum, ve kterém už nechci bydlet [Advertising a House I Don't Want to Live In Anymore].   Prague, Mladá fronta, 1965.
Automat svět.   Prague, Mladá fronta, 1966; as *The Death of Mr. Baltisberger*, New York, Doubleday, 1975.
Morytáty a legendy [Fair Ditties and Legends].   Prague, Československý spisovatel, 1968.
Postřižiny [The Haircut].   N.p., samizdat, 1970; Prague, Československý spisovatel, 1976; as *Cutting It Short*, London, Scribner, 1992.
Sklenice grenadýny [A Glass of Grenadine].   N.p., samizdat, 197–?
Obsluhoval jsem anglického krále.   Prague, samizdat, 1971; as *Jak jsem obsluhoval anglického krále*, Cologne, Index, 1980; as *I Served the King of England,* San Diego, Harcourt Brace, and London, Chatto and Windus, 1989.
Něžný barbar [Tender Barbarian].   N.p., samizdat, 1973; Prague, Dilia, and Cologne, Index, 1981.
Příliš hlučná samota.   Prague, samizdat, 1976; Cologne, Index, 1980; as *Too Loud a Solitude*, San Diego, Harcourt Brace, 1990; London, Deutsch, 1991.
Krasosmutnění [Lovely Wistfulness].   Prague, Československý spisovatel, 1977.
Mestecko ve kterém se zastavil čas [The Town Where Time Stood Still].   Innsbruck, Comenius, 1978.
Tři teskné grotesky, 1944–1953 [Three Melancholy Grotesques].   N.p., samizdat, 1979.
Každý den zázrak [A Miracle Every Day].   Prague, Československý spisovatel, 1979.
Kluby poezie [The Poetry Club].   Prague, Mladá fronta, 1981.
Harlekýnovy milióny [The Harlequin's Millions].   Prague, Československý spisovatel, 1981.
Poupata [Burgeoning].   Toronto, 68 Publishers, 1982(?).
Svatby v Domě [Weddings in the House].   Prague, samizdat, 1984; Toronto, 68 Publishers, 1987.
Hovory lidí [Selected Stories].   Prague, Československý spisovatel, 1984.
Proluky [Vacant Sites].   Prague, samizdat, and Toronto, 68 Publishers, 1986.
Vita nuova: kartinky [Vita nuova: Episodes].   Prague, samizdat, and Toronto, 68 Publishers, 1987.
Můj svět [My World].   Prague, Československý spisovatel, 1988.
Kouzelná flétna [Magic Flute].   Prague, Československý spisovatel, 1990.

Plays

Closely Watched Trains (translation of screenplay), with Jiří Menzel.   New York, Simon and Schuster, 1971; as *Closely Observed Trains*, London, Lorrimer, 1971.

Screenplays: *Fádní odpoledne* (*A Boring Afternoon*), with Ivan Passer, 1965; *Ostře sledované vlaky* (*Closely Watched Trains*; *Closely Observed Trains*), with Jiří Menzel, 1967; *Postřižiny* [The Haircut], 1980; *Něžný barbar* (*Tender Barbarian*), from his own novel, with Václav Nyvlt, 1989.

Verse

Bambino di Praga.   Prague, Dilia, 1978; with *Barvotisky* and *Krásná Poldi*, Prague, Československý spisovatel, 1991.

Chcete vidět zlatou Prahu? výbor z povídek.   Prague, Mladá
fronta, 1989.
Ztracena ulička.   Prague, Melantrich, 1991.

Other

Toto město je ve společné péči obyvatel [This Town Is in the
Joint Care of All Its Inhabitants].   Prague, Československý
spisovatel, 1967.
Slavnosti sněženek [Celebration of Snowdrops].   Prague,
Československý spisovatel, 1978.
Domácí úkoly z pilnosti [Voluntary Homework] (miscellany).
Prague, Československý spisovatel, 1982.
Život bez smokingu [Life Without a Dinner Jacket].   Prague,
Československý spisovatel, 1986.
Pražská ironie [Prague Irony].   Kersko, samizdat, 1986.
Životopis trochu jinak [A Biography Done Differently].
Prague, samizdat, 1986.
Ponorné říčky [Subterranean Streams].   Prague, Pražska
imaginace, 1990.
Kličky na kapesníku: román-interview [Knots in a Hand-
kerchief].   Prague, Práce, 1990.
Schizofrenické evangelium, 1949–1952 [Schizophrenic
Gospel]. Prague, Melantrich, 1990.
Slavná Vantochova legenda.   Prague, Nejemší Nakl, 1991.

Editor, *Výbor z české prózy* [Selected Czech Prose].   Prague,
Mladá fronta, 1967.

*

Critical Study: *"The Haircutting* and *I Waited on the King of
England*: Two Recent Works by Bohumil Hrabal" by George
Gibian, in *Czech Literature Since 1956: A Symposium*, edited
by William E. Harkins and Paul I. Trensky, New York,
Bohemica, 1980.

*   *   *

Although Bohumil Hrabal was trained for a career in law, he
preferred to try a wide variety of occupations, mostly of the
kind that sedate and reputable people avoid if they can. He
would explain that having to approach prospective customers
with a travelling salesman's pitch, for instance, helped him to
overcome his innate shyness. However, the ever-changing
environment must also have helped to quench his thirst for the
illuminating experience, for movement, for the sudden flash of
beauty, while long years spent in the company of compulsive
talkers, more often than not fortified by Czech beer, provided
him with a treasure-trove of tales and anecdotes. All that was
left for him to do, so he alleged, was to transcribe, arrange, and
collate what he had seen and heard.

If this claim is to be believed, then it is the most fortunate
coincidence that the raw material thus collected happened to
fall into his hands. It would never have achieved literary
significance had it not been shaped by Hrabal's perception,
which, in turn, had been honed by his fascination with art,
particularly modern art. He absorbed the influence of an
almost indiscriminately wide range of diverse styles and added
it to his grounding in philosophy, both ancient and contemporary.

In Hrabal's prose, the presence of this vast, although largely
unstructured knowledge lurks in the background and is hardly
noticed. The originality and the extraordinary appeal of his
work lie primarily in his peculiar vision, zany and grotesque,
and equally in the uncommon characters, as they are paraded,
for instance, in his short stories. Most of these characters are

from the fringes of respectable society, the misfits, the failures,
those who did not quite make it. What they lack in worldly
success, they compensate for with fantasy, fuelled by drink and
congenial company. In their bragging, imagination lends
magic even to the greyness of everyday life so that for a
moment it glows with vivid and unexpected colours. Obsessed
with the delight and the pain of life, they endow their
uninspiring personal histories with meaning by creating them
anew from discarded bits and pieces. Even in the lowliest and
most pathetic of them a "pearl in the deep" can be found, a
spark of human individuality that is never quite extinguished.

Hrabal's tales seldom have clearly defined plots. He claims
that he writes in the same way that he talks. The subject
accumulates and lingers long in his mind, but when the time is
ripe, it rushes out in one piece like a long breath. Events,
episodes, scraps of observation are either related in a continuous stream, as in *Taneční hodiny pro starší a pokročilé*
(Dancing Lessons for the Advanced and the Elderly), written
in a single unfinished sentence, or are connected by subconscious links like a surrealist collage. Often his work is
reminiscent of the pictures of Pieter Brueghel or contemporary
Sunday painters that are filled with seemingly unconnected
action on every plane and in every corner of the canvas, yet in
fact present a unified and integrated view.

Some critics believe they have traced in Hrabal's writing the
application of sophisticated literary skills. However, it seems
instead that he has been guided by intuition and that any
refined technique has been assimilated without much conscious effort. Such opinion is confirmed by the fact that
whenever Hrabal has attempted to conform to conventional
standards, as in *Ostře sledované vlaky* (*A Close Watch on the
Trains* or *Closely Watched Trains*), the result has proven to be
inferior to his less selfconscious writing. When he was exposed
in the 1970s and 1980s to particular pressures from a political
system that frowned upon any artistic eccentricity and nonconformity, on several occasions he consented to mutilate his
work in order to secure its publication. After the overthrow of
Communism in Czechoslovakia in 1989, Hrabal admitted
responsibility for what others had thought was the work of
censors or cautious editors. His readiness to oblige the
authorities was motivated not only by his ambition to see his
books in print, but also by his dread of the secret police,
chillingly described in "Total Fears" and often referred to in
his three-volume autobiography. The latter work is in many
respects a remarkably frank account of his life. By employing
the device of ostensibly telling the story through his wife,
Hrabal could treat even his own weaknesses with amused
detachment.

In his autobiography Hrabal indicates that he prefers his
prose to retain the rough texture and unfinished quality that his
thoughts assume in his mind when they first frantically strive to
project themselves onto paper. Of course, such facile spontaneity could also be only one step removed from the pitfall of
rambling self-indulgence, in which much of his recent work has
been trapped.

Looking back, it appears that Hrabal wrote best when not
distracted by hopes of publication and publicity. Most of his
work which first appeared in the 1960s and brought him fame
had been written in the immediately post-Stalinist 1950s when
it was still inconceivable that writing as non-conformist as his
would see the light of day. Similarly, two of the best books of
his later years, *Příliš hlučná samota* (*Too Loud a Solitude*) and
Obsluhoval jsem anglického krále (*I Served the King of
England*), were written while his works were temporarily
banned in the early 1970s; they first appeared in samizdat
underground publishing, and had to wait many years for full
and undistorted publication in Czechoslovakia. The former

told from the perspective of a scrap-paper yard, presents near-apocalyptic views of the wholesale destruction of the printed products of civilization, in which horror is sublimated into beauty, but by implication it also questions social morality. The latter, the grotesque history of a cunningly selfish, ambitious dwarf, poses questions about the morals of the individual. In both books Hrabal's singular vision and headlong narrative style are combined in what will probably remain his greatest accomplishments.

—Igor Hájek

———

HUSSEIN, Abdullāh. Pseudonym for Muhammad Khān. Born in Rawalpindi, in 1931. Has lived in Pakistan, India, and Canada, and in England since the 1960s. Recipient: Adamjee prize, 1963/64. Address: c/o South Asia Books, P.O. Box 502, Columbia, Missouri 65205, U.S.A.

PUBLICATIONS

Fiction

Udās naslē [Sad Generations].   Lahore, Naya Adarah, 1963.
Naś eb [Descent].   Lahore, Qausain, 1981.
Qaid [Imprisonment].   1982.
Bāgh [The Tiger].   Lahore, Qausain, 1982.
Sāt raṅg [Seven Colours].   New Delhi, Shaoor, 1982.
Nadī [River].   Lahore, Nusrat, 1984.
Night and Other Stories.   New Delhi, Orient Longman, 1984.
Downfall by Degrees and Other Stories.   Toronto, TSAR, and Columbia, Missouri, South Asia Books, 1987.

*   *   *

Abdullāh Hussein is a prominent figure among contemporary writers of Urdu fiction. His work explores the nature of exile and alienation in many forms. For Hussein's characters the state of innocence ends at an early age as adulthood starts; every human being thus becomes an exile from his or her childhood freedom. Some of his characters find themselves in an alien country, but more often it is the change in their state of being which causes a loss of identity and the creation of a new and troubled self.

His early short stories are fatalistic. Most of the protagonists, failing to create any kind of balance between their conscious and unconscious selves, are drawn to commit suicide. They do not, however, succumb without a struggle. They seek survival, through love and through self-reliance; they try strenuously to cleanse themselves of their sense of guilt. The act of purification is presented through images and symbols of running water, especially the sea. In "Night," when Śaukat realizes that his identity and his very existence have been obliterated, he follows a hawk which is flying towards the sea. This incident occurs when, after finishing his meal in a restaurant, in "a vacuous" moment of calm, he is watching the sea gulls on the beach. Suddenly a hawk appears, and the gulls take flight in panic. The bird of prey exists not to catch the gulls, merely to scatter them. In an intense, overpowering moment, Śaukat sees his vision of transcendental freedom:

Even from where he sat, he could see clearly the hawk's agile, strong pinions and its sharp, preying eyes. Colour flushed across his pale, bleached face and the familiar exuberant gleam returned to his eyes. All of a sudden, the turbid, viperous bluish-green mist that seemed to assault him relentlessly everywhere these days dissolved like vapour in the sun, leaving only the sandy white beach, the foaming, uproarious sea, the bright sunshine and a clear blue sky. In that warm, effulgent honey-coloured expanse, everything appeared so lucid, snug and fit in its own place. His heart felt strangely light and at ease . . .

Outside, he saw the hawk with its wings fully spread, flying toward deeper waters, self absorbed, unconcerned, free! Mesmerized, his gaze fixed upon the bird, he began to follow it.

The people in the restaurant "stood terrified and breathless as they watched the water rising up to his knees, and then swirling around his waist."

Hussein's characters usually live in a haze of colours, emblematic of their moods and lifestyles. Yellow light is associated with richness and ripeness. Close to yellow is gold — the colour of nostalgia and good times. Opposed to these are "bluish-green," which suggests unpleasantness, depression, and melancholy.

As Hussein has matured in his art, so have his protagonists. They no longer have the fatalistic approach of the adolescents depicted in "Night" and "The Little Brook." They have now reached a stage in their lives where they are able to come to terms with their loss of innocence and exile, and create a new beginning, albeit a modest one. "Sea," however, shows a state of transition. The events of the story occur on a liner crossing the Atlantic. The sea, though at times choppy, creates a sense of joy, and seems to act as an adviser, which even speaks to the characters, and urges them to "enjoy and celebrate beauty." In "Sea" Ahmad Firoz, despite his inability to establish a relationship with the woman he loves, is possessed of an inner calmness which will prevent him taking any drastic or self-destructive action.

Love and marriage are also seen as causes of alienation and exile. So in "The Rose," Sarwat, after being married to a man she did not love for 10 years, and having yearned for her childhood love for 32 years, succeeds in fulfilling her love in one night of intense intimacy. The effects on the two participants in this encounter are quite different, despite their both acknowledging more forcefully their true state of exile. For Naim, who has seen Sarwat as an utterly sexless woman for so long, it comes initially as a shock, then as a revelation:

. . . so amazingly incandescent, so vibrant with life that she had carried him to the summit of unimaginable bliss instantly. When love and a woman come together, a miracle is born. One gets to experience a segment of life through this miracle. Be it sublime or low, it is momentous all the same, because of its truly exquisite power to transform and exalt man — even to immortality . . . When passion has run its course, and the blood has chilled, *love* is what remains behind — like the memory of a good time, a memory more enduring and pleasant than the time itself. Or like the fugitive scent of a rose: no matter how intangible, it is still more real than its bloom . . .

But for Sarwat the experience is completely different. She had finally learned that one didn't suffer from one's own fate or deeds in life, but from the chance of birth.

Desires — fulfilled or unfulfilled — what did they give us? They only made us poorer. We had to suffer them equally. Once two hearts have gone out of harmony, they drift apart. Nothing can bring them back together, not even the sacrifice of body.

The realization that man can not be free from his actual or inner state of exile is a constant theme in Hussein's fiction, but what is important for him is the way his characters try to survive in their own peculiar tragic situations. Hussein examines man's limits of endurance, through a stylized idiom, which is at once both eloquent and expressive.

—Parvin Loloi

———

HYDER, Qurratulain. *See* **HAIDAR, Qurratulain.**

———

HYVRARD, Jeanne.   French.   Teacher at a lycée in Paris. Address: 13 rue Descombes, 75017 Paris, France.

PUBLICATIONS

Fiction

Les Prunes de Cythère.   Paris, Minuit, 1975.
Mère la mort.   Paris, Minuit, 1976; as *Mother Death*, Lincoln, University of Nebraska Press, 1988.
La Meurtritude.   Paris, Minuit, 1977.
Les Doigts du figuier.   Paris, Minuit, 1977.
Le Corps défunt de la comédie: traité d'économie politique.   Paris, Seuil, 1982.
Auditions musicales certains soirs d'été.   Paris, Des Femmes, 1984.
Canal de la Toussaint.   Paris, Des Femmes, 1985.
Ton Nom de végétal.   Paris, Des Femmes, 1992.

Verse

Le Silence et l'obscurité, réquiem littoral pour corps polonais 13–28 décembre 1981.   Paris, Montalba, 1982.
La Baisure; Que se partagent encore les eaux.   Paris, Des Femmes, 1984.

Other

Le Cercan: essais sur un long et douloureux dialogue de sourds.   Paris, Des Femmes, 1987.
La Pensée corps.   Paris, Des Femmes, 1989.
La Jeune Morte en robe de dentelle.   Paris, Des Femmes, 1990.

*

Critical Studies: "Jeanne Hyvrard: The Writing of the Night" by Marguerite Le Clézio, in *Revue de l'Université d'Ottawa*, 54(1); *Jeanne Hyvrard* by Maïr Verthuy and Jennifer Waelti-Walters, Amsterdam, Rodopi, 1988, and "Transnational Thought: Michel Butor and Jeanne Hyvrard" by Waelti-Walters, in *Dalhousie French Studies* (Halifax, Nova Scotia), Fall/Winter 1989.

*   *   *

Since she published her first book, *Les Prunes de Cythère* (The Plums of Cythera) in 1975 Jeanne Hyvrard has been considered by critics primarily as a literary figure. Indeed she writes in densely metaphorical language, with rhythms, repetitions, and tone that bring to mind prophecy rather than the linear development of rational thought. The narrator in her early works, *Les Prunes de Cythère*, *Mère la mort* (*Mother Death*), *La Meurtritude* (Batteritude) — is fighting a madness imposed upon her by those around her while searching for a language which permits her to express her certainty that the multitudinous elements of the world must be thought together rather than named, separated, limited, and rendered static by logic. In her later writing — *Le Corps défunt de la comédie* (The Corps of the Comedy), *Canal de la Toussaint* (All Saints' Day Strait), *La Jeune morte en robe de dentelle* (The Dead Girl in a Lace Dress) — that language has been formulated and results in works that are elegant, fluid, lyrical, and structured with mathematical precision.

The symbolic forms and languages of literature are a vehicle, however, for Hyvrard's political and economic thought — a poetics of the female body politic. Her writing offers a criticism of Western economic hegemony and a reconceptualization of Western culture. She is a political commentator who writes in the metaphorical tradition of subversives in previous centuries and other continents because her view point is unacceptable to the dominant group and because, as a woman, she has no recognized right to a voice in the public arena of power. Her closest literary peers are perhaps Madeleine Gagnon and Nicole Brossard in Quebec. By profession she is a teacher of political economy in a "lycée technique" in Paris so that her writing is informed by economic, political, and philosophical studies and by constant contact with the realities of immigration, racism, sexism, poverty, the effects of the media — all elements inherent in and rendered invisible by "classical" economics and politics. (To this day she claims that *Les Prunes de Cythère* is primarily a report on the economic state of Martinique.)

She claims roots in Marx and Freud, but rather than using psychoanalysis as do her peers in French feminist thought (e.g., Julia Kristeva, Hélène Cixous (*q.v.*), and Luce Irigaray), Hyvrard sees Freud as an arbiter of social norms. Particularly as a result of the new translation of Freud's work currently being done in France, she sees him as a thinker in the Jewish tradition — a tradition which she feels has also influenced her own development through the writings of Simone Weil, Emmanuel Lévinas, André Chouraqui's new translation of the *Bible* into French, and recently Claude Lanzmann's work *Shoah*.

She is and acknowledges herself to be a product of her time and context; a student in the Paris of 1968, her writing goes hand-in-hand with direct political protest. Her education has trained her in abstract thought and political attitudes. She looks at Africa, Eastern Europe, North America from a point of view based in Western Europe and a perspective particular to France. From that place Hyvrard questions the assumptions and underpinnings of "high culture" — economic theory, political elitism, literary tradition, correct language, seeing them all as vehicles of oppression of the "bio-mass" which includes women and the Third World. She writes about the legacy of colonialism, the links between multinational power and the ethnic awareness, the cybernetic revolution, and its effects on the "bio-mass," the dehumanization of the modern world and the entry of "bionomics" (the management of human beings as elements in a consumer economy) into economic and political practice, about the social significance of female madness, of scapegoats — all in the context of the need for a new sense of the sacred.

Hyvrard sees herself as the product of a specific socio-economic circumstance and her books as both products of and interventions in her particular moment of history. Writing as a woman she recognizes that in France she has no right to a public political voice and hence her perspective is necessarily that of the silenced and marginalized members of society. Her works are studies of the lines of power and domination in the modern world, systems and strategies of oppression both public and private: colonialism, racism, sexism, gender, modes of thought and language (all her neologisms are defined in *La Pensée corps* [Body of Thought], the dictionary of her political economy), family relations, the destruction of identity and of the body. She uses the female body as a constant metaphor of the body-politic as she moves out from personal to public, transnational, and global issues, calling into question all the underpinnings of capitalism and the traditions of "high culture" as she goes. Hyvrard is a revolutionary thinker of increasing importance who has not as yet received the attention she deserves.

—Jennifer Waelti-Walters

I

IBUSE Masuji. Japanese. Born in Kamo, Hiroshima Prefecture, 15 February 1898. Educated at Fukuyama Middle School, 1912–17; Waseda University, 1917–1922; also studied painting at Japanese School of Art. Served in the Japanese Army as a war correspondent during World War II. Married Akimoto Setsuyo in 1927; four children. Recipient: Japanese Arts Academy prize, 1956; Yomiuri prize, 1960; Noma prize, 1966; Order of Cultural Merit, 1966; Naoki prize. Elected to Japanese Arts Academy, 1960. *Died 10 July 1993.*

PUBLICATIONS

Fiction

Sazanami gunki. 1930; as *Waves: A War Diary*, in *Waves: Two Short Novels*, 1986.
Shūkin ryokō [The Travelling Debt Collectors]. 1935.
Keirokushū [Miscellany]. 1936.
Jon Manjirō hyōryūki: furai hyomin kitan. Tokyo, Kawade Shobō, 1937; as *John Manjiro, the Castaway: His Life and Adventures*, Tokyo, Hokuseido, 1940; as *John Manjiro: A Castaway's Chronicle*, in *Castaways: Two Novels*, 1987.
Tajinko mura. 1939; as "Tajinko Village," in *Lieutenant ookeast, and Other Stories*, 1971.
Kawa to tanima [Rivers and Ravines]. Tokyo, Sōgensha, 1939.
Hana no machi [City of Flowers]. 1942.
Wabisuke. 1946; as *Isle-on-the-Billows*, in *Waves: Two Short Novels*, 1986.
Hikkoshi-yatsure [Always Moving]. 1947.
Kashima ari [Room for Rent]. 1948.
Sankyōfūbutsushi [Notes on Scenery of the Ravine]. 1948.
Honjitsu kyūshin. 1949; with *Yōhai taichō* (bilingual edition), as *No Consultations Today/Honjitsu kyūshin*, Tokyo, Hara Shobō, 1964.
Yōhai taichō. 1950; with *Honjitsu kyūshin* (bilingual edition), as *A Far-Worshipping Commander/Yōhai taichō*, Tokyo, Hara Shobō, 1964; as *Lieutenant Lookeast*, in *Lieutenant Lookeast, and Other Stories*, 1971.
Nanatsu no kaidō [Seven Roads]. 1952.
Hyōmin Usaburō [Usaburo the Castaway]. 1954.
Ekimae ryokan [The Station Hotel]. 1956.
Chimpindō shujin [The Curio Dealer]. Published in *Chūō kōron* (Tokyo), January 1959.
Bushū hachigata [The Hachigata Castle of Musahi]. 1961.
Kuroi ame. 1965; as *Black Rain*, Tokyo and New York, Kōdansha International, 1969; London, Secker and Warburg, 1971.
Two Stories. Tokyo, Hokuseido, 1970.
Lieutenant Lookeast, and Other Stories. Tokyo and New York, Kōdansha International, and London, Secker and Warburg, 1971; as *Salamander and Other Stories*, Tokyo and New York, Kōdansha International, 1981.
Chōyō chū no koto [Under Arms]. Published in *Umi* (Tokyo), September 1977–January 1980.

Ogikubo fudoki [An Ogikubo Almanac]. Published in *Shinchō* (Tokyo), February 1981–June 1982.
Tomonotsu chakaiki [The Record of Tea Parties at Tomonotsu]. Published in *Kaien* (Tokyo), July 1983–April 1985.
Waves: Two Short Novels. Tokyo and New York, Kōdansha International, 1986.
Castaways: Two Short Novels. Tokyo and New York, Kōdansha International, 1987.

Verse

Shi to zuihitsu (includes essays). 1948.
Yakuyoke shishu. 1952.

Other

Ibuse Masuji zuihitsu zenshū. 3 vols., 1941.
Ibuse Masuji zenshū. 9 vols., 1948.
Ibuse Masuji sakuhinshū. 6 vols., 1953.
Ibuse Masuji zenshū. Tokyo, Chikuma Shobō, 14 vols., 1964–75.
Hanseiki [The First Half of My Life]. 1970.
Yakimono zakki. Tokyo, Bunka Suppankyoku, 1985.
Ibuse Masuji jisen zenshū. Tokyo, Shinchōsha, 13 vols., 1985–86.
Yomo. Tokyo, Sakuhinsha, 1985.
Dazai Osamu. Tokyo, Chikuma Shobō, 1989.
Bunshi no fūbō. Tokyo, Fukutake, 1991.

Translator, with Gishu Nakayama, *Heike monogatari*. 1958.

*

Critical Studies: "*Black Rain*" by Robert J. Lifton, in *Death in Life: Survivors of Hiroshima*, New York, Simon and Schuster, 1967; "Ibuse's *Black Rain*," "Carp," and "Pilgrims' Inn," all in *Approaches to the Modern Japanese Novel*, edited by K. Tsuruta and T. Swann, Tokyo, Waseda University Press, 1976, and "*The River*: Ibuse's Poetic Cosmology," in *Essays on Japanese Literature*, edited by Takeda Katsuhiko, Tokyo, Waseda University Press, 1977, all by Anthony V. Liman; "Tradition and Contemporary Consciousness: Ibuse, Endo, Kaiko, Abe" by J. Thomas Rimer, in *Modern Japanese Fiction and Its Traditions*, Princeton, New Jersey, Princeton University Press, 1978; "The Theme of Survival in John Hersey's *Hiroshima* and Ibuse Masuji's *Black Rain*" by John T. Dorsey, in *Tamkang Review* (Taibei), 14(1–4), 1984; *Pools of Water, Pillars of Fire: The Literature of Ibuse Masuji* by John Whittier Treat, Seattle, University of Washington Press, 1988.

* * *

Ibuse Masuji's international reputation is based principally on *Kuroi ame* (*Black Rain*), his novel about the bombing of Hiroshima. As a novel it is a towering achievement, arguably the only work in any language which comes near to dealing adequately with the horror of that first use of nuclear weapons.

Ibuse wrote *Black Rain* when he was in his 60s, and although he continued to produce good work in the quarter century since then, it is difficult not to think of the novel as the pinnacle of his literary career, since it seems to draw together so many of the techniques and preoccupations of his writing.

The story of the novel is essentially that of a single family — husband, wife, and niece — and their experiences in the few days between the dropping of the bomb and the Japanese surrender. It opens, however, several years after the end of the war when the husband, Shigematsu Shizuma, is anxious to scotch rumours that his niece was close to ground zero when the bomb dropped and is suffering from radiation sickness — rumours that have persistently cut short all marriage negotiations. He begins to copy the journal she kept during those terrible days, and is then inspired to recopy his own journal of the same period. Gradually other records and memoirs of the aftermath work themselves into the book so that it becomes a patchwork of different perspectives. Moreover, since the story returns intermittently to the present and to Shigematsu's own continuing battle against radiation sickness, we are constantly reminded that the aftermath is not over — a fact further poignantly underlined when, at the end of the book, the niece Yasuko does indeed show symptoms of the disease and it is clear that she will soon die.

The village where the Shizuma family live is in Eastern Hiroshima Prefecture, the area where Ibuse himself grew up. A sense of place is important in his works and, as one might expect, the country and its inhabitants are valued because they preserve something of the old traditions and attitudes. Yet the countryside is not portrayed only as a peaceful refuge. Ibuse's native region figures prominently in the turbulent history of Japan, and ruins and remains of former times constantly crop up in his stories as reminders that suffering and loss have never long been absent from the land.

Many of his works are historical and many, like *Black Rain*, are cast in the form of journals or chronicles. Author of a Japanese translation of *Robinson Crusoe*, Ibuse is particularly interested in the narratives of refuge and castaways, those making their way in new and hostile surroundings. He wrote several accounts of castaways in the Edo era, such as *Jon Manjirō hyōryūki* (*John Manjiro: A Castaway's Chronicle*), and *Hyōmin Usaburō* (Usaburo the Castaway), while *Sazanami gunki* (*Waves: A War Diary*) is the fragmented diary of a prince of the defeated Heike clan, in the late 12th century, being harried among the islands of the inland sea.

Of course, a distinction might also be drawn between those works like *Jon Manjiro* which were largely a reworking of existing documents, and *Waves: A War Diary* which was almost entirely invented. Yet in all cases, the story progresses by describing signficant individual incidents in the lives of the protagonists, whom the reader grows to understand through these intensely realized narrative moments.

Ibuse also used this technique in works set in contemporary Japan, such as the policeman's diary in "Tajinko Mura" ("Tajinko Village") and the chronicles of a small private hospital in *Honjitsu kyūshin* (*No Consultations Today*). It might be seen as a way of producing longer works by extending the methods of the short story — Ibuse's other main area of literary endeavour. His first published short story, "Yuhei" ("Confinement"), later reworked and given the title "Sanshouo" ("The Salamander"), concerns itself with individual moments in the life of a salamander, trapped forever in a cave which it has grown too large to swim out of. This has been read as an allegory on many levels about the embowered consciousness of the artist, or the restrictions placed on the

ordinary individual in Japanese society, or even the long isolation of Japan as a whole.

Although Ibuse's fictional accounts do span many eras, the period of Japanese history to which he most frequently returns to is that of the Shogunate, the 250-odd years from the 17th century onward during which Japan was effectively closed off from the rest of the world. In a country where the people were so strictly monitored, travellers, however involuntary the reasons for their voyage, were automatically regarded with suspicion by the authorities, and in all of Ibuse's works bullying officialdom bears down hard on the ordinary people.

Ibuse's salamander has been seen as a prototype of the outcasts of whom Ibuse was to write so often. But this role is perhaps more properly allotted to the other character in the story, a frog which the salamander forces to share its solitude. At the very end of the story the frog, on the point of death, declares: "even now I am not really angry with you." Oppressed so long, he is unable to express his outrage towards his oppressor even at the last.

Not all of Ibuse's characters let themselves be ground down so easily, and their discreet but stubborn resistance to those on high is the soil that nourishes Ibuse's distinctive irony, present for example in "Wabisuke," "Kuchisuke no iru tanima," and other stories.

This irony also plays a part in *Black Rain*, helping to humanize the horrors of the bombing. Early in the book Shizuma remembers hearing how the local volunteer force were drawn up by their headman and harangued as they were about to go and look for survivors. His speech ended: "I must request you above all, therefore, to take care not to drop those symbols of your invincible determination to fight on to the bitter end — your bamboo spears." This image of a corps going to confront the ravages of modern mass destruction with bamboo spears can seem only pathetic; but a paragraph later we find that the volunteers, stolidly unimpressed by the head man's rhetoric, fast disencumber themselves of these patriotic props and go to tackle the job as practically as they can.

In the descriptions that follow the diary technique provides both immediacy and distance. As readers we confront the terrors of the bomb in a piecemeal, human way and, like the protagonists, temporarily forget one ghastly moment as the next brings practical problems for us to attend to. Yet all the while an aching sense of the pity and waste of it is inexorably building.

The ending, though sad, is infused with the unassuming dignity of Shigematsu and his family, a quality exhibited by characters in other of Ibuse's works when faced with manmade and natural disasters. Here, though, it is raised to an almost transcendental level by the greatness of the subject. It is as though, when it happened on his own ground, Ibuse's fiction, with its compassion for all victims, its respect for ordinariness, and its quiet irony rose to meet the defining event of the 20th century.

—James Raeside

IONESCO, Eugène. French. Born in Slatina, Romania, 26 November 1912 (some sources say 13 November 1909); grew up in France. Educated at the University of Bucharest, agrégation de lettres. Married Rodica Burileanu in 1936; one daughter. Taught French in Bucharest from age 18; worked as a proofreader in Paris after World War II; then freelance writer. Recipient: Tours Festival prize, for film, 1959; Italia prize, 1963; Society of Authors theatre prize (France), 1966; National grand prize for theatre, 1969; Monaco grand prize, 1969; Austrian state prize for European literature, 1970; Jerusalem prize, 1973; T. S. Eliot award, 1985. Honorary doctorate: New York University, 1971; universities of Louvain, Warwick, Tel Aviv. Officier de l'Ordre des Arts et des Lettres, 1961; Chevalier, Légion d'Honneur, 1970; member, French Academy, 1971. Agent: Société des Auteurs Dramatiques, 9–11 rue Ballu, 75009 Paris, France. Address: 96 boulevard du Montparnasse, 75014 Paris, France.

PUBLICATIONS

Plays

La Cantatrice chauve (produced Paris, 1950). Included in Théâtre I, 1954; as The Bald Soprano (produced London, 1956; New York, 1958), in Plays I, 1958; as The Bald Prima Donna, London, French, 1961,

La Leçon (produced Paris, 1951). Included in Théâtre I, 1954; as The Lesson (produced London and New York, 1958), in Plays I, 1958.

Les Chaises (produced Paris, 1952). Included in Théâtre I, 1954; as The Chairs (produced London, 1957; New York, 1958), in Plays I, 1958.

Sept Petits Sketches (includes Les Grandes Chaleurs; Le connaissez-vous?; Le Rhume onirique; La Jeune Fille à marier; Le Maître; Le Nièce-Épouse; Le Salon de l'automobile) (produced Paris, 1953). La Jeune Fille à marier included in Théâtre II, 1958, as Maid to Marry, in Plays III, 1960; Le Maître included in Théâtre II, 1958, as The Leader, in Plays IV, 1960; La Nièce-Épouse translated as The Niece-Wife, in Ionesco by Richard N. Coe, 1971; Le Salon de l'automobile included in Théâtre IV, 1966, as The Motor Show, in Plays V, 1963.

Victimes du devoir (produced Paris, 1953). Included in Théâtre I, 1954; as Victims of Duty (produced New York, 1960), in Plays II, 1958.

Théâtre I (includes La Cantatrice chauve; La Leçon; Jacques, ou, La Soumission; Les Chaises; Victimes du devoir; Amédée, ou, Comment s'en débarrasser). Paris, Gallimard, 1954.

Amédée; ou, Comment s'en débarrasser (produced Paris, 1954). Included in Théâtre I, 1954; as Amédée (produced New York, 1955), in Plays II, 1958.

Jacques; ou, La Soumission (produced Paris, 1955). Included in Théâtre I, 1954; as Jack (produced New York, 1958), in Plays I, 1958.

Le Nouveau Locataire (produced Helsinki, 1955; Paris, 1957). Included in Théâtre II, 1958; as The New Tenant (produced London, 1956; New York, 1960), in Plays II, 1958.

Le Tableau (produced Paris, 1955). Included in Théâtre III, 1963; as The Picture (produced New York, 1969), in Plays VII, 1968.

L'Impromptu de l'Alma; ou, Le Caméléon du berger (produced Paris, 1956). Included in Théâtre II, 1958; as Improvisation; or, The Shepherd's Chameleon (produced New York, 1960), in Plays III, 1960.

L'Avenir est dans les œufs; ou, Il faut tout pour faire un monde (produced Paris, 1957). Included in Théâtre II, 1958; as The Future Is in Eggs; or, It Takes All Sorts to Make a World, in Plays IV, 1960.

Impromptu pour la Duchesse de Windsor (produced Paris, 1957).

Plays I (includes The Chairs; The Bald Soprano; The Lesson; Jack, or, Obedience). London, Calder, 1958; as Four Plays, New York, Grove Press, 1958.

Théâtre II (includes L'Impromptu de l'Alma, ou, Le Caméléon du berger; Tueur sans gages; Le Nouveau Locataire; L'Avenir est dans les œufs, ou, Il faut tout pour faire un monde; Le Maître; La Jeune Fille à marier). Paris, Gallimard, 1958.

Tueur sans gages (produced Paris, 1959). Included in Théâtre II, 1958; as The Killer (produced New York, 1960), in Plays III, 1960.

Plays II (includes Amédée, or, How to Get Rid of It; The New Tenant; Victims of Duty). New York, Grove Press, 1958; London, Calder, 1961.

Rhinocéros (produced Düsseldorf, 1959; Paris, 1960). Included in Théâtre III, 1963; in English (produced London, 1960; New York, 1961), in Plays IV, 1960.

Scène à quatre (produced Spoleto, 1959). Included in Théâtre III, 1963; as Foursome (produced London, 1970), in Plays V, 1963.

Apprendre à marcher (ballet scenario; produced Paris, 1960). Included in Théâtre IV, 1966; as Learning to Walk, in Plays IX, 1973.

Plays III (includes The Killer; Improvisation, or, The Shepherd's Chameleon; Maid to Marry). New York, Grove Press, 1960; London, Calder, 1962.

Plays IV (includes Rhinoceros; The Leader; The Future Is in Eggs, or, It Takes All Sorts to Make a World). New York, Grove Press, 1960; London, Calder, 1963.

Délire à deux (produced Paris, 1962). Included in Théâtre III, 1963; as Frenzy for Two, in Plays VI, 1965.

Le Roi se meurt (produced Paris, 1962). Paris, Gallimard, 1963; as Exit the King (produced London, 1963; Ann Arbor, Michigan, 1967), New York, Grove Press, 1963; in Plays V, 1963.

Le Piéton de l'air (produced Düsseldorf, 1962; Paris, 1963). Included in Théâtre III, 1963; as A Stroll in the Air (produced New York, 1964), in Plays VI, 1965.

Théâtre III (includes Rhinocéros; Le Piéton de l'air; Délire à deux; Le Tableau; Scène à quatre; Les Salutations; La Colère). Paris, Gallimard, 1963.

Plays V (includes Exit the King; The Motor Show; Foursome). London, Calder, 1963.

Les Salutations (produced London, 1970). Included in Théâtre III, 1963; as Salutations, in Plays VII, 1968.

La Soif et la faim (produced Düsseldorf, 1964; Paris, 1966). Included in Théâtre IV, 1966; as Hunger and Thirst (produced Stockbridge, Massachusetts, 1969), in Plays VII, 1968.

La Lacune (produced Paris, 1965). Included in Théâtre IV, 1966; as The Oversight, in Plays VIII, 1971.

Plays VI (includes A Stroll in the Air; Frenzy for Two). London, Calder, 1965; New York, Grove Press, 1968.

Pour Préparer un Œuf dur (produced Paris, 1966). Included in Théâtre IV, 1966.

Théâtre IV (includes Le Roi se meurt; La Soif et la faim; La Lacune; Le Salon de l'automobile; L'Œuf dur; Pour préparer un œuf dur; Le Jeune Homme à marier; Apprendre à marcher). Paris, Gallimard, 1966.

Leçons de Français pour Américains (produced Paris, 1966). As Exercices de conversation et de diction française pour étudiants américains, in Théâtre V, 1974.

Plays VII (includes Hunger and Thirst; The Picture; Anger; Salutations). London, Calder, 1968; New York, Grove Press, 1969.

Jeux de massacre (produced Düsseldorf and Paris, 1970). Paris, Gallimard, 1970; as *Killing Game* (as *Wipe-Out Game*, produced Washington, D.C., 1971), New York, Grove Press, 1974; as *Here Comes a Chopper* (produced London, 1990), in *Plays VIII*, 1971.

La Vase (television play; broadcast 1970). Included in *Théâtre V*, 1974.

The Duel (produced Paris, 1971; produced as part of *O Calcutta*, London, 1974). In *Plays XI*, 1979.

Double Act (produced Paris, 1971; produced as part of *Carte blanche*, London, 1976). Included *Plays XI*, 1979.

Plays VIII (includes *Here Comes a Chopper*; *The Oversight*; *The Foot of the Wall*). London, Calder and Boyars, 1971.

Macbett (produced Paris, 1972). Paris, Gallimard, 1972; in English, in *Plays IX*, 1973.

Plays IX (includes *Macbett*; *The Mire*; *Learning to Walk*). London, Calder and Boyars, 1973.

Ce Formidable Bordel (produced Paris, 1973). Paris, Gallimard, 1973; as *A Hell of a Mess*, New York, Grove Press, 1975; as *Oh What a Bloody Circus*, in *Plays X*, 1976.

Théâtre V (includes *Jeux de massacre*; *Macbett*; *La Vase*; *Exercices de conversation et de diction françaises pour étudiants américains*). Paris, Gallimard, 1974.

L'Homme aux valises (produced Paris, 1975). Paris, Gallimard, 1975; as *Man with Bags* (produced Baltimore, 1977), New York, Grove Press, 1977; as *The Man with the Luggage*, in *Plays XI*, 1979.

Plays X (includes *Oh What a Bloody Circus*; *The Hard-Boiled Egg*). London, Calder and Boyars, 1976.

Plays XI (includes *The Man with the Luggage*; *The Duel*; *Double Act*). London, Calder, 1979.

Théâtre VII (*Voyages chez les morts: thèmes et variations*). Paris, Gallimard, 1981; as *Plays XII* (*Journeys among the Dead*) (produced New York, 1980; London, 1987), London, Calder, and New York, Riverrun, 1985.

Screenplays: "La Colère" episode in *Les Sept Péchés capitaux*, 1962; *Monsieur Tête* (animated film), 1970.

Ballet Scenarios for Television, with Fleming Flindt: *La Leçon*, 1963; *Le Jeune Homme à marier*, 1965; *The Triumph of Death*, 1971.

Television Play: *La Vase*, 1971.

Fiction

La Photo du Colonel. Paris, Gallimard, 1962; as *The Colonel's Photograph*, London, Faber, 1967; New York, Grove Press, 1969.

Le Solitaire. Paris, Mercure de France, 1973; as *The Hermit*, New York, Viking Press, 1974; London, Deutsch, 1975.

Other

Elegii pentru fiinti mici. Craiova, Romania, Scirsul Romanesc, 1931.

Nu! Bucharest, Vremea, 1934; as *Non*, Paris, Gallimard, 1986.

Notes et contre-notes. Paris, Gallimard, 1962; revised edition, 1966; as *Notes and Counter-Notes*, New York, Grove Press, 1964.

Entretiens avec Claude Bonnefoy. Paris, Belfond, 1966; as *Conversations with Ionesco*, London, Faber, 1970; New York, Holt Rinehart, 1971.

Journal en miettes. Paris, Mercure de France, 1967; as *Fragments of a Journal*, New York, Grove Press, and London, Faber, 1968.

Présent passé, passé présent. Paris, Mercure de France, 1968; as *Present Past, Past Present*, New York, Grove Press, 1971; London, Calder and Boyars, 1972.

Conte pour enfants. Paris, Quist, 4 vols., 1969–75; as *Story for Children*, New York, Quist, 1968–75.

Découvertes, illustrated by the author. Geneva, Skira, 1969.

Mise en train: première année de Français, with Michael Benamou. New York, Macmillan, 1969.

Monsieur Tête (animated film text). Munich, Bruckmann, 1970.

Discours de réception á l'Académie française . . . Paris, Gallimard, 1971.

Entre la vie et la rêve: entretiens avec Claude Bonnefoy. Paris, Belfond, 1977.

Antidotes. Paris, Gallimard, 1977.

Un Homme en question. Paris, Gallimard, 1979.

Le Noir et le blanc. St. Gallen, Erker, 1980.

Hugoliade. Paris, Gallimard, 1982; as *Hugoliad; or, The Grotesque and Tragic Life of Victor Hugo*, New York, Grove Press, 1987.

Pourquoi J'écris. Konstanz, Universitätsverlag, 1986.

La Quête intermittente (from his diary). Paris, Gallimard, 1987.

*

Bibliographies: *Eugène Ionesco: a Bibliography* by Griffith R. Hughes and Ruth Bury, Cardiff, University of Wales Press, 1974; *Bibliographie et index thématique des études sur Eugène Ionesco* by Wolfgang Leiner, Fribourg, Éditions Universitaires, 1980.

Critical Studies: *Eugène Ionesco* by Richard N. Coe, New York, Grove Press, 1961, revised edition, London, Methuen, 1971; *Eugène Ionesco* by Leonard C. Pronko, New York, Columbia University Press, 1965; *Ionesco and Genet* by Josephine Jacobsen and William Randolph Mueller, New York, Hill and Wang, 1968; *Brecht and Ionesco: Commitment in Context* by J. H. Wulbern, Urbana, University of Illinois Press, 1971; *Eugène Ionesco* by Ronald Hayman, London, Heinemann, 1972; *Eugène Ionesco* by Allan Lewis, New York, Twayne, 1972; *Eugène Ionesco: A Collection of Critical Essays* edited by Rose C. Lamont, Englewood Cliffs, New Jersey, Prentice Hall, 1973, and *The Two Faces of Ionesco* edited by Lamont and M. J. Friedman, Troy, New York, Whitston, 1978; *Eugène Ionesco's Dramatic Modes and Their Sources* by Margarett McElroy Powell, 1978; *The Dream and the Play: Ionesco's Theatrical Quest*, edited by Moshe Lazar, Malibu, California, Undena, 1982.

*   *   *

Like some other members of the new drama movement which burst on the French stage in the early 1950s, such as Samuel Beckett and Arthur Adamov, Eugène Ionesco was an outsider: a Romanian who did not come from an orthodox French literary background. His first play, *La Cantatrice chauve* (*The Bald Soprano*), created a sensation when it was put on in a small theatre in Paris, and the so-called "theatre of the absurd" was suddenly born. At least, not quite suddenly; there had been a few lone forerunners, like *Ubu Roi*, Alfred Jarry's iconoclastic play of 1896, or Guillaume Apollinaire's *Les Mamelles de Tirésias*, a quixotic plea for repopulation uttered in the darkest years of World War I, but they did not have much of a following. Ionesco's dazzling comedy about a couple who discover, after a long and increasingly zany conversation, that they are husband and wife, changed all that. It came like a bolt from the blue, not surprisingly, since it was not based on anything which had gone before in the theatre, but on the eminently actable exchanges on a Linguaphone record which Ionesco had bought in an attempt to teach himself English conversation.

That simple initial stroke of genius — to perceive theatricality where no one else had thought to look for it — launched Ionesco on a controversial but lucrative career which has brought him many honours, of which the one he most prizes is perhaps election to that élite literary establishment in France, the Académie Française. He has, however, missed the Nobel prize — Beckett won it instead — which indicates no doubt the extent and limitations of his achievement: that he is a prolific and inventive writer but not a great one, whose best work was done in the earlier part of his career.

La Leçon (*The Lesson*), for instance, is a superb piece of theatre, in which a girl's private lesson turns into ritual rape and murder as the tutor "assaults" her with words which pour unstoppably from his lips. *Les Chaises* (*The Chairs*) is also concerned with proliferation, something of an Ionesco trade mark: in this case chairs fill the stage as an elderly couple welcome an invisible audience to listen to the wisdom of an orator who turns out to be dumb. In *Victimes du devoir* (*Victims of Duty*) one character is stuffed with food he does not want and another dies a "victim of duty" in a black comedy which disturbs and amuses the audience simultaneously. This gift — of treating serious matters with unsettling levity — is exercised to perfection in *Amédée*, perhaps Ionesco's finest work. Amédée is host to a corpse which he cannot rid his flat of (hence the subtitle "how to get rid of it"); indeed, it starts instead to grow, and mushrooms spring up from his floors. Hilariously incapable of disposing of the suffocating nuisance, Amédée (who, it is revealed, is a failed playwright) floats away from it all to the consternation of his long-suffering wife and the dismay of a passing policeman, who laments the loss to literature of such a promising writer.

There is a unique charm about the plays which Ionesco wrote in the early 1950s that disappears from *Tueur sans gages* (*The Killer*, 1958) onwards, when the writing becomes more didactic and less dramatically inventive. *The Killer* is about a character called Bérenger, who stands for Ionesco himself and all decent, ordinary people; this man is overwhelmed by evil he cannot control in the shape of an assassin who ignores all his honest and liberal words and bears down mercilessly upon him as the curtain falls. Bérenger is also the protagonist in *Rhinocéros*, a play about crowds and power, the gullibility of the masses and the insidiousness of propaganda, and becomes a kind of spokesman for Ionesco's own anti-totalitarian political position. This is all very worthy, but it makes for tiresome watching in the theatre. The same applies to the long plays which followed, *Le Roi se meurt* (*Exit the King*), *La Soif et la faim* (*Hunger and Thirst*), and *Macbett*, the last of which is in the same line as Edward Bond's *Lear* or Tom Stoppard's *Rosencrantz and Guildenstern Are Dead*, all meditations upon or adaptations of Shakespeare.

The recent plays have been put on in major theatres by prestige companies — a far cry from the pocket theatres which launched Ionesco in the early 1950s — but the critics' reactions have been mixed. There was always a tendency in this playwright to verbosity, but whereas in *The Lesson* the exuberant language was almost a character in its own right, in the later plays it becomes mere windy rhetoric. This should not, however, detract from the magnitude of the achievement represented by the sheer inventiveness of the early work; besides, Ionesco is not merely a playwright. His meditations on the art of theatre, collected in *Notes et contre-notes* (*Notes and Counter-Notes*), are a major contribution to the theory of drama, a not unworthy successor to Antonin Artaud's *The Theatre and Its Double* (1938) which has had such an important influence on the sort of theatre which Ionesco took a leading part in creating, a theatre in which traditional notions of stagecraft are abandoned in favour of a more dream-like conception of plot and character.

Ionesco is also a poet (his earliest writings are in Romanian), a short story writer of some power (especially in tales which deal in concentrated form with the dream situations subsequently elaborated into full-length stage works), and a charming autobiographer and essayist. He is just the sort of prolific, elegant, and versatile writer whom l'Académie Française likes to recruit, and it is very much to his credit that he achieved election to this body notwithstanding his foreign origins. He is a fine if not a great writer, and thanks to *The Bald Soprano*, which so astonished Paris first-nighters on 11 May 1950, he is assured for ever of an honourable place in theatre history.

—John Fletcher

————

INFANTE, G. Cabrera. *See* **CABRERA INFANTE, G.**

————

J

JABRĀ, Jabrā Ibrāhīm. Palestinian. Born in Bethlehem, 28 August 1920. Educated at the Arab College, Jerusalem, 1938; Exeter University, Devon; Fitzwilliam House, Cambridge, B.A. in English literature 1943, M.A. 1948; Harvard University, Cambridge, Massachusetts, 1952–54. Married Lamia Barqi al-Askari in 1952; two sons. Teacher of English literature, Rashidiya College, Jerusalem, 1944–48, and College of Arts and Sciences, Baghdad, 1948–52; lecturer, Queen Aliya College, Baghdad, 1948–52; senior staff member, 1954–60, and head of employee communications, later publications, 1960–72, Iraq Petroleum Company, Baghdad; part-time lecturer, College of Arts, Baghdad, 1956–64; head of Information and Publications Office, 1972–74, and of Translation Office, 1974–77, Iraq National Oil Company; visiting lecturer, University of California, Berkeley, 1976; senior staff member, Ministry of Information and Culture, Baghdad, 1977–84. President, Arts Club, Jerusalem, 1944–48; founder, with Jewad Selim, Baghdad Modern Art Group, 1951; editor-in-chief, *Funūn Arabiyyah* [Arab Arts], London, 1982–84; president, Art Critics Association, Iraq, 1982–90. Recipient: Rockefeller Foundation research fellowship, 1952–54; Targa Europa prize for culture, 1983; Kuwait Foundation for the Advancement of Science prize, 1987; Saddam prize, 1988; Jerusalem Medal, 1990; Sultan al Oweis prize, 1990; Medal of Merit (Tunisia), 1991; Thorton Wilder prize for translation, 1991. Honorary member, Iraqi Translators Society and Iraqi Artists Society. Address: 55/11/601 Al Mansour, Baghdad, Iraq.

PUBLICATIONS

Fiction

Surakh fī lail tawīl [A Cry in a Long Night]. Baghdad, 1955.
Arrak and Other Short Stories. Beirut, 1956.
Hunters in a Narrow Street. London, Heinemann, 1960; Washington, D.C., Three Continents Press, 1990.
Al-safīnah. Beirut, 1970; as *The Ship,* Washington, D.C., Three Continents Press, 1985.
Al-baḥth 'an Walīd Mas'ūd [In Search of Walid Mas'ud]. Beirut, Dār al-Adāb, 1978.
'Ālam bi-la khara' iṭ [World Without Maps], with Abdal Rahman Munīf. Beirut, al-Mu'assasah al-'Arabiyyah lil-Dirāsāt wa-al-Nashr, 1982.
Al-ghuraf al-ukhrā [The Other Rooms]. Beirut, al-Mu'assasah al-'Arabiyyah lil-Dirāsāt wa-al-Nashr, 1986.
Yawmiyyāt Sarab Affān [The Diary of Saraab Affan]. Beirut, 1991.

Verse

Tammūz fī al-madīnah [Tammūz in the City]. Beirut, 1959.
Al-madār al-mughlaq [Closed Circuit]. Beirut, 1964.
Law'at al-shams [Sun's Passion]. Baghdad, 1979.
Complete Poetical Works (in Arabic). London, 1990.

Plays

Al malik al shams [The Sun King] (screenplay). Baghdad, 1985.
Sanawat al uqāb [The Years of the Eagle] (screenplay). Baghdad, 1988.

Other

Al hurriya wal tūfan [Freedom and the Deluge]. Beirut, 1960.
Art in Iraq Today. London, Embassy of the Republic of Iraq, 1961.
Al rihla al thāmina [Eighth Voyage]. Beirut, 1967.
Iraqi Art Today (bilingual edition). Baghdad, 1972.
Jewad Selīm wa nasb al-ḥurriya [Jewad Selim and the Liberty Monument]. Baghdad, 1974.
Al-nār wal-Jawhar [Fire and Essence]. Beirut, Dār al-Quds, 1975.
Yanabi' al-ru'ya [Fountains of Vision]. Beirut, 1979.
Usṭūrah wa-al-ramz: dirāsāt naqdīyah li-khamsah 'ashar naqdan. Beirut, al-Mu'assasah al-'Arabiyyah lil-Dirāsāt wa-al-Nashr, 1980.
Al-Adīb wa-sina'atuh: dirasat fial-adab wa-al-naqd. Beirut, al-Mu'assasah al-'Arabiyyah lil-dirāsāt wa-al-Nashr, 1983.
The Grass-Roots of Iraqi Art. Baghdad, 1983; in Arabic, 1985.
Al-fan wal-ḥulum wal-fi'l [Art, Dream, and Action]. Baghdad, 1985.
Al bi'r al ūla [The First Well]. London, Riad el-Rayyes, 1987.
Baghdad bayn al ams wal yawm [Baghdad, Past and Present], with Ihsan Fathi. Baghdad, 1987.
A Celebration of Life: Essays on Literature and Art. Baghdad, Dār al-Ma'mūn, 1988.
Ta'ammulāt fī bunyān marmari [Reflections on a Marble Monument]. London, Riad el-Rayyes, 1989.
Mu'āyashat al namira [Living with the Tigress]. Beirut, 1991.
Aqni' at al haqīqa wa aqni' at al khayāl [Masks of the Real and the Unreal]. Beirut, 1992.

Has translated into Arabic works by William Shakespeare, Sir James Frazer, William Faulkner, Alexander Elliot, Germaine Brée, Eric Bentley, Edmund Wilson, Jan Kott, Janet Dillon, Samuel Beckett, Dover Wilson, Oscar Wilde, and others.

* * *

Jabrā Ibrāhīm Jabrā is a man of many talents, in each of which his thought, his personality, and his values are exhibited. A poet, short-story writer, novelist, literary critic, essayist, translator, painter and art critic, he has been creative for a period of about half a century, during which the Arab world has witnessed dramatic social and political change. Now in his seventies, he has been a witness to many upheavals in the Middle East, none of which is perhaps as deeply ingrained in him as the loss of Palestine, his homeland. The feeling of being an exile pervades his poetry and fiction, but he does not permit it to be bitter and destructive. Nostalgic memories of the homeland abound in his poetry, to be sure, and fictional characters searching for their identity and roots recur in his short stories and novels. But as a writer, he transcends personal feelings to arrive at a universal vision of man in the 20th century, indeed to arrive at an understanding of the human condition in modern times.

His education in the West and his deep knowledge of Western culture and thought have made of him a force for change in an Arab world that is currently experiencing the pull of modernity. Strongly grounded in Arab culture with its long history of great achievements, he does not want it to be smothered by its own tradition that has in recent centuries become constraining and inhibiting. He rather wants Arab culture to grow and develop, not by imitating the West or even the great Arab masters of the past, but by daringly rising to its own potential and creatively adding to its own past accomplishments. He does not want the Arabs to be only part of the modern world, he wants them to participate in its modern civilization and contribute to it by their creative additions. This is one of the most significant values that Jabrā's works stand for and defend. His essays and literary criticism give expression to these opinions, and his poetry and fiction implement them creatively.

Writing in an age when urban growth has become a pronounced feature of modern developments in the Arab world as elsewhere, Jabrā focuses most of his attention on the Arab city, its people, its problems, its opportunities and challenges, and its power to crush individuals and values as it develops its own urban rules of living. His first collection of poems, *Tammūz fī al-madīnah* (Tammūz in the City), laments the spiritual death that prevails in the city as its people move away from life-giving principles in their search for material gain and power. His second collection, *Al-madār al-Mughlaq* (Closed Circuit), decries the constraints imposed on people undergoing dramatic change in the city and being forced to lose their natural selves and their real voice. His third collection, *Law' at al-shams* (Sun's Passion), reveals the evils that enslave humans caught in the mesh of city life, from which nothing but love can redeem them. As a symbol of modern civilization, the city — like T. S. Eliot's wasteland — needs a revivifying force to bring back fertility and happiness to it. In all his poetry, Jabrā has opted for free verse, away from traditional meters and rhyme schemes, in order to convey in prose and in fresh language a vision of the new world of harmony and wholeness that he would like to build.

With greater elaboration, though with similar poetic symbols, Jabrā deals with the Arab city in his fiction. His characters in his short stories and novels are in search of themselves, their identity, their individual salvation, their long-cherished goals of social and national well-being. Whether rich or poor, they are frustrated and mercilessly put down by unseen forces that the structures of the city blindly manipulate. Some individuals try to run away from the city to escape its oppressive power, only to be overcome by the oppression they carry away within them, as did the characters in his novel *Al-safīnah* (The Ship), one of whom commits suicide on board the ship taking them on a cruise in the Mediterranean. Others try to find shelter in the past, in some romance, or in rebellion against dominant mores as did the characters in his *Hunters in a Narrow Street*. Others find themselves being led willy-nilly into an uncharted world they understand little, and into endless labyrinthian situations they understand even less, as does the main character in Jabrā's novel *Al-ghuraf al-ukhrā* (The Other Rooms).

Jabrā is telling his readers that something is basically wrong with the modern city and with civilization as it is developing, and he is suggesting that the solutions people are attempting are futile because they lack fundamental principles that are essential for human happiness. Tammūz must come to the city to renew and revive it, love must return to its people to recreate strong bonds of human relations, self-sacrifice rather than self-aggrandizement must prevail in its rules of morality and ethics. Walīd Mas'ūd, the hero of Jabrā's novel *Al-baḥth 'an Walīd Mas'ūd* (In Search of Walīd Mas'ud), is one character of mythical proportions who identifies with such values. A Palestinian in exile who amassed a large fortune, he mystifies his friends in Baghdad when he secretly abandons the city and all his wealth. His car is found on the Iraqi-Syrian borders with a tape-recording of Mas'ūd's final rambling words, and one rumor has it that he has returned to occupied Palestine to fight for his people's freedom.

Although Jabrā does not prescribe solutions, he lets his readers arrive at them by internal conviction through his compelling fiction and poetry. There is always a feeling in his writings that life is essentially tragic, that man is in a state of permanent siege from which he constantly attempts to break out. Freedom, salvation, love are ultimately the great human values that Jabrā's works of creative writing are all about.

—Issa J. Boullata

————

JACCOTTET, Philippe. Swiss. Born in Moudon, Switzerland, 30 June 1925. Educated at the University of Lausanne, 1944–46, graduated 1946. Married Anne-Marie Haesler in 1953; one son and one daughter. Translator for Mermod publishers, Lausanne, 1946–53. Since 1953 has lived in Grignan, France. Recipient: Hermès prize, 1962; Voss prize, for translation, 1966; Lausanne prize, 1970; Ramuz prize, 1970; Montaigne prize (Hamburg), 1972; Halpérine-Kaminsky prize, for translation, 1973; Larbaud prize, 1978. Address: c/o Éditions Gallimard, 5 rue Sébastien-Bottin, 75007, Paris, France.

PUBLICATIONS

Verse

Requiem. Lausanne, Mermod, 1947.
L'Effraie et autres poésies. Paris, Gallimard, 1953.
L'Ignorant: poèmes 1952–1956. Paris, Gallimard, 1958.
Airs: poèmes 1961–1964. Paris, Gallimard, 1967.
Leçons. Lausanne, Payot, 1969.
Poésie 1946–1967. Paris, Gallimard, 1971.
Chants d'en bas. Lausanne, Payot, 1974.
Breathings, translated by Cid Corman. New York, Grossman, 1974.
À la Lumière d'hiver; Leçons; Chants d'en bas. Paris, Gallimard, 1977.
Pensées sous les nuages. Paris, Gallimard, 1983.
Selected Poems, translated by Derek Mahon. London, Viking, 1987; Winston-Salem, North Carolina, Wake Forest University Press, 1988.
Cahier de verdure (includes prose). Paris, Gallimard, 1990.
Libretto. Geneva, Dogana, 1990.

Fiction

L'Obscurité: récit. Paris, Gallimard, 1961.

Other

La Promenade sous les arbres: proses.   Lausanne, Mermod, 1957.

Éléments d'un songe: proses.   Paris, Gallimard, 1961.

La Semaison:
   vol. 1: *Carnets 1954–1962.*   Lausanne, Payot, 1963; revised edition, as *Carnets 1954–1967*, Paris, Gallimard 1971; as *Seedtime*, New York, New Directions, 1977.
   vol. 2: *Carnets-journées, 1968–1975.*   Lausanne, Payot, 1977.
   vols. 1 and 2 revised as *Carnets 1954–1979*, Paris, Gallimard, 1984.

Paysages de Grignan.   Lausanne, Bibliothèque des Arts, 1964.

Autriche.   Lausanne, Rencontre, 1966.

L'Entretien des muses: chroniques de poésie.   Paris, Gallimard, 1968.

Paysages avec figures absentes: proses.   Paris, Gallimard, 1970.

Rilke par lui-même.   Paris, Seuil, 1971.

À Travers un Verger.   Montpellier, Fata Morgana, 1975; as *Through an Orchard*, Portree, Isle of Skye, Aquila, 1978.

Adieu à Gustave Roud, with Maurice Chapaz and Jacques Chessex.   Vevey, Galland, 1977.

Beauregard.   Paris, Maeght, 1981.

Gustave Roud.   Fribourg, Éditions Universitaires, 1982.

Des Histoires de passage: prose 1948–1978.   Lausanne, À l'Enseigne du Verseau, 1983.

Dans la Lumière de Vaucluse: carnets de Michel Steiner et de Philippe Jaccottet.   Avignon, Galerie G. Guerre, 1983.

À Travers un Verger; Les Cormorans; Beauregard.   Paris, Gallimard, 1984.

Une Transaction secrète: lectures de poésie.   Paris, Gallimard, 1987.

Autres Journées.   Fontfroide-le-Haut, Fata Morgana, 1987.

Pages retrouvées-inédits-entretiens-dossier critique-bibliographie, edited by Jean-Pierre Videl.   Lausanne, Payot, 1989.

Editor, *Élégies et autres vers*, by Francis Jammes.   Lausanne, Mermod, 1946.

Editor, *Gustave Roud.*   Paris, Seghers, 1968.

Editor, *Haut-Jorat*, by Gustave Roud.   Lausanne, Payot, 1978.

Editor and Translator, *Essais, conférences, critique, aphorismes et réflexions* (selected works), by Robert Musil.   Paris, Seuil, 1984.

Editor, with Doris Jakubec, *Lectures*, by Gustave Roud.   Lausanne, l'Aire, 1988.

Translator, *La Mort à Venise*, by Thomas Mann.   Lausanne, Mermod, 1946.

Translator, *L'Odyssée*, by Homer.   Paris, Club Français du Livre, 1955.

Translator, *L'Homme sans qualités*, by Robert Musil.   Paris, Seuil, 1957.

Translator, *Hyperion*, by Friedrich Hölderlin.   Lausanne, Mermod, 1957.

Translator, *Trois Femmes*, by Robert Musil.   Paris, Seuil, 1963.

Translator, *Œuvres*, by Giacomo Léopardi.   N.p., Del Duca, 1964.

Translator, *Les Désarrois de l'élève Törless*, by Robert Musil.   Paris, Livre de Poche, 1967.

Translator, *Le Vaisseau des morts*, by B. Traven.   Paris, Livre de Poche, 1967.

Translator, *Œuvres complètes*, by Friedrich Hölderlin.   Paris, Gallimard, 1967.

Translator, *Innocence et mémoire*, by Giuseppe Ungaretti.   Paris, Gallimard, 1969.

Translator, *La Femme du dimanche*, by Carlo Fruttero.   Paris, Seuil, 1973.

Translator, *Correspondance* by Rainer Maria Rilke.   Paris, Seuil, 1976.

Translator, *Le Banquet*, by Plato.   Lausanne, l'Aire, 1979.

Translator, *Journaux*, by Robert Musil.   Paris, Seuil, 3 vols., 1981.

Translator, *Les Solitudes*, by Luis de Góngora y Argote.   Geneva, la Dogana, 1984.

Also translator of works by Carlo Cassola, Eugenio Montale, Novalis, and many others.

*

Critical Studies: "Swords Above the Trees: The Poetics of Philippe Jaccottet" by Michael Bishop, in *Swiss-French Studies* (Wolfville, Ontario), May 1980; "Landscape and Loss in Yves Bonnefoy and Philippe Jaccottet," in *French Forum* (Lexington, Kentucky), 5, 1980, and "The Unseizable Landscape of the Real: The Poetry and Poetics of Philippe Jaccottet," in *Studies in 20th-Century Literature* (Manhattan, Kansas), Winter 1989, both by Richard Stamelman; "Philippe Jaccottet: '. . . je n'ai fait que passer, accueillir'" by Andrea Cady, in *Swiss-French Studies* (Wolfville, Ontario), May 1982; "Philippe Jaccottet: The Itinerary of a Post-War Poet" by Peter Low, in *New Zealand Journal of French Studies* (Palmerston North), May 1983.

*   *   *

In 1946, while travelling through Italy, the Swiss poet and translator Philippe Jaccottet met and befriended the poet Giuseppe Ungaretti (1888–1970), whom he greatly admires and whose works he has translated into French. Jaccottet has described Ungaretti's poetry as "a passionate song for light" in the midst of "nothingness, darkness, boredom, fog, threatening clouds, night, shipwreck, opacity and blindness" (from *Une Transaction secrète* [A Secret Transaction]). This description can equally well be applied to Jaccottet's own work.

In his teens, and then at the University of Lausanne, Jaccottet read and studied with predilection the Greek and Roman philosophers (his own translation of Plato's *Banquet* was published in 1979), and the German Romantic and idealist authors (Friedrich Hölderlin, Rainer Maria Rilke), whom he read in the original and also in Gustave Roud's French translations. Like Ungaretti, Roud (1897–1976), a Swiss poet of the preceding generation, exerted a strong formative influence on Jaccottet and it was he perhaps who pointed the way not only to an ascetic style of writing, but also to a reclusive lifestyle. After spending a few years in Paris (1946–53), Jaccottet settled permanently, in 1953, in Grignan, a village in the Drôme (Rhône-Alpes) in southern France.

Jaccottet's poetic output is relatively small, but his translation work is colossal, and he tackles only the most demanding of authors. Translating is for Jaccottet a literary and intellectual passion as well as an economic necessity. Having decided that he would neither teach to earn a living nor write poetry for financial reward, translation work became for this highly gifted linguist the obvious professional choice.

Jaccottet's poetry is haunted by the presence of death, by the unshakeable feeling that he, the poet, is nothing but a passerby to-ing and fro-ing between the visible and the invisible, between — precisely — life and death. Over and over again, in his poems, prose, and critical writing Jaccottet endeavours to come to terms with death. "To die? We do nothing else from the moment we open our eyes to the blinding evidence of nothingness." (*L'Obscurité* [Darkness]). His work, he writes, is nothing but "a cry of utter despair" (*Revue Sud*, 32/33, 1981). But Jaccottet expresses his anguish with restraint and simplicity, even reticence: his poetry is, in Simon Watson Taylor's felicitous judgement, made of "an artlessly artful simplicity." He positions himself at a point equally distant from Samuel Beckett's monomaniac obsessiveness with the void and what he considers to be Saint-John Perse's triumphant lyricism. His modest aim is to "hold the unknown at bay, to drive away the fear" (*La Semaison* [*Seedtime*]). Jaccottet is enemy of all doctrines, of all systems, even — or, rather, especially — in literature. His attitude towards literary creation is highly ambivalent: he considers a poem as the only human creation which comes anywhere near the truth and, yet, the futility of playing with words is all too obvious: "Words are nothing but words. Facile. At certain moments, when I am confronted by certain realities, they anger and disgust me" (*À Travers un Verger* [Through An Orchard]). A 1974 poem from *Chants d'en bas* (Songs from Below) has a characteristically pessimistic ending: "To speak is to lie, or worse: a craven/insult to grief or a waste/of the little time and energy at our disposal."

In 1960 Jaccottet published a review of R. H. Blyth's *History of Haïku*. The discovery of that minimal art form, which Blyth calls "self-obliterating," was a revelation for Jaccottet: these short traditional Japanese poems of syllables illuminate exquisitely the most obscure existences and recapture the most fleeting moments of human consciousness. *Mutatis mutandi* Jaccottet and his Japanese counterparts pursue the same aim: "The poet must look out, like a shepherd, and evoke all these little things which might get lost if he fell asleep" (*L'Ignorant* [Ignorance]). Jaccottet's minimalism is neither a retreat from the world nor a comfortable aloofness: for him, a closed, but dry completeness, like a lyrical and ebullient ejaculation, would be a betrayal of reality in its fleeting evanescence, its ever-changing fragmentation, its endless questioning. As he writes in *Éléments d'un songe* [Fragments of Dream], if questions open doors, answers close them for ever.

Against the ever greater encroachment of modern technology (representing order, the negation of life), poetry breathes and creates life, it expresses the inexpressible, it sees the invisible, it listens to the silence: it captures that which cannot be captured. Jaccottet teaches us to remain silent, to meditate, to reflect. His poetry speaks to the soul, not the senses; it is composed of restrained whispers and never allows itself to exult, in joy or in despair. Much has been said of Jaccottet's reticence, of his "Swiss" or "Calvinist" reluctance to open up, to embrace profusely. Such criticism is ill applied: it is as illogical as expecting a cherry tree to bring forth peaches. A single stroke, a single note are enough for this poet to create the picture, the atmosphere which haunt him and his power of evocation are unsurpassed: "Nothing at all, a footfall on the road,/yet more mysterious than guide or god."

If, as George Steiner says, "music speaks of the otherness of reality," then Jaccottet's poetry belongs to the realm of music as he mysteriously guides his reader along the uncharted road of life, a road studded with small but invaluable jewels to be admired along the way, despite (or perhaps

enhanced by) the knowledge that death will ultimately obliterate all.

—Claude Schumacher

———

JACOBSEN, Rolf. Norwegian. Born in Oslo, 8 March 1907. Educated at the University of Oslo. Served in the Norwegian Army for six weeks, 1927. Married Petra Tendø in 1940; two sons. Formerly journalist for local newspaper, Hamar. Member, Norwegian Academy of Language and Literature. Recipient: Norwegian Critics' prize, 1960; Riksmål prize, 1965; Swedish Academy Doubloug prize, 1968, and Nordic prize, 1989. Agent: Gyldendal Norsk Forlag, Postboks 6860, St. Olavs Plass, 0130 Oslo 1, Norway. Address: Skappelsgt. 2, 2300 Hamar, Norway.

PUBLICATIONS

Verse

Jord og jern [Soil and Iron].   Oslo, Gyldendal, 1933.
Vrimmel [Crowd].   Oslo, Gyldendal, 1935.
Fjerntog [Long-Distance Trains].   Oslo, Gyldendal, 1951.
Hemmelig liv (Secret Life).   Oslo, Gyldendal, 1954.
Sommeren i gresset [The Summer in the Grass].   Oslo, Gyldendal, 1956.
Brev til lyset [Letter to the Light].   Oslo, Gyldendal, 1960.
Stillheten efterpå.   Oslo, Gyldendal, 1965; as *The Silence Afterwards*, translated by Roger Greenwald, Princeton, New Jersey, Princeton University Press, 1985.
Headlines.   Oslo, Gyldendal, 1969.
Pass for dørene, dørene lukkes [Stand Clear of the Doors, Please].   Oslo, Gyldendal, 1972.
Samlede dikt [Collected Poems].   Oslo, Gyldendal, 1973; revised edition, 1977, 1982, 1986.
Pusteøvelse.   Oslo, Gyldendal, 1975; as *Breathing Exercise*, translated by Olav Grinde, Buffalo, New York, White Pine Press, 1985.
Twenty Poems, translated by Robert Bly. Madison, Minnesota, Seventies Press, 1977.
Tenk på noe annet [Think About Something Else].   Oslo, Gyldendal, 1979.
Nattåpent [Open at Night].   Oslo, Gyldendal, 1985.
Alle mine dikt [All My Poems].   Oslo, Gyldendal, 1990.

*

Critical Studies: "The Poetry of Rolf Jacobsen" by Harald Naess, in *American-Scandinavian Review*, 62(3), 1974; "Interview with Rolf Jacobsen" by Olav Grinde, in *South Dakota Review* (Vermillion), 21(1), 1983.

Rolf Jacobsen comments:
I am, by many, called "the Green Poet" in Norwegian literature. The title of my first work *Jord og Jern* (Soil and Iron) points to a certain theme: the balance between nature and technology. Man has conquered nature. But the technology he cannot master. I was probably the first who used what we call "verse libre" (free verse) in Norwegian poetry (1933).

*   *   *

Rolf Jacobsen has published 12 collections of poetry since he made his debut in 1933. These collections, together with numerous editions of his *Samlede dikt* (Collected Poems), have secured him a place as one of the two or three most important Norwegian poets of his generation.

Jacobsen published two collections of poetry in the 1930s: *Jord og jern* (Soil and Iron) and *Vrimmel* (Crowd), then was silent for 16 years. The two early collections nonetheless established Jacobsen as a spokesman for a new generation of poets, who wrote about the big city and showed a fascination with machines and modern life. But his poems are not limited to this subject alone; they celebrate the richness and multitude of experience in the modern world. The poet writes about the opposition between nature and civilization, and is clearly in favour of man's ability to control nature through modern technology. During World War II Jacobsen worked as a journalist, and his next collection of poems, *Fjerntog* (Long-Distance Trains), did not appear until 1951. Most critics claim that little development or growth took place in this long silent period. This may be correct in one sense, since the poems of *Fjerntog* are traditional in form. At the same time, however, the celebration of the machine has given way to descriptions of rough and lonely Norwegian scenery through which the train, the collection's central symbol, runs, and some of the poems mention human misery and loneliness. In his next collection, *Hemmelig liv* (Secret Life), Jacobsen found the form of poetic expression which he was to perfect. The tone of the poems has changed; he has become a strong critic of life in the city, of machines and so-called progress, although he is never polemic or propagandistic. His emotions are always controlled, although there is no mistaking the intensity behind them. His subjects are always objects and phenomena in the outside world. His poems describe minute changes which, taken together, reveal how a world is lost and replaced by a new, less friendly one. But there are still things of beauty and value in the modern world, and Jacobsen invests some of them with strange poetic qualities.

Sommeren i gresset (The Summer in the Grass) is evidently the product of the rich imagination of a poet in love with the world around him, despite its tendencies to regulate, control, and curb personal freedom. Negativity is not allowed to dominate, and Jacobsen's warm humour and mild irony are always present.

In later collections Jacobsen confirms and secures his position as one of the best Norwegian poets of his time, and one of the most widely read and recited. The poems in *Brev til lyset* (Letter to the Light) and *Stillheten efterpå* (The Silence Afterwards) may still be about machines, cars, and life in the big city, but they all show, in their shifting images and elaborate contrasts, that new technology and the consumer society threaten traditional human values. It becomes increasingly difficult to lead a decent and meaningful life when the smell of timber or the softness of the grass are so far away and are replaced by income tax returns, neon lights, and marketing analyses. The "message" is nevertheless not a simple one, and becomes more complex in Jacobsen's more recent collections, *Headlines*, *Pass for dørene, dørene lukkes* (Stand Clear of the Doors, Please) and *Pusteøvelse* (Breathing Exercise). Jacobsen's *Samlede dikt* (Collected Poems) were published for his 70th birthday in 1977, and *Alle mine dikt* (All My Poems), a beautifully illustrated edition of extracts from all his books of poems, sold spectacularly in 1990, leaving no doubt about Jacobsen's position in Norwegian literature.

The special quality of Jacobsen's poetry has to do with his probing examination of the ways of the modern world. He may be critical of what he sees, but the rich implications of his poetic language show that there are no easy solutions, no simple attitudes. At times his language is almost clinical — the poems are simply a list of images, comparisons, contrasts; at times it is filled with compassion and love for the seemingly unimportant and small things around us, without which life would be even more lonely. His collections of poems over a period of more than 50 years also provide a good starting point for those who want to familiarize themselves with Norwegian poetry in the 20th century. Although Jacobsen's poetry clearly bears his personal stamp, it is very much related to his observations of the almost complete change from the old world to a new and modern one in his native country.

—Hans H. Skei

JAKOBSDÓTTIR, Svava. Icelandic. Born in Neskaupsstaður, 4 October 1930. Educated at Smith College, Northampton, Massachusetts, A.B.; Somerville College, Oxford; University of Uppsala. Member, Icelandic Parliament, 1971–79. Recipient: Icelandic Writers' Fund literary prize, 1968. Address: c/o Iðunn, Braeðraborgarstíg 16, Pósthólf 294, 101 Reykjavík, Iceland.

PUBLICATIONS

Fiction

Tólf konur [12 Women].   Reykjavík, Almenna Bókafélagið, 1965.
Veisla undir grjótvegg [Dinner Party by a Stone Wall].   Reykjavík, Helgafell, 1967.
Leigjandinn [The Lodger].   Reykjavík, Helgafell, 1969.
Gefið hvort öðru [Given to Each Other].   Reykjavík, Iðunn, 1982.
Undir eldfjalli [At the Volcano's Foot].   Reykjavík, Forlagið, 1986.
Gunnlaðar saga [The Story of Gunnlöð].   Reykjavík, Forlagið, 1987.
Smásögur [Short Stories].   Reykjavík, Helgafell, 1987.

Plays

Hvað er í blýhólknum [What's in the Lead Pipe?] (produced Iceland, 1970).
Friðsæl veröld [A Peaceful World] (produced Iceland, 1974).
Æskuvinir [Childhood Friends] (produced Iceland, 1976).
Lokaæfing [Dress Rehearsal] (produced Faroe Islands, 1900). Reykjavík, Iðunn, 1983.

Radio Play: *Í takt við tímana* [In Step with the Times], 1980.

Other

Translator, *Öskubuska í austri og vestri* [Cinderella East and West], by Anna Birgitta Rooth. Reykjavík, Iðunn, 1982.

*

Critical Studies: "The Icelandic Short Story: Svava Jakobsdóttir" by Sigurður A. Magnússon, in *Scandinavian Studies* (Madison, Wisconsin), 49(2), 1977; "Women's Predicament: Svava Jakobsdóttir Interviewed" by Evelyn S. Firchow, in *Icelandic Writing Today*, edited by Sigurður A. Magnússon, 1982.

*   *   *

The titles of Svava Jakobsdóttir's first two collections of short stories, *Tólf konur* (12 Women) and *Veisla undir grjótvegg* (Dinner Party by a Stone Wall) indicate two major themes of her work: the position of women in society, and the implied contrast of modern urban living with a more traditional, rural existence. Related themes, reflected in the titles of her short-story collections *Gefið hvort öðru* (Given to Each Other) and *Undir eldfjalli* (At the Volcano's Foot), are marriage and life's precariousness. Yet another is the nuclear threat, seen as largely the product of male sociopolitical domination. Realistic though her work is in large measure, it also has a strong element of magic realism: in one of her stories, "Saga handa börnum" (A Story for Children), a woman "lives" through the experiences of having her brain sawn out by her children and her heart cut out by her doctor, finally keeping both organs in jars on a shelf in her house.

Jakobsdóttir's first novel, *Leigjandinn* (The Lodger), tells of a foreigner lodging at the flat of an Icelandic couple preoccupied with building their own house. Such is the fascination he holds for them that they effectively decamp from their sitting room to the hallway where he lives. Eventually they succumb to his offer of financial assistance and move with him into their new house, where the wife for snobbish reasons, and against the lodger's will, insists on him having a room to himself. They then notice a stranger lingering near the house, who the husband discovers is a stateless person. He resists the pressure from his wife to ask the stranger to leave; at the same time she notices that husband and lodger are limping in the right and left leg respectively. Finally, at Christmas, the stranger knocks at their door. When husband and lodger rise in response, their bodies appear to have grown together, leaving only two legs between them, and the wife's arm turns to stone and falls as she raises it to open the door. The message here seems to be that the Icelanders, occupied by British and American troops during World War II, and now, as members of NATO, hosts to an American air base, are so open to foreign influence as to be in danger of having nothing left of their own to offer to those who might look to them for asylum.

In the play *Lokaæfing* (Dress Rehearsal) a husband and wife agree to spend a month in the husband's carefully built nuclear shelter, behaving exactly as if a nuclear attack had occurred. In the mind of the husband, at least, this "rehearsal" becomes reality, as appears when he breaks his ankle and refuses to let his wife get help, and when, at the end of the play, he shoots dead a young piano pupil of his wife's who happens upon their hiding place.

The background to Jakobsdóttir's second novel, *Gunnlaðar saga* (The Story of Gunnlöð), is partly explained in a scholarly article by her published in 1988 in *Skírnir*, the journal of the Icelandic Literary Society, where she argues that the obscure stanzas 104–10 of the anonymous medieval Eddic poem *Hávamál* (Words of the High One) describe the typical kingship inauguration ritual of a pre-Viking Scandinavian matriarchal society, with the difference that the traditional pattern of the king (represented by Oðinn) receiving a drink signifying royal power from the fertility goddess (represented by Gunnlöð) is here disrupted by Oðinn's treacherous theft of the Grail-like vessel in which the drink is contained. This vessel turns up in the novel, linking together its two alternating plots, which deal respectively with the attempts of an Icelandic mother to help her daughter, Dís, who is accused of stealing the vessel from the National Museum of Denmark, and with the vessel's early history, into which Dís is drawn, as though in a dream, as she views it in the museum. The ancient world in which Dís thus finds herself is a waste land, whose infertility signifies that its kingship has failed. This is because Oðinn has stolen from Gunnlöð the vessel earlier used in the sacred marriage of king and goddess. No longer deigning to receive the royal power as a gift from the goddess, Oðinn has initiated by this theft a new age, an Iron Age of weapons and warfare, an age in which men, rather than women, rule, and which has lasted to the present day — witness the Chernobyl disaster, news of which reaches Denmark in the course of the novel's other main plot. It has thus become necessary for a woman to reclaim the vessel, and this explains not only the theft with which Dís is charged, but also the development that takes place in the character of her mother, who learns from the experience of helping her daughter in Copenhagen that she herself — with her middle-class Reykjavík background and a husband with business interests involving the American base — is very much a product of the kind of society that Oðinn has brought into being. Significantly, when mother and daughter arrive back in Iceland after the Danish court has found Dís insane, the mother is arrested at the airport when the vessel, which had been used in evidence at the trial, is found in her hand luggage.

In an interview published in 1990 in the other major Icelandic literary journal, *Tímarit Máls og menningar*, Jakobsdóttir claims that she has "never been given to dualism." This may explain why the contrasts in her work are implied rather than explicit, with equal attention not always being paid to both elements in the contrast. Her work nevertheless thrives on a preoccupation with many different kinds of contrast: the solitary and the social, the local and the cosmopolitan, the rigid and the flexible, the pacific and the military; fertile and sterile, ancient and modern, old and young, woman and man.

—Rory McTurk

JANSSON, Tove (Marika). Finnish (Swedish language). Born in Helsinki, 9 August 1914. Studied at art schools in Stockholm, Helsinki, and Paris. Writer and artist: creator of the Moomins in cartoon and book form; cartoon strip *Moomin* appeared in *Evening News*, London, 1953–60; several individual shows. Recipient: Lagerlöf Medal, 1942, 1972; Finnish Academy award, 1959; Andersen Medal, 1966; Finnish state prize, 1971; Swedish Academy prize, 1972. Address: c/o Schildts Förlagsaktiebolag, Nylandsgatan 17 B 27, 00120 Helsinki, Finland.

PUBLICATIONS

Fiction

Lyssnerskan [The Listener].   Stockholm, Bonnier, 1971.
Sommarboken.   Stockholm, Bonnier, 1972; as *The Summer*

Book, New York, Pantheon, and London, Hutchinson, 1975.

Solstaden. Stockholm, Bonnier, 1974; as *Sun City*, New York, Pantheon, 1976; London, Hutchinson, 1977.

Dockskåpet och andra berättelser [The Doll's House and Other Stories]. Stockholm, Bonnier, 1978.

Den ärliga bedragaren [The Honest Cheat]. Stockholm, Bonnier, 1982.

Stenåkern [The Stony Field]. Stockholm, Bonnier, and Helsinki, Schildt, 1984.

Resa med lätt bagage [Travelling Light]. Stockholm, Bonnier, 1987.

Rent spel [Fair Play]. Stockholm, Bonnier, 1989.

Other

Småtrollen och den stora översvämningen [The Small Troll and the Large Flood]. 1945.

Mumintrollet och Kometen. Helsinki, Söderstrom, 1946; as *Comet in Moominland*, London, Benn, 1951; New York, Walck, 1967.

Trollkarlens Hatt. Helsinki, Schildt, 1949; as *Finn Family Moomintroll*, London, Benn, 1950; as *The Happy Moomins*, Indianapolis, Bobbs Merrill, 1951.

Muminpappans bravader. Helsinki, Schildt, 1950; as *The Exploits of Moominpappa*, London, Benn, 1952; New York, Walck, 1966.

Hur Gick det Sen? Helsinki, Schildt, 1952; as *Moomin Mymble and Little My*, London, Benn, 1953.

Farlig midsommar. Helsinki, Schildt, 1954; as *Moominsummer Madness*, London, Benn, 1955; New York, Walck, 1961.

Trollvinter. Helsinki, Schildt, 1957; as *Moominland Midwinter*, London, Benn, 1958; New York, Walck, 1962.

Vem Ska trösta knyttet? Helsinki, Schildt, 1960; as *Who Will Comfort Toffle?*, London, Benn, 1960.

Det Osynliga Barnet och andra berättelser. Helsinki, Schildt, 1962; as *Tales from Moominvalley*, London, Benn, 1963; New York, Walck, 1964.

Pappan och Havet. Helsinki, Schildt, 1965; as *Moomin Pappa at Sea*, London, Benn, 1966; New York, Walck, 1967.

Muminpappans memoarer. Stockholm, Gebers, 1968.

Bildhuggarens dotter (autobiography). Stockholm, Almqvist & Wiksell, 1968; as *Sculptor's Daughter*, London, Benn, 1969.

Sent i November. Helsinki, Schildt, 1970; as *Moominvalley in November*, London, Benn, and New York, Walck, 1971.

Den farliga resan. Stockholm, Bonnier, 1977; as *The Dangerous Journey*, London, Benn, 1978.

Vå berättelser från havet [Our Tales from the Sea] (for children). Stockholm, Bonnier, 1984.

Brev från Klara [Letters from Klara]. Stockholm, Bonnier, 1991.

*

Critical Studies: *Tove Jansson: Papan och Havet* (in English), Hull, University of Hull Department of Scandinavian Studies, 1979, "Tove Jansson: Themes and Motifs," in *Proceedings of the Conference of Scandinavian Studies in Great Britain and Northern Ireland*, Guildford, University of Surrey, 1983, and *Tove Jansson*, Boston, Twayne, 1984, all by W. Glyn Jones; "Tove Jansson: The Art of Travelling Light" by Marianne Bargum, in *Books from Finland* (Helsinki), 21(3), 1987; "Equal to Life: Tove Jansson's Moomintrolls" by Nancy Lyman Huse, in *Webs and Wardrobes: Humanist and Religious World Views in Children's Literature*, edited by Joseph O'Beirne Milner

and Lucy Floyd Morcock Milner, Lanham, Maryland, University Press of America, 1987.

*   *   *

As the author of the Moomin books, Tove Jansson is internationally famous. However, even at an early stage in the Moomin stories, an adult element begins to emerge, centred on obsession, the limit to contact between different creatures, the problems of the artist. In *Trollvinter* (*Moominland Midwinter*) the childish element is already beginning to recede, and Jansson is concerned with the phenomenon of change in living beings and with the question of establishing the nature of reality. The collection of short stories entitled *Det Osynliga Barnet och andra berättelser* (*Tales from Moomin valley*) moves directly into these central themes in stories which are only superficially for children. The last two of the Moomin books continue this process, and it is doubtful whether children can any longer really understand them. The themes are adult, though they are presented in the guise of children's stories.

Jansson then takes the logical step of moving into adult literature proper, originally with semi-autobiographical stories with a simple charm which should not blind the reader to the deeper implications. The account of her childhood as a sculptor's daughter gives scope for consideration of the artist's problem, while the account of a child's relationship with an ageing grandmother allows an exploration of the extent and limit of human contact.

Subsequent works show an increasing interest in the abnormal sides of human nature, in the frightening power of the imagination, and in the loneliness of the individual. The most important volume of short stories, *Dockskåpet* (The Doll's House), moves yet further into the realm of the abnormal in a series of gripping and disturbing stories in which the predatory nature of artistic inspiration is added to the earlier themes. One particular aspect of Jansson's psychological preoccupations is senility, and this she makes the central motif in a novel about life in an American community for the aged, *Solstaden* (*Sun City*). All the old people living in one house are portrayed with both humour and warm sympathy. The symbolism in this novel seems to imply the need for some kind of dream on which to survive.

Den ärliga bedragaren (The Honest Cheat) returns to the themes of the predatory nature of certain human relationships and the difficulty of establishing contact between two radically different and unusual personalities; the problems of the artist form a dramatic background.

Jansson is now established as a major writer of penetrating and highly idiosyncratic adult fiction, an author who has made the very difficult transition from a writer of children's fantasies to books completely beyond the comprehension of children. Taken as a whole, her work shows an impressive thematic unity transcending the two genres in which she has excelled. The honours bestowed on her betoken the esteem in which she is held both at home and abroad.

—W. Glyn Jones

JERSILD, P(er) C(hristian). Swedish. Born in Katrineholm, 14 March 1935. Educated at the Karolinska Institute, 1955–62, M.D. 1962. Married Ulla Flyxe in 1960; two sons. Contracted tuberculosis, 1955; staff member, Institute of

Social Medicine, Stockholm, 1963–66, and Stockholm Civil
Service Welfare Department, 1966–74; social psychiatrist,
Huddinge Hospital, Stockholm, 1974–78; Assistant Professor
of social and preventive medicine, and medical consultant,
National Government Employee Administration Board.
Recipient: Swedish Society for Promotion of Literature grand
prize, 1981; Swedish Academy award, 1982. Address: Rosens-
dalsv. 20, 19454 Uppl. Vasby, Sweden.

PUBLICATIONS

Fiction

Räknelära [Algebra].   Stockholm, Bonnier, 1960.
Till varmare länder [To Warmer Climes].   Stockholm,
    Bonnier, 1961.
Ledig lördag [Free Saturday].   Stockholm, Bonnier, 1963.
Calvinols resa genom världen [Calvinol's Journey Through the
    World].   Stockholm, Bonnier, 1965.
Prins Valiant och Konsum [Prince Valiant and Konsum].
    Stockholm, Bonnier, 1966.
Grisjakten [The Pig Hunt].   Stockholm, Bonnier, 1968.
Drömpojken: en paranoid historia [The Dream Boy: A
    Paranoid Story].   Stockholm, Bonnier, 1970.
Vi ses i Song My [See You at Mai Lai].   Göteborg,
    Författarförlaget, 1970.
Uppror bland marsvinen [Revolt Among the Guinea Pigs].
    Göteborg, Författarförlaget, 1972.
Djurdoktron.   Stockholm, Bonnier, 1973; as *The Animal
    Doctor*, New York, Pantheon, 1975.
Stumpen [The Remnant].   Solna, Kulturfront, 1973.
Barnens ö.   Stockholm, Bonnier, 1976; as *Children's Island*,
    Lincoln, University of Nebraska Press, 1986.
Babels hus.   Stockholm, Bonnier, 1978; as *The House of
    Babel*, Lincoln, University of Nebraska Press, 1987.
En levande själ.   Stockholm, Bonnier, 1980; as *A Living Soul*,
    Norwich, Norvik Press, 1988.
Efter floden.   Stockholm, Bonnier, 1982; as *After the Flood*,
    New York, Morrow, 1986.
Den femtionde frälsaren [The Fiftieth Savior].   Stockholm,
    Bonnier, 1984.
Tre berättelser [Three Stories].   Stockholm, Månaden, 1984.
Geniernas återkomst [Return of the Geniuses].   Stockholm,
    Bonnier, 1987.
Holgerssons [The Holgerssons].   Stockholm, Bonnier, 1991.

Plays

Pyton [Python], with Lars Ardelius (produced 1966).
Fänrik Duva [Lieutenant Duva].   Published in *Refuserat: fyra
    pjäser*, Stockholm, Bonnier, 1969.
Moskvafeber [Moscow Fever], with Frei Lindqvist, adaptation
    of a story by Anton Chekhov (produced 1977).
Gycklarnas Hamlet [The Players' Hamlet]; *Och monologerna
    Balans och en rolig halvtimme.*   Stockholm, Norstedt, 1980.
Lit de parade: svart komedi [Lying in State: A Black
    Comedy].   Stockholm, Bonnier, 1983.

Television Play: *OBS! Sammanträde pågår* [Notice: Meeting in
Progress], 1967.

Other

*Recovery in Schizophrenia: A Clinical and Sociopsychiatric
    Study*, with Gunnar and Maj-Britt Inghe.   Stockholm,
    Läromedelsförlag, 1970.

Den elektriska kaninen: en midsommarsaga [The Electric
    Rabbit] (for children).   Göteborg, Författarförlaget,
    1974.
Professionella bekännelser [Professional Confessions].
    Göteborg, Författarförlaget, 1981.
Geniernas åkterkomst: kronika [Return of the Geniuses].
    Stockholm, Bonnier, 1987.
Ryktet smittar: en monolog an AIDS [The Rumour Spreads:
    A Monologue on AIDS].   Stockholm, Bonnier, 1988.
Fem hjärten i en tändsticksask [Five Hearts in a Matchbox]
    (autobiography).   Stockholm, Bonnier, 1989.
Ett ensamt öra [A Solitary Ear].   Stockholm, Carlsen/if,
    1989.
Humpty Dumptys Fall.   Stockholm, Bonnier, 1990.
Slutet: om dödens höghet och låghet [The End: On Death's
    Highs and Lows], with Lars Ardelius.   Stockholm,
    Legenda, 1990.

*

Critical Studies: Jersild issue of *Swedish Book Review*
(Lampeter, Wales), supplement, 1983; "Dehumanization
and the Bureaucracy in Novels by P. C. Jersild," in
Scandinavica (Norwich), 23(1), 1984, "The Battle for the
Self in P. C. Jersild's *En levande själ*," in *Scandinavian
Studies* (Madison, Wisconsin), 56(3), 1984, and
"P. C. Jersild's *Efter floden* and Human Value(s)," in
Scandinavica (Norwich), 27(1), 1988, all by Ross Shideler.

*   *   *

Since his debut as a writer at the beginning of the 1960s,
P. C. Jersild has been popular with the general reading public in Sweden, and film or television versions have been
made of several of his works. The farcical, satirical, and
absurd books and plays by this qualified physician, now a
full-time writer, are attacks on modern society and often
take the form of red tape and bureaucratic stupidity presenting a threat to the dignity and integrity of the individual. His
experience of social medicine, his post in the Stockholm
Civil Service Welfare Department, and his work as a social
psychiatrist have given him insight into the functioning of
bureaucratic institutions and jargon, which he satirizes in a
masterly fashion.
    Although Jersild is now best known as a novelist, he
started as a short-story writer with the collection *Räknelära*
(Algebra), embodying some of the themes that were to appear in later works and already showing some of the characteristics that were to be his trademark: ordinary everyday
life is depicted, but suddenly reality is turned upside down
by some bizarre happening. In the novel *Ledig lördag* (Free
Saturday), for instance, a couple on their way home from a
company party find themselves trapped for a week-long
nightmare in a Stockholm underground train. Although
Ledig lördag attracted critical acclaim, Jersild describes it as
the one of his works he likes least in *Professionella bekännelser* (Professional Confessions), where he reflects upon
his career as a writer, discusses his own works, and
emphasizes that he finds his writing a trial-and-error activity
in which it is more usual for him to hit his head against the
labyrinth wall than to find an exit. Even more absurd, and
very typical of the early 1960s in Sweden, is Jersild's first
novel, *Till varmare länder* (To Warmer Climes), involving
an ambulance expedition to Hell in order to save its burns
victims. *Calvinols resa genom världen* (Calvinol's Journey
Through the World) is another fantastic experiment in which
he gives his imagination free rein to depict an adventurer

who never dies. It is a burlesque novel in 13 more or less free-standing chapters, ranging widely in time and international settings, and was described by the author as "an ecstatic writing experience."

The next few years saw the publication of brilliant satirical novels on bureaucracy, society, and the drawbacks of the welfare state which reveal Jersild's outstanding narrative originality. *Grisjakten* (The Pig Hunt) chronicles in diary form the "final solution" by government decree to eradicate all pigs on the island of Gotland in true Nazi fashion, a task given to the perfect bureaucrat and duty-bound civil servant Lennart Siljeberg. Here Jersild made good use of his experiences within a government department, and admitted there were traces of himself in his main character, suggesting there is something of an Auschwitz commandant in all of us. *Djurdoktron* (*The Animal Doctor*), published in 1973 but depicting events in 1988–89, was set far enough in the future to allow new perspectives while being close enough in time for contemporary readers to recognize their own world, increasingly dominated by the computerized state establishment which inevitably crushes the innocent individual. *Barnens ö* (*Children's Island*) chronicles the adventures of 11-year-old Reine, the runaway boy, alone and abandoned in the jungle that is the city of Stockholm: violence, isolation, and the struggle to survive are the dominant features of the world Reine encounters in his search for purity and the meaning of life, and his efforts never to become an adult. *Babels hus* (*The House of Babel*) is perhaps Jersild's most realistic work, describing a huge, fictitious Stockholm hospital and the human problems associated with the public health service machinery; it also serves as a symbol of today's rationalized society and the inherent inability of people to communicate with one another on any level.

Jersild's next two novels come under the heading of science fiction. *En levande själ* (*A Living Soul*), described by the author as "a tale in lab surroundings," is a first-person narrative told by a disembodied human brain, floating in an aquarium and subjected to various experiments. The implications are far-reaching: is this human organ actually a human being, a "living soul," since in spite of everything he is still able to record emotions like love and fear, and to be aware of his personal identity? It is a frightening and pessimistic vision of what medical research and bioengineering might result in when coupled with crass profit-making motives, which decide the experiment is to be terminated: the power supply which keeps the brain alive is abruptly cut off, and the narrative suddenly ceases. *Efter floden* (*After the Flood*) is set 30 years after a nuclear catastrophe has destroyed life on earth, and describes the pitiful human wrecks that still survive, in a fashion, before being finally destroyed by a virus carried ironically by doves. Everything is reduced to the primary need of survival, but here and there are glimpses of what life was like before the unthinkable took place.

The declining culture of late 18th-century Venice is depicted in the fascinating novel *Den femtionde frälsaren* (The Fiftieth Saviour), while the chronicle *Geniernas återkomst* (Return of the Geniuses), a succession of untitled and unconnected narratives, is a history of the evolution of culture and human development, full of variety and inventiveness in its reflections and comments on reality. *Holgerssons* (The Holgerssons) takes Selma Lagerlöf's turn-of-the-century boy hero Nils Holgersson and describes his adventures in more recent Sweden, including the grandiose world takeover plans of his midget offspring, designed to save the earth's resources. Despite the promising subject-matter, most critics felt *Holgerssons* was not one of Jersild's most successful works; at his best, however, he is a significant

writer, dealing with existential problems and social follies, and endowed with a lively imagination and an exceptional aptitude for telling tales.

—Birgitta Thompson

JOHANNESSEN, Matthías (Haraldsson). Icelandic. Born in Reykjavík, 3 January 1930. Educated at the University of Iceland, M.A. in Icelandic literature and philology 1955; University of Copenhagen, 1955–56. Married Jóhanna Kristveig Ingólfsdóttir in 1953; two sons. Journalist, 1952–59, and editor-in-chief, since 1959, *Morgunblaðið*, Reykjavík. Member of the board, since 1972, and chair, since 1985, Cultural Council of Iceland; chair, Society of Icelandic Writers, 1969–70, Union of Icelandic Authors, 1970–72, Committee for 1100 Years of Settlement in Iceland, 1974, and Council of Icelandic Writers, 1976; member, Almenna Bókafélagið literary council. Recipient: Icelandic Language Foundation prize, 1983. Address: Reynimel 25A, Reykjavík, Iceland.

PUBLICATIONS

Verse

Borgin hló [The City Laughed]. Reykjavík, Helgafell, 1958.
Hólmgöngul jóð [Duelling Poems]. Reykjavík, Helgafell, 1960.
Jörð úr ægi [Earth from the Sea]. Reykjavík, Helgafell, 1961.
Vor úr vetri [Spring Follows Winter]. Reykjavík, Helgafell, 1963.
Fagur er dalur [Fair Is the Dale]. Reykjavík, Almenna Bókafélagið, 1966.
Vísur um vötn [Lake Poems]. Reykjavík, Bókaútgáfa Guðjóuð, 1971.
Mörg eru dags augu [Many Are the Eyes of Day]. Reykjavík, Almenna Bókafélagið, 1972.
Dagur ei meir [Day No Longer]. Reykjavík, Almenna Bókafélagið, 1975.
Morgunn í maí [A Morning in May]. Reykjavík, Almenna Bókafélagið, 1978.
Tveggja bakka veður [Uncertain Weather Outlook]. Reykjavík, Almenna Bókafélagið, 1981.
Veður ræður akri [The Weather Rules the Field]. Reykjavík, Bókaútgáfa Guðjóuð, 1981.
Flýgur örn yfir [The Eagle Flies Over]. Reykjavík, Skákprent, 1984.
Three Modern Icelandic Poets. Selected Poems of Steinn Steinarr, Jón úr Vör and Matthías Johannessen, translated by Marshall Brement. Reykjavík, Iceland Review, 1985.
Hólmgónguljóð. Reykjavík, Almenna Bókafélagið, 1985.
Dagur af degi [One Day After Another]. Reykjavík, Almenna Bókafélagið, 1988.
The Naked Machine: Selected Poems. London, Forest, 1988.
Sálmar á atómöld [Psalms for the Atomic Age]. Reykjavík, Almenna Bókafélagið, 1991.
Fuglar og annað fólk [Birds and Others]. Reykjavík, Iðunn, 1991.
'Arstíðaferðum innvi mann. Reykjavík, Iðunn, 1992.

Fiction

Nítján smápættir [19 Small Pieces]. Reykjavík, Þjóðsaga, 1981.
Spunnið um Stalín [Weaving About Stalin]. Published in *Morgunblaðið* (Reykjavík), March-April, 1983.
Konungur af Aragon og aðrar sögur [A King of Aragon and Other Stories]. Reykjavík, Almenna Bókafélagið, 1986.
Sól á heimsenda [The Sun at the World's End]. Reykjavík, Almenna Bókafélagið, 1987.

Plays

Sólmyrkvi [Solar Eclipse]. Reykjavík, Helgafell, 1962.
Jón gamli [Old Jón] (produced Reykjavík, 1967).
Eins og þér sáið [As You See] (produced Reykjavík, 1967).
Fjaðrafok [All in a Flutter] (produced Reykjavík, 1969). Included in *Fjaðrafok og önnur leikrit*, 1975.
Fjaðrafok og önnur leikrit [All in a Flutter and Other Plays]. Reykjavík, GuðjónÓ, 1975.

Radio Plays: *Sókrates*, 1974; *Guðs reiði* [God's Wrath], 1984.

Television Plays: *Jón gamli* [Old Jón], 1964; *Ófelía* [Ophelia]; *Glerbrot* [Broken Glass]; *Sjóarinn* [The Fisherman], 1992.

Other

Njála í íslenzkum skáldskap [*Njáls saga* in Icelandic Poetry]. Reykjavík, Hið íslenzka Bókmenntafélag, 1958.
Í kompaníi við allífið [With the Life Spirit for Company] (interviews), with Þórbergur Þórðarson. Reykjavík, Helgafell, 1959.
Svo kvað Tómas [Thus Spake Tómas]. Reykjavík, Almenna Bókafélagið, 1960.
Hundaþúfan og hafið [The Mound Where the Dogs Go and the Ocean]. Reykjavík, Bókfellsúlgátan, 1961.
Hugleiðingar og viðtöl [Reflections and Interviews]. Reykjavík, Helgafell, 1963.
Í dag skein sól. Reykjavík, Bókfellsútgáfan, 1964.
Kjarvalsker (on the painter Kjarval). Reykjavík, Helgafell, 1968; abridged in English, Helgafell, 1981.
Bókin um Ásmund [On Ásmundur Sveinsson]. Reykjavík, Helgafell, 1971.
Klofningur Sjálfstæðisflokksins gamla [The Split in the Old Independence Party]. Reykjavík, Árvakur, 1971.
Skeggræður gegnum tíðina [Interviews over the Years], with Halldór Laxness. Reykjavík, Helgafell, 1972.
Gunnlaugur Scheving. Reykjavík, Helgafell, 1974.
Sculptor Ásmundur Sveinsson: An Edda in Shapes and Symbols (abridged in English). Reykjavík, Iceland Review, 1974.
Sverrir Haraldsson (editions in Icelandic and English). Reykjavík, Myndamót, 1977.
Samtöl I–V [Conversations I–V]. Reykjavík, Almenna Bókafélagið, 5 vols., 1977–85.
Erró: An Iceland Artist, with Bragi Ásgeirsson. Reykjavík, Iceland Review, 1978.
Ólafur Thors I og II, ævi og störf [The Life and Achievement of Ólafur Thors in Two Volumes]. Reykjavík, Almenna Bókafélagið, 2 vols., 1981.
Kjarval: malari lands og vætta, with Aðalsteini Ingólfssyni. Reykjavík, Iceland Review, 1981; as *Kjarval: A Painter of Iceland*, Iceland Review, 1981.
Félagi Orð: greinar, samtöl og ljóð [Comrade Word: Articles, Conversations, and Poems]. Reykjavík, Þjoðsaga, 1982.

Ferðarispur, ferðalýsingar og ljóð [Travelogues, Travel Accounts, and Poems]. Reykjavík, Almenna Bókafélagið, 1983.
Bókmennta Pættir [Essays on Literature]. Reykjavík, Almenna Bókafélagið, 1985.
Í kompaníi við Þórberg [In Þórbergur's Company]. Reykjavík, Almenna Bókafélagið, 1989.
Veröld Þín [Your World]. Reykjavík, Iðunn, 1989.
Vökunótt fuglsins [The Bird's Vigil]. Reykjavík, Almenna Bókafélagið, 1990.
Ævisaga hugmynda [The Biography of Ideas]. Reykjavík, Iðunn, 1990.
Þjóðfélagið [Society]. Reykjavík, Iðunn, 1992.

*   *   *

Matthías Johannessen has long been one of the foremost literary figures in Iceland. He has been a prolific writer in a number of forms: poetry, fiction, short stories, drama, history, biography, and criticism. He has been a journalist — editor-in-chief of his country's largest daily newspaper (*Morgunblaðið*) — and an academic. Johannessen has always regarded his poetry as his most important work. Icelandic society continues to have a profound familiarity with, and respect for, its great poetic tradition and, although Johannessen is certainly a knowledgeable reader of the foreign (and native) "modernists," his work is deeply rooted in his country's tradition. Johannessen's sensibility, though not his poetic manner, has been nourished by his knowledge of the medieval poetic and prose Eddas, and of the work of such figures as Hallgrímur Pétursson and Jónas Hallgrímsson. A characteristic example is "jörð úr ægi" (Earth from the Sea), aspects of which are a kind of rewriting of elements from the Eddic poem "Völuspá", though there is much in the poetic idiom which is distinctly modern and demotic. This is not to suggest that the interests of Johannessen's work are in any sense merely parochial. His landscapes are often specifically Icelandic, but he "reads" them in religious, moral, and emotional terms which are profound and universal. His allusions may sometimes be rightly those of his own culture, but the emotional intensity they serve guarantees that such references never exclude other readers:

> You
> are the day that vanished
> with our joy into the glacier
> like Helgi Hundingsbane
> with Sigrún's grief into the grave-mound
> . . .
> O you who are as young in my heart
> as the mountains are blue on the heath
> it is long since you came with me to the window
> it is long since we have held hands
> looking at the sun tiptoe along the roof-tops
> creep across the bleeding bay.

At the core of Johannessen's work is a religious vision of the world. He can write very beautifully of the moment at Icelandic twilight when:

> everything becomes alive and the land changes
> into a letter from God and grass and heather
> and water bringing us a message from him.
> . . .
> We see the sky with the dead
> eyes of water.
> Life and Death in one element
> inseparable.

In his "Sálmar á atómöld" (Psalms for the Atomic Age) Johannessen's fierce judgement of much in present-day society and politics is made in the context of a determined affirmation of life's possibilities and a faith in human value. Images of human endurance are located against a sea and sky which belong both to a geographically-real Iceland and to a universal, almost allegorical realm:

> My life is a boat
> leaky from the sun and the long summer.
> And the sea awaits.
>
> With no other choice
> I sail over the sea
> in your name.

Indeed, Johannessen writes especially well of light and its movements, and of the sea, combining precise observation with the articulation of human emotion, as in poems such as "Veglaust haf" (The Trackless Sea) and "Myndspá" (Vision).

Johannessen's essential subjects are the great subjects of poetry — love, mutability, and death. His poetic idiom's basic simplicity finds room for a very real sophistication of mind. At times there is an almost minimalist quality to his work, as in the "fragments" (as he describes them) of "Flýgur örn yfir" (The Eagle Flies Over):

> The mountains are newly shorn,
> it is summer.

or

> White
> transparent
> shadows
> rise
> from the sea
> toward the sky
>
> mountains walk
> unseen
> into the sea-blue
> waters
> of your eyes.

The attempt to develop an argument in the elegiac "Lennon" is perhaps less successful; there is a certain flatness, even banality of statement in places; nor are the explicit political poems of "Erlendar fréttir" (News from Abroad) very convincing. Johannessen is at his most striking and effective when his poetry is at its most visual. Not, of course, that he is ever a merely descriptive poet; but he is a poet whose response to the human condition is inextricably bound up with his response to the natural world, and who is most successful when the two are most completely integrated in his words. At its best Johannessen's is a highly distinctive and rewarding poetic voice.

—Glyn Pursglove

———

JOYAUX, Philippe. *See* **SOLLERS, Philippe.**

———

JUHÁSZ, Ferenc. Hungarian. Born in Bia, 16 August 1928. Educated at Lajos Kossuth Business High School, Budapest, diploma 1946; Attila József College, Budapest, 1948–49; University of Budapest, from 1951. Married in 1948. Worker, French-Hungarian Cotton Factory, Budapest; part-time editor, Szépirodalmi publishing company, from 1951; editor, *Új Írás* [New Writings]. Recipient: Kossuth prize, 1950. Address: c/o Szépirodalmi Kiadó, Lenin Körút 9–11, 1063 Budapest, Hungary.

PUBLICATIONS

Verse

Szárnyas csikó [The Winged Colt]. Budapest, Franklin Könyvkiadó Nemzeti Vállalat, 1949.
Apám [My Father]. Budapest, Szépirodalmi, 1950.
A Sántha család: költemény [The Sántha Family: Poem]. Budapest, Hungária, 1950.
Új versek [New Poems]. Budapest, Szépirodalmi, 1951.
Óda a repüléshez [Ode to Flight]. Budapest, Szépirodalmi, 1953.
A tékolzló ország [The Prodigal Country]. Budapest, Szépirodalmi, 1954.
A virágok hatalma [The Power of Flowers]. Budapest, Magvető, 1955.
A tenyészet országa: összegyűjtött versek 1946–1956 [The Breeding Country]. Budapest, Szépirodalmi, 1956.
Virágzó világfa: válogatott versek [Flowering World Tree]. Budapest, Szépirodalmi, 1965.
A nap és a hold elrablása: verses mesék [Stealing the Sun and the Moon: Fairytales in Verse]. Budapest, Ifjusági, 1965.
Harc a fehér báránnyal [War with the White Lamb]. Budapest, Szépirodalmi, 1965.
A szent tűzözön regéi [Tales of the Sacred Fire]. Budapest, Szépirodalmi, 1969.
Anyám [My Mother]. Budapest, Szépirodalmi, 1969.
Vázlat a mindenségről [Draft of the Universe]. Budapest, Szépirodalmi, 1970.
The Boy Changed into a Stag: Selected Poems 1949–1967, translated by Kenneth McRobbie and Ilona Duczynska. Toronto, New York, and London, Oxford University Press, 1970.
Selected Poems, translated by David Wevill, with *Selected Poems* by Sandor Weöres. London, Penguin, 1970.
A mindenség szerelme: összegyűjtott versek, 1946–1970 [The Love of Humanity: Collected Poems, 1946–1970). Budapest, Szépirodalmi, 2 vols., 1971–72.
A halottak királya [The King of the Dead]. Budapest, Szépirodalmi, 1971.
A megváltó aranykard [The Redeeming Golden Sword]. Budapest, Szépirodalmi, 1973.
Három éposz [Three Epic Poems]. Budapest, Szépirodalmi, 1975.
Versek és époszok [Poems and Epic Poems] (includes prose). Budapest, Szépirodalmi, 1978.
Művei [Works]. Budapest, Szépirodalmi, 3 vols., 1978.
Csikóellés. Budapest, Móra, 1978.
Remény a halálig: 35 vers [Hope Until Death: 35 Poems]. Budapest, Szépirodalmi, 1983.
A boldogság: új versek [Happiness: New Poems]. Budapest, Szépirodalmi, 1984.
Halott feketerigó [The Dead Blackbird]. Budapest, Szépirodalmi, 1985.
A csörgőkigyó hőszeme [The Glowing Eye of the Rattlesnake]. Budapest, Szépirodalmi, 1987.

Fekete saskirály [Black Eagle King]. Budapest, Szépirodalmi, 1988.
A hazatérő halott [Return of the Dead]. Békéscsaba, Új Aurora, 1988.
A tizmilliárd éves sziv [10-Billion-Year-Old Heart]. Budapest, Szépirodalmi, 1989.

Other

Panelos építési mód: munkások, művezetők számára [Building Methods for Blocks of Flats: For Builders and Site Foremen], with Mihály Rikker. Budapest, Építésügyi Dok. Iroda, 1965.
A motiváció szerepe a nevelésben [The Role of Motivation in Education]. Budapest, Tankönyvkiadó, 1967.
Mit tehet a költő? [What Can the Poet Do?]. Budapest, Szépirodalmi, 1967.
Irás egy jövendő őskoponyán [Writing on a Future Ancient Skull]. Budapest, Szépirodalmi, 1974.
Szerelmes hazatántorgás [Staggering Home in Love]. Budapest, Szépirodalmi, 1977.
Veszprém, with Emil Balogh and Tibor Berki. Budapest, Kossuth, 1983.

Editor, *A teremtett világ* [The Created World], by István Vas. Budapest, Magvető, 1956.
Editor, *Munka és szerelem* [Work and Love], by Ferenc Kis. Budapest, Szépirodalmi, 1974.
Editor, with Béla Pomogáts, *Mai magyar költők antológiája* [An Anthology of Contemporary Hungarian Poets]. Budapest, Kozmosz, 1974.

*

Critical Studies: "Two Hungarian Poets" by George Gömöri, in *Mosaic* (Winnipeg, Manitoba), 5(1), 1971; "Ferenc Juhász at 50" by László Ferenczi, in *New Hungarian Quarterly* (Budapest), Summer 1979; "Beyond Nature with a Human Face? Ferenc Juhász's 'Homage to Karl Marx'" by Kenneth McRobbie, in *Canadian Slavonic Papers* (Edmonton, Alberta), 23(3), 1981.

* * *

Some of Ferenc Juhász's first work was passionate in its enthusiasm for the communist régime, pedantic in its adherence to the canons of social realism. Disenchantment was first powerfully expressed in his mock-epic of 1951, "A jégvirág kakasa" (The Frost Flower's Cockerel). His work thereafter took a new direction; he became a hymnist of individuality, and his work increasingly addressed itself to the perennial poetic subjects of Love and Death, rather than Collective Farms and Economic Plans or, indeed, the tractor (as in *Szárnyas csikó* [The Winged Colt]). He developed an idiom which while superficially subjective was in fact deeply rooted in myth and the archetypal. For Juhász, to write about oneself is to write about one's past; to write about one's past is to write about one's family, and that, in turn, is to write about the identity of one's nation and, indeed, of one's species.

Juhász writes of his childhood in prose both passionate and exquisite. Prose poems such as "Brief Confessions About Myself" and, especially striking, "At Childhood's Table" are remarkable for their evocation of people and things, for the richness of their metaphorical invention, and for the almost visionary intensity of their self-awareness. So Juhász and other youngsters making their way to school are presented thus:

In the ice-crunching, white covered winter dawn, yellow rock-bulb moon's halo-ribbon tied around space, we used to trudge along with frosty faces, iced nostril-hairs, ice-straw eye-brows, breathing out white tongues of vapour like the damned. Above us the transparent corpse of dissected space sprawled from the world-island out to islands of other substances: wrenched-apart joints, bone growths, glimmering muscle-clusters, weary muscle-ribbons, ribs, steaming viscera, withered blue heart-valve shells, and the huge brain's yellow rind in the blood-rimmed skull-cavity, beside the sawn-off skull's top: moon with phosphorescent convolutions.

The juxtaposition of the everyday and "unpoetic" (nostril-hairs, for example), with the cosmic ("the transparent corpse of dissected space") is a characteristic effect.

The bonds of family similarly underlie "The Boy Changed into a Stag Cries Out at the Gate of Secrets," not unreasonably described by W. H. Auden as "one of the greatest poems written in my time" (in his Foreword to *The Plough and the Pen*, 1963). Juhász's power in the creation of the "mythical" is at its most powerful here, in a lyrical quasi-narrative of developing individualisation, of home and mother, and of the father's death. Much in the poem is directly autobiographical, but all is universalised, achieving the power of dream and myth in the finished text:

There he stood on the renewing crags of time,
stood on the ringed summit of the sublime
universe, there stood the boy at the gate of secrets,
his antler prongs were playing with the stars,
with a stag's voice down the world's lost paths
he called back to his life-giving mother:
    mother, my mother, I cannot go back,
pure gold seethes in my hundred wounds,
day by day a hundred bullets knock me from my feet
and day by day I rise again, a hundred times more complete,
. . .
each branch of my antlers is a dual-based pylon,
each prong of my antlers a high-tension wire,
. . .
each of my cells is a factory, my arms are solar systems
sun and moon swing in my testicles, the Milky Way is my
    bone marrow,
each point in space is one part of my body,
my brain's impulse is out in the curling galaxies.

Consciousness is the exclusive human privilege — and burden. However much a man is in contact with "nature" he remains apart from it; "as a man I am removed,/set apart from dews/or Pleiades" ("Farm, at Dark, on the great Plain"); "Plant cannot guess — nor planet — the knowledge a human bears" he declares in the same poem. The poet's role is to articulate that consciousness to be the "web of life's nervous system" ("The Grave of Attila József"). All men are lonely; all men are part of the same community. In the seeming paradox lies much of Juhász's vision, and much of his poetry is rooted in the exploration of that paradox. So too his poetry is driven by the perception he expresses as a kind of credo: "I believe in death and I do not believe in annihilation" ("At Childhood's Table"). Poetry is a form of social memory, and a means of dialogue with the dead themselves. The sense of human mortality is never far from the surface of Juhász's work; it is no surprise that a poet who writes so frequently of both childhood and death should be an admirer of Dylan Thomas.

Juhász is a sophisticated individual. His work makes extensive use of scientific imagery, he has travelled extensively, and he has worked as a literary editor and a publisher's reader. As a poet, however, his achievement is inseparable from his intuitive closeness to the traditions of the Hungarian people. This is expressed in the use of both traditional forms in some poems (e.g., "The Foaling Time") and subtle reworkings of motifs from folklore. It is not unreasonable that Juhász should more than once have been compared with Béla Bartók (by András Diószegi and by A. Alvarez, for example). In both one sees a consummate fusion of the sophisticated and the "naïve," the learned and the "primitive," the individual and the traditional, so handled that the quintessentially national becomes of international significance.

—Glyn Pursglove

K

KAHANA-CARMON, Amalia. Israeli. Born in Ein Harod, Palestine (now Israel), in 1930. Educated at the School of Librarianship, Hebrew University, Jerusalem, B.A. in literature and librarianship. Served in the Negev Brigade during the Israeli War of Independence, 1948. Married Aryeh Carmon in 1951; one daughter and two sons. Assistant to the Military Attaché, then worked for the BBC, London, 1950; lived in West Germany, 1951–58; librarian, Tel Aviv University Central Library; chief librarian, Israeli Petroleum Institute; guest writer, Tel Aviv University, 1974–75, and Oxford Centre for Post-Graduate Hebrew Study, 1978–79; participated in International Writers Program, University of Iowa, Iowa City; lectured at many U.S. universities. Member of executive board, Hebrew Writers' Association, 1977–79, 1982–84. Recipient: Ammot award, 1964; B'nai B'rith award for librarianship, 1964; baMachaneh writer of the year, 1964–65; S. D. Steinberg award (Zurich), 1967; Prime Minister's creative writing award, 1971; Aricha award, 1981; Brenner prize, 1985. Address: 12 Zlochisty Street, Tel Aviv 62994, Israel.

PUBLICATIONS

Fiction

Bichefifah achat [Under One Roof]. Tel Aviv, Shomer haTsa'ir, 1966.
Veyareyach be'emek Ayalon [And Moon in the Valley of Ayalon]. Tel Aviv, Hakibuts haMe'uchad, 1971.
Sadot magnetiyim [Magnetic Fields]. Tel Aviv, Hakibuts haMe'uchad, 1977.
Lema'alah beMontifer [Up in Montifer]. Tel Aviv, Hakibuts haMe'uchad, 1984.
Liviti otah baderech leveytah [I Accompanied Her Home]. Tel Aviv, Hakibuts haMe'uchad, 1991.

Play

Ket'a lebamah beta'am hasignon hagadol [A Piece for the Stage in the Grand Manner]. 1976.

*

Critical Studies: "Amalia Kahana-Carmon and the Plot of the Unspoken" by Leon I. Yudkin, in his 1948 and After: Aspects of Israeli Fiction, Manchester, University of Manchester Press, 1984; "Gynographic Re-Visions: Amalia Kahana-Carmon" and "Self-Conscious Heroism: And Moon in the Valley of Ayalon," in her Israeli Mythogynies: Women in Contemporary Hebrew Fiction, Albany, State University of New York Press, 1987, and "Amalia Kahana-Carmon and Contemporary Hebrew Women's Fiction," in Signs (Durham, North Carolina), 13(2), 1988, all by Esther Fuchs; "A Re-Reading: 'First Axioms': A Writer's Attempt at Self-Definition" by Sonia Grober, in Modern Hebrew Literature (Ramat-Gan, Israel), 13(3–4), 1988.

*   *   *

Already in her first published volume, a collection of stories, Bichefifah achat (Under One Roof), Amalia Kahana-Carmon marked out for herself a distinctive mode in Israeli fiction, deviating sharply from the norms then prevalent. The authorial voice is mature and decisive, relating primarily to the emotional life of the self and to the contact and romantic attraction between individuals. This attraction is seen as ungraspable, perhaps irrational and even mystical, but still more significant than any other human emotion invoked in her writing. Little social, political, or historical context emerges — not much that is overtly or quintessentially Israeli. The language of the stories is condensed, intricate, and elliptical. Sentences are short, and the phraseology alludes little to classical Hebrew sources. The narratives here explore the relationships and feelings of narrator or subject with a growing intensity, often highlighting the disjunction between such feelings and objective reality. The person to whom such feeling attaches may be totally unaware of what is happening. Such an infatuation is always modified by the narrative irony of an alternative voice; the commentator remains behind or at the side of the action. The implied question is — what is the true reality? Is it the subject's version of the inner event, or is it another version, that attaching to the object of attention and description?

In Kahana-Carmon's subsequent work, the novel Veyareyach be'emek Ayalon (And Moon in the Valley of Ayalon), material from an earlier short story here becomes part of the extended, on-going narrative. The third-person account of Mrs. Talmor now incorporates this first-person account from an earlier phase of her life. So we see her both within and from without, sometimes wavering between accounts appropriate to the limited focus of a single character on the one hand, or those within the province of the omniscient narrator on the other. The novel contrasts the hopes of youth, the sense of limitless possibilities, with the resignation, sobriety, and disappointments of middle age. The novel's unusual title is taken from Joshua 10:12, and refers to the stopping of the sun and moon in their tracks in order to give time to the Israelites to overcome the Amorites within the space of a single day. Events, specifically romantic attachments, once to her husband Asher (from the youth section) and now to the visiting Philip, are unrepeatable and evanescent. The source of the attraction is mysterious; Philip, for example, is the "messenger from the regions of brightness." But Mrs. Talmor also recognizes the inevitable disappointment that will follow. Her story, as the conclusion of the novel indicates, is incomplete.

The overall title of the triptych Sadot magnetiyim (Magnetic Fields) in itself presents the author's concern with the attraction between man and woman. The metaphor is suggestive of the observable truth that this attraction is neither consistent nor predictable. These magnetic fields delimit the range of the two individual paths. As often as not, Kahana-Carmon describes the encounter from the male point of view, as in the main unit of the triptych, "Sham hadar hahadashot" (The Newsroom Is over There). In this case, the American girl Wendy argues that the two lovers exist in two separate fields. As they are not magnetically held, they must part.

Kahana-Carmon explores themes of attraction, support, and dependence in her later work, *Lema'alah beMontifer* (Up in Montifer) and in *Liviti otah baderech leveytah* (I Accompanied Her Home). In the first, the main section has a mediaeval setting, so the archaic language favoured by the author seems ever more appropriate. The narrator is a Jewess, subject to the Christian Peter, previously a torture victim but now ruminating her fate and her relationship to the master, who has free access to Montifer. Her own account of the past and present situation is both realistic and masochistic. The other stories in the volume have a contemporary setting, and again deal with the nature of male/female relationships. The two see this relationship differently, but it is part of the author's art to get the characters to articulate this nature, and so spell out the difference. She wants him very much, but, for him, she is a passing interlude. Her view is that her attitude must be articulated, even if "life" mitigates against this stance. Attraction between the sexes involves clash of sexes, and the material of the stories is the nature of this meeting as transcribed.

This sort of analysis is continued in *Liviti otah baderech leveytah*, although here all disguises and wrappings have been replaced by a transparent and contemporary review of a relationship. Again we have two points of view, and, again, the inevitable clash of views, attitudes, postures, and levels of attachment. Kahana-Carmon seems to have moved further away from fiction into a prosaic reconstruction of an affair, with its necessarily attendant bitterness and recrimination. But the level of craftsmanship has been reduced.

Kahana-Carmon's work is path-breaking in Israeli narrative, for its close analysis of relationships and for its condensed yet metaphorical and unusual language. This strength is also its limitation, and may indeed be the product of such contraction of theme and view. It is this limited focus that has to be treated with circumspection, wit, and depth.

—Leon I. Yudkin

———

KAMLESHWAR. *See* **KAMLEŚVAR.**

———

KAMLEŚVAR. Also Kamleshwar. Indian. Born in Mainpuri, 6 January 1932. Educated to M.A. Married to Gayatri; one daughter. Has worked for Indian television since 1960; director-general for television, New Delhi, 1980–82. Associate editor, *Kuhānī*, editor, *Naī Kajuanīyā*, 1963–66, *Sarika*, 1967–78, and *Ingit, Naī Dhārā, Srī Varṣā,* and *Kathāyātrā.* Address: 28 Parag Apartments, Jayaprakash Road, Versova, Bombay 400061, India.

PUBLICATIONS

Fiction

Rājā nirbansiyā [The Issueless King]. New Delhi, Hind Pocket Books, 1957.

Kasbe kā ādmī [Small-Town Man]. New Delhi, Rājkamal, 1957.
Lauṭte hue musāfir [Travellers on the Way Home]. New Delhi, Hind Pocket Books, 1957.
Ḍāk bungalow. New Delhi, Rājkamal, 1961.
Tīsrā ādmī [The Third Man]. New Delhi, Hind Pocket Books, n.d.
Khoyī huī diśaē [Lost Directions]. Benares, Bhārtīy Jñānpīṭh, 1963.
Śreṣṭha kahāniyā [Best Stories], edited by Rājendra Yādav. New Delhi, Rājpāl & Sons, 1964.
Mās kā dariyā [The River of Flesh]. New Delhi, Akṣar, 1966.
Badnām galī. New Delhi, Pañjābī Pustak Bhaṇḍār, 1968; as *The Defamed Alley*, New Delhi, India Paperbacks, 1977.
Samudra mē khoyā huā ādmī [A Man Lost in the Sea]. Allahabad, Rām Nārāyaṇ Lāl Benīprasād, 1969.
Zindā murde [The Living Dead]. New Delhi, Rājpāl & Sons, 1970.
Merī priy kahāniyā [My Favourite Short Stories]. New Delhi, Rājpāl & Sons, 1972.
Bayān tathā anya kahāniyā [A Statement and Other Stories]. Allahabad, Lokbhārtī, 1972.
Kālī ādhī [Black Storm]. New Delhi, Rājpāl & Sons, 1974.
Āgāmī atīt [The Forthcoming Past]. New Delhi, Śabdākar, 1976.
Kamleśvar kī śreṣṭh kahāniyā [Great Short Stories of Kamleśvar]. New Delhi, Parāg, 1976.
Summer Days. New Delhi, Himalaya, 1977.
Ek saṛak sattāvan galiyā [One Road and 57 Lanes]. New Delhi, Rājpāl & Sons, 1979.
Vahī bāt [The Same Talk]. New Delhi, Śabdākar, 1980.
Jārj Pañcam kī nāk [George V's Nose]. New Delhi, Rājpāl & Sons, 1985.
Itne acche din [Such Pleasant Days]. New Delhi, Rājpāl & Sons, 1989.

Plays

Adhūrī āvāz [The Incomplete Voice]. New Delhi, Ātmarām & Sons, 1962.
Lahar lauṭ ā gaī [The Wave Has Come Back]. New Delhi, Rājpāl & Sons, 1985.

Other

Nāṭakkār Aśk [Ask the Playwright], with Gopāl Kṛṣṇa Kaul. Allahabad, Nīlābh, 1954.
Nayī kahānī kī bhūmikā [Introduction to the New Short Story]. New Delhi, Akṣar, 1966.
Merā pannā [My Page]. New Delhi, Śabdākar, 1978.
Gardiś ke din [Hard Times]. New Delhi, Rājpāl, 1980.
Apnī nigāh mē [In My Own View]. New Delhi, Śabdākar, 1982.
Subah-dopahar-śām [Morning, Afternoon, Night]. New Delhi, Rājpāl & Sons, 1982?
Uske bad [After That] (film script). New Delhi, Rājpāl & Sons, 1986.
Registān [Desert]. New Delhi, Rājpāl & Sons, 1988.

Editor, *Samāntar* [Parallels] (short stories). Allahabad, Lokbhārtī Prakāśan, 1972.

Has translated works by Rabindranath Tagore and Bertolt Brecht.

*   *   *

Kamleśvar began writing in the 1950s and holds a place of eminence in Hindi literature, having distinguished himself as a writer of short stories, novels, and essays. He has published five collections of short stories and five novels so far. Several of his short stories have been filmed.

For Kamleśvar the story is a living experience. His characters, who belong to the lower middle class of north Indian society, are products of a complex culture, constantly facing the realities of a society in transition. He narrates their experiences in a matter-of-fact way, without offering explanations, theories, or solutions of his own. He takes them through the struggles, sufferings, and humdrum events of the world they live in. They face the world and do not run away. Yet his characters do not rebel against the values of their society, nor do they hanker after an ideal.

Kamleśvar was the first editor of the Hindi magazine *Naī Kahāniyā̃*, which served as a mouthpiece for the "new story" movement of the same name that began in the 1960s. The writers of this school reject the past; instead they place the individual in the context of the changing ethos of post-independence India. On the one hand they find that a whole new world is waiting to be explored; on the other they see the disintegration of contemporary Indian society, where the centrality of the individual has become untenable in the face of nagging social problems.

For Kamleśvar, as he himself puts it, "A glorious past is dying like a dog. Emerging from it is an incomprehensible present standing face to face in nameless, unprotected, primordial form . . . and man is standing in the midst of all this, is crying out for his language, faith, his mental and material world . . ."

Like other short-story writers of this movement, Kamleśvar's sensibility reacts more and more acutely to the throb of complex Indian social and material life all around him, full of anxiety and apprehension. Kamleśvar successfully penetrates deeper into the life of his characters to identify the elements that cause the anxiety and apprehension.

Kamleśvar's writing confirms the general view that the Indian lower middle class is defeated and repressed by its own false sense of dignity and imaginary responsibilities, combined with economic deficiency. In this particular class man is often lonely and helpless, his identity overshadowed by nagging elements such as financial strain, social tensions, loneliness, estrangement, urban anonymity, bureaucratic indifference, and general loss or absence of individual personality.

The preference for rural life over the hustle and bustle of urban life is an old theme of Hindi writers. In the 1960s the alienation and loneliness was more noticeable when writers began to portray the individual lost in big cities. Kamleśvar highlights these problems in various ways in several of his stories. In "Fāltū ādmī" (The Disposable Man), the man is an exiled self — a man left alone in the alien world, with no hope, no faith, no future. For such a man the ultimate escape from his fate is his transcendence to God. But God is dead. In "The Alien City" Kamleśvar writes:

Whenever any festival draws near, Sukh Bir begins to feel restless. It's fifteen years now since he started living in Delhi, yet he does not feel that he belongs to the place, he just cannot call it his own . . . and who does? Talk to anyone, and he will begin to remember his own town or village, and an alien look will come into his eyes.

The problem of poverty is also an inexhaustible topic for Hindi writers. In "Rājā nirbansia" (The King with No Progeny), Kamleśvar highlights how economic factors can create conjugal tensions in an ordinary lower-middle-class man. The story brings out the effect of poverty, showing a man so degenerated that he helplessly accepts his wife's pregnancy by another man.

Kamleśvar's treatment of love and sex highlights the alienation of his characters. In "Khoī huī dis'āē" (Lost Directions), for example, his characters are lonely even after making love:

Chandra looks at Nirmala lying lazily at his side. He again starts feeling lonely . . . terribly lonely. Keeping his hands on her shoulders he wants her to turn towards him, but finds that his fingers don't work. For a few moments he keeps watching her in the dark, greatly dismayed, and doesn't know when he, too, falls asleep.

But Kamleśvar's stories are generally not a reaction against the earlier romantic, nationalist, or Marxist type of story. In his works the hero is nameless and his background and surroundings, expressed in short, simple, and sometimes humorous sentences, are snapshots of social realities, often lacking the perspective which could penetrate much deeper and raise the wider question of human destinies.

Among his novels *Kālī ādhī* (Black Storm) stands out as it unmasks the dark face of the dehumanised politics of India. Kamleśvar shows that the world's largest democracy suffers contradictions and delusions, particularly at the time of general elections.

Kamleśvar's writing is a mirror of a complex and changing society.

—Satyendra Śrīvāstava

KEMAL, Yaşar (Yaşar Kemal Gökçeli). Also Yashar Kemal. Turkish. Born in Adana, in autumn 1922. Educated at schools in Kadirli. Married Thilda Serrero in 1952; one son. Worked as farmhand, cobbler's apprentice, construction worker, clerk, and petition writer in southern Turkey; reporter, *Cumhuriyet* newspaper, Istanbul, 1951–63; then full-time writer. Editor, *Ant* Marxist weekly, in 1960s; on Central Committee of Turkish Labour Party; arrested and tried for Communist propaganda, 1950, and imprisoned briefly for political views, 1971. Former president, Turkish Writers Union. Recipient: Varlik prize, 1956; Iskender award, 1966; International Theatre Festival prize (Nancy), 1966; Madarali award, 1973; Foreign book prize (France), 1979; Cino del Duca prize (France), 1982; Simavi Foundation award, 1985. Honorary doctorate: University of Strasbourg, 1991. Commandeur, Légion d'Honneur, 1984. Address: P.K. 14, Basınköy, Istanbul 34820, Turkey.

PUBLICATIONS

Fiction

Sari sicak [Yellow Heat].   Istanbul, Varlĭk, 1952.
Ince Memed.   Istanbul, Remzi, 1955; as *Memed, My Hawk*, New York, Pantheon, and London, Collins, 1961.
Teneke [The Drumming-Out].   Istanbul, Varlĭk, 1955.
Ortadirek.   Istanbul, Remzi, 1960; as *The Wind from the Plain*, London, Collins, 1963; New York, Dodd Mead, 1969.

Yer demir, gök bakir.   Istanbul, Guven, 1963; as *Iron Earth, Copper Sky*, London, Collins, 1974; New York, Morrow, 1979.

Üç Anadolu efsanesi [Three Anatolian Legends].   Istanbul, Ararat, 1967.

Bütün hikâyeler.   Istanbul, Ararat, 1967; translated in part as *Anatolian Tales*, London, Collins, 1968; New York, Dodd Mead, 1969.

Ince Memed II.   Istanbul, Ant, 1969; as *They Burn the Thistles*, London, Collins, 1973; New York, Morrow, 1977.

Ölmez otu.   Istanbul, Ant, 1969; as *The Undying Grass*, London, Collins, 1977; New York, Morrow, 1978.

Ağridaği efsanesi.   Istanbul, Cem, 1970; as *The Legend of Ararat*, London, Collins, 1975.

Binboğalar efsanesi.   Istanbul, Cem, 1971; as *The Legend of the Thousand Bulls*, London, Collins, 1976.

Çakircali efe [The Bandit Çakircali].   Istanbul, Ararat, 1972.

Akçasazin Ağalari [The Lords of Akchasaz]:
1. *Demirciler çarşisi cinayeti.*   Istanbul, Cem, 1974; as *Murder in the Ironsmiths Market*, London, Collins, 1979; New York, Morrow, 1980.
2. *Yusufçuk Yusuf* [Yusuf, Little Yusuf].   Istanbul, Cem, 1975.

Yilani Öldürseler.   Istanbul, Cem, 1976; as *To Crush the Serpent*, London, Collins Harvill, 1991.

Al gözüm seyreyle salih.   Istanbul, Cem, 1976; as *The Saga of a Seagull*, London, Collins, 1981; as *Seagull*, New York, Pantheon, 1981.

Kuşlar da gitti.   Istanbul, Milliyet, 1978; as *The Birds Have Also Gone*, London, Collins Harvill, 1987.

Deniz küstü.   Istanbul, Milliyet, 1978; as *The Sea-Crossed Fisherman*, London, Collins Harvill, and New York, Braziller, 1985.

Kimsecik [A Little Nobody].   Istanbul, Tekin, 1980.

Hüyükteki nar ağaci [Pomegranate on the Knoll].   Istanbul, Toros, 1982.

Ince Memed III.   Istanbul, Toros, 1984.

Kale kapısı [The Castle Gate].   Istanbul, Toros, 1985.

Ince Memed IV.   Istanbul, Toros, 1987.

Kanın sesi [The Voice of Blood].   Istanbul, Toros, 1991.

Plays

Teneke [The Drumming-Out], from his own novel (produced Istanbul, 1965).

Yer demir, gök bakir [Iron Earth, Copper Sky], from his own novel (produced Nancy, 1966; Istanbul, 1967).

Other

Yanan ormanlarda elli gün [50 Days in Burning Forests].   Istanbul, Türkiye Ormancilar Cemiyeti, 1955.

Çukurova yana yana [Chukurova Up in Flames].   Istanbul, Yeditepe, 1955.

Peri bacalari [Fairy Chimneys].   Istanbul, Varlïk, 1957.

Tas çatlasa [The Stones Cry Out].   Istanbul, Atac, 1961.

Bu diyar baştan başa [This Country from Top to Bottom].   Istanbul, Cem, 1972.

Bir bulut kayniyor [A Cloud Is Churning].   Istanbul, Cem, 1974.

Baldaki tuz [Salt in the Honey].   Istanbul, Cem, 1974.

Filler sultani ile kirmizi sakalli topal karinca [The Sultan of the Elephants and the Red-Bearded Lame Ant].   Istanbul, Cem, 1977.

Allahin askerleri [God's Soldiers].   Istanbul, Milliyet, 1978.

Ağacin çürüğü [Dry Rot in the Tree].   Istanbul, Milliyet, 1980.

*

Critical Studies: Kemal issue of *Edebiyat: A Journal of Middle Eastern Literatures* (Philadelphia), 5(1–2), 1980.

*   *   *

"Traditionally and temperamentally," Yaşar Kemal (Yashar Kemal) wrote in the early 1970s, "I feel drawn to the art of Homer and Cervantes." Although it is difficult to detect any links between him and Miguel de Cervantes, an imaginative critic can divine Kemal's aspiration to create a modern saga in the spirit of the Homeric epic. Aspects of his fiction invite comparison with Leo Tolstoi, Thomas Hardy, John Steinbeck, Ignazio Silone, and William Faulkner. Kemal himself has often paid tribute to "Father Faulkner," drawing analogies between Yoknapatawpha County and his own Chukurova, the fertile plains of southern Turkey where the dramatic events of most of Kemal's major novels take place.

Frequently mentioned as a candidate for the Nobel prize for literature, Kemal enjoys immense popularity in Turkey. He has been extensively translated into all major and some minor languages (his first novel, *Ince Memed* [*Memed, My Hawk*], is available in no less than 25 languages). Particularly in France, the Scandinavian countries, and many Socialist nations, his works have drawn critical praise and achieved wide circulation.

Kemal's youthful literary interests were moulded by poetry and oral narrative. His first publication was a collection of elegies from southern Turkey, and his earliest writings that brought him to national attention were short vivid journalistic pieces published in the influential daily *Cumhuriyet*. His early predilections are discernible in his fiction in many refined and compelling ways: the narrative style has a strong affinity to the Turkish oral tradition and a penchant for poetic devices, often dominated by an elegiac tone. Many of the scenes are suffused with the heightened effects that had characterized the author's early journalistic writing — sharp focus on events and characters, an unmistaking ear for rhythms of speech, and a masterful description of locale and action.

Memed, My Hawk (made into a film by Peter Ustinov) is an action-filled novel about a brigand who becomes a folk hero by taking up arms against the exploiters of the poor. This novel, and virtually all the other works of fiction Kemal published until the mid-1970s, are among the masterworks of Turkey's so-called "Village Literature," which depicts the plight of peasants living in abject poverty in the grip of a feudal system. His second novel, *Ortadirek* (*The Wind from the Plain*), although less popular than *Memed, My Hawk*, is likely to endure as the author's best. Compared by some critics to Steinbeck's *Grapes of Wrath*, it is a moving saga of destitute peasants trudging along in search of work. The trilogy comprising *The Wind from the Plain*, *Yer demir, gök bakir* (*Iron Earth, Copper Sky*), and *Ölmez otu* (*The Undying Grass*) represents the zenith of Kemal's achievement and has somewhat overshadowed his other multi-volume novels as well as his fiction about coastal towns and city life since the mid-1970s.

Kemal's later novels display a stronger reliance on the lyrical style and stream-of-consciousness techniques and a tendency to blend realistic depictions with myth and fantasy. In some, sprawling narration tends to lose the power that characterizes his earlier crisp style. The storylines, however, are less involuted and cumbersome. Psychological portrayals have become far more powerful, introspective, and in some cases profound. In his fifties, Kemal began to shift his locale from rural villages into the urban areas, from rural society exposed to inner worlds unfurled, from the received tradition of legends to his own creation of mythic reality. Certainly, volumes II, III, and IV of *Ince Memed* sustain the hallmarks of Kemal's early novelistic art and as such appear conventional. Much of his fiction since the 1970s, principally *Al gözüm seyreyle salih* (*The Saga of a Seagull*), *Kuşlar da gitti* (*The Birds Have Also Gone*), and *Deniz Küstü* (*The Sea-Crossed Fisherman*), and *Kimsecik* (*A Little Nobody*), contain new dimensions of Kemal's tragic vision, blend of realism and myth, interplays of superstition and gossip, flashback techniques, and human conflict. His ideology now tends to express itself in less combative terms although the central drama in his narratives continues to be exploitation and socio-economic injustice. His late work has introduced two new emphases: one is cultural, in which he faults entrenched traditions and reactionary beliefs as a major deterrent to dignified life. The other is ecological, whereby he identifies pollution as a heinous threat against life itself.

Raymond Williams describes Kemal as a prime example of a novelist of social change. In an intensely personal formulation, Kemal unfurls, almost in poetic terms, the harsh reality of the countryside, with its beauties and brutalities, with its myths and passions. His entire work stands as an indictment of an archaic, unjust system and reaffirms his faith and optimism in the eventual triumph of the human spirit.

—Talat S. Halman

———

KHĀN, Muhammad. *See* **HUSSEIN, Abdullāh.**

———

KIRSCH, Sarah. German. Born Ingrid Bernstein in Limlingerode, 16 April 1935. Educated at the University of Halle, diploma in biology 1959; Literaturinstitut, Leipzig; R. Becher Institute for Literature, 1963–65. Married Rainer Kirsch in 1958 (some sources say 1960) (divorced 1968 [some sources say 1966]); one son (by Karl Mickel). Expelled from Socialist Unity party and Writers Union, 1976, as a result of protesting the revocation of GDR citizenship of Wolf Biermann (*q.v.*); left East Germany for West Berlin, 1977; travelled to Italy, France, and the United States. Lives in Schleswig-Holstein. Recipient: Heine prize, 1973; Petrarca prize, 1976; Villa Massima grant; Austrian Critics' prize, 1981; Gandersheim prize, 1983; Hölderlin prize, 1984; Gold Medal, Literature prize, 1986; Schleswig-Holstein art prize, 1987; City of Mainz prize, 1988. Address: c/o Deutsche Verlags-Anstalt, Neckarstraße 121–125, 7000 Stuttgart 1, Germany.

PUBLICATIONS

Verse

Gespräch mit dem Saurier, with Rainer Kirsch. Berlin, Neues Leben, 1965.
Gedichte. Leipzig, Reclam, 1967.

Landaufenthalt. Berlin, Aufbau, 1967; revised edition, as *Gedichte*, Ebenhausen, Langewiesche-Brandt, 1969.
Zaubersprüche. Berlin, Aufbau, 1973.
Es war dieser merkwürdige Sommer: Gedichte. Berlin, Berliner Handpresse, 1974.
Rückenwind. Berlin, Aufbau, 1976.
Musik auf dem Wasser. Leipzig, Reclam, 1977.
Katzenkopfpflaster. Munich, Deutscher Taschenbuch, 1978.
Wintergedichte: Poetsiche Wandzeitung. Ebenhausen, Langewiesche-Brandt, 1978.
Sommergedichte: Poetische Wandzeitung. Ebenhausen, Langewiesche-Brandt, 1978.
Drachensteigen: vierzig neue Gedichte. Ebenhausen, Langewiesche-Brandt, 1979.
Papiersterne: 15 Lieder für Mezzosopran und Klavier, music by Wolfgang von Schweinitz. Stuttgart, Deutsche Verlags-Anstalt, 1981.
Erdreich. Stuttgart, Deutsche Verlags-Anstalt, 1982.
Poems, translated by Jack Hirschman. Santa Cruz, California, Alcatraz, 1983.
Der Winter. Hauzenberg, Pongratz, 1983.
Katzenleben. Stuttgart, Deutsche Verlags-Anstalt, 1984.
Mädchen, pfeif auf den Prinzen!, with Günter Grass. Cologne, Diederichs, 1984.
Hundert Gedichte. Ebenhausen, Langewiesche-Brandt, 1985.
Landwege: Eine Auswahl, 1980–1985. Stuttgart, Deutsche Verlags-Anstalt, 1985.
Conjurations: The Poems of Sarah Kirsch, translated by Wayne Kvam. Athens, Ohio University Press, 1985.
Three Contemporary German Poets: Wolf Biermann, Sarah Kirsch, Reiner Kunze, edited by Peter J. Graves. Leicester, Leicester University Press, 1985.
Luft und Wasser, with Ingo Kühl. Göttingen, Steidl, 1988.
Schneewärme. Stuttgart, Deutsche Verlags-Anstalt, 1989.
Tiger im Regen, with Song Hyun-Sook. Ravensburg, Ravensburger Buchverlag, 1990.
The Brontës Hats, translated by Wendy Mulford and Anthony Vivis. Cambridge, Street, 1991.

Fiction

Die Pantherfrau: 5 unfrisierte Erzählungen aus dem Kassetten-Recorder. Berlin, Aufbau, 1973; as *Die Pantherfrau: 5 Frauen in der DDR*, Reinbek, Rowohlt, 1978; as *The Panther Woman*, Lincoln, University of Nebraska Press, 1989.
Die ungeheuren bergehohen Wellen auf See. Berlin, Eulenspiegel, 1973.
Spreu. Göttingen, Steidl, 1991.
Schwingrasen. Stuttgart, Deutsche Verlags-Anstalt, 1991.

Play

Die Betrunkene — Der Stärkste (radio play), with Rainer Kirch. Berlin, Staatliches Rundfunkkomitee, 1963.

Other

Berlin-Sonnenseite: Deutschlandtreffen der Jugend in der Hauptstadt der DDR Berlin, with Rainer Kirsch. Berlin, Neues Leben, 1964.
Hänsel und Gretel: Eine illustrierte Geschichte für kleine und grosse Leute nach der gleichnamigen Märchenoper von Adelheid Wette und Engelbert Humperdinck. Leipzig, Peters, 1972.

Caroline im Wassertropfen (for children).   Berlin, Junge
    Welt, 1975.
Zwischen Herbst und Winter (for children).   Berlin,
    Kinderbuchverlag, 1975.
Wiepersdorf.   Ebenhausen, Langewiesche-Brandt, 1977.
Wind, illustrated by Kota Taniuchi.   Hamburg, Wittig, 1978.
Ein Sommerregen, illustrated by Kota Taniuchi.   Hamburg,
    Wittig, 1978.
Schatten, illustrated by Kota Taniuchi.   Hamburg, Wittig,
    1979.
Sieben Häute.   Berlin, Anabis, 1979.
La Pagerie (diary; includes prose poems).   Stuttgart,
    Deutsche Verlags-Anstalt, 1980.
Hans mein Igel, adaptation of a story by the Brothers
    Grimm.   Cologne, Middlehauve, 1980.
*Geschlechtertausch: drei Geschichten über die Umwandlung
    der Verhältnisse*, with Irmtraud Morgner and Christa Wolf.
    Neuwied, Luchterhand, 1980.
Landleben, photographs by Olaf Plotz.   Breitenberg,
    Katzenvilla, 1984.
Irrstern: Prosa.   Stuttgart, Deutsche Verlags-Anstalt, 1986.
Galoschen: immerwährender Kalender.   Bremen, Neue
    Bremer Presse, 1987.
Allerlei-Rauh: Eine   Chronik.   Stuttgart,   Deutsche
    Verlags-Anstalt, 1988.

Editor, *Trost: Gedichte und Prosa*, by Elke Erb.   Stuttgart,
    Deutsche Verlags-Anstalt, 1982.
Editor, *Annette von Droste-Hülshoff.*   Munich, Goldmann,
    1988.

Translator, with Rainer Kirsch, *Ein niedagewesener Herbst*, by
    Anna Akhmatova.   Berlin, Kultur und Fortschritt, 1967.
Translator, with Eckhard Ulrich, *Gedichte*, by Novella
    Matveeva.   Berlin, Neues Leben, 1967.
Translator, with Ilse Krätzig, *Gedichte*, by Lavissa Vasil'eva.
    Berlin, Neues Leben, 1971.
Translator, *Laiko, Piff und Onkel Wertscho*, by Radka
    Aleksandrova.   Sofia, Bulgarski Hdoshnik, 1972.
Translator, *Das fliegende Regenschirmchen*, by Jordan
    Drumnikov.   Sofia, Bulgarski Hdoshnik, 1973.
Translator, *Der kleine hellblane Luftballon und die Puppe mit
    dem rosa Kleidchen*, by Leda Mileva.   Sofia, Bulgarski
    Hdoshnik, 1973.

*

Bibliography: by Walter Helmut Fritz, in *Kritisches Lexikon
zur deutschsprachigen Gegenwartsliteratur*, edited by Heinz
Ludwig Arnold, Munich, Text und Kritik, 1985.

Critical Studies: "Authorial Voice in Sarah Kirsch's *Die
Pantherfrau*" by Ann Clark Fehn, in *Erkennen und Deuten:
Essays zur Literatur und Literaturtheorie, Edgar Lohner in
memoriam*, edited by Martha Woodmansee and Walter
Lohnes, Berlin, Schmidt, 1983; "The Poetry of Sarah Kirsch"
by Laura Post, in *The Rackham Journal of the Arts and
Humanities* (Ann Arbor, Michigan), 1986; "Landscape as
Writing and Revelation in Sarah Kirsch's 'Death Valley'" by
Charlotte Melin, in *Germanic Review* (New York), Fall 1987.

* * *

In the 1960s the German Democratic Republic experienced
what became known as a "lyrical wave." Such an exotic term
may seem incongruous when applied to such a dour state, but it
aptly describes the remarkable outpouring of poetic activity
among young East German writers at that time. Into a
literature marked hitherto by stagnation and defensiveness
there came a new generation, born in the 1930s, who were
committed to the socialist order and eager to have their say in
its construction. They brought with them not only fresh vigour
and a willingness to experiment, but also the confidence to ask
awkward questions and a refusal to transmit prefabricated
harmonies dispensed from above. Although their work was a
joint undertaking in that it was sustained by a common impulse
and a network of friendships, each poet had a distinctive voice,
and one of their main concerns was precisely the role of
individuality within a collective society. Among this loose
grouping were such as Reiner Kunze, Wolf Biermann, and
Volker Braun (*qq.v.*). The leading lady was Sarah Kirsch.

It is the way with waves that they are uncontrollable. In the
case of Kirsch it was the highly subjective nature of her poetry
which raised official concern. The starting point in many of her
poems may be the familiar world of people, places, and
objects, but the reader is then led on an inward journey in
which a series of associated images or scenes passes before the
imagination in fanciful sequence, culminating in some new
vision or perception. This projection onto the real world of a
private emotion or fancy has remained a major hallmark of
Kirsch's writing, but in the GDR it was seen by some critics as
marking a shift away from political involvement towards
introspection and self-absorption. Nevertheless, she also had
her defenders, and her poetry was published in the GDR in
volumes such as *Landaufenthalt* (Visit to the Country),
Zaubersprüche (Magic Charms), and *Rückenwind* (Following
Wind).

Although the natural world is usually present in her writing
as a backdrop, or even as active participant, the main focus is
upon personal, at times indeed intimate, experience. Much of
her East German verse, for instance, reflects the crises of her
own life, the strain of an unsympathetic social environment or
the distress of a broken marriage. Evocations of physical union
convey not only the intensity of that act but also its transience,
and there remains deep hunger for a stable relationship within
a fractured world. Occasional images of fulfilment do occur,
and despair never dominates, but the prevailing atmosphere is
one of dislocation. In 1977 this acquired a new reality when, by
now thoroughly disillusioned with socialism and having
protested publicly against the expatriation of Wolf Biermann
the previous year, she left the GDR and moved to West
Germany.

The transition from East to West posed few problems to her
as a writer: "I do not intend to die of homesickness" was the
defiant assertion in one poem written after her move. Initially
the canvas of her work broadened with the new freedom to
travel, but otherwise the continuity is unmistakable. Her
poetry derives its primary inspiration not so much from topical
events or from situations specific to one kind of society, but
from universal experiences independent of nationality or else
from visual and sensuous impressions of the physical world.
Dominating her work now is the windswept northern land
scape of Schleswig Holstein, her home since 1981. Fragile in its
austere beauty, it is a fitting mirror for the restlessness of
human existence, also for the dangers facing the planet, an
awareness greatly intensified by the accident at the nuclear
plant at Chernobyl in 1986. Although still writing poetry, in
recent years Kirsch has also published prose, most notably
Allerlei-Rauh (the title is taken from the Grimms' fairytale of
that name, "Thousandfurs"), a chronicle with strongly autobiographical reference. She is not an overtly political poet, but she
has never disguised her disdain for the ideology she left behind,
and here she is overtly critical of former colleagues in East
Germany who had hoped, and worked, for the resurrection

of socialism in renewed form. Another prose work, *Schwingrasen* (Marsh Grass), contains a reminder in its title that appearance can be deceptive and the ground underfoot treacherous, but there is also a greater note of contentment here, a quiet humour, a hesitant stability, as the poet indulges her writing, cares for her animals, and performs the various duties of country life.

Kirsch's works are not transparent or explicit: they invite the reader's involvement and leave much scope for imaginative interpretation. Hers is a world of ambiguity and shifting contours, where even apparently fixed reference points are liable to dissolve into startling and unexpected shapes. Her language too blends the archaic and the colloquial, a whimsical mix that hovers on the brink of affectation but miraculously never falls. This sense of flux is heightened in her poetry by the free structure of the verse, as rhythm and meaning flow within and across lines largely uninterrupted by punctuation. Despite the prominence given to nature, she offers no retreat into idyll or romanticism. Hers is a vision that longs for harmony but recognizes discord. It is also a poetry of involvement, not of withdrawal, and with its suggestive imagery and evocative associations it exerts a haunting appeal.

—Peter J. Graves

KLÍMA, Ivan. Czech. Born in Prague, 14 September 1931. Spent over three years in concentration camp at Terezín as a child. Educated at Charles University, Prague, graduated 1956. Married Helena Klíma in 1958; one son and one daughter. Editor of periodicals, 1956–59; deputy editor-in-chief, *Literární noviny* [Literary Journal], 1964–68; Visiting Professor, University of Michigan, Ann Arbor, 1969–70; also worked as an ambulance man, messenger, and surveyor's assistant. Writings banned in Czechoslovakia, 1970–89. President, Czech PEN, since 1990. Recipient: Hostovsky award, 1986. Agent: (prose) Brombergs Bokförlag, Radmansgatan 72, Box 45151, 104 30 Stockholm, Sweden; (theatre) Projekt, Theater & Medien Verlag, Karolingerring 31, 5000 Cologne 1, Germany. Address: Nad lesem 8, 147 00 Prague 4, Czech Republic.

PUBLICATIONS

Fiction

Bezvadný den [The Wonderful Day]. Prague, Mladá fronta, 1960.
Hodina ticha [Hour of Silence]. Prague, Československý spisovatel, 1963.
Milenci na jednu noc [Lovers for One Night]. Prague, Československý spisovatel, 1964.
Kokrhací hodiny a jiné příběhy z Vlašských Klobouk a podobných Tramtárii. Prague, Státní nakladatelství dětské knihy, 1965.
Loď jménem naděje. Prague, Československý spisovatel, 1969; as *A Ship Named Hope: Two Novels* (*The Jury*; *A Ship Named Hope*), London, Gollancz, 1970.
Markétin zvěřinec. Prague, samizdat, 1973; Recklinghausen, Germany, 1978.
Malomocní [The Lepers]. Prague, samizdat, 1974.

Stojí, stojí šibenička. Prague, samizdat, 1976(?); as *Soudce z milosti*, London, Rozmluvy, 1986; as *Judge on Trial*, London, Chatto and Windus, 1991.
Má vesela jitrá. Prague, samizdat, 1978; Toronto, 68 Publishers, 1979; as *My Merry Mornings*, London and New York, Readers International, 1985.
Milostné léto. Toronto, 68 Publishers, 1979; as *A Summer Affair*, London, Chatto and Windus, 1987.
Moje první lásky. Toronto, 68 Publishers, 1985; as *My First Loves*, London, Chatto and Windus, 1986; New York, Harper, 1988.
Láska a smetí. Prague, samizdat, 1986; London, Rozmluvy, 1988; as *Love and Garbage*, London, Chatto and Windus, 1990; New York, Knopf, 1991.
Moje zlatá řemesla. Brno, Atlantis, 1990; as *My Golden Trades*, London, Granta, 1992.
Ostrov mrtvých králů [The Island of the Dead Kings]. Prague, Rozmluvy, 1992.
Milenci na jeden den [Lovers for One Day]. Prague, Rozmluvy, 1992.

Plays

Zámek (produced Prague, 1964). Prague, Dilia, 1964; as *The Castle* (produced Ann Arbor, Michigan, 1968).
Mistr. Prague, Divadlo, 1967; as *The Master* (produced St. Louis).
Porota [The Jury] (produced Prague, 1969). Prague, Dilia, 1968.
Klára a dva páni. With *Cukrárna Myriam*, Prague, Dilia, 1968; as *Klára and Two Men* (produced New York, 1968).
Cukrárna Myriam. With *Klára a dva páni*, Prague, Dilia, 1968; as *A Sweetshop Myriam* (produced New York, 1968).
Ženich pro Marcelu. Prague, Dilia, 1968; as *Bridegroom for Marcela* (produced New York, 1969).
Theaterstücke (includes *Zámek*; *Klára a dva páni*; *Cukrárna Myriam*; *Ženich pro Marcelu*; *Pokoj pro dva*). Lucerne, n.p., 1971.
Pokoj pro dva a jiné hry (includes *Pokoj pro dva*; *Hromobití*; *Ministr a anděl*) [The Double Bedroom; The Thunderstorm; The President and the Angel]. Prague, samizdat, 1973.
Hry. Prague, samizdat, 1974; as *Games* (produced Vancouver, 1981; London, 1990).
Franz a Felice. Prague, samizdat, 1983; as *Kafka and Felice*, published in *Cross Currents* (Ann Arbor, Michigan), 5, 1986.

Radio Plays: *Porota*, 1968, as *The Jury*; *Ženich pro Marcelu*, 1969 (banned; original recording broadcast Prague, 1990); *Minstr a anděl*, 1984, as *The President and the Angel* (UK); *Hromobití* [The Thunderstorm], 1990.

Television Plays: *Pokoj pro dva* [The Double Bedroom], 1990; *Minstr a anděl* [The President and the Angel], 1992; *Franz a Felice* [Franz and Felice], 1992; *Markétin zvěřinec*, 1993.

Other

Mezi třemi hranicemi [Between Three Borders]. Prague, Československý spisovatel, 1960.
Karel Čapek. Prague, Československý spisovatel, 1962.
Návštěva u nesmrtelné tetky: Polské zápisky [Visit to an Immortal Auntie]. Prague, Mladá fronta, 1965.
Už se blíží [The Swords Are Approaching]. Prague, Novinář, 1990.

*

Critical Studies: *The Silenced Theatre: Czech Playwrights Without a Stage* by Marketa Goetz-Stankiewicz, Toronto, University of Toronto Press, 1979; "Profile: Ivan Klíma" by Igor Hájek, in *Index on Censorship* (London), 12(2), 1983.

Ivan Klíma comments:

My favourite writer probably is Graham Greene. And also: Böll, Dürrenmatt . . . Their books have something in common. They bring an important message about our position, our role in the contemporary world. At the same time they bring some entertainment. My intention is to follow this path. In my opinion our stories have to address our readers, bring them some kind of hope in our hopeless world. Hope which is connected with our way of life, with our values and not with any external conditions, with any kind of goods, with politics. At the same time I try to keep in my mind my readers: to bring them some entertainment, not to bore them.

The critics have found that I am interested in the problems of justice, of unfaithfulness, of honesty, of loneliness, of Kafka's type of absurdity, of oppression of religious uplift, of dilapidated totalitarian regimes, but I would simply say that I am interested in the problems (or rather in the fate) of a man.

*   *   *

To put it mildly, Ivan Klíma's luck has not been particularly good, though his perseverance has finally assured his talents a measure of the success and recognition they deserve. Three years of Klíma's childhood were spent in the concentration camp at Terezín. After a good education in literature and philosophy at Charles University, Klíma contributed his editorial work, his narrative writings, and his plays to the socialist reform energies that produced the Prague Spring. After the reversal of power in 1968 his writings were banned. He chose to return to Prague in 1969, despite holding an academic post at the University of Michigan, and continued to write while undertaking a variety of other jobs. Since the revolution of 1989 he has emerged as one of the most credible spokesmen in contemporary Czechoslovak intellectual culture.

The first book Klíma wrote, *Mezi třemi hranicemi* (Between Three Borders), was a travel book on Slovakia. And his first novel, *Hodina ticha* (Hour of Silence), took advantage of those sympathetic observations by presenting the plight of Slovak farmers, whose ideas about socialism were vastly different from those of the bureaucrats overseeing the collectivization of their farms. Klíma also went to Poland to compose another travelogue, *Návštěva u nesmrtelné tetky* (Visit to an Immortal Auntie). Travel then emerged as an allegorical conceit in his *Loď jménem naděje* (A Ship Named Hope); a diffident man named Jacob, mistaken for a priest, undertakes to lead the resistance on a voyage to nowhere, captained by an autocrat and undertaken in the false name of a salvation that appears more and more to be a baroque impossibility. Klíma's identification with this range of outsiders in a supposedly just, classless society gave him a vantage point that allowed him to express increasingly critical judgements about the government's questionable moral behavior — opinions which, in the climate of relative thaw, earned him a series of editorial advancements and literary prizes.

Among Klíma's later, more characteristic themes are trials and, more generally, social games. Perhaps his most ambitious intellectual projects are his meditations on justice. The title story of his first collection, *Bezvadný den* (The Wonderful Day), concerned the way a character who resembled Klíma's friend Josef Vyhrozek was drummed out of the Communist Party after publishing a critical account of a politically correct

novel. His radio play *Porota* (*The Jury*), written in 1968, was converted to a novella in which the hero, a renaissance historian, discovers that his earnest considerations of an accused man's fate are part of a show trial; when he eventually casts a "not guilty" vote, it scarcely matters, for the man was already executed in jail, and the vote of dissent only tends to confer an illusion of fairness on the rigged proceedings. The trial theme recently reached its culmination in *Soudce z milosti* (*Judge on Trial*), about a good judge mired in the contradictions of his role in the Party system. Scrupulously observed, sad and eloquent, it took Klíma 13 years to write before it was published abroad in 1986. The mock trial, the ruthless execution, and several other related rituals are dramatized in more cynical, relativist terms in Klíma's play *Hry* (*Games*). These works, like the play *Zámek* (*The Castle*) about the government writers' home in Dobris, or Klíma's dramatic adaptations of *Amerika* and *Franz a Felice* (*Kafka and Felice*), most clearly bear the imprint of Klíma's omnipresent Jewish precursor in Prague, Franz Kafka, of whom he has said, "a creator who knows how to reflect his most personal experiences deeply and truthfully also touches the suprapersonal and political spheres."

Klíma's generation of writers, including Josef Škvorecký and Milan Kundera (*qq.v.*), tended to equate sexual adventure with political liberation. Consequently Klíma's other books play out the possibilities of resistance and genuine human contact that can be found in those relationships that communism was reluctant to legislate, that is, in Prague's intimate games of love and chance. In the 1960s Klíma wrote a set of stories that were eventually collected into companion volumes, *Milenci na jednu noc* (Lovers for One Night) and *Milenci na jeden den* (Lovers for One Day).

In later stories and novels Klíma's version of love grows more bittersweet, more as a context for frustration and regret than for fulfillment. *Moje první lásky* (*My First Loves*), for example, begins with a story about a young woman in the camp at Terezin who develops a crush on the Klíma-like narrator; she gives him extra rations of milk, though both seem to suspect, even at their young age, that any attempt at romance in the camps must surely end badly. These stories, in which sentiment and desire are fused with clear, engaging narratives of disappointment, are like the powerful, lyric tales of Bohumil Hrabal (*q.v.*), the humble dean of Czech novelists whom Klíma has repeatedly called "one of the greatest living European prose writers."

In another collection of stories, *Má vesela jitrá* (*My Merry Mornings*), the fables are more in the way of fantastic irony, like the story of a literary intellectual's failed efforts to become a blackmarket Christmas carp broker. When the narrator, desperate to read something that is not tainted by the "jerkish" idiom of propaganda, turns to the *Canine News*, no Czech reader can fail to recall the ridiculous fabulations of Jaroslav Hašek, who spent much of his early career inventing nonsense about imaginary dogs and ante-diluvian fleas. Love in this collection is more like physical sex than emotional upheaval; romance becomes an effort by the characters to claim some independence, which they can only feel through their grotesque eagerness to indulge, in any situation, in the little freedoms of carnal pleasure that everyday Soviet life still allowed.

But the greatest stylistic influence on Klíma is surely Karel Čapek, whose ambitious range of work and ingenuous tone of voice he most nearly imitates. Klíma does not have the luxury of Čapek's charm, the melodic lines and accessible philosophical narratives that Klíma described in his critical monograph of 1962 on Čapek, but in Klíma's recent, mature work he seems to have found a way of adapting Čapek's intimate style of domestic observation and familiarity of tone into novels that capture the lingering feeling of oppression, of hope against hope, that characterized life in the two decades after 1968.

In *Milostné léto* (*A Summer Affair*), a build-up of unresolved ambitions, of professional and family confinement, causes an otherwise sober, intelligent junior scientist to pursue an affair with a capricious, apparently confident girl of dubious understanding. Rather than celebrating such a private escape, the story ends quite credibly with the hero squandering his chances for a foreign research appointment, alienating his wife and family, and discovering the suicide of his confused young lover. Bracketed by funerals, the novel concludes with a touch that might have come from Čapek; the hero buys a bouquet for the lover's burial from a shy, beleaguered florist, then orders a second set of flowers and hands them back to the plain shop girl. She stands on tiptoe to kiss his forehead, and "as her lips touched him, he felt a gigantic rock of pain detaching itself within him."

Láska a smetí (*Love and Garbage*), Klíma's last novel published before the revolution, is also the most complete blend of these stylistic pleasures with an implied criticism of the structures of everyday life. Clearly autobiographical, the book records with fascinating frankness the small temptations, pleasant distractions, and abiding sense of dread that comprised the experience of Czech dissident writers. In this deceptively artless book, the work of creation itself provides little solace, yet literature alone can tell about the moments of true experience shared by people, that microcosmic paradise "in which the soul feels clean." Klíma followed that book with a set of narrative reflections, *Moje zlatá řemesla* (*My Golden Trades*), written in 1988 but published freely in Czechoslovakia in 1990.

Klíma was sustained by his membership in the dissident samizdat community, by his close relation with his brilliant wife, the social psychologist Helena Klimova, and by his contacts with foreign writers like Philip Roth and the emigré publishing house Rozmluvy in London. Like many of the writers who continued to produce without an audience, his novels are now enjoying an enthusiastic reception at home, as well as an expanding reputation abroad. His dramatic works, which have received solid support in critical summaries like Marketa Goetz-Stankiewicz's *The Silenced Theatre* (1979), are still in search of a devoted audience. In the solitary work after 1968, during his greatest test of character, Klíma seems also to have produced his best writing; his honesty, humanity, and enormous understanding should provide him a secure place in the future of Czech literature as well.

—Michael L. Quinn

KONESKI, Blaže. Macedonian. Born in Nebregovo, near Prilep, 19 December 1921. Educated at the University of Belgrade, 1939–41; University of Sofia, 1941–44, degree in Slavonic philology. Speech consultant, Macedonian National Theatre, Skopje, 1944; member, Commission for Macedonian Language and Orthography, from 1945; head of Cultural Department, Ministry of Education, 1945–46; member of editorial staff, *Osten* magazine, from 1945; co-founder, *Nov den* journal, 1945; lecturer in history of Macedonian language, School of Philosophy, from 1946, head of Department of South Slavonic Languages, from 1949, and rector, 1968–70,

University of Skopje; co-founder, 1950, and chief editor, 1950–72, *Makedonski jazik* linguistic journal. President, Yugoslav Writers' Union, 1961–65; corresponding member, Yugoslav Academy of Arts and Sciences, 1962, and Serbian Academy, 1963; member, 1967, and president, 1967–75, Macedonian Academy of Arts and Sciences. Recipient: Njegoš prize, 1965; Union of Soviet Writers prize, 1967; Herder prize, 1971; Struga Golden Wreath, 1981; Anti-Fascist Council for National Liberation prize. Honorary doctorate: University of Chicago, 1968; University of Wrocław, 1973. Address: c/o Misla, Gradski zid, Blok 2, Poštanski fah 460, 91000 Skopje, Macedonia.

PUBLICATIONS

Verse

Mostot [The Bridge]. Skopje, Kultura, 1945.
Od borbata: pesni [From the Conflict: Poems]. Skopje, Državno Knigoidatelstvo na Makedonija, 1947.
Zemjata i ljubovta: pesni [Land and Love: Poems]. Skopje, Državno Knigoidatelstvo na Makedonija, 1948.
Pesni [Poems]. Skopje, Kočo Racin, 1953.
Vezilka: pesni [The Embroideress: Poems]. Skopje, Kultura, 1955; enlarged edition, 1961.
Pesni [Poems]. Skopje, Kočo Racin, 1963.
Poezija: izbor [Poetry: A Selection]. Skopje, Kultura, 1965.
Stena [Rock]. Skopje, Misla, 1966.
Reke = Reki [Rivers] (bilingual edition in Macedonian and Serbo-Croatian). Skopje, Kultura, 1968.
Rakuvan'a [Handshakes]. Skopje, Misla, 1969.
Pesme = Pesni [Poems] (bilingual edition in Macedonian and Serbo-Croatian). Belgrade, Narodna Knjiga, 1974.
Stara loza [Old Vine] (bilingual edition in Macedonian and Serbo-Croatian). Cačak, Gradska Biblioteka, 1978.
Poems: Blaže Koneski, translated by Andrew Harvey and Anne Pennington. London, Deutsch, 1979.
Stari i novi pesni [Old and New Poems]. Prilep, Stremež, 1979.
Pesni i poemi [Poems and Longer Poems]. Skopje, Misla, 1980.
Pesni = Poems (bilingual edition), translated by Andrew Harvey and Anne Pennington. Struga, Struške Večerina Poezijata, 1981.
Mesta i migovi [Places and Moments]. Skopje, Misla, 1981.
Igra so dete [Game with a Child]. Skopje, Misla, 1982.
Tvrdjava: izabrane pjesme [Fortress: Selected Poems]. Cetinje, Obod, 1982.
The Fountains (in Macedonian). 1984.
Crkva [Church]. Skopje, Misla, 1988.
Zlatovrv [Golden Peak]. Skopje, Makedonska Kniga, 1989.
Seizmograf [Seismograph]. Skopje, Misla, 1989.

Fiction

Lozje: raskazi [Grapes: Stories]. Skopje, Kočo Racin, 1955.
Lozje i pesni vo proza [Grapes and Poems in Prose]. Skopje, Misla, 1981.
Sredba vo rajot [Meeting in Paradise]. Skopje, Misla, 1988.

Other

Makedonskata literatura i makedonskiot literaturen jazik Skopje, Kultura, 1945.
Po povod najnoviot napad na našiot jazik. Skopje, Zemskio odbor na Narodniot front na Makedonija, 1948.

Makedonskite učebnici od 19 vek: eden prilog kon istorijata na makedonskata prerodba. Skopje, Glavniot odbor na Narodniot front na Makedonija, 1949; as *Kon makedonskata prerodba: makedonskite učebnici od 19 vek*, Skopje, Institut za Nacionalna Istorija, 1959.

Makedonski pravopis, so pravopisen rečnik, with K. Tošev. Skopje, Državno Knigoizdatelstvo na Makedonija, 1950.

Makedonskata literatura vo 19 vek: kratok pregled i tekstovi. Skopje, Državno Knigoizdatelstvo na Makedonija, 1950.

Za makedonskiot literaturen jazik. Skopje, Kočo Racin, 1952.

Gramatika na makedonskiot literaturen jazik. Skopje, Skopje, Državno Knigoizdatelstvo na Makedonija, 2 vols., 1952–54.

Towards the Macedonian Renaissance: Macedonian Textbooks of the 19th Century. Skopje, Institute of Natural History, 1961.

Makedonski tekstovi 10–20 vek, with O. Jašar-Nasteva. Skopje, Sojuzot na Društvata za Makedonski Jazik i Literatura, 1966.

Izbrani dela (includes 1: *Poezija*; 2: *Prepevi*; 3: *Lozje*; 4: *Za makedonskata literatura*; 5: *Za makedonskiot literaturen jazik*; 6: *Gramatika na makedonskiot literaturen jazik*; 7: *Istorija na makedonskiot jazik*). Skopje, Kultura, 7 vols., 1967; revised edition, 1981.

Makedonskiot jazik vo razvojot na slovenskite literaturni jazici. Skopje, Kultura, 1968; as *The Macedonian Language in the Development of the Slavonic Literary Languages*, Kultura, 1968.

Jazikot na makedonska narodna poezija. Skopje, Makedonska Adademija na Naukite i Umetnostite, 1971.

Besedi i ogledi. Skopje, Makedonska Kniga, 1972.

Zapisi [Essays]. Skopje, Makedonska Kniga, 1974.

Od istorijata na jazikot na slovenskata pismenost vo Makedonija. Skopje, Makedonska Kniga, 1975.

Jazični temi. Skopje, Misla, 3 vols., 1981.

Makedonskiot XIX vek: jazični i kniževnoistoriski prilozi. Skopje, Kultura, 1986.

Dnevnik po mnogu godini. Skopje, Makedonska Kniga, 1988.

Editor, *Zbirka na makedonski narodni pesni.* Skopje, Državno Knigoizdatelstvo na Makedonija, 1945.

Editor, *Skazni i storenija*, by M. Cepenkov. Skopje, Kočo Racin, 1954.

Editor, *Vranešički apostol.* Skopje, Institut za Makedonski Jazik, 1956.

Editor, *Slovo za praznicite*, by K. Pejčinovik. Skopje, Kultura, 1956.

Editor, *Makedonska književnost.* Belgrade, Srpska Književna Zadruga, 1961.

Editor, *Rečnik na makedonskiot jazik so srpskohrvatski tolkuvan'a.* Skopje, Univerzitetska P-ca, 3 vols., 1961–66.

Editor, *Izbrani tekstovi*, by J. Krčovski. Skopje, Kočo Racin, 1963.

Editor, *Izbrani tekstovi*, by K. Pejčinovik. Skopje, Kočo Racin, 1963.

Editor and Translator, *Poezija: izbor*, by A. Blok. Skopje, Kultura, 1966.

Editor, with Dimitar Mitrev and Aleksandar Spasov, *Makedonska književnost XIX veka . . .* Novi Sad, Matica Srpska, 1978.

Editor, with T. Dimitrovski and T. Stamatoski, *About the Macedonian Literary Language.* Skopje, Krste Misirkov Institute of the Macedonian Language, 1978.

Editor, with Božidar Vidoeski and B. Korubin, *Referati od X zasedanie na Meǵunarodnata komisija za izučuvanje na gramatičkata struktura na slovenskite literaturni jazici.* Skopje, Makedonska Akademija na Naukite i Umetnostite, 1979.

Editor, *The Progressive Palatalization of Common Slavic*, by H. G. Lunt. Skopje, Makedonska Akademija na Naukite i Umetnostite, 1981.

Editor, *Blažena gora zelena: antologija na makedonskata narodna lirika* [Blessed Green Forest: Anthology of Macedonian Folk Lyric Poetry]. Skopje, Makedonska Kniga, 1986.

Editor, *Svečen sobir posveten na 125-godišninata od izleguvanjeto na Zbornikot na Miladinovci.* Skopje, Makedonska Akademija na Naukite i Umetnostite, 1987.

Editor, *Izbrani stranici*, by Hadži Konstantinov-Džinot. Skopje, Misla, 1987.

Editor, *Svečen sobir posveten na 150-godišninata od raǵanjeto na Konstantin Miladinov.* Skopje, Makedonska Akademija na Naukite i Umetnostite, 1988.

Editor, with Božidar Vidoeski and Peter Hr. Ilievski, *Kirilo-metodievskiot (staroslovenskiot) period i kirilo-metodievskata tradicija vo Makedonija.* Skopje, Makedonska Akademija na Naukite i Umetnostite, 1988.

Translator, *Gorski venac*, by P. P. Njegoš. Skopje, Državno Kigoizdatelstvo na Makedonija, 1947.

Translator, with N. Koneski, *Brigadata*, by V. Kaleb. Skopje, Nopok, 1950.

Translator, *Novi raskazi*, by Ivo Andrić. Skopje, Kočo Racin, 1951.

Translator, *Lirsko intermeco*, by Heinrich Heine. Skopje, Kočo Racin, 1952.

Translator, *Otello*, by William Shakespeare. Skopje, Kočo Racin, 1953; new translation, Skopje, Kultura, 1967; new translation, Skopje, Makedonska Kniga, 1971.

Translator, *Sredbi i spomeni*, by R. Čolaković. Skopje, Kultura, 1959.

Translator, with others, *Izbor*, by Ivo Andrić. Skopje, Kočo Racin, 1963.

*

Bibliography: *Blaže Koneski: A Bibliography* by Garth M. Terry, Nottingham, Astra, 1983.

Critical Studies: "Blazhé Koneski — The Founder of Modern Macedonian Linguistics" by A. Dzhukeski, in *Macedonian Review* (Skopje), 9(2), 1979; "The Poetry of Blazhé Koneski" by Andrew Harvey and Anne Pennington, in *Macedonian Review* (Skopje), 10(1), 1980; "Blaže Koneski: The Right Man in the Right Place at the Right Time" by Yvonne Burns, in *Makedonski Jazik* (Skopje), 1981–82; "The Historiographic Thought of Blazhé Koneski" by Hristo Andonov-Polyanski in *Macedonian Review* (Skopje), 14(1), 1984.

* * *

Blaže Koneski is the most significant Macedonian literary figure in the post-war development of Macedonian literature from the time, in 1945, when Macedonians were first granted the freedom to publish books and newspapers in their own language, and each of his publications has been received as an important event in the Macedonian literary scene. He has received the highest awards and is honoured throughout the world.

He began his literary career while still at high school, and had already been writing poetry in Macedonian before the beginning of World War II, but his primary task when the war was over was the scholarly one of codifying the Macedonain language, and his published work is the reflection of his preoccupation with the task of laying a firm and unimpeachable foundation for the emerging Macedonian literature. He has made a lasting contribution with his scholarly work extending over more than half a century, in every possible aspect of linguistics and literature relevant to Macedonian language and literature, from the earliest Slavonic manuscripts to the latest printed books.

Koneski's first book of poetry was *Mostot* (The Bridge), a cycle of poems that describes the rebuilding of a bridge destroyed by the Germans, symbolising the destruction and rebuilding of Macedonia itself. The sixth poem of the cycle concludes: "Blood lies in the foundations. But such/ neither time can destroy, nor storms o'erwhelm," alluding to the folk legend of the need to enclose a human sacrifice in the foundations of a building to prevent evil forces destroying at night what had been built during the day. It also represents the bridge between Macedonia's past and its future. It is a rallying call, rousing the nation to join in the work of reconstruction.

His third book, the collection *Zemjata iljubovta* (Land and Love), contains the magnificent poem "Teškoto," the name of the most virile and exciting Macedonian dance, and is a hymn of victory. "Ilinden Melodies" and the ballad "The Sun's Column" glorify the sacrifices made in the past and more recent struggles for freedom, while other poems such as "A Spring Song" speak of the joy of victory. In "Appointment with Žinzifov," Koneski evokes the dead Žinzifov in Moscow. A variant of this literary form is the dialogue between Kole Nedelkovski and Kočo Racin in "A Handshake." Koneski clearly feels in close touch with his forerunners whose lives and works he has been studying.

The underlying theme of these two collections is the memory of what it had been like for the Macedonian people before they won their freedom. The books were first published during the period of Social Realism of the immediate post-war epoch, when the people's collective enthusiasm, which had successfully driven out the occupying forces, needed to be maintained in order to create a new infrastucture to support Macedonia's new status as a Republic, and its newly acquired right to its own language and literature.

By 1950, however, a new cultural and literary climate emerged in which the principle of freedom of expression was proclaimed, and new publishing opportunities were founded. This made possible the confrontation of the old by the new, the traditional by the avant-garde, realism by modernism. It also meant that the best modern writing from abroad could be obtained and read in the original and could be translated by the first generation to have had the advantage of a Macedonian university education.

Koneski had been much engaged in his academic work since his appointment in 1946 as lecturer and then Professor in the newly formed Department of Macedonian Language in the University of Skopje: by 1952 he had published eight important volumes on the Macedonian language and translations into Macedonian verse of important works by P. P. Njegoš, Ivo Andrić, and Heinrich Heine. The following year his translation of Shakespeare's *Othello* was published.

Koneski then published in 1953 *Pesni* (Poems), a new collection in which with his lyric forms and rich vocabulary he confirmed the newly introduced intimate style of poetry. While displaying influences of poets he had translated such as Heine and Alexander Blok, it is clear that these poems could only have been written by Koneski. "Game with a Child," com-

pletely modern in form, with an apparent simplicity that only a great artist can produce, is terrifying in its evocation of that cold premonition that can come to us in moments of bliss: that our joy, and ourselves, are but mortal.

The second half of the 1950s saw the fruit of attempts of the previous decade to bring the youthful Macedonian literature into the stream of world literature. An environment conducive to the expression of new ideas, the opening of lively communication with the rest of the world, and the increasing availability of world literature in translation made the development of the so-called aesthetic pluralism possible. Nevertheless, nothing remains static, and it was not long before the newly introduced style of writing often developed into sentimentalism.

Koneski was the first to take a stand against this trend, with the publication of his collection *Vezilka* (The Embroideress) in 1955. He writes metaphorically of the poet writing a poem as an embroideress makes a cloth by weaving red and black threads. He puts the question: "Embroideress, tell me how is a precise/and austere Macedonian song born?" In this volume the poetry is turned almost completely towards the inner world of the poet — not by exploring personally intimate information, but rather by telling stories about exterior real objects. In these "stories" we can always recognise the human being with all his joys and sorrows. The exterior object may also be a mythical being or a hero of experiencing folk legends familiar emotions such as pain, fear, or astonishment.

Koneski's was not a lone voice, and, with other eminent poets quickly taking the same stand a year later, 1956 became a turning point in Macedonian poetry, which from that time moved onwards, exploring richer fields.

Koneski also published in 1955 his first collection of short stories, *Lozje* (Grapes). It was immediately acclaimed as a mature work, dealing with real people in real circumstances, and it has continued to be one of the most successful and appreciated collections of Macedonian short stories.

Koneski is an innovator. His lively and precise mind experiments, looks for problems to tackle, and solves them. He likes to cover a variety of subjects and groupings in one collection, to retain the interest of the reader. He is also deeply self-critical and wants to be sure the time is right for publication. As A. Spasov has said, Koneski published his poetry only when "it was not possible to postpone publication any longer."

Koneski prefaced the volume *Stari i novi pesni* (Old and New Poems) with four short essays he had written about poetry; they have been quoted many times by critics over the years. In the arrangement of this volume he introduced no fewer than four new cycles, regrouping some poems previously published. The most important and productive new cycle is called "Proložni Žitija" (Eulogies), each poem written in memory of a dearly loved relative or friend.

Koneski looks back to examine his sources in *The Fountains* In 12 sonnets, all with 11-syllable lines and the rhyme scheme *adab cdcd efefef*, he writes a tribute to Kočo Racin, the tragi prophet who was his forerunner, and vividly reminisces abou his youth (when, as Cane Andreevski points out, Konesk wrote precise verses like these, carefully counting th syllables), but suddenly reminds himself that "youth is on alive in the dream," nothing comforts him, "this sorro remains."

Recent collections, including *Crkva* (Church), *Zlatovr* (Golden Peak), and *Seizmograf* (Seismograph), have all bee welcomed and appreciated. The latter collection is name after the instrument that measures the tremors of the earth as graph. All the poems in the collection had to be in their fin form in 30–40 days. Only a few were in rough outline form the start, but all of them were ready within the deadline. T result is like some seismograph that followed continuous

Koneski's mental state of excitements and shocks during that time.

In his poetry Koneski chooses just the right word for his purpose. From his linguistic studies he has a rich vocabulary which he knows how to use effectively to strengthen the atmosphere he wishes to create. Each poem has its especial beauty because of its form, rhythm, and the musical nature of the phrases. The poems' apparent simplicity hide more complex ideas; that which may appear simple at first glance always appears more complicated in the end. As Koneski himself has said, anyone who thinks it is easy should try writing poetry.

—Yvonne Burns

KONRAD, George. *See* **KONRÁD, György.**

KONRÁD, György. Also George Konrad. Hungarian. Born in Debrecen, 2 April 1933. Educated at Debrecen Reform College; Madách Gymnasium, Budapest, 1947–51; Lenin Institute, Budapest; Loránd Eötvös University, Budapest, degree in teaching literature 1955. Married to Judit Lakner; three sons and one daughter. Teacher, general gymnasium, Csepel, 1956; editor, *Életképek* [Life Scenes], 1956, and *Magyar Helikon*, 1960–66; social worker, Budapest, 1959–65; sociologist, City Planning Research Institute, 1965–73; arrested and imprisoned for six days, Budapest, 1974; Visiting Professor of comparative literature, Colorado Springs College, 1986. Also worked at the Institute for Literary Scholarship for several years. Currently president, International PEN. Corresponding member, Bayerische Academy. Recipient: Herder prize, 1984; Veillon prize, 1986; Fredfonden Peace Foundation prize (Copenhagen), 1986; German Critics' prize, 1986; Kossuth prize, 1990. Address: Torockó utca, 3, 1026 Budapest, Hungary.

PUBLICATIONS (books in English published as George Konrád)

Fiction

A látogató. Budapest, Magvető, 1969; as *The Case Worker*, New York, Harcourt Brace, 1974; London, Hutchinson, 1975.

A városalapító. Budapest, Magvető, 1977; as *The City Builder*, New York, Harcourt Brace, 1977; London, Sidgwick and Jackson, 1980; revised (uncensored) edition, Budapest, Magvető, 1992.

The Loser. San Diego, Harcourt Brace, 1982; London, Allen Lane, 1983; as *A cinkos*, New York, Püski, 1986.

Agenda: Kerti mulatság. Budapest, Magvető, 1989; as *A Feast in the Garden*, San Diego, Harcourt Brace, 1992.

Other

Az új lakótelepek szociológiai problémái [Sociological Problems in the New Housing Development], with Iván Szelényi. Budapest, Akadémiai Kiadó, 1969.

Az értelmiség útja az osztályhatalomhoz: esszé, with Iván Szelényi. Paris, Európai Protestáns Magyar Szabadegyetem, 1978; as *The Intellectuals on the Road to Class Power*, New York, Harcourt Brace, and Brighton, Harvester, 1979.

Az autonómia kísértése: kelet-nyugati utigondolatok 1977–1979 [The Temptation of Autonomy]. Paris, Magyar Füzetek, 1980.

Antipolitics. San Diego, Harcourt Brace, and London, Quartet, 1984; as *Antipolitika*, with *Az autonómia kísértése*, Budapest, Codex, 1989.

Európa köldökén: esszék 1979–1989 [At the Navel of Europe]. Budapest, Magvető, 1990.

Az ujjászületés melankóliája [The Melancholy of Rebirth]. Budapest, Magvető, 1992.

Editor, *A francia "új regény".* Budapest, Európa, 1967.

*

Critical Studies: "György Konrád's Novel *A látogató*" by Paul Varnai, in *International Fiction Review* (Fredericton, New Brunswick), 1(1), 1974; "Freedom's Captives: Notes on George Konrád's Novels" by Ivan Sanders, in *World Literature Today* (Norman, Oklahoma), 57(2), 1983; "György Konrád: On the Front Line" by Elizabeth Heron, in *Index on Censorship* (London), 14(2), 1985.

*   *   *

With his first novel György Konrád started a new chapter in the history of Hungarian literature. *A látogató* (*The Case Worker*), published in 1969, immediately established him as an important writer of modern fiction. Written in the first-person singular, this short novel is the sum of diverse, often horrific experiences of a social worker in a Central European city in the 1960s. It deals with people whose lives have not been touched by "the Socialist transformation of man," who exist on the fringe of society, often in subhuman circumstances; it also asks searching questions about the limits of empathy. Although it is a "social critical" novel in one sense, *The Case Worker* is alluring for its masterful style, full of poetic metaphors. The American critic Irving Howe believed that with this one book Konrád placed himself "in the forefront of contemporary European literature."

Konrád is an autobiographical writer in a sense: having studied Hungarian literature at university, for a time he worked as a social worker in Budapest — an experience that provided material for *The Case Worker*. His second novel, *A városalapító* (*The City Builder*), delayed for years and published only in a censored version in 1977 (the uncensored version was published in Hungary only in 1992), is also based on Konrád's work experience at the City Planning Research Institute. *The City Builder* can be read on two levels: as a stylistic *tour de force*, and as a critique of the "planners" who constantly interfere with other people's lives.

From the exploration of deviant psychology and sociology Konrád moved back into the domain of history in his third novel *A cinkos* (*The Loser*). The narrative in this story is more conventional than in the two previous books, but the dualism observed in the novels is equally present here in the form of two heroes, T. and his younger brother Dani. The plot moves back and forth through flashbacks, illuminating 50 years of East Central European history. T.'s life includes all the stages through which a typical Jewish intellectual born around 1920 would have passed, from the initial social rebellion against unjust society, through turbulent and often bizarre war experiences, to participation in the post-war Communist bureaucracy, and finally, to a rejection of Communism after 1956.

Konrád's latest novel, *Kerti mulatságok* (*A Feast in the Garden*), part of the *Agenda* series (Novel and Working Diary), notes a return to the autobiographical mode: the main character's experiences during and after the war roughly correspond with Konrád's own biography. The book also includes Konrád's present impressions and meditations, many of which relate to Budapest, where Konrád lives and which he loves with the passion of an adopted son. After the publication of this novel Konrád was awarded the prestigious Kossuth prize in 1990.

Apart from fiction Konrád also writes essays in a literary, cultural, or political vein. His first venture in this field was the controversial (and in Hungary banned) treatise *Az értelmiség útja az osztályhatalomhoz* (*The Intellectuals on the Road to Class Power*), written with the sociologist Ivan Szelényi. His less theoretical (and therefore more enjoyable) essays have been published in four volumes, beginning with *Az autonómia kísértése* (The Temptation of Autonomy) through *Antipolitika* (*Antipolitics*) and *Európa köldökén* (At the Navel of Europe), to the recent *Az ujjászületés melankóliája* (The Melancholy of Rebirth). In these essays Konrád makes a plea for the rights of the individual, taken for granted in western societies but systematically violated in less fortunate parts of Europe. He is a broad-minded, intelligent, liberal observer of social change and the search for national identity which has been a central issue in countries formerly belonging to the now defunct Soviet empire. As President of the International PEN Club he has been working toward more international cooperation in the spirit of respect for different lifestyles and diverse values.

—George Gömöri

KONWICKI, Tadeusz. Polish. Born in Nowa Wilejka, near Vilnius, 22 June 1926. Educated at the University of Warsaw, and Jagiellonian University, Cracow, 1945–49. Served in the Resistance during World War II, 1944–45. Married Danuta Lenica in 1949; two daughters. Full-time writer and journalist; also screenwriter and film director. Member of editorial staff, *Nowa Kultura*, 1950–57. Recipient: State prize for literature, 1950, 1954, 1966; Knight's Cross, 1954, and Officer's Cross, 1964, Order of Polonia Restituta; Medal of 10th Anniversary of People's Poland, 1955; for films: Venice Festival prize, 1958; Mannheim Festival prize, 1962; San Remo Festival prize, 1972; Mondello prize (Italy), 1980. Address: ul. Górskiego, 1 m. 68, 00–033 Warsaw, Poland.

PUBLICATIONS

Fiction

Przy budowie [At the Building Site].   Warsaw, Czytelnik, 1950.
Godzina smutku [The Hour of Sadness].   Warsaw, Czytelnik, 1954.
Władza [Power].   Warsaw, Czytelnik, 1954.

Z oblężonego miasta [From the Besieged Town].   Warsaw, Iskry, 1956.
Rojsty [The Marshes].   Warsaw, Czytelnik, 1956.
Dziura w niebie [A Hole in the Sky].   Warsaw, Iskry, 1959.
Sennik współczesny.   Warsaw, Iskry, 1963; as *A Dreambook for Our Time*, Cambridge, Massachusetts, MIT Press, 1969.
Wniebowstąpienie [Ascension].   Warsaw, Iskry, 1967.
Nic albo nic [Nothing or Nothing].   Warsaw, Czytelnik, 1971.
Kronika wypadków miłosnych [The Chronicle of Love Events].   Warsaw, Czytelnik, 1974.
Kalendarz i klepsydra [A Calendar and a Water-Clock].   Warsaw, Czytelnik, 1976.
Kompleks polski.   Published in *Zapis 3* (samizdat), 1977; as *The Polish Complex*, New York, Farrar Straus, 1982.
Mała apokalipsa.   Published in *Zapis 10* (samizdat), 1979; as *A Minor Apocalypse*, London, Faber, and New York, Farrar Straus, 1983.
Wschody i zachody księżyca.   Published in *Zapis 21* (samizdat), 1982; London, Index on Censorship, 1982; as *Moonrise, Moonset*, New York, Farrar Straus, 1987; London, Faber, 1988.
Rzeka podziemna, podziemne ptaki [Underground River, Underground Birds].   Samizdat, 1984; London, Aneks, 1985.
Kronika wypadków miłosnych [The Chronicle of Love Events].   Warsaw, Czytelnik, 1985.
Nowy Świat i okolice.   Warsaw, Czytelnik, 1986; as *New World Avenue and Vicinity*, New York, Farrar Straus, 1991.
Bohiń.   Warsaw, Czytelnik, 1987; as *Bohin Manor*, New York, Farrar Straus, 1990; London, Faber, 1991.

Plays

Ostatni dzień lata [The Last Day of Summer] (screenplays; includes *Zaduszki* [Halloween]; *Salto*; *Matura* [Matriculation Examination]; *Zimowy zmierzch* [Winter Dusk]).   Warsaw, Iskry, 1966; enlarged edition (includes *Jak daleko stąd, jak blisko* [So Far, So Near]), 1973.

Screenplays: *Zimowy zmierzch* [Winter Dusk], 1957; *Ostatni dzień lata* [The Last Day of Summer] (also director), 1958; *Matka Joanna od Aniołów* (Joan of the Angels), with Jerzy Kawalerowicz, 1961; *Zaduszki* [Halloween] (also director), 1961; *Faraon* [Pharaoh], with Jerzy Kawalerowicz, 1965; *Salto* (also director), 1965; *Matura* [Matriculation Examination], 1965; *Jowita* (*Jovita*), 1967; *Jak daleko stąd, jak blisko* [So Far, So Near] (also director), 1971; *Dolina Issy* [The Issa Valley] (also director), 1982; *Austeria*, with Jerzy Kawalerowicz and Julian Stryjkowski, 1983; *Lawa* [Lava] (also director), 1989.

Other

Zwierzoczłekoupiór.   Warsaw, Czytelnik, 1969; as *The Anthropos-Specter-Beast*, New York, Phillips, and London, Oxford University Press, 1977.
Dlaczego kot jest kot [Why a Cat Is a Cat].   Warsaw, KAW, 1976.
Pół wieku czyśćca: Rozmowy z Tadeuszem Konwickim [Half a Century of Purgatory: Conversations with Tadeusz Konwicki], with Stanisław Nowicki.   Warsaw, Przedświt (samizdat), and London, Aneks, 1986.

*

Critical Studies: "The Haunted World of Tadeusz Konwicki," in *Books Abroad*, 48, 1974, and "The Polish Complex," in *Polish Review* (New York), 25(1), 1980, both by Jerzy

R. Krzyżanowski; "The Polish Complex" by Stanisław Barańczak, in *Partisan Review* (Boston), 51(3), 1984; "Beyond Aesthetics of Censorship: Tadeusz Konwicki's Ordinary Politicking" by Michael Szporer, in *Modern Fiction Studies* (West Lafayette, Indiana), Spring 1986.

* * *

Since the publication of *Sennik współczesny* (*A Dreambook for Our Time*) in 1963, Tadeusz Konwicki has been universally considered one of the most prominent novelists of post-war Poland. His popularity reached its peak, however, in the late 1970s, when Konwicki, unable to reconcile with the communist censor's attempts at bowdlerizing his novel *Kompleks polski* (*The Polish Complex*), turned to the underground publishing network (samizdat), which subsequently issued this and his next three books. Besides *The Polish Complex*, the novel *Mała apokalipsa* (*A Minor Apocalypse*) is particularly characteristic of Konwicki's peculiar imagination, morbid humor, and narrative skills. He has also been highly successful as a screenwriter and director of films based mostly on his own scripts.

Konwicki was born into a worker's family in 1926 near the city of Vilna (now Vilnius) in the part of Lithuania that then belonged to Poland. He attended a high school in Vilna and, under the Nazi occupation, continued his study in a clandestine study group. In July 1944, he joined a guerilla unit which fought both the retreating Nazis and the approaching Soviet troops. In 1945, his native region having been annexed by the Soviet Union, he went to Cracow, where he managed to conceal his anti-communist past and began to study Polish literature at the Jagiellonian University. In 1948 he moved to Warsaw, where he has lived ever since.

It might seem that, like the majority of Polish writers of his generation, Konwicki went through a period of infatuation with the Stalinist ideology and Socialist Realist style in his youth before he was able to find an independent stance and a more authentic voice of his own. In fact, however, he had found this voice long before he was able to make it resound publicly. During the early post-war years he led a double life as a writer: while publishing propagandistic novels, short stories, and reportage, he was secretly writing a novel about his guerilla experience, *Rojsty* (The Marshes), which he only managed to publish eight years after its completion. Since 1956, the year of the general "thaw" in Polish political and cultural life, he has continued the kind of writing that this early work had initiated.

Beginning with *A Dreambook for Our Time*, the constant thematic focus of his novels has been on the reality of contemporary Poland, but reality seen highly subjectively, through the eyes of an individual who obsessively confronts it with his personal memories and with what he knows about his nation's historical past. Moreover, Konwicki frequently uses a first-person narrator who does not fully belong in the reality he describes; the narrator's primary task is to find a key to a world that seems alien and absurd to him. This strategy is carried out in a variety of ways. The narrator, for example, may be a child whose perversely naive way of seeing things as they are exposes the hypocrisy of adults (*Zwierzoczłekoupiór* [*The Anthropos-Specter-Beast*]); he may be a man who mysteriously wakes up in a remote town where he has never been before (*A Dreambook for Our Time*), or who regains consciousness after having been beaten up by hooligans in the center of Warsaw, only to discover that he has lost his memory (*Wniebowstąpienie* [Ascension]). The common effect of these various situations is to create the cognitive and narrative position of an *outsider*, who perceives the surrounding realm of everyday life as utterly absurd and incomprehensible. The existing world (and particularly the reality of Poland under Communist rule) appears to him as both grotesque and apocalyptic; the absurdity he encounters provokes nervous laughter as well as eschatological fear. A world so absurd cannot possibly exist for long, and thus there is only one conclusion: Doomsday must be nigh.

Only in the late 1970s, however, did Konwicki begin to speak without inhibition and without spending his artistic energy on finding intricate ways to confuse the censor. The first two novels he published underground are arguably his best works to date and have remained the most popular among his readers both in Poland and abroad. In both *The Polish Complex* and *A Minor Apocalypse*, the narrator is closely identified with Konwicki himself, the narration is often interrupted by quasi-essayistic digressions expressing the author's point of view, and the reality presented is clearly that of communist Poland, despite occasional elements of caricatural exaggeration (and also despite the fact that the action of *A Minor Apocalypse* takes place ostensibly in an unspecified future). Nevertheless, both novels are not chiefly political; their aim is rather to offer a condensed artistic image of a certain society in a certain country at a certain time. In both novels, this aim is achieved in the first place by highly eccentric yet highly convincing opening situations which provide a point of departure for the plot as well as the key metaphor for each novel.

In *The Polish Complex* such a key appears on the very first page. The narrator stands 23rd in a long queue in front of a state jewelry shop. (In Poland of the 1970s, suffering rapid inflation, gold was a highly valued and sought-after commodity.) The waiting for merchandise (cheap Soviet rings) drags on, and in the queue, which contains a cross-section of society, social acquaintances as well as sympathies and antipathies form. The class differences and opposing political views are, however, less essential than the problem of how to win a better place in the queue: the desire to obtain unattainable goods seems to be the only element left that still unites society.

The contemporary plot of the novel constitutes only one of its layers, though. Another layer consists of lengthy digressions and even separate short stories inserted in the narrative. In particular, two such stories, both referring to the defeat of one of the many spurts of liberation in Polish history, the 1863 Uprising, apparently bear no relation to the main line of the plot, yet they present another version of the familiar motif of "amnesia," in demonstrating the degree to which the contemporary citizen of a socialist state has become alienated from ethical imperatives.

While the action of *The Polish Complex* occasionally shifts back to the historical past, the action of *A Minor Apocalypse* is moved forward, to some unspecified (though ominously near) future. The reality presented here is again that of Poland in the 1970s, yet it is subject to dreamlike distortion and grotesque, often darkly comic hyperbole. Communism appears here as a still powerful system, but it is powerful by the force of inertia; its true condition can only be defined as one of prolonged collapse.

This novel opens, too, with a startlingly absurd, yet in a sense plausible, situation: The narrator-author is visited by two literary acquaintances, both known as prominent dissidents, who seriously propose that, as a respected and famous Polish writer, he should set himself on fire in front of the Party Central Committee building as an act of protest against the incorporation of Poland into the Soviet Union, which is to take place that very day. Understandably shocked at first, the narrator grudgingly acknowledges their point and sluggishly sets off in search of unavailable gasoline and matches. His weary progress through Warsaw streets, apartments, and restaurants mirrors, in a self-mocking way, the Stations of the Cross, and the end of the novel is deliberately inconclusive: the reader can only guess that the act of self-immolation finally does take place.

This deliberately bizarre plot is matched throughout the novel with the recurrent motif of shabbiness, corruption, and self-destruction of virtually anything the narrator encounters. Bridges fold down and buildings collapse without attracting anybody's attention; the general erosion of the public's morale has come to the point where even the proposed annexation of Poland to the Soviet Union is met with cynical indifference. In this diagnosis of the state of Polish society, *A Minor Apocalypse* — written toward the end of the 1970s — appeared more bitter than any of Konwicki's previous works and (as the course of historical events was to prove very soon) it offered a clearly exaggerated picture. Still, it was precisely the ingenious use Konwicki makes of the novelist's right to exaggerate and to observe things from his subjective vantage point that makes his best novels so memorable and continues to force their readers to look self-critically at themselves as society.

—Stanisław Barańczak

—————

KROETZ, Franz Xaver. German. Born in Munich, 25 February 1946. Studied acting in Munich, 1961–63, and at Reinhardt Seminar, Vienna, 1964–66. Has one daughter and one son. Actor in Munich, 1966–70; playwright-in-residence, Heidelberg Theater, 1972–73; has also worked as a labourer, truck driver, nurse, and banana cutter; co-founder, Franz Xaver Koetz Dramatik publishing house; actor in *Kir Royal* television series, 1987; journalist in Seoul for Olympic Games, *Die Welt* newspaper, 1988. Recipient: Thoma Medal, 1970; Suhrkamp-Dramatiker stipendium, 1970; Fontane prize, 1972; Critics prize (Germany), 1973; Hanover Drama prize, 1974; Lübke prize, 1975; Drama prize (Mühlheim), 1976; tz-Rose, 1983; Grimme prize, 1987. Address: Kirchberg 3, 8226 Altenmarkt, Germany.

Publications

Plays

Oblomov, adaptation of a novel by Ivan Goncharov (produced Munich, 1968).
Julius Caesar, adaptation of the play by William Shakespeare (produced Munich, 1968).
Hilfe, ich werde geheiratet (produced Rottach/Egern, 1969). In *Weitere Aussichten*, 1976.
Hartnäckig (produced Munich, 1971). Included in *Drei Stücke*, 1971.
Männersache (produced Darmstadt, 1972). Included in *Drei Stücke*, 1971; revised version, as *Ein Mann, ein Wörterbuch* (produced Vienna, 1977); as *A Man, A Dictionary* (produced Northampton, Massachusetts, 1979), in *Farmyard and Four Plays*, 1976; as *Wer durchs Laub geht* (produced Marburg, 1981), included in *Drei neue Stücke*, 1979; as *Through the Leaves* (produced Los Angeles, 1983; New York, 1984; Edinburgh and London, 1985), New York, Theatre Communications Group, 1983.

Drei Stücke (includes *Männersache*; *Heimarbeit*; *Hartnäckig*). Frankfurt, Suhrkamp, 1971.
Wildwechsel (produced Dortmund, 1971). Wollerau, Lentz, 1973.
Michis Blut (produced Munich, 1971). Included in *Gesammelte Stücke*, 1975; as *Michi's Blood* (produced New Haven, Connecticut, 1975), in *Farmyard and Four Plays*, 1976.
Heimarbeit, und Hartnäckig (produced Munich, 1971). Included in *Drei Stücke*, 1971; *Heimarbeit* translated as *Homeworker* (produced London, 1974); as *Home Work* (produced London, 1990), in *Gambit* (London), 39–40, 1982.
Dolomitenstadt Lienz (produced Bochum, 1972). Frankfurt, Suhrkamp, 1974.
Globales Interesse (produced Munich, 1972).
Herzliche Grüße aus Grado (televised 1972; produced Düsseldorf, 1976).
Stallerhof (produced Hamburg, 1972). Included in *Vier Stücke*, 1972; in English, (produced London, 1974), in *Bauer, Fassbinder, Handke, Kroetz*, London, Eyre Methuen, 1977; as *Farmyard*, in *Farmyard and Four Plays*, 1976.
Oberösterreich (produced Heidelberg, 1972). Frankfurt, Suhrkamp, 1974; as *Morecambe* (produced Edinburgh and London, 1975).
Wunschkonzert (produced Stuttgart, 1973). Included in *Vier Stücke*, 1972; as *Request Concert* (as *Request Programme*, produced Edinburgh, 1974; as *Request Concert*, produced New York, 1981), in *Farmyard and Four Plays*, 1976.
Geisterbahn (produced Vienna, 1975). Included in *Vier Stücke*, 1972; in English (produced London, 1975).
Lieber Fritz (produced Darmstadt, 1975). Included in *Vier Stücke*, 1972.
Gute Besserung (radio play broadcast 1972; stage adaptation produced Munich, 1982).
Bilanz (radio play broadcast 1972; stage adaptation produced Sommerhausen, 1980).
Vier Stücke (includes *Stallerhof*; *Wunschkonzert*; *Geisterbahn*; *Lieber Fritz*). Frankfurt, Suhrkamp, 1972.
Münchner Kindl (produced Munich, 1973). Frankfurt, Suhrkamp, 1974.
Maria Magdalena, from the play by Friedrich Hebbel (produced Heidelberg, 1973). Frankfurt, Suhrkamp, 1974.
Die Wahl fürs Leben (broadcast 1973; produced Munich, 1980). Included in *Weitere Aussichten*, 1976.
Weitere Aussichten (televised, 1974; produced Karl-Marx-Stadt, 1975). Included in *Weitere Aussichten*, 1976.
Das Nest (produced Munich, 1975). Included in *Weitere Aussichten*, 1976.
Reise ins Glück (broadcast 1975; produced Zurich 1976). Included in *Weitere Aussichten*, 1976.
Gesammelte Stücke. Frankfurt, Suhrkamp, 1975.
Weitere Aussichten: Ein Lesebuch, edited by Thomas Thieringer. Cologne, Kiepenheuer und Witsch, 1976.
Farmyard and Four Other Plays (includes *Farmyard*; *Request Concert*; *Michi's Blood*; *Men's Business*; *A Man, Dictionary*). New York, Urizen, 1976.
Agnes Bernauer, from the play by Friedrich Hebbel (produced Leipzig, 1977). Included in *Weitere Aussichten*, 1976.
Sterntäler, with Peter Zwetkoff (produced Braunschweig, 1977).
Verfassungsfeinde (produced Dresden, 1977). With *Nicht Fisch nicht Fleisch* and *Jumbo Track*, Frankfurt, Suhrkamp, 1981.

Mensch Meier (produced Düsseldorf, 1978); as *Mensch Meier: A Play of Everyday Life* (produced Seattle, 1982; New York, 1984), New York, Theatre Communications Group, 1983.
Drei neue Stücke. Frankfurt, Suhrkamp, 1979.
Der stramme Max (produced Recklinghausen, 1980). Included in *Drei neue Stücke*, 1979.
Nicht Fisch nicht Fleisch (produced Düsseldorf, 1981). With *Verfassungsfeinde* and *Jumbo-Track*, Frankfurt, Suhrkamp, 1981.
Stücke. Berlin, Henschel, 1981.
Jumbo-Track, with Floh de Cologne (produced Tübingen, 1983). With *Nicht Fisch nicht Fleisch* and *Verfassungsfeinde*, Frankfurt, Suhrkamp, 1981.
Furcht und Hoffnung der BRD, with Alexandra Weinert-Purucker (produced Bochum and Düsseldorf, 1984). Frankfurt, Suhrkamp, 1984.
Bauern Sterben: Materialien zum Stück (produced Hamburg, 1985). Reinbek, Rowohlt, 1985.
Help Wanted (produced Los Angeles, 1985; New York, 1986).
Stücke. Frankfurt, Suhrkamp, 4 vols., 1989.
Bauerntheater. Frankfurt, Suhrkamp, 1991.
Deal Soil (produced Leicester, 1992).

Radio Plays: *Inklusive*, 1972; *Bilanz*, 1972; *Gute Besserung*, 1972; *Die Wahl fürs Leben*, 1973; *Oberösterreich*, 1973; *Reise ins Glück*, 1975; *Globales Interesse*, 1976; *Das Nest*, 1976.

Television Plays: *Der Mensch Adam Deigl und die Obrigkeit*, from a work by Josef Martin Bauer, 1972; *Herzliche Grüße aus Grado*, 1972; *Weitere Aussichten*, 1974; *Muttertag*, 1975; *Verfassungsfeinde*, 1976; *Das Nest*, 1976, 1979; *Oberösterreich*, 1976.

Fiction

Der Mondscheinknecht. Frankfurt, Suhrkamp, 1981.
Der Mondscheinknecht: Fortsetzung (sequel). Frankfurt, Suhrkamp, 1983.

Other

Weitere Aussichten: Ein Lesebuch, edited by Thomas Thieringer. Cologne, Kiepenheuer und Witsch, 1976; as *Ein Lesebuch: Stücke, Polemik, Gespräche, Filme, Hörspiele, Analysen*, Reinbek, Rowohlt, 1982.
Chiemgauer Geschichten: Bayerische Menschen erzählen. Cologne, Kiepenheuer und Witsch, 1977.
Frühe Prosa, Frühe Stücke. Frankfurt, Suhrkamp, 1983.
Nicaragua Tagebuch. Hamburg, Konkret, 1985.
Mythos und Politik: über die magischen Gesten der Rechten, with Peter Glotz. Hamburg, VSA, 1985.
Brasilien-Peru-Aufzeichnungen. Frankfurt, Suhrkamp, 1991.

*

Critical Studies: "Kroetz' *Heimarbeit*: The Stratification of Language" by Margaret Herzfeld-Sander, in *Teaching Language Through Literature* 14(?), 1974; "The Theatre of Franz Xaver Kroetz" by Dragan Kalić, in *Yale/Theatre* (New Haven, Connecticut), 6(1), 1974; "Franz Xaver Kroetz Checklist" by Hugh Rorrison, in *Theatrefacts*, 3(2), 1976; "*Mitleid* and *Engagement*: Compassion and/or Political Commitment in the Dramatic Works of Franz Xaver Kroetz" by Susan L. Cocalis, in *Colloquia Germanica* (Lexington, Kentucky), 14(3), 1981; *Franz Xaver Kroetz: The Emergence of a Political Playwright* by R. W. Blevins, New York, Lang, 1983; *The Theater of Confinement: Language and Survival in the Milieu Plays of Marieluise Fleißer and Franz Xaver Kroetz* by Donna L. Hoffmeister,

Columbia, South Carolina, Camden House, 1983; "Kroetz's *Nicht Fisch nicht Fleisch*: A Good Red Herring?" by Elizabeth Boa, in *German Life and Letters* (London), July 1985; "Love at the Margin: Franz Xaver Kroetz's *Through the Leaves*" by Colette Brooks, in *Before His Eyes: Essays in Honor of Stanley Kauffmann*, edited by Bert Cardullo, Lanham, Maryland, University Press of America, 1986; "'Dreams Against the Cold': Characterization in Kroetz's *Help Wanted*" by Scott T. Cummings, in *Modern Drama* (Toronto), December 1986; "Theatre Work: *Request Concert* Project" by Rustom Bharucha, in *Performing Arts Journal* (New York), 11(1[31]), 1988; "Subject, Politics, Theatre — Reflections on Franz Xaver Kroetz" by Moray McGowan, in *A Radical Stage: Theatre in Germany in the 1970s and 1980s*, edited by W. G. Sebald, Oxford, Berg, 1988; "Franz Xaver Kroetz's *Michi's Blood* and the Representation of Violence" by Paul Walsh, in *Enclitic* (Los Angeles), 10(1[19]), 1988.

*   *   *

Franz Xaver Kroetz, one of the most frequently played modern German dramatists, is also one of the most controversial. His earliest work in the 1950s drew heavily on the theatre of Eugène Ionesco (*q.v.*) and Samuel Beckett, but theatrical collaboration with Rainer Werner Fassbinder opened up for him the folk-theatre traditions of his native Bavaria and of Austria, portraying peasant and working-class life. Kroetz's portrayals, however, have an even harsher socio-critical edge than those of modern precursors like Marieluise Fleisser or Ödon von Horváth. Kroetz is not concerned with depicting a cosy folksiness or a sentimental or satirical "superiority" of ordinary folk to their "betters." As a sometime member of the German Communist Party and an admirer of Bertolt Brecht, Kroetz focuses on the socially conditioned latent violence of the underprivileged. As a result, his writing often seems to sail perilously close to melodramatic sensationalism. In fact — following Brecht to some extent — he is primarily concerned with the way in which injustices in the system show themselves most seriously in their effects on personal relationships, and very directly in linguistic deprivation. Kroetz's characters do not communicate effectively, not because they consciously or deliberately retreat into themselves, nor simply because they are often illiterate. He shows them as having no grasp of or access to the wider social causes of their misery, and for this reason it is often hard for Kroetz to indicate what those causes actually are. Unlike Georg Büchner for instance, another precursor, Kroetz does not depict direct class oppression, and a number of his plays hover rather uncomfortably between angled social criticism, where characters are seen as victims of socialization processes, and the merely anthropological or pictorial. In this aesthetic problem, as in its everyday proletarian realism, Kroetz's work is reminiscent of Naturalism nearly a century earlier.

Nevertheless, his use of language especially encourages the reader to probe more deeply. He is not in fact attempting a naturalistic phonographic record, and himself states that there is to be just a South German flavour in performance of his dialogue; that is, the realist/illusionist aspect of theatre is present, but very carefully managed and directed. That is evident in his use of setting: there is frequently a pointed contrast between the apparently bucolic or cosily familial context, given in outline, and the action which is violent and crude. Thus Kroetz seems to draw our attention to received notions of the "natural" and "unnatural," showing that what we might deem uncivilized, even bestial, is in another sense paradoxically "normal," because induced in the underprivileged by a society of which they are the helpless victims. It is society that brutalizes, and Kroetz's almost minimalist stage style starkly reveals that what a bourgeois audience might class as the "exceptional" are the bare and inescapable facts of life for the deprived.

A striking example of his work in *Wildwechsel* (Wild Animals), where a 13-year-old girl from an apparently normal working-class home gets pregnant and induces her boyfriend to attempt the murder of her father, who has threatened them with prosecution. What at first may seem a tale of merely pathological brutality is in fact a study of emotional deprivation within a family context ruled by unthinking response to both physical urges and social stereotypes. "Shocking" details like showing the father urinating on stage set precisely the level of unreflecting, reactive behaviour typical of the family. They simply accept incongruous external models, whether for their moral sanctions or their sentimental ideals. The text is a powerful study of reliance on cliché at all levels, from buying lotto tickets because otherwise watching the Saturday-night television draw is boring, to defining parent/child relationships. Violence is always close to the surface, as a substitute for the differentiated self-awareness and verbal control not open to these poorly educated, media-dependent characters. The unseen Court, to which the "lovers" are led at the end, is merely an externalization of their total subjection to a depersonalized lifestyle. To such people the fixed norms and rules of society are not a guarantee of freedom, but another form of oppression. If the play has a weakness, it is that the degree to which broader socio-economic underprivilege rather than mere conformism produces this clichéd linguistic prison remains a shade unclear, though there are many hints of a class-typical uncertainty in a fast-changing world, as of the pressures of having only just enough to live "decently."

In later plays Kroetz is more explicitly analytical, particularly where he deals with peasant life. He deconstructs the traditional bourgeois idyllic vision of country life, showing the amputation of personality that results from unremitting hard physical labour. Relative poverty and resultant economic dependence, emotional backwardness and undeveloped social skills, inherited prejudices and crude notions of "normality" defined by lack of education and the central importance of "usefulness": all these are causes of the brutality that derives from the sheer struggle to survive within a social system of "care" that categorizes just as crudely. Such figures can only respond to the mechanics of society with self-mutilation.

Many works continue and adapt these themes, with obvious Brechtian influence as Kroetz became increasingly Marxist in his literary-theoretical views, and this led him away from conventional theatre for a time to work with smaller, often working-class groups. His political views on Germany after the end of the socialist-liberal coalition are powerfully evident in *Furcht und Hoffnung der BRD* (Fear and Hope in the Federal Republic), whose title alone is a tribute to Brecht. He also attacks the emptiness of bourgeois ideology by confronting the 19th-century tradition of *Bürgerliches Trauerspiel* (Bourgeois Tragedy) in plays such as *Maria Magdalena*. Subsequent works have shown him seeking stylistic renewal, experimenting with a mixture of the real and surreal in *Nicht Fisch nicht Fleisch* (Neither Fish Nor Fowl), but his most striking works remain his direct portrayals of lower-class life, into whose effective theatricality some of Kroetz's own experience as an actor has perhaps fed.

—Mary E. Stewart

———

KROLOW, Karl (Gustav Heinrich). German. Born in Hanover, 11 March 1915. Educated at the universities of Göttingen and Breslau, 1935–41. Married Luize Gaida in 1941; one child. Visiting Lecturer in poetry, University of Frankfurt, 1960–61, and University of Munich, 1964; town clerk of Bergen-Enkheim, 1975–76. Vice president, 1966–75, and president, 1972–75, German Academy of Speech and Poetry. Recipient: Büchner prize, 1956; Grosse Niedersächsischer Kunstpreis, 1965, 1975; Goethe-Plak, 1975; City of Darmstadt Silver Verdienstplak, 1975; Rilke prize, 1975; State of Hesse art prize, 1983; Bavarian Academy of Fine Arts award, 1985; Hölderlin prize, 1988. Honorary doctorate: Technical University of Darmstadt, 1975. Address: Park Rosenhöhe 5, 6100 Darmstadt, Germany.

PUBLICATIONS

Verse

Gedichte.   Constance, Süd, 1948.
Heimsuchung.   Berlin, Volk und Welt, 1948.
"Auf Erden".   Hamburg, Ellermann, 1949.
Die Zeichen der Welt.   Stuttgart, Deutsche Verlags-Anstalt, 1952.
Wind und Zeit: Gedichte 1950–1954.   Stuttgart, Deutsche Verlags-Anstalt, 1954.
Tage und Nächte.   Düsseldorf, Diederich, 1956.
Fremde Körper.   Frankfurt, Suhrkamp, 1959; as *Foreign Bodies*, translated by Michael Bullock, Athens, Ohio University Press, 1969.
Unsichtbare Hände: Gedichte 1959–1962.   Frankfurt, Suhrkamp, 1962; as *Invisible Hands*, translated by Michael Bullock, London, Cape Goliard Press, 1969.
Ausgewählte Gedichte.   Frankfurt, Suhrkamp, 1963.
Reise durch die Nacht.   Darmstadt, Bläschke, 1964.
Gesammelte Gedichte.   Frankfurt, Suhrkamp, 1965.
Landschaften für mich.   Frankfurt, Suhrkamp, 1966.
Alltägliche Gedichte.   Frankfurt, Suhrkamp, 1968.
Minuten–Aufzeichnungen.   Frankfurt, Suhrkamp, 1968.
Leave-Taking and Other Poems, translated by Herman Salinger.   Austin, Texas, n.p., 1968.
Poems Against Death, translated by Herman Salinger.   Washington, D.C., Charioteer Press, 1969.
Bürgerliche Gedichte (as Karol Kröpcke).   Hamburg, Merlin, 1970.
Nichts weiter als Leben.   Frankfurt, Suhrkamp, 1970.
Zeitvergehen.   Frankfurt, Suhrkamp, 1972.
Gesammelte Gedichte 2.   Frankfurt, Suhrkamp, 1975.
Ein Lesebuch (includes prose), edited by Walter Helmut Fritz.   Frankfurt, Suhrkamp, 1975.
Der Einfachheit halber.   Frankfurt, Suhrkamp, 1977.
Sterblich.   Pfaffenweiler, Pfaffenweiler Presse, 1980.
Gedichte.   Frankfurt, Suhrkamp, 1980.
Herbstsonett mit Hegel.   Frankfurt, Suhrkamp, 1981.
Pomologische Gedichte.   Usingen, Petri-Presse, 1981.
Zwischen Null und Unendlich.   Frankfurt, Suhrkamp, 1982.
Glanz aus dem Glas.   Usingen, Petri-Presse, 1982.
Schönen Dank und vorüber.   Frankfurt, Suhrkamp, 1984.
On Account Of: Selected Poems, translated by Stuart Friebert   Oberlin, Ohio, Oberlin College, 1985.
Gesammelte Gedichte 3.   Frankfurt, Suhrkamp, 1985.
Gedichte, illustrated by Thomas Duttenhoefer   Iserhagen/Hanover, Galerie Lüpfert, 1986.
Die andere Seiteder Welt.   Pfaffenweiler, Pfaffenweiler Presse, 1987.
Als es soweit war.   Frankfurt, Suhrkamp, 1988.

Wenn die Schwermut Fortschritte macht. Leipzig, Reclam, 1990.
Sätze in die Nacht, with Uta Franck. Frankfurt, Fischer, 1990.
Meine Gedichte: Eine Auswahl. Frankfurt, Suhrkamp, 1990.

Fiction

Das andere Leben. Frankfurt, Suhrkamp, 1979.
Im Gehen. Frankfurt, Suhrkamp, 1981.
Melanie: Geschichte eines Namens. Munich, Nymphen-burger, 1983.
Nacht-Leben, oder, Geschonte Kindheit. Frankfurt, Suhrkamp, 1985.

Other

Von nahen und fernen Dingen: Betrachtungen. Stuttgart, Deutsche Verlags-Anstalt, 1953.
Tessin, photographs by Fritz Eschen. Munich, Knorr und Hirth, 1959.
Aspekte zeitgenössischer deutscher Lyrik. Gütersloh, Mohn, 1961.
Im Rheinpark zu Köln, with J. J. Hässlin. Cologne, Verkehrsamt der Stadt, 1961.
Die Rolle des Autors im experimentellen Gedicht. Mainz, Akademie der Wissenschaften und der Literatur, 1962.
Schattengefecht. Frankfurt, Suhrkamp, 1964.
Corrida de toros, photographs and illustrations by Helmut Lander. Darmstadt, Peter-Presse, 1964.
Abglanz einer Residenz, illustrated by Annelise Reichmann. Darmstadt, Roether, 1964.
Laudatio auf Fritz Usinger. Friedberg, Usinger, 1965.
Poetisches Tagebuch. Frankfurt, Suhrkamp, 1966.
Das Problem des langen und kurzen Gedichts heute. Wiesbaden, Akademie der Wissenschaften und der Literatur, 1966.
Flug über Heide, Moor und grüne Berge: Niedersachsen, Nordhessen, Ostwestfalen. Braunschweig, Westermann, 1969.
Deutschland, deine Niedersachsen: Ein Land, das es nicht gibt. Hamburg, Hoffmann und Campe, 1972.
Zu des Rheins gestreckten Hügeln. Cologne, Grote, 1972.
Ein Gedicht entsteht: Selbstdeutungen, Interpretationen, Aufsätze, with others. Frankfurt, Suhrkamp, 1973.
Bremen Color, with Jochen Mönsch. Bremen, Röver, 1976.
Herodot, oder, Der Beginn von Geschichte. Waldbrunn, Heiderhoff, 1983.
Gedichte und poetologische Texte. Stuttgart, Reclam, 1985.
Unumwunden. Schondorf, Babel, 1985.
Darmstadt. Hanau, Peters, 1986.
Joseph von Eichendorff. Cologne, Kiepenheuer und Witsch, 1987.
In Kupfer gestochen: Observationen. Frankfurt, Suhrkamp, 1987.

Editor, *Gedichte*, by Paul Verlaine. Frankfurt, Insel, 1957.
Editor, *Spanische Gedichte des XX. Jahrhunderts.* Frankfurt, Insel, 1962.
Editor, *Unter uns Lesern.* Darmstadt, Roether, 1967.
Editor, *Miteinander.* Darmstadt, Bläschke, 1974.
Editor, *Gedichte*, by Wilhelm Lehmann. Frankfurt, Suhrkamp, 1977.
Editor, with Fritz Deppert and Wolfgang Weyrauch, *Literarischer März.* Munich, List, 2 vols., 1979–81.
Editor, *Deutsche Gedichte.* Frankfurt, Insel, 1982.

Editor, *Vorlieben.* Darmstadt, Ges. Hess. Literaturfreunde, 1984.

Translator, *Nachdichtungen aus fünf Jahrhunderten französischer Lyrik.* Hanover, Beeck, 1948.
Translator, *Die Barke Phantasie: Zeitgenössische französische Lyrik.* Düsseldorf, Diederich, 1957.
Translator, *Bestiarium: 25 Gedichte*, by Guillaume Apollinaire. Gessen, Walltor, 1959.

*

Bibliography: *Karl-Krolow-Bibliographie* by Rolf Paulus, Frankfurt, Athenäum, 1972.

Critical Study: "Karl Krolow: A Portrait: Introduction and Poems," in *Mundus Artium*, 12–13, 1980–81.

* * *

Karl Krolow's long literary career as one of Germany's foremost poets has accompanied the development of German literature from the very inception of the post-war West German state right up until the present day. His contribution to modern German lyric poetry resides not simply in the accumulated achievement of over 30 volumes of verse but also in his tireless activity as a champion and critic of other German poets and in his work as a translator, principally from French and Spanish. Through his activity in these three spheres — practitioner, interpreter, and promoter of the work of younger German poets, and as a distinguished mediator between German and foreign poetry — Krolow has done much to develop the taste and intelligence of the poetry-reading public in West Germany. It is not without significance, too, that poetry also forms an important topic within his creative opus, and to this extent Krolow has taken up a position at odds with the utilitarian view of literature and poetry often preached — but not always practised — by Bertolt Brecht.

Although most critics rightly focus on the achievement of Krolow from the late 1950s and the appearance of such works as *Tage und Nächte* (Days and Nights) and *Fremde Körper* (*Foreign Bodies*), works which gave clear evidence of his technical and lyrical assuredness, Krolow's first and vital service to modern German poetry is to be found much earlier. It is today difficult to appreciate the importance of Krolow's immediate post-war poetry but in the three volumes published in the years 1948 and 1949 his work represented one of the few rays of hope for the first generation of younger German poets emerging from a defeated Germany. While his contemporaries betrayed in their work all the technical defects and aesthetic limitations of a generation stunted by its upbringing and education in Nazi Germany, Krolow's poetry was singularly impressive in its openness to developments in European poetry that had yet to be absorbed by a nation that had lost contact with most advances in art and literature for well over a decade. Krolow's earlier work was further distinguished by its lightness and sureness of touch, in stark contrast to much of the bombastic and technically inept poetry produced in Germany in the wake of Hitler's defeat.

Krolow's sense of play in poetry and his structural dexterity have remained with him throughout his career. They have allowed him to display a remarkable ability to absorb and recreate in his own fashion the many streams making up post-war European poetry. It has been a virtuosity, however, that has not been without its critics, and Krolow has often been reproached for a chameleon-like rapidity in adapting to innovations and new styles. Such charges contain the underlying assumption that Krolow lacks any strong personal convictions or perspectives on either his art form or on society. While it is true that Krolow's poetry (he has written relatively little prose) has come under the influence of many of the major trends in German and European literature, it is important to note at the same time the extent to which Krolow has also modified and advanced those movements, and in many instances has actually stood in opposition to the dominant literary moods of the day. Nor are the many styles to be found in Krolow's work surprising in view of the man's longevity and productivity.

One of the earliest and initially most tenacious influences on his poetry was the work of the German nature poets, and in particular the work of Wilhelm Lehmann, whose verse had in part stirred Krolow to become a poet during World War II. Yet far from displaying an epigonal fidelity to the master of this uniquely German school of poetry, Krolow dared to break the mould of the nature poets by demythologising the form and bringing it back from the idealised state that threatened to ossify the genre. Krolow's outgrowing of Lehmann ran parallel to his awareness that German poetry was failing to make contact with the most potent elements in foreign poetry. He responded by translating the work of many of the leading French and Spanish poets, especially of the late 19th and early 20th centuries. His own poetry also reflected the degree to which he had been influenced by these contacts outside his own native German tradition. The work of the Spanish Surrealists can be detected in the opening lines of his poem "Drei Orangen, Zwei Zitronen" (Three Oranges, Two Lemons).

> Three oranges, two lemons:–
> Equation that will soon no longer be hidden,
> Formulae that inhabit the air,
> Algebra of ripe fruits!

Krolow's involvement with Surrealism was no doubt rooted in his overriding and abiding fascination with metaphor in poetry. Metaphor as *the* premise to all his poetry was admitted by Krolow in his contribution to Hans Bender's seminal volume of poets writing on their poetry, *Mein Gedicht ist mein Messer* (My Poem Is My Knife) (1955), in which Krolow saw metaphor as the controlling element in poetry, and although Krolow's work has long since developed beyond his concern with Surrealism and Dadaism and has shown him at times close to the laconic and realistic tone of more recent German poetry, he has never abandoned his belief in the primacy of metaphor. (The noun-centred nature of Krolow's poetic language—precisely because of his use of metaphor—explains some of the obstacles faced in translating his work for an English-speaking audience.)

Krolow's later poetry, often ironic and sometimes scatological, together with his pursuit of stricter verse forms, may have isolated him from the influential school of political and committed writing within German literature, yet this primacy of form over content could yet outlast the alternative work of his detractors, for Krolow's poetic gifts, developed to perfection in almost half a century of writing, reveal an unrivalled mastery of his medium in post-war Germany.

—Anthony Bushell

KU SANG. Korean. Born Sang-jun in Seoul, 16 September 1919. Moved to Wŏnsan, northern Korea (now North Korea) as a child. Educated at a seminary, briefly; University of Japan, Tokyo, degree in religion. Married. Journalist, *Puksŏn maeil*, from 1942; forced to flee to southern Korea before Korean War; imprisoned for a time after war because of writings; staff member and chief editorialist, *Yongham Ilbo* newspaper; head of Tokyo bureau, *Kyunghyang Daily News*; Professor (now Emeritus), Chungang University, Seoul; exchange professor, University of Hawaii, Honolulu, 1970. Former president, Catholic Writers' Association, and Korean PEN Section. Recipient: Seoul City cultural award for literature, 1957. Address: c/o Samseong Publishing, 340–2 Yongdungpo, P.O. Box 237, Tangsan-dong 6-9a, Yongdungpo-gu, Seoul 150-046, Republic of Korea.

PUBLICATIONS

Verse

Condensed Perfume (in Korean).   Wŏnsan, n.p., 1946.
Ku Sang.   1951.
Wasteland Poems (in Korean).   1953.
Wastelands of Fire (in Korean).   1956.
Diary of the Fields (in Korean).   1967.
The Reality of Language (in Korean).   1980.
The Crow (in Korean).   1981.
As He Walked Alone (in Korean).   1981.
From Dreyfus's Beach (in Korean).   1984.
Even the Knots on Quince Trees Tell Tales (in Korean).   1984.
Selected Poems (in Korean).   1984.
Mokkwa ongduri edo sayon i.   Seoul, Hondae Munhaksa, 1984.
Choguk songga, with Sol Ch`ang-su.   Seoul, Hongsongsa, 1986.
St. Christopher's River (in Korean).   Enlarged edition, 1986.
Wastelands of Fire, translated by Anthony Teague.   London, Forest, 1989.
Infant Splendour, translated by Brother Anthony (i.e., Anthony Teague).   Seoul, Samseong, 1990.
A Korean Century: Rivers and Fields, translated by Brother Anthony (i.e., Anthony Teague).   London, Forest, 1991.

Other

Sarang iyo, pit illera.   Seoul, Kongsongsa, 1982.
Han`guk ui mot.   Seoul, Hanlguk ui Mot Sa, 1984.
Han ch`ot pul irado k`yonun kot i.   Seoul, Munuma, 1985.
Samsimnyondae ui modonijum.   Seoul, Pom Yangsa, Ch`ulp`anbu, 1987.
Siin Kongch`o O Sang-sun.   Seoul, Chayu, 1988.
Hyondaesi ch`angjak immun.   Seoul, Hyondae Munhak, 1988.
Si wa salm ui not`u: Ku Sang esai.   Seoul, Chayu Munhaksa, 1988.

*

Critical Study: "Ku Sang: Authenticity and Commitment" by Anthony Teague, in *Korea Journal* (Seoul), 29(3), 1989.

* * *

Ku Sang has written essays and plays, but his chief importance is as a poet. The special distinctiveness of Ku Sang's work lies in his achievement of a profound simplicity out of a background characterised by a heterogeneity one would not have expected to be conducive to such a virtue of mind or art.

Korea has always felt the influence of both Chinese and Japanese traditions; in modern times, of course, it has been a battlefield, literally and metaphorically, for two competing western philosophies. Ku Sang has responded to and registered this multiplicity of influences. His own life has been very varied. He was born into a Catholic family (his elder brother was a priest who "disappeared" after the Communist takeover of North Korea). Ku Sang did not complete his own studies at minor seminary and later studied at the University of Japan in Tokyo. He has been by turns a journalist, and a political prisoner, a teacher, and an essayist. To his Catholicism has been added an alert responsiveness to the Buddhist and Confucian thinking and practices around him — as well as to both the Communist and American presences in his country. In his autobiographical sequence "Even the Knots on Quince Trees" Lao Tzu and Chuang Tzu rub shoulders with Rainer Maria Rilke, Vincent Van Gogh, Friedrich Nietzsche, and La Rochefoucauld. Out of all this, Ku Sang has emerged with a personal vision of great clarity and a poetic idiom of corresponding simplicity.

For the modern Western reader what will perhaps be most striking is the almost complete absence of irony in Ku Sang's work. Ku Sang feels no need of the protective colouring which irony offers; he is unembarrassed by the certainties of his convictions, and is similarly unafraid of the large statement or the conventionally beautiful. His "Midday Prayer" is for the gifts of "wonder, tears and prayer" and for "eternal life/as a radiancy of purity." Some of the most attractive of his work is to be found in those poems in which he celebrates the glimpses of that radiance to be found in *this* life. He finds God "when, above a shimmering pond, a dreamlike butterfly gently descends" or "within the inborn joy/of swarms of fish flashing in jade-green streams" ("In All Places"). Primary colours are named with a ringing confidence that paints vivid pictures:

> In the orchard white with snow
> like sprinkled salt,
> a plum tree raises thick black branches
> in a victory sign
>   ("In a Winter Orchard")

or

> Above your deep blue skirts,
> over your silken breasts
> a white towel lies stretched
> and your heart vibrates heat,
> a golden light as from a furnace,
> and the whole universe is glorious.
> Miles of bright sand!
>   ("Seaside in a lost homeland")

Certain repeated motifs function in Ku Sang's poetic language as reminders of the divine radiancy — flowers, butterflies, snow (the crow stands as a kind of symbolic counterpoint to such images). Flowers are tokens of "Mysterious wealth" — "full-blown petunias in pots on verandas,/ . . . strike me as infinitely new, astonishing and miraculous." In their infinite newness, flowers are, for Ku Sang, remembrances (and proofs) of resurrection:

> . . . the newly-opened forsythia flowers
> in one corner of the hedge beyond my window
> entrance me utterly,
> like seeing a model of Resurrection.
>   ("The True Appearance of the Word")

Ku Sang writes with particular exquisiteness of butterflies, with both an apprehension of their fragile beauty and delicacy of movement (e.g., "Meditation") and a comprehension of their sturdy role in the ecological cycle (e.g., "Within Creation"). Indeed, his sense of the purposefulness of the butterfly is part of the reason for that sense of fallen man's alienation from his proper role which many poems articulate:

> Ah, every creature, every one,
> knows the meaning of here, and tomorrow,
> and so they live in togetherness,
> assisting each other with all their hearts;
> so how is it that I, a man, stand here
> this night, all alone, like a rotting stick in a fence,
> understanding nothing?
>
>   ("Within Creation")

Ku Sang is no facile optimist, no happy sentimentalist. For all the ecstatic quality of some of his work, poems in which he is "overwhelmed in rapture," his experience of life has been too complete to allow him any hint of complacency. He can lacerate his own failure to follow the model of Christ ("Rehearsal for a Death-Bed Scene"); he can be compassionate towards the sufferings of others — and suffering is certainly not a reality he seeks to deny (e.g., "Before a War Cemetery of North Korean Dead"). He is not without a certain dry wit — "a poet's income being what it is,/I avoid funerals" he tells us in "News of Death." His political consciousness — inseparable from his religious sense — is evident both in his poetry and in the essays of his *Democratic Accusations* which led to his imprisonment in the 1950s.

Ku Sang's "simplicity" is no matter of simple naïvety. It has been hard won through experience and reflection, achieved through a life that has been far from sheltered. His poetic range is greater than might at first appear, and in sequences such as "Diary of the Fields" and "St. Christopher's River" he shows himself well able to sustain and develop poetic ideas. He is a poet of a type not readily imaginable in the contemporary West, and especially to be valued for that.

—Glyn Pursglove

KUMBEL. *See* **HEIN, Piet.**

KUNDERA, Milan. Czech and French. Born in Brno, Czechoslovakia, 1 April 1929; emigrated to France, 1975, became French citizen, 1981. Educated at Charles University, Prague; Academy of Music and Dramatic Arts Film Faculty, Prague, 1956. Married Věra Hrabánková in 1967. Assistant Professor of film, Academy of Music and Dramatic Arts, Prague, 1958–70; Professor of comparative literature, University of Rennes, France, 1975–80. Since 1980 Professor, École des Hautes Études, Paris. Member of the editorial board, *Literární noviny* [Literary Journal], 1956–59, 1963–68, and *Literární listy*, 1968–69. Recipient: Writers' Publishing

House prize, 1961, 1969; Klement Lukeš prize, 1963; Czechoslovak Writers' Union prize, 1968; Medicis prize (France), 1973; Mondello prize (Italy), 1978; Commonwealth award (USA), 1981; Europa prize, 1982; Los Angeles *Times* award, 1984; Jerusalem prize, 1984; Académie Française Critics prize, 1987; Nelly Sachs prize, 1987; Osterichischeve state prize, 1987; *Independent* award for foreign fiction (UK), 1991. Honorary doctorate: University of Michigan, Ann Arbor, 1983. Member, American Academy; Officier, Légion d'Honneur. Address: École des Hautes Études, 54 Boulevard Raspail, 75006 Paris, France.

PUBLICATIONS

Fiction

Směšné lásky [Laughable Loves]; *Druhý sešit směšných lásek* [A Second Book of Laughable Loves]; *Třetí sešit směšných lásek* [A Third Book of Laughable Loves].   Prague, Československý spisovatel, 3 vols., 1963–69; revised and collected as *Směšné lásky*, 1970; as *Laughable Loves*, New York, Knopf, 1974; London, Murray, 1977.
Žert.   Prague, Československý spisovatel, 1967; as *The Joke*, New York, Coward McCann, and London, Macdonald, 1969; revised edition, London, HarperCollins, 1992.
La Vie est ailleurs.   Paris, Gallimard, 1973; as *Life Is Elsewhere*, New York, Knopf, 1974; London, Faber, 1986; as *Život je jinde*, Toronto, 68 Publishers, 1979.
La Valse aux adieux.   Paris, Gallimard, 1976; as *The Farewell Party*, New York, Knopf, 1976; London, Murray, 1977; as *Valčík na rozloučenou*, Toronto, 68 Publishers, 1979.
Le Livre du rire et de l'oubli.   Paris, Gallimard, 1979; as *The Book of Laughter and Forgetting*, New York, Knopf, 1980; London, Faber, 1982; as *Kniha smíchu a zapomnění*, Toronto, 68 Publishers, 1981.
L'Insoutenable Légéreté de l'être.   Paris, Gallimard, 1984; as *The Unbearable Lightness of Being*, New York, Harper, and London, Faber, 1984; as *Nesnesitelná lehkost bytí*, Toronto, 68 Publishers, 1985.
L'Immortalité.   Paris, Gallimard, 1990; as *Immortality*, London, Faber, and New York, Grove Weidenfeld, 1991.

Plays

Majitelé klíčů [The Owners of the Keys] (produced Prague, 1962).   Prague, Československý spisovatel, 1962.
Dvě uši dvě svatby [Two Ears and Two Weddings].   Prague, Dilia, 1968; as *Ptákovina* [Cock-a-Doodle-Do] (produced Prague, 1969).
Jakub a pán (produced Zagreb, 1980); as *Jacques et son maître: hommage à Denis Diderot* (produced Paris, 1981; London, 1984), Paris, Gallimard, 1981; as *Jacques and His Master* (produced London, 1985; Cambridge, Massachusetts, 1985), New York, Harper, 1985; London, Faber, 1986.

Screenplays: *Žert* [The Joke], from his own novel, with Jaromil Jires, 1968; *Já Truchlivý Bůh* [I the Sad God], 1969.

Verse

Člověk zahrada širá [Man: A Broad Garden].   Prague, Československý spisovatel, 1953.
Poslední máj [The Last May].   Prague, Československý spisovatel, 1955; revised edition, 1961, 1963.
Monology [Monologues].   Prague, Československý spisovatel, 1957; revised edition, 1964, 1965, 1967, 1969.

Other

Umění románu: cesta Vladislava Vančury za velkou epikou [The Art of the Novel: Vladislav Vančura's Road in Search of the Great Epic].   Prague, Československý spisovatel, 1960.
L'Art du roman.   Paris, Gallimard, 1987; as *The Art of the Novel*, New York, Grove Press, and London, Faber, 1988; *Milan Kundera and the Art of Fiction*, edited by Aron Aji, New York, Garland, 1992.

*

Bibliography: *Milan Kundera: An Annotated Bibliography* by Glen Brand, New York, Garland, 1988.

Critical Studies: *Milan Kundera: A Voice from Central Europe* by Robert Porter, Aarhus, Arkona, 1981; Kundera issue of *Salmagundi* (Saratoga Springs, New York), 73, 1987, and *Review of Contemporary Fiction* (Elmwood Park, Illinois), 9(2), 1989; *Terminal Paradox: The Novels of Milan Kundera* by Maria Němcová Banerjee, New York, Grove Weidenfeld, and London, Faber, 1991; *Milan Kundera and the Art of Fiction*, edited by Aron Aji, New York, Garland, 1992.

*   *   *

Milan Kundera's development as a writer has been strongly influenced by historical events. During World War II and in the brief, dynamic years which followed he was committed to the Communist cause; he later justified his enthusiasm with the explanation, "Communism enthralled me in much the way Stravinsky, Picasso and Surrealism had. It promised a great, miraculous metamorphosis, a totally new and different world" (New York Times Book Review). But in the 1960s, while still a member of the Communist Party, he became uneasy about its actual practice, including the policy concerning censorship. Kundera was one of a number of writers who refused to make changes in the articles they wrote and so ran the risk of remaining unpublished, but who eventually won greater freedom in the material which they did succeed in publishing.

The predominant theme in Kundera's writing is that of identity: not simply the identity of the inner self, but with whom and with what a person identifies his or her self. In the work Kundera completed while living in Czechoslovakia this theme has three strands: identification with (or commitment to) an ideology; identification with (or desire for) an idealised self-image; and identification with a history and a tradition.

In the mid-1950s Kundera was known to the Czech reading public as a poet, author of three collections: *Člověk zahrada širá* (Man: A Broad Garden), *Poslední máj* (The Last May), and *Monology* (Monologues). *Poslední máj* is particularly remarkable as an apparent sanctification of the Communist journalist Julius Fučík, who was executed by the Nazis.

Kundera's first published fiction, the short stories *Směšné lásky* (*Laughable Loves*), deal with the idealised self-image. The characters in the stories pride themselves on being able to manipulate the world around them and live out their self-images. In reality, however, they have no control over their lives; they can be humiliated by a simple chain of events or by another victim of chance. These hedonists are very different from the subject of Kundera's first full-scale work, *Umění románu: cesta Vladislava Vančury za velkou epikou* (The Art of the Novel: Vladislav Vančura's Road in Search of the Great Epic). (This is a different book from his 1987 work, *L'Art du roman*). Vančura had been a member of the pre-war avant-garde, a writer and a Communist, who was executed by the Nazis at the end of the war. Kundera placed Vančura's work in the context of the world novel: of Henry Fielding, Sir Walter Scott, Leo Tolstoy, Honoré de Balzac, Gustave Flaubert, and Anatole France. Vančura, both in his commitment to Communism and his place in European culture, represented the antithesis of the ephemeral subjects of *Laughable Loves*.

Kundera's first play, *Majitelé klíčů* (The Owners of the Keys), also presents a contrast between material comfort and a commitment to history. The setting is a provincial town during the German occupation; the (positive) hero has to decide whether he will rejoin the (Communist) resistance — a decision which will mean the betrayal of his wife and her petit bourgeois parents to the Nazis. However, although the play was effective in dramatic terms, its content was conventional Socialist Realism. More significant was Kundera's first novel, *Žert* (The Joke), which tells the story of Communism in Czechoslovakia between the years 1948 and 1965. Through the experiences of its characters it traces the loss of idealism, the hopeless reliance on hollow images. Paradoxically, the character who remains inwardly most loyal to Communist ideals also values the folk traditions of the country's past.

Before August 1968, the Theatre on the Balustrade in Prague had commissioned a play from Kundera which was produced there in May 1969. *Ptákovina* (Cock-a-Doodle-Do) is set in a school staffed by cringing or sadistic teachers; the action is triggered by a crude practical joke played by the headmaster that eventually rebounds on him. The theme of the play is moral degradation in a society which has lost its values. *Jakub a pán* (Jacques and His Master), on the other hand, was written as an "homage to Diderot," a variation on Diderot's *Jacques le fataliste*. Kundera later claimed that when he wrote it, he saw the shadow of encroaching Asian hordes falling across the western world, and felt that he was trying to hold on to the disappearing civilisation of Diderot's world.

The subject of the novel *La Vie est ailleurs* (Life Is Elsewhere) is the degeneration which brought the West close to disintegration. The young poet, Jaromil — a precocious surrealist and Party hack poet — thinks of himself as an intellectual descendant of Arthur Rimbaud; to Kundera, he is a forerunner of the pretentious students revolting in the streets of Paris in May 1968. In *La Valse aux adieux* (The Farewell Party) the theme is death. The action follows five days in the life of a popular jazz trumpeter who tries to persuade a young nurse to abort the child which she claims is his; it is a picture of a society in the grip of a life-denying force which seeks to suppress and condemn every natural, irrational or "mystical" experience.

In July 1967, during the run-up to the Prague Spring, Kundera, together with Ivan Klíma, Václav Havel, and Ludvík Vaculík (qq.v.), made a speech at the Congress of the Czechoslovak Writers' Union which was regarded by Party functionaries as a political outrage. Kundera appealed to writers to consider the role of literature in the wider context of Czech history. He described how the writers of the 19th century had helped to shape Czechoslovakia's destiny, and asked whether today's writers were prepared to let the decline into provincialism and officially sanctioned vandalism continue.

In Spring 1970, 18 months after the Russian occupation, the Communists embarked on a systematic humiliation of those considered to be in any way responsible. Early in 1970 Kundera lost his lectureship in world literature at the Prague Film Academy. At this time he did not expect to be published again in Czechoslovakia in his lifetime, and in 1975 accepted the post of Professor of comparative literature at the University of Rennes in France. Soon afterwards he was notified of the confiscation of his Czechoslovak citizenship. Ironically, the exile and the loss of his nationality led him to reassess his position, and to consider himself as a European rather than a Czechoslovak writer.

It was in France that Kundera wrote the two novels that enhanced his international fame — *Le Livre du rire et de l'oubli* (The Book of Laughter and Forgetting) and *L'Insoutenable Légéreté de l'être* (The Unbearable Lightness of Being). In these novels he abandons continuous narrative for a structure which resembles film collage. He juxtaposes one narrative with another, moves backward and forward in time, fictionalises historical characters, and treats fictional characters as real by bringing them into dialogue with the author-narrator. In *The Book of Laughter and Forgetting* the central character is Tamina, an exiled Czech working as a waitress in a provincial French town, who tries to remember her dead husband and to regain the diary and letters she left behind in Prague. In *The Unbearable Lightness of Being* Kundera contrasts the fate of two exiles, Tereza and Sabina: the one drawn back to her homeland and her death; the other who floats free and drifts to America. The novel weaves a web of chance encounters, uncertainties, and betrayals, both political and personal. The third member of the triangle is Tomas, husband of Tereza and lover of (among many other women) Sabina. Tomas is a surgeon who returns with Tereza to "normalised" Prague where, harassed by the secret police, he becomes a window cleaner. He and Tereza take "the only escape open to them," life in the countryside, where those who no longer have anything to lose have nothing to fear. They die together, when the weight of Tomas's badly maintained truck crushes their bodies into the earth. Sabina, abandoning one lover in Geneva on her way to Paris, with a final destination of America, is aware of emptiness all around her: "Until that time, her betrayals had filled her with excitement and joy, because they opened up new paths to new adventures of betrayal. But what if the paths came to an end? One could betray one's parents, husband, country, love, but when parents, husband, country and love were gone — what was left to betray?"

The theme of identity powerfully re-emerges in Kundera's most recent novel, *L'Immortalité* (Immortality). It is not the immortal soul that Kundera is thinking of, but earthly immortality; as Laura says: "After all, we want to leave something behind!" only to be challenged by her sister Agnes's "sceptical astonishment." Although Agnes's life forms the axis of the novel, around it revolve other stories, fantasies, and feuilletons. Central to the theme is the story of Bettina von Arnim, who created her own immortality out of two or three meetings and an exchange of letters with Goethe. The structure of *Immortality* is built on echo and reflection, gesture and memory. Kundera contrasts the reality experienced by his grandmother in her Moravian village community with the "reality" seen by the average Parisian businessman on his evening TV news. Immortality is not in the roles we create for ourselves, the images we set up for posterity, but in the continuity of life and the fragile survival of our culture.

History is for Kundera the land and its traditions, which have shaped lives for generations. His exile from his country has shaped his awareness of the disintegration of European society. In his writing he tries to recapture and hold on to the last remnants of a vanishing western civilisation.

—Barbara Day

KUNERT, Günter. German. Born in Berlin, 6 March 1929. Educated at the Academy of Applied Arts, Berlin-Weißensee, 1946–49. Married Marianne Todten in 1952. Staff member, *Ulenspiegel*, 1949; Visiting Associate Professor, University of Texas, Austin, 1972; writer-in-residence, University of Warwick, Coventry, 1975, Town of Bergen-Enkheim, 1983–84, and City of Mainz, 1989. Recipient: Heinrich Mann prize, 1962; Becher prize, 1973; Confederation of German Industry award, 1980; Heinrich Heine prize, 1985; Hölderlin prize, 1991; Curtius prize, 1991. Honorary doctorate: Allegheny College, Pennsylvania, 1988. Member, Academy of Arts, Berlin, 1976, and German Academy of Languages and Literature, 1982. Address: Schulstrasse 7, 2216 Kaisborstel, Germany.

PUBLICATIONS

Verse

Wegschilder und Mauerinschriften.   Berlin, Aufbau, 1950.
Unter diesem Himmel.   Berlin, Neues Leben, 1955.
Tagwerke.   Halle, Middeldeutschen, 1960.
Das Kreuzbrave Liederbuch.   Berlin, Aufbau, 1961.
Erinnerung an einen Planeten.   Munich, Hanser, 1963.
Der ungebetene Gast.   Berlin, Aufbau, 1965.
Verkündigung des Wetters.   Munich, Hanser, 1966.
Unschuld der Natur.   Berlin, Aufbau, 1966.
Poesiealbum acht.   Berlin, Neues Leben, 1968.
Warnung vor Spiegeln.   Munich, Hanser, 1970.
Notizen in Kreide.   Leipzig, Reclam, 1970.
Offener Ausgang.   Berlin, Aufbau, 1972.
Im weiteren Fortgang.   Munich, Hanser, 1974.
Das kleine Aber.   Berlin, Aufbau, 1976.
Unterwegs nach Utopia.   Munich, Hanser, 1977.
Verlangen nach Bomarzo: Reisegedichte.   Munich, Hanser, 1978.
Unruhiger Schlaf.   Munich, Deutscher Taschenbuch, 1979.
Abtötungsverfahren.   Munich, Hanser, 1980.
Stilleben.   Munich, Hanser, 1983.
Abendstimmung: Gedichte — Holzschnitte, with Heinz Stein. Hauzenberg, Pongratz, 1983.
Vor der Sintflut: das Gedicht als Arche Noah: Frankfurter Vorlesungen.   Munich, Hanser, 1985.
Berlin beizeiten.   Munich, Hanser, 1987.
Gedichte.   Stuttgart, Reclam, 1987.
Die befleckte Empfängnis.   Berlin, Aufbau, 1988.
Ich, du, er, sie, es: Gedichte.   Ravensburg, Maier, 1988.
Fremd daheim.   Munich, Hanser, 1990.

Plays

Der Kaiser von Hondu (television play).   Berlin, Aufbau, 1959.
Ein anderer K: Hörspiele.   Berlin, Aufbau, 1977.

Screenplay: *Beethoven: Tag aus einem Leben*, 1976.

Radio Plays: *Mit der Zeit ein Feuer*; *Ehrenhändel: Ein anderer K.*

Television Plays: *Fetzers Flucht*, 1962; *Karpfs Karriere*, 1970; *King Arthur*, 1990; *An Obituary in the Wall*, 1991; *Endstation: Harembar*, 1991.

Fiction

Der ewige Detektiv und andere Geschichten.   Berlin, Eulenspiegel, 1954.
Tagträume.   Munich, Hanser, 1964.
Im Namen der Hüte.   Munich, Hanser, 1967.
Die Beerdigung findet in aller Stille statt.   Munich, Hanser, 1968.
Kramen in Fächern.   Berlin, Aufbau, 1969.
Tagträume in Berlin und andernorts.   Munich, Hanser, 1972.
Gast aus England.   Munich, Hanser, 1973.
Der Hai: Erzählungen und kleine Prosa, edited by Dietrich Bode.   Stuttgart, Reclam, 1974.
Keine Affäre.   Berlin, Berliner Handpresse, 1976.
Kinobesuch.   Leipzig, Insel, 1977.
Drei Berliner Geschichten.   Berlin, Aufbau, 1979.
Zurück ins Paradies.   Munich, Hanser, 1984.
Aus vergangener Zukunft.   Berlin, Aufbau, 1990.

Other

Kunerts lästerliche Leinwand.   Berlin, Eulenspiegel, 1965.
Betonformen, Ortsangaben.   Berlin, Literarisches Colloquium, 1969.
Ortsangaben.   Berlin, Aufbau, 1971.
Die geheime Bibliothek.   Berlin, Aufbau, 1973.
Der andere Planet: Ansichten von Amerika.   Berlin, Aufbau, 1974.
Der Mittelpunkt der Erde.   Berlin, Eulenspiegel, 1975.
Warum schreiben: Notizen zur Literatur.   Munich, Hanser, 1976.
Jeder Wunsch ein Treffler (for children).   Cologne, Middelhauve, 1976.
Berliner Wände, photographs by Thomas Höpker.   Munich, Hanser, 1976.
Camera obscura.   Munich, Hanser, 1978.
Heinrich von Kleist: Eine Modell.   Berlin, Akademie der Kunst, 1978.
Ein englisches Tagebuch.   Berlin, Aufbau, 1978.
Die Schreie der Fledermäuse (miscellany), edited by D. R. Zimmer.   Gütersloh, Bertelsmann, 1978.
Ziellose Umtriebe.   Berlin, Aufbau, 1979.
Ulenspiegel: Zeitschrift für Literatur, Kunst, und Satire, edited by Kunert and H. Sandberg.   Munich, Hanser, 1979.
Acht bunte Blätter.   Berlin, Eulenspiegel, 1979.
Kurze Beschreibung eines Momentes der Ewigkeit.   Leipzig, Reclam, 1980.
Verspätete Monologe.   Munich, Hanser, 1981.
Diesseits des Erinnerns.   Munich, Hanser, 1982.
Die letzten Indianer Europas.   Hauzenberg, Pongratz, 1983.
Leben und Schreiben.   Pfaffenweiler, Pfaffenweiler Presse, 1983.
Windy Times (verse and prose).   New York, Red Dust, 1983.
Auf der Suche nach der wirklichen Freiheit.   Berlin, Berliner Handpresse, 1983.
Kain und Abels Brüderlichkeit.   Hauzenberg, Pongratz, 1984.
Der Wald.   Hamburg, Ellert und Richter, 1985.
Berliner Nächte: Laternenbilder, with Michael Engler.   Hamburg, Ellert und Richter, 1986.
Toskana, photographs by Klaus Bossemeyer.   Hamburg, Ellert und Richter, 1986.
Zeichnungen und Beispiele, edited by Joseph A. Kruse.   Düsseldorf, Droste, 1987.
Lesarten.   Munich, Piper, 1987.
Auf Abwegen und andere Verirrungen.   Munich, Hanser, 1988.

In Schleswig-Holstein: zwischen den Meeren, photographs by Joachim Kürtz.   Freiburg, Eulen, 1990.

Editor, *Kriegsfibel*, by Bertolt Brecht.   Berlin, Eulenspiegel, 1955.

Editor, *Gedichte*, by Nikolaus Lenau.   Frankfurt, Fischer, 1969.

Editor, *Über die irdische Liebe und andere gewisse Welträtsel in Liedern und Balladen*, by Bertolt Brecht.   Berlin, Eulenspiegel, 1970.

Editor, *Dimension* (East German literature).   Austin, University of Texas Press, 1973.

Editor, *Jahrbuch für Lyrik vol. 3*.   Frankfurt, Athenäum, 1981.

Editor, with Jürgen Manthey and Delf Schmidt, *Die Literatur blüht im Tal*.   Reinbek, Rowohlt, 1981.

Editor, *Mein Lesebuch*.   Frankfurt, Fischer, 1983.

Editor, *Gedicht die "Zeit"*.   Munich, Piper, 1987.

Editor, *Aus fremder Heimat: zur Exil-situation heutiger Literatur*.   Munich, Hanser, 1988.

Editor, *Dichter predigen: Reden aus der Wirklichkeit*.   Stuttgart, Radius, 1989.

Translator, with Ernst Jandl, *Wie wir Grossmutter zum Markt bringen*, by Christopher Middleton.   Stierstadt, Eremiten-Presse, 1970.

*

Critical Studies: "Orpheus in the East: Günter Kunert's Orpheus Cycle" by Lisa Kahn, in *Modern Language Quarterly* (Seattle), 38, 1977; "An Analysis of Günter Kunert's 'Schatten entziffern'" by Clark W. Kenyon, in *University of Dayton Review* (Dayton, Ohio), 13(2), 1978; "Günter Kunert's *Der Hai*: Socialist Realism and Beyond" by Alan D. Latta, in *Seminar* (Kingston, Ontario), 1980; "Cultural Politics and the Literary Avant-Garde in East Germany: The Case of Günter Kunert" by James R. Reece, in *Selecta* (Corvallis, Oregon), 2, 1981; "Faltering Steps: Günter Kunert's *Unterwegs nach Utopia*," in *Germanic Review* (New York), Winter 1982, and "Günter Kunert and Socialism: A 'Classic Experiment' in New Perspective," in *Germanic Review* (New York), Spring 1986, both by Erich P. Hofacker, Jr.; "Günter Kunert's Image of the USA: Another Look at *Der andere Planet*" by Nancy A. Lauckner, in *Studies in GDR Culture and Society, III: Selected Papers from the Eighth International Symposium on the German Democratic Republic*, edited by Margy Gerber and others, Lanham, Maryland, University Press of America, 1983; "Günter Kunert, a Contemporary German Consciousness: A Study of His Poetry and Poetics" by Agnes Stein, in *Modern Language Studies* (Providence, Rhode Island), Winter 1983; "The 'Uneven Mirrors' of Art and Science: Kunert and Escher" by Valerie D. Greenberg, in *Mosaic* (Winnipeg, Manitoba), Spring 1989.

Günter Kunert comments:

The poems are at the centre of my writing. For me they are its essence. The smaller prose works are grouped around this centre, then the stories, travel writings, and essays. This variety was the result of different intentions and inspirations. Apart from these works I also write screenplays for television, radio plays, and reviews: not only to earn a living but also because in these genres one can make more topical statements about the time or the state of the world. Although I live in the country I do not live in an ivory tower. I observe very clearly — and sometimes with complete despair — what is happening on our planet. And I can only deal with these daily, routine atrocities by reflecting on them and by freeing myself of them

again and again through writing. Yet this freedom only ever lasts a short while. So writing is for me an attempt to escape, which I have to repeat again and again and which never ends.

* * *

Poetry and literary criticism, short stories and television plays — Günter Kunert has written in almost every genre. His real talent undoubtedly lies in the more concise forms: his one novel is of uneven quality. In his best poems and short stories, on the other hand, Kunert achieves a stylistic virtuosity and intellectual sharpness hardly rivalled in East German writing.

Kunert's often biting irony, his command of the aphorism, and his extensive use of the parable all reveal the influence of Bertolt Brecht on his work. He has taken the latter's dialectical approach to reality a step further, however, in according the concept of the paradox an important place in much of his poetry. Kunert demonstrated its function in the essay "Paradoxie als Prinzip" by analysing one of his first poems to employ the technique: in "Ikarus 64" the reader is encouraged to "spread his arms" and fly — and then told this is, of course, impossible. "Flight," Kunert explains, is here a metaphor for flight from the past — which in fact cannot be escaped, but whose baleful influence can be lessened if the attempt is nonetheless made. The paradoxical formulation of this problem is intended to provoke the reader into looking more critically at society.

Kunert's negative view of the past, engendered by his experience of fascism and the war, forms a leitmotif in his work. His first collection of poems, *Wegschilder und Mauerinschriften* (Signposts and Wall Inscriptions) contains a number which warn against the danger of the recent war being repeated: in one, a survivor crawls from a bombed house vowing "never again" — only to add (in an ironic afterthought typical of Kunert) "at least, not straightaway." The tenor of these so-called "warning poems" changed, however, in the 1960s from one of admonition to growing disillusionment. In poems from the collection *Der ungebetene Gast* (The Uninvited Guest) to *Warnung vor Spiegeln* (Warning Against Mirrors), Kunert insisted with growing emphasis that far from being dead the past was still at work in the distortions of East German socialism. Thus in "Hoffnungsvolle Entdeckung" he shows the emergence of a soulless bureaucracy, in which mountains of files squeeze the blood from the citizens registered in them. Above all, Kunert began to depict in both poems and stories an insidious alienation of the individual in society, extending from the workplace to his private life.

This trend in Kunert's work inevitably led to repeated attacks on him from Party critics in the GDR. In 1963 some of his poems were described as "lumps of dirt"; in 1966 he was accused of displaying un-Marxist "despair"; and in 1969 a volume of short stories was similarly condemned. His situation worsened in the 1970s as his poems became more pessimistic (the Utopia aspired to by socialism reveals itself in one poem to be an "El Dorado," a chimera) and their irony more vitriolic. His involvement in a series of cultural-political controversies further strained his relations with the Party, so that in 1979 he finally left East Germany. His work in the 1980s was informed by an uncompromisingly resigned tone which, although it could verge on affectation, more frequently displayed both formal and philosophical subtlety. It will be interesting to gauge any change in his tone with the reunification of Germany.

—Neil Jackson

KUNZE, Reiner. German. Born in Oelsnitz/Erzgebirge, 16 August 1933. Educated at the University of Leipzig, 1951–55, diploma in journalism 1955. Married 1) Inge Kunze in early 1950s (divorced), one son; 2) Elisabeth Mifka in 1961, one daughter. Lecturer, University of Leipzig, early 1950s: denounced by colleague as counterrevolutionary; suffered heart attack, 1959; factory worker, one year; lived in Czechoslovakia, 1960–62; resigned from Socialist Unity party, 1968, in protest at Soviet invasion of Czechoslovakia; expelled from the Writers Union, 1976, in response to protesting the GDR revocation of citizenship of Wolf Biermann, *q.v.*; emigrated to West Germany, 1977; writer-in-residence, Mainz. Recipient: Czech Writers' Society translation prize, 1968; German book prize for children's literature, 1971; Bavarian Academy of Fine Arts prize, 1973; Mölle prize (Sweden), 1973; Trakl prize (Austria), 1977; Gryphius prize, 1977; Büchner prize, 1977; Bavarian film prize, 1978; Geschwister-Scholl prize, 1981; Eichendorff award, 1984; Federal Cross of Merit, 1984; Ostbayerischer Kulturpreis, 1988; Weichmann prize, 1990; Schleyer prize, 1991. Member, Academy of Arts, Berlin, and German Academy for Languages and Literature. Address: Am Sonnenhang 19, 8391 Obernzell-Erlau, Germany.

PUBLICATIONS

Verse

Die Zukunft sitzt am Tische: 26 Gedichte, with Egon Günther. Halle, Mitteldeutscher, 1955.
Vögel über dem Tau: Liebesgedichte und Lieder. Halle, Mitteldeutscher, 1959.
Aber die Nachtigall jubelt. Halle, Mitteldeutscher, 1962.
Widmungen. Bad Godesberg, Hohwacht, 1963.
Reiner Kunze: Poesiealbum 11. Berlin, Neues Leben, 1968.
Sensible Wege: 48 Gedichte und ein Zyklus. Reinbek, Rowohlt, 1969.
Zimmerlautstärke. Frankfurt, Fischer, 1972; as *With the Volume Turned Down, and Other Poems*, translated by Ewald Osers, London, London Magazine Editions, 1973; as *Zimmerlautstärke: With the Volume Down Low*, translated by Lori Fischer, Amherst, Massachusetts, Swamp Press, 1981.
Brief mit blauem Siegel. Leipzig, Reclam, 1973.
Die Bringer Beethovens. Düsseldorf, Eremiten-Presse, 1976.
Das Kätzchen (for children). Frankfurt, Fischer, 1979.
Wo wir wohnen. Weilheim, Deutschlehrer am Gymnasium Weilheim, 1981.
Auf eigene Hoffnung. Frankfurt, Fischer, 1981.
Gespräch mit der Amsel: Frühe Gedichte; Sensible Wege; Zimmerlautstärke. Frankfurt, Fischer, 1984.
Three Contemporary German Poets: Wolf Biermann, Sarah Kirsch, Reiner Kunze, edited by Peter J. Graves. Leicester, Leicester University Press, 1985.
Eines jeden einziges Leben. Frankfurt, Fischer, 1986.
Selbstgespräch für andere (includes prose). Stuttgart, Reclam, 1989.
Wohin der Schlaf sich schlafen legt (for children). Frankfurt, Fischer, 1991.
Am Krankenbett des Tierbildhauers Heinz Theuerjahr. Hauzenberg, Pongratz, 1991.

Fiction

Der Löwe Leopold: Fast Märchen, fast Geschichten (for children). Frankfurt, Fischer, 1970.

Der Dichter und die Löwenzahnwiese (for children). Berlin, Berliner Handpresse, 1971.
Die wunderbaren Jahre. Frankfurt, Fischer, 1976; as *The Wonderful Years*, New York, Braziller, 1977; as *The Lovely Years*, London, Sidgwick and Jackson, 1978.
Eine stadtbekannte Geschichte (for children). Olten, Walter, 1982.

Play

Die wunderbaren Jahre, adapted from his novel (screenplay; produced 1980). Frankfurt, Fischer, 1979.

Other

Wesen und Bedeutung der Reportage. Berlin, Deutscher Schriftstellerverband, 1960.
Wintereisenbahnerhochzeit: über das poetische in einem Bild von Jan Balet. Altwindeck, Windecker Winkelpresse, 1978.
Erfriggen von den Messen Mozarts. Hauzenberg, Pongratz, 1981.
In Deutschland Zuhaus. Hauzenberg, Pongratz, 1984.
Zurückgeworfen auf sich selbst: Interviews 1983–1988. Hauzenberg, Pongratz, 1989.
Das weisse Gedicht: Essays. Frankfurt, Fischer, 1989.
Deckname "Lyrik". Frankfurt, Fischer, 1990.
Mensch ohne Macht. Hauzenberg, Pongratz, 1991.

Editor, with Edith Nell, *Die Sonne den anderen*. Berlin, Aufbau, 1959.
Editor, with Heinz Knobloch, *Mir gegenüber*. Halle, Mitteldeutscher, 1960.
Editor, *Das Brot auf dieser Erden*, by Kurt Heinze. Weimar, Volksverlag Weimar, 1962.
Editor, *Über, o über dem Dorn*. Frankfurt, Fischer, 1986.

Translator, *Der Wind mit Namen Jaromir*, by Jan Skácel. Berlin, Volk und Welt, 1961.
Translator, *Die Schlüsselbesitzer*, by Milan Kundera. Berlin, Bloch, 1962.
Translator, *Die Tür: Nachdichtungen aus dem Tschechischen*. Bad Godesberg, Hohwacht, 1964.
Translator, *Der Schatz der Hexe Funkelauge*, by Ladisław Dvorsky. Prague, Dilia, 1964.
Translator, *Neugier*, by Ludvik Kundera. Kassel, Bärenreiter, 1966.
Translator, *Fastnacht*, by Josef Topol. Berlin, Henschel, 1966.
Translator, *Fährgeld für Charon*, by Jan Skácel. Hamburg, Merlin, 1967.
Translator, *Der Abend aller Tage*, by Ludvik Kundera. Prague, Dilia, 1967.
Translator, *Nacht mit Hamlet*, by Vladimir Holan. Hamburg, Merlin, 1969.
Translator, *Wunderschöne Sträflingskugel*, by Antonín Brousek. Darmstadt, Bläschke, 1970.
Translator, *Vor eurer Schwelle*, by Vladimir Holan. Darmstadt, Bläschke, 1970.
Translator, *Eine Tafel, blau wie der Himmel*, by Milos Macourek. Hauzenberg, Pongratz, 1982.
Translator, *Sommertraum: Gedichte in Prosa*, by Vit Obrtel. Hauzenberg, Pongratz, 1982.
Translator, *Wundklee*, by Jan Skácel. Frankfurt, Fischer, 1982.
Translator, *Erdlast*, by Jaroslav Seifert. Hauzenberg, Pongratz, 1985.

Translator, *Das blaueste Feuilleton*, by Jan Skácel. Hauzenberg, Pongratz, 1989.

Translator, *Die Letzte fahrt mit der Lokalbann*, by Jan Skácel. Hauzenberg, Pongratz, 1991.

*

Bibliographies: in *Reiner Kunze, Materialien zu Leben und Werk*, edited by Heiner Feldkamp, Frankfurt, Fischer, 1987, and *Sichtbar Machen* by Feldkamp, Hauzenberg, Pongratz, 1991.

Critical Study: "Reiner Kunze, a Poet from 'Prussia': A Preface with Some Stories" by Martin Esslin, in *Encounter* (London), July 1978.

*   *   *

The power of Reiner Kunze's work is belied by its softness of tone and its comparatively small scale. In the eyes of the Stasi, the East German state security service, this gentle poet was considered sufficient threat to merit, as the opening of the files has shown, some 12 volumes of documentation totalling nearly 3,500 pages. Kunze has published extracts in *Deckname "Lyrik"* (Code-Name "Lyric"), and they reveal in chilling detail how the authorities in the German Democratic Republic, not content with keeping him under observation, launched a covert operation to break him psychologically and hound him out of the state. Yet Kunze had begun his literary career in the 1950s as a staunch defender of East German socialism, and his early work is scarcely different from the flaccid and deferential verse characteristic of the time. But growing experience of the way in which the regime treated divergent opinions led to what he has described as his "great political disillusionment, the dreadful recognition that I had been deceived and betrayed." After the Warsaw Pact invasion of Czechoslovakia in 1968 he resigned from the Party; in 1977 he moved to the West.

Immediately striking in Kunze's poetry is the economy with which he operates. His verse is often the distillation of just one thought or idea, and characteristically this is compressed into a terse allegory, or a pithy observation, or a single pregnant metaphor. The title of one of his collections, *Zimmerlautstärke* (*With the Volume Turned Down*), is derived from a poem comparing, in just six short lines, the fate of writers under the Nazis and the Communists, but it applies equally well to a poetic style marked by understatement and ellipsis. Kunze's dominant theme is concern for individual integrity within a hostile world. In its deepest sense this relates to the conviction that, although life is ultimately devoid of meaning, individuals may still affirm their humanity by confronting and resisting the absurdity of existence. This is a position derived, as Kunze has acknowledged many times, from Albert Camus, but matching the existentialist impulse of his poetry is a parallel desire to defy that sense of helplessness engendered by human agency, particularly the abuse of political power. This received its most forceful expression in *Die wunderbaren Jahre* (*The Lovely Years* or *The Wonderful Years*), a collection of short pieces which, though written in prose, display all the suggestiveness, and the same limpid expression, as his poetry. The title of the book refers to childhood and the teenage years in East Germany, but it is heavy with irony, for the young citizen must survive within a system which demands a Prussian-like conformity to the prevailing line and punishes the smallest expression of individuality. The narrative voice throughout remains calm and restrained, letting the idiocy and inhumanity of the system and the humourless inflexibility of some of its servants speak for themselves, but the cumulative impact is

overwhelming. It is therefore perhaps no surprise that the response of the East German authorities was to unleash the Stasi upon the author and his family.

Unlike some East German writers who moved to West Germany and proclaimed that they were in exile, Kunze declared, in a poem called "I have arrived": "This too is my country/I shall find the light-switch/in the dark." The process of adjustment, however, was not straightforward. Whereas many of his fellow emigrants were reticent in their comments on the GDR, or turned their fire on targets in the West, Kunze followed Alexander Solzhenitsyn (*q.v.*) in warning against the continuing dangers of Marxism. This brought accusations that he was a reactionary, but the charge was wholly misplaced. He never concealed his appreciation of the West's freedoms, particularly that as a writer he was no longer expected to purvey untruth, but to deduce from this an affirmation of all that Western society stands for was to overlook not just his repeated stress on artistic independence but also his clear repudiation of materialistic values.

Some critics also questioned whether so condensed a style, appropriate perhaps for East German readers attuned to oblique messages, would survive in a society geared to abundance and consumption. It is true that parts of his first post-GDR collection, *Auf eigene Hoffnung* (To Personal Hope), showed Kunze looking back with some bitterness at times past and groping for direction in the unfamiliar present. His next volume, however, *Eines jeden einziges Leben* (Each Individual's Only Life), containing poems written between 1982 and 1985, proved beyond doubt that he had regained his artistic footing. The aphoristic style is unmistakably the same, as is the poet's continued commitment to the upholding of human dignity, whether the threat to it comes from political oppression or the materialistic pressures of the marketplace. But there is a fresh conviction and vitality in these verses. Although echoes of his own vulnerability still vibrate beneath the surface, the dominant mood is quietly positive. Through the metaphorical transformation of quite ordinary scenes he celebrates the small, unexpected joys that give meaning to existence and make up, as the title affirms, the uniqueness of individuality. It is an unpretentious but appealing vision, wrought with precise craftsmanship and seasoned in places by a mischievous humour.

Kunze is also a distinguished translator of Czech poetry, has written books of children's stories and verse, and in 1989 published a collection of perceptive essays on literary topics. But it is above all as a poet that he remains one of the most sensitive, meticulous, and uncompromisingly humane writers in contemporary Germany.

—Peter J. Graves

KUSHNER, Aleksandr (Semenovich). Also Alexander Kushner. Russian. Born in Leningrad, 14 September 1936. Educated at Gertsen Leningrad Pedagogic Institute, 1954–59. Married Elena Vsevolodovna Nevzgliadova in 1982; one son. Teacher of Russian literature for senior schools, 1959–70. Since 1970 full-time writer. Member of Union of Soviet Writers, since 1965, and PEN, since 1987. Address: Koluzhskii pereulok 9, Kv.48, 193015 St. Petersburg, Russia.

PUBLICATIONS

Verse

Pervaia vstrecha [First Meeting].   1957.
Pervoe vpechatlenie [First Impression].   Leningrad, Sovetskii
    pisatel', 1962.
Nochnoi dozor [Night Patrol].   Leningrad, Sovetskii pisatel',
    1966.
Primety [Signs].   Leningrad, Sovetskii pisatel', 1969.
Zavetnoe zhelanie [Cherished Desires].   Leningrad, Detskaia
    literatura, 1973.
Pis'mo [Letter].   Leningrad, Sovetskii pisatel', 1974.
Priamaia rech' [Direct Speech].   Leningrad, Lenizdat, 1975.
Bol'shaia novost' [Big News].   Leningrad, Detskaia liter-
    atura, 1975.
Gorod v podarok.   Leningrad, Detskaia literatura, 1976.
Golos [Voice].   Leningrad, Sovetskii pisatel', 1978.
Velosiped [The Bicycle].   Leningrad, Detskaia literatura,
    1979.
Kanva [Canvas].   Leningrad, Sovetskii pisatel', 1981.
Tavricheskii sad [Tauride Garden].   Leningrad, Sovetskii
    pisatel', 1984.
Stikhotvoreniia [Poems].   Leningrad,   Khudozhestvennaia
    literatura, 1986.
Dnevnie sny [Daytime Dreams].   Leningrad, Lenizdat, 1986.
Srok liubvi [Time of Love].   Published in *Novyi mir*
    (Moscow), 8, 1987.
Zhivaia izgorod' [Hedge].   Leningrad, Sovetskii pisatel',
    1988.
Pamiat' [Memory], with I. Auzin'.   Riga, Liesma, 1989.
Chetyre stikhotvoreniia [Four Poems].   Published in *Novyi
    mir* (Moscow), 6, 1990.
Novye stikhi [New Poems].   Published in *Oktiabr'* (Moscow),
    1, 1990.
Iz liriki [From Poems].   Published in *Druzhba narodov*
    (Moscow), 7, 1990.
Novyi Orfei [New Orfei].   Published in *Znamia* (Moscow), 1,
    1990.
Nochnaia muzyka [Night Music].   Leningrad, Lenizdat, 1991.
Apollo in the Snow, translated by Paul Graves and Carol
    Ueland.   New York, Farrar Straus, 1991; London, Collins
    Harvill, 1992.
Novye stikhi [New Poems].   Published in *Ogonek* (Moscow),
    42/43, 1992.
So zvezdoi v oblakakh [With the Star in the Clouds].   Pub-
    lished in *Novyi mir* (Moscow), 4, 1992.

Other

Zametki na poliakh.   Published in *Voprosy literatury*
    (Moscow), 10, 1981.
Vtoraia real'nost [Second Reality].   Published in *Liter-
    aturnaia gazeta*, 29 August 1984.
Inye, luchshie mne dorogi prava . . .   Published in *Novyi mir*
    (Moscow), 1, 1987.
Apollon v snegu [Apollo in the Snow] (essays).   Leningrad,
    Sovetskii pisatel', 1991.

Has translated Armenian, Georgian, and Latvian poets, and
also Philip Larkin and Robert Frost into Russian.

*

Aleksandr Kushner comments:
    Poetry for me is the quickest and most effective means of
giving meaning to life. In poetry thought is speeded up, the
poetic word, warmed by feeling, is plugged in to the high
tension network of all of world poetry: at my back I sense the
great shades of Catullus and Ovid, but above all of Pushkin,
Tiutchev, Annenskii, Mandel'shtam.
    Lyric verse is largely poetry of a small scale (18–20–24 lines)
which permits the attainment of the greatest possible intensity
of thought and feeling; this is why I do not write long poems
since I consider them an old-fashioned genre. We live in a time
of lyric consciousness when mankind has become aware of the
value of each and every human life.
    Poetry is a means of arresting the moment: even misfortune
and sadness with the help of rhythm and rhyme are capable of
inspiring the reader with a feeling of happiness. Poetry is a
reminder of the possibility of happiness, despite all the tragedy
of existence. Not only love, death, the soul's link with Divinity,
the beauty of nature, the starry sky above us, the greatness and
horror of history, but even the simplest things such as the cloth
on the table or the pattern on the wallpaper are subjects
worthy of poetic attention. My favourite prose writer is Proust.
The deepest and most unexpected poetic thoughts often
originate from the most insignificant cause. No kind of
premeditated grandiose projects, a poetic thought is born out
of trivialities, grows like a pearl in a sea shell; the less pathetic
intention and loud proclamation the better.
    In my case the renewal of poetic language is linked with the
renewal of poetic themes which are no longer embarrassed at
being situational, momentary, a part of everyday surroundings
(a telephone conversation, a newspaper item, a visit to an
exhibition, looking at photographs, drinking tea at table,
fastening buttons on my coat, etc.) without at the same time
forgetting for an instant the tragic experience which has been
man's lot in Russia in the 20th century.
    I believe that my poetry is not easily translatable because its
verbal fabric is rooted in the Russian poetic tradition and in a
large measure based upon these associations, linked to the
verse of my predecessors: these links are not visible to the
foreign reader; but if there is a special charm to be found in my
verse, it is largely based on the unexpected nature of the
elaboration and transformation of an earlier model.

*   *   *

    Aleksandr Kushner belongs to the talented group of
"Leningrad" (perhaps, in keeping with the renaming of the city
and their own predilections, better termed "Petersburg")
poets, only a few years apart in age, whose formative years
came during the 1950s. Along with Kushner, the pleiad
includes Evgenii Rein, Vladimir Ufliand, Mikhail Erëmin, Lev
Losev, and of course Iosif Brodskii (*q.v.*). Indeed, were it not
for Brodskii, Kushner would almost surely be regarded as the
leading poet to emerge during the second half of the 20th
century from the city that Anna Akhmatova and Osip
Mandel'shtam once called home.
    Until the coming of glasnost (and the subsequent collapse of
the Soviet state) Leningrad's poets had not fared well in their
own country. The sufferings of the previous generation are
well documented; most of the younger group remained
virtually unpublished at home. Kushner was an exception to
the rule in that collections of his poetry have appeared
regularly since 1962, but he too was long denied the critical
recognition he deserved. By his own testimony, his favorite
poets include Aleksandr Pushkin and Fedor Tiutchev from the
19th century, Innokentii Annenskii and Mandel'shtam from
the 20th. The list is instructive: Kushner too is a highly erudite
lyrical poet with a strong philosophical bent: references to

antiquity, mythology, and world culture pervade his verse. He is not, therefore, a poet "for the masses," to be read easily or quickly, and the very qualities for which he is now so highly admired — his ability to take the most ordinary phenomena and make them the "stuff" of poetry, the parallels he is able to draw between widely separate eras and locales — earned him the obloquy of party-line Communist critics. Thus a review of his collections *Kanva* (Canvas) and *Tavricheskii sad* (Tauride Garden), which appeared in the 17 April 1985 issue of *Pravda*, said that Kushner had abandoned reality for his own "hermetic, archaically artificial and microscopic" world.

Kushner himself, in an article on Pushkin published in the January 1987 issue of *Novyi mir*, indirectly answered this attack. "The breath of freedom," he said, "always lives in [poetry] . . . Poetry is man's confidence in the possibility of his freedom. And this assurance comes about, perhaps, just because poetry in its choice of subject does not take into account the demands and notions of the moment." Kushner goes on to assert that there are no minor or major themes, but only false and true verse; a counterfeit poem, no matter how large its theme, is not poetry. Once the strictures of censorship had fallen away in his country, Kushner showed that his world was far from hermetic and that he himself was willing to comment on life around him. Thus in "Vospominaniia" (Memoirs), which could be published only some years after it was written, the first-person voice (older than Kushner) tells of the childhood friends who fell victim to the Revolution, the Civil War, and the purges, effectively destroying a generation. The more recent "I was Sitting in the Trojan Horse," first published in 1992, unexpectedly shifts from its classical imagary to a mention of the Russian invasion of Czechoslovakia.

But as both his critic and Kushner himself indicate, he most often begins with seemingly insignificant topics. In such relatively early poems as "Starik" (The Old Man) and "Po sravnen'iu s primetami zim" (By Comparison with the Signs of Winters) he describes, respectively, an old man entering a hospital and the frost at dawn, but quickly moves on to his true concerns. In a few short (iambic trimeter) lines he manages to sketch possibilities for the old man's past and shows him set off against the nature that outlives him; in the second poem he goes from the signs of winter to the barely visible signs of the soul's immortality. Kushner in fact does take on the large themes; the precise, concrete descriptions of objects nearly always lead to meditations on the nature of love and happiness, or, as here, to probing the boundary between life and death, to examining the very essence of existence.

Throughout his career the city of Leningrad (Petersburg) and its surroundings have regularly provided him with inspiration for his verse; he is one of the most recent in a long line of writers who has added to the mystique of Peter the Great's creation. In "Na Peterburgskikh starinnykh graviurakh" (On

Antique Etchings of Petersburg) the poet looks at the old depictions and thinks about what was still to come in those far-off days, all the writers who had not yet been born, all the projects not yet built. For Kushner the classical architecture and sculpture of Petersburg frequently recalls antiquity and myth; the references to other ages in turn provide a commentary on the city's past and present. His intimate knowledge not only of the famous buildings and avenues, but also of the parks, the canals, and the hidden byways provides the impetus for contemplations on the individual's position in the world, on ways in which the past can teach us about the present.

While known primarily as a poet, since 1970 or so Kushner has written numerous literary essays, most often on poetry. The first two decades worth of these writings are collected in *Apollon v snegu* (Apollo in the Snow — not to be confused with the English language collection of his poetry bearing this title); here he intersperses his prose with poems on similar topics, creating an original resonance between the works in the two genres.

Kushner has indicated a distaste for narrative verse, preferring instead the "book of poems," which he has described as a new genre. Each of his volumes, therefore, while retaining the general features of his poetry, can be said to have its own special flavor, to emphasize certain topics and certain attitudes over others. There have been formal changes in his verse as well. Unlike many modern Russian poets, Kushner has strongly preferred the strictly regulated meters and rhymes of 18th- and 19th-century Russian poetry. Yet even a quick glance at his verse from about the mid-1970s on reveals at least one basic change: the short, generally self-contained lines of his earlier verse have often given way to longer lines (iambic hexameter, amphipbrachic pentameter), which themselves do not quite seem able to accommodate his thoughts — many of his poems are notable for their frequent use of enjambement. A closer look reveals occasional approximate rhymes and metrical irregularities as well; in this regard Kushner admits a more contemporary aesthetic into his poetry. But these formal features also fulfill a semantic purpose: the rhythm of his verse is less smooth than the underlying metrical structure would predict, in keeping with the ultimately disturbing quality of his poetry. From the most commonplace of phenomena Kushner's observant (and often ironical) eye gleans hidden meanings, showing both the fragility of human existence and the delicate threads that link the local with the universal, the present with the past, the individual with nature.

—Barry P. Scherr

L

LAFORET (Díaz), Carmen. Spanish. Born in Barcelona, 6 September 1921. Grew up in the Canary Islands. Educated at the University of Barcelona, 1939–42; University of Madrid, from 1942. Married Manuel González Cerezales in 1946 (separated 1970); three daughters and two sons. Recipient: Nadal prize, 1945; Fastenrath prize, 1949; Menorca prize, 1955; Cervantes prize, 1956. Address: c/o Editorial Planeta, Córcega 273–277, 08008 Barcelona, Spain.

PUBLICATIONS

Fiction

Nada. Barcelona, Destino, 1945; in English, New York, Oxford University Press, and London, Weidenfeld and Nicolson, 1958; as *Andrea*, New York, Vantage, 1964.
La muerta. Madrid, Rumbos, 1952.
La isla y los demonios. Barcelona, Destino, 1952.
El piano. Madrid, Rollan, 1952.
Un noviazgo. Madrid, Novela del Sabado, 1953.
La niña. Madrid, Cid, 1954.
El viaje divertido. Madrid, Cid, 1954.
La llamada. Barcelona, Destino, 1954.
La mujer nueva. Barcelona, Destino, 1955.
Mis páginas mejores. Madrid, Gredos, 1956.
Un matrimonio. Madrid, Mon, 1956.
Novelas. Barcelona, Planeta, 1957.
La insolación. Barcelona, Planeta, 1963.
La niña, y otros relatos. Madrid, Magisterio Español, 1970.

Other

Gran Canaria. Barcelona, Noguer, 1961; as *Grand Canary*, Noguer, 1964.
Paralelo 35. Barcelona, Planeta, 1967.

*

Critical Studies: "Carmen Laforet: A Tentative Evaluation" by Cyrus C. DeCoster, in *Hispania* (Los Angeles), 40, 1957; "The Moral Structure of Carmen Laforet's Novels" by Pierre L. Ullman, in *The Vision Obscured: Perceptions of Some Twentieth Century Catholic Novelists*, New York, Fordham University Press, 1970; "Structural and Thematic Tactics of Suppression in Carmen Laforet's *Nada*" by Ruth El Saffar, in *Symposium* (Washington, D.C.), 28, 1974; "Carmen Laforet's *Nada* as an Expression of Woman's Self-Determination" by Celita Lamar Morris, in *Letras Femeninas* (Lincoln, Nebraska), 1, 1975; "The Solstitial Holidays in Carmen Laforet's *Nada*: Christmas and Mid Summer" by Wilma Newberry, in *Romance Notes* (Chapel Hill, North Carolina), 17, 1976; "*Nada*: Initiation into Bourgeois Patriarchy" by Elizabeth Ordóñez, in *Analysis of Hispanic Texts: Current Trends in Methodology*, edited by Mary Ann Beck and others, New York, Bilingual Review Press, 1976; "Carmen Laforet and the Spanish Spinster" by Carolyn Galerstein, in *Revista de Estudios Hispánicos* (Poughkeepsie, New York), 11, 1977; "Animal Imagery in *Nada*" by Kathleen Glenn, in *Revista de Estudios Hispánicos* (Poughkeepsie, New York), 11, 1977; "Symbolic Portals in Laforet's *Nada*" by Michael D. Thomas, in *Anales de la Novela de Posguerra*, 3, 1978; "Dialectical Movement as Feminist Technique in the Works of Carmen Laforet" by Margaret Jones, in *Studies in Honor of Gerald E. Wade*, Madrid, Porrúa, 1979; *Carmen Laforet*, Boston, Hall, 1981, and "Light and Morality in Carmen Laforet's *La insolación*," in *Letras Femeninas* (Lincoln, Nebraska), 12, 1986, both by Roberta Johnson; "Portraits of the *Femme seule* by Laforet, Matute, Soriano, Martín Gaite, Galvarriato, Quiroga and Medio" by Janet Pérez, in *Feminine Concerns in Contemporary Spanish Fiction by Women*, edited by Roberto C. Manteiga, Carolyn Galerstein, and Kathleen McNerney, Potomac, Maryland, Scripta Humanística, 1988.

* * *

The first woman to achieve literary fame in postwar Spain, Carmen Laforet is essentially a realist whose forté is the portrayal of women and children, especially adolescents. Her studies of adolescent psychology and depictions of the "rites of passage" to maturity abound in characters with emotional disturbances and psychological abnormalities. Typically, her protagonists begin with many childish or adolescent illusions and, through exposure to realities of the adult world, lose their "innocence" while maturing socially and emotionally in the process. Adult protagonists are usually women, usually alone (literally or figuratively and existentially), and must search within themselves for the strength to overcome the egocentricity, insensitivity and neglect of family members, employers, and others around them.

Much of Laforet's fiction has an autobiographical substrata, and some of her characters may legitimately be viewed as masks or alter egos of the author, although plot details and many incidents are fictitious. Specifically, her childhood in the Canary Islands and her sojourn to Barcelona at the end of the Spanish Civil War to live with her grandparents and attend the university provide the setting, point of departure, and much descriptive background for her first two novels. Absence of the mother is crucial for the adolescent protagonists of her long novels, and her personal religious crisis in 1951 inspired *La mujer nueva*.

When only 23, Laforet won the first Nadal prize (for many years, the country's most prestigious prize for new fiction) for her novel *Nada* (*Andrea*). The Spanish title (literally, "Nothing") made allusion to the existential absurdity abounding in postwar European literature, and *Nada*'s numerous anguished, alienated characters seemed to support conjectures of existentialist intent; however, the novel probably lacks the philosophical profundity originally attributed to it. Andrea, an 18-year-old from the Canary Islands, arrives in postwar Barcelona to live with relatives while attending the university there. The year spent in the war-ravaged city, with hunger, overcrowding, repression, frustration, filth, and despair end with her departure for Madrid to live with a more fortunate classmate, having learned much of life in the interim. *Nada* begins and ends with a journey, but lacks definitive closure. *La isla y los demonios* (The Island and the Demons) constitutes a "prequel" to *Nada* insofar as it ends with the adolescent protagonist's departure for Barcelona and the university. The characters are different, and erotic deviance is more noticeable, but the psychological and emotional problems are much the same. Both girls are motherless (like Laforet); Andrea's mother had died, while her younger counterpart Marta discovers that her mother, hopelessly insane, is confined to the attic.

La mujer nueva (The New Woman) is allegedly the result of Laforet's "conversion," a rekindling of her faith in the Catholicism into which she was born. Via flashbacks, Pauline, the mature feminine protagonist, recalls her youthful freedom under the "licentious" Republic two decades before, a civil marriage (no longer recognized), and the Franco regime's restrictions on women, all in the context of a struggle to decide between her present, unsatisfying marriage and the possible return to the love of her youth. Reaffirmation of traditional Catholic values need not make bad literature, but this novel has not pleased Laforet's critics, despite its receiving the Menorca prize. *La insolación* (Sunstroke) of 1963 was originally billed as the first volume in a trilogy (never completed); it is Laforet's last novel to date. Although written near the end of the Franco era, it deals with the early years, and is the only one of Laforet's novels to have a masculine protagonist-narrator. Martin recalls three carefree summers (1940–42) of his adolescence spent in a Mediterranean resort and the acquaintances and events which led to his being accused of homosexuality, violently rejected by his father, and cast out into the harsh realities of the postwar adult world.

Laforet's many short stories and seven novelettes are masterful, often surpassing in artistry her novels. Psychological characterization is outstanding in these basically realistic pieces which often feature expressionistic distortion in descriptive passages as a way of externalizing the emotions of the protagonists. *La muerta* (The Dead Woman) includes several feminist tales written in the 1940s that emphasize how women's aspirations were subordinated to patriarchal values. *La llamada* (The Call) brings together four short novels written in 1952 and 1953, which reflect the same intense involvement with Christianity that inspired *La mujer nueva*, composed at the same time. The themes of charity and self-sacrifice predominate in many of the novelettes and the later short stories. *La niña, y otros relatos* (The Girl, and Other Stories), an anthology of previously published stories, adds an interesting authorial prologue. *Paralelo 35* (The 35th Parallel) is non-fiction, offering journalistic commentary on Laforet's 1965 trip to the United States at the invitation of the State Department, and is the last "new" volume she has published.

—Janet Pérez

LALIĆ, Ivan V. Serbian. Born in Belgrade, in 1931. Educated at the University of Zagreb, degree in law. Married. Correspondent, Radio Zagreb; currently senior editor, Nolit publishers, Belgrade. Address: c/o Nolit Publishing House, Terazije 27/II, Poštanski fah 369, 11000 Belgrade, Serbia.

PUBLICATIONS

Verse

Bivši dečak [One-Time Schoolboy].   Zagreb, Sykos, 1955.
Vetrovito proleće [Windy Spring].   Zagreb, Društvo Knjizevnika Hrvatske, 1956.
Velika vrata mora [The Great Gate of the Sea].   Belgrade, Nolit, 1958.
Melisa.   Zagreb, Lykos, 1959.
Vreme, vatre, vrtovi [Time, Fire, Gardens].   Novi Sad, Matica, 1961.
Argonauti i druge pesme [The Argonauts and Other Poems].   Zagreb, Naprijed, 1961.
Čin [Act].   Belgrade, Prosveta, 1963.
Istria and Kvarner [Istria and the Quamero].   Belgrade, Jugoslavija, 1966.
Krug [Circle].   Belgrade, Nolit, 1968.
Izabrane i nove pesme [Selected and New Poems].   Belgrade, Srpska Književna Zadruga, 1969.
Four Yugoslav Poets: Ivan V. Lalić, Brank Miljković, Milorad Pavić, Ljubomir Simović, edited and translated by Charles Simic.   New York, Lillabulero Press, 1970.
Fire Gardens, edited and translated by Charles Simic and C. W. Truesdale.   New York, New Rivers Press, 1970.
Smetnje na vezama [Trouble on the Line].   Belgrade, Srpska Književna Zadruga, 1975.
Izabrane pesme [Selected Poems].   Belgrade, Srpska Književna Zadruga, 1979.
The Works of Love: Selected Poems of Ivan V. Lalić, translated by Francis R. Jones.   London, Anvil Press Poetry, 1981.
Strasna mera.   Belgrade, Nolit, 1984; part as *Last Quarter*, translated by Francis R. Jones, London, Anvil Press Poetry, 1987; whole as *The Passionate Measure*, translated by Jones, Anvil Press Poetry, 1989.
Pesme [Poems].   Belgrade, Prosveta, 1987.
O delima ljubavi ili Vizantija [The Works of Love or Byzantium].   N.p., n.p., 1987.
Roll Call of Mirrors: Selected Poems of Ivan V. Lalić, translated by Charles Simic.   Middletown, Connecticut, Wesleyan University Press, 1988.
Pismo [Letter]. Belgrade, Srpska Književna Zadruga, 1992.

Play

Majstor Hanuš [Master Hanuš] (verse drama).   1964.

Other

O poeziji dvanaest pesnika [The Poetry of 12 Poets].   Belgrade, Slovo Ljubve, 1980.

Editor, with Josip Pupačić, *Vrata vremena* [The Door of Time].   Zagreb, Poslijeratni Jugoslavenski Pjesnici, 1958.
Editor, *Milutin Bojić*.   Belgrade, Narodna, 1974.
Editor and Translator, *Pjesme* [Poems], by Silvije Strahimir Kranjčević.   Belgrade, Slovo Ljubve, 1978.
Editor, *Studije, ogledi i kritike* [Studies, Essays, and Criticism], by Aleksandar Spasov.   Belgrade, Narodna, 1978.

Translator, *Antologija moderne americke poezije* [Anthology of Modern American Poetry].   Belgrade, Prosveta, 1972.

*   *   *

Ivan V. Lalić is the leading poet of the second post-war Serbian "reserve" (*Sveta Lukić*) generation. He began publishing poetry as early as 1951, but his first book, *Bivši dečak* (One-Time Schoolboy), came out in 1955, to be followed at regular intervals by 13 others.

Whereas the majority of modernist poets of the Serbian post-war period consciously emphasized their break with the language and poetic norms of the poets of an earlier age, Lalić represents a link with the Serbian Parnassians of the first part of the century, in particular Jovan Dučić and Milutin Bojić. He is not averse to making use of traditional metre and form, and he displays a richness of expression, a fine musicality, and a remarkable balance between rhythm, language, and content. Nevertheless, he has remained a modernist poet in outlook and has known how to add a new freshness to the older traditional mould. Especially original is his striking imagery:

> And behind us the rain has rusted the woods . . .
> ("Smederevo")

> Tyrrhenian Sea,
>   a perfumed rag of blue
> torn by thousands of hooves of sinewy air.
>   ("Tirensko more")

> In the acetylene flash of lightning (lame thunder
> Lags behind, not reaching the picture).
>   ("Marina V")

As the critic Petar Džadžić said in a review in 1961: "his form is polished and finely honed, his verse is ennobled by the combination of rhythm, music and meaning, his ear is wide open to the artistic nuance of words."

But there is more to Lalić than smoothness of form and originality of image. At a deeper level he is a meditative poet of reflective ideas — his first influences were Rainer Maria Rilke and Friedrich Hölderlin — and his inspiration is often to be found in the passing of great civilizations and the consequent tragic loss of man's cultural heritage. In particular, he is concerned with the course of history in Europe, Ancient Greece, Rome, Byzantium, and the Serbian medieval "Golden Age," continued through Dubrovnik to the Renaissance: it is this historico-mythological background that provides him with a large part of the substance of his poetry. Lalić has chosen these means for his own exploration of his country's roots. As Jovan Hristić noted in his Introduction to Lalić's *Izabrane i nove pesme* (Selected and New Poems) in 1969: "Most of all Byzantium represents our link not only to a part of our own tradition from which we were artificially severed, but also to a link with the tradition of all traditions, Greece. It is a sign of our belonging to and participating in Mediterranean culture, the touchstone of all European culture . . . Byzantium is a route by which we can renew classical values in a way both completely natural and spontaneous."

Lalić has a whole and as yet incomplete cycle of evocative poetry inspired entirely by Byzantium. And from Byzantium and the early Eastern Church, like many Serbs he traces a direct line to the tragic end of his own people's golden moment of history, the destruction of Tsar Dušan's former empire before the onslaught of the advancing Turks. This historical progression serves as a setting for different facets of the symbol which Lalić uses to focus on the tragedy of time passing, the transience of human endeavour and achievement, the poignancy of beauty lost. Typical of the atmosphere he creates is the poem "Smederevo," the fortified town on the Danube which was the last Serbian bastion to fall to the Turks in 1459:

> We raised up a town Ivoje, a city of stone
> And we steeped the shadows of square-sided towers
> In the wide grey river. Now the town's on the right bank
> The wind's on the left. Autumn has come
> And behind us the rain has rusted the woods.
> Men stand guard by night at the heavy gates
> Under arms, and dark in armour like scarabs,
> Warming their frozen hands at the red-glowing fires.
> We wait and with us the twenty-four towers
> Exposed to time, as to rain, we here,
> I think we shall not be forgotten, ever,
> We in the last town on the river's right bank,
> Though we shall not turn to stone by its towers,
> Enough that we are those who wait, listening
> For the echo of thousands of hooves that swells in the night
> Beneath the indifferent stars. Our Lord the Despot
> Drinks wine as gold as the carp in the river,
> But his beard has gone gray like his ancestors' glory:
> May the Lord God grant him his end before the end.
> We are the last. If we sleep by these towers
> Who will awake us? The fires burn low.
> The town on the right bank, the wind on the left.

If a record of the events of history represents a guarantee against the transience of things, history's surviving, more tangible reminders — places, buildings, works of art — add a further solid line of defence against the passing of time. As Lalić says in "Pohvala Dubrovniku" (In Praise of Dubrovnik): "History dies without stone." Indeed, Dubrovnik, after Byzantium and Medieval Serbia, is the third most powerful symbol of beauty in Lalić's work: some of his finest writing is to be found in the cycle "Dubrovnik, zimska priča" (Dubrovnik, a Winter's Tale): ". . . town, Beauty with no comparative dictionary,/The uncreatable created."

These Dubrovnik poems are good examples of Lalić's poetic technique, but there are also many others where the act of writing down in verse, creating a verbal image of the poet's own reaction to a scene or object of beauty, are equally indicative examples of Lalić's self-imposed poetic task, of condensing the very essence of such beauty and thus enhancing its chance of survival.

Given the richness of Lalić's language and imagery, it is not surprising that his poetry is also frequently stimulated by visual art. Once again he is especially fond of early Christian (Byzantine and Balkan) motifs, as in the poems "Freska" (Fresco), "Jahač" (Horseman), and the fine "Joana iz Ravene" (Joanna from Ravenna): "Joanna, time's sister, gleams on ./ These words recall her . . ."

Lalić is often inspired also by places with echoes of great events or people still clinging to them, and such settings are used as vehicles for his own purpose — for example, the poem "Mocartov grob" (Mozart's Grave), where the poverty and anonymity of Mozart's funeral is contrasted with the immortality of his music. Other poems explore the inspiration of an intense moment of experience, a fleeting moment of perfect harmony almost achieved, yet frozen into the poem, as in "Zapis u srebru mora" (Written in the Silver of the Sea):

> And yet we were once so close
> Beside our birthplace,
>   just on the other side
> Of the thinned air; we used to listen
> To swift-winged words, sense perceived
> In lightning's crude translation;
> Frightened we fled into time's
> Illusion, into false equilibrium —
> The truest pictures recalled are at waking:

Wild fig and chestnut tree, the slow flame
In the ruins,
        all we call memory
Shines on the tip of a long bright needle
Where the taste of fire is mixed with the silence
In the air up above the shortlived silver
Of the sea between storms.

The scope of Lalić's poetry is wide, extending from poems on classical and mythological subjects, poems of personal experience, poems which are statements of the poet's calling, poems of love, poems inspired by places and their allusions, poems from Serbian folklore, to poems involving everyday scenes and their consequences. But the overall impression of his verse is its mellifluous harmony of language, the richness and originality of its poetic imagery, and Lalić's profound emotional and artistic involvement.

Lalić recently suffered a deep personal tragedy and his latest poems bear the stamp of his sadness and grief. One of the best, "Plavna grobnica" (Blue Grave), carries a direct, textual allusion to Milutin Bojić's well-known poem of the same title which is generally interpreted as a requiem for his fellow poet Vladislav Petković-Dis, and also for the whole devastated generation of Serbian youth of 1914–18. Lalić's poem, ostensibly inspired by the sea off Corfu where Dis was drowned, is a parallel lament for that same lost generation:

of a long past, still half unsung war.

. . . . requiem,
I whisper it to myself, not to be crazy
In the eyes of the guide who routinely burbles
On about Nausica, quite out of place
For my requiem and the miserable lot of the Serbs.

It acquires an even deeper and more moving significance when taken in conjunction with the circumstances of the death of the poet's own son.

Long acknowledged as an accomplished artistic craftsman, Lalić with his recent book, *Pismo* (Letter), shows that he has now matured into a deeper metaphysical poet of European stature.

—Bernard Johnson

LANGEVIN, André. Canadian. Born in Montreal, Quebec, 11 July 1927. Educated at the Collège de Montréal. Worked as a clerk, farm hand, tavern worker; messenger, then journalist for 2 years, *Le Devoir* newspaper, Quebec; in charge of literary section for *Le Temps* newspaper, 1947–48; worked for Radio Canada, Canadian Broadcasting Corporation, from 1948. Recipient: Cercle du Livre de France prize, 1951, 1953; Théâtre du Nouveau Monde prize, 1958; Canada Council senior fellowship, 1959; Liberté prize, 1967; Montreal grand prize, 1973. Address: c/o McClelland and Stewart Ltd., 481 University Avenue, Toronto, Ontario M5G 2E9, Canada.

PUBLICATIONS

Fiction

L'Évadé de la nuit. Montreal, Cercle du Livre de France, 1951.

Poussière sur la ville. Montreal, Cercle du Livre de France, 1953; as *Dust over the City*, Toronto, McClelland and Stewart, 1954.
Le Temps des hommes. Montreal, Cercle du Livre de France, 1956.
L'Élan d'Amérique. Montreal, Cercle du Livre de France, 1972.
Une Chaîne dans le parc. Paris, Julliard, 1974; as *Orphan Street*, Toronto, McClelland and Stewart, 1976; Philadelphia, Lippincott, 1977.

Plays

Une Nuit d'amour (produced Montreal, 1954).
L'Œil du peuple (produced Montreal, 1958). Montreal, Cercle du Livre de France, 1958.

Radio Plays: *Une Neige en octobre*, 1968; *Les Semelles du vent*, 1972.

*

Critical Studies: "Alain Dubois's Commitment: A Reading of *Poussière sur la ville*" by Paul Socken, in *International Fiction Review* (Fredericton, New Brunswick), 4, 1977; "Time and Space in André Langevin's *L'Élan d'Amérique*" by Richard G. Hodgson, in *Canadian Literature* (Vancouver), Spring 1981; *The Temptation of Despair: A Study of the Quebec Novelist André Langevin* by David J. Bond, Fredericton, New Brunswick, York Press, 1982.

* * *

Although his last novel was published in 1974, André Langevin is one of contemporary Quebec's most important novelists. Using such basic themes of Quebec literature as isolation, suffering, and death, Langevin has produced two major novels, *Poussière sur la ville* (*Dust over the City*) and *L'Élan d'Amérique*, three other novels (which have unfortunately received very little critical attention), three short stories, and two plays. The evolution of Langevin's novelistic technique from *Dust over the City* to *L'Élan d'Amérique* illustrates very graphically the fundamental changes which have occurred in the Quebec novel since the 1950s.

In *Dust over the City*, Langevin used the first-person narrative of a young doctor practicing in an asbestos-mining town whose wife's adulterous affair leads to tragedy as the framework for an extremely moving examination of some of the metaphysical and other problems of modern man. In addition to the fundamental themes of solitude and alienation, *Dust over the City* poses the question of the meaning of physical suffering and of "the burning sense of inner anguish" felt by the doctor in a way which is very reminiscent of the novels of Albert Camus. Indeed, Langevin refers explicitly to the existentialist concepts of absurdity, divine injustice, and revolt. But it is not just because of its treatment of such themes that Langevin's novel is one of the major landmarks in Quebec fiction since World War II. Langevin's mastery of the first-person narrative form and his highly effective symbolic use of space to reflect the innermost feelings of the human heart make *Dust over the City* one of the best novels ever published in Canada.

Langevin's other major contribution to the contemporary Quebec novel, *L'Élan d'Amérique*, is a very different work, both in form and in content. Borrowing heavily from the stream-of-consciousness techniques of the French "new" novelists, Langevin set out, in writing this novel, to study the disillusionment and frustration felt by the Quebec people in the period immediately following the October crisis of 1970, during which the Ottawa government invoked the War Measures Act to suppress a separatist uprising. As in *Dust over the City*, space has a vitally important symbolic function in this novel, which consists of the interior monologues of the two main characters, Claire Peabody, the Franco-American wife of an American industrialist, and Antoine, a modern version of the archetypal *coureur de bois* ("woods man"). Like most of Langevin's characters, Claire and Antoine are orphans, but their lack of family is but one form of their isolation and alienation, which take on, as in all of Langevin's novels, both a physical and a spiritual dimension. Startlingly innovative at the level of narrative techniques and structures. *L'Élan d'Amérique* also marks an important stage in the awakening of the Quebec consciousness.

In these two novels, and in the other three (*L'Évadé de la nuit*, *Le Temps des hommes*, and *Une Chaîne dans le parc* [*Orphan Street*], Langevin seeks to provide answers to some of the fundamental questions concerning the human condition which have always been his chief preoccupation. His novels are firmly rooted in the context of modern Quebec culture but at the same time they deal eloquently with universal literary themes centering around the social and metaphysical dilemmas facing modern man.

—Richard G. Hodgson

LAXNESS, Halldór (Kiljan). Pseudonym for Halldór Guðjónsson. Icelandic. Born in Reykjavík, 23 April 1902. Educated at the grammar school, Reykjavík; lived in Benedictine monastery, Luxembourg; Jesuit school, Champion House, Osterley, England, 1923–24. Married 1) Ingibjörg Einarsdóttir in 1930, one son; 2) Auður Sveinsdóttir in 1945, two daughters. Lived in Europe, then in the United States, 1927–29, and in Iceland since 1930. Recipient: International Peace Movement prize, 1953; Nobel prize for literature, 1955; Sonning prize, 1969. Honorary doctorate: Aabo University, 1968; University of Iceland, 1972; Eberhaar-Karls University, Tübingen, 1982. Honorary member, Union of Icelandic Artists. Address: Gljúfrasteinn, 270 Mosfellsbaer, Iceland; or c/o Vaka-Helgafell hf., Siðumúli 6, 108 Reykjavík, Iceland.

PUBLICATIONS

Fiction

Barn náttúrunnar [Child of Nature]. Reykjavík, Höfundurinn, 1919.
Nokkrar sögur [Several Stories]. Reykjavík, Isafoldarprentsmiðja, 1923.
Undir Helgahnúk [Under the Holy Mountain]. Reykjavík, Ársæll Arnason 1924.
Vefarinn mikli frá Kasmír [The Great Weaver from Kashmir]. Reykjavík, Prentsmiðjan Acta, 1927.
Salka Valka (Pu vínviður hreini, Fuglinn í fjörunni). Reykjavík, Bokádeild Menningarsjoðs, 2 vols., 1931–32; in English, Boston, Houghton Mifflin, 1936; London, Allen and Unwin, 1963.

Fótatak manna [Footsteps of Men]. Akureyri, Jónsson, 1933.
Sjálfstætt fólk. Reykjavík, Briem, 2 vols., 1934–35; as *Independent People*, London, Allen and Unwin, 1945; New York, Knopf, 1946.
Þórður gamli halti [Old Þhórður the Lame]. 1935.
Heimsljós. Reykjavík, Helgafell, 2 vols., 1955; as *World Light*, Madison, University of Wisconsin Press, 1969.
   1. *Ljós heimsins* [The Light of the World]. Reykjavík, Heimskringla, 1937.
   2. *Höll sumarlandsins* [The Palace of the Summerland]. Reykjavík, Heimskringla, 1938.
   3. *Hús skáldsins* [The Poet's House]. Reykjavík, Heimskringla, 1939.
   4. *Fegurð himinsins* [The Beauty of the Sky]. Reykjavík, Heimskringla, 1940.
Gerska æfintýrið [The Russian Adventure]. Reykjavík, Heimskringla, 1938.
Sjö töframenn [Seven Magicians]. Reykjavík, Heimskringla, 1942.
Trilogy:
   1. *Íslandsklukkan* [Iceland's Bell]. Reykjavík, Helgafell, 1943.
   2. *Hið ljósa man* [The Bright Maiden]. Reykjavík, Helgafell, 1944.
   3. *Eldur í Kaupinhafn* [Fire in Copenhagen]. Reykjavík, Helgafell, 1946.
Atómstöðin. Reykjavík, Helgafell, 1948; as *The Atom Station*, London, Methuen, 1961; Sag Harbor, New York, Second Chance Press, 1982.
Gerpla. Reykjavík, Helgafell, 1952; as *The Happy Warriors*, London, Methuen, 1958.
Brekkukotsannáll. Reykjavík, Helgafell, 1957; as *The Fish Can Sing*, London, Methuen, 1966; New York, Crowell, 1967.
Ungfrúin góða og Husið [The Honor of the House]. Reykjavík, Helgafell, 1959.
Paradísarheimt. Reykjavík, Helgafell, 1960; as *Paradise Reclaimed*, London, Methuen, and New York, Crowell, 1962.
Sjöstafakverið. Reykjavík, Helgafell, 1964; as *A Quire of Seven*, Reykjavík, Iceland Review, 1974; Forest Grove, Oregon, Hydra, 1981.
Kristnihald undir Jökli. Reykjavík, Helgafell, 1968; as *Christianity at the Glacier*, Helgafell, 1972.
Guðsgjafaþula [A Narration of God's Gifts]. Reykjavík, Helgafell, 1972.
Seiseijú, mikil ósköp [Oh Yes! By Jove]. Reykjavík, Helgafell, 1977.
Dagar hjá múnkum [Day Spent with Monks]. Reykjavík, Helgafell, 1987.

Plays

Straumrof [Short Circuit]. Reykjavík, Heimskringla, 1934.
Snæfríður Islandssól [Snaefriður, Iceland's Sun]. Reykjavík, Helgafell, 1950.
Silfurtúnglið [The Silver Moon]. Reykjavík, Helgafell, 1954.
Strompleikurinn [The Chimney Play]. Reykjavík, Helgafell, 1961.
Prjónastofan Sólin [The Sun Knitting Shop]. Reykjavík, Helgafell, 1962.
Dúfnaveislan. Reykjavík, Helgafell, 1966; as *The Pigeon Banquet*, Helgafell, 1973.
Úa. Reykjavík, Helgafell, 1970.
Norðanstulkan [The Girl from the North]. Reykjavík, Helgafell, 1972.

Verse

Kvaeðakver [A Sheaf of Poems]. Reykjavík, Prentsmidjan Acta, 1930.

Other

Kapólsk viðhorf [Catholic Views]. Reykjavík, Arnasonar, 1925.
Althýðubókin [The Book of the Plain People]. Reykjavík, Alþýðuprentsmiðjan, 1929.
Í austurvegi [On the Eastern Road]. Reykjavík, Sovétvina-félag Islands, 1933.
Dagleið á fjöllum: greinar [Day's Journey in the Mountains]. Reykjavík, Heimskringla, 1937.
Vettvangur dagsins [Forum of the Day]. Reykjavík, Heimskringla, 1942.
Sjálfsagðir hlutir [Things Taken for Granted]. Reykjavík, Helgafell, 1946.
Reisubókarkorn [A Little Travel Book]. Reykjavík, Helgafell, 1950.
Heiman eg fór [I Went from Home]. Reykjavík, Helgafell, 1952.
Dagur í senn [A Day at a Time]. Reykjavík, Helgafell, 1955.
Gjörningabók [Miscellany]. Reykjavík, Helgafell, 1959.
Skáldatími [Poets' Time]. Reykjavík, Helgafell, 1963.
Upphaf mannúðarstefnu [The Origin of Humanism]. Reykjavík, Helgafell, 1965.
Íslendíngaspjall [Talk of Icelanders]. Reykjavík, Helgafell, 1967.
Vínlandspúnktar [Vineland Notes]. Reykjavík, Helgafell, 1969.
Innansveitarkronika [A Parish Chronicle]. Reykjavík, Helgafell, 1970.
Yfirskygðir staðir [Overshadowed Places]. Reykjavík, Helgafell, 1971.
Þjóðhátiðarrolla [Book of National Celebration]. Reykjavík, Helgafell, 1974.
Í túninu heima [In the Hayfields of Home]. Reykjavík, Helgafell, 1975.
Úngur eg var [Young I Was]. Reykjavík, Helgafell, 1976.
Sjömeistarasagan [The Story of the Seven Masters]. Reykjavík, Helgafell, 1978.
Grikklandsárið [The Year in Greece]. Reykjavík, Helgafell, 1980.
Við heygarðshornið. Reykjavík, Helgafell, 1981.
N. Tryggvadóttir: Serenity and Power, with Hrafnhildur Schram. Reykjavík, Iceland Review, 1982.
Og árin líða [And the Years Pass]. Reykjavík, Helgafell, 1984.
Af menníngarástandi [On the Cultural Situation] (selected articles). Reykjavík, Helgafell, 1986.
Sagan af brauði nu dýra. As *The Bread of Life*, Reykjavík, Helgafell, 1987.

Editor, *Grettissaga* [The Saga of Grettir the Strong]. Reykjavík, Helgafell, 1946.
Editor, *Laxdæla saga* [The Laxdalers' Saga]. Reykjavík, Helgafell, 1973.

Translator, *Aðventa* [Advent], by Gunnar Gunnarsson. Reykjavík, Heimskringla, 1939.
Translator, *Alexandreis; Það, Er Alexanders saga mikla* [Alexandreis; That Is, the Saga of Alexander the Great]. Reykjavík, Helgafell, 1945.

Also translator of *A Farewell to Arms* and *A Moveable Feast* by Hemingway and *Candide* by Voltaire.

*

Bibliographies: by Haraldur Sigurðsson, in *Landsbókasafn Íslands: Árbok*, 1971, and in *Skirnir 146*, 1972; "Halldór Laxness and America: A Bibliography" by Fred R. Jacobs, in *The Serif* (Kent, Ohio), 10(4), 1973.

Critical Studies: "Halldór Kiljan Laxness" by Lawrence S. Thompson, in *Books Abroad* (Norman, Oklahoma), 28, 1954; "Halldór Kiljan Laxness: Iceland's First Nobel Prize Winner," in *American-Scandinavian Review* (New York), 44, 1956, and "The World of Halldór Laxness," in *World Literature Today* (Norman, Oklahoma), 6(33), 1992, both by Sigurður A. Magnússon; "Christianity in the Slopes of the Glacier" by Richard N. Ringler, in *Books Abroad* (Norman, Oklahoma), 44, 1970; *Halldór Laxness*, New York, Twayne, 1971, and "Halldór Laxness and the Icelandic Sagas," in *Leeds Studies in English*, 13, 1982, both by Peter Hallberg; Laxness issue of *Scandinavica* (Norwich), 11(2), 1972; "Beyond *The Atom Station*" by Hermann Pálsson, in *Ideas and Ideologies*, Reykjavík, University of Iceland, 1975; "Halldór Kiljan Laxness and the Modern Scottish Novel: Some Sociolinguistic Parallels" by Harry D. Watson, in *Scandinavica* (Norwich), 21(2), 1982; "Eldorado and the Garden in Laxness' *Paradísarheimt*" by George S. Tate, in *Scripta Islandica* (Uppsala), 36, 1985.

*   *   *

Halldór Laxness made his breakthrough in 1923 with the novel *Vefarinn mikli frá Kasmír* (The Great Weaver from Kashmir). It is a conversion novel, inspired by the spirit, if not the facts, of Laxness's own conversion to Roman Catholicism. It confronts a baffling number of conflicting views of the world with each other, and makes clear that in turning to religion, Steinn Elliði is renouncing human claims.

Thus it represents an important element in Laxness's work: the problem of the individual vis-à-vis a monolithic authority, the claims of the individual conscience as opposed to the conformative nature of the major ideologies.

Laxness subsequently spent a period in America where under the influence of Upton Sinclair and Sinclair Lewis he developed a sense of social injustice resulting in his becoming a communist. One fruit was the major novel *Salka Valka* concerning the establishment of a trade union in a fishing village and describing the effect this has on the environment, and in particular on Salka Valka herself. Social novels continued with *Sjálfstætt fólk* (*Independent People*), portraying the individualist peasant who believes he is free but is in fact being exploited by society, and *Heimsljós* (*World Light*), about a visionary pauper persecuted by his fellows.

In 1943 Laxness turned to the historical novel with *Íslandsklukkan* (Iceland's Bell), about Jón Hreggviðsson's battle with the authorities. Unjustly condemned to death, he pursues a prolonged and finally successful struggle against bureaucracy. There are distinct national overtones, but also a poetical element centred on the main female character. The novel can be seen as a glorification of the Icelandic character, but it also represents the individual confronted with an impersonal bureaucracy. Similar ideas are found in *Atómstöðin* (*The Atom Station*) and *Gerpla* (*The Happy Warriors*).

The national theme, though with universal overtones, appears in *Paradísarheimt* (*Paradise Reclaimed*), about a poor Icelandic farmer tempted by a Mormon bishop to emigrate to the earthly paradise of Salt Lake City. In a touching, but sometimes bitingly satirical novel, Steinar experiences the unswerving faith of an ideology, but fails to accept it fully himself, and he returns to his home in Iceland, *his* paradise.

More recently, Laxness has moved from the long epic to the more concentrated, pithy novel, closely related to the plays with which he has also experimented. Outstanding is *Kristnihald undir Jökli* (*Christianity at the Glacier*), a humorous but nevertheless serious and philosophical novel about a bishop who sends an assistant to examine the state of Christianity in an outlying village. The result, when he finds a priest who cannot be bothered to bury the dead, preferring to shoe horses and offer his congregation practical help, a doctor who has given up a brilliant career to study the skies, and a pastor's wife who has been both nun and prostitute, is a picture of humankind in all its diversity.

In portraying the individual's confrontation with societies and ideologies, Laxness constantly takes the side of the individual. He examines both Catholicism and communism, but ultimately it is probably Taoism, with its demand for tolerance and humanity, that attracts him most. He weds his philosophical considerations to his intense national feeling and gives the two a universal significance.

—W. Glyn Jones

———

LE CLÉZIO, J(ean)-M(arie) G(ustave). French. Born in Nice, 13 April 1940. Educated at schools in Africa, 1947–50, and Nice, 1950–57; Bristol University, England, 1958–59; University of London, 1960–61; Institut d'Études Littéraires, Nice, 1959–63, licence-es-lettres 1963; University of Aix-en-Provence, M.A. 1964; University of Perpignan, docteur-ès-lettres 1983. Married Rosalie Piquemal in 1961 (divorced), one daughter; remarried, one daughter. Teacher, Buddhist University, Bangkok, 1966–67, University of Mexico, Mexico City, 1967, and at Boston University, University of Texas, Austin, and University of New Mexico, Albuquerque; lived with Embera Indians, Panama, 1969–73. Since 1973 has been based in Nice. Recipient: Renaudot prize, 1963; Larbaud prize, 1972; Académie Française Morand prize, 1980. Chevalier de l'Ordre des Arts et des Lettres. Address: c/o Éditions Gallimard, 5 rue Sébastien-Bottin, 75007 Paris, France.

PUBLICATIONS

Fiction

Le Procès-Verbal.   Paris, Gallimard, 1963; as *The Interrogation*, London, Hamish Hamilton, and New York, Atheneum, 1964.
Le Jour où Beaumont fit connaissance avec sa douleur.   Paris, Mercure, 1964.
La Fièvre.   Paris, Gallimard, 1965; as *Fever*, London, Hamish Hamilton, and New York, Atheneum, 1966.
Le Déluge.   Paris, Gallimard, 1966; as *The Flood*, London, Hamish Hamilton, 1967; New York, Atheneum, 1968.
Terra amata.   Paris, Gallimard, 1968; in English, London, Hamish Hamilton, and New York, Atheneum, 1969.

Le Livre des fuites.   Paris, Gallimard, 1969; as *The Book of Flights*, London, Cape, 1971; New York, Atheneum, 1972.
La Guerre.   Paris, Gallimard, 1970; as *War*, London, Cape, and New York, Atheneum, 1973.
Les Géants.   Paris, Gallimard, 1973; as *The Giants*, London, Cape, and New York, Atheneum, 1975.
Voyages de l'autre côté.   Paris, Gallimard, 1975.
Voyage aux pays des arbres.   Paris, Gallimard, 1978.
Mondo et autres histoires.   Paris, Gallimard, 1978; as *Mondo*, New York, Riverrun, 1990.
Désert.   Paris, Gallimard, 1980.
La Ronde et autres faits divers.   Paris, Gallimard, 1982.
Le Chercheur d'or.   Paris, Gallimard, 1985.
Villa aurore; Orlamonde.   Paris, Gallimard, 1985.
Balaabilou.   Paris, Gallimard, 1985.
Printemps et autres saisons: nouvelles.   Paris, Gallimard, 1989.
Onitsha.   Paris, Gallimard, 1991.

Other

L'Extase matérielle.   Paris, Gallimard, 1966.
Haï.   Geneva, Skira, 1971.
Mydriase.   Montpellier, Fata Morgana, 1973.
L'Inconnu sur la terre.   Paris, Gallimard, 1978.
Vers les Icebergs.   Montpellier, Fata Morgana, 1978.
Trois Villes saintes.   Paris, Gallimard, 1980.
Lullaby (for children).   Paris, Gallimard, 1980.
Celui qui n'avait jamais vu la mer; La Montagne du dieu vivant (for children).   Paris, Gallimard, 1984.
Voyage à Rodrigues.   Paris, Gallimard, 1986.
Les Années Cannes: 40 ans de festival.   Paris, Hatier, 1987.
Le Rêve mexicain, ou, La Pensée interrompue.   Paris, Gallimard, 1988.
Sirandanes; Un Petit Lexique de la langue créole et des oiseaux.   Paris, Seghers, 1990.

Translator, *Les Prophéties du chilam Balam.*   Paris, Gallimard, 1976.
Translator, *Relation de Michocan.*   Paris, Gallimard, 1984.

*

Critical Study: *J.-M. G. Le Clézio* by Jennifer Waelti-Walters, Boston, Twayne, 1977.

*   *   *

J.-M. G. Le Clézio is connected to none of the modern movements in French literature. He stands by himself, expressing his anguish and his quest in powerfully lyric prose which breaks the traditional bounds of the novel and creates an epic of consciousness rather than of deeds. His world is a mysterious place that he must struggle to understand but from which he is separated by a growing multitude of manmade objects, which is rapidly becoming intolerable and from which his characters try to escape. They do this by flight: flight from the city in quest of the natural world; flight from everyday perception in quest of a greater understanding (by meditation, walking, emotion, drugs), in a series of books that become progressively less violent until the flight leads into the world of the imagination, the world of children, and of very simple happenings. (Le Clézio's own "flight" leads him frequently to Central America and the cultures of Panama and Mexico influence his thought patterns and symbolism.)

An alteration of quest and flight controls the works which are built on a series of juxtapositions of opposites: the city and the natural world, the sun and the sea, male and female. All man's thought is centred on the sun for it is the source of revelation and around its image Le Clézio creates his structures. The complementary influence is water, symbol both of woman and of death. Indeed the books express a version of the Icarus myth, for the metaphors that dominate them when taken chronologically are the sea and death, falling, the sun, soaring up to the light, and the city as labyrinth and womb.

Juxtaposition of alternatives provides the form as well as the content of the works. The use of subject pronouns is unstable; narration moves frequently from "I" to "you" to "he" without apparent motivation — a technique which both alienates readers and forces them to share the alienation of narrator and protagonist. It should be noted that a strong vein of humour runs through the novels as well. Many of the novels have little or no plot, and in many cases the sections within a book have no apparent order, yet they are very clear to read as they are made up of a series of situations which illustrate a major theme from different angles. These can be complementary or contradictory, developing the theme further or offering another possibility, a different interpretation, so that the effect is that of a number of tableaux rather than of continuous narration. The same effect is created between the books, for each is complete in itself and yet is linked to the world of the other books by a system of recurrent detail, repetition of images, new or further treatment of themes and problems. Hence all Le Clézio's writings are woven together into a single growing structure in which each strand reinforces the others, and adds to their combined impact and power.

—Jennifer Waelti-Walters

———

LEM, Stanisław. Polish. Born in Lvov, 12 September 1921. Educated at Lvov Medical Institute, 1939–41, 1944–45; Jagiellonian University, Cracow, 1946–48. Married Barbara Leśniak in 1953; one son. Garage assistant during World War II; assistant in Science Circle, Jagiellonian University, 1947–49; contributor, *Życie Nauki* [Life of Science] magazine, 1947–49; full-time writer from 1949. Since 1973 part-time lecturer, University of Cracow. Co-founder, Polish Astronautical Society. Recipient: Polish Ministry of Culture award, 1965, 1973; Polish State prize, 1976; Austrian State prize for European literature, 1985; Jurzykowski Foundation award, 1987; Kafka award (Austria), 1991. Honorary Ph.D.: University of Wrocław, 1981. Agent: Franz Rottensteiner, Marchettigasse 9/17, 1060 Vienna, Austria. Address: ul. Narwik 66, 30–436 Cracow, Poland.

PUBLICATIONS

Fiction

Człowiek z Marsa [A Man from Mars]. Serialized in *Nowy Świat Przygód* [New World of Adventure], 1946.
Astronauci [The Astronauts]. Warsaw, Czytelnik, 1951.
Sezam i inne opowiadania [Sesame and Other Stories]. Warsaw, Iskry, 1954.

Obłok Magellana [The Magellan Nebula]. Warsaw, Iskry, 1955.
Dzienniki gwiazdowe. Warsaw, Iskry, 1957; as *The Star Diaries*, London, Secker and Warburg, and New York, Seabury Press, 1976; as *Memoirs of a Space Traveller: Further Reminiscences of Ijon Tiehy*, Secker and Warburg, and New York, Harcourt Brace, 1982.
Czas nieutracony [Time Not Wasted]: *Szpital przemienienia*; *Wśród umarłych* [Among the Dead]; *Powrót* [Return]. Cracow, Wydawnictwo Literackie, 3 vols., 1957; translated as *Hospital of the Transfiguration*, San Diego, Harcourt Brace, 1988; London, Deutsch, 1989.
Śledztwo. Warsaw, Wydawnictwo Ministerstwa Obrony Narodowej, 1959; as *The Investigation*, New York, Seabury Press, 1974.
Inwazja z Aldebarana [Invasion from Aldebaran]. Cracow, Wydawnictwo Literackie, 1959.
Eden. Warsaw, Iskry, 1959; in English, San Diego, Harcourt Brace, 1989; London, Deutsch, 1990.
Powrót z gwiazd. Warsaw, Czytelnik, 1961; as *Return from the Stars*, London, Secker and Warburg, and New York, Harcourt Brace, 1980.
Solaris. Warsaw, Wydawnictwo Ministerstwa Obrony Narodowej, 1961; in English, New York, Walker 1970; London, Faber, 1971.
Pamiętnik znaleziony w wannie. Cracow, Wydawnictwo Literackie, 1961; as *Memoirs Found in a Bathtub*, New York, Seabury Press, 1973.
Księga robotów [Book of Robots]. Cracow, Wydawnictwo Literackie, 1961.
Noc księzycowa [Lunar Night]. Cracow, Wydawnictwo Literackie, 1963.
Niezwyciężony i inne opowiadania. Warsaw, Wydawnictwo Ministerstwa Obrony Narodowej, 1964; as *The Invincible*, London, Sidgwick and Jackson, and New York, Seabury Press, 1973.
Bajki robotów [Robot Fables]. Cracow, Wydawnictwo Literackie, 1964; in *Mortal Engines*, 1977.
Cyberiada. Cracow Literackie, 1965; as *The Cyberiad*, New York, Seabury Press, 1974; London, Secker and Warburg, 1975.
Polowanie [The Hunt]. Cracow, Wydawnictwo Literackie, 1965.
Wysoki zamek [The High Castle]. Warsaw, Wydawnictwo Ministerstwa Obrony Narodowej, 1966.
Ratujmy Kosmos i inne opowiadania [Let Us Save the Cosmos and Other Stories]. Cracow, Wydawnictwo Literackie, 1966.
Głos pana. Warsaw, Czytelnik, 1968; as *His Master's Voice*, London, Secker and Warburg, 1983; New York, Harcourt Brace, 1984.
Opowieści o pilocie Pirxie. Cracow, Wydawnictwo Literackie, 1968; part as *Tales of Pirx the Pilot*, New York, Harcourt Brace, 1979; London, Secker and Warburg, 1980; part as *More Tales of Pirx the Pilot*, New York, Harcourt Brace, 1982; London, Secker and Warburg, 1983.
Opowiadania [Stories]. Cracow, Wydawnictwo Literackie, 1969.
Bezsenność [Insomnia]. Cracow, Wydawnictwo Literackie, 1971; part as *The Futurological Congress*, New York, Seabury Press, 1974; London, Secker and Warburg, 1975.
Doskonała próznia. Warsaw, Czytelnik, 1971; as *A Perfect Vacuum*, London, Secker and Warburg, and New York, Harcourt Brace, 1979.
Opowiadania wybrane [Selected Stories]. Cracow, Wydawnictwo Literackie, 1973.

Wielkość urojona.   Warsaw, Czytelnik, 1973; as *Imaginary Magnitude*, New York, Harcourt Brace, 1984; London, Secker and Warburg, 1985.
Maska [The Mask].   Cracow, Wydawnictwo Literackie, 1976; part in *Mortal Engines*, 1977.
Suplement [Supplement].   Cracow, Wydawnictwo Literackie, 1976.
Katar.   Cracow, Wydawnictwo Literackie, 1976; as *The Chain of Chance*, London, Secker and Warburg, and New York, Harcourt Brace, 1978.
Mortal Engines   New York, Seabury Press, 1977.
Powtórka [Repetition].   Warsaw, Iskry, 1979.
Golem XIV.   Warsaw, Iskry, 1981; in *Imaginary Magnitude*, 1984.
The Cosmic Carnival of Lem, edited by Michael Kandel. New York, Continuum, 1981.
Wizja lokalna [Eyewitness Account].   Cracow, Wydawnictwo Literackie, 1982.
Biblioteka XXI wieku.   Cracow, Wydawnictwo Literackie, 1986; as *One Human Minute*, San Diego, Harcourt Brace, and London, Deutsch, 1986.
Fiasko.   Cracow, Wydawnictwo Literackie, 1987; as *Fiasco*, San Diego, Harcourt Brace, and London, Deutsch, 1987.
Dzienniki gwiazdowe [Star Diaries].   Warsaw, Gebethner i Ska, 1991.

Plays

Jacht Paradise, with Roman Hussarski.   Warsaw, Czytelnik, 1951.

Screenplay: *Przekładaniec* [Roly Poly].

Other

Dialogi [Dialogues].   Cracow, Wydawnictwo Literackie, 1957.
Wejście na orbitę [Getting into Orbit].   Cracow, Wydawnictwo Literackie, 1962.
Summa technologiae.   Cracow, Wydawnictwo Literackie, 1964.
Filozofia przypadku: literatura w świetle empirii [The Philosophy of Chance: Literature Considered Empirically].   Cracow, Wydawnictwo Literackie, 1968.
Fantastyka i futurologia [Science Fiction and Futurology].   Cracow, Wydawnictwo Literackie, 1970.
Rozprawy i szkice [Essays and Sketches].   Cracow, Wydawnictwo Literackie, 1975.
Prowokacja [Provocation].   Cracow, Wydawnictwo Literackie, 1984.
Microworlds: Writings on Science Fiction and Fantasy, edited by Franz Rottensteiner.   New York, Harcourt Brace, 1984; London, Secker and Warburg, 1985.
Pokój na ziemi [Peace on Earth].   Cracow, Wydawnictwo Literackie, 1987.
Rozmowy ze Stanisławem Lemem [Conversations with Stanisław Lem], with Stanisław Berés.   Cracow, Wydawnictwo Literackie, 1987.
Ciemność i pleśń [Darkness and Mildew].   Cracow, Wydawnictwo Literackie, 1988.

*

Critical Studies: "A Writer in No-Man's Land" by Małgorzata Szpakowska, in *Polish Perspectives* (Warsaw), 14(10), 1971; "Stanisław Lem on Men and Robots" by Michael A. Kandel, in *Extrapolation* (Kent, Ohio), 14, 1972; "*Solaris* and the

Illegitimate Suns of Science Fiction" by David Ketterer, in *Extrapolation* (Kent, Ohio), 14, 1972; "European S[cience] F[iction]: Rottensteiner's Anthology, and the Strugatskys, and Lem" by Ursula K. Le Guin, in *Science-Fiction Studies* (Montreal), 1(3), 1974; Lem issues of *Science-Fiction Studies* (Montreal), 4, 1977, 5, 1978, and 13, 1986; "Cybernetics and a Humanistic Fiction: Stanisław Lem's *The Cyberiad*," in *Research Studies*, 45, 1977, "Having Everything Is Having Nothing: Stanisław Lem versus Utiliterianism," in *Southwest Review* (Dallas), Summer 1981, "The Ghost in the Machine: Stanisław Lem's *Mortal Engines*," in *Liberal and Fine Arts Review*, January 1984, and "'Memoirs Found in a Bathtub': Stanisław Lem's Critique of Cybernetics," in *Mosaic* (Winnipeg, Manitoba), Fall 1984, all by John Rothfork; "*The Investigation*: Stanisław Lem's Pynchonesque Novel" by Stanley Vogel, in *Riverside Quarterly* (Lake Charles, Louisiana), 6, 1977; "Stanisław Lem's Fiction and the Comic Absurd" by Reuel K. Wilson, in *World Literature Today* (Norman, Oklahoma), 51, 1977; "'The Genius of the Sea': Wallace Stevens' 'The Idea of Order at Key West,' Stanisław Lem's *Solaris*, and the Earth as a Muse" by David L. Lavery, in *Extrapolation* (Kent, Ohio), 21, 1980; "Threats to Rationalism: John Fowles, Stanisław Lem, and the Detective Story" by Frank Occiogrosso, in *Armchair Detective* (New York), 13, 1980; "Stanisław Lem and John Dickson Carr: Critics of the Scientific World-View" by Edmund Miller, in *Armchair Detective* (New York), Fall 1981; "Stanisław Lem's Detective Stories: A Genre Extended" by T. R. Steiner, in *Modern Fiction Studies* (West Lafayette, Indiana), Autumn 1983; "Earth Mothers or Male Memories: Wilhelm, Lem, and Future Women" by Patrice Caldwell, in *Women Worldwalkers: New Dimensions of Science Fiction and Fantasy*, edited by Jane B. Weedman, Lubbock, Texas Tech Press, 1985; "The Book Is the Alien: On Certain and Uncertain Readings of Lem's *Solaris*" by Istvan Csicsery, in *Science-Fiction Studies* (Montreal), March 1985; "'Today's Exception Becomes Tomorrow's Rule': Stanisław Lem's *The Chain of Chance*," in *Publications of the Mississippi Philological Association*, 1985, and *Stanisław Lem*, Mercer Island, Starmont House, 1990, both by J. Madison Davis; "The Gods Must Be Crazy: On the Utility of Playful Chaos in the Universe of Stanisław Lem" by Tony Meesdom, in *Just the Other Day: Essays on the Suture of the Future*, edited by Luk de Vos, Antwerp, EXA, 1985; *Stanisław Lem* by Richard E. Ziegfeld, New York, Ungar, 1985; "Noise, Information and Statistics in Stanisław Lem's *The Investigation*" by Geroge R. Guffey, and "The Cybernetic Paradigms of Stanisław Lem" by Robert M. Philmus, in *Hard Science Fiction*, edited by George E. Slusser and Eric S. Rabkin, Carbondale, Southern Illinois University Press, 1986; "Understanding Lem: *Solaris* Revisited" by Abraham Yossef, in *Foundation* (Dagenham, Essex), Autumn 1989.

*   *   *

   The most widely translated and one of the most prolific among contemporary Polish writers, Stanisław Lem is known internationally as a highly original author of science fiction. He entered the narrow elite of the modern masters of the genre in the early 1970s with the publication of foreign translations of his novel *Solaris*, a collection of "robot tales" *Cyberiada* (*The Cyberiad*), and other works. The SF label, however, encompasses only the most conspicuous aspect of Lem's writing, and only a part (albeit a large one) of his output. In his works of non-fiction he appears a profound philosopher, literary theorist, and observer of contemporary civilization; besides science fiction, his fictional oeuvre also includes genre ranging from the traditionally realistic, panoramic novel (*Czas nieutracony* [Time Not Wasted]) or the mystery (*Śledztwo* [*The Investigation*]), to the philosophical parable (*Pamiętnik znaleziony w wannie* [*Memoirs Found in a Bathtub*]). Finally, even those works that can be roughly subsumed under the heading "science fiction" are in fact so varied in theme, tone, and approach — from the dark vision and sparse narrative style of *Solaris* to the grotesque humor and fireworks of parodistic stylization in *The Cyberiad* — as to stretch the heading well beyond its usual capacity. Moreover, as if this versatility were not enough for him to express his creative breadth, Lem can even be credited with inventing new literary genres, such as the one introduced in *Doskonała próznia* (*A Perfect Vacuum*) and *Wielkość urojona* (*Imaginary Magnitude*) — the review of a book which does not exist (although it should).

Lem was born in the city of Lvov, which in the interwar period belonged to Poland until it was seized by Soviet troops at the outset of World War II. In 1940, he began his study of medicine at the clandestine Polish university, continuing it, after the war ended, in Lvov and Cracow, where he settled in 1946. After his graduation in 1948 he worked as a medical researcher and even published a number of articles in the professional press. These interests, however, co-existed with an increasingly serious commitment to literature, which soon made Lem embark on the career of a full-time fiction writer. His extremely wide scientific knowledge, broadened and deepened over the years thanks to his voracious reading habits, has been a relevant factor in his writing ever since.

Lem's first published novel was a fairly typical SF piece titled *Człowiek z Marsa* (A Man from Mars) and serialized in 1946 in a teen magazine. It was, however, the appearance in 1951 of his first book, *Astronauci* (The Astronauts), that brought him wide critical recognition and popularity with readers. At the time of his debut, he had already completed his three-volume autobiographical and realistic novel *Czas nieutracony*, written in 1948–49, but published only in 1957. This delay in publishing was due to political circumstances: although the trilogy assumed an increasingly Socialist-Realist outlook, its first volume, *Szpital przemienienia* (*Hospital of the Transfiguration*), in particular raised the censor's objections with its unconventional portrayal of the fate of the contemporary Polish intelligentsia. These censorship troubles may have played a part in prompting Lem to switch from realism to science fiction as an outlet that allowed for more criticism of the surrounding reality under the guise of a cautionary tale about the future, while also being safer from the censor's red pencil. His early science-fiction novels, especially *Astronauci* and *Obłok Magellana* (The Magellan Nebula), were still marked with the presence of the obligatory optimistic, progressivist, and "internationalistic" ideology of Socialist Realism, but at the same time they managed to pose a number of disquieting questions concerning the nature of human civilization and the ethical complications involved in the mind's triumphs over matter.

In Lem's early work, this kind of concealment of contemporary concerns under the veil of the imaginary vision of the future could still be seen as, more than anything else, a device designed to fool the censor. With Communist Poland entering a new, relatively more liberal phase of its existence in the wake of the political and cultural "thaw" of 1956, Lem's persistent use of that device could not, however, be explained any longer in such a one-sided manner. In particular, his purely nonsensical satires, actually hilarious parodies of the adventurous plots and space-travel settings of typical science fiction (the best example being *Dzienniki gwiazdowe* [*Memoirs of a Space Traveller*]), have, apart from their obvious antitotalitarian satirical edge, also a broader significance. Quite contrary to

what the reader of science fiction might expect, they emphasize the essential immutability of human nature and human existence. Evolution provided by history is, for Lem, merely a consoling myth: he visualizes the future only to find more proof to support his suspicion that human fate has remained and will remain essentially the same, regardless of all the successes of technology and social progress. In his "robot tales" he suggests half-jokingly that even artificial intelligence, if created by humans, is bound to inherit human flaws. This conviction finds its amusing reflection in the peculiar mixture of the archaic and the super-modern that characterizes both the world represented and the language used to describe it. In *The Cyberiad*, Lem's masterpiece of the "robot" genre, the crucial stylistic device is the ingenious word construction best exemplified in the book's title by the hybridizing of "cybernetics" with "The Iliad." Moreover, the characters — named, analogously, "cyberknights" — are products of crossbreeding of the most traditional roles of epic heroes or villains and ultra-futuristic technological advancement.

Lem argues the same point in a different manner but with equal force in his apparently "more serious" works of fiction, such as *Solaris*, *Memoirs Found in a Bathtub*, and *Głos pana* (*His Master's Voice*). In *Solaris*, for instance, his omnipresent theme of modern man shown as a sorcerer's apprentice, who in the course of the evolution of technology has unleashed forces beyond his control and his capacity to understand, is viewed, thanks to an imaginative quasi-science-fiction plot, from a highly revealing vantage point. Confronted, on another planet, with a form of intelligent life whose nature cannot possibly be grasped by their innate ways of reasoning and acquired experience, the novel's characters demonstrate, in a variety of ways, the unavoidable limitations imposed on mankind's cognition — and, as a result, the limits of adaptability to changing circumstances — by the flaws inherent in human nature itself. In the final analysis, it is the fundamental question of what actually does constitute the human identity that has informed Lem's work from the start. The generic convention of science fiction is, for him, just a handy means to locate this profound problem in a perspective which has a double advantage of attracting the readers' attention while also making them reflect on issues far weightier than literary entertainment could possibly touch upon.

—Stanisław Barańczak

LENZ, Siegfried. German. Born in Lyck, East Prussia (now Elk, Poland), 17 March 1926. Educated at the University of Hamburg, 1945–48. Served in the navy during World War II. Married Lieselotte Lenz in 1949. Reporter, 1948–50, and editor, 1950–51, *Die Welt* newspaper, Hamburg. Since 1951 freelance writer. Visiting Lecturer, University of Houston, Texas, 1969. Member, Gruppe 47. Campaign speaker for Social Democratic party, from 1965. Recipient: Schickele prize, 1952; Lessing prize, 1953; Hauptmann prize, 1961; Mackensen prize, 1962; Schickele prize, 1962; City of Bremen prize, 1962; State of North Rhine-Westphalia arts prize, 1966; Gryphius prize, 1979; German Free Masons prize, 1979; Thomas Mann prize, 1984; Raabe prize, 1987; Federal Booksellers peace prize, 1988; Galinsky Foundation prize, 1989. Honorary doctorate: University of Hamburg, 1976. Address: Preußerstraße 4, 2000 Hamburg 52, Germany.

PUBLICATIONS

Fiction

Es waren Habichte in der Luft. Hamburg, Hoffmann und Campe, 1951.
Duell mit dem Schatten. Hamburg, Hoffmann und Campe, 1953.
So zärtlich war Suleyken. Hamburg, Hoffmann und Campe, 1955.
Der Mann im Strom. Hamburg, Hoffmann und Campe, 1957.
Dasselbe. Hamburg, Hoffmann und Campe, 1957.
Jäger des Spotts. Hamburg, Hoffmann und Campe, 1958; as *Jäger des Spotts, und andere Erzählungen*, edited by Robert H. Spaethling, New York, Norton, 1965.
Brot und Spiele. Hamburg, Hoffmann und Campe, 1959.
Das Feuerschiff. Hamburg, Hoffmann und Campe, 1960; title story as *The Lightship*, New York, Hill and Wang, and London, Heinemann, 1962.
Das Wunder von Striegeldorf: Geschichten. Frankfurt, Hirschgraben, 1961.
Stimmungen der See. Stuttgart, Reclam, 1962.
Stadtgespräch, adapted from his play *Zeit der Schuldlosen*. Hamburg, Hoffmann und Campe, 1963; as *The Survivor*, New York, Hill and Wang, 1965.
Der Hafen ist voller Geheimnisse: Ein Feature in Erzählungen und zwei masurische Geschichten. Lübeck, Matthiesen, 1963.
Lehmanns Erzählungen; oder, So schön war mein Markt: Aus den Bekenntnissen eines Schwarzhändlers. Hamburg, Hoffmann und Campe, 1964.
Der Spielverderber. Hamburg, Hoffmann und Campe, 1965.
Begegnung mit Tieren, with Hans Bender and Werner Bergengruen. Hamburg, Hamburger Lesehefte, 1966.
Das Wrack, and Other Stories, edited by C. A. H. Russ. London, Heinemann, 1967.
Die Festung und andere Novellen. Stockholm, Läromedelsförlaget, 1968.
Deutschstunde. Hamburg, Hoffmann und Campe, 1968; as *The German Lesson*, London, Macdonald, 1971; New York, Hill and Wang, 1972.
Hamilkar Schass aus Suleyken. Lübeck, Mattiesen, 1970.
Lukas, sanftmütiger Knecht. Stuttgart, Klett, 1970.
Gesammelte Erzählungen. Hamburg, Hoffmann und Campe, 1970.
So war es mit dem Zirkus: Fünf Geschichten aus Suleyken. Hamburg, Hoffmann und Campe, 1971.
Erzählungen. Frankfurt, Büchergilde Gutenberg, 1972.
Meistererzählungen. Stuttgart, Europaische Bildungsgemeinschaft, 1972.
Ein Haus aus lauter Liebe. Stuttgart, Klett, 1973.
Das Vorbild. Hamburg, Hoffmann und Campe, 1973; as *An Exemplary Life*, New York, Hill and Wang, and London, Secker and Warburg, 1976.
Der Geist der Mirabelle: Geschichten aus Bollerup. Hamburg, Hoffmann und Campe, 1975.
Einstein überquert die Elbe bei Hamburg. Hamburg, Hoffmann und Campe, 1975.
Die Kunstradfahrer und andere Geschichten. Hamburg, Agentur des Rauhen Hauses, 1976.
Heimatmuseum. Hamburg, Hoffmann und Campe, 1978; as *The Heritage*, New York, Hill and Wang, and London, Secker and Warburg, 1981.
Der Verlust. Hamburg, Hoffmann und Campe, 1981.
Der Anfang von etwas. Leipzig, Reclam, 1981.
Ein Kriegsende. Hamburg, Hoffmann und Campe, 1984.

Exerzierplatz. Hamburg, Hoffmann und Campe, 1985; as *Training Ground*, London, Methuen, 1991.
Der Verzicht. Neu-Isenburg, Tiessen, 1985.
Die Erzählungen: 1949–1984. Munich, Deutscher Taschenbuch, 3 vols., 1986.
Das serbische Mädchen. Hamburg, Hoffmann und Campe, 1987.
Geschichten ut Bollerup. Hamburg, Quickborn, 1987.
Motivsuche. Berlin, Aufbau, 1988.
The Selected Stories of Siegfried Lenz. New York, New Directions, 1989.
Die Klangprobe. Hamburg, Hoffmann und Campe, 1990.

Plays

Das schönste Fest der Welt (radio play). Hamburg, Hans Bredow-Institut, 1956.
Zeit der Schuldlosen; Zeit der Schuldigen (radio play). Hamburg, Hans Bredow-Institut, 1961; stage adaptation (in German), London, Harrap, 1966.
Das Gesicht: Komödie (produced Hamburg, 1964). Hamburg, Hoffmann und Campe, 1964.
Haussuchung (radio play). Hamburg, Hoffmann und Campe, 1967.
Die Augenbinde; Schauspiel; Nicht alle Förster sind froh: Ein Dialog. Reinbek, Rowohlt, 1970.
Drei Stücke. Hamburg, Hoffmann und Campe, 1980.
Zeit der Schuldlosen und andere Stücke. Munich, Deutscher Taschenbuch, 1988.

Radio Plays: *Zeit der Schuldlosen/Zeit der Schuldigen*, 1961; *Das schönste Fest der Welt.*

Other

So leicht fängt man keine Katze. Hamburg, Agentur des Rauhen Hauses, 1954.
Der einsame Jäger. Gütuersloh, Rufer, 1955.
Das Kabinett der Konterbande. Hamburg, Hoffmann und Campe, 1956.
Flug über Land und Meer: Nordsee—Holstein—Nordsee, with Dieter Seelmann. Brunswich, Westermann, 1967; as *Wo die Möwen schreien: Flug über Norddeutschlands Küsten und Länder*, Hamburg, Christian, 1976.
Leut von Hamburg: Satirische Porträts. Hamburg, Hoffmann und Campe, 1968.
Versäum nicht den Termin der Freude. Memmingen, Visel, 1970.
Lotte soll nicht sterben (for children). Copenhagen, Grafisk, and St. Paul, EMC, 1970; as *Lotte macht alles mit*, Munich, Lenz, 1978.
Beziehungen: Ansichten und Bekenntnisse zur Literatur. Hamburg, Hoffmann und Campe, 1970.
Die Herrschaftssprache der CDU. Kiel, Wählerinitiative Nord, 1971.
Verlorenes Lang—gewonnene Nachbarschaft: zur Ostpolitik der Bundesregierung. Kiel, Wählerinitiative Nord, 1972.
Der Amüsierdoktor. Mainz, Eggebrecht, 1972.
Der Leseteufel. Stammheim, Rossipaul, 1972(?).
Elfenbeinturm und Barrikade: Schriftsteller zwischen Literatur und Politik. Hamburg, Hoffmann und Campe, 1976.
Die Wracks von Hamburg: Hörfunk-Features. Oldenburg, Stalling, 1978.
Himmel, Wolken, weites Land: Flug über Meer, Marsch, Geest und Heide, with Dieter Seelmann. Hamburg, Christian, 1979.

Waldboden: Sechsunddreissig Farbstiftzeichnungen, illustrated by Liselotte Lenz.   Hamburg, Knaus, 1979.
Gespräche mit Manès Sperber und Leszek Kołakowski, edited by Alfred Mensak.   Hamburg, Hoffmann und Campe, 1980.
Über Phantasie: Siegfried Lenz, Gespräche mit Heinrich Böll, Günter Grass, Walter Kempowski, Pavel Kohout, edited by Alfred Mensak.   Hamburg, Hoffmann und Campe, 1982.
Fast ein Triumph: aus einem Album.   Hamburg, Otto-Rohse-Presse, 1982.
Elfenbeinturm und Barrikade: Erfahrungen am Schreibtisch.   Hamburg, Hoffmann und Campe, 1983.
Manès Sperber, sein letztes Jahr, with Manès and Jenka Sperber.   Munich, Deutscher Taschenbuch, 1985.
Etwas über Namen (address).   Hamburg, Hoffmann und Campe, 1985.
Kleines Standgut, illustrated by Liselotte Lenz.   Hamburg, Hoffmann und Campe, 1986.
Am Rande des Friedens.   Frankfurt, Büchergilde Gutenberg, 1989.

Editor, with Egon Schramm, *Wippchens charmante Scharmützel*, by Julius Stettenheim.   Hamburg, Fischer, 1960.

*

Critical Studies: "From the Gulf Stream in the Main Stream: Siegfried Lenz and Hemingway" by Sumner Kirshner, in *Research Studies*, June 1967; "Narrowing the Distance: Siegfried Lenz's *Deutschstunde*" by Robert H. Paslick, in *German Quarterly* (St. Louis, Missouri), March 1973; "The Macabre Festival: A Consideration of Six Stories by Siegfried Lenz" by Colin Russ, in *Deutung und Bedeutung: Studies in German and Comparative Literature*, edited by Brigitte Schludermann and others, The Hague and Paris, Mouton, 1973; "How It Seems and How It Is: Marriage in Three Stories by Siegfried Lenz" by Esther N. Elstun, in *Orbis litterarum* (Copenhagen), 29(2), 1974; "Ironic Reversal in the Short Stories of Siegfried Lenz," in *Neophilologus* (Groningen), 58(4), 1974, and *Siegfried Lenz*, London, Wolff, 1978, both by Brian O. Murdoch; "Siegfried Lenz's *Deutschstunde*: A North German Novel," in *German Life and Letters* (London), July 1975, and "The 'Lesson' in Siegfried Lenz's *Deutschstunde*," in *Seminar* (Kingston, Ontario), February 1977, both by Peter Russell; "Zygmunt's Follies? On Siegfried Lenz's *Heimatmuseum*" by Geoffrey P. Butler, in *German Life and Letters* (London), January 1980; "Captive Creator in Siegfried Lenz's *Deutschstunde*: Writer, Reader, and Response" by Todd Kontje, in *German Quarterly* (St. Louis, Missouri), 53, 1980; "The Interlocutor and the Narrative Transmission of the Past: On Siegfried Lenz's *Heimatmuseum*" by Marilyn Sibley Fries, in *Monatshefte* (Madison, Wisconsin), Winter 1987; "The Eye of the Witness: Photography in Siegfried Lenz's Short Stories" by Hanna Geldrich-Leffmann, in *Modern Language Review* (London), April 1989.

*   *   *

The similarities between the fortunes and careers of Siegfried Lenz and Günter Grass (*q.v.*) are remarkable. Both were born within a year, in the eastern part of the German-speaking areas of Europe that after 1945 became part of Poland. Towards the end of World War II they were both drafted, and after their release from prisoner-of-war camps of the Western allies, they both ended up in the Federal Republic where they became best-selling novelists with a strong social and political

engagement. Lenz's experiences under the Nazi regime, as a teenage soldier, and the resettlement after the loss of his homeland all contributed to his development and made him one of Germany's most prominent writers.

Lenz can be described as a realist-symbolist writer whose fiction deals with contemporary topics. In an interview (*Die Zeit*, 12 November 1982) he said that one of his guiding stylistic principles is to put himself inside his characters "until the last possible moment." Although he could hardly be called an innovator, the themes of his books make him a very significant figure in post-war German literature.

Lenz has written some radio and stage plays, most noteworthy *Zeit der Schuldlosen* (Time of the Guiltless), but he had his major success as a prose writer. A member of the influential Gruppe 47, Lenz published his first novel *Es waren Habichte in der Luft* (Hawks Were in the Air) in 1951. The book was followed by a string of short novels and a number of short stories, of which *So zärtlich war Suleyken* (So Tender Was Suleyken) is of particular interest as it pays homage to Lenz's lost homeland of Masuria in East Prussia.

While his first few works are somewhat existentialist in nature, discussing the dilemmas of the human condition, Lenz soon turned his attention to more specific political and social problems of the emerging West German state. He shared this critical role with some of his contemporaries, especially Heinrich Böll and Martin Walser (*q.v.*). Lenz's strong concerns about the political development of the Federal Republic led to his active participation — along with Grass — as a campaign speaker in Willy Brandt's 1969 federal election bid.

Certain novels mark the stages in his artistic development. The early *Es waren Habichte in der Luft* portrays the role of the humanistic, freedom-seeking individual in conflict with a totalitarian ideology. Stenka, the protagonist who has been falsely accused of murder, tries to flee the country in the company of a young man whose fiancée has been killed by a madman. In the end Stenka is shot dead while his companion survives. The largely symbolic work — the ever-present birds of prey set the tone — carries the fatalistic message that we must follow our convictions regardless of success and that in the end no one will escape. *Der Mann im Strom* (The Man in the River) turns to a more concrete social issue. The novel relates the fate of an aging diver who, under the harsh competitive conditions of the emerging German "economic miracle," forges his birthdate on a document to secure a job meant for younger workers. Portrayed is a basically honest man who is driven to deceit, in contrast to members of the younger generation who are unscrupulous in their desire to make fast money.

While Lenz's earlier works were short novels and several collections of short stories (many have argued that the latter are his true forte) he surprised his critics in 1968 by publishing *Deutschstunde* (*The German Lesson*), a tome of some 500 pages and an immediate bestseller. This novel also marked his international breakthrough, being translated into over 20 languages and selling well over a million copies. It is Lenz's most significant attempt to come to terms with the German past and makes a contribution to what is sometimes misleadingly called *Vergangenheitsbewältigung* (overcoming the past). In this book he seeks to find the roots of the crimes of the Third Reich in an unusual and convincing way. Rather than depicting the Nazi era in its most brutal detail as others have done, he takes a much more subtle approach. The father of the protagonist, Siggi Jepsen, is a subordinate policeman who does nothing but what he considers his duty when enforcing a ban on a childhood friend whose paintings are not acceptable to the regime. This policeman does not commit any atrocities, nor does he help to deport Jews or participate in any other of the notorious Nazi crimes. But it is precisely in the unquestioning sense of duty of the minor players that Lenz's psychologically probing character study finds the source of an attitude which made possible the perversion of a whole nation by a criminal regime. Years later Siggi is in jail in the new democratic Germany for arson. He suffers from a serious psychological disorder which is the direct result of having observed his father's actions during the Nazi era. The irony of the novel's central idea lies in the fact that Siggi produces this character study of his father while writing a required essay on "The Joys of Duty." Thus *The German Lesson* becomes "a lesson for Germans" who are implored to stop inoculating young people with the disavowed notion that the blind execution of duty is of any intrinsic value.

More recent novels by Lenz such as *Das Vorbild* (*An Exemplary Life*) and *Exerzierplatz* (*Training Ground*) continue in a similar vein by questioning the moral and educational value systems of contemporary Germany.

—Manfred K. Kremer

LI FEIKAN. *See* **BA JIN.**

LI YAOTANG. *See* **BA JIN.**

LIANG JINGUANG. *See* **HAO RAN.**

LIDMAN, Sara (Adela). Swedish. Born in Missenträsk, 30 December 1923. Educated at the University of Uppsala, Ph.D. 1949. Freelance journalist: reported on Vietnam war for Swedish newspapers. Travelled in South Africa, 1960–61, and Kenya, 1962–64. Member of De Nio Swedish literary society, 1955–63. Honorary doctorate: University of Umeå, 1978. Address: c/o Bonniers Förlag, Box 3159, 103 63 Stockholm, Sweden.

PUBLICATIONS

Fiction

Tjärdalen [The Tar Pit]. Stockholm, Bonnier, 1953.
Hjortronlandet [Cloudberry Country]. Stockholm, Bonnier, 1955.

Regnspiran. Stockholm, Bonnier, 1958; as *The Rain Bird*, New York, Braziller, 1962; London, Hutchinson, 1963.
Bära mistel [Wearing the Mistletoe]. Stockholm, Bonnier, 1960.
Jag och min son [My Son and I]. Stockholm, Bonnier, 1961.
Med fem diamanter [With Five Diamonds]. Stockholm, Bonnier, 1964.
Norrland Suite.
   Din tjänare hör [Thy Servant Heareth]. Stockholm, Bonnier, 1977.
   Vredens barn [Anger's Child]. Stockholm, Bonnier, 1979.
   Nabots sten. Stockholm, Bonnier, 1981; as *Naboth's Stone*, Norwich, Norvik Press, 1989.
   Den underbare mannen [The Miracle Man]. Stockholm, Bonnier, 1983.
Järnkronan [The Iron Crown]. Stockholm, Bonnier, 1985.

Plays

Job Klockmakares dotter [Job the Watchmaker's Daughter] (produced 1954).
Aina (produced 1956).
Marta, Marta: en folksaga. Stockholm, Bonnier, 1970.

Other

Mitt första besök i Skellefteå [My First Visit to Skellefteå]. Stockholm, Skellefteå, 1955.
Misteldans [Mistletoe Dance]. Stockholm, Bonnier, 1960.
Samtal över en klyfta [Conversations About a Split], with Bo Gustafsson. Stockholm, Clarté, 1965.
Från kolonialism till socialism: en essä om ekonomisk utveckling [From Colonialism to Socialism: An Essay on Economic Development], with Bo Gustafsson. Stockholm, Clarté, 1966.
Samtal i Hanoi [Conversations in Hanoi]. Stockholm, Bonnier, 1966.
Till den annamitiska ungdomen. Stockholm, Giai Phong, 1967.
Gruva [Mine]. Stockholm, Bonnier, 1968.
Vänner och u-vänner [Friends and Developing Friends]. Stockholm, Bonnier, 1969.
Politisk asyl åt Vietnamkrigsvägrare [Political Asylum for Vietnamese Refugees]. Stockholm, Stockholms Forskn.-Kollektiv, 1971.
Fåglarna i Nam Dinh [The Birds of Nam Dinh]. Eneryda, DFFG/Ordfront, 1972.
Varje löv är ett öga [Every Leaf Is an Eye]. Stockholm, Bonnier, 1980.
Bröd men också rosor [Bread But Also Roses], with Per Frostin and Henry Cöster. Stockholm, Rabén & Sjögren, 1985.
Och trädet svarade [And the Tree Replied]. Stockholm, Bonnier, 1988.

*

Critical Studies: "Sara Lidman's Progress: A Critical Survey of Six Novels," in *Scandinavian Studies* (Madison, Wisconsin), 39(2), 1967, and "Sara Lidman, Novelist and Moralist," in *Svensk Litteraturtidskrift* (Stockholm), 36(1), 1973, both by Harold Borland; "Eyvind Johnson, Per Olof Sundman and Sara Lidman: An Introduction" by Lars Bäckström, in *Contemporary Literature* (Madison, Wisconsin), 12, 1971; "An Interview with Sara Lidman" by L. S. Dembo, in *Contemporary Literature* (Madison, Wisconsin), 12, 1971; "The Inadequacy of Literature: Jan Myrdal and Sara Lidman" by

Janet Mawby, in her *Writers and Politics in Modern Scandinavia*, London, Hodder and Stoughton, 1978; "In Defense of People and Forests: Sara Lidman's Recent Novels" by Helena Scott, in *World Literature Today* (Norman, Oklahoma), 58(1), 1984; "Sara Lidman's Chronicles of Norrland" by Diana W. Wormuth, in *Swedish Book Review* (Lampeter, Wales), 2, 1984.

*   *   *

The superficial course of Sara Lidman's career from neo-provincialism in the 1950s to internationalist solidarity in the 1960s and back to provincialism in the 1970s and 1980s is misleading. It is noteworthy that Norrland, the distant and sparsely populated northern half of Sweden from which she came and in which most of her novels are set, was subject to such extremes of economic exploitation in the 19th century and into this century that it has been suggested its situation mirrors the pattern of exploitation being practised on an international scale by the imperial powers in their African and Asian colonies. One might also say that the break in Lidman's literary career from the mid 1960s to the mid 1970s is likewise more apparent than real, for during that period she continued to be engaged in the discussion of the themes that are central to her fiction, but that she chose areas other than fiction as the arena for debate. *Gruva* (Mine) and *Samtal i Hanoi* (Conversations in Hanoi) — the documentary and reportage books of those years — as well as her political involvement as speaker and campaigner against the American presence in Vietnam are a direct-action equivalent of the concerns of her fiction.

Central to Lidman's writing from the start have been questions of social morality, of individual and collective responsibility, of the rights of outsiders and the oppressed — those that she herself has referred to as "the unloved." She has been called "the social conscience of the welfare state" by Ingemar Algulin in *Litteraturens historia i Sverige* (1987), even though almost all of the fiction she has written is set in geographical zones or historical phases outside the Sweden of the welfare state. Thus the main characters in her novels of the 1950s, set in Norrland, are all in one way or another situated on the fringes of their communities, whether as outcasts, as rejecters of community norms, or as more talented than the rest. And the communities themselves are similarly on the fringe of the larger national and international society. Unlike the African novels that followed them — *Jag och min son* (My Son and I) and *Med fem diamanter* (With Five Diamonds) — these novels are not in any overt sense socially tendentious: the community they portray is viewed as so enclosed that, except in the case of individuals, any external perspective bearing the possibility of change is absent. The African novels, however, with their clear revelation of the exploitation of the native by the outsider, make manifest the subtext of the Norrland novels — that, from the social aspect, it is oppression by external forces that has corrupted the concept of community. In Lidman's finest body of work — the five novels beginning with *Din tjänare hör* (Thy Servant Heareth) which make up the Norrland Suite — the building of the railway that opened up the northern interior of Sweden in the last decades of the 19th century serves as a double-edged symbol in that it brings with it both corruption and a widening of possibilities.

Lidman's writing exists broadly within the great Swedish tradition of social realism, a tradition that has always found room for a deepening of the psychological, social, and existential perspectives by the use of the symbolic and the grotesque. There is in her works, however, none of the tendency to idealize character to be found, for instance, in works of the social realists of the 1930s, where sympathy for the oppressed can paradoxically lead to something close to a mythology of the beneficial effects of deprivation. But like many other Norrland writers the registers of Lidman's realism have been augmented by everpresent elements of oral storytelling, biblical allusion, provincial myth, and graphic naivism. Her frequent use of dialect, in particular, functions on one level to reinforce the realism of the narration but on another to impart distance between the reader and the harsh exoticism of that which is narrated.

There is another sense, too, in which it is impossible to confine Lidman's fiction within the boundaries of social realism. In spite of the active campaigning stance adopted in her extra-literary activities, the novels reveal an unremitting fatalism that allows for no secure release from the cycle. Lidman's novels present the problems without offering solutions, wonder at the resilience of humanity without positing relief. The world she portrays is ultimately one where the Lord gives and the Lord takes away, blessed be the name of the Lord. In this Old Testament ethos lies the true voice of both international solidarity and of her own province.

—Peter Graves

————

LILAR, Françoise. *See* **MALLET-JORIS, Françoise.**

————

LINDGREN, Astrid (Anna Emilia, née Ericsson). Swedish. Born in Vimmerby, 14 November 1907. Married Sture Lindgren in 1931 (died 1952); one son and one daughter. Worked as a secretary in Stockholm; children's book editor, Rabén & Sjögren publishers, Stockholm, 1946–70. Member, De Nio literary society, 1963. Recipient: Nolgersson Medal, 1950; Swedish State award, 1957; Hans Christian Andersen award, 1958; Boys' Clubs of America award, 1961; New York *Herald Tribune* award, 1959; Swedish Academy Gold Medal, 1971; International Book Committee award, 1993. Honorary doctorate: University of Linköping, 1973; University of Leicester, 1978; University of Warsaw, 1989. Fellow, International Institute of Arts and Letters, 1975. Address: c/o Rabén & Sjögren, Box 45022, 104 30 Stockholm, Sweden.

PUBLICATIONS

Fiction (for children)

Britt-Mari lättar sitt hjärta [The Confidences of Britt-Mari]. Stockholm, Rabén & Sjögren, 1944.
Kerstin och jag [Kerstin and I]. Stockholm, Rabén & Sjögren, 1945.
Pippi Långstrump. Stockholm, Rabén & Sjögren, 1945; as *Pippi Longstocking*, New York, Viking, 1950; London, Oxford University Press, 1954.
Pippi Långstrump går ombord. Stockholm, Rabén & Sjögren, 1946; as *Pippi Longstocking Goes Aboard*, London, Oxford University Press, 1956; as *Pippi Goes on Board*, New York, Viking, 1957; London, Puffin, 1977.
Mästerdetektiven Blomkvist. Stockholm, Rabén & Sjögren,

1946; as *Bill Bergson, Master Detective*, New York, Viking, 1952.

Alla vi barn i Bullerbyn. Stockholm, Rabén & Sjögren, 1947; as *The Six Bullerby Children*, London, Methuen, 1963.

Känner du Pippi Långstrump?: bilderbok. Stockholm, Rabén & Sjögren, 1947.

Pippi Långstrump i Söderhavet. Stockholm, Rabén & Sjögren, 1948; as *Pippi in the South Seas*, London, Oxford University Press, 1957; New York, Viking, 1959.

Mera om oss barn i Bullerbyn [More About the Bullerby Children]. Stockholm, Rabén & Sjögren, 1949.

Nils Karlsson-Pyssling. Stockholm, Rabén & Sjögren, 1949.

Kajsa Kavat. Stockholm, Rabén & Sjögren, 1950.

Kajsa Kavat hjälper mormor. Stockholm, Rabén & Sjögren, 1950; as *Brenda Brave Helps Grandmother*, St. Louis, Webster, 1961; as *Brenda Helps Grandmother*, London, Burke, 1966.

Kati i Amerika. Stockholm, Rabén & Sjögren, 1950; as *Kati in America*, Leicester, Brockhampton Press, 1964.

Jag vill också gå i skolan. Stockholm, Rabén & Sjögren, 1951; as *I Want to Go to School Too*, London, Methuen, 1980; New York, R & S Books, 1987.

Mästerdetektiven Blomkvist lever farligt. Stockholm, Rabén & Sjögren, 1951; as *Bill Bergson Lives Dangerously*, New York, Viking, 1954.

Boken om Pippi Långstrump. Stockholm, Rabén & Sjögren, 1952.

Bara roligt i Bullerbyn [Having Fun in Bullerby]. Stockholm, Rabén & Sjögren, 1952.

Kati pä Kaptensgatan. Stockholm, Rabén & Sjögren, 1952; as *Kati in Italy*, New York, Grosset, 1961; Leicester, Brockhampton Press, 1962; as *Kati i Italien*, Rabén & Sjögren, 1971.

Kalle Blomkvist och Rasmus. Stockholm, Rabén & Sjögren, 1953; as *Bill Bergson and the White Rose Rescue*, New York, Viking, 1965.

Kati i Paris. Stockholm, Bonnier, 1953; as *Kati in Paris*, New York, Grosset, 1961; Leicester, Brockhampton Press, 1966.

Mio, min Mio. Stockholm, Rabén & Sjögren, 1954; as *Mio, My Son*, New York, Viking, 1956.

Jag vill också ha ett syskon. Stockholm, Rabén & Sjögren, 1954; as *That's My Baby*, London, Methuen, 1979; as *I Want a Brother or Sister*, New York, Harcourt Brace, 1981.

Lillebror och Karlsson på taket. Stockholm, Rabén & Sjögren, 1955; as *Eric and Karlsson-on-the-Roof*, London, Oxford University Press, 1958; as *Karlsson on the Roof*, New York, Viking, 1971; London, Methuen, 1975.

Rasmus på luffen. Stockholm, Rabén & Sjögren, 1956; as *Rasmus and the Vagabond*, New York, Viking, 1960; as *Rasmus and the Tramp*, London, Methuen, 1961.

Korea, ofredens land [Korea, a Country at War]. Stockholm, Rabén & Sjögren, 1956.

Nils Karlsson-Pyssling flyttar in. Stockholm, Rabén & Sjögren, 1956; as *Simon Small Moves In*, London, Burke, 1965.

Barnen på Bråkmakargatan. Stockholm, Rabén & Sjögren, 1956; as *The Children on Troublemaker Street*, New York, Macmillan, 1964; as *The Mischievous Martens*, New York, Macmillan, 1964; London, Methuen, 1968.

Rasmus, Pontus och Toker [Rasmus, Pontus, and Toker]. Stockholm, Rabén & Sjögren, 1957.

Noriko-San, Girl of Japan. London, Methuen, 1958.

Sia bor på Kilimandjaro. Stockholm, Rabén & Sjögren, 1958; as *Sia Lives on Kilimanjaro*, New York, Macmillan, and London, Methuen, 1959.

Pjäser för barn och ungdom. Stockholm, Rabén & Sjögren, 1959.

Sunnanäng. Stockholm, Rabén & Sjögren, 1959; as "Summer Meadow," in *Mio, My Son*, 1956.

Mina svenska kusiner. Stockholm, Rabén & Sjögren, 1959; as *My Swedish Cousins*, Stockholm, Swedish Institute, 1959; New York, Macmillan, 1960; London, Methuen, 1961.

Lilibet, cirkusbarn. Stockholm, Rabén & Sjögren, 1960; as *Lilibet, Circus Child*, London, Methuen, 1960; New York, Macmillan, 1961.

Madicken. Stockholm, Rabén & Sjögren, 1960; as *Mischievous Meg*, New York, Viking, 1962; as *Madicken*, London, Oxford University Press, 1963; as *Mardie*, London, Methuen, 1979.

The Tomten. New York, Coward McCann, 1961; London, Constable, 1962.

Jul i stallet. Stockholm, Rabén & Sjögren, 1961.

Bullerby boken. Stockholm, Rabén & Sjögren, 1961; as *The Children of Noisy Village*, New York, Viking, 1962; as *Cherry Time at Bullerby*, London, Methuen, 1964; part translated as *Happy Times in Noisy Village*, New York, Viking, 1963; part translated as *Happy Days at Bullerby*, London, Methuen, 1965.

Lotta på Bråkmakargatan. Stockholm, Rabén & Sjögren, 1962; as *Lotta on Troublemaker Street*, New York, Macmillan, 1963; as *Lotta Leaves Home*, London, Methuen, 1969.

Karlsson på taket flyger igen. Stockholm, Rabén & Sjögren, 1962; as *Karlsson Flies Again*, London, Methuen, 1977.

Christmas in the Stable. New York, Coward McCann, 1962.

Marko bor i Jugoslavien. Stockholm, Rabén & Sjögren, 1962; as *Marko Lives in Yugoslavia*, New York, Macmillan, 1963.

Emil i Lönneberga. Stockholm, Rabén & Sjögren, 1963; as *Emil in the Soup Tureen*, Chicago, Follett, and Leicester, Brockhampton Press, 1970; as *Emil's Pranks*, Follett, 1971.

Jul i Bullerbyn. Stockholm, Rabén & Sjögren, 1963; as *Christmas in Noisy Village*, New York, Viking, 1964; as *Christmas at Bullerby*, London, Methuen, 1964.

Jackie bor i Holland. Stockholm, Rabén & Sjögren, 1963; as *Dirk Lives in Holland*, New York, Macmillan, 1963.

Vi på Saltkråkan. Stockholm, Rabén & Sjögren, 1964; as *Seacrow Island*, Edinburgh, Oliver and Boyd, 1968; New York, Viking, 1969.

Vår i Bullerbyn. Stockholm, Rabén & Sjögren, 1965; as *Springtime in Noisy Village*, New York, Viking, 1966; as *Springtime in Bullerby*, London, Methuen, 1980.

Randi bor i Lofoten. Oslo, Gyldendal, 1965; as *Randi Lives in Norway*, New York, Macmillan, 1965; as *Gerda Lives in Norway*, London, Methuen, 1966.

Jag vill inte gå och lägga mej. Stockholm, Rabén & Sjögren, 1965.

Barnens dag i Bullerbyn. Stockholm, Rabén & Sjögren, 1966; as *A Day at Bullerby*, London, Methuen, 1967.

Nya hyss av Emil i Lönneberga. Stockholm, Rabén & Sjögren, 1966; as *Emil's Pranks*, Chicago, Follett, 1971 Leicester, Brockhampton Press, 1973.

Noy bor i Thailand. Stockholm, Rabén & Sjögren, 1966; a *Noy Lives in Thailand*, New York, Macmillan, an London, Methuen, 1967.

The Tomten and the Fox. New York, Coward, 1966; as *Th Fox and the Tomten*, London, Constable, 1966.

Skrållan och sjörövarna. Stockholm, Rabén & Sjögren 1967; as *Skrållan and the Pirates*, New York, Doubleday 1969.

Karlsson på taket smyger igen. Stockholm, Rabén & Sjögren, 1968; as *The World's Best Karlsson*, London, Methuen, 1980.

Matti bor i Finland. Stockholm, Rabén & Sjögren, 1968; as *Matti Lives in Finland*, New York, Macmillan, and London, Methuen, 1969.

Passaules labakais Karlssons. Stockholm, Gramatu Draugs, 1969.

Pippi flytar in, with Ingrid Vang Nyman. Stockholm, Rabén & Sjögren, 1969.

Pippi ordnar allt, with Ingrid Vang Nyman. Stockholm, Rabén & Sjögren, 1969.

Än lever Emil i Lönneberga. Stockholm, Rabén & Sjögren, 1970; as *Emil and Piggy Beast*, Chicago, Follett, 1973; as *Emil and His Clever Pig*, London, Hodder and Stoughton, 1974.

All About the Bullerby Children. London, Methuen, 1970.

Visst kan Lotta cykla. Stockholm, Rabén & Sjögren, 1971; as *Of Course Polly Can Ride a Bike*, Chicago, Follett, 1972; as *Lotta's Bike*, London, Methuen, 1973.

Mina påhitt: ett urval från Pippi till Emil. Stockholm, Rabén & Sjögren, 1971.

Den där Emil. Stockholm, Rabén & Sjögren, 1972.

Allrakäraste syster. Stockholm, Rabén & Sjögren, 1973.

Bröderna Lejonhjärta. Stockholm, Rabén & Sjögren, 1973; as *The Brothers Lionheart*, New York, Viking, and Leicester, Brockhampton Press, 1975.

Madicken och Junibackens Pims. Stockholm, Rabén & Sjögren, 1976; as *Mardie to the Rescue*, London, Methuen, 1981.

När Emil skulle dra ut Linas tand. Stockholm, Rabén & Sjögren, 1976; as *Emil and the Bad Tooth*, London, Hodder and Stoughton, 1976.

Visst kan Lotta nästan allting. Stockholm, Rabén & Sjögren, 1977; as *Of Course Polly Can Do Almost Anything*, Chicago, Follett, 1978; as *Lotta's Christmas Surprise*, London, Methuen, 1978; New York, R & S Books, 1990.

Pippi Långstrump har julgransplundring [Pippi's Christmas]. Stockholm, Rabén & Sjögren, 1979.

Sagorna: en samlingsvolym. Stockholm, Rabén & Sjögren, 1980.

Ronja Rövardotter. Stockholm, Rabén & Sjögren, 1981; as *Ronia, the Robber's Daughter*, New York, Viking, 1983; as *The Robber's Daughter*, London, Methuen, 1983.

En bunt visor: för Pippi, Emil och andra. Stockholm, Rabén & Sjögren, 1981.

Från Pippi till Ronja: valda skrifter. Stockholm, Rabén & Sjögren, 1982.

Smålandsk tjurfäktare, och andra berättelser: en samlingsvolym. Stockholm, Rabén & Sjögren, 1982.

Allas vår Madicken. Stockholm, Rabén & Sjögren, 1983.

Titta, Madicken, det snöar! Stockholm, Rabén & Sjögren, 1983; as *The Runaway Sleigh Ride*, London, Methuen, and New York, Viking, 1984.

När lilla Ida skulle göra hyss. Stockholm, Rabén & Sjögren, 1984; as *Emil's Little Sister*, London, Hodder and Stoughton, 1985.

Spelar min lind sjunger min näktergal. Stockholm, Rabén & Sjögren, 1984; as *My Nightingale Is Singing*, London, Methuen, 1985; New York, Viking Kestrel, 1986.

Emils hyss nr 325. Stockholm, Rabén & Sjögren, 1985; as *Emil's Sticky Problem*, London, Hodder and Stoughton, 1986.

Allt om Karlsson på taket. Stockholm, Rabén & Sjögren, 1985.

Draken med de röda ögonen. Stockholm, Rabén & Sjögren, 1985; as *The Dragon with Red Eyes*, London, Methuen, 1986; New York, Viking Kestrel, 1987.

Skinn Skerping, hemskast av all spöken i Småland. Stockholm, Rabén & Sjögren, 1986; as *The Ghost of Skinny Jack*, London, Methuen, and New York, Viking Kestrel, 1988.

Assar Bubbla. Stockholm, Rabén & Sjögren, 1987.

Jag vill inte gå och lägga mig! Stockholm, Rabén & Sjögren, 1988; as *I Don't Want to Go to Bed*, New York, R & S Books, 1988.

När Bäckhultarn for till stan [When the Bäckhultars Drove to Town]. Stockholm, Rabén & Sjögren, 1989.

Visst är Lotta en glad unge [Of Course Lotta Is a Happy Child]. Stockholm, Rabén & Sjögren, 1990.

Other (for adults)

Samuel August från Sevedstorp och Hanna i Hult [Samuel August from Sevedstorp and Hanna in Hull] (biography of parents). Stockholm, Bokvännerna, 1973.

*

Critical Studies: "The Love Story of Astrid Lindgren" by Ralph Slayton, in *Scandinavian Review*, 63(4), 1975; "The Screening of Pippi Longstocking" by Harriette A. Andreadis, in *Children's Novels and the Movies*, edited by Douglas Street, New York, Ungar, 1983; *Astrid Lindgren*, Stockholm, Swedish Institute, 1987, and "Pippi Longstocking: Chaos and Postmodernism," in *Swedish Book Review* (Lampeter, Wales), supplement, 1990, both by Vivi Edström; "The Ultimate Fantasy: Astrid Lindgren's *The Brothers Lionheart*" by Clara Juncker, in *The Fantastic in World Literature and the Arts*, edited by Donald E. Morse, Westport, Connecticut, Greenwood, 1987; "Astrid Lindgren — The Child Who Refuses to Grow Up" by Birgitta Thompson, in *Swedish Book Review* (Lampeter, Wales), 2, 1987; "Astrid Lindgren's *The Robber's Daughter*: A 20th-Century Fairy Tale" by Eva-Maria Metcalf, in *The Lion and the Unicorn: A Critical Journal of Children's Literature* (Brooklyn, New York), 12(2), 1988.

*   *   *

Astrid Lindgren is probably better known outside her native Sweden than any other living writer in Swedish, and yet she writes exclusively for children. Her Pippi Longstocking books have inspired generations of children throughout the world since 1945, but they created something of a scandal when they first appeared. Conservative critics thought the naughty little girl who lived in an untidy house of her own with no parental control, who taunted and mishandled policemen, told enormous whoppers of lies, and led well-behaved children astray was the epitome of decadence, signalling the end of civilisation as they knew it.

In a sense, this was true. In the first half of the 20th century, children's literature in Sweden had been dominated by stories in the tradition of the Elsa Beskow books, about well-groomed little boys and girls who flourished when they were seen but not heard, did as they were told, and respected their elders and betters. Pippi Longstocking typified the new anti-authoritarian ideal — and was immediately an enormous success. Nevertheless, those who hoped Lindgren would spearhead a socio-political crusade were disappointed: when asked about the aims of her books, her answers were disarmingly simple, and probably reveal why she was so successful:

All I can say is that I never had any purpose at all, either with Pippi or any other book. I write to amuse the child in myself and can only hope that in that way other children will also have some fun . . . I try to be "true" in the artistic sense when I write and that is the only guideline I have . . . I don't consciously try to influence the children who read my books. All I dare hope for is that they may contribute a little bit towards a humane and democratic view of the world in the children who read them.

Many of Lindgren's early books were based on her own childhood experiences in a rural area of southern Sweden near the small town of Vimmerby, but the attitudes and pranks of the children are universal. Probably the best-known of them are the ones about Emil, which first appeared in the 1960s. Set at the turn of the century (and actually based on her father rather than herself), they are generally recognised to be her funniest creations. As with Pippi, Emil's appeal to children is based on his anarchic behaviour, his outrageous exploits, his enormous strength, and the ridiculous, often farcical situations in which he finds himself.

Lindgren tried her hand at most children's genres, and always succeeded in imbuing them with new vigour. The trilogy of books about the detective Bill Bergson introduce increasingly complex plots, and lead to a situation when readers are not merely following the exciting trail of a super-sleuth, but confronting questions about the nature of Good and Evil. A similar confrontation occurs in the often horrific *Mio, min Mio* (*Mio, My Son*), which was widely praised as a renewal of the fairy tale and teems with references to the genre, and to mythology. Asked by a journalist in 1985 whether *Mio, My Son* was really a rather nasty book, Lindgren's reply was: "Of course, that's why children love it."

Death is a taboo subject, but has been introduced in several of Lindgren's books. Few writers would have considered making it the central theme of a book for children, but Lindgren did just that in *Bröderna Lejonhjärta* (*The Brothers Lionheart*). Seen by some as a natural development from *Mio, My Son*, it is a brave and remarkable novel which vacillates between reality and fantasy. The author avoids sentimentality, and relies on the fundamental honesty and good sense of children in bringing them face-to-face with the sorrows and mysteries of death and bereavement. It fascinates readers of various ages, all of whom bring to the story reactions commensurate with their experience. The style and indeed the purpose are very different from those of the early books, but there are grounds for arguing that this is Lindgren's finest achievement.

Others will give that accolade to *Ronja Rövardotter* (*Ronia, the Robber's Daughter*), in which feuding robber bands are reconciled thanks to the growing friendship between the son and daughter of the two chieftains. The natural common sense of the children arouses the finer instincts of their parents, and love and decency triumph in the end; but before that can happen, Ronia and Birk run away and live in a cave in the depths of a forest, experiencing danger, brutality, fear, and terror, but also the glory of spring and summer in the wild. Adults recognise hints of classical mythology and the sagas, while children like the excitement and adventure, revel in the air of mystery, intrigue, and fear, and even enjoy the constant threat of tragedy which is nevertheless avoided in the end.

Lindgren's successfulness as a writer for children is that she understands thoroughly the nature of her prospective readers and treats them with respect, never writing down to them, never worrying about whether certain themes or topics are what adults think children ought to be reading about. As she put it, she writes for the child in herself. Birgitta Thompson aptly summarises Lindgren's achievements thus (*Swedish Book Review*, 2, 1987): "She writes about fear, aggression, sorrow and bliss, and the need for love, respect and understanding, the need to overcome one's fear of loneliness, of the great unknown, of death itself. These strong and intense feelings are balanced by her humour and everyday language, pitched at exactly the right level for the particular narrative."

One might wonder whether Lindgren's storytelling genius and her ability to write in a wide range of styles and genres could have made her an outstanding novelist for adults, but she has never been tempted to try.

—Laurie Thompson

LIPSKA, Ewa (Aleksandra). Polish. Born in Cracow, 8 October 1945. Educated at the Academy of Fine Arts, Cracow, 1963–65; International Writing Program, University of Iowa, Iowa City, 1975–76. Poetry editor, Wydawnictwo Literackie publishers, Cracow, 1970–80, and *Pismo*, Cracow, 1981–83; associated with the Deutschen Akademie Austauschdienstes, Berlin, 1983. Currently deputy director, Institute of Polish Culture, Vienna. Recipient: Łódź Poetry Festival prize, 1972; Kościelski Foundation prize, 1973; Andrzej Bursa prize, 1973; Robert Graves prize, 1979. Address: Polnisches Institut, Am Gestade 7, 1010 Vienna, Austria.

PUBLICATIONS

Verse

Wiersze [Poems]. Warsaw, Czytelnik, 1967.
Drugi zbiór wierszy [Second Book of Poems]. Warsaw, Czytelnik, 1970.
Trzeci zbiór wierszy [Third Book of Poems]. Warsaw, Czytelnik, 1972.
Czwarty zbiór wierszy [Fourth Book of Poems]. Warsaw, Czytelnik, 1974.
Piąty zbiór wierszy [Fifth Book of Poems]. Warsaw, Czytelnik, 1978.
Dom spokojnej młodości: wiersze wybrane [The House of Peaceful Youth: Selected Poems]. Cracow, Wydawnictwo Literackie, 1979.
Poezje wybrane [Selected Poems]. Warsaw, Ludowa Spółdzielnia Wydawnicza, 1981.
Such Times. Toronto, Hounslow Press, 1981.
Nie o śmierć tutaj chodzi, lecz o biały kordonek [It Is Not About Death Here, It Is About the White Thread]. Cracow, Wydawnictwo Literackie, 1982.
Przechowalnia ciemności [Storage Room for Darkness]. Warsaw, Przedświt-Warszawska Niezależna Oficyna Poetów i Malarzy (samizdat), 1985.
Utwory wybrane: 1967–1984 [Selected Works 1967–1984]. Cracow, Wydawnictwo Literackie, 1986.
Poet? Criminal? Madman?, translated by Barbara Plebanek and Tony Howard. London, Forest, 1991.

Novel

Żywa śmierć. Cracow, Wydawnictwo Literackie, 1979.

*

Critical Study: introduction to selection of translated poems, by Magnus J. Krynski, in *Polish Review* (New York), 25(3–4), 1980.

* * *

The name of Ewa Lipska is often quoted in one breath with those of Julian Kornhauser, Ryszard Krynicki, or Adam Zagajewski, poets of her age who made themselves known in the late 1960s or early 1970s as the most promising representatives of the so-called "New Wave," known also as the "Generation of '68." In reality, even though Lipska has shared the chief concerns of her generation — in particular, the necessity of the defense of the human individual against collectivist manipulation — her position in contemporary literature has always been somewhat apart. Similarly, although she has been close to the New Wave's type of poetic diction (one relying squarely on modern colloquial speech yet also sensitive to language's hidden semantic potential), her style has always maintained the uniqueness which it first revealed in her youthful debut, the collection *Wiersze* (Poems).

Lipska was born in Cracow and has lived there most of her life, except for extended periods of travel to Western Europe and America and the recent few years spent in Vienna, where she currently works as vice-director of the Institute of Polish Culture. She graduated from Cracow's Academy of Fine Arts, where she studied art history and painting. In th 1970s and 1980s she made her living by working as an editor in a publishing house. It was in those years, however, that she fell seriously ill and, as a result, spent a total of six years in various hospitals before being cured. This biographical circumstance explains the prominence given to the theme of death in her later poetry. By no means does the shadow of death appear as a license for self-pity or sentimental outbursts; on the contrary, it is being constantly woven into the fabric of life, as something that hangs over everyone and can fall on us anytime. Our being alive is, actually, a result of thousands of narrow escapes we perform unwittingly every day, and, ironically, being thus spared means not much more than being exposed to renewed threats: "Nothing saved me. I'M ALIVE," realizes the speaker in one of Lipska's poems.

The feeling of death's omnipresence is, however, merely one among many shapes in which the oppression of the individual materializes. In Lipska's best poems, the existential perspective co-exists with the historical and social ones. Just as we have to face our individual deaths alone, we are also doomed to loneliness imposed on us by life spent within a society in which the attitude of indifference is constantly and deliberately instilled in every individual by means of skillful manipulation of his or her fears and hidden resentments. Ironically again, the more crowded the world is, the more lonely is the individual bound to feel. "My loneliness/is peopled," a phrase pronounced in another poem, seems to have a paradoxical ring to it, but on closer look is a direct statement of fact.

The kind of society, totalitarian or otherwise, which is founded not so much on fanatical faith or blind obedience as on indifference and inability to communicate is a specter which haunts Lipska's poems. In her collection *Przechowalnia ciemności* (Storage Room for Darkness), published underground a few years after the imposition of martial law in Poland in 1981, this premonition seems already to have come true. Yet, for Lipska, the destruction of interhuman ties, regardless of whether it is caused by existential loneliness or political oppression, is never tantamount to the silencing of the voice of poetry. The more hopeless human misery appears, the more vital is the need for the word that has not lost its meaning; as a result, the poet's wish made by Lipska in her four-line poem "Envoy" as "To write so that a beggar/would take it for money/And the dying/would take it for birth" expresses, in fact, a sense of obligation rather than merely an impossible dream.

—Stanisław Barańczak

LIU BINYAN. Chinese. Born in Changchun, Jiliang Province, 15 January 1925. Grew up in Harbin; moved to Beijing in 1940. Married Zhu Hong in 1951; one son and one daughter. Joined the Communist Party in 1944; teacher, Yaohua Middle School, Tianjin, 1945–46; journalist, *China Youth News*, 1950–58, 1961–66; accused of being a rightist, 1958, and sent to countryside for rehabilitation, 1958–61; rehabilitated, but then accused again, 1966, and sent to May Seventh Cadre School, Henan, 1969–77; rehabilitated, 1979; journalist, *People's Daily*, 1979–85; columnist, *Encounter Monthly* literary magazine, from 1985; vice president, Writers' Union of China, 1985–87; expelled from Communist Party, 1987; visited the United States, 1988; exiled from China, June 1989. Address: c/o Harvard University Press, 79 Garden Street, Cambridge, Massachusetts 02138, U.S.A.

PUBLICATIONS

Fiction

Fragrant Weeds: Chinese Short Stories Once Labelled as "Poisonous Weeds", with others.   Hong Kong, Joint Publishing, 1983.
Yinwei wo ai [Because I Love].   Beijing, Gongren, 1984.
Liu Binyan chuan qi [Romances by Liu Binyan].   Taibei, Shiying Publishing House, 1987.

Other

Jiannandeqifei [Difficult Start].   Shanghai, Hunan People's Publishing House, 1982.
People or Monsters? and Other Stories and Reportage from China After Mao, edited by Perry Link.   Bloomington, Indiana University Press, 1983.
Yi ge nu daxuesheng de ziji [Traces of a Female University Student].   Chengdu, Sichuan People's Publishing House, 1984.
Guangdong qi ren zhuan: baogao wenxue [A Biography of the Odd Person from the Northeast].   Beijing, China Wen Lian Publishing House, 1984.
Di er zhong zhongcheng [A Second Kind of Loyalty].   Hong Kong, Jing Bao Cultural Enterprise, 1985.
Gaosu ni yi ge mimi [I'll Tell You a Secret].   Beijing, Writers' Publishing House, 1986.
Liu Binyan zuopin jing xuan [Selected Works by Liu Binyan].   Jiulong, Literary Research Publishing House, 1986(?).
Wo de riji [My Diary].   Shanghai, Hunan People's Publishing House, 1986.
Liu Binyan renlun ji [Selected Speeches by Liu Binyan].   Hong Kong, Xianggang Publishing House, 1988–.

Liu Binyan zixuanji [Selected Works by Liu Binyan].   Beijing, China Wenlian Publishing House, 1988.
Tell the World: What Happened in China and Why, with Ruan Ming and Xu Gang.   New York, Pantheon, 1989.
China's New Revolution. Cambridge, Massachusetts, Harvard University Press, 1989.
China's Crisis, China's Hope.   Cambridge, Massachusetts, Harvard University Press, 1990.
A Higher Kind of Loyalty: A Memoir by China's Foremost Journalist.   New York, Pantheon, and London, Methuen, 1990.

*

Critical Study: "Liu Binyan and the Texie" by Rudolf Wagner, in *Modern Chinese Literature* (San Francisco), 2(1), 1986.

*   *   *

Liu Binyan's record of courage and integrity has made him an exceptional figure on the Chinese literary scene. Since 1949 there have been severe controls on what can be published in China. Liu Binyan took advantage of a period of comparative liberalisation in 1956 to publish what he saw as loyal critiques of abuses of the Party's power. In 1979, he emerged from over 20 years of persecution to express through his writing the same concerns and rather greater reservations about China's political system.

Liu Binyan is best known for his reportage, a hybrid form of writing which takes a real-life incident as its base, "reports" on it using verbatim dialogue, but allows the author to fictionalise the detail of the story in order to make an often didactic point. The form has been much favoured by propaganda writers in China, and when Liu Binyan, a Communist Party member and an editor of *China Youth News*, China's official journal for young people, published his first pieces of reportage in the 1950s, like the propaganda writers he also wrote to convey a clear political message. However, his pieces were not adulatory; instead they focused on the dark side of life in China and made outspoken protests against corruption, injustice, and hypocrisy.

"At the Bridge Construction Site" (1956) portrays a chief engineer and a head of construction in charge of a major construction site. They have become complacent, fear change, and are out above all to look after their own interests. As they are long-time Party members who served in the revolution with distinction, one implication of the story is that power and privilege may corrupt, a dangerous message in China. There is a suggestion box for criticisms on the site, but symbolically it, too, has decayed, its lock rusted shut. When an enthusiastic young engineer arrives and tries to speed up construction his efforts get him into trouble. Inevitably he is transferred, leaving the site to the bureaucratic bungling of the older men.

"An Inside Story," another piece published in 1956, concerns a young woman reporter who has applied to join the Communist Party. Her truthful and critical reports about the local mine are an obstacle; the reader understands that she will be allowed to join only if she becomes a less truthful reporter. In this environment the people who succeed are those who are so apathetic or so self-seeking that they take no risks.

In 1958 Liu Binyan was severely criticised for his authorship of "At the Bridge Construction Site" and "An Inside Story." He was condemned as the mouthpiece of the "bourgeois rightists within the Party" and sent to the countryside to do manual labour among the peasants for three years. He returned to the city to work as a researcher and translator in 1961, and was rehabilitated in 1966, only to be disgraced again two months later at the outbreak of the Cultural Revolution. A second exile, at a cadre school in the countryside where he underwent political education, lasted from 1969 to 1977. He was rehabilitated once more in 1979, in the more liberalised climate created by Deng Xiaoping's reforms, and began to publish after a silence of over 20 years.

"People or Monsters?," a lengthy piece of reportage which appeared in 1979, returned to his old theme of corruption and bureaucracy. Its exposure of layer upon layer of bribery, corruption, and abuse of power by arrogant officials was welcomed by a generation disillusioned by the Cultural Revolution. Liu Binyan's writings during this period are also an impressive testimony to his determination. After two decades of great personal suffering, he pursued with even greater conviction the very themes which had first got him into trouble.

In the early 1980s his writing still reflected his strong Marxist faith, which set him aside from many of the younger writers of that period of literary renaissance and experimentation. He has since commented reflectively on his own evolution. In his first exile, he had made a real attempt to accept the judgement of the Party and his own need for political reform. However, the poverty and sufferings of the peasants, so different from the rosy picture of their lives promoted in the official press, convinced him that the writer ultimately had to "listen to the voice of the people" and to write the truth as he saw it. The discovery that the price for doing this in the People's Republic was social and psychological isolation and physical suffering led him to more fundamental criticisms of the system. He came to see the absolute power of the Party as producing and encouraging abuses. By protecting itself from honest criticism, he warned, the Party would create the conditions for its own destruction. "Without the supervision of the people, a good person will turn bad, and an honest official will turn corrupt." He expressed these ideas in another piece of reportage, *Di er zhong zhongcheng* (A Second Kind of Loyalty), which tells the story of two ordinary men for whom loyalty to principle comes first. Their steadfastness is contrasted with the behaviour of those who "loyally" follow the Party line, whatever its vicissitudes and inconsistencies. However, even at this stage Liu Binyan remained a member of the Communist Party and offered no challenge to its central goals. His stance was in striking contrast to that of the young radicals of the Democracy Movements of the late 1970s and the late 1980s who often rejected the whole communist project.

Like the orthodox political writers of Communist China, Liu Binyan has an unsophisticated and straightforward view of literature and its purposes. He is not, even in his fictional writing, primarily concerned with creativity, imagination, or aesthetic effect. Unlike the Party hacks, however, he is a writer of conscience and produces writing which though didactic is also realistic. He seeks to inform as well as to form opinion. He believes in his art not for its own sake, but for its social and political purposes. He argues that literature is a mirror. "When literature shows us things which are not very pretty, or that fall short of our ideals, it is wrong to blame the mirror. Instead we should root out and destroy those conditions that disappoint us. Mirrors show us the true appearance of things. Literary mirrors speed the progress of society."

Liu Binyan could be tolerated in the intellectual climate of the early 1980s because the existence of a loyal but critical voice within the Chinese Communist Party helped to distance the reform leadership from the narrowness and intolerance of the Cultural Revolution in the minds of the public. By the mid-1980s, however, the political climate was changing, and in 1987 Liu Binyan was expelled from the Party. Abroad at the time of the Tiananmen massacre in 1989, he did not return

China. He has associated himself with China's democracy movement in exile, and remains one of the most interesting commentators on China's recent history.

—Delia Davin

LIU HSIN-WU. *See* **LIU XINWU.**

LIU PIN-YEN. *See* **LIU BINYAN.**

LIU XINWU. Chinese. Born in Chengdu, Sichuan Province, 4 June 1942. Educated at Beijing Normal University, graduated 1961. Married Lu Xiaoge in 1970; one son. High school teacher, 1961–76; editor, Beijing Publishing House, 1976–80; chief editor, *People's Literature* journal, Beijing, 1987–90 (dismissed because of support for Democracy Movement). Recipient: National prize, for short story, 1978, 1979; National prize, for children's writing, 1979, 1988; Mao Dun literature prize, 1985. Address: 8th Floor, No. 1404, Anding Menwai Dongheyan, Beijing 100011, China.

PUBLICATIONS

Fiction

Prize-Winning Stories from China 1978–1979, with others. Beijing, Foreign Languages Press, 1981.
Ruyuan [The Wish]. Beijing, Dian Ying, 1983.
Dao yuanchu qu fa xin [Posting Letters from Distant Places]. Chengdu, Sichuan People's Publishing House, 1984.
Zhong gu lou [Bell and Drum Towers]. Beijing, People's Publishing House, 1985.
Jialingjiang liujin xueguan [Jialing River Runs in the Veins]. Xian, Shanxi People's Publishing House, 1985.
Richeng jinpo [Tight Schedule]. Beijing, Qun Zhong, 1985.
Li ti jiao ta chao [Overpass]. Beijing, People's Publishing House, 1986.
Mubian shi jie zhi [A Fossilized Ring]. Xining, Qinghai People's Publishing House, 1986.
5.19 changjingtou [Zooming in on 19 May 1985]. Sichuan, Literature and Arts Publishing House, 1987.
Black Walls and Other Stories, edited by Don J. Cohn. Hong Kong, Chinese University of Hong Kong, 1990.
Feng guo er [Overheard]. N.p., China Qingnian Publishing House, 1992.

Plays

Television Plays: *Gonggongchiche yongtandiao* [Bus Aria], 1986; *Zhong gu lon* [Bell and Drum Towers], 1986.

Other

Tong wenxue qingnian duihua [Children's Literature and Teenagers' Dialogues]. Beijing, Wenhua yi shu, 1983.
Yi pian lü ye dui ni shuo [Talking to You About a Green Leaf] (essays). N.p., Hebei Education Publishing House, 1989.

*

Critical Studies: "Youth and Education in the Short Stories of Liu Xin-wu" by Kam Louie, in *Westerley* (Nedlands, Western Australia), 26(3), 1981; "Liu Xinwu: In Search of a Dewdrop" by Helena Kolenda, in *Phi Theta Papers* (Berkeley, California), 17, 1987; article by Frances LaFleur, in *World Literature Today* (Norman, Oklahoma), 1991.

Liu Xinwu comments:

Because the story "The Class Counsellor," published in 1977, gave rise to the Chinese movement of "Scar Literature," some people called me the father of Scar Literature. "I Love Every Green Leaf," *Ruyuan* (The Wish), and "The Overpass" attracted people's attention by reflecting vividly and deeply Chinese contemporary real life and expressing a strong humanitarian spirit. The novel *Zhong gu lou* (Bell and Drum Towers) won the highest prize for literature in China, the Mao Dun literature prize, for the book reckoned to be the most important "Beijing flavour novel" (having Beijing regional characteristics and skilfully using the language of Beijing townspeople). At present the creative force is still vigorous, and new works are continually published.

* * *

Liu Xinwu first attracted attention as a writer in the late 1970s, although he had begun to write and publish in 1959 when still a teenager and continued to produce stories and essays when he became a middle-school teacher. In 1977, when he was working as an editor, his short story "Banzhuren" (The Class Counsellor) was published. It is about a middle-school teacher responsible for students who face personal and psychological difficulties resulting from the 10 years of the Cultural Revolution (1966–76). Among them is a young criminal who has to be "remoulded" and a young girl who is a good student but is also narrow-minded, dogmatic, and censorious, thinking, for example, that it is bourgeois to wear a flowery blouse and skirt, to go to a dance, or to read Western literature. Although there is an impressive range of types among the young people presented in this story, the characterization is not especially profound. Moreover, the style is marred by jargon and a rather wooden style. The story owed its considerable success less to literary merit than to the timing of its publication. It contains the sort of condemnation of ultra-leftism that had hitherto been taboo and was just becoming permissible. Liu Xinwu said what everyone wanted to say but had not quite dared to. Furthermore, the story drew attention to the need to impose discipline and reinstil moral values in a generation profoundly disturbed by the Cultural Revolution. It contains an impassioned appeal by the teacher to "rescue the kids poisoned by the Gang of Four." This was a message which the reformist post-Mao government was happy to have spread.

Liu Xinwu subsequently published several more short stories such as "Xinglai ba, Didi" (Wake Up, Brother) and "Aiqingde weizhi" (The Place of Love), still focusing on the dreadful long-term aftermath of the Cultural Revolution. Thus concern about the fragmented nature of society and people's crippled mental attitudes have been Liu Xinwu's main themes. The power of his works comes from his sensitivity to social problems, and to the main social concerns of the particular historical moment. This has become the hallmark of his writings.

After his initial success, Liu Xinwu began to shift his focus to Beijing: the life and customs in the city and the state of mind of its people. During this period he experimented with quite different techniques. In his novella *Ruyuan* (The Wish) he strives to reveal the inner world of working people. In *Li ti jiao ta chao* (Overpass) he gives thumb-nail sketches of a wide range of characters to convey the rich variety of human nature. His short story "Hei qiang" ("Black Walls") highlights the more absurd aspects of Chinese life. The protagonist shocks his neighbours by painting his walls black. They call a meeting to discuss how to deal with this "problem." They are sure that black walls must be bad, but bereft of the certainties of the Cultural Revolution, they are not quite sure why. Perhaps because the story satirizes aspects of Chinese society which seem completely natural in China, critics were puzzled by the story when it first appeared. His "5.19 changjingtou" ("Zooming in on 19 May 1985") is based on a real incident of football violence in Beijing. Liu Xinwu attempts to explain the psychology of his characters as well as expounding his own views on the state of China and the world.

In 1984 Liu Xinwu published his first novel, *Zhong gu lou* (Bell And Drum Towers). It describes the daily lives of 40 typical Beijing citizens, all connected to nine families who share a single courtyard. All face their own particular problems in a time of rapid change, and each can look back on different experiences in the past. This "cross section" method enabled him to explore the full variety of life in the capital today, and to reflect the full gamut of emotions—happiness, grief, anger, and joy. Liu Xinwu appears to be moving away from the social and political concerns which informed his earlier work, and to be focusing more closely on the inner world of his characters.

None of his later writing has attracted the attention given to his first stories, perhaps due to a lack of literary power and depth. However, his use of the pithy language of Beijing is outstanding, and will ensure him a place among the local writers of the capital.

—David Jiang and Li Ruru

LLOSA, Mario Vargas. *See* **VARGAS LLOSA, Mario.**

LØVEID, Cecilie. Norwegian. Born in Mysen, 21 August 1951. Recipient: Prix Italia, for radio play, 1983. Address: c/o Gyldendal Norsk Forlag, Postboks 6860, St. Olavs Plass, 0130 Oslo 1, Norway.

PUBLICATIONS

Fiction

Most. Oslo, Gyldendal, 1972.

Tenk om isen skulle komme [What If the Ice Should Come]. Oslo, Gyldendal, 1974.
Alltid skyer over Askøy [Always Clouds over Askøy]. Oslo, Gyldendal, 1976.
Mørkets muligheter [The Dark's Possibilities]. Oslo, Gyldendal, 1976.
Fanget villrose [Imprisoned Wild Rose]. Oslo, Gyldendal, 1977.
Sug. Oslo, Gyldendal, 1979; as *Sea Swell*, London, Quartet, 1986.

Plays

Måkespisere (radio play; also includes *Vinteren revner; Du, bli her!* [The Ice Breaks Up; Stay Here!]). Oslo, Gyldendal, 1983; as *Seagull Eaters*, in *New Norwegian Plays*, Norwich, Norvik Press, 1989.
Vinteren revner [The Ice Breaks Up] (produced 1983). Included in *Måkespisere*, 1983.
Dusj-1 opera for 2 [Shower-1 Opera for 2] (produced Bergen 1984).
Balansedame [Tightrope Lady] (produced 1984). Oslo, Gyldendal, 1984.
Fornuftige dyr [Rational Animals]. Oslo, Gyldendal, 1986.
Dobbel nytelse [Double Delight] (produced 1990). Oslo, Gyldendal, 1988.

Radio Play: *Måkespisere* [Seagull Eaters], 1982.

Other

Vift: en barnesang [Puff: A Children's Song]. Oslo, Solum, 1985.

Editor, with Lars Saabye Christensen and Gunnar Sivertsen, *Når det tause får ord på seg . . .: studentnoveller*. Oslo, Universitetsforlaget, 1983.

*

Critical Studies: "Dreams and Discontent: The Female Voice in Norwegian Literature" by Janet E. Rasmussen, in *Review of National Literatures: Norway* (New York), 12, 1983; "One Day We will Find a Path That Has Heart" by Jofrid Karner Smidt, in *News from the Top of the World* (Oslo), 1, 1988.

*   *   *

Cecilie Løveid's texts are often difficult to assign to any particular genre; she mixes prose and poetry, dramatic and epic techniques, and is frequently involved in a performance where her text is linked with musical and visual art to form a whole which cannot be conveyed in the pages of a book. Her works are in continual evolution, and the published versions of them are often a rather arbitrary choice from a number of possible texts. She draws on other authors and other texts from classical allusion to modern graffiti, in such a way that her text at times seems to be a collage of overlapping references, and realistic plot gives way to a succession of images and tableaux from which, nevertheless, a story emerges. The subject of her works is nearly always woman, both in the literal sense that her central characters are women and in the more general sense that they are written around women's bodies and women's desire. Here if anywhere one can find in Norwegian literature an equivalent of the writing of the female body, the *jouissance* that Hélène Cixous (*q.v.*) and other French writers advocate.

Broadly speaking, there is a development in Løveid's writing from lyrical/epic texts to more dramatic ones. Her early works, like *Most* and *Alltid skyer over Askøy* (Always Clouds over Askøy), announce themes which recur throughout her work: that of abandonment by or absence of a man, who may variously be husband/lover/father, and that of the sea; the two are often linked in the figure of the absent sailor. These themes coalesce in her best-known non-dramatic work, *Sug* (*Sea Swell*), a collection of texts (called a "novel") with a central character Kjersti, who confronts her absent sailor-father from the past as well as trying to cope with the lover who abandons her in the present. The Norwegian title *Sug* means literally "Suck," and has clear sexual overtones; Kjersti's coming to terms with her own sexuality involves a re-enactment of (fantasized?) abuse/incest with her father as well as a struggle out of dependence on the lover towards an affirmation of autonomy. The novel ends with a new meeting with a man, and a desire for a new language which will not carry with it the contaminations of the old one: "So many languages. Is it easier to have a language without words? Without colour? One with a fine 'touch me' structure? One with warm 'come into me' calls. Or a language which rises up like a racing cycle in a rainy street in town."

More recently, Løveid has concentrated on writing for dramatic performance. Her radio play *Måkespisere* (*Seagull Eaters*), which won the Prix Italia in 1983, is about a poor Bergen girl who dreams of becoming a great actress, but without money or sponsorship has no chance. On the brink of starvation during the German occupation in the 1940s, she is seduced by a rich grocer, and then bullied into giving her baby to the "Give the Führer a child" campaign. Her wretched fate is interwoven with many other voices, the most insistent being that of Henriette Schønberg Erken, the Mrs. Beeton of Norway, whose elegant domestic advice becomes an ironic commentary on the way Kristine is gradually stripped of anything that makes life worth living.

Although she has written many plays for the stage and had them performed in Bergen and Oslo, Løveid has had problems with the Norwegian theatre; both theatre managers and critics complain that she is too experimental for a public who are still more readily drawn to an Ibsen play or a foreign musical. She is not a commercial success, despite sparkling performances of plays like *Vinteren revner* (The Ice Breaks Up), *Balansedame* (Tightrope Lady) and *Dobbel nytelse* (Double Delight).

Dobbel nytelse is a good example of her recent writing. It centres on a triangular relationship between Guy, a medieval archaeologist, his wife Siri, and Katarina, who believes herself to be Siri's little sister but is in fact her daughter. An Oedipal conflict arises as Katarina tries to lure Guy away from Siri; it is played out as a power battle between the two women, with Guy as a passive character who is ultimately unable to make love to Katarina, seeing her as an untouchable Madonna. In this play it is the father figure who is killed/conquered in the end, unlike earlier plays where it is often the mother; the final tableau suggests a female tradition of birth and rebirth to which man is incidental.

Other characters and themes are interwoven with this central trio; the action takes place at the medieval nunnery of St. Katarina, and the modern Katarina is linked with the medieval saint as well as with a feline predator (her name abbreviates to Cat). Two dancers, Tutti and Frutti, provide a balletic accompaniment to the action, and the scenes are linked by a grotesquely androgynous pig, who sings melancholy Provençal troubadour songs while accompanying himself on the lute. The language of the play is exuberant and inventive; there are dialogues which consist of a competition to produce the most absurd rhyming words, and others where

sexual innuendo and double entendre produce pun after pun, which makes reading the text itself a double delight.

Løveid is the most exciting of contemporary Norwegian dramatists. At the same time her multi-layered, non-realistic texts have given her the reputation of being a "difficult" author. Her subject is, as she says herself, "first and foremost language"; she is trying to write in a new way which gives intimate expression to women's experiences. A new language has to struggle to create an audience for its message.

—Janet Garton

LUCEBERT. Pseudonym for Lubertus Jacobus Swaanswijk. Dutch. Born in Amsterdam, 15 September 1924. Educated at Institute for Arts and Crafts, Amsterdam, 1938. Artist: member of Dutch Experimental Group, 1949, and Cobra, 1949; group and individual shows since 1948; retrospective exhibition, Stedelijk Museum, Amsterdam, 1969, 1987. Has lived in Bergen, North Holland, since 1953. Recipient: Anut poetry prize, 1954; Biennale de la Jeunesse prize, 1959; Biennale Internazionale di Scultura prize, 1959; Marzotto prize, 1962; Biennale Carrara graphic art prize 1962; Venice Biennale Cardazzo prize, 1964; Hooft prize, 1967; Triennial State literary prize, 1983. Address: Boendermakerhof 10, 1861 TB Bergen, The Netherlands.

PUBLICATIONS

Verse

Triangel in de jungle [Triangle in the Jungle]. The Hague, Stols, 1951.
Apocrief [Apocryphal]. Amsterdam, Bezige Bij, 1952.
Van de afground en de luchtmens [Of the Abyss and the Airman]. The Hague, Stols, 1953.
Alfabel. Amsterdam, Bezige Bij, 1955.
De Amsterdamse school. The Hague, Stols, 1955.
Amulet. Amsterdam, Bezige Bij, 1957.
Val voor vliegengod [A Trap for a God of the Flies]. Amsterdam, Bezige Bij, 1959.
Lithologie: Tien gedichten, tien litho's [Lithology: 10 Poems, 10 Lithographs]. Hilversum, De Jong, 1959.
De gebroken rietlijn [The Broker Reed]. Amsterdam, Instituut voor Kunstnijverheidsonderwijs, 1959.
Dag en nacht [Day and Night]. Hilversum, van Saane, 1959.
Januari [January]. Amsterdam, Bezige Bij, 1964.
Gedichten 1948–1963 [Poems]. Amsterdam, Bezige Bij, 1965.
Seizoen [Season]. Amsterdam, Wereldbibliotheek, 1968.
Drie lagen diep [Three Layers Deep]. Amsterdam, Stedelijk Museum, 1969.
Verzamelde gedichten [Collected Poems], edited by C. W. van der Watering. Amsterdam, Bezige Bij, 1974.
The Tired Lovers They Are Machines, translated by Peter Nijmeijer. Deal, Kent, Transgravity, 1974.
Beelden in het heden [Pictures in the Present]. Utrecht, Knippenberg, 1977.
Chambre-Antichambre, with Bert Schierbeek. The Hague, BZZTôH, 1978.

Voor vrienden dieren [For Animal Lovers].   's-Gravenhage, Lanschot Bankiers-Nouvelles Images, 1979.

Mooi uitzicht en andere kurioziteiten [Nice View and Other Curiosities].   Amsterdam, Bezige Bij, 1980.

Oogsten in de dwaaltuin [Harvesting in the Maze]. Amsterdam, Bezige Bij, 1981.

Paradijs [Paradise].   The Hague, Nouvelles Images, 1981.

De moerasruiter uit het paradÿs [The Marsh-Rider from Paradise].   Amsterdam, Bezige Bij, 1982.

5 litho's en 5 gedichten [Five Lithographs and Five Poems]. Amsterdam, Printshop, 1982.

Haar lichaam heeft haar typograaf [Her Body Has Her Typography].   Groningen, Verkruissen, 1982.

Ongebundedelde gedichten [Scattered Poems].   Amsterdam, Bezige Bij, 1983.

Dagelijks een schitterend kind gewint de zon [Daily a Shimmering Child Yields the Sun].   Terhorst, Ser J.L. Prop, 1984.

Horror.   Bedum, Exponent, 1986.

Troost de hysterische robot: gedichten en een oratorium [Console the Hysterical Robot: Poems and an Oratorio].   Amsterdam, Bezige Bij, 1989.

Play

De perfekte misdaad [The Perfect Crime].   The Hague, Bert Bakkar, 1968.

Other

Dames en heren [Ladies and Gentlemen].   Amsterdam, Bezige Bij, 1976.

. . . En morgen de hele wereld [And Tomorrow the Whole World].   Amsterdam, Bezige Bij, 1984.

Het hart van de zoeker [Heart of the Searchers].   Amsterdam, Bezige Bij, 1987.

Lucebert: Early Works: Drawings and Gouaches 1942–1949 (exhibition catalogue).   Amsterdam, Picaron, 1990.

*

Critical Studies: *Lucebert* edited by Lucebert, London, Marlborough Art, 1963; *The Experimental Artists* by Bert Schierbeek, Amsterdam, Meulenhoff, 1963; *Lucebert* (in English) by J. Eijkelboom, Amsterdam, Meulenhoff, 1964.

*   *   *

Lucebert's distinctiveness and stature as a poet have become clearer with the passage of time. As "Emperor" and principal spokesman of the 1950s generation of experimentalists, the *Vijftigers*, he was to some a standard-bearer in the iconoclastic assault on pre-war complacency and provincialism in much Dutch poetry, to others a pretentious and often incoherent literary vandal and demagogue. Neither image did justice to Lucebert's richly synthetic craftsmanship which, despite the startling and seemingly impenetrable "newness" of parts of it in a Dutch context, was informed from the first by a profound sense of literary and intellectual continuity.

The early collections bear the clear traces of his involvement as a painter with the Cobra movement, whose dislike of abstractions and admiration of the primitive directness of children's art he shares. Kaleidoscopically suggestive images, bewildering associative leaps, multi-layered neologisms and ambiguous syntax assail and challenge the reader one moment, suggesting links with surrealism and Dada (Hans Arp is cited as a revered master), while the next a naively transparent,

programmatic pronouncement proclaims that the poet's goal is to use "simplicity's enlightened waters/to give expression to the whole expanse and fulness of life" ("School of Poetry"). Lucebert's poetry does indeed evoke the great themes of birth, love, death, war, destruction, and regeneration and simplicity and complexity co-exist in it. To achieve his stated aim, he draws on sources as diverse as Dutch predecessors like Herman Gorter (who is echoed in the title of the poem quoted), Friedrich Hölderlin, Bertolt Brecht, and Chinese classical verse (as in the serene "Fisherman by Ma Yuan").

Though unashamedly and often scathingly anti-elitist and anti-bourgeois, Lucebert's political and lyrical subversiveness is never simplistic propaganda; the irony and self-mockery of the "nimble con-man" reeling off his "little revolution" are apt to escape many of his critics. At the level of form, his break with the past is less radical than may appear from his abandonment of punctuation, capitalisation, and regular line-length in much of his work: his are not arbitrary word-clusters, but are bound together by such traditional elements as assonance, alliteration, and even internal rhyme — for all his dismissal of the "rhyme rats" of a previous generation. The poet himself regards the ultimate determinant of line-structure as the pattern of the breath, and his poems' resonance is best felt when they are read aloud.

His very choice of pseudonym is a revealing example of the way in which by dismantling and reassembling morphological units he transforms the familiar and banal — in this case his own Christian name — and achieves dense allusiveness: both its roots, one Latin and one Germanic, mean "light," while the combination evokes the fallen angel Lucifer. Both associations are very relevant; light, both literal and figurative, is a constant preoccupation for this painter-poet, who, moreover, like the great modernist Paul van Ostaijen (1898–1928), sees poetry as "a game with words anchored in metaphysics," an heroic mystical journey finally doomed because of human imperfection.

Some disillusion with the medium of language, at a time when experimentalism had lost much of its freshness and had itself become, in the hands of lesser imitators, the mannerism of an elite, may account for Lucebert's relatively small poetic output in the 1960s and 1970s, during which period he devoted himself mainly to painting. However, the collection *Oogsten in de dwaaltuin* (Harvesting in the Maze), though sober, somber, and even bleak in comparison with earlier work, showed the hand of a mature master. Its promise is fulfilled in the collection *Troost de hysterische robot* (Console the Hysterical Robot), at once densely crafted and transparent. The "just man," one of the solo parts in the oratorio with which the collection concludes, has three lines which could serve as a motto for an impressive oeuvre: "What is lost must be sought/ What cannot be said/May be sung incomprehensibly."

—Paul Vincent

———

LUSTIG, Arnošt. Czech and American. Born in Prague, 21 December 1926. Held in concentration camps at Terezín, Auschwitz, and Buchenwald during World War II: escaped 1945. Educated at the College of Political and Social Sciences, Prague, M.A. 1951, Ing. degree 1954. Married Věra Weislitzová in 1949; one son and one daughter. Arab-Israeli war correspondent, Radio Prague, 1948–49; correspondent in

Europe, Asia, and North America, Czechoslovak Radio Corporation, 1950–68; screenwriter, Barandov Film Studios, Prague, 1960–68, and Jadran Film Studio, Zagreb, 1969–70; moved to United States, 1970: naturalized citizen, 1979; member of International Writers Program, 1970–71, and Visiting Professor, 1971–72, University of Iowa, Iowa City; Visiting Professor, Drake University, Des Moines, Iowa, 1972–73. Since 1973 Professor of literature and film, American University, Washington, D.C. Correspondent for literary magazines in Czechoslovakia, 1950–58; editor, *Mladý svět* [Young World] magazine, 1958–59. Head of Czechoslovak film delegation to San Sebastian Film Festival, 1968; member of jury, Karlovy Vary International Film Festival, 1968. Honorary president, Kafka Society, since 1990. Recipient: Mladá fronta publishing house prize, 1962; Locarno Film Festival prize, 1963; Mannheim prize, for film, 1964; Monte Carlo Film Festival prize, 1966; Czechoslovak Radio Corporation prize, 1966, 1967; Gottwald prize, 1967; B'nai B'rith prize, 1974; National Jewish Book award, 1980, 1986; Emmy award, 1986. Honorary doctorate in Hebrew letters: Spertus College of Judaica, Chicago, 1986. Address: 4000 Tunlaw Road, N.W., Apt. 825, Washington, D.C. 20007, U.S.A.

PUBLICATIONS

Fiction

Ulice ztracených bratří.   Prague, Mladá fronta, 1949; as *The Street of Lost Brothers*, Evanston, Illinois, Northwestern University Press, 1990.
Můj známý Vili Feld [My Acquaintance Willi Feld].   Prague, Mladá fronta, 1949.
Children of the Holocaust.   Washington, D.C., Inscape, 2 vols., 1976.
  Noc a naděje.   Prague, Naše Vojsko, 1958; as *Night and Hope*, New York, Dutton, and London, Hutchinson, 1962.
  Tma nemá stín.   As *Darkness Casts No Shadow*, Washington, D.C., Inscape, 1978; London, Quartet, 1989.
Démanty noci.   Prague, Mladá fronta, 1958; as *Diamonds of the Night*, Prague, Artia, 1962; Washington, D.C., Inscape, 1978; London, Quartet, 1989.
Dita Saxová.   Prague, Československý spisovatel, 1962; as *Dita Sax*, London, Hutchinson, 1966.
Noc a den (includes *Noc a naděje*; *Démanty noci*; *Můj známý Vili Feld*).   Prague, Československý spisovatel, 1962.
Nikoho neponížíš [Nobody Will Be Humiliated].   Prague, Naše Vojsko, 1963.
Modlitba pro Kateřinu Horovitzovou.   Prague, Československý spisovatel, 1964; as *A Prayer for Katerina Horovitzova*, New York, Harper, 1973; London, Quartet, 1990.
Vlny v řece [Waves in the River]   Prague, Československý spisovatel, 1964.
Bílé břízy na podzim [The White Birches in September].   Prague, Československý spisovatel, 1966.
Hořká vůně mandlí [The Bitter Smell of Almonds].   Prague, Mladá fronta, 1968.
Miláček [Darling].   Prague, Československý spisovatel, 1969.
Nemilovaná: z deníku sedmnáctileté Perly Sch.   Toronto, 68 Publishers, 1979; as *The Unloved: From the Diary of Perla S.*, New York, Arbor, 1985; London, Macmillan, 1986.

Indecent Dreams (includes *Indecent Dreams*; *Blue Day*; *The Girl with the Scar*).   Evanston, Illinois, Northwestern University Press, 1988.

Plays

Screenplays: *Transport z ráje* [Death Camp from Paradise], from his stories *Noc a naděje* (*Night and Hope*), 1962; *Diamonds of the Night*, 1964; *Ditá Saxova*, 1968; *The Precious Legacy*, 1984.

Radio Plays: *Prague Crossroads*, 1966; *A Man the Size of a Postage Stamp*, 1967.

Television Plays: *The Blue Day*, 1960; *Names for Which There Are No People*, 1960; *A Prayer for Katerina Horovitzova*, from his novel, 1965; *Theresienstadt* (*Terezin*), with Ernest Pendrell, 1965; *Stolen Childhood*, 1966.

Other

První stanice štěstí: reportáže [The First Stop of Happiness: Reportage].   Prague, Mladá fronta, 1961.

*   *   *

At the very core of Arnošt Lustig's writing lies his experience during World War II. As a Jew, he was at the age of 16 sent first to the Nazi ghetto town of Terezín (Theresienstadt) and from there to the extermination camps of Auschwitz and Buchenwald. Incredibly he survived, unlike millions of others, and he felt, as many other survivors did, that it was his duty to render a testimony of the genocide. Like them, he was to find that owing to the enormity of the experience, mere reporting of it was ineffectual. Conventional writing was inadequate to convey the horrors he had witnessed and he was not skilled enough to achieve more. When his first book was accepted for publication, he withdrew it from the publishers, dissatisfied with his performance.

It was not until the mid-1950s tht Lustig found the right approach to his subject, inspired by the work of William Faulkner and Ernest Hemingway and by the dictum that "man can be destroyed, but not vanquished." When two volumes of his short stories, *Noc a naděje* (*Night and Hope*) and *Démanty noci* (*Diamonds of the Night*) appeared in quick succession in 1958, it was recognized that he presented the Holocaust not just as a crime against Jews, but as an attack on humanity.

Lustig's stories lack the sense of drama one may expect to develop in a setting such as that of a concentration camp. In fact, there is little movement and hardly any action in his stories. Mostly they are static studies of incidents in which people find themselves under extreme pressure, such as only other human beings can devise for them. The unimaginable horror of the conditions they have to live in and the situations they face is not implied through a colourful evocation of gruesome details. On the contrary, it is hardly mentioned — it has become a part of everyday life that is being taken for granted, and besides, there is no escape. A terrifying picture is created of ordinary life in absolute hell.

Amazingly, Lustig brings back from these lowest reaches of inhumanity a message which is essentially optimistic. Even when placed in a position which makes demands upon them beyond endurance, people in his short stories still behave with moral dignity. Many of his characters are children who had little opportunity to digest any social rules and those that they have learned they see trodden into the dust every minute of the day. Yet when they are faced with a decision, they demonstrate that even in such circumstances the spark of true humanity has survived in them and they choose good over evil, however complex the choice may be.

Lustig's short story "A Bite to Eat" is regarded as an outstanding example of this faith in the innate strength of human beings. A young boy, after a bitter inner struggle, desecrates the corpse of his father to obtain from it a gold tooth which he exchanges for food that will, he hopes, save his ailing sister and starving mother.

There remains of course the question of the innate qualities of the perpetrators of these horrors, the Nazis. By blending them into the grey, featureless background, Lustig seems to suggest that they simply cannot be considered as belonging to the human race, and sees no need to concern himself with their motives or psychology. Their deeds speak for them.

In the books that followed the first two volumes, Lustig mainly enlarges upon his essential theme with various degrees of success. Perhaps most remarkable among them is *Modlitba pro Kateřinu Horovitzovou* (*A Prayer for Katerina Horovitzova*), an ingenious combination of two real events: the blackmailing by the Nazis of a group of Jewish prisoners with large accounts in foreign banks and an act of revolt carried out by a beautiful Polish actress at the gas chamber door.

A stylistic perfectionist, Lustig quite often rewrote and amplified his stories so that more than one version exists of some of them. Rewriting his earlier work became something of an escape activity when he found himself in political exile in the United States after 1968. Only one entirely new work has been added to his oeuvre in the past 20 years, a long short story, *Nemilovaná: z deníku sedmnáctileté Perly Sch.* (*The Unloved: From the Diary of Perla S.*), in which a Jewish prostitute in the Terezín ghetto camp takes an appropriately fiendish revenge on her Nazi customer and tormentor. It is once again a study of human behaviour *in extremis*, of the child-like prostitute's reaction when she grasps the immensity of the evil that surrounds her.

—Igor Hájek

LUZI, Mario. Italian. Born in Castello, near Florence, 20 October 1914. Educated at schools in Florence and Siena; University of Florence, 1930–36. Married Elena Monazi in 1942; one child. Teacher in various cities, including Parma, Urbino, San Miniato, Rome, and Florence, 1938–55; Professor of French, University of Florence, from 1955. Recipient: Carducci prize, 1953; Marzotto prize, 1957; Etna-Taormina prize, 1964; Fiuggi prize, 1971; Viareggio prize, 1978; Mondello award, 1985; Librex Guggenheim, 1986. Honorary doctorate: Queen's University, Belfast, 1987. Address: c/o Rizzoli Libri, Via Angelo Scarsellini 17, 20161 Milan, Italy.

PUBLICATIONS

Verse

La barca.   Modena, Guanda, 1935.
Avvento notturno.   Florence, Vallecchi, 1940.
Un brindisi.   Florence, Sansoni, 1946.
Quaderno gotico.   Florence, Vallecchi, 1947.

Primizie del deserto.   Milan, Schwarz, 1952.
Onore del vero.   Venice, Pozza, 1957.
Il giusto della vita.   Milan, Garzanti, 1960.
Nel magma.   Milan, Scheiwiller, 1963; revised edition, 1966.
Dal fondo delle campagne.   Turin, Einaudi, 1965.
Su fondamenti invisibili.   Milan, Rizzoli, 1971.
Poesie.   Milan, Garzanti, 1974.
In the Dark Body of Metamorphosis and Other Poems, translated by Isidore Lawrence Salomon. New York, Norton, 1975.
Al fuoco della controversia.   Milan, Garzanti, 1978.
Semiserie.   Salerno, Galleria "Il Catalogo," 1979.
Tutte le poesie: Il giusto della vita, 1934–57; Nell'opera del mondo, 1957–78.   Milan, Garzanti, 2 vols., 1979; enlarged edition, 1 vol., 1988.
Reportage: un poemetto; seguito dal, Taccuino di viaggio in Cina, 1980.   Milan, All'Insegna del Pesce d'Oro, 1984.
Per il battesimo dei nostri frammenti.   Milan, Garzanti, 1985.
L'alta, la cupa fiamma.   Milan, Rizzoli, 1990.
Frasi e incisi di un canto salutare.   Milan, Garzanti, 1991.
Spazio, stelle, voce: il colore della poesia, edited by D. Fazoli. Milan, Leonardo, 1992.

Plays

Ipazia.   Milan, Scheiwiller, 1973.
Libro di Ipazia.   Milan, Rizzoli, 1979.
Rosales.   Milan, Rizzoli, 1983.
Hystrio.   Milan, Rizzoli, 1987.
Corale della città di Palermo per S. Rosalia.   Genoa, S. Marco dei Giustiniani, 1989.
Il Purgatorio; *La notte lava la mente*; *Drammaturgia di un'ascensione.*   Genoa, Costa & Nolan, 1990.

Other

L'opium chrétien.   Modena, Guanda, 1938.
Un'illusione platonica e altri saggi.   Florence, Edizioni di Rivoluzione, 1941; revised edition, Bologna, Boni, 1972.
Biografia a Ebe.   Florence, Vallecchi, 1942.
L'inferno e il limbo.   Florence, Marzocco, 1949; revised edition, Milan, Il Saggiatore, 1964.
Studio su Mallarmé.   Florence, Sansoni, 1952.
Aspetti della generazione napoleonica ed altri saggi di letteratura francese.   Modena, Guanda, 1956.
Lo stile di Constant.   Milan, Il Saggiatore, 1962.
Trame.   Lecce, Quaderni del Critone, 1963; revised edition, Milan, Rizzoli, 1982.
Tutto in questione.   Florence, Vallecchi, 1965.
Poesia e romanzo, with Carlo Cassola.   Milan, Rizzoli, 1973.
Vicissitudine e forma.   Milan, Rizzoli, 1974.
Discorso naturale.   Siena, Quaderni di Messapo, 1980.
Il silenzio, la voce.   Florence, Sansoni, 1984.
Cronache dell'altro mondo.   Genoa, Marietti, 1989.
Scritti, edited by G. Quiriconi. Venice, Arsenale, 1989.
De quibis.   Montichiari, Zanetti, 1991.
Non sono sazi della loro vita, with Anna M. Bartolini. Florence, Festina Lente, 1992.

Editor, with Tommaso Landolfi, *Anthologie de la poésie lyrique française.*   Florence, Sansoni, 1950.
Editor, *L'idea simbolista.*   Milan, Garzanti, 1959.
Editor and Translator, *Francamente (versi dal francese).* Florence, Vallecchi, 1980.

Translator, *Vita e letteratura*, by Charles du Bos.   Padua, Cedam, 1943.

Translator, *Poesia e prose*, by Samuel Coleridge.   Milan,
  Cederna, 1949.
Translator, *Andromaca*, by Jean Racine.   In *Teatro francese
  del Grande Secolo*, Rome, ERI, 1960.
Translator, *Cantico delle colonne*, by Paul Valéry.   Milan,
  Scheiwiller, 1960.
Translator, *La fonte*, by Jorge Guillén.   Milan, Scheiwiller,
  1961.
Translator, *Riccardo II*, by William Shakespeare.   Turin,
  Einaudi, 1966.
Translator, *La cordigliera delle Ande*.   Turin, Einaudi, 1983.

*

Critical Studies: "The Anti-Oracle in Mario Luzi's Recent
Poetry" by Bruce Merry, in *Modern Language Review*
(London), 68, 1973; "Mario Luzi" by W. Craft, in *Books
Abroad* (Norman, Oklahoma), Winter 1975; "The Dark Body
of Metamorphosis" by Radcliffe Squires, in *Michigan
Quarterly Review* (Ann Arbor), Winter 1975; "Poets' 'Stories':
Trame by Mario Luzi" by Alberto Frattini, in *Italian Books
and Periodicals* (Rome), 25(1), 1982; "Poetry and Theatre: An
Interview with Mario Luzi" and "Poetic Horizons: Spatial
Configurations in Mario Luzi's 'Nel corpo oscuro della
metamorfosi,'" both in *Stanford Italian Review* (California),
4(2), 1984, and "Corporal Controversy: Mario Luzi's 'In corpo
vile'," in *MLN* (Baltimore, Maryland), 100(1), 1985, all by
Keala Jane Jewell; "The Difficult Hope of Mario Luzi" by
Mario Specchio, in *The Dialectic of Discovery*, edited by John
D. Lyons and Nancy J. Vickers, Lexington, Kentucky,
French Forum, 1984; "Mario Luzi's Latest Poetry" by
G. Singh, in *World Literature Today* (Norman, Oklahoma),
59(3), 1985.

*   *   *

Since Eugenio Montale's death, Mario Luzi has been
commonly regarded — and with some justification — as the
most important living Italian poet. Since 1935, when he
published his first volume of poetry — *La barca* (The Boat) —
he has written a quite substantial body of both verse and
criticism that is impressive for its individuality and, at times,
for its originality. During the lifetime of Giuseppe Ungaretti,
Montale, and Salvatore Quasimodo, Luzi had succeeded in
creating a particularly personal line of poetry, with a characteristic vein and timbre. For all his admiration of Ungaretti and
Montale, who may have to some extent influenced him, Luzi is
something more than a continuator of what these poets
represent, and in his own lifetime has become an important
part of his country's rich, illustrious poetic tradition.

Because he is an admirer of such culturally and artistically
diverse poets as Guido Cavalcanti, Gabriele D'Annunzio, and
Vincenzo Cardarelli on the one hand, and Samuel Coleridge
and Paul Eluard on the other, and of Oriental philosophy and
mysticism as well as the religious philosophy of the West,
Luzi's poetry achieves a fruitful synthesis between what is
symbolic and realistic, mystical and experimental, and the very
tone of his poetry, at its most characteristic, registers a perfect
fusion between the reflective and the discursive, the lyrical and
the philosophical, the subjective and the universal.

It is due to this synthesis that Luzi's poetic imagery too has
such evocative potency, exploiting both what is conventional
and what the poet arrives at by exploratory thought and
creative perception, which serves to underline the intrinsically

reflective and meditative, mystical and philosophical character
of his poetry, with its creative interplay between what is within
time and what is timeless, what is contingent and what is
eternal, what is empirically realized and what is beyond
experience. Thus a certain symbolism underlies much of Luzi's
poetry — a symbolism that owes more to Eliot than to the
French Symbolists, as his later volumes of poetry — *Onore del
vero* (To Tell the Truth), *Il giusto della vita* (The Fairness of
Life), *Nel magma* (In the Magma), and *Dal fondo delle
campagne* (From the Depths of the Countryside) — amply
illustrate. In these volumes Luzi's strength and individuality
are revealed through such qualities as his neo-religio-
philosophical humanism, the moral intensity of his thought
expressed by means of a discursive lyricism, his inner calm and
self-control which are both moral and creative, and his artistic
and technical mastery which is synonymous with a rare kind of
sincerity and integrity.

In one of his earlier poems ("A un compagno" [To a
Comrade], 1944) Luzi said: "per me essere è non dimenticare"
(for me to live means not to forget), which may be taken as an
epigraph for all his poetic *oeuvre*, summing up, as it does, the
introspective, morally charged, and poetically realized
existentialism underlying his verse and his temperament.

In three later books of poetry — *Al fuoco della controversia*
(In the Heat of the Debate), *Per il battesimo dei nostri
frammenti* (On the Baptism of Our Fragments), and *Frasi e
incisi di un canto salutare* (Phrases and Clauses of a Salutary
Song) — Luzi's art has acquired a more subtle kind of lyric
sophistication, intuitive clairvoyance, and moral depth. For
instance, his exploration of reality and of the relation between
the inner and the outer, time and timelessness is dealt with in
terms of such luminous, evocative concepts as "sfacelo delle
memoria" (the disintegration of memory), the timelessness of
hope, "il silenzio della mente/e quello della campagna/e delle
acque" (the silence of the mind/and that of the countryside/and
of the waters), "luce nella luce,/ . . . musica in fondo della
musica" (light within light,/ . . . music at the heart of music),
and love with its "indicibile potenza" (inexpressible potency).
Thus the lyric vein in Luzi almost always prevails over any
other vein — be it religious, metaphysical, or speculative —
and the union between thought and poetry acquires a new
depth and a new dimension in his hand.

—G. Singh

————

LYNCH, B. Suárez. *See* **BIOY CASARES, Adolfo.**

————

————

LYNCH DAVIS, B. *See* **BIOY CASARES, Adolfo.**

————

M

MĀGHŪT, Muhammad al-. Syrian. Born in 1934. Has lived in Damascus, Beirut, and in the Gulf; cultural editor, *Al-Khalij* [The Gulf] newspaper. Address: c/o Three Continents Press, 1901 Pennsylvania Avenue, N.W., Suite 407, Washington, D.C. 20006, U.S.A.

PUBLICATIONS

Verse

Sorrow in the Moonlight (in Arabic).   1960.
A Room with a Million Walls (in Arabic).   1973.
Joy Is Not My Profession (in Arabic).   1973.
Al-'āthār al-kāmilah (includes a play). Beirut, Dār al-'Awdah, 1981.
The Fan of Swords, translated by May Jayyusi and Naomi Shihab Nye.   Washington, D.C., Three Continents Press, 1991.

Play

Al-'uṣfūr al-aḥdab [The Hunchbacked Bird].   1973.

Other

Sa' akhūnū waṭanī: haẓayan fī al-ru'b wa-al-hurriyah [I Will Betray My Country].   London, Riad el-Rayyes, 1987.
Al-Urjūha [The Swing].   London, Riad el-Rayyes, 1991.

*   *   *

A poet of the avant-garde, Muhammad al-Māghūt has played a significant role in developing the genre of prose poetry in contemporary Arabic literature. The language of his prose poetry is simultaneously simple, and rich in allegory and symbol. Through an unusual mixture of metaphors and images, he succeeds in highlighting the social and cultural problems of the Arab world. His tone is satirical and ironic, with occasional outbursts of the comic.

Al-Māghūt, along with many others poets, is deeply involved with the tragic situation of the Arab world. His sense of despair and anguish is brilliantly expressed through the juxtaposition of paradoxes, through the use of both serious and trivial images. Naturally, the defeat of the Palestinians and the betrayal of a nation, which caused the painful breakdown of Arab pride and honour, made poets question the traditional values of the political and religious establishments. Al-Māghūt's anger and despair find an outlet in poems such as "An Arab Traveller in a Space Ship" and "The Postman's Fear." With a futuristic note, in the first poem the poet begs the scientists to give him a ticket to a spaceship, so that he might reach God, and put "a whip in his hand/That he may rouse us to revolt!" The second of these poems shows the influence of the French Existentialists. Its anger questions even the justice of God:

Prisoners everywhere,
send me all you've seen
of horror and weeping and boredom —
Fishermen on every shore,
send me all you know
of empty nets and whirling seas —
. . .
I am preparing a huge portfolio
on human suffering
to present to God
as soon as it is signed by the lips of the hungry
and the eyelids of the waiting.
But oh, you miserable ones everywhere,
I have a fear
that God may be "illiterate".

In his well-known poem "When the Words Burn," al-Māghūt deftly turns the heroic language of the past against itself; thus romantic classical vocabulary serves to emphasize the tragic and sombre imagery. Here, with simple and familiar words, his satire is, at the same time, both painfully shocking and amusing. The poet mocks his own traditional heroic role, because in the face of the devastation and human suffering surrounding him, his artistic achievement seems worthless, and his words sound like "the wind laden with bells." The poem starts with a striking paradox:

Poetry, this immortal carcass, bores me.
Lebanon is burning —
It leaps, like a wounded horse at the edge of the desert
and I am looking for a fat girl
to rub myself against on the tram,
for a bedouin-looking man to knock down somewhere.
. . .
The goddess of poetry
stabs my heart like a knife
when I think I am singing poems to an unknown girl,
to a voiceless motherland
that eats and sleeps with everyone.
I can laugh till the blood runs from my lips.

Yet, despite all the painful agony and desperation, the poetic act itself is a catalyst which allows for the possibility of continuing life and hope:

Over the faces of mothers and captive women,
over the decaying verses and meters
I will spurt fountains of honey,
I will write about trees or shoes, roses or boys.
Tell the misery to depart . . .

Although al-Māghūt does not see himself as a poet-prophet (unlike some other Arab poets), the possibility that his words may be "adjacent to the words of Christ" does not escape him. The tone of "From the Threshold to the Sky" is softer and more hopeful. It is still sardonic, but there flows from it a calm resignation to human fate. The poem ends on a romantic note of faith and hope: "Let us wait then for the sky to let fall its tears/Oh my love!"

One of the most striking images employed by al-Māghūt is the symbol of grass to represent the simplicity of the pre-industrial Arab world. In "The Plateau," the poet will return to his village on foot, and throw himself "on the grass and the river bank/like a horseman after an exhausting battle."

Al-Māghūt is also a pioneer of the long poem in Arabic, such as his poem "The Dead Man." His play *Al-'uṣfūr al-aḥdab* (The Hunchbacked Bird) is highly surrealist, but his collection of essays which is included in his book *Sa'akhūnū waṭanī* (I Will Betray My Country) deals mainly with the political and everyday life of the Arab world. Al-Māghūt's work employs a variety of genres, but his predominant tone is satirical.

Despite the occasional archaism, al-Māghūt's language belongs to the modern literary Arabic of the newspapers and the educated, which makes it accessible to the international Arab community. He is one of the few Arab poets who believes in the use of conversational speech rhythms in poetry; through such rhythms he expresses the full complexity of human emotion in an age of political repression and war.

—Parvin Loloi

MAHFOUZ, Naguib. *See* **MAHFŪZ, Nagīb.**

MAHFŪZ, Nagīb (Abdel Azīz al-Sabilgi). Also Naguib Mahfouz. Egyptian. Born in Gamaliya, Cairo, 11 December 1911. Educated at the University of Cairo, 1930–34, degree in philosophy 1934, post-graduate study 1935–36. Married 'Aṭiyya 'Alla' in 1954; one son and one daughter. Secretary, University of Cairo, 1936–38; journalist: staff member, *Ar-Risāla*, and contributor to *Al-Hilāl* and *Al-Ahrām*; civil servant, Ministry of Islamic Affairs, 1939–54; director of censorship, Department of Art; director of Foundation for Support of the Cinema for the State Cinema Organization, 1959–69; consultant for cinema affairs to the Ministry of Culture, 1969–71; retired from civil service, 1971. Member of board, Dār al/Ma'āref publishing house. Recipient: Egyptian state prize, 1956; National prize for letters, 1970; Collar of the Republic (Egypt), 1972; Nobel prize for literature, 1988. Named to Egyptian Order of Independence and Order of the Republic. Agent: c/o Donald E. Herdeck, Three Continents Press, 1636 Connecticut Avenue, N.W., Washington, D.C. 20009, U.S.A. Address: Al-Ahrām, Al Jalā' Street, Cairo, Egypt.

PUBLICATIONS

Fiction

Hams al-junūn [The Whisper of Madness]. Cairo, Misr, 1939.
'Abāth al aqdār [The Mockery of Fate]. Cairo, Misr, 1939.

Radubis. Cairo, Misr, 1943.
Kifaḥ Ṭība [Thebes' Struggle]. Cairo, Misr, 1944.
Khān al-Khalīli. Cairo, Misr, 1945.
Al-Qāhira al-jadīda [New Cairo]. Cairo, Misr, 1946.
Zuqāq al-Midaqq. Cairo, Misr, 1947; as *Midaq Alley*, Beirut, Khayāts, 1966; revised edition, London, Heinemann, and Washington, D.C., Three Continents Press, 1975.
Al-sarāb [Mirage]. Cairo, Misr, 1949(?).
Bidāya wa-nihāya. Cairo, Misr, 1949; as *The Beginning and the End*, Cairo, American University in Cairo Press, 1985; New York, Doubleday, 1989; London, Doubleday, 1990.
Al-thulāthiya [The Cairo Trilogy]:
  Bayn al-Qasrayn. Cairo, Misr, 1956; as *Palace Walk*, New York and London, Doubleday, 1990.
  Qasr al-shawq. Cairo, Misr, 1957; as *Palace of Desire*, New York and London, Doubleday, 1991.
  Al-sukkariya. Cairo, Misr, 1957; as *Sugar Street*, New York and London, Doubleday, 1992.
Al-liṣ wa-l-kilāb. Cairo, Misr, 1961; revised edition, as *The Thief and the Dogs*, Cairo, American University in Cairo Press, 1984; New York, Doubleday, 1989; London, Doubleday, 1990.
Al-sammān wa-l-kharīf. Cairo, Misr, 1962; as *Autumn Quail*, Cairo, American University in Cairo Press, 1985; New York and London, Doubleday, 1990.
Dunya Allah [The World of God]. Cairo, Misr, 1963.
Al-Ṭarīq. Cairo, Misr, 1964; as *The Search*, Cairo, American Univesity in Cairo Press, 1987; New York and London, Doubleday, 1991.
Al-shaḥḥāẓ. Cairo, Misr, 1965; as *The Beggar*, Cairo, American University in Cairo Press, 1986; New York and London, Doubleday, 1990.
Bayt sayyi' al-sum'a [A House of Ill-Repute]. Cairo, Misr, 1965.
Tharthara fawq al-Nīl [Chit-Chat on the Nile]. Cairo, Misr, 1966.
Awlād ḥāratina. Beirut, Dār al-Adāb, 1967; as *Children of Gebelawi*, London, Heinemann, and Washington, D.C., Three Continents Press, 1981.
Miramār. Cairo, Misr, 1967; in English, Cairo, American University in Cairo Press, London, Heinemann, and Washington, D.C., Three Continents Press, 1978.
Khammārat al-qiṭṭ al-aswad [The Black Cat Tavern]. Cairo, Misr, 1968.
Taḥt al-miḍhalla [Under the Awning]. Cairo, Misr, 1969.
Ḥikāya bi-la bidāya wa-la nihāya [A Story Without Beginning or End]. Cairo, Misr, 1971.
Shahr al-'asal [Honeymoon]. Cairo, Misr, 1971.
Al-marāya. Cairo, Misr, 1972; as *Mirrors*, Minneapolis, Bibliotheca Islamica, 1977.
Al-ḥubb taḥta al-maṭar [Love in the Rain]. Cairo, Misr, 1973.
God's World: An Anthology of Short Stories, edited by Akef Abadir and Roger Allen. Minneapolis, Bibliotheca Islamica, 1973.
Al-jarīma [The Crime]. Cairo, Misr, 1973.
Al-karnak. Cairo, Misr, 1974; in English, in *Three Contemporary Egyptian Novels*, Fredericton, New Brunswick, York Press, 1979.
Ḥikāyāt ḥāratina. Cairo, Misr, 1975; as *Fountain and Tomb*, Washington, D.C., Three Continents Press, 1988.
Qalb al-layl [In the Heart of the Night]. Cairo, Misr, 1975.
Ḥaḍrat al-muḥtaram. Cairo, Misr, 1975; as *Respected Sir*, London, Quartet, 1986; Cairo, American University in Cairo Press, 1987; New York, Doubleday, 1990.
Modern Egyptian Short Stories, with Yusuf Idrīs and Sa'd al-Khādim. Fredericton, New Brunswick, York Press, 1977.

Malḥamat al ḥarāfīsh.   Cairo, Misr, 1977.
Al-ḥubb fawqa Haḍabat al-Haram [Love on Pyramid Mount].
   Cairo, Misr, 1979.
Al-shayṭān ya'iḍ [Satan Preaches].   Cairo, Misr, 1979.
'Asr al-ḥubb [Age of Love].   Cairo, Misr, 1980.
Layāli alf laylah [A Thousand and One Nights].   Cairo, Misr,
   1981.
Afrāḥ al-qubbah.   Cairo, Misr, 1981; as *Wedding Song*, re-
   vised and edited by Mursi Saad el-Dīn and John Rodenbeck,
   Cairo, American University in Cairo Press, 1984; New
   York, Doubleday, 1989; London, Doubleday, 1990.
Ra'aytu fīma yara al-na'im [I Have Seen What a Sleeper
   Sees].   Cairo, Misr, 1982.
Bāqi min al-zaman sā'ah [One Hour Left].   Cairo, Misr,
   1982.
Amāma al'arsh [In Front of the Throne].   Cairo, Misr, 1982.
Riḥlat Ibn Faṭṭūmah.   Cairo, Misr, 1983; as *The Journey of
   Ibn Fattouma*, New York and London, Doubleday, 1992.
Al-tanḍhīm al-sirri [The Secret Organization].   Cairo, Misr,
   1984.
Al-ā'ish fī al-ḥaqīqah [Living with the Truth].   Cairo, Misr,
   1985.
Yawm qutila al-za'im.   Cairo, Misr, 1985; as *The Day the
   Leader Was Killed*, Cairo, General Egyptian Book Organ-
   ization, 1989.
Ḥadīth al ṣabāh wa-al-masā' [Morning and Evening
   Talk].   Cairo, Misr, 1987.
Ṣabāh al-ward [Good Morning].   Cairo, Misr, 1987.
Qushtumor.   Cairo, Misr, 1989.

Plays

One-Act Plays.   Cairo, General Egyptian Book Organization, 1989.

Other

Nagīb Maḥfuz-yataẓakkar [Mahfouz Remembers], edited by
   Jamāl al-Ghītani.   Beirut, Dār al-Masīrah, 1980.

*

Critical Studies: *The Changing Rhythm: A Study of Nagib
Mahfuz's Novels* by Sasson Somekh, Leiden, Brill, 1973;
"Reality, Allegory and Myth in the Work of Najib Mahfuz" by
Mehahern Milson, in *African and Asian Studies*, 11, 1976;
'Mahfuz's *Al-karnak*: The Quiet Conscience of Nassir's Egypt
Revealed" by T. Le Gassick, in *Middle Eastern Journal*, 31(3),
1977; *Religion, My Own: The Literary Works of Nagib Mahfuz*
by Matityahu Peled, New Brunswick, New Jersey, Transac-
tion, 1983; *Critical Perspectives on Naguib Mahfouz* edited by
Trevor Le Gassick, Washington, D.C., Three Continents
Press, 1989; *Naguib Mahfouz, Nobel 88: Egyptian
Perspectives: A Collection of Critical Essays*, Cairo, General
Egyptian Book Organization, 1989.

*   *   *

Crowned with the Nobel prize for literature, Nagīb Mahfūz
(Naguib Mahfouz) reigns over 20th-century Arabic prose
literature like an influential but unassuming constitutional
monarch. The current success of translations of his works in
many languages is unprecedented for a modern Arab author.
His novels and collections of short stories portray different
strata and aspects of Egyptian society, most frequently those of
contemporary Cairo, although four are pharaonic novels.

Al-thulāthiya (The Cairo Trilogy), consisting of *Bayn al-
Qasrayn* (*Palace Walk*), *Qasr al-shawq* (*Palace of Desire*), and
Al-sukkariya (*Sugar Street*), is thought by many critics to be his
masterpiece. It is a massive but intimate account of the
emotional and intellectual development from childhood to
maturity of the hero, Kamal, and of the adventures of his
parents, siblings, and — in the third volume — his nephews
and nieces. Part of the fascination of the Trilogy is the mirror
that the fortunes and misfortunes of this family provide for
those of Egypt as a whole during the period from 1917 to 1944.
In the Trilogy and elsewhere, Mahfūz has been able to reveal
the universal dimensions of chance events and of eccentric
characters, thus introducing outsiders to some of Cairo's secret
worlds while at the same time reintroducing readers to
themselves.

Known for his sympathetic portrayals of female characters,
this author's most typical hero, however, is the male civil
servant — whether a teacher like Kamal or an office clerk like
his libidinous brother Yasin — who is making his way through
life none too surely, pushed in many different directions by the
demands of family, sex, ambition, religion, modernity, tradition, and idealism. He has chronicled the full range of human
possibilities, including the most sexually confused (for
example in *Al-sarāb* [Mirage]) or corruptly degraded, in a
sympathetic way that does not seem judgmental. If Mahfūz has
a typical villain, it is time.

Mahfūz is an author who may weep at the tragedies of his
characters without once moderating the blows he administers
to them on behalf of fate. Although his works are often
flavored with a melancholy pessimism, there is usually a life-
affirming thread in the fabric. Novels by Mahfūz frequently
depict the comic or pathetic attempts of human beings to make
sense of those fleeting moments of consciousness that constitute our allotment of the pulsing surge of evolutionary life.
Traditional conservatism and revolutionary experiments are
merely rival extremes in an endless dialectic that presses
humanity toward a tantalizing but unreachable synthesis.
Paternalism, no matter how affectionate and benevolent, is
doomed to tragic failure, but so too is liberalism, understood as
surrender to sensual or intellectual appetites.

An autobiographical author, Mahfūz tends to identify not
with any one character, except perhaps for Kamal, but with the
sum of all character traits presented. Trained as a philosopher,
he has allowed his heroes to brood about deep questions,
without forgetting that the job of an author is to tell stories.

Besides the Cairo Trilogy, several other works by Mahfūz
have acquired many fans. In *Miramār*, thought by some to be
his best work, residents of a *pension* that has seen better days
reveal their outlook and backgrounds as they react to a
beautiful woman who joins the staff. *Zuqāq al-Midaqq* (*Midaq
Alley*), a racy slice of working-class life in Cairo during World
War II, asks readers whether the heroine should elect to be a
prostitute for British forces stationed in Cairo or the wife of a
nice but dull alley barber. *Al-Qāhira al-jadīda* (New Cairo)
records the exploits of some school friends, one of whom
willingly sacrifices his honor to further his career. Like many of
his other novels, some of which have also been successfully
adapted for the stage, it has been made into a popular film. *Al-
liṣ wa-l-kilāb* (*The Thief and the Dogs*) is a brief and grim
account of a convicted felon who attempts to take revenge on
the powerful man who betrayed him. *Awlād ḥaratina* (*Children of Gebelawi*), a book banned in Egypt, draws on the
heritage of the Abrahamic religions to create an allegory about
mankind's continuing search for spiritual values. In *Ḥikāya
ḥaratina* (*Fountain and Tomb*) as in other works Mahfūz has
utilized elements of Islamic mysticism, here as part of the
framework for a series of lively vignettes of back-street life.

If Mahfūz has rarely shown the stylistic brilliance in Arabic of Ibrahim Abd al-Qadir al-Mazini or the natural simplicity of Tawfiq al-Hakim, he has demonstrated an awesome and deft mastery of the Arabic language, which in its vast potential resembles an enormously complicated pipe organ. Even so, Mahfūz is more noteworthy for his psychological penetration and his ability to make even minor characters convincing and appealing, no matter how disgusting, than for the poetry of his language. In his more recent fiction, Mahfūz, who has been amazingly prolific through the years, has tended to abandon the detailed social realism that first made his reputation, favoring instead experiments in more rapid delivery of stories stripped to their psychological core or attempts to return to a more traditional, Islamic form of storytelling. Yet from the very beginning of his career with his first historical novels set in ancient Egypt, Mahfūz has been experimenting with different literary forms. The Cairo Trilogy, for all its traditional social realism, must have seemed to him a giant experiment.

—William M. Hutchins

MAILLET, Antonine. Canadian. Born in Bouctouche, New Brunswick, 10 May 1929. Educated at the Collège Notre-Dame d'Acadie, Moncton, New Brunswick, B.A. 1950; University of Moncton, M.A. 1959. Taught at the Collège Notre-Dame d'Acadie, 1954–60, University of Moncton, 1965–67, and Collège des Jésuites Québec, 1968–69; Professor, University of Laval, Quebec, 1971–74, and University of Montreal, 1974–75; Visiting Professor, University of California, Berkeley, 1983; Chancellor, University of Moncton, 1989. Recipient: Dominion Drama Festival prize, 1958; Champlain prize, 1960; Council of Arts prize, 1960; Governor-General's award, 1972; City of Montreal grand prize, 1973; Volcans prize (France), 1975; France-Canada prize, 1975; Littéraire de la Presse prize, 1976; Four Juries prize, 1978; Goncourt prize, 1979; Chalmers prize, 1980. D.H.L.: University of Moncton, 1972; Saint Mary's University, 1980; Windsor University, 1980; Acadia University, 1980; University of Laurentienne, 1981; McGill University, 1982; St. Thomas University, 1986; University of St. Anne, 1987; Mount St. Vincent University, 1987; Bowling Green University, 1988; University of Laval, 1988; Simon Fraser University, 1989; Concordia University, 1990; University of Maine at Fort Kent, 1990. Litt.D.: Carleton University, 1978; Mount Allison University, 1979. LL.D.: University of Alberta, 1979; University of Dalhousie, 1981; University of Toronto, 1982; Queen's University, Kingston, 1982; St Francis Xavier University, 1984; University of Lyon, 1989; University of British Columbia, 1991. Officier, 1976, and Compagnon, 1982, de l'Ordre du Canada; Officier des Palmes Académiques Françaises, 1980; Chevalier de l'Ordre de la Pléiade, Fredericton, New Brunswick; member of l'Académie Canadienne-Française; Officier de l'Ordre des Arts et des Lettres (France), 1985; Officier de l'Ordre National du Québec, 1990; member of l'Académie des Grands Montréalais, 1991. Address: 735 Antonine Maillet Avenue, Montreal, Quebec H2V 2Y4, Canada.

PUBLICATIONS

Plays

Les Crasseux (produced Montreal, 1974). Montreal, Holt, 1968; revised version, Montreal, Leméac, 1974.
La Sagouine (produced Montreal, 1972). Montreal, Leméac, 1971; in English, Toronto, Simon and Pierre, 1979.
Gapi (produced Montreal, 1977). Published as *Gapi et Sullivan*, Montreal, Leméac, 1973; as *Gapi and Sullivan*, Toronto, Simon and Pierre, 1987.
Mariaàgélas, from her own novel (produced Montreal, 1974).
La Sagouine II (produced Montreal, 1975).
Évangéline Deusse (produced Montreal, 1976). Montreal, Leméac, 1975; as *Evangeline the Second*, Toronto, Simon and Pierre, 1987.
La Veuve enragée (produced Montreal, 1978). Montreal, Leméac, 1977.
Le Bourgeois Gentilhomme, adaptation of the play by Molière (produced Montreal, 1978). Montreal, Leméac, 1978.
Emmanuel à Joseph à Dâvit, from her own novel (produced Montreal, 1979).
La Contrebandière (produced Montreal, 1981). Montreal, Leméac, 1981.
La Joyeuse criée (produced Montreal, 1983).
Les Drôlatiques, horrifiques et épouvantables aventures de Panurge, ami de Pantagruel, d'après Rabelais (produced Montreal, 1983). Montreal, Leméac, 1983.
Garrochés en Paradis (produced Montreal, 1986). Montreal, Leméac, 1986.
Margot la Folle (produced Montreal, 1987). Montreal, Leméac, 1987.
Les Fantastiques, translation of the play by Tom Jones (produced Ottawa, 1988).
Richard III, translation of the play by William Shakespeare (produced Ottawa, 1990). Montreal, Leméac, 1989.
William S (produced Montreal, 1991). Montreal, Leméac, 1991.

Radio Play: *La Sagouine.*

Television Play: *La Sagouine.*

Fiction

Pointe-aux-Coques. Montreal, Fidès, 1958.
On a mangé la dune. Montreal, Beauchemin, 1962.
Don l'Original. Montreal, Leméac, 1972; as *The Tale of Don l'Original*, Toronto, Clarke Irwin, 1978.
Par Derrière chez Mon Père. Montreal, Leméac, 1972.
Mariaàgélas. Montreal, Leméac, 1973; in English, Toronto, Simon and Pierre, 1986.
Emmanuel à Joseph à Dâvit. Montreal, Leméac, 1975.
Les Cordes de Bois. Montreal, Leméac, 1977.
Pélagie-la-Charrette. Montreal, Leméac, 1979; in English, London, Calder, 1982; as *Pélagie: The Return to a Homeland*, New York, Doubleday, 1982.
Cent Ans dans les bois. Montreal, Leméac, 1981.
La Gribouille. Paris, Grasset, 1982.
Crache-à-Pic. Montreal, Leméac, 1984; as *The Devil Is Loose!*, Toronto, Lester and Orpen Dennys, 1986; New York, Walker, 1987.
Le Huitième Jour. Montreal, Leméac, 1986; as *On the Eighth Day*, Toronto, Lester and Orpen Dennys, 1989.
L'Oursiade. Montreal, Leméac, 1990.

Other

Rabelais et les traditions populaires en Acadie. Quebec, Presses de l'Université de Laval, 1971.
L'Acadie pour quasiment rien: guide touristique. Montreal, Leméac, 1973.
Christopher Cartier de la Noisette, dit Nounours (for children). Paris, Hachette, and Montreal, Leméac, 1981; as *Christopher Cartier of Hazelnut, Also Known as Bear*, Toronto and London, Methuen, 1984.

*

Critical Studies: "Antonine Maillet: The Search for a Narrative Voice" by Margorie A. Fitzpatrick, in *Journal of Popular Culture* (Bowling Green, Ohio), Winter 1981; "The Mythical Dimension of *Pélagie-la-Charrette*" by Karolyn Waterson, in *Francophone Literatures of the New World*, edited by James P. Gilroy, Denver, University of Denver, 1982; "The Anatomy of a Translation: *Pélagie-la-Charrette*" by Philip Stratford, in *Translation in Canadian Literature*, edited by Camille R. La Bossière, Ottawa, University of Ottawa Press, 1983; "Antonine Maillet and the Epic Heroine" by Marjorie A. Fitzpatrick, in *Traditionalism, Nationalism, and Feminism: Women Writers of Quebec*, edited by Paula Gilbert Lewis, Westport, Connecticut, Greenwood, 1985; Maillet issue of *Québec Studies* (Montreal), 4, 1986; "*Pélagie-la-Charrette* and Antonine Maillet's Epic Voices" by Bernard Arésu, in *Explorations: Essays in Comparative Literature*, edited by Matoto Ueda, Lanham, Maryland, University Press of America, 1986; "The Bible and Myth in Antonine Maillet's *Pélagie-la-Charrette*" by Paul G. Socken, in *Studies in Canadian Literature* (Fredericton, New Brunswick), 12(2), 1987; "Antonine Maillet's *Évangéline Deusse*: Historical, Popular and Literary Elements" by Janis Pallister, in *American Review of Canadian Studies*, Summer 1988.

*   *   *

Antonine Maillet is the most important author in the history of French-speaking Acadia, the first French colony in North America, comprising most of today's Maritime Provinces of Canada. She has also been the most eloquent advocate of Acadian culture, language, and traditions.

Maillet's literary beginnings were tentative, her fifth published work, the monodrama *La Sagouine* being the first to achieve critical or popular acclaim. Initially a series of 16 short sketches written for local French-language radio in Moncton, New Brunswick, *La Sagouine* soon captured national attention in its stage and television versions in the early 1970s, in French and in English. Audiences were mesmerized first of all by the unfamiliar accent and authentic diction of its eponymous character ("Sagouine" is an Acadian term suggesting a slovenly woman), who speaks a dialect rich in archaic idioms accessible, however, to most educated speakers of standard French. This is the language in which virtually all of Maillet's prolific literary creation is steeped, and her knowledge of it is unsurpassed (her Ph.D. dissertation is a fascinating study of the survival of Rabelaisian influences in the speech and popular oral traditions of modern Acadia).

72 years old, illiterate and ailing, La Sagouine has had to sell her labour — and sometimes her body — in order to survive. But not her soul: candid and courageous, she reflects, with rueful and often mordant humour, on the injustices she and her people have suffered, on the follies, prejudices, and ingrained hypocrisy of contemporary society and its principal institutions, most notably the Catholic Church. La Sagouine

was immediately perceived as a symbol of Acadia itself, of a tiny nation economically deprived and politically marginalized by the Anglophone majority, but determined to do whatever is necessary to retain its ancient identity.

This is the achievement of which Maillet is most proud, for the mythical symbol of Acadia which *La Sagouine* helped to displace was that of Longfellow's Evangeline, the passive, plangent heroine of the American author's romantic poem. This vital task of subverting a dated, cumbersome myth in order to replace it with a more appropriate one was furthered considerably a few years later through another play, significantly entitled *Évangéline Deusse* (*Evangeline the Second*). The dynamics of this work constantly oppose Longfellow's 18th-century heroine (his poem is referred to explicitly in Maillet's text) and a contemporary Evangeline, in this case an 80-year-old Acadian grandmother living in impatient exile in Montreal. As stubbornly loyal to her language and history as La Sagouine, Evangeline the Second is one of the most memorable of the strong female characters who populate Maillet's compelling literary universe.

The novels which have earned for Maillet international acclaim are firmly anchored in her native culture as well. Between 1958 and 1973 three of these won important Canadian literary awards, although the author continued to be recognized mainly as a dramatist. Full international recognition came for her novel *Pélagie-la-Charrette* (*Pélagie: The Return to a Homeland*), winner of France's prestigious Goncourt prize in 1979. Based largely on historical fact, this is a novel of messianic quest in which complex layers of popular oral legend, recondite history, Rabelaisian reference, surreal allegory, and biblical symbolism intertwine effectively to create a truly epic adventure — *the* epic of Acadia's Long March, after the Deportation of 1755.

After 15 years of difficult subsistence in the Georgian colony the heroine has gathered about her a few exiled remnants of her nation. They set out, by foot and by ox-cart (the *charrette* of the French title), for their native land, half a continent away. Their odyssey lasts the entire decade of the 1770s, as Pélagie leads her ragged troupe through countless perils, seen and unseen (they are constantly followed by the black cart of Death, visible only to the eldest among them, the 100-year-old seer Bélonie), through the British Colonies about to achieve their own nationhood (Pélagie's band, its numbers swelled as it encounters other exiles on its way, arrives in Philadelphia in July 1776), back towards their ancestral territory. On their arrival they learn that the original Acadian lands are now occupied by British settlers. The returnees must settle elsewhere, in the coastal regions and tidal plains of New Brunswick, where their numbers still predominate today. Pélagie herself dies soon after their arrival, for her mission has been accomplished. The Acadian nation will henceforth survive through the courage of one determined, enterprising woman, a new Mother Courage who replaces once and for all Longfellow's ineffectual Evangeline.

La Sagouine and *Pélagie*, in the opinion of most critics, represent the apogee of Maillet's career to date. A sequel to the latter, *Cent Ans dans les bois* (A Hundred Years in the Woods), set in Acadia a century after Pélagie's return, is decidedly less effective, although its skilful blending of diverse narrative techniques has evoked admiration. None of her several novels published since then has been of comparable stature. Her theatre also is perceived by critics as increasingly predictable; indeed, several of her more recent plays have merely been adaptations of her own novels.

An objective reassessment of Maillet's place in French literature, in Canada and abroad, is now taking place. Her impassioned commitment to the cause of Acadia, initially an attraction for readers unfamiliar with its colourful history and language, has sometimes been an impediment to its reception outside Canada. This is unfortunate, for once the slight linguistic hurdle has been passed, the memorable characters and situations she depicts become thoroughly, poignantly universal. It would appear that the author herself is well aware of the disadvantages of unrelieved provincialism, since her most recent works (*Le Huitième Jour* [*On the Eighth Day*]; *L'Oursiade* [*Saga of the Bear*]; her adaptation of Shakespeare's *Richard III*) clearly indicate a search for broader horizons.

—Leonard E. Doucette

* * *

MALLET-JORIS, Françoise. Pseudonym for Françoise Lilar. French. Born in Antwerp, Belgium, 6 July 1930; now a French citizen. Educated in Antwerp; Bryn Mawr College, Pennsylvania, 1947–48; the Sorbonne, Paris, 1949. Married 1) Robert Amadou in 1947 (divorced 1948), one son; 2) Alain Joxe in 1952 (dissolved); Jacques Delfau in 1958, one son and two daughters. Reader, from 1952, and director of "Nouvelles" collection, 1960–65, Julliard publishers, Paris; Reader, Grasset publishers from 1965; television columnist, *Panorama chrétien*, 1967; member of Prix Fémina jury, 1969; member, 1970, and vice-president, 1973, Goncourt Academy; member of the Board of Directors, TF–1 television station, since 1980. Songwriter for Marie-Paule Belle. Recipient: French Booksellers prize, 1957; Fémina prize, 1958; Julliard prize, 1963; Monaco grand prize, 1965; Ordre National du Mérite, 1986. Address: c/o Flammarion et Cie, 26 rue Racine, 75278 Paris cedex 06, France.

PUBLICATIONS

Fiction

Le Rempart des Béguines. Paris, Julliard, 1951; as *The Illusionist*, New York, Farrar Straus, 1952; as *Into the Labyrinth*, London, W. H. Allen, 1953.
La Chambre rouge. Paris, Julliard, 1955; as *The Red Room*, New York, Farrar Straus, and London, W. H. Allen, 1956.
Cordélia. Paris, Julliard, 1956; as *Cordelia and Other Stories*, New York, Farrar Straus, and London, W. H. Allen, 1965.
Les Mensonges. Paris, Julliard, 1956; as *House of Lies*, New York, Farrar Straus, 1957; London, W. H. Allen, 1958.
L'Empire Céleste. Paris, Julliard, 1958; as *Café Céleste*, London, W. H. Allen, 1959; New York, Farrar Straus, 1962.
Les Personnages. Paris, Julliard, 1961; as *The Favourite*, New York, Farrar Straus, and London, W. H. Allen, 1962.
Les Signes et les prodiges. Paris, Grasset, 1966; as *Signs and Wonders*, New York, Farrar Straus, and London, W. H. Allen, 1967.
Trois Âges de la nuit: histoires de sorcellerie. Paris, Grasset, 1968; as *The Witches: Three Tales of Sorcery*, New York, Farrar Straus, 1969; London, W. H. Allen, 1970.

Le Jeu du souterrain. Paris, Grasset, 1973; as *The Underground Game*, London, W. H. Allen, 1974; New York, Dutton, 1975.
Allegra. Paris, Grasset, 1976.
Dickie-Roi. Paris, Grasset, 1979.
Un Chagrin d'amour et d'ailleurs. Paris, Grasset, 1981.
Le Clin d'œil de l'ange. Paris, Gallimard, 1983.
Le Rire de Laura. Paris, Gallimard, 1985.
La Tristesse du cerf-volant. Paris, Flammarion, 1988.
Adriana Sposa. Paris, Flammarion, 1989.
Divine. Paris, Flammarion, 1991.

Plays

Un Goût de miel, with G. Arout, from play by Shelagh Delaney. Paris, L'Avant-Scène, 1960.

Screenplays: *Le Gigolo*, 1962; *Le Rempart des Béguines*, 1972.

Verse

Poèmes du dimanche (as Françoise Lilar). Brussels, Artistes, 1947.

Other

Lettre à moi-même. Paris, Julliard, 1963; as *A Letter to Myself*, New York, Farrar Straus, and London, W. H. Allen, 1964.
Marie Mancini: le premier amour de Louis XIV. Paris, Hachette, 1964; as *The Uncompromising Heart: A Life of Marie Mancini, Louis XIV's First Love*, New York, Farrar Straus, and London, W. H. Allen, 1964.
Enfance, ton regard. Paris, Hachette, 1966.
La Maison de papier. Paris, Grasset, 1970; as *The Paper House*, New York, Farrar Straus, and London, W. H. Allen, 1971.
À Propos de Madame de Sévigné. Liège, Dynamo, 1971.
Le Roi qui aimait trop les fleurs (for children). Paris, Casterman, 1972.
Les Feuilles mortes d'un bel été (for children). Paris, Grasset, 1973.
Le Cirque. Paris, Mouret, 1974.
J'aurais voulu jouer de l'accordéon. Paris, Julliard, 1975.
Juliette Greco, with Michel Grisolia. Paris, Seghers, 1975.
Jeanne Guyon. Paris, Flammarion, 1978.
Marie-Paule Belle. Paris, Seghers, 1987.

Editor, *Nouvelles*. Paris, Julliard, 1957.
Editor, *Le Rendez-vous donné par Françoise Mallet-Joris à quelques jeunes écrivains*. Paris, Julliard, 1962.
Editor, *Lettres*, by Madame de Sévigné. Paris, Rombaldi, 1969.

*

Critical Studies: "Françoise Mallet-Joris and the Anatomy of the Will" by Rima Drell Reck, in *Yale French Studies* (New Haven, Connecticut), Summer 1959; "Mirrors and Masks in the World of Françoise Mallet-Joris" by Geneviève Delattre, in *Yale French Studies* (New Haven, Connecticut), Spring 1961; *Françoise Mallet-Joris* by Lucille Frackman Becker, Boston, Twayne, 1985.

* * *

The eminent French critic Pierre-Henri Simon called Fran-çoise Mallet-Joris one of the most gifted writers of her generation. Her first novel, *Le Rempart des Béguines* (*The Illusionist*), published in 1951 when the author was 21 years old, is the story of an adolescent who enters into a lesbian relationship with her father's mistress. The protagonist of the novel is the prototype of all of the author's subsequent heroines; she is an independent, brave, and resolute young girl, created in the author's own image, who refuses to play the role assigned to her by society and who revolts against the hypocrisy and constraints of her milieu. Her rebellion is directed solely against family and society without reference to the human condition.

While the behavior of the heroines of *The Illusionist*, of its sequel *La Chambre rouge* (*The Red Room*), and of the short stories of *Cordélia* is motivated by a search for truth, that of the males is characterized by a flight from truth. The men in Mallet-Joris's work are, for the most part, inauthentic beings who have directed their efforts towards creating an image of themselves that will free them from the existentialist imperative of creating their own essence. The danger of such behavior is made manifest in *Les Mensonges* (*House of Lies*) and *L'Empire Céleste* (*Café Céleste*), where the male protagonists find ultimately that the personas they have created have destroyed their authentic being, leaving nothing in its stead. In these two novels, the author changes from first- to third-person narration. Interior monologues, dialogues, and individual perceptions provide the multiple points of view that were lacking in the preceding works.

Mallet-Joris presents her prototypical heroine against historical backgrounds in two novels, *Les Personnages* (*The Favourite*) and *Trois Âges de la nuit* (*The Witches*), and two biographical works, *Marie Mancini* and *Jeanne Guyon*. The women who are the protagonists of these works are called "personnes" (authentic beings) by the author because they remain true to their inner selves. She contrasts them with characters she refers to as "personnages" (personae), because they hide behind masks and play prescribed roles. While each of the heroines revolts in a different way against society, all of them are similarly conspired against and attacked on all sides by hostile forces. In these works, the author's denunciation of the plight of the heroine develops into a more sweeping indictment of the condition of women in general, expressing a feminine bias that will become more pronounced in her subsequent novels. Emphasis is also placed in these works on spiritual preoccupations which often take precedence over social concerns and which will constitute the essence of Mallet-Joris's later works.

Lettre à moi-même (*A Letter to Myself*) is an autobiographical work in which the author tells the story of her search for God and her religious conversion. This work provides the key to all of Mallet-Joris's later works, for it is the search for an absolute that motivates the characters of the novels *Les Signes et les prodiges* (*Signs and Wonders*), *Allegra*, *Dickie-Roi*, *Un Chagrin d'amour et d'ailleurs*, *Le Rire de Laura*, *La Tristesse du cerf-volant*, and *Divine*, as well as the short stories of *Le Clin d'œil de l'ange*.

Mallet-Joris's novels remain within the framework of the traditional novel with their emphasis on plot and characterization. At the same time, her emphasis on visual detail and her use of certain techniques of the new novel place her within the mainstream of modern fiction.

—Lucille Frackman Becker

MANET, Eduardo. Cuban and French. Born in Santiago de Cuba, 19 June 1930 (as stated by Manet; some sources say 1927). Educated at the University of Havana; studied theatre in Paris and Italy. Associated with mime troupe of Jacques Lecoq. Returned to Cuba in 1960; director, Cuban Drama Center, 1960–65; film director, Cuban Institute of Cinema, 1965–68; exiled from Cuba, 1968; French citizen since 1979. Recipient: Lugné-Poë prize, 1969; Off-Avignon Festival prize, 1986. Address: c/o Flammarion, 26 rue Racine, 75278 Paris Cedex 06, France.

PUBLICATIONS

Plays

Scherzo (produced Havana, 1948). With *Presagio* and *La infanta que no quiso tener ojos verdes*, 1949.
Presagio (produced Havana, 1949[?]). With *Scherzo* and *La infanta que no quiso tener ojos verdes*, 1949.
Scherzo; Presagio; La infanta que no quiso tener ojos verdes. Havana, Prometeo, 1949.
La santa (produced Havana, 1964).
Helen viendra nous voir de Hollywood et nous lui ferons la plus belle des fêtes parties (produced Montreal, 1968).
Las monjas. As *Les Nonnes* (produced Paris, 1969), Paris, Gallimard, 1969; as *The Nuns* (produced Brighton, 1970), London, Calder and Boyars, 1970.
Eux, ou La Prise du pouvoir (produced Paris, 1992). Paris, Gallimard, 1971.
Sur la Piste (produced Paris, 1972).
Holocaustum, ou Le Borgne (produced France, 1972). Paris, Gallimard, 1972.
L'Autre Don Juan (produced Montreal, 1974). Paris, Gallimard, 1973.
Madras, la nuit où . . . (produced Avignon, 1974). Paris, Gallimard, 1975.
Lady Strass (produced Paris, 1977). Published in *L'Avant-Scène* (Paris), 613, 1977; in English (produced Toronto, 1982).
Les Ménines de la Mer Morte (produced Geneva, 1977).
Le Jour où Mary Shelley rencontra Charlotte Brontë (produced Paris, 1979). Published in *L'Avant-Scène* (Paris), 654, 1979; as *The Day Mary Shelley Met Charlotte Brontë* (produced Los Angeles, 1991).
Un Balcon sur les Andes (produced Nice, 1979). Paris, Stock, 1979.
Les Gozzi (produced Nice, 1981).
Sacrilèges (produced Paris, 1981).
Mendoza, en Argentine . . . (produced Paris, 1984). Paris, Recherche-Action Théâtre Ouvert, 1983; in English (produced London, 1986).
Un Balcon sur les Andes; Mendoza, en Argentine; Ma'Déa. Paris, Gallimard, 1985.
Ma'Déa (produced Paris, 1986). With *Un Balcon sur les Andes* and *Mendoza, en Argentine*, 1985.
Histoire de Maheu le boucher (produced Avignon, 1986). Paris, Gallimard, 1986.
Les Chiennes. Paris, Recherche-Action Théâtre Ouvert, 1987.
Le Primerissimo (produced Malaucène, 1988).
Les Couples et les paravents (produced Melun-Sénart, 1992).
Deux Siècles d'amour (produced Paris, 1992).

Radio and Television Plays: *Mirage dans un miroir sans reflects*, 1974; *Bolivar et Le Congrès de Panama*, 1976;

Topologies d'une cité fantôme, 1979; *Les Poupées en noir*, 1990, as *The Dolls in Black*, 1991 (United Kingdom).

Fiction

Les Étrangers dans la ville.   Paris, Julliard, 1960.
Un Cri sur le rivage.   Paris, Julliard, 1963.
La Mauresque.   Paris, Gallimard, 1982.
Zone interdite.   Paris, Gallimard, 1984.
L'Île au lézard vert.   Paris, Flammarion, 1992.

*

Critical Studies: "*Godot* Surpassed — Eduardo Manet's *Holocaustum, ou Le Borgne*" by Judith D. Suther, in *Research Studies*, 43, 1975; "Politics as Metatheatre: A Cuban-French View of Latin America," in *Latin American Theatre Review* (Lawrence, Kansas), 23(2), 1990, "Cinematic Devices in Cuban-French Theatre of Eduardo Manet," in *Studies in Modern and Classical Languages and Literatures*, 3, 1990, "Eduardo Manet, Hispanic Playwright in French Clothing?," in *Modern Language Studies* (Providence, Rhode Island), 22(1), 1992, "Interlingual Metatheatricalism: Manet's *L'Autre Don Juan*," in *Symposium* (Washington, D.C.), 45(4), 1992, and "Nuns in Drag: Manet's Cross-Gender Casting," in *TDR (The Drama Review)* (Cambridge, Massachusetts), 36(4), 1992, all by Phyllis Zatlin.

Theatrical Activities:
Director: **Films** — *El negro*, 1960; *Realengo 18*, 1960; *Napoleón gratis*, 1961; *Tránsito*, 1961; *En la playa*, 1961; *Portocarrero*, 1963; *El solar*, 1965; *El huesped*, 1967; *Show*, 1967; *Alicia*, 1968. **Plays** — some of his own, and several others.

*   *   *

As a teenager and university student in Havana, Eduardo Manet began publishing poetry and film reviews, as well as collaborating in a theatre group. His first staged plays date from the late 1940s and were written in his native Spanish. In 1951 he went to Paris to continue his theatre studies. Because of increasing repression under President Fulgencio Batista, he remained in Europe for a full decade, returning to Cuba only after Fidel Castro had achieved power and urged exiled intellectuals to come home.

For an eight-year period in Havana, Manet first headed the national drama center and then devoted himself to the direction of films for the Cuban Institute of Cinema. He also published his first two novels, in French, including *Un Cri sur le rivage* (A Cry from the Shore), which deals directly with the Cuban Revolution. Manet drafted many plays in the 20 years following his first youthful productions but, dissatisfied with the result, tore them up. In 1967, however, he finally found his voice as a playwright with *Las monjas* (*The Nuns*), a macabre tragifarce that ostensibly dealt with the 1804 black rebellion in Haiti but actually spoke metaphorically of the contemporary situation in Cuba. When Castro sided with the Soviet invasion of Czechoslovakia in 1968, Manet opted for exile in France. In Paris in 1969 the renowned avant-garde director Roger Blin staged Manet's own French version of *The Nuns*. The play's immediate triumph established the Cuban's international reputation and launched his new career, ultimately making him the most successful Latin American-born author of the French stage.

The title characters of Manet's grotesque comedy are to be played by men. At no time does the text reveal whether the audience should perceive men disguised as nuns or male actors cast in female roles. The ambiguity underscores the metatheatrical nature of the play. Led by the Mother Superior, the nuns create roles within their roles in order to deceive a wealthy Señora whom they murder for her jewels. However, the story of an impending black revolt, invented by the Mother Superior to frighten her victim, turns out to be true. To the sound of drumbeats without, the increasingly frantic nuns find themselves entrapped in their basement convent.

The Nuns introduces elements that are repeated in several of Manet's dramatic texts of the 1970s: the characters, caught in some kind of enclosure, resort to metatheatrical games, either to control one another or to recreate an idealized past. Typically the unseen, outside world represents revolution or other danger. The plays tend towards small casts, single sets, and a highly theatrical mode that features cinematographic acting styles, lighting, and use of soundtrack. These early works include *Eux, ou La Prise du pouvoir* (Them, or Taking Power), *Holocaustum, ou Le Borgne* (Holocaustum, or The One-Eyed Man), *Madras, la nuit où . . .* (That Night in Madras . . .), and *Lady Strass*.

Lady Strass, like *The Nuns*, premiered under the direction of Roger Blin and continues to be staged internationally. The cast consists of two would-be thieves — a middle-aged Frenchman and a younger Central American mestizo — and an eccentric old Englishwoman, who lives out her fantasies in a boarded-up house in Belize. The original French dialogue incorporates lines of Spanish and English as the characters switch between languages. Such multilingual games are common in Manet's theatre, reaching their maximum development in two metaplays that contain bilingual (French/Spanish) scenes: *L'Autre Don Juan* (The Other Don Juan) and *Un Balcon sur les Andes* (A Balcony over the Andes).

First staged in Montreal in 1974, *L'Autre Don Juan* is Manet's version of a Golden Age play from Spain: Ruiz de Alarcón's *Las paredes oyen* (The Walls Have Ears). Manet creates a wildly farcical frame play in which to place the French performance of the classic comedy. Among the actors in the French troupe is Ruiz de Alarcón himself, whose protests over the changes to his text lead him to begin speaking his lines in the original Spanish. In *Un Balcon sur les Andes*, a French theatrical troupe tours Latin American dictatorships; the lines of their plays within the play are often provided with interpretation to Spanish for the benefit of the audience within the play.

The extensive use of an intertext in *L'Autre Don Juan* is repeated in *Le Jour où Mary Shelley rencontra Charlotte Brontë* (The Day Mary Shelley Met Charlotte Brontë), a clever comedy that reflects Manet's love both of British literature and of Hollywood movies. The four-actor cast includes the two women writers and the characters from whom they cannot escape: Frankenstein's Monster and Jane Eyre. The characters force their authors into writing sequel novels that will free them to be their idealized selves.

Un Balcon sur les Andes, on the other hand, introduces another aspect of Manet's theatre: history plays in a Brechtian mode that require cinematographic staging for their episodic action. While this text, as well as the later *Histoire de Maheu le boucher* (The Story of Maheu the Butcher), is structured as farce, *Mendoza, en Argentine . . .* (Mendoza, in Argentina . . ,) is a serious indictment of political torture and exploitation of the indigenous population. Like *Ma'Déa*, a modernization of the Medea story set in Haiti, *Mendoza, en Argentine . . .* rises in tone to the level of Greek tragedy.

Manet's five novels may be classified in two groups. *Les Étrangers dans la ville* (Strangers in the City), *Un Cri sur le rivage*, and *Zone interdite* (Forbidden Territory), while varying widely in setting, all present panoramic accounts of society at times of great stress. *La Mauresque* (The Moorish Lady), and its sequel *L'Île au lézard vert* (The Island of the Green Lizard), are fictional autobiographies based on Manet's childhood experiences in Cuba.

—Phyllis Zatlin

———

MAR, Florentina del. *See* **CONDE, Carmen.**

———

MARAINI, Dacia. Italian. Born in Florence, 13 November 1936. Held in a concentration camp in Japan during World War II. Married 1) Alberto Moravia in 1963 (divorced); 2) Lucio Pozzi (divorced). Film director of *Conjugal Love*, 1970. Founder, Il Teatro La Maddalena feminist theatrical association, 1973. Recipient: Formentor prize, 1963; Saint Vincent prize, 1973; Riccione prize, 1975, 1976, 1978, 1981; Arta Terme prize, 1983; Freggene prize, 1985; Campiello prize, 1990; Calabria prize, 1991; Apollo prize, 1991; Quadrivio prize, 1991. Address: Via Beccaria 18, 00196 Rome, Italy.

PUBLICATIONS

Fiction

La vacanza. Milan, Lerici, 1962; as *The Holiday*, London, Weidenfeld and Nicolson, 1966.
L'età del malessere. Turin, Einaudi, 1963; as *The Age of Malaise*, New York, Grove Press, 1963; as *The Age of Discontent*, London, Weidenfeld and Nicolson, 1963.
A memoria. Milan, Bompiani, 1967.
Mio marito. Milan, Bompiani, 1968.
Memorie di una ladra. Milan, Bompiani, 1972; as *Memoirs of a Female Thief*, London, Abelard Schuman, 1973.
Donna in guerra. Turin, Einaudi, 1975; as *Woman at War*, London, Lighthouse, 1984; New York, Italica Press, 1988.
Lettere a Marina. Milan, Bompiani, 1981; as *Letters to Marina*, London, Camden Press, 1987; Freedom, California, Crossing Press, 1988.
Il treno per Helsinki. Turin, Einaudi, 1984; as *The Train*, London, Camden Press, 1989.
Isolina, la donna tagliata a pezzi. Milan, Mondadori, 1985.
La lunga vita di Marianna Ucrìa. Milan Rizzoli, 1990; as *The Silent Duchess*, London, Owen, 1992.

Plays

La famiglia normale (produced Italy, 1967). Included in *Il ricatto a teatro e altre commedie*, 1970.
Il ricatto a teatro (produced Italy, 1968). Included in *Il ricatto a teatro e altre commedie*, 1970.

Cuore di mamma (screenplay), with Salvatore Samperi. Milan, Forum, 1969.
Recitare (produced Italy, 1969). Included in *Il ricatto a teatro e altre commedie*, 1970.
Il manifesto dal carcere (produced Rome, 1969). As *Il manifesto*, in *Il ricatto a teatro e altre commedie*, 1970; as *Manifesto* (produced San Francisco, 1979).
Il ricatto a teatro e altre commedie (includes *La famiglia normale*; *Il ricatto a teatro*; *Recitare*; *Il manifesto*). Turin, Einaudi, 1970.
Centocelle, gli anni del fascismo (produced Rome, 1970s?). Included in *Fare teatro*, 1974.
Viva l'Italia (produced Italy, 1973?). Turin, Einaudi, 1973.
La donna perfetta (produced Venice, 1974). With *Il cuore di una vergine*, Turin, Einaudi, 1975.
Don Juan (produced Rome, 1977). Turin, Einaudi, 1976.
Dialogo di una prostituta con un suo cliente (produced Rome, 1978). Padua, Mastrogiacomo, 1978; as *Dialogue Between a Prostitute and One of Her Clients* (produced London, 1980); with *Giovanni Tenorio*, as *Sexual Acts* (produced Sydney, 1988).
Due donne di provincia (produced Rome, 1978). Included in *I sogni di Clitennestra e altre commedie*, 1981.
I sogni di Clitennestra (produced Prato, 1978). Included in *I sogni di Clitennestra e altre commedie*, 1981; as *The Dreams of Clitennestra* (produced New York, 1989).
Una casa di donne (produced Bologna, 1979). Included in *I sogni di Clitennestra e altre commedie*, 1981.
Suor Juana (produced Rome, 1980). Turin, La Rosa, 1980.
Dramma d'amore al Circo Bagno Balò (produced Rome, 1980s).
Maria Stuarda (produced Messina, 1980). Included in *I sogni di Clitennestra e altre commedie*, 1981; as *Mary Stuart* (produced London, 1984; Sydney, 1985).
Fede o della perversione matrimoniale (produced Italy, 1981?). Included in *I sogni di Clitennestra e altre commedie*, 1981.
I sogni di Clitennestra e altre commedie (includes *I sogni di Clitennestra*; *Due donne di provincia*; *Zena*; *Una casa di donne*; *Donna Lionora Giacubina*; *Maria Stuarda*; *Fede o della perversione matrimoniale*). Milan, Bompiani, 1981.
Mela (produced Ancona, 1982). Included in *Lezioni d'amore e altre commedie*, 1982.
Felice sciosciammocca (produced Italy, 1982). Included in *Lezioni d'amore e altre commedie*, 1982.
Lezioni d'amore. Included in *Lezioni d'amore e altre commedie*, 1982; as *Lesson in Love* (produced Melbourne).
Lezioni d'amore e altre commedie (includes *Lezioni d'amore*; *Felice sciosciammocca*; *Bianca garofani*; *Mela*). Milan, Bompiani, 1982.
Madre saginata (produced Rome, 1983). N.p., Ridotto, 1983.
Le figlie del colonello (produced Rome, 1985).
Netocka (produced Rome, 1986).
Norma '44 (produced Montevideo and Rome, 1986).
Stravaganza (produced Rome, 1987). Rome, Serarcangeli, 1987; in English (produced Canberra, 1988).
Delitio. Lungro, Marco, 1990.

Screenplays and Screen Adaptations: *Cuore di mamma*, with Salvatore Samperi, 1969; *Storia di Piera*, with Piera Degli Esposti and Marco Ferreri, 1983; *Sweet Movie*; *Solaris*; *La merlettaia*; *Trash*; *Anni di piombo*; *Paura e amore*; *Il futuro è donna*; *Il fiore delle mille e una notte*.

Radio Plays: *Mussomeli-Düsseldorf*, 1991 (Canada); *La sigaretta*.

Verse

Crudeltà all'aria aperta.   Milan, Feltrinelli, 1966.
Donne mie.   Turin, Einaudi, 1974.
Mangiami pure.   Turin, Einaudi, 1978; as *Devour Me Too*,
    Montreal, Guernica, 1987.
Dimenticato di dimenticare.   Turin, Einaudi, 1982.
Viaggiando con passo di volpe.   Milan, Rizzoli, 1991.

Other

E tu chi eri? interviste sull'infanzia.   Milan, Bompiani, 1973.
Fare teatro.   Milan, Bompiani, 1974.
Parlare con Dacia Maraini (interview), with Ileana Montini.
    Verona, Bertani, 1977.
Storia di Piera (interview), with Piera Degli Esposti.   Milan,
    Bompiani, 1980.
Il bambino Alberto, with Alberto Moravia.   Milan,
    Bompiani, 1986.
La bionda, la bruna e l'asino.   Milan, Rizzoli, 1987.
Uomo tatuato — Pomeriggio, with Giada Menichella.   Naples,
    Guida, 1990.
Fabio Rieti.   Milan, Appiani Arte Trentadue, 1991.
Sulla vecchiezza, with Alberto Oliverio and Eide
    Spedicato.   Chieti, Vecchio Faggio, 1991.

Editor, with Michiko Nojiri, *La protesta poetica del
    Giappone.*   Rome, Officina, 1968.

Translator, *Commedia ripugnante di una madre*, by Stanisław
    Ignacy Witkiewicz.   Rome, Bulzoni, 1970.

*

Critical Studies: "Dacia Maraini: From Alienation to Femi-
nism" by Augustus Pallotta, in *World Literature Today*
(Norman, Oklahoma), 58(3), 1984; "An Interview with Dacia
Maraini" by Grazia Weinberg, in *Tydskrif vir Letterkunde*
(Pretoria), 27(3), 1989.

*   *   *

Dacia Maraini is Italy's leading feminist creative writer.
Since 1962 when, at the age of 26 her first novel *La vacanza*
(*The Holiday*) was published, she has published 10 major
fictional works, five volumes of poetry, four volumes of plays,
a biographical collaboration with the actress Piera Degli
Esposti, an interview with Alberto Moravia, and a collection
of essays. She has also been active in the theatre; she ran the
Women's Theatre in Rome, Il Teatro Maddalena, and wrote
Fare teatro (Making Theatre); and she has contributed numerous essays to leading journals and to two sociological studies,
one on women prisoners (1969), the other on old age (1991).

In all her creative writing Maraini combines formal experiment with political analysis. Her poetry broke through the
dominant lyrical mode with a deliberately personal and
vigorous style very different from the cool, intellectual poetic
interrogations of the innovatory male poets of the "Gruppo 63,"
as exemplified in the dramatic analysis of her relationship with
her father in *Crudeltà all'aria aperta* (Cruelty in the Open Air);
her most famous play *Dialogo di una prostituta con un suo cliente*
(*Dialogue Between a Prostitute and One of Her Clients*)
combines moving drama with consciousness-raising when the
action pauses to allow discussion between audience and actors.

It is, however, as a novelist that Maraini has made her major

contribution both to modern Italian and to European feminist
literature. Her novels combine an analysis of a carefully
defined political period — for instance, the last phases of
Fascism in *The Holiday* — and the period after the industrial
boom in *Donna in guerra* (*Woman at War*), with an unremitting exposition of an androcentric society that marginalizes
and victimizes women. A writer who interrogates rather than
describes reality, Maraini draws her material from social
observations (*Memorie di una ladra* [*Memoirs of a Female
Thief*], for instance, was taken from her work on female
prisoners), which are filtered through her commitment to a
new socialism (a classless society which incorporates both
sexual equality and sexual difference) and a strong
coordinating imagination.

The most emblematic of the women victims in Maraini's
fiction is the absent heroine of the documentary novel *Isolina*,
subtitled *la donna tagliata a pezzi*, "the woman cut into
pieces." Maraini recreates the story of a young woman who
lived in Verona at the turn of the century, whose sawn-up body
was recovered from the Adige River, probably the victim of an
abortion attempt by her soldier-lover and his mates. Maraini's
attempts to document this story reveal not merely the invisibility of women, but their "invisibilization": Maraini's research led her to suggest that the army, in protecting its own,
denied both justice and memory to the female victim. Others
of Maraini's oppressed protagonists speak in their own voice:
Enrica in *L'età del malessere* (*The Age of Malaise* or *The Age of
Discontent*), Teresa Numa in *Memoirs of a Female Thief*,
Giovanna Magro in *Woman at War*, Bianca in *Lettere a Marina*
(*Letters to Marina*) are all first-person narratives, a technique
Maraini uses with consummate skill. This deliberately restrictive form of storytelling enables the writer both to include the
protagonist's personal viewpoint and to depict a panorama of
deprivation. It is most successful in *Memoirs of a Female Thief*
and *Woman at War*. In the former, a truly "choral picture of
the proletariat of women sufferers" (Bruce Merry, *Women in
Modern Italian Literature*, 1990), Maraini exposes through
Teresa Numa, the thief, the lives of the lower proletariat and
the appalling conditions of Italy's prisons in the 1970s, while
also celebrating through her lively storytelling Teresa's resilience, humour, personal ethics, and capacity for love. In
Woman at War the reader is privy to Giovanna's diary as she
records her odyssey towards self-knowledge and self-expression which takes her on a holiday island near Naples, where the
privileged, "the beautiful people," rub shoulders with the
people of the island, Naples itself, and the suburbs of Rome.
The passages where Giovanna records her visits to a
Neapolitan hospital, and the interrogation of a prison director
by the revolutionary group with which she has become
involved, are documentary essays in themselves in this ambitious and powerful novel, but they are nevertheless carefully
held within the first-person narration. Here, as elsewhere,
Maraini maintains a fine balance between exposing corrupt
capitalism and celebrating its victims, between documentary
accuracy and emblematic example.

Emblem is an important characteristic of Maraini's art of
communication. In the novel that won the Campiello prize in
1990, *La lunga vita di Marianna Ucrìa* (*The Silent Duchess*),
the protagonist is, unusually for Maraini, a member of the
aristocracy, destined either to marry and enrich the estate or to
become a nun. Set in Palermo and its environs in the first half
of the 18th century, and written in the third person, this novel
of an aristocratic deaf-mute woman who communicates by
messages written on a tiny desk affixed to her waist can be seen
as an emblem of the female condition. Meticulously researched and evocatively written, *The Silent Duchess* is a
testament to Maraini's seemingly inexhaustible capacity for

innovation and stylistic development. Each of her novels is a literary experiment, a new exploration of the art of narration.

Apart from the two early novels, *The Holiday* and *The Age of Discontent*, where the monotonous and repetitious style used to convey the alienation of the young protagonists runs into the danger of alienating the reader, Maraini's acute ear for the idiolects of her characters is one of her important contributions to Italian fiction and the modern Italian language. Her novels form part of the documentation of a developing national language that is no longer dominated by the conservative hold of the Tuscan literary tradition. By conveying in literary form the language of, for example, a woman thief, the young people of a left-wing revolutionary group, a prison officer, and a young car mechanic she has broadened the linguistic consciousness of her country. Here too sensitivity and ideology combine: authentic female speech includes neologisms and variants on traditional words as women work to describe their condition in a language they alter to make their own.

Maraini's writing has been compared to that of Alberto Moravia as contributor to the socially committed Italian post-war literature. It is important, however, also to see her as an important voice in what is becoming recognized as an Italian female narrative tradition. As others have pointed out, her writing can be seen as a development from that seminal early 20th-century text, *A Woman* by Sibilla Aleramo.

—Jennifer Lorch

MÁRQUEZ, Gabriel García. *See* **GARCÍA MÁRQUEZ, Gabriel.**

MARTÍN GAITE, Carmen. Spanish. Born in Salamanca, 8 December 1925. Educated at the University of Salamanca, licenciada in Roman philology 1949; University of Madrid, doctorate in history 1972. Married Rafael Sánchez-Ferlosio in 1953 (separated 1970); one son and one daughter (both deceased). Writer-in-residence, University of Virginia, Charlottesville, 1982. Recipient: Café Gijón prize, 1954; Nadal prize, 1958; National Literature prize, 1978; Anagrama essay prize, 1987; Booksellers' Guild Golden Book award, 1987. Address: c/o Editorial Anagrama, Calle Pedró de la Creau 58, 08034 Barcelona, Spain.

PUBLICATIONS

Fiction

El balneario.   Madrid, Afrodisio Aguado, 1954.
Entre visillos.   Barcelona, Destino, 1958; as *Behind the Curtains*, New York, Columbia University Press, 1990.
Las ataduras.   Barcelona, Destino, 1960.
Ritmo lento.   Barcelona, Seix Barral, 1963.

Retahílas.   Barcelona, Destino, 1974.
Fragmentos de interior.   Barcelona, Destino, 1976.
Cuentos completos.   Madrid, Alianza, 1978.
El cuarto de atrás.   Barcelona, Destino, 1978; as *The Back Room*, New York, Columbia University Press, 1983.
Nubosidad variable.   Barcelona, Anagrama, 1992.

Verse

A rachas.   Pamplona, Peralta, and Madrid, Ayuso, 1976.

Other

El proceso de Macanaz: historia de un empapelamiento. Madrid, Moneda y Crédito, 1969; as *Macanaz, otro paciente de la Inquisición*, Madrid, Taurus, 1975.
Usos amorosos del dieciocho en España.   Madrid, Siglo Veintiuno, 1972; as *Love Customs in 18th-Century Spain*, Berkeley, University of California Press, 1991.
La búsqueda de interlocutor y otras búsquedas.   Madrid, Nostromo, 1973.
El castillo de las tres murallas (for children).   Barcelona, Lumen, 1982.
El cuento de nunca acabar: apuntes sobre la narración, el amor y la mentira (includes fiction).   Madrid, Trieste, 1983.
El Conde de Guadalhorce: su época y su labor.   Madrid, Turner, 1983.
El pastel del diablo (for children).   Barcelona, Lumen, 1985.
Dos relatos fantásticos (includes *El castillo de las tres murallas* and *El pastel del diablo*) (for children).   Barcelona, Lumen, 1986.
Usos amorosos de la postguerra español.   Barcelona, Anagrama, 1987.
Desde la ventana: enfoque femenino de la literatura española. Madrid, Espasa-Calpe, 1987.
Lo que queda enterrado (for children).   London, Murray, 1987.
Caperusita Manhattan (for children).   Madrid, Siruela, 1990.

Editor, with Andrés Ruiz Tarazona, *Ocho siglos de poesía gallega: antología bilingüe*.   Madrid, Alianza, 1972.

*

Critical Studies: "*El balneario* by Carmen Martín-Gaite: Conceptual Aesthetics and 'l-étrange pur'," in *Journal of Spanish Studies: Twentieth Century*, 6, 1978, "A Fantastic Mirror: Technique and History in *El cuarto de atrás*," in *Anales de la Literatura Española Contemporánea* (Boulder, Colorado), 6, 1981, "The Nonconformist Character as Social Critic in the Novels of Carmen Martín-Gaite," in *Romance Quarterly* (Lexington, Kentucky), 28, 1981, "*Tiempo de silencio* and *Ritmo lento*: Pioneers of the New Social Novel in Spain," in *Hispanic Review* (Philadelphia), 50(1), 1982, "One Autobiography, Twice Told: Martín-Gaite's *Entre visillos* and *El cuarto de atrás*," in *Hispanic Journal* (Indiana, Pennsylvania), 7(2), 1986, *Secrets from the Back Room: The Fiction of Carmen Martín-Gaite*, University, Mississippi, Romance Monographs, 1987, "*El cuarto de atrás*: Metafiction and the Actualization of Literary Theory," in *Hispanófila* (Chapel Hill, North Carolina), 30(3), 1987, "The Challenge of Martín-Gaite's Woman Hero," in *Feminine Concerns in Contemporary Spanish Fiction by Women*, edited by Roberto Manteiga, Carolyn Galerstein, and Kathleen McNerney, Potomac, Maryland, Scripta Humanística, 1988, and "Carmen Martín-Gaite: Reaffirming the Pact Between Reader and Writer," in *Women Writers of Contemporary Spain: Exiles in* the Homeland, edited by Joan Lipman Brown, Cranbury, New Jersey, Associated University Presses, 1991, all by Joan Lipman Brown; "The Decoding and Encoding of Sex Roles in Carmen Martín-Gaite's Retahílas" by Elizabeth Ordóñez, in Romance Quarterly (Lexington, Kentucky), 27, 1980; From Fiction to Metafiction: Essays in Honor of Carmen Martín-Gaite, edited by Mirella Servodidio and Marcia L. Welles, Lincoln, Nebraska, Society of Spanish and Spanish-American Studies, 1983; "The Metafictional Codes of Don Julián versus the Metafictional Mode of El cuarto de atrás" by Robert C. Spires, in Revista Canadiense de Estudios Hispánicos, 7(2), 1983; "Shaping the Chaos: Carmen Martín-Gaite and the Never- Ending Tale," in International Fiction Review (Fredericton, New Brunswick), 11(1), 1984, and "Redeeming Loss: Reflections on Carmen Martín Gaite's The Back Room," in Revista de Estudios Hispánicos (Poughkeepsie, New York), 20(1), 1986, both by Ruth El Saffar; "Martín Gaite, Todorov and the Fantastic" by Kathleen Glenn, in The Scope of the Fantastic: Theory, Technique, Major Authors, Westport, Connecticut, Greenwood Press, 1985; "War as Rite of Passage in El cuarto de atrás" by Catherine Bellver, in Letras Femeninas (Lincoln, Nebraska), 12(1–2), 1986; "El cuarto de atrás as Autobiography" by Jean Chittenden, in Letras Femeninas (Lincoln, Nebraska), 12(1–2), 1986; "Ritual and Repression in Carmen Martín Gaite's Entre visillos" by Roxanne B. Marcus, in Studies in Honor of Gustavo Correa, Potomac, Maryland, Scripta Humanistica, 1986; "Never-Ending Story: Carmen Martín Gaite's The Back Room" by Debra A. Castillo, in PMLA (New York), 102(5), 1987; "Fragmentos de interior: Patterns and Pieces," in Hispanófila (Chapel Hill, North Carolina), 31(1), 1987, and Narrative Authority and Homeostasis in the Novels of Doris Lessing and Carmen Martín-Gaite, New York, Garland, 1990, both by Linda E. Chown; "Female Archetypes in Carmen Martín Gaite's Entre visillos" by Lynn K. Talbot, in Anales de la Literatura Española Contemporánea (Boulder, Colorado), 12(1–2), 1987; "Philologist, Scholar, Theorist, and Feminist," in Contemporary Women Writers of Spain, Boston, Hall, 1988, and "Plant Imagery and Feminine Dependency: Josefina Aldecoa, Carmen Martín-Gaite and Maria Antónia Oliver," in In the Feminine Mode: Essays on Hispanic Women Writers, edited by Noël Valis and Carol Maier, Cranbury, New Jersey, Associated University Presses, 1990, both by Janet Pérez; "Carmen Martín Gaite's A rachas: Dreams of the Past and Memories of the Future, Text[ure]s Woven of Many Colored Threads" by Margaret Persin, in Monographic Review/Revista Monográfica (Odessa, Texas), 6, 1990; "A palo seco by Carmen Martín Gaite: Metatheatrical Discourse and Creative Process" by Mirella Servodidio, in Anales de la Literatura Española Contemporánea (Boulder, Colorado), 15(1–3), 1990; "A Never-Ending Autobiography: The Fiction of Carmen Martín-Gaite" by Concha Alborg, in Redefining Autobiography in Twentieth-Century Women's Fiction: An Essay Collection, edited by Janice Morgan, Colette T. Hall, and Carol Snyder, New York, Garland, 1991; interview by Marie-Lise Gazarian Gautier, in Interviews with Spanish Writers, edited by Manuel Alvar, Elmwood Park, Illinois, Dalkey Archive Press, 1991.

*   *   *

Carmen Martín Gaite has always treated feminist themes, but her literary mode has changed from the neo-realist "social literature" of the 1950s and 1960s in Spain to one of literary and linguistic experimentation in the 1970s and thereafter. Fantasy, visible at times in Retahílas, and increasingly important in El cuarto de atrás, is not new in Martín Gaite's writing; her first major narrative, El balneario (The Spa), blends reality and fantasy in a Kafkaesque atmosphere with a protagonist,

the drab, middle-aged narrator Matilde, whose perceptions range from the hallucinatory to psychoneurotic before Martín Gaite finally opts for a realistic explanation by revealing that the entire narrative has been a dream. The surrealistic air of the isolated, decrepit hotel and bizarre behavior of other characters contrast starkly with the dull, conformist monotony of the frustrated spinster's bourgeois waking world.

Most of Martín Gaite's fiction centers on female characters, from adolescence through maturity, portraying both the social and psychological constraints repressing women under the patriarchal, conservative Franco regime. Regardless of the literary mode, the background (temporal and historical, socio-economic and politico-geographical) is resolutely realistic and rooted in autobiographical acquaintance and experience. By preference, the ambients painted are those of feminine experience, and thus frequently involve interiors and enclosed spaces — domestic enclosures which also serve the function of encloisterment and occasionally hint at imprisonment. Titles such as Entre visillos (Behind the Curtains), Las ataduras (The Bonds), Fragmentos de interior (Indoor Fragments), and El cuarto de atrás (The Back Room) are revealing of the encierro (harem-like existence) of Spanish women; significantly, perhaps, the only novel by Martín Gaite which features a male protagonist, Ritmo lento (Slow Motion), also involves enforced enclosure: the alienated, anguished intellectual is confined to an asylum for the mentally ill. One of this writer's essays speaks of the condición ventanera (window location) as typifying Spanish women of the period: they perceive life from the window — shut in and looking out — not as participants so much as spectators, an analogy which applies particularly to the several female characters in Behind the Curtains.

The Back Room, Martín Gaite's last major novel to date, and Behind the Curtains, her first long novel, both offer an authentic depiction of the life of girls growing up in the provincial, oppressive atmosphere of postwar Spain and thus have an especially significant autobiographical substrata. The characters and plot are fictitious in the earlier novel, which employs the visillos (curtains) as a symbol of entrapment for the feminine figures whose lives unfold behind them, bound by conventions not permitting them to pursue a career. In The Back Room, the guise of fiction is stripped away and real names and events appear. What is fictitious is the framing narrative, set in the present: the novelist's midnight meeting with a mysterious interviewer dressed in black; her recollections, sparked by the encounter, are memoir or autobiography, inserted within the novel. Martín Gaite's interest in history makes of this novel an informal treatise on feminine social and cultural history as well as a parody of the novela rosa (pulp romance) and fascinating meditation on literary creativity.

The novelette Las ataduras presents the plight of an intellectual young Spanish woman, the only daughter of schoolteachers, who manages through prolonged struggle to escape to attend the university, hoping to avoid the fate of "all decent Spanish women" — marriage and motherhood or the convent. Infatuated with a French professor, she runs away with him to Paris, only to end up an exhausted housewife with two small children, unmarried, in an unstable liaison, far from the support of her family. Many of Martín Gaite's short stories also emphasize the dilemma facing Spanish women under a regime which preferred not to educate them for careers, professions, or any independent existence, preparing them instead from an early age to live only for their husbands and children. The lack of liberty, boredom, and mental inertia to which females were thus condemned constitutes a recurring theme with numerous variations, and the other side of the coin — the desperation of the woman facing spinsterhood, the tedious routine of the elderly spinster — is a major sub- theme in Behind the Curtains.

Retahílas (Threads of Conversation), written in the last years of the dictatorship, presents an educated, middle-aged woman of some means who is separated from her husband (also the situation of the novelist at that time, although the plot is not autobiographical). While the novel foregrounds oral discourse and the near-magical powers of language to create, to rescue from oblivion, and to explore, the attentive reader must realize the plight of the protagonist, essentially condemned to living indefinitely in limbo (divorce did not exist in Spain under the Franco regime, and the married woman living apart from her husband did not escape social stigma). Eulalia is thus reduced to having little or nothing to do, few friends, and large amounts of time on her hands during a sweltering summer in Madrid. Impulsively dropping in on her grandmother (from whom she has been partially estranged), she finds the old woman on her deathbed and accedes to her request to take her back home to Galicia to die. When her brother declines to accompany her, her nephew takes his place; their nightlong conversation—or more precisely, parallel monologues—become the major focus of the novel, an oral revival of times past.

Martín Gaite's best-known novel, winner of the 1979 National prize for literature, *The Back Room* has been the favorite of critics and professional Hispanists. In addition to its recreation of the intrahistorical nuances of growing up female under the repressive, Fascist regime, the novel explores the creative process in true metaliterary fashion, providing a mosaic of intertextual references, drawn from literature and popular culture, at the same time that it undertakes a self-referential investigation of Todorov's theory of the fantastic, Martín Gaite's own prior writing, and a melange of contemporary critical theory.

Considerable coherence exists between this writer's fiction and her essays, as two major historical works, *Usos amorosos del dieciocho en España* (*Love Customs in 18th-Century Spain*) and *Usos amorosos de la postguerra español* (Love Customs of the Spanish Postwar Era) focus on male-female relationships, viewing the relevant social mores from a feminine perspective. Two other essay collections, *La búsqueda de interlocutor y otras búsquedas* (The Search for an Interlocutor and Other Searches) and *El cuento de nunca acabar* (The Never-Ending Tale) both center around her concern for the reader (or listener, as her narrative theory uses the oral storyteller and the interlocutor as essential building-blocks); for this reason, Martín Gaite's narrative style, as well as that of her essays, is not simply conversational but orally based, a masterful recreation of colloquial discourse whose intellectual profundity and literary sophistication belie its quotidian appearance.

—Janet Pérez

————

MATTHÍAS JOHANNESSEN. *See* **JOHANNESSEN, Matthías.**

————

MATUTE (Ausejo), Ana María. Spanish. Born in Barcelona, 26 July 1926. Educated at Damas Negras French Nuns College

and schools in Barcelona and Madrid. Married Ramón Eugenio de Goicoechea in 1952 (separated 1963); one son. Member of the Turia literary group, with Juan Goytisolo (*q.v.*) and others, Barcelona, 1951. Visiting Professor, Indiana University, Bloomington, 1965–66, and University of Oklahoma, Norman, 1969; writer-in-residence, University of Virginia, Charlottesville, 1978–79. Recipient: Café Gijón prize, 1952; Planeta prize, 1954; National Critics' prize, 1959; March Foundation grant, 1959; Cervantes prize, 1959; Nadal prize, 1960; Lazarillo prize, for children's writing, 1965; Fastenrath prize, 1969. Honorary Fellow, American Association of Teachers of Spanish and Portuguese; corresponding member, Hispanic Society of America, 1960. Address: Provenza, 84-At. 3A, Barcelona 29, Spain.

PUBLICATIONS

Fiction

Los Abel.   Barcelona, Destino, 1948.
Fiesta al noroeste.   Madrid, Aguado, 1953.
La pequeña vida.   Madrid, Prensa Española, 1953.
Pequeño teatro.   Barcelona, Planeta, 1954.
En esta tierra.   Barcelona, Exito, 1955.
Los cuentos, Vagabundos.   Barcelona, G.P., 1956.
Los niños tontos.   Madrid, Arion, 1956.
El tiempo.   Barcelona, Mateu, 1957.
Los hijos muertos.   Barcelona, Planeta, 1958; as *The Lost Children*, New York, Macmillan, 1965.
Los mercaderes:
   1. *Primera memoria.* Barcelona, Destino, 1959; as *Awakening*, London, Hutchinson, 1963; as *School of the Sun*, New York, Pantheon, 1963; London, Quartet, 1991.
   2. *Los soldados lloran de noche.* Barcelona, Destino, 1964.
   3. *La trampa.* Barcelona, Destino, 1969.
Tres y un sueño.   Barcelona, Destino, 1961.
A la mitad del camino.   Barcelona, Rocas, 1961.
Historias de la Artámila.   Barcelona, Destino, 1961.
El arrepentido.   Barcelona, Rocas, 1961.
El río.   Barcelona, Argos, 1963.
Algunos muchachos y otros cuentos.   Barcelona, Destino, 1968; as *The Heliotrope Wall and Other Stories*, New York, Columbia University Press, 1989.
La torre vigía.   Barcelona, Lumen, 1971.
Olvidado rey Gudu.   Barcelona, Lumen, 1980.
Diablo vuelve a casa.   Barcelona, Destino, 1980.
La vírgen de Antioquía y otros relatos.   Madrid, Mondadori, 1990.

Other

El país de la pizarra (for children).   Barcelona, Molino, 1957.
Paulina, el mundo, y las estrellas (for children).   Barcelona, Garbo, 1960.
El saltamontes verde; El aprendiz (for children).   Barcelona, Lumen, 1960.
Libro de juegos para los niños de los otros, photographs by Jaime Buesa.   Barcelona, Lumen, 1961.
Caballito loco; Carnavalito (for children).   Barcelona, Lumen, 1962.
El polizón del "Ulises" (for children).   Barcelona, Lumen, 1965.
Obra completa.   Barcelona, Destino, 5 vols., 1971–77.
Sólo un pie descalzo (for children).   Barcelona, Lumen, 1983.

Sino España. Madrid, Compañía Europa de Comunicación y Información, 1991.

Translator, *Frederick; Nadarín* (for children), by Leo Lionni. Barcelona, Lumen, 2 vols., 1986.

*

Critical Studies: "Antipathetic Fallacy: The Hostile World of Ana María Matute's Novels," in *Romance Quarterly* (Lexington, Kentucky), 13 (Supplement), 1967, and *The Literary World of Ana María Matute*, Lexington, University Press of Kentucky, 1970, both by Margaret E. W. Jones; *The World of Ana María Matute* by M. Weitzner, Lexington, University Press of Kentucky, 1970; *Ana María Matute* by Janet W. Díaz, New York, Twayne, 1971; "Forms of Alienation in Ana María Matute's *La trampa*" by Elizabeth Ordóñez, in *Journal of Spanish Studies: 20th Century*, 4, 1976; "Adolescent Friendship in Two Contemporary Spanish Novels" by Phyllis Zatlin-Boring, in *Hispanófila* (Chapel Hill, North Carolina), 60, 1977; "Retrospection as a Technique in Ana María Matute's *Los hijos muertos* and *En esta tierra*" by J. Townsend Shelby, in *Revista de Estudios Hispánicos* (Poughkeepsie, New York), 14(2), 1980; "Trace-Reading the Story of María/Matute in *Los mercaderes*" by Michael Scott Doyle, in *Revista de Estudios Hispánicos* (Poughkeepsie, New York), 19(2), 1985; "Privation in Ana María Matute's Fiction for Children," in *Symposium* (Washington, D.C.), 39(2), 1985, "Codes of Exclusion, Modes of Equivocation: Ana María Matute's *Primera memoria*," in *Ideologies and Literature* (Minneapolis), 1(1–2), 1985, and "Stranger than Fiction: Fantasy in Short Stories by Matute, Rodoreda, Riera," in *Monographic Review/Revista Monográfica* (Odessa, Texas), 4, 1988, all by Geraldine Cleary Nichols; "*Los hijos muertos*: The Spanish Civil War as a Perpetrator of Death" by Eunice D. Myers, in *Letras Femeninas* (Lincoln, Nebraska), 12(1–2), 1986; "From Freedom to Enclosure: 'Growing Down' in Ana María Matute's *Primera memoria*" by Lucy Lee-Bonanno, in *Kentucky Philological Review* (Highland Heights), 13, 1986; "Notes of Hans Christian Andersen Tales in Ana María Matute's *Primera memoria*" by Suzanne Gross Reed, in *Continental, Latin-American and Francophone Women Writers*, edited by Eunice D. Myers and Ginette Adamson, Lanham, Maryland, University Press of America, 1987; "Two Mourners for the Human Spirit: Ana María Matute and Flannery O'Connor" by Mary S. Vásquez, in *Monographic Review/Revista Monográfica* (Odessa, Texas), 4, 1988.

*   *   *

Ana María Matute has written a number of major prize-winning novels as well as collections of short stories and fiction for children. Her major emphasis concerns the process of growing up and the loss of illusion and innocence by anguished adolescents who seek in vain for love and beauty in an ugly and terrifying adult world. Fusing fantasy and reality, Matute paints a portrait of a materialistic, petrified Spain, filled with social and ethical problems and victimized by fratricidal strife, but she evinces great maternal tenderness toward alienated orphan children.

In many of her novels Matute deforms nature to reflect the fatalistic elements of a hateful, violent world and its citizens. At times she affects an involuted, baroque style; at others she overwhelms the reader with a rich and delicate sensory imagery. She uses interior monologue, flashbacks, first-person narrative, free association, and temporal jumps, fusing subjective lyricism with committed literature much as she dichotomizes and coalesces fantasy and reality.

In an early novelette, *Fiesta al noroeste* (Celebration in the Northeast), an excellent psychological analysis of the all-powerful local overlord, Juan Midinao, she exposes the hypocrisy of traditional Spanish values and explores the need for freedom from political oppression, the Cain-Abel theme, the plight of brutalized children, and existential loneliness and inability to communicate.

Los hijos muertos (*The Lost Children*), her most complex and ambitious novel, deals with the generation gap, the tragic legacy of the Spanish Civil War, and the lack of love and charity. The protagonist, Daniel Corvo, loses his life, like so many others in his idealistic generation which dreams of justice in the face of a repressive, decadent, and sterile tradition.

Primera memoria (*School of the Sun*), the first volume of the trilogy *Los mercaderes* (The Merchants), achieved an even greater critical acclaim. Matia, the young protagonist, loses her innocence, remaining silent in the face of injustice. In the second volume the merchants of this world continue to exploit others, and Manuel, a victim earlier of adult hypocrisy, fruitlessly sacrifices himself in the last days of the civil war. Bourgeois mentality, fear, and hatred continue in the final volume, set some 30 years later. Matia, guilt-ridden, betrayed by those she loved, nonetheless hopes for the future even in a degraded world of sexual repression which denies woman her moral and psychological liberty.

In *La torre vigía* (The Look-Out Tower), Matute abandons the civil war, its aftermath and consequences, and retreats in time to the Middle Ages. Utilizing a mixture of reality and fantasy, she creates a magical, sensual setting for a young apprentice whose experiences in his quest to become a knight serve as a kind of allegory.

Typical of Matute's many short-story collections, *Historias de la Artámila* (Stories from the Artámila) contains sketches of childhood, real and imagined, in a fantasy town between the Pyrenees and the Ebro. Her everyday scenes do not disguise the existential isolation found in an unjust world.

Matute's protagonists, trapped by time, unable to communicate, often dream of a lost Paradise. But the author's world of oppressed children lacks Christian charity, and sooner or later, abandoning fantasy, they must react to false values and lack of comprehension and learn to explore the disparate values of a brutalized and tragic world.

—Kessel Schwartz

———

MAURIAC, Claude. French. Born in Paris, 25 April 1914; son of the writer François Mauriac. Educated at Lycée Janson-de-Sailly; University of Paris, doctorate in law, 1943. Married Marie-Claude Mante in 1951; two sons and one daughter. Private secretary to de Gaulle, 1944–49; founding director, *Liberté de l'Esprit* magazine, Paris, 1949–53; critic and columnist ("La Vie des Lettres"), *Le Figaro*, Paris, 1946–77, and film critic, *Figaro Littéraire*, 1947–72; film critic, *Vendredi Samedi Dimanche*, Paris, from 1977; columnist, *Matin*, from 1986. Recipient: Sainte Beuve prize, 1949; Medicis prize, 1959. Officier, Légion d'Honneur. Address: 24 Quai de Béthune, 75004 Paris, France.

PUBLICATIONS

Fiction

Le Dialogue intérieur:
  Toutes les femmes sont fatales.   Paris, Michel, 1957; as *All Women Are Fatal*, New York, Braziller, 1964; as *Femmes fatales*, London, Calder and Boyars, 1966.
  Le Dîner en ville.   Paris, Michel, 1959; as *The Dinner Party*, New York, Braziller, 1960; as *Dinner in Town*, London, Calder, 1963.
  Le Marquise sortit à cinq heures.   Paris, Michel, 1961; as *The Marquise Went Out at Five*, New York, Braziller, 1962; London, Calder and Boyars, 1967.
  L'Agrandissement.   Paris, Michel, 1963.
Les Infiltrations de l'invisible:
  L'Oubli.   Paris, Grasset, 1966.
  Le Bouddha s'est mis à trembler.   Paris, Grasset, 1979.
  Un Coeur tout neuf.   Paris, Grasset, 1980.
  Radio nuit.   Paris, Grasset, 1982.
  Zabé.   Paris, Gallimard, 1984.
  Trans-amour-étoiles.   Paris, Grasset, 1989.

Plays

La Conversation (produced Paris, 1966).   Paris, Grasset, 1964.
Les Parisiens du dimanche (produced Montreal, 1967). Included in *Théâtre*, 1968.
Ici, maintenant (produced Paris, 1971).   Included in *Théâtre*, 1968.
Le Cirque (produced Paris, 1982).   Included in *Théâtre*, 1968.
Théâtre (includes *La Conversation*; *Ici, maintenant*; *Le Cirque*; *Les Parisiens du dimanche*; *Le Hun*).   Paris, Grasset, 1968.

Screenplays: *Les Sept Péchés capitaux* (*The Seven Deadly Sins*), with others, 1962; *Thérèse*, with François Mauriac and Georges Franju, 1963.

Other

Introduction à une mystique de l'enfer.   Paris, Grasset, 1938.
La corporation dans l'état.   Bordeaux, Bière, 1941.
Aimer Balzac.   Paris, Table Ronde, 1945.
Jean Cocteau; ou, La Vérité du mensonge.   Paris, Lieutier, 1945.
La Trahison d'un clerc.   Paris, Table Ronde, 1945.
Malraux; ou, Le Mal du héros.   Paris, Grasset, 1946.
André Breton: essai.   Paris, Flore, 1949.
Conversations avec André Gide: extraits d'un journal.   Paris, Michel, 1951; revised edition, 1990; as *Conversations with André Gide*, New York, Braziller, 1965.
Hommes et idées d'aujourd'hui.   Paris, Michel, 1953.
Marcel Proust par lui-même.   Paris, Seuil, 1953.
L'Amour du cinéma.   Paris, Michel, 1954.
Petite Littérature du cinéma.   Paris, Cerf, 1957.
L'Alittérature contemporaine.   Paris, Michel, 1958; revised edition, 1969; as *The New Literature*, New York, Braziller, 1959.
De la Littérature à l'alittérature.   Paris, Grasset, 1969.
Une Amitié contrariée.   Paris, Grasset, 1970.
Un Autre de Gaulle: journal 1944–1954.   Paris, Hachette, 1971; as *Aimer de Gaulle*, Paris, Grasset, 1978; as *The Other de Gaulle: Diaries 1944–1954*, New York, Day, and London, Angus and Robertson, 1973.

Le Temps immobile:
  1. *Le Temps immobile*.   Paris, Grasset, 1974.
  2. *Les Espaces imaginaires*.   Paris, Grasset, 1975.
  3. *Et Comme l'Espérance est violente*.   Paris, Grasset, 1976.
  4. *La Terrasse de Malagar*.   Paris, Grasset, 1977.
  5. *Aimer de Gaulle*.   Paris, Grasset, 1978.
  6. *Le Rire des pères dans les yeux des enfants*.   Paris, Grasset, 1981.
  7. *Signes, rencontres, et rendez-vous*.   Paris, Grasset, 1983.
  8. *Bergère ô tour Eiffel*.   Paris, Grasset, 1985.
  9. *Mauriac et fils*.   Paris, Grasset, 1986.
  10. *L'Oncle Marcel*.   Paris, Grasset, 1988.
Une Certaine Rage.   Paris, Laffont, 1977.
L'Éternité parfois.   Paris, Belfond, 1978.
Laurent Terzieff.   Paris, Stock, 1980.
Qui peut le dire?   Lausanne, l'Age d'Homme, 1985.
François Mauriac, sa vie, son œuvre.   Paris, Birr, 1985.
Le Temps accompli.   Paris, Grasset, 1991.

Editor, *Proust*.   Paris, Seuil, 1953.

*

Critical Studies: "Structure in the Novels of Claude Mauriac" by S. Johnston, in *French Review 38*, February 1965; "Silence as an Element of Dialogue in Claude Mauriac's *L'Agrandissement*" by Sandra M. Boschetto, in *International Fiction Review* (Fredericton, New Brunswick), 7, 1980.

* * *

Writing in the limelight of the fascinating problems and techniques underscored by the French New Novel, and by the 20th-century novel in general, Claude Mauriac is largely concerned in his work with the conception and incubation of creative inspiration, along with the dilemma of choice resulting from the infringement of multiple subject-matter upon any delimitation of time and space. Beyond the ontological, psychological, and moral planes, Mauriac measures his art against metaphysical dimensions. For Mauriac communication has become buried under an almost unsupportable burden of self-consciousness. Language is experienced not merely as something shared but as something corrupted, weighted down by historical accumulation. There is a devaluation of language and character in Mauriac's work. Characters who in the hands of former writers had some fictional relief now lose artistic dimension.

In his tetralogy, titled significantly *Le Dialogue intérieur*, Mauriac examines silence as an element of dialogue, of communication and knowledge. Silence for Mauriac is merely the furthest extension of that reluctance to communicate, that ambivalence about making contact with an audience or a character, which is a leading motif of modern art, with its tireless commitment to the new and esoteric. *L'Agrandissement* (The Enlargement or The Blow-Up, a term borrowed from photography) is the last novel of the series, which, like the preceding ones, is *nouveau* by virtue of its technical similarities with the work of Nathalie Sarraute and Michel Butor (*qq.v.*), among others. But in *L'Agrandissement* Mauriac becomes for the first time a pioneer by writing what may be described as an essay on the novel in the form of a novel. The tetralogy has been compared to Samuel Beckett's trilogy (*Molloy, Malone Dies, The Unnamable*) in the single respect that each succesive novel narrows the scope allowed to its predecessor. In Beckett's series there is a progressive constriction of space and number of characters; in Mauriac's, the narrowing affects only time. *L'Agrandissement* is not only an absorbing picture of a novelist's mind at work and a fascinating commentary on the three preceding novels, but an entertainment full of humorous quirks. To indicate that it forms an uninterrupted interior monologue, the book, although conventionally punctuated, consists of a single enormous paragraph — some 200 pages in length!

Mauriac, borrowing from the New Novelists, is concerned primarily with art and fiction as means of grasping reality. He is preoccupied with depicting a reality consisting of simultaneous thoughts, spoken words, and tacit communication. As an introverted essayist and literary theorist who disguises his form as "novelistic," Mauriac prefigures what some critics have recently observed: that most art in our time has been experienced by audiences as a move into silence, unintelligibility, invisibility, or inaudibility.

—Sandra Maria Boschetto-Sandoval

MELO NETO, João Cabral de. Brazilian. Born in Recife, 9 January 1920. Married Stella Barbosa de Oliveira in 1947. Entered diplomatic service, 1945: posts in Spain, England, and Switzerland; dismissed, 1952, but reinstated; administrative officer in Ministry of Agriculture, from 1960. Recipient: Anchieta prize, 1954; Brazilian Academy of Letters prize, 1955. Member, Brazilian Academy of Letters, 1969. Address: Ministry of Agriculture, Esplanada dos Minesterios, Block D, 8th Floor, 70043 Brasilia D.F., Brazil.

PUBLICATIONS

Verse

Pedro do sono.   Privately printed, 1942.
O engenheiro.   Rio de Janeiro, Amigos da Poesia, 1945.
Psicologia da composição, com a Fábula de Anfion e Antiode.   Barcelona, O Livro Inconsútil, 1947.
O ção sem plumas.   Privately printed, 1950.
Poemas reunidos.   Rio de Janeiro, Orfeu, 1954.
O Rio.   São Paulo, Comissão do IV Centenário da Cidade de São Paulo, 1954.
Pregão turístico.   Recife, Magalhães, 1955.
Duas águas.   Rio de Janeiro, Olympio, 1956.
Aniki Bobó.   Recife, Magalhães, 1958.
Quaderna 1956–1959.   Lisbon, Guimarães, 1960.
Dois parlamentos 1958–1960.   Privately printed, 1961.
Terceira feira.   Rio de Janeiro, Editôra do Autor, 1961.
Poemas escolhidos.   Lisbon, Portugalia, 1963.
Antologia poética.   Rio de Janeiro, Editôra do Autor, 1963; revised edition, Rio de Janeiro, Sabiá, 1967, 1973.
Morte e vida severina.   São Paulo, Teatro da Universidade Católica de São Paulo, 1965.
A educacão pela pedra.   Rio de Janeiro, Editôra do Áutor, 1966.
Morte e vida severina, e outros poemas em voz alta.   Privately printed, 1966; revised edition, Rio de Janeiro, Sabiá, 1967, 1973.
The Rebounding Stone, translated by A. B. M. Cadaxa.   London, Outposts, 1967.

Funeral de um lavrador.   São Paulo, Musical Arlequim, 1967.
Poesias completas 1940–1965.   Rio de Janeiro, Sabiá, 1968; revised edition, 1975, 1979.
Museu de tudo: poesia 1966–74.   Rio de Janeiro, Olympio, 1975.
A escola das facas.   Rio de Janeiro, Olympio, 1980.
Poesia crítica: antologia.   Rio de Janeiro, Olympio, 1982.
Auto do frade: poema para vozes.   Rio de Janeiro, Olympio, 1984.
O cão sem plumas, photographs by Maureen Bisilliat.   Rio de Janeiro, Nova Fronteira, 1984.
Os melhores poemas (selection).   São Paulo, Global, 1985.
Agrestes: poesia (1981–1985).   Rio de Janeiro, Nova Fronteira, 1986.
Poesia completa 1940–1980.   Lisbon, Imprensa Nacional-Casa de Moeda, 1986.
Crime na calle Relator.   Rio de Janeiro, Nova Fronteira, 1987.
Poemas pernambucanos.   Rio de Janeiro, Nova Fronteira, 1988.
Museu de tudo e depois (1967–1987).   Rio de Janeiro, Nova Fronteira, 1988.
Sevilha andando.   Rio de Janeiro, Nova Fronteira, 1989.

English translations of his poetry published in *Modern Brazilian Poetry* edited by John Nist, Bloomington, Indiana University Press, 1962, and *An Anthology of Twentieth Century Brazilian Poetry* edited by Elizabeth Bishop, Middletown, Connecticut, Wesleyan University Press, 1972.

Other

Joan Miró.   Barcelona, Edicions de 10c, 1950.
O arquivo das Índias e o Brasil.   Rio de Janeiro, Min. de Relacões Exteriores, 1966.
Poesa e composição: a inspiração e o trabalho de arte.   Coimbra, Fenda, 1982.

*

Critical Studies: in *Tongues of Fallen Angels* by Selden Rodman, New York, New Directions, 1974; "Sleep, Poetry and João Cabral's 'False Book': A Revaluation of *Pedra do sono*" by John A. Gledson, in *Bulletin of Hispanic Studies* (Liverpool), 55, 1977; "An Allegorical Interpretation of João Cabral de Melo Neto's *Morte e vida severina*" by Jon M. Tolman, in *Hispania* (Los Angeles), 61, 1977; "The Geography-Anatomy Metaphor in João Cabral de Melo Neto's *Morte e vida severina*" by Paul B. Dixon, in *Chasqui* (Provo, Utah), 11(1), 1981; "João Cabral: From Pedra to Pedra" by Stephen Reckert, in *Portuguese Studies* (London), 2, 1986; "João Cabral de Melo Neto: An Engineer of Poetry" by Richard Zenith, in *Latin American Literary Review* (Pittsburgh), 15(30), 1987; "Cabral de Melo Neto's English Poets" by Ashley Brown, in *World Literature Today* (Norman, Oklahoma), 65(1), 1991.

*   *   *

As the acknowledged leader of the Generation of 1945, João Cabral de Melo Neto began by reacting against the verbosity, vehemence, and ethnocentrism of the 1922 Modernists; he was, however, strongly influenced by two older Brazilian poets, Manuel Bandeira and Carlos Drummond de Andrade, as well as by Marianne Moore and Paul Valéry. His first collection of verse, *Pedra do sono*, contained highly personal and frequently surrealistic poems based primarily upon free association.

During the next five years, Melo Neto moved rather rapidly towards a quite different poetic stance, striving to create a new theory of the poetic process and to describe and exemplify that theory in his works. As the title of his 1945 book, *O engenheiro* (The Engineer), suggests, he defined poetry as an intensely conscious and self-conscious enterprise, in which all personal associations and all traditional poetic connotations are painstakingly chiseled off the surfaces of every word, revealing the Platonic essence — the elemental force whose expression is the word's paramount function; these basic building-blocks of discourse are then carefully arranged in patterns designed, as Melo Neto put it, to recreate "the indifferent perfection of geometry, like magazine reproductions of Mondrian, seen from a distance."

Melo Neto was very much aware, however, that this kind of intellectualized poetic minimalism could lead to an amoral, socially exclusive hermeticism; his physical isolation from the reality of Brazilian life during his years of diplomatic service abroad may well have intensified his disquiet about an ivory-tower aesthetics far removed from the dust-dry landscapes and the overcrowded shanty towns and cemeteries of his ancestral and spiritual homeland, the Brazilian Northeast. One result of this preoccupation is Melo Neto's best-known work, *Morte e vida severina*, a verse drama drawn from Northeastern folk traditions. He has attemped to synthesize minimalist aesthetics and social consciousness in other ways, however, and his efforts have provided important models for a number of younger Brazilian poets.

The basis fo synthesis, as Melo Neto sees it, is the image and the reality of the stone. His own "Education by Stone," his effort to strip away superficiality of thought and discourse in order to reach the elemental, simply parallels a process which occurs naturally and inevitably among the poorest inhabitants of the Northeast's barren and stony landscapes: "you don't learn the stone, there; there, the stone/born stone, penetrates the soul." As a result of this convergence through the stone, the painfully purified language of the poet and the painfully experienced life of the Northeastern peasant meet on common ground, and both identification and communication are possible:

> That's why the man from up-country says little:
> the stone words ulcerate the mouth
> and it hurts to speak in the stone language;
> those to whom it's native speak by main force.
> Furthermore, that's why he speaks slowly:
> he has to take up the words carefully,
> he has to sweeten them with his tongue, candy them;
> well, all this work takes time.

—David T. Haberly

MEMMI, Albert. Tunisian. Born in Tunis, 15 December 1920. Educated at the Lycée Carnot, Tunis; University of Algiers, Licence ès philosophie 1943; L'École Pratique des Hautes Études, Paris, Docteur ès lettres 1970. Interned in a labour camp during World War II (1942–43). Married Germaine Dubach in 1946; two sons and one daughter. Teacher at a technical college, from 1949; philosophy teacher, Lycée Carnot, Tunis, 1953–56; director, Center of Educational Research, Tunis, 1953–57; researcher, National Center of Scientific Research, Paris, 1957; maître de conférence, École Pratique des Hautes Études, Paris, from 1958 Since 1958 Professor of cultural studies, l'École des Hautes Études Commerciales, Paris; maître de conférence, 1970, then Professor of sociology, University of Paris, Nanterre; Walker Ames Professor, University of Seattle, Washington, 1972. Vice-president, PEN (France), 1976–79, and International Federation of Francophone Writers, 1985. Recipient: Carthage prize, 1953; Fénéon prize, 1954; Simba prize; Commandeur de l'Ordre de Nichan Iftikhar (Tunisia); Officier de la Légion d'Honneur; Officier de l'Ordre de la République Tunisienne, 1984; Officier de l'Ordre des Arts et des Lettres; Officier des Palmes Académiques. Address: 5 rue St. Merri, 75004 Paris, France.

PUBLICATIONS

Fiction

La Statue de sel.   Paris, Corréa, 1953; as *The Pillar of Salt*, New York, Criterion, 1955; London, Elek, 1956.
Agar.   Paris, Corréa 1955; as *Strangers*, London, Elek, 1958; New York, Orion Press, 1960.
Le Scorpion, ou, La Confession imaginaire.   Paris, Gallimard, 1969; as *The Scorpion, or, The Imaginary Confession*, New York, Grossman, 1971.
Le Désert; ou, La Vie et les aventures de Jubaïr Ouali El-Mammi.   Paris, Gallimard, 1977.
Le Pharaon.   Paris, Julliard, 1988.

Verse

Le Mirliton du ciel.   Paris, Julliard, 1990.

Other

Portrait du colonisé, précédé du Portrait du colonisateur.   Paris, Buchet/Chastel, 1957; revised edition, Montreal, L'Étincelle, 1972; as *The Colonizer and the Colonized*, New York, Orion Press, 1965; London, Souvenir Press, 1974.
Portrait d'un juif (includes *L'Impasse*; *La Libération d'un juif*).   Paris, Gallimard, 2 vols., 1962; as *Portrait of a Jew*, New York, Orion Press, 1962; London, Eyre and Spottiswood, 1963; vol. 2 published separately as *The Liberation of the Jew*, Orion Press, 1966.
Les Français et le racisme, with Paul Hassan Maucorps and J. F. Held.   Paris, Payot, 1965.
L'Homme dominé.   Paris, Gallimard, 1968; as *Dominated Man: Notes Towards a Portrait*, New York, Orion Press, 1968.
Juifs et arabes.   Paris, Gallimard, 1974; as *Jews and Arabs*, Chicago, J. Philip O'Hara, 1975.
Albert Memmi: un entretien avec Robert Davies, suivi de Itinéraire de l'expérience vécue à la théorie de la domination (interview).   Montreal, Réedition Québec, 1975.
La Terre intérieure: entretiens avec Victor Malka (interviews).   Paris, Gallimard, 1976.
La Dépendance: esquisse pour un portrait du dépendant.   Paris, Gallimard, 1979; as *Dependence*, Boston, Beacon Press, 1984.
Le Racisme: description, définition, traitement.   Paris, Gallimard, 1982.
Ce que je crois.   Paris, Grasset, 1985.

L'Écriture colorée, ou, Je vous aime en rouge.   Paris, Périple, 1986.

Editor, *La Poèsie algérienne de 1830 à nos jours: approche socio-historique*, by Jean Dejeux.   Paris, Mouton, 1963.

Editor, *Anthologie des écrivains maghrébins d'expression française*.   Paris, Présence Africaine, 2 vols., 1964; revised edition, Paris, La Haye, 1965.

Editor, *Bibliographie de la littérature nord-africaine d'expression française, 1945–1962*, by Jacqueline Arnaud.   Paris, Mouton, 1965.

Editor, *Écrivains Francophones du Maghreb*.   Paris, Seghers, 1985.

*

Critical Studies: "The Zionism of Albert Memmi" by Mitchell Cohen, in *Midstream*, November 1978; "Memmi's Introduction to History: *Le Désert* as Folktale, Chronicle and Biography," in *Philological Quarterly* (Iowa City), Spring 1982, and *Albert Memmi*, Philadelphia, Revue Celfan/Celfan Review, 1987, both by Judith Roumani; "Du *Scorpion* au *Désert*: Albert Memmi Revisited," in *STCL*, Fall 1982, and "Ethics and Aesthetics in Albert Memmi's *Le Scorpion*," in *Africana Journal*, 13(1–4), 1982, both by Isaac Yetiv.

* * *

While Tunisia's contribution to North African Francophone literature has been less extensive than that of Algeria and Morocco, it has in Albert Memmi a writer who not only played a key role in initiating that literature but has been ever since a distinguished participant in intellectual and cultural debate in both the Maghreb and beyond. While Memmi eventually left Tunisia for France, his career as a university researcher in sociology was in no way to prove at odds with his creative writing. The issues that are dominant in his published studies of social behaviour, identity, and racism have also informed his novels. Indeed it was in works of fiction that they first received expression, Memmi declaring in *France-Observateur* in 1959 that: "Seule la forme romanesque . . . semble assez riche pour exprimer, pour permettre de rendre compte de l'extraordinaire richesse de l'aventure humaine" (only the novel form . . . seems rich enough to express, to permit an account of the extraordinary richness of the human adventure).

Memmi's highly acclaimed first novel, *La Statue de sel* (*The Pillar of Salt*), published in 1953 and therefore one of the earliest novels written in French by a Maghrebian, already shows Memmi's preference for using autobiographical material as a springboard for fictional elaboration. In type it is a *bildungsroman*, with the narrator, Benillouche, relating his development from early childhood in Tunis until his departure to South America as a young man and including the standard ingredients of family influences, education, sexual initiation, and gradual discovery of the wider world. The particular interest of Memmi's text comes from the specific nature of those ingredients, for Benillouche's situation (mirroring Memmi's) is unusually complex. He is an *acculturé*, a native North African who is accorded the privilege of a French-style education but then finds himself rejected by the country with whose language and culture he has come to identify.

Memmi's sympathetic but lucid portrayal of the *acculturé* was to be echoed in many later novels by North African writers, but another dimension of Benillouche's situation found fewer imitators. For Benillouche is also a Jew and, given the traditional hostility of Muslim to Jew, feels endangered even within his Tunisian identity. Eventually Benillouche's quest becomes one of establishing for himself what constitutes identity, and it is noticeable that in evaluating his experiences he highlights the satisfaction of the senses, thus contesting the tendency of Western civilization to privilege the intellect. This enables Memmi to offer a very original view of Jewishness. The writing of *The Pillar of Salt* had, Memmi claims in *Portrait d'un Juif* (*Portrait of a Jew*), been motivated by his reading of Jean-Paul Sartre's *Réflexions sur la question juive* (Reflections on the Jewish Question) which argues that there is no such thing as Jewish identity and that the Jew is only invented by others. Memmi uses *The Pillar of Salt* to affirm that Jewishness does exist, but he sets out to show that it is not determined by Judaism but is instead a psychological reality deriving from a particular way of relating to the physical world.

The novels that followed *The Pillar of Salt* varied considerably in type and quality. *Agar* was also based on autobiographical material but was narrower in scope, concentrating on the marriage of a North African Jew to a Protestant Frenchwoman that founders because of their failure to reconcile their different ways of relating to the world. Neither *The Pillar of Salt* nor *Agar* reveals any of the interest in experimentation with form that was evident in other North African writers of the 1950s, and it was therefore a new departure for Memmi when, in his third novel *Le Scorpion* (*The Scorpion*), he rejected conventional linear narration for a polyphonic structure combining different kinds of subject-matter, narrative manner, and typography. *The Scorpion* becomes a meditation not only on the nature of reality but also on that of literature. Memmi even suggests that the most appropriate method of writing the book would have been to use different inks for the different sections (an idea later elaborated in the essay *L'Écriture colorée* [Coloured Writing]).

Memmi's remaining two novels have moved further away from autobiographical inspiration. The historical tale *Le Désert* (The Desert) seeks to recreate the distant past of North Africa although continuing Memmi's search for roots since the narrator is one El-Mammi. The novel depicts the fatuity of conquest, since empires rise only to fall in their own turn, and suggests that the only worthwhile dominion is over self. *Le Désert* is, however, a somewhat colourless tale with characters of little substance, underlining Memmi's need for the stimulus of personal experience for his fiction.

His most recent novel, *Le Pharaon* (The Pharaoh), shows a return to 20th-century North Africa, although the central character is not obviously a mirror-image of Memmi. There is a degree of reference to contemporary political events not attempted by Memmi since *The Pillar of Salt*'s evocation of the impact of World War II on North Africa. *Le Pharaon* sets the romantic involvement of its central figure against the background of the 1950s' decolonisation struggles in the Maghreb. Memmi raises some interesting questions about literary realism as his cast of characters combines fictional figures with real-life personalities from the forefront of French and North African politics.

Memmi's contribution to North African Francophone literature goes beyond his own novelistic production. He has published two useful anthologies, one of native-born Maghrebian writers and the other of French-born writers who have written about the Maghreb, and, as an insider, comments illuminatingly on the works of both groups. He has also, with his academic career drawing to a close, found more time for a side interest, poetry. *Le Mirliton du ciel* (Heaven's Kazoo), a mixture of poems, anecdotes, and philosophical reflections, is a joyful celebration of Tunisia, affections, the physical world, things Jewish and — surprisingly, in view of Memmi's earlier lack of interest — God.

—Carys Owen

———

MIHALIĆ, Slavko. Croatian. Born in Karlovac, in 1928. Journalist and writer; founder, *Tribina* and *Knjižena tribina* literary journals; editor, *Telegram*; currently chief editor, *Forum* literary journal. Address: c/o Prosveta, Dobračina 30, 11000 Belgrade, Serbia.

PUBLICATIONS

Verse

Komorna muzika [Chamber Music]. 1954.
Put u nepostojanje [Road into Non-Existence]. Zagreb, Lykos, 1956.
Početak zaborava [Beginning of Oblivion]. Zagreb, Mala, 1957.
Darežljivo progonstvo [Generous Exile]. Zagreb, Lykos, 1959.
Ljubav za stvarnu zemlju [Love for the Real Land]. Zagreb, Mala, 1964.
Prognana balada [Exiled Ballad]. Kruševac, Bagdala, 1965.
Izabrane pjesme [Selected Poems]. Zagreb, Matica Hrvatska, 1966; revised edition, Matica Hrvatska, 1980.
Posljednja večera [Last Supper]. Zagreb, Kolo, 1969.
Vrt crnih jabuka [Orchard of Black Apples]. Zagreb, Studenski Centar Sveučilišta, 1972.
Krčma na vogalu [Inn on the Corner]. Trieste, Zalažništvo Tržaškega Tiska, 1974.
Djevojčica i pjesma [Girl and Poem]. Zagreb, Naprijed, 1975.
Klopka za uspomene [A Trap for Memories]. Zagreb, Znanje, 1977.
Pohvala praznom džepu [Praise of an Empty Pocket]. Zagreb, SNL, 1981.
Atlantida [Atlantis]. Belgrade, Prosveta, 1982.
Atlantis: Selected Poems, 1953–1982, translated by Charles Simic and Peter Kastmiler. Greenfield Center, New York, Greenfield Review Press, 1983.
Black Apples: Selected Poems, 1954–1987, translated by Bernard Johnson. Toronto, Exile, 1989.

Fiction

Novele: teleći odresci [Short Stories: Slices of Veal]. Zagreb, Matica Hrvatska Zora, 1967.

Other

Iskrišta u tmini: zapisi umobolnih: knjigu priredio [Sparks in the Darkness: Writings of the Mentally Disturbed]. Zagreb, Lykos, 1957.

Editor, *Knjiga sedmorice* [Book of the Seven]. Zagreb, Lykos, 1957.
Editor, *Put bratstva i jedinstva* [The Road of Fraternity and Unity]. Belgrade, Lykos, 1959.

Editor, with J. Pupačić and A. Šoljan, *Antologija hrvatske poezije dvadesetog stoleća, od Kranjčevića do danas* [Anthology of Croatian Poetry of the 20th Century: Kranjčević to the Present Day]. Zagreb, Znanje, 1966.
Editor, *Kameni brid* [Stone Blade], by Dubravko Škurla. Zagreb, Matica, 1970.
Editor, with Ivan Kušan, *La Poésie croate, des origines à nos jours*. Paris, Seghers, 1972.
Editor, with Gane Todorovski, *Novata hrvatska poezija* [New Croatian Poetry]. Skopje, Misla, 1973.
Editor and Translator, *Moja kratka vječnost* [My Short Eternity], by Ciril Zlobec. Zagreb, Ausut Cesarec, 1982.

Translator, *Strava: izabrane pjesme* [Fear: Selected Poems], by Edvard Kocbek. Zagreb, Matica, 1970.

*

Critical Study: "The Poetry of Slavko Mihalić" by Bernard Johnson, in *South Slavonic Perspectives* (Krusevac and London), 1989.

* * *

Slavko Mihalić has been Croatia's most consistent poet since the publication of his first book, *Komorna muzika* (Chamber Music), in 1954 up to the present day. His verse shows an enormous diversity of theme and subject-matter, which widens with each new volume. Nevertheless, his style and use of everyday colloquial language has remained constant. He seems to be an entirely "home grown" poet in the sense that he appears to have been little affected by contemporary mainstream poetic currents, the only detectable influence on his writing being that of the inter-war Croatian existentialist poet, A. B. Šimić. The label most often attached to Mihalić's verse is also "existentialist," but this seems hardly justifiable. Mihalić is a highly original poet whose poetic world is built from a sequence of reflective and often highly unusual ideas which progress from sometimes banal, sometimes significant incidents, scenes, or topics towards an unexpected conclusion which often questions fundamental concepts. Frequently this poetic reasoning is turned inwards towards the poet's own experience, but sometimes the perspective is more generalised. Some of his best poems are satirical and/or covertly or indirectly political. And although he is not a "personal" poet, and his sense of humour is pessimistic, his poems can contain considerable depths of emotion, especially nostalgia for the past. A whole book, *Vrt crnih jabuka* (Orchard of Black Apples), is written in this nostalgic mode. Because of this wide scope to be found in his poetry, it is difficult to fit Mihalić into any poetic movement or specific category.

The constant thread in Mihalić's verse is the poet's own reality, which links the diversity of his themes and his wide range of subject-matter. It is particularly evident in the early books, such as *Komorna muzika* and *Put u nepostojanje* (Route into Non-Existence), where the poet illuminates an ordinary and often trivial moment or event of everyday life with the light of his own perception, and his imagination changes and develops it into an episode of immense importance to the poet's inner experience. The reality developed in the poem derives from the poet's inward contemplation and is often a means of arriving at an insight into universal human experience. Reality is less important than its projection in the poet's own perception:

I'm trying to stop time
For a reckless driver and a frightened deer

To give form to an exceptional event in the street
Which only half happened.

The vision Mihalić often creates for himself is one
of impending menace. In the poem "Metamorfoza"
(Metamorphosis), the poet feels transformed by a chance
moment in the street into a highly receptive state for which the
image is a glassy lake. Yet at the same time he is aware of the
negative side of this image for his inner reality:

> I pass along the street, head bent, as if
> some other lake, but mainly sombre
> and poisonous; we do not speak of those
> vile creatures crawling in its depths.

In poems such as this which make use of an imaginative
development of an initial situation or idea, Mihalić is very
aware of the contrast between the two halves of the poet-
magician's psyche, the base and the inspired components of his
reality which, like Ariel and Caliban, make up his power. With
Mihalić, it is often Caliban who has the last word. This
heightened intensity of perception triggered by an initial real
stimulus is typical of Mihalić's poetic technique.

Much has been said about the fundamentally sombre nature
of Mihalić's poetic inspiration, and there can be no doubt that
the reader is left with an overall impression of pessimism. But
this is not the mannered despair of romanticism, nor the self-
destructive, morbid fascination with death and corruption that
was the hallmark of turn-of-the-century symbolism. for
Mihalić's generation the violence and atrocities of war and
revolution were very much part of the material reality of their
youth, and few Yugoslavs who survived the 1940s and their
aftermath were not marked by the cruelty, suffering, and
devastation they had seen around them. And although
Mihalić's poetic universe has less apparent horror and violence
in its makeup than others of his contemporaries, one does not
have to dig very deep beneath the surface to discover the
effects of the events and experiences of the poet's adolescence
that have left their indelible trace on his sensibility. Lines from
the poem "Silazak" (Descent) illustrate this background to his
times: "Went down . . ./A whole people/With bullet-torn
memories in their pouches."

While this despondent tone varies from poem to poem, it
seems that the constant in much of Mihalić's writing is his
concern for the tragic nature of man's condition and destiny:
his awareness of the fragility of life and man's inevitable
mortality are never far away. Hence a recurring theme is that
of fear, insecurity, and uncertainty about the future:

> Fear, no more of others than ourselves
> We feel there's someone larger welling up inside us
> Impossible to look him in the eyes
> Which recognise no obstacles.

Such inner fear is independent of man's will, irrational and
uncontrollable:

> Oh, it's pointless to walk round the tombstones seeking your
> grave
> Death will catch you unready, when you forget for a moment
> In some alien town, in your cups, or with some unworthy
> love.

The obverse side of Mihalić's fear of the future and
awareness of the ever-menacing presence of death is his
heightened nostalgia for the past, for rose-tinted impressions
and situations which take on an aura of wishful tranquillity.

Among the most powerful of such nostalgic vistas is the
eponymous poem of the collection *Klopka za uspomene* (A
Trap for Memories), with its gently sensual souvenirs of
adolescence, and the evocative "Zimski krajobraz" (Winter
Landscape):

> In fact you love your long-past childhood
> in wet shoes
> the fabulous parade of colours at New Year and Christmas.
> You long madly for something that might have happened.
> It was so close.
> Your dream floats
> in the place you left it
> and everything's once more resplendent.

Mihalić has never been a directly political poet. But the
times and place where he has lived have made it impossible for
him to remain uninfluenced by and entirely uninvolved in the
main political events going on around him and their consequences for the problems and tragedies of Eastern Europe and
Yugoslavia. Poems like "Ne nadaj se" (Don't Hope), "Još
malo neka smo" (Just a Little Longer Let Us Be), "Prognan se
vratio" (The Exile's Return), and "Majstore, ugasi svijeću"
(Maestro, Put Out the Candle) among many others contain
their own comments on specific situations and events. He feels
very strongly attached to his homeland but rarely does he
concern himself directly with what his fellow Croatians see as
their country's deep-rooted political problems. But there are
two fine poems that can be cited in which by means of allegory
and analogy he makes important and sensitive statements that
reveal his deep concern for the nation and people to which he
belongs. These are *Atlantida* (Atlantis) and "S Guliverovih
putovanja" (From Gulliver's Travels). The latter is an eloquent satirical poem which relates Gulliver's dilemma to the
confusion of Mihalić's own time and the contradictory nature
of his own, or any other society:

> The natives always talk of something else,
> never of what they really have in mind. They walk
> backwards, rejoicing when they run into
> some hard thing with their heads.
>
> And then, secretly, by night
> they're digging up their houses. At first I thought
> they must be seeking gold. But that's not it. It seems to be
> their work. It looks as though each one
> has to outsmart himself. The best he can. For his own
>   ruination.
>
> I've no idea:
> where are their temples? Who serves whom?
> Who gives the orders? One thing's certain
> here reason is a disadvantage.
> Each one works hard for his own downfall,
> and more besides. They help each other.

But all this topsy-turvy world seems so real that Gulliver
himself feels part of it. It is no accident that Mihalić chooses
Swift as his point of reference and his gift for the grotesque and
unexpected, for parody and satire, echo those of his original.

In *Atlantida*, by making use of the parallel of the mythical
fate of Atlantis, the poet gives an insight into the historical and
psychological paradox facing his country: the problem of a
people of considerable cultural achievement and potential,
eager to play an important role on the wider historical stage,
but doomed always to suffer their own frustrations and the
world's unawareness:

Never, never shall we be discovered,
never, never shall our existence begin,
nor even Columbus, a single Columbus escape from the curse;
the world will die helpless in sight of Atlantis.

Mihalić is neither a profoundly philosophical nor a "musical" poet, but he makes up for this by the originality of his imagination, the crispness of his language, and the precision with which he carries an idea through to his own poetic conclusion. He can be expected to develop further against the background of his country's new circumstances.

—Bernard Johnson

———

MIŁOSZ, Czesław. Polish and American. Born in Szetejnie, Lithuania, 30 June 1911; came to the United States in 1960; naturalized citizen, 1970. Educated at the High School, Vilna (now Vilnius); University of Stefan Batory, Vilna, M. Juris. 1934; studied in Paris, 1934–35. Took part in the Polish Resistance during World War II. Programmer, Polish National Radio, 1935–39; member of the Polish Diplomatic Service, Washington, D.C., and Paris, 1945–50; defected to the West, 1951; freelance writer, Paris, 1951–60; Visiting Lecturer, 1960–61, Professor of Slavic languages and literatures, 1961–78, and since 1978 Professor Emeritus, University of California, Berkeley. Co-founder of the literary periodical *Zagary*, 1931. Recipient: European literary prize, 1953; Kister award, 1967; Jurzykowski Foundation award, 1968; Creative Arts fellowship, 1968, and University citation, 1978, University of California; Polish PEN. Club award, for translation, 1974; Guggenheim fellowship, 1976; Neustadt International prize, 1978; Nobel prize for literature, 1980; Bay Area Book Reviewers prize, 1985; National Medal of Arts (United States), 1989. Litt.D.: University of Michigan, Ann Arbor, 1977; honorary doctorate; Catholic University, Lublin, 1981; Brandeis University, Waltham, Massachusetts, 1983; Harvard University, Cambridge, Massachusetts, 1989; Jagiellonian University, Cracow, 1989. Member, Polish Institute of Letters and Sciences in America, American Academy of Arts and Sciences, and American Institute of Arts and Letters. Address: c/o Department of Slavic Languages and Literature, University of California, Berkeley, California 94720, U.S.A.

PUBLICATIONS

Verse

Poemat o czasie zastygłym [A Poem on Time Frozen]. Vilnius, 1933.
Trzy zimy [Three Winters]. Vilnius, Union of Polish Writers, 1936.
Wiersze [Poems] (as J.Syruć). Warsaw, 1940.
Ocalenie [Rescue]. Warsaw, Czytelnik, 1945.
Światło dzienne [Daylight]. Paris, Instytut Literacki, 1953.
Traktat poetycki [Treatise on Poetry]. Paris, Instytut Literacki, 1957.
Kontynenty [Continents]. Paris, Instytut Literacki, 1958.
Król Popiel i inne wiersze [King Popiel and Other Poems]. Paris, Instytut Literacki, 1962.

Gucio zaczarowany [Bobo's Metamorphosis]. Paris, Instytut Literacki, 1965.
Wiersze [Poems]. London, Oficyna Poetów i Malarzy, 1967.
Lied vom Weltende [A Song for the End of the World]. Cologne, Kiepenheuer und Witsch, 1967.
Miasto bez imienia [City Without a Name]. Paris, Instytut Literacki, 1969.
Selected Poems. New York, Seabury Press, 1973; revised edition, New York, Ecco Press, 1981.
Gdzie wschodzi słońce i kiedy zapada [From Where the Sun Rises to Where It Sets]. Paris, Instytut Literacki, 1974.
Utwory poetyckie [Selected Poems]. Ann Arbor, University of Michigan Slavic Publications, 1976.
Bells in Winter, translated by the author and Lillian Vallee. New York, Ecco Press, 1978; Manchester, Carcanet, 1980.
Poezje [Poems]. Warsaw, Czytelnik, 1981.
Moja wierna mowo [My Faithful Tongue]. Toruń, Oficyna Drukarska Książnicy Miejskiej im. M. Kopernika, 1981.
Wiersze wybrane [Selected Poems]. Warsaw, Państwowy Instytut Wydawniczy, 1981.
Traktat moralny [A Moral Treatise]. Lublin, Krajowa Agencja Wydawnicza, 1981.
Poezje [Poems]. Paris, Instytut Literacki, 1982.
Hymn o perle [Hymn to the Pearl]. Ann Arbor, University of Michigan Slavic Publications, 1982.
Wiersze [Poems]. Warsaw, Ludowa Społdzielnia Wydawnicza, 1983.
The Separate Notebooks, translated by Robert Hass and Robert Pinsky. New York, Ecco Press, 1984.
Nieobjęta ziemia. Paris, Instytut Literacki, 1984; as *The Unattainable Earth*, translated by Robert Hass, New York, Ecco Press, 1986.
Wiersze [Poems]. Wrocław, Wydawnictwo Literackie, 1985.
The View, translated by the author and Lilian Vallee. New York, Whitney Museum of American Art, 1985.
Dziewięć wierszy [Nine Poems], with Karl Dedecius. Lódź, Correspondance des Arts II, 1987.
Kroniki [Chronicles]. Paris, Instytut Literacki, 1987.
The Collected Poems 1931–1987. New York, Ecco Press, 1988.
Świat/The World (bilingual edition). San Francisco, Arion Press, 1989.

Fiction

Zdobycie władzy. Paris, Instytut Literacki, 1955; as *The Seizure of Power*, New York, Criterion, 1955; London, Sphere, 1985; as *The Usurpers*, London, Faber, 1955.
Dolina Issy. Paris, Instytut Literacki, 1955; as *The Issa Valley*, London, Sidgwick and Jackson, and New York, Farrar Straus, 1981.

Other

Zniewolony umysł (essays). Paris, Instytut Literacki, 1953; as *The Captive Mind*, New York, Knopf, and London, Secker and Warburg, 1953.
Rodzinna Europa. Paris, Instytut Literacki, 1959; as *Native Realm: A Search for Self-Definition*, New York, Doubleday, 1968; London, Sidgwick and Jackson, 1981.
Człowiek wśród skorpionów: studium o Stanisławie Brzozowskim [A Man Among Scorpions: A Study of Stanisław Brzozowski]. Paris, Instytut Literacki, 1962.
The History of Polish Literature. New York, Macmillan, and London, Collier Macmillan, 1969; revised edition, Berkeley, University of California Press, 1983.

Widzenia nad Zatoką San Francisco. Paris, Instytut Literacki, 1969; as *Visions from San Francisco Bay*, Manchester, Carcanet, and New York, Farrar Straus, 1982.
Prywatne obowiązki [Private Obligations]. Paris, Instytut Literacki, 1972.
Mój wiek: pamiętnik mówiony [My Century: An Oral Diary] (interview with Alexander Wat), edited by Lidia Ciołkoszowa. London, Polonia Book Fund, 2 vols., 1977.
Emperor of the Earth: Modes of Eccentric Vision. Berkeley, University of California Press, 1977.
Ziemia Ulro. Paris, Instytut Literacki, 1977; as *The Land of Ulro*, New York, Farrar Straus, 1984; Manchester, Carcanet, 1985.
Ogród nauk [The Garden of Knowledge]. Paris, Instytut Literacki, 1980.
Dzieła zbiorowe [Collected Works]. Paris, Instytut Literacki, 1980–.
Nobel Lecture. New York, Farrar Straus, 1981.
Swiadectwo poezji: sześć wykładów o dotkliwości naszego wieku. Paris, Instytut Literacki, 1983; as *The Witness of Poetry* (lectures), Cambridge, Massachusetts, Harvard University Press, 1983.
Poszukiwania: wybór publicystyki rozproszonej 1931–1983 [Search: Selection of Essays from 1931–1938]. Warsaw, CDN (samizdat), 1985.
Zaczynając od moich ulic. Paris, Instytut Literacki, 1985.
Conversations with Czesław Miłosz, with Ewa Czarnecka and Aleksander Fiut. San Diego, Harcourt Brace, 1987.
Czesława Miłosza autoportret przekorny [Czesław Miłosz's Willful Self-Portrait] (interviews), with Aleksander Fiut. Cracow, Wydawnictwo Literackie, 1988.
Exiles, photographs by Josef Koudelka. New York, Apenture Foundation, 1988.
Metafizyczna pauza [Metaphysical Interval]. Cracow, Znak, 1989.
Rok myśliwego [The Year of the Hunter]. 1990.

Editor, with Zbigniew Folejewski, *Antologia poezji społecznej* [Anthology of Social Poetry]. Vilnius, 1933.
Editor, *Pieśń niepodległa* [Invincible Song]. Warsaw, 1942.
Editor and Translator, *Drogami klęski* [On the Roads of Defeat], by Jacques Maritain. Warsaw, 1942.
Editor and Translator, *Polityka i rzeczywistość* [Politics and Reality], by Jeanne Hersch, Paris, Instytut Literacki, 1955.
Editor and Translator, *Praca i jej gorycze* [Work and Its Discontents], by Daniel Bell. Paris, Instytut Literacki, 1957.
Editor and Translator, *Wybór pism* [Selected Works], by Simone Weil. Paris, Instytut literacki, 1958.
Editor, *Kultura masowa* [Mass Culture]. Paris, Instytut Literacki, 1959.
Editor, *Węgry* [Hungary]. Paris, Instytut Literacki, 1960.
Editor and Translator, *Postwar Polish Poetry: An Anthology*. New York, Doubleday, 1965; London, Penguin, 1970; revised edition, Berkeley, University of California Press, 1983.
Editor, *Lettres inédites de O.V. de L. Milosz à Christian Gauss*. Paris, Silvaire, 1976.

Translator, with Peter Dale Scott, *Selected Poems*, by Zbigniew Herbert. London, Penguin, 1968.
Translator, *Mediterranean Poems*, by Alexander Wat. Ann Arbor, Michigan, Ardis, 1977.
Translator, *Ewangelia według św. Marka* [The Gospel According to St. Mark]. Cracow, Znak, 1978.
Translator, *Księga Hioba* [The Book of Job]. Paris, Dialogue, 1980.

Translator, *Ksiega psalmów* [The Book of Psalms]. Paris, Dialogue, 1980.
Translator, *Księgi pięciu Megilot*. Lublin, Katolicki Uniwersytet Lubelski, 1984.
Translator, *Happy as a Dog's Tail*, by Anna Swir. San Diego, Harcourt Brace, 1985.
Translator, *Mowa wiązana* [Poetry Language]. Warsaw and Paris, Państwowy Instytut Wydawniczy, 1986.
Translator, with Leonard Nathan, *With the Skin: The Poems of Aleksander Wat*. New York, Ecco Press, 1989; London, Penguin, 1991.

*

Critical Studies: Miłosz issues of *World Literature Today* (Norman, Oklahoma), 52, 1978, and *Ironwood* (Tucson, Arizona), 18, 1981; *Czesław Miłosz and the Insufficiency of Lyric* by Donald Davie, Cambridge, Cambridge University Press, 1986; *Between Anxiety and Hope: The Poetry of Czesław Miłosz*, edited by Edward Możejko, Edmonton, University of Alberta Press, 1988; *The Eternal Moment: The Poetry of Czesław Miłosz* by Aleksander Fiut, Berkeley, University of California Press, 1990; *The Poet's Work: An Introduction to Czesław Miłosz* by Leonard Nathan and Arthur Quinn, Cambridge, Massachusetts, Harvard University Press, 1991.

*   *   *

Czesław Miłosz is an outstanding figure of 20th-century Polish literature. In his youth he belonged to the so-called "Second Vanguard," the poetry of which was characterized by neo-symbolistic tendencies of a "catastrophist" kind. Miłosz's poetry before World War II suggests the nearness of some kind of a cataclysm; there is a "thorn of prophecy" in these otherwise carefully structured, distant, and allusive poems. During the war the poet's perception of reality and with it his poetic language underwent a substantial change — in the cycle *Świat* (*The World*) and even more so in the collection *Ocalenie* (Rescue), he dropped many of his poetic adornments of the 1930s and tried to redefine the world in terms of compassion and hope. At the same time he was profoundly disturbed by the brutality of totalitarianism and the savagery of war, as in "Dedication":

> What is poetry which does not save
> Nations or people?
> A connivance with official lies,
> A song of drunkards whose throats
> will be cut in a moment.

The antinomies of Miłosz's poetry are between "immoral" beauty and "moral" truth, between chaos and order, nature and civilization. His poetry is pervaded by a strong historicism and a constant awareness of transience, and the poet himself seems to oscillate between his "private cares" and contemplations and his historical, even social preoccupations. This is reflected by the "polyphony" of Miłosz's poetic voices, stressed by Jan Blonski in his essay in *World Literature Today* (Summer 1978); he sometimes speaks with different voices within the same poem. Nevertheless, his longer poems *Traktat moralny* (A Moral Treatise) and *Traktat poetycki* (Treatise on Poetry) are didactic in a way which has not been attempted since Cyprian Norwid. *Traktat poetycki* is a multi-faceted, ironic survey of Polish literature since the end of the 19th century.

In California Miłosz's poetry became more introspective and absorbed elements of Surrealism in poems such as "Album snów" (Album of Dreams) and "Po ziemi naszej" (Throughout Our Lands). The most representative piece of his Californian period, the long polyphonic poem *Gdzie wschodzi słońce i kiedy zapada* (From Where the Sun Rises to Where It Sets) blends memories of the poet's childhood and youth with the imagery of American nature and with eschatological expectations of the Last Judgement.

Miłosz's reputation as a writer of fiction rests on a number of novels of which the compelling *Dolina Issy* (*The Issa Valley*), a Manichean tale of the poet's childhood in densely wooded Lithuania, is the most accomplished. *Rodzinna Europa* (*Native Realm*) is also written in the autobiographical vein but with the purpose of tracing the author's intellectual development from his university years in Vilna (through Paris) to his settling down in Warsaw. Nonetheless, it was *Zniewolony umysł* (*The Captive Mind*) that made Miłosz best known outside Poland. Written soon after his break with the Communist Polish authorities in 1951, this book is an incisive and rather pessimistic analysis of the intricate mechanism of the Polish intelligentsia's adaptation to Communist ideology. Miłosz has also written several books of essays on Polish and American themes — of these *Widzenia nad Zatoką San Francisco* (*Visions from San Francisco Bay*), written "to exorcise the evil spirit of contemporary times," should have the greatest appeal to the general reader.

Miłosz is the author of a comprehensive and challenging history of Polish literature, *The History of Polish Literature*, and an excellent translator. He has translated into Polish among other things T. S. Eliot's and Simone Weil's writings and published an anthology of Polish poetry in English translation, *Postwar Polish Poetry*. In recent years his most interesting prose publication has been the "literary diary" of *Rok myśliwego* (The Year of the Hunter), which records Miłosz's thoughts, memories, comments, and travels throughout the year 1987–1988. It shows that advancing age has impaired neither Miłosz's critical judgement nor his ability to assist in the political transformation for which Central and East European intellectuals have been striving.

—George Gömöri

MIRANDA, Javier. *See* **BIOY CASARES, Adolfo.**

MIŚRA, Vaidyanāth. *See* **NĀGĀRJUN.**

MŇAČKO, Ladislav. Slovak. Born in Valašské Klobouky, Czechoslovakia, 29 January 1919. Fought as a partisan during World War II: injured by bullet wound to spine. Journalist, *Rudé Právo* newspaper, Prague, 1945–48; reporter at iron works, Košice, 1950–51; member, National Assembly, Bratislava, 1954–57; editor-in-chief, Slovak Writers' Union *Kulturný Život* journal, 1956, 1964. Joined Communist Party after World War II: expelled for protesting against Party policy towards Israel, and defected to Israel, 1967; returned to Czechoslovakia, Spring 1968, and reinstated in Party; defected to Austria, Summer 1968. Lives in Austria and Israel. Recipient: Merited Artist, 1953, 1956; Gottwald prize. Address: c/o Langen-Müller Verlag, Thomas-Wimmer-Ring 11, 8000 Munich 22, Germany.

PUBLICATIONS

Fiction

Vpád: rok na stavbe HUKO [Invasion: A Year in the Construction of HUKO]. Bratislava, Tatran, 1952.
Marxova ulica [Marx Street]. Bratislava, Mladé letá, 1957.
Smrt' sa volá Engelchen. Bratislava, Slovenské Vydavateľstvo Politickej Literatúry, 1959; as *Death Is Called Engelchen*, Prague, Artia, 1961.
Ja, Adolf Eichmann [I, Adolf Eichmann]. Bratislava, Slovenské Vydavateľstvo Politickej Literatúry, 1961.
Oneskorené reportáže [Belated Reports]. Bratislava, Slovenské Vydavateľstvo Politickej Literatúry, 1963.
Nočný rozhovor [Conversation at Night]. Bratislava, Slovenské Vydavateľstvo Politickej Literatúry, 1966.
Wie die Macht schmeckt. Vienna, Molden, 1967; as *The Taste of Power*, London, Weidenfeld and Nicolson, and New York, Praeger, 1967; as *Ako chutí moc*, Bratislava, Slovenský spisovateľ, 1968.
Der Vorgang. Munich, Kindler, 1970.
Súdruh Münchhausen [Comrade M.]. Cologne, Index, 1972.
Einer wird überleben. Munich, List, 1973.
Der Gigant. Munich, Langen-Müller, 1978.

Play

Mosty na východ [Bridges to the East]. Martin, Osveta, 1953.

Verse

Piesne ingotov [The Songs of Ingots]. Bratislava, n.p., 1950.
Bubny a činely [Drums and Symbols]. Bratislava, Slovenský spisovateľ, 1954.

Other

Izrael [Israel]. Bratislava, Nakladeľstvo Pravda, 1949.
Albanská reportáž [Reportage from Albania]. Bratislava, Nakladateľstvo Pravda, 1950.
Dobrodružstvo vo Vietname. Bratislava, n.p., 1954.
Vody Oravy [The Waters of the Orava]. Prague, Mladá fronta, 1955.
Ďaleko je do Whampoa [It Is Far to Whampoa]. Bratislava, Slovenské Vydavateľstvo Politickej Literatúry, 1958.
Čo nebolo v novinách [What Was Not in the Newspapers]. Bratislava, Slovenské Vydavateľstvo Politickej Literatúry 1958.
U-2 sa nevracia [It Is Not Coming Back]. Bratislava, Slovenské Vydavateľstvo Politickej Literatúry, 1960.
Slovakia Yesterday and Today, photographs by Karol Kállay. Prague, Artia, 1961.

A Marx utca. Bratislava, Slovenské Vydavateľstvo Politickej Literatúry, 1961.
Kde končia prašné cesty [Where the Dusty Road Ends]. Bratislava, Osveta, 1963.
De kinõajutsia kurni dorohy. Priašiv, Slov. Pedag. Vydav., 1964.
Dlhá, biela, prerušovaná čiara [The Long White Dotted Line]. Bratislava, Slovenský spisovateľ, 1965.
Rozprával ten kapitán [What the Captain Told Me]. Bratislava, Slovenské Vydavateľstvo Politickej Literatúry, 1965.
Die siebente Nacht. Vienna, Molden, 1968; as *The Seventh Night*, London, Dent, and New York, Dutton, 1969.
Die Aggressoren. Vienna, Molden, 1968.
Hanoi-Report. Hamburg, Holsten, 1972.
Die Festrede: Satiren. Munich, List, 1976.
Jenseits von Intourist: satirische Reportagen. Munich, Langen-Müller, 1979.

*

Bibliography: *Ladislav Mňačko: Eine Bibliographie* by Suzanne L. Auer, Munich, Sagner, 1989.

Critical Study: "The Case of Ladislav Mňačko" by Frank Osvald, in *Survey: A Journal of Soviet and East European Studies*, 55, 1965.

*   *   *

During the 1960s Ladislav Mňačko was both the most read and the most controversial Slovak writer of fiction. He was a Communist and his writing supported Communism, indeed supported Stalinism in the 1950s; his important works all in some way or another discuss the guilt of all Communists for what had happened during the Stalin era. Mňačko was, then, controversial because of his subject-matter. He is no stylist; on the whole he writes fiction as though it were journalism and, as he states in *Die siebente Nacht* (*The Seventh Night*), his memoirs on 30 years of Party life, all his fiction is directly or indirectly based on his personal experience, usually as a reporter. When he writes straight fiction, as in *Einer wird überleben* (One Will Survive), it is not of a high standard.

"I have written only one novel proper, *Death Is Called Engelchen*, but even here I was not concerned with fiction," Mňačko states in *The Seventh Night*, and in fact, like Mňačko the novel's narrator has a bullet-wound in his spine. *Smrť sa volá Engelchen* (*Death Is Called Engelchen*) concerns the partisan war following the Slovak National Uprising in 1944, which was one of the main subjects of Slovak literature from the 1940s to the end of the 1970s; the setting, though, is the Slovak-Moravian border, not Central Slovakia where most Uprising novels are set. It centres on one group of partisans who are unusually ordinary people, with the exception of their Russian leader, whose suicide is an ambiguous blend of the heroic and unheroic. A member of the group is playing with a new type of grenade, which suddenly explodes and deprives the leader of a leg and his genitalia; he shoots himself either because of his emasculation or because of his failure to maintain discipline. Equally unusual for a Slovak war novel is the attention Mňačko pays to the psychology of the partisans; indeed the psychology makes the novel, redeeming its tendency towards sentimentality, uninventive structure and language, and clichéd imagery. The pictures of the Moravian Czechs' brutality towards the Germans after their defeat and of a minor collaborator who becomes a self-heroising patriot perhaps break political taboos, but the novel's pro-Communist

tone and its mawkish eulogy of the Red Army keep it well in line.

Although *Death Is Called Engelchen* is by far Mňačko's most accomplished work from a literary point of view, politically most important is his collection of 11 pieces of fictionalised journalism, *Oneskorené reportáže* (Belated Reports), which sold 300,000 copies within two months of publication. The stories depict the corruption in industry and in the judicial system during the Stalinist régime in Slovakia. Mňačko writes in his Introduction: "I am a Communist and I love my Party [. . .] I have written this book for and on behalf of my Party and as a Party-member [. . .] In it I also intended to document my share of the guilt for the events that took place." As a loyal Party man, he refused to have this book published abroad. The criminals portrayed here are bigoted lawyers and judges, wheeler-dealer construction-site bosses, and narrow-minded and frightened bureaucrats. The victims tend to be good, pure Communists, often with a record of war-time valour. In one case a man is expelled from the Party simply because he has the same name as a bourgeois villain in a propaganda film.

While the stories in *Oneskorené reportáže* primarily concern the moral violence of Stalinist arbitrary rule, in the neatly constructed and vividly narrated novella *Nočný rozhovor* (Conversation at Night), Mňačko turns to the problem of physical violence under Nazism. He intends to show that the violence of SS camp commandants and guards was unjustifiable, whereas the violence of the Allied carpet-bombing of Dresden could be justified. His ill-argued assertion is that any amount of physical violence is acceptable if it is for a good cause. He appears here to regret that the Soviet Union had not occupied the whole of Germany and suggests that West Germany is riddled with ex-Nazi businessmen and industrialists.

Mňačko returns to Stalinism in *Wie die Macht schmeckt* (*The Taste of Power*), which concerns a Party leader, called simply the Great Man, who dies just before he was to be toppled by one Galovič (whose name echoes that of the Slovak chief of the secret police, Šalgovič, but whose characteristics, for example calling Vietnam "Vitnam," are taken from the most powerful man in the Slovak Party in the 1950s, Pavol David). This somewhat overwrought stream-of-consciousness novel is a study of the corruption of power, in which a solid, honourable, uneducated but very brave young revolutionary is perverted into a vain monster by the power bestowed on him by his position as "Great Man" in a Stalinist régime.

With *Súdruh Münchhausen* (Comrade M.) Mňačko turns to satire in his picture of the neo-Stalinism introduced by Husák after the fall of Dubček. Unfortunately he demonstrates that he has little imagination when describing what he has not experienced himself. Most of the satire is directed at Party jargon, and instead of irony, Mňačko seems only to produce irate sarcasm. His satirical pictures of corruption and opportunism are less incisive than his journalistic analyses of such ills had been in the early 1960s.

The main themes of Mňačko's writing in the 1960s and 1970s are violence, guilt, and Jewishness. Apart from the violence of war and, in *Einer wird überleben*, criminal violence, most of the violence Mňačko writes about is moral. In *The Seventh Night* he informs us that he had himself been somewhat free with his fists when making a point in the 1950s. Most striking perhaps is the amount of sexual violence in his writing; sexual intercourse tends to have a sadomasochistic tinge, and one of the grimmest parts of *The Taste of Power* concerns the Great Man's persecution of the man who had saved him from death in the war after the Great Man has tried to rape the other's daughter. As in the Introduction to *Oneskorené reportáže* Mňačko declares himself guilty by association, and in his fiction such guilt is punished. For example, in *Death Is Called Engelchen* a thoroughly decent German officer is shot by the narrator because the copy of the *Forsyte Saga* he is reading had previously belonged to a Jew. The Hamburg girl who inspires the central narrative of *Nočný rozhovor* in a journey to Dresden tries and fails to find expiation for her father's guilt; he had been hanged by the British as a war criminal. Mňačko also touches on a still delicate subject, the Slovak Army's participation in German atrocities in the Ukraine (*Oneskorené reportáže* and *The Seventh Night*). In *Oneskorené reportáže*, however, he cannot bring himself to blame personally the 1950s police and prison officers who tortured their victims: "Were not those who set up the trials, who tortured and persecuted innocent people Communists? Are not they in their own way victims of erroneous methods and of an erroneous interpretation of the erroneous doctrine of the class struggle? After all, they were loyal, devoted to the Party, and once dauntless fighters for socialism!"

Mňačko himself was attacked as a Jew, though he is not Jewish; he has, however, always been concerned about anti-Semitism. He explains 1950s Party anti-Semitism to be the result of the Communists' disappointment that Israel had not become a socialist state, after the Communists had supported the Jews against the Arabs and the British. The bravest of the resistance fighters in *Death Is Called Engelchen* is a Jewess, who becomes a prostitute to German officers in order to get information for the partisans; after the war she commits suicide. Another Jewish partisan woman is persecuted by the Communists in *Oneskorené reportáže*, and the jolly Jewish boxer who runs the blackmarket in war-time Dresden is betrayed to the Germans by his Prague landlady because she does not want to lose the few knick-knacks he had asked her to look after for him. In *Súdruh Münchhausen* Mňačko mocks the new Party anti-Semitism of the early years of the Husák régime. Mňačko has always been a defender of victims in his writing, but, at least while in Czechoslovakia, never became fully aware that, as an influential Communist, he himself was a victimiser.

—Robert B. Pynsent

MODIANO, Patrick. French. Born in Boulogne-sur-Seine, 30 July 1945. Educated at the Collège Saint-Joseph, Thônes; Lycée Henri-IV, Paris. Married Dominique Zehrfuss in 1970; two daughters. Recipient: Nimier prize, 1969; Fénéon prize, 1969; Académie Française grand prize, 1972; French Booksellers prize, 1976; Goncourt prize, 1978; Monaco prize, 1984; Prix Relais H du Roman d'Évasion, 1990. Chevalier de l'Ordre des Arts et des Lettres. Address: c/o Éditions Gallimard, 5 rue Sébastien-Bottin, 75007 Paris, France.

PUBLICATIONS

Fiction

La Place de l'étoile. Paris, Gallimard, 1968.
La Ronde de nuit. Paris, Gallimard, 1969; as *Night Rounds*, New York, Knopf, 1971; London, Gollancz, 1972.
Les Boulevards de ceinture. Paris, Gallimard, 1972; as *Ring Roads*, London, Gollancz, 1974.

Villa Triste. Paris, Gallimard, 1975; in English, London, Gollancz, 1977.
Livret de famille. Paris, Gallimard, 1977.
Rue des boutiques obscures. Paris, Gallimard, 1978; as *Missing Person*, London, Cape, 1980.
Une Jeunesse. Paris, Gallimard, 1981.
Memory Lane (in French). Paris, Hachette/POL, 1981.
De si braves garçons. Paris, Gallimard, 1982.
Quartier perdu. Paris, Gallimard, 1984; as *A Trace of Malice*, Henley-on-Thames, Ellis, 1988; Boston, Godine, 1990.
Dimanches d'août. Paris, Gallimard, 1986.
Remise de peine. Paris, Seuil, 1988.
Vestiaire de l'enfance. Paris, Gallimard, 1989.
Voyage de noces. Paris, Gallimard, 1990; as *Honeymoon*, London, Collins Harvill, 1992.
Fleurs de ruine. Paris, Seuil, 1991.

Plays

La Polka (produced Paris, 1974).
Lacombe Lucien (screenplay), with Louis Malle. Paris, Gallimard, 1974; in English, New York, Viking, 1975.
Poupée blonde, with Pierre Le-Tan. Paris, POL, 1983.

Screenplay: *Lacombe Lucien*, with Louis Malle, 1974.

Other

Emmanuel Berl interrogatoire, with *Il fait beau, allons au cimetière*, by Emmanuel Berl. Paris, Gallimard, 1976.
Une Aventure de Choura (for children). Paris, Gallimard, 1986.
Une Fiancée pour Choura (for children). Paris, Gallimard, 1987.
Catherine Certitude (for children). Paris, Gallimard, 1988.
Paris tendresse, photographs by Brassaï. Paris, Hoëbecke, 1990.

Editor, *Paris*. Paris, Fixot, 1987.

*

Critical Studies: "Anthology as Art: Modiano's *Livret de famille*" by C. W. Nettelback and P. A. Hueston, in *Australian Journal of French Studies* (Clayton, Victoria), May–August 1984; "Re-Membering Modiano, or Something Happened" by Gerald Prince, in *Sub-Stance* (Santa Barbara, California), 49, 1986; "Originality and Narrative Nostalgia: Shadows in Modiano's *Rue des boutiques obscures*" by Marja Warehime, in *French Forum* (Lexington, Kentucky), September 1987; "Collaboration, Alienation, and the Crisis of Identity in the Film and Fiction of Patrick Modiano" by Richard J. Golsan, in *Film and Literature*, edited by Wendell Aycock, Lubbock, Texas Tech University Press, 1988; "Patrick Modiano's *La Place de l'étoile*: Why Name a Narrator 'Raphaël Schlemilovitch'?" by Charles O'Keefe in *Literary Onomastics Studies* (Brockport, New York), 15, 1988.

* * *

Patrick Modiano is a novelist obsessed with the problem of personal identity. His father was Jewish, his mother was half-Belgian, half-Hungarian, and his childhood, by his own account, was insecure. These circumstances helped shape both the obsessive nature of his fiction and its retrospective slant. Fascinated by the German Occupation of France, in which he located a metaphorical setting for the uncertainties he felt driven to explore, Modiano acquired such mastery of a period of which he had no personal knowledge that his first three novels convey an uncanny impression of lived rather than vicarious experience. His apparent ability to remember, rather than recast, places and events led to his being credited with pioneering the *mode rétro* (the upsurge of interest in the "black years" of the Occupation) of the 1970s. His association with the trend was confirmed by his collaboration on the script of Louis Malle's much remarked film, *Lacombe Lucien*.

La Place de l'étoile (The Place of the Star) was prefaced by an anecdote which captures the playful seriousness of Modiano's first, highly acclaimed novel. In June 1942, a German officer asks a young man to point out the famous Paris landmark; the young man indicates the place, over his heart, where Jews were required to display the star of David. The ambiguity raises both a smile and a wince and sets the tone for the freewheeling story of Raphaël Schlemilovitch who sets out to discover the nature of his Jewishness. He assumes various roles, guises, and identities and moves unimpeded through time and space. He plays the Jewish snob, the servile Jew, the Jewish wartime collaborator, and even catches tuberculosis because Kafka had suffered from the disease. He tries out both anti-French attitudes and anti-semitism, and from his many theatrical incarnations acquires a clearer view of "the Jewish question." Yet he never ceases to be a wanderer and his unfruitful search for roots is a cipher for his equally anchorless creator, whose biography he shares. Swing Troubadour, the hero of *La Ronde de nuit* (*Night Rounds*; the title contains an allusion to Rembrandt's "The Night Watch"), is a *gestapiste* who is ordered to join the Resistance which in turn sends him to infiltrate the Gestapo. As a double agent, he is uncertain of who he is. Unable to be a traitor, he cannot be a hero and is doomed to be the victim of his tenuous hold on his identity. The world of wartime collaboration also provides the setting of *Les Boulevards de ceinture* (*Ring Roads*) which shows how, through imagined memories, Serge Alexandre travels in time in search of his father, who might be a black market trafficker or possibly a hunted Jew. His quest proves to be both fruitless and illusory, for its object is not his absent father but himself.

Modiano has indicated that his first three novels may be taken as a loose trilogy, a triple mirror reflecting the same images. His wartime Paris is not a real place, in spite of the striking immediacy with which it is evoked, but an imaginary landscape ideally suited to explorations of the themes which fascinate him: personal identity, time, memory, and the vanity of autobiography. But his fictions also embody the search for lost values, authority, and morality, and tell us more about the present than about the past. Yet the obsessiveness with which Modiano returned to the same themes and mechanisms in these early fictions clearly indicate their role as exercises in self-exorcism.

Villa Triste, set in Switzerland in the 1960s, sends Victor Chmara in search of family ties. The tale seems uncomplicated until a wrong name or a memory lapse casts doubt upon the truth of what is remembered, the perception of the past, and the reality of the quest. The less unified *Livret de famille* (Family Record) also casts doubts on the reality of "Switzerland" as a satisfying destination but strikes a more optimistic note in the reality of family ties. The excellent *Rue des boutiques obscures* (*Missing Person*) features an amnesiac detective who sets his professional skills the task of finding out who he is. More than a successful pastiche of a popular genre, it offers a more relaxed meditation on the uses of the past, and signals a lowering of the intensity of Modiano's compulsive preoccupation with identity. By the time *Une Jeunesse* (Young Lives) appeared in 1981, Modiano had a family of his own and in his subsequent work has continued to explore the same themes — interchangeable places, retrospection, searches for missing persons which turn out to be quests for the self — in a mood of greater detachment. *Dimanches d'août* (Sundays in August) is a slightly ghostly tale of a man and a woman who are simultaneously running away and pursuing. The novelist hero of *Vestiaire de l'enfance* (The Cloakroom of Childhood) again shares Modiano's biography and, in what might be Mexico or North Africa, can neither jettison the past nor accept the present.

Modiano's eternally tumescent fiction — the play of time and memory recurs with variations in *Fleurs de ruine* (Flowers of Decay) — asserts that the truth about ourselves exists somewhere, in a continuum which may be glimpsed through the real or false memories of a past which we can never possess fully enough to let us be who we are. His heroes work out their obsessions in a process of perpetual self-discovery which is much less "difficult" than at first appears. It is true that Modiano's early work, in the manner of the New Novel, abandoned conventional chronology, linear plots, and palpable "characters." Yet such techniques did not signal allegiance to experimental fiction which Modiano dismisses: "What I dislike about the 'nouveau roman' is that it lacks both tone and life. I am opposed to disembodied literature." Hence the absence of formal and linguistic experiment in a body of work which now, less anguished but no less challenging, has acquired the sobriety and elegance of the classic tradition.

—David Coward

MØRCH, Dea Trier. *See* **TRIER MØRCH, Dea.**

MOREN, Halldis. *See* **VESAAS, Halldis Moren.**

MROŻEK, Sławomir. Polish. Born in Borzęcin, 26 June 1930. Studied architecture, oriental culture, and painting in Cracow. Married 1) Maria Obremba in 1959 (died 1969); 2) in 1987. Journalist, 1950–54, cartoonist, then full-time writer; lived in Western Europe, 1963–72, 1975–88; now lives in Mexico; film director and producer, S.D.R., Stuttgart, 1977, 1979. Recipient: Black Humour prize (France), 1964; Austrian State prize for European literature, 1972. Agent: Diogenes Verlag, Sprecherstraße 8, 8032 Zurich, Switzerland.

PUBLICATIONS

Plays

Policja (produced Warsaw, 1958). Included in *Utwory sceniczne* 1963; as *The Policeman* (produced New York, 1961;

London, 1964), in *Six Plays*, 1967; as *The Police* (produced London, 1990).

Męczeństwo Piotra O'Heya (produced Cracow, 1959). Included in *Utwory sceniczne*, 1963; as *The Martyrdom of Piotr Ohey*, in *Six Plays*, 1967.

Indyk [The Turkey] (produced Cracow, 1960). Included in *Utwory sceniczne*, 1963.

Na pełnym morzu (produced Zakopane, 1961). Included in *Utwory sceniczne* 1963; as *Out at Sea* (produced New York, 1962; Edinburgh, 1965), in *Six Plays*, 1967; as *Out to Sea* (produced London, 1989).

Striptease (produced Zakopane, 1961). Included in *Utwory sceniczne*, 1963; in English (produced Lawrence, Kansas, 1964; London, 1969), in *Three Plays*, 1972.

Karol (produced Zakopane, 1961). Included in *Utwory sceniczne*, 1963; as *Charlie* (produced Edinburgh, 1964; London, 1989), in *Six Plays*, 1967.

Zabawa (produced Wrocław, 1963). Included in *Utwory sceniczne*, 1963; as *The Party* (produced Edinburgh, 1964; London, 1975), in *Six Plays*, 1967.

Kynolog w rozterce [Dog Lover in a Dilemma] (produced Cracow, 1967). Included in *Utwory sceniczne*, 1963.

Czarowna noc (produced Cracow, 1963). Included in *Utwory sceniczne*, 1963; as *Enchanted Night* (produced Edinburgh, 1964; London, 1971), in *Six Plays*, 1967.

Smierć porucznika [Death of the Lieutenant] (produced Warsaw, 1963). Included in *Utwory sceniczne*, 1963.

Utwory sceniczne (includes *Policija*; *Męczeństwo Piotra O'Heya*; *Indyk*; *Na pełnym morzu*; *Karol*; *Striptease*; *Zabawa*; *Kynolog w rozterce*; *Czarowna noc*; *Smierć porucznika*; *Tango*; *Testarium*; *Drugie danie*; *Woda*; *Dom na granicy*). Cracow, Wydawnictwo Literackie, 2 vols., 1963–73.

Tango (produced Warsaw, 1964). Included in *Utwory sceniczne*, 1973; in English (produced London, 1966; New York, 1969), London, Cape, and New York, Grove Press, 1968.

Six Plays (includes *The Policeman*; *The Martyrdom of Piotr Ohey*; *Out at Sea*; *Charlie*; *The Party*; *Enchanted Night*). London, Cape, and New York, Grove Press, 1967.

Poczwórka [The Quarternion] (produced Gdansk, 1967). Published in *Dialog* (Warsaw), 1, 1967.

Dom na granicy [The House on the Frontier] (produced Cracow, 1968). Included in *Utwory sceniczne*, 1973.

Vatzlav (produced in English, Stratford, Ontario, 1970; London, 1973; New York, 1982). New York, Grove Press, 1970; London, Cape, 1972.

Testarium. Included in *Utwory sceniczne*, 1973; as *The Prophets* (produced Glasgow, 1970), in *Three Plays*, 1972.

Three Plays (includes *Striptease*; *Repeat Performance*; *The Prophets*). New York, Grove Press, 1972.

Drugie danie (produced Łódź, 1979). Included in *Utwory sceniczne*, 1973; as *Repeat Performance*, in *Three Plays*, 1972.

Szczęśliwe wydarzenie [A Happy Event] (produced Warsaw, 1973). Published in *Dialog* (Warsaw), 4, 1973.

Rzeźnia [The Abattoir] (produced Warsaw, 1975). Published in *Dialog* (Warsaw), 9, 1973.

Utwory sceniczne nowe [New Plays] (includes *Rzeźnia*; *Emigranci*; *Wyspa róż*). Cracow, Wydawnictwo Literackie, 1975.

Emigranci (produced Warsaw, 1975). Included in *Utwory sceniczne nowe*, 1975; as *The Emigrés* (produced London, 1976; New York, 1979); as *The Emigrants*, New York, French, 1984.

Garbus [The Hunchback] (produced Cracow, 1975). Included in *Amor*, 1979.

Serenada [Serenade] (produced Warsaw, 1977). Included in *Amor*, 1979.

Lis filozof [Fox the Philosopher] (produced Warsaw, 1977). Included in *Amor*, 1979.

Polowanie na lisa [The Fox Hunt] (produced Zabrze, 1977). Included in *Amor*, 1979.

Krawiec [The Tailor] (produced Szczecin, 1978). Included in *Amor*, 1979.

Lis aspirant [Fox the Aspirant]. Included in *Amor*, 1979.

Amor (teleplay; includes *Amor*; *Krawiec*; *Polowanie na lisa*; *Serenada*; *Lis filozof*; *Lis aspirant*). Cracow, Wydawnictwo Literackie, 1979.

Pieszo [On Foot] (produced 1980). Warsaw, Czytelnik, 1983.

Ambasador, with *Vatzlav*. Paris, Instytut Literacki, 1982; as *The Ambassador*, New York, Institute for Contemporary Eastern European Drama and Theatre, 1984.

Alfa. Paris, Instytut Literacki, 1984.

A Summer's Day (produced London, 1985).

Wybór dramtów [Selected Drama]. Cracow, Wydawnictwo Literackie, 1987.

Fiction

Opowiadania z Trzmielowej Góry [Stories from Bumble Bee Hill]. Warsaw, 1953.

Połpancerze praktyczne [Practical Half-Armors]. Cracow, Wydawnictwo Literackie, 1953.

Maleńkie lato [The Small Summer]. Cracow, Literackie, 1956.

Słoń. Cracow, Wydawnictwo Literackie, 1957; as *The Elephant*, London, Macdonald, 1962; New York, Grove Press, 1963.

Wesele w Atomicach [A Wedding in Atomtown]. Cracow, Wydawnictwo Literackie, 1959.

Ucieczka na południe [Escape Southward]. Warsaw, Iskry, 1961.

Deszcz [Rain]. Cracow, Wydawnictwo Literackie, 1962.

Opowiadania [Stories]. Cracow, Wydawnictwo Literackie, 3 vols., 1964–81.

The Ugupu Bird (selection). London, Macdonald, 1968.

Dwa listy i inne opowiadania [Two Letters and Other Stories]. Paris, Instytut Literacki, 1970.

Parabellum. Warsaw, Ludowa Spółdzielnia Wydawnicza, 1979.

Moniza Clavier. Cracow, Wydawnictwo Literackie, 1983.

Wybór opowiadań, 1982–1985 [Selected Stories, 1982–1985]. Cracow, Biblioteka Promienistych (samizdat), 1985.

Opowiadania [Stories]. Lublin, samizdat, 1985.

Other

Polska w obrazach [Poland in Pictures] (cartoons). Cracow 1957.

Postępowiec [The Progressive] (cartoons). Warsaw, Iskry 1960.

Przez okulary [Through Sławomir Mrożek's Glasses (cartoons). Warsaw, Iskry, 1968.

Małe listy [Little Letters]. Cracow, Wydawnictw Literackie, 1982.

Rysunki [Drawings]. Warsaw, Iskry, 1982.

Donosy [Denunciations]. London, Puls, 1983.

*

Critical Studies: "Mrożek's Family" by Jan Kott, in *Encounter* (London), 25(6), 1965; Mrożek issue of *Drama at Calgary* (Calgary, Alberta), 3(3), 1969; "Sławomir Mrożek: Jester in Search of an Absolute," in *Canadian Slavic Studies*, 3(4), 1969, and "Sławomir Mrożek: The Seeker of Absolutes," in *Contemporary Polish Theater and Drama (1956–1984)*, Westport, Connecticut, Greenwood, 1988, both by E. J. Czerwinski; "The Absurdist Vision of Sławomir Mrożek's *Striptease*" by Frank S. Galassi, in *Polish Review* (New York), 17(3), 1972; "Sławomir Mrożek and the Polish Tradition of the Absurd" by Barbara Kejan-Sharratt, in *New Zealand Slavonic Journal* (Wellington), 1, 1974; "Mrożek and the Form Theory Revised" by Anthony J. Bednarczyk, in *Polish Review* (New York), 23(1), 1978; *Mrożek* by Jan Kłossowicz, Warsaw, Authors Agency/Czytelnik, 1980; "Sławomir Mrożek: The Moulding of a Polish Playwright" by Marketa Goetz-Stankiewicz, in *The Tradition of Polish Ideas*, London, Orbis, 1981; "A Collage of History in the Form of Mrożek's *Tango*" by Michael C. O'Neill, in *Polish Review* (New York), 28(2), 1983; "Contexts for *Vatzlav*: Mrożek and the Eighteenth Century" by Daniel Gerould, in *Modern Drama* (Toronto), March 1984; "Sławomir Mrożek: From Satire to National Drama" by Halina Stephan, in *Polish Review* (New York), 34(1), 1989.

*   *   *

Sławomir Mrożek is contemporary Poland's most penetrating and popular writer. He combines steely, precise language with sharp irony and surrealism, and thus elevates the absurd situations that typify a modern totalitarian state to more than just benign or malignant satire.

As a product of the limited thawing of intellectual life following the 1956 "Polish October," Mrożek's work was published intermittently, when the censor felt like proving his tolerance. As a result of such state anti-patronage the Polish public has seen staged plays dealing with areas of enormous sensitivity, such as the police, exile, or the state bureaucracy, but in a way that no direct references are made to specific national figures or countries. That the Polish political status quo has also actively interfered with people's lives is purely "coincidental." His other main target has been his disaffected but apathetic audience whose neuroses and phobias he dissects and blames for the continuing malaise, in conceding so much to "Big Brother."

Mrożek's obvious success rests particularly with his plays, hitting a suppressed nerve again and again: *Policja* (*The Policeman*) first found that nerve as it depicted the mind-boggling inanity of the thugs elevated to the guardianship of law and order. While the characters are stereotyped and the plot absurd, Mrożek's technique is clear: he invites comparison between the universal (*policja*) and the particular (the Polish *milicja obywatelska*). The audience reads these many levels into such works, used as it is to many decades of censorship.

Tango firmly established Mrożek's reputation. It is a witty representation of the problems of the generation gap, and "revolting" children. Artur, son of the family, fights for the re-establishment of traditional values and ambitions in the face of his parents' dated ideals of spontaneous performance art, free love, and revolutionary freedom. *Tango* reveals the forces willing to profit from such "power struggles" when the mother's boorish lover stages a *coup d'état* and imposes his vision of social progress on his hosts — dancing the tango. While the intellectuals argue, the workers seize the freedoms promised.

Despite other plays, his dramatic work was extended again by his experiences during his brief exiles abroad. The product of these travels was *Emigranci* (*The Emigrés*), where the plot centres around two exiles, living in constant conflict, a rapacious *gastarbeiter* of peasant stock, and a cynical, disillusioned intellectual. The tension between them leads to a murder attempt, and the acceptance of the immutability of their sentences to exile, economic and political.

In all his plays, his collections of short stories (particularly *Słoń* [*The Elephant*] and *Deszcz* [Rain]), and even in his irreverent cartoons published in the weekly *Szpilki*, Mrożek paints a bleak picture of humanity and, by implication, of his fellow Poles. These snapshots of personal or national obsessions have imprisoned people in a deadly logic of action (or inaction). While that logic (which is absurd) may be humorous when represented, Mrożek is warning his audiences that a break has to be made in the vicious circle of survival and power. For that reason, Mrożek is one of the few Polish writers today whose work is relevant even to non-Polish audiences.

—Donald Pirie

———

MULISCH, Harry (Kurt Victor). Dutch. Born in Haarlem, 29 July 1927. Educated at Haarlem Lyceum. Married Sjoerdje Woudenberg in 1971; two daughters. Writer; founder-editor, *Randstad* magazine; member of the Board, De Bezige Bij publishers, Amsterdam. Recipient: Reina Prinsen Geerligs prize, 1951; Bijenkorf prize, 1957; Anne Frank prize, 1957; Visser Neerlandia prize, 1960; Athos prize, 1961; Constantijn Huygens prize, 1977; Hooft Prize, 1977. Knighted, Order of Orange-Nassau, 1977. Address: Leidsekade 103, 1017 PP Amsterdam, Netherlands.

PUBLICATIONS

Fiction

Tussen hamer en aambeeld [Between Hammer and Anvil]. Amsterdam, Arbeiderspers, 1952.
Archibald Strohalm. Amsterdam, Bezige Bij, 1952.
Chantage op het leven [Blackmailing Life]. Amsterdam, Bezige Bij, 1953.
Di diamant [The Diamond]. Amsterdam, Bezige Bij, 1954.
De sprong der paarden en de zoute zee [The Horses' Leap and the Salt Sea]. Amsterdam, De Beuk, 1955.
Het mirakel [The Miracle]. Amsterdam, Arbeiderspers, 1956.
Het zwarte licht [The Black Light]. Amsterdam, Bezige Bij, 1056.
De versierde mens [The Decorated Man]. Amsterdam, Bezige Bij, 1957.
Het stenen bruidsbed. Amsterdam, Bezige Bij, 1959; as *The Stone Bridal Bed*, New York and London, Abelard Schuman, 1962.
Quauhquauhtinchan in den vreemde: een sprookje [Quauhquauhtinchan Abroad: A Fairytale]. Amsterdam, Bezige Bij, 1962.
Wat gebeurde er met Sergeant Massuro?. Amsterdam, Bezige Bij, 1972; as "What Happened to Sergeant Massuro," in *The Modern Image: Outstanding Stories from the Hudson Re-*

view, edited by Frederick Morgan, New York, Norton, 1965.

De verteller [The Narrator]. Amsterdam, Bezige Bij, 1970.

De grens [The Limit]. Amsterdam, Loeb, 1975.

Twee vrouwen. Amsterdam, Bezige Bij, 1975; as *Two Women*, London, Calder, 1980; New York, Riverrun, 1981.

Verzamelde verhalen 1947–1977 [Collected Stories]. Amsterdam, Anthenaeum-Polak & Van Gennep, 1977; as *De verhalen 1947–1977*. Amsterdam, Bezige Bij, 1981.

Oude lucht: Drie verhalen [Stale Air: Three Stories]. Amsterdam, Bezige Bij, 1977.

Symmetrie en andere verhalen [Symmetry and Other Stories]. Utrecht, Knippenberg, 1982.

De aanslag. Amsterdam, Bezige Bij, 1982; as *The Assault*, London, Collins Harvill, and New York, Pantheon, 1985.

De gezochte spiegel [The Sought Mirror]. Zutphen, ten Bosch, 1983.

The Decorated Man (7 novellas). London, Calder, 1984.

De kamer [The Room]. Nieuwervaart, d'Onderkruiper, 1984.

Hoogste tijd. Amsterdam, Bezige Bij, 1985; as *Last Call*, London, Collins Harvill, 1987; New York, Viking, 1989.

De pupil [The Pupil]. Amsterdam, Bezige Bij, 1987.

De elementen [The Elements]. Amsterdam, Bezige Bij, 1988.

Voorval: variatie op een thema [Incident: Variation on a Theme]. Amsterdam, Bezige Bij, 1989.

Plays

Tanchelijn: Kroniek van een ketter [Tanchelijn: Chronicle of a Heretic]. Amsterdam, Bezige Bij, 1960.

De knop: Gevolgd door Stan Laurel & Oliver Hardy [The Button: Followed by Stan Laurel & Oliver Hardy]. Amsterdam, Bezige Bij, 1961.

Reconstructie [Reconstruction], with others (produced Amsterdam, 1969). Amsterdam, Bezige Bij, 1969.

Oidipous Oidipous, from the play by Sophocles. Amsterdam, Bezige Bij, 1972.

Bezoekuur [Visiting Time]. Amsterdam, Bezige Bij, 1974.

Volk en vaderliefde: een koningskomedie [The People and Paternal Love: A Royal Comedy]. Amsterdam, Bezige Bij, 1975.

Axel, from the play by Villiers de l'Isle-Adam. Amsterdam, Bezige Bij, 1977.

Theater 1960–1977. Amsterdam, Bezige Bij, 1988.

Verse

Woorden, woorden, woorden [Words, Words, Words]. Amsterdam, Bezige Bij, 1973.

De vogels: drie balladen [The Birds: Three Ballads]. Amsterdam, Athenaeum-Polak & Van Gennep, 1974.

Tegenlicht [Light in the Eyes]. Amsterdam, Athenaeum-Polak & Van Gennep, 1975.

Kind en kraai [Kinfolk]. Amsterdam, Eliance Pers, 1975.

De wijn is drinkbaar dank zij het glas [The Wine Is Drinkable Because of the Glass]. Amsterdam, Bezige Bij, 1976.

De taal is een ei [Language Is an Egg]. Amsterdam, Athenaeum, 1976.

Wat poëzie is: een leerdicht. Amsterdam, Athenaeum, 1978; as *What Poetry Is*, Merrick, New York, Cross Cultural, 1981.

Opus gran. Amsterdam, De Harmonie, 1982.

Egyptisch [Egyptian]. Amsterdam, Bezige Bij, 1983.

De gedichten: 1974–1983 [The Poems 1974–1983]. Amsterdam, Bezige Bij, 1987.

Other

Manifesten [Manifestoes]. Zaandijk, Heijnis, 1958.

Voer voor psychologen [Fodder for Psychologists]. Amsterdam, Bezige Bij, 1961.

Wenken voor de bescherming van uw gezin en uzelf, tijdens de jongste dag [Tips for the Protection of Your Family and Yourself, at the Day of Judgement]. Amsterdam, Bezige Bij, 1961.

De zaak 40/61: een reportage [The Eichmann Case: A Report]. Amsterdam, Bezige Bij, 1962.

Nol Gregoor in gesprek met Harry Mulisch [Nol Gregoor in Conversation with Harry Mulisch]. Amsterdam, Bezige Bij, 1965.

Bericht aan de rattenkoning [Report to King Rat]. Amsterdam, Bezige Bij, 1966.

Wenken voor de Jongste Dag [Tips for the Day of Judgement]. Amsterdam, Bezige Bij, 1967.

Het woord bij de daad: getuigenissen van de revolutie op Cuba [Words After Deeds: Testimony on the Cuban Revolution]. Amsterdam, Bezige Bij, 1968.

Israël is zelf een mens [Israel Is Human Too]. The Hague, Bakker, 1969.

Paralipomena Orphica. Amsterdam, Bezige Bij, 1970.

Over de affaire Padilla [The Padilla Affair]. Amsterdam, Bezige Bij, 1971.

De verteller verteld [The Story of "The Narrator"]. Amsterdam, Bezige Bij, 1971.

De toekomst van gisteren [The Future of Yesterday]. Amsterdam, Bezige Bij, 1972.

Soep lepelen met een vork [Eating Soup with a Fork]. Amsterdam, Bezige Bij, 1972.

Het sexuele bolwerk [The Sexual Bastion]. Amsterdam, Bezige Bij, 1973.

Mijn getijdenboek [My Book of Hours]. Amsterdam, Landshoff, 1975.

Het ironische van de ironie: over het geval G. K. van het Reve [The Irony of Irony: On the Case of G. K. van het Reve]. Amsterdam, Manteau, 1976.

Vergrote raadsels: verklaringen, paradoxen, mulischesken [Magnified Riddles: Explanations, Paradoxes, Mulischesques], edited by Gerd de Ley. Nijmegen, Gottmer, 1976.

Paniek der onschuld [Panic of Innocence]. Amsterdam, Bezige Bij, 1979.

De compositie van de wereld [The Composition of the World]. Amsterdam, Bezige Bij, 1980.

De mythische formule: dertig gesprekken 1951–1981 [The Mythical Formula: Thirty Conversations 1951–1981]. Amsterdam, Bezige Bij, 1981.

Het boek [The Book]. Amsterdam, Bezige Bij, 1984.

Het ene: Huizinga-lezing 1984 [The One: Huizinga-Reading 1984]. Amsterdam, Athenaeum, 1984.

Wij uiten wat wij voelen, niet wat past [We Say What We Feel Not What Is Appropriate]. Amsterdam, Bezige Bij, 1984.

Vaders en toverballen [Fathers and Magic Balls]. Kolderveen, De Maffer, 1984.

Aan het woord: zeven toespraken [On the Word: Seven Speeches]. Amsterdam, Bezige Bij, 1986.

Bijlage bij de eerste druk van "De compositie van de wereld" [Appendix to the First Impression of "The Composition of the World"]. Amsterdam, Bezige Bij, 1986.

Grondslagen van de mythologie van het schrijverschap [Foundations of the Mythology of Writing]. Amsterdam, Thoth, 1987.

Het licht [The Light]. Amsterdam, Bezige Bij, 1988.

Oedipus als Freud: naar aanleiding van Jung [Oedipus as Freud]. Rotterdam, Lemniscaat, 1988.
Het beeld en de klok [The Picture and the Clock]. Amsterdam, Bezige Bij, 1989.
De zuilen van Hercules [The Pillars of Hercules]. Amsterdam, Bezige Bij, 1990.

*

Bibliography: *Harry Mulisch: een bibliografie* by Marita Mathijsen, The Hague, BZZTôH, 1979.

Critical Studies: "Coming to Terms with the Past and Searching for an Identity: The Treatment of the Occupied Netherlands in the Fiction of Hermans, Mulisch and Vestdijk" by John Michielsen, in *Canadian Journal of Netherlandic Studies* (Windsor, Ontario), 7(1–2), 1986; "An Interview with Harry Mulisch" by Kristina R. Sazaki, in *New German Review* (Los Angeles), 2, 1986; "The Prolog in Mulisch's *aanslag*: A Novel in a Nutshell" by Marcel Janssens, in *The Berkeley Conference on Dutch Literature 1987: New Perspectives on the Modern Period*, edited by Johan D. Snapper and T. F. Shannon, Lanham, Maryland, University Press of America, 1989.

*   *   *

Though chronologically Harry Mulisch belongs to the "war generation" which also produced Willem Frederik Hermans, Gerard Reve, and Jan Wolkers (*qq.v.*), his wide-ranging output of fiction, drama, autobiographical and philosophical essays, superior political journalism, and, more recently, poetry distinguishes itself from the essential naturalism and introverted pessimism of these contemporaries by its playful life-assertiveness and its magico-mythical vision of man, history, and art.

A collection of autobiographical pieces and artistic manifestoes, published in 1961 under the typically provocative title *Voer voor psychologen* (Fodder for Psychologists), illuminates Mulisch's underlying motivations and concerns as an artist. For him the act of writing is akin to alchemy, at once a transformatory rather than a descriptive process, and a quest for the Philosophers' Stone of an all-embracing explanatory principle underlying the surface chaos of existence. In his novels, stories, and plays of the 1950s, with their bizarre juxtapositions of banal realism and supernatural flights of fancy, that principle is often his very personal reading of the Oedipus myth (he was later to adapt Sophocles's version for the Dutch stage), in which God the Father represents the tyranny of death and time. Many of his protagonists, like the visionary puppeteer and charlatan Archibald Strohalm in his first novel and the heretical title-figure of the play *Tanchelijn*, are also significantly themselves artists of a kind, who try to usurp the authority of that God and are destroyed, though their very destruction is a form of identification.

In *Het stenen bruidsbed* (*The Stone Bridal Bed*), arguably the most successful work of Mulisch's "first period," in which an American participant in the Allied bombing of Dresden returns to the city after the war and is caught up in a nightmare of guilt and retribution, the realistic surface is disturbed by mythical and historical undercurrents, most strikingly in the typographically distinct passages of Homeric prose-poetry.

During the 1960s fiction took a back seat, as Mulisch became increasingly involved with contemporary political reality, in turn warning against the dehumanising effect of runaway technology (*De zaak 40/61* [The Eichmann Case]), extolling the anarchistic Dutch Provo movement (*Bericht aan de rattenkoning* [Report to King Rat]), attacking the nuclear arms race (*Wenken voor de Jongste Dag* [Tips for the Day of Judgement]), celebrating the first heady days of the Cuban revolution (*Het woord bij de daad* [Words After Deeds]), and participating in a collaborative opera project on the life of Che Guevara, performed as *Reconstructie* [Reconstruction] in 1969. His subsequent disillusion with utopianism of all kinds is recorded in *De toekomst van gisteren* (The Future of Yesterday), an account of a significantly unwritten work on the fate of Europe after a Nazi victory.

De verteller (The Narrator), a bewildering collage of narrative fragments, riddles, formulae, etc., so cryptic as to require its own key, marked a return to Mulisch's perennial concern with his own creative processes as a storyteller, for whom, he succinctly and dogmatically put it, "the problem is never *what* to write about, but *how* to write about it." By comparison the bestselling *Twee vrouwen* (*Two Women*), which was later filmed, has a deceptively conventional, even trite, storyline, featuring a love triangle and a violent denouement, but subtly evokes a mythical dimension — here that of the Orpheus legend.

Some of Mulisch's recent poetry, often dream-like and tantalisingly hermetic, is reminiscent of his admired predecessor Gerrit Achterberg.

The ambitious and long-gestated philosophical study *De compositie van de wereld* (The Composition of the World), which attempts to account for the whole of human existence and history in terms of the musical octave, met with a mixed reception, and was criticised as pretentious and simplistic. However, if read primarily as literature, the work is entirely consistent with the oeuvre of this eternal enthusiast and dilettante, whose next publication may be (or may not be, since he has been repeatedly distracted in the past) an historical-philosophical novel on which he has worked for over 20 years, to be called *The Discovery of Moscow*.

In fact, research on the former project led to the conception of the war novel *De aanslag* (*The Assault*), which was to become Mulisch's most widely read work to date. In a prologue and five episodes stretching from 1945 to the 1980s it chronicles the aftermath of a wartime assassination and subsequent reprisals through the eyes of a survivor. Fons Rademakers's film adaptation won an Oscar. *Hoogste tijd* (*Last Call*) is the poignant story of the swan song of a veteran musical-hall performer with a shady wartime past who is invited to play Prospero in Shakespeare's *The Tempest*. The elegant novella *De elementen* (The Elements), set on Crete, combines Mulisch's familiar mythical and philosophical preoccupations with expert and ingenious narration.

Reading Mulisch is a constant imaginative and intellectual adventure — one may often dissent, but one is seldom bored.

—Paul Vincent

———

MÜLLER, Heiner. German. Born in Eppendorf, Saxony, 9 January 1929. Married Inge Müller (died 1966). Bookshop worker, then journalist and freelance writer: editor, *Junge Kunst* magazine; staff member, Berliner-Maxim-Gorki-Theater, 1958–59, Berliner Ensemble 1970–76, and Berlin Volksbühne from 1976. Recipient: Heinrich Mann prize, 1959; Erich Weinert Medal, 1964; BZ Critics prize, 1970, 1976; Lessing prize, 1975. Address: c/o Reclam-Verlag, Nonnenstraße 38, 7031 Leipzig, Germany.

PUBLICATIONS

Plays

Zehn Tage die die Welt erschütterten, with Hagen Müller-Stahl, from a work by John Reed (produced Berlin, 1957). Leipzig, Hofmeister, 1958.

Der Lohndrücker, with Inge Müller (produced Leipzig, 1958). Berlin, Henschel, 1958.

Die Korrektur (produced Berlin, 1958). Berlin, Henschel, 1959; as *The Correction*, in *Hamletmachine and Other Texts*, 1984.

Die Umsiedlerin (produced Berlin, 1961). Berlin, Rotbuch, 1975; revised version, as *Die Baueren* (produced Berlin, 1975), in *Stücke*, 1975.

Herakles 5 (produced Berlin, 1974). With *Philoktet*, Frankfurt, Suhrkamp, 1966.

Philoktet (produced Munich, 1968). With *Herakles 5*, Frankfurt, Suhrkamp, 1966; as *Philoctetes* (produced Edinburgh, 1986), Lincoln, University of Nebraska Press, 1981.

Ödipus Tyrann, from the work by Friedrich Hölderlin (produced Berlin, 1967). Berlin, Aufbau, 1968.

Die Aristokraten, with Benno Besson (produced Berlin, 1968).

Wie es euch gefällt, from the play *As You Like It* by Shakespeare (produced Munich, 1968). Included in *Kopien*, 1977.

Drachenoper, from the opera *Lancelot* by Paul Dessau (produced Berlin, 1969). Included in *Theater-Arbeit*, 1975.

Horizonte, from a work by Gerhart Winterlich (produced Berlin, 1969). Included in *Theater-Arbeit*, 1975.

Prometheus (produced Zurich, 1969). Included in *Geschichten aus der Produktion 2*, 1974.

Weiberkomödie, from a radio play by Inge Müller (produced Magdeburg, 1970). Included in *Theater-Arbeit*, 1975.

Arzt wider Willen, with Benno Besson (produced Berlin, 1970).

Die Möwe, with Ginka Tscholakowa, from a work by Anton Chekhov (produced Berlin, 1972).

Macbeth, from the play by Shakespeare (produced Magdeburg, 1972). Included in *Stücke*, 1975.

Der Horatier (produced Berlin, 1972). Included in *Stücke*, 1975; as *The Horatian*, in *Minnesota Review*, 1976.

Zement, from a work by Fyodor Gladkov (produced Berlin, 1973). Included in *Geschichten aus der Produktion 2*, 1974; as *Cement* (produced Wivenhoe Park, Essex, 1981), in *New German Critique 16*, Winter 1979.

Traktor (produced Neustrelitz, 1974–75). Included in *Geschichten aus der Produktion 2*, 1974.

Geschichten aus der Produktion 1–2. Berlin, Rotbuch, 2 vols., 1974.

Der Bau (produced Berlin, 1980). Included in *Geschichten aus der Producktion 1*, 1974.

Die Schlacht (produced Berlin, 1975). Berlin, Henschel, 1977; as *The Battle*, in *The Battle: Plays, Prose, Poems*, 1989.

Mauser, from the novel *And Quiet Flows the Don* by Sholokhov (produced Austin, Texas, 1975). Included in *Mauser* (collection), 1978.

Theater-Arbeit. Berlin, Rotbuch, 1975.

Stücke. Berlin, Henschel, 1975.

Kopien: 3 Versuche, Shakespeare zu töten. Frankfurt, Suhrkamp, 1977.

Leben Gundlings Friedrich von Preussen Lessings Schlaf Traum Schrei (produced Frankfurt, 1979). With *Die Schlacht*, 1977; as *The Life of Gundling*, New York, Performing Arts, 1984.

Hamlet, with Matthias Langhoff, from the play by Shakespeare (produced Berlin, 1977). Included in *Shakespeare Factory 2*, 1980.

Germania Tod in Berlin (produced Munich, 1978). Berlin, Rotbuch, 1977.

Fatzer (produced Hamburg, 1978).

Mauser (collection). Berlin, Rotbuch, 1978.

Die Hamletmaschine (produced Paris, 1979). Included in *Mauser*, 1978; as *Hamletmachine* (produced New York, 1984; London, 1987), in *Hamletmachine and Other Texts*, 1984.

Shakespeare Factory 2. Frankfurt, Suhrkamp, 1980; revised and enlarged edition, as *Shakespeare Factory 1–2*, 2 vols., 1985–89.

Der Auftrag (produced Berlin, 1980). With *Der Bau* and *Herakles 5*, 1981; as *The Mission; or, Memory of a Revolution* (produced London, 1982), in *Gambit* (London), 39-40, 1982; as *The Assignment*, New York, Performing Arts, 1984; as *The Task* (produced London, 1989), in *Hamletmachine and Other Texts*, 1984.

Der Auftrag; Der Bau; Herakles 5. Berlin, Henschel, 1981.

Quartett, from the novel *Les Liaisons dangereuses* by Choderlos de Laclos (produced Bochum, 1982). Frankfurt, Autoren, 1981; as *Quartet* (produced London, 1983; New York, 1985), in *Hamletmachine and Other Texts*, 1984.

Verkommenes Ufer Medeamaterial Landschaft mit Argonauten (produced Bochum, 1982). Berlin, Henschel, 1982; as *Despoiled Shore Medeamaterial Landscape with Argonauts*, in *Hamletmachine and Other Texts*, 1984; as *Medea Plays: Medea Game and Waterfront Wasteland* (produced London, 1990).

Herzstück. Berlin, Rotbuch, 1983; as *Heartpiece*, in *Hamletmachine and Other Texts*, 1984.

Bildbeschreibung (produced Graz, 1985). Berlin, Henschel, 1984.

Hamletmachine and Other Texts for the Stage. New York, Performing Arts, 1984.

Wolokolamsker Chaussee 1 (produced East Berlin, 1985). Berlin, Henschel, 1985.

The CIVIL warS. a tree is best measured when it is down, with Robert Wilson (produced Cologne, 1985).

Anatomie Titus Fall of Rome (produced Bochum, 1985). Included in *Shakespeare Factory 2*, 1989.

Quai West, from a work by Bernard-Marie-Koltès (produced Bochum, 1986).

Wolokolamsker Chaussee II: Wald bei Moskau, from a work by Alexander Bek (produced Potsdam, 1986). Included in *Shakespeare Factory 2*, 1989.

Prologue to *Alcestis* (produced Cambridge, Massachusetts, 1986).

Wolokolamsker Chaussee III: Das Duell, from a work by Anna Seghers (produced Potsdam, 1987). Included in *Shakespeare Factory 2*, 1989.

Revolutionsstücke, edited by Uwe Wittstock. Stuttgart, Reclam, 1988.

Stücke: Texte über Deutschland (1957–1979), edited by Frank Hörnigk. Leipzig, Reclam, 1989.

Kopien 1–2. Berlin, Rotbuch, 2 vols., 1989.

Other

"Ich bin ein Neger": Diskussion mit Heiner Müller, with Eva-Maria Viebeg. Darmstadt, Büchner, 1986.

Gesammelte Irrtümer: Interviews und Gespräche. Frankfurt, Autoren, 1986.

Sprach-Spiel-Spaß: . . . manchmal in Fraktur. Horneburg/ Niederelbe, Persen, 1988.
Explosion of a Memory and Other Writings (includes plays), edited and translated by Carl Weber. New York, Performing Arts, 1989.
Ein Gespräch: geführt am 16.10.1987 in Frankfurt, with Erich Fried.   Berlin, Alexander, 1989.
The Battle: Plays, Prose, Poems, edited and translated by Carl Weber.   New York, Performing Arts, 1989.
Heiner Müller Material: Texte und Kommentare, edited by Frank Hörnigk.   Göttingen, Steidl, 1989.
Heiner Müller "zur Lage der Nation" (interview), with Frank M. Raddatz.   Berlin, Rotbuch, 1990.
Ein Gespenst verläßt Europa, photographs by Sibylle Bergemann.   Cologne, Kiepenheuer und Witsch, 1990.

*

Critical Studies: "Heiner Müller and Other East German Dramaturgs" by Joel Schlechter, in *Yale/Theatre* (New Haven, Connecticut), 8(2–3), 1977; "*Cement*: From Gladkov's Monumental Epos to Müller's Avant-Garde Drama" by Halina Stephan, in *Germano-Slavica* (Waterloo, Ontario), 3, 1979; "The Gender of Authorship: Heiner Müller and Christa Wolf" by Helen Fehervary, in *Studies in 20th-Century Literature* (Manhattan, Kansas), Fall 1980; "'Reject It, in Order to Possess It!': On Heiner Müller and Bertolt Brecht" by Theo Girshausen, in *Modern Drama* (Toronto), January 1981; *The Silence of Entropy of Universal Discourse: The Postmodernist Poetics of Heiner Müller*, New York, Lang, 1985, and "*Der Auftrag* and *Die Maßnahme*: Models of Revolution in Heiner Müller and Bertolt Brecht," in *German Quarterly* (St. Louis, Missouri), Winter 1986, both by Arlene Akiko Teraoka; "Life on the Wall: An Interview with Heiner Müller" by Elinor Fuchs and James Leverett, in *Art and Cinema*, Summer 1986; "'The Rebellion of the Body Against the Effect of Ideas': Heiner Müller's Concept of Tragedy" by Julie Klassen, in *Within the Dramatic Spectrum*, edited by Karelisa V. Hartigan, Lanham, Maryland, University Press of America, 1986; "On Myth and Marxism: The Case of Heiner Müller and Christa Wolf" by Herbert A. Arnold, in *Colloquia Germanica* (Lexington, Kentucky), 21(1), 1988; "Müller's *Cement*: Fragments of Heroic Myth" by Max Harris, in *Modern Drama* (Toronto), September 1988; "A Conversation with Robert Wilson and Heiner Müller" by Arthur Holmberg, in *Modern Drama* (Toronto), September 1988; "Homburg-Machine — Heiner Müller in the Shadow of Nuclear War" by J. H. Reid, in *A Radical Stage: Theatre in Germany in the 1970s and 1980s*, edited by W. G. Sebald, Oxford, Berg, 1988; "Heiner Müller's *Der Lohndrücker*" by Marc Silberman, in *Theater* (New Haven, Connecticut), Summer-Fall 1988; "Post-Modernism and the Multi-Media Sensibility: Heiner Müller's *Hamletmachine* and the Art of Robert Wilson" by Nicholas Zurbrugg, in *Modern Drama* (Toronto), September 1988.

*   *   *

The plays of Heiner Müller could be organized within two basic periods: the Brechtian period from 1956 to 1968 and the avant-garde period from 1968 to the present. As "the new Brecht," Müller concentrated on the historical development of state socialism in the GDR. These early plays are composed of character types and classical verse forms, depicting the move of history through contradiction and error, a style regarded as both formative and unacceptable by the official Cultural Policy in the East and as Marxist model as well as pessimistic individualism in the West.

In 1968, concurrent with the Soviet invasion of Czechoslovakia, Müller's plays adopt a darker tone. History is no longer their subject-matter, but merely a theatrical element, mixed with classical themes, horrifying fantasies, and personal dreams. *Zement* (*Cement*) provides an example of this style: set in the Soviet Revolution, fantasy scenes of Prometheus and Heracles are interspersed with those of historical events. The play ends in scenes of Party expulsions. Subsequent to *Cement*, the plays of the late 1970s are composed of fragmentary scenes and sentences, cast in a postmodern text of metaphor and allusion. These plays indict theatrical conventions as allies of state politics. *Die Hamletmaschine* (*Hamletmachine*) illustrates this indictment: Hamlet is a prince of both state and theatrical imperialist organizations with the playwright as the hidden power behind the throne. The language of the stage is portrayed as exclusionary and oppressive. The play calls for a revolution against its own production.

Müller's avant-garde plays require a new production style, combining the stage traditions of the Absurdists with those of Performance Art. The plays suggest visual spectacles which clarify their basic meanings, but which have an obtuse relationship with the words of the text. The process of discovering the production elements in both aesthetic and political in its technique. Because of this unique sense of production, Müller began to direct his own plays in the 1980s. In production, he combined the elements of Erwin Piscator's and Brecht's political theaters with those of Samuel Beckett and Robert Wilson.

In spite of the major change in Müller's work from his early to his late plays, certain themes run through his entire opus. The theme of sexual politics develops throughout his plays, allied with themes of the sexual ownership of women and the sexual roles in which both theater and state have cast them. The theme of imperialism develops through capitalism, state socialism to theatrical convention. The theme of the individual as subject or object of the political process is portrayed through early collectives to postmodern autobiographical dreams.

Müller enjoys an international reputation as an innovator of dramatic form, a master of German dramatic language, and a crucial political voice on the stage.

—Sue-Ellen Case

———

MUNĪF, 'Abd al-Rahmān. Saudi Arabian. Born in Amman, Jordan, in 1933. Educated in Egypt. Worked as an oil economist in Baghdad, and for OPEC. Exiled; since mid-1980s has lived in Damascus. Address: c/o Quartet Books, 27–29 Goodge Street, London W1P 1FD, England.

PUBLICATIONS

Fiction

Al-ashjār wa-ightiyāl Marzūq [The Trees and the Assassination of Marzūq].   1973.
Qiṣṣat ḥubb majūsiyyah [Magian Love Story].   1974.
Sharq al-Mutawasiṭ [East of the Mediterranean].   1975.
Al-nihāyāt.   1978; as *Endings*, London, Quartet, 1988.
Sibāq al-masāfāt al-ṭawīlah [Long-Distance Race].   1979.

'*Ālam bi-lā kharā' iṭ* [World Without Maps], with Jabrā
  Ibrāhīm Jabrā. Beirut, al-Mu'assasah al-'Arabiyyah lil-
  Dirāsāt wa-al-Nashr, 1982.
Mudun al-milḥ [Cities of Salt], quintet.
  Al-tīh. Beirut, Arab Institute for Research and Publishing,
    1984; as *Cities of Salt*, New York, Random House, 1987;
    London, Cape, 1988.
  Al-ukhdūd [Farrow]. 1985.
  Taqāsīm al-layl wa-al-nahār [Variations on Night and Day].
    1989.
  Al-munbatt [The Uprooted]. 1989.
  Bādiyat al-ẓulumāt [The Desert of Darkness]. 1989.
Hina tarakna al-jisr [When We Left the Bridge]. n.d.
Al-ān hunā [Here and Now]. 1991.

Other

Al-dīmuqrāṭiyya awalan, al-dīmuqrāṭiyya dā'iman [Demo-
  cracy First, Democracy Always]. Beirut, Al-Mu'ssasah al-
  'Arbiyyah lil-Dirāsāt wa-al-Nashr, 1992.

*   *   *

'Abd al-Rahmān Munīf is the most important writer to
emerge from the Arabian peninsula, and one of the major
Arab writers of the last two decades. He was born in Amman
(Jordan) of a Saudi father and Iraqi mother and spent large
periods of his life in Jordan, Iraq, Syria, and Lebanon. This
first-hand experience of many Arab countries was the result of
a varied career, for he started as a law student and political
activist in the Ba'th Party, then graduated in economics and
became an oil specialist and journalist. Unlike many writers of
his generation he started writing late in his life: his first novel,
Al-ashjār wa-ightiyāl Marzūq (The Trees and the Assassination of Marzūq), appeared when he was 40 years old.
This wide experience coupled with the late start gave his
writing pan-Arab relevance and maturity.

The appearance of his first novel in 1973, the year of the
October War and oil boom, coincided with the rejuvenation of
the Arabic novel and the exploration of untrodden paths of
human experience. The change in literary sensibility towards
modernistic writing which took roots in the previous decade
liberated Arabic literature from the constraints of monophonic
narration. Instead it was directed towards the sophistication of
polyphonic narrative with its pluralist perspectives and density
of voices contending to shed doubt on one another's accounts
of the plot. The syllogistic progression which, in the past,
created the coherence of narrative and developed the novel's
plot was replaced by dynamically dialectic progression and use
of the text's internal memory. New novels suppressed their
subject- matter or submerged it in an elaborate labyrinth of
narrative strategies. The writer became more aware of the
constant interaction between the form and content of his work
and developed a sensitive approach to the motivations of his
technical devices. In addition, the concept of the individual
hero and central plot gave way to an elaborate network of
relationshps in which all characters attain equal importance.

These changes are all evident in Munīf's novels, which are at
the forefront of modernistic narrative. Since his first novel and
through to his latest, *Al-ān huna* (Here and Now), Munīf
abandoned the outmoded concept of the individual hero and
selected his protagonists from the marginalised and violated.
He tried to establish his unique fictional space which is capable
of capturing the contradictory nature of the Arab world. Like
Hardy's Wessex or Faulkner's Yoknapatawpha County, Munīf

created his imaginary desert town, Thebes, from his first
novel and elaborated it in *Al-nihāyāt* (*Endings*), changing its
name to *wādi al-'uyūn* in the Cities of Salt quintet. In this
imaginary place, which stands as a metaphor for the whole of
the Arab world, Munīf elaborates the impotent, backward,
and defeated Arab world in which a number of impossibly
romantic characters struggle to attain simple dreams. One
such character is 'Assāf, the enigmatic hero, or rather anti-
hero, of *Endings*, with its haunting and poetic atmosphere
and fascinating binary structure of two interconnected but
semi-autonomous narratives. His simple and impossible
dream is nothing less than the preservation of the essence of
life, of humanity, in a nightmarish reality redolent with
symbolism.

A similar atmosphere is invoked in '*Ālam bi-lā kharā' iṭ*
(World Without Maps), which he wrote with Jabrā Ibrāhīm
Jabrā (*q.v.*). The novel investigates the impact of the transformation of space on the modes of human existence and
types of interaction. It endeavours to record the
metamorphosis of the Arab city over the last 25 years. The
deformation of the city goes hand-in-hand with the deterioration of the hero's tribal background. So the tribal escape
is eliminated as an option, and the city becomes man's destiny
and his doom. Here its contradictory character is at its height.
It has liberated man from the bonds of the closed, almost
incestuous relations of the tribal mode of existence, yet its
constant transformation undermines the positive aspects of
that freedom. The process of urbanisation is a product of
human endeavour, and a manifestation of its limits. In this
novel one encounters the city as a contemporary labyrinth.
The various textual strategies at work in this novel attempt to
show that the labyrinthine and nightmarish nature of the
modern Arab city are detectable in both the novel's theme
and its structure.

But Munīf's most comprehensive metaphor of the Arab
condition and its metamorphosis is his quintet, *Mudun al-
Milḥ* (Cities of Salt). It is the epic of contemporary Arabic
novel *par excellence*, and the contemporary heir of the
archetypal Arab narrative of *The Arabian Nights*. Unlike
Nagīb Mahfūz's (*q.v.*) Cairo trilogy with its Cairene world
and family saga, Munīf's quintet is a novel about the historical, cultural, and moral transformation of Arabia. The
structure of the novel is akin to that of *The Arabian Nights* in
which stories generate other stories in an endless sequence
whose main character is time. On the surface level, it tells the
story of the collective transformation of a Bedouin society
from the state of tribal existence into oil boom consumerism
and modern state apparatus. The constant violations of triba
ethics and rebellion against its taboos are coupled with an
inherent respect for them, a condition that enhances tension
and sustains the nightmare. But beneath this surface one see:
the dynamics of the impact of modernity on traditionalism
the development of the oppressive state machine, the inne
mechanism of the American control over the Arabian penin
sula, and the disintegration of the old cultural and mora
ethos of Arabia.

Another recurring theme in Munīf's novels is politica
coercion, which is woven into the fabric of his narrative. It i
the main theme of *Sharq al-Mutawasiṭ* (East of the Mediterra
nean), and his most recent novel, *Al-ān hunā*. In these work
the whole of the Arab world stretching to the east and th
south of the Mediterranean seems like a vast political priso
in which suffering equally befalls those in prison and tho:
outside its immediate walls, the victim and the torturer. I
these novels terror reins supreme and every attempt to sta\
off its tyrannical power is futile. However, despite the nigh
marish atmosphere in most of Munīf's novels (save *Qiṣ*

ḥubb majūsiyyah [Magian Love Story] and *Sibāq al-masāfāt al-ṭawīlah* [Long-Distance Race]), there is always a glimmer of hope and a strong belief that while it may be possible to crush man, it is impossible to defeat him.

—Sabry Hafez

MURAKAMI Haruki. Japanese. Born in 1949. Educated at Waseda University. Married to Yoko Takahashi. Owner of jazz club, Tokyo, for seven years. Has lived in Greece, 1986–89, and Italy. Visiting fellow, Princeton University, New Jersey, 1991. Lives in Princeton. Recipient: Shinjin Bungaku prize, 1980; Tanizaki prize, 1985. Address: c/o Kōdansha International, 114 Fifth Avenue, New York, New York 10011, U.S.A.

PUBLICATIONS

Fiction

Hear the Wind Sing (in Japanese). 1979.
Pinball 1973.   Tokyo, Kōdansha, 1980.
Hitsuji o meguru bōken.   Tokyo, Kōdansha, 1982; as *A Wild Sheep Chase*, New York, Kōdansha International, 1989; London, Hamish Hamilton, 1990.
Kaiten mokuba no deddo hīto.   Tokyo, Kōdansha, 1985.
Sekai no owari to hādo-boirudo wandārando.   Tokyo, Shinchōsha, 1985; as *Hard-Boiled Wonderland and the End of the World*, Tokyo, New York, and London, Kōdansha International, 1991.
Noruuei no mori [Norwegian Wood].   Tokyo, Kōdansha, 2 vols., 1987.
Dansu, dansu, dansu [Dance Dance Dance].   Tokyo, Kōdansha, 1988.
Murakami Haruki zensakuhin, 1979–1989.   Tokyo, Kōdansha, 8 vols., 1990–91.
The Elephant Vanishes.   New York, Knopf, 1993.

Other

Murakami Asahidō, with Anzai Mizumaru.   Tokyo, Wakabayashi Shuppan Kikaku, 1984.
Tōi taiko.   Tokyo, Kōdansha, 1990.

Has translated into Japanese works by F. Scott Fitzgerald, Truman Capote, Raymond Carver, Paul Theroux, John Irving, and others.

*   *   *

Several critics have cited Murakami Haruki's writing as a turning point in Japanese literature. While earlier Japanese writers have concentrated on Japan's traditional heritage, as well as been, as Murakami himself describes it, "addicted to the beauty of the language," Murakami displays a westernised sensibility set in an only vaguely Japanese landscape, written in an understated, prosaic style. Indeed, it is easy to forget that his stories and novels *are* set in Japan; only offhand references to Tokyo and other Japanese cities remind us that this is not America. Culturally there are many more references to American literature, films, and music than to anything Asian.

And the psychological make-up of his characters is more familiar to Western readers as a kind of late 20th-century disenfranchisement common among the young in the West. While it may be an authentic portrayal of the new generation in Japan, it is a very new perspective of the Japanese for the rest of the world.

Murakami began writing in the 1970s after owning a jazz club for several years. His first two novels, *Hear the Wind Sing* and *Pinball 73* (the latter winning Kodansha publisher's Shinjin Bungaku prize for best newcomer in 1980), are "weak" according to Murakami, and are unlikely to be translated into other languages. They did, however, introduce the nameless protagonist who was to become more familiar to readers in Murakami's third novel, the bestselling *Hitsuji o meguru bōken* (*A Wild Sheep Chase*). The novel is a bizarre tale about the search for a sheep with special powers — a premise never really questioned by the protagonist, who pursues the sheep as much out of boredom with his life as from pressure to do so from a mysterious, powerful gangster figure. The hero is rootless, faceless, distanced, and reminiscent of Raymond Chandler heroes — one of Murakami's favourite writers. His emotional vulnerability — his wife leaves him at the beginning of the novel, and *à la* Chandler he doesn't keep the girl in the end either — does not warm readers to him, in part because the narrative's laconic style does not encourage identification with him. However, he can be very funny and entertaining, frequently bringing up metaphysical questions about his predicament. In fact, in the minds of the characters the sheep itself takes on metaphysical qualities, ultimately representing a kind of life force that can engender both good and evil. *Dansu, dansu, dansu* [Dance, Dance, Dance], the sequel to *Wild Sheep*, continues the story in the same vein.

Murakami's other novel that has been translated into English, *Sekai no owari to hādo-boirudo wandārando* (*Hard-Boiled Wonderland and the End of the World*), is a kind of science-fiction story made up of two separate but interwoven tales, representing the conscious and unconscious mind. In the first, *Hard-Boiled Wonderland* part, set in a futuristic Tokyo, the protagonist displays a curious ability to "launder" information in his unconscious mind, shuffling data from one side of his brain to the other. Various commercial elements would like to exploit his talent, and the story chronicles his attempts to escape them. *The End of the World* section is set in a walled town where the residents appear incapable of thought, and to which the hero's unconscious has been banished. The link between the two parts is subtle and satisfying, with various images echoing back and forth. However, ultimately there is something flat about the novel — it fails to communicate beyond a certain point. As reviewer Nick Hornby explained, "For all Murakami's ambitions as a late twentieth-century myth-teller, the myths steadfastly refuse to resonate, and the entire inventive network refers only to itself."

Murakami's most popular novel in Japan has also been his most realistic and straightforward, *Noruuei no mori* (*Norwegian Wood*, after the Beatles song) is set in Tokyo of the late 1960s, and follows the story of a young man in love with an unhappy girl who is hospitalised and eventually commits suicide. Interestingly, for all the book's popularity in Japan (over four million copies sold), Murakami and his publishers have expressed reluctance to have it translated into other languages, saying it is too "simple" and "sentimental" for western readers.

Clearly Murakami relishes the role he has created for himself as a new voice of Japan — detached, questioning its place in the world, embracing American culture. He now lives in the United States, and it will be interesting to see if he can and will sustain his chosen voice there.

—Theresa Werner

MYRDAL, Jan. Swedish. Born in Stockholm, 19 July 1927. Married 1) Nadja Wiking in 1948; 2) Maj Liedberg in 1953; 3) Gun Kessle in 1956; one son and one daughter. Columnist, *Stockholms-Tidningen*, 1963–66, and *Aftonbladet*, 1966–72; publisher and chair, 1971–72, and since 1972 columnist, *Folket i Bild/Kulturfront*. Chair, Sino-Chinese Organisation, 1968–71; member, 1971–73, and chair, 1973, Sino-Swedish Association. D.Litt.: Upsala College, New Jersey, 1980. Chevalier de l'Ordre des Arts et des Lettres (France), 1990. Address: Fagervik, 150 30 Mariefred, Sweden.

PUBLICATIONS

Fiction

Hemkomst [The Homecoming].   Stockholm, Tiden, 1954.
Jubelvår [The Joys of Spring].   Stockholm, Tiden, 1955.
Att bli och vara [To Become and To Be].   Stockholm, Tiden, 1956.
Badrumskranen [The Bathroom Tap].   Stockholm, Norstedt, 1957.
Karriär [Career].   Stockholm, Norstedt, 1975.

Plays

Folkets hus: samtal vid en invigning [Town Hall: Conversations at an Opening] (produced 1953).   Stockholm, Seelig, 1953.
Moraliteter [Moralities] (produced 1967).   Stockholm, Norstedt, 1967.
Är Inga Eriksson människa? [Is Inga Eriksson a Person?] (radio play).   Stockholm, Sveriges Radio, 1969.
Garderingar [Safeguards] (produced 1969).   Stockholm, Norstedt, 1969.
B. Olsen löper livet ut: ett svenskt tvärgrepp i 13 bilder [B. Olsen Lives Life to the Full: A Cross-Section of Sweden in 13 Pictures] (produced 1972).   Stockholm, Norstedt, 1972.

Screenplays: *Myglaren* [The Fixer], with Rune Hassner, 1966; *Hjälparen* [The Helper], 1968; *Balzac or the Triumphs of Realism*, 1975.

Television Documentaries: *Democratic Kampuchea*, 1978–79; *China*, 1979; *Guerilla Base Area of Democratic Kampuchea*, 1979.

Other

Kulturers korsväg: en bok om Afghanistan.   Stockholm, Norstedt, 1960; as *Kulturers korsväg: resa i Afghanistan*, 1960; as *Gates to Asia: A Diary from a Long Journey*, New York, Pantheon, 1971; London, Chatto and Windus, 1972.
Rescontra: utdrag ur avräkningsbok för personliga conti [Journey Through].   Stockholm, Norstedt, 1962.

Bortom berg och öknar [Beyond Mountains and Deserts].   Stockholm, Bonnier, 1962.
Rapport från kinesisk by.   Stockholm, Norstedt, 1963; as *Report from a Chinese Village*, London, Heinemann, 1965; New York, New American Library, 1966.
Samtida bekännelser av en europeisk intellektuell.   Stockholm, Norstedt, 1964; revised edition, as *Confessions of a Disloyal European*, London, Chatto and Windus, and New York, Pantheon, 1968; as *En illojal europés bekännelser*, Norstedt, 1983.
Chinese Journey, photographs by Gun Kessle.   London, Chatto and Windus, and New York, Random House, 1965; as *Kinesisk resa*, Stockholm, Norstedt, 1966.
Söndagsmorgon [Sunday Morning].   Stockholm, Norstedt, 1965.
Nordisk trio [Nordic Trio], with Carl Scharnberg and Sigurd Evensmo.   Oslo, Pax, 1966.
Turkmenistan: en revolutions övergångsår [The Transition of a Revolution], photographs by Gun Kessle.   Stockholm, Norstedt, 1966.
Skriftställning 1–14 [Writing Posture].   Stockholm, PAN/Norstedt, 13 vols., 1968–83; vol. 14 published, Solna, Kulturfront, 1987.
Ansikte av sten: staden Angkor i Kambodja, photographs by Gun Kessle.   Stockholm, PAN/Norstedt, 1968; as *Angkor: An Essay on Art and Imperialism*, New York, Pantheon, 1970; London, Chatto and Windus, 1971.
Albansk utmaning, photographs by Gun Kessle.   Stockholm, PAN/Norstedt, 1970; as *Albania Defiant*, New York, Monthly Review Press, 1976; London, Stage 1, 1978.
Kina: revolutionen går vidare, photographs by Gun Kessle.   Stockholm, PAN/Norstedt, 1970; as *China: The Revolution Continued*, London, Chatto and Windus, and New York, Pantheon, 1970.
Tal om hjälp: anteckningar om hjälp och hjälpare 1959–1971 på förekommen anledning publicerade [Talk About Aid: Notes on Help and the Helpers 1959–1971 Published out of Necessity].   Stockholm, PAN/Norstedt, 1971.
Ett femtiotal [About 50].   Stockholm, Gidlund, 1972.
Den onödiga samtiden [The Unnecessary Contemporary World], with Lars Gustafsson.   Stockholm, PAN/Norstedt, 1974.
Solidaritet med Tjeckoslovakiens folk [Solidarity with the Czechoslovakian People], with Lars Gustafsson.   Stockholm, Oktober, 1975.
Lag utan ordning [Law Without Order].   Stockholm, Gidlund, 1975.
Kineskika frågor från Liu Ling 1975.   Stockholm, Norstedt, 1975; with *Kina efter Mao Tsetung*, as *China Notebook, 1975–1978*, Chicago, Liberator Press, 1979.
Ondskan tar form [The Evil Takes Shape], photographs by Gun Kessle.   Stockholm, PAN, 1976.
Tyska frågor [German Questions].   Stockholm, Oktober, 1976.
Avgörande år: svenska frågor 1975–1977 [Decisive Years: Swedish Questions 1975–1977].   Stockholm, Oktober, 1977.
Sidenvägen, photographs by Gun Kessle.   Stockholm, Norstedt, 1977; as *The Silk Road: A Journey from the High Pamirs and Ili Through Sinkiang and Kansu*, New York, Pantheon, 1979; London, Gollancz, 1980.
En världsbild [A Conception of the World], photographs by Gun Kessle.   Stockholm, Norstedt, 1977.
Kina efter Mao Tsetung.   Stockholm, Ordfront, 1977; with *Kineskika frågor från Liu Ling 1975*, as *China Notebook, 1975–1978*, Chicago, Liberator Press, 1979.
Kampuchea hösten 1979.   Stockholm, PAN/Norstedt, 1979.

Kampucheas heliga Angkor [Kampuchea's Holy Angkor], photographs by Gun Kessle. Stockholm, Oktober, 1979.

Indien väntar, photographs by Gun Kessle. Stockholm, Norstedt, 1980; as *India Waits*, Madras, Sangam, 1984; Chicago, Lake View Press, 1986.

Strindberg och Balzac: essayer kring realismens problem [Strindberg and Balzac: Essays on the Problem of Reality]. Stockholm, Norstedt, 1981.

Barndom. Stockholm, Norstedt, 1982; as *Childhood*, Chicago, Lake View Press, 1991.

Bortom bergen [Beyond the Mountain], photographs by Gun Kessle. Stockholm, Norstedt, 1983.

Kinesisk by 20 år senare: rapport med frågetecken. Stockholm, Norstedt, 1983; as *Return to a Chinese Village*, New York, Pantheon, 1984.

Kampuchea: krigen, politiken, diplomatin [Kampuchea: Wars, Politics, Diplomacy], with Per Axelsson and Gunnar Bergström. Stockholm, Ordfront, 1983.

En annan värld [Another World]. Stockholm, Norstedt, 1984.

Rapporter från kinesisk by: Liu Lin 1962–1982 [Reports from a Chinese Village: Liu Lin 1962–1982], photographs by Gun Kessle. Stockholm, Norstedt, 1985.

Ord och avsikt: ett resonemang [Words and Intentions: A Discussion]. Stockholm, Norstedt, 1986.

Brev från en turist [Letters from a Tourist], photographs by Gun Kessle. Stockholm, Norstedt, 1987.

Den albanska utmaningen 1968–1986 [The Albanian Challenge 1968–1986], photographs by Gun Kessle. Stockholm, Norstedt, 1987.

En Meccanopojke berättar: eller Anteckningar om ett borgerligt förnuft [A Meccano Boy Recounts, or, Notes on Bourgeois Sense]. Höganäs, Wiken, 1988.

3 × Sovjet: kommenterade resor från åren 1960, 1965 och 1988, photographs by Gun Kessle. Stockholm, Askelin & Hägglund, 1988.

En annan ordning: litterärt & personligt [A New State of Affairs: Literary and Personal]. Stockholm, Norstedt, 1988.

Pubertet: en samling utskriven hösten 1946 [Puberty: A Collection Written During Autumn 1946]. Stockholm, Norstedt, 1988.

Tolv på det trettonde: en berättelse [12 on the 13th: a Story]. Stockholm, Norstedt, 1989.

Franska revolutionens bilder [Pictures of the French Revolution]. Stockholm, Askelin & Hägglund, 1989.

Editor, *Fallet myglaren* [The Case of the Wheeler-Dealer]. Stockholm, Norstedt, 1967.

Editor, *Ordet i min makt: läsebok för underklassen* [The Word in My Power], by August Strindberg. Stockholm, PAN/Norstedt, 1968.

*

Bibliography: *Jan Myrdal: en kronologisk bibliografi 1943–1976* by Britta-Lena Jansson, Stockholm, Oktober, 1977.

*   *   *

As the son of two internationally renowned, Nobel prize-winning parents, Jan Myrdal has always been a public person. Brought up in a sophisticated intellectual environment, he has been a firm believer in the value of rational thinking and in the necessity of making conscious choices. As he says in one of his early novels: "You can shape your own life . . . If it all goes to hell, it's your own fault." Like his parents, but in a totally different way, he has always been deeply concerned with global problems, especially those concerning the relationship between the rich Western countries and the Third World.

After an insignificant play debut in 1953, Myrdal wrote a number of novels of little distinction in which his critical attitude to the Swedish "people's home" created by the Social Democrats can already be sensed.

In 1960 he found a literary form — "faction" rather than fiction — that better suited his avid thirst for knowledge. In his first travel account, *Kulturers korsväg: resa i Afghanistan* (*Gates to Asia: A Diary from a Long Journey*) as in his other travelogues, many of them excellently photo-illustrated by his wife Gun Kessle, he tries to describe social and cultural conditions from an Asiatic rather than a European perspective, suggesting rational explanations for what Westerners tend to regard as exotic manifestations.

His breakthrough came in 1963 with *Rapport från kinesisk by* (*Report from a Chinese Village*), which has become something of an international standard work on the "basic" situation in communist China. Anxious to be "the interpreter, not the falsifier of reality," Myrdal here provides a number of human documents based on interviews made in a village in northern Shensi. Not altogether unlike a collective novel, the book aims to give an objective presentation of the reality experienced by the villagers. A semi-documentary work, it introduces the interview as a "literary" genre. Seven years later the results of the cultural revolution were observed in *Kina: revolutionen går vidare* (*China: The Revolution Continued*). Other travelogues concern Albania, India, and Turkmenistan; in the last case Myrdal unveils the Soviet suppression of the native culture.

In 1964 Myrdal launched another highly influential book: *Samtida bekännelser av en europeisk intellektuell*, four years later issued in a revised English version entitled *Confessions of a Disloyal European*. On the private level the book deals with Myrdal's inability to prevent a friend from committing suicide. This inability becomes a pregnant symbol for the impotence of the group to which he belongs — the Western intelligentsia — with regard to the fascism of the 1930s. Identifying himself with Western intellectuals Myrdal declares: "We have analysed all wars even before they were declared. But we did not prevent them . . . We described the torture and we put our names under manifestoes against torture, but we did not prevent it . . . We are not the carriers of consciousness. We are its whores." Myrdal feels the intelligentsia has failed in its duty to make the masses conscious of what is really happening in societies behind what seems to be happening. Undoubtedly one of the crucial books of the 1960s, *Confessions* has proved seminal for the confessional genre that, in a more private fashion, was to become so popular in the next decade.

Myrdal has occasionally also tried his hand at radio and television plays, and film. Especially in the film *Myglaren* (The Fixer), made together with Rune Hassner, he effectively satirised the means used by the pillars of society to promote themselves, so much so that the noun *myglare* and the corresponding verb *mygla* since then have become incorporated in the Swedish language as words standing for manipulating careerism.

Myrdal's essential contribution to the confessional genre came in the 1980s, when he brought out a highly praised series of autobiographical works. In these books Myrdal attempts to see everything from the growing child's point of view. The images of childhood are recreated without the filtering censorship of the grown-up mind. The first of the series, *Barndom* (*Childhood*), was immediately acclaimed as a masterpiece. At the same time the book caused much uproar because of its violent attack on little Jan's parents. Both parents protested against what they considered a falsification of reality. Myrdal's two sisters subsequently published books in which they give a very different picture of the Myrdal family, notably of their mother Alva.

With his ambition to inform his readers about historical backgrounds and socio-political conditions, Myrdal has written many polemical newspaper articles. Taken together they provide a continuous ideological muck-raking and a vivid exposé of the development of leftist attitudes in the past decades. Many of them have been gathered in his *Skriftställningar* (Writing Postures), published more or less annually since 1968.

Throughout his work, be it fiction, non-fiction, or faction, Myrdal has focussed on "the gap between words and deeds."

Like the intellectual giants he likes to identify himself with, he is well aware of the power of the word, both in a negative and a positive sense. In many ways the most Strindbergian of today's Swedish writers, he has significantly brought out an anthology of the "red" Strindberg's radical writings under the title *Ordet i min makt* (The Word in My Power).

For decades both Swedish literature and Swedish society have sensed the impact of the protean writer and agitator Jan Myrdal.

—Egil Törnqvist

N

NĀGĀRJUN. Pseudonym for Vaidyanāth Miśra. Also writes in Maithili as "Yātrī" [Traveller]. Indian. Born in Darbhanga district, Bihar, in 1911. Educated in his village, then in Benares and Calcutta. Married; four sons. Lived in the Panjab, then at Kelaniya University, Sri Lanka, 1935–37; became Buddhist monk, 1936; travelled to Lhasa, Tibet, 1938. Editor, *Viśvabandhu* weekly, Lahore, 1942–43; took part in the Kisān Sabhā activities in Bihar, 1940s, and went to jail; jailed again after taking part in Jay Prakas' Nārāyaṇ movement, 1974–78. Lives in New Delhi and his village. Recipient: Sāhitya Akādemī award, 1968. Address: c/o Vāṇī Prakashan, 4697/5, 21-A Daryaganj, New Delhi 110002, India.

PUBLICATIONS

Verse

Citrā (in Maithili). Allahabad, n.p., 1948.
Canā jorgaram [Nice Hot Chick Peas]. Allahabad, Hans Prakāśan, n.d.
Yugdhārā [Current of the Age]. Allahabad, n.p., 1953.
Sātraṅge pankhōvālī [Rainbow-Coloured Wings]. Calcutta, Yātrī, 1959.
Pyāsī pathrāī āṅkhē [The Yearning in Dull Eyes]. Allahabad, Yātrī, 1962.
Patrahīn nagnagāch [Leafless Wedding-Tree] (in Maithili). 1967.
Bhasmāṅkur [Sprouting from Ashes]. New Delhi, Rājkamal, 1971.
Tālāb kī machliyā̃ [Fishes from the Pond]. Bhinda, Lokāyan Saṃskṛtik Sansthān, 1974.
Cādnā [Light]. 1976.
Tumne kahā thā [You Had Said]. New Delhi, Vāṇī, 1980.
Khicṛī viplav dekhā hamne [A Hotchpotch Revolt We've Seen]. 1980.
Hazār hazār bāhōvālī [The Thousand-Armed]. New Delhi, Rādhākṛṣṇa, 1981.
Purānī jutiyō kā chorus [Chorus of the Worn Shoes]. New Delhi, Vāṇī, 1983.
Ratnagarbhā [The Jewel in the Womb]. New Delhi, Vāṇī, 1984.
Aise bhī ham kyā! Aise bhī tum kyā! [After All, What Are We, What Are You!]. 1985.

Fiction

Pāro (in Maithili). Darbhanga, Granthālay, 1946.
Ratīnāth kī cācī [Ratīnāth's Aunt]. Allahabad, Kitāb Mahal, 1948.
Balcanmā. Allahabad, Kitāb Mahal, 1952.
Bābā Baṭesarnāth. New Delhi, Rājkamal, 1954.
Navturiā (in Maithili). Darbhanga, Vidyāpati Prakāśan, 1954; as *Naī paudh* [The New Plant], Allahabad, Kitāb Mahal, 1957.
Dukhmocan. New Delhi, Rājkamal, 1956.
Varuṇ ke beṭe [The Sons of the Sea]. 1957.

Kumbhīpāk. New Delhi, Ātmarām & Sons, 1960.
Hīrak jayantī [The Golden Jubilee]. New Delhi, Ātmarām & Sons, 1962.
Ugratārā. New Delhi, Rājpāl & Sons, 1963.
Imratiyā. As *Jāmanīya ke bābā*, Allahabad, Kitāb Mahal, 1969; as *The Holy-Man from Jamaniya*, Calcutta, Writers' Workshop, 1977.
Abhinandanā [Felicitation]. New Delhi, Vāṇī, 1979.
Tīna ahadī. New Delhi, Vāṇī, 1979.
Āsmān mē cād taire [The Moon Is Swimming in the Sky] (as "Yātrī"). New Delhi, Vāṇī, 1979.
Garībdās. New Delhi, Vāṇī, 1981.

Other

Annahīnam kriyahīnam. New Delhi, Vāṇī, 1983.
Nāgārjun: cunī huī racnāē [Selected Works], edited by Sobhākānt Miśra. New Delhi, Vāṇī, 2 vols., 1985.

Editor, *Vidyāpati ke git* [Songs of Vidyapati]. New Delhi, Vāṇī, 1979.

Translator, *Meghaduta*. Patna, Rāṣṭrīy, 1956.
Translator, *Gītagovinda*. New Delhi, Vāṇī, 1979.

*   *   *

Nāgārjun's significance is as a leading Hindi writer whose work reflects changing attitudes in north India around the time of India's independence. His early literary work was in poetry, and it illustrates perhaps more clearly than his individual novels the extent of conflict possible between traditional Indian cultural values (as acquired in his case from a brahminical education and reinforced by his interest in Buddhism) and new political alternatives. The latter were represented on the one hand by the Congress Party, and on the other by the ideals of the Kisān Sabhā (Farmers' Association, established 1926) and the Progressive Writers' Association (established 1935), which were prevailingly understood in a Marxist sense.

Nāgārjun's novels reveal him to be a pioneer, and the first major exponent of Hindi regional (*āṁcalik*) fiction. Regional environment and identity are specifically emphasised in this genre, usually at the expense of plot and often of character development. By contrast, a village community as a whole may in a regional novel (as in Nāgārjun's *Naī paudh*) acquire a status resembling that of a major character, subject to tensions, growth, and change. Nāgārjun's approach, essentially a development of the progressive writing of the 1930s, lends itself to close treatment of social and political issues. It is greatly encouraged by the impact of independence, which freed thought and emotion to turn from a preoccupation with nationwide politics to particular, smaller-scale issues — the actual concerns of daily life. The strong local traditions of Mithila (North Bihar), Nāgārjun's home region, evidently fostered such an approach.

Nāgārjun's two anthologies *Yugdhārā* (Current of the Age) and *Hazār hazār bāhōvālī* (The Thousand-Armed) are representative of his poetic production. They attest a clear shift in his perspective in the course of the 1940s, with an early subjective consciousness of the world's beauty and life's promise (as expressed in "Bādal to ghirte dekhā hai" [I Saw the Clouds Drifting]) giving way to disillusionment over the evident ills of society, and a resolve to work for reform following paths other than those of belles lettres or promotion of Sanskritic culture ("Ravi Ṭhākur" [Tagore]). Veneration for Mahatma Gandhi, a strong motivating force for Nāgārjun at first, was overtaken after Gandhi's assassination in 1948 by a sense of despair at the self-seeking, cynicism, and hypocrisy of officialdom, and at the widespread abuses of land tenure. The poet's earlier vein of angry independence was increasingly obscured by a polemical tone. By the mid-1950s Gandhi's ideals were seen by Nāgārjun as having been betrayed.

In the earlier part of his career Nāgārjun appears as a promising poet of some originality, able to turn traditional subject-matter and style to his own purposes and to speak powerfully in his own voice. His concerns were too practical and pragmatic, however, to allow verse to remain his major field of expression. He produced four collections apart from those already mentioned: *Citrā* (the name of a constellation) in Maithili, *Sātraṇge pàkhōvālī* (Rainbow-Coloured Wings), *Pyāsī pathrāī ā̃khē̃* (The Yearning in Dull Eyes), and *Patrahīn nagnagāch* (The Leafless Wedding-Tree).

Of Nāgārjun's 10 Hindi novels produced between 1948 and 1968 the second, *Balcanmā*, has received most attention. The eponymous hero of this work expresses in his character the optimism and sense of opportunity of the early independence years, but his story is about the insuperable difficulties of remedying the burdens of life facing the village and urban poor. The plot concerns a sequence of events befalling the cowherd Balcanmā in his village and in nearby Patna, where he supports in vain the interests of the socialists and the Kisān Sabhā. Though Balcanmā's hopes are doomed to disappointment — as were those of Horī, the archetypal peasant hero of Premcand's *Godān* (1936) — Balcanmā displays a self-reliance that marks him out as a modern personality. Yet as in many of Premcand's novels, the realism of this work is distorted to some extent by Nāgārjun's insinuation of his own political views. His next novel, *Naī paudh* (The New Plant), is by contrast a refreshingly undoctrinaire approach to a traditional (and uncontroversial) subject. The successful arrangement in inauspicious family circumstances of a suitable marriage for a young Maithil girl is related here with a similar technique to that employed in other regional novels, against a background of personalities and events of contemporary Bihar village life. The local attitudes of conservatism and slowly evolving modernity are brought out and contrasted with skill. Nāgārjun makes it clear that, in this village context, he approves of a slow rate of social change. The plot of *Naī paudh* remains in unusually clear focus for a regional novel and the leading characters are analysed with exceptional insight, making this work, although by no means the best known of Nāgārjun's novels, perhaps the best realized and most successful.

In the sharply contrasting *Dukhmocan* an eponymous (and artificially named) hero devotes himself idealistically to village reform. This subject-matter reflects a growing disappointment at the pace of progress since independence. In *Kumbhīpāk* and *Ugratārā* Nāgārjun is concerned with changing social attitudes to women. *Hīrak jayantī* (The Golden Jubilee) satirises corruption in politics and in the Hindi literary world. The last novel, *Imratiyā*, also published

as *Jāmanīya ke bābā* (*The Holy-Man from Jamaniya*), deals with corruption in religious establishments and strikes a strongly pessimistic note.

—Stuart McGregor

NIEVA, Francisco. Spanish. Born in Valdepeñas, 21 January 1927. Educated at the School of Fine Arts, Madrid, 1942–48; also studied art in Paris, from 1948. Artist and set designer. Lived in Paris, 1950s–60s; lived in Venice and East Berlin for periods in 1960s; lived in Madrid, from 1964. Since 1970 Professor of design, School of Fine Arts and School of Dramatic Arts, Madrid. Since 1984 regular contributor, *ABC* newspaper. Recipient: Polignac prize, for art works, 1963; Mayte prize, 1976; National Theatre prize, 1980; National Critics' prize, 1982; Prince of Asturias prize for literature, 1992. Elected to the Spanish Royal Academy, 1986. Address: c/o Ediciones Cátedra, Calle Josefa Valcárel 27, 28027 Madrid, Spain.

PUBLICATIONS

Plays

Es bueno no tener cabeza (produced Madrid, 1971). Published in *Primer Acto* (Madrid), 132, 1971.
Tórtolas, crepúsculo y . . . telón. Madrid, Escelicer, 1972.
Teatro furioso, with *Representación de Don Juan Tenorio* by Luis de Riaza y de Garnacho. Madrid, Safer, 1972.
Danzón de exequias, adaptation of the play by Ghelderode (produced Vigo, 1973).
Teatro furioso (includes *La carroza de ploma candente*; *Combate de Opalos y Tasia*; *El fandango asombroso*). Madrid, Libros de Teatro, 1973.
Combate de Opalos y Tasia (produced Madrid, 1976). Included in *Teatro furioso*, 1973.
La carroza de plomo candente (produced Madrid, 1976). Included in *Teatro furioso*, 1973; as *The Carriage of White-Hot Lead*, New Brunswick, New Jersey, Rutgers University, 1982.
Teatro furioso (includes *Teatro furioso*; *Pelo de tormenta*; *Nosferatu*; *Coronada y el toro*; *Teatro de farsa y calamidad*; *El rayo colgado y peste de loco amor*; *El paño de injurias*; *El baile de los ardientes*; *Claves excendentes*). Madrid, Akal, 1975.
Coronada y el toro (produced Madrid, 1982). Included in *Teatro furioso*, 1975; as *Coronada and the Bull*, in *Drama Contemporary: Spain*, New York, Performing Arts Journal Publications, 1985.
El rayo colgado (produced Vitoria, 1980). Included in *Teatro furioso*, 1975.
Sombra y quimera de Larra (produced Valencia, 1976). Madrid, Fundamentos, 1976.
La paz: celebración grotesca sobre Aristófanes (produced Mérida, 1977). Published in *La Farsa* (Madrid), 1980.
Delirio del amor hostil (produced Madrid, 1978). With *Malditas sean Coronada y sus hijas*, Madrid, Cátedra, 1980.
Los baños de Argel, adaptation of a play by Miguel de Cervantes (produced Madrid, 1979). Madrid, Centro Dramático Nacional, 1980.

La señora Tártara (produced Madrid, 1980).   Madrid, MK, 1980.

Maldítas sean Coronada y sus hijas; Delirio del amor hostil. Madrid, Cátedra, 1980.

Don Alvaro, o La fuerza del sino, adaptation of a work by Duque de Rivas (produced Madrid, 1983).

Casandra, adaptation of the work by Benito Pérez Galdós (produced Madrid, 1983).   Madrid, MK, 1983.

Las aventuras de Tirante el Blanco (produced Madrid, 1987).   Published in *Primer Acto* (Madrid), 219, 1987.

Fantasía, humor y terror: no es verdad, el espectro insaciable, El corazón insaciable.   Madrid, Verdugo, 1987.

Corazón de arpía (produced Madrid, 1989).   Published in *El Público* (Madrid), 21, 1987.

Te quiero, zorra (produced Madrid, 1988).   Madrid, Machado, 1989.

No es verdad (produced Madrid, 1988).

La magosta.   Madrid, Alhambra, 1988.

Trilogia italiana: Salvator Rosa o El Artista; Los españoles bajo tierra.   Madrid, Cátedra, 1988.

En baile de los ardientes (produced Madrid, 1990).

Teatro completo, edited by Jesús Martín Rodríguez.   Junta Castilla-La Mancha, n.p., 2 vols., 1992.

Other

Análisis de cinco comedias, with Andrés Amorós and Marina Mayoral.   Madrid, Castalia, 1977.

El tela de juicio: la literatura y la vida, la moda y el teatro. Madrid, Arnao, 1988.

El rayo colgado.   Madrid, Arnao, 1989.

Esencia y paradigma del "Género chico".   Madrid, Comunidad de Madrid, 1990.

*

Bibliography: in *España: bibliografía de un teatro "silenciado"* by L. Teresa Valdivieso, Lincoln, Nebraska, Society of Spanish and Spanish-American Studies, 1979.

Critical Studies: "Francisco Nieva: Spanish Representative of the Theater of the Marvelous" by Emil G. Signes, in *The Contemporary Spanish Theater: A Collection of Critical Essays*, edited by Martha T. Halsey and Phyllis Zatlin, Lanham, Maryland and London, University Press of America, 1988; "Masculine, Feminine and Androgynous Sex Roles in Nieva's Theater: The Case of *Coronada y el toro*" by Iride Lamartina-Lens, and "Francisco Nieva in the Shadow of Goya, Valle-Inclán, and the Aesthetic of the *Esperpento*" by Claudia Schaefer, both in *Estreno* (University Park, Pennsylvania), 15(2), 1989; "Metatheatricalism and Nieva's *Sombra y quimera de Larra*," in *Gestos* (Irvine, California), 4(7), 1989, and "Defamiliarizing the *Zorra*: Nieva's *vodevil superrealista*," in *Estreno* (University Park, Pennsylvania), 15(2), 1989, both by Phyllis Zatlin.

*   *   *

Francisco Nieva's original theatre is noted for its verbal and visual imagination and for its spirit of transgression. Highly metatheatrical and theatricalist, often erotic, and always wildly funny, it is anti-realistic and anti-illusionist. Within the context of the contemporary Spanish stage, it defies classification; Nieva is frequently labeled the most European of the playwrights residing in Spain. In the 1950s, when key Spanish authors like Antonio Buero Vallejo and Alfonso Sastre (*qq.v.*) were exploring social realism, Nieva lived in France. His work reflects his deep knowledge of Artaud, Bataille, and Jean Genet but yet falls within the great Spanish tradition of grotesque, baroque art that encompasses *La Celestina*, Miguel de Cervantes, Francisco Quevedo, Francisco José de Goya, Ramón María del Valle-Inclán, and Fernando Arrabal (*q.v.*). In Nieva's approach to the performance text and total theatre, there is likewise an admitted influence of Brechtian staging techniques.

As a writer, Nieva has received his nation's highest recognition: election, in 1986, to the Royal Spanish Academy, and, in 1992, the Prince of Asturias prize for literature. Nevertheless, for decades his play manuscripts gathered dust while he became famous as Spain's pre-eminent set designer. His original theatre was virtually unknown until 1971, when a student group staged *Es bueno no tener cabeza* (It's Nice to Be Without a Head) and *Primer Acto*, a major theatre journal, published the text.

By the early 1970s, Nieva had divided his plays into two groups: *Furious Theatre* and *Theatre of Farce and Calamity*. The works under the first label emphasize linguistic and visual effects and have little plot or character development; the furies they unleash are those of unrestricted freedom of expression and exploration of forbidden ecstasies. Under the second category, Nieva placed somewhat more conventional works which he mistakenly thought would be more acceptable to the Franco-era censors. Rather than exalting freedom, the farces tend to trace the disillusionment of a protagonist who is subjected to a repressive environment. Both groups are cast in the surrealistic mode and are marked by their humor.

Nieva's first invitation to stage a work in a major theatre, however, was not for one of his own texts but for an adaptation of a 19th-century play by Mariano José de Larra. The resulting *Sombra y quimera de Larra* (Shadow and Delusion of Larra) was not a mere version but rather a complex example of metatheatre in which the source text becomes a play-within-the-play. It introduced a series of innovative adaptations, including the 1979 *Los baños de Argel* (The Baths of Algiers), a spectacular reworking of Cervantes, that earned Nieva a National Theatre prize.

In April 1976, only a month after the opening of *Sombra y quimera de Larra*, Nieva finally achieved a major production of original texts. Two representative, short works of his *Furious Theatre* — *Combate de Opalos y Tasia* (The Battle of Opalos and Tasia, written in 1953) and *La carroza de plomo candente* (*The Carriage of White-Hot Lead*, written in 1971) — suddenly established Nieva as one of Spain's most creative writers for the stage. The first is a bawdy farce in which two "ladies" from the "kingdom of beggars," accompanied by their "pages," resort to insults and blows as they fight over a young man, for whose physical attributes they both express eloquent admiration. The second one-act play presents a surrealistic and grotesque image of an imaginary Spanish king, the silly and impotent Luis III. Central to the action is his bed, which becomes magically transformed during a night of witchcraft. The dark ritual, intended to help Luis III produce an heir, includes the wedding of a bullfighter and a she-goat, who is turned into a charming — and nude — Venus. To be sure, neither work could have been staged before the new freedoms of democratic Spain.

Coronada y el toro (*Coronada and the Bull*) is another well-known example of Nieva's *Furious Theatre*. The text attacks "Black Spain" and its perpetuation of stereotypical sex roles. Coronada, the mayor's sister, rebels against her brother's repressive rule, as does Marauna, a reluctant bullfighter. They are aided in their efforts by the androgynous and mystical Nun Man of the Intermingled Order. In an apocalyptic ending, the old world disappears while the victims of machismo are resurrected from their tomb.

Representative of the *Theatre of Farce and Calamity*, *La señora Tártara* (The Woman from the Nether Land) nevertheless shares the apocalyptic vision of *Coronada and the Bull*. The title character, Death, like the Nun Man, is a sexually ambiguous figure. The setting is a vague moment in the past, and the atmosphere is oddly reminiscent of both fairytales and political satires. Ary, an idealistic and poor young man, creator of whimsical inventions, discovers that he has the power to kill others with his disdain. The only survivor of Ary's unintentional massacre is the humble waitress in the rustic inn where the final scenes take place.

Although many of Nieva's plays are short, for the publication of his complete theatre he created a new category of brief texts (*Teatro en clave de brevedad*), including some from the 1960s and some written in the 1980s specifically for theatre students. Emphasizing themes of fantasy, humor, and terror, these one-act plays are often deliberately reminiscent of romantic films. *No es verdad* (It's Not True) and *Te quiero, zorra* (I Love You, Foxy), staged together in 1988, both are vaguely set in 19th-century France. The former deals with characters who have either gone mad or joined a wolf pack. The latter is an extended visual pun on the meaning in Spanish of female fox as a woman of easy virtue. The "fox" in this case is horrified to find that she has grown a foxtail; nevertheless her metamorphosis — revealed gradually in the fashion of classic farce — only makes her more attractive to her upperclass lover.

Nieva's theatre represents a unique blend of Spanish literary tradition with the European avant-garde and of verbal creativity with the plastic arts.

—Phyllis Zatlin

NORDBRANDT, Henrik. Danish. Born in Copenhagen, 21 March 1945. Educated at the University of Copenhagen. Married Anneli Nordbrandt Fuch in 1977 (divorced 1983). Literary critic and travel writer for periodicals, newspapers, and Denmark Radio. Has lived in Turkey, Greece, and Italy. Recipient: Hvedekorn Jubilæum prize, 1966; Danish State Art Foundation 3-year stipend, 1967, and lifelong grant, from 1980; Nalbandian award, 1971; Ewald award, 1974; Drachmann award, 1974; Benzon award, 1976; Nathansen award, 1976; Victor B. Andersen award, 1976; Aarestrup Medal, 1979; Danish Academy prize, 1980; Litteraturkritikernes Lav prize, 1984; Gyldendal prize, 1987; Nielsen award, 1987; Swedish Academy Nordic prize, 1990. Address: Plaza Santa Cruz 9, 29700 Vélez-Malaga, Spain.

PUBLICATIONS

Verse

Digte [Poems]. Copenhagen, Gyldendal, 1966.
Miniaturer [Miniatures]. Copenhagen, Gyldendal, 1967.
Syvsoverne [The Seven Sleepers]. Copenhagen, Gyldendal, 1969.
Omgivelser [Surroundings]. Copenhagen, Gyldendal, 1972.

Opbrud og ankomster [Departures and Arrivals]. Copenhagen, Gyldendal, 1974.
Ode til blæksprutten og andre kærlighedsdigte [Ode to the Octopus and Other Love Poems]. Copenhagen, Gyldendal, 1975.
Glas [Glass]. Copenhagen, Gyldendal, 1976.
Guds hus. Copenhagen, Augustinus, 1977; as *God's House*, translated by the author and Alexander Taylor, Willimantic, Connecticut, Curbstone Press, 1979.
Istid [Ice Age]. Copenhagen, Gyldendal, 1977.
Selected Poems, translated by the author and Alexander Taylor. Willimantic, Connecticut, Curbstone Press, 1978.
Spøgelseslege [Ghost Games]. Copenhagen, Gyldendal, 1979.
Rosen fra Lesbos [The Rose from Lesbos]. Copenhagen, Swing, 1979.
Gratiernes befrielsesfront [The Liberation Front of the Graces]. Hørsholm, Nyborg, 1979.
Forsvar for vinden under døren [Defence of the Wind Under the Door]. Copenhagen, Brøndum, 1980.
Udvalgte digte [Selected Poems]. Copenhagen, Gyldendal, 1981.
Armenia. Copenhagen, Gyldendal, 1982; in English, translated by Alexander Taylor, Willimantic, Connecticut, Curbstone Press, 1984.
84 Digte [84 Poems]. Copenhagen, Gyldendal, 1984.
Violinbyggernes by [The Violin Maker's Town]. Copenhagen, Gyldendal, 1985.
Håndens skælven i november [The Trembling of the Hand in November]. Copenhagen, Brøndum, 1986.
Under mausolæet [Under the Mausoleum]. Copenhagen, Gyldendal, 1987.
Vandspejlet [The Mirror of the Water]. Copenhagen, Gyldendal, 1989.
Glemmersteder [Forgotten Places]. Copenhagen, Brøndum, 1991.

Fiction

Finckelsteins blodige bazar [Finckelstein's Bloody Bazaar]. Copenhagen, Gyldendal, 1983.
Nissen flytter med [The Nisse Moves with You]. Copenhagen, Gyldendal, 1988.

Other

Historier om Hodja [Stories About Hodja]. Copenhagen, Lindhardt og Ringhof, 1973.
Breve fra en ottoman [Letters from a Couch]. Copenhagen, Gyldendal, 1978.
Tifanfaya (for children). Copenhagen, Dansklærerforeningen, 1990.

*   *   *

"The words I write only exist unwritten." This line sums up Henrik Nordbrandt's poetic creation — his poems are journeys between inspiration and language. In "Broncerelief i olielampeskær" (Bronze Relief in the Light of an Oil Lamp) from *Glas* (Glass), the words are oarsmen made of bronze who never reach shore, and the land from which they set out vanishes when, listening to their own singing, they understand who they are and from where they come.

Melancholy, frustration, and despair pervade Nordbrandt's works; even the affirmative Mediterranean poetry has an undercurrent of sadness. His poems, inspired by North American poets such as Wallace Stevens and Ezra Pound, consist of elaborate images implying an absent perfection. The early works abound in images of decadence, labyrinthine, paradoxical metaphors with a life of their own. What begins as a simple comparison develops asymmetrically, generating new images and incorporating the poet into the poem on terms dictated by the words themselves. Later the metaphors become simpler and sharper, and negation is introduced as an alternative device to express the inexpressible.

Nordbrandt's first collection of poetry, *Digte* (Poems), appeared in 1966. The setting of these poems is Denmark, often in late autumn, grey, dingy, and decaying. An absence of purity, of perfection, is intimated, an impossible meeting with the "you" that is always elsewhere, in another time, and the poet suffers because everything is now "too late." In "Tornerose" (The Sleeping Beauty) the Sleeping Beauty plays Mozart, lost in a world of her own, with icicles hanging from her forehead, while the baroque angels on the ceiling sprinkle their gilt as dust onto the withered rosebed. But in the last stanza it is the poet who wakes, unable to tell whether she has left him or is about to arrive. She is absent from the present tense of the poem, and all he can do for her is "blow [her] absence full of dust."

In *Miniaturer* (Miniatures) the season is winter. The poet seeks the source of a distant singing, but loses his way in dense forests or blizzards. In "De dødes vejskilt" (The Signpost of the Dead) he comes across a signpost, but there is no name on it, and the towns at the end of the roads have disappeared. The language of winter contains no words and the objects without names no longer exist. The language has no name for the lost poet and the signpost points inwards, singing about itself. "Dødsikon" (Icon of Death) sums up the first phase of Nordbrandt's work, depicting poetry as imprisoning reality and depriving it of life. The poems are icons of death.

A poem from Lao Tzu's *Tao Te Ching* is used as an epigraph in *Syvsoverne* (The Seven Sleepers), which marks a transitional stage between the first and second phases of Nordbrandt's work. "Kina betragtet gennem græsk regnvejr i café turque" (China Observed Through Greek Rain in Turkish Coffee) illustrates the new orientation, which penetrates the darkness, creating a transparency that makes possible the merging of cultures.

Nordbrandt has studied Chinese, Turkish, and Arabic and has translated poems by Djelaleddin Rûmi (d.1273) from Turkish into Danish. His next four collections, which were written in Turkey and Greece, are influenced both by Rûmi and by the Turkish Sufi mystic Yunus Emre (1240–1320). Nordbrandt quotes Emre in *Ode til blæksprutten og andre kærlighedsdigte* (Ode to the Octopus and Other Love Poems): "Take my I-ness from me, and fill it with your you-ness." The poem "Konya" conveys this loss of identity:

> Now it has filled me, o Djelaleddin,
> the sea of love you speak of.
> On three shores she whom I call mine
> found my body, and I was her, one and empty.

Greek poetry, in particular Cavafy (1863–1933), was also a source of inspiration. Part of Cavafy's poem "Ithaka" is quoted as an introduction to *Opbrud og ankomster* (Departures and Arrivals):

> But don't hurry the journey at all.
> Better it lasts for years,
> so you are old by the time you reach the island . . .

The journey is the central theme of *Opbrud og ankomster*. In the last poem, "Landgang" (Landfall), the poet has arrived, but not at his death; after many futile voyages, he has finally found a language in which every word is a declaration of love. The relationship between poet and words is reversed. They force him to sing and he submits to their enchantment, to the creativity that compels him to invent countries he has never seen. He celebrates his own inconsequential death because it forces him to live. The celebratory second phase represents life as a journey of continuous departures and arrivals, where dying and being born are synonymous.

Istid (Ice Age), written during a lengthy stay in Denmark, shatters this perfection. An awareness of a growing global crisis, caused by the collapse of culture and endangering the survival of mankind, is reflected in poems that are cries of despair: "In February even the boundless despair/has outlines so sharp that no misunderstanding is possible."

Schizophrenia and the disintegration of the self are dominant themes in this most recent phase of Nordbrandt's poetry. His concerns and the complexity of his poems are well exemplified by "Dværgen betragter sig selv i et medbragt lommespejl" (The Dwarf Observes Himself in a Pocket Mirror He Has Brought Along) in *84 digte* (84 Poems), in which the speaker is variously identified as the poet's double, as dwarf, toad, court jester or Hamlet and Odysseus in a single body. The central images are shadows, doubles, and mirror reflections. Art is a mirror and a shadow, and when the blackened dwarf drowns in the blackness of his mirror (art), the poet's voice takes over, warning his readers that he will cast so dark and sharp a shadow over their lives that they too will drown in reality.

—Bente Elsworth

NORÉN, Lars. Swedish. Born in Stockholm, 9 April 1944. Has two daughters. Lives in Stockholm. Recipient: Swedish Dramatist of the Year, 1983; Swedish Theatre Critics' prize, 1984. Address: c/o Bonniers Förlag, Box 3159, 103 63 Stockholm, Sweden.

PUBLICATIONS

Plays

Box ett [Box One] (radio play).   Stockholm, Sveriges Radio, 1972.
Fursteslickaren [The Prince's Bootlicker] (produced Stockholm, 1973).
Orestes (produced Stockholm, 1980).
Modet att döda (television play).   Included in *Tre skådespel*, 1980; as *Courage to Kill* (stage version produced Mold, North Wales, 1984).
Tre skådespel: Modet att döda; Akt utan nåd; Orestes [Three Plays: The Courage to Kill; Act Without Mercy; Orestes]. Stockholm, Bonnier, 1980.
Underjordens leende [The Smile of the Underworld] (produced Copenhagen, 1980; Stockholm, 1982).
En fruktansvärd lycka [A Terrible Happiness] (produced Stockholm, 1981).
Natten är dagens mor [Night Is the Mother of Day] (produced Malmö, 1982).   Included in *Två skådespel*, 1983.

Kaos är granne med Gud [Chaos Is God's Neighbour] (produced Gothenborg, 1983). Included in *Två skadespel*, 1983.

Två skådespel: Natten är dagens mor; Kaos är granne med Gud. Stockholm, Bonnier, 1983.

Demoner [Demons] (produced Stockholm, 1984).

Nattvarden [Holy Communion] (produced Stockholm, 1985).

Stillheten [The Stillness] (produced Stockholm, 1986).

München-Aten (television play). As *Munich-Athens* (stage version produced London, 1987).

Endagsvarelser [Dragonflies] (produced Kassel, Germany, 1989). Stockholm, Bonnier, 1990.

Hebriana (produced The Hague, 1989).

Autumn and Winter (produced Copenhagen, 1989).

Och ge oss skuggorna [And Grant Us the Shadows] (produced in Norwegian, as *Under ödets stjärnor* [Under the Stars of Destiny], Oslo, 1991; in Swedish, Stockholm, 1991).

Radio Plays: *Box ett* [Box One], 1972; *Röster* [Voices], 1973; *Akt utan nåd* [Act Without Mercy], 1978; *När dom brände fjärilar på lilla scenen* [When They Burned Butterflies on the Small Stage], 1983.

Television Plays: *Kingsdon Hotel*, 1968; *En hungersaga* [A Hunger Story], 1970; *Amalia, Kamala*, 1971; *Modet att döda* [Courage to Kill], 1978; *München-Aten* [Munich-Athens], 1983; *Komedianter* [Strolling Players], 1987.

Verse

Syrener, snö [Lilacs, Snow]. Stockholm, Bonnier, 1963.

De verbala resterna av en bildprakt som förgår [The Verbal Remains of a Vanishing Pictorial Splendor]. Stockholm, Bonnier, 1964.

Inledning n:r 2 till schizz [Introduction No. 2 to Schizz (ofrenia)]. Stockholm, Bonnier, 1965.

Encylopedi: Mémoires sur la fermentation 1–3 [Encyclopedia]. Stockholm, Bonnier, 1966.

Stupor: Nobody Knows You When You're Down and Out. Stockholm, Bonnier, 1968.

Revolver. Stockholm, Bonnier, 1969.

Solitära dikter [Solitary Poems]. Stockholm, Bonnier, 1972.

Viltspeglar [Mirror of the Wild]. Göteborg, Författarförlaget, 1972.

Kung Mej, och andra dikter [King Mej, and Other Poems]. Stockholm, Bonnier, 1973.

Dagliga och nattliga dikter [Daily and Nightly Poems]. Stockholm, Bonnier, 1974.

Dagbok augusti-oktober 1975 [Diary August-October 1975]. Stockholm, Bonnier, 1976.

Nattarbete: del 2 [Night Work: Part 2]. Stockholm, Bonnier, 1976.

Hans Bellmer: bilder från åren 1934–1950 [Hans Bellmer: Pictures from the Years 1934–1950], with prose by Ragner von Holten. Stockholm, Norstedt, 1978.

Order [The Command]. Stockholm, Bonnier, 1978.

Murlod [Wall Plumbing]. Stockholm, Bonnier, 1979.

Den ofullbordade stjärnan [The Incomplete Star]. Stockholm, Bonnier, 1979.

Hjärta i hjärta [Heart to Heart]. Stockholm, Bonnier, 1980.

Fiction

Salome — Sfinxerna [Salome — The Sphinxes]. Stockholm, Bonnier, 1968.

Biskötarna [The Beekeepers]. Stockholm, Bonnier, 1970.

I den underjordiska himlen [In the Underground Sky]. Stockholm, Bonnier, 1972.

*

Critical Studies: "Lars Norén: A Working Process for the Director" by Suzanne Osten, in *Not Only Strindberg*, edited by Egil Törnqvist, Amsterdam, 1985; "Theatre with the Intoxication of Insight: Notes on Lars Norén" by Lotta Neuhauser, in *Theatre (Yale)* (New Haven, Connecticut), 22(1), 1991; "Strindberg, O'Neill, Norén: A Swedish-American Triangle" by Egil Törnqvist, in *Eugene O'Neill Review* (Boston), 1991.

*   *   *

Lars Norén is one of the most prolific as well as the most challenging of contemporary Swedish writers. His career thus far embraces two principal genres, and falls roughly into two halves. For although he has written some fine novels, including in *Biskötarna* (The Beekeepers) a compelling and personal account of the modern metropolitan underclass of junkies, gays, and whores, his writing up until the end of the 1970s was dominated by poetry; since then, however, he has virtually abandoned verse, and is now established as the most significant Swedish dramatist since August Strindberg.

Norén's early poetry displays an almost overwhelming need for self-expression. Beginning in the early 1960s in the modernist tradition, his first books, including the concrete poetry of *Inledning n:r 2 till schizz* (Introduction No. 2 to Schizz[ofrenia]), project a chaotic world, and bombard the reader with an almost unbearable flood of language, at times suggesting the automatic writing of Surrealism, at others a psychotic, almost psychedelic, universe with moments of sudden and frightening calm. This poetry is closely bound up with Norén's own experience. In what is perhaps his major collection of the decade, *Stupor*, which has the subtitle *Nobody Knows You When You're Down and Out*, and is the second of an autobiographical sequence embracing *Encyclopedi* (Encyclopedia) and *Revolver* as well, he has consciously recreated the whirlwind of voices, impulses, and images that circulate in the vacuum of the title, a medical term for a form of catatonic schizophrenia. Beginning with *Kung Mej, och andra dikter* (King Mej, and Other Poems), however, his poetry becomes more restrained, though no less powerful; the language is now concentrated, and in the often brief, almost laconic verse of *Order* (The Command), *Murlod* (Wall Plumbing), and *Hjärta i hjärta* (Heart to Heart), he allies himself with considerable success to the major Central European tradition of Friedrich Hölderlin, Rainer Maria Rilke, and Paul Célan.

However, notwithstanding the disastrous reception of his first play *Fursteslickaren* (The Prince's Bootlicker), Norén eventually made the transition from poetry to drama, in part because, as he remarked, he longed to see bodies and words in a definite place. Almost without exception the setting of Norén's theatre is an enclosed room from which the characters can only escape by way of the tightly structured vehicle of the play, in admitting or denying the possibility of change. ("I want to describe meetings that inspire change," Norén has remarked, "that cause characters to grow, and that reveal their nakedness.") Thus a play like *Akt utan nåd* (Act Without Mercy) initially recalls Harold Pinter, for the audience is confronted with an apparently chance encounter between strangers in a shabby room, speaking an ambivalent dialogue that is freighted with half-truths, hermeneutic puzzles, and rapid shifts between loquacity and taciturnity. But Norén's major plays belong more specifically within the tradition of heightened, sometimes hallucinatory, naturalism of Strindberg and Eugene O'Neill, while also elevating the particular and local into subjects of general concern, in the manner of Henrik Ibsen and Anton Chekhov.

According to Norén it is in the nature of drama to illuminate the writer's life in an almost psychoanalytical manner: the past is objectified upon the stage, enabling the dramatist to understand his own and other people's behaviour, and the audience to witness a situation in which they may recognize themselves. Recurring themes and reappearing configurations of characters, images, and stage objects transform the scenic space into an inner chamber of great personal significance where, as (supposedly) in analysis, the pressure of the situation will ultimately compel the characters to reveal themselves. This is most clearly the case in the concentrated family dramas in which Norén observes a classic compression of time and place. In plays like *Modet att döda* (*Courage to Kill*), and the sequence of dramas *Natten är dagens mor* (Night Is the Mother of Day), *Kaos är granne med Gud* (Chaos Is God's Neighbour), and *Stillheten* (The Stillness), he explores both real and fictional memories with great power and concentration. The constellation of alcoholic father, mortally ill mother, brash older brother, and younger son on the edge of psychosis, represent perhaps the most considerable achievement of this kind since their acknowledged model, O'Neill's *Long Day's Journey into Night*. While they may have enabled Norén to discover something about himself, these plays have also been performed widely, and with great success, in both Holland and Germany, and it is likely that his most recent play, *Och ge oss skuggorna* (And Grant Us the Shadows), which extends his personal analysis into an account of a day in the life of O'Neill himself, will now introduce his work to a wider audience in Britain and the United States.

A less autobiographical dimension of Norén's playwriting is the series of dramas in which he presents the abrupt and seemingly inconsequential turns of thought of characters caught up in the vacuum of contemporary urban life. The three plays *En fruktansvärd lycka* (A Terrible Happiness), *När dom brände fjärilar på lilla scenen* (When They Burned Butterflies on the Small Stage), and *Underjordens leende* (The Smile of the Underworld) portray the rootless lives of contemporary Swedish intellectuals, the materially if not spiritually solvent class which the title of a more recent play dubs *Endagsvarelser* (Dragonflies). For them, language is a substitute for feeling and Norén is adept at capturing the unconscious speech rhythms of such characters: though often violent the language of these plays is also musical, and in combination with the stage images that Norén requires of his performers, it sustains a drama that is at once painful and yet both moving and exhilarating.

—Michael Robinson

O

OCAMPO, Silvina. Argentinian; sister of the writer Victoria Ocampo. Born in Buenos Aires, in 1906. Studied painting in Paris with Giorgio de Chirico and Fernand Léger. Married Adolpho Bioy Casares (*q.v.*) in 1940; one daughter. Writer and painter. Recipient: Municipal prize for poetry, 1945; National Poetry prize, 1962; Club de los XIII prize, 1988; PEN Club Gold Pen. Address: Posadas 1650, 1112 Buenos Aires, Argentina.

PUBLICATIONS

Fiction

Viaje olvidado. Buenos Aires, Sur, 1937.
Los que aman, odian, with Adolfo Bioy Casares. Buenos Aires, Emecé, 1946.
Autobiografía de Irene. Buenos Aires, Sur, 1948.
La furia y otros cuentos. Buenos Aires, Sur, 1959.
Las invitadas. Buenos Aires, Losada, 1961.
El pecado mortal. Buenos Aires, Universitaria, 1966.
Informe del cielo y del infierno. Caracas, Monte Avila, 1970.
Los días de la noche. Buenos Aires, Sudamericana, 1970.
Canto escolar. Buenos Aires, Fraterna, 1979.
Y así sucesivamente. Barcelona, Tusquets, 1987.
Leopoldina's Dream. Markham, Ontario, New York, and London, Penguin, 1988.
Cornelia frente al espejo. Barcelona, Tusquets, 1988.

Verse

Enumeración de la patria, y otros poemas. Buenos Aires, Sur, 1942.
Espacios métricos. Buenos Aires, Sur, 1945.
Los sonetos del jardín. Buenos Aires, Sur, 1946.
Poemas de amor desesperado. Buenos Aires, Sudamericana, 1949.
Los nombres. Buenos Aires, Emecé, 1953.
Pequeña antología. Buenos Aires, Ene, 1954.
Lo amargo por dulce. Buenos Aires, Emecé, 1962.
Amarillo celeste. Buenos Aires, Losada, 1972.
Arboles de Buenos Aires, with Aldo Sessa. Buenos Aires, Librería la Ciudad, 1979.

Plays

Los traidores, with Juan Rudolfo Wilcock (drama-in-verse). Buenos Aires, Losada, 1956.
No solo el perro es mágico (for children; produced Buenos Aires, 1958).

Other

El caballo alado (for children). Buenos Aires, Flor, 1972.
El cofre volante (for children). Buenos Aires, Estrada, 1974.
El tobogán (for children). Buenos Aires, Estrada, 1975.

La naranja maravillosa: cuentos para chicos grandes y para grandes chicos (for children). Buenos Aires, Orión, 1977.
La continuación y otras páginas. N.p., Centro Editor de América Latina, 1981.
Breve santoral. Buenos Aires, Ediciones de Arte Gaglianone, 1984.
Páginas (selections). Buenos Aires, Celtia, 1984.

Editor, with Jorge Luis Borges and Adolfo Bioy Casares, *Antología de la literatura fantástica.* Buenos Aires, Sudamericana, 1940; as *The Book of Fantasy*, New York, Viking, and London, Xanadu, 1988.
Editor, with Jorge Luis Borges and Adolfo Bioy Casares, *Antología poética argentina.* Buenos Aires, Sudamericana, 1941.

*

Critical Studies: "The Initiation Archetype in Arguedas, Roa Bastos and Ocampo" by Barbara A. Aponte, in *Latin American Literary Review* (Pittsburgh), 11(21), 1982; "A Portrait of the Writer as Artist: Silvina Ocampo," in *Perspectives on Contemporary Literature* (Lexington, Kentucky), 13, 1987, "The Twisted Mirror: The Fantastic Stories of Silvina Ocampo," in *Letras Femeninas* (Lincoln, Nebraska), 13(1–2), 1987, and "The Mad Double in the Stories of Silvina Ocampo," in *Latin American Literary Review* (Pittsburgh), 16(32), 1988, all by Patricia N. Klingenberg; *From the Ashen Land of the Virgin: Conversations with Bioy Casares, Borges, Denevi, Etchecopar, Ocampo, Orozco, Sabato* by Raul Galvez, Oakville, Ontario, Mosaic Press, 1989.

*   *   *

Silvina Ocampo has occupied a central position in the literary circle of Argentina whose distinguished members include her sister Victoria, husband Adolfo Bioy Casares (*q.v.*), and friend and collaborator Jorge Luis Borges, but the fame accorded others in the group has so far eluded her. Judging from attitudes expressed in certain of Ocampo's works and in rare interviews with her, however, the relative obscurity in which she has worked may reflect a deliberate strategy on her part. As she states in the introduction to *Leopoldina's Dream*, a collection of her short stories translated into English, "But I did not hope to be known: that seemed the most horrible thing in the world to me. I will never know what I was hoping for. A beggar who sleeps under a tree without anything in the world to shelter him is happier than a famous man . . ." John King, in a recent essay devoted to Victoria Ocampo, describes her sister Silvina as "the most underrated of all Argentinian writers, whose mature work can stand comparison with that of Borges" (*Knives and Angels: Women Writers in Latin America* edited by Susan Bassnett, 1990). This belated recognition and the comparison with Borges provides the inevitable starting point for an appraisal of Silvina Ocampo's complex and fascinating work.

Ocampo began her artistic career studying painting; she spent several years in Paris as a student of both Fernand Léger and Giorgio de Chirico, and a 1940 exhibit in Buenos Aires included her paintings as well as those of Xul Solar and Norah Borges. A review of the exhibition, published in *Sur* (Buenos Aires, 1940), compared her canvases to the works of Rodin, Gauguin, and Manet; her subjects were reported to be female nudes and mothers with children, painted in a robust, ample style reminiscent of sculpture. After this date her attention turned to literature, but the subject-matter which originally attracted her and a painterly attention to detail reappear as essential aspects of her fiction. Ocampo collaborated with Bioy Casares on a detective novel, *Los que aman, odian* (Those Who Love, Hate), and with Juan Rudolfo Wilcock on a drama-in-verse, *Los traidores* (The Traitors). But her mature work, like that of Borges, has been devoted to poetry and the short story. Unlike Borges, her poetry began with quite traditional themes, including extensive references to historical, biblical, and mythological figures, and traditional structures, such as the *cuarteto* and the sonnet. Experimentation with free verse and more personal subject-matter appear only relatively late in her career.

Like both Borges and Bioy Casares, with whom she collaborated on the influential *Antología de la literatura fantástica* (*The Book of Fantasy*), Ocampo is known primarily as a writer of short stories of the fantastic. Her fictional works have sought to unsettle readerly expectations of reality and to question our ability to know either existential truth or a consistent personal identity. Whereas Borges plays with conventions of detective fiction and academic literary critical and philosophic discourses, Ocampo works with myth, fairytales, and conventions of feminine romance fiction. Unlike either of her more famous associates, Ocampo situates her subversive vision within a carefully created domestic scene. Her fictional doubles, predictions of the future, metamorphoses, and telekinetic powers are carried out within upper-class households by servants, children, pets, and myriad seemingly innocuous household objects. Ocampo's interest in the grotesque, which ranges in her works from the subtly ironic to the macabre, gives political significance to her work and differentiates it sharply from that of her distinguished male colleagues. In his study of the literary group under discussion, *Oligarquía y literatura* (Oligarchy and Literature, 1975), Blas Matamoro finds in Ocampo's fiction alone a class tension which gives revolutionary bite to her fantastic vision. The magically wicked children, servants, animals, and objects seem to mount a rebellion against oppressive parents and masters which transcends the psychological slant Ocampo frequently gives it and amounts to an insurrection of global proportions. "The Velvet Dress," originally published in *La furia y otros cuentos* (The Fury and Other Stories), exemplifies the complex forces at work in Ocampo's stories. A little girl and a seamstress arrive at a wealthy woman's home for her final fitting of a most unusual dress. This exquisite three-page story evokes the menace of the black velvet dress with its sensuous sequined dragon embroidered down one side, the boorish insensitivity of the fretful woman, the oppressive heat, and the gleeful fascination of the child narrator who seems to intuit (or cause) the ensuing tragedy. The story's brevity, its black humor, its empowerment of a child narrator, its social tension, and its carefully suggested but never confirmed supernatural intrusion mark the best of Ocampo's fantastic stories.

Feminist literary theories should prove extremely useful in mapping the ways in which Ocampo's fiction seeks to subvert standard representations of human experience. No other writer has explored more penetratingly the limitations of our concepts of class, of gender, of adult and child, even of human and animal. Ocampo does more than simply defy or transgress normal boundaries — she questions basic assumptions about the location of power, the definition of success, of beauty, and of self. The cruelty, perversity, and shocking sexual themes found in numerous stories, as well as narrative ambiguity and complexity, may have impeded their critical reception. Whether Ocampo depicts the female as victim, sometimes as disturbingly compliant ones, or as perpetrator of violence, the ironic or even humorous narrative voice serves to amplify, rather than to mitigate, the reader's horror. By detailing the madness at the very center of the oligarchy (and patriarchy), Ocampo has created some of the most powerful critiques of current social and literary arrangements to have appeared in this rich era of Argentine letters. Ocampo concentrates on the wonder and horror of mundane existence, finding in everyday people and things a source simultaneously of the transcendent and the absurd.

—Patricia N. Klingenberg

ŌE Kenzaburō. Japanese. Born in Ōse village, Shikoku island, 31 January 1935. Educated at Tokyo University, 1954–59, B.A. in French literature 1959. Married Itami Yukari in 1960; three children. Freelance writer. Travelled to China as member of Japan-China Literary Delegation, 1960; travelled to Eastern and Western Europe, 1961, United States, 1965, Australia and U.S., 1968, and Southeast Asia, 1970; Visiting Professor, Collegio de México, Mexico City, 1976. Recipient: May Festival prize, 1954; Akutagawa prize, 1958; Shinchōsha prize, 1964; Tanizaki prize, 1967; Noma prize, 1973; Osaragi Jirō award. Address: 585 Seijo-machi, Setagaya-ku, Tokyo, Japan.

PUBLICATIONS

Fiction

Shisha no ogori [The Arrogance of the Dead] (collection). Tokyo, Bungei Shunjū, 1958.
Miru mae ni tobe [Leap Before You Look] (collection). Tokyo, Shinchōsha, 1958.
Memushiri kouchi [Pluck the Flowers, Gun the Kids]. Tokyo, Kōdansha, 1958.
Warera no jidai [Our Age]. Tokyo, Chūō Kōronsha, 1959.
Seinen no omei [The Young Man's Stigma]. 1959.
Kodoku na seinen no kyūka. 1960.
Okurete kita seinen [The Youth Who Arrived Late]. Published in *Shincho* (Tokyo), September 1960–February 1962; Tokyo, Shinchōsha, 1962.
Sevuntiin [17]. Published in *Bungakukai* (Tokyo), January 1961.
Seiji shōnen shisu [The Death of a Political Boy]. Published in *Bungakukai* (Tokyo), February 1961.
Sakebigoe [Outcries]. Published in *Gunzō* (Tokyo), November 1962; Tokyo, Kōdansha, 1963.
Seiteki ningen [The Sexual Man]. Tokyo, Shinchōsha, 1963.
Nichijō seikatsu no bōken [Adventures of Everyday Life]. 1963.

Kojinteki na taiken.   Tokyo, Shinchōsha, 1964; as *A Personal Matter*, New York, Grove Press, 1968; London, Weidenfeld and Nicolson, 1969.

Sora no kaibutsu Aguii.   1964; as *Aghwee the Sky Monster*, in *Teach Us to Outgrow Our Madness: Four Short Novels*, 1977.

Man'en gannen no futtobōru.   Tokyo, Kōdansha, 1967; as *The Silent Cry*, Tokyo, Kōdansha, 1974; London, Serpent's Tail, 1988.

Warera no kyoki o iki nobiru michi o oshieyo.   1969; augmented edition, 1975; as *Teach Us to Outgrow Our Madness*, in *Teach Us to Outgrow Our Madness: Four Short Novels*, 1977.

Waga namida o nuguitamū hi.   Tokyo, Kōdansha, 1972; as *The Day He Himself Shall Wipe My Tears Away*, in *Teach Us to Outgrow Our Madness: Four Short Novels*, 1977.

Kōzui wa waga tamashii ni oyobi [The Flood Has Reached My Soul].   Tokyo, Shinchōsha, 2 vols., 1973.

Pinchiranna chōsho [The Pinch-Runner Memorandum].   Tokyo, Shinchōsha, 1976.

Teach Us to Outgrow Our Madness: Four Short Novels (includes *Teach Us to Outgrow Our Madness*; *The Day He Himself Shall Wipe My Tears Away*; *Prize Stock*; *Aghwee the Sky Monster*).   New York, Grove Press, 1977; London, Boyars, 1978.

Dōjidai gemu [The Game of Contemporaneity].   Tokyo, Shinchōsha, 1979.

Gendai denkishū [Modern Tales of Wonder].   Tokyo, Iwanami Shoten, 1980.

"Ame no ki" o kiku onnatachi [Women Listening to "Rain Tree"].   Tokyo, Shinchōsha, 1982.

Atarashi hito yo mezameyo [Rouse Up O Young Men of the New Age!].   Tokyo, Kōdansha, 1983.

Natsukashii toshi e no tegami [Letters to the Lost Years].   Tokyo, Kōdansha, 1986.

Chiryō no tō [Tower of Healing].   Tokyo, n.p., 1991.

Other

Sekai no wakamonotachi.   1962.

Hiroshima nōto [Hiroshima Notes].   Tokyo, Iwanami Shinsho, 1965.

Genshuku na tsunawatari [The Solemn Tightrope Walking].   Tokyo, Bungei Shunjū, 1965.

Ōe Kenzaburō zensakuhin [Collected Works].   Tokyo, Shinchōsha, 6 vols., 1966–67; 2nd series, 6 vols., 1977–.

Jizokusuru kokorozashi [Enduring Volition].   Tokyo, Bungei Shunjū, 1968.

Kowaremono to shite no ningen [Fragile Human].   1970.

Okinawa nōto [Okinawa Notes].   Tokyo, Iwanami Shinsho, 1970.

Kakujidai no sōzōryoku [The Imagination of the Nuclear Age].   Tokyo, Shinchō Sensho, 1970.

Genbakugo no ningen [Homo sapien After the A-Bomb].   Tokyo, Shinchō Sensho, 1971.

Kujira no shimetsusuru hi [The Day the Whales Shall Be Annihilated].   Tokyo, Bungei Shunjū, 1972.

Dōjidai to shite no sengo [Post-War as the Contemporaneity].   1973.

Jōkyō e [Toward Situations].   Tokyo, Shoten, 1974.

Bungaku nōto [Literary Notes].   Tokyo, Shinchōsha, 1974.

Kotoba ni yotte: Jōkyō/Bungaku [Via Words: Situations/ Literature].   Tokyo, Shinchōsha, 1976.

Shōsetsu no hōhō [The Method of a Novel].   Tokyo, Iwanami Gendai Sensho, 1978.

Ōe Kenzaburō dōjidaironshū [An Essay on the Contemporary Age].   Tokyo, Iwanami Shoten, 10 vols., 1981.

Shomotsu — sekai no in'yu, with Yujiro Nakamura and Masao Yamaguchi.   Tokyo, Iwanami Shoten, 1981.

Chūshin to shūen, with Yujiro Nakamura and Masao Yamaguchi.   Tokyo, Iwanami Shoten, 1981.

Bunka no kasseika, with Yujiro Nakamura and Masao Yamaguchi.   Tokyo, Iwanami Shoten, 1982.

Hiroshima kara Oiroshima e: '82 Yōroppa no hankaku heiwa undō o miru.   Tokyo, Iwanami Shoten, 1982.

Kaku no taika to "ningen" no koe [The Nuclear Conflagration and the Voice of "Man"].   Tokyo, Iwanami Shoten, 1982.

Ika ni ki o korosu ka [How to Kill a Tree].   Tokyo, Bungei Shunjū, 1984.

Nihon gendai no yumanisuto Watanabe Kazuo o yomu.   Tokyo, Iwanami Shoten, 1984.

Ikikata no teigi: futatabi jokyo e.   Tokyo, Iwanami Shoten, 1985.

Shōsetsu no takurami chi no tanoshimi.   Tokyo, Shinchōsha, 1985.

Kaba ni kamareru.   Tokyo, Bungei Shunjū, 1985.

M/T to mori no fushigi no monogatari.   Tokyo, Iwanami Shoten, 1986.

Atarashii bungaku no tame no.   Tokyo, Iwanami Shoten, 1988.

Kirupu no gundan.   Tokyo, Iwanami Shoten, 1988.

Saigo no shōsetsu.   Tokyo, Kōdansha, 1988.

Editor, *Itami Mansaku essei shū*, by Mansaku Itami.   1971.

Editor, *Atomic Aftermath: Short Stories About Hiroshima-Nagasaki.*   Tokyo, Shueisha Press, 1984; as *The Crazy Iris and Other Stories of the Atomic Aftermath*, New York, Grove Press, 1985; as *Fire from the Ashes: Short Stories About Hiroshima and Nagasaki*, London, Readers International, 1985.

*

Critical Studies: "Circles of Shame: 'Sheep' by Ōe Kenzaburō" by Frederick Richter, in *Studies in Short Fiction* (Newberry, South Carolina), 11, 1974; in *The Search for Authenticity in Modern Japanese Literature*, Cambridge, Cambridge University Press, 1978, and *Oe Kenzaburo and Contemporary Japanese Literature*, Oxford, Nissan Institute, 1986, both by Hisaaki Yamanouchi; "The 'Mad' World of Ōe Kenzaburō" by Iwamoto Yoshio, in *Journal of the Association of Teachers of Japanese*, 14(1), 1979; "Toward a Phenomenology of Ōe Kenzaburō: Self, World, and the Intermediating Microcosm" by Earl Jackson, Jr., in *Transactions of the International Conference of Orientalists in Japan*, 25, 1980; "Ōe's Obsessive Metaphor, Mori the Idiot Son: Toward the Imagination of Satire, Regeneration, and Grotesque Realism" by Michiko N. Wilson, in *Journal of Japanese Studies* (Seattle, Washington), 7(1), 1981; "Kenzaburo Oe: A New World of Imagination" by Yoshida Sanroku, in *Comparative Literature Studies* (University Park, Pennsylvania), 22(1), 1985; *The Marginal World of Oe Kenzaburo: A Study in Themes and Techniques* by Michiko N. Wilson, Armonk, New York, and London, Sharpe, 1986; in *Off Center* by Miyoshi Masao, Cambridge, Massachusetts, Harvard University Press, 1991; *Escape from the Wasteland: Romanticism and Realism in the Fiction of Michima Yukio and Oe Kenzaburo* by Susan J. Napier, Cambridge, Massachusetts, Harvard-Yenching Institute Monograph Series, 1991.

*   *   *

Ōe Kenzaburō, one of Japan's most important writers and essayists, is known for his works celebrating the marginal and the outcast, in often violent opposition to a central establishment. It is perhaps not surprising, therefore, that Ōe was born in a mountain village on Shikoku, the smallest and still most rural of Japan's four major islands. Although Ōe now lives and writes in Tokyo, the village in the valley and the forest surrounding it have been a major source for Ōe's fictional imagination. Works highlighting a rural background range from his early so-called "pastoral fiction," such as his 1958 Akutagawa prize-winning story "Shiiku" ("Prize Stock and The Catch") to his nostalgic 1986 novel *Natsukashii toshi e no tegami* (Letters to the Lost Years). While his pastoral works were largely realistic in their treatment of the village and the valley, Ōe's later fiction increasingly began to attach a mythological significance to these places. In the 1968 *Man'en gannen no futobōru* (The Silent Cry), a novel which Ōe describes as "a turning point," two urban brothers return to their village in the mountains to forge new lives: the older brother searches for a "thatched hut," a retreat away from the world, while the younger brother mixes village history and legends to empower himself as leader of the increasingly apathetic villagers.

The possibilities inherent in rural folk legends became increasingly important in Ōe's fiction in the 1970s and 1980s, leading to his controversial 1979 novel *Dōjidai gemu* [The Game of Contemporaneity], which describes a hidden mountain village's relentless opposition towards what they call the Greater Japanese Empire. *Dōjidai gemu* offers the inspiration of the folklore and legends of the village as a substitute to what Ōe considers to be the pernicious influence of the elitist myths of the Japanese emperor system.

In fact, Ōe's strong opposition to the emperor system has been another important element in his writing, often combined with the events of the summer of 1945, the summer when Japan acknowledged defeat and the emperor admitted that he was not a god. Ōe's Japanese critics have pointed to 1945 as a watershed year in the young Ōe's life, creating a bifurcation in Ōe's personal ideology, between the "patriotic boy" who had loved the emperor and the "democratic boy" who believed in the liberal principles fostered by the American Occupation. Many of his early novels display this bifurcation. Some range obsessively over the frightening yet attractive aspects of war and violence, while others contain protagonists who have a love-hate relationship with the emperor. Ōe's angry satire *Sevuntiin* (17), published in 1961 and based on an incident that had occurred the previous year, tells the story of a pathetic young adolescent's attempted assassination of a socialist politician in the name of the emperor.

Perhaps Ōe's most fascinating fictional comment on the emperor system is his brilliant 1970 novella *Waga namida o nuguitamū hi* (The Day He Himself Shall Wipe My Tears Away). Inspired by the emperor-oriented suicide of Ōe's fellow novelist and personal bête noire Mishima Yukio, the novella is a savage attack on both the emperor system and the insane romanticism that lay behind Mishima's death. At the same time, however, the novella betrays a certain empathy towards that very romanticism, suggesting that traces of the "patriotic boy" still remain in Ōe's personality, although the present-day Ōe is a committed leftwing humanist.

Indeed, Ōe's portraits of romantic protagonists, lost in dreams of violence or escape, are among his effective, even when they are not overtly ideological. Perhaps his most successful characterization of this sort is contained in his 1964 novel *Kojinteki na taiken* (A Personal Matter). A darkly humorous, yet extraordinarily affecting account of a young man's struggle to come to terms with having fathered a brain-damaged child, *A Personal Matter* contains strongly autobiographical elements. But Bird, as the young father is called, is

ultimately far more than Ōe's alter ego. A passive dreamer who initially wants only to escape his marriage and travel to Africa, Bird grows up in the course of the book through a series of grotesque and memorable encounters that range from the erotic — a marathon sex session with an old girl-friend — to the comic — the hungover Bird's breaking down and vomiting in front of his students in an English class. *A Personal Matter* is one of Ōe's funniest and most moving novels and its hero, irritating and self-pitying though he may be, remains with the reader as one of the most brilliantly realized characters in modern Japanese fiction.

The theme of father and brain-damaged son begun in *A Personal Matter* has also remained an important element in Ōe's fiction, from the surreal fantasy *Sora no kaibutsu Aguii* (Aghwee the Sky Monster), in which a father is unable to overcome his guilt for having murdered his brain-damaged baby, to the 1976 carnivalesque epic *Pinchiranna chōsho* (The Pinch-Runner Memorandum), in which a father and idiot son lead an army of marginals and grotesques against the Japanese establishment. *Pinchiranna* thus exemplifies some of the most important elements of Ōe's work: its opposition to the centre and to the emperor system, its privileging of the marginal in the duo of outcast father and son, and its celebration of the liberating aspects of the violent and the grotesque.

In recent years Ōe's work has continued to mine these themes, although the tone has become increasingly elegiac rather than angry. Thus, the aforementioned *Natsukashii toshi e no tegami* revolves around the protagonist's guilt-ridden acceptance that he can no longer return to the valley of his childhood except in dreams and fiction. Ōe's recent work, especially the 1991 science fiction novel *Chiryō no tō* (Tower of Healing), set in a dystopian future where a hidden valley exists as a final escape, suggests that his favorite themes may increasingly be combined with new departures. Whatever Ōe's next direction will be, it seems certain that he will remain committed to producing politically controversial and highly imaginative fiction, an increasing rarity in the Japanese literary scene these days.

—Susan J. Napier

ONETTI, Juan Carlos. Uruguayan. Born in Montevideo, 1 July 1909. Married Dolly Muhr in 1955; one son and one daughter. Lived in Buenos Aires, 1930–34; editor, *Marcha*, Montevideo, 1939–42, and *Vea y Lea*, Buenos Aires, 1946–55; editor for Reuters, Montevideo, 1941–43, and Buenos Aires, 1943–46; manager of an advertising firm, Montevideo, 1955–57; director of municipal libraries, Montevideo, 1957; lived in Spain, from 1975. Recipient: National Literature prize, 1962; William Faulkner Foundation Ibero American award, 1963; Casa de las Americas prize, 1965; Italian-Latin American Institute prize, 1972. Address: c/o Editorial Sudamericana, Humberto 531 — 1° piso, 1103 Buenos Aires, Argentina.

PUBLICATIONS

Fiction

El pozo. Montevideo, Signo, 1939; as *The Pit*, with *Tonight*, London, Quartet, 1991.

Tierra de nadie.   Buenos Aires, Losada, 1941.
Para esta noche.   Buenos Aires, Poseidon, 1943; as *Tonight*, with *The Pit*, London, Quartet, 1991.
La vida breve.   Buenos Aires, Sudamericana, 1950; as *A Brief Life*, New York, Grossman, 1976.
Un sueño realizado y otros cuentos.   Montevideo, Número, 1951.
Los adioses.   Buenos Aires, Sur, 1954; as *Goodbyes*, in *Goodbyes and Other Stories*, 1990; as *Farewells*, with *A Grave with No Name*, London, Quartet, 1992.
Una tumba sin nombre.   Montevideo, Marcha, 1959; as *A Grave with No Name*, with *Farewells*, London, Quartet, 1992.
La cara de la desgracia.   Montevideo, Alfa, 1960.
El astillero.   Buenos Aires, Fabril, 1961; as *The Shipyard*, New York, Scribner, 1968; London, Serpent's Tail, 1992.
El infierno tan temido.   Montevideo, Asir, 1962.
Tan triste como ella.   Montevideo, Alfa, 1963.
Juntacadáveres.   Montevideo, Alfa, 1964; as *Body Snatcher*, London, Quartet, and New York, Pantheon, 1991.
Jacob y el otro, Un sueño realizado y otros cuentos.   Montevideo, Banda Oriental, 1965.
Tres novelas (includes *La cara de la desgracia*; *Tan triste como ella*; *Jacobo y el otro*).   Montevideo, Alfa, 1967.
Cuentos completos.   Buenos Aires, Centro Editor de America Latina, 1967; revised edition, Buenos Aires, Corregidor, 1974.
Novelas [and *Cuentos*] *cortas completas.*   Caracas, Monte Avila, 2 vols., 1968.
La novia robada y otros cuentos.   Buenos Aires, Centro Editor de America Latina, 1968.
Los rostros del amor.   Buenos Aires, Centro Editor de America Latina, 1968.
Obras completas.   Mexico City, Aguilar, 1970.
La muerte y la niña.   Buenos Aires, Corregidor, 1973.
Tiempo de abrazar y los cuentos de 1933 a 1950.   Montevideo, Arca, 1974.
Tan triste como ella y otros cuentos.   Barcelona, Lumen, 1976.
Dejemos hablar al viento.   Barcelona, Bruguera, 1979.
Cuentos secretos: Periquito el Aguador y otras máscaras.   Montevideo, Biblioteca de Marcha, 1986.
Presencia y otros cuentos.   Madrid, Almarabu, 1986.
Cuando entonces.   Madrid, Mondadori, and Buenos Aires, Sudamericana, 1987.
Goodbyes and Other Stories.   Austin, University of Texas Press, 1990.

Other

Requiem por Faulkner.   Montevideo, Arca, 1976.

*

Bibliographies: "Contribución a la bibliografía de Juan Carlos Onetti" by Hugo J. Verani, in *Onetti*, edited by Jorge Ruffinelli, Montevideo, Marcha, 1973; "Bibliografía de Onetti" by Aurora Ocampo, in her *Novelistas iberoamericanos contemporáneos*, Mexico City, Universidad Nacional Autónoma de México, 1981.

Critical Studies: *The Formal Expression of Meaning in Juan Carlos Onetti's Narrative Art* by Yvonne P. Jones, Cuernavaca, Cidoc, 1971; Onetti issues of *Crisis*, 6, 1974, and *Review* (New York), 16, 1975; *Three Authors of Alienation: Bombal, Onetti, Carpentier* by M. Ian Adams, Austin, University of Texas Press, 1975; *Juan Carlos Onetti* by Djelal

Kadir, Boston, Twayne, 1977; *Reading Onetti: Language, Narrative and the Subject* by Mark Millington, Liverpool, Cairns, 1985; "Juan Carlos Onetti and the Auto-Referential Text" by Bart L. Lewis, in *Hispanófila* (Chapel Hill, North Carolina), 96, 1989.

*   *   *

The high regard in which the contemporary Latin American novel is held by both critics and readers can be traced in considerable measure to the contribution of Uruguay's most respected prose writer, Juan Carlos Onetti, whose novels, *nouvelles*, and short stories bring eminence to the practice of modernist auto-referentiality in Latin America. The neglect into which his early works fell, the delayed recognition of his narrative talents, his posed, sullen detachment from the literary community all define the figure who was to bring Uruguayan, and Latin American, literature from forbidding plain and jungle onto the cerebral battlefield of modern urban life.

The signal year 1939 marks two events that were to set the course for Onetti's own career and to initiate his long-range influence on Latin American prose: his appointment as editor of *Marcha*, a weekly journal of fiction, criticism, and opinion, and the publication of his first novel, *El pozo* (*The Pit*). His early essays in *Marcha* are urgent calls for the establishment of a Latin American aesthetic identity, based not on quaint scenes of restless, overpowering Nature, but born rather of an intense devotion to the enterprise of *art* and its untold, unending variations, a call that would be increasingly heeded into the 1940s and 1950s. And *The Pit* — a short, sour examination of a 40-year-old life, adrift and contemptuous, in the manner of Fedor Dostoevskii, Albert Camus, and Jean-Paul Sartre — prefigures the Latin American "Boom" novel of shadowy introspection and modernist technique, prompting Mario Vargas Llosa (*q.v.*) to date the birth of Latin America's "creative novel" precisely from the publication of *The Pit* (*La crítica de la novela iberoamericana* [*Criticism of the Latin American Novel*], 1973). Over a 50-year career, characterized by alternating periods of steady productivity and silent inertia, Onetti has formed fictions that set feckless, self-absorbed characters against the means of their creation, an author/narrator and his power to imagine. Onetti's official acceptance is now assured with the awarding to him in 1980 of Spain's prestigious Cervantes literary prize, and one of the Boom's principal initiators has thus lived to see the full flowering of his continent's literature.

Onetti's principal concern as a writer is the act of artistic creation, the narrated, studied crafting of a literary text. After his early experiments with narration as its own subject such as *The Pit*, he brought into being in his 1950 masterpiece *La vida breve* (*A Brief Life*) his definitive narrator, the imaginative, besieged Juan María Brausen, screenplay writer and dreamer of other worlds. Brausen, who also takes the fictitious identity of Juan María Arce in order to dissolve into yet another life, that of the woman next door, creates a baleful, middle-aged doctor, Díaz Grey, and places him into the heterocosm of Santa María. From *A Brief Life* onward, Brausen is the divine figure alluded to by characters in other works, the creator to whom they owe their full, if grudging, allegiance. Onetti's metafictional project — writing as proposal, as small, saving victory, as the promise of mimetic "adventures" — structures and distinguishes the novels, *nouvelles*, and short stories which are his contribution to the respected body of contemporary Latin American fiction.

In addition to Onetti's other well-known and skillfully metafictional novels such as *El astillero* (*The Shipyard*) and *Juntacadáveres* (*Body Snatcher*), and such representative short stories as "A Dream Come True," "The House on the Sand," "Hell Most Feared," and "The Stolen Bride," three works distinctly mark the range of his auto-referential production. *Los adioses* (*Goodbyes*) is the least metafictional of all his works: there is a vividly depicted setting, a recognizable plot, and a heroic moral dilemma. Only the presence of a deceitful, manipulative narrator, akin to Brausen, allies this book to the others. *Una tumba sin nombre* (*A Grave with No Name*), at the other extreme, is Onetti's most overtly self- conscious work, in which metafiction is born not of narrational authority, but rather from the complicity of several characters, among them the ubiquitous Díaz Grey, who affirms characteristically: "the only thing that matters is that when I finished writing this story I felt at peace." Finally, Onetti's 1979 novel *Dejemos hablar al viento* (Let Us Allow the Wind to Speak) would appear to close out his metafictional career: the novel's enigmatic, contradictory "adventures" are interspersed with paragraphs, chapters, titles, and allusions from a great many other Onetti works, a palimpsest of fictions, pure form. But Onetti does not stop there; his 1987 *nouvelle Cuando entonces* (When Then) seems to extend the Onettian range even further. Together with the expected matter of elaborately getting the tale under way, humor, avuncular wisdom, real geography, and the introduction of a detective tale characterize this most recent work, and promise further creativity.

Onetti's uneven, troubled career has resolved itself into a large body of critically admired prose that, finally, hews to a single driving artistic impulse: the necessary predominance of writing as process. Onetti's anguished, detached narrators, creators of public worlds and private torments, brought Latin American fiction out of its provincial stasis at a time when talent, opportunity, and attention were poised to grant it greatness, and the Latin American novel from the 1940s onward stands as the heir to Onetti's artistic, self-examining vision.

—Bart L. Lewis

OUSMANE, Sembène. Senegalese. Born in Ziguinchor, Casamance, 8 January 1923. Educated at a technical school; Gorki Film Studios, Moscow, 1962. Served in the Free French Forces fighting in Africa, 1942–46. Married Carrie Moore in 1974. Worked as a fisherman, Casamance, and as a plumber, mechanic's helper, and bricklayer, Dakar, before World War II; docker and stevedore, Marseilles, from 1948; Secretary General of black workers organization in France. Since 1963 filmmaker. Founding editor, *Kaddu* newspaper, 1972. Recipient: Dakar Festival of Negro Arts prize, 1966; Cannes Film Festival prize, 1967, Venice Film Festival prize, 1969; Atlanta Film Festival prize, 1970. Address: c/o P.O. Box 8087, YOFF, Dakar, Senegal.

PUBLICATIONS

Fiction

Le Docker noir.   Paris, Nouvelles Éditions Debresse, 1956; as *Black Docker*, London, Heinemann, 1987.

O Pays, mon beau peuple!   Paris, Presses de la Cité, 1957.
Les Bouts de bois de Dieu.   Paris, Le Livre Contemporain, 1960; as *God's Bits of Wood*, New York, Doubleday, 1962; London, Heinemann, 1970.
Voltaïque.   Paris, Présence Africaine, 1962; as *Tribal Scars, and Other Stories*, London, Heinemann, and Washington D.C., INSCAPE, 1974.
Référendum.   Paris, Présence Africaine, 1964.
Véhi-Ciosane; ou, Blanche-Genèse; Le Mandat.   Paris, Pre´sence Africaine, 1965; as *The Money Order; White Genesis*, London, Heinemann, 1972.
Xala [Impotence].   Paris, Présence Africaine, 1973; in English, London, Heinemann, and Westport, Connecticut, Hill, 1976.
Le Dernier de l'empire.   Paris, L'Harmattan, 2 vols., 1981; as *The Last of the Empire*, London, Heinemann, 1983.
Niiwan; Taaw.   Paris, Présence Africaine, 1987.

Plays

Screenplays (also director): *Borom Sarret*, 1963; *Niaye*, 1964; *La Noire de . . .*, from his own story, 1966, as *The Black Girl from . . .* (US), 1969; *Mandabi*, from his novella *The Money Order*, 1968; *Tauw*, 1970; *Emitai*, 1971; *Xala* [Impotence], from his novel, 1974; *Ceddo* [The People], 1977; *Camp de Thiaroye*, 1987.

*

Critical Studies: "Ousmane Sembène: His Films, His Art," in *Black Art* (Hollywood, Florida), 3(3), 1979, "Myths, Traditions and Colonialism in Ousmane Sembène's *Emitai*," in *CLA Journal* (Atlanta, Georgia), 24(3), 1981, "Three Faces of Africa: Women in *Xala*," in *Jump Cut* (Berkeley, California), 27, 1982, and *The Cinema of Ousmane Sembène: A Pioneer of African Film*, Westport, Connecticut, Greenwood, 1984, all by Françoise Pfaff; *Evolution of an African Artist: Social Realism in the Work of Ousmane Sembène* by Carrie Dailey Moore, Ann Arbor, University of Michigan Press, 1984; *Ousmane Sembène, Contemporary Griot* by Jonathan Peters, Washington, D.C., Three Continents Press, 2 vols., 1990–91.

*   *   *

Throughout his career as novelist, short story writer, and filmmaker, Sembène Ousmane has displayed a compassionate understanding of the sufferings of the powerless and dispossessed of his native Senegal. In contrast to the *négritude* espoused by fellow Senegalese writer Léopold Senghor (*q.v.*) that exalted black culture and experience, Ousmane has adopted a more critical attitude towards West African culture, showing that it is not only the colonialist's racism that causes brutal injustice, but also the institutions of pre- and post-colonial black Africans which can stunt the individual's development.

Ousmane's work draws on his own remarkable experience. Largely self-taught, Ousmane was born into a family of fishermen, and worked as a soldier, bricklayer, and docker, before beginning a career as writer and film director. All his major work has been written in French rather than in his indigenous Wolof to ensure publication and readership. His first novel, *Le Docker noir* (*Black Docker*) was written after he had been a trade union leader in the docks of Marseilles. An account of a young black worker's (and would-be novelist's) exploitation by whites, Ousmane's novel shows great sympathy for the exploited migrant workers of the French shipyards, and an awareness of social oppression and racial prejudice that is present throughout his work.

Ousmane came to critical attention with his assured novel of 1957, *O Pays, mon beau peuple!* (Oh Country, My Beautiful People), which depicts a return to a native land marred by interracial and intergenerational hostilities. Faye, a soldier who has served in World War II, returns to his home region of Casamance in southern Senegal, complete with white wife, Isabelle. He bears a renewed sense of devotion to serve his country through regeneration of the land, and a desire to break with some of his parents' social and religious practices. Caught between progress and tradition, black prejudices and white racism, African and European mentalities, Faye encounters great difficulties in establishing his farm, la Palmeraie. The novel ends with Faye's tragic murder marking an abrupt end to his plans to cultivate his native soil. *O Pays, mon beau peuple!* displays an acute awareness of social structures and relations, with Ousmane very sensitively indicating the different social allegiances and beliefs of the various ranks and age groups of Casamancian society under French rule.

An ability to sketch in the social and economic circumstances of a whole society is well evident in Ousmane's distinguished third novel, *Les Bouts de bois de Dieu* (*God's Bits of Wood*). This epic novel, like Zola's *Germinal*, depicts the life of a strike, namely the 1947 strike action by railroad workers on the Senegal to French Sudan line. Using many different perspectives on the strike from workers and their families of various ethnic groups along the 1,000 miles of line, Ousmane skilfully opens up a complete social panorama, offering us individual case histories within a collective context. The various stages of industrial action from downing of tools right through to the French employers' attempts at strike-breaking, and the betrayal of the strikers by returning workers, are very clearly developed, providing a compelling account of a historical event. Even more decidedly than in *O Pays, mon beau peuple!*, Ousmane in his multi-voiced work shows how those without power, here women and children, often become the unwitting victims of historical change.

A more ironic narrative distinguishes the novel *Xala* from its predecessors. Voiced laconically and in quasi-anthropological terms, Ousmane's work dissects the vanities, weaknesses and corrupt practices of Senegal's prosperous business class. The novel (also made into a film by Ousmane) guides us through the fears and miseries of a Dakar businessman and proud member of the Chamber of Commerce and Industry, who in order to impress the business community takes a young woman as his third wife. Unfortunately El Hadji Abdou Kader discovers he has been struck down by the curse of impotence, the *xala*, a condition that he goes to ridiculous lengths to cure.

Le Dernier de l'empire (The Last of the Empire), like *Xala*, is set in a not-so-fictitious Senegal after French rule, and again looks with considerable irony at the ways that the country's black professional elites have betrayed the hopes and ideals of African independence. Written as a political thriller, this work concerns the rumoured disappearance of the President, and the subsequent machinations among remaining ministers to gain power. As in earlier works, Ousmane displays an acute awareness of social nuance and position, and provides a masterly examination of the less honourable aspirations of some of the politicians who took over power when the French left Senegal. Ousmane's exasperation at the silk-shirted and Fifth Avenue-clad *arrivistes* whose goal is self-aggrandisement is voiced here by the elder statesman figure of the Minister of Justice. Being as old as the century and a party to all major changes in the country's history, he has always been a model of political accommodation until faced by this new ruthless generation whose "hyena fangs are greedy for power."

Ousmane's accomplished short stories also expose brutal treatment and corruption, and plead eloquently for the defenceless. Most of these pieces are socially realistic with colonial and post-colonial settings. Some, though, are written as folktales, such as "The False Prophet," which deals with human willingness to believe in an obvious charlatan, and the impressive "Tribal Scars," which in Kipling-like fashion ponders on the origin of West African facial and bodily scars, tracing them to an attempt to remain free in the advent of slave traders. Other outstanding short stories in the collection *Voltaïque* (*Tribal Scars, and Other Stories*) include the moving "Her Three Days," the account of a third wife's loss of favour with her polygynous husband, and there are several stories set in France about black immigrant experiences. "Letters from France" is a wail from a lonely exile's heart as she recounts her life in France with an elderly, unemployed husband far from the lively communality of the African world, and "The Promised Land" provides a harrowing account of a black woman's life as an underpaid and taunted nursemaid, cook, and washerwoman in a France she cannot recognise from the descriptions she heard back home.

Ousmane has also written extended short stories. *Le Mandat* (*The Money Order*), a comic account of how a rather pompous head of family is caught in a maze of bureaucracy, false promises, and open theft in his attempts to cash a money order from Paris, anticipates the sardonic tone of Ousmane's most recent novels. *Blanche-Genèse* (*White Genesis*), which in its introduction contains Ousmane's disassociation from the idealising tendencies in *négritude*, shows Ousmane as a modern *griot*, with his retelling of a sad tale of the fall of a noble family and his hopes for its surviving child.

Ousmane's work deserves to be wider known, and can quite rightly be considered alongside that of outstanding English-language West African writers such as Chinua Achebe, Buchi Emecheta, and Wole Soyinka for its ability to chronicle the social and psychological burdens of colonialism and the subsequent transfer of power to native rule.

—Anna-Marie Taylor

OYÔNÔ-MBIA, Guillaume. Cameroonian. Born in Mvoutessi, in 1939. Educated at the Collège Evangélique, Libamba; University of Keele, Staffordshire, 1964–69. Lecturer in English, University of Yaoundé; head of cultural affairs division, Ministry of Information and Culture, 1972–75. Recipient: El Hadj Ahmadou Ahidjo prize; Inter-African theatre competition prize, 1969. Address: Department of English, University of Yaoundé, BP 337, Yaoundé, Cameroon.

<small>PUBLICATIONS</small>

Plays

Trois Prétendants . . . un mari (produced Cameroon) Yaoundé, Clé, 1964; as *Three Suitors: One Husband*, with *Until Further Notice*, London, Methuen, 1968; in *Faces of African Independence: Three Plays*, Charlottesville, University Press of Virginia, 1988.

Le Train spécial de Son Excellence = His Excellency's Train (bilingual edition; produced Cameroon; broadcast, 1969). Yaoundé, Clé, 1979.

Jusqua'à Nouvel Avis, from his radio play. Yaoundé, Clé, 1970; as *Until Further Notice*, with *Three Suitors: One Husband*, London, Methuen, 1968; in *Faces of African Independence: Three Plays*, Charlottesville, University Press of Virginia, 1988.

Notre Fille ne se mariera pas!, from his radio play. Paris, ORTF-DAEC, 1971.

Radio Plays: *His Excellency's Special Train*, (in English) 1969, (in French) 1975; *Notre Fille ne se mariera pas!*, 1969; *Jusqu'à Nouvel Avis*.

Fiction

Chroniques de Mvoutessi 1–3. Yaoundé, Clé, 3 vols., 1971–72.

*

Critical Studies: "Drama as Social Criticism: The Case of Oyônô-Mbia's *Trois Prétendants . . .*" by Cyril Mokwenye, in *Ufahamu* (Los Angeles), 14(2), 1985; "The Double Irony of Culture-Conflict in Guillaume Oyônô-Mbia's *Jusqu'à Nouvel Avis*" by Janice S. Spleth, in *West Virginia University Philological Papers* (Morgantown), 33, 1987.

* * *

Although the author of three volumes of short stories, Guillaume Oyônô-Mbia is better known as a prize-winning and widely performed playwright. His first work for the theatre, *Trois Prétendants . . . un mari (Three Suitors: One Husband)* was written in 1960 to entertain his fellow students at the Collège Évangélique de Libamba. In 1961 it became the first modern Cameroonian play to be staged in the country's capital, Yaoundé. The preface to the second (French) edition of the play contains what may be regarded as Oyônô-Mbia's credo as a dramatist. In it, he indicates just how little hope he had of the play's being publicly performed when he first wrote it. As he explains, theatres and permanent theatre companies were extremely rare in Cameroon at that time. Oyônô-Mbia's success gave clear encouragement to a younger generation of writers, and he may be regarded as a founding father of contemporary theatre in that country.

Oyônô-Mbia's reputation as a dramatist does not, however, rest solely on his historic role in the development of modern Cameroonian theatre. His plays themselves show him to be a knowledgeable, skilled, and highly versatile dramatist, who can write for both stage and radio. The latter medium has been crucially important for those wishing to reach a mass audience in Africa, and three of Oyônô-Mbia's four plays were first written for it. He is equally at home in English and in French, writing in both languages and habitually translating his own work. Oyônô-Mbia is also clearly familiar with world theatre. The influence of Molière is apparent in his early theatrical style (especially in the five-act *Three Suitors: One Husband*) and seems also to have shaped his view of the dramatist's mission — essentially a restatement of Molière's undertaking to "amuse and educate." And the self-consciousness of a later work, *Notre Fille ne se mariera pas!* (Our Daughter Must Not Get Married), is reminiscent of Pirandello.

However, Oyônô-Mbia is never merely imitative or derivative. On the contrary, he displays a remarkable ability to address cultural and social issues of national significance in a highly personal idiom. His main preoccupations centre on the conflict between tradition and modernity in contemporary Africa. His subjects include the dowry system, the practice of polygamy, the generation gap, the impact of education on African society, the drift from the land to the cities, and the lure — for some — of Europe.

Oyônô-Mbia is skilled in the art of dramatic construction, exploiting to the full the tensions inherent in his themes. He habitually creates suspense by the relatively simple device of making us await the advent of a key individual, on whom the resolution of the play's central conflict crucially depends. Moreover, he is an excellent comic writer, with particular strengths in farce and satire.

Although intent on presenting his chosen issues with clarity, Oyônô-Mbia's treatment of them is subtle and multifaceted. He has recorded his embarrassment at being lauded as the champion of the emancipation of African women, a theme he handles in *Three Suitors: One Husband*. And he is courageous enough to show some of the negative aspects of what has occasionally passed for emancipation, in the form of female characters whose aspirations for careers lead merely to their becoming bar-room singers or mistresses of minor bureaucrats. His critique of polygamy is similarly balanced. He illustrates the wrongs and absurdities of the practice, and yet also suggests that what at times has replaced it may be even more exploitative of women. Oyônô-Mbia's characterizations are similarly nuanced. Though constantly depicting the lives and opinions of simple, country people, he refrains from doing so in a simplistic manner.

Like most of Oyônô-Mbia's work, his second play, *Jusqu'à Nouvel Avis (Until Further Notice)*, is set in his birthplace, Mvoutessi, in eastern Cameroon. Here, Abessolo and his family await the return home of his daughter Matalina and her husband. Both have spent several years studying medicine in Europe. In the end they fail to turn up, but send instead a large hamper of food and drink. This greatly delights the villagers, with the sole exception of Cecilia, Abessolo's wife. Superficially, Cecilia may be dismissed as uneducated and even reactionary; she is mocked even by her own husband as "uncivilized." She spends much of her time offstage in her kitchen and is scandalized to learn that her daughter does not see cooking her husband's food as her prime duty. She is at the centre of a comic scene in which her son Mezoe seeks unsuccessfully to explain to the older members of the family what is meant by the concept "Africa." Yet Cecilia's role in the play is much more complicated than simply being the butt of the joke. Her regret that Matalina's husband has decided to take up a career not as a doctor but as a civil servant is deplored by the rest of her family. But it is her apparent naïvety that allows Oyônô-Mbia to examine the role of the educated individual in a developing country, and indeed to raise the wider question of African identity. In the French version of the play in particular, she becomes a sad, silent commentator on a changing world. It is this combination of genuine reflectiveness with sheer comic verve that constitutes Oyônô-Mbia's real contribution to the theatre.

—Tim Lewis

———

OZ, Amos. Israeli. Born in Jerusalem, 4 May 1939. Educated at Hebrew University, Jerusalem, B.A. in Hebrew literature and philosophy 1963. Served in the Israeli Army, 1957–60; fought as reserve soldier in tank corps in Sinai, 1967, and in the Golan Heights, 1973. Married Nily Zuckerman in 1960; two daughters and one son. Teacher of literature and philosophy, Hulda High School, Kibuts Hulda, and Regional High School, Givat Brenner, 1963–86; also tractor driver, youth instructor, Kibuts Hulda; visiting fellow, St. Cross College, Oxford, 1969–70; writer-in-residence or Visiting Professor, Hebrew University, Jerusalem, 1975, University of California, Berkeley, 1980, Colorado College, Colorado Springs, 1984–85, Boston University, 1987, and Hebrew University, Jerusalem, 1990. Since 1987 Professor of Hebrew literature, Ben Gurion University, Beersheva. Recipient: Holon prize, 1965; Israel-American Cultural Foundation Award, 1968; B'nai B'rith award, 1973; Brenner prize, 1976; Ze'ev award for children's books, 1978; Bernstein prize, 1983; Bialik prize, 1986; H. H. Wingate award, 1988; Prix Femina Étranger (France), 1988; German Publishers' Union international peace prize, 1992. Honorary doctorate: Hebrew Union College, Cincinnati, 1988; Western New England College, Springfield, Massachusetts, 1988; Tel Aviv University, 1992. Chevalier de l'Ordre des Arts et des Lettres (France), 1984. Member, Catalan Academy of the Mediterranean, Barcelona, 1989, and Academy of Hebrew Language, 1991. Address: Arad 80700, Israel.

PUBLICATIONS

Fiction

Artsot hatan. Tel Aviv, Massade, 1965; as *Where the Jackals Howl, and Other Stories*, San Diego, Harcourt Brace, and London, Chatto and Windus, 1981.
Makom acher. Tel Aviv, Sifriyat Po'alim, 1966; as *Elsewhere, Perhaps*, New York, Harcourt Brace, 1973; London, Secker and Warburg, 1974.
Micha'el sheli. Tel Aviv, Am Oved, 1968; as *My Michael*, New York, Knopf, and London, Chatto and Windus, 1972.
Ahavah me'ucheret. Tel Aviv, Sifriyat Po'alim, 1971; as *Unto Death*, New York, Harcourt Brace, 1975; London, Chatto and Windus, 1976.
Laga'at bamayim, laga'at baruach. Tel Aviv, Am Oved, 1973; as *Touch the Water, Touch the Wind*, New York, Harcourt Brace, 1974; London, Chatto and Windus, 1975.
Anashim acherim [Different People]. Tel Aviv, Hakibuts haMe'uchad, 1974.
Har ha'etsah hara'ah. Tel Aviv, Am Oved, 1976; as *The Hill of Evil Counsel*, New York, Harcourt Brace, and London, Chatto and Windus, 1978.
Menuchah nechonah. Tel Aviv, Am Oved, 1982; as *A Perfect Peace*, San Diego, Harcourt Brace, and London, Chatto and Windus, 1985.
Kufsah shechorah. Tel Aviv, Am Oved, 1987; as *Black Box*, San Diego, Harcourt Brace, and London, Chatto and Windus, 1988.
Lada'at ishah. Jerusalem, Keter, 1989; as *To Know a Woman*, San Diego, Harcourt Brace, and London, Chatto and Windus, 1991.
Hamatsav hashelishiy [The Third Condition]. Jerusalem, Keter, 1991.

Other

Soumchi (for children). Tel Aviv, Am Oved, 1978; in English, New York, Harper, and London, Chatto and Windus, 1980.

Be'or hakelet he'azah [Under This Blazing Light]. Tel Aviv, Sifriyat Po'alim, 1979.
Po vesham b'eretz Yisra'el. Tel Aviv, Am Oved, 1983; as *In the Land of Israel*, San Diego, Harcourt Brace, and London, Chatto and Windus, 1983.
Mimordot haLevanon. Tel Aviv, Am Oved, 1987; as *The Slopes of Lebanon*, San Diego, Harcourt Brace, 1989; London, Chatto and Windus, 1990.

Editor, with Richard Flantz, *Until Daybreak: Stories from the Kibbutz*. Tel Aviv, Institute for the Translation of Hebrew Literature, 1984.

*

Bibliography: by Y. Yerushalmi, Tel Aviv, Am Oved, 1984.

Critical Studies: "On Amos Oz: Under the Blazing Light" by Dov Vardi, in *Modern Hebrew Literature* (Ramat-Gan, Israel), 5(4), 1979; "The Jackal and the Other Place: The Stories of Amos Oz" by Leon I. Yudkin, in his *1948 and After: Aspects of Israeli Fiction*, Manchester, University of Manchester Press, 1984; "An Interview with Amos Oz" by Anita Susan Grossman, in *Partisan Review* (Boston), 53(3), 1986; "The Mythic Pattern in the Fiction of Amos Oz" by Avraham Balaban, and "*My Michael* — from Jerusalem to Hollywood via the Red Desert" by Nurith Gertz, both in *Modern Hebrew Literature in English Translation*, edited by Leon I. Yudkin, New York, Wiener, 1987; "Amos Oz in Arad: A Profile" by Shuli Barzilai, in *Southern Humanities Review* (Auburn, Alabama), 21(1), 1987; "Amos Oz: The Lack of Conscience" by Esther Fuchs, in her *Israeli Mythogynies: Women in Contemporary Hebrew Fiction*, Albany, State University of New York Press, 1987; "Amos Oz: Off the Reservation" by Chaim Chertok, in his *We Are All Close: Conversations with Israeli Writers*, New York, Fordham University Press, 1989; in *The Arab in Israeli Literature* by Gila Ramras-Rauch, Bloomington, Indiana University Press, and London, Tauris, 1989; in *Voices of Israel* by Joseph Cohen, Albany, State University of New York Press, 1990; "Amos Oz" (interview) by Eleanor Wachtel, in *Queens Quarterly* (Kingston, Ontario), 98(2), 1991.

*   *   *

Amos Oz is Israel's most popular and internationally acclaimed novelist. In addition to novels, he has written short stories, novellas, children's stories, literary criticism and political essays.

The stories in his first published volume, *Artsot hatan* (*Where the Jackals Howl*), had already made a considerable impact when they were published individually. The plots are original and often shocking, challenging stereotypes of Israeli society and human behaviour, paradoxical in dénouement, pointing up the dark side of behavioural tendencies. In this first volume, for example, the jackal, in both reality and metaphor, embodies the threat to settled society. The prophet Jeremiah had already forecast that Jerusalem would become a "habitation of jackals" (*Jeremiah* 10:22), and this city, the author's own, figures often in the writing as subject to challenge and threat from those hills which surround it and whence the dark forces emanate.

But the character of the threat is ambivalent. For the object of the threat, this source is dangerous but also captivating. Pain is also sometimes desired. In the title story, Gelilah is both fascinated and terrified by Damkov. When she remembered his invitation, "she was filled with revulsion and gaiety. Sh thought of his gripping ugliness . . ." The narrative description breaks down the division between the animate and the inanimate. And human nature, as we see here, is divided, and thus captured well by oxymoron.

Some of Oz's best-known novels and the characters within them, particularly the women, are prey to such inexplicable and divided motives and impulses. These things baffle logical analysis, and things are never as they seem. The author's first novel, *Makom acher* (*Elsewhere, Perhaps*), tests surface appearance against hidden reality, the apparently sedate, rational, and ordered life of the kibbutz against the forces that actually operate among those who inhabit this space. We are not quite sure what these "other" forces are, but they are subsumed under the overall character of the literal sense of the novel's title, the "other place." The other place, mentioned 11 times in the novel, is the metaphorical shadow of man, the object of yearning, but also of dread, the source of threat and unacknowledged desire. The conventional wisdom, that officially propagated by the kibbutz and its ideologues, is opposed by another, officially rejected reality that is ultimately more powerful and decisive. In this novel the apparently rational force is defeated in the struggle over the nubile Noga, who is drawn to the sinister visitor from Germany, Siegfried, rather than stay with her upright father, Reuben.

Although the sober, rational view of reality usually takes precedence over the unstable, unpredictable, and demented view, this does not prevent Oz from at times presenting an unstable consciousness as a dominant perspective. The novel *Micha'el sheli* (*My Michael*) adopts the voice and enters the mind of Hannah, the leading female protagonist and narrator. Two sorts of story are presented in parallel. One is a chronological account of the years 1950–60 surrounding Hannah and Michael, their meeting, engagement, marriage, family, social and public life. The other account consists of Hannah's fantasies surrounding Arab twins, of rape and terror, and her fantasies surrounding herself, of both helplessness and domination. The final description is one of ultimate destruction (her own suicide?), a fantasy of general and self-annihilation. Told in the form of a memoir, this is also an account of a mind in the process of disintegration against the backdrop of Jerusalem's reality in the first decade of Israel's independent existence. That the story lacks causality in elements of the plot (for example, that Hannah married Michael in the first place, that she agrees to leading a standard, bourgeois life clearly against her own deeper inclinations) only adds to the hold exercised by this unreliable narrator. The reader must always question and doubt Hannah's account of events, and yet this is the only account available.

The world of Oz's fiction moves between Israel's overt social reality and the personal fantasies of individuals beyond that sphere. The author himself is careful to distinguish between his fictional and political writing. When he wants to comment on the political scene, he insists on doing so in the appropriate manner and genre. This does not mean of course that his fiction lacks the ingredients of recognisable social reality, whether in a contemporary or older historical setting. On the contrary, Oz's fictions are set within familiar surroundings, and it is from these that the fictional figures derive their mental images. But they also move beyond. Oz's fiction sometimes explicitly notes the mystical yearning, as in *Laga'at bamayim, laga'at baruach* (*Touch the Water, Touch the Wind*), but often the plot begins in a more conventional setting, as in two recent novels, *Lada'at ishah* (*To Know a Woman*), and *Hamatsav hashelishiy* (The Third Condition). Both novels tell conventional stories, with recognisable, contemporary, Israeli settings. But in both too there is a mystery at the heart of the main characters. In the first, the woman, the now dead wife of the hero, Yoel, presents a problem of which Yoel is only now aware, at the onset of the novel. Much of the plot is recapped and retold, but the puzzle, of his own life as much as hers, remains. In the second novel, it is precisely this "third condition," the condition that would move the novel's hero beyond the immediate concerns of his life, that interests him. Yoel too in *To Know a Woman* had to shed something of his own selfish concern in order to move into another sphere and to become something more.

Oz's writing appears accessible, and it is indeed always marvelously constructed and readable. But it also constantly strains to reach for, and sometimes attain, extra elements in another dimension.

—Leon I. Yudkin

P

PA CHIN. *See* BA JIN.

————

PACHECO, José Emilio. Mexican. Born in Mexico City, 30 June 1939. Educated at the National Autonomous University of Mexico, Mexico City. Married to Cristina Pacheco; two daughters. Lecturer, University of Maryland, College Park, University of Illinois, Urbana, universities in Toronto and New York, and University of Essex, Wivenhoe. Former editor, *Diálogos* critical review, and cultural sections of *Excelsior* and *Novedades* newspapers. Recipient: Enrique Lihn prize, 1966; Magda Donato prize, 1968; National poetry prize, 1969; Guggenheim fellowship, 1970; Xavier Villaurrutia prize, 1973. Elected to the Colegio Nacional, 1986. Address: c/o Ediciones Era, Apdo 74–092, 09080 Mexico City, Mexico.

PUBLICATIONS

Verse

Los elementos de la noche. Mexico City, Universidad Nacional Autónoma de México, 1963.
El reposo del fuego. Mexico City, Fondo de Cultura Económica, 1966.
No me preguntes cómo pasa el tiempo: poemas, 1964–1968. Mexico City, Mortiz, 1969; as *Don't Ask Me How the Time Goes By: Poems, 1964–1968*, translated by Alastair Reid, New York, Columbia University Press, 1978.
Arbol entre dos muros/Tree Between Two Walls (bilingual edition), translated by Edward Dory and Gordon Brotherston. Los Angeles, Black Sparrow Press, 1969.
Irás y no volverás. Mexico City, Fondo de Cultura Económica, 1973.
Islas a la deriva. Mexico City, Siglo Veintiuno, 1976.
Ayer es nunca jamás. Caracas, Monte Avila, 1978.
Desde entonces: poemas 1975–1978. Mexico City, Era, 1980.
Tarde o temprano (includes translations of other poets' work). Mexico City, Fondo de Cultura Económica, 1980.
Signals from the Flames, translated by Thomas Hoeksema, edited by Yvette Miller. Pittsburgh, Latin American Literary Review Press, 1980.
Los trabajos del mar. Mexico City, Era, 1983.
Fin de siglo y otros poemas. Mexico City, Cultura SEP, 1984.
Alta traición. Madrid, Alianza, 1985.
Miro la tierra: poemas 1983–1986. Mexico City, Era, 1986.
José Emilio Pacheco: selecciones, edited by Luis Antonio de Villena. Madrid, Júcar, 1986.
Selected Poems (bilingual edition), edited by George McWhirter. New York, New Directions, 1987.
Ciudad de la memoria: poemas 1986–1989. Mexico City, Era, 1989.

Fiction

La sangre de Medusa. Mexico City, Porrúa, 1958.
El viento distante. Mexico City, Era, 1963.
Morirás lejos. Mexico City, Mortiz, 1967.
El principio del placer. Mexico City, Mortiz, 1972.
Las batallas en el desierto. Mexico City, Era, 1981; as *Battles in the Desert and Other Stories*, New York, New Directions, 1987.
La sangre de Medusa y otros cuentos marginales. Mexico City, Era, 1990.

Plays

Screenplays (all with Arturo Ripstein): *El castillo de la pureza*, 1972; *El santo officio*, 1975; *Fox Trot*, 1975.

Other

The Lost Homeland: Notes on Francisco Xavier Clavijero and the "National Culture" of Mexico. Toronto, University of Toronto, 1976(?).
Poesía modernista. Mexico City, SEP/Universidad Nacional Autónoma de México, 1982.
Album de zoología. Guadalajara, Cuarto Menguante, 1985.
Crónica del puerto de Veracruz, with Fernando Benitez. Xalapa, Gobierno del Estado de Veracruz, 1986.

Editor, *La poesía mexicana del siglo XIX: antología*. Mexico City, Empresas, 1965.
Editor, *Universidad, política y pueblo*, by Alfonso Reyes. Mexico City, Universidad Nacional Autónoma de México, 1967.
Editor, *Antología del modernismo (1884–1921)*. Mexico City, Universidad Nacional Autónoma de México, 2 vols., 1970.
Editor, with Gabriel Zaid, *El otoño recorre las islas: obra poética, 1961–1970*, by José Carlos Becerra. Mexico City, Era, 1973.
Editor, *Diario di Federico Gamboa, 1892–1939*. Mexico City, Siglo Veintiuno, 1977.
Editor, *Antología mínima*, by Alexis Saint-Léger Léger. Mexico City, Universidad Nacional Autónoma de México, 1977(?).
Editor, *Textos y pretextos*, by Xavier Villaurrutia. Mexico City, Universidad Nacional Autónoma de México, 1988.

Translator, *Comment C'est* [How It Is], by Samuel Beckett. 1966.
Translator, with Salvador Barros, *¡Que viva México!*, by Sergei M. Eizenshtein. Mexico City, Era, 1971.
Translator, *El frijol mágico*. Mexico City, PROMEXA, 1982.
Translator, *Aladino y la lámpara maravillosa* [Aladdin and His Magic Lamp]. Mexico City, Promociones Editoriales Mexicanas, 1982.
Translator, *El valiente soldadito de plomo* [The Steadfast Tin

Soldier], by Hans Christian Andersen.   Mexico City, Promociones Editoriales Mexicanas, 1982.
Translator, *Aproximaciones*.   Mexico City, Penélope, 1984.

*

Bibliography: in *Mexican Literature: A Bibliography of Secondary Sources* by David William Foster, Metuchen, New Jersey, Scarecrow Press, 1992.

Critical Studies: "José Emilio Pacheco: Signals from the Flames," in *Latin American Literary Review* (Pittsburgh), 5, 1973, and "A Poetry of Extremes," in *Review* (New York), 23, 1978, both by Thomas J. Hoeksema; "Four Contemporary Mexican Poets: Marco Antonio Montes de Oca, Gabriel Zaid, José Emilio Pacheco, Homero Aridjis" by Merlin H. Forster, in *Tradition and Renewal: Essays on 20th-Century Latin American Literature and Culture*, Urbana, University of Illinois Press, 1975; "Dreams and Distance in Recent Poetry of José Emilio Pacheco" by Agnes M. Gullón, in *Latin American Literary Review* (Pittsburgh), 11, 1977; "The Themes of Isolation and Persecution in José Emilio Pacheco's Short Stories," in *Ibero-Amerikanisches Archiv* (Berlin), 4(3), 1978, and "The Novel as Poem and Document: José Emilio Pacheco's *Morirás lejos*," in *Ibero-Amerikanisches Archiv* (Berlin), 6(4), 1980, both by J. Ann Duncan; "Documentation, Conjecture, and Reader Participation in José-Emilio Pacheco's [*sic*] *Morirás lejos*," in *Selecta* (Corvallis, Oregon), 1, 1980, and "Perfecting a Text: Authorial Revisions in José Emilio Pacheco's *Morirás lejos*," in *Chasqui* (Provo, Utah), 14(2–3), 1985, both by Joel Hancock; "Immutable Humanity Within the Hands of Time: Two Short Stories by José Emilio Pacheco" by Russell M. Cluff, in *Latin American Literary Review* (Pittsburgh), 20, 1982; "The Fantastic as a Vehicle of Social Criticism in José Emilio Pacheco's 'La fiesta brava'" by Cynthia Duncan, in *Chasqui* (Provo, Utah), 14(2–3), 1985; "Inspiration and Its Agents" by Helene J. F. de Aguilar, in *Parnassus* (New York), 14(2), 1988; "José Emilio Pacheco: An Overview of the Poetry" by Michael J. Doudoroff, in *Hispania* (Los Angeles), 72, 1989.

*   *   *

José Emilio Pacheco began his writing career working on *Estaciones*, a literary magazine that was hostile to Mexico's great poet and essayist Octavio Paz (*q.v.*). An 18-year-old Pacheco attacked Paz in 1957 for being "contaminated" by Parisian surrealism. However, a few years later in 1961 Pacheco publicly declared that Paz's exposure to surrealism had resulted in his best poetry. Pacheco collaborated in Paz's innovative anthology *Poesía en movimiento* (1966) (*New Poetry of Mexico*), in the prologue to which Paz both criticized and praised Pacheco's overintellectualized and static early poetry. From his collaboration in Paz's fertile rereading of the Mexican poetic tradition, Pacheco moved into an area of writing that is completely his own, distancing himself politically from and owing little to Paz.

The book of poems that heralded this change in tone was *No me preguntes cómo pasa el tiempo* (*Don't Ask Me How the Time Goes By*). Its title proclaims Pacheco's particular vision of life and art as grounded in the inexorable passing of time, one of the great lyrical and emotional themes of poetry and one which Pacheco explores in fascinating ways. One strand that typifies his work is the emphasis placed on dismissing the traditional poet's ego. Pacheco has consistently refused to glorify himself, dislikes giving interviews, and places the poem above its creator. He is a keen translator of poetry, and usually includes translations of others' poems in his own collections. He often impersonates a historical character, puts on a mask, and employs ironic set phrases, leading critics to talk of his "collage" technique.

While Pacheco has great respect for the lyric tradition, at the same time he is aware that poetry is not read much anymore and that it has lost its cultural importance, thus affirming an ambivalent feeling about the "survival of the genre." His poem "Critique of Poetry" reveals this in parentheses: "(The corrupt bitch, flea-bitten poetry,/a laughable version of neurosis,/the price which some men pay/for not knowing how to live./Oh sweet, eternal, luminous poetry.)" In a confessedly post-Borgesian way Pacheco is aware that poetry only happens in a written poem, that he is a poet only when he writes a poem. This anti-Romantic stance remains subversive.

Another consequence of Pacheco's exploration of the passing of time is his sense of relativity. The poet is a chronicler who comments on events from the limitations of his period. Fashions change, and history accelerates (a title of a short poem) so that the passing of time undermines any certainties, any "truths." Pacheco's poetry is littered with references from the 1960s youth culture and from political positions. As a chronicler he has commented on the Vietnam war, on the massacre of students in Tlatelolco in 1968, on the ecological disaster that is Mexico City, and most recently on the 1985 earthquake in Mexico. The titles of his collections confirm this complex investigation into time and art, from *Desde entonces* (Since Then) to *Tarde o temprano* (Sooner or Later). In 1986 he published *Miro la tierra* (I Look at the World), hinting at the way he coolly observes life, followed in 1989 by *Ciudad de la memoria* (City of Memory). His is one of the most distinctive voices in contemporary Latin American poetry, at odds with the more literal and obvious political poets, as well as those who still affirm the prestige and magic of art.

Pacheco began his career as a short-story writer with *La sangre de Medusa* (Medusa's Blood), followed in 1963 by *El viento distante* (The Distant Wind). Again, passing time underlies most of these deceptively simple stories, many of them about growing up, and narrated by children. An example is "You Will Not Understand," in which a father cannot explain racist violence to his daughter after watching a gang of boys in a park in Mexico City. In 1981 Pacheco published *Las batallas en el desierto* (*Battles in the Desert*), whose title refers to a game in a boy's school. This subtle novella follows the growing up of a Mexican boy, Carlitos, in Mexico City during Miguel Alemán's presidency. Pacheco reconstructs this period through news flashes, brand names, slang, and songs. The novel hints at the violent changes that Mexico has undergone since its 1910 revolution; the boy's period of maturation is now preserved only in the words of the story as his past, its schools, and buildings have all been demolished. We are given crisp descriptions of family life, a rightwing brother, the narrator's crush on Mariana, the sexy mother of his best friend, of how he plays truant from school to declare his love, how he meets a school friend forced to become a street seller, and finally how Mariana commits suicide. The novel ends with a manifesto of Pacheco's view on passing time: "They demolished the school, they demolished Mariana's house, they demolished my home, they demolished the Roma district. That city is over. That country is finished. There is nothing left to remember the Mexico of those years . . ."

Earlier in 1967 Pacheco published his novel *Morirás lejos* (You Will Die Far Away), an experimental novel about imagining evil. It plays with a Borgesian hypothesis about the identity of the narrator, and how to penetrate the mind and personal history of a character called "M." It is also a study of an ongoing racial hatred — anti-Semitism — that cuts across recorded history, for Pacheco recreates in numbered fragments the sacking of Jerusalem by Roman forces parallel with the annihilation of the Warsaw Ghetto by the Nazis. A man watches another man sitting on a park bench, and the novel offers a series of hypotheses about his identity. It is a typical self-conscious novel of the 1960s, describing its own process of creation and doubt about what fiction can explain. The model for this strange and difficult story about vengeance and racism is Jorge Luis Borges's short story "Death and the Compass."

Pacheco is also an astute literary critic, an excellent anthologist, and a translator of many poets and playwrights, including Samuel Beckett and Harold Pinter. Although he has written in several genres, he is essentially a poet commenting on his world, aware of its and his own inevitable ephemerality.

—Jason Wilson

PADILLA (Lorenzo), Heberto. Cuban. Born in Puerta de Golpe, Pinar del Río, 20 January 1932. Educated at the University of Havana, 1952–56. Married 1) Berta Hernández in 1956 (divorced 1968), two daughters and one son; 2) Belkis Cuza Malé in 1968, one son. Radio commentator, WMIE-Radio, Miami, 1957; Spanish and French instructor, Berlitz School, New York, 1958; journalist for Prensa Latina government press agency, New York, 1959, London, 1960–61, and Moscow, 1962–63; contributing editor, *Lunes de Revolución*, Havana, 1959–63; director, Cubartimpex cultural import-export agency, 1964–66; Lecturer in literature, University of Havana, 1969–70; arrested, imprisoned, and forced to confess to political misdeeds, 1971; citrus farmer, near Cumanayagua, Las Villas, 1971; translator, Cumanayagua, 1971–80; allowed by Fidel Castro to immigrate to United States, 1980; fellow, New York Institute for the Humanities, New York University, 1980–83; since 1982 founder and editor, *Linden Lane Magazine*, Princeton, New Jersey. Co-founder, 1960, and director of literature section, 1966, Cuban Union of Writers and Artists; member of editorial board, *Unión*, 1966; executive director, Center for Hemispheric Affairs, Institute for Contemporary Studies, San Francisco, 1986–87. Recipient: Union of Cuban Writers and Artists poetry prize, 1968; Julián del Casal prize, 1968. Address: 103 Cuyler Road, Princeton, New Jersey 08540, U.S.A.

PUBLICATIONS

Verse

El justo tiempo humano.   Havana, Ediciones Unión/Poesía, 1962.
La hora.   Havana, Cuadernos de Poesía, 1965.
Fuera del juego.   Havana, Ediciones Unión, 1968.
Sent off the Field: A Selection from the Poetry of Heberto Padilla, translated by J. M. Cohen. London, Deutsch, 1972.
Provocaciones.   Madrid, La Gota de Agua, 1973.
Poesía y política: poemas escogidos de Heberto Padilla/Poetry and Politics: Selected Poems of Heberto Padilla (bilingual edition), translated by Frank Calzón. Madrid, Playor, 1974; Washington, D.C., Georgetown University Cuban Series, 1977.

El hombre junto al mar.   Barcelona, Seix Barral, 1981; as *Legacies: Selected Poems* (bilingual edition), translated by Alastair Reid and Andrew Hurley, New York, Farrar Straus, and London, Faber, 1982.
A Fountain, a House of Stone (bilingual edition), translated by Alastair Reid and Alexander Coleman.   New York, Farrar Straus, 1991.

Fiction

En mi jardín pastan los héroes.   Barcelona, Argos Veraga, 1981; as *Heroes Are Grazing in My Garden*, New York, Farrar Straus, 1984.

Other

Autoretrato del otro: la mala memoria.   Madrid, Plaza & Janés, 1989; as *Self-Portrait of the Other: A Memoir*, New York, Farrar Straus, 1990; London, Faber, 1991.

Editor, with Luis Suardíaz, *Cuban Poetry, 1959–1966.*   Havana, Book Institute, 1967.

Translator, *Un arcoiris para el occidente cristiano: poema-misterio-vodú* by René Depestre.   Havana, Casa de las Américas, 1967.
Translator, *Poesías para los que no leen poesías.*   Barcelona, Seix Barral, 1972.
Translator, *Poesía romántica inglesa.*   Havana, Arte y Literatura, 1979.

*

Critical Studies: "The Case of Heberto Padilla" by José Yglesias, in *New York Review of Books*, 16(10), 1971; "*Fuera del juego*: A Poet's Appraisal of the Cuba Revolution" by Luis Manuel Quesada, in *Latin American Literary Review* (Pittsburgh), 6, 1975; *Case of the Cuban Poet Heberto Padilla* by Scott Johnson, Gordon Press, 1978.

*   *   *

The poetry of Heberto Padilla treats primarily four basic themes: man's relationship to history and his role in society; marginality, exile, and nostalgia for the lost innocence of the past; love; and what might be called occasional poetry, dealing with an immediate place or situation and the poet's response to it.

The early poems, collected in *El justo tiempo humano* (The Just Human Time; the title was taken from Quasimodo) reflect the anguish and disillusionment so common to the "disconsolate child of the West," as Padilla calls the member of his generation. Man does not choose the historical moment in which he lives; rather it is imposed upon him, and unfortunately, he has been condemned to live in difficult trying times. In the poem "Gifts" he addresses his "other self" and laments:

> You were not given the time of love
> Nor the time of tranquility. You couldn't read
> the clear book your grandparents told you about.
> A furious wind rocked you from childhood,
> an air of destroyed springtime.

In another poem he declares:

He does not want to be a hero,
not even a romantic
around whom we might
weave a legend
He is sentenced to this life, and, what terrifies him more,
condemned irretrievably to his own time.

However, in 1960 his anguish turns to hope as he celebrates the Cuban Revolution as a time of justice and humanity. Although he finds himself far from Cuba, he rallies to her cause and returns to serve his country: "Motherland/couldn't help but remember you/ at a moment like this." Unfortunately, his revolutionary fervor soon cooled as the demands of the collective society began to impinge upon the freedom of the individual. He became especially uncomfortable with the concept of the New Man entirely at the service of the New Society. As he explains in one of his poems: "Ideologies create fanatics/Fanatics don't think. They follow rules," and since he was no longer able or willing to follow the rules of the new revolutionary society, he was *Fuera del juego* (Out of the Game or *Sent Off the Field*), the title of the collection of poetry which won him the coveted Union of Cuban Writers and Artists poetry prize in 1968. This collection of poems, along with another volume, *Provocaciones* (Provocations), cost him his job at the University of Havana and landed him in jail, giving rise to what was to be known as the Padilla Affair, a political *cause célèbre* which was to bring his poetry to world attention but haunt him forever after. Padilla has lost faith in a system which annihilates the individual, demands blind allegiance, and makes thought a perilous act. Borrowing a line from the Catalan poet Salvador Espriu he declares:

At times it is necessary and unavoidable
that a man die for his country,
but never should a people all have to die
for one man only.

He laments the fact that "Cuban poets no longer dream" and he urges them to

Tell the truth
Tell, at least, your truth,
And afterwards
Let anything happen:
let them tear up your beloved page,
let them stone your door . . .

Padilla's disenchantment with Fidel Castro and the Cuban Revolution produced two prose volumes as well: *En mi jardín pastan los héroes* (*Heroes Are Grazing in My Garden*), an autobiographical novel, and *Autoretrato del otro* (*Self-Portrait of the Other*), memoirs of his life under Castro.

In 1980 Padilla was finally allowed to leave Cuba to live in the United States. He hoped to leave the Padilla Affair behind, but for many years it haunted him; condemning him to be labelled The Cuban Exile. He begged the media and his readers to let him be himself and begin anew:

The Right praises me
       (In no time they will defame me)
The Left has given me a name
       (have they not begun to have doubts?)
. . .
Give me room, now.
Don't greet me, I beg you.
Don't even speak to me.
If you see me, keep to one side.

Finally, he made peace with his past and began to sing from the present:

Best
to begin this minute to celebrate
the delight of fulfilled dreams
and forget the world of my ancestors.
For them ashes, for me life.

Padilla's poetry is highly lyrical and autobiographical in nature. Even before his political exile, one of his main themes was the feeling of being uprooted. After his political exile, when life in Cuba was no longer bearable for him, he still felt the weight of his destiny: he was Cuban no matter where he actually lived. As he said in one of his most moving poems:

I live in Cuba. I've always
lived in Cuba. Those years of wandering
throughout the world so many have talked about
are my lies, my falsification.

Because I have always been in Cuba.

And although he was living happily in the United States, he would often recall with nostalgia his native Cuba, his family, his childhood, and he lamented: "My God, have pity on the wanderer/for in the wandering lies the pain."

Many of Padilla's poems respond to his historical, geographical, and cultural context. He has written poems to Octavio Paz (*q.v.*), Anne Frank, William Blake, Lezama Lima, and many others. He has written about London, Greece, Spain, Florida, and Princeton, New Jersey.

In his latest works, in addition to recognizing his place in history, Padilla finds a sense of belonging in his personal circumstances. His relationship with his wife, the poet Belkis Cuza Malé, affords him an identity, a refuge from his historical destiny:

nor are there countries living in my memory
more intensely than this body resting at my side;
besides, the best ground
for a man to be on
is his own ground, his garden, his own house . . .

Many of the poems of his most recent volumes celebrate their love and the happiness of the simple trivial minutiae of their life together.

Padilla's poetry uses simple, direct, everyday language. The tone is often conversational, an oral quality intensified by his constant use of the apostrophe to express his ideas. He addresses the reader, his beloved, his political opponents, Death, and even himself. Although many poems are written in the first person, even more are written in the second person, creating an immediacy where the reader is witness to a conversation, albeit one-sided. In fact, it can be said that Padilla's poetry is a conversation, a highly personal conversation with History, with one's loved ones, and above all, with oneself.

—Marlene Gottlieb

PAMUK, Orhan. Turkish. Born in 1952. Educated at Robert College, Istanbul; International Writing Program, University of Iowa, Iowa City. Recipient: *Independent* award for foreign fiction, 1990. Address: Teşvikiye Cad. 131/1, Nişantaşı, Istanbul, Turkey.

PUBLICATIONS

Fiction

Cevdet Bey ve oğulları [Jevdet Esquire and Sons].   Istanbul, Can, 1982.
Sessiz ev [The Quiet House].   Istanbul, Can, 1983.
Beyaz kale. Istanbul, Can, 1985; as *The White Castle*, Manchester, Carcanet, 1990.
Kara kitap [Black Book].   Istanbul, Can, 1990.

Play

Gizli yüz [Hidden Face] (screenplay).   Istanbul, Can, 1992.

*

Critical Studies: "Being Oneself and Another," in *The World of I* (Washington, D.C.), June 1991, and article in *World Literature Today* (Norman, Oklahoma), 1992, both by Güneli Gün.

*   *   *

Orhan Pamuk has emerged on the world literary scene not only as the major innovator of contemporary Turkish fiction but also as a contributor to the new international voice. His third novel, *Beyaz kale* (*The White Castle*), has garnered critical acclaim in the West, not only because it provides an entry into Turkish literature, but because it is part of a discourse that goes beyond national boundaries, concerned with philosophical and aesthetic themes that the proponents of a timeless, metapersonal literature have taught the world (under the tutelage of Jorge Luis Borges, the master illusionist).

Although Pamuk's early work has its roots in modernist novels, via 19th-century realism, his later fiction develops in the discourse that has come to be loosely termed postmodernism. *The White Castle* masquerades as a historical novel in which the two protagonists are mirror-images of one another, *doppelgängers* — one of whom is ostensibly Ottoman, the other Venetian — but in fact serve as a metaphor for the dissolution of the self into the other. This is one of Pamuk's major themes, which he picks up and elaborates in his later novel, *Kara kitap* (forthcoming in English as *Black Book*), concerning the dichotomy between self/other, reader/author, East/West, lover/beloved, reality/illusion, knowledge/mystery, being/nothingness, sign/signified, fragmentation/totality, and, ultimately, seeker/sought, which in all cases dissolve into each other.

In the myth of the Double, integration of the shadow into the self can succeed only if the process is mutual and voluntary. The Venetian slave and the Ottoman master in *The White Castle* can redeem their joint identity only when they are willing to part with their most cherished self-images as Ottoman (persona) or Venetian (shadow), or vice versa. Yet, lest his readers think there is a "real" Ottoman and a "real" Venetian character in the book, Pamuk makes sure it is understood that his Venetian comes from fictions about Venetians which he has read, digested, and incorporated. Nor

is his Ottoman a real Ottoman but a composite of everything that is taught about Ottomans in his country's primary and secondary schools, seen through the cultural lens of a modern Turk. As is the case with all good writers, behind Pamuk's fiction there is a wondering adolescent who quests after the polarities of his imagination. Transcendence comes only when the writer, through his characters, gives up, although with accompanying sadness, the adolescent desire of wanting to be someone else, or else putting up with the shame of not being, inviolably and authentically, oneself: "I loved him the way I loved that helpless wretched ghost of my own self I saw in my dreams, as if choking on the shame, rage, sinfulness, and melancholy of that ghost . . . And perhaps most of all I loved Him with the stupid revulsion and stupid joy of knowing myself."

His first novel, *Cevdet Bey ve oğulları* (Jevdet Esquire and Sons) narrates the three-generation saga of a wealthy Istanbul family. Formally, it employs the strategies and procedures of European realism although it is in itself the culmination of the modern Turkish novel, which is concerned with telling Turks about themselves. Yet this is a book about "the way we were," considering that it is set in the period when Ottoman Empire ends and the new Turkish Republic begins, a period well before Pamuk's time. What delights his compatriots is the young novelist's comprehensive insight into recent Turkish history, the innocence and the ignorance of the forever-young Turks who shaped it.

Pamuk's second novel, *Sessiz ev* (The Quiet House), is told from five different perspectives and deals with a week spent by three siblings, who represent three generations and ideologies, at their dying grandmother's country house where their dwarf bastard-uncle attends on the old lady. Set during a particularly dark period in Turkish politics (1981), when generations and ideologies were at each others' throats, The Quiet House is the metaphor for The Quiet Country: Turkey, where the violence of the Ottoman past is visited on the violence of the "modern" present behind closed doors.

Kara kitap (*Black Book*), his fourth and most complex book, is a stunning fruition of Pamuk's fictional concerns where the subject-matter is the mystery of the cosmos, although its working premise comes from the popular genre of the mystery novel. The protagonist, who is married to his first cousin, is seeking his beloved, mysteriously beautiful wife who has vanished into the maze of Istanbul, perhaps in the company of her half-brother with whom both the husband and the missing wife have been in love since they were children. Sleuthing for his lost heart, the protagonist is inevitably lured into mysteries that are mystical and literary, cultural and universal, idealized and incestuous. As the writer re-invents Istanbul with its mazes above and below the ground, the quest is intertextual and intercultural. Not only does the hero's love sickness for his missing wife reflect Marcel's anguish over his runaway Albertine in Marcel Proust's *The Sweet Cheat Gone*, it also is drawn from the 17th-century Ottoman mystic poet Sheikh Galip's verse novel *Love and Beauty*, as well as a thousand other sources both from the East, which Pamuk inherits by birthright, and the West, which he has acquired through his own erudition. The double, mirrors, reflection of reflections, infinite regression into nothingness are themes that baffle and delight not only the Western Man — they have also been the consuming passion for the Easterner both in traditional and Gnostic thought.

Pamuk, a writer for whom the pleasure of the text is the ultimate high, taps into Sufi mystic material and its accompanying mysteries that mirrors the book in the sense that the Sufi quest for "the beloved," which is seeking for absolute state of union with God by dissolving into Nothingness. To fin

God, in other words, is to become God: to find Oneself, one has to become Another, which makes the self, of course, the ultimate mystery. Mystery is the "center" of the universe, which is "the self," which is the emblematic center of the book. Writing is a self-centred occupation.

Yet here Pamuk creates self-referent fictions within fictions which constantly reveal their techniques and objectives on every page, thereby instructing the reader not only how to read the book but to become someone else, i.e.: the author. ("What is reading but acquiring someone else's memory bank?") Lest we take anything he says as gospel truth, however, Pamuk keeps pulling the rug from under our feet, warning that what we are falling for is a fiction: a construction whose only relation to "the truth" is its own internal logic. Identity is not inherent but constructed. Love is not natural but learned by imitation, mainly by reading other texts, and the same goes for writing fictions — as well as murder, which also needs models, not to mention inspiration from mystery novels.

Pamuk has a very good idea that all fiction is incestuous; it is a love affair between the precursor and the successor in which the precursor is both the parent and the beloved. Moreover, the precursor and the successor are both after the same dame, who changes names and guises (be it Beatrice or Leila, La Belle Dame Sans Merci, Albertine, or Rüya, *Black Book*'s "muse" whose name means "Dream"), but whose real name is Lady Literature. Dissolving into another then is no longer an unpleasant and frightening prospect, but, as is the case with Pamuk's protagonist who "becomes" his cousin (who is a writer as well as the rival for the missing beloved's affections), it provides the required distance and objectivity, as well as the necessity, for inventing elaborate fictions.

Black Book might have easily been titled "Book of Paradoxes." While the book is black because it mirrors the chaotic, mysterious Black Hole of the universe, every fragment of the book itself is emblematic and reflective of the whole as a work of art. In a world of appearances, surfaces, faces, mirror images, photographs, where the "hidden" refuses to manifest itself, Pamuk practices skepticism about the nature of knowledge while simultaneously, by sleight of hand or fictional device, he produces reality, meaning, and depth. Where signs are empty and road maps are misleading, he finds fictional significance and arrives at his destination while having a very good time along the way. Memory is fickle, chaotic, and subject to loss, but even as memory dissolves into forgetfulness, it also liberates the power of invention. Given a world where man is unable to comprehend reality or solve the mystery, fiction, for Orhan Pamuk, is not everything, it is the only thing.

—Güneli Gün

* * *

PARRA, Nicanor. Chilean. Born in San Fabián, 5 September 1914. Educated at the University of Chile, Santiago, degree in mathematics and physics 1938; studied advanced mechanics, Brown University, Providence, Rhode Island, 1943–45; studied cosmology at Oxford University (British Council grant), 1949–51. Married 1) Ana Troncoso in 1948 (marriage dissolved); 2) Inga Palmen; seven children. Taught in secondary school, 1938–43; since 1948 director of School of Engineering, and since 1952 Professor of theoretical physics, University of Chile. Visiting Professor, Louisiana State University, Baton Rouge, 1966, and New York, Columbia, and Yale universities, 1971. Recipient: City of Santiago prize, 1937, 1954; Writers' Union prize, 1954; National literature prize, 1969; Guggenheim fellowship, 1972. Address: c/o Julia Bernstein, Parcela 272, Lareini, Santiago, Chile.

PUBLICATIONS

Verse

Cancionero sin nombre. Santiago, Nascimento, 1937.
Poemas y antipoemas. Santiago, Nascimento, 1954.
La cueca larga. Santiago, Editorial Universitaria, 1958.
Anti-Poems. San Francisco, City Lights, 1960.
Versos de salón. Santiago, Nascimento, 1962.
La cueca larga y otros poemas, edited by Margarita Aguirre and Juan Agustín Palazuelos. Buenos Aires, Editorial Universitaria, 1964.
Poems and Antipoems, edited by Miller Williams. New York, New Directions, 1967; London, Cape, 1968.
Canciones rusas. Santiago, Editorial Universitaria, 1967.
Poesía rusa contemporanea. Santiago, Ediciones Nueva Universidad, 1967.
Obra gruesa. Santiago, Editorial Universitaria, 1969; as *Emergency Poems*, translated by Miller Williams, New York, New Directions, 1972; London, Boyars, 1977.
Poemas. Havana, Casa de las Américas, 1969.
Los profesores. New York, Antiediciones Villa Miseria, 1971.
Antipoemas: antologia 1944–1969. Barcelona, Seix Barral, 1972.
Artefactos. Santiago, Universidad Católica de Chile, 1972.
Sermones y prédicas del Cristo de Elqui. Santiago, Universidad de Chile Estudios Humanisticos, 1977.
Nuevos sermones y prédicas del Cristo de Elqui. Valparaiso, Ganymedes, 1979.
Poema y antipoema a Eduardo Frei. Santiago, América del Sur, 1982.
El anti-Lázaro. Santiago, Gráfica Marginal, 1982.
Coplas de navidad. Santiago, Ediciones del Camaleón, 1983.
Poesía política. Santiago, Bruguera, 1983.
Chistes para desorientar a la poliesía. Santiago, Galería Epoca, 1983.
Hojas de Parra, edited by David Turkeltaub. Santiago, Ganymedes, 1985.
Antipoems: New and Selected, edited by David Unger. New York, New Directions, 1985.
Fotopoemas sobre textos de Nicanor Parra, photographs by Sergio Marras. Santiago, Ornitorrinco, 1986.
Nicanor Parra: biografía emotiva (selected poems), edited by Efraín Szmulewicz. Santiago, Ediciones Rumbos, 1988.

Other

La evolución del concepto de masa. 1958.
Discursos, with Pablo Neruda. Santiago, Nascimento, 1962.

Editor, *Poesía soviética rusa.* Mexico City, Progreso, 1965.

Translator, *Fundamentos de la física* [Foundations of Physics], by R. D. Lindsay and Henry Margenau. 1967.

*

Critical Studies: "In Defense of Antipoetry: An Interview with Nicanor Parra" by Patricio Lerzundi, in *Review* (New York),

4–5, 1971–72; "The Artefactos of Nicanor Parra: The Explosion of the Antipoem" by Karen S. Van Hooft, in *Bilingual Review* (Tempe, Arizona), 1, 1974; *The Antipoetry of Nicanor Parra* by Edith Grossman, New York, New York University Press, 1975; "Nicanor Parra: Antipoetry, Retraction and Silence" by George Melnykovich, in *Latin American Literary Review* (Pittsburgh), 3(6), 1975; "Generic Composition in Latin American Poetry: Nicanor Parra and Diatribe" by Geoffrey R. Barrow, in *Selected Proceedings of the 35th Annual Mountain Interstate Foreign Language Conference*, Greenville, South Carolina, 1987.

*   *   *

Nicanor Parra is recognized in contemporary Latin American poetry as the founder of antipoetry, a term the poet himself popularized to distinguish his poetry from the rhetoric of the Romantic/Symbolist concept of the poet as prophet and the mystical power of the word as sensation. In his poem "Manifesto" Parra declared that "the poets have come down from Olympus." Parra proposes that poetry be written in the language of everyday life and incorporate commercials, slogans, clichés, and phrases taken from all the diverse "languages" in which man expresses himself, thus forming a kind of linguistic collage of disparate levels of discourse designed to mirror the absurdity of human existence and shock the reader into consciousness, eliciting a kind of simultaneous reaction of laughter and tears. This is an iconoclastic poetry in which all the sacred values of western civilization are ridiculed: God and religion, education, love, family, art, poetry. Irony and black humor are its trademarks.

Parra began publishing the antipoems which were to be his hallmark in 1948. The first antipoems were long, prosaic, free verse, anecdotal poems in which the narrator, easily identifiable with the poet himself, recounts several humiliating encounters in an absurd and hypocritical world: his adulterous love affair with a materialistic, conniving woman he calls "the viper"; his miserable life in the "tunnel" of his elderly aunts' house, where he was subjected to their every whim until one day he peeked through a keyhole only to discover that his poor paralytic aunt could walk perfectly well. He even gives us a self-portrait of a defeated, impoverished, grotesque schoolteacher, who leads a senseless existence. Among the most noteworthy poems of this period (collected in *Poems and Antipoems*) is the "The Individual's Soliloquy," in which the individual recounts the entire history of mankind from the Stone Age to the 20th century only to conclude:

> Perhaps I better go back to that valley,
> To that rock that was home
> And start scratching all over again,
> Scratching out everything backward,
> The world in reverse.
> But life doesn't make sense.

As the antipoem evolves, the verses become shorter, the syntax simpler. The anecdote is replaced by disconnected ideas, lists of images relating to a specific topic (dreams, women, current events) with titles such as "Telegrams," "Isolated Verses," "Phrases." Some of the images have an oneiric, surrealist quality. Gradually the biographical poet disappears from the text and is replaced by a series of characters, some of whom are marginal, antisocial figures (beggars, muggers); others are recognizable, historic figures whose discourse is created by Parra (God, the Pope, Domingo Zárate, a Chilean wandering preacher). These characters speak directly to the reader/listener/spectator, often eliciting

the reader's participation. This adds not only a dramatic element to the antipoem, but also intensifies the oral quality of the text. The language is highly colloquial and filled with slang and regional expressions, which are adeptly counterposed with bureaucratic phrases and legal terms and encased in an unexpected framework. The poet's *ars poetica*, for example, is presented as a test in which the reader is asked to place an X next to the definition of antipoetry he/she considers correct. The Lord's Prayer is ingeniously modified resulting in the inversion of roles between God and his followers: "Padrenuestro que estás en el cielo/lleno de toda clase de problemas . . ./tienes que darte cuenta/de que los dioses no son infalibles/y que nosotros perdonamos todo." (Our Father Who art in Heaven/Full of all sorts of problems . . ./You have to realize/that gods are not infallible/and that we forgive all). *Sermones y prédicas del Cristo de Elqui* (Sermons and Preachings of the Christ of Elqui) present a wandering preacher from the 1920s whose comments are clearly relevant to the Pinochet dictatorship of the 1970s. In fact, this use of masks is an ideal technique on the part of the poet to elude censorship, allowing him to make statements without taking full responsibility for them, for as Parra himself has repeatedly said: "You can't blame Cervantes for Sancho's vulgarities." *Hojas de Parra* (a play on words based on the double meaning of hoja as both page and leaf and Parra, the poet's name and the word for fig, thus resulting in the ambiguous title of "Parra's Pages" or "Fig Leaves") continues in this dramatic vein and contains two masterpieces of antipoetry: the "Anti-Lazarus," in which Parra advises Lazarus to remember how miserable his life had been and not to allow himself to be resurrected, and a response to that poem, "Rest in Peace," in which even the dead don't escape misery:

> Sure — rest in peace
> but what about the damp?
>   and the moss?
>   and the weight of the tombstone?
> and the drunken gravediggers?
> and the people who steal the flowerpots?
> and the ants gnawing at the coffins?
> and the damned worms
> crawling in everywhere
> they make death impossible for us . . .

In 1972 Parra embarked upon another experiment: the artifact, a short poem of one to four lines, accompanied by an illustration (for which Parra commissions an artist). These artifacts, as Parra explains, are the resulting fragments of the explosion of the antipoem. They are grenades which attack everything and everyone, from the Pope and the Roman Catholic Church to the political Left as well as the Right. The first collection of artifacts is published as a box of postcards, each postcard has an illustration accompanied by a text. In all other respects it is an ordinary postcard, ready to be sent by mail, thus passing from hand to hand in a most original version of collective and public poetry. More recently Parra has written a series of artifacts known as ecopoems, in which he demonstrates his growing concern over the destruction of our natural environment, as well as several political jibes under the title of *Chistes para desorientar a la poliesía* (Jokes to Mislead the Police).

The evolution of Parra's antipoetry is characterized by the poet's overriding fear of taking himself too seriously and becoming a "solemn fool" (an allusion perhaps to fellow Chilean Pablo Neruda?) and his never-ending search to revitalize his poetry so that it remains fresh and unpredictable.

As the poet said in one of his artifacts: "You never finish being born."

—Marlene Gottlieb

PASO, Fernando del. Mexican. Born in 1935. Lived in London, 14 years: worked for BBC. Diplomat: cultural attaché, Mexican Embassy, Paris. Recipient: Xavier Villaurrutia prize, 1966; Prix du Meilleur Roman Étranger (France), 1975; Rómulo Gallegos prize (Venezuela). Address: c/o Editorial Diana, Roberto Gayol 1219, Apdo 44–986, 03100 Mexico City, Mexico.

PUBLICATIONS

Fiction

José Trigo. Mexico City, Siglo Veintiuno, 1966.
Palinuro de México. Madrid, Alfaguara, 1977; as *Palinuro of Mexico*, London, Quartet, 1990.
Noticias del imperio. Mexico City, Diana, 1987.

Verse

Sonetos de lo diario. Mexico City, n.p., 1958.

*

Bibliography: in *Mexican Literature: A Bibliography of Secondary Sources* by David William Foster, Metuchen, New Jersey, Scarecrow Press, 1992.

Critical Studies: "The Function of Myth in Fernando del Paso's *José Trigo*" by Dagoberto Orrantia, in *Tradition and Renewal: Essays on 20th-Century Latin American Literature and Culture*, Urbana, University of Illinois Press, 1975; "*Palinuro de México*: A World of Words," in *Bulletin of Hispanic Studies* (Liverpool), 58, 1981, "*Palinuro de México* and *Ulysses*," in *Estudios Angloamericanos*, 5–6, 1981, "Beyond the Unquiet Grave and the Cemetery of Words: Myth and Archetype in *Palinuro de México*," in *Ibero-Amerikanisches Archiv* (Berlin), 8(3), 1982, and "James Joyce and Fernando del Paso," in *Insula*, 455, 1984, all by Robin W. Fiddian.

*   *   *

Fernando del Paso, undoubtedly the outstanding novelist of his generation in Mexico, has dedicated his creative literary gift to probing and restructuring artistically the history of his beloved country. His quest has focused on capturing the essence of Mexican culture and civilization. In effect, it is a quest for self-fulfillment. In order to accomplish his mission, fact and fiction are interwoven within the fabric of his eventful accounts to depict the past as an undying, ever-present organism that reflects the Mexican way of life, emphasizing its foibles as well as its feats. Amazingly detailed in the recreation of past events, del Paso writes with profound understanding and compassion for all people who have been actors in the drama that is Mexico, and especially so for the legendary outcasts and foreign "interlopers" who have been condemned by historians as "enemies of the State." On the other hand, there are no "sacred cows" who escape the novelistic, ironic process of humanization. Even Benito Juárez, who occupies the loftiest position among patriotic heroes, is envisaged as quite human: while honored for his truly formidable personal and political achievements, at the same time his unseemly qualities are also noted and recorded.

Born in Mexico in 1935, del Paso has had a varied career in his country and abroad. For some 14 years he lived in London, where he worked for the BBC. He has also been a member of the Mexican diplomatic corps, and has risen to the coveted position of cultural attaché of the Mexican Embassy in Paris, traditionally considered in Latin America as a mecca for writers and other artists. To be sure, the appointment reflects in most cases the high esteem in which an artist is held in his country. (Occasionally, however infrequently, such appointments have also served as a convenient, decorous exile.) Nonetheless, political recognition notwithstanding, it is as a writer that del Paso has established himself. His awards for creative accomplishments have steadily multiplied.

Del Paso first made his literary debut as a poet in 1958 with the publication of his *Sonetos de lo diario* (Sonnets of Daily Existence). In 1966 his first novel appeared. It bore the allegorical, generic title of *José Trigo* (Joseph Wheat), and was soon recognized as valuable, original work, winning the Xavier Villaurrutia prize. In the novel del Paso captures the essence of the uncommon "common man" in Mexico with masterful poetic imagery. All aspects of José Trigo's existence are encompassed within a vision of respect and admiration. Yet the account does not degenerate into a sociological plea for reform, as has been the case with many Latin American novels.

Del Paso's second novel, *Palinuro de México* (*Palinuro of Mexico*), is a frightening, beautiful fantasy that celebrates the ambiguities of human existence, its horrors and its delights. The panoramic view encompasses acts of both unspeakable cruelty and tenderness. Love, which prevails in the final analysis, assumes many configurations, while eroticism serves as a contrapuntal musical movement to humanity's penchant for destruction. While del Paso assures us that his creation is but a work of fiction, he further explains that some of its characters may resemble "real people" just as real people may resemble characters in a novel. Thus, he adds, "while no one has the right to feel included in the book, neither does any one have the right to feel excluded." To del Paso human experience and fiction are inexorably and irreducibly intertwined; indeed, the novel envisages historical figures of an era long past interacting with fictional characters of the present. Del Paso's powerful prose makes such a phenomenon seem believable, at least momentarily.

Del Paso's masterpiece bears the title of *Noticias del imperio* (News from the Empire). Published in 1987 after some 10 years of preparation, the novel is a monumental work which brings to life an unusual but believable perspective of history not often found in texts. (When asked in 1988 if what he wrote were *true*, del Paso replied, "if it is not true, neither is it a lie.") The work is a daring exposition of Mexican history, and tangentially a history of Europe since 1864, the year Maximilian and Carlotta were sent to Mexico, charged by "little Napoleon" with the task of establishing a Hapsburg dynasty there. And a task it proved to be for the unfortunate monarchs!

Noticias del imperio reads more easily than del Paso's two earlier novels. It depicts Carlotta at the age of 86 recounting her memoirs as she addresses her late husband, who had been put to death by order of Benito Juárez almost 60 years before. From the insane asylum in which she has resided since becoming a widow Carlotta brings history up to date for the benefit of her departed spouse. At the same time as berating him for his personal shortcomings, she recognizes his qualities of valour and nobility. For Benito Juárez, understandably, she has fewer words of praise, especially for his lack of compassion towards the invaders. In the literary tradition long ago established by Miguel de Cervantes, Carlotta's madness gives her license to delve into the inner reality of humanity and destroy socially accepted mythological beliefs. And not only are the figures of Mexican history divested of their striking garments — the process is extended to all political leaders of a period that spanned 60 years. The Hapsburgs, in particular, fare badly. *Noticias del imperio* is a bold undertaking for del Paso, some of whose compatriots have not taken kindly to his focus on two foreigners who came to Mexico as usurpers of a legally established national government. However, for his portrayal of the Royal House of Austria, del Paso will be blessed by most Mexicans — and possibly others.

—Robert Kirsner

PAVIĆ, Milorad. Serbian. Born in Belgrade, in 1929. Taught at the Sorbonne, Paris, and in Germany; currently Professor of the history of literature, University of Belgrade. Address: Department of Literature, University of Belgrade, Studentski trg 1, 11001 Belgrade 6, Serbia.

PUBLICATIONS

Fiction

Gvozdena zavesa [The Iron Curtain]. Novi Sad, Matica Srpska, 1973.
Konji Svetoga Marka [The Horses of Saint Mark]. Belgrade, Prosveta, 1976.
Hazarski rečnik: roman leksikon u 100,000 reči. Belgrade, Prosveta, 1984; as *Dictionary of the Khazars: A Lexicon Novel in 100,000 Words*, New York, Knopf, 1988; London, Hamish Hamilton, 1989.
Ruski hrt i nove priče [The Borzoi and New Stories]. Belgrade, Književne Novine, 1986.
Predeo slikan čajem: roman za ljubitelje ukrštenih reči. Belgrade, Prosveta, 1988; as *Landscape Painted with Tea: A Novel for Lovers of Crossword Puzzles*, London, Hamish Hamilton, 1989; New York, Knopf, 1990.
Izvrnuta rukavica [Inside-Out Glove]. Novi Sad, Matica Srpska, 1989.

Verse

Palimpsesti [Palimpsests]. Belgrade, Nolit, 1967.
Duše se kupaju poslednji put [Souls Bathe for the Last Time]. Novi Sad, Matica Srpska, 1982.

Other

Vojislav Ilić (1860–1894). Belgrade, Prosveta, 1961.
Vojislav Ilić, njegovo vreme i delo [Vojislav Ilić, His Time and Work]. Belgrade, Rad, 1962.
Gavril Stefanović Venclović. Belgrade, Zadruga, 1972.

Istorija srpske književnosti klasicizma i predromantizma: klasicizam [A History of Serbian Literature of Classicism and Pre-Romanticism: Classicism]. Belgrade, Nolit, 1979.
Nove beogradske priče [New Belgrade Stories]. Belgrade, Nolit, 1981.
Radanje nove srpske književnosti: istorija srpske književnosti klasicizma i predromantizma [The Birth of New Serbian Literature: A History of New Serbian Literature of Classicism and Pre-Romanticism]. Belgrade, Zadruga, 1983.
Jezičko pamćenje i pesnički oblik [Language Remembrance and Poetic Form]. Novi Sad, Matica Srpska, 2 vols., 1985.
Stari srpski zapisi i natpisi [Old Serbian Engravings and Inscriptions]. Belgrade, Prosveta, 1986.
Kratka istorija Beograda [A Short History of Belgrade]. Belgrade, Prosveta, 1990.

Editor, *Drame; poeme; pesme*, by Aleksandr Pushkin. Belgrade, Prosveta, 1963.
Editor, *Vojislav Ilić.* Belgrade, Rad, 1963.
Editor, *Memoari XVIII i XIX veka* [Memoirs of the 18th and 19th Centuries]. Novi Sad, Matica, 1964.
Editor, *Od baroka do klasicizma* [From Baroque to Classicism]. Belgrade, Nolit, 1966.
Editor, *Crni bivo u srcu* [Black in the Heart], by Gavril Stefanović Venclović. Belgrade, Prosveta, 1966.
Editor, *Pesme* [Poems], by Vojislav Ilić. 1968.

*   *   *

Milorad Pavić has published numerous volumes of literary and academic works. He is a professor at Belgrade University who specialises in 18th-century Serbian literature. The value of his contribution to literature lies in his stylistic experimentation which tests the limits of narrative structures. He mounts his challenge to the conventions of the literary prose form by foregrounding linguistic patterns and textual associations over the coherency of story or plot. His fresh, innovative approach is evident from his earliest collections of short stories *Gvozdena zavesa* (The Iron Curtain) and *Konji Svetoga Marka* (The Horses of Saint Mark), which appeared in the early and mid-1970s. He has continued to elaborate on this basic path in his longer works published later such as *Hazarski rečnik* (*Dictionary of the Khazars*) and *Predeo slikan čajem* (*Landscape Painted with Tea*). His works project meanings through an accumulation of associations betweeen different layers of the text. His collections of short stories read like excerpts taken from more substantial works; they are incomplete when taken individually, particularly in view of the instability of the fabula construction, but when taken together they echo one another. Stories take up themes and motifs from other stories and develop them further. Each story represents a framework in which other stories will intrude and form cycles of interruption, recall, and anticipation. These cycles extend beyond the individual collections: for example, the first story of the third collection, *Ruski hrt* (The Borzoi), refers to a character first mentioned in one of the stories from the second collection. Each story becomes part of a larger whole which then suggests an extension into an infinity of textual production.

Alongside the fragmentation of plot, time, and character are undermined as constitutive elements of narrative structure. Time in Pavić's work is rarely the relationship of duration and succession which determines the order of events. Psychological, historical, and mythic time are interwoven without differentiating between the conceptual bases on which they are founded. All concepts are presented as conventions in language open to speculative question. For example, the names of the days of the week can be transposed such that Wednesday could follow Thursday, as suggested in the story "Crveni kalendar" (The Red Calendar). The idea of a literary character as representative of a human personality is undermined by a lack of psychological motivation and the detachment of characters from the consequences of events. Pavić's fictional worlds do not rely on relationships of cause and effect, but on contingency. This freedom from the demands of mimesis gives his work the flavour of fantasy typical of magical realism, which hovers over the borderline between the possible and the impossible. He incorporates a number of styles and genres, including the evocative language of dream, with references to classical mythology and Serbian history accompanied by scenes from contemporary Belgrade life. This kind of textual integration does not always sit easily; however, Pavić is not concerned with coherency, but rather with the representation of different orders of reality. He strives to represent the artifice of writing in narratives which otherwise aim to give order to the chaos of experience.

The title of the *Dictionary of the Khazars* implies a work of definitions based on etymological principles. Sense and meaning can be deduced from careful exploration of the past. However, this view assumes the possibility that truth is a factor which can be assimilated and reproduced. Pavić questions this view by producing a semiologically based enigma. The work is divided into three books, each of which represents the history of the mythic race of the Khazars from a Jewish, Christian, and Muslim point of view. Each book is the reproduction of an original work from the 17th century, now lost, and divided into sections which take their titles according to the main protagonists or significant events in the history of the Khazars, who themselves have disappeared without trace. The different sections overlap and contradict one another, while their alphabetic ordering dissects the chronological evolution of historical processes into so many isolated episodes. It is a work which challenges the reader by fragmenting narrative structures and re-assembling them throughout the three books, juxtaposing different writing styles and generic conventions from the historical novel to the detective story. Pavić stretches his enigmatic approach to writing and desire to go beyond the familiar world of literature and publishing by offering the reader two editions of *Dictionary of the Khazars*: a male and a female edition with the difference between them contained in one paragraph. Similarly, *Landscape Painted with Tea* is subtitled *A Novel for Lovers of Crossword Puzzles*. Chapters are labelled as "down" or "across" sections and they follow different but connected stories. Pavić forces the reader to rise to the challenge of his literary montages.

Pavić's work constantly tests the potential of the literary narrative. His aim is indicative of a trend particularly strong in the history of the novel from Laurence Sterne in the 18th century, through the Romantics, the Modernists, and the present generation of Postmodernists. This trend has experimented in different ways with the relationship between art and reality, aware of the artifice which attempts to impose order on chaos. The strange juxtapositions and fragmented elements become recast in Pavić's work to produce a tenuous order in a semiotic game. Each word develops multiple associations through its contact with the varied genres. Each genre or style of writing then begins to influence the other, further disrupting the reader's expectations. There are no strict divisions between Pavić's representations of reality. His work demands, like all literature, that readers suspend belief and surrender themselves to the text. Paradoxically, Pavić's resistance to traditional generic classification is a recognition of their power.

He employs genres in new ways, thereby contributing to the pluralism on which the vitality of the prose form, particularly the novel, has always depended.

—David A. Norris

PAVLOVIĆ, Miodrag. Serbian. Born in Novi Sad, 29 November 1928. Educated at the School of Medicine, University of Belgrade, 1947–54, diploma 1954. Military service, one year, after 1954. Married Marlen Müller in 1961; two daughters. Physician at a clinic in Belgrade, 1950s; drama director, National Theatre, Belgrade, 1960–61; editor, Prosveta publishing house, Belgrade, 1961–84; Professor of literary history, Ohio State University, Columbus; Lecturer at Universities of Munich, Novi Sad, and Belgrade. Recipient: Yugoslav Writers' Union prize, 1952; October prize, 1963, 1991; Town of Novi Sad "Zmajeva nagrada," 1969; Struga Golden Wreath, 1970; Town of Niš Branko Miljković prize, 1979; Djordje Jovanović prize, for theory and literary criticism, 1979; Medal for editorial achievements, 1986; Nolit prize, 1987; 7th of July prize, 1988; Golden Key prize, 1989. Member, Academy of Sciences and Arts, Belgrade, since 1978; Officier de l'Ordre des Arts et des Lettres (France), 1986. Address: Wagenstraße 4, 72 Tuttlingen 14, Germany.

PUBLICATIONS

Verse

87 pesama [87 Poems]. Belgrade, Nolit, 1952.
Stub sećanja [Pillar of Memory]. Belgrade, Novo Pokoljenje, 1953.
Oktave [Octaves]. Belgrade, Nolit, 1956.
Mleko iskoni [Milk of Yore]. Belgrade, Prosveta, 1963.
Velika Skitija [Great Scythia]. Sarajevo, Svjetlost, 1969.
Hododarje [Pilgrimage]. Belgrade, Nolit, 1971.
Svetli i tamni praznici [Light and Dark Holy Days]. Novi Sad, Matica Srpska, 1971.
Velika Skitija i druge pesme [Great Scythia and Other Poems]. Belgrade, Srpska Književna Zadruga, 1972.
Zavetine [Spells]. Belgrade, Rad, 1976.
The Conqueror in Constantinople, translated by Joachim Neugroschel. New York, New Rivers Press, 1976.
Karike [Links]. Kragujevac, Svetlost, 1977.
Pevanje na viru. Belgrade, Slovo Ljubve, 1977; as *Singing at the Whirlpool* (bilingual edition), translated by Barry Callaghan, Toronto, Exile, 1983.
Vidovnica [Propheters]. Belgrade, Narodna Knjiga, 1979.
Bekstva po Srbiji [Flight Through Serbia]. Belgrade, Slovo Ljubve, 1979.
Izabrane pesme [Selected Poems]. Belgrade, Rad, 1979.
Divno čudo [A Divine Miracle]. Belgrade, Nolit, 1982.
Zlatna zavada [Golden Catch]. Niš, Gradina, 1982.
Nova pevanja na viru [New Singing at the Whirlpool]. Belgrade, Centar za Umetnost i Kulturu RU, 1983.
The Slavs Beneath Parnassus, translated by Bernard Johnson. London, Angel, and St. Paul, Minnesota, New Rivers Press, 1985.
Glas pod kamenon/A Voice Locked in Stone (bilingual edition), translated by Barry Callaghan. Toronto, Exile, 1985.

Sledstvo [Consequence]. Belgrade, Srpska Književna Zadruga, 1985.
Poezija [Poetry]. Belgrade, Prosveta, 1986.
Svetogorski dani i noći [Mount Athos Days and Nights]. Priština, Jedinstvo, 1987.
On [Him]. Novi Sad, Matica Srpska, 1989.
Links, translated by Bernard Johnson. Toronto, Exile, and Leek, Staffordshire, Aquila, 1989.
Knjiga staroslovna [Book of Love]. Belgrade, Srpska Književna Zadruga, 1989.
Ulazak u Kremonu [Entry into Cremona]. Belgrade, Nolit, 1989.
Bezazlenstva [Innocence]. Valjevo, Milić Rakić, 1989.
Cosmologia profanata [Cosmology of the Profane]. Belgrade, Grafos, 1990.
Pesme o detinjstvu i ratovima [Poems of Childhood and Wars]. Belgrade, Srpska Književna Zadruga, 1992.

Fiction

Most bez obala [Bridge Without Shore]. Novi Sad, Matica Srpska, 1956.

Plays

Igre bezimenih [Games Without Names]. Belgrade, Prosveta, 1963.
Koraci u podzemlju [Steps in the Underworld] (produced Belgrade, 1967). Novi Sad, Matica Srpska, 1991.

Radio Plays: *Kuća ljubavi* [The House of Love]; *Bdenje* [Vigil]; *Koraci u drugoj sobi* [Steps in the Other Room].

Other

Rokovi poezije [Poetic Timespans]. Belgrade, Srpska Književna Zadruga, 1959.
Osam pesnika [Eight Poets]. Belgrade, Prosveta, 1964.
Dnevnik pene [Diary of Foam]. Belgrade, Slovo Ljubve, 1972.
Poezija i kultura: ogledi o srpskim pesnicima XIX i XX veka [Poetry and Culture: Essays on Serbian Poets]. Belgrade, Nolit, 1974.
Poetika modernog [Poetry of the Modern]. Belgrade, Grafos, 1978.
Ništitelji i svadbari [Destroyers and Wedding Guests]. Belgrade, Beogradski Izdavačko-Grafički Zavod, 1979.
Izabrana dela [Selected Works]. Belgrade, Vuk Karadžić, 1981.
Kina — oko na putu [China — Travel Impressions]. Niš, Gradina, 1982.
Prirodni lik i oblik: likovni ogledi [Natural Shape and Form: Essays on Art]. Belgrade, Nolit, 1984.
Obredno i govorno delo [Ritual and Oral Work]. Belgrade, Prosveta, 1986.
Govor o ničem [Discourse on Nothingness]. Niš, Gradina, 1987.
Poetika žrtvenog obreda [The Poetics of Sacrificial Ritual]. Belgrade, Nolit, 1987.
Hram i preobraženje: jedna knjiga [Temple of Transfiguration]. Belgrade, Sfairos, 1989.
Čitanje zamišljenog [Reading of the Imagined]. Novi Sad, Bratstvo-Jedinstvo, 1990.
Putevi do hrama [Routes to the Temple]. Niš, Gradina, 1991.

Editor and Translator, with Svetozar Brkić, *Antologija moderne engleske poezije* [Anthology of Modern English Poetry]. Belgrade, Nolit, 1957.
Editor, *Antologija srpskog pesništva* [Anthology of Serbian Verse]. Belgrade, Srpska Književna Zadruga, 1964.
Editor, *Izabrana dela* [Selected Works], by Momčilo Nastasijević. Belgrade, Prosveta, 1966.
Editor, *Pesništvo evropskog romantizma* [Poetry of European Romanticism]. Belgrade, Prosveta, 1969.
Editor, *Pesništvo od Vojislava do Bojića* [Poetry from Vojislav Ilić to Bojić]. Belgrade, Nolit, 1972.
Editor and Translator, *Pesme* [Poems], by Petre Andreevski. Belgrade, Prosveta, 1977.
Editor, *Antologija lirske narodne poezije* [Anthology of Lyric Folk Poetry]. Belgrade, Vuk Karadžić, 1982.

Translator, *Slova i natpisi* [Characters and Inscriptions], by Stefan Lazarević. Belgrade, Slovo Ljubve, 1979.
Translator, *Na Kirkinom ostrvu* [On Circe's Island], by Robert Marteau. Niš, Gradina, 1984.

*

Bibliographies: *Miodrag Pavlovitch* by Robert Marteau, Paris, Recueil, 1985; "Poezija Miodraga Pavlovića" [The Poetry of Miodrag Pavlović] by Ljubomir Simović, in *Bezazlenstva*, Valjevo, Milić Rakić, 1989.

Critical Studies: "Poetry of Miodrag Pavlović" by Bernard Johnson, and "Three Principles of the Creative Universe: The Poetry of Miodrag Pavlović" by Bogdan A. Popović, both in *Relations* (Belgrade), Autumn 1986.

* * *

Miodrag Pavlović is one of the two most outstanding poets of the first post-war Serbian (Yugoslav) generation. Trained as a doctor, he gave up medicine to become a full-time writer and editor in the early 1960s, by which time his reputation was already well established. He is now an eminent Serbian academician with translations of his work in a number of other languages.

Initially he was a member of the "modernist" group whose poetry represented a reaction against the dominant pre-war currents in Serbian poetry, the lyrico-traditional and the surrealist, although later he was to include the influence of both these in his writing. For a time he was close to Vasko Popa, but soon his poetry was to develop in an entirely different and original direction. Pavlović's immediate and most lasting influences, to which he himself has paid tribute, were those of the post-symbolist school, notably W. E. Yeats and T. S. Eliot, but as a talented linguist he was familiar with most of the major European currents of poetry, in particular French, German, and Italian in addition to English.

There have been four basic currents or "cycles" in Pavlović's poetry, each one reflecting a new preoccupation and development in his expanding poetic horizons. In his early poems *87 pesama* (87 Poems) and *Stub sećanja* (Pillar of Memory) he uses short, elliptical, almost aphoristic forms, creating a forceful impact on his reader. Brought up against the background of war and violence and consequent to his medical studies as a young man, he had experienced at first-hand the harsh realities of life and death, and his early poems are full of stark and immediate violent images and a sense of ever-present menace.

This time
someone close has died

Requiem
in a grey park
under a closed-in sky . . .

You feel
the world has become lighter
by one human brain . . . ("Requiem")

A meadow of blood
flows from this hand

A blinded bird
singing of flowers

Man's misunderstanding
with his own image . . . ("Suicide")

By the mid-1950s literature in Yugoslavia had gone a long way to casting off the limitations of the political straitjacket which still applied to most of Eastern Europe. But still a little uncertain, many Serbian writers were to make use of satire which for a time became the dominant mode. Pavlović adapted the genre to his own needs in a quite original way.

Never an overtly political poet, his next books of poetry reflected his interest in the historical and oral traditions so strong in Serbian folk poetry and dating back to a much earlier tradition. Pavlović turned first to the universal myths which have survived from pre-history: beginning with Ancient Greece, the subject-matter of Pavlović's three major works between 1963 and 1971 continued with the Byzantine Eastern Empire and the earliest Slav presence in the Balkans, culminating in the rise of the medieval Serbian kingdom, the reign of Tsar Dušan and the eventual catastrophic defeat at the hands of the advancing Turks at Kosovo in 1389. The third volume deals with episodes in the lives of figures from the Old and New Testaments and saints and martyrs of the early Eastern Church. In *Mleko iskoni* (Milk of Yore), *Velika Skitija* (Great Scythia), and *Svetli i tamni praznici* (Light and Dark Holy Days), Pavlović sees the passage of centuries in the Balkans as a continuous rising current of civilization, cut short by the intrusion of an alien culture. Its abrupt and untimely destruction at the hands of the Turks lies at the root of the historical tragedy suffered by the Serbs. In this process of defeat, they became the saviours of the rest of Europe from a similar fate.

But this traditional "victory out of defeat" motif is only the first layer at which the poetry functions. By combining a method of viewing epic mythological and historical themes and events through the eyes of an often confused and ordinary contemporary observer, Pavlović arrives at a poetic vehicle which he uses as subtle satire, relevant also to the present-day situation. At the same time, he stresses the unbroken currents of myth, so in "Prince's Daughter Weaving" the poem relates the Persephone story to that of a Serbian princess carried off captive by the Turks. And in poems such as "Prince's Supper" and "A Beheaded Prince Remembers" he continues the traditional parallel between Prince Lazar and the figure of Christ. This symbolic use of myth and traditional image is rounded off by a more generalised philosophical progression, often tinged with the anticlimax of irony. One of the finest poems of *Svetli i tamni praznici*, "Dragonslayer," is a good illustration of Pavlović's style and method:

Every year he comes down from the mountain
on a steed as white as the lily
a dragonfly girded with a breastplate of iron
and rises up before the silver veil that looks on him in tears.

The scallop-shell of his palm touches the harp
and the trembling lips of the prince's daughter.
Then he goes out to the serpent
which, as is known, has come
out of some festering corner of the universe
and whose strength is made up of the unity
of a multitude of death in a hundred-headed monster.
And so this knight of valour, with his beauty
and with his lance, kills the abomination
and a choir of maidens from on high
sings to his glory.

With his head on the dawn's shoulder
he modestly goes on his way
and rests in the narrow shade of a cedar.
There he is set upon by spiders and their henchmen
who tear his body into sheaves
taking his head with special care
into their workshop to torture.

And now at the sight of his life-springs
— seek rhyme or reason in this world —
he who severed the Tsar Serpent's head,
the favoured of the gods,
can be dissolved in ant's acid.

Pavlović's poetic medium, an amalgam of colloquial Serbian, semi-archaic religious forms and expressions, and images taken from folk poetry presents an original and at the same time highly evocative picture to the Serbian reader: the poet is very adept at adapting the language of his verse to its subject-matter.

Pavlović continued his involvement with history with three longer poems: "Apocalypse," "Flight Through Serbia" and "A Divine Miracle." At the first level they are concerned with a symbolic interpretation of his country's destruction by the Turks, search for a new beginning and eventual rebirth, but by now Pavlović had travelled widely (notably to India and China) and these poems, epic in conception, contain many elements of recurring myths which he had found in Eastern cultures and identified in Serbian folk tradition, but here used as stylised symbols. In "A Divine Miracle," it is the poet himself who leads us through and explains the meanings of the poem's metaphysical theme, and it is his task to experience and interpret the trials and suffering of his people and their painful renascence through the continuing cycles of death and rebirth. This is entirely in accord with Pavlović's view of the poet as the direct descendant of the seer-priest of early ritual and the custodian of his race's deeper truths and true values.

The discovery of an important Mesolithic settlement at Lepenski Vir on the middle Danube in the early 1970s stimulated Pavlović's interest to search even further back in time for the ritual beginnings of poetry, and he was to publish several books of essays in this area, notably *Poetika žrtvenog obreda* (The Poetics of Sacrificial Ritual). The river civilization contained many archeological finds of importance — among them artefacts, including ritual objects and primitive carvings of apparent fish-god heads. Pavlović's fourth cycle of poetry returns to shorter, terse forms and is inspired initially by this early civilization. *Pevanje na viru* (Singing at the Whirlpool), and *Nova pevanja na viru* (New Singing at the Whirlpool) are written from the viewpoint of primitive people, of the objects that surround them and their mystical relation to the year's natural cycles. *Links* and *Zavetine* (Spells) in the same vein attempt to link the world of these primitive Balkan ancestors with that of their historical Serbian descendants. Pavlović sees an unbroken development encompassing natural phenomena, the land and human civilization, and poetry, with its beginnings in stylized ritual worship, as the means of its preservation. Essential here is the role of the poet through the generations as priest, interpreter and guardian of the traditional mysteries and values of man's spiritual heritage. So in "Prorok" (Prophet) from *Singing at the Whirlpool*:

> While others sleep
> he goes on striving
> he climbs up
> to where rain flows
> where others
> try to make out
> number and reason
> he weaves words . . .

As well as poetry, Pavlović has also written plays, short stories, and a number of critical works on poetry dealing both with Serbian and European writers. He has compiled a number of important anthologies, notably *Antologija moderne engleske poezije* (Anthology of Modern English Poetry) in 1957 which was highly influential in introducing contemporary English verse, much of which had not been published before in translation, to Serbian readers. His *Antologija srpskog pesništva* (Anthology of Serbian Verse) broke new ground in its conceptual selection and has subsequently become the definitive work of its kind.

Very much a "poet of ideas," Pavlović's work has emphasized a new artistic perception of his country's cultural roots and history and gone much further in attempting to trace the universals of poetry through the roots of European and eastern civilization still further back into the condensed rituals of primitive societies. He is a poet of considerable significance whose influence has been handicapped hitherto by the relative inaccessibility of the language in which he writes.

—Bernard Johnson

PAZ, Octavio. Mexican. Born in Mexico City, 31 March 1914. Educated at the National Autonomous University of Mexico, Mexico City, 1932–37. Married 1) Elena Garro (*q.v.*) in 1937 (divorced), one daughter; 2) Marie José Tramini in 1964. Founder or editor of literary reviews *Barandal*, 1931, *El Popular*, late 1930s, *Taller*, 1938–41, *El Hijo Pródigo*, 1943–46, and *Plural*, later called *Vuelta*, 1971–75. Secretary, 1946, and extraordinary and plenipotentiary minister, 1959–62, Mexican Embassy, Paris; chargé d'affaires, 1951, later posted to Secretariat for External Affairs, 1953–58, Mexican Embassy, Tokyo; Mexican Ambassador to India, 1962–68 (resigned). Visiting Professor of Spanish American literature, University of Texas, Austin, and University of Pittsburgh, 1968–70; Simón Bolívar Professor of Latin American studies, 1970, and Fellow of Churchill College, 1970–71, Cambridge University; Charles Eliot Norton Professor of poetry, Harvard University, Cambridge, Massachusetts, 1971–72; Regent's Fellow, University of

California, San Diego. Recipient: Guggenheim fellowship, 1944; International grand prize for poetry (Belgium), 1963; Jerusalem prize, 1977; Critics' prize (Spain), 1977; National prize for letters, 1977; Grand Aigle d'Or (Nice), 1979; Yoliztli prize, 1980; Cervantes prize, 1982; Neustadt international prize, 1982; Heinse Medal (Germany), 1984; Federation of German Book Trade Peace prize, 1984; Gran Cruz de Alfonso X el Sabrio, 1986; Ingersoll Foundation T. S. Eliot award, 1987; Institut de France De Toqueville prize, 1988; Nobel prize for literature, 1990. Honorary member, American Academy of Arts and Letters, 1972. Address: c/o Revista Vuelta, Amigos del Arte A.C., Avenida Contreras 516, Piso 3, Col. San Jéronimo Lidice, 10200 Mexico City, Mexico.

PUBLICATIONS

Verse

Luna silvestre.   Mexico City, Fabula, 1933.
¡No pasarán!   Mexico City, Simbad, 1936.
Raíz del hombre.   Mexico City, Simbad, 1937.
Bajo tu clara sombra y otros poemas sobre España.   Valencia, Españolas, 1937; revised edition, Valencia, Tierra Nueva, 1941.
Entre la piedra y la flor.   Mexico City, Nueva Voz, 1941.
A la orilla del mundo y primer dia: Bajo tu clara sombra, Raíz del hombre, Noche de resurrecciones.   Mexico City, Compañía Editora y Librera Ars, 1942.
Libertad bajo palabra.   Mexico City, Tezontle, 1949.
¿Aguila o sol?   Mexico City, Tezontle, 1951; as *Eagle or Sun?*, translated by Eliot Weinberger, New York, October House, 1970; London, Owen, 1990.
Semillas para un himno.   Mexico City, Tezontle, 1954.
Piedra de sol.   Mexico City, Tezontle, 1957; as *Sun Stone*, translated by Muriel Rukeyser, New York, New Directions, 1963; as *The Sun Stone*, translated by Donald Gardner, York, Cosmos, 1969.
La estación violenta.   Mexico City, Fondo de Cultura Económica, 1958.
Agua y viento.   Bogota, Mito, 1959.
Libertad bajo palabra: obra poética 1935–1958.   Mexico City, Fondo de Cultura Económica, 1960; revised edition, 1968.
Salamandra 1958–1961.   Mexico City, Mortiz, 1962.
Selected Poems, translated by Muriel Rukeyser. Bloomington, Indiana University Press, 1963.
Viento entero.   New Delhi, Laxton Press, 1965.
Vrindaban, Madurai.   New Delhi, Laxton Press, 1965.
Blanco.   Mexico City, Mortiz, 1967; in English, translated by Eliot Weinberger, New York, The Press, 1974.
Disco visuales.   Mexico City, Era, 1968.
Ladera este (1962–1968).   Mexico City, Mortiz, 1969.
La centana: poemas 1935–1968.   Barcelona, Seix Barral, 1969.
Configurations.   New York, New Directions, and London, Cape, 1971.
Renga, with others.   Paris, Gallimard, 1971; in English, translated by Charles Tomlinson, New York, Braziller, 1972; London, Penguin, 1980.
Topoemas.   Mexico City, Era, 1971.
Early Poems 1935–1955.   New York, New Directions, 1973.
Pasado en claro.   Mexico City, Fondo de Cultura Económica, 1975.
Vuelta.   Barcelona, Seix Barral, 1976.
A Draft of Shadows and Other Poems.   New York, New Directions, 1979.

Selected Poems, translated by Charles Tomlinson. London, Penguin, 1979.

Airborn/Hijos del aire, with Charles Tomlinson. London, Anvil Press, 1981.

Poemas 1935–1975. Barcelona, Seix Barral, 1981.

Poemas recientes. N.p., Institución Cultural de Cantabria de la Diputación Provincial de Santander, 1981.

Instante y revelación, photographs by Manuel Alvarez Bravo. Mexico City, Circulo, 1982; bilingual edition, New York, Grove Weidenfeld, 1985.

Selected Poems, edited by Eliot Weinberger. New York, New Directions, 1984.

Cuatro chopos/The Four Poplars, translated by Eliot Weinberger. Purchase, State University of New York, 1985.

Nineteen Ways of Looking at Wang Wei, with Eliot Weinberger. Mt. Kisko, New York, Moyer Bell, 1987.

The Collected Poems of Octavio Paz, 1957–1987, edited by Eliot Weinberger. New York, New Directions, 1987; Manchester, Carcanet, 1988.

Arbol adentro. Barcelona, Seix Barral, 1987; as *A Tree Within*, New York, New Directions, 1988.

Lo mejor de Octavio Paz: el fuego de cada día. Barcelona, Seix Barral, 1989.

Play

La hija de Rappaccini, from the story by Nathaniel Hawthorne (produced Mexico, 1956). Published in *Primera antología de obras en un acto*, edited by Maruxa Vilalta, Mexico City, Collección Teatro Mexicano, 1959.

Other

El laberinto de la soledad. Mexico City, Cuadernos Americanos, 1950; revised edition, Mexico City, Fondo de Cultura Económica, 1959; as *The Labyrinth of Solitude: Life and Thought in Mexico*, New York, Grove Press, 1961; London, Allen Lane, 1967.

El arco y la lire: el poema, la revelación poética, poésia e historia. Mexico City, Fondo de Cultura Económica, 1956; revised edition, 1967; as *The Bow and the Lyre: The Poem, The Poetic Revelation, Poetry and History*, Austin, University of Texas Press, 1973.

Las peras del olmo. Mexico City, Universidad Nacional Autónoma de México, 1957.

Tamayo en la pintura mexicana. Mexico City, Universidad Nacional Autónoma de México, 1959.

Cuadrivio (on Darío, López Verlarde, Pessoa, Cernuda). Mexico City, Mortiz, 1965.

Los signos en rotación. Buenos Aires, Sur, 1965.

Puertas al campo. Mexico City, Universidad Nacional Autónoma de México, 1966.

Claude Lévi-Strauss; o, El nuevo festín de Esopo. Mexico City, Mortiz, 1967, as *Claude Lévi-Strauss: An Introduction*, Ithaca, New York, Cornell University Press, 1970; as *On Lévi-Strauss*, London, Cape, 1970.

Corriente alterna. Mexico City, Siglo Veintiuno, 1967; as *Alternating Current*, New York, Viking Press, 1973; London, Wildwood House, 1974.

Marcel Duchamp; o, El castillo de la pureza. Mexico City, Era, 1968; as *Marcel Duchamp; or, The Castle of Purity*, New York, Grossman, and London, Cape Goliard, 1970.

México: la última década. Austin, University of Texas Institute of Latin American Studies, 1969.

Conjunciones y disyunciones. Mexico City, Mortiz, 1969; as *Conjunctions and Disjunctions*, New York, Viking Press, 1974; London, Wildwood House, 1975.

Posdata. Mexico City, Siglo Veintiuno, 1970; as *The Other Mexico: Critique of the Pyramid*, New York, Grove Press, 1972.

Las cosas en su sitio: sobre la literatura española del siglo XX, with Juan Marichal. Mexico City, Finisterre, 1971.

Los signos en rotación y otros ensayos, edited by Carlos Fuentes. Madrid, Alianza, 1971.

Traducción: literatura y literalidad. Barcelona, Tusquets, 1971.

Apariencia desnuda: la obra de Marcel Duchamp. Mexico City, Era, 1973; as *Marcel Duchamp: Appearance Stripped Bare*, New York, Viking Press, 1979.

El signo y el garabato. Mexico City, Mortiz, 1973.

Solo a dos voces, with Julián Ríos. Barcelona, Lumen, 1973.

Teatro de signos/transparencias, edited by Julián Ríos. Madrid, Fundamentos, 1974.

Versiones y diversiones (translations). Mexico City, Mortiz, 1974.

Los hijos del limo: del romanticismo a la vanguardia (lectures). Barcelona, Seix Barral, 1974; as *Children of the Mire: Modern Poetry from Romanticism to the Avant-Garde*, Cambridge, Massachusetts, Harvard University Press, 1974.

El mono gramático. Barcelona, Seix Barral, 1974; as *The Monkey Grammarian*, New York, Seaver, 1981.

La búsqueda del comienzo: escritos sobre el surrealismo. Madrid, Fundamentos, 1974.

The Siren and the Seashells and Other Essays on Poets and Poetry. Austin, University of Texas Press, 1976.

Xavier Villaurrutia en persona y en obra. Mexico City, Fondo de Cultura Económica, 1978.

El ogro filantrópico: historia y política 1971–1978. Barcelona, Seix Barral, 1979.

Rufino Tamayo: Myth and Magic. New York, Guggenheim Foundation, 1979.

México en la obra de Octavio Paz, edited by Luis Mario Scheider. Mexico City, Promexa, 1979; Mexico City, Fondo de Cultura Económica, 3 vols., 1987.

Rufino Tamayo, with Jacques Lassaigne. Barcelona, Poligrafia, 1982; in English, New York, Rizzoli, 1982.

Sor Juana Inés de la Cruz, o, Las trampas de la fe. Mexico City, Fondo de Cultura Económica, 1982; as *Sor Juana: Her Life and World*, London, Faber, 1988; as *Sor Juana, or, The Traps of Faith*, Cambridge, Massachusetts, Bel Knap Press, 1988.

Tiempo nublado. Barcelona, Seix Barral, 1983; as *One Earth, Four or Five Worlds: Reflections on Contemporary History*, San Diego, Harcourt Brace, and Manchester, Carcanet, 1985.

Sombras de obras: arte y literatura. Barcelona, Seix Barral, 1983.

Günter Gerzo (in Spanish, English, and French), with John Golding. Neuchâtel, Griffon, 1983; Montclair, New Jersey, Abner Schram, 1984.

Hombres en su siglo y otros ensayos. Barcelona, Seix Barral, 1984; as *On Poets and Others*, New York, Seaver, 1986; Manchester, Carcanet, 1987.

Pasión crítica: conversaciones con Octavio Paz, edited by Hugo J. Verani. Barcelona, Seix Barral, 1985.

The Labyrinth of Solitude, The Other Mexico, Return to the Labyrinth of Solitude, Mexico and the United States, and The Philanthropic Ogre. New York, Grove Press, 1985.

Convergences: Essays on Art and Literature. San Diego, Harcourt Brace, and London, Bloomsbury, 1987.

Generaciones y semblanzas: escritores y letras de México. Mexico City, Fondo de Cultura Económica, 1987.

El pelegrino en su patria: historia y política de México. Mexico City, Fondo de Cultura Económica, 1987.

Los privilegios de la vista: arte de México. Mexico City, Fondo de Cultura Económica, 1987.

Primeras letras, 1931–1943. Barcelona, Seix Barral, 1988.

One Word or the Other. Mansfield, Texas, Latitudes Press, 1989.

Poesía, mito, revolución. Coyoacán, Vuelta, 1989.

La otra voz: poesía y fin de siglo. Barcelona, Seix Barral, 1990; as *The Other Voice*, Manchester, Carcanet, 1992.

Editor, *Voces de España.* Mexico City, Letras de Mexico, 1938.

Editor, with others, *Laurel: antología de la poésia moderna en lengua española.* Mexico City, Séneca, 1941.

Editor, *Anthologie de la poésie mexicaine.* Paris, Nagel, 1952.

Editor, *Antología poética.* Mexico City, Revista Panoramas, 1956.

Editor, *Anthology of Mexican Poetry*, translated by Samuel Beckett. Bloomington, Indiana University Press, 1958; London, Thames and Hudson, 1959; as *Mexican Poetry: An Anthology*, New York, Grove Press, 1985.

Editor, *Tamayo en la pintura mexicana.* Mexico City, Imprenta Universitaria, 1959.

Editor, *Magia de la risa.* Xalapa, Universidad Veracruzana, 1962.

Editor, *Antología*, by Fernando Pessoa. Mexico City, Universidad Nacional Autónoma de México, 1962.

Editor, with Pedro Zekeli, *Cuatro poetas contemporáneos de Suecia: Martinson, Lundkvist, Ekelöf, y Lindegren.* Mexico City, Universidad Nacional Autónoma de México, 1963.

Editor, with others, *Poesía en movimiento: Mexico 1915–1966.* Mexico City, Siglo Veintiuno, 1966; as *New Poetry of Mexico*, edited by Mark Strand, New York, Dutton, 1970; London, Secker and Warburg, 1972.

Editor, with Roger Caillois, *Remedios varo.* Mexico City, Era, 1966.

Editor, *Antología*, by Xavier Villaurrutia. Mexico City, Fondo de Cultura Económica, 1980.

Translator, with E. Hayashiya, *Sendas de Oku*, by Basho. Mexico City, Universidad Nacional Autónoma de México, 1957.

Translator, *Veinte poemas*, by William Carlos Williams. Mexico City, Era, 1973.

Translator, *15 poemas*, by Guillaume Apollinaire. Mexico City, Latitudes, 1979.

*

Bibliographies: *Bibliografía selecta y crítica de Octavio Paz* by Juan O. Valencia and Edward Coughlin, Cincinnati, University of Cincinnati, 1973; *Octavio Paz: bibliografía crítica* by Hugo J. Verani, Mexico City, Universidad Nacional Autónoma de México, 1983; in *Mexican Literature: A Bibliography of Secondary Sources* by David William Foster, Metuchen, New Jersey, Scarecrow Press, 1992.

Critical Studies: *The Poetic Modes of Octavio Paz* by Rachel Phillips, London, Oxford University Press, 1972; *The Perpetual Present: The Poetry and Prose of Octavio Paz* by Ivar Ivask, Norman, University of Oklahoma Press, 1973; *Octavio Paz: A Study of His Poetics*, Cambridge, Cambridge University Press, 1979, and *Octavio Paz*, Boston, Twayne, 1986, both by Jason Wilson; Paz issue of *World Literature Today* (Norman, Oklahoma), 56, 1982; *Octavio Paz: The Mythic Dimension* by Frances Chiles, New York, Lang, 1986; *Toward Octavio Paz: A Reading of His Major Poems 1957–1976* by John M. Fein, Lexington, University Press of Kentucky, 1986.

*   *   *

Within the intellectual landscape of the 20th century, in an increasingly specialized and divided world, Octavio Paz is a writer of exceptional and diverse interests, of prodigious versatility, unusual erudition and imagination, recognized as one of the major poets of our time (underlined by his 1990 Nobel prize for literature) and as a lucid interpreter of modernity. His critical thought includes a bewildering number of fields of human activity — art, aesthetics, philosophy, Oriental religion, anthropology, psychology, political ideology. The preoccupations that cross the writing of Octavio Paz — the search for lost unity and the reconciliation of man with himself and the universe, the celebration of love and of freedom of thinking, the merging of contraries, the reviving of the poetic word — converge in the reflexive prose of his essays and in a poetry that assumes the form of self-criticism and incessant interrogation, two sides of an organic whole of inseparable unity in its diversity, that constitutes an uncommon and passionate testimony of humanity.

Paz is primarily a poet, considered (along with Pablo Neruda and César Vallejo) as one of the truly outstanding Spanish American poets of the century. Paz sees poetry as a path towards the revelation of man, as a means to restore authenticity. Poetic creation and erotic love are the only ways to reconcile the opposing forces of the world, the only ways to transcend solitude and reach spiritual fulfillment.

Paz's extensive travels throughout the world have affected the many phases and transformations of his poetry. His first trip to Spain in 1937, during the Civil War, introduced him to the Spanish tradition, particularly the Baroque world of Francisco Gómez de Quevedo and Luis de Góngora, poets who left a deep mark on his early writing. His stay in the United States (1944–45) enabled him to read the great poets of the Anglo-American tradition (T. S. Eliot, Ezra Pound, E. E. Cummings); he came to share with them the representation of the dissociated image of the world and the self through fragmentation and simultaneity, through the suppression of logical ties. During the five years that he lived in France (1946–51), he participated in the surrealist movement and developed a lifelong affinity with its tenets. Paz sees surrealism as an activity of the human spirit based on the idea of rebellion, love, and freedom, as a total subversion, as a movement meant to recapture the natural innocence of man. His debt to surrealism can best be found in *La estación violenta* (The Violent Season), where his poetry becomes more hermetic, and indulges in complex oneiric images and occasional automatic writing. The conjunction of ancient Mexican mythology and surrealism ("telluric surrealism," as termed by the French poet Benjamin Péret) guides his quest for eternal values, his desire to transcend the contradictions of humanity. "Hymn among the Ruins" and, above all, *Piedra de sol* (*Sun Stone*) are the masterpieces of this period of his poetry. In Japan (1952) he was ready to explore Japanese poetry, primarily the Haiku, a form of poetry that stresses condensation, ellipsis, and imagery. After a stay in Mexico (1953–58) he resided in France again (1959–62), where he deepened his interest in structuralism. Finally, he became Ambassador to India (1962–68), a country that profoundly affected his vision of the world and his approach to poetry. Many concepts of Oriental thought were incorporated into his poetics: detachment from the outside world, the illusory nature of the world, the stress on natural man, the illusion of the ego, sudden illumination, transcendence through the senses, rebellion against all systems. *Ladera este* (The East Slope) and *Blanco* include the major poems of this period.

Since the early 1960s the most significant constants of Paz's poetic work are experimentation with space and the use of visual effects. Faced with the disconcerting, fragmentary, and dissociated character of reality, he questions all certainty and converts natural relationships into multiple, unconnected moments, which are regrouped in a space that reveals the fragmented consciousness of modern man, the loss of cosmic harmony, and the ancient, coherent image of reality. The most important poems of the 1960s ("Whole Wind," *Blanco*) are constellations of juxtaposed fragments and of voices in perpetual rotation in which the simultaneity of times and spaces is the point of confluence in an inexhaustible net of relations that enrich the analytical reading of the text. In his poetry the spatial-temporal markings disappear, and all ages converge in a privileged moment, in that evanescent and fleeting, atemporal and archetypal present. Paz liberates language from the illusion of representing an empirical reality: spaces, times, and distant cultures interweave without explicit transition and give the poem a plural meaning.

Paz is also a major essayist. Few Spanish-American writers, if any, have developed a critical system that encompasses the main intellectual currents of modern times. In over 20 volumes of essays, from his early reflections on Mexican society (*El laberinto de la soledad* [The Labyrinth of Solitude]) and on poetic theory (*El arco y la lire* [The Bow and the Lyre]), his studies on structuralism and modern art (the books on Lévi-Strauss and Marcel Duchamp), the meditations on eroticism (*Conjunciones y disyunciones* [Conjunctions and Disjunctions]), and on diverse artistic manifestations, to the revision of the modern poetic tradition (*Los hijos del limo* [Children of the Mire]), of political ideology (*El ogro filantrópico* [The Philanthropic Ogre]), and his monumental book on Sor Juana Inés de la Cruz, critical reflexion is one of the central preoccupations of Octavio Paz, a product of a lucid and passionate meditation on the culture of the modern times. Paz sees himself, and all writers, as dissidents, as outsiders: "Our civilization has been founded on the notion of criticism: there is nothing sacred or untouchable except the freedom to think. Without criticism, that is to say, without rigor and without experimentation, there is no science; without criticism there is no art or literature. I would also say that without criticism there is no healthy society. The writer is not the servant of the Church, the State, a political party, a country, the people, or social morals: he is the servant of language. But he really serves it only when he questions it: modern literature is above all criticism of language."

For over half a century Octavio Paz has adhered, then, to two fundamental premises: the questioning of all established truths and, above all, the passionate search for human dignity and the defense of the freedom of the human being, principles whose aim is always in Paz a recovery of the essential values of humanism.

—Hugo J. Verani

PENDSE, Śrīpad Nārāyaṇ. Indian. Born in Murdi, Ratnagiri District, 5 January 1913. Educated at Bombay University, B.Sc. Married Kamal Marathe in 1943; one son and two daughters. French teacher, M.H. High School, Thane, Bombay, 1933–38; primary teacher, Bombay Municipality, 1938–42; clerk, 1942–64, and deputy public relations officer, 1964–68, Bombay Electric Supply and Transport Company. Since 1968 full-time writer. Recipient: five state awards; Rockefeller Foundation travelling fellowship, 1955–56; Sāhitya Akādemī award, 1964. Address: 10 Tukaram Niketan, Mahim, Bombay 400016, India.

PUBLICATIONS

Fiction

Elgar.   Mumbai, Mauja, 1949.
Haddapar [Exile].   Mumbai, Mauja, 1950.
Garambītsā Bāpū.   Mumbai, Mauja, 1952; as *Wild Bapu of Garambi*, New Delhi, Sāhitya Akādemī, 1969.
Hatyā.   Mumbai, Mauja, 1954.
Yaśodā.   Mumbai, Mauja, 1957.
Kalandar [Calendar].   Mumbai, Mauja, 1959.
Rathacakrà [The Chariot Wheel].   Mumbai, Mauja, 1962.
Lavhali [The Bending Reed].   Mumbai, Mauja, 1966.
Jumman.   1966.
Octopus.   Mumbai, Mauja, 1972.
Akānta [Outcry].   Mumbai, Mauja, 1981.
Tumbadtse Khot [The Khots of Tumbad].   Pune, Kontinentala, 2 vols., 1987.

Plays

Mahāpur [Flood].   Mumbai, Mauja, 1961.
Rājemastar, from his novel *Haddapar*.   1964.
Yaśodā, from his own novel.   Mumbai, Mauja, 1965.
Garambītsā Bāpū, from his own novel.   Mumbai, Mauja, 1965.
Sambhusanca calit.   Mumbai, Mauja, 1967.
Asa zhala ani ujadla.   1969.
Cakravyuha. Mumbai, Mauja, 1970.
Paṇḍita! ata tari sahane vha!   Mumbai, Mauja, 1978.
Rathacakrà, from his own novel.   Mumbai, Mauja, 1980.

Television Play: *Rathacakrà*, from his own novel, 1989.

Other

Khadakavaril hirval [Grass upon the Rocks] (sketches).   1941.
The B.E.S.T. Story.   Bombay, Bombay Electric Supply and Transport Undertaking, 1972.
Śrī Nāth Peṇḍse, lekhak ani manuṣ (autobiography).   1974.

Translator, *Prayaścit* [The Scarlet Letter], by Nathaniel Hawthorne.   1969.

*

Śrīpad Nārāyaṇ Peṇḍse comments:
I am a middle-class writer. My father died when I was 24 and all the responsibility for eight people — seven brothers and sisters and my mother — fell on me. We had always been poor and now we became even poorer. I had to keep our family going by working 13 or 14 hours a day and there was hardly any time for reading or writing. Still I wrote whenever I could and had to wait until I was 37 before I attracted the attention of the

critics. From then until now I have been constantly writing and am now considered to be in the first rank of Marathi novelists. I have written plays in order to make money but nobody thinks much of me as a playwright, even though two of my plays have had over a thousand performances and one or two others have had a reasonable success. I have written some short stories which have been noticed and also an autobiography, but people think of me as essentially a novelist.

The world about which I write is that of the middle class. My sole aim is to seek out the essential humanity of man. When I am first engaged on a novel it is always the characters that I see first. Afterwards the world that they inhabit begins to appear.

I have faith in a few things: that man is basically good and that he appears in various forms because of the social situations in which he lives. I don't believe in any god. The world was created by man, by accident and by chance. All my life I have given first place to the principles of honesty and gratitude.

*   *   *

Śrīpad Nārāyaṇ Peṇḍse is recognised throughout India as the leading Marathi novelist of the first decades of India's independence. He was brought up in considerable poverty, the eldest of a Brahmin family from the lush but backward Konkan, the coastal strip south of Bombay. Although the family moved to Bombay city when he was still quite young, it was the Konkan, and especially the region west of Dapoli in Ratnagiri District, that Peṇḍse used as the background for all of his early novels. Replacing a literary tradition which had been substantially confined to the urban centres of Bombay and Poona, he effectively introduced the regional novel to Marathi readers.

Peṇḍse's earliest work, *Khadakavaril hirval* (Grass upon the Rocks), is a collection of pen portraits originally published in the many monthly magazines of the time. But he first came to the notice of the literary world with *Elgar*, a powerful novel which treats the Hindu-Muslim riots of wartime India as they spread from Bombay to corrupt the peaceful co-existence of the two faiths in the coastal villages of Ratnagiri District. Among the early novels, *Haddapar* (Exile) is the story of an unconventional but still highly orthodox village school teacher, while *Garambītsā Bāpū* (*Wild Bapu of Garambi*) takes unconventionality to lengths which were slightly shocking in their time. Bapu, the illegitimate son of the village headman, or *Khot*, flouts all the rules of deference to authority that are ingrained in the Indian villager, turning himself into a successful businessman and marrying a widow from a non-Brahmin caste after living with her for a number of years. The reputation earned by *Wild Bapu* brought Peṇḍse a year-long Rockefeller travelling fellowship through which he and his wife were able to visit Europe, the United States, and the Far East in 1955–56, and the novel was subsequently selected by Unesco for the list of works to be translated under the representative world literature scheme.

The following novels and the play *Mahāpur* (Flood) made less impact, though *Yaśodā*, which is actually a novelette plus three short stories, continued the Bapu theme by going back to the earlier story of his mother. It was *Rathacakrà* (The Chariot Wheel) in 1962 which earned him the Sāhitya Akādemī award and an all-India reputation. Set once again in a Konkan village, very like the one in which Peṇḍse was born, it tells the story of a woman married into an orthodox Brahmin family whose husband is a natural ascetic for whom sex is a guilt-ridden but occasionally unavoidable experience. After having four children with her he finally disappears, and the following years are punctuated by continual rumours that he has been sighted as a *sadhu* (holy man) in some of the holy places of India. She is

supposed to revere his saintliness while seeing her children neglected and exploited within the large Hindu joint family in which she has been abandoned. Her second son is obviously intelligent, and with some assistance from her eldest and absentee brother-in-law the woman defies convention in order to move with her children to the nearest town to give her son a decent education. For this action she gets no credit from her neighbours, who are only interested in the holiness of her missing husband, or even from the son who cannot understand her indifference to his father. His education and future prospects secured, the son ends by rejecting her and she throws herself into a well, the traditional last resort of the oppressed Indian woman. However, the novel ends enigmatically with her still alive, supported by the buckets of the Persian wheel and staring up into the bright sky framed by the well's mouth. Peṇḍse, a declared atheist, has great faith in the indestructability of the human spirit, but none in divine intervention.

In Peṇḍse's later work he increasingly turns to Bombay as his setting, partly no doubt in order to prove that he is not just a regional novelist. *Lavhali* (The Bending Reed) is in diary form and more obviously autobiographical than anything else that he has written — except, of course, his own biography which he published in the guise of a third-person narrative by "A Friend." *Lavhali* actually uses quotations from the diaries that Peṇḍse has kept all his life to tell the story of a poor Brahmin clerk, living in a Bombay chawl; struggling to pass exams while supporting himself and his family by elementary teaching; dreaming of marriage, which he cannot afford, and a decent job which continually eludes him — almost exactly like Peṇḍse's own life in Bombay in the late 1930s and 1940s. In *Octopus* and *Akānta* (Outcry) Peṇḍse attempted novels set in the more sophisticated life of Bombay, touching on homosexuality and the vices of high life, but these did not find much favour with the public. Recently he has returned to the Konkan with a long two-volume novel *Tumbadtse Khot* (The Khots of Tumbad), about the rise and fall of a landed family.

Peṇḍse has turned a number of his own novels into plays, notably *Wild Bapu of Garambi*, which has had many performances and continual revivals on the flourishing Marathi stage, and has also written a number of other successful independent plays. Peṇḍse is a natural dramatist: dialogue makes up nine-tenths of his novels and short stories. In spite of his famous regionalism, his descriptions of the setting in which his characters move are perfunctory — a deficiency, if it is a deficiency, that he shares with most Marathi fiction writers. Peṇḍse actually prides himself on not describing his protagonists, rather allowing their characters and perhaps a few brief indications of their appearance to be made manifest in their words and in the references made to them by others. It is the vividness and bite of the dialogue, tinged with Konkani dialect or Bombay demotic, that has made his work so popular with educated urban readers.

—Ian Raeside

PERI ROSSI, Cristina. Uruguayan and Spanish. Born in Montevideo, November 1941. Educated to licenciada in comparative literature. Literature teacher and journalist, Montevideo; since 1972 has lived in exile in Barcelona; Professor of comparative literature, Autonomous University of Barcelona. Recipient: Arca prize, 1968; *Marcha* prize,

1969; Inventarios Provisionales prize, 1974; City of Palma de Mallorca prize, 1976; Benito Pérez Galdós prize, 1980; City of Barcelona prize, 1991. Agent: International Editors, Rambla de Cataluña 63, 3 piso, Barcelona 08007, Spain. Address: Travessera de Les Corts 171, 4 piso 1a, Barcelona 08007, Spain.

PUBLICATIONS

Fiction

Viviendo. Montevideo, Alfa, 1963.
El libro de mis primos. Montevideo, Biblioteca de Marcha, 1969.
Los museos abandonados. Montevideo, Arca, 1969.
Indicios pánicos (includes poetry). Montevideo, Nuestra América, 1970.
La tarde del dinosaurio. Barcelona, Planeta, 1976.
La rebelión de los niños. Caracas, Monte Avila, 1980.
El museo de los esfuerzos inútiles. Barcelona, Seix Barral, 1983.
La nave de los locos. Barcelona, Seix Barral, 1984; as *The Ship of Fools*, London, Allison and Busby, and Columbia, Louisiana, Readers International, 1989.
Una pasión prohibida. Barcelona, Seix Barral, 1986.
Solitario de amor. Barcelona, Grijalbo, 1988.
Cosmoagonías. Barcelona, Laia, 1988.
La última noche de Dostoievski. Madrid, Mondadori, 1992.

Verse

Evohé: poemas eróticos. Montevideo, Girón, 1971.
Descripción de un naufragio. Barcelona, Lumen, 1974.
Diáspora. Barcelona, Lumen, 1976.
Lingüística general. Valencia, Prometeo, 1979.
Europa después de la lluvia. Madrid, Banco Exterior de España, 1987.
Babel bárbara. Caracas, Angria, 1990.

Other

Fantasías eróticas. Madrid, Temas de Hoy, 1991.

Editor, *Antología*, by Homero Aridjis. Barcelona, Lumen, 1976.

*

Bibliography: by Fernando Burgos, in *Antología del cuento hispanoamericano*, Mexico City, Porrua, 1991.

Critical Studies: "Cristina Peri Rossi and the Other Side of Reality" by Amaryll B. Chanady, in *Antigonish Review* (Nova Scotia), 54, 1983; "(De)ciphering Reality in 'Los extraños objetos voladores'" by Debra A. Castillo, in *Letras Femeninas* (Lincoln, Nebraska), 13(1–2), 1987; "Gender and Exile in Cristina Peri Rossi" by Amy Kaminsky, in *Continental, Latin American and Francophone Writers*, edited by Eunice Myers and Ginette Adamson, Lanham, Maryland, University Press of America, 1987; "Oneiric Riddles in Peri Rossi's *La nave de los locos*," in *Romance Languages Annual*, 1, 1989, and "Cristina Peri Rossi, *Solitario de amor*," in *Journal of Interdisciplinary Literary Studies* (Santa Monica, California), 2(1), 1990, both by Mercedes M. de Rodríguez; "Enigmas and Subversions in Cristina Peri Rossi's *La nave de los locos* [*Ship of Fools*]" by Gabriela Mora, in *Splintering Darkness: Latin American Women Writers in Search of Themselves*, Pittsburgh, Latin American Literary Review Press, 1990; "A Satiric Perspective on the Experience of Exile in the Short Fiction of Cristina Peri Rossi" by Cynthia A. Schmidt, in *The Americas Review* (Houston), 18(3–4), 1990.

Cristina Peri Rossi comments:
According to the dictionary (the only book which is constantly rewritten), "evidence" is an action or sign that reveals something hidden. The dictionary adds charmingly that "circumstantial evidence" is evidence which consists of details that strongly suggest something, but do not provide direct proof of it.

Man is a hunter of evidence; evidence provides the clues, the guidelines he needs to interpret life, to interpret reality — it's impossible to imagine an existence without this interpretation. We are all private detectives, looking out for the signs that surround us, come close to us, the ones that are hidden from us, only banality being transparent. Our task is to organize the dispersion and disparity of clues and guidelines, and this is also, specifically, the task of the writer. We live surrounded by evidence: our dreams, the details of our daily lives, anecdotes, presences and absences, our fantasies, dialogues — they're all specific to each individual, of course, but they are also the key to something more profound. No catastrophe, no feeling, no idea is surprising or unpredictable in itself; there is always evidence that we didn't know how to interpret or didn't allow ourselves to recognize. So reality is a palimpsest which we read only superficially, either through laziness or cowardice, comfort or clumsiness, making do with the most obvious signs or using incorrect sensual information, although this sensual information is not always incorrect.

To read these signs (and we never know whether one reading is correct over all other possible ones), to be able to unravel them means possessing a vision of the world without which the kaleidoscope of experience is baffling, or at the very least contradictory and always hazardous. There is not one sole correct reading, then, and the possible evidence is infinite, all-embracing. That allows for the plurality of books and paintings and poems. A world governed by just one reading of the evidence would be unbearable, and that is something that politicians, visionaries, and mystics sometimes fail to understand.

At a certain point of my life (I was more than 25 and less than 30) it seemed to me that I had the necessary aptitude to uncover the evidence (which is always either material or immaterial, the remains or traces of something) of what was around me, of my country Uruguay. It is something that sometimes happens to people when they are young, as I was. This aptitude did not depend, I supposed, on circumstances, although these were especially propitious at that time. (It was still six years before the military coup but there was already a rarified atmosphere in the city, an atmosphere full of foreboding). If that evidence was worth anything, it was in revealing something more than just the deterioration of one reality; it seemed to me to be the symbol, the allegory, and the metaphor of existence itself. (from the Prologue to *Indicios pánicos*, 2nd edition, 1980)

*   *   *

Cristina Peri Rossi is one of the finest and most important Latin American writers at work today. A versatile and prolific writer, she has distinguished herself in short fiction, the novel, and poetry, having produced in fewer than three decades a corpus of consistently high quality.

In Montevideo, Peri Rossi began her career in her early twenties with the publication of three short stories under the title *Viviendo* (Living). In these stories she shows her concern for women's passivity and the marginal place they occupy in society. This collection raised considerable controversy in its portrayal of lesbian relationships. A second book of stories, *Los museos abandonados* (The Abandoned Museums), marks her departure from realism in literature, and establishes her preference for the allegorical mode in which she expresses concern for and involvement in the social and political issues of her country. However, her works transcend a solely Latin American focus: her perspective is universal rather than regional. She is often compared with Jorge Luis Borges and Julio Cortázar, not only because of her universal vision, but also for her elliptic, allegorical style, and a demonstrated flair for abstraction. In *Los museos abandonados* a feeling of precariousness pervades the stories, with their apocalyptic vision of a world crumbling, in their rural and their urban environments. These traits are also present in her prophetic stories entitled *Indicios pánicos* (Signs of Panic), which foreshadow the military takeover in Uruguay in 1973. In the Spanish reissue of the book in 1981 Peri Rossi reflects in the prologue on this premonition, saying that at a certain time, in her youth, she believed that she had the ability to read signs in the world that surrounded her.

Her first novel, *El libro de mis primos* (The Book of My Cousins), appeared in 1969, a year before *Indicios pánicos*. It presents a satirical view of the bourgeoisie, a social world created by patriarchy and populated by useless, stagnant adults: passive, frivolous women, and greedy, incestuous men. Wise and uninhibited children seem to hold the key to the future, a new generation that would bring a new order. Children frequently populate Peri Rossi's fiction; they are wise beyond their years, sharp observers of reality, and even revolutionaries: children whose mere glance can shred an obstinate society refusing to acknowledge its true nature. This opinion by Julio Cortázar in his prologue to Peri Rossi's *La tarde del dinosaurio* (The Afternoon of the Dinosaur) is an apt commentary on her literary intent. Dreams, intertextual allusions, parody, puns, shifting perspectives, typographical devices, and the mixing of prose and poetry in her narratives are all part of Peri Rossi's repertoire of stylistic devices.

In the prologue to the 1989 edition Peri Rossi explains her aesthetic reasons for mixing prose and poetry in *El libro de mis primos* and says that her purpose was to bring together that which the reader frequently finds apart: a union of fictive narrative and lyricism, prose and poetry. This literary amalgamation has become a recurrent form of textual construction in her works.

In 1971, shortly after the publication of *Indicios pánicos*, Peri Rossi published *Evohé* (the name comes from the Greek Bacchae's call in the Dionysian mysteries), her first book of poems, and the last of her works to appear in Montevideo before she went into exile in 1972. The poems celebrate the erotic physicality of the female body and at the same time extol lesbian love. The seeds of Peri Rossi's oeuvre are — stylistically and thematically — found in these early works. To the recurrent motifs of the plight of the oppressed and the power of the oppressor, alienation, demythification of taboos (homosexual love, incest), and the search for identity, another central theme is added related to her own personal circumstances: the theme of exile with its related journey (the oceanic voyage, airports, strange cities), isolation, and time. Peri Rossi's characters confront the absurdity of their existence, and at times are reminiscent of the characters of Franz Kafka, as in "La grieta" (The Crack), where a man observes a crack in a wall as he is on the stairs of a metro station and becomes disoriented, forgetting whether he was going up or down. His hesitation causes chaos in the crowded stairs, and he is apprehended and interrogated for hours about what made him stop.

Peri Rossi elaborates further on the erotic tradition and the theme of lesbian love in her subsequent poetry — *Diáspora, Lingüística general* (General Linguistic), *Babel bárbara* (Barbarian Babel) — in many of her short stories, and especially in her latest novel, *Solitario de amor* (Lonely for Love). The latter is a celebration of the female body and lesbian ardor, a novel that parallels sexual passion and literary creation. Peri Rossi's powerful images and metaphors exalt woman as archetypal figure, mother and motherland.

The ever-prevalent theme of exile reappears in Peri Rossi's books of poems *Diáspora* and *Descripción de un naufragio* (Description of Shipwreck). The latter is an homage to the lost revolution and depicts the aftermath of the military takeover in Uruguay in 1973. In her short fiction, particularly in various stories from *El museo de los esfuerzos inútiles* (The Museum of Useless Efforts), the theme of the exile is also present. "El viaje inconcluso," from this collection, prefigures her most important novel to date, *La nave de los locos* (The Ship of Fools), a multidimensional work, whose main theme is the essence of exile and the loss of paradise: "A stranger. [X]. Estranged. Expelled from the womb of earth. Eviscerated: once more to give birth."

The ludic element combines understated irony with angst in most of Peri Rossi's works, as in her stories in *Cosmoagonías* (Cosmic/Agonies) — for example, "Suicidios, S. A." (Suicides, Ltd.), where we find a city with special areas reserved for suicide. Such elements are also found in the stories from the recently published *La última noche de Dostoievski* (Dostoevskii's Last Night), where gambling acquires erotic and mystical qualities.

Peri Rossi has lived in Spain since 1972, where she has been a journalist. She has added the essay to her considerable literary accomplishments, with the publication in 1991 of *Fantasías eróticas* (Erotic Fantasies). Her dedication to her craft, her love for words, and her insight in the human condition make her an extraordinary writer still searching for new forms and aspects to become part of her literary world.

—Mercedes Mazquiarán de Rodríguez

PETRI, György. Hungarian. Born in Budapest, 22 December 1943. Educated: received high school certificate 1962; Loránd Eötvös University, Budapest, 1966–71. Since 1974 freelance writer. Recipient: Attila József prize, 1990. Address: 17 Budakeszi út, 1021 Budapest, Hungary.

PUBLICATIONS

Verse

Magyarázatok M. számára [Explanations for M.].   Budapest, Szépirodalmi, 1971.
Körülírt zuhanás [Circumscribed Fall].   Budapest, Szépirodalmi, 1974.
Örökhétfő [Constant Monday].   Budapest, AB (samizdat publishers), 1981.

Hólabda a kézben [Snowball in Hand]. New York, HHRF/CHRR, 1984.

Azt hiszik . . . [They Drink . . .]. Budapest, AB (samizdat publishers), 1985.

Valahol megvan [Somewhere It Exists]. Budapest, Szépirodalmi, 1989.

Ami kimaradt [Whatever Was Left Out]. Budapest, Aura Kiadó, 1989.

Night Song of the Personal Shadow: Selected Poems, translated by Clive Wilmer and George Gömöri. Newcastle-upon-Tyne, Bloodaxe, 1989.

Valami ismeretlen [Something Unknown]. Jelenkor, Pécs, 1990.

Összes versei [Collected Poems]. Budapest, Szépirodalmi, 1991.

Other

Editor and Translator, *Volker Braun versei*. Budapest, Európa, 1986.

*

Critical Studies: "The First Hungarian Samizdat Poetry Collection" by Sándor Radnóti, in *Formations* (Evanston, Illinois), 3(1), 1986; "György Petri: The New Poetics of Tension in the Hungarian Context" by Kenneth McRobbie, in *World Literature Today* (Norman, Oklahoma), 62(1), 1988.

*   *   *

György Petri is an outstanding poet of the generation that grew up after the 1956 Hungarian uprising. He studied philosophy in the 1960s and his first book of poetry *Magyarázatok M. számára* (Explanations for M.) was published in 1971. Already that collection indicated that Petri is more interested in expressing what he considers to be "true" than simply seeking beauty — in other words, that he is a moralist. Such an approach, translated into the language of politics, meant a rejection of the bribes offered by the post-1956 Kádár régime; in his first collection Petri judges not only the Stalinist past ("By an Unknown Poet from Eastern Europe") but also the present, which he sees as a mixture of half-truths and tactical compromises ("This life of ours bled dry"). There are more personal poems in the second collection, *Körülírt zuhanás* (Circumscribed Fall), which is permeated by an existentialist mood of seeking freedom through sex and in the context of death. Petri's negations are not only political: he has a thinly veiled contempt for the kind of life led by the average citizen, whether it be a bourgeois or proletarian philistinism. He also finds traditional love poetry disingenuous: in his poems about lovemaking he reaches a level of sincerity earlier unheard of in Hungarian poetry. While these poems occasionally seem harsh, almost brutal, there is also much tenderness in Petri's approach and in his lyrical diagnoses of human relations.

Between 1975 and 1989 Petri's work (with few exceptions) was banned in Hungary and could be read only in samizdat. In other words, he made a definite choice: no more "cooperation" with the censor, even if it meant a limited audience. The several samizdat collections Petri brought out through the independent illegal presses in Hungary (his former illegal publisher is now the Mayor of Budapest) contain some of his best, most striking political poetry. Some of these poems reflect upon a specific event or discussion (e.g., "The Under-Secretary makes a Statement" refers to the political tension in the Solidarity period in Poland in 1980–81), while others are an expression of Petri's deep philosophical opposition to the Communist regime. For instance, in the poem "Electra" Petri speaks with the voice of an Electra whose motifs are misunderstood: "Well, that's why! That's why!/Because of disgust, because it all sticks in my craw,/revenge has become my dream and my daily bread." However, most poems from this period are satirical, often self-ridiculing in their tone. A two-liner from the late 1970s sums up Petri's ambivalent feelings about the "milder" form of tyranny prevailing in Kádár's Hungary: "I glance down at my shoes and — there's the lace!/This can't be gaol then, can it, in that case."

Petri as a poet expresses the spirit of the concluding decade of the 20th century through his complex and sophisticated use of the poetic language. His verse shows a constant awareness of both Classical and modernist models (Horace and Juvenal just as much as Cavafy and Brecht) and his recent work leads a "hidden dialogue" with the most lonely and alienated Hungarian poet of our century, Attila József. While Petri's poems are constructed in a matrix of literary allusions, his skill in using both rhetoric and anti-rhetoric, "high" metaphors and contemporary slang, including scatological expressions, is remarkable. Clive Wilmer characterized him as "perhaps the outstanding verse satirist of his generation in any European language."

—George Gömöri

PETRUSHEVSKAIA, Liudmila (Stefanovna). Also Lyudmila Petrushevskaya. Russian. Born in Moscow, 26 May 1938. Educated at Moscow University Faculty of Journalism. Journalist, 1961–70; teacher of improvisation, Gosudarstvennyi Institut Teatra i Satira (GITIS); editor for central television studios, 1972. Address: c/o Izdatel'stvo Iskusstvo, Sobinovskii bul'var' 3, 103009 Moscow, Russia.

PUBLICATIONS

Plays

Seti i lovushki. Published in *Avrora* (Leningrad), 4, 1974; as *Nets and Traps*, in *Four*, 1984; as *Nets and Snares*, in *Cinzano: Eleven Plays*, 1991.

Dva okoshka [Two Windows]. Moscow, VAAP, 1975.

Bystro khorosho ne byvaet, ili chemodan chepukhi [Things Don't Get Better Quickly, or the Suitcase of Nonsense]. Published in *Odnoaktnye p'esy*, 1978.

Prokhodite v kukhniu. Published in *Odnoaktnye p'esy*, 1979; as *Come into the Kitchen*, in *Four*, 1984.

Vse ne kak u liudei [Different from People]. Published in *Odnoaktnye komedii*, 1979.

Liubov' (produced 1980). Published in *Teatr* (Moscow), 3, 1979; as *Love*, in *Four*, 1984.

Ozelenenie [Making It Green]. Published in *Odnoaktnye p'esy*, 2, 1980.

Uroki muzyki (produced Moscow, 1983). Included in *P'esy*, 1983; as *Music Lessons*, in *Cinzano: Eleven Plays*, 1991.

Tri devushki v golubom. Published in *Sovremennaia dramaturgiia* (Moscow), 3, 1983; as *Three Girls in Blue* (produced Leeds, 1992), in *Cinzano: Eleven Plays*, 1991.

P'esy [Plays] (includes *Uroki myzyki*), with Viktor Slavkin. Moscow, Sovetskaia Rossiia, 1983.

Stakan vody (produced Moscow, 1983). As *A Glass of Water*, in *Cinzano: Eleven Plays*, 1991.

Lestnichnaia kletka. 1983; as *The Stairwell*, in *Cinzano: Eleven Plays*, 1991.

Four (includes *Love*; *Come into the Kitchen*; *Nets and Traps*; *The Violin*). New York, Institute for Contemporary Eastern European Drama and Theatre, 1984.

Kvartira Kolombiny [Columbine's Apartment] (produced Moscow, 1985).

Cinzano (produced Soviet Union, 1987; in English, Glasgow and Louisville, Kentucky, 1989). Included in *Cinzano: Eleven Plays*, 1991.

Pesni XX veka [20th-Century Songs] (includes *Uroki muzyki*; *Kvartira Kolombiny*; *Monologi*; *Temnaia komnata*). Moscow, RSFSR Union of Theatre Workers, 1988.

Andante. 1988.

Syraia noga ili vstrecha druzei. Published in *Sovremennaia dramaturgiia* (Moscow), 2, 1989; as *The Meeting*, in *Cinzano: Eleven Plays*, 1991.

Novye Robinzony: khronika XX veka [The New Robinsons: Chronicle of the Twentieth Century]. Published in *Novyi mir* (Moscow), 8, 1989.

Krokhmal' E Razmyshlenii u razbitogo koryta . . . Published in *Grani* (Frankfurt), 157, 1990.

Krokhmal' E Chernaia koshka v "temnoi komnate". Published in *Grani* (Frankfurt), 158, 1990.

Cinzano: Eleven Plays (includes *Cinzano*; *Smirnova's Birthday*; *Music Lessons*; *Three Girls in Blue*; *The Stairwell*; *Love*; *Nets and Snares*; *The Execution*; *The Meeting*; *A Glass of Water*; *Isolation Box*). London, Hern, 1991.

Fiction

Smotrovaia ploshchadka [Review Square]. Published in *Druzhba narodov* (Moscow), 1, 1982.

Cherez polia [Across the Fields]. Published in *Avrora* (Leningrad), 5, 1983.

Bessmertnaia liubov' [Undying Love]. Moscow, Moskovskii rabochii, 1988.

Svoi krug. Moscow, Pravda, 1990.

Other

Translator, *Moi chetyre kolesa*, by T. Dzhumagel'dev. Moscow, VAAP, 1975.

*

Critical Studies: "In 'Cinzano' veritas: The Plays of Liudmila Petrushevskaia" by M. T. Smith, in *Recent Polish and Soviet Theatre and Drama*, edited by J. A. Phillips, Stony Brook, New York, Slavic Culture Press, 1985; "About Brothers and Sisters, Fathers and Sons," in *Soviet Theatre*, 2, 1988, and "An Interview with Liudmila Petrushevskaya," in *Theater* (New Haven, Connecticut), 20(3), 1989, both by Victoria Vainer.

*   *   *

In Liudmila Petrushevskaia's stories and plays voices burst forth that have never been seen in print or heard on the stage in Russian before. They belong above all to Russian women — single mothers, fighting for their own and their children's very existence (*Tri devushki v golubom* [Three Girls in Blue]), young women traumatized by abortion (*Smirnova's Birthday*), proletarian punks and romantic virgins (*Uroki muzyki* [Music Lessons]), women dabbling in prostitution (*Lestnichnaia kletka* [The Stairwell]), others destroyed by it (*Takaia devochka* [That Kind of Girl], part of *Monologi*), middle-aged women struggling with their husbands' compulsive philandering (*Stakan vody* [A Glass of Water]), a terminally ill old woman communicating with her granddaughter beyond the grave (*Isolation Box*), and many more. There are male voices in Petrushevskaia — men drinking themselves unconscious (*Cinzano*), men desperate for love (*Pesni XX veka* [20th-Century Songs]), even a man condemned to death (*Syraia noga ili vstrecha druzei* [The Meeting]) — but the men are almost always idle, faithless, and egotistical. As one character puts it: "the family no longer exists. There's just the female tribe with their young ones, and lone males" (*The Stairwell*).

Most of Petrushevskaia's subjects were taboo before Mikhail Gorbachev's presidency, and collectively her work presents a damning picture of Soviet society. But she is not a perestroika playwright. Her focus is not social (or feminist). Rather, she is engrossed in the individual speech of her characters and the way in which they talk their highly detailed worlds out. *Cinzano*, for example, has been interpreted in the West as a rambling portrait of Russian alcoholism, but is in fact a very precisely paced study of a man (Pasha) struggling through words and drink to come to terms with the death of his mother earlier that day. He never tells the other two men that she has died, but through all the drunken talk about unrelated subjects one of them gradually understands, and it looks as though he will stay with Pasha until the funeral. Similarly, in *Three Girls in Blue* the women bitch and argue endlessly over living space and the behaviour of each other's children, but by the end a kind of resolution has been achieved not so much by logic as through the very act of close verbal communication. Nearly all Petrushevskaia's people live on the edge of a black hole, but miraculously as long as they can keep talking they are not sucked into it.

Monologues are prominent, then, in Petrushevskaia, but they are not of the confessional, self-indulgent type. Usually they narrate highly absorbing personal stories in a Russian that is taut, utterly individual, and full of surprises. The effect is often comic. There are few obscenities, but Petrushevskaia's command of slang and intonation is masterly. Moreover, some characters have a penchant for exotic words that verges on the fantastic: in *Three Girls in Blue* a Party careerist seriously claims he was treated in London for flu with a medicine called "Brobdingnag," and one of the girls (who seems to live by selective prostitution) says she teaches Gaelic, Manx, Welsh, and Cornish!

A particularly exhilarating feature of Petrushevskaia's theatre writing is her ability to generate a sense of play on the stage. In *Kvartira Kolombiny* (Columbine's Apartment), for example, an actress of a certain age in a Russian experimental theatre company appears to have invited a young actor (Pierrot) to her flat for a square meal and some professional advice. Brilliantly inventive dialogue develops into a seduction masquerading as an improvization of *Romeo and Juliet*, with the man playing Juliet in some of the actress's clothes. The "improvisers" are then surprised by the actress's "man," the company's director Harlequin, but he enters into the game to even more hilarious effect.

Although the departure point of Petrushevskaia's writing might be said to be Soviet "reality," it often ends in the surreal. In the closing minutes of the precisely observed *Music Lessons* one of the two rejected girlfriends produces a baby she claims was born with no head and both girls are lowered on trapezes to divebomb members of the calculating, insensitive "proletarian" family below. In *The Execution* a taxi-driver is hired to deliver two boxes — one (the head) to a crematorium, and the other (the body) to a medical institute.

The abiding reality in Petrushevskaia's work, however, is what one might call anthropological or biological. In the cultural, ethical, and economic vacuum that has been Russia, life is sustained by speech, by bewilderingly complex patterns of kinship and sexual relationships, and by the act of birth. The women live for their children. They hate abortion as the only means of contraception available to them. They grieve for the foetuses they have lost and the children who were stillborn. A man murders the family who forced their unmarried daughter to abort "his" unborn child (*The Meeting*). Sex, birth, and death are the chief preoccupations of Petrushevskaia's world. They give it an almost tribal quality, but it is a world also touched by women's love and forgiveness, by humour, and by Petrushevskaia's own deep spiritual empathy with her speakers.

—Patrick Miles

PETRUSHEVSKAYA, Lyudmila. *See* **PETRUSHEVSKAIA, Liudmila.**

PINGET, Robert. Swiss and French. Born in Geneva, 19 July 1919. Educated Collège de Genève; school of law, Geneva, law degree; École des Beaux-Arts, Paris. Practiced law, 1944–46; moved to France in 1946, and worked as painter; taught drawing and French in England. Since 1951 freelance writer in Paris. Recipient: Ford Foundation grant, 1960; Critics prize (France), 1963; Fémina prize, 1965. Address: c/o Éditions de Minuit, 7 rue Bernard-Palissy, 75006 Paris, France.

PUBLICATIONS

Fiction

Entre Fantoine et Agapa (stories). Jarnac, Tour de Feu, 1951; as *Between Fantoine and Agapa*, New York, Red Dust, 1983.
Mahu; ou, Le Matériau. Paris, Minuit, 1952; as *Mahu; or, The Material*, London, Calder and Boyars, 1966; New York, Riverrun, 1985.
Le Renard et la boussole. Paris, Gallimard, 1953.
Graal Flibuste. Paris, Minuit, 1956; revised edition, 1966.
Baga. Paris, Minuit, 1958; in English, London, Calder and Boyars, 1967; New York, Riverrun, 1985.
Le Fiston. Paris, Minuit, 1959; as *No Answer*, London, Calder, 1961; as *Monsieur Levert*, New York, Grove Press, 1961.
Clope au dossier. Paris, Minuit, 1961.
L'Inquisitoire. Paris, Minuit, 1962; as *The Inquisitory*, London, Calder and Boyars, and New York, Grove Press, 1966.
Quelqu'un. Paris, Minuit, 1965; as *Someone*, New York, Red Dust, 1984.

Le Libéra. Paris, Minuit, 1968; as *The Libera Me Domine*, London, Calder and Boyars, 1972; New York, Red Dust, 1978.
Passacaille. Paris, Minuit, 1969; as *Recurrent Melody*, London, Calder and Boyars, 1975; New York, Riverrun, 1988; as *Passacaglia*, New York, Red Dust, 1978.
Fable. Paris, Minuit, 1971; in English, London, Calder, and New York, Red Dust, 1980.
Cette Voix. Paris, Minuit, 1975; as *That Voice*, New York, Red Dust, 1982.
L'Apocryphe. Paris, Minuit, 1980; as *The Apocrypha*, New York, Red Dust, 1987.
Monsieur Songe. Paris, Minuit, 1982; in English, New York, Red Dust, 1989.
Le Harnais. Paris, Minuit, 1984.
Charrue. Paris, Minuit, 1985.
L'Ennemi. Paris, Minuit, 1987.
Du Nerf. Paris, Minuit, 1990.
Théo ou le temps neuf. Paris, Minuit, 1991.

Plays

Lettre morte, from his novel *Le Fiston* (produced Paris, 1960). Paris, Minuit, 1959; as *Dead Letter* (produced Bromley, Kent, 1961), in *Plays 1*, 1963.
La Manivelle/The Old Tune (radio play; bilingual edition; produced as play Paris, 1962). Paris, Minuit, 1960; as *The Old Tune* (produced Edinburgh, 1964; London, 1972), in *Plays 1*, 1963.
Ici ou ailleurs; Architruc; L'Hypothèse. Paris, Minuit, 1961.
Ici ou ailleurs, from his novel *Clope au dossier* (produced in German, Zurich, 1961). Included in *Ici ou ailleurs* (collection), 1961; as *Clope* (produced London, 1964), in *Plays 1*, 1963.
Architruc (produced Paris, 1962). Included in *Ici ou ailleurs* (collection), 1961; as *Architruc* (produced London, 1967), in *Plays 2*, 1967.
L'Hypothèse (produced Paris, 1965). Included in *Ici ou ailleurs* (collection), 1961; as *The Hypothesis* (produced London, 1967), in *Plays 2*, 1967.
Plays 1 (includes *The Old Tune*; *Clope*; *Dead Letter*). London, Calder, 1963; as *Three Plays*, New York, Hill and Wang, 1966.
Autour de Mortin (radio play). Paris, Minuit, 1965; as *About Mortin*), in *Plays 2*, 1967.
Plays 2 (includes *Architruc*; *The Hypothesis*; *About Mortin*). London, Calder and Boyars, 1967; as *Three Plays*, New York, Hill and Wang, 1968.
Identité (produced Paris, 1972). With *Abel et Bela*, 1971.
Abel et Bela (produced Paris, 1971). With *Identité*, 1971; as *Abel and Bela*, New York, Red Dust, 1987.
Identité; Abel et Bela. Paris, Minuit, 1971.
Paralchimie; Architruc; L'Hypothèse; Nuit. Paris, Minuit, 1973.
Lubie (radio play). Published in *Présence Francophone 22*, Spring 1981; Paris, Minuit, 1986.
Un Testament bizarre; Mortin pas mort; Dictée; Sophisme et sadisme; Le Chrysanthème; Lubie. Paris, Minuit, 1986; *Un Testament bizarre* published as *A Bizarre Will*, New York, Red Dust, 1989.

Other

Cette Chose, with Jean Deyrolle. Paris, Deyrolle, 1990.

*

Critical Studies: "Robert Pinget's Agapa Land" by Marilyn G. Rose, in *Forum* (Houston), 8(1), 1970; "The House Metaphor in Pinget's *The Inquisitory*" in *Critique* (Washington, D.C.), 14(3), 1972, and *Robert Pinget: The Novel as Quest*, University, University of Alabama Press, 1979, both by Robert M. Henkels, Jr.; "A New Mode of Reading: Pinget's *Passacaille*" by Peter Broome, in *Nottingham French Studies*, 12, 1973; "Scoring Twice: Pinget's *La Manivelle* and Beckett's *The Old Tune*" by Clas Zilliacus, in *Moderna Språk* (Stockholm), 68, 1974; "Pinget's Fable, récit: An Allegory in the Style of the New, New Novel" by Enid G. Marantz, in *20th-Century Literature* (Hempstead, New York), 23, 1977; "Fiction Under Interrogation: Pinget's *L'Inquisitoire*" by Beverly Livingston, in *Romanic Review* (New York), May 1981; Pinget issue of *Review of Contemporary Fiction* (Elmwood Park, Illinois), Summer 1983; "Robert Pinget's Polyvalent Use of Parody in *Abel et Bela*, *Identité*, and *Nuit*" by Germaine Bavil, in *Degré Second* (Blacksburg, Virginia), July 1983; "Pinget's *Passacaille*: The Endless Sonata of the Dead" by Victor Carrabino, in *Neophil*, January 1985; "The Force of Consciousness: A Study of Pinget's *Passacaille* and *Fable*" by J. P. Szarka, in *Nottingham French Studies*, June 1987; "Pinget's Others" by Anthony Cheal, in *Paragraph* (Cambridge), March 1989.

*   *   *

Robert Pinget's is one of the most distinctive voices of the so-called French "new novel": an explorer of forms and patterns within the partial vacuum that has been left, in what Nathalie Sarraute (*q.v.*) calls our "era of suspicion," by the collapse of faith in many of the inherited conventions of fiction. No one could better illustrate the novel as insecurity, as abolished definition: the text cut adrift from its traditional supports and comforting illusions, with its author/writer/ scribe seeking to establish a footing, a purpose, and a justification in the swirling potentialities and impotences of language, as it vainly aspires to something higher or more durable than itself. Pinget's earliest works *Entre Fantoine et Agapa* (*Between Fantoine and Agapa*) and *Mahu; ou, Le Matériau* (*Mahu; or, The Material*) evoke the perplexed and paradoxical situation of the artist, seeking truth through falsehood, querying the limits and hypothetical virtues of his fictions, wondering how and to what extent he can identify with them, found a personal value within them. They are symptomatic of a fictional crisis where the would-be writer, having jettisoned the irrelevant paraphernalia of an outworn or discredited system, now arrives in a place of doubt: where all the pitfalls and deceptions of authorship and readership open before him, where creative freedom is more an abyss than an adventure, and where the only viable raw material left to him is not the "real" stuff of life, the servant of some misguided notion of "realism," but the revolving patterns of language itself indulging, perhaps gratuitously, in its pure inventions and linguistic play.

Pinget's work shows, not "man-in-his-acts" as seen in the existentialist era of André Malraux, Jean-Paul Sartre, or Albert Camus, but "man-in-his-language": a more introverted subject, perhaps, but one which poses the same fundamental questions of human definition in the absence of transcendent values and the corrosive underlying presence of death. His novels investigate words and the void behind words, words on the loose, having lost their one-to-one relationship with anything. One is made aware of words and their runaway, renegade nature, and that all language is a kind of discrepancy of language, doomed to the peripheral and the centrifugal. As language does its best to cope with the elusive, multi-layered nature of reality, it seems to be never far from a state of breakdown (hence the breakdown van, which may have nothing but a verbal existence, which recurrently traverses the text of *Passacaille* [*Recurrent Melody*]). Pinget's narrators — if one can isolate them clearly as narrators, so much does their role shade into those of character, reader, and listener — are like a sorcerer's apprentice manipulating an instrument beyond their control. They cannot stop using it, causing it to proliferate, to exercise itself *ad infinitum*, fictionalizing itself as it goes, erasing itself as truth, but without which there would be nothing but the encroachments of a deathly silence. The theme of the missing manuscript runs strongly through Pinget's writing: a kind of textual abyss, an inaccessible myth of completeness, invalidating or at least relativizing the formations of the actual text secreted on to the page. So too does the idea of correspondence which never reaches its destination, to the extent that one wonders if it was actually written or only conjectured. So, one is caught in a limbo of language, a strangely disorientating but fascinating, and at times hauntingly beautiful, zone of absence and presence.

The traditional mainstays of the novel — recognizable characters, the contours of plot, and the stabilizing framework of time and space — are almost non-existent in Pinget's works. Though many of his characters have memorable names and recur from work to work as if they had some hypertextual transcendence, they seem to be vanishing silhouettes or disembodied voices, lacking identifying features, disturbingly interchangeable, tentatively stitched together with aberrant words, not compact enough to hold them together or keep them apart: a hollow, porous "I" (or several superimposed and blurring each other) grappling with the hydra of the impossible autobiography. Plot, such as it exists, is made largely of hearsay and hypothesis, rarely materializing as fact. It is erratic and disrupted, branching into detours, variants, and alternative versions, and therefore undermining its own solidity as it advances. Time becomes a jumbled chronology, a defiant metamorphosis, a succession of uncontrollable expansions and contractions, a shuttle service obeying no fixed hours; while space, though familiar from book to book in that they are often set in the same village or country area, with recurrent place names and recognizable landmarks, seems to fluctuate to mental rhythms and textual accidents.

Jean Roudaut has divided Pinget's writing into three broad phases, which he calls, with an appropriate degree of tentativeness, "pseudo-cycles." The first, including *Mahu*, *Graal Flibuste* (Grail Freebooter), and *Baga*, is the period of fantasy, parody, absurdist invention, humorous surrealistic effect. The second, including *L'Inquisitoire* (*The Inquisitory*), *Autour de Mortin* (*About Mortin*), and *Quelqu'un* (*Someone*), moves into a more earnest, probing confrontation with language, from quest to inquest, using interviews and dialogues to track the obscurities and resistances of the verbal process. The third, stretching from *Le Libéra* (*The Libera Me Domine*), *Recurrent Melody*, *Fable*, and *Cette Voix* (*That Voice*) onwards, allows words themselves to pursue their permutations and arabesques, their butterfly forms, their intricate and lovely flightpaths, weaving and unweaving mirages of meaning before the reader's eye. But, through all these evolutions, the broad characteristics and preoccupations are the same. They are too in Pinget's plays, *Lettre morte* (*Dead Letter*), *La Manivelle* (*The Old Tune*) or *L'Hypothèse* (*The Hypothesis*): a minimal theatre reminiscent of that of Beckett, with its semi-derelicts in harness, failed dialogues on different wavelengths, absurdities of language, treacheries of memory, threatened identities and gulfs of silence.

A main difference between Pinget's world and that of a "new novelist" like Alain Robbe-Grillet (*q.v.*) with his so-called "école du regard" (school of the look) is that Pinget is concerned with the "school of hearing": listening for tones of voice, the authenticity of spoken language, the "live" snatches of everyday gossip and cliché. And in this way, although his work may seem to risk dissolving into a fluidity of tenuous, inconclusive sonorities, it acquires an almost naturalistic realism, a common touch, a distinctly human appeal.

It is also a work of great humour, ranging from the tongue-in-cheek sagas of *Baga* and *Mahu*, to outrageous inventiveness in *Graal Flibuste*, to the comic slips, discrepancies, errors, and misapprehensions of language as it goes off the track, to a deeper self-contemplating, self-eroding irony.

Far from being an abstract, technical exercise, haunted by the narcissism of language looking simply at itself, Pinget's work gives the deepest, most poignant insight into the pains and dilemmas of human communication in the face of time and death, as his latest works *L'Ennemi* (The Enemy) and *Théo ou le temps neuf* (Theo or Time Anew) intuitively illustrate.

—Peter Broome

PIÑÓN, Nélida. Brazilian. Born in Rio de Janeiro, May 1936. Educated at a German Colégio; Faculty of Philosophy, Pontífica Universidade Católica, Rio de Janeiro. Taught at Federal University of Rio de Janeiro, Columbia University, New York, Johns Hopkins University, Baltimore, Maryland, and University of Miami. Former vice president, Sindicato de Escritores. Recipient: Castelao Medal; Galícia Medal. Elected to Ordem do Cruzeiro do Sul, and Lazo de Dama de Isabel La Católica; member, Brazilian Academy, since 1989. Agent: Agencia Carmen Balcells, Diagonal 580, 08021 Barcelona, Spain. Address: Av. Rodolfo Amoedo, 418 apto. 201, Barra da Tijuca, 22620 Rio de Janeiro, Brazil.

PUBLICATIONS

Fiction

Guia mapa de Gabriel Arcanjo.   Rio de Janeiro, G.R.D., 1961.
Madeira Feita Cruz.   Rio de Janeiro, G.R.D., 1963.
Tempo das frutas.   Rio de Janeiro, Álvaro, 1966.
Fundador.   Rio de Janeiro, Álvaro, 1969.
A casa da paixão.   Rio de Janeiro, Mário de Andrade, 1972.
Sala de armas.   Rio de Janeiro, Sabiá, 1973.
Tebas do meu coração.   Rio de Janeiro, Olympio, 1974.
A força do destino.   Rio de Janeiro, Record, 1977.
O calor das coisas.   Rio de Janeiro, Nova Fronteira, 1980.
A república dos sonhos.   Rio de Janeiro, Alveo, 1984; as *The Republic of Dreams*, New York, Knopf, 1989.
A doce canção de Caetana.   Rio, Guanabara, 1987; as *Caetana's Sweet Song*, New York, Knopf, 1992.

*

Critical Study: "Note on the Fiction of Nelida Piñon" by Giovanni Pontiero, in *Review* (New York), 19, 1976.

*   *   *

Until fairly recently, Nélida Piñón was one of Brazil's hidden treasures: revered and acclaimed at home but little known beyond the borders except to specialists of Brazilian literature and to admiring fellow writers such as Gabriel García Márquez and Mario Vargas Llosa (*qq.v.*) (who dedicated *La guerra del fin del mundo* [*The War of the End of the World*] [1981] to her). Like her friend and compatriot Clarice Lispector, Nélida Piñón had already produced a considerable body of work before attaining international recognition but, unlike Lispector, Piñón's accomplishments are being widely recognized during her lifetime, principally in France, Spain, and most recently in the United States.

Although Piñón's eight novels and three collections of short stories are mostly set in and interwoven with the reality of 20th-century Brazil, they are nonetheless universal and timeless in their poetically piercing depiction of the "human adventure" in its myriad manifestations. Piñón's style is a masterful blend of metaphor and myth, archetypes and illusions, dreams and political realities. She combines a vivid sense of history (European as well as Brazilian) with a keen understanding of contemporary politics and a deep commitment to human rights, then proceeds to season the mixture with dozens of different spices. These include an early and rich exposure to music, theatre, and opera; the viewpoint of a Galician immigrant's daughter eager to understand her dual patrimony; an attunement to the psychological forces underlying human relationships; an imaginary world that encompasses simultaneously a variety of spatial and temporal realities. Piñón's style is rich in form and content; each sentence is carefully crafted with little regard for traditional rules of syntax. "The gerund is the verb form of America," she declared in a recent interview: ". . . it mobilizes sentiments," seducing author and reader alike. The originality of Piñón's use of language, her love affair with the human voice, is inevitably linked to the Brazilian Portuguese language in which she writes, but her carefully chosen translators have succeeded in transferring many of the nuances of her enchantingly luminous style into French, Spanish, and English.

Within her own country Piñón's recognition as a singular voice in Brazilian letters came with the publication of her first novel, *Guia mapa de Gabriel Arcanjo* (Guide Map of Gabriel Archangel) in 1961. Her first collection of short stories, *Tempo das frutas* (Season of Fruits), introduces a type of character, the distracted or absent-minded woman, who remained a hallmark of Piñón's fiction until *A república dos sonhos* (The Republic of Dreams). Piñón calls these women "modest and silent guerrillas." Unable to lose themselves in the social practices of daily life to which society would relegate them, they invalidate that reality in a very revolutionary manner that "contaminates" the consciousness of those around them, especially the men in their lives. In "I Love my Husband" from *O calor das coisas* (The Heat of Things), the protagonist experiences her marriage with silent irony. In her interior monologue we find the allegory of a woman who, by defining her oppression ironically, in the words of Sara Castro-Klarén (1991), "widens the cracks in the social structures that had so far bound and blindfolded her life."

Although she does not consider herself to be one, Piñón, like many feminists, depicts and celebrates feminine *jouissance* or sexual fulfillment. In *A casa da páixao* (The House of Passion), her beautifully erotic novel of a young girl's awakening to the consciousness of her own body and its potential for passion, Piñón's four characters are archetypal figures living out primordial relationships. As Naomi Hoki Moniz stated in a 1984 article, "[in this novel Piñón] presents a rare allegorical image of the search for the masculine/ feminine essence in its most profound aspect, as well as suggesting a revision of sexual politics."

Desire and vengeance are the passions celebrated in *A força do destino* (The Force of Destiny). Based on Verdi's opera, the novel is transformed by the addition of one character, Piñón herself. Through an ironic goading of Verdi's characters, and an invitation to the reader/spectator to participate in the novelistic creation, Piñón puts into contemporary perspective her youthful appreciation for the magnificence of Verdi's opera as sung by Renata Tebaldi in a "parodic exaltation" that counterbalances reality and melodrama.

The Republic of Dreams, Piñón's first novel to be translated into English, is her masterwork to date. This saga of four generations of a Brazilian family from its Galician roots at the turn of the century to the present time has been compared to García-Márquez's *Cien años de soledad* (*One Hundred Years of Solitude*) (1967) and *La casa de los espiritus* (*The House of the Spirits*) (1982) by Isabel Allende (*q.v.*). The two central figures are the patriarch Madruga, who arrives in Brazil as a young man in search of a fortune, and Venâncio, a dreamer and skeptic whom he meets on the voyage and who, despite their opposing views on practically everything, remains his lifelong friend. The archetype of the self-made man, Madruga is also the depository of the legends of Galicia passed on to him by his grandfather Xan. These he will in turn bequeath, not to any of his four children who view him with varying degrees of fear, greed, and loathing, but to his granddaughter Breta, the female protagonist and future storyteller. Loosely circumscribed on one level by the week that lapses between the time that Madruga's wife Eulalia announces her imminent death and her funeral ceremonies, the narrative actually spans more than 80 years. Moving back and forth across the Atlantic, backwards and forwards through several decades of time, and related by three distinct narrative voices, this chronicle presents, in Piñón's own words, "the dream of Brazil seen by immigrants from outside, [and] inside . . . a corrupted and degraded dream marked by disillusionment." Piñón's language resonates with poetry and metaphor as she searches the far reaches of collective memory to explain Brazil's European legacy and its existential reality, ". . . to explain my country to myself."

In her latest book, *A doce canção de Caetana* (*Caetana's Sweet Song*), Piñón returns to a theatrical, operatic setting. A wealthy small-town cattle rancher, Polidoro, does his best to grant the dearest wish of his former mistress, Caetana, an itinerant actress who suddenly reappears after an absence of 20 years. Caetana wants, for one night, to sing like her idol Maria Callas. Polidoro provides her with a theatre, an audience, and the illusion of greatness, but disaster strikes and Caetana disappears once again. Colorful, humorous, and passionate, the novel is a symbolic portrayal, on several levels, of what Piñón calls "the aging of dreams."

In her recreation of language and syntax, the singularity of her style, and the poetic richness of her imagery, Nélida Piñón continues to incarnate the statement she made in an interview 20 years ago, "Si admito límites, cancelo la creación" (If I were to recognize limitations, I would abort creation).

—Celita Lamar

PIRES, José Cardoso. *See* **CARDOSO PIRES, José.**

POIRIER, Louis. *See* **GRACQ, Julien.**

PONIATOWSKA (Amor), Elena. Mexican. Born in Paris, 19 May 1933; brought to Mexico at the age of eight. Educated at Liceo de México, one year; Convent of the Sacred Heart's Eden Hall, Torresdale, Pennsylvania, two years; Manhattanville College, Bronx, New York. Married Guillermo Haro (died 1988); two sons and one daughter. Member of staff, *Excelsior*, 1954–55, and *Novedades*, Mexico City, since 1955; member of editorial board, *fem.* feminist journal. Co-founder, Editorial Siglo Veintiuno, Cineteca Nacional Mexican film library, and Taller Literario; teacher at Injuve. Recipient: Centro de Escritores fellowship, 1957; Turismo Francés prize, 1965; Mazatlán prize, 1970; Xavier Villaurrutia prize, 1970 (refused); *Revista Siempre* prize, 1973; National Journalism prize, 1979. D.H.C.: University of Sinaloa. Address: Cerrada del Pedregal 79, Coyoacán, Z.P. 21, Mexico City, Mexico.

PUBLICATIONS

Fiction

Lilus Kikus.   Mexico City, Los Presentes, 1954.
Los cuentos de Lilus Kikus.   Xalapa, Universidad Veracruzana, 1967.
Hasta no verte, Jesús mío.   Mexico City, Era, 1969; as *Until We Meet Again*, New York, Pantheon, 1987.
Querido Diego, te abraza Quiela.   Mexico City, Era, 1978; as *Dear Diego*, New York, Pantheon, 1986.
De noche vienes.   Mexico City, Grijalbo, 1979.
La "Flor de Lís".   Mexico City, Era, 1988.
Tinísima.   Mexico City, Era, 1992.

Plays

Melés y teleo: a puntes para una comedia.   Published in *Revista Panoramas* (Mexico City), 2, Summer 1956.

Screenplay: *Hasta no verte, Jesus mio*.

Other

Palabras cruzadas: crónicas.   Mexico City, Era, 1961.
Todo empezó el domingo.   Mexico City, Fondo de Cultura Económica, 1963.
México visto a ojo de pájaro.   Mexico City, Colibrí/SEP, 1968.
La noche de Tlatelolco: testimonios de historia oral.   Mexico City, Era, 1971; as *Massacre in Mexico*, New York, Viking, 1975.
La vendedora de nubes.   Mexico City, Colibrí, 1979.

Gaby Brimmer, with Gaby Brimmer.   Mexico City, Grijalbo, 1979.

Fuerte es el silencio.   Mexico City, Era, 1980.

La casa en la tierra, photographs by Mariana Yampolsky.   Mexico City, INI-Fonapas, 1980.

Domingo siete.   Mexico City, Océano, 1982.

El último guajolote.   Mexico City, Fondo Cultura Económica, 1982.

¡Ay vida, no me mereces!: Carlos Fuentes, Rosario Castellanos, Juan Rulfo, la literatura de la onda.   Mexico City, Mortiz, 1985.

La raíz y el camino, illustrated by Mariana Yampolsky.   Mexico City, Fondo de Cultura Económica, 1985.

Estancias del olvido, photographs by Marian Yampolsky.   Mexico City, INI-Centro Hidalguense de Investigaciones Históricas, 1986.

Serena y alta figura.   Mexico City, Océano, 1986.

Tlacotalpan, photographs by Marian Yampolsky.   Mexico City, n.p., 1987.

Hablando en plata, with David Maawad.   Mexico City, Centro Hidalguense de Investigaciones Históricas, 1987.

México sin retoque, with Héctor García.   Mexico City, Universidad Nacional Autónoma de México, 1987.

Nada, nadie: las voces del tremblor.   Mexico City, Era, 1988.

Juchitán de las mujeres, with Graciela Iturbide.   Mexico City, Toledo, 1989.

Compañeras de México.   Riverside, University of California, 1990.

*

Bibliography: in *Mexican Literature: A Bibliography of Secondary Sources* by David William Foster, Metuchen, New Jersey, Scarecrow Press, 1992.

Critical Studies: "Elena Poniatowska's *Hasta no verte, Jesús mío*" by Charles M. Tatum, in *Latin American Women Writers: Yesterday and Today*, Pittsburgh, Latin American Literary Review Press, 1977: "Interview with Elena Poniatowska" by Grace M. Bearse, in *Hispania* (Los Angeles), 64, 1981; "Breaking the Silence: Elena Poniatowska, Writer in Transition," in *Literatures in Transition: The Many Voices of the Caribbean Area: A Symposium*, Gaithersburg, Maryland, Hispanamérica, 1982, and "Elena Poniatowska: Witness for the People," in *Contemporary Women Authors of Latin America*, Brooklyn, Brooklyn College Press, 1983, both by Elizabeth D. Starčević; "Elena Poniatowska: The Feminist Origins of Commitment," in *Women's Studies International Forum* (Elmsford, New York), 6(5), 1983, and "Subverting the Dominant Text: Elena Poniatowska's *Querido Diego*," in *Knives and Angels: Women Writers in Latin America*, edited by Susan Bassnett, London, Zed, 1990, both by Juan Bruce-Novoa; "Elena Poniatowska's *Hasta no verte, Jesús mío*: The Remaking of the Image of Women" by Joel Hancock, in *Hispania* (Los Angeles), 66(3), 1983; "The New Journalism in Mexico: Two Women Writers" by Dolly J. Young and William D. Young, in *Chasqui* (Provo, Utah), 12(2–3), 1983; "Visions of Women: Symbolic Physical Portrayal as Social Commentary in the Short Fiction of Elena Poniatowska" by Mónica Flori, in *Third Woman* (Berkeley, California), 2(2), 1984; "The Transformation of Privilege in the Work of Elena Poniatowska" by Bell Gale Chevigny, in *Latin American Literary Review* (Pittsburgh), 26, 1985; "An Invitation to Understanding Among Poor Women of the Americas: *The Color Purple* and *Hasta no verte, Jesús mío*" by Lisa Davis, in *Reinventing the Americas: Comparative Studies of Literature in the United States and Spanish America*, New York, Cambridge University Press, 1986; "The Marginated Narrator: *Hasta no verte, Jesús mío* and the Eloquence of Repression" by Edward H. Friedman, in his *The Antiheroine's Voice: Narrative Discourse and Transformations of the Picaresque*, Columbia, University of Missouri Press, 1987; "Invention, Convention, and Autobiography in Elena Poniatowska's *Querido Diego, te abrazo Quiela*" by John Berry, in *Confluencia* (Greeley, Colorado), 3(2), 1988.

*   *   *

Born in France with French as her first language, Elena Poniatowska came to Mexico at the age of eight. Her position as an outsider in Mexican society has given her freedom as both an observer and a writer, and she has used it to great effect in her works. She has been most influential in her books of testimony which have shown the continuing oppression and poverty which characterize the lives of many in Mexico, especially women from the lower classes.

Out of her work as a journalist, Poniatowska has written several books of oral history in which the raw material from her interviewees is shaped and given a meaningful framework by the author. In *Gaby Brimmer*, for example, Poniatowska tells the story of a woman's struggle with cerebral palsy, based on interviews with the woman's mother and nanny as well as direct correspondence with her. The result is a mixture of voices which amply conveys the drama and potential richness of one woman's life as she struggles against adversity.

More wide-ranging books of oral history are *La noche de Tlatelolco* (*Massacre in Mexico*), which deals with the 1968 student movement that culminated in a massacre of hundreds of students by troops in Tlatelolco square in the capital, and *Nada, nadie* (Nothing, Nobody), which concerns the 1985 earthquake in Mexico City and the grassroots organizations that sprang up afterwards to try to rebuild the thousands of lives shattered by the disaster. Once again Poniatowska's concern is for the victims, whose views she portrays in a series of voices linked by an unobtrusive editorial voice. Out of the juxtaposition of witnesses' views, newspaper reports, police files, official speeches, and other material which includes extracts from indigenous chronicles on the conquest of Mexico by the Spaniards, Poniatowska conveys much of the complexity surrounding a single historical event. *Massacre in Mexico* is still regarded by many as Poniatowska's finest achievement.

In addition however, she has written several novels, which also have their starting points in true stories. Her first novel, *Hasta no verte, Jesús mío* (*Until We Meet Again*), originated from interviews with a woman resident of one of Mexico City's slums. The protagonist Jesusa tells of the hard life she has led since being born with the century in 1900, and Poniatowska manages skilfully to convey her strength, independence, and contradictions with subtle conviction.

Her next novel, *Querido Diego, te abraza Quiela* (*Dear Diego*), consists of 12 letters written to the famous Mexican painter Diego Rivera by a lover, Quiela. Although the pair were in fact lovers in Paris for almost a decade, the letters are fictional. As the critic Beth E. Jorgensen has written: "Quiela arouses both sympathy and impatience in the reader as she fluctuates between attempts at self-affirmation through her own painting and her self-destructive obsession with Diego, a godlike figure of power and creativity."

A further novel, *La "Flor de Lis"* (The "Fleur de Lis"), turns directly to autobiographical material. The heroine is born in France and brought to Mexico at the age of nine. Poniatowska here presents an effective portrait of the growth of a powerful if confused consciousness, which ends with a movement towards liberty and an acceptance of the risks that a closer involvement with the struggles of her time entails.

Poniatowska has returned to Mexico history for the central character of her latest novel, the 500-page *Tinísima*. It centres on the life and revolutionary times of the Italian photographer Tina Modotti, who like Diego Rivera was part of the left-wing artistic avant-garde in Mexico several decades ago. In *Tinísima* Poniatowska is again concerned to portray the development of consciousness in a strong, talented woman.

In giving a voice to women and the dispossessed of Mexican society, Poniatowska has opened important spaces for writing in Mexico and thus encouraged both journalists and other writers of fiction.

—Nick Caistor

————

PRISCO, Michele. Italian. Born in Torre Annunziata, 18 January 1920. Educated at the University of Naples, law degree 1942. Served in the Scuola Allievi Ufficiali di Complemento, 1942–43. Married Sarah Buonomo in 1951; two daughters. Freelance writer; journalist, *Risorgimento* and *Nuovo Corriere*; founding director, *Le Ragioni Narrative*, Naples, 1961–62. Vice president, National Union of Writers, 1960–69. Recipient: Venice prize, 1950; Cervia prize, 1960; Naples prize, 1962; Sardinia prize, 1968; Hemingway prize, 1985; Verga prize, 1985; Fiuggi prize, 1985. Address: Via Stazio 8, 80122 Naples, Italy.

PUBLICATIONS

Fiction

La provincia addormentata. Milan, Mondadori, 1949; revised edition, Milan, Rizzoli, 1969.
Gli eredi del vento. Milan, Rizzoli, 1950; as *Heirs to the Wind*, London, Verschoyle, 1953.
Figli difficili. Milan, Rizzoli, 1954.
Fuochi a mare. Milan, Rizzoli, 1957.
La dama di piazza. Milan, Rizzoli, 1961.
Punto franco. Milan, Rizzoli, 1965.
Una spirale di nebbia. Milan, Rizzoli, 1966; as *A Spiral of Mist*, New York, Dutton, and London, Chatto and Windus, 1969.
I cieli della sera. Milan, Rizzoli, 1970.
Inventario della memoria. Milan, Rizzoli, 1970.
Gli ermellini neri. Milan, Rizzoli, 1975.
Il colore del cristallo. Milan, Rizzoli, 1977.
Le parole del silenzio. Milan, Rizzoli, 1981.
Lo specchio cieco. Milan, Rizzoli, 1984.
I giorni della conchiglia. Milan, Rizzoli, 1989.

Other

Il romanzo italiano contemporaneo. Florence, Cesati, 1983.
La porta segreta (for children). Turin, Società Editrice Internazionale, 1986.

*

Critical Study: Prisco issue of *Italian Quarterly* (New Brunswick, New Jersey), 29, 1988.

*   *   *

Born in Torre Annunziata, Naples in 1920, Michele Prisco has made the south, and in particular his part of the south, the focus of his fiction. But Prisco is not a "regional" writer in the traditional sense. Nor is he a new realist, though his first works were published when Neo-Realism was flourishing: he does not use dialect in his fiction, there are no emotive descriptions of poverty, nor does his writing carry any hint of overt political commitment to change. Naples or other southwestern Italian towns figure repeatedly in his novels and stories, but the narrative techniques are European, deriving from, and in his later work, interrogating the naturalist and psychological traditions. The influences on his work are extensive: among them, 19th-century European fiction (Giacinto Spagnoletti, in his essay on Prisco in *Letteratura italiana: i contemporanei*, 1974, has called particular attention to the English novel and Gustave Flaubert), Marcel Proust, Matilde Serao, Walt Whitman, Katherine Mansfield, Jorge Luis Borges. Writing when the *nouveau roman* was in vogue, and when it was fashionable to be difficultly experimental, Prisco defended his own form of innovation in an interview published in *Ragguaglio librario* (December 1971): his was a stylistic experimentation, he argued, that gave attention to the manipulation of point of view, emphasis to the inner life of his characters, and investigated the workings of memory. In the past novelists made spectators of their readers, whereas now the tendency was to make them into collaborators, he wrote; his aim was other — to "immerse the reader in the page." To this end Prisco has concentrated on evolving a style of long, slowly unfolding sentences, quite often containing phrases in parentheses which draw attention to psychological details, textures, nuances of sound, and play of light. The reader becomes enfolded in that reality, or semblance of reality, which Prisco seems to want to caress with his prose.

In fact, perhaps more than any other writer of his time, Prisco's writing seems engendered by love: affection for place, a loving search for that elusive reality which hovers tantalisingly before him (an important motif that becomes more dominant in his later work), and a deep commitment to words and syntax. In each novel there are clear themes: *La dama di piazza* (The Society Woman), for instance, is an almost sociological analysis of social climbing during the interwar years in Naples: in *Una spirale di nebbia* (A Spiral of Mist), matrimonial incompatibility suggests a plea for divorce, before divorce was an available option in Italy; in *Lo specchio cieco* (The Blind Mirror), Prisco depicts the gradual emergence of the middle-class southern woman as an autonomous person, and his most recent novel *I giorni della conchiglia* (The Days of the Shell) investigates the question of personal identity. Running through them all, however, is the theme of the impossibility of epistemological clarity in the quietly insistent questioning of the nature of truth.

In each of his novels there is an element of *giallo*, the Italian term for detective story, that contributes to the reader's pleasure in the text but also conveys without ostentation, through its inability to come to a water-tight solution, the failure of rationality and the claims of the Enlightenment to offer an adequate version of reality, let alone the truth. At the beginning of *A Spiral of Mist*, Fabrizio Sangermano, on holiday with his wife and children near Naples, is seen one Sunday afternoon bringing back the body of his wife Valeria, killed by a gunshot. Was she murdered, or was it an accident? In *I cieli della sera* (The Evening Skies) the first-person narrator David is drawn back to his native area in the vicinity of Vesuvius to find out how and why his parents died. In *Lo specchio cieco* attention is focussed on how Margherita Attanasio changed from an insignificant, oppressed, and servile creature into an attractive and competent businesswoman. In *I giorni della conchiglia* the detective story motif is given a different orientation, more in the manner of an Ibsen play: the first-person narrator is undergoing psychoanalysis during the course of the story, but it is a long time before the reader is allowed to know why. However, Prisco's major interest is not in looking afresh at the "who dunnit," but in giving expression to the contingent and the symbolic, in attempting to catch in a meticulously crafted prose the details of that reality which he knows can have no linguistic expression. Unlike some other writers whose writing yields a similar theme (Luigi Pirandello, Italo Calvino, and Jorge Luis Borges come to mind) Prisco is not a ludic writer: his fiction conveys a melancholy celebration of life's textures rather than an exuberant fascination with game-playing.

In contrast too with some other southern Italian writers Prisco peoples his fiction predominantly with the moderately wealthy bourgeoisie. Working-class people are usually present as servants in affluent households. Nor are the middle classes presented satirically or with any tendency to grotesque caricature, as, for instance, other writers might have made of the police officer Nicola Mazzù in *Gli eredi del vento* (*Heirs to the Wind*); the lives, thoughts, and feelings of the middle class are taken seriously. Even in more panoramic novels, in particular, *La dama di piazza* (The Society Woman) in which Prisco employs a narrative form where the fiction is historically placed with careful detail in the 20 years between the two world wars, the emphasis is on the effect of the historical events only when they touch individual characters' lives. In this respect, Prisco is a conservative novelist, and has become increasingly so over the years. His attention has always been focussed on the family but in earlier fiction, for example in the short stories of his first published volume *La provincia addormentata* (The Sleeping Province), and in *Fuochi a mare* (Fires at Sea), the characters were drawn from a wider social sphere. Yet his experimental concern with the form of the novel remains unabated. Prisco's is a lone, original, and distinctive voice, at its best when maintaining and renewing the tradition of the European psychological novel.

—Jennifer Lorch

PRITAM, Amritā. Indian (Panjabi). Born in 1919. Married at age 16 (separated 1960); one daughter and one son. Worked for All-India Radio, Lahore, and Delhi Radio. Editor, *Nāgmaṇi* Panjabi monthly, from 1966; member of Executive Committee, Sāhitya Akādemī, 1968–73. Recipient: Sāhitya Akādemī award, 1956; Bhārtīy Jñānpīṭh award, 1981; Padmaśrī. D. Litt.: University of Delhi, 1973. Nominated member, Rājya Sabha (Upper House), since 1986. Address: c/o Vikas Publishing House, 5 Ansari Road, Daryaganj, New Delhi 110002, India.

PUBLICATIONS

Fiction

Chabbī varhe bād [26 Years Later]. 1943.
Kuñjiyā [A Bunch of Keys]. 1944.

Jai Śrī. 1946.
Daktar Dev [Dr. Dev]. 1949.
Piñjar [Skeleton]. 1950.
Ālhaṇā [The Nest]. New Delhi, Navyug, 1952.
Aśū. New Delhi, Navyug, 1958.
Ik savāl [A Question]. New Delhi, Navyug, 1959.
Bulāvā [The Call]. New Delhi, Navyug, 1960.
Band darvāzā [Closed Door]. New Delhi, Navyug, 1961.
Canan dā hauka [The Sigh of Light]. 1962.
Raṅg dā pattā [Trump Card]. 1963.
Ik sī Anītā [Once There Was an Anita]. New Delhi, Navyug, 1964.
Cakknambar chattī [Village Number 36]. 1964; as *A Line in Water*, New Delhi, Arnold Heinemann, 1975.
Dhartī, sāgar te sippiyā [Earth, Sea, and Shells]. New Delhi, Navyug, 1965.
Nāgmaṇi [The Jewel in the Snake's Hood] (in Hindi). New Delhi, Hind Pocket Books, 1967.
Eskimo Smile. 1967.
Dillī diyā galiyā [Delhi Lanes]. New Delhi, Navyug, 1968.
Ekte te Aerial. 1968; as *The Aerial, and Other Stories*, Calcutta, United Writers, 1978.
Jilāvatan [The Exiled]. 1968.
Ajnabī [Stranger]. New Delhi, Navyug, 1970.
Ākharī rāt [The Last Night]. New Delhi, Navyug, 1970.
Pañj varhe lambī saṛak [A Five-Year-Long Road]. New Delhi, Nāgmaṇi, 1971.
Yātrī [Traveller]. New Delhi, Nāgmaṇi, 1971.
Jebkatre [Pickpockets]. 1971; as *Flirting with Youth*, New Delhi, Sterling, 1973.
Ag dā būṭā [The Fire Plant]. 1972.
Pakkī havelī [The Mansion]. New Delhi, Nāgmaṇi, 1972.
Do raṅg [Two Colours] (in Hindi). New Delhi, Hind Book Centre, 1974.
Ag dī lakīr [A Line of Fire]. New Delhi, Nāgmaṇi, 1974.
Kaccī saṛak [Unpaved Road]. New Delhi, Nāgmaṇi, 1975.
Unkī kahānī [Their Story]. New Delhi, Star Publications, 1975.
Koī nahī jāndā. New Delhi, Nāgmaṇi, 1975; as *Nobody Knows*, with *Time and Beyond* (2 short novels), New Delhi, Himalay Books, 1977.
Yahā kahā nahī hai [Nowhere Here] (in Hindi). New Delhi, Parāg, 1976.
Akṣarō kī chāyā mē [In the Shadow of Letters] (in Hindi). New Delhi, Parāg, 1977.
Hīre dī kani [Diamond Earrings]. New Delhi, Nāgmaṇi, 1977.
Ih sac hai aur Dūsrī manzil [One Is True, and Another Aim]. New Delhi, Nāgmaṇi, 1977; as *A Statement of Agony*, New Delhi, Vision, 1979.
Latīā dī chokrī. New Delhi, Nāgmaṇi, 1977.
Terahvā sūraj [The Thirteenth Sun]. New Delhi, Nāgmaṇi, 1978.
Tīsrī aurat [The Third Woman]. New Delhi, Nāgmaṇi, 1978.
Unīñjā din [The Forty-Ninth Day]. New Delhi, Nāgmaṇi, 1979.
Sāgar aur sipiyā [The Shells and the Sea]. New Delhi, Hindi Book Centre, 1979.
Forty-Nine Days. New Delhi, Chanakya, and Columbia, Missouri, South Asia Books, 1981.
Kore kāgaz [Waste Paper]. New Delhi, Nāgmaṇi, 1982.
Hardatt dā zindagīnāmā [The Life Story of Hardatta]. Amritsar, Loa, 1983.
Na Rādhā, na Rukmiṇī [Neither Rādhā, nor Rukmiṇī] (in Hindi). New Delhi, Hindi Book Centre, 1985(?).

Verse

Ṭhandiyā kirnā [Cool Rays].   1935.
Amṛt lehrā [Nectar Waves].   1936.
Jiundā jīvan [Pulsating Life].   1939.
Trel dhote phūl [Dew-Drenched Flowers].   1941.
O gītvāliā [O Song Giver].   1942.
Badlān de palle vich [In the Skirt of the Clouds].   Prīt Nagar
    (Amritsar), Prīt Maṇḍal, 1943.
Sañjh dī lālī [Sunset].   1943.
Lok pīr [People's Pain].   1944.
Patthar gīk [Pebble Playthings].   1946.
Lammiyā vaṭā [Long Journeys].   Amritsar, Lok Sāhit, 1949.
Sargī velā [Morning Time].   1951.
Sunehre [Messages].   1955.
Aśok ceti.   Amritsar, Lok Sāhit, 1957.
Kasturi [Musk].   New Delhi, Navyug, 1959.
Navin rut: cōvī kavitā (in Urdu script).   Lahore, Al-Jadid,
    1960(?).
Nāgmaṇī [Serpent's Jewel].   New Delhi, Navyug, 1964.
Black Rose (selection of poems).   New Delhi, Nāgmaṇī, 1967.
Ce ruttā.   New Delhi, Navyug, 1971.
Kāgaz te canvas [From Paper to Canvas].   New Delhi,
    Navyug, 1971.
Time and Time Again and Other Poems.   Calcutta, United
    Writers, 1975.
Ik udās kitāb [A Sad Book].   New Delhi, Nāgmaṇī, 1976.
Maī jamha tūm.   New Delhi, Nāgmaṇī, 1977.
Alone in the Multitude: Selected Poems, translated by Suresh
    Kohli.   New Delhi, Indian Literary Review, 1979.
Amrita Pritam: Selected Poems, edited by Khushwant Singh.
    New Delhi, Bhārtīy Jñānpīṭh, 1982.
Cetarnāmā.   New Delhi, Nāgmaṇī, 1983.
141 kavitavā [141 Poems].   New Delhi, Nāgmaṇī, 1984.

Other

Bāriyā jharokhe [Through Windows Big and Small] (trave-
    logue).   1961.
Kirmicī lakīrā [Crimson Lines].   New Delhi, Navyug, 1965.
Kālā gulāb [Black Rose] (autobiography).   New Delhi,
    Navyug, 1968.
Ikkī pattiyā dā gulāb [The 21-Petalled Rose].   1968.
Aurat: ik dṛṣtikoṇ [The Woman: A Point of View] (essays). New
    Delhi, Nāgmaṇī, 1975.
The Revenue Stamp: An Autobiography.   New Delhi, Vikas,
    1977; New York, Advent, 1983; as *Rasīdī ticket: ātmacaritra,*
    Pune, Śrī Vidyā, 1984.
Apne apne cār varhe [Our Four Years].   New Delhi, Nāgmaṇī,
    1978.
Dastavez [Documents].   New Delhi, Prakāśana, 1978.
Kaun-sī zindagī? Kaun-sā sāhitya? [Which Life? Which
    Literature?].   New Delhi, Parāg, 1979; as *Kiharī zindagī?,*
    kihar sāhit? (in Panjabi), New Delhi, Nāgmaṇī, 1979.
Muhabbatnāmā [Love Story].   New Delhi, Sarasvatī Vihār,
    1981.
Tīsrī ākh [The Third Eye] (interviews).   New Delhi, Kitāb,
    1983.
Sāt savāl [Seven Questions].   New Delhi, Kitāb Ghar, 1984.
Amṛtā dī ḍairī [Amṛtā's Diary].   New Delhi, Nāgmaṇī, 1984.
Ik thī Sārā (biography of Pakistani Urdu poet Sārā Śāhgufta; in
    Urdu).   New Delhi, Kitāb Ghar, 1988.
Life and Times.   New Delhi, Vikas, and New York, Advent,
    1989.

Editor, *Pañjāb dī āvāz* [Voice of the Panjab] (collection of folk
    songs).   1952.

Editor, *Maulī te mehendī* [Sacred Thread and Henna] (collec-
    tion of folk songs).   1955.
Editor, *Convī pañjābī kavitā* (anthology of poems).   New
    Delhi, Sāhitya Akādemī, 1957.
Editor, *Aśma* (folk songs).   1960.
Editor, *Āj dī pañjābī kahānī* [Today's Panjabi Short Stories].
    New Delhi, Sāhitya Akādemī, 1971.
Editor, *Pañjābī ke tīn upanyās* [Three Panjabi Novels].   New
    Delhi, Parāg, 1975.
Editor, *Maī aur maī* [I and I] (self-assessment of some Indian
    writers).   New Delhi, Parāg, 1978.
Editor, *Pauriā ate hora yādagārī balgārian kahāniā* (Bulgarian
    short stories).   New Delhi, Nāgmaṇī, 1979.
Editor, *Aur nadī bahtī rahī* [And the River Kept
    Flowing].   New Delhi, Parāg, 1979.
Editor, *Aur bāt sulagtī rahī* [And the Issue Kept Burning]. New
    Delhi, Viśāl Sāhitya Sadan, 1979.
Editor, *Maī sassi maī sahidhan.*   New Delhi, Prakāśak, 1980.
Editor, *Kacce akṣava.*   New Delhi, Sarasvatī Vihār, 1980.
Editor, *Merā kamrā* [My Room].   New Delhi, Hindi Book
    Centre, 1980.
Editor, *Karī dhūp kā safar* [Journey Under Scorching Sun].
    New Delhi, Rājpāl & Sons, 1982.

*

Bibliography: "A Bibliography of Major Works by Amrita
Pritam," in *Mahfil,* 5(3), 1968–69.

Critical Studies: Pritam issue of *Mahfil,* 5(3), 1968–69; "Then,
Will Be, and Now: or How the Woman Becomes Contempor-
ary in Amrita Pritam's Fiction" by Renu Juneja, in *South
Asian Review* (Jacksonville, Florida), 1981.

*   *   *

Amritā Pritam's renown revolves around a series of paradoxes. She is above all famous as a poet; interpretation of her
verse, written in her native Panjabi, is all too often confused
with her personal image as a liberated, convention-defying
woman, an advocate of secularism and free love, though she
actually encompasses a variety of themes from the political to
the metaphysical and mythological. Much of her vast creative
output is in a variety of prose genres, and it is for her fiction in
Hindi translation that she gained a massive (in Indian terms)
popular readership. Originally primarily concerned with the
destinies of women, both rural and urban, Pritam's novels —
notably brief, they are actually novellas — have increasingly
adopted male perspectives and shifted their preoccupations to
the social construction of gender in a specifically Indian
context. An obsession with mythological motifs seems to
imply her involvement in the search for an authentic Indian
metaphysic.

The fictions in her *Chune hue upanyas* (Selected Novels)
may be seen as emblematic, since they provide an index both to
her preoccupations and her range of styles. Of these, *Piñjar*
(Skeleton) is arguably the finest, with a compression and depth
that Pritam has rarely been able to replicate. Through the
figure and radical choices of her central protagonist, Puro,
Pritam explores the issues around the partition of India in
1947. Presented as a rural love story, it stages questions of
national, religious, and gender identity through the sensibilities of the rural women who become victims of social and
political upheavals and of history itself. Sparely narrated in the
third person, it also reveals Pritam's insight into and intimacy
with the rural Panjab and its customs and folklore.

If *Piñjar* is distinguished, above all, by its sensitive handling of the tangled connections of gender and history, *Cakknambar chatti* (Village Number 36, translated as *A Line in Water*) scores a first in contemporary Indian fiction for its daring portrayal of a woman whose sexual choices — potent metaphors for autonomy and freedom of expression — place her beyond bourgeois respectability: her decisions are seen as positive, and the artist to whom she gives her body is depicted as the weaker one of the couple, demonstrating Pritam's evolving belief in women's superior strength. (In the earlier *Ik sí Anītā* [Once There Was an Anita] the middle-class heroine, admittedly an autobiographical projection, is a victim of her own unfulfilled sexual desires.) As is often the case, Pritam reworks and amplifies the theme of the transgressing woman in *Dhartī, sāgar te slppiyā* (Earth, Sea, and Shells), in which the heroine chooses to give birth to an illegitimate child, an unbearable stigma in the middle-class India of the 1960s.

Yātrī (Traveller) is a shift in direction to a male perspective and first-person narration, though the focus remains on women — specifically, male attitudes towards women. Here the narrator's identity is tied up with the question of his parentage and his mother's decisions. Couched in the language of legend and myth, this exploration of adolescent sexuality with its oedipal subtext indicates Pritam's quest for a new idiom crafted from a Pan-Indian, not to say Hindu, heritage, a quest that recurs in several other works, though it is handled here with humour verging on farce and an almost surreal lyricism. In *Ak de patte* (*Time and Beyond*) Pritam repeats the male perspective and mythical motif: here the narrator uncovers the ugly truth of his sister's murder by vengeful relatives and the aura of silence that surrounds violence to women's bodies. In these fictions, women who cross the boundaries of sexual propriety pay the price with their lives or at the very least the love of their men. The most charming and socially aware of these, *Jebkatre* (*Flirting with Youth*), tells of the varying destinies — marriage, political protest, prison — of a group of college students; the narrator's voice is inspired by Pritam's son.

Pritam's productions of the 1970s were marked, within a fairly narrow thematic range, by formal experimentation. *Koī nahī̃ jāndā* (*Nobody Knows*) borrows the tone of the village storyteller to narrate, in ballad-like fashion, a tale of love, honour, banditry, and sacrifice, displaying Pritam's ease with traditional narrative forms; the protagonist is once again a rural woman, but the novel's vague sense of history deprives it of the strength of *Piñjar*, which it in part resembles. Here the woman, though circumscribed by her class and status, refuses to be a victim or to abjure her passion for her lost lover.

The novel sequence *Terahvā̃ sūraj* (The Thirteenth Sun) and *Uñīñja din* (The Forty-Ninth Day) focuses on the struggles, friendships, and loves of a writer, one of Pritam's most sympathetic male protagonists. Here her reflections on creativity combine with her increasing obsession with arcane lore and esoteric terminology, but the second volume marks a welcome return to social issues as Pritam deals with the efforts of groups who form collectives to beat the rising tide of materialism and capitalist competitiveness. *Kore kāgaz* (Waste Paper) marks no significant advance on previous work; though elegantly narrated in the first person by its male hero, it deals once again with the problems of male identity — tied up with class origins and legitimate birth — and the position of the unmarried (lost) mother in Hindu society.

Pritam has also turned to lightly fictionalised biographies of public personae — a Marxist who lives in Russia, a romantic painter — adding the lyrical colour of dreams, fantasy, and nostalgia to socio-historical subjects. This experimental technique ripens and bears fruit in her innovative biography of the Pakistani poet Sārā Śāhgufta, which is composed of letters between the women, journal entries, reminiscences, and the writer's reflection on the younger woman's tragic suicide at the age of barely 30. As a poet and as a feminist Pritam is eminently qualified to do justice to a portrayal of a woman striving for creative and personal expression in a harshly patriarchal society. Though uneven and carelessly structured — like her autobiography, *Life and Times*, which is a patchwork of memories, impressions, and dreams — this dialogic work has the intensity of Pritam's best fiction with a passion underlined by hard fact. A pervasive sense of regret would seem to indicate a deep identification of the tragic poet Sārā with herself, or a hidden woman within her; the contrast between the two poets, survivor and suicide, reflects the polarity between Pritam's fictional women who alternately fight and fall.

—Aamer Hussein

Q

QABBĀNI, Nizār. Syrian. Born in Damascus, 21 March 1923. Educated at the University of Damascus, LL.B. 1945. Married Balqīs ar-Rāwi (died); two children from a previous marriage. Diplomat, 1945–66: Syrian chargé d'affaires, Cairo, 1945–48; former ambassador in Ankara, 1948, London, 1952, Beijing, Beirut, and Madrid, 1965. Has lived in Beirut since 1966; founder, Manshurāt Nizār Qabbāni publishing house, Beirut, 1967. Address: Mar Mansour Street, Banque Beyrouth et des Pays Arabes Building, P.O. Box 6250, Beirut, Lebanon.

PUBLICATIONS

Verse

Qālat lī al-samara [The Brunette Said to Me]. 1942.
Tufūlat nahd [The Childhood of a Breast]. 1948.
Anti lī [You Are Mine]. 1950.
Sāmba. 1951.
Qasā'id min Nizār Qabbāni [Poems from Nizār Qabbāni]. 1956.
Ḥabībatī [My Beloved]. 1961.
Al-shi'r qindīl akhḍar [Poetry Is a Green Lamp]. 1964.
Al-rasm bi-al-kalimāt [Drawing with Words]. 1966.
Al-A'māl al-shi'riyya al-kāmila (collected works). Beirut, Manshurāt Nizār Qabbāni, 1967.
'A la hāmish dafter al-naksa [In the Margin of the Book of Defeat]. Beirut, 1967.
Yawmiyyat imra'a la-mubāliya [The Diary of a Blasé Woman]. 1968.
Al-Mumaththilūn, al-istijwāb [The Actors, Interrogation]. 1969.
Kitāb al-ḥub [The Book of Love]. 1970.
Lā [No]. 1970.
Qasā'id mutawaḥḥisha [Wild Poems]. 1970.
Ash'ār khārija 'ala al-qānūn [Outlawed Poems]. 1972.
Qāmūs al-'ashiqīn [Lover's Dictionary]. Beirut, Manshurāt Nizār Qabbāni, 1981.
Al-'asafīr laha ta'shīrāt dukhūl [Birds Need Visas]. Beirut, Manshurāt Nizār Qabbāni, 1981.
Qasīdat Balqīs [Balqīs Poems]. Beirut, Manshurāt Nizār Qabbāni, 1982.
Ash'ār majnūnah [Crazy Poems]. Beirut, Manshurāt Nizār Qabbāni, 1983.
Al-ḥubb lā yaqif 'ala al-daw' al-aḥmar [Love Does Not Stop at the Red Light]. Beirut, Manshurāt Nizār Qabbāni, 1983.

Play

Jumhūriyyat Junūnstan (Lubnān sābiqan): masraḥiyya [Craziness Republic (Former Lebanon): A Play]. Beirut, Manshurāt Nizār Qabbāni, 1988.

Other

Al-a'māl al-siyāsiyya [Political Works]. 1974.
Al-kitāba 'amal inqilābi [Writing Is a Process of Change]. 1978.

Shay' min al-nathr [Some Prose]. Beirut, Manshurāt Nizār Qabbāni, 1979.
Al-Sirah al-ẓātiyah li-sayf 'Arabi [Bibliography of an Arab Sword]. London, Riad el-Rayyes, 1987.

*

Critical Studies: "Nizar Qabbani, the Poet and His Poetry" by Z. Gabay, in *Middle Eastern Studies* (London), 9(2), 1973; "Poetry as a Social Document: The Social Position of the Arab Woman as Reflected in the Poetry of Nizar Qabbani" by A. Loya, in *Muslim World* (Hartford, Connecticut), 63(1), 1973.

*   *   *

Nizār Qabbāni has been hailed as the most popular love poet of the Arab world, as well as raising a strong voice in support of women's social position in a deprived and male-dominated society. His sociopolitical poetry considers some of the most acute problems of the present-day Arab world.

Qabbāni's early poetry deals mainly with the physical attractiveness of women, and the poet's desire to fulfil his own sexual needs. Despite the erotic nature of these poems, Qabbāni succeeds in depicting the bourgeois milieux of his heroines, their empty and superficial ways of life, as well as showing the chauvinistic attitudes of men towards women — their ego-boosting conquests and their pride in their own virility. Even at this early stage in his poetic development, his compassion for women and the wrongs done to them by men is discernible.

It is not, however, until his fifth volume of poetry, *Qasā'id min Nizār Qabbāni* (Poems from Nizār Qabbāni), that we meet the mature poet's most outstanding achievements. In three of the poems — "Pregnant," "A Letter from a Spiteful Lady," and "The Vessels of Pus" — the poet assumes a female persona, through which the exasperations and resentments of women towards men are expressed. The soliloquy in the first-person feminine is a device used in much of Qabbāni's later verse.

The most famous of his social poems is also included in this book. In "Bread, Hashish and Moon" Qabbāni criticises the apathy of the Arab society, when on "the mountaintops/They all sell, they all buy fallacies /and illusions . . ." For Qabbāni poverty and polygamy are among the main causes of the weaknesses of the Arab world:

> In the nights of the East and when
> the moon grows full
> the East is stripped of all dignity
> and initiative to struggle.
> And the millions who run barefoot
> and who believe in having four wives
> and in the Day of Judgement,
> those millions who enjoy the taste of bread
> only in the imagination
> and dwell in the night in

cough-ridden houses,
knowing no medicine,
are corpses, reclining under the light.

Qabbāni continued to be the spokesman for Arab women in his next book, *Ḥabībatī* (My Beloved). His love poems here show a much greater maturity. Devoid of eroticism, the poems reflect a deeper understanding of women, and instead of extolling every part of the female body, the poet now seeks friendship with her. He urges women to rebel against their status in society, and to try to gain their freedom and self-respect. In his poem "Love and Petroleum" the female voice asserts itself in anger:

When will you understand?
O unbridled camel of the desert
. . .
That I will not be here
Ashes in your cigarettes
. . .
A breast on the marble of which
You leave the form of your fingerprints
When will you understand?

When will you understand?
That you will never numb me
By your wealth and your princedoms . . .

After the devastating defeat of the Arabs in the Six-Day War in 1967, Qabbāni turned his attention to nationalistic poetry. His poem "Marginal Notes on the Book of Defeat" is a scathing attack on the intellectuals and the leaders of the Arab world.

It is not strange that we should lose a war:
we enter them
with all our Eastern arts of rhetoric
and heroism, which never killed a blackfly.
We enter
with the logic of the drum and the rebab

My master Sultan,
You have lost the war twice
because half of our people have no tongues.
And what is the worth of a voiceless people?
Half of us
are besieged like ants and rats
inside the walls.
If someone would grant me passage
through the Sultan's guard
I would say to him: You have lost the war twice
because you have stood apart from every human condition.

Influenced by Western Romanticism, especially the French poets, as well as T. S. Eliot, Qabbāni's language is simple and free from rhetorical and symbolic ambiguities. Although much of his early poetry is written in the classical form of two hemistiches, his role in establishing free verse in contemporary Arabic poetry is also significant. In much of his free verse, Qabbāni employs a quasi-conversational tone, using language which is close to the vernacular. His use of material from folklore gives his poetry great vitality. Indeed, influenced by the Italian philosopher Benedetto Croce, he sees a poem as a painting, and expects his readers to read his poems as though they were looking "at the moon." One of the volumes of his poetry is aptly entitled *Al-rasm bi-ul-kallmat* (Drawing with Words). He sees the role of the poet as that of an artist who paints social and political scenes without seeking any cause or effect, and without offering any solution to the problems questioned.

Although many of Qabbāni's love poems are superficially repetitive, his artistic achievement lies, in a manner familiar from classical Arabic poetry, in the creation of variations on the same theme — through its musicality, and in its variety of tone. Above all he has trodden ground where no Arab poet had dared to step before — seeking to revolutionize women's attitude towards their own sexuality. Against a background of despondency and defeat, "his abundant love poetry is," in the words of Salma Khaḍra Jayyūsi, "the major source of hope that the human heart can finally transcend pain and dare to assert its capacity to summon joy and engage passion . . . In his political verse, loud-toned and angry, he asserts the need for freedom and liberty, but strengthens it significantly when he shows, in his erotic verse, that the freedom of the body is a path to the freedom of the spirit."

—Parvin Loloi

QIAN ZHONGSHU. Chinese. Born in Wuxi, Jiangsu Province, 21 November 1910. Educated at St. John's University Affiliated High Schools in Suzhou and Wuxi; Qinghua University, Beijing, 1929–33; Exeter College, Oxford, 1935–37; studied in Paris, 1937–38. Married Yang Jiang in 1935; one daughter. Taught at Guanghua University, Shanghai, 1933–35, National Southwest Associated University, Kunming, 1938–39, Lantian Normal College, Baoqing, Hunan, 1939–41, Aurora Women's College, Shanghai, 1941–45, Qinan University, Shanghai, 1946–48, and Qinghua University, Beijing, 1949–52; editor, *Philobiblion* English-language periodical, Nanking, 1946–48; Senior Fellow, Chinese Literature Institute, 1982–85; since 1985 vice president, Chinese Social Sciences Academy. Address: No. 2–6, Building 6, Nanshagou, Salihe Road, Beijing 100045, China.

PUBLICATIONS

Fiction

Ren, shou, gui [Men, Beasts, Ghosts]. Shanghai, Enlightenment Press, 1946.
Wei cheng. Shanghai, Aurora Press, 1947; as *Fortress Besieged*, Bloomington, Indiana University Press, 1979.

Other

Xie zai renshengbian shang [In the Margin of Life]. Shanghai, Enlightenment Press, 1941.
Tan yi lu [On Poetry and Poetics]. Shanghai, Enlightenment Press, 1948; revised edition, Beijing, Zhonghua, 1984.
Guan zhui bian [Partial Views: Essays on Letters and Ideas]. Beijing, Zhonghua, 4 vols., 1979–81.
Jiuwen si pian [Four Old Essays]. Shanghai, Chinese Classics Publishing House, 1979.
Lin Shu de fanyi [The Translations of Lin Shu 1852–1924]. Beijing, Shangwu, 1981.
Ye shi ji [Some Essays]. Hong Kong, Wide Angle Press, 1984.

Qi zhu ji [Seven Essays].   Shanghai, Shanghai Classics Publishing House, 1985.

Editor, *Songshi xuanzhu* [Critical Anthology of Sung Poetry]. Beijing, People's Literature Publishing House, 1958; revised edition, 1979.

*

Critical Study: *Qian Zhongshu* by Theodore Huters, Boston, Twayne, 1982.

*   *   *

Qian Zhongshu is one of the most brilliant and erudite comparers of Chinese and Western cultures in the 20th century. Having early on written what is among China's greatest modern novels, *Wei cheng* (*Fortress Besieged*), he has maintained an honored position in contemporary Chinese letters. However, he has written relatively little fiction (none after 1949) and in the past 40 years has concentrated on scholarship. Since the late 1970s he has met with foreign scholars and friends and has continued to impress people with an astounding depth of memory and perception about Chinese and European culture.

In the 1930s and 1940s he published essays in both English and Chinese, some scholarly and others primarily satirical. His most famous pre-1949 study is *Tan yi lu* (On Poetry and Poetics), examination of the style and diction of a broad range of traditional Chinese poets. He also wrote short stories in which he reflected his responses to the social and intellectual scene in China leading up to the Japanese invasion. There are humorous caricatures and satirical vignettes, many of which focus on one of his favorite targets, the pseudo-modernized or Westernized intellectual. Some of these stories were anthologized in his 1946 volume, *Ren, shou, gui* (Men, Beasts, Ghosts).

His major work of fiction, *Fortress Besieged*, is a novel about a student returning from Europe and witnessing, in somewhat picaresque fashion, the panorama of China's pre-war condition. He is isolated by the fact of his heightened but ineffective awareness of the world beyond China and of the hypocrites, imposters, and incompetents that people his native land. In the confrontation between old and new worlds, he repeatedly discovers that whatever is modern and advanced always ends up seeming as equally hollow and ludicrous as the thing it supplants.

One of the novel's outstanding accomplishments is its portrayal of love and marriage. The returned student, Fang Hung-chien, is at loose ends and takes up with whomever accidentally falls in his way. However, at the same time that he is driven to marital attachment, he is also inherently detached and ultimately finds nothing but misunderstanding and entrapment. The "forteresse assiégiée" is thus Qian Zhongshu's metaphor for marriage: "Those who are outside want to get in, and those who are inside want to get out."

The novel strikes most readers as an exuberant work always worth remembering for this or that brilliantly comic scene. But at times it suffers from an excess of topical satire and a tendency to lampoon; this fault is especially characteristic of his stories. In addition, the novel seems to have a pointedly vague sense of political or ideological identity, a factor that undoubtedly contributed to the extreme criticism he and his works received after the communist revolution. Had Qian Zhongshu continued to write fiction he very possibly would have corrected the first of these defects (the progress from his stories to the novel is already clear). As for the second, to write a novel as full of irony as *Fortress Besieged* is impossible in the People's Republic of China today.

Since 1949 Qian Zhongshu has worked as a teacher and scholar in Beijing. He has published numerous works, including *Guan zhui bian* (Partial Views), a lengthy study of major classical Chinese works such as the *Book of Changes*, the *Classic of Poetry*, and others. He has written this book in an elegant, literary style, and has included both philological and cross-cultural comments about what he considers the most important aspects of the Chinese past. Such a style and focus are part of a post-Cultural Revolution revival of interest in the classical past.

—Keith McMahon

———

QUEIROZ, Rachel de. Brazilian. Born in Fortaleza, 17 November 1910. Educated at the Colégio da Imaculada Conceição, Fortaleza, 1921–25; completed training as a primary school teacher at age 15. Married. Teacher, 1925–30; joined Communist Party, 1931: expelled 1933; weekly newspaper and magazine columnist, from early 1940s; served in United Nations Assembly and on Commission on the Rights of Man. Recipient: Fundação Graça Aranha prize, 1931; Sociedade Felipe d'Oliveira prize; Saci prize, 1953; Brazilian Academy of Letters prize, 1957; Machado de Assis prize, 1958; Instituto Nacional do Livro theatre prize, 1959; Roberto Gomes prize, 1959. Elected member of Brazilian Academy of Letters, 1977. Address: c/o José Olympio Editora, CP 9018, 22251 Rio de Janeiro RJ, Brazil.

PUBLICATIONS

Fiction

O quinze.   Rio de Janeiro, Olympio, 1930.
João Miguel.   Rio de Janeiro, Schmidt, 1932.
Caminho de pedras.   Rio de Janeiro, Olympio, 1937.
As três Marias.   Rio de Janeiro, Olympio, 1937; as *The Three Marias*, Austin, University of Texas Press, 1963.
Brandão entre o mar e o amor, with Jorge Amado, José Lins do Rêgo, Graciliano Ramos, and Anibal M. Machado.   São Paulo, Martins, 1942.
3 romances.   Rio de Janeiro, Olympio, 1948.
O galo de ouro.   Rio de Janeiro, Olympio, 1950.
Dôra, Doralina.   Rio de Janeiro, Olympio, 1975.
O jogador de sinuca e mais historinhas.   Rio de Janeiro, Olympio, 1980.

Plays

Lampião (produced Rio de Janeiro and São Paulo, 1953).   Rio de Janeiro, Olympio, 1953.
A beata Maria do Egito (produced Rio de Janeiro, 1958).   Rio de Janeiro, Olympio, 1958.

Other

A donzela e a moura torta: crônicas e reminiscências.   Rio de Janeiro, Olympio, 1948.
100 crônicas escolhidas.   Rio de Janeiro, Olympio, 1958.

O brasileiro perplexo: historías e crônicas. Pôrto Alegre, Autor, 1963.

O caçador de tatu. Rio de Janeiro, Olympio, 1967.

O menino mágico (for children). Rio de Janeiro, Olympio, 1969.

Meu livro de Brasil, 3,4,5: livro-guia, with Nilda Bethlem. Rio de Janeiro, Olympio, 1973.

As menininhas e outras crônicas. Rio de Janeiro, Olympio, 1976.

Teresa de Jesus. Rio de Janeiro, Tecnoprint, 1985(?).

Cafute & Pena-de-prata (for children). Rio de Janeiro, Olympio, 1986.

Mapinguari: crônicas. Rio de Janeiro, Olympio, 1989.

Translator, *Náufragos,* by Erich Maria Remarque. Rio de Janeiro, Olympio, 1942(?).

Translator, *Os Carolinos,* by Verner von Heidenstam. Rio de Janeiro, Delta, 1963.

Translator, *O romance da mumia: um romance do tempo dos faraões,* by Theophile Gautier. Rio de Janeiro, n.p., 1972.

Translator, *O lobo do mar* [The Sea-Wolf], by Jack London. Rio de Janeiro, n.p., 1972.

Translator, *Miguel Strogoff, o correio do Czar,* by Jules Verne. Rio de Janeiro, n.p., 1972.

Translator, *Memorias,* by Leo Tolstoy. São Paulo, Global, 1983.

Translator, *Mansfield Park,* by Jane Austen. São Paulo, Global, 1983.

Translator, *O castelo do homem sem alma* [Hatter's Castle], by A. J. Cronin. Rio de Janeiro, Record, 1985(?).

Translator, *A mulher diabólica* [At Bertram's Hotel], by Agatha Christie. Rio de Janeiro, Olympio, 1985.

Translator, *Uma razão por dia para ser feliz* [Onedayreason to Be Happy], by Laura Archera Huxley. Rio de Janeiro, Olympio, 1988.

*

Critical Studies: *Brazil's New Novel: Four Northeastern Masters* by Fred P. Ellison, Berkeley, University of California Press, 1954; "Three Contemporary Brazilian Novels: Some Comparisons and Contrasts" by G. D. Schade, in *Hispania* (Los Angeles), 39, 1956; "The Art of Rachel de Queiroz" by B. M. Woodbridge, Jr., in *Hispania* (Los Angeles), 40, 1957; "The Santa María Egipciaca Motif in Modern Brazilian Letters" by C. R. Reynolds, in *Romance Notes* (Chapel Hill, North Carolina), 13, 1971; "*A beata Maria do Egito*: Anatomy of Tyranny," in *Chasqui* (Provo, Utah), 13(2–3), 1984, "The Problematic Heroines in the Novels of Rachel de Queiroz," in *Luso-Brazilian Review* (Madison, Wisconsin), 22(2), 1985, and "*Dôra, Doralina*: The Sexual Configuration of Discourse," in *Chasqui* (Provo, Utah), 20(1), 1990, all by Joanna Courteau; "The Singular Encounter" by James Dauphiné, in *Romanian Review* (Bucharest), 40(2), 1986; "A Woman's Place: Rachel de Queiroz's *Dôra, Doralina*" by Renata R. Mautner Wasserman, in *Brasil/Brazil,* 2, 1989.

* * *

A metaphor frequently used by professors of Brazilian literature is perhaps the best statement on the place of Rachel de Queiroz in Brazilian letters: if José Américo de Almeida were the St. John the Baptist of the 1930s novel of social protest, de Queiroz was its Virgin Mary. The appearance of her *O quinze* (The Year Fifteen) in 1930, rather than the publication of *Bagaceira* (Trash) by Almeida in 1928, is considered to be the starting point for what Fred P. Ellison has called "Brazil's new novel."

O quinze lays out all the major elements that the Brazilian novel will explore in the decade: the Northeastern *sertão* or "backlands" as the setting; the rural masses — especially the *retirante* who is victimized by the drought of the Northeastern region, as the collective character; the social conditions in the region — with degrading imbalance of wealth distribution and chronic cultural backwardness — and the need for social reform, which functions as the central motif for many of the novels. A strong memorialistic presence is also evident, whose temporal settings often correspond to the rural childhood of the authors. Regional fiction, with noticeable roots in 20th-century writers like Afonso Arinos, is resumed at a different level of intention, with the ideological replacing the descriptive. De Queiroz is unique among writers of this period in that her story plots center on strong women protagonists.

Stylistically, *O quinze* sets the tone for the prose writing of the period. The trendy experimentation of the historical avant-garde that dominated the 1920s is abandoned and an earlier tradition of direct and natural expression is resumed. Colloquial language — a conquest of the avant-garde — is adapted by the young author to serve a more sober, almost humorless manner.

With *João Miguel* de Queiroz expands the feminine presence. Although the title indicates that the main character is a man, who has been jailed for a common crime, the narrative point of view displaces the focus of interest to the woman who visits the prisoner, her lover. As the character's needs grow and she matures into awareness, the social and economic problems of the Brazilian Northeastern region become no more than a backdrop for an extended analysis the author makes of the female condition.

In *Caminho de pedras* (Road of Stones), de Queiroz continues to explore the female presence in the Northeast. This novel, whose reception at the time of publication was lukewarm, and which continues to be the least successful of her major works, shifts from rural Brazil to the city. Working primarily with autobiographical material, the author emphasizes political activism as its theme and female independence as its goal. Its basic failure comes from a technical flaw: the lack of distance in the narration gives way to a sentimental tone less compelling than the starkness of her previous narratives.

With her fourth novel, *As três Marias* (*The Three Marias*), de Queiroz fuses her personal experiences with her observations on the plight of women in Brazil. The struggle of middle-class women to find independence within the boundaries of a traditional society is portrayed in three parallel stories. Their different endings, although encompassing only a very limited range of possibilities, imply the existence of change and improvement in the female condition. By using first-person narration, and by creating a character who serves the double role of actor and observer, the author issues a strong indictment of the social prejudices against women. Critics have been unanimous in considering *The Three Marias* her best work.

The Three Marias closes the first cycle of de Queiroz's literary life as a novelist. She returned to writing novels sporadically — as for example, with her attempt at popular literature, *O galo de ouro* (The Golden Rooster), set in the urban context of Rio de Janeiro's slums; and with *Dôra, Doralina*, in which she tries to resuscitate the themes of female identity and liberation. Neither of these novels was well-received by the critics. Despite their attempts to deal with some of the issues present in her previous novels, they suffer from a "journalistic" style of writing that has little aesthetic preoccupation.

De Queiroz also wrote several short stories, which have been published in the collection *O jogador de sinuca* (The Snooker Player). They neither add nor detract from the rest of her fictional work: the themes are similar, as are the settings and the language.

After 1939 journalism and theater became her major literary concerns. She became one of the best-known writers of *crônicas*, a literary genre akin to the newspaper column but with a broader range of artistic interest. She brings to the *crônica* much of her experience as a novelist, and together with fellow *cronistas* Rubem Braga and Carlos Drummond de Andrade, she helped to elevate the form to an accepted literary genre in contemporary Brazilian literature. As with her novels, the Northeast and the female condition are favorite themes in her *crônicas*.

It is, however, as a playwright, that de Queiroz best followed up the success of her earlier novels. *Lampião* is a forceful portrayal of banditry in rural Brazil. By stressing psychological instead of political interplay, she creates one of the most powerful roles in contemporary Brazilian theater. Her views on religious fanaticism in the Northeastern region, as represented by *A beata Maria do Egito* (The Pious Mary of Egypt), combines her concern with social problems and the female experience. Both plays use the same stark, colloquial language found in her earlier novels.

In the broad picture of Brazilian 20th-century letters, de Queiroz is a major figure by virtue of the range of her output, the influence of her writing on others, and the originality of her approach. She continues and enlarges the tradition of Júlia Lopes de Almeida and opens the path for Clarice Lispector.

—Heitor Martins

QUIROGA (de Abarca), Elena. Spanish. Born in Santander, 26 October 1921 (as stated by Quiroga; some sources say 1919 or 1920). Married Dalmiro de la Válgoma in 1950. Recipient: Nadal prize, 1951; National Critics' prize, 1961. Elected to the Spanish Royal Academy, 1983. Address: c/o Agencia Carmen Balcells, Diagonal 580, 08021 Barcelona, Spain.

PUBLICATIONS

Fiction

La soledad sonora.   Madrid, Espasa-Calpe, 1949.
Viento del norte.   Barcelona, Destino, 1951.
La sangre.   Barcelona, Destino, 1952.
Trayecto uno.   Madrid, Tecnos, 1953.
La otra ciudad.   Madrid, Prensa Española, 1953.
Algo pasa en la calle.   Barcelona, Destino, 1954.
La enferma.   Barcelona, Noguer, 1955.
La careta.   Barcelona, Noguer, 1955.
Plácida, la joven y otras narraciones.   Madrid, Prensa Española, 1956.
La última corrida.   Barcelona, Noguer, 1958.
Tristura.   Barcelona, Noguer, 1960.
Escribo tu nombre.   Barcelona, Noguer, 1965.
Presente profundo.   Barcelona, Destino, 1973.

Other

Presencia y ausencia de Alvaro Cunqueiro: discurso leído el 8 de abril en su recepción pública.   Madrid, Real Academia Española, 1984.

*

Bibliography: in *Las mejores novelas contemporáneas*, edited by Joaquín de Entrambasaguas, Barcelona, Planeta, 1971.

Critical Studies: "The Novels of Elena Quiroga" by Albert Brent, in *Hispania* (Los Angeles), 42, 1959; "The Novelistic Style of Elena Quiroga," in *Kentucky Foreign Language Quarterly* (Lexington), 9, 1962, and "Sensory Images in the Galician Novels of Elena Quiroga," in *Kentucky Foreign Language Quarterly* (Lexington), 10, 1963, both by Lucile K. Delano; *Elena Quiroga*, Boston, Twayne, 1977, "Faulkner in Spain: The Case of Elena Quiroga," in *Comparative Literature Studies* (Eugene, Oregon), 14, 1977, "Divorce in Franco Spain: Elena Quiroga's *Algo pasa en la calle*," in *Mosaic* (Winnipeg, Manitoba), 17(1), 1984, "Elena Quiroga's *Tristura*: The Anguish of Silence and Absence," in *Modern Language Studies* (Providence, Rhode Island), 18, 1988, and "Writing Against the Current: The Novels of Elena Quiroga," in *Women Writers of Contemporary Spain: Exiles in the Homeland*, edited by Joan L. Brown, Newark, University of Delaware Press, and London and Toronto, Associated University Presses, 1991, all by Phyllis Zatlin-Boring; "Elena Quiroga's *Yo* Voice and the Schism Between Reality and Illusion," in *Anales de la Novela de Posguerra*, 5, 1980, and "Time in the Novels of Elena Quiroga," in *Hispania* (Los Angeles), 64, 1981, both by Martha Alford Marks.

*   *   *

Elena Quiroga gained national recognition in Spain when her second novel, *Viento del norte* (Northwind), was awarded the Nadal prize for 1950. She is grouped by scholars with other important, prize-winning women novelists who emerged in the early post-war period: Carmen Laforet (*q.v.*), Dolores Medio, Carmen Martín Gaite (*q.v.*), and Ana María Matute (*q.v.*). Her election to the Spanish Royal Academy in 1983 nevertheless came as a surprise to some, no doubt because of the long silences between works since the mid-1960s. In supporting the novelist's candidacy, poet Carmen Conde (*q.v.*), the first woman member of the Academy, clarified that Quiroga had dared to take risks and speak of taboo topics during the difficult years of the Franco dictatorship.

Viento del norte, still Quiroga's most widely-read novel and one that also gained popularity as a movie, takes place in rural Galicia (northwestern Spain) and is written in a traditional novelistic structure, with an omniscient third-person narrator. Although it is atypical of the author's work in general, it introduces elements that permeate all of her texts: penetrating psychological analysis, creation of authentic characters within a given sociohistorical circumstance, poetic style, and themes of orphanhood, alienation, and class prejudice.

Quiroga's later works of the 1950s become increasingly experimental and Faulknerian. While *Viento del norte* was rejected by some critics for being "19th-century" in its narrative strategies, paradoxically the innovative novels that followed also ran against the dominant current of social realism. Subjective, stream-of-consciousness narrations that utilized multiple perspectives and temporal fluidity, they required sophisticated readers. Their difficulty precluded immediate popularity but also facilitated Quiroga's treatment of subjects generally prohibited by official censorship: divorce, sexuality, atrocities committed during the Spanish Civil War (1936–1939), and postwar political retribution and moral degeneracy.

Foremost among these novels of the 1950s are *Algo pasa en la calle* (Something's Happening in the Street) and *La careta* (The Mask). The former is a multiple-perspective probing of the relationships of a liberal, idealistic philosophy professor with his two wives, and the long-term effects of his divorce, granted during the Second Republic. The latter is a compelling stream- of-consciousness exploration of one man's inner world; it finally uncovers his guilt stemming from the horrible moment during his childhood in Republican Madrid when his parents were killed by Communist soldiers.

In Franco Spain, not only was the Republican divorce law repealed, but both divorces and civil marriages were annulled retroactively. Ventura, whose accidental death at the novel's beginning is the catalyst for the various subjective strands of *Algo pasa en la calle*, had married Presencia before the birth of their son. In Franco Spain, however, she has been repudiated as an immoral woman, their child is considered illegitimate, and the long-estranged Esperanza is still Ventura's legal wife. With consummate psychological sensitivity, Quiroga explores both the intellectual and sexual incompatibility that led to Ventura's separation from his wealthy first wife and the impact on their daughter Agata, who grows up deprived of a father. Her portrait of Presencia, the "other woman," is a sympathetic one, even though the younger woman neither believes in God nor conforms to her society's outward moral standards. Quiroga reveals a hidden level of degeneracy and hypocrisy under that surface morality and suggests, contrary to Catholic doctrine, that a good divorce is better than a bad marriage. In Franco Spain the subject of divorce was so silenced that a generation of Spaniards was unaware that its country had ever had a divorce law. In that context, Quiroga's novel is daring indeed.

La careta is tied to existential psychiatry in its approach to time: for Moisés, the moment of his parents' death is not the past but rather a deeper present that remains always with him and informs his reality. When the soldiers discover his father in his hiding place, a 12-year-old Moisés flees in terror. The soldiers kill his father, wound his mother, and leave. The child, fearing they will return, prevents his mother from calling for help and hence causes her to bleed to death. The fictive present of the novel is one evening in the present, but within Moisés's mind there is a constant flux between that present, the recent past, and 20 years earlier. In Proustian fashion, sensations in the present trigger associations to the past. The reader must enter the protagonist's thoughts in order to unscramble the dialogue and scenes and hence reconstruct the chronology of events and the cause of Moisés's alienation and degeneracy.

Tristura (Sadness) and *Escribo tu nombre* (I Write Your Name) are part of a planned trilogy that traces the experiences of Tadea, a motherless child raised by maternal relatives in Santander, her years as a boarder at a convent school, and the war years behind the lines in Galicia. Although not intended to be purely autobiographical, the Tadea novels do share much of Quiroga's own life. Given its linear structure, *Tristura* appears superficially to be a much simpler novel than some of the author's preceding works, but in subtle ways it is perhaps more challenging. The perspective is that of a young child, eight to nine years old, who provides only the information known to her and who is unable to communicate, even to herself, the loss she feels from the absence of love. The reader is left to fill in not only what the child narrator leaves unsaid but also the gaps and silences of a household ruled by a rigidly moral aunt. By her adolescent years in *Escribo tu nombre*, Tadea has become rebellious; the name she wishes to write is that of Liberty.

Quiroga's most recent novel, *Presente profundo* (Profound Present), dealing with society in the early 1970s, incorporates multiple perspectives in a fragmentary structure that somewhat recalls *Algo pasa en la calle*. Again she explores marital, parent-child, and love relationships, developing both traditional and non-traditional female characters. Like *La careta*, the action shifts between Galicia and cosmopolitan Madrid, providing a full view of contemporary Spain.

—Phyllis Zatlin

———

QUOIREZ, Françoise. *See* **SAGAN, Françoise.**

———

QURRATULAIN HAIDAR. *See* **HAIDAR, Qurratulain.**

———

R

RABIKOVITZ, Dahlia. *See* **RAVIKOVITCH, Dahlia.**

RADZINSKII, Edvard (Stanislavovich). Also Edward Radzinsky. Russian. Born in Moscow, 23 September 1936. Educated at the Moscow Historical Archive Institute, 1959. Married several times; one son. Agent: Lynn C. Franklin, 386 Park Avenue South, New York, New York 10016, U.S.A. Address: Ulitsa Usievicha N 8, Kvartira 96, 125319 Moscow, Russia.

PUBLICATIONS

Plays

Mechta moia, Indiia [India, My Dream] (produced Leningrad, 1960).
Vam 22, stariki [You Are 22, Old Men] (produced Moscow, 1962).
104 stranitsy pro liubov [104 Pages About Love] (produced Moscow, 1964). Published in *Teatr* (Moscow), 12, 1964.
Snimaetsia kino [The Filmmaker]. Published in *Teatr* (Moscow), 1, 1966.
104 stranitsy pro liubov [104 Pages About Love] (collection). Moscow, Sovetskii pisatel', 1968.
Obol'stitel' Kolobashkin [The Seducer Kolobashkin]. Published in *Teatr* (Moscow), 1, 1968.
Peizazh s rekoi i krepostnymi stenami [Landscape with a River and Fortress Walls] (produced as *Turbaza* [Tourist Centre], Moscow, 1973). Included in *Besedy s Sokratom* (collection), 1981.
Monolog o brake [Monologue About Marriage] (produced Leningrad, 1973).
Snimaetsia kino [The Filmmaker] (collection). Moscow, Sovetskii pisatel', 1974.
Besedy s Sokratom (produced Moscow, 1975). Included in *Besedy s Sokratom* (collection), 1981; as *Conversations with Socrates* (produced New York, 1986).
"A sushchestvuet li liubov?" sprashivaiut pozharniki [Does Loves Really Exist? Ask Firemen] (produced Moscow, 1978).
Lunin, ili, Smert' Zhaka, zapisannaia v prisutstvii khoziaina (produced Moscow, 1978). Published in *Teatr* (Moscow), 3, 1979; as *I, Mikhail Sergeevich Lunin* (produced New York, 1985), New York, Institute for Contemporary Eastern European Drama and Theatre, 1982.
Prodolzhenie Don Zhuana [Don Juan Continued] (produced Moscow, 1979). Moscow, VAAP, 1979; as *Okonchanie Don Zhuana* [The Last Return of Don Juan], in *Teatr vremen*, 1986.
Besedy s Sokratom [Conversations with Socrates] (collection). Moscow, Sovetskii pisatel', 1981.

Ona v otsutstvii liubvi i smerti [She in the Absence of Love and Death]. Published in *Teatr* (Moscow), 6, 1982.
Ia stoiu u restorana (produced Moscow, 1982). As *To Kill a Man (I'm Standing by a Restaurant)* (staged reading, New York, 1987).
Teatr vremeni Nerona i Seneki (produced Copenhagen, 1984). Published in *Sovremennaia dramaturgiia* (Moscow), 1, 1982; as *Theatre in the Time of Nero and Seneca* (produced New York, 1984).
Priiatnaia zhenshchina s tsvetkom i oknami na sever [Pleasant Woman with a Flower and Windows to the North]. Published in *Teatr* (Moscow), 7, 1983.
Staraia aktrisa na rol' zheny Dostoevskogo. Published in *Sovremennaia dramaturgiia*, 1, 1984; as *Comedienne d'un certain âge pour jouer la femme de Dostoievski* (produced Paris, 1986), in *L'Avant Scène* (Paris), 1986; as *An Old Actress in the Role of Dostoevsky's Wife* (produced New York, 1992).
Teatr vremen [The Theatre of Time] (collection). Moscow, Iskusstvo, 1986.
Sportivnye stseny 1981 goda (produced Moscow, 1987). Published in *Sovremennaia dramaturgiia* (Moscow), 4, 1986; as *Jogging (Sporting Scenes 1981)* (staged reading, New York, 1987).
Nash Dekameron [Our Decameron], from his own novel (produced Moscow, 1989). Moscow, Pravda, 1988.

Screenplays: *Ulitsa N'iutona, d. 1* [One, Newton Street], 1961; *Eshche raz pro liubov* [Once More About Love], from his play *104 stranitsy pro liubov* [104 Pages About Love], 1969.

Fiction

Nash Dekameron: ispoved' pasynka veka [Our Decameron]. Published in *Biblioteka Ogonek* (Moscow), 39, 1988; Moscow, Moskovskii rabochii, 1990.
Posledniaia iz doma Romanovykh [The Last Girl of the Romanov House]. Moscow, Moskovskii rabochii, 1989.
Gospodi . . . spasi i usmiri Rossiiu [Lord . . . Save and Pacify Russia]. Published in *Druzhba narodov* (Moscow), 9, 1991.

Other

The Last Tsar: The Life and Death of Nicholas II. New York, Doubleday, 1992.

Critical Studies: "Edvard Radzinskii's *Don Juan Continued*: The Last Return of Don Juan?," in *Slavic and East European Arts* (Stony Brook, New York), 3(1), 1985, "*Monologue About Love*: The Plays of Edvard Radzinskii," in *Soviet Union/Union Soviétique* (Atlanta, Georgia), 12(3), 1985, and "In Search of a Synthesis: Reflections on Two Interpretations of Edward Radzinskii's *Lunin or the Death of Jacques Recorded in the Presence of the Master*," in *Studies in 20th*

Century Literature (Manhattan, Kansas), 13(2), 1989, all by Maia Kipp.

*   *   *

Edvard Radzinskii (Edward Radzinsky) emerged as the leading Russian playwright of the critical intelligentsia during the period of so-called "mature socialism" of the Brezhnev era. His dramas dominated the Moscow theatrical scene for much of the 1970s and early 1980s and were often produced abroad.

During the radical changes of the late 1980s and early 1990s, in conjunction with perestroika and the disintegration of the Soviet Union, Radzinskii turned his attention to prose fiction, publishing *Nash Dekameron* (Our Decameron), and to history, producing *The Last Tsar: The Life and Death of Nicholas II*, a ground-breaking work on the final days and murder of Nicholas II and his family. In this book the Soviet regime's culpability in their murders serves as an indictment of the banality of evil.

This return to historical-ethical topics by the mature Radzinskii represented in many ways a matter of continuity, linking together his early education as historian and archivist, the historical-philosophical themes of his mature dramas, and the concerns of the intelligentsia as it pondered the costs and consequences of seven decades of Soviet power. Radzinskii came to drama through history. In fact, his first dramatic effort in 1958 was a historical play, *Mechta moia, Indiia* (India, My Dream). During his mature period Radzinskii devoted himself to a systematic investigation of historical-philosophical topics as a way of exploring the human dilemma. History became a continuous dialogue between various historical epochs concerning the continuity of human spirit in a never-ending struggle against both authoritarian oppression and the pervasive banality of life. The most important works of this period are *Besedy s Sokratom* (*Conversations with Socrates*), *Lunin, ili* (*I, Mikhail Sergeevish Lunin*), *Teatr vremeni Nerona i Seneki* (*Theatre in the Time of Nero and Seneca*) — plays which form what Radzinskii himself defined as "a historical-philosphical trilogy" — and *Prodolzheni Don Zhuana* (Don Juan Continued), later renamed *Okonchanie Don Zhuana* (The Last Return of Don Juan).

Radzinskii's development as a playwright and thinker over the last three decades is marked by ever-growing intellectualsm and deepening pessimism. The dramatist speaks of his plays as "apocalyptic." Indeed, the world that Radzinskii's characters inhabit is both grotesque and terrifying. God is dead, and so Don Juan of the 20th century is an atheist. Without God man is alone, confronted with his own self-doubts and individual fantasies, unable and unwilling to act. Thus, Radzinskii's Don Juan is not able to perform his eternal function. Since there is no god there is also no damnation, salvation, or resurrection; therefore at the end of the play the Commander never arrives. Consequently, Don Juan's return to life, this time in Moscow of the 20th century, must be his last return. There is also no tragedy, for without God, Don Juan is not a tragic hero but an absurd one: in Radzinskii's play he walks on stilts rather than *coturns*. Yet this farce is horrifying banality rules the world, and Leporello is the one who inherits the name and, hence, the legend. Disguised as Don Juan, he goes about in his new role, unrecognized by Donna Anna: seduction and betrayal go on, but there is no divine justice to give ethical meaning to the tale.

In this universe, human relations can be reduced to a simple formula, "victim versus executioner," the theme that runs through all of Radzinskii's drama, whether about love *Monolog o brake* [Monologue About Marriage]), or the struggle pitting the intellectual against totalitarian authority (*Theatre in the Time of Nero and Seneca*), or art (*Staraia aktrisa na rol' zheny Dostoevskogo* [*An Old Actress in the Role of Dostoevsky's Wife*]). The whole of human history can be summed up in the story of "Cain-Abel-Caesar." Victims cooperate with their executioners, and so "whole nations willingly follow their butchers to the slaughter house." The accomplishments and sacrifices of the few heroic figures, such as Christ, Socrates, or Lunin, go unnoticed, or worse, are condemned by those for whose sake they die on the cross. Thus, the Old Man in Radzinskii's *Theatre in the Time of Nero and Seneca* has been crucified before, and will be crucified again and again, as if to prove that Dostoevskii's Grand Inquisitor was right — the gladiators indulge in orgies, only to be butchered in tomorrow's fight.

Radzinskii's major prose work, *Nash Dekameron*, represents a summation of main ideas and motifs of his drama. The apocalyptic vision of the Soviet world finds its expression in the title, which alludes to Boccaccio's (and Pushkin's) "Feast in the Time of Black Death." The subtitle *ispoved' pasynka veka* (A Confession of the Step-Child of the Century) points to Alfred de Musset's *La Confession d'un enfant du siècle* (1836). Yet, 150 years separate the two confessions, and Radzinskii's story is that of an unwanted, mistrusted, and alienated child of the end of the 20th century. In fact, this is the postmodern *Man from the Underground*. Its central character, the narrator, decides to kill himself. In the face of his approaching death which he "freely" chooses, he feels liberated of all lies and conventions of society of which he is a product. He wallows in self-revelations and self-disgust, only to discover that actually he has been dead all along. He had killed his own "I" long ago. All these years he has been his own Mozart and his own Salieri, his own Don Juan and his own Leporello, his own victim and his own executioner. It remains to be seen whether in Russia of the post-perestroika period this man can rise from the dead and begin a new life or, like Andreev's Eliazar, he will rise dead and will continue to walk among us bringing destruction to anyone who dares to look into his dead eyes.

—Maia Kipp

————

RADZINSKY, Edward. *See* **RADZINSKII, Edvard.**

————

RAMÍREZ (Mercado), Sergio. Nicaraguan. Born in Masatepe, 5 August 1942. Educated at the National Autonomous University of Nicaragua, León, 1959–64, law degree. Married to Gertrudis Guerrero Mayorga; one son and two daughters. Secretary general, Consejo Superior Universitario C.A., 1964–79; member of the Government Committee for National Reconstruction, 1979–85; Vice President of Nicaragua, 1985–90; head of the Sandinista block of the National Assembly. Recipient: Imagen international prize (Venezuela), 1971; Bruno Kreisky prize for defense of human rights (Austria), 1988; Giacalone di Monreale cultural prize (Italy), 1988; Dashiell Hammett international prize, 1989. Honorary doctorate: Central University of Ecuador, Quito, 1984.

Agent: Hortensia Campanella, Madrid, Spain. Address: Apartado Postal RP 24, Managua, Nicaragua.

PUBLICATIONS

Fiction

Cuentos.   Managua, Editorial Nicaragüense, 1963.
Nuevos cuentos.   León, Editorial Universitaria, 1969.
Tiempo de fulgor.   Guatemala City, Editorial Universitaria de Guatemala, 1970.
De tropeles y tropelías.   San Salvador, Editorial Universitaria de El Salvador, 1973.
Charles Atlas también muere.   Mexico City, Mortiz, 1976; as *Stories*, London and New York, Readers International, 1986.
¿Te dio miedo la sangre?   Caracas, Monte Avila, 1977; as *To Bury Our Fathers*, London and New York, Readers International, 1984.
Castigo divino.   Madrid, Mondadori, 1988.

Plays

El pajaro del dulce encanto (produced Managua, 1992).
Cuando calienta el sol (produced Managua, 1992).

Radio Play: *Sandino* (The Netherlands), 1992.

Screenplay: *Sandino*, 1976.

Other

Mis dias con el rector.   León, Ventana, 1965.
La narrativa centroamericana.   San Salvador, Editorial Universitaria de El Salvador, 1969.
Mariano fiallos: biografía.   León, Editorial Universitaria, 1971.
Biografía de Sandino.   Managua, Ministerio de Educación, 1979.
El muchacho de Niquinohomo.   Managua, Unidad Editorial "Juan de Dios Muñoz," 1981.
La edad presente es de lucha = The Present Age Is One of Struggle, with Julio Cortázar.   Managua, JGRN, 1983.
El alba de oro: la historia viva de Nicaragua.   Mexico City, Siglo XXI, 1983.
Nicaragua Answers Reagan.   Chicago, New Patriot Alliance, 1984(?).
Balcanes y volcanes y otros ensayos y trabajos.   Managua, Nueva América, 1985.
Seguimos de frente.   Caracas, Centauro, 1985.
Estás en Nicaragua.   Barcelona, Muchnik, 1985.
Julio, estás en Nicaragua.   Buenos Aires, Nueva América, 1986.
Las armas del futuro.   Havana, Editorial de Ciencias Sociales, 1987.
La marca del zorro.   Managua, Nueva Nicaragua, 1989.
Confesión de amor.   Managua, Nicarao, 1991; as *Election Night in Nicaragua*, London, Granta, 1991.

Editor, *El pensamiento vivo de Sandino*.   San José, Costa Rica, EDUCA, 1975; revised and enlarged edition, EDUCA, 1980; revised edition, as *Sandino: Testimony of a Nicaraguan Patriot 1921–1934*, Princeton, New Jersey, Princeton University Press, 1990.
Editor, *El cuento nicaragüense*.   Managua, El Pez y La Serpiente, 1976.

Editor, with Carlos Martínez Rivas, *Antología*, by Ernesto Gutiérrez.   San José, Costa Rica, EDUCA, 1976.
Editor, *Antología del cuento centroamericano*.   San José, Costa Rica, EDUCA, 1977.
Editor, *El ángel del espejo y otros relatos*, by Salarrué.   Caracas, Ayacucho, 1977.
Editor, *Hombre del Caríbe: memorias*, by Abelardo Cuadra.   San José, Costa Rica, EDUCA, 1977.
Editor, *Pensamiento politico*, by Augusto César Sandino.   Caracas, Ayacucho, 1988.

*

Critical Studies: "History, Textuality, Revolution: Sergio Ramírez's *To Bury Our Fathers*" by E. San Juan, Jr., in *Likha*, 11(2), 1989–90; "The Politician as Novelist: Sergio Ramírez's *Castigo divino*" by Peter Ross, in *Antípodas*, 3, 1991.

Sergio Ramírez comments:

When I was 14, *La Prensa Literaria* (The Literary Press), the only Nicaraguan cultural supplement there was in 1956, published my first story, which recreated a traditional legend from my childhood, *La carreta nagua*, the nagua — or probably nahuatl [one of the original American languages] — wagon: the phantom wagon that conveys souls in torment at midnight, a wagon rather than a ship, driven by a ferryman like Caron. So I did not start out as a poet, as is the norm in Nicaragua, but as a teller of traditional tales. There were already too many poets.

After the massacre of 23 July 1959, when Somoza's army fired on a student demonstration, I learned to divide my life between the occupations of writer and politician, something which is not easy to explain, as to many people, and to me most of all, the two appear incompatible; but in me — and the revolution itself explains it better than any other argument — they have been united, having as their root the same vision, the same conviction, the same experiences, the same motive, and the results of the same power of feeling. I have always been careful to separate the two, in methodological terms, via a strict working discipline, and this even during those years of the war of aggression which were the worst of times.

And with these twin aspects to my life, I have been determined to safeguard my occupation as a writer, a professional writer, not an amateur. Neither, I should say, am I an amateur politician, having lived, of course, for a cause — and I insist on using the word "cause" because in spite of the bitter winds now blowing, my cause will never be discredited. So I return to my childhood, because I grew up between the classes of my town, between those of the upper and lower classes, and it is from there that my common feeling for both poetry and politics came. My two causes are not just any causes but my very reason for being and are, in my life, both inseparable and of the same substance.

My stories, when they manage to detach themselves from the primitive attraction of the vernacular, lean towards an ironic treatment of cultural alienation, but not deliberately, for political reasons, as something done deliberately is never successful, but as a way of explaining my country through fiction.

*   *   *

As vice president of the Sandinista government which ruled Nicaragua for 10 years after 1979, Sergio Ramírez was charged with formulating the artistic policy of the revolution. He insisted that the only guiding principle must be that of complete freedom for the individual artist, as this was in his view the only way of remaining true to the guiding spirit of the Sandinista revolution, which he saw as operating creatively on Nicaraguan reality to transform it from top to bottom. He has always applied this principle to his own work, often surprising his fellow Sandinistas with his insistence on writing about topics and themes far removed from the turbulent political events he was living through. He has frequently described himself as a writer who felt impelled to take part in politics, since, as with other creative writers such as Václav Havel or Mario Vargas Llosa (qq.v.), he sees the two activities as springing from the same source rather than as contradicting each other. In this sense, all Ramírez's writing is "political," however distant it may seem from events playing themselves out in contemporary Nicaragua.

Ramírez's writing career began with short stories. He composed most of them while living in exile in Costa Rica, and many deal with themes of the loss of country, or the oppressive political conditions in Nicaragua under the regime of the Somoza family, such as "Centerfielder," a convincing description of how a despotic regime can affect every aspect of life. What enlivens these stories is Ramírez's sense of humour, which comes to the fore in stories such as "Charles Atlas Also Dies." Here, the cultural dependency of a country like Nicaragua is engagingly illustrated through the story of one man's fascination with the American strongman, whom he finally gets to meet when Atlas is on his deathbed. Ramírez's ironic portrayal of what might easily be too obvious a political message saves it from being hackneyed. In other stories, such as "Saint Nikolaus," Ramírez succeeds in movingly illustrating the situation of lonely Latin American exiles caught up in situations they can hardly understand, let alone control; here pathos and sympathy add to the emotional weight of the stories.

Exile is also at the heart of ¿Te dio miedo la sangre? (To Bury Our Fathers), Ramírez's first major novel translated into English. The book presents a kaleidoscopic vision of the lives of a group of would-be revolutionaries who spend their whole lives dreaming of returning in triumph to their native Nicaragua, but who fail in their attempt at explosive action, and in the end are left only with memories of what might have been. Ramírez's technique of intermingling the characters' different stories and destinies adds to the sense of confusion and lack of direction that they experience: the book as a whole offers a perhaps surprisingly negative assessment of the possibilities for change in Central America, placing more emphasis on the warmth of comradeship than on decisive action, on the nostalgic recounting of events rather than on the experience itself.

To Bury Our Fathers was based around real incidents, as was Ramírez's next novel, Castigo divino (Divine Punishment). A famous case of poisoning in Ramírez's home city of León in Nicaragua in the 1930s once again serves as the springboard for a complex exploration of the interpenetration of everyday events and the political context in which they take place. The novel is divided into over 50 chapters which tell the story of the trial of the person suspected of the murders from many different points of view. Events leading up to the trial, and what happens during the hearings themselves show Ramírez's concern with the way our own version of the truth is constructed from a wide array of versions, none of which is complete in itself. The reader is presented with the courtroom transcripts of the trial, the way the local reporters write of what has been happening, letters between the protagonists, and so on, leaving the reader to decide for himself whether or not the accused is guilty, whether or not one can ever establish the truth of events beyond the language used to describe them.

Another important element in Castigo divino is the painstakingly detailed description Ramírez gives of life in this provincial city of Nicaragua in the 1930s. Perhaps because of the distortions which both cultural dependency and years of dictatorship inflict upon a country such as Nicaragua, Ramírez takes very seriously this role of the writer as social historian. This idea is prominent too in his novel in progress, based on the life of the Nicaraguan poet Rubén Darío, regarded as the founder of modern Latin American poetry. In looking back to the life of a prominent Nicaraguan in the early years of this century, Ramírez is continuing with his task of constructing a history of the creative endeavours of his own people.

—Nick Caistor

RASPUTIN, Valentin (Grigorevich). Russian. Born in Ust-Uda, Irkutsk Oblast, 15 March 1937. Educated at Irkutsk State University, graduated in literature and history 1959. Journalist in Siberia, 1959–61. Since 1961 full-time writer. Member of the editorial staff, Nash sovremennik [Our Contemporary], Moscow, 1975. Member, 1975, and member of the board, 1981, Union of Soviet Writers. Elected a People's Deputy, 1989; member of Mikhail Gorbachev's Presidential Council, 1990–91. Recipient: State prize, 1977, 1987; Hero of Socialist Labour, 1987. Address: 5th Army Street 67, Apt. 68, 664000 Irkutsk, Russia.

PUBLICATIONS

Fiction

Ia zabyl sprosit' u Leshki [I Forgot to Ask Leshka].   1961.
Krai vozle samogo neba [The Land at the Edge of Heaven Itself].   Irkutsk, Vostochno-Sibirskoe Knizhnoe izdatel'stvo, 1966.
Chelovek s etogo sveta [A Man from This World].   Krasnoiarsk, Knizhnoe izdatel'stvo, 1967.
Den'gi dlia Marii.   Moscow, Molodaia gvardiia, 1968; as Money for Maria, with Borrowed Time, St. Lucia, University of Queensland Press, and London, Quartet, 1981.
Poslednii srok.   Published in Nash sovremennik (Moscow), 1970; as Borrowed Time, with Money for Maria, St. Lucia, University of Queensland Press, and London, Quartet, 1981.
Vniz i vverkh po techeniiu [Down and Up Stream].   Moscow, Sovetskaia Rossiia, 1972.
Zhivi i pomni.   Moscow, Sovremennik, 1975; as Live and Remember, New York, Macmillan, 1978.
Povesti [Short Stories].   Moscow, Molodaia gvardiia, 1976.
Proshchanie s Materoi.   Moscow, Molodaia gvardiia, 1976; as Farewell to Matyora, New York, Macmillan, 1979.
Na reke Angare [On the River Angara].   Moscow, Malysh, 1980.
Money for Maria, and Borrowed Time: Two Village Tales.   St. Lucia, University of Queensland Press, and London, Quartet, 1981.
Uroki frantsuzskogo [French Lessons].   Moscow, Sovetskaia Rossiia, 1981.
Vek zhivi — vek liubi: rasskazy.   Moscow, Molodaia gvardiia, 1982, as You Live and Love and Other Stories, London, Granada, and New York, Vanguard Press, 1985.
Chetyre povesti [Four Novels],   edited Aleksandr Dyrdin.   Leningrad, Lenizdat, 1982.

Zemlia rodiny [The Earth of the Motherland]. Moscow, Malysh, 1984.

Izbrannye proizvedeniia v 2-kh tomakh [Selected Works in Two Volumes]. Moscow, Molodaia gvardiia, 1984.

Povesti i rasskazy [Novels and Stories]. Moscow, Sovremennik, 1984.

Poslednii srok: proshchanie s materio: povesti i rasskazy. Moscow, Sovetskii pisatel', 1985.

Pozhar [The Fire]. Published in *Nash sovremennik* (Moscow), 7, 1985.

Chto v slove, chto za slovom? [What's in a Word, What's for a Word?]. Irkutsk, Vostochno-Sibirskoe Knizhnoe izdatel'stvo, 1987.

V taige, nad Baikalom [In the Taiga, Above Baikal]. Moscow, Malysh, 1987.

Zemlia otchizny [The Earth of One's Country]. Kiev, Vesela, 1987.

Chto peredat' vorone? [What to Give to the Crow?]. Moscow, Detskaia literatura, 1988.

Siberia on Fire: Stories and Essays. DeKalb, Northern Illinois University Press, 1989.

Sibir', sibir'... [Siberia, Siberia...]. Novosibirsk, Knizhnoe izdatel'stvo, 1990.

Vospominaniia sovremennikov [Recollections of Contemporaries]. Moscow, VTsPKhL, Lit-konsul'tativ-tsentr, 1990.

Blizhnii svet izdaleko: k 600-letiiu prestavleniia prepodobnogo Sergiia Radonezhskogo. Moscow, Molodaia gvardiia, 1992.

Other

Essays, with *Valentin Rasputin* by Nikolai Kotenko. Moscow, Raduga, 1988.

*

Bibliography: "A Bilingual Bibliography of Works by and About Valentin Rasputin" by Suzan K. Burks, in *Russian Literature Triquarterly* (Ann Arbor, Michigan), 22, 1988.

Critical Studies: "For Truth and Goodness: The Stories of Valentin Rasputin" by Vladimir Vasil'ev, and "To Live and to Remember: Comments on Valentin Rasputin's Prose" by E. Starikova, both in *Soviet Studies in Literature* (Armonk, New York), 14, 1978; "Valentin Rasputin: A General View" by Deming Brown, in *Russian Literature and Criticism*, edited by Evelyn Bristol, Berkeley, California, Berkeley Slavic Specialties, 1982; "Religious Symbolism in Valentin Rasputin's Tale *Live and Remember*" by Gerald E. Mikkelson, in *Studies in Honor of Xenia Gasiorowska*, edited by Lauren Leighton, Columbus, Ohio, Slavica, 1982; "Valentin Rasputin: The Human Race Is Not Accidental" by Alexander Afanasyev, in *Soviet Literature* (Brooklyn, New York), 7[424], 1983; "Childhood and the Adult World in the Writing of Valentin Rasputin," in *Modern Language Review* (Providence, Rhode Island), 80(2), 1985, and *Valentin Rasputin and Soviet Russian Village Prose*, London, Modern Humanities Research Association, 1986, both by David C. Gillespie; "Home or Shelter? Notes on Valentin Rasputin's Story 'The Fire'" by Fyodor Chapchakov, in *Soviet Literature* (Brooklyn, New York), 7[460], 1986; "The Mother Theme in Valentin Rasputin" by Robert Porter, in *Canadian Slavonic Papers* (Edmonton, Alberta), 28(3), 1986; "Fate?" by Elizabeth Rich, and "Soundness of Moral Character" (in reply to Rich's article) by Nikolai Kotenko, both in *Soviet Literature* (Brooklyn, New York), 3[468], 1987; "'Live and Love': The Spiritual Path of Valentin Rasputin" by Margaret Winchell, in

Slavic and East European Journal (Minneapolis), 31(4), 1987; *Valentin Rasputin* (in English) by Nikolai Kotenko, Moscow, Raduga, 1988; *The Novellas of Valentin Rasputin: Genre, Language and Style* by Teresa Polowy, New York, Peter Lang, 1989; "Valentin Rasputin: Then and Now: *Soviet Literature*'s Round Table," in *Soviet Literature* (Brooklyn, New York), 5[494], 1989.

*   *   *

Valentin Rasputin rapidly became one of the leading figures in the so-called "village prose" movement, which arose in the late 1950s and for the next two decades or so embraced much of the best contemporary writing in the Soviet Union. Rasputin's first stories, from the early and mid-1960s, originally appeared in local Siberian publications, but his work quickly attracted national interest. Since 1970 his writings — both fiction and, increasingly, non-fiction — have appeared regularly in the Moscow journal *Nash sovremennik* (Our Contemporary), which has maintained a strong commitment to the village writers; it has also become a leading voice for the nationalistic, "Russophile" movement. Long active as an environmentalist, Rasputin has come to express in his essays an antipathy toward the forces that he feels have harmed rural Russia. In the pre-glasnost era he and the other village prose writers were almost universally praised for their willingness to express harsh truths about life in the Soviet Union. With glasnost and the subsequent fall of the Soviet state, Rasputin, along with such figures in the movement as Viktor Astafiev and Vasilii Belov, has frequently been accused of espousing intolerance toward those not of Russian nationality; the resulting controversy has at times overshadowed his literary reputation.

Like all those who have at one time or another been categorized as village prose writers, Rasputin belongs to the movement not just because his own origins and the settings for his stories happen to be outside the main urban centers, but also because the set of themes that recurs throughout his work expresses a particular outlook. Either explicitly or implicitly, he constantly compares life in the city with that in the country, to the usual detriment of the latter, and he shows those in the country victimized by the complexities and demands of modern society. Thus in his first major work, *Den'gi dlia Marii* (*Money for Maria*), the central figure is a semi-literate peasant woman, in charge of a village store, who somehow must come up with the thousand rubles that an inspector has found to be missing or face jail. The story begins with the contrast between implacable authority and the simple honesty of Maria, and in later scenes it goes on to draw equally sharp distinctions between peasants and city dwellers in general. There appears to be no bridge between the two worlds, and, typically for Rasputin, it remains unclear at the end whether the needed money will be obtained.

That village life is changing irrevocably becomes clear in *Poslednii srok* (*Borrowed Time*), where a dying peasant woman realizes that the countryside has changed greatly during her lifetime and that the four children who come to visit her (two from the city, but also the two who have remained in the country) no longer share her values — and indeed the four end up leaving before she dies. A sign of Rasputin's growing maturity as a writer was his ability here to present the divergent personalities and the web of relationships among the five central characters, at the same time that he offered a psychological study of the way imminent death affects not just the dying but also others in a family. The depth of Rasputin's concern for village life is revealed in *Proshchanie s Materoi* (*Farewell to Matyora*), which depicts the period just before a small island village is to be flooded as part of a huge hydroelectric project. The story is permeated with nostalgia for an older way of life and also for an older set of values, when people lived more in accordance with their conscience. Both the modern bureaucrats and the new settlement of apartments to which the villagers are to be moved are revealed as cold and lacking the spirit of the peasants and their beloved village. This novel, which was made into a popular film, resonates both backward and forward within Rasputin's oeuvre. The earlier story "Downstream" described a visit by the narrator, a writer, to his native village, displaced by a dam. Since Rasputin himself was born on the upper Angara River, which in fact flooded a number of villages when the huge Bratsk hydroelectric project was completed, his concerns touch very close to home. *Pozhar* (The Fire), Rasputin's third work on this theme and his only novella-length piece of fiction in the decade and a half since *Farewell to Matyora*, presents perhaps his most bitter indictment of the damage wreaked in the name of progress. His protagonist is an upright worker whose life has been devoted to hard work, but the removal of his native village has undermined individual morality and destroyed the community fabric. The fire, which destroys a huge warehouse containing supplies for the entire village, provides both a symbolic (after the flood, the "fire next time") and a literal embodiment of the punishment inflicted on those who have lost their roots.

Rasputin's literary reputation has been established on the basis of a relatively modest output. Never very prolific, his writing slowed markedly after the mid-1970s. Nor has he been close to the centers of literary activity. Residing in Irkutsk, he has remained physically apart from other writers. And the locales of his stories, which are most often set near the banks of the Angara river flowing northward from Lake Baikal, are hardly likely to be familiar to the majority of his readers. Yet his literary skills are difficult to ignore, and his themes did strike a nerve in the popular imagination. Nowhere is his talent more in evidence than in his novella *Zhivi i pomni* (*Live and Remember*), where a Siberian soldier, wounded during the waning days of World War II, decides after his recovery to return to his village instead of to the front. But the work is less about him than about his wife, who aids him in his hiding, eventually becomes pregnant, and, tortured by the suspicions of her fellow villagers, finally commits suicide. Rasputin's ability to capture the nuances of Siberian peasant speech, the sympathy and depth he lends to his depiction of the wife (here as in most of his important works the central and most sympathetic character is a woman), the mastery with which he weaves a complex yet engaging narrative that includes shifting points of view as well as the use of flashback and dreams — all these are the mark of a fine literary craftsman.

— Barry P. Scherr

RATUSHINSKAIA, Irina (Georgievna). Also Irina Ratushinskaya. Russian and British. Born in Odessa, Ukraine, 4 March 1954. Educated at Odessa University, M.A. in physics 1976. Married Igor Gerashchenko in 1979. Teacher at primary school, Odessa, 1975–78; worked at Odessa Pedagogical Institute, from 1977; arrested September 1982, sentenced to seven years hard labour for political activities: spent four years in labour camps in Mordovia, 1982–86, transferred to KGB investigation camp, Kiev, June 1986;

released October 1986 as a result of international pressure leading up to summit in Reykjavík between President Mikhail Gorbachev and U.S. President Ronald Reagan; moved to England; lost Russian citizenship, 1987. Founder, Democracy and Independence Group, 1989. Recipient: Institute on Religion and Democracy Religious Freedom award, 1987. Agent: Andrew Nurnberg Associates, Clerkenwell House, 45–47 Clerkenwell Green, London EC1 0HT, England.

PUBLICATIONS

Verse

Stikhi [Poems]. Published in *Grani* (Frankfurt), 123, 1982; 129, 1983; 132, 1984; 137, 1985.
Stikhi [Poems] (trilingual edition in Russian, English, and French). Ann Arbor, Michigan, Hermitage, 1984.
Vne limita: izbrannoe. Frankfurt, Posev, 1986; as *Beyond the Limit* (bilingual edition), translated by Frances Padorr Brent and Carol J. Avis, Evanston, Illinois, Northwestern University Press, 1987.
Ia dozhivu: stikhi [I'll Survive: Poems]. New York, Cultural Center for Soviet Refugees, 1986.
No, I'm Not Afraid, translated by David McDuff. Newcastle-upon-Tyne, Bloodaxe, 1986.
Pencil Letter. Newcastle-upon-Tyne, Bloodaxe, 1988; New York, Knopf, 1989.
Rodina, ty mne vrastaesh' v rebra . . . [Motherland . . . You Raised Me on the Edge]. Published in *Druzhba narodov* (Moscow), 1, 1990.
Dance with a Shadow. Newcastle-upon-Tyne, Bloodaxe, 1992.

Fiction

O smysle zhizni: golos [About the Idea of Life: Voice]. Published in *Grani* (Frankfurt), 126, 1982.
Skazka o trekh golovakh: rasskazy-pritchi [A Tale of Three Heads: Short Stories] (bilingual edition). Ann Arbor, Michigan, Hermitage, 1986.

Other

Grey Is the Colour of Hope (memoir). New York, Knopf, and London, Hodder and Stoughton, 1988; as *Ser'ii: tsvet nadezhd'i*, London, Overseas Publications Interchange, 1989.
In the Beginning. London, Hodder and Stoughton, 1990; New York, Knopf, 1991.

*

Critical Studies: "Making Up for Lost Time," in *Index on Censorship* (London), 14(5), 1985; "The Poetry of Irina Ratushinskaya" by Raymond Cooke, in *Journal of Russian Studies* (Rugby, Warwickshire), 3, 1987, *Irina* by Dick Rodgers, Tring, Lion, 1987; "What Does a Six-Winged Seraphim Taste Like?" by David M. Bethea, in *Parnassus* (New York), 14(2), 1988; *Poet Against the Lie: Irina Ratushinskaya Talks of Her Experience as a Russian Dissident*, n.p., Grosvenor/For a Change, 1991.

*   *   *

Irina Ratushinskaia first came to prominence in the West as a writer of "protest" poems against the conditions of imprisonment in Soviet labour camps during the 1970s and 1980s. However, this theme of protest, though undoubtedly one of the principal features of her work, is by no means its only one. Together with Iosif Brodskii and Aleksandr Kushner (*qq.v.*), Ratushinskaia is one of the few genuine inheritors of the poetic tradition represented by the so-called "quartet" of Osip Mandel'shtam, Boris Pasternak, Marina Tsvetaeva, and Anna Akhmatova; her concerns, though perhaps not quite as broad and deep as theirs, nonetheless go far beyond the scope of purely political poetry, and include a number of religious and metaphysical themes.

Ratushinskaia's early poetry shows the influence of Russian folk verse and popular song. Even in these early lyrics, there is a sense of foreboding and of a sacrifice that awaits somewhere in the future. Many of the poems have a ballad-like form, and involve the telling of fortunes and the presaging of a young couple's destiny:

> "Tell me, gypsy woman, is it true
> That our fate is on our palms?"
> "Give me your hand. He loves you.
> And this means a far-away road."

There is also, however, the influence of contemporary Polish poetry. Being herself of Polish extraction, Ratushinskaia obviously felt an affinity with poets such as Wysława Szymborska (*q.v.*), and quite a few of Ratushinskaia's early poems dispense with strict rhyme and metre, or are written in completely free verse — something comparatively rare in Russian poetry.

Another feature of the early work, and one which characterizes much of the poet's output in general, is a fondness for and sensitivity to the idioms and expressive modes of children's verse. In Ratushinskaia's work of the early 1970s there are poems about cats, hide-and-seek, a "Waltz with Umbrella, Hurdy-Gurdy and Pie," and *shurshavchiki* ("rustlers," a kind of self-invented mythical creature), and at times the whimsicality of such verse can seem excessive. Yet there is a deeper purpose here: Ratushinskaia is a committed Christian, and in her poems she often invokes the reality of childhood in order to underline her faith that there does exist a simple, childlike path to God:

> The road to Him, how discover?
> With what measure the hope, pain and grief?
> People seek God, a kind one.
> God grant they may find and believe.

But the core of Ratushinskaia's mature poetry is represented by the large body of verse written in and about the Soviet prison camps in which she was held as a prisoner of conscience during the early 1980s, in particular the KGB prison in Kiev and the "Small Zone" of Camp Zh/Kh 285/34, special women's prison in the Mordovian "Dubrovlag." These poems not only give the poet's individual reaction to the harsh conditions of her imprisonment and that of her fellow-inmates, they also document those conditions with a sane objectivity that renders the subjective, lyrical statements of the poems all the more moving and truthful. Through Ratushinskaia's eyes and ears we experience the reality of the camp and the solidarity between the women prisoners. Some of the most powerful poems describe incidents of violence and torture, as when the poet had her head "slammed against a trestle," and later, in solitary confinement in a freezing cell, saw the "rainbow ice" form on the window, in a vision of almost ethereal, fairytale beauty, strangely incongruous in the circumstances, but believable and spiritually penetrating:

Only a blue radiance on a tiny pane of glass,
A cast pattern — none more beautiful could be dreamt!
The more clearly you looked, the more powerfully blossomed
Those brigand forests, campfires and birds!

Ratushinskaia writes in the best tradition of Russian poetry — like Mandel'shtam, she maintains her sanity and sense of humour even when her situation was at its most intolerable, and like Akhmatova she is concerned to bear witness, to provide an indelible record of the suffering that is not only her own but that of her "hateful motherland." From Tsvetaeva she learned how to make the spoken voice, with its rhythms and cross-beats, resound in her poems, and from Pasternak she derived a facility with images which in their concision and clarity contain a spiritual strength that is the strength of the individual consciousness and conscience. As Brodskii has written, Ratushinskaia "is a remarkably genuine poet, a poet with faultless pitch, who hears historical and absolute time with equal precision. She's a full-fledged poet, mature, with a voice of her own, piercing but devoid of hysteria . . . Whatever bad luck Russia may have had in this century, it has been extraordinarily lucky with its poetry. Ratushinskaia's poems confirm the fact that the luck holds. The price of this luck, however, has been frightful, as is confirmed by her fate."

Since her emigration to England in 1986, Ratushinskaia has continued to write poetry. Some of the more recent poems seem to look back to the beginning of her poetic career, containing the same elements of childlike whimsy and romantic nostalgia; but others reflect on the experience of exile and imprisonment with a depth and awareness that spring from a religious vision that has been tempered and clarified by suffering. One looks forward to see how her poetic gift will develop, and whether new themes and images will eventually appear in her poems.

—David McDuff

RATUSHINSKAYA, Irina. *See* **RATUSHINSKAIA, Irina.**

RAVIKOVITCH, Dahlia. Also Dahlia Rabikovitz. Israeli Born in Ramat-Gan, Palestine (now Israel), 17 Novembe 1936. Has one son. Teacher, 1959–63; journalist. Address: c/ Hakibuts haMe'uchad Publishing House, P.O. Box 16040, 3 Hayetzirah Street, Tel Aviv 61160, Israel.

PUBLICATIONS

Verse

Ahavat tapuach hazahav [The Love of an Orange].   Tel Avi
    Sifriyat Po'alim, 1959.
Mivchar shirim udevarim al yetsiratah [Selected Poems ar
    Comments on Her Work].   Tel Aviv, Machbarot leShira
    1962.

Hachalil vahachetz [The Flute and the Sorrow].   Tel Aviv, La-Dori, 1963(?).
Choref kasheh [A Hard Winter].   Tel Aviv, Dvir, 1964.
Hasefer hashelishiy [Third Book].   Tel Aviv, Levine-Epstein, 1969.
Kol mishbarecha vegalecha [All Thy Breakers and Waves]. Tel Aviv, Hakibuts haMe'uchad, 1972.
Tehom kore [Deep Calleth unto Deep].   Tel Aviv, Hakibuts haMe'uchad, 1976.
A Dress of Fire, translated by Chana Bloch. London, Menard Press, 1976.
Ahavah amitit [Real Love]. Tel Aviv, Hakibuts haMe'uchad, 1986.
The Window: New and Selected Poems, translated by Chana and Ariel Bloch.   New York, Sheep Meadow Press, 1989.

Other

Mavet bamishpachah [Death in the Family].   Tel Aviv, Am Oved, 1976.
Me'alilot Dedi hamufl'a [The Deeds of Dedi the Wonderful] (for children).   Tel Aviv, Hakibuts haMe'uchad, 1977.

Editor, *The New Israeli Writers: Short Stories of the First Generation*.   New York, Funk and Wagnalls, 1990.

*

Critical Studies: in *The Modern Hebrew Poem Itself*, edited by Stanley Burnshaw, T. Carmi, and Ezra Spicehandler, New York, Holt Rinehart, 1965, revised edition, Cambridge, Massachusetts, Harvard University Press, 1989; "Closing Distances: Three Modern Hebrew Poets" by Yossi Gamzu, in *Poetry Australia* (Berrima, New South Wales), 66, 1978; "Besieged Feminism: Contradictory Rhetorical Themes in the Poetry of Daliah Rabikovitz" by Yair Mazor, in *World Literature Today* (Norman, Oklahoma), 58(3), 1984.

*   *   *

Dahlia Ravikovitch is Israel's leading woman poet. She is one of the first generation of poets who, in Stanley Burnshaw's words, were "born into both the language and the landscape" of Israel (*The Modern Hebrew Poem Itself*, 1965). In Ravikovitch's poetry, one senses the emotional dimensions of this landscape, the vicissitudes of living with "no resting place for my eyes/from one end of the sky to the other" ("King over Israel"). Bleakness, weariness, and loss resound in the poems, and their speaker is often quite alone. Yet the voice in these poems — astringent, self-aware, and at times self-mocking — conveys a survivor's strength.

Ravikovitch's poems are deeply felt and intensely personal, yet reject sentimentality and the excess of more "confessional" poetry. In many of her poems, as Arieh Sachs notes in *The Modern Hebrew Poem Itself*, "the deeply personal hurt assumes the impersonal forms of myth and hallucination." Even poems about failed love (such as "Heron" and "Hills of Salt") have an emblematic quality, as if the speaker is not referring to an actual loved one, but continuing a discourse with herself. This is poetry anchored not in relationship to specific landscapes or people but in the loneliness and richness of the imagination.

The poems' use of natural imagery reinforces this sense. Recurring images of trees, grass, birds, and flowers do not root the speaker in the world as much as they loom above and diminish her, and leave her longing for connection. In "Night Sorrow," "The stars, the planets swarm./Night drops into the sea of nights . . ." "The way is so long/and the new moon's like hammered tin/and above it, whiter than milk, that light/streaming/like salvation." Allusions to biblical figures and verses also recur, adding an ancient undertone to Ravikovitch's stark vision. In Psalm 19, "Day unto day utters speech" in God's praise; in the poem "Even a Thousand Years," "Day unto day and day unto night declare nothing." Yet an unfulfilled yearning calls from "the deep" in Ravikovitch's poems, despite the overall bleakness of her landscape and her own attempts to dismiss it.

Ravikovitch's books of poetry reveal an evolution in her use of language and her themes. In her earliest books, *Ahavat tapuach hazahav* (The Love of an Orange) and *Choref kasheh* (A Hard Winter), the poems have the "once-upon-a-time" tint of children's stories or the enigmatic quality of parables. Through the dreamlike surfaces of these poems, depths of feeling glow. Robert Alter, in his foreword to *The Window*, describes the poet's child-like "sense of wonder and terror" and adds, "The Hebrew Ravikovitch uses in her first two volumes of poetry is an apt vehicle for such a sense of reality precisely because of its ostentatiously literary, uncolloquial character." Tightly structured and highly musical, the early poems have an incantatory quality, as in "Buba Memukenet" ("Clockwork Doll," a poem widely anthologized in English), in which the poet's alienation is seen through her identification with a mechanical doll. A longing to escape to "The Land of the Setting Sun," to "sail around the whole world in one night" ("Time Caught in a Net") is darkened in these poems by the loneliness of ". . . no companion at all,/only the dust/came along with me" ("Dust").

In the laconically titled *Hasefer hashelishiy* (Third Book), Ravikovitch forfeits fantasy for the equally lonely task of confronting the "real" world. As the poet addresses a more complex reality, she simplifies her language, turning at last to more colloquial Hebrew and abandoning formally structured, rhymed stanzas. In contrast to earlier works, these poems do not hesitate to make outright claims: "Pain has no use,/I assure you" ("A Personal Opinion"); "I tell you, even rocks crack ,/and not because of age" ("Pride"). Instead of fairytale lands, the poet names actual places — Australia, Manchuria, Chad, and Cameroon, still exotic, but far less hospitable. The surreal is not entirely absent from Ravikovitch's vision, however. In "A Dress of Fire," a dialogue about a burning dress reveals that the poet herself is on fire; memory breaks "from the depths of the earth/bright red as a poppy" ("Pure Memory"); an apocalyptic vision of the poet in Hong Kong ends: "I am not in Hong Kong/and Hong Kong is not in the world" ("Hong Kong Was Destroyed"). In "The Marionette," the poet considers the life of "a pale slender doll of porcelain,/held by threads. . . . A marionette —/she too is real./She has memories . . ." Yet in contrast to "Clockwork Doll," the poet never merges with the puppet, and her tone reveals the impossibility of becoming that dehumanized again.

The concern with life's harshness in *Hasefer hashelishiy* presages Ravikovitch's most recent book of poems, *Ahavah amitit* (Real Love). Published four years after Israel's war with Lebanon, the book includes Ravikovitch's first explicitly political work. Some of these "protest poems" were first published in the Israeli press during the war. The poet's translators, Chana and Ariel Bloch, note: "These poems, which Ravikovitch herself calls 'newspaper verse,' have aroused much debate in Israel . . ." Regardless of their controversy, and even regardless of their merit as literary works, they are a vivid sign of the poet's struggle to confront her own complicity in the horrors of her time and place. One of the best-known poems from this collection is "Hovering at a Low Altitude," in which the speaker repeatedly insists "I am not here," yet is positioned "not with my feet on the ground, and not flying —/hovering" over a violent scene that she is unable to escape.

Ravikovitch's poems contain an almost overwhelming vision of a world that lacks "sense," in which death waits for "everything beautiful" ("Even a Thousand Years"). Yet the voice in these poems is that of a survivor, whose stubborn and even proud existence is no small triumph. And the "infinite treasures" of the imagination ("Surely You Remember"), although no substitute for love or justice, burn through Ravikovitch's poems.

—Merle Lyn Bachman

REVE, Gerard (Kornelis van het). Dutch. Born in Amsterdam, 14 December 1923. Educated at Vossius Gymnasium, Amsterdam; school for graphic design. Reporter, *Het Parool*, Amsterdam, 1945–47; lived in London, studying drama and working as a mental nurse, 1952–57; editor, *Tirade* magazine from 1957; has lived in France since 1969. Recipient: Hooft prize, 1968. Address: La Grâce, Le Poët-Laval, 26160 La Bégude de Mazenc, France.

PUBLICATIONS

Fiction

De avonden: een winterverhaal [The Evenings: A Winter's Tale]. Amsterdam, Bezige Bij, 1947.
Werther Nieland. Amsterdam, Bezige Bij, 1949.
De ondergang van de familie Boslowits [The Downfall of the Boslowits Family]. Amsterdam, Bezige Bij, 1950.
The Acrobat and Other Stories (written in English). Amsterdam and London, Van Oorschot, 1956; as *Vier wintervertellingen* [Four Winter Tales], Amsterdam, Van Oorschot, 1963.
Tien vrolijke verhalen [Ten Cheerful Stories]. Amsterdam, Van Oorschot, 1961.
Op weg naar het einde [Approaching the End]. Amsterdam, Van Oorschot, 1963.
Nader tot u [Nearer to You]. Amsterdam, Van Oorschot, 1966.
A Prison Song in Prose (written in English). Amsterdam, Athenaeum-Polak & Van Gennep, 1968.
De taal der liefde [The Language of Love]. Amsterdam, Athenaeum-Polak & Van Gennep, 1972.
Onze vrienden [Our Friends]. Amsterdam, Athenaeum-Polak & Van Gennep, 1972.
Lieve jongens [Dear Boys]. Amsterdam, Athenaeum-Polak & Van Gennep, 1973.
Lekker kerstbrood [Lovely Christmas Cake]. Amstelveen, Peter Loeb, 1973.
Rietsuiker [Cane Sugar]. Amstelveen, Peter Loeb, 1974.
Het lieve leven [Dear Life]. Amsterdam, Athenaeum-Polak & Van Gennep, 1974.
Ik had hem lief [I Loved Him]. Amsterdam, Elsevier, 1975.
Een circusjongen [A Circus Boy]. Amsterdam, Athenaeum-Polak & Van Gennep, 1975.
Oud en eenzaam [Old and Alone]. Amsterdam, Elsevier, 1978.

Moeder en zoon [Mother and Son]. Amsterdam, Manteau, 1980.
De vierde man [The Fourth Man]. Amsterdam, Manteau, 1981.
Wolf. Amsterdam, Manteau, 1983.
De stille vriend [The Silent Friend]. Amsterdam, Manteau, 1984.
Bezorgde ouders. Utrecht, Veen, 1988; as *Parents Worry*, London, Fourth Estate, 1990.

Plays

Commissaris Fennedy. Amsterdam, Bezige Bij, 1962.
Proloog/epiloog. Gripsholm, Donkeremaanpers, 1985.

Verse

Zes gedichten [Six Poems]. Amsterdam, Polak & Van Gennep, 1965.
Gezicht op Kerstmis, en andere geestelijke liederen [Prospect of Christmas, and Other Spiritual Poems]. Amsterdam, Fritz Boer, 1965.
Credo. Zandvoort, Eliance, 1973.
Trouw [Faithful]. Zandvoort, Eliance, 1973.
Het zingend hart [The Singing Heart]. Amsterdam, Athenaeum-Polak & Van Gennep, 1973.
Elf gedichten [Eleven Poems]. Amsterdam, The Publishers, 1973.
Ernstjan Engels geeft voor zijn bengels een heel fijn feest [Ernstjan Engels Throws a Fine Party for His Hanging Things]. N.p. n.p., 1974.
Cubaans bidprentje [Cuban Devotional Picture]. Amsterdam, Loeb & Van der Velden, 1978.
Vergeten gedichten [Forgotten Poems]. Amsterdam, Bibliotheca Reviana, 1979.
(Selection in English), in *Dutch Crossing 12*, December 1980.
Quattuor poemata [Four Poems]. N.p., Prelum cui nomen Brakmoron, 1982.
Het fijne leven [The Fine Life]. N.p., J.S.-NVSC, 1984.
Verzamelde gedichten [Collected Poems]. Amsterdam, Van Oorschot, 1987.

Other

Verzameld werk [Collected Work]. Amsterdam, Van Oorschot, 1956.
Veertien etsen van Frans Lodewijk Pannekoek [Fourteen Etchings by Frans Lodewijk Pannekoek]. Amsterdam, Rap, 1967.
Uit de kunst: brieven aan Simon Carmiggelt [A Work of Art: Letters to Simon Carmiggelt]. Zandvoort, Eliance Pers, 1970.
Vier pleidooien [Four Pleas]. Amsterdam, Athenaeum-Polak & Van Gennep, 1971.
Drie toespraken [Three Public Addresses]. Amsterdam, Peter Loeb, 1976.
Brieven aan kandidaat katholiek A 1962–1969 [Letters to Prospective Catholic A]. Amsterdam, Rap, 1976.
Een eigen huis [A House of One's Own]. Amsterdam, Manteau, 1979.
Brieven aan Wimie 1959–1963 [Letters to Wimie]. Utrecht, Veen, 1980.
Het boek van het violet en van de dood [The Book of the Violet and of Death]. Amsterdam, Manteau, 1980.

Gerard Reve en S. Carmiggelt in gesprek [Gerard Reve and S. Carmiggelt in Conversation]. Amsterdam, Van der Velden, 1980.

Drie woorden [Three Words]. Utrecht, Reflex, 1981.

Brieven aan Josine M 1959–1975 [Letters to Josine M]. Amsterdam, Van Oorschot, 1981.

Brieven aan Bernard S 1965–1975 [Letters to Bernard S], edited by Sjaak Hubregtse. Utrecht, Veen, 1981.

Archief Reve 1931–1980, edited by Pierre H. Dubois, annotated by Sjaak Hubregtse. Baarn, Prom, 2 vols., 1981–82.

Brieven aan Simon C 1971–1976 [Letters to Simon C]. Amsterdam, Van Oorschot, 1982.

Zeergeleerde vrouwe [Well-Educated Women]. Utrecht, Veen, 1982.

Aan Sint Vincentius [To Saint Vincentius]. Yde, De Breukenpers, 1982.

In gesprek [In Conversation] (interviews). Baarn, de Prom, 1983.

Brieven aan Wim B 1968–1975 [Letters to Wim B]. Utrecht, Veen, 1983.

Een vieze oude kale mann [A Dirty Old Bald Man]. Utrecht, Utrechtse Dom-pers, 1983.

Album Reve, edited by Joost Schafthuizen. Amsterdam, Elsevier, 1983.

De overschatting [The Reassessment]. Utrecht, Het Mortier, 1984.

Schon schip: 1945–1984. Amsterdam, Manteau, 1984.

Brieven aan Frans P: 1965–1969 [Letters to Frans P]. Utrecht, Veen, 1984.

Interview over roofdrukken [Interview on Looting]. Schiedam, Het Schaftlokaal, 1985.

De sociale positie van Sinterklaas [The Social Position of Father Christmas]. Waspik, "De Gulden Roede," 1985.

Roomse Heisa. Amsterdam, Manteau, 1985.

Vier brieven [Four Letters], with Jotie T' Hooft. Rotterdam, Bébert, 1985.

Brieven aan geschoolde arbeiders [Letters to Educated Workers]. Utrecht, Veen, 1985.

Wordt het geen tijd . . .? [Is It Not Time?]. Amsterdam, n.p., 1985.

Zelf schrijver worden [Becoming a Writer]. Leiden, Nijhoff, 1986.

Dagsluiting [Close of Day]. Rotterdam, Bébert, 1986.

Brieven aan Ludo P 1962–1980 [Letters to Ludo P]. Amsterdam, Van Oorschot, 1986.

Klein gebrek geen bezwaar: een keuze uit zijn brieven [Little Use, No Objection]. Utrecht, Veen, 1986.

Droom [Dream]. Rotterdam, Bébert, 1986.

Roeping [Calling]. Rotterdam, Bébert, 1986.

Je brief kwam net te laat [Your Letter Was Just Too Late], with Rudy Kousbroek. Rotterdam, Bébert, 1986.

Oompje beer en jihn vriendjes [Uncle Bear and His Friends]. Amstelveen, AMO, 1987.

Het geheim van Louis Couperus [Louis Couperus's Secret]. Utrecht, Veen, 1987.

Buitenland trekt onze meisjes aan: weten zij wel, waar ze terechtkomen? [The Outside World Attracts Our Girls: Do They Know Where They Will End Up?] Bedum, Exponent, 1988.

Het zesde jaar [The Sixth Year]. Amstelveen, AMO, 1989.

Geen intellectuelenpoëzie [No Intellectual Poetry]. Bedum, Exponent, 1990.

Hoe zwaar weegt een been?: open brief aan Rudy Kousbroek [How Heavy Is a Leg?: Open Letter to Rudy Kousbroek]. Oosterhesselen, De Klencke, 1991.

Translator, *Het verjaardagsfeest* [The Birthday Party]; *De huisbewaarder* [The Caretaker]; *De collectie* [The Collection], by Harold Pinter. Amsterdam, Bezige Bij, 1980.

*

Bibliography: *Bibliografie von Reve* by Gerrit Heuvelman and Peter Willems, privately printed, 1980.

Critical Studies: "The Greatest Show in Church" by J. H. W. Veenstra, in *Tirade* (Amsterdam), 14, 1970; "G. K. van het Reve's English Prose Style" by Felix J. Douma, in *Spektator* (Amsterdam), 3, 1973; "From Cronus to Janus: The Problem of Time in Gerard (Kornelius van het) Reve's Work," in *Dutch Studies*, 3, 1977, "Gerard Reve's Window of Vulnerability," in *Papers from the Third Interdisciplinary Conference on Netherlandic Studies*, edited by Ton J. Broos, Lanham, Maryland, University Press of America, 1988, and "Reve's Early Protagonists: Between the Pages and the Sheets," in *The Berkeley Conference on Dutch Literature 1987: New Perspectives on the Modern Period*, edited by Johan D. Snapper and T. F. Shannon, Lanham, Maryland, University Press of America, 1989, all by Johan D. Snapper; Reve issue of *Tirade* (Amsterdam), December 1983.

* * *

Gerard Reve is widely regarded as the supreme stylist among living Dutch prose writers, though his literary career since the 1960s has made him, artistically, morally, and politically, a controversial figure.

His early, naturalistic, work derives its impact from an understated, deadpan formality of tone, used to telling effect in his first novel, *De avonden* (The Evenings), which became a classic of the war generation and has enjoyed enduring popularity since. The book, whose "hero," a school dropout in his early twenties still living at home, spends an aimless 10 days between Christmas and New Year conversing but not communicating with family and friends, reflecting on his lot, and finally appealing *de profundis* to a God he may or may not believe in, is punctuated by a series of nightmares in which his repressed anxieties surface. Equally impressive is the novella *Werther Nieland*, a study of boyhood obsession and ritual.

A period spent in England (where his contacts included Angus Wilson), produced a collection of eerie stories in English, *The Acrobat*, and an involvement with English theatre as student, critic, and translator (of, among others, Harold Pinter, Edward Albee, and Brendan Behan). His own activity as a playwright was short-lived: only one play, reminiscent of Tennessee Williams, was performed, while a second, called *Moorlandshuis*, though commissioned and awarded a literary prize, was never published.

Two widely acclaimed books of "open letters," *Op weg naar het einde* (Approaching the End) and *Nader tot u* (Nearer to You) (the latter containing a number of striking poems), mark a major turning point. Freed from the constraints of a traditional plot, Reve blurs the boundaries of fiction and autobiography (the explicit treatment of his own homosexuality broke an important taboo in the post-war Netherlands), in a style switching constantly from the solemnly exalted and archaic to the grossly colloquial, often to riotous effect. In *Nader tot u*, under the influence of Mario Praz's work, he finds his mission as a Romantic Decadent dedicated to celebrating the sacred trinity of Love, Sex, and Death (such capitalising of key concepts is to become a hallmark) in the context of a very individual brand of Roman Catholicism, to which he was converted in 1966. The much-publicised conversion, exploited with the flair of a natural showman, helped make him a national figure with a mass readership, as well as incurring the disapproval of some of the literary establishment and a conviction for blasphemy, against which he appealed eloquently and successfully.

The cult of "Revism" (a play on the shortened form of his name and its associations with *rêve*), using frame narrative to weave a bizarre tapestry of fact and fantasy, was carried further in *De taal der liefde* (The Language of Love), in which a queen figure strongly suggestive of the actual Dutch monarch acts as confidante and muse, and in its sequel *Lieve jongens* (Dear Boys), which was subsequently filmed. *Een circusjongen* (A Circus Boy) made virtuoso use of kitsch elements, but in lesser books his writing tended to become overly mannered and repetitive.

Reve made a comeback in a more sober vein with *Oud en eenzaam* (Old and Alone), in which he ingeniously combines an account of a homosexual pursuit in present-day France with a flashback to a heterosexual episode in the London of the 1950s, and confirmed it two years later in *Moeder en zoon* (Mother and Son), which traces his religious development, culminating, in a sublimely comic passage, in his improbable acceptance into the Catholic Church.

Bezorgde ouders (*Parents Worry*), to quote its blurb (a genre which Reve has turned into a minor art form), is "the largely historical story of one day in the ravaged life of the poet Hugo Treger, who sees the dire straits humanity and the world are in and who desperately searches for a way out and for the truth. The way to truth, however, leads through pain, cruelty, and suffering. 'Per Dolorem ad Veritatem,' muses our hero: 'Through Pain to Truth.'" The book marks a new high point in Reve's pursuit of a unique blend of camp and high seriousness.

For Reve, the self-professed Romantic, the outer world is ultimately merely decor, and as such is to be treated with appropriate scepticism. His conservative political stance, as expressed both in his work and in a notorious newspaper interview in the 1980s, have led to widespread public outrage and to charges of fascism and racialism. His pronouncements in this field may be seen as reactions partly to a childhood spent in a fanatically Communist family and partly to the rhetoric of progressive conformism which attended the post-1960s wave of "democratisation" in the Netherlands. Admirers would claim that the element of irony and self-parody is as difficult to gauge as it is with a writer like Jorge Luis Borges.

Certainly, Reve continues to have as many adherents as detractors, witness the growth in recent years of a veritable "Reve industry" of secondary literature, archive material, and letters, a monument during the author's own lifetime to 40 years' diverse and often distinguished literary achievement.

—Paul Vincent

RIBEIRO, João Ubaldo (Osório Pimentel). Brazilian. Born on Island of Itaparica, All Saints Bay, Bahia, 23 January 1941. Educated at the Federal University of Bahia, 1959–62, LL.B. 1962; University of Southern California, Los Angeles, 1964–65, M.S. in public administration 1965. Married 1) Maria Beatriz Gordilho Moreira Caldas (divorced); 2) Mónica Maria Roters (divorced), two daughters; 3) Berenice de Carvalho Batella, one son and one daughter. Professor of political science, Federal University of Bahia, and Catholic University of Salvador, Bahia; editor-in-chief, *Tribuna da*

Bahia newspaper, Salvador, Bahia; journalist or editor for various other newspapers; participated in International Writers Program, University of Iowa, Iowa City. Recipient: State of Rio de Janeiro Golfinho de Ouro [Golden Dolphin] prize; Brazilian Book Chamber Jabuti [Tortoise] prize (twice); José Lins do Rego prize; São Paulo Association of Art Critics award; Brazilian National Foundation for Literature for Young People award; Gulbenkian Foundation (Portugal) scholarship. Commander, Order of Merit of Portugal. Agent: Thomas Colchie, 324 85th Street, Brooklyn, New York 11209, U.S.A. Address: Rua General Urquiza 147, ap.401, 22431 Rio de Janeiro, R.J., Brazil.

PUBLICATIONS

Fiction

Setembro não tem sentido.   Rio de Janeiro, Álvaro, 1968.
Sargento Getúlio.   Rio de Janeiro, Civilização Brasileira, 1971; as *Sergeant Getúlio*, Boston, Houghton Mifflin, 1978; London, Deutsch, 1980.
Vencecavalo e o outro povo.   Rio de Janeiro, Artenova, 1974.
Vila real.   Rio de Janeiro, Nova Fronteira, 1979.
Viva o povo brasileiro.   Rio de Janeiro, Nova Fronteira, 1984; as *An Invincible Memory*, New York, Harper, and London, Faber, 1989.
Livro de histórias.   São Paulo, Círculo do Livro, 1985.
O sorriso do lagarto.   Rio de Janeiro, Nova Fronteira, 1989; as *The Smile of the Lizard*, New York, Atheneum, 1992.

Plays

Radio Plays: *História de pescaria* (Germany); *Viva a Novo Mundo* (Germany).

Other

Política: quem manda, por que manda, como manda.   Rio de Janeiro, Nova Fronteira, 1981.
Vida e paixão de Pandonar, o Cruel.   Rio de Janeiro, Nova Fronteira, 1983.
Nunca aos domingos.   Rio de Janeiro, Nova Fronteira, 1988.

*

Critical Study: "Chthonian Visions and Mythic Redemption in João Ubaldo Ribeiro's *Sergeant Getúlio*" by Robert Di Antonio, in *Modern Fiction Studies* (West Lafayette, Indiana), 32(3), 1986.

*   *   *

It is not merely physically that the vast territory of Brazil has yielded to man's conquest: the literary imagination of its writers is still grappling with its sprawling, complex geography and its equally complicated history and social evolution. João Ubaldo Ribeiro is one of Brazil's contemporary writers who has shown the keenest appetite to explore these riches.

Ribeiro came of age as a writer during the 1970s, when the main challenge to Brazilian society and the individual psyche was seen to be the threat from the widespread abuse of authority, symbolised by the military rule imposed after 1964. His second novel *Sargento Getúlio* (*Sergeant Getúlio*) situates this struggle in the figure of a lowly official who is gradually transformed into an unfeeling monster by the role he finds himself playing in repressing his own kind. As author, Ribeiro does something similar in reverse, by convincingly projecting himself into the voice of repression, suggesting in this way how each and every one in a repressive society comes to incorporate the language and attitudes of dictatorship into their own personal experience.

It was, however, in Ribeiro's next novel *Viva o povo brasileiro* (*An Invincible Memory*) that his ambition to encompass the whole of Brazilian history and experience was most clearly demonstrated. This 500-page book traces a wide panorama of life in Brazil from the 1640s to the 1970s, seen largely through the experiences of the white settlers on the one hand, and the black slaves and their descendants on the other. Paradoxically perhaps, Ribeiro maintains that it is the slaves brought to Brazil against their will who were more able to claim the land as their own. Ribeiro attributes this to the fact that they worked directly on the land in the sugar and coffee plantations, used the products of Brazil's nature to cook for their masters, and brought with them strong beliefs that offered them brotherhood rather than a sense of alienation from their surroundings. By the end of the novel Ribeiro is declaring his faith in the "Spirit of Man" to bring hope for Brazil's future; with hindsight, this spirit and the optimism revealed in the vast scope of *An Invincible Memory* are an expression of the period in the 1980s when the military regimes were finally giving way to civilian rule, and a whole new generation of Brazilians felt they could start society anew.

Such hopes have been largely frustrated, and once again the spirit of the country has been reflected in Ribeiro's writing, which has taken on a much darker tone. Environmental concerns and a fear of a natural apocalypse have been more recent themes in his work, with solutions being found only on a local scale. Ribeiro has now adopted a more modest belief in the possibilities for salvation: "the spirit of man" is still functioning, but the earlier ambition to explore and uncover new worlds has been replaced by one of trying to preserve what has already been achieved.

Ribeiro lived and taught for many years in the United States. He has translated his own novels into English, creating a kind of language no native English speaker would use. This phenomenon reflects the need Ribeiro feels to convey the Brazilian experience without intermediary so that the reader is offered a more authentic version of the vast world he is venturing into.

—Nick Caistor

RIFBJERG, Klaus (Thorvald). Danish. Born in Copenhagen, 15 December 1931. Educated at Princeton University, New Jersey, 1950–51; University of Copenhagen, 1951–55. Married Inge Gerner Andersen in 1955; one son and two daughters. Film director, 1955–57; critic and columnist, *Information* newspaper, 1957–59, and *Politiken*, 1959–71; editor, with Villy Sørensen (*q.v.*), *Vindrosen*, 1959–63; literary director, Gyldendal publishers, Copenhagen, 1984–92; Adjunct Professor, Danish Lærerhøjskole, 1986; Honorary Doctor, Lund University, from 1992. Recipient: Aarestrup Medal, 1964; Danish Critics award, 1965; Danish Dramatists award, 1966; Danish Academy prize, 1966; Danish Booksellers' Association Golden Laurels, 1967; Gyldendal prize, 1969; Nordic Council prize, 1970; Danish Writers Guild prize, 1973; "Nissen-flytter-med-Medaljen," 1973; Nathansen prize, 1976;

Poul Henningsen prize, 1979; Holberg Medal, 1979; Victor B. Andersen award, 1981; Blicher prize, 1985; Hans Christian Andersen award, 1988. Address: Kristianiagade 22 3.th., 2100 Copenhagen Ø, Denmark.

PUBLICATIONS

Verse

Under vejr med mig selv [Getting Wind of Myself]. Copenhagen, Schønberg, 1956.
Efterkrig [Postwar]. Copenhagen, Schønberg, 1957.
Konfrontation [Confrontation]. Copenhagen, Schønberg, 1960.
Camouflage. Copenhagen, Gyldendal, 1961.
Voliere [Aviary]. Copenhagen, Gyldendal, 1962.
Portræt [Portrait]. Copenhagen, Gyldendal, 1963.
Boi-i-ing' 64. Copenhagen, Gyldendal, 1964.
Amagerdigte [Poems from Amager]. Copenhagen, Gyldendal, 1965.
Drømmen om København og andre digte fra byen [The Dream About Copenhagen and Other Poems from the City]. Copenhagen, Gyldendal, 1967.
Fædrelandssange [Patriotic Songs]. Copenhagen, Gyldendal, 1967.
(*Selection*), photographs by Flemming Arnholm. Copenhagen, Rhodos, 1969.
I skyttens tegn: digte i udvalg 1956–67 [Sagittarius: Selected Poems 1956–67]. Copenhagen, Gyldendal, 1970.
Mytologier [Mythologies]. Copenhagen, Gyldendal, 1970.
Scener fra det daglige liv [Scenes from Daily Life]. Copenhagen, Gyldendal, 1973.
25 desperate digte [25 Desperate Poems]. Copenhagen, Gyldendal, 1974.
En hugorm i solen [Viper in the Sun]. Copenhagen, Gyldendal, 1974.
Selected Poems, translated by Nadia Christensen and Alexander Taylor. Willimantic, Connecticut, Curbstone Press, 1975.
Den søndag [That Sunday]. Copenhagen, Brøndum, 1975.
Stranden [The Beach]. Copenhagen, Sommersko, 1976.
Livsfrisen [The Frieze of Life]. Copenhagen, Gyldendal, 1979.
Spansk motiv [Spanish Motif]. Copenhagen, Gyldendal, 1980.
Landet Atlantis [The Land of Atlantis]. Copenhagen, Gyldendal, 1981.
3 Poems, translated by Alexander Taylor. Willimantic, Connecticut, Curbstone Press, 1982.
Det svævende træ [The Floating Tree]. Copenhagen, Gyldendal, 1983.
Udenfor har vinden lagt sig: prosadigte [Outside the Wind Has Dropped: Prose Poems]. Copenhagen, Brøndum, 1984.
Septembersang [September Song]. Copenhagen, Gyldendal, 1988.
Digte [Poems]. Copenhagen, Reitzel, 1986.
Byens tvelys [The Town's Double Light]. Copenhagen, Gyldendal, 1987.
150 korte og meget korte tekster [150 Short and Very Short Texts]. Copenhagen, Gyldendal, 1991.
Bjerget i himlen [The Mountain in the Sky]. Copenhagen, Gyldendal, 1991.

Plays

Weekend (*Filmmanuskript*). Copenhagen, Danske Filmmuseum, 1962.

Hvá skal vi lave? [What Shall We Do?] with Jesper Jensen. Copenhagen, Gyldendal, 1963.

Diskret ophold [Discreet Stay], with Jesper Jensen. Copenhagen, Gyldendal, 1965.

Udviklinger: et skuespil for fire jazz-musikere, fire skueskillere, og lille teater (produced Stockholm, 1965). Copenhagen, Gyldendal, 1965; as *Developments: A Play for Four Jazz Musicians, Four Actors, and a Little Theater, in Modern Nordic Plays*, Oslo, Universitetsforlaget, 1974.

Hvad en mand har brug for [What a Man Needs]. Copenhagen, Gyldendal, 1966.

Der var engang en krig: en film [Once There Was a War], with Palle Kjaerulff-Schmidt. Copenhagen, Gyldendal, 1966.

Voks [Wax]. Copenhagen, Gyldendal, 1968.

År [Years]. Copenhagen, Gyldendal, 1970.

Narrene [Fools]. Copenhagen, Gyldendal, 1971.

Svaret blaeser i vinden [The Answer Is Blowing in the Wind]. Copenhagen, Gyldendal, 1971.

Privatlivets fred: et filmmanuskript [Peace of Private Life: A Filmscript]. Copenhagen, Gyldendal, 1974.

Sangen om sengen [The Song About the Bed]. Copenhagen, Gyldendal, 1982.

Intet nyt fra køkkenfronten [No News from the Kitchen Front]. Copenhagen, Gyldendal, 1984.

Screenplays: *Danske billeder* [Danish Pictures], 1970; *Ved vejen* [At the Road], 1988.

Radio Plays: *De beskedne 1–20* [The Modest 1–20] (series), 1975–76.

Television Plays: *Hele den tyrkiske musik* [All the Turkish Music], 1970; *Premiere*, 1970; *Ferien* [The Holiday], 1971; *Den frygtelige fiesta* [The Terrible Fiesta], 1971; *Laila Løvehjerte* [Laila Lionheart], 1972; *På vej til Hilda* [On the Way to Hilda], 1972; *Gibs*, 1973; *Privatlivets fred* [Peace of Private Life], 1973; *Brudstykker af en landsbydegns dagbog* [Fragments of a Parish Clerk's Diary], 1975; *Ludvigsbakke* [Ludvigshill], with Jonas Cornell, 1978; *Vores år 1–4* [Our Years 1–4], 1980; *Falsk forår* [False Spring], 1989.

Fiction

Den kroniske uskyld [Chronic Innocence]. Copenhagen, Schønberg, 1958.

Og andre historier [And Other Stories]. Copenhagen, Gyldendal, 1964.

Operaelskeren [The Opera Lover]. Copenhagen, Gyldendal, 1966.

Arkivet [The Archives]. Copenhagen, Gyldendal, 1967.

Lonni og Karl [Lonni and Karl]. Copenhagen, Gyldendal, 1968.

Anna (jeg) Anna. Copenhagen, Gyldendal, 1969; as *Anna (I) Anna*, Willimantic, Connecticut, Curbstone Press, 1982.

Rejsende [Traveller]. Copenhagen, Gyldendal, 1969.

Marts 1970 [March]. Copenhagen, Gyldendal, 1970.

Brevet til Gerda [The Letter to Gerda]. Copenhagen, Gyldendal, 1972.

R.R. Copenhagen, Gyldendal, 1972.

Den syende jomfru og andre noveller [The Sewing Virgin and Other Stories]. Copenhagen, Gyldendal, 1972.

Dilettanterne [The Dilettantes]. Copenhagen, Gyldendal, 1973.

Spinatfuglene [The Spinach Birds]. Copenhagen, Gyldendal, 1973.

Du skal ikke være ked af det, Amalia [Don't Be Sad, Amalia]. Copenhagen, Gyldendal, 1974.

Sommer [Summer]. Copenhagen, Gyldendal, 1974.

En hugorm i Solen [A Viper in the Sun]. Copenhagen, Gyldendal, 1974.

Vejen ad hvilken [The Road Along Which]. Copenhagen, Gyldendal, 1975.

Det korte af det lange [In Short]. Copenhagen, Gyldendal, 1976.

Twist. Copenhagen, Gyldendal, 1976.

Kiks [Miss]. Copenhagen, Gyldendal, 1976.

De beskedne: en familiekrønike [The Modest: A Family Chronicle]. Copenhagen, Gyldendal, 4 vols., 1976.

Et bortvendt ansigt [Averted Face]. Copenhagen, Gyldendal, 1977.

Drengene [The Boys]. Copenhagen, Gyldendal, 1977.

Tango. Copenhagen, Gyldendal, 1978.

Joker. Copenhagen, Gyldendal, 1979.

Odysseus fra Amager [Odysseus from Amager]. Copenhagen, Vindrose, 1981.

De hellige aber. Copenhagen, Gyldendal, 1981; as *Witness to the Future*, Seattle, Washington, Fjord Press, 1987.

Kesses krig [Kesse's War]. Copenhagen, Gyldendal, 1981.

Jus, og/eller, Den gyldne middelvej [Jus, and/or, The Golden Mean]. Copenhagen, Gyldendal, 1982.

Mænd og kvinder [Men and Women]. Copenhagen, Gyldendal, 1982.

Patience, eller, Kortene å bordet: en Beckett-idyl [Patience, or, The Cards on the Table: A Beckett-Idyll]. Copenhagen, Gyldendal, 1983.

En omvej til Klostret [The Long Way Round to the Cloister]. Copenhagen, Vindrose, 1983.

Hvad sker der i kvarteret? [What Is Happening in the Quarter?]. Copenhagen, Gyldendal, 1983.

Falske forår [False Spring]. Copenhagen, Gyldendal, 1984.

Harlekin skelet [Harlequin Skeleton]. Copenhagen, Gyldendal, 1985.

Borte tit [Often Gone]. Copenhagen, Gyldendal, 1985.

Som man behager [As One Wishes]. Copenhagen, Gyldendal, 1986.

Engel [Angel]. Copenhagen, Gyldendal, 1987.

Det ville glæde [It Would Please]. Copenhagen, Gyldendal, 1989.

Det svage køn [The Weak Sex]. Copenhagen, Gyldendal, 1989.

Rapsodi i blåt [Rhapsody in Blue]. Copenhagen, Gyldendal, 1991.

Other

Rifbjerg: KR-journalistik, edited by Hanne Marie Svendsen. Copenhagen, Gyldendal, 1967.

I medgang og modgang [Good and Bad Luck], illustrated by Lilli Friis. Copenhagen, Gyldendal, 1970.

Leif den Lykkelige jun [Leif, the Happy Junior]. Copenhagen, Gyldendal, 1971.

Lena Jørgensen, Klintevej 4, 2650 Hvidovre. Copenhagen, Gyldendal, 1971.

Dengang det var før: Syv kronikker [When It Was Before: Seven Articles]. Copenhagen, Gyldendal, 1971.

Til Spanien [To Spain]. Copenhagen, Gyldendal, 1971.

Rifbjergs lytterroman, edited by Ole Larsen and others. Copenhagen, Gyldendal, 1972.

Tak for turen [Thank You for the Trip]. Copenhagen, Gyldendal, 1975.

Deres Majestaet! åbent brev til Dronning Margrethe II af

Danmark [You, Majesty: Open Letter to Queen Margrethe II of Denmark]. Copenhagen, Corsaren, 1977.

Dobbeltgaenger; eller, Den Korte, inderlige men fuldstaendig sande beretning om Klaus Rifbjergs liv [The Double; or, The Short, Intimate But Completely Truthful Story of Klaus Rifbjerg's Life]. Copenhagen, Gyldendal, 1978.

Det sorte hul [The Black Hole]. Copenhagen, Gyldendal, 1980.

Vores år [Our Year]. Copenhagen, Gyldendal, 2 vols., 1980.

Rifbjerg rundt: en montage [Around Rifbjerg: A Montage]. Copenhagen, Gyldendal, 1981.

Jeg skal nok [I Shall]. Copenhagen, Gyldendal, 1984.

Japanske klip [Japanese Cuts], photographs by Georg Oddner. Copenhagen, Brøndum, 1987.

Linda og baronen [Linda and the Baron]. Copenhagen, Gyldendal, 1989.

Da Oscar blev tosset [When Oscar Went Mad]. Copenhagen, Gyldendal, 1990.

En udflugt [An Excursion]. Copenhagen, Gyldendal, 1990.

Den hemmelige kilde [The Secret Source]. Copenhagen, Gyldendal, 1991.

Editor, *Min yndlingslaesning* [My Favourite Reading]. Copenhagen, Vendelkaer, 1965.

Editor, with Jørgen Gustava Brandt and Uffe Harder, *Anthologie de la poésie danoise contemporaine*. Paris, Gallimard, 1975.

*

Bibliography: *Klaus Rifbjerg: nogle litteraturhenvisninger* by Aage Jørgensen, Aarhus, privately printed, 1973.

Critical Studies: "Klaus Rifbjerg: A Contemporary Writer," in *Books Abroad* (Norman, Oklahoma), 45, 1975, and *Klaus Rifbjerg*, Westport, Connecticut, Greenwood, 1986, both by Charlotte Schiander Gray; "*Anna I Anna*: A Novel by Klaus Rifbjerg" by Lisa Alther, in *Denmarkings* (Copenhagen), 1982; "Repetition in Klaus Rifbjerg's *Arkivet*" by Jørgen Steen Veistand, in *Edda: Scandinavian Journal of Literary Research* (Bergen, Norway), 2, 1988.

* * *

Klaus Rifbjerg is the quintessential modern Danish literary artist. From being an angry — and very articulate — young Dane in the 1950s he has become the grand old man of the Danish literary world, a writer who fears no genre and can boast success in most that he has tried. For all his versatility, his real achievement is most evident in his poetry: his ability to forge a new poetic language, capable of expressing the experience of life in a modern, secular, materialistic world, and an exploration of his personal experience so carefully carried out that personal impressions become expressions of much more general experience. *Konfrontation* (Confrontation) marked the breakthrough not only of Rifbjerg himself as a major poet but also of the new, international Modernist movement in Denmark. In a direct manner and in imagery that is almost tangible, his poetry confronts the reality of a world "empty, empty, empty — blissfully empty . . . of all but things" ("Frihavnen" [Free Port]). In *Camouflage* and *Portræt* (Portrait) he further explored the associative and creative power of language to the extent that he seemed to go beyond the point where language communicates in any conventional sense, but *Amagerdigte* signalled a new approach. Dealing, as he had in *Camouflage*, with personal experience, he used a more straightforward style to encourage readers to share his

recollections of childhood rather than simply sharing the linguistic form of his poetry. As later collections make clear — e.g., *Mytologier* (Mythologies) and *Livsfrisen* (The Frieze of Life) — this change implied no rejection of experimentation; rather, it showed his ability to develop his medium and respond to the mood of his time.

Rifbjerg has written for the stage: his first play was *Udviklinger* (*Developments*), a Pirandellian exploration of identity and illusion, and he has tried his hand at various dramatic genres at different stages in his career. Most immediately popular are his films and his two series for radio and television respectively: *De beskedne* (The Modest) and *Vores år* (Our Years), chronicling the progress of the Danes through the post-war world.

However, the novel seems increasingly to have become his preferred medium. His first novel, *Den kroniske uskyld* (Chronic Innocence), is typical of his prose work in that its formative artistic impulse derives from a single central theme: the formative processes and points of crisis in the life of a human being. His awareness of the deceptive nature of surface realism and of his own position as a creator of his own fictional universe is evident in his first collection of short stories, *Og andre historier* (And Other Stories), where his play with points of view and varying degrees of identification with characters successfully expresses the complexity of human experience. Rifbjerg's mastery of language ensures that in the best of his prose and poetry, language is no mere vehicle through which to express experience: it *becomes* that experience itself.

Gradually, Rifbjerg has moved away from the subjective view of childhood and youth to a more detached treatment of the whole of human life. A later novel, *De hellige aber* (*Witness to the Future*), shows that his analysis of childhood becomes a search for human values in an increasingly dehumanized world. Rifbjerg tends to find those human values and to base his work not on their absence but on his own demonstration that there are still people such as himself looking for them, capable of adapting — like the central character in the "Anglo-Danish" novel *Falsk forår* (False Spring) — and of being fascinated by the very stuff of human existence, as he himself is in his description of a real and personally experienced robbery in Spain, in *En udflugt* (An Excursion). The real and the fictional are never far apart in the work of this writer, and his own ability to change and adapt is very clear.

—Hans Christian Andersen

ROA BASTOS, Augusto (Antonio). Paraguayan. Born in Iturbe, Guairá, 13 June 1917. Educated at a military school, Asunción. Served in the Paraguayan Army during Chaco War against Bolivia. Journalist for newspapers, Asunción, early 1940s; correspondent in Europe and North Africa, mid-1940s; cultural attaché for Paraguay, Buenos Aires, 1946; exiled to Argentina and France, 1947–89; Professor of Guaraní (Indian language of Paraguay) and Spanish American studies, University of Toulouse, until 1985; returned to Paraguay, 1989. Recipient: Fellow of British Council, 1944, Editorial Losada prize, 1959, Guggenheim fellow, 1970; Concurso Internacional de Narrativa, 1959; Cervantes prize, 1989. Address: Berutti 2828, Martínez, Buenos Aires, Argentina.

PUBLICATIONS

Fiction

El trueno entre las hojas.   Buenos Aires, Losada, 1953.
Hijo de hombre.   Buenos Aires, Losada, 1960; as *Son of Man*, London, Gollancz, 1965; New York, Monthly Review Press, 1988.
El baldío.   Buenos Aires, Losada, 1966.
Madera quemada.   Santiago, Universitaria, 1967.
Los pies sobre el agua.   Buenos Aires, Centro Editor de América Latina, 1967.
Moriencia.   Caracas, Monte Ávila, 1969.
Cuerpo presente, y otros textos.   Buenos Aires, Centro Editor de América Latina, 1972.
Yo, el Supremo.   Buenos Aires, Siglo XXI, 1974; as *I the Supreme*, New York, Knopf, 1986; London, Faber, 1987.
Kurupí.   Published in *Noveletas criollistas latino-americanas*, Havana, Arte y Literatura, 1975.
Antología personal.   Mexico City, Nueva Imagen, 1980.
Contar un cuento, y otros relatos, edited by Ana Becciú.   Buenos Aires, Kapelusz, 1984.

Plays

Screenplays: *El trueno entre las hojas*, 1955; *Hijo de hombre*, 1960; *Shunko*, 1960; *Alias Gardelito*, 1963; *Castigo al traidor*, 1966; *El señor presidente*, 1966; *Don Segundo Sombra*, 1968.

Verse

El ruiseñor de la aurora, y otros poemas.   Asunción, Nacional, 1942.
El naranjal ardiente, nocturno paraguayo: 1947–1949. Asunción, Diálogo, 1960.

Other

El génesis de los Apapokura-Guaraní.   Asunción, Alcor, 1971.
El pollito de fuego (for children).   Buenos Aires, Flor, 1974.
Los juegos.   Buenos Aires, Flor, 2 vols., 1979.
Lucha hasta el alba.   Asunción, Arte Nuevo, 1979.
Rafael Barrett.   Stockholm, Estudios Latinoamericanos, 1981.
Escritos políticos, edited by Marta Teresa Casteros.   Buenos Aires, Instituto de Estudios de Literatura Latinoamericano, 1984.
Carta abierta a mi pueblo.   Buenos Aires, Frente Paraguayo en Argentina, 1986.
El tiranosaurio del Paraguay da sus últimas boqueadas. Buenos Aires, Frente Paraguayo en Argentina, 1986.
On Modern Latin American Fiction, edited by John King. New York, Noonday Press, 1989.

*

Bibliography: *Augusto Roa Bastos* by Rubén Bareiro Saguier, Montevideo, Trilce, 1989.

Critical Studies: *The Myth of Paraguay in the Fiction of Augusto Roa Bastos*, Chapel Hill, University of North Carolina Press, 1969, "Augusto Roa Bastos's *I the Supreme*: The Image of a Dictator," in *Latin American Literary Review* (Pittsburgh), 7, 1975, and *Augusto Roa Bastos*, Boston, Twayne, 1978, all by David William Foster; "Time and Transportation in *Hijos de hombre*" by W. A. Luchting, in *Research Studies*, 41, 1973; "The Initiation Archetype in Arguedas, Roa Bastos and Ocampo" by Barbara A. Aponte, in *Latin American Literary Review* (Pittsburgh), 11(21), 1982.

*   *   *

Since the first days of European conquest, Latin America has often been identified with possible utopias. Unfortunately, history has equally often thwarted this vision, making of the continent a place where utopia seems like nothing more than an unrealizable dream. Yet this dream has inspired not only revolutionaries, but many of its most outstanding writers. The Paraguayan author Augusto Roa Bastos is one of their number, constantly measuring the gulf between dream and reality in his short stories and powerful, influential novels. Roa Bastos himself has written: "The complacent supporters of submission and oppression may consider utopia as the expression of irreality, of hopeless projects and endless frustration, but the temper of our oppressed but undefeated peoples sees precisely in utopia the model for and the path to their liberation made reality in the essence of their being, with the impulse of their acts" (*Marcha* [Montevideo], 8 July 1973).

The political inspiration behind this necessary search for utopia is explored at length in Roa Bastos's early novel *Hijo de hombre* (*Son of Man*). The continual resistance by the poor peasants of the Paraguayan countryside to almost ceaseless repression is movingly conveyed as the nine sections of the book chronicle their past, present, and hopes for the future. At this stage in his career, Roa Bastos was interested above all in creating a literature that would be able to express this collective sense of rebellion, allying himself with those who rebelled in a way that would free him from the condition of being an "artist" writing in an alienated fashion for a reduced number of educated readers. The fact that Roa Bastos lived for over 40 years in exile from his home country of Paraguay only served to exacerbate this awareness of the isolation of the novel writer in modern society; it is plain from *Son of Man* that he is trying to regain the voice of epic narrative that can reduce the distance between the writer and those he writes about. Roa Bastos himself has expressed this wish in the following manner: "literary activity once again means the necessity of embodying a destiny, the will to inscribe oneself in the vital reality of a collectivity in its true moral environment and social structure, in the complex system of relationships of contemporary reality, that is to say, projecting itself towards the universal world of man . . ." (*Journeys Through the Labyrinth* by Gerald Martin, 1989).

If this desire can be seen as utopic, Roa Bastos's other major novel to date, *Yo, el Supremo* (*I, the Supreme*) presents the reader with the opposite extreme, the rule of despotic dystopia. *I, the Supreme* is a 500-page monologue from the mouth (and mind) of the 19th-century Paraguayan dictator José Gaspar de Francia. As with his literary colleagues Alejo Carpentier or Gabriel García Márquez (*q.v.*), Roa Bastos felt in the 1970s that his most pressing need was to examine the meaning and relevance of the typical Latin American figure of the dictator, which had first appeared in the early years of the Latin American countries' struggle to establish themselves after independence from Spanish colonial rule, but which in the 1970s was being rapidly updated in brutal regimes throughout the continent.

Roa Bastos's dictator is far from being simply a portrayal of brutal repression, however. What most fascinates Roa Bastos, and provides for an optimistic reading of the work which thus links it to his earlier concerns as expressed in *Son of Man*, is that the dictator's quest for the absolute must of necessity be doomed to failure. Roa Bastos uses the novel to argue that meaning and truth are by definition a process of negotiation between individuals freely constructing their own ideas, whereas the dictator's sole aim is to crush and silence the voice of the other. In doing so, he condemns himself to silence, and with it the complete loss of any means by which to judge the meaning of his own achievements. It is in this location of the most fundamental aspects of human existence in a definite, though constantly menaced, reality, that Roa Bastos affirms his belief in both the value of that existence and the worth of literature as the most sensitive explorer of its potentialities.

—Nick Caistor

————

ROBBE-GRILLET, Alain. French. Born in Brest, 18 August 1922. Educated at Lycée de Brest, and lycées Buffon and St Louis, Paris; National Institute of Agronomy, Paris, diploma 1944. Sent to work in German tank factory during World War II. Married Catherine Rstakian in 1957. Engineer, National Statistical Institute, Paris, 1945–49, and Institute of Colonial Fruits and Crops, Morocco, French Guinea, Guadeloupe, and Martinique, 1949–51; then full-time writer; since 1955, literary consultant, Minuit publishers, Paris. Recipient: Fénéon prize, 1954; Critics prize (France), 1955; del Duca bursary, 1956; Delluc prize, 1963; Berlin Festival prize, for screenplay 1969; Mondello prize, 1982. Officer, Order of Merit; Chevalier, Légion d'Honneur. Address: 18 Boulevard Maillot, 92200 Neuilly-sur-Seine, France.

PUBLICATIONS

Fiction

Les Gommes. Paris, Minuit, 1953; as *The Erasers*, New York, Grove Press, 1964; London, Calder and Boyars, 1966.
Le Voyeur. Paris, Minuit, 1955; as *The Voyeur*, New York, Grove Press, 1958; London, Calder, 1959.
La Jalousie. Paris, Minuit, 1957; as *Jealousy*, New York, Grove Press, and London, Calder, 1959.
Dans le Labyrinthe. Paris, Minuit, 1959; as *In the Labyrinth*, New York, Grove Press, 1960; London, Calder and Boyars, 1968.
L'Année dernière à Marienbad. Paris, Minuit, 1961; as *Last Year at Marienbad*, New York, Grove Press, and London, Calder and Boyars, 1962.
Instantanés. Paris, Minuit, 1962; as *Snapshots*, with *Towards a New Novel*, London, Calder and Boyars, 1965; published separately, New York, Grove Press, 1968.
L'Immortelle. Paris, Minuit, 1963; as *The Immortal One*, London, Calder and Boyars, 1971.
La Maison de rendez-vous. Paris, Minuit, 1965; in English, New York, Grove Press, 1966; as *The House of Assignation*, London, Calder and Boyars, 1970; as *Le Rendez-vous* (in French), New York, Holt Rinehart, 1981; in English, London, Methuen, 1987.
Projet pour une révolution à New York. Paris, Minuit, 1970; as *Project for a Revolution in New York*, New York, Grove Press, 1972; London, Calder and Boyars, 1973.
Glissements progressifs du plaisir. Paris, Minuit, 1974.

Topologie d'une cité fantôme. Paris, Minuit, 1976; as *Topology of a Phantom City*, New York, Grove Press, 1977; London, Calder and Boyars, 1978.
Souvenirs du triangle d'or. Paris, Minuit, 1978; as *Recollections of the Golden Triangle*, London, Calder, 1984; New York, Grove Weidenfeld, 1986.
Un Régicide. Paris, Minuit, 1978.
Djinn. Paris, Minuit, 1981; in English, New York, Grove Press, 1982; London, Calder, 1983.

Plays

Screenplays: *L'Année dernière à Marienbad* (*Last Year at Marienbad*), 1961; *L'Immortelle*, 1963; *Trans-Europ-Express*, 1967; *L'Homme qui ment* (*The Man Who Lies*), 1968; *L'Eden et après*, 1970; *Glissements progressifs du plaisir*, 1973; *Le Jeu avec le feu*, 1975; *La Belle Captive*, 1983.

Other

Pour un Nouveau Roman. Paris, Minuit, 1963; revised edition, 1970; as *Towards a New Novel*, with *Snapshots*, London, Calder and Boyars, 1965; as *For a New Novel: Essays on Fiction*, New York, Grove Press, 1966.
Rêves de jeunes filles, photographs by David Hamilton. Paris, Laffont, 1971; as *Dreams of a Young Girl*, New York, Morrow, 1971; as *Dreams of Young Girls*, London, Collins, 1971.
Les Demoiselles d'Hamilton, photographs by David Hamilton. Paris, Laffont, 1972; as *Sisters*, New York, Morrow, 1973; London, Collins, 1976.
Construction d'un temple en ruines à la déesse Vanadé, etchings by Paul Delvaux. Paris, le Bateau Lavoir, 1975.
La Belle Captive, illustrated by René Magritte. Paris, Bibliothèque des Arts, 1976.
Temple aux miroirs, photographs by Irina Ionesco. Paris, Seghers, 1977.
Le Miroir qui revient. Paris, Minuit, 1985; as *Ghosts in the Mirror*, London, Calder, 1988; New York, Grove Weidenfeld, 1991.
Angélique; ou, l'Enchantement. Paris, Minuit, 1987.
George Segal, invasion blanche. Paris, la Différence, 1990.

*

Bibliography: *Alain Robbe-Grillet: An Annotated Bibliography of Critical Studies 1953–1972* by Dale W. Fraizer, Metuchen, New Jersey, Scarecrow Press, 1973.

Critical Studies: *Alain Robbe-Grillet and the New French Novel*, Carbondale, Southern Illinois University Press, 1964, *Alain Robbe-Grillet: The Body of the Text*, Rutherford, New Jersey, Fairleigh Dickinson University Press, and London, Associated University Presses, 1985, and *Alain Robbe-Grillet: Life, Work and Criticism*, Fredericton, New Brunswick, York Press, 1987, all by Ben Frank Stoltzfus; *The French New Novel: Claude Simon, Michel Butor, Alain Robbe-Grillet* by John Sturrock, London, Oxford University Press, 1969; *Narrative Consciousness: Structure and Perception in the Fiction of Kafka, Beckett, and Robbe-Grillet* by G. H. Szanto, Austin, University of Texas Press, 1972; *The Novels of Alain Robbe-Grillet*, Ithaca, New York, Cornell University Press, 1975, and *Intertextual Assemblage in Robbe-Grillet from Topology to the Golden Triangle*, Fredericton, New Brunswick, York Press, 1979, both by Bruce Morrissette; *The Film Career of Alain Robbe-Grillet* by William F. Van Wert, London, Prior, 1977; *The Films of Alain Robbe-Grillet* by Roy

Armes, Amsterdam, Benjamins, 1981; *Realism, Reality, and the Fictional Theory of Alain Robbe-Grillet* by Patricia A. Deduck, Lanham, Maryland, University Press of America, 1982; *Alain Robbe-Grillet* by John Fletcher, London, Methuen, 1983; *Alain Robbe-Grillet* by Ilona Leki, Boston, Twayne, 1983.

* * *

The best known of the so-called *nouveaux romanciers* in France — writers who have attempted to find a new path for the novel in radical distinction to the methods of classic authors like Balzac — Alain Robbe-Grillet began life as an agricultural scientist, and turned to literature only after illness brought his research career in the field to an end. He thus comes from a background which is different from that of the normal French person of letters, and explains to some extent the iconoclastic impact he made on the literary scene when his second novel, *Les Gommes* (*The Erasers*), was published in Paris in 1953 (his first novel, *Un Régicide*, appeared only in 1978).

The Erasers is a detective story based on the legend of Oedipus. A sleuth called Wallas arrives in a provincial town to investigate a murder which, 24 hours to the second later, he himself commits: and the man he accidentally shoots is his own father who had managed to survive a similar attack the previous evening. This complex, enigmatic story is typical of Robbe-Grillet, who followed it, in *Le Voyeur*, with a novel about a travelling salesman who visits the offshore island of his birth and (perhaps) commits a sadistic rape and murder before leaving scot-free some days later; the reason why it is necessary to say "perhaps" is because the crime may have been enacted in the protagonist's sick mind only.

La Jalousie (*Jealousy*) turns on a French pun: *jalousie* means both jealousy and slatted blinds. The workings of the sick mind of the protagonist now actually become the text, so that the novel itself constitutes a fit of jealousy in which the narrator watches his wife obsessively through slatted blinds as she plans (or so he believes) a night away from home in the company of a neighbouring planter who is a frequent visitor to the house. The jealous frenzy subsides — and the novel ends — only with the return of the (errant?) wife and the (apparent) discomfiture of the neighbour, whom the wife teases for his clumsiness as a motor mechanic, a remark the narrator naturally interprets in a bawdy sense.

Robbe-Grillet has declared on a number of occasions how much he owes to Kafka, and so it is not surprising that *Dans le Labyrinthe* (*In the Labyrinth*) should be Kafkaesque in inspiration. A soldier is wandering in a snow-covered town looking for a man to whom he wants to deliver the effects of a dead comrade after a major military disaster, and he ends up dying from wounds himself. What is not clear is how far the whole story is elaborated by the narrator on the basis of a picture called "The Defeat at Reichenfels," that is to what extent, like jealousy in the previous novel, it is a construct of the fantasising consciousness.

During the next few years Robbe-Grillet concentrated on making or helping to make a number of films, of which the best known is *L'Année dernière à Marienbad* (*Last Year at Marienbad* directed by Alain Resnais), the story of a man who succeeds in persuading a woman that she agreed, the year before in Marienbad, to meet him in the resort where they presently are staying and leave her husband for him. As in *Jealousy*, there is at the heart of *Marienbad* ambiguity about what precisely is real, what exactly happened, and who is mesmerising whom. Robbe-Grillet then proceeded to make a number of films himself, one of which, *L'Immortelle* (based on the Orpheus and Eurydice legend: a man dies with the woman

he loves after he has already succeeded once in "resurrecting" her from the dead) is, for all its amateurish clumsiness of technique, a considerable work of art.

Robbe-Grillet returned to the novel in *La Maison de rendez-vous* (*The House of Assignation*), a witty parody of James Bond stories set in an exotic Hong Kong where women's flesh "plays a large part" in the protagonist's dreams, and *Projet pour une révolution à New York* (*Project for a Revolution in New York*), a more self-indulgently sadistic fantasy about an imaginary wave of terrorism in Manhattan. Since then the preoccupation with sadism and voyeurism has become almost totally obsessive, and more recent novels and films are tedious reading and viewing, as are the "soft-porn" books like *Les Demoiselles d'Hamilton* and *Temple aux miroirs* with which he has been closely associated. The detachment which characterised the analysis of the diseased or tortured mind in *The Voyeur* and *Jealousy* is replaced in his later work by a modish and self-indulgent exhibition of something disturbingly close to the fantasies which the protagonist of *The Voyeur* luxuriated in.

Robbe-Grillet has also made a considerable reputation for himself as a theorist of fiction, and his collected articles in *Pour un Nouveau Roman* are widely admired. They contain a clear statement of his position, which is that in a world without God, in which the universe is not hostile to mankind (as Albert Camus tended to suppose) but merely indifferent, the novelist should avoid what he stigmatises as anthromorphism, that is, the illusion that there is a sly complicity between humanity and things, which leads to writing overladen with sentimental metaphors such as "the lowering sky" or "the cruel sea." People who steer clear of this sort of thing, Robbe-Grillet argues, write fiction which makes none of the outworn and even discredited assumptions about coherence of plot and solidity of character, and which accepts that time is a fluid, not stable medium.

It is clear why his novels, based as they are on this philosophy, seemed so radical, even iconoclastic, when they first appeared. Now that many of his theoretical arguments have been accepted — it was no less a writer than John Fowles who said that we live in the age of Robbe-Grillet — the genuine part of his achievement can more easily be separated from the spurious, and on that basis it is clear that his best work is contained in the three mature novels of his middle period, *The Voyeur*, *Jealousy*, and *In the Labyrinth*, works which will remain important in the history of 20th-century literature long after the polemics which surrounded their publication have been forgotten.

—John Fletcher

———

ROCHEFORT, Christiane. French. Born in Paris, 17 July 1917. Journalist; press secretary, Cannes film festival, 15 years, until late 1960s. Recipient: Nouvelle Vague prize, 1958; Prix du Roman Populiste, 1961; Medicis prize, 1988. Address: c/o Éditions Grasset, 61 rue des Sts.-Pères, 75006 Paris, France.

PUBLICATIONS

Fiction

Le Repos du guerrier. Paris, Grasset, 1958; as *Warrior's Rest*, New York, McKay, 1959; London, Hamilton, 1960.

Les Petits Enfants du siècle.   Paris, Grasset, 1961; as *Children of Heaven*, New York, McKay, 1962; as *Josyane and the Welfare*, London, Macdonald, 1963.
Les Stances à Sophie.   Paris, Grasset, 1963; as *Cats Don't Care for Money*, New York, Doubleday, 1965; London, Cresset, 1966.
Une Rose pour Morrison.   Paris, Grasset, 1966.
Printemps au parking.   Paris, Grasset, 1969.
Archaos, ou, Le Jardin étincelant.   Paris, Grasset, 1972.
Encore Heureux qu'on va vers l'été.   Paris, Grasset, 1975.
Quand Tu vas chez les femmes.   Paris, Grasset, 1982.
Le Monde est comme deux chevaux.   Paris, Grasset, 1984.
La Porte du fond.   Paris, Grasset, 1988.

Other

C'est bizarre, l'écriture.   Paris, Grasset, 1970.
Les Enfants d'abord.   Paris, Grasset, 1976.
Journal de printemps: récit d'un livre.   Montreal, Étincelle, 1977.
Ma Vie revue et corrigée par l'auteur, with Maurice Chavardes. Paris, Stock, 1978.

Translator, with Rachel Mizrahi, *John Lennon en flagrant délire*, by John Winston Lennon.   Paris, Laffont, 1965.
Translator, with the author, *Le Cheval fini*, by Amos Kenan. Paris, Grasset, 1966.
Translator, *Les Tireurs de la langue*, by Amos Kenan.   Paris, Yves Rivière, 1974.
Translator, *Holocauste II*, by Amos Kenan.   Paris, Flammarion, 1976.

*

Critical Studies: "What Rest for the Weary" by Joseph H. McMahon, in *Yale French Studies* (New Haven, Connecticut), 27, 1961; Rochefort issue of *Biblio* (Tübingen), November 1965; "Christiane Rochefort's *Ma Vie revue et corrigée par l'auteur*: Autobiography *à la dérive*" by Helen Bates McDermott, in *French Literature Series* (Columbia, South Carolina), 12, 1985; "Effects of Urbanization in the Novels of Christiane Rochefort" by Anne D. Cordero, in *Faith of a (Woman) Writer*, edited by Alice Kessler-Harris and William McBrien, Westport, Connecticut, Greenwood, 1988.

*   *   *

Christiane Rochefort was over 40 when her first book was published in 1958, but she has made up for this late start by producing books at regular intervals ever since. Many readers are surprised on learning her age, for her books give the impression that she belongs to a much younger age group. It is true that the cheerful anarchy characterizing much of Rochefort's writing suggests someone who has not yet had to yield to social pressures.

Rochefort's resistance to those pressures has its source, however, in diligent observation of the workings of society. What she has found increasingly necessary to condemn is the determination of present-day society to make the behaviour of its individual members conform to models which are presented as "normal" and which exclude the exceptional. For Rochefort this is a matter not simply of blatantly ignoring the rich variety of human potential but also of actively damaging individuals psychologically and physically by rendering their personal fulfilment impossible. She has used her books to show how individuals may challenge the oppressive structures found in a wide range of areas of social existence: personal and sexual

relationships, education, employment, medicine, the environment, the military, commerce, the media and advertising. Of course, many of these aspects of social existence were under attack in a number of Western countries in the 1960s, but it can be argued that Rochefort was not imitating but rather helping to initiate the movement of protest. Even her earliest novels vigorously contest conditions of modern life; and, two years before the famous events of May 1968, she foreshadowed the events in *Une Rose pour Morrison* (A Rose for Morrison), which creates a vision of mass protest marches filling the streets of Paris and uniting students, schoolchildren, and workers.

Rochefort is particularly concerned with the structures society imposes on personal and sexual relationships, and her themes have included marriage, homosexuality, the sexual activity of minors, oral sex, sado-masochism, and incest. There is, however, no hint of pornographic titillation, explicit details being assiduously omitted; Rochefort is much more interested in the roles individuals are required to play. Inevitably, she considers this issue particularly from the standpoint of a woman, and has contributed significantly to the propagation of modern feminist ideas by persistently questioning conventions of gender. Although Simone de Beauvoir's *Le Deuxième Sexe* (The Second Sex) had appeared in 1949, fiction produced by women in the years immediately afterwards bore little witness to her theory of the cultural construction of femininity. Rochefort was one of the first modern women writers to use the novel to contest conventional perceptions of female experience. *Le Repos du guerrier* (*Warrior's Rest*) questions the traditional conception of female sexuality. *Les Petits Enfants du siècle* (*Children of Heaven*; also published as *Josyane and the Welfare*) illustrates the consequences of the material conditions of women's lives, including the generous French State child allowances that reduce women to childbearing machines. *Les Stances à Sophie* (*Cats Don't Care for Money*) considers, in much the same way as Betty Friedan's *The Feminine Mystique* (published in the same year), the targeting of women by economic forces that promote an ideal of femininity in the interests of consumerism. Remarkably, already in the 1960s Rochefort raises certain issues now more often identified with the kind of feminism that developed after 1970; *Cats Don't Care for Money*, for example, considers both the struggle of women against the medical establishment to regain control over their bodies and the role that language plays in the disempowering of women.

Rochefort's awareness of the need to challenge the dominant discourse of society in order to allow oppressed groups to express their own needs and values has encouraged her to use innovative fictional forms. She may, to some degree, be labelled a realist writer, certain of her texts constituting graphic records of life in various contemporary contexts. Other texts, however, move away from realism to imaginary constructions, *Une Rose pour Morrison* being a dystopian vision of a highly policed society of the future, and *Archaos, ou, Le Jardin étincelant* (Archaos, or, The Sparkling Garden) portraying a Utopia in which individuals thrive on the abolition of conventions of behaviour. A different kind of affirmation of "otherness" appears in *Cats Don't Care for Money*, which borrows its storyline from a well-known medical students' song of the same name, but then systematically subverts the song's values by presenting the situation from the point of view of the female protagonist rather than that of the male.

Rochefort's style incorporates popular idiomatic expressions and a syntax that reflects the loosely structured patterns of oral speech. As a result, traditionally minded critics have sometimes seized on the alleged negligence of her writing in order to classify her as a lightweight writer with little to say to her readers. Rochefort has, however, suggested in *C'est* bizarre, l'écriture (Writing's Odd) that her choice of style is quite conscious and enables her to reach a far wider public than she might have done had she chosen a more elevated manner of expression. In fact, the unsophisticated character of her writing is part of her technique of subversion. The popular expressions are a source of considerable comedy, which punctures the pompous attitudes of conventional society. The conversational effect also strongly invites reader response, so that the novel is no longer the unchallenged voice of authority but an active dialogue between writer and reader. Finally, Rochefort's insistence on the right to use such a style represents a victory for women since they are no longer being restricted to the traditional "lady-like" language which has limited them intellectually, emotionally, and imaginatively.

—Carys Owen

ROOKE, Katerina Anghelaki. *See* **ANGHELAKI-ROOKE, Katerina.**

ROSSI, Cristina Peri. *See* **PERI ROSSI, Cristina.**

RÓŻEWICZ, Tadeusz. Polish. Born in Radomsko, 9 October 1921. Educated at Jagiellonian University, Cracow, 1948–53. Served in the Polish Resistance Home Army during World War II. Married; two sons. Lived in Gliwice until 1968, then in Wrocław. Recipient: State prize, 1955, 1966; Cracow prize, 1959; Minister of Culture prize, 1962; Jurzykowski Foundation award, 1966; Wrocław prize, 1972; Medal of 30th Anniversary of People's Poland, 1974; Minister of Foreign Affairs prize, 1974, 1987; Order of Banner of Labour, 1977; Austrian State prize, 1982; Golden Wreath prize (Yugoslavia), 1987. Commander of the Cross, Order of Polonia Restituta, 1970. Corresponding member, Bavarian Academy of Fine Arts, since 1982. Address: ul. Januszewicka 13 m. 14, 53–136 Wrocław, Poland.

PUBLICATIONS

Plays

Kartoteka (produced Warsaw, 1960). With *Zielona róza*, Warsaw, Państwowy Instytut Wydawniczy, 1961; as *The Card Index* (as *The Dossier*, produced New York, 1961; as *The Card Index*, produced Oxford, 1967; London, 1968), in *The Card Index and Other Plays*, 1969.
Świadkowie. Included in *Nic w płaszczu Prospera*; 1962; as *The Witnesses*, in *The Witnesses and Other Plays*, 1970.

Grupa Laokoona [Laocoön Group]. Included in *Nic w płaszczu Prospera*, 1962.
Utwory dramatyczne (includes *Kartoteka*; *Grupa Laokoona*; *Śmieszny staruszek*; *Spaghetti i Miecz* [Spaghetti and the Sword]; *Wyszedł z domu*; *Akt przerywany*). Cracow, Wydawnictwo Literackie, 1966.
Moja coreczka [My Little Daughter] (produced 1966).
Stara kobieta wysiaduje. Published in *Dialog* (Warsaw), 8, 1968; as *The Old Woman Broods* (produced United States, 1971), in *The Witnesses and Other Plays*, 1970.
The Card Index and Other Plays. London, Calder and Boyars, 1969; New York, Grove Press, 1970.
Wyszedł z domu. As *Gone Out*, in *The Card Index and Other Plays*, 1969.
Akt przerywany. As *The Interrupted Act*, in *The Card Index and Other Plays*, 1969.
Śmieszny staruszek. As *The Funny Old Man* (produced London, 1973), in *The Witnesses and Other Plays*, 1970.
The Witnesses and Other Plays. London, Calder and Boyars, 1970.
Na czworakach [On All Fours]. Published in *Dialog* (Warsaw), 9, 1971.
Sztuki teatralne [Theatrical Plays]. Wrocław, Ossolineum, 1972.
Białe małżeństwo (produced Wrocław). Included in *Białe małżeństwo, i inne utwory sceniczne*, 1975; as *The White Marriage* (produced Port Jefferson, New York, 1975; New Haven, Connecticut, 1977); as *Mariage Blanc*, with *The Hungry Artist Departs*, London, Boyars, 1983.
Białe małżeństwo i inne utwory sceniczne [White Marriage and Other Plays]. Cracow, Wydawnictwo Literackie, 1975.
Odejście głodomora [Exit of the Starving Man]. Published in *Dialog* (Warsaw), September 1976.
Do piachu [To the Boneyard] (produced Warsaw, 1979). Published in *Dialog* (Warsaw), February 1979.
Teatr niekonsekwencji [The Inconsistent Theatre]. Wrocław, Ossolineum, 1979.
Pułapka. Warsaw, Czytelnik, 1983; as *The Trap* (produced Bergen, Norway, 1983; London, 1990), New York, Institute for Contemporary Eastern European Drama and Theatre, 1984.
Mariage Blanc, and The Hungry Artist Departs. London, Boyars, 1983.
Teatr [Theatre]. Cracow, Wydawnictwo Literackie, 2 vols., 1988.

Fiction

Opadły liście z drzew [The Leaves Have Fallen from the Trees]. Warsaw, Państwowy Instytut Wydawniczy, 1955.
Przerwany egzamin [The Interrupted Examination]. Warsaw, Państwowy Instytut Wydawniczy, 1960.
Wycieczka do muzeum [An Excursion to a Museum]. Warsaw, Czytelnik, 1966.
Opowiadania wybrane [Selected Stories]. Warsaw, Czytelnik, 1968.
Śmierć w starych dekoracjach [Death amid Old Stage Props]. Warsaw, Państwowy Instytut Wydawniczy, 1970.
Opowiadania traumatyczne [Traumatic Stories]. Cracow, Wydawnictwo Literackie, 1979.
Tarcza z pajęczyny. Cracow, Wydawnictwo Literackie, 1980.
Echa leśne. Warsaw, Państwowy Instytut Wydawniczy, 1985.
Prozal [Prose]. Cracow, Wydawnictwo Literackie, 1990.

Verse

Niepokój [Anxiety]. Cracow, Przełom, 1947.

Czerwona rękawiczka [The Red Glove]. Cracow, Wydawnictwo Książka, 1948.

Czas który idzie [The Time Which Goes By]. Warsaw, Czytelnik, 1951.

Wiersze i obrazy [Poems and Images]. Warsaw, Czytelnik, 1952.

Równina [The Plain]. Cracow, Wydawnictwo Literackie, 1954.

Uśmiechy [Smiles]. Warsaw, Czytelnik, 1955.

Srebrny kłos [Silver Grain]. Warsaw, Czytelnik, 1955.

Poemat otwarty [An Open Room]. Cracow, Wydawnictwo Literackie, 1956.

Poezje zebrane [Selected Poems]. Cracow, Wydawnictwo Literackie, 1957.

Formy [Forms]. Warsaw, Czytelnik, 1958.

Rozmowa z księciem [Conversation with a Prince]. Warsaw, Państwowy Instytut Wydawniczy, 1960.

Głos anonima [The Anonymous Voice]. Katowice, Śląsk, 1961.

Zielona róża; Kartoteka [Green Rose; Card Index]. Warsaw, Państowy Instytut Wydawniczy, 1961; *Zielona róża* as *Green Rose*, translated by Geoffrey Thurley, Darlington, Western Australia, John Michael, 1982.

Nic w płaszczu Prospera [Nothing in Prospero's Cloak] (includes the plays *Świadkowie* and *Grupa Laokoona*). Warsaw, Państwowy Instytut Wydawniczy, 1962.

Niepokój: Wybór wierszy 1945–1961. Warsaw, Państwowy Instytut Wydawniczy, 1963.

Twarz [The Face]. Warsaw, Czytelnik, 1964.

Twarz trzecia [The Third Face]. Warsaw, Czytelnik, 1968.

Regio [That Area]. Warsaw, Państwowy Instytut Wydawniczy, 1969.

Faces of Anxiety, translated by Adam Czerniawski. London, Rapp and Whiting, 1969.

Wiersze [Poems]. Warsaw, Państwowy Instytut Wydawniszy, 1974.

The Survivor and Other Poems, translated by Magnus I. Krynski and Robert A. Maguire. Princeton, New Jersey, Princeton University Press, 1976.

Selected Poems, translated by Adam Czerniawski. London, Penguin, 1976.

Poezje zebrane [Collected Poems]. Warsaw, Zakład Narodowy Imienia Ossolińskich, 1976.

Unease, translated by Victor Contoski. St. Paul, Minnesota, New Rivers Press, 1980.

Conversation with the Prince and Other Poems, translated by Adam Czerniawski. London, Anvil Press Poetry, 1982; revised edition, as *They Came to See a Poet*, 1991.

Na powierzchni poematu i w środku: nowy wybór wierszy [On the Surface of Poem and Inside: New Selection of Poems]. Warsaw, Czytelnik, 1983.

Poezje wybrane [Selected Poems]. Warsaw, Ludowa Spoldielnia Wydavinicza, 1984.

Poezje [Poems]. Wrocław, Wydawnictwo Dolnośląskie, 1987.

Poezja [Poetry]. Cracow, Wydawnictwo Literackie, 2 vols., 1988.

Płaskorzeźba. Wrocław, Wydawnictwo Dolnośląskie, 1991.

Selected Poems/Poezjezebrane, translated by Adam Czerniawski. Cracow, Wydawnictwo Literackie, 1991.

Other

Kartkł z Wegler [Notes from Hungary]. Warsaw, Czytelnik, 1953.

Przygotowanie do wieczoru autorskiego [Preparations for a Poetry Reading]. Warsaw, Państwowy Instytut, Wydawniczy, 1971.

Proza [Prose]. Wrocław, Ossolineum, 1973.

Poezja, dramat, proza [Poetry, Drama, Prose] (collected works). Warsaw, Zaklad Narodowy Imienia Ossolińskich, 1973.

Duszyczka [A Little Soul]. Cracow, Wydawnictwo Literackie, 1977.

Próba rekonstrukcji [A Trial of Reconstruction]. Wrocław, Ossolineum, 1979.

Editor, *Kto jest ten dziwny nieznajomy* [Who Is This Odd Stranger], by Leopold Staff. Warsaw, n.p., 1964.

*

Critical Studies: "The Natural World of Tadeusz Różewicz" by Victor Contoski, in *Books Abroad*, 29(3), 1965; "A Context for Tadeusz Różewicz" by Richard Lourie, in *Polish Review* (New York), 12, 1967; "The Poetics of Tadeusz Różewicz" by Magnus John Krynski and Robert A. Maguire, in *Polish Review* (New York), 16(4), 1971; "Różewicz Abroad" by Mieczysław Orski, in *Polish Perspectives* (Warsaw), 18(10), 1975; *Tadeusz Różewicz* by Henryk Vogler, Warsaw, Authors' Agency/Czytelnik, 1976; "Tadeusz Różewicz and the Poetics of Pessimism" by Robert Hauptmann, in *North Dakota Quarterly* (Grand Forks), 50(3), 1982; "Laocoön at the Frontier, or the Limit of Limits" by Daniel Gerould, in *Modern Drama* (Toronto), 29(1), 1986; "Tadeusz Różewicz: The Reluctant Jester" by E. J. Czerwinski, in his *Contemporary Polish Theater and Drama (1956–1984)*, Westport, Connecticut, Greenwood, 1988; "On Różewicz" by András Fodor, in *Acta Litteraria*, 30(1–2), 1988; *A Laboratory of Impure Forms: The Plays of Tadeusz Różewicz* by Halina Filipowicz, Westport, Connecticut, Greenwood, 1991.

*   *   *

Tadeusz Różewicz is one of those poets whose artistic development was shaped by history in a decisive way. He was under 20 when World War II broke out and his war experiences — he belonged to the underground Home Army and fought in the Resistance — set the tone of the early poetry. His first collections of verse, *Niepokój* (Anxiety) and *Czerwona rękawiczka* (The Red Glove) were characterized by a stark, almost bare style of great simplicity dispensing with rhymes and metaphors; in these books Różewicz created an anti-poetic model. His style reflected his conviction that the wartime collapse of traditional values led to a situation in which the poet had to re-establish the meaning of ordinary words and had to start building from the foundations: "Create a new [poetry]/which builds/from common feelings/from simple words/Let it take away from man/all that is animal/and divine." After writing a number of anti-war poems and trying to force upon himself an optimistic mood in accordance with the expectations of the post-war Communist regime, in the 1960s Różewicz's attention became focused on what he saw as the crisis of European culture and civilization. While aware of the bankruptcy of certain Socialist ideals ("the new man/that's him there/yes it's that/sewage pipe/which lets through/everything"), he attacked the mindless consumerism of the West in equally bitter terms. In his mature poetry — as Magnus Kryński and Robert Maguire point out in their introduction to an English selection of his work — there is a tension "between a highly emotional tone . . . and the 'objective' presentation of seemingly factual data." Especially in the collections *Twarz*

(The Face) and *Regio* (That Area) Różewicz made frequent use of the collage technique, sprinkling his poems with foreign names and quotations, often in another language.

For all his distinction as a poet, Różewicz is probably better known as a playwright both in and outside Poland. His first two plays, *Kartoteka* (*The Dossier* or *The Card Index*) and *Świadkowie* (*The Witnesses*), were hailed as — apart from Sławomir Mrożek (*q.v.*) — the most interesting examples of the Polish theatre of the absurd. In *The Dossier* the life of the nameless hero is simultaneously intersected by people who knew him at different ages and in various roles; *The Witnesses* (subtitled "Our Little Stabilization") begins with a dialogue recited by a nameless man and a woman which reflects the author's unease about the post-1956 adaptation of Polish society to "normal" petty-bourgeois standards, an adaptation which is in any case illusory: "Perhaps our little stabilization/is nothing but a dream." *Akt przerywany* (*The Interrupted Act*) consists mainly of stage directions and the author's self-mocking commentaries on the subject of his stagecraft. Already here a note of admiration for Samuel Beckett can be detected which becomes even more obvious in *Stara kobieta wysiaduje* (*The Old Woman Broods*). Part of this play takes place on a huge rubbish heap after a devastating war or cataclysm of the future, while another part is filled with the gluttonous old woman's endless (and largely meaningless) monologues. In later years Różewicz scored his greatest theatrical success with the play *Białe małżeństwo* (*The White Marriage* or *Mariage Blanc*), an amusing, and heavily Freudian, interpretation of young girls' fears and phantasies. Różewicz's prose fiction is, by and large, restricted to short stories written in a terse, laconic style; his *Śmierć w starych dekoracjach* (*Death Amid Old Stage Props*) is a longer story which takes place in a Rome polluted by vulgarity and consumerism.

—George Gömöri

RUIBAL (Argibay), José. Spanish. Born near Pontevedra, Galicia, 27 October 1925. Military service in Madrid. Married to Consuelo Vazquez de Parga; two children. Lived in Argentina and Uruguay in the 1950s and 1960s; taught at the State University of New York, Albany, 1972, 1973, University of Minnesota, Minneapolis, 1973, 1974, 1976, and Syracuse University, New York, 1978. Recipient: Modern International Drama prize, 1969; March Foundation grant, 1972. Address: Olivar, 3, 3D, Madrid 12, Spain.

PUBLICATIONS

Plays

Los mendigos y seis piezas de café-teatro (includes *La secretaria*; *Los mutantes*; *El rabo*; *Los ojos*; *El padre*; *El supergerente*). Madrid, Escelicer, 1969; book was almost immediately banned, and reissued as *El mono piadoso y seis piezas de café-teatro*, 1969; *Los mendigos* translated as *The Beggars*, in *Drama and Theatre*, 7(1), 1968; *El rabo* translated as *Tails*, in *Drama Review*, Summer 1969; *El mono piadoso* (produced 1970).

La máquina de pedir; El asno; La ciencia de birlibirloque. Madrid, Siglo Veintiuno, 1970; *El asno* translated as *The Jackass* (produced Binghamton, New York, 1971; New York City, 1972), in *The New Wave Spanish Drama*, edited by George E. Wellwarth, New York, New York University Press, 1970; *La máquina de pedir* translated as *The Begging Machine*, in *Modern International Drama*, 1975.

Teatro difícil (includes *Curriculum vitae*; *El bacalao*). Madrid, Escelicer, 1971; *El bacalao* translated as *The Codfish*, in *Modern International Drama*, 1972.

Teatro sobre teatro. Madrid, Cátedra, 1975.

El hombre y la mosca. Madrid, Fundamentos, 1977; as *The Man and the Fly* (produced Binghamton, New York, 1971; New York, 1982), in *The New Wave Spanish Drama*, edited by George E. Wellwarth, New York, New York University Press, 1970.

Otra vez las avestruces. Murcia, University of Murcia, 1991.

*

Critical Studies: *Spanish Underground Drama*, University Park, Pennsylvania State University Press, 1972, and "José Ruibal: Dramatic Symbolist," in *Estreno* (University Park, Pennsylvania), 1, 1975, both by George E. Wellwarth; "José Ruibal: Feminist Unaware in *La secretaria*?" by Patricia W. O'Connor, in *Revista de Estudios Hispánicos* (Poughkeepsie, New York), 8, 1974.

*   *   *

José Ruibal first achieved prominence outside Spain during the latter years of the Franco regime. He and a group of other dramatists, principally Antonio Martínez Ballesteros, José María Bellido, and Juan Antonio Castro, founded what came to be known as the "Spanish Underground Drama." This was a catch-all term that was first used in the United States and shortly afterwards in England, West Germany, and other European countries to describe drama that was considered politically subversive by the Franco regime and was consequently censored in Spain, where it could neither be published nor performed.

The principal characteristic of Ruibal's theatre was its use of symbolism and a technique of deliberately distancing the audience from the action by setting it in mythical countries and by giving the characters non-Hispanic names. This was done partially in the hope of fooling the censors, never very intelligent readers of literature, into thinking that the play lacked direct references to the Spanish situation, partially in order to universalize the plays (the demise of Spanish totalitarianism has by no means caused them to lose their pertinence), and partially in order to enable the spectator to think about the action — i.e., objectify it — rather than be emotionally caught up in it.

Ruibal's initial success, like that of his fellow dramatists of the "underground" such as, in addition to those mentioned above, Miguel Romero Esteo, Luis Matilla, Jerónimo López Mozo, Angel García Pintado, Eduardo Quiles, Luis Riaza and the very important Catalan writers Manuel de Pedrolo and Josep Benet, came in the United States through publication in various anthologies (e.g., *Modern Spanish Theatre*, *New Wave Spanish Drama*, *New Generation Spanish Drama*, *Three Catalan Dramatists*) and in journals such as *Modern International Drama* as well as through productions in university theatres. Subsequently Ruibal spent several years in the United States as a guest lecturer at numerous colleges and universities.

Ruibal's major works are *El hombre y la mosca* (*The Man and the Fly*) and *La máquina de pedir* (*The Begging Machine*). Although he had written a number of interesting plays prior to the former, such as *El rabo* (*Tails*), *Los mendigos* (*The Beggars*), and *El asno* (*The Jackass*), it is with *The Man and the Fly* that Ruibal created the most trenchant satire of totalitarianism that the Spanish Underground Drama has produced. The focus of the play is on the tendency — as Lord Acton put it — of absolute power to become absolutely corrupt, in this case through an attempt at self-deification by means of a putatively eternal series of doubles. The fragility and ridiculousness of the attempt is depicted by a setting almost overloaded with symbolism: a crystal dome decorated with stained-glass panels and hunting trophies on a foundation of skulls, indestructible from the outside, fragile on the inside, and incapable of ever being completed.

Ruibal's other major play, *The Begging Machine*, concerns the hypocrisy of charity and the mechanization of life. Its principal symbol is a Begging Machine that not only begs but steals as well. Ruibal makes use of surrealistic techniques by making one of his chief characters a yellow octopus that gives birth constantly to oil tankers and by showing the ruling powers of the world as hybrid machine-men, their heads in the form of miniature computers if they are civilians and in the form of weapons if they are in uniform.

It is hard to predict Ruibal's future as a dramatist at this point. He has the talent and the versatility to accomplish almost anything in the theatre and the maturity and insight to treat any subject. Of that there can be no question.

—George E. Wellwarth

RUSAN, Otilia Valeria. *See* **BLANDIANA, Ana.**

S

SABATO, Ernesto (R.). (Author does not use accent on surname.) Argentinian. Born in Rojas, 24 June 1911. Educated at the Colegio Nacional, 1924–28; National University of La Plata, 1929–37, Ph.D. in physics 1937; Joliot-Curie Laboratory, Paris, 1938; Massachusetts Institute of Technology, Cambridge, 1939. Married Matilde Kuminsky-Richter in 1934; two sons. Professor of theoretical physics, National University of La Plata, 1940–45; dismissed because of conflict with government; held executive post, Unesco, 1947 (resigned after two months); editor, *Mundo Argentino*, from 1955; director of cultural relations, Ministry of Foreign Relations and Culture, 1958–59 (resigned). Chair, National Commission of the Disappearance of Persons, 1983. Also a painter. Recipient: Argentine Association for the Progress of Science fellowship, 1937; Argentine Writers Society sash of honor, 1945, and grand prize, 1974; Buenos Aires Municipal prize, 1945; Institute of Foreign Relations prize (West Germany), 1973; Consagració Nacional prize, 1974; Argentine Society of Writers prize of honour, 1974; Prix du Meilleur Livre Étranger (France), 1977; Gran Cruz al Mérito Civil (Spain), 1979; Gabriela Mistral prize, 1984; Cervantes prize, 1985; Jerusalem prize, 1989. Chevalier de l'Ordre des Arts et des Lettres (France), 1964; Chevalier, 1979, and Commandeur, 1987, de la Légion d'Honneur (France). Address: Langeri 3135, 1676 Santos Lugares, Buenos Aires Province, Argentina.

PUBLICATIONS

Fiction

El túnel. Buenos Aires, Sur, 1948; as *The Outsider*, New York, Knopf, 1950; as *The Tunnel*, New York, Ballantine, and London, Cape, 1988.
Sobre héroes y tumbas. Buenos Aires, Fabril, 1961; excerpt as *Un dios desconocido: romance de la muerte de Juan Lavalle (de "Sobre héroes y tumbas")*, Buenos Aires, Dabini, 1980; as *On Heroes and Tombs*, Boston, Godine, 1981; London, Cape, 1982.
Obras de ficción. Buenos Aires, Losada, 1966.
Abaddón, el exterminador. Buenos Aires, Sudamericana, 1974; as *The Angel of Darkness*, New York, Ballantine, 1991.
Narrativa completa. Barcelona, Seix Barral, 1982.

Other

Uno y el universo. Buenos Aires, Sudamericana, 1945.
Hombres y engranajes: reflecciones sobre el dinero, la razón y el derrumbe de nuestro tiempo. Buenos Aires, Emecé, 1951.
Heterodoxia. Buenos Aires, Emecé, 1953.
El otro rostro del peronismo: Carta abierta a Mario Amadeo. Buenos Aires, López, 1956.
El caso Sabato: torturas y libertad de prensa — Carta abierta al Gral. Aramburu. Buenos Aires, privately printed, 1956.
Tango: discusión y clave. Buenos Aires, Losada, 1963.

El escritor y sus fantasmas. Madrid, Aguilar, 1963.
Pedro Henriquez Ureña. Buenos Aires, Ediciones Culturales Argentinas, 1967.
Tres aproximaciones a la literatura de nuestro tiempo: Robbe-Grillet, Borges, Sartre. Santiago, Universitaria, 1968.
La convulsión política y social de nuestro tiempo. Buenos Aires, Edicom, 1969.
Itinerario (includes fiction). Buenos Aires, Sur, 1969.
Obras: ensayos. Buenos Aires, Losada, 1970.
La cultura en la encrucijada nacional. Buenos Aires, Ediciones de Crisis, 1973.
Diálogos, with Jorge Luis Borges. Buenos Aires, Emecé, 1976.
Los libros y su misión enla liberación e integración de la América Latina. Buenos Aires, Embajada de Venezuela, 1978.
Apologías y rechazos. Barcelona, Seix Barral, 1979.
Cuatro hombres de pueblo, illustrated by Antonio Berni. Buenos Aires, La Ciudad, 1979.
La robotización del hombre y otras páginas de ficción y reflexión. Buenos Aires, Centro Editor del América Latina, 1981.
Páginas de Ernesto Sabato. Buenos Aires, Celtia, 1983.
La cultura en la encrucijada nacional. Buenos Aires, Sudamericana, 1985.
L'Écrivain et la catastrophe. Paris, Seuil, 1986; enlarged edition, as *The Writer in the Catastrophe of Our Time*, Tulsa, Oklahoma, Council Oak, 1990.
Entre la letra y la sangre: conversaciones con Carlos Catania. Barcelona, Seix Barral, 1989.
Lo mejor de Ernesto Sabato. Barcelona, Seix Barral, 1989.

Editor, *Mitomagia: los temas del misterio*. N.p., Ediciones Latinoamericanas, 1969.
Editor, with Anneliese von der Lipper, *Viaje a los mundos imaginarios*. Buenos Aires, Legasa, 1983.

*

Bibliography: "Bibliografía crítica completa de Ernesto Sabato, con un índice temático" by Nicasio Urbina, in *Revista de Critica Literaria Latinoamericana* (Lima), 14(27), 1988.

Critical Studies: "Magical Realism in Spanish American Fiction" by Angel Flores, in *Hispania* (Los Angeles), May 1955; "*El túnel*: Portrait of Isolation" by Beverly J. Gibbs, in *Hispania* (Los Angeles), September 1965; "Sabato's *El túnel*: More Freud than Sartre" by John Fred Petersen, in *Hispania* (Los Angeles), May 1967; "Dostoevsky's *Notes from the Underground* and Sabato's *El túnel*," in *Hispania* (Los Angeles), 51, 1968, and "Metaphysical Revolt in Ernesto Sabato's *Sobre heroes y tumbas*," in *Hispania* (Los Angeles), 52, 1969, both by Tamara Holzapfel; "Ernesto Sabato's Sexual Metaphysics: Theme and Form in *El túnel*" by Thomas C. Meehan, in *Modern Language Notes* (Baltimore, Maryland), 83, 1968; *Ernesto Sábato* by Harley Dean Oberhelman,

Boston, Twayne, 1970; "Fernando as Hero in Sabato's *Sobre héroes y tumbas*" by Raymond D. Souza, in *Hispania* (Los Angeles), 55, 1972; "The Integral Role of 'El informe sobre ciegos' in Sabato's *Sobre héroes y tumbas*," in *Romance Notes* (Chapel Hill, North Carolina), 14, 1972, and *Currents in the Contemporary Argentine Novel: Arlt, Mallea, Sabato and Cortázar*, Columbia, University of Missouri Press, 1975, both by David W. Foster; "Sabato's Fiction: A Jungian Interpretation" by Richard J. Callan, in *Bulletin of Hispanic Studies* (Liverpool), 51, 1974; "The Characterization of the Ontologically Insecure in *El túnel*" by Henry J. Richards, in *Romance Quarterly* (Lexington, Kentucky), 24, 1977; "*El túnel*: The Novel as Psychic Drama" by Robert H. Scott, in *The American Hispanist* (Clear Creek, Indiana), 2(14), 1977; "The Structural and Thematic Elements in *Abaddón, el exterminador* (Abbadon the Exterminator)" by Nivia Montenegro, in *Latin American Literary Review* (Pittsburgh), 12, 1978; "*Abaddón, el exterminador*: Sabato's Gnostic Eschatology" by Salvador Bacarisse, in *Contemporary Latin American Fiction*, Edinburgh, Scottish Academic Press, 1980; "Sabato's Tombs and Heroes" by William Kennedy, in *Review* (New York), 29, 1981; "Psychic Integration and the Search for Meaning in Sabato's *El túnel*" by Armand F. Baker, in *Hispanic Journal* (Indiana, Pennsylvania), 5(2), 1984; "'Report on the blind': Sabato's Journey into the Fantastic" by Margaret G. Redd, in *The Scope of the Fantastic*, edited by Robert A. Collins and Howard D. Peaze III, Westport, Connecticut, Greenwood, 1985; "Contemporary Poets to the Rescue: The Enigmatic Narrator in Sabato's *El túnel*" by Luis T. González-del-Valle and Catherine Nickel, in *Rocky Mountain Review* (Boise, Idaho), 40(1–2), 1986; "Sabato's *El túnel* and the Existential Novel" by William Nelson, in *Modern Fiction Studies* (West Lafayette, Indiana), 32(3), 1986.

* * *

After completing his doctorate in physics in 1937 Ernesto Sabato won a scholarship to do research at the Curie laboratory in Paris, where he befriended some of the Parisian surrealists, especially the Canary Islands painter Oscar Domínguez (who reappears as a character in Sabato's last novel). Back in Argentina, Sabato lectured at La Plata University before undergoing a crisis that led to his renunciation of science in favour of writing. His first published works were lucid, didactic essays concerning the crisis of culture after the war, and the bankruptcy of scientific reason. Over the years Sabato has become a great popularizer of ideas, measuring himself against the luminaries of his day like Jean-Paul Sartre, and culminating in a defence of the novel called *El escritor y sus fantasmas* (The Writer and His Ghosts), about the way a writer makes contact with primordial, dark forces, his demons. All the concerns manifested in his essays resurface in the three novels that Sabato has published in his lifetime.

His first novel *El túnel* (*The Outsider* or *The Tunnel*) opens with the paranoid painter Pablo Castel in prison justifying his murder of Maria Iribarne, the only person he ever loved and who really understood him. Clearly the actual murder is not what this short, hectic novel is about. From prison Castel returns in memory to the gallery where his painting called "Maternity" was being exhibited, and an enigmatic woman who stares at it. He eventually begins an affair with her dominated by his jealousy that she has her own life, a blind husband, and possibly other lovers. Through Castel's paranoid mind we see, in the shadow of Perón's fascism, a Buenos Aires that is vividly evoked and topographically exact. We also penetrate Castel's obsessive, split mind, his rational self-justifications, and prejudices against conventions, other writers, psychoanalysts, beaches, football, and bureaucrats. The title alludes to Castel's sense of despair and loneliness, of being trapped in his own tunnel. Sabato was aiming at a parable of the times, close to Albert Camus's *L'Étranger* where Castel echoes Sabato's own crisis of identity and profession confronted with the "dark labyrinth" inside the mind. *The Tunnel* is best read today not as a philosophical novel but as a satirical, localized story about a doomed love affair, an urban romance, with its chance meetings in cafés and bars and country estates.

Sabato's next novel *Sobre héroes y tumbas* (*On Heroes and Tombs*) appeared 13 years later in 1961, and its size alone suggests its ambitions. Again Sabato sets his novel in Buenos Aires, with scenes in recognizable bars and parks like the Parque Lezama. Again the novel is structured round several doomed love affairs, especially the naïve young Martin and the intuitive and rebellious Alejandra Vidal from a decadent patrician family. Her father Fernando Vidal contributes an eerie "Report on the Blind," a novel within the novel, reiterating a paranoid view of a conspiracy organized by the mafia of the blind. *On Heroes and Tombs* opens with the discovery of Alejandra and Fernando dead in a burnt-out house in June 1955. Through Martin, Alejandra, Fernando, and Bruno, an intellectual commentator often identified with Sabato himself, the reader is led through a series of set scenes that explore the enigma of contemporary Argentina, with vivid scenes going back to the English invasion of 1806, then Lavalle's 1841 defeat against the dictator Juan Manuel Rosas, and forward to Peronist church burnings of the early 1950s where history is an oscillation between "heroes" and tombs. Sabato has cleverly embedded in this fiction many discussions between the characters, where he can air his contradictory ideas about art, loneliness, sex, and Argentine identity. As in his earlier novel these café chats are linked to mordant satire and a sense that the present moment is a fall from grace. The novel can be portentous, with coincidences, false symbols, and forced allusions, especially between characters and Argentina, and the existential concerns of the time (lack of communication, alienation, etc.) have dated, but in general it does succeed as fiction.

The explicit models for Sabato's explorations are Franz Kafka and especially Fedor Dostoevskii, whose passionate, formless novels encouraged Sabato to develop ideas in an organic and Romantic way, untrammeled by plot. He views life as "overflowing rigid schemas, contradictory and paradoxical, driven by unreasonableness not reason," and the function of art is to reveal life's "secrets."

In 1974 Sabato published his third novel *Abaddón, el exterminador* (*The Angel of Darkness*). This sprawling, plotless novel, set in Buenos Aires during the crisis year of 1973, tries to capture the complex unfolding of Argentine history as an embodiment of evil. Sabato himself is one of the main characters, and interacts with his earlier novelistic characters such as Bruno, Alejandra, Castel, and Martin. Part of the novel dramatizes Sabato's own problems of being famous, of what he said or did not say in a lecture about Sartre. Radical students accuse him of being frivolous. The plot includes torture scenes, episodes dealing with the lure of revolutionary violence, a long description of Argentine Che Guevara's last days in Bolivia, and a subplot about an evil world organisation. The novel reaches back to 1938 and Sabato's encounter with the surrealist painter Oscar Domínguez. The autobiographic vein makes *The Angel of Darkness* an eye-witness novel ranging essay-like over problems about creativity to discussions about science, meat-eating, terrorism, etc. This highly self-conscious, experimental work does not live up to its visionary intentions and remains readable only because of

Sabato's earlier reputation. Following this novel Sabato renounced fiction and turned to painting, with recent one-man shows in Buenos Aires and Madrid.

—Jason Wilson

SACASTRU, Martin. *See* **BIOY CASARES, Adolfo.**

SA'DĀWI, Nawal al-. Also Nawal el-Saadawi. Egyptian. Born in Kafr Tahla, 27 October 1931. Educated at the University of Cairo, M.D. 1955; Columbia University, New York, M.P.H. 1966; Ain Shams University, 1973–75. Married 1) Ahmed Halmy in 1955 (divorced 1956), one daughter; 2) Sherif Hetata in 1964, one son. Physician, University of Cairo, 1955–56, and Rural Health Center, Tahla, 1956–58; director of health education, Ministry of Health, Cairo, 1958–72 (dismissed on publication of *Al-ma'ra wa-al-jins* [Women and Sex]); writer, High Institute of Literature and Science, Cairo, 1973–78; director of African Training and Research Center for Women, United Nations Economic Commission for Africa, Addis Ababa, 1978–80; adviser for women's programs, UN Economic Commission for West Asia, Beirut, 1978–80; since 1980 practicing psychiatrist. Arrested under Egyptian "Law for the Protection of Values from Shame," imprisoned for two months, 1981. Editor-in-chief, *Health* magazine, 1968–72 (dismissed). Co-founder, African Women's Association for Research and Development, 1977. Books banned in Egypt and some other Arab countries. Recipient: High Council of Literature award, 1974; Literary Franco-Arab Friendship award (France), 1982. Address: 25 Murad Street, Giza, Egypt.

PUBLICATIONS

Fiction

Ta'lamt al-ḥub [I Learned to Love]. Cairo, Maktabet al Nahda, 1958.
Moẓakkerat ṭabība. Cairo, Dār al Ma'āref, 1958; as *Memoirs of a Woman Doctor*, London, Al-Saqi, 1988; San Francisco, City Lights, 1989.
Ḥanān qalīl [Little Tenderness]. Cairo, Al Kitāb al Ẓahabi, 1959.
Laḥḍhat ṣidq [A Moment of Truth]. Cairo, Al Kitāb al Ẓahabi, 1962.
Al ghayib [The Absent]. Cairo, Al Kitāb al Ẓahabi, 1965.
Imra'atān fī imra'ah. Cairo, Dār al Kitab, 1968; as *Al-baḥitha 'an al-hub*, Cairo, Al Ḥaya al Miṣriya al-'Ama Lilkitāb, 1974; as *Two Women in One*, London, Al-Saqi, 1985.
Al-khaiṭ wa'ayn al-ḥayāt [The Thread and the Wall of Life]. Cairo, Al Shaab, 1972.
Kānat hiya al-aḍ'af. Cairo, Al Shaab, 1972; as *She Has No Place in Paradise*, London, Methuen, 1987.
Al-khaiṭ wa-al jidār [The Thread and the Wall]. Cairo, Al Shaab, 1972.

Emra'a 'inda nuqṭat al-ṣifr. Beirut, Dār al-Ādāb, 1975; as *Woman at Point Zero*, London, Zed, 1983.
Mawt al-rajul al-waḥīd 'ala al-arḍ. Beirut, Dār al-Ādāb, 1976; as *God Dies by the Nile*, London, Zed, 1985.
Ughniyat al-atfāl al dā'iriyah. Beirut, Dār al-Ādāb, 1977; as *The Circling's Song*, London, Zed, 1989.
Mawt ma'āli al wazīr sābiqan. Beirut, Dār al-Ādāb, 1979; as *Death of an Ex-Minister*, London, Methuen, 1987.
Ferdaous: une voix en enfer. Paris, Des Femmes, 1982.
Ṣuqūṭ al-Imām. Cairo, Dār al Mostaqbal al-'Ārabi, 1987; as *The Fall of the Imam*, London, Methuen, 1988.
Ganah wa iblīs [Paradise and Lucifer]. Beirut, Dār al-Ādāb, 1992.
The Spring of Life. London, Methuen, 1992.
The Innocence of the Devil. London, Methuen, 1993.

Plays

Al-insān [The Human Being]. Cairo, Maktabet Madbouli, 1983; as *Ethna ashra Imra'a fi zinzanah* [12 Women in One Call], Maktabet Madbūli, 1983.
Izis [Izis]. Cairo, Dār al-Mustaqbal al-'Ārabi, 1986.

Other

Al-mar'a wa-al-jins [Women and Sex]. Cairo, Al Shaab, 1971.
Al-rajul wa-al-jins [Man and Sex]. Beirut, Al-Mu'assasah al-'Arabiyyah lil-Taḥrīr wa-al-Nashr, 1973.
Al-mar'a hiy al-aṣl [The Essentiality of the Woman]. Beirut, Al-Mu'assasah al-'Arabiyyah lil-Taḥrīr wa-al-Nashr, 1975.
Al mar'a wal sirā' al-nafsī [Woman and Psychological Conflict]. Beirut, Al-Mu'assasah al-'Arabiyyah lil-Taḥrīr wa-al-Nashr, 1976.
Al-wajh al-'ārī lil-mar'ah al-'Arabiyyah. Beirut, Al-Mu'assasah al-'Arabiyyah lil-Dirāsat wa-al-Nashr, 1977; as *The Hidden Face of Eve: Women in the Arab World*, London, Zed, 1980; Boston, Beacon Press, 1982.
Muẓakkirāti fī sijn al-nisa'. Cairo, Dar al-Mustaqbal al-'Ārabi, 1983; as *Memoirs from the Women's Prison*, London, Women's Press, 1986.
Riḥlati hawla al-'ālam. Cairo, Dar al-Hilāl, 1986; as *My Travels Around the World*, London, Methuen, 1991.
Dirāsāt 'an al-mar'ah wa-al-rajul fī al-mujtama' al-'Arabi [Studies on the Arabic Woman and Man in the Arab Society]. Beirut, Al-Mu'assasah al-'Arabiyyah lil-Dirāsāt wa-al-Nashr, 1986.

*

Critical Study: *Woman Against Her Sex: A Critique of Nawal al Saadawi, with a Reply by Nawal al Saadawi* by Georges Tarabishi, London, Al-Saqi, 1988.

* * *

Nawal al-Sa'dāwi (Nawal el-Saadawi) is probably the most famous Arab woman writer outside Egypt. Her crusade for the liberation of Arab women earned her fame in the West as the major Arab feminist. She started her career as a medical doctor, which gave her insight into both the individual and social aspects of her society, and greatly benefited her when she turned to literature a few years later. She started writing in the late 1950s, but her early works went unnoticed for nearly 10 years. She first attained wide acclaim in the Arab world when she published daring studies on sexuality, particularly on female sexuality. These coincided with the rise of the international feminist movement in the 1970s, furthering interest in her work and enabling her to devote her time entirely to her writing. The major theme in her novels, short stories, essays, and studies is the protest against the standards and values of the patriarchal society and its implicit system which mitigates against women. From the outset of her career, al-Sa'dāwi realized that literary discourse plays a significant part in the social and political life of her nation and became aware of its function as a propagator of a "world view" and hence of its vital role in passifying the oppressed or inciting them to revolt against their lot. For without altering women's perception of themselves and their role, it is difficult to motivate them to change.

Her first novel, *Moẓakkerat ṭabība* (*Memoirs of a Woman Doctor*), has a strong autobiographical tone. It portrays a young Egyptian woman in conflict with her own femininity and the prevalent perception of the female in her immediate surroundings. The quest for recognition as an equal in the world of men forms the core of the work. Her achievements at school, in the Faculty of Medicine, and later as a working doctor are portrayed as being a direct result of her suppression of her own sexuality. Her first marriage, in which she was sought as a mother figure rather than as a wife and companion, collapsed. Working close to nature in the countryside (and here one finds the roots of al-Sa'dāwi's environmental concern) strengthens her individuality, and her close affinity with underprivileged peasants and victims of rape develops her social consciousness. Thus when the heroine meets a musician and falls in love with him her affair has the ingredient of a more fulfilling relationship. Yet the ending shows us the militant heroine melting in his arms and expressing her affection by baking him a cake and cleaning the flat. This happy ending sees the taming of the shrew, the transformation of a confused woman into a more traditional one who falls head over heels in love as soon as she meets the right man who is capable of penetrating the skin-deep feminism to reveal the traditional woman underneath, ready to seek his protection.

Reading the book as a mixture of narrative and autobiography enables the reader to accept and sympathize with its heroine in her struggle to come to terms with her own sexuality. *Memoirs*'s subjectivity is accepted as an inherent part of a true record of the author's controversial and often problematic struggle to invert social perceptions of male and female roles and standings. The contradictions of the text and the subjective exaggerations in its depiction of social ills and the double standard of morality continue to prevail in many of her subsequent works. In *Emra'a 'inda nuqṭat al-ṣifr* (*Woman at Point Zero*), *Mawt al-rajul al-waḥīd 'ala al-arḍ* (*God Dies by the Nile*), and *Imra'atān fī imra'ah* (*Two Women in One*), the more the feminist rebels against the prevalent norms, the more attractive she becomes to the establishment, which is in the habit of co-opting the propagators of change. The heroines of these works fight against the limitations imposed on them by society and attempt to take power into their hands. They identify with rebellious and subversive characters, as in *Two Women in One* and *Al ghayib* (The Absent), and revolt against any manifestation of patriarchy, as in *Memoirs* and *Woman at Point Zero*.

The main characteristic of the feminist narrative discourse in these works, namely its desire to subvert patriarchal control of the distribution of roles, aims at opening new venues for women and enhancing their place in the society. Yet many of these texts reveal a peculiar tendency to invert the prevalent patriarchal order without a clear understanding of the dangers involved. The inversion of an unjust order retains the inherent contradictions of its original system, albeit in an inverse form. They are taking on the ideology of the system they sought to repudiate.

This is evident in al-Sa'dāwi's recent novel, *Ṣuqūṭ al-Imām* (*The Fall of the Imam*), which brings together elements of al-Sa'dāwi's feminism and her political and public role. It relates the story of an illegitimate woman who discovers that her real father is the Imam, a political leader who exploits religion for his own ends. The structure of the novel is one of equivocation, selective and controlled by both the account of the public assassination of the Imam and preparations for his official funeral and the flashes of subjective memory which punctuate the current events and provide them with their historical dimension.

On one level of interpretation, the novel is a female *bildungsroman* which elects to maximise the obstacles and constraints in the path of its female protagonist in order to elaborate the process of her cultural and sexual formation. The revelation of the heroine's identity poses a threat to her father, the Imam, and his corrupt authority. The power of the Imam, or in other words of patriarchy, is based on the suppression of the identity of his daughter. The conflict between the woman's desire for self-expression and the realisation of her identity and the institution of patriarchy is given added weight by making the Imam the ultimate symbol of power and the seat of political, cultural, and religious authority. In order to posit her heroine as the counter power in this multidimensional conflict and give her added religious significance, al-Sa'dāwi presents her heroine as a female version of Christ. The novel's challenge to patriarchy requires a reinforcement of the heroine's bonds with her father, while the added religious significance demands the weakening of these bonds. This structural equivocation is a product of the author imposing her ideology on her narrative.

On another level of interpretation, *The Fall of the Imam* is a political allegory based on the era of Anwar Sadat's presidency and made of thinly disguised characters which lack inner motivation and have little symbolic value. The fictional world of the novel strives for plausibility and derives it from its constant reference to extrinsic data. However, for those who cannot relate its events or characters to their historical referents, *The Fall of the Imam* appears as an ambiguous fantasy marked by a burdensome authorial presence which generates a heavy sense of didacticism and reproduces one of the worst aspects of patriarchal narrative. What unfolds in the book is not a multitude of characters and fates but a group of fragmentary characters who are objects of authorial discourse, and not subjects of their own directly signifying discourse. Although the allegorical nature of the text and its ideological implications necessitate a rich dialogue between the various arguments and viewpoints, al-Sa'dāwi's discourse is monological rather than dialogical. Unlike the polyphonic narrative which unifies highly heterogeneous and incompatible material, al-Sa'dāwi's monophonic narrative reduces the plurality of consciousness to an ideological common denominator.

However, al-Sa'dāwi's road to literary creativity is paved with good causes and honourable intentions. She aspires to achieve justice and fights for her sisters' rights, equality, and self-determination in a traditional and highly patriarchal society.

—Sabry Hafez

SAER, Juan José. Argentinian. Born in Serodino, in 1937. Educated at the Instituto de Cinematografía, Universidad Nacional del Litoral, Santa Fé. Left Argentina in 1968; lives in France. Recipient: Nadal prize (Spain). Address: c/o Edicions Destino, Consell de Cent 425, 08009 Barcelona, Spain.

PUBLICATIONS

Fiction

Responso. Buenos Aires, Alvarez, 1964.
Unidad de lugar. Buenos Aires, Galerna, 1967.
Cicatrices. Buenos Aires, Sudamericana, 1969.
El limonero real. Barcelona, Planeta, 1974.
Nadie nada nunca. Mexico City, Siglo Veintiuno, 1980.
La mayor. Buenos Aires, Centro Editor de América Latina, 1982.
Narraciones. Buenos Aires, Centro Editor de América Latina, 1983.
El entenado. Mexico City, Folios, 1983; as *The Witness*, London, Serpent's Tail, 1990.
Glosa. Buenos Aires, Alianza, 1986.
La ocasión. Barcelona, Destino, 1988.

Other

En la zona, 1957–1960. Santa Fé, Castellví, 1960.
Una literatura sin atributos. Santa Fé, Universidad Nacional del Litoral, 1986.
Juan José Saer (selected works). Buenos Aires, Celtia, 1986.
El arte de narrar. Santa Fé, Universidad Nacional del Litoral, 1988.

* * *

Juan José Saer has lived outside his home country of Argentina since 1968. Being cut off from his own country has resulted in the paradox that his work is much better known in translation in his adopted country of France (where it has won several prizes) than in Argentina itself. Only since winning the prestigious Spanish Nadal literary prize has Saer become regarded as a writer worthy of critical attention in Argentina, where literature is particularly susceptible to the swings of fashion.

For all that, Saer's work is deeply rooted in Argentina, and in particular in the part of the vast grasslands or pampas of the province of Santa Fé where he lived during his formative years. His first writings followed the 1960s fashion in Argentine literature for "committed" work, which at that time meant an alliance of the aspirations of Peronist nationalism with left-wing ideas. However, already in a novel such as *Cicatrices* (Scars) there are signs of a more personal voice emerging, with a deeper concern for language as the means of exploring inner realities in fiction rather than conveying a straightforward realism.

This development was first successfully explored in the novel *El limonero real* (The Royal Lemon Tree). The novel revolves around 24 hours in the life of Wenceslao, an inhabitant of the Argentine pampas. The events of the day are trivial: he visits his relations, has lunch, kills a sheep for a barbecue, which he then enjoys, and eventually retires to bed with his wife. What is foregrounded in the telling of these events is how difficult it is for writing to convey convincingly even something as apparently simple as these events: the attempts are constantly overwhelmed by memories or even intrusions from the past, speculation and plans for the future — the constant seeping

away of reality. Saer skilfully illustrates this difficulty by on the one hand giving a vivid portrayal of a specific, well-defined world, that of provincial Argentina, while at the same time showing how cumbersome all language, with its in-built linear construction of meaning, is to convey adequately our sense of being in that world.

Two further novels, *La ocasión* (The Event), and *El entenado* (*The Witness*), examine similar ideas in different historical periods. *La ocasión* tells the story of Bianco, a magician who is forced by rational science and the positivists to flee from 19th-century Paris, and ends up in the Argentine pampas. There he gradually loses his reason, becoming obsessed with the vision of a woman and of his past powers. Once again Saer is interested in how his protagonist's grip on reality slowly loosens, and how language is both his lifeline and his betrayer.

The Witness is a story told by a cabin boy of the time he spent among cannibalistic natives after being one of the few survivors from one of the early Spanish expeditions to Latin America (he too in fact may have been left stranded on the Argentine coast). Though horrified at the time by what seemed to him the barbaric practices of the native people he is forced to live with, in later life he comes to realise what a privileged position he had been in to experience a completely different way of constructing the world, and once again the primordial role language plays in that construction. In this novel too, Saer's writing is convincing thanks to his ability to combine elements of description and action with a more philosophical level of enquiry.

This side of his work is at its most pronounced — and most successful — in the novel *Glosa* (Gloss), which has been described as Saer's version of Plato's Banquet. In this novel we are once again in Santa Fé, but here more than ever the setting is merely a point of departure. The novel tells how two young men, Angel Leto and "The Mathematician," meet and walk along in conversation. The subject of their talk is a famous barbecue held in honour of a local poet. Neither was actually at the barbecue, and they have to rely on the account of it given by a third person, Bouton (which in Argentine slang means "grass," or "police informer"), who is notoriously unreliable in what he says. The pair are reduced to conjecturing as to whether it is ever possible to get at the truth of the "banquet" which undeniably took place, and yet which they find almost impossible to describe accurately.

These books show Saer to be undoubtedly one of the finest contemporary writers from the Río de la Plata, building on the tradition of writers such as Jorge Luis Borges or Juan Carlos Onetti (*q.v.*). His years of living abroad seem to have freed him from the narrowness of much of what has been written in the past two decades in Argentina itself, while he has shown that it has in no way diminished his bold, probing use of the Spanish language.

—Nick Caistor

SAGAN, Françoise. Pseudonym for Françoise Quoirez. French. Born in Carjac, 21 June 1935. Educated at a lycée in Paris, graduated 1952; the Sorbonne, Paris. Married 1) Guy Schoeller in 1958 (divorced 1960); 2) Robert Westhoff in 196_ (divorced 1963), one son. Involved in near-fatal car accident 1957; convicted for cocaine possession, 1990. Recipien_

Critics' prize, 1954; Monaco prize, 1985. Address: c/o Jean-Jacques Pauvert, 8 rue de Nesle, 75006 Paris, France.

PUBLICATIONS

Fiction

Bonjour Tristesse. Paris, Julliard, 1954; in English, New York, Dutton, and London, Murray, 1955.

Un Certain Sourire. Paris, Julliard, 1956; in English, London, Murray, 1956; as *A Certain Smile*, New York, Dutton, 1956.

Dans un Mois, dans un an. Paris, Julliard, 1957; as *Those Without Shadows*, New York, Dutton, and London, Murray, 1957.

Aimez-Vous Brahms? Paris, Julliard, 1959; in English, New York, Dutton, and London, Murray, 1960.

Les Merveilleux Nuages. Paris, Julliard, 1961; as *Wonderful Clouds*, London, Murray, 1961; New York, Dutton, 1962.

La Chamade. Paris, Julliard, 1965; in English, New York, Dutton, and London, Murray, 1966.

Le Garde du cœur. Paris, Julliard, 1968; as *The Heart-Keeper*, New York, Dutton, and London, Murray, 1968.

Un Peu de soleil dans l'eau froide. Paris, Flammarion, 1969; as *A Few Hours of Sunlight*, New York, Harper, 1971; as *Sunlight on Cold Water*, London, Weidenfeld and Nicolson, 1971.

Des Bleus à l'âme. Paris, Flammarion, 1972; as *Scars on the Soul*, New York, McGraw Hill, and London, Deutsch, 1974.

Un Profil perdu. Paris, Flammarion, 1974; as *Lost Profile*, New York, Delacorte, and London, Deutsch, 1976.

Des Yeux de soie. Paris, Flammarion, 1976; as *Silken Eyes*, New York, Delacorte/Friede, and London, Deutsch, 1977.

Le Lit défait. Paris, Flammarion, 1977; as *The Unmade Bed*, New York, Delacorte/Friede, and Henley-on-Thames, Ellis, 1978.

Le Chien couchant. Paris, Flammarion, 1980; as *Salad Days*, New York, Dutton, 1984; as *Le Chien couchant* (in English), London, Allen, 1985.

Musiques de scènes. Paris, Flammarion, 1981; as *Incidental Music*, New York, Dutton, 1983; London, Allison and Busby, 1989.

La Femme fardée. Paris, Pauvert, 1981; as *The Painted Lady*, New York, Dutton, and London, Allen, 1983.

Un Orage immobile. Paris, Pauvert, 1983; as *The Still Storm*, London, Allen, 1984; New York, Dutton, 1986.

De Guerre lasse. Paris, Gallimard, 1985; as *A Reluctant Hero*, New York, Dutton, 1987; as *Engagements of the Heart*, London, Allison and Busby, 1988.

La Maison de Raquel Vega: Fiction d'après le tableau de Fernando Botero. Paris, La Différence, 1985.

Un Sang d'aquarelle. Paris, Gallimard, 1987; as *Painting in Blood*, Henley-on-Thames, Ellis, 1988.

La Laisse. Paris, Julliard, 1989; as *The Leash*, London, Allison and Busby, 1991.

Les Faux-fuyants. Paris, Julliard, 1991.

Plays

Le Rendez-vous manqué (ballet), with Michel Mange (produced Monte Carlo, 1958).

Château en Suède (produced Paris, 1960). Paris, Julliard, 1960; as *Castle in Sweden* (produced in English, 1962).

Les Violons parfois (produced Paris, 1961). Paris, Julliard, 1962.

La Robe mauve de Valentine (produced Paris, 1963). Paris, Julliard, 1963.

Landru (screenplay), with Claude Chabrol. Paris, Julliard, 1963.

Bonheur, impair et passe (produced Paris, 1964). Paris, Julliard, 1964.

Le Cheval évanoui; L'Écharde (produced Paris, 1966). Paris, Julliard, 1966; as *The Dizzy Horse* (produced in English, 1968).

Un Piano dans l'herbe (produced Paris, 1970). Paris, Flammarion, 1970.

Le Sang doré des Borgia (screenplay), with Jacques Quoirez. Paris, Flammarion, 1977.

Il fait beau jour et nuit (produced Paris, 1978). Paris, Flammarion, 1979.

L'Excès contraire (produced Paris, 1987). As *Opposite Extremes* (produced in English, 1987).

Screenplay: *Encore un Hiver*, 1979.

Other

Toxique. Paris, Julliard, 1964; in English, New York, Dutton, 1964; London, Souvenir Press, 1965.

Mirror of Venus, with Federico Fellini, photographs by Wingate Paine. New York, Random House, and London, Nelson, 1966.

Il est des parfums, with Guillaume Hanoteau. Paris, Dullis, 1973.

Réponses, 1954–1974. Paris, Pauvert, 1974; as *Réponses: The Autobiography of Françoise Sagan*, Godalming, Surrey, Ram, 1979; as *Night Bird: Conversations with Françoise Sagan*, New York, Clarkson Potter, 1980.

Brigitte Bardot, photographs by Christian Dussart. Paris, Flammarion, 1975; in English, New York, Delacorte, 1976.

Avec Mon Meilleur Souvenir. Paris, Gallimard, 1984; as *With Fondest Regards*, New York, Dutton, 1985; London, Allen, 1986.

Sarah Bernhardt: Le Rire incassable. Paris, Laffont, 1987; as *Dear Sarah Bernhardt*, New York, Seaver, 1987; London, Macmillan, 1988.

La Sentinelle de Paris. Paris, Laffont, 1988.

Au marbre: chroniques retrouvées 1952–1962, with Guy Dupré and François Nourissier. Paris, Désinvolture, 1988.

The Eiffel Tower, with Winnie Denker. London, Deutsch, and New York, Vendome, 1989.

Editor, *Sand & Musset: lettres d'amour*. Paris, Hermann, 1985.

*

Bibliography: by John Robert Kaiser, in *Bulletin of Bibliography and Magazine Notes*, July–September 1973.

Manuscript Collection: Pennsylvania State University Library, University Park.

Critical Studies: interview by Blair Fuller and Robert B. Silvers, in *Writers at Work: The Paris Review Interviews*, edited by Malcolm Cowley, New York, Viking, 1958; *Françoise Sagan* by Judith Graves Miller, Boston, Twayne, 1988.

*   *   *

Bonjour Tristesse sold more than half a million copies within a year of its publication in 1954 and won its teenage author the prestigious Critics' prize and an enormous reputation. But if readers almost the whole world over were delighted by the freshness and immediacy of this very personal account of a girl's transition from adolescence to adulthood during a summer holiday by the sea, the critical establishment refused to be impressed. Perhaps it was because the novel in its emotions and settings was deemed to be just a little too close to popular fiction and the sort of stories that are published in a certain type of women's magazine; or because the very straightforward narrative technique appeared to have no relationship with the French novel as it was developing in post-war years; or because the concentration on the affairs of the heart seemed irrelevant when social and political involvement and philosophical *angst* were the order of the day. Another explanation might simply be an unwillingness to take very seriously a girl from a well-heeled bourgeois background who had not even been to university and who was thought by many to quarry her fiction from either her personal experience or adolescent dreams. Though, strictly speaking, biographical considerations should not be allowed to cloud the criticism of texts, there can be little doubt that graphic newspaper reports of Françoise Sagan's rather glamorous lifestyle and of the misfortunes to which it inevitably led did nothing to endear her to those already antipathetic to her and everything she was taken to stand for.

Despite certain personal problems, Sagan has, however, continued to write quite prolifically, apparently not very much troubled by the reservations that some feel obliged to go on expressing about her work. She has several plays to her credit, and she has made it clear that she has found genuine professional satisfaction and emotional contentment from close involvement in all the practical and technical aspects of working in the boulevard theatre. But it is not for plays like *Château en Suède* (*Castle in Sweden*), with its title that offers a quirky variant of the idiom "Castles in Spain," that Sagan will be best remembered. What has always attracted most attention are her novels and short stories, and these, paradoxically enough for the work of a writer who first came to the fore as a representative of the bright young things of the rising generation, have taken on what now can be interpreted as something like period charm.

Nothing, it is fair to say, interests Sagan so much as the classic issue of the interplay of the two sexes, and this she presents, above all, in two different settings. The first is the world of French middle-class people, well-to-do and goodlooking, sociable and at least outwardly polite to one another, generally not much troubled about conventional morality, and essentially selfish as they search for their own happiness in love. But if in portraying the affairs of the heart in such situations Sagan may be drawing on what she herself knows best, she also gives scope to her imagination as she sets her tales in what she presents as overtly romantic settings, such as the French past, Italy, and a piquantly aristocratic England.

After *Bonjour Tristesse*, *Un Certain Sourire* (*A Certain Smile*) was regarded, not without some justification, as little more than an attempt to continue in much the same vein, but *Aimez-Vous Brahms?* was recognised as evidence of some maturing in both sensibility and novelistic technique. *Un Orage immobile* (*The Still Storm*) owes quite a lot to an historical setting, and indeed in the way it is narrated the story seems to belong, not to the late 20th century, but to the early decades of the 19th which it evokes, as its male narrator describes how the regular routines of his life as a country notary are shattered by his growing emotional involvement with the aristocratic Flora de Margelasse, whose personal magnetism is reflected in her romantic name. Sagan turns to the traumatic period of the German occupation of France in 1942 for *Un Sang d'aquarelle* (*Painting in Blood*) in which, however, love still remains the major concern.

Many readers may well find that, after *Bonjour Tristesse*, short stories are the most satisfactory part of Sagan's output. Brief, striking, and varied, they present a beguiling blend of cynicism and romanticism with skill and, sometimes, humour, and never outstay their welcome. In *Musiques de scènes* (*Incidental Music*) we have, for instance, in "Aftermath of a Duel" the highly charged emotional climate of the officer caste in *fin-de-siècle* Austria, and "La Futura" has searing passions in a context of cruelty and class distinctions. "The Exchange," quaintly located in Fontleroy Castle, is very neatly handled. "Third-Person Singular" brings us back to all the difficulties of the French bourgeoisie in a deftly told story, and in "A Question of Timing" Sagan displays a very French mixture of insight, cynicism, and humanity.

—Christopher Smith

ŠALAMUN, Tomaž. Slovene. Born in Zagreb, 4 July 1941. Educated at the University of Ljubljana, M.A. in art history 1965; studied art history in Paris and Rome, 1967; International Writing Program, University of Iowa, Iowa City, 1971–73. Served in the Yugoslav Army, 1966. Married 1) Maruša Krese in 1969 (divorced 1975), one daughter and one son; 2) Metka Krese in 1979. Assistant curator, Modern Gallery, Ljubljana, 1969–70; Assistant Professor, Academy of Art, Ljubljana, 1970–72; since 1972 freelance writer. Residences at Yaddo and MacDowell colonies, United States, 1973, 1974, 1979, 1986, and 1987. Exhibitor at Conceptual Artists Show, Museum of Modern Art, New York, 1970. Recipient: Fulbright grant, 1986–87. Address: Masarykova 28, 61000 Ljubljana, Slovenia.

PUBLICATIONS

Verse

Poker. Ljubljana, samizdat, 1966; Ljubljana, Cankarjeva Zalpžba, 1989.
Namen Pelerine [The Intention of the Pelerine]. Ljubljana, samizdat, 1968.
Romanje za Maruško [Pilgrimage for Maruška]. Ljubljana, Cankarjeva Zalpžba, 1971.
Bela Itaka [White Ithaca]. Ljubljana, Državna Založba Slovenije, 1972.
Amerika. Maribor, Obzorja, 1973.
Arena. Koper, Lipa, 1973.
Turbines, translated by Anselm Hollo and Elliott Anderson. Iowa City, Windhover Press, 1973.
Snow. West Branch, Iowa, Toothpaste Press, 1973.
Sokol [Falcon]. Ljubljana, Mladinska Knjiga, 1974.
Imre. Ljubljana, Državna Založba Slovenije, 1975.
Druidi [Druids]. Koper, Lipa, 1975.
Turbine [Turbines]. Maribor, Obzorja, 1975.
Praznik [Holiday]. Ljubljana, Cankarjeva, 1976.
Zvezde [Stars]. Ljubljana, Državna Založba Slovenije, 1977.

Metoda angela [Angel's Method]. Ljubljana, Mladinska Kniga, 1978.
Po sledeh divjadi [On the Track Game]. Koper, Lipa, 1979.
Zgodovina svetlobe je oranžna [The History of Sight Is Orange]. Maribor, Obzorja, 1979.
Pesmi [Poems], with Svetlana Makarović and Niko Grafenauer. Ljubljana, Mladinska Kniga, 1979.
Pesmi [Poems]. Ljubljana, Državna Založba Slovenije, 1980.
Maske [Masks]. Ljubljana, Mladinska Kniga, 1980.
Balada za Metko Krašovec [Ballad for Metko Krašovec]. Ljubljana, Državna Založba Slovenije, 1981.
Analogije svetlobe [Anthologies of Light]. Ljubljana, Cankarjeva Založba, 1982.
Glas [Voice]. Maribor, Obzorja, 1983.
Sonet o mleku [Sonnet on Milk]. Ljubljana, n.p., 1984.
Soy realidad [I Am Reality]. Koper, Lipa, 1985.
Ljubljanska pomlad [Ljubljana Spring]. Ljubljana, Državna Založba Slovenije, 1986.
Mera časa. Ljubljana, Cankarjeva Založba, 1987.
Ziva rana, živi sok [Living Wound]. Maribor, Obzorja, 1988.
The Selected Poems of Tomaž Šalamun, edited and translated by Charles Simic. New York, Ecco Press, 1988.
Otrok in jelen [Boy and Stag]. Celovec, n.p., 1990.

*

Critical Studies: "Tomaž Šalamun and Slovenian Poetry" by Michael Biggins, in *Boulevard*; "The Elegies of Style" by Richard Jackson, in *Georgia Review* (Athens), 42(4), 1988; article by Aleš Debeljak, in *Poetry Miscellany* (Chattanooga, Tennessee), 20(6), 1989.

*   *   *

Tomaž Šalamun's poetry, like that of T. S. Eliot's in English, represents a crucial formally aesthetic turning point in the development of modern Slovene poetry. Since the early 1960s he has tried to demolish the classical type of poetry by postulating poetic play as the paramount principle of the sarcastic and at times cynical parody of Slovene literary and historical tradition and thus breaking into a delayed avant-garde movement (dadaism and surrealism). Šalamun is exceptionally prolific and much translated, widely acclaimed especially in the United States. His disruptive eclecticism — the sense of loose improvisation and play in the poems, the disjunctions, the fast jottings of what is going on at the moment, puns, neologisms and various lexical and syntactical innovations in the Slovene language — is clearly the result of his reading the German expressionists, the French surrealists, the Russian futurists, Arthur Rimbaud, Lautréamont, Frank O'Hara, John Ashbery, and William Carlos Williams.

Today a well-loved participant in public poetry readings and prestigious world poetry gatherings, Šalamun entered Slovene poetry in the 1960s as a phoenix with the collection of verse *Poker*, which came as a shock to many of his compatriots for its sarcastic Apollinaire-like rejection of the Slovene "tribe," an exile he sought as an exponent of Slovene experimental poetry, following the traditions of the European avant-garde. In *Poker* the poet did not directly accept the parodied and satirical texts, because the greater part of the poems were rooted in two inclinations. The first was of an ethical nature, trying to reveal the truth of the world and existence, while the second was aesthetic and endeavoured to incorporate the content into the sphere of word expression.

Considered in a broader literary perspective, he can be said to belong to the generation of Eastern European poets, including Joseph Brodsky (*q.v.*) from Russia and Adam Zagajewski from Poland, whose verse also emerged in the 1960s. He shares with them a sense of history and a strong commitment to the freedom of his art, which is essentially playful, full of egotistical self-mythologizing, and marked by a sense of the absurd bordering on anger. Like them he is not marked by the experience of war and its aftermath, but rather by the post-war years of intellectual dishonesty and almost Stalinistic cultural suffocation, although his is not really a poetics of revolution or even revolt.

In contrast to his first book, Šalamun's second and third collections of verse, *Namen Pelerine* (The Intention of the Pelerine) and *Romanje za Maruško* (Pilgrimage for Maruška), for example, are much less unified in expression. These poems clearly belong to pop art and are constructed on surrealistic principles of form, while also aspiring towards narrativeness. The poet's narcissistic poetic bravado, mixed with self-undercutting irony, is characterized by the amassment of literalized figures of speech, hyperbole, improbable causalities, postmodern juxtapositions of trivial and historical detail, and purely associative leaps and bounds.

The extreme modernism of Šalamun's lyrics is mostly designated with a shapelessness of form, evident in the absence of punctuation marks, demolished syntax, and the mixing of lexemes and syntaxemes. Still, this apparent disorder is substantiated in the author's unique and original poetic stance. Šalamun visualizes the word as a ready-made thing, and creates outrageous juxtapositions by combining seemingly incongruous contexts. One of the great problems he attempts to solve in his poems is how to commence and how to end a (modernist) poem. To this end he establishes a certain spatial poetic form, enabling a multi-layered reading whereby a poem can be "entered" at any ontological level, at the beginning, in the middle, or at the end.

The ironic mysticism and expressive personal inconography from *Balada za Metko Krašovec* (The Ballad for Metka Krašovec) has gradually given way to the topography of love, through which it is revealed that the poetry of love is always the poetry of mental and physical rifts, climaxes, torments, longing, and metaphysical search for personal and poetic freedom. Šalamun's poem "Who Is Who?" characteristically deals with the Whitmanesque building of the mythology of the self by beginning, "Tomaž Šalamun you are a genius/you are wonderful you are a joy to behold/you are great you are a giant . . ."

Šalamun has written nearly 30 books of poems, and a selection of English translations was published in 1988. It was edited by Charles Simic, who found a fresh, regenerative poetic expression of the Slovene language. Šalamun is right in saying that he himself and "Every true poet is a monster./He destroys people and their speech/His singing elevates a technique that wipes out/the earth so we are not eaten by worms . . ."

—Igor Maver

———

SĀLIH, al-Tayyib. Also Tayeb Salih. Sudanese. Born in Dabba, northern Sudan, in 1928. Educated at Khartoum University, B.A.; Exeter University, Devon; University of

London, degree in education. Briefly a teacher; head of drama, BBC Arabic Service, 12 years; technical adviser, Sudan Broadcasting Service, Khartoum; director general of Ministry of Information, Katar; consultant to Unesco. Address: c/o Three Continents Press, 1901 Pennsylvania Avenue, N.W., Suite 407, Washington, D.C. 20006, U.S.A.

PUBLICATIONS

Fiction

Dawmat wad ḥamid. 1962.
'Urs az-Zen. 1964; as *The Wedding of Zein*, in *The Wedding of Zein and Other Stories*, 1968.
Mawsim al-hijrah ila al-shamāl. 1966; as *Season of Migration to the North*, London, Heinemann, 1969; Washington, D.C., Three Continents Press, 1978.
The Wedding of Zein and Other Stories. London, Heinemann, 1968; Washington, D.C., Three Continents Press, 1978.
Bandar Shah. 1971.

* * *

The intellectual make-up of al-Tayyib Sālih (Tayeb Salih) represents a process of bringing together, but not necessarily fusing or synthesizing, the techniques of European fiction and Arabic narrative art. The more powerful influence on his work has undoubtedly been his upbringing within the deeply rooted traditions of Sufism which he has inherited from his family of religious leaders and mystics.

Sālih's work burst onto the literary scene in the Arab world in the late 1960s, ushering in a new phase in modernist writing in Arabic and giving the realistic novel a new lease of life. Coming at a time of great political upheaval and ideological fervour, Sālih's work appeared to be flowing in a stream of its own, almost oblivious to the political and ideological turmoils all around it and exploring issues of a more universal nature such as identity, sexuality, spirituality and materialism, modernity and change, the meaning and function of traditional modes of existence in the modern world, the tensions and conflicts which shape the relationship of the so-called Third World to the West, and the nature and language of narrative and its potential power. At a time when nationalism, socialism, and secularism were major issues in Arabic writing, and when political authority and political leaders such as Nasser were at the centre of everything from consciousness to literary production, Sālih's work assigned ideology and political authority a very marginal place. In more senses than one, he was reversing, or inverting, the order of things and deconstructing the geo-cultural realities of the Arab world by ignoring its central issues and the centrality of its major metropolises and transforming the distant margins into the centre of his fictional world. African rather than Arab identity, social, cultural, and artistic issues rather than political and ideological ones, the community rather than the State, ordinary people rather than intellectuals, popular culture rather than official culture, religious and mystical belief rather than secularism, the Sudanese dialect rather than Standard Arabic, and the small village rather than the great metropolis — these are the constituent elements of his fictional world. Edward Said sees Sālih as a counter-narrator who "appropriate(s) for (his) fiction such great *topoi* of colonial culture as the quest and the voyage into the unknown, claiming them for (his) own, post-colonial purposes." Sālih reverses the direction of the invasion and the invading hero: Conrad depicts Europe invading Africa, Sālih Africa invading Europe.

Nevertheless, Sālih's fiction is that of penetration and withdrawal — of return to the origins and the roots. In *Mawsim al-hijrah ila al-shamāl* (*Season of Migration to the North*) the knife Mustafa Said sticks into the body of the English woman then withdraws covered with blood, and his sexual penetration of the bodies of so many European women form a structural representation of Sālih's narrative: Said penetrates Europe and withdraws from it in an act of violence and blood letting to lead a different life in his homeland, a life which substitutes the materiality of the land and the intimacy of the network of social relations for the cerebrality of life in the West and the one-dimensionality of the human relations he experiences in it. The nameless narrator goes through the same journey and withdrawal but with none of the violence of Said's invasion; he too returns to his homeland seeking an organic, purposeful, and meaningful mode of existence. The return to the native culture, however, fails to secure lasting happiness and ends in tragedy. It is as though the very act of penetrating the body of Europe, even though it is followed by a final and total withdrawal from it, turns into a curse that chases its victim and inflicts destruction on him. The response to the colonialist invasion, Sālih's fiction seems to argue, should not be a counter-invasion but a total immersion in the authentic history and cultural and social practice of the "native" culture and the devotion of energy to the construction of a narrative of this history and culture which reveals their coherence, validity, and dynamism in a space *un*connected (rather than *dis*connected) to the West and its colonial history. This might imply a rejection of the outside world; yet nowhere is there a closed or antagonistic attitude to that world: identity in Sālih's work is neither exclusive nor aggressive; it is a simple, natural aspect and constituent of reality. It is also an open identity which receives the other into its space, accepts him, and incorporates him into its being.

Of the many issues that preoccupy Sālih's fiction, nothing is more vital than the desire to demonstrate the inner coherence, meaningfulness, and validity of the world of his culture and to offer a vital and involved representation of its history and creative energies in a world which has forgotten or marginalized it. The progression of Sālih's work reveals a powerful tendency to give priority to the exploration of this world in its own terms and in isolation from the impact and intrusion of the Other, particularly the Western Other. While his first novel, *Season of Migration to the North*, involved a journey of discovery, a violent invasion of the West and an ambiguous withdrawal from it into the "native" culture, his subsequent fiction positions itself entirely in the place and time of that culture, turning its back to the West completely. Significantly it is at this point in his work that Sālih began to use the Sudanese dialect in the dialogue sections of his fiction. He has not yet emerged out of these depths. And this might be responsible for his extraordinary silence over the past two decades: producing new fiction might depend on finding a new direction within, or out of, these closed spaces of imaginative geography.

In the coherent world Sālih explores, man is an extension of nature and history. The individual is an integral part of the body of the community, despite the conflicts which arise between them or between different groups and generations within that community. Problems and tragedies are accepted and accommodated as an organic part of life. Oppositions dissolve into each other as though they were governed by some eternal law of mediation, reconciliation, and harmony. Furthermore, in this coherent world everything has meaning and functions as a natural and necessary part in a complex reality: man, life, the river, death, language, narrative, wealth, sex, the real and the imaginary, the fantastic and the ordinary, the religious and mystical as well as the skeptical and unholy. Sex is a powerful and creative impulse. It is the manifestation of the lust for life, continuity, and survival. Yet the lust for life is matched only by the total acceptance of death. The river, for instance, is the source of both life and death, and in both roles it is accepted, loved, and glorified by the community; many die in — or rather *into* — its body. Religion is a mode of existence, a constituent of a distinctive identity and a vital history; it is a regulating and worldly force, but it is not allowed to exert an oppressive power over life or to throttle its passionate expression of itself.

As opposed to institutionalized religion, Sufism and Sufi figures constitute an active and shaping force in this organic universe. The mystical is a source of magical, transforming powers which help to resolve many of the tensions and contradictions in the life of the community; it grants its mysterious bliss to those individuals who seem to be organically rooted in their culture and its traditions, who are as natural and innocent as the earth and the river themselves, or who possess that superhuman power of selflessness, charity, and sacrificial love. Mysticism gives existence a sense of purpose and imbues it with faith in the justness, validity, and harmony of human life. Yet the religious and the mystical co-exist side by side in the village; there is room for both and each has its necessary function.

The timeless, organic world of the village is ultimately disrupted by the intrusion into it of Mustafa Said returning from the North of frost and death, but it is also disrupted by its own inner contradictions and tensions. Said dissolves into this world and becomes very much a part of it, achieving a degree of understanding of it which he had never possessed before his journey to the north. But his presence has deeper effects on this world than could be immediately realized. He disrupts his wife's life as well as that of the nameless narrator. After his death, his widow appears to have been transformed into a different woman; she refuses to submit to the timeless traditions of the village, by refusing to marry the old man Wadd al-Rayyis; and when she is forced to do so, she refuses to sleep with him. Eventually she kills him and herself in a violent act which invokes the violence of Said himself in his European labyrinth. In subsequent novels, the structure of authority in the village is challenged by a new generation and the old order is threatened by a rising tide of new ideas and figures.

Thus Sālih's narrative does not resolve the contradictions and tensions; it rather articulates and brings to a climax the forces and oppositions which shatter the structure of reality, either arising from within this reality or impinging on it and threatening it from without.

But what gives Sālih's fiction its special excellence is his mastery of narrative: the shifting times of narration, the different tones, the variety of narrative modes, the richly evocative imagery, the multiplicity of linguistic levels, the changing rhythm, and, above all, the brilliance with which he reveals his fantastic characters. He is a true heir of the techniques of the Arabic narrative: the magical and fantastic traditions of *The Arabian Nights* and popular and mystical narration. His real power lies in the way he weaves all these strands into the texture of realistic narrative and the manner in which he juxtaposes two linguistic levels into the same structure and allows them to interact and interlace to form a signifying space. Because of these and other qualities of his work, Sālih can be credited with being one of the early pioneers of the narrative techniques and structures which are now associated with Latin American magic realist fiction.

Sālih is a master of the discontinuous and fragmented narrative as well as the more familiar linear, diachronic narrative of the realistic novel. In each of his novels, the narrative techniques seem to arise naturally from his vision of the structure of the reality he is narrating. Thus, the narrative modes of *'Urs az-Zen* (*The Wedding of Zein*) and *Bandar Shah* contrast sharply with *Season of Migration*. In the former, the coherent world of the culture and the intimately interlaced life of the community are embodied in closely knit, coherent narrative structures from within which rise naturally the fantastic and supernatural (both as aspects of reality and as modes of narration). In *Season*, the narrative is told in fragments. Moreover, it is constituted by two overlapping narratives which are fundamentally different: Mustafa Said's narrative is incoherent, ambiguous, and discontinuous, whereas the nameless narrator narrates himself diachronically and unambiguously, thereby giving a concrete expression to the underlying feeling that his is an organic existence with a linear, meaningful, and purposeful historical progression; his life has actually followed a clear, positive trajectory. Thus, fragmented narrative stands in opposition to coherent narrative to embody two different characters and two contrasting worlds. Fragmentation here is not merely an artistic device but a genuine embodiment of a fragmented world and a discontinuous narrative, both of which lack inner coherence and unity. The discontinuity of Said is not a property of the narrative of his life, but of his very existence. The text closes with huge gaps in our, as well as the narrator's, knowledge of Said and his life. The narrator is not the all-knowing, omnipresent figure we encounter in much fragmented fiction. In *Season*, the narrator knows much less and is present in many fewer places than is customary in fiction, and his narration of his characters embodies, almost graphically, this lack of knowledge and infrequency of presence. Sālih's fiction had thus destroyed the authority of the all-knowing narrator years before this notion became a stylish and often artificial construct in much postmodernist fiction and critical jargon.

—Kamal Abu-Deeb

———

SARAMAGO, José (de Sousa). Portuguese. Born in Azinhaga, 16 November 1922. Married to Pilar del Río; one child. Recipient: Grinzane Cavour prize; Mondello prize; Flaliano prize. Honorary doctorate: universities of Turin and Seville, 1991. Agent: Ray-Güde Mertin, 1 Friedrichstrasse, 6380 Hamburg 1, Germany. Address: R. Dos Ferreiros a Estrela, 32-1.°, 1200 Lisbon, Portugal.

PUBLICATIONS

Fiction

Manual de pintura e caligrafia. Lisbon, Moraes, 1976.
Objecto quase. Lisbon, Moraes, 1978.
Levantado do chão. Lisbon, Caminho, 1980.
Memorial do convento. Lisbon, Caminho, 1982; as *Baltasar and Blimunda*, San Diego, Harcourt Brace, 1987; London, Cape, 1988.
O ano da morte de Ricardo Reis. Lisbon, Caminho, 1984; as *The Year of the Death of Ricardo Reis*, San Diego, Harcourt Brace, 1991.
A jangada de pedra. Lisbon, Caminho, 1986.
História do Cerco de Lisboa. Lisbon, Caminho, 1989.

O Evangelho Segundo Jesus Cristo.   Lisbon, Caminho, 1991.

Verse

Os poemas possíveis.   Lisbon, Portugália, 1966.
Provavelmente Alegria.   Lisbon, Horizonte, 1970; revised
    and enlarged edition, Lisbon, Caminho, 1985.
O ano de 1993.   Lisbon, Futura, 1975.

Plays

A noite.   Lisbon, Caminho, 1979.
Que farei com este livro?   Lisbon, Caminho, 1980.
A segunda vida de Francisco de Assis.   Lisbon, Caminho,
    1987.
Blimunda (opera libretto), adaptation of his novel *Memorial
    de convento*, music by Azio Corghi (produced Milan, 1990).

Other

Deste mundo e do outro.   Lisbon, Arcádia, 1971.
A bagagem do viajante.   Lisbon, Futura, 1973.
O embargo.   Lisbon, Estúdios Cor, 1973.
Os opiniões que o D.L. teve.   Lisbon, Seara Nova, 1974.
Os apontamentos.   Lisbon, Seara Nova, 1976.
Viagem a Portugal.   Lisbon, Círculo de Leitores, 1981.

Editor, *O poeta perguntador*, by Armindo Rodrigues.
    Lisbon, Caminho, 1979.

*

Critical Study: "A View of 18th-Century Portugal: José
Saramago's *Memorial do convento*" by Richard A. Preto-
Rodas, in *World Literature Today* (Norman, Oklahoma),
61(1), 1987.

*   *   *

Poet, columnist, playwright, and essayist, José Saramago
has made greatest impact as a novelist. In the past decade he
has won international recognition as Portugal's most distinguished and influential contemporary man of letters.

Although remarkably varied in theme and inspiration,
Saramago's major novels bear all the hallmarks of great
fiction. Like the great 19th-century novelists he favours a
broad canvas which allows him to explore every conceivable
facet of human experience. A deep love and knowledge of his
native Portugal goes hand in hand with a keen awareness of
cultural differences beyond the Iberian peninsula.

Saramago was already in his fifties when he wrote his first
novel *Manual de pintura e caligrafia* (Manual of Painting and
Calligraphy), which conveys from the outset his constant
preoccupation with the relationship between life and art. The
narrator is the anonymous H, a second-rate artist commissioned by a wealthy client to paint a family portrait. As H
reflects on the artist's struggle to survive in a world of material
bourgeois values, he clings to his ideals in a world obsessed
with status and affluence. H's penetrating eye begins to disturb
his sitters and the more he works on the portrait, the deeper
the animosity and resentment which surface. H's portrait
leaves his sitters feeling uncomfortably exposed. H comments:
"I believe biography is to be found in everything we do and say,
in our every gesture, in the way we sit, the way we walk and
stare, the way we turn our head or pick up an object from the
floor. And that is what the painter must try to capture." And
presumably by extension the novelist too. H's reflections on

people and things within his immediate circle soon expand
into closer analysis of wider issues concerning aesthetics and
ethics. Diary entries during a tour of Italian museums and art
galleries confirm the painter's belief that the critic's role,
whatever his medium, is not merely to observe but, above all,
to understand. Serious and biting in turn, Saramago can elicit
overwhelming perceptions about fate and circumstance from
the most banal details. The commission is abruptly cancelled
and financial compensation offered but H prefers to keep his
unfinished portrait and go unpaid rather than sacrifice his
principles. Creative truth is seen to be more important than
material rewards.

Saramago's second novel *Levantado do chão* (Raised from
the Ground), which he himself defined as a "social novel,"
exposes the sinister methods of repression during the Salazar
dictatorship (1936–68), a dark chapter in Portugal's history
which silenced writers and opponents of the regime.

Two years later, Saramago established his reputation with
Memorial do convento (*Baltasar and Blimunda*) which many
critics consider to be his greatest achievement. This takes a
satirical view of power and politics in Portugal during the first
half of the 18th century. Evoking an age of pomp and
ceremony when Portugal still exercised considerable influence in Europe, Saramago pillories both the monarchy and
the Church for their vanity and greed while thousands of
ordinary men and women suffer poverty and hardship in
order to satisfy the whims of kings and prelates who rule by
force and the cruel instrument of the Inquisition. This grim
picture of human fortunes is mitigated on the one hand by
dreamers and visionaries such as Padre Bartolomeu Lourenço
de Gusmão who invented a flying machine in the form of a
huge bird and, on the other, by the haunting love affair
between a disabled ex-soldier Baltasar Mateus (nicknamed
"Seven Suns" because he can only see in the light) and the
mysterious Blimunda (also known as "Seven Moons" because
she can see in the dark) who has inherited her mother's
Jewish blood and clairvoyant powers. Baltasar and Blimunda
represent two vastly different worlds locked within the same
historical reality. Richly textured with multiple layers of
meaning, this is a novel in the grand manner which brings
fresh insights and discoveries with every reading. The Italian
composer Azio Corghi composed a three-act opera *Blimunda*
based on the Italian translation of the novel. The first
performance was given at La Scala, Milan, in May 1990 and
more recently the work has been performed in Lisbon and
Turin.

A jangada de pedra (The Stone Raft) speculates on the
dramatic separation of the Iberian peninsula from the rest of
Europe when a crack suddenly opens the entire length of the
Pyrenees. This inexplicable phenomenon allows the author to
voice his own misgivings about the excessive influence of
France, Germany, and England over European politics and
to launch a vigorous defence of small and poorer nations
within the European Community. The panic that ensues as
the Iberian peninsula floats off into the Atlantic has elements
of farce and pathos. Politicians and bureaucrats are thrown
into confusion by this threat to their supremacy, and experts
and advisors consult their textbooks in vain while faceless
men and women try to make a new life for themselves amidst
the chaos. Ironically, the latter are better equipped to cope
with crisis than the powerful and privileged.

História do Cerco de Lisboa (The History of the Siege of
Lisbon) finds Saramago at his most introspective. Closer to
essay than fiction, this perusal of Portugal's past reveals a
subtle game of counterpoint between the real and the imagined, between history and literature.

O ano da morte de Ricardo Reis (*The Year of the Death of*

Ricardo Reis) is rightly considered to be Saramago's most ambitious novel to date. Set in Lisbon in the 1930s, the novel probes every imaginable aspect of Portugal's history and culture by means of lengthy dialogues between the fictional narrator Ricardo Reis, newly returned from political exile in Brazil, and Portugal's most celebrated poet Fernando Pessoa (1888–1935). Wide-ranging discussions touch on life and art, history and politics, philosophy and religion as interpreted by their generation. As in all of Saramago's novels, poetry and reflection overlap. Pessoa and Reis are to some extent mirror images of the author himself who reminds the reader: "We all suffer from some essential malaise, inseparable from what we are . . . because of that malaise we are so little, because of it we succeed in being so much." Saramago sees the world as one great theatrical arena where men and women play out games of life and death, each and every one of us irresistibly drawn to our own destiny. Intimations of transcience, solitude, and nothingness remind us that human existence is at once prodigious and tragic. The vision of mankind presented here is complex and all-embracing. An astute observer of human nature and its foibles, Saramago guides us through the ages of man as his characters bare their souls and eventually discover that "human nature with its endless contradictions and misunderstandings is not to be trusted." A master of satire, he has an unsparing eye for the sham and hypocritical. Things human and divine are challenged, complacent values overturned. The author's portrait of Lisbon in 1936 has been compared with Flaubert's descriptions of Paris in 1848 and Joyce's vision of Dublin at the turn of the century.

Saramago's latest novel, *O Evangelho Segundo Jesus Cristo* (The Gospel According to Jesus Christ), will certainly be remembered as his most controversial. This powerful and moving account of Christ's earthly mission from Bethlehem to Gethsemane makes a spirited attack on traditional interpretations. Saramago faithfully traces out the key episodes in the Gospels, but bland, edifying narration is replaced with startling intimacies about the main protagonists in the greatest of all dramas. The emotional and spiritual ties between Jesus and his parents, between God the Son and God the Father are ambivalent, tense, and often hostile. A troubled Jesus implacably questions the role he has been coerced into playing. An uncompromising champion of mankind, Saramago's Christ challenges Divine Authority, rejects the dubious nature of Providence, and mocks God's justice. As his end approaches, Jesus acknowledges that he has learned as much from Satan as from God. 33 years on Earth have not been enough to ask all the questions or to receive any of the answers he so badly needed. God the Father, as portrayed by Saramago, is intransigent to the point of irrationality, his designs obscure to the point of perversity. In the final confrontation between Father and Son, Jesus has to be satisfied with "the only reply silence can give." Radical scepticism has rarely been voiced with such passion and poetry.

Fluent and persuasive, Saramago passes effortlessly from description to commentary, from philosophical conceits to popular wisdom, from elaborate metaphors to simple human statements. Traditional elements of symmetry and counterpoint are combined with avant-garde techniques. Punctuation is strictly limited to commas and full-stops to serve the author's pursuit of "verbal music."

—Giovanni Pontiero

SARDUY, Severo. Cuban. Born in Camagüey, 25 February 1937. Briefly studied medicine in Havana; art history at L'École du Louvre, Paris, from 1960. Editor of Latin American list, Seuil publishers, Paris, from 1966; adviser to various French publishing companies; editor of *Tel Quel* journal. Recipient: Medicis prize, 1972; Guggenheim fellowship, 1975; Italia prize; Paul Gilson prize. Agent: Agencia Carmen Balcells, Diagonal 580, 08021 Barcelona, Spain. Address: 2 rue Lakanal, 92330 Secaux, Paris, France.

PUBLICATIONS

Fiction

Gestos.   Barcelona, Seix Barral, 1963.
De dónde son los cantantes.   Mexico City, Mortiz, 1967; as *From Cuba with a Song*, in *Triple Cross: Three Short Novels*, New York, Dutton, 1972.
Cobra.   Buenos Aires, Sudamericana, 1972; in English, New York, Dutton, 1975.
Maitreya.   Barcelona, Seix Barral, 1978; in English, Hanover, New Hampshire, Norte, 1986.
Colibrí.   Barcelona, Argos Vergara, 1984.
El Cristo de la rue Jacob.   Barcelona, Mall, 1987.
Cocuyo.   Barcelona, Tusquets, 1990.

Plays

La playa (produced Kassel, 1971; Paris, 1977).   Paris, Cahiers Renauld-Barrault, 1965.
Para la voz (includes *La playa*; *La caída*; *Relato*; *Los matadores de hormigas*).   Madrid, Fundamento, 1978; as *For Voice* (includes *The Beach*; *Fall*; *Re-Cite*; *The Ant-Killers*), Pittsburgh, Latin American Literary Review Press, 1985.

Radio Plays: *La caída*, 1974; *Relato*, 1974; *Los matadores de hormigas*, 1976.

Verse

Flamenco.   Stuttgart, Manus-Presse, 1969.
Mood Indigo.   Stuttgart, Manus-Presse, 1969.
Merveilles de la nature.   Paris, Pauvet, 1971.
Overdose.   Las Palmas, Mallorca, Inventarios Provisionales, 1972.
Big Bang, para situar en órbita cinco máquinas, pour situer en orbite cinq machines de Ramon Alejandro.   Montpellier, Fata Morgana, 1973; Barcelona, Tusquets, 1974.
Daquirí.   Santa Cruz, Tenerife, n.p., 1980.
Un testigo fugaz y disfrazado.   Barcelona, Mall, 1985.

Other

Escrito sobre un cuerpo: ensayos de crítica.   Buenos Aires, Sudamericana, 1969; as *Written on a Body*, New York, Lumen, 1989.
Barroco.   Buenos Aires, Sudamericana, 1974.
La doublure.   Paris, Flammarion, 1981.
La simulación.   Caracas, Monte Avila, 1982.
Micro-opera de Benet Rossell, with Annemieke van de Pas.   Barcelona, Ambit, 1984.
Nueva inestabilidad.   Mexico City, Vuelta, 1987.
Ensayos generales sobre el Barroco.   Mexico City, Fondo de Cultura Económica, 1987.

*

Bibliographies: "Para una bibliografía de y sobre Severo Sarduy (1955–1971)," in *Revista Iberoamericana*, 38, 1972, and in *La ruta de Severo Sarduy*, Hanover, New Hampshire, Norte, 1987, both by Robert González Echevarría.

Critical Studies: "'Total' Reality in Severo Sarduy's Search for *Lo Cubano*" by Donald R. Johndrow, in *Romance Notes* (Chapel Hill, North Carolina), 13, 1972; Severo issue (focus on *Cobra*) of *Review* (New York), Winter 1974; "Baroque Endings: Carpentier, Sarduy and Some Textual Contingencies" by Eduardo González, in *Modern Language Notes* (Baltimore, Maryland), 92, 1977; "Severo Sarduy: Vital Signs" by Alfred MacAdam, in *Modern Latin American Narratives: The Dreams of Reason*, Chicago, University of Chicago Press, 1977; "Literature, History, and Literary History: A Cuban Family Romance" by Andrew Bush, and "Textual Politics: Severo Sarduy" by Enrico Mario Santí, both in *Latin American Literary Review* (Pittsburgh), 8(16), 1980; "Severo Sarduy's Strategy of Irony: Paradigmatic Indecision in *Cobra* and *Maitreya*" by Gustavo Pellón, in *Latin American Literary Review* (Pittsburgh), Fall-Winter 1983; "The Ambivalent Fiction of Severo Sarduy" by René Prieto, in *Symposium* (Washington, D.C.), 1, 1985; *The Name Game: Writing/Fading Writer in "De dónde son los cantantes"* by Oscar Montero, Chapel Hill, University of North Carolina Press, 1988; *Severo Sarduy and the Religion of the Text* by Rolando Perez, Lanham, Maryland, University Press of America, 1988.

*   *   *

As for so many Hispanic writers, for Severo Sarduy exile has been not only the loss of family, culture, and sense of place, but the loss of language. Spanish, specifically Cuban Spanish, begins to fade for the writer the moment he leaves Cuba. For 30 years, Sarduy's works have reconstructed that original loss of a native idiom. Through the many characters and voices he has created, Sarduy can be sentimental, nostalgic, grotesque, mocking, visionary, and often brilliant.

Although there are many points of contact between the work of Sarduy and that of his Spanish American contemporaries— Carlos Fuentes, Gabriel García Márquez, José Donoso, Mario Vargas Llosa (*qq.v.*), and Julio Cortázar being perhaps the best-known ones—Sarduy's work is closer to that of Jean Genet and William S. Burroughs. His literary roots are in the Spanish baroque, in the picaresque novel, and in Cuban literature — José Martí and Julián del Casal in the 19th century, and certainly in the work of 20th- century Cuban writer José Lezama Lima, whose audacious, provocative use of language echoes throughout Sarduy's work.

Sarduy's writing is particularly concerned with the uses and abuses of cultural representations. The relationship between writing and painting, between the graphic trace and the image, is often dramatized in his fictional works, and his book-length essay *La simulación* (Simulation) is a subjective, imaginative treatment of the topic of mimesis.

Sarduy's first novel *Gestos* (Gestures) appropriates some of the techniques of the French *nouveau roman*, particularly its descriptive objectivity, but it may be more accurately described as the collision of two disparate texts: painting and political action. The protagonist, a black nightclub singer, must set off a bomb at the main electric plant in pre- revolutionary Havana, yet she moves through a landscape composed of shreds from a Jackson Pollock painting. A witty syncretism characterizes all of Sarduy's writing. His second novel, *De dónde son los cantantes* (*From Cuba with a Song*), blends the meditations on the subject of French psychoanalyst Jacques Lacan with a veritable cultural potpourri. In the novel, notions of self and national identities, a prestigious tradition in Cuban culture, are at once mocked and affirmed through the pilgrimage of the double main characters, a set of transvestites or transsexuals whose metamorphoses resurface in Sarduy's later work.

Cross-dressing is in fact one of the ruling conceits of Sarduy's work. For the cross-dresser, or more accurately the "drag queen," sexual, and therefore spiritual and cultural, identity is a question of surfaces and effects; so is writing for Sarduy a question not of essences or themes to be communicated but of representations to be carried off as effectively as possible. In his third novel, *Cobra*, the setting is a theater where the characters are at once dolls, sex-changed hookers, leather hustlers, and reincarnations of the Buddha. The novel is in a sense the fictional side of the essay *Barroco* (Baroque), a meditation on the way that the cosmology of the baroque period impacts on our own. *Barroco* is the most complete treatment of Sarduy's influential notion of a post-modern neo-baroque, further developed in *Nueva inestabilidad* (New Instability). Sarduy refuses to accept the modern rift between astronomy and astrology, between the objectivity of science and the subjectivity of vision. In his poetry, especially in the texts that make up *Big Bang*, he combines musings on the origins of the universe with lyrical versions of explicit sexual encounters. *El Cristo de la rue Jacob* (Christ on the Rue Jacob) is made up of flashes, epiphanies, furtive meetings with truck drivers, provoked by the desire to write the story of the scars left on the body.

An aspect of the carnivalesque that is certainly pertinent to Sarduy's work is its irreverent blending of the sacred and the profane. The theatrical rituals of Tibetan Buddhism are at the core of *Maitreya*, Sarduy's fourth novel. Named after the future Buddha, *Maitreya* is the story of the funeral rites of a departed master, an explicit reference to the death of Lezama Lima; the novel is also the visionary transformation of Lezama's Catholic notion of *telos*, or final cause, into *karma*, or contingent cause. Sarduy's festive epiphanies ultimately skirt a dreaded void, but their result is less existential angst than the resigned acceptance of those who have entered the path, meaning those who understand something of the nature of Buddhist enlightenment.

In a sense, both *Colibrí* (Hummingbird) and *Cocuyo* (Firefly), Sarduy's latest novels, are mock *Bildungsromans*, where the biographical is no less a simulacrum than the most extravagant antics of his fictional creatures. *Colibrí* turns the Latin American house of fiction, set in the proverbial jungle, into a den of hustlers ruled by a grand queen, a direct heir of a Genet madam. The "sacred jungle" of the Spanish American literary tradition, the novelistic versions of the self-liberating journey, in short, the novel of redemption and renewal become the painted backdrops for nothing more than a backwater spectacle for a bar full of obese queens. For Sarduy, that representation is not only Latin American culture, always removed from its dearest sources, but culture itself, a house of cards claiming to be a castle or a fortress, all the more precious because it is so fragile and so fleeting.

Cocuyo is the adventure of a Caribbean boy, homicidal, precocious, and perverse. Displaying a style that is now synonymous with his name, Sarduy's novel is something of a self-portrait, distorted in the process of reproduction of course, a portrait of an angry young man, an extravagant queer, a perennial outsider, a *pícaro*, a "fleeting, masked witness," and a dazzling writer.

—Oscar Montero

SARRAUTE, Nathalie (née Tcherniak). French. Born in Ivanovo, Russia, 18 July 1900; moved to France in 1908. Educated at Lycée Fénelon, Paris; the Sorbonne, Paris, licence in English 1920; Oxford University, 1921; University of Berlin, 1921–22; École de Droit, Paris, law degree 1925. Married Raymond Sarraute in 1925; three daughters. Member of the French Bar, 1926–41. Since 1941 full-time writer. Recipient: International Publishers prize, 1964; Formentor prize, 1964. Honorary doctorate: Trinity College, Dublin, 1976; University of Kent, Canterbury, 1980; Oxford University, 1991. Address: 12 Avenue Pierre I de Serbie, 75116 Paris, France.

PUBLICATIONS

Fiction

Tropismes. Paris, Denoël, 1939; revised edition, Paris, Minuit, 1957; as *Tropisms*, with *The Age of Suspicion*, London, Calder, 1963; published separately, New York, Braziller, 1967.
Portrait d'un inconnu. Paris, Marin, 1948; as *Portrait of a Man Unknown*, New York, Braziller, 1958; London, Calder, 1959.
Martereau. Paris, Gallimard, 1953; in English, New York, Braziller, 1959; London, Calder, 1964.
Le Planétarium. Paris, Gallimard, 1959; as *The Planetarium*, New York, Braziller, 1960; London, Calder, 1961.
Les Fruits d'or. Paris, Gallimard, 1963; as *The Golden Fruits*, New York, Braziller, 1964; London, Calder, 1965.
Entre la Vie et la mort. Paris, Gallimard, 1968; as *Between Life and Death*, New York, Braziller, 1969; London, Calder and Boyars, 1970.
Vous les entendez? Paris, Gallimard, 1972; as *Do You Hear Them?*, New York, Braziller, 1973; London, Calder and Boyars, 1975.
"disent les imbéciles." Paris, Gallimard, 1976; as *"fools say,"* New York, Braziller, and London, Calder, 1977.
L'Usage de la parole. Paris, Gallimard, 1980; as *The Use of Speech*, New York, Braziller, 1982; London, Calder, 1983.
Tu ne t'aimes pas. Paris, Gallimard, 1989; as *You Don't Love Yourself*, New York, Braziller, 1990.

Plays

Le Silence; *Le Mensonge* (produced Paris, 1967). Paris, Gallimard, 1967; as *Silence*, and *The Lie* (produced London, 1972), London, Calder and Boyars, 1969.
Isma (produced Paris, 1973). With *Le Silence* and *Le Mensonge*, Paris, Gallimard, 1970; as *Izzuma*, in *Collected Plays*, 1980.
C'est beau (produced Paris, 1975). Included in *Théâtre*, 1978; as *It's Beautiful*, in *Collected Plays*, 1980.
Elle est là (produced Paris, 1978). Included in *Théâtre*, 1978; as *It Is There*, in *Collected Plays*, 1980.
Théâtre (Includes *Elle est là*; *C'est beau*; *Isma*; *Le Mensonge*; *Le Silence*). Paris, Gallimard, 1978; as *Collected Plays* (includes *It Is There*; *It's Beautiful*; *Izzuma*; *The Lie*; *Silence*). London, Calder, 1980; New York, Braziller, 1981.
Pour un Oui ou pour un non (produced Paris, 1986; London [in French], 1987). Paris, Gallimard, 1982; as *For No Good Reason* (produced New York, 1985).
Childhood, from her autobiography (produced New York, 1985).

Other

L'Ère de soupçon. Paris, Gallimard, 1956; as *The Age of Suspicion*, New York, Braziller, 1963; with *Tropisms*, London, Calder and Boyars, 1963.
Enfance (autobiography). Paris, Gallimard, 1983; as *Childhood*, New York, Braziller, and London, Calder, 1984.
Paul Valéry et l'enfant d'éléphant; *Flaubert le précurseur* (two essays). Paris, Gallimard, 1986.
Nathalie Sarraute, qui êtes-vous?: conversations avec Simone Benmussa. Lyon, la Manufacture, 1987.

*

Bibliography: *Nathalie Sarraute: A Bibliography* by Sheila M. Bell, London, Grant and Cutler, 1982.

Critical Studies: *Nathalie Sarraute* by Ruth Z. Temple, New York, Columbia University Press, 1968; *Nathalie Sarraute* by Gretchen Rous Besser, Boston, Twayne, 1979; *Nathalie Sarraute and the War of the Words: A Study of Five Novels* by Valerie Minogue, Edinburgh, Edinburgh University Press, 1981; *Sarraute: "Le Planétarium"* by Roger McClure, London, Grant and Cutler, 1987; *Sarraute: "Portrait d'un inconnu" and "Vous les entendez?"* by Sheila M. Bell, London, Grant and Cutler, 1988.

*   *   *

Not a prolific writer, Nathalie Sarraute has, to date, composed eight novels, two volumes of studies akin to prose poems, and six short plays. She has also produced many influential critical essays and commented on her own work and literature in general in many interviews, notably a book-length interview with Simone Benmussa, *Nathalie Sarraute, qui êtes-vous?* published in 1987. Her essays on Paul Valéry and Gustave Flaubert, first published in 1947 and 1965 respectively, were republished in book form in 1986. The essays collected in *L'Ère du soupçon* (*The Age of Suspicion*) provided an early manifesto for the literary movement dubbed the New Novel, or *nouveau roman*, in whose emergence in the late 1950s Sarraute played a leading role. The essays, deriving not from abstract theorising but from the demands of a new subject-matter, reject the conventions of the traditional novel and defend the novelist's need for formal experimentation. Her first work, *Tropismes* (*Tropisms*), begun in 1932, was first published in 1939 and republished in the more welcoming climate of 1957; these evocative sketches already show the preoccupation with the unspoken undertow of human discourse which makes Sarraute's work quite distinct from that of other New Novelists and keeps it, for all its radical innovations, more fundamentally attached to the realist mimetic tradition. This undertow she has variously termed "tropisms" (taking the word from the Natural Sciences where it denotes movement in response to stimulus), "sub-conversation," "infra-psychology," "pre-language," and "le ressenti" (the "felt" or "experienced").

The plays, originally written for radio and broadcast in many countries, have also been successfully performed on stage: like *Tropisms*, they enlarge specific moments in human encounters, so that the actors speak words which would normally remain unspoken, and formulate feelings that would normally be no more than the twitching of a muscle or a tiny eye movement. The most recent and perhaps the most dramatically intense of the plays, *Pour un Oui ou pour un non* (*For No Good Reason*), focuses on the pronunciation and tone of a single phrase spoken by one of two friends. Perceived as a symptom of a profound rift, it becomes the source of a fully articulated confrontation that goes well beyond the bounds of any conventional realism and into what Sarraute has called "the invisible texture of our lives." *L'Usage de la parole* (*The Use of Speech*) returns to the prose poem form of *Tropisms*, and with its intricate unfurlings of the movements preceding and following speech, testifies to the constancy of Sarraute's attention to tropistic undercurrents. Finding traces of similar undercurrents in many literary predecessors, notably Fyodor Dostoevsky and Marcel Proust, Sarraute acknowledges her decision to follow a Proustian direction, discarding the conventional demands of the novel to give herself space and time enough to slow down, enlarge, and deepen the subterranean feelings Prouts briefly suggests or retrospectively analyses. In Sarrautean fiction, they do not occur in the interstices of the action, nor are they viewed in retrospect, but constitute the action, and the poetic prose which recreates rather than describes them invites the reader to participate in their immediacy. Sarraute's option for the microscopic inevitably excludes large-scale frames of reference — to broad social, political, or moral issues — but offers a penetrating view of interpersonal encounters at a universal level.

Communication of these elusive particles of feeling demanded not only a style able to defeat the petrifying and categorising tendency inherent in language, but a new approach to the novel form. Sarraute's fictional works reflect, along with a maturing stylistic technique, a critique of, and progressive liberation from, the conventions of the novel. The boundaries between "observation" and creation are shown to be uncertain; the relation between "observer" and "observed" is problematic; certain sequences are "replayed" with different tonalities, and the authority of the narrator is radically undermined; each new voice becomes a suspect narrative source, striving to impose its own plot and characterisation on the world about it. In *Portrait d'un inconnu* (*Portrait of a Man Unknown*) an unnamed first-person narrator struggles to observe an old man and his daughter (inspired by Honoré de Balzac's Eugénie Grandet and her miserly father), but the constantly changing figures refuse to be converted into consistent characters, and the narrator refuses to "cheat" by giving them names. The narrative of *Martereau* takes up where *Portrait* leaves off. Starting with the seemingly defined and solid character of Martereau, it subjects him to scrutiny and speculation till he is only a perplexing bundle of possibilities. *Le Planétarium* sees the dispossession of the first-person narrator: an aspiring writer becomes only one among a number of voices relating domestic conflicts and the clashes of bourgeois and intellectual attitudes. *Les Fruits d'or* (*The Golden Fruits*) is a discussion by many voices of the changing fortunes of a novel called "The Golden Fruits": in a mixture of self-definition and literary comment they not only provide a brilliantly funny satire of Parisian literary circles but show the fundamental uncertainty of all literary values. *Entre la Vie et la mort* (*Between Life and Death*) takes the reader into the consciousness of the writer in the act of writing, oscillating between the self-abnegation of creativity and the self-consciousness that intrudes to make him "play the writer." *Vous les entendez?* (*Do You Hear Them?*), the most tenderly ironic of the novels, focuses on the love, anger, hopes, exasperations, and doubts of a father hearing, interpreting, and reinterpreting his children's laughter. *"disent les imbéciles"* (*"fools say"*) again centres on characterisation and categorisation as features of intellectual terrorism. *Enfance* (*Childhood*), autobiographical in origin, is arguably the summit of Sarraute's later work. It submits the novelist's early memories to the same probing scrutiny found in the novels, with a similar insistence on the fluidity of experience: it is a richly poetic patchwork of childhood fragments. *Tu ne t'aimes pas* (*You Don't Love Yourself*) explores the inner dramas of the beleaguered self whose myriad voices refuse unification and defy definition. From Sarraute's ironic attacks on narrative features (the meshing of events into "plot," the reduction of fluctuating beings to "characters") that bedevil literature and life alike, the positive values that emerge are humility, compassion, and humour. They are the qualities that help to make Sarraute one of France's greatest living writers.

In Sarraute's hesitant pages with their question marks, trails of dots, and broken syntax, the trivia of everyday life — an unexplained silence, a mispronunciation, a bar of soap, marks of screw-holes in a door, and intrusive "My dear" in a conversation — become focal points for doubt and mortal anguish, but the ironic disproportion between the trivia and the feelings they carry maintains a precarious and poetic balance between the tragic and the comic.

—Valerie Minogue

SASTRE (Salvador), Alfonso. Spanish. Born in Madrid, 20 February 1926. Educated at the universities of Madrid and Murcia. Married Eva Forest in 1955; two sons and one daughter. Co-founding director, Arte Nuevo theatre group, 1945–48; founder, Teatro de Agitación Social (often censored; imprisoned, 1956, 1961), and, with José María de Quinto, Realistic Theatre Group, 1960. Theatre editor, *La Hora*, 1948–50. Recipient: Viareggio-Versilia prize, 1976. Address: c/o Ediciones Cátedra, Calle Josefa Valcárcel 27, 28027 Madrid, Spain.

PUBLICATIONS

Plays

Uranio 235 (produced Madrid, 1946).   Included in *Teatro de vanguardia*, 1949.
Ha sonado la muerte, with Medardo Fraile (produced Madrid, 1946).   Included in *Teatre de vanguardia*, 1949.
Cargamento de sueños (produced Madrid, 1948).   Included in *Teatro de vanguardia*, 1949.
Teatro de vanguardia (includes *Uranio 235*; *Cargamento de sueños*; with Medardo Fraile, *Ha sonado de muerte* and *Comedia sonámbula*).   Madrid, Permán, 1949.
Escuadra hacia la muerte (produced Madrid, 1953).   Included in *Teatro*, 1960; edited by Farris Anderson, with *La mordaza*, Madrid, Clásicos Castalia, 1975.
La mordaza (produced Madrid, 1954).   Madrid, Escelicer, 1965; edited by Farris Anderson, with *Escuadra hacia la muerte*, Madrid, Clásicos Castalia, 1975.
La sangre de Dios (produced Valencia, 1955).   Madrid, Escelicer, 1959.
Ana Kleiber (produced Athens, 1960).   Madrid, Escelicer, 1957; in English (produced Belfast, 1967), in *The New Theatre of Europe*, edited by Robert W. Corrigan, New York, Dell, 1962.
El pan de todos (produced Barcelona, 1957).   Madrid, Escelicer, 1960.
El cuervo (produced Madrid, 1957).   Madrid, Escelicer, 1960.
Medea (produced 1958).   Madrid, Escelicer, 1963.

Muerte en el barrio (produced Madrid, 1959). Included in *Teatro*, 1960.

La cornada (produced Madrid, 1960). Madrid, Escelicer, 1965; as *Death Thrust*, in *Masterpieces of the Modern Spanish Theatre*, edited by Robert W. Corrigan, New York, Collier, 1967.

Teatro (includes *Escuadra hacia la muerte*; *Tierra roja*; *Ana Kleiber*; *Muerte en el barrio*; *Guillermo Tell tiene los ojos tristes*; *El cuervo*). Buenos Aires, Losada, 1960.

Tierra roja (produced Montevideo). Included in *Teatro*, 1960.

Guillermo Tell tiene los ojos tristes (produced Madrid, 1965). Included in *Teatro*, 1960; as *Sad Are the Eyes of William Tell*, in *The New Wave Spanish Drama*, edited by George E. Wellwarth, New York, New York University Press, 1970.

En la red (produced Madrid, 1961). Madrid, Escelicer, 1961.

Cuatro dramas de la revolución. Madrid, Bullon, 1963.

Cargamento de sueños; Prólogo patético; Asalto nocturno. Madrid, Taurus, 1964.

Asalto nocturno (produced Barcelona, 1965). With *Cargamento de sueños*, 1964.

Prólogo patético. With *Cargamento de sueños*, 1964; as *Pathetic Prologue*, in *Modern International Drama*, March 1968.

Teatro selecto. Madrid, Escelicer, 1966.

Obras completas (plays). Madrid, Aguilar, 1967.

Oficio de tinieblas (produced Madrid, 1967). Madrid, Alfil, 1967.

El circulito de tiza (produced in part, Alicante, 1969). Included in *Obras completas*, 1967.

El escenario diabólico: *El cuervo, Ejercicios de terror, Las cintas magnéticas*. Barcelona, Saturno, 1973.

Las cintas magnéticas (produced Lyons, France, 1973). Included in *El escenario diabólico*, 1973.

Ejercicios de terror (produced in part, Murcia, 1981). Included in *El escenario diabólico*, 1973.

Askatasuna! (televised, 1974). Included in *Teatro político*, 1979.

M.S.V.; o, La sangre y la ceniza (produced Barcelona, 1976). With *Crónicas romanas*, Madrid, Cátedra, 1979.

Teatro político (includes *Askatasuna!*; *El camarada oscuro*; *Análisis espectral de un Comando al servicio de la Revolución Proletaria*). Donostia, Hordago, 1979.

Crónicas romanas (produced Avignon, France, 1982). With *M.S.V.*, Madrid, Cátedra, 1979.

Ahola no es de leil (produced Madrid, 1979). Madrid, Vox, 1980.

Tragedia fantástica de la gitana Celestina (produced Rome, 1979). With *La taberna fantástica*, Madrid, Cátedra, 1990.

El hijo único de Guillermo Tell. Published in *Estreno 9*, Spring 1983.

La taberna fantástica, edited by Mariano de Paco. Murcia, Cuadernos de la Cátedra de Teatro de la Universidad de Murcia, 1983.

Asalto a una ciudad, adaptation of a play by Lope de Vega. Castilla y León, Junta de Castilla y León, Consejería de Cultura y Bienestar Social, 1988.

Los hombres y sus sombras: terrores y miserias del IV Reich. Murcia, University of Murcia, 1988.

Los últimos días de Emmanuel Kant contados por Ernesto. Madrid, Instituto Nacional de Artes Escénicas y de la Música, 1989.

Demasiado tarde para Filoctetes. Bilbao, Arquitaletxe Hiru, 1990.

Dónde estas, Ulalume, dónde estas? Bilbao, Arquitaletxe Hiru, 1990.

El viaje infanto de Sancho Panza. Bilbao, Arquitalctxc Hiru, 1991.

Irlanda, Irlanda. Bilbao, Arquitaletxe Hiru, 1991.

Revelaciones inesperadas sobre Moisés. Bilbao, Arquitaletxe Hiru, 1991.

Television Play: *Askatasuna!*, 1974.

Fiction

Las noches lúgubres. Madrid, Horizonte, 1964.
El paralelo 38. Madrid, Alfaguara, 1965.
Flores rojas para Miguel Servet. Madrid, Rivadeneyra, 1967.
Lumpen, marginación, y jerigonca. Madrid, Legasa, 1980.
El lugar del crimen — Unheimlich. Barcelona, Vergara, 1982.

Verse

Balada de Carabanchel y otros poemas celulares. Paris, Ruedo Ibérico, 1976.
El español al alcance de todos. Madrid, Sensemayá Chororó, 1978.
TBO. Madrid, Zero Zyx, 1978.

Other

Drama y sociedad. Madrid, Taurus, 1956.
Anatomía del realismo. Barcelona, Seix Barral, 1965; revised edition, 1974.
La revolución y la crítica de la cultura. Barcelona, Grijalbo, 1970.
Crítica de la imaginación. Madrid, Cátedra, 1978.
Escrito en Euskadi: revolución y cultura (1876–1982). Madrid, Revolución, 1982.
Crónica de una marginación: conversaciones con Alfonso Sastre, with Francisco Caudet. Madrid, Torre, 1984.
"Frankenstein" en Hortaleza: argumento para un film. N.p., n.p., 1986.

Translator, with José Sastre, *El retrato de Dorian Gray*, by Oscar Wilde. Madrid, Edaf, 1988.

Translator, with José Sastre, *Novelas y cuentos; Teatro; Poemas en prosa; Ensayos; Cartas y otros escritos*, by Oscar Wilde. Madrid, Edaf, 1988.

*

Bibliography: *Antonio Buero Vallejo and Alfonso Sastre: An Annotated Bibliography* by Marsha Forys, Metuchen, New Jersey, Scarecrow Press, 1988.

Critical Studies: "Sastre on Brecht: The Dialectics of Revolutionary Theater," in *Comparative Drama* (Kalamazoo, Michigan), 3, 1969–70, and *Alfonso Sastre*, New York, Twayne, 1971, both by Farris Anderson; "Alfonso Sastre on Alfonso Sastre" by N. Vogely, in *Hispania* (Los Angeles), 64, 1981; *Censorship and Social Conflict in the Spanish Theatre: The Case of Alfonso Sastre* by T. Avril Bryan, Lanham, Maryland, University Press of America, 1982; "The Function and Meaning of Dramatic Symbol in *Guillermo Tell tiene los ojos tristes*" by S. Harper, in *Estreno* (University Park, Pennsylvania), 9(1), 1983.

* * *

Alfonso Sastre represents an almost clinically objective case of the creative dramatist in absolute conflict with the demands of popular taste and the limitations which severe political censorship have imposed on his work. His dedication to a revolutionary view of theatre dates from his early university affiliation with young radical groups, his wide reading of French, German, and American plays and dramatic theory, and his own unyielding vision of theatre as a social and existentialist statement. The writer was not yet 20 when he began to write short plays of somewhat cryptic social message (*Uranio 235* [Uranium 235] and *Cargamento de sueños* [Cargo of Dreams]) and participated in the founding of a theatrical group, Arte Nuevo. In 1950, the playwright helped draft and co-signed a manifesto proclaiming the establishment of a "Theatre of Social Agitation." This creative movement failed to attract much interest save that of the police and the censors of Spain's socially repressive government. Sastre was effectively prohibited from producing the plays he continued to write, except in the most restricted media: small university groups, with inadequate staging and inexperienced actors and directors.

Three years later his best-known work, *Escuadra hacia la muerte* (Death Squad), was produced by a student group in a major theatre in Madrid, but censorship closed the play after three performances. This was sufficient to attract international attention to Sastre's theatre and to originate the legend of the dramatic genius denied voice by a repressive dictatorship. The author has indeed suffered incarceration and other civil indignities for no more aggressive acts than the expression of his ideas, and he has generally been denied access in Spain to the major theatres and professional companies that would certainly have produced his work. He continued to write, and most of his plays have by now been published in Spain and abroad. Several of his works were produced initially outside Spain: in France, Italy, Greece, Czechoslovakia, and despite frequent revocation of his passport by Spanish authorities, the author has traveled to openings of his work abroad and to literary congresses as distant as Sweden and Cuba. He has frequently been invited to lecture and teach courses in American universities, but has invariably been denied the necessary visa for entry into the United States.

Sastre is as much a critical theorist of contemporary drama as he is a playwright; he has written as much *about* theatre as he has written theatre, and a great deal on his own work and creative revolutionary stance. His guiding principle is a sort of analytic social realism. For Sastre, revolution must and will come to pass, but it will create as many problems of human conscience and co-existence as it corrects or eliminates. His many articles on dramatic theory, some incorporated in two books (*Drama y sociedad* [Drama and Society] and *Anatomía del realismo* [Anatomy of Realism]) detail dramatic and social esthetics that are often contradictory and at times close to unintelligible. A lack of linear coherence is found in much of his more recent drama. Sastre's international success is based on his more straightforward plays (*Escuadra hacia la muerte*, *La mordaza* [The Gag], *Guillermo Tell tiene los ojos tristes* [*Sad Are the Eyes of William Tell*], *Tierra roja* [Red Earth]), all written in the early and mid-1950s. An important facet of his work has been the adaptation of plays by August Strindberg, Peter Weiss, Henrik Ibsen, Sean O'Casey, and Jean-Paul Sartre. This activity, along with his foreign productions, places Sastre in a European milieu, and it is difficult to think of him now as an exclusively Spanish dramatist.

Sastre has moved ever farther from the structure of a traditional "bourgeois" theatre. The author had never modeled his work on the three-act formula typical of both classical and modern Spanish drama. He has preferred to write in *cuadros*, relatively short scenes of varying number. He frequently complicates his dramatic exposition with flashbacks, overlapping of time, enforced audience participation, taped sounds and voices, disruptive use of lights and music, and calculated interruptions of the action.

Sastre is undeniably a major intellectual and artistic figure in contemporary European theatre, and we can only surmise what his work would have been, conceived in a more open, less frustrating social context. As it is, his has been the most persistently contentious dramatic voice raised in several decades of post-war Spain.

—James Russell Stamm

SCHOULTZ, Solveig von (née Segerstråle). Finnish (Swedish language). Born in Borgå (Porvoo), 5 August 1907. Educated: teacher's diploma 1926. Married 1) Sven von Schoultz in 1930 (divorced 1961), two daughters; 2) Erik Bergman in 1961. Teacher in several schools, 1928–72. Member of the board, Finlands Svenska Författareförening, 1947–69. Recipient: De Nios prize, 1959; Swedish Academy prize, 1970; Pro Finlandia Medal, 1980; Finnish Evangelical Church prize, 1981; Finnish State prize, 1984; Södergran prize, 1984; Bellman prize, 1986; Ferlin prize, 1988. Honorary doctorate, 1986. Address: Bergg. 22 C, 52 00100 Helsinki, Finland.

PUBLICATIONS

Fiction

Petra och silverapan [Petra and the Silver Monkey]. Helsinki, Schildt, 1932.
Ingenting ovanligt [Nothing Special]. Helsinki, Schildt, 1947.
Närmare någon [Nearer to Someone]. Helsinki, Schildt, 1951.
Ansa och samvetet [Ansa and Conscience]. Helsinki, Schildt, 1954.
Den blomstertid [That Time of Flowers]. Helsinki, Schildt, 1958.
Även dina kameler [Thy Camels Too]. Helsinki, Schildt, 1965.
Rymdbruden [The Space Bride]. Helsinki, Schildt, 1970.
Där står du [There You Stand]. Helsinki, Schildt, 1973.
Somliga mornar [Some Mornings]. Helsinki, Schildt, 1976.
Kolteckning, ofullbordad [Charcoal Drawing, Unfinished]. Helsinki, Schildt, 1983.
Ingen dag förgäves: noveller 1947–1983 [No Day in Vain, Novellas 1947–1983]. Helsinki, Schildt, 1984.
Heartwork: Selected Short Stories. London, Forest, 1989.
Nästa dag [Next Day]. Helsinki, Schildt, 1991.

Verse

Min timme [My Hour]. Helsinki, Schildt, 1940.
Den bortvända glädjen [The Shy Joy]. Helsinki, Schildt 1943.
Eko av ett rop [Echo of a Cry]. Helsinki, Schildt, 1945.
Nattlig äng [Nocturnal Meadow]. Helsinki, Schildt, 1949.

Allt sker nu [Everything Happens Now].   Helsinki, Schildt, 1952.

Nätet [The Net].   Helsinki, Schildt, 1956.

Terrassen: tankasvit [The Terrace: A Suite of Tankas]. Helsinki, Schildt, 1959.

Sänk ditt ljus [Lower Your Light].   Helsinki, Schildt, 1963.

Klippbok [Scrapbook].   Helsinki, Schildt, 1968.

De fyra flöjt spelarna [The Four Flute Players].   Helsinki, Schildt, 1975.

Bortom träden hörs havet [A Single Minute].   Helsinki, Schildt, 1980.

En enda minut: dikter 1940–1980 [A Single Minute: Poems 1940–1980].   Helsinki, Schildt, 1981.

Poems 1940–1980, translated by Jeremy Parsons.   Helsinki, Finnish Literature Information Service, 1982.

Vattenhjulet [The Water Wheel].   Helsinki, Schildt, 1986.

Alla träd väntar fåglar [All Trees Await Birds].   Stockholm, Alba, 1988; Helsinki, Schildt, 1989.

Ett sätt att räkna tiden [One Way to Count Time].   Helsinki, Schildt, 1989.

Snow and Summers (Poems 1940–1989), translated by Anne Born.   London, Forest, 1989.

Plays

Parkbänk [Park Bench] (produced 1958).

Passgångaren [The Ambler] (produced 1960).

Radio Plays: *Luftombyte* [Change of Air], 1950; *Vänta* [Wait], 1953; *Tessi kan vänta* [Tessi Can Wait], 1957; *Halv sex en morgon* [Half Past Five One Morning], 1965; *Situationen* [The Situation], 1967; *Pulli*, 1968; *Nästa dörr* [The Next Door], 1969; *Amaryllis*, 1972; *Weekend i oktober* [Weekend in October], 1973; *Ostkupan* [The Cheese Bell], 1975; *Katri*, 1980.

Television Plays: *Javisst, kära du* [Of Course, My Dear], 1967; *Ett rum för natten* [A Room for the Night], 1971.

Other

De sju dagarna: två barn skapar sin värld [The Seven Days: Two Children Create Their World].   Helsinki, Schildt, and Stockholm, Wahlström & Widstrand, 1942.

Nalleresan [The Teddy-Bear Trip] (for children).   Helsinki, Schildt, and Stockholm, Wahlström & Widstrand, 1944.

Millaskolan [Milla School] (for children).   Stockholm, Rabén & Sjögren, 1961.

Porträtt av Hanna [Portrait of Hanna].   Helsinki, Schildt, 1978.

*

Critical Studies: "Solveig von Schoultz: A Sense of Order: Poems" by Thomas Warburton, in *Books from Finland* (Helsinki), 21(2), 1987; "The Narrative of Solveig von Schoultz" by George C. Schoolfield, in *Swedish Book Review* (Lampeter, Wales), 1, 1989.

Solveig von Schoultz comments:

During my long literary life I have preferred the concentrated forms, lyrical poetry and short stories. I have felt a need to express my thoughts in both poetry and prose because they speak about different things and come from different sections of the mind. In my short stories human relations are the main theme. In the poems nature is very near; they also express inner experiences. I have often tried to catch and to keep the precious present minute. All my books are written in Swedish; I belong to the Swedish-speaking minority in Finland.

*   *   *

Solveig von Schoultz is an accomplished writer of both prose and verse. Her prose works include not only the short stories for which she is famous, but also autobiographical (or semi-autobiographical) writings. *Dje sju dagarna* (The Seven Days) is a beautifully observed account of the childhood of her two daughters; *Porträtt av Hanna* (Portrait of Hanna) is a remarkable account of her mother, the painter Hanna Frosterus-Segerstråle. The book offers far more, however, than merely an account of the life and works of the writer's mother; it is effectively a double portrait, as well as a sensitive analysis of a mother-daughter relationship. It counterpoints generations, even dedications to different arts. It is characteristic of Schoultz that her final emphasis should be upon the complexities of the relationship between two individuals. It is there that the centre of art as a writer can perhaps be located. She is an unspectacular writer, dealing more in nuances than in the grand effect. The title of one of her early collections of stories, *Ingenting ovanligt*, can be translated as "Nothing Special," and the title may be taken as symptomatic of her particular interest, as a writer, in the hidden significance of the apparently "ordinary." The best stories, such as those in *Ansa och samvetet* (Ansa and Conscience) or *Somliga mornar* (Some Mornings), have a quiet authority, a certainty of insight and knowledge, which are very impressive. In *Ansa och samvetet* she uses material from both her own youth, and that of her daughters, in the creation of an interlocking series of stories which adds up to a fascinating study of adolescence, of a young girl's journey of self-discovery as she enters the confusing (and confused) world of adult values, of guilt and love, fear and comfort. The stories of *Somliga mornar* are compassionate studies of family life and its disruptions, mother and child, wife and lover, husband and wife. The emotional lives of women are usually the focal point, and the dominant interest is in psychology rather than external event.

Schoultz herself sees her short stories and her poems as closely related, in both manner and matter, and the perception is surely a just one. There is about most of her poetry the same sense of the moment of perception, when the unspectacular is made to yield up its secrets. Her characteristic themes of time and memory (e.g. "A Way to Measure Time," "The Water-wheel," "Five-Finger Exercise"), and of female roles and lives (e.g. "Frau Bach," "Woman Cleaning Fish," "The Dolls") are articulated in language that is highly economical but fertile in metaphorical significance:

The rain shook its hair out carelessly over the streets.
I stood in a doorway thinking of you.
The lamp whipped up thin threads of fire
before they plunged blindly to oblivion's foot.
Thus, lit by my heart
the darkness streamed out of you
past past

fallen into the dark.

Openness and receptivity become positive values in Schoultz's work, the means to knowledge and self-knowledge alike. In "The Room by the River," for example, the wish is for a process of self-purification which will strip away self-awareness and make possible access to a more profound level of reality:

Here all illusion will be washed away
in wicked little swirls
and day and night sluice away
small pieces of myself.
Until I'm bare and hard as the floor by the river,
till what's makeshift lifts
like clouds of autumn finches,
till I stand open like a window
to the brown sun of change.

One of Schoultz's best-known poems, "Tree," speaks of a similar kind of inner strength, a recognition of one's *true* nature which is seen as independent of external circumstances. To wish to be anything other is, in both senses of the word, a mere vanity:

> There is nothing for it but to become more tree.
>
> . . .
>
> For ever nailed to this: immobility
> move in the tree's direction:
> deeper down.
>
> Can a tree that loves the storm become storm?
> . . .
> There is nothing for it but to become more tree.

There is nothing specifically "feminist" about "Tree," but it is a poem which makes a clear statement about woman's realization of her own selfhood. This is perhaps Schoultz's most abiding concern as a writer. Such problems of feminine self-knowledge and identity underlie the deceptive simplicities of a poem such as "Three Sisters":

> The woman bent down to pick up her child
> and her hair fell over her face
> and inside her a little old woman
> clear-eyed, dry
> and doddery
> bent down for her knitting
> and inside her
> a girl bent down for her doll
> with gentle hands
>
> three sisters
> who would never see each other.

Schoultz's voice is never doctrinaire or stridently feminist. Yet all her work, in prose and verse, addresses itself to many of feminism's most central concerns — with the especial quality of feminine identities, with the female role in society, with female self-awareness and relationships — in an especially intelligent and subtle manner. Such a description should not be allowed to suggest that her work belongs in any special or exclusive category of "women's writing." Insofar as such a category has any reductive implications, Schoultz is too universal, and too interesting, a writer to be reduced thus.

—Glyn Pursglove

———

SEMBÈNE, Ousmane. *See* **OUSMANE, Sembène.**

———

SENGHOR, Léopold (Sédar). Senegalese. Born in Joal, 9 October 1906. Educated at a Catholic school, Ngasobil, 1914–23; Libermann Junior Seminary, Dakar, 1923–26; secondary school in Dakar (later Lycée Van Vollenhoven), 1926–28; Lycée Louis-le-Grand, Paris, 1928–31; the Sorbonne, Paris, agrégation 1935. French military service, 1934–35; served in the French Army, 1939–42: prisoner of war, 1940–42; active in the Resistance, 1942–45. Married 1) Ginette Eboué in 1946 (divorced 1956), two sons (one deceased); 2) Colette Hubert in 1957, one son (deceased), Teacher, Lycée Descartes, Tours, 1935–38 and Lycée Marcelin-Berthelot, Saint-Maur des Fossés, 1938 and 1942–45; Professor, École Nationale de la France d'Outremer, 1944–60; representative for Senegal in the two French constituent assemblies, 1945–46, and Deputy for Senegal in the French National Assembly, 1946–59; United Nations delegate, 1950–51; Secretary of State for scientific research, representative to Unesco conferences, 1955–56, member of consultative assembly, 1958, minister-counsellor to Ministry of Cultural Affairs, Education, and Justice, 1959–60, and advisory minister, from 1960, all for French government, Paris; mayor of Thies, Senegal, from 1956; elected representative, Senegalese Territorial Assembly, Paris, from 1957; founder and head of Union Progressiste Sénégalaise, from 1958; president of Federal Assembly, Mali Federation of Senegal and Sudan, 1959–60; First President of Republic of Senegal, 1960–80; minister of defense, 1968–69. Founder, with Lamine Gueye, Bloc Africaine, 1945; official grammarian for writing of French Fourth Republic's new constitution, 1946; founder, Bloc Démocratique Sénégalais, Dakar, 1948; chair, Organisation Commune Africaine et Malgache, 1972–74; established West African Economic Community, 1974; chair, ECONAS, 1978–79; chair, Socialist Inter-African, from 1980; vice-president, Haut Conseil de la Francophonie, from 1985. Founder, with Aimé Césaire (*q.v.*) and Léon Damas, *L'Étudiant Noir*, Paris, 1934. Recipient: French Friendship prize, 1961; French Language prize, 1963; Dag Hammarskjoeld international prize, 1965; Marie Noel poetry prize, 1965; Red and Green international grand prize, 1966; German Book Trade freedom prize, 1968; International grand prize for poetry, 1970; Knokke Biennial international poetry grand prize, 1970; Grenoble Gold Medal, 1972; Haile Selassie African research prize, 1973; Monaco grand prize, 1977; Cino del Duca prize, 1978; Euroafrique prize, 1978; Unesco international book award, 1979; de Vigny prize, 1981; Aasan world prize, 1981; Nehru award, 1984; Athinai prize, 1985. Member, Academy of Overseas Sciences, 1971, Black Academy of Arts and Sciences, 1971. Académie Française, 1984, and American Academy; Commandeur, Ordre des Arts et des Lettres, 1973; Grand Cross, Légion d'Honneur; many honorary memberships and degrees. Address: 1 square de Tocqueville, 75017 Paris, France.

PUBLICATIONS

Verse

Chants d'ombre.   Paris, Seuil, 1945.
Hosties noires.   Paris, Seuil, 1948.
Chants pour Naëtt.   Paris, Seghers, 1949.
Éthiopiques.   PARIS, Seuil, 1956.
Nocturnes.   Paris, Seuil, 1961; in English, London Heinemann, 1969; New York, Third Press, 1971.
Poèmes.   Paris, Seuil, 1964.

Selected Poems, edited by John Reed and Clive Wake. London, Oxford University Press, and New York, Atheneum, 1964.

Elégie pour Alizés. Paris, Seuil, 1969.

Lettres d'hivernage. Paris, Seuil, 1973.

Selected Poems, translated by Craig Williamson. London, Rex Collings, 1976.

Selected Poems, edited by Abiola Irele. London, Cambridge University Press, 1977.

L. S. Senghor, poète sénégalais (selected poems). Paris, Nathan, 1978.

Poems of a Black Orpheus, translated by William Oxley. London, Menard Press, 1981.

Ndesse, translated by William Oxley. London, Menard Press, 1981.

Poèmes. Paris, Seuil, 1984.

She Chases Me Relentlessly, translated by William Oxley. London, Menard Press, 1986.

Oeuvre poétique. Paris, Seuil, 1990.

Play

Chaka (dramatic poem), music by Akin Euba (produced London, 1986).

Other

La Communauté impériale française, with Robert Lemaignen and Prince Sisowath Youtevang. Paris, Alsatia, 1945.

Commémoration du centenaire de l'abolition de l'esclavage, with Gaston Monnerville and Aimé Césaire. Paris, Presses Universitaires de France, 1948.

Pierre Teilhard de Chardin et la politique africaine. Paris, Seuil, 1952.

La Belle Histoire de Leuk-le-lièvre, with *Abdoulaye Sadji*. Paris, Hachette, 1953.

Future Role of Western European Union in the Political, Economic, Cultural and Legal Fields. Paris, n.p., 1957.

Rapport sur la doctrine et le programme du parti. Paris, Présence Africaine, 1959; as *Report on the Principles and Programme of the Party*, 1959; abridged edition, as *African Socialism*, n.p., American Society of African Culture, 1959.

Rapport sur la politique générale. Senegal, n.p., 1960(?).

Rapport sur la doctrine et la politique générale; ou, Socialisme, unité africaine, construction nationale. Dakar, n.p., 1962.

Liberté:
1. *Négritude et humanisme*. Paris, Seuil, 1964; selections translated as *Freedom I: Negritude and Humanism*, Providence, Rhode Island, n.p., 1974.
2. *Nation et voie africaine du socialisme*. Paris, Seuil, 1971; as *Nationhood and the African Road to Socialism*, 1962; abridged edition, as *On African Socialism*, London, Pall Mall Press, and New York, Praeger, 1964.
3. *Négritude et civilisation de l'universel*. Paris, Seuil, 1977.
4. *Socialisme et planification*. Paris, Seuil, 1983.

Théorie et pratique du socialisme sénégalais. Dakar, n.p., 1964.

Prose and Poetry, edited and translated by John Reed and Clive Wake. London, Oxford University Press, 1965.

Latinité et négritude (in Portuguese, French, and Spanish). Dakar, University of Dakar, 1966.

Négritude, arabisme, et francité: réflexions sur le problème de la culture. Beirut, Dar al-Kitab Allubnani, 1967; as *Les Fondements de l'Africanité; ou, Négritude et arabité*, Paris, Présence Africaine, 1967; as *The Foundations of "Africanité"; or, Négritude and "Arabité"*, 1971.

Exécution du deuxième plan quadriennal de développement économique et social. Dakar, Édition Unité Africaine, 1967(?).

Politique, nation, et développement moderne: rapport de politique générale. Rufisque, Imprimerie Nationale, 1968.

Le Plan du décollage économique: ou, La Participation responsable comme moteur du développement. Dakar, Union Progressiste Sénégalaise, 1970.

Pourquoi une idéologie négro-africaine? (lecture). Abidjan, University of Abidjan, 1971.

La Négritude est un humanisme du vingtième siècle: Senghor à Bruxelles. Dakar, Ministry of Information, 1971.

La Néo-Traite des nègres; ou, La Deuxième Guerre de l'independance. Dakar(?), n.p., 1973.

La Parole chez Paul Claudel et chez les négro-africains. Dakar, Nouvelles Éditions Africaines, 1973.

Problèmes de développement dans les pays sous-développés. Ottawa, University of Ottawa, 1975(?).

Paroles (addresses). Dakar, Nouvelle Éditions Africaines, 1975.

Pour une Société sénégalaise socialiste et démocratique: rapport sur la politique générale. Dakar, Nouvelles Éditions Africaines, 1976.

Le Problème de la faim: allocution. Gembloux, Faculté des Sciences Agronomiques de l'État à Gembloux, 1976.

Africa. Montrouge, Draeger, 1976.

Pour une relecture africaine de Marx et d'Engels. Dakar, Nouvelles Éditions Africaines, 1976.

La Bibliothèque comme instrument du développement. Brussels, s.n., 1977.

La Place des langues classiques dans les humanités sénégalaises. Paris, privately printed, 1978.

Élégies majeures: dialogue sur la poésie francophone. Paris, Seuil, 1979.

La Poésie de l'action, with Mohamed Aziza. Paris, Stock, 1980.

Pour une Lecture négro-africaine de Mallarmé. Paris, Diffusion, 1981.

Discours de remerciement et de réception à l'Académie Française, with Edgar Fauré. Paris, Seuil, 1984.

African Sojourn, photographs by Uwe Ommer. Santa Barbara, California, Arpel Graphics, 1986.

Black Ladies, photographs by Uwe Ommer. Paris, Jaguar, 1986.

Ce que je crois: négritude, francité, et civilisation de l'universel. Paris, Grasset, 1988.

Espaces: à la recherche d'une écologie de l'esprit. Luxembourg, Euroeditor, 1989.

Editor, *Anthologie de la nouvelle poésie nègre et malgache de langue française*. Paris, Presses Universitaires de France, 1948.

*

Bibliography: *Léopold Senghor: Bibliographie* by Bureau de Documentation de la Présidence de la République, Dakar, Fondation L. S. Senghor, 1982.

Critical Studies: *Léopold Senghor and the Politics of Negritude* by Irving L. Markovitz, London, Heinemann, 1969; *The African Image in the Work of Léopold Senghor* by Barend Van Niekerk, Cape Town, Balkema, 1970; *Léopold Senghor: An Intellectual Biography* by Jack Hymans, Edinburgh, Edinburgh University Press, 1971; *The Poetry of Léopold Senghor* by S. Okechukwu Mezu, London, Heinemann, 1973; *The Concept of Négritude in the Poetry of Léopold Senghor* by

Sylvia Washington Bâ, Princeton, New Jersey, Princeton University Press, 1973; *A Dance of Masks: Senghor, Achebe, Soyinka* by Jonathan Peters, Washington, D.C., Three Continents Press, 1978; *Black, French, and African: A Life of Léopold Sédar Senghor* by Janet G. Vaillant, Cambridge, Massachusetts, Harvard University Press, 1990.

*   *   *

A man who made distinguished contributions in the sphere of politics in Africa during the era of decolonisation as well as in the world of literature, Léopold Senghor reveals in his literary works the complex interplay of cultural forces which makes *négritude* such a problematic concept. After a childhood in Senegal in an environment where Catholicism was dominant and French values were rated highly, he completed his education in Paris and continued to move in French intellectual circles until the outbreak of World War II. He came under the influence of Paul Claudel's sensuous mystic lyricism. He was also attracted by the religious and philosophical speculations of Emmanuel Mounier and Pierre Teilhard de Chardin. Ironically enough, it was also a French novel — *Les Déracinés* (The Uprooted) which Maurice Barrès had written in 1897 to stir up French public opinion over the Prussian occupation of Lorraine — which brought Senghor to an appreciation of his own need to preserve and develop his cultural identity as a black African. He was by no means persuaded that he should jettison all that he had learned to respect and cherish in metropolitan France, but rather sought to assimilate it with the insights and attitudes of his homeland.

Interest in Africa, aroused by the publication of André Gide's *Voyage au Congo* (Journey to the Congo) in 1927 and *Le retour du Tchad* (Return from Chad) a year later, was further stimulated by the Paris Colonial Exhibition in 1931. The time was ripe for the black intellectuals in Paris to assert themselves, and Senghor, along with Aimé Césaire (*q.v.*) from Martinique who is credited with coining the word *négritude*, played a leading part. In particular he became associated with *L'Étudiant Noir* (The Black Student) which aimed at raising black consciousness while at the same time breaking down barriers between writers and students from different colonies, whether in Africa or the West Indies. The culmination of Senghor's efforts to demonstrate the vitality of black literature in French came with the publication in 1940 of his *Anthologie de la nouvelle poésie nègre et malgache de langue française*. With an important introduction with the title "Orphée noir" (Black Orpheus) by Jean-Paul Sartre, the anthology made a strong impact and has been reprinted several times.

As well as an advocate of black poetry, Senghor is a gifted poet in his own right. *Chaka* is an extended poem on the theme of Shaka, a more or less legendary Zulu king from precolonial days; though not properly a dramatic work, it has been staged and broadcast with some success. Generally Senghor did not work on such a large scale, producing a number of collections of lyric poems in which the influence of Paul Claudel and Saint-John Perse are unmistakeable, *Chants d'ombre* (Songs of Shadow), *Hosties noires* (Black Host), *Éthiopiques*, and *Nocturnes*. As the titles themselves hint, Senghor is a poet of twilight and darkness, which he explores in every manifestation, from womb to grave, as the reservoir of true energy. He takes the primordial themes of love and nature and expresses them with rich vocabulary and the grant rhetoric which Claudel reintroduced into French poetry with his *Odes*. Lyric in the traditional senses of the term, Senghor's poems are often conceived as for recitation or chanting to the accompaniment of an African drum or stringed or wind instrument.

In recent years Senghor has, in addition to playing a role in politics, continued to champion the cause of francophone African literature. His reputation as a creative writer, however, still stands on his earlier works.

—Christopher Smith

SHĀMLŪ, Ahmad. Has also written as Alef Bamdad and Alef Sobh. Iranian. Born in Tehran, 12 December 1925. Imprisoned at age 16 for year and a half during Allied occupation of Iran during World War II. Married to Ayda Shāmlū. Imprisoned at age 29 for one year because of membership of Communist Tudeh Party; arrested and/or jailed several more times; left Iran in 1976 for voluntary exile: lived in Princeton, New Jersey, 1976–77, and London, 1977–79; editor, *Iranshahr* newspaper, London; returned to Iran, 1979. Founder and editor of many artistic and literary journals. Address: c/o Sāzman-i Publishers, 99, First Floor, Mirdamad Avenue, Tehran, Iran.

PUBLICATIONS

Verse

Ahangha-ye faramush shodeh [Forgotten Songs].   1947.
Bist-o seh [23].   1951.
Qat'nāmeh [Manifesto].   1951.
Ahanhā va ehsās [Irons and Emotion].   1953.
Havā-ye tāzeh [Fresh Air].   1957.
Bagh-e ayeneh [The Garden of Mirrors].   1960.
Ayda dar ayeneh [Aida in the Mirror].   1964.
Ayda: derakht-o khanjar-o khatereh [Aida: The Tree, the Dagger, and a Memory].   1965.
Qaqnus dar bārān [Phoenix in the Rain].   1966.
Marsiyeh'hā-ye khāk [Elegies of the Earth].   1969.
Shekoftan dar meh [Blossoming in the Mist].   1970.
Ebrāhīm dar ātash [Abraham in the Fire].   1973.
Deshneh dar dīs [Dagger in the Dish].   1977.
Tarāneh'ha-ye kuchak-e ghorbat [Small Songs of Exile].   1980.
Kāshifān-i furūtan-i shawkarān [The Humble Explorers of Shawkarā].   Tehran, Sāzmān-i, 1981.

English translations of his poems published in various journals and anthologies, including "Major Voices in Persian Literature" issue of *Literature East and West* (Austin, Texas), 20 (1–4), 1976, and *An Anthology of Modern Persian Poetry*, Boulder, Colorado, Westview Press, 1978.

Other

Ketāb-e kūcheh: farhang-i lughāt, estelāhāt, ta'bīrāt, zarb al-masal-hā-yi Fārsī (dictionary of colloquial Persian). Tehran, n.p., 5 vols., 1978–81.

*

Critical Studies: "A Well amid the Waste: An Introduction to the Poetry of Ahmad Shamlu" by Ahmad Karimi-Hakkak, in *World Literature Today* (Norman, Oklahoma), 51, 1977;

"Mayakovsky and the 'New Poetry' of Iran in the Works of Ahmad Shamlu'" by V. B. Klyashtorina and Mary Lee Schnieders, in *Critical Perspectives on Modern Persian Literature*, Washington, D.C., Three Continents Press, 1984; "Ahmad Shamlu: The Rebel Poet in Search of an Audience" by Leonard P. Alishan, in *Iranian Studies* (New York), 18(2–4), 1985.

*   *   *

One of the most influential living poets of Iran, Ahmad Shāmlū came to prominence with the publication of his third collection, *Havā-ye tāzeh* (Fresh Air), in 1957. A prolific writer, his continual experimentalism in form, language, and themes has given contemporary Persian poetry a new vitality. His poetry is deeply influenced by such modern Western writers as Paul Eluard, Rainer Maria Rilke, and Federico García Lorca. His early work clearly reflects such an indebtedness. However, he soon developed his own particular style and language, creating an innovative and highly individual poetic idiom.

From the very beginning of his poetic career, Shāmlū has been concerned with the injustices of society. He seeks to arouse the ordinary, predominantly superstitious people to take their lives into their own hands and not to wait for a Messiah; this is expressed with vivid anger in the "Tablet":

> I yelled out to them: "You, devoid of courage
> in vain you wait, this is the very last Coming."
>
> And I cried out: "Gone are the days
> of mourning some crucified Christ
> for today every woman is another Mary
> and every Mary has a Jesus upon the cross . . .

But with his "words the crowd ignored," the poet finds himself in a desperate state of hopelessness; the only possible survival is in love.

Shāmlū's love poetry is among the most lyrical and sensitive of the century. Love, for him is a starting point: "Never did a man so ruinously rise/to kill himself/as I settled to the task of living." In a world of chaos and injustice, love brings harmony and peace. "Aida in the Mirror," for example, expresses vividly the poet's ennobling experiences of love:

> Your lips, delicate as poetry
> turn the most voluptuous kiss
> into such coyness
> that the cave-animal uses it
> to become human.
>   . . .
> And your eyes are the secret of fire
> and your love
> is the victory of man
> when he rushes to battle against his fate.

Shāmlū's love poetry does not, however, ignore the dilemmas of society. It is the juxtaposition of the ugliness and vice of society with the purity and beauty of love, in fresh and vivid imagery, which gives his love poetry its individual lyrical beauty. The tone of his later love poems is closer to epic, for "Where love is not a lyric/it is an epic," because it encompasses humanity, not merely the individual. Death preoccupies the poet's mind alongside love. He expresses his fear of death in many of his poems. He fears not physical death, but rather "Dying in a world where the fees of the grave-digger/are higher/than man's freedom."

One of the most striking features of Shāmlū's poetry is his repeated (but various) employment of the image of the mirror, which also plays an important role in classical, particularly mystical, Persian poetry. Shāmlū sees the face of his beloved Aida as a mirror which can reflect a more sublime beauty and truth:

> Your forehead is a tall mirror
> luminous and high
> in which the Seven Sisters stare
> to realize their beauty.

Above all, for Shāmlū it is poetry itself which acts as a mirror to reflect the poet's mind and soul in an uncertain and troublesome world. His fascination with mirrors is further reflected in his language and style. His poem "Hamlet" begins thus: "To be/or not to be,/this is not the question/this is the evil temptation." It ends with a more vivid and emphatic mirror image of this opening: "Not a question/but an evil temptation, this/to be/or/not to be."

Shāmlū's interest in Persian translations of the Old and New Testaments has had an influence, both in language and content, on his own poetry. His poem "Marg-e Nāserī" (The Death of the Nazarene), included in his volume *Qaqnus dar bārān* (Phoenix in the Rain), is a particularly moving and beautiful poem on the crucifixion of Christ. It is an allegory of the defeat of goodness and pure love by a world full of evil and darkness. While in the "Tablet" the poet identifies himself with Christ, here he sees himself being dragged to the Cross by a mob of ignorant people, who seek the truth "only in legends." The poem also shows the marks of Western existentialism, as elsewhere in his work. Here, however, Shāmlū reiterates the uselessness of Christ's death, and therefore states, symbolically, that "God is dead"; nevertheless, as the title of the poem also suggests by way of allusion (*Nāsir* also means defender, [God] giver of victory), the poet has succeeded in creating a new form of freedom — poetry — from the "dead legends." Shāmlū's keen interest in "The Song of Songs" is evident in his love poetry; he has also produced an eloquent and beautiful Persian translation of the text. Shāmlū's other translations include powerful versions from Lorca.

Shāmlū's fascination with folklore and his ceaseless poetic experimentation have led to some particularly distinctive work, such as "Parlīyā" (The Fairies), a masterfully formed poem which juxtaposes the colloquial idiom of folklore with "high" literary language. Its rhythm is varied and irregular, yet harmonious. It fuses tones both of despair and hope.

Much of Shāmlū's early poetry is written in classical forms. He is also greatly indebted to Nīmā Yūshīj, the father of modernist Persian poetry. Shāmlū, however, is best known for his development of free verse. It is in this form that he is unquestionably a master. His free verse is devoid of the uneasy rhythm and awkward language of some of his earliest poetry. Aware of the Imagists, his imagery is precise, sharp, and vivid; his language is concise and inventive, in a manner both colloquial and poetic. The result is a poetic voice unique in contemporary Persian.

—Parvin Loloi

SHAYKH, Ḥanān al-. Lebanese. Born in Beirut, 12 November 1945. Educated at Alamiliah traditional Muslim girls' primary school, Beirut; Ahliyyah School, Beirut; American College for Girls, Cairo, 1963–66. Married Fu'ād Malūf in 1968; one son and one daughter. Journalist, *Al-Ḥasna'* women's magazine, 1966–68, and *Al-Nahār* literary supplement, 1968–75; left Lebanon because of civil war, 1976: lived in Saudi Arabia for six years, then moved to London, 1982. Agent: David Higham Associates, 5–8 Lower John Street, Golden Square, London W1R 4HA, England. Address: 7 Grosvenor Square, Flat 16, London W1X 9LA, England.

PUBLICATIONS

Fiction

Intiḥār rajul mayyit [Suicide of a Dead Man].   Beirut, Dār al-Nahār li al-Nashr, 1970.
Faras al-shaiṭān [Praying Mantis].   Beirut, Dār al-Nahār li al-Nashr, 1975.
Ḥikāyat Zahrah.   Beirut, Ḥanān al-Shaykh and N. Ṭāher, 1980; as *The Story of Zahrah*, London, Quartet, 1986.
Wardat al-ṣahra [The Desert Rose].   Beirut, al-Mu'assasah al-Jāmi'iyya li al-Dirāsāt wa al-Nashr wa al-Tawzī', 1982.
Misk al-ghazāl.   Beirut, Dār al-Ādāb, 1988; as *Women of Sand and Myrrh*, London, Quartet, 1989.
Barīd Bairūt [Poste Restante Beirut].   Cairo, Dār al-Hilāl, 1993.

*

Critical Studies: in *War's Other Voices — Women Writers on the Lebanese Civil War* by Miriam Cooke, Cambridge, Cambridge University Press, 1987; in "Sexuality, War and Literature in Lebanon" by Evelyne Accad, in *Tulsa Studies in Women's Literature* (Tulsa, Oklahoma), 8, Winter 1989; "The Fiction of Ḥanān Al-Shaykh, Reluctant Feminist" by Charles Larson, in *Literary Quarterly of the University of Oklahoma* (Tulsa), 1, Winter 1991; "An Interview with Ḥanān Al-Shaykh," in *The Middle East: Michigan Quarterly Review*, Fall 1992, and "Gender, Violence and Sexuality: Female Narrators in *Women of Sand and Myrrh*," in *Phoebe* (Fairfax, Virginia), Spring 1993, both by Paula W. Sunderman.

Ḥanān al-Shaykh comments:

I started writing when I was 16 years old in an attempt to release my anger and frustration towards my father and brother because they had a hold over me and were able to restrict my freedom. As my writing developed I moved away from this immediate reason, and writing became a necessity to me in my desire to understand life and death. I found that only in reading and writing could I hope to achieve this understanding.

Writing fiction makes me feel that I am not alone. I am cushioned by my characters and by readers who can enter a world they weren't aware of before and share it with me.

Writing fiction has become a way of life to me.

*   *   *

The varied life that took Ḥanān al-Shaykh from the south of Lebanon to Beirut, Cairo, the Arabian Gulf, and then to London and Paris has provided her with a unique perspective on the life of her own country and fellow Arab women. It has enabled her to interweave first-hand experience with a comparative and multicultural outlook. From a very early stage in

her journalistic career at the prestigious newspaper, *Al-Nahār*, she wrote short stories and novels and was soon recognized as one of the most talented female writers of her generation.

Her first novel, *Intiḥār rajul mayyit* (Suicide of a Dead Man), established her unique style of writing, profoundly dislodging the patriarchal system without ostensibly challenging it. Unlike most first novels by Arab women writers, which draw on autobiographical experience and are related through the female voice, al-Shaykh's novel is narrated by a middle-aged married man probing his life in the light of his obsessive desire for a 16-year-old girl. The first-person narrative internalizes the male perspective in order to subvert the patriarchal control over the realm of discourse from within. It apparently reproduces the patriarchal order, giving the middle-aged male the monopoly over discourse and making the young female voiceless. The female heroine Dānyā shows her talent through a medium, painting, that conforms to the patriarchal image of the silent female. The narrative is occupied mainly with the story of the narrator's affair with the young girl, the opposition he meets from his wife, and his attempt to consummate the relationship. But beneath this preoccupation and the apparent reproduction of the dominant power relations, the author conducts her subtle deconstruction of the ethos of patriarchy. The unnamed narrator is captivated by the fresh innocence of the young woman, taken by her talent, beauty, and freedom, yet is incapable of making love to her. The narrator's impotence is presented as an ideological stance rather than a physical condition, for outside his immediate social context he is capable of performing with foreign women. Before his encounter with the heroine, he was virile and in total control over his wife and numerous mistresses. But as soon as he fails to make love to the talented young painter, his impotence manifests itself with both his wife and his mistress. The impotence induced by his encounter with the young liberated woman is a metaphor for the inability of patriarchy to deal with the untapped talent of liberated women.

In her second novel, *Faras al-Shaiṭān* (Praying Mantis), al-Shaykh explores the social and cultural education of one of these women, the heroine of the novel, Sārah, in her search for liberty and fulfilment. The prevalent narrative voice in the novel is that of the heroine, which oscillates between the probing of her individual psyche and the reconstruction of her social past. The past serves as the internal memory and collective history of both the text and the southern Lebanese community from which she comes, and provides both the cultural and personal background against which she acts. The examination of the self furnishes the motivation for both characterisation and action and delineates the heroine's views and feelings. Although the novel appears as a female *bildungsroman*, sketching the journey of its heroine through adverse circumstances, it avoids the traditional causal narrative and consecutive time and resorts to the accumulation of tales and disconnected fictional vignettes to illustrate the heroine's search for herself and her happiness.

This search acquires a wider and more sophisticated dimension in her much admired novel, *Ḥikāyat Zahrah* (*The Story of Zahrah*). Indeed it was *Zahrah* that established al-Shaykh's name in the forefront of modern Arabic literature, which was an active participant in the shaping of modern sensibility. As a modernist novel in which the sexual and political aspects are inscribed into every facet of its textual strategies, *Zahrah* works on many different levels. It is the story of the oppression endured by Lebanese and Arab women throughout the centuries in their "degraded search" for their voice. The suppressed female voice is the major image that permeates every aspect of the text, and the struggle to articulate her voice earns the novel a prominent place in feminist discourse. Th novel posits the female body as both a symbol of the physical world and a metaphor for war-torn Lebanon. On a certain level of interpretation, the story of *Zahrah* is also the story of Lebanon's quest for national identity and political legitimacy which erupted in the brutality of the civil war. This is enhanced by the novel's resort to polyphonic narrative in which many voices, languages, and ideologies are fused into a highly complex stratagem of conflicts and interests. In *Zahrah*, the inherent contradictions of patriarchy are seen as destructive to both women and country and as the source of the havoc which manifests itself in the fatal fascination of violence that leads to the annihilation of the self. The novel ends in an act of double suicide in which the sniper, the symbol of warring Lebanon and the cause of its doom, kills the pregnant Zahrah who carries his own child and with her the country and any hope for a future.

Al-Shaykh's fourth novel, *Misk al-ghazāl* (*Women of Sand and Myrrh*), is a fascinating work both thematically and artistically. It is a novel of four women living in unnamed desert society, who come from different social and cultural backgrounds. Two, Nur and Tamr, are from the unnamed desert society but represent the two ends of its social spectrum. The other two are foreigners: Suha, a Lebanese who is escaping from the civil war, is undergoing a difficult cultural transition that affects her own identity in a harsher way than the war she left at home; and Suzanne, an American, who is there in search of adventure and wealth, has been hypnotized by the fatal attraction of the new society, and is sleep-walking into disaster. Yet the conditions in which they live bring elements of similarity and contrast into their lives, portrayed as both a material reality and a human and psychological phenomenon, a function of the way women and men perceive one another and themselves. Under the restrictive conditions of the climate and the socially constructed environment, foreign, even Western, women do not fare any better than local ones. The narrative is charged with subtle criticism of the gender-based system and its oppressive nature without resorting to any of the hackneyed jargon in this domain. Feminism is inscribed as much into the elaborate details of the narrative structure as in the social predicament of the four characters.

As the title of the novel reflects through the juxtaposition of sand with its associations of beauty, emptiness, and even sterility, and myrrh with its richly exotic connotations of luxurious promises being the gift offered to Christ in his cradle, the novel is redolent with symbols and allusions rich in tension and contradictions. The elaborate network of first-person narrative, in which the text allows the four women to speak in turn giving voice to the voiceless, reflects in its structure the compartmentalization of women and their struggle to break out of all forms of social confinement. The very structure of the novel in which each section conveys a sense of independence while at the same time being an integral part of a whole reflects the degree of sophistication in the author's feminist vision.

This technique is also used in al-Shaykh's most recent novel, *Barīd Bairūt* (Post Restante Beirut), in which the fragmentary narrative structure of the novel corresponds to the devastation of war-torn Lebanon. The discourse of the disparate letters of the heroine, Asmahān, which have little or no hope of reaching their destination, is of one of solitude and siege, and at the same time an unequivocal cry for help for an escape from the madness of war. The 11 letters which comprise the novel can be seen as various attempts to find logic in a world of madness, posit human memory in the face of destruction and doom, capture in the intricacy of writing the splendid past of the country, and restore the fascinating and rich tapestry of its culture. In this novel, the writing of war involves a war against traditional modes of writing and thinking and an endeavour to create a new discourse that will rise like a phoenix from the ashes of the old. The sensitive eye of the woman writer, with its life-giving force, breathes new life into the ashes of self-devastation and national suicide. In a narrative technique reminiscent of *The Arabian Nights*, al-Shaykh generates a rich web of stories emerging endlessly one out of the other, weaving together the destiny of the Palestinians and the Lebanese, the memory of the past and the events of the present, the ordeal of the hostages and the fate of the fighters, and the various shreds of a war-torn country. What holds all this together is the recurring image of Asmahān, the woman, mother earth, and Lebanon that has been afflicted by war for so long, but is still endowed with humanity and an endless capacity to celebrate life and engender joy.

—Sabry Hafez

SHEN RONG. Chinese. Born in Hankou, Hubei Province, October 1935. Educated at Beijing Russian College, 1954–57. Sales assistant, Gongren Publishing House bookshop, from 1951; music editor and Russian interpreter, People's Central Broadcast Station, from 1957; sent to countryside for rehabilitation during the Cultural Revolution; Russian teacher, Fifth High School, Beijing, from 1973. Member, China Writers' Association, Beijing Writers' Association, China International Exchange Association, and China PEN. Address: c/o China PEN, Shatan Beije 2, Beijing, China.

PUBLICATIONS

Fiction

Wan qingnian [Evergreen].   1973.
Guangming yu heian [Brightness and Darkness].   Beijing, People's Literature Publishing House, 1978.
Yongyuan shi chuntian [Everlasting Spring].   Published in *Harvest*, 1979.
Bing zhong [In Sickness].   Shanghai, Wenhui Zengkan, 1980.
Ren dao zhongnian.   Published in *Harvest*, 1980; as *At Middle Age*, Beijing, Chinese Literature/Panda, 1987.
Fannao de xingqin [A Distracting Sunday].   1980.
Xin [Heart].   1980.
Meiguise de wancai [A Rose-Coloured Evening Meal].   1980.
Zhoumo [Weekend].   Beijing, People's University Publishing House, 1980.
Baixue [Snow].   N.p., Shi Yue, 1980.
Tongkuzhong de jueze [A Painful Decision].   N.p., Wen Yibao, 1981.
Zan ge [Songs of Praise]   Published in *Harvest*, 1981.
Guanyu zizhu guodong wenti [How Piglets Spend the Winter].   N.p., Dangdai, 1981.
Tuise de xin [The Faded Letter].   Beijing, People's University Press, 1981.
Zhenzhen jiajia [True and False].   Published in *Harvest*, 1982.
Ye suan zhanwang [Also a Prospect].   Beijing, Beijing Literature, 1982.
Duzi zen sheng de hei [How Could I Become Black by Myself].   Beijing, People's University Press, 1982.

Taizi cun de mimi [The Secret of Crown Prince Village]. N.p., Dangdai, 1982.

Wanwan de yueliang [The Crooked Moonlight]. Beijing, People's University Press, 1982.

Da gongji beixiju [Tragicomedy of a Big Rooster]. Beijing, People's Literature Publishing House, 1984.

Sandan de ren [The Scatty Person]. Published in *Xiaoshuo Monthly*, 1985.

Jianqu shi sui [Reducing My Age by 10 Years]. Beijing, People's Literature Publishing House, 1986.

Sheng si qian hou [Before and After Life and Death]. Beijing, People's Literature Publishing House, 1987.

Dengdai dianhua [Waiting for the Phone]. Published in *Xioashuo Monthly*, 1987.

Lande lihun [Too Lazy to Get a Divorce]. Published in *Xioashuo Monthly*, 1987.

Baba conghezheng [Eight Eight Syndrome]. Beijing, People's Literature Publishing House, 1989.

De hu? Shi hu? [Won? Or Lost?]. N.p., Zhongpian xiaoshuo xuankan, 1989.

Ti xiao jie fei [Neither Laughing Nor Crying]. N.p., Zhongpian xiaoshuo xuankan, 1989.

Hua kai hua luo [Flowers Blossom Flowers Wither]. Published in *Zhong Shan*, 5, 1991.

Other

Ye suan zhanwang [Also a Prospect]. Beijing, Beijing Literature, 1982.

Yang YueYue yu Sartre zhi yanjiu [Research into Yang YueYue and Sartre]. 1983.

Cong Lu Wenting dao Jiang Zhuying [From Lu Wenting to Jiang Zhuying]. N.p., Guangming Daily, 1983.

*   *   *

Shen Rong belongs to a group of writers acclaimed in China in the late 1970s and early 1980s for their treatment of subjects which had long been forbidden territory. Like most Chinese writers, she sees herself as having a responsibility to observe, comment on, and influence her society. Working in a period when the strictest Maoist constraints on literature had been abandoned, and the follies and outrages of the Cultural Revolution were being exposed by officials and writers alike, she has been able to write both more realistically and more critically than authors of the preceding generation. She is especially interested in the problems of intellectuals. Her themes include bureaucracy, hypocrisy, and conformity in Chinese official culture, the use of the back door and corruption, the heavy work burden suffered by middle-aged intellectuals, tensions between the generations, and the stresses imposed on family life and relationships when individuals suffer political criticism or disgrace.

Shen Rong became famous for her novella *Ren dao zhongnian* (*At Middle Age*), which sold over three million copies and was made into a very successful film. It portrays a conscientious woman doctor who struggles to reconcile the conflicting demands of work and family. Dr. Lu's dedication to duty is overzealous; for example, when her daughter gets pneumonia Lu finishes seeing her own patients before going to the kindergarden to collect the child and does not consider taking time off work to care for her. When her husband seems to find the family burden too much, she suggests that he might move into his institute, leaving her to cope with the children alone. This superhuman selflessness is reminiscent of the crude characterisations found in the literature of the Cultural Revolution era. However, when it first appeared in 1980, *At*

Middle Age made an impression partly because it flouted so many of the formulaic rules of the years when literature had "served politics." The heroine is an intellectual rather than a worker or a peasant, she and her husband recite the poetry of the Hungarian poet Sándor Petőfi to each other, and though dedicated to medicine, she comes from a "bad" class background and is not a Party member. Furthermore, her foil, the wife of a high Party official, is conspicuously lacking in proletarian selflessness. She is self-important, smug, and secure in the confidence conferred by her membership of the privileged Party elite. A subplot of the novel involves another doctor and her husband who, unable to endure the harsh living and working conditions in China any longer, are preparing to emigrate to Canada. By contrast, Dr. Lu works herself into a near-fatal heart attack but recovers apparently not because her husband devotedly sits at her bedside reading poetry, nor because her sick child needs her, but because she feels she cannot desert her patients. Perhaps Shen Rong could not allow her to die. A "happy" ending is frequently tacked onto works of critical realism in China to protect their authors from the charge of negativism.

The novella is clearly a call to improve the treatment of intellectuals; indeed, so hazy are the boundaries between literature and life in China that it was often cited as evidence by those campaigning for better pay and living conditions for professionals. Its points seem innocuous enough today, but when the story first appeared it provoked considerable reaction. Intellectuals were pleased with its vindication of their role in society, whereas Party hardliners condemned both its satirical depiction of the "Marxist Leninist old lady" and its neutral attitude towards the couple who were "deserting China" by emigrating.

The sentimentality of *At Middle Age* and its sympathetic portrayal of intellectuals ensured it a particular success with China's reading public, yet some of Shen Rong's later pieces of satire have greater vigour. Another novella, *Taizi cun de mimi* (The Secret of Crown Prince Village), recounts the story of a village which has aroused suspicion by successfully raising agricultural production year after year despite all the changes in policy as left and right vied for control in Beijing. Its secret, revealed only in the last pages, is that its enterprising brigade leader has consistently followed rational economic strategies but has used ruses which fit the current political line to justify or cover up his actions when they might otherwise have been criticised. The moral seems to be that in recent times in China it has not been possible for a straightforward person to do a good job. Readers are left to decide for themselves whether things have changed.

Shen Rong's short story *Zhenzhen jiajia* (True and False) is set in an Institute for the Study of Foreign Literature. Working in such a politically sensitive area, its members have developed considerable skills in the art of phoney self-criticism, meaningless verbiage, and ambiguous statements to get them through the endless political meetings they are obliged to attend. Most of them have so internalised the prohibitions of earlier years that despite a recent Party directive calling for more independent thinking, they dare not oppose the political commissar's attack on an article on Western modernism by one of their colleagues. At first only a young woman who missed out on an education when schools were closed during the Cultural Revolution and understands nothing of the content of the article dares to assert that the attack is nonsense. Ironically, she gained her post in spite of her lack of qualifications, because her father is a high official: a family background which allows her to express total cynicism without fear of repercussions. Finally, after a struggle with himself, the head of the institute also defends the article, urging his colleagues to recognise that there is no need to lie any more. The implication is that intellectuals must cease the self-censorship that keeps them from questioning and criticising.

Fannao de xingqin (A Distracting Sunday) deals with the very prevalent problem of back-doorism. Mu, the Party secretary at a university, is preparing to take his grandson to the park for a Sunday outing. To the increasing fury of the little boy he is delayed by a stream of visitors who arrive one after another to intercede for Ding, a student who wants to stay in Beijing but is about to be assigned to a job in his own province. We are given an unsympathetic picture of Ding who apparently pulled strings to get into university in the first place and is now trying to improve his career prospects by the same means. We then learn that his parents have nearly ruined themselves to get him so far, and are made to see him as a sort of underdog who may lose out because others have more money and better strings to pull. The story ends on an apparently positive note with Mu resolving to show no favour to Ding, yet its deeper message is that in a society where back-doorism is rife, anyone, however principled, may be drawn into practising it in order to assist those whom they regard as deserving.

Shen Rong's best work was very much of its own period, dealing with the problems thrown up by the reform process from the perspective of a supporter of reform. When public confidence that the Party could adequately reform China's political and economic system was eroded by developments in the late 1980s, such themes began to seem outmoded.

—Delia Davin

SIMON, Claude (Eugène Henri). French. Born in Tananarive, Madagascar, 10 October 1913. Educated at Collège Stanislas, Paris; Lycée Saint-Louis (for naval career: dismissed); at Cambridge and Oxford universities for a short time; studied painting with André Lhote. Served in the French Cavalry, 1934–35 and 1939–40: captured, but escaped, 1940; joined resistance movement in Perpignan. Married 1) Yvonne Ducuing in 1951 (dissolved); 2) Réa Karavas in 1978. Lives in Paris and in Salses, Pyrenees. Recipient: Express prize, 1960; Médicis prize, 1967; Nobel prize for Literature, 1985. D.Litt.: University of East Anglia, Norwich; D.H.C.: University of Bologna, 1989. Address: c/o Éditions de Minuit, 7 rue Bernard-Palissy, 75006 Paris, France.

PUBLICATIONS

Fiction

Le Tricheur. Paris, Sagittaire, 1945.
Gulliver. Paris, Calmann Lévy, 1952.
Le Sacre du printemps. Paris, Calmann Lévy, 1954.
Le Vent: tentative de restitution d'un rétable baroque. Paris, Minuit, 1957; as *The Wind: Attempted Restoration of a Baroque Masterpiece*, New York, Braziller, 1959.
L'Herbe. Paris, Minuit, 1958; as *The Grass*, New York, Braziller, 1960; London, Cape, 1961.
La Route des Flandres. Paris, Minuit, 1960; as *The Flanders Road*, New York, Braziller, 1961; London, Cape, 1962.
Le Palace. Paris, Minuit, 1962; as *The Palace*, New York, Braziller, 1963; London, Cape, 1964.

Histoire. Paris, Minuit, 1967; in English, New York, Braziller, 1968; London, Cape, 1969.
La Bataille de Pharsale. Paris, Minuit, 1969; as *The Battle of Pharsalus*, New York, Braziller, and London, Cape, 1971.
Les Corps conducteurs. Paris, Minuit, 1971; as *Conducting Bodies*, New York, Viking Press, 1974; London, Calder and Boyars, 1975.
Triptyque. Paris, Minuit, 1973; as *Triptych*, New York, Viking Press, 1976; London, Calder, 1977.
Leçon de choses. Paris, Minuit, 1975; as *The World About Us*, Princeton, New Jersey, Ontario Review Press, 1983.
Les Géorgiques. Paris, Minuit, 1981; as *The Georgics*, London, Calder, and New York, Riverrun, 1989.
L'Acacia. Paris, Minuit, 1989; as *The Acacia*, New York, Pantheon, 1991.

Play

La Séparation, from his novel *L'Herbe* (produced Paris, 1963).

Other

La Corde raide. Paris, Sagittaire, 1947.
Femmes, illustrated by Joan Miró. Paris, Maeght, 1966; as *La Chevelure de Bérénice*, Paris, Minuit, 1983.
Orion aveugle. Geneva, Skira, 1970.
Discours de Stockholm. Paris, Minuit, 1987.
L'Invitation. Paris, Minuit, 1987; as *The Invitation*, Elmwood Park, Illinois, Dalkey Archive Press, 1991.

*

Critical Studies: *The French New Novel: Claude Simon, Michel Butor, Alain Robbe-Grillet* by John Sturrock, London, Oxford University Press, 1969; *Claude Simon* by Salvador Jimenez-Fajardo, Boston, Twayne, 1975; *The Novels of Claude Simon* by J. A. E. Loubère, Ithaca, New York, Cornell University Press, 1975; *Claude Simon and Fiction Now* by John Fletcher, London, Calder and Boyars, 1975; *Claude Simon's Mythic Muse* by Karen Gould, York, South Carolina, French Literature Publications, 1979, and *Orion Blinded: Essays on Simon* edited by Gould and Randi Birn, Lewisburg, Pennsylvania, Bucknell University Press, 1981; *Practices of the New Novel in Claude Simon's "L'Herbe" and "La Route des Flandres"* by Doris Y. Kadish, Fredericton, New Brunswick, York Press, 1979; *John Fowles, John Hawkes, Claude Simon: Problems of Self and Form in the Post-Modernist Novel* by Robert Burden, Würzburg, Könishausen Neumann, 1980; *Claude Simon: New Directions: Collected Papers*, edited by Alastair B. Duncan, Edinburgh, Scottish Academic Press, 1985; *Claude Simon: Writing the Visible* by Celia Britton, Cambridge, Cambridge University Press, 1987; *Claude Simon and the Transgressions of Modern Art* by Michael Evans, London, Macmillan, 1988; *Understanding Claude Simon* by Ralph Sarkonak, Columbia, University of South Carolina Press, 1989.

*   *   *

Considered by many to be the greatest of the group of writers loosely linked by the French literary movement known as the *nouveau roman*, Claude Simon took longer than some of the others to achieve prominence. His first novel, *Le Tricheur* (The Cheater), written about the same time as Albert Camus's much more famous book *L'Étranger*, although published a few years later, reflects a similar world of chance and absurdity; the title refers to the fact that mankind struggles in vain to correct ("cheat") destiny. In its overt imitation of the style of "hard-boiled" American novels, and in its bold use of sudden time shifts, it foreshadows major features of Simon's later, more mature writing.

He then wrote two very different works, *Gulliver* represented an unsuccessful attempt to produce a popular book in the Faulkner manner, and *Le Sacre du printemps* (The Rite of Spring) explored for the first time Simon's experiences in the Spanish civil war when he engaged in some gun-running for the republican side. With *Le Vent* (*The Wind*) he joined the lists of Alain Robbe-Grillet's (*q.v.*) publisher, the Éditions de Minuit, with whom he has remained ever since. *The Wind*, set in the wind-swept Pyrenean region where he spends part of every year, is the first work of his which has clear affinities with the *nouveau roman* style of narrative, but *L'Herbe* (*The Grass*) represents a more powerful breakthrough into a personal idiom. The title, taken from a remark made by Boris Pasternak to the effect that it is no more possible to watch history unfolding than it is to observe the grass growing, introduces the story of a woman who changes her mind about leaving her husband and running off with her lover, although neither she nor the reader is able to pinpoint the moment when her decision was taken.

The action of *La Route des Flandres* (*The Flanders Road*) (the death of a cavalry officer on a country road during the Battle of the Meuse in 1940) occupies only a few minutes of real time, but the narrating voice which explores and develops this simple incident weaves a fabric which fills the entire book. *Le Palace* (*The Palace*) returns to personal memories of civil war Barcelona deployed to more tragic effect than in *Le Sacre du printemps*, and *Histoire* is a dense, sombre story of a family and its misfortunes which "grows" out of a collection of postcards which the narrator's mother received during her protracted engagement to the man who was to become the narrator's father. Since this book Simon has relied heavily on objective materials of this kind; *La Bataille de Pharsale* (*The Battle of Pharsalus*) is constructed around extracts from Roman historians and novelists, and *Les Corps conducteurs* (*Conducting Bodies*) and *Leçon de choses* (*The World About Us*) are based on real objects like cigar-box labels and snapshots. *Triptyque* (*Triptych*) and *Les Géorgiques* (*The Georgics*) exploit in addition personal memories or family history, such as the true story of one of Simon's ancestors who took an active part in the French revolution and served as a general under Napoleon. *L'Acacia* (*The Acacia*) continues this tendency: the novel tells how the young Claude Simon and his mother went in search of his officer father's grave after the armistice in 1918, and how the adult Claude Simon escaped from a POW camp in 1940 and returned incognito to the ancestral home in southern France.

Simon writes in a rich and sensuous style, composed of long, complex sentences with a higher-than-average proportion of present participles, which owes a lot to American writing, Faulkner's in particular, in its attempt to encompass the bewildering flux of life. Like Faulkner's, too, Simon's vision is pessimistic, even tragic; he shows mankind powerless to compete with the continually renewed vigour of the natural world. In *The Georgics* for instance, the alternation of the seasons, of rain and sun and springtime, continue as if indifferent to human tragedy, and men attempt in vain to transcend their condition through frenetic military and political activity.

—John Fletcher

SINIAVSKII, Andrei (Donatovich). Also Andrei Siniavsky, Andrej Sinjavskij. Also writes as Abram Terts (also Tertz). Russian. Born in Moscow, 8 October 1925. Educated at Moscow University, degree 1949, candidate of philological sciences 1952. Served in the Soviet Army. Married to Maria Rozanova-Kruglikova; one son. Senior research fellow, Gorky Literary Institute, Moscow, until 1966; lecturer in Russian literature, Moscow University, until 1965; arrested for alleged anti-Soviet writings, 1965, sentenced to seven years' hard labour, 1966: released from prison, 1971; emigrated to France, 1973; Assistant Professor, then Professor of Slavic studies, the Sorbonne, Paris, from 1973. Founder, *Sintaksis* literary journal. Russian citizenship restored, 1990. Recipient: Grolier Club Bennett award, 1978. Address: c/o Sintaksis, 8 rue Boris Vilde, 92260 Fontenay-aux-Roses, France.

PUBLICATIONS

Fiction (as Abram Terts)

Sud idet. Published in *Kultura* (Paris), 1960; as *The Trial Begins*, New York, Pantheon, and London, Collins, 1960.
Fantasticheskie povesti. Paris, Instytut Literacki, 1961; as *Fantastic Stories*, New York, Pantheon, 1963; as *The Icicle, and Other Stories*, London, Collins and Harvill, 1963.
Liubimov. Published in Polish as *Lubimow*, Paris, Instytut Literacki, 1963; in Russian, Washington, D.C., Filipoff, 1964; as *The Makepeace Experiment*, New York, Pantheon, and London, Collins Harvill, 1965.
Spokoinoi nochi. Paris, Sintaksis, 1984; as *Goodnight!*, New York, Penguin, 1989; London, Viking, 1990.

Other

Kto kak zashchishchaetsia [Who Defends Oneself Thus]. Alma-Ata, Kazgoslitizdat, 1953.
"Chto takoe sotsialisticheski realizm?" (as Abram Terts). Published in *L'Esprit* (Paris), February 1959; as *On Socialist Realism*, New York, Pantheon, 1961.
Pikasso [Picasso], with I. N. Golomshtok. Published in *Znanie* (Moscow), 1960.
Istoriia russkoi sovetskoi literatury [History of Soviet Russian Literature]. 1961.
Za poeticheskuiu aktivnost' (zametki o poezii molodykh) [For Poetical Activity (Notes About the Poetry of the Young)], with A. N. Menshutin. Published in *Novyi mir* (Moscow), 1, 1961.
Davaite rovorit' professional'no [Let's Speak Professionally]. Published in *Novyi mir* (Moscow), 8, 1961.
Lysukha (Naturalist Stories). Alma-Ata, Kazgoslitizdat, 1961.
Poeziia pervykh let revoliutsii, 1917–20 [The Poetry of the First Years of the Revolution], with A. N. Menshutin. Moscow, Nauka, 1964.
Mysli vrasplokh (as Abram Terts). New York, Rausen, 1966; as "Thought Unaware," in *New Leader* (New York), 19 July 1965; as *Unguarded Thoughts*, London, Collins Harvill, 1972.
Druzhnaia semeika [Friendly Family]. Alma-Ata, Kainar, 1966.
Fantasticheskii mir Abrama Tertsa [Fantastic World of Abram Terts] (as Abram Terts). Paris, Inter-Language Literary Associates, 1967.
Medvezhonok Taimyr [The Bear Cub Taimyr]. Alma-Ata, Kainar, 1969.

Khrabryi tsyplenok [The Brave Chicken]. Alma-Ata, Zhazushy, 1971.

For Freedom of Imagination. New York, Holt, 1971.

V nochnom zooparke [In the Night Zoo]. Alma-Ata, Zhazushy, 1973.

Golos iz khora (as Abram Terts). London, Stenvalley, 1973; as *A Voice from the Chorus*, New York, Farrar Straus, and London, Collins Harvill, 1976.

Literaturnyi protsess v Rossii [Literary Process in Russia]. Published in *Kontinent* (Paris), 1, 1974.

Progulki s Pushkinym [Strolls with Pushkin] (as Abram Terts). London, Overseas Publications Exchange, 1975.

V teni Gogolia [In the Shadow of Gogol] (as Abram Terts). London, Overseas Publications Interchange, 1975.

Kroshka Tsores [Little Tsores] (as Abram Terts). Paris, Sintaksis, 1980.

Syntaxis: réflexion sur le sort de la Russe et de la culture russe. Paris, Michel, 1981.

"Opavshie list'ia" V. V. Rozanova [V. V. Rozanov's Fallen Leaves]. Paris, Sintaksis, 1982.

Osnovy sovetskoi tsivilizatsii. As *La Civilisation Soviétique*, Paris, Albin Michel, 1989; as *Soviet Civilization: A Cultural History*, New York, Arcade, 1992.

Sny na pravoslavnuiu Paskhu [Dreams of Orthodox Pashka]. Moscow, Sovetskii pisatel', 1991.

Pokhvala emigratsii: rech' pri vruchenii premii "Pisatel' v izgnanii" [Emigration Commended: Speech During the Award Ceremony For "The Writer in Exile"]. Published in *Stolitsa* (Moscow), 40, 1992.

*

Critical Studies: *On Trial: The Case of Sinyavsky — Tertz — and Daniel — Arzhak*, edited by Leopold Labedz and M. Hayward, New York, Harper, and London, Harvill, 1966, revised edition, Westport, Connecticut, Greenwood Press, 1980; "Sinyavsky in Two Worlds: Two Brothers Named Chénier" by Richard Pevear, in *Hudson Review* (New York), 25, 1972; *Andrei Siniavsky and Julii Daniel', Two Soviet "Heretical" Writers* by Margaret Dalton, Würzburg, Jal, 1973; "Andrei Siniavskii: The Chorus and the Critic" by Walter F. Kolonsky, in *Canadian-American Slavic Studies* (Bakersfield, California), 9, 1975; "The Sense of Purpose and Socialist Realism in Terz's *The Trial Begins*" by W. J. Leatherbarrow, in *Forum for Modern Language Studies* (St. Andrews, Scotland), 11, 1975; *Letters to the Future: An Approach to Sinyavsky-Tertz* by Richard Lourie, Ithaca, New York, Cornell University Press, 1975; "On Abram Tertz's *A Voice from the Choir*" by Laszlo M. Tikos, in *International Fiction Review* (Fredericton, New Brunswick), 2, 1975; "The Literary Criticism of Abram Tertz" by Albert Leong, in *Proceedings of the Pacific Northwest Conference on Foreign Languages*, 28(1), 1977; "The Bible and the Zoo in Andrey Sinyavsky's *The Trial Begins*" by Richard L. Chapple, in *Orbis Litterarum* (Copenhagen), 33, 1978; "Narrator, Metaphor and Theme in Sinjavskij's *Fantastic Tales*" by Andrew R. Durkin, in *Slavic and East European Journal* (Minneapolis), 24, 1980; "'The Icicle' as Allegory" by Grace Anne Morsberger, in *Odyssey*, 4(2), 1981; "Andrei Sinyavsky's 'You and I': A Modern Day Fantastic Tale" by Catharine Theimer Nepomnyashchy, in *Ulbandus Review*, 2(2), 1982; "The Writer as Alien in Sinjavskij's 'Pkhens'" by Ronald E. Peterson, in *Wiener Slawistischer Almanach* (Vienna), 12, 1983; "Conflicting Imperatives in the Model of the Russian Writer: The Case of Tertz/Sinyavsky" by Donald Fanger, in *Literature and History: Theoretical Problems and Russian Case Studies*, edited by Gary Saul Morson, Stanford, California,

Stanford University Press, 1986; "*Spokojnoj noci*: Andrej Sinjavskij's Rebirth as Abram Terc" by Olga Matich, in *Slavic and East European Journal* (Minneapolis), 33(1), 1989.

*   *   *

Prior to his arrest and imprisonment in 1965, Andrei Siniavskii led two lives: one as a respected literary critic, the other, under the pseudonym Abram Terts, as the author of literature that could not be published in the Soviet Union for reasons of both its manner and its message. Siniavskii established his second identity with the programmatic essay, *On Socialist Realism*, in which he put his knowledge of Russian literary history to good use. Here he employs the same devices that were to appear in his fiction — irony and satire — to undermine the foundations of socialist realism, the method that from the 1930s until the 1980s was, in theory at least, supposed to guide Soviet writers in the thematic and the formal aspects of their writing. Pointing out that no logical connection exists between the terms "socialism" and "realism," Siniavskii goes on to show that the supposedly atheistic Marxism in fact bears numerous resemblances to Christian dogma, and that writing purporting to advocate socialism or any other set of beliefs turns out to share more affinities with romanticism than realism. Further, attempts to impose an ideology result in a static literary tradition, within which writers are not free to express their inner selves or to explore the ambiguities that are the hallmark of great literature.

The career of Siniavskii/Terts, therefore, has served as an antipode to both socialism and realism. His first novel, *Sud idet* (*The Trial Begins*), already contains shifts in narrative voice along with elements of fantasy and the grotesque that mark a determined break with the realistic tradition. An exuberant style, exaggerated depictions, and sexual frankness (all to a greater or lesser extent taboo under socialist realism) are employed to reveal a variety of attitudes, from outright resistance to enthusiastic conformity, toward the demands of a rigid ideology. In showing the stolid determination with which the secret police track down and arrest those guilty of dissent, Siniavskii both evokes the atmosphere of a totalitarian state and provides an eerie foreshadowing of his own fate.

Liubimov (*The Makepeace Experiment*), the other novel written by Siniavskii before his arrest, is equally inventive and perhaps the greater literary achievement. His technique is similar, but here the attack on socialism is presented in near-mythic terms. The protagonist uses magical powers to impose on his backwater town a caricature of a socialist regime, which eventually collapses under its own weight. Opposed to the would-be ruler's secular miracles are the simple but sincere beliefs of his mother and the spirituality of a village priest. A non-dogmatic religious sensibility provides something far more lasting than the ultimately ephemeral promises of material wealth. In the autobiographical novel, *Spokoinoi nochi* (*Goodnight!*), composed after he had already settled in France but once again signed with the nom de plume Terts, Siniavskii explores his own apostasy from Communism and the subsequent cat-and-mouse game he played with the state. The most ambitious of his writings, it presents not only his personal history, but also a discourse on the nature of Stalinism and an inquiry into the meaning of guilt and responsibility under a coercive regime. The biographical framework makes *Goodnight!* more accessible than much of his other fiction; however, the often bizarre digressions show that he has lost none of his imaginativeness, and the work as a whole reveals the full breadth of his interests in philosophy, history, religion, and myth.

Siniavskii's shorter fiction is generally less political than his novels, but the protagonists are again nearly always alienated from society. The grotesque and the fantastic emerge even more strongly in the stories, where they serve to highlight extreme psychological states. It is often hard to be sure whether a given scene belongs to the realm of fantasy or represents a character's distorted view of the world; at times Siniavskii appears to be purposefully ambiguous. The story "You and I" is among his most obscure; much of it employs a second-person narration, which addresses the "You" of the title directly. Some critics feel the work depicts a single figure, who suffers from both paranoia and schizophrenia, while others believe that the relationship being described is more that between some godlike figure and the "You" — it is possible to find evidence to support any of several interpretations. For all their unreal elements and references to technology, few of Siniavskii's stories seem to bear a close affinity to science fiction; however, "Pkhentz," perhaps the most widely anthologized of his short stories, provides an exception. It describes the lonely fate of an alien creature stranded on our planet, detailing the revulsion that this being, who must contort his body into a human shape to hide his true identity, feels toward such basic human activities as sex and eating. The first-person narrative, more straightforward than is usually the case in the stories, can be seen both as an allegory for the way in which society seems to demand conformity, or, on a more personal level, for the dilemma faced by the writer Terts (a name that bears some resemblance to Pkhentz) who similarly had to mask his actual nature from those around him.

The critical pieces that Siniavskii produced under his own name before his imprisonment lack the stylistic inventiveness of his stories, but they already reveal him as a probing and sensitive critic, most notably in the long introduction he wrote for a major 1965 collection of Boris Pasternak's poetry (an English version of which can be found in *For Freedom of Imagination*). In the years following his arrest and his emigration Siniavskii has emerged as an important essayist as well. Interestingly, he has employed the pseudonym Terts for many of these works, as though to emphasize their imaginative (and often polemic) qualities. His *Progulki s Pushkinym* (Strolls with Pushkin) has created controversy both when it was first published in the West and again when, under glasnost, it finally became possible for the work to appear in the Soviet Union: his seemingly irreverent treatment of Russia's greatest poet has been difficult for many to accept. A major work that has appeared under his own name is *Osnovy sovetskoi tsivilizatsii* (*Soviet Civilization: A Cultural History*), where he develops some of the ideas outlined in both his fiction and his earlier essays. He details the nature of the "civilization" that the Soviet leadership attempted to impose on its people, the reasons why their utopian vision degenerated into terrorism, and the effect that the new state had on literature, the arts, the spiritual life of the people, and even on language.

Siniavskii is by nature an enemy of the comfortable. His writings are challenging both in their form and in their message; if at one time their purpose seemed specifically to question the tenets of the Soviet state, he can now be seen as a writer whose broader goal is to test general assumptions about culture and morality at the same time that he probes the effects of dogma on individuals and on the arts.

—Barry P. Scherr

SINIAVSKY, Andrei. *See* SINIAVSKII, Andrei.

SIRCAR, Badal. Indian. Born Sudhīndra Sircar in Calcutta, 15 July 1925. Educated at Calcutta University, B.E. 1947, diploma in town and regional planning 1952; University of London, 1957–59, diploma in town planning; town planning training in France, 1963–64. Engineer in Nagpur, Maithin, and Calcutta, 1947–57; principal town planning officer, East Nigerian Government, Enugu, 1964–67; founder, Śatābdī theatre group, 1967, and Aṅganmañc theatre group, 1972, both Calcutta; training adviser, then chief town planner, Calcutta Metropolitan Planning Organisation, 1968–71; Jawaharlal Nehru Fellow, 1971–73; director of planning, Comprehensive Area Development Corporation, Calcutta, 1974–77. Toured United Kingdom and Pakistan giving theatre workshops and lectures, 1980s. Recipient: Giriś Nāṭya Pratiyogitā award, 1963; Saṅgīt Nāṭak Akādemī award, 1968; Padma Śrī, 1972. Address: 1A Peary Row, Calcutta 700006, India.

PUBLICATIONS

Plays

Solution X (produced 1956).
Baṛo piṣimā [Aunt] (produced Calcutta, 1959).
Śanibār [Saturday] (produced 1959).
Rām Śyām Jadu (produced 1961).
Samabritta (produced 1961).
Evam Indrajīt (produced 1963; Calcutta, 1965). Calcutta, Oxford University Press, 1974; as *And Indrajīt Too* (produced Madras, 1970), in *Three Modern Indian Plays*, New Delhi, Oxford University Press, 1989.
Shārā rāttrī [The Whole Night] (produced 1963; Calcutta, 1969).
Ballabpurer rūpkathā [Ballabpurer's Fable] (produced 1963; Calcutta, 1970).
Pare kono din [Then Someday] (produced 1966).
Jadi ār ekbār [If There Were Another Chance], adaptation of *Dear Brutus* by J. M. Barrie (produced 1966).
Paglā ghoṛā [Mad Horse] (produced Calcutta, 1967).
Kabi-kahinī [A Poet's Tale] (produced Calcutta, 1968).
Bāgh [Tiger], adaptation of the play by Murray Schisgal (produced Calcutta, 1968).
Bicitra anusthān [Variety Programme] (produced Calcutta, 1968).
Pralāp [Mad Speech], adaptation of *Next Time I'll Sing to You* by James Saunders (produced Calcutta, 1968).
Śeṣ neī (produced Calcutta, 1970). As *There's No End*, published in *ENACT* (New Delhi), 59, 1971.
Marital: A Mini Play (produced Calcutta, 1970). Published in *ENACT* (New Delhi), 44/45, 1970.
Sagino Mahto, adaptation of a story by Gour Kiśore Ghoṣ (produced Calcutta, 1971).
Abu Hossain, adaptation of a play by Giriś Candra Ghoṣ (produced Calcutta, 1972).
Spartacus, adaptation of the novel by Howard Fast (produced Calcutta, 1973).
Prastāb [Proposition] (produced Calcutta, 1973).
Muktamelā [Open Fair] (produced Calcutta, 1973).

Michil (produced Calcutta, 1974).   As *Procession*, in *Three Plays*, 1985.

Triṅgśā śatābdī [The 30th Century] (produced Calcutta, 1974).

Lakṣmīcharar pañcalī (produced Calcutta, 1974).

Bhanumatik khel [Bhanumatik's Magic] (produced Calcutta, 1974).

Nidhirāmer rājya [Nidhirām's Kingdom] (produced Calcutta, 1974).

Rūpkathār keleṅkari, adaptation of a story by Premendra Mitra (produced Calcutta, 1975).   As *Scandal in Fairyland*, with *Beyond the Land of Hattamala*, Calcutta, Seagull, 1992.

Bhomā (produced Calcutta, 1976).   In English, in *Three Plays*, 1985.

Sukhapathya bhāratu itihās [Indian History Made Easy] (produced Calcutta, 1976).

Bhaṅga manuṣ (produced Calcutta, 1977).

Mani-kañcen [Jewel] (produced Calcutta, 1977).

Hattamālār oparey (produced Calcutta, 1977).   As *Beyond the Land of Hattamālā*, with *Scandal in Fairyland*, Calcutta, Seagull, 1992.

Bākī itihās (produced Calcutta, 1977).   As *That Other History*, published in *ENACT* (New Delhi), 123–124, 1977.

Goṇḍi, adaptation of *The Caucasian Chalk Circle* by Bertolt Brecht (produced Calcutta, 1978).   Calcutta, Sri Aurobindo Press, 1978.

Bāsī khabar (produced Calcutta, 1979).   As *Stale News*, in *Three Plays*, 1985.

Ekṭi hatyār naṭyakathā, adaptation of *Marat/Sade* by Peter Weiss (produced Calcutta, 1980).

Manuṣey, manuṣey [Man-Man] (produced Calcutta, 1981).

Naginī kanyā kahini [Snake's Daughter], adaptation of a story by Arashanker Bandyopadhyāy (produced Calcutta, 1982).

Khaṭ mat kning (produced Calcutta, 1983).

Sīrī [Stairway] (produced Calcutta, 1985).

Three Plays (includes *Procession*; *Bhoma*; *Stale News*). Calcutta, Seagull, 1985.

Janmabhūmi āj [Poetry Montage], with B. Chattopadhya and M. Bhattacharya (produced Calcutta, 1986).

Sādo-kālo [White and Black], adaptation of *Woza Albert!* by Barney Simon, Mtongeni Ngema, and Percy Mtwa (produced Calcutta, 1987).

Curhā prithivī [Fragmented World] (produced Calcutta, 1988).

Bioscope (produced Calcutta, 1989).

Bhūl rāstā [The Wrong Way] (produced Calcutta, 1989).

Padmā nadīr mājhī [Boatman of the River Padma], adaptation of a novel by Manik Bandyopadhyāy (produced Calcutta, 1990).

Androcles o sinha, adaptation of *Androcles and the Lion* by G. B. Shaw (produced Calcutta, 1991).

Other

The Third Theatre.   Privately printed, 1978.

The Changing Language of Theatre.   New Delhi, Indian Council for Cultural Relations, 1982.

Thiyetarer bhāṣā.   Kolkātā, Paribeśak Nab Grantha Kuṭīr, 1983.

*

Critical Studies: in *Rehearsals of Revolution: The Political Theater of Bengal*, Calcutta, Seagull, 1983; *Performative Circumstances from the Avant Garde to Ramlila* by Richard Schechner, Calcutta, Seagull, 1983.

*   *   *

The Bengali playwright, director, and actor Badal Sircar's work with his Calcutta-based theatre group Satabdi has been among the most significant and influential of contemporary Indian drama since the late 1960s.

The transition in Sircar's writing following the national prominence he gained with *Evam Indrajīt* (*And Indrajit Too*) in 1962 was stimulated by his desire to move away from the confines of the conventional proscenium arch stage towards the discovery of non-traditional performance spaces, and a concomitant emphasis on the fundamental importance of a direct relationship between performer and spectator. Performance places have included the intimate setting of a room or small hall in buildings such as the Academy of Fine Arts in Calcutta, as well as outdoor venues such as Curzon Park where Satabdi's productions over the years have attracted a popular audience of many thousands of spectators.

In *Evam Indrajīt*, several of the characters who people the imagination of a central figure of The Writer are literally drawn out from the audience. Amal, Kamal, Vimal, and Indrajīt are perhaps more "types" than characters, caught up in the pursuit of middle-class ambitions of educational achievement, career moves, materialism, and marriage prospects. This early example already indicates Sircar's disinterest in the psychology of his dramatic creations and instead his concern with social and economic factors which determine choices and lives. While the different kinds of responsibility facing the creative artist and the frequent misunderstandings by others provide one aspect of the play's theme, Sircar's construction of a special, symbiotic relationship between Indrajīt and The Writer sets up a simple theatrical metaphor for the dialectic between the public and private selves of a single individual experiencing alienation from the expected norms of the society in which he finds himself. The play has been located in absurdist traditions, though the pessimism of the final note, as Indrajīt's three contemporaries drift into the anonymity of conventional bourgeois existence, is muted by the redemptive power of the conscience which The Writer manages to engender in his last remaining creation.

It would be impossible to ignore the impact of Sircar's exposure in the late 1960s to European and American theatre practice, by way of cultural exchange programmes to the U.S.S.R., Poland, and Czechoslovakia (where he had the opportunity of seeing productions by Yuri Lyubimov and Jerzy Grotowski, among others) and through his later stay in New York where he encountered Julian Beck's Living Theatre and the work of Richard Schechner. Yet, ironically perhaps, these visits served to emphasise the intrinsic value of the direct communication of the Indian folk theatre and dance forms Sircar had left behind and which the western practitioners were at that time "discovering." Sircar's ideas found synthesis in *The Third Theatre*, a research project completed with a Jawaharlal Nehru fellowship which identified the possibilities of bridging the rural-urban divide in India through the use of theatre workshops and performances, liberated from the physical constraints of the city's proscenium arch and the ideological constraints inherent in village folk and traditional theatres' absence of contemporary, relevant social themes.

Sircar's work is not explicitly politically partisan insofar as he refuses to align himself with any one political party, preferring instead to preserve the integrity that this independence affords him. Sircar's motivation for writing has become characterised by a passionate personal response to the injustices and oppressions endured in the lives of the poor and disenfranchised, both by his own country and beyond. The themes of his plays are located in struggle against the inertia of complacency and ignorance. Yet his plays do not have the revolutionary rhetoric of his Bengali contemporary and uncompromising Marxist Utpal Dutt. They depend instead on a recognition that responsibility for change must rest at an individual level before a collective response is possible.

At a time when India was developing its own nuclear capability, Sircar wrote a trilogy of plays which derived its impetus from the devastation of Hiroshima and Nagasaki. *Bākī itihās* (*That Other History*), *Triṅśā śatābdī* (*The 30th Century*), and *Śeṣ neī* (*There's No End*) examine crimes against humanity and the guilt and responsibility which accompany them.

In many ways Sircar's theatre form has become inextricably linked to the notion that the "message" is more important than the aesthetic means by which it is conveyed. In this sense his theatre is "poor," stripped of any excesses of decorative embellishments, elaborate costumes, scenery, lights, and so on. *Sagino Mahto* was the first of many plays to be produced in this way, charting the rise and fall of a committed worker attempting to achieve improvements in the working conditions of his colleagues. Similarly, Sircar's adaptation of Howard Fast's novel *Spartacus* proved to be greatly enhanced by the powerful theatrical simplicity of its staging, the Satabdi actors choreographed into a striking physicality to convey the toil of the Romans' slaves, rhythmically accompanied by *dhol* (drum) percussion and song, ubiquitous features of Sircar's plays. Sircar's use of chorus is vital, stressing the universal nature of the characters he creates in his plays as the actors fluidly take on roles and then merge back into the group.

Michil (*Procession*) has proved an immensely successful play, using the noisy, chaotic, evocation of Calcutta's crowded streets in a theatrical setting which incorporates an audience on pathways around the acting arena in a fast-moving satirical tragicomedy of police repression, establishment hypocrisy, race riot, and personal loss of direction. Sircar's skill is often in placing snatches of colloquial conversation overheard on crowded buses, at the street corner, or the market place, in ironic juxtaposition with the dry language of power from the mouths of politicians or from along the corridors of bureaucratic offices. Such sound collages have a poetic intensity about them, yet Sircar's intention is never a purely aesthetic one.

In recent years Sircar has organised *parikrama*, or shows taken to the rural areas, in the Sundarbans and other Bengali districts. Plays such as *Bhomā* have been created from this contact, dealing specifically with the difficulties encountered by impoverished villagers. Performed in Calcutta, such plays deny an urban audience the opportunity to turn away from their responsibilities, however remote. Sircar's own writing, and adaptations of George Bernard Shaw, Bertolt Brecht, and Peter Weiss, among others, continues to be driven by his passionate belief in the medium of a "free" theatre as being the most direct means of conveying his ideas to the widest possible audience.

—Chris Banfield

SKÁRMETA, Antonio. Chilean. Born in Antofagasta, 7 November 1940. Educated at the University of Chile, Santiago; Columbia University, New York, M.A. Married Cecilia Boisier in 1964 (divorced); two sons. Professor of contemporary Latin American literature, University of Chile,

early 1970s; left Chile after military coup in 1973; Professor of screenwriting, Film and Television Academy, West Berlin, 1978–81; since 1981 freelance writer and filmmaker. Recipient: Fulbright fellowship; Casa de las Américas prize, 1969; Daniel Belmar prize, 1969; Biarritz Film Festival prize, 1983; Huelva Film Festival prize, 1983; Guggenheim fellowship, 1986. Agent: Carmen Balcells Literary Agency, Diagonal 580, 08021 Barcelona, Spain.

PUBLICATIONS

Fiction

El entusiasmo.   Santiago, Zig-Zag, 1967.
Desnudo en el tejado.   Buenos Aires, Sudamericana, 1969.
Tiro libre.   Buenos Aires, Siglo XXI, 1973.
El ciclista del San Cristóbal.   Santiago, Quimantú, 1973.
Soñé que la nieve ardía.   Barcelona, Planeta, 1975; as *I Dreamt the Snow Was Burning*, London, Readers International, 1985.
Novios y solitarios.   Buenos Aires, Losada, 1975.
Chileno!   New York, Morrow, 1979.
La insurrección.   Hanover, New Hampshire, Ediciones del Norte, 1982; as *The Insurrection*, Ediciones del Norte, 1983.
No pasó nada y otros relatos.   Santiago, Pehuén, 1985.
Ardiente paciencia.   Buenos Aires, Sudamericana, and Hanover, New Hampshire, Ediciones del Norte, 1985; as *Burning Patience*, New York, Pantheon, 1987; London, Methuen, 1988.
Match Ball (in Spanish).   Buenos Aires, Sudamericana, 1989.
Watch Where the Wolf Is Going.   London, Readers International, 1991.

Plays

Screenplays: *Es herrscht Rue im Land*; *La insurrección*, from his novel; *Ardiente paciencia*, from his novel, 1983.

Other

Translator, with Cecilia Boisier, *La casa en París* [The House in Paris], by Elizabeth Bowen.   Santiago, Zig-Zag, 1969.

*

Critical Studies: "'La cencienta en San Francisco' by Antonio Skármeta," in *Revista de Estudios Hispánicos* (Poughkeepsie, New York), 21(2), 1987, "Fictional Technique in Skármeta's *La insurrección*," in *Antípodas*, 3, 1991, and "The Structure of Antonio Skármeta's *Soñé que la nieve ardía*," in *The Americas Review* (Houston), 18(3–4), 1990, all by Donald L. Shaw; "Toward a Revolutionary Writing: Antonio Skármeta's *La insurrección*" by Jonathan Tittler, in *Literature and Revolution*, edited by David Bevan, Amsterdam, Rodopi, 1989.

*   *   *

Like many young writers of the 1960s in Latin America Antonio Skármeta was first drawn to literature through short stories. In his case, these stories revolved around everyday situations in which the characters dreamed of other possibilities, only to be defeated by the absurdities of life. At the end of the 1960s, Skármeta became swept up in the political events when Salvador Allende's Popular Unity government attempted to take his native Chile along its own path toward socialism. Skármeta's stories became more overtly political, in support of the changes taking place. With the military coup that toppled Allende in 1973, Skármeta left Chile to live in exile, and it was then that he began to write novels, coloured by his political experiences and by living outside of his native country.

The first of these novels, *Soñé que la nieve ardía* (*I Dreamt the Snow Was Burning*), was first published in 1975. The title is taken from a popular song of the Allende period, and the book's events take place around the meeting of a non-politically-minded footballer, Arturo, who comes from the provinces, with a group of politically active youngsters in the capital. Skármeta attempts to convey the different components of a society involved in trying to make a revolution work, but his message is a sombre one, since the city youngsters are killed after the 1973 military takeover, while Arturo returns disillusioned and apparently none the wiser to his home province. Skármeta's strengths appear to be in capturing popular speech and the new ideas being debated at that time, along with a talent for the humorous observation of incongruity which is not allowed free rein by the tragic circumstances described in the novel.

These are also the strong points of Skármeta's novel *Ardiente paciencia* (*Burning Patience*), whose title is a quotation from the work of the famous Chilean poet Pablo Neruda. The book imagines that the poet meets and becomes interested in the local postman at his seaside home of Isla Negra. Since the poet is the only person in the place who can read and receive letters, the postman is a regular visitor with plenty of time on his hands. He "borrows" the poet's verses to help him in his amorous conquests, and later repays his debt when the poet himself is far from his beloved home in Paris. Contrasts of language and scenes of absurdity are once again to the fore; one critic has written of the book "this conflict between literate and non-literate cultures allows for some amusing reflections on the role of the written word as a vehicle for popular aspirations, the suggestion being that the written word has to be translated into oral performance in order to become an 'act'."

Skármeta's other novels of exile also stress the importance of language, as he tried in his writing to keep his native country alive for himself. *Chileno!* dealt with a Chilean adolescent in Berlin, while *La insurrección* (*The Insurrection*) describes a village rising against the oppression of the Somoza dynasty in Nicaragua. Gradually, though, the years abroad left Skármeta starved of contact with his first real inspiration, the spoken language of his own country. This was reflected in a falling-off in his literary production, as he turned to writing screenplays and to teaching creative writing. More recently, after the return of an elected civilian government, Skármeta has returned to Chile. It is to be hoped that this reunion with his country will lead to a renewed exploration of the evolving popular language and ideas of a new generation.

—Nick Caistor

ŠKVORECKÝ, Josef (Václav). Has also written as Jan Zábrana. Czech and Canadian. Born in Náchod, Czechoslovakia, 27 September 1924; became Canadian citizen, 1976. Educated at Charles University, Prague, Ph.D. 1951. Served in the Czechoslovak Army Tank Corps, 1951–53. Married Zdena Salivarová in 1958. Editor, State Publishing House, Prague, 1953–56, and 1959–63, and *Světová Literatura* [World Literature] magazine, Prague, 1956–59; freelance writer, Prague, 1963–68; Visiting Lecturer, 1969–70, writer-in-residence, 1970–71, Associate Professor of English, 1971–75, Professor of English, 1975–90, and since 1990 Professor Emeritus, University of Toronto; writer-in-residence, Northwestern University, Evanston, Illinois, 1984, University of British Columbia, Vancouver, 1984, and Amherst College, Massachusetts, 1985–86. Since 1973 editor, 68 Publishers, Toronto; since 1973 lecturer on literary topics, Voice of America; member of the Board of Directors, Toronto Arts Council, 1984–85; member of Board of Consultants to the Czechoslovak President, from 1990. Recipient: Czechoslovak Writers Union award, 1967; Canada Council grant, 1978; Neustadt International prize, 1980; Guggenheim fellowship, 1980, Governor-General's award, 1985; City of Toronto Book award, 1985; Ontario Bicentennial Medal; Foundation for the Advancement of Canadian Letters award, 1988; František Martin Pelcl Medal, 1990; Palacký University Medal, 1990; Echoing Green Foundation prize, 1990. D.H.L.: State University of New York, 1986; Doctor scientiae artium honoris cause: Masaryk University, Brno, 1991. Fellow, Royal Society of Canada, 1984; Order of the White Lion (Czechoslovakia), 1990; Honorary Citizen, City of Prague, 1990, and town of Náchod, 1990. Agent: Louise Dennys, Lester and Orpen Dennys Inc., 78 Sullivan Street, Toronto, Ontario M5T 1C1, Canada. Address: 487 Sackville Street, Toronto, Ontario M4X 1T6, Canada.

PUBLICATIONS

Fiction

Divák v únorové noci [The Viewer in the February Night]. Prague, samizdat, 1948; Prague, Listy, 1989.
Zbabělci. Prague, Československý spisovatel, 1958; as *The Cowards*, New York, Grove Press, and London, Gollancz, 1970.
Vražda pro štěstí [Murder for Luck] (as Jan Zábrana). Prague, Mladá fronta, 1962.
Legenda Emöke. Prague, Československý spisovatel, 1963; as *Emöke*, in *The Bass Saxophone*, 1977.
Sedmiramenný svícen [The Menorah]. Prague, Naše Vojsko, 1964.
Vražda se zárukou [Guaranteed Murder] (as Jan Zábrana). Prague, Mladá fronta, 1964.
Ze života lepší společnosti [The Life of High Society]. Prague, Mladá fronta, 1965.
Smutek poručíka Borůvky. Prague, Mladá fronta, 1966; as *The Mournful Demeanour of Lieutenant Boruvka*, London, Gollancz, 1974; New York, Norton, 1987.
Bassaxofon. Prague, Svobodné Slovo, 1967; as *The Bass Saxophone* (includes *Emöke*), Toronto, Anson Cartwright, 1977; London, Chatto and Windus, 1978; New York, Knopf, 1979; as *Dvě legendy* [Two Legends], Toronto, 68 Publishers, 1982.
Babylonský příběh [A Babylonian Story]. Prague, Svobodné Slovo, 1967.
Konec nylonového věku [The End of the Nylon Age]. Prague, Československý spisovatel, 1967.
Vražda v zastoupení [Murder by Proxy] (as Jan Zábrana). Prague, Mladá fronta, 1967.
Farářuv konec [End of a Priest] (novelization of screenplay). Hradec Králové, Kruh, 1969.
Lvíče. Prague, Československý spisovatel, 1969; as *Miss Silver's Past*, New York, Grove Press, 1974; London, Bodley Head, 1976.

Hořkej svět: povídky z let 1946–1967 [The Bitter World: Selected Stories 1946–1967]. Prague, Odeon, 1969.
Tankový prapor [The Tank Battalion]. Prague, Československý spisovatel, 1969; Toronto, 68 Publishers, 1971.
Mirákl. Toronto, 68 Publishers, 1972; London, Rozmluvy, 1986; as *The Miracle Game*, London, Faber, and New York, Knopf, 1991.
Oh, My Papa! Tokyo, Asahi Press, 1972.
Hříchy pro pátera Knoxe. Toronto, 68 Publishers, 1973; as *Sins for Father Knox*, Toronto, Lester and Orpen Dennys, 1988; London, Faber, and New York, Norton, 1989.
Konec poručíka Borůvky. Toronto, 68 Publishers, 1975; as *The End of Lieutenant Boruvka*, Toronto, Lester and Orpen Dennys, 1989; London, Faber, and New York, Norton, 1990.
Prima sezóna. Toronto, 68 Publishers, 1975; as *The Swell Season: A Text on the Most Important Things in Life*, Toronto, Lester and Orpen Dennys, and London, Chatto and Windus, 1983; New York, Ecco Press, 1986.
Příběh inženýra lidských duší. Toronto, 68 Publishers, 2 vols., 1977; as *The Engineer of Human Souls*, Toronto, Lester and Orpen Dennys, and New York, Knopf, 1984; London, Chatto and Windus, 1985.
Návrat poručíka Borůvky. Toronto, 68 Publishers, 1981; as *The Return of Lieutenant Boruvka*, Toronto, Lester and Orpen Dennys, and London, Faber, 1990; New York, Norton, 1991.
Scherzo capriccioso: veselý sen o Dvořákovi. Toronto, 68 Publishers, 1984; as *Dvořák in Love*, Toronto, Lester and Orpen Dennys, and London, Chatto and Windus, 1986; New York, Knopf, 1987.
Ze života české společnosti [The Life of the Czech Society]. Toronto, 68 Publishers, 1985.
Nevěsta z Texasu [A Bride from Texas]. Toronto, 68 Publishers, 1992.

Plays

Bůh do domu [God in Your House] (produced Toronto, 1980). Toronto, 68 Publishers, 1980.

Screenplays: *Zločin v dívčí škole* [Crime in a Girls' School], 1966; *Zločin v šantánu* [Crime in a Nightclub], 1968; *Farářův konec* [End of a Priest], 1968; *Flirt se slečnou Stříbrnou* [Flirtations with Miss Silver], 1969; *Šest černých dívek* [Six Brunettes], 1969.

Radio Play: *The New Men and Women*, 1977 (Canada).

Television Plays: *Revue proj banjo* [The Banjo Show], 1965; *Vědecké metody poručíka Borůvky* series [The Scientific Methods of Lieutenant Boruvka], 1967–68.

Verse

Nezoufejte! [Do Not Despair!]. Munich, Poezie mimo domov, 1980.
Dívka z Chicaga a jiné hříchy mládí: básně z let 1940–1945 [A Girl from Chicago and Other Sins of Youth: Poems from 1940–1945]. Munich, Poezie mimo domov, 1980.

Other

Nápady čtenáře detektivek [Reading Detective Stories]. Prague, Československý spisovatel, 1965.
Táňa a dva pistolníci [Tanya and the Two Gunmen] (for children). Prague, Svě Sovětu, 1966.

O nich — o nás [They – Which Is We] (essays on American literature). Hradec Králové, Kruh, 1968.
All the Bright Young Men and Women: A Personal History of the Czech Cinema. Toronto, Peter Martin Associates, 1971.
Na brigádě [Working Overtime] (essays on contemporary Czech writers), with Antonin Brousek. Toronto, 68 Publishers, 1979.
Velká povídka o Americe (1969) [A Tall Tale about America]. Toronto, 68 Publishers, 1980.
Jiří Menzel and the History of the Closely Watched Trains. Boulder, Colorado, East European Monographs, 1982.
Útěky [Escapes] (ghostwritten autobiography of Lída Baarová). Toronto, 68 Publishers, 1983.
Talkin' Moscow Blues, edited by Sam Solecki. Toronto, Lester and Orpen Dennys, 1988; New York, Ecco Press, and London, Faber, 1989; revised edition, as *Franz Kafka, jazz a jiné marginálie*, Toronto, 68 Publishers, 1988.
Hlas z Ameriky [A Voice from America] (book reviews). Toronto, 68 Publishers, 1989.

Editor, with Lubomír Dorůžka, *Tvář jazzu* [The Face of Jazz]. Prague, Státní Hudební Vydavatelství, 2 vols., 1964–66.
Editor, with Lubomír Dorůžka, *Jazz ová inspirace* [The Jazz Inspiration]. Prague, Odeon, 1966.
Editor, *Nachrichten aus der ČSSR* [News from Czechoslovakia]. Frankfurt, Suhrkamp, 1968.
Editor, *Miss Rosie*, by Bartoš Bittner. Toronto, 68 Publishers, 1986.

Translator of works by Ray Bradbury, Henry James, Ernest Hemingway, William Faulkner, Sinclair Lewis, Alan Sillitoe, Dashiell Hammett, Raymond Chandler, and William Styron.

*

Critical Studies: Škvorecký issue of *World Literature Today* (Norman, Oklahoma), 54, 1980; "The Language and Style of Škvorecký's *The Cowards*" by Václav Pletánek, in *Canadian Slavonic Papers* (Edmonton, Alberta), 23(4), 1981; "An Interview with Josef Škvorecký" by Geoffrey Hancock, in *Canadian Fiction Magazine* (Toronto), 1982–83; "A Literary Bridge Between Canada and Central Europe: Thoughts on the Translation of Josef Škvorecký's New Novel *The Engineer of Human Souls*," in *Translation in Canadian Literature*, edited by Camille R. La Bossière, Ottawa, University of Ottawa Press, 1983, and "Literary Mirrors," in *Canadian Literature* (Vancouver), 110, 1986, both by Marketa Goetz-Stankiewicz; "An Interview with Josef Škvorecký" by Kerry Regier, in *West Coast Review*, 21(3), 1987; "The Bittersweet Fruits of Exile: George Jonas and Josef Škvorecký" by Peter Buitenhuis, in *Cross Cultural Studies: American, Canadian and European Literatures: 1945–1985*, edited by Mirko Jurak, Ljubljana, Filozofska Fakulteta, 1988; "'Where Is My Home?': Some Notes on Reading Josef Škvorecký in 'America'" by Sam Solecki, in *Canadian Literature* (Vancouver), 120, 1989; *The Fiction of Josef Škvorecký* by Paul I. Trensky, New York, Macmillan, 1991.

*   *   *

"You're playing about the same thing all the time," a mother is said to have complained to her saxophonist son. Unwittingly, she pronounced a comment that fits jazz as well as nearly all literature. It certainly applies to the work of the Czech writer Josef Škvorecký. Since his earliest and perhaps most successful novel, *Zbabělci* (*The Cowards*), written in 1948 but published 10 years later, he has pursued an ever elusive main theme: the magic of the world when it is young and the eternal game of love that young men and women play in it. Even when he deviated from his preoccupation to examine other subjects, this theme's presence could still be felt under the surface.

Over the years, Škvorecký has explored the theme in various contexts and settings. The backbone of his work consists of several books which follow the adventures of Danny Smiřický, in whom it is not difficult to recognize the author's alter ego, created of both reality and fantasy. As his life story proceeds, Danny ages, but his principal attitudes remain those of a young man. He first appears in *The Cowards*, just turned 20, and, with an irreverence and cynicism quite natural and appropriate to his age, views the hypocritical antics of his senior fellow Czechoslovak citizens as they struggle to keep their respectability and positions at the end of World War II. Following in his author's footsteps, Danny turns up in his latest incarnation in *Příběh inženýra lidských duší* (*The Engineer of Human Souls*), far from his native Czechoslovakia as a middle-aged professor of English and American literature at a Canadian university. He still regards the world with some disdain, albeit tinged now with amused resignation.

In between lies a historical epoch, nearly three decades of the turbulent 20th century. Danny has had his share of it: soon after the end of the Nazi occupation of Czechoslovakia came the Stalinist years, then new hope in the 1960s cut short by the Soviet invasion in 1968, followed by exile in Canada. This entire period comes to life in Škvorecký's novels. Service in the People's Army in the 1950s has been recorded in the hilariously satirical *Tankový prapor* (The Tank Battalion) and the sadly failed attempt to combine socialism and freedom in *Mirákl* (*The Miracle Game*).

Those, however, are only the surface features of the social, temporal, and physical landscapes through which Danny passes on his pilgrimage. Deceptive as the great *theatrum mundi* may be, Danny is endowed with a perception that allows him to unveil the true nature of the roles that people play in it. Retold by him, it looks more like a farce than a drama. But only a very inexperienced reader would miss the serious note, the bittersweet and sometimes tragic ostinato under the thrilling, joyful tones. The world is wonderful, but deadly.

On the other hand, there are ways to escape the constant reminder of this inevitability. In the midst of the cruelty, betrayal, baseness, and ordinary stupidity that corrupt the world, Škvorecký finds several points of reassurance and security, to which he returns again and again. He is particularly attached to the memories of the times and place where we first meet young Danny (Czechoslovakia in the late 1940s), and he revisits those years frequently in his stories, notably in *Prima sezóna* (*The Swell Season*). On such occasions, Škvorecký's own kind of nostalgia becomes prominent, even in those novels and short stories where other characters besides Danny are the central figure or narrator.

Another source of reassurance is jazz. *The Cowards* is a jazz novel not just because it turns around a youthful jazz band; neither is *Bassaxofon* (*The Bass Saxophone*) exclusively the celebration of one musical instrument. The spirit of the music underlies Škvorecký's writing. His style has been affected by the clipped phrases of the trumpet and the smooth runs of the saxophone, and his outlook shaped by the yearning and the ecstasy that can be heard in jazz. In Nazi-occupied Europe it was the symbol of freedom; in the Stalinist years it signified irrepressible creativity; in happier times it has been the provider of elation. In the words of the composer George

Handy, "jazz originated as the outgrowth of the emotions of a frustrated people; but these emotions belong to all of us."

Škvorecký continued to transform these emotions into prose even after Danny was finally left behind; it was difficult to imagine that much more could be added to his life story so exhaustively covered in *The Engineer of Human Souls*. American music, however, still resounds in the pages of a historical novel based on a completely different personality: *Scherzo capriccioso* (*Dvořák in Love*) deals with the composer's sojourn in the United States, and like his music, the mood of the writing is almost exuberant. Škvorecký's most recent book, *Nevěsta z Texasu* (A Bride from Texas), is another historical novel, set during the American Civil War. At the centre of a complex story is a group of Czech volunteers fighting for the Union. It would take a few decades yet before jazz would emerge, but its roots are already there, in the songs of the black slaves for whose freedom the young Czech farmers are laying down their lives. Although the novel is based on solid and detailed research, only Škvorecký's humour and compassion could bring these people to life. It is also an apotheosis of the democratic spirit of America and indirectly of the freedom once again enjoyed by Škvorecký's native country.

—Igor Hájek

———

SOBOL, Joshua. *See* **SOBOL, Yehoshua.**

———

SOBOL, Yehoshua. Also Joshua Sobol. Israeli. Born Tel Mond, Palestine, in 1939. Educated at the Tikhon-Chadash, Tel Aviv; the Sorbonne, Paris, 1965–70, degree in philosophy. Served in the Nahal (kibuts military service). Member of Kibuts Shamir, 1957–65; journalist for the *Al haMishmar* socialist newspaper. Founder of theatre company specifically for the production of Israeli work, 1977; teacher of aesthetics and workshop director, Tel Aviv University, Seminar Hakibutsim, and Beit Tzvi Drama Schools; artistic director, Haifa Municipal Theatre, 1984–88. Recipient: Aharon Meskin prize, 1983; German Critics' Poll award, 1985; London *Evening Standard* drama award, 1989; London Theatre Critics' award, 1990. Address: c/o Or-Am Publishing House, P.O. Box 22096, Tel Aviv 61220, Israel.

PUBLICATIONS

Plays

The Days to Come (produced in Hebrew, Haifa, 1971).
Status Quo Vadis (produced Haifa, 1973).
Sylvester 1972 [New Year's Eve 1972] (produced Haifa, 1974).
The Joke (produced in Hebrew, Haifa, 1975).
Nerves (produced in Hebrew, Haifa, 1976).

Leyl ha'esrim (produced Haifa, 1976).   Tel Aviv, Prozah, 1977; as *The Night of the Twentieth* (produced London, 1978), Tel Aviv, Institute for the Translation of Hebrew Literature, 1978.

Gog and Magog Show (produced in Hebrew, Haifa, 1977).

Repentance (produced in Hebrew, Haifa, 1977).

The Tenants (produced in Hebrew, Haifa, 1978).

Beyt Kaplan [The House of Kaplan] (trilogy; produced Israel, 1978–79).

Halaylah ha'acharon shel Oto Vaininger [The Last Night of Otto Weininger].   Tel Aviv, Or-Am, 1982; as *Nefesh yehudi* (produced Haifa, 1982); as *The Soul of a Jew* (produced Edinburgh and London, 1983).

Ghetto (produced Haifa and Berlin, 1984; Los Angeles, 1986; London and New York, 1989).   Tel Aviv, Or-Am, 1984; in English, Tel Aviv, Institute for the Translation of Hebrew Literature, 1986; London, Hern, 1989.

Hapalestina'it [The Palestinian Woman] (produced Haifa, 1985).   Tel Aviv, Or-Am, 1985.

Sindrom Yerushalayim [Jerusalem Syndrome] (produced Haifa and Tel Aviv, 1987).   Tel Aviv, Or-Am, 1987.

Adam [Man] (produced Tel Aviv, 1989).   Tel Aviv, Or-Am, 1989.

Bamartef [In the Cellar].   Tel Aviv, Or-Am, 1990.

Solo (produced Tel Aviv and The Hague, 1991).   Tel Aviv, Or-Am, 1991.

Girls of Toledo, lyrics by Sobol, music by Shosh Reisman (produced Jerusalem, 1992).

*

Critical Studies: interview by Clive Sinclair, in *Index on Censorship* (London), 14(1), 1985; "Zionism: Neurosis or Cure? The 'Historical' Drama of Yehoshua Sobol" by Yael S. Feldman, in *Prooftexts* (College Park, Maryland), 7(2), 1987; "When Choosing Good Is Not an Option: An Interview with Joshua Sobol" by Douglas Langworth, in *Theater (Yale)* (New Haven, Connecticut), 22(3), 1991.

*   *   *

Drama has been the least favoured of the genres in Israeli literature. Because Hebrew as a vernacular has only been revived fairly recently, Hebrew speech has lagged behind the written word in power, variety, and expressiveness. Early Hebrew drama in Palestine was written in a necessarily archaic language, remote from the natural rhythms of speech. And even within the early Israeli theatre, there was always a disjunction between the medium of performance and the reality that was supposed to act as the model. The solution proposed by earlier Hebrew drama was to distance the play from reality in a deliberately non-naturalistic theatre, as, for example, in the writings of Nissim Aloni. But more recently, the language of Hebrew drama has come considerably closer to living Hebrew speech. Thus the range of options has been broadened, and, in this new context, contemporary Israeli playwrights can elect to use either the vernacular or literary allusion, and also combine both as required.

From the 1970s, Yehoshua Sobol (Joshua Sobol) began producing a series of dramatic re-creations centring on choice, decision, and action at key moments of Jewish history. His plays combine a theatre of ideas, where abstract and ideological notions are proposed and challenged, with a theatre of alienation where the characters stand back from the material represented, which is then distanced, encapsulated, and sometimes rendered in song.

Sobol deploys the common language of speech in the creation of a naturalistic frame, but does so within a given historical context, often far removed in time and place from contemporary Israel. One of his early plays, *Leyl ha'esrim* (*The Night of the Twentieth*), places the scene in the yishuv (Jewish Palestine) of 20 October 1920, where a small group of young people are making a crucial decision to create a new settlement the following day. Not only will the decision to be significant to the future of Jewish settlement and what is to become the State of Israel, but, and more crucially here, for their own future as human beings. This is to be a foundation experience, a sort of rebirth. The drama of the situation derives from a clarification of beliefs and values within a group situation, and it becomes a sort of group experience with its own dynamic. Four young men and three young women, all from central Europe, are now becoming Middle Eastern, Hebrews, future Israelis, farmers, and they will also constitute a new society. They may relish the opportunity to be removed from a decaying Europe and to create something different *ab initio*, but this is their last opportunity to probe the genuine and deeper motives, as tomorrow and beyond the immediate task will obliterate all such possibility.

Sobol, in his function as playwright, rigorously eschews judgement. Although he presents conflict and options, he does not as an author decide in favour of one or the other, and neither does he imply, implicitly or explicitly, that one argument is better than another or that one view of history is more correct than another. This is true also for the play *Ghetto*, where we see the Vilna ghetto in the process of liquidation during the years 1942–43. Various options are being proposed and debated by various parties and individuals on the best way to survive. There are views proposed by collaborationists in the interests of survival, by Zionists, who of course hope to get out, by revolutionary Bundists, and by members of the resistance. In the light of our own historical knowledge, we may be tempted to come to the conclusion that all this argument is wasted breath as the same end is inevitable, whatever course of action is to be adopted. This, however, is not the dramatic reality, either in this play and or in the two successive plays of the trilogy (as yet unpublished) which investigate further episodes within this context. *Ghetto* creates both a naturalistic context and also a distance through the convention of building the play on the fortunes of a Jewish (Yiddish) theatre that is set up during the liquidation.

Sobol often plays on the dual aspect of reality and fantasy. *Hapalestina'it* (The Palestinian Woman) is a play about putting on a play, including some of the material of the play itself. We see each character in two aspects, in their own lives and in the parts they assume. The nature of the conflict between private and political life is thus raised, as is the more general question about the nature of truth, and seeing things from both within and without.

In all Sobol's plays, in those with a contemporary (or near contemporary setting) and those set in the recent or more distant past, the conflicts are presented and concretised by character. While not resolved or concluded, they are fully explored.

—Leon I. Yudkin

SOKOLOV, Sasha (Aleksandr Vsevolodovich Sokolov). Russian and Canadian. Born in Ottawa, Ontario, Canada,

6 November 1943. Educated at the Military Institute of Foreign Languages, Moscow, 1962–65; Moscow University, B.A. in journalism 1971. Married; one daughter. Staff writer, *Novorossiiskii rabochii* [The Novorossiisk Worker], 1967, *Kolkhoznaia pravda* [Kolkhoz Truth], Morky, 1967–68, *Literaturnaia Rossiia* [Literary Russia], Moscow, 1969–71, *Studencheskii meridian* [The Student Meridian], summers 1970–71, and *Leninskaia pravda* [Leninist Truth], Georgievsk, 1974; went on hunger strike to obtain exit visa from Soviet authorities following ban on his marriage; emigrated to Canada, 1976; writer-in-residence and instructor in Russian, Grand Valley State College, Allendale, Michigan, from 1977; returned to Russia, 1989–90; now lives in Canada. Address: c/ o Ardis Publishers, 2901 Heatherway, Ann Arbor, Michigan 48104, U.S.A.

PUBLICATIONS

Fiction

Shkola dlia durakov. Ann Arbor, Michigan, Ardis, 1976; as *A School for Fools*, Ardis, 1977.
Mezhdu sobakoi i volkom [Between Dog and Wolf]. Ann Arbor, Michigan, Ardis, 1980.
Palisandriia. Ann Arbor, Michigan, Ardis, 1985; as *Astrophobia*, New York, Grove Weidenfeld, 1989.

*

Bibliography: in *Canadian-American Slavic Studies* (Bakersfield, California), 21(3–4), 1987.

Critical Studies: "A Structural Analysis of Sasha Sokolov's *School for Fools*: a Paradigmatic Novel," in *Fiction and Drama in Eastern and Southeastern Europe: Evolution and Experiment in the Postwar Period*, edited by H. Birnbaum and T. Eekman, Columbus, Ohio, Slavica, 1980, "Sasha Sokolov's *Palisandrija*," in *Slavic and East European Journal* (Minneapolis), 30, 1986, "Sasha Sokolov's Twilight Cosmos: Themes and Motifs," in *Slavic Review* (Austin, Texas), 45, 1986, "Sasha Sokolov: The New Russian Avant-Garde," in *Critique: Studies in Modern Fiction* (Washington, D.C.), 30, 1989, and "The Galoshes Manifesto: A Motif in the Novels of Sasha Sokolov," in *Oxford Slavonic Papers*, 22, 1989, all by D. Barton Johnson; "Sasha Sokolov's *Palisandriia*: History and Myth" by Olga Matich, in *Russian Review* (Columbus, Ohio), 45, 1986; Sokolov issue of *Canadian-American Slavic Studies* (Bakersfield, California), 21(3–4), 1987; "Incarnations of the Hero Archetype in *School for Fools*" by C. Simmons, in *The Supernatural in Slavic and Baltic Literature: Essays in Honor of Victor Terras*, Columbus, Ohio, Slavica, 1989; "Aberration or the Future: The Avant-Garde Novels of Sasha Sokolov" by Arnold McMillan, in *From Pushkin to Palisandriia: Essays on the Russian Novel in Honor of Richard Freeborn*, edited by McMillan, London, Macmillan, 1990.

*   *   *

Sasha Sokolov is the leading avant-garde stylist to emerge in Russian literature in the late 1970s and 1980s. His first novel, *Shkola dlia durakov* (*A School for Fools*), which appeared concurrently with the author's emigration in 1976, was hailed by Vladimir Nabokov as "an enchanting, tragic, and touching book." Widely translated, the experimental novella has become a minor modernist classic. A second novel, *Mezhdu sobakoi i volkom* (Between Dog and Wolf), a dazzling, stylistic

tour de force that remains untranslated (and untranslatable), has been called a Russian *Finnegans Wake*. A third book, *Palisandriia* (*Astrophobia*), is perhaps the first Russian postmodern novel. Sokolov's novels, all initially published in the West, have now appeared in Russia where, together with his essays, they are playing a role in the rebirth of literary modernism in post-Soviet Russian literature.

Sokolov's three novels radically differ from each other in subject-matter, social ambience, temporal setting, tone, and style. *A School for Fools*, a chamber work, is set among the Soviet professional classes circa 1960 and depicts that world through the eyes and pure if eccentric language of a schizophrenic youth who is a student at a "special" school. The plotless narrative consists of exchanges between the two halves of the boy's personality and focuses on a small number of scenes that recur in evolving variants. The novella's central conflict is between the forces that oppress the boy, i.e., his misanthropic father who is a public prosecutor, the boy's psychiatrist and the hospital, and the bureaucracy of the special school and, on the other side, two teachers whom the boy idolizes. The latter are identified with nature and, above all, the liberating force of the wind, promising freedom and creativity. *Mezhdu sobakoi i volkom* recreates the timeless miasma of the remote upper Volga. The title, an idiom meaning "twilight," also refers to the book's central event — the murder of the narrator in revenge for his maiming of a hunter's dog that he has drunkenly mistaken for a wolf. The two men may be father and son, as well as lovers of the same woman. The novel is partly in the form of letters penned by a near-illiterate whose colorful phraseologisms, rich regional vocabulary, and erratic syntax give pause to even sophisticated Russian readers. *Astrophobia*, a picaresque mock epic, paints a hilariously revisionist picture of life among the Kremlin elite. Its episodes, featuring famous historical figures, range over a century as the bizarre hero, Palisander, rises from Kremlin orphan to ruler of the empire. His adventures parody several sorts of popular fiction including sensational autobiography, thrillers, and pornography. The writing reflects many stylistic registers, but a playful imperial baroque is one of the major tonalities. Although Sokolov has been fortunate in his English translators, much of the stylistic richness of his language is inevitably diluted in translation.

The heterogeneity of content and setting in Sokolov's novels is impressive, but from the formal point of view their most striking common feature is their dislocation of language and traditional narrative form. Each book represents a unique and often extreme form of stylization. With the parodic exception of *Astrophobia*, they are plotless and lack the traditional points of orientation that guide readers through works of art. In spite of their diversity and difficulty, Sokolov's novels display a single, consistent set of concerns that order his fictional universe and define its thematic cosmology. Time and memory, death and sex are major themes in all of the novels. Time is the most pervasive of Sokolov's themes and underlies other, seemingly bizarre aspects of his work. Sokolovian time is not linear, but random and circumambient. In a universe with multiple concurrent time dimensions, memory, Sokolov's second theme, is no longer retrospective but, rather, atemporal. Characters "remember" selectively and erratically, and alternate versions of events are equally possible. Where linear time does not exist, memory is supplanted by imagination. Since Sokolov's novels are, for the most part, first-person accounts narrated from "memory," the described metaphysic has radical consequences for their structure. It is a primary source of the novels' difficulty and strange enchantment. Sokolov's second pair of themes, sex and death, is also marked by an unusual sensibility. Common sense dictates that sex and death be seen as opposites. For Sokolov, however, they are complementary. Their conjunction is vividly embodied in the recurrent figure of "that woman" who haunts the novels. The image is that of the temptress, a seductress, who lures men to their doom. Almost all of Sokolov's female characters partake of this mythic image. Sokolovian death, however, is not what we might think, for in a timeless universe, the distinction between the living and the dead is indeterminate.

The phenomena of time, memory, sex, and death are fundamental organizing concepts of human existence. They are the coordinates of consciousness that supply the contexts and reference points that we use in understanding real and fictional universes. We assume time to be linear and divided into past, present, and a problematic future. Memory recalls the past, not the future. Personal identity is more or less fixed. Sex entails differentiation into male and female. Incest is avoided. One is either dead or alive. Sokolov's novels systematically violate all of these assumptions and do so without warning or explanation. Although the reader's basic coordinates of consciousness are dislocated in Sokolov's novels, each foregrounds a particular theme: *A School for Fools* is told by a schizophrenic who does not believe in time; *Mezhdu sobakoi i volkom* is narrated by a murdered man in a world where the living and the dead are indistinguishable; *Astrophobia*'s incestuous narrator is both male and female. The fixed points of existence are destabilized; the boundaries are erased, and we are in a twilight universe. The reader who enters Sokolov's fictional cosmos encumbered by purely commonplace notions of time, memory, sex, and death is likely to find it a disorienting, if exhilarating experience. Style and linguistic elegance are the only reality in Sokolov's art.

—D. Barton Johnson

SOLDATI, Mario. Italian. Born in Turin, 17 November 1906. Educated at Jesuit schools in Turin; Istituto Superiore di Storia dell'Arte, Rome; University of Turin, degree in literature 1927; Columbia University, New York, 1929–31. Married twice; three children. Full-time writer; also film director; contributed regularly to *Il Giorno* and *Il Corriere della Sera*. Currently president, ANGEAT (National Association of Journalists in Cenology, Gastronomy, and Agritourism); president, Centro Pannunzio, Turin, from 1988. Recipient: San Babila prize, 1949; Strega prize, 1954; Campiello prize, 1970; Bagutta prize, 1976; Naples prize, 1978; Giarre-Taormina prize, 1979; Hemingway prize, 1986; Viareggio prize, 1987; Amici dei Latini prize. Address: Via Cavour 34, 10123 Turin, Italy.

PUBLICATIONS

Fiction

Salmace. Novara, La Libra, 1929.
La verità sul caso Motta. Milan, Rizzoli, 1941.
L'amico gesuita. Milan, Rizzoli, 1943.
A cena col commendatore. Milan, Garzanti, 1950; as *The Commander Comes to Dine*, London, Lehmann, 1952; as *Dinner with the Commendatore*, New York, Knopf, 1953.

Le lettere da Capri. Milan, Garzanti, 1954; as *The Capri Letters*, London, Hamish Hamilton, 1955; New York, Knopf, 1956; as *Affair in Capri*, New York, Berkley, 1957.
La confessione. Milan, Garzanti, 1955; as *The Confession*, New York, Knopf, and London, Deutsch, 1958.
Il vero Silvestri. Milan, Garzanti, 1957; as *The Real Silvestri*, London, Deutsch, 1960; New York, Knopf, 1961.
I racconti. Milan, Garzanti, 1957.
La messa dei villeggianti. Milan, Mondadori, 1959.
I racconti (1927–1947). Milan, Mondadori, 1961.
Storie di spettri. Milan, Mondadori, 1962.
Le due città. Milan, Garzanti, 1964; as *The Malacca Cane*, London, Deutsch, and New York, St. Martin's Press, 1973.
La busta arancione. Milan, Mondadori, 1966; as *The Orange Envelope*, London, Deutsch, and New York, Harcourt Brace, 1969.
I racconti del Maresciallo. Milan, Mondadori, 1967.
Fuori. Milan, Mondadori, 1968.
L'attore. Milan, Mondadori, 1970.
55 novelle per l'inverno. Milan, Mondadori, 1971.
Lo smeraldo. Milan, Mondadori, 1974; as *The Emerald*, New York, Harcourt Brace, 1977.
La sposa americana. Milan, Mondadori, 1977; as *The American Bride*, London, Hodder and Stoughton, 1979.
44 novelle per l'estate. Milan, Mondadori, 1979.
Addio diletta Amelia. Milan, Mondadori, 1979.
La carta del cielo: racconti. Turin, Einaudi, 1980.
L'incendio. Milan, Mondadori, 1981.
La casa del perché. Milan, Mondadori, 1982.
Nuovi racconti del maresciallo. Milan, Rizzoli, 1984.
L'architetto. Milan, Rizzoli, 1985.
L'albero. Milan, Rizzoli, 1985.
L'avventura in Valtellina. Rome, Laterza, 1986.
El paseo de Gracia. Milan, Rizzoli, 1987.

Plays

Pilato. Turin, Società Editrice Internazionale, 1925.

Screenplays: *Gli uomini, che mascalzoni!*, 1932; *Il signor Max*, 1937; *La principessa Tarakanova*, 1938; *La signora di Montecarlo*, 1938; *Due milioni per un sorriso*, 1939; *Dora Nelson*, 1939; *Tutto per la donna*, 1940; *Piccolo mondo antico (Old-Fashioned World)*, 1941; *Tragica notte*, 1941; *Malombra*, 1942; *Quartieri alti*, 1943; *Le miserie del signor Travet (His Young Wife)*, 1945; *Eugenia Grandet*, 1946; *Daniele Cortis*, 1947; *Fuga in Francia (Flight into France)*, 1948; *Quel bandito sono io!*, 1949; *Botta e risposta*, 1950; *Donne e briganti (Of Love and Bandits)*, 1950; *Il sogno di Zorro*, 1951; *E l'amor che mi rovina*, 1951; *O.K. Nerone (O.K. Nero)*, 1951; *Le avventure di Mandrin*, 1952; *I tre corsari*, 1952; *Jolanda — La figlia del corsaro nero*, 1952; *La provinciale (The Wayward Wife)*, 1953; *La mano dello straniero (The Stranger's Hand)*, 1953; *Questa è la vita (Of Life and Love)*, 1954; *La donna del Fiume (Woman of the River)*, 1955; *Era di venerdì 17 (The Virtuous Bigamist)*, 1957; *Italia piccola*, 1957; *Policarpo — Ufficiale di scrittura*, 1959.

Other

America, primo amore. Forence, Bemporad, 1935.
Ventiquattro ore in uno studio cinematografico. Milan, Corticelli, 1945.
Fuga in Italia. Milan, Longanesi, 1947.
L'accalappiacani. Rome, Atlante, 1953.
To Plan or Not to Plan? A Short Talk. Rome, n.p., 1959.
Canzonette e viaggio televisivo. Milan, Mondadori, 1962.

Vino al vino. Milan, Mondadori, 1969.
I disperati del benessere: viaggio in Svezia. Milan, Mondadori, 1970.
Gloria dell'uomo, with Colomba Russo. Florence, Cremonese, 1973.
Da spettatore. Milan, Mondadori, 1973.
Un prato di papaveri: diario 1947–1964. Milan, Mondadori, 1973.
The Octopus and the Pirates (for children). London, Deutsch, 1974.
Lo specchio inclinato: diario 1965–1971. Milan, Mondadori, 1975.
Piemonte e Valle d'Aosta, illustrated by Folco Quilici. Milan, Silvana, 1978.
Lo scopone, with Maurizio Corgnati. Milan, Mondadori, 1982.
Conversazione in una stanza chiusa con Mario Soldati, with Davide Lajolo. Milan, Frassinelli, 1983.
24 ore in uno studio cinematografico. Palermo, Sellerio, 1985.
Ah! Il Mundial! Milan, Rizzoli, 1986.
Regione regina. Rome, Laterza, 1987.
Rami secchi. Milan, Rizzoli, 1989.
Opere, vol. 1: racconti autobiografici. Milan, Rizzoli, 1991.

* * *

In any consideration of Mario Soldati's literary work, it is useful to note several facts: first, he was born in Turin in 1906 of middle-class Catholic parents; second, from an early age he was as much interested in the fine arts as in literature; third, he spent an influential period of his early manhood in the United States; and fourth, he was for many years involved in the Italian film industry. All tend to be strongly reflected in his writing.

Although Soldati's first public piece, the comic play *Pilato* (Pilate), attracted little attention, a collection of short stories, *Salmace*, published in 1929 while he was still a post-graduate student at Columbia University in New York, established his reputation as a promising young writer of fiction. That helped him, on his return from the United States, to be taken on as a scriptwriter with the film production centre in Rome, Cines. Although Soldati is best-known today as a novelist, the earlier part of his career was dominated by his activities in the Italian film industry, and these need briefly to be sketched here as they provided the background to several of his later novels.

Soldati began by scripting scenarios for several of the most distinguished Italian directors of the 1930s, like Alessandro Blasetti, with whom he worked on *La tavola dei poveri* (The Table of the Poor), and Mario Camerini, for whom he did *Gli uomini, che mascalzoni!* (Men) and *Il signor Max* (Mr. Max). He then graduated to direction, co-directing with F. Ozep *La principessa Tarkanova* (Princess Tarkanova), and although he turned increasingly to novel writing after the success of his later 1930s fiction, like *La verità sul caso Motta* (The Motta Affair), he maintained his contacts with the film industry through to the 1960s. Perhaps appropriately for one whose prime interest lay in writing, as a film director he proved to be particularly good at handling adaptations of literary texts, especially those with a nostalgic bent. In the post-war period, influenced by the then dominant mode in Italian serious filmmaking, Neo-Realism, he attempted, if with only modest success, to apply something of the new realist manner to materials drawn from middle-class life, as in an adaptation of his own short story, *Fuga in Francia* (Flight into France), and in a version of Alberto Moravia's novel, *La provinciale* (The

Wayward Wife). In the 1950s and 1960s Soldati was also very active in television.

Some recent critics have seen in Soldati's early stories an ironic and sceptical treatment of bourgeois values under Fascism, rather comparable to the stance and tone of other young writers of the 1930s, like Alberto Moravia. But this reading is rather forced, for there is little overt attempt in his early work to engage with politics; although it may contain implicit social and political criticism, his interests are essentially private, engaged much more with the interior life, and with personal relationships, than with expressly public concerns. Most of his work of the 1930s seems to underscore the truth of Cesare Pavese's view that the largely non-prescriptive nature of the Italian regime towards the arts encouraged many to cultivate an apolitical individualism, for the prime emphasis in many of Soldati's novels and short stories is on the psychology and sensibilities of individuals, preoccupations which in part perhaps explain the comparative neglect of his work in much post-war Italian literary criticism, which has tended to favour writing of firm political commitment.

Much of Soldati's writing appears to have a strong autobiographical dimension: this is seen as much in an early non-fiction work, like *America, primo amore* (America, First Love), as in a much later novel, *The American Bride* (The American Bride). The former, rooted in the observations of his post-graduate years in the United States, sifts myth and reality in European conceptions of the American way of life; its implicit nationalism struck a particularly strong cord in a nation where, following the wave of emigration in the early years of the century, most families had friends or relatives, and won for Soldati his first major literary success, *The American Bride*, one of his last novels, re-explores some of the issues of cultural difference he had examined from various perspectives in a number of stories, and is a sensitive account (if overly marked by a resort to the melodramatic) of irresolvable tensions and misunderstandings in a marital relationship.

Themes rooted in childhood and adolescent experience, more particularly the personal and moral implications of a sexually repressive education, inform some of his best work. Translation of such experience into fictional terms is seen in *L'amico gesuita* (The Jesuit Friend) and *La confessione* (The Confession). The 14-year-old protagonist of the latter novel, Clemente Perrier, is at school in an academically demanding but morally rigorous and austere Jesuit college in Turin, rather as Soldati himself had been. Disturbed by the awakening of sexual instincts, and plagued by a sense of guilt, Clemente reveals his confused feelings to his spiritual director, the gentle and considerate Father Genovesi. With the best of intentions, but governed by his own austere religious beliefs, the priest counsels the suppression of all such impulses in favour of a rigorously disciplined celibacy. But these impulses, first aroused in the young Clemente by the alluring femininity of a woman briefly encountered in a hotel lift in Florence, are not so easily stilled, and are further aroused while the family is on holiday by a friend of his mother, Jeanette, and by a young girl, Mareska. Seeking to reject the temptation of mortal sin, Clemente is drawn instead into a sexual relationship with a local boy, Luisito. The tale is told with some sensitivity and psychological perception, and with a wry irony characteristic of much of Soldati's writing, but does not wholly stave off the reader's impatience with the spiritual earnestness of Clemente.

As this novel indicates, there is a sense in which Soldati can be seen as a Catholic novelist, but characteristically his is not an overt engagement, for in most of his novels the concern is not with relationships profoundly complicated by commitment to the faith, in the manner of, say, Graham Greene, but with the ways in which lives are subtly affected by religious attitudes and assumptions, and how faith can operate in mundane ways to condition actions. Thus one of Soldati's best novels, *Le lettere da Capri* (*The Capri Letters* or *Affair in Capri*), while not a Catholic novel in any conventional sense of the phrase, is nonetheless one in which belief, rather like nationality, is seen almost incidentally to be an inextricable part of the climate of lives. The complex narrative concerns the fascination of an American art historian, Harry Perkins, working for Unesco on the preservation of Italian works of art, with a prostitute, Dorotea. In recounting that relationship, it imaginatively interweaves the flashback recollections of its Italian narrator, Mario, an apparently autobiographical scenario sent to him by Harry, and a series of letters written by Harry's American Catholic wife Jane. While Harry leads a double life with Jane and Dorotea, in need of both women, Jane meets through Dorotea a young Italian, Aldo, with whom she has an affair, recounted in letters to him which later become instruments of blackmail. On Jane's death, Harry marries Dorotea and takes her to America, but his fascination with her evaporates as she accommodates happily to the comforts of bourgeois consumerist life. At the root of the novel, which is crafted like a tale of suspense and revelation, is what Soldati apparently takes to be an irresolvable conflict between Italian sensuality and Anglo-Saxon repression, which dooms those in its toils to frustration and disillusionment.

Many of Soldati's novels are concerned with self-deception in relationships. The tightly written novella *Il vero Silvestri* (*The Real Silvestri*) juxtaposes the opposed views held of a mutual friend by a middle-class lawyer and an attractive working-class woman: for the latter, Silvestri is a cheat and blackmailer, while the former remembers him only as the very model of kindness, consideration, and personal honesty. Gradually the lawyer appreciates how impossibly idealised was his memory of his friend, but comes to understand and feel for him all the more by accepting his human failings.

Notwithstanding that his plots can exploit the bizarre and the extraordinary, Soldati chronicles the human ordinariness in the romantic deceptions and misunderstandings of friendship, marriage, and the intrigues of love relationships. There is, too, an element of the erotic in his work, the more powerful for never being overt or exploitative. The romantic dimension, reinforced by the sure sense of the storyteller, helped to win for several of his novels in the 1950s and 1960s a wide readership in Italy and abroad. Although at times overly rhetorical, and not always persuasive in handling the psychology of relationships, Soldati shows an impressive stylistic mastery in his skilful intermingling of the formal and the colloquial; his work is eminently readable.

—Francesca Ross

SOLLERS, Philippe. Pseudonym for Philippe Joyaux. French. Born in Bordeaux, 28 November 1936. Educated at the Lycées Montesquieu et Montaigne, Bordeaux; École Sainte-Geneviève, Versailles. Married Julia Kristeva in 1967; one son. Editor, *Tel Quel* journal, Éditions du Seuil, Paris, 1960–83. Since 1983 editor, *L'Infini* journal, Paris; since 1990 member of the advisory board, Gallimard publishers. Recipient: Fénéon prize, 1958; Medicis prize, 1961; City of Paris grand prize, 1988. Address: c/o *L'Infini*, 5 rue Sébastien-Bottin, 75007 Paris, France.

PUBLICATIONS

Fiction

Une Curieuse Solitude. Paris, Seuil, 1958; as *A Strange Solitude*, New York, Grove Press, 1959; London, Eyre and Spottiswoode, 1961.
Le Parc. Paris, Seuil, 1961; as *The Park*, London, Calder and Boyars, 1968; New York, Red Dust, 1969.
Drame. Paris, Seuil, 1965; as *Event*, New York, Red Dust, 1987.
Nombres. Paris, Seuil, 1968.
Lois. Paris, Seuil, 1972.
H. Paris, Seuil, 1973.
Paradis. Paris, Seuil, 1981.
Femmes. Paris, Gallimard, 1983; as *Women*, New York, Columbia University Press, 1990; London, Quartet, 1991.
Portrait du joueur. Paris, Gallimard, 1984.
Paradis II. Paris, Gallimard, 1986.
Le Coeur absolu. Paris, Gallimard, 1987.
Les Folies françaises. Paris, Gallimard, 1988.
Le Lys d'or. Paris, Gallimard, 1989.
La Fête à Venise. Paris, Gallimard, 1991.

Verse

La Seconde Vie de Shakespeare; Paradis (includes prose). Paris, Cercles, 1980.

Other

Le Défi. Paris, Seuil, 1957.
L'Intermédiaire. Paris, Seuil, 1963.
Logiques. Paris, Seuil, 1968.
Entretiens avec Francis Ponge. Paris, Seuil, 1970.
L'Écriture et l'expérience des limites. Paris, Seuil, 1971; as *Writing and the Experience of Limits*, New York, Columbia University Press, 1983.
Sur le Matérialisme: de l'atomisme à la dialectique révolutionnaire. Paris, Seuil, 1974.
Au-delà du dialogue, with Edgar Faure. Paris, Balland, 1977.
Délivrance (interviews), with Maurice Clavel. Paris, Seuil, 1977.
Vision à New York (interviews), with David Hayman. Paris, Grasset, 1980.
Alain Kirili (exhibition catalogue), with Donald Kuspit. Paris, Maeght, 1984.
Théorie des exceptions. Paris, Gallimard, 1986.
Les Surprises de Fragonard. Paris, Gallimard, 1987.
Rodin: dessins érotiques, with Alain Kirili. Paris, Gallimard, 1987.
De Kooning, vite. Paris, La Différence, 2 vols., 1988.
Sade contre l'Être suprême. Paris, Quai Voltaire, 1989.
Carnet de nuit. Paris, Plon, 1989.
Girodias, l'insoumis, with *L'Affaire Kissinger*, by Maurice Girodias. Paris, La Différence, 1990.

Banlieux, photographs by Marc Riboud, Patrick Zachmann, and Roland Laboye.   Paris, Denoël, 1990.
Improvisations.   Paris, Gallimard, 1991.

Editor, *Francis Ponge, ou la raison à plus haut prix*.   Paris, Seghers, 1963.
Editor, *Théorie d'ensemble*.   Paris, Seuil, 1968.
Editor, *Roland Barthes*.   Paris, Seuil, 1971.
Editor, *Artaud; Bataille*.   Paris, Union Générale d'Éditions, 2 vols., 1973.
Editor, *Colloque "Vers une Révolution culturelle"*.   Paris, Union Générale d'Éditions, 2 vols., 1974.
Editor, *Literatura, política y cambio*.   Buenos Aires, Calden, 1976.
Editor, with Alain Jouffroy, *Le Gué: Machiavel, Novalis, Marx*.   Paris, Bourgois, 1977.
Editor, *Photos licencieuses de la Belle Époque*.   Paris, Éditions 1900, 1987.

Translator, *Cobra*, by Severo Sarduy.   Paris, Seuil, 1972.

*

Critical Studies: "An Interview with Philippe Sollers," in *TriQuarterly* (Evanston, Illinois), Winter 1977, and "Nodality or Plot Displaced: The Dynamics of Sollers' *H*," in *Sub-Stance* (Santa Barbara, California), 43, 1984, both by David Hayman; *Sollers écrivain* by Roland Barthes, Paris, Seuil, 1979, translated as *Sollers Writer*, London, Athlone Press, 1987; "Paradise Lost? An Interview with Philippe Sollers" by Shushi Kao, in *Sub-Stance* (Santa Barbara, California), 30, 1981; "Philippe Sollers and the Scene of Writing" by Betty R. McGraw, in *American Journal of Semiotics* (Davis, California), 3(2), 1984; *The Fictional Encyclopedia: Joyce, Pound, Sollers* by Hilary Clark, New York, Garland, 1990.

*   *   *

Philippe Sollers is regarded variously as a wilfully "difficult," even unreadable product of Parisian intellectualism at its most perverse, or as a seminal figure in the literary and theoretical avant-garde of the Fifth Republic. In 1960, the precocious author of a book of essays and a fairly conventional "rites of passage" novel, he became a founder member of *Tel Quel* journal, which was to exert a potent force on intellectual postmodernism into the 1980s. It published experimental writing as well as essays on philosophy, culture, literary theory, language, politics, and psychoanalysis, and Sollers's development as a writer is mirrored in its evolving preoccupations which in many ways he helped to stage manage. He also directed *Tel Quel*'s fiction list, published by Seuil. When the magazine ceased publication in 1983, he became editor of its less uncompromising successor, *L'Infini*.

Le Parc (*The Park*), the first shot in Sollers's war against the humanist tradition of realistic fiction, abandons conventional character and linearity of plot and sows narrative motifs which undermine "meaning" and constitute a dispersed, de-centred zone of self-referencing fragments. The even bolder *Drame* (*Event*) is made up of 64 sequences, the number of squares on a chessboard. Two narrative voices, "I" and "He," evoke fleeting glimpses of events and places — a train, a forest fire, a car skidding, flotsam and jetsam in water — which may be remembered or dreamed, real or invented. Time is uncertain and place problematic, and the reader negotiates the sequences in a complicated series of horizontal and vertical manoeuvres which dramatise, not anecdotal experience, but the processes of literary creation. The same denial of mimesis

and language as means of expressing human experience characterises the 100 numbered sequences of *Nombres* (Numbers) which may be read continuously or serially. Three of the sections are written in the third person and the past tense and are likened to three sides of an auditorium. The fourth, "open" sequence is directed at the reader in the first person of the present tense, a process which denies the "closure" of the artistic project, and makes the act of reading the site of a creative process in which meaning eludes our learned responses, and requires our complicity in an ideological rearrangement of language and subjectivity as instruments of apprehending the uncertainties and complexities of the world.

After 1968, Sollers continued to use the novel to dramatize the creative processes of fiction. Subject-matter is banished to the edges of perception and protagonists, emptied of Newtonian reality, inhabit regions made immanent by interchangeable voices. *Lois* (Laws) is a compendium of pastiche, narrative strands, and quotation and, like all Sollers's work before 1980, replaces the figure of the novelist by a text which "reads and writes itself." *H* places the weight of exposition almost entirely on language. A verbal continuum, without punctuation or semantic units, its reflections on a wide range of literary and intellectual matters are accessible only through the rhythms and intonations of spoken discourse. *Paradis* (Paradise) revived this near-Joycean "interior monologue" which, however, is multi-vocal and, in Sollers's phrase, an "exterior polylogue."

By the time *Tel Quel* closed, Sollers had undergone a profound philosophical and literary sea change. His bleak landscapes acquired a recognisable population, narrative themes abandoned their abstract mythicism, and his polemical habits became more direct and pungent. *Femmes* (*Women*) was overtly misogynistic, and the novels which followed confirmed a return to linear plot lines which deal plainly with a semi-autobiographical figure who resists all attempts to invade his personality. Often taking the form of pastiches of established genres (thriller, pornography), they are regularly spiced with satirical commentaries on a range of topics: political militancy, the new avant-garde, sex, the commercial exploitation of art, and the vulgarity of the age as indicated by the title of *Les Folies françaises* (French Follies). Thus *La Fête à Venise* (Carnival in Venice), which has the makings (but no more) of a thriller involving the theft of a Watteau painting, castigates the IT revolution, instant knowledge and advertising, but argues that art alone has the power to communicate the uniqueness of the human spirit. If Sollers's manner has changed, his purpose has not.

His critics have taxed him with hitching his literary ambitions to every passing fashion. At first, he threw in with the *nouveau roman* which pointedly abandoned plot, character, and the other mainstays of bourgeois realism. His disaffection with literary formalism, conventional expressivity, and committed literature was subsequently linked to Marxism and, during the early 1970s, to psychoanalysis, semiology, structuralism, and Maoism, which he abandoned after 1976 when, in common with *Tel Quel*, he warmed to the United States as fertile ground for a new dissidence. By the early 1980s, he declared himself to be "spontaneously attached to Catholicism," abandoned non-representation, and acquired a much wider readership. Since then, with the sophisticated venom of "a left-wing renegade," he has proceeded to round on the libertarian causes he had once defended.

Sollers makes a virtue of being a natural rebel. He was expelled from school, dismissed from the army, and has continued to reject affiliation with groups, even those which he himself helped to form. He has always consciously rejected the clammy grip of the normal and the predictable — "family, school, religion, sexual desire, work, philosophy, politics" — which limit the writer's freedom to respond spontaneously to changing climates. "A writer's business is to get himself thrown out of everything, because otherwise he becomes integrated and the great adventure is over," he says in *Vision à New York* (Vision in New York). Stated thus, his apparent compromises are redefined as intellectual and artistic consistency, a continuing dialectic of a mind determined to keep all options open.

—David Coward

SOLÓRZANO, Carlos. Guatemalan and Mexican. Born in San Marcos, Guatemala, Mexico, 1 May 1922; moved to Mexico in 1939. Educated at the National Autonomous University of Mexico, Mexico City, B.A. 1939, M.A. 1945, Ph.D. 1948; the Sorbonne, Paris, 1948–50. Married Beatrice Caso in 1946; one son and two daughters. Artistic director, Teatro Universitario, 1952–62, Professor, 1960–85, and since 1985 Professor Emeritus, National Autonomous University of Mexico; executive director, reorganization of the Mexican National Theatre, 1976–85. Visiting Professor, University of Southern California, Los Angeles, and University of Kansas, Lawrence. Former theatre critic, *Siempre!* magazine. Recipient: Rockefeller grant, 1958–60. Address: Condor 199, Col. Alpes Tlacopac, Mexico City 01010, D.F. Mexico.

PUBLICATIONS

Plays

Doña Beatriz, la sin ventura (produced 1952).   Published in *Teatro guatemalteco contemporáneo*, Madrid, Aguilar, 1964.
El hechicero: tragedia en tres actos (produced 1954).   Mexico City, Cuadernos Americanos, 1955.
Las manos de Dios (produced Mexico City, 1956).   Published in *El teatro hispanoamericano contemporáneo*, Mexico City, Fondo de Cultural Económica, 1964; as *The Hands of God* (produced Hiram, Ohio, 1968).
Mea culpa (produced 1956).   Included in *Teatro breve*, 1977.
Dos obras, with Carlos Prieto.   1957.
Los fantoches (produced 1958; Paris, 1963).   Included in *Teatro*, 1972.
El crucificado (produced 1958).   Included in *Teatro*, 1972.
Cruce de vías (produced 1959).   Included in *Teatro breve*, 1977.
Tres actos.   Mexico City, El Unicornio, 1959.
El sueño del ángel (produced 1960).   Included in *Teatro*, 1972.
El censo.   1962.
Los falsos demonios.   1963.
El zapato (produced 1966).   Included in *Teatro breve*, 1977.
El visitante (produced 1966).
Teatro (includes *Los fantoches*; *El crucificado*; *Las manos de Dios*; *El sueño del ángel*).   San José, Costa Rica, Universitaria Centroamericana, 1972.
Teatro breve (includes *El zapato*; *Cruce de vías*; *El sueño del ángel*; *Mea culpa*; *El crucificado*; *Los fantoches*).   Mexico City, Mortiz, 1977.

Fiction

Los falsos demonios, from his own play.   Mexico City, Mortiz, 1966.
Las celdas.   Mexico City, Mortiz, 1971.

Other

Del sentimiento de lo plástico en la obra de Unamuno.   Mexico City, n.p., 1944.
Espejo de novelas.   1945.
Unamuno y el existencialismo.   1946.
Novelas de Unamuno.   1948.
Teatro latinoamericano del siglo XX.   Buenos Aires, Nueva Visión, 1961; revised edition, New York, Macmillan, 1963.
Tesimonios teatrales de México.   Mexico City, Universidad Nacional Autónoma de México, 1973.

Editor, *Teatro guatemalteco contemporáneo*.   Madrid, Aguilar, 1964.
Editor, *El teatro hispanoamericano contemporáneo*.   Mexico City, Fondo de Cultura Económica, 2 vols., 1964.
Editor, *Teatro breve hispanoamericano contemporáneo*.   Madrid, Aguilar, 1970.
Editor, *El teatro actual latinoamericano*.   Mexico City, Andrea, 1972.

*

Bibliographies: "Carlos Solórzano — bibliografía" by Pedro Frank de Andrea, in *Comunidad Latinoamericano de Escritores Boletín*, 7, March 1970; "Carlos Solórzano: cronología bibliográfica mínima" by O. Rodríguez, in *Chasqui* (Provo, Utah), 1(1), 1972; in *Mexican Literature: A Bibliography of Secondary Sources* by David William Foster, Metuchen, New Jersey, Scarecrow Press, 1992.

Critical Studies: "The Drama of Carlos Solórzano" by F. Dauster, in *Modern Drama* (Toronto), 7, 1968–69; "Solórzano's Tormented Puppets" by D. Radcliff-Umstead, in *Latin American Theatre Review* (Lawrence, Kansas), 4(2), 1971; "The Mexican Existentialism of Solórzano's *Los fantoches*" by Katharine C. Richards, in *Latin American Literary Review* (Pittsburgh), 9, 1976; "The Ritual of Solórzano's *Las manos de Dios*" by John R. Rosenberg, in *Latin American Theatre Review* (Lawrence, Kansas), 17(2), 1984; "Myth and Theatricality in Three Plays by Carlos Solórzano" by Wilma Feliciano, in *Latin American Theatre Review* (Lawrence, Kansas), 25(1), 1991.

*   *   *

Carlos Solórzano is widely known and greatly respected throughout the theatre world of Latin America for his work as a playwright as well as for his work as a critic and editor. Born in San Marcos, Guatemala, he moved to Mexico in 1939 to pursue studies in architecture and literature. In 1948 he earned the degree Doctor en Letras from the National Autonomous University of Mexico (UNAM) and then continued with specialized studies in dramatic art in France under the auspices of a Rockefeller grant. During the many years in which he served as director of the Teatro Universitario in Mexico, and later as professor of dramatic art at UNAM, he actively and passionately promoted the theatre through histories, anthologies, articles, lectures, and festivals.

Solórzano's theatre is a reflection of his existentialist approach to contemporary situations. His anguished characters strive to establish meaningful communication and relationships within a world of alienation. Steeped in the works of Michel de Ghelderode and Albert Camus during his years in Paris, Solórzano established close relationships with the two writers and admits having inherited from them a predilection for a symbolic and philosophical theatre.

The freedom to be oneself is perhaps the basic tenet of all Solórzano's theatre. "Men are born free. It's other men who make them prisoners afterwards," says the Devil in *Las manos de Dios*. For Solórzano freedom is a complex, multifaceted concept; individuals should have freedom of election in their political, social, moral, and religious structures. His plays underscore in theme and technique the processes that accompany an existentialist view of freedom of choice.

His career as a playwright was launched in 1952 with the premiere of *Doña Beatriz, la sin ventura* ("The Unfortunate"), wife of Pedro de Alvarado, who was sent by Hernán Cortés to conquer Guatemala. Doña Beatriz suffers the indignities of the New World where she is a creature out of time and space. Bound by traditions and the Church, her loyalties remain with Spain as she struggles to maintain her identity. The structural oppositions between Beatriz and Pedro's *mestiza* daughter Leonor, as well as between Don Pedro and Beatriz's brother Rodrigo, emphasize the conflicts and the struggle for power in this hostile environment. The psychological anguish apparent throughout the play is in the end exacerbated by the forces of nature when Beatriz, long estranged from her profligate and ambitious husband, admits defeat and surrenders to the flood that carries her away. Beatriz's death and Leonor's survival can be seen as symbols of the end of an old world order and the beginning of a new society.

In 1954 Solórzano's second play, *El hechicero* (The Sorcerer), he continued his fascination with earlier times and other places to dramatize his concept of freedom. Set in "these Middle Ages which have not yet ended," the play presents the struggle of Merlin the magician to find the secret of the philosopher's stone in order to change lead into gold. This discovery will enable him to purchase the freedom of his townspeople from the Duke, whose troops occupy the village and will not be withdrawn until each of the inhabitants pays the tribute demanded. The conflict involves Merlin's daughter Beatriz and his wife, who plots to kill him, steal the secret, and marry her husband's brother. This configuration allows Solórzano the artistic license to explore issues of economic freedom, physical freedom from incarceration, and freedom from irrational action without a sense of responsibility.

Solórzano's master work is *Las manos de Dios* (*The Hands of God*), which became an instant success when it opened in 1956. In a tightly knit conflict, the young protagonist Beatriz is challenged to steal jewels from the Church in order to bribe the jailer to free her brother. The forces in conflict are expressed dramatically by the Devil who provokes Beatriz and by the authoritarian figures of the Church, who represent traditional values. The townspeople waver symbolically like a Greek chorus between the opposing forces. While attacking both Church and State for keeping people enslaved in a state of ignorance, Solórzano dramatizes the plight of the individual who must make decisions that are critical for his or her own self-realization. In attempting to secure the freedom of her brother (who represents Mankind), Beatriz achieves the freedom that comes from commitment without regret (existential choice). Her death at the end is inconsequential in proportion to her existential victory. The play provides a superb integration of theme and technique and is considered one of the classics of the contemporary theatre.

In addition to these three major plays, Solórzano is the author of six one-act plays, most of which continue similar preoccupations. In *Los fantoches* (The Puppets), a play built around the use of Mexican fireworks in religious celebrations, the Big-Head determines the fate of the other puppets by random selection. The central figure functions metaphorically as a god disposing human lives without love or compassion. In *El crucificado* (The Crucified) a drunken Mexican peasant is crucified to re-enact the passion of Christ, and predictably those who participate later deny responsibility for their actions. *El sueño del ángel* (The Angel's Dream) pairs a woman with her Guardian Angel who insists she must expiate her sin, an act of adultery committed years before. *Mea culpa* is a weaker play also dealing with fear and guilt produced by religious imbalance. *Cruce de vías* (Railroad Crossing) epitomizes hopelessness through a missed encounter. A man and a woman search for each other in a scene with touches of a silent movie while the switchman serves as a foil to their existentialist game. The other very short play, *El zapato* (The Shoe), takes the metaphor of an old shoe that hurts the young boy's foot to explore not only a sinister and perhaps incestuous relationship with his mother but also the guilt and recrimination that he experiences before his father, a god-like figure who insists on subjugation, guilt, and repentance.

Carlos Solórzano has made extraordinary contributions not only to the Latin American theatre but also to critical study of the theatre: he was the author of two books that provided the first panoramic views of Latin American theatre as an entity.

—George Woodyard

———

SOLOUKHIN, Vladimir (Alekseevich). Russian. Born in Alepino Stavrovsky, Vladimir region, 14 June 1924. Educated at the Vladimir Engineering Technicum, 1938–42, graduated in tool mechanics; Gorky Literary Institute, Moscow, 1946–51. Served in the army until 1945. Married to Rosa Soloukhin. Magazine feature writer; joined Communist Party, 1952; member of editorial staff, Molodaia gvardiia publishing house, Moscow, 1964–81. Member of the board of Union of Soviet Writers, from 1959. Recipient: State prize, 1979. Address: c/o Union of Writers, Ulitsa Vorovskogo 52, Moscow, Russia.

PUBLICATIONS

Fiction

Rozhdenie Zernograda [The Birth of Zenograd]. Moscow, Pravda, 1955.
Z sin'-moriami. Moscow, Molodaia gvardiia, 1956
Kaplia rosy [A Dewdrop]. Moscow, Molodaia gvardiia, 1960.
Otkrytki iz V'etnama [Postcards from Vietnam]. Moscow, Molodaia gvardiia, 1961.
Liricheskie povesti [Lyrical Stories]. Moscow, Moskovskii rabochii, 1961.
Karavai zavarnogo khleba: rasskazy [Round Loaf of Scalded Bread]. Moscow, Pravda, 1963.
Svidanie v Viaznikakh [Appointment in Viaznik]. Moscow, Molodaia gvardiia, 1964.

Vremena goda: kartiny russkoi prirody [Time of Years: Pictures of Russian Nature].   Moscow, Sovetskaia Rossiia, 1964.

Slavianskaia tetrad' [Slavic Notebook].   Moscow, Sovetskaia Rossiia, 1965.

Mat'-machekha [Mother-Stepmother].   Moscow, Sovetskii pisatel', 1966.

Rabota [Work].   Moscow, Sovetskaia Rossiia, 1966.

Zimnii den' [A Winter's Day] (includes *Chernie doski* [Blackboards]).   Moscow, Sovetskii pisatel', 1969.

Serafima.   Tbilisi, Nakaduli, 1969.

Zakon nabata [The Law of the Alarm].   Moscow, Sovremennik, 1971.

Belaia trava.   Moscow, Progress, 1971; as *White Grass*, Moscow, Progress, 1971.

Olepinskie prudy [The Ponds of Olepino].   Moscow, Sovremennik, 1973.

Solomennyi kordon [Straw Cordon].   Moscow, Sovremennik, 1974.

Prigovor [The Sentence].   Published in *Moskva* (Moscow), 1, 1975.

Rybii bog [Fish God].   Moscow, Sovetskaia Rossiia, 1975.

Poseshcheniie Zvanka [Visit to Zvanka].   Published in *Moskva* (Moscow), 7, 1975.

Buinaia kura.   Moscow, Khudozhestvennaia literatura, 1976.

Prekrasnaia Adygene [Beautiful Adygene].   Moscow, Sovetskii pisatel', 1976.

Krutaia Marina [Stern Marina].   Moscow, Sovremennik, 1978.

Pod odnoi kryshei [Under One Roof].   Iaroslavl', Verkh-Volzh. knizhnoe izdatel'stvo, 1979.

Kolokol, pervoe poruchenie [The Bell, the First Assignment].   Published in *Grani* (Frankfurt), 118, 1980.

Prodolzhenie vremeni; Pis'ma iz raznykh mest [The Continuation of Time; Letters from Various Places].   Moscow, Published in *Nash sovremennik* (Moscow), 1, 1982.

Sobranie sochinenii [Collected Works].   Moscow, Khudozhestvennaia literatura, 4 vols., 1983–84.

Rasskazy; Prigovor [Stories; The Sentence].   Moscow, Khudozhestvennaia literatura, 1984.

Bedstvie s golubiami: rasskazy i ocherki [Disaster with Blues].   Moscow, Sovetskii pisatel', 1984.

Byvali chelovek.   Moscow, Sovetskii pisatel', 1986.

Pokhorony Stepanidy Ivanovny [The Funeral of Stepanida Ivanovna].   Published in *Novyi mir* (Moscow), 9, 1987.

Scenes from Russian Life.   London, Owen, 1988.

Lugovaia gvozdichka [Meadow Carnations].   Moscow, Sovetskaia Rossiia, 1989.

Verse

Dozhd v Stepi [Rain on the Steppes].   1953.

Razryv-trava [Cut Grass].   Moscow, Molodaia gvardiia, 1956.

Ruch'i na asfal'te [Stream on Asphalt].   Moscow, Sovetskii pisatel', 1958.

Kolodets [The Well].   Moscow, Pravda, 1959.

Zhuravlikha [Cranes].   Moscow, Moskovskii rabochii, 1959.

Kak vypit' solntse [How to Drink the Sun].   Moscow, Sovetskii pisatel', 1961.

Imeiushchii v rukakh tsvety [Flowers in His Hands].   Moscow, Sovetskii pisatel', 1962.

Stikhi [Poems].   Tbilisi, Sabchota mtserali, 1962.

Zhit' na zemle [To Live on Earth].   Moscow, Sovetskii pisatel', 1965.

Ne priach'tes' ot dozhdia [Don't Hide from the Rain].   Moscow, Pravda, 1967.

Sorok zvonkikh kapelei; Osennie list'ia [Forty Drops Ringing; Autumn Leaves].   Moscow, Molodaia gvardiia, 1968.

Izbrannaia lirika [Selected Lyrics].   Moscow, Molodaia gvardiia, 1970.

Argument.   Moscow, Sovetskii pisatel', 1972.

Venok sonetov [A Garland of Sonnets].   Moscow, Molodaia gvardiia, 1975.

Lirika [Lyrics].   Moscow, Sovetskaia Rossiia, 1975.

Sedina [Grey Hair].   Moscow, Sovetskii pisatel', 1977.

Derevo nad vodoi: poeticheskie perevody [The Tree Above the Water].   Moscow, Sovetskaia Rossiia, 1979.

Stikhotvoreniia [Poems].   Moscow, Sovremennik, 1982.

V chistom pole [In a Clean Field].   Moscow, Sovetskii pisatel', 1988.

Smekh za levym plechom.   Published in *Grani* (Frankfurt), 147, 1988, and Frankfurt, Posev, 1988; as *Laughter over the Left Shoulder*, London, Owen, 1990.

Chitaia Lenina [Reading Lenin].   Published in *Rodina*, 10, 1989; Frankfurt, Posev, 1989.

Iz novoi knigi [From a New Book].   Published in *Grani* (Frankfurt), 152, 1989.

Masterskaia [Workshop].   Moscow, Sovremennik, 1990.

Severnye berezy [Northern Silver Birches].   Moscow, Molodaia gvardiia, 1990.

Drevo [Tree].   Moscow, Molodaia gvardiia, 1991.

Other

Zolotoe dno [Golden Bottom].   Moscow, Sovetskii pisatel', 1956.

Vladimirski Proselki.   Moscow, Goslitizdat, 1958; as *A Walk in Rural Russia*, London, Hodder and Stoughton, 1966; New York, Dutton, 1967.

Veter stranstvii [The Wind of Travelling] (essays).   Moscow, Sovetskii pisatel', 1960.

Bibliuteka proizbedenii sovetskikh pisatelei.   Moscow, Molodaia gvardiia, 5 vols., 1964.

S liricheskikh pozitsii [From Lyrical Points of View] (essays).   Moscow, Sovetskii pisatel', 1965.

Pis'ma iz russkogo muzeia; Chernye doski; Vremia sobirat' kamni [Letters from the Russian Museum; Blackboards; Time to Collect Stones].   Moscow, Molodaia gvardiia, 1966; *Chernye doski* as *Searching for Icons in Russia*, London, Harvill Press, 1971; New York, Harcourt Brace, 1972.

Nozhichek skostianoi ruchkoi [The Little Knife Knocked Out of the Hand].   Moscow, Detskaia literatura, 1966.

Rodnaia krasota [Native Beauty].   Moscow, Sovetskii khudozhnik, 1966; London, Iskander, 1969.

Tret'ia okhota [Third Hunt] (nature writings).   Moscow, Sovetskaia Rossiia, 1968.

0,0001. Odna stotysiachnaia.   Minsk, Belarus', 1971.

Po griby.   Moscow, n.p., 1974.

Znakomyi neznakomets [The Known Unknown].   Minsk, Mastatskaia literatura, 1974.

Izbrannye proizvedeniia [Selected Works].   Moscow, Khudozhestvennaia literatura, 2 vols., 1974.

Slovo zhivoe i mertvoe (o vremeni i o sebe) [The Word Living and Dead (About Time and Self)].   Moscow, Sovremennik, 1976.

Kameshki na ladoni [A Handful of Pebbles].   Moscow, Sovetskaia Rossiia, 1977.

Med na khlebe.   Moscow, Molodaia gvardiia, 1978; as *Honey on Bread*, Moscow, Progress, 1982.

Pisatel' i khudozhnik [Writer and Artist].   Moscow, Izobrazitel'noe Iskusstvo, 1979.

Vremia sobirat' kamni: ocherki [A Time to Collect Stones: Essays].   Moscow, Sovremennik, 1980.

Trava (Etiudy o prirode) [Grass (Studies on Nature)].   Riga, Zvaigzne, 1983.

Volshebnaia palochka [Magical Cane] (essays).   Moscow, Moskovskii rabochii, 1983.

Sozertsanie chuda [The Contemplation of a Miracle] (essays).   Moscow, Sovetskaia Rossiia, 1984.

Priiti i poklonit'sia [Come and Bow Down].   Moscow, Pravda, 1986.

Vozvrashchenie k nachulu [Returning to the Beginning].   Moscow, Sovremennik, 1990.

Rasstavanie s idolom [Parting with an Idol].   N.p., S.Sh.A., 1991.

Nastala ochered' moia [My Turn Has Come].   Moscow, Golos, 1992.

Pri svete dnia [Before the Light of Day].   Moscow, n.p., 1992.

Editor, *Tsotne, ili padenie i vozvyshenie Gruzin*, by Grigol Abashidze.   Tbilisi, Merani, 1977.

Editor, *Prevyshenie skorosti*, by Liliana Stefanova.   Moscow, Progress, 1982.

Editor, with Sergeia Podelkova, *Nastuplenie leta*, by Aleksei Kulakovskii.   Moscow, Sovremennik, 1986.

Translator, *Moi Dagestan*, by R. Gamzatov.   Moscow, Molodaia gvardiia, 1972.

Translator, *Slomannaia podkova*, by A. Keshokov.   Moscow, Molodaia gvardiia, 1973.

*

Critical Studies: *A History of Post-War Soviet Writing: The Literature of Moral Opposition* by G. Svirskii, Ann Arbor, Michigan, Ardis, 1981; "A Brief Survey of Vladimir Soloukhin's Works" by N. G. Kosachov, in *Russian Language Journal*, 121–122, 1981; "Energy and Talent" by Andrei Turkov, in *Soviet Literature* (Brooklyn, New York), 6[435], 1984.

*   *   *

Vladimir Soloukhin gained prominence in the 1960s as a member of the "village prose" school of Soviet Russian literature, in particular as a consequence of his defence of religion and his advocacy for State-sponsored maintenance of old buildings, especially churches. He writes both poetry and prose, but it is for his prose, and in particular his non-fiction, that he is chiefly known. His works focuses on the lyrical evocation of nature, reflections on the Russian past, and anxiety at the needless delapidation or destruction of architectural monuments.

Soloukhin was born and brought up in a village in the Vladimir region in northern Russia. He attended the Gorky Literary Institute, published his first works (poems) under Stalin, but is best known for a few longer, first-person narratives, published between 1957 and 1988. He first attracted attention with *Vladimirski Proselki* (*A Walk in Rural Russia*), a work of fresh and vivid imagery, full of the joy and exhilaration of "rediscovering" the Russian countryside. The book is crammed with descriptions of birds, wildlife, trees and plants, as well as the peaceful rhythms of peasant life in the north of Russia, seemingly undisturbed by the cataclysms of recent history. He develops his interest in the Russian past in subsequent works such as *Chernye doski* (*Searching for Icons in Russia*). Here Soloukhin deplores the destruction of the old buildings and icons, and the subsequent loss of the Russian

spiritual heritage, and his anger approaches a full-blown critique of Soviet state policies towards religion, the church, and the Russian past — writing that met with official criticism and disapproval.

Soloukhin has anticipated many cultural concerns, especially in the glasnost years: his essay "Vremia sobirat' kamni" (A Time to Collect Stones) is about the destruction of the famous Optina Pustyn' monastery; in *Pis'ma iz russkogo muzeia* (Letters from the Russian Museum) he condemns the demolition of the Church of Christ the Saviour in Moscow to make way for a huge outdoor swimming pool. The fate of both these symbols of Russian spirituality has since 1988 been forthrightly condemned and deplored in various sections of the Soviet and post-Soviet media.

Throughout Soloukhin's writing the first-person narrative is dominant, and his subject-matter is generally based on his own experience. Soloukhin seldom has need of a narrator or protagonist, but even when he does, this character conveys directly to the reader Soloukhin's own views, thoughts, and feelings. Several commentators (Grigorii Svirskii and Kathleen Parthé, for instance) have noted with disapproval the extreme self-centredness of Soloukhin's writing, where the reader is forced to accept the self-declared importance of the author's own stance and experience. Moreover, in comparison with the other village prose writers (Valentin Rasputin [*q.v.*], Viktor Astaf'ev, Fedor Abramov, and Vasilii Belov, for instance), until his very latest, post-glasnost period, Soloukhin's fiction lacks the specific historical dimension that is characteristic of village prose as a whole.

Soloukhin's fictional subject-matter differs little from that of his fellow *derevenshchiki* (village prose writers). The short story "Pasha" is about an old woman of that name who in the course of her life has suffered gang-rape, revolution, war, material deprivation, and, in her old age, alienation from her town-based daughter, but whose spirit remains strong. She belongs to the gallery of modern Russian peasant heroines that includes Aleksander Solzhenitsyn's (*q.v.*) Matrena, Rasputin's peasant women Natasha, Anna, and Dar'ia, and the old women of Astaf'ev and Vladimir Lichutin. In another story, "Dvadsat' piat' na dvadsat' piat'" (25 on to 25), the central character, now a middle-aged professor, returns to the village of his childhood and youth to find many of the old ways disappearing, and the younger generation preferring music played on Sony tape-recorders to actually making music on the traditional accordion (the title refers to a type of accordion). Everything that reminds him of the modern world — motorcycles, political slogans, television sets — arouses his sadness at the loss of the past. Such nostalgia is also clearly within the village prose tradition.

Soloukhin's most important work may well prove to be *Smekh za levym plechom* (*Laughter over the Left Shoulder*), one of the few examples of village prose to be published abroad before being published in the Soviet Union. It is a virtual rewriting of his earlier autobiographical novel *Kaplia rosy* (A Dewdrop), which omitted important details of collectivization in Soloukhin's native village of Olepino. Both works are tales of a rural childhood, full of wondrous descriptions of nature and peasant life, and bemoaning the ills of modern, urban life. In the later work, however, the callous randomness of the policy of dekulakization and collectivization is emphasized. The author rails not only against the ravages of Stalinism, but shows clearly that Lenin is himself to blame. Soloukhin in this work shows that he has undoubtedly been influenced by the writings of Solzhenitsyn.

Soloukhin remains a writer of both integrity and contradictions. On the one hand, he is respected by many for his fearless advocacy of protecting the Russian cultural and spiritual heritage; on the other, he has also recommended the prohibition of church services if such an action would preserve church buildings. He was one of the writers who attacked Pasternak in 1958 for publishing *Doctor Zhivago* abroad, and yet 30 years later did exactly that himself with *Laughter over the Left Shoulder*. He is a well-travelled man (he often describes in detail his trips to foreign lands, a trait that would not endear him to the majority of Soviet readers deprived of any such opportunity), but is also an ardent nationalist of neo-Slavophile convictions. This seeming dichotomy extends to his narrative persona: in his publicism he is strident and emphatic, while his lyrical voice is gentler and more reflective.

—David Gillespie

SOLZHENITSYN, Aleksandr (Isaevich). Also Alexander Solzhenitsyn. Russian. Born in Kislovodsk, 11 December 1918. Educated at school in Rostov-on-Don; University of Rostov, 1936–41, degree in mathematics and physics 1941; correspondence course in philology, Moscow University, 1939–41. Served in the Soviet Army, 1941–45: captain; decorated twice; arrested and stripped of rank, 1945. Married 1) Natalia Alekseevna Reshetovskaia in 1940 (divorced), remarried in 1957 (divorced 1973), three sons; 2) Natalia Svetlova in 1973, one stepson. Physics teacher, secondary school, Morozovsk, 1941; sentenced to eight years imprisonment for anti-Soviet agitation, 1945: in prisons in Moscow, 1945–50, and labour camp in Kazakhstan, 1950–53; released from prison, and exiled to Kok-Terek, Siberia: mathematics teacher, 1953–56; released from exile, 1956, and settled in Ryazan, 1957, as teacher, then full-time writer; unable to publish from 1966; charged with treason and expelled from U.S.S.R., 1974; lived in Zurich, 1974–76, and in Cavendish, Vermont, since 1976; reinstated to Union of Soviet Writers, 1989; Soviet citizenship restored, 1990; treason charges formally removed, 1991. Recipient: Foreign book prize (France), 1969; Nobel prize for literature, 1970; Templeton prize, 1983. D.Litt.: Harvard University, Cambridge, Massachusetts, 1978. Member, American Academy of Arts and Sciences, 1969; Honorary Fellow, Hoover Institution on War, Revolution, and Peace, 1975; Address: c/o Harper and Row, 10 East 53rd Street, New York, New York 10022, U.S.A.

PUBLICATIONS

Fiction

Odin den' Ivana Denisovicha. London, Flegon Press, 1962; as *One Day in the Life of Ivan Denisovich*, New York, Praeger, and London, Gollancz, 1963.
Dlia pol'zy dela. Chicago, Russian Language Specialties, 1963; as *For the Good of the Cause*, New York, Praeger, 1964; London, Bodley Head, 1971.
Sluchai na stantsii Krechetovka; Matrenin dvor. London, Flegon Press, 1963; as *We Never Make Mistakes*, Columbia, University of South Carolina Press, 1963.
Etudy i krokhotnye rasskazy. Frankfurt, Posev, 1964; as *Stories and Prose Poems*, New York, Farrar Straus, 1971; as *Prose Poems*, London, Bodley Head, 1971; as *Matryona's House and Other Stories*, London, Penguin, 1975.

V kruge pervom. Frankfurt, Fischer, 1968; as *The First Circle*, New York, Harper, and London, Harvill, 1968; restored complete edition, Paris, YMCA Press, 1978.
Rakovyi korpus. Milan, Mondadori, 1968; complete edition, London, Bodley Head, 1968; as *Cancer Ward*, 2 vols., Bodley Head, 1968–69; as *The Cancer Ward*, New York, Farrar Straus, 1969.
Six Etudes. Northfield, Minnesota, College City Press, 1971.
Avgust chetyrnadtsatogo. London, Flegon Press, 1971; as *August 1914*, New York, Farrar Straus, and London, Bodley Head, 1972; expanded version, as *Krasnoe koleso 1*, in *Sobranie sochinenii*, 11–12, 1983; revised edition, as part of *Krasnoe koleso*, 1983–86.
Krasnoe koleso: povestvovan'e v otmerennykh srokakh [The Red Wheel].
  Uzel 1: Avgust chetyrnadtsatogo. Paris, YMCA Press, 2 vols., 1983; as *The Red Wheel: A Narrative in Discrete Periods of Time*, New York, Farrar Straus, and London, Bodley Head, 1989.
  Uzel 2: Oktiabr'shestnadtsatogo. Paris, YMCA Press, 2 vols., 1984.
  Uzel 3: Mart semnadtsatogo. Paris, YMCA Press, 2 vols., 1986.
  Uzel 4: Aprel' semnadtsatogo. Paris, YMCA Press, 1991.
Rasskazy [Short Stories]. Moscow, Sovremennik, 1990.

Plays

Olen' i shalashovka. London, Flegon Press, 1968; as *The Love-Girl and the Innocent* (produced London, 1981), London, Bodley Head, and New York, Farrar Straus, 1969; as *Respublika truda*, published in *Sobraniye sochineniy*, 8, 1981.
Svecha na vetru. London, Flegon Press, 1968; as *Candle in the Wind*, Minneapolis, University of Minnesota Press, and London, Bodley Head-Oxford University Press, 1973; as *Svet, koroty, v tebe*, published in *Sobranie sochinenii*, 8, 1981.
Pir podebitelei. Published in *Sobranie sochinenii*, 8, 1981; as *Victory Celebrations* (produced Liverpool, 1990), London, Bodley Head, 1983; New York, Farrar Straus, 1984.
Plenniki. Published in *Sobranie sochinenii*, 8, 1981; as *Prisoners*, London, Bodley Head, 1983; New York, Farrar Straus, 1984.
P'esy i kinostsenarii (plays and film scripts). Paris, YMCA Press, 1981.
The Love-Girl and the Innocent (includes *Prisoners*; *Victory Celebration*). London, Faber, 1986.

Verse

Prusskie nochi: poema napisannaia v lagere v 1950. Paris, YMCA Press, 1974; as *Prussian Nights,* translated by Robert Conquest, New York, Farrar Straus, and London, Collins, 1977.

Other

Sobranie sochinenii [Collected Works]. Frankfurt, Posev, vols., 1969–70.
Les Droits de l'écrivain. Paris, Seuil, 1969.
Nobelevskaia lektsiia po literature. Paris, YMCA Press, 1972; as *Nobel Lecture*, edited by F. D. Reeve, New York, Farrar Straus, 1972; as *One Word of Truth*, London, Bodley Head, 1972.

Arkhipelag Gulag. Paris, YMCA Press, 3 vols., 1973–76; as *The Gulag Archipelago*, New York, Harper, and London, Collins, 3 vols., 1974–78; abridged edition in 1 vol., edited by Edward Ericson, Jr., New York, Harper, 1985; London, Collins Harvill, 1986.

Iz-pod glyb. Paris, YMCA Press, 1974; as *From Under the Rubble*, Boston, Little Brown, and London, Collins, 1975.

Mir i nasilie [Peace and Violence]. Frankfurt, Posev, 1974.

Pis'mo vozhdiam Sovetskogo soiuza. Paris, YMCA Press, 1974; as *Letter to the Soviet Leaders*, New York, Harper, and London, Collins, 1974.

A Pictorial Autobiography. New York, Farrar Straus, 1974.

Solzhenitsyn, the Voice of Freedom (two speeches). Washington, D.C., AFL-CIO, 1975.

Bodalsia telenok s dubom (autobiography). Paris, YMCA Press, 1975; as *The Oak and the Calf*, London, Collins, and New York, Harper, 1980.

Lenin v Tsiurikhe. Paris, YMCA Press, 1975; as *Lenin in Zurich*, New York, Farrar Straus, and London, Bodley Head, 1976.

Detente: Prospects for Democracy and Dictatorship. New Brunswick, New Jersey, Transaction, 1975.

America, We Beg You to Interfere (speeches). Wheaton, Illinois, Church League of America, 1975.

Amerikanskie rechi [American Discourse]. Paris, YMCA Press, 1975.

Warning to the Western World (interview). New York, Farrar Straus, and London, Bodley Head-BBC Publications, 1976.

A World Split Apart (address). New York, Harper, 1978.

Alexander Solzhenitsyn Speaks to the West (speeches). London, Bodley Head, 1978.

Sobranie sochinenii [Collected Works]. Paris, YMCA Press, 1978–.

The Mortal Danger: How Misconceptions About Russia Imperil the West. New York, Harper, and London, Bodley Head, 1980.

East and West (miscellany). New York, Harper, 1980.

Issledovaniia noveishei russkoi istorii. Paris, YMCA Press, 1980–.

Publitsistika: stat'i i rechi (articles and speeches). Paris, YMCA Press, 1981.

Kak nam obustroit' Rossiiu [How Are We to Put Russia in Order?]. Paris, YMCA Press, 1990.

Rebuilding Russia: Toward Some Formulations. New York, Farrar Straus, and London, Harper Collins, 1991.

Les Invisibles. Paris, Fayard, 1992.

Nashi pliuralisty: otryvok iz vtorogo toma "Ocherkov literaturnoi zhizni" (Mai 1982). Published in *Novyi mir* (Moscow), 4, 1992.

Editor, *Russkii slovar' iazykovogo rasshireniia.* Moscow, Nauka, 1990.

*

Bibliography: *Alexander Solzhenitsyn. An International Bibliography of Writings by and About Him* by Donald M. Fiene, Ann Arbor, Michigan, Ardis, 1973.

Critical Studies: *Alexander Solzhenitsyn* by George Lukács, London, Merlin, 1970, Cambridge, Massachusetts, M.I.T. Press, 1971; *Alexander Solzhenitsyn: The Major Novels* by Abraham Rothberg, Ithaca, New York, Cornell University Press, 1971; *Alexander Solzhenitsyn* by David Burg and George Feifer, New York, Stein and Day, 1973; *Alexander Solzhenitsyn: Critical Essays and Documentary Materials* edited by John B. Dunlop and others, Belmont, Massachusetts, Nordland, 1973, revised edition, 1975; *Alexander Solzhenitsyn* by Christopher Moody, Edinburgh, Oliver and Boyd, 1973, revised edition, Oliver and Boyd, and New York, Harper, 1976; *Alexander Solzhenitsyn: A Collection of Critical Essays* edited by Kathryn Feuer, Englewood Cliffs, New Jersey, Prentice Hall, 1976; *Solzhenitsyn: Politics and Form* by Francis Barker, London, Macmillan, 1977; *The Politics of Solzhenitsyn* by Stephen Carter, London, Macmillan, 1977; *Alexander Solzhenitsyn* by Steven Allaback, New York, Taplinger, 1978; *Solzhenitsyn and the Secret Circle* by Olga Andreyev Carlisle, New York, Holt Rinehart, and London, Routledge, 1978; *Solzhenitsyn Studies: A Quarterly Survey* (journal) (Hamilton, New York), from Spring 1980; *Solzhenitsyn and Dostoevsky: A Study in the Polyphonic Novel* by Vladislav Krasnov, London, Prior, 1980; *Solzhenitsyn, Tvardovsky and "Novy mir"* by Vladimir Lakshin, Cambridge, Massachusetts, M.I.T. Press, 1980; *Solzhenitsyn: The Moral Vision* by Edward E. Ericson, Grand Rapids, Michigan, Eerdmans, 1982; *Alexander Solzhenitsyn's Traditional Imagination* by James Curtis, Athens, University of Georgia Press, 1984; *Solzhenitsyn* by Georges Nivat, London, Overseas Publications Interchange, 1984; *Alexander Solzhenitsyn: A Biography* by Michael Scammell, New York, Norton, 1984, London, Hutchinson, 1985; *Alexander Solzhenitsyn in Exile: Critical Essays and Documentary Material* edited by John B. Dunlop, Richard S. Haugh, and Michael Nicholson, Stanford, California, Hoover Institution Press, 1985; *Alexander Solzhenitsyn: Myth and Reality* by A. Flegon, London, Flegon Press, 1986.

*   *   *

Aleksandr Solzhenitsyn figures not only as Russia's most important living writer, but as a prominent political personage, historian, and moral and social philosopher. He ranked with Andrei Sakharov as Soviet Russia's leading dissident and, as one of his own characters would put it, has played the role of Russia's "second government." This public persona has often obscured Solzhenitsyn's literary creation. Indeed, the headline-grabbing content of much of his early fiction itself overshadowed his artistic achievement, as did his battles with the Soviet literary establishment, the politicized circumstances of his 1970 Nobel prize for literature, and his 1974 expulsion from his homeland. In exile, Solzhenitsyn has devoted his prodigious energies and literary gifts to deliberately programmatic work, significant more for its political and historical substance than for its artistic merit, even when cast as fiction. At his best, however, Solzhenitsyn is a formidable artist, an old-fashioned realist who commands the panoramic breadth and dramatic force, if not, finally, the depth or artistic genius of Fedor Dostoevskii and Leo Tolstoi, giants with whom he often is compared.

Solzhenitsyn's debut in 1962 constitutes perhaps *the* signal event of post-Stalin Russian culture before glasnost. *Odin den' Ivana Denisovicha* (*One Day in the Life of Ivan Denisovich*), the first public treatment of Stalin's forced-labor camps — a subject previously *and* subsequently taboo — appeared only through the intervention of Nikita Khrushchev, who was attracted both to the sympathetic portrait of the "Everyman" peasant hero, and to the story's potential for revitalizing his own anti-Stalin campaign. *Ivan Denisovich*, however, demands attention not merely for its sensational content, which takes the paradoxical form of a matter-of-fact account of one average day in the Soviet gulag. This work also subverts both the cliché-ridden bombast of official Soviet discourse and the sentimentality and self-congratulatory pomposity of Soviet socialist realism by focusing on the minutiae of everyday life as recorded from Ivan's limited perspective; by utilizing the colloquial hodgepodge of prison camp idiom for its third-person narrative; and by implicitly presenting the prison camp's pointless labor and its guards' malevolent authority as metaphors for Stalinist society at large. Moreover, *Ivan Denisovich* carries an important thematic subtext which suggests that while Ivan's struggle for material survival (literally for his daily bread) justly evokes in readers terror and pity, it ultimately is misguided in its blindness to spiritual survival, to the needs of the soul — a religious underpinning which has remained a Solzhenitsyn constant. Also to remain constants in Solzhenitsyn's prose fiction were efforts to revivify the Russian literary language with popular speech, archaisms, folk sayings, and proverbs, and a thematic preoccupation with language's uses and abuses.

With *Ivan Denisovich* Solzhenitsyn established the paradigm of constricted spatial and temporal frameworks which has characterized all his most successful work. Within these frameworks single events or circumstances stand as metaphors for larger entities, be they geopolitical (a cancer ward or labor camp representing Soviet society at large), ethical (the question of collaboration with an evil system and the meaning and value of freedom and responsibility), or existential (the struggle for survival and the meaning of life). Thus, Solzhenitsyn's second important publication, the story "Matryona's House," offers in the portrait of a simple peasant woman an emblem of "that one righteous person without whom no village can stand. Nor the world." The story's symbolically weighty events, wherein the selfless Matryona, helping her drunken relatives dispossess her of her own home, is killed by a train travelling backwards at night with its lights out, suggests Russia's martyrdom to blind historical forces tragically imposed on her by agents of the materialistic, spiritually bankrupt West. Here Solzhenitsyn reveals deeply conservative, neo-Slavophile sympathies which recall those of contemporary Russian "village prose" writers who bemoan the destruction of their nation's traditional ways and values.

"Matryona's House" was to be the last important work Solzhenitsyn would publish in the Soviet Union until the final days of its existence. The first of his banned books to be published abroad was *V kruge pervom* (*The First Circle*), a lengthy novel which centers on the life-and-death moral choices faced by all citizens of the Stalinist state, be they great or humble, jailer or jailed. As is true of nearly all Solzhenitsyn's fiction, it is based closely on autobiographical material, typically taken from the watershed experience of the author's life — his eight years' imprisonment in the Soviet gulag for obliquely disparaging Stalin in letters to a friend. *The First Circle* draws specifically on Solzhenitsyn's stay in a special camp where scientists performed technical slave labor. Also typically, *The First Circle* engages in dialogue with literary classics, most obviously in this instance with Dante's *Inferno*, but also with works by Tolstoi, Dostoevskii, Anton Chekhov, and others. *Rakovyi korpus* (*Cancer Ward*), Solzhenitsyn's second long fiction, grew out of the author's own experience as a cancer patient. Both works have been described by their author as "polyphonic," meant not in the Bakhtinian sense *per se*, but as "a novel without a hero" where each of the many characters "becomes the central one while he is in the field of action." The novels' "meaning" accrues through ironic juxtaposition of episodes wherein the several "central characters," covering a cross-section of society, face similar ethical and existential crises, responding variously in what amounts structurally to a "multi-voiced" chorus.

Solzhenitsyn continues work on his massive *Krasnoe koleso* (*The Red Wheel*), the novel he has been planning since 1936 and which he considers "the most important thing" of his life. It offers a predetermined investigation into the meaning and causes of the revolution of 1917 and Russia's derailment from its true historical path. Solzhenitsyn's culprits, again, are the poisonous Western ideas imported by Russia's liberals throughout the 19th and early 20th centuries, which later were applied ruthlessly by dogmatic revolutionaries, unwittingly abetted by a weak Tsar and a corrupt incompetent leadership. Solzhenitsyn expounds and illustrates his historical theories in what he terms "knots" (*uzel*) — long narratives covering critical historical junctures where multiple destinies intersect; junctures such as the disastrous military campaign described in *Avgust chetyrnadtsatogo* (*August 1914*), the only "knot" as yet translated into English. While *The Red Wheel* incorporates "experimental" features such as montage, review chapters, and cinematic scripts, its dominant device is historical documentation, including verbatim transcripts of archival materials and quotations from contemporary newspapers — documentation which, comprising as much as three-quarters of an entire knot, engulfs the plot and results, in the opinion of some, in overkill. While Solzhenitsyn never truly allowed for intellectual or existential ambiguity in his art, the diverse narrative viewpoints in earlier works did create the appearance of openness, even objectivity. *The Red Wheel*, however, lacks much sense of genuine dialogue on issues: the author's moral and intellectual authority is palpable, pervasive, and nearly monolithic.

A work others are more likely to consider Solzhenitsyn's most important is the equally huge *Arkhipelag Gulag* (*The Gulag Archipelago*), a non-fictional chronicle of Soviet repression which its author describes as "an experiment in literary investigation." *Gulag* organizes personal memories, historical documents, and the testimony of hundreds of witnesses by the techniques of literary fiction — metaphor, dramatization, irony, and narrative exhortations — to restore to society's consciousness and indict a long suppressed historical reality.

Of considerable importance to understanding Solzhenitsyn's character is his *Bodalsia telenok s dubom* (*The Oak and the Calf*), an idiosyncratic memoir. While Solzhenitsyn's prose masterfully exploits the structures and techniques of drama, his plays themselves, which explore war and prison themes, are less successful. His verse's interest lies primarily in the circumstances of its secret composition and commitment to memory in the camps. Despite mixed response to his most recent work, Solzhenitsyn remains a colossus of 20th-century Russian literature.

—Richard C. Borden

SOMMER, Piotr. Polish. Born in Wałbrzych, 13 April 1948. Educated at the University of Warsaw, M.A. in English 1973. Married Jolanta Sommer in 1972; two sons. Anglo-American poetry editor, 1976–80, and since 1980 Anglo-American editor, *Literatura na Świecie* [World Literature], Warsaw; contributing editor, *Res Publica*, since 1987, and *Tygodnik Literacki*, 1990–91, both Warsaw. Visiting writer, Washington and Lee University, Lexington, Virginia, Spring 1983, and Amherst College, Massachusetts, 1987–88, Spring 1992; Visiting Professor, University of Nebraska, Lincoln, summers

1988 and 1989, Mount Holyoke College, South Hadley, Massachusetts, Fall 1988, and Wesleyan University, Middletown, Connecticut, and Amherst College, both Spring 1989; translator-in-residence, University of Warwick, Coventry, Spring 1991. Recipient: Sadowska Foundation prize, 1988; Kościelski Foundation prize, 1988; *Literatura na Świecie* poetry translation prize, 1988. Address: ul. Moniuszki 9/11, 05-070 Sulejówek, Poland.

PUBLICATIONS

Verse

W krześle [In the Chair].   Cracow, Wydawnictwo Literackie, 1977.
Pamiątki po nas (1973–1976) [Remembrance of Us (1973–1976)].   Cracow, Wydawnictwo Literackie, 1980.
Przed snem [Before Going to Bed] (for children).   Warsaw, Nasza Księgarnia, 1981.
Kolejny świat [A Subsequent World].   Warsaw, Czytelnik, 1983.
Czynnik liryczny [The Lyrical Factor].   Cracow, Oficyna Literacka, 1986.
Czynnik liryczny i inne wiersze [The Lyrical Factor and Other Poems].   London, Aneks, 1988.
Things to Translate and Other Poems.   Newcastle-upon-Tyne, Bloodaxe, 1991.

Other

Wywiady z poetami brytyjskimi [Interviews with British Poets].   Warsaw, Czytelnik, 1985.
Zapisy rozmów [Recorded Conversations].   Warsaw, Czytelnik, 1985.

Editor and Co-Translator, *Antologia nowej poezji brytyjskiej* [An Anthology of New British Poetry].   Warsaw, Czytelnik, 1983.
Editor and Translator, *Twoja pojedynczość* [Your Singularity], by Frank O'Hara.   Warsaw, Państwowy Instytut Wydawniczy, 1987.
Editor and Translator, *Graffiti*, by Charles Reznikoff. Sanok, Sanocki Dom Kultury, 1991.

Translator, *Słoń i kwiat* [The Elephant and the Flower], by Brian Patten.   Warsaw, Krajowa Agencja Wydawnicza, 1982.
Co-Translator, *Poezje*, by Robert Lowell.   Cracow, Wydawnictwo Literackie, 1986.

*

Piotr Sommer comments:
I'm mostly interested in the tonalities of the sentence.

*   *   *

Having emerged, with the publication of his second collection, as one of the most original young poets of the early 1980s, Piotr Sommer has so far published five books of poems (as well as a volume of poems for children), of which the latest one, *Czynnik liryczny i inne wiersze* (The Lyrical Factor and Other Poems), provides a particularly convincing argument for considering him a major presence in today's Polish poetry. He is also one of the most active and influential translators of modern British and American poetry into Polish. Besides his large *Antologia nowej poezji brytyjskiej* (An Anthology of New British Poetry), which in 1983 first acquainted the Polish reader with the work of such poets as Seamus Heaney, Douglas Dunn, Paul Muldoon, Tony Harrison, Derek Mahon, and Craig Raine, he has also published *Zapisy rozmów* (Recorded Conversations), a collection of interviews with British and Irish poets and critics. More recently, his separate selections of the work of Frank O'Hara and Charles Reznikoff have appeared, and he has also translated extensively the poetry of Robert Lowell, John Berryman, and many others. He lives near Warsaw and over the past decade has made his living as an editor at the Warsaw-based monthly *Literatura na Świecie* (World Literature), besides several stints as a Visiting Professor at British and American universities.

As an original poet, Sommer's uniqueness has much to do with his choices of poets and poems to translate. These choices have reflected his own poetic program but, at the same time, they themselves have influenced Sommer's program quite considerably, if only by providing him with an initial stimulus to go in a specific direction, toward the direction of colloquial speech and ordinary reality. Over the past half century Poland has had an abundance of poets who explored such "low" subjects and levels of style, but in doing so, very few have gone to the lengths as Sommer has. In that respect he has perhaps just one Polish predecessor, the great poet Miron Białoszewski (1922–1983); still, he seems to be even more indebted to the respective examples of casual, low-key, spontaneous, quasi-oral poetic speech offered by O'Hara on the one hand and Berryman on the other. Just like these predecessors, Sommer aims at the sort of poetic utterance which is based on spontaneity without lapsing into disorganized randomness, colloquial without turning into empty social chit-chat, anti-conventional without being incommunicative. The poems he writes are uniformly "talk poems," devoid of any singsong quality yet faithfully preserving all the melodies and rhythms of colloquial speech. Events and objects of ordinary, everyday reality are related and described by the speaker in a deliberately deadpan manner, yet a closer look at the language he uses, with all its ironic inflexions and subtle "intermeanings" (Sommer's own term, from his poem "Niedyskrecje" — "Indiscretions"), reveals that in fact the poem's message should be identified more with the way it is being spoken than with what it apparently says. "Between these intermeanings the whole man is contained,/squeezing in where he sees a little space."

—Stanisław Barańczak

———

SØRENSEN, Villy.   Danish. Born in Copenhagen, 13 January 1929. Educated at the Vestre Borgerdydskole, graduated 1947; University of Copenhagen, 1947–51; University of Freiburg, Baden, 1952–53. Editor, with Klaus Rifbjerg (*q.v.*), *Vindrosen*, 1959–63; editor, *På vej*, 1978–81, and Gyldendal Kulturbibliotek, 1987–91. Recipient: Danish Critics prize, 1959; Danish Academy prize, 1962; Gyldendal prize, 1965; Nathansen award, 1969; Holberg Medal, 1973; Brandes prize, 1973; Steffens prize, 1974; Nordic Council prize, 1974; Amalienborg prize, 1977; Weekendavisen prize, 1982; Hans Christian Andersen award, 1983; Swedish Academy Nordic prize, 1986; Poul Henningsen prize, 1987; Wilster prize, 1988. Honorary doctorate: University of Copenhagen, 1979. Address: Skovvej 6, 2930 Klampenborg, Denmark.

PUBLICATIONS

Fiction

Sære historier. Copenhagen, Gyldendal, 1953; as *Strange Stories*, London, Secker and Warburg, 1956; as *Tiger in the Kitchen and Other Strange Stories*, New York, Abelard Schuman, 1957.
Ufarlige historier. Copenhagen, Gyldendal, 1955; as *Harmless Tales*, Norwich, Norvik Press, 1991.
Formynderfortællinger. Copenhagen, Gyldendal, 1964; as *Tutelary Tales*, Lincoln, University of Nebraska Press, 1988.
Ragnarok. Aarhus, Centrum, 1982; as *The Downfall of the Gods*, Lincoln, University of Nebraska Press, 1989.
De mange og De enkelte og andre småhistorier. Copenhagen, Brøndum, 1986; as *Another Metamorphosis and Other Fictions*, Seattle, Fjord Press, 1990; part as *Four Biblical Tales*, Seattle, Mermaid Press, 1991.
Den berømte Odysseus [The Famous Ulysses]. Copenhagen, Gyldendal, 1988.
Apollons oprør [The Revolt of Apollo]. Copenhagen, Vindrose, 1989.

Other

Digtere og dæmoner: fortolkninger og vurderinger [Poets and Demons: Interpretation and Criticism]. Copenhagen, Gyldendal, 1959.
Hverken-eller: kritiske betragtninger [Neither-Nor: Critical Reflections]. Copenhagen, Gyldendal, 1961.
Nietzsche. Copenhagen, Gad, 1963.
Kafkas digtning [Kafka's Work]. Copenhagen, Gyldendal, 1968.
Mellem fortid og fremtid [Between Past and Future]. Copenhagen, Gyldendal, 1969.
Schopenhauer. Copenhagen, Gad, 1969.
Uden mål — og med: moralske tanker [Without Aim or Purpose: Moral Reflections]. Copenhagen, Gyldendal, 1973.
Seneca: humanisten ved Neros hof. Copenhagen, Gyldendal, 1976; as *Seneca: The Humanist at the Court of Nero*, Edinburgh, Canongate, and Chicago, University of Chicago Press, 1984.
Oprør fra midten, with Niels I. Meyer and K. Helveg Petersen. Copenhagen, Gyldendal, 1978; as *Revolt from the Center*, London, Boyars, 1981.
Den gyldne middelvej og andre debatindlaeg fra 70erne [The Golden Mean and Other Contributions to Debate in the 1970s]. Copenhagen, Gyldendal, 1978.
Vejrdage [Weather Days]. Copenhagen, Gyldendal, 1980.
Tilløb: dagbøger 1949–53 [Beginnings: Diary 1949–53]. Copenhagen, Gyldendal, 1988.
Demokratiet og kunsten [Democracy and Art]. Copenhagen, Gyldendal, 1989.
Forløb: dagbøger 1953–61 [Continuation: Diary 1953–61]. Copenhagen, Gyldendal, 1990.
Jesus og Kristus [Jesus and Christ]. Copenhagen, Gyldendal, 1992.
Den frie vilje [Free Will]. Copenhagen, Reitzel, 1992.

Editor, *Begrebet Angest* [The Concept of Dread], by Søren Kierkegaard. Copenhagen, Gyldendal, 1960.
Editor, *Økonomi og filosofi* [Economics and Philosophy], by Karl Marx. Copenhagen, Gyldendal, 1962.
Editor, *Haabløse Slægter* [Hopeless Generations], by Herman Bang. Copenhagen, Gyldendal, 1965.

Editor, *Eventyr og historier* [Tales and Stories], by H. C. Andersen. Copenhagen, Gyldendal, 1965.
Editor, *Skuespil* [Plays], by William Shakespeare. Copenhagen, Gyldendal, 1966.
Editor, *Kunsten og revolutionen* [Art and Revolution], by Richard Wagner. Copenhagen, Gyldendal, 1983.
Editor, *Tine*, by Herman Bang. Copenhagen, Borgen, 1986.
Editor, *Tunge melodier* [Sad Melodies], by Herman Bang. Copenhagen, Gyldendal, 1987.
Editor, *Enten-eller* [Either-Or], by Søren Kierkegaard. Copenhagen, Gyldendal, 1988.
Editor, *Demokratiske visioner* (Democratic Vistas), by Walt Whitman. Copenhagen, Gyldendal, 1991.

Translator, with Anne Born, *The Book*, by Martin A. Hansen. Copenhagen, Wind-Flower Press, 1978.
Translator, with Anne Born, *The Dream of the Woman*, by Knud Hjortø. Copenhagen, Wind-Flower Press, 1980.
Translator, with Anne Born, *The Mountains*, by H. C. Branner. Copenhagen, Wind-Flower Press, 1982.

Also translator of works by Broch, Kafka, Hoffmann, von Horvath, Thomas Mann, Erasmus, and Seneca.

*

Villy Sørensen comments:
I have written short stories, biographies, essays on literary, philosophical, and political subjects, and treated the same subject (individual versus society, guardianship, and liberation) in those different genres. Poets consider me sort of a philosopher, philosophers consider me sort of a poet, both of them are right. I feel indebted to the humanism of a Seneca and an Erasmus (and translated them into Danish), and recognized (my own) modern problems in the conflict of Seneca as a poet, a thinker, and a statesman. I have had no political career, but was co-author of a Danish Utopia, which caused a heated discussion for several years. After that I have withdrawn to the wisdom of the old — Nordic, Greek, and Jewish-Christian — myths. I have sought continuity and coherence — and am not sure that people have found it in my books.

*   *   *

When Villy Sørensen made his debut in 1953, he went relatively unnoticed. Today, he is established as one of Denmark's most distinguished writers.
Although his work can be divided into two categories, the fiction and the philosophy, Sørensen himself has refused to distinguish between the two, preferring to see them as complementary. Nor does the literary historian find it easy to make an absolute distinction: the short stories *are* fiction, but they also express a philosophy, while some of the philosophical writings are at times close to the work of a creative writer. In both categories Sørensen stands as a linguistic innovator, making frequent play on words, less for the sake of the immediate effect than to emphasise and to create a new perspective by using an expression that at first appears to be cliché, but turns out to be innovatory.
With the early short stories, *Sære historier* (*Strange Stories*) and *Ufarlige historier* (*Harmless Tales*), Sørensen introduced the absurd into Danish literature. Franz Kafka's influence particularly obvious in "Mordsagen" ("The Murder Case") about a police commissioner seeking to solve a murder which concerns him closely, but about which he knows absolutely nothing. The force of these stories taken as a whole is that man is subject to a disharmony which it is useless to seek

suppress. Rather, a way must be found of living with it. The innocence of childhood must give way to adult lack of innocence, as in the story of the two little boys who, in an effort to save the life of another child, saw off his leg and thus kill him. Death has entered their world, and reality has to be interpreted in a different way. Evil in man must be accepted, as is demonstrated in "Duo," in which Siamese twins have an operation to remove one half, the evil half, with a resultant disharmony in the "good" half, the implications being that both were necessary.

Disharmony in human nature extends to cultural and social disharmony, receiving philosophical treatment in *Digtere og dæmoner* (Poets and Demons) and ultimately in *Oprør fra midten* (*Revolt from the Center*).

The 1960s saw the publication of commentaries and translations, in which Sørensen's own philosophical purpose is apparent—an introduction to Søren Kierkegaard's *Concept of Dread*, a translation of Kafka's short stories, and works on Friedrich Nietzsche and Arthur Schopenhauer, as well as eager participation in the social and political debate of that time.

In 1976 came *Seneca*, pursuing further the examination of the myth as expressing man's disharmony, and at the same time interpreting a complex personality and culture. It is at once a scholarly examination of Seneca and his work and an explanation of the apparent contradiction between Seneca's principles and actions. Nero's court is a mirror of modern society, and no one reading this impressive book can fail to see its application to the present century.

In *Vejrdage* (Weather Days), in a series of brief, poetical pieces, Sørensen gives a direct expression to his philosophy, while in *Ragnarok* (*The Downfall of the Gods*) he retells the old Nordic myths in such a way as to make the futility of the Gods' behaviour relevant to the modern world.

—W. Glyn Jones

SORESCU, Marin. Romanian. Born in Bulzeşti, Dolj, 19 February 1936. Educated at Iaşi University, 1955–60, B.A. in philology 1960. Married in 1981. Literary critic, *Luceafărul* review, Bucharest, 1960–66; editor, *Viaţa studenţească*, 1960–62; editor-in-chief, *Ramuri* literary review, 1970–91, and *Literatrul* journal, since 1991; participated in International Writing Program, University of Iowa, Iowa City, 1971–72; visiting writer, West Berlin, 1973–74, 1990; director, Animafilm Studios. Recipient: Writers' Union prize, 1965, 1968, 1974; International Poetry Festival Gold Medal (Naples), 1969; Romanian Academy prize, 1970 (and several other times); Academia delle Muze prize (Italy), 1978; Fernando Riello poetry prize (Spain), 1983; Herder prize (Austria), 1991. Corresponding member, Mallarmé Academy, Paris, since 1983, member, Romanian Academy, since 1991. Address: Strade Grigore Alexandrescu 43, Bucharest 71128, Romania.

PUBLICATIONS

Verse

Singur printre poeţi [Alone Among the Poets]. Bucharest, Editura pentru Literatură, 1964.

Poeme; versuri [Poems; Verses]. Bucharest, Editura pentru Literatură, 1965.
Moartea ceasului [The Death of the Watch]. Bucharest, Editura Tineretului, 1966.
Poeme [Poems]. Bucharest, Editura pentru Literatură, 1967.
Tinereţea lui Don Quijote. Bucharest, Editura Tineretului, 1968; as *Don Quijote's Tender Years*, translated by Stavros Deligiorgis, Bucharest, Carta Românească, and Iowa City, Corycian Press, 1979; as *The Youth of Don Quixote*, translated by John F. Deane, Dublin, Dedalus, 1987.
Unghi [Angle]. Bucharest, Carta Românească, 1970; as *Ram = Frames, 25 Poems* (bilingual edition), translated by Roy MacGregor Hastie, Bucharest, Eminescu, 1972.
O aripă şi-un picior: despre cum era să zbor [A Wing and a Foot] (for children). Bucharest, Albatros, 1970.
Tuşiţi [Cough]. Bucharest, Eminescu, 1970.
Suflete, bun la toate [Oh, Soul, Good for Everything]. Bucharest, Albatros, 1972.
La Lilieci [In the Village Lilieci]. Bucharest, Eminescu, 3 vols., 1973–79.
Astfel [So]. Iaşi, Junimea, 1973.
Norii [The Clouds]. Craiov, Scrisul Românesc, 1975.
Descîntoteca [Conjuring Book]. Craiov, Scrisul Românesc, 1976.
Poeme [Poems]. Bucharest, Albatros, 1976.
Sărbători itinerante [Feats with Changing Dates]. Bucharest, Carta Românească, 1978.
Ceramiča [Ceramics]. Bucharest, Militařa, 1979.
This Hour, translated by Michael Hamburger. Durango, Colorado, Logbridge-Rhodes, 1982.
Symmetries: Selected Poems, translated by John Robert Colombo and Petronela Negoşanu. Toronto, Hounslow Press, 1982.
Fîntîni în mare [Fountains in the Sea]. Bucharest, Eminescu, 1982.
Selected Poems, translated by Michael Hamburger. Newcastle-upon-Tyne, Bloodaxe, 1983.
Drumul [The Road]. Bucharest, Minerva, 1984.
Abendrot Nr. 15. Bucharest, n.p., 1985.
Let's Talk About the Weather, translated by Andrea Deletant and Brenda Walker. London, Forest, 1985.
The Biggest Egg in the World. Newcastle-upon-Tyne, Bloodaxe, 1987.
Ecuatorul şi polii. Timişoara, Facla, 1989.
Hands Behind My Back: Selected Poems, translated by Gabriela Dragnea, Stuart Friebert, and Adriana Varga. Oberlin, Ohio, Oberlin College Press, 1991.

Plays

Iona (produced Bucharest, 1968). Bucharest, Editura pentru Literatură, 1968; as *Jonah*, in *The Thirst of the Salt Mountain*, 1985.
Paraclisierul (produced Bucharest, 1970). Bucharest, Eminescu, 1970; as *The Verger*, in *The Thirst of the Salt Mountain*, 1985.
Matcă (produced Bucharest, 1973). Bucharest, Eminescu, 1976; as *The Matrix*, in *The Thirst of the Salt Mountain*, 1985.
Setea muntelui de sare (includes *Iona*; *Paraclisierul*; *Matcă*). Bucharest, Carta Românească, 1974; as *The Thirst of the Salt Mountain* (includes *Jonah*; *The Verger*; *The Matrix*), London, Forest, 1985.
Răceala (produced Bucharest, 1977). Bilingual edition, as *Răceala = A Cold*, Iaşi, Junimea, 1978.

A treia ţeapă [The Third Stake] (produced Cluj, 1978). In-
cluded in *Teatru*, 1980; as *Vlad Dracula the Impaler*
(produced Exeter, Devon, 1991), London, Forest, 1987.
Teatru (includes *Răceala*; *A treia ţeapă*). Craiova, Scrisul
Românesc, 1980.
Ieşirea prin cer [The Exit Through the Sky]. Bucharest,
Eminescu, 1984.

Fiction

Teoria sferelor de influenţă [The Theory of the Spheres of
Influence]. Bucharest, Eminescu, 1969.
Trei dinţi din faţă [Three Teeth in Front]. Bucharest,
Eminescu, 1977.
Viziunea vizuinii [Vision of the Burrow]. Bucharest, Alba-
tros, 1982.

Other

Unde fugim de-acasă [Where Do We Run Away from Home?]
(for children; includes poetry, prose, and plays). Bucharest,
Editura Tineretului, 1966.
Insomnii [Insomnia]. Bucharest, Albatros, 1971.
Ocolul infinitului mic, pornind de la nimic [Around the Small
Infinity, Starting from Nothing]. Bucharest, Ion Creangă,
1973.
Stare de destin [The State of Destiny]. Iaşi, Junimea, 1976.
Uşor cu pianul pe scări [Carefully with the Pianoforte Up-
stairs]. Bucharest, Carta Românească, 1985.
Tratat de inspiraţie [Treaty of Inspiration]. Craiova, Scrisul
Românesc, 1985.
Dracula, Prince of Many Faces: His Life and Times. Boston,
Little Brown, 1991.

Editor, *Ruinurile Tîrgoviştii*, by Cîrlova. Craiova, Scrisul
Românesc, 1975.

*

Critical Study: "A New Dramatist: Marin Sorescu" by Ion
Pascadi, in *Romanian Review* (Bucharest), 23(4), 1970.

* * *

Marin Sorescu is an ironist, even a joker, in whose work the
metaphysical and the ordinary cohabit. Poem after poem
challenges the comfortable assumption; poem after poem is
marked by a striking discontinuity between the matter-of-fact,
unsurprised diction and the spiralling absurdities of subject-
matter. Unexpected propositions are offered as the most
commonplace tokens of shared experience:

> To the dead
> eternity seems
> longer
> because they're forbidden
> to smoke

or

> When at night in bed
> I can't get to sleep
> I take an historical atlas
> with a mouthful of water.

Each of these instances constitutes the opening of a poem.
What follows develops both their banal and their fantastic

qualities. It is in the interaction of the two that Sorescu's
particular apprehension of the absurd is located. There is a
recognizable affinity with his fellow Romanian Eugène
Ionesco (*q.v.*).

Sorescu first came to the fore as part of the revival of
Romanian literature in the 1960s, along with such figures as
Nichita Stanescu and Ioan Alexandru. His first volume —
Singur printre poeţi (Alone Among the Poets) — was a
collection of parodies, an early indication of his refusal of the
solemn or wholly serious. His mature manner is frequently
self-deprecatory. We may call him an observer of the ironies
and absurdities of the human condition, but the word "observer" must not be allowed to suggest that Sorescu is ever guilty
of imagining himself to be above, or immune to, such ironies.
His role as a poet in communist Eastern Europe is hilariously
evoked in "Impulse," for example:

> Evening after evening
> I collect all the available chairs
> in the neighbourhood
> and read them poems.
>
> Chairs are most receptive
> to poetry,
> if the seating order is right.

Typically, Sorescu avoids the limitations of the specific — the
fable of "Impulse" may, of course, be read as a larger
statement about poetry, or about the very activity of human
communication, not as making a merely political point. Even
in plays such as *Există nervi* (There Are Nerves) or *Vlad
Dracula the Impaler* (originally *A treia ţeapă* [The Third
Stake]), the unmissable allegorical application to the rule of
the Ceaucescus does not exclude many other, less politically
specific, resonances. Sorescu is far too wise to imagine that
betrayal, suffering, and injustice could ever usefully be
thought of as merely local phenomena.

There are few unchallenged certainties in Sorescu's world.
The Roman past and the Orthodox Church function as more or
less fixed points of reference, but they do not escape his irony.
His Ovid is a permanent exile on the Black Sea, since those in
power like his elegies — "but only from a distance." (Modern
Romania has, of course, a long history of distinguished poets in
exile: Tristan Tzara, Eugène Ionesco, Isidore Isou, Aron
Cotruş, etc.) Sorescu's Seneca is "inexpressibly bored" as his
bathwater gets warm and must wait another "full four hours"
before he can slash his veins. Sorescu's irony is a serious
business — as a form of sanity in an insane world it could hardly
be otherwise.

It must be said, however, that Sorescu's "seriousness" is
never altogether distinct from his sense of the comic, just as it is
often difficult to decide whether the stance of particular poems
might better be described as naïve or as sophisticated. "Twice"
may tell us "I look at everything/Twice,/Once to be
cheerful/And once to be sad," but there is no such simple
disjunction in the way the poems actually operate. The
humour of "Skittles" is decidedly disquieting:

> Without doubt, the earth
> Is a great
> Bowling alley.
>
> Because there aren't enough
> Trees,
> People stand
> As well.

Someone throws the ball
From far away
And marks with chalk
Those who fall.

It's a society game
Of course,
Just as fine
As duelling.

The apparent dogmatism of the opening is a characteristic strategy; so is the counterpoint between the assumed certainty and the open-ended exactness of "someone." In a Preface specially written for the English translation of his dramatic trilogy *Setea muntelui de sare* (*The Thirst of the Salt Mountain*), Sorescu comments "I have tried in these monodramas to ask myself a few 'searching' questions without pretending to know the answers." Everywhere is the refusal of any pretence to certainty in works which offer a quizzical consideration of fundamental questions. (Given its particular openness it is not surprising that Sorescu's work should have lent itself so readily and effectively to the variations played on it by many British poets in that remarkable volume of translations and adaptations *The Biggest Egg in the World*.)

The problems of language and identity are the source of many a riddling parable in Sorescu's work:

Look . . . objects
Are cut in two,
On one side — the objects,
On the other — their names.

There is a vast space between them,
Space for running.
For life.

("Look . . .")

The world plays many tricks on human perception — as in "Sentence" where "Each traveller in the tram/Looks identical to the one who sat there before him/On that very seat."

Virgil Nemoianu has (in the *Times Literary Supplement*, 9 October 1987) well described the special quality of Sorescu's voice: "he represents the voice of a community that has had to respond to sore trials and pressures without recourse to heroism or to a tragic sense of life. His rueful jocularity and the good natured cynicism are responses frequent among Romanians and perfectly crystallized in Sorescu's poetry." But it is of more than just his own people that Sorescu speaks; he speaks of and from the human sense of a life not adequately described as either grandly tragic or simply comic.

—Glyn Pursglove

———

SOW FALL, Aminata. *See* FALL, Aminata Sow.

———

ŚRĪVĀSTAVA, Satyendra. Indian. Born in Azamgarh, Uttar Prades, 5 August 1935. Educated at the University of Poona, 1953–57; University of London, 1962–77, Ph.D. 1978. Married Mriṇālinī Śrīvāstava in 1973. Lecturer, University of Toronto, 1969–71; since 1980 senior language teaching officer, University of Cambridge. Columnist, *Sunday Mail*, India. Address: Faculty of Oriental Studies, University of Cambridge, Sidgwick Avenue, Cambridge CB3 9DA, England.

PUBLICATIONS

Verse

Jaltaraṅg [Harmonica]. Vārāṇasī (Benares), Śrī Kailāś, 1952.
Ek kiraṇ ek phūl [For Every Flower a Sun]. Vārāṇasī, Śrī Nareś, 1954.
Sthir yātrāē [Stationary Voyages]. New Delhi, Parāg, 1975.
Mrs. Jones aur vah galī [Mrs. Jones and Her Street]. New Delhi, Abhivyañjanā, 1978.
Satah kī gahrāī [Below the Surface]. New Delhi, Abhivyañjanā, 1980.

Plays

Śahīd Udham Singh [The Martyr Udham Singh]. New Delhi, Abhivyañjanā, 1991.

Radio Play: *Patthar gātā hai* [The Stone Sings], 1956.

Other

Kandhō par indradhanuṣ [A Rainbow on My Shoulder]. New Delhi, Pustkāyan, 1989.

*

Satyendra Śrīvāstava comments:
I write poetry in both Hindi and English. My English poems appear in leading English magazines and periodicals.
I think poetry is the best medium to talk to anyone heart-to-heart and share or invoke views and feelings. It makes you reveal what has always been there, but not always recognized, either by you or by others. Then suddenly it is expressed — expressed in a language which is yours yet sometimes not — you become and act as only a conveyer — a medium of someone or something which is part of you as you are part of something bigger, deeper, greater, and more substantial.

*   *   *

Satyendra Śrīvāstava is a Hindi writer who has lived most of his adult life in western countries and who, while always conscious of his Indian identity and background, has actively sought to assimilate his western experience to it. His poetry expresses both the outward content of a bi-cultural experience and, to a high degree, the inner effort of integrating its parts. He brings a combination of imaginative insight, historical understanding, and self-awareness to the interpretation of his varied subject-matter. Śrīvāstava's work thus appears as a poet's commentary on a representative human experience of the late 20th century, and with its author's tolerance and balanced sense of optimism contributes fruitfully to a sense of the changing dimensions of the world for many, and of dilemmas herein posed for the individual. Śrīvāstava's main work to date is *Mrs. Jones aur vah galī* (Mrs. Jones and Her

Street). Apart from this and the other collections of verse discussed below he has produced a volume of essays. *Kandhō par indradhanuṣ* (A Rainbow on My Shoulder), describing experiences in different parts of the world. This, along with his column "London kī ciṭṭhī" [Letters from London] in the *Sunday Mail* (Delhi, Calcutta, and Bombay), has contributed to knowledge of his poetry among the many in South Asia interested in the kind of experiences that underlie it. He has also written original poetry in English which has won favourable recognition.

Śrīvāstava's two early collections *Jaltaraṅg* (Harmonica) and *Ek kiraṇ ek phūl* (For Every Flower a Sun) strike a lyrical tone, with personal feeling not yet applied to the later range of experience. Longing and desire predominate here, yet with a sense that an unattainable ideal can, somehow, be reached: hope is just over the horizon. Śrīvāstava's poetic style, built on essentially simple language used in accordance with well-understood conventions of Urdu and Hindi verse, contributes greatly to the communicability (*sampreṣaṇīytā*) of feeling that has been remarked on in his writing. *Ek kiraṇ ek phūl* shows a freer verse style. The author begins now to define more clearly the urban, regional, and historical parameters of his Indian identity.

The two later collections of short poems develop the author's reactions to life in both worlds. *Sthir yātrāē* (Stationary Voyages) displays his concern with worldwide social and political issues and his desire to find interpretations that are meaningful in Indian terms. Change and the passage of time are now constant preoccupations, with the individual's position in the onward flow of life a prominent theme, and stress laid on the importance of the present moment, as well as on the pathos this can contain when seen against the background of the past. *Satah kī gahrāī* (Below the Surface) chiefly presents fleeting emotions of day-to-day life. A sense of life's difficulties and frustrations is strongly present, counterbalanced by consciousness of the worth and strength of the individual.

In *Mrs. Jones aur vah galī* Śrīvāstava finds a larger theme: the history of a small East London street during the 20th century, and of changing attitudes and patterns of interaction among its residents. In this long work of more than a hundred pages the author asks, using the form of a descriptive monologue often strongly dramatised, what these changes mean in human terms. He stresses the evolutionary aspect of his subject, defining its scope typologically in terms of representatives of English, Irish, Jewish, West Indian, and Indian communities who have settled in the street during the long period of residence of an Englishwoman born in the Victorian age, herself an early "immigrant" to the street. Mrs. Jones is presented with great imaginative insight. She struggles in old age to reconcile memories of the past with the confusing present: a time when old values have weakened and loneliness is accentuated by the impersonality of the city. Yet change also brings renewal. She is baffled by the newest (Indian) immigrants yet warms to their friendliness which rekindles the self-esteem of her earlier days. They for their part live with their own problems of adaptation: how to take up the social freedom in prospect in their new lives when far from home without family support, and with little background in that freedom; how to reconcile themselves to drastic change in the next generation; and how to relate successfully to new neighbours. Śrīvāstava tells us that the individuals making up any community can thrive only by accepting growth and change and the stresses therein entailed. They must at the same time acknowledge their own identity: to become "Romans in Rome" is no answer to the immigrant's dilemma. At the end of the poem Śrīvāstava looks to the prospect of regeneration of a single new community in Mrs. Jones's street, when members of the different groups come together to preserve the street from demolition. The complexities of life need not stop men of good will from moving forward into a new age: like the Victorian streetlight that symbolised a golden age to Mrs. Jones, the old ideas and assumptions of every community can often be safely left behind.

—Stuart McGregor

STANGERUP, Henrik. Danish. Born in Copenhagen, 1 September 1937. Educated at Stenhus, graduated 1956; University of Copenhagen, 1956–60; Institut des Hautes Études Cinématographiques, Paris, 1964. Married 1) Lotte Tarp in 1967 (divorced 1976); 2) Susanne Krage in 1982. Staff member, *Kristeligt Dagblad*, 1957, *Den konservative Generalkorrespondence*, 1958–59, *Ekstrabladet*, 1960–64, *Politiken*, 1965–69, *Berlingske Tidende og Samvirke*, 1978–80, and *Ekstrabladet og Politiken*, from 1985; co-founder, Collagetruppen, 1963; journalist in Paris, 1964–65; co-editor, *Kosmorama*, 1967–69, and *Weekend* radio program, 1970–71. Member of the representative body of the Danish Film Institute, 1974–75; co-founder, Gulliver author forum, Amsterdam, 1987. Recipient: Danish State Art Foundation 3-year stipend, 1970, and lifelong grant, 1984; Danish Booksellers' Association Golden Laurels, 1972; Danish Critics prize, 1981; Amalienborg prize, 1982; P. W. Lund Medal (Brazil), 1983; Pontoppidan award, 1985; Danish Academy prize, 1986; Rio de Janeiro cultural prize, 1992; Nathansen prize, 1992. Address: Jordbærvej 5, 4772 Langebæk, Denmark.

PUBLICATIONS

Fiction

Grønt og sort [Green and Black].   Fredensborg, Arena, 1961.
Veritabel Pariser [Veritable Parisian].   Fredensborg, Arena/Forfatternes, 1966.
Slangen i brystet [The Viper in the Bosom].   Copenhagen, Gyldendal, 1969.
Løgn over løgn [Lie upon Lie].   Copenhagen, Gyldendal, 1971.
Manden der ville være skyldig.   Copenhagen, Gyldendal, 1973; as *The Man Who Wanted to Be Guilty*, New York and London, Boyars, 1982.
Fjenden i forkøbet [Stealing a March on the Enemy].   Copenhagen, Gyldendal, 1978.
Vejen til Lagoa Santa.   Copenhagen, Gyldendal, 1981; as *The Road to Lagoa Santa*, New York and London, Boyars, 1984.
Det er svært at dø i Dieppe.   Copenhagen, Gyldendal, 1985; as *The Seducer: It Is Hard to Die in Dieppe*, New York and London, Boyars, 1990.
Broder Jacob.   Copenhagen, Lindhardt og Ringhof, 1991; as *Brother Jacob*, London, Boyars, 1992.

Plays

Jorden er flad eller Erasmus Montanus [The Earth Is Flat or Erasmus Montanus] (screenplay).   Copenhagen, Gyldendal, 1976.

Screenplays: *Asta Nielsen*, 1966; *Giv Gud en chance om søndagen* [Give God a Chance on Sundays], 1970; *Farlige kys* [Dangerous Kisses], 1972; *Jorden er flad* [The Earth Is Flat], 1977.

Television Play: *Pelouse interdite*, 1970 (France).

Other

Kunsten at være ulykkelig [The Art of Being Unhappy]. Copenhagen, Gyldendal, 1974.
Mens tid var: kronik og journalistik 1961–1977 [When There Was Time: Articles and Journalism 1961–1977]. Copenhagen, Gyldendal, 1978.
Retten til ikke at høre til: Paris foran fiserne [The Right Not to Belong: Paris Before the Eighties]. Copenhagen, Berlingske, 1979.
Fangelejrens frie halvdel [The Free Half of the Prisoner's Camp]. Copenhagen, Berlingske, 1979.
Tag din seng og gå: en personlig beretning [Take Your Bed and Leave: A Personal Account]. Copenhagen, Gyldendal, 1986.
Den kvarte sandhed: fra et tiår [The Quarter Truth: From a Decade]. Copenhagen, Lindhardt og Ringhof, 1989.

Editor, *Vi er selv historie* [We Are History Ourselves], by Poul Henningsen. Copenhagen, Thaning & Appel, 1963.
Editor, with Ole Grünbaum, *Kulturkampen* [Culture Battle]. Copenhagen, Fremad, 1968.
Editor, with Roger Poole, *The Laughter Is on My Side: An Imaginative Introduction to Kierkegaard*. Princeton, New Jersey, Princeton University Press, 1989.
Editor, with Roger Poole, *A Kierkegaard Reader*. London, Fourth Estate, 1989.

*

Critical Study: "Henrik Stangerup: In the Shadow of Northern Lights" (interview), in *Encounter* (London), 63, 1984.

*   *   *

There have so far been two stages on Danish writer Henrik Stangerup's literary path. The first stage, which ended in 1978, can be described as the struggle against the enemy. The period since then has been occupied by his writing of the Kierkegaardian trilogy, the third part of which, *Broder Jacob* (*Brother Jacob*), appeared in 1991.

Dominant themes in the early phase are fear and guilt. Stangerup's novels from this period address a deep-rooted personal guilt complex originating in his childhood. As a boy he met much hatred and derision because his father, Professor Hakon Stangerup, had acquired a bad reputation during World War II. Although innocent, the son was treated as if guilty, and gradually the guilt became part of his character. This guilt was also the result of the exceedingly high expectations that this brilliant father had of his son.

In the 1960s Stangerup distanced himself from the modernism that dominated the literary scene in Denmark, and his first novel belongs in the realist tradition with a plot that develops chronologically. In *Slangen i brystet* (The Viper in the Bosom) the main character is a foreign correspondent with a Danish newspaper in Paris, a profession Stangerup knows from personal experience, having worked for Danish newspapers in Paris in 1964–65. The novel gives a well-informed and detailed picture of the protagonist's work, the pressure created by deadlines, and the need to be innovative. Max

Mollerup is 10 years older than Stangerup, and the promising future that once awaited him has not materialized. His creativity has dried up, and he sees the expectations and demands that he cannot meet as enemies. A gradual regression begins, during which his personality gradually breaks up, ending in paranoia. The final chapter describes Mollerup sitting in a small room in Paris, marking the positions and manoeuvres of his enemy on a large ordinance map.

"I have always been fascinated by madness — from a philosophical point of view. How can we avoid going mad? When people go mad, isn't it just a way of escaping from something which is even madder — a world devoid of meaning?" Stangerup says in an interview with Iben Holk (*Henrik Stangerup*, 1986). The enemy that destroys Mollerup represents the same feeling of guilt that possesses Stangerup. In *Løgn over løgn* (Lie upon Lie) he also fictionalizes his guilt complex, describing its worst imaginable consequences, in order to exorcise it.

In the 1970s, when the political debate in Denmark was dominated by Marxist ideology, Stangerup extolled pluralism, the right of the individual to be different, opposing any kind of utopian totalitarianism. *Manden der ville være skyldig* (*The Man Who Wanted to Be Guilty*) reflects this philosophical orientation. The main character Torben kills his wife in a fit of temper. Society, however, refuses to place the blame for the murder on him, as his aggression is believed to be caused by circumstances. The state believes it can prevent any crime by mounting compulsory aggression-combating courses. The essence of human nature, however, is the ability to distinguish between good and evil, and Torben insists on his own guilt for the evil he knows he has committed. When his helpers declare that his attitude is asocial and a relic from a past that paid homage to individualism and the integrity of the personality, Torben goes mad.

Stangerup wrote his fourth novel, *Fjenden i forkøbet* (Stealing a March on the Enemy), during an existential crisis. It is a novel about fear, guilt, and inner torment. At the end of the first part the main characters from his first three novels say to Stangerup with one voice: "Your turn, old boy! Your evil chapter has already started! And it will be longer than you think!" The protagonist is thus Stangerup, and at this point it is unknown whether he will suffer the same fate as his fictional characters. The process of writing about his traumas, experienced as evil forces, enables him to overcome the crisis, and his rediscovery of the creativity and existential force possessed by language gives him the strength to break "the demonic spell."

While Stangerup journeys deeper and deeper into his own soul during this first stage in his development as a writer, in the second stage he transports himself away from his own time, identifying with historical characters from past centuries. The three novels that form the Kierkegaardian trilogy are a mixture of history and fiction, biography and autobiography. *Vejen til Lagoa Santa* (*The Road to Lagoa Santa*) represents Kierkegaard's theory of the second stage on the path of life. The scientist, Peter Wilhelm Lund (1801–1880), is the ethical man who sees his life as a vocation. With his voyage of exploration in Brazil he aims to discover God's plan of creation through the classification of all his creatures. However, the European man of the intellect becomes captivated by the material he set out to record. Incapable of surrendering to the mysterious otherness, the world of the senses that Brazil represents, he falls into depression.

The writer and critic Peter Ludvig Møller (1814–1865) is Stangerup's aesthete (Kierkegaard's first stage). *Det er svært at dø i Dieppe* (*The Seducer: It Is Hard to Die in Dieppe*) depicts his restless pursuit of ideal female beauty that drives him towards greater intensity of enjoyment and stronger intoxication, and away from boredom, repetition, and commitments, finally to die, mentally deranged. In death, however, he meets the perfection that eluded him in life.

Brother Jacob deals with Kierkegaard's religious stage. The religious character is the Danish mendicant friar and king's son, Brother Jacob, who leaves Lutheran Denmark, ending up in Mexico, where he remains among Tarask Indians until his death at the age of 82. His attempts to adapt Catholicism to the culture of the Indians provoked the anger of the colonial Spanish Catholic Church, and the case brought by the Church against Brother Jacob resulted in severe punishment. His goodness, however, makes him greater than the Church and the various forms of punishment are turned into blessings.

—Bente Elsworth

STRAUSS, Botho. German. Born Naumburg/Saale, 2 December 1944. Educated at the universities of Cologne and Munich. Editor, *Theater heute* periodical, 1967–70; dramatic adviser, Schaubühne am Halleschen Ufer theatre company, 1970–75. Recipient: Hanover dramatists' prize, 1975; Villa Massimo grant, 1976; Schiller prize, 1977; Bavarian Academy of Fine Arts prize, 1981; Bayerische Academy prize, 1981; Mülheim dramatists' prize, 1982; Jean Paul prize, 1987; Büchner prize, 1989. Address: Keithstraße 8, 1000 Berlin 30, Germany.

PUBLICATIONS

Plays

Die Hypochonder (produced Hamburg, 1972). Frankfurt, Autoren, 1972; as *The Hypochondriacs* (produced Glasgow, 1992).
Bekannte Gesichter, gemischte Gefühle (produced Stuttgart, 1975). With *Die Hypochonder*, Munich, Hanser, 1979.
Trilogie des Wiedersehens (produced Hamburg, 1977). Munich, Hanser, 1976; as *Three Acts of Recognition*, in *West Coast Plays*, Berkeley, California Theatre Council, 1981.
Groß und klein (produced Berlin, 1978). Munich, Hanser, 1978; as *Big and Little* (produced New York, 1979), New York, Farrar Straus, 1979; as *Great and Small* (produced London, 1983).
Kalldewey, Farce (produced Hamburg, 1982). Munich, Hanser, 1981.
Der Park (produced Freiburg, 1984). Munich, Hanser, 1983; as *The Park* (produced New York and London, 1988), Sheffield, Sheffield Academic Press, 1988.
Die Fremdenführerin (produced Berlin, 1985). Munich, Hanser, 1986; as *The Tourist Guide* (produced London, 1987), London, Chancery, 1987.
Sieben Türen. Included in *Besucher*, 1988; as *Seven Doors* (produced London, 1992).
Besucher (includes *Besucher*; *Sieben Türen*; *Die Zeit und das Zimmer*). Munich, Hanser, 1988.
Fragmente der Undeutlichkeit (includes *Jeffers-Akt*; *Sigé*). Munich, Hanser, 1989.
Schlußchor (produced Munich, 1991). Munich, Hanser, 1991.
Angelas Kleider. Munich, Hanser, 1991.

Theaterstücke (vol. 1 includes *Die Hypochonder*; *Bekannte Gesichter, gemischte Gefühle*; *Das Sparschwein* by Eugène Labiche, translated by Strauss; *Sommergäste* by Maxim Gorky, translated by Strauss and Peter Stein; *Trilogie des Wiedersehens*; *Gross und klein*; vol. 2 includes *Kalldewey*; *Der Park*; *Die Fremdenführerin*; *Misanthrop* by Molière, translated by Strauss; *Besucher*; *Die Zeit und das Zimmer*; *Sieben Türen*; *Schlußchor*; *Angelas Kleider*). Munich, Hanser, 2 vols., 1991.

Fiction

Schützenehre. Düsseldorf, Eremiten-Presse, 1975.
Marlenes Schwester (collection). Munich, Hanser, 1975.
Die Widmung. Munich, Hanser, 1977; as *Devotion*, New York, Farrar Straus, 1979; London, Chatto and Windus, 1980.
Rumor. Munich, Hanser, 1980; as *Tumult*, Manchester, Carcanet, 1984.
Paare, Passanten. Munich, Hanser, 1981.
Der junge Mann. Munich, Hanser, 1984.
Niemand anderes. Munich, Hanser, 1987.

Verse

Diese Erinnerung an einen, der nur einen Tag zu Gast war. Munich, Hanser, 1985.

Other

Versuch, ästhetische und politische Ereignisse zusammenzudenken: Texte über Theater, 1967–1986. Frankfurt, Autoren, 1987.
Kongress: die Kette der Demütigungen. Munich, Matthes und Seitz, 1989.
Beginnlosigkeit: Reflexionen über Fleck und Linie. Munich, Hanser, 1992.

Editor, with Ellen Hammer and Karl Ernst Herrmann, *Peer Gynt, ein Schauspiel aus dem neunzehnten Jahrhundert*. Berlin, n.p., 1971.
Editor and Translator, *Das Sparschwein*, by Eugène Labiche. Frankfurt, Autoren, 1973.
Editor, *Briefwechsel*, by Moses Mendelssohn. Stuttgart, Frommann-Holzboog, 1974.

Translator, *Molières Misanthrop*. Berlin, Schaubühne am Lehniner Platz, 1987.

*

Critical Studies: "Subjectivity Reconsidered: Botho Strauss and Contemporary West German Prose," in *New German Critique* (Ithaca, New York), Fall, 1983, "Botho Strauss Pays Tribute to the Bomb: On *Paare, Passanten* and the Collective Survival," in *German Quarterly* (St. Louis, Missouri), Spring 1984, and *Crisis of Subjectivity: Botho Strauss's Challenge to West German Prose of the 1970's*, Amsterdam, Rodopi, 1984, all by Leslie A. Adelson; "Tumult, Horn and Double Bass" by Michael Hulse, in *The Antigonish Review* (Antigonish, Nova Scotia), Summer-Autumn 1986; "Myth and Mythology in the Drama of Botho Strauss" by Irmela Schneider, in *A Radical Stage: Theatre in Germany in the 1970s and 1980s*, edited by W. G. Sebald, Oxford, Berg, 1988.

*   *   *

For English-speaking theatre audiences used to the critical realism of modern German-language playwrights such as Bertolt Brecht, Friedrich Dürrenmatt, and Franz Xaver Kroetz (*q.v.*), the inward-looking plays of Botho Strauss must seem part of a very different writing tradition. For this reason, perhaps, stagings of even his more accessible plays such as *Groß und klein* (*Great and Small* or *Big and Little*) and *Der Park* (*The Park*) have baffled London theatre critics.

These protestations of incomprehension may reflect a certain Anglo-Saxon intransigence in face of things Teutonic. However, similar bewilderment and critical antagonism have accompanied performances of Strauss's work in the German theatre; from his first work, involving lust and murder among the German middle classes at the time of the Boer War, *Die Hypochonder* (*The Hypochondriacs*) right through to his recent response to German unification, *Schlußchor* (Final Choir). The difficulties in responding to Strauss's work have much to do with the author's selfconscious mode of writing, his demanding investigation of what constitutes social, personal, and artistic reality, and his own "inner emigration" — a retreat into the self which a number of critics have seen as Strauss's response to living in a post-revolutionary period after the failure of the student movements of the late 1960s and early 1970s.

Strauss's dramatic work of the 1970s is certainly marked by a desire to come to terms with the failed expectations, lack of solidarity, and artificial lives of his peers among the West German educated middle classes. An early work, *Bekannte Gesichter, gemischte Gefühle* (Familiar Faces, Mixed Feelings), depicts the dreams of seven inhabitants of a small hotel that is under threat of closure. *Trilogie des Wiedersehens* (*Three Acts of Recognition*) portrays with wit the fears, aspirations, and foibles of chic West Berliners in an art gallery, while *Great and Small* follows the quest of a graphic artist for self-affirmation and human warmth in various social situations. Although Strauss often chooses to record the behaviour (and in particular the verbal usages) of groups of Germans, his characters are almost always seen as isolated beings, outside a shared sense of community. Hence Lotte's search for sympathy and humanity in *Great and Small* is seen as absurd, as she moves from location to location as if in a modern German morality play. But this is a dramatic world devoid of religious belief and a common culture, which communicates by designer names, holidays without pleasure, and seeks solace in drugs, alcohol, and medical diagnosis. *Three Acts of Recognition* gives us a view of secondhand emotions and prosaic existences that are cloaked by fashionable utterances or not recognised through self-absorption. 18 characters move on and off stage, regrouping in front of the pictures that are part of the ironically titled "Capitalist Realism" exhibition. As in *Great and Small*, these meetings are seen to be devoid of real contact. Individual feelings are expressed in the form of monologues, with Strauss trying to translate the cinema's full-frame, close-up shots into stage practice in order to penetrate his characters' personal realities.

The visitors to the art gallery are all personalised by their various modes of speech, their words indicating the tension between their inner experiences and the social situation they are in. The satirical *Kalldewey, Farce* also records the linguistic habits of several West German social groupings, from comfortable members of the middle classes and office workers, to lesbian separatists and anarchists. This play, first performed successfully (as was much of Strauss's work) at Berlin's Schaubühne, introduces a mythical/folkloric element into his writing. Kalldewey of the title is a trickster figure, resembling the Pied Piper of Hamelin, who provides a carnivalesque aspect to the play. No real attempt is made to naturalise

Kaldewey within the social frameworks of the play, as it is clear that Strauss now is questioning the nature of theatricality, and exploring the boundaries of stage writing and theatrical presentation.

The Park is perhaps the best example of this exploration. Here Strauss reworks Shakespeare's *A Midsummer Night's Dream* in the spirit of his deracinated and materialistic times. Oberon and Titania return to a West German city, seeking sexual joy and true love within the confines of a debris-strewn park, eventually shedding their divinity to lead mediocre human lives. As in the original, Strauss explores sexual mayhem, when the two central couples (who are, as we might expect, middle-class professionals, apart from an American trapeze artist) change allegiances. In this version, love is controlled by the laws of the marketplace, as evident in the amulets that Strauss's addition, the artist Cyprian, manufactures. The confrontation of Shakespeare's text and the world of Greek myths with Strauss's present consumerist society gives rise to an allusive and tantalising meditation on the loss of power of older belief systems and their replacement by the power of money, correct behaviour, and a faith in rational thought. Furthermore, Strauss demonstrates in his juxtaposition of mythical creatures with sad reality that there is no unifying cultural tradition, our perceived past being composed of shards of previous artistic works.

Die Fremdenführerin (*The Tourist Guide*) also contrasts a classical heritage with the rootless present. This two-hander concerns the relationship between a young German tourist guide at the Olympia Stadium and an older school teacher. Strauss shows us a relationship that like his theatre can go anywhere and develop anyhow, and that takes place amid classical references. We expect some kind of transfiguration or re-enactment of classical legend. However, the lovers share no common discourse, and their relationship ends in anti-climax and disappointment for both characters and audience, showing perhaps that the Greek heritage can no longer offer cultural resonance or any point of cohesion.

Subsequent plays have experimented with form and content, and include the (for Strauss) almost realistic *Besucher* (Visitors) which deals with the nature of the rehearsal process. This drama returns to different generations of actors at odds with one another (as briefly sketched in *Trilogie des Wiedersehens*). Strauss uses the figure of Karl Joseph, a survivor of Goebbels's patronage, as the representative of the older generation, echoing Klaus Mann's creation of Hendrik Höfgen in *Mephisto* (1936). *Sieben Türen* (*Seven Doors*) is a more experimental piece, illustrating the chance encounters of various unnamed figures as seven different doors are opened. The short poetic drama, *Fragmente der Undeutlichkeit* (Fragments of Obscurity), awarded that year's Büchner prize, explores the correspondence between literary criticism and creative experience. Rather surprisingly, Strauss chooses an actual rather than imagined subject, the early 20th-century American poet Robinson Jeffers, who in this version has become impatient with his poetry. Strauss's most recent plays include the quasi-realistic *Angelas Kleider* (Angela's Clothes) and the aforementioned *Schlußchor*. The latter has attracted controversy not only because of its use of unrelated scenes, but also because of its voicing of uncomfortable sentiments, not least in its depiction of stereotypical but unimpressed *Ossis*. Strauss's private response to German unification results in a disquieting articulation of German attitudes, a striking feature of his drama over the last 20 years. German history is presented in this play as a series of fractured experiences, as are human relationships, that, in the words of one representative of Germany's present, need "an interpreter, who knows more than foreign languages, and who could fluently translate what people are no longer able to understand about one another."

Strauss is best known outside Germany as a playwright. He has, however, also written a number of prose works which elaborate upon the ideas prominent in his plays. Freed from the plasticity of the stage, Strauss has been able in his novels and essays to develop his concern with what constitutes reality and the relationship between art and life. The two short stories, "Marlenes Schwester" (Marlene's Sister) and "Theorie der Drohung" (Threat Theory), are representative of his narrative method, for here Strauss conflates the act of writing and the construction of a recognisable social reality, constantly intervening and breaking the illusion of the stories. "Marlenes Schwester" deals with the bond between sisters, mainly from the perspective of one seriously ill sister, but with interspersed vignettes about the nature of friendship. "Theorie der Drohung" is a more complex narrative about an imagined relationship with a woman, which rather like Paul Auster's *The New York Trilogy* (1985) leads back to its author as the source of enunciation.

Die Widmung (*Devotion*) is probably Strauss's most successful prose work. Set in the hot summer of 1976 in West Berlin, the novella traces a bookseller's desire to win back his girlfriend Hannah. Possessed of a Wertherian sensibility and devotion, Richard Schroubek records his feelings and thoughts in the hope that Hannah, on reading his notebook, will return. Schroubek's intense emotions, his morbidity, and renunciation of food, work, and bourgeois orderliness are placed in among the banal trappings of West Berlin life. Eventually he meets up with Hannah once more, and as in most of Strauss's works, the grand moment of passion and romantic surrender turns to bathos, when it becomes clear she only wants to borrow money, and then leaves his notebook behind, unread, in a taxi.

Rumor (*Tumult*) deals with an employee of the Kafka-esque "Institute for News and Information," a business that peddles ready-to-use knowledge (a ridiculous place of certitude in Strauss's literature of hesitancy and reflection), who meets up with his daughter after a long separation. This novel traces the awkward relationship between the two, delineating a desire to reclaim a love object reminiscent of *Devotion*. Family relations are also scrutinised in *Der junge Mann* (The Young Man), an attempt at a *Bildungsroman*. *Paare, Passanten* is a collection of observations about contemporary West German life, which returns to Strauss's preoccupation with the disappearance of genuine feeling under modern consumer capitalism.

The possibilities of thought and apprehension are discussed in *Beginnlosigkeit: Reflexionen über Fleck und Linie* (Lack of Beginning: Reflections About Place and Line), where Strauss grapples with ideas from modern physics on human perception. "Everything that is anything occurs under our skulls," claims Strauss. And, indeed, throughout his sophisticated, sensitive, and often puzzling work, Strauss points to the primacy and power of thought and perception, indicating that in a world bereft of human contact and shared experience, imagination and the act of writing can provide pleasure and meaning.

—Anna-Marie Taylor

SUÁREZ LYNCH, B. *See* **BIOY CASARES, Adolfo.**

SÜSKIND, Patrick. German. Born in Ambach, 26 March 1949. Educated at the universities of Munich and Aix-en-Provence. Television scriptwriter, 10 years. Recipient: Gutenberg prize, 1987. Agent: Tanja Howarth, 19 New Row, London WC2N 4LA, England. Address: c/o Diogenes Verlag, Sprecherstraße 8, 8032 Zurich, Switzerland.

PUBLICATIONS

Fiction

Das Parfum: die Geschichte eines Mörders. Zurich, Diogenes, 1985; as *Perfume: The Story of a Murderer*, London, Hamish Hamilton, and New York, Knopf, 1986.
Die Taube. Zurich, Diogenes, 1987; as *The Pigeon*, London, Hamish Hamilton, and South Yarmouth, Massachusetts, Curley, 1988.
Die Geschichte vom Herrn Sommer. Zurich, Diogenes, 1991; as *The Story of Mr. Sommer*, London, Bloomsbury, 1992.

Plays

Der Kontrabaß (produced Munich, 1981). Bad Homburg, Hunzinger/Bühnen, 1983; as *The Double Bass*, London, Hamish Hamilton, and New York, Viking Penguin, 1987.
Monaco Franze: der ewige Stenz (television series), with Helmut Dietl. Hamburg, Knaus, 1983.
Kir Royal (television series), with Helmut Dietl. Hamburg, Knaus, 1986.

*

Critical Study: "Tradition vs. Optical Innovation in Patrick Süskind's *Die Taube*: A Classical Novelle or an Extended Story on a Kafka Model?" by David B. Fiero, in *Germanic Notes* (Bemidji, Minnesota), 20(1), 1989.

*   *   *

In more rarefied academic circles, popularity and literary merit are often regarded as being incompatible. With his enthralling narratives, distinctive prose style, and powerfully imagined characterisations, Patrick Süskind has succeeded in writing works that have appeared on many a European bestseller list; yet they are sophisticated literary creations.

Süskind's first published work of literature was a one-man play, *Der Kontrabaß* (*The Double Bass*). This extended, and ironically voiced monologue explores the fears and miseries of a double-bass player, as he muses on love, life, and the tortuous relationship he has to his instrument. In a circumlocutory fashion, and aided by more than the occasional beer, the central character presents his opinions on the history of classical music, the hierarchical state of the orchestra, and the nature of music. Again and again, though, *der Jemand* (the somebody) returns to his "mark of Cain," the double bass, which he describes as "the most dreadful, clumsiest and least elegant instrument ever invented," even offering quasi-Freudian reasons, relating to his rejection of his mother, for the adoption of such an instrument.

The double-bassist's Manichaean sense of the world, as being divided between the lightness, beauty, and fame of the other instrumentalists, and the gracelessless, lack of attraction, and insignificance of his own position, is carried through into Süskind's best-known work, *Das Parfum* (*Perfume*). Like the musician in *The Double Bass*, the main figure in this novel is an outsider who craves social recognition and acceptance, yet has an undisguised contempt for his fellow humans. The orphan Jean-Baptiste Grenouille, whose mother gave birth to him on the foulest and rankest spot in the whole of Paris, is kept apart from everyday social interaction not only through physical repulsiveness but also because he has been born without any personal odour. However, he has been born with the most acute sense of smell, possessing the ability to identify and distinguish between all odours, vegetable and human.

In his main character Süskind creates a hideous outcast, worthy of inclusion in any literary gallery of Grand Guignol monsters. Grenouille's abnormal sense of smell and his psychopathic desire for dominance results in a diabolical plan to make himself adored. By distilling the scent of a large number of beautiful virgins (to be slaughtered by Grenouille), ". . . they would love him as they stood under the spell of his scent, not just accept him as one of them, but love him to the point of insanity, or self-abandonment, they would quiver with delight, scream, weep for bliss, they would sink to their knees just as if under God's cold incense, merely to be able to smell *him*, Grenouille!"

This ecstatic, overblown passage is typical of the tone of much of Süskind's remarkable novel, which fuses a Hoffmann-esque tale of terror with an imaginative recreation of the social circumstances of the perfume trade in mid-18th-century France. Süskind's novel is particularly skilled at provoking a sensuous response, and attempts the impossible with no mean success — that is, the communication of perfumes and odours from the written word. Influenced perhaps by recent European historians' work on public displays and group communion, and with a not-too-distant glance at Germany's own troubled past, Süskind is also very adept at conveying frenzied mass behaviour.

While Grenouille craves power and fame, Jonathan Noel in the novella *Die Taube* (*The Pigeon*) has done his best to live as inconspicuous a life as possible. Having survived a childhood that came to an abrupt end when his parents were taken off to concentration camps, and after a short, unsuitable marriage, Jonathan has allowed no doubt or uncertainty in his life. For 20 years his existence has been completely without incident. He has worked as a bank guard in Paris, and has inhabited a small maid's room in the Rue de la Planche, surrounded by familiar and neatly organised possessions. For no explicable reason, this modest bank employee's existence falls apart when he discovers a pigeon has got into the sixth floor of his building. Irrationally frightened of the bird, he finds that he can no longer consider his beloved Room 24 safe. Unlike *Perfume*'s grandiose doings and overembellished prose, *The Pigeon* is characterised by its lack of event and reticence. Jonathan sees a pigeon, goes to work, rips his trousers slightly, fails to get them mended, and does not spend a full night in a hotel. But, in recounting such non-events, Süskind manages to summon up a tragic and unfulfilled life, and to indicate the complex psychology of the central figure, eventually shaping a moving ending when Jonathan relives and recognises the pain and loss of his childhood.

Süskind's interest in the motivations and behaviour of the outsider is seen once more in his most recent work, *Die Geschichte vom Herrn Sommer* (*The Story of Mr. Sommer*). This recollection of a post-war childhood, which can be best described as a *Bildungsnovelle*, focuses on the eccentric figure of Herr Sommer who spends his days (and some of his nights) walking in a frantic fashion from village to village, hardly ever exchanging a word and brandishing an extraordinary, long walking stick. The narrator recalls his childhood, and the way he developed knowledge of the adult world, in terms of encounters with the curious but ever-present ambulatory figure. Climbing trees, a crush on a haughty schoolgirl, piano lessons with a tyrannical teacher, learning to ride a bike — all the minutiae of a comfortable, rural childhood, so cruelly denied Jonathan in *The Pigeon*, are related with charm and affection. However, the puzzling death of the wandering misfit forces the child-narrator to recognise the responsibilities of life beyond childhood, and to learn that suffering and distress exist outside the boy's seemingly contented life.

As far as his writing goes, Süskind is a masterly storyteller, and the irony, elegance, and lucidity of his language give the reader great pleasure. However, why his portrayals of eccentric outsiders, above all the repellent serial killer Grenouille and the solitary walker Sommer, should have engaged the imagination of so large a reading public is a question that cannot be easily answered.

—Anna-Marie Taylor

SÜTŐ, András. Romanian (Hungarian language). Born in Pusztakamarás, Transylvania, 17 June 1927. Educated at Bethlen Gábor College, Nagyenyed (now Aiud, Romania); Reformed College, Kolozsvár (now Cluj, Romania). Married Éva Szabó in 1949; two sons. Journalist, *Világosság* [Light] newspaper, Cluj; journalist, then editor-in-chief, *Falvak Népe* [Village Folk], Tirgu Mures, 1949–54; deputy chief editor, *Igaz Szó* [True Word] journal, 1955–57; chief editor, *Új Élet* [New Life], 1957–89. Member, Romanian Communist Party, from 1946: candidate member of Party Central Committee, 1967–84; member of Executive Bureau, Council of Hungarian Working People, 1969–85; vice president, Writers' Federation of Romania, 1973–81. Recipient: Romanian State prize, 1953, 1954; Herder prize, 1979. Address: Str. Mărăşti Nr. 36, Tirgu Mures (Marosvásárhely), Romania.

PUBLICATIONS

Plays

Mezitlábos mennyasszony [The Barefoot Bride] (screenplay). Kolozsvár, RNK Irószövetségének Irodalmi és Művészeti Kiadója, 1950.
Fecskeszárnyú szemöldök [Swallow-Tailed Eyebrow]. Bucharest, n.p., 1960.
Szerelem, ne siess! [Love, Don't Hurry!]. Bucharest, n.p., 1961.
Tékozló szerelem [Lavish Love]. Bucharest, n.p., 1963.
Pompás Gedeon [Magnificent Gedeon] (produced Kaposvár, 1972). Bucharest, n.p., 1968; included in *Advent a Hargitán*, 1987.
Egy lócsiszár virágvasárnapja [The Palm Sunday of a Horse Dealer] (produced Kaposvár, 1974). With *Csillag a máglyán*, Budapest, Magvető, 1976.
Csillag a máglyán [Star at the Stake] (produced Budapest, 1975). With *Egy lócsiszár virágvasárnapja*, Budapest, Magvető, 1976.
Itt állok, másként nem tehetek [Here I Stand, I Cannot Do Otherwise]. Bucharest, Kriterion, 1975.
Káin és Ábel [Cain and Abel] (produced Budapest, 1978). Budapest, Magvető, 1978.

Vidám sirató egy bolyongó porszemért [Cheerful Lament for a Wandering Speck of Dust] (produced Szeged, 1978). As *Vidám sirató*, included in *Advent a Hargitán: három játék*, 1987.

Három dráma [Three Dramas] (includes *Egy lócsiszár virágvasárnapja*; *Csillag a máglyán*; *Káin és Ábel*). Bucharest, Kriterion, 1978.

A szuzai mennyegző [The Wedding Feast of Susa]. Budapest, Szépirodalmi, 1981.

Advent a Hargitán: három játék [Advent at Hargita: Three Plays] (includes *Advent a Hargitán*; *Vidám siratók*; *Pompás Gedeon*). Budapest, Szépirodalmi, 1987.

Álomkommandó [Dream Command] (produced Budapest, 1987).

Színművek [Plays] (includes *Pompás Gedeon*; *Egy lócsiszár virágvasárnapja*; *Csillag a máglyán*). Budapest, Szépirodalmi, 1989.

Screenplay: *Mezítlábos mennyasszony* [The Barefoot Bride], 1950.

Fiction

Anikónén' felébred [Oun' Anikó Wakes Up]. Bucharest, n.p., 1950.

Emberek indulnak [People Are Starting Off]. Bucharest, n.p., 1953.

Egy pakli dohány [A Packet of Tobacco]. Bucharest, n.p., 1954.

Az új bocskor [The New Sandals]. Bucharest, n.p., 1954.

Októberi cseresznye [October Cherries]. Bucharest, n.p., 1955.

Félrejáró salamon [The Salamon, Who Steps Aside]. Budapest, Új Magyar Kiadó, 1956.

A nyugalom bajnoka [The Champion of Tranquillity]. Bucharest, n.p., 1959.

Tártkarú világ: válogatott elbeszélések [The World of Open Arms: Short Stories]. Bucharest, Allami Irodalmi és Művészeti Kiadó, 1959.

Az ismeretlen kérvényező [The Unknown Petitioner]. Bucharest, n.p., 1961.

Misi, a csillagos homlokú [Misi with the Star-Studded Forehead]. Bucharest, n.p., 1969.

Nyugtalan vizek: válogatott írások [Restless Waters: Selected Writings]. Bucharest, Ion Creangă, 1974.

Engedjétek hozzám jönni a szavakat: jegyzetek hómezőn es porban [Let the Words Come to Me]. Bucharest, Kriterion, 1977.

A lőtt lábú madár nyomában [Tracking a Bird]. Budapest, Szépirodalmi, 1988.

Other

Hajnali győzelem [Dawn Victory]. Bucharest, Kolozsvár, 1949.

Egy képviselő levelei [Letters of a Deputy]. Bucharest, n.p., 1954.

Rigó és apostol [Thrush and Apostle]. Bucharest, Kriterion, 1970.

Anyám könnyű álmot ígér [My Mother Promises Easy Dreams]. Bucharest, Kriterion, 1970(?).

Istenek és falovacskák: esszék, újabb úti tűnődések [Gods and Little Wooden Horses]. Bucharest, Kriterion, 1973.

Félszárnyú asszonyok [Half-Winged Woman]. Bucharest, n.p., 1975.

Nagyenyedi fügevirág: esszék, tűnődések [Flowering Fig-Tree of Nagyenyed]. Budapest, Szépirodalmi, 1978.

Évek — hazajáró lelkek: cikkek, naplójegyzetek (1953–1978) [Years — Returning Spirits: Articles, Diary Notes]. Bucharest, Kriterion, 1980.

Gyermekkorom tükörcserepei [Fragments of Childhood Memories]. Budapest, Móra, 1982.

Az idő markában: esszék, naplójegyzetek [In the Grip of Time: Essays, Diary Notes]. Budapest, Szépirodalmi, 1984.

Sikaszói fenyőforgácsok: cikkek, naplójegyzetek [Pine Shavings of Sikaszó]. Budapest, Ifjúsági Lap-és Könyvkiadó Vállatat, 1987.

Sütő András munkái [Works]. Budapest, Szépirodalmi, 1989–.

Omló egek alatt: arcképvázlatok és tűnődések [Under Collapsing Skies: Portraits and Reflections]. Budapest, Szépirodalmi, 1990.

Translator, *Fehér szerecsen*, by Ion Creangă. Budapest, Ifjabb Kiadó, 1953.

Translator, with Jenő Kiss, *Gyermekkorom emlékei*, by Ion Creangă. Bucharest, Creangă, and Budapest, Móra, 1986.

*

Critical Study: "Tragedies of National Fate: A Comparison Between Brian Friel's *Translation* and Its Hungarian Counterpart, András Sütő's *A szuzai menyegző*" by Csilla Bertha, in *Irish University Review* (Dublin), 17(2), 1987.

*   *   *

András Sütő is a major representative of Hungarian literature written outside the borders of present-day Hungary and has become a spokesman for the Hungarian minority of Romania. Living and writing in Transylvania, he looks back on the distinctive tradition of that land. As a spokesman for national values he joins predecessors such as Sándor Petőfi and Gyula Illyés, but in his essays he addresses the universal question of the freedom of the individual and the abuse of power, and particularly the problem of survival for a minority group. While this particular orientation stems from the late 1960s, Sütő from the beginning of his literary career had examined the relation of the individual to society. The film script *Mezítlábos mennyasszony* (The Barefoot Bride) of 1950 as well as the essays of this period examined changes in the village society of Transylvania as a result of the imposition of communist rule following World War II. At first a supporter of the socialist system, he soon criticized its abuses, particularly in the hero of *Pompás Gedeon* (Magnificent Gedeon), a stageplay written in 1968.

In 1970, with the publication of his *Anyám könnyű álmot ígér* (My Mother Promises Easy Dreams), he entered universal Hungarian literature. He also found a genre best suited to conveying his concerns: a mix between essay and diary which he variously calls "journal thoughts," or "diary entries." As he states in an interview, he followed his mother's advice in writing this work: "If you would write about us, son, write the truth." In subsequent essay collections, and more recently in his major dramas, Sütő has been led by this dictum even when the setting and ideas have transcended the world of his native Pusztakamarás society.

The particular in Sütő's work reflects his birthplace, Pusztakamarás (Cămăraşu) and the Mezőség region of Transylvania. But his observations on this region are grounded in a deep knowledge of history and literature and constitute profound philosophical essays. Sütő has said that he is like the peasant women of his region who never travel without their eyt, 1968.

spinning: his own home-spinning permeates even comments on ancient Persia and the United States of the 1980s. "I spoke not about them or to them, but for them," he has stated of his relationship to the people. But, while rooted in the particular of his own family, town, and nation, the scope of his work expands beyond his own world. In an era of fragmentation he offers the unifying force of language and culture; in a world seeking moral and ethical standards, he offers the evolving, understanding, yet prescriptive standards of the community; in a totalitarian dictatorship, he argued for human rights and individual dignity. The focal point in this struggle is the family, for the enduring rules and values are, he maintains, enforced through loyalty to language and nationality (ethnicity). The essay *Nagyenyedi fügevirág* (Flowering Fig-Tree of Nagyenyed) expresses Sütő's concern for his native land and the responsibility he has taken upon himself for its fate.

The question Sütő asks in his essays is: how can this ethnic group survive? That is why Gábor Bethlen fascinated him, for this Transylvanian ruler of the 17th century had faced the same problem and found the solution in tolerance. *Nagyenyedi fügevirág* takes as its point of departure Sütő's arrival at the famous school founded by Bethlen in a long address to the erstwhile ruler who had supported the various cultural and religious groups of his realm in the "intolerant" 1600s while the "enlightened" 20th-century rulers engage in cultural genocide. Ostensibly addressing the problems of the Hungarian population of Romania in the 1940s, it gives voice to universal concerns of human rights: the closing of schools, destruction of national memory through falsification of history, forcible assimilation. The essay "Perzsák" (The Persians) is also the result of the fortuitous joining of historical studies and personal experience. A trip to the site of Persepolis serves as a catalyst for both the essays and the later drama, *A szuzai mennyegző* (The Wedding Feast of Susa) in which he reiterates that a nation cannot be conquered as long as it has its secrets: the Persian maidens, forced to marry the Greek soldiers, will sing lullabies to the children in their own language and about their own gods.

The 1970s also mark the development of Sütő's dramatic genius. In *Csillag a máglyán* (Star at the Stake) Calvin, the reformer and erstwhile rebel, turns on his friend Servetius. Sütő suggests that ideals can be subverted in the name of so-called practical demands. Eternal vigilance is the only guarantee of freedom: "one can forgive . . . an individual's relationship with himself; but one cannot close one's eyes to the behavior of an individual to the community. This is especially true when the individual has an influence on the community."

Sütő's dramas attracted the most attention when censorship in Romania forced him to publish in Hungary, and led to his plays being premiered there. They have since been performed in various European cities and in English in New York. Sütő honed his analytical skills and came to see his own Hungarian minority through historical lenses. Thus the vague socialist and internationalist slogans of his earlier plays received a reality and context: misuse of power and arbitrariness were no longer abstractions but were tied to individual dignity. As he had said many years earlier: "the past is one of Mohács and Sodom, a series of great and heroic deeds and of failures; we cannot do without its lessons and great intellectual values in the interest of personal goals; the historical novel, the historical drama is needed by society."

This task is addressed in the trilogy represented by *Egy lócsiszár virágvasárnapja* (The Palm Sunday of a Horse Dealer), *Csillag a máglyán*, and *Káin és Ábel* (Cain and Abel). In the first he juxtaposes revolution and evolution; in the second he inveighs against fanaticism that abrogates to itself the supreme judgement of right and wrong; in the last he champions human dignity in the face of a power that only asks for submission.

Sütő is a consummate master of language, and his works reflect his mastery of the Hungarian idiom. He relies to a great extent on folk poetry, on the Bible as translated by Gáspár Károlyi, and on Hungarian classical writers such as János Arany. The result is a conciseness and explicitness that has few parallels.

—Enikő Molnár Basa

SUTZKEVER, Abraham. Israeli. Born in Smorgon, Lithuania, 15 July 1913. Educated at Vilna (Vilnius University). Leader of Young Vilna group in 1930s; lived in Vilna Ghetto, 1941–43; partisan, 1943–44. Married to Freydl Sutzkever; two daughters. Editor, *Di Goldene Keyt* [The Golden Chain] Yiddish literary journal, Tel Aviv. Recipient: Association of Yiddish Writers in the Vilna Ghetto prize, 1942; World Jewish Congress prize, 1950, 1956; *Le Petit Parisien* prize, 1950; Itsik Manger prize, 1969; Sholem Aleichem prize; Yakov Fichman prize; New York Culture Congress prize; Zvi Kessel prize (Mexico); Shmuel Niger prize; B'nai B'rith prize, 1979; Israel prize, 1985; David Hofshteyn prize, 1987. Honorary doctorate: Teachers' Seminar, New York. Freeman of the City of Tel Aviv. Address: c/o *Di Goldene Keyt*, 30 Weizman Street, Tel Aviv, Israel.

PUBLICATIONS

Verse

Lider [Poems]. Warsaw, Bibliotek fun Yidishn Pen-klub, 1937.
Valdiks [From the Forest]. Vilnius, Yidisher Literatur-Fareyn un Pen-klub, 1940.
Di festung [The Fortress]. New York, Yikuf-farlag, 1945.
Lider fun geto [Poems from the Ghetto]. New York, Yikuf-Farlag, 1946.
Yidishe gas [The Jewish Quarter]. New York, Farlag Matones, 1948.
Geheymshtot [Secret City]. Tel Aviv, n.p., 1948.
In fayer-vogn [In the Fiery Chariot]. Tel Aviv, Di Goldene Keyt, 1952.
Sibir. Jerusalem, n.p., 1952; as *Siberia*, translated by Jacob Sonntag, London, Abelard Schuman, 1961.
Ode tsu der toyb [Ode to the Dove]. Tel Aviv, Di Goldene Keyt, 1955.
In Midber Sinay [In the Sinai Desert]. Tel Aviv, Farlag Perets-bibliotek, 1957; bilingual edition, Providence, Rhode Island, Ziggurat Press, 1987.
Oazis [Oasis]. Tel Aviv, Farlag Y.L. Perets, 1960.
Gaystike erd [Spiritual Soil]. New York, Der Kval, 1961.
Poetische verk [Poetic Works]. Tel Aviv, Yoyvl-komitet, 2 vols., 1963.
Lider fun Yam-hamoves [Poems from the Dead Sea]. Tel Aviv and New York, Farlag Bergen-Belzen, 1968.
Firkantike oysyes un mofsim [Square Letters and Magical Signs]. Tel Aviv, Di Goldene Keyt, 1968.

Tsaytike penemer [Mature Faces]. Tel Aviv, Farlag Y.L. Perets, 1970.

Di fidlroyz [The Fiddle Rose]. Tel Aviv, Di Goldene Keyt, 1974.

Lider fun togbukh [Poems from a Diary]. Tel Aviv, Di Goldene Keyt, 1977.

Di ershte nakht in get [The First Night in the Ghetto]. Tel Aviv, Di Goldene Keyt, 1979.

Burnt Pearls: Ghetto Poems of Abraham Sutzkever, translated by Seymour Mayne. Oakville, Ontario, Mosaic, 1981.

Fun alte un yunge ksav-yadn [From Old and Young Manuscripts]. Tel Aviv, Farlag Yisroel-bukh, 1982.

Tsviling-bruder [Twin Brother]. Tel Aviv, Di Goldene Keyt, 1986.

Di nevue fun shvartsaplen [Prophecy of the Inner Eye]. Jerusalem, Hebrew University, 1989.

The Fiddle Rose: Poems 1970–1972 (bilingual edition), edited and translated by Ruth Whitman. Detroit, Wayne State University Press, 1990.

A. Sutzkever: Selected Poetry and Prose, translated by Barbara and Benjamin Harshav. Berkeley, University of California Press, 1991.

Der yoyresh fun regn [The Heir of the Rain]. Tel Aviv, Di Goldene Keyt, 1992.

Fiction

Griner akvariyum [Green Aquarium]. Tel Aviv, Committee for Yiddish Culture in Israel, 1975.

Dortn vu es nekhtikn di shtern [Where the Stars Spend the Night]. Tel Aviv, Farlag Yisroel-bukh, 1979.

Other

Vilner geto 1941–1944 [Vilna Ghetto 1941–1944]. Paris, Farband fun di Vilner in Frankraykh, 1946; Buenos Aires, Farlag Yikuf, 1947.

Fun Vilner geto [Vilna Ghetto]. Moscow, Ogiz Melukhe-Falag "Der emes," 1946.

*

Bibliography: *Avrom Sutskever bibliografiye* by Abraham Novershtern, Tel Aviv, Farlag Yisroel-bukh, 1976.

Critical Studies: *Abraham Sutzkever, Partisan Poet* by Joseph Leftwich, Cranbury, New Jersey and London, Yoseloff, 1971; "The Poetry of Abraham Sutzkever," in *Lines Review* (Loanhead, Midlothian, Scotland), 102, 1987, and "Changing Perspectives on Two Poems by Sutzkever," in *The History of Yiddish Studies*, edited by Dov-Ber Kerler, New York, Harwood Academic, 1991, both by Heather Valencia.

*   *   *

Abraham Sutzkever's work encompasses two cultures. He is a Jewish poet, and the heir of the flowering of modern Yiddish literature, but has also been profoundly influenced by the European literary tradition. From youth he was familiar with the Russian and Polish Romantics, and only later with Yiddish poetry. Strong influences on his work are the American Yiddish Introspectivists, who had roots in the Romantic and Expressionist movements, but striking affinities with Rainer Maria Rilke and with the French Symbolist poets are also evident.

Sutzkever also straddles two eras: society before and after the Holocaust. This division has even greater significance for a Yiddish poet than for other writers because of the virtual destruction not only of his society, but also of his language. Sutzkever's poetry originated in a community with a common language and culture, but continues in a society devoid of the integral community of readers; even his language is threatened with extinction.

Sutzkever's themes mirror these ambiguities. In the formative years there is tension between his inner aesthetic impulse and the ethical exigencies of the time. The Holocaust, both in a personal and public dimension, underlies not only the "ghetto-poems," but all his writing, and from the late 1930s onward his poetry considers the role of the poet in a time of moral and physical catastrophe. The affirmative answer to these doubts is the keystone of his mature poetry. Sutzkever constructs a poetic universe in which the word has equal reality to that of tangible objects, and is imbued with a magical, nourishing, and protective power. The aesthetic and the ethical are fused in his private mysticism: the poet as witness communicates with the dead, with those as yet unborn, and with inanimate things, which share in the life of sentient beings:

> I shall seek out between the desert's cliffs
> That word-free alphabet, which will be understood
> By locust and by rain. Mighty revelation:
> The dead shall answer and a stone shall smile!

This conviction constitutes his poetic vocation, and even during the darkest days, the metapoetic theme — the attempt to discover and express *through* poetry the essence of poetry itself — underlies all his work.

Though the Jewish God is strangely absent from Sutzkever's writing — his religious perception is also part of his *poetic* universe — two important aspects of his poetry reveal the essential Jewishness of his world-view. The first is his unwavering commitment to the Jewish people and the continuity of the "golden chain" of the generations. This manifests itself in the importance of the idea of Israel, the land "where every stone is my grandfather," and in countless images from Jewish religious tradition and history. The second is his belief in the substantiality and holiness of the word. The veneration of the written word in Jewish religious and secular life gives the concept of the *word* its particular resonance in Sutzkever's poetry. One of the great paradoxes of his work is his rejection of inadequate human words ("scrape off my words from me/ They are rotting flesh"), while at the same time it is *through* words that he seeks the essence of poetry, attempting to capture it in a variety of metapoetic images: "the sparkling essence," the "word soul," or "the stillness." In this search, the poetic "I" is imbued with almost divine power and perception ("I read texts which no human hand is capable/Of writing").

Three main genres make up Sutzkever's extensive *oeuvre*: prose, shorter lyric poetry (*lider*), and longer, epic poems (*poemes*). The prose pieces, collected in *Griner akvariyum* (Green Aquarium) and *Dortn vu es nekhtikn di shtern* (Where the Stars Spend the Night), and continuing in the Yiddish journal he edits, *Di Goldene Keyt* (The Golden Chain), are poetic prose with surrealistic, mystical imagery through which he probes themes from the Holocaust. (The prose work *Vilner geto* (Vilna Ghetto), on the other hand, is one of the most vivid of the ghetto diaries which give witness to these events.) The *poemes* develop on a monumental scale the public and private themes of the *lider*: "Geheymshtot" (Secret City) depicts the existence of 10 survivors in the sewers of Vilna: the setting of the work within the framework of the poet's vocation to be a "living witness/Of pain which must be transformed into light" testifies to the poem's importance in Sutzkever's struggle to unite poetic individualism with the ethical imperative of the time. Two *poemes*, *Sibir* (Siberia) and *Ode tsu der toyb* (Ode to the Dove), are devoted to the metapoetic theme: the former, exploring the origins of the poet's inspiration in his vision of his Siberian childhood, introduces many seminal images which recur throughout his work. The ode is a turning point, where previous inner conflict is resolved, and a serene, Apollonian harmony is reached, leading into the mature aestheticism of the later poetry.

The lyric poetry moves from the Romanticism of the early *Lider* (Poems) to the powerful anguish of *Di festung* (The Fortress). After the war, the encounters with the land of Israel and with the primordial environment of Africa bring poetic renewal, realized in the biblical mysticism of *In fayer-vogn* (In the Fiery Chariot) and in the celebration of savage, untamed nature in "Helfandn bay nakht" (Elephants at Night). Through these transformations of experience, the poet seems to liberate himself from the burden of the past, and his later poetry, particularly the collections *Di fidlroyz* (The Fiddle Rose) and *Lider fun togbukh* (Poems from a Diary), creates a mystical universe, where he delves ever more deeply into the essence of the inexpressible Word and the nature of the poetic self.

Sutzkever's poetry is unified by a network of permanent images. Many are universal symbols, either emanating from Jewish and biblical sources, or with strong affinities to Jungian archetypes. Other images, however (snow and fire, the fiddle, the dove, the volcano, granite, pearls, grasses, cherries, tiny insects, and many others), gradually develop a private metapoetic significance; they change, develop, and combine to form new concepts — for example, the mysterious "fiddle rose," symbol of the resurrective power of poetry. The Baudelairean synaesthesia inherent in the imagery conveys Sutzkever's perception of the equivalence of all entities, animate and inanimate.

Formally, Sutzkever combines traditional and modern characteristics. In contrast to much 20th-century poetry, a rhetorical style, strong metres, and complex rhyme schemes are fundamental to his work. He is, however, a daring modernist in his innovative enrichment of the Yiddish literary language, through evocative melody, wordplay, ironic wit, and brilliant neologisms.

Sutzkever is probably the last great Yiddish poet, and undoubtedly one of the great 20th-century poets. Poetry has sustained him throughout his eventful life, and he believes it to be humanity's only ultimate food:

> And at the end of days
> Thus it shall be:
> Man will not take into his hungry mouth
> Bread or meat, fig or honey;
> But will merely try a word or two
> And will be satisfied.

—Heather Valencia

SVAVA JAKOBSDÓTTIR. *See* **JAKOBSDÓTTIR, Svava.**

SWAANSWIJK, Lubertus Jacobus. *See* **LUCEBERT.**

SZYMBORSKA, Wisława. Polish. Born in Bnin (now a part of Kórnik), near Poznań, 2 July 1923. Educated at Jagiellonian University, Cracow, 1945–48. Poetry editor and columnist, *Życie Wydawnictwo Literackie* [Literary Life], Cracow, 1953–81. Member, 1952–83, and member of the General Board, 1978–83, Polish Writers' Association. Recipient: Cracow literary prize, 1954; Gold Cross of Merit, 1955; Minister of Culture prize, 1963; Knight's Cross, Order of Polonia Resituta, 1974; Goethe award, 1991. Address: ul. 18 Stycznia 82/89, 30-079 Cracow, Poland.

PUBLICATIONS

Verse

Dlatego żyjemy [That's Why We Are Alive].   Warsaw, n.p., 1952.
Pytania zadawane sobie [Questioning Oneself].   Warsaw, n.p., 1954.
Wołanie do Yeti [Calling the Yeti].   Warsaw, n.p., 1957.
Sól [Salt].   Warsaw, Państwowy Instytut Wydawniczy, 1962.
Wiersze wybrane [Selected Poems].   Warsaw, Państwowy Instytut Wydawniczy, 1964.
Sto pociech [A Hundred Joys].   Warsaw, Państwowy Instytut Wydawniczy, 1967.
Poezje wybrane [Selected Poems].   Warsaw, Ludowa Spółdzielnia Wydawnicza, 1967.
Poezje [Poems].   Warsaw, Przedmowa Jerzego Kwiatkowskiego, 1970.
Wybór poezji [Selected Poems].   Warsaw, Czytelnik, 1970.
Wszelki wypadek [There But for the Grace].   Warsaw, Czytelnik, 1972.
Wybór wierszy [Selected Poems].   Warsaw, Państwowy Instytut Wydawniczy, 1973.
Tarsjusz i inne wiersze [Tarsius and Other Poems].   Warsaw, Krajowa Agencja Wydawnicza, 1976.
Wielka liczba [A Great Number].   Warsaw, Czytelnik, 1976.
Sounds, Feelings, Thoughts: 70 Poems, translated by Magnus J. Krynski and Robert A. Maguire.   Princeton, New Jersey, Princeton University Press, 1981.
Poezje wybrane (II) [Selected Poems II].   Warsaw, Ludowa Spółdzielnia Wydawnicza, 1983.
Ludzie na moście.   Warsaw, Czytelnik, 1986; as *People on a Bridge*, translated by Adam Czerniawski, London, Forest, 1990.
Poezje = Poems [bilingual edition], translated by Magnus J. Krynski and Robert A. Maguire.   Cracow, Wydawnictwo Literackie, 1989.

Other

Lektury nadobowiązkowe [Non-Compulsory Reading].   Cracow, Wydawnictwo Literackie, 1973.

*

Critical Studies: in *Contemporary Polish Poetry, 1925–1975* by Madeleine G. Levine, Boston, Twayne, 1981; "'In the Abscence [*sic*] of Witnesses': The Poetry of Wisława Szymborska" by Jonathan Aaron, in *Parnassus* (New York), 11(2), 1984; "The Possibilities and Limitations of Poetry: Wisława Szymborska's *Wielka liczba*" by John Freedman, in *Polish Review* (New York), 31(2–3), 1986.

* * *

One of Wisława Szymborska's finest collections takes its title from her poem "Ludzie na moście" — "People on a Bridge." The poem takes as its starting point a famous Japanese print by Hiroshige Utagawa. It opens thus:

> A strange planet with its strange people.
> They yield to time but don't recognise it.
> They have ways of expressing their protest.
> They make pictures, like this one for instance . . .

The picture is seen as essentially subversive, insofar as

> Here time has been stopped.
> Its laws have been ignored.
> It's been denied influence on developing events.
> It's been insulted and spurned.

The quiet subversiveness of art is a recurrent theme of Szymborska's work. Her poetry, unsurprisingly, attempts little explicit political subversiveness (though it contains a good deal that is implicit — "Apolitical poems are political too" she notes in "Children of This Age"); rather it subverts a whole range of conventional presuppositions about the nature of the world (of which any specific political system could only be an instance), in a philosophically quizzical fashion. For her our world is, indeed, a "strange planet."

The image which clearly attracted the poet to Utagawa's print is to be found elsewhere in Szymborska's work too. It is central to "Rachunek elegijny" ("An Elegiac Account"), for example, where the poet reflects on all those, now dead, she has known who have "crossed the threshold,/have run across this bridge,/if it is a bridge —." To call life a "bridge" may be to recognise something of its incomplete nature — bridges, after all, only exist to join two things more "important" than themselves. But Szymborska has no confidence that she can have any knowledge of quite what it is that *this* bridge ("if it is a bridge" — the strategy of constant qualification is a wholly characteristic one) joins:

> How many after a briefer or longer life
> . . .
> have found themselves on the other shore,
> if they have found themselves
> and the other shore exists —
>
> I have not been granted certitude
> regarding their further fate . . .

Nor can life on the bridge be a matter of any certainty. Knowing what is "real" is only possible in her ironic "Utopia": "an island where everything becomes clear." This "Utopia" (approached by no bridge) contains "the dazzlingly straight tree of Understanding" and "the Valley of Obviousness." Here "whatever the doubt, the wind blows it away." Yet the island is unpeopled; such footprints as are to be found on its beaches all point out to sea:

> As though people always went away from here
> and irreversibly plunged into the deep.
> In life that's inconceivable.

In a world characterised by the inconceivable and the uncertain, a fresh twist is necessarily given to many an old topos. All the world may be a stage, but Szymborska finds life to be not a well-scripted and plotted masterwork, but a sustained exercise in improvisation:

> I am ignorant of the role I perform.
> All I know is it's mine, can't be exchanged.
>
> What the play is about
> I must guess promptly on stage.

This particular "revolving stage's been turning for quite some time," the poet drily observes.

Szymborska writes frequently of works of art — of pictures, of "Wrażenia z teatru" ("Theatrical Impressions") — because they offer a kind of alternative model by the side of which one might seek to understand "reality." So do dreams — another favourite subject. Reality is certainly the "greater puzzle" since "Dreams have keys/Reality opens on itself/and won't quite shut." The interplay of dream and reality gives poignancy to a number of poems, notably in the tender love poetry of "I Am Too Near":

> I am too near to be dreamt of by him.
> I do not fly over him, do not escape from him
> under the roots of a tree. I am too near.
> . . .
> I slide my arm from under the sleeper's head
> and it is numb, full of swarming pins,
> on the tip of each, waiting to be counted,
> the fallen angels sit.

A view of the world such as Szymborska's necessarily leads to a questioning of the adequacy of language itself, of its capacity to delineate the world we live in (e.g., "View with a Grain of Sand"). Szymborska can be very amusing in her treatment of the human tendency to reduce language to an effectively meaningless system of exchangeable tokens, for instance in "Funeral." She is endlessly alert to language's paradoxical capacity to be both unthinking custodian of the lazy preconception and a means for the challenging of all conventional codes of values.

Szymborska is a lucid and direct poet. She belongs to the generation of Tadeusz Różewicz and Zbigniew Herbert (*qq.v.*). Seamus Heaney in *The Government of the Tongue* (1988) praised Herbert's work in terms of "the exactions of its logic, the temperance of its tone, and the extremity and equanimity of its recognitions." While Szymborska may not be a poet of quite the same range or depth as Herbert, these are phrases that are not without their appropriateness in her case. But it would be wrong to think of her merely a lesser Herbert. Szymborska's is a distinctive voice in its own right — the voice of an entertaining fabulist, a provocative and witty thinker whose work overturns preconceived expectations. Hers is an accomplished examination of ideas, rooted at all times in a sense of the particular:

> Four billion people on this earth of ours,
> but my imagination is unchanged.
> It does not do well with great numbers.
> It is still moved by what is individual.
>
>   ("Wielka liczba" — "A Great Number")

—Glyn Pursglove

T

TABUCCHI, Antonio. Italian. Born in Pisa, in 1943. Educated at the University of Pisa; Scuola Normale Superiore, Pisa. Married to Maria José Lancastre; two children. Lecturer in literature, University of Genoa, until 1987; staff member, Italian Institute of Culture, Lisbon, until 1991. Since 1991 Professor of Portuguese, University of Siena. Recipient: Inedito prize, 1975; Pozzale Luigi Russo prize, 1981; Medicis prize, 1987. Address: Department of Portuguese, University of Siena, Banchi di Sotto 55, 53100 Siena, Italy.

PUBLICATIONS

Fiction

Piazza d'Italia. Milan, Bompiani, 1975.
Il piccolo naviglio. Milan, Mondadori, 1978.
Il gioco del rovescio. Milan, Feltrinelli, 1981.
Donna di Porto Pim. Palermo, Sellerio, 1983; as *Woman of Porto Pim*, with *Vanishing Point* and *The Flying Creatures of Fra Angelico*, London, Chatto and Windus, 1991.
Notturno indiano. Palermo, Sellerio, 1984; as *Indian Nocturne*, London, Chatto and Windus, 1988; New York, New Directions, 1989.
Piccoli equivoci senza importanza. Milan, Feltrinelli, 1985; as *Little Misunderstandings of No Importance*, New York, New Directions, 1987; London, Chatto and Windus, 1988.
Il filo dell'orizzonte. Milan, Feltrinelli, 1986; as *The Edge of the Horizon*, New York, New Directions, 1990; as *Vanishing Point*, with *Woman of Porto Pim* and *The Flying Creatures of Fra Angelico*, London, Chatto and Windus, 1991.
I volatili del Beato Angelico. Palermo, Sellerio, 1987; as *The Flying Creatures of Fra Angelico*, with *Vanishing Point* and *Woman of Porto Pim*, London, Chatto and Windus, 1991.
Le mappe del desiderio. Milan, Idea Books, 1989.
L'angelo nero. Milan, Feltrinelli, 1991.
Requiem: un'allucinazione. Milan, Feltrinelli, 1992.

Play

I dialoghi mancati. Milan, Feltrinelli, 1988.

Other

Il teatro portoghese del dopoguerra. Rome, ABETE, 1976.
Il gioco del rovescio. Milan, Il Saggiatore, 1981; as *Letter from Casablanca*, New York, New Directions, 1986.
Il Poeta e la finzione. Genoa, Tilgher-Genova, 1983.
Pessoana mínima: escritos sobre Fernando Pessoa. Lisbon, Nacionat Casa de Moeda, 1984.
Tanti saluti, with Tullio Pericoli. N.p., Archinto, 1988.
Baule pieno di gente: scritti su Fernando Pessoa. Milan, Feltrinelli, 1990.

Editor, *Una sola moltitudine*, by Fernando Pessoa. Milan, Adelphi, 1979.

Editor and Translator, *Sentimento del mondo*, by Carlos Drummond Andrade. Turin, Einaudi, 1987.

Translator, *Zero*, by Ignácio de Loyola. Milan, Feltrinelli, 1974.
Translator, *Il treno di Recife*, by José Lins do Rego. Milan, Longanesi, 1974.

* * *

Antonio Tabucchi belongs to the tradition of Italian short story writers with a strong sense of the writer as liar. He is also Professor of Portuguese at the University of Siena and his fascination for Portugal, and particularly the writer Fernando Pessoa (1888–1935), constitutes one of his major themes.

His hallmark is a teasing, hoodwinking approach, where suspense and patterning go together in a feast of ultra-postmodern trickery. We are not dealing with fantasy in the manner of Dino Buzzati or Italo Calvino, however. Tabucchi's world keeps abreast of the calamitous 20th century and expresses movingly and starkly the nature of its tragedies. In his early collection of stories, *Il gioco del rovescio* (The Backwards Game), the title story marks the whole with a sense of reversal, that "something seen one way, could also be seen another way round." It is based on the narrator's return journey to Lisbon on the death of a woman he had loved and had helped during the Resistance. The guiding mood is one of *saudade*, Portuguese for yearning, nostalgia, which was the theme of Pessoa and his contemporaries' answer to Italian Futurism. To achieve its impact in story form at least two periods in time must be overlaid by means of memory and dreams. In Italian literature one is reminded of the biographies with which Alessandro Manzoni foreshadows some of the chief characters in *I promessi sposi* (*The Betrothed*), Cesare Pavese's myth of the return in *La luna e i falò* (*The Moon and the Bonfires*), and Elio Vittorini's "twice real" effect in *Conversazione in Sicilia* (*Conversation in Sicily*), all of which give further emotional depth to a psychological and historical situation. Tabucchi adds uncertainty and pattern play to this mixture: perhaps the woman, Maria do Carmo, is not dead and her husband was merely seeing the lover off. The key to the story turns out to be Velasquez's painting *Las Meninas*, which can also be read backwards, for the main figure is at the back of the scene, and in any case, as a picture it can be turned back to front and seen from behind, as perhaps Maria do Carmo now sees it. Another remarkable story in this collection is "Dolores Ibarruri versa lacrime amare" (Dolores Ibarruri Sheds Bitter Tears). A mother is being interviewed after the death of her son in a terrorist incident. The monologue covers issues such as the Spanish Civil War, Fascism, Jewish refugees, and Communism and its break-up, as well as Italian terrorism, while the mother remembers the caring relationship between father and son during her husband's last illness. The suffering is encapsulated in the untutored words of the widow spoken into the reporter's tape recorder.

Tabucchi likes to use modern gadgetry to give a realistic edge to his tales. Records of old hits and old films are peculiarly evocative of the spirit of *saudade*, as are photographs, sometimes studied in minute detail in mock detective stories, and telephone answering machines which record teasing messages. Guide books and maps can also set the agenda, as in *Donna di Porto Pim* (*Woman of Porto Pim*), with its background in the whaling industry in the Azores, and *Notturno indiano* (*Indian Nocturne*), redolent again of the Portuguese diaspora as well as the Raj, with the narrator questing for a hazy Conradian double.

The best-known collection of stories translated into English is *Piccoli equivoci senza importanza* (*Little Misunderstandings of No Importance*). The title story takes in the Red Brigades era. The "misunderstanding" explains how one of the narrator's two friends came to read law at university through a clerical error, and so in later life came to be prosecuting the other friend in a big terrorist trial, with the narrator reporting the event for his newspaper. Meanwhile the girl they were all in love with is operated on for breast cancer. Here the cinematic technique of flashback, or even flash forward, implicit in the operation of *saudade*, telescopes the lives of four people. And when all is over the whole can be frozen and packed away as a still snapshot in the memory of narrator and reader.

Tabucchi's novel *Il filo dell'orizzonte* (*Vanishing Point* or *The Edge of the Horizon*) is in the detective story mode. The search is for the identity of a dead man, who turns out to bear the name Carlo Noboldi or Nobodi, Tabucchi being no stranger to English and American fiction. The "detective" is called Spino, which a note points out is reminiscent of Spinoza, a Portuguese Jew who carried the edge of the horizon (*il filo dell'orizzonte*) in his eyes. It is not surprising to see him launching out for the "vanishing point" at the edge of the world at the end of his futile search.

In *L'angelo nero* (The Black Angel) the stories centre around more sinister compulsions. A game of picking up odd sentences overheard around the Leaning Tower in Pisa becomes the hope of a sinister rendezvous with the ghost of an old Portuguese poet friend alone at the top of the Tower at dusk ("Voci portate da qualcosa, impossibile dire cosa," Voices carried by something, impossible to say what). Temptation assails an old poet, as it might be a Montale or Pavese figure, longer-lived, and dreaming of the 1930s and 1940s, when faced with an attractive young literary critic over dinner ("La trota che guizza fra le pietre mi ricorda la tua vita," The trout flashing between the stones reminds me of your life). The final story, "Capodanno" (New Year), is a gripping re-evocation of the last Fascist Republic of Salò and the Partisans, with the subsequent effects on a young middle-class boy brought up on Jules Verne.

The full-length *Requiem* is a monument to Tabucchi's identification with Portugal and Pessoa, even to the extent of having first been written in Portuguese. Even language itself can be a fiction. The subtitle is *un'allucinazione*, "a hallucination," and the structure recalls James Joyce's *Ulysses*, in that it is an account of meetings with real and ghostly characters in and around Lisbon one July Sunday. The visionary quest culminates with dinner with Pessoa at a postmodern restaurant with a literary *nouvelle cuisine* menu. Ulysses was the legendary founder of Lisbon and one might well suspect that the Ulysses of Homer, Virgil, and Dante has been a presence throughout much of Tabucchi's work, with his passive and active temptations and his silver tongue.

—Judy Rawson

TAFDRUP, Pia. Danish. Born in Copenhagen, 29 May 1952. Educated at the University of Copenhagen. Married to Bo Hakon Jørgensen; two sons. Recipient: Danish State Art Foundation lifelong grant, from 1981, and 3-year stipend, 1984; Drachmann award, 1986; Nathansen award, 1987; Rung award, 1987; Tagea Brandt award, 1989. Agent: (poetry) Borgens Forlag, Valbygårdsvej 33, 2500 Valby, Denmark; (plays) Paul Opstrup, Købmagergade 5, 1150 Copenhagen K, Denmark. Address: Rudmevej 110, 5750 Ringe DK, Denmark.

PUBLICATIONS

Verse

Når der går hul på en engel [When an Angel's Been Grazed]. Copenhagen, Borgen, 1981.
Intetfang [No Hold].   Copenhagen, Borgen, 1982.
Den inderste zone [The Innermost Zone].   Copenhagen, Borgen, 1983.
Springflod.   Copenhagen, Borgen, 1985; as *Spring Tide*, translated by Anne Born, London, Forest, 1989.
Hvid feber [White Fever].   Copenhagen, Borgen, 1986.
Sekundernes bro [The Bridge of Moments].   Copenhagen, Borgen, 1988.
Ten Poems.   Toronto, Cloudberry Foundation, 1989.

Plays

Døden i bjergene [Death in the Mountains] (produced Odense, 1988).   Graasten, Teaterforlaget Dansk Drama, 1988.
Jorden er blå [The Earth Is Blue] (produced Odense, 1991).   Graasten, Teaterforlaget Dansk Drama, 1991.

Screenplay: *Døden i bjergene* [Death in the Mountains], 1990.

Other

Over vandet går jeg: skitse til en poetik [Walking Above the Water: Sketches for a View of Poetics].   Copenhagen, Borgen, 1991.

Editor, *Konstellationer: en antologi af dansk lyrik 1976–1981* [Constellations: An Anthology of Danish Poems 1976–1981].   Herning, Systime, 1982.
Editor, *Transformationer: poesi 1980–1985* [Transformations: Poetry 1980–1985].   Herning, Systime, 1985.

*

Pia Tafdrup comments:
My view of poetics could be called "floating poetics," since all significance comes from within. Reality is only reality. It is given depth and dimension by entry into it. Thus exterior reality depends on interior emotional reality. By floating I am not thinking either of a seraphic position or of escapism but of the felicitous uplift the weight and gravity of images can give, the momentary clarity a poem can reveal. Art must be more than merely attractive, it has to contain passion. To me, writing poems is a process that lifts and opens, gives me a feeling of walking above water. And perhaps the poem may grip the reader firmly enough to make him or her float for a moment?

What I hope for is to connect words so they take on an aura of significance. That the significance comes from within and that the detail must always emanate from me, implies solitude, but no other person can receive my vision, just as a certain amalgam of biological circumstances is necessarily mine alone. No one else can wake from my sleep, no one else can die my death. I belong to myself. Carry my destiny.

There are few human beings who can tolerate being alone with themselves, but the further into solitude I go, the less alone I am.

*   *   *

Danish creative writing changed from the 1970s to the 1980s, and one of the central names involved in that change was the poet Pia Tafdrup. The 1970s had seen a profusion of socially and politically orientated poetry. It was a decade of exploration, in prose, poetry, and drama, but the exploration took place mainly at the level of the community, not at that of the individual. The individual had to be seen in its context, and the emphasis was strongly on the latter; human beings were best understood when seen from the outside, as it were. Writers explored their personal experience as evidence of trends in contemporary society, poetic language was reduced to accessible prose-derivatives, and creative writing acquired purpose, namely that of guiding its readers towards a better future, whether as women, men, workers, or whatever.

That changed in the 1980s. Pre-eminently in lyrical poetry, but also in the theatre, a new interest in the individual emerged. One might put it down simply to the cyclical development of literary taste, but more likely the reason was a new uncertainty about the relationship between people and their society, brought on by the escalating economic crisis and increased unemployment in Denmark. That the poets were "getting it right" was proved by sales figures: lyrical poetry became the literary genre of the decade.

The close relationship between individual and society suddenly seemed more complicated and a new generation of poets started their own exploration of that relationship, this time seen from "inside" rather than outside the individual. At the extreme, the result was narcissism, but for the majority of the new generation it was more a question of creating through language a more physical, sensuous relationship between the poet and her surroundings.

It is the very physicality of Tafdrup's poetry that immediately strikes the reader in her first collection, *Når der går hul på en engel* (When an Angel's Been Grazed). In one poem, "Yesterday's Tea," an apparently trivial, everyday phenomenon is elevated to universal significance:

The set surface
cracking subtly
on yesterday's tea

already a matt membrane
gathering dust

already a painting of the past
the oil cracking

mirroring
in the morning
September's clouds sailing
over red hawthorn berries

mirroring
at noon
the rain riding
baling out across the sky

not given to
speculation about the future
but to reflections on
that which must be
at the moment
when it is
— an angel, perhaps, in my cup?

What strikes the reader is the attention to physical detail in the poet's immediate surroundings, and simple images that set that detail in the context of other, physical and natural phenomena, widening the meaning of the original image. But even more characteristic, of both Tafdrup and her contemporaries, is the rejection of simple, all-embracing significance in the poem. There is no hidden Utopia in this work; the poet claims only to deal with that which is, here and now. Immediacy is the key word. That is not to say that some level of universality is not hinted at. Indeed, the last line suggests — humorously, perhaps — that universality and significance may appear within the poet's reach but not how it might manifest itself; nor is there any guarantee that there will be any universality beyond that which lies in the poet's own surroundings.

Typical of her writing is the linking, in the imagery, of nature and the body. One senses a struggle for wholeness, albeit without any concrete hope of finding it. And there is an acceptance of the physical universe, including the body itself with its potential for close human contact, but at the same time the erotic experience becomes ambiguous rather than a means of salvation for the individual. She continues to develop this theme in her later collections, among them *Intetfang* (No Hold), *Den inderste zone* (The Innermost Zone), and *Springflod* (*Spring Tide*).

But first and last there is a denial of the modernist movement and its insistence that reality is unknowable and that language cannot express it. Like her colleagues, Tafdrup insists that reality at the very least must be the subject of human investigation and conversation, and it must be explored outside the constraints of ideological endeavour. This is not to say that she does not believe poetry is a public phenomenon, addressing contemporary issues, but her voice is that of an artist rather than an ideologue, and when she speaks outside her poetry it is as a critic and — more recently — as a dramatist rather than as a politician.

—Hans Christian Andersen

TARDIEU, Jean. French. Born in Saint-Germain-de-Joux, 1 November 1903; raised in Paris from 1905. Educated at Lycée Condorcet and the Sorbonne, both Paris. Married Marie-Laure Blot in 1932; one daughter. Joined Radio-diffusion-Télévision Française (RTF), Paris, 1944: head of Drama, 1944–45; director, "Club d'Essai" experimental drama studios, 1945–60; program director, 1954–64; Council Member, 1964–74. Recipient: grand prize for poetry, 1972; Critics prize (France), 1976; City of Paris grand prize for poetry, 1981; SACEM grand prize, 1989. Officier, Légion d'Honneur; Commandeur de l'Ordre des Arts et des Lettres. Address: 72 Boulevard Arago, 75013 Paris, France.

PUBLICATIONS

Plays

Qui est là? (produced Anvers, 1949). Included in *Théâtre de chambre*, 1966; as *Who Goes There?*, in *The Underground Lovers*, 1968.

La Politesse inutile (produced Brussels, 1950). Included in *Théâtre de chambre*, 1966; as *Courtesy Doesn't Pay*, in *The Underground Lovers*, 1968.

Un Mot pour un autre (produced Paris, 1950). Paris, Gallimard, 1951.

Faust et Yorick (as *Mi-figure, mi-raisin*, produced Paris, 1951). Included in *Théâtre de chambre*, 1966; as *Faust and Yorick*, in *The Underground Lovers*, 1968.

Oswald et Zénaïde (produced Paris, 1951). Included in *Théâtre de chambre*, 1966.

Ce que parler veut dire (produced Paris, 1951). Included in *Théâtre de chambre*, 1966.

Il y avait foule au manoir (produced Paris, 1951). Included in *Théâtre de chambre*, 1966; as *The Crowd up at the Manor*, in *The Underground Lovers*, 1968.

Un Geste pour un autre (produced Paris, 1951). Included in *Théâtre de chambre*, 1966.

Conversation-sinfonietta (produced Paris, 1951). Included in *Théâtre de chambre*, 1966; as *Conversation-Sinfonietta*, in *The Underground Lovers*, 1968.

Eux seuls le savent (produced Paris, 1952). Included in *Théâtre de chambre*, 1966; as *They Alone Knew*, in *The Underground Lovers*, 1968.

Les Amants du métro (produced Paris, 1952). Included in *Poèmes à jouer*, 1969; as *The Lovers in the Metro* (produced New York, 1962); as *The Underground Lovers* (produced London, 1969), in *The Underground Lovers* (collection), 1968.

Le Meuble (produced Bienne, 1954). Included in *Théâtre de chambre*, 1966; as *The Contraption* (produced Edinburgh, 1980), in *The Underground Lovers*, 1968.

La Serrure (produced Paris, 1955). Included in *Théâtre de chambre*, 1966; as *The Keyhole* (produced New York, 1962; London, 1980).

Le Guichet (produced Paris, 1955). Included in *Théâtre de chambre*, 1966; as *The Enquiry Office* (as *The Information Bureau*, produced New York, 1962), in *The Underground Lovers*, 1968.

La Société Apollon (produced Paris, 1955). Included in *Théâtre de chambre*, 1966; as *The Apollo Society*, in *The Underground Lovers*, 1968.

Théâtre de chambre. Paris, Gallimard, 1955; augmented edition (includes *Qui est là?*; *La Politesse inutile*; *Le Sacre de la nuit*; *Le Meuble*; *La Serrure*; *Le Guichet*; *Monsieur Moi*; *Faust et Yorick*; *La Sonate et les trois messieurs*; *La Société Apollon*; *Oswald et Zénaïde*; *Ce que parler veut dire*; *Il y avait foule au manoir*; *Eux seuls le savent*; *Un Mot pour un autre*; *Un Geste pour un autre*; *Conversation-sinfonietta*), 1966.

Une Voix sans personne (produced Paris, 1956). Included in *Poèmes à jouer*, 1969.

Les Temps du verbe (produced Paris, 1956). Included in *Poèmes à jouer*, 1969.

Rythme à trois temps (produced Paris, 1959). Included in *Poèmes à jouer*, 1969.

Poèmes à jouer. Paris, Gallimard, 1960; augmented edition (includes *L'A.B.C. de notre vie*; *Rythme à trois temps*; *Une Voix sans personne*; *Les Temps du verbe*; *Les Amants du métro*; *Tonnerre sans orage*; *Des Arbres et des hommes*; *Trois Personnes entrées dans des tableaux*; *Malédictions d'une Furie*), 1969.

Monsieur Moi. Included in *Théâtre de chambre*, 1966; as *Mr. Me* (produced London, 1972), in *The Underground Lovers*, 1968.

La Sonate et les trois messieurs. Included in *Théâtre de chambre*, 1966; as *The Sonata and the Three Gentlemen* (produced London, 1972), in *The Underground Lovers*, 1968.

The Underground Lovers and Other Experimental Plays (includes *Who Goes There?*; *Courtesy Doesn't Pay*; *The Contraption*; *The Enquiry Office*; *Mr. Me*; *Faust and Yorick*; *The Sonata and the Three Gentlemen*; *The Apollo Society*; *The Crowd up at the Manor*; *They Alone Knew*; *Conversation-Sinfonietta*). London, Allen and Unwin, 1968.

Une Soirée en Provence (includes *Une Soirée en Provence*; *Un Clavier pour un autre*, music by Claude Arrieu; *Souper*, music by Marius Constant; *Le Club Archimède*). Paris, Gallimard, 1975.

Le Professeur Froeppel. Paris, Gallimard, 1978.

La Cité sans sommeil et autres pièces (includes *Le Rite du premier soir, ou, Le Petit Voleur*; *Pénombre et chuchotements*; *L'Épouvantail*; *De Quoi s'agit-il?, ou, La Méprise*; *La Galerie, ou, Comment parler peinture*; *Un Film d'art et d'aventures, ou, L'Art à la portée de tous*). Paris, Gallimard, 1984.

La Triple Mort du client. Paris, Gallimard, 1987.

La Comédie de la comédie; *La Comédie des arts*; *Poèmes à jouer*. Paris, Gallimard, 1990.

L'Archipel sans nom. Paris, Avant-Scène, 1991.

Verse

Le Fleuve caché. Paris, Schiffrin, 1933.

Accents. Paris, Gallimard, 1939.

Le Témoin invisible. Paris, Gallimard, 1943.

Poèmes. Paris, Seuil, 1944.

Les Dieux étouffés. Paris, Seghers, 1946.

Le Démon de l'irréalité. Neuchatel, Ides et Calendes, 1946.

Jours pétrifiés. Paris, Gallimard, 1948.

Monsieur monsieur. Paris, Gallimard, 1951.

Une Voix sans personne (includes prose). Paris, Gallimard, 1954.

L'Espace et la flûte, illustrated by Picasso. Paris, Gallimard, 1958.

Histoires obscures. Paris, Gallimard, 1961.

Choix de poèmes (1924–1954). Paris, Gallimard, 1961.

Le Fleuve cache (poésies 1938–1961). Paris, Gallimard, 1968.

Formeries. Paris, Gallimard, 1976; in English, Ann Arbor, Michigan, Ardis, 1983.

Comme ceci, comme cela. Paris, Gallimard, 1979.

L'Accent grave et l'accent aigu; poèmes 1976–1983. Paris, Gallimard, 1986.

Margeries: poèmes inédits 1940–1985. Paris, Gallimard, 1986.

The River Underground: Selected Poems and Prose, translated by David Kelley. Newcastle-upon-Tyne, Bloodaxe, 1991.

Other

Figures. Paris, Gallimard, 1944.

Bazaine, Estève, Lapicque, with André Frénaud and Jean Lescure. Paris, Carré, 1945.

Il était une fois, deux fois, trois fois. Paris, Gallimard, 1947.

La Première Personne du singulier. Paris, Gallimard, 1952.

Farouche à quatre feuilles, with others. Paris, Grasset, 1954.

De la Peinture abstraite. Lausanne, Mermod, 1960.

Hollande.   Paris, Maeght, 1963.
Pages d'écriture.   Paris, Gallimard, 1967.
Les Portes de toile.   Paris, Gallimard, 1969.
Grandeurs et faiblesses de la radio.   Paris, Unesco, 1969.
La Part de l'ombre.   Paris, Gallimard, 1972.
Obscurité du jour.   Geneva, Skira, 1974.
Bazaine, with Jean-Claude Schneider and Viveca Bosson.
   Paris, Maeght, 1975.
Les Tours de Trébizonde et autres textes.   Paris, Gallimard,
   1983.
Causeries devant la fenêtre (interviews), with Jean-Pierre
   Vallotton.   Lausanne, Pingoud, 1988.
La Prononciation de l'anglais.   Paris, Presses-Pocket, 1989.
On vient chercher Monsieur Jean.   Paris, Gallimard, 1990.

*

Critical Studies: "Jean Tardieu and the Structure of the
Grotesque," in *Romance Notes* (Chapel Hill, North Carolina),
19, 1978, "The Theater of Jean Tardieu: Experiments in the
Grotesque," in *Savage Comedy: Structures of Humor,* edited
by Kenneth S. White, Amsterdam, Rodopi, 1978, "The
Dynamics of Tardieu's *Le Meuble,*" in *Transformations in
Literature and Film,* edited by Leon Golden, Tallahassee,
University of Florida, 1982, and *"In lustris scaena/Scaena
inlustris*: On Jean Tardieu's *La Serrure,*" in *Bulletin of the
Midwest Modern Language Association,* Spring 1983, all by
Sylvie Debevec Henning; "From Visual to Verbal in Jean
Tardieu's *Les Portes de toile*" by Adelaide M. Russo, in
SubStance (Santa Barbara, California), 14(1), 1985; "Surreal-
ism and the Theater of Jean Tardieu" by Nancy Lane, in *South
Atlantic Review* (Tuscaloosa, Alabama), November 1987;
"Language and Its Comic Effect: An Introduction to the
Theatre of Jean Tardieu" by Marilyn Sparks Severson, in
European Studies Journal (Cedar Falls, Iowa), 5(1), 1988.

*   *   *

Jean Tardieu is a writer who belongs to no literary movement and is identified with no particular philosophy, a position
unusual for any writer and peculiarly so for a French one. If
Tardieu may be said to have an intellectual position in his plays
it is a tongue-in-cheek satiric attitude toward the arbitrary
illogicalities of social intercourse. Combined with this is a
sardonic tendency to follow situations to their ultimate logical
conclusions. Both of these attitudes lead to the production of
some outlandishly witty scenes that bear a stamp that is
unmistakably Tardieu's. His principal contribution to dramatic literature, however, consists of his use of language as
form rather than as semantic instrument. Words provide
atmosphere and feeling instead of analyzable meaning.

Tardieu's use of language as form is best seen in *La Sonate et
les trois messieurs* (*The Sonata and the Three Gentlemen*). In
this play Tardieu tries to imitate the musical sonata form, using
words as sounds. Three players sit on stools on a bare stage and
talk dreamily, rhythmically, meaninglessly as they use speech
to simulate the cadences of music. Tardieu's other experiments
of this kind are *Les Amants du métro* (*The Lovers in the
Metro*), *Rythme à trois temps* (Rhythm in Three-Time), *Une
Voix sans personne* (A Voice Without Anyone), and *Conversation-sinfonietta.*

In *La Serrure* (*The Keyhole*) Tardieu plays with the concept
of logic taken to its ultimate conclusion. *The Keyhole* is a
sophisticated *grand guignol* skit shot through with a macabre
humour. A timid little pervert comes to a whorehouse in order
to see a woman undress. He is strictly a voyeur — personal
contact with the woman does not interest him. The madam

arranges matters so that he can watch one of her girls undress
through a huge keyhole. We are given to understand that this
occasion is the culminating point of the man's life — something he has been looking forward to and working for since an
early age. Ecstatically the man watches the woman strip
naked, but she does not stop. She takes out her eyes, pulls off
her lips, peels off her flesh. Finally, when only a skeleton is
left, the man drops dead. Other plays in this genre include *Le
Guichet* (*The Enquiry Office*) and *Le Meuble* (*The Contraption*).

Tardieu's satire of the conventions of social behaviour finds
its high point in *Un Geste pour un autre* (One Gesture for
Another), where he exposes the basic meaninglessness of the
little automatic gestures required by society by simply inventing a society the same as ours in all respects except that these
gestures are reversed. In the Nameless Archipelago, where
the play takes place, when a guest arrives at a party he puts
his hat on and takes his shoes and socks off, making the
hostess a present of the latter. Then he kisses her foot.
During the party the guests amuse themselves by coughing
and spitting and insulting each other.

Most of Tardieu's plays are a satiric protest against the
enslavement of the human mind by social pressure. The
theme of human helplessness in the face of authority — an
authority that is, ironically, also purely human — appears
again and again in his works. Tardieu sees the human race as
pressed down flat by the weight of the social institutions that
it has itself built up. Mentally, man has no initiative anymore;
physically, he is timid and ulcer-ridden. The tragedy is that he
has been brought to a state where his one wish is not to break
the ring that he has put through his own nose but to hook it to
something — anything. Tardieu's vision is of a world where
logic leads to death, language is as semantically ephemeral as
music, and everyday behaviour is grotesquely pointless and
arbitrary.

—George E. Wellwarth

———

TELLES, Lygia Fagundes. Brazilian. Born in São Paulo,
19 April 1924. Educated at various institutions: holds a teach-
ing credential and degrees in physical education and law.
Married 1) Gofredo da Silva Telles (divorced 1961); 2) Paulo
Emílio Salles Gomes (died 1977). Recipient: Afonso Arinos
prize, 1949; Instituto Nacional do Livro prize, 1958; Boa
Leitura prize, 1961; Cannes Festival grand prize for short
fiction, 1969; Guimarães Rosa prize, 1972; Brazilian
Academy of Letters award, 1973; Pedro Nava award, 1989.
Elected to Brazilian Academy of Letters. Address: c/o
Livraria José Olympio Editora, CP 9018, 22251 Rio de
Janeiro RJ, Brazil.

PUBLICATIONS

Fiction

Porão e sobrado.   São Paulo, n.p., 1938.
Praia viva.   São Paulo, Martins, 1944.
O cacto vermelho.   Rio de Janeiro, Mérito, 1949.
Cirunda de pedra.   Rio de Janeiro, Nova Fronteira, 1954; as
   The Marble Dance, New York, Avon, 1986.

Histórias do desencontro.   Rio de Janeiro, Olympio, 1958.
Histórias escolhidas.   São Paulo, Boa Leitura, 1961.
Verão no aquário.   São Paulo, Martins, 1963.
A confissão de Leontina.   Sá de Bandeira, Angola, 1964.
O jardim selvagem.   São Paulo, Martins, 1965.
Antes do baile verde.   Rio de Janeiro, Bloch, 1970; revised
    and enlarged edition, Rio de Janeiro, Olympio, 1971.
Seleta.   Rio de Janeiro, Olympio, 1971.
As meninas.   Rio de Janeiro, Olympio, 1973; as *The Girl in
    the Photograph*, New York, Avon, 1982.
Seminário dos ratos.   Rio de Janeiro, Olympio, 1977; as
    Tigrela and Other Stories, New York, Avon, 1986.
Filhos pródigos.   São Paulo, Livraria Cultura, 1978.
A disciplina do amor: fragmentos.   Rio de Janeiro, Nova
    Fronteira, 1980.
Mistérios: ficçoes.   Rio de Janeiro, Nova Fronteira, 1981.
Os melhores contos, edited by Eduardo Portella.   São Paulo,
    Global, 1984.
10 contos escolhidos.   Brasília, Horizonte, 1984.
Venha ver o por-do-sol & outros contos.   São Paulo, Ática,
    1988.
As horas nuas.   Rio de Janeiro, Nova Fronteira, 1989.

Other

Lygia Fagundes Telles (selected works and criticism).   São
    Paulo, Abril Educação, 1980.

*

Critical Studies: "New Fiction: Lygia Fagundes Telles" by Jon
M. Tolman, in *Review* (New York), 30, 1981; "The Baroness
of Tatui" by Edla Van Steen, in *Review* (New York), 36, 1986;
"The Guerrilla in the Bathtub: Telles's *As Meninas* and the
Irruption of Politics" by Renata R. Wasserman, in *Modern
Language Studies* (Providence, Rhode Island), 19(1), 1989.

*   *   *

Lygia Fagundes Telles is the most typical fiction writer of the
so-called Brazilian "Generation of 1945." As a result of her
precocity — she published her first book, *Porão e sobrado*
(Basement and Second Floor), in 1938, when she was 15 years
old — she is actually the first author of this "generation." In
spite of her tendency to adapt to new literary trends, she has
been quite faithful to the early tenets of her formative years.
She repudiated her first book long ago, and lists *Praia viva*
(Living Beach) of 1944 as her debut. Despite the considerable
difference in quality between these two works, it is difficult to
perceive any essential variation in their tone, ideology,
thematic interests, or basic psychological, analytical line. Since
the beginning of her career, Telles has made the description
and analysis of the mores and psychology of the urban middle
and upper classes the center of her literary pursuit.

A change in her perception of reality follows the most
violent political upheaval in Brazilian history, beginning in
1964. The decorous chronicler of São Paulo upper classes
becomes perplexed by the events and the transformations
happening around her. The specific part of the upper classes
that she depicts — the economically decadent former rural
landowners — is one that is the most affected by the political
events of the period. At this point Telles begins to reflect on
the validity of certain social institutions (family, marriage) that
she had considered almost immutable in her earlier works. The
author sees these institutions suffering a heavy toll as the result
of violations of civil rights by the two decades of military
dictatorship. A small but noticeable change also occurs in her

style: a more colloquial language is adopted, and the
vulgarisms of today's youth creep in.

Within the generation of 1945, Telles sides with those fiction
writers — such as Autran Dourado, Breno Acioli, Almeida
Fischer, and Samuel Rawet — who preferred to distance
themselves from the experimental line represented by Clarice
Lispector, Murilo Rubião, and Dalton Trevisan. In that sense,
she continues a tradition whose direct ascendants are Érico
Veríssimo and Lúcio Cardoso, novelists for whom psychological analysis is of primary interest, and who were broadly
influenced by Fedor Dostoevskii and Julian Green (*q.v.*).

Telles's best fiction is written in a synthetic manner,
representative of a "slice-of-life" technique — for instance in
"Apenas um Saxofone", from *Antes do baile verde* (Before the
Green Ball) which appears as "Just a Saxophone" in *One
Hundred Years After Tomorrow* (1992). This technique seems
especially suitable to the variety of themes the author handles,
in both her short stories and novels: betrayal and adultery ("O
menino" [The Boy], from *O cacto vermelho* [The Red
Cactus]); prostitution ("A confissão de Leontina" [Leontina's
Confession], from the same collection); political militancy
under a military dictatorship (*As meninas* [*The Girl in the
Photograph*]); drug addiction among the Brazilian youth
(same novel); conflicts among generations, social maladjust-
ments, maturity and aging (*Verão no aquário* [Summer in the
Aquarium] and *As horas nuas* [The Naked Hours]); and the
influence of economic changes on the family structure and on
social mores (*Ciranda de pedra* [*The Marble Dance*]).

By emphasizing this technique, Telles establishes a
meaningful distance between herself as narrator and the
characters she depicts. Added to other narrative qualities
(precision, consistency, fantasy, discernment), the technique
produces works that are obsessive in their presentation of
psychological truth. In Telles's vision, under the refined and
sophisticated manners of a decadent part of wealthy society,
there always lies some kind of disturbing reality. In her later
works — *Seminário dos ratos* (*Tigrela and Other Stories*), *As
horas nuas* — this reality is reminiscent of some surrealist
experiments, with the appearance of a world inhabited by
insect imagery and anthropomorphic beasts.

As a woman who writes fiction, Telles has been frequently
considered as a "feminine writer." However, prior to the 1970s
it is difficult to detect in her work any deep-seated characteristics that would substantiate such an assessment. There are a
number of female narrators in her fiction, but there are also
many stories with a male central protagonist. A majority of her
themes affect equally men and women, and she seems to make
it clear that *human* rather than *feminine* condition is her
preoccupation. In the 1970s, however, a clear interest emerges
in a literature that represents a "female experienced vision." In
The Girl in the Photograph, a novel narrated by three young
women in a boarding school during a student strike, Telles
presents the reader with a panoramic view of the possibilities
of growth open to women in urban Brazilian society at the
close of the century. This novel is in some ways reminiscent of
Rachel de Queiroz's (*q.v.*) masterpiece, *As três Marias* (*The
Three Marias*, 1939), which was set in similar political times.
As horas nuas deals with a traditional cliché in fiction about
women: the aging theatrical star whose success in the past was
based in her now fading physical beauty, who is unable to cope
with the reality of old age, and sinks into alcoholism. Telles
gives life to this familiar plot line by adding an abundance of
new elements to the narrative, thus diverting from the cliché
and raising the story to a higher level of perception. The
presence of an anthropomorphic cat, who "remembers" part
of the story, adds an uncanny interference reminiscent of a
surrealist style.

In some ways Telles represents the social class that is her subject. Starting from the sedate climate of optimism after World War II, through the years of brutal rightwing military dictatorship of the 1960s and 1970s, she finally arrives at an awareness of present-day Brazilian reality. She also represents well the aesthetic range of this period: her work was tradition-bound in the beginning, and later became suffused with conflicting demands, at both the thematic and stylistic levels. As a fiction writer, Telles has responded to these demands by emphasizing a "woman's vision" and by accepting the linguistic changes that mark contemporary Brazilian literature.

—Heitor Martins

TEN BERGE, H. C. *See* **BERGE, H. C. ten.**

TERTS, Abram. *See* **SINIAVSKII, Andrei.**

TERTZ, Abram. *See* **SINIAVSKII, Andrei.**

THOR VILHJÁLMSSON. *See* **VILHJÁLMSSON, Thor.**

ÞORÐARSON, Agnar. Icelandic. Born in Reykjavík, 11 September 1917. Educated at the University of Iceland, 1937–45, M.A. 1945; Oxford University, 1947–48; Yale University School of Drama, New Haven, Connecticut (Fulbright scholar), 1960–61. Married Hildigunnur Hjálmarsdóttir in 1947; three sons. Secretary to British Press Attaché, Reykjavík, 1941–43, and Ministry of Information, London, 1942; librarian, National Library of Iceland, Reykjavík, 1951–86. Recipient: British Council scholarship, 1947–48. Address: Sólheimar 23, 104 Reykjavík, Iceland.

PUBLICATIONS

Plays

Þeir koma í haust [They're Coming This Fall] (produced Reykjavík, 1955).
Kjarnorka og kvenhylli (produced Reykjavík, 1955). Reykjavík, Menningarsjóður, 1957; as *Atoms and Madams*, in *Fire and Ice*, edited by Einar Haugen, Madison, University of Wisconsin Press, 1967.

Spretthlauparinn [The Sprinter] (produced Reykjavík, 1958). Reykjavík, Menningarsjóður, 1959.
Gauksklukkan [The Cuckoo Clock] (produced Reykjavík, 1958). Reykjavík, Helgafell, 1962.
Víxlar með afföllum [Notes at Discount] (produced Selfoss, 1963).
Sannleikur í gifsi [Truth in Plaster] (produced Reykjavík, 1965).
Hundadagakóngurinn [The Dog Day King], from his radio play *Hæstráðandi til sjós og lands* [King of Sea and Land]. Reykjavík, Helgafell, 1969.
Lausnargjaldið [The Ransom] (produced Reykjavík, 1973).
Kona [A Woman] (produced Reykjavík, 1978).
Sandur [Sand] (produced Reykjavík, 1978).

Radio Plays: *Förin til Brasilíu* [Voyage to Brazil], 1953; *Spretthlauparinn* [The Sprinter], 1954; *Andri*, 1955; *Tónsnillingurinn* [The Musical Genius], 1955; *Víxlar með afföllum* [Notes at Discount], 1958; *Goðorðamálið* [The Chieftaincy], 1959; *Ekið fyrir stapann* [The Auto Accident], 1960; *Hæstráðandi til sjós og lands* [King of Sea and Land], 1965; *Mangi grásleppa* [Poor Old Mangi], 1969; *Baráttusætið* [The Seat of the Battle], 1970; *Lausnargjaldið* [The Ransom], 1973; *Sandur* [Sand], 1974; *Ungur maður með skegg* [Young Man with Beard], 1977; *Jarðarberin* [The Strawberries], 1980; *Úlfaldinn* [The Camel], 1980; *Þyrnirós vaknar* [Sleeping Beauty Awakes], 1981.

Fiction

Haninn galar tvisvar [The Cock Crows Twice]. Reykjavík, Helgafell, 1949.
Ef sverð þitt er stutt. Reykjavík, Mál og Menning, 1953; as *The Sword*, New York, Irvington, 1970.
Hjartað í borði, from his radio play *Ekið fyrir stapann* [The Auto Accident]. Reykjavík, Almenna Bókafélagið, 1968; as *A Medal of Distinction*, New York, Hippocrene, 1984; Sawtry, Cambridgeshire, Dedalus, 1988.
Kallaður heim [Summoned Home]. Reykjavík, Almenna Bókafélagið, 1983.
Sáð í sandinn [Sown in the Sand]. Reykjavík, Menningarsjóður, 1988.
Stefnumótið [The Rendezvous]. Reykjavík, Frjálst Framtak, 1989.

Other

Kallað í Kremlarmúr: ferð um Sovétríkin sumarið 1956 með Steini Steinar og fleirum [Sounding Out the Kremlin: A Tour of the Soviet Union in the Summer of 1956 with Steinn Steinar and Others]. Reykjavík, Almenna Bókafélagið, 1978.

Translator, *Ibsensrannsakendur og Henrik Ibsen* [Ibsen Scholars and Henrik Ibsen], by Harald L. Tvetevås. Reykjavík, n.p., 1980.

*   *   *

Just as the Gospels imply that before the cock crows a third time, Peter will have a chance to redeem himself for his denial of Christ, so does Agnar Þorðarson's first novel, *Haninn galar tvisvar* (The Cock Crows Twice), leave the impression that the full story of its hero has not been told. Ingjaldur has rejected his upper-class background, cuckolded the friend who introduced him to communism, and further compromised his integrity by marrying a rich woman he does not love. The novel ends with his wedding, at which he gets drunk, and with the teasing ambiguity of his wife's comment, "he'll recover." The sense that the narrative is only partly complete does not make it any the less readable, and indeed one often has the feeling, on finishing a novel or short story by Þorðarson of wishing that there had been more of it, not least because his narratives seem to reflect so convincingly the tantalising uncertainties and unexplained loose ends of reality.

This is indeed true of his one autobiographical work, *Kallað í Kremlarmúr* (Sounding Out the Kremlin), an account of a visit with some other Icelanders to the Soviet Union in 1956, where he leaves open the question of what would have happened if he had visited the third in a cluster of three farmhouses near Tbilisi, and not been discouraged by his hostile reception — by a dog and an old woman respectively — at the first two. His short story "Þjófurinn" (The Thief) poses the question of why, precisely, a man who at his wife's insistence has called in the police after apprehending an intruder in the building where they live, and where various belongings of theirs had previously gone missing, withdraws charges on discovering that the intruder is from a home for the disadvantaged. Is it purely because of sympathy for the intruder, or because he now feels he has proved himself sufficiently in his wife's eyes?

Uncertainty in the minds of the protagonists as to the exact course of past events affecting their destinies is the subject of Þorðarson's second and third novels, *Ef sverð þitt er stutt* (The Sword) and *Hjartað í borði* (A Medal of Distinction). In the former, a *Hamlet*-like story of preoccupation with revenge, the narrator is driven to madness and the point of murder by his suspicions as to the circumstances of his father's death. The narrator of the latter, after his acute status-consciousness (symbolised by a Portuguese medal inherited from and dubiously acquired by his father) has led him into gambling, embezzlement, and involvement in a car accident resulting in his wife's death, finally acknowledges a need for myth-making about the past in handing on the medal to his son.

Þorðarson's fourth novel, *Kallaður heim* (Summoned Home), a third-person narrative like the first and set in the Westman Islands off the south coast of Iceland at the time of the volcanic eruption in 1973, also has uncertainty about the past as one of its themes. Is Sara, the girl with whom the young poet Andri has an affair, really his half-sister, as his mother would have him believe? Typical of Þorðarson's method is the fact that, when Sara changes her name to Gríma, her new name is said to have three meanings, of which we are told only two. Leaving us to guess at the third meaning with the knowledge that the first two are "night" and "mask" is an effective way of emphasizing her enigmatic character.

It is however as a playwright that Þorðarson is best known in Iceland and is most prolific. Status-consciousness is a major theme of his comedy *Spretthlauparinn* (The Sprinter), in which a Reykjavík housewife originally from the country, feeling that her motor mechanic husband is not good enough for her, plays off against each other as possible alternatives a recently widowed Englishman and an Icelandic country parson originally from Reykjavík. When the Englishman reveals himself as a conceited snob and the parson's mistress arrives from the country to claim him, the housewife settles for her husband with all his faults, which include a certain economy with the truth about his past success as a sprinter. The country vs. town, Iceland vs. abroad oppositions also occur in the comedy *Kjarnorka og kvenhylli* (Atoms and Madams), in which a bogus Canadian physicist pretends to have discovered uranium in a mountain in Iceland. A member of the Icelandic Parliament, taken in by the fraud, plans to buy the mountain from the farmer who owns it. Later, after the fraud is exposed and its perpetrator has fled, the farmer offers hospitality to the parliamentarian's daughter, whom the supposed physicist has made pregnant.

A rather more sombre play is *Gauksklukkan* (The Cuckoo Clock), in which a Reykjavík bank clerk, once a promising pianist, is inspired by a composer friend, who has sensationally gate-crashed a dinner party he and his wife are giving in his boss's honour, to abandon his job and his middle-class way of life — symbolised by the cuckoo clock of the title — in the hope of resurrecting his musical talent. His rebellion is short-lived, however, and by the end of the play he has rejoined the ratrace — though with great reluctance, and mainly for the sake of his wife and adopted child.

A number of Þorðarson's plays are on subjects from Icelandic history. One of them, *Hundadagakóngurinn* (The Dog Day King), concerns Jörgen Jörgensen, a paroled Danish prisoner-of-war of the British, who gave Iceland a brief foretaste of independence in July and August 1809 by declaring himself its protector after he and the London merchant Samuel Phelps had sailed there to open the market for British goods in defiance of the Danish trade monopoly.

Foreign influences are certainly apparent in Þorðarson's work, notably in the stream-of-consciousness passages in his first three novels and in the flashback technique of *Gauksklukkan*. With the subjects he chooses, however, and with his keen sense of plot, of character revealed through dialogue, and of what to omit as well as include, he is a writer most at home in the tradition of Icelandic storytelling.

—Rory McTurk

THORUP, Kirsten (née Christensen). Danish. Born in Gelsted, Fyn, 2 February 1942. Educated at Fredericia Gymnasium, graduated 1961. Married Ib Thorup in 1963 (divorced 1976); one daughter. Lived in England, 1961–62; office assistant, Copenhagen, 1962–70; literary consultant to publishing companies. Recipient: Danish State Art Foundation 3-year stipend, 1970–73; Gelsted memorial award, 1974; Pegasus prize, 1979; Hans Christian Andersen award, 1980; Danish Critics prize, 1982; Danish Booksellers' Association Golden Laurels, 1982; Poul Henningsen prize, 1985; Gelsted-Kirk-Scherfig prize, 1987; Gyldendal prize, 1987; Danish Writers' Association Woman Writer prize, 1987; FTF cultural prize, 1988; LO (Workers Association) cultural prize, 1988; Nathansen award, 1991; Oehlenschläger award, 1991. Address: Carl Bernhards Vej 15A, 1817 Frederiksberg C, Denmark.

PUBLICATIONS

Fiction

I dagens anledning [In Honour of the Occasion]. Copenhagen, Gyldendal, 1968.
Baby. Copenhagen, Gyldendal, 1973; in English, Baton Rouge, Louisiana State University Press, 1980.
Lille Jonna [Little Jonna]. Copenhagen, Gyldendal, 1977.
Den lange sommer [The Long Summer]. Copenhagen, Gyldendal, 1979.

Himmel og helvede [Heaven and Hell]. Copenhagen, Gyldendal, 1982.
Marie. Buffalo, New York, Top Stories, 1982.
Den yderste grænse [The Final Frontier]. Copenhagen, Gyldendal, 2 vols., 1987.

Plays

Romantica (produced Herning, 1983). Copenhagen, Gyldendal, 1983.
Sidste nat før kærligheden [Last Night Before Love] (produced Copenhagen, 1989). Copenhagen, Gyldendal, 1989.

Radio Plays: *Historien om Mally* [The Story of Mally], 1973; *Længslen efter tatovørens nål* [The Longing for the Tattooist's Needle], 1989.

Television Plays: *Sæsonen slutter* [The Season Is Over], 1971; *Frisørinden* [The Hairdresser], 1971; *Hvornår dør Maria?* [When Is Maria Dying?], 1972; *Helte dør aldrig* [Heroes Never Die], 1976; *Else Kant I-II*, 1978; *Du er smuk: jeg elsker dig* [You Are Beautiful: I Love You], 1981; *Krigsdøtre 1. del* and *5. del* [War Daughters Parts 1 and 5], with Li Vilstrup, 1981.

Verse

Indeni-udenfor [Inside-Outside]. Copenhagen, Gyldendal, 1967.
Love from Trieste. Copenhagen, Gyldendal, 1969; in English, translated by Alexander Taylor and Nadia Christensen, Willimantic, Connecticut, Curbstone Press, 1980.
Idag er det Daisy [It's Daisy Today]. Copenhagen, Gyldendal, 1971.

*

Critical Studies: "Thoughts About Kirsten Thorup's *Baby*" by Elizabeth Hardwick, in *Denmarkings* (Copenhagen), 1982; "It's Thorup Today" by Torben Brostrøm, in *Out of Denmark: Isak Dinesen/Karen Blixen 1885–1985 and Danish Women Writers Today*, edited by Bodil Wamberg, Copenhagen, Danish Cultural Institute, 1985; "Identity and Narrative Structure in Kirsten Thorup's Novels" by Charlotte Schiander Gray, in *Scandinavian Studies* (Provo, Utah), 63(2), 1991.

*   *   *

It does not fall to every writer to portray the significant experiences of her lifetime and become known and popular for doing so. But Kirsten Thorup has become one of the voices of her generation in Denmark: those who reached adulthood during the challenging 1960s, the decade of social welfare and political turmoil. Hers is the voice of the new, liberated women of the post-war generation, whose lives were changed irrevocably when women escaped from complete physical and economic dependence on men.

Thorup's focus is not so much on feminism as on the individual (mainly individual woman) in a changing social environment. She writes from experience. Her works reflect her own ability to explore that experience honestly and her style of writing proves her determination to express her opinions in a complex and varied way, which may well account for her popularity among readers of both sexes.

She came to modern, gender-orientated realism in a far from straightforward way. indeed, she personifies a development in Danish literature as such away from 1960s modernism, with its doubts about the meaning of life and the power of language to

express it, to a rather firmer belief in the 1970s that the need to talk about and explain the purpose of human existence is an essential part of life itself.

Her earliest work, in verse and prose, display much of the aesthetic self-consciousness and philosophical relativism that characterized Danish poetry of the 1960s. *Indeni-udenfor* (Inside-Outside) and *Love from Trieste* reveal a fragmented picture of the world, seen through the unreliable prism of human perception: the world may not be unknowable but it cannot be easily pinned down.

But Thorup's own perspective on the world soon becomes evident. Her first novel, *Baby*, was much of its time in laying bare some of the effects of the modern consumer society. But it now became clear that the fragmented world picture had its roots in a particular kind of social organization which tended to objectify everything, turning even human beings into things and giving them equal status with all other objects. Thorup's favoured style of writing was solidifying: she is essentially "dramatic," allowing her characters to reveal themselves through their thoughts and actions rather than through authorial comment. But more significant was the interest that was becoming evident in a particular theme: the fate of the dispossessed, the invisible class in the modern, Danish welfare state.

With hindsight, the reader can see her building up to her monumental trilogy about post-war life, with its central character Jonna, whose experiences are partly based on the author's own childhood. Jonna exemplifies the fate of the young woman who grows up in the Danish countryside without enjoying any of the material benefits of a booming agricultural industry. It is a world close to the roots of most modern Danes, but one from which Thorup's increasingly city-orientated contemporaries have distanced themselves. The reader, seeing this world through the sharp eye of little Jonna, appreciates why even Jonna eventually takes the opportunity to escape from her parochial background, as described in *Lille Jonna* (Little Jonna), as she moves towards the city, where she finds herself in *Den lange sommer* (The Long Summer).

The author continued her description of modern Denmark in the mammoth novels *Himmel og helvede* (Heaven and Hell) and *Den yderste grænse* (The Final Frontier), where the multifarious experience of modern Danes continue to be described in increasingly realistic tones. But Thorup is never entirely realistic. There is always a streak of the poetic in her writing, to reassure the modern reader that she has taken in all of the lessons of modern, 20th-century realism and has the range to describe any facet of life.

—Hans Christian Andersen

———

TIŠMA, Aleksandar. Serbian. Born in Horgoš, 16 January 1924. Educated at the University of Belgrade, diploma 1952. Served in the Yugoslav Army, 1944–45. Married Sonia Tišma in 1952; one son. Journalist and editor, Novi Sad publishing house, 1945–49; director, Matica Srpska publishing house; editor-in-chief, *Letopis Matice srpske*, from 1958. Secretary, Academy of Sciences and Arts, Vojvodina, from 1984. Agent: Liepman AG, Maienburgweg 23, 8044 Zurich, Switzerland. Address: c/o Zeisler, 6 rue des Princes, 92000 Boulogne, France.

PUBLICATIONS

Fiction

Krivice [Guilt].   Novi Sad, Matica, Srpska, 1961.
Nasilje [Violence].   Belgrade, Prosveta, 1965.
Za crnom devojkom [In Pursuit of the Dark Girl].   1969.
Knjiga o blamu [The Book of Shame].   Belgrade, Nolit, 1971.
Mrtvi ugao [Blind Comer].   Novi Sad, Radivoj Ćirpanov, 1973.
Upotreba čoveka.   Belgrade, Nolit, 1976; as *The Use of Man*, San Diego, Harcourt Brace, 1988; London, Faber, 1989.
Povratak miru: pripovetke [Return to Peace: Stories].   Belgrade, Nolit, 1977.
Skola bezbožništva: pripovetke [School of Atheism: Stories].   Belgrade, Nolit, 1978.
Bez krika: pripovetke [Without a Cry: Stories].   Belgrade, Nolit, 1980.
Vere i zavere [Faiths and Conspiracies].   Belgrade, Nolit, 1983.
Hiljadu i druga noć: izbrane pripovetke [The One Thousand and Second Night: Selected Stories].   Belgrade, Srpska Književna Zadruga, 1987.
Kapo.   Belgrade, Nolit, 1987.
Široka vrata [The Wide Door].   Belgrade, Nolit, 1989.
Koje volimo [Who We Love].   Sarajevo, Svjetlost, 1990.

Play

Cena laži [Price of a Lie].   1953.

Other

Naseljeni svet [Populated World].   Belgrade, Matica Srpska, 1956.
Krčma [Inn].   Novi Sad, Progres, 1961.
Drudge [Elsewhere].   1969.
Begunci [Fugitives].   Titograd, Pobjeda, 1981.
Pre mita [Before Myth].   Banjaluka, Glas, 1989.

*

Critical Study: "Alcksandar Tišma's 'Personality': A Feminist Critique" by Barbara Heldt, in *Essays in Poetics* (Oxford), 12(2), 1987.

*   *   *

Aleksandar Tišma is best known for his prose works, which deal with events and experiences based on World War II. Poetry figures strongly among his earlier publications, but his real talent is expressed in the short story and the novel. Writing about his own work in the essay "Nenapisana priča" (The Unwritten Story) Tišma considers that even where the theme of war is not immediately evident it nevertheless forms the background against which the narrative unfolds. He is concerned with both the specific situation of the war in Yugoslavia, complicated by the many factions composed of different nationalities at odds with each other, and with war as a universal experience in which human behaviour is pushed to extremes. The strength of Tišma's work lies on three levels. Firstly, he considers the events of the war in relation to characters' experiences both before and after the actual period of hostilities. Secondly, he focuses on the harsh reality of a situation in which all normal values have been suspended. Thirdly, his language and narrative style are governed by a restraint made remarkable by the otherwise powerful and often emotionally intense subject-matter.

Those who suffered in the wake of World War II had lives before hostilities broke out. By linking the fates of his characters with their pre-war selves Tišma focuses on the impact of the war on individual lives without losing sight of the momentous scale of the historical event. Sredoje Lazukić in *Upotreba čoveka* (*The Use of Man*) is reckless and selfish as an adolescent before the war. These attributes make him a danger to those with whom he comes into contact later when he utilises these negative traits in order to survive the mass destruction. The main character and narrator of *Široka vrata* (The Wide Door) is sentenced to death by a partisan court for an offence he commits as a result of feeling threatened by the possible consequences of a friendship which he had ingenuously fostered before the war. Tišma's characters are not changed by the war; rather it serves to emphasise their strengths and weaknesses. The greater timescale of his narratives also extends to the post-war world. Vera Kroner in *The Use of Man* is morally and spiritually destroyed by her experiences in the concentration camp. She cannot integrate herself into the post-war world and eventually kills herself. It is not possible to return to a social structure in which the emotional and mental tempo of life is not determined by the constant fear of death. Post-war society is portrayed as bureaucratic and dominated by party functionaries as in the short story "Stan" (The Flat). Tišma's panoramic view from pre-war to post-war years refuses to isolate the war years; such a sense of perspective almost offers a note of coherency as the characters attempt to come to terms with the pain of their personal experiences.

In many works of war literature the horrors of mass destruction and individualised terror are often counterbalanced by idyllic memories of the past and hopes for the future. Tišma, however, rejects this possibility and concentrates on the different paths his characters follow in order to cope with their situations. Some, like Vera Kroner, try to retreat into themselves in order to escape reality. Others yield to the pressure and become part of the impersonal machinery of destruction. One of Tišma's most graphic studies of this extreme form of behaviour is contained in his story "Škola bezbožništva" (The School of Godlessness). The story begins as a duel between the interrogator Dulič and his victim Ostojin, a young communist. Dulič tortures him most cruelly, driven on by the prisoner's refusal to reveal the name of his accomplices. He is then informed that the authorities have gained the necessary information from another source. Dulič, crossing the line between rationality and insanity, reacts as if his victim has been transformed into a victor and proceeds to kill him in a barbarous manner. At the same time his thoughts constantly flit back to his son who is lying dangerously ill, and he even imagines Ostojin as an incarnation of him. Fear and evil become mixed with guilt and the desire to kill in the torturer's deranged psychology. His murder of Ostojin is followed by the news that his son will recover. Tišma's nightmare world of the war is a godless place where there is no justice to reward good and evil in equal measure. Individual human beings are not held responsible for the vast scale of the event, yet the war is fought by them. Moral restraint is lost in a world devoid of moral responsibility, and all that remains is the bare struggle to survive. Tišma artistically transposes the absurdity of war without metaphysics or judicial evaluation. The tragedy of war is the brutal reality itself.

Tišma's art is to draw the reader into a circle of intimacy with survivors and victims of the war. The brutality tells its own story through the details of the events themselves. The lack of commentary and the matter-of-fact approach to scenes of the most startling cruelty communicate the anonymity of war. O the other hand, his tendency to narrate a scene as seen through the eyes of one of his characters or through dialogue gives his work the emotional immediacy which only the participants can reveal. This controlled use of language and point of view of the characters as they try to extract some semblance of truth about themselves from the chaos into which they are thrown contributes to that element in Tišma's work which makes what is abnormal appear almost normal. The characters' attempts to justify themselves and to make sense of their experiences leave the reader with the uncomfortable feeling that until human nature is no longer capable of making the unthinkable into a reality, the horror of war will be repeated.

—David A. Norris

TOLSTAIA, Tatiana (Nikitinichna). Also Tatyana Tolstaya. Russian; great-grand-niece of Leo Tolstoi; granddaughter of Aleksandr Nikolaevich Tolstoi. Born in Leningrad, 3 May 1951. Educated at Leningrad State University, 1968–74, degree in philology 1974. Married Andrei Lebedev in 1974; two sons. Junior editor, Eastern literature division, Nauka publishing house, Moscow, 1974–83; writer-in-residence, University of Richmond, Virginia, 1988, and Texas Tech University, Lubbock, 1990; Senior Lecturer in Russian literature, University of Texas, Austin, 1989. Agent: Andrew Wylie, 250 West 57th Street, Suite 2106, New York, New York 10107, U.S.A. Address: 37 B. Polianka No. 2, 109180 Moscow, Russia.

PUBLICATIONS

Fiction

Na zolotom kryl'tse sideli. Moscow, Molodaia gvardiia, 1987; as *On the Golden Porch and Other Stories*, New York, Knopf, and London, Virago, 1989.
Limpopo. Published in *Znamia* (Moscow), 11, 1991.
Sleepwalker in a Fog. New York, Knopf, and London, Virago, 1992.

*

Critical Study: "Tat'iana Tolstaia's 'Dome of Many-Colored Glass': The World Refracted Through Multiple Perspectives" by Helena Goscilo, in *Slavic Review* (Austin, Texas), 47(2), 1988.

*   *   *

The reigning divinities of Tatiana Tolstaia's iridescent, complex fictional universe are language, time, and imagination. With the aid of myth, folklore, and numerous intertexts, her inordinately condensed narratives offer meditations on eternal universal concerns: the elusive significance of a given life ("Sonia," "Most Beloved," "Sleepwalker in a Fog"); the isolation of the individual personality ("Peters," "The Moon Came Out," "Sweet Dreams, Son," "The Circle"); the conflicting claims of spirit and matter ("Hunting the Woolly Mammoth," "Fire and Dust," "The Poet and the Muse"); the complex nature of, and interplay between, perception and language ("On the Golden Porch," "The Fakir," "Night," "Loves Me, Loves Me Not"); and the transforming power of imagination and memory ("On the Golden Porch," "Date with a Bird," "Okkervil River," "Dear Shura").

Throughout her oeuvre, as Tolstaia herself has acknowledged, style dominates over thematic novelty and psychological insight. Her narratives move at an irregular pace, combining minimal plots and sparse dialogue with extravagant poetic description as they slip unobtrusively in and out of temporal frames and characters' thoughts through quasi-direct discourse. Those characters, often situated at the two extremes of the age spectrum, are rendered memorable through Tolstaia's vividly grotesque depiction of their simultaneously risible and pitiable features: e.g., the little girl in "Loves Me, Loves Me Not," the aged protagonists of "Sweet Shura," "Most Beloved," and "Okkervil River."

A comparably synthetic technique for portraying "losers" in amorous endeavors allows Tolstaia to demythologize romance ("Peters," "The Moon Came Out"), just as multiple perspectives on a given individual destabilize a single, unilinear interpretation of character. Tolstaia's fiction teems with dreamers, self-abnegators, failures, pragmatists, egotists, and misanthropes shuttled between largely unrealizable dreams and brute reality. That gap may be bridged by the transfiguring capacities of the imagination, which flourishes virtually unchecked in childhood, but diminishes with time's passage (e.g., "On the Golden Porch," "Date with a Bird") — hence the melancholy sense of loss and helplessness that permeates Tolstaia's texts.

Tolstaia compensates for her protagonists' deprivations by conjuring up for the reader an Aladdin's cave of stylistic riches. To enter Tolstaialand is to step simultaneously into the magical realm of the fairytale and the oppressive dinginess of a grimy kitchen. The endless array of startling contrasts yields not only sensual pleasure, but also fresh perspectives on phenomena that acquire multiple dazzling hues. Scrambling temporal and spatial categories, alternating poetic lyricism with satirical irony, shifting from one narrative perspective to another, leaping from colloquialism and popular slogans to elevated diction and citations from "sacrosanct" sources, Tolstaia packs her kaleidoscopic narratives to the brim.

Readers and critics alike have responded above all to the bold originality of her metaphors, which sometimes swell to Homeric proportions; to her breathtakingly unconventional, subversive juxtapositions; to her idiosyncratic, garrulous Sternian narrator; and to her skill at creating a densely palpable atmosphere through eloquent detail and accumulation of rhetorical devices. Her iridescent, luxurious prose — laden with colorful tropes, apostrophes, exclamations, rhetorical questions, and allusions — isolates her stylistically from the majority of contemporary Russian writers. It allies her with such creative innovators of the 1920s in Russia as Iurii Olesha (1899–1960) and Isaak Babel (1894–1941), as well as Nikolai Gogol (1809–52), Andrei Belyi (1880–1934), and Vladimir Nabokov (1899–1977). Moreover, it corroborates Tolstaia's claim that the desire to display the spectacular range of the Russian language, to explore its boundless expressive powers, was the chief stimulus for her metamorphosis into a writer.

Early in her career Tolstaia focused on the lost paradise of childhood, relying on the Edenic myth as algorithm. Whatever the diversity of her subsequent narratives, including experiments in moral allegory ("Serafim," "A Clean Sheet"), they never addressed nakedly political issues or engaged in topical debates. In that regard, her latest publications, "Limpopo" and "Siuzhet" (Plot), signal a dramatic re-orientation. Longer, more digressive, and less tightly constructed than any of her previous stories, "Limpopo" verges on a novella and offers transparently ironic commentary on Russia's current condition of impotent chaos and spiritual indigence: crushed by a compromised past, Russians foresee no tenable future and dwell in anomie. Its verbal pyrotechnics and hilariously comic passages notwithstanding, "Limpopo" has affinities with the apocalyptic strain of literature that proliferated during President Gorbachev's policy of glasnost.

Since her debut in 1983, Tolstaia's texts have grown progressively longer. One could reasonably classify two of her most recent publications — "Sleepwalker in a Fog" and "Limpopo" — as novellas rather than short stories. Moreover, during the last two years Tolstaia has devoted her energies to journalism instead of fiction. With time her writing has taken an unexpected turn away from her signature genre of short story.

If Tolstaia's professed intention of authoring a novel in the near future signals a search for new directions, then the first phase of her creative development unequivocally guarantees her status as the stylistically more venturesome, nuanced, modernist practitioner of the short story in Russia during the 1980s. Although relatively modest in quantity, her oeuvre amply justifies Iosif Brodskii's (*q.v.*) assertion that Tolstaia is "[t]he most original, tactile, luminous voice in Russian prose today."

—Helena Goscilo

TOLSTAYA, Tatyana. *See* **TOLSTAIA, Tatiana.**

TORGA, Miguel. Pseudonym for Adolfo Correia da Rocha. Portuguese. Born in São Martinho da Anta, 12 August 1907. Educated at schools in São Martinho da Anta, and in Brazil, 1913–16, 1924–25; University of Coimbra, graduated as doctor 1933. Practicing physician: in São Martinho da Anta, Vila Nova de Miranda do Corvo, Leiria, and since 1940, in Coimbra. Recipient: International grand prize for poetry (Belgium), 1976; Montaigne prize; Morgado de Mateus prize; Almeida Garrett prize; *Diário de Notícias* prize; Camões prize, 1989; Association of Portuguese Writers Vide Literária prize, 1992; Prémio do Correspondentes Estrangeiros, 1992. International Miguel Torga prize named for him. Address: Rua Fernando Pessoa 3, Coimbra, Portugal.

PUBLICATIONS (privately printed unless otherwise noted)

Verse

Ansiedade (as Adolfo Correia da Rocha). Coimbra, Imprensa Académica, 1928.
Rampa. Coimbra, Presença, 1930.
Tributo. 1931.
Abismo. 1932.
O outro livro de Job. 1936.
Lamentação. 1943.

Libertação. 1944.
Odes. 1946; revised edition, 1951, 1956, 1977.
Nihil Sibi. 1948.
Cântico do homen. 1950.
Alguns poemas ibéricos. 1952.
Penas do Purgatório. 1954.
Orfeu rebelde. 1958; revised edition, 1970.
Câmara ardente. 1962.
Poemas ibéricos. 1965.
Antologia poética. 1981; revised edition, 1985.
Miguel Torga (selection). Lisbon, Fundação Calouste Gulbenkian, 1988.

Plays

Teatro: Terra firme, Mar. 1941; revised edition of *Mar*, 1977, 1983.
Terra firme (produced Coimbra, 1947). Included in *Teatro*, 1941; revised edition, 1977.
Sinfonia. 1947.
O Paraíso. 1949.

Fiction

Pão ázimo. 1931.
A criação do mundo: Os dois primeiros dias. 1937; revised edition, 1948, 1969, 1981.
O terceiro dia da Criação do mundo. 1938; revised edition, 1952, 1970.
O quarto dia da Criação do mundo. 1939; revised edition, 1971.
Bichos. 1940; revised edition, 1970; as *Farrusco the Blackbird and Other Stories*, London, Allen and Unwin, 1950; New York, Arts Inc., 1951.
Montanha: contos. 1941; enlarged edition, as *Contos da montanha*, 1955, 1969, 1976, 1982.
Rua: contos. 1942; revised edition, 1967.
O senhor Ventura. 1943; revised edition, 1985.
Novos contos da montanha. 1944; enlarged edition, 1952, 1959, 1967, 1975, 1977, 1978, 1979, 1980, 1981, 1982, 1984.
Vindima. 1945; revised edition, 1965, 1971.
Pedras lavradas. 1951; revised edition, 1958.
O quinto dia da Criação do mundo. 1974.
O sexto dia da Criação do mundo. 1981.

Other

A terceira voz. 1934.
Diário 1–15. 1941–90.
Portugal. 1950; revised edition, 1967.
Traço de união. 1955; revised edition, 1969.
Fogo preso. 1976.
Lavrador de palavras e ideias. Lisbon, Ministerio da Comunicação Social, 1978.
Trás-os-Montes, illustrated by Georges Dussaud. Paris, Équinoxe, 1984.
Camões. 1987.

*

Bibliographies: in *Biblos*, 1979; *Ensaio bibliográfico de Miguel Torga* by Maria de Lurdes Gouveia, Castelo Branco, Câmara Municipal, 1979; *Miguel Torga: ensaio biobibliofotográfico* by José de Melo, Aveiro, Lions Clube de Aveiro, 1983.

Critical Studies: *Humanist Despair in Miguel Torga* by Eduardo Lourenço, Coimbra, n.p., 1955; "Miguel Torga: A

New Portuguese Poet," in *Dublin Review*, 229, 1955, and "The Art and Poetry of Miguel Torga," in *Sillages* (Poitiers, France), 2, 1973, both by Denis Brass; "The Portuguese Revolution Seen Through the Eyes of Three Contemporary Writers" by Alice Clemente, in *Proceedings of the Fourth National Portuguese Conference*, Providence, Rhode Island, Multilingual Multicultural Resource and Training Center, 1979; "Madwomen, Whores and Torga: Desecrating the Canon?" by Maria Manuel Lisboa, in *Portuguese Studies* (London), 7, 1991.

*   *   *

Miguel Torga, the *doyen* of Portuguese letters, and Portuguese candidate for the Nobel prize, has shown over almost 60 years a consistency of courage and artistic purpose rarely equalled among his national contemporaries. This has led him into clashes with authorities during the Salazar period, and he did his stint in prison. His early experience in a seminary, from which he fled to Brazil as a poor peasant boy to eke out an existence as a menial on a coffee estate, has marked his writing. He has rejected his childhood Catholicism, but retained the imagery. With the Revolution of 1974 he achieved almost guru status with the new socialist government, and published his political writings under the title *Fogo preso*. His fame rests, however, on a substantial corpus of poetry, and on his several collections of short stories which have been acclaimed as some of the finest in the language. "Torga found himself with a twofold problem. On the one hand he wanted to find real living types, that, while keeping the peninsular fire of their own condition, would have a universal message and at the same time remain Portuguese. On the other hand he had to create a style that could interpret this message in the drama and dynamism of our own times. And so he took the language to pieces and built it anew, taking in idioms and vocabulary of his own region, charged with dramatic content. And so, his is the short sentence and the significant word. An approach to cine technique" (introduction by Denis Brass to *Farrusco the Blackbird*).

The key to his work is his intense, even sensual relationship with his birthplace in Trás-os-Montes. His anguish is that the people there, for whom he wrote in the first place, are, many of them, illiterate, and cannot appreciate his work. Torga is a passionate traveller in his own and in other countries; many journeys are recorded in his *Diaries*. He recognizes the importance of the sea for the history and the economy of his country, and in his *Poemas ibéricos* (Iberian Poems) he addresses the peninsular explorers who set out to till the sea against an uncertain harvest. The sea is also the title of one of his theatre pieces, *Mar* (Sea), where he treats a favourite theme of the prodigal, the man who is lost in shipwreck, or who goes overseas abandoning family, and who may or may not return. Torga sees himself as a kind of smuggler on the frontier between two worlds — Agarez (his birthplace) — and the rest. Agarez symbolizes the whole Iberian peninsula. He set out to explore that other world — Europe — but he always returned to "my hot peninsular night." He is very conscious of his mission as a peninsular writer. His world, he says, finishes only at the Pyrenees, that great barrier that saves his Don Quixote from the temptations of the *Folies Bergères*.

Torga has the "uncontaminated vision" of the countryman and the hunter. Hunting is his recreation and it informs several of his stories. He is a practising doctor, and his observation has been helped by his experience in the consulting room. He sees link between the healing mission of the doctor, the priest, and the poet, all intent on saving or praising life, a mission wonderfully portrayed in the short story "Viaticum" (*O senhor

Ventura). The poet's alternating moods of hope and despair find utterance in the two longer poems *Lamentação* and *Libertação*. His poet's faith and optimism are boldly proclaimed in the title poem of the collection *Orfeu rebelde* (Orpheus in Revolt).

—Denis Brass

———

TOURNIER, Michel (Édouard). French. Born in Paris, 19 December 1924. Educated at Collège Saint-Erembert and Collège Municipal, Saint-Germain-en-Laye; the Sorbonne; University of Tübingen. Producer and director, Radiodiffusion-Télévision Française (RTF), Paris, 1949–54; press attaché, Europe No. 1 radio, 1955–58; director of literary services, Plon publishers, Paris, 1958–68. Television host, *La Chambre Noir* television series, 1960–65. Recipient: Académie Française grand prize for novel, 1967; Goncourt prize, 1970. Chevalier, Légion d'Honneur; Commandeur, Ordre Nationale du Mérite; member, Académie Goncourt, since 1972. Address: Le Presbytère, Choisel, 78460 Chevreuse, France.

PUBLICATIONS

Fiction

Vendredi; ou, Les Limbes du Pacifique. Paris, Gallimard, 1967; revised edition, 1978; as *Friday; or, The Other Island*, London, Collins, and New York, Doubleday, 1969; edition for children as *Vendredi; ou, La Vie sauvage*, Paris, Flammarion, 1971; as *Friday and Robinson: Life on Esperanza Island*, New York, Knopf, and London, Aldus, 1972.
Le Roi des Aulnes. Paris, Gallimard, 1970; as *The Erl-King*, London, Collins, 1972; as *The Ogre*, New York, Doubleday, 1972.
Les Météores. Paris, Gallimard, 1975; as *Gemini*, London, Collins, and New York, Doubleday, 1981.
Le Coq de bruyère (stories). Paris, Gallimard, 1978; as *The Fetishist and Other Stories*, London, Collins, 1983; New York, Doubleday, 1984.
Gaspard, Melchior et Balthazar. Paris, Gallimard, 1980; as *The Four Wise Men*, London, Collins, and New York, Doubleday, 1982; revised edition, as *Les Rois mages*, Gallimard, 1983.
Gilles et Jeanne. Paris, Gallimard, 1983; as *Gilles and Jeanne*, London, Methuen, 1987.
La Goutte d'or. Paris, Gallimard, 1985; as *The Golden Droplet*, London, Collins, and New York, Doubleday, 1987.
Le Médianoche amoureux. Paris, Gallimard, 1989; as *The Midnight Love Feast*, London, Harper Collins, 1991.

Play

Le Fétichiste (produced Paris, 1974). As *The Fetishist* (produced New York, 1984; Edinburgh, 1987), New York, Ubu Repertory Theater, 1983.

Other

Le Nain rouge.   Montpellier, Fata Morgana, 1975.
Le Vent Paraclet.   Paris, Gallimard, 1977; as *The Wind Spirit: An Autobiography*, Boston, Beacon Press, 1988; London, Collins, 1989.
La Famille des enfants (photo collection; commentary by Tournier).   Paris, Flammarion, 1977.
Canada: journal de voyage, photographs by Edouard Boubat.   Montreal, La Presse, 1977; as *Journal de Voyage au Canada*, Paris, Laffont, 1984.
Des Clefs et des serrures.   Paris, Chêne, 1979.
Le Vol du vampire.   Paris, Mercure, 1981.
Pierrot et les secrets de la nuit (for children).   Paris, Gallimard, 1981.
Vues de dos, photographs by Edouard Boubat.   Paris, Gallimard, 1981.
Barbedor (for children).   Paris, Gallimard, 1982.
L'Aire de Muguet (for children).   Paris, Gallimard, 1982.
François Mitterrand, with Konrad R. Müller.   Paris, Flammarion, 1983.
Sept Contes (for children).   Paris, Gallimard, 1984.
Le Vagabond immobile, designs by Jean-Max-Tombeau.   Paris, Gallimard, 1984.
Marseille, ou, Le Présent incertain (photo collection; commentary by Tournier).   Paris, PUF, 1985.
Le Tabor et le Sinaï: essais sur l'art contemporain.   Paris, Belfond, 1988.

*

Critical Studies: *Michel Tournier* by William Cloonan, Boston, Twayne, 1985; *Michel Tournier* by David Bevans, Amsterdam, Rodopi, 1986; *Michel Tournier: Philosophy and Fiction* by Colin Davis, Oxford, Clarendon Press, 1988.

* * *

Among recent French novelists, Michel Tournier stands apart in his determination to revitalize the genre by means of an imaginative faculty that is both unorthodox and powerful. His novels are populated by nomadic characters belonging to strikingly diverse epochs. His work thereby represents a conscious break with the expectation that modern French novelists will explore milieux of which they have first-hand experience, though, as the examples of Marguerite Yourcenar and Patrick Modiano (*q.v.*) illustrate, Tournier is not alone in turning his back on the contemporary world. His fertile imagination leads to knowingly perverse transformations of some of the most familiar images bequeathed by our civilization. Taken together, his fictions suggest nothing less than a project to rewrite our relationship with that civilization.

In harnessing the novel to a faith in the power of the imagination, Tournier is consciously reacting against the non-representational nature of the French "new novel." The popularity of his work is witness to his unfashionable concern for readability. He seeks to emulate the qualities that leave the child-reader of fiction spellbound, lamenting the fact that when he is below his best, he produces works that only adults can read. He has become increasingly drawn to the naïve appeal of the short story and has claimed that his novels had always been an entanglement of individual tales. His compositions are nevertheless by no means straightforwardly representational. For all their immediate appeal, their complexity issues the reader with a difficult challenge. Moreover, they are designed to disturb, highlighting, as they do, paedophilia, the scatalogical, and, in *Le Roi des Aulnes* (*The Erl-King*), an

imaginative reworking of some of the worst excesses of Nazi cruelty.

On closer inspection, Tournier's imaginative verve is, like everything in his fictional universe, part of a duality. Despite the impression his works give of randomness, Tournier's formal training as a philosopher informs much of his practice as a novelist. His first novel, *Vendredi; ou, Les Limbes du Pacifique* (*Friday; or, The Other Island*), the most overtly philosophical of his fictions, is a sustained attempt to explore the limitations of human reason, but all his novels invite readings in terms of categories taken from the various philosophers who together have exerted an influence on him greater than that of more purely literary writers.

Tournier's reputation rests chiefly on his first three novels, all of which are grounded in myth. *Friday* is a reworking of the story of *Robinson Crusoe*, but with Friday as the hero who makes possible the initiatory experience that allows Tournier's Crusoe to break out of his insistent rationalism. In *The Erl-King*, Tournier's invention of a myopic garage-mechanic-cum-ogre (Abel Tiffauges) combines the legend celebrated by Goethe with the story of St. Christopher. In *Les Météores* (*Gemini*), it is the myth of Castor and Pollux (or twinship) that spawns the ideal schema against which to measure the shortcomings of the lone individual. His more recent novels make less marked use of specific myths, but both *Gaspard, Melchior et Balthazar* (*The Four Wise Men*) (to the three Magi is added Taor, a prince who, after his encounter with Caspar, Melchior, and Balthazar, is led to self-sacrifice and eventual peace in the world beyond) and *Gilles et Jeanne* (*Gilles and Jeanne*) (in which Tournier makes use of the story of Joan of Arc to illuminate the evil crimes of Gilles de Rais) continue his practice of taking well-known stories which are then distorted for his particular ends.

In *La Goutte d'or* (*The Golden Droplet*), Tournier turns aside from existing fictional models and invents Idriss, a North African immigrant. Through Idriss, Tournier is able to explore, unexpectedly, what he discovers to be at stake for him in the act of writing. Yet Idriss, by virtue of his marginal status and nomadic existence, is the kinsman of his creator's other heroes. Habitually finding themselves at the margins of society, Tournier's characters experience a solitude that is heightened by their sense of the world being the embodiment of disorder. Robinson, Tiffauges, and Paul in *Gemini* are impelled to seek complementary figures who will release them from their solitude. Within the closed worlds they inhabit, they are possessed by a totalizing desire. Robinson is led through a rejection of rationalism to a form of mysticism. Tiffauges is obsessed by his conviction that everything in the world is a sign. Paul searches for his lost twin in order to regain entry to the privileged wholeness of childhood. In all these cases, the initiatory experiences possess a disturbing duality, presented as they are in terms of benign and malign inversions. The double-sided nature of all experience remains Tournier's fundamental concern.

Tournier's novels are anthropological fictions in which the heroes' mental and physical states and the writing itself present the reader with a potentially infinite number of (imperfect) copies of an original model. For Tournier, writing can only ever be rewriting, not just the rewriting of key myths, but also conscious and unconscious intertextuality. The rewriting of *Friday* for children is merely the most obvious example of a compulsion to rework his fictional narratives.

The reader is faced with paradox at every turn. Tournier's fictions present an indissoluble mixture of order and disorder, the familiar and the strange. They offer comfort, yet disturb; they both fascinate and disgust. Tournier's pursuit of what he calls "white humour," a synthesis of the comic and the cosmic, and his delight in puns and other forms of ludic activity in situations that, viewed more conventionally, would exclude the possibility of laughter, are further evidence that he considers the artist's role to be subversive. His works can be read as explorations of self and other, of language and reality, and as attempts to answer the question "what is knowledge?" Yet they owe their originality and power to Tournier's readiness to break with taboos and engage with the fact that certain responses we may wish to keep separate are intimately related. As a "philosopher," Tournier is derivative, but the boldness with which his works involve us in confronting the perverse activity that ensues from our solitude authorizes us to see his writing as following on from Jean-Paul Sartre and Albert Camus in holding up a mirror in which is reflected an image that, for all its evident exaggeration and distortion, cannot easily be dismissed by us as belonging totally to another.

—Michael Tilby

TRANSTRÖMER, Tomas (Gösta). Swedish. Born in Stockholm, 15 April 1931. Educated at the University of Stockholm, degree 1956. Married Monica Bladh in 1958; two daughters. Psychologist, Psykotekniska Institutionen, Stockholm, 1957–59, Ungdomsanstalten, Roxtuna, 1960–65, Parådetin, Västerås, from 1966, and Arbmarkninst, Västerås, from 1980. Recipient: Aftonbladets prize, 1958; Bellman prize, 1966; International Poetry Forum Swedish award, 1971; Övralids prize, 1975; Boklotteriets prize, 1981; Petrarca prize, 1981; Swedish Academy Nordic prize, 1991. Address: c/o Bonniers Förlag, Box 3159, 103 63 Stockholm, Sweden.

PUBLICATIONS

Verse

17 dikter [17 Poems]. Stockholm, Bonnier, 1954.
Hemligheter på vägen [Secrets on the Way]. Stockholm, Bonnier, 1958.
Den halvfärdiga himlen [The Half-Finished Heaven]. Stockholm, Bonnier, 1962.
Klanger och spår [Soundings and Tracks]. Stockholm, Bonnier, 1966.
Three Poems. Lawrence, Kansas, Williams, 1966.
Kvartett [Quartet]. Stockholm, Bonnier, 1967.
Mörkerseende. Gothenburg, Författarförlaget, 1970; as *Night Vision*, translated by Robert Bly, Ithaca, New York, Lillabulero Press, 1971; London, London Magazine Editions, 1972.
Twenty Poems, translated by Robert Bly. Madison, Minnesota, Seventies Press, 1971.
Windows and Stones: Selected Poems, translated by May Swenson and Leif Sjöberg. Pittsburgh, University of Pittsburgh Press, 1972.
Stigar [Paths]. Gothenburg, Författarförlaget, 1973.
Elegy, Some October Notes, translated by Robert Bly. Rushden, Northamptonshire, Sceptre Press, 1973.
Ostersjöar. Stockholm, Bonnier, 1974; as *Baltics*, translated by Samuel Charters, Berkeley, California, Oyez, 1975; also translated by Robin Fulton, London, Oasis, 1980.

Selected Poems, translated by Robin Fulton. London, Penguin, 1974; Ann Arbor, Michigan, Ardis, 1981.
Citoyens, translated by Robin Fulton. Rushden, Northamptonshire, Sceptre Press, 1974.
Friends, You Drank Some Darkness, with Harry Martinson and Gunnar Ekelöf, translated by Robert Bly. Boston, Beacon Press, 1975.
Sanningsbarriären. Stockholm, Bonnier, 1978; as *Truth Barriers*, translated by Robert Bly, San Francisco, Sierra Club, 1980; as *The Truth Barrier*, translated by Robin Fulton, London, Oasis, 1984.
Dikter 1954–1978. Stockholm, Bonnier, 1979.
How the Late Autumn Night Novel Begins, translated by Robin Fulton. Knotting, Bedfordshire, Sceptre Press, 1980.
Det vilda torget. Stockholm, Bonnier, 1983; as *The Wild Square*, translated by Robin Fulton, London, Oasis, 1984; as *The Wild Marketplace*, translated by John F. Deane, Dublin, Dedalus, 1985.
Collected Poems, translated by Robin Fulton. Newcastle-upon-Tyne, Bloodaxe, 1987; Chester Springs, Pennsylvania, Dufour, 1988.
Selected Poems, 1954–1986, edited by Robert Hass. New York, Ecco Press, 1987.
The Blue House/Det blå huset (bilingual edition), translated by Göran Malmqvist. Houston, Texas, Thunder City Press, 1987.
För levande och döda [For the Living and the Dead]. Stockholm, Bonnier, 1989.
Four Swedish Poets: Tranströmer, Ström, Sjögren, Espmark, translated by Robin Fulton. Buffalo, New York, White Pine Press, 1990.

*

Bibliography: *Tomas Tranströmer: en bibliografi* by Lennart Karlström, Stockholm, Kungliga Biblioteket, 1990.

Critical Studies: by Birgita Steene, in *Scandinavian Studies* (Madison, Wisconsin), 37, 1965; by Robin Fulton, in *Lines Review*, 35, December 1970; "The Values of Contemporary European Poetry" by Alan Williamson, in *American Poetry Review* (Philadelphia), 13(1), 1984; "Tomas Tranströmer" by Gavin Orton, in *Aspects of Swedish Literature*, edited by Irene Scobbie, Norwich, Norvik Press, 1988.

*   *   *

On the strength of two slim volumes of poetry Tomas Tranströmer became almost a cult figure in the 1950s. Although he followed in the Swedish tradition of nature poetry and was a successor to the surrealists, his metaphorical virtuosity inclined neither to romantic ambiguity nor the absurd but to clarity, precision, and striking images — a giant oak is a "petrified elk"; "a dog's bark hangs like a hieroglyph over the garden"; at midnight "the spruce stands like the hand of a clock, spiked." Tranströmer state in an interview that he viewed existence as a great mystery which in certain moments has a religious character, and it is this mystery he attempts to capture in his poetry. In the state between dreaming and waking he suggests a vision of the world experienced fleetingly: "In the first hours of the day our consciousness enfolds the world/like a hand holding a sun-warmed stone." As a psychologist he can use the dream to reach our subconscious but it also becomes the entrance to a visionary transcendental world: "But the writer is halfway into his image, there/he travels, at the same time eagle and mole." The tensions of his world arc reflected often in antithesis: movement-stasis; light-darkness;

interior-exterior ("Under the buzzard's hovering point of stillness/the roaring sea surges forward in the light"; or "There is peace in the forging prow"). There are often religious overtones — God is "unchanging and thus seldom noticed here" (*17 dikter* [17 Poems]), or in *Hemligheter på vägen* (Secrets on the Way) we can feel "God's energy rolled up in the dark." The dreamer at the point of waking, the lover, and the musician come closest to realising the vision of cosmic harmony. For the lovers in *Den halvfärdiga himlen* (The Half-Finished Heaven) "all questionmarks began to sing about God's existence," and in *Det vilda torget* (*The Wild Square* or *The Wild Marketplace*) the night sky lows and they "secretly milk the cosmos."

Activists criticised Tranströmer in the 1960s for lack of political commitment. Several of his poems bear political references — the Berlin Wall, the Algerian War, for instance — but as part of the flow of history. Man's role is to observe, listen, and sympathise with the victims; only the faces of the victims change. French atrocities in Algeria conjure up Dreyfus. A newspaper "full of events" lying outside for months is "on the way to becoming a plant . . . to being united with the earth. Just as a memory is slowly transmuted into your own self." Even urban pollution can be assimilated on this time scale. "Factories brood/the buildings sink two millimetres/per year — the ground is devouring them slowly." In *Ostersjöar* (*Baltics*) the Baltic symbolises peoples of many ages co-existing in the present. It unites and divides countries and social systems but has wider connotations of eternity, solitude, and, in magic moments, of peace. At his best Tranströmer conjures up clear contours of our world in a new perspective, making it familiar and yet strange, and can convey his sense of wonder at our universe.

—Irene Scobbie

TREMBLAY, Michel. Canadian. Born in Montreal, Quebec, 25 June 1942. Educated at the Institut des Arts Graphiques. Linotypist, 1963–66. Since 1964 writer. Recipient: Radio Canada prize, 1964; Méritas Trophy, 1970, 1972; Canada Council award, 1971; Chalmers award, 1972, 1973, 1974, 1975, 1978, 1986, 1989; Victor Morin prize, 1974; Canadian Film Festival award, 1975; Ontario Lieutenant-Governor's Medal, 1976 (twice); Quebec Ministry of International Relations France-Quebec prize, 1981, 1985; Festival du Théâtre des Ameriques award, 1985; City of Montreal grand prize, 1989; Prix du Public, 1990; Grand Prix du Public, 1990; Jacques-Cartier Lyon prize, 1991. Chevalier, 1984, and Officier, 1991, de l'Ordre des Arts et des Lettres (France). Honorary doctorate: Concordia University, 1990; McGill University, 1991. Agent: Agence Goodwin, 839 est, rue Sherbrooke, Suite 2, Montreal, Quebec H2L 1K6, Canada.

PUBLICATIONS

Plays

Le Train (broadcast on radio, 1964; produced Montreal, 1965). Montreal, Leméac, 1990.
Messe noir, from his stories in *Contes pour buveurs attardés* (produced Montreal, 1965).

Cinq (includes *Berthe*; *Johnny Mangano and His Astonishing Dogs*; *Gloria Star*; first produced Montreal, 1966). Revised version, as *En Pièces détachées* (produced Montreal, 1969), with *La Duchesse de Langeais*, Montreal, Leméac, 1970; in English, Vancouver, Talon, 1975; as *Like Death Warmed Over* (produced Winnipeg, Manitoba, 1973), Toronto, Playwrights Co-op, 1973; as *Montreal Smoked Meat* (produced Toronto, 1974); as *Broken Pieces* (produced Vancouver, 1974); television adaptation as *Trois Petit Tours* (broadcast 1969), Montreal, Leméac, 1971; in *La Duchesse de Langeais and Other Plays*, 1976.
Les Belles-Soeurs (produced Montreal, 1968). Montreal, Holt, 1968; in English, Vancouver, Talon, 1974; as *The Guid Sisters* (produced Toronto and Glasgow, 1987), Toronto, Exile, 1988; London, Hern, 1991.
Lysistrata, with André Brassard, adaptation of the play by Aristophanes (produced Ottawa, 1969). Montreal, Leméac, 1969.
Les Paons (produced Ottawa, 1971). Montreal, CEAD, 1969.
L'Effet des rayons gamma sur les vieux-garçons, adaptation of *The Effect of Gamma Rays on Man-in-the-Moon Marigolds* by Paul Zindel (produced Montreal, 1970). Montreal, Leméac, 1970.
La Duchesse de Langeais (produced Montreal, 1970). With *En Pièces détachées*, Montreal, Leméac, 1970; in *La Duchesse de Langeais and Other Plays*, 1976.
". . . Et Mademoiselle Roberge boit un peu . . .", adaptation of *And Miss Reardon Drinks a Little* by Paul Zindel (produced Montreal, 1972). Montreal, Leméac, 1971.
Le Pays du dragon, adaptation of four one-act plays by Tennessee Williams (produced Montreal, 1971).
À Toi, pour toujours, ta Marie-Lou (produced Montreal, 1971). Montreal, Leméac, 1971; as *Forever Yours, Marie-Lou* (produced Toronto, 1974), Vancouver, Talon, 1975.
Demain Matin Montréal m'attend (produced Montreal, 1972). Montreal, Leméac, 1972.
Hosanna (produced Montreal, 1973; Toronto, 1974; New York; Birmingham and London, 1981). With *La Duchesse de Langeais*, Montreal, Leméac, 1973; in English, Vancouver, Talon, 1974.
Mistero buffo, translation of the play by Dario Fo (produced Montreal, 1973).
Bonjour, là, bonjour (produced Ottawa, 1974). Montreal, Leméac, 1974; in English (produced 1975), Vancouver, Talon, 1975.
Mademoiselle Marguerite, adaptation of *Aparaceu a Margarida* by Roberto Athayde (produced Ottawa, 1976). Montreal, Leméac, 1975.
Les Héros de mon enfance (produced Eastman, Quebec, 1975). Montreal, Leméac, 1976.
Surprise! Surprise! (produced Montreal, 1975). With *Damnée, Manon, sacrée Sandra*, Montreal, Leméac, 1977; in English, in *La Duchesse de Langeais and Other Plays*, 1976.
Sainte-Carmen de la Main (produced Montreal, 1976). Montreal, Leméac, 1976; as *Saint Carmen of the Main* (broadcast BBC Radio, 1987), Vancouver, Talon, 1981.
La Duchesse de Langeais and Other Plays (includes *La Duchesse de Langeais*; *Berthe*; *Johnny Mangano and His Astonishing Dogs*; *Gloria Star*; *Surprise*). Vancouver, Talon, 1976.
Damnée, Manon, sacrée Sandra (produced Montreal, 1977). With *Surprise! Surprise!*, Montreal, Leméac, 1977 (produced in the U.S., 1981) in English, Vancouver, Talon, 1981; as *Sandra/Manon* (produced Edinburgh and London, 1984).

L'Impromptu d'Outremont (produced Montreal, 1980). Montreal, Leméac, 1980; as *The Impromptu of Outremont* (produced in English, 1981), Vancouver, Talon, 1981.
Les Grandes Vacances (produced Montreal, 1981).
Les Anciennes Odeurs (produced Montreal, 1981). Montreal, Leméac, 1981; as *Remember Me*, Vancouver, Talon, 1984.
Oncle Vania, adaptation of the play by Anton Chekhov, with Kim Yaroshevskaya. Montreal, Leméac, 1983.
Albertine en cinq temps (produced Ottawa, 1984). Montreal, Leméac, 1984; as *Albertine in Five Times* (produced Toronto, Edinburgh, and London, 1986), Vancouver, Talon, 1987; London, Hern, 1991.
Le Gars de Québec, adaptation of *Le Revizor* by Nikolai Gogol (produced Montreal, 1985). Montreal, Leméac, 1985.
Six Heures au plus tard, adaptation of the play by Marc Perrier. Montreal, Leméac, 1986.
Le Vrai Monde? (produced concurrently in Ottawa and Montreal, 1987). Montreal, Leméac, 1987; as *The Real World* (produced London, 1990), Vancouver, Talon, 1988.
Nelligan (opera libretto; produced Montreal, 1990). Montreal, Leméac, 1990.
La Maison suspendue (produced Montreal, 1990). Montreal, Leméac, 1990; in English, Vancouver, Talon, 1991.
Théâtre I. Arles, Actes Sud, 1991.

Screenplays: *Françoise Durocher, Waitress*, with André Brassard, 1972; *Il était une fois dans l'est*, with André Brassard, 1973; *Parlez-Vous d'amour*, 1976; *Le Soleil se lève en retard*, 1977; *Le Cœur découvert*, 1986; *Le Grand Jour*, 1988; *Six Heures plus tard*, 1988; *Le Vrai Monde?*, 1991.

Radio Plays: *Le Train*, 1964; *Saint Carmen of the Main*, 1987 (U.K.).

Television Plays: *Trois Petits Tours*, from his plays, 1969.

Fiction

Contes pour buveurs attardés. Montreal, Jour, 1966; as *Stories for Late Night Drinkers*, Vancouver, Intermedia Press, 1977.
La Cité dans l'œuf. Montreal, Jour, 1969.
C't'à ton tour, Laura Cadieux. Montreal, Jour, 1973.
La Grosse Femme d'à côté est enceinte. Montreal, Leméac, 1978; as *The Fat Woman Next Door Is Pregnant*, Vancouver, Talon, 1981; London, Serpent's Tail, 1991.
Thérèse et Pierrette à l'école des Saints-Anges. Montreal, Leméac, 1980; as *Therese and Pierrette and the Little Hanging Angel*, Toronto, McClelland and Stewart, 1984.
La Duchesse et le roturier. Montreal, Leméac, 1982.
Des Nouvelles d'Édouard. Montreal, Leméac, 1984.
Le Cœur découvert: Roman d'amours. Montreal, Leméac, 1986; as *The Heart Laid Bare*, Toronto, McClelland and Stewart, 1989; as *Making Room*, London, Serpent's Tail, 1990.
Le Premier Quartier de la lune. Montreal, Leméac, 1989.
Les Vues animées. Montreal, Leméac, 1990.

Other

Québec, trois siècles d'architecture, with Claude Paulette and Luc Noppen. Montreal, Libre Expression, 1979.

*

Bibliography: by P. Lavoie, in *Voix et Images* (Montreal), Winter 1982.

Manuscript Collection: Bibliothèque Nationale du Canada, Ottawa.

Critical Studies: "Michel Tremblay's Seduction of the 'Other Solitude'" by Catherine McQuaid, in *Canadian Drama* (Guelph, Ontario), 2, 1976; *Stage Voices: Twelve Canadian Playwrights Talk About Their Lives and Work*, edited by Geraldine Anthony, New York, Doubleday, 1978; "Five Short Plays by Tremblay" by Bruce Serafin, in *Essays on Canadian Writing* (Toronto), 11, 1978; "Where to Begin the Accusation" (interview), and "The Tremblay Opus: Unity in Diversity," both in *Canadian Theatre Review* (Toronto), 24, 1979, and *Michel Tremblay: A Critical Study*, Vancouver, Douglas and McIntyre, 1982, all by Renate Usmiani; "From Alienation to Transcendence: The Quest for Selfhood in Michel Tremblay's Plays" by John Ripley, in *Canadian Literature* (Vancouver), 85, 1980; "Michel Tremblay and the Fantastic of Violence" by Ruth B. Antosh, in *Aspects of Fantasy*, edited by William Coyle, Westport, Connecticut, Greenwood, 1986; "Structures of Impasse in Michel Tremblay's *Albertine en cinq temps*" by Elaine Hopkins Garrett, in *Québec Studies* (Montreal), 4, 1986; "An Eye for an Ear: *Fifth Business* and *La Grosse Femme d'à côté est enceinte*" by Gregory J. Reid, in *Studies in Canadian Literature*, 14(2), 1989.

*   *   *

Long acknowledged as the most important playwright in the history of French Canada, Michel Tremblay has now achieved international recognition as well for the power and originality of his dramatic and — more recently — novelistic creations. In an apparent paradox, most of his plays are firmly rooted, by language, setting, and cultural reference, in the narrowly confined world of Montreal's working-class slums; yet they transcend place, language, and time to appeal to audiences and readers everywhere.

The performance in 1968 of his best-known work, *Les Belles-Soeurs* (The Sisters-in-Law) immediately brought Tremblay to national attention. The play, and the warm controversy it aroused, are now seen as an apogee in the cultural awakening of Quebec known as the Quiet Revolution. Set in a tawdry flat in east-end Montreal, *Les Belles-Soeurs* has the sparest of plots: the central character, Germaine (there are only female roles — 15 of them — in the play), having won a million trading-stamps in a contest, has invited relatives and friends to help her paste them in booklets for redemption. Her good fortune leads the others to reflect individually and collectively on their own pervasive frustrations. By play's end the guests have stolen Germaine's stamps, booklet by booklet, leaving her more deprived and despairing than ever.

It was not the plot but the language which aroused vehement reaction, for the play makes exclusive use of *joual*, the impoverished, anglicized popular speech of urban Quebec — the only speech appropriate for these characters in this setting. Critics were scandalized, since critics write for the social classes which in Quebec had long preferred to ignore the very existence of *joual* (the term, pejorative in intention, comes from a distorted pronunciation of *cheval*, "horse"), despite its prevalence among their economically and socially under-privileged compatriots. For generations theatre audiences had accepted a bloodless "international" French onstage, however Canadian the setting of the play. Critics were thus correct in assessing the cultural and even political importance of Tremblay's linguistic innovation: of working-class origin himself, he was challenging the artificial tradition of "correct" French, in itself symptomatic of the radical alienation so many of his countrymen felt so intensely.

For months the debate continued, obscuring the innate merits of *Les Belles-Soeurs*. But in the end even the most illiberal critics had to concede that this was the most compellingly original play yet composed in Quebec. For the sordid, naturalistic setting and the unpleasant but realistic diction of its characters represent only the first and more accessible level of this complex work. It is in fact intensely theatrical, with recurring alienation techniques that force the audience to recoil and reflect upon what is being enacted onstage. "I don't want to offer people a pleasant evening out," the author explains, "I want them to react, to be afraid, to weep, to laugh, to tell themselves 'things have got to change!'" Thus purposely "stagy," anti-realistic monologues express individual anguish, and stylized choruses, and choreographed diversions intrude, heightened by complex lighting and sound effects. Profoundly pessimistic in tone, the play exudes nevertheless an intense and unexpected lyrical quality not unlike that of classical tragedy. In fact *Les Belles-Soeurs* is now recognized as a "classic" in more than one sense, its status amply confirmed by translation into more than 20 languages and performances in a dozen countries, most recently in Japanese in Tokyo and in Scots dialect (the translation is entitled *Guid Sisters*) in Glasgow and Toronto. Sales of the text are approaching 100,000 copies, more than for any contemporary play in French anywhere in the world, and it is the only foreign play on the compulsory reading list for secondary schools in France.

On the foundations of this play Tremblay has since constructed a literary opus unlike any other. *Les Belles-Soeurs* is the door to a coherent universe, where characters in one play or novel may assume leading roles in another: the children, Manon and Carmen, in *À Toi, pour toujours, ta Marie-Lou* (*Forever Yours, Marie-Lou*), for example, reappear as title characters in *Sainte-Carmen de la Main* (*Saint Carmen of the Main*) and *Damnée Manon, sacrée Sandra* (Damned Manon, Holy Sandra). What they have in common is their desire — always ultimately frustrated — to transcend the moral and physical universe in which they find themselves trapped. Comprising 12 plays, Tremblay's first dramatic cycle, from *Les Belles-Soeurs* to *Damnée Manon, sacrée Sandra*, depicts domestic tragedies (notably *Forever Yours, Marie-Lou*) and singular anti-heroes, often transvestites (*Hosanna*; *La Duchesse de Langeais*) struggling, like Quebec itself (the author himself underlines the parallel) to affirm their troubled identities in a constraining universe they cannot comprehend. Some seek salvation in the cheap entertainments of Montreal's bars, like the heroines of *Demain Matin Montréal m'attend* (Tomorrow Morning Montreal Awaits Me) and *Saint Carmen of the Main*; some revert to traditional religious belief (*Damnée Manon, sacrée Sandra* neatly juxtaposes the two impulses); others seek all-encompassing sexual commitment (nearly all the male characters in Tremblay's plays are homosexual). But are all doomed to failure and the crushing existential *angst* which, in the author's perspective, defines the universal human condition.

There have been visible changes in the shape and focus of Tremblay's writing since the mid-1970s, the most obvious being his growing preference for the novelistic form. His novels generally have strong autobiographical bases, as well as explicit connections with the dramatic universe first presented in *Les Belles-Soeurs*. Four of them are loosely grouped in a cycle the author identifies as "The Chronicles of Plateau Mont-Royal." In the first of these, set in the 1940s, *La Grosse Femme d'à côté est enceinte* (*The Fat Woman Next Door Is Pregnant*), Tremblay himself is the child the Fat Woman will bear. A critical and commercial success, it was followed by the others at two-year intervals, all less well received than the first. In them he extends the world of his plays, fleshing out minor characters, providing a social and familial context for each. More recently novels such as *Le Cœur découvert* (*The Heart Laid Bare*) and *Le Premier Quartier de la lune* (The First Quarter of the Moon) leave his familiar universe behind, dwelling exclusively on what is perennial in human nature. His theatre shows major thematic shifts as well, as he moves away from proletarian characters and setting towards middle-class concerns and more universal themes, in *L'Impromptu d'Outremont* (*The Impromptu of Outremont*), *Les Grandes Vacances* (Summer Vacation), and his major success of the 1980s, *Albertine en cinq temps* (*Albertine in Five Times*), a compelling portrait of a troubled elderly woman in dialogue with herself at five different stages of her life. *La Maison suspendue* (The Suspended House), on the other hand, returns to Tremblay's well-known universe as it presents three generations of the same family in their relentless but futile pursuit of meaning and identity.

Author of two musical comedies and an historical opera (*Nelligan*), Tremblay has also translated and adapted for performance plays by authors as diverse as Aristophanes and Chekhov, written short stories and a dozen film and television scenarios. Prolific and versatile, he continues to voice the frustrations and the aspirations of his native Quebec even as he formulates a universal human search for values in an apparently inhumane world.

—Leonard E. Doucette

———

TRIER MØRCH, Dea. Danish. Born in Copenhagen 9 December 1941. Educated at the Academy of Fine Arts Copenhagen, 1957–64; academies of fine arts in Warsaw Cracow, Belgrade, Leningrad, and Prague, 1964–67. Married Troels Trier in 1976 (divorced 1979); two daughters and one son. Artist: many group and individual exhibitions, since 1961 Co-founder and member, Røde Mor [Red Mother] artists collective, 1969–77; member, Danish Communist Party, until 1982; chair, Danish Writers' Association, Copenhagen 1990–91; member, Arte por la Vida international artists group 1990. Recipient: Danish Author of the Year, 1977; Danish State Art Foundation lifelong grant, from 1985; Hvass Foundation award, 1985; Peter Sabroe children's prize, 1987; Tagea Brand award, 1988. Agent: Line Schmidt Madsen, Gyldendal Klareboderne 3, 1001 Copenhagen K, Denmark. Address Jens Juelsgade 7, 2100 Copenhagen Ø, Denmark.

PUBLICATIONS

Fiction

Vinterbørn. Copenhagen, Gyldendal, 1976; as *Winter Child*, London, Serpent's Tail, and Lincoln, University of Nebraska Press, 1986.
En trekant [A Triangle]. Copenhagen, Brøndum, 1977.
Ind i verden [Into the World]. Copenhagen, Gyldendal, 197
Kastaniealléen [Chestnut Avenue]. Copenhagen, Gyldendal 1978.
Den indre by [Inner City]. Copenhagen, Vindrose, 1980.
Aftenstjernen. Copenhagen, Vindrose, 1982; as *Evening Star* London, Serpent's Tail, and Lincoln, University of Nebraska Press, 1988.

Morgengaven [Morning Gift].   Copenhagen, Vindrose, 1984;
one chapter as "The Wedding," in *No Man's Land: An
Anthology of Modern Danish Women's Literature*,
Norwich, Norvik Press, 1987.
Skibet i flasken [The Ship in the Bottle].   Copenhagen,
Vindrose, 1988.

Other

Sorgmunter socialisme [Bittersweet Socialism]. Copenhagen,
Rhodos, 1968.
Polen [Poland].   Copenhagen, Rhodos, 1970.
Da jeg opdagede Amerika [When I Discovered America].
Copenhagen, Vindrose, 1986.
Barnet uden navn [The Child with No Name].   Copenhagen,
Det Etiske Råd, 1990.
Pengene eller livet [The Money and the Life] (for children).
Copenhagen, Gyldendal, 1990.

*

Bibliography: *Dea Trier Mørch: en bibliografi* by Hanne Hørl
Hansen, Copenhagen, Danmarks Biblioteksskole, 1988.

Manuscript Collection: The Royal Library, Copenhagen.

Critical Study: "Dea Trier Mørch: A Journey in the Soul" by
Erik Vagn Jensen, in *Out of Denmark: Isak Dinesen/Karen
Blixen 1885–1985 and Danish Women Writers Today*, edited by
Bodil Wamberg, Copenhagen, Danish Cultural Institute,
1985.

Dea Trier Mørch comments:

To give birth is like travelling in a foreign country. That was
how I experienced it, when in the course of a few years, I had
my own three children. But it is a country which is different
from all other countries, in that you can't return to it. Because I
was afraid that this country would disappear irrevocably, I
wrote and illustrated the novel *Vinterbørn* (*Winter's Child*).
Through text and pictures I will try to encapsulate the
country's geography, inhabitants, and past — I will try to
remember all details — before it forever sinks into the ocean
like the country Atlantis.

Winter's Child is divided into three parts: an antenatal ward,
a delivery ward, and a postnatal ward. The frame is the
University Hospital, called Rigshospitalet, in my own town,
Copenhagen, Denmark. The main characters are the women
giving birth. The minor characters are hospital staff, relatives
of the patients, and the newborn babies. In the book I try to
describe the contradictory conditions that a woman lives
through, such as anxiety mixed with confidence, despair with
expectation, sadness with happiness.

The book indirectly draws a picture of Danish society. There
are women from all sectors of society on the maternity ward
which traditionally takes in unmarried, pregnant women and
women whose pregnancy for various reasons is problematic.
At this hospital, having children is free. The births are being
paid for by the state, that is, through taxpayers' contributions.

I have all together written and illustrated 14 books, but this
book has had the strangest and most wonderful fate of all. It
immediately caused a stir, because for the first time it was
possible to talk completely openly about the great mystery of
giving birth. The book was soon translated into many
languages, including English, German, French, Italian,
Portuguese, Hungarian, Polish, Greek, Greenlandic,
Hebrew, Russian, and Japanese. The book has taken me out
into the world and men and women in many countries have
told me about the births of their children. Through these
conversations, I have realized that in Denmark, we have a
quite satisfactory and humane environment in which to give
birth and a good tradition for educating midwives.

One more of my novels has been translated into English. It is
called *Aftenstjernen* (*Evening Star*) and is in direct counterpoint to *Winter's Child*, as its theme is Death. The process of
dying, which takes place within a Danish family of three
generations, extends over nine months like a backward birth
into oblivion.

*   *   *

Dea Trier Mørch is a writer and illustrator who shares with
other Danish women writers the view of art as a medium for
expressing the conflict between work and domestic life.

Although she began her career as an artist, Trier Mørch
turned to writing when she became aware of the conflicts
between her own needs and those of her children. She first
published two books based on her time spent travelling and
studying in East European countries. *Sorgmunter socialisme*
(Bittersweet Socialism) and *Polen* (Poland) are characterised
by short, simple sketches which capture the immediacy of the
author's experiences, her frame of mind, and the atmosphere
of the settings.

Danish critic Gunhild Agger writes that whereas Trier
Mørch's books on Eastern Europe are characterized by a
narrative distance, written from a foreigner's perspective, her
three novels *Vinterbørn* (*Winter's Child*), *Kastaniealléen*
(Chestnut Avenue), and *Den indre by* (Inner City) are
characterized by a narrative closeness and empathy. All three
novels are set in Denmark and deal with problems in domestic
life.

The highly successful *Winter's Child* is about the process of
pregnancy and birth. The main character Marie Hansen is
required to stay in hospital during the final month of her
pregnancy. This period is usually called "expecting"; however,
Trier Mørch points out that this is not a time of expectation but
one which involves re-evaluation of priorities. World and local
politics give way to the problems surrounding the origins of
life. The changes in a pregnant woman's body and mind
become her central concerns; she must also prepare herself
psychologically for the child, and she feels anxiety about labor
and delivery.

The perspective of *Winter's Child* is narrow and concentrated, as reflected in the hospital setting, a place where world
and class conflicts are de-emphasized. Marie can see busses
passing by, people walking home from work, and can listen to
news about the war in Vietnam on the radio, but such things
represent another reality. The patients in Marie's hospital
room are all concerned about their unborn children, creating a
solidarity between the women that transgresses class and
language barriers. Agger points out that this alliance between
the women is part of a vision of an alternative society with
other values and other ways of bringing people together than
those of contemporary society. Trier Mørch uses the conflict
between the everyday world and the hospital world to criticise
contemporary society, which can afford to see to it that all
children are born equal, but cannot afford to give them equal
chances for a good upbringing.

In *Kastaniealléen* Trier Mørch writes about early childhood
and the relationship between grandparents and grandchildren.
Once again the world she depicts is narrow and condensed.
The focus this time is from the perspective of children, who
constantly try to expand their field of experience.

Kastaniealléen is about three young children from Copenhagen who visit their maternal grandparents. Their father is a patient in a tuberculosis sanatorium, and their mother is working in Copenhagen. The children are not particularly depressed by these circumstances, but find security in interaction with each other, and in their relationship to their grandparents, especially their grandmother. The relationship between grandparents and children is depicted as secure and stable, free from the friction between parents and children.

Through a series of everyday and holiday situations, Trier Mørch captures the way children absorb the world around them — their assessment of language, social norms, and ideas. Agger writes that Trier Mørch presents the children's way of absorbing the world by, on the one hand, acceptance, and on the other, distorting and ridiculing language and norms of adults. However, their acceptance and ridicule of the grandparent's norms never conflicts with that which has the grandmother's approval. What is essential here is the foundation of a (sometimes overidealized) mutual respect and harmony between the two generations.

Trier Mørch's third novel *Den indre by* (Inner City) is, in a way, an extension of elements from *Winter's Child* and *Kastaniealléen*. Marie, the main character in *Winter's Child*, is also central to *Den indre by*. In fact the title of this novel is taken from the last words of *Winter's Child* when Marie leaves the hospital, and is on her way to Copenhagen's inner city. Its perspective, however, is wider than the previous novels and includes political activism and its conflict with domestic life.

In 1977 Trier Mørch published a short story called *En trekant* (A Triangle), which deals with the conflicts between woman, man, and child when the child is a newborn baby. This theme is also explored in *Den indre by*. In addition, the novel explores the world of children by registering their independent language and life, their assessment of adult values, and their reactions. In contrast to *Kastaniealléen*, *Den indre by* deals with the relationship between parents and children — and it is not presented as harmonious.

The main character, Lulu, a 36-year-old housewife, is experiencing a crisis, which the novel explores as a widespread condition afflicting women who live as spouses and who have reached a certain age. It arises when a woman's desire for an independent life conflicts with work, on the one hand, and the demands made by her children and her husband's attitude on the other. It is antagonized by a multitude of stressful everyday situations, in which the relationship between the spouses is desexualised.

"Inner city" refers to the area in Copenhagen where the main characters live, but it also implies that Lulu has her own "inner city," a number of mental blocks and problems. It also refers to the inner city office of DKP, the Danish communist party, where Lulu's husband is politically active and unable to balance this with his role as a parent.

Marie introduces Lulu to the women's movement, and although she finds the movement's political platform too theoretical, it appeals to her emotionally. Whereas the women's movement opens up Lulu, the political party in her life, the DKP, has the opposite effect by blocking and inhibiting her development.

Trier Mørch has written three more novels, *Aftenstjernen* (*Evening Star*), *Morgengaven* (Morning Gift), and *Skibet i flasken* (The Ship in the Bottle). She has also written the travel book *Da jeg opdagede Amerika* (When I Discovered America), a children's book *Pengene eller livet* (The Money and the Life), and numerous essays and debate articles.

Trier Mørch has made women's experiences and problems visible in a way that has attracted a larger reading audience than most socialist writers in Denmark. She raises questions about women's desire for independence in conflict with domestic expectations, and the need to find a way to balance several of life's elements — work outside the home, political activism, sexuality, and small children. Her strength in composition lies in her power of observation rather than in in-depth, complex analysis.

—Deborah Fronko

———

TS'AO YÜ. *See* **CAO YU.**

———

TSUSHIMA Yūko. Japanese. Born Tsushima Satoko in Tokyo, 30 March 1947. Educated at Shirayuri Women's College, M.A. in English literature 1969. Has one daughter. Recipient: Izumi Kyōka prize, 1977; Women's Literature award, 1978; Kawabata Yasunari prize, 1983; Yomiuri prize, 1987. Agent: English Agency, no. 305, 4-11-28, Nishiazabu, Minato-ku, Tokyo 106, Japan. Address: no. 602, 6-15-16, Hongomagome, Bunkyo-ku, Tokyo 113, Japan.

PUBLICATIONS

Fiction

Dōji no kage [Shadow of Child].   Tokyo, Kawade Shobō, 1973.
Mugura no haha [The Mother in the House of Grass]. Tokyo, Kawade Shobō, 1975.
Yorokobi no shima [Island of Joy].   Tokyo, Chūō Kōronsha, 1978.
Chōji.   Tokyo, Kawade Shoboshinsha, 1978; as *Child of Fortune*, Tokyo and New York, Kōdansha International, 1983; London, Women's Press, 1986.
Hikari no ryōbun [Territory of Light].   Tokyo, Kōdansha, 1979.
Yama o hashiru onna.   Tokyo, Kōdansha, 1980; as *Woman Running in the Mountains*, New York, Pantheon, 1991.
Moeru kaze [Burning Wind].   Tokyo, Chūō Kōronsha, 1980
Suifu [City in the Water].   Tokyo, Kawade Shobō, 1982.
Hi no kawa no hotori de [On the Bank of the Fire River] Tokyo, Kōdansha, 1983.
Danmariichi [The Silent Traders].   Tokyo, Shinchōsha, 1984.
Ōma monogatari [Twilight Stories].   Tokyo, Kōdansha 1984.
Yoru no hikari ni owarete [Driven by the Light of Night] Tokyo, Kōdansha, 1986.
Mahiru e [Toward Noon].   Tokyo, Shinchōsha, 1988.
Yume no kiroku [Record of Dreams].   Tokyo, Bunge Shunjū, 1988.
The Shooting Gallery and Other Stories.   New York, Pantheon, and London, Women's Press, 1988.
Kusamura: jisen tanpenshū.   Tokyo, Gakugei Shorin, 1989.
Oinaru yume yo, hikari-yo [Enormous Dream, Light!] Tokyo, Kōdansha, 1991.

*

Critical Study: in *Off Center* by Miyoshi Masao, Cambridge, Massachusetts, Harvard University Press, 1991.

*   *   *

In a society which until very recently saw women writers as a distinct and narrowly defined category, Tsushima Yūko was one of the first to be recognised as simply a representative writer of her generation. Part of this is undoubtedly due to her skill at her craft. Her short stories range from the intimate, domestic, and confessional to the chilling and fantastic, blending Japanese folklore with comic realism. Her novels, which often employ female narrators, rarely present women as suffering and passive victims; rather, they offer sharply observed and offbeat depictions of modern family life and sexual relationships.

Much of Tsushima's early fiction draws upon personal experience, seducing her readers into complicity: the fatherless daughter, the sister of a mentally handicapped boy, the single or divorced mother, the independent working woman of her fiction — such as the sequence *Hikari no ryōbun* (Territory of Light), which portrays a newly divorced woman's life with her child, or the novel *Yama o hashiru onna* (*Woman Running in the Mountains*), in which a woman escapes into her imagination from the dull routine, precisely detailed, of day-to-day existence — are all autobiographical projections. She often uses the first person in the prevalent modern Japanese mode of the "I-novel," inviting identification. But along with her unique brand of domestic realism, Tsushima frequently displays another talent: her stories, even when they do not contain explicitly supernatural events, often play with the dark underbelly of everyday life: the menace at the edge of town, the concealed suicide or murder, the gaping psychic wound behind the silken urban armour. This technique is best exploited in such stories as "An Embrace," in which virtual strangers are drawn together by the shared trauma of parental suicide, and "The Silent Traders" (the title story of the collection *Danmariichi*), in which a young mother's loneliness leads her to imagine that her children are trafficking with the wild animals in a wood, in a silent bargain for survival. "The Marsh" and "The Chrysanthemum Beetle" both use legendary motifs of hauntings, suicides, and revenges to cast light on the effect of the past on present relationships.

Tsushima's is an inhospitable world: the rather random sexual encounters of her women are mostly transitory, the gap between the genders virtually unbridgeable, families are responsible for repression and mental pain, and even friendships are inconstant and competitive. Women, however independent, are particularly susceptible. And yet there are flashes of compassion, solidarity, and affection, even between men and women, as the long title story of *Mugura no haha* ("The Bed of Grass") reveals: in the floating Tokyo world of transient contacts, the heroine's sense of humour, and her friendship with a single mother and a simple, alienated Thai student, help her survive a futile relationship with a chauvinistic and potentially violent lover. A sense of humour also irradiates *Chōji* (*Child of Fortune*), the story of a 36-year-old divorced mother who, when she finds herself pregnant by her lover, decides against an abortion. (Not, in the Western sense, a radical feminist, Tsushima here implicitly takes the side of the unborn against restrictive social norms, in a context which differs from its Western counterpart.) The novel ends, as does "The Bed of Grass," in an encounter with another woman's child: children, who often represent secrets and hostile resistance in Tsushima's fiction, just as often symbolise love, resilience, and hope. *Child of Fortune*, like many of her

stories, attributes her experiences, if not her talent and autonomy, to Koko, her heroine; but the third-person perspective she employs allows for detachment and an affectionately comical portrayal.

Tsushima's fiction is remarkable not only for its structural economy and coherence but also for its innovative and original use of imagery. The most trivial and banal domestic objects can acquire a sinister or menacing significance, leading to an onrush of memory or a deluge of paranoia; landscapes are appropriated to match inner states, as in *Hi no kawa no hotori de* (On the Bank of the Fire River), a story of father-daughter incest described by Geraldine Harcourt, Tsushima's usual translator, as her most complex work to date.

Younger writers have continued to inject innovative techniques into Japanese literature, but Tsushima's work — especially her short fiction — continues to have an impact beyond the timely and topical, partly because underneath its flippant modern surfaces lie signs of something deeper, and an awareness of the grand literary heritage from which it has emerged.

—Aamer Hussein

———

TUSQUETS (Guillen), Esther. Spanish. Born in Barcelona, 30 August 1936. Educated at the Colegio Alemán, Barcelona; universities of Barcelona and Madrid, licenciada in philosophy and letters. Has one daughter and one son. Since 1960 director, Editorial Lumen, Barcelona. Recipient: City of Barcelona prize, 1979. Agent: Mercedes Casanovas, Calle Teodora Lamadrid 29, 08022 Barcelona, Spain. Address: Ps° de la Bonanova 92–94, 08017 Barcelona, Spain.

PUBLICATIONS

Fiction

El mismo mar de todos los veranos. Barcelona, Lumen, 1978; as *The Same Sea as Every Summer*, Lincoln, University of Nebraska Press, 1990.
El amor es un juego solitario. Barcelona, Lumen, 1979; as *Love Is a Solitary Game*, London, Calder, 1985.
Varada tras el último naufragio. Barcelona, Lumen, 1980; as *Stranded*, Elmwood Park, Illinois, Dalkey Archive Press, 1991.
Siete miradas en un mismo paisaje. Barcelona, Lumen, 1981.
Para no volver. Barcelona, Lumen, 1985.

Other

La conejita Marcela (for children). Barcelona, Lumen, 1980.

*

Critical Studies: "The Barcelona Group: The Fiction of Alós, Moix, and Tusquets" by Elizabeth Ordóñez, in *Letras femeninas* (Lincoln, Nebraska), Spring 1980; "The Language of Eroticism in the Novels of Esther Tusquets" by Catherine G. Bellver, in *Anales de la Literatura Española Contemporánea* (Boulder, Colorado), 9(1–3), 1984; "Reading, Rereading, Misreading and Rewriting the Male Canon: The Narrative Web of Esther Tusquets" by Linda Gould Levine, in *Anales de la Literatura Española Contemporánea* (Boulder, Colorado), 12, 1987; *Foucault, Feminism, and Power: Reading Esther Tusquets* by Nina Molinaro, Lewisburg, Pennsylvania, Bucknell University Press, 1991; "The Prison-House (and Beyond): *El mismo mar de todos los veranos*" by Geraldine Cleary Nichols, in *Romanic Review* (New York), 75; "Esther Tusquets's Fiction: The Spinning of a Narrative Web" by Mirella Servodidio, in *Women Writers of Contemporary Spain: Exiles in the Homeland*, edited by Joan L. Brown, Newark, University of Delaware Press, 1991; *The Sea of Becoming: Approaches to the Fiction of Esther Tusquets*, edited by Mary S. Vásquez, Westport, Connecticut, Greenwood Press, 1991.

*   *   *

Esther Tusquets enjoys a long-standing connection with the literary world — she has been the director of the Lumen publishing house since the 1960s — but her career as a fiction writer began at age 42, with the publication of *El mismo mar de todos los veranos* (*The Same Sea as Every Summer*), an unusually mature first novel whose themes and style set a pattern for later works, which are complex and highly original variations on the original story. In addition, this novel represents the literature of post-Franco Spain in its intermingling of universal and national themes viewed from the critical, ironic perspective of the postmodernist. Tusquets also plays an important role in the development of Spanish women's fiction, disclosing both surface and hidden realities of women's lives and roles in modern Spain, opening new avenues of expression through an emphasis on female eroticism (lesbian relationships, woman's sexuality and pleasure, female erotic imagery), and in general both directly and indirectly revealing opposition to phallocentric patterns that deny self-realization.

The Same Sea . . . is a quest novel, narrated by an unnamed middle-aged woman who seeks to refashion her unhappy life through a relationship with Clara, a young student in her literature class. Together they embark on a journey of self-discovery, which includes a re-evaluation of the narrator's past: conflict with her mother, alienation from the Catalan bourgeoisie, the unexplained suicide of her first love. The unselfish love of these women seems to offer the means to recapture lost innocence and create a world free of power and subordination, but the narrator ultimately repeats the very paradigm she was desperately trying to subvert: betrayal of the loved one, which she effects by inexplicably returning to her unfaithful husband and her former, unhappy life. This circular narrative also defuses contemporary Spanish history and social values and adds a feminist slant that depicts women's passive role in a society controlled (scripted) by men, women's friendship, the importance of mother-daughter bonding (one of the basic problems in this novel, because it is unrealized), and glimpses of a new world-order through a lesbian relationship. However, the end suggests that traditional structures still hold sway in contemporary society. Other complex issues arise from the highly literary nature of the work: the narrator patterns her life on literary models; intertextual underpinnings of myth and fairytale foretell the immutable nature of the text of life; her attempts to rescript her life and change the ending of her "story" are doomed to failure.

Shifting relationships, betrayal, and the search for authenticity continue in *El amor es un juego solitario* (*Love Is a Solitary Game*). The unusual components of this title foretell the unconventional involvement that defines the "players"; the desire for power and control mark changes in alliances. The characters bear an uncanny resemblance to those in the earlier novel — an older, unhappy woman (Elia), a worshiping young girl, and the addition of a young man, whom Elia initiates sexually. Their decadent games offer sexual rather than spiritual or existential satisfaction. Intertextuality, role-playing, and scripting on many levels emphasize themes of life reflected through literature.

Although Tusquets has considered *Varada tras el último naufragio* (*Stranded*) as the last novel of a trilogy that includes the previous two works, it could also be successfully paired with her latest novel, *Para no volver* (Never to Return), published five years after *Stranded*. Shifting relationships, the exploration of love and its betrayal, rebellion, alienation, an obsession with aging and the passage of time, the interweaving of life and text — all elements associated with Tusquets's earlier works — are recombined and elaborated in a slightly different way. Here quest is circumscribed by an increased emphasis on self- definition through retrospection and self-analysis; as a result, each woman gains a greater measure of independence and thus the possibility of a more promising future. In *Stranded* a middle-aged writer tries to pull the pieces of her life together after the trauma of a failed marriage; *Para no volver* describes the stages of self-recovery through a more focussed process. This paradigmatic "heroine" is again cut loose from her safe moorings: family changes (marital problems, independence of her children), the realization of her aging, and a sense of alienation create a crisis situation which Elena tries to resolve through psychoanalysis. This experience allows scope for airing personal, social, and national concerns. Elena rebels against traditional intertexts which fix power at almost inaccessible levels ("Papa Freud's" ideas on women and analysis, her role in the patriarchal text which scripted her as the "perfect wife").

A story for children (*La conejita Marcela* [Marcela the Bunny Rabbit]) and a book of short stories (*Siete miradas en un mismo paisaje* [Seven Looks at a Same Landscape]) complete Tusquets's fiction to date. The latter describes seven separate episodes in the life of a single protagonist, presented in nonchronological order. An increased emphasis on social problems adds a new dimension to the major themes.

Tusquets's fiction concentrates on the inner life of her characters, generally mature women who must come to grips with unhappiness, alienation, aging, and failing relationships in varying degrees. Their quest for fulfillment parallels complex and shifting alliances which may involve a third party who changes the dynamics in both sexual and existential ways. Erotic experiences (heterosexual, bisexual, and homosexual) are often attempts to locate or define the authentic self.

Tusquets's complex narratives reflect postmodern textual strategies: experimental form, fragmentary presentation, recondite style, allusive content, ambiguity, ironic overlay, and particularly, the constant use of literature and games in the development of the work. The individual is seen in relationship to the text: reading one's script elicits attempts to rewrite it; characters try to subvert "fixed" texts (for example, patterns learned from fairytales and myths). Intertextuality on all levels complements these concerns.

Although Tusquets has attenuated the intensely lyrical, emotional style of her first novel, the issues she addresses have become even more complex, as each heroine confronts the texts of her life and attempts to interpret and rewrite them.

—Margaret E. W. Jones

U

UGREŠIĆ, Dubravka. Croatian. Born in Kutina, in 1949. Educated at the University of Zagreb, B.A. and M.A. in Russian literature. Formerly worked at Institute for the Theory of Literature; newspaper columnist; taught Russian literature in the United States. Lives in Zagreb. Address: c/o August Cesarec, Prilaz JA 57, 41000 Zagreb, Croatia.

PUBLICATIONS

Fiction

Poza za prozu [A Pose for Prose]. Zagreb, Centar Druš-venih Djelatnosti, 1978.
Štefica Cvek u raljama života: Patchwork Story. Zagreb, Grafički Zavod Hrvastske, 1981; as *In the Jaws of Life*, London, Virago, 1992.
Život je bajka [Life Is a Fairytale]. Zagreb, Grafički Zavod Hrvastske, 1983.
Forsiranje romana-reke. Zagreb, August Cesarec, 1989; as *Fording the Stream of Consciousness*, London, Virago, 1991.

Plays

Screenplays: *Za sreću je potrebno troje* [Three Are Needed for Happiness], with Rajko Grlić; *Štefica Cvek u raljama života* [Steffie Speck in the Jaws of Life], from her own novel, 1984.

Other

Fili i Srećica [Philip and Little Luck] (for children). N.p., n.p., 1979.
Mali plamen [A Small Flame] (for children). Zagreb, Mladost, 1981.

Editor, with Aleksandar Flaker, *Pojmovnik avangarde* series.

*   *   *

The main focus of Dubravka Ugrešić's fiction to date has been the whole business, in all senses and from various angles, of creative writing. Like other consciously postmodern writers, Ugrešić draws on a close familiarity with a range of literary genres from the traditional canon of "high" literature, to the "trivial": romance, thriller, and fantasy. Features of all these occur side by side in her work. Implicit in this approach is a fundamental irony, the distinguishing characteristic of which is its inclusive nature: since it is the writing of fiction that is the central focus of her mocking wit, the writer herself and her own endeavour are themselves her targets.

Ugrešić's first important work, *Poza za prozu* (A Pose for Prose), represents a kind of hypothetical sketchbook for her future writing, trying out and rejecting various possible styles and approaches. Typically, its title already suggests an ironic deflation of the "high seriousness" of literature. The first part, entitled "Love Story," takes as its epigraph a quotation from

Gabriel García Márquez (*q.v.*): "I write in order to be better loved . . ." Taking this statement literally, Ugrešić then develops the piece as a series of texts created by the first-person narrator in an effort to please a lover. The interpretation of the statement thereby acquires another dimension: because of the narrator's sex, her writing becomes simply a manifestation of women's destiny — the struggle for acceptance and approval by men. Thus both material and narrator are objects of mockery: all the exchanges between the two characters about literature become allegories of a sexual game.

Ugrešić's first short "novel," *Štefica Cvek u raljama života* (In the Jaws of Life), explores the interrelationship of fiction and reality and the extent to which human beings are trapped within fictions: the heroine's outward life is constrained and shaped entirely by cliché. The work is an elaborate evocation of the parameters of the "woman's world" as defined particularly by women's magazines, illustrating the way women are seen and encouraged to live in a world of folklore. Within this multi-layered and touchingly comic context, what engages the reader's attention is the heroine's inability to be completely defined by its terms; her bewilderment offers the only scope she has for a minimal rebellion.

Ugrešić's next work, *Život je bajka* (Life Is a Fairytale), develops parody, one of the possibilities suggested in the earlier "sketchbook" and suggested indeed by her whole ironic stance. It consists of five pieces, each of which may stand on its own, but the whole is enhanced by the brief "introductory" notes that appear at the end of the work, describing the point of transformation of other writings or fragments into these stories. The notes are themselves part of the text, beginning with a mock scholarly explanation in the style of Jorge Luis Borges of the origin of the word "métaterxies," defined as "metatextual-therapeutic tales." The stories draw on a variety of writers and genres, including Nikolai Gogol, Leo Tolstoy, Borges, Lewis Carroll, Amos Tutuole, and newspaper clippings.

Ugrešić's first full-length novel, *Forsiranje romana-reke* (*Fording the Stream of Consciousness*), was published in 1988. Like many of her other writings, the surface and immediate appeal of this work consists of an elaborate game concerning many aspects of the whole business of writing, both from the inside (the use of different styles, genres, etc.), and here also from the outside: an account of all the paraphernalia of criticism, commercialism, and the international literary community. The setting is an international literary conference in Zagreb, attended by writers and critics from East and West Europe and the United States. The shape of the work is provided by the genre of the detective story with additional elements of tales of espionage, with all the standard requisites of suspense, unsolved mysteries, and intrigue. Within this frame, the representatives of different genres and cultures enable the author to treat each of them in the appropriate style. The result is a source of endless delight in the wealth of references and quotation, the use of different styles from different literary traditions, and informed comment on the whole international literary scene. All of this is deftly and wittily controlled. As is the case with all Ugrešić's works, the meta-literary function of the novel, its intertextual references, and its ultimately rather sombre implications for European culture do not detract from the reader's involvement in what is, on its most immediate level, a thoroughly engaging story, or rather series of individual stories. The majority of the characters, while subject as ever to mockery, are treated with a degree of understanding and sympathy which is an important element of the flavour of this writer's work. It has been suggested that this quality is usually associated with 20th-century Czech writing, from Jaroslav Hašek to Václav Havel (*q.v.*), and it is clear from many of Ugrešić's works that she feels a special affinity with this tradition. She is never solemn, but nevertheless the surface charm of her writing is not the whole "story." Her irony is not arbitrary, but springs from a clearsighted rejection of all pretensions, self-importance, and sham, aiming at the demystification of the writer's trade. At the same time, she does not dismiss all earlier literature, but draws on it, identifying what is still fruitful and giving it new life. Since Ugrešić refers so frequently to herself as exploiting the fashionable literary device of allusion, it might perhaps be appropriate to define her essential procedure by the late 20th-century catchword of "recycling." The connotations of well-intentioned earnestness, a clumsy and naive unworldliness that the word may have in English would be entirely appropriate for a writer who so clearly includes herself in her profoundly good-natured mockery.

—Celia Hawkesworth

V

VACULÍK, Ludvík. Czech. Born in Brumov, Moravia, 23 July 1926. Educated at the Commerce Academy for International Business, 1944–46; High School for Social and Political Sciences, Prague, 1946–51, B.Soc. and Pol.Sci. 1951. Served in the Czechoslovak Armed Forces, 1951–53. Married Marie Komarkova in 1949; three sons. Worker, Bata shoe factory, Zlin and Zurc, 1941–43; teacher in vocational school, until 1949; tutor, Ceskoslovenska Kolben-Danek machine works, Prague, 1950–51; editor, Rude pravo publishers, 1953–57, *Beseda venkovske rodiny*, 1957–59, Czechoslovak Radio, Prague 1959–66, Czechoslovak Writers' Union *Literární noviny* [Literary Journal] weekly, 1966–69 (magazine banned 1969), and *Literární listy*, 1968–69, all Prague; member of Communist Party, from 1946, expelled 1967; wrote intellectuals' proclamation "2000 Words," June 1968: banned; main organizer, Edice Petlice [Padlock Editions] samizdat series; arrested for television interview given to the BBC, 1973: passport revoked. Recipient: State award, 1964; Československý spisovatel publishers award, 1967; George Orwell prize, 1976. Address: c/o Mladá fronta, Panská 8, 11222 Prague 1, Czech Republic.

PUBLICATIONS

Fiction

Rušný dům [The Busy House]. Prague, Československý spisovatel, 1963.
Sekyra. Prague, Československý spisovatel, 1966; as *The Axe*, New York, Harper, and London, Deutsch, 1973.
Die Meerschweinchen. Lucerne, Bucher, 1971; as *Morčata*, Prague, Edice Petlice (samizdat), 1973; Toronto, 68 Publishers, 1977; as *The Guinea Pigs*, New York, Third Press, 1973; London, London Magazine Editions, 1974.
Český snář [A Czech Dreambook]. N.p., samizdat, 1980; Toronto, 68 Publishers, 1983.

Other

Na farmě mládeže [The Youth Farm]. Prague, Státní Nakladatelství Politické Literatury, 1958.
The Relations Between Citizen and Power. London, Liberal International [British Group], 1968.
Milí spolužáci! Výbor písemných prací 1939–1979: 1. Kniha indiánská; 2. Kniha dělnická [Dear School-Fellows! A Choice of Written Work 1939–1979. 1. Indian Book; 2. A Worker's Book]. Cologne, Index, 2 vols., 1986.
A Cup of Coffee with My Interrogator: The Prague Chronicles of Ludvík Vaculík. London, Readers International, 1987.
Jaro je tady: fejetony z let 1981–1987 [Spring Is Here: Columns from 1981–1987]. Cologne, Index, 1988.
Srpnový rok: fejetony z roku 1988 [August Year: Columns from 1988]. Prague, Pražská imaginace, 1989.
Stará dáma se baví [The Old Lady Is Enjoying Herself]. Prague, Lidové noviny, 1990.

Editor, with Jiří Gruša and Milan Uhde, *Hodina naděje: almanach české literatury 1968–1978* [Hour of Hope: Anthology of Czech Literature]. Lucerne, Reich, 1978; Toronto, 68 Publishers, 1980.
Editor, *Hlasy nad rukopisem Vaculíkova Českého snáře* [Views on the Manuscript of Vaculík's *Český snář*]. Prague, Torst, 1991.

*

Critical Studies: "Ludvík Vaculík's *The Axe*: A Quest for Human Dignity" by Herbert Eagle, in *Books Abroad* (Norman, Oklahoma), 49, 1975; "Ludvík Vaculík and His Novel *The Axe*" by Antonin J. Liehm, in *Czech Literature Since 1956: A Symposium*, edited by William E. Harkins and Paul I. Trensky, New York, Bohemica, 1980; "The Semantic Gesture in *The Guinea Pigs*" by K. Mercks, in *Vozmi na radost': To Honour Jeanne von der Eng-Liedmeier*, Amsterdam, n.p., 1980; *Czech Writers and Politics 1945–1969* by A. French, Boulder, Colorado, East European Monographs, 1982; "*Guinea Pigs* and the Czech Novel 'Under Padlock' in the 1970s: From the Modern Absolutism to the Postmodernist Absolute," in *Rocky Mountain Review of Language and Literature* (Boise, Idaho), 37(1–2), 1983, and "*The Guinea Pigs* by Ludvík Vaculík: Codes, Metaphors and Compositional Devices," in *Slavic Review: American Quarterly of Soviet and East European Studies* (Austin, Texas), 43(1), 1984, both by Bronislava Volek.

* * *

Ludvík Vaculík is probably the most provocative contemporary Czech novelist and, at the same time, the most egocentric. Gradually since the mid-1970s confessional literature has become a major part of mainstream Czech literature — for instance Milan Kundera's *Life Is Elsewhere* (q.v.), Václav Havel's *Letters to Olga* (q.v.), Pavel Kohout's *Kde je zakopán pes* (There's the Rub), Jana Boučková's *Indiánský běh* (Red Indian Run), Jana Brabcová's *Daleko od stromu* (Off the Old Block) — but Vaculík's have been confessional since his debut novel *Rušný dům* (The Busy House) in 1963. For today's general readership Vaculík is best known for his *feuilletons*, and these, too, tend towards the confessional. The latest volume of these, *Stará dáma se baví* (The Old Lady Is Enjoying Herself), written in 1967–68, portrays Vaculík as a radical loner, perhaps an "old-fashioned conservative"; the *feuilletons* trace his deepening disillusion with Communism and express scepticism about Dubček and his "socialism with a human face" as well as contemporary Czechs' capacity for "democracy."

Vaculík's four novels follow the development of an intelligent, streetwise countryman from Communist enthusiasm in *Rušný dům*, to wry quizzicality about the deformation and degradation engendered by the Communist Party in *Sekyra* (The Axe), to a parodic analysis of the rule of fear and inaccessibility of knowledge under Communism in *Morčata* (The Guinea Pigs), and finally, in *Český snář* (A Czech

Dreambook), to the recognition of freedom as lying in love and responsibility, and being indifferent to the régime. One might say, then, that together the novels depict the formation of a self.

Rušný dům, where the narrator-hero is a tutor in an apprentices' hostel, is essentially a Communist idyll, and its vigorous, plain style successfully evokes the Party enthusiasm of its temporal setting (1951–53). Though the author is a true believer, he is not blind to the failings of the régime. Few of the young workers are interested in the building of the worker state; examination methods are ludicrous (candidates are asked to quote either the first or the last sentence of the Communist Manifesto); the hostel charwomen are punctiliously bureaucratic. Furthermore, the narrator's non-Communist wife is a better educator towards socialism than any of the Communist tutors.

The Axe has no story; the framework consists of the journalist narrator's trip to see his brother, but what action there is concerns the narrator's kindhearted, but rather stupid carpenter father, his work in Iran before the war, his promotion through the collective-farm bureaucracy (and unpopularity with the peasants) and, eventually, after he has read about such things in a magazine about Soviet life, his volunteering for an experimental brain operation to aid the cause of socialism. *The Axe* is a novel about memory and is constructed as the sort of collage that memory constitutes. Thus it is chronologically disjointed; dates of events are given by reference to a person's age or to their temporal relationship to some other event. Moreover, the language used is a mix of ordinary literary Czech, Moravian dialect (not only in dialogue), parodic bureaucratic language, lyrical diction (Vaculík sometimes uses rhyming phrases or sentences), mock proverbs ("a good excuse is better than dog-shit"), grotesque alliteration, literary allusion. Disconnected events are sometimes linked by refrains, which also may be used to prefigure some event which comes much later in the novel. Though the end-product is an absurd tragicomedy of rural life, particularly in the 1950s, and an expression of profound love for the countryside, there is nothing anti-régime about *The Axe*; by far the most attractive human being is the narrator's hard-line Communist father.

From memory of childhood and youth Vaculík turns to present anxiety in *The Guinea Pigs*, an anxiety he is determined not to submit to. The novel is a satirical fairytale which includes elements of the horror story. In *Rušný dům* and *The Axe* the narrator has had occupations Vaculík himself had pursued, but in *The Guinea Pigs* he is a bank clerk. Vaculík chooses that occupation as a parody of his own time as a cog in the reform Communist machine, a bureaucrat who, like the character of the bank clerk, muses about and seeks out what he should not. The bank clerk's violent death or "disappearing" marks the end of Vaculík's role as a cog. The guinea pigs appear to represent the manipulable or apathetic citizens of a socialist state, and the bank clerk's glimpse of this state secret no doubt ultimately leads to his death. Vaculík uses a simple, naive, and lucid style to create a both sinister and frivolous narrative, whose motto might be the following words from chapter two: "Most difficult of all, boys and girls, is to change your life of your own free will. Even when you have the most wonderful feeling that you're the driver of your locomotive, someone else always comes along and changes the points."

Český snář is ostensibly a genuine diary of a year of life under police surveillance (January 1979–February 1980), including the narrator's dreams, his wife's and his mistress's, but sometimes the borderline between dream and reality is unclear, and some events are invented or so disguised they appear invented. The pictures the author-narrator gives of

fellow dissidents are bluntly affectionate or hostile. He describes his erotic life decently, but openly, even ostentatiously, much as he describes his monthly meetings with his secret-police desk officer, Major Fišer. The very ostentatiousness of the novel might be seen simply as arrogant and tactless, even coarse. On the other hand, it is the statement of a proud, private man. When the state deprives one of all privacy (at one point the police confine his mistress in a VD clinic as punishment for being his mistress), one literary protest may be to fling one's privacy in the state's face. Furthermore, by attempting to write a totally nonfictional novel, Vaculík has in fact written an extreme form of fiction (or metafiction). He drove his point home by circulating the typescript among a few critics and the fellow dissidents he had written about (he also gave it to Major Fišer) and asked them for written responses. He published these responses as *Hlasy nad rukopisem Vaculíkova Českého snáře* (Views on the Manuscript of Vaculík's *Český snář*). This work is a kind of continuation of the novel, for the responses constitute: reactions to the novel as a novel about a novel; corrections, objections, and concurrences of "characters" in the novel; and an account of the general (noisy) reception of the novel. The result is that *Český snář* becomes a novel where author, narrator, characters, and readers play potentially equal roles. Thus in this innovative way Vaculík has continued on his path of bold self-advertisement and rebellious truthfulness.

—Robert B. Pynsent

VALENZUELA, Luisa. Argentinian. Born in Buenos Aires, 26 November 1938. Educated at Belgrano Girls' School; Colegio Nacional Vicente Lopez, Buenos Aires; University of Buenos Aires, B.A. Married Théodore Marjak in 1958 (divorced); one daughter. Lived in Paris, 1958–61; assistant editor of Sunday supplement, *La Nación*, Buenos Aires, 1964–69; freelance journalist in the United States, Europe, and Mexico, 1970–73, and Buenos Aires, 1973–79; writer-in-residence, Columbia University, New York, 1980–83; Visiting Professor, New York University, 1984–89; Fellow, New York Institute for the Humanities. Lived in New York, Buenos Aires, and Tepoztlán, Mexico, 1978–89; now lives in Buenos Aires. Recipient: Fondo Nacional de las Artes award, 1966, 1973; Fulbright fellowship, 1969–70; Instituto Nacional de Cinematografía award, 1973; Guggenheim fellowship, 1983. Honorary doctorate: Knox College, Illinois, 1991. Address: La Pampa 1202, 1428 Buenos Aires, Argentina.

PUBLICATIONS

Fiction

Hay que sonreír. Buenos Aires, Américalee, 1966; as *Clara*, in *Clara: 13 Short Stories and a Novel*, 1976.
Los heréticos. Buenos Aires, Paidós, 1967; as "The Heretics," in *Clara: 13 Short Stories and a Novel*, 1976.
El gato eficaz. Mexico City, Mortiz, 1972.
Aquí pasan cosas raras. Buenos Aires, Flor, 1975; translations in *Strange Things Happen Here: 26 Short Stories and a Novel*, 1979.

Clara: 13 Short Stories and a Novel. New York, Harcourt Brace, 1976.
Como en la guerra. Buenos Aires, Sudamericana, 1977; as *He Who Searches*, in *Strange Things Happen Here: 26 Short Stories and A Novel*, 1979.
Strange Things Happen Here: 26 Short Stories and a Novel. New York, Harcourt Brace, 1979.
Libro que no muere. Mexico City, Universidad Nacional Autónoma de México, 1980.
Cambio de armas. Hanover, New Hampshire, Ediciones del Norte, 1982; as *Other Weapons*, Ediciones del Norte, 1985.
Cola de lagartija. Buenos Aires, Bruguera, 1983; as *The Lizard's Tail*, New York, Farrar Straus, 1983; London, Serpent's Tail, 1987.
Donde viven las águilas. Buenos Aires, Celtia, 1983; as *Up Among the Eagles*, in *Open Door*, 1988.
Open Door. San Francisco, California, North Point Press, 1988; London, Serpent's Tail, 1992.
Novela negra con argentinos. Hanover, New Hampshire, Ediciones del Norte, 1990.
Blame. New York, Simon and Schuster, 1992.

Plays

Realidad nacional desde la cama. Buenos Aires, Grupo Editor Latinoamericano, 1990.

Screenplay: *Hay que sonreír.*

*

Critical Studies: "Women Writing About Prostitutes: Amalia Jamilis and Luisa Valenzuela" by Amy Kaminsky, in *The Image of the Prostitute in Modern Literature*, New York, Ungar, 1984; "Luisa Valenzuela: From *Hay que sonreír* to *Cambio de armas*," in *World Literature Today* (Norman, Oklahoma), 58, 1984, "Luisa Valenzuela's *Cambio de armas*: Subversion and Narrative Weaponry," in *Romance Quarterly* (Lexington, Kentucky), 1986, and *Reflections/Refractions: Reading Luisa Valenzuela*, New York, Lang, 1988, all by Sharon Magnarelli; "Luisa Valenzuela's *The Lizard's Tail*: Deconstruction of the Peronist Mythology" by Z. Nelly Martínez, in *El Cono Sur*, edited by Rose S. Minc, Upper Montclair, New Jersey, Montclair State College, 1985; Valenzuela issue of *Review of Contemporary Fiction* (Elmwood Park, Illinois), Fall 1986; "Fragmentation in Luisa Valenzuela's Narrative" by Patricia Rubia in *Salmagundi* (Saratoga Springs, New York), 82–83, 1989.

*   *   *

Throughout her literary career, Luisa Valenzuela has focused on politics, discourse, and women. Her deadly serious games with language demonstrate how dominant groups use discourse to oppress, first by distracting from those issues that disadvantage them and then by creating a perception of reality that benefits them. At the same time, she shows political tyranny to be a macrocosmic manifestation of the oppression and hierarchism that mark many interpersonal and particularly male-female relationships.

With the passage of time, Valenzuela's works have become more intricate and perhaps less readable, according to Miguel de Cervantes's *desocupado lector* (lazy, uninvolved reader), for she has moved from the thematics of the personal and a naturalistic style into the thematics of the political and a more lyrical, metaphoric, or oneiric style. Nevertheless, as she demonstrated in *Cambio de armas* (*Other Weapons*) or more recently in *Novela negra con argentinos* (Mystery Novel with Argentines) and *Realidad nacional desde la cama* (National Reality from the Bed), the personal is political and the metaphoric or oneiric is often all too real.

Her preoccupation with politics, discourse, and women is already apparent in her first novel, *Clara*. A young prostitute, Clara passes through the hands of a series of men who exploit her and mold her into a reflection of their desires. Clara is a symbol of all who are degraded and metaphorically prostituted as they are denied access to a world in which both mind and body can be used without contradiction. Her ostensibly private journey is in fact a confrontation with the mores of patriarchal society and religion, inculcated and perpetuated through discourse.

The theme of society and institutionalized religion which, in Western culture at least, provides us with most of our beliefs about women, is continued in *Los heréticos* (*The Heretics*). Here religion plays the role that politics will assume in her later works as Valenzuela amusingly debunks the Judeo-Christian perception of women as agents and perpetuators of sin.

In *El gato eficaz* (The Efficacious Cat) the female narrator's sin has been to allow the evils of the world to escape, in the form of "black cats of death." Playful and serious at the same time, this innovative work toys with and repudiates the dialectical structure of language as it plays on antonyms such as dog and cat, life and death, demonstrating that language itself generates or magnifies the bipolar oppositions we believe we perceive.

Written in Argentina near the height of the political terrorism of the 1970s, *Aquí pasan cosas raras* (*Strange Things Happen Here*) focuses on oppression and our apparently limitless capacity for double thinking and double speaking. In one story, "Unlimited Rapes United, Argentina," we learn that it is for his wife's sake that the husband pays high dues to an agency, whose duties include raping his wife. Revealingly, she is ever grateful to him for the "sacrifices" he makes for her and for "defending" her (rhetoric also employed by the military regime). Thus, the morpheme, *defend* (like countless others), is stripped of its normal significance (metaphorically raped) and inverted so that on both a personal and a political level what is labeled "defending" is in fact codified rape. Nonetheless, the victim has so internalized the rhetoric that she not only fails to recognize her victimization but perceives her rape as an honor bestowed upon her.

Like so many Valenzuela texts, *Como en la guerra* (*He Who Searches*) is a novel that demands to be read a number of ways: as a parody of the classical mythic structure, as a journey in search of the self or origins (but significantly the self the male narrator seeks via his journey, both linguistic and spatial, is a female self), and as a search for truth. The text proposes, however, that our truths are inevitably influenced by the seeker, the human mind, and emotions. The novel demands yet another reading once we focus on the two political dramas that frame it: the final one in which the searcher finds himself in tyrannized Argentina, performing terrorist activities, and the initial one, on "page zero" (omitted in the Spanish edition) in which he is being interrogated, tortured, and raped with a gun barrel, presumably also in Argentina in the 1970s. In this manner, Valenzuela underlines the brutality of a political reality that cannot be erased by our mythic impulses. The metaphoric suggestion is that we continually begin at page one, but that we need to go back to page zero to seek that which has been silenced.

As the title suggests, *Donde viven las águilas* (*Up Among the Eagles*) often takes us to the high plateau of Mexico, with its hazy, magical ambience. Even those stories that do not take place in this magical world still focus on the inexplicable. In one, the law-abiding security guard enigmatically steals the money he was guarding and disappears from the face of the earth. In another, a censor becomes so well-trained and zealous in his job that he condemns himself and is shot at dawn. The potential victim is converted to victimizer and, in turn, becomes his own victim.

In *Other Weapons* the personal and the political intermingle in the erotic, which in turn functions as a metaphor or synecdoche for the political and as a shield behind which the subtext, the political, lurks. In "Fourth Version" the narrator attempts to rewrite Bella's love story, but that love story proves to be a political tale. The narrative technique, which piles layer upon layer of language, truth, and fiction, underscores the impossibility of expressing truth via discourse as it highlights the inevitable identification between narrator and protagonist, reader and character. "Other Weapons" centers on a former terrorist who is physically and erotically enslaved by the army colonel she had earlier attempted to assassinate. Having managed to erase her past and even her language while imposing his own on her, he has tried to make her totally dependent on him. The strategy has worked only partially, however, for in the final gesture of the text, she aims at him with the thing *he calls* a revolver, perhaps prepared to use his weapons (discursive or otherwise) against him.

The metaphoricity of *Cola de lagartija* (*The Lizard's Tail*) in no way detracts from its trenchant and scathing criticism of the Argentine military regime and its use of language and rhetoric to distort. The central character is a political figure, who, unlike other mere mortals, is endowed with three testicles, ostensibly a surplus of masculinity. Paradoxically, however, his third testicle is a female, his sister Estrella, a pure egg, which he will inseminate and from which he will give birth to himself. The novel concludes as he explodes in a bloody overabundance of self-generated arrogance and exaggeration.

Although a detective novel on some level, *Novela negra con argentinos* is concerned, not with "whodunit," which we know from the opening page, but with the more philosophical and less answerable questions: why did he do it, and has anything really happened here, the latter an overt reference to the Dirty War and the disappeared in Argentina in the 1970s. Unlike traditional detective novels, however, the questions are not answered. Agustín's violent act, like the more widespread violence in Argentina, defies logic and rationality.

Finally, *Realidad nacional desde la cama* abolishes the separation between actors and spectators and considers the role of the spectator in the theatre of national politics. Indeed, the text dramatically demonstrates that as spectators we see very little and to see is not to know, for what we see is often nothing more than spectacle — theatrical, discursive creation. Here, as perhaps throughout her recent work, Valenzuela posits that our perception of reality is a composite of fact and fiction, just as contemporary Argentina is its poverty, its military, its inflation, but also its recollection of things past and hope for things future, both this side and the other of that ubiquitous looking glass of literature.

—Sharon Magnarelli

VALKEAPÄÄ, Nils Aslak. Finnish (Sámi). Born in Enontekiö, Finland, 23 March 1943. Educated at a teachers' training school, Kemijärvi. Writer, visual artist, photo-

grapher, performer, and actor. First cultural coordinator, World Council of Indigenous Peoples. Painter: individual exhibitions — Oulu, Finland, 1973; Rovaniemi, Finland, 1975; Harstad, Norway, 1991; Torshavn, Faroe Islands, 1992; Tromsoe, Norway, 1992; Copenhagen, 1992. Also musician (yoiker: Sámi folk music): has made several recordings. Active with DAT Sámi publishing company, Guovdageaidnu, Norway. Recipient: Nordic Council prize, 1991. Address: 99470 Gáresavvon/Kaaresuvanto, Finland; or, P.O. Box 91, 9048 Ivgubahta, Skibotn, Norway.

PUBLICATIONS

Verse

Ruoktu váimmus [My Home Is in My Heart].   Guovdageaidnu, Norway, DAT, 1985.
   Giða i jat čuovgadat [The Nights of Spring So Full of Light]. Guovdageaidnu, Norway, DAT, 1974.
   Lávllo vizár biellocizáš [Bluethroat, Sing and Twitter]. Guovdageaidnu, Norway, DAT, 1976.
   Ádjaga silbasuonat [The Spring's Silver Veins]. Guovdageaidnu, Norway, DAT, 1981.
Beaivi, áhčážan [The Sun, My Father].   Guovdageaidnu, Norway, DAT, 1988.

Translations of verse by David McDuff, published in *Books from Finland* (Helsinki), 1, 1991, and by Lars Norström and Ralph Salisbury, in *WRIT* (Toronto), 23/24, 1991–92.

Other

Terveisiä Lapista.   Helsinki, Otava, 1971; as *Greetings from Lapland: The Sami — Europe's Forgotten People*, London, Zed, 1983.

Editor, *Paulus Utsi: Don čanat mu alccesat.*   Guovdageaidnu, Norway, DAT, 1992.

*   *   *

Nils Aslak Valkeapää is the most important living Sámi poet; since his receipt of the Nordic Council literature prize in 1991, his work has become more widely read and known. He began his literary career in 1971 with a pamphlet, *Terveisiä Lapista* (*Greetings from Lapland*), in which he protested against the environmental exploitation of Lapland and the linguistic oppression of the Sámi people. As an artist and musician he has worked as a performer of the traditional Sámi *joig* chants in concert halls around the world, and in recordings, and the *joig* has had a decisive influence on his poetry, which is close to the oral traditions of Lapland and to the "musical glissando-speech" of its chants. The *joig* has been characterized as being concerned not primarily with communication, but rather with repetitive, elementary movements of the solitary mind, unravellings of mental images, and songs to the self, animals, and nature; these are also the features and subjects of the poems Valkepää published between 1974 and 1988 in the three collections that make up *Ruoktu váimmus* (My Home Is in My Heart). A leading Finnish critic has characterized these poems as describing "a herdsman's thoughts as he follows his reindeer through the mountains, the alternation of the seasons, and of a man's longing for love; there are also stories about the old people of the tribe and their self-sufficient, now threatened, way of life. In some of the more concentrated poems, perceptions of nature crystallise into images reminiscent of classical Japanese or Chinese poetry." *Ruoktu váimmus* is expected to be published in English.

But Valkeapää's most important achievement to date is the extended, obscurely autobiographical poem *Beaivi, áhčážan* (The Sun, My Father). This major work, which was published both in the original Lapp and in Swedish and Norwegian translation, and concerns a gifted Sámi who cannot continue his forefathers' means of livelihood, represents a synthesis of Valkeapää's activities as a poet and as an ethnographically oriented documenter of his people's life and history. The poems are accompanied by almost 500 photographs collected from various sources by the poet himself, and these depict and chronicle the society out of which and against whose background the subjective meditations of the individual consciousness move. The poems themselves have an Ungaretti-like brevity and concision, giving a sense of inner concentration and meditative space that is in harmony with a wider, external world:

> life was fond of us, the sun
> in heaven's space
> and the earth
> sought in its arms
> gifts
> the reindeer roamed the salmon climbed
> the grouse laughed the geese flew
> the cloudberry ripened

Behind all the poems there is the consciousness of modern "civilization," which has forced the people to which the poet belongs to change or abandon old ways of living; yet the poems also invoke the ancient Sámi gods and customs, and by doing so keep them alive. What Valkeapää appears to be saying is that the new order of society brought about — in Lapland, sometimes with brutal cruelty — by technological innovation is only one more challenge to the Sámi people, of a kind they have faced before in their history. By sustaining within themselves their language, customs, and religion, they may survive in the new world as they have survived other threats. The *joig* itself, after all, was for a long time even before the 20th century considered not only by their Norwegian, Swedish, and Russian masters but by the Sámi people themselves to be something evil — an inevitable consequence of the fact that many Sámi were executed (by beheading) for joiging. This was all part of the aggressive Christianization of the Sámi at the beginning of the 18th century, a process that has now more or less ceased. The Sámi are now able to reclaim this important psycho-social art form for their own, and in his poems Valkeapää explores its origins and significance. In his meditations on the ornamented shamanic Sámi drum, used to accompany the *joig*, the poet sees the drum as a means of fixing not only his own identity, but also the identity of the whole Sámi people:

> and now,
>   now I drum
>   draw myself
>   whole, only now
>   accomplished
>
> and from this image
> I do not turn back
> any more
>
> from this image
> I do not move
>
> no

Beaivi, áhčážan is remarkable in presenting through a number of different media a complete picture of the Sámi experience. In particular, the role played by nature in the lives of the ordinary people is made vividly clear, and the way in which, for example, birdsong is seen as existing on a par with human song, and birds in the same frame of reference as human beings, moving from one region to another according to the seasons and the time of year. Sámi culture, being one of the most northerly in the world, inevitably has points of contact with others — notably Norwegian, Swedish, Finnish, Russian, and Canadian — yet in Valkeapää's poems and in the photographs he has collected, it emerges as quite distinct from these. It is somewhat akin to North American Indian or Samoyed culture, and the poems about tents and magical images relating to family tend to emphasize this resemblance; but in the end it has a territorial separateness that is also marked by a universal character, best summed up in the words that conclude Valkeapää's poem "Eanan, eallima eadni" — "the earth, life's mother."

—David McDuff

VALLEJO, Antonio Buero. *See* **BUERO VALLEJO, Antonio.**

VARELA, Blanca. Peruvian. Born in Lima, in 1926. Married Fernando de Syzlo (separated); has children. Lived in Paris for several years, and in the United States. Currently director, Fondo de Cultura Económica, Lima branch. Address: c/o Fondo de Cultura Económica, Ave Universidad 975, Apdo 44975, 03100 Mexico City 12, Mexico.

PUBLICATIONS

Verse

Ese puerto existe, y otros poemas. Xalapa, Universidad Veracruzana, 1959.
Luz de día. Lima, La Rama Florida, 1963.
Canto villano. N.p., Arybalo, 1978.
Camino a Babel. Lima, Municipalidad de Lima Metropolitana, 1986.
Canto villano: poesia reunida, 1949–1983. Mexico City, Fondo de Cultura Económica, 1986.

*

Critical Study: in *History of Peruvian Literature* by James Higgins, Liverpool, Cairns, 1987.

*   *   *

Blanca Varela is one of an outstanding generation of Peruvian poets who began writing in the 1950s. Since the publication of her first book in 1959, her more-or-less consistent view of the world has found an increasingly more accomplished artistic expression. The dominant note of her poetry is one of rebellious dissatisfaction with the conditions of life. With a mixture of sadness and irony, her lucid consciousness cuts through the veil of comfortable illusions to lay bare life's unpleasant underside. Yet that same lucidity never allows her to lapse into facile romantic posturing, but forces her to recognise the contradictory nature of the world and of human beings, to question and criticise her own attitudes, and to face up to life with honesty and resilience. Her poetic style is characterised by a starkly austere language whose concision creates an effect of great emotional intensity.

In a Peruvian literary scene traditionally dominated by men, Varela stands out as a profoundly feminine poet who writes from her experience as a woman. "Antes del día" (Before Day), for example, employs imagery of childbirth to convey her view of existence as a constant struggle to create something meaningful out of the sterility of our lives, while "Casa de cuervos" (House of Crows) voices the conflicting emotions of a mother whose son has grown up and left home to fend for himself. And even in poems that do not deal with a specifically female experience, the perspective Varela communicates is essentially a feminine one.

That is not to say that Varela is a feminist. In "Vals del Angelus" (The Angelus Waltz) the female persona rebels against the model of womanhood encapsulated in the Angelus prayer, bitterly denouncing a male God whose unjust creation has condemned her to subordination and the arrogant male who exercises dominance as if he were a god. Typically, though, the poem subverts itself even as it subverts male assumptions. On the one hand, the title puts the poetic persona's complaints on the level of the maudlin laments of the Peruvian popular song and her masochistic servility insinuates that women collaborate in their own subjection by their passiveness and their vocation for martyrdom. On the other, the laconic last line undermines her earlier estimate of the male, as she comes to see her own vulnerability mirrored in his and to recognise that they are both victims of their human condition. Ultimately, Varela's major concern is not the relationship between the sexes but humanity's relationship with the world.

Central to Varela's world view is her ambivalent relationship with her native environment. In "Puerto Supe" the eponymous seaside town where she spent childhood summers is evoked as a mythical space of timeless happiness, but it is also recalled as the scene of a confused adolescence in which rebelliousness alternated with anguished apprehension. Thus, if Puerto Supe stands as an image of her emotional identification with her roots, it is also a metaphor for her dissatisfaction with life and for her sense of inadequacy in face of it. "Valses" (Waltzes) is a long poem dealing with her re-encounter with Lima after a prolonged absence in the United States. The text is based on a contrast between her nostalgic image of an earthly paradise and the drab reality of Third World underdevelopment that greets her on her return. The city, in fact, becomes a metaphor for human frustration, and a series of personifications represent it as a child born of her imaginings, a lover idealised from afar, and, finally, a shameless tramp of a mother. Yet her rejection of this unworthy mother provokes a contradictory reaction of guilty affection and she ends by proclaiming an illogical attachment to a home town that fails to live up to her expectations.

Other poems deal with the human condition in a more general sense. "Auvers-sur-Oise" is addressed to Vincent Van Gogh, treating him ironically as the embodiment of the contradictions of a modern humanity that persists in striving after an illusory ideal of transcendence in a world which it itself has desacramentalised. Yet if his art is thus seen as being based on a fiction, the poet herself lapses into contradiction by celebrating it as an example of the human spirit's refusal to be bound by limitations. "Camino a Babel" (Road to Babel) consists of seven sections corresponding to the various stages in the development of an existential philosophy. The poem is both a parody of the spiritual pilgrimage of the mystics, in that it suggests that the search for meaning in life inevitably leads to awareness of its senseless absurdity, and a secular version of it, in that it implies that such awareness is positive if assumed as an existential position. Hence the Tower of Babel stands as a symbol not only of the absurd but of the construction of a personal *raison d'être* free of metaphysics, a solution which Varela recognises as provisional and one which must constantly be renewed.

Ultimately, Varela regards life as a question of coping with despair. The female protagonist of "Secreto de familia" (Family Secret), the indomitable support of the household during the day, is assailed in the night by a nightmare which reflects her loneliness and vulnerability. "Lady's Journal" presents an ambiguous image of the housewife who suppresses her critical faculty in order to maintain an illusion of order and stability, an image which is ironic yet at the same time hints that such strategies are necessary to enable life to go on. In effect, Varela views existence as an art form which consists of inventing fictions in order to survive, of living life as if it were meaningful while all the time being conscious that it is not. This tenacity in the face of life is closely linked to women's domestic experience and confirms the profound femininity of her poetry.

—James Higgins

VARGAS LLOSA, (Jorge) Mario (Pedro). Peruvian. Born in Arequipa, 28 March 1936. Educated in Bolivia, to 1945; Leoncio Prado Military Academy, Lima, 1950–52; Colegio Nacional San Miguel de Piura, 1952; University of San Marcos, Lima, B.A. 1957; University of Madrid, 1957–59, Ph.D. 1959. Married 1) Julia Urquidi in 1955 (divorced); 2) Patricia Llosa in 1965, two sons and one daughter. Journalist, *La Industria*, Piura, and for Radio Panamericana and *La Crónica*, both in Lima; journalist, Agence-France-Presse, and broadcaster, French National Radio Network, in 1960s; lecturer or Visiting Professor, Queen Mary College and King's College, University of London, 1966–68, University of Washington, Seattle, 1968, University of Puerto Rico, Río Piedras, 1969, Columbia University, New York, 1975, Cambridge University, 1977, Florida International University, Miami, 1991, and Wissenschaftskolleg, Berlin, 1991–92; fellow, Woodrow Wilson Center, Washington, D.C., 1979–80. Director, *Captain Pantoja and the Special Service*, 1976 (film; banned). Fredemo (Democratic Front) candidate for president of Peru, 1990. Recipient: Alas prize, 1959; Biblioteca Breve prize, 1962; Rómulo Gallegos prize (Venezuela), 1967; National Critics prize (Spain), 1967; National prize, 1967; Ritz Paris Hemingway award, 1985; Scottish Arts Council Neil Gunn International Fellow, 1986; Prince of Asturias prize (Spain) 1986. Agent: Agencia Carmen Balcells, Diagonal 580, 08021 Barcelona, Spain. Address: Malecón Paul Harris 194, Lima 4 Peru.

PUBLICATIONS

Fiction

Los jefes. Barcelona, Rocas, 1959; in English, in *The Cubs and Other Stories*, 1979.

La ciudad y los perros. Barcelona, Seix Barral, 1963; as *The Time of the Hero*, New York, Grove Press, 1966; London, Cape, 1967.

La casa verde. Barcelona, Seix Barral, 1966; as *The Green House*, New York, Harper, 1968; London, Cape, 1969.

Los cachorros. Barcelona, Lumen, 1967; as *The Cubs*, in *The Cubs and Other Stories*, 1979.

Conversación en La Catedral. Barcelona, Seix Barral, 1969; as *Conversation in the Cathedral*, New York, Harper, 1975.

Obras escogidas. Madrid, Aguilar, 1973.

Pantaleón y las visitadoras. Barcelona, Seix Barral, 1973; as *Captain Pantoja and the Special Service*, New York, Harper, and London, Cape, 1978.

La tía Julia y el escribidor. Barcelona, Seix Barral, 1977; as *Aunt Julia and the Scriptwriter*, New York, Farrar Straus, 1982; London, Faber, 1983.

The Cubs and Other Stories. New York, Harper, 1979; London, Faber, 1991.

La guerra del fin del mundo. Barcelona, Seix Barral, 1981; as *The War of the End of the World*, New York, Farrar Straus, 1984; London, Faber, 1985.

Historia de Mayta. Barcelona, Seix Barral, 1984; as *The Real Life of Alejandro Mayta*, New York, Farrar Straus, and London, Faber, 1986.

¿Quien mató a Palomino Molero? Barcelona, Seix Barral, 1986; as *Who Killed Palomino Molero?*, New York, Farrar Straus, 1987; London, Faber, 1988.

El hablador. Barcelona, Seix Barral, 1987; as *The Story-teller*, New York, Farrar Straus, 1989; London, Faber, 1990.

Elogio de la madrastra. Barcelona, Tusquets, 1988; as *In Praise of the Stepmother*, New York, Farrar Straus, 1990; London, Faber, 1991.

Plays

La huida del Inca (produced Piura, Peru, 1952).

La señorita de Tacna. Barcelona, Seix Barral, 1981; as *The Senorita from Tacna* (produced New York, 1983); as *The Young Lady from Tacna* (produced Los Angeles, 1985), included in *Three Plays*, 1990.

Kathie y el hipopótame. Barcelona, Seix Barral, 1983; as *Kathie and the Hippopotamus* (produced Edinburgh, 1986; London, 1987), included in *Three Plays*, 1990.

La Chunga (produced in English, New York, 1986; London, 1988). Barcelona, Seix Barral, 1986; included in *Three Plays*, 1990.

Three Plays (includes *The Young Lady from Tacna*; *Kathy and the Hippopotamus*; *La Chunga*). London, Faber, 1990.

Other

La novela en América Latina: dialogo, with Gabriel García Márquez. Lima, Carlos Milla Batres, 1968.

La literatura en la revolución y revolución en la literatura, with Julio Cortázar and Oscar Collazos. Mexico City, Siglo Veintiuno, 1970.

Historia secreta de una novela. Barcelona, Tusquets, 1971.

Gabriel García Márquez: historia de un deicidio. Barcelona, Seix Barral, 1971.

La novela y el problema de la expresión literaria en Peru. Buenos Aires, América Nueva, 1974.

La orgía perpetua: Flaubert y "Madame Bovary." Madrid, Taurus, 1975; as *The Perpetual Orgy: Flaubert and "Madame Bovary,"* New York, Farrar Straus, 1986; London, Faber, 1987.

José María Arguedas: entre sapos y halcones. Madrid, Cultura Hispánica del Centro Iberoamericano de Cooperación, 1978.

La utopia arcaica. Cambridge, Cambridge University Centre of Latin American Studies, 1978.

Art, Authenticity and Latin American Culture. Washington, D.C., Woodrow Wilson Center, 1981(?).

Entre Sartre y Camus. Río Pedras, Huracán, 1981.

Contra vientro y marea (1962–1982). Barcelona, Seix Barral, 1983.

La cultura de la libertad, la libertad de la cultura. Santiago, Fundación Eduardo Frei, 1985.

Dialogo sobre la novela latinoamericana, with Gabriel García Márquez. Lima, Perú Andino, 1988.

— *Sobre la vida y la politica* (interview), with Ricardo A. Setti. Buenos Aires, Intermundo, 1989.

La verdad de las mentiras: ensayos sobre literatura. Barcelona, Seix Barral, 1990; as *A Writer's Reality*, Syracuse, New York, Syracuse University Press, 1990; London, Faber, 1992.

Letra de batalla por Tirant lo Blanc. Barcelona, Seix Barral, 1991.

Editor, with Gordon Brotherston, *Seven Stories from Spanish America.* Oxford, Pergamon Press, 1968.

*

Critical Studies: *Mario Vargas Llosa's Pursuit of the Total Novel* by Luis A. Diez, Cuernavaca, Cidoc, 1970; *Mario Vargas Llosa: A Collection of Critical Essays* edited by Charles Rossman and Alan Warren Friedman, Austin, University of Texas Press, 1978; *Literary Analysis: Reflections on Vargas Llosa's "The Green House"* by M. J. Fenwick, Minneapolis, Institute for the Study of Ideologies and Literatures, 1981; *From Lima to Leticia: The Peruvian Novels of Mario Vargas Llosa* by Marvin A. Lewis, Lanham, Maryland, University Press of America, 1983; *Novel Lives: The Fictional Autobiographies of Guillermo Cabrera Infante and Mario Vargas Llosa* by Rosemary Geisdorfer Feal, Chapel Hill, University of North Carolina Press, 1986; *Mario Vargas Llosa* by Raymond Leslie Williams, New York, Ungar, 1986; *Understanding Mario Vargas Llosa* by Sara Castro-Klarén, Columbia, University of South Carolina Press, 1989.

*   *   *

Of the writers associated with "Boom" in Latin American literature in the 1960s, Mario Vargas Llosa was the youngest and the principal Peruvian. Attentive to the lessons of European and Anglo-American modernism, Vargas Llosa fused the panoramic realism characteristic of the 19th-century novel with the dynamic techniques found in the 20th-century novel: multiple points of view, interior monologues and internalized dialogues; suspended identifications of characters; montage effects; discontinuous, fragmented, and intertwined narrative lines. His themes echo his narrative experiments. A promise of freedom, exhilarating and tantalizing, ends with disillusion as those established in power re-impose their authority by violence or as those devoid of power adopt and accept more tacit but no less forceful social constraints. In his more recent fiction, the power of storytelling subverts such constraints without denying their power over reality. Not surprisingly, in an increasingly extensive body of criticism, Vargas Llosa speaks eloquently for the view that fictions repair reality and make it possible to "endure the burden of life."

From his first published work, a collection of short stories spare in style and dramatic in construction, *Los jefes* (The Bosses), to his masterwork, *Conversación en La Catedral* (*Conversation in the Cathedral*), Vargas Llosa's fiction pursued a trajectory of increasing narrative complexity. His more recent fiction and plays exploit the same devices, but more simply and, with the notable exception of *La guerra del fin del mundo* (*The War of the End of the World*), more briefly. While *The War of the End of the World*, based on Euclides Da Cunha's *Rebellion in the Backlands* (1902), shares the totalizing impulse of Vargas Llosa's earlier fiction, the later works usually isolate specific social, political, or amorous conflicts intertwined with a literary problem or puzzle. Plot has become the explicit vehicle for the difficulty of representation, the impossibility of historical accuracy, the deceptiveness of any single statement or perspective, the false certainties imposed by the irresistible necessity of choice. In addition, his most recent fiction dramatizes the relation between autobiography and art that has long been a theme of his criticism, relative both to his own work, as in *Historia secreta de una novela* (The Secret History of a Novel), and to the work of others, as in *Gabriel García Márquez: historia de un deicidio*.

His first novel, *La ciudad y los perros* (*The Time of the Hero*), set in Lima's Colegio Militar Leoncio Prado, where Vargas Llosa had been a student, was doubly distinguished by a Spanish literary prize and a public burning in the school's courtyard. Using the school as a claustrophobic microcosm of Peruvian society, the novel explores the brutalizing effects of the military discipline of the school and the codes of honor the students impose on themselves. His second novel, *La casa verde* (*The Green House*), extended the opposition between city and school geographically to an opposition between the green freedoms of the Amazonian jungle and the dusty constraints of Piura. A temporal contrast compounded the physical contrast, with both locations possessed of a mythic past invaded and altered by the present, an effect achieved by the shuffling of five interconnected narratives taking place over a 40-year span. In *Conversation in the Cathedral*, Vargas Llosa returned to Lima, and, still intercutting narrative lines, elaborated an unwinding, circular structure affined to the detective story. Masterly in its narrative coherence, the novel ranges through social, sexual, and political corruption at all levels during the Odria regime of the 1950s, with the unaccountable murder of a prostitute as the absent center on which the narrative turns.

The autobiographical element, submerged source material in his earlier fiction, made its way to the surface in the comic novel *La tía Julia y el escribidor* (*Aunt Julia and the Scriptwriter*). Not political corruption but the paradoxes of daily life, love, and writing play into and against one another as Vargas Llosa intercuts "Marito"'s courtship of his own Aunt Julia and the extravagant, but socially representative soap operas of the scriptwriter Pedro Camacho. (Aunt Julia, Vargas Llosa's first wife, has written a reply to that novel.) In *El hablador* (*The Storyteller*), Vargas Llosa moves beyond the inclusion of bits of biography (recognizable principally to those who know him) to include references to his earlier work (recognizable to all who read him). The practice makes explicit the uncertain, shimmering relation between reality and fiction, as one passes into the other, changing form and status as it goes and putting into question the status of the fiction.

Descending from the meditative structure of *Conversation in the Cathedral*, later works such as *The Storyteller* and *Historia de Mayta* (*The Real Life of Alejandro Mayta*) address

particular political and economic problems through the medium of a narrator juggling obscure and contradictory evidence to construct an account of a man, hero or fool, who resisted the powers of the present. *The Real Life of Alejandro Mayta* reconstructs an earlier, failed terrorist episode in a Peru still struggling with the *Sendero Luminoso* armed opposition group, while *The Storyteller* weighs, without resolving, the conflicting claims of traditional Amazonian cultures and modernization. In each, the narrator's activities provide the matrix within which others act and multiple meanings and alternatives proliferate. The strength of such texts is the equal play they give to the processes of narrative and to the ongoing, still unsolved political choices that will, in spite of fiction, be resolved in one unsatisfactory way or another.

Doing without the foregrounded narrator, other fiction uses the more dramatic narrative shuffling of *The Green House*, though it abandons temporal shifts for simple linearity. *Elogio de la madrasta* (*In Praise of the Stepmother*), a comic novel significantly more wicked than *Aunt Julia* or *Pantaleón y las visitadoras* (*Captain Pantoja and the Special Service*), introduces paintings, reproduced as plates in the text, to complicate the levels of reality and systems of interpretation the reader encounters. Somewhat oddly, Vargas Llosa's plays incorporate the meditating narrator instead of proceeding by purely dramatic means. In *La señorita de Tacna* (*The Young Lady from Tacna*), the grandson Belisario writes as the young lady and her family age and decay; in *Kathie y el hipopótame* (*Kathy and the Hippopotamus*), the characters invent and act multiple roles.

In this criticism, Vargas Llosa is engagingly frank about the deficiencies of life and the consequent demands he places on literature for order, excitement, erotic and imaginative stimulation (much the same thing). As he puts it in *La orgía perpetua* (*The Perpetual Orgy*), *Madame Bovary* endures partly for its exploitation of violence, sex, and melodrama. Vargas Llosa's own project is a literature that agitates, stirs up, and questions as it explores the fissures between life as it is lived, life as it is reconstructed by memory and desire, and the mysterious alchemy of art that uses and transforms those materials. To achieve it, he engages the disasters of reality as subject-matter (corruption sexual and political; violence sexual and political, religious and historical) through a literary technique that implicates the reader, struggling to connect narrative strands, puzzling over juxtapositions, laughing aloud at the surprises produced by those juxtapositions, startled and horrified at the springing of a sudden narrative trap. As in life, both reader and writer are trapped in a downward spiral, but the text between them enlivens, distracts, and gives form and value to the journey.

—Regina Janes

VARMĀ, Nirmal. Also Nirmal Verma. Indian; younge[r] brother of painter and writer Rām Kumār. Born in Śimlā, i[n] 1929. Educated at St. Stephen's College, University of Delhi M.A. in history 1951; Prague Oriental Institute. Lived i[n] Prague, 1959–68; correspondent, *The Times of India*, London until 1972; Fellow, Indian Institute for Advanced Studie[s] Śimlā; participated in the International Writing Progra[m] University of Iowa, Iowa City, 1977; Nirālā Chair, Bhāra[t] Bhavan, Bhopal, 1981–83; Yaśpāl Chair, Śimlā, 1988. Rec[i] pient: Sāhitya Akādemī award, 1988. Address: c/o Rājkamal Prakāśan, 1B Netaji Subhas Marg, New Delhi 110002, India.

PUBLICATIONS

Fiction

Parinde. New Delhi, Rājkamal, 1958; as *The Hill Station and Other Stories*, Calcutta, Writers Workshop, 1962.
Jaltī jhāṛī [Burning Bush]. New Delhi, Rājkamal, 1964.
Ve din. New Delhi, Rājkamal, 1964; as *Days of Longing*, New Delhi, Hind Pocket Books, 1972.
Itne baṛe dhabbe [Such Large Stains]. New Delhi, Rādhākṛṣṇa, 1966.
Māyā-darpaṇ. Benares, Bhārtīy Jñānpīṭh, 1967; as *Maya Darpan and Other Stories*, New Delhi and Oxford, Oxford University Press, 1986; as *The World Elsewhere and Other Stories*, London and New York, Readers International, 1988.
Pichlī garmiyō mē [Last Summer]. New Delhi, Rājkamal, 1968.
Merī priy kahāniyā [My Favourite Stories]. New Delhi, Rājpāl & Sons, 1970.
Lāl ṭīn kī chat [The Red Tin Roof]. New Delhi, Rājkamal, 1974.
Ek cithṛā sukh [A Patch of Happiness]. New Delhi, Rājkamal, 1979.
Kavve aur kālā pānī. New Delhi, Rājkamal, 1983; as *The Crows of Deliverance*, London and New York, Readers International, 1991.
Merī kahāniyā [My Stories]. Delhi, Diśā, 1985.
Pratinidhi kahāniyā [Representative Stories]. New Delhi, Rājkamal, 1988.
Rāt kā reporter [Night Reporter]. New Delhi, Rājkamal, 1989.

Play

Tīn ekānt [Three Solitudes]. New Delhi, Rājkamal, 1976.

Other

Cīrō par cādnī [Moonlit Pines]. New Delhi, Rājkamal, 1962.
Har bāriś mē [With Every Rain]. New Delhi, Rādhākṛṣṇa, 1970.
Bīc bahas mē [Discussions]. Hapur, Sambhāvnā, 1971.
Śabd aur smṛti. New Delhi, Rājkamal, 1976; as *Word and Memory*, Bikaner, Vagdevi, 1988.
Dusrī duniyā [The Other World: Collected Essays]. Hapur, Sambhāvnā, 1978.
Kalā kā zokhim [The Risk of Art]. New Delhi, Rājkamal, 1981.
Dhalān se utarte hue. New Delhi, Rājkamal, 1987.
India aur Europe. New Delhi, Rājkamal, 1991.
Itihās smṛti akānkśā. New Delhi, National Publishing House, 1992.

Has translated Kuprin, Karel Čapek, Mihail Sadoveanu, and *Romeo and Juliet* by William Shakespeare into Hindi.

*

Critical Study: *Nirmal Varmā* edited by Aśok Vajpeyī, New Delhi, Rājkamal, 1990.

*   *   *

An acknowledged writer of "poetic prose," Nirmal Varmā made his reputation in the 1950s with his first collection of short stories, *Parinde* (*The Hill Station and Other Stories*), alongside the "New Story" movement in modern Hindi literature. Through several subsequent collections, novels, travelogues, and essays, he has of late emerged as a staunch critic of modern western civilization. Critics have hailed him as the pioneer of the "new story," but he stands almost alone in his light-and-shade play of language, reflective and self-reflexive mode of narration, metaphorical and imagistic composition, and sonorous yet deeply disturbing voice. "I was there . . . hearing voices in the other room coming over to me from across the threshold. I could not catch the words, hence the voices — primordial, limpid, naked — such that I could directly recognize them . . . For the first time I realized that words are what you can only hear, but voices can be seen. They are the frescoes on the wall of a fierce solitude, with the plaster of anger, pain and remorse mouldering away amidst them; there the silence has its own colours, laughter its own glow, brooding its own space" (*Ek cithṛā sukh* [A Patch of Happiness]).

Initially he looked up to Anton Chekhov and Ivan Turgenev, and Rainer Maria Rilke, T. S. Eliot, and Paul Eluard, apart from "Ajñeya," the multivalent modernist pioneer in Hindi literature. A long stay at Prague enabled Varmā to settle accounts with his early Marxist leanings, ending with the Prague Spring 1968, which, according to him, was an intimate revelation of "the end of history," a closure of dreams wrought by 19th-century humanity. Marxism, in any case, rarely impinged on him creatively; it was confined to an intellectual plane. His Chekhovian mould witnessed earlier also foreshadowed an engagement with the existentialist angst over the human condition and human destiny, an essential loneliness, soon enmeshed with the peculiarly East European variant of tormenting irony, disillusion, and despair.

Ve din (*Days of Longing*), *Jaltī jhāṛī* (Burning Bush), and the travelogue *Cīrō par cādnī* (Moonlit Pines) published during his Czech sojourn established him as an internationalist-modernist writer, distinguished from his coeval realist moderns such as Phaṇiśvar Nath Renu and Kṛṣṇa Sobtī who focussed more on their immediate, local contexts, milieux, and traditions undergoing shocking changes. In terms of locale, environs, and characters, Varmā has had a penchant for — with all the fine, rich, and sensuous detail of a master narrator — essentialist abstraction. Distance, both temporal and spatial, seems interwoven in the very fabric of his sensibility. The "felt reality," which he sees as the core of his artistic-creative moment, has a rather complex relationship with time-consciousness. Even dwelling in the "eternal present," as he discards the past and the future as redundant categories, the present still comes steeped in memory. Memory to Varmā discharges a highly complex function. It is an artistic device, a perennial repository of creativity and self-renewal, an entity that overcomes the delimiting and debilitating "history," at the same time performing what "mythic consciousness" is unable to perform in the modern times.

As if to capture the primal moment of innocence before the Fall, Varmā often deploys a child or an (invalid) adolescent as his narrator. In the novel *Ek cithṛā sukh* a sick boy witnesses the void in the network of relationships, etched against the backdrop of the world of theatre. Similarly, a girl in another novel, *Lāl ṭīn kī chat* (The Red Tin Roof), gazes into the mysteries of existence. In "Under Cover of Darkness," an ill child observes the estrangement between his parents. Though engaging characters from all age groups, Varmā most effectively projects through such characters an "absolute" sense of time and experience. "Nothing can console a child when he weeps. He weeps absolutely," Varmā says. "The World Elsewhere," another famous short story and the culmination of the author's specific search and style, recreates an eerie, unreal world, yet very real to the little girl living alone with her mother. The childhood motif perhaps also signifies the first stage of garnering bits and pieces for memory, the perennial source of creativity. Thus an adult in "A Splinter of the Sun" explains: "Certain snatches of conversation, certain glimpses, certain sounds, which, though later lost in the maze of routine-bound years, return as if with a vengeance, just when a person, unawares, walks down a street or waits for a bus or lies in bed over a moment suspended between sleep and wakefulness. You hardly know what has struck. I know it. It has happened with me, too."

The rigorous Hindi critic Nityānand Tivārī points out "new" elements entering Varmā's writing. His growing inclination towards Indian tradition leads him to explore the path of renunciation, which is "the way of knowledge" in contrast to the popular path of devotion (bhakti) to God/s with worldly attributes. Thus, in the title story of Kavve aur kālā pānī (The Crows of Deliverance), the author's long-held "ideology" of impossibility and fragility of relationships seems curiously to correspond to and unite with the traditional world-view of detachment. On the other hand, his story "Guest for a Day" wades through relationships gone sour under specific socio-historical circumstances, and thus calls for a reappraisal of his a priori pessimism.

The colonial and post-colonial savaging of an ancient tradition by the West propels Varmā the cultural critic to reject modern western civilization with its core of violence manifest in technologism, consumerism, and the vain enlightenment-humanism. His prized philosophies — Vedānta and Buddhism — are primarily concerned with the "Self." While the former preaches transcendence to, and merging with, the ultimate reality, the latter negates any ontic "Self." Most of Varmā's metaphors, including the ever-recurring darkness, would seem poised or torn between these opposite choices. Both his fiction and criticism are inescapably yet subtly tinged with such debates.

Even as he veers closer to the positions of postmodernism, Varmā still has doubts in regard to its future course. Intellectually, he would like to see a new synthesis along Gandhian lines — of man and nature, self and other, religion and politics. However, his recent, semi-articulated sympathies for BTP, the Hindu fundamentalist party, have aroused, perhaps unjustifiably, some unease among secular-humanistic circles.

—Girdhar Rathi

————————

VEGA, Ana Lydia. Puerto Rican. Born in 1946. Professor of French and literature, University of Puerto Rico, Río Piedras. Recipient: Casa de las Américas prize, 1982; Juan Rulfo international prize, 1984; Guggenheim fellowship, 1989. Address: c/o Casa de las Américas, Calle Gy3 Tercera y G, Vedado, Havana, Cuba.

PUBLICATIONS

Fiction

Vírgenes y mártires, with Carmen Lugo Filippi.   Río Piedras, Antillana, 1981.

Encancaranublado y otros cuentos de naufragio.   Havana, Casa de las Américas, 1982.
Pasión de historia y otras historias de pasión.   Buenos Aires, Flor, 1987.

English translations of stories published in: *Reclaiming Medusa: Short Stories by Contemporary Puerto Rican Women*, edited by Diana Vélez, San Francisco, Spinsters/Aunt Lute, 1988; *Short Stories by Latin American Women: The Magic and the Real*, edited by Celia Correas de Zapata, Houston, Arte Público, 1990; *Scents of Wood and Silence: Short Stories by Latin American Women Writers*, edited by Kathleen Ross and Yvette Miller, special issue of *Latin American Literary Review* (Pittsburgh), 19(37), 1991; and other anthologies.

Play

Screenplay: *La gran fiesta*, 1986.

Other

Editor, *El Tramo anda: ensayos puertorriqueños de hoy*.   Río Piedras, Editorial de la Universidad de Puerto Rico, 1988.

*

Critical Studies: "From a Woman's Perspective: The Short Stories of Rosario Ferré and Ana Lydia Vega" by Margarite Fernández Olmos, in *Contemporary Women Authors of Latin America*, Brooklyn, Brooklyn College Press, 1983; "Pollito Chicken: Split Subjectivity, National Identity and the Articulation of Female Sexuality in a Narrative by Ana Lydia Vega" by Diana Vélez, in *The Americas Review* (Houston), 14(2), 1986; "The Reproduction of Ideology in Ana Lydia Vega's 'Pasión de historia' and 'Caso omiso'" by Becky Boling, in *Letras Femeninas* (Lincoln, Nebraska), 17(1–2), 1991.

*   *   *

As a short story writer, Ana Lydia Vega is important as a lively representative of the new generation of committed Puerto Rican writers, who use the form to convey both personal and more general political messages. At her best, her work is saved from being pamphleteering through a combination of humour, genuine interest in the characters she creates, and an inventive use of the contemporary Spanish language. These strengths are evident from her first book of stories *Vírgenes y mártires* (Virgins and Martyrs), written in collaboration with the writer Carmen Lugo Filippi. Vega's contributions to the book show young women in Puerto Rico trying to deal with the machismo of their male contemporaries, getting together on their own, struggling both to live in the modern city and to express themselves in a language that has inevitably become infiltrated by English from the United States. "Pollito Chicken" in this volume is a hilarious exposition of this kind of dilemma.

A political accent dominated her second book of stories, "Encancaranublado y otros cuentos de naufragio" (the title being a children's tongue-twister without much meaning). Here Vega explores the roots of domination in the Caribbean, and looks at the ways the Puerto Rican experience is similar to that of other islands sharing its mixed heritage. The anger of the slaves on the islands is expressed in a story such as "Pateco's Little Prank," where the presence of their African gods is used metaphorically to depict the destruction of an unjust system. Elsewhere, Vega further explores the mixture of Spanish, African, and North American influences on contemporary Caribbean society.

Pasión de historia y otras historias de pasión (A Passion for History and Other Stories of Passion) marks a return to more intimate themes. Here Vega uses the detective genre to explore crimes of passion, in which the women usually emerge the victors. Once again, irony and out-and-out slapstick leaven the stories. In her forthcoming book, however, *Falsas crónicas del sur* (False Accounts from the South) Vega turns her attention back to a concern for history, this time investigating the way history and folk memory interact. Other stories in the volume reflect once again the difficulties of life in a tough place like San Juan de Puerto Rico. In most of these stories, however, as in her earlier work, Vega's exuberance and basic optimism with regard to life shine through and make for thoroughly entertaining reading.

—Nick Caistor

———

VENTSEL', Elena Sergeevna. *See* **GREKOVA, I.**

———

VERMA, Nirmal. *See* **VARMĀ, Nirmal.**

———

VESAAS, Halldis Moren. Norwegian. Born in Trysil, 18 November 1907. Educated at a teacher's college, 1928. Married the writer Tarjei Vesaas in 1934 (died 1970); one son and one daughter. Secretary in Switzerland, 1930–33; teacher, Vinje primary school, 1941–43. Member, National Theatre Board, 1949, Norwegian Language Advisory Board, 1952, and Norwegian Cultural Council, 1965–73. Recipient: Dobloug prize, 1961; Norsk Kulturåds Ærespris, 1982. Address: c/o Aschehoug & Co., Postboks 363, Sentrum, 0102 Oslo 1, Norway.

PUBLICATIONS

Verse

Harpe og dolk [Harp and Dagger] (as Halldis Moren).   Oslo, Aschehoug, 1929.
Morgonen [The Morning] (as Halldis Moren).   Oslo, Aschehoug, 1930.
Dyr og dikt (as Halldis Moren).   Oslo, Norsk Lithografisk Officin, 1930.
Strender [Beaches] (as Halldis Moren).   Oslo, Aschehoug, 1933.
Lykkelege hender [Joyful Hands].   Oslo, Aschehoug, 1936.
Tung tids tale [Words from a Heavy Time].   Oslo, Aschehoug, 1945.
Treet [The Tree].   Oslo, Aschehoug, 1947.

Tidleg på våren [In Early Spring].   Oslo, Aschehoug, 1949.
I ein annan skog [In Another Forest].   Oslo, Aschehoug, 1955.
Utvalde dikt [Selected Poems].   Oslo, Aschehoug, 1957; revised edition, 1974.
Ord over grind [Words over the Gate].   Oslo, Den Norske Bokklubben, 1965.
Dikt i samling [Collected Poems].   Oslo, Aschehoug, 1977.

Fiction

Hildegunn.   Oslo, Aschehoug, 1942.
Så nær deg [So Close to You].   Oslo, Aschehoug, 1987.

Other

Du får gjera det, du [You'd Better Do It, Then] (for children).   Oslo, Aschehoug, 1935.
Den grøne hatten [The Green Hat] (for children).   Oslo, Aschehoug, 1938.
Sven Moren og heimen hans [Sven Moren and His Home] (biography).   Oslo, Aschehoug, 1951.
Sett og levd [Seen and Lived].   Oslo, Aschehoug, 1967.
Gudefjellet [The Mountain of the Gods].   Oslo, Aschehoug, 1970.
Det store nashornet [The Big Rhinoceros] (for children).   Oslo, Det Norske Samlaget, 1970.
I Midtbøs bakkar [On Midtbø's Hills] (autobiography).   Oslo, Aschehoug, 1974.
Båten om dagen: minne frå eit samliv 1946–1970 [The Boat in the Daytime] (autobiography).   Oslo, Aschehoug, 1976.
Den gode gåva: segna om Demeter [The Good Gift: The Legend of Demeter] (for children).   Oslo, Det Norske Samlaget, 1987.

Editor, *Nynorsk novellekunst*.   Oslo, Det Norske Samlaget, 1965.
Editor, *Nynorske noveller*.   Oslo, Det Norske Samlaget, 1969.
Editor, *I grenselandet* [On the Border].   Oslo, Den Norske Bokklubben, 1969.
Editor, *Dikt i urval*, by Sigmund Skard.   Oslo, Gyldendal, 1973.
Editor, *Trær: treet i norsk lyrikk: en antologi*.   Oslo, Den Norske Bokklubben, 1977.
Editor, with Asbjørn Gimse, *Leva här bland alla andra: finlandssvensk lyrikk*.   Oslo, Den Norske Bokklubben, 1978.
Editor, *Med eiga lyre*, by Hartvig Kiran.   Oslo, Det Norske Samlaget, 1979.
Editor, with Simen Skjønsberg and Idar Stegane, *Noveller i samtiden*.   Oslo, Aschehoug, 1981.
Editor, *Blomster og brød: dikt om kjærleik*.   Oslo, Den Norske Bokklubben, 1983.

Translator, *Barn av Hiroshima*, edited by Arata Osada. Oslo, Det Norske Samlaget, 1961.
Translator, *Djedneskniven og andre soger*, by Rasmus Løland.   Oslo, Det Norske Samlaget, 1961.
Translator, *Hundre år*, by Rasmus Løland.   Oslo, Det Norske Samlaget, 1961.
Translator, *Kvitegbjørnen*, by Rasmus Løland.   Oslo, Det Norske Samlaget, 1961.
Translator, *Berre ein hund og andre soger*, by Per Sivle. Oslo, Det Norske Samlaget, 1963.
Translator, *Natta og eg*, by Sigurd Kvåle.   Oslo, Det Norske Samlaget, 1967.

Translator, *Lærde damer* [Les Femmes Savantes], by Molière.
Oslo, Det Norske Samlaget, 1984.
Translator, *Bérénice*, by Jean Racine. Oslo, Det Norske
Samlaget, 1989.

*

Critical Study: "When the Rose Becomes a Sword: The
Beginnings of a Tradition of Women's Poetry in Norway" by
Tone Selboe, in *New Comparison* (London), 4, 1987.

*   *   *

Halldis Moren Vesaas has often somewhat ruefully complained that she has sat on cultural committees beyond count
because she represents several "minority" interests in Norway,
being a) a woman, b) a *nynorsk* writer, and c) from a rural
area, in a country where cultural life is dominated by male
writers from Oslo whose language is *bokmål*. Nynorsk (New
Norwegian) is Norway's second language, spoken by less than
a fifth of the population, but one that has been used by a fair
number of writers. When you add to this list the fact that
Vesaas is not only a woman writer but also a poet, it becomes
clear that she is a rare phenomenon indeed.

The events of Vesaas's life are not outwardly dramatic; from
her marriage to fellow author Tarjei Vesaas and settling in
Telemark in 1934, it seems to have flowed smoothly. Over 26
years she published several volumes of poetry, which trace
stages on life's way; we follow her development from early
youth into maturity, marriage, and motherhood, and then into
a more reflective and troubled period of middle life. Outside
events impinge more and more, as the rumblings of political
upheaval in the 1930s are followed by war and occupation. Yet
the poems never become propaganda; even her war poetry
expresses the same warm sympathy for all life which prefers to
understand rather than to judge.

With her first collection, *Harpe og dolk* (Harp and Dagger),
Vesaas was the first woman poet to make an appearance in
Norwegian literature for almost a generation. She wrote with a
frankness which startled critics about female sexual desire,
about a lovemaking in which the whole of the natural earth
seems a participant:

> You come and pull me close with your brown hands
> and speak to me in words so wild and sweet.
> Bewitched, I lie with you. Oh, I can sense
> Through all my joy how rich you smell of earth!
> ("Scent of Earth")

Nature is constantly present in her writing, not as a framework
or a sympathetic echo in the Romantic sense, but as an
inextricable part of a relationship. Trees are a recurrent image,
and convey a sense of permanence and belonging. The same
tone continues in *Lykkelege hender* (Joyful Hands), a celebration of young marriage and childbirth. Vesaas writes the first
Norwegian poems which express the physical feeling of
carrying a child.

World War II brought darker poems in *Tung tids tale* (Words
from a Heavy Time), in which the dominant emotion is sadness
— not only at the suffering of her country, but at the waste of
life on both sides. The image of a woman planting a tree as a
tremor of destruction runs through the earth expresses both
hope for the future and an awareness of the fragility of that
hope. Trees dominate too in her final collection of poetry, *I ein
annan skog* (In Another Forest), in which the forest of early
youth, with its tall, straight trees, has been left behind, and the

poet finds herself in an altogether darker and more
threatening place, which she yet feels may challenge her to
greater effort:

> Here it is narrow and dark
> with peculiar twisted trees,
> storm-tossed, bent and broken —
> never was I in such a forest.
> Can it be here that my heart
> must seek — and find its peace?
> ("The Other Forest")

Death is a constant presence in these poems, no longer as a
distant peace at the end of a working day, as it had appeared
earlier, but as a much more immediate reality. Several of
Vesaas's writing colleagues had died in the 1940s and 1950s
— some by their own choice — and awareness of this lies
behind several poems. Yet when she looked back over her
poetry a decade later, she summed up its dominant emotion
as love for "all that we living possess."

Since 1955 Vesaas has written little poetry; it has no
longer come to her spontaneously. Yet she has been continually active in a wide cultural circle as one of Norway's
most popular "travelling artists," talking and reading her
poems around the world. As well as all her cultural and
educational activities, she has written a great deal in other
genres. She has been active as a translator of plays since
1940, translating from English, French, and German, including Shakespeare, Goethe, Kafka, Racine, Molière, Claudel,
Pirandello. She has published essays, articles, travel reports,
and two volumes of autobiography, *I Midtbøs bakkar* (On
Midtbø's Hills) and *Båten om dagen* (The Boat in the Day-
time). The latter two books chronicle the life of the "author-
apparatus" Vesaas until her husband's death in 1970, and
document so rich an artistic interchange across national
borders that they practically read like a cultural history of
modern Scandinavia.

In her 80th year, Vesaas published a collection of four
stories, *Så nær deg* (So Close to You). All four stories are
concerned with the relationships between mother and
daughter, and all work through a crisis to a reconciliation;
they were intended, as the author explained, to "act as a
kind of positive counterweight to all the negative mother/
daughter relationships in contemporary literature." It is the
kind of resolution which emerges from most of what Vesaas
has written, be it fact or fiction, where "nothing which is
natural is really bad."

—Janet Garton

———

VIK, Bjørg (Turid). Norwegian. Born in Oslo, 11 September 1935. Educated at a journalism school. Married
Hans Jørgen Vik in 1957; three children. Worked as a journalist in Porsgrunn, five years. Recipient: Riksmål prize,
1972; Aschehoug prize, 1974; Norwegian Critics' prize,
1979; Porsgrunn prize, 1981; Cappelen prize, 1982;
Booksellers' prize, 1988; Ibsen prize, 1992; Skomvær prize,
1992. Agent: J. W. Cappelens Forlag, Boks 350, Sentrum,
Oslo 1, Norway. Address: Furustadvn 10, 3900 Porsgrunn,
Norway.

PUBLICATIONS

Fiction

Søndag ettermiddag [Sunday Afternoon].   Oslo, Cappelen, 1963.
Nødrop fra en myk sofa [Cries for Help from a Soft Sofa].   Oslo, Cappelen, 1966.
Det grådige hjerte [The Greedy Heart].   Oslo, Cappelen, 1968.
Gråt, elskede mann [Weep, Beloved Man].   Oslo, Cappelen, 1970.
Kvinneakvariet.   Oslo, Cappelen, 1972; as *An Aquarium of Women*, Norwich, Norvik Press, 1987.
Fortellinger om frihet [Tales of Freedom].   Oslo, Cappelen, 1975.
En håndfull lengsel.   Oslo, Cappelen, 1979; as *Out of Season and Other Stories*, London, Sinclair Brown, 1983.
Snart er det høst [Soon It Will Be Autumn].   Oslo, Cappelen, 1982.
En gjenglemt petunia [A Forgotten Petunia].   Oslo, Cappelen, 1985.
Når en pike sier ja [When a Girl Says Yes].   Oslo, Cappelen, 1985.
Små nøkler store rom [Small Keys Large Rooms].   Oslo, Cappelen, 1988.
Poplene på St. Hanshaugen [The Poplars on St. Hanshaugen].   Oslo, Cappelen, 1991.

Plays

To akter for fem kvinner [Two Acts for Five Women].   Oslo, Cappelen, 1974; as *Wine Untouched* (produced New York).
Hurra, det ble en pike! [Hurray — It's a Girl!].   Oslo, Cappelen, 1974.
Sorgenfri: fem bilder om kjærlighet [Free from Sorrow: Five Pictures of Love].   Oslo, Cappelen, 1978.
Det trassige håp [Defiant Hope] (radio plays).   Oslo, Cappelen, 1981.
Fribillett til Soria Moria [Free Ticket to Soria Moria].   Oslo, Cappelen, 1984.
Døtre (radio play). As *Daughters*, in *New Norwegian Plays*, Norwich, Norvik Press, 1989.
Vinterhagen [The Winter Garden].   Oslo, Cappelen, 1990.
Reisen til Venezia [The Trip to Venice].   Oslo, Cappelen, 1991.

Radio Plays: *Døtre* (*Daughters*), 1979; *Myrtel* [Myrtle], 1981.

Television Play: *Fribillett til Soria Moria* [Free Ticket to Soria Moria].

Other

Gutten som sådde tiøringer [The Boy Who Sowed Pennies] (for children).   Oslo, Pax, 1970.
Jørgen Bombasta (for children).   Oslo, Cappelen, 1987.

*

Critical Study: "The Norwegian Short Story: Bjørg Vik" by Carla Waal, in *Scandinavian Studies* (Madison, Wisconsin), 49, 1977.

*   *   *

Bjørg Vik is a popular Norwegian author, who has had considerable success both as a fiction writer (of novels and short stories) and as a dramatist, on radio, television, and in the theatre. Her plays and stories are meticulously observed realistic studies of contemporary life. She began writing in the 1960s, and her stories from that time are the first to give expression to the "new wave" feminism which did not gain momentum in Norway until the following decade.

The short story, with its concentration and precision, was her preferred form from the start; she learned much from Cora Sandel. Her early collections, such as *Søndag ettermiddag* (Sunday Afternoon) and *Nødrop fra en myk sofa* (Cries for Help from a Soft Sofa), are sometimes optimistic stories of women discovering their own sexuality, sometimes low-key studies of quiet desperation, in which indignation lies below the surface.

Indignation is more clearly articulated in some of her works from the following decade, such as *Kvinneakvariet* (*An Aquarium of Women*). This is a cycle of nine short stories, divided into three sections. The first section deals with young girls on the threshold of adolescence, becoming aware of how their freedom of action is restricted by social pressures embodied in their ever-watchful mothers. The second section follows the women into adult life, and depicts the unbearable stresses caused by the impossible conflict of demands from work and family. "Emilie" charts the breakdown of a woman trying to combine a "privileged" career as a librarian with the care of a sick child; "Liv" is a rare study of working-class drudgery, depicting the numbing combination of boring, repetitive work and an endless struggle to make the money go around. In the third section, the subjects are women who are trying to live more independently, outside the traditional set-up; but they still have to fight convention, like the woman in "After All the Words" whose lover cannot accept the fact that she will not declare him her one and only love.

This collection was followed by a play, *To akter for fem kvinner* (Two Acts for Five Women), which continues the theme; the play depicts a reunion between five former school friends, who have all taken different paths in life and who are all brought to face the compromises they have made or the price they have paid for their freedom. It is not just a topical feminist statement, however, but a well-written play which has been translated into around 20 languages and successfully performed in many countries. The dialogue tends towards stichomythia; Vik has mastered the art of making her characters talk past one another in a way which gives the impression of spontaneous conversation, while blending into a pattern of theme and cross reference where one comment illuminates the next.

This technique is also in evidence in her popular radio plays, such as *Døtre* (*Daughters*), a study of the relationships between three generations of women, a grandmother, mother, and daughter. It is a study of the failure of communication, of the way in which people talk past one another and fail to express what they mean; although all three generations mean well, they cannot really approve of the way the others are living their lives.

Since the mid-1970s Vik has continued to write a mixture of plays and short stories, as well as two autobiographical novels. She has distanced herself somewhat from the feminist movement, partly because she grew tired of being regarded as a figurehead, and partly because she disagreed with what she saw as the narrow politicization and middle-class domination of the Norwegian women's movement. Women are still the central characters of her stories, but the tone has become softer and more resigned. Several of the stories in *En håndfull lengsel* (*Out of Season*), for example, are about women past their first youth, carrying on courageously with lives in which there is little sunshine. Yet all is not bleak; the story "The Widows," about two old women with little left to wait for but death, becomes paradoxically the most positive story in the collection, as contact is established with the next generation and fear of isolation is overcome by solidarity.

There is a tendency for Vik's characters to grow older as she herself grows older; many of the stories in collections like *Snart er det høst* (Soon It Will Be Autumn) and *En gjenglemt petunia* (A Forgotten Petunia) have an autumnal feel to them. Yet there are also stories in these collections which experiment with different narrative techniques and unusual subjects, like "Amandabakken," a collective study of the life of a whole street, and "Call Me Jutta," a bleak study of stunted sexuality with a male central character.

In the 1980s the critical spotlight shifted away from Vik; it was her deliberate decision to be a less public figure. Yet her books continue to sell well and to win prizes, and her plays are welcomed by theatres and the public. Her autobiographical novels are finely-observed records of life in Oslo in the postwar years. Her most recent play, *Reisen til Venezia* (The Trip to Venice), subtitled "A Melancholy Comedy," is about a married couple nearing the end of their long life together; yet the threatening morbidity of the subject is dispelled by the indomitable spirit of the pair, who refuse to give in quietly, and whose outrageous behaviour communicates itself to the young people who come in contact with them.

—Janet Garton

VILHJÁLMSSON, Thor. Icelandic. Born in Edinburgh, 12 August 1925. Educated at the University of Iceland, Reykjavík, 1944–46; University of Nottingham, 1946–47; the Sorbonne, Paris, 1947–52. Librarian, National Library of Iceland, Reykjavík, for several years. Former president, Union of Icelandic Artists. Recipient: Nordic Council prize, 1988; Swedish Academy Nordic prize, 1992. Address: c/o Mál og menning, PO Box 392, 121 Reykjavík, Iceland.

PUBLICATIONS

Fiction

Maðurinn er alltaf einn [Man Is Always Alone].   Reykjavík, Prentsmiðjan Hólar, 1950.
Dagar mannsins [The Days of Man].   Reykjavík, Heimskringla, 1954.
Andlit í spegli dropans.   Reykjavík, Helgafell, 1957; as *Faces Reflected in a Drop*, Helgafell, 1966.
Fljótt fljótt, sagði fuglinn.   Reykjavík, Helgafell, 1968; as *Quick Quick Said the Bird*, Kapuskasing, Ontario, Penumbra Press, 1987.
Óp bjöllunnar [The Beetle's Cry].   Reykjavík, Helgafell, 1970.
Folda [Mother Land].   Reykjavík, Ísafold, 1972.
Fuglaskottís [Birds Dancing the Polka].   Reykjavík, Ísafold, 1975.
Mánasigð [Crescent Moon].   Reykjavík, Ísafold, 1976.
Skuggar af skýjum [Shadows of Clouds].   Reykjavík, Ísafold, 1977.

Turnleikhúsið [The Tower Theatre].   Reykjavík, Iðunn, 1979.
Grámosínn glóir [The Grey Moss Glows].   Reykjavík, Svart á Hvítu, 1986.
Náttvíg [Killing by Night].   Reykjavík, Mál og Menning, 1989.

Verse

The Deep Blue Sea, Pardon the Ocean.   Northeast Harbor, Maine, LoonBooks, 1981.

Plays

Horfðu reiður um öxl, translation of *Look Back in Anger* by John Osborne (produced Reykjavík, 1959).   Reykjavík, n.p., 1959.
Á yztu nöf, translation of a play by Thornton Wilder (produced Reykjavík, 1959).
Ætlar blessuð manneskjan að gefa upp andann? [Is the Poor Creature Going to Give Up the Ghost?] (produced 1963).
Allt hefur sinn tíma [Everything at Its Proper Time] (produced 1967).
Dagleiðin langa inn í nótt, with Guðmundur Andri Thorsson, translation of *Long Day's Journey into Night* by Eugene O'Neill (produced Reykjavík, 1982).   Reykjavík, Menningarsjóður, 1983.

Other

Undir gervitungli [Under an Artificial Moon].   Reykjavík, n.p., 1959.
Regn á rykið: ferðaþættir og fleira [Rain on the Dust].   Reykjavík, Helgafell, 1960.
Svipir dagsins, og nótt [Night and Aspects of the Day].   Reykjavík, Helgafell, 1961.
Kjarval.   Reykjavík, Helgafell, 1964.
Hvað er San Marínó? [What Is San Marínó?].   Reykjavík, Ísafold, 1973.
Fiskur í sjó, fugl úr beini [Fish in the Sea, Bird of Bone].   Reykjavík, Ísafold, 1974.
Faldafeykir [Blow-About].   Reykjavík, Lystræninginn, 1979.
Tryggvi Ólafsson, with Halldór B. Runólfsson.   Reykjavík, Listasafn, 1987.

Translator, *Dáið þér Brahms* [Aimez-Vous Brahms?], by Françoise Sagan.   1959.
Translator, *Saga úr dýragarðinum* [The Zoo Story], by Edward Albee.   1963.
Translator, *Ótrygg er ögurstund*, by Edward Albee.   1973.
Translator, *Hlutskipti manns* [La Condition humaine], by André Malraux.   Reykjavík, Svart á Hvítu, 1983.
Translator, *Nafn rósarinnar* [The Name of the Rose], by Umberto Eco.   Reykjavík, Svart á Hvítu, 1984.

*

Critical Study: "The One Who Sees: The Icelandic Writer Thor Vilhjálmsson" by Peter Hallberg, in *Books Abroad* (Norman, Oklahoma), 47(1), 1973.

*   *   *

The Icelandic novel begins in the 19th century with a pastoral tendency which may be explained partly as a reaction against the heroic literature of the Middle Ages, and partly in terms of a deeply felt need to idealize Icelandic rural life in contrast to the urban life that foreign influence must sooner or later inevitably bring in its train. Linked with this tendency is a new one which has developed with the growth of the capital city of Reykjavík, particularly since World War II: towards the creation, not yet fully achieved, of an Icelandic urban novel. Thor Vilhjálmsson, who as well as being a novelist writes short stories, poems, travel books, and plays, seems in his early works to have largely dissociated himself from either of these tendencies. The title of his first book, *Maðurinn er alltaf einn* (Man Is Always Alone), a collection of short works mainly in prose, emphasizes the precarious nature of man's relationship to any kind of environment, and while his second and third books, *Dagar mannsins* (The Days of Man) and *Andlit í spegli dropans* (*Faces Reflected in a Drop*), resemble the first not only in consisting mainly of short prose pieces but also in often describing urban scenes, the latter are invariably European and continental rather than Icelandic.

His sixth book, *Svipir dagsins, og nótt* (Night and Aspects of the Day) is a fascinating account of travel by train — itself a phenomenon foreign to Iceland, where there are no passenger trains — in Europe near the end of the 1950s, involving visits to countries in which momentous changes have since taken place, notably Germany and Yugoslavia. While this is a relatively straightforward travelogue, Vilhjálmsson allows himself the modernist techniques of leaving open the question of from whose point of view, precisely, the experiences are being described, and of moving unexpectedly from the present to the historical past, as with his greater concentration on Erasmus of Rotterdam than on the modern Netherlands. Also noteworthy is the fact that opportunities for comparison with Icelandic customs and traditions — as with the account of farming in Yugoslavia — are almost pointedly missed; in retrospect it seems as though the author was deliberately educating himself in non-Icelandic European culture before confronting Icelandic subjects.

His first two novels, *Fljótt fljótt, sagði fuglinn* (*Quick Quick Said the Bird*) and *Óp bjöllunnar* (The Beetle's Cry), also show a break with tradition with their highly pictorial descriptions and lyrical style, their relative lack of consistently drawn characters or of events arranged in structures recognizable as plots, and in their deep preoccupation with travel abroad, whether literally or in the mind. More traditional in their consistent adherence to plot and characterization are the novel *Fuglaskottís* (Birds Dancing the Polka) and *Folda* (Mother Land), a satirical sequence of three fictionalised travel accounts, set in Iceland, China, and a Mediterranean holiday resort respectively. Here Icelandic and foreign culture are amusingly juxtaposed; the discovery by the travellers in the first account that a river into which they had fallen and by whose current they had been borne along was in fact the urine of a giantess — a motif borrowed from the prose Edda of the medieval Icelandic writer, Snorri Sturluson — is seen in relation to a cautious investigation by an Icelandic tourist couple in the third account of whether or not there is a bidet in their hotel bathroom. Rail travel is a unifying feature of the novel *Mánasigð* (Crescent Moon), in which apparently random thoughts from past and present occur in the mind of the traveller, while in *Turnleikhúsið* (The Tower Theatre), the first of Thor's novels to be set in Iceland, the Icelandic National Theatre is used as a framework for introducing dreamlike glimpses of many different cultures: Japanese, North and South American, and ancient Greek.

It is nevertheless in his two most recent novels that Vilhjálmsson embraces Icelandic culture most fully. In *Grámosinn glóir* (The Grey Moss Glows), which won the 1988 Nordic Council literary prize, a poet mystically preoccupied with the unification of apparent irreconcilables finds himself confronted, in his capacity as a district magistrate, with a horrifying unity of life, love, death, and hatred in trying a case of incest involving a rape victim who, after finding happiness in a sexual relationship with her half-brother, kills her child by him out of fear for its future and later commits suicide. Based on an episode in the life of the Icelandic poet and lawyer Einar Benediktsson (1864–1940), who, like his counterpart in the novel, had lived abroad prior to the trial in question, the novel is partly an examination of that poet's ideas, and also, more generally, of Icelandic in relation to foreign culture. With his vivid descriptions of Icelandic nature as apprehended by the *yrkjandi auga* or "poetic eye" of his hero, who compares what he sees to Mantegna's paintings, Vilhjálmsson brings his well-travelled cultural experience to bear on the pastoral tradition in the Icelandic novel.

In *Náttvíg* (Killing by Night) a Reykjavík taxi-driver recalls two experiences: a woman's arrest following her admittance to having killed a man, and the hijacking of his taxi by three criminals who use it in the violent robbery of an elderly couple. Their dialogue is blood-curdlingly convincing, though more assured than might be expected of real Icelandic gangsters, who are still an emergent breed. Vilhjálmsson's contribution to the Icelandic urban novel is thus to give Reykjavík even more of an urban feel than it has already acquired in reality. Whether or not this is to be read as a socio-political warning is of small importance; more significant is the confirmation by these last two novels that in Vilhjálmsson's hands the Icelandic language is more than capable of transforming creatively whatever themes foreign or domestic culture, ancient or modern, may have to offer it. The award to him in 1992 of the Swedish Academy's Nordic prize — its next most prestigious award after the Nobel prize — is richly deserved.

—Rory McTurk

VILLUM, Kjartan. *See* **FLØGSTAD, Kjartan.**

VINAVER, Michel. French. Born Michel Grinberg in Paris, in 1927. Formerly business executive, Gillette International. Chair of drama committee, Centre National des Lettres, from 1983. Recipient: Fénéon prize, 1952; Ibsen prize, 1986; Kleist prize, 1986. Address: c/o Actes Sud, Passage du Mejan, 13200 Arles, France.

PUBLICATIONS

Plays

Les Coréens (produced as *Aujourd'hui, ou, Les Coréens*, Lyon, 1956). Paris, Gallimard, 1956.
Les Huissiers. Published in *Théâtre Populaire*, March 1958; revised version (produced Lyon, 1980), in *Le Livre des huissiers*, n.p., Limage/Avila, 1981.

La Fête du cordonnier, adaptation of a play by Thomas Dekker
(produced Paris, 1959).
Iphigénie Hôtel, part an adaptation of a novel by Henry Green
(produced Paris, 1977).   Paris, Gallimard, 1963.
Par-dessus bord (produced Villeurbanne, 1973).   Paris,
L'Arche, 1972.
La Demande d'emploi (produced Avignon, 1972).   Paris,
L'Arche, 1973; as *Situation Vacant* (produced Richmond,
Surrey, 1989).
Théâtre de chambre (includes *Dissident, il va sans dire*; *Nina,
c'est autre chose*; produced Paris, 1978).   Paris, L'Arche,
1978.
Les Travaux et les jours (produced Paris, 1980).   Paris,
L'Arche, 1979; as *A Smile on the End of the Line* (produced
Richmond, Surrey, 1987); as *Blending In* (produced
Edinburgh, 1989).
À la Renverse (produced Paris, 1980).   Lausanne, L'Aire,
1980.
L'Ordinaire (produced Paris, 1983).   Lausanne, L'Aire,
1982.
Les Estivants, adaptation of *Datchniki* by Maxim Gorkii
(produced Paris, 1983).   Included in *Théâtre*, vol. 2, 1986.
Le Suicidé, adaptation of the play by Nicolaï Erdman (pro-
duced Paris, 1984).   Included in *Théâtre complet*, vol. 2,
1986.
Théâtre complet (vol. 1 includes *Les Coréens*; *Les Huissiers*;
La Fête du cordonnier; *Iphigénie Hôtel*; *Par-dessus bord*; *La
Demande d'emploi*; vol. 2 includes *Dissident, il va sans dire*;
Nina, c'est autre chose; *Les Travaux et les jours*; *À la
Renverse*; *Le Suicidé*; *L'Ordinaire*; *Les Estivants*; *Les
Voisins*; *Portrait d'une femme*).   Arles, Actes Sud, 2 vols.,
1986.
Les Voisins (produced Paris, 1986).   Included in *Théâtre
complet*, vol. 2, 1986; as *The Neighbours*, New York, Ubu
Repertory, 1988.
Portrait d'une femme (produced Paris, 1988).   In *Théâtre
complet*, vol. 2, 1986; as *Portrait of a Woman* (produced in
English, 1988), in *New French Plays*, edited by David
Bradby and Claude Schumacher, London, Methuen, 1989.
Le Compte rendu d'Avignon.   Arles, Actes Sud, 1987.
Le Dernier Sursaut.   Arles, Actes Sud, 1990.
L'Émission de télévision (produced Paris, 1990).   Arles,
Actes Sud, 1990.

Fiction

Lataume, ou, La Vie quotidienne.   Paris, Gallimard, 1950.
L'Objecteur.   Paris, Gallimard, 1951.
Les Histoires de Rosalie.   Paris, Flammarion, 1980.

Other

Écrits sur le théâtre, edited by Michelle Henry.   Lausanne,
L'Aire, 1982.

Translator, *Amour*, by Henry Green.   Paris, Gallimard,
1954.
Translator, *Jules César*, by William Shakespeare.   Arles,
Actes Sud, 1990.

*

Critical Studies: "The Medium Is Not the Message: Myth in
Vinaver's *Iphigénie Hôtel*" by Judith D. Suther, in *French
Review* (Oxford), 45, 1972; "'Entre le mythique et la ques-
tion': Myth in the Theatre of Michel Vinaver" by David
Bradby, in *Myth and Its Making in the French Theatre*,

Cambridge, Cambridge University Press, 1988; "'Des Petits
Ébranlements capillaires . . .': The Art of Michel Vinaver" by
Rosette Lamont, in *Modern Drama* (Toronto), September
1988.

*   *   *

Michel Vinaver, one of France's leading playwrights, has
been working in theater since 1955. He has written more than
20 original plays and adaptations, as well as a number of critical
articles, and in 1983 was appointed to chair the drama
committee of the Centre National des Lettres, which published
a perceptive report on the state of the playwright in the French
theater industry. In 1986, his ardent and innovative work
earned him the Ibsen prize; his play *Les Voisins* (The
Neighbors), written in 1984, won the Kleist prize for the year's
best production, and his collected plays were published in two
volumes (noteworthy since it was the first publication of the
complete works of a living dramatist to appear in France for a
decade).

Vinaver was born in Paris in 1927 into a family of Russian
Jewish émigrés, who moved to the "Free Zone" in the South of
France, then to New York during the Nazi Occupation of
France. Returning to Europe, he translated T. S. Eliot's *The
Waste Land* into French and wrote two novels, *Lataume, ou,
La Vie quotidienne* (Lataume, or, Everyday Life) and
L'Objecteur (The Objector). As an author, Michel Grinberg
took his mother's name and became Michel Vinaver. Although *L'Objecteur* won the Fénéon prize in 1951, Vinaver
feels that his style of writing in dialogues is better suited to
theater. Inspired by Eliot's *The Waste Land*, the counterpoint
of music, the multi-layering of the painter Jean Dubuffet, and
the cubist multiple viewpoint, Vinaver's plays intertwine and
juxtapose independent motifs drawn from contemporary
French economics and politics.

Les Coréens (The Koreans) contrasts the daily life of
peasants in a South Korean village with the reactions to war of
a platoon of ordinary French soldiers from the United Nations'
expeditionary forces active in Korea. *Les Huissiers* (The
Ushers) and *Iphigénie Hôtel* (Hotel Iphigenia) center on the
Algerian war, and underline Vinaver's commitment to theater
that makes connections between the politics of individual
concerns and the wider context of national and international
politics.

His later plays, which focus on a spectrum of socio-political
issues and give vivid representations of capitalism, recreate
some of the economic changes he witnessed in his career as an
executive in a multinational company. *Par-dessus bord* (Overboard), a monster play with 50 characters and 29 sets, and
lasting from four to nine hours, gives an inside look at the
mechanisms of capitalist consumer society through the confrontation of two toilet-paper manufacturing companies: a
dynamic large-scale American firm and a traditional French
family business. The large cast and numerous sets caused
problems for Roger Planchon, the director, and Vinaver's next
play, *La Demande d'emploi* (*Situation Vacant*) continues the
focus of *Par-dessus bord* in a more concise and practical way.
Les Travaux et les jours (*A Smile on the End of the Line*; also
produced as *Blending In*), *À la Renverse* (Backwards), and
L'Ordinaire (The Ordinary) pursue the theme of capitalist
growth, highlighting a pivotal change in the business world. In
these later plays monopolistic, multinational administration
gradually replaces astute marketing campaigns of competitive
capitalism. The changes give capitalism a much broader base,
but the drive to dominate the world market alienates those in
charge of the companies from their employees, and management's confidence withers.

Vinaver's precise portrait of day-to-day life in the corporate or domestic world is instantly recognizable. However, drama which encompasses the contours of daily routine can create a reality that an audience might prefer to shut out. During a debate following a performance of *Les Travaux et les jours*, a play centered around the constantly ringing telephones and fragmented conversations of five workers in the After-Sales Service Department of Cosson, a coffee-grinder manufacturing company in the process of being bought out by a European competitor, a member of the audience wondered why the audience should want to spend its evening watching its work-day routine.

Vinaver tries to avoid the banality of everyday life through a montage of fragmentary, ambiguous elements, which generate meaning through ironic collisions and reverberations. In his socio-political canvas, Vinaver dramatizes the realities of French bourgeois democracy adapting to vigorous American business methods. He reveals neither a triumphant free enterprise *à la* Milton Friedman, nor a deprived, exploited proletariat in a struggle against capitalist bosses. Caught in the economy's web, the characters forge their links with the world not through divine or social sanctions but through the economy.

In *Dissident, il va sans dire* (Dissident, It Goes Without Saying) and *Nina, c'est autre chose* (Nina, That's Something Else), Vinaver invites us to consider the extension of marketplace values into the home, as well as the political implications of family conflicts. Amid seemingly banal household activities and mundane dialogue, the plays give political insights into our lives and times.

Portrait d'une femme (*Portrait of a Woman*), on the other hand, is the only Vinaver play set in the past. It is closely based on newspaper accounts of the 1951 case of a medical student who murdered her lover. Constructed with courtroom evidence and flashbacks, Vinaver's play reminds us that the politics of the judicial system revolve around the capacity to depict.

Vinaver's montage technique interrupts the smooth flow of narrative by the juxtaposition of illogical and discontinuous dialogue, and dividing plays into *morceaux* (bits) rather than scenes. Vinaver creates a social canvas made up of ordinary, almost anonymous characters who do not stand out individually. The resultant group voice makes a political statement by giving a critical picture of the petty bourgeoisie and working class lost in a stifling, arid, enclosed world. If his technique puts him on the cutting edge of French theater, however, in truth he straddles a line between "avant-garde" and the theatrical canon. He has earned the title of the "French Chekhov," and is well versed in theatrical tradition; he has a long-standing interest in Greek theater, and has translated Elizabethan and early 20th-century Russian dramatic works. Greek mythology and theater technique imbue much of his work; moreover, lately Vinaver has moved towards the French canon by writing two *comédies* and an *impromptu*.

With an ironic wink at Molière's *L'Impromptu de Versailles* (The Rehearsal at Versailles, 1663), Vinaver's *impromptu*, *Le Dernier Sursaut* (The Latest Surprise) lampoons protests in France at Martin Scorcese's film *The Last Temptation of Christ*. Vinaver's *comédies* also have Molièresque touches. Like Molière's *L'Avare*, *Les Voisins* (The Neighbors) plunges us into the daily concerns of a bourgeois household where all activities and thoughts are closely linked with finances, and parents seek to maintain property and family dynasty by marrying their children to prosperous bourgeois.

The brilliance of *Les Voisins* lies in the subversion of the comedic genre. Similarly, *L'Émission de télévision* (The Television Program) stages a critique of television in an ironic pastiche of television techniques. Vinaver pays particular attention to the way "human interest" programs present distressing material in a demobilizing fashion. By contrast, Vinaver's parody of T.V. technique provokes. His open-ended montage, combining a parody of the detective story genre, Molièresque situations, T.V. show format, and the cruelties of daily life, creates a striking, funny, and poignant drama in which Vinaver dismantles the conventional representations of social reality and undermines any listless acceptance of *télé-réalité*.

Into his social canvases of the political and economic system, Vinaver weaves intimate depictions of individuals battling rejection by the system and fighting for social integration; he endeavors to explode restrictive monolithic portrayals in favor of diverse representations of the individual and collective forces at work in society.

—Kevin Elstob

VOINOVICH, Vladimir (Nikolaevich). Russian. Born in Dushanbe, Tadzhikistan, 26 September 1932. Educated at Moscow Pedagogical Institute, 1957–59. Served in the Soviet Army, 1951–55. Married 1) Valentina in 1957, one daughter and one son; 2) Irina Braude in 1965, one daughter. Worked as a herdsman, factory hand, locksmith, construction and railroad worker, carpenter, aircraft mechanic, and director of radio programmes. Since 1956 freelance writer in Moscow: expelled from Union of Soviet Writers, 1974; went to the West, 1980, and deprived of Soviet citizenship, 1981; taught Russian literature, Princeton University, New Jersey, 1982–83; Soviet citizenship restored, 1990. Member, Bavarian Academy of Fine Arts, Serbian Academy of Sciences and Arts, and honorary member, Mark Twain Society. Agent: Georges Borchardt, 136 East 57th Street, New York, New York 10022, U.S.A. Address: Hans-Carossastrasse 5, 8035 Stokdorf, Germany; and Astrakhanskii Pereklok 10/36, Kv. 62, Moscow, Russia.

PUBLICATIONS

Fiction

My zdes' zhivem [We Live Here].   Published in *Novyi mir* (Moscow), 1, 1961; Moscow, Sovetskii pisatel', 1963.
Khochu byt' chestnym: povesti [I Want to Be Honest].   Published in *Novyi mir* (Moscow), 2, 1963; Moscow, Moskovskii rabochii, 1989.
Dva tovarishcha [Two Comrades].   Published in *Novyi mir* (Moscow), 1, 1967.
Zhizn' neobychnye prikliucheniia soldata Ivana Chonkina.   Part 1 published in *Grani* (Frankfurt), 72, 1969; parts 1 and 2 published Paris, YMCA Press, 1975; as *The Life and Extraordinary Adventures of Private Ivan Chonkin*, New York, Farrar Straus, and London, Cape, 1977.
Stepen' doveriia [A Degree of Trust].   Moscow, Politizdat, 1972.
Povesti [Novellas].   Moscow, Sovetskii pisatel', 1972.
Putem vzaimnoi perepiski.   In *Grani* (Frankfurt), 87–88, 1973; Paris, YMCA Press, 1979; as *In Plain Russian*, London, Cape, 1980.

Pretendent na prestol: novye prikliucheniia soldata Ivana Chonkina. Paris, YMCA Press, 1979; as *Pretender to the Throne: The Further Adventures of Private Ivan Chonkin,* New York, Farrar Straus, and London, Cape, 1981.
Moskva 2042. Ann Arbor, Michigan, Ardis, 1987; as *Moscow 2042,* San Diego, Harcourt Brace, 1987; London, Cape, 1988.
Shapka. London, Overseas Publications Interchange, 1988; as *The Fur Hat,* San Diego, Harcourt Brace, 1989; London, Cape, 1990.

Plays

Fiktivnii brak [Fictitious Wedding].   Published in *Vremia i my* (Jerusalem), 72, 1983.
Tribunal: sudebnaia komediia v trekh deistviiakh. London, Overseas Publications Interchange, 1985.

Other

Proisshastvie v 'Metropole' [Incident in the Metropol].   Published in *Kontinent* (Paris), 5, 1975.
Ivankiada: ili rasskaz o vselenii pisatelia Voinovicha v novuiu kvartiru. Ann Arbor, Michigan, Ardis, 1976; as *The Ivankiad: The Tale of the Writer Voinovich's Installation in His New Apartment,* New York, Farrar Straus, 1977; London, Cape, 1978.
Antisovetskii sovetskii soiuz. Ann Arbor, Michigan, Ardis, 1985; as *The Anti-Soviet Soviet Union,* San Diego, Harcourt Brace, 1986.
Nulevoe reshenie [Zero Decision] (essays).   Moscow, Pravda, 1990.

*

Critical Studies: "Vladimir Voinovich and the Comedy of Innocence" by Robert Porter, in *Forum for Modern Language Studies* (St. Andrews, Scotland), April 1980; "Vladimir Voinovich's *Pretender to the Throne*" by John B. Dunlop, in *Literature and American Critics: In Honor of Deming B. Brown,* edited by Kenneth N. Bostrom, Ann Arbor, University of Michigan, 1984.

*   *   *

Vladimir Voinovich was highly regarded in the 1960s for stories such as "Knochu byt' chestnym" ("I Want to Be Honest") and "Dva tovarishcha" ("Two Comrades"), which showed a high degree of frankness regarding urban life, the pressures on the individual to conform, and the unorthodox values of some unsophisticated characters. To a degree his early work can be classified as belonging to the "young prose" school, whose chief exponent was Vasilii Aksenov (*q.v.*). Rebelliousness and individualism are portrayed in a racy style, and in the 1960s it was these qualities which marked these authors out from the traditional practitioners of Socialist Realism and the rising school of "village prose" writers. Wit, perception, and vigorous moral awareness are the hallmarks of Voinovich's work. Occasional lighthearted verse, the lyrics to a hugely popular song about Soviet astronauts (the author claims that it took him just 14 minutes to write it), an historical novel about Vera Figner, all illustrate Voinovich's wide range and show him to be at once entertaining and serious. Highly irreverent satire is his forte, and his literary lineage might include Mikhail Zoshchenko and I'lf and Petyrov from the Soviet period. In his most mature work the legacy of Gogol is clearly in evidence. Many commentators have seized on

Jaroslav Hašek's *The Good Soldier Švejk* as a starting point for any discussion of Voinovich's masterpiece *Zhizn'i neobychnye prikliucheniia soldata Ivana Chonkina* (*The Life and Extraordinary Adventures of Private Ivan Chonkin*).

Chonkin's adventures remain to date unfinished, but the book — in four parts to date, with a fifth long promised — has already achieved a commendable place in Russian literature. Utterly at variance with the mainstream of Soviet literature on World War II, this work, which owes something to the picaresque novel, shows Russia to be more at war with herself than with the Germans. Hitler and Stalin are strikingly similar and the Soviet Union seems to be run entirely by self-deluding incompetents, duped by ideology, pseudo-science, and myopic self-interest. Chonkin, the village simpleton and willy-nilly Red-Army-man, manages to confound all the institutions he comes into contact with by his uncomprehending innocence. The Ivan-the-Fool of Russian folk stories is at the back of Private Chonkin, who, though constantly falling foul of his superiors, can on occasion be a fine soldier, if left to his own devices, and equally proves to be a good husband, farmer, or embroiderer. His dreams and fantasies provide a valuable counterfoil to the official "real" world. In the time-honoured fashion of comic writers, the author frequently denigrates his own story and his own ability to tell it ("If you think it's not interesting, or boring, or even stupid, then just spit and pretend I haven't told you anything at all."). The subversive nature of the comedy was something that the authorities were emphatically unable to ignore, and the book remained banned in Russia until well into the era of glasnost. In Voinovich's world dreams, daydreams, naïvety, and spontaneity are ultimately the surest path to an authentic and more moral existence. Behind the bawdiness and the fun there is the author's sustained moral commitment — one might detect in the latter parts an increasing anger, for the author was persistently harassed throughout the late 1970s and was finally forced into emigration in 1980. A number of open letters and the autobiographical *Ivankiada* (*The Ivankiad*) (the story of Voinovich's acquisition of a promised apartment despite the attempts by a greedy bigwig to have it for himself) document with wit and irony the author's confrontations with the authorities.

Voinovich's military service in the immediate post-war years seems to have been most formative as far as creative writing is concerned — some of his experiences are recounted in a collection called *Putem vzaimnoi perepiski* (*In Plain Russian*). "By Means of Mutual Correspondence" is a delightful but somewhat chilling account of a penpal romance going awfully wrong once the less-than-candid partners come face to face. "A Circle of Friends" gives another example of the author's ability to illustrate the yawning gaps between appearances and reality. Stalin and his cronies burn the midnight oil in the Kremlin, arguing over a crossword, as Hitler launches operation Barbarossa. Stalin has a dummy of himself placed in the one lit Kremlin window — to further the myth of his working while the people sleep.

In emigration Voinovich's main works have been *Antisovetskii sovetskii soiuz* (*The Anti-Soviet Soviet Union*) (a collection of feuilletons and other pieces), and the full-length novel *Moskva 2042* (*Moscow 2042*), which satirises Western affluence, political extremists of all persuasions, certain Russian emigrés (one in particular bears a strong resemblance to Aleksandr Solzhenitsyn [*q.v.*]), and even the hero's own anomalous position as a dissident writer, who in emigration cannot altogether master German, and who is financed by all sorts of clandestine organisations to go on a time-travel excursion. The story is only superficially science fiction, and the hero, on arriving in the Moscow of the future from the present-day (1982) West, is inadvertently commenting on a Soviet Union and an international scene that is not so unfamiliar. Perhaps one of the major preoccupations of this novel is the question of one's own identity and status. Seasoned by the vagaries of official grace in real life and of public opinion, Voinovich is practising a form of self-defence in *Moscow 2042*. Flattery is perceived by the hero for the comforting lie that it is. He has a dream in which Communism has at last been achieved, there is an abundance of material and spiritual wealth, and there is perfect happiness. All this contrasts with the sordid and run-down Moscow of 2042, which boasts, among other things, self-service brothels. Banality and philistinism are rife in the West, and it would seem that the only constant the author can cling to is literature itself. A splendid short novel entitled *Shapka* (*The Fur Hat*) similarly raises questions of an author's worth.

At his best, Voinovich is much more than a satirist, for he perceives the essential absurdity of man, who is always a prey to vanity or delusion. The modesty, humour, and common sense on display in Voinovich's more publicistic works are also to be found in his fiction, and indeed, they add up to a philosophy — if one can pause for reflection between the laughs.

—Robert Porter

VOLPONI, Paolo. Italian. Born in Urbino, 6 February 1924. Educated at schools in Urbino; University of Urbino, 1943–47, law degree. Social services consultant, Calabria and Sicily, 1950–53, and Rome, 1953–55; social services consultant, 1956–71, and director of business reports, 1966–71, Olivetti, Ivrea; worked for FIAT, 1972–76; elected Senator, Independent Committee, 1983, re-elected 1987; currently member of Foreign Affairs and Emigration Committee in the Senate; member of Parliamentary Supervisory Committee for Radio-Television Services. Associated with *Officina* magazine, 1950s. Recipient: Viareggio prize, for poetry, 1960, for fiction, 1975; Strega prize, 1965. Address: Piazza Madama 1, 00186 Rome, Italy.

PUBLICATIONS

Fiction

Memoriale. Milan, Garzanti, 1962; as *My Troubles Began*, New York, Grossman, 1964; as *The Memorandum*, London, Calder and Boyars, 1967.
La macchina mondiale. Milan, Garzanti, 1965; as *The Worldwide Machine*, New York, Grossman, 1967; London, Calder and Boyars, 1969.
Corporale. Turin, Einaudi, 1974.
Il sipario ducale. Milan, Garzanti, 1975.
Il pianeta irritabile. Turin, Einaudi, 1978.
Il lanciatore del giavellotto. Turin, Einaudi, 1981.
Le mosche del capitale. Turin, Einaudi, 1989.

Verse

Il ramarro. Urbino, Istituto d'Arte, 1948.
L'antica moneta. Florence, Vallecchi, 1955.
Le porte dell'Appennino. Milan, Feltrinelli, 1960.
Poesie e poemetti 1946–66, edited by Gualtiero De Santi. Turin, Einaudi, 1980.

(Selection) in English, in *The New Italian Poetry*, edited and translated by Lawrence R. Smith. Berkeley, University of California Press, 1981.
Con testo a fronte: poesie e poemetti 1967–1985. Turin, Einaudi, 1986.

Other

Il principio umano della pittura-scienza. Milan, Rizzoli, 1968.
Pier Paolo Pasolini nel dibattito culturale contemporaneo, with others. Pavia, Amministrazione Provinciale di Pavia, 1977.
Scrittori di "Attraverso l'Italia," 1930/1972. Milan, Touring Club Italiano, 1984.
Archivi privati e ricerca storica: Perugia, Palazzo Donini, 19 dicembre 1985, with Dante Magnini and Arnaldo D'Addario. Perugia, Grafica Perugia, 1986.

*

Critical Studies: "The Narrator-Protagonist and the Divided Self in Paolo Volponi's *Corporale*" by Rocco Capozzi, in *Forum Italicum*, 10, 1976; "Interview with Paolo Volponi," in *Italian Quarterly* (New Brunswick, New Jersey), 25, 1984, and "The Quest for Self-Fulfillment in Paolo Volponi's Fiction," in *Canadian Journal of Italian Studies* (Hamilton, Ontario), 9(33), 1986, both by Peter N. Pedroni; "The Play of Literary Self-Consciousness in Paolo Volponi's Fiction: Violence and the Power of the Symbol" by Gregory L. Lucente, in *World Literature Today* (Norman, Oklahoma), 61(1), 1987.

*   *   *

In Paolo Volponi's development as a writer two factors are of particular interest: his association, from 1956 to 1971, with the firm Olivetti as a social services consultant; and his involvement, in the late 1950s, with *Officina*, an avant-garde review which advocated a close relationship between literature and the social sciences, consistent with Marxist thought mediated and brought into the context of Italian culture through the writings of Antonio Gramsci. Both experiences are discernible in Volponi's early narrative, which draws attention to the changes in the fabric of Italian society stemming from the rapid industrial expansion of the early 1960s — the years of the "economic miracle."

Significant, in this respect, are the novels *Memoriale* (*My Troubles Began* or *The Memorandum*) and *La macchina mondiale* (*The Worldwide Machine*) in which the impetus of industrialization is viewed in problematic terms, essentially as a dehumanizing force tied to the advances of neo-capitalism. Yet these works can hardly be characterized as a simplistic condemnation of technology. Volponi's heightened realism and his projection of contemporary life through the vicissitudes of eccentric, neurotic characters essentially unrepresentative of the working class point chiefly, and in a quasi-Orwellian fashion, to the abuses and potential consequences of misguided scientific progress. It is more accurate to say that Volponi's early fiction suggests a reformist view of technology, implicit in his concern for an equilibrium between human needs (freedom, individuality, creativity) and the rigid, impersonal make-up of the industrial system.

The social content of Volponi's work unfolds in unison with lucid character studies of disoriented individuals afflicted with various forms of mental disorder. Their opposition to the regimented structure of factory life gives rise to extreme reactions: defeatist sentiments leading to withdrawal and suicide in *The Memorandum*; an anthropocentric approach to technology which, in *The Worldwide Machine*, is translated into utopian designs for the betterment of humanity. This sociological perspective plays a lesser role in *Corporale* (Corporeal) where the main focus is on introspective analysis and the narrative process that generates it. The condition of a schizoid character wrestling with deep anxieties is examined within a structural context in which the act of writing, through a skillful progression from first- to third-person narrative, tests its own resources and limitations as it subjects the divided self of the protagonist to intense psychoanalytical scrutiny.

The prospect of a nuclear cataclysm, foreshadowed in *Il sipario ducale* (The Ducal Curtain), takes on the semblance of a factual occurrence in *Il pianeta irritabile* (The Irritable Planet). The work, an allegorical fable with foreboding allusions to the present, is set in 2293 in the aftermath of a nuclear conflagration which has destroyed virtually all forms of life on earth. Moving against the background of a ravaged landscape, four survivors — a gorilla, an elephant, a goose, and a circus midget — undertake the difficult journey toward a new land blessed with "harmonious living."

Il lanciatore del giavellotto (The Javelin Thrower) marks a return to the familiar grounds of socially deviant behavior and psychological analysis, placed in evidence here by the story of an adolescent whose feelings of sexual inadequacy and the progressive manifestation of a tormenting Oedipus complex pave the way for a tragic ending. While the frame of Volponi's fiction rests on the constants of social consciousness and introspection, the constituent structures point to consistent renewal and diversity. Thus the work in question, departing from the problematic of industrial life, examines with discerning ability the experience of Fascism in a provincial town. What is reiterated with systematic and disturbing frequency in Volponi's novels is the pathological condition of his characters — a leitmotif through which the metaphor of disease asserts its value as the emblematic sign of our time.

A fresh disenchantment with industrialization is apparent in *Le mosche del capitale* (The Money Flies) in which Volponi reiterates the failures of capitalism as a social and economic system. However, what distinguishes this from earlier novels is the writer's despairing pessimism which offers little hope that technology and industry can be made to fulfill human needs. The protagonist, a businessman who reflects much of Volponi's professional background, grows bitter and disillusioned as he witnesses firsthand one-dimensional striving for capital acquisition and essential disregard for social concerns.

Volponi's verse, collected in the volume *Poesie e poemetti 1946–66*, draws its strength from a process of renewal and intellectual maturity attested by a fluid dialectical interaction between the poetic persona and his native countryside. Youthful impressionism, structured with sensual and idyllic images of rural living, gives way in the course of time to the projection of an alienated, pensive self drawn time and again to the privileged place of his birth to examine the contingencies of life in the light of immanent, ancestral forms of a primitive culture.

The second volume, *Con testo a fronte: poesie e poemetti 1967–1985* (Parallel Text), harbors structural forms ideologically attuned to Volponi's novels but deemed unsuited to their internal design. Thus many of the poems issue from a sociological matrix and dwell on the dehumanizing effects of industrialization. Religious symbols bear as their ideological

sign the projection of a humane, Christian socialism mindful of Ignazio Silone.

—Augustus Pallotta

VON SCHOULTZ, Solveig. *See* **SCHOULTZ, Solveig von.**

VOZNESENSKII, Andrei (Andreevich). Also Andrei Voznesensky, Andrej Voznesenskij. Russian. Born in Moscow, 12 May 1933. Educated at the Institute of Architecture, Moscow, graduated 1957. Married Zoia Boguslavskaia in 1965; one son. Writer and painter. Member of the board, Union of Soviet Writers, since 1967; chair, Commission on the Legacy of Pasternak, 1987; vice president, Soviet PEN, since 1989. Recipient: International award for distinguished achievement in poetry, 1978; State prize, 1978; State prize for poetry, 1979; Order of the Red Banner of Labour. Member, American Academy, 1972, Bavarian Academy of Fine Arts, and French Academy Mérime. Address: Kotelnicheskaia nab. 1/15, Korp. B, Apt. 62, 109240 Moscow, Russia.

PUBLICATIONS

Verse

Mozaika [Mosaic].   Vladimir, Knizhnoe izdatel'stvo, 1960.
Parabola.   Moscow, Sovetskii pisatel', 1960.
Pishetsia kak liubitsia [I Write as I Love] (in Russian and Italian).   Milan, Feltrinelli, 1962.
40 liricheskikh otstuplenii iz poemy "Treugol'naia grusha" [40 Lyrical Digressions from the Poem "The Triangular Pear"].   Moscow, Sovetskii pisatel', 1962.
Menia pugaiut formalizmom [They Frighten Me with Formalism].   London, Flegon Press, 1963.
Selected Poems, translated by Anselm Hollo.   New York, Grove Press, 1964.
Antimiry.   Moscow, Molodaia gvardiia, 1964; as *Antiworlds*, New York, Basic Books, 1966; augmented edition, as *Antiworlds and the Fifth Ace*, New York, Doubleday, 1967.
Selected Poems, translated by Herbert Marshall.   New York, Hill and Wang, and London, Methuen, 1966.
Akhillesovo serdtse [An Achilles Heart].   Moscow, Khudozhestvennaia literatura, 1966.
Moi liubovnyi dnevik [My Diary of Love].   London, Flegon Press, 1966.
Stikhi [Poems].   Moscow, Khudozhestvennaia literatura, 1967.
Rossiia — rodina moia [Russia Is My Native Land].   1967.
Svetovye gody [Light Years].   Riga, Liesma, 1968.
Ten' zvuka [The Shadow of Sound].   Moscow, Molodaia gvardiia, 1970.
Vzgliad [Look].   Moscow, Sovetskii pisatel', 1972.
Dogalypse.   San Francisco, City Lights, 1972.
Little Woods: Recent Poems.   Melbourne, Sun, 1972.

Vypusti ptitsu! [Release the Bird!]. Moscow, Molodaia gvardiia, 1974.

Integral ot sireni [Integral from Lilac]. Tallin, Eesti raamat, 1974.

Dubovyi list violonchel'nyi [Violoncello Oak Leaf]. Moscow, Khudozhestvennaia literatura, 1975.

Vitrazhnykh del master [Maker of Stained-Glass Windows]. Moscow, Molodaia gvardiia, 1976.

Nostalgia for the Present. New York, Doubleday, 1978; Oxford, Oxford University Press, 1980.

Izbrannaia lirika [Selected Lyrics]. Moscow, Detskaia literatura, 1979.

Soblazn' [Temptation]. Moscow, Sovetskii pisatel', 1979.

Nebom edinym [To United Heaven]. Minsk, Mastatsannaia literatura, 1980.

Bezotchotnoye [Unaccountable]. Moscow, Sovetskii pisatel', 1981.

Izbrannoe (collection). Alma-Ata, Zhazushy, 1981.

Sobranie sochinenii [Collected Works]. Moscow, Khudozhestvennaia literatura, 3 vols., 1983–84.

Stikhotvoreniia. Moscow, Khudozhestvennaia literatura, 2 vols., 1983–84.

Proraby dukha [Clerks of Works to the Spirit]. Moscow, Sovetskii pisatel', 1984.

Iverskii svet [Iberian Light]. 1984.

An Arrow in the Wall: Selected Poetry and Prose, edited by F. D. Reeve and William Jay Smith. New York, Holt, and London, Secker and Warburg, 1987.

Rov [The Ditch]. Moscow, Sovetskii pisatel', 1987.

Tri stikhotvoreniia [Three Poems]. Published in *Znamia* (Moscow), 1, 1989.

Aksioma samonska [Axiom]. Moscow, SP "IKRA," 1990.

On the Edge: Poems and Essays from Russia, translated by Richard McKane. London, Weidenfeld and Nicolson, 1991.

Rossiia [Russia]. Moscow, n.p., 1991.

Stikhotvoreniia [Poems]. Moscow, Molodaia gvardiia, 1991.

Plays

Save Your Faces (produced Moscow, 1971–72).

Television Play: *Juno and Avos*, music by Alexei Rybnikov, translated by Adrian Mitchell, 1983.

Fiction

Povest pod parusami. 1971; as *Story Under Full Sail*, New York, Doubleday, 1974.

Petrovo Gnezdo. Leningrad, Khudozhestvennaia literatura, 1990.

Other

Pis'mo v redaktsii gazetu "Pravda" [A Letter to the Editor of the Newspaper "Pravda"]. Published in *Grani* (Frankfurt), 66, 1967.

Editor, *Poesiia Evropy* [Poetry of Europe]. Moscow, Khudozhestvennaia literatura, 3 vols., 1978–79.

*

Critical Studies: "*Antiworlds* by Andrei Voznesensky on the Stage of the Moscow Theatre" by Tatiana Skianczenko, in *Drama & Theatre*, 7, 1969; "A Look Around: The Poetry of Andrey Voznesensky" by W. G. Jones, in *Major Soviet Writers*, edited by E. J. Brown, London, Oxford University Press, 1973; "The Verse of Andrej Voznesenskij as an Example of Present-Day Russian Versification" by James Bailey, in *Slavic and East European Journal* (Minneapolis), 17, 1974; "Voznesensky's Dystopia" by J. A. Harvie, in *New Zealand Slavonic Journal* (Wellington), 2, 1974; "The Functions of Tonality and Grammar in a Voznesenkii Poem" by Dennis Ward, in *International Journal of Slavic Linguistics and Poetics*, 17, 1974; "Andrey Voznesensky: Between Pasternak and Mayakovsky" by R. D. B. Thomson, in *Slavonic and East European Review* (London), 54, 1976; "On the Art of Linguistic Opportunism" by Dennis Mickiewicz, in *Russian Literature*, 8, 1980; "Refresh My Tongue, Contemporary Muse" by Valeri Dementyev, in *Soviet Literature* (Brooklyn, New York), 5[422], 1983; "Oliver Friggieri Talks to Andrej Voznesenskij" (interview), in *Skylark* (India), 64, 1988; "Finding the Proper Equivalent: Translating the Poetry of Andrei Voznesensky" by William Jay Smith, in *Translating Poetry: The Double Labyrinth*, edited by Daniel Weissbort, Iowa City, University of Iowa Press, 1989.

*   *   *

Andrei Voznesenskii will always be associated in the minds of many with his almost exact contemporary, Evgenii Evtushenko (*q.v.*). Both men came to fame as leading representatives of the post-Stalin "Thaw" generation of young poets. Both have travelled widely, on one occasion visiting the United States together in 1960. They share a conviction that poetry is for the ear rather than the eye and their public renditions of their poetry are famous. Both, despite brushes with the Soviet literary bureaucracy, continued to publish, and even flourished, during the Brezhnev era. Because of this, both are viewed with some suspicion by younger, more radical writers, especially in the post-Communist era.

It is Voznesenskii's early poetry which is, and will probably remain, his best-known. The much anthologised and much performed "Goya" exemplifies many features of Voznesenskii's poetry. Extensive alliteration and assonance dominate the poem to such an extent that its semantic meaning — the artist's attitude to human suffering — is in danger of being submerged.

The use of a historical figure to illustrate a contemporary truth has always been a feature of Voznesenskii's poetry. Nowhere is this better illustrated than in the two dedications to the poem "Craftsmen," where Michelangelo, Dante, and Barma, the architect of St. Basil's cathedral, are used to illustrate the theme of the artist's perennial struggle against tyranny. That Voznesenskii should personify the artist by examples from the world not only of poetry but also of sculpture and architecture is also typical. He has, of course, consistently championed poetry, particularly the work of Robert Lowell (whom he has translated), T. S. Eliot, and Boris Pasternak, and on the pages of the journal *Ogonek* he has brought poets repressed by Stalin, such as Iurii Kublanovskii, to the notice of Russian readers. Among painters, Marc Chagall has had a decisive influence on Voznesenskii (see "Chagall's Cornflowers"), as has American pop art, particularly that of Robert Rauschenberg. Voznesenskii has also found inspiration in the avant-garde music of John Cage and in the pioneering theatrical work of Moscow's Taganka Theatre.

The bulk of Voznesenskii's work consists of short poems, but, in addition to the occasional excursion into prose, such as the portentous and obscure "O," he has produced a number of important *poemy* or narrative poems. Most important among these are "Oza," "Ice-69," "Perchance," "Andrei Polisadov," and "The Ditch." In these works Voznesenskii mixes syllaboaccentual verse, free verse, prose, dialogue, and historical document and uses registers as diverse as Old Church Slavonic, 18th-century poetic, modern technological, and contemporary popular music. The thematic content of these poems is just as diverse: the pollution of the environment ("Ice-69"), love and death ("Perchance"), the poet's own ancestry ("Andrei Polisadov"), and the atrocities of war ("The Ditch").

The importance of these narrative poems can be judged from the fact that there is strong evidence to suggest that the book *Ten' zvuka* (The Shadow of Sound), which marked the revival of Voznesenskii's fortunes, was constructed from sections of "Ice-69" detached from the journal version of the poem. *Vzgliad* (Look), too, is similarly based on a narrative poem and, like *Ten' zvuka*, is conceived as an integrated whole. The key to *Vzgliad* is the narrative poem "Perchance," the name of a ship which, in Russian (*Avos*), punningly alludes to Voznesenskii himself. The ostensible hero is Nikolai Rezanov, a Russian explorer who, in 1806, married the daughter of the governor of Spanish California. The underlying theme of the poem, which was turned into a successful, if derivative, rock opera, is the isolation of the individual in a hostile world, subjected to constant scrutiny, looks, stares. The poem stresses the difficulty of communication with other human beings and the need for the artist to look within himself and at the world around him in order to create. This idea is most clearly expressed in a prose section of *Vzgliad* entitled "Oh Vancouver!":

Have you ever seen people taking photographs with a mirror? The man puts the camera to his stomach or to his chest and looks into it, his head bowed. From the side it seems as if the man is examining himself, as if he is engrossed in the study of his own navel. But no! The process of recording reality is under way.

The poet is just such a mirror: the world, filtered through his innermost being, takes on a different aspect.

Hence, creative work is looking into oneself, studying one's inner world. Always through an intermediary. Through one's own personality.

Voznesenskii has had his critics, both in Russia and in the West. His penchant for monosyllabic onomatopeia, particularly in "Ice-69," was brilliantly parodied in the pages of *Literaturnaia gazeta* and his later work has been unfavourably compared with such early poems as "Longjumeau" and "Autumn in Sigulda." R. D. B. Thomson (1976) found the faults of Voznesenskii's early work — superficiality, vulgarity, name-dropping — accentuated in *Ten' zvuka* and *Vzgliad* and hoped that Voznesenskii would establish a mature style. Glasnost has given him that opportunity and *Rov* (The Ditch) has become one of the key documents of the Gorbachev era. This account of the desecration of a mass grave combines thematic power and linguistic restraint in a manner which confirms Voznesenskii's position at the forefront of Russian literature and justifies Evtushenko's eloquent defence of him against accusations of "foreign-ness": "The poetry of Voznesenskii in no way infringes the traditions of Russian poetry but is a unique development of these traditions in new conditions."

—Michael Pursglove

————

VOZNESENSKY, Andrei. *See* **VOZNESENSKII, Andrei.**

————

W

WALSER, Martin. German. Born in Wasserburg, 24 March 1927. Educated at Gymnasium, Lindau, 1938–44; Philosophisch-Theologische Hochschule, Regensburg, 1946–48; University of Tübingen, 1948–51, Ph.D. 1951. Served in the Deutsche Wehrmacht, 1944–45. Married Käthe Jehle in 1950; four daughters. Radio and television director Süddeutscher Rundfunk, Stuttgart, 1949–57; Visiting Professor or Fellow, Middlebury College, Vermont, and University of Texas, Austin, 1973, Warwick University, Coventry, 1975, University of West Virginia, Morgantown, 1976, Dartmouth College, Hanover, New Hampshire, 1979, Princeton University, New Jersey, 1981, and University of California, Berkeley, 1983. Founder, with Rolf Hochhuth (q.v.), Meersburg Summer theatre festival. Recipient: Gruppe 47 prize, 1955; Hesse prize, 1957; Hauptmann prize, 1962; Schiller prize, 1965; Bodensee prize, 1967; Schiller prize, 1980; Heine Medal, 1981; Büchner prize, 1981; Grand Federal Cross of Merit, 1987; Bayerischer Academy of Fine Arts grand literature prize, 1990. Honorary doctorate: University of Constance, 1983. Agent: Suhrkamp Verlag, Postfach 101945, 6000 Frankfurt am Main, Germany. Address: Zum Hecht 36, 777 Überlingen 18, Germany.

PUBLICATIONS

Fiction

Ein Flugzeug über dem Haus und andere Geschichten. Frankfurt, Suhrkamp, 1955.
Ehen in Philippsburg. Frankfurt, Suhrkamp, 1957; as *The Gadarene Club*, London, Longman, 1960; as *Marriage in Philippsburg*, New York, New Directions, 1961.
Halbzeit. Frankfurt, Suhrkamp, 1960.
Lügengeschichten. Frankfurt, Suhrkamp, 1964.
Das Einhorn. Frankfurt, Suhrkamp, 1966; as *The Unicorn*, London, Calder and Boyars, 1971.
Fiction. Frankfurt, Suhrkamp, 1970.
Die Gallistl'sche Krankheit. Frankfurt, Suhrkamp, 1972.
Der Sturz. Frankfurt, Suhrkamp, 1973.
Jenseits der Liebe. Frankfurt, Suhrkamp, 1976; as *Beyond All Love*, New York, Riverrun, 1982; London, Calder, 1983.
Ein fliehendes Pferd. Frankfurt, Suhrkamp, 1978; as *Runaway Horse*, New York, Holt Rinehart, and London, Secker and Warburg, 1980.
Seelenarbeit. Frankfurt, Suhrkamp, 1979; as *The Inner Man*, New York, Holt Rinehart, 1985; London, Deutsch, 1986.
Das Schwanenhaus. Frankfurt, Suhrkamp, 1980; as *The Swan Villa*, New York, Holt Rinehart, 1982; London, Secker and Warburg, 1983.
Selected Stories. Manchester, Carcanet Press, 1982.
Brief an Lord Liszt. Frankfurt, Suhrkamp, 1982; as *Letter to Lord Liszt*, New York, Holt Rinehart, 1985.
Gesammelte Geschichten. Frankfurt, Suhrkamp, 1983.
Brandung. Frankfurt, Suhrkamp, 1985; as *Breakers*, New York, Holt Rinehart, and London, Deutsch, 1987.

Dorle und Wolf. Frankfurt, Suhrkamp, 1987; as *No Man's Land*, New York, Holt Rinehart, 1989.
Jagd. Frankfurt, Suhrkamp, 1988.
Armer Nanosh, with Asta Scheib. Frankfurt, Fischer, 1989.
Die Verteidigung der Kindheit. Frankfurt, Suhrkamp, 1991.

Plays

Ein grenzenloser Nachmittag, in *Hörspielbuch 1955.* Frankfurt, Europäischer Verlag-sanstalt, 1955.
Der Abstecher (produced Munich, 1961). Frankfurt, Suhrkamp, 1961; as *The Detour* (produced Edinburgh 1964; London, 1967), with *The Rabbit Race*, London, Calder, 1963.
Eiche und Angora: Eine deutsche Chronik (produced Berlin, 1962). Frankfurt, Suhrkamp, 1962; as *The Rabbit Race* (produced Edinburgh, 1963), with *The Detour*, London, Calder, 1963.
Überlebensgross Herr Krott: Requiem für einen Unsterblichen (produced Stuttgart, 1963). Frankfurt, Suhrkamp, 1964.
Der Schwarze Schwan (produced Stuttgart, 1964). Frankfurt, Suhrkamp, 1964.
Die Zimmerschlacht (produced Munich, 1967). Frankfurt, Suhrkamp, 1967; as *Home Front* (produced London, 1971), in *The Contemporary German Theatre*, New York, Avon, 1972.
Wir werden schon noch handeln (as *Der schwarze Flügel*, produced Berlin, 1968). Munich, Hanser, 1968.
Ein Kinderspiel (produced Stuttgart, 1972). Frankfurt, Suhrkamp, 1970.
Aus dem Wortschatz unserer Kämpfe (as *Ein reizender Abend*, produced Luxembourg, 1972). Stierstadt, Eremiten-Presse, 1971.
Gesammelte Stücke. Frankfurt, Suhrkamp, 1971.
Der Menschenfreund, from the play *The Philanthropist* by Christopher Hampton (produced Berlin, 1971). Published in *Theater Heute*, February 1971.
Die Wilden, from the play *Savages* by Christopher Hampton (produced Bochum, 1974). Published in *Theater Heute*, February 1974.
Das Sauspiel: Szenen aus dem 16. Jahrhundert (produced Hamburg, 1975). Frankfurt, Suhrkamp, 1975.
In Goethes Hand: Szenen aus dem 19. Jahrhundert (produced Vienna, 1982). Frankfurt, Suhrkamp, 1982.
Säntis (radio play). Stuttgart, Radius, 1986.
Die Ohrfeige (produced Darmstadt, 1986). Frankfurt, Suhrkamp, 1986.
Stücke. Frankfurt, Suhrkamp, 1987.
Nero läßt grüssen, oder, Selbstportrait des Künstlers als Kaiser: ein Monodram; Alexander und Annette: ein innerer Monolog. Eggingen, Isele, 1989.
Das Gespenst von Gattnau (radio play). Frankfurt, Suhrkamp, 1991.
Hilfe kommt aus Bregenz (radio play). Frankfurt, Suhrkamp, 1991.
Lindauer Pietà (radio play). Frankfurt, Suhrkamp, 1991.

Die Verteidigung von Friedrichshafen (radio play). Frankfurt, Suhrkamp, 1991.
Zorn einer Göttin (radio play). Frankfurt, Suhrkamp, 1991.

Verse

Der Grund zur Freude: 99 Sprüche zur Erbauung des Bewußtseins. Düsseldorf, Eremiten-Presse, 1978.

Other

Lese-Erfahrungen mit Proust. Frankfurt, Suhrkamp, 1960.
Hölderlin auf dem Dachboden. Frankfurt, Suhrkamp, 1960.
Beschreibung einer Form: Versuch über Franz Kafka. Munich, Hanser, 1961.
Mitwirkung bei meinem Ende. Biberach an der Riss, Wege und Gestalten, 1962.
Erfahrungen und leseerfahrungen. Frankfurt, Suhrkamp, 1965.
Theater, Theater: Ein Bilderbuch des Theaters, with Karl Chargesheimer. Velber, Friedrich, 1967.
Heimatkunde. Frankfurt, Suhrkamp, 1968.
Hölderlin zu entsprechen (address). Biberach an der Riss, Thomae, 1970.
Wie und wovon handelt Literatur: Aufsätze und Reden. Frankfurt, Suhrkamp, 1973.
Was zu bezweifeln war: Aufsätze und Reden 1958–1975, edited by Klaus Schuhmann. Berlin, Aufbau, 1976.
We ist ein Schriftsteller? Aufsätze und Reden. Frankfurt, Suhrkamp, 1978.
Heimatlob: Ein Bodensee-Buch, with André Ficus. Friedrichshafen, Gessler, 1978.
Die Würde am Werktag. Frankfurt, Fischer, 1980.
Heines Tränen: Essay. Düsseldorf, Eremiten, 1981.
Selbstbewußtsein und Ironie: Frankfurter Vorlesungen. Frankfurt, Suhrkamp, 1981.
Versuch, ein Gefühl zu verstehen, und andere Versuche. Stuttgart, Reclam, 1982.
Liebeserklärungen. Frankfurt, Suhrkamp, 1983.
Goethes Anziehungskraft. Constance, Universitäts-verlag, 1983.
Variationen eines Würgegriffs: Bericht über Trinidad und Tobago. Stuttgart, Radius, 1985.
Messmers Gedanken. Frankfurt, Suhrkamp, 1985.
Die Amerikareise: Versuch, ein Gefühl zu verstehen, with André Ficus. Ravensburg, Weingarten, 1986.
Geständnis auf Raten. Frankfurt, Suhrkamp, 1986.
Grimmige Märchen, with Ilse Aichinger, edited by Wolfgang Mieder. Frankfurt, Fischer, 1986.
Heilige Brocken: Aufsätze, Prosa, Gedichte. Weingarten, Drumlin, 1986.

Editor, *Die Alternative; oder, Brauchen wir eine neue Regierung?* Reinbek, Rowohlt, 1961.
Editor, *Vorzeichen II: Neun neue deutsche Autoren.* Frankfurt, Suhrkamp, 1963.
Editor, *Er: Prosa*, by Kafka. Frankfurt, Suhrkamp, 1963.
Editor, *Die Würde am Werktag: Literatur der Arbeiter und Angestellten.* Frankfurt, Fischer, 1980.

Translator, with Edgar Selge, *Antigone*, by Sophocles. Frankfurt, Insel, 1989.

*

Bibliography: *Martin Walser: Bibliographie* 1952–1970 by Heinz Saueressig and Thomas Beckermann, Biberach an der Riss, Wege und Gestalten, 1970.

Critical Studies: *Wife and Mistress: Women in Martin Walser's Anselm Kristlein Trilogy* by Kathryn Rooney, Coventry, University of Warwick, 1975; *Martin Walser: The Development as Dramatist 1950–1970*, Bonn, Bouvier, 1978, *Martin Walser*, Munich, Beck, 1980, and "Productive Paradoxes and Parallels in Martin Walser's *Seelenarbeit*," in *German Life and Letters* (London), April 1981, all by Anthony Waine; "Martin Walser: The Nietzsche Connection" by R. Hinton Thomas, in *German Life and Letters* (London), July 1982; "Martin Walser's *Ein fliehendes Pferd* and the Tradition of Repetitive Confession" by Donald P. Haase, in *Selected Proceedings: 32nd Mountain Interstate Foreign Language Conference*, edited by Gregorio C. Martín, Winston-Salem, North Carolina, Wake Forest University, 1984; *Martin Walser: International Perspectives*, edited by Jürgen E. Schlunk and Armand E. Singer, New York, Lang, 1987, and "Fictional Response to Political Circumstance: Martin Walser's *The Rabbit Race*" by Schlunk, in *Text and Presentation*, edited by Karelisa Hartigan, Lanham, Maryland, University Press of America, 1988; "A Literary Collage: Martin Walser's *Brandung*" by Kurt Fickert, in *International Fiction Review* (Fredericton, New Brunswick), Summer 1988.

Martin Walser comments:

Writing is experienced as something inevitable: what I need just comes into my mind. Thus writing is to a large degree involuntary, and this gives the impression of inevitability. This is something which must be said, as otherwise novels can fall under suspicion of having historical/philosophical ambitions.

A novel does not seek to prove anything; its only aim is to narrate around something experienced until the event no longer seems real but appears in a bearable form. This is where comedy comes into play. And everyone does the same in everyday life, even if they do not write it: they relate in the evening the events of the day in order not to have to live, or go to sleep, with them. Everyday life is a struggle and an adventure. The novelist pursues his project of self-awareness or escape entirely unreflectively within the bounds of the adventure novel. This is perhaps even where we originated. Now we narrate existence, love, and death under conditions of dependence, competition, and impotence within a society in which self-determination seems to be possible. The novel reacts to the difference between reality and appearance.

I cannot narrate what has happened to me. This would be to repeat the unbearable. But I have to give an answer to what has happened to me. It is for this reason that I write.

*   *   *

Short-story writer, radio playwright, dramatist, novelist, literary critic, essayist, and theorist — Martin Walser's roles since he first began writing in the late 1940s have been manifold. Even within an individual genre he eschews writing to a standard formula or adhering to a German tradition. For example, *Ein fliehendes Pferd* (*Runaway Horse*), first published in 1978, introduces the reader to the grammar school teacher Helmut Halm via the well-tried and tested German literary route of the novella, whereas seven years later, when we encounter the same protagonist at a Californian university, the narrative of *Brandung* (*Breakers*) adopts the Anglo-American model of the so-called campus novel. Similarly, in his dramatic *oeuvre,* he hijacks the Brechtian political parable for *Eiche und Angora* (*The Rabbit Race*) in 1962 while only a few years later he reverts to the form of the one-act domestic comedy for *Die Zimmerschlacht* (*Home Front*). As these two widely differing plays from the 1960s show, Walser is just as confident dealing with the subject-matter of the recent German past and its legacy for the public mentality of post-war Germany as he is in exposing the social and sexual mores of middle-class marriages manifest in the aptly named *Home Front*.

Indeed, to judge by the subject-matter of this play and the aforementioned *Runaway Horse*, Walser might well be described as the marriage counsellor to West German society. In both works the terrain of marriage is reconnoitred and found to be a minefield of biological, psychological, and social conflicts. Common to both the play and the novella (and indeed to several other works by the author) are the themes of sexuality, ageing, role-playing, ritual, and socially determined pressures. Not only do these works portray the male attracted to and repulsed by the female, but also the male in league and in competition with other males. The male is exposed to an awesome combination of threats to his identity, both from within himself and from external forces, but these works along with so many others right up to and including the recent *Jagd* (The Hunt) end with a guardedly optimistic view that the husband can best overcome his identity crises by truthfully communicating his problems to his wife.

Not surprisingly, therefore, women loom large in the works of Walser, and invariably the reader-spectator is made to feel some sympathy with them. Anna, the working-class housewife in Walser's first stage success, *Der Abstecher* (*The Detour*), has once been so badly hurt, emotionally, by the smoothtalking middle-class businessman Hubert that when he looks her up several years later (with decidedly carnal intentions) she sets up her own one-woman court to bring him to justice and threatens to electrocute him. But, typically and ironically, Hubert manages to extricate himself, thanks to the solidarity of Anna's own husband. This farce ends with the two men setting off on a pub crawl, leaving the poor woman alone, embittered and still the victim of male manipulations. In the course of Walser's works, however, the females gradually cease being the objects of male chauvinism to assert themselves quietly yet effectively against men's stratagems. The real power they hold over their subjects can be beautifully and comically appreciated in Walser's latest bestselling epic *Die Verteidigung der Kindheit* (Defence of Childhood), in which Alfred Dorn's seemingly oedipal relationship with his mother is the theme.

Yet it is not only within the sphere of private relationships that man's identity is put under strain; his professional work exerts perhaps even more pressure on the individual's sense of self. Invariably this sphere of his life compels him to adopt values which run counter to his own nature and involve him in relationships which compromise his independence. It is symptomatic therefore that one relationship which recurs frequently in Walser's dramas and novels is that of the master and servant, usually clothed in some modern guise such as the company director and his chauffeur, as in *The Detour* and *Seelenarbeit* (*The Inner Man*). In some works written approximately before 1970, that relationship is static, but after 1970 Walser begins to demonstrate how the affected individual can and does gain insights into the mechanisms which, from childhood to adulthood, have conditioned in him a subservient, dependent state of mind and he shows, furthermore, how through self-awareness the "inferior" human being can begin to emancipate himself. It is important to note that this process of emancipation is not brought about from outside, through changed political conditions or political activities, for Walser is too much of a realist to posit such a Utopian ideal.

Instead it begins within the traumatised psyche of the individual — and proceeds, not uncommonly, with a little help from his female friends.

Unfortunately, such a positive development happened a fraction too late for Walser's most illustrious and illustrative anti-hero, Anselm Kristlein, the central figure of the 2000-page trilogy *Halbzeit* (Half-Time), *Das Einhorn* (*The Unicorn*), and *Der Sturz* (The Fall). Anselm's social rise and fall against the backdrop of West Germany's "economic miracle" contains a trenchant critique of many false and negative traits of post-war German society: the competition ethic, greed, egotism, opportunism, sexual permissiveness. Anselm helps to promote all these "values" until he is finally destroyed by them. Walser, however, manages to depict Anselm's fate both humorously and critically, and it is one of his great strengths as a writer that we can also laugh at and learn from the tragedies which befall his impressive assortment of petit bourgeois representatives.

Indeed Walser's figures, right from the arriviste Hans Beumann in *Ehen in Philippsburg* (*Marriage in Philippsburg* or *The Gadarene Club*) onwards, are acutely if not pathologically class-conscious. Helmut Halm articulates this class consciousness in *Runaway Horse* when he exclaims: "If I am anything at all, I'm a petit bourgeois. And if I'm proud of anything at all, it's of that." Walser excels in the evocation of this middle-class world by detailing its myriad everyday phenomena. In fact he once described himself as an "historian of the everyday world." Yet, equally Walser, certainly in the works written since the early 1980s, has not only been actively documenting seismographically the implosions of the middle-class consciousness but also the latent tremors of the German national consciousness. In speech after speech, essay after essay, Walser has been articulating, without self-pity, without ideological ulterior motives, without rancour, his emotionally rooted belief in and hope for a Germany which is no longer divided. Such an apparently "conservative" sentiment had earned him much scorn and anger from liberal and left-wing quarters. Now, of course, with hindsight, Walser's pan-German yearnings have assumed a prophetic import.

These yearnings can be seen as one facet of, arguably, the overriding theme of Walser's richly diverse work: the search for a sense of belonging to and identification with a community (encapsulated in the emotive German word *Heimat*) which, more than that of almost any other nation, has been riven by crisis, conflict, and upheaval. Walser's characters, including his very latest creation, the Dresden-born Alfred Dorn in *Die Verteidigung der Kindheit*, have been engaged in a fundamentally existential odyssey, through which they seek that state of being when class, culture, character, and chance finally conspire to produce a sense of oneness with self and with history — in short, a state of harmony. His work never lets us lose sight of this elusive goal, towards which his very secular pilgrims progress.

—Anthony Waine

WAN JIABAO. *See* **CAO YU.**

WANG MENG. Chinese. Born in Beijing, 15 October 1934. Educated at Pinmin Middle School, 1945–48; Hebei Middle School, 1948–49. Married Cui Ruifang in 1957; two sons and one daughter. Member of Beijing Municipal Committee, Communist Youth League, 1949–62; teacher, Beijing Teacher's College, 1962–63; criticized, 1957–76, and sent to countryside: editor and farmer, Xinjiang, 1964–78; rehabilitated, 1979; Minister of Culture, 1986–89. Vice president, China PEN, Beijing, since 1982, and Chinese Association for International Understanding, Beijing, since 1985; vice chair, Chinese Writers Association, Beijing, since 1985; alternate member, 12th Central Committee, 1982, member, 12th Central Committee, 1985, and member, 13th Central Committee, 1987–92, all Chinese Communist Party. Recipient: National prize, for short story, 1978, 1979, 1980, for novel, 1981, 1982, for reportage, 1986. Address: Ministry of Culture, Donganmen Street A83, Beijing, China.

PUBLICATIONS

Fiction

Buli. 1978; as *Bolshevik Salute: A Modernist Chinese Novel*, Seattle, University of Washington Press, 1989.
Qingchun wansui [Long Live Spring]. Beijing, People's University Press, 1979.
Dong yu [Winter Rain]. Beijing, People's University Press, 1980.
Prize-Winning Stories from China 1978–79, with others. Beijing, Foreign Languages Press, 1981.
Xiang jian zhi nan. Beijing, China Qingnian Publishing House, 1982; as *The Strain of Meeting*, Beijing, Foreign Languages Press, 1989.
Shen de hu [The Deep Lake]. N.p., Huacheng Publishing House, 1982.
The Butterfly and Other Stories. Beijing, Chinese Literature, 1983.
Muxiang shenchu de zichou huafu [The Jacket in the Bottom of the Trunk]. Shanghai, Shanghai Literature and Arts Publishing House, 1984.
Zai Yili, danhuise de yanchu [Light Grey Eyes in Yili]. Beijing, Writers' Publishing House, 1984.
Zhao ze de pang de bu luo, with Zhang Shijun. Chengdu, Sichuan People's Publishing House, 1984.
Juhuangse de meng [The Orange Dream]. Tianjin, Baihua Literature and Arts Publishing House, 1984.
Wang Meng zhongpian xiaoshuo ji [Selected Novelettes by Wang Meng]. Shanghai, Hunan People's Publishing House, 1985.
Miao Xiao An jianying [A Sketch of Miao An Shan]. Tianjin, Baihua Literature and Arts Publishing House, 1985.
Huodong bian renxing [Movable Parts]. Beijing, People's University Press, 1986.
Wang Meng Ji [Selected works of Wang Meng]. N.p., Haixia Literature and Arts Publishing House, 1986.
Jianada de yueliang [Canadian Moonlight]. Beijing, Writers' Publishing House, 1986.
Wang Meng xuanji [Selected Works of Wang Meng]. Tianjin, Baihua Literature and Arts Publishing House, 1986.
Hudie [The Butterfly]. Taibei, Taiwan Yuanying Publishing House, 1988.
Xue qiu ji. As *Snowball: Selected Works of Wang Meng*, Beijing, Foreign Languages Press, 1989.
Qiu xing qi yuji [The Adventure of the Moon and the Stars]. Beijing, People's University Publishing House, 1990.

Honglou qishilu [Honglou Apocalypse]. N.p., Sanlian Shudian, 1991.
Zhongguo dangdai zuojia xianji congshu, Wang Meng Ji [Selected Works of Contemporary Writers: Wang Meng]. Beijing, People's Literature Publishing House, 1991.

Verse

Xuanzhuan de qiuqian [The Spinning Swing]. Chengdu, Sichuan People's Publishing House, 1988.

Other

Dang ni naqi bi [When You Pick up the Pen]. Beijing, Beijing Publishing House, 1981.
Wang Meng xiaoshuo baogao wenxuexuan [Selected Reportage Novels by Wang Meng]. Beijing, Beijing Publishing House, 1981.
De Mei jixing [Travel Notes from Germany and the U.S.A.]. Hangzhou, Zhejiang Publishing House, 1982.
Mantan xiaoshuo chuangzuo [Informal Discussion on Writing Novels]. Shanghai, Shanghai Literature Publishing House, 1983.
Wang Meng tan chuangzuo [Wang Meng on Writing]. N.p., China Wenlian Publishing House, 1983.
Zouxiang wenxue zhi lu [On the Road of Literature]. Shanghai, Hunan People's Publishing House, 1983.
Chuangzuo shi yi zhong ranshao [Creativity Is a Kind of Fire]. Beijing, People's Literature Publishing House, 1985.
Wenxue chuangzuo bitan [Notes on Creative Writing], with Bai Hua and Chin Mu. Chongqing, Chongqing Publishing House, 1985.
Fan Su xin chao [Surging Thoughts and Emotions When Visiting the U.S.S.R.]. Shanghai, Shanghai Literature and Arts Publishing House, 1986.
Wenxue de youhuo [The Attractions of Literature]. Shanghai, Hunan Literature and Arts Publishing House, 1987.
Ming yi Liang You zhi chuanqiir [Legend of the Famous Doctor Liang Youzhi]. Hong Kong, Shanghai Shuju, 1988.
Zai Fenglengcui ji Foluolunsa yi ge zhuming can guan chi ye far di jing li. Beijing, China Huaqiao Publishing House, 1989.
Fengge Sanji [Notes on Style]. Beijing, People's Literature Publishing House, 1991.

*

Critical Studies: "The Writer Wang Meng" by Zhaoyang Qin, in *Chinese Literature* (Beijing), 7, 1980; "Wang Meng, Stream-of-Consciousness, and the Controversy over Modernism" by Cornelius C. Kubler, in *Modern Chinese Literature* (San Francisco), 1(1), 1984; "Modernism and Social Realism: The Case of Wang Meng" by William Tay, in *World Literature Today* (Norman, Oklahoma), 63(3), 1991.

* * *

Wang Meng survived 20 years of political disgrace to emerge as one of China's most important literary figures in the 1980s. His work reflects with unusual honesty both his country's turbulent recent history and his own tragic experiences over four decades. He shuns the predictable formulae still all too common in Chinese writing and favours innovative stylistic techniques. Most strikingly he allows questions and ambiguities which negate the crude demand, widely accepted in China until very recently, that literature's primary purpose should to offer moral and political instruction. Wang Meng's best writing achieves a considerable depth and power.

Like Liu Binyan (*q.v.*), with whom his name is often associated, Wang Meng became well known for an attack on bureaucratism published in the comparatively relaxed period of 1956. Also like Liu Binyan, he was the victim of a political campaign the following year against writers who had criticised the Party, was declared a rightist, ceased to publish for 20 years, and suffered a prolonged exile. The story for which Wang Meng was attacked, "The Young Newcomer in the Organisation Department," recounts the experiences of a naïve, idealistic youth assigned to work in the District Office of the Communist Party. He becomes increasingly frustrated as his efforts to dislodge an inefficient and lazy factory manager are blocked by bureaucratic forces of which he is, at first, hardly aware. By later standards the criticism of Party bureaucracy implicit in the story is muted and gentle. Although the protagonist gradually comes to accept that successes cannot be achieved as quickly as he had at first hoped, he still manages to preserve his ideals. The piece was nonetheless singled out for criticism as a destructive, anti-Party, anti-socialist work, and Wang Meng was sent to do hard labour in Xinjiang in the far northwest of China.

When Wang Meng was rehabilitated and returned to Beijing in 1979, he soon established himself as a writer willing to deal courageously and honestly with life as it had been in Mao Zedong's China and with the problems of the post-Cultural Revolution years. He still consistently selects issues of social importance as his themes but has abandoned the straightforward narratives of his earlier stories. He uses flashbacks to deal with the inner world of his characters, their thought processes and mental conflicts, exploring the larger problems of life in China through a focus on the individual which would have been condemned as bourgeois in earlier years. In stories such as "Voices of Spring" and "Eyes of Night" he experimented with stream-of-consciousness writing in a way political critics condemned as "decadent and outmoded." A prolific writer, he wrote over a million and a half words between 1976 and 1982.

Wang Meng's novella *Hudie* (*The Butterfly*) deals with a senior official who shows no sympathy at all for his young wife when she is criticised in 1957 for having praised a short story which attacked bureaucracy. (Here Wang Meng is drawing very closely on life; the story could very well have been his own "Young Newcomer in the Organisation Department"). She is politically disgraced and they divorce. The official's insufferable political smugness is finally punctured when he himself comes under attack in the Cultural Revolution. His ex-wife commits suicide and his son rejects him. He suffers a nightmarish sense of unreality as he works through all the consequences of his fall: divorce from his ambitious second wife, the loss of his home, exile to a poor remote village, hard physical toil, and low status. After the Cultural Revolution he undergoes another bewildering reversal when he is rehabilitated and made a government vice-minister. Yet this official advancement is not matched by any reconstruction of his personal life. First his son, with whom he has long since been reconciled, rejects his father's attempts to draw him back to Beijing from his village exile; then the village doctor whom he had come to love also declines to give up her own life to join him in the capital. The story ends, like others of Wang Meng's, on a note of moderate and not altogether convincing optimism as the official comes to terms with life on his own.

The theme of the rehabilitated intellectual was understandably a popular one among educated Chinese of the 1980s, many of whom had endured political disgrace and exile. Wang Meng's stories were well-received by them, and his appointment as Minister of Culture in 1986 was understood as

signalling some commitment to a liberal cultural policy. Although he was relieved of this post only three years later, in the wake of the Tiananmen Square massacre, he retained his seat on the Central Committee until October 1992. In 1991, he began to probe the limits of cultural freedom in an entirely new way by attempting to bring a libel case against a literary paper controlled by political hardliners. This paper had published a political attack on Wang Meng which claimed that a story he had published early in 1989 had been intended as a satire on China's reform policies. He demanded damages and an apology. Had he succeeded, the implications for freedom of expression in China would have been immense. Fear of the sort of attack which had been made on Wang Meng still keeps many writers silent. Unfortunately no court could take the case. However, as many newspapers defied an order banning them from reporting on this affair and its details are well-known among the Chinese intelligentsia, Wang Meng's challenge to the cultural hegemony of the hardliners is perhaps as much admired as his writing.

—Delia Davin

WÄSTBERG, Per (Erik). Swedish. Born in Stockholm, 20 November 1933. Educated at Harvard University, Cambridge, Massachusetts, B.A. 1955; University of Uppsala, Ph.D. 1962. Married 1) Anna-Lena Eldh in 1955 (ended 1969); 2) Margareta Ekström in 1970 (ended 1986), one daughter and one son; 3) Anita Theorell in 1987. Critic and columnist, since 1953, and editor-in-chief, 1976–82, *Dagens Nyheter* newspaper; founder and chair, Swedish South Africa Committee, Stockholm, 1960–76; founder and vice president, Swedish Amnesty International, Stockholm, 1963–71; president, Swedish PEN, 1967–78, and International PEN, 1979–86, and 1989–90; board member, Scandinavian Institute of African Studies, Uppsala, 1980, and University of Uppsala, since 1991; vice chair, Stockholm City Council Committee on Environment and Preservation, since 1983. Recipient: Swedish Academy prizes; Swedish Booksellers prize, 1969; St. Erik award, 1979. Member, European Academy of Arts and Sciences, since 1980. Agent: Kerstin Kvint, Kammakarg 40, 111 60 Stockholm, Sweden. Address: Kammakarg 4, 111 40 Stockholm, Sweden.

PUBLICATIONS

Fiction

Pojke med såpbubblor [Boy with Soap Bubbles]. Stockholm, Wahlström & Widstrand, 1949.
Enskilt arbete [Private Writings]. Stockholm, Wahlström & Widstrand, 1952.
Ett gammalt skuggspel [An Old Shadowplay]. Stockholm, Wahlström & Widstrand, 1952.
Halva kungariket [Half of the Kingdom]. Stockholm, Wahlström & Widstrand, 1955.
Arvtagaren [The Heir]. Stockholm, Wahlström & Widstrand, 1958.
Vattenslottet. Stockholm, Wahlström & Widstrand, 1968; as *The Water Castle*, with *The Air Cage*, New York, Delacorte Press, 1972; London, Souvenir Press, 1973.

Luftburen. Stockholm, Wahlström & Widstrand, 1969; as *The Air Cage*, with *The Water Castle*, New York, Delacorte Press, 1972; London, Souvenir Press, 1973.

Jordmånen. Stockholm, Wahlström & Widstrand, 1972; as *Love's Gravity*, London, Souvenir Press, 1977.

Eldens skugga [Shadow of Fire]. Stockholm, Wahlström & Widstrand, 1986.

Bergets källa [A Source of the Mountain]. Stockholm, Wahlström & Widstrand, 1987.

Ljusets hjärta [The Heart of Light]. Stockholm, Wahlström & Widstrand, 1991.

Vindens låga [Flame of the Wind]. Stockholm, Wahlström & Widstrand, 1993.

Verse

Tio atmosfärer [Ten Atmospheres]. Stockholm, Wahlström & Widstrand, 1963.

Enkel resa [Single Journey]. Stockholm, Wahlström & Widstrand, 1964.

En avlägsen likhet [A Distant Affinity]. Stockholm, Wahlström & Widstrand, 1983.

Frusna tillgångar [Frozen Assets]. Stockholm, Wahlström & Widstrand, 1990.

Other

Klara. Stockholm, Norstedt, 1957.

Förbjudet område [Forbidden Territory]. Stockholm, Wahlström & Widstrand, 1960.

På svarta listan [On the Black List]. Stockholm, Wahlström & Widstrand, 1960.

Angela-Moçambique, with Anders Ehnmark. Lund, Cavefors, 1961; as *The Case Against Portugal*, London, Pall Mall Press, 1963.

Östermalm. Stockholm, Wahlström & Widstrand, 1962.

Innen gaslågan slocknade [Before the Gaslight Expired]. Stockholm, Billberg, 1963.

Ernst och Mimmi [Ernst and Mimmi]. Stockholm, Nordiska Museet, 1964.

En dag på världsmarknaden [A Day at the World's Market]. Stockholm, Wahlström & Widstrand, 1967.

Afrikas moderna litteratur [Modern African Literature]. Stockholm, Wahlström & Widstrand, 1969.

Röda huset [The Red House], with Anna-Lena Wästberg. Stockholm, Wahlström & Widstrand, 1970.

Humlegårdsmästaren [The Hop Garden Master]. Stockholm, Bonnier, 1971.

Afrika — ett updrag. Stockholm, Wahlström & Widstrand, 1976; as *Assignments in Africa*, New York, Farrar Straus, and London, Olive Press, 1986.

Berättarens ögonblick [The Moment of the Narrator]. Stockholm, Wahlström & Widstrand, 1977.

Ett hörntorn vid Riddargatan [A Tower at Knight Street]. Stockholm, Wahlström & Widstrand, 1980.

Obestämda artiklar [Indefinite Articles]. Stockholm, Wahlström & Widstrand, 1981.

Bestämda artiklar [Definite Articles]. Stockholm, Wahlström & Widstrand, 1982.

Tal i Röda rummet [A Speech in the Red Room]. Stockholm, Höjering, 1982.

Frukost med Gerard [Breakfast with Gerard]. Stockholm, Wahlström & Widstrand, 1992.

Editor, *Afrika berättar* [Africa Tells]. Lund, Cavefors, 1961.

Editor, *The Writer in Modern Africa.* Uppsala, Scandinavian Institute of African Studies, 1968.

Editor, *Kära Hjalle, Kära Bo* (letters), by Bo Bergman and Hjalmar Söderberg. Stockholm, Bonnier, 1969.

Editor, *Afrikansk lyrik* [African Lyric]. Stockholm, Bonnier, 1970.

Editor, *Hjalmar Söderbergs skrifter* [Hjalmar Söderberg's Writings]. Stockholm, Liber, 9 vols., 1977–78.

Editor, *An Anthology of Modern Swedish Literature.* Merrick, New York, Cross Cultural Communications, 1979.

*

Bibliography: *Per Wästbergs skrifter 1943–73* and *1973–83* by Anders Ryberg, Stockholm, Wahlström & Widstrand, 2 vols., 1973–83.

Per Wästberg comments:

A year in southern Africa (1959) became a turning point in my life and letters. Everything I have written since is permeated by the interconnecting themes of freedom-oppression, travel-roots, chaos-order, love-cruelty. I have worked in most genres and published 35 volumes in a joint printing of 2.3 million copies. My first trilogy of novels (1968–72) became a widely discussed generation document about different forms of love and of life together in the turbulent society of the late 1960s. My quartet of novels (1986–93) try to penetrate the shifts of sensual experience, the different faces of love as well as love's stages of ecstasy, clearsightedness, and constant discovery. The setting is Stockholm, London, Cameroon, the characters a female city architect and an undersecretary of state in the Foreign Office. In books of poems, prose poems, aphorisms I have sketched a fragmented autobiography. In four monographs of Stockholm I have traced the history, the destinies and the everyday life patterns of four parts of Stockholm, looking at my home city as Livingstone saw Africa: as if for the first time — the only true recipe for a writer.

*   *   *

The 1950s is a rather calm period in Swedish literature, marked by a renewed, somewhat nostalgic interest in small, provincial communities and with little concern for the world outside Sweden. To the writers of the next decade with its demand for political commitment, those of the 1950s seemed far too introvertly romantic and idyllic in their preoccupation with the personal and the intimate.

Per Wästberg is often considered to be a typical representative of the "lyrical" 1950s. His writing is well-balanced and sensible and, though the searching quality is apparent, some critics find it too tentative and not passionate enough to engage the reader deeply.

Wästberg was only 15 when he made his debut with a collection of short stories, *Pojke med såpbubblor* (Boy with Soap Bubbles) published in 1949. In *Halva kungariket* (Half of the Kingdom), his breakthrough, the youthful main character sends his son Felix out on a summer trip close to home, suggesting that it is not necessary to travel widely to gain experience of life. In *Arvtagaren* (The Heir), another young protagonist sets out on an educational tour of Europe. Here, by contrast, it is recognized that there is knowledge to be gained which you could not have found close to home. The people Mattias meets on his journey have firsthand experience of war-torn Europe. He sees the need for sharing their experience and for redefining his own.

Wästberg's own travels in southern Africa were to result in penetrating and sensitive reports. His visit to Rhodesia in

1959 resulted in the documentary *Förbjudet område* (Forbidden Territory). This was followed by *På svarta listan* (On the Black List), based on his impressions of South Africa. Both are — even in an international perspective — surprisingly early and perceptive descriptions about life in the shadow of apartheid. With his concern for racial and political discrimination (he has been very active within Amnesty International) Wästberg preceded the writers of the politically committed 1960s. Having introduced African fiction to the Swedish public in the anthology *Afrika berättar* (Africa Tells), he has remained an ardent reporter on African culture, not least in his capacity of cultural editor of Scandinavia's largest daily, *Dagens Nyheter*.

Reports of a very different kind are the books in which Wästberg, in collaboration with various photographers, documents environments in and around Stockholm. Here the author listens with a nostalgic ear to what old people have to say about their lives in a rapidly changing city.

In the late 1960s Wästberg began a trilogy of novels which seemed on one level to be advocating the new liberated view of eroticism. But like most of Wästberg's fictional works, *Vattenslottet* (*The Water Castle*), *Luftburen* (*The Air Cage*), and *Jordmånen* (*Love's Gravity*), are essentially about people who are compelled to find their place in a widening world where their native Sweden seems too safe a haven. The central character, Jan Backman, is an air traffic controller at Stockholm international airport. His carefully timed job personality contrasts with another side of him, his tendency to daydream and his feeling of vulnerability. Of the two women surrounding him one, Gertrud, is his half-sister, with whom he lives in an incestuous relationship, while the other, Jenny, signals his need to find an alternative to his outgrown role as brother/lover. Professionally a well-defined member of society but in his personal life an outsider, Backman's predicament is sensitively expressed in slow-moving prose which is either descriptive in a most accurate, almost scientific way or loses itself in long, imaginary sequences triggered off by a detail in the landscape or a momentary association.

The lovers' choice in these novels is not between freedom and security. Leaving social convention behind, they are able to experience both and yet remain reasonably safe in their privileged middle-class world. Of the three novels, *The Air Cage* in particular caused debate among the Swedish critics. Those with a Marxist leaning — and in 1969 they actually dominated the Swedish cultural scene — found it blinkered and narrow, dealing with the luxury problems of a privileged class.

14 years after the publication of *Love's Gravity* Wästberg returned to fiction with *Eldens skugga* (Shadow of Fire), *Bergets källa* (A Source of the Mountain), and *Ljusets hjärta* (The Heart of Light). *Vindens låga* (Flame of the Wind), the fourth volume in this planned tetralogy, will be published in 1993.

The central character is again an intellectual who lives an ordinary life. The theme is again love and the elusiveness of love. A broken marriage makes Johan-Fredrik Victorin realize that in a life together with someone he might successively come to know the other person less and less. Here the mature, sensible, middle-class man is faced with a situation where he needs to rethink everything. The new element in these novels is the presence of a teenage daughter, representing the next generation, who with her clarity of thought and strength of feeling offers hope for the future. Yet in structure and theme the planned tetralogy does not seem radically different from the previous trilogy. Once more Wästberg explores a human being's potential for understanding him- or herself, for understanding other human beings and the world at large. The search goes on.

—Kerstin Petersson

———

WIESEL, Elie(zer).   American.   Born in Sighet, Romania, 30 September 1928; became American citizen, 1963. Interned in Auschwitz, 1944–45, and Buchenwald concentration camp, 1945. Educated at the Sorbonne, Paris, 1948–51. Married Marion Erster Rose in 1969; one son. Foreign correspondent, *L'Arche*, Paris, from 1949, *Yedioth Ahronoth*, Tel Aviv, from 1952, and *Jewish Daily Forward*, New York, from 1957; Professor of Judaic studies, City College of City University of New York, 1972–76. Since 1976, Andrew Mellon Professor in the Humanities, and since 1988 Professor of philosophy, Boston University. Henry Luce Visiting Scholar in the Humanities and Social Thought, Yale University, New Haven, Connecticut, 1982–83. Chair, U.S. Holocaust Memorial Council. Recipient: Rivarol prize, 1963; Remembrance award, 1965; Epstein award, 1965; Jewish Heritage award, 1966; Medicis prize, 1969; Bordin prize, 1972; Eleanor Roosevelt memorial award, 1972; American Liberties Medallion, 1972; Cohen award, 1973; Martin Luther King Jr. award, 1973; Joseph prize for human rights, 1978; Shazar award, 1979; Prix Livre-International, 1980; Jabotinsky award, 1980; Librarians' prize (France), 1981; Shcharansky Humanitarian award, 1983; City of Paris grand prize, 1983; Royal Academy of Belgium international literary prize for peace, 1983; Congressional Gold Medal of Achievement, 1984; Anne Frank award, 1985; Medal of Jerusalem, 1986; Nobel Peace prize, 1986; Edelman award, 1989; Weil award, 1990; many other awards. Litt.D.: Jewish Theological Seminary, 1967; Marquette University, 1975; Simmons College, 1976; Anna Maria College, 1980; Yale University 1981; Wake Forest University, and Haverford College, both 1985; Capital University, 1986; the Sorbonne, 1987; University of Connecticut, Storrs, 1988; Wittenberg University, and Wheeling Jesuit College, both 1989. D.H.L.: Hebrew Union College, 1968; Manhattanville College, 1972; Yeshiva University, 1973; Boston University, 1974; College of St. Scholastica, 1978; Wesleyan University, 1979; Anna Maria College, and Brandeis University, both 1980; Kenyon College, and Hobart and William Smith Colleges, both 1982; Emory University, Florida International University, Siena Heights College, Fairfield University, Dropsie College, and Moravian College, all 1983; Colgate University, 1984; State University of New York at Binghamton, Lehigh University, and University of Hartford, all 1985; College of New Rochelle, Georgetown University, Hamilton College, Tufts University, University of Haifa, Long Island University, and Rockford College, all 1986; Villanova University, College of St. Thomas, Lycoming College, University of Denver, Walsh College, and Loyola College, all 1987; Ohio University, and University of Central Florida, both 1988; Concordia College, New York University, Fordham University, and Connecticut College, all 1990; Upsala College, Dusquesne University, and Roosevelt University, all 1991; Hunter College, City University of New York, 1992. Doctor of Hebrew Letters: Spertus College of Judaica, 1973; Doctor of Philosophy: Bar-Ilan University, 1973; Ben-Gurion University of the Negev, 1988. LL.D.: Hofstra University, 1975; Talmudic University, 1979; University of Notre Dame,

1980; LaSalle University, 1988. Doctor of Science: Chicago Medical School, 1989. Doctor of Humanities: Brigham Young University, 1989. Doctor of Theology: University of Åbo Akademi, 1990. Grand Officier de la Légion d'Honneur (France). Agent: Georges Borchardt, 136 East 57th Street, New York 10022, U.S.A. Address: Department of Religion, Boston University, 745 Commonwealth Avenue, Boston, Massachusetts 02215, U.S.A.

PUBLICATIONS

Fiction

Night; Dawn; The Accident: Three Tales.   New York, Hill and Wang, 1972; London, Robson, 1974; as *The Night Trilogy: Night, Dawn, The Accident*, Hill and Wang, 1987.
Un di Velt Hot Geshvign [And the World Has Remained Silent].   Buenos Aires, Central Farbond Fun Poylishe Yidn in Argentina, 1956; revised and abridged edition, as *La Nuit*, Paris, Minuit, 1958; as *Night*, New York, Hill and Wang, and London, MacGibbon and Kee, 1960.
L'Aube.   Paris, Seuil, 1960; as *Dawn*, New York, Hill and Wang, and London, MacGibbon and Kee, 1961.
Le Jour.   Paris, Seuil, 1961; as *The Accident*, New York, Hill and Wang, 1962.
La Ville de la chance.   Paris, Seuil, 1962; as *The Town Beyond the Wall*, New York, Atheneum, 1964; London, Robson, 1975.
Les Portes de la forêt.   Paris, Seuil, 1964; as *The Gates of the Forest*, New York, Holt, 1966; London, Heinemann, 1967.
Le Mendiant de Jérusalem.   Paris, Seuil, 1968; as *A Beggar in Jerusalem*, New York, Random House, and London, Weidenfeld and Nicolson, 1970.
Vingt Ans après Auschwitz (includes *Zalmen*; *Le Mendiant de Jérusalem*).   Paris, Center for Contemporary Jewish Documentation, 1968.
Le Serment de Kolvillag.   Paris, Seuil, 1973; as *The Oath*, New York, Random House, 1973.
Le Testament d'un poète juif assassiné.   Paris, Seuil, 1980; as *The Testament*, New York, Summit, and London, Allen Lane, 1981.
Le Cinquième Fils.   Paris, Grasset, 1983; as *The Fifth Son*, New York, Summit, 1985; London, Viking, 1986.
Le Crépuscule au loin.   Paris, Grasset, 1987; as *Twilight*, New York, Summit, and London, Viking, 1988.
L'Oublié.   Paris, Seuil, 1989; as *The Forgotten*, New York, Summit, 1992.

Plays

Zalmen; ou, La Folie de Dieu.   Paris, Seuil, 1968; as *Zalmen; or, The Madness of God* (produced Washington, D.C., 1974), New York, Holt, 1968.
Ani Maamin: Un Chant perdu et retrouvé (cantata), music by Darius Milhaud.   Paris, Seuil, 1973; as *Ani Maamin: A Song Lost and Found Again* (produced New York, 1973), New York, Random House, 1974.
Le Procès de Shamgorod tel qu'il se déroula le 25 février 1649: Pièce en trois actes (produced Paris).   Paris, Seuil, 1979; as *The Trial of God (as It Was Held on February 25, 1649, in Shamgorod): A Play in Three Acts* (produced in English, 1988), New York, Random House, 1979.
The Haggadah, new version of the traditional text (performed New York, 1980).   New York, French, 1982.
A Song for Hope, music by David Diamond (cantata; performed New York, 1987).

Other

Les Juifs du silence.   Paris, Seuil, 1966; as *The Jews of Silence: A Personal Report on Soviet Jewry*, New York, Holt, 1966; London, Valentine Mitchell, 1968.
Le Chant des morts.   Paris, Seuil, 1966; as *Legends of Our Time*, New York, Holt, 1968.
Entre Deux Soleils.   Paris, Seuil, 1970; as *One Generation After*, New York, Random House, 1970; London, Weidenfeld and Nicolson, 1971.
Célébration hassidique: portraits et légendes.   Paris, Seuil, 1972; as *Souls on Fire: Portraits and Legends of Hasidic Masters*, New York, Random House, and London, Weidenfeld and Nicolson, 1972.
Célébration biblique: portraits et légendes.   Paris, Seuil, 1975; as *Messengers of God: Biblical Portraits and Legends*, New York, Random House, 1976.
Un Juif aujourd'hui: récits, essais, dialogues.   Paris, Seuil, 1977; as *A Jew Today*, New York, Random House, 1978.
Four Hasidic Masters and Their Struggle Against Melancholy.   Notre Dame, Indiana, University of Notre Dame Press, 1978.
Images from the Bible.   New York, Overlook Press, 1980.
Five Biblical Portraits.   Notre Dame, Indiana, University of Notre Dame Press, 1981.
Inside a Library; and, The Stranger in the Bible.   Cincinnati, Hebrew Union College/Jewish Institute of Religion, 1981.
Contre la Mélancolie: célébration hassidique II.   Paris, Seuil, 1981; as *Somewhere a Master: Further Hasidic Portraits and Legends*, New York, Summit, 1982; with *Souls on Fire*, London, Penguin, 1984.
Paroles d'étranger.   Paris, Seuil, 1982.
The Golem: The Story of a Legend as Told by Elie Wiesel.   New York, Summit, 1983.
Against Silence: The Voice and Vision of Elie Wiesel, edited by Irving Abrahamson.   New York, Holocaust Library, 3 vols., 1985.
Signes d'exode.   Paris, Grasset, 1985.
Job, ou, Dieu dans la tempête, with Josy Eisenberg.   Paris, Grasset, 1986.
The Nobel Address: Hope, Despair and Memory (Nobel peace prize acceptance speech).   New York, Summit, 1986; as *Discours d'Oslo*, Paris, Grasset, 1987.
Le Mal et l'exil.   Paris, Nouvelle Cité, 1988; as *Evil and Exile*, Notre Dame, Indiana, University of Notre Dame Press, 1990.
The Six Days of Destruction: Meditations Towards Hope, with Albert H. Friedlander.   Mahwah, New Jersey, Paulist Press, and Oxford, Pergamon Press, 1988.
Silences et mémoire d'hommes.   Paris, Seuil, 1989.
A Journey of Faith, with John Cardinal O'Connor.   New York, Donald I. Fine, 1989.
From the Kingdom of Memory.   New York, Summit, 1990.
Sages and Dreamers.   New York, Summit, 1991.
Célébration talmudique.   Paris, Seuil, 1991.

*

Bibliography: *Elie Wiesel: A Bibliography* by Molly Abramowitz, Metuchen, New Jersey, Scarecrow Press, 1974.

Manuscript Collection: Boston University.

Critical Studies: *Elie Wiesel: A Small Measure of Victory* by Gene Koppel and Henry Kaufmann, Tucson, University of Arizona Press, 1974; *Harry James Cargas in Conversation with Elie Wiesel*, New York, Paulist Press, 1976; *Responses to Elie*

Wiesel: Critical Essays by Major Jewish and Christian Scholars, edited by Harry James Cargas, New York, Persea, 1978; *Confronting the Holocaust: The Impact of Elie Wiesel*, edited by Alvin H. Rosenfeld and Irving Greenberg, Bloomington, Indiana University Press, 1978; *The Vision of the Void: Theological Reflections on the Works of Elie Wiesel* by Michael Berenbaum, Middletown, Connecticut, Wesleyan University Press, 1979; *A Consuming Fire: Encounters with Elie Wiesel and the Holocaust* by John King Roth, Atlanta, Knox Press, 1979; *Elie Wiesel* by Ted L. Estess, New York, Ungar, 1980; *Legacy of Night: The Literary Universe of Elie Wiesel* by Ellen S. Fine, Albany, State University of New York Press, 1982; *Elie Wiesel: Witness for Life* by Ellen N. Stern, Hoboken, New Jersey, Ktav, 1982; *Elie Wiesel: Messenger to All Humanity* by Robert McAfee Brown, Notre Dame, Indiana, University of Notre Dame Press, 1983; *Religious Melancholy or Psychological Depression? Some Issues Involved in Relating Psychology and Religion as Illustrated in a Study of Elie Wiesel* by Christopher J. Frost, Lanham, Maryland, University Press of America, 1985; *Abraham Joshua Heschel and Elie Wiesel, You Are My Witnesses* by Maurice Friedman, New York, Farrar Straus, 1987; *Elie Wiesel: A Challenge to Theology* by Graham B. Walker, Jefferson, North Carolina, McFarland, 1988; *Elie Wiesel: Between Hope and Memory* by Carol Rittner, New York, New York University Press, 1990; *In Dialogue and Dilemma with Elie Wiesel* by David Patterson, Wolfeboro, New Hampshire, Longwood Academic, 1991.

Elie Wiesel comments:

In his novels as in his works on the Bible, the Talmud, or Hasidism, the writer in me wants to assume the role of the witness.

His aim is to establish links between the ancient past and the so-called modern generation, between yesterday's dead and today's world, in order to save them from another death, one which comes with forgetting.

He rarely escapes from his difficulties: how to write on events that defy language. But also, how to write about other things, which in the light or in the shadow of such events, can only pale in comparison.

To speak is impossible; to keep quiet is inconceivable. So, as a last resort, "en désespoir de cause" as Samuel Beckett would say, the writer in me comments on the Bible or the Talmud in order not to talk about himself. Or, put another way, in talking about the writings of the Ancients, he talks about himself.

*   *   *

When Elie Wiesel received the Nobel Peace prize on 10 December 1986, his friends were surprised — he had been expected to receive it in literature, and is still nominated for that prize. The Nobel Peace citation explains, "Wiesel is a messenger to mankind. His message is one of peace and atonement and human dignity. The message is in the form of a testimony, repeated and deepened through the works of a great author."

His writings and his life come together in a profound teaching which begins with the Holocaust and the continuance of evil in the world, but which culminates within a religious dimension from which humanity is not excluded. Over 30 books have appeared to date: novels, plays, reportage, studies of biblical figures and of the Hasidic masters, a cantata (with Darius Milhaud), and children's books. The basic theme of all of his works is the struggle against evil, but it would be a mistake to think of him primarily as a Holocaust writer. Wiesel is, first of all, a storyteller who weaves old and new legends

together with a deceptively simple style which is "a statement by understatement."

It is difficult to place Wiesel within the context of a language. Born in Sighet, Romania, in 1928, his first language was Yiddish. He now writes primarily in French, with his wife Marion serving as the main translator into English. At one time he lived in Israel and worked as a journalist, writing in Hebrew. As the Andrew Mellon Professor in the Humanities at Boston University, Wiesel is a quiet, charismatic teacher who lives within the English language; and his always over-subscribed lectures at the 92nd Street Young Men's Hebrew Association (YMHA) in New York showcase his superb English style which is, nevertheless, reminiscent of the Yiddish *darshan* and *maggid* (storyteller and preacher).

Wiesel's experiences as a child in Auschwitz, where he saw his family die, were first recorded in his first novel *Un di Velt Hot Geshvign* (And the World Was Silent) in 1956, published in a shorter French version as *La Nuit* and translated into English as *Night*. The images of that work, notably the three gallows with the child hanging in the middle and dying more slowly, have received more commentary from theologians, literary critics, and various scholars than many modern texts. Was it God dying at Auschwitz, or God taking his place among the persecuted and rejecting the perpetrators? Wiesel's own thoughts here have changed from deepest doubt to quiet affirmation of God.

The Auschwitz dimension of Wiesel's work, and his role as witness, inform his next novel *L'Aube* (*Dawn*); in a scene in Israel of resistance and killing he says, "We shall be bound together for all eternity by the tie that binds a victim and his executioner" — a thought echoed in *Le Jour* (*The Accident*), a novel which forms a trilogy with *Night* and *Dawn*. Questions about Auschwitz and its aftermath continue to be voiced in *La Ville de la chance* (*The Town Beyond the Wall*) and *Le Serment de Kolvillag* (*The Oath*), both of which feature the enigmatic Moshe the Madman, a recurring figure throughout Wiesel's work who represents the Jew who cannot live with God in this world, but cannot live without him either.

Slowly a new theme begins to develop in Wiesel's writings: the solitude and the suffering of God. In one of his latest novels, *Le Crépuscule au loin* (*Twilight*), set in a sanatorium filled with those who identify themselves as biblical figures, including God, the narrator is asked to cry for God:

What? Cry for Him too? Save Him too? Cry not only to God but for God? Could God need His creatures as much as they need Him? . . . Ecclesiastes . . . this desperate book refers not to man but to the King of the Universe. "For all my days are but sorrow!" That is not man howling, but God.

An autobiographical element can be found also in Wiesel's writings about the Hasidic tradition — Wiesel himself is descended from Hasidic masters, and maintains a close relationship with various Hasidic communities. His main works on the subject are *Célébration hassidique: portraits et légendes* (*Souls on Fire: Portraits and Legends of Hasidic Masters*), *Four Hasidic Masters and Their Struggle Against Melancholy*, and *Contre la Mélancholie: célébration hassidique II* (*Somewhere a Master: Further Hasidic Portraits and Legends*). In fact, almost every book Wiesel has written contain Hasidic stories. In contrast to Martin Buber who tended to beautify and edit the Hasidic tales, but also against the historians of Hasidism and their scholarly seriousness, Wiesel's excursions into this field are joyous celebrations illuminated by deep psychological insights. The *Kotzker rebbe*, or the Seer of Lublin, are seen in all their complexity. The narrative is punctuated by the stories in which the masters reveal themselves in all their despair and hope. Wiesel uses them to complete his images of humanity between darkness and hope, as from *Somewhere a Master*:

> Lublin, during the darkest hours, became a center for torment and death. Lublin, an ingathering place for condemned Jews, led to the nearby concentration camps at Belzec and Majdanek. Lublin meant the great fall, not of one man, nor of one people, but of mankind.
>
> And yet, and yet . . .
>
> Hasidism is a movement out of despair, away from despair — a movement against despair. Only Hasidism? Judaism too. Who is a Jew? A Jew is he — or she — whose song cannot be muted, whose joy cannot be killed by the enemy . . . ever.

From early childhood, Wiesel lived within a community which considered itself to be a living commentary on the Bible: every ritual act had to be traced back to the Torah, and every Talmudic law was anchored in a biblical text. In *Le Chant des morts* (*Legends of Our Time*), Wiesel explores the inter-relationship between the generations throughout time. Cain prefigures Titus, and the sacrifice of Isaac heralds the Holocaust. Jacob chooses exile so that Moses can choose liberty; and even God studies the Torah. In a later book, *Célébration biblique* (*Messengers of God*), Wiesel moves beyond the standard commentaries and rabbinic interpretations towards mysticism. The "chain of transmission" includes the mystic *Book of Creation* and the tales remembered by the disciples of Rabbi Nachman, the "Dead Hasidim." But the messengers which pass to and fro in Wiesel's novels are all Elijah, in one form or another.

The land of Israel, and Jerusalem, is central to both the Bible and Wiesel. His passionate and poetic novel *Le Mendiant de Jérusalem* (*A Beggar in Jerusalem*) expresses a love for a Jerusalem in which the biblical, Talmudic, Hasidic, and Israeli dimensions join together upon the sacred hill which is the foundation of that city: Mt. Moriah, the place of Abraham's testing and of Isaac's near sacrifice. The master of that tale, about to die with all his community, summons up Abraham, Isaac, and Jacob and puts God on trial — a theme which is repeated in various Wiesel works. The biblical image that keeps recurring is of Abraham addressing God: the dialogue between man and God is a recurrent theme; but so is silence — God's silence, and the silence of humanity.

In a liturgy for *Yom Ha-Shoah* (Holocaust Memorial Day), Wiesel wrote (together with a rabbi) six stories which all end in death, commemorating the six million Jews killed in the Holocaust (*The Six Days of Destruction*). In the first story, a woman writes a letter to God which she places in her prayerbook. The story ends: "She hid the letter in her prayerbook. And when, with her family, she was taken to a ghetto far away in the East, she did not forget to take it with her. And so she was able to deliver it in person."

Each new book by Wiesel is filled with the concern for humanity which earned him the Nobel Peace prize. Each book is a letter addressed both to humanity and God. When one understands this, one begins to understand Elie Wiesel and his message.

—Albert H. Friedlander

WILLEMS, Paul. Belgian. Born in Missembourg, Edegem, 4 April 1912. Educated at the Lycée d'Anvers; Free University of Brussels, doctorate in law 1936. Served in the Belgian Army, 1937–40. Married Elza de Groodt in 1942; one son and one daughter. Lawyer, Antwerp, 1937–40; director of maritime fishing, Ministry of Rationing, Brussels, 1941–46; Secretary General, then Director General and delegated administrator, Palais des Beaux-Arts, Brussels, 1947–84. Secretary General, Fédération Internationale des Jeunesses Musicales; founder, with the Baron de Voghel, Europalia festival, 1969. Recipient: Belgian state prize, 1963, 1970, 1980; Latin Theatre prize (Barcelona), 1965; Marzotto prize, 1966. Member of l'Académie Royale (Belgium); C.B.E. (Commander, Order of the British Empire), 1969; Officier in de Orde van Oranje-Nassau (Pays-bas), 1973; Grand-Officier of l'Ordre de Léopold (Belgium), 1975; Das grosse Verdienstkreuz der Bundesrepublik Deutschland, 1979. Agent: (for French language) Société des Auteurs et Compositeurs Dramatiques, 29 Avenue Jeanne, 1050 Brussels, Belgium; (all other languages) Frau Dr. Maria Sommer, Kiepenheuerbühnenvertrieb Schweinfurthstrasse 60, 1000 Berlin-Dahlem 33, Germany. Address: 396 Mechelsesteenweg, 2650 Edegem, Belgium.

PUBLICATIONS

Plays

Le Bon Vin de Monsieur Nuche (produced Brussels, 1949). Brussels, Cahiers du Rideau, 1983.
Lamentable Julie (produced Brussels, 1949).
Peau d'ours (produced Brussels, 1951). Brussels, Artistes, 1958.
Off et la lune (produced Brussels, 1955).
Il pleut dans ma maison (produced in German, Vienna and Cologne, 1958; in French, Brussels, 1962). Brussels, Cahiers du Rideau, 1962; as *It's Raining in My House*, in *Dreams and Reflections*, 1992.
La Plage aux anguilles (produced Brussels, 1959). Brussels, Le Théâtre en Belgique, 1964.
Warna (produced Brussels, 1962). Brussels, Cahiers du Rideau, 1963; revised version, as *Warna, ou, Le Poids de la neige*, Brussels, Didascalies, 1984; as *The Weight of the Snow*, in *Dreams and Reflections*, 1992.
Le Marché des petites heures (produced in German, Salzburg, 1964; in French, Brussels, 1966). Brussels, Didscalies, 1983.
La Ville à voile (produced Brussels, 1967). Paris, Gallimard, 1967; as *The Sailing City*, in *Dreams and Reflections*, 1992.
Le Soleil sur la mer (produced Brussels, 1970).
Les Miroirs d'Ostende (produced Brussels, 1974). Brussels, Jacques Antoine, 1974.
Nuit avec ombres en couleurs (produced Brussels, 1983). Brussels, Didascalies, 1983.
Elle disait dormir pour mourir (produced Brussels, 1983). Brussels, Cahiers du Rideau, 1983; as *She Confused Sleeping and Dying*, in *Dreams and Reflections*, 1992.
La Vita breve (produced Spa, 1991). With *La Ville à voile*, Brussels, Labor, 1989.
Dreams and Relections: Plays of Paul Willems. New York, Garland, 1992.

Radio Play: *Plus de danger pour Berto*, 1966.

Television Play: *L'Écho*, 1963.

Fiction

Tout est réel ici.   Brussels, Toison d'Or, 1941.
Blessures.   Paris, Gallimard, 1945.
La Chronique du cygne.   Paris, Plon, 1949.
La Cathédrale de brume.   Montpellier, Fata Morgana, 1983.
Le Pays noyé.   Fontfroide-le-Haut, Fata Morgana, 1990.

Other

L'Herbe qui tremble.   Brussels, Toison d'Or, 1942.
Le Monde de Paul Willems (includes texts, interviews, and critical studies on Willems), edited by Paul Émond, Henri Ronse, and Fabrice van de Kerckhove.   Brussels, Labor, 1984.
Un Arrière-pays.   Louvain, Presses Universitaires de Louvain, 1989.

*

Paul Willems comments:

I hate abstraction. Writing is an act fuelled by desire, fear, anxiety, joy, anger, or by nostalgia for the horizon, a nostalgia familiar to those who have sailed and who have seen the line where the sky and the sea meet recede day after day.

To write is also to name. An act of faith that is always disappointed. The desired horizon is never reached, or even neared, and the thing we believe we've grasped vanishes the moment we name it. If our illusions were not inexhaustible, we wouldn't write. Therefore, disappointed act of faith, useless voyage.

Each person's voyage is different. Mine uses a situation and the moment. I always remain concrete. I start from a situation — for example, I bring three characters together and I wait. From this first situation a second will emerge, which in its turn will create a third. Memory is added to this formula, preferably unconscious memory, which in its turn nourishes the situation. You will not find abstraction in my work, nor Cartesian-like systems of thought. To that, my doors are shut.

*   *   *

Due to changing linguistic politics in Belgium, Paul Willems is the last of the great Belgian dramatic poets, such as Maurice Maeterlinck and Fernand Crommelynck, who were Flemings by birth but whose literary life has been conducted in French. Like his predecessors, Willems reveals in his work the allegorical tendencies and blend of earthiness and mysticism characteristic of Belgian literature.

Critics note that other influences on Willems's writing include German Romanticism, Surrealism, and Dadaism. In *The Theatre in French-Speaking Belgium Since 1945* (1991), Marc Quaghebeur characterizes Willems's drama as allied to magic realism. The author himself, however, insists he creates his works independent of any literary movement, the most precious gift known to man being total freedom of thought.

Willems began his literary career with novels and poetic essays — *Tout est réel ici* (Everything Here Is Real), *L'Herbe qui tremble* (Trembling Grass), *Blessures* (Wounds) — which bear the imprint of his hereditary family chateau, the Rousseau-esque retreat Missembourg, with its legendary ghost and gardens. Like his mother, poetess Marie Gevers, Willems celebrates intense sensory experiences that open a passage to "lost paradise," a recurring theme in his work. "I left the city and came to dream of paradise," says a character in *La Chronique du cygne* (The Swan's Chronicle). "It's not necessary to dream. Paradise is all around me; I find it in the colors of the world." Paradise, for Willems, resembles an Edenic garden of childhood innocence, unsullied by modern civilization and man's inhumanity to man.

In Willems's poetic vision, nature's ever-changing moods — the music of wind and rain and stormy seas, the silence of ponds, the whisper of trembling grass — contrast with the agony of cities, wherein the author depicts men building skyscrapers of illusory immortality to defend themselves from death. A self-proclaimed fatalistic pessimist who rejects religious orthodoxy, Willems nonetheless meditates with both irony and mystical delight on the nameless beauty of the Ephemeral. In the title story of *La Cathédrale de brume* (The Fog Cathedral), he recounts the parable of a famous architect who tires of building with stubborn stone (whose only destiny is to last) and instead creates a fog cathedral in which pilgrims commune with the Void, experiencing "a kind of healing emptiness, as if that man who lives inside us, who questions and judges us, were absent." After the architect dies of grief when war's ravages destroy his masterpiece, the narrator wryly notes, his friends betray his vision by erecting a stone memorial.

Turning to the theatre with *Le Bon Vin de Monsieur Nuche* (Good Wine, a Comedy for Springtime) in 1949, Willems translates into theatrical terms the rhythmic musicality and sensory imagery of the novels. Like Jean Giraudoux, with whom he shares verbal virtuosity and a taste for German Romanticism, Willems has preferred to collaborate with a "soul mate" director — first Pierre Laroche and more recently, Henri Ronse. Willems's dramas have also enjoyed popularity on German stages, several premiering in that country.

Raised in a Belgium torn by linguistic-cultural political battles between Flemings and francophone Walloons, the dramatist explains in *Le Monde de Paul Willems* (1984) that he has "always lived between two tongues." Thus his Romantic obsession with dualities interweaves with a thoroughly contemporary ambiguity towards the power of language and frustration at the failure of human communication. In his perennially popular *Il pleut dans ma maison* (It's Raining in My House) all the opposites (city and country dweller, man and woman, the living and the dead) speak different languages, and the gardener Bulle, knowing that "a raven is not a raven," attempts to translate between lovers. A tree growing inside a living room serves as a reminder of lost Eden. With psychological insight, Willems spins a poetic healing ritual: the reconciliation on the archetypal level of the original male/female split between the ghost couple Georges and Aunt Madeleine is reflected on the mundane level; all the opposites are reconciled and the garden returned to its rightful owners. The play ends with Bulle's ode to the Ephemeral and to the reflections that allow us to see ourselves and thus to grow. If this is a fairytale ending, Willems views fairytales as an "initiation" into life's mysteries. In our time, he proclaims, what we need is not demystification but "re-mythification."

While critics were initially misled by the poetic whimsy in Willems's plays, the more astute among them eventually realized, as Anne-Marie Glasheen notes in *Four Belgian Playwrights* (1986), that "Behind the fantasy, is cruelty; in the reflection of the water hides death." Willems's plays probe psychic wounds. His later plays are constructed, as Marc Quaghebeur observed in *Le Monde de Paul Willems*, as "a cruel game of mirrors." Underneath the humor and fanciful wordplay of Willems's theatrical fairytales lurks the darkness of the Brothers Grimm, as Willems sardonically watches our world lurch towards a fate best described by the name he gives his feline narrator of *Nuit avec ombres en couleurs* (Night with Colored Shadows) — Cat Astrophe.

Sexual love often appears as the serpent in Willems's garden — not because of biblical scruples but because Willems's lovers tend to prefer an image of the beloved to the beloved herself. Through multiple metaphors of mirrors, doubles, and life-sized dolls, Willems reflects a narcissistic world in which the individual is trapped in his own consciousness, unable truly to love. For instance, *La Ville à voile* (The Sailing City) portrays mortally ill Josty chasing his dream of happiness, the lost past drifting out of his grip. He marries young Anne-Marie, the exact replica of the shop mannequin that in his childhood Josty had fantasized as his future wife — but spurns her when she succumbs to his attempted rape, revealing herself as "a woman, nothing more."

Willems's post-Edenic world seethes with sexual perversion: incestuous fantasies, sadism, and murder. *La Vita breve* (The Short Life) probes the paradoxical intertwining of guilt and innocence, love and hate, sexuality and violence. Obsessed with the death of a Neapolitan courtesan, the Captain of Le Fameux Findor sets sail for Naples to track down her murderer. A "sailor's doll," a life-sized duplicate of the courtesan, provokes the unmasking of all the characters' capacity for brutal sexual jealousy. "It's not the guilty we must find," cries the Captain. "It's the innocent." Sexual jealousy finally leads to the disintegration of a country enamored of death in Willems's most recent novel, *Le Pays noyé* (The Drowned Country).

Willems's cruelty is far from gratuitous. As Max Lüthi notes in *Once Upon a Time* (1970), "Fairy tales concern themselves not with just happiness and light but quite often with privation and suffering, cruelty and betrayal, murder and death." Those who know Willems find the cruelty in his literature in contradiction with the almost angelic gentleness of his personality, but the voyages of self-confrontation he mirrors inspire us, his audiences and readers, to face the evil in ourselves.

—Suzanne Burgoyne

WITTIG, Monique. French. Born in Haut Rhin, Alsace, in 1935. Spokeswoman for Féministes Révolutionnaires association, from 1970. Lives in Paris. Recipient: Medicis prize, 1964. Address: c/o Éditions de Minuit, 7 rue Bernard-Palissy, 75006 Paris, France.

PUBLICATIONS

Fiction

L'Opoponax. Paris, Minuit, 1964; as *The Opoponax*, London, Owen, and New York, Simon and Schuster, 1966.
Les Guérillères. Paris, Minuit, 1969; in English, London, Owen, and New York, Viking, 1971.
Virgile, non. Paris, Minuit, 1985; as *Across the Acheron*, London, Owen, 1987.

Play

Le Voyage sans fin (produced Goddard College, Vermont, and Paris). Paris, Vlasta, 1985.

Verse

Le Corps lesbien. Paris, Minuit, 1973; as *The Lesbian Body*, translated by David Le Vay, London, Owen, and New York, Morrow, 1975.

Other

Brouillon pour un dictionnaire des amantes, with Sande Zeig. Paris, Grasset, 1976; as *Lesbian Peoples: Materials for a Dictionary*, New York, Avon, 1979; London, Virago, 1980.
The Straight Mind and Other Essays. Boston, Beacon Press, 1992.

Translator, with the author, *L'Homme unidimensionnel*, by Herbert Marcuse. Paris, Minuit, 1968.
Translator, with Vera Alves da Nobrega and Evelyne Le Garrec, *Nouvelles Lettres portugaises*, by Maria I. Barreno. Paris, Seuil, 1974.

*

Critical Studies: "Nouvelle, nouvelle autobiographie: Monique Wittig's *Le Corps lesbien*" by Lynn Higgins, in *SubStance* (Santa Barbara, California), 14, 1976; "Myth and Ms.: Encroachment and Liberation in Monique Wittig's *Les Guérillères*" by Mary Pringle Spraggins, in *International Fiction Review* (Fredericton, New Brunswick), January 1976; "Cannibalism and Fiction: Love and Eating in Fielding, Mailer, Genet and Wittig" by C. J. Rawson, in *Genre* (Norman, Oklahoma), Summer 1978; "Circle Games in Monique Wittig's *Les Guérillères*" by Jennifer R. Waelti-Walters, in *Perspectives on Contemporary Literature*, 6, 1980; "Language and the Vision of a Lesbian-Feminist Utopia in Wittig's *Les Guérillères*" by Marthe Rosenfeld, in *Frontiers* (Boulder, Colorado), Spring-Summer 1981; "The Text as Body/Politics: An Appreciation of Monique Wittig's Writings in Context" by Hélène Vivienne Wenzel, in *Feminist Studies* (College Park, Maryland), Summer 1981; "Amazons and Mothers? Monique Wittig, Hélène Cixous and Theories of Women's Writing" by Diane Griffin Crowder, in *Contemporary Literature* (Madison, Wisconsin), Summer 1983; "Language and Childhood: *L'Opoponax* by Monique Wittig," in *Forum for Modern Language Studies* (St. Andrews, Fife), October 1983, and "Women and Language in *Les Guérillères* by Monique Wittig," in *Stanford French Review* (California), Winter 1983, both by Jean H. Duffy; "By Myriad Constellations: Monique Wittig and the Writing of Women's Experience" by Winnie Woodhull (and a reply by Patricia S. Yaeger), in *Power, Gender, Values*, edited by Judith Genova, Edmonton, Alberta, Academic, 1987; "The Ontology of Language in a Post-Structuralist Feminist Perspective: Explosive Discourse in Monique Wittig" by Lois Oppenheim, in *Poetics of the Elements of the Human Condition, II*, edited by Anna-Teresa Tymienicka, Dordrecht, Kluwer, 1988; "Writing Feminism: Myth, Epic and Utopia in Monique Wittig's *Les Guérillères*" by Lawrence M. Porter, in *L'Esprit Créateur* (Baton Rouge, Louisiana), Fall 1989.

*   *   *

Of all the French feminists who have taken as their clarion call Simone de Beauvoir's celebrated statement "One is not born a woman," Monique Wittig offers probably the most radical response. If her mission is to overturn a society that is patriarchal in both its practice and its discourse, she is not content merely to deconstruct a phallocentric universe but proceeds to a Utopian reconstruction based on what she sees as the nature of the female subject. She also parts company with other contemporary French feminists, notably Hélène Cixous (*q.v.*), in her determination to assail the historical and material basis of women's oppression. A preoccupation with language is to be found in all her work, since the alternative world she seeks to create must invent its own vocabulary and discourse so as to avoid recuperation by the phallocratic society she seeks to destroy. Whereas Beauvoir had assigned a prominent place in her work to autobiographical writing, Wittig has divulged little of her own history and personality. For the success of her mission depends on the avoidance of all established forms of writing, since she considers these contaminated by the masculine world that sanctions them.

Wittig's fictions seek progressively to exclude men from their precincts and to give expression to a celebration of the female body. She sees her task as being to reappropriate woman's body from the masculine, fetishizing gaze. This involves her in intimate descriptions of the female genitalia but in terms that contrast absolutely with the male language of pornography. On offer to women is not only an increased pleasure, with the source of femininity being appreciated for its own sake rather than in relation to possession by the male, but also the achievement of a new female subjectivity rooted in a sense of wholeness. Lesbianism duly emerges from being a relatively discreet presence in *L'Opoponax* (*The Opoponax*) to a choice explored unrelentingly in *Le Corps lesbien* (*The Lesbian Body*). Wittig's opposition to heterosexuality is total. As she insists in her essay entitled "Paradigm" in *Homosexualities and French Literature*, 1979): "Heterosexuality is a cultural construct designed to justify the whole system of social domination based on the obligatory reproductive function of women." Unlike many feminists, she mounts a virulent attack on psychoanalysis for its questionable assumption that sexual fulfilment can ensue only from heterosexual intercourse.

Paradoxically, Wittig insists that her lesbians are not women. Instead, the lesbian is an idealized being she places in opposition to "woman," the latter being the economic, political, and ideological invention of men. "Men" and "women" are reduced to the status of anachronisms. In *Brouillon pour un dictionnaire des amantes* (*Lesbian Peoples: Materials for a Dictionary*), "women" are duly replaced by "amazons" and *amantes* ("female lovers"). The narrator in *Les Guérillères* shows the Amazons to be aware that the recuperative male enemy dismisses their revolt as the desire merely to appropriate the phallus. She goes on to incant their commitment to breaking with traditional oppositions:

The women say, I refuse henceforward to speak this language, I refuse to mumble after them the words lack of penis lack of money lack of insignia lack of name. I refuse to pronouce the names of possession and non-possession. They say, If I take over the world, let it be to dispossess myself of it immediately, let it be to forge new links between myself and the world.

Wittig's Utopianism could indeed never be content with a mere transference of power that left the structures of the world unchanged.

The Opoponax is Wittig's most conventional work and caused her to be hailed in 1964 as following in the steps of Alain Robbe-Grillet (*q.v.*) and his fellow "new novelists." Those who looked beyond the rejection of traditional notions of character and the unrelieved flow of neutral descriptive statements invariably saw the content as reflecting "every-body's childhood," thereby obscuring Wittig's conviction that the world which so baffles Catherine Legrand (the surname is carefully chosen to connote the masculine) before being rejected by her in favour of her own "opoponax" or private symbolic world, is unambiguously patriarchal. In retrospect, even the "nought" that she receives in class can be related to Wittig's celebration of the vulval circle. Wittig's other novels leave the reader in no doubt as to their purpose. For structure, they rely on the subversion of familiar literary genres that have perpetuated phallocractic power. *Les Guérillères* (a feminine neologism highlighting the "ll" present in the subject pronoun "elle") rewrites the traditional epic poem. *The Lesbian Body* rewrites the Song of Songs and Western mythology, offering for our delectation such figures as Ulyssa and Christa. *Lesbian Peoples: Materials for a Dictionary* undermines the most normative of all literary productions, the lexicon. *Virgile, non* (*Across the Acheron*) is a parody of Dante's Inferno.

The need to avoid the phallocentric entails constant experimentation. Wittig's compositions seem more like avant-garde narrative poems than novels. Her deconstructive approach to personal and social identity involves a rejection of the conventional use of pronouns and possessive adjectives that sometimes places insuperable difficulty in the way of English translators. Already in *The Opoponax*, the child's view of herself is expressed in terms of the impersonal pronoun "on," or by referring to herself as "Catherine Legrand." Only in the final sentence, in her recognition of her love for her classmate Valérie Borge, is she able to voice the subject pronoun "I." In *Les Guérillères*, the collective third-person pronoun "elles" is used throughout; only when the successful campaign has led to a sense of unity, symbolized by the singing of the "Internationale," is the narrator able to say "we." No such reticence is observed in the purely female world of *The Lesbian Body*, but, here, all the first-person pronouns and possessive adjectives are rent in two by an attention-catching use of the slash, indicating, in the words of one sympathetic commentator, "the split nature of any female who attempts to constitute herself as the subject of her own discourse."

The ideology of liberation underlying Wittig's Utopian vision is easily assimilated and goes well beyond narrowly feminist concerns. But if the terms of her attack on phallocracy are vulnerable to the charge of being naïve and simplistic, her innovative discourse may nevertheless convince even sceptical readers that women's writing about themselves has been — and continues to be — strikingly incomplete.

—Michael Tilby

———

WOHMANN, Gabriele (née Guyot). German. Born in Darmstadt, 21 May 1932. Educated at the University of Frankfurt, 1951–53. Married Reiner Wohmann in 1953. Teacher, Langeoog island, and Darmstadt, 1953–56. Recipient: Villa Massimo grant, 1967–68; City of Bremen prize, 1971; Order of Merit, 1980; Hessischer prize, 1988. Member, Academy of Arts, Berlin 1975, and German Academy for Languages and Literature, 1980. Address: Ludwig-Engel- Weg 11, Park Rosenhöhe, 6100 Darmstadt, Germany.

PUBLICATIONS

Fiction

Jetzt und nie. Darmstadt, Luchterhand, 1958.
Mit einem Messer (as Gabriele Guyot). Stierstadt, Eremiten-Presse, 1958.
Sieg über die Dämmerung. Munich, Piper, 1960.
Trinken ist das Herrlichste. Darmstadt, Roether, 1963.
Erzählungen: Im Auftrage des Volksbundes für Dichtung, edited by Reinhold Siegrist. Karlsruhe, Volksbund für Dichtung, 1964.
Abschied für länger. Olten, Walter, 1965.
Erzählungen: Eine Auswahl 1965–1966. Ebenhausen, Langewiesche-Brandt, 1966.
Ein unwiderstehlicher Mann: Erzählungen. Ebenhausen, Langewische-Brandt, 1966.
Die Bütows. Stierstadt, Eremiten-Presse, 1967; revised edition, 1971.
Ländliches Fest und andere Erzählungen. Neuwied, Luchterhand, 1968.
Sonntag bei den Kreisands: Erzählungen. Stierstadt, Eremiten-Presse, 1970.
Ernste Absicht. Neuwied, Luchterhand, 1970.
Treibjagd: Erzählungen, edited by Heinz Schöffler. Stuttgart, Reclam, 1970.
Übersinnlich. Düsseldorf, Eremiten-Presse, 1972.
Alles für die Galerie: Erzählungen. Berlin, Aufbau, 1972; as "Everything for the Gallery and Other Stories," in *Dimension,* 4(1), 1971.
Gegenangriff. Neuwied, Luchterhand, 1972.
Habgier: Erzählungen. Düsseldorf, Eremiten-Presse, 1973.
Paulinchen war allein zu Haus. Neuwied, Luchterhand, 1974.
Dorothea Wörth: Erzählung. Düsseldorf, Eremiten-Presse, 1975.
Schönes Gehege. Neuwied, Luchterhand, 1975.
Ein Fall von Chemie: Erzählung. Düsseldorf, Eremiten-Presse, 1975.
Ausflug mit der Mutter. Neuwied, Luchterhand, 1976.
Alles zu seiner Zeit: Erzählungen. Munich, Deutscher Taschenbuch, 1976.
Böse Streiche und andere Erzälungen. Düsseldorf, Eremiten-Presse, 1977.
Das dicke Wilhelmchen: Erzählungen. Düsseldorf, Eremiten-Presse, 1978.
Frühherbst in Badenweiler. Neuwied, Luchterhand, 1978.
Die Nächste bitte!: Erzählung. Düsseldorf, Eremiten-Presse, 1978.
Nachrichtensperre. Berlin, Aufbau, 1978.
Erzählungen. Ebenhausen, Langewiesche-Brandt, 1978.
Streit: Erzählungen. Düsseldorf, Eremiten-Presse, 1978.
Ausgewählte Erzählungen aus zwanzig Jahren. Neuwied, Luchterhand, 2 vols., 1979.
Knoblauch am Kamin: Erzählung. Düsseldorf, Eremiten-Presse, 1979.
Paarlauf: Erzählungen. Neuwied, Luchterhand, 1979.
Ach wie gut, dass niemand weiss. Neuwied, Luchterhand, 1980.
Vor der Hochzeit: Erzählungen. Reinbek, Rowohlt, 1980.
Wir sind eine Familie: Erzählungen. Düsseldorf, Eremiten-Presse, 1980.
Violas Vorbilder: eine Erzählung. Düsseldorf, Eremiten-Presse, 1980.
Guilty. Düsseldorf, Eremiten-Presse, 1980.
Komm donnerstags. Munich, Deutscher Taschenbuch, 1981.
Stolze Zeiten: Erzählungen. Düsseldorf, Claassen, 1981.
Das Glücksspiel. Neuwied, Luchterhand, 1981.

Ein günstiger Tag: Erzählungen. Düsseldorf, Eremiten-Presse, 1981.
Einsamkeit: Erzählungen. Neuwied, Luchterhand, 1982.
Das Trugbild: Erzählung. Hauzenberg, Pongratz, 1982.
Der kürzeste Tag des Jahres: Erzählungen. Neuwied, Luchterhand, 1983.
Verliert, oder?: Erzählungen. Neuwied, Luchterhand, 1983.
Goethe hilf! Erzählungen. Düsseldorf, Eremiten-Presse, 1983.
Bucklicht Männlein: Erzählungen. Berlin, Aufbau, 1984.
Der Kirschbaum: Erzählung. Düsseldorf, Eremiten-Presse, 1984.
Der Irrgast. Neuwied, Luchterhand, 1985.
Gesammelte Erzählungen aus dreißig Jahren. Neuwied, Luchterhand, 3 vols., 1986.
Der Flötenton. Neuwied, Luchterhand, 1987.
Ein russischer Sommer: Erzählungen. Neuwied, Luchterhand, 1988.
Kassensturz. Neuwied, Luchterhand, 1989.
Er Saß in dem Bus, der seine Frau überfuhr. Hamburg, n.p., 1991.
Das Salz, bitte! Munich, n.p., 1992.

Plays

Große Liebe und andere Liebesgeschichten von heute. Munich, Desch, 1968.
Große Liebe (television play). Bad Homburg, Tsamas, 1971.
Die Gäste (radio play). Basel, Lenos Presse, 1971.
Die Witwen, oder, Eine vollkommene Lösung (television play). Stuttgart, Reclam, 1972.
Entziehung: Materialien zu einem Fernsehfilm. Neuwied, Luchterhand, 1974.
Heiratskandidaten (television play and three radio plays). Munich, Piper, 1978; adapted for stage (produced Augsburg, 1981).
Der Nachtigall fällt auch nichts Neues ein: ein Dialog. Düsseldorf, Eremiten-Presse, 1978; enlarged edition, Munich, Deutscher Taschenbuch, 1979.
Wanda Lords Gespenster (radio play). Düsseldorf, Eremiten-Presse, 1979; adapted for stage (produced Darmstadt, 1980), Bad Homburg, Hunzinger-Bühnen, 1980.
Plötzlich in Limburg: Komödie in 4 Bildern. Bad Homburg, Hunzinger-Bühnen, 1981.
Nachkommenschaften (television play). Düsseldorf, Eremiten-Presse, 1981.
Hilfe kommt mir von den Bergen (radio play). Düsseldorf, Eremiten-Presse, 1982.
Hebräer 11.1 (radio play). Düsseldorf, Eremiten-Presse, 1985.
Darmstadt: Unterwegs gehöre ich nach Haus (television play). Freiburg, Eulen, 1986.
Plötzlich in Limburg: Komödie in vier Bildern. Munich, Piper, 1989.

Radio Plays: *Norwegian Wood,* 1967; *Der Fall Rufus,* 1969; *Tod in Basel,* 1972; *Wanda Lords Gespenster,* 1979; *Hebräer 11.1,* 1981; *Es geht mir gut, ihr Kinder,* 1988; *Drück mir die Daumen,* 1991.

Television Plays: *Das Rendezvous,* 1965; *Große Liebe,* 1966; *Die Witwen,* 1972; *Entziehung,* 1973; *Heiratskandidaten,* 1975; *Nachkommenschaften,* 1977; *Paulinchen war allein zu Haus,* 1981; *Unterwegs,* 1985; *Schreiben müssen,* 1990.

Verse

So ist die Lage. Düsseldorf, Eremiten-Presse, 1974.
Grund zur Aufregung. Neuwied, Luchterhand, 1978.
Ich weiss das auch nicht besser. Munich, Deutscher Taschenbuch, 1980.
Komm lieber Mai. Neuwied, Luchterhand, 1981.
Gesammelte Gedichte 1964–1982. Neuwied, Luchterhand, 1983.
Passau, Gleis 3. Neuwied, Luchterhand, 1984.
Das könnte ich sein: sechzig neue Gedichte. Düsseldorf, Eremiten-Presse, 1989.

Other

Theater von innen: Protokoll einer Inszenierung. Olten and Freiburg, Walter, 1966.
In Darmstadt leben die Künste: Feuilleton. Darmstadt, Schlapp, 1967.
Selbstverteidigung: Prosa und anderes. Neuwied, Luchterhand, 1971.
Der Fall Rufus: Ein Elternabend. Stierstadt, Eremiten-Presse, 1971.
Endlich allein, endlich zu zwein. Düsseldorf, Eremiten-Presse, 1976.
Materialienbuch. Neuwied, Luchterhand, 1977.
Feuer bitte! Düsseldorf, Eremiten-Presse, 1978.
Meine Lektüre: Aufsätze über Bücher. Neuwied, Luchterhand, 1980.
Geschwister, photographs by John Harding. Frankfurt, Fricke, 1982.
Ich lese, ich schreibe: Autobiographische Essays. Neuwied, Luchterhand, 1984.
Begegnung mit zwei Eichen. Munich, Delphin, 1985.
Glücklicher Vorgang. Düsseldorf, Eremiten-Presse, 1986.
Unterwegs: ein Tagebuch. Neuwied, Luchterhand, 1986.
Darmstadt: Unterwegs gehöre ich nach Haus, photographs by Roman Grösser. Freiburg, Eulen, 1986.
Fensterblicke. Isernhagen/Hanover, Galerie Lüpfert, 1989.

Editor, *Anton Cechov.* Cologne, Kiepenheuer und Witsch, 1985.

*

Critical Studies: "The Short Stories and Novels of Gabriele Wohmann" by H. M. Waidson, in *German Life and Letters* (London), 26(3), 1973; "The Short Fiction of Gabriele Wohmann" by Kenneth Hughes, in *Studies in Short Fiction* (Newberry, South Carolina), 13(1), 1976; "Gabriele Wohmann: A Thematic Approach to Alienation" by Gisela G. Strand, in *Michigan Academician* (Ann Arbor), Spring 1977; "Quotation and Literary Echo as Structural Principles in Gabriele Wohmann's *Frühherbst in Badenweiler*" by Walter H. Sokel, in *Studies in Twentieth-Century Literature* (Manhattan, Kansas), Fall 1980; "Portrait and Self-Portrait: Gabriele Wohmann's *Ausflug mit der Mutter*" by Yvonne Holbeche, in *Seminar* (Kingston, Ontario), 20(3), 1984.

Gabriele Wohmann comments:

"Artist, do not talk, create!" Goethe's exhortation is as close to my heart as Chekhov's "autobiography phobia": he consistently refused to make pronouncements about himself. I have indeed answered questions in many interviews — but my instinct warns me against explaining my own work. I write about people, and to do this I use empathy, observation, and imagination — leaving interpretation to those for whom it is a necessary part of reading. I do not find myself difficult to understand.

*   *   *

Gabriele Wohmann has suffered rather than profited from her reputation as one of the most prolific writers in Germany today. In a culture which has traditionally made a sharp distinction between serious and popular authors, Wohmann's prodigious output and wide readership have outstripped her critical reception. As early as the 1970s certain sections of the West German literary establishment were already prepared to dismiss her work, which had begun to appear in the late 1950s, as thematically restricted and structurally repetitive.

Her work is indeed relentlessly focused on the world of the everyday; her characters present an unremitting parade of the failed or the unfulfilled, a kaleidoscope of men and women who inhabit the contradictory world of the post-war Federal Republic of Germany, a society which superficially offers a degree of economic freedom to the individual unmatched in Europe's history yet remains incapable of allowing its citizens to slip the fetters imposed by that society in order to find personal happiness. Those restrictions are not presented as abstract treatises but are revealed concretely through what may be regarded as Wohmann's obsessive preoccupation with endless case studies of particular fictional lives which all illustrate the same tenet.

In novels, radio plays, verse, scripts for television and, above all and most characteristically, in hundreds of short stories, Wohmann offers her readers the fragments of overtly insignificant lives. Typically, many of these stories begin with the coordinating conjunction "and," the very arbitrariness of such openings suggesting the aimlessness and inconclusiveness of the existences led by her characters. If gathered together, the sum total of all these lives should represent for the reader something akin to a *comédie humaine* on modern German society, yet they fall short of that because Wohmann is reluctant to engage explicitly and in detail with the outer world engulfing the lives of her characters. (References to the Chernobyl disaster in her more recent novel *Der Flötenton* [The Sound of the Flute] represented a major departure from her conscious practice of withholding social, political, or historical references, and Wohmann has always struggled against the wish to see her work more tangibly linking her characters' fate with specific events in the real world.) Wohmann's unhappy wives, tired and middle-aged employees, fading actresses, minor artists, and damaged children are not offered as parts of a richer mosaic. Their lives are as dull as the world these characters recognise themselves as inhabiting. And in revealing contrast to Marie Luise Kaschnitz, the leading German woman writer of the previous generation, who also concentrated on the world of ordinary people, Wohmann does not permit her creations the possibility of grace to imbue their lives with significance. What motivates Wohmann to write, as she confessed in an essay of 1971, "Jemand der schreibt" (Someone Who Writes), is her observation of that which she finds in the daily grind of existence, namely "death's variations in the midst of life."

If they cannot be transfigured, Wohmann's creations at least delude themselves that they can be transformed, and the wish for transformation becomes a survival technique. The reader soon grows alert to the basic configurations within Wohmann's fiction; she concentrates on those points and stages in life where society, or habit, engulf and stifle individual aspirations: in marriage, at the work place or at that moment where childhood confronts the adult world. Because society will not allow itself to be changed, its victims give up any effort to interact with the real world and instead adopt purely illusory strategies to change their lives. Thus in the short story "Parkverbot" (Parking Prohibited) ageing actress Winnie Täufer responds to the lack of recognition in her life by answering an urgent message over a station loudspeaker for a Frau Heinz to report to the station master immediately. Winnie sees here the chance to slip into a new identity, a last possibility in life to experience some dangerous adventure. Instead she is greeted by the request to remove an illegally parked car. In the short prose piece "Dinner at 8" the narrator cannot deceive either herself or her reader for very long that what she portrays as a luxury hotel set in the countryside with attentive uniformed servants and waiters is in fact an institution for the mentally ill.

The marked lack of action or plot in Wohmann's writing is compensated for by what must be seen as the hallmark of all her fiction: the torrent of words that all her characters pour out over their frustrated lives. In a seemingly endless stream of vocabulary that betrays a debt both to Marcel Proust and James Joyce, Wohmann's characters smother the insignificance of their world with reflections, imagined dialogues, and altercations which by their very virtuosity make good the missing momentum caused by the absence of a story line.

As if to anticipate the charge of one-dimensionalism in her writing, Wohmann has provided what might be termed the philosophical foundation and justification to her approach, her obsession with the immediate and her avoidance of the abstract. Her recent book *Schreiben müssen* (Must Write) contained the text to her film *Jetzt ist nur jetzt* (Now Is Only Now); here she offers her creed:

Today is today and only today. Today is not the day before yesterday and not the day after tomorrow, and now is only now, now it is quiet, a moment before and a moment afterwards is not now, and in this moment NOW I try to be completely here, and not there or there . . .

To this she adds the conviction that: "Truly, in the specific moment we understand the meaning of the eternal." Wohmann, the pastor's daughter, may have shown, after all, that in her case ceaseless writing is as much a mission as it is a condition.

—Anthony Bushell

WOLF, Christa. German. Born in Landsberg an der Warthe, Germany (now Gorzow, Poland), 18 March 1929. Educated at a school in Bad Frankenhausen, graduated 1949; universities of Jena and Leipzig, 1949–53, diploma 1953. Married Gerhard Wolf in 1951; two daughters. Secretary to the mayor of Gammelin, after 1945; technical assistant, East German Writers' Union, 1950s; editor, *Neue deutsche Literatur*; reader for Mitteldeutscher Verlag, Halle, 1959–62, and Verlag Neues Leben, Berlin; worked in a freight car manufacturing company, 1959–62. Member of the German Communist Party (resigned 1989); candidate member of central committee, SED, 1967–68. Recipient: Heinrich Mann prize, 1963; National prize, 1964; Raabe prize, 1972; Fontane prize, 1972; City of Bremen prize, 1978; Büchner prize, 1980; Schiller prize, 1983. Member, Academy of Arts, Berlin. Address: Friedrichstraße 133, 1040 Berlin, Germany.

PUBLICATIONS

Fiction

Moskauer Novelle. Halle, Mitteldeutscher, 1961.
Der geteilte Himmel. Halle, Mitteldeutscher, 1963; as *Divided Heaven*, Berlin, Seven Seas, 1965; New York, Adler, 1976.
Nachdenken über Christa T. Halle, Mitteldeutscher, 1968; as *The Quest for Christa T.*, New York, Farrar Straus, 1970; London, Hutchinson, 1971.
Till Eulenspiegel: Erzählung für den Film. Berlin, Aufbau, 1972.
Unter den Linden: Drei unwahrscheinliche Geschichten. Berlin, Aufbau, 1974.
Kindheitsmuster. Berlin, Aufbau, 1976; as *A Model Childhood*, New York, Farrar Straus, and London, Virago, 1982.
Kein Ort, Nirgends. Berlin, Aufbau, 1979; as *No Place on Earth*, New York, Farrar Straus, 1982; London, Virago, 1983.
Gesammelte Erzählungen. Neuwied, Luchterhand, 1980.
Kassandra. Neuwied, Luchterhand, 1983; as *Cassandra: A Novel and Four Essays*, New York, Farrar Straus, and London, Virago, 1984.
Erzählungen. Berlin, Aufbau, 1985.
Neue Lebensansichten eines Katers; *Juninachmittag: Erzählungen.* Leipzig, Reclam, 1986.
Störfall: Nachrichten eines Tages. Berlin, Aufbau, 1987; as *Accident: A Day's News*, New York, Farrar Straus, and London, Virago, 1989.
Sommerstück. Berlin, Aufbau, 1989.
Was bleibt: Erzählung. Neuwied, Luchterhand, 1990.
What Remains and Other Stories. New York, Farrar Straus, 1993.

Verse

Das Leben der Schildkröten in Frankfurt am Main: ein Prosagedicht. Leipzig, Sisyphos, 1989.

Other

Lesen und Schreiben: Aufsätze und Prosastücke. Berlin, Aufbau, 1972; revised edition, 1981; as *The Reader and the Writer*, Berlin, Seven Seas, 1977; New York, International, 1978.
Fortgesetzter Versuch: Aufsätze, Gespräche, Essays. Leipzig, Reclam, 1979.
Voraussetzungen einer Erzählung: Kassandra. Neuwied, Luchterhand, 1983.
Ins Ungebundene gehet eine sehnsucht: Gesprächsraum Romantik, with Gerhard Wolf. Berlin, Aufbau, 1985.
Die Dimension des Autors: Essays und Aufsätze, Reden und Gespräche, 1959–1985. Berlin, Aufbau, 2 vols., 1986; selections published as *The Fourth Dimension: Interviews with Christa Wolf*, London, Verso, 1988.
Ansprachen. Neuwied, Luchterhand, 1988.
Essays of Christa Wolf. New York, Holmes and Meier, 1990.
Reden im Herbst. Berlin, Aufbau, 1990.
The Author's Dimension: Selected Essays. New York, Farrar Straus, 1993.

Editor, with Gerhard Wolf, *Wir, unsere Zeit.* Berlin, Aufbau, 1959.
Editor, *In diesen Jahren: Deutsche Erzähler der Gegenwart.* Leipzig, Reclam, 1959.

Editor, *Proben junger Erzähler: Ausgewählte deutsche Prosa*. Leipzig, Reclam, 1959.

Editor, *Glauben an Irdisches*, by Anna Seghers. Leipzig, Reclam, 1969.

Editor, *Verzeichnis der Hochschullehrerder TH Darmstadt*. Darmstadt, Verlag des Historischen Vereins für Hessen, 1977.

Editor, *Der Schatten eines Traumes*, by Karoline von Günderrode. Neuwied, Luchterhand, 1979.

Editor, *Die Günderrode*, by Bettina von Arnim. Leipzig, Insel, 1981.

Editor, *Materialienbuch*, with Klaus Sauer. Neuwied, Luchterhand, 1983.

Editor, *Ausgewahlte Erzählungen*, by Anna Seghers. Neuwied, Luchterhand, 1983.

Editor, *Historischer Verein für Hessen, 1934–1983*. Darmstadt, Verlag des Historischen Vereins für Hessen, 1983.

*

Critical Studies: "The Gender of Authorship: Heiner Müller and Christa Wolf" by Helen Fehervary, in *Studies in 20th-Century Literature* (Manhattan, Kansas), Fall 1980; "'Tacit Knowledge' in *Der geteilte Himmel* and *Nachdenken über Christa T*" by Doris Brett, in *Colloquia Germanica* (Lexington, Kentucky), 17(3–4), 1984; *The Death of Socialist Realism in the Novels of Christa Wolf* by George Bühler, New York, Lang, 1984; "Christa Wolf" by Sneja Gunew, in *Meanjin* (Parkville, Victoria), March 1985; "The Politics of Love: Ideology and Romance in Christa Wolf's *Der geteilte Himmel*" by Steven Joyce, in *New German Studies* (Hull), Spring 1985; "Generational Patterns in Christa Wolf's *Kindheitsmuster*" by David Dollenmayer, in *German Life and Letters* (London), April 1986; "'Scratching Away the Male Tradition': Christa Wolf's *Kassandra*," in *Contemporary Literature* (Madison, Wisconsin), Spring 1986, and "Christa Wolf's *Cassandra*: Parallels to Feminism in the West," in *Critique* (Washington, D.C.), Spring 1987, both by Linda Schelbitzki-Pickle; "Appropriating Romantic Consciousness: Narrative Mode in Christa Wolf's *Kein Ort, Nirgends*" by Linda Dietrick, in *Echoes and Influences of German Romanticism*, edited by Michael Batts, Anthony W. Riley, and Heinz Wetzel, New York, Lang, 1987; "Christa Wolf's *Kassandra*: Myth or Anti-Myth?" by Jürgen Lieskonnig, in *Theoria* (Natal), October 1987; "*Nachdenken über Christa T* and the Bildungsroman" by Roman Struc, in *Echoes and Influences of German Romanticism*, edited by Michael Batts, Anthony W. Riley, and Heinz Wetzel, New York, Lang, 1987; "Prophecy in Search of a Voice: Silence in Christa Wolf's *Kassandra*" by Edith Waldstein, in *Germanic Review* (New York), Fall 1987; "Divisions and Transformations: Christa Wolf's *Störfall*," in *German Life and Letters* (London), October 1987, and "'These Drowsy Approaches of Sleep': Christa Wolf and the Hypnagogic Dream," in *New German Studies* (Hull), 14(3), 1986–87, both by Andrew Winnard; "The Transsexual as Anders in Christa Wolf's 'Self-Experiment'" by Anne Herrmann, in *Genders* (Boulder, Colorado), November 1988; *Christa Wolf's Utopian Vision: From Marxism to Feminism*, edited by Anna K. Kuhn, Cambridge, Cambridge University Press, 1988; *Difficulties of Saying "I": The Narrator as Protagonist in Christa Wolf's "Kindheitsmuster" and Uwe Jonson's "Jahrestage"* by Robert K. Shirer, New York, Lang, 1988; "Christa Wolf and Anna Seghers" by Colin Smith, in *German Life and Letters* (London), April 1988; "Probing the Blind Spot: Utopia and Dystopia in Christa Wolf's *Störfall*" by Ute Brandes, in *Selected Papers from the Fourteenth New Hampshire Symposium on the German Democratic Republic*, edited by Margy Gerber and others, Lanham, Maryland, University Press of America, 1989; "The *Kassandra* of Christa Wolf (1983)" by Russell E. Brown, in *Classical and Modern Literature* (Terre Haute, Indiana), Winter 1989; *Responses to Christa Wolf*, edited by Marilyn Sibley Fries, Detroit, Wayne State University Press, 1989.

* * *

Christa Wolf is one of the few writers of the former German Democratic Republic to make a major reputation not only in the other half of Germany, but, in translation, in the rest of Europe and the United States. In her case it is difficult to separate biography and literary output, not only because her lifetime spans the crucial period of German history from the Nazi seizure of power to the "gentle revolution" and subsequent reunification of Germany, but also because she propounded an influential theory of "subjective authenticity" to underpin her chosen novelistic position, as a counter to the variants of official Socialist Realism. It foregrounds the author's experience of that history, not in terms of public event, but as it affects the deepest layers of her own psyche.

In this respect she took on, or was awarded by her readers, the function of representative voice for her half of a divided Germany. "How did we become what we are today?" is the key question of her deeply self-scrutinizing autobiographical novel *Kindheitsmuster* (*A Model Childhood*). The discoveries she makes from encountering her own buried life-history — models of authority and obedience, responses of self-division and bad faith — made therapeutic reading for readers behind the Berlin Wall ready to question the moral and psychological bases of their own society. That "we" is characteristic, not only of the sense of intimate identification she offers to and draws from her readers, but also of her strong sense of solidarity with the GDR from its inception — one which became more critical and self-critical as the years of "really existing Socialism" went by.

Wolf began her literary career in fiction with *Moskauer Novelle* (*Moscow Novella*), an obedient exercise in Socialist Realism. In it a German woman doctor years after the war on a friendship mission to USSR re-encounters a liberating Russian officer now blinded as a result of her adolescent hostility; this brief encounter ends in an emblematic act of reconciliation on behalf of two former enemy states. Wolf now dismisses it as naïve and has never had it reprinted.

Her next story, *Der geteilte Himmel* (*Divided Heaven*), made her early reputation. It is a modest enough love story of the girl from the country who proves herself a good citizen by working valiantly in the railway wagon workshop, and by choosing, at great personal cost, to stay there when her lover, an older engineer of bourgeois origins, rebuffed in his career, urges her to leave for the West with him. The ambivalence of the "little work" (on the one hand the heroine's choice represents a bow to official judgement; on the other, she is brought close to suicide in making it) set a pattern for Wolf's later, greater achievements. So did the overreaction of its reception: on the one hand it was attacked for having represented a divided Germany in terms of inner conflict — and what is more, West German critics had begun to notice a new talent; on the other, new talent was not so common that it could be dismissed. Indeed, she was awarded the Heinrich Mann prize.

Wolf could have turned into a literary functionary. She had enough talent, commitment, and favour in high places, in 1967 she actually became a candidate member of the Zentralkommittee of the German Socialist Unity Party (SED). But her defence of offending writers at the 1965 Plenum of the Central Committee (ZK) — a rare voice at a time when the authorities were redoubling their insistence on the writer's function as ideological instrument — ensured her removal a year later. These years also mark a major shift in her writing style. In *Nachdenken über Christa T.* (*The Quest for Christa T.*) she abandons the kitsch of the ideal figures and happy endings required by the socialist plot for the figure of the imaginative outsider, for projected self-divisions, and for her characteristic internalised reflective mode and procedural narration which activate the reader to collaborate in the making of meaning. The narrator goes in search of the life story of her dead friend, but out of the process of mourning comes self-confrontation; the lost Christa's non-conforming values of conscience, imagination, and openness are internalised and regained by her survivor just in time. The novel ends with a challenge to the reader too: "When, if not now!" "Now" was 1968, the year of the Prague Spring. But GDR soldiers joined the Russian tanks invading Czechoslovakia, and the novel had a rough ride through the censorship.

It was followed by the searching *A Model Childhood*, also a quest for an integral self. It appeared as the Wolf Biermann (*q.v.*) affair was breaking: the critical songwriter, long a thorn in the side of the GDR authorities, finally had his citizenship withdrawn while he was in West Germany, performing for the first time in years. Wolf was one of a group of writers to protest, and though the terms of their protest seem cautious enough now, it ushered in a period when it was made brutally clear to Wolf and her colleagues that they had nothing to offer the GDR state. Wolf's answer was the poetic novel *Kein Ort, Nirgends* (*No Place on Earth*), a coded imaginary dialogue between two writers of the Romantic period, Heinrich von Kleist and Karoline von Günderode, who exemplify the alienation their successors were to experience. Its last words are: "We know what is coming."

What came for Wolf was surveillance by the Stasi and near-paralysis as a writer. She wrote a frozen account of the experience which she could not publish until after the end of the GDR.

But for a fruitful time Wolf found a new solidarity outside the GDR as much as within it during the last years of the Cold War, in the international women's movement and in her reworking of the ancient tale of Troy. Their products are her Frankfurt Lectures in Poetics of 1982 and the story whose preconditions they (partially) tell, *Kassandra* (*Cassandra*). The lectures (published as *Voraussetzungen einer Erzählung: Kassandra*) pursue the question of the distinctive nature of women's writing. Deftly she subsumes the essentialist and the historical-relativist views by her characteristic appeal to experience: ". . . to the extent that for biological and historical reasons women experience a different reality from men." In the internalised monologue of *Cassandra* itself she takes on the major masculine epic and dramatic traditions of the Western world (Homer and Aeschylus), rewriting the heroics from the point of view of the women, as objects, complicit or rebellious, of marriage treaty, barter, and lust. It is also the story of the painful disengagement of a loyalty. Cassandra, once the favourite daughter of the ruling house, refuses to tell its truths, which are her lies; is cast out, finds brief respite and a glimpse of Utopian possibility among the women's community outside the pale, but, with the Greeks at the gate, returns to become at the end Agamemnon's booty. In her representation of Cassandra's conflict of loyalties at the gradual corruption of Troy behind its protective wall, Wolf bids a tragic farewell to her earlier commitment. But in theme and choice of vehicle,

Cassandra enabled her to transcend the walls of the GDR. It provided the catharsis that the hidden manuscript had not been able to, proving Wolf's point in her argument long ago with Anna Seghers's dictum: "What has become narratable is already overcome." "No," said Wolf, "What still has to be overcome should be narrated."

There followed *Störfall* (*Accident*), a short "day in the life of a woman writer." But the Day is the day of her brother's operation for a brain tumour and the Day Chernobyl exploded, and the writer, out in the countryside even as it becomes despoiled, loses faith in her craft. It is a work with the theme of disintegration at its core. Its composition interrupted that of a longer lyrical novel full of images of foreboding, *Sommerstück* (*Summer Piece*), a dark Chekovian dance of uneasy relationships among a group of her contemporaries escaping to the countryside but not from themselves.

Then came the collapse of the regime. Wolf's first public efforts were to use her reputation to help hold a reformed GDR together. When that failed, she was the first GDR writer to risk entering the changed cultural and political scene, revising the numb "Day in the life of a woman writer under surveillance" under the title *Was bleibt* (*What Remains*). In the event, it became the occasion for the first all-German debate on the position writers had held in the former socialist state. Wolf was joyfully attacked as the representative of a privileged and powerful elite, and the publication of *Was bleibt* as opportunistic. On the other hand she was also defended as a moralist and humanist whose coded criticism over the years had been heard and understood by readers who became peaceful revolutionaries. The debate continues through the traumas of unification.

—Joyce Crick

WOLKERS, Jan (Hendrik). Dutch. Born in Oegstgeest, 26 October 1925. Studied painting and sculpture in Amsterdam and Salzburg, and in Paris under Ossip Zadkine. Married twice. Individual exhibition: Stedelijk Museum De Lakenhal, Leiden, 1986. Recipient: City of Amsterdam literature prize, 1962. Address: Huize "Pomona," Rozendijk 23, Westermiend, 1791 PD Den Burg (Texas), The Netherlands.

PUBLICATIONS

Fiction

Serpentina's Petticoat. Amsterdam, Meulenhoff, 1961.
Kort Amerikaans [Crew Cut]. Amsterdam, Meulenhoff, 1962.
Gesponnen suiker [Cotton Candy]. Amsterdam, Meulenhoff, 1963.
Een roos van vlees. Amsterdam, Meulenhoff, 1963; as *A Rose of Flesh*, London, Secker and Warburg, 1967.
De hond met de blauwe tong [The Dog with the Blue Tongue]. Amsterdam, Meulenhoff, 1964.
Terug naar Oegstgeest [Back to Oegstgeest]. Amsterdam, Meulenhoff, 1965.

Horrible tango. Amsterdam, Meulenhoff, 1967; in English, London, Secker and Warburg, 1970.

Turks fruit. Amsterdam, Meulenhoff, 1969; as *Turkish Delight*, London, Calder and Boyars, 1974; New York, Boyars, 1983.

De walgvogel [The Dodo]. Amsterdam, Meulenhoff, 1974.

De kus [The Kiss]. Amsterdam, Meulenhoff, 1977.

De doodshoofdvlinder [The Death's-Head Moth]. Amsterdam, Bezige Bij, 1979.

De perzik van onsterfelijkheid [The Peach of Immortality]. Amsterdam, Bezige Bij, 1980.

Brandende liefde [Burning Love]. Amsterdam, Bezige Bij, 1981.

Alle verhalen [All the Stories]. Amsterdam, Meulenhoff, 1981.

De junival [Windfalls]. Amsterdam, Bezige Bij, 1982.

Gifsla [Poison Ivy]. Amsterdam, Bezige Bij, 1983.

De ontbrekende verhalen [The Missing Story]. N.p., RoSa, 1984.

De onverbiddelijke tijd [The Inexorable Time]. Amsterdam, Bezige Bij, 1984.

22 sprookjes, verhalen en fabels [22 Fairytales, Stories, and Fables]. Amsterdam, Bezige Bij, 1985.

Kunstfruit en andere verhalen [Fake Fruit and Other Stories]. Amsterdam, Meulenhoff, 1988.

Jeugd jaagt voorbij: verhalen [Youth Flies By: Stories]. Amsterdam, Meulenhoff, 1989.

Dominee met strooien hoed [Clergyman with Straw Hat]. Amsterdam, Meulenhoff, 1990.

Op de vleugelen der profeten/On the Wings of the Prophets (bilingual edition). Deventer, Ypse Fecit, 1990.

Plays

Wegens sterfgeval gesloten [Closed on Account of Death]. Amsterdam, Meulenhoff, 1963.

De Babel. Amsterdam, Bezige Bij, 1963.

Other

18 composities. 1966.

Het afschuwelijkste uit Jan Wolkers [The Most Gruesome Bits of Jan Wolkers]. Amsterdam, Meulenhoff, 1969.

Zwarte advent [Black Advent]. Utrecht, Motion, 1969.

Groeten van Rottumerplaat [Greetings from Rottumerplaat]. Amsterdam, Elsevier, 1971.

Werkkleding [Working Clothes]. Amsterdam, Elsevier, 1971.

Verzen [Songs]. N.p., RoSa, 1985.

Jan Wolkers, schilder, beeldhouwer [Jan Wolkers, Painter, Sculptor] (exhibition catalogue). Amsterdam, Bezige Bij, 1986.

Een paradijsvogel boven het aardappelloof [A Bird of Paradise Over the Potato Plants]. Breda, De Geus, 1987.

De bretels van Jupiter [Jupiter's Braces]. Breda, De Geus, 1988.

De drijfschaal van Van Gogh [The Floating Flower-Bowl of Van Gogh]. Rotterdam, Van Hezik-Fonds 90, 1990.

Tarzan in Arles. Amsterdam, Bezige Bij, 1991.

*   *   *

Since his comparatively late debut (a decade or more after those of his most famous contemporaries, Willem Frederik Hermans, Gerard Reve, and Harry Mulisch (*qq.v.*), Jan Wolkers has established himself as one of the Netherlands' most widely read authors; two novels, *Turks fruit* (*Turkish Delight*) and *Kort Amerikaans* (Crew Cut), have been filmed and he has been, for a Dutch writer, much translated.

Wolkers's popular appeal derives from a number of interrelated sources. His powerful depiction of a severely orthodox Calvinist upbringing and the hedonistic but guilt-laden rebellion against it, tapped a rich fund of common experience in his home country for the first time in postwar fiction; Wolkers has since been emulated, though not surpassed, by a number of younger talents. Storytelling skill combines with a vigorous plasticity of style, worthy of a painter and sculptor- turned-writer, to produce indelible images, full of Bosch-like distortions and biblical echoes.

The "shock effect" of his penchant for grotesque and horrific detail and his sexual explicitness, which caused a moral outcry in some quarters when his first books appeared, can be seen with hindsight as both a contribution to and a symptom of the "liberated" Dutch 1960s.

Many of the themes that were to dominate his later work (including his two stylised plays), were already present in concentrated form in the story collections *Serpentina's Petticoat* and *Gesponnen suiker* (Cotton Candy), which remain peaks in his career so far. In them, a young, isolated, impressionable, and (over-)imaginative protagonist (often a first-person narrator) confronts various forms of death "in the midst of life," as the Bible has it, though death is here, emphatically not in the gateway to eternity, but final and frequently messy extinction. Sexuality is sometimes an assertion of life over death, but in Wolkers's vision remains essentially akin to it. Conflict with authority and consuming guilt are both commonly associated with an elder brother figure, mentor and rival, who does not survive. A deep love of nature exists alongside gruesome cruelty to animals, which make ritualistic atonement for the larger cruelties inflicted by man, that "degenerate ape" as Wolkers sees him, on his fellow-men. *Kort Amerikaans* expands on the theme of despairing and ultimately impotent sexuality, while *Horrible tango* explores betrayal and guilt in the relationship between two men.

Charges of literary machismo were levelled at Wolkers from the time of the appearance of *Een roos van vlees* (*A Rose of Flesh*) onwards; the latter novel's presentation of woman as part sex-object, part predator was found widely offensive. The bestselling *Turkish Delight*, in which a tumultuous love affair terminates in the heroine's death of a brain tumour, smacked of formula pulp fiction and provoked comparisons with the sentimentality of, for example, Erich Segal's *Love Story*. While there is no doubt that virility looms large in much later fiction and non-fiction, as in the case of the scrapbook *Werkkleding* (Working Clothes), and is even flaunted, Norman Mailer-style, the core of his preoccupation is the essential vulnerability of his macho figures.

What began as a political undercurrent in the work of a writer among whose formative experiences had been the Depression of the 1930s, paternalistic denominational government, war and occupation, and the ignominious loss of empire, became explicit anti-colonialism in *De kus* (The Kiss) and anti-capitalism in *De perzik van onsterfelijkheid* (The Peach of Immortality), and led to such gestures as the much-publicised return of a literary award on political grounds.

Two of Wolkers's artistically most successful books were written in a more sober vein: *Terug naar Oegstgeest* (Back to

Oegstgeest) switches back constantly from present to past and attempts (hopelessly) to come to terms with childhood traumas, while *De doodshoofdvlinder* (The Death's-Head Moth) is a moving treatment of bereavement. Some recent work is uneven and repetitive, and occasionally, as with *De junival* (Windfalls), both contrived and maudlin, but throughout his work Wolkers shows himself, for better or worse, a passionate, intemperate writer who can sometimes be undis-

ciplined, vulgar, and overblown, but who is almost always a compellingly readable original.

—Paul Vincent

Y

YĀDAV, Rājendra. Indian. Born in Agra, 28 August 1929. Educated at Agra College; holds M.A. Married to the writer Mannū Bhaṇḍārī; one daughter. Founder, Akṣar Prakāśan publishing house; runs *Hans* monthly, New Delhi. Address: 2/36 Ansari Road, Daryanganj, New Delhi 110002, India.

PUBLICATIONS

Fiction

Pret bolte haĩ [Ghosts Speak]. New Delhi, Progressive Publishers, 1952; as *Ukhṛe hue log* [The Uprooted], Bombay, Rājkamal, 1956.
Devtāõ kī mūrtiyā̃ [Gods' Images]. New Delhi, Ālok, 1953.
Jahā̃ Lakṣmī kaid hai [Where Lakṣmī Is a Prisoner]. New Delhi, Rājkamal, 1957.
Kulṭā [Fallen Woman]. Agra, Viśva Sāhitya, 1958.
Śah aur mat [Victory and Defeat]. Benares, Bhārtīy Jñānpīṭh, 1959.
Abhimanyu kī ātmahatyā [Abhimanyu's Suicide]. Agra, Viśva Sāhitya, 1959.
Choṭe choṭe Tāj Mahal [Many Tiny Tāj Mahals]. New Delhi, Rājpāl & Sons, n.d.
Pratīkṣā [Waiting]. New Delhi, Hind Pocket Books, 1960.
Sārā ākāś [The Whole Sky]. New Delhi, Rājkamal, 1960.
Ek inĉ muskān [An Inch of a Smile], with Mannū Bhaṇḍārī. New Delhi, Akṣar, 1963.
Andekhe anjān pul [Unseen, Unknown Bridges]. New Delhi, Rājpāl & Sons, 1963.
Kināre se kināre tak [From One Edge to the Other]. New Delhi, Rājpāl & Sons, 1963.
Khel-khilaune [Games and Toys]. Benares, Bhārtīy Jñānpīṭh, 1964.
Śreṣṭh kahāniyā̃ [Best Short Stories]. New Delhi, Rājpāl & Sons, 1966.
Ṭūṭnā [Breaking]. New Delhi, Akṣar, 1966.
Mantra-viddha [Under Spell]. New Delhi, Akṣar, 1967.
Ḍhol aur anya kahāniyā̃ [Drum and Other Stories]. New Delhi, Akṣar, 1972.
Merī priy kahāniyā̃ [My Favourite Stories]. New Delhi, Rājpāl & Sons, 1973.
The Flirt. New Delhi, Hind Pocket Books, 1975.
Pratinidhi kahāniyā̃ [Representative Stories]. New Delhi, Rājkamal, 1985.
Caukhaṭē ṭorte trikon [Triangles Breaking Quadrangles]. New Delhi, Akṣar, 1987.
Yahā̃ tak [Up to Now] (collected short stories). New Delhi, National, 2 vols., 1990.

Verse

Āvāz terī hai [It's Your Voice]. Benares, Bhārtīy Jñānpīṭh, 1960.

Other

Kahānī: svarūp aur sanvednā [The Short Story: Outlook and Sensibility]. New Delhi, National Publishing House, 1968.
Premcand kī virāsat aur anya nibandha [Premcand's Heritage and Other Essays]. New Delhi, Akṣar, 1978.
Aurō ke bahāne: saṃsleṣaṇ [Using Others as an Excuse]. New Delhi, Akṣar, 1980.
Aṭhārah upanyās [18 Novels]. New Delhi, Akṣar, 1981.

Editor, *Śreṣṭha kahāniyā̃* [Best Stories], by Kamleśvar. New Delhi, Rājpāl & Sons, 1964.
Editor, *Ek duniyā: samanāntar* [One World: Parallels] (anthology of contemporary Hindi short stories). New Delhi, Akṣar, 1966.
Editor, *Kathāyātrā* [A Journey in Stories] (anthology of Hindi short stories). New Delhi, Akṣar, 1969.

Has translated Anton Chekhov, Ivan Turgenev, Mikhail Lermontov, John Steinbeck, and Albert Camus.

* * *

Rājendra Yādav is one of the main proponents of the post-independence era of Indian short-story writing, in particular the *Naī Kahānī* ("New Story") movement. He is an alert, socially conscious, sensitive story teller who is eager to create magical effects in his writing. Yādav believes that the ideal of a writer should be to see things as they are and describe them with the utmost integrity. The writer should be someone "above all principles, politics, philosophies, and social responsibility, committing himself to nothing — or at least to nothing but himself."

Like other new writers in the 1960s, Yādav rejects the past. Instead, the period of transition immediately after Indian independence forms the backdrop of his writing. He would admit that previous realities may not have been so different from the present ones, but the contemporary writers of this period faced "almost no ordered tradition" and the past values of humanism, patriotism, leadership, truth, and pride in history were now considered impractical, unscientific, and reactionary, and amounted to "scraps of useless conviction."

The characters in Yādav's stories are mainly urban, middle-class people trying to survive the breakdown in middle-class life and the crisis of values under the pressure of modernity. They have the capacity to cope with this crisis, are forward-looking and liberal towards change and values, and are alert to new social awareness.

For Yādav the state of mind and feelings of his characters are more important than what happens to them outwardly. As he says, "The experience and sensed moment of one's environment is today's reality." His characters are thus committed "only to that present reality which is part of their consciousness . . . There is no past or future."

The destruction of the relationship between husband and wife recurs constantly in Yādav's stories. It may be due to clashes of personality or financial circumstances — money plays a large part in changing human relationships. In his story "Ṭūṭnā" (The Break Up), a man and woman marry for love rather than as a "good match." The woman's father is a rich tax commissioner and the lover is only a poor college tutor, intimidated by the wealth and power of the girl's father. After getting married the wife tries to improve her husband's way of life by changing his pronunciation, his behaviour, the way he dresses, and by making him aware of "modern life." Convinced that she does all this at her father's bidding as a way of ridiculing him, the man begins to suffer from an inferiority complex that eventually destroys the marriage. Nevertheless the man *is* changed and works hard to become rich. One day he hears that the woman's father has died and writes to her, saying that those hands which had challenged him to a trial of strength were not his wife's but her father's; she was "only a pawn."

As a writer mainly of urban life, Yādav sees this environment as narrow and unsympathetic to the human condition. This is particularly visible in *Choṭe choṭe Tāj Mahal* (Many Miniature Tāj Mahals), where both characters, the man and the woman, are like Taj Mahals — the mausoleum represents the coldness of their frozen blood and their anger where no warmth, spirit, or strength remains. This coldness has robbed them of life and paved the way for separation.

Yādav takes account of external circumstances as well, where people face injustice and the horror of economic disparity in society, where the rich are becoming richer and the poor poorer. In *Abhimanyu kī ātmahatyā* (Abhimanyu's Suicide), he shows how the lack of material comfort and poverty can hurt a man's ego so deeply that he sees suicide as the only way out.

In his novels Yādav also portrays the complexities of urban life, where people seek their own answers and mostly find only fear, neurosis, and feelings of loneliness and alienation. He studies the psychological complexities of his characters and tries to probe the roots of their problems. *Ukhṛe hue log* (The Uprooted) is an outstanding novel about a capitalist leader engaged in underhand practices and ugly doings, hiding behind the mask of his mild and gentle behaviour. This character, like many leaders, pretends to follow Mahatma Gandhi and the teachings of Gita. He projects himself as a social benefactor and servant of the people, but in fact he is a debauched and unscrupulous capitalist who corrupts and coerces women. In the end, however, Yādav is more hopeful for the new generation than he has been in his stories. They cannot support capitalism, are afraid of communism, yet they are prepared to put up a fight.

Yādav's writing is a vivid reflection of a changing society.

—Satyendra Śrīvāstava

YANG CHANGYE. *See* **YANG MO.**

YANG LIAN. Chinese. Born in Berne, Switzerland, 22 February 1955; moved to China, 1956. Educated at primary and middle schools, 1962–73. Sent to Changping County near Beijing as part of movement to send educated youths to learn from the peasants, 1974–77; staff member of literature unit, Central Broadcasting Station, Beijing, from 1977. Member,

Jintian [Today] literary group, and Jintian Wenxue Yanjiuhui [Today Literature Research Society], from 1980, and Beijing Writers' Association, from 1981; co-founder, The Survivors Poets' Club, 1988. Address: c/o China Writers' Association, Shatan Beijie 2, Beijing 100720, China.

PUBLICATIONS

Verse

Shichuan de guo du [Lost Land].   Published underground in China, 1980.
Hai bian de haizi [Child by the Sea].   Published underground in China, 1982.
Xizang [Tibet].   Published underground in China, 1984.
Shi zhe [Flux].   Published underground in China, 1985.
Li hun [Ritualisation of the Soul].   Xi An, Shanxi dangdai zhongguo qingnian shiren congshu, 1985.
Huang hun [Desolate Soul]. Shanghai, Shanghai wenyi chubanshe, 1986.
Huang [Yellow].   Beijing, People's Literature Publishing House, 1989 (published but circulation withheld).
In Symmetry with Death.   Canberra, ACT, Australian National University, 1989.
Masks and the Crocodile: A Contemporary Chinese Poet and His Poetry, translated by Mabel Lee. Sydney, Wild Peony, 1990; London, Wellsweep Press, 1992.
The Dead in Exile.   Canberra, ACT, Tiananmen Publications, 1990.
Taiyang yu ren [The Sun and People].   Hunan, Hunan wenyi chubanshe, 1991.

English translations of many of his poems have appeared in *Renditions* (Hong Kong), 1983–85.

Other

Ren de zijue [Man's Self-Awakening].   Sichuan, Sichuan People's Publishing House, n.d. (published but circulation withheld).

*   *   *

The poet Yang Lian is one of many Chinese writers for whom a temporary sojourn abroad became a long-term exile after the Tiananmen Square massacre of June 1989. Yang Lian gained his reputation as one of a group of young "modernist" poets associated with the Democracy Movement of the late 1970s who rejected socialist realism in favour of self-expression. This group was called "modernist" because they broke away from the rigid literary conventions of Maoist China and asserted the artist's sovereignty over subject-matter, form, and technique. Yang Lian's subjects are contemporary, and he certainly does not observe the strict rules of classical poetry, but his writing shows a great awareness of the past and a sense of connection with it. Unusually for a child of his generation he was encouraged to study classical poetry, an influence that shows in the rich tonal quality of his lines when read aloud, the esoteric references he likes to make, and his advocacy of the freedom of the spirit.

Death, decay, and the importance of the past are preoccupations in all of his poetry; indeed one of his important works, a group of 16 poems which traces the journey of the poet through life, is entitled "In Symmetry with Death." Ruins are for him a metaphor for death and loss:

I often strain to catch voices wafted from afar
Faint snatches, dead leaves, white snow
Drifting down from a remote dream world,
Often in the rainbow wandering in after rain
I seek the shadow of the Great Wall, proud and comforting;
But the roaring wind only tells me new tales of ruin
Mud and rubble have silted
The canal, my arteries no longer pulse,
My throat no longer sings.

The aged century bares its brow,
Shakes its wounded shoulders;
Snow covers the ruins — white and restless
Like surf — moving among the pitch-black trees;
A lost voice is transmitted across time
There is no road
Through this land that death has lent mystery.
                                           ("The Burden")

In December 1989, the Chinese government banned the publication of Yang Lian's writing on the grounds that he had engaged in counter-revolutionary activities abroad. He had in fact participated in protest meetings in New Zealand where he happened to be at the time of the Tiananmen Square massacre, and with fellow poet Gu Cheng had written a prose poem "In Memory of the Dead":

Armoured vehicles ploughed across your bodies splattering your brains everywhere. Bullets pursued you, carts for carrying the dead pursued you, helicopters and petrol throwers pursued you. Your skin turned black, cracking open as it burned; the wounded and the dead were incinerated together.

Another poem from this period is a savage commentary on the reports that Beijing people were forced to make after the massacre on their own activities during the democracy movement. Their confessions, written in the spirit of fear produced by conformity, denied everything:

But you were not in the Square. In the confessions everybody testified that they were not there. In June there was no-one in the Square . . .
It is absolutely certain that this person had not been running about in the Square, slipped over, called for help, heard the dull thud of bullets striking bodies . . .
It is absolutely certain that no-one had lived, crowded together or died here . . .
So you too are an accomplice in slaughtering in the month of June. You had to write and you wrote: This year there was no June. The Square did not exist in June.
                                           ("The Square")

Like most writers who grew up when the Maoist straitjacket was at its tightest, Yang Lian at first rejected the notion that a writer should have a political mission or that his writing should serve politics. By a historical irony he was ultimately driven to take stands and produce overtly political writing.

As Yang Lian is all too well aware, exile is a tragedy for creative writers, cutting them off from their audience and often too from their source of inspiration. In July 1989 he wrote, "For me the inseparable bond between language and the land is so crucial that it is impossible to believe in world literature. Thus 'Tiananmen' for me was death and whether or not after

'In Memory of the Dead' there will be a rebirth remains to be seen."

                                           —Delia Davin

———

YANG MO. Chinese. Born Yang Chengye in Beijing, August 1914. Educated at Beijing Wenquan Girls' Middle School, from 1928. Married Y.C. Li in 1989; two sons and one daughter. Worked as a primary school teacher, private tutor, and bookshop assistant; joined the Chinese Communist Party, 1936; worked in women's programs in Japanese-occupied areas, 1937–49. Committee member, China Writers' Association, Beijing, since 1988; chair, Beijing Federation of Literature and Arts Circles, Beijing, since 1989. Representative at 3rd, 5th, 6th, and 7th National People's Congress. Address: Hong yilou 3, Beijing shi fandaxui, Beijing 100088, China.

PUBLICATIONS

Fiction

Wei tang ji shi [The Story of the Reed Pond].   Beijing, Beijing Writers' Publishing House, 1950.
Qing chun zhi ge.   1958; revised edition, 1960; as *The Song of Youth*, Beijing, Foreign Languages Press, 1964.
Dongfang yu xiao [Dawn in the East].   1970s.
Honghong de shandanhua [The Red Morning Star Lily].   Beijing, Beijing Publishing House, 1978.
Yang Mo duanpian xiaoshuo [Short Stories of Yang Mo].   Hunan, Hunan People's Publishing House, 1982.

Play

Screenplay: *Qing chun zhi ge* (*The Song of Youth*), 1960.

Other

Bushi riji de riji [It Is Not the Diary's Diary].   Hunan, Hunan People's Publishing House, 1980.
Yang Mo sanwen xuan [Selected Prose of Yang Mo].   Hunan, Hunan People's Publishing House, 1981.
Da he yü langhua [The Great River and the Spindrift].   Hunan, Hunan People's Publishing House, 1982.
Zibai — wo de riji [Confession — My Diary].   Guangzhou, Huacheng Publishing House, 1985.

———

Yang Mo, originally named Yang Chengye, published writings in left-wing newspapers and journals from 1934 onwards, but was not widely known until her first novel *Qing chun zhi ge* (*The Song of Youth*) appeared in 1958. This book was enormously popular and was greeted as an outstanding example of the new Chinese literature in the late 1950s and early 1960s when Chinese literature and art was supposed to be guided by the doctrine of socialist realism.

The story of *The Song of Youth* takes place between 1931, on the eve of all-out Sino-Japanese War when the Japanese had just occupied northeast China, and 1935, when the patriotic students' movement began in Beijing. Lin Daojing, the heroine, is a sentimental girl student. After running away from her morally corrupt and financially ruined family, she supports herself with various jobs. She falls in love with a student, but later realizes that the gallant knight of her first perception is actually a selfish snob. She encounters numerous financial, physical, and mental difficulties. Lin is frustrated with her own situation and uncertain of her country's future until she meets with the members of the Communist underground working in the universities, who convince her to support Marxism and revolution. She joins the Communist underground movement and eventually becomes a revolutionary.

This novel has sold approximately five million copies in China since it first appeared. It has also been translated into major European languages as well as Japanese, Korean, Vietnamese, and Arabic. The film version, its screenplay written by the author herself, was released in 1960, and later became one of the few films allowed by the Government censors to be shown abroad. Lin Daojing came to symbolize the young female intellectual revolutionary, while the other fictional characters in the story were so convincingly portrayed in their fight against the Japanese invaders and Guomindang (KMT) that thousands of young people, trying to show their veneration for them, went in vain every year to search for their graves in the cemetery of the martyrs of the revolution in Nanjing. Readers from abroad also wrote to express their admiration for the Chinese revolutionary cause.

The success of *The Song of Youth* was largely due to the author's faithful portrayal of her own experience. Unlike other writers at this time, Yang Mo did not try to fabricate a proletarian hero according to a certain pattern advocated by the Party; she wrote instead about the sort of people with whom she was familiar, although such characters were regarded as petty bourgeois by doctrinaire critics. In Lin Daojing there is a great deal of Yang Mo herself. Almost all the incidents and feelings described in the book — Lin's flight from home to escape the fate of becoming a concubine, her attempted suicide, her infatuation with the sea, her experiences as a primary school teacher, the insults she suffered from a rich man, her separation from her first sweetheart, and her acceptance of the Communist Party — are taken directly from the author's life. Yang Mo denies that *The Song of Youth* is an autobiographical novel, since she declares that she is a disciple of socialist realism and always tries to create "a typical character in typical circumstances" (Engels), yet because the novel is based on real experience, it is less stereotypical and dogmatic, and contains less revolutionary jargon than other literary works of this period. Its scenes of student life in the first half of the 1930s were so realistic that many of her older readers could still identify with the world she depicted. This made the book especially remarkable in the 1960s, when literature was dominated by stilted, unconvincing productions, written to political formulae. The author shares with her readers her real feelings about her friends and enemies, her loves and hatreds, her frustrations and expectations. The heroine's sentimentality, depression, hesitation, and fanaticism make her seem more true to life than other heroes or heroines of the period. However, this attempt to reflect reality, and the fact that Lin is portrayed as a still-maturing intellectual revolutionary rather than an already perfect proletarian fighter brought blistering attacks on the novel from leftist critics. Yang Mo's response was to write seven additional chapters about Lin Daojing's experiences in the countryside with the revolutionary peasants for a new edition of the novel. These chapters, lacking in authenticity, are unconvincing to readers. Yang Mo once wrote in her diary in a rather self-deprecating tone: "Even in a battle surrounded by the smoke of gunpowder, I still feel I am less a fighter than a poet" (26 May 1947). Perhaps because of this conviction, she kept sufficient integrity as a writer to enable her to produce a piece of fiction comparatively free of artificial political formulae.

In the period of comparative cultural liberalisation after Mao Zedong's death, Yang Mo published several short stories, some reportage, and one novel, *Dongfang yu xiao* (Dawn in the East), but nothing of the quality of *The Song of Youth*. However, she produced one book worth discussing, entitled *Zibai — wo de riji* (Confession — My Diary). Yang Mo has kept a diary since she was at primary school, and never stopped, even when she was fighting as a Communist guerrilla. The early diaries were lost during the war, but she managed to preserve all the volumes written since 1945. Some give very interesting insights; for instance, she criticized herself during Land Reform for having been too sympathetic towards a landlord when his home was sacked by enraged peasants; she complained about a two-year delay in the publication of her novel, simply because she was an unknown woman writer; and she had to be persuaded that many political campaigns were necessary and timely. The diaries reveal that from 1953 to 1957 she lived through 22 months of meetings and various campaigns, spent 10 months living with peasants and workers in order to get to know them, took nine months to write *The Song of Youth*, and devoted 22 months to writing film scripts, most of which came to a halt midway when the film studio for which she worked told her to change the theme and content. Although we do not know how much it was edited for publication, this 38-year diary is important because it offers readers a rare chance to share the experience of a Party intellectual in years of great change and upheaval, and to see the history of the People's Republic through her eyes.

—Li Ruru

YASUOKA Shōtarō. Japanese. Born in Kōchi City, Shikoku island, 30 May 1920 (according to author, day and month probably incorrect; no records kept). Educated at Tokyo City Secondary School; Keio University. Served in the Japanese Army, 1944–45. Married. Recipient: Akutagawa prize, 1953; Rockefeller Foundation fellowship, 1958; Noma prize, 1959; Ministry of Education Mombusho prize, 1960(?); Mainichi prize, 1967/68; Yomiuri prize, 1973/74; Japanese Grand prize for literature, 1981/82. Address: c/o Kōdansha Ltd., 17-14, Otowa 1-chome, Bunkyo-ku, Tokyo 112, Japan.

PUBLICATIONS

Fiction

Umibe no kōkei. Published in *Gunzō* (Tokyo), November–December 1959; as *A View by the Sea*, New York, Columbia University Press, 1984.
Shichiya no nyōbo. Published in *Bungei Shunjū* (Tokyo), May 1960; Tokyo, Shinchōsha, 1966; as "The Pawnbroker's Wife," in *Japan Quarterly* (Tokyo), 8(2), 1961; in *New Writing in Japan*, London, Penguin, 1972.

Hanamatsuri [Buddha's Birthday Festival].   Tokyo, Shin-
chōsha, 1962.
Maku ga orite kara [After the Curtain Falls].   Published in
Gunzō (Tokyo), March 1967.
Tsuki wa higashi ni [The Moon Is to the East].   1971.
Ryūritan [Tales of Wanderings].   Tokyo, Shinchōsha, 1981.

Other

Amerika kanjō ryokō [Sentimental Journeys in the United
States].   1962.
Shisō onchi no hassō.   Tokyo, Haga, 1966.
Yasuoka Shōtarō zenshū [Collected Works].   Tokyo,
Kōdansha, 4 vols., 1971.
Boku no shōwa shi.   Tokyo, Kōdansha, 3 vols., 1984–88.
Daiseikimatsu.   Tokyo, Asahi Shinbunsha, 1984.
Kotoba no naka no tabi.   Tokyo, Asahi Shinbunsha, 1984.
*Saisai nennen: nennen saisai hana ainitari, saisai nennen hito
onajikarazu*.   Tokyo, Kōdansha, 1989.
Sakaya e sanri tōfuya e niri.   Tokyo, Fukutake Shoten, 1990.
Katsudō-goya no aru fūkei.   Tokyo, Iwanami Shoten, 1990.

Translator (into Japanese), *Roots*, by Alex Haley.

*

Critical Studies: in *The Sting of Life: Four Contemporary
Japanese Novelists*, New York, Columbia University Press,
1989, and "The Voice of the Doppelgänger," in *Japan
Quarterly* (Tokyo), 28(2), 1991, both by Van C Gessel.

*   *   *

Yasuoka Shōtarō's breakthrough into the Japanese literary
world in 1951, with his nomination, albeit unsuccessful, for the
prestigious Akutagawa prize for literature, was viewed by
some as recognition as much of the author's perseverance in
the face of illness and adversity as of the innate literary merit of
the works included in the citation. But by the time the prize
was conferred on him in 1953 for two remarkable short stories,
"Bad Company" and "Gloomy Pleasures," Yasuoka was well
and truly established as a prominent member of the group of
writers seeking through their literature to come to terms with
the confusion and pain engendered by defeat in 1945 and the
ignominy of life under Allied occupation.

The material for these and other Yasuoka stories of the time
is drawn heavily from autobiographical experience — and in
this, the author can be seen staking out the terrain that would
provide the backdrop for so much of his ensuing literary
production: as he confessed in a more recent work, "Autobiographical Journey", it was his "unhappy" and "unsuccessful"
childhood that was to be the "primary influence on [his]
personality and literary sensibility." In sharp contradistinction
to the majority of his contemporaries whose *après guerre*
literature he dismissed as "over-idealistic," Yasuoka was
forced to adopt a far more realistic attitude as a result of
personal circumstances, in which the inability of his recently
demobilised father to readjust successfully to post war reality
had led to increasing evidence of nervous tension on the part of
his mother and a consequently enhanced responsibility
accruing to the young Yasuoka to preserve the family stability.

The bewildered and self-conscious protagonists of these
earlier stories appear destined to "assume the pose of the
weakling" (Yasuoka's own assessment) and to withdraw ever
further into their own little worlds. The result, in Yasuoka's
later works, is a series of uprooted protagonists for whom
"loss" — especially that of the most basic bond in society, the

family tie — has come to represent the norm. In this, they
mirror faithfully the view expressed by Yasuoka: "Even
though I considered myself unreliable, I couldn't depend on
anything outside myself either. I had no choice but to cling to
my unreliability as long as I lived."

The trait is epitomised in the portrayal of Shintarō, protagonist of Yasuoka's masterpiece, *Umibe no kōkei* (*A View by the
Sea*), a young man whose propensity for escape has rendered
him totally bereft of self-confidence and seemingly incapable
of forming any lasting relationship — even with his own family
members. By this stage in his career, however, Yasuoka had
come to assume a narrative perspective that enables his reader
to maintain a more detached and critical posture towards the
events narrated. Through skillful manipulation of his third-
person narrator and through a carefully controlled infusion of
ironic distance, the author is able to hint at a deeper level of the
narrative in which Shinkichi, the father on whom Shintarō
heaps nothing but scorn, ultimately emerges as seeming far
more deserving of sympathy than his son would have us
believe, and where Shintarō, for whom the demise of his
mother would appear to represent the very liberation he had
been craving, appears unable to cope with his new-found
freedom. Significantly, it is only with the final scene of the
novel that the author intimates that all is not as his third-person
narrator has suggested: "All across the unrippled surface of the
bay, now calmer than a lake, there stood hundreds upon
hundreds of stakes, looming blackly out of the water as far as
[Shintarō] could see . . . As he looked at the rows of stakes
standing like the teeth of an upturned comb, like tombstones,
it was a death he held in his own hands that he saw."

The attitude towards society and life in general of the
Yasuoka protagonist — the portraits of a young man torn by an
inferiority complex and by a sense of victimization — are
reminiscent of the *shishōsetsu*, the style of writing traditionally
translated as the "I-novel," that so dominated the pre-war
literary scene in Japan. In common with his "I-novelist"
precursors, Yasuoka's ability to depict images of both past and
present with convincing accuracy is readily apparent. But
whereas his predecessors so often lacked the ability to organise
these vignettes of autobiographical experience, to adequately
assess their implications and to make of them something of
more universal significance, Yasuoka proves a master at
undercutting his surface narrative and at exploring the distance
between the limited viewpoints of his protagonists and the
more analytical authorial perspective.

Without recognition of such ironic detachment, much of
Yasuoka's fiction could be dismissed as the records of failed
individuals. The legacy of Yasuoka's oeuvre lies in his skill at
highlighting, behind the surface depictions of the awkward
adolescent and incompetent parents, the subtext, described by
Van C. Gessel in *The Sting of Life* (1989) as focusing on the
inability of the Yasuoka protagonist to "fulfill the minimal
requirements for membership in human society." In this he
was not entirely alone, and it is as an integral member of the
group known in Japanese literary history as the "Third
Generation of New Writers" that Yasuoka is best remembered. In contrast to the preceding generation of writers,
whose left-wing orientation was a direct result of having cut
their literary teeth during the political turmoil of the 1930s and
who consequently advocated a focus on broader social,
political, and historical concerns, the writings of this younger
generation, whose experience of adult life began with the
Pacific War years, are informed by a sense of ambivalence and
loss in which the themes of collapse of the family and loss of
self-confidence predominate. Taking advantage of their "vivid
powers of perception" (Hirano Ken), these writers sought to
capture in their literature the "gnawing sense of inferiority and

guilt" that persisted in Japan even after the onset of the "economic miracle" of post-war Japan (Gessel). Their success in this venture is widely heralded, leading Ōe Kenzaburō (*q.v.*), one of the leading contemporary Japanese novelists, to remark of them: "They do not merely capture one small corner of society — but the social changes of a period. They were also better able to capture people than their predecessors . . . This is their strength."

For the reader in search of the reality of daily life in post-war Japan, however, it is Yasuoka more than any other member of this "new generation" who best captured the indignities and degradation of the times. His creative literary impulse, heavily dependent upon his own sense of "crisis" (significantly, the vast majority of his output since his "establishment" on the literary scene has been of a non-fictional nature), Yasuoka has never wavered from his belief in the need to remain honest to his personal observation of human nature and society and thereby to "fill the holes left by the passing bulldozer of contemporary fiction in Japan." The result is a body of works that echoes as powerfully as any the sense of loss of a generation and that consequently touches the reader with its distinctive kind of humanity.

—Mark Williams

YE JUNJIAN. Chinese. Born in Hongan, Hubei Province, 7 December 1914. Educated at Wuhan University; King's College, Cambridge. Married Yuan Yin in 1942; two children. Professor of literature, Chongqing University, Zhongyang University, and Fudan University, 1940–44, and Furen University, 1950–52. Honorary Lecturer, King's College, Cambridge; Honorary Professor, Shanxi University, Anhui University, and Beijing University of Science. Recipient: Order of Dannebrog [Denmark]. Agent: Jennifer Kavanagh, 39 Camden Park Road, London NW1 9AX, England. Address: 6 Gongjian Hutong, Di An Men, Beijing 100009, China.

PUBLICATIONS

Fiction

The Ignorant and the Forgotten.   London, Sylvan Press, 1946.
Three Seasons and Other Stories.   London, Staples Press, 1946.
Jijing de qunshan [Quiet Are the Mountains].   Beijing, China Wenlian Publishing House, 2 vols., 1986.
   The Mountain Village.   London, Sylvan Press, and New York, Putnam, 1947.
   The Open Fields.   London, Faber, 1988.
   A Distant Journey.   London, Faber, 1989.
They Fly South.   London, Sylvan Press, 1948.
Kaikenzhi de mingyun [Pioneers' Fate].   Beijing, Youth Publishing House, 1960.
Huohua [The Sparks].   Beijing, People's Publishing House, 1980.
Ziyou [Freedom].   Beijing, People's Publishing House, 1981.
Shuguang [Dawn].   Beijing, People's Publishing House, 1982.
Ye Junjian xiaoshuo xuan [Stories by Ye Junjian].   Nanjing, Jiangsu People's Publishing House, 1983.

Zai caoyuan shang [On the Steppes].   Tianjin, Baihua Publishing House, 1984.
Du shu yu xin shang [Reading and Rejoicing].   Wuhan, Wuhan University Press, 1985.
Kuang ye [Wilderness].   Beijing, China Wenlian Publishing House, 1986.

Other

Yuanxing Ji [West Pavilion Essays].   Nanchang, Baihua Zhou Publishing House, 1962.
Hong ye [Red Leaves] (essays).   Nanchang, Baihua Zhou Publishing House, 1965.
Jie jie Lupa [Sister Luoba] (for children).   Chengdu, Sichuan People's Publishing House, 1981.
Chongfan Jian Qiao [Returning to Cambridge].   Beijing, Shenghuo, dushu, xin zhi san lian shudian, 1983.
Gu ren xin shi ji.   Hong Kong, Shenghuo, dushu, xin zhi san lian shudian, 1984.
Bu chou de chouxiaoya [The Ugly Duckling Who Wasn't Ugly] (for children).   Shanghai, Hunan shaonian ertong Publishing House, 1984.

*   *   *

A contemporary, albeit somewhat younger, of such luminaries of modern Chinese literature such as Ding Ling and Ba Jin (*q.v.*), Ye Junjian has produced his major works in Chinese only in the aftermath of the Cultural Revolution, during which he was severely criticised, subjected to physical indignities, and forced to work at the lowliest menial tasks. Unlike most of his younger contemporaries of the "wounded generation," he has not, as yet, written of his experiences of those years: interested readers are referred to the last volume of Han Suyin's memoirs, *Phoenix Harvest* (1980), in which Ye plays a leading part. However, those years served as a gestation peroid in which Ye planned and drafted his first trilogy, The Land, which chronicles the rise of rural rebellion in the early years of this century and the consequent slow erosion of feudalism at the close of the Qing dynasty. With the commencement of this work he seems to have committed himself to the task of recording, in his rich, powerful novels, the history of China in the 20th century, largely from the perspective of the rural population which played an essential part in the events that broke down the feudal bastions of centuries.

Ye skilfully adapts the techniques of classical Chinese narrative in his novels, and employs a vast canvas and cast of characters. An admirer of 19th-century French and Russian realism, his fascination with exact reconstruction may also owe a little to Gustave Flaubert, but the real source of his inspiration is to be found in many traditional Chinese literary genres: the classical lyric, the tightly constructed Tang dynasty tale, the voluminous vernacular novel, (the 18th-century novel *The Scholars* by Wu Jizi is a particular favourite). Praising the economy and precision of the traditional story, Ye has pointed out the indebtness of Chinese fiction to folklore and oral traditions; his own prose borrows from a panoply of techniques, intertwining the imagistic obliquity of verse with the storyteller's robust rustic directness.

His best-known work, the trilogy *Jijing de qunshan* (Quiet Are the Mountains), narrated by the adolescent Chunsheng, is interspersed with allusions to myth, ritual, and legend, and constantly dissolves into other first-person accounts. Counterspectives create a many-layered narrative, in the distinctive Chinese manner. Ironically, the first volume of the trilogy, *The Mountain Village*, was originally written in English and published to critical acclaim in Britain and the United States in 1947. But Ye, after producing two collections of stories and a fantasy novel in English, returned to China in 1949, for he had a deep, if not unquestioning, sympathy for the Communists and their radical reforms, which richly informs the trilogy. *The Mountain Village* is written in the kind of English prose that is often described as artless, though it is actually subtle and carefully evokes the cadences and imagery of Chinese poetry. Focusing on the small joys and sorrows that shape the lives of Ye's mostly illiterate protagonists, each episode has the ring of authentic personal experience: Ye has evidently drawn much of the material from his memories of his native Dabei mountains. Beginning in the mid-1920s, the novel chronicles the slow erosion of a way of life and a set of values eroded by the events that eventually transform the history of a nation. Chunseng, caught up in the struggle between landlord and landless peasant, slowly awakened to the possibility of revolution though sheer and brutal need, arrives at the brink of uneasy and premature adulthood. A memorable community of characters caught up in the struggle between new ideologies and old peasant superstitions is introduced: peasants, wily priests, pious widows, bourgeois intellectuals ready to sacrifice their lives in the service of their Marxist tenets and ideals, and the storyteller Lao Liu, the trilogy's most colourful character, whose metamorphosis from local lovesick vagabond to committed revolutionary propagandist represents the awakening political consciousness of the dispossessed peasant.

The second volume of the trilogy, *The Open Fields*, written several decades later, picks up the threads of the preceding novel, continuing the story of the adolescent Chunsheng, his family and friends. Several of the earlier novel's characters reappear, including Lao Liu, whose observations provide an impromptu metafictional commentary throughout the novels, debating the need for literature to adapt itself to the ideological requirements of a period of upheaval, and serve as a repository of information for readers. In keeping with the collective revolutionary spirit it articulates, *The Open Fields*, if less intimate and spontaneous, is a bolder work than its precursor; presented on a far wider canvas, it is also more complex in composition and execution. The maturing perceptions of its narrator, coupled with the author's access to retrospective insight, contribute a higher level of political awareness and debate to the novel. Ye skilfully deploys multiple voices in the service of historical authenticity: scholars, peasants, landlords, and soldiers tell their own stories, enriching and amplifying Chunsheng's limited perspective.

The predominatly oral nature of Ye's narrative technique makes demands on readers used to the pleasures of intimate and introspective prose, and the novel's political agenda adds a severity to its prose in marked contrast to the gentle lyricism of the earlier work. Recurring metaphors of hope — a male child born in winter, visions and portents of spring — fade in the trilogy's third volume, *A Distant Journey*. The most stirringly dramatic of the three novels, it depicts the defeats and betrayals within the revolutionary ranks, the senseless sacrifice of remarkable women and men and the marginalisation of others, and the barbarism of the Kuomintang troops in their determination to wipe out all traces of revolutionary activity from China's rural hinterlands. Ye's literary achievement in the trilogy — to date, his representative work and claim to international recognition — rests on his commitment to remembering the simple martyrs and unsung heroes of his land. A conscientious witness to his century, he has reached beyond his own memory into the past in The Land, and in *Jijing de qunshan* reminds the younger generations of the great toll paid in lives to achieve the freedom from hunger and want

which was the true goal of the revolution. While Ye deals with history he is equally concerned with displacement, loss, poverty, and the slow and painful acquisition of maturity; his restrained, sober methods, while they may remain, in content if not in style, deeply connected to the mainstream of modern Chinese realism, place an emphasis on truths and doubts beyond the sloganeering and theorising he recognises and so effectively portrays.

—Aamer Hussein

———

YEH CHUN-CHAN. *See* **YE JUNJIAN.**

———

YEHOSHUA, A(braham) B. Israeli. Born in Jerusalem, 9 December 1936. Educated at Jerusalem Hebrew Gymnasium; Hebrew University, Jerusalem, B.A. 1961; Teachers College, graduated 1962. Served in the Israeli Army, 1954–57. Married Rivka Kirsninski in 1960; one daughter and two sons. Teacher, Hebrew University High School, Jerusalem, 1961–63; director, Israeli School, Paris, 1963–64; secretary-general, World Union of Jewish Students, Paris, 1963–67. Dean of students, 1967–72, and since 1972 Professor of comparative literature, Haifa University. Visiting fellow, St. Cross College, Oxford, 1975–76; Guest Professor, Harvard University, Cambridge, Massachusetts, 1977, University of Chicago, 1988, and Stanford University, California, 1990. Member of board of art, Haifa Municipal Theatre; adviser to drama editorial board, Israeli Television Network; member of editorial board, *Keshet* literary magazine, 1967–74; editorial consultant, *Siman Kria*, *Tel-Aviv Review*, and *Mifgash*. Recipient: Akum prize, 1961; Municipality of Ramat-Gan prize, 1968; University of Iowa fellowship, 1969; Prime Minister's prize, 1972; Brenner prize, 1983; Alterman prize, 1986; Bialik prize, 1989; National Jewish Book award (U.S.A.), 1990; Israeli Booker prize, 1992. Honorary doctorate: Hebrew Union College, Cincinnati, Ohio, 1990. Address: Department of General Literature, Haifa University, Mount Carmel, Haifa 31999, Israel.

PUBLICATIONS

Fiction

Mot hazaken [Death of the Old Man]. Tel Aviv, n.p., 1962.
Mul haye'arot [Facing the Forests]. 1968.
Three Days and a Child. New York, Doubleday, 1970; London, Owen, 1971.
Tishah sipurim [Nine Stories]. 1970.
Sheney sipurim. Jerusalem, Machlakah, 1970–71.
Bithilat kayits 1970. Jerusalem, Schocken, 1972; as *Early in the Summer of 1970*, New York, Doubleday, 1977; London, Heinemann, 1980.
Ad choref 1974: mivchar. Tel Aviv, Hakibuts haMe'uchad, 1975.

Hame'ahev. Tel Aviv, Hakibuts haMe'uchad, 1977; as *The Lover*, New York, Doubleday, 1978; London, Heinemann, 1979.
Gerushim me'ucharim. Tel Aviv, Hakibuts haMe'uchad, 1982; as *A Late Divorce*, New York, Doubleday, and London, Harvill, 1984.
Molcho. Tel Aviv, Hakibuts haMe'uchad, 1987; as *Five Seasons*, New York, Doubleday, and London, Collins, 1989.
The Continuing Silence of a Poet. London, Halban, 1988.
Mar Maniy. Tel Aviv, Hakibuts haMe'uchad, 1990; as *Mr. Mani*, New York, Doubleday, 1992; London, Halban, 1993.

Plays

Laylah beMai (produced Tel Aviv, 1969). As *A Night in May*, in *Two Plays*, 1974.
Tipolim acharonim (produced Haifa, 1973). As *Last Treatment*, in *Two Plays*, 1974.
Two Plays: A Night in May and Last Treatment. New York, Schocken, 1974.
Chafetsim [Possessions] (produced Haifa, 1986).
Tinokot laylah [Children of the Night] (produced Tel Aviv, 1992).

Screenplays: *Sheloshah yamim veyeled* [Three Days and a Child], 1967; *Hame'ahev* [The Lover], 1986; *The Continuing Silence of a Poet* (Germany), 1987.

Other

Bizechut hanormaliyut. Tel Aviv, Hakibuts haMe'uchad, 1980; as *Between Right and Right*, New York, Doubleday, 1981.
Israel, with Frederic Brenner. New York, Harper, and London, Collins Harvill, 1988.
Hakir vehahar: metsi'uto hasifrutit shel hasofer beYisrael [The Wall and the Mountain: The Literary Reality of the Writer in Israel]. Tel Aviv, Zemorah-Bitan, 1989.

*

Bibliography: *A. B. Yehoshua*, Tel Aviv, Sifriyat Po'alim, 1980.

Manuscript Collection: National Library, Jerusalem.

Critical Studies: "An Appraisal of the Stories of Avraham B. Yehoshua" by Baruch Kurzweil, in *Literature East and West* (Austin, Texas), 14(1), 1970; "A. B. Yehoshua as Playwright" by Anat Feinberg, in *Modern Hebrew Literature* (Ramat-Gan, Israel), 1, 1975; "A Touch of Madness in the Plays of A. B. Yehoshua" by Eli Pfefferkorn, in *World Literature Today* (Norman, Oklahoma), 51, 1977; "Distress and Constriction" by Haim Shoham, in *Ariel* (Calgary, Alberta), 41, 1976; "Multiple Focus and Mystery" by Leon I. Yudkin, in *Modern Hebrew Literature* (Ramat-Gan, Israel), 3, 1977; "A Great Madness Hides Behind All This" by Gershon Shaked, in *Modern Hebrew Literature* (Ramat-Gan, Israel), 8(1–2), 1982–83; "Casualties of Patriarchal Double Standards: Old Women in Yehoshua's Fiction," in *South Central Bulletin* (College Station, Texas), 43(4), 1984, and "The Sleepy Wife: A Feminist Consideration of A. B.Yehoshua's Fiction," in *Hebrew Annual Review* (Columbus, Ohio), 8, 1984, both by Esther Fuchs; "Possessions as a Death Wish" by Gideon Ofrat, in *Modern Hebrew Literature* (Ramat-Gan, Israel), 12(1–2), 1986; "A. B. Yehoshua: Dismantler" by Chaim Chertok, in his *We Are All Close: Conversations with Israeli Writers*, New York, Fordham Uni-

versity Press, 1989; "A. B. Yehoshua" in *The Arab in Israeli Literature*, Bloomington, Indiana University Press, and London, IB Tauris Press, 1989, and "A. B. Yehoshua and the Sephardic Experience," in *World Literature Today* (Norman, Oklahoma), 65(1), 1991, both by Gila Ramras-Rauch; "Yehoshua's 'Sound and Fury': *A Late Divorce* and Its Faulknerian Model" by Nehama Aschkenasy, in *Modern Language Studies* (Providence, Rhode Island), 21(2), 1991.

A. B. Yehoshua comments:

My writings began in 1958 with short stories that were abstract in their essence; their meanings were divorced from any specific Israeli reality. The reality that emerged in them was obscure and remote. These short stories, in essence, deal with abstract and refined human situations, as in a laboratory experiment. Then I began to make my stories approximate Israeli reality more and more, and tried out new ideas about the complex human situations which arise even within the conventional human, social, and political views. This was achieved in the four novellas which form the collection *Mul haye'arot* (Facing the Forests).

After the Six Day War in 1967, political reality began to impinge more and more upon all of us. Issues such as the identity of Israeli national borders, the relationship with the Arabs, and the problems of the Territories changed the national consciousness into that of rulers, and also showed up in literature, especially in mine. The big political conflicts began to penetrate my literature, beginning with drama and later in novellas. Then, in the middle 1970s, when I was approaching the age of 40, I felt ready to write a novel. Until then I had perhaps too much respect for the genre to try and write a novel, a feeling to which I still relate. And so the novels, which came one after another, were born: *Hame'ahev* (*The Lover*), *Gerushim me'ucharim* (*A Late Divorce*), *Molcho* (*Five Seasons*), and *Mar Maniy* (*Mr. Mani*). The common factor between three of these novels — *The Lover*, *A Late Divorce*, and *Mr. Mani* — is the polyphonic nature of the story. The books are presented by different voices sometimes telling the same story from different angles. This folk-narrative technique appeared to me to be the most suitable for presenting the fracture that began to appear in the centre of Israeli ideology, with the buckling of the national consensus and the radical splits in the interpretation of that phenomenon.

In *Mr. Mani* I try to examine this split not only in the present, but also through an investigation of the past. Using the technique of incomplete dialogue I built five conversations that proceed backward from the present of 1982 to the past, to 1848. The book investigates the vital junctures in the history of the nation and Zionism by way of five generations of a Jerusalemite Sephardi family, similar to my father's family, which arrived in Jerusalem in the mid 19th century. Certainly the fact that this family is Sephardi means that they view reality differently from non-Sephardis. In the novel *Five Seasons* I try to deal in detail with the cultural intricacies that differentiate the West and the Orient, by examining Molcho's marriage after the death of his first wife who came from Germany.

It is possible that reference to Israel's many national and social problems will be a bit misleading for a reader of my comments here because the emotional and experiential basis of my work deals with the soul of a person as a topic sufficient to itself. Using the profound revelations uncovered by Freud and his pupils, I try to examine the workings of the unconscious by means of literature. After all, ideology is only a super structure, resting on human foundations, even if bound to our psyches organically.

*   *   *

A. B. Yehoshua is an Israeli writer of stories (specialising in novellas), novels (four to date), plays, and essays. He began publishing stories in 1957, and his first collection, *Mot hazaken* (Death of the Old Man), had an immediate impact on Israeli readership, taken aback by the ferocity and shocking paradox of the writing. Characteristic stylistic features are already discernible in his early work, although these have undergone conscious modification, change, and transformation in his subsequent fiction. Such early stories are distinguished by the starkness of the sentences, abrupt transitions, surprising shifts in plot, neutrality of the narrator, symbolic actions and names of characters, and overall allegorisation.

These features were carried over and refined in the second collection of novellas, *Mul haye'arot* (Facing the Forests), still considered by many to be Yehoshua's major achievement. On the whole, allegorisation gives way to metaphor, which works on both the concrete level in the specific narrative context as well as in the transforming suggestion. The title story, for example ("Facing the Forests"), tells of an aging student who seeks an environment where he can continue his studies. He takes on work as a forest guard, but becomes partially and ambiguously responsible for the fire which breaks out and burns down the forest. Personal traits and character — here the ambivalence of the student — are shaped to fit the larger framework of a story with historical and political implications.

Yehoshua is adept at setting up extreme and ambivalent situations indicating characters' mixed and contrasting motives. In *Bithilat kayits 1970* (*Early in the Summer of 1970*), a father tells of the death of his own son, victim of the on-going war. However, it later transpires that there has been a case of mistaken identity; the corpse discovered is not that of his son. We then see that he, the "bereaved" father, is in love with that role and finds it difficult to function without it. The manifest narrative features in *Early in the Summer of 1970* are role reversal, shock, surprise, psychological undermining, and indication of national implications. The style is marked by short, stenographic sentences, unexpected images, and extreme language. The narrator is as much a victim of surprise as the reader. In fact, it is his complicity that leads the reader astray and then brings him back to a reversed realisation, in the manner of a detective story. It is indeed a mystery story, but one with psychological and national content and character.

In all his work Yehoshua has displayed a preoccupation with form. *Early in the Summer of 1970* is constructed in a circular pattern, where the final chapter repeats the first, with added variations, as though time could be played with. When the author began to write novels, this concern was dominant. His first novel, *Hame'ahev* (The Lover), consists of a series of monologues spoken by separate people, where each successive section takes up the story from the conclusion of the previous section. Here again we have a mystery, of motivation and impulse. Who is the "lover" of the title? Why was he adopted, not only by the wife Asya, who takes him as a lover, but by the betrayed husband Adam as well? Does he obtrude into the family situation, or is he invited in? How do the subplots relate to the main story? What is the relationship of private concerns to the national situation, to the on-going war, to Israel as a state, and to the Arabs, one of whom, Naim, plays a major part in the novel?

Even clearer in its national and radical connotations is *Gerushim me'ucharim* (A Late Divorce), where the "divorce" planned and projected by the old man, living in America but arriving in Israel where his wife lives to finalise matters, is paralleled by a national, Jewish issue, the relationship between Israel and the diaspora. Can the old man once and for all effect the divorce and break off his ties with Israel? In fact he does manage to secure that divorce, but then replaces his wife and puts on her clothes. The two elements, personal and national, are inextricably linked, and the reader may have difficulty in disentangling the surface, narrative elements from the metaphorical and allegorical indicators. Just as the couple can not split up despite the formalised proceedings, so the elements of the story are entwined.

In a later novel, *Molcho* (*Five Seasons*), Yehoshua attempts to return to a more traditional form, writing a third-person narrative about the eponymous hero Molcho, recently widowed, who attempts to make a new life for himself in late middle age. Absent here are the characteristic elements of the author's prose — the odd images, shock reverses, surprising developments, and allegorical leads. Here we have a tale of a very average, not to say boring man, in his routine ambition and attempted re-engagement. Molcho is a man removed from history, or perhaps someone, who, in terms of Yehoshua's declared ideology in his political essays, has been liberated of his Jewish neurosis by Israeli "normality."

In *Mar Maniy* (*Mr. Mani*), both the obsessional pursuit after the meaning of Israeli, Jewish history and the interest in technique return. Here the structure adopted is of the telephone conversation where we hear only one side of a dialogue and have to infer the other. An even greater surprise is the direction of the narrative. Spaced over 200 years or so, in five episodes, the story begins in the present, in the early 1980s, and goes back, marked by key episodes in Jewish history, always to the accompaniment of a member of the Mani family. Mani, unlike Molcho (so unrelated to significant episodes in history) is always at the side of great events, although he himself does not forge them. The first of the Manis to appear chronologically (paradoxically, in the final chapter) wonders whether he is to be the last of the line. In this case technique, in pursuit of meaning, has shunted meaning aside, and put a question to which such answer as there can be has been offered in earlier chapters.

—Leon I. Yudkin

YEVTUSHENKO, Yevgeny. *See* **EVTUSHENKO, Evgenii.**

YOSHIOKA Minoru. Japanese. Born in Tokyo, in 1919. Served in the military forces in China, 1941–45. Worked for publishing house before World War II; editor after the war until 1978. Recipient: Mr. H. prize, 1958. Address: c/o Katydid Books, Department of English, Oakland University, Rochester, Michigan 48309-4401, U.S.A.

PUBLICATIONS

Verse

Ekitai [Liquid].   Tokyo, Sōzensha, 1941.

Seibutsu [Still Life].   Privately printed, 1955.
Sōryo [The Monks].   Tokyo, Eureka, 1958.
Bōsuikei [The Spindle-Shape].   Tokyo, Sōzensha, 1962.
Shizukana ie [The Quiet House].   Tokyo, Shinchōsha, 1968.
Shinpitekina jidai no shi [Poetry in a Mystical Age].   Tokyo, Yukawa Shobō, 1974.
Safuran tsumi [Saffron Gathering].   Tokyo, Seidōsha, 1976.
Lilac Garden, translated by Hiroaki Sato.   Chicago, Chicago Review Press, 1976.
Natsu no utage [Summer Banquet].   Tokyo, Seidōsha, 1979.
Kusudama [Scene Bag].   Tokyo, Shoshi Tamada, 1983.
Celebration in Darkness: Selected Poems of Yoshioka Minoru, with *Strangers' Sky: Selected Poems of Iijima Koichi*, translated by Onuma Tadayoshi.   Rochester, Michigan, Katydid, 1985.
A Play of Mirrors.   Rochester, Michigan, Katydid, 1987.
Hiji kata tatsumi sho.   Tokyo, Chikuma Shobo, 1987.

*   *   *

Reading *Seibutsu* (Still Life), Yoshioka Minoru's second collection of poems, one is tempted to baptize him a "poet of the egg," so obsessively recurrent is the image. With a consummate skill of imagistic juxtaposition, the poet creates a world of strange silence and slow disintegration where "the bones/temporarily placed in the fish/now extricate themselves out of the starry sea/and secretly dissolve/on the plate . . ." It is amid this world of "putrefying time" that he places a lonely egg, which, admirably refusing to be sentimentalized or mythologized, becomes a symbol of profound unrest as well as of autistic peace. The seeming stability of sculpturesque surface is such that a hasty reader might get a deceptive impression of "classicism," though it should be impossible not to sense something underneath that "tilts" (the poet's favourite word) towards uncanniness.

In the next volume, *Soryo* (The Monks), uncanniness shifts with a jerk into mercilessness, the static into the dynamic, as if the painter in Yoshioka had developed into a curious dramatist. The title poem reads almost like a scenario of the theatre of the absurd, depicting as it does, in a hitherto unprecedented spare style, the life of four monks — their obscene grotesqueries, their works and meals, their writings, and their suicide ("their bones just as thick as winter trees/hand dead till some day the ropes snap"). "The Coolie," a poem generated out of a memory of wartime experience in China, physically vibrates with powerful motions of a horse, incorporating at the same time an acute insight into Japan's recent history of political follies. Another important poem is an attempt at defining this world of ours as a system of dealing with "Dead Children" (the poem's title); its savage indignation is riveting, and yet there is an incandescent beauty of an autonomous poetic form.

Soryo, winning the coveted Mr. H. prize for poetry of the year, publicly announced the advent of a poet whose dislocation of poetic grammar was more radical than any experiments by other post-war poets while it maintained a fierce tension with his innate sense of form. The degree to which he rejected humanistic lyricism and exposed himself to the anxiety of identity was also unique.

It cost Yoshioka years of trials and errors to break himself free from the yoke imposed by the perfected style of *Soryo*, only three slim volumes of verses in 15 years and two years of complete silence. He finally emerged triumphantly in 1976 with a volume entitled *Safuran tsumi* (Saffron Gathering) as a poet who has acquired a new mobility, an agility which thrives on appropriation of the vocabulary external to the poet's own, such as proper nouns, foreign words, and quotations. Interestingly it was Lewis Carroll's photographed girls who triggered off this new mode by inspiring him to write a poem on them. Though he remains as unpredictable and disconcerting as ever, Yoshioka's renewed productivity would seem to confirm our belief that he is probably the best successor to the deceased master poet, Junzaburo Nishiwaki.

—Takahashi Yasunari

Z

ZÁBRANA, Jan. *See* ŠKVORECKÝ, Josef.

ZACH, Nathan. Israeli. Born in Berlin, in 1930; moved to
Palestine in 1935. Educated at Hebrew University, Jerusalem;
University of Essex, Wivenhoe, 1967–70, Ph.D. Repertory
director, Ohel trade union theatre, to 1967; adviser to the
Chambre Theatre, Tel Aviv, to 1967; lived in London, 1967–
79; London news editor, Jewish Telegraphic Agency, to 1979.
Currently Professor of comparative literature, Haifa University. Co-editor, *Likrat*, and *Yochani* literary journal; co-
founder, Achshav publishing house. Recipient: Bialik prize,
1981. Address: c/o Hakibuts haMe'uchad Publishing House,
P.O. Box 16040, 34 Hayetzirah Street, Tel Aviv 61160, Israel.

PUBLICATIONS

Verse

Shirim rishonim [First Poems]. Jerusalem, n.p., 1955.
Shirim shonim [Different Poems]. Tel Aviv, n.p., 1960.
Natan Zach, mivchar shirim (Selected poems). Tel Aviv,
  Machbarot laShirah, 1962.
Bimkom chalom [Instead of a Dream]. Tel Aviv, Galeriyah
  Masadah, 1966.
Kol hechalav vehadevash [All the Milk and Honey]. Tel
  Aviv, Am Oved, 1966.
Against Parting, translated by Jon Silkin. London, Royal
  Press, 1967.
Dekalim utemarim [Palms and Dates: Arab Folksongs]. 1967.
Shirim shonim [Various Poems]. Tel Aviv, Hakibuts
  haMe'uchad, 1968.
Mivchar [The Best]. Tel Aviv, Hakibuts haMe'uchad, 1974.
Tsefonit mizrachit [North Easterly]. Tel Aviv, Hakibuts
  haMe'uchad, 1979.
The Static Element: Selected Poems, translated by Peter
  Evermine and Schulamit Yasny-Starkman. New York,
  Atheneum, 1982.
Anti mechichon [Hard to Remember]. Tel Aviv, Hakibuts
  haMe'uchad, 1984.
Beyt sefer lerikudim: album kolot [Dancing School]. Tel
  Aviv, Hakibuts haMe'uchad, 1985.
Shirim al kelev vekalbah [Poems About a Dog and a Bitch]. Tel
  Aviv, Hakibuts haMe'uchad, 1990.

Other

*Kavey avir: al haromantikah basifrut haYisre'elit ve'al nos'im
  acherim: sichot milu'im* [Lines in the Air: On Romanticism
  in Israeli Literature and Other Topics]. 1983.

Editor, with Moshe Dor, *The Burning Bush: Poems from
  Modern Israel*. London, Allen, 1977.
Editor and Translator, *Kadish veshirim acherim*, by Allen
  Ginsberg. Tel Aviv, Am Oved, 1988.

Translator, *Dominoes*, by Chanoch Levine. London, n.p.,
  1974.

*

Critical Studies: in *The Hebrew Poem Itself*, edited by
Stanley Burnshaw, T. Carmi, and Ezra Spicehandler, New
York, Holt Rinehart, 1965, revised edition, Cambridge,
Massachusetts, Harvard University Press, 1989; "Elements
of Poetic Self- Awareness in Modern Poetry" by Shimon
Levy, in *Modern Hebrew Literature* (Ramat-Gan, Israel), 3,
1976.

* * *

Nathan Zach began writing poetry in the early 1950s, publishing in such avant-guarde journals as *Likrat*, *Achshav*,
and *Yochani*. He deliberately set his face against the earlier
prevalent modes of Palestinian/Israeli Hebrew poetry, with
its high language and literary allusiveness, against the
dominant expression of poets like Avraham Shlonsky and
Nathan Alterman. He more than anyone, and together with
Yehudi Amichai (*q.v.*), introduced a low-key, conversational language into poetry, eschewing for the most part
formal metre and rhyme. The poem derives from the dramatic structure in the authentic tracing of the mind and its
movement, an ambition parallel with that of the stream-of-
consciousness novel, highly individual, non-rhetorical, and
even anti-nationalistic.

His first collection of poems, *Shirim rishonim* (First
Poems), marks out this simple, personal, insistently repetitive, internally rhythmic, and idiomatic tone. The end of
love is marked not by great verbal flourishes, but by understated remarks, approaching the banal: "That's that," as he
concludes the poem "Final Separation." As in an everyday
conversation, when overheard or taken out of context, the
words seem abrupt and incomplete, demanding amplification
and comment. But the poem is left hanging, sometimes even
lacking punctuation that would indicate an ending.

Shirim shonim (Different Poems) makes more intensive use
of dramatic confrontation. We, as it were, interrupt the
speaker in midstream while he is trying to clarify or explicate a
situation. As the conversation has a context, known to the
speakers for which the way has presumably been paved by
previous such conversations and meetings, by unaccompanied
gestures and non-verbal indicators, the words themselves seem
partial and have to be filled out by the reader. Not only are the
poems sometimes open-ended literally, they can also be
ambiguous, as in the famous poem "Levado" (By Himself).
The title and first line of the poem: "It is not good for man to be
by himself" constitute a quotation from *Genesis* 2:18, when

God, after creating man, asserts that he should have a companion. Following the quotation, the poem here makes the counter assertion that man is alone in any event, whatever the circumstances. The continuation of this short poem invokes Messianic language, specifically the formulation by Maimonides of the 13th principle of faith that, even if delayed, the Messiah will eventually come, and that we should await him constantly. In the Zach poem, however, it is the subject of the poem himself who does the waiting, who is alone, and who, he assuredly knows, will eventually come. But the poem ends in mid-sentence, and the reader is provided with no further information or context. When and whither will he come? The combination of two confident oracles of divine origin, assuring man of a spouse, and then promising him ultimate redemption through His agency, are turned into an assurance that . . . What? Something will happen. He will surely come. To death? That seems to be the only thing of which he can be reliably assured. But that is hardly in the line of the Messianic future, one of whose functions is to "swallow up death for ever." Assurances are given in Zach's poems, but these assurances are not spelled out. What emerges, indeed, is that there is a truth behind and beyond the word. In another of these dramatic sections, one side of a dialogue: "keshetsiltsalt raad qolekh" (When you spoke your voice trembled), the word of the telephone conversation is indeed never spoken. He, the dramatic voice, articulating the situation in the poem, is already in a state of mourning, and has no need to hear either what the woman on the line has to say or even his own voice. The whole truth is in the tremor, and then in her subsequent absence.

Zach's subsequent poems continue to investigate personal moods, changes of mood, and life's expectations. Genuine heroism, for the poem, lies in the apparently small achievement, "the courage to wait," as from the poem "Gadol hu haomets lehakoth" (Great Is the Courage to Wait), in the volume, Kol hechalav vehadevash (All the Milk and Honey). Greater admiration is awarded to restraint and self-control than to unrestrained confession and self-indulgence. From this control, it appears, can come poetry itself, asserts a poem, offering an *ars poetica* in the poem "Keshebedidut eynah pahad" (When Loneliness Is Not Fear), whose first lines assert: "When loneliness is not fear/Poetry is born . . ." And the poem ends, again inviting the reader's conclusion: "Only/Then." The poet wants the poem to linger; as he says of his tailor in another poem, he is "against parting." The poems, then, linger and link up, forming a dramatic monologue with an implied interlocutor.

The Anglo-Saxon attitudes manifest in the understatement carefully cultivated, in the qualifications that are modified even at the point of expression, were expressed ever more directly in the volume that was a product of his extended residence in England, *Tsefonit mizrachit* (North Easterly), a reaction to England itself. The poems are indeed concerned with ambivalence, with the borderline between two tendencies, in reaction to the English landscape, climate, people, and moods. In passing by some workmen, it seems that they did not know "whether to bless or curse." All is a shade of grey, which can either brighten up or darken quite suddenly, depending on both external factors and the subject's perception.

The poet is often only a potential presence in the enacted scene, waiting on the sidelines of the action, longing for the proper moment and the appropriate gesture. Perhaps this moment will never arrive, that moment when he will be able "to speak some soothing words to you." Zach's poetry depends on tact, wit, and the fitting language. The rhythm is internal, sometimes intertextual, very different from Amichai's imagism. It is in all a finely balanced expression.

—Leon I. Yudkin

———

ZANZOTTO, Andrea. Italian. Born in Pieve di Soligo, near Treviso, 10 October 1921. Educated at the University of Padua, degree in literature 1942. Took part in the Resistance during World War II. Worked as a school teacher, and headmaster of local high school, Pieve di Soligo, for over 40 years. Recipient: Saint Vincent prize, 1950; Chianciano prize, 1962; Etna-Taormina prize, 1977; Viareggio prize, 1979; Montale-Librex prize, 1983. Address: c/o Musumeci Editore, Via de Maistre 12, 11100 Aosta, Italy.

PUBLICATIONS

Verse

Dietro il paesaggio. Milan, Mondadori, 1951.
Elegia e altri versi. Milan, Meridiana, 1954.
Vocativo. Milan, Mondadori, 1957; revised and enlarged edition, 1981.
IX Ecloghe. Milan, Mondadori, 1962.
La beltà. Milan, Mondadori, 1968.
Gli sguardi, i fatti e senhal. Pieve di Soligo, Bernardi, 1969.
A che valse? (versi 1938–1942). Milan, Scheiwiller, 1970.
Pasque. Milan, Mondadori, 1973.
Poesie (1938–1972), edited by Stefano Agosti. Milan, Mondadori, 1973.
Selected Poetry of Andrea Zanzotto, edited and translated by Ruth Feldman and Brian Swann. Princeton, New Jersey, Princeton University Press, 1975.
Filò per il Casanova di Fellini. Venice, Ruzante, 1976.
Sovraesistenze. Avelling Pergola, 1977.
Il galateo in bosco. Milan, Mondadori, 1978.
Mistieròi. Feltre, Arte Castaldi, 1979.
Filò e altre poesie. Rome, Lato Side, 1981.
Fosfeni. Milan, Mondadori, 1983.
Idioma. Milan, Mondadori, 1986.
Poesie (1938–1986). Turin, Arzana, 1987.

Other

Sull'altopiano (racconti e prose 1942–1954). Vicenza, Neri Pozza, 1964.
La storia della Zio Tonto (for children). Teramo, Lisciani & Giunti, 1980.
Credibilità che, with Giuseppe Santomaso. St. Gallen, Erker, 1988.
Cori per il film "E la nave va". Milan, Scheiwiller, 1988.
Ferruccio Gard: geometrie 1978–1988, with Piero Dorazio. Mantova, Casa del Mantegna, 1988.
Attraverso l'evento, with Giosetta Fioroni. Mirano, Eidos, 1988.
Racconti e prosa. Milan, Mondadori, 1990.
Fantasie di avvicinamento. Milan, Mondadori, 1991.
Sulla poesia, with Attilio Bertolucci and Vittorio Sereni. Parma, Pratiche, 1991.

Editor, with Nico Naldini, *Poesie e pagine ritrovate*, by Pier Paolo Pasolini. Rome, Lato Side, 1980.

Editor, *Mondo in bottiglia*, by Mario Marzi. Milan, All'Insegna del Pesce d'Oro, 1988.

Translator, *Una gazzella per te*, by Malek Haddad. Milan, Mondadori, 1960.

Translator, with Alberto Pescetto, *Giamilja e altri racconti*, by Chingiz Aitmatov. Milan, Mondadori, 1961.

Translator, *Età d'uomo*, by Michel Leiris. Milan, Mondadori, 1966.

Translator, *Nietzsche, il culmine e il possible* [Sur Nietzsche], by Georges Bataille. Milan, Rizzoli, 1970.

Translator, *La letteratura e il male* [La Littérature et le mal], by Georges Bataille. Milan, Rizzoli, 1973.

Translator, *La ricerca dell'assoluto*, by Honoré de Balzac. Milan, Garzanti, 1975.

Translator, *Il compagno segreto* [The Secret Agent], by Joseph Conrad. Milan, Rizzoli, 1975.

Translator, *Studi di sociologia dell'arte* [Études de sociologie de l'art], by Pierre Francastel. Milan, Rizzoli, 1976.

Translator, *Il medico di campagna*, by Honoré de Balzac. Milan, Garzanti, 1977.

*

Bibliography: "Saggio di bibliografia per Andrea Zanzotto (1951–1984)" by Piero Falchetta, in *Quaderni Veneti*, 4, 1987.

Critical Studies: "An Interview with Andrea Zanzotto" by Wallace P. Sillanpoa, in *Yale Italian Studies* (New Haven, Connecticut), 2, 1978; "The Poetry of Andrea Zanzotto" by P. R. J. Hainsworth, in *Italian Studies* (Leeds), 37, 1982; Zanzotto issue of *Stanford Italian Review* (California), 4(2), 1984; "Andrea Zanzotto: From the Language of the World to the World of Language" by Thomas J. Harrison, in *Poesis*, 5(3), 1984; "From Babel to Pentecost: The Poetry of Andrea Zanzotto," in *World Literature Today* (Norman, Oklahoma), 58(3), 1984, and *The Poetry of Andrea Zanzotto: A Critical Study of "Il galateo in bosco"*, Rome, Bulzoni, 1987, both by John P. Welle; *Andrea Zanzotto: The Language of Beauty's Apprentice* by Beverly Allen, Berkeley, University of California Press, 1988.

* * *

Italian poet Andrea Zanzotto was born in 1921 in Pieve di Soligo, where he has spent most of his life. Few poets after Thomas Hardy have been so deeply rooted in the culture, dialect, and landscape of their birthplace as Zanzotto. Together with Mario Luzi (*q.v.*), he is the most distinguished contemporary Italian poet, and author of some of the best books of Italian poetry to appear in the second half of this century.

Zanzotto's poetry, like much modern Italian poetry, is subjective, symbolically as well as hermetically personal, and, at its best, incandescently lyrical. This, however, doesn't exclude the probing, analytical, and exploratory nature of his preoccupation with himself and his alter-ego — of which the landscape in particular and the external world in general are both an embodiment and a spokesman, a prey as well as subject-matter. To some extent, this may be seen as a compensation for the unhappy influence that Freud and Freudianism have had on Zanzotto's development and sensibility as a poet — an influence that, for one thing, lets loose the flow of the subconscious at the expense of the curbing, disciplining, and organising role of the conscious. Hence the

criteria of what form and substance, theme and meaning, style and technique in poetry mean are largely irrelevant to Zanzotto's poetry.

Zanzotto's language is at times limpid like a running brook, at times as abstract and abstruse as a theorem or an insoluble conundrum, and at times both too personal and too disintegrated. This makes his genially luminous and happily inspired details, images, and metaphors all the more telling and significant — as, for instance, "il fiore marcito in un riflesso" (a flower rotting in a reflection), "il mio cuore trafitto dal futuro" (my heart transfixed by the future) , or "vuoto di ragnatele/ per valli e fessure,/ vuoto di nascita e sangue" (Valleys and fissures/ devoid of cobwebs/ devoid of birth and blood). There is something at once puzzling and haunting, evocative and abstruse about such verses which bear the unmistakeable stamp of Zanzotto's poetic brilliance and originality.

But Zanzotto's dealings with the multi-layered complexity of language are conditioned as well as brought about by an awareness of himself and of the world around him being in a state of perpetual neurosis. His creative originality is to be measured in terms of his brilliant verbal, stylistic, and technical experimentalism. His imagery can be daring ("i bianchi vermi con occhi di sole" — white worms with their sun-like eyes) or tender (birdies which "indugiano audacemente/ tra gli equilibri delle dita" — are audaciously poised/ on their balanced fingers). His mastery over naturalistic detail in its hallucinatory vividness and realism is apparent in lines such as "avanza il sole col precario" (the sun advances with its precarious footsteps), and his conceptual subtlety and delicacy are equally impressive, as in the lines: "Io pensavo che il mondo così concepito/ con questo super-cadere super-morire/ il mondo così fatturato/ fosse soltanto un io male sbozzalato/ fossi io indigesto male fantasticante/ male fantasticato mal pagato" (I thought that the world so conceived/ with this super-falling super-dying/ the world so adulterated/ was only an ill-cocooned me/ unbearable ill daydreaming me/ ill dreamt about ill paid).

In short, Zanzotto's singularly creative use of the language of poetry is what ultimately accounts for his originality — the originality of one confessedly imprisoned in the world of his own neurosis, poetic as well as moral, linguistic as well as psychological. And inspiring as well as dictating all his linguistically frenzied efforts to overcome this chronic sense of neurosis is his irrepressible desire to communicate, communicate not so much to others as to himself. "We write poetry," said C. Day Lewis, "not in order to be understood, but in order to understand ourselves." Zanzotto could have said the same.

And yet for all his linguistic innovations and complexities, there are gems of transparent lyricism where the poet's mastery over himself happily combines with his mastery over the language as well as over the world of neurosis. For instance, while talking of his own writings and how he left them behind "tra il grano e tra il vento" (amidst the grain and the wind), he tells them how "vi ho lasciato lassù perché salvaste/ dalle ustioni della luce/ il mio tetto incerto/ i comignoli disorientati/ la terrazza ove cammina impazzita la grandine" (I left you up there so that/ you might save from the burns of light/ my precarious roof/ the disorientated chimneys/ the terrace exposed to the raging hail-storm) — a superb example of how one needs all the strength to uphold and safeguard something humdrum, domestic, and fragile.

One particular device Zanzotto uses often and effectively is that of an inexhaustibly rich and evocative epithet — "deluso autunno" (disappointed autumn), "vagabonde uve" (vagrant grapes), "luce plurifonte" (light springing from various founts) — which offset other less lyrical devices such as a play of words, assonances, consonances etc. used apparently for their own sake: "quella luce limitata, limata" (that limited, polished light), or a series of almost mechanically worked out variants used for the sake of emphasis: "mi distinguo m'isolo m'isso m'attenaglio all'appiglio" (I differentiate myself isolate myself hoist myself grip myself to the hold).

While a certain degree of obscurity is inevitable in modern poetry, in Zanzotto's case it doesn't always seem to be so; at times it even seems to be willed or contrived, and not dictated from within. Perhaps Zanzotto's need to communicate what is at heart incommunicable gets the better of him and his ability to give it, if not a body and a name, at least a form and a substance. Despite that, one can admire and appreciate the indubitable wealth and intensity of his similes, metaphors, imagery, and details for what they are, without always being able to grasp what the poem they form an integral part of is really about.

"Go in fear of abstractions," cautioned Ezra Pound. As far as chunks of Zanzotto's poetry are concerned, such a caution seems to have gone completely unnoticed. But there are occasions when his linguistic dexterity, poetic inspiration, and the charged significance of what he has to say achieve a poignantly haunting expression, as, for instance, in the lines: "Mi è mancato così poco per vivere/ Così poco per sfuggire alla vita" (I needed so little in order to live/ So little in order to escape life). This may not be Zanzotto at his most characteristic, but this is certainly Zanzotto at his lyrically best.

—G. Singh

ZHANG AILING. Also Eileen Chang. Chinese. Born in Shanghai, 30 September 1920 (some sources say 1921). As a child lived in Beijing and Tianjin; returned to Shanghai in 1929. Educated at the University of Hong Kong, 1939–42; returned to Shanghai in 1942 because of war. Worked for *The Times* and *Twentieth Century*, Shanghai; moved to Hong Kong in 1952; worked for *The World Today*; moved to the United States in 1955; associated with Chinese Study Centre, University of California, Berkeley, from 1955; visiting writer, Cambridge University, 1967, and Miami University, Oxford, Ohio; associate scholar, Radcliffe Institute for Independent Study, Cambridge, Massachusetts. Address: c/o People's Literature Publishing House, 166 Chaoyangmen Nei Pajie Street, Beijing, China.

Publications

Fiction

Chenxiangxie [Bits of Incense Ashes]. Shanghai, Shanghai Violet, 1943.
Moli xiangpian [Jasmine Tea]. Shanghai, Shanghai Violet, 1943.
Xinjing [Heart Sutra]. Shanghai, Shanghai huang xiang, 1943.
Qingcheng zhi lian [Love in a Fallen City]. N.p., Shi Yue Publishing House, 1943.
Fengsuo [Sealed Off]. Shanghai, Shanghai tiandi Monthly, 1943.
Liuli pian [Glazed Tiles]. N.p., Huang Xiang, 1943.

Jin suo ji [The Golden Cangue]. 1943.
Deng [Waiting]. 1943.
Hongyingxi [Happiness]. 1943.
Hua diao [Withered Flowers]. 1943.
A Xiao bei qiu [A Xiao's Sad Autumn]. 1943.
Lianhuan tao [Chain of Rings]. N.p., Huang Xiang, 1944.
Nianqing de shihou [Time of Youth]. 1944.
Hong meigui bai meigui. 1944; as *Red Rose and White Rose*, Washington, D.C., American University, 1978.
Chuanqi xiaoshuo ji [Selected Romances]. Shanghai, Shanghai Zaji she, 1944.
Yinbao yan song hualouhui. 1944.
Sanwen ji [Selected Prose]. N.p., Jiedeng shubaoshe, 1945.
Liu qing [Mercy]. 1945.
Chuang shiji [Genesis]. 1945.
Chuanqi [Romances]. 1947.
Jidi zhi lian. As *Naked Earth*, Hong Kong, World Today, 1954.
Zhang Ailing Xiaoshuoji [Selected Short Stories by Zhang Ailing]. Hong Kong, Tian Feng Publishing House, 1954.
Yang ko. As *The Rice Sprout Song*, New York, Scribner, 1955.
Wu si yi shi [Remnants from May 4th Movement]. Taibei, n.p., 1958.
Yuan nu [The Embittered Woman]. Hong Kong, Hongkong Xingdao Evening Paper, 1966.
The Rouge of the North. London, Cassell, 1967.
Wang ran ji [Disappointment]. Taibei, Taibei Huangguan, 1968.
Liu yan [Gossip]. Taibei, Taibei Huangguan, 1969.
Zhang kan [Zhang's View]. Taibei, Taibei Huangguan, 1976.
Xiao tuanyuan [Reunion]. 1976.
Se jie [Threshold of Eroticism]. N.p., China Shibao renjian fukan supplement, 1979.
Haishanghua liezhuan [Biography of Prostitutes]. Taibei, Taibei Huangguan 1981.
Zhang Ailing juan [Zhang Ailing]. Taibei, Taibei Yuanjing Publishing House, 1982.
Lian zhi bei ge. Taibei, Lanyu Publishing House, 1983.
Yin Bao Yan kan Hualouhui. N.p., Lianhe, 1983.
Sheng ming de yue zhang [Music of Life], with Lin Haiyin. Jiulong, Wen kuang, 1983.
Qingcheng zhi lian: Zhang Ailing duanpian xiaoshuo xuan [Love in a Fallen City: Zhang Ailing's Short Stories]. Yinchuan Shi, Ningxia People's Publishing House, 1985.
Chuanqi [Romance]. Beijing, People's Literature Publishing House, 1986.
Si yu [Whispers]. N.p., Huacheng Publishing House, 1990.

Other

Shi ba chun [Spring of 18]. 1948.

Translator, *Fool in the Reeds*, by Chen Chi-ying. Hong Kong, Rainbow Press, 1959.

*

Critical Studies: in *A History of Modern Chinese Fiction, 1917–1957*, New Haven, Connecticut, Yale University Press, 1961, and *Modern Chinese Stories and Novellas: 1919–1949*, New York, Columbia University Press, 1981, both by C. T. Hsia; "Eileen Chang's Bridges to China" by Jeannine Bohlmeyer, in *Tamkang Review* (Taibei), 5(1), 1972; "Themes and Techniques in Eileen Chang's Stories" by Stephen Cheng.

in *Tamkang Review* (Taibei), 8(2), 1977; "Fiction and Autobiography: Spatial Form in *The Gold Cangue* and *The Woman Warrior*" by Lucien Miller and Hui-chuan Chang, in *Tamkang Review* (Taibei), 15(1–4), 1984–85; "Moon, Madness and Mutilation in Eileen Chang's English Translation of *The Golden Cangue*" by Shirley J. Paolini and Chen-Shen Yen, in *Tamkang Review* (Taibei), 19(1–4), 1988–89.

*   *   *

Zhang Ailing (Eileen Chang), an eminent fiction writer and translator, has been recognized by critic C. T. Hsia in *Modern Chinese Stories and Novellas: 1919–1949* (1981) as the most talented Chinese writer of the 1940s. Since she is proficient in Chinese and English, she is able to translate her own works. Among Zhang Ailing's major works is the brilliant novelette *Jin suo ji* (The Golden Cangue), which has in turn spawned two further versions: *Yuan nu* (The Embittered Woman) and *The Rouge of the North*. Departing from classical inspiration, Zhang Ailing's tragic novel *Yang ko* (The Rice Sprout Song) is set in China during the land reform in the 1950s. On a similar note, *Jidi zhi lian* (*Naked Earth*) chronicles Communist rule in China from the land reform period through the Korean War. Broader in scope than *The Rice Sprout Song*, the novel deals with adversity, friendship, and love. She has also written short stories of note.

Some universal themes in Zhang Ailing's fiction include survival and suffering, the elusiveness of romantic love, the importance of family, and the clarification of individual identity with respect to the group. Duty and convention rankle against self-fulfillment or self-indulgence. In her works she presents generational clashes between mothers and daughters-in-law and conflicts between spouses and brothers and sisters. She shows the hierarchical structure of Chinese families, be they mandarins or farmers, and depicts the world of servants, concubines, and slaves. Often her stories use Shanghai or its environs as their locale.

In *The Rice Sprout Song*, for example, Zhang Ailing creates the predicament of village folk in the countryside outside of Shanghai. In simple, direct language she relates the tale of Chinese villagers who suffer from poverty and hunger after Mao Zedong's revolution, and exposes the hypocrisy of the government which officially proclaims its achievements in the countryside while the people starve. She portrays an authentic picture of the familial and social interactions of Chinese villagers, demonstrating the interrelationships between generations, mothers-in-law and new brides, spouses, and parents and children. She lifts the veil of lies perpetuated by Comrade Wong, the village official of the Communist Party. Events reach crisis proportions when Moon Scent, the heroine, having earned some money working in Shanghai, is forced by Wong to part with her nest egg to donate food for the families of the People's Liberation Army. When Comrade Wong asks for further sacrifices from the peasants, Gold Root, Moon Scent's spouse, leads the resistance and a riot ensues. When Gold Root and his daughter are killed, Moon Scent burns down a government storehouse in retaliation, but loses her life in the fire. Ironically, the filmmaker Ku finds inspiration in the couple's story for his new film, but he will alter the story so as to conform to Party dictates. The "truth" of the villagers' revolt, which was precipitated by hunger and rage, will be altered for political expediency. With candour Zhang Ailing powerfully exposes hypocrisy and lies. She uncovers the reality under Party rhetoric: her truth is the hunger and desperate condition of the people despite the government's efforts to gloss over its problems.

While *The Rice Sprout Song* focuses upon the poor, *Jin suo ji* illustrates the decadence of the idle rich. Located in Shanghai, the novelette unfolds the step-by-step degeneration of Ch'i-ch'iao and her family. The "golden cangue" symbolizes the destructiveness of the protagonist who, while metaphorically bearing the frame used to hold prisoners in old China, is both imprisoned and imprisoning. She uses the golden cangue as a way of mutilating others psychologically while this instrument ironically stands for her own exploitation. The motifs of moon, madness, and mutilation and the themes of exploitation, moral degeneration, and destruction merge with images and symbols of moon, gold, and green, and the cangue. Tragically, the heroine of humble origins, who marries a physically handicapped man, suffers an unhappy and unfulfilled life. Lacking love and consumed by her opium habit, she lashes out at those around her, particularly her hapless daughter-in-law and her daughter. At the conclusion of the story, Ch-i-ch'iao lies in an opium stupor, reflecting upon her ruined life and the hatred of those around her.

Developed from the story of *Jin suo ji*, *The Rouge of the North* is an in-depth study of the heroine Yindi (Ch'i-ch'iao), a woman of lowly origins who marries into the rich Yao family, and struggles to be accepted by her mother-in-law, the Old Mistress. After a brief liaison with her brother-in-law, Yindi attempts suicide but survives. (No such suicide occurs in the first story.) Like the heroine of *Jin suo ji*, Yindi falls victim to her opium habit, manipulates the life of her only son after her invalid spouse dies, and finally achieves independence. Similarities occur in both stories when the heroines fail to find fulfillment in love or marriage, and dominate their sons and daughters-in-law. *The Rouge of the North* is more fleshed out with details of the characters' habits and backgrounds than *Jin suo ji* and offers information on family social structure, styles of living, and conversation. While focusing upon the theme of love lost, *The Rouge of the North* lacks the symbolism and brevity of *Jin suo ji*, which paints a more devastating picture of its protagonist's destructiveness.

Zhang Ailing's body of work succeeds in revealing family relationships, especially the plight of her female protagonists as they attempt to work out their conflicts. Her heroines are strong, memorable characters. Whether mandarins or villagers, her characters are drawn in sharp, deft strokes, and she captures conversation with a practiced ear in a realistic and descriptive style.

—Shirley J. Paolini

———

ZHANG JIE. Chinese. Born in Beijing, 27 April 1937. Educated at China People's University, Beijing, 1956–60, B.A. in economics 1960. Married Sun Youyu in 1986; one daughter. Staff member, State Bureau of Industry, from 1960; former staff member, Beijing Film Studios. Visiting Professor, Wesleyan University, Middletown, Connecticut, 1989–90. Vice chair, Beijing Association of Writers. Recipient: National prize, for short story, 1978, 1979, 1983, for novella, 1985; Mao Dun prize, 1985; Malaparte literary prize (Italy), 1989. Honorary member, American Academy and Institute of Arts and Letters. Address: International Department, China Writers' Association, Shatan Beijie 2, Beijing 100720, China.

PUBLICATIONS

Fiction

Ai shi bu neng wangji de.   Guangzhou, Guangdong People's Publishing House, 1980; as *Love Must Not Be Forgotten*, San Francisco, China Books, and Beijing, Panda, 1986.
Chenzhong de chibang.   Beijing, People's Literature Publishers, 1982; as *Leaden Wings*, London, Virago, 1987; as *Heavy Wings*, New York, Grove Weidenfeld, 1989.
Zai nei lu cao dishang [On a Green Lawn].   N.p., Literature Association Publishing, 1983.
Fangzhou [The Ark].   Beijing, Beijing Publishing House, 1983.
Zumu lu [Emerald].   Tianjin, Baihua Publishing House, 1985.
Zhi you yi ge taiyang [Only One Sun].   Beijing, Writers' Publishing House, 1988.
As Long as Nothing Happens, Nothing Will.   London, Virago, 1988.

*   *   *

Zhang Jie is one of the most versatile of the writers to emerge in China after the death of Mao Zedong in 1976. In much of her work, like other women writers of her generation, she is concerned with subjects such as love and marriage in Chinese society. She exposes the generally negative attitudes towards divorce which lead many couples to continue hypocritically in unhappy relationships because they fear the public condemnation which a breakup would produce. Her story *Ai shi bu neng wangji de* (*Love Must Not Be Forgotten*) is narrated by a young woman whose divorced mother was passionately in love with a married man for many years. He returned her love, but they knew that they could never act on their feelings and their relationship did not develop. When she learns of her mother's story, the daughter resolves to remain single if she does not meet anyone she can marry for love. This story was highly controversial at a time when China was just breaking free of the Cultural Revolution, for not only does it focus on love, it argues that political life should not always take precedence over personal life. Critics accused Zhang Jie of undermining public morality by her sympathetic presentation of extramarital love.

Zhang Jie shows particular sympathy for the female victims of repressive social attitudes and attacks the misogynist morality of feudal tradition. In her novella *Fangzhou* (The Ark), one of her best-known works, she explores with real sympathy the problems of three divorced women who try to build independent lives, showing the stress that social pressures put them under and the sexism and suspicion they meet from colleagues and neighbours. In this, as in other stories, she implies that the Party has not been able to put all the wrongs of Chinese society right, nor will it ever be able to.

In *Chenzhong de chibang* (*Leaden Wings* or *Heavy Wings*) Zhang takes on new themes. The novel is set in the Ministry of Heavy Industry, and its main focus is on the modernisation of Chinese industry and industrial management. She shows the old guard in the Ministry bitterly opposing the young reformers who are trying to raise efficiency. Zhang Jie trained as an economist and worked in industry for some years. She wrote this novel as a Party member who believed that China could not make progress without the introduction of more scientific and democratic approaches. Unlike most of the best of reform literature, including most of Zhang Jie's own work, it goes beyond the criticism and satire of Chinese society to present a vision of how things could change. When it was attacked by conservatives within the Chinese literary establishment for being "anti-Party and anti-Socialism," Zhang Jie defended herself by saying, "I wrote that book precisely because I am for socialism and China's modernisation." Perhaps because of its didactic mission, some passages of the novel have a turgid quality reminiscent of the politicised literature of the Cultural Revolution era. Nonetheless the novel can be read as a plea for more liberal individual values. It is concerned with private as well as with public worlds, and it contains, like so much of Zhang Jie's work, portraits of stale, unhappy marriages, which their victims preserve in order to retain their social and political positions.

Possibly influenced by trips to the West and by more extensive contacts with Western literature and Western tastes, Zhang Jie seems to have become less sentimental and less idealistic in her later writing. She continues to employ satire but has also introduced the fantastic into stories such as her work as in "What's Wrong with Him?," a sketch of life in a poorly equipped, underfunded hospital where exhausted doctors hallucinate, badly nourished nurses faint, and patients die when broken lifts cause delays. The world outside China impinges increasingly on Zhang Jie's plots. In "Professor Meng Abroad," a distinguished academic on a trip to the West develops a bladder problem. As all the money for the delegation is held by the interpreter, young Miss Ding, he is forced to humiliate himself by asking for coins each time he needs a lavatory. To make matters worse, she complains that he is using more than his fair share of the funds. The tragicomedy can be read as a metaphor for the suffocating control still exerted by the Party over even the most private areas of life. In "The Other World," an unknown small-town artist is suddenly summoned to the big city to be lionised by the artistic establishment and by various rather shady females. It turns out that a rich foreign patron of the arts admires his work and wishes to organise a foreign tour for him. All his new friends are trying to climb on the bandwagon. When the invitation is revoked, the artist is dropped by all these admirers and returns to his hometown, happy to be going back, but still confused by all that has happened to him. On the train he begins to itch and discovers that he is infested with lice.

Zhang Jie is more interested in and concerned with the literary world outside China than many contemporary Chinese writers. She once complained that the regulation and control of Chinese writers in the past prevented them from producing world class literature. In "The Other World," however, she seems also to warn that Chinese creative artists may lose their integrity if they concentrate too much on pleasing foreign audiences.

—Delia Davin

————

ZHANG KANGKANG. Chinese. Born in Hangzhou, Zhejiang Province, 3 July 1950. Educated at Heilongjiang Province School of Art; China Luxun School for Literary Studies, from 1980. Married Lü Jin Min (second marriage); one son. Vice chair, Heilongjiang Writers' Association, since 1986. Recipient: National prize, for short story, 1980, for novella, 1986; Heilongjiang Province Government prize, for novel; Heilongjiang short story award. Agent: Yang Xiany Waiwenju, Baiwanzhuang, Beijing, China. Address Huayuancun 2, Fuwai dajie, Beijing, China.

PUBLICATIONS

Fiction

Deng [The Light].   Published in *Jie fang ri bao* [Liberation Paper] (Shanghai), October 1972.
Fenjiexian [Border Line].   Shanghai, Shanghai People's Publishing House, 1975.
Xia [Summer].   Heilongjiang, Heilongjiang People's Publishing House, 1981.
Zhang Kangkang zhongpian ji [Selected Novelettes of Zhang Kangkang].   N.p., China Qingnian Publishing House, 1983.
Hong yingsu [Red Poppy].   Heilongjiang, Heilongjiang Literature and Arts Publishing House, 1985.
Ta [Pagoda].   Sichuan, Sichuan Literature and Arts Publishing House, 1985.
Yinxing banlü [The Invisible Companion].   Beijing, Beijing Writers' Publishing House, 1986.
Tuoluo Sha [Tuoluo Building].   Beijing, Hua Yi Publishing House, 1991.
Shujia de kalaok [Summer Holiday Karaoke].   Shanghai, Shanghai People's Publishing House, 1991.

Verse

Ganlan [The Olive].   Shanghai, Shanghai Literature and Arts Publishing House, 1982.
Diqui ren duihua [Dialogues of People from All over the World].   Beijing, China Huaqiao Publishing House, 1990.
Yewei [Game].   Tianjin, Baihua Literature and Arts Publishing House, 1990.

*

Manuscript Collection: Wanshou si [Longevity Temple], Beijing.

Zhang Kangkang comments:

There is no novel in which qualities of form and content are as indivisible as in the psychological novel. When the levels of consciousness have been grasped, then the novel obtains its correct form. When the obscure chaos of the levels of consciousness have been seen and very carefully described, only then does the novel have a sound psychological content.

If literature were not created to express people's experiences and battles with the tragedies of life, would it continue to exist? (from *Wen yi bao* [Literature and Art], 29 August 1987)

* * *

Like other writers of her generation, in much of her writing Zhang Kangkang is concerned with the hard lives of the young city people sent down to the countryside during the Cultural Revolution, with corruption and the abuse of power, and with the search of those who became disillusioned with the political orthodoxy they had been taught from childhood for some other code which might give meaning to life. Unusually for one of the writers in this group, she had published a first novel, *Fenjiexian* (Border Line), in 1975 when many Cultural Revolution policies were still in force and before she herself had completed her eight years in China's equivalent to Siberia, the Great Northern Waste. The book adopted the rosy tone obligatory at the time, and she was later to dismiss it.

Her first successful short story, "The Right to Love," is profoundly critical of Chinese society. A brother and sister have been affected differently by the tragic deaths of their parents during the Cultural Revolution. In this, as in other stories, Zhang Kangkang seems to imply that self-assertion is difficult for everyone in China, but especially so for women. The sister has become so timid that she suppresses the love she feels for a student. Life has taught her that love makes you vulnerable and ends in tragedy. Arguing that she is wrong, her brother insists that love is the right of citizens in a socialist society. "The Wasted Years" concerns a young man who has run away from his family to escape their demands that he take a dead-end job which would give him money but no chance to study for university entrance exams. He is living on a tiny salary but has a "room of his own," albeit a miserable one, and time to study. The narrator, who is a teacher, discovers the young man's hideout. Despite the sympathy that he feels for the young man, he is uncertain who is right in this conflict between family and self, and wonders whether to tell the parents where to find the young man. In another early story, "The Tolling of a Distant Bell," a mother comes to accept her son's right to make his own decisions in love, even though she fears that his relationship with the daughter of a high cadre is doomed. Where much literature of the 1980s in China merely condemned the Cultural Revolution and the repressive mentality that too often survived it, Zhang Kangkang's writing implies a more analytic critique based on a notion of human rights and individual responsibility.

Like other young writers of the 1980s, Zhang Kangkang experimented with imported literary forms such as the use of dreams and soliloquy, stream-of-consciousness narration, and the story as a metaphor. Most characteristic of her style is the use of a first-person or third-person narrator who tells the story through perceptions of the protagonist. Locked into the consciousness of a single character, the reader sees other characters only in one dimension. In a sense this is obviously a limitation of her fiction, yet the narrow focus on the inner life of a single character also gives a striking strength and intensity especially to her treatment of extreme emotional states. It is extraordinarily effective in conveying the nature of the paranoid state in "Bitter Dreams," the story of a man who fails to rise through nepotism because he lacks connections and cannot succeed through initiative because he is timid. The changes of the reform period are profoundly disturbing for him — he becomes bitterly jealous of colleagues who are promoted, and seeks psychological help from a woman doctor. Because we follow the story only through him, the border between reality and his tortured imaginings are never clear, and we get drawn into the world of the insane. The story ends as the man discovers the clinic he visited has vanished, leaving us uncertain if it ever existed.

Zhang Kangkang stands out from other writers of her background for the quality of her writing and her impressive output, but above all her insistence, revolutionary in the Chinese context, on the right and need of individuals to make their own decisions and even their own mistakes in life.

—Delia Davin

ZHANG XIANLIANG. Chinese. Born in Nanjing, 8 December 1936. Educated at schools in Beijing, expelled 1954. Divorced; one son. Farm labourer in Ningxia region, 1955; teacher, school for government cadres, 1956; imprisoned for writing: sent to labour camps, state farms, and prisons, 1957–79. Committee member, China People's Consultative Conference, 1983, and China Writers' Association, 1986; chair, Ningxia Federation of Literary and Art Circles, since 1986. Recipient: National prize, 1980. Address: Ningxia Federation of Literary and Art Circles, Wenhua Street, Yinchuan, Ningxia, China.

PUBLICATIONS

Fiction

Ling yu rou [Body and Soul]. Tianjin, Baihua Literature and Arts Publishing House, 1981.
Nanren de fengge [Men's Style]. Tianjin, Baihua Literature and Arts Publishing House, 1983.
He de zisun [The Descendants of the River]. Tianjin, Baihua Literature and Arts Publishing House, 1983.
Long zhong [The Seed of the Dragon]. Tianjin, Baihua Literature and Arts Publishing House, 1984.
Xiaoerbulake. Shanghai, Shanghai Literature and Arts Publishing House, 1984.
Nanren de yiban shi nüren. Beijing, China Wenlian Publishing House, 1985; as *Half of Man Is Woman*, New York and London, Viking, 1988.
Lühua shu. Beijing, Shi yue Literature and Arts Publishing House, 1985; as *Mimosa*, in *Mimosa and Other Stories*, 1985.
Prize-Winning Stories from China, 1980–1981, with others. Beijing, Foreign Languages Press, 1985.
Mimosa and Other Stories. Beijing, Chinese Literature/Panda, 1985.
Ganqing de licheng [The Course of Love]. Zhongguo, Writers' Publishing House, 1986.
Zao-an pengyou [Good Morning Friend]. Taibei, Taiwan Yuanjing Publishing House, 1987.
Xiguan siwang. Tianjin, Baihua Literature and Arts Publishing House, 1989; as *Getting Used to Dying*, New York and London, Harper Collins, 1991.

Plays

Screenplays: *Yi xiang tian kai* [Indulge in the Wildest Fantasy], 1986; *Women shi shijie* [We Are the World], 1988.

Other

Zhang Xianliang zixuanji [Selected Works by Zhang Xianliang]. Yinchuan, Ningxia People's Publishing House, 1986.
Fei yue Ouluoba [Flying over Ouluoba]. Tianjin, Baihua Literature and Arts Publishing House, 1986.

*   *   *

Zhang Xianliang is perhaps China's best-known writer of gulag literature. He rose to prominence with a collection of short stories, *Ling yu rou* (Body and Soul), but his best-known works are his novels based on the 22 years he spent in jails and labour camps in northwestern China. The first of these, *Lühua shu* (*Mimosa*), concerns the experiences of the protagonist, Zhang Yonglin, over a two-month period in 1961 when he is transferred from a prison camp to a state farm. It is the time of a great famine; he has earlier been left for dead and has had to "crawl out of a pile of corpses." The camp doctor, recording Zhang's weight at 44 kilos, congratulates him on being alive. As Zhang has used his wits to obtain the tiny amount of extra food that can make survival possible, it is indeed an achievement. The reader rejoices with him when he scrounges extra buns, and shares his devastation when they are eaten by rats. However, Zhang himself wonders if his scheming over food does not confirm that he is indeed a "bourgeois rightist," the charge which sent him to the gulag. He is not resentful or indignant about his punishment, nor is he certain that it is wrong; the key to understanding what has happened lies, he feels, in a better understanding of Marxism. Some critics accused the author of deliberately making the main character acceptable in order to get the book published, but Zhang Xianliang has retorted that intellectuals under political attack in China really did behave in this way.

Nanren de yiban shi nüren (*Half of Man Is Woman*) continues the story of Zhang Yonglin from 1966 to 1976, as he moves from a labour camp to a state farm. Zhang marries, and his wife has made for him what seems like a cosy, happy home, but on their wedding night he is struck by impotence. His wife finally loses patience and has an affair, assaulting Zhang's male pride. Zhang then joins the peasants in fighting a flood and demonstrates great heroism. When he returns home he has recovered his sexual powers. Zhang's impotence is symbolic of the impotence of the Chinese people who, it is implied, had lost the power to think or act for themselves during the Cultural Revolution in which the book is set. The use of sex to stand for politics is a recurring device in Zhang Xianliang's work. His explicit treatment of lust and impotence, unprecedented in modern Chinese literature, made him very popular with young Chinese readers, although they did not necessarily understand the metaphor. The authorites have decried his overt descriptions of sex as vulgar. More sophisticated critics see his view of sexuality as an exclusively male one and accuse him of objectifying his female characters.

The third of Zhang's autobiographical novels, *Xiguan siwang* (*Getting Used to Dying*), is the most complex. It is narrated in two voices, which belong to the same person, and this divided self produces a divided or uncertain reality. The novel is set in various American cities, in Paris, and in China; most of the time it is set in the present, but there are many flashbacks and one chapter is set in the year 2000. Realism vies with surrealism. The narrator's matter-of-fact treatment of terrifying events in China makes them seem all the more surreal. For example, in 1970 he was brought into town from the labour camp to be executed. The old carter who transports him explains that after the execution he'll take advantage of this unusual opportunity to do some shopping for his wife. When they arrive at the execution ground, guards seize the carter in error. The narrator, who as a political prisoner is accustomed to being always in the wrong, enjoys daring to correct them as he calls out, "Young comrades, I am the one to be executed, not him." A big crowd is waiting to watch the mass execution. Indeed the guards reproach the party from the state farm for keeping so many waiting. Parents have brought their children along to the spectacle. (Here, in an excursion to the present, Zhang Xianliang observes sardonically that these days when people criticise the influence that all the sex in his novels may have on China's youth, he agrees. How utterly inappropriate it is for children under 18 to read his books, how much better it would be for them to see as many executions as possible. Not only are executions entertaining, they also have great educational value.) Again Zhang turns out to be one of the lucky ones. When the shots ring out the majority of the prisoners are killed; the few who are not hit are told that they were chosen to "accompany to the execution ground." This expression describes a "normal" practice in modern China intended to frighten prisoners into working harder on reforming themselves.

Most of the book is set in the United States and Paris where Zhang Xianliang is being lionised as one of China's "new writers." Juxtaposed to what is normality for the narrator — the harsh, frightening, and yet internally logical world of China of the political outcast — the prosperous self-indulgence of the West appears ridiculous, uncaring, and surreal.

For some time after the Tiananmen Square massacre of 1989, Zhang Xianliang's books were not obtainable in China. Proof that he could publish again came with the appearance in 1992 of a memoir of his prison life. He is perhaps the best known of China's contemporary novelists outside China. Flawed and wordy as his writing sometimes is, it can also be immensely powerful. His harrowing accounts of prison life and his affirmation that self can be preserved in the most adverse conditions are not easily forgotten.

—Delia Davin

ZHANG XINXIN. Chinese. Born in Nanjing, 4 October 1953. Joined Cultural Revolution and spent time as a peasant worker and as a nurse in the People's Liberation Army, from 1966. Educated at China Central Drama School, from 1979. Since 1984 director, Beijing People's Art Theatre; hostess, China Central Television Station, and China Central People's Broadcasting Station. Visiting writer, Cornell University, Ithaca, New York, 1988. Address: c/o Beijing People's Art Theatre, Beijing, China.

PUBLICATIONS

Fiction

Zhang Xinxin xiaoshuo ji [Selected Short Stories by Zhang Xinxin]. Harbin, Beifang Literature and Arts Publishing House, 1985.
Zhang Xinxin zhongduanpian xiaoshuo ji [Collected Works of Zhang Xinxin]. Sichuan, Sichuan Literature and Arts Publishing House, 1985.
Wutai [The Stage]. Published in *Xiaoshuo Monthly*, 1988.

Other

Jie hou jie [Back Streets]. Hong Kong, Bo yi chuban jituan, 1986.

Beijing ren, with Sang Ye. As *Chinese Profiles*, Beijing, Chinese Literature/Panda, 1986; as *Chinese Lives*, with Sang Ye, edited by William J. Jenner and Delia Davin, New York, Pantheon, and London, Macmillan, 1987.
Nu wei yueji zhe rong [Women Make up for Those Who Make Them Happy]. Beijing, People's Literature Publishing House, 1987.

* * *

Zhang Xinxin was one of the new generation of writers to emerge in the cultural liberalisation that followed the death of Mao Zedong in 1976. Her early writing was concerned with the unique experience of her generation in China which, born after the establishment of the People's Republic in 1949, grew up among the certainties of Communist orthodoxy until it was caught up in the maelstrom of the Cultural Revolution of 1966–76. Zhang Xinxin's own formal education ended with the closure of all schools when she was 13. At 16, like millions of other young people, she was sent to the countryside to farm. Her posting was to the Great Northern Waste, a poor barren area often known as China's Siberia. After a year there she became an army nurse. Later, ill health took her back in Beijing where two years as an invalid gave her time for extensive reading and reflection before she started nursing again. In 1979, after a prolonged struggle to resume her education, she became a student in a drama institute and began to publish short stories.

In the years that followed, like other writers of her age, Zhang Xinxin reflected the feelings of those who felt they had become China's lost generation. She wrote of the courage and idealism of young city people sent to the countryside, but also of their loneliness and disillusion, of their struggles to return to the city, to get jobs and qualifications, and of the corruption and nepotism they encountered as they did so. Writing that exposed the irrationality of the Cultural Revolution and the sufferings of its victims received some official encouragement because it legitimised the reform regime. However, her writings seemed increasingly critical of the present, portraying young people who despite the reforms suffered feelings of spiritual emptiness, alienation, and uncertainty about the meaning of life. Her characters' search for personal happiness seems doomed to disappointment.

In "On the Same Horizon," the novella which first made her famous, Zhang Xinxin explored the emotional turmoil and pain of two young people involved in a divorce. Although in China divorce was still scarcely acceptable, she forced her readers to relate to the feelings of those involved in it. The story can also be read as a criticism of the opportunistic calculations often made in the formation of relationships in contemporary Chinese society. As her writing became more alienated, it also became more experimental in style. She attempted stream of consciousness, alternate narration, and the use of fables and fantasy to convey symbolic meanings. With such techniques she moved a long way from the social realism that has dominated modern Chinese fiction. She also aroused the ire of conservative cultural forces. In the 1983 "Campaign to Oppose Spiritual Pollution" she was accused of individualism, negativism, and mysticism, and condemned for having made her characters selfish and self-serving, thus portraying reform China in a negative light.

Accepting that she would be unable to publish fiction for the time being, she began collaboration with Sang Ye, a young journalist, on an oral history project influenced by the work of the American writer-interviewer Studs Terkel. They collected over 100 life stories of Chinese of all ages and classes, which were published in serial form in various literary journals and later in a collection entitled *Beijing ren* (*Chinese Profiles* or *Chinese Lives*). Reprinted in Chinese in Taiwan and translated into many languages, the book has been very successful outside China where it is recognised as a lively, multi-faceted portrait of Chinese life with considerable literary merit. In China, Zhang Xinxin's move away from fiction was less acclaimed and readers complained that the life histories were mundane. Nonetheless she continued to write reportage with *Returning Home*, an account of a visit to her father's backward home village where she found both a sense of belonging and a sense of her own distance and difference as a city intellectual.

—Delia Davin

————

ZHAO ZHENKAI. *See* **BA JIN.**

————

NATIONALITY INDEX

Entrants are listed by both past and current nationalities.

ALGERIAN
Marie Cardinal (now French)

AMERICAN
Iosif Brodskii
Julien Green (now French)
Arnošt Lustig
Elie Wiesel

ARGENTINIAN
Adolfo Bioy Casares
Griselda Gambaro
Silvina Ocampo
Ernesto Sabato
Juan José Saer
Luisa Valenzuela

AUSTRIAN
Ilse Aichinger
Peter Handke

BELGIAN
Hugo Claus
Paul Willems

BRAZILIAN
Jorge Amado
João Cabral de Melo Neto
Nélida Piñón
Rachel de Queiroz
João Ubaldo Ribeiro
Lygia Fagundes Telles

BRITISH
G. Cabrera Infante
Elias Canetti
Irina Ratushinskaia

BULGARIAN
Blaga Dimitrova

CAMEROONIAN
Guillaume Oyônô-Mbia

CANADIAN
Marie-Claire Blais
Nicole Brossard
Anne Hébert
André Langevin
Antonine Maillet
Josef Škvorecký
Sasha Sokolov
Michel Tremblay

CHILEAN
Isabel Allende
Jorge Díaz
José Donoso
Ariel Dorfman
Nicanor Parra
Antonio Skármeta

CHINESE
Ba Jin
Bei Dao
Cao Yu
Feng Jicai
Hao Ran
Liu Binyan
Liu Xinwu
Qian Zhongshu
Shen Rong
Wang Meng
Yang Lian
Yang Mo
Ye Junjian
Zhang Ailing
Zhang Jie
Zhang Kangkang
Zhang Xianliang
Zhang Xinxin

COLOMBIAN
Gabriel García Márquez

CROATIAN
Slavko Mihalić
Dubravka Ugrešić

CUBAN
G. Cabrera Infante (now British)
Eduardo Manet (now French)
Heberto Padilla
Severo Sarduy

CZECH
Václav Havel
Miroslav Holub
Bohumil Hrabal
Ivan Klíma
Milan Kundera
Arnošt Lustig (now American)
Josef Škvorecký (now Canadian)
Ludvík Vaculík

DANISH
Anders Bodelsen
Suzanne Brøgger
Piet Hein
Henrik Nordbrandt
Klaus Rifbjerg
Villy Sørensen
Henrik Stangerup
Pia Tafdrup
Kirsten Thorup
Dea Trier Mørch

DUTCH
H. C. ten Berge
Willem Frederik Hermans
Judith Herzberg
Lucebert
Harry Mulisch

TITLE INDEX

The following list includes the titles of all the books listed in the Fiction, Plays, and Verse sections of the book, as well as a few important titles from the Other section. The name in parentheses after the title is meant to direct the reader to the appropriate entry, where full publication information is given. For the purpose of alphabetization, all diacritical marks (whether for pronunciation or stress) have been ignored, and roman letter equivalents have been assumed for the following letters outside the roman alphabet: æ = ae; œ = oe; ð = d; þ = th; ß = ss. Titles beginning with numerals have been inserted in the alphabetical sequence as if the numbers were spelled out (in the language of the title).

A cena col commendatore (Soldati), 1950
À cœur joual (Blais), 1974
A este lado de la eternidad (Conde), 1970
A la epopeya, un gajo (Carballido), 1983
A la estrella por la cometa (Conde), 1961
'A la hāmish dafter al-naksa (Qabbāni), 1967
À la Lumière d'hiver (Jaccottet), 1977
A la mitad del camino (Matute), 1961
A la orilla de un pozo (Chacel), 1936
A la orilla del mundo y primer día (Paz), 1942
A la pata de palo (Cela), 1965–67
A la pintura (Alberti), 1945
À la Renverse (Vinaver), 1980
A l'Insu du souvenir (Ben Jelloun), 1980
A' māl al-shi' riyya al-kāmila (Qabbāni), 1967
A memoria (Maraini), 1967
A rachas (Martín Gaite), 1976
"A sushchestvuet li liubov?" sprashivaiut pozharniki (Radzinskii), 1978
À Toi, pour toujours, ta Marie-Lou (Tremblay), 1971
À Tout Regard (Brossard), 1989
A Xiao bei qiu (Zhang Ailing), 1943
Aan de evenaar (Claus), 1973
Aanslag (Mulisch), 1982
Abaddón, el exterminador (Sabato), 1974
Abahn Sabana David (Duras), 1970
Abārīq muhashshamah (Bayāti), 1954
'Abāth al aqdār (Mahfūz), 1939
ABC (Hauge), 1986
Abeille (Guillevic), 1979
Abel (Matute), 1948
Abel and Bela (Pinget), 1987
Abel et Bela (Pinget), 1971
Abendrot Nr. 15 (Sorescu), 1985
Abendstimmung (Kunert), 1983
Aber die Nachtigall jubelt (Kunze), 1962
Abhimanyu kī ātmahatyā (Yādav), 1959
Abhinandanā (Nāgārjun), 1979
Abierto a todas horas (Alberti), 1964
Abismo (Torga), 1932
About Face (Fo), 1983
About Mortin (Pinget), 1967
Abrazo del Winnipeg (Díaz), 1989
Abschied für länger (Wohmann), 1965
Absence (Handke), 1990
Abstecher (Walser), 1961
Abtötungsverfahren (Kunert), 1980
Abu Hossain (Sircar), 1972
Abwāb ila al-bayt al-dayyiq (Ḥaydari), 1990
Abwesenheit (Handke), 1987
Aç yazı (Dağlarca), 1951

Acacia (Simon), 1989
Acapulco, los lunes (Carballido), 1969
Accent grave et l'accent aigu (Tardieu), 1986
Accents (Tardieu), 1939
Accident (Wiesel), 1962
Accident (Wolf), 1989
Accidental Death of an Anarchist (Fo), 1979
Accidente (Alberti), 1987
Ach, Butt, dein Märchen geht böse aus (Grass), 1983
Ach wie gut, dass niemand weiss (Wohmann), 1980
Achat hi li (Carmi), 1985
Achilles a želva (Holub), 1960
Achshav bara'nsh (Amichai), 1968
Achshav ubayamin na'acherim (Amichai), 1955
Acht liederen van angst en vertwijfeling (Berge), 1987
Açıl susam açıl (Dağlarca), 1967
Ačkoli (Holub), 1969
Acrobat (Reve), 1956
Across (Handke), 1986
Across the Acheron (Wittig), 1987
Acrópolis (Chacel), 1984
Acuario (Alegría), 1955
Ad alot hashachar (Guri), 1950
Ad choref 1974 (Yehoshua), 1975
Ad kav nesher (Guri), 1975
Adam und Eva (Hacks), 1973
Adams dagbok (Faldbakken), 1978
Adam's Diary (Faldbakken), 1988
Ādarś aur yathārtha (Aśk), 1953
Addio diletta Amelia (Soldati), 1979
Adefesio (Alberti), 1944
Aden made (Endō), 1954
Adhikār kī rakṣak (Aśk), 1938
Adhūrī āvāz (Kamleśvar), 1962
Ādi mārg (Aśk), 1950
Adioses (Onetti), 1954
Ádjaga silbasuonat (Valkeapää), 1981
Adoni hanahar (Appelfeld), 1971
Adriana Sposa (Mallet-Joris), 1989
Adrienne (Green), 1990
Adrienne Mesurat (Green), 1927
Adŗśya nadī (Aśk), 1977
Adult Orgasm Escapes from the Zoo (Fo), 1983
Advent a Hargitán (Sütő), 1987
Adventures of a Photographer in La Plata (Bioy Casares), 1989
Adversos milagros (Bioy Casares), 1969
Aerial (Pritam), 1978
Aerial Letter (Brossard), 1988
Æskuvinir (Jakobsdóttir), 1976

605

Buffalo Bill (Breytenbach), 1984
Bůh do domu (Škvorecký), 1980
Buinaia kura (Soloukhin), 1976
Bulāvā (Pritam), 1960
Buli (Wang Meng), 1978
Bullerby Children series (Lindgren), from 1947
Bumazhnyi peizazh (Aksenov), 1983
Bunkócska (Határ), 1972
Burannyi polustanok (Aitmatov), 1981
Burial of the Sardine (Arrabal), 1965
Buried Mirror (Fuentes), 1991
Burn (Aksenov), 1984
Burning Patience (Skármeta), 1987
Burnt Pearls (Sutzkever), 1981
Burnt Water (Fuentes), 1981
Burro-em-pé (Cardoso Pires), 1978
Bushū hachigata (Ibuse), 1961
Busta arancione (Soldati), 1966
Bustān 'Ā'isha (Bayāti), 1989
But What (Herzberg), 1988
Butt (Grass), 1977
Butterfly (Wang Meng), 1983
Butts (Chraïbi), 1983
Bürgerliche Gedichte (Krolow), 1970
Bütows (Wohmann), 1967
Bütün hikâyeler (Kemal), 1967
Byen uden ildebrande (Bodelsen), 1989
Byens tvelys (Rifbjerg), 1987
Bystro khorosho ne byvaet (Petrushevskaia), 1978
Byvali chelovek (Soloukhin), 1986

Cabalgata (Hernández), 1988
Cabeza de la hidra (Fuentes), 1978
Cabeza del cordero (Ayala), 1949
Cācā Rāmditā (Aśk), 1981
Cacáu (Amado), 1933
Cachondeos, escareos y otros meneos (Cela), 1991
Cachorros (Vargas Llosa), 1967
Cacto vermelho (Telles), 1949
Cād aur ṭūṭe hue log (Bhārtī), 1965
Cadastre (Césaire), 1961
Cadaveri si spediscono e le donne si spogliano (Fo), 1962
Cādnā (Nāgārjun), 1976
Cādnī rāt aur ajgar (Aśk), 1952
Caetana's Sweet Song (Piñón), 1992
Café Céleste (Mallet-Joris), 1959
Café des artistas (Cela), 1953
Cage (Hébert), 1990
Cahier de verdure (Jaccottet), 1990
Cahier d'un retour au pays natal (Césaire), 1947
Cai xia ji (Hao Ran), 1963
Caída (Sarduy), 1974
Caifanes (Fuentes), 1967
Caimán (Buero Vallejo), 1981
Caja de cristal (Ferré), 1982
Caja vacía (Carballido), 1962
Cajón de sastre (Cela), 1957
Çakırcalı efe (Kemal), 1972
Çakırın destanı (Dağlarca), 1945
Cakknambar chattī (Pritam), 1964
Cakravyuha (Peṇḍse), 1970
Cal y canto (Alberti), 1929
Călcîiul vulnerabil (Blandiana), 1966
Calende greche (Bufalino), 1992
Call of the Fledgling (Hao Ran), 1974
Call of the Toad (Grass), 1992
Call Yourself Alive? (Cassian), 1988

Calle de la gran ocasión (Hernández), 1962
Calle de los balcones azules (Conde), 1985
Calling for Help (Handke), 1972
Calor das coisas (Piñón), 1980
Calviniste (Chessex), 1983
Calvinols resa genom världen (Jersild), 1965
Camaleón solteiro (Cela), 1991
Câmara ardente (Torga), 1962
Camarada oscuro (Sastre), 1979
Cambio de armas (Valenzuela), 1982
Cambio de piel (Fuentes), 1967
Caminheiros (Cardoso Pires), 1949
Caminho de pedras (Queiroz), 1937
Camino (Delibes), 1950
Camino a Babel (Varela), 1986
Camion (Duras), 1977
Camouflage (Rifbjerg), 1961
Camp (Gambaro), 1971
Camp de Thiaroye (Ousmane), 1987
Campagne (Frénaud), 1967
Campaign (Fuentes), 1991
Campaña (Fuentes), 1990
Campo (Gambaro), 1967
Canā jorgaram (Nāgārjun), n.d.
Çanakkale destanı (Dağlarca), 1965
Canal de la Toussaint (Hyvrard), 1985
Canaletto (Berge), 1969
Canan dā hauka (Pritam), 1962
Cancer Ward (Solzhenitsyn), 1968–69
Canción de cuna para un decapitado (Díaz), 1966
Cancionero de la Alcarria (Cela), 1987
Cancionero sin nombre (Parra), 1937
Canciones de nana y desvelo (Conde), 1985
Canciones del alto valle del Aniene (Alberti), 1972
Canciones par Altair (Alberti), 1989
Canciones rusas (Parra), 1967
Cāṅdi Begum (Haidar), 1990
Candle in the Wind (Solzhenitsyn), 1973
Canne à pêche (Hébert), 1959
Cannibals (Heym), 1958
Can't Pay? Won't Pay! (Fo), 1981
Canta, gallo acorralado (Gala), 1973
Cantar de ciegos (Fuentes), 1964
Cantar de Santiago para todos (Gala), 1974
Cantate d'octobre à la vie et à la mort du commandant
    Ernesto Che Guevara (Depestre), 1968
Cantatrice chauve (Ionesco), 1950
Cántico cósmico (Cardenal), 1989
Cântico do homen (Torga), 1950
Canto a un país que nace (Cardenal), 1978
Canto ceremonial contra un oso hormiguero (Cisneros), 1968
Canto de siempre (Alberti), 1980
Canto escolar (Ocampo), 1979
Canto nacional (Cardenal), 1973
Canto villano (Varela), 1978
Canzoni e ballate (Fo), 1974
Cão sem plumas (Melo Neto), 1950
Caos (Bioy Casares), 1934
Caperucita en la zona rosa (Argueta), 1977
Capitães de Areia (Amado), 1937
Capri Letters (Soldati), 1955
Captain Nemo's Library (Enquist), 1992
Captain Pantoja and the Special Service (Vargas Llosa), 1978
Captains of the Sands (Amado), 1988
Car Cemetery (Arrabal), 1962
Cara de la desgracia (Onetti), 1960
Carabas (Chessex), 1971

Dance with a Shadow (Ratushinskaia), 1992
Daneshvar's Playhouse (Dāneshvar), 1989
Dangerous Journey (Jansson), 1978
Daniele Cortis (Soldati), 1947
Danmariichi (Tsushima), 1984
Dans l'Arbre ténébreux (Frénaud), 1956
Dans le Labyrinthe (Robbe-Grillet), 1959
Dans le Leurre de seuil (Bonnefoy), 1975
Dans les flammes (Butor), 1965
Dans un Mois, dans un an (Sagan), 1957
Dans van de reiger (Claus), 1962
Danse de mort (Duras), 1970
Danse des korrigans (Guillevic), 1976
Danske billeder (Rifbjerg), 1970
Dansu, dansu, dansu (Murakami), 1988
Dantons dood (Claus), 1958
Danza del urogallo múltiple (Hernández), 1971
Danza que sueña la tortuga (Carballido), 1957
Danzig Trilogy (Grass), 1987
Danziger Trilogie (Grass), 1980
Danzón de exequias (Nieva), 1973
Dao yuanchu qu fa xin (Liu Xinwu), 1984
Dapim mimachazor nesher (Guri), 1974
Daquirí (Sarduy), 1980
Dar la vuelta (Gambaro), 1980s
Där står du (Schoultz), 1973
Dårarnas natt (Aspenström), 1966
D'Arcs de cycle la dérive (Brossard), 1979
Darežljivo progonstvo (Mihalić), 1959
Dark Journey (Green), 1929
Dark Room of Damocles (Hermans), 1962
Dark Stranger (Gracq), 1951
Darkness Casts No Shadow (Lustig), 1989
Darmstadt (Wohmann), 1986
Dasselbe (Lenz), 1957
Dat het 's ochtends ochtend wordt (Herzberg), 1974
Daughters (Vik), 1989
Daughters of Egalia (Brantenberg), 1985
Davar acher (Carmi), 1970
David (Cisneros), 1962
David Sterne (Blais), 1967
Davor (Grass), 1969
Dawmat wad ḥamid (Sālih), 1962
Dawn (Wiesel), 1961
Dawn: Red and Black (Arrabal), 1971
Day He Himself Shall Wipe My Tears Away (Ōe), 1977
Day Is Dark (Blais), 1967
Day Lasts More than a Hundred Years (Aitmatov), 1983
Day Mary Shelley Met Charlotte Brontë (Manet), 1991
Day the Leader Was Killed (Mahfūz), 1989
Day They Let the Lions Loose (Carballido), 1971
Daydream Mechanics (Brossard), 1980
Days in the Trees (Duras), 1966
Days of Longing (Varmā), 1972
Days to Come (Sobol), 1971
De amor y de sombra (Allende), 1984
De dónde son los cantantes (Sarduy), 1967
De Guerre lasse (Sagan), 1985
De hu? Shi hu? (Shen Rong), 1989
De la costilla de Eva (Belli), 1987
De la prairie (Guillevic), 1970
De l'hiver (Guillevic), 1971
De îndurare (Cassian), 1981
De noche vienes (Poniatowska), 1979
De Quoi s'agit-il?, ou, La Méprise (Tardieu), 1984
De raptos, violaciones y otras inconveniencias (Ayala), 1966
De si braves garçons (Modiano), 1982

De Singes et de mouches (Dupin), 1983
De Tous les Horizons (Chraïbi), 1958
De tropeles y tropelías (Ramírez), 1973
De un momento a otro (Alberti), 1937
Dead in Exile (Yang Lian), 1990
Dead Letter (Pinget), 1961
Dead Love (Carballido), 1970
Dead Soil (Kroetz), 1992
Deaf to the City (Blais), 1981
Dear Diego (Poniatowska), 1986
Death and the Maiden (Dorfman), 1991
Death as a Way of Life (Ayala), 1964
Death Is Called Engelchen (Mňačko), 1961
Death of a Beekeeper (Gustafsson), 1981
Death of an Ex-Minister (Saʿdāwi), 1987
Death of Artemio Cruz (Fuentes), 1964
Death of Mr. Baltisberger (Hrabal), 1975
Death Thrust (Sastre), 1967
Debut (Brodskii), 1973
Début et fin de la neige (Bonnefoy), 1991
Decir sí (Gambaro), 1981
Decorated Man (Mulisch), 1984
Dedans (Cixous), 1969
Deep Blue Sea, Pardon the Ocean (Vilhjálmsson), 1981
Defamed Alley (Kamleśvar), 1977
Déficient mental (Hébert), 1960
Degningsælið (Heinesen), 1953
Degrees (Butor), 1961
Degrés (Butor), 1960
Dehors (Dupin), 1975
Dejemos hablar al viento (Onetti), 1979
Dekalim utemarim (Zach), 1967
Del Miño al Bidasoa (Cela), 1952
Del obligado dolor (Conde), 1984
Del sol naciente (Gambaro), 1984
Delfim (Cardoso Pires), 1968
Delicado equilibrio (Gala), 1969
Delice böcek (Dağlarca), 1957
Délices de la chair (Arrabal), 1984
Delicioso domingo (Carballido), 1978
Delima ljubavi ili Vizantija (Lalić), 1987
Délire à deux (Ionesco), 1962
Delirio del amor hostil (Nieva), 1978
Delitio (Maraini), 1990
Deliver Us from Love (Brøgger), 1976
Déluge (Le Clézio), 1966
Demain Matin Montréal m'attend (Tremblay), 1972
Demain n'existe pas (Green), 1985
Demande d'emploi (Vinaver), 1972
Démanty noci (Lustig), 1958
Demasiado tarde para Filoctetes (Sastre), 1990
Demirciler çarşisi cinayeti (Kemal), 1974
Democracy (Brodskii), 1990
Demokratiia (Brodskii), 1990
Démon de l'irréalité (Tardieu), 1946
Demoner (Norén), 1984
Den' pervogo snegopada (Aksenov), 1990
Den søndag (Rifbjerg), 1975
Deng (Zhang Ailing), 1943
Deng (Zhang Kangkang), 1972
Dengdai dianhua (Shen Rong), 1987
Den'gi dlia Marii (Rasputin), 1968
Deniz küstü (Kemal), 1978
Denkmal (Braun), 1991
Denní služba (Holub), 1958
Deobe (Ćosić), 1961
Dépossessions (Garelli), 1968

Dinner Party (Mauriac), 1960
Dinner with the Commendatore (Soldati), 1953
Dinossauro excelentíssimo (Cardoso Pires), 1972
Dios desconocido (Sabato), 1980
Dios no nos quiere contentos (Gambaro), 1979
Dīp jalegā (Aśk), 1950
Diqui ren duihua (Zhang Kangkang), 1990
Dirk Lives in Holland (Lindgren), 1963
Dışardan gazel (Dağlarca), 1965
Disciplina do amor (Telles), 1980
Disciplina harfei (Cassian), 1965
Disco visuales (Paz), 1968
Discorsi sul terrorismo e la repressione (Fo), 1989
Discours du chameau (Ben Jelloun), 1974
Discours sur le colonialisme (Césaire), 1950
Discourse on Colonialism (Césaire), 1972
"disent les imbéciles" (Sarraute), 1976
Di-si bingshi (Ba Jin), 1946
Diskret ophold (Rifbjerg), 1965
Disparu (Blais), 1971
Disputado voto del señor Cayo (Delibes), 1978
Dissident, il va sans dire (Vinaver), 1978
Distant Journey (Ye Junjian), 1989
Distant Lands (Green), 1990
Distant Lover (C. Hein), 1989
Distant Relations (Fuentes), 1982
Dita Sax (Lustig), 1966
Dita Saxová (Lustig), 1962
Dito nell'occhio (Fo), 1953
Divák v únorové noci (Škvorecký), 1948
Divided Heaven (Wolf), 1965
Divine (Mallet-Joris), 1991
Dívka z Chicaga a jiné hříchy mládí (Škvorecký), 1980
Divno čudo (Pavlović), 1982
Divorced (Bergman), 1951
Dix Heures et demi du soir en été (Duras), 1960
Dizzy Horse (Sagan), 1968
Djävulens öga (Bergman), 1960
Djevojčica i pjesma (Mihalić), 1975
Djinn (Robbe-Grillet), 1981
Djurdoktron (Jersild), 1973
Dlaczego kot jest kot (Konwicki), 1976
Dlatego żyjemy (Szymborska), 1952
Dlia pol'zy dela (Solzhenitsyn), 1963
Dmitri (Braun), 1982
Dnevnie sny (Kushner), 1986
Dni cherni i beli (Dimitrova), 1975
Do dhārā (Aśk), 1949
Do piachu (Różewicz), 1979
Do raṅg (Pritam), 1974
Do utre (Dimitrova), 1959
Do You Hear Them? (Sarraute), 1973
Dobbel nytelse (Løveid), 1988
Doble historia del Doctor Valmy (Buero Vallejo), 1976
Doce canção de Caetana (Piñón), 1987
Docker noir (Ousmane), 1956
Dockskåpet (Jansson), 1978
Døden i bjergene (Tafdrup), 1988
Døden ikke heller (Fløgstad), 1975
Dog Years (Grass), 1965
Dogalypse (Voznesenskii), 1972
Dogg og dagar (Hauge), 1964
Doigts du figuier (Hyvrard), 1977
Dois parlamentos (Melo Neto), 1961
Dōji no kage (Tsushima), 1973
Dōjidai gemu (Ōe), 1979
Doktor Faustina (Dimitrova), 1971

Doktor Mabuses Nya Testamente (Enquist), 1982
Dolina Issy (Konwicki), 1982
Dolina Issy (Miłosz), 1955
Dollar Road (Fløgstad), 1989
Dolls in Black (Manet), 1991
Dolomitenstadt Lienz (Kroetz), 1972
Dol'she veka dlitsia den' (Aitmatov), 1981
Dom na granicy (Mrożek), 1968
Dom spokojnej młodości (Lipska), 1979
Dominee met strooien hoed (Wolkers), 1990
Domino (Bodelsen), 1984
Don Alvaro, o La fuerza del sino (Nieva), 1983
Don Juan (Maraini), 1976
Don l'Original (Maillet), 1972
Don Quijote's Tender Years (Sorescu), 1979
Don Segundo Sombra (Roa Bastos), 1968
Doña Beatriz, la sin ventura (Solórzano), 1952
Dona Flor and Her Two Husbands (Amado), 1969
Dona Flor e seus dois maridos (Amado), 1966
Dónde estas, Ulalume, dónde estas? (Sastre), 1990
Donde viven las águilas (Valenzuela), 1983
Dong yu (Wang Meng), 1980
Dongfang yu xiao (Yang Mo), 1970s
Donkere kamer van Damokles (Hermans), 1959
Donna del Fiume (Soldati), 1955
Donna di Porto Pim (Tabucchi), 1983
Donna in guerra (Maraini), 1975
Donna Lionora Giacubina (Maraini), 1981
Donna perfetta (Maraini), 1974
Donne e briganti (Soldati), 1950
Donne mie (Maraini), 1974
Don't Ask Me How the Time Goes By (Pacheco), 1978
Don't Give Me the Whole Truth (Hauge), 1985
Don't Pay! Don't Pay! (Fo), 1985
Dood en weggeraakt (Hermans), 1980
Doodshoofdvlinder (Wolkers), 1979
Dôra, Doralina (Queiroz), 1975
Dora Nelson (Soldati), 1939
Dorando la pildora (Dorfman), 1985
Dorle und Wolf (Walser), 1987
Dormir al sol (Bioy Casares), 1973
Doroga nomer odin (Evtushenko), 1972
Doroga, ukhodiashchaia vdal' (Evtushenko), 1979
Dorothea Wörth (Wohmann), 1975
Dört kanatlı kuş (Dağlarca), 1970
Dortn vu es nekhtikn di shtern (Sutzkever), 1979
Dos fantasías memorables (Bioy Casares, as Bustos
    Domecq), 1946
Doskonała próznia (Lem), 1971
Dossier (Różewicz), 1961
Døtre (Vik), 1989
Double Act (Ionesco), 1971
Double Bass (Süskind), 1987
Double Case History of Doctor Valmy (Buero Vallejo), 1968
Double Impression (Brossard), 1984
Dove in Santiago (Evtushenko), 1982
Downfall (Enquist), 1986
Downfall by Degrees (Hussein), 1987
Downfall of the Gods (Sørensen), 1989
Dozhd v Stepi (Soloukhin), 1953
Dra en nit (Bergman), 1948
Drachenblut (C. Hein), 1983
Drachenoper (Müller), 1969
Drachensteigen (Kirsch), 1979
Dra-Dra (Biermann), 1970
Draft of Shadows (Paz), 1979
Dragon with Red Eyes (Lindgren), 1986

Ek saṛak sattāvan galiyẵ (Kamleśvar), 1979
Ekho mira (Aitmatov), 1985
Ekið fyrir stapann (Þórðarson), 1960
Ekimae ryokan (Ibuse), 1956
Ekitai (Yoshioka), 1941
Eklips (Breytenbach), 1983
Eko av ett rop (Schoultz), 1945
Ekspeditsiya kum idniya den (Dimitrova), 1964
Ekte te Aerial (Pritam), 1968
Ekṭī hatyār naṭyakathā (Sircar), 1980
El erets acheret (Carmi), 1977
El Salvador (Argueta), 1990
El' — Zhaleika (Akhmadulina), 1958
Élan d'Amérique (Langevin), 1972
Eldens skugga (Wästberg), 1986
Eldur í Kaupinhafn (Laxness), 1946
Electroshock para gente de orden (Díaz), 1973
Elefántcsorda (Határ), 1972
Elegia (Zanzotto), 1954
Elegia na odejście (Herbert), 1990
Elegia tis Oxopetras (Elytis), 1991
Elégie pour Alizés (Senghor), 1969
Élégie, soleil du regret (Chessex), 1976
Élégies (Guillevic), 1946
Elegy, Some October Notes (Tranströmer), 1973
Elegy to John Donne (Brodskii), 1967
Elementen (Mulisch), 1988
Elementos de la noche (Pacheco), 1963
Eleonor (Blais), 1962
Elephant (Mrożek), 1962
Elgar (Peṇḍse), 1949
Eliza, Eliza (Aichinger), 1965
Elizabeth: Almost by Chance a Woman (Fo), 1986
Elle disait dormir pour mourir (Willems), 1983
Elle est là (Sarraute), 1978
Elmaradt lázálom (Csoóri), 1982
Elogio de la madrastra (Vargas Llosa), 1988
Else Kant I–II (Thorup), 1978
Elseneur (Butor), 1979
Elsewhere, Perhaps (Oz), 1973
Embarquement de la Reine de Saba (Butor), 1989
Emberek indulnak (Sütő), 1953
Embrasure (Dupin), 1969
Emerald (Soldati), 1977
Emergency Poems (Parra), 1972
Emigranci (Mrożek), 1975
Emigrants (Mrożek), 1984
Emigrés (Mrożek), 1976
Emil series (Lindgren), from 1963
Emily L. (Duras), 1987
Émission de télévision (Vinaver), 1990
Emitai (Ousmane), 1971
Emmanuel à Joseph à Dâvit (Maillet), 1975
Emöke (Škvorecký), 1977
Empire Céleste (Mallet-Joris), 1958
Emploi du temps (Butor), 1956
Emra'a 'inda nuqṭat al-ṣifr (Saʿdāwi), 1975
En el costado de la luz (Argueta), 1968
En esta tierra (Matute), 1955
En État de poésie (Depestre), 1980
En la ardiente oscuridad (Buero Vallejo), 1950
En la red (Sastre), 1961
En la tierra de nadie (Conde), 1960
En manos del silencio (Conde), 1950
En mi jardín pastan los héroes (Padilla), 1981
En/of (Herzberg), 1984
En Pièces détachées (Tremblay), 1969

En toch . . . was de machine goed (Hermans), 1982
En un mundo de fugitivos (Conde), 1960
Enantios Erotas (Anghelaki-Rooke), 1982
Encancaranublado Encantador solitario (Aridjis), 1972
Encanto, tendajón mixto (Garro), 1958
Enchancré (Dupin), 1991
Enchanted Night (Mrożek), 1964
Enclos (Gatti), 1962
Encoches (Guillevic), 1970
Encore en Hiver (Sagan), 1979
Encore Heureux qu'on va vers l'été (Rochefort), 1975
Encyclopedi (Norén), 1966
End of Lieutenant Boruvka (Škvorecký), 1989
End Papers (Breytenbach), 1986
Enda minut (Schoultz), 1981
Endagsvarelser (Norén), 1989
Ende des Flanierens (Handke), 1976
Endings (Munīf), 1988
Endstation: Harembar (Kunert), 1991
Enemigo íntimo (Gala), 1960
Enfant (Blais), 1980
Enfant chargé de songes (Hébert), 1992
Enfant du sable (Ben Jelloun), 1983
Enfant-rat (Gatti), 1960
Enfants du sabbat (Hébert), 1975
Enferma (Quiroga), 1955
Engagements of the Heart (Sagan), 1988
Engedjétek hozzám jönni a szavakat (Sütő), 1977
Engel (Rifbjerg), 1987
Engenheiro (Melo Neto), 1945
Engineer of Human Souls (Škvorecký), 1984
Enkel resa (Wästberg), 1964
Ennemi (Green), 1954
Ennemi (Pinget), 1987
Énorme Figure de la Déesse Raison (Frénaud), 1950
Enquête au pays (Chraïbi), 1981
Enquiry Office (Tardieu), 1968
Ensemble (Guillevic), 1942
Entenado (Saer), 1983
Enterrement de la sardine (Arrabal), 1961
Entre Deux Soleils (Wiesel), 1970
Entre el clavel y la espada (Alberti), 1941
Entre Fantoine et Agapa (Pinget), 1951
Entre la piedra y la flor (Paz), 1941
Entre la Vie et la mort (Sarraute), 1968
Entre pícaros (Díaz), 1983
Entre visillos (Martín Gaite), 1958
Entusiasmo (Skármeta), 1967
Entziehung (Wohmann), 1974
Enumeración de la patria (Ocampo), 1942
Envahisseur (Blais), 1972
Envie de vivre (Guillevic), 1951
Envois (Butor), 1980
Épaves (Green), 1932
Épervier (Dupin), 1960
Epigramas (Cardenal), 1961
Epilogos Aeras (Anghelaki-Rooke), 1990
Epitaffio (Bassani), 1974
Épouvantail (Tardieu), 1984
Equación (Díaz), 1979
Er Hu (Chen Ruoxi), 1985
Er saß in dem Bus, der seine Frau überfuhr (Wohmann), 1991
Er svært at dø i Dieppe (Stangerup), 1985
Era di venerdi 17 (Soldati), 1957
Erasers (Robbe-Grillet), 1964
Erdreich (Kirsch), 1982

Já Truchlivý Bůh (Kundera), 1969
Ja vi slutter (Brantenberg), 1978
Ja wiem, że to niesłuszne (Barańczak), 1977
Jaar van de kreeft (Claus), 1972
Jacht Paradise (Lem), 1951
Jack (Ionesco), 1958
Jack hos skådespelarna (Bergman), 1946
Jackass (Ruibal), 1970
Jackie bor i Holland (Lindgren), 1963
Jacob the Liar (Becker), 1975
Jacob y el otro (Onetti), 1965
Jacques and His Master (Kundera), 1985
Jacques et son maître (Kundera), 1981
Jacques; ou La Soumission (Ionesco), 1954
Jadi ār ekbār (Sircar), 1966
Jag måste till Berlin (Aspenström), 1967
Jag och min son (Lidman), 1961
Jag vill inte gå och lägga mej (Lindgren), 1965
Jag vill också gå i skolan (Lindgren), 1951
Jag vill också ha ett syskon (Lindgren), 1954
Jagd (Walser), 1988
Jahā Lakṣmī kaid hai (Yādav), 1957
Jahrmarktfest zu Plundersweilern (Hacks), 1975
Jai Śrī (Pritam), 1946
Jak daleko stąd, jak bliko (Konwicki), 1971
Jak jsem obsluhoval anglického krále (Hrabal), 1980
Jakob der Lügner (Becker), 1969
Jakub a pán (Kundera), 1980
Jalousie (Robbe-Grillet), 1957
Jaltaraṅg (Śrīvāstava), 1952
Jaltī jhāṛī (Varmā), 1964
Jambes du fils de Dieu (Dadié), 1980
Jamilia (Aitmatov), 1960
Jan de Lichte (Claus), 1981
Jangada de pedra (Saramago), 1986
Janglestrå (Hauge), 1980
Janmabhūmi āj (Sircar), 1986
Jansenisme (Claus), 1977
Januari (Lucebert), 1964
Jarðarberin (Þórðarson), 1980
Jardim selvagem (Telles), 1965
Jardin dans la tempête (Blais), 1990
Jardín de al lado (Donoso), 1981
Jardín de las delicias (Ayala), 1971
Jardín de las malicias (Ayala), 1988
Jardin des délices (Arrabal), 1969
Jardinero y los pájaros (Carballido), 1960
Jarīma (Mahfūz), 1973
Jaskinia filozofów (Herbert), 1970
Jaune le soleil (Duras), 1971
Javisst, kära du (Schoultz), 1967
Jay-parājay (Aśk), 1937
Jäger des Spotts (Lenz), 1958
Järnkronan (Lidman), 1985
Jāmanīya ke bābā (Nāgārjun), 1969
Jārj Pañcam kī nāk (Kamleśvar), 1985
Jā-ye khālī sūlūch (Dawlatābādi), 1982
Jdi a otevři dveře (Holub), 1962
Je est un autre (Green), 1954
Jealousy (Robbe-Grillet), 1959
Jebkatre (Pritam), 1971
Jede Zeit baut Pyramiden (Hochhuth), 1988
Jednym tchem (Barańczak), 1970
Jefes (Vargas Llosa), 1959
Jeffers-Akt (Strauss), 1989
Jeg kommer til at løbe (Bodelsen), 1987
Jenseits der Liebe (Walser), 1976

Jessica! (Claus), 1977
Jetzt und nie (Wohmann), 1958
Jeu avec le feu (Robbe-Grillet), 1975
Jeu de lettres/Character (Brossard), 1986
Jeu du souterrain (Mallet-Joris), 1973
Jeugd jaagt voorbij (Wolkers), 1989
Jeûne de huit nuits (Chessex), 1966
Jeune Fille à marier (Ionesco), 1958
Jeune Morte en robe de dentelle (Hyvrard), 1990
Jeunes Barbares d'aujourd'hui (Arrabal), 1975
Jeunesse (Modiano), 1981
Jeunesse illustrée (Arrabal), 1967
Jeux de massacre (Ionesco), 1970
Jew Today (Wiesel), 1978
Jews of Silence (Wiesel), 1966
Jia (Ba Jin), 1931
Jia (Cao Yu), 1942
Jia bu chuqu de sha yatou (Hao Ran), 1985
Jialingjiang liujin xueguan (Liu Xinwu), 1985
Jianada de yueliang (Wang Meng), 1986
Jiandan pian (Cao Yu), 1962
Jiangjun (Ba Jin), 1933
Jianqu shi sui (Shen Rong), 1986
Jidi zhi lian (Zhang Ailing), n.d.
Jijing de qunshan (Ye Junjian), 1986
Jilāvatan (Pritam), 1968
Jiliu trilogy (Ba Jin), 1931–40
Jin suo ji (Zhang Ailing), 1943
Jinguang da dao (Hao Ran), 1972–74
J'irai comme un cheval fou (Arrabal), 1973
Jiundā jīvan (Pritam), 1939
João Miguel (Queiroz), 1932
Job Klockmakares dotter (Lidman), 1954
Job, ou, Dieu dans la tempête (Wiesel), 1986
Jogador de sinuca e mais historinhas (Queiroz), 1980
Jogging (Sporting Scenes 1981) (Radzinskii), 1987
Jogos de azar (Cardoso Pires), 1963
Johan Padan a la descoverta de le Americhe (Fo), 1991
Johannes Buchholtz's urolige hjerte (P. Hein), 1977
John Manjiro, the Castaway (Ibuse), 1940
Johnny Mangano and His Astonishing Dogs (Tremblay), 1966
Joint (Gatti), 1975
Joke (Kundera), 1969
Joke (Sobol), 1975
Joker (Rifbjerg), 1979
Jolanda (Soldati), 1952
Jón gamli (Johannessen), 1967
Jon Manjirō hyōryūki (Ibuse), 1937
Jona (Hacks), 1989
Jonah (Sorescu), 1985
Jonas (Chessex), 1987
Jonk (Aśk), 1939
Jord og jern (Jacobsen), 1933
Jörð úr ægi (Johannessen), 1961
Jorden er blå (Tafdrup), 1991
Jorden er flad (Stangerup), 1976
Jordmånen (Wästberg), 1972
Jordvagga — himmelstak (Aspenström), 1973
José Trigo (Paso), 1966
Jóslás a te idődről (Csoóri), 1979
Josyane and the Welfare (Rochefort), 1963
Joualonais, sa joualonie (Blais), 1973
Jouets du vent (Butor), 1985
Jour (Wiesel), 1961
Jour de silence à Tanger (Ben Jelloun), 1990
Jour est noir (Blais), 1962

Mala nochebuena de don Etcétera (Díaz), 1964
Malacca Cane (Soldati), 1973
Maladie de la mort (Duras), 1983
Malady of Death (Duras), 1986
Malasangre (Gambaro), 1982
Malazgirt ululaması (Dağlarca), 1971
Mal'chik s pal'chik (Aitmatov), 1985
Maldítas sean Coronada y sus hijas (Nieva), 1980
Maldito amor (Ferré), 1986
Male minore (Erba), 1960
Malemort (Glissant), 1975
Maleńkie lato (Mrożek), 1956
Malen'kii Garusov (Grekova), 1970
Malen'kii kit (Aksenov), 1965
Malfaiteur (Green), 1956
Malhamat al harāfīsh (Mahfūz), 1977
Malik al shams (Jabrā), 1985
Malombra (Soldati), 1942
Malomocní (Klíma), 1974
Mama i neitronaiia bomba (Evtushenko), 1983
Mamlakat al-sunbulah (Bayāti), 1979
Mammifères (Guillevic), 1981
Man, A Dictionary (Kroetz), 1979
Man and the Fly (Ruibal), 1971
Man Closing Up (Guillevic), 1973
Man of God (Göncz), 1990
Man the Size of a Postage Stamp (Lustig), 1967
Man Who Lies (Robbe-Grillet), 1968
Man Who Wanted to Be Guilty (Stangerup), 1982
Man with an Umbrella (Bergman), 1946
Man with Bags (Ionesco), 1977
Man with the Luggage (Ionesco), 1979
Mánasigð (Vilhjálmsson), 1976
Mandabi (Ousmane), 1968
Mandat (Ousmane), 1965
Manden der ville være skyldig (Stangerup), 1973
Man'en gannen no futtobōru (Ōe), 1967
Mange og De enkelte (Sørensen), 1986
Mangi grásleppa (Þórðarson), 1969
Mangiami pure (Maraini), 1978
Manifestación (Díaz), 1979
Manifesto (Maraini), 1979
Manifesto dal carcere (Maraini), 1969
Mani-kañcen (Sircar), 1977
Manivelle (Pinget), 1960
Mann, ein Wörterbuch (Kroetz), 1977
Mann im Strom (Lenz), 1957
Manne aux Mandelstams aux Mandelas (Cixous), 1988
Mannen på trottoaren (Enquist), 1979
Mannenschrik (Berge), 1984
Männersache (Kroetz), 1971
Mano dellostraniero (Soldati), 1953
Manos de Dios (Solórzano), 1956
Mantra-viddha (Yādav), 1967
Manual de pintura e caligrafia (Saramago), 1976
Manuscripts of Pauline Archange (Blais), 1970
Manuscrito carmesí (Gala), 1990
Manuscrits de Pauline Archange (Blais), 1960
Manuşey, manuşey (Sircar), 1981
Many Dogs and the Dog (Akhmadulina), 1982
Mappe del desiderio (Tabucchi), 1989
Maqām 'Aṭiyyah (Bakr), 1986
Máquina de pedir (Ruibal), 1970
Mar (Torga), 1941
Mar Maniy (Yehoshua), 1990
Mar morto (Amado), 1936
Marāya (Mahfūz), 1972

Marble Dance (Telles), 1986
Marbles (Brodskii), 1989
March of the Musicians (Enquist), 1985
Marché des petites heures (Willems), 1966
Marche royale (Arrabal), 1973
Märchen vom kleinen Herrn Moritz (Biermann), 1972
Marcolfa (Fo), 1962
Mardie series (Lindgren), from 1979
Marea conjugare (Cassian), 1971
Margarete in Aix (Hacks), 1969
Margeries (Tardieu), 1986
Marginalia (Buero Vallejo), 1984
Margot la Folle (Maillet), 1987
María Carmen Portela (Alberti), 1956
María de mi corazón (García Márquez), 1983
Maria Magdalena (Kroetz), 1973
Maria Nefeli (Elytis), 1978
Maria Sabina (Cela), 1967
Maria Stuarda (Maraini), 1980
Mariaàgélas (Maillet), 1973
Mariage Blanc (Różewicz), 1983
Mariazuehren (Grass), 1973
Marie (Thorup), 1982
Marie Antoinette (Endō), 1979
Maries Baby (Hacks), 1985
Marijuana della mamma è la più bella (Fo), 1976
Marilyn Monroe (Cardenal), 1975
Marin de Gibraltar (Duras), 1952
Marinero en tierra (Alberti), 1925
Mariscalito (Díaz), 1979
Marital (Sircar), 1970
Market Day in Plundersweilen (Hacks), 1982
Markétin zvěřinec (Klíma), 1973
Markleys breiðist nú fyri tær fold (Heinesen), 1983
Marko bor i Jugoslavien (Lindgren), 1962
Marko Lives in Yugoslavia (Lindgren), 1963
Marks of Identity (J. Goytisolo), 1969
Marlenes Schwester (Strauss), 1975
Mar'ot Geychazi (Guri), 1974
Marquise sortit à cinq heures (Mauriac), 1961
Marquise Went Out at Five (Mauriac), 1962
Marriage in Philippsburg (Walser), 1961
Marsiyeh'hā-ye khāk (Shāmlū), 1969
Mart semnadtsatogo (Solzhenitsyn), 1986
Marta, Marta (Lidman), 1970
Martereau (Sarraute), 1953
Marts 1970 (Rifbjerg), 1970
Martyrdom of Piotr Ohey (Mrożek), 1967
Marxova ulica (Mňačko), 1957
Mary My Dearest (García Márquez), 1983
Mary Stuart (Maraini), 1984
März (Grass), 1966
Mãs kā dariyä (Kamleśvar), 1966
Mas'a leNinveh (Amichai), 1962
Ma'sāt al-Nirjis wa-malhat al-fiddah (Darwīsh), 1989
Mascara (Dorfman), 1988
Máscaras (Dorfman), 1988
Moooulin grammaticale (Brossard), 1974
Maska (Lem), 1976
Maske (Šalamun), 1980
Maskebajō ka svarg (Aśk), 1951
Masks and the Crocodile (Yang Lian), 1990
Második születésem (Csoóri), 1967
Mas'ot Binyamin ha'acharon mitudelah (Amichai), n.d.
Masrah wa'l marāya (Adūnīs), 1968
Massacre in Mexico (Poniatowska), 1975
Masscheroen (Claus), 1967

Moerasruiter uit het paradÿs (Lucebert), 1982
Moeru kaze (Tsushima), 1980
Moi, Laminaire (Césaire), 1982
Moi liubovnyi dnevik (Voznesenskii), 1966
Moi, Tituba, sorcière noire de Salem (Condé), 1986
Moia rodoslovnaia (Akhmadulina), 1963
Moja coreczka (Różewicz), 1966
Moja wierna mowo (Miłosz), 1981
Moje první lásky (Klíma), 1985
Moje zlatá řemesla (Klíma), 1990
Mokkwa ongduri edo sayon i (Ku Sang), 1984
Molcho (Yehoshua), 1987
Moli xiangpian (Zhang Ailing), 1943
Molino de viento (Cela), 1956
Moment of True Feeling (Handke), 1977
Mon doux royaume saccagé (Arrabal), 1981
Mona que le pisaron la cola (Ferré), 1981
Monaco Franze (Süskind), 1983
Monde est comme deux chevaux (Rochefort), 1984
Mondo et autres histoires (Le Clézio), 1978
Mondscheinknecht (Kroetz), 1981
Mondscheinknecht: Fortsetzung (Kroetz), 1983
Money for Maria (Rasputin), 1981
Money Order (Ousmane), 1972
Monika (Bergman), 1953
Moniza Clavier (Mrożek), 1983
Monjas (Manet), n.d.
Mono piadoso y seis piezas de café-teatro (Ruibal), 1969
Monogramma (Elytis), 1972
Monolog o brake (Radzinskii), 1973
Monologi (Petrushevskaia), 1988
Monólogo de la casta Susana (Cisneros), 1986
Monólogos de la hija (Conde), 1959
Monology (Kundera), 1957
Monsieur Levert (Pinget), 1961
Monsieur Moi (Tardieu), 1966
Monsieur monsieur (Tardieu), 1951
Monsieur Songe (Pinget), 1982
Monsieur Tête (Ionesco), 1970
Monsieur Thôgô-Gnini (Dadié), 1969
Monsieur Toussaint (Glissant), 1961
Monstres (Arrabal), 1971
Montanha (Torga), 1941
Mont-Cinère (Green), 1926
Montreal Smoked Meat (Tremblay), 1974
Mood Indigo (Sarduy), 1969
Mooi uitzicht (Lucebert), 1980
Moomin series (Jansson), from 1951
Moon in the Mirror (Donoso), n.d.
Moonrise, Moonset (Konwicki), 1987
Moraliteter (Bergman), 1948
Moraliteter (Myrdal), 1967
Morambong (Gatti), 1958
Morčata (Vaculík), 1973
Mordaza (Sastre), 1954
Mordet i Barjärna (Bergman), 1952
Mordre en sa chair (Brossard), 1966
More (Evtushenko), 1985
More Tales of Pirx the Pilot (Lem), 1982
Morecambe (Kroetz), 1975
Morgane Madrigal (Chessex), 1990
Morgengaven (Trier Mørch), 1984
Morgonen (Vesaas, as Moren), 1930
Morgunn í maí (Johannessen), 1978
Moriencia (Roa Bastos), 1969
Morirás lejos (Pacheco), 1967
Morituri (Claus), 1968

Moritz Tassow (Hacks), 1965
Mørk lægning (Bodelsen), 1988
Mørkets muligheter (Løveid), 1976
Moros en la costa (Dorfman), 1973
Mort au Canada (Chraïbi), 1974
Mort d'Ivan Ilytch (Green), 1965
Mort d'Oluwémi d'Ajumako (Condé), 1973
Mortaja (Delibes), 1969
Mortal Engines (Lem), 1977
Morte accidentale di un anarchico (Fo), 1970
Morte e a morte de Quincas Berro d'Água (Amado), 1962
Morte e resurrezione di un pupazzo (Fo), 1971
Morte e vida severina (Melo Neto), 1965
Mortin pas mort (Pinget), 1986
Morto da vendere (Fo), 1962
Morytáty a legendy (Hrabal), 1968
Mosche del capitale (Volponi), 1989
Moscow 2042 (Voinovich), 1987
Moskauer Novelle (Wolf), 1961
Moskovskaia saga (Aksenov), 1991
Moskva 2042 (Voinovich), 1987
Moskvafeber (Jersild), 1977
Most (Løveid), 1972
Most bez obala (Pavlović), 1956
Mostot (Koneski), 1945
Mosty na východ (Mňačko), 1953
Mot hazaken (Yehoshua), 1962
Mot pour un autre (Tardieu), 1951
Motes and Beams (P. Hein), 1973
Motet (Claus), 1969
Mother (Fo), 1984
Mother Comes of Age (Chraïbi), 1984
Mother Death (Hyvrard), 1988
Mother-Earth (Aitmatov), 1965
Mother Spring (Chraïbi), 1989
Motifs (Guillevic), 1987
Motivsuche (Lenz), 1988
Motor Show (Ionesco), 1953
Mots pour le dire (Cardinal), 1975
Motýl na anténě (Havel), 1975
Mountain Village (Ye Junjian), 1947
Mournful Demeanour of Lieutenant Boruvka (Škvorecký), 1974
Mouroir (Breytenbach), 1983
Mouvement brownien (Butor), 1968
Mozaika (Voznesenskii), 1960
Mozakkerat ṭabība (Saʿdāwi), 1958
Moïra (Green), 1950
Mörg eru dags augu (Johannessen), 1972
Mörkerseende (Tranströmer), 1970
Möwe (Müller), 1972
Mramor (Brodskii), 1984
Mrtvi ugao (Tišma), 1973
M.S.V. (Sastre), 1976
Mubian shi jie zhi (Liu Xinwu), 1986
Mudanza (Garro), 1958
Mudun al-milh quintet (Munīf), 1984–89
Muero, luego existo (Díaz), 1990
Muerta (Laforet), 1952
Muerte de Artemio Cruz (Fuentes), 1962
Muerte en el barrio (Sastre), 1959
Muerte y la niña (Onetti), 1973
Muertes de perro (Ayala), 1958
Mugura no haha (Tsushima), 1975
Muḥākama fī Nīsabūr (Bayāti), 1963
Muḥāwalah raqm sabʿah (Darwīsh), 1973
Můj svět (Hrabal), 1988

Můj známý Vili Feld (Lustig), 1949
Mujer de malas (Carballido), 1978
Mujer habitada (Belli), 1988
Mujer nueva (Laforet), 1955
Mujer sin Edén (Conde), 1947
Mujeres, animales, y fantasías mecánicas (Arreola), 1972
Mukhṛā badal gayā (Aśk), 1980
Muktamelā (Sircar), 1973
Mul haye'arot (Yehoshua), 1968
Mûle de Corbillard (Cardinal), 1963
Müller von Sanssouci (Hacks), 1958
Mum vechalom (Carmi), 1951
Mumaththilūn, al-istijwāb (Qabbāni), 1969
Mumin series (Jansson), from 1946
Munbatt (Munīf), 1989
München-Aten (Norén), 1983
Münchhausen (Haavikko), 1958
Münchner Kindl (Kroetz), 1973
Mündel will Vormund sein (Handke), 1969
Muñeca rusa (Bioy Casares), 1991
Munich-Athens (Norén), 1987
Murder in the Ironsmiths Market (Kemal), 1979
Murdō kā gāv (Bhārtī), 1946
Murlod (Norén), 1979
Murmures (Blais), 1976
Murs (Guillevic), 1950
Musen (Hacks), 1981
Museo de los esfuerzos inútiles (Peri Rossi), 1983
Museo d'ombre (Bufalino), 1982
Museos abandonados (Peri Rossi), 1969
Museu de tudo (Melo Neto), 1975
Museu de tudo e depois (Melo Neto), 1988
Music (Duras), 1966
Music Lessons (Petrushevskaia), 1991
Music of Human Flesh (Darwīsh), 1980
Musica (Duras), 1965
Música cercana (Buero Vallejo), 1989
Musica deuxième (Duras), 1985
Musik auf dem Wasser (Kirsch), 1977
Musikanternas uttåg (Enquist), 1978
Musiques de scènes (Sagan), 1981
Mussomeli-Düsseldorf (Maraini), 1991
Mutantes (Ruibal), 1969
Muttertag (Kroetz), 1975
Muxiang shenchu de zichou huafu (Wang Meng), 1984
Muẓakkirāti fī sijn al-nisā' (Sa'dāwi), 1983
My First Loves (Klíma), 1986
My Foot My Tutor (Handke), 1971
My Golden Trades (Klíma), 1992
My House Is on Fire (Dorfman), 1990
My Merry Mornings (Klíma), 1985
My Michael (Oz), 1972
My Nightingale Is Singing (Lindgren), 1985
My Swedish Cousins (Lindgren), 1959
My Troubles Began (Volponi), 1964
My zdes' zhivem (Voinovich), 1961
Myglaren (Myrdal), 1966
Myriel (Vik), 1981
Mystère de la parole (Hébert), 1975
Mystères de Paris (Frénaud), 1944
Mytologier (Rifbjerg), 1970

Na czworakach (Różewicz), 1971
Na ispytaniakh (Grekova), 1967
Na otkrito (Dimitrova), 1956
Na pełnym morzu (Mrożek), 1961
Na polputi k lune (Aksenov), 1962

Na powierzchni poematu i w środku (Różewicz), 1983
Na Rādhā, na Rukmiṇī (Pritam), 1985(?)
Na reke Angare (Rasputin), 1980
Na zolotom kryl'tse sideli (Tolstaia), 1987
Naar Archangel (Herzberg), 1971
Naar Magnitogorsk (Hermans), 1990
Naboth's Stone (Lidman), 1989
Nabots sten (Lidman), 1981
Nach der ersten Zukunft (Becker), 1980
Nachdenken über Christa T. (Wolf), 1968
Nachkommenschaften (Wohmann), 1981
Nachlaß I (Biermann), 1977
Nachmittag eines Schriftstellers (Handke), 1987
Nachricht vom Tag (Aichinger), 1970
Nachrichtensperre (Wohmann), 1978
Nachruf auf einen Handschuh (Grass), 1982
Nächste bitte (Wohmann), 1978
Nachtfahrt und früher Morgen (C. Hein), 1982
Nachtigall fällt auch nichts Neues ein (Wohmann), 1978
Nacht-Leben, oder, Geschonte Kindheit (Krolow), 1985
Nada (Laforet), 1945
Nader tot u (Reve), 1966
Nadī (Hussein), 1984
Nadī pyāsī thī (Bhārtī), 1954
Nadie nada nunca (Saer), 1980
Naginī kanyā kahinī (Sircar), 1982
Nāgmaṇī (Pritam), 1964
Nahui Ollin (Carballido), 1977
Naī paudh (Nāgārjun), 1957
Naismetsa (Haavikko), 1981
Naissance (Gatti), 1968
Naissance à l'aube (Chraïbi), 1986
Naked Earth (Zhang Ailing), 1954
Naked Machine (Johannessen), 1988
Naked Night (Bergman), 1953
Name of Oedipus (Cixous), 1991
Name of the Rose (Eco), 1983
Namen Pelerine (Šalamun), 1968
Names for Which There Are No People (Lustig), 1960
Nanatsu no kaidō (Ibuse), 1952
Nanhī-sī lau (Aśk), 1979
Nanna-ya (Condé), 1985
Nanren de fengge (Zhang Xianliang), 1983
Nanren de yiban shi nüren (Zhang Xianliang), 1985
Naopak (Holub), 1982
Nap és a hold elrablása (Juhász), 1965
Napis (Herbert), 1969
När Bäckhultarn for till stan (Lindgren), 1989
Når der går hul på en engel (Tafdrup), 1981
När dom brände fjärilar på lilla scenen (Norén), 1983
Når en pike sier ja (Vik), 1985
När lilla Ida skulle göra hyss (Lindgren), 1984
Nära livet (Bergman), 1958
Nār wa-al-kalimāt (Bayāti), 1964
Naranjal ardiente, nocturno paraguayo (Roa Bastos), 1960
Närmare någon (Schoultz), 1951
Narrateur et personnages (Brossard), 1971
Narratori della pianura (Celati), 1985
Narrene (Rifbjerg), 1971
Näsan (Aspenström), 1971
Naśeb (Hussein), 1981
Nash Dekameron (Radzinskii), 1988
Nasilje (Tišma), 1965
Nasledniki Stalina (Evtushenko), 1963
Nästa dag (Schoultz), 1991
Nästa dörr (Schoultz), 1969
Nastro di Moebius (Erba), 1980

Opus gran (Mulisch), 1982
Or vehakutonet (Appelfeld), 1971
Ora de nisip (Blandiana), 1983
Ora marítima (Alberti), 1953
Oración por Marilyn Monroe (Cardenal), 1965
Orage immobile (Sagan), 1983
Oraison (Arrabal), 1958
Orange Envelope (Soldati), 1969
Orange sur le Mont de Vénus (Arrabal), 1976
Oratorio de Fuenterrabía (Gala), 1976
Oráculo sobre Managua (Cardenal), 1973
Orchestration théâtrale (Arrabal), 1960
Orchids in the Moonlight (Fuentes), 1982
Ord over grind (Vesaas), 1965
Ordbok (Aspenström), 1976
Orden de los factores (Hernández), 1983
Order (Norén), 1978
Ordinaire (Vinaver), 1982
Ordinary Day (Fo), 1988
Ordine! Per Dio.000.000.000 (Fo), 1972
Ördögpille (Csoóri), 1957
Orestes (Claus), 1976
Orestes (Norén), 1980
Orfeu rebelde (Torga), 1958
Orgástula (Díaz), 1970
Oriflama (Hernández), 1988
Orilleros (Bioy Casares), 1955
Orinoco! (Carballido), 1982
Orison (Arrabal), 1961
Orlamonde (Le Clézio), 1985
Ormens ägg (Bergman), 1977
Ornis de oro (Cardenal), 1991
Örökhétfő (Petri), 1981
Orphan Street (Langevin), 1976
Orquídeas a la luz de la luna (Fuentes), 1982
Ortadirek (Kemal), 1960
Örtlich betäubt (Grass), 1969
Őrző könyve: Egregor (Határ), 1974
Os anxos cómense crús (Díaz), 1973
Osadeni na lyubov (Dimitrova), 1967
Oscuras raíces (Conde), 1954
Oscuro vuelo compartido (Díaz), 1982
Osennie list'ia (Soloukhin), 1968
Osennii krik iastreba (Brodskii), 1990
Ostanovka v pustyne (Brodskii), 1970
Ostatni dzién lata (Konwicki), 1958
Ostersjöar (Tranströmer), 1974
Ostkupan (Schoultz), 1975
Ostrov Krym (Aksenov), 1981
Ostrov mrtvých králů (Klíma), 1992
Ostře sledované vlaky (Hrabal), 1965
Oswald et Zénaïde (Tardieu), 1951
Osynliga Barnet (Jansson), 1962
Otan to Soma (Anghelaki-Rooke), 1988
Other One (Green), 1973
Other Shore (Alberti), 1981
Other Weapons (Valenzuela), 1985
Otklonenie (Dimitrova), 1967
Otkrytki iz V'etnama (Soloukhin), 1961
Otkuda rodom ia (Evtushenko), 1983
Otoko to kyūkanchō (Endō), 1963
Otoño del patriarca (García Márquez), 1975
Otoño, otra vez (Alberti), 1960
Otpadnik (Ćosić), 1986
Otra ciudad (Quiroga), 1953
Otra orilla (Díaz), 1988(?)
Otra vez las avestruces (Ruibal), 1991

Otro Cristobal (Gatti), 1962
Otro fútbol (Delibes), 1982
Otrok in jelen (Šalamun), 1990
Ottsovskii slukh (Evtushenko), 1975
Otvetstvennost' pered budushchim (Aitmatov), 1967
Otvůd liubovta (Dimitrova), 1987
Où vont mourir les oiseaux (Chessex), 1980
Oubli (Mauriac), 1966
Oublié (Wiesel), 1989
Oud en eenzaam (Reve), 1978
Oude lucht (Mulisch), 1977
Ouï-dire (Deguy), 1966
Our Golden Ironburg (Aksenov), 1988
Our Vietnam War (Dağlarca), 1966
Oursiade (Maillet), 1990
Out at Sea (Mrożek), 1962
Out of Season (Vik), 1983
Out to Sea (Mrożek), 1989
Outro livro de Job (Torga), 1936
Outsider (Sabato), 1950
Ouvert obscur (Chessex), 1967
Ouverture orang-outan (Arrabal), 1978
Ovanligt fall (Aspenström), 1963
Over regnbuen (Bodelsen), 1982
Overdose (Sarduy), 1972
Overgangsriten (Berge), 1992
Overgebleven gedichten (Hermans), 1968
Overhøring (Bodelsen), 1979
Oversight (Ionesco), 1971
Overtreding (Claus), 1985
Owl's Insomnia (Alberti), 1973
Ozelenenie (Petrushevskaia), 1980
Özgürlük alanı (Dağlarca), 1960
Ozhog (Aksenov), 1980
Oznob (Akhmadulina), 1968

På ørnetuva (Hauge), 1961
På svarta listan (Wästberg), 1960
På vej til Hilda (Rifbjerg), 1972
Paal en perk (Claus), 1955
Pa'amonim verakavot (Amichai), n.d.
Paare, Passanten (Strauss), 1981
Paarlauf (Wohmann), 1979
Pabellón de reposo (Cela), 1943
Pábitelé (Hrabal), 1964
Pablo Neruda viene volando (Díaz), 1991
Padmā nadīr mājhī (Sircar), 1990
Padre (Ruibal), 1969
Pagaré a cobrar (Alegría), 1973
Paglā ghoṛā (Sircar), 1967
Pagne noir (Dadié), 1955
Pahelī (Aśk), 1939
Painted Lady (Sagan), 1983
Painting in Blood (Sagan), 1988
Paintre (Aśk), 1952
País do carnaval (Amado), 1931
Paisaje andaluz con figuras (Gala), 1984
Paisaje con figuras (Gala), 1985
Paisajes después de la batalla (J. Goytisolo), 1982
Pájara pinta (Alberti), 1931(?)
Pajaro del dulce encanto (Ramírez), 1992
Pakkā gānā (Aśk), 1950
Pakkī havelī (Pritam), 1972
Pakli dohány (Sütő), 1954
Palabra tuya (Conde), 1988
Palabras cruzadas (Carballido), 1955
Palabras en la arena (Buero Vallejo), 1949

Schaamte (Claus), 1972
Schatten und Licht (Heym), 1960
Schauspiel (Lenz), 1970
Scherzo (Manet), 1948
Scherzo capriccioso: veselý sen o Dvořákovi (Škvorecký), 1984
Schlacht (Müller), 1975
Schlacht bei Lobositz (Hacks), 1956
Schlaflose Tage (Becker), 1978
Schlangenei (Bergman), 1977
Schlötel, oder Was solls (C. Hein), 1974
Schlußchor (Strauss), 1991
Schmähschrift; oder, Die Königin gegen Defoe (Heym), 1970
Schmitten (Braun), 1981
Schneewärme (Kirsch), 1989
Schommelpaard (Claus), 1988
Schöne Helena (Hacks), 1964
Schönen Dank und vorüber (Krolow), 1984
Schönes Gehege (Wohmann), 1975
Schönste Fest der Welt (Lenz), 1956
School of the Sun (Matute), 1963
Schreiben müssen (Wohmann), 1990
Schuhu und die fliegende Prinzessin (Hacks), 1966
Schützenehre (Strauss), 1975
Schwanenhaus (Walser), 1980
Schwarze Flügel (Walser), 1968
Schwarze Schwan (Walser), 1964
Schwarzenberg (Heym), 1984
Schweinekopfsülze (Grass), 1969
Schwingrasen (Kirsch), 1991
Scorpion, or, The Imaginary Confession (Memmi), 1971
Scorpion, ou, La Confession imaginaire (Memmi), 1969
Sculptor's Daughter (Jansson), 1969
Se jie (Zhang Ailing), 1979
Sea and Poison (Endō), 1972
Sea-Crossed Fisherman (Kemal), 1985
Sea la luz (Conde), 1947
Sea of Troubles (Duras), 1953
Sea Swell (Løveid), 1986
Sea Wall (Duras), 1952
Seacrow Island (Lindgren), 1968
Seagull (Kemal), 1981
Seagull Eaters (Løveid), 1989
Search (Mahfūz), 1987
Season in Paradise (Breytenbach), 1980
Season in Rihata (Condé), 1988
Season in the Congo (Césaire), 1968
Season in the Life of Emmanuel (Blais), 1966
Season of Migration to the North (Sālih), 1969
Second Sous-sol (Butor), 1976
Second Thoughts (Butor), 1958
Seconde Vie de Shakespeare (Sollers), 1980
Secret Life of Saeed, the Pessoptimist (Ḥabībi), 1982
Secretaria (Ruibal), 1969
Secrets of Women (Bergman), 1952
Secuestro (García Márquez), 1982
Sedmiramenný svícen (Škvorecký), 1964
Seducer: It Is Hard to Die in Dieppe (Stangerup), 1990
See Under: Love (Grossman), 1989
Seedtime (Jaccottet), 1977
Seelenarbeit (Walser), 1979
Sefer hadikduk hapenimiy (Grossman), 1991
Sefer hameshug'a (Guri), 1971
Sefer hashelishiy (Ravikovitch), 1969
Ségou (Condé), 1984
Ségou II (Condé), 1985
Segu (Condé), 1987

Seibutsu (Yoshioka), 1955
Seiji shōnen shisu (Ōe), 1961
Seinen no omei (Ōe), 1959
Seint rødnar skog i djuvet (Hauge), 1956
Seis problemas para don Isidro Parodi (Bioy Casares, as Bustos Domecq), 1942
Seiseijú, mikil ósköp (Laxness), 1977
Seisoen in die paradys (Breytenbach), 1976
Seiteki ningen (Ōe), 1963
Seizmograf (Koneski), 1989
Seizoen (Lucebert), 1968
Seizure of Power (Miłosz), 1955
Séjour des morts (Chessex), 1977
Sekai kikō (Endō), 1975
Sekai no owari to hādo-boirudo wandārando (Murakami), 1985
Sekonden (Enquist), 1971
Sekundernes bro (Tafdrup), 1988
Sekyra (Vaculík), 1966
Sel noir (Glissant), 1960
Selaginela (Carballido), 1957
Selbstbezichtigung (Handke), 1966
Selbstgespräch für andere (Kunze), 1989
Self-Accusation (Handke), 1969
25 desperate digte (Rifbjerg), 1974
Semana de colores (Garro), 1964
Semelles du vent (Langevin), 1972
Semillas para un himno (Paz), 1954
Semiserie (Luzi), 1979
Séneca, o el beneficio de la duda (Gala), 1987
Séneca, ratón de biblioteca (Díaz), 1979
Senecas Tod (Hacks), 1978
Sennik wspołczesny (Konwicki), 1963
Senorita from Tacna (Vargas Llosa), 1983
Sens apparent (Brossard), 1980
Sensible Wege (Kunze), 1969
Sent i November (Jansson), 1970
Sent off the Field (Padilla), 1972
Señal que se espera (Buero Vallejo), 1952
Señas de identidad (J. Goytisolo), 1966
Señor presidente (Roa Bastos), 1966
Señora de rojo sobre fondo gris (Delibes), 1991
Señora en su balcón (Garro), 1970
Señora Tártara (Nieva), 1980
Señorita de Tacna (Vargas Llosa), 1981
Separate Notebooks (Miłosz), 1984
Séparation (Simon), 1963
Sept Petits Sketches (Ionesco), 1953
Sept Péchés capitaux (Mauriac), 1962
7 Possibilités du train 713 en partance d'Auschwitz (Gatti), 1989
Septembersang (Rifbjerg), 1988
Serapio y Yerbabuena (Díaz), 1964
Serbische Mädchen (Lenz), 1987
Seremoniar (Fløgstad), 1969
Serenada (Mrożek), 1977
Serenade (Claus), 1984
Serment d'amour (Dadié), 1965
Serment de Kolvillag (Wiesel), 1973
Sermones y moradas (Alberti), 1959
Sermones y prédicas del Cristo de Elqui (Parra), 1977
Serpentina's Petticoat (Wolkers), 1961
Serpent's Egg (Bergman), 1977
Serrure (Tardieu), 1955
Şeş neī (Sircar), 1970
Sessiz ev (Pamuk), 1983
Šest černých dívek (Škvorecký), 1969

Setea muntelui de sare (Sorescu), 1974
Settimo, ruba un po' meno (Fo), 1964
Seven Doors (Strauss), 1992
Seventh Commandment: Thou Shalt Steal a Bit Less (Fo),
 1973
Seventh Seal (Bergman), 1957
Sevuntiin (Ōe), 1961
Sexual Acts (Maraini), 1988
Şeyh Galib'e çiçekler (Dağlarca), 1986
Sezam (Lem), 1954
Sguardi, i fatti e senhal (Zanzotto), 1969
Sha ding (Ba Jin), 1932
Shadows and Lights (Heym), 1963
Shaga (Duras), 1968
Shaḥḥāẓ (Mahfūz), 1965
Shahr al-'asal (Mahfūz), 1971
Shahrī chon behesht (Dāneshvar), 1961
Shahwa tataqadam fi kharā'iṭ al-mādda (Adūnīs), 1987
Shakespeare Factory 2 (Müller), 1980
Shame (Bergman), 1968
Shan shui qing (Hao Ran), 1980
Shanim vesha'ot (Appelfeld), 1974–75
Shārā rāttrī (Sircar), 1963
Sharq al-Mutawasiṭ (Munīf), 1975
Shayṭān ya' iḍ (Mahfūz), 1979
She Chases Me Relentlessly (Senghor), 1986
She Confused Sleeping and Dying (Willems), 1992
She Has No Place in Paradise (Sa'dāwi), 1987
She'at hachesed (Amichai), 1982
Shekoftan dar meh (Shāmlū), 1970
Sheleg bi-Yrushalayim (Carmi), 1956
Sheloshah yamim veyeled (Yehoshua), 1967
Shen bian (Feng Jicai), 1984
Shen de hu (Wang Meng), 1982
Shen, gui, ren (Ba Jin), 1935
Shendeng (Feng Jicai), 1981
Sheney sipurim (Yehoshua), 1970–71
Sheng ming de yue zhang (Zhang Ailing), 1983
Sheng si qian hou (Shen Rong), 1987
Shi to zuihitsu (Ibuse), 1948
Shi zhe (Yang Lian), 1985
Shichiya no nyōbō (Yasuoka), 1960
Shichuan de guo du (Yang Lian), 1980
Shikai no hotori (Endō), 1973
Shinpitekina jidai no shi (Yoshioka), 1974
Ship (Jabrā), 1985
Ship Bound for India (Bergman), 1947
Ship Named Hope (Klíma), 1970
Ship of Fools (Peri Rossi), 1989
Shipyard (Onetti), 1968
Shi'r qindīl akhḍar (Qabbāni), 1964
Shirei chotam (Guri), 1954
Shirey Yerushalayim (Amichai), 1987
Shirim al kelev vekalbah (Zach) , 1990
Shirim min ha-'azuvah (Carmi), 1988
Shirim shonim (Zach), 1960
Shiroi hito (Endō), 1955
Shisha no ogori (Ōe), 1959
Shizukana ie (Yoshioka), 1968
Shooting Gallery (Tsushima), 1988
Short Day's Anger (Carballido), 1970
Short Letter, Long Farewell (Handke), 1974
Shoshanat haruchot (Guri), 1960
Shot (Buero Vallejo), 1989
Shuguang (Ye junjian), 1982
Shūkin ryokō (Ibuse), 1935
Shunko (Roa Bastos), 1960

Shut Up, You Plucked Chickens (Carballido), 1969
Si J'étais vous (Green), 1947
Sia bor på Kilimandjaro (Lindgren), 1958
Sia Lives on Kilimanjaro (Lindgren), 1959
Siameses (Gambaro), 1967
Sibāq al-masāfāt al-ṭawīlal (Munīf), 1979
Siberia (Sutzkever), 1961
Sibir (Sutzkever), 1952
Sichu de taiyang (Ba Jin), 1930
Sidenvägen (Myrdal), 1977
Sidste nat før kærligheden (Thorup), 1989
Sieben Türen (Strauss), 1988
Sieg über die Dämmerung (Wohmann), 1960
Siegfried (Braun), 1986
Siestas con viento sur (Delibes), 1957
Siete miradas en un mismo paisaje (Tusquets), 1981
Sifr al-faqr wa-al-thawrah (Bayāti), 1965
Sigaretta (Maraini), n.d.
Sigé (Strauss), 1989
Sigismund (Gustafsson), 1976
Sign of the Hamster (Claus), 1986
Signals from the Flames (Pacheco), 1980
Signes d'exode (Wiesel), 1985
Signes et les prodiges (Mallet-Joris), 1966
Signes, recontres, et rendez-vous (Mauriac), 1983
Signor Max (Soldati), 1937
Signora di Montecarlo (Soldati), 1938
Signora è da buttare (Fo), 1967
Signos del día (Alberti), 1978
Signs and Wonders (Mallet-Joris), 1967
Silence (Bergman), 1963
Silence (Endō), 1969
Silence (Sarraute), 1967
Silence Afterwards (Jacobsen), 1985
Silence et l'obscurité, réquiem littoral pour corps polonais
 13–28 décembre 1981 (Hyvrard), 1982
Silences et mémoire d'hommes (Wiesel), 1989
¡Silencio, pollos pelones . . .! (Carballido), 1963
Silent Cry (Ōe), 1974
Silent Day in Tangier (Ben Jelloun), 1991
Silent Duchess (Maraini), 1992
Silent Partner (Bodelsen), 1978
Silent Rooms (Hébert), 1974
Silfurtúnglið (Laxness), 1954
Silk Road (Myrdal), 1979
Silken Eyes (Sagan), 1977
Sillat (Haavikko), 1984
Simple Past (Chraïbi), 1990
Simplex Deutsch (Braun), 1980
Sin mors hus (Faldbakken), 1969
Sinfonía doméstica (Carballido), 1953
Sîngele (Cassian), 1966
Singer and the Moon (Bayāti), 1976
Singing at the Whirlpool (Pavlović), 1983
Singur printre poeţi (Sorescu), 1964
Sinkende skip blou te verf (Breytenbach), 1972
Sinking of the Titanic (Enzensberger), 1980
Sinking Ship Blues (Breytenbach), 1977
Sinrazón (Chacel), 1960
Sins for Father Knox (Škvorecký), 1988
Sipario ducale (Volponi), 1975
Sīrī (Sircar), 1985
Široka vrata (Tišma), 1989
Sírónevető (Határ), 1972
Śiśe ke ghar (Haidar), 1952
Sista paret ut (Bergman), 1956
Siste landhandleren (Faldbakken), 1981

Vieja se muere la alegría (Gala), 1968
Vieja señorita del Paraíso (Gala), 1981
Viejo venís y florido . . . (Conde, as del Mar), 1963
Viejos amigos (Cela), 1960–61
Viejos olivos (Alberti), 1960
Viento del norte (Quiroga), 1951
Viento distante (Pacheco), 1963
Viento entero (Paz), 1965
Vier neue Lieder (Biermann), n.d.
Vier wintervertellingen (Reve), 1963
Vierde man (Reve), 1981
Vierge rouge (Arrabal), 1986
Vietnam körü (Dağlarca), 1970
Vietnam savaşımız (Dağlarca), 1966
Vieux pays (Frénaud), 1967
View (Miłosz), 1985
View by the Sea (Yasuoka), 1984
View of Dawn in the Tropics (Cabrera Infante), 1978
Vigilias (Alegría), 1953
Viiniä, kirjoitusta (Haavikko), 1976
Viinin karsimykset Venajalla (Haavikko), 1981
Viisi sarjaa nopeasti virtaavasta elämästä (Haavikko), 1987
Vijanden (Claus), 1967
Viking Vistas (P. Hein), 1983
Vila real (Ribeiro), 1979
Világ emlékművei (Csoóri), 1989
Vilda torget (Tranströmer), 1983
Villa aurore (Le Clézio), 1985
Villa Natacha (Elytis), 1973
Villa Sunset (Bodelsen), 1964
Villa Triste (Modiano), 1975
Village of God and the Devil (Alegría), 1990
Ville (Guillevic), 1969
Ville à voile (Willems), 1967
Ville de la chance (Wiesel), 1962
Ville dont le prince était une princesse (Arrabal), 1984
Ville glæde (Rifbjerg), 1989
Ville ou nul ne meurt (Dadié), 1968
Villes (Dadié), 1934
Vilner geto 1941–1944 (Sutzkever), 1946
Viltspeglar (Norén), 1972
Vindens låga (Wästberg), 1993
Vingermaan (Breytenbach), 1980
Vingt Ans après Auschwitz (Wiesel), 1968
Vinterbørn (Trier Mørch), 1976
Vinteren revner (Løveid), 1983
Vinterhagen (Vik), 1990
Violas Vorbilder (Wohmann), 1980
Violinbyggernes by (Nordbrandt), 1985
Violons parfois (Sagan), 1961
Virágok hatalma (Juhász), 1955
Virágzó világfa (Juhász), 1965
Viraje (Cassian), 1978
Vírgen de Antioquía (Matute), 1990
Vírgenes y mártires (Vega), 1981
Virgile, non (Wittig), 1985
Virgin Spring (Bergman), 1960
Vîrstele anului (Cassian), 1957
Virtudes del pájaro solitario (J. Goytisolo), 1988
Virtues of the Solitary Bird (J. Goytisolo), 1991
Virtuous Bigamist (Soldati), 1957
Virtuous Burglars (Fo), 1992
Visionnaire (Green), 1934
Visions d'Anna, ou, Le Vertige (Blais), 1982
Visitaciones del diablo (Carballido), 1965
Visitante (Solórzano), 1966
Viskningar och rop (Bergman), 1973

Víspera del degüello (Díaz), 1970
Visperas de Fausto (Bioy Casares), 1949
Vista del amanecer en el trópico (Cabrera Infante), 1974
Vísur um vötn (Johannessen), 1971
Vita breve (Willems), 1989
Vita nuova (Hrabal), 1987
Viudas (Dorfman), 1981
Viva la muerte (Arrabal), 1971
Viva l'Italia (Maraini), 1973(?)
Viva o povo brasileiro (Ribeiro), 1984
Viva Sandino (García Márquez), 1982
Vivāh ke din (Aśk), 1940
Viviendo (Peri Rossi), 1963
Vivientes de los siglos (Conde), 1954
Vivir para ver (Aridjis), 1977
Vivre en poésie (Guillevic), 1980
Vivre l'orange (Cixous), 1979
Vivre! Vivre! (Blais), 1969
Víxlar med afföllum (Þórðarson), 1958
Viziunea vizuinii (Sorescu), 1982
Vlad Dracula the Impaler (Sorescu), 1987
Vliegen (Herzberg), 1970
Vlny v řece (Lustig), 1964
Vluchtende Atalanta (Claus), 1977
Vocativo (Zanzotto), 1957
Voetskrif (Breytenbach), 1976
Vögel (Hacks), 1975
Vögel über dem Tau (Kunze), 1959
Vogels (Mulisch), 1974
Voice Locked in Stone (Pavlović), 1985
Voices at the Late Hour (Carpelan), 1988
Voices from the Plains (Celati), 1989
Voices of Dissent (Göncz), 1989
Voisins (Vinaver), 1986
Voix dans le vent (Dadié), 1969
Voix la nuit (Chessex), 1957
Voix sans personne (Tardieu), 1954
Voks (Rifbjerg), 1968
Volatili del Beato Angelico (Tabucchi), 1987
Volcano (Endō), 1978
Vole-Moi un petit milliard (Arrabal), 1977
Voliere (Rifbjerg), 1962
Volk en vaderliefde (Mulisch), 1975
Volksbuch vom Herzog Ernst (Hacks), 1967
Voltaïque (Ousmane), 1962
Vom hungrigen Hennecke (C. Hein), 1974
Voor Pierre (Claus), 1987
Voor vrienden dieren (Lucebert), 1979
Voorval (Mulisch), 1989
Vor der Hochzeit (Wohmann), 1980
Vor der Sintflut (Kunert), 1985
Vor úr vetri (Johannessen), 1963
Vorbild (Lenz), 1973
Vores år 1–4 (Rifbjerg), 1980
Vorgang (Mňačko), 1970
Vorläufiges (Braun), 1966
Vorzüge der Windhühner (Grass), 1956
Vossejacht (Claus), 1972
Votre Faust . . . (Butor), 1962
Vous les entendez? (Sarraute), 1972
Voyage aux pays des arbres (Le Clézio), 1978
Voyage de noces (Modiano), 1990
Voyage du Grand Tchou (Gatti), 1960
Voyage sans fin (Wittig), 1985
Voyages de l'autre côté (Le Clézio), 1975
Voyageur sur la terre (Green), 1927
Voyageurs sacrés (Blais), 1966

NOTES
ON
ADVISERS
AND
CONTRIBUTORS

ABU-DEEB, Kamal. Professor of Arabic, University of London. Previously taught at Columbia University, New York, and the universities of San'aa, Yarmouk, Pennsylvania, California (Berkeley), and Oxford. Also poet and critic. **Essays:** Adūnīs; al-Tayyib Sālih.

ALLAN, Robin. Queen Alexandra Lecturer in Danish, University College London. Author of "The Novels of Jens Pauli Heinesen," in *Proceedings of the Conference of Scandinavian Studies in Great Britain*, Guildford, University of Surrey, 1983, "Fiction and Fact in the Faroese Novel," in *Bradford Occasional Papers* (University of Bradford), 6, 1984, and publications on the Danish language. **Essay:** Jens Pauli Heinesen.

ANDERMAN, Gunilla M. Head of Swedish and Director of Programme in Translation and Language Studies, University of Surrey, Guildford. Editor of *New Swedish Plays*, 1992. Translator of Swedish plays into English. **Essay:** Per Olov Enquist.

ANDERSEN, Hans Christian. Lecturer in marketing, Newcastle Business School, Newcastle upon Tyne Polytechnic. Author of *Hans Christian Andersen and Thalia: Love's Labours Lost?*, 1992, articles on Scandinavian literature to *Scandinavica* and *Durham University Journal*, and publications on Danish theatre and on marketing for non-profit-making organizations. **Essays:** Klaus Rifbjerg; Pia Tafdrup; Kirsten Thorup.

ARNOLD, A. James. Professor of French, University of Virginia, Charlottesville. Author of *Paul Valéry and His Critics: A Bibliography*, 1970, *"Les Mots" de Sartre*, 1973, and *Modernism and Negritude: The Poetry and Poetics of Aimé Césaire*, 1981. Editor of *Caligula (1941)* by Albert Camus.

BACHMAN, Merle Lyn. M.F.A. candidate in creative writing, Mills College, Oakland, California. Author of poetry published in a number of small American press journals. **Essay:** Dahlia Ravikovitch.

BANFIELD, Chris. Lecturer in Department of Drama and Theatre Arts, University of Birmingham. **Essay:** Badal Sircar.

BARAŃCZAK, Stanisław. See his own entry. **Essays:** Tadeusz Konwicki; Stanisław Lem; Ewa Lipska; Piotr Sommer.

BASA, Enikő Molnár. Librarian, Library of Congress, Washington, D.C. Author of *Sándor Petőfi*, 1980, "Kata Szidonia Petroczy," in *Women Writers of the 17th Century*, "Bibliography of the Hungarian Revolution," in *First War Between Socialist States*, 1984, and 10 essays in *Dictionary of Continental Women Writers*, 1990. Editor, Hungarian Section, Twayne World Authors Series; guest editor, Council of National Literatures volume on Hungary, 1992. **Essays:** Péter Esterházy; András Sütő.

BASSNETT, Susan. Professor of comparative literature and Director, Centre for British and Comparative Cultural Studies, University of Warwick, Coventry. Author of *Translation Studies*, 1980, *Feminist Experiences: The Women's Movement in Four Cultures*, 1986, *Sylvia Plath*, 1987, *Elizabeth I*, 1988, and *Comparative Literature: A Critical Introduction*, 1993. Editor of *Knives and Angels: Women Writers in Latin America*, 1990, and *Translation, History and Culture* (with André Lefevere), 1990. Translator of *Ariadne's Thread: An Anthology of Contemporary Polish Women Poets* (with Piotr Kuhiwczak), 1988, *Family Tree* by Margo Glantz, 1990, and *The Flame* by D'Annunzio, 1991.

BECKER, Lucille Frackman. Professor of French, Drew University, Madison, New Jersey. Author of *Henry de Montherlant*, 1970, *Louis Aragon*, 1971, *Georges Simenon*, 1977, *Françoise Mallet-Joris*, 1985, and *Twentieth-Century French Women Novelists*, 1989. **Essay:** Françoise Mallet-Joris.

BERGIN, Thomas G. Sterling Professor of Romance Languages Emeritus, Yale University, New Haven, Connecticut. Author of many books, including *Giovanni Verga*, 1931, *Dante*, 1965 (as *An Approach to Dante*, 1965), *A Diversity of Dante*, 1969, *Petrarch*, 1970, and *Boccaccio*, 1981. Editor, with Jennifer Speake, *Encyclopedia of the Renaissance*, 1987; editor or translator of works by Dante, Petrarch, Vico, Shakespeare, William of Poitou, Quasimodo, and editor of collections of Italian and French literature.

BOND, David J. Professor of French and Head of the Department of French and Spanish, University of Saskatchewan, Saskatoon. Author of *The Fiction of André Pieyre de Mandiargues*, 1982, *The Temptation of Despair: A Study of the Quebec Novelist André Langevin*, 1982, and articles in *Canadian Literature, Esprit Créateur, Mosaic, Romanic Review*, and other journals. **Essay:** Jacques Chessex.

BORDEN, Richard C. Formerly Associate Professor of Slavic languages and literatures, Harvard University, Cambridge, Massachusetts. Author of *The Art of Writing Badly: Russian Literary Mauvisme*, 1992. **Essay:** Aleksandr Solzhenitzyn.

BOSCHETTO-SANDOVAL, Sandra Maria. Associate Professor of Spanish, Michigan Technological University, Houghton. Author of articles on Claude Mauriac, Luigi Pirandello, Miguel de Unamuno, Giorgio Saviane, Azorín, and José Donoso, in *International Fiction Review, Selecta, Hispania*, and other journals. Editor of *Claribel Alegría and Central American Literature: Critical Essays* (with Marcia P. McGowan), 1993. **Essays:** Claribel Alegría; Claude Mauriac.

BOULLATA, Issa J. Professor of Arabic literature and language, McGill University, Montreal. Editor of *Mundus Arabicus*, since 1981, and *Oral Tradition*, since 1985; former editor of *The Muslim World* and *Al-'Arabiyya*. Author of *Al Rūmantīqiyya*, 1960, *Badr Shākir al-Sayyāb*, 1971, and *Trends and Issues in Contemporary Arab Thought*, 1990. Editor and translator of *Modern Arab Poets 1950–1975*, 1976, and editor of *Critical Perspectives on Modern Arabic Literature*, 1980. **Essays:** 'Abd al-Wahhāb al-Bayāti; Jabrā Ibrāhīm Jabrā.

BRASS, Denis. Professor Extraordinary in the University of Coimbra, Portugal. Author of *Portugal*, 1960, *António Vieira: O Nosso Contemporâneo*, 1973, *The Rounding of Cape Bojador*, 1974, and many critical articles on Miguel Torga and other writers. Translator of *Farrusco the Blackbird*, 1950, and other works by Torga. Formerly Senior Lecturer in Spanish and Portuguese, University of Bristol. **Essay:** Miguel Torga.

BROOME, Peter. Professor of French, Queen's University, Belfast. Co-author of *The Appreciation of Modern French Poetry 1850–1950*, 1976, *Henri Michaux*, 1977, and *André Frénaud*, 1987. Co-editor of *An Anthology of Modern French Poetry 1850–1950*, 1976, and editor of *Au pays de la magie* by Michaux, 1977, and *Les Caves du Vatican* by André Gide, 1993. **Essays:** André Frénaud; Robert Pinget.

BROTHERSTON, Gordon. Professor of literature, University of Essex, Wivenhoe. Author of *Manuel Machado: A Revalua-*

tion, 1968, *Latin American Poetry: Origins and Presence*, 1975, *The Emergence of the Latin American Novel*, 1977, and *Image of the New World*, 1979. Editor or co-editor of *Selected Poems* by César Vallejo, 1976, *Ficciones* by Jorge Luis Borges, 1976, and collections of Spanish American fiction and poetry.

BURGOYNE, Suzanne. Associate Professor of theatre, University of Missouri, Columbia. Author of articles in *Theatre Topics*, *Theatre Journal*, and *American Drama*. Editor and translator of two plays in *Dreams and Reflections: Plays of Paul Willems*, 1992. **Essay:** Paul Willems.

BURNE, Glenn S. Formerly Professor of English, University of North Carolina, Chapel Hill. Author of *Rémy de Gourmont: His Ideas and Influence in England and America*, 1963, *Julien Green*, 1972, and *Richard F. Burton*, 1985. **Essay:** Julien Green.

BURNS, Yvonne. Freelance writer. **Essay:** Blaže Koneski.

BUSHELL, Anthony. Head of German, Saint David's University College, University of Wales, Lampeter. Author of *The Emergence of West German Poetry from the Second World War into the Early Post-War Period*, 1989, and numerous articles on aspects of modern German and Austrian literature and culture. **Essays:** Karl Krolow; Gabriele Wohmann.

CACHIA, Pierre. Formerly Professor of Arabic, Columbia University, New York. Author of *Al-Arif: A Dictionary of Grammatical Terms*, 1974, *Popular Narrative Ballads of Modern Egypt*, 1989, and *Overview of Modern Arabic Literature*, 1990.

CAIRNS, Christopher. Reader in Italian drama, University College of Wales, Aberystwyth. Editor of *Commedia dell-Arte from the Renaissance to Dario Fo*, 1989. **Essay:** Dario Fo.

CAISTOR, Nick. Editor, BBC World Service, London. Editor of *Facing the Sea: An Anthology for Caribbean Schools* (with Anne Walmsley), 1986, *The Faber Book of Contemporary Latin American Short Stories*, 1989, and *Columbus' Egg: New Latin American Stories on the Conquest*, 1992. **Essays:** Manlio Argueta; Juan José Arreola; Adolfo Bioy Casares; Elena Poniatowska; Sergio Ramírez; João Ubaldo Ribeiro; Augusto Roa Bastos; Juan José Saer; Antonio Skármeta; Ana Lydia Vega.

CASE, Sue-Ellen. Member of the English Department, University of California, Riverside. Author of *Feminism and Theatre*, 1987, and various articles on German theatre and playwrights. Editor of *Performing Feminisms: Feminist Critical Theory and Theatre*, 1990. **Essay:** Heiner Müller.

CAWS, Mary Ann. Distinguished Professor of French and comparative literature, City University of New York Graduate Center. Author of many books, including *The Poetry of Dada and Surrealism*, 1970, *The Inner Theatre of Recent French Poetry*, 1972, *The Eye in the Text*, 1981, *A Metapoetics of the Passage*, 1981, *Reading Frames in Modern Fiction*, 1985, *Textual Analysis: Some Readers Reading*, 1986, *Perspectives on Perception: Philosophy, Art and Literature*, 1989, *The Art of Interference: Stresses Readings in Verbal and Visual Texts*, 1990, *Women of Bloomsbury*, 1990, and books on Yves Bonnefoy, André Breton, René Char, Robert Desnos, and Pierre Reverdy. Editor or translator of works by Tristan Tzara, Char, Reverdy, Mallarmé, Breton, and Saint-John

Perse, and editor of critical collections on French writing. **Essays:** Yves Bonnefoy; Jacques Garelli.

COHN, Ruby. Freelance writer. Associate editor of several drama reviews. Professor Emeritus of comparative drama, University of California, Davis. Author of *Samuel Beckett: The Comic Gamut*, 1962, *Currents in Contemporary Drama*, 1969, *Edward Albee*, 1969, *Dialogue in American Drama*, 1971, *Back to Beckett*, 1974, *Modern Shakespeare Offshoots*, 1976, *Just Play: Beckett's Theatre*, 1980, *New American Dramatists 1960–1990*, 1991, and *Retreat from Realism in Recent English Drama*, 1992.

COWARD, David. Reader in French literature, University of Leeds. Author of *The Philosophy of Restif de la Bretonne*, 1991, and *Marcel Pagnol: "Les Souvenirs d'enfance"*, 1992. Translator of *The Misfortunes of Virtue* by Sade, 1992, and *Mlle Fifi and Other Stories*, 1993. **Essays:** Marguerite Duras; Eugène Guillevic; Patrick Modiano; Philippe Sollers.

CRICK, Joyce. Senior Lecturer in German, University College London. **Essay:** Christa Wolf.

DAVIN, Delia. Senior Lecturer in Chinese studies, University of Leeds. Author of *Woman-Work: Women and the Party in Revolutionary Russia*, 1976. Co-editor of *Chinese Lives: An Oral History of Contemporary China* by Zhang Xinxin and Sang Ye, 1987. **Essays:** Chen Ruoxi; Hao Ran; Liu Binyan; Shen Rong; Wang Meng; Yang Lian; Zhang Jie; Zhang Kangkang; Zhang Xianliang; Zhang Xinxin.

DAY, Barbara. Director, Jan Hus Educational Foundation. Editor of *Czech Plays*, 1993. **Essay:** Milan Kundera.

DONAHUE, Thomas J. Professor of modern languages, St. Joseph's University, Philadelphia. Author of *The Theatre of Fernando Arrabal: A Garden of Earthly Delights*, 1980, *Structures of Meaning: A Semiotic Guide to the Dramatic Text*, 1992, and articles on Samuel Beckett, and Ariane Mnouchkine and the popular theatre movement in the 20th century. **Essay:** Fernando Arrabal.

DOUCETTE, Leonard E. Professor of French, University of Toronto. Author of *Emery Bito*, 1970, *Theatre in French Canada*, 1984, and many articles on the literature of French Canada. Co-editor of *Theatre History in Canada/Histoire du théâtre au Canada*. **Essays:** Antonine Maillet; Michel Tremblay.

ELSTOB, Kevin. Assistant Professor, Cleveland State University, Ohio. **Essay:** Michel Vinaver.

ELSWORTH, Bente. Lector in Danish. Author of the entry on Danish studies in *The Year's Work in Modern Language Studies*. **Essays:** Henrik Nordbrandt; Henrik Stangerup.

FLETCHER, John. Professor of European literature, University of East Anglia, Norwich. Author of *The Novels of Samuel Beckett*, 1964, *Samuel Beckett's Art*, 1967, *New Directions in Literature*, 1968, *Claude Simon and Fiction Now*, 1975, *Novel and Reader*, 1980, and *Alain Robbe-Grillet*, 1983. Translator of *The Georgics* by Claude Simon, 1989. **Essays:** Eugène Ionesco; Alain Robbe-Grillet; Claude Simon.

FOWLIE, Wallace. Professor Emeritus of French, Duke University, Durham, North Carolina. Author of many books, including studies of Villon, Mallarmé, Rimbaud, Claudel,

Proust, Gide, Cocteau, Stendhal, and Lautréamont, general books on French literature, and four volumes of memoirs. Editor or translator of many works by French writers.

FREEMAN, Michael. Professor of French, University of Leicester. Author of articles on Guillaume Coquillart, Étienne Jodelle, Pierre de Larivey, François Villon, and medieval and Renaissance theatre, and on Fernando Pessoa and other Portuguese topics. Editor of works on Coquillart, 1975, *Les Esprits* by Larivey, 1987, *Eugène* by Jodelle, 1987, and co-editor of the *Actes* of the colloquium held in Paris 1989 on Villon, 1993.

FRIEDLANDER, Albert H. Dean, Leo Baeck College. Rabbi, Westminster Synagogue, London. Author of *The Six Days of Destruction* (with Elie Wiesel), 1988, and *A Thread of Gold*, 1990. Editor of *European Judaism*. **Essays:** Aharon Appelfeld; Elie Wiesel.

FRONKO, Deborah. Freelance writer and translator in Sweden. Author of articles and interviews published in Swedish newspapers and journals. Assistant editor of *Café Existens: tidskrift för nordisk litteratur* [Literary Journal for Nordic Literature], 1984–85. **Essays:** Suzanne Brøgger; Dea Trier Mørch.

GADJIGO, Samba. Associate Professor of French, Mount Holyoke College, South Hadley, Massachusetts. Author of *École blanche, Afrique noire*, 1980. **Essay:** Aminata Sow Fall.

GARTON, Janet. Senior Lecturer in Scandinavian studies, University of East Anglia, Norwich; editor of *Scandinavica*; director of Norvik Press. Author of *Writers and Politics in Modern Scandinavia*, 1978, *Jens Bjørneboe*, 1985, *Norwegian Women's Writing 1850–1990*, 1993, and several articles on modern Scandinavian literature. Translator of modern Norwegian literature. **Essays:** Gerd Brantenberg; Cecilie Løveid; Halldis Moren Vesaas; Bjørg Vik.

GILLESPIE, David. Lecturer in Russian, Bath University. Author of *Valentin Rasputin and Soviet Russian Village Prose*, 1986. **Essay:** Vladimir Soloukhin.

GODARD, Barbara. Associate Professor of English and women's studies, York University, North York, Ontario. Founding co-editor of *Tessera* feminist theoretical journal. Author of *Talking About Ourselves: The Cultural Productions of Canadian Native Women*, 1985, and *Audrey Thomas: Her Life and Work*, 1989. Editor of *Gynocritics/Gynocritiques: Feminist Approaches to the Writing of Canadian and Quebec Women*, 1987. Translator of *Picture Theory* by Nicole Brossard, 1991, and *The Tangible Word* by France Théoret, 1991. **Essay:** Nicole Brossard.

GOETZ-STANKIEWICZ, Marketa. Professor of comparative literature and Germanic studies, University of British Columbia, Vancouver. Author of *The Silenced Theatre: Czech Playwrights Without a Stage*, 1979. Editor of *Drama Contemporary: Czechoslovakia*, 1985, *The Vaněk Plays: Four Authors One Character* by Václav Havel, 1987, and *Goodbye Samizdat: Twenty Years of Czechoslovak Underground Writing*, 1992. **Essay:** Václav Havel.

GÖMÖRI, George. Lecturer in Slavonic studies, Cambridge University. Author of *Polish and Hungarian Poetry 1945 to 1956*, 1966, and *Cyprian Norwid*, 1974. Editor, with others, of *Love of the Scorching Wind* by László Nagy, 1973, *Forced*

March by Miklós Radnóti, 1979, and *Night Song of the Personal Shadow* by György Petri, 1991. **Essays:** Stanisław Barańczak; Árpád Göncz; Győző Határ; Zbigniew Herbert; György Konrád; Czesław Miłosz; György Petri; Tadeusz Różewicz.

GOSCILO, Helena. Chair of the Slavic Department, University of Pittsburgh. Author of *Russian and Polish Women's Fiction*, 1985, *Balancing Acts*, 1991, *The Wild Beach and Other Stories* (with Byron Lindsey), 1992, *Fruits of Her Plume: Essays in Contemporary Russian Women's Culture*, 1993, *Lives in Transit*, 1993, and forthcoming monographs on recent women's fiction, Tatiana Tolstaia, and Liudmila Petrushevskaia. Editor of *Glasnost: An Anthology of Literature* (with Byron Lindsey), 1990. **Essay:** Tatiana Tolstaia.

GOTTLIEB, Marlene. Chair, Department of Romance Languages, Herbert Lehman College, City University of New York, Bronx. Author of *No se termina nunca de nacer: la poesía de Nicanor Parra*, and *Nicanor Parra, antes y después de Cristo*, 1993. **Essays:** Herberto Padilla; Nicanor Parra.

GRAVES, Peter. Head of Department of Scandinavian Studies, University of Edinburgh. Author of *Jan Fridegard: Lars Hard*, 1977, and many articles on and translations of Swedish literature. **Essay:** Sara Lidman.

GRAVES, Peter J. Head of German Department, Leicester University. Author of "Three Contemporary German Poets: Wolf Biermann, Sarah Kirsch, Reiner Kunze," 1985, and numerous other articles on contemporary German literature; regular reviewer for *The Times Literary Supplement* on German literature and politics. **Essays:** Christoph Hein; Sarah Kirsch; Reiner Kunze.

GREEN, Brita. Part-time lecturer in Swedish, York University. Author of articles on poetic language in *Nysvenska Studier* and *Proceedings of Conferences of Teachers of Scandinavian Studies*. Translator of poetry, articles, and reviews in *Proof*, *Lyrikvännen*, *Swedish Books*, and *Swedish Book Review*. **Essay:** Werner Aspenström.

GÜN, Güneli. Writer and translator. Author of *Book of Trances*, 1979, and *On the Road to Baghdad*, 1992. Translator of *Night* by Bilge Karasu, 1993, and *Black Book* by Orhan Pamuk, forthcoming. **Essay:** Orhan Pamuk.

HABERLY, David T. Professor of Portuguese, University of Virginia, Charlottesville. Author of *Three Sad Races: Racial Identity and National Consciousness in Brazilian Literature*, 1983, and numerous articles on Brazilian, Portuguese, Spanish American, and comparative literature. **Essay:** João Cabral de Melo Neto.

HAFEZ, Sabry. Member of the Department of Near and Middle East, School of Oriental and African Studies, University of London. Editor, with Catherine Cobham, *Reader of Modern Arabic Short Stories*, 1988. **Essays:** Salwā Bakr; Mahmūd Darwīsh; Imīl Habībī; 'Abd al-Rahmān Munīf; Nawal al-Sa'dāwi; Hanān al-Shaykh.

HÁJEK, Igor. Senior Lecturer in Czechoslovak studies, University of Glasgow. Co-editor and contributor, *Modern Slavic Literature 2*, 1976, and *Dictionary of Czech Writers 1948–1979*, 1982; author of numerous articles and reviews.

Essays: Miroslav Holub; Bohumil Hrabal; Arnošt Lustig; Josef Škvorecký.

HALMAN, Talat S. Professor of Turkish studies, New York University. Formerly Turkey's Minister of Culture and Ambassador for Cultural Affairs. Author of *The Humanist Poetry of Yunus Emre*, 1972, *Modern Turkish Drama*, 1976, *Shadows of Love*, 1979, *Contemporary Turkish Literature*, 1982, *Mevlana Celaleddin Rumi and the Whirling Dervishes*, 1983, *Süleyman the Magnificent — Poet*, 1987, *Living Turkish Poets*, 1989, *A Last Lullaby*, 1990, *Turkish Legends and Folk Poems*, 1992, and 30 more volumes in Turkish and English. **Essays:** Fazıl Hüsnü Dağlarca; Yaşar Kemal.

HAWKESWORTH, Celia. Senior Lecturer in Serbo-Croat, School of Slavonic and East European Studies, University of London. Author of *Ivo Andrić: Bridge Between East and West*, 1984, and *Colloquial Serbo-Croat*, 1986. Editor of *The Damned Yard* by Ivo Andrić, 1992, and *Literature and Politics in Eastern Europe*, 1992. Translator of *The Days of the Consuls*, 1992, and co-translator of *Conversation with Goya, Bridges, Signs*, 1992, both by Andrić; translator of *In the Jaws of Life* by Dubravka Ugrešić, 1992. **Essays:** Dobrica Ćosić; Dubravka Ugrešić.

HERTZ-OHMES, Peter. Professor of German and humanities, State University of New York, Oswego. Author of "Turning the Postmodern Corner: A Personal Epilogue," in *Twentieth Century Art Theory*, 1990, and "If Gods Were Hormones: Fractals, Catastrophes and Other Good Things in Homer's *Odyssey*," in *Mythologies*, 1992. Translator of *On the Way to Language* by Martin Heidegger, 1971. **Essay:** Lars Gustafsson.

HERZBERGER, David K. Professor of Spanish, University of Connecticut, Storrs. Editor of *Siglo XX/20th Century*. President of Twentieth-Century Spanish Studies Association of America, 1992–95. Author of *The Novelistic World of Juan Benet*, 1977, and *Jesús Fernández Santos*, 1984. **Essay:** Luis Goytisolo.

HIGGINS, James. Professor of Latin American literature, University of Liverpool. Author of *The Poet in Peru*, 1982, *A History of Peruvian Literature*, 1987, *César Vallejo: A Selection of His Poetry*, 1987, *César Vallejo en su poesia*, 1990, and *Cambio social y constantes humanas: la narrativa corta de Ribeyro*, 1991. **Essays:** Antonio Cisneros; Blanca Varela.

HODGSON, Richard G. Associate Professor of French, University of British Columbia, Vancouver. Author of "Un roman à métamorphoses: éléments baroques dans *Neige noire* d'Hubert Aquin," in *Présence Francophone*, Autumn 1981, and "Time and Space in André Langevin's *L'Élan d'Amérique*," in *Canadian Literature*, Spring 1981. **Essay:** André Langevin.

HOLT, Marion Peter. Professor of theatre, City University of New York. Author of *The Contemporary Spanish Theatre (1949–1972)*. Editor of *DramaContemporary: Spain*. Translator of *Three Plays* by Antonio Buero Vallejo. **Essay:** Antonio Buero Vallejo.

HUSSEIN, Aamer. Freelance writer, and book reviewer for *The Times Literary Supplement*, London. Editor of *Tigers and Butterflies: Selected Writings on Politics, Culture, and Society* by Han Suyin, 1990. **Essays:** Tahar Ben Jelloun; Qurratulain Haidar; Amritā Pritam; Tsushima Yūko; Ye Junjian.

HUTCHINS, William M. Professor of English and comparative literature, American University in Cairo. Translator of *Plays, Prefaces, and Postscripts*, 2 vols., 1981–83, and *Return of the Spirit*, 1990, both by Tawfiq al-Hakim, *Al-Mazini's Egypt*, 1984, and *Nine Essays of al-Jahiz*, 1989. Principal translator of the Cairo trilogy by Nagīb Mahfūz, 1990–92. **Essay:** Nagīb Mahfūz.

HUTCHINSON, Peter. Fellow of Trinity Hall, Cambridge. Author of *Literary Presentations of Divided Germany*, 1977, *Games Authors Play*, 1983, and *Stefan Heym: The Perpetual Dissident*, 1992. **Essay:** Stefan Heym.

JACKSON, Neil. Lector for English, University of Munich. Author, with Barbara Saunders, of "Christa Wolf's *Kindheitsmuster*: An East German Experiment in Political Autobiography," in *German Life and Letters*, July 1980. **Essay:** Günter Kunert.

JANES, Regina. Professor of English, Skidmore College, Saratoga Springs, New York. Author of *Gabriel García Márquez: Revolutions in Wonderland*, 1981, *"One Hundred Years of Solitude": Modes of Reading*, 1991, and articles on 18th-century British and modern Latin American literature in journals such as *Salmagundi*, *Hispanófila*, *World Literature Today*, *Journal of the History of Ideas*, and *Representations*. **Essays:** Gabriel García Márquez; Mario Vargas Llosa.

JIANG, David. Freelance director and researcher. Author of "Diversified Drama and Diversified Acting," in *Dramatic Arts* (China), 1987, and "New Concept of Acting Styles," in *Dramatic Arts* (China), 1988. Editor of *On Acting* (in Chinese), 1982, and *The Directing Skills of Zhuduanjun* (in Chinese), 1984. Professional director and actor in China. **Essays:** Ba Jin; Feng Jicai (with Li Ruru); Liu Xinwu (with Li Ruru).

JOHNSON, Bernard. Director of Language Studies Centre, London School of Economics. Translator of works by several Yugoslav poets. **Essays:** Ivan V. Lalić; Slavko Mihalić; Miodrag Pavlović.

JOHNSON, D. Barton. Professor of Russian, University of California, Santa Barbara. Author of *Worlds in Regression: Some Novels of Vladimir Nabokov*, 1985. Editor and contributor to special journal issues on Sasha Sokolov, in *Canadian-American Slavic Studies* (Bakersfield, California), 21(3–4), 1987, and on Vladimir Nabokov, in *Russian Literature Triquarterly* (Ann Arbor, Michigan), 24, 1991. **Essay:** Sasha Sokolov.

JONES, Margaret E. W. Professor of Spanish, University of Kentucky, Lexington. Author of *The Literary World of Ana María Matute*, 1970, *Dolores Medio*, 1974, and *The Contemporary Spanish Novel, 1939–1975*, 1986. Translator of *The Same Sea as Every Summer* by Esther Tusquets, 1990. **Essay:** Esther Tusquets.

JONES, W. Glyn. Professor of Scandinavian studies, University of East Anglia, Norwich. Author of *Johannes Jörgensen*, 1969, *Denmark*, 1970, *William Heinesen*, 1974, *Danish: A Grammar* (with K. Gade), 1981, *Tove Jansson*, 1984, *Denmark: A Modern History*, 1986, and two books in Danish. Editor of *Selected Letters* by Georg Morris Cohen Brandes, 1970. Translator of *Seneca: The Humanist at the Court of Nero* by Villy Sørensen, 1984. **Essays:** Tove Jansson; Halldór Laxness; Villy Sørensen.

KALSI, A. S. Lecturer in Hindi and Urdu, School of Oriental and African Studies, University of London. **Essay:** Gyānrañjan.

KAMINSKY, Amy. Associate Professor of women's studies, University of Minnesota, Minneapolis. Author of *Reading the Body Politic: Latin American Women Writers and Feminist Criticism*, 1992. Associate editor of *Signs*. **Essay:** Gioconda Belli.

KIPP, Maia. Staff member of the Department of Slavic Languages and Literatures, University of Kansas, Lawrence. **Essay:** Edvard Radzinskii.

KIRSNER, Robert. Professor Emeritus of Spanish, University of Miami, Coral Gables, Florida. Author of *The Novels and Travels of Camilo José Cela*, 1964, *Veinte años de matrimonio en la novela de Galdós*, 1983, and texts and numerous articles on Spanish and Spanish American language and literature. Former associate editor of *Caribe*. **Essays:** Camilo José Cela; Carlos Fuentes; Fernando del Paso.

KLINE, George L. Milton C. Nahm Professor Emeritus of Philosophy and former Chairman, Department of Russian, Bryn Mawr College, Pennsylvania. Author of *Spinoza in Soviet Philosophy*, 1952, *Religious and Anti-Religious Thought in Russia*, 1968, and several articles on Iosif Brodskii, including "Variations on the Theme of Exile," 1990. Translator of *Boris Pasternak: Seven Poems*, 1969, and *Selected Poems*, 1973, and *A Part of Speech*, 1980 (with others), both by Brodskii. **Essay:** Iosif Brodskii.

KLINGENBERG, Patricia N. Associate Professor of Spanish, Illinois Wesleyan University, Bloomington. Author of "Portrait of the Writer as Artist: Silvina Ocampo," in *Perspectives in Contemporary Literature*, 1987, "The Mad Double in the Short Stories of Silvina Ocampo," in *Latin American Literary Review* (Pittsburgh), 1988, and "The Feminine 'I': Silvina Ocampo's Fantasies of the Subject," in *Romance Languages Annual*, 1989. **Essay:** Silvina Ocampo.

KLOPP, Charles. Associate Professor of Romance languages, Ohio State University, Columbus. Author of "'Peregrino' and 'Errante' in the *Gerusalemme liberata*," in *Modern Language Notes* (Chapel Hill, North Carolina), 1979, *Gabriele D'Annunzio*, 1988, and articles on Italian literature. Editor and translator of *Ghisola* by Federigo Tozzi, 1990. **Essay:** Giorgio Bassani.

KREMER, Manfred K. Professor of German, University of Guelph, Ontario. Author of *Die Satire bei Johann Beer*, 1964, and various articles on German writers. **Essays:** Günter Grass; Siegfried Lenz.

LAMAR, Celita. Associate Professor of French and Associate Chair of Department of Foreign Languages and Literatures, University of Miami, Coral Gables, Florida. Member of the editorial board, *Dalhousie Studies* journal. Author of *Our Voices, Ourselves: Women Writing for the French Theatre*, 1991. **Essay:** Nélida Piñón.

LEFEVERE, André. Professor of Germanic languages, University of Texas, Austin. Author of *Translation, Rewriting, and the Manipulation of Literary Fame*, 1992, and *Translating Literature*, 1992. Editor of *Translation, History and Culture* (with Susan Bassnett), 1990. **Essays:** H. C. ten Berge; Breyten Breytenbach.

LEVIN, Harry. Formerly Irving Babbitt Professor of Comparative Literature, Harvard University, Cambridge, Massachusetts. Author of many critical boks, most recently *The Gates of Horn: A Study of Five French Realists*, 1986, and *Playboys and Killjoys: An Essay on the Theory and Practice of Comedy*, 1987. Editor of works by Jonson, Rochester, Joyce, Shakespeare, and Hawthorne, and of anthologies.

LEWIS, Bart L. Professor of Spanish, California State University, San Marcos. Author of "Pubis angelical: la mujer codificana," in *Revista Iberoamericana* (Pittsburgh), September 1983, and "Tales Told: Narrator, Character, and Theme in Juan Carlos Onetti's *Junta cadaveres*," in *Chasqui* (Williamsburg, Virginia), May 1991. Past President of Southwest Council of Latin American Studies. **Essays:** Jorge Díaz; Juan Carlos Onetti.

LEWIS, Tim. Director of Modern Languages Teaching Centre, University of Sheffield. **Essays:** Bernard Dadié; Guillaume Oyônô-Mbia.

LI Ruru. Lecturer in East Asian studies, University of Leeds. Also Lecturer at Shanghai Academy of Drama. Author of "Traditional Chinese Theatre and Shakespeare," in *Asian Theatre Journal* (Honolulu), 1988, "Study on Contemporary German Theatre," in *Dramatic Arts*, 1988, and "Shakespeare Translation in China," in *Leeds East Asia Papers*, 1991. **Essays:** Cao Yu; Feng Jicai (with David Jiang); Liu Xinwu (with David Jiang); Yang Mo.

LOLOI, Parvin. Writer and translator. Translator of *Poems from the Divan of Hafiz* (with William Oxley), forthcoming. **Essays:** Sīmīn Dāneshvar; Mahmūd Dawlatābādi; Buland al-Haydari; Abdullāh Hussein; Muhammad al-Māghūt; Nizār Qabbāni; Ahmad Shāmlū.

LONDRÉ, Felicia Hardison. Curators' Professor of Theatre, University of Missouri, Kansas City; dramaturg, Missouri Repertory Theatre. Author of *Tennessee Williams*, 1979, *Tom Stoppard*, 1981, *Federico García Lorca*, 1984, and *The History of World Theater: From the English Restoration to the Present*, 1991. **Essays:** Emilio Carballido; Griselda Gambaro.

LORCH, Jennifer. Lecturer in Italian, University of Warwick, Coventry. Author of *Mary Wollstonecraft, the Making of a Radical Feminist*, 1990. Editor of *Yearbook of Society for Pirandello Studies*, 1984–90, and *Journal of Society for Italian Studies*, since 1991. **Essays:** Dacia Maraini; Michele Prisco.

MAGNARELLI, Sharon. Professor, Department of Foreign Languages, Albertus Magnus College, New Haven, Connecticut. Author of *The Lost Rib: Female Characters in the Spanish American Novel*, 1985, *Reflections/Refractions: Reading Luisa Valenzuela*, 1988, and *Understanding José Donoso*, 1992. **Essay:** Luisa Valenzuela.

MARTINS, Heitor. Professor of Spanish and Portuguese, University of Indiana, Bloomington. Author of *Neoclassicismo*, 1982, and *Do Barroco a Guimarães Rosa*, 1983. **Essays:** Rachel de Queiroz; Lygia Fagundes Telles.

MAVER, Igor. Assistant Professor of English and American literature, University of Ljubljana, Slovenia. Author of works on cross-cultural studies, contemporary American literature, Australian literature, and English Romanticism. **Essay:** Tomaž Šalamun.

MAZQUIARÁN de RODRÍGUEZ, Mercedes. Associate Professor of Spanish, Hofstra University, Hempstead, New York. Author of *Hacia el siglo XXI, Hispanoamérica: pensamiento y realidad*, 1984, "Oneiric Riddles in Peri Rossi's *La nave de los locos*," 1989, "*Para no volver*: Humor vs. Phallocentrism," 1990, "Narrative Strategies in the Novels of Esthers Tusquets," 1991, and several other articles on women writers. **Essay:** Cristina Peri Rossi.

McDOUGALL, Bonnie S. Professor of Chinese, University of Edinburgh. Editor and translator of *The August Sleepwalker*, 1988, and *Old Snow*, 1991, both by Bei Dao, and *The Yellow Earth* (screenplay) by Chen Kaige, 1991. **Essay:** Bei Dao.

McDUFF, David. Writer and translator. Translator of *The House of the Dead*, 1985, *Crime and Punishment*, 1991, and *The Brothers Karamazov*, 1993, all by Fedor Dostoevskii. **Essays:** Bo Carpelan; Paavo Haavikko; Irina Ratushinskaia; Nils Aslak Valkeapää.

McGREGOR, Stuart. Lecturer in Hindi, Cambridge University. Author of *Language of Indrajit of Orcha: Study of Early Braj Bhasa Prose*, 1968, *Hindi Literature from Its Beginnings to the 19th Century*, 1984, and Hindi grammar books. Editor of *The Oxford Hindi-English Dictionary*, 1993. Translator of *The Round Dance of Krishna and Uddhar's Message*, 1973. **Essays:** Upendranāth "Aśk"; Nāgārjun; Satyendra Śrīvāstava.

McMAHON, Keith. Associate Professor, University of Kansas, Lawrence. **Essay:** Qian Zhongshu.

McMURRAY, George R. Professor of Spanish, Colorado State University, Fort Collins. Book review editor of *Chasqui*. Author of *Gabriel García Márquez*, 1977, *Jorge Luis Borges*, 1980, *Spanish-American Writing Since 1941*, 1987, and many articles on Spanish and Latin American literature. Editor of *Critical Essays on Gabriel García Márquez*, 1987. **Essay:** Rosario Ferré.

McTURK, Rory. Senior Lecturer in English and Supervisor of Icelandic studies, University of Leeds. Author of *Studies in Ragnars Saga Loðbrókar and Its Major Scandinavian Analogues*, 1991. Contributor to *The Year's Work in English Studies*, 1974–77. Co-editor of *Saga-Book of the Viking Society for Northern Research*, since 1992. **Essays:** Svava Jaokobsdóttir; Agnar Þórðarson; Thor Vilhjálmsson.

MEYER, Doris. Professor of Hispanic studies, Connecticut College, New London. Author of *Victoria Ocampo: Against the Wind and the Tide*, 1979. Editor of *Contemporary Women Authors of Latin America*, 1983, and *Lives on the Line: The Testimony of Contemporary Latin American Authors*, 1988. Translator of *Cartucho and My Mother's Hands* (with Irene Matthews) by Nellie Campobello, 1988.

MILES, Patrick. Senior research associate, Cambridge University. Author of *Chekhov: The Early Stories 1880–1888*, 1982, and *Chekhov on the British Stage 1909–1987*, 1987. **Essay:** Liudmila Petrushevskaia.

MINER, Earl. Townsend Martin Professor of English and Comparative Literature, Princeton University, New Jersey. Author of *An Introduction to Japanese Court Poetry*, 1968, *Literary Uses of Typology*, 1977, *Japanese Linked Poetry*, 1979, *Principles of Classical Japanese Literature*, 1985, *Com-*

parative Poetics: An Intercultural Essay on Theories of Literature, 1990, and several other books.

MINOGUE, Valerie. Research Professor of French, University College, Swansea. Author of *Proust: du côté de chez Swann*, 1973, *Nathalie Sarraute and the War of the Words*, 1981, *Zola: L'Assommoir*, 1991, and articles on the modern French novel. General editor of *Romance Studies*. **Essay:** Nathalie Sarraute.

MITCHELL, Michael. Lecturer in German, University of Stirling. Author of *Peter Hacks: Drama for a Socialist Society*, 1990. **Essay:** Peter Hacks.

MONTERO, Oscar. Professor of Spanish American literature, Herbert Lehman College, City University of New York, Bronx. Author of *The Name Game: The Semiotic Intertext of "De dónde son los cantantes"*, 1988, and *Erotismo y representación en Julián del Casal*, 1993. **Essay:** Severo Sarduy.

MULLEN, Anne W. Lecturer in Italian studies, University of Strathclyde, Glasgow. Author of "An Honest Writer in a Difficult Land" (on Leonardo Sciascia), in *PN Review* (Manchester), 72, November 1989, and an article on Vincenzo Consolo, in *Edinburgh Review*, August 1991. **Essays:** Gesualdo Bufalino; Gianni Celati.

NAPIER, Susan J. Assistant Professor of Japanese, University of Texas, Austin. **Essay:** Ōe Kenzaburō.

NIGRO, Kirsten F. Associate Professor of Spanish, University of Cincinnati, Ohio. Member of the editorial board, *Latin American Theatre Review*; editor of *Studies in Latin American Chicano and U.S. Latino Theatre*. Author of articles on modern Latin American theatre and literature, women writers and feminist theory, José Triana, Vicente Leñero, Griselda Gambaro, Luisa Josefina Hernández, Carlos Fuentes, José Ignacio Cabrujas, and Rosario Castellanos for various journals. **Essay:** Luisa Josefina Hernández.

NORRIS, David A. Lecturer in Serbian and Croatian studies, University of Nottingham. Author of *The Novels of Miloš Crnjanski: An Approach Through Time*, 1990, and an article on Crnjanski. **Essays:** Milorad Pavić; Aleksandar Tišma.

ODBER de BAUBETA, Patricia Anne. Lecturer in Hispanic studies and Director of Portuguese studies, University of Birmingham. Author of *Anticlerical Satire in Medieval Portuguese Literature*, 1992, and several articles on Portuguese literature. Founder and commissioning editor of the *Portuguese Plays in Translation* series. **Essay:** Jorge Amado.

O'LEARY, John. Writer. **Essay:** Ariel Dorfman.

OPPENHEIM, Lois. Staff member of French Department, Montclair State College. Author of *Intentionality and Intersubjectivity: A Phenomenological Study of Butois' "La Modification"*, 1980, and numerous articles on phenomenological aesthetics, comparative and French studies. Editor and translator of *Three Decades of the New French Novel*, 1986. Acting managing editor of *Journal of Philosophy*; co-editor of *The Beckett Circle*. **Essay:** Michel Deguy.

OWEN, Carys. Lecturer in French, University of Leeds. **Essays:** Driss Chraïbi; Albert Memmi; Christiane Rochefort.

PALLOTTA, Augustus. Professor of Italian, Syracuse University, New York. Author of articles on modern and contemporary Italian writers in *Forum Italicum*, *Italica*, *Italian Quarterly*, and other journals; regular contributor to the annual *The Romantic Movement: A Selective and Critical Bibliography*. **Essays:** Luciano Erba; Paolo Volponi.

PAOLINI, Shirley J. Professor of literature and Dean of School of Human Sciences and Humanities, University of Houston, Clear Lake, Texas. Author of *Creativity, Culture and Values: Comparative Essays in Literary Aesthetics*, 1990, "Desert Metaphors in Patrick White's *Voss*," 1991, and "Western Modernist Influences in Eileen Chang's *The Golden Cangue* and Li Ang's *The Butcher's Wife*," 1991. General editor of *New Connections: Studies in Interdisciplinarity*. **Essay:** Zhang Ailing.

PECKHAM, Robert Shannan. Ph.D. candidate in the Department of Modern Greek and Byzantine Studies, King's College, London. Author of numerous articles on Greek and comparative literatures in *Encounter*, *The Independent*, *Journal of the Hellenic Diaspora*, *London Magazine*, *Mediterraneans*, *The Times Literary Supplement*, and other journals, magazines, and newspapers. **Essays:** Katerina Anghelaki-Rooke; Jacques Dupin; Odysseus Elytis.

PÉREZ, Janet. Paul Whitfield Horn Professor of Spanish, Texas Tech University, Lubbock. Author of *The Major Themes of Existentialism in the Works of José Ortega y Gasset*, 1970, *Ana María Matute*, 1971, *Miguel Delibes*, 1972, *Gonzalo Torrente Ballester*, 1984, *Women Writers of Contemporary Spain*, 1988, and numerous articles on contemporary Spanish literature. Editor of *Novelistas femeninas de la postguerra española*, 1983, *Critical Studies on Gonzalo Torrente Ballester*, 1988, *The Spanish Civil War in Literature*, 1990, and *Dictionary of the Literature of the Iberian Peninsula*, 1992. **Essays:** Francisco Ayala; Rosa Chacel; Carmen Conde; Carmen Laforet; Carmen Martín Gaite.

PETERSSON, Kerstin. Lecturer in Scandinavian studies, University of East Anglia, Norwich. Author of bibliographical articles in *The Year's Work in Modern Language Studies*, since 1979. **Essay:** Per Wästberg.

PIKE, Christopher R. Senior Lecturer in Russian studies, University of Keele, Staffordshire. Former editor of *Essays in Poetics* journal. Author of "Formalist and Structuralist Approaches to Dostoevsky," in *New Essays on Dostoevsky* edited by Malcolm V. Jones and Garth M. Terry, 1983. Editor of *The Futurists, The Formalists and the Marxist Critique*, 1980.

PIRIE, Donald. Lecturer in Polish, University of Glasgow. **Essay:** Sławomir Mrożek.

POLUKHINA, Valentina. Lecturer in Russian, University of Keele, Staffordshire. Author of *Joseph Brodsky: A Poet for Our Time*, 1989. Editor of *Joseph Brodsky's Poetics and Aesthetics* (with Lev Lozeff), 1990. **Essay:** Evgenii Evtushenko.

PONTIERO, Giovanni. Reader in Latin American literature, University of Manchester. Translator of the major novels of José Saramago and Clarice Lispector, and of works by Daniel Moyano, Lya Luft, Ana Miranda, and Lygia Bojunga Nuñes. **Essay:** José Saramago.

PORTER, Robert. Senior Lecturer in Russian studies, University of Bristol. Author of *Understanding Soviet Politics Through Literature*, 1984, and *Four Contemporary Russian Writers*, 1989. Editor of *Seven Soviet Poets*, 1988. Translator of *The Soul of a Patriot* by Evgenii Popov, 1993. **Essays:** Chingiz Aitmatov; Vladimir Vionovich.

PRIELAIDA, Sabrina. Ph.D. candidate in theatre history and dramatic criticism, School of Drama, University of Washington, Seattle. **Essays:** Hélène Cixous; Armand Gatti.

PURSGLOVE, Glyn. Editor of *The Swansea Review*. Senior Lecturer in English, University College, Swansea. Author of *Francis Warner and Tradition: An Introduction to the Plays*, 1981, and *Francis Warner's Poetry*, 1988. Editor of *Distinguishing Poetry: Writings on Poetry by William Oxley*, 1989, *Tasso's "Aminta" and Other Poems* by Henry Reynolds, and *Selected Poems* by Richard Niccols. **Essays:** Ernesto Cardenal; Nina Cassian; Aimé Césaire; Blaga Dimitrova; Matthías Johannessen; Ferenc Juhász; Ku Sang; Solveig von Schoultz; Marin Sorescu; Wisława Szymborska.

PURSGLOVE, Michael. Lecturer in Russian, University of Exeter. Author of *D. V. Grigorovich: The Man Who Discovered Chekhov*, 1987, and *Anton; The Peasant: Two Stories of Surfdom*, 1991. **Essay:** Andrei Voznesenskii.

PUVAČIĆ, Dušan. Lecturer in Serbian and Croatian studies, School of Slavonic and East European Studies, University of London. Author of *Tragom teksta*, 1989, and *Ugovor s davolom*, 1990. Editor of *Kritički radovi Branka Lazarevića*, 1975. Translator into Serbo-Croat of many works of English and American literature. Member of the editorial board, *Književne Novine*, 1962–69, *Savremenik*, 1970–73, and *Mostovi*, since 1992.

PYNSENT, Robert B. Professor of Czech and Slovak literature, University of London. Author of *Julius Zeyer: The Path to Decadence*, 1973, and *Conceptions of Enemy: Three Essays on Czech and Slovak Literature*, 1988. Editor of *Decadence and Innovation*, 1989, *Modern Slovak Prose-Fiction Since 1954*, 1990, and *The Everyman Companion to East European Literature*, 1992. **Essays:** Ladislav Mňačko; Ludvík Vaculík.

QUINN, Michael L. Assistant Professor of drama, University of Washington, Seattle. Author of *The Semiotic Stage: Prague School Theater Theory*, 1992. **Essay:** Ivan Klíma.

RAESIDE, Ian. Retired Senior Lecturer in Marathi and Gujarati, School of Oriental and African Studies, University of London. Author of *Marathi Reading Course* (with B. V. Nemade), 1991. Translator of *The Rough and the Smooth*, 1966, *Wild Bapu of Garambi* by Śripad Nārāyaṇ Peṇḍse, 1969, *The Decade of Panipat*, 1984, and *Gadyarāja*, 1988. **Essay:** Śripad Nārāyaṇ Peṇḍse.

RAESIDE, James. Lecturer, Keio University. Author of numerous articles and reviews on Japanese literature and other topics. Former literary editor of *Asahi Evening News*. **Essay:** Ibuse Masuji.

RAGUSA, Olga. Da Ponte Professor of Italian, Columbia University, New York. Author of several books on Italian literature, most recently *Luigi Pirandello: An Approach to His Theatre*, 1980, and *Comparative Perspectives on Manzoni*, 1986.

RATHI, Girdhar. Editor of National Academy of Letters *Samkālīn Bhāratīya Sāhitya* quarterly; managing editor of *Alternatives*. Author of *Bāhar bhītar*, 1980, and *Unīnde kī lorī*, 1985. Co-editor of *Ten Indian Poets*. Translator into Hindi of poems of Bertolt Brecht and Nicholas Guillén. **Essay:** Nirmal Varmā.

RAWSON, Judy. Senior Lecturer and Chair of the Department of Italian, University of Warwick, Coventry. Editor of *Fontamara* by Ignazio Silone, 1977. **Essay:** Antonio Tabucchi.

ROBINSON, Michael. Professor of drama, University of Birmingham. Author of *The Long Sonata of the Dead: A Study of Samuel Beckett*, 1969, *Sven Delblanc's Aminne*, 1981, and *Strindberg and Autobiography: Writing and Reading a Life*, 1987. **Essay:** Lars Norén.

ROCK, David. Lecturer in modern languages, Keele University, Staffordshire. Author of "In Defence of Bärlach," in *Modern Languages* (Rugby, Warwickshire), 1982, "Some Thoughts on the Role of Chance in Dürrenmatt," in *Modern Languages* (Rugby, Warwickshire), 1987, and "Interior Landscapes: Narrative Perspective in Hauptmann," in *Modern Languages* (Rugby, Warwickshire), 1989. Co-editor of *Bahnwärter Thiel* by Gerhardt Hauptmann, 1989. **Essay:** Jurek Becker.

ROSS, Francesca. Freelance writer living in Germany. **Essays:** Umberto Eco; Peter Handke; Mario Soldati.

RUBIO, Patricia. Associate Professor of Spanish, Skidmore College, Saratoga Springs, New York. Author of *Carpentier ante la critica*, 1985, "Niveles y sujetos de focalización en Pedro Paramo," 1986, "El concepto de focalización: su aplicación a la cuentistica de O. J. Cardoso," 1987, "Funciones del nivel descriptivo en *Los recuerdos del porvenir*," 1987, "La fragmentación: principio ordenador en la ficción de Luisa Valenzuela," 1989, and "Carmen Naranjo," 1989. **Essay:** Elena Garro.

RUDOLF, Anthony. Editor and chair, Menard Press, London. Author of *The Same River Twice*, 1976, and *At an Uncertain Hour: Primo Levi's War Against Oblivion*, 1991. Co-editor of *Voices Within the Ark: The Modern Jewish Poets* (with Howard Schwartz), 1980, and *Selected Poems* by Yves Bonnefoy, 1993. Translator of *Tyorkin, and The Stovemakers* by Aleksandr Tvardovskii, 1974.

RYDEL, Christine A. Professor of Russian, Grand Valley State University, Allendale, Michigan. Author of *A Nabokov's Who's Who*, 1992. Editor of *The Ardis Anthology of Russian Romanticism*, 1983. **Essays:** Bella Akhmadulina; Natalia Gorbanevskaia.

SCHERR, Barry P. Professor of Russian, Dartmouth College, Hanover, New Hampshire. Author of *Russian Poetry: Meter, Rhythm, and Rhyme*, 1986, *Maxim Gorky*, 1988, "Beginning at the End: Rhyme and Enjambment in Brodsky's Poetry," 1990, and "Pasternak, Hegel, and Christianity: Religion in *Doctor Zhivago*," 1991. Co-editor of *Russian Verse Theory: Proceedings of the 1987 Conference at UCLA*, 1989. **Essays:** Vasilii Aksenov; I. Grekova; Aleksandr Kushner; Valentin Rasputin; Andrei Siniavskii.

SCHULMAN, Grace. Professor at Baruch College, City University of New York. Author of two books of poetry, *Marian Moore: The Poetry of Engagement*, 1987, and poems,

essays, and translations in various journals and anthologies. Translator of works by T. Carmi and Pablo A. Cuadra. **Essay:** T. Carmi.

SCHUMACHER, Claude. Reader in French theatre studies, Glasgow University. Editor of *Theatre Research International*. Author of *Jarry and Apollinaire*, 1984, *Artaud on Theatre*, 1989, and *Zola's Thérèse Raquin*, 1990. **Essay:** Philippe Jaccottet.

SCHWARTZ, Kessel. Professor Emeritus of modern languages and literatures, University of Miami, Coral Gables. Author of *The Contemporary Novel of Ecuador*, 1953, *Introduction to Modern Spanish Literature*, 1968, *Vicente Aleixandre*, 1970, *The Meaning of Existence in Contemporary Hispanic Literature*, 1970, *Juan Goytisolo*, 1970, *A New History of Spanish American Fiction*, 1972, and *Studies on Twentieth-Century Spanish and Spanish American Literature*, 1983; co-author of *A New History of Spanish Literature*, 1967 (revised 1991). Co-editor of *A New Anthology of Spanish Literature*, 1967. **Essays:** Rafael Alberti; Miguel Delibes; Juan Goytisolo; Ana María Matute.

SCOBBIE, Irene. Reader Emeritus in Scandinavian studies, University of Edinburgh. Author of *Pär Lagerkvist: An Introduction*, 1963, *Sweden: Nation of the Modern World*, 1972, *Pär Lagerkvist's Gäst hos verkligheten*, 1974, and articles on Lagerkvist, Strindberg, P. O. Sundman, Stig Claesson, and other writers. Editor and contributor, *Aspects of Swedish Literature*, 1988; editor of *Northern Studies*. **Essay:** Tomas Tranströmer.

SILENIEKS, Juris. Professor Emeritus, Carnegie Mellon University, Pittsburgh. Author of *Themes and Dramatic Forms in the Theater of Armand Salacrou*, 1967, and *L'Image des États-Unis dans les œuvres des auteurs noirs de langue française*, 1974. Editor of *Monsieur Toussaint* by Édouard Glissant, 1982. **Essay:** Édouard Glissant.

SINGH, G. Professor of Italian, Queen's University, Belfast. Author of *Leopardi and the Theory of Poetry*, 1964, *Leopardi e l'Inghilterra*, 1968, *Montale: A Critical Study of His Poetry, Prose and Criticism*, 1973, and *Ezra Pound*, 1979. Editor of *It Depends: A Poet's Notebook* by Montale, 1980, and *Collected Essays of Q. D. Leavis*, vol. 1, 1983. Translator of *New Poems* by Montale, 1976. **Essays:** Mario Luzi; Andrea Zanzotto.

SKEI, Hans H. Professor of comparative literature, University of Oslo. Editor of *NLÅ* annual, since 1989. Author of *William Faulkner: The Short Story Career*, 1981, *William Faulkner: The Novelist as Short Story Writer*, 1984, *Ålese litteratur*, 1992, and *Vagen til bøkene*, 1993. **Essays:** Knut Faldbakken; Kjartan Fløgstad; Olav H. Hauge; Rolf Jacobsen.

ŠKVORECKÝ, Josef. See his own entry.

SMITH, Christopher. Senior Lecturer, School of Modern Languages and European History, University of East Anglia, Norwich. Editor of *Seventeenth-Century French Studies*. Author of many articles and reviews of the performing arts. Editor of works by Antoine de Montchrestien, Jacques de la Taille, and Pierre Matthieu. **Essays:** Marie Cardinal; Julien Gracq; Françoise Sagan; Léopold Senghor.

SOUZA, Raymond D. Professor of Spanish, University of Kansas, Lawrence; assistant editor, *Latin American Theatre Review*. Author of *Major Cuban Novelists: Innovation and*

Tradition, 1976, *Lino Novás*, 1981, and *The Poetic Fiction of José Lezama Lima*, 1983. **Essay:** G. Cabrera Infante.

ŚRĪVĀSTAVA, Satyendra. See his own entry. **Essays:** Dharmvīr Bhārtī; Kamleśvar; Rājendra Yādav.

STAMM, James Russell. Professor of Spanish and Portuguese, New York University. Author of *A Short History of Spanish Literature*, 1966 (revised 1979), and numerous articles on the early Spanish novel and theatre. Editor of *Dos novelas cortas: Miguel de Unamuno* (with Herbert E. Isar), 1967. **Essay:** Alfonso Sastre.

STEWART, Mary E. Fellow and University Lecturer in German, Robinson College, Cambridge. Contributor to *Rejection and Emancipation: Writing in German-Speaking Switzerland 1945–91*, edited by M. Butler and M. Pender, 1991, and to *Beyond Realism*, edited by D. Midgley, 1993. **Essay:** Franz Xaver Kroetz.

SUBIOTTO, Arrigo V. Emeritus Professor of German and Honorary Fellow, Institute for Advanced Research in the Humanities, University of Birmingham. Author of *Bertolt Brecht's Adaptations for the Berliner Ensemble*, 1975, and numerous articles on German writers. Editor of *Hans Magnus Enzensberger: Poems*, 1985. **Essays:** Wolf Biermann; Volker Braun; Rolf Hochhuth.

SWANSON, Philip. Lecturer in Hispanic studies, University of Edinburgh. Author of *José Donoso: The "Boom" and Beyond*, 1988, *Landmarks in Modern Latin American Fiction*, 1990, and *Cómo leer a Gabriel García Márquez*, 1991. **Essay:** José Donoso.

TAKAHASHI Yasunari. Formerly Professor of English, University of Tokyo. Author of *The Genealogy of Ecstasy: From Donne to Beckett*, 1966, *Samuel Beckett*, 1971, and *Summa Nonsensologica*, 1977. **Essay:** Yoshioka Minoru.

TAYLOR, Anna-Marie. Lecturer in drama, University College of Wales, Aberystwyth. Author of articles on modern drama and contemporary literature. **Essays:** Ilse Aichinger; Elias Canetti; Sembène Ousmane; Botho Strauss; Patrick Süskind.

THOMPSON, Birgitta. Lecturer in Swedish, Saint David's University College, Lampeter. Author of "Swedish Views on Franz Kafka," in *Humanismen som salt och styrka* (Stockholm), 1987, and various articles in *Swedish Book Review* (Lampeter), 1983–90. **Essay:** P. C. Jersild.

THOMPSON, Laurie. Head of the School of Modern Languages, Saint David's University College, Lampeter. Author of *Stig Dagerman*, 1983. Editor of *Swedish Book Review*. **Essays:** Ingmar Bergman; Astrid Lindgren.

THOMSEN, Bjarne T. Lecturer in Scandinavian studies, University of Edinburgh. **Essay:** Anders Bodelsen.

TILBY, Michael. Fellow and Senior Tutor, Selwyn College, Cambridge. Editor of *Les Faux-Monnayeurs* by André Gide, 1981, and *Beyond the Nouveau Roman: Essays on the Contemporary French Novel*, 1990. **Essays:** Michel Tournier; Monique Wittig.

TÖRNQVIST, Egil. Professor of Scandinavian studies, University of Amsterdam. Author of *A Drama of Souls: Studies in*

O'Neill's Super-Naturalistic Technique, 1969, *Strindbergian Drama*, 1982, and *Transposing Drama*, 1991. **Essay:** Jan Myrdal.

VALENCIA, Heather. Lecturer in German, University of Stirling. Author of articles on Yiddish literature and poets in various journals. **Essay:** Abraham Sutzkever.

VERANI, Hugo J. Professor of Spanish American literature, University of California, Davis. Author of *Narrativa contemporánea*, 1979, *Onetti: el ritual de la impostura*, 1981, and *Octavio Paz: bibliografía crítica*, 1983. **Essay:** Octavio Paz.

VERTHUY, Maïr. Professor of French and Founding Principal of the Simone de Beauvoir Institute, Concordia University, Montreal. Author of numerous books and articles on feminist issues and the writings of contemporary writers in French. Currently working on a biography of Hélène Parmelin, an assessment of Simone de Beauvoir's works, and a study of immigrant women writers in Quebec. Past editor of *Canadian Women Studies*, and various conference proceedings. **Essays:** Marie-Claire Blais; Anne Hébert.

VINCENT, Paul. Formerly Senior Lecturer in Dutch, University College London. Co-editor of *Modern Dutch Studies*, 1988. **Essays:** Hugo Claus; Willem Frederik Hermans; Judith Herzberg; Lucebert; Harry Mulisch; Gerard Reve; Jan Wolkers.

WAELTI-WALTERS, Jennifer. Director of the Women's Studies Programme and Professor of French, University of Victoria, British Columbia. Author of *Alchimie et littérature*, 1975, *J.-M. G. Le Clézio*, 1977, *Michel Butor*, 1977, *Icare ou l'évasion impossible: étude psycho-mythique de J.-M. G. Le Clézio*, 1981, *Fairytales and the Female Imagination*, 1982, *Jeanne Hyvrard*, 1988, *Feminist Novelists of the Belle Epoque*, 1990, *French Feminisms of the Belle Epoque*, 1992, and *Michel Butor*, 1992. **Essays:** Michel Butor; Jeanne Hyvrard; J.-M. G. Le Clézio.

WAINE, Anthony. Lecturer in German studies, University of Lancaster. Author of *Martin Walser: The Development as Dramatist 1950–1970*, 1978, *Martin Walser*, 1980, and numerous articles about 20th-century German literature and society. Editor of *Brecht in Perspective* (with Graham Bartram), 1982, and *Culture and Society in the GDR*, 1984. **Essays:** Hans Magnus Enzensberger; Martin Walser.

WARNER, I. Robin. Lecturer in Hispanic studies, University of Sheffield. **Essay:** José Cardoso Pires.

WEISSBORT, Daniel. Professor of comparative literature and Director of the Translation Workshop, University of Iowa, Iowa City; co-founding editor, with Ted Hughes, of *Modern Poetry in Translation*. Author of five books of poetry. Editor and translator of many books, including works by Natalia Gorbanevskaia, Nikolai Zabolotskii, Andrei Amalrik, Evgenii Vinokurov, Evgenii Evtushenko, Patrick Modiano, Claude Simon, and of collections of Russian poetry. **Essay:** Yehuda Amichai.

WELLWARTH, George E. Professor of theatre and comparative literature, State University of New York, Binghamton; co-editor of *Modern International Drama*. Author of *The Theater of Protest and Paradox*, 1964 (new edition 1974),

Spanish Underground Drama, 1972, and *Modern Drama and the Death of God*, 1986. Editor or translator of *Concise Encyclopaedia of the Modern Drama*, 1964, *Modern French Theatre*, 1964, *Postwar German Theatre*, 1967, *Modern Spanish Theatre*, 1968, *The New Wave Spanish Drama*, 1970, *German Drama Between the Wars*, 1972, *Themes of Drama*, 1972, *New Generation Spanish Drama*, 1976, and *Three Catalan Dramatists*, 1976. **Essays:** José Ruibal; Jean Tardieu.

WERNER, Theresa. Freelance writer and editor in London. **Essays:** Ana Blandiana; Maryse Condé; Sándor Csoóri; René Depestre; Piet Hein; Murakami Haruki.

WILLIAMS, Mark. Lecturer in Japanese studies, University of Leeds. Author of "Life After Death? The Literature of an Undeployed Kamikaze Squadron Leader," in *Japan Forum*, 1992. Translator of *Ryugaku* by Endō Shūsaku, 1989. **Essays:** Endō Shūsaku; Yasuoka Shōtarō.

WILSON, Jason. Lecturer in Hispanic poetry, University College London. Author of *Octavio Paz: A Study of His Poetics*, 1979, *Octavio Paz*, 1986, *An A-Z of Modern Latin American Literature in English Translation*, 1989, and *Traveller's Literary Companion to Latin America*, 1992. **Essays:** Isabel Allende; Homero Aridjis; José Emilio Pacheco; Ernesto Sabato.

WOODYARD, George. Professor of Spanish, University of Kansas, Lawrence; editor of *Latin American Theatre Review*. Author of articles on Latin American theatre. Editor of *The Modern Stage in Latin America: Six Plays*, 1971, *Dramatists in Revolt: The New Latin American Theatre* (with Leon F. Lyday), 1976, and *A Bibliography of Latin American*

Theatre Criticism, 1940–1974, 1976. **Essay:** Carlos Solórzano.

YOUNG, David. Longman Professor of English, Oberlin College, Ohio; editor of *Field: Contemporary Poetry and Poetics*. Author of many collections of poems, three books about Shakespeare, and one book about Yeats. Editor of several anthologies of stories and poems. Translator of poems by Wang Wei, Li Ho, Rainer Maria Rilke, Günter Eich, Miroslav Holub, Pablo Neruda, and others.

YUDKIN, Leon I. Lecturer in Hebrew, University of Manchester. Author of *Isaac Lamdam: A Study in Twentieth-Century Hebrew Poetry*, 1971, *Escape into Siege*, 1974, *Jewish Writing and Identity in the 20th Century*, 1982, *1948 and After: Aspects of Israeli Fiction*, 1984, *On the Poetry of U. Z. Greenberg*, 1987, *Else Lasker-Schueler: A Study in German Jewish Literature*, 1991, and *Beyond Sequence: Current Israeli Fiction and Its Context*, 1992. Editor of *Jews in Modern Culture* monograph series. **Essays:** David Grossman; Haim Guri; Amalia Kahana-Carmon; Amos Oz; Yehoshua Sobol; A. B. Yehoshua; Nathan Zach.

ZATLIN, Phyllis. Professor of Spanish, State University of New Jersey, Rutgers. Associate editor of *Estreno* journal. Author of *Elena Quiroga*, 1977, *Víctor Ruiz Iriarte*, 1980, *Jaime Salom*, and *Cross-Cultural Approaches to Theatre: The Spanish-French Connection*, 1993, and numerous scholarly articles on Spanish theatre, Spanish women writers, cross-cultural approaches to theatre, and other topics. Translator of *Going Down to Marrakesh* by J. L. Alonso de Santos, 1992, *A Bonfire at Dawn* by Jaime Salom, 1992, and *Lady Strass* by Eduardo Manet, 1992. **Essays:** Antonio Gala; Eduardo Manet; Francisco Nieva; Elena Quiroga.

ISBN 1-55862-200-4